The Good Pub Guide 2004

Edited by Alisdair Aird

Deputy Editor: Fiona Stapley

Managing Editor: Karen Fick
Assistant Editor: Elizabeth Adlington
Associate Editor: Robert Unsworth
Editorial Assistance: Fiona Wright

EBURY PRESS
LONDON

Please send reports on pubs to

The Good Pub Guide
FREEPOST TN1569
WADHURST
East Sussex
TN5 7BR

or contact our website:
www.goodguides.com

Good Guide publications are available at special discounts for bulk purchases or for sales promotions or premiums. Special editions, including personalized covers, excerpts of existing Guides and corporate imprints, can be created in large quantities for special needs. Enquiries should be sent to the Sales Development Department, Random House, 20 Vauxhall Bridge Road, London SW1V 2SA (020 7840 8400).

This edition first published in 2003 by Ebury Press,
Random House, 20 Vauxhall Bridge Road,
London SW1V 2SA

The Random House Group Limited Reg. No. 954009

www.randomhouse.co.uk

3 5 7 9 10 8 6 4

Copyright © 2003 The Random House Group Ltd.
Maps copyright © 2003 PerrottCartographics
Cover design by 2H Design
Cover photographs © 2003 Getty Images

A CIP catalogue record for this book is available from the British Library.

ISBN 0 09 188897 2

Typeset from author's disks by Clive Dorman & Co.
Edited by Pat Taylor Chalmers
Printed and bound in Great Britain by Cox and Wyman Ltd, Reading, Berkshire

Contents

Introduction

We pride ourselves on the diversity of the pubs included in this *Guide*, each with their own special strengths – the quality of their beer or wine, the appeal of their food, the warmth of their welcome, for instance. Here, we pick out the front-runners for each main quality, and name the top award winners.

Over 40 of the main entries (and dozens of the pubs in the Lucky Dip sections) now brew their own beers. The brews are often favourites with beer-minded readers: the Brewery Tap in Peterborough (Cambridgeshire), the Bentley Brook at Fenny Bentley and John Thompson near Melbourne (Derbyshire), the Fountain Head at Branscombe (Devon), the Flower Pots at Cheriton (Hampshire), the Victory in Hereford (Herefordshire), the Swan on the Green at West Peckham (Kent), the Marble Arch in Manchester (Lancashire chapter), the Exeter Arms at Barrowden, Bell at East Langton and Grainstore in Oakham (Leicestershire), the Blue Cow at South Witham (Lincolnshire), the Dipton Mill Inn at Diptonmill (Northumbria), the Six Bells in Bishop's Castle (Shropshire), the Burton Bridge Inn in Burton upon Trent (Staffordshire), the Plough at Coldharbour (Surrey), the Gribble at Oving (Sussex), the Beacon in Sedgley (Warwickshire), the New Inn at Cropton, Turkey at Goose Eye, Sair in Linthwaite and Fat Cat in Sheffield (Yorkshire), the Fox & Hounds in Houston (Scotland), and the White Hart at Llanddarog (Wales). Top of the brewing tree, the Flower Pots at Cheriton (Hampshire) is **Own Brew Pub of the Year 2004.**

Most of our main entries have an enjoyable choice of well kept 'real' (cask-conditioned) ales, and many have a very wide choice of 10 or so interesting real ales from smaller specialist brewers. In each chapter, we name the local breweries to look out for in that area. A few pubs stand out for the way that, month after month, readers have been reporting back very favourably on the quality of the beers on offer, the choice, and the help they have had from knowledgeable staff: the Bhurtpore at Aston (Cheshire), the Blisland Inn in Blisland and Old Ale House in Truro (Cornwall), the Watermill at Ings (Cumbria), the Brunswick in Derby (Derbyshire), the Bridge in Topsham (Devon), the Fat Cat in Norwich (Norfolk), the Victoria in Beeston and Vat & Fiddle in Nottingham (Nottinghamshire), the Turf Tavern in Oxford (Oxfordshire), the Crown at Churchill (Somerset), the Griffin at Shustoke (Warwickshire), the Fat Cat in Sheffield (Yorkshire), and the Guildford Arms in Edinburgh (Scotland). For its great carefully explained choice the Watermill at Ings (Cumbria) is **Beer Pub of the Year 2004.**

Hook Norton, a small Oxfordshire brewer based in the small town of that name, owns several appealing main entries. Its main claim on our affections, though, is the good value pricing of its beers. Over 50 of our main entries have a Hook Norton beer as their cheapest real ale. This is not just in their home county, but in 10 other English counties, and in Wales. These are nice beers (their strong Old Hooky is a favourite of many), made very traditionally – a steam engine still powers the brewery. Hook Norton is **Brewer of the Year 2004.**

It is easier for a pub to build up a good collection of whiskies than it is to keep a fine range of real ales or of wines – as whiskies, true to their Scottish character, are not so fussy about how they are kept, and as they don't have a short life in the way that a cask of beer or an opened bottle of wine does. In Scotland, most good pubs keep a worthwhile range of single malt whiskies. However, in England and Wales it is less easy to find malt whiskies that are at all out of the ordinary. There are some noble exceptions, which have splendid ranges: the Crown & Horns at East Ilsley (Berkshire), the Bhurtpore at Aston (Cheshire), the Hardwick Inn at Hardwick Hall (Derbyshire), the Nobody Inn at Doddiscombsleigh (Devon), the Britons Protection in Manchester (Lancashire chapter), the Bulls Head at Clipston (Northamptonshire), the Victoria in Beeston (Nottinghamshire), the Fox & Hounds at Great Wolford (Warwickshire), the Marton Arms at

Thornton in Lonsdale (Yorkshire), and in Scotland the Bow Bar in Edinburgh, the Fox & Hounds in Houston, the Stein Inn on Skye, and the Eilean Chraggan at Weem. The champion for whisky enthusiasts is the Bulls Head at Clipston, which now has a staggering array of over 600: it is **Whisky Pub of the Year 2004.**

Nowadays, with most good pubs offering a decent range of perfectly drinkable wines by the glass, it's extraordinary to remember that just a very few years ago pub wine was in general pretty ghastly. This transformation certainly suits the customer: a great many of our readers prefer wine to beer – and know more about it. And while not so long ago many landlords seemed to think it wasn't quite the done thing for a publican to know about or like wine, many now take real pride in tracking down an interesting choice. A long shortlist of pubs with an exceptional range of wines includes the Bell at Boxford (Berkshire), the Crooked Billet at Newton Longville and Five Arrows in Waddesdon (Buckinghamshire), the Trengilly Wartha near Constantine (Cornwall), the Punch Bowl at Crosthwaite (Cumbria), the Nobody Inn at Doddiscombsleigh (Devon), the Village Pub at Barnsley (Gloucestershire), the Wykeham Arms in Winchester (Hampshire), the Stagg at Titley (Herefordshire), the Olive Branch at Clipsham (Leicestershire), the Crown at Colkirk (Norfolk), the Caunton Beck at Caunton (Nottinghamshire), the Royal Oak at Ramsden and Trout at Tadpole Bridge (Oxfordshire), the Blue Ball at Triscombe (Somerset), the Cornwallis at Brome and Crown in Southwold (Suffolk), the Vine Tree at Norton and Pear Tree at Whitley (Wiltshire), and the White Swan in Pickering (Yorkshire). The small Brunning & Price and Huntsbridge groups, each with several main entries, both have a fine choice of wines in all their pubs. The Olive Branch at Clipsham, with friendly staff happy to guide you through their enticing blackboard selection of interesting wines, is **Wine Pub of the Year 2004.**

Over a hundred of the main entry pubs in this edition – about one in 12 – have qualified for our Bargain Award. You can get a decent main dish for £5.75 or less in these. Mostly, you can't expect anything very special at that price level. However, a few pubs do cook interesting food at prices this low. Ones which stand out for this are the Sweeney & Todd in Reading (Berkshire), the Old Ale House in Truro (Cornwall), the Black Dog at Belmont and Britons Protection in Manchester (Lancashire chapter), the Lincolnshire Poacher in Nottingham (Nottinghamshire), the Basketmakers in Brighton (Sussex), and the Fat Cat and New Barrack in Sheffield (Yorkshire). The Fat Cat concentrates on its good beers, but its remarkably cheap food, with strong vegetarian leanings, is so tasty that we name the Fat Cat in Sheffield **Bargain Food Pub of the Year 2004.**

In each county chapter we have named that county's best pub for food. The decision has rarely been simple: several pubs have usually been in contention for this top award. The standard at this level is now exceptionally high, with dedicated chefs putting great imagination and energy into creating delicious meals using top-quality local produce. The hundred or so best dining pubs in this book are all very rewarding places for a special meal out – their outstanding cooking stands comparison with many of this country's most respected restaurants. Ones which have been giving particular pleasure this year are the Pheasant at Keyston and Three Horseshoes at Madingley (Cambridgeshire), the Plume of Feathers at Mitchell (Cornwall), the Punch Bowl at Crosthwaite and Drunken Duck near Hawkshead (Cumbria), the Drewe Arms at Broadhembury and Dartmoor Inn at Lydford (Devon), the White Horse at Frampton Mansell and Bell at Sapperton (Gloucestershire), the Stagg at Titley (Herefordshire), the Dove at Dargate and Harrow at Ightham Common (Kent), the Olive Branch at Clipsham (Leicestershire), the Rose & Crown at Snettisham (Norfolk), the Falcon at Fotheringhay (Northamptonshire), the County in Aycliffe (Northumbria), the Kings Head at Aston Cantlow (Warwickshire), the Star at Harome and Three Acres in Shelley (Yorkshire), and for its fresh seafood the Applecross Inn up in Scotland. Some of this year's newcomers look extremely promising on the food front, too, notably the Spread Eagle at Sawley (Lancashire), the Boat near Lichfield (Staffordshire), the Appletree at Marton (Yorkshire), and Brickys in Montgomery (Wales). Our mouths still water when we think of our inspection meal at the Dartmoor Inn at Lydford (Devon): it is **Dining Pub of the Year 2004.**

People keep saying that unspoilt traditional pubs are disappearing fast. This is probably one of the most persistent myths in pub history – exactly the same sort of thing was being said 50 years ago, 100 years ago, and over 150 years ago. Of course pubs evolve over the years, and we have seen many changes in the country's best pubs over the last couple of decades in which we have been producing this *Guide*. But one thing is certain: there are still plenty of splendidly unspoilt pubs to be tracked down. Some favourites are the Cock at Broom (Bedfordshire), the Bell at Aldworth (Berkshire), the Queens Head at Newton (Cambridgeshire), the Bear at Alderwasley and Barley Mow at Kirk Ireton (Derbyshire), the London at Molland, Bridge in Topsham and Northmore Arms at Wonson (Devon), the Digby Tap in Sherborne and Square & Compass at Worth Matravers (Dorset), the Red Lion at Ampney St Peter and Boat at Ashleworth Quay (Gloucestershire), the Flower Pots at Cheriton and Harrow at Steep (Hampshire), the Carpenters Arms at Walterstone (Herefordshire), the Red Lion at Snargate (Kent), the Three Horseshoes at Warham (Norfolk), the Victoria in Durham (Northumbria), the Star in Bath, Carew Arms at Crowcombe, Tuckers Grave at Faulkland and Rose & Crown at Huish Episcopi (Somerset), the Yew Tree at Cauldon (Staffordshire), the Royal Oak at Wineham (Sussex), the Beacon in Sedgley and Case is Altered at Five Ways (Warwickshire and West Midlands chapter), the Birch Hall at Beck Hole, Whitelocks in Leeds and Laurel at Robin Hood's Bay (Yorkshire), and the Cresselly Arms at Cresswell Quay and Plough & Harrow at Monknash (Wales). The Bell at Aldworth up on the Berkshire downs, in the same family for over two centuries, is **Unspoilt Pub of the Year 2004.**

Over 80 of the main entries are new this year. Ones which particularly stand out for their all-round appeal are the Live & Let Live at Pegsdon (Bedfordshire), the Eagle & Child in Stow-on-the-Wold (Gloucestershire), the Vine in Hambledon (Hampshire), the Cat Head at Chiselborough (Somerset), the Anchor at Nayland (Suffolk), the Horse & Groom at East Ashling (Sussex), the Neeld Arms at Grittleton (Wiltshire), the Admiral Rodney at Berrow Green and Nags Head in Malvern (Worcestershire), the Appletree at Marton (Yorkshire), and the Brunant Arms at Caio and Corn Mill in Llangollen (Wales). The attractively placed Brunant Arms at Caio, interesting and warmly welcoming, with good food and a fine range of well kept beers, is **Newcomer of the Year 2004.**

The pubs which generate most enthusiasm among our readers are surprisingly varied. Some of the places which delight virtually everyone are very simple, while others are decidedly upscale. At both extremes, the vital thing is a real sense of welcome for all, and an atmosphere of thorough enjoyment. This comes across strongly in the Bell at Aldworth (Berkshire), the Dysart Arms at Bunbury (Cheshire), the Halzephron near Helston and Roseland at Philleigh (Cornwall), the Britannia at Elterwater (Cumbria), the Masons Arms at Branscombe and Five Bells at Clyst Hydon (Devon), the Royal Oak in Cerne Abbas (Dorset), the Brushmakers Arms at Upham (Hampshire), the Inn at Whitewell (Lancashire), the Welby Arms at Allington and George of Stamford (Lincolnshire), the Victoria in Beeston (Nottinghamshire), the Lamb in Burford, Chequers in Chipping Norton and Sun in Hook Norton (Oxfordshire), the Horseshoe at Ebbesbourne Wake (Wiltshire), the Abbey Inn at Byland Abbey, Star at Harome and St Vincent Arms at Sutton upon Derwent (Yorkshire), the Plockton Hotel at Plockton (Scotland), and the Bear in Crickhowell (Wales). The Star at Harome is an exceptionally good dining pub, and a fine place to stay in, but what makes it special for us and for the dozens of readers who have been praising it so highly to us is the relaxed and informal pubby atmosphere which its young enthusiastic owners have worked so hard to keep. The Star at Harome in Yorkshire is **Pub of the Year 2004.**

Several of these top pubs are also delightful places to stay in: the Halzephron near Helston (Cornwall), the Inn at Whitewell (Lancashire), the George of Stamford (Lincolnshire), the Lamb in Burford (Oxfordshire), the Abbey Inn at Byland Abbey and Star at Harome (Yorkshire), the Plockton Hotel at Plockton (Scotland), and the Bear in Crickhowell (Wales). Other lovely places to stay include the Pheasant at Bassenthwaite Lake and Drunken Duck near Hawkshead (Cumbria), the Feathers in Ledbury (Herefordshire), the Nevill Arms at Medbourne (Leicestershire), the Fishermans Arms at Winterton-on-Sea (Norfolk), the Rose & Crown at Romaldkirk (Northumbria), the White Swan in Pickering (Yorkshire), and the Stein Inn on Skye (Scotland). The Bear in Crickhowell (Wales), convivial and civilised with its blazing log fires, is **Inn of the Year 2004**.

To excel in any of the categories we have mentioned so far, takes a very special person. The landlords and landladies who are behind all these pubs have put a great deal of energy and individuality into their success. Sometimes, a pub's character seems almost inseparable from its licensee. Landlords and landladies who stand out for their commitment and personality are Angela Thomas of the Halzephron near Helston (Cornwall), Jamie Stuart and Pippa Hutchinson of the Duke of York at Iddesleigh (Devon), Jane and Simon Hudson of the Weighbridge near Nailsworth and Peter and Assumpta Golding of the Horse & Groom at Upper Oddington (Gloucestershire), Lucille and Barry Carter of the Woolpack at Terrington St John (Norfolk), Maggie Chandler of the George in Kilsby (Northamptonshire), Kathy Jones of the Rose at Thorington Street (Suffolk), Alan Stoneham of the Compasses at Chicksgrove and Charlie and Boo West of the Neeld Arms at Grittleton (Wiltshire), Andy and Sue Cole of the Wombwell Arms at Wass (Yorkshire), and the Key family at the Nags Head in Usk (Wales). Always cheerful and on the case, Kathy Jones of the Rose at Thorington Street in Suffolk is **Landlady of the Year 2004**.

It is very rare indeed for the *Guide* to rate every single pub in one group worthy of a main entry. And it has never before happened that a group with as many as 11 pubs has secured this uniform success. This year all 11 pubs in the Brunning & Price group are main entries: properly pubby, but with up-to-date food alongside good beers and wines, helpful young staff, and a relaxed and informal décor. Sweeping the board, Brunning & Price are **Pub Group of the Year 2004**.

Beer prices

As usual, this year we have investigated beer prices throughout the country. Our annual national price survey shows that the price of a pint of real ale has jumped the £2 barrier now, averaging £2.07. Major beers from the big international brewing combines, Tetleys, John Smiths, Theakstons, Boddingtons, Worthington and Flowers, hover closely around the £2 mark. When their other beers including more expensive brands such as Bass and Courage are counted in, these international combines average out bang on the national norm of £2.07, showing how their beers still dominate pub pricing.

Often, the best way of getting value for money on the beer front is to choose a beer from one of the smaller brewers. The Table which follows shows how smaller brewers compare with the £2.07 national average price. We have included only those brewers whose beers we found offered as the cheapest by at least two pubs, and we have excluded Channel Islands brewers, which work under a slightly more lenient tax regime. The number in brackets after each name shows the number of pubs we found offering their beer as its cheapest – obviously, the more pubs, the more reliable our price.

£/pint

£1.42	Sam Smiths (5)
£1.60	Barnsley (2)
£1.63	Castle Rock (4)
£1.67	Holts (2)
£1.70	Hydes (2)
£1.71	Burton Bridge (4)
£1.79	Lees (2)
£1.85	Tomos Watkins (2)
£1.87	Hobsons (11)
£1.90	Robinsons (9), Yates (2)
£1.91	Wye Valley (9)
£1.92	Thwaites (3), Burtonwood (2)
£1.93	Donnington (4), Hardys & Hansons (3)
£1.94	Jennings (16), Batemans (5)

£1.95	Grainstore (4), Branscombe Vale (3), Mansfield (3), Nethergate (2), Whim (2)
£1.97	Teignworthy (6), Archers (3), Goachers (3)
£1.98	Ridleys (4), Skinners (2)
£2.00	Moles (2), Moorhouses (2), Summerskills (2)
£2.01	Banks's (14)
£2.02	Brains (7)
£2.03	Princetown (5), Wickwar (3), Wychwood (2)
£2.04	Cotleigh (10)
£2.05	Black Sheep (35), Butcombe (16), Marstons (7), Hop Back (3), Becketts (2), Itchen Valley (2), Smiles (2)
£2.08	Hook Norton (54), Otter (18), Sharps (15), Leatherbritches (2), Vale (2)
£2.09	Belhaven (4)
£2.10	Bath (2), Mauldons (2)
£2.11	Wadworths (24), St Austell (16), Palmers (8)
£2.13	Shepherd Neame (16), Gales (8), Ventnor (3)
£2.14	Greene King (102), Ringwood (21), Exmoor (8), Cheriton (7)
£2.15	Oakham (3), Goddards (2)
£2.16	Timothy Taylors (7)
£2.18	Fullers (26), Caledonian (11)
£2.19	Badger (23)
£2.20	Cottage (2), Rother Valley (2), Wylam (2)
£2.22	Adnams (74), Youngs (19), West Berkshire (7)
£2.23	Charles Wells (10), Larkins (5), Woodfordes (4)
£2.26	St Peters (4)
£2.27	King (3)
£2.28	Harveys (19), Broughton (2), Orkney (2)
£2.29	Brakspears (24)
£2.33	Morrells (2)
£2.34	Isle of Skye (2)

Other beers we found at extremely low prices, but just in single pubs, were Wyre Piddle, Bathams, Barngates, York, Clarks, Bullmastiff and Goffs. All these were £1.80 a pint or less. Averaging £1.81 a pint, pubs brewing their own beer are also very good value.

The cheapest area for drinks is now Nottinghamshire – a hair's breadth cheaper even than Lancashire, the traditional home of cheap beer. In our survey of prices in 1,186 pubs nationwide, we found beer there was typically 23p a pint cheaper than the national average. The Table below shows how much extra people in other areas now have to pay for their beer:

How much extra you pay per pint

Lancashire	1p
Staffordshire	4p
Cheshire	7p
Cumbria, Yorkshire	8p
Herefordshire, Shropshire	10p
Northumbria, Worcestershire	13p
Wales	14p
Derbyshire	15p
Warwickshire	18p
Gloucestershire	19p
Devon	20p
Cornwall, Leicestershire	22p
Wiltshire	23p
Lincolnshire, Northamptonshire, Somerset	24p
Bedfordshire, Essex	26p
Dorset	27p
Norfolk	29p

Hertfordshire, Isle of Wight	30p
Cambridgeshire, Hampshire, Suffolk	33p
Kent, Oxfordshire, Sussex	34p
Scotland	35p
Buckinghamshire	38p
Surrey	43p
Berkshire	45p
London	49p

The agony column

Sometimes we feel as if we have become the agony aunt of the pub world. The great bulk of our postbag consists of recommendations, for pubs that are in the *Guide* already or ones that people feel should be added to it. But we also get hundreds of letters describing often really dreadful experiences in pubs. Sometimes the experience is so ghastly that our correspondents refrain from describing it – simply warning us against the establishment, in the strongest possible terms (as one put it, 'If Shropshire evacuates its bowels, this is where the product exits').

This year we have had nearly 600 of these sob stories – needless to say, not one of the pubs which features in them features in this edition of the *Guide*, even as a Lucky Dip. To give you some idea of the delights you are missing by sticking to our current recommendations, here is a selection of readers' comments:

Waiter, there's a stalk in my soup

Sausages too tough to cut, chef's hair in the soggy frozen vegetables, beer awful!

There was no draught beer available (had the landlord not paid the brewery?) and the bottled beer that I asked for must have been past its sell-by date, as it was flat as a pancake. My wife asked for a glass of red wine, which she returned because there were at least seven flies swimming around on the surface.

Very poor food (two different pitta melts, both burnt), didn't fancy the cockerel walking around inside, either; unprofessional service (public debate about who was actually to deliver our meals).

Could not understand a word the girl taking our order was saying, and service was inefficient. The food was slow in coming, the poached salmon was full of bones and not tender, beans were not cooked and there were stalks on them.

The customer is never right

My parents stayed last week, and we met them for a meal. The cod was undercooked. When we made this known to the manager at the end of the meal, he accused us: 'you are the type who always complain', and 'you should have brought your own fish in'. He then made it clear that if I did not leave he would throw me out; I then left. My parents who were sitting outside were not party to this. They later retired to their bedroom, only to be woken by banging on their door, and were told in no uncertain terms to leave.

The unpleasant manageress became aggressive when she realised my wife had queried the taste of the lemon sole – she insisted that it was 'fresh and expensive', although the chef reported that there could be a problem, and my wife and I and two strangers from an adjoining table all agreed it was past its best. The bill presented was for another table, and when I pointed this out the landlady said 'What's the matter with the bill now? Don't you want to pay the bill? Well don't, just go' – so we did!

When my wife wanted to make a complaint about cold food the landlord swore at us and threatened violence at us in front of our children.

We look forward to seeing you again soon, Madam

It is not a pub, it is a greasy spoon café licensed to sell alcohol, and has all the atmosphere of a school canteen. Food was barely passable and service was slow; tables were far too close together. My biggest complaint is against the landlord and bar staff. I have never come across a more surly, disagreeable and bad-tempered pair. Our pot of tea was almost thrown at us and it was other customers, not the bar staff, who helped me find sugar, teaspoons, cutlery. We were given only one tea bag for two of us, and when I queried this I was told it was a 'two-cup' bag which it was not; my mackerel was tough and greasy, and salad was just a few blackened-at-the-edges leaves and a couple of slices of cucumber and tomato.

While it's 'pretty-pretty olde-worlde', it's also incompetently run, the prices are outrageous, the service is shoddy, and they can't find room on the bar to serve you for all the piles of used glasses. Ugh!

Food orders when NOT busy anything up to 45 mins. Customers constantly complaining. One lady came in from the beer garden, threw all the knives and forks on the bar and demanded their money back... they had been waiting so long. Plate of food (burnt) just dumped on table, served by schoolchildren without any cutlery etc. No evidence of any cutlery. My wife had to go to the kitchen and demand cutlery. No salt available but 12 (yes 12) pepper containers! Constant chaos. Overheard conversation that when the beer runs out, there won't be any more. Disaster of the year!

A night to remember

We were surprised to find a smelly room with window panes missing (one 'mended' with strips of Sellotape), very lumpy mattress, no waste bin, tiny shower room with dirty grouting, no toiletries other than a piece of already-used soap. Back downstairs the general atmosphere was not exactly welcoming. Bar staff cliquey with regulars and each other. Feeling a bit dismayed, we headed to our room. In the middle of the night we were woken by the fire alarm and, as it continued, realised we'd better get dressed and out of there. There were no fire instructions in the room at all, so we just went downstairs, where we found staff deliberating how to turn it off. Exhausted, we went back to bed (amazingly no-one else had bothered to get up!). In the morning no apologies for the alarm received and slow service at breakfast. The whole experience was not a good start to our holiday and at £80 per room, really a rip-off.

Please wash your hands after using this pub

The stair carpet and upstairs landing carpet had not been cleaned for some time. The room smelled of stale cooking smells from the kitchen immediately below. The carpet was so dirty I hesitated to put my feet on it. There was no wardrobe as the doors had come off leaving an open alcove with a rail. I have suspicions that the bedding had not been changed since the last occupant. There were dead insects on the windowsills. The bathroom carpet was filthy. The toilet had not been cleaned and someone had vomited in it. The wash basin had a filthy rim around it. The shower tray was filthy. Our complaint was dealt with by a cursory clean. The bar was none too clean and the settle on which we sat had stuffing coming out of the tears in the fabric. The glass my wife was given was dirty. We arrived late on Easter Saturday and could not find anywhere else with a vacancy at that time of day otherwise we would have left. As it was, we did not stay for breakfast as we could imagine the standards of hygiene in the rest of the premises. Unsurprisingly the landlord expects payment on arrival!

A middle-aged woman leapt out of the front door, retched noisily, and returned. Rather warily we entered the pub to discover that the afore-mentioned lady was the landlady. Needless to say we only stopped for a quick pint. Too much like the *League of Gentlemen* for comfort.

Two of the worst pubs I have had the misfortune to frequent. Both dirty, glasses and rubbish all over the garden, and the second has the added bonus of dog pooh all over the garden.

Ghastly, I think it has changed hands. The seat covers appeared to be so old and dirty my wife washed her jeans when she got home.

The revolving landlord syndrome

We could have probably forgiven the appalling wine and slow service, but not the totally inflexible attitude of the 'jobs-worth' manager whose complete lack of charm and 'we are right' attitude was a total turn-off. May he move on to his next mass food chain job as soon as possible.

No atmosphere, all charming features disappeared (*another pub that has changed hands*), appalling service, licensee had arguments with staff so loudly the entire pub could hear, wrong wine, lamb cold and almost inedible, steak brought without sauce, staff arguments continued all evening, and when we went to bed through the carpetless floorboards of our bedroom.

Really rather scruffy; two run-of-the-mill beers, plus pictures of the landlord in nothing but a thong advertising himself as a stripper.

Food prices

Quite a few readers have been complaining to us about food price increases recently. So we have taken a sample of 331 pubs in 12 areas, from Cambridgeshire to Cornwall, from Berkshire to Wales, from Kent to Yorkshire. For each pub we took one typical dish, then compared its price now with what that pub was charging for it two years ago. If they did not have exactly the same dish, we selected two dishes which were of a closely comparable nature – the sort of thing that the same person might have chosen in that pub then and now.

Our hope was that we would be able to reassure readers, by finding that price increases had been no higher than the general rate of inflation over the same period, which has of course been low. Over the period of our price comparison, from May 2001 to May 2003, the Retail Price Index (RPI), excluding housing, rose by just under 3% – to be exact, 2.67%.

In fact, we found that over this same period pub food has gone up in price by an average of 13%. This increase is nearly five times as high as the RPI.

This is of course quite a small survey. But it is country-wide, and it does put some figures to the widespread feeling among our readers that quite a few pubs are getting greedy about their food pricing; and it seems to support that feeling. Certainly, at a time when other high street prices have been almost at a standstill, price increases on this scale do get noticed – and do hurt customers' pockets.

Some pubs have held their food prices steady, with no increase over this period, and some others have made only very modest increases. But at the other extreme, in one in seven pubs the price has jumped by 25% or more.

In some cases, a sharp jump in food prices has coincided with a takeover by new owners. This may well be accompanied by a quantum leap in quality; but equally, it may not. So an obvious lesson is to be on your guard when you see that proud notice 'Under New Management', or an advertisement in the local paper announcing a new landlord trained by some famous chef.

Our snapshot survey was concerned mainly with hot dishes. But we also know that many readers feel bulldozed into having – and paying for – something rather fancier than the simple lunchtime snack or sandwich that they really want. Either a sandwich comes with a few pence' worth of unwanted chips, crisps or salad, bumping the price up by a pound or two. Or the sandwich has blown up into a huge baguette, or trendified into a pannini or a ciabatta or even a wrap. Of course these are popular in their own right; but they should never be seen as substitutes for proper sandwiches.

Smoke

It seems to us likely that within a few years smoking in pubs will be banned. In his most recent annual report on public health the Government's Chief Medical Officer has called for a ban on smoking in public places, particularly to safeguard the health of people who are exposed to others' smoke at their place of work, especially in bars and restaurants. This follows many other calls for a ban on smoking in public places, for example from the British Medical Association (and of course similar bans already in places overseas, most famously in New York and California). The TUC has even claimed that a blanket ban on smoking in pubs and restaurants, as well as protecting the health of people working in them, would increase profits by attracting extra customers who at the moment stay away because of the smoke.

We rather doubt whether the TUC is right about that, at least as far as pubs are concerned. Our readers rarely stay away from smoky pubs, even when they complain to us about them (and they do complain, particularly when smoke drifts into a nominal no smoking area). In their letters to us, readers almost never raise the passive-smoking health issue (though that will be what eventually ends smoking in pubs). Their concern is simply that it makes the atmosphere unpleasant, particularly if they are eating.

Most of the pubs in this *Guide* do make some provision for people who want to be smoke-free. But nearly one in three still allows smoking throughout. Given that 60% of the people who use pubs don't smoke, it seems clear that while smoking is still allowed in pubs, any truly customer-friendly pub should confine it to properly segregated areas, certainly separated from eating areas. Moreover, as non-smokers are now a clear majority, and very few smokers smoke all the time, it makes sense for the smoking room to be relatively small.

Staying in pubs

Two out of five of the pubs in this *Guide* have bedrooms, and the proportion increases each year. If you have not stayed in a pub recently, you may well have the wrong idea about the sort of accommodation they have. Mostly, you can now expect a good level of comfort and facilities, and as much seclusion as you want. And forget about padding down a corridor to a shared bathroom: more than 19 out of 20 pubs with accommodation now have bedrooms with their own bathrooms.

Tipping and credit cards

Tipping is still not expected in the vast majority of pubs, though many people like to leave something for waiting staff after a meal, perhaps up to 10% or so, to reward better or more helpful service than normal.

A few restauranty places try to encourage you to tip, by putting a note on the menu or the bill about Service being At Your Discretion. Remember that it certainly is: that sort of prompt should never make you feel obliged to be more generous than you feel truly inclined to be. Recently one or two have started adding a 10% service charge to bills, sometimes even if you order your food yourself from the bar. Readers have even had this charge added to the cost of drinks they have got from the bar themselves: rather topsy-turvy – the logical thing would be a discount for self-service, instead. The right thing to do is always to ask for this service charge to be removed; alas, very few of us have the courage to do that – certainly, your Editor would never dare. But we do count it as a black mark against a pub which tries this on.

> From a reader's letter: *Our experience on Saturday night was dreadful. Three hours for two courses, rude staff and no separation between dining and drinking areas leaving our table as a dumping ground for drinks. When we asked for service to be removed, we had our credit card thrown back at us and were told 'If you can't afford it, get out and don't come back.' Please don't be tempted to feature this dreadful pub in a forthcoming Guide.*

Still on this general topic, a few pubs still try to make customers hand over a credit or debit card, to be kept behind the bar, if they are 'running a tab' for payment of their bill at the end of a meal. This is a bad practice. The card issuing banks strongly discourage it. They say that if you are asked to do this you should object and resist. They have even suggested to us that, in theory (we hope not in practice), if someone's card was used fraudulently by the staff who had retained it, the card holder could be held responsible, for negligently letting the card leave their sight. Our own view is a lot simpler. If the staff expect you to act fraudulently by doing a runner, what does that say about them? Follow the card companies' guidance, and never risk letting anyone get away with this. If you are still happy to do business with people who are treating you as a potential fraud and thief, let them swipe your card (as many hotels do), but make sure you get it back.

What is a Good Pub?

The main entries in this book have been through a two-stage sifting process. First of all, some 2,000 regular correspondents keep in touch with us about the pubs they visit, and nearly double that number report occasionally. We are now also getting quite a flow of reports through our **www.goodguides.com** web site. This keeps us up-to-date about pubs included in previous editions – it's their alarm signals that warn us when a pub's standards have dropped (after a change of management, say), and it's their continuing approval that reassures us about keeping a pub as a main entry for another year. Very important, though, are the reports they send us on pubs we don't know at all. It's from these new discoveries that we make up a shortlist, to be considered for possible inclusion as new main entries. The more people that report favourably on a new pub, the more likely it is to win a place on this shortlist – especially if some of the reporters belong to our hard core of about 500 trusted correspondents whose judgement we have learned to rely on. These are people who have each given us detailed comments on dozens of pubs, and shown that (when we ourselves know some of those pubs too) their judgement is closely in line with our own.

This brings us to the acid test. Each pub, before inclusion as a main entry, is inspected anonymously by the Editor, the Deputy Editor, or both. They have to find some special quality that would make strangers enjoy visiting it. What often marks the pub out for special attention is good value food (and that might mean anything from a well made sandwich, with good fresh ingredients at a low price, to imaginative cooking outclassing most restaurants in the area). The drinks may be out of the ordinary (pubs with several hundred whiskies, with remarkable wine lists, with home-made country wines or good beer or cider made on the premises, with a wide range of well kept real ales or bottled beers from all over the world). Perhaps there's a special appeal about it as a place to stay, with good bedrooms and obliging service. Maybe it's the building itself (from centuries-old parts of monasteries to extravagant Victorian gin-palaces), or its surroundings (lovely countryside, attractive waterside, extensive well kept garden), or what's in it (charming furnishings, extraordinary collections of bric-a-brac).

Above all, though, what makes the good pub is its atmosphere – you should be able to feel at home there, and feel not just that *you're* glad you've come but that *they're* glad you've come. A good landlord or landlady makes a huge difference here – they can make or break a pub.

It follows from this that a great many ordinary locals, perfectly good in their own right, don't earn a place in the book. What makes them attractive to their regular customers (an almost clubby chumminess) may even make strangers feel rather out-of-place.

Another important point is that there's not necessarily any link between charm and luxury – though we like our creature comforts as much as anyone. A basic unspoilt village tavern, with hard seats and a flagstone floor, may be worth travelling miles to find, while a deluxe pub-restaurant may not be worth crossing the street for. Landlords can't buy the Good Pub accolade by spending thousands on thickly padded banquettes, soft music and menus boasting about signature dishes nesting on beds of trendy vegetables drizzled by a jus of this and that – they can only win it by having a genuinely personal concern for both their customers and their pub.

Using the *Guide*

THE COUNTIES

England has been split alphabetically into counties, mainly to make it easier for people scanning through the book to find pubs near them. Each chapter starts by picking out the pubs that are currently doing best in the area, or are specially attractive for one reason or another.

The county boundaries we use are those for the administrative counties (not the old traditional counties, which were changed back in 1976). We have left the new unitary authorities within the counties that they formed part of until their creation in the most recent local government reorganisation. Metropolitan areas have been included in the counties around them – for example, Merseyside in Lancashire. And occasionally we have grouped counties together – for example, Rutland with Leicestershire, and Durham with Northumberland to make Northumbria. If in doubt, check the Contents.

Scotland and Wales have each been covered in single chapters, and London appears immediately before them at the end of England. Except in London (which is split into Central, East, North, South and West), pubs are listed alphabetically under the name of the town or village where they are. If the village is so small that you probably wouldn't find it on a road map, we've listed it under the name of the nearest sizeable village or town instead. The maps use the same town and village names, and additionally include a few big cities that don't have any listed pubs – for orientation.

We always list pubs in their true locations – so if a village is actually in Buckinghamshire that's where we list it, even if its postal address is via some town in Oxfordshire. Just once or twice, when the village itself is in one county but the pub is just over the border in the next-door county, we have used the village county, not the pub one.

STARS ★

Really outstanding pubs are picked out with a star after their name. In a few cases, pubs have two stars: these are the aristocrats among pubs, really worth going out of your way to find. The stars do NOT signify extra luxury or specially good food – in fact some of the pubs which appeal most distinctively and strongly of all are decidedly basic in terms of food and surroundings. The detailed description of each pub shows what its particular appeal is, and this is what the stars refer to.

FOOD AND STAY AWARDS 🍽 🛏

The knife-and-fork rosette shows those pubs where food is quite outstanding. The bed symbol shows pubs which we know to be good as places to stay in – bearing in mind the price of the rooms (obviously you can't expect the same level of luxury at £40 a head as you'd get for £100 a head). Pubs with bedrooms are marked on the maps as a square.

♀

This wine glass symbol marks out those pubs where wines are a cut above the usual run, and/or offer a good choice of wines by the glass.

◖

The beer tankard symbol shows pubs where the quality of the beer is quite exceptional, or pubs which keep a particularly interesting range of beers in good condition.

£

This symbol picks out pubs where we have found decent snacks at £2.30 or less, or worthwhile main dishes at £5.75 or less.

RECOMMENDERS

At the end of each main entry we include the names of readers who have recently recommended that pub (unless they've asked us not to).

Important note: the description of the pub and the comments on it are our own and not the recommenders'; they are based on our own personal inspections and on later verification of facts with each pub. As some recommenders' names appear quite often, you can get an extra idea of what a pub is like by seeing which other pubs those recommenders have approved.

LUCKY DIPS

The Lucky Dip section at the end of each county chapter includes brief descriptions of pubs that have been recommended by readers, with the readers' names in brackets. As the flood of reports from readers has given so much solid information about so many pubs, we have been able to include only those which seem really worth trying. Where only one single reader's name is shown, in most cases that pub has been given a favourable review by other readers in previous years, so its inclusion does not depend on a single individual's judgement. In all cases, we have now not included a pub in the list unless readers' descriptions make the nature of the pub quite clear, and give us good grounds for trusting that other readers would be glad to know of the pub. So the descriptions normally reflect the balanced judgement of a number of different readers, increasingly backed up by similar reports on the same pubs from other readers in previous years. Many have been inspected by us. In these cases, LYM means the pub was in a previous edition of the *Guide*. The usual reason that it's no longer a main entry is that, although we've heard nothing really condemnatory about it, we've not had enough favourable reports to be sure that it's still ahead of the local competition. BB means that, although the pub has never been a main entry, we have inspected it, and found nothing against it. In both these cases, the description is our own; in others, it's based on the readers' reports. This year, we have deleted many previously highly rated pubs from the book simply because we have no very recent reports on them. This may well mean that we have left out some favourites – please tell us if we have!

Lucky Dip pubs marked with a ☆ are ones where the information we have (either from our own inspections or from trusted reader/reporters) suggests a firm recommendation. Roughly speaking, we'd say that these pubs are as much worth considering, at least for the virtues described for them, as many of the main entries themselves. Note that in the Dips we always commend food if we have information supporting a positive recommendation. So a bare mention that food is served shouldn't be taken to imply a recommendation of the food. The same is true of accommodation and so forth.

The Lucky Dips (particularly, of course, the starred ones) are under consideration for inspection for a future edition – so please let us have any comments you can make on them. You can use the report forms at the end of the book, the report card which should be included in it, or just write direct (no stamp needed if posted in the UK). Our address is The Good Pub Guide, FREEPOST TN1569, WADHURST, East Sussex TN5 7BR. Alternatively, you can get reports to us immediately, through our web site **www.goodguides.com**.

MAP REFERENCES

All pubs outside the big cities are given four-figure map references. On the main entries, it looks like this: SX5678 Map 1. Map 1 means that it's on the first map (see first colour section). SX means it's in the square labelled SX on that map. The first figure, 5, tells you to look along the grid at the top and bottom of the SX square for the figure 5. The third figure, 7, tells you to look down the grid at the side of the square to find the figure 7. Imaginary lines drawn down and across the square from these figures should intersect near the pub itself.

The second and fourth figures, the 6 and the 8, are for more precise pin-pointing, and are really for use with larger-scale maps such as road atlases or the Ordnance Survey 1:50,000 maps, which use exactly the same map reference system. On the relevant Ordnance Survey map, instead of finding the 5 marker on the top grid you'd find the 56 one; instead of the 7 on the side grid you'd look for the 78 marker. This makes it very easy to locate even the smallest village.

Where a pub is exceptionally difficult to find, we include a six-figure reference in the directions, such as OS Sheet 102 map reference 654783. This refers to Sheet 102 of the Ordnance Survey 1:50,000 maps, which explain how to use the six-figure references to pin-point a pub to the nearest 100 metres.

MOTORWAY PUBS

If a pub is within four or five miles of a motorway junction, and reaching it doesn't involve much slow traffic, we give special directions for finding it from the motorway. And the Special Interest Lists at the end of the book include a list of these pubs, motorway by motorway.

PRICES AND OTHER FACTUAL DETAILS

The *Guide* went to press during the summer of 2003. As late as possible, each pub was sent a checking sheet to get up-to-date food, drink and bedroom prices and other factual information. By the summer of 2004 prices are bound to have increased a little – to be prudent, you should probably allow around 5% extra by then. But if you find a significantly different price please let us know.

Breweries or independent chains to which pubs are 'tied' are named at the beginning of the italic-print rubric after each main entry. That generally means the pub has to get most if not all of its drinks from that brewery or chain. If the brewery is not an independent one but just part of a combine, we name the combine in brackets. When the pub is tied, we have spelled out whether the landlord is a tenant, has the pub on a lease, or is a manager. Tenants and leaseholders of breweries generally have considerably greater freedom to do things their own way, and in particular are allowed to buy drinks including a beer from sources other than their tied brewery.

Free houses are pubs not tied to a brewery, so in theory they can shop around to get the drinks their customers want, at the best prices they can find. But in practice many free houses have loans from the big brewers, on terms that bind them to sell those breweries' beers. So don't be too surprised to find that so-called free houses may be stocking a range of beers restricted to those from a single brewery.

Real ale is used by us to mean beer that has been maturing naturally in its cask. We do not count as real ale beer which has been pasteurised or filtered to remove its natural yeasts. If it is kept under a blanket of carbon dioxide to preserve it, we still generally mention it – as long as the pressure is too light for you to notice any extra fizz, it's hard to tell the difference. (For brevity, we use the expression 'under light blanket pressure' to cover such pubs; we do not include among them pubs where the blanket pressure is high enough to force the beer up from the cellar, as this does make it unnaturally fizzy.) If we say a pub has, for example, 'Whitbreads-related real ales', these may include not just beers brewed by the national company and its subsidiaries but also beers produced by independent breweries which the national company buys in bulk and distributes alongside its own.

Other drinks: we've also looked out particularly for pubs doing enterprising non-alcoholic drinks (including good tea or coffee), interesting spirits (especially malt whiskies), country wines (elderflower and the like), freshly squeezed juices, and good farm ciders. So many pubs now stock one of the main brands of draught cider that we normally mention cider only if the pub keeps quite a range, or one of the less common farm-made ciders.

Bar food refers to what is sold in the bar, not in any separate restaurant. It means a place serves anything from sandwiches and ploughman's to full meals, rather than pork scratchings or packets of crisps. We always mention sandwiches in the text if we know that a pub does them – if you don't see them mentioned, assume you can't get them.

The *food listed* in the description of each pub is an example of the sort of thing you'd find served in the bar on a normal day, and generally includes the dishes which are currently finding most favour with readers. We try to indicate any difference we know of between lunchtime and evening, and between summer and winter (on the whole stressing summer food more). In winter, many pubs tend to have a more restricted range, particularly of salads, and tend then to do more in the way of filled baked potatoes, casseroles and hot pies. We always mention barbecues if we know a pub does them. Food quality and variety may be affected by holidays – particularly in a small pub, where the licensees do the cooking themselves (May and early June seems to be a popular time for licensees to take their holidays).

What we call OAP meals are usually available for all 'seniors', not only people of pensionable age.

Any separate *restaurant* is mentioned. But in general all comments on the type of food served, and in particular all the other details about bar food at the end of each entry, relate to the pub food and not to the restaurant food.

Children's Certificates exist, but in practice *children* are allowed into at least some part of almost all the pubs included in this *Guide* (there is no legal restriction on the movement of children over 14 in any pub, though only people over 18 may get alcohol). As we went to press, we asked the main-entry pubs a series of detailed questions about their rules. *Children welcome* means the pub has told us that it simply lets them come in, with no special restrictions. In other cases we report exactly what arrangements pubs say they make for children. However, we have to note that in readers' experience some pubs make restrictions that they haven't told us about (children only if eating, for example). Also, very occasionally pubs which have previously allowed children change their policy altogether, virtually excluding them. If you come across this, please let us know, so that we can clarify the information for the pub concerned in the next edition. Beware that if children are confined to the restaurant, they may occasionally be expected to have a full restaurant meal. Also, please note that a welcome for children does not necessarily mean a welcome for breast-feeding in public. If we don't mention children at all, assume that they are not welcome. All but one or two pubs (we mention these in the text) allow children in their garden or on their terrace, if they have one. In the Lucky Dip entries we mention children only if readers have found either that they are allowed or that they are not allowed – the absence of any reference to children in a Dip entry means we don't know either way.

We asked all main entries what their policy was about *dogs*, and if they allow them we say so. Generally, if you take a dog into a pub you should have it on a lead. We also mention in the text any pub dogs or cats (or indeed other animals) that we've come across ourselves, or heard about from readers.

Parking is not mentioned if you should normally be able to park outside the pub, or in a private car park, without difficulty. But if we know that parking space is limited or metered, we say so.

We now say if a pub does **not** accept *credit cards*; some which do may put a surcharge on credit card bills, as the card companies take quite a big cut. We also say if we know that a pub tries to retain customers' credit cards while they are eating. This is a reprehensible practice, and if a pub tries it on you, please tell them that all banks and card companies frown on it – and please let us know the pub's name, so that we can warn readers in future editions.

Telephone numbers are given for all pubs that are not ex-directory.

Opening hours are for summer; we say if we know of differences in winter, or on particular days of the week. In the country, many pubs may open rather later and close earlier than their details show unless there are plenty of customers around (if you come across this, please let us know – with details). Pubs are allowed to stay open all day Mondays to Saturdays from 11am (earlier, if the area's licensing magistrates have permitted) till 11pm. However, outside cities most English and Welsh pubs close during the afternoon. Scottish pubs are allowed to stay open until later at night, and the Government has announced plans to allow later opening in England and Wales too, and it's just possible that the law will be changed during the currency of this edition. We'd be very grateful to hear of any differences from the hours we quote. You are allowed 20 minutes' drinking-up time after the quoted hours – half an hour if you've been having a meal in the pub.

Bedroom prices normally include full English breakfasts (if these are available, which they usually are), VAT and any automatic service charge that we know about. If we give just one price, it is the total price for two people sharing a double or twin-bedded room for one night. Otherwise, prices before the / are for single occupancy, prices after it for double. A capital B against the price means that it includes a private bathroom, a capital S a private shower. As all this coding packs in quite a lot of information, some examples may help to explain it:

£65	on its own means that's the total bill for two people sharing a twin or double room without private bath; the pub has no rooms with private bath, and a single person might have to pay that full price.
£65B	means exactly the same – but all the rooms have private bath
£50(£65B)	means rooms with private baths cost £5 extra
£35/£50(£65B)	means the same as the last example, but also shows that there are single rooms for £35, none of which have private bathrooms

If there's a choice of rooms at different prices, we normally give the cheapest. If there are seasonal price variations, we give the summer price (the highest). During the winter, many inns, particularly in the country, will have special cheaper rates. And at other times, especially in holiday areas, you will often find prices cheaper if you stay for several nights. On weekends, inns that aren't in obvious weekending areas often have bargain rates for two- or three-night stays.

MEAL TIMES

Bar food is commonly served from 12-2 and 7-9, at least from Monday to Saturday (food service often stops a bit earlier on Sundays). If we don't give a time against the *Bar food* note at the bottom of a main entry, that means that you should be able to get bar food at those times. However, we do spell out the times if we know that bar food service starts after 12.15 or after 7.15; if it stops before 2 or before 8.45; or if food is served for significantly longer than usual (say, till 2.30 or 9.45).

Though we note days when pubs have told us they don't do food, experience suggests that you should play safe on Sundays, and check first with any pub before planning an expedition that depends on getting a meal there. Also, out-of-the-way pubs often cut down on cooking during the week, especially the early part of the week, if they're quiet – as they tend to be, except at holiday times. Please let us know if you find anything different from what we say!

NO SMOKING

We say in the text of each entry what, if any, provision a pub makes for non-smokers. Pubs setting aside at least some sort of no smoking area are also listed county by county in the Special Interest Lists at the back of the book.

DISABLED ACCESS

Deliberately, we do not ask pubs questions about this, as their answers would not give a reliable picture of how easy access is. Instead, we depend on readers' direct experience. If you are able to give us help about this, we would be particularly grateful for your reports.

PLANNING ROUTES WITH THE GOOD PUB GUIDE

Computer users may like to know of a route-finding programme, Microsoft® MapPoint™ European Edition, which shows the location of *Good Pub Guide* pubs on detailed maps, works out the quickest routes for journeys, adds diversions to nearby pubs – and shows our text entries for those pubs on screen.

OUR WEB SITE (**www.goodguides.com**)

Our Internet web site combines material from *The Good Pub Guide* and its sister publication *The Good Britain Guide* in a way that gives people who do not yet know the books at least a taste of them. The site is being continually improved and expanded, and we hope to use it to give readers of the books extra information. You can use the site to send us reports – this way they get virtually immediate attention.

CHANGES DURING THE YEAR – PLEASE TELL US

Changes are inevitable, during the course of the year. Landlords change, and so do their policies. And, as we've said, not all returned our fact-checking sheets. We very much hope that you will find everything just as we say. But if you find anything different, please let us know, using the tear-out card in the middle of the book (which doesn't need an envelope), the report forms at the back of the book, or just a letter. You don't need a stamp: the address is The Good Pub Guide, FREEPOST TN1569, WADHURST, East Sussex TN5 7BR. As we have said, you can also send us reports by using our web site **www.goodguides.com**.

Author's Acknowledgements

The *Guide* relies to a huge degree on the extraordinarily generous help we have from the many thousands of readers who report to us on the pubs they visit, often in great detail. For the special help they have given us this year, I am deeply grateful to Richard Lewis, Ian Phillips, George Atkinson, Kevin Thorpe, LM, Steve Whalley, Tracey and Stephen Groves, Michael Doswell, CMW, JJW, Susan and John Douglas, Michael and Jenny Back, Phyl and Jack Street, the Didler, Tom Evans, Martin and Karen Wake, Guy Vowles, Jenny and Brian Seller, John Beeken, Gerry and Rosemary Dobson, Dennis Jenkin, Dr and Mrs M E Wilson, Paul and Ursula Randall, Rona Murdoch, Joan and Michel Hooper-Immins, Ann and Colin Hunt, Pete Baker, Howard Dell, Peter and Audrey Dowsett, W W Burke, E G Parish, Peter Scillitoe, Derek and Sylvia Stephenson, Michael Dandy, Tony and Wendy Hobden, B and K Hypher, Peter Meister, Roger and Jenny Huggins, Dave Irving, Tom McLean, Ewan McCall, Val and Alan Green, Joe Green, Pat and Tony Martin, John Foord, John and Judy Saville, Alan and Paula McCully, Simon Collett-Jones, John Evans, J R Ringrose, G Coates, Andy and Jill Kassube, MDN, Charles and Pauline Stride, Comus and Sarah Elliott, Pamela and Merlyn Horswell, Neil and Anita Christopher, MLR, Mike Ridgway, Sarah Miles, Mayur Shah, Joyce and Maurice Cottrell, Tina and David Woods-Taylor, Michael Butler, Nick Holding, Lynn Sharpless, B Newman, Margaret Dickinson, Bob and Maggie Atherton, Eric Larkham, Andrew Crawford, Peter F Marshall, Mr and Mrs Colin Roberts, Mr and Mrs G S Ayrton, Paul Humphreys, Pete and Rosie Flower, Ted George, B and M Kendall, J F M and M West, Mike and Mary Carter, John Wooll, Ian and Nita Cooper, Marjorie and David Lamb, R T and J C Moggridge, JHBS, Dick and Madeleine Brown, Stephen, Julie and Hayley Brown, KC, E D Fraser, Lorraine and Fred Gill, Brian and Anna Marsden, Alan Thwaite, Martin Jennings, Anthony Longden, Paul A Moore, Keith and Chris O'Neill, Mike Gorton, Bruce Bird, David Crook, Martin Grosberg, Ron Shelton, Alan M Pring, Dave Braisted, Esther and John Sprinkle, Duncan Cloud, Gill and Tony Morriss, Malcolm Taylor, Phil and Sally Gorton, Dr and Mrs A K Clarke, M G Hart, Tim and Ann Newell, Roy and Lindsey Fentiman, Len Banister and Richard Stancomb.

Warm thanks too to John Holliday of Trade Wind Technology, who built and looks after our state-of-the-art database; and above all to the thousands of devoted publicans, who give us all so much pleasure.

Alisdair Aird

England

Bedfordshire

It's now a lot easier to find a good pub lunch here than it used to be, from honest homely cooking as under the new landlord in the Three Tuns at Biddenham, at the Chequers in Keysoe, or the splendidly unspoilt old Cock at Broom, to something more unusual, like the steaks sold by weight at the very cheerful Fox & Hounds at Riseley. And there is a growing choice of pubs for a really special meal out. Perhaps the best food of all is to be found in the Knife & Cleaver at Houghton Conquest – best to go there in a restaurry frame of mind. But this year two other contenders for our main accolade here are pubs that have burst on to the dining scene more recently: the Hare & Hounds in the attractive village of Old Warden, new to the Guide this year, and the Five Bells at Stanbridge, a main entry for not much longer. You can also eat most enjoyably at another new entry, the Live & Let Live at Pegsdon, flourishing after a good revamp by its expert new landlord. The Five Bells does very good imaginative and up-to-date food in contemporary surroundings. The Hare & Hounds food is so delicious, using top-quality ingredients cooked with great care, that it comes straight in with a Food Award, yet keeping a warmly pubby atmosphere; it's the Hare & Hounds at Old Warden which takes the title of Bedfordshire Dining Pub of the Year. In the Lucky Dip section at the end of the chapter, the Black Horse at Ireland is another pub well worth noting for reliable food. Drinks prices are around the national average here; the county's major brewer is Charles Wells.

BIDDENHAM TL0249 Map 5
Three Tuns

Village signposted from A428 just W of Bedford

Tidied up since the last edition of the *Guide*, this thatched village pub is popular for its very reasonably priced enjoyable food – so you may need to book, particularly at lunchtime. The comfortably decorated low-beamed lounge has country paintings, with dark wood tables, wheelback chairs, window seats and pews on a red turkey carpet. A simpler green-carpeted public bar has photographs of local sports teams, darts, table skittles and dominoes, and the dining room is no smoking. As we went to press there were plans to add a conservatory. Served in good helpings the homely food includes dishes such as soup (£2.50), sandwiches (from £2.50; soup and sandwich £4), ploughman's or ham and egg (£4), home-made dishes such as beef and ale pie or lamb shanks in red wine and mint (£6.50), meat or vegetable lasagne (£7.50), steaks (from £9.50), puddings (£3), and children's menu (£3). On handpump, Greene King IPA and Abbot are well kept alongside a guest such as Everards Tiger. There are seats in the attractively sheltered spacious garden, and a big terrace has lots of picnic-sets. The very good children's play area has swings for all ages. *(Recommended by Colin and Janet Roe, Maysie Thompson)*

Greene King ~ Tenant Kevin Bolwell ~ Real ale ~ Bar food (12-2, 6-9; not Sun evening) ~ (01234) 354847 ~ Children in eating area of bar and restaurant ~ Dogs allowed in bar ~ Open 11.30-2.30, 6-11; 12-3, 7-10.30 Sun

BROOM TL1743 Map 5
Cock ★

High Street; from A1 opposite northernmost Biggleswade turn-off follow Old Warden 3,
Aerodrome 2 signpost, and take first left signposted Broom

The four quietly cosy rooms at this welcoming 17th-c pub have remained almost
untouched over the years – simple and unspoilt. Original latch doors lead from one
little room to another, where you'll find warming winter log fires, low ochre
ceilings, stripped panelling, and farmhouse tables and chairs on antique tiles.
There's no bar counter, and the very well kept Greene King IPA, Abbot and
Ruddles County are tapped straight from casks by the cellar steps off a central
corridor. Enjoyable straightforward bar food includes sandwiches (from £2.85),
home-made soup (£2.95), ploughman's (from £4.55), vegetarian lasagne (£6.25),
scampi or filled yorkshire puddings (£6.95), breaded plaice filled with prawns and
mushrooms or large cod (£6.95), cajun chicken (£7.25), 8oz sirloin steak (£8.95),
and Sunday roast (£6.95). The restaurant is no smoking; piped (perhaps classical)
music, darts, table skittles, cribbage and dominoes. There are picnic-sets and flower
tubs on the terrace by the back lawn, and a fenced-off play area; caravanning and
camping facilities are available. *(Recommended by the Didler, J D M Rushworth,
S F Parrinder, Quentin and Carol Williamson, P Smith, Kevin Thorpe, JWAC, Paul Humphreys,
W W Burke, Pete Baker, Ian Phillips)*

*Greene King ~ Tenants Gerry and Jean Lant ~ Real ale ~ Bar food (not Sun evening)
~ Restaurant ~ (01767) 314411 ~ Children in restaurant ~ Dogs allowed in bar ~
Open 12-3(4 Sat), 6-11; 12-4, 7-10.30 Sun*

HOUGHTON CONQUEST TL0441 Map 5
Knife & Cleaver ⊕ ♀ ⇌

Between B530 (old A418) and A6, S of Bedford

While some readers find this attractive 17th-c dining pub too restauranty for their
tastes, others are grateful to find such well prepared food in an area where pubs
serving really good meals are a little thin on the ground. Beware that it does get
very busy, and on Saturday evening and Sunday lunchtime if the restaurant is fully
booked they may not serve bar meals. Dishes are stylishly presented, imaginative
and fully flavoured, taking the same care over ingredients and cooking as with the
separate more elaborate restaurant menu: soup of the day such as carrot and ginger
(£3), ploughman's (£4), filled breads such as chicken and bacon ciabatta (£5.95), a
dish of the day which might include duck confit crêpes with spiced plum chutney
(£6.50), steamed chicken and bacon pudding (£6.95), moules marinière (£7.25) and
puddings such as lime tart in coconut pastry with gin and lime sorbet, and sticky
toffee apple pudding with calvados toffee sauce (£3.50), and there's a proper
cheeseboard (£4). The comfortably civilised bar has dark panelling which is reputed
to have come from nearby ruined Houghton House, as well as maps, drawings and
old documents on the walls, and a blazing fire in winter. The airy white-walled no
smoking conservatory restaurant has rugs on the tiled floor and lots of hanging
plants. There's also a no smoking family room. Service is really welcoming and
efficient. Well kept Bass and Batemans XB on handpump, Stowford Press farm
cider, around 30 good wines by the glass, and over 20 well aged malt whiskies;
unobtrusive piped music. There are tables on the terrace in a neatly kept garden,
and the church opposite is worth a look. *(Recommended by Phil and Heidi Cook,
Peter and Anne-Marie O'Malley, Sue Forder, Maysie Thompson, Karen and Graham Oddey,
Mr and Mrs P L Haigh)*

*Free house ~ Licensees David and Pauline Loom ~ Real ale ~ Bar food (12-2.30
(2 Sat), 7-9.30; not Sun or bank hol evenings; but see text about wknds) ~ Restaurant
~ (01234) 740387 ~ Children welcome ~ Dogs allowed in bedrooms ~ Open 12-2.30
(2 Sat), 7-10.30(11 Sat); closed Sun evening ~ Bedrooms: £53B/£63B*

KEYSOE TL0762 Map 5
Chequers
Pertenhall Road, Brook End (B660)

Usually fairly quiet at lunchtime (unless a group is in), the two neat and simple beamed rooms at this pleasant village local are divided by an unusual stone-pillared fireplace. Comfortable seats in one room and piped local radio or music lends a homely 1960s air, and the friendly licensees go out of their way to make customers feel at home. Bar food includes sandwiches, plain or toasted (£2.50), home-made soup (£2.75), garlic mushrooms on toast (£3.75), ploughman's (£4), chilli (£6), home-made steak and ale pie or scampi (£6.50), chicken breast stuffed with stilton in chive sauce (£8.25), steaks (from £9.75) and blackboard specials such as sweet and sour chicken (£6.50) and tomato, orange and lamb casserole (£7). The handpumps on the stone bar counter serve well kept Fullers London Pride and Hook Norton Best, and they have some malt whiskies, and mulled wine in winter; darts, shove-ha'penny and dominoes. Tables and chairs on the back terrace look over the garden, which has a play tree and swings. *(Recommended by Michael and Jenny Back, Maysie Thompson)*

Free house ~ Licensee Jeffrey Kearns ~ Real ale ~ Bar food (12-2, 7-9.45) ~ (01234) 708678 ~ Children in no smoking room ~ Open 11.30-2.30, 6.30-11; 12-2.30, 7-10.30 Sun; closed Tues

ODELL SP9658 Map 4
Bell
High Street/Horsefair Lane; off A6 S of Rushden, via Sharnbrook

Of the five little low-ceilinged rooms which loop around a central servery at this lovely old stone and thatched village pub, the ones at the front have the pleasantest atmosphere. Some areas have shiny black beams, there's a log fire in one big stone fireplace, and two coal fires elsewhere. It's furnished with handsome old oak settles, bentwood chairs and neat modern furniture on slightly worn red carpets, and has countryside prints on the walls. Reasonably priced bar food includes sandwiches (from £2.60), ploughman's (from £5.10), ham, egg and chips (£6.55), liver and bacon (£6.95), and daily specials such as mediterranean vegetable lasagne (£6.25), spicy pork sausages (£7.65), lamb or chicken curry (£7.95), braised lamb shank (£8.95), and puddings such as cheesecake or treacle sponge and custard (£3.25); well kept Greene King IPA, Abbot and Ruddles County and a guest such as Wadworths 6X on handpump, and piped radio. The garden is rather lovely, with picnic-sets on the flower-filled terrace overlooking a wooded part that makes an attractive walk down through a wild area to a bridge over the Great Ouse. Children are well entertained by the garden roamings of Lucy the 12-year-old goose, and the golden pheasants, cockatiels and canaries in their aviary. Further along the road is a very pretty church, and the pub is handy for the local country park. *(Recommended by E J and M W Corrin, CMW, JJW, Maysie Thompson)*

Greene King ~ Tenants Derek and Doreen Scott ~ Real ale ~ Bar food (12-2, 7-9.30; not Sun evening) ~ (01234) 720254 ~ Children welcome in area away from counter ~ Open 11-2.30, 6-11; 12-2.30, 7-10.30 Sun

OLD WARDEN TL1343 Map 5
Hare & Hounds 🍴 ♀
Village signposted off A600 S of Bedford and B658 W of Biggleswade

Bedfordshire Dining Pub of the Year

Doing particularly well under its current licensees, this welcoming old pub was a delight on our midsummer evening visit, when the happy chatter was disturbed only by the sound of popping corks and gentle birdsong. It's a popular spot, and though there's an ample car park, they sometimes need to commandeer the grounds of the village hall as an overflow. There's a glorious sloping garden, with picnic-sets stretching up to pine woods behind, and a warmly friendly atmosphere in the comfortably refurbished rooms, but the main draw these days is the excellent food, thoughtfully prepared by a chef who has impressed at a couple of other main entries in the past. Freshly cooked using local ingredients (including pork from the surrounding Shuttleworth estate, and their own breads and ice cream), the changing menu might include soup (£3.95), smoked haddock risotto or tea-smoked duck (£5.95), grilled focaccia topped with tomatoes, basil and mozzarella (£6.95), a pie of the day (£7.95), roasted vegetable tart (£8.95), roast pork belly or whole bass roasted with lemon and rosemary (£12.95), and puddings such as panna cotta with Drambuie-soaked raspberries or warm bitter chocolate pudding with white chocolate ice cream (£4.95). Readers have enjoyed the scallops on their Thursday fish nights. Rambling around a central servery, and painted a warmly cosy red, the four beamed rooms have dark standing timbers, fresh flowers on the bar, an open fire, and plenty of prints and photographs of the historic aircraft in the Shuttleworth Collection just up the road. A table in one of the two smaller rooms is in a big inglenook. Well kept Charles Wells Eagle and Bombardier on handpump, with a guest such as Adnams Broadside or Greene King Old Speckled Hen; the half dozen or so wines by the glass include some from the local Southill estate. Service is attentive and friendly, from consistently well turned out staff. Two rooms are no smoking. There are more tables at the side on a small terrace, and a couple more in front. The village itself is part of the Shuttleworth estate, and was built about 200 years ago in a Swiss style. Its 19th-c Swiss Garden is appealing, and there are more substantial walks nearby. *(Recommended by Neil Coburn, Colin and Janet Roe, John Redfern, Maysie Thompson, Tom Gondris, Michael Dandy)*

Charles Wells ~ Lease Jane Hasler ~ Real ale ~ Bar food (12-2, 6-9.30; 12-4 Sun) ~ Restaurant ~ (01767) 627225 ~ Open 12-3, 6-11; 12-10.30 Sun; closed Mon except bank hols

PEGSDON TL1130 Map 5
Live & Let Live ♀ 🍺
B655 W of Hitchin

The landlord who took over here last year is no stranger to the *Guide*; he previously enjoyed huge success at the Green Man in nearby Great Offley, and more recently at the Red Lion in Milton Bryan in Buckinghamshire. He's running this in much the same way, and it's already a popular spot for a very good, well prepared meal. It's been much extended from its snugly traditional tiled and panelled core, with a big beamed dining room behind the cosier salmon-painted rooms at the front, separated by a double-sided fireplace. There are fresh flowers on the tables, rustic pictures on the walls, and a nice, chatty feel, with obviously happy staff. In summer the big back garden has a startling array of hanging baskets and flowers, as well as cast-iron tables and chairs on a terrace, and picnic-sets on the long lawn, with views of the Chiltern Hills (a track leads straight up almost opposite). There's just as much colour in the winter, when the bars are transformed by particularly good decorations at Christmas. Upmarket without being overpriced, bar food includes sandwiches (from £3.25), filled baked potatoes (from £3.50), ploughman's (£3.95), mediterranean vegetable and cheese wellington (£8.50), chicken tikka or turkey and ham pie (£9.50), fresh fish such as tuna with cajun spices (£11.95), bass (£12.95) and dover sole (£15.95), with changing specials such as fillet steak stir fry (£11.75), pork with orange and walnut cream (£12.95), and duck with fruits of the forest sauce (£13.95). Service is particularly friendly and efficient, though there may be a wait for meals at the busiest periods. Well kept Brakspears, Marstons Pedigree, Theakstons Best and a changing guest such as Old Mill on handpump, and a comprehensive wine list with plenty by the glass. Most parts are no smoking; piped music. Though the pub's postal address is Hertfordshire, it's actually in Bedfordshire, which bulges down here almost as if it's determined just to capture this nice pub. *(Recommended by Mrs Diane M Hall, Steve and Stella Swepston)*

Free house ~ Licensees Ray and Maureen Scarbrow ~ Real ale ~ Bar food (12-2, 6-9.30) ~ Restaurant ~ (01582) 881739 ~ Children welcome ~ Dogs allowed in bar ~ Open 11.30-3(4 Sat), 6-11; 12-10.30 Sun

RISELEY TL0362 Map 5
Fox & Hounds
High Street; village signposted off A6 and B660 N of Bedford

The speciality at this very welcoming pub, which is cheerily run by its jovial landlord, is steaks. You choose the piece of meat you want and how you want it cooked, and you're charged by the weight – say, £11.60 for 8oz rump, £12.60 for 8oz of sirloin and £14.20 for fillet. Blackboards show other dishes such as beef and onion soup (£3.25), juniper salmon (£4.25), home-made steakburgers (from £5.50), wild mushroom lasagne (£7.95), steamed fillet of plaice (£8.50), steak and stilton pie (£9.50), and traditional puddings such as spotted dick or treacle pudding (£3.75). Even if you don't see anything you fancy, it's worth asking: they're very obliging here, and will try to cope with particular food requests. It's a cheerfully bustling place, and does get busy; as they don't take bookings on Saturday night be prepared for a long wait for your table, and your food. A relaxing lounge area, with comfortable leather chesterfields, lower tables and wing chairs, contrasts with the more traditional pub furniture spread among timber uprights under the heavy low beams; unobtrusive piped classical or big band piped music. Charles Wells Eagle and Bombardier with perhaps a changing guest such as Marstons Pedigree are kept well on handpump, alongside a decent collection of other drinks including bin-end wines and a range of malts and cognacs. An attractively decked terrace with wooden tables and chairs has outside heating, and the pleasant garden has shrubs and a pergola. *(Recommended by Michael Dandy, Margaret and Roy Randle, Bob and Maggie Atherton)*

Charles Wells ~ Managers Jan and Lynne Zielinski ~ Real ale ~ Bar food (12-1.45, 6.30-9.30 (no steaks Sat lunchtime)) ~ Restaurant ~ (01234) 708240 ~ Children welcome ~ Dogs allowed in bar ~ Open 11.30-2.30, 6.30-11; 12-3, 7-10.30 Sun

STANBRIDGE SP9623 Map 4
Five Bells
Station Road; pub signposted off A5 N of Dunstable

Stylish décor at this smartly relaxed old country pub gives it a fresh, contemporary feel. Earthy colours on the walls and ceilings look well with the very low exposed beams, and careful spotlighting creates quite different moods around the various areas (of which perhaps the cosiest is the small corner by the fireplace). Rugs on wooden floors, armchairs and sofas, and candles on the neatly polished tables all add luxury. Airily decorated in cream, the brighter elegant no smoking restaurant leads into a large garden with plenty of good wooden tables and chairs, and big perfectly mown lawns with fruit trees. Five real bells form the pub sign, and the cream frontage with its striking grey woodwork is a backdrop to more tables nestling under a big tree. The chefs here trained at hotels such as the Lanesborough in London, and on gourmet nights really show off what they can do, while the well trained staff look good in their modern uniforms. There's always quite an emphasis on the imaginative food, which might include soup (£3.75), contemporary sandwiches (£4), chicken tikka salad with mint yoghurt dressing (£4.75), filled baked potatoes (£5.50), lasagne or chilli (£6.95), beef and potato stew with a puff pastry case (£7.25) from the bar menu, and roast vegetable tower with a trio of cheeses and basil cream sauce (£9), confit of duck on parsnip mash with balsamic jus (£12.75) and baked cod on spinach crushed potato with dill and lemon dressing (£13) from the restaurant menu (which is also available in the bar). Well kept Bass and Black Sheep, a guest such as Hook Norton on handpump and a good range of wines by the glass; piped music. *(Recommended by Susan and John Douglas, Ian Phillips, Bob and Maggie Atherton)*

Traditional Freehouses ~ Licensee Andrew MacKenzie ~ Real ale ~ Bar food (12-9) ~ Restaurant ~ (01525) 210224 ~ Children in eating area of bar and restaurant ~ Open 12-11; 11-11 Sat; 12-10.30 Sun

TURVEY SP9452 Map 4
Three Cranes ◗

Just off A428 W of Bedford

Friendly new licensees have chosen to change little at this friendly stone-built 17th-c coaching inn. The airy two-level carpeted bar (with piped music, and a solid-fuel stove) is quietly decorated, with old local photographs and Victorian-style prints, and an array of stuffed owls and other birds in the no smoking main dining area, which has sensible tables with upright seats. There are picnic-sets in a neatly kept sheltered garden with a climbing frame, and in summer, the pub frontage attractively overflows with colourful hanging baskets and window boxes. Pleasant bar food includes lunchtime sandwiches (from £3.50), filled baked potatoes (£4.45) and ploughman's (£4.75), as well as sausage and mash (£6.75), cottage pie (£6.95) and lamb in garlic and rosemary (£7.95). Taking a step away from the obvious, three guest beers might include Batemans Godivas Gold, St Austell HSD and Thwaites Lancaster Bomber, alongside the house beers, Greene King IPA and Abbot, all kept well on handpump; cribbage. *(Recommended by Maysie Thompson, George Atkinson, Blaise Vyner, Michael Dandy, Mike Ridgway, Sarah Miles)*

Greene King ~ Managers Paul and Sheila Linehan ~ Real ale ~ Bar food (12-2.30, 6.30-9; 12-9.30(8 Sun) Sat) ~ (01234) 881305 ~ Children welcome ~ Dogs allowed in bedrooms ~ Open 11.30-11; 12-10.30 Sun; 11.30-3, 6-11 Mon-Fri in winter ~ Bedrooms: £35S/£45S

Lucky Dip

Besides the fully inspected pubs, you might like to try these Lucky Dips recommended to us and described by readers (if you do, please send us reports):

BIGGLESWADE [TL1844]
Brown Bear [Hitchin St; from A6001 follow sign for Hitchin Street shops]: Local worth knowing for its wide range of real ales *(Ian Phillips, LYM, Pete Baker)*
Wheatsheaf [Lawrence Rd]: Unpretentious local, as they used to be a few decades ago; one

small very friendly room, well kept Greene King ales inc Mild, darts, dominoes and cards, TV for horseracing, no food or music *(Pete Baker)*
BROMHAM [TL0050]
Swan [Bridge End; nr A428, 2 miles W of Bedford]: Friendly and comfortable beamed

family dining pub, good choice of food from sandwiches to seafood specials, quick service, lots of pictures, well kept Greene King IPA and Abbot, decent ales, evening log fire; quiet piped music; public bar with darts and fruit machine, provision for children, garden *(M and G Rushworth)*

CARDINGTON [TL0847]
Kings Arms [The Green; off A603 E of Bedford]: Extended Brewers Fayre, usual food not too expensive, real ales such as Flowers Original and Wadworths 6X, airship photographs; sheltered picnic-sets under weeping willows *(Maysie Thompson)*

COLMWORTH [TL1057]
☆ *Cornfields* [Wilden Rd]: Early 17th-c, restaurant rather than pub, but with well kept Adnams and Bass as well as interesting stylish food, helpful young waitresses, good house wines; big log fire and low armchairs in small low-beamed bar; front picnic-sets, small garden, large comfortable well equipped bedrooms in new extension *(Anthony Barnes)*

EATON BRAY [SP9620]
☆ *White Horse* [Market Sq]: Wide choice of good fresh food and welcoming licensees in well run and relaxing old low-beamed and timbered dining pub, suit of armour in one room, real ales, decent wines, reasonable prices; ranks of tables on back lawn, good walking nearby *(A R Hawkins)*

FANCOTT [TL0227]
Fancott Arms [B579 3 miles from M1 junction 12, via Toddington]: Steep-tiled three-room cottagey pub with dining extension, decent food all day, two real ales; piped music, TV, fruit machines; disabled lavatory, picnic-sets in front with lots of flowers, big back garden with play area and short wknd/holiday children's train rides *(CMW, JJW)*

GREAT BARFORD [TL1351]
Anchor [High St; off A421]: Recently refurbished pub by medieval bridge and church, generous food from sandwiches and baked potatoes up, wider evening choice, Charles Wells Bombardier, Eagle and a changing guest such as Naked Gold, good wine choice, quick friendly service, open-plan bar with small no smoking area down steps and back restaurant; piped music may obtrude; bedrooms, roadside picnic-sets overlooking River Ouse *(Michael Dandy)*

HENLOW [TL1738]
Engineers Arms [High St]: Fine choice of changing real ales inc rarities, a seasonal regular from the Bass Museum, fine log fire, daily papers, breweriana, two friendly dogs, back bar with juke box, TV, games inc table football and lots of old soccer posters and photographs; piped radio, occasional live music, quarterly bank hol beer festivals; back terrace *(Kevin Thorpe)*

IRELAND [TL1341]
☆ *Black Horse* [off A600 Shefford—Bedford]: Busy and attractive dining pub consistently reliable for wide choice of good value plentiful piping hot food, good fresh ingredients, up-to-

date presentation and interesting light dishes, recently refurbished small bar in sizeable smart lounge, two charming dining rooms, well kept ales such as Greene King IPA and Old Speckled Hen and Fullers London Pride, good range of wines and good coffee, attentive service from very helpful friendly staff; plenty of tables in neat front garden with play area, cottage bedrooms – peaceful and attractive rural setting *(Anthony Barnes, Maysie Thompson, V Green, BB, Gordon Tong, Dr DJ Darby, Brian Root, Bob and Maggie Atherton, Eithne Dandy)*

LEIGHTON BUZZARD [SP9225]
Stag [Heath Rd]: Cosy, comfortable and relaxing, traditional home cooking inc some scottish dishes, full Fullers beer range kept well, changing guests such as Everards Butser, welcoming efficient service, candles at night; Tues quiz night *(MP)*

LINSLADE [SP9126]
☆ *Globe* [off A4146 nr bridge on outskirts]: 19th-c pub nicely set below Grand Union Canal, tables up on embankment and in garden or good well fenced play area, lots of rooms, beams and flagstones, log and coal fires, well kept Greene King IPA, Abbot and Ruddles and a guest such as Everards Tiger, usual food (not winter Sun evening), no smoking restaurant; piped music may obtrude; children welcome in eating areas, open all day *(Ian Phillips, John and Judy Saville, LYM)*
Hare [Bunkers Lane, Southcott]: Three intimate linked areas, sofa, two roaring fires, local pictures and bare boards; three well kept ales and a weekly changing guest beer, bar food, welcoming landlady and efficient staff *(MP)*
Hunt [Church Rd]: Big traditional pub refurbished by new owner, well kept Fullers ales, Tetleys and another guest beer, home-made food in restaurant *(MP)*

MAULDEN [TL0538]
Dog & Butcher [Clophill Rd]: Attractive and friendly thatched village pub, good choice of good value food (best to book wknds), nice wines; tables in front garden *(Mrs Diane M Hall)*

MILTON BRYAN [SP9730]
Red Lion [Toddington Road, off B528 S of Woburn]: Beamed dining bar with some stripped brickwork, boards and flagstones, well kept ales such as Hook Norton and Greene King IPA, Old Speckled Hen and Ruddles County, decent wines, friendly efficient staff, usual food inc OAP lunch; children welcome, plenty of tables in garden with terrace and climbing frame *(June and Malcolm Farmer, LYM, Ian Phillips, Teresa and David Waters)*

NORTHILL [TL1446]
Crown [Ickwell Rd; village signed from B658 W of Biggleswade]: Busy black and white thatched pub with traditional food inc Sun lunch (and some interesting fashion plates) in extended restaurant, low-beamed main bar, huge open fire, well kept Greene King ales,

good service; front seats by village pond, play area in huge back garden, tranquil village not far from the Shuttleworth Collection *(Bob and Maggie Atherton, Colin and Janet Roe, Maysie Thompson, Pete Baker)*

ROXTON [TL1554]

Royal Oak [High St]: Small recently refurbished L-shaped bar with Charles Wells beers, food from sandwiches and generous baguettes (lunchtime only) to steaks, quick efficient service, darts; piped music may obtrude; Post Office and small shop in new back extension *(Michael Dandy)*

SANDY [TL1749]

Sir William Peel [High St, opp church]: Open-plan pub with old paintings on flock wallpaper above panelled dado, a real ale from their Old Stables microbrewery out behind, several guest beers, games end; can get smoky when packed; open all day (not Sun) *(Kevin Thorpe)*

SHARPENHOE [TL0630]

☆ *Lynmore*: Woodburner and lots of old local photographs, prints and bric-a-brac in long low-beamed rambling family lounge and big back no smoking dining area (good views of The Clappers), plentiful quick consistently good value food inc fresh veg and children's, well kept Bass, Fullers London Pride and Hancocks HB, good service; good garden for children, big wendy house; popular with walkers *(Phil and Heidi Cook)*

SHEFFORD [TL1439]

Brewery Tap [North Bridge St]: No-nonsense bare-boards L-shaped bar notable for its well kept B&T Two Brewers, Shefford, Dark Mild and Dragon Slayer brewed nearby, with a guest such as Everards Tiger; beer bottle collection filling all the ledges, brewery posters and advertisements, chatty staff, cheap rolls or pasties; live music Fri, open night Weds; picnic-sets out behind, open all day *(Kevin Thorpe, Ian Phillips, Pete Baker)*

SHILLINGTON [TL1234]

Musgrave Arms [Apsley End Rd, towards Pegsdon and Hexton]: Low-beamed village local with settles, tables, prints and horsebrasses in friendly and civilised lounge, woodburner in comfortable public bar, small no smoking dining room, wide choice of generous home-made usual food inc Tues steak night and good Sun roast, Greene King IPA and Abbot and a guest beer tapped from cooled casks, cheerful service; big back garden with picnic-sets *(Barry and Marie Males, Phil and Heidi Cook)*

SILSOE [TL0835]

Star & Garter [High St]: Smart two-bar pub by village church, usual bar food from sandwiches and baked potatoes up, evening restaurant, Adnams, Black Sheep, B&T Shefford and Youngs; darts and piped music; nice seating area outside *(V Green, Michael Dandy)*

SOULDROP [SP9861]

☆ *Bedford Arms* [High St; off A6 Rushden—Bedford]: Several bright and cheerful biggish room areas with large central stone fireplace, good range of interesting food esp fish, well

kept Greene King ales, brasses, settles and prints, children welcome (play fort in back garden); piped music; very peaceful village; may close outside advertised times *(George Atkinson, BB)*

SOUTHILL [TL1542]

White Horse [off B658 SW of Biggleswade]: Comfortable country pub with extensive eating area, wide food choice, Fullers London Pride and Greene King IPA and Old Speckled Hen; lots of tables in large pleasant garden with good play area *(LYM, Michael Dandy)*

STEPPINGLEY [TL0135]

☆ *French Horn* [Church End]: Two-bar beamed pub, partly carpeted, part flagstones or bare boards, enjoyable food from sandwiches and baked potatoes up inc more interesting evening dishes in bar and fairly sizeable restaurant, quick friendly service, good choice of wines by the glass, Greene King IPA and Abbot, woodburner, plenty of brass and pictures; small village *(Michael Dandy)*

STREATLEY [TL0728]

Chequers [just off A6 N of Luton; Sharpenhoe Rd]: Popular partly panelled open-plan L-shaped local, mix of chairs and table sizes, old-fashioned prints and old local photographs, good value food inc some inventive dishes (and doorstep sandwiches or omelettes till late), Greene King IPA, Abbot, Jubilee, Old Speckled Hen and Ruddles County, cheerful staff, open fire; nostalgic piped music, Tues quiz night; garden with Sun lunchtime jazz *(Phil and Heidi Cook)*

TOTTERNHOE [SP9721]

☆ *Cross Keys* [off A505 W of A5; Castle Hill Rd]: Charming low-beamed thatched and timbered local below remains of a motte and bailey fort, friendly new management, small public bar and slightly larger lounge bar, good value straightforward food (not Sun evening), well kept Adnams Broadside, Greene King IPA and Old Speckled Hen and a guest such as Wadworths 6X, no smoking restaurant; may be piped music; a real welcome for children, good views from big attractive garden, extensive play area in orchard below, open all day wknds *(David and Anthea Eeles, LYM)*

TURVEY [SP9452]

Three Fyshes [Bridge Street]: As we went to press, we heard that this attractive pub, nicely placed next to the River Ouse, has closed *(LYM)*

WOBURN [SP9433]

Bell [Bedford St]: Small area by bar, longer lounge/dining area up steps, pleasant furnishings, warm woodburner, settles and hunting prints; friendly helpful staff, generous food from baguettes and ploughman's to steaks, well kept Greene King IPA and Abbot, good choice of wines by the glass, good coffee, roomy restaurant; children welcome at lunchtime; tables outside, hotel part across road, handy for Woburn Park *(Michael Dandy)*

☆ *Black Horse* [Bedford St]: Spacious 19th-c food pub, wide choice from sandwiches and baked potatoes to steaks and fish cut to order and grilled in the bar, also children's and special orders, several room areas, steps down to pleasant back restaurant; well kept Greene King IPA, Abbot and Old Speckled Hen with a guest such as St Austell Tribute, good choice of wines by the glass; children in eating areas, open all day, summer barbecues in attractive sheltered courtyard, bedrooms across road *(LYM, JHBS, Michael Dandy)*

'Children welcome' means the pub says it lets children inside without any special restriction. If it allows them in, but to restricted areas such as an eating area or family room, we specify this. Places with separate restaurants usually let children use them, hotels usually let them into public areas such as lounges. Some pubs impose an evening time limit – let us know if you find this.

Berkshire

The stand-out pub here this year is the Bell at Aldworth, a very special unspoilt place with no frills but a great welcome – just how the best pubs have been, for centuries. Other pubs here doing particularly well this year are the civilised Bell at Boxford (a tremendous range of wines by the glass), the interesting old Bel & the Dragon in Cookham (imaginative food and good service), the Pot Kiln at Frilsham (a nice old place in a charming rural spot, with its own good beer), the Crown & Garter at Inkpen (a new entry this year, with good food and beer, and a warm welcome for people of all ages), the Dundas Arms by the canal at Kintbury (years since this was last in the Guide – doing well these days, with good food, wines and beer), the cosily old-fashioned Two Brewers in Windsor (good food, with sandwiches not forgotten), and the interestingly decorated Winterbourne Arms at Winterbourne (good value lunches). For a special meal out, the Dundas Arms and Winterbourne Arms, the Horns at Crazies Hill, the restauranty Red House at Marsh Benham and the smart Royal Oak at Yattendon all appeal; it is the Horns at Crazies Hill which gains our title of Berkshire Dining Pub of the Year. Judging by the flow of readers' reports, Berkshire's pubs have been rather over-represented among the main entries in recent editions of the Guide, in comparison with some other counties in the region. So this year we have trimmed the numbers down. But there's no denying that Berkshire has a good many fine pubs, so the Lucky Dip section at the end of the chapter is now particularly strong. Our current pick there would be the Four Points at Aldworth, Flower Pot at Aston, Thatched Tavern at Cheapside (only a lack of reader reports keeping it out of the main entries), Star and Swan both at East Ilsley, White Hart at Hamstead Marshall (too restauranty for the main entries now), Green Man at Hurst, Bird in Hand at Knowl Hill, Union in Old Windsor, Royal Oak at Paley Street, Bull in Sonning and Five Bells at Wickham. Drinks cost far more in Berkshire than most other places, with a pint of beer costing over 20p more than the national average; the Hobgoblin in Reading and the Bell up on the downs at Aldworth both stand out as having much fairer prices, and beer from the local West Berkshire brewery, available much more widely this year, tends to be good value.

ALDWORTH SU5579 Map 2
Bell ★ ♀ ◗ £

A329 Reading—Wallingford; left on to B4009 at Streatley

'It's hard to drag yourself away' writes one reader of this tremendously unspoilt 14th-c country pub, while another refers to it as 'probably the nicest pub in the country'. Superbly run by the same welcoming family for over 200 years, it makes you feel immediately at home, whether you're a walker, part of a family, or lucky enough to be a local. It is simply furnished with benches around the panelled walls, an ancient one-handed clock, beams in the shiny ochre ceiling, and a woodburning stove; rather than a bar counter for service, there's a glass-panelled hatch. The ban on games machines, mobile phones and piped music helps along the convivial atmosphere. The quiet, old-fashioned pub garden is by the village cricket ground, and behind the pub is a paddock with farm animals. Very good value bar food is confined to filled hot crusty rolls such as honey-roast ham, wild mushroom and port pâté, mature cheddar, stilton or brie (£1.80), smoked salmon, crab, tuna or salt beef (£1.95), and ploughman's (from £3 to £5); in winter they have home-made soup (£2.95). Reasonably priced Arkells BBB and Kingsdown are especially well kept alongside, from the local West Berkshire brewery, Old Tyler, Dark Mild, and a monthly guest on handpump (no draught lager); good house wines and winter mulled wine (£1.50). Darts, shove-ha'penny, dominoes, and cribbage. It's worth visiting at Christmas when local mummers perform in the road by the ancient well-head (the shaft is sunk 400 feet through the chalk), while in summer morris dancers visit sometimes. It tends to get busy at weekends; dogs must be kept on leads. *(Recommended by Peter B Brown, Jeremy Woods, Susan and John Douglas, Catherine Pitt, Dick and Madeleine Brown, N Bayley, A P Seymour, Paul Hopton, the Didler, J R Reayer, Anthony Longden, Kevin Thorpe)*

Free house ~ Licensee H E Macaulay ~ Real ale ~ Bar food (11-2.45, 6-10.45; 12-2.45, 7-10.15 Sun) ~ No credit cards ~ (01635) 578272 ~ Children must be well behaved ~ Dogs welcome ~ Open 11-3, 6-11; 12-3, 7-10.30 Sun; closed Mon exc bank hols, 25 Dec

ASHMORE GREEN SU5069 Map 2
Sun in the Wood

NE of Newbury, or off A4 at Thatcham; off A34/A4 roundabout NW of Newbury, via B4009 Shaw Hill, then right into Kiln Road, then left into Stoney Lane after nearly ½ mile; or get to Stoney Lane sharp left off Ashmore Green Road, N of A4 at W end of Thatcham via Northfield Road and Bowling Green Road.

Surrounded by tall trees, this country pub has a great setting, yet it's only a few minutes away from the centre of Newbury. The big woodside garden has plenty of picnic-sets, and there's a play area with slide and climber. Inside, the high-beamed front bar has bare boards on the left, carpet on the right, with a mix of old bucket chairs, padded dining chairs and stripped pews around sturdy tables. It opens into a big back dining area which has the same informal feel, candles on tables, and some interesting touches like the big stripped bank of apothecary's drawers. There's a small conservatory sitting area by the side entrance. The good bar food is deservedly popular and, besides freshly baked lunchtime baguettes (from £3.60, not Sunday), could include starters such as home-made soup (£3.55), smoked haddock florentine (£5.20) or steamed salmon and crab sausage with chardonnay and crab claw sauce (£5.25), and main dishes such as steak and kidney pudding with red onion gravy and bubble and squeak cake (£9.95), chargrilled marinated venison steak with garlic mash and red wine and thyme sauce (£12.95), and grilled bass fillets on a spring onion and smoked haddock fishcake with light lemon sauce (£13.50), while the delicious puddings could be dark chocolate mousse cake and chocolate roulade with white chocolate sauce or lemon tart with lemon sorbet and strawberries (£4.25). They've a children's menu (£4.25), and they do roasts on Sundays; service can sometimes slow when it's very busy. Part of the bar and the restaurant are no smoking. Along with good house wines, they've well kept Wadworths IPA and 6X, and a guest such as Badger Tanglefoot on handpump. More reports please. *(Recommended by June and Robin Savage, Ian Phillips, Mike and Mary Carter)*

Wadworths ~ Tenant Philip Davison ~ Real ale ~ Bar food ~ Restaurant ~ (01635) 42377 ~ Children welcome ~ Open 12-2.30(3 Sat), 6-11; 12-4, 7-10.30 Sun; closed Mon (exc Christmas)

We checked prices with the pubs as we went to press in summer 2003. They should hold until around spring 2004 – when our experience suggests that you can expect an increase of around 10p in the £.

BOXFORD SU4271 Map 2
Bell ♀

Back road Newbury—Lambourn; village also signposted off B4000 between Speen and M4 junction 14

This civilised mock-Tudor inn has an incredible choice of around 60 wines by the glass, and 12 champagnes by the flute. The generously served bar food is another huge draw, and the extensive menu could include sandwiches and toasties (from £3.95), soup (£3.95; with a sandwich £6.25), snacks to share such as vegetable tempura (£5.25), filled baked potatoes (from £6.95), vegetarian mixed grill (£7.95), pizzas made to order (from £7.95), battered haddock or various curries (£8.95), and home-made pies (£9.95); puddings could be chocolate brownie with home-made vanilla ice cream or bread and butter pudding (£4.95). Most people eat in the rather smart, no smoking restaurant area on the left, but you can also dine on the attractive covered and heated terrace (prettily lit at night). The bar is quite long but snug, with a nice mix of racing pictures, old Mercier advertisements, red plush cushions for the mate's chairs, some interesting bric-a-brac, and a coal-effect fire at one end. Changing beers (under light blanket pressure) such as Badger IPA, Bass, Courage Best and Morrells Oxford Blue on handpump, and they stock a wide range of whiskies. Pool, cribbage, shove-ha'penny, and dominoes, plus a fruit machine, TV, and piped music. Service is friendly, and the long-standing landlord skilfully manages to keep a relaxed, country-local atmosphere. The side courtyard has white cast-iron garden furniture. *(Recommended by Sheila and Robert Robinson, Dr P J W Young, Martin and Karen Wake, Dr Paull Khan, John and Tania Wood)*

Free house ~ Licensee Paul Lavis ~ Real ale ~ Bar food ~ Restaurant ~ (01488) 608721 ~ Children in eating area of bar and restaurant ~ Dogs allowed in bar and bedrooms ~ Open 11-3, 6-11; 12-4, 6.30-11 Sun ~ Bedrooms: £40S/£60S

BRAY SU9079 Map 2
Crown

1¾ miles from M4 junction 9; A308 towards Windsor, then left at Bray signpost on to B3028; High Street

Three log fires make this pleasant 14th-c pub especially cosy in winter. Throughout, there are lots of beams (some so low you have to mind your head), and plenty of old timbers conveniently left at elbow height where walls have been knocked through. The partly panelled main bar has a good mix of customers, oak tables, leather-backed armchairs, and a roaring fire. One dining area has photographs of World War II aeroplanes. The emphasis is on the enjoyable (though not cheap) food, and drinkers may have problems finding a seat at busy lunchtimes. Cooked to order, dishes could be home-made soup (£3.95), pâté of the day (£5.85), wild boar sausages with onion gravy and mashed potatoes (£9.75), home-made beef and Guinness pie or coriander and chilli crab cakes with rocket salad and lime and mango dressing (£10.95), oriental warm chicken salad (£11.50), and scotch sirloin steak with green peppercorn sauce (£15.85). They serve well kept Brakspears Special and Courage Best and Directors on handpump, and there's a fair choice of wines; friendly efficient service. In fine weather you can sit at the tables and benches in the attractive, sheltered flagstoned front courtyard (which has a flourishing grape vine), or under cocktail parasols in a large back garden. *(Recommended by Tom and Ruth Rees, John Robertson, Susan and John Douglas, Ian Phillips, Michael Dandy, Bob Turnham, Alison Hayes, Pete Hanlon)*

Scottish Courage ~ Tenants John and Carole Noble ~ Real ale ~ Bar food (not Sun or Mon evenings) ~ Restaurant ~ (01628) 621936 ~ Children in eating area of bar and restaurant ~ Open 11-3, 6-11; 12-3, 7-10.30 Sun; closed 25-26 Dec and 1 Jan

COOKHAM SU8884 Map 2

Bel & the Dragon

High Street; B4447 N of Maidenhead

The three thoughtfully furnished rooms at this bustling old dining pub have comfortable seats, heavy Tudor beams and open fires – quite a contrast to the hand-painted cartoons on the pastel walls and up-to-date low voltage lighting. The interesting, well presented (though not cheap) food is what draws the crowds. Served quickly by the friendly staff (and there are plenty of them), dishes could include soup (£3.95), delicious country breads with roast garlic, olive oil and olives (£4.25), creamy wild mushroom and baby spinach risotto topped with parmesan shavings and crispy pancetta (£6.95), chargrilled chicken skewers wrapped in parma ham with mango salsa (£7.95), chargrilled salmon fillet with sautéed asparagus and basil noodles with saffron and dill butter sauce, slow-roasted lamb shoulder with mashed potatoes and cranberry and orange jus or fried veal escalope with two fried eggs and basil linguini (all £14.95), and chargrilled bass fillets with fennel and green bean salad and red pepper coulis (£17.95). At lunchtime they also do sandwiches and baguettes; readers warn us the dining area can get noisy. Well kept Brakspears Bitter, Courage Best, and Marstons Pedigree are served from the wooden bar counter, and there's a good choice of wines, whiskies, liqueurs and fruit juices. Street parking can be very difficult, though there's a car park on Cookham Moor. The rewarding Stanley Spencer Gallery is almost opposite. *(Recommended by J and B Cressey, Prof H L Freeman, Tracey and Stephen Groves, Mrs Ailsa Wiggans, Paul Humphreys, Susan and John Douglas, Simon Collett-Jones)*

Free house ~ Licensees Andrea Mortimer and Daniel Macdonald ~ Real ale ~ Bar food (12-2.30, 7-10; 12-3, 7-9.30 Sun, not Mother's Day) ~ Restaurant ~ (01628) 521263 ~ Children welcome ~ Dogs allowed in bar ~ Open 11-11; 12-10.30 Sun

CRAZIES HILL SU7980 Map 2

Horns 🍴

From A4, take Warren Row Road at Cockpole Green signpost just E of Knowl Hill, then past Warren Row follow Crazies Hill signposts

Berkshire Dining Pub of the Year

The gentrified country atmosphere at this tiled and whitewashed cottage is helped by the fact that there's no juke box, fruit machine or piped music. The comfortable bars have rugby mementoes on the walls, exposed beams, open fires and stripped wooden tables and chairs, while the no smoking barn room is opened up to the roof like a medieval hall. The new garden bar, with another open fire, gives access to a big landscaped garden, where they've recently put in a play area. The popular bar menu has fresh fish specials from Billingsgate, such as chargrilled tuna steak with lemon and basil butter and poached salmon fillet with creamy white wine and bay leaf sauce (around £13.95). Aside from lunchtime baguettes, other very well prepared dishes could include asparagus and lemon soup (£4.25), bacon salad with avocado, stilton and mushrooms in a special dressing (£5.95), sweet pepper and asparagus pasta bake (£7.25), beef, mushroom and Guinness pie (£7.95), fried calves liver with black pudding and red wine gravy or delicious slow-roasted lamb shoulder with mint and basil gravy (£12.95), and a nicely cooked fillet steak with creamy peppercorn sauce (£15.95); puddings such as apple and cinnamon pie (£4.25). It is essential to book a table at weekends, and it gets particularly busy on Sunday lunchtimes. Well kept Brakspears Bitter, Special, and seasonal ales on handpump; there's also a thoughtful wine list, several malt whiskies, and they make a good bloody mary. *(Recommended by Ian Phillips, Simon Collett-Jones, Guy Charrison, Brian England, Jeremy Woods, J and B Cressey, C A Hall, David Rule, T R and B C Jenkins, Paul Humphreys, Mike and Sue Richardson, June and Robin Savage, John and Penny Spinks)*

Brakspears ~ Tenant A J Hearn ~ Real ale ~ Bar food (not Sun evening) ~ Restaurant ~ (0118) 940 1416 ~ Dogs allowed in bar ~ Open 11.30-2.30(3 Sat), 6-11; 12-5.30, 7-10.30 Sun; closed winter Sun evening

EAST ILSLEY SU4981 Map 2
Crown & Horns 🍺 🛏
Just off A34, about 5 miles N of M4 junction 13

The cosy atmosphere at this well liked old pub really appeals to readers. It's set right in the heart of horse-training country, and the side bar may have locals (including stable lads) poring over the day's races on TV; lots of interesting racing prints and photographs to look at on the walls. Promptly and cheerfully served bar food includes reasonably priced sandwiches, toasties, french bread or baps (from £2.80), and enjoyable dishes such as home-made soup (£3.25), lots of filled baked potatoes (from £4.50), ploughman's (from £5.75), steak and mushroom pie (£6.75), meaty or vegetable lasagne (£7.25), chicken in stilton and mushroom sauce or seafood pancake (£9.95), rump steak (£10.50), and daily specials such as crispy duck salad (£5.95) and lamb noisettes with port sauce and spinach (£10.95); puddings could include toffee apple cheesecake or treacle tart (£3.25). The rambling set of snug beamed rooms is relaxed and unpretentious, with soft lighting, a blazing log fire, tables tucked into intimate corners, and (ideal for a small party) there's a no smoking snug with one big oval table. There are also two more formal dining rooms. Four handpumps serve a wide range of regularly changing and well kept ales such as Black Sheep, Brakspears, Hook Norton Old Hooky and Wadworths 6X; also 160 whiskies from all over the world (some of the bottles have clearly been there for ages). Fruit machine and piped music. Under two chestnut trees, there are tables in the pretty paved stable yard, and the surrounding countryside is laced with tracks and walks. *(Recommended by Ian Phillips, W W Burke, R Huggins, D Irving, E McCall, T McLean, Lynn Sharpless, SLC, Mike and Mary Carter, Gill and Keith Croxton, Tom McLean, Dick and Madeleine Brown, Nigel and Sue Foster, Susan and John Douglas)*

Free house ~ Licensees Chris and Jane Bexx ~ Real ale ~ Bar food (12-2.30, 6-10; not 25 Dec) ~ Restaurant ~ (01635) 281545 ~ Children away from bar ~ Dogs welcome ~ Open 11-11; 12-10.30 Sun ~ Bedrooms: £60S/£70B

FRILSHAM SU5573 Map 2
Pot Kiln ★ 🍺
From Yattendon take turning S, opposite church, follow first Frilsham signpost, but just after crossing motorway go straight on towards Bucklebury ignoring Frilsham signposted right; pub on right after about half a mile

This welcoming brick pub is in a charming rural spot, and picnic-sets in the big suntrap garden have good views of the nearby woods and meadows. There's a buoyant chatty atmosphere in the three basic yet comfortable bar areas, which have wooden floorboards, bare benches and pews, and good winter log fires. It's well run with friendly, efficient staff, and at weekends especially it does get busy. From a hatch in the panelled entrance lobby (which has room for just one bar stool), they serve well kept Brick Kiln Bitter, Dr Hexters Healer and a monthly guest, all from the West Berkshire brewery which started life here at the pub, though it's run separately and has now expanded to a bigger brewhouse up the road in Yattendon; they also have Arkells BBB and Greene King Morlands Original. The public bar has darts, dominoes, shove-ha'penny, table skittles, and cribbage; the back room is no smoking. As well as tasty filled hot rolls (from £2), good home-made soup (£3.25), and ploughman's (from £4), decent straightforward bar food (served with fresh vegetables) could include roast vegetable tart (£7.25), various casseroles (from £7.50), grilled salmon (£8.95), and sirloin steak (£10.70), with puddings such as hot jam sponge pudding (£3.65). On Sundays they serve rolls only. By the time we go to press, they hope to be able to accept credit cards. There are plenty of opportunities for good walks nearby. *(Recommended by Dick and Madeleine Brown, Mick Simmons, the Didler, Richard Gibbs, N Bayley, Mike and Sue Richardson)*

Own brew ~ Licensee Philip Gent ~ Real ale ~ Bar food (not Tues) ~ (01635) 201366 ~ Well behaved children in back room ~ Dogs allowed in bar ~ Irish music first Sun of month ~ Open 12-2.30, 6.30-11; 12-3, 7-10.30 Sun; closed Tues lunchtimes; and 25 Dec, evening 26 Dec

HOLYPORT SU8977 Map 2
Belgian Arms

1½ miles from M4 junction 8/9 via A308(M), A330; in village turn left on to big green, then left again at war memorial (which is more like a bus shelter)

While you relax in this cheery pub's charming garden (which looks out over a duck pond towards the village green), you'll have difficulty believing you're so close to the M4. Readers like the chatty bustling atmosphere here, and the staff are welcoming. The cosy L-shaped, low-ceilinged bar has interesting framed postcards of belgian military uniform and other good military prints, and some cricketing memorabilia on the walls, a china cupboard in one corner, a variety of chairs around a few small tables, and a roaring log fire. Well kept Brakspears Bitter and Special on handpump, and a few good malt whiskies; the bar can get smoky. The straightforward menu includes sandwiches (from £2.50), tasty ploughman's (£4.95), cheesy potato skins with bacon and egg (£5.95), home-made beefburgers (£6.95), chilli con carne, lasagne or pizzas with various toppings (from £6.95), good steaks (from £9.95), and evening dishes such as duck breast with various sauces (£11.95), with puddings (£3.95); they also do a Sunday roast (£8.95). *(Recommended by Alyson and Andrew Jackson, Howard Dell, Julie and Bill Ryan, Simon Collett-Jones, Susan and John Douglas, June and Robin Savage, BKA, Alan and Paula McCully, Mrs G R Sharman, Jeremy Woods, Bob Turnham, Ian Phillips, Anthony Longden, Michael Dandy, Brian England)*

Brakspears ~ Tenant Alfred Morgan ~ Real ale ~ Bar food (12-2, 6.30-9.30; not Sun evening) ~ Restaurant ~ (01628) 634468 ~ Children in eating area of bar ~ Dogs allowed in bar ~ Open 11-3, 5.30(6 Sat)-11; 12-3, 7-10.30 Sun

INKPEN SU3864 Map 2
Crown & Garter 🍺 🛏

Inkpen signposted with Kintbury off A4; in Kintbury turn left into Inkpen Road, then keep on into Inkpen Common

Tucked away up its narrow country lane, this brick-built pub is surprisingly substantial for somewhere so remote-feeling. Dating from the 16th c, it has an appealing low-ceilinged bar, its few black beams liberally draped with hops, and an attractive variety of mainly old prints and engravings on walls painted cream or shades of pink. The relaxed central bar has well kept Arkells Moonlight and West Berkshire Mr Chubbs and Good Old Boy on handpump, and service is friendly and helpful, with a real welcome for families. Three areas radiate from here; perhaps the nicest is the parquet-floored part by the raised log fire, with a couple of substantial old tables, a huge old-fashioned slightly curved settle, and a neat little porter's chair decorated in commemoration of the Battle of Corunna (a favourite seat of the cats – they've three). Other parts are carpeted, with a good mix of well spaced tables and chairs, and nice lighting. A good blackboard choice of reasonably priced home-made food, imaginative without being too way out, includes soup (£3.45), chicken liver parfait with toast and red onion marmalade (£4.45), home-made lasagne (£7.95), gammon and two eggs (£8.45), and steak (from £12.95), with specials such as shepherd's pie or chilli con carne (£7.95), thai marinated tuna steak with noodles and stir-fried vegetables (£8.95), and saddle of rabbit with mustard cream sauce (£9.50), and puddings such as chocolate bread and butter pudding with custard (£3.95). A Friday OAP bargain lunch gives a popular choice of two or three courses (£7.95 or £9.95). The long side garden has picnic-sets and a play area, by shrubs and a big oak tree. The bedrooms are in a separate single-storey building making an L around another pretty garden; this is handy for good downland walks. Please note the opening times; they serve food only to residents Sunday-Tuesday evenings. *(Recommended by Philip Atkins, A P Seymour, Simon Cooke)*

Balaclava Pub Group ~ Licensee Gill Hern ~ Bar food (not evenings Sun-Tues) ~ Restaurant ~ (01488) 668325 ~ Children in eating area of bar and restaurant ~ Dogs allowed in bar ~ Open 12-3, 6.30(6 Sat)-11; 12-3, 7-10.30 Sun; closed Mon and Tues lunchtime ~ Bedrooms: £45B/£65B

KINTBURY SU3866 Map 2
Dundas Arms ♀ 🛏

Village signposted off A4 Newbury—Hungerford; Station Road, before you reach the village itself

This old-fashioned pub depends on its waterside setting for much of its charm – so a visit in summer is especially pleasant, when you can choose between seats on the canalside jetty or the river patio. Built for canal workers in the early 19th c, it stands between the River Kennet and the Kennet & Avon Canal, surrounded by lots of ducks (and in spring banks of daffodils); there's a lock just beyond the hump-backed bridge. Inside, the partly panelled and carpeted bar is popular with locals, and one of the walls has a splendid collection of blue and white plates. They serve well kept Butts Barbus Barbus, Greene King Morlands Original, West Berkshire Good Old Boy and a guest such as Adnams from handpump, and there's a good range of wines. Tasty bar food such as soup (£3.95), ploughman's (£4.95), thai fishcakes with chilli sauce (£4.95), spinach and red pepper lasagne (£7), steak and kidney pie or moroccan spicy lamb casserole (£9.75), and grilled monkfish with crab risotto (£13.95), while puddings could include bread and butter pudding (£4.25); children's meals (£3.95). There's a pleasant evening restaurant. The former barge-horse stables have been converted into comfortable bedrooms, which look out through french windows on to a secluded terrace. *(Recommended by Robin Tandy, Alan and Paula McCully, Ian Walker, Peter and Jean Hoare, Jim Bush, Angus and Rosemary Campbell, Mrs J H S Lang)*

Free house ~ Licensee David Dalzell-Piper ~ Bar food (not Sun, or Mon evening) ~ Restaurant ~ (01488) 658263 ~ Children in eating area of bar ~ Open 11-2.30, 6-11; 12-2.30 Sun; closed Sun evening ~ Bedrooms: /£80B

MARSH BENHAM SU4267 Map 2
Red House 🍴 ♀

Village signposted from A4 W of Newbury

This smartly renovated thatched dining pub is the kind of place you'd come to for a special meal, rather than a quick pint. Their imaginative and modern (but not cheap) menu includes dishes such as tomato and mozzarella tart with pesto dressing or beef carpaccio with rocket and parmesan (£6.95), seared tuna loin marinated in lime, ginger and coriander with lime and coconut risotto (£14.75), roast rack of welsh lamb with artichokes, baby onions, lardons of bacon, and white truffle sauce (£14.95), fried veal escalope with garlic mash and mushroom sauce (£15.25), and fried sea bream with roasted jerusalem artichokes and a red pepper compote, fresh tapenade and lemon oil (£15.50), while puddings could be vanilla crème brûlée or white chocolate and raspberry parfait with passion fruit soufflé and crushed berry sauce (£4.95); vegetables are from £2.50 extra. The comfortable bar has a light stripped wood floor and magenta walls, and a mix of Victorian and older settles. The appealing library-style front restaurant (which is no smoking) is lined with bookcases and hung with paintings. A terrace with teak tables and chairs overlooks the long lawns that slope down to water meadows and the River Kennet. They have good wines, lots of malt whiskies, and quite a few brandies and ports along with Brakspears and Fullers London Pride on handpump; piped music, pleasant service. *(Recommended by C S Samuel, Ian Phillips, T R and B C Jenkins, Colette Annesley-Gamester, Jonathan Harding, Neil and Karen Dignan)*

Free house ~ Licensee Xavier Le-Bellego ~ Real ale ~ Bar food (12-2.15, 7-10) ~ Restaurant ~ (01635) 582017 ~ Children in eating area of bar, must be over 6 in restaurant ~ Open 12-11; 12-2.15 Mon; 12-3.30 Sun; closed Sun and Mon evenings

---

Post Office address codings confusingly give the impression that some pubs are in Berkshire, when they're really in Oxfordshire or Hampshire (which is where we list them).

READING SU7272 Map 2
Hobgoblin ◀

Broad Street

At this basic but cheerful pub, beer mats cover practically every inch of the walls and ceiling of the simple bare-boards bar – a testament to the enormous number of brews that have passed through the pumps over the past few years (around 3,954 at last count). The eight well kept real ales can change by the day, but a typical selection could include Wychwood Fiddlers Elbow and Hobgoblin and West Berkshire Good Old Boy, as well as brews such as Butts Barbus Barbus, Church End Pooh Beer, Fisherrow Mick the Ticks 15,000th Tick, Houston Blonde, Oakleaf Yodel Weiss, Rebellion Round Avoider and West Berkshire Magnificent; ask the friendly, knowledgeable landlord if you're flummoxed by the choice. They also have a good range of bottled beers, czech lager on tap, Weston's farm cider, and country wines. Even though it gets very busy (especially at weekends), the atmosphere is friendly. Up a step is a small seating area, but the best places to sit are the three or four tiny panelled rooms reached by a narrow corridor leading from the bar; cosy and intimate, each has barely enough space for one table and a few chairs or wall seats, but they're very appealing if you're able to bag one; the biggest also manages to squeeze in a fireplace. Please note that they don't do any food at all, and they don't allow children or mobile phones. Piped music (very much in keeping with the rough and ready feel of the place), TV. *(Recommended by Richard Lewis, Catherine Pitt, Bernie Adams, Paul Hopton, R T and J C Moggridge)*

Balaclava Pub Group ~ Manager Paul Campbell ~ Real ale ~ No credit cards ~ (0118) 950 8119 ~ Open 11-11; 12-10.30 Sun

Sweeney & Todd £

10 Castle Street; next to Post Office

Hidden behind a baker's shop, this unusual café cum pub is a pie-lover's paradise. With a variety of imaginative combinations such as partridge and pear, steak and oyster, chicken, honey and mustard, the rugby-influenced five nations (a tasty blend of beef, Guinness, garlic, mustard and leeks), hare and cherry, duck and apricot or goose and gooseberry (all £4), the only problem is choosing which pie to have. Other amazingly good value, generously served food includes soup (£3), a choice of ploughman's (from £3.90), casseroles (£5.70), and roasts (£6.50). Behind the counter and down some stairs in the lively bar (it can get quite noisy), a surprising number of tiny tables squeeze into one long thin room, most of them in rather conspiratorial railway-carriage-style booths separated by curtains, and each with a leather-bound menu to match the leather-cushioned pews. Old prints line the walls, and the colonial-style fans and bare-boards floor enhance the period feel. From the small bar, they serve well kept Adnams Best, Badger Tanglefoot, Wadworths 6X and a changing guest on handpump; also various wines and a range of liqueurs and cigars. You can buy the pies in the shop to take away until 10.30pm (all £2). *(Recommended by Andy and Yvonne Cunningham, Paul Hopton, CMW, JJW, D J and P M Taylor, R T and J C Moggridge, Susan and John Douglas)*

Free house ~ Licensee Mrs C Hayward ~ Real ale ~ Bar food (served all day) ~ Restaurant ~ (0118) 958 6466 ~ Children in restaurant ~ Open 11-11; closed Sun and bank hols

STANFORD DINGLEY SU5771 Map 2
Bull

From M4 junction 12, W on A4, then right at roundabout on to A340 towards Pangbourne; first left to Bradfield, and at crossroads on far edge of Bradfield (not in centre) turn left signposted Stanford Dingley; turn left in Stanford Dingley

The half-panelled lounge bar of this attractive 15th-c brick pub reflects the motorsport and classic car interests of the licensees, and on some summer Saturdays owners of classic cars and motorcycles gather in the grounds. The beamed tap room is firmly divided into two by standing timbers hung with horsebrasses. The main part has an old brick fireplace, cushioned seats carved out of barrels, a window settle, wheelback chairs on the red quarry tiles, and an old station clock; a carpeted section has an exposed wattle and daub wall. Service is excellent, and the atmosphere is welcoming. Reasonably priced for the area, the five well kept real ales on handpump could include Bass, Brakspears Bitter and West Berkshire Good Old Boy, Dr Hexters Healer, and Skiff. Besides well presented lunchtime (and Sunday evening) snacks such as home-made soups (from £3.50), sandwiches or baguettes (from £3.50, toasted 25p extra), ploughman's (£5), and chilli con carne (£7), they do enjoyable daily specials such as oriental pork burger (£8.50), turkey and mushroom pie (£9.50) and monkfish and parma ham in herb sauce (£13). In the evening, the menu could include salmon and broccoli tartlet (£4.50), lamb shank on garlic and rosemary mash (£12) and seared bass with pea mash and lime butter sauce (£14); home-made puddings (£4.25, readers recommend the lime and blackberry brûlée). They also do children's dishes (from £4.50), Sunday roasts (£8), and on Monday nights a two-course oriental special (£10). The dining room (and saloon bar at weekends) is no smoking; ring the bull and piped music. In front of the building are some big rustic tables and benches, and to the side the big garden has plenty of seats. Morris men visit in August and on New Year's Day. *(Recommended by Liz and Brian Barnard, Mr and Mrs S Felstead, Mike and Sue Richardson, Lynn Sharpless, Neil and Karen Dignan)*

Free house ~ Licensees Robert and Kate Archard, Robin and Carol Walker ~ Real ale ~ Bar food (12-2.30, 6.30-9.30; 12-2.30, 7-9 Sun) ~ Restaurant ~ (0118) 974 4409 ~ Children in eating area of bar and restaurant ~ Dogs allowed in bar ~ Open 12-3, 6-11; 12-3, 7-10.30 Sun ~ Bedrooms: £55S(£65B)/£70S(£80B)

Old Boot

Off A340 via Bradfield, coming from A4 just W of M4 junction 12

With pleasant rural views, the tranquil sloping back garden and terrace of this stylish 18th-c pub are good places to relax in fine weather. The neatly kept beamed bar has fine old pews, settles, old country chairs, and tables smelling nicely of good wax polish, attractive fabrics for the old-fashioned wooden-ring curtains, some striking pictures and hunting prints, two welcoming fires (one in an inglenook), and bunches of fresh flowers. Whether you're a local, a visitor or part of a family, you'll be made to feel welcome here. Three well kept beers such as Bass, Brakspears and West Berkshire Good Old Boy on handpump, and (generously poured) good wine. A tempting choice of tasty bar food might include home-made soup (£3.50), filled baguettes (£4.95), various home-made curries and pies or beef stroganoff (£8.50), game pie (£8.95), and fresh battered cod and chips (£9.50), with home-made puddings (£4.50); the dining conservatory is no smoking. There are more tables out in front of the pub too. More reports please. *(Recommended by Dr P J W Young, James Woods, Dick and Madeleine Brown)*

Free house ~ Licensees John and Jeannie Haley ~ Real ale ~ Bar food ~ Restaurant ~ (0118) 974 4292 ~ Children welcome ~ Dogs allowed in bar ~ Open 11-3, 6-11

WEST ILSLEY SU4782 Map 2
Harrow ♀

Signposted at East Ilsley slip road off A34 Newbury—Abingdon

The knocked-through bar of this white-painted village pub has terracotta and green walls, mainly hung with Victorian prints, and a mix of antique oak tables, unpretentious old chairs, and a couple of more stately long settles. Look out for the unusual stripped twin-seated high-backed settle between the log fire and the bow window. Good well presented bar food changes regularly, but could include home-made soup (£4.50), warm goats cheese with black pudding (£4.95), lemon and sun-dried tomato risotto with parmesan shavings (£4.95), home-made pork and leek sausages with wholegrain mustard mash, red cabbage and caramelised onion gravy

(£8.75), lambs liver and bacon topped with black pudding with horseradish mash and red wine gravy (£9.25), salmon and coriander fishcakes on tomato and pesto ragoût with lemon cream sauce (£10.95), and aberdeen angus steak (£13.95) with puddings such as pear and cinnamon crumble or brioche bread and butter pudding with white chocolate ice cream (£4.95); they do lunchtime filled french rolls from Tuesday to Saturday (£5.95). Greene King Abbot, IPA and Morlands Original are well kept on handpump, and there are decent wines. In summer, you can choose between the picnic-sets in the big garden, or the seats under cocktail parasols looking out over the duck pond and cricket green. More reports please. *(Recommended by Ian Phillips, RB)*

Greene King ~ Lease Alan Berry ~ Real ale ~ Bar food ~ Restaurant ~ (01635) 281260 ~ Children in eating area of bar and restaurant ~ Dogs allowed in bar ~ Open 11-3, 6-11; 12-4.30 Sun; closed Sun evening

WINDSOR SU9676 Map 2
Two Brewers ♀ ◖

Park Street, off High Street next to Mews

Rambling around a central servery, each of the three quaint but cosily civilised bare-board rooms at this appealingly old-fashioned pub has a different feel, but all share the same relaxed atmosphere. Our favourite is the red room on the left, with a big armchair and wooden floors, sizeable piles of magazines, and a rarely used, discreetly tucked-away TV. Chalkboards record events of the day in history, and there are distinctive old pews and tables. The back bar leading off has something of a champagne theme; hundreds of corks line the walls, particularly around a big mirror above the fireplace. It's the kind of place where no space is wasted, and there's heaps to look at; around the bar are lots of tickets, for everything from Royal Ascot to the final of *Pop Idol*. The bar on the right has stripped tables, and a stack of daily papers; friendly service, and piped jazz throughout. Although all the tables are given over to diners, it's best to book if you want to eat the good home-made bar food. Besides excellent lunchtime sandwiches (from £4), the menu could include home-made soup (£3), fried brie wedges with cranberry sauce (£4.50), chilli con carne with cheese and sour cream (£7.50), fishcakes or grilled smoked haddock (£8), lamb shank with minted gravy and mashed potato (£8.50), and a choice of Sunday roasts (£7.50). Most dishes have a £1 surcharge in the evening. Well kept Courage Best, Wadworths 6X and a guest such as Marstons Pedigree on handpump. The fairly priced, wide-ranging wine list has several by the glass (including champagne), and they also sell a fine range of havana cigars. Out in front, under an array of hanging baskets, there are a few tables; they provide a big bowl of water for dogs. It's handily situated next to the entrance to Windsor Great Park's Long Walk (plenty of big car parks nearby), and one of the three cosy little rooms has photographs of the neighbours (the Royal Family) passing by on state occasions. Note they don't allow children. *(Recommended by Val Stevenson, Rob Holmes, Ian Phillips, Simon Collett-Jones, R T and J C Moggridge)*

Free house ~ Licensee Robert Gillespie ~ Real ale ~ Bar food (12-2.30, 6.30-10 Mon-Thurs; 12-2.30 Fri; 12-4 wknds) ~ Restaurant ~ (01753) 855426 ~ Dogs welcome ~ Open 11-11; 12-10.30 Sun

WINTERBOURNE SU4572 Map 2
Winterbourne Arms ⑪

3.7 miles from M4 junction 13; A34 S, then cutting across to B4494 Newbury—Wantage from first major slip road, and follow Winterbourne signs

The peaceful view over the rolling fields from the big bar windows of this pleasant countryside pub cleverly avoids the quiet road, which is sunken between the pub's two lawns. In summer, flowering tubs and hanging baskets brighten up the picnic-sets, and there's a big weeping willow in the garden. The bars are interestingly decorated with a collection of old irons around the fireplace, early prints and old photographs of the village, and a log fire; piped music. The little no smoking restaurant area was once a bakery, and you can still see the original bread ovens. Excellent value lunchtime bar food includes sandwiches (made with home-baked bread; £4.75), roasted vegetable gateau with avocado and herb salad (£4.50), beer-battered cod fillets (£6.50), juicy pork and leek sausage with butternut squash mash and onion gravy (£6.95), and steak, mushroom and ale pie (£7.50); mouth-watering dishes (from the evening à la carte menu) could include good home-made tomato and chilli soup (£3.50), home-made king prawn spring rolls with spicy tomato relish (£6.50), grilled swordfish steak (£12.50), and seared duck breast on a sweet potato and savoy cabbage rösti with fresh mango compote (£14.95), and puddings such as home-made fruit cheesecake (£4.75). They've a decent wine list (served in elegant glasses), and West Berkshire Good Old Boy is well kept on handpump alongside a couple of guests such as Greene King Old Speckled Hen and Wadworths 6X; the staff are helpful. It's in a charming spot, and there are nearby walks to Snelsmore and Donnington. *(Recommended by John Hale, Maysie Thompson, John and Judy Saville, Bob and Maggie Atherton, Paul Humphreys, Evelyn and Derek Walter, R T and J C Moggridge, Mrs S Fry, Philip Meek, Alan and Paula McCully, Sharon and Alan Corper, W W Burke)*

Free house ~ Licensee Claire Owens ~ Real ale ~ Bar food ~ Restaurant ~ (01635) 248200 ~ Children in restaurant ~ Dogs allowed in bar ~ Open 12-3, 6-11; 12-3 Sun; closed Sun evening, all day Mon – exc bank hols

WOODSIDE SU9270 Map 2
Rose & Crown

Woodside Road, Winkfield; A332 Ascot—Windsor, about ½ mile N of A330 roundabout, turn left down small lane, then bear right through village

There's an appealingly thriving atmosphere in this attractive white dining pub, handy for Ascot. The low-beamed bar has been extended and refurbished, giving more seating in the no smoking dining area. Although most of these tables are set for diners, it's still somewhere that regulars drop into for a drink, and on a big race day you'll probably find a lively group in a corner around the TV; the licensees are friendly. Popular well presented bar food includes lunchtime sandwiches and filled baguettes (£3.95), home-made pie of the day or lasagne (£6.95), and rib-eye steak (£8.95), with evening dishes such as beef chilli with cheese, bangers and mash or home-made fishcakes (£6.95), or you can choose from the more elaborate restaurant menu, which contains dishes such as thai spiced king prawns with asian salad and thai dressing (£6.95), wild mushroom risotto (£9.95), fish mixed grill (£13.95), and roast duck breast with fondant potatoes, braised sweet red cabbage and red onion, with roast garlic jus (£14.95); puddings could include fresh raspberries and cream or home-made apple pie (£3.75). Well kept Greene King IPA and Morlands Original and a guest such as Charles Wells Bombardier on handpump; piped music and fruit machine. The side garden has tables and a swing, and the setting backed by woodland is peaceful and pretty. *(Recommended by Bob Turnham, John and Glenys Wheeler, Alistair Forsyth, Andy and Yvonne Cunningham, Richard Marjoram, Bob and Margaret Holder)*

Greene King ~ Tenant Mr Morris ~ Real ale ~ Bar food (12-2.30, 7-9.30; Sun 12-4, not Mon evenings) ~ Restaurant (evening) ~ (01344) 882051 ~ Children in eating area of bar ~ Open 11-11; 12-7 Sun; closed Sun evening

YATTENDON SU5574 Map 2
Royal Oak ♀ 🍽

The Square; B4009 NE from Newbury; turn right at Hampstead Norreys, village signposted on left

The panelled and prettily decorated brasserie/bar is a good place to enjoy the well prepared food at this handsome and rather upmarket inn; there's a marvellous log fire and striking flower arrangements, and the atmosphere is relaxed. In summer, you can eat at tables in the pleasant walled garden, and there are more in front by the quiet and appealing village square. The imaginative menu could include soup

(£4.25), smoked salmon canelloni with a quail egg (£5.95), baked cod with bubble and squeak (£13.50), smoked haddock kedgeree with a poached egg and curry cream (£13.75), roast loin of pork with fondant potatoes, carrot purée and a morrel mushroom jus with chervil oil or goats cheese salad (£14.50), puddings such as vanilla crème brûlée with compote of rhubarb and shortcake biscuit (from £5.99); vegetables are extra. It's best to book for the (more expensive) no smoking restaurant. Well kept real ales such as West Berkshire Good Old Boy and Wadworths 6X, and a good wine list; piped music. Some of the attractive, well appointed bedrooms (not cheap) overlook the garden. The pretty village is one of the few still privately owned, and poet Robert Bridges once lived here. More reports please. (Recommended by W K Wood, the Didler, Peter B Brown, Neil and Karen Dignan)

Regal-Corus ~ Manager Corinne Macrae ~ Real ale ~ Bar food ~ Restaurant ~ (01635) 201325 ~ Children in eating area of bar ~ Dogs allowed in bar and bedrooms ~ Open 11-11; 11-10.30 Sun ~ Bedrooms: £105B/£130B

Lucky Dip

Besides the fully inspected pubs, you might like to try these Lucky Dips recommended to us and described by readers (if you do, please send us reports: www.goodguides.com).

ALDWORTH [SU5579]
☆ *Four Points* [B4009 towards Hampstead Norreys]: Doing well under current welcoming regime, with good value home-made food from baguettes up, well kept Adnams Best and Wadworths 6X, quick service, tidy array of polished tables in long low-beamed bar and dining area partly divided by standing timbers, no piped music, games room; children very welcome, neat garden over road (Pat and Robert Watt, LYM, Michael and Jenny Back, Tim and Carolyn Lowes)

ASTON [SU7884]
☆ *Flower Pot* [small signpost off A4130 Henley—Maidenhead at top of Remenham Hill]: Roomy old-fashioned two-bar pub with lots of picnic-sets giving quiet country views from nice big orchard garden (dogs allowed there), side field with chickens, ducks and guinea fowl; well kept Brakspears inc a seasonal beer, good unusual reasonably priced food from sandwiches to lots of fish and game in season, cheerful welcoming staff, endless stuffed fish and other river-inspired decorations in bright bare-boards public bar and (children allowed here) bigger blue-carpeted saloon, tiled-floor adult dining area; may be unobtrusive piped music, friendly siamese cats and spaniel, busy with walkers and families wknds, when service can slow (Simon Collett-Jones, Michael Porter, Mike and Sue Richardson, M Borthwick, Brian England, BB, Mark Percy, Lesley Mayoh)

BEECH HILL [SU6964]
☆ *Elm Tree* [3½ miles from M4 junction 11: A33 towards Basingstoke, turning off into Beech Hill Rd after about 2 miles]: Five carefully decorated rooms, one with dozens of clocks, hollywood photographs and a woodburner, nice views especially from conservatory, barn-style restaurant, enjoyable generous food (all day wknds) from toasties and baked potatoes to alluring puddings, well kept Fullers London Pride, Greene King IPA and Old Speckled Hen and a guest beer, quick service; children welcome away from bar; benches and tables on front terrace, open all day (Michael Dandy, LYM, Neil and Karen Dignan)

BINFIELD [SU8271]
Bullfinch [B3034 W]: Effectively refurbished, with attentive friendly staff, enjoyable food with good interesting choice, Adnams Broadside, Fullers London Pride, good house wines and coffee; plenty of garden tables (Ian and Barbara Rankin)
Stag & Hounds [B3034]: Comfortable 14th-c pub, often very busy (food service may take a while), with interesting array of low-beamed bars inc large no smoking room, open fires, antiques, brass, wide changing food choice, well kept ales such as Courage Best and Directors, Theakstons XB and Wadworths 6X, decent wines, friendly young staff, daily papers; piped music; children allowed in eating area, tables out on front terrace and in back garden (Andy and Yvonne Cunningham, Joy and Harold Dermott, LYM, Lesley and Peter Barrett, Ian and Barbara Rankin)

BRAY [SU9079]
☆ *Hinds Head* [High St]: Handsome Tudor beams and panelling, sturdy oak furniture, leather porter's chairs and other comfortable seating, two blazing log fires, plenty of memorabilia and nice pictures, good helpings of decent food from sandwiches, baguettes and baked potatoes up, well kept Greene King IPA and Old Speckled Hen and a guest beer, good wines, friendly locals and staff, upstairs restaurant; tables on suntrap front terrace (Peter and Giff Bennett, LYM, John and Glenys Wheeler, Michael Dandy)

BURCHETTS GREEN [SU8381]
☆ *Crown* [side rd from A4 after Knowl Green on left, linking to A404]: Comfortable restauranty dining bar with high-backed chairs and soft piped music, very wide choice of generous if not cheap mainstream food (service charge added), very small plain bar with one or two

tables for casual customers, well kept Bass and Greene King IPA, lots of wines by the glass, chirpy service; friendly cats, tables out in pleasant quiet garden *(Jeremy Woods, Brian Root, T R and B C Jenkins, Joan Thorpe, DHV, Simon Collett-Jones, Paul Humphreys, LYM, Stephen and Jean Curtis)*

CHEAPSIDE [SU9469]

☆ *Thatched Tavern* [off A332/A329, then off B383 at Village Hall sign]: Civilised dining pub with big inglenook, low beams and polished flagstones in cottagey core, three smart dining rooms off with deep carpet, crisp linen and big church candles, good interesting up-to-date food priced as you'd expect in this prime spot so handy for Virginia Water, friendly service, well kept Brakspears, Courage Best and Fullers London Pride, lots of wines, daily papers, no games or piped music; children in restaurant, rustic tables on attractive sheltered back lawn, open all day wknds *(Andy and Yvonne Cunningham, LYM, John and Joyce Snell)*

CHIEVELEY [SU4773]

☆ *Olde Red Lion* [handy for M4 junction 13 via A34 N-bound; Green Lane]: Bustling local with good value straightforward food (Weds steak night, Thurs fish and chip night), helpful staff, well kept Arkells beers, comfortable low-beamed L-shaped bar with well worn furnishings, lots of brasses around walls, couple of old sewing machines, roaring log fire, back restaurant; piped music, fruit machine, pool, TV; parking immediately outside can be a squeeze – easier in overflow opp *(R T and J C Moggridge, BB)*

COOKHAM DEAN [SU8785]

☆ *Uncle Toms Cabin* [off A308 Maidenhead—Marlow; Hills Lane, towards Cookham Rise and Cookham]: Snug and unpretentious low-beamed local with old-fashioned furnishings and a coal fire in its small rooms, long a main entry, but as we went to press plans were uncertain following the landlord's recent death; it's had tasty and sensibly priced pubby bar food from sandwiches to steaks, well kept Brakspears, Fullers London Pride and a guest beer, and pub games; children in eating areas, attractive sheltered sloping back garden, open all day Sun and perhaps summer Sats *(Brian Root, David Tindal, Paul Humphreys, John and Glenys Wheeler, Tracey and Stephen Groves, LYM)*

COOKHAM RISE [SU8885]

Old Swan Uppers [B4447 Cookham—Maidenhead]: Flagstones, low beams, log fire and a real unspoilt feel; friendly management, good range of real ales, bar food, restaurant, unobtrusive piped music; bedrooms *(David Tindal, LYM)*

CURRIDGE [SU4871]

☆ *Bunk* [3 miles from M4 junction 13: A34 towards Newbury, then first left to Curridge, Hermitage, and left into Curridge at Village Only sign]: More restaurant than pub, with wide choice of interesting food (not cheap, not Sun evening), four well kept ales inc Fullers London Pride, good choice of wines, buoyant atmosphere, smart stripped-wood tiled-floor

bar, dining conservatory overlooking meadows and woods; tables in neat garden, fine woodland walks nearby *(Angus and Rosemary Campbell, J R Reayer, BB, Peter and Jean Hoare, Neil and Karen Dignan)*

EAST ILSLEY [SU4980]

☆ *Star* [leaving village southwards]: Partly 15th-c, attractively and comfortably refurbished for even more of a sense of welcome, with good value fresh traditional food in dining room, bar with beams and black woodwork, well kept Brakspears and Fullers London Pride, good choice of other drinks, welcoming new licensees, inglenook log fire, books, board games and shove-ha'penny; children and dogs welcome, garden behind with picnic-sets and play area, good well uprated bedrooms *(Edward and Ava Williams, BB, Stan Edwards, Lisa-Marie Hunter)*

☆ *Swan* [High St]: Spacious, neat and well decorated dining pub, with civilised layout and pleasantly informal atmosphere, wide range of good bar food inc interesting vegetarian dishes, friendly attentive service, well kept Greene King IPA and Abbot, daily papers; no smoking restaurant, busy with families Sun – best to book; tables in courtyard and walled garden with play area, excellent bedrooms, some in house down road *(Stan Edwards, LYM, Val and Alan Green, David Crook)*

ETON [SU9677]

George [High St]: Recently refurbished with new furniture on stripped wood floor, efficient quick service, Brakspears, Fullers London Pride and Wadworths 6X, good choice of wine, food from lunchtime sandwiches and burgers up *(Michael Dandy)*

☆ *Gilbeys* [High St]: Not a pub, but well worth knowing for good imaginative home-cooked light bar meals, nice sensibly priced house wines, friendly unstuffy family service; can be very busy if there's an event at the school, best to book for light and airy back restaurant down long corridor *(Mike and Sue Richardson, Terence Boley, BB)*

FARLEY HILL [SU7564]

Fox & Hounds [Church Rd]: Unspoilt beamed and flagstoned village local with well kept Greene King and guest ales, young welcoming landlord, usual food lunchtime and Thurs-Sat evening, log fire, dogs and walkers welcome (good walks nearby), skittle alley; soft piped music, can get smoky when crowded *(Mr and Mrs R Drury)*

FINCHAMPSTEAD [SU7963]

Queens Oak [Church Lane]: Good value food in bar and separate restaurant (where children allowed), pleasant helpful staff, particularly well kept Brakspears ales, no smoking area; garden with play area and Sun lunchtime barbecues *(Andy and Yvonne Cunningham, June and Robin Savage)*

GREAT SHEFFORD [SU3875]

Swan [2 miles from M4 junction 14 – A338 towards Wantage]: Low-ceilinged bow-windowed pub now part of new small chain (formed by one of the Eldridge Pope family), popular food (not Tues evening, and stops promptly at lunchtime) from baguettes up, well kept real ale, good wine choice, civil attentive service, good log fire, daily papers and magazines, river-view restaurant; good wheelchair access, children in eating areas, tables on quiet waterside lawn and terrace *(A and B D Craig, Sebastian Leach, M J Park, Jill McLaren, Gerald Wilkinson, Andy and Yvonne Cunningham, Pauline and Philip Darley, Pamela and Merlyn Horswell, Michael Cross, Mayur Shah, LYM, Dick and Madeleine Brown)*

HALFWAY [SU4068]

☆ *Halfway Inn* [A4 Hungerford—Newbury]: Nicely done Badger dining pub named for its position between London and Bath, with daily papers and log fire in attractive rambling traditional bar, softly lit well divided back dining area, wide choice of enjoyable imaginative food from lunchtime ciabattas and baked potatoes up, fresh veg, good children's dishes (and children's helpings of most main ones), well kept Best and Tanglefoot, good range of wines and beers, friendly helpful staff, log fire; may be faint piped pop music; picnic-sets on side terrace and neat back lawn *(Peter Scillitoe, Meg and Colin Hamilton, BB)*

HAMPSTEAD NORREYS [SU5376]

White Hart [Church St]: Low-beamed local under very friendly new management, easy chairs and sofa around the fire, good range of blackboard food, good-sized dining area, well kept real ales; children welcome, darts, pool and fruit machine in well patronised public bar, back terrace and garden *(Stan Edwards)*

HAMSTEAD MARSHALL [SU4165]

☆ *White Hart* [off A4 W of Newbury]: Long a main entry, with good service and good authentic italian food (not Sun) using home-grown herbs and sometimes vegetables, this comfortable place now doesn't serve drinks unless you eat, so can't really qualify any more as a pub, but does have Hook Norton Best and Wadworths 6X alongside decent italian wines, and a log fire; children welcome, no smoking restaurant, pretty tree-sheltered walled garden, quiet and comfortable beamed bedrooms in a converted barn, cl 2 wks in summer *(Alistair Forsyth, Ian Phillips, LYM, Neil and Karen Dignan)*

HARE HATCH [SU8077]

☆ *Queen Victoria* [Blakes Lane; just N of A4 Reading—Maidenhead]: Two relaxed and chatty low-beamed and panelled bars with nice décor and friendly local atmosphere, enjoyable fairly priced food from sandwiches up, well kept Brakspears PA, SB, Old and a seasonal beer, a fair choice of wines by the glass, cheerful helpful service, pub games, flower-filled no smoking conservatory; children in eating area, one or two tables outside, open all day Sun *(Lesley Bass, Tom Evans, LYM, Doreen and Haydn Maddock, Rona Murdoch)*

HUNGERFORD [SU3368]

Bear [3 miles from M4 junction 14; town signed at junction]: Jarvis hotel worth knowing for varied, reasonably priced and plentiful bar food, pleasant period atmosphere, fantastic huge clock, open fires, well kept real ales such as Wadworths 6X, efficient service; restaurant, bedrooms comfortable and attractive *(LYM, Meg and Colin Hamilton)*

John o' Gaunt [Bridge St (A338)]: Comfortable, attractive and restful, with good choice of food from cold or hot baguettes up, helpful staff, Greene King IPA, Abbot and Ruddles, decent daily papers; quiet piped music; pleasant small outside seating area with play things *(Ken Flawn, LYM, Ian Phillips, Meg and Colin Hamilton)*

HURLEY [SU8183]

Black Boy [A4130 E of Henley]: Old-fashioned cottagey pub concentrating on freshly cooked food (not cheap but enjoyable) from sandwiches up; a few tables for drinkers, with very well kept Brakspears PA, Mild and SB, decent house wines, friendly atmosphere, open fire; picnic-sets in garden by paddock (road noise), walks to Thames *(K Drane, Bob and Laura Brock, John and Glenys Wheeler, Jeremy Woods)*

Dew Drop [small yellow sign to pub off A4130 just W]: Two crisply refurbished bars in country pub tucked away in nice rustic setting, popular food from sandwiches (not Sun) to enjoyable meals, well kept Brakspears PA, SB and seasonal ales, quite a few malt whiskies, darts, shove-ha'penny, backgammon and dominoes; children in eating area, french windows to courtyard and attractive sloping garden with barbecue, good walks *(LYM, John and Glenys Wheeler, Jeremy Woods)*

Red Lion [A4130 SE, just off A404]: Comfortable Vintage Inn recently refurbished with four separate areas and neat bar, two log fires, amiable service, decent food from sandwiches and generous starters to steak and bass, Bass, good wine choice; picnic-sets in garden behind *(Michael Dandy)*

HURST [SU8074]

☆ *Green Man* [Hinton Rd, off A321 just outside village]: Softly lit cosily old-fashioned low-beamed bar with log fires, snug little lower room with just four tables, lighter and airier no smoking area, wide range of enjoyable well prepared blackboard food, well kept Brakspears, good choice of wines by the glass, pleasant service, pub games; cast-iron tables out on heated terrace, picnic-sets in attractive garden under big oak trees, sturdy play area *(Peter Needham, Richard Endacott, D J and P M Taylor, BB)*

INKPEN [SU3564]

☆ *Swan* [Lower Inkpen; coming from A338 in Hungerford, take Park St (first left after railway bridge, coming from A4)]: Rambling beamed country pub with cosy corners, three log fires, Butts, Hook Norton and organic Caledonian Golden Promise, local farm cider, organic wines and champagne, home-made sloe gin, and organic produce featuring strongly in the food, from sandwiches and pubby food to more ambitious restaurant dishes – the farming owners have an organic shop next door; flagstoned games room, piped music; well behaved children welcome in eating areas, picnic-sets out in front, small quiet garden, well equipped bedrooms, open all day in summer *(Lynn Sharpless, Alan and Paula McCully, Alan and Gill Bull, David Crook, Mrs Romey Heaton, Pat and Tony Martin, Betsy and Peter Little, LYM, Bill and Jessica Ritson)*

KNOWL HILL [SU8178]

☆ *Bird in Hand* [A4, quite handy for M4 junction 8/9]: Relaxed civilised atmosphere and good home-made food even Sun evening from sandwiches and baguettes up (two big bright menu boards, also fixed price buffet) in spacious beamed main bar and restaurant; splendid log fire, cosy alcoves, much older side bar; well kept Braxspears and Fullers London Pride, good wines by the glass, good choice of other drinks, polite efficient staff in colourful waistcoats, no smoking buffet area – where children allowed; tables out on new front terrace, clean and tidy modern bedrooms *(Mrs E A Macdonald, Ron and Sheila Corbett, Simon Collett-Jones, June and Robin Savage, LYM)*

LAMBOURN [SU3278]

George [Market Pl]: Unpretentious old pub with plenty of character, cheap food, well kept Arkells, friendly efficient service *(John Brightley)*

Hare & Hounds [Lambourn Woodlands, well S of Lambourn itself]: Smart but friendly dining pub with several nicely individual rooms, lunchtime food from filled baguettes to aberdeen angus steak, more elaborate evening menu inc seasonal local game, well kept Wadworths IPA or 6X and a guest beer, nice wines; piped music; children welcome, garden behind with decent play area, cl Sun evening *(Peter Wrobbel, John and Judy Saville, M Hounsell, LYM)*

MAIDENHEAD [SU8881]

Hand & Flowers [Queen St]: Lively bar, straightforwardly old-fashioned despite the chocolate-and-mirrors décor and bare boards, noisily chatty (not just the parrot), with well kept Braxspears, decent wine choice and coffee, various cocktails, interesting lunchtime food, friendly prompt service; soft piped music *(Simon Collett-Jones)*

MIDGHAM [SU5566]

Coach & Horses [Bath road (N side)]: Friendly comfortably refurbished main-road pub with helpful licensees, masses of bric-a-brac from safes and brassware to masks and spears from New Zealand, wide choice of reasonably priced food from lunchtime sandwiches up, Fullers London Pride and West Berkshire Good Old Boy; garden behind *(BB, Ian Phillips)*

NEWBURY [SU4767]

☆ *Lock Stock & Barrel* [Northbrook St]: Popular modern pub standing out for canalside setting, with suntrap balcony and terrace looking over a series of locks towards handsome church; clean and spacious wood-floored bar with antique-effect lights and fittings, and quite a sunny feel – lots of windows; good choice of reasonably priced food all day, well kept Fullers beers, plenty of newspapers, lots of tables and chairs; no smoking back bar; busy with young crowds at wknds, upstairs lavatories; canal walks *(BB, Charles and Pauline Stride)*

OAKLEY GREEN [SU9276]

Olde Red Lion [B3024 just W of Windsor]: Cosy old low-beamed dining pub with good interesting reasonably priced food from wide sandwich range up, welcoming helpful staff, Bass, Courage Best and Flowers IPA in small bar, mix of seating from homely old chairs to trendy modern ones; comfortable bedrooms, good breakfast, pleasant garden *(Susan and John Douglas, June and Robin Savage, Simon Collett-Jones)*

OLD WINDSOR [SU9874]

Jolly Gardeners [St Lukes Rd]: Good value food in unpretentious friendly local, real ale inc a Mild, pleasant service *(R A Watson)*

☆ *Union* [Crimp Hill Rd, off B3021 – itself off A308/A328]: Friendly and comfortable old pub, good traditional bar food from sandwiches up, well kept ales such as Braxspears SB, Courage Best and Fullers London Pride or Marstons Pedigree, consistently good service from long-serving staff, log fire in big fireplace, lots of black and white show-business photographs, bank notes on beams, good value attractive copper-decorated restaurant; soft piped music, fruit machine; white plastic tables under cocktail parasols on sunny front terrace (heated in cooler weather), country views; comfortable bedrooms with own bathrooms *(BB, Ian Phillips, Jeremy Woods, Gordon Prince, Susan and John Douglas)*

PALEY STREET [SU8676]

☆ *Royal Oak* [B3024 W]: Friendly and obliging service in simply but stylishly refurbished restaurant pub, well kept Fullers London Pride and good wide choice of wines by the glass (vintage port at a price), good food, smallish front part by bar with easy chairs and piano, pleasantly relaxed gingham-and-linen country eating area stretching back with bare boards, flagstones and some stripped brick, cricketing prints mixed with photographs of celebrity friends of landlord's father Michael Parkinson; piped jazz *(Simon Collett-Jones, Susan and John Douglas, Bob and Maggie Atherton, BB)*

PANGBOURNE [SU6376]

Swan [Shooters Hill]: Attractive pub dating from 17th c and worth knowing for its Thames-side location, with picnic-sets on terrace overlooking the weir and moorings, river-view dining balcony and conservatory (food all day); Greene King ales, decent wines, piped music, sports TV *(Hugh Spottiswoode, Roger and Pauline Pearce)*

READING [SU7272]

☆ *Fishermans Cottage* [Kennet Side – easiest to walk from Orts Rd, off Kings Rd]: Friendly local in nice spot by canal lock and towpath (gasometer view), with waterside tables, lovely big back garden and light and airy conservatory; modern furnishings of character, pleasant stone snug behind woodburning range, good value lunches inc lots of hot or cold sandwiches (very busy then but service quick), full Fullers beer range kept well, small choice of wines, small darts room, SkyTV; dogs allowed (not in garden) *(R T and J C Moggridge, the Didler)*

George [Loddon bridge, Earley; A329 E towards Wokingham]: Well run Chef & Brewer with good choice of enjoyable food inc impressive specials, friendly helpful staff, well kept beer; waterside setting by River Loddon *(Andy and Yvonne Cunningham, Gerald Wilkinson)*

Griffin [Church Rd, Caversham]: Roomy chain dining pub with good varied blackboard choice, Courage, Theakstons and a guest beer, good friendly service, separate areas with several log fires; tables in courtyard, beautiful spot on Thames overlooking swan sanctuary *(Chris and Jo Nicholls, Tony and Wendy Hobden)*

REMENHAM [SU7682]

Little Angel [A4130, just over bridge E of Henley]: Good atmosphere in low-beamed dining pub popular with business people, attractive panelled restaurant area with darkly bistroish décor and extension into big mexican-theme conservatory, small simple front bar, enjoyable food from tapas and steak sandwich up, friendly helpful unhurried service, splendid range of wines by the glass, well kept Brakspears PA; floodlit terrace *(Rob Jarvis, Michael Dandy, LYM)*

SHINFIELD [SU7367]

Magpie & Parrot [A327 S; handy for M4 junction 11, via B3270]: Endearing combination of pub and nursery, homely beamed bar with Fullers London Pride, no food or music, charming landlady and chatty locals, settee and comfortable chairs (one for Spencer the dog), open fire, old beer posters, paintings for sale, model cars, gramophone, and old bottles; bird-filled garden, open 12-7, Sun 12-3 *(Kevin Thorpe)*

SHURLOCK ROW [SU8274]

Royal Oak [Hungerford Lane]: Unpretentious décor like a homely dining room, enjoyable food inc all-year plum pudding, well kept beer *(Andy and Yvonne Cunningham)*

SONNING [SU7575]

☆ *Bull* [off B478, by church; village signed off A4 E of Reading]: Attractive old-fashioned inn in pretty setting nr Thames, low heavy beams, cosy alcoves, cushioned antique settles and low-slung chairs, inglenook fireplaces, no smoking back dining area (children allowed), well kept Gales GB, HSB and Butser and a guest such as Fullers London Pride, lots of country wines, separate ordering for pricy bar lunches from baguettes and baked potatoes to steaks (they may try to keep your credit card), charming courtyard; open all day summer wknds, bedrooms *(John and Glenys Wheeler, Ian Phillips, LYM, DHV, Val Stevenson, Rob Holmes, Paul Humphreys, Tim and Jane Charlesworth)*

STRATFIELD MORTIMER [SU6764]

☆ *Fox & Horn* [The Street; 4 miles W of A33]: Good unusual changing food from light lunches up, inc some inspired puddings, in roadside pub done up for dining by Californian licensees, largely dark green and buff décor, open-plan big-windowed front bar with log fire, well kept Fullers London Pride, Hook Norton Best and Wadworths 6X, good choice of wines in big glasses, espresso machine, comfortable two-room no smoking restaurant; may be piped music; tables on lawn neat as a bowling green *(Richard Foskett, Stephanie Lang, BB, Ian Phillips)*

SUNNINGHILL [SU9367]

Dog & Partridge [Upper Village Rd]: Well kept beer, good range of wines and enjoyable reasonably priced food in newly refurbished local *(Ron and Pam Higgins)*

SWALLOWFIELD [SU7264]

Crown [The Street]: Well kept Greene King Morlands and a guest beer, well priced pub food, friendly service, good local atmosphere *(R T and J C Moggridge)*

☆ *George & Dragon* [Church Rd, towards Farley Hill]: Relaxed cottagey dining pub with stripped beams, red walls, rugs on flagstones and big log fire, plenty of character and atmosphere, food using fresh seasonal produce and normally hitting the mark with good interesting recipes, well kept Fullers London Pride and one or two other beers such as Flowers IPA, good wines; service by welcoming and charming young staff can be erratic or slow, piped music; well behaved children welcome, open all day *(Andy and Debs Thorne, KC, Robert F Smith, Susan and John Douglas, Ian Phillips, J R Reayer, LYM, M J Bastin)*

THEALE [SU6168]

Winning Hand [A4 W, opp Sulhamstead turn]: Friendly pub with good service, well kept Arkells and Hook Norton, varied wine list, wide choice of enjoyable food from sandwiches, baguettes and light meals to very substantial dishes, restaurant; quiet piped music; bright gardens, four bedrooms *(Mike and Sue Richardson, Geoff Palmer)*

WALTHAM ST LAWRENCE [SU8376]

☆ *Bell*: Handsome heavy-beamed and timbered village pub with big sofa, daily papers and log fire in panelled lounge, no smoking front snug, cheery local public bar, two well kept West Berkshire beers and three interesting guests, plenty of malt whiskies, good wine, good value bar food (not Sun evening) from sandwiches up; children in eating areas and family room, tables in back garden with extended terrace, open all day *(LYM, Prof Chris Bucke, John and Judy Saville, Paul Humphreys, June and Robin Savage, Tracey and Stephen Groves)*

WARGRAVE [SU7878]

☆ *Bull* [off A321 Henley—Twyford; High St]: Good friendly atmosphere in cottagey low-beamed two-bar pub popular for interesting and enjoyable food esp good value lunchtime filled baguettes and hot dishes, well kept Brakspears, good wine choice, friendly staff, good log fires; tables on neat partly covered terrace, bedrooms *(LYM, Paul Humphreys, Michael Dandy)*

St George & Dragon [High St]: Large pleasant Vintage Inn, decent food inc smaller dishes, friendly service; attractive terrace overlooking Thames *(J and B Cressey)*

WICKHAM [SU3971]

☆ *Five Bells* [3 miles from M4 junction 14, via A338, B4000; Baydon Rd]: Neatly kept local in racehorse-training country, big log fire, tables tucked into low eaves, inviting good value food from generous baguettes up, well kept ales inc Greene King Old Speckled Hen and Ringwood, friendly landlord, good lunchtime mix from regulars to family groups; children in eating area, garden with good play area and rabbit hutches, good value bedrooms *(LYM, Esther and John Sprinkle)*

WINNERSH [SU7870]

☆ *Wheelwrights Arms* [off A329 Reading—Wokingham at Winnersh crossroads by Sainsbury's, signed Hurst, Twyford; then right into Davis Way]: Traditional beamed bar with big woodburner, bare black boards and flagstones, cheerful and bustling local atmosphere (can be a bit smoky by bar), well kept Wadworths IPA and 6X, good guest beers, enjoyable lunchtime food from huge doorstep sandwiches up, quick friendly service, cottagey no smoking dining area; picnic-sets in smallish garden with terrace, disabled parking

and facilities *(John Baish, June and Robin Savage, D J and P M Taylor, BB)*

WOKINGHAM [SU8168]

Broad Street Tavern [Broad St]: Old building smartly but not over-trendily done up with stripped wood, good range of filling lunchtime food, well kept Wadworths IPA, 6X and guest beers tapped from the cask, low prices, very friendly service, nice local atmosphere, quarterly beer festivals *(Dr and Mrs A K Clarke, Matthew Shackle)*

Crooked Billet [Honey Hill]: Busy country pub with pews, tiles, brick serving counter, crooked black joists, generous enjoyable plain lunchtime food, well kept Brakspears ales; nice outside in summer, very busy wknds *(Andy and Yvonne Cunningham, LYM, Dr and Mrs Jackson)*

WOODSIDE [SU9271]

Duke of Edinburgh [Woodside Rd, off A332 Windsor—Ascot S of B3034]: Busy local with wide choice of reasonably priced meals and snacks, well kept Arkells 2B, 3B and Kingsdown, cheerful welcoming service; quiz night, children welcome, tables in pleasant garden *(John Hale)*

WRAYSBURY [TQ0074]

Perseverance [High St]: Friendly staff, comfortable bar areas, enjoyable sensibly priced food here or in small restaurant, quick service, real ale; tables in back garden *(Mrs W Mabilat)*

Real ale to us means beer which has matured naturally in its cask – not pressurised or filtered. We name all real ales stocked. We usually name ales preserved under a light blanket of carbon dioxide too, though purists – pointing out that this stops the natural yeasts developing – would disagree (most people, including us, can't tell the difference!)

Buckinghamshire

Though this is a smart county, it has a good many properly pubby unspoilt traditional pubs too, such as the Old Ship at Cadmore End (cheap beer for the area), the Bell at Chearsley, the Prince Albert at Frieth (good food under its friendly new licensees), the bustling White Horse at Hedgerley (one of the best), the splendidly old-fashioned Crown at Little Missenden, and the Chequers at Wheeler End. Other pubs on fine form include the well run Red Lion at Chenies (a fine all-rounder), the marvellous old Royal Standard of England at Forty Green, the nicely set and bustling Full Moon on Hawridge Common (getting organically grown meat now), the chatty Swan at Ley Hill (enjoyable uncomplicated food using local produce), the Polecat at Prestwood (another excellent well run all-rounder, with nice food), the Frog at Skirmett (consistently good food, and caters well for all sorts), and a pub that's back in the Guide under new licensees, after quite a break, the Walnut Tree at Fawley (much loved by walkers, good food too). If it's a really special meal you're after, two new entries spring to mind: the Royal Oak at Bovingdon Green, attractively reworked as a relaxed country dining pub, and the more brasserie-style Boot at Soulbury – both have most enjoyable food now. Other places with top-notch food are the Mole & Chicken at Easington, the Green Dragon at Haddenham, and the very civilised Five Arrows in Waddesdon (excellent wines here, too); all are first-class dining pubs. It is the Green Dragon at Haddenham, with its warm welcome and temptingly imaginative food, which gains the award of Buckinghamshire Dining Pub of the Year. In the Lucky Dip section at the end of the chapter, pubs we'd focus particular attention on are the Old Thatched Inn at Adstock, Chester Arms at Chicheley, Swan in Denham, Chequers at Fingest, Pink & Lily near Lacey Green, Angel in Long Crendon (a restaurant really now), Crown at Penn, Hit or Miss at Penn Street, Old Swan at The Lee, George & Dragon in West Wycombe and Clifden Arms at Worminghall. Drinks prices are generally quite a bit higher here than the national average.

BENNETT END SU7897 Map 4

Three Horseshoes

Horseshoe Road; from Radnage follow unclassified road towards Princes Risborough and turn left into Bennett End Road, then right into Horseshoe Road

After quite a few changes, this unpretentious old country inn has now re-opened. There are three new ensuite letting bedrooms, much work has gone into uncovering old beams and original brickwork, a wooden floor in the main bar has been exposed, and lots of sporting prints and antiques have been added. There are high wooden settles, a few seats tucked around an antique range, and Brakspears and Fullers London Pride, with guests such as Greene King Old Speckled Hen and Wadworths 6X on handpump. Good bar food now includes lunchtime sandwiches, steak in ale pie or vegetable and cashew nut stir fry (£6.95), chicken stuffed with mozzarella and sun-dried tomatoes (£7.95), pork loin with apple compote (£8.95), swordfish steak in a thai green curry sauce (£9.95), and half roast duck with sage and onion stuffing or halibut steak with prawns in lemon butter sauce (£12.95).

What was the lounge has become part of the extended restaurant. This is a lovely tranquil spot (with its surroundings made particularly distinctive by a red phone box rising inexplicably from the fenced-off duck pond) and the licensees tell us there are lots of kites circling overhead. No children. More reports please. *(Recommended by Tim and Ann Newell)*

Free house ~ Licensee Richard Howard ~ Real ale ~ Bar food ~ Restaurant ~ No credit cards ~ (01494) 483273 ~ Open 11-11; 12-10.30 Sun ~ Bedrooms: £55S/£70B

BOVINGDON GREEN SU8286 Map 2
Royal Oak

¾ mile N of Marlow, on back road to Frieth signposted off West Street (A4155) in centre

Well organised and civilised, but a nicely laid-back place to relax in, this rambling country pub has been stylishly transfomed by the same people who run the Alford Arms in Frithsden (see Hertfordshire main entries). There's a similar emphasis on the excellent food, from a changing blackboard menu that might include oak-smoked bacon on bubble and squeak with hollandaise and poached egg (£5.75 starter, £11.50 main course), sautéed duck liver on sweetcorn pancake with harissa and crème fraîche (£5.75), and baked gilthead bream with jersey royals and herb butter sauce or chargrilled rib-eye steak with portabella mushrooms (£13.75); Sunday roasts. Several attractively decorated areas open off the central bar, the half-panelled walls variously painted in pale blue, green or cream: the cosiest part is the low-beamed room closest to the car park, with three small tables, a woodburner in an exposed brick fireplace, and a big pile of logs. Throughout there's a mix of church chairs, stripped wooden tables and chunky wall seats, with rugs on the partly wooden, partly flagstoned floors, co-ordinated cushions and curtains, and a very bright, airy feel. Thoughtful extra touches set the tone: a big, square bowl of olives on the bar, smart soaps and toiletries in the lavatories, and carefully laid out newspapers. A good few tables may have reserved signs (it's worth booking ahead); most have fresh flowers or candles. A terrace with good solid tables leads to an appealing garden with plenty more, and there's a smaller garden at the side as well. All the staff get a shift looking after the garden. Well kept Brakspears, Fullers London Pride and Marlow Rebellion on handpump; helpful, polite service, piped music. The owners now also run the Swan at Denham. *(Recommended by Susan and John Douglas, Simon Collett-Jones, T R and B C Jenkins)*

Enterprise ~ Lease Trasna Rice-Giff ~ Real ale ~ Bar food (12-2.30(3 Sun), 7-10) ~ (01628) 488611 ~ Children welcome ~ Dogs allowed in bar ~ Open 11-11; 12-10.30 Sun; closed 26 Dec, evenings 31 Dec/1 Jan

CADMORE END SU7892 Map 4
Old Ship ◀

B482 Stokenchurch—Marlow

A new licensee has taken over this carefully restored, 17th-c tiled cottage, but happily has made few changes. There's plenty of unpretentious character and charm, and the tiny low-beamed two rooms of the bar are separated by standing timbers and simply furnished with scrubbed country tables and bench and church chair seating (one still has a hole for a game called five-farthings); cribbage, and dominoes. Bar food now includes home-made soup or pâté (£3.95), filled baguettes with chips (£4.95), local ham and eggs (£6.95), home-made steak and mushroom pie, caramelised red onion and goats cheese tart or salmon and dill lasagne (£7.95), and puddings such as treacle sponge or spotted dick (£2.95). Up to five well kept ales tapped from the cask: Brakspears Bitter and Tetleys with guests such as Greene King Abbot, St Austell HSD, and Vale Black Beauty Porter. There are seats in the sheltered garden with a large pergola and a terrace at the end of the bar with cushioned seats and clothed tables. Parking is on the other side of the road. More reports on the new regime please. *(Recommended by Brian Root, Tracey and Stephen Groves, the Didler, Pete Baker)*

Free house ~ Licensee Philip Butt ~ Real ale ~ Bar food (not Sun evening or Mon lunchtime) ~ (01494) 883496 ~ Children in eating area of bar ~ Dogs allowed in bar ~ Open 11-3, 5.30-11; 12-4, 7-10.30 Sun; closed 25 Dec

CHEARSLEY SP7110 Map 4
Bell

The Green; minor road NE of Long Crendon and N of Thame

Very popular locally, this bustling pub has a cosy bar with mugs and tankards hanging from the beams, a collection of plates at one end of the room, an enormous fireplace and handsome counter, and a good traditional feel; there are usually batches of local eggs for sale and often competitions such as pumpkin weighing. Well kept Fullers Chiswick, London Pride and seasonal brews, and a small but well chosen choice of wines by the glass. Much of the simple decent bar food is made from local ingredients and might include home-made soup (£3.95), lunchtime sandwiches such as bacon on chunky local bread topped with a local fried egg (£3.95), mushroom and tomato risotto (£6.25), local butcher's ham with local farm eggs and chips (£7.45), and lamb casserole with apricot dumpling (£8.95). You can't book tables, so there's ample space for drinkers, but it's best to get there early if you intend to eat. Prompt friendly service; cribbage, dominoes. Play equipment such as slides, a rope bridge, wendy house, climbing frames and the like fill the spacious back garden, which has rabbits in one corner. There are plenty of tables out here, with more on a paved terrace, where there may be barbecues in summer. A couple of tables in front overlook the very grassy village green. *(Recommended by John and Glenys Wheeler, Andrew Scarr, Gill and Keith Croxton, Jill McLaren, Mr and Mrs A Stansfield, Heather Couper, B H and J I Andrews, Dr R C C Ward)*

Fullers ~ Tenants Peter and Sue Grimsdell ~ Real ale ~ Bar food (12-1.45, 7-9; not winter Sun evening, not Mon (exc bank hols)) ~ (01844) 208077 ~ Children in eating area of bar until 9pm ~ Dogs welcome ~ Open 12-11; 12-11 Sat; 12-10.30 Sun; 12-2.30, 6-11 in winter; 12-3, 7-10.30 Sun in winter; closed Mon lunchtime

CHENIES TQ0198 Map 3
Red Lion ★

2 miles from M25 junction 18; A404 towards Amersham, then village signposted on right; Chesham Road

This is a very well run and friendly pub with a warm welcome for visitors and a bustling, pubby atmosphere. The unpretentious L-shaped bar has comfortable built-in wall benches by the front windows, other traditional seats and tables, and original photographs of the village and traction engines; there's also a small no smoking back snug and a dining room. From an extensive menu, the good, enjoyable home-made food includes baguettes or wholemeal baps with fillings such as bacon and turkish delight, smoked chicken breast with mango and brie or steak and onions (from £3.50), pasta with roasted peppers, cherry tomatoes, parmesan, pine nuts and optional italian sausage (£4.75; main course £6.95), smoked haddock bake (£5.50; main course £7.50), prawns and mushrooms in garlic butter and cream (£5.50; main course £7.95), pies such as lamb, thai fish curry or bison in red wine (from £7.25), bangers and mash surprise (£8.95), fresh salmon marinated in teriyaki and apricots (£10.95), chicken breast stuffed with bacon and mushrooms in a honey crumb (£11.25), steaks (from £11.50), and puddings (from £2.75). Well kept Benskins Best, Marlow Rebellion Lion Pride (brewed for the pub), Wadworths 6X, and a guest beer on handpump. The hanging baskets and window boxes are pretty in summer, and there are picnic-sets on a small side terrace. No children, games machines or piped music; handy for the M25. *(Recommended by Peter Saville, John and Judy Saville, Howard Dell, John and Glenys Wheeler, Peter and Giff Bennett, Christopher and Elise Way, Charles Gysin)*

Free house ~ Licensee Mike Norris ~ Real ale ~ Bar food (12-2, 7-(9.30 Sun)10) ~ (01923) 282722 ~ Dogs allowed in bar ~ Open 11-2.30, 5.30-11; 12-3, 6.30-10.30 Sun; closed 25 Dec

EASINGTON SP6810 Map 4
Mole & Chicken ⏸ ♀ ⟷

From B4011 in Long Crendon follow Chearsley, Waddesdon signpost into Carters Lane opposite the Chandos Arms, then turn left into Chilton Road

Although customers do drop in for just a drink (and there are up to four real ales on handpump), this is very much a friendly dining pub and somewhere for a special meal out. The open-plan layout is very well done, so that all the different parts seem quite snug and self-contained without being cut off from what's going on, and the atmosphere is chatty and relaxed. The beamed bar curves around the serving counter in a sort of S-shape, and there are pink walls with lots of big antique prints, flagstones, and (even at lunchtime) lit candles on the medley of tables to go with the nice mix of old chairs; good winter log fires. From an imaginative menu, the particularly good food might include sandwiches, home-made soup (£3.50), roasted field mushrooms with spinach and cheese (£5.95), chilli mussels, thai-style salmon and smoked haddock fishcake with a mild curry sauce or king prawns in garlic butter (£6.95), asparagus, bean and broccoli pasta with a lime, artichoke and parmesan oil or popular duck and bacon salad with a warm plum and red wine sauce (£8.95), rack of ribs in barbecue sauce (£9.95), chargrilled steak with shoestring chips or thai prawn curry with poppadums (£12.95), shoulder of slow roasted lamb (£13.95), and beef wellington stuffed with gorgonzola cheese wrapped in puffy pastry and served with a watercress and cream sauce (£15.95); daily specials and fish dishes are listed separately. You must book to be sure of a seat. Decent french house wines (and a good choice by the bottle), over 40 malt whiskies, and well kept Fullers London Pride, Greene King IPA and Old Speckled, and Morrells Oxford Blue on handpump. The garden, where they sometimes hold summer barbecues and pig and lamb roasts, has quite a few tables and chairs. *(Recommended by Michael Jones, Maysie Thompson, Mike and Heather Watson, MP, Karen and Graham Oddey, Mr and Mrs A Stansfield, Richard Siebert, Susan and John Douglas)*

Free house ~ Licensees A Heather and S Ellis ~ Real ale ~ Bar food ~ Restaurant (12-2, 7-10; 12-9.30 Sun) ~ (01844) 208387 ~ Children in eating area of bar and restaurant ~ Open 12-3, 6-11; 12-9 Sun; closed 25 Dec ~ Bedrooms: /£65B

FAWLEY SU7586 Map 2
Walnut Tree ♀

Village signposted off A4155 or B480, N of Henley

Beautifully placed with the Chilterns all around, this is a well run dining pub, popular with a wide mix of customers – those popping in for a drink and a chat, hungry and thirsty walkers and ramblers, and customers out for a special meal. Of the two main areas, one is the saloon bar offering lighter style meals, and there's also a main lounge bar which offers a comprehensive menu with enjoyable modern dishes. The dining conservatory is no smoking and is open on two sides with lovely country views, with the no smoking restaurant next door. Outside on the big lawn around the front car park are seats and tables with more in a covered extension, and this year, a new terrace, lit up at night, has been added. From the lounge bar menu, there might be home-made soup (£4.25; main course £5.95), home-made crab, lime and ginger fishcakes with Malibu cream sauce (£6.50; main course £9.95), fried portabello mushroom on toasted brioche with grilled marinated goats cheese (£6.95), 4oz sirloin steak sandwich with mustard mayonnaise and french fries (£8.95), barnsley lamb chop marinated in fresh mint or grilled sardines served portuguese style (£9.95), pork and sage sausages on mustard mash (£10.95), calves liver on grain mustard mash with a smoked bacon and rich red wine jus (£12.95), and puddings like chocolate fondant with mascarpone cream and chocolate sauce, whisky and marmalade bread and butter pudding with crème anglaise or pink grapefruit tart with crème fraîche (£4.95). Well kept Brakspears Bitter and Special on handpump, and a nice little wine list. *(Recommended by Lesley Bass, Derek and Priscilla Coley, T R and B C Jenkins, Simon Collett-Jones, Dick and Madeleine Brown, June and Robin Savage)*

Brakspears ~ Lease Sean and Tina Mayberry ~ Real ale ~ Bar food ~ Restaurant ~ (01491) 638360 ~ Children in eating area of bar and restaurant ~ Dogs allowed in bar ~ Jazz first Sun of each month ~ Open 12-3, 6-11; 12-11 Sat; 12-4, 7-10.30 Sun; closed Sun evening, all day Mon

FORTY GREEN SU9292 Map 2
Royal Standard of England

3½ miles from M40 junction 2, via A40 to Beaconsfield, then follow sign to Forty Green, off B474 ¾ mile N of New Beaconsfield; keep going through village

This is a fascinating old place and one reader was delighted to find it as good as he remembered on his last visit 40 years earlier. It has enormous appeal, both in the layout of the building itself and in the marvellous collection of antiques which fill it. The rambling rooms have huge black ship's timbers, finely carved old oak panelling, roaring winter fires with handsomely decorated iron firebacks, and there's a massive settle apparently built to fit the curved transom of an Elizabethan ship; also, rifles, powder-flasks and bugles, ancient pewter and pottery tankards, lots of brass and copper, needlework samplers, and stained glass. The main dining bar and one other area are no smoking. Enjoyable bar food includes danish-style sandwiches (which come with a choice of chips and salad or soup) such as bacon, brie and rocket or smoked salmon, prawns and herbed crème fraîche (all £5.75), home-made soup (£3.95), chicken liver pâté with a red berry coulis (£4.50), smoked salmon and hake fishcakes with warm dill cream sauce (£4.95), lunchtime ploughman's (£6.50), tagliatelle with wild mushrooms and a tomato and basil sauce or speciality sausages with red onion gravy (£7.95), home-made beef in ale pie (£8.50), slow-cooked spring lamb marinated in mild ale and mead (£9.90), steaks (from £12.95), daily specials like scallops breton (£7.95), skate with black butter sauce (£8.25) or crispy duck with plum and pea sauce (£12.95), and puddings such as white chocolate and cream cheese tart or gooseberry fool (£3.95). Well kept Brakspears Bitter, Fullers London Pride, Greene King Old Speckled Hen, Marstons Pedigree, and a guest such as Adnams or Vale Notley Ale on handpump, and country wines and mead. There are seats outside in a neatly hedged front rose garden, or in the shade of a tree. *(Recommended by Tracey and Stephen Groves, the Didler, Susan and John Douglas, Michael Porter, Kevin Blake, Peter and Giff Bennett, Anthony Longden, Lesley Bass, Alison Hayes, Pete Hanlon, David and Higgs Wood, John and Tania Wood)*

Free house ~ Licensees Cyril and Carol Cain ~ Real ale ~ Bar food ~ (01494) 673382 ~ Children in two rooms ~ Open 11-3, 5.30-11; 12-3, 7-10.30 Sun

FRIETH SU7990 Map 2
Prince Albert

Village signposted off B482 in Lane End; turn right towards Fingest just before village

Friendly and helpful new licensees have taken over this old-fashioned and cottagey Chilterns pub, and while the menu has changed (Mr Newman is the chef), no major alterations are planned. On the left, there are low black beams and joists, brocaded cushions on high-backed settles (one with its back panelled in neat squares), a big black stove in a brick inglenook, and a leaded-light built-in wall cabinet of miniature bottles. The slightly larger area on the right has more of a medley of chairs and a big log fire. Good bar food includes home-made soup (£2.95), baguettes (£4.95), mussels of the day (£5.95; main course £7.95), lemon and asparagus risotto (£6.50), fresh cod in beer batter with mushy peas (£6.95), lamb steak with redcurrant and mint gravy (£8.95), duck breast with hoisin, red wine and cream (£9.95), and puddings like blackberry and apple crumble or toffee pecan sticky pudding (£3.95). Well kept Brakspears Bitter, Old and Special with a guest like Batemans Mild on handpump. By the time this book is printed, Trebor the pointer should have arrived. A nicely planted informal side garden has views of woods and fields, and there are plenty of nearby walks. *(Recommended by Tracey and Stephen Groves, the Didler, Charles Harvey, Brian England, John Roots, Dennis Jenkin,*

Pete Baker, R K Phillips, Mike and Kathryn Budd)

Brakspears ~ Tenant Dan Newman ~ Real ale ~ Bar food (not Mon) ~ No credit cards ~ (01494) 881683 ~ Children in eating area of bar ~ Dogs welcome ~ Open 12-3, 5.30-11; 12-10.30 Sun

GREAT HAMPDEN SP8401 Map 4
Hampden Arms
Village signposted off A4010 N and S of Princes Risborough

New licensees have taken over this quietly set pub, opposite the village cricket pitch and on the edge of Hampden Common, and apart from some light refurbishment, no major changes are planned. The green-walled front room has broad dark tables with a few aeroplane pictures and country prints, and the back room has a slightly more rustic feel, with its cushioned wall benches and big woodburning stove. Bar food now includes sandwiches (from £4.25), home-made pâté (£5.50), seafood pasta (£7.95), chicken with pancetta and avocado sauce or lambs liver (£8.25), lasagne (£8.50), steaks (from £12.95), and puddings like home-made tiramisu or bread and butter pudding (£3.50). A small corner bar has well kept Adnams and Brakspears on handpump, and maybe Addlestone's cider. There are tables out in the tree-sheltered garden. More reports on the new regime, please. *(Recommended by John Roots, Martin Burgess, Mike and Sue Richardson, Peter Saville)*

Free house ~ Licensees Louise and Constantine Lucas ~ Real ale ~ Bar food ~ (01494) 488255 ~ Children welcome ~ Dogs welcome ~ Open 12-3, 6-11; 12-3, 7-10.30 Sun

HADDENHAM SP7408 Map 4
Green Dragon 🍴 🍷
Village signposted off A418 and A4129, E/NE of Thame; then follow Church End signs

Buckinghamshire Dining Pub of the Year

Readers travel many miles to visit this particularly well run pub, both for the friendly welcome from the licensees and for the especially good food. The opened-up bar, in colours of pale olive and antique rose, has an open fireplace towards the back of the building and attractive furnishings throughout, and the dining area has a fine mix of informal tables and chairs. From an imaginative menu, dishes might include home-made soup (£3.75), salmon and crab fishcake with a fresh herb and tartare dressing (£6; main course £9), confit of duck glazed with local honey and black pepper with pineapple chutney (£6.75), calves liver on pesto-roasted vegetables, rosemary sautéed potatoes and caramelised baby onion sauce (£8.95), carrot and courgette roulade, orange infused ratatouille and mozzarella (£9.25), home-made steak and kidney suet pudding (£9.50), fillets of bass on roasted red pepper, parmesan and basil risotto cake with garlic tiger prawns (£12), rump of lamb on a garlic potato croquette with a sage and wild mushroom jus (£12.50), daily specials like pork and leek sausage with onion gravy or chargrilled chicken and pear with a red pepper mayonnaise (£8.50), and puddings such as home-made sticky toffee pudding or home-made lemon and lime tart with raspberry sorbet (£4.95). The main eating area is no smoking. Well kept real ales from the Vale Brewery on handpump, and sensibly priced well chosen wines including a few by the glass. A big sheltered gravel terrace behind the pub has white tables and picnic-sets under cocktail parasols, with more on the grass, and a good variety of plants. This part of the village is very pretty, with a duckpond unusually close to the church. *(Recommended by Tracey and Stephen Groves, MP, Maysie Thompson, Mike and Sue Richardson, Dr R C C Ward, Jestyn Phillips, John Hale, Colin Whipp, Neil and Karen Dignan)*

Whitbreads ~ Lease Peter Moffat ~ Real ale ~ Bar food ~ Restaurant ~ (01844) 291403 ~ Children in eating area of bar and in restaurant lunchtime only ~ Open 11.30-2.30, 6.30-11; 12-3 Sun; closed Sun evening

HAMBLEDEN SU7886 Map 2
Stag & Huntsman ◗

Turn off A4155 (Henley—Marlow Road) at Mill End, signposted to Hambleden; in a mile
turn right into village centre

The Hambleden Estate, which includes this attractive brick and flint pub, is up for
sale along with most of the village and 1,600 acres of the surrounding Chilterns.
But as we went to press, there was no news of any immediate changes and readers
were enjoying their visits as much as ever. The half-panelled, L-shaped lounge bar
has a cheerful, lively atmosphere, low ceilings, a large fireplace, and upholstered
seating and wooden chairs on the carpet. Popular bar food might include home-
made soup (£3.95), a bowl of chilli or ploughman's (£5.95), spinach and
mushroom lasagne (£7.25), fresh salmon fishcakes (£8.50), home-made venison
sausages (£8.75), breast of local pheasant with cumberland sauce or fresh haddock
fillet in beer batter (£8.95), steaks (from £12.25), and puddings like wild berry and
apple strudel (£3.95). Well kept Rebellion IPA, Wadworths 6X, and a guest beer
from Rebellion or Smiles on handpump, farm ciders, and good wines are served by
friendly staff in the attractively simple public bar; darts, dominoes, cribbage, shove-
ha'penny, and piped music. There's a dining room, and a cosy snug at the front.
Seats in the spacious and neatly kept country garden are quickly snapped up in
good weather. The pub is set opposite the church on the far edge of one of the
prettiest Chilterns villages, and it's just a field's walk from the river. (Recommended
by John Roots, Simon Collett-Jones, Eric Locker, John Hale, Anthony Longden, Tracey and
Stephen Groves, June and Robin Savage, Brian England, D and M T Ayres-Regan, John and
Glenys Wheeler)

Free house ~ Licensees Hon. Henry Smith and Andrew Stokes ~ Real ale ~ Bar food
(not Sun evenings) ~ (01491) 571227 ~ Children in eating area of bar and restaurant
~ Dogs allowed in bar ~ Open 11-2.30(3 Sat), 6-11; 12-3, 7-10.30 Sun; closed
25 Dec, evenings 26 Dec and 1 Jan ~ Bedrooms: £58B/£68B

HAWRIDGE COMMON SP9406 Map 4
Full Moon

Hawridge Common; left fork off A416 N of Chesham, then follow for 3½ miles towards
Cholesbury

In summer, you can sit at seats on the terrace (which has an awning and outside
heaters for cooler evenings) and gaze over the windmill nestling behind this
attractively set little country local; plenty of walks over the common from here.
Inside, it's bustling and friendly, and the low-beamed rambling bar is the heart of
the building, with oak built-in floor-to-ceiling settles, ancient flagstones and
flooring tiles, hunting prints, and an inglenook fireplace. They have six well kept
real ales on handpump, with regulars such as Bass, Boddingtons, Brakspears
Special, and Fullers London Pride, and weekly changing guests like Shepherd
Neame Spitfire and Wells Bombardier; good service. Enjoyable, reasonably priced
food at lunchtime includes sandwiches (from £3.50), home-made soup (£4),
ploughman's (£6.95), home-cooked ham and egg (£7.25), chilli (£7.75), a
vegetarian dish of the day (£7.95), and cumberland sausage with bubble and
squeak or fresh fish of the day (£8.95), with evening dishes like portuguese sardines
or smoked chicken and pine nut salad with a honey and lemon dressing (£5.25),
chicken and prawn thai curry or duck breast with Cointreau and kumquat sauce
(£10.95), and a trio of seafood with a Pernod cream sauce (£11.95). The meat,
poultry and game come from an organic butcher. Both the restaurants are no
smoking; piped music. (Recommended by Andrea and Guy Bradley, Tracey and
Stephen Groves, Marjorie and David Lamb, Peter and Giff Bennett, John Roots, Tim Maddison)

Enterprise ~ Lease Peter and Annie Alberto ~ Real ale ~ Bar food (12-2, 6-9; no food
Sun evening) ~ Restaurant ~ (01494) 758959 ~ Children in eating area of bar and
restaurant ~ Dogs allowed in bar ~ Open 12-3, 5.30-11; 12-11 Sat; 12-10.30 Sun;
closed 25 Dec

HEDGERLEY SU9686 Map 2
White Horse 🍺

2.4 miles from M40 junction 2: at exit roundabout take Slough turn-off then take Hedgerley Lane (immediate left) following alongside M40. After 1½ miles turn right at T junction into Village Lane

This is a proper country local with a wonderful jolly atmosphere – lots of beers and regular ale festivals, warmly friendly service from the long-standing licensees, and plenty of character. The cottagey main bar has lots of beams, brasses and exposed brickwork, low wooden tables, some standing timbers, jugs, ball-cocks and other bric-a-brac, a log fire, and a good few leaflets and notices about future village events. The fine range of seven or eight real ales, all tapped from the cask in a room behind the tiny hatch counter, alongside good farm cider, might include Greene King IPA and Marlow Rebellion, but the rest could be from anywhere in the country. At lunchtimes staff busily serve sandwiches (from £3.25) and things like quiche, ploughman's (from £4.50), and tandoori chicken from a cold cabinet in the corner, with a changing range of simple home-cooked hot dishes (from £5.45); service is cheery and relaxed. There is a little flagstoned public bar on the left. On the way out to the garden, which has tables and occasional barbecues, they have a canopy extension to help during busy periods. In front are lots of hanging baskets, with a couple more tables overlooking the quiet road. There are good walks nearby, and the pub is handy for the Church Wood RSPB reserve. It can get very busy at weekends. *(Recommended by the Didler, Lesley Bass, LM, Susan and John Douglas, Simon Collett-Jones, Anthony Longden, Tracey and Stephen Groves, Kristian Brodie, Martin and Karen Wake)*

Free house ~ Licensees Doris Hobbs and Kevin Brooker ~ Real ale ~ Bar food (lunchtime only) ~ (01753) 643225 ~ Children allowed in special area ~ Dogs allowed in bar ~ Open 11-2.30, 5.30-11; 11-11 Sat; 12-10.30 Sun

LEY HILL SP9802 Map 4
Swan 🍺

Village signposted off A416 in Chesham

It's not easy to combine an old-fashioned pubby atmosphere with a very good restaurant, but the friendly licensees have managed to do just that in this charming little timbered 16th-c pub. The main bar has black beams (mind your head) and standing timbers, an old working range, a log fire and a collection of old local photographs, a cosy snug, and a chatty mix of locals and visitors. The restaurant is no smoking. Using fine quality local produce, enjoyable lunchtime food might include open sandwiches or filled baguettes (from £3.25), filled baked potatoes (from £3.75), home-made soup (£3.90), warm salads like aromatic duck or garlic mushrooms and blue stilton (from £4.95), ploughman's (£5.50), spicy king prawns (£6.50), and home-baked ham and eggs (£7.50); evening dishes such as warm goats cheese and vegetable tartlet (£4.95), sesame seed-battered scampi with chilli dip (£5.95), a vegetarian dish of the day (from £7.95), steak and kidney pie (£8.25), baked loin of pork with apple charlotte and cider cream sauce (£12.50), aberdeen angus steaks (from £12.50), and half a honey-roast norfolk duckling with cranberry, red wine and orange sauce (£15.95). Well kept Adnams, Fullers London Pride, Marstons Pedigree, Timothy Taylors Landlord on handpump, 10 wines by the glass, and Addlestone's cider. Picnic-sets in front of the pub amongst the flower tubs and hanging baskets, with more in the large back garden. There's a cricket pitch, a nine-hole golf course, and a common opposite. *(Recommended by Martin Price, Tracey and Stephen Groves, David and Ruth Shillitoe, Peter and Giff Bennett, John and Glenys Wheeler, Matthew Edworthy, Heather Couper, Geoff and Sylvia Donald)*

Punch ~ Lease Joy and Carol Putland ~ Real ale ~ Bar food (bar snacks lunchtime only) ~ Restaurant ~ (01494) 783075 ~ Children in eating area of bar and in restaurant but no small children in evening ~ Open 12-3, 5.30-11; 12-11 Sat; 12-3, 7-10.30 Sun

LITTLE HAMPDEN SP8503 Map 4
Rising Sun

Village signposted from back road (ie W of A413) Great Missenden—Stoke Mandeville; pub at end of village lane; OS Sheet 165 map reference 856040

In a delightful setting, this comfortable, totally no smoking dining pub has an opened-up bar mainly dominated by dining tables; there's a woodburning stove and log fire to add to the cosiness in winter. This year, several new ensuite bedrooms have been opened. Most customers come to enjoy the very good food: wild mixed mushrooms with a creamy stilton sauce served in a puff pastry case (£4.95), curried prawns on a mango and orange salad (£5.95), chicken satay (£6.50), ploughman's (£6.95), baked red snapper catalan style with tomatoes, anchovies, olives and capers or dressed crab topped with a creamy cheese and mustard sauce (£9.75), roast home-smoked pork joint with a red wine and plum sauce or roast shoulder of lamb with a rosemary and honey sauce (£9.95), deben duck with an apricot and brandy sauce or sirloin steak with béarnaise sauce (£10.95), and puddings like bitter sweet flummery with raspberries in syrup, butterscotch dumplings with vanilla ice cream or chocolate rum cheesecake with chocolate sauce (all £4.25). Well kept Adnams, Brakspears Bitter and a seasonal beer from Shepherd Neame on handpump, with home-made mulled wine and spiced cider in winter, and a short but decent wine list; piped music. There are some tables on the terrace by the sloping front grass. Despite the pub's being surrounded by fine woodland tracks, walkers' boots – dry or otherwise – are not welcome. *(Recommended by R T and J C Moggridge, Peter Saville, Mrs J Smythe, Brian Root, Peter Shapland, Mike and Sue Richardson, David and Ruth Shillitoe, Julia and Richard Tredgett, Peter and Jan Humphreys, Peter and Giff Bennett, Mike and Heather Watson, Tracey and Stephen Groves)*

Free house ~ Licensee Rory Dawson ~ Real ale ~ Bar food (not Sun evening, not Mon) ~ Restaurant ~ (01494) 488360 ~ Children must be well behaved ~ Open 11.30-3, 6.30-10(11 Sat); 12-3 Sun; closed Sun evenings and all Mon (open bank hols) ~ Bedrooms: £45B/£70B

LITTLE MISSENDEN SU9298 Map 4
Crown ★ ◖

Crown Lane, SE end of village, which is signposted off A413 W of Amersham

Spotlessly kept and with a fine traditional and proper pubby feel, this unspoilt country brick cottage has been run by the same family for over 90 years. The bustling bars are more spacious than they might first appear, with old red flooring tiles on the left, oak parquet on the right, built-in wall seats, studded red leatherette chairs, a few small tables, and a complete absence of music and machines; a good mix of customers adds to the chatty relaxed atmosphere. Well kept Adnams, Black Sheep Special, Fullers London Pride, and a guest from breweries such as Gales, Hop Back or Vale on handpump, and decent malt whiskies. Popular straightforward home-made bar food includes a decent choice of generous very good value sandwiches (from £2.75), as well as buck's bite (a special home-made pizza-like dish £4.50), steak and kidney pie (£4.95), and ploughman's (from £5); darts, shove-ha'penny, cribbage, and dominoes. The attractive sheltered garden behind has picnic-sets and other tables, and the pretty village has an interesting church. No children. *(Recommended by Brian England, D and M T Ayres-Regan, R T and J C Moggridge, Tracey and Stephen Groves, Anthony Longden, Derek and Sylvia Stephenson)*

Free house ~ Licensees Trevor and Carolyn How ~ Real ale ~ Bar food (lunchtime only; not Sun) ~ No credit cards ~ (01494) 862571 ~ Open 11-2.30, 6-11; 12-3, 7-11 Sun

---

People named as recommenders after the main entries have told us that the pub should be included. But they have not written the report – we have, after anonymous on-the-spot inspection.

MENTMORE SP9119 Map 4
Stag
Village signposted off B488 S of Leighton Buzzard; The Green

The small civilised lounge bar in this pretty village pub has a relaxed atmosphere, low oak tables, attractive fresh flower arrangements, and an open fire; the more simple public bar leading off has shove-ha'penny, cribbage and dominoes. Well kept Wells Eagle, IPA and Bombardier, with a guest from Adnams or Fullers on handpump, 50 wines by the glass, and champagne cocktails; friendly service. Nicely presented, reasonably priced lunchtime bar food includes interesting sandwiches (£4), salads (£5), and hot meals such as smoked haddock with welsh rarebit cheese, steamed oriental trout or spicy sausages with onion gravy (all £6). In the evening, there might be pasta with leek and mushrooms or chicken curry (£6), and calves liver with red wine jus, confit of duck and pork with spiced vegetable salad or greek lamb platter (all £8). Part of the restaurant is no smoking; piped music. There are seats out on the pleasant flower-filled front terrace looking across towards Mentmore House, and a charming, well tended, sloping garden. More reports please. *(Recommended by Karen and Graham Oddey, George Atkinson, MP, N J Dack)*

Charles Wells ~ Lease Jenny and Mike Tuckwood ~ Real ale ~ Bar food (not Mon evenings) ~ Restaurant ~ (01296) 668423 ~ Children in restaurant but must be over 10 in evening ~ Dogs allowed in bar ~ Occasional live jazz ~ Open 12-3, 6-11; 12-11 Sat; 12-10.30 Sun

NEWTON LONGVILLE SP8430 Map 4
Crooked Billet ♀
Off A421 S of Milton Keynes; Westbrook End

Though the focus in this brightly modernised thatched pub, in a slightly unusual position by a modern housing estate, is very much on the food, it still feels like a proper pub, and the extended bar has beam and plank ceilings, some partly green-painted walls, sporting trophies on the shelves, and usually a few chatting locals. Well kept Batemans XXXB, Greene King IPA and Abbot, and Wychwood Hobgoblin on handpump, and all 300 wines are offered by the glass; also, 30 malt whiskies, and 30 cognacs and armagnacs. Most customers come to enjoy the ambitious food which includes lunchtime sandwiches (from £4.25; toasted bocatta with roast chicken, maple cured bacon and salad £7.25), cream of wild mushroom soup with crispy sage, crème fraîche, and white truffle oil (£4.75), avocado, comice pear, mixed leaves with garlic and parmesan croutons and chargrilled orange and avocado oil dressing (£5), crayfish pasta with mild sweet red chilli, tomato, garlic and lemon and olive oil (£5.75; main course £9.50), smoked haddock and bubble and squeak fishcake, poached egg, bacon and hollandaise (£9), beef meatball with fried potato cake, spiced red cabbage and caramelised onion (£10), garlic roast chicken breast with wilted spinach, colcannon and roast baby carrots (£11), pork loin with sage and onion crust, cauliflower and horseradish purée, green beans and parma ham (£13), goose three ways (fried breast with fondant potato, goose and wild mushroom sausage, and foie gras with wilted spinach, £16), and puddings such as rich dark chocolate tart with green tea ice cream or gooseberry blancmange, sweet wine and grape jelly and spiced madeleines (from £5). They don't take bookings at lunchtimes (except on Sundays), but in the evening restaurant tables need to be reserved well in advance – up to a month some weekends. The restaurant is no smoking; piped music. There are a few tables out on the lawn. *(Recommended by Ian Phillips, Andrea and Guy Bradley, Bob and Maggie Atherton, Mike Turner, John and Judy Saville, Karen and Graham Oddey, Mr and Mrs John Taylor)*

Greene King ~ Lease John and Emma Gilchrist ~ Real ale ~ Bar food (snacks lunchtime only, no food Mon) ~ (01908) 373936 ~ Children in restaurant ~ Dogs allowed in bar ~ Open 12-2.30, 5.30-11; 12-11 Sat; 12-4, 7-10.30 Sun; closed Mon lunchtime, 25-26 Dec, 1 Jan

PRESTWOOD SP8700 Map 4

Polecat

170 Wycombe Road (A4128 N of High Wycombe)

There's always a good bustling atmosphere and plenty of cheerful customers at this particularly well run and friendly pub. Opening off the low-ceilinged bar, there are several smallish rooms with an assortment of tables and chairs, various stuffed birds as well as the stuffed white polecats in one big cabinet, small country pictures, rugs on bare boards or red tiles, and a couple of antique housekeeper's chairs by a good open fire; the Gallery Room is no smoking. At lunchtime there tend to be chatty crowds of middle-aged diners, with a broader mix of ages in the evening. As well as lunchtime snacks such as sandwiches (from £3.20), filled baked potatoes (from £4.60), and ploughman's (£4.95), there might be home-made soup (£3.50), chicken, pork, liver and brandy pâté with red onion marmalade (£4.60), flaked haddock, chives and cream baked in filo pastry (£4.90), spiced lentil roast with onion purée (£7.50), home-made venison and rabbit pie (£7.90), salmon fishcakes with a herby tomato sauce (£8.20), chicken with cep mushrooms, pearl onions, bacon and parmentier potatoes (£8.90), and braised lamb shank (£9.40), with daily specials like terrine of chicken and asparagus wrapped in parma ham and served with charred olive bread (£4.60), spiced chick pea and vegetable fritters with stewed peppers, onion and tomato (£7.90) or magret of duck with cherry and orange sauce (£11.40), and puddings like raspberry shortcake with raspberry coulis or profiteroles with chocolate sauce (£3.95). Well kept Bass, Flowers IPA, Greene King Old Speckled Hen, and Marstons Pedigree on handpump at the flint bar counter, nine wines by the glass, and a good few malt whiskies; piped music. The garden is most attractive, with lots of bulbs in spring, and lovely summer hanging baskets, tubs, and herbaceous plants; there are quite a few picnic-sets under parasols on neat grass out in front beneath a big fairy-lit pear tree, with more on a big well kept back lawn. *(Recommended by Lesley Bass, Roy and Lindsey Fentiman, Mike and Heather Watson, Simon Collett-Jones, Marion Turner, John and Glenys Wheeler)*

Free house ~ Licensee John Gamble ~ Real ale ~ Bar food (12-2, 6.30-9; not Sun evening) ~ Restaurant ~ No credit cards ~ (01494) 862253 ~ Dogs welcome ~ Open 11.30-2.30, 6-11; 12-3 Sun; closed Sun evening, evening 24 Dec, 25-26 Dec, evening 31 Dec

SKIRMETT SU7790 Map 2

Frog 🛏

From A4155 NE of Henley take Hambleden turn and keep on; or from B482 Stokenchurch—Marlow take Turville turn and keep on

What makes this bustling country inn special is the way it caters for all sorts of customers, and the friendly licensees go out of their way to make all feel welcome. Although brightly modernised, it still has something of a local feel with leaflets and posters near the door advertising raffles and so forth. The neatly kept beamed bar area has a mix of comfortable furnishings, a striking hooded fireplace with a bench around the edge (and a pile of logs sitting beside it), big rugs on the wooden floors, and sporting and local prints around the salmon painted walls. The function room leading off, with a fine-looking dresser, is sometimes used as a dining overflow. To be sure of a table, you must book in advance for the consistently good, popular food: sandwiches, home-made soup (£3.50), caesar salad with bacon, croutons, citrus chicken and home-made caesar dressing (£5.75), watercress pancake filled with smoked haddock glazed with saffron sauce (£6.25), warm potato rösti, black pudding and smoked salmon with a poached egg salad (£6.75), lasagne of wild mushrooms and asparagus with a chervil cream sauce (£9.50), grilled escalope of salmon with onion marmalade or roast chicken breast with wild mushrooms, tarragon and garlic potatoes (£10.95), baked bass fillets marinated in thai spices, chilli and soy dressing (£11.25), honey-glazed shank of lamb with rosemary infused jus (£12.50), and grilled sirloin steak with port and stilton sauce (£12.95). The restaurant is no smoking; piped music. Well kept Adnams, Fullers London Pride,

Hook Norton, and a weekly changing guest like Black Sheep or Rebellion IPA on handpump, a good range of wines, quite a few whiskies, and various coffees. A side gate leads to a lovely garden with a large tree in the middle and unusual five-sided tables, well placed for attractive valley views. The bedrooms are engaging and make a nice base for the area. Henley is close by, just down the road is the delightful Ibstone windmill, and there are many surrounding hiking routes. *(Recommended by Mike and Sue Richardson, Boyd Catling, Brian England, Peter Saville, Piotr Chodzko-Zajko, J V Dadswell, Di and Mike Gillam, Tracey and Stephen Groves)*

Free house ~ Licensees Jim Crowe and Noelle Greene ~ Real ale ~ Bar food (12-2.30, 6.30-9.30; not winter Sun evening) ~ Restaurant ~ (01491) 638996 ~ Children welcome ~ Dogs allowed in bar ~ Open 11-3, 6.30(6 Sat)-11; 12-4, 6-10 Sun; closed Sun evening Oct-May ~ Bedrooms: £55B/£65B

SOULBURY SP8827 Map 4
Boot ♀

B4032 W of Leighton Buzzard

Brightly modernised over the last few years (and winning its parent company's Pub of the Year award as a result), this civilised village pub is particularly liked for its interesting well prepared food, especially the fresh fish, delivered every day. A board makes clear the choice of fillets, whole fish or shellfish, with a typical menu taking in salmon (£10.95) or mahi-mahi, whole bass (£14.50) and trout; all are grilled, and served with a butter of the day, such as lemon and parsley or garlic. Other dishes might include lunchtime sandwiches, braised lamb shank with rosemary and redcurrant sauce (£10.50), vegetarian dishes, and roast beef fillet with field mushrooms and red wine sauce (£13.95). They don't usually do fish on Sundays. Even on a dull day the partly red-tiled bar has a light, sunny feel, thanks mainly to its cream ceilings and pale green walls, and there's a nice mix of smart and individual furnishings, as well as sporting prints and houseplants, and neat blinds on the windows. Behind the modern, light wood bar counter are plenty of bottles from their well chosen wine list; they do a dozen by the glass. Well kept Greene King IPA and a changing beer such as Courage Directors; good service from friendly, smartly dressed staff. One end of the room, with a fireplace and wooden floors, is mostly set for diners, then at the opposite end, by some exposed brickwork, steps lead down to a couple of especially cosy rooms for eating, a yellow one with beams and another fireplace, and a tiny red one. All the eating areas are no smoking; piped music. There are tables behind in a small garden overlooking peaceful fields, and a couple more in front. *(Recommended by J Iorwerth Davies, B H and J I Andrews)*

Pubmaster ~ Lease Greg Nichol ~ Real ale ~ Bar food (12-2.30(4 Sun), 6-9.30) ~ (01525) 270433 ~ Children welcome ~ Open 11-11; 12-10.30 Sun; closed 25 Dec

WADDESDON SP7417 Map 4
Five Arrows ★ ⓘ ♀ 🛏

A41 NW of Aylesbury

Happily, little changes at this elegant and civilised place so you can be sure of a consistently friendly welcome and an excellent meal. A series of light and airy high-ceilinged rooms makes up the unstuffy open-plan pubby bar, with family portrait engravings, lots of old estate-worker photographs, heavy dark green velvet curtains on wooden rails, and mainly sturdy cushioned settles and good solid tables on parquet flooring. Newspapers and copies of *Country Life* are kept in an antique magazine rack. Very good food from an interesting menu might include coriander and parsley pancake filled with spiced vegetables and served with a yoghurt and mango dressing (£5.25; main course £11.50), salmon fishcakes with coriander jam or chicken livers with artichoke hearts (£5.95), thai marinated fillet of red mullet on soy noodles (£6.50; main course £13.70), steamed hoki fish with ginger, spring onions, sesame and fragrant rice (£12.50), chargrilled breast of chicken with tomato and parmesan polenta and rosemary jus (£13), slow braised lamb shank with mint and sage gravy (£13.50), and mushroom mille feuille with garlic and roquefort dressing (£14.25); also, lunchtime specials such as bacon, cheese and tomato tart (£5.50), pork sausages with onion gravy or ploughman's (£5.95), and steak in ale pie (£6.95). The country-house-style restaurant is no smoking on one side; must book at busy times. The formidable wine list runs to Rothschild first-growth clarets as well as lesser-known Rothschild Estate wines. Well kept Fullers London Pride on handpump, many malt whiskies, champagne by the glass, proper cocktails, and freshly squeezed orange juice. The sheltered back garden has attractively grouped wood and metal furnishings. This is an ideal base for visiting Waddesdon Manor. *(Recommended by B N F and M Parkin, Lesley Bass, Richard and Margaret Peers, Simon Reynolds, Val Stevenson, Rob Holmes, Chris Chaplin, Andrew McHardy, Karen and Graham Oddey, Neil and Karen Dignan)*

Free house ~ Licensees J A Worster and F Bromovsky ~ Real ale ~ Bar food (12-2.30, 7-9.30; 12-2, 7.30-8.30 Sun) ~ Restaurant ~ (01296) 651727 ~ Children at designated tables in restaurant ~ Open 11-3, 5.30 (6 Sat)-11; 12-3, 7-10.30 Sun ~ Bedrooms: £65S(£70B)/£85B

WHEELER END SU8093 Map 4
Chequers ◀

Off B482 in Lane End NW of Marlow, then first left also signposted Wheeler End

The low-ceilinged bar in this neatly kept 17th-c pub has what might be called an inherently friendly layout: it's so small, and shaped in such a way, that you can't help but feel part of the general conversation. It angles back past the inglenook fireplace, and a little roomlet, to the bigger back no smoking restaurant with its candlelit tables and hunting prints on the walls. Well kept Fullers London Pride, ESB, and a guest on handpump; dominoes and cribbage. Good bar food includes sandwiches (from £3.50; croque monsieur £5; ciabattas and baguettes £5), mussels cooked in cumin, ginger, white wine and cream or eggs à la benedictine (£5), warm pigeon breast with apple salad (£5.50), baked goats cheese, pine nut and spinach filo parcel with a tomato and tarragon sauce (£9), chargrilled steaks (from £11), roast salmon supreme on a wilted spinach salad with an orange butter and green peppercorn sauce (£12), and a medley of seafood flamed with Pernod and finished with cream (£14.50), with specials such as roast pepper and tomato soup or gammon, egg and chips (£5.50), wild boar and apple sausages on scallion mash (£7), artichoke and sun-dried tomato pasta in a cream and basil sauce (£8), and venison pie (£9), and puddings like lemon tart with fresh raspberries and clotted cream or chocolate parfait with nougat and blackcurrant (£3.50). There are two neat gardens, and Harvey the dog will share doggy biscuits and his water bowl. More reports please. *(Recommended by John and Glenys Wheeler, John Hale, Tracey and Stephen Groves)*

Fullers ~ Lease Anna Kaiser and Stephen Warner ~ Real ale ~ Bar food (12-2.30, 7-10) ~ Restaurant ~ (01494) 883070 ~ Children in eating area of bar and restaurant ~ Dogs allowed in bar ~ Open 11-3, 5.30-11; 11-11 Sat; 12-10.30 Sun

WOOBURN COMMON SU9187 Map 2
Chequers 🛏

From A4094 N of Maidenhead at junction with A4155 Marlow road keep on A4094 for another ¾ mile, then at roundabout turn off right towards Wooburn Common, and into Kiln Lane; if you find yourself in Honey Hill, Hedsor, turn left into Kiln Lane at the top of the hill; OS Sheet 175 map reference 910870

Although many customers are drawn from the thriving hotel and restaurant side, the low-beamed, partly stripped-brick bar offers a friendly welcome to its mix of customers. There are standing timbers and alcoves to break the room up, comfortably lived-in sofas on its bare boards, a bright log-effect gas fire, and various pictures, plates, a two-man saw, and tankards; one room is no smoking. Changing daily, the bar menu might include sandwiches, vegetable soup with pesto (£3.95), game sausages with onion gravy, home-made burger with bacon and cheese, and fishcake with poached egg, spinach and béarnaise sauce (£8.95), tagliatelle of mussels, tomatoes and olives, chicken curry, and grilled lamb leg steak with rosemary jus (£9.95), breast of guinea fowl (£10.50), sirloin steak with café de paris butter (£14.95), and puddings (£3.95). Well kept Greene King IPA, Original, and Ruddles County on handpump, a sizeable wine list (champagne and good wine by the glass), and a fair range of malt whiskies and brandies; piped music. The spacious garden, set away from the road, has cast-iron tables. Attractive stripped-pine bedrooms are in a 20th-c mock-Tudor wing. More reports please.

(Recommended by Mrs Ailsa Wiggans, Peter and Giff Bennett, Chris Glasson, Lesley Bass, Ian Phillips)

Free house ~ Licensee Peter Roehrig ~ Real ale ~ Bar food (12-2.30, 6-9.30; all day Sat/Sun) ~ Restaurant ~ (01628) 529575 ~ Children welcome ~ Dogs allowed in bar ~ Open 10.30-11; 10.30-10.30 Sun ~ Bedrooms: £99.50B/£107.50B

Lucky Dip

Besides the fully inspected pubs, you might like to try these Lucky Dips recommended to us and described by readers (if you do, please send us reports: www.goodguides.com).

ADSTOCK [SP7330]
☆ *Old Thatched Inn* [Main St, off A413]: Beams and flagstones, cosy corners and open fires, part pubby, and part with easy chairs and settees leading to modern restaurant; friendly and comfortable, with generous food from interesting sandwiches to game and theme nights, well kept Bass and Hook Norton Best, decent wines, good service; seats out in sheltered back garden, children in restaurant and eating area *(B H and J I Andrews, LYM, Peter and Anne Hollindale, Karen and Graham Oddey, Arthur Baker)*
AKELEY [SP7037]
☆ *Bull & Butcher* [just off A413]: Genuine village pub with three good fires in long open-plan beamed bar, red plush banquettes and lots of old photographs, good value sandwiches and sensibly priced main dishes, well kept Fullers Chiswick and London Pride with a guest such as Jennings Cumberland, good house wines, traditional games, TV; children allowed in eating area, tables in pleasant small back garden, handy for Stowe Gardens *(LYM, George Atkinson)*
AMERSHAM [SU9597]
Crown [Market Sq]: Small peaceful modernised hotel bar, beams and polished wood floors, neat tables all set for dining, interesting 16th-c features in comfortable lounge, short choice of bar food from sandwiches up, afternoon teas, good restaurant, cheery helpful staff, Bass and Hancocks HB, good house wine; nearby parking may be difficult; attractive split-level outside seating area with cobbled courtyard and plant-filled garden, comfortable bedrooms *(John and Glenys Wheeler, BB, Reg J Cox, Howard Dell)*
☆ *Saracens Head* [Whielden St (A404)]: Friendly unspoilt 17th-c local, neat, clean and largely no smoking, with beams, gentle lighting, massive inglenook with roaring fire in ancient decorative fire-basket, interesting décor,

enjoyable generous fresh food from baguettes to full meals, well kept Greene King IPA, Old Speckled Hen and Ruddles Best and Hook Norton Old Hooky, winter mulled wine, pleasant staff, cheery chatty landlord; soft piped music; little back terrace, bedrooms *(LYM, Betty Laker, Jarrod and Wendy Hopkinson)*
ASTON CLINTON [SP8811]
Duck In [London Rd]: Vintage Inn with enjoyable reasonably priced food inc lighter lunchtime dishes, nice variety of furnishings with flagstones and dark brown and dark cream paintwork; picnic-sets under trees in garden *(Matthew Shackle, Mel Smith)*
☆ *Oak* [Green End St]: Cosy and attractively refurbished beamed Fullers pub, good bar and plenty of dining room, friendly efficient service, enjoyable home-made food (not Sun pm) cooked to order inc good value lighter lunches, decent wines, real fire, no music or machines *(John and Glenys Wheeler)*
AYLESBURY [SP7510]
Bottle & Glass [A418 some miles towards Thame, beyond Stone]: This friendly thatched pub with its attractive low-beamed rambling layout was gutted by fire in April 2003; news please *(LYM)*
BISHOPSTONE [SP8010]
Harrow: Welcoming country pub with good food in bar and restaurant (steaks particularly good), real ales such as Flowers and Charles Wells Bombardier, candles and mahogany tables, dark red walls; pub games, piped music; big well kept garden with barbecues, picturesque village *(Dr R C C Ward, Neil and Karen Dignan)*
BLEDLOW [SP7702]
Lions of Bledlow [off B4009 Chinnor—Princes Risboro; Church End]: Low 16th-c beams, attractive oak stalls, antique settle, ancient tiles, inglenook log fires and a woodburner, and fine views from bay windows; well kept ales such as Courage Best, Marlow Rebellion

and Wadworths 6X, bar food from sandwiches up, no smoking restaurant; well behaved children allowed, tables out on sheltered terrace and small sloping lawns, nice setting, good walks *(LYM, Tracey and Stephen Groves, the Didler, John Roots)*

BLEDLOW RIDGE [SU7997]

Boot [Chinnor Rd]: Light and pleasant tiled bar (walkers brush boots at back entrance), enjoyable food, well kept Fullers London Pride *(Peter Shapland)*

BOLTER END [SU7992]

☆ *Peacock* [just over 4 miles from M40 junction 5, via A40 then B482]: Pleasantly set Chilterns pub, brightly modernised bar with nice little bolt-hole down to the left, no smoking room, good log fire, well kept Brakspears and generous food inc familiar favourites and fresh veg; picnic-sets in garden, has been cl Sun evening *(Tracey and Stephen Groves, E B Ireland, LYM, John and Glenys Wheeler)*

BOURNE END [SU8887]

Bounty [Cockmarsh; reached over railway bridge from Bourne End, or towpath from Cookham]: Friendly pub tucked away in outstanding setting on the opposite bank of the Thames, well kept local beers, decent unpretentious food; children and walkers welcome, tables out on the grass *(David Tindal)*

Garibaldi [Hedsor Rd]: Cheerful and very welcoming new Irish landlord in 18th-c beamed pub with sofa and assorted rustic furniture on bare boards, log fire, bright yellow walls; country views from garden tables *(Susan and John Douglas)*

BRILL [SP6513]

Pheasant [off B4011 Bicester—Long Crendon; Windmill St]: Unpretentious simply furnished beamed pub in marvellous spot looking over to ancient working windmill, nearby view over nine counties, good choice of food, well kept Marstons Pedigree and Tetleys, good value house wines, attractive dining room up a step; piped music, no dogs; children welcome, tables in verandah and garden with terrace, bedrooms, open all day wknds *(K H Frostick, Tim and Ann Newell, LYM)*

CHACKMORE [SP6835]

Queens Head [Main St]: Comfortable village pub by Stowe Gardens, with welcoming landlord, good value varied lunchtime food from toasties and baguettes up, well kept real ales, nice local feel in bar, small separate dining room *(Brian Root, Guy Vowles)*

CHALFONT ST GILES [SU9895]

☆ *Ivy House* [A413 S]: Smart and attractively laid out 18th-c open-plan dining pub, comfortable armchairs by fire in elegantly cosy L-shaped tiled bar, lighter flagstoned no smoking extension full of tables set for eating; wide range of good freshly cooked food, not cheap but generous, well kept changing ales such as Brakspears and Everards Tiger, good wines by glass, espresso machine; pleasant terrace and sloping garden (can be traffic noise) *(Anthony Longden, BB)*

White Hart [Three Households]: Well run

traditional pub with wide range of good generous food in bar and restaurant, well kept real ales, good choice of wines, friendly owners and staff; children welcome, big garden, comfortable bedrooms with own bathrooms in barn at the back *(Mr and Mrs P Lally)*

CHICHELEY [SP9045]

☆ *Chester Arms* [quite handy for M1 junction 14]: Cosy and pretty beamed pub with rooms off semi-circular bar, log fire, comfortable settles and chairs, wide choice of good popular home-made food from sandwiches to daily fresh fish (they do lobster with notice) and aberdeen angus beef, children's helpings, friendly service, Greene King IPA, decent wines, daily papers, back dining room down steps; darts, fruit machine, quiet piped music; picnic-sets in small back garden *(Michael Dandy, Gerry and Rosemary Dobson, David and Mary Webb, Maysie Thompson, Sarah Markham, John Saul, BB)*

COLESHILL [SU9495]

Red Lion: Early 20th-c pub quietly placed well off the road, one room with a few dining tables for the good reasonably priced home-made blackboard food Mon-Sat, two or three well kept changing ales such as Banks's, Greene King IPA and Vale Wychert, amiable helpful landlord; picnic-sets out in front and in back garden with sturdy climbing frames outside, good walks *(Howard Dell)*

COLNBROOK [TQ0277]

☆ *Ostrich* [1¼ miles from M4 junction 5 via A4/B3378, then 'village only' rd]: Striking Elizabethan pub, modernised and plans for further work but still signs of its long and entertaining history (even has a life-sized stuffed ostrich); good log fire, well kept Courage Best and Directors and the accurately named Charles Wells Banana Bread, prompt friendly service, though emphasis primarily on food side – good range of bar food, good upstairs restaurant; quiet piped music, and they may try to keep credit cards as security *(LYM, Susan and Nigel Wilson, Susan and John Douglas, John and Glenys Wheeler)*

CUBLINGTON [SP8322]

Unicorn [High St]: Thriving 16th-c beamed pub in centre of village, supposedly haunted, long rustic bare-boards room with wooden seating and attractive fireplace at one end, good generous increasingly imaginative food, five interesting changing real ales, prompt friendly service; picnic-sets in peaceful attractive enclosed garden behind *(MP, Marjorie and David Lamb)*

CUDDINGTON [SP7311]

☆ *Crown* [village signed off A418 Thame—Aylesbury; Spurt St]: Small convivial village pub, olde-worlde with candles and open fire, prompt friendly service, unusual choice of good food inc interesting hot sandwiches and specials, Fullers Chiswick, London Pride and ESB, curry night Thurs, summer mediterranean nights *(Graham Parker, John and Glenys Wheeler, Mr and Mrs A Stansfield, Marjorie and David Lamb)*

DAGNALL [SP9916]
Golden Rule [Main Rd S]: Comfortable, friendly and bustling small local, wide changing range of real ales, occasional beer festivals, low-priced tapas-style food; good walk to Whipsnade *(MP)*

DENHAM [TQ0486]
Falcon [Village Rd]: Warm and friendly open-plan pub doing well under current licensees, freshly cooked original dishes with emphasis on fish (more limited choice Sun lunchtime), also cheaper light dishes, well kept ales such as Brakspears, Flowers, Marstons Pedigree and Timothy Taylors Landlord, bare boards and quarry tiles, old painted woodwork, coal-effect gas fires with inglenook fireside seats below ancient cupboards, lower no smoking back dining area, steps up to entrance, lavatories upstairs; teak tables and comfortable chairs out on terrace *(Ian Phillips, John and Glenys Wheeler, Simon Collett-Jones, Ilse Ryder, P J Keen)*
Green Man: Warm and lively 18th-c pub, beams and flagstones in original part, conservatory dining extension, food from sandwiches and baked potatoes to generous good value main dishes, well kept Fullers London Pride, Greene King IPA and Abbot and Charles Wells Bombardier, cheerful willing service; picnic-sets on small back terrace, many more in quiet garden beyond *(Howard Dell)*
☆ *Swan* [¾ mile from M40 junction 1; follow Denham Village signs]: Pretty pub in lovely village, taken over by good new licensees (who also run the main entries at Bovingdon Green, and in Herts at Frithsden) and reworked in the current style of chapel chairs, plain tables and bare boards, with attentive emphasis on the food side – good interesting cooking beautifully presented, with light dishes as well as main courses, and puddings from traditional ones to more exotic home-made tartes; efficient service, Courage Best and Directors and Tetleys, decent house wine, open fires, picture windows overlooking splendid floodlit back garden with picnic-sets and play area; may be thumpy piped music *(John Branston, John and Glenys Wheeler, Ian Phillips, LYM, Peter Saville, Stan Edwards, Howard Dell)*

DINTON [SP7611]
Seven Stars [signed off A418 Aylesbury—Thame, nr Gibraltar turn-off; Stars Lane]: Pretty pub with inglenook bar, comfortable beamed lounge and spacious dining room, well kept Fullers London Pride, food (not Sun evening) from sandwiches and baked potatoes to traditional puddings, prompt service; cl Tues, tables under cocktail parasols in sheltered garden with terrace, pleasant village, handy for Quainton Steam Centre *(Andrea and Guy Bradley, LYM, Dr R C C Ward, Marjorie and David Lamb)*

DORNEY [SU9278]
☆ *Palmer Arms* [B3026, off A4, 2 miles from M4 junction 7]: Friendly and roomily extended early 20th-c pub with colourful carpet in smallish dark green bar and pleasant stripped brick back dining room, pine and dark wood,

food inc good value generous lunches from ciabattas and flatbreads up, smaller children's and OAP helpings, wider evening choice (newish Thai manageress cooks her national cuisine on Mon night), well kept Greene King IPA, Abbot and Old Speckled Hen, 10 wines by the glass, good attentive service, no smoking area; solid garden furniture in good mediterranean-feel garden behind, open all day Sat *(I D Barnett, DC, Martin and Karen Wake, Simon Collett-Jones, Susan and John Douglas, Michael Dandy)*
Pineapple [off A4 Maidenhead—Cippenham by Sainsbury's; Lake End Rd]: Old-fashioned beamery and panelling, gleaming bar, simple furniture, great range of sandwiches, other food inc Sun roasts, well kept Flowers Original, Fullers London Pride and Tetleys, decent house wine, friendly staff; verandah, picnic-sets in garden, good walks *(Ian Phillips)*

DRAYTON PARSLOW [SP8328]
Three Horseshoes [Main Rd]: Good reasonably priced food inc classic steak and kidney pie and some interesting puddings, good choice of beers, friendly helpful service *(V Green, Marjorie and David Lamb)*

FARNHAM ROYAL [SU9584]
King of Prussia [Blackpond Lane]: Small and civilised vine-covered pub back to its original name after many decades as Emperor of India, wide range of interesting food from good choice of sandwiches and baguettes to excellent fish, several well kept real ales; cosy corners, buoyant atmosphere, back restaurant with barn as overflow, well kept garden *(Anthony Longden)*

FINGEST [SU7791]
☆ *Chequers* [signed off B482 Marlow—Stokenchurch]: Proper traditional pub with several rooms around old-fashioned Tudor core, roaring fire in vast fireplace, sunny lounge by good-sized charming country garden with lots of picnic-sets, small no smoking room, interesting furniture, Brakspears full range kept well, dominoes and cribbage, wholesome lunchtime food (not Mon) from sandwiches up, reasonable prices, quick friendly service, attractive restaurant; children in eating area; interesting church opp, picture-book village, good walks – can get crowded wknds *(Tony Middis, Mark Percy, Lesley Mayoh, the Didler, Chris Smith, Tracey and Stephen Groves, Martin and Karen Wake, LYM, Howard Dell)*

FORD [SP7709]
Dinton Hermit [SW of Aylesbury]: This neat little stone cottage, with its inglenook log fire and appealing furnishings, was popular with many readers for its good food, beers and wines, and an attractive sheltered country garden with play area, but was closed in late 2002, with plans for redevelopment probably including half a dozen bedroom units; news please *(LYM)*

FRIETH [SU7990]
Yew Tree [signed off B482 N of Marlow]: Enjoyable if not cheap traditional food in peaceful bar and pleasant dining conservatory

(service charge), well kept ales such as
Brakspears PA and Fullers London Pride,
friendly landlord and exemplary service, huge
log fire, scrubbed pine tables; shame about the
piped music; walkers with dogs welcome,
lovely setting *(LYM, Tracey and
Stephen Groves, Kerry and Tricia Thomas,
Susan and John Douglas)*

FULMER [SU9985]
Black Horse [Windmill Rd]: Small traditional
stepped bar areas, beams, woodburner,
chequered tables, some sofas, well kept Greene
King IPA and Abbot and Hook Norton,
popular food from sandwiches and baguettes
up, good décor; small garden, attractive village
(LM, Dr and Mrs A K Clarke)

GAWCOTT [SP6831]
Crown [Hillesden Rd]: Traditional beamed
village pub lifted from ordinary by good
cooking by Italian chef-landlord, from
sandwiches and home-made pasta through
intensely flavoured main dishes to exemplary
tiramisu; well kept Adnams and a guest such as
Greene King Old Speckled Hen, good italian
wines; long back garden with swings
(Howard and Margaret Buchanan, BB)

GREAT BRICKHILL [SP9029]
☆ *Red Lion* [Ivy Lane]: Friendly two-roomed
traditional pub popular with families in school
hols, Flowers Original, Fullers London Pride
and Greene King IPA, reasonably priced nicely
presented food in bar and restaurant, good
service; fabulous view over Buckinghamshire
and beyond from the enclosed back lawn *(Ian
Phillips, LYM)*

GREAT HORWOOD [SP7630]
Swan [B4033 N of Winslow]: Former coaching
inn, friendly open-plan lounge and dining area,
large attractive inglenook, well kept Bass,
Greene King IPA and Hook Norton Best, usual
food, small back bar with pool and darts; nice
side garden, open all day wknds
(Karen and Graham Oddey)

GREAT KIMBLE [SP8206]
☆ *Bernard Arms* [Risborough Rd (A4010)]:
Plushly upmarket but friendly, with some nice
prints (and photographs of recent Prime
Ministers dropping in for a drink), daily
papers, good if not cheap imaginative food in
bar and restaurant, four changing real ales,
decent wines, good range of malt whiskies and
bottled beer, games room; no dogs, attractive
fairy-lit gardens, well equipped bedrooms
(K Drane, John and Glenys Wheeler)
Swan & Brewer [Grove Lane (B4009, nr
A4010)]: Attractive pub with beamed and tiled
tap room, wide choice of good reasonably
priced fresh food, well kept ales such as
Adnams, Fullers London Pride and Hook
Norton Best, good welcoming service, pleasant
end dining area; well behaved children
allowed, tables out on village green
(Marjorie and David Lamb, B Brewer)

GREAT MISSENDEN [SP8901]
☆ *Cross Keys* [High St]: Cheerful and old-
fashioned beamed bar divided by standing
timbers, bric-a-brac and traditional
furnishings, big open fire, well kept Fullers

Chiswick, London Pride and ESB, good wines,
enjoyable modern food from tasty baguettes
up; children in attractive restaurant, back
terrace *(Kent Barker, Mike Turner, LYM)*

GRENDON UNDERWOOD [SP6820]
Swan [Main St]: Divided open-plan pub with
warm welcome, wide choice of good value
home-made food, good service, Courage real
ales, simple pine furniture on bare floor, back
games area with darts and pool
(Marjorie and David Lamb)

IVINGHOE [SP9416]
☆ *Rose & Crown* [Vicarage Lane, off B489 opp
church]: Cosy and spotless low-ceilinged
L-shaped bar with back lounge up a few
steps, wholesome reasonably priced freshly
made food, well kept ales such as Adnams,
Brakspears, Everards Organic and Tetleys, nice
wine, quick friendly service, separate dining
area, children welcome; quiet piped music, no
muddy boots – nr one end of Ridgeway long-
distance path; small secluded suntrap terrace
with wendy house, pleasant village
*(Christopher and Jo Barton, John and
Glenys Wheeler, Ian Phillips)*

KINGSWOOD [SP6919]
☆ *Plough & Anchor* [Bicester Rd (A41 NW of
Aylesbury)]: Very good food in plain but smart
bar/restaurant, beams and flagstones, heavy
tables, friendly staff, well kept ales such as
Greene King Old Speckled Hen, Tetleys and
Wadworths 6X, good wine list
(H O Dickinson, Brian Root)

LACEY GREEN [SP8201]
☆ *Pink & Lily* [from A4010 High Wycombe—
Princes Risboro follow Loosley sign, then Gt
Hampden, Gt Missenden one]: Charming little
old-fashioned tap room (celebrated sillily by
Rupert Brooke – poem framed here) in much-
extended Chilterns pub with airy and plush
main dining bar, well presented good food;
well kept Brakspears and other changing beers,
good well priced wines, friendly attentive
service, log fires, dominoes, cribbage, ring the
bull; piped music, children over 5 welcome if
eating; conservatory, big garden – and good
free range eggs from next-door farm
*(the Didler, LYM, K Drane, Kerry and
Tricia Thomas, Heather Couper)*

LAVENDON [SP9153]
Horseshoe [A428 Bedford—Northampton;
High St]: Sizeable spotlessly kept low-beamed
village pub with restaurant off small lounge,
enjoyable food from baguettes and baked
potatoes to lots of fish, well kept Charles Wells
ales, small but interesting wine list, quick
efficient service, skittles in public bar;
appealing good-sized garden with play area.
(John Saul, BB, Michael Dandy)

LEDBURN [SP9022]
Hare & Hounds [off B488 Ivinghoe—Leighton
Buzzard, S of Linslade]: Country-style bar and
no smoking back restaurant, bigger than it
looks, with wide range of generous reasonably
priced food, Greene King real ales with a guest
such as Hook Norton, quick friendly down-to-
earth service even when busy, memorabilia of
Great Train Robbery; pleasant back garden,

handy for Ascott (NT) *(Marjorie and David Lamb, MP)*

LITTLE HORWOOD [SP7930]

Old Crown [Mursley Rd]: Friendly old thatched and beamed village pub, small bar, dining area with small room off, good value freshly made food (not Sun evening, Mon lunch) inc children's, real ales, daily papers; juke box, fruit machine, TV, quiz nights; picnic-sets in side garden *(Marjorie and David Lamb)*

☆ *Shoulder of Mutton* [Church St; back road 1 mile S of A421 Buckingham—Bletchley]: New management again in partly thatched timbered pub with rambling bar, promising food (best to book if you don't want a long wait for a table), welcoming sofas and easy chairs on the way in, woodburner in huge inglenook, french windows to pleasant back garden with plenty of tables *(Karen and Graham Oddey, LYM)*

LITTLE KINGSHILL [SU8999]

☆ *Full Moon* [Hare Lane]: Picturesque hidden-away country pub with big helpings of well served food all freshly cooked, changing real ales, friendly landlord, buoyant atmosphere, no piped music; neat attractive garden *(Mr and Mrs David Johnson)*

LITTLE MARLOW [SU8788]

☆ *Kings Head* [A4155 about 2 miles E of Marlow; Church Rd]: Long low flower-covered pub with homely open-plan beamed bar, wide choice of generous food from substantial good value sandwiches to some unusual main dishes, children's menu, smart red dining room, no smoking areas, quick pleasant service, well kept ales such as Brakspears, Marlow Rebellion and Timothy Taylors Landlord; big garden behind popular with families, nice walk down to church *(Mike Turner, BB)*

Queens Head [Church Rd/Pound Lane; cul de sac off A4155 nr Kings Head]: Small and attractive quietly placed pub with current licensees doing interestingly varied good food (not Mon/Tues evening), well kept Marstons Pedigree and Charles Wells Bombardier; darts and TV in public bar, may be jazz Tues; picnic-sets in pleasant front garden, a couple more tables on secluded terrace across lane – short walk from River Thames *(Paul Humphreys, Howard Dell)*

LITTLE MISSENDEN [SU9298]

Red Lion: Small 15th-c local, two coal fires, well kept real ales, decent wines, generous good value standard food, preserves for sale; piped music; tables (some under awning) and busy aviary in sunny side garden by river with ducks, swans and fat trout *(Ken and Jenny Simmonds, John and Glenys Wheeler)*

LITTLEWORTH COMMON [SP9386]

☆ *Blackwood Arms* [3 miles S of M40 junction 2; Common Lane, OS Sheet 165 map ref 937864]: Smartly renovated country pub, blinds and mulberry décor fitting surprisingly well with the traditional furnishings, roaring log fire and handsome oak counter serving well kept Brakspears and guests such as Coniston; friendly atmosphere, prompt pleasant service,

good home cooking inc game and lunchtime bargains, roaring log fire; quiet piped music, dogs welcome; tables in pleasant garden, lovely spot on edge of beech woods – good walks *(Tracey and Stephen Groves, John and Glenys Wheeler, C and R Bromage, Simon Collett-Jones, LYM)*

Jolly Woodman [2 miles from M40 junction 2; off A355]: Busy pub by Burnham Beeches, buildings of varying ages carefully knocked through to give one rambling and cottagey area, beams, timbers, farm tools and hurricane lamps, wide food choice, crisp linen on dining tables, Bass, Brakspears, Flowers Original, Fullers London Pride, Gales HSB and Timothy Taylors Landlord, quick attentive service, useful tourist leaflets; unobtrusive piped music, jazz Mon; tables out in front, picnic-sets in garden behind *(John and Glenys Wheeler, LYM, Susan and John Douglas)*

LONG CRENDON [SP6808]

☆ *Angel* [Bicester Rd (B4011)]: Partly 17th-c restaurant-with-rooms rather than pub – a place for a special treat, with most enjoyable interesting meals (lunchtime open sandwiches and baguettes too), fish and puddings particularly good, friendly and crisply organised service, good no smoking dining areas inc a conservatory, comfortable pre-meal lounge with sofas; well kept Hook Norton and Ridleys, good house wines; may be piped music; tables in garden, good bedrooms *(LYM, Douglas Smart, Mr and Mrs A Stansfield, Bob and Maggie Atherton)*

MAIDS MORETON [SP7035]

☆ *Wheatsheaf* [Main St, just off A413 Towcester—Buckingham]: Cosy thatched and low-beamed pub with keen young landlord, wide choice of good attractively priced food from sandwiches up, well kept Hook Norton Best and a guest beer, farm cider, decent choice of wines, lots of pictures and bric-a-brac in old part, two inglenooks, settles and chairs, friendly atmosphere and service, conservatory restaurant with woodburner; unobtrusive piped music; pleasant quiet enclosed garden behind *(Graham and Elizabeth Hargreaves, D C T and E A Frewer)*

MARLOW [SU8486]

Claytons [Quoiting Sq, Oxford Rd]: Popular tapas bar, not pub, several beer taps (inc Brakspears – not on handpump), nice wines, pleasant atmosphere, friendly staff, good tapas, smooth piped jazz – may be louder piped music evenings, and crowds of young people then; heated terrace *(the Didler, John and Glenys Wheeler)*

☆ *Two Brewers* [St Peter St; first right off Station Rd from double roundabout]: Busy low-beamed pub with most tables set for its good food (may have to book Sun lunch), shiny black woodwork, nautical pictures, gleaming brassware, an unusual crypt-like area, well kept Bass, Brakspears, Fullers London Pride and Marlow Rebellion, good wines, welcoming service, relaxed atmosphere; children in eating area, unobtrusive piped music; tables in sheltered back courtyard with more in converted garage, front seats with glimpse of the Thames (pub right on Thames Path) *(Simon Collett-Jones, Michael Dandy, LYM, John and Glenys Wheeler)*

MARSH GIBBON [SP6422]

☆ *Greyhound* [West Edge]: Traditional furnishings, stripped beams and stonework, and surprisingly good fresh interesting thai food, half-price for children (no under-6s), in bar and two-room restaurant with oriental statuary; well kept Fullers London Pride, Greene King Abbot and IPA, decent house wines, handsome woodburner, dominoes, cribbage, and classical piped music; tables outside with play area *(Karen and Graham Oddey, LYM)*

MOULSOE [SP9041]

☆ *Carrington Arms* [1¼ miles from M1 junction 14: A509 N, first right signed Moulsoe; Cranfield Rd]: Interesting if not cheap pub featuring meats and fresh fish sold by weight from refrigerated display then cooked on indoor barbecue, with wide range of other food, even a lobster tank and separate oyster and caviar bar; well kept Bass, Caledonian Deuchars IPA and Theakstons Best, champagnes by the glass, friendly and helpful new management, comfortable mix of wooden chairs and cushioned banquettes; open all day Sun, children allowed, long pretty garden behind *(W K Wood, Colin Mason, Brian Root, Mrs Catherine Draper, Ian Phillips, John and Judy Saville, LYM)*

NAPHILL [SU8497]

Black Lion [Woodlands Dr]: Good choice of reasonably priced food from generous baguettes and baked potatoes to good value specials, real ales and friendly efficient staff in comfortable open-plan bar with aircraft pictures (Strike Command HQ nearby), and conservatory dining extension; maybe piped music; picnic-sets in good-sized garden with swings and slides, nearby Chilterns walks; has been open all day *(John and Glenys Wheeler, LYM)*

NEWTON BLOSSOMVILLE [SP9251]

Old Mill Burnt Down [4 miles from M1 junction 14; off A428 at Turvey – Clifton Rd]: Cheery homely beamed open-plan pub, tiled and carpeted, rafters and red plush seating, chatty staff, Courage Best and a couple of guest beers, good value usual food inc children's, small no smoking restaurant, steps up to skittles room; small informal back walled garden, bedrooms *(Mike Ridgway, Sarah Miles)*

OLNEY [SP8851]

☆ *Swan* [High St S]: Cosy and civilised beamed and timbered pub, with good choice of excellent value generous food inc plenty of baked potatoes and fish, a bargain daily special, well kept real ales such as Adnams, Fullers London Pride and Hook Norton, lots of good value wines, quick pleasant service; very busy and popular at lunchtime, several rooms off bar, candles on pine tables, log fires, small no smoking back bistro dining room (booking advised for this); no under-10s;

marsh views from roomy bedrooms, garden with tables in courtyard, one under cover *(Stephen, Julie and Hayley Brown, George Atkinson, Michael Dandy, O J Barlow, BB, Roger Braithwaite)*

OVING [SP7821]

Black Boy [off A413 Winslow rd out of Whitchurch]: Quietly friendly and interesting old pub nr church, more spacious inside than it looks; attractive old tables, magnificent collection of jugs, log fire, well kept real ales, well presented generous food esp fish, good children's choice, cheerful service, superb views from extended back dining area over pleasant terrace and big sloping garden; TV in small bar *(Karen and Graham Oddey)*

PENN [SU9193]

☆ *Crown* [B474 Beaconsfield—High Wycombe]: Friendly and accommodating Chef & Brewer, no 'chain pub' feel, good-humoured prompt service even when packed, and interesting uncontrived décor and attractive furnishings in the various areas carefully extended from its low-ceilinged medieval core; wide choice of good generous food all day from sandwiches up, well kept Courage Best, decent wine choice, two roaring log fires, children very welcome, air conditioning; fruit machine, trivia; perched opp 14th-c church on high ridge with distant views, lots of tables in attractive gardens with good play area, wknd barbecues, open all day *(LYM, John and Glenys Wheeler, Peter Saville, Tracey and Stephen Groves, Martin and Karen Wake, Gill and Keith Croxton, Howard Dell, Jenny and Brian Seller, Simon Collett-Jones)*

Red Lion [Elm Rd]: Low-ceilinged traditional bar with vast log fire and plenty of bric-a-brac, no smoking area, separate games room, growing local reputation for wide choice of generous well priced food showing imagination, five real ales inc Marlow Rebellion seasonal ones, friendly landlord and efficient service; children welcome, nice spot opp green and duck pond *(Tracey and Stephen Groves)*

PENN STREET [SU9295]

☆ *Hit or Miss* [off A404 SW of Amersham, then keep on towards Winchmore Hill]: Well laid out low-beamed pub with own cricket ground, pleasant atmosphere in three clean linked rooms, welcoming bustle and helpful service, well kept Badger ales, decent wines, good if not cheap food inc tasty lunchtime snacks, log fire, charming décor inc interesting cricket and chair-making memorabilia, well behaved children over 5 allowed, good-sized no smoking area; may be soft piped music; picnic-sets out in front, pleasant setting *(Peter Saville, Tracey and Stephen Groves, LYM, Graham Chamberlain)*

SAUNDERTON [SU8198]

Rose & Crown [Wycombe Rd]: Pub/hotel with nice log fires, big winged leather chairs and some quirky touches, good choice of wines and guest beers, friendly staff, restaurant with good food from fine kedgeree to well presented contemporary dishes, comfortable coffee lounge; well placed for Chilterns walks, comfortable bedrooms *(David and Belinda Devine, Neil and Karen Dignan)*

SHERINGTON [SP8946]

White Hart [off A509; Gun Lane]: Fair choice of good food from sandwiches up, four well kept real ales, friendly attentive landlord, bright fire, two-room bar and pleasantly rustic restaurant; may be quiet piped radio; children and dogs welcome, picnic-sets in garden with terrace, pretty hanging baskets *(CMW, JJW, Mr and Mrs John Taylor)*

STOKE GREEN [SU9882]

Red Lion [off B416 signed Wexham and George Green]: Rambling and roomy refurbished Vintage Inn, lots of little separate areas with plenty of character and pleasant relaxed atmosphere, well presented good value food, well kept Bass and Tetleys, good choice of decent wines, attentive helpful service, log fires, no smoking room, children welcome; soft piped music; tables outside, may be summer barbecues, open all day *(Simon Collett-Jones, LYM, June and Robin Savage, Dr and Mrs A K Clarke)*

STONE [SP7912]

Bugle Horn [Hartwell; A418 SW of Aylesbury]: Long low whitewashed stone-built Vintage Inn, warm and friendly series of comfortable rooms, pleasant furnishings, good choice of decent food, usual large range of wines by the glass, well kept Bass and Tetleys, log fire and prettily planted well furnished conservatory; no under-21s unless eating; lovely trees in large private garden, horses grazing in meadows beyond *(Tim and Ann Newell, Mel Smith)*

STONY STRATFORD [SP7840]

Fox & Hounds [High St]: 17th-c pub with pictures and photographs, fresh flowers, well kept ales such as Adnams, Crouch Vale High Tide and Everards Tiger, cheerful chef/landlord doing decent cheap lunchtime food from sandwiches and baked potatoes to bargain specials in no smoking lounge area; piped radio, games area with hood skittles, darts, folk, blues or jazz Thurs, Sat and first Tues; tables in walled garden *(George Atkinson, Pete Baker)*

THE LEE [SP8904]

☆ *Old Swan* [Swan Bottom, back rd ¾ mile N of The Lee]: Charming civilised 16th-c dining pub, with very good interesting food esp seafood cooked by long-serving landlord (sandwiches too); four simply but attractively furnished linked rooms, low beams and flagstones, cooking-range log fire in inglenook, particularly well kept Adnams and Brakspears, decent wines, friendly relaxed service; spacious prettily planted back lawns with play area, good walks *(LYM, J M Hunting, Mrs P J Pearce, Piotr Chodzko-Zajko)*

THORNBOROUGH [SP7433]

☆ *Lone Tree* [A421 4 miles E of Buckingham; pub named on OS Sheet 165]: Nicely converted old roadside house, open-plan but not large, with two side areas and unspoilt feel, wide choice of home-made traditional food

such as curried parsnip soup, sardines on toast and kedgeree, well kept changing ales such as Brains St Davids, Fullers London Pride, Hook Norton Steaming On and Shepherd Neame, friendly service, big log fire *(George Atkinson, LYM, Dave Braisted)*

TURVILLE [SU7691]

☆ *Bull & Butcher* [off A4155 Henley—Marlow via Hambleden and Skirmett]: The licensees who stamped their considerable character on this civilised black and white timbered pub were leaving as we went to press, so with no firm news of a successor we have had to suspend it (we hope temporarily) from the main entries; it's a Brakspears pub, so will have their real ales, if not the fantastic range of wines by the glass it's had up to now, or the good interesting bar food; in any event, it's an appealing place, with an inglenook fireplace in one of its two low-beamed rooms, and a lovely Chilterns valley setting; news please *(LYM, Bob and Margaret Holder)*

WENDOVER [SP8607]

☆ *Red Lion* [High St]: Bustling and friendly 17th-c inn with wide choice of good value changing food, generous and imaginative, inc fish specialities, Sun lunch and children's dishes in refurbished oak-beamed flagstoned bar and adjacent good value restaurant, four well kept ales inc one brewed for the pub, good wines, many by the glass, efficient service; can get smoky, dogs allowed till 7; walker-friendly (on Ridgeway Long Distance Path), tables and heaters out behind, with colourful flowering tubs; comfortable bedrooms *(BB, John Branston, John and Glenys Wheeler)*

WEST WYCOMBE [SU8394]

☆ *George & Dragon* [High St; A40 W of High Wycombe]: Handsome and popular centrepiece of beautifully preserved Tudor village, comfortably worn-in rambling bar with massive beams, sloping rust-coloured walls, interesting 1890s village picture over its big log fire, well kept ales such as Courage Best and Charles Wells Bombardier, food from fresh lunchtime sandwiches and wraps to some exotic specials, small no smoking family dining room (wknd children's menu); spacious peaceful garden with fenced play area, bedrooms (magnificent oak staircase), handy for West Wycombe Park *(Susan and John Douglas, Tracey and Stephen Groves, LYM, Mr and Mrs A Mills, Ian Phillips, Simon Collett-Jones)*

WESTON UNDERWOOD [SP8650]

☆ *Cowpers Oak* [signed off A509 in Olney; High St]: Charming wisteria-covered old pub, beams, dark panelling and more stripped masonry after very recent refurbishment, well kept changing ales such as Arundel Cold Willie, Fullers London Pride, Theakstons Old Peculier and Wye Valley Dorothy Goodbodys Winter Tipple, farm cider, generous good value food (all day wknds) inc good soup and hearty sandwiches, no smoking back restaurant, nice medley of old-fashioned furnishings, log fire, good games room with darts, bar billiards, hood skittles and table football, daily papers, friendly black cat; piped music, TV; children very welcome, dogs in main bar; small suntrap front terrace, more tables on new decking and in big attractive orchard garden (no dogs) with play area and farm animals, bedrooms, open all day wknds, pretty thatched village *(Maysie Thompson, LYM, George Atkinson, John and Judy Saville, Ian Phillips, J I Davies)*

WOOBURN COMMON [SU9387]

☆ *Royal Standard* [about 3½ miles from M40 junction 2]: Thriving low-ceilinged two-bar local with friendly and obliging staff, wide choice of enjoyable good value straightforward food, well kept changing ales such as Badger K&B, Caledonian Deuchars IPA, Gales Butser, Greene King Old Speckled Hen and Rebellion Blond, well chosen wines, lots of daily papers,

open fire, popular dining area; picnic-sets on pretty front terrace and in back garden *(LYM, Ian Phillips, Susan and John Douglas)*

WORMINGHALL [SP6308]

☆ *Clifden Arms* [Clifden Rd]: Archetypal 16th-c beamed, timbered and thatched pub in pretty gardens, old-fashioned seats, rustic memorabilia and roaring log fires, attractive lounge bar leading to further no smoking dining area, decent food inc bargain wkdy lunches, well kept real ales inc four interesting guest beers, relaxed friendly service, traditional games in public bar, children allowed; good play area, aunt sally; attractive village *(Dick and Madeleine Brown, Tim and Ann Newell, LYM, Richard Fendick, John and Glenys Wheeler)*

Stars after the name of a pub show exceptional character and appeal. They don't mean extra comfort. And they are nothing to do with food quality, for which there's a separate knife-and-fork symbol. Even quite a basic pub can win stars, if it's individual enough.

Cambridgeshire

Pubs on fine form here include the handsome old Eagle in Cambridge (friendly new licensees), the cheerful Black Horse at Elton (good interesting food here, edging towards a Food Award now, and a big new garden), the friendly Ancient Shepherds at Fen Ditton (enjoyable food), the civilised Chequers at Fowlmere (consistently good for a special meal out), the Blue Bell at Helpston (a new entry – nice all round under its excellent new landlord), the well run Pheasant at Keyston (exceptional food, super wines), the Queens Head at Newton (first-class unspoilt pub, a readers' favourite since our very first edition), Charters in Peterborough (lots of real ales on this converted dutch barge), the Bell at Stilton (really enjoyed for its food, and a bigger bar this year), the White Swan at Stow cum Quy (another new entry, a proper village pub very popular for its good value lunches), the Anchor at Sutton Gault (plenty of atmosphere in this good dining pub), and the Green Man at Thriplow (nice all round, with a happy balance between comfortable pub and smart restaurant). The Chequers, the Pheasant and the Anchor are by no means the only top-drawer dining pubs in this favoured county. In the same small group as the outstanding Pheasant – which for the second year running gains the title of Cambridgeshire Dining Pub of the Year – are the Old Bridge in Huntingdon (a civilised small hotel) and the Three Horseshoes at Madingley (perhaps the most restaurant of the group). In the Lucky Dip section at the end of the chapter, pubs to note particularly are the Lion in Buckden, Free Press in Cambridge, John Barleycorn at Duxford, George & Dragon at Elsworth, Leeds Arms at Eltisley, Golden Pheasant at Etton, Green Man in Grantchester, Pheasant at Great Chishill, Blue Lion at Hardwick, Cock at Hemingford Grey and Red House at Longstowe. Drinks prices in the county are somewhat higher than the national average. The Brewery Tap in Peterborough deeply undercuts prevailing local beer price levels with its own good Oakham ales, as does Charters, its sister ship there. The local Milton beers also tend to be good value, and Adnams, from Suffolk, is often sold more cheaply here than competing national brands.

CAMBRIDGE TL4658 Map 5
Cambridge Blue 🍺 £

85 Gwydir Street

Completely no smoking and free of piped music (mobile phones are discouraged too), this quiet back street pub has two simple uncluttered rooms with old-fashioned bare-boards style furnishings, candles on the tables, a big collection of oars and such a nice selection of rowing photographs that you feel you're browsing through someone's family snaps; cribbage and dominoes. The seven regularly changing well kept real ales on handpump are picked from mostly East Anglian breweries such as Adnams, Elgoods, Iceni, Mauldons, Milton, Nethergate, Potton or Woodfordes; they also have a decent choice of wines and malt whiskies. Reasonably priced straightforward bar food is served in an attractive little conservatory dining area, and might include home-made soup (from £2.95), filled ciabatta rolls (from £3.50), mediterranean vegetable bake or sausage and onion gravy (£5), fish pie, meat pudding or filled giant yorkshire puddings (£6), a cold table with game or picnic pies, nut roast, and various quiches, and puddings (from £2.25). Children like the surprisingly large back garden, which has rabbits and a boules pitch. *(Recommended by John Wooll, the Didler, Michael and Marion Buchanan, Tina and David Woods-Taylor, Mr and Mrs T B Staples, Pat and Tony Martin, Peter J Holmes, Paul Hopton, Dr and Mrs Jackson)*

Free house ~ Licensees Chris and Debbie Lloyd ~ Real ale ~ Bar food (12-2.30, 6-9.30) ~ (01223) 361382 ~ Children welcome in conservatory till 9pm ~ Dogs welcome ~ Open 12-2.30(3 Sat), 5.30-11; 12-3, 6-10.30 Sun; closed evenings 25-26 Dec

Eagle ♀ £

Bene't Street

There's plenty to look at in this lively old stone-front coaching inn including the new plaque celebrating 50 years since the discovery of DNA – Mr Watson was at the ceremony. The five rambling rooms have many charming original architectural features: lovely worn wooden floors and plenty of original pine panelling, two fireplaces dating back to around 1600, two medieval mullioned windows, and the remains of two possibly medieval wall paintings. The creaky old furniture is nicely in keeping. Don't miss the high dark red ceiling which has been left unpainted since World War II to preserve the signatures of British and American airmen worked in with Zippo lighters, candle smoke and lipstick. There is a no smoking room. Under the friendly new licensee, straightforward bar food at lunchtime includes filled baguettes (from £4.70), vegetarian quiche (£4.95), and steak in ale pie, ham and eggs or lasagne (£5.50), while in the evenings, there might be bangers with bubble and squeak (£6.25), tagliatelle with chicken and bacon or with wild mushrooms (£6.75), giant battered cod (£6.95), and steaks (from £7.95). Well kept Greene King IPA, Abbot, Old Speckled Hen, and Ruddles County, and a guest such as Caledonian 80/- or Wadworths 6X on handpump. An attractive cobbled and galleried courtyard, screened from the street by sturdy wooden gates and with heavy wooden seats and tables and pretty hanging baskets, takes you back through the centuries – especially at Christmas, when they serve mulled wine and you can listen to the choristers from King's College singing here. No children inside. *(Recommended by Dr Andy Wilkinson, Mike Turner, B N F and M Parkin, Eric Locker, Anthony Barnes, Terry Mizen, John and Judy Saville, Chris Flynn, Wendy Jones, Tim and Ann Newell, the Didler, M Borthwick)*

Greene King ~ Managers Steve Ottley and Sian Crowther ~ Real ale ~ Bar food (12-3.30, 5-9; not Sat or Sun evenings) ~ (01223) 505020 ~ Open 11-11; 12-10.30 Sun

Live & Let Live ◧ £

40 Mawson Road; off Mill Road SE of centre

Unpretentious and friendly, this bustling little local has a good range of real ales with regulars such as Adnams Bitter, Everards Tiger and Nethergate Umbel, and guests from independent brewers such as Milton, Oakham and Tring on handpump too, as well as several malts. The heavily timbered brickwork rooms have sturdy varnished pine tables with pale wood chairs on bare boards, real gas lighting, lots of interesting old country bric-a-brac, and posters about local forthcoming events; piped music, cribbage, dominoes. The eating area of the bar is no smoking until 9pm, and basic but good value food (unchanged by the new licensee) includes hot filled baguettes (£3.50), popular giant filled yorkshire puddings (£4.95, choose from beef, pork, lamb, sausage or chicken), one or two specials (from £3.95 to £5.95), a Saturday morning breakfast (£4.95), and a Sunday roast (£5.25). More reports please. *(Recommended by Paul Hopton, Dr and Mrs Jackson)*

Burlison Inns ~ Lease Peter Wiffin ~ Real ale ~ Bar food (no food Sun evening) ~ (01223) 460261 ~ Children in eating area of bar ~ Dogs welcome ~ Folk music most Sun evenings ~ Open 11.30-2.30, 5.30(6 Sat)-11; 12-3, 7-10.30 Sun

ELTON TL0893 Map 5
Black Horse

B671 off A605 W of Peterborough and A1(M); Overend

New for this popular dining pub this year is a huge garden plus two acres of grass for children to safely play in; super views across the park. Inside, there are roaring fires, hop-strung beams, a homely and comfortable mix of furniture (no two tables and chairs seem the same), antique prints, and lots of ornaments and bric-a-brac including an intriguing ancient radio set. Dining areas at each end of the bar have parquet flooring and tiles, and the stripped stone back lounge towards the partly no smoking restaurant has an interesting fireplace. Enjoyable food served by welcoming staff includes filled baked potatoes (from £3.25), home-made soup (£3.95), sandwiches (from £4.50), filled baguettes (from £6.25), salads or ploughman's (from £6.95), and home-made pie of the day (£8.95), with changing specials such as home-made pâté with onion marmalade (£4.95), thai mussels or caesar salad with chicken breast, anchovies, croutons and parmesan cheese (£5.25; main course £10), deep-fried filo prawns with sweet chilli and soy sauce (£5.95; main course £10.50), bangers and mash with crispy bacon and red wine jus (£10.95), steaks (from £12.95), cannon of lamb with gooseberry and mint chutney (£13.95), and duck breast with roasted mediterranean vegetable medley or fillet of bass with hollandaise and prawn sauce (£14.95). Well kept Bass, Everards Tiger, Nethergate Suffolk County, and a monthly guest from Nethergate on handpump, and good value wines. There are tables, some shaded by horse chestnut trees, in a garden that's prettily divided into separate areas. Behind the low-built pub is Elton Hall, and this attractive bypassed village has a lovely Saxon church. *(Recommended by Gerry and Rosemary Dobson, Lorraine and Fred Gill, Stephen, Julie and Hayley Brown, Gordon Theaker, M and G Rushworth, Roy Bromell)*

Free house ~ Licensee John Clennell ~ Real ale ~ Bar food (not Sun evening) ~ Restaurant ~ (01832) 280240 ~ Children welcome ~ Dogs allowed in bar ~ Open 12-3, 6-11; 12-11 Sat; 12-6 Sun

ELY TL5380 Map 5
Fountain ⬛

Corner of Barton Square and Silver Street

Close to the cathedral, this genteel, if basic, town corner pub somehow manages to escape the tourists. Very simple and traditional with no music, fruit machines or even food, it's the type of place that's nice to come to for a chat. You'll find a real mix of age groups, and the atmosphere is pleasant and inclusive. They serve well kept Adnams Bitter and Broadside, Fullers London Pride and a changing guest such as Timothy Taylors Landlord on handpump. Old cartoons, local photographs, regional maps and mementoes of the neighbouring King's School punctuate the elegant dark pink walls, and neatly tied-back curtains hang from golden rails above the big windows. Above one fireplace is a stuffed pike in a case, and there are a few antlers dotted about – not to mention a duck at one end of the bar; everything is very clean and tidy. A couple of tables are squeezed on to a tiny back terrace. Note the limited opening times. *(Recommended by Stephen, Julie and Hayley Brown, the Didler, Dr Andy Wilkinson, C J Fletcher)*

Free house ~ Licensees John and Judith Borland ~ Real ale ~ No credit cards ~ (01353) 663122 ~ Children welcome until 8pm but away from bar and must not run around ~ Dogs welcome ~ Open 5-11; 12-2, 6-11 Sat; 12-2, 7-10.30 Sun

Post Office address codings confusingly give the impression that some pubs are in Cambridgeshire, when they're really in the Leicestershire or Midlands groups of counties (which is where we list them).

FEN DITTON TL4860 Map 5

Ancient Shepherds

Off B1047 at Green End, The River signpost, just NE of Cambridge

This is a well liked place for an enjoyable midweek lunch and you can be sure of a friendly welcome from the helpful staff. Perhaps the nicest room is the central one, with lots of fat dark red button-back leather settees and armchairs, low solid indonesian tables, heavy drapes around a window seat with big scatter cushions, and a warm coal fire. Above a black dado the walls (and ceiling) are dark pink, and decorated with little steeplechasing and riding prints, and comic fox and policeman ones, and the lighting is soothing. On the right the smallish convivial bar serves Adnams and Greene King IPA on handpump, and there's another coal fire, while on the left is a pleasant no smoking restaurant (piped music in here). Good bar food includes home-made soup (£3.75), filled granary rolls or baguettes (from £4.25), ploughman's (from £5.95), spicy prawn potato cake with sweet chilli sauce (£6.25), home-baked ham and eggs (£6.95), wild mushroom lasagne (£8.95), and specials like crab salad (£5.50), spinach and ricotta cheese cannelloni (£8.95), home-made beef and Guinness pie (£9.95), and whole lemon sole (£13.95). The friendly pub dog is called Hugo (who may not be around during meal times).
(Recommended by John and Judy Saville, George Atkinson, Bob Turnham)

Pubmaster ~ Tenant J M Harrington ~ Real ale ~ Bar food (not Sun evening) ~ Restaurant ~ (01223) 293280 ~ Children in eating area of bar and restaurant ~ Dogs allowed in bar ~ Open 12-3, 6-11; 12-5.30 Sun; closed Sun evening

FEN DRAYTON TL3368 Map 5

Three Tuns

Signposted off A14 NW of Cambridge at Fenstanton; High Street

The heavy-set moulded Tudor beams and timbers in this well preserved ancient thatched building were certainly built to last, and it may be that this once housed the guildhall for the pretty village. The relaxed and friendly bar has a pair of inglenook fireplaces, there are comfortable cushioned settles, and a nice variety of chairs here and in the appealing partly no smoking dining room. The enjoyable food, served by helpful well trained staff, includes bar snacks such as lunchtime sandwiches, various omelettes (£5.95), home beer-battered cod or home-made steak, Guinness and mushroom pie (£6.95), home-made lasagne (£7.25), and steaks (from £8.95), as well as more elaborate dishes like home-made pâté or thai fishcakes with sweet chilli sauce (£4), japanese filo prawns with an orange, mango and coriander dressing (£4.50), pork, apple and cider sausages on apple mash with onion gravy (£8.95), and duck breast on basil mash with a honey and balsamic jus or braised lamb shank (£10.50). Well kept Greene King IPA and Ruddles Best with a guest like Batemans XXXB or Black Sheep on handpump; piped music, sensibly placed darts, and a fruit machine. A well tended lawn at the back has tables under cocktail parasols, a covered dining area, and a good play area. More reports please.
(Recommended by Steve Riches, Michael and Marion Buchanan, JWAC, Ian Phillips, Peter J Holmes)

Greene King ~ Tenants Tim Cook and Marianne Cook ~ Real ale ~ Bar food ~ Restaurant ~ (01954) 230242 ~ Children welcome ~ Open 12-2.30, 6-11; 12-3, 7-10.30 Sun; closed evenings 25 and 26 Dec, lunchtime 1 Jan

FORDHAM TL6270 Map 5

White Pheasant

Market Street; B1085, off A142 and A11 N of Newmarket

This is a friendly place for either a drink or an enjoyable meal, and the smallish but airy bar has a mix of nicely spaced out big farmhouse tables and chairs, a couple of turkey rugs on the bare boards, some stripped brickwork, and a cheery log fire at one end. One or two steps lead down to a small similarly furnished green-carpeted room. Well kept Adnams Best, Greene King Abbot, and a beer from Elgoods or Woodfordes on handpump from the horseshoe bar that faces the entrance, and there's a carefully chosen wine list. Good bar food includes home-made soup (£4.50), crispy whitebait (£4.75), sandwiches (from £5.25), sausages with mustard mash and red onion gravy (£7.50), and big breakfasts (£9.95), with more elaborate dishes such as sun-dried tomato and spring onion crab cakes (£6.50), seared smoked salmon cutlet with watercress and couscous salad and spring onion crème fraîche (£6.25), king scallops wrapped in bacon (£6.95), wild mushroom tortellini (£10.95), spinach and leek stuffed chicken supreme (£14.95), and barbary duck breast with sweet potato mash and spicy honey gravy (£15.95). There are seats outside in the redeveloped garden. *(Recommended by J D M Rushworth, John and Judy Saville, Ian Phillips, Stephen, Julie and Hayley Brown, Michael Dandy)*

Free house ~ Licensee Elizabeth Meads ~ Real ale ~ Bar food (12-2.30, 7-9) ~ Restaurant ~ (01638) 720414 ~ Children in eating area of bar ~ Open 12-3, 6-11.30(7-10.30 Sun); closed 25 Dec

FOWLMERE TL4245 Map 5
Chequers (🍴) ♀

B1368

In 1660, Pepys had dinner in this 16th-c coaching inn – roast veal and a bottle of port – and today, this civilised place remains somewhere special for a good meal out. Two warm and comfortably furnished communicating rooms downstairs have an open log fire (there's a priest's hole above the bar), while upstairs there are beams, wall timbering and some interesting moulded plasterwork above the fireplace. The airy no smoking conservatory overlooks white tables under cocktail parasols among flowers and shrub roses in an attractive well tended floodlit garden – in summer overhead you might see historic aeroplanes flying from Duxford. From an imaginative menu, dishes might include roast chicken and shi-itake mushroom broth (£3.60), pork and duck pâté with juniper and apricot chutney or fried greek halloumi cheese with marinated roast peppers (£5.20), smoked haddock with chopped chives and tomatoes in a cream and cheese sauce or ploughman's with home-made chutney (£5.40), marinated roast chicken breast topped with pesto (£8.90), a mix of mushrooms and parmesan with pasta (£9.80), grilled calves liver on horseradish mash with caramelised red onion gravy (£10.40), prawn and mango curry with won ton crisps and spicy saffron rice (£10.80), beef and prune tagine (£11.20), and puddings such as hot date sponge with sticky toffee sauce or fried bananas with muscovado sugar and Tia Maria, served with vanilla ice cream and chocolate shavings (from £3.90). The thoughtful selection of attractively priced fine wines by the glass includes vintage and late-bottled ports. There's also a good list of malt whiskies, well kept Adnams with a guest such as Nethergate Old Growler or Oakham Bishops Farewell on handpump, freshly squeezed orange juice, and several brandies. *(Recommended by Bob and Maggie Atherton, A J Bowen, Gordon Prince, Noel and Judy Garner, Ian Phillips, Dr and Mrs D A Blackadder, SH, Dr Andy Wilkinson, Pat and Tony Hinkins, R C Wiles, Mary Anne Wright, Chris Flynn, Wendy Jones, WAH, Adele Summers, Alan Black, Tony and Shirley Albert)*

Free house ~ Licensees Norman and Pauline Rushton ~ Real ale ~ Bar food ~ Restaurant ~ (01763) 208369 ~ Well behaved children allowed lunchtimes in the conservatory ~ Open 12-2.30, 6-11; 12-2.30, 7-10.30 Sun; closed 25 Dec

GODMANCHESTER TL2470 Map 5
Exhibition

London Road

The main bar in this bustling brick house comes as rather a surprise, given the somewhat straightforward-looking frontage. The walls have been decorated with re-created shop-fronts – a post office, gallery, and wine and spirit merchant – complete with doors and stock in the windows. Some large plants have a few white fairy lights, and it's a cosy room, with big flagstones on the floor, cushioned wall benches, and fresh flowers and candles on each of the tables. As well as light lunches – including filled baguettes – the interesting food here might include soup (£3.95), smoked chicken and beetroot fritters on vegetable linguini with red pepper oil (£3.50), marinated seafood with saffron and lemon risotto (£4.50), chicken, pork and olive terrine with tomato concasse (£4.75), pasta of the day with fresh parmesan (£7.25), home-made vegetable spring rolls with mango, coriander and chilli salsa (£7.95), chargrilled bass fillet marinated in fresh herbs served on antipasto salad with toasted olive oil ciabatta (£11.95), chargrilled lamb gigot steak with parsnip mash, steamed pak choi and ginger and soy sauce (£12.75), and braised medallions of beef in a red wine and shallot jus with dauphinoise potatoes and glazed french beans (£13.25). The dining room, with smart candelabra and framed prints, is no smoking. Well kept Fullers London Pride, Greene King IPA and a changing guest beer like Timothy Taylors Landlord on handpump, a good wine list and several malt whiskies. There are picnic-sets on the back lawn, and a couple in front as well, and they hold barbecues in summer. Every year the Exhibition and its sister pub, the nearby White Hart, organise a gathering of steam engines. More reports please. *(Recommended by Michael Dandy)*

Free house ~ Licensee Willem Middlemiss ~ Real ale ~ Bar food (12-2.15, 6.30-9.45; 12.30-2.30, 6.30-9.30 Sun) ~ Restaurant ~ (01480) 459134 ~ Children in eating area of bar, restaurant and family room ~ Monthly live jazz or blues on Tues ~ Open 11.30-3, 5.30-11; 11.30-11 Sat; 12-10.30 Sun

HELPSTON TF1205 Map 5
Blue Bell 🍺
Woodgate; off B1443

The landlord made plenty of friends among our readers at his last pub, the Millstone at Barnack, before he moved here with his loyal and cheerful team in spring 2003. People who knew that pub will recognise some of the pictures on the bar's dark brown panelling-effect walls here; a nice collection of antique and country prints, alongside some big china ornaments, lots of tankards, mugs and horsebrasses overhead, and an enormous brass platter above the small fireplace. There is plenty of red plush, including cushions for the three oak settles. The corner bar counter has well kept Adnams, Everards Tiger and Old Original and a guest such as Moles Holy Moley on handpump, and the good coffee comes with fresh cream; piped music, cribbage and dominoes. Good honest food includes sandwiches (£2.95), baguettes (£3.45), fishcakes or pâté (£3.55), home-made steak in ale pie, stilton and vegetable crumble or fresh battered fish (£7.25), chicken in tarragon (£7.45), barbecued ribs (£7.50), and puddings such as home-made crumbles (£3.45). The comfortable flagstoned no smoking dining room on the right, with stripped joists and some stripped stone, gives the greatest impression of the building's age; John Clare the early 19th-c peasant poet was born next door, and originally worked here. Wheelchair access; there may be faint piped pop music. A sheltered terrace has plastic garden tables under outdoor heaters. *(Recommended by Michael and Jenny Back, Des and Jen Clarke)*

Free house ~ Licensee Aubrey Sinclair Ball ~ Bar food (not Sun, Mon or Tues evenings) ~ Restaurant ~ (01733) 252394 ~ Children in eating area of bar and restaurant ~ Open 11.30-2.30, 5(6 Sat)-11; 12-3.30, 7-10.30 Sun

HEYDON TL4340 Map 5
King William IV 🍽️
Off A505 W of M11 junction 10

Even a dedicated meat-eater would be hard-pushed not to enjoy one of the 10 or so imaginative vegetarian dishes here: tempura of summer vegetables with a trio of oriental dips or bubble and squeak with sweet chestnut potato cakes and wholegrain mustard sauce (£8.95), mushroom wheel filled with mediterranean fruits topped with a swiss gruyère crust and a tomato and basil sauce (£9.25), lattice puff filled with ripe brie, sun-dried tomatoes and courgette with a roasted pepper coulis (£9.45), and goats cheese and vegetable wellington with saffron sauce (£9.95). There's also home-made soup (£3.95), chicken caesar salad (£5.95), lobster and crab thai fishcakes with oriental jam (£6.45), steak and kidney pudding or chicken and pistachio curry (£9.25), and baked scottish salmon wrapped in prosciutto and served with a prawn, pea, basil and mint risotto (£11.95); daily specials, lighter lunchtime bar snacks, and puddings such as chocolate and peppermint torte or sticky toffee pudding (from £5.25). Part of the restaurant is no smoking. Warmed in winter by a log fire, the nooks and crannies of the beamed rambling rooms are crowded with a charming jumble of rustic implements like ploughshares, yokes and iron tools, as well as cowbells, beer steins, samovars, cut-glass, brass or black wrought-iron lamps, copper-bound casks and milk ewers, harness, horsebrasses, smith's bellows, and decorative plates and china ornaments. Well kept real ales such as Adnams Best, Greene King IPA, Fullers London Pride, City of Cambridge Boathouse Bitter, and a beer from Woodfordes named for the pub on handpump; they also do cocktails. Fruit machine. A wooden deck has teak furniture and outdoor heaters, and there are more seats in the pretty garden. *(Recommended by DRH and KLH, M R D Foot, Bob Turnham, WAH, Bob and Maggie Atherton, George Atkinson, Dr and Mrs D A Blackadder, Sarah Davis, Rod Lambert, Andrew and Samantha Grainger, Peter and Joan Elbra, J D M Rushworth, Ian Arthur)*

Free house ~ Licensee Elizabeth Nicholls ~ Real ale ~ Bar food (till 10 Sat) ~ Restaurant ~ (01763) 838773 ~ Children in snug at any age but must be over 12 in restaurant ~ Dogs allowed in bar ~ Open 12-2.30(3 Sat), 6.30(6 Sat)-11; 12-3, 7-10.30 Sun; closed 25 Dec

HINXTON TL4945 Map 5
Red Lion
Between junctions 9 and 10, M11; just off A1301 S of Great Shefford

This pretty pink-washed and twin-gabled old pub is a popular place to eat, though they do keep four real ales, too. The dusky mainly open-plan bustling bar is no smoking, and has leather chesterfields on wooden floors, and perhaps George the chatty amazon parrot; cribbage. The smart restaurant is filled with mirrors, pictures, grandfather and other assorted clocks. Served by friendly staff, the lunchtime snacks might include sandwiches (from £2.50; chargrilled steak, red onion and black pepper £5.95), home-made soup (£3.95), and filled baked potatoes (from £3.95), as well as chicken satay (£4.75), home-made chicken liver, port and brandy pâté with onion marmalade (£4.95), thai prawn, bean sprout and red chilli fritters with sweet chilli sauce (£5.95), chicken or vegetable madras (£6.95), lasagne (£7.95), steak in ale pie (£8.95), oven-roasted pork escalope layered with a mushroom, red onion and tarragon sauce (£10.75), steaks (from £11.95), and puddings like home-baked apple pie or banoffi pie (from £4.25). Real ales on handpump include Adnams, Greene King IPA, Woodfordes Wherry and perhaps guests such as Adnams Regatta, kept in good condition. In the tidy, attractive garden there's a pleasant terrace with picnic-sets. The pub is not far from the Imperial War Museum, Duxford. *(Recommended by Andrew and Samantha Grainger, Eric Locker, Pat and Tony Martin, Mike and Shelley Woodroffe, Dr and Mrs D A Blackadder, Jason Caulkin, John Wooll, Oliver and Sue Rowell)*

Free house ~ Licensees Jim and Lynda Crawford ~ Real ale ~ Bar food ~ Restaurant ~ (01799) 530601 ~ Children in restaurant and family room ~ Open 11-2.30, 6-11; 12-2.30, 7-10.30 Sun; closed 25 and 26 Dec

HUNTINGDON TL2371 Map 5
Old Bridge Hotel ★ ⑪ ♀ ⇔
1 High Street; ring road just off B1044 entering from easternmost A14 slip road

Civilised and not too big, this attractive hotel is tucked away in a good spot by the River Great Ouse with its own landing stage, and tables on the waterside terraces. The main emphasis is on the excellent imaginative food, which you can eat in the big no smoking airy Terrace (an indoor room, but with lovely verdant murals suggesting the open air) or in the slightly more formal panelled no smoking restaurant. Changing monthly, the menu might include spinach and lentil soup with crème fraîche (£4.75), risotto of the day (£5.50; main course £10), seared scallops with roast artichoke and vegetables à la grecque (£8.75), deep-fried cod with pease pudding (£11.50), braised pork belly with parsnip purée, savoy cabbage and caramelised apple (£13.50), corn-fed goosnargh chicken with boulangère potato, morel mushrooms and leeks (£14.75), loin of cornish lamb with sweetbreads and braised young fennel (£18), and puddings such as liquorice floating island, cardamom and carrot pancakes with cape gooseberry compote and vanilla ice cream or hot Valrhona chocolate fondant with jersey double cream (from £4.50); they also offer hot and cold sandwiches (from £5), and a Monday-Saturday two-course bargain lunch for £12. They excel too in their wine list which includes a fine choice by the glass; there's also freshly squeezed orange juice, smoothies, and good coffee. The bar, with its fine polished floorboards, good log fire, and quietly chatty atmosphere, serves well kept Adnams, Timothy Taylors Landlord, and a guest such as Batemans or Wadworths 6X on handpump. There are seats in the neat garden (unfortunately there may be some traffic noise, too). More reports please. *(Recommended by Philip J Cooper, David and Judith Stewart, J F M and M West, Gordon Theaker, R C Wiles, Pamela and Merlyn Horswell, Andy and Ali, David R Crafts, Joe Green; also in the Good Hotel Guide)*

Huntsbridge ~ Licensee Martin Lee ~ Real ale ~ Bar food (12-2, 7-10(9.30 Sun)) ~ Restaurant ~ (01480) 424300 ~ Children welcome ~ Dogs allowed in bar and bedrooms ~ Open 11-11; 12-10.30 Sun; closed first Sun after 25 Dec ~ Bedrooms: £95B/£125B

KEYSTON TL0475 Map 5
Pheasant 🍴 ♀

Village loop road; from A604 SE of Thrapston, right on to B663

Cambridgeshire Dining Pub of the Year

This neatly kept and thatched white building has come a long way since it was the village smithy. It's now a civilised dining pub with courteous and smart young staff and exceptional food. As well as sandwiches, the menu might include squid and sweetcorn soup with chilli oil (£4.95), deep-fried brie de meaux with roast onion jam (£5.95), carpaccio of aberdeenshire beef with radicchio and aged balsamic (£7.95), south coast crab with fresh pasta and chilli (£7.95; main course £12.95), bangers and mash with white onion sauce (£8.95), chicken with herbs, potato purée, mousseron mushrooms and spinach (£13.95), whole bass cooked in a bag with roast vegetables or navarin of spring lamb with sautéed lamb sweetbreads and spring vegetables (£14.95), aberdeenshire steaks (from £14.95), and puddings like crème brûlée with lime leaves and lemon grass with strawberry juice and strawberry sorbet or hot chocolate fondant with crème fraîche (from £5.50); there's a bargain lunch for £5 per course on Monday-Saturday lunchtimes. One dining area is no smoking. The excellent wine list includes an interesting choice of reasonably priced bottles and around 20 wines by the glass (plus two champagnes); fine port and sherry too. There's also well kept Adnams Bitter with changing guests like Nethergate Augustinian or Potton Shambles or Village Bike on handpump, and freshly squeezed juices. The atmosphere in the oak-beamed spreading bar is relaxing, and there are open fires, simple wooden tables and chairs, guns on the pink walls, and country paintings. Seats out in front of the building. *(Recommended by Ian and Jane Irving, J F M and M West, Gordon Theaker, J R Bird, O K Smyth, Stephen, Julie and Hayley Brown, Oliver and Sue Rowell, Dr Alan Sutton, Marjorie and Bernard Parkin, R C Wiles)*

Huntsbridge ~ Licensee Clive Dixon ~ Real ale ~ Bar food (12-2, 6.30-9.30; 12-2, 7-8.45 Sun) ~ Restaurant ~ (01832) 710241 ~ Children welcome ~ Dogs allowed in bar ~ Open 12-3, 6-11; 12-3, 7-10.30 Sun; closed 25/26 Dec, 1 Jan evenings

You can send us reports through our web site: www.goodguides.com

KIMBOLTON TL0967 Map 5
New Sun ♀

High Street

In a lovely village main street, this seems to be somewhere that readers drop into on a regular basis, whether for a pint, a morning coffee or to enjoy the very good food. The low-beamed front lounge is perhaps the cosiest, with a couple of comfortable armchairs and a sofa beside the fireplace, standing timbers and exposed brickwork, books, pottery and brasses, and maybe mid-afternoon sun lighting up the wonkiest corners. This leads into a narrower locals' bar, with well kept Wells Bombardier and Eagle, and a guest such as Greene King Old Speckled Hen, and over a dozen wines by the glass; fruit machine and piped music. Opening off here are a dining room and a bright, busy tiled conservatory, with wicker furniture, an unusual roof like a red and yellow striped umbrella, and plenty of tables for eating. As well as lunchtime sandwiches and filled baked potatoes, the menu might include feta cheese, baby fig and sunblush tomato salad with raspberry vinegar dressing (£4.75), kiln roasted salmon with dill and whisky sauce (£5.50), king prawns in hot garlic and ginger oil (4 for £6), steak and kidney pudding with cabbage and bacon and roast gravy (£7.50), fresh spring vegetable risotto with parmesan, mint oil and leaf salad (£8.50), chicken supreme with potato rösti, curly kale, goats cheese and pancetta sauce (£10.75), steaks (from £11.25), fried bass and tiger prawns with wilted spinach, parisienne potatoes and salsa verde (£12.25), and wild boar cutlet, roast baby vegetables, basil crushed potatoes and calvados jus (£13.95). Service is friendly and attentive. There's a very pleasant garden behind, with plastic tables and chairs. Some of the nearby parking spaces have a 30-minute limit. More reports please. *(Recommended by George Atkinson, P Abbott, John Picken)*

Charles Wells ~ Tenant Stephen Rogers ~ Real ale ~ Bar food (12-2.15(2.30 Sun), 7-9.30; not Sun, Mon evenings) ~ Restaurant ~ (01480) 860052 ~ Children in eating area of bar and restaurant ~ Dogs allowed in bar ~ Open 11(11.30 Sat)-2.30, 6(6.30 Sat)-11; 12-10.30 Sun

MADINGLEY TL3960 Map 5
Three Horseshoes 🍴 ♀

Off A1303 W of Cambridge

Perhaps this elegant thatched place is the most restauranty of this little chain of pubs, yet it still has a pleasantly relaxed if civilised atmosphere, and does offer a couple of real ales. To be sure of a table it's best to book well in advance. From an innovative menu and served in the bar or conservatory-restaurant, the daily changing dishes might include pea and bean salad with shaved pecorino, dandelion, mint and olive oil (£5.75), risotto of crab, chilli, parsley, chardonnay and crème fraîche (£6.75), antipasti of cured duck, parma ham and salami with shaved fennel, dill and lemon salad (£7.75), chargrilled breast of chicken with roasted courgettes, new potatoes, marjoram and pancetta with green chilli and lemon peel salsa (£14.50), chargrilled strips of lambs kidney and liver, roast red onions, green beans, lentils, and salsa verde (£15.50), whole roast bass with garlic and rosemary baked new potatoes, wild mixed mushrooms, rocket and lemon (£16.50), fillet of beef with roast butternut squash, leeks, thyme and garlic with olive oil mash, and aged balsamic (£18.50). Not just the food but the wine list too is outstanding, with around 20 wines by the glass, plus sweet wines and ports. The pleasantly relaxed little no smoking airy bar has an open fire, simple wooden tables and chairs on the bare floorboards, stools at the bar and pictures on the green walls. Well kept Adnams plus a guest such as Everards Tiger or Wadworths 6X on handpump. More reports please. *(Recommended by Pamela Goodwyn, Terry Mizen, Michael Dandy, Maysie Thompson, R C Wiles, Brian Root)*

Huntsbridge ~ Licensee Richard Stokes ~ Real ale ~ Bar food (12-2(2.30 Sun), 6.30-9.30) ~ Restaurant ~ (01954) 210221 ~ Children welcome ~ Open 11.30-3, 6-11; 12-2.30 Sun; closed Sun evening

NEWTON TL4349 Map 5

Queens Head ★ ◀ £

2½ miles from M11 junction 11; A10 towards Royston, then left on to B1368

'May this pub never change' is the plea from one of our long-standing readers. The licensees have been here for over 26 years and always offer a genuinely friendly welcome to all their customers, and it is this real hospitality plus the simple and unspoilt feel of the place that appeals to so many. The well worn main bar has a low ceiling and crooked beams, bare wooden benches and seats built into the walls, paintings on the cream walls, and bow windows. A curved high-backed settle stands on yellow tiles, a loudly ticking clock marks the unchanging time, and a lovely big log fire cheerily warms the place. The little carpeted saloon is similar but even cosier. Adnams Bitter and Broadside are tapped straight from the barrel, with Regatta in summer, Old Ale in winter and Tally Ho at Christmas, Crone's and Cassell's ciders, and organic apple juice. Darts in a no smoking side room, with shove-ha'penny, table skittles, dominoes, cribbage, and nine men's morris. There's a limited range of hearty straightforward food which includes toast and beef dripping (£2), good value lunchtime sandwiches (from £2, including things like banana with sugar and lemon or herb and garlic), a mug of lovely home-made brown soup (£2.50), and filled baked potatoes (£2.70); in the evening and on Sunday lunchtime you can get plates of excellent cold meat, smoked salmon, cheeses and pâté (from £3.50). There are seats in front of the pub, with its vine trellis. (*Recommended by Dr Emma Disley, Mr Biggs, Susan and Nigel Wilson, Ian Phillips, Michael and Marion Buchanan, R C Wiles, Charles Gysin, JWAC, Minda and Stanley Alexander, Tim Maddison*)

Free house ~ Licensees David and Juliet Short ~ Real ale ~ Bar food (not 25 Dec) ~ No credit cards ~ (01223) 870436 ~ Very well behaved children in games room ~ Dogs welcome ~ Open 11.30-2.30, 6-11; 12-2.30, 7-10.30 Sun; closed 25 Dec

PETERBOROUGH TL1999 Map 5

Brewery Tap ◀ £

Opposite Queensgate car park

The threat of being turned into a parking complex still hangs over this cavernous pub, said to be one of the largest microbreweries in Europe. They keep up to a dozen real ales on handpump, and a huge glass wall on one side of the building gives a view of the massive copper-banded stainless brewing vessels that produce the very good Oakham beers: Bishops Farewell, Helterskelter, JHB and White Dwarf from the brewery here, with guests from breweries scattered all over the country. There's an American style to the place which is a striking conversion of an old labour exchange, with blue-painted iron pillars holding up a steel-corded mezzanine level, light wood and stone floors, and hugely enlarged and framed newspaper cuttings on its light orange or burnt red walls. It's stylishly lit by a giant suspended steel ring with bulbs running around the rim, and steel-meshed wall lights. A band of chequered floor tiles traces the path of the long sculpted light wood bar counter, which is boldly backed by an impressive display of bottles in a ceiling-high wall of wooden cubes. A new sofa seating area downstairs and padded upstairs seating make this already relaxed, friendly and comfortable venue popular with a surprisingly mixed bunch of customers. It gets very busy in the evening, and there's a DJ on Friday and Saturday nights, when there may be an entry fee. The thai bar food, prepared by Thai chefs, includes snacks (£1.50-£3.95), stir fries (£4.95-£6.50), curries (£4.95-£5.95), and set menus (from £10.95) and buffets (from £11.95). It's owned by the same people as Charters. (*Recommended by Rona Murdoch, Richard Lewis, Ian and Nita Cooper, the Didler, Peter and Pat Frogley, Pat and Tony Martin*)

Own brew ~ Licensees Stuart Wright and Emma Walker ~ Real ale ~ Bar food (all day Fri/Sat) ~ (01733) 358500 ~ DJ Fri/Sat evenings ~ Open 12-11(till 1.30am Fri/Sat); 12-10.30 Sun

Charters 🍺 £

Town Bridge, S side

Apart from the fact that this lively pub offers a dozen real ales (enough of a draw for that alone), it's worth a visit for the novelty value, as this unusual place is housed in a remarkable conversion of a sturdy 1907 commercial dutch grain barge. As well as four permanent real ales such as Bass, Hop Back Summer Lightning, their own Oakham JHB, and Timothy Taylors Landlord, they keep eight quickly changing guests from many widely spread breweries. There's plenty of seating in the well timbered sizeable nautically themed bar, which is down in the cargo holds, and above deck a glazed oriental restaurant replaces the tarpaulins that used to cover the hold; piped music. Good value asian-style lunchtime bar food includes snacks like crispy seaweed, prawn toasts or spring rolls (from £1.50), pitta bread filled with oriental duck, beef in black bean sauce, thai stir fry or sweet and sour vegetables (£3.65), and singapore chicken curry or lamb rendang curry (£5.65). The pub also boasts one of the biggest pub gardens in the city. *(Recommended by the Didler, Peter F Marshall, Rona Murdoch)*

Free house ~ Licensees Stuart Wright and Emma Walker ~ Real ale ~ Bar food (12-2.30) ~ Restaurant ~ (01733) 315700 ~ Children in restaurant ~ Dogs welcome ~ Live bands Fri/Sat ~ Open 12-11(10.30 Sun; till 2am Fri/Sat)

STILTON TL1689 Map 5

Bell 🍴 🍷 🛏

High Street; village signposted from A1 S of Peterborough

By the time this book is published, the Village Bar in this elegant 16th-c stone coaching inn will have doubled in size. Neatly kept, this extended room and the residents' bar have bow windows, sturdy upright wooden seats on flagstone floors as well as plush button-back built-in banquettes, and there's a good big log fire in one handsome stone fireplace. The partly stripped walls have big prints of sailing and winter coaching scenes, and a giant pair of blacksmith's bellows hangs in the middle of the front bar; backgammon, dominoes and piped music. Generously served and popular, the good bar food includes sandwiches, stilton and broccoli soup (£3.50), chicken liver pâté with onion jam (£4.50), mussels in a creamy garlic and thyme sauce (£5.50; main course £10.50), wild smoked salmon with potato pancake and crème fraîche (£5.95), pasta with mediterranean vegetables and goats cheese or chicken supreme on crushed potatoes with a smoked bacon, brie and mushroom sauce (£9.50), grilled lamb rack cutlets with redcurrant glaze or whole baked bass with pesto couscous (£10.50), chargrilled 10oz sirloin steak with stilton or pepper sauce (£13.45), daily specials, and puddings. The eating area of the bar and lower part of the restaurant are no smoking, and service is friendly and obliging. Well kept Bass, Greene King IPA and Abbot, and Oakham JHB on handpump, and a decent choice of wines by the glass. Through the fine coach arch is a lovely sheltered courtyard with tables, and a well which supposedly dates back to Roman times; attractive chintzy bedrooms. *(Recommended by Gordon Theaker, B and M Kendall, David and Betty Gittins, Anthony Barnes, Tony Gayfer, Barry Collett, P R Morley, Mrs Joy Griffiths, Bob Turnham, David and Brenda Tew)*

Free house ~ Licensee Liam McGivern ~ Real ale ~ Bar food (12-2, 6.30-9.30; 12-2.30 Sun lunchtime) ~ Restaurant ~ (01733) 241066 ~ Well behaved children in eating area of bar at lunchtime only ~ Open 12-2.30(3 Sat), 6-11; 12-3, 7-10.30 Sun; closed 25 Dec ~ Bedrooms: £72.50B/£96.50B

STOW CUM QUY TL5260 Map 5

White Swan 🍺

Off A14 just E of Cambridge; from B1102 through village turn off at Bottisham sign

This is a proper village local, bustling at lunchtime for its popular and straightforward home cooking, from a good choice of baguettes (from £3), some with hot fillings, and ham or cheese ploughman's (£4.75) to piping hot main dishes brought through by the friendly chef, such as soup (£2.95), hot goats cheese salad (£3.95), liver and bacon (£6.50), fishcakes or beef and ale pie (£6.95) and steaks (£10.50), with a choice of Sunday roasts (£7.50). The carpeted bar, with traditional cushioned wall seats and wheelback chairs, has a coal-effect stove in its big fireplace; the dining room on the left is no smoking, with flowers on its tables. They have a couple of changing guest beers on handpump, often including interesting seasonal ones, besides their regular well kept Adnams, Greene King IPA and Woodfordes Wherry; welcoming service. There are picnic-sets out on the terrace. *(Recommended by Terry Mizen, Michael and Marion Buchanan, Peter J Holmes)*

Free house ~ Licensee Melanie Rowlatt ~ Bar food ~ Restaurant ~ (01223) 811821 ~ Children in restaurant ~ Dogs allowed in bar ~ Open 11-3, 5.30-11; 12-3, 7-10.30 Sun; closed Mon lunchtime in winter

SUTTON GAULT TL4279 Map 5
Anchor ★ ⑪ ♀
Village signed off B1381 in Sutton

Before or after a lunchtime visit to this popular dining pub, you can enjoy a walk along the high embankment, and the birdwatching is said to be good, too; pleasant seats outside. Inside, there are four heavily timbered stylishly simple rooms with a nicely pubby and informal atmosphere, three log fires, antique settles and well spaced scrubbed pine tables on the gently undulating old floors, good lithographs and big prints on the walls, and lighting by gas and candles. Most customers do come to enjoy the particularly good (though not cheap) food, and to be sure of a table, it's best to book. During the week, there's a light lunch menu with toasted chicken and bacon club sandwich or ploughman's (£5.95), eggs benedict (£5.95; main course £8.95), salad of buffalo mozzarella, bayonne ham and rocket with a honey dressing (£7.50), and ham hock with creamy mustard sauce (£7.95), as well as home-made soup (£4.50), warm red onion and goats cheese tart with celeriac salad (£5.25; main course £10.50), baked ramekin of smoked haddock with spinach, egg, mashed potato and saffron cream sauce (£6.50), saffron and pumpkin risotto (£11), fillets of gilt head bream with asparagus and lemon butter sauce (£14.50), braised shoulder of lamb with cannellini bean stew and rosemary gravy or calves liver with bacon and mushroom mash and creamy onion sauce (£14.95), scotch rump steak with béarnaise sauce (£15), and puddings like thin baked french apple tart with calvados ice cream, sticky toffee pudding with caramel sauce and home-made vanilla ice cream or chocolate nemesis with crème fraîche (from £3.95); good cheeses, and three-course Sunday lunch (£19.95). A thoughtful wine list (including a wine of the month and eight by the glass), winter mulled wine and freshly squeezed fruit juice, and a real ale tapped from the cask from a brewer such as City of Cambridge; friendly, helpful staff. *(Recommended by Gordon Theaker, A J Bowen, Bob and Maggie Atherton, O K Smyth, M and G Rushworth, Adele Summers, Alan Black, John and Judy Saville, D L Parkhurst, David Green, Sharon and Alan Corper, Anthony Longden, DC)*

Free house ~ Licensee Robin Moore ~ Real ale ~ Restaurant ~ (01353) 778537 ~ Children welcome ~ Open 12-3, 7(6.30 Sat)-11(10.30 Sun); closed 25 Dec evening, and 26 Dec ~ Bedrooms: £50S(£65B)/£75S(£95B)

THRIPLOW TL4346 Map 5
Green Man
3 miles from M11 junction 10; A505 towards Royston, then first right; Lower Street

They've managed to strike a happy balance between comfortable pub and smart restaurant in this well liked Victorian pub. There's a good mix of furniture, mostly sturdy stripped tables and attractive high-backed dining chairs and pews on a flowery red carpet, and shelves with pewter mugs and decorated china. To the right of the bar a sweet and cosy little room has comfortable sofas and armchairs, while two arches lead through to a no smoking restaurant on the left. A very short lunchtime bar menu includes home-made soup (£2.95), a dipping plate of hummous and tzatsiki with marinated black olives and toasted fingers of pitta bread (£4.50), freshly baked organic baguettes with salad and a choice of fillings (from £4.50), and fresh pasta with anchovies, capers, chilli, onion and coriander or home-made burger (£4.95); in the evening, there are starters (£5.75) such as ceviche of scallops, chicken liver parfait with raisin and whisky chutney or grilled and roasted vegetable salad, main courses (£15.50) like goats cheese and spinach soufflé, roast rack of spring lamb with braised butter beans, bacon and basil or bouillabaissse, and puddings (£5.25) like crème brûlée with home-made shortbread, creamed rice pudding or a plate of sliced seasonal fruit with mint and vanilla syrup and strawberry sorbet. Regularly changing real ales from brewers such as Batemans, Oakham, Oldershaw, Milton, and Wolf. You can sit outside (there's an outdoor heater). *(Recommended by Malcolm and Jennifer Perry, Neville and Anne Morley, Maureen and Bill Sewell, Ian Phillips, S Horsley, Roger Everett, David R Crafts, Francis Johnston, Kevin Thorpe)*

Free house ~ Licensee Ian Parr ~ Real ale ~ Bar food (lunchtime only; not Mon) ~ Restaurant ~ (01763) 208855 ~ Children welcome ~ Open 12-3, 6-11; closed Sun evening, all Mon

WANSFORD TL0799 Map 5
Haycock ♀ ⇌

Village clearly signposted from A1 W of Peterborough

Under new ownership just as we went to press, this handsome and much extended old coaching inn is a useful place to take a break from the busy A1, though of course many customers tend to stay overnight. The main entrance hall has a fine flagstone floor with antique hunting prints, seats and a longcase clock, and this leads into a smart panelled main bar with dark terracotta walls, a sturdy rail above a mulberry dado, and old settles. Through two comely stone arches is another attractive area, while the comfortable front sitting room has some squared oak panelling by the bar counter, a nice wall clock, and a big log fire. The airy stripped brick Orchard Room by the garden has dark blue and light blue basketweave chairs, pretty flowery curtains and nice modern prints; doors open on to a big sheltered courtyard with lots of tables and cream italian umbrellas; piped music. Good food includes chicken liver pâté with spiced tomato chutney (£4.95), cod and crab fishcakes with a lightly spiced coconut sauce (£5.25; main course £10.30), smashing sandwiches (from £5.25), toasted open ciabatta (from £6), ploughman's (£7.25), scrambled egg and smoked salmon (£7.95), sausage and mash with onion gravy (£7.95), mushroom and leek with pasta in a creamy garlic sauce (£9.95), battered fish with mushy peas (£12.25), and roast duck breast with a cinnamon and cassis sauce (£16.95); the restaurant is no smoking. Well kept Adnams and Bass on handpump and a good wine list. More reports on the new regime, please. *(Recommended by Norma and Keith Bloomfield, Gordon Theaker)*

Free house ~ Licensee Pierre Marechal ~ Real ale ~ Bar food (10-9) ~ Restaurant ~ (01780) 782223 ~ Children in eating area of bar and restaurant ~ Dogs allowed in bar and bedrooms ~ Open 11-11; 12-10.30 Sun ~ Bedrooms: £90B/£100B

Lucky Dip

Besides the fully inspected pubs, you might like to try these Lucky Dips recommended to us and described by readers (if you do, please send us reports: www.goodguides.com).

ABBOTSLEY [TL2256]
Jolly Abbot [High Street/St Neots Rd]: Roomy, relaxed and comfortable open-plan pub with chef/landlord doing good interesting food using carefully chosen ingredients, restaurant sectioned off by standing timbers, leather banquettes, chesterfields and stools, Greene King real ales, decent wines, welcoming service, nice atmosphere *(Anthony Barnes)*

ABINGTON PIGOTTS [TL3044]
Pig & Abbot: Thriving L-shaped bar with four real ales inc Adnams and Fullers London Pride, food inc good hot beef baguettes *(JHBS)*

BARNACK [TF0704]
Millstone [off B1443 SE of Stamford, via School Lane into Millstone Lane]: Timbers, high beams and stripped stone, with no smoking conservatory extension and converted cellar area; the landlord who made it a popular main entry for its enjoyable food, good beer and cheerful atmosphere has just moved to the nearby Blue Bell at Helpston (see main entries) – too recently for us to form a view on the new team here *(LYM)*

BARRINGTON [ST3818]
☆ *Royal Oak* [turn off A10 about 3¾ miles SW of M11 junction 11, in Foxton; West Green]: New licensees in rambling thatched Tudor pub with tables out overlooking classic village green, heavy low beams and timbers, lots of character, enjoyable food in bar and pleasant no smoking dining conservatory, friendly prompt service, well kept real ales, children welcome; discreet piped music *(P and D Carpenter, Gordon Theaker, LYM)*

BOXWORTH [TL3464]
Golden Ball [High St]: Attractive pub/restaurant with enjoyable food, well kept real ales, helpful service; piped music; big well kept garden, nice setting *(Gordon Theaker, Roche Bentley)*

BRAMPTON [TL2170]
Grange [High St]: Imposing hotel with leatherette chairs and sofas in back bar used by locals, good food from sandwiches and more substantial bar meals (not Sun evening) to fine restaurant meals (not Sun evening or Mon), welcoming landlord, good service, Greene King IPA; comfortable bedrooms *(BB, Gordon Theaker)*

BRINKLEY [TL6254]
Red Lion [High St]: Large bar with log fire, nice no smoking dining room, enjoyable food inc good fresh veg and set lunches, friendly efficient service *(Adele Summers, Alan Black)*

BUCKDEN [TL1967]
☆ *Lion* [High St]: Handsome partly 15th-c coaching inn, black beams and big inglenook log fire in airy and chattily relaxed bow-windowed entrance bar with plush bucket seats and wing armchairs, panelled restaurant beyond latticed window partition, decent well presented bar food, neat quick staff, good choice of wines, Greene King IPA, no music or machines; bedrooms with own bathrooms *(Michael Dandy, Gordon Theaker, Mr and Mrs J Glover, Susan Lee, Darly Graton, Graeme Gulibert, BB)*

BURROUGH GREEN [TL6355]
Bull [B1061 Newmarket—Sturmer]: Attractive traditional country pub, cosy and warm, with friendly landlord and good service, well kept Greene King, varied home-made food, interesting farm tools behind nice woodburner, no smoking dining room *(Adele Summers, Alan Black)*

BYTHORN [TL0575]
☆ *White Hart* [just off A14]: Attractively relaxed dining pub with good generous bistro food in homely bar and several smallish interestingly furnished linked no smoking rooms off; thoughtfully chosen affordable wines, well kept ales such as Greene King IPA and Abbot, excellent coffee, friendly service, children welcome; cl Sun evening and Mon *(Stephen, Julie and Hayley Brown, LYM, David and Mary Webb)*

CAMBRIDGE [TL4458]
Anchor [Silver St]: Well laid out pub worth knowing for its beautiful riverside position by a punting station, with fine river views from its upper bar and suntrap terrace; Flowers IPA, bar lunches till 4, evening baguettes, children in eating areas, open all day *(Mark Walker, Tim and Ann Newell, Dr and Mrs Jackson, LYM)*

☆ *Castle* [Castle St]: Large, airy and well appointed, with full Adnams range kept well and guests such as Wadworths, enjoyable generous quickly served food, no smoking area with easy chairs upstairs, friendly staff; can be crowded, may be piped pop music; picnic-sets in good garden *(the Didler, P and D Carpenter)*

Champion of the Thames [King St]: Small cosy local with particularly well kept Greene King IPA and Abbot, plenty of character, decorated windows, padded walls and seats, painted Anaglypta ceiling, lots of woodwork, no music, welcoming atmosphere, may be lunchtime sandwiches *(the Didler)*

☆ *Free Press* [Prospect Row]: Charmingly unpretentious proper pub, no smoking throughout, no piped music, machines or mobile phones; plain wooden tables and benches on bare boards, open fires, short choice of cheap ample tasty food inc plenty of vegetarian dishes, well kept Greene King IPA, Abbot and Mild and a guest beer, decent wines, friendly service, cribbage and dominoes; small sheltered paved back garden *(the Didler, John Wooll, Terry Mizen, LYM, Bob Turnham, Dr and Mrs Jackson, David Edwards)*

Kingston Arms [Kingston St]: Large popular U-shaped pub with 10 real ales inc several of their own Lidstones brews, good wines by the glass, decent choice of food (can take a time), pleasant service, no music, machines or children inside; small enclosed torch-lit back garden *(Ged Lithgoe, David Edwards, Mike and Mary Carter, John Wooll)*

Pickerel [Magdelene St]: Spacious pub with low beams and cosy corners, friendly staff, well kept beers, limited lunchtime food inc good baguettes; heated courtyard *(M Borthwick)*

Six Bells [Covent Garden]: Small slightly modernised two-roomed local with vibrant atmosphere, friendly service, bargain food, well kept Greene King ales *(John A Barker)*

CHATTERIS [TL3986]

Cross Keys [Market Hill]: Attractive 16th-c coaching inn opp church in fenland market town, warm and welcoming, relaxing open fire in long bar (part public and part comfortable armchairs), decent reasonably priced food in bar and comfortable candlelit restaurant inc good Sun lunches, friendly service, Greene King beers, inexpensive wine, tea and coffee; pleasant back courtyard, comfortable bedrooms *(Michael and Marion Buchanan, Bob Turnham, Mr and Mrs T B Staples)*

CONINGTON [TL3266]

☆ *White Swan* [signed off A14 (was A604) Cambridge—Huntingdon; Elsworth Rd]: Attractive and friendly quietly placed country local with well kept Greene King IPA and Abbot and guest beers tapped from the cask, good home-made food (not Sun evening) inc fish and children's, quick service, cheerful traditional bar, eating areas inc no smoking ones on right, games inc bar billiards and darts on left; good big front garden with play area and play house, open all day *(J Maskell, Peter J Holmes)*

CROYDON [TL3149]

☆ *Queen Adelaide* [off A1198; High St]: Big beamed dining area very popular for wide range of attractively priced food, well kept ales such as Boddingtons and Greene King, impressive array of spirits, efficient friendly service, standing timbers dividing off part with settees, banquettes and stools; garden, play area *(Margaret and Roy Randle, P and D Carpenter)*

DULLINGHAM [TL6357]

☆ *Kings Head* [Stetchworth Rd]: Cosy dining pub in pretty village, wide range of tasty reasonably priced food, coal fires, well kept real ales, good choice of fairly priced wines, friendly helpful staff, children in no smoking restaurant and separate family room; fairy-lit seats out above broad village green, adventure playground *(LYM, Adele Summers, Alan Black, P and D Carpenter)*

DUXFORD [TL4745]

☆ *John Barleycorn* [off A1301; Moorfield Rd, pub at far end]: Welcoming food pub in thatched and shuttered early 17th-c cottage, good home-made food all day (cooked to order, so may be a wait), Greene King IPA and Abbot and a guest beer, decent wines, helpful service, softly lit spotless but relaxed bar with old prints, decorative plates and so forth; may be piped music; tables out among flowers,

open all day *(David Twitchett, C and G Fraser, Mr and Mrs T B Staples, LYM)*

EATON SOCON [TL1658]

☆ *Crown* [B4128, nr A1/A428 interchange]: Welcoming civilised bustle in Chef & Brewer with low beams and separate areas inc no smoking, good choice of moderately priced food (not Sun) from sandwiches up, well kept ales, two coal-effect gas fires, restaurant (good steaks); piped music; garden, comfortable bedroom block *(John and Judy Saville, Michael Dandy)*

☆ *White Horse* [B4128]: Rambling, comfortable and interestingly furnished low-beamed rooms dating from 13th c, relaxing atmosphere, well kept ales inc Greene King Abbot, Tetleys and Wadworths 6X, decent wines, quick friendly service and enjoyable fresh food from sandwiches to tender steaks; nice high-backed traditional settles around fine log fire in end room; play area in back garden, children in eating areas, bedrooms in more recent back extension *(LYM, Bob and Maggie Atherton, Michael Dandy)*

ELSWORTH [TL3163]

☆ *George & Dragon* [off A14 NW of Cambridge, via Boxworth, or off A428]: Neatly furnished restauranty pub, very popular with older people for landlord/chef's good range of enjoyable food (OAP wkdy lunchtime discount card), panelled main bar and back dining area, well kept Greene King IPA, Old Speckled Hen and Ruddles Best, decent wines, friendly attentive service, open fire; disabled access (step down to lavatories); nice terraces, play area in garden, attractive village *(Michael and Jenny Back, Bill and Doreen Sawford, O K Smyth, Maysie Thompson, LYM, Gordon Theaker, Mr and Mrs T B Staples, M Borthwick, P and D Carpenter)*

Poacher [Brockley Rd]: Reopened 17th-c thatched pub with softly lit and comfortably plush beamed lounge, lots of carving inc nicely done birds on bar front, well kept changing ales mainly from East Anglia, welcoming landlord and friendly staff, enjoyable food in bar and similarly furnished no smoking restaurant; plenty of tables in pretty garden with play area and barbecues, good walks *(BB, Neil Woods)*

ELTISLEY [TL2659]

☆ *Leeds Arms* [signed off A428; The Green]: Knocked-through pleasantly old-fashioned beamed bar overlooking peaceful village green, huge log fire, close-set tables for very popular substantial food from nicely presented sandwiches to more adventurous evening dishes, well kept Adnams Broadside and Greene King IPA, Stowford Press cider, quick friendly service, no smoking restaurant; darts, unobtrusive piped music; children in eating area, attractive garden with play area, simple comfortable bedrooms in separate block *(D and M T Ayres-Regan, P and D Carpenter, Brian Root, LYM, Michael Dandy)*

ELTON [TL0893]

☆ *Crown* [Duck St]: Carefully rebuilt stone pub with above-average varied food from good chunky sandwiches (wknd baguettes instead) to enjoyable hot dishes and tempting puddings trolley, well kept ales such as Adnams, Greene King IPA and Woodfordes Wherry, cheerful helpful uniformed staff, banknotes on low beams, watercolours and drawings for sale, big log fire, large dining conservatory (cl Sun pm and Mon); steps up to no smoking back restaurant and lavatories; opp green in beautiful small village *(Michael and Jenny Back)*

ETTON [TF1406]

☆ **Golden Pheasant** [just off B1443 N of Peterborough, signed from nr N end of A15 bypass]: Looks like the 19th-c private house it once was, notable for consistently well kept ales usually inc Adnams Broadside, Batemans XXXB, Cottage Goldrush, Greene King IPA, Kelham Island Pale Rider, Timothy Taylors Landlord and six weekly guests; homely plush bar, airy glass-walled no smoking family side room, tasty food in bar and restaurant, quick charming service, pub games; well reproduced piped music, friendly dogs; good-sized well kept garden with soccer pitch, floodlit boules pitch, interesting aviary, adventure playground and marquee; bedrooms, open all day at least in summer *(Tom Evans, Des and Jen Clarke, BB)*

FARCET FEN [TL2493]

Plough [B1095 SE of Peterborough]: L-shaped bar with real fire, three well kept ales such as Oakham JHB, pictures, lots of brass and pub games at one end, dining room the other with good reasonably priced food *(Derek and Sylvia Stephenson)*

FULBOURN [TL5156]

Bakers Arms [Hinton Rd]: Picturesque pub in pleasant village, popular with local business lunchers and wknd families for good choice of generous enjoyable food, good service, Greene King ales; roomy conservatory, good-sized garden *(Adele Summers, Alan Black)*

GIRTON [TL4262]

Old Crown [High St]: Roomy and tastefully refurbished restaurant/pub, antique pine on polished boards, good generous food with fish emphasis, prompt smiling service, well kept Greene King IPA, good wine choice, real fires; children welcome, disabled facilities, pleasant terrace overlooking countryside *(P and D Carpenter)*

GOREFIELD [TF4111]

Woodmans Cottage [Main St; off B1169 W of Wisbech]: Spacious bar with brocaded banquettes, stripped brick side eating area and pitched-ceiling restaurant, beams and open fires, good value pubby food from sandwiches to vast array of home-made puddings, Greene King IPA and Abbot and a couple of guests from central servery, games area; piped music; children in eating areas, tables on front verandah and sheltered back terrace, play area *(Mike and Lynn Robinson, Michael and Jenny Back, LYM, R C Wiles, June and Malcolm Farmer)*

GRANTCHESTER [TL4355]

Blue Ball [Broadway]: Small bare-boards

village local, the oldest in the area, log fire, well kept Greene King IPA and enjoyable local food (must book Sun lunch); Thurs music night *(Brian Attmore)*

☆ **Green Man** [High St]: Attractively laid out, interesting and welcoming, with individual furnishings, lots of beams, good choice of food, Adnams Bitter and Broadside and Greene King IPA, impressive service, log fire, no smoking dining room, no music; disabled facilities, plenty of tables in lovely garden behind, nice village, a short stroll from lovely riverside meadows *(DC, Ian Phillips, Tim and Ann Newell, LYM)*

GREAT CHISHILL [TL4239]

☆ **Pheasant** [follow Heydon signpost from B1039 in village]: Good home-made food in beamed split-level flagstoned and timbered bar with some elaborately carved though modern seats and settles, friendly staff, real ales such as Adnams, Courage Best and Directors and Theakstons, Stowford Press cider, good choice of wines by the glass, small dining room, darts, cribbage, dominoes; piped music; children welcome, charming back garden with small play area *(Abi Benson, LYM, Keith and Janet Morris, E Smeeten)*

GUYHIRN [TF3903]

☆ **Oliver Twist** [follow signs from A47/A141 junction S of Wisbech]: Comfortable open-plan lounge with cheerful welcoming landlord, well kept sturdy furnishings, good range of home-made generous food from huge crusty warm rolls to steaks, well kept Everards Beacon and Tiger with a weekly guest beer, big open fires, restaurant; may be piped music *(BB, Barry Collett)*

HADDENHAM [TL4675]

Three Kings [Station Rd]: Popular village pub with particularly well kept Greene King IPA and Old Speckled Hen, enjoyable varied home-made food, friendly service *(Nick and Ginny Law, Michael Williamson)*

HARDWICK [TL1968]

☆ **Blue Lion** [signed off A428 (was A45) W of Cambridge; Main St]: Friendly and attractive old local with lots of beams, open fire and woodburner, good food from lunchtime sandwiches and baguettes to wide choice of cooked dishes in bar and extended restaurant area (evening booking recommended), cheerful service, well kept Greene King IPA and Abbot tapped from the cask, old farm tools, two cats, conservatory; may be piped music; pretty roadside front garden, handy for Wimpole Way walkers *(Roy Bromell, P and D Carpenter, BB, Keith and Janet Morris)*

HEMINGFORD GREY [TL2970]

☆ **Cock** [village signed off A14 eastbound, and (via A1096 St Ives rd) westbound; High St]: Small uncluttered bar with woodburner and well kept ales such as Adnams, Elgoods Black Dog, Oakham JHB and Woodfordes Wherry, mid-Aug beer festival, steps down to more seating below black beams; stylishly simple restaurant on right with pale bare boards and canary walls above powder-blue dado, good food from traditional dishes with a touch of flair to plenty of fish (must book wknds), good affordable wines, quick friendly service; tables out behind in neat garden by gravel car park, pretty village *(Robin Thain, David Collins, David and Judith Stewart, C Woodhams, BB)*

HILDERSHAM [TL5448]

☆ *Pear Tree* [off A1307 N of Linton]: Friendly pub in picturesque thatched village, odd crazy-paved floor and plenty of curios, generous changing home cooking from ploughman's up, cheerful service, well kept Greene King IPA, Abbot and Ruddles Best, daily papers, board games; children welcome, tables in garden behind, aviary with finches and canaries *(Dr and Mrs D A Blackadder, BB, Michael and Jenny Back)*

HISTON [TL4363]

Red Lion [High St]: Popular and friendly, with plain public bar, comfortably well used lounge, several real ales inc Greene King (beer festivals and other events), good value pub food; big garden *(Keith and Janet Morris, JHBS)*

HOUGHTON [TL2772]

Three Jolly Butchers [A1123, Wyton]: Good atmosphere, friendly attentive service, well kept ales such as Bass and Greene King IPA and Abbot, beams and brasses, good food from sandwiches to restaurant dishes; huge back garden, play area and occasional barbecues, lovely village *(Gordon Theaker)*

HUNTINGDON [TL2371]

☆ *George* [George St]: Quiet and comfortable hotel lounge bar, decent straightforward food, well kept real ales, good coffee, magnificent galleried central courtyard; bedrooms comfortable *(LYM, Joe Green)*

LEVERINGTON [TF4410]

Rising Sun [just NW of Wisbech; Dowgate Rd]: Decent food inc bargain three-course meal Mon-Thurs, very helpful and efficient chef/landlord, well kept Elgoods *(Mike and Lynn Robinson)*

LONGSTOWE [TL3154]

☆ *Red House* [Old North Road; A1198 Royston—Huntingdon, S of village]: Relaxed rambling bar with big log fire, easy chairs and settees, horsey décor, well kept Greene King IPA and interesting changing guest beers, enjoyable food from sandwiches to mixed grill, children welcome in neat restaurant area on left; may be quiet piped jazz; picnic-sets in sheltered and attractive little garden, cl Mon lunchtime *(Derek and Sylvia Stephenson, LYM, Clive Jones)*

LONGTHORPE [TL1698]

Fox & Hounds [just W of Peterborough]: Popular chain dining pub with well prepared blackboard food, well kept real ales *(Peter Scillitoe)*

MARHOLM [TF1402]

Fitzwilliam Arms [Stamford Rd]: Handsome thatched stone-built Vintage Inn, its rambling three-room bar comfortably opened up and modernised, good value food from interesting sandwiches up, efficient service, Bass; good big garden *(Tom Evans)*

MILTON [TL4763]

Waggon & Horses [off A10 N of Cambridge;

High St]: Welcoming mock-Tudor local with L-shaped lounge, good value food, faultlessly kept Elgoods ales, cheerful efficient service, games corner with darts and bar billiards, friendly dalmatian, lots of hats; attractive garden with slide and swing, apple trees, barbecues, picnic-sets and boules *(Pete Baker)*

PARSON DROVE [TF3808]

Five Bells [Main Rd]: Good value home-made food (not Mon-Weds lunchtimes), three well kept real ales, friendly efficient service *(Mike and Lynn Robinson)*

PETERBOROUGH [TL1897]

Coalheavers Arms [Park St, Woodston]: Small friendly traditional flagstoned pub, now owned by Milton with their real ales, farm cider, good range of continental imports and malt whiskies *(the Didler)*

College Arms [Broadway]: Technical college building that became a large open-plan Wetherspoons instead of a university, well kept ales for central bar, good value varied food inc bargains, friendly helpful staff, comfortable seating inc upstairs, side alcoves and no smoking areas, bookshelves and paintings; open all day, may be doormen Fri/Sat night *(Beryl and Bill Farmer, Richard Lewis)*

Goodbarns Yard [St Johns St, behind Passport Office]: Two-room pub with good changing real ale choice, annual beer festival, food wkdy lunchtime, big conservatory; open all day *(the Didler)*

Palmerston Arms [Oundle Rd]: 16th-c stone-built pub with old tables, chairs, benches and a sofa in carpeted lounge, tiled-floor public bar, lots of well kept ales tapped from casks behind hop-hung counter, even organic lager, good pork pies, friendly landlord, no music or machines; step down into pub, steps to lavatory; small garden, open all day, but at busy times, esp wknds, they may lock doors and restrict access to locals only *(the Didler)*

REACH [TL5666]

☆ *Dykes End* [off A14 via B1102, and signed from Swaffham Prior; Fair Green]: Comfortable L-shaped bar and upstairs evening restaurant, tastefully redeveloped by village consortium; wide range of food from lunchtime sandwiches, baguettes and other bar food to local game, well kept Adnams, Greene King and guests such as Woodfordes Wherry, good atmosphere, friendly staff, quiz nights *(Chris Butt, Michael and Marion Buchanan, Pam and David Bailey, C J Fletcher)*

SAWSTON [TL4849]

Greyhound [High St (Cambridge Rd)]: Smart grey banquettes in cosy L-shaped bar, light and airy high glass-roofed dining room overlooking good big garden, generous prompt food from sandwiches up, Boddingtons, Fullers London Pride, Nethergate and Wadworths 6X, pleasant obliging staff, big open fires, games room down steps, good facilities for children *(Francis Johnston)*

SPALDWICK [TL1372]

George [just off A14 W of Huntingdon]: Refurbished 16th-c village inn which has been a popular main entry for the good value, well cooked food esp fish in its three linked no smoking dining rooms (children allowed), with well kept real ales, decent wines, good coffee, lots of pictures, brasses and dried flowers, and a proper chatty public bar with pool; but the friendly and helpful landlord who has worked so hard to make it a success is selling, probably to one of the big chains *(LYM)*

ST NEOTS [TL1859]

Chequers [St Marys St, Eynesbury]: Charming 16th-c beamed inn, interesting antique furnishings in small bar, well kept Tetleys and guest beers such as Greene King Old Speckled Hen, Nethergate Suffolk and Oakham JHB, good varied bar food from sandwiches and baked potatoes to steaks, welcoming staff, restaurant; sheltered terrace and garden *(Michael Dandy)*

SUTTON [TL4478]

Chequers [(B1381 W of Ely); High St]: Good atmosphere in bright and attractive L-shaped bar and dining room, good genuine home cooking from home-made bread to tempting puddings, well kept Greene King ales, friendly licensees, log fire, comfortable wall banquettes, World War II local bomber photographs, lots of decorative china; may be piped classical music, monthly folk night 4th Weds; small garden, a few picnic-sets out in front with colourful hanging baskets *(DJH, Fiona Wynn, Pete Stroud)*

SWAFFHAM PRIOR [TL5764]

☆ *Red Lion* [B1102 NE of Cambridge; High St]: Attractive and interesting local in pleasant village, well kept Greene King Old Speckled

Hen and Abbot, wide range of generous and reliable fresh food from sandwiches, baked potatoes and exemplary ploughman's to steaks, comfortably divided dining area, prompt friendly service; tables in courtyard *(Mr and Mrs J E C Tasker, Anthony Barnes)*

WARESLEY [TL2454]

Duncombe Arms [Eltisley Rd (B1040, 5 miles S of A428)]: Comfortable and welcoming old pub, long main bar, fire one end, good range of generous reasonably priced food from lunchtime sandwiches to imaginative good value main dishes and roasts, consistently well kept Greene King IPA, Abbot and Ruddles, good service, no smoking back room and restaurant; picnic-sets in garden *(Rev John Hibberd, Colin McKerrow, Gerry and Rosemary Dobson)*

WICKEN [TL5670]

Maids Head [High St]: Neatly kept dining pub in lovely village-green setting, huge helpings of reasonably priced good food in bar and no smoking restaurant, friendly local atmosphere, well kept Bass and related beers with a changing guest ale, fair-priced wines, quiet piped music; tables outside, handy for Wicken Fen nature reserve (NT) *(Stephen and Jean Curtis, M and G Rushworth)*

WILLINGHAM [TL4070]

Three Tuns [Church St]: Welcoming old two-bar village local, attractively priced home cooking (not Mon) inc bargain steak and kidney pie, well kept Greene King ales inc Mild, darts, cards and dominoes; live music Fri *(Pete Baker)*

Please tell us if the décor, atmosphere, food or drink at a pub is different from our description. We rely on readers' reports to keep us up to date. No stamp needed: The Good Pub Guide, FREEPOST TN1569, Wadhurst, E Sussex TN5 7BR.

Cheshire

Pubs on fine form here are the Grosvenor Arms at Aldford (the original flagship of the small Brunning & Price group of good civilised interestingly furnished and decorated dining pubs), the Bhurtpore at Aston (good all round – and great for beer), the timeless old thatched White Lion at Barthomley, the Dysart Arms at Bunbury (another Brunning & Price pub, and one of the best), the canalside Old Harkers Arms in Chester (yet another), the Fox & Barrel at Cotebrook (nice atmosphere, good food), the Pheasant at Higher Burwardsley (terrific views, and it gains a Food Award this year), the 16th-c Sutton Hall Hotel near Macclesfield (a good interesting all-rounder), the Legh Arms in Prestbury (a new entry – good food and service in an appealing old pub), the good value Rising Sun in Tarporley (another nice all-rounder), the Boot & Slipper at Wettenhall (good all round too – surprisingly few people know about this friendly hideaway), the Ship at Wincle (nice for walkers and one of Cheshire's most ancient pubs, it has a new landlord this year) and the canalside Dusty Miller at Wrenbury (this handsome converted mill is well on its way to a Food Award now). Though as you can see from this listing there is plenty of competition for the title, the Dysart Arms at Bunbury is the Cheshire Dining Pub of the Year. Pubs that currently stand out in the Lucky Dip section at the end of the chapter are the Stanley Arms at Bottom of the Oven, Bears Head at Brereton Green, Boot and Mill both in Chester, Alvanley Arms at Cotebrook, Thatch at Faddiley, Harrington Arms at Gawsworth, Chetwode Arms at Lower Whitley, Spread Eagle in Lymm, Roebuck in Mobberley, Legs of Man at Smallwood and Swan at Wybunbury. Robinsons is the most prominent regional brewer here; the local Burtonwood beers are generally available, and Storm and Weetwood beers are becoming quite widely available too. This thriving independent brewing scene means that drinks prices in the area are a lot lower than the national average; the civilised Dog at Peover Heath stands out with its cheap Hydes beer.

ALDFORD SJ4259 Map 7
Grosvenor Arms ★ 🍴 ♈ 🍺

B5130 Chester—Wrexham

Spacious and open plan, this well liked pub has a traditional feel, and an enjoyably chatty atmosphere reigns in the huge panelled library. Tall book shelves line one wall, and lots of substantial tables are well spaced on the handsome board floor. Several quieter areas (ideal for relaxing with the papers) are well furnished with good individual pieces, including a very comfortable parliamentary-type leather settle. Lighting is welcoming, and there are plenty of interesting pictures; cribbage, dominoes, Trivial Pursuit and Scrabble. The airy terracotta-floored conservatory has lots of huge low hanging flowering baskets and chunky pale wood garden furniture, and opens on to a large elegant suntrap terrace and neat lawn with picnic-sets, young trees and a tractor. Five well kept real ales on handpump include guests such as Weetwood Old Dog and Woodfordes Wherry alongside Flowers IPA, Caledonian Deuchars IPA and Robinsons Best. A fine choice of whiskies includes 100 malts, 30 bourbons, and 30 from Ireland, and all 20 wines (largely new world) are served by the glass. Enjoyable well presented bar food from a tempting menu could include mushroom soup (£3.50), sandwiches (from £3.75), baked macaroni cheese with spinach and poached egg (£4.95), ploughman's (£5.95), coriander and lime stuffed chicken breast with mushroom and spicy chorizo linguini (£9.75), tandoori lamb chops with roasted peppers, salad and yoghurt dressing (£10.95), with puddings such as caramelised banana rice pudding (£3.75) or dark chocolate truffle torte (£4.25); best to book on weekend evenings. *(Recommended by Chris Flynn, Wendy Jones, Richard and Jean Phillips, Revd D Glover, W K Wood, Mike and Wendy Proctor, Lorraine and Fred Gill, Andrea and Guy Bradley, Jean and Richard Phillips, Paul Boot, Graham and Lynn Mason, John Knighton)*

Brunning & Price ~ Managers Gary Kidd and Jeremy Brunning ~ Real ale ~ Bar food (12-10(9 Sun); not 25 Dec) ~ (01244) 620228 ~ No children inside after 6pm ~ Dogs allowed in bar ~ Open 11.30-11; 12-10.30 Sun; closed 25 Dec evening

ASTBURY SJ8461 Map 7
Egerton Arms 🛏️
Village signposted off A34 S of Congleton

By the middle of 2004 all the bedrooms at this welcoming village inn will have their own bathrooms, and readers are pleased with them anyway. It's set in a pretty spot overlooking an attractive old church, and has a few well placed tables out in front, and a play area with wooden fort. There's a cheerily pubby feel in the brightly yellow-painted rooms that ramble round the bar. Around the walls are the odd piece of armour, shelves of books, and mementoes of the Sandow Brothers, who performed as 'the World's Strongest Youths' (one of them was the landlady's father). In summer dried flowers fill the big fireplace. Parts of the bar and restaurant are no smoking; piped music, fruit machine, TV. Robinsons Best, Frederics and Hartleys Cumbria Way are well kept on handpump; look out for the sociable pub dogs. Served by friendly helpful staff, the straightforward bar food (which you can eat in either the bar or the restaurant) could include soup (£2.40), sandwiches (from £2.80), brie, courgette and almond crumble or chilli con carne (£5.99), mediterranean pasta with chicken and pancetta (£6.50), and steaks (from £10.99), with puddings such as toffee trifle (£2.95); OAP lunches Mon-Thurs (two courses £4.25, three £5.25) and children's menu (£2.80). Even though they've a large car park, at Sunday lunchtime you might struggle to get a place. It was originally a farmhouse, and some parts date back to the 16th c. *(Recommended by K M Crook, E G Parish, Mike and Wendy Proctor, Maurice and Della Andrew, Stephen Buckley)*

Robinsons ~ Tenants Alan and Grace Smith ~ Real ale ~ Bar food (11.30-2, 6.30-9) ~ Restaurant ~ (01260) 273946 ~ Children away from bar till 8.30pm ~ Open 11.30-11; 12-3, 6.30-10.30 Sun ~ Bedrooms: £45S/£55S

ASTON SJ6147 Map 7
Bhurtpore ★ ♀ 🍺
Off A530 SW of Nantwich; in village follow Wrenbury signpost

The 11 handpumps at this excellent roadside pub serve up to 1,000 different superbly kept real ales a year, including some really unusual ones. The rotating choice might include Abbeydale Absolution, Durham Magus, Hanbys Drawwell, Marston Moors Mongrel, Oakham JHB, Storm Beauforts, Salopian Shropshire Gold and Weetwood Oasthouse, plus continental beers such as Bitburger Pils or Timmermans Peach Beer. They also have dozens of good bottled beers, fruit beers and a choice of farm ciders and perries. Their growing wine list includes some fine wines (and fruit wines), and you can choose from 100 different whiskies. The pub takes its name from the town in India, where local landowner Lord Combermere won a battle, and the carpeted lounge bar bears some indian influences, with an expanding collection of exotic artefacts (one turbaned statue behind the bar proudly sports a pair of Ray-Bans), as well as good local period photographs, and some attractive furniture. The enjoyable menu includes about six very good home-made indian curries (£7.50-£7.95), alongside reasonably priced dishes such as sandwiches (from £2.25, hot filled baguettes £3.95), cheese and leek cakes with creamy dijon sauce (£7.50), steak and kidney pie (£7.95), salmon fillet in pastry with creamy basil sauce or braised lamb shoulder with mint and sherry gravy (£8.95), and perhaps a seasonal game dish such as venison casserole with blueberry and sloe wine sauce (£8.95), and puddings such as rhubarb crumble (£3.25); readers warn us they stick to food service times quite strictly. The cheerful staff cope well on weekends when it can get packed; at lunchtime or earlyish on a weekday evening the atmosphere is cosy and civilised. Tables in the comfortable public bar are reserved for people not eating, and the snug area and dining room are no smoking. Darts, dominoes, cribbage, pool, TV, fruit machine.

(Recommended by Mike and Wendy Proctor, Sue Holland, Dave Webster, E G Parish, the Didler, Martin Grosberg, Margaret and Allen Marsden, Mr and Mrs S Felstead, G Coates, Andy Chetwood, Rick Capper, Richard Lewis)

Free house ~ Licensee Simon George ~ Real ale ~ Bar food (12-2, 7-9; 12-9 Sun) ~ Restaurant ~ No credit cards ~ (01270) 780917 ~ Well behaved children lunchtime and early wkdy evenings ~ Dogs allowed in bar ~ Open 12-2.30(3 Sat), 6.30-11; 12-10.30 Sun; closed 25-26 Dec, 1 Jan ~ Bedrooms: £30S/£40S

BARTHOMLEY SJ7752 Map 7
White Lion ★ £

A mile from M6 junction 16; from the A500 towards Stoke-on-Trent, take B5078 Alsager road, then Barthomley signposted on left

'The way old pubs should be' sums up the reaction of most readers to this lovely black and white thatched pub. Seats and picnic-sets on the cobbles outside have a charming view of the attractive village, and the early 15th-c red sandstone church of St Bertiline across the road is well worth a visit. Inside, the main bar feels timeless (no noisy games machines or music), with its blazing open fire, heavy oak beams dating back to Stuart times, attractively moulded black panelling, Cheshire watercolours and prints on the walls, latticed windows, and wobbly old tables. Up some steps, a second room has another open fire, more oak panelling, a high-backed winged settle, a paraffin lamp hinged to the wall, and shove-ha'penny, cribbage and dominoes; local societies make good use of a third room. From a short and straightforward chalkboard menu, the good value lunchtime bar food could include cheese and onion oatcakes with beans and tomatoes (£2.50), sandwiches (from £3.75), home-made steak and kidney pie or sausages and mash (£4.90), daily roasts (£5) and stilton and local roast ham ploughman's (£5.50); to be sure of a table, get here early on the weekends. The staff are friendly and efficient. Well kept real ales on handpump include Burtonwood Bitter and Top Hat, alongside a couple of guests such as Coach House Dick Turpin and Hook Norton Old Hooky. The cottage behind the pub is available to rent. *(Recommended by MLR, E G Parish, the Didler, John Dwane, Mike Rowan, Ewan and Moira McCall, Dave Irving, Dr D J and Mrs S C Walker, Karen Eliot, F H Saint, Hilary Forrest, Sue Holland, Dave Webster, Stephen Buckley, S and R Gray, Paul Humphreys, Mike and Wendy Proctor)*

Burtonwood ~ Tenant Terence Cartwright ~ Real ale ~ Bar food (lunchtime only, not Thurs) ~ (01270) 882242 ~ Children welcome away from public bar ~ Dogs welcome ~ Open 11.30-11(5-11 only Thurs); 12-10.30 Sun

BICKLEY MOSS SJ5650 Map 7
Cholmondeley Arms ♀

Cholmondeley; A49 5½ miles N of Whitchurch; the owners would like us to list them under Cholmondeley Village, but as this is rarely located on maps we have mentioned the nearest village which appears more often

Handy for Cholmondeley Castle Gardens, this imaginatively converted Victorian schoolhouse has lots for you to look at. The cross-shaped high-ceilinged bar is filled with objects such as old school desks above the bar on a gantry, and there are masses of Victorian pictures (especially portraits and military subjects), over one of the side arches is a great stag's head, and there are gothic windows and huge old radiators too. A medley of seats runs from cane and bentwood to pews and carved oak settles, and the patterned paper on the shutters matches the curtains. Outside, there are seats on the sizeable lawn. Ten or so interesting and good value wines by the glass are listed on a blackboard; they do good coffees (liqueur ones too), and some speciality teas. Well kept Adnams, Banks's, Marstons Pedigree and perhaps a guest such as Charles Wells Bombardier on handpump. You'll have to book at weekends for the bar food which, served by friendly staff, could include soup (£3.25), sandwiches (£3.95), duck and brandy pâté (£4.95), game pie (£7.95), rack of lamb with garlic and thyme sauce (£9.95), or fried calves liver with red onion and sage confit (£10.50), with puddings such as syrup tart (£4.25); children's menu (£3.95). *(Recommended by Revd D Glover, John Kane, Joyce and Geoff Robson, Ray and Winifred Halliday, Karen Eliot, E G Parish, Paul Humphreys, Mike and Wendy Proctor, Rod Stoneman)*

Free house ~ Licensees Guy and Carolyn Ross-Lowe ~ Real ale ~ Bar food (12-2.15, 6.30-9.30) ~ Restaurant ~ (01829) 720300 ~ Children in eating area of bar and restaurant ~ Dogs welcome ~ Open 11-3, 6-11; closed 25 Dec ~ Bedrooms: £50S/£65B

BUNBURY SJ5758 Map 7
Dysart Arms ★ ⑪ ♀

Bowes Gate Road; village signposted off A51 NW of Nantwich; and from A49 S of Tarporley – coming this way, coming in on northernmost village access road, bear left in village centre

Cheshire Dining Pub of the Year

Very popular locally – and no wonder, the food here is first class, and the friendly staff work hard to maintain the pub's reputation. From a frequently changing menu, imaginative dishes could include spicy beef potato cake with chilli dressing (£4.95), ploughman's (£6.25), smoked haddock rarebit with tomato and scallion salad (£9.95), fried chicken breast wrapped in bacon with red wine sauce (£9.95), duck confit with stir-fried vegetables and honey and blackbean sauce (£10.95), and braised shoulder of lamb with minted gravy and dauphinoise potatoes (£11.50), while puddings could be glazed apple tart or golden treacle sponge (£4.25); they also do sandwiches (from £4.50) and a bonus is their good changing selection of british cheeses (£5.95). Drinkers are not neglected, and besides interesting wines by the glass, they serve well kept Flowers IPA, Timothy Taylors Landlord and a couple of guests such as Moorhouses Black Cat and Worfield Shropshire Pride on handpump. Nicely laid out spaces ramble around the pleasantly lit central bar. Under deep venetian red ceilings, the knocked-through cream-walled rooms have red and black tiles, some stripped boards and some carpet, a comfortable variety of well spaced big sturdy wooden tables and chairs, a couple of tall bookcases, some carefully chosen bric-a-brac, properly lit pictures, and warming fires in winter. One area is no smoking, and they have dominoes. They've lowered the ceiling in the more restaurant end room (with its book-lined back wall), and there are lots of plants on the window sills. The tables on the terrace and in the immaculately kept slightly elevated garden are very pleasant in summer, with views of the splendid church at the end of the pretty village, and the distant Peckforton Hills beyond. *(Recommended by E G Parish, Revd D Glover, Sue Holland, Dave Webster, Paul Boot, Mike Schofield, Gill and Keith Croxton, Rita and Keith Pollard, Kevin Blake, Brenda and Stuart Naylor, JES, Stephen Buckley, Mr and Mrs J E C Tasker, MLR)*

Brunning & Price ~ Managers Darren and Elizabeth Snell ~ Real ale ~ Bar food (12-2.15, 6-9.30; 12-(9 Sun)9.30 Sat) ~ (01829) 260183 ~ No children under 10 after 6pm ~ Dogs allowed in bar ~ Open 11.30-11; 12-10.30 Sun

---

Post Office address codings confusingly give the impression that some pubs are in Cheshire, when they're really in Derbyshire (and therefore included in this book under that chapter) or in Greater Manchester (see the Lancashire chapter).

CHESTER SJ4166 Map 7
Albion ★ ◧
Park Street

Throughout the rooms of this old-fashioned corner pub, you'll find an interesting collection of World War I memorabilia. Big engravings of men leaving for war, and similarly moving prints of wounded veterans, are among the other more expected aspects – flags, advertisements and so on. The post-Edwardian décor is charmingly muted, with floral wallpaper, appropriate lamps, leatherette and hoop-backed chairs, a period piano, a large mangle, and cast-iron-framed tables; there's an attractive side dining room too. The atmosphere is peacefully relaxed and chatty; the lack of piped music, noisy machines and children makes the pub especially popular with older visitors. Service is friendly, though they don't like people rushing in just before closing time, and discourage race-goers; readers tell us it can get smoky. Banks's Mild, Timothy Taylors Landlord and perhaps a couple of weekly guest beers are well kept on handpump, and they've around 30 malt whiskies and fresh orange juice; the wines are new world. As well as doorstep sandwiches (£3), the menu could include generously served dishes such as corned beef hash, boiled gammon with creamed potatoes and goats cheese, and pesto ravioli with tomato and chilli sauce (all £5.95), with specials such as spicy thai chicken curry (£5.95), and puddings such as fresh lemon and lime cheesecake (£2.95); it can get very busy at lunchtime. The long-awaited new bedrooms should be open by the beginning of 2004, when they hope to extend their opening and food service times. It's tucked away in a quiet part of town just below the Roman Wall. *(Recommended by E G Parish, MLR, Peter F Marshall, SLC, Sue Holland, Dave Webster, the Didler, Catherine Pitt, Tracey and Stephen Groves, Joe Green)*

Pubmaster ~ Lease Michael Edward Mercer ~ Real ale ~ Bar food (12-2, 5(6 Sat)-8; 12-2, 7-8 Sun) ~ No credit cards ~ (01244) 340345 ~ Dogs allowed in bar ~ Open 11.30-3, 5(6 Sat)-11; 11.30-11 Fri; 12-3, 7-10.30 Sun

Old Harkers Arms ♀ ◧
Russell Street, down steps off City Road where it crosses canal – under Mike Melody antiques

Whether you're eating or just in for a chatty drink, this is a relaxing place to spend an afternoon. The nicely decorated bar has attractive lamps, interesting old prints on the walls, and newspapers and books to read from a well stocked library at one end. Though the tables are carefully arranged to create a sense of privacy, the lofty ceiling and tall windows give an appealing sense of space and light. As well as Harkers Superbrew (brewed especially for the pub by Roosters), they serve around four well kept real ales on handpump, such as Boddingtons, Fullers London Pride, Thwaites and Weetwood Best; around 50 malt whiskies too, and decent well described wines. It's a popular place for a meal or just a snack, and good dishes from a changing menu could include sandwiches (from £3.25), soup (£3.50), toasted ciabattas and baguettes (from £3.95), steamed mussels in cream and pink peppercorn sauce (£4.50), thai chicken noodles with nan bread (£6.95), grilled smoked haddock with bacon (£7.95), and caribbean chicken with grilled sweet potato or steak and mushroom pie (£8.95); puddings such as apple and blueberry cobbler with custard (£3.95). The pub is right next to the canal and was a Victorian warehouse; the bar counter is apparently constructed from salvaged doors. It's especially popular with younger visitors Friday and Saturday evenings, when it gets very busy. *(Recommended by Kevin Blake, Mrs J Thomas, Peter F Marshall, SLC, Sue Holland, Dave Webster)*

Brunning & Price ~ Managers Barbie Hill and Catryn Devaney ~ Real ale ~ Bar food (12-2.30, 5.30-9.30; 12-9.30 Sat, 12-9 Sun) ~ (01244) 344525 ~ Children till 7pm ~ Open 11.30-11; 12-10.30 Sun

COTEBROOK SJ5865 Map 7

Fox & Barrel 🍽

A49 NE of Tarporley

There's an enjoyably buoyant atmosphere at this well run bar and restaurant, and the uniformed staff are welcoming and attentive whether you're here for a three-course meal or just a quick drink. The snug distinct areas are interestingly furnished, with good mix of tables and chairs including two seats like Victorian thrones, an oriental rug in front of a very big log fireplace, a comfortable banquette corner, and a part with shelves of rather nice ornaments and china jugs; silenced fruit machine, unobtrusive piped music. Beyond the bar is a huge uncluttered candlelit dining area (no smoking) with varying-sized tables, comfortable dining chairs, attractive rugs on bare boards, rustic pictures above the panelled dado, and one more extensively panelled section. Lots of people come here for the superbly cooked food, which is served in very generous helpings. The enticing menu changes every few months, but might include well presented dishes such as home-made soup (£3.25), sandwiches and baguettes (from £3.75), grilled sardines with garlic butter (£4.55), home-made lasagne (£5.75), chicken fajita (£6.75), home-made steak and kidney pie (£8.45), fried bass fillets with caper, lemon and chive dressing (£10.95), and 8oz fillet steak (£14.95); it's a good idea to book for Sunday lunch. Well kept John Smiths, Marstons Pedigree and a couple of guests such as Flowers IPA and Timothy Taylors Landlord served (through a sparkler, though you can ask for it to be taken off) by handpump; you'll also find a decent choice of wines. *(Recommended by Olive and Ray Hebson, Revd D Glover, Kevin Blake, Ray and Winifred Halliday, E G Parish, Simon J Barber, Derek and Margaret Underwood, Mrs G Coleman, Mrs P J Carroll, MLR)*

Inn Partnership (Pubmaster) ~ Tenant Martin Cocking ~ Real ale ~ Bar food (12-2.30, 6.30(6 Sat)-9.30; 12-9 Sun) ~ Restaurant ~ (01829) 760529 ~ Children in restaurant ~ Trad jazz band Mon evening ~ Open 12-3, 5.30-11; 12-(11 Sat)10.30 Sun; closed 25 Dec

DARESBURY SJ5983 Map 7

Ring o' Bells 🍺

1½ miles from M56 junction 11; A56 N, then turn right on to B5356

From the front of this comfortable pub you can see the church where Lewis Carroll's father was vicar – one window shows all the characters in *Alice in Wonderland*. The pub is set in a pretty village and, although there are plenty of tables in the long partly terraced garden, in summer you may struggle to get a seat. Inside, they've managed to combine a spacious and airy atmosphere with a cosy, homely feel, and there's a good variety of places to sit. On the right is a comfortable, down-to-earth part where walkers from the nearby canal can relax, while the left has more of a library style, and some reflection of its 19th-c use as a magistrates' court; there's a nice coal fire in winter. All rooms have wheelchair access. The long bar counter has well kept Courage Directors, Greenalls Bitter and Mild, Theakstons, and perhaps a couple of guests such as Gales Frolic or Mauldons Black Adder on handpump. All their wines are available by the glass, and they've a dozen malt whiskies; pleasant young staff. Bar food could include soup (£2.95), sandwiches (from £2.95), baked potatoes (from £3.50), ploughman's (from £4.20), fish and chips (£5.95), beef and Theakstons pie (£6.80), lemon chicken and almond couscous (£7.75), with puddings such as treacle sponge pudding (£2.95); the dining rooms are no smoking. This is a Chef & Brewer, and there's piped music and a fruit machine. *(Recommended by David Field, E G Parish, Pat and Tony Martin, Graham and Lynn Mason, Roy and Lindsey Fentiman, Hugh A MacLean, Bernie Adams, Hilary Forrest, J Roy Smylie)*

Scottish Courage ~ Manager Martin Moylon ~ Real ale ~ Bar food (12-(9.30 Sun)10) ~ Restaurant ~ (01925) 740256 ~ Children in restaurant ~ Open 11-11; 12-10.30 Sun

FRODSHAM SJ5277 Map 7
Ring o' Bells ◗ £

Just over 2 miles from M56, junction 12; 2 Bellemonte Road – from A56 in Frodsham take B5152 and turn right (uphill) into Overton at Parish Church signpost

The friendly pub cats Ambrose, Flora and Tilly may curl up next to you as you enjoy a drink at this friendly and relaxed 17th-c pub. An old-fashioned hatch-like central servery dispenses the three continually changing real ales by handpump (say, Black Sheep Special, Fullers London Pride and Youngs Special), and they also keep about 85 malt whiskies. A couple of the little rambling rooms have pleasant views over a stone-built church and the Mersey far below. The room at the back has some antique settles, brass-and-leather fender seats by the log fire, and old hunting prints on its butter-coloured walls; a beamed room with antique dark oak panelling and stained glass leads through to a darts room (there's also a TV, dominoes, cribbage, and other board games). Up on blackboards, the good value lunchtime menu includes sandwiches and toasties (from £2.50), baked potatoes (£3.10), and enjoyable straightforward dishes such as steak and mushroom pie, chicken tikka masala or cumberland sausage and mash (£4.25), and lamb chump in honey and garlic sauce (£4.95), with puddings such as blackberry and apple crumble (from £1.90). There's one no smoking room, and a secluded garden at the back has tables and chairs, a pond, and lots of trees. In summer when it's festooned with a mass of colourful hanging baskets, the pub is quite a sight. More reports please.
(Recommended by Mike Schofield, GSB)

Pubmaster ~ Tenant Shirley Wroughton-Craig ~ Real ale ~ Bar food (lunchtime only, not 25-26 Dec) ~ No credit cards ~ (01928) 732068 ~ Children in eating area of bar ~ Dogs allowed in bar ~ Folk group fourth Tues in month ~ Open 12-3, 5.30-11; 12-4, 6-11 Sat; 12-4, 7-10.30 Sun

HAUGHTON MOSS SJ5855 Map 6
Nags Head

Turn off A49 S of Tarporley into Long Lane, at 'Beeston, Haughton' signpost

The big neat garden of this immaculate black and white country pub has well spaced picnic-sets, a good little adventure playground, and even a bowling green. Inside, black and white tiles gleam by the serving counter, with pews and a heavy settle by the fire in a small quarry-tiled room on the left, and button-back wall banquettes in the carpeted room on the right, which also has logs burning in a copper-hooded fireplace. Below the heavy black beams are shelves of pewter mugs, attractive Victorian prints and a few brass ornaments. On the right is a sizeable carpeted dining area, and a new extension has a dining room and conservatory with oak beams; there may be very quiet piped music. Besides snacks (served till 4.30) such as sandwiches (£3.50), filled baked potatoes (£3.95), omelettes (£3.60) and ploughman's (£5.20), they do an all day brunch for £6 (not Sunday), and there's a good value self-service buffet (12-2 weekdays; £5.85). Other popular home-made bar food could include soup (£2.95), fishcakes (£3.95), mushroom stroganoff (£7.10), fried or grilled trout (£7.60), and half a roast duck with orange sauce (£12.90); as well as various ice creams (£2.95), there's a puddings trolley. The American landlord has well chosen generous wines alongside Boddingtons and Fullers Original on handpump, and service is efficient. The front window of the pub is full of charmingly arranged collector's dolls. More reports please.
(Recommended by E G Parish)

Free house ~ Licensees Rory and Deborah Keigan ~ Real ale ~ Bar food (12-9; 12-10 Fri and Sat) ~ Restaurant ~ (01829) 260265 ~ Children in eating area of bar and restaurant ~ Open 12-11(10.30 Sun); closed evening 25 Dec

---

The ◗ symbol shows pubs which keep their beer unusually well or have a particularly good range.

HIGHER BURWARDSLEY SJ5256 Map 7

Pheasant 🍴 🛏

Burwardsley signposted from Tattenhall (which itself is signposted off A41 S of Chester) and from Harthill (reached by turning off A534 Nantwich—Holt at the Copper Mine); follow pub's signpost on up hill from Post Office; OS Sheet 117 map reference 523566

The bar of this half-timbered and sandstone 17th-c pub has a bright modern feel, with wooden floors and light-coloured furniture. The see-through fireplace is said to house the largest log fire in the county, and there's a pleasant no smoking conservatory. Very good imaginative bar food might include pea, pear and mint soup (£3.95), sandwiches (from £3.95), scallops and black pudding (£7.25), poached seafood sausages with creamed leeks in saffron sauce (£8.50), roasted red mullet fillets (£11.25), and chargrilled rib-eye steak or roasted lightly curried cod fillet (£12.95), with puddings such as caramelised lime tart with chilli and ginger ice cream (from £4); service is prompt. Their four very well kept ales on handpump are all from the local Weetwood brewery, and they've more than 30 malts. A big side lawn has picnic-sets, and on summer weekends they sometimes have barbecues. The views from here are amazing, and on a clear day the telescope on the terrace lets you make out the pier head and cathedrals in Liverpool, while from inside you can see right across the Cheshire plain. The pub is well placed for the Sandstone Trail along the Peckforton Hills. *(Recommended by Chris Hutt, Tracey and Stephen Groves, B A Jackson, F H Saint; also in the* Good Hotel Guide*)*

Free house ~ Licensee Simon McLoughlin ~ Real ale ~ Bar food (12-2.30, 6.30-9.30; Sun 12-5, 6.30-8.30) ~ Restaurant ~ (01829) 770434 ~ Children welcome away from bar ~ Open 11.30-11; 12-10 Sun ~ Bedrooms: £55B/£70B

LANGLEY SJ9569 Map 7

Hanging Gate

Meg Lane, Higher Sutton; follow Langley signpost from A54 beside Fourways Motel, and that road passes the pub; from Macclesfield, heading S from centre on A523 turn left into Byrons Lane at Langley, Wincle signpost; in Sutton (½ mile after going under canal bridge, ie before Langley) fork right at Church House Inn, following Wildboarclough signpost, then 2 miles later turning sharp right at steep hairpin bend; OS Sheet 118 map reference 952696

This old drover's inn is set high on a Peak District ridge, and seats out on the crazy-paved terrace give spectacular views over a patchwork of valley pastures to distant moors, and the tall Sutton Common transmitter above them. It's a welcoming place, and service is very friendly and attentive. The three cosy low-beamed rambling rooms are simply and traditionally furnished with some attractive old prints of Cheshire towns, and big coal fires; piped music. Down some stone steps, there's an airy garden room; the blue room is no smoking. Besides well kept Hydes Bitter, Jekylls Gold and a guest from the brewery on handpump, they've got quite a few malt whiskies. The bar food is popular (readers recommend booking on weekends) and could include soup (£2.45), prawns in filo parcels or deep-fried camembert (£3.95), fried cod (£7.45), steaks (from £8.95), and lamb chops (£10.50), with puddings such as crème caramel (£2.95). The pub was first licensed around 300 years ago, but is thought to have been built long before that. *(Recommended by Sheila and Phil Stubbs, Stephen Buckley, Mr and Mrs Colin Roberts, Doug Christian, the Didler, R F Grieve, Derek and Sylvia Stephenson, John Hillmer, Derek Manning, Mike and Wendy Proctor, Nick and Lynne Carter)*

Hydes ~ Tenants Peter and Paul McGrath ~ Real ale ~ Bar food (not Sun evening) ~ (01260) 252238 ~ Children in eating area of bar ~ Open 12-3, 7-11; 12-11 Sat; 12-10.30 Sun

---

Ideas for a country day out? We list pubs in really attractive scenery at the back of the book – and there are separate lists for waterside pubs, ones with really good gardens, and ones with lovely views.

LOWER PEOVER SJ7474 Map 7
Bells of Peover ★
The Cobbles; from B5081 take short cobbled lane signposted to church

This gorgeous wisteria-covered old Chef & Brewer is idyllically set in a peaceful hamlet. Seats on the crazy-paved terrace in front overlook a fine black and white 14th-c church, while at the side a spacious lawn beyond the old coachyard spreads down through trees and under rose pergolas to a little stream. The cosy tiled bar has side hatches for its serving counter, toby jugs and comic Victorian prints, and the original lounge has antique settles, high-backed windsor armchairs and a spacious window seat, antique china in the dresser, and pictures above the panelling. There are two small coal fires, and one room is no smoking; dominoes, cribbage and piped music. Well kept real ales such as Courage Directors, Greenalls and Theakstons on handpump. Bar food could include sandwiches (from £2.95), filled baked potatoes (from £3.95), ploughman's (from £4.20), smoked chicken and pesto penne (£8.50) and steak (£10.50), with specials such as chicken stuffed with haggis (£10.15), and fried duck breast with sweet and sour raspberry sauce (£11.25); puddings such as hot chocolate truffle pudding (£4.50). *(Recommended by Darly Graton, Graeme Gulibert, the Didler, Andrew Scarr, Revd D Glover, Steve Whalley, Brenda and Stuart Naylor, Stephen Buckley)*

Scottish Courage ~ Manager Richard Casson ~ Real ale ~ Bar food (11-10; 12-9 Sun) ~ (01565) 722269 ~ Children in family room ~ Open 11-11; 12-10.30 Sun

MACCLESFIELD SJ9271 Map 7
Sutton Hall Hotel ★ 🛏
Leaving Macclesfield southwards on A523, turn left into Byrons Lane signposted Langley, Wincle, then just before canal viaduct fork right into Bullocks Lane; OS Sheet 118 map reference 925715

This 16th-c baronial hall strikes exactly the right balance: although it's undoubtedly a civilised place, the atmosphere is relaxed and service is friendly. The bar (divided into separate areas by tall oak timbers) has some antique squared oak panelling, lightly patterned art nouveau stained-glass windows, broad flagstones around the bar counter (carpet elsewhere), and a raised open fire. It's mostly furnished with straightforward ladderback chairs around sturdy thick-topped cast-iron-framed tables, but there are a few unusual touches such as a suit of armour by a big stone fireplace, a longcase clock, a huge bronze bell for calling time, and a brass cigar-lighting gas taper on the bar counter itself. Readers enjoy the bar food, which could include soup (£3.25), sandwiches (from £3.75), chicken and leek pancake with cheese sauce (£5.25), mushroom stroganoff (£6.55), daily specials such as lamb balti (£7.25), sautéed tuna steak in black bean sauce (£8.95) or fillet steak medallions with stilton sauce (£10.95), and puddings such as crème brûlée and sticky toffee pudding (£3.50). They serve well kept Bass, Greene King IPA, Marstons Best and a guest on handpump; also over 40 malt whiskies, decent wines, freshly squeezed fruit juice, and proper Pimms. It's in lovely grounds with tables on the tree-sheltered lawn, and ducks and moorhens swimming in the pond. For residents, they can arrange clay shooting, golf or local fishing and there's access to canal moorings at Gurnett Aqueduct 200 yards away. *(Recommended by the Didler, Wendy and Bob Needham, Dr W J M Gissane, Hugh A MacLean, Mr and Mrs B Hobden, Kevin Blake, Tracey and Stephen Groves, June and Ken Brooks)*

Free house ~ Licensee Robert Bradshaw ~ Real ale ~ Bar food (12-2.30(2 Sun), 7-10) ~ Restaurant ~ (01260) 253211 ~ Children in family room wknds and bank hol lunchtimes, any time in restaurant ~ Dogs allowed in bedrooms ~ Open 11-11(10.30 Sun) ~ Bedrooms: £79.95B/£94.95B

PEOVER HEATH SJ7973 Map 7

Dog 🛏

Off A50 N of Holmes Chapel at the Whipping Stocks, keep on past Parkgate into Wellbank Lane; OS Sheet 118 map reference 794735; note that this village is called Peover Heath on the OS map and shown under that name on many road maps, but the pub is often listed under Over Peover instead

This popular civilised pub has such a comfortable bar that you may find it hard to drag yourself away. Along with over 50 malt whiskies, they've well kept Hydes, Moorhouses Black Cat, and Weetwood Best and Old Dog on handpump, and Addlestone's cider too; darts, pool, dominoes, TV, a juke box and piped music. The main bar has inviting easy chairs and wall seats (including one built into a snug alcove around an oak table), and two wood-backed seats built in either side of a coal fire, opposite which logs burn in an old-fashioned black grate. Outside, the attractive garden is nicely lit on summer evenings, and underneath pretty hanging baskets there are picnic-sets on the quiet lane. Generous helpings of enjoyable bar food include home-made soup (£2.50), sandwiches (from £2.85), warm smoked chicken salad (£4.50), ploughman's (from £4.95), steak and mushroom pie (£9.95), and halibut and spinach mornay (£10.95), with changing specials such as ravioli provençale (£4.50) or ham shank with parsley sauce (£10.95), and puddings such as sticky toffee (£3.50). The dining room is no smoking, and booking is a good idea at weekends. It's a pleasant walk from here to the Jodrell Bank Centre and Arboretum. (Recommended by Arthur Baker, Mr and Mrs Colin Roberts, JES, Derek and Sylvia Stephenson, Doug Christian, Dr Paull Khan, R Pring, JWAC)

Free house ~ Licensee Steven Wrigley ~ Real ale ~ Bar food (12-2.30, 6-9; 12-8.30 Sun; not evenings 25 or 26 Dec) ~ Restaurant ~ (01625) 861421 ~ Children in eating area of bar, restaurant and family room ~ Dogs allowed in bar ~ Theme night one Friday in month ~ Open 11.30-3, 5(5.30 Sat)-11; 12-10.30 Sun ~ Bedrooms: £55B/£75B

PLUMLEY SJ7175 Map 7

Smoker

2½ miles from M6 junction 19: A556 towards Northwich and Chester

The pub takes its name from a favourite racehorse of the Prince Regent, and an Edwardian print of a hunt meeting outside shows how little its appearance has changed over the centuries. Nowadays, it's a good haven from the M6; the sizeable side lawn has roses and flower beds, and the extended garden has a children's play area. Inside, the three connecting rooms are well decorated, with dark panelling, open fires in impressive period fireplaces, military prints, and a collection of copper kettles. Comfortable furnishings include deep sofas, cushioned settles, windsor chairs, and some rush-seat dining chairs. With an emphasis on local produce (their beef comes from the farm next door), tasty dishes could include home-made soup (£2.75), sandwiches (from £3.55), baked potatoes (£3.75), home-made seafood pancake or breaded mushrooms (£4.75), mackerel fillets with tomato and white wine sauce (£7.95), pork fillet in calvados (£8.95), baked duck breast with plum sauce (£10.55), and specials such as home-made cottage pie or turkey à la king (£7.25), with puddings such as home-made sherry trifle (£3.95). The same menu covers the bar and restaurant; service can sometimes slow at busy times. Robinsons Best and Old Stockport on handpump are well kept alongside a guest such as Cwmbran Double Hop; 30 malt whiskies too, and a good choice of wines including around 11 by the glass. There are no smoking areas in the bar; piped music, fruit machine. (Recommended by Nigel and Sue Foster, Richard and Wendy Harris, Karen Eliot, E G Parish, M S Catling, Andrew Crawford)

Robinsons ~ Tenants John and Diana Bailey ~ Real ale ~ Bar food (11.30-2.15, 6-9.30; 12-9.15 Sun) ~ Restaurant ~ (01565) 722338 ~ Children away from bar ~ Open 11.30-3, 6-11; 12-10.30 Sun

PRESTBURY SJ8976 Map
Legh Arms
A538, village centre

Doing well under its new landlord (a well known restaurateur in Manchester), this civilised 16th-c building combines good inventive food in its bar and restaurant with an appealing and interesting interior and a chatty and relaxed atmosphere. Opened up inside, it is well divided, with several distinctive areas: muted tartan fabric over a panelled dado on the right, with ladderback dining chairs, good solid dark tables, elegant french steam train prints, italian costume engravings and a glass case of china and books; brocaded bucket seats around similar tables, antique steeplechase prints, staffordshire dogs on the stone mantelpiece and a good coal fire on the left; a snug panelled back part with cosy wing armchairs and a grand piano; a narrow side offshoot with pairs of art deco leather armchairs around small granite tables, and more antique costume prints, of french tradesmen. The bar, towards the back on the left, has well kept Robinsons Best on handpump and nice house wines, good coffee, and usually genial regulars chatting on the comfortable leather bar stools; this part looks up to an unusual balustraded internal landing. There are daily papers on a coffee table, and an antique oak dresser with magazines below and menus on top. Bar food we or readers have enjoyed recently includes fish broth (£4.50), a big plate of mussels with leek, garlic, wine and cream sauce (£4.75), a bacon and blue cheese burger (with thai nuances; £6.25), stir-fried king prawns on thai noodles (£6.50), and authentic-tasting thai beef (£7.50); their breads are excellent, and other things might include soup (£2.95), sandwiches (from £4.25), and baked goats cheese with roast mediterranean salad (£6.95). There is a more elaborate choice in the comfortable and attractive restaurant. Service by uniformed staff is pleasantly informal and friendly; there may be fairly inoffensive piped music. A garden behind has tables and chairs. In 2004, they hope to open eight bedrooms. *(Recommended by Mrs P J Carroll)*

Robinsons ~ Tenant Peter Myers ~ Real ale ~ Bar food (12-2, 7-10; 12-9.30) ~ Restaurant ~ (01625) 829130 ~ Children in eating area of bar and restaurant ~ Open 12-11

TARPORLEY SJ5563 Map 7
Rising Sun
High Street; village signposted off A51 Nantwich—Chester

In summer this welcoming pub is a mass of hanging baskets and flowering tubs, while in winter the rooms are lovely and cosy, with three open fires. Well chosen tables are surrounded by eye-catching old seats including creaky 19th-c mahogany and oak settles, and there's also an attractively blacked iron kitchen range, sporting and other old-fashioned prints on the walls, and a big oriental rug in the back room. Service is friendly and helpful, and readers very much enjoy the good value bar food. As well as a selection of tasty pies (from £6.50) and a good variety of vegetarian dishes (all £8.15), the extensive menu includes soup (£2.20), sandwiches (from £2.50), toasties and filled baked potatoes (from £2.95), avocado and prawns (£4.45), fruit beef curry and scampi mornay (£8.10), and steaks (from £10.95). Well kept Robinsons Best, Hartleys Cumbria Way and Hatters Mild on handpump. Tarporley is a picturesque village. *(Recommended by Mike and Wendy Proctor, Ken Richards, F H Saint, Maurice and Della Andrew, E G Parish, the Didler)*

Robinsons ~ Tenant Alec Robertson ~ Real ale ~ Bar food (11-2, 5.30-9.30; 12-9 Sun) ~ Restaurant (evening) ~ (01829) 732423 ~ Children lunchtime away from bar, restaurant only in the evening ~ Open 11-3.30, 5.30-11; 11.30-11 bank hols; 11-11 Sat; 12-10.30 Sun

---

Though we don't usually mention it in the text, most pubs will now make coffee or tea – always worth asking.

WESTON SJ7352 Map 7
White Lion 🍺

3½ miles from M6 junction 16; A500 towards Crewe, then village signposted on right

Originally a Tudor farmhouse though much modernised since, this pretty black and white timbered inn has a friendly and relaxed atmosphere. Divided into smaller areas by very gnarled black oak standing timbers, the low-beamed main room is usually bustling. There's a good choice of seats from cushioned modern settles to ancient oak ones, with plenty of smaller chairs, and in a smaller room on the left are three fine settles, carved in 18th-c style. The two side rooms are no smoking; dominoes, TV and piped music. Straightforward bar food, generously served, includes soup (£1.95), sandwiches (from £3.20), filled baguettes (from £4.20), vegetarian pancakes (£5.75), scampi, roast local chicken or chilli con carne (£5.95), and a daily special such as cottage pie (£5.75); as well as puddings they serve ice-cream sundaes. Please note that they stop serving lunch at 1.45 on Sunday. You'll find Bass and Jennings Cumberland on handpump, and they've a sizeable wine list. By a sheltered lawn with picnic-sets, the hotel even has its own bowling green. *(Recommended by Philip and June Caunt, K H Frostick, John Hale, Martin Grosberg, D J Hulse, Brenda and Stuart Naylor)*

Free house ~ Licensee Alison Davies ~ Real ale ~ Bar food (12-2, 6(6.30 Sat, 7 Sun)-9.30) ~ Restaurant ~ (01270) 500303 ~ Children in eating area of bar and restaurant ~ Open 11-3, 5(6.30 Sat)-11; 12-3, 7-10.30 Sun ~ Bedrooms: £58S/£68B

WETTENHALL SJ6261 Map 7
Boot & Slipper 🍺

From B5074 on S edge of Winsford, turn into Darnhall School Lane, then right at Wettenhall signpost: keep on for 2 or 3 miles; OS Sheet 118 map reference 625613

There's a friendly relaxed atmosphere in the knocked-through beamed main bar of this pleasant old pub, with three shiny old dark settles, more straightforward chairs, and a fishing rod above the deep low fireplace with its big log fire. The modern bar counter also serves the left-hand communicating beamed room with its shiny pale brown tiled floor, cast-iron-framed long table, panelled settle and bar stools; darts, dominoes, and piped music. An unusual trio of back-lit arched pseudo-fireplaces forms one stripped-brick wall, and there are two further areas on the right, as well as an attractive back restaurant with big country pictures. The charming landlady and friendly staff are genuinely welcoming, and readers enjoy eating here. Aside from lunchtime sandwiches (from £3.40), good well presented food could include home-made soup (£3.25), salmon and asparagus tartlet in cream sauce topped with a brie melt (£4.95), pie of the day (£7.95), leek and potato bake or home-made beef or vegetable lasagne (£8.25), seared tuna steak with chinese-style spring onion and red pepper with sweet and sour sauce or grilled chicken stuffed with stilton and leeks with white wine and cream sauce (£9.95), and steaks (from £13.25), with puddings such as home-made apple pie or sherry trifle (£3.50); children's meals (£3.80). They also do an excellent value two-course lunch special (£6.95); it's best to book on weekends. Well kept Bass and Tetleys on handpump, a good choice of malt whiskies and a decent wine list. Outside, there are picnic-sets on the cobbled front terrace by the big car park; children's play area. *(Recommended by E G Parish, Leo and Barbara Lionet)*

Free house ~ Licensee Joan Jones ~ Real ale ~ Bar food (12-2(2.30 Sun), 6-9) ~ Restaurant ~ (01270) 528238 ~ Children under 8 in restaurant and in eating area of bar till 8.30 ~ Open 12-3, 5.30-11; 12-11(10.30 Sun) Sat ~ Bedrooms: £36S/£48S

'Children welcome' means the pub says it lets children inside without any special restriction. If it allows them in, but to restricted areas such as an eating area or family room, we specify this. Some pubs may impose an evening time limit.

WILLINGTON SJ5367 Map 7
Boot

Boothsdale, off A54 at Kelsall

In a terrific setting on wooded hillside (with views across the Cheshire Plain to the Welsh hills), this enjoyable dining pub has been carefully converted from sandstone cottages. The raised stone terrace outside with picnic-sets is lovely in summer, when it's a real suntrap; the three donkeys, golden retriever H, and Sooty and Sweep (the cats) are popular with children. Inside, it's been opened up, leaving small unpretentiously furnished room areas around the central bar with its woodburning stove; an extension with french windows overlooks the garden. Besides tasty regularly changing specials such as lamb hotpot or grilled pork chops (£6.95), and dressed crab (£9.95), good dishes could include soup (£2.75), sandwiches (from £3.50), baguettes (from £5.80), steak and kidney pie or breaded plaice (£6.95), asparagus and brie bake or lamb chops (£8.95), and steaks (from £11.50); puddings (£3.95). The charming restaurant (with a roaring log fire) has wheelback chairs around plenty of tables on its flagstones. They've well kept Bass, Cains, Timothy Taylors Landlord and a guest from the local Weetwood brewery on handpump, a decent wine list, and over 30 malt whiskies. *(Recommended by E G Parish, F H Saint, John and Angela Main, Leo and Barbara Lionet, MLR)*

Pubmaster ~ Lease Mike Gollings and Liz Edwards ~ Real ale ~ Bar food (11-2.30, 6-9.30; 11-9.30 wknds and bank hols) ~ Restaurant ~ (01829) 751375 ~ Children in restaurant and snug until 8.30pm ~ Open 11-3, 6-11; 11-11 Sat; 11-10.30 Sun

WINCLE SJ9666 Map 7
Ship ◗

Village signposted off A54 Congleton—Buxton

Since our last edition, this pleasant pub has been taken over by a new landlord, and it's still a great place to refuel or relax after a bracing walk. Good bar food could include home-made soup (£2.95), lunchtime sandwiches (£4.25), gnocchi with creamy wild mushroom sauce (£4.95), steak and ale pie (£9.50), roast lamb rump with apple mash and mixed bean and rosemary ragu (£11.95), and specials such as smoked haddock on a muffin with poached egg (£5.95) or fried ox liver with black pudding mash in red wine gravy (£12.95), with home-made puddings such as crème brûlée (£3.95). Saturday evenings and Sunday lunchtimes (when it's best to book) it can get busy, and you might have to park on the steep, narrow road outside. The pub dates from the 16th c and is said to be one of Cheshire's oldest. The two old-fashioned and simple little tap rooms (no piped music or games machines) have thick stone walls, and a coal fire; dominoes. On handpump, four well kept ales include Moorhouses Premier and Timothy Taylors Landlord alongside guests such as RCH Pitchfork and Storm Windgather; they also have fruit wines. A small garden has wooden tables and swings. It's tucked away in scenic countryside, and they sell their own book of local walks (£3). *(Recommended by Mike and Wendy Proctor, Ian Phillips, the Didler, John Hillmer, P Abbott, Stephen Buckley)*

Free house ~ Licensee Giles Henry Meadows ~ Real ale ~ Bar food (12-2.30, 7(6 Fri)-9.30; 12-(8 Sun)9.30 Sat; not Mon exc all day bank hols) ~ Restaurant ~ (01260) 227217 ~ Children in family room ~ Dogs allowed in bar ~ Open 12-3, 7-11; 12-11 Sat; 12-10.30 Sun; closed Mon (exc bank hols)

WRENBURY SJ5948 Map 7
Dusty Miller

Village signposted from A530 Nantwich—Whitchurch

There's quite an emphasis on dining at this handsomely converted 19th-c mill. Enjoyable dishes are made with mostly local ingredients, and could include home-made soup (£2.95 – readers recommend the cauliflower and cheese), local black pudding with smoked back bacon (£4.95), cod fillet in lemon butter sauce or chargrilled chicken fillet with crispy smoked bacon and coronation mayonnaise

(£9.95), braised lamb shank with tomato and garlic sauce (£10.25), and local steak (£12.75); as well as puddings such as sticky toffee pudding (£3.75), they do a selection of british cheeses (£4.25). The restaurant and five tables in the bar are no smoking; friendly staff and fresh flowers on tables. In fine weather (when it can get very crowded) picnic-sets on the gravel terrace, among rose bushes by the water, are a pleasant place to sit; you get to them either by the towpath or by a high wooden catwalk over the River Weaver. Inside you get a good view of the striking counterweighted drawbridge going up and down, from a series of tall glazed arches. The modern main bar area is comfortable, with long low-hung hunting prints on green walls, and the mixture of seats flanking the rustic tables includes tapestried banquettes, an ornate church pew and wheelback chairs; further in is a quarry-tiled standing-only part by the bar counter. Well kept Robinsons ales such as Best, Frederics, Hatters Mild, and in winter Old Tom on handpump; piped music, dominoes. The pub enjoys an appealingly peaceful setting by the Shropshire Union Canal. *(Recommended by David Carr, E G Parish, Mike Schofield, Amanda Eames, Dave Braisted, Brenda and Stuart Naylor)*

Robinsons ~ Tenant Mark Sumner ~ Real ale ~ Bar food (not Mon in winter) ~ Restaurant ~ (01270) 780537 ~ Children in eating area of bar ~ Dogs allowed in bar ~ Open 11.30-3(not Mon), 6(6.30 in winter)-11; 12-3, 7-10.30 Sun

Lucky Dip

Besides the fully inspected pubs, you might like to try these Lucky Dips recommended to us and described by readers (if you do, please send us reports: www.goodguides.com).

ACTON BRIDGE [SJ5974]
Hazel Pear [Hill Top Rd]: Country pub with enjoyable sensibly priced food, Marstons Pedigree and Timothy Taylors Landlord, good wine choice, pleasant attentive service; children welcome, open all day *(Andrew Crawford)*
ALPRAHAM [SJ5859]
Tollemache Arms [Chester Rd (A51)]: Extended family pub with country décor, interesting pictures and bric-a-brac, cheerful bar, separate dining areas, reasonably priced food all day, real ales inc Greene King Old Speckled Hen, good service, open stove; big play area outside *(E G Parish)*
Travellers Rest [A51 Nantwich—Chester]: Chatty four-room country local with veteran landlady (same family for three generations), particularly well kept Tetleys Bitter and Mild, leatherette, wicker and Formica, some flock wallpaper, fine old brewery mirrors, darts, back bowling green; no machines, piped music or food (apart from crisps and nuts), cl wkdy lunchtimes *(the Didler, Pete Baker)*
ALSAGER [SJ8054]
Manor House [Audley Rd]: Part of hotel complex, cosy and charming oak-beamed lounge bar, relaxing atmosphere, good choice of food inc lunchtime salad bar, comfortable upstairs restaurant (pianist at Sun lunch), friendly staff, Flowers Original; good bedrooms *(E G Parish)*
BARBRIDGE [SJ6156]
Barbridge Inn [just off A51 N of Nantwich]: Well run and lively open-plan family dining pub done out in olde-worlde style with tiled floors, faded woodwork, hessian curtains, country prints and artefacts; pretty setting by

lively marina at junction of Shropshire Union and Middlewich canals, with play area in busy riverside garden, flagstoned conservatory with washtub tables, no smoking area, friendly helpful staff, simple well cooked food, well kept Boddingtons, Cains and Greenalls, games room, quiet piped music; good disabled facilities, open all day, quiz Tues, jazz Thurs, barbecue *(E G Parish, LYM)*
BELL O' TH' HILL [SJ5245]
Blue Bell [just off A41 N of Whitchurch]: Cosy and attractive two-roomed heavily beamed partly 14th-c country local; the American-born landlord with his Russian-born wife who made this an interesting laid-back main entry with well kept real ales and decent food left in spring 2003 and we have no news yet on their successors, but it's a nice place, with a pleasant garden and surroundings; reports please *(LYM)*
BOLLINGTON [SJ9377]
☆ *Church House* [Church St]: Small village pub with wide choice of good value properly home-made lunchtime food inc interesting dishes (can book tables for busy lunchtimes), quick friendly service, well kept ales such as Flowers, Theakstons and Timothy Taylors Landlord, good range of wines, furnishings inc pews and working sewing-machine treadle tables, roaring fire, separate dining room, provision for children; *(DJH, Dr W J M Gissane, Stephen Buckley)*
Poachers [Mill Lane]: Friendly stone-built village local, three changing well kept ales, decent wines, home-made food with appealingly priced lunches attracting older people and more upscale evening choice,

helpful and attentive young licensees; attractive secluded garden and terrace behind, pretty setting, handy for walkers *(Stephen Buckley, MLR)*

BOTTOM OF THE OVEN [SJ9872]

☆ *Stanley Arms* [A537 Buxton—Macclesfield, 1st left past Cat & Fiddle]: Isolated moorland pub, small, friendly and cosy, lots of shiny black woodwork, plush seats, dimpled copper tables, open winter fires in all rooms inc dining room, generous well cooked traditional food, well kept Marstons and guest beers; children welcome, piped music; picnic-sets on grass behind, may close Mon in winter if weather bad *(LYM, Stephen Buckley, Mike and Wendy Proctor, Richard Waller)*

BRADFIELD GREEN [SJ6859]

☆ *Coach & Horses* [A530 NW of Crewe]: Attractive and comfortably cottagey, good value properly cooked food from good sandwiches up, children's dishes and OAP bargains, perfect veg, well kept real ales, good value house wine, friendly obliging service, horse-racing pictures; discreet piped music *(E G Parish, Sarah Worth)*

BRERETON GREEN [SJ7864]

☆ *Bears Head* [handy for M6 junction 17; set back off A50 S of Holmes Chapel]: Handsome old heavily timbered inn pleasantly reworked as a comfortable brasserie-style Vintage Inn, welcoming warren of small balustraded rooms with old-fashioned furniture, flagstones, carpets and hop-hung low beams, good choice of well prepared enjoyable fresh food, well kept Bass and Tetleys, cheerful log fires, good service, daily papers; open all day, good value bedrooms in modern block *(Ian Phillips, Roger Cass, LYM, E G Parish)*

BROXTON [SJ4858]

Egerton Arms [A41/A534 S of Chester]: Large neatly kept chain pub with well polished old furniture, antique plates and prints in roomy dark-panelled bar, warmly decorated no smoking dining area off; wide choice of food from sandwiches up inc lots for children, efficient staff, well kept Burtonwood and a guest beer, decent wines, children very welcome, colouring materials; discreet piped music; picnic-sets out under cocktail parasols, play area, balcony terrace with lovely views, open all day, comfortable bedrooms – breakfast extra *(Graham and Lynn Mason, LYM, R Davies, E G Parish)*

CHELFORD [SJ8175]

Egerton Arms [A537 Macclesfield—Knutsford]: Good Chef & Brewer, candles on oak tables, bottles on shelves, bric-a-brac, wide choice of blackboard food, Theakstons; garden tables, open all day *(Graham and Lynn Mason)*

CHESTER [SJ4166]

☆ *Boot* [Eastgate Row N]: Down-to-earth and relaxed atmosphere in lovely 17th-c Rows building, heavy beams, lots of dark woodwork, oak flooring and flagstones, even some exposed Tudor wattle and daub, black-leaded kitchen range in lounge beyond good value food servery, no smoking oak-panelled upper

area popular with families (despite hard settles), good service, cheap well kept Sam Smiths; piped music, downstairs can be smoky, children allowed *(Kevin Blake, Joe Green, the Didler, Mr and Mrs Colin Roberts, LYM, Sue Holland, Dave Webster)*

☆ *Falcon* [Lower Bridge St]: Striking and substantial ancient building, with good bustling atmosphere, handsome beams and brickwork, well kept Sam Smiths, well thought out reasonably priced food (not Sun), fruit machine, piped music; children allowed lunchtime (not Sat) in airy upstairs room; open all day Sat (can get packed then, with lunchtime jazz) *(Mr and Mrs S Felstead, LYM, Sue Holland, Dave Webster, Tracey and Stephen Groves, E G Parish)*

☆ *Mill* [Milton St]: A dozen or more changing well kept and well priced ales from smaller breweries inc a Mild (and blackboard for real ale requests) in neat and comfortably carpeted sizeable bar off smart hotel reception, relaxed mix of customers from teenagers to older folk and ladies lunching (good value ciabattas and enjoyable hot dishes, till late evening), friendly efficient staff, restaurant overlooking canal (good value Sun lunch); quiet piped music, big-screen SkyTV, jazz Mon; good with children, waterside benches, boat trips; good bedrooms *(Sue Holland, Dave Webster, BB, the Didler, Andy Chetwood, Rick Capper, Joe Green, Tracey and Stephen Groves, Edward Leetham)*

Olde Kings Head [Lower Bridge St]: Fine old timbered building, lots of woodwork, beams and bric-a-brac, coal fires, low lighting, friendly efficient bar service, well kept Greenalls, lunchtime bar food; upstairs restaurant and hotel part, comfortable bedrooms *(Kevin Blake)*

Pied Bull [Upper Northgate St]: Roomy open-plan carpeted bar, attractive mix of individual furnishings, divided inner area with china cabinet and lots of pictures, nice snug by pillared entrance, imposing intriguingly decorated fireplace; wide choice of generous reasonably priced food inc afternoon teas, real ales, attentive welcoming staff, no smoking area; fruit machines, may be piped music; open all day, handsome Jacobean stairs up to bedrooms *(Kevin Blake, E G Parish, BB)*

Telfords Warehouse [Tower Wharf, behind Northgate St nr railway]: Converted canal building, bare brick and boards, high pitched ceiling, big wall of windows overlooking water, massive iron winding gear in bar, some old enamelled advertisements, good photographs for sale; several well kept ales such as Timothy Taylors Landlord, good wine choice, up to date freshly made generous food, steps to heavy-beamed restaurant area with more artwork; live music Fri/Sat, tables out by water *(BB, Martin and Rose Bonner)*

Union Vaults [Francis St/Egerton St]: Old-fashioned corner alehouse with three quietly interesting and friendly split-level rooms, enthusiastic staff, well kept and reasonably priced Greenalls, Plassey and unusual changing beers and stouts (guest beer suggestions book), bar billiards and bagatelle, back room with pool; may be sandwiches, piped music; open all day *(the Didler, Joe Green, Sue Holland, Dave Webster)*

☆ **White Lion** [off A41 S of M53 junction 5; New Rd]: Low two-room whitewashed pub, old-fashioned and unpretentious, with well kept Thwaites Bitter, Mild and Lancaster Bomber, enjoyable well priced value lunches, welcoming staff, open fire, framed matchbooks, no music or machines; tables out in sheltered area behind, swings in nice quiet front garden *(MLR)*

CHRISTLETON [SJ4565]

Plough [Plough Lane]: Attractive country local dating from 1700s, interlinked lounge areas with lots of bric-a-brac and pictures, no smoking eating area, enjoyable generous well priced food, well kept real ales; garden with play area *(Myke and Nicky Crombleholme)*

CHURCH MINSHULL [SJ6660]

Badger [B5074 Winsford—Nantwich; handy for Shrops Union Canal, Middlewich branch]: Village pub concentrating on enjoyable food in bar and restaurant, OAP lunches Mon-Thurs, carvery every lunchtime (till 5 Sat, bargains for two Sun), friendly staff, roomy comfortable furnishings; tables in garden behind, pretty village, open all day wknds *(E G Parish, LYM)*

CLOTTON [SJ5263]

Bulls Head [A51 Chester—Nantwich]: Attractive building, spaciously refurbished, with civilised but friendly atmosphere, well presented food inc interesting dishes, good service, John Smiths, pool room; country views *(E G Parish)*

CONGLETON [SJ8663]

Beartown Tap [Willow St]: Light and airy tap for nearby Beartown small brewery, their well priced beers from six handpumps, farm cider, bare boards in friendly bar and two pleasant rooms off, another upstairs *(the Didler, Bernie Adams)*

COTEBROOK [SJ5765]

☆ **Alvanley Arms** [A49/B5152 N of Tarporley]: Handsome sandstone inn, 16th-c behind its Georgian façade, with three pleasant beamed rooms (two no smoking areas), big open fire, chintzy little hall, shire horse décor (plenty of tack and pictures – adjacent stud open in season), good generous food with extra lunchtime snack choice and good value specials, Robinsons Best and a seasonal beer, good service; garden with pond and trout, seven good bedrooms with own bathrooms *(Olive and Ray Hebson, T R Emdy, LYM, E G Parish, MLR)*

CREWE [SJ7053]

Albion [Pedley St]: Backstreet local with well kept Tetleys Bitter and Dark Mild, friendly staff, lively bar with sports chat, darts, dominoes, TV and pool room, railway-theme lounge; piped music, quiz night Weds *(E G Parish)*

Borough Arms [Earle St]: Nine or ten interesting changing ales in top condition, four

belgian beers on draught and dozens in bottle, two real lagers, friendly and dedicated landlord; railway theme, green décor, plans for basement microbrewery; games machine, TV, has been cl wkdy lunchtimes, may be wknd evening doorman *(Richard Lewis, the Didler, E G Parish, Andy Chetwood, Rick Capper)*

Crown [Earle St]: Popular recently refurbished high-ceilinged local with welcoming landlady, well kept Robinsons, traditional snug with service bell pushes, back games area; handy for Railway Heritage Centre *(Pete Baker, E G Parish)*

Express [Mill St]: Comfortable local with well kept ale, sports TV *(E G Parish)*

Three Lamps [Earle St, by town hall]: Very popular combination of good eating place with comfortably pubby bar, lots of woodwork and attractive prints, relaxed atmosphere, friendly staff; back food area, well kept Banks's ales inc Mild; piped music, games machines, live music some nights; open all day, overlooking Town Lawn and handy for Lyceum Theatre; very busy lunchtime, esp market days – Mon, Fri, Sat *(E G Parish)*

CROFT [SJ6393]

General Elliot [Lord St]: Painstaking newish landlord, well kept Timothy Taylors Landlord and three or four guest beers such as Jennings, good value fresh food inc authentic greek dishes; well chosen piped music *(Jack Clark)*

DAVENHAM [SJ6670]

Bulls Head [London Rd]: Picturesque old coaching inn with several rooms inc upstairs no smoking dining room, sympathetic décor, interesting prints, large blackboard choice of enjoyable food inc light dishes, Greenalls and Theakstons, good big wine glasses, pleasant helpful staff *(Stuart Paulley, Mrs P J Carroll)*

DUDDON [SJ5164]

Headless Woman [A51 NW of Tarporley]: Neatly enlarged country pub, oak beams and gleaming brass, impression of several little rooms, old timbers worked into walls, wide choice of food from good baguettes up, real ale; play area, open for food all day wknds and bank hols *(E G Parish, Graham and Lynn Mason)*

EATON [SJ8765]

Plough [A536 Congleton—Macclesfield]: Smart and prettily extended 17th-c inn under enthusiastic new management, cosy fires, friendly staff, wide choice of enjoyable food from snacks up, attractive raftered back barn restaurant, well kept real ales inc Hydes, decent wine; piped music; pleasant annexe bedrooms with own bathrooms *(Arthur Baker)*

FADDILEY [SJ5753]

☆ **Thatch** [A534 Wrexham—Nantwich]: Attractive thatched, low-beamed and timbered dining pub carefully extended from medieval core, open fires, candelit barn-style dining room with no smoking area (children allowed); friendly helpful service under new landlord, relaxing atmosphere, well kept real ales inc local Weetwood, enjoyable food (all day Sun) inc children's helpings; charming country garden, open all day Sun *(E G Parish, LYM,*

Myke and Nicky Crombleholme)
GAWSWORTH [SJ8969]

☆ *Harrington Arms* [Church Lane]: Ancient farm pub with two small basic rooms (children allowed in one), bare boards and panelling, fine carved oak bar counter, Robinsons Best and Hatters Mild on handpump, friendly service, pickled eggs or onions, pork pies, fresh chunky lunchtime sandwiches; sunny benches on small front cobbled terrace *(LYM, the Didler, Des and Jen Clarke, R F Grieve, MLR)*

HANDLEY [SJ4758]

☆ *Calveley Arms* [just off A41 S of Chester]: Cosy alcove seating in black and white beamed country pub licensed since 17th c, enjoyable changing food from sandwiches and baguettes to interesting specials and fish dishes, courteous welcoming service (they even keep a visitors' book), well kept Boddingtons and Theakstons Black Bull with occasional guest beers and interesting soft drinks, open fire, traditional games; piped music; very well behaved children allowed, secluded garden with boules *(A and B D Craig, Paul Boot, Mr and Mrs A H Young, E G Parish, LYM)*

HANKELOW [SJ6645]

White Lion [A529 Audlem—Nantwich]: Well organised sympathetically renovated pub opp village green and pond, well prepared food in comfortable dining areas, good young licensees, open fires *(E G Parish)*

HOUGH [SJ7151]

White Hart [A500 3 miles from M6 junction 16]: Pleasant surroundings, good home cooking (all day wknd) inc children's helpings, local and guest beers, decent wines *(D L Mayer)*

KELSALL [SJ5268]

Olive Tree [Chester Rd (A54)]: Former Morris Dancer, roomy and civilised yet cosy, with two bars, wine bar area and restaurant, low beams and comfortable country-style furniture, enjoyable food inc interesting dishes (service can slow on Sun), pleasant relaxing atmosphere, well kept local real ale, decent wines, log fires *(Derek and Margaret Underwood, E G Parish)*

LACH DENNIS [SJ7072]

Duke of Portland [B5082]: Roomy country pub with attractive L-shaped bar, balustraded eating areas (one no smoking), enjoyable fresh food using local suppliers from good sandwiches to theme nights (best to book Sun lunch), two-course wkdy bargain lunch, good service, Banks's and Marstons Pedigree, good value house wines *(E G Parish)*

LANGLEY [SJ9471]

☆ *Leathers Smithy* [off A523 S of Macclesfield, OS Sheet 118 map ref 952715]: Pleasant relaxing atmosphere in isolated two-bar pub up in fine walking country, enjoyable bar food (all day Sun) from sandwiches to good steaks, open fires, winter glühwein and lots of whiskies, well kept ales such as Courage Directors, Marstons Pedigree, Storm Windgather and RCH Pitchfork, farm cider, good service, family room *(LYM, Stephen*

Buckley, Mr and Mrs Colin Roberts, MLR)
LITTLE BARROW [SJ4769]

☆ *Foxcote* [B5152, between A51 and A56 E of Chester]: Big largely no smoking L-shaped eating place specialising in good freshly cooked seafood (a separate board just for mussels dishes), early-evening bargains, good choice of wines by the glass, courteous efficient staff, relaxed and cheerful pubby atmosphere despite the gingham tablecloths on all tables and lack of real ales, seafood and country prints on hessian walls, classy flower arrangements, end tables with picture-window country views *(Jean and Douglas Troup, Mrs P J Carroll, Lynette and Stuart Shore, BB)*

LITTLE BOLLINGTON [SJ7286]

☆ *Swan With Two Nicks* [2 miles from M56 junction 7 – A56 towards Lymm, then first right at Stamford Arms into Park Lane; use A556 to get back on to M56 westbound]: Welcoming bustle in refurbished beamed village pub full of brass, copper and bric-a-brac, snug alcoves, some antique settles, log fire, good choice of generous popular food from filling baguettes up, well kept ales inc Boddingtons, Greene King Old Speckled Hen and Timothy Taylors Landlord, decent wines, cheerful quick staff; tables outside, open all day, attractive hamlet by Dunham Hall deer park, walks by Bridgewater Canal *(LYM, Stephen Buckley, Mr and Mrs Colin Roberts)*

LITTLE BUDWORTH [SJ5965]

Red Lion [Vicarage Lane]: Pleasant pub in unspoilt spot, handy for country strolls; welcoming licensees, good choice of well prepared food (all day Sun), comfortable lounge bar, well kept beers, sensibly priced wines; good bedrooms with own bath *(Mrs Sandria Parker)*

LITTLE LEIGH [SJ6076]

Leigh Arms [A49 by swing bridge]: Riverside pub next to Acton swing bridge, beams and flagstone, tile or wood floors, interesting pictures, leather chesterfields and armchairs, country kitchen tables and chairs, wide food choice from good generous ploughman's up, Burtonwood and a guest such as Elgoods Pageant, welcoming service; children's corner with play things in one room, music nights Thurs-Sat; waterside garden with play area *(Lynda Payton, Sam Samuells)*

LOWER WHITLEY [SJ6178]

☆ *Chetwode Arms* [just off A59, handy for M56 junction 10; Street Lane]: Family dining pub with traditional layout, solid furnishings all clean and polished, friendly local atmosphere in front bar, wide choice of good varied original food in side bar and other rooms (cheaper dishes not served evenings), generous helpings, warm coal fires, four real ales, good wines by the glass, good service; immaculate bowling green, play area, has been open all day Sat *(LYM, Simon J Barber)*

LYMM [SJ6787]

☆ *Spread Eagle* [not far from M6 junction 20; Eagle Brow]: Long rambling beamed village pub, big comfortable two-level lounge with good value home-made food all day from sandwiches and baguettes through two-course bargains to steaks, proper drinking area by central bar, particularly well kept Lees Bitter and Red Dragon, good choice of wines, cheery atmosphere and good service, coal fire, separate games room with pool; bedrooms, attractive village *(Derek and Sylvia Stephenson, Pete Baker, MLR)*

MACCLESFIELD [SJ9273]

☆ *Castle* [Church St]: Deceptively large unchanging local in narrow cobbled street, two lounges, small public bar, plenty of character and lots of nooks and crannies in and out glass-roofed area up steps, well kept Courage Directors and Theakstons Bitter and Mild, simple lunchtime food inc proper chips *(E G Parish, the Didler, BB)*

Dolphin [Windmill St, just off A523 S]: Friendly traditional three-room pub left unspoilt by sympathetic refurbishment, good home-made lunchtime food at bargain prices, well kept Robinsons, darts and cards *(Pete Baker)*

Sun [Mill Lane/London Rd]: Beams and bare boards in two basic rooms off central servery, one with games, well kept Burtonwood, Cains and three changing guest beers, coal fires, friendly landlord may knock up a sandwich for you; open all day Sat *(Pete Baker)*

MARTON [SJ8568]

Davenport Arms [A34 N of Congleton]: Clean and spaciously modernised, with warmly friendly atmosphere and service, generous good value home-made food in bar and restaurant inc popular Sun lunch, well kept real ales inc a Mild, no smoking area; nr ancient half-timbered church (and Europe's widest oak tree) *(Dr D J and Mrs S C Walker)*

MOBBERLEY [SJ7879]

Bulls Head [Mill Lane]: Comfortable low-beamed pub with old pictures, soft lighting, enjoyable straightforward reasonably priced food inc hot baguettes and children's, well kept ales such as Boddingtons, Timothy Taylors Landlord and Tetleys Bitter and Mild, quick friendly service, central open fire and another one end, games room; piped music; immaculate bowling green *(Michael and Jenny Back, Mr and Mrs Colin Roberts, BB)*

Church Inn [opp church]: Popular lunchtime for enjoyable fresh food from good baguettes up, well kept real ales, big log fire, cheerful service, friendly atmosphere; children welcome, tables outside, play area, own bowling green *(Pat and Robert Watt, Crystal and Peter Hooper)*

Frozen Mop [Faulkners Lane]: Comfortable Brewers Fayre dining pub with good value food, well kept ales such as Boddingtons and Marstons Pedigree, popular family area *(Mr and Mrs Colin Roberts)*

☆ *Roebuck* [Mill Lane; down hill from sharp bend on B5085 at E edge of 30mph limit]: Spacious and appealing open-plan bar with brasses, pews, polished boards, panelling and alcoves; good fresh food from lunchtime sandwiches to interesting modern hot dishes, very welcoming young staff, well kept real ales, no smoking area, upstairs restaurant; children

welcome, can get busy Sat night; pretty outside, with tables in cobbled courtyard and pleasant extended garden behind, play area *(Doug Christian, Mrs P J Carroll, LYM, Suzanne Miles, R F Grieve)*

NANTWICH [SJ6552]

☆ *Black Lion* [Welsh Row]: Three little rooms alongside main bar, old-fashioned nooks and crannies, beams and bare floors, big grandfather clock; four changing real ales inc well kept local Weetwood brews and a guest beer, farm cider, cheap sandwiches, very friendly cat, chess; occasional live music; heated marquee outside, open all day *(Edward Leetham, Pete Baker, BB)*

☆ *Crown* [High St, free public parking behind]: Striking three-storey timbered Elizabethan hotel with overhanging upper galleries, cosy rambling beamed bar with antique tables and chairs on sloping creaky floors, decent bar lunches from sandwiches and baked potatoes to steak, italian evening restaurant (and all day Sat), Boddingtons and Flowers IPA, helpful service; very busy wknd evenings, piped music, fruit machine and TV; children welcome, open all day, comfortable bedrooms *(E G Parish, David Carr, LYM)*

Globe [Audlem Rd]: Traditional landlady and home cooking (all day wknds) inc lunchtime and early evening bargains, Flowers real ale, good wine choice, very welcoming and helpful staff, comfortable seating inc some small room areas, good civilised pub atmosphere, quaint rooms with old prints; tables in garden, pretty floral displays *(E G Parish)*

Oddfellows Arms [Welsh Row]: Recently reworked in pleasantly rustic low-ceilinged style, real fires, friendly staff, Burtonwood Top Hat and Weetwood, reasonably priced generous food; garden tables, lovely street, antique shops *(Graham Burns)*

NESTON [SJ2976]

☆ *Harp* [Quayside, SW of Little Neston; keep on along track at end of Marshlands Rd]: Well kept real ales such as Fullers London Pride, Greene King Abbot, Holts, Ind Coope Burton, Moorhouses Black Cat Mild and Timothy Taylors Landlord, good malt whiskies, woodburner in pretty fireplace, local atmosphere, pale quarry tiles and simple furnishings (children allowed in room on right), lunchtime food; picnic-sets up on grassy front sea wall look out over the Dee marshes to Wales, glorious sunsets with wild calls of wading birds; open all day from noon *(MLR, Sue and Keith Campbell, BB)*

OVER PEOVER [SJ7674]

☆ *Whipping Stocks* [Stocks Lane]: Several neatly kept rooms, good oak panelling and fittings, solid furnishings, well kept cheap Sam Smiths, wide choice of low-priced popular straightforward food all day from good sandwiches up, friendly smartly dressed staff, log fires; children in eating area, picnic-sets in good-sized garden with safe play area, easy parkland walks *(LYM, E G Parish)*

PARKGATE [SJ2878]

Boathouse [village signed off A540]: Black and

white timbered dining pub with several interesting connecting rooms and big conservatory (booking needed wknds), spectacular views to Wales over silted grassy estuary behind, generous food inc children's and popular Sun lunch, well spaced tables, well kept Tetleys tapped from the cask, good friendly service; nearby marshes good for birdwatchers *(E G Parish)*

☆ *Red Lion* [The Parade (B5135)]: Comfortable and neatly kept local on attractive waterfront, big windows look across road to silted grassy estuary with Wales beyond, typical pub furnishings, shiny brown beams hung with lots of china, copper and brass, good value food inc sandwiches and OAP lunches, well kept Adnams, Ind Coope Burton and Tetleys, flame-effect fire in pretty Victorian fireplace, good games room off public bar; picnic-sets out on small front terrace, open all day *(BB, MLR, Sue and Keith Campbell)*

RAINOW [SJ9576]

☆ *Highwayman* [A5002 Whaley Bridge—Macclesfield, NE of village]: Timeless unchanging moorside pub with small rooms, low 17th-c beams, well kept Thwaites ales, bar food inc good sandwiches and ideal black pudding, good winter fires (electric other times), plenty of atmosphere, lovely views *(LYM, the Didler, Dr D J and Mrs S C Walker, Stephen Buckley)*

RODE HEATH [SJ8057]

Royal Oak [A533; a walk from Trent & Mersey Canal, Bridge 141/142]: Friendly pub with wide choice of food inc bargain Sun lunch, various areas off central bar inc back games room, real ales such as Adnams Broadside, Bass and Tetleys Bitter and Dark Mild, plenty of brass, ornaments and pictures *(Richard Lewis)*

SMALLWOOD [SJ7861]

☆ *Legs of Man* [A50 S of Sandbach]: Good home-cooked food inc some imaginative dishes and a suggestion of spanish or portuguese influence inc comfortable roadside pub with carefully matched chairs, banquettes, carpet, curtains and wallpaper, fin de siècle tall white nymphs on columns, lush potted plants, well kept Robinsons Best, Frederics and Hatters Mild, good friendly service even when busy; restaurant, children truly welcome; well spaced tables on side lawn with play area *(BB, Mrs P J Carroll, E G Parish)*

SPROSTON GREEN [SJ7366]

Fox & Hounds [nr M6 junction 18 – A54 towards Middlewich]: Attractive and welcoming low-beamed and flagstoned pub with good choice of food in bar and dining area, well kept Courage Directors and Greenalls *(Nigel and Sue Foster)*

STOAK [SJ4273]

Bunbury Arms [Little Stanney Lane; 1 mile from M53 junction 10, A5117 W then first left]: Small snug and big but cosy beamed lounge with interesting antique furniture, lots of pictures and books, friendly staff and locals, enjoyable home-made food (all day Sun) with unusual starters making good light lunches

(very popular wkdys with local business people), well kept Cains; tables on grass by car park (M-way noise), short walk for canal users from bridge 136 or 138, handy for Cheshire Oaks shopping outlet *(Graham and Lynn Mason)*

SWETTENHAM [SJ8067]

Swettenham Arms [off A54 Congleton—Holmes Chapel or A535 Chelford—Holmes Chapel]: Attractive old country pub very popular for its pretty setting next to the Quinta (scenic wildlife area), wide choice of good food in charming series of individually furnished rooms from sofas and easy chairs to no smoking dining area (must book Sun), well spaced tables, well kept ales such as Beartown, Hydes, Jennings and Tetleys, farm cider, picnic-sets on quiet side lawn; children welcome, live music Weds *(Doug Christian, LYM, E G Parish, Brenda and Stuart Naylor)*

TARPORLEY [SJ5561]

☆ *Red Fox* [A49/A51, 1 mile S]: Sympathetically extended and attractively decorated country pub with comfortable and spacious low-beamed bar, wide range of good reasonably priced interesting food, well kept real ales, friendly staff, pleasant conservatory; children welcome, bedrooms, handy for Beeston and Peckforton castles, open all day Sun *(Colin Harrison, Sue Holland, Dave Webster)*

WALKER BARN [SJ9573]

Setter Dog [A537 Macclesfield—Buxton]: Stone-built pub in great moorland setting with windswept Pennine views, handy for Teggs Nose Country Park, but closed from autumn 2002, future uncertain; news please *(BB)*

WARRINGTON [SJ6188]

Blue Bell [Horsemarket St]: Welcoming town pub, lots of dark wood in smallish rooms off central bar, wide choice of generous low-priced food, well kept Greenalls, exemplary service *(Mr and Mrs Colin Roberts)*

WHEELOCK [SJ7559]

Commercial [off new A534 bypass; Game St]: Old-fashioned unspoilt local, two smaller rooms (one no smoking) off high-ceilinged main bar, unaltered décor, Boddingtons, Marstons Pedigree, Thwaites and perhaps a guest beer, real fire, firmly efficient service, no food; pool in games room, may be Thurs folk night, open from 8 evenings only, and Sun lunchtime *(the Didler, Pete Baker)*

WHITELEY GREEN [SJ9278]

Windmill [Hole House Lane; village signposted off A523 a mile N of B5091 Bollington turn-off]: Big open-plan pub extended from heavy-beamed core, good-sized no smoking area, well kept Greene King Old Speckled Hen, Tetleys and sometimes a guest beer, usual food; TV, piped music; children in eating areas, big attractive garden with plenty of picnic-sets and summer bar, open all day wknds *(Andrew Scarr, Stephen Buckley, Doug Christian, LYM, Brian and Anna Marsden)*

WILLINGTON CORNER [SJ5366]

Willington Hall [signed off A51 N of Tarporley]: Small country hotel with good value bar food and nice choice of beers in spacious public and lounge bars, big windows with pleasant views, friendly staff, enjoyable restaurant; tables out on attractive terrace, bedrooms *(Gill and Keith Croxton)*

WINCLE [SJ9467]

Wild Boar: Traditional moorland pub with food lunchtimes and evenings from sandwiches to steaks, Robinsons Bitter, coal fire in comfortable bar, separate restaurant; open all day wknds, cl Tues, two newly done bedrooms *(MLR, BB, Mike and Wendy Proctor)*

WINTERLEY [SJ7557]

Forresters Arms [A534]: Cosy and friendly low-beamed village local with warmly welcoming attentive landlord, inventive good value bar lunches, well kept Tetleys ales inc Dark Mild; darts and quiz night, Weds raffle; pleasant garden with dovecote and retired tractor *(E G Parish, Sue Holland, Dave Webster, John Hulme)*

WRENBURY [SJ5948]

Cotton Arms [Cholmondeley Rd]: Welcoming beamed and timbered pub in popular spot by canal locks and boatyard, with good value food in two large comfortable dining areas, friendly staff, well kept real ales inc a guest beer, lots of brass, open fire, side games room *(E G Parish, Andy Chetwood, Rick Capper, Mike Schofield)*

WYBUNBURY [SJ6950]

☆ *Swan* [B5071]: Spotless family-friendly bow-windowed pub popular for good home-made food at reasonable prices, well kept ales inc Jennings, good house wines, efficient helpful service, nooks and crannies in homely rambling lounge, snug dining areas inc no smoking one, pleasant public bar, plenty of bric-a-brac; tables in garden by beautiful churchyard, bedrooms *(Mike and Wendy Proctor, Mrs P J Carroll, Sue Holland, Dave Webster, LYM)*

Real ale may be served from handpumps, electric pumps (not just the on-off switches used for keg beer) or – common in Scotland – tall taps called founts (pronounced 'fonts') where a separate pump pushes the beer up under air pressure. The landlord can adjust the force of the flow – a tight spigot gives the good creamy head that Yorkshire lads like.

Cornwall

Cornwall's pubs have come on in leaps and bounds in recent years. Pub food here is now so much better than it used to be, there are good real ales (with lots of support for the local Sharps and Skinners, joining the veteran St Austell brewery), and hardworking friendly landlords and landladies are making the most of buildings of real character, often in lovely waterside settings. Four newcomers to the main entries this year are the nicely set and welcoming Blisland Inn (hearty food and lots of real ales), the Coombe Barton at Crackington Haven (great position), the Gurnards Head Hotel (good all round, in another great spot) and the Old Success at Sennen Cove (also by the sea, on Cornwall's very tip). Other pubs doing particularly well here this year are the Olde Plough House at Duloe (good all round), the Halzephron near Helston (an absolute smasher, doing brilliantly under its very special landlady), the well run Halfway House at Kingsand (though it may be changing hands), the Royal Oak in Lostwithiel (the best sort of town pub), the Plume of Feathers at Mitchell (super food, nice bedrooms and very hard-working licensees), the Roseland at Philleigh (one of the West Country's top all-rounders), the Ship in Porthleven (a harbourside gem), the Turks Head on St Agnes (it would be a top pub anywhere, but its idyllic island setting makes it very special indeed), the Falcon at St Mawgan (particularly popular for its food, and a nice place to stay), the Springer Spaniel at Treburley (new licensees settling in well, good food), the Driftwood Spars at Trevaunance Cove (fine position, good beers including one it brews itself, decent traditional food), and the cheerful Old Ale House in Truro (its name says it all). For a special meal out, the Halzephron and the Plume of Feathers both have great appeal; the Plume of Feathers at Mitchell gains the title of Cornwall Dining Pub of the Year. The Lucky Dip section at the end of the chapter is particularly rich in pubs that, for the qualities we applaud, are really of main entry quality. Ones we would note specially are the Old Albion at Crantock, Smugglers Den at Cubert, Old Quay House at Devoran, Quayside Inn in Falmouth, King of Prussia in Fowey, Fishermans Arms at Golant, Ferry Boat at Helford Passage, Blue Anchor in Helston, Lamorna Wink at Lamorna, Ship at Lerryn, Top House at Lizard, White Hart at Ludgvan, Bush at Morwenstow, Fort in Newquay, Victoria at Perranuthnoe, Royal Oak at Perranwell, Weary Friar at Pillaton, Three Pilchards in Polperro, Plume of Feathers at Portscatho, Railway Inn in St Agnes, Ring o' Bells in St Issey, Sloop in St Ives, Victory in St Mawes, Crooked Inn at Trematon and New Inn at Veryan.

BLISLAND SX0973 Map 1
Blisland Inn 🍺

Village signposted off A30 and B3266 NE of Bodmin

Nicely set on the pretty tree-lined village green, this welcoming local is best known for its ever-changing range of perfectly kept real ales. By the time of our visit in spring 2003 they had stocked 1,777 over the last eight and a half years, and the evidence is everywhere: every inch of the beams and ceiling is covered with beer mats (or their particularly wide-ranging collection of mugs), and the walls are similarly filled with beer-related posters and memorabilia. A blackboard lists the day's range, which has a firm emphasis on brews from Cornwall. They also have a changing farm cider, and fruit wines. Above the fireplace another blackboard has the choice of enjoyable, hearty home-made food, which might include sandwiches, a number of good home-made pies (£6.45 – the gravy for the steak and ale is made purely from beer, without any water), simple basket meals, changing fresh fish, and a popular Sunday lunch (£5.45, including pudding and coffee, booking advisable); service is chatty and friendly. No smoking at mealtimes, the partly flagstoned and carpeted lounge has a number of clocks and barometers on one wall, a rack of daily newspapers for sale, a few standing timbers, and a good chatty atmosphere; occasional piped music. Note children are allowed only in the separate, plainer family room (with darts, euchre and pool), though there are plenty of picnic-sets outside. The Camel Trail cycle path is close by. As with many pubs in this area, it's hard to approach without negotiating several single-track roads. *(Recommended by Peter Salmon, D and M T Ayres-Regan, Dr and Mrs M E Wilson, Dr D J Groves, P R and S A White, Sue Spencer-Hurst, JP, PP, the Didler, Joan and Michel Hooper-Immins, DAV, Margaret Mason, David Thompson)*

Free house ~ Licensees Gary and Margaret Marshall ~ Real ale ~ Bar food (12-2, 6.30-9) ~ (01208) 850739 ~ Children in family room ~ Dogs welcome ~ Live music Sat evening ~ Open 11.30-11; 12-10.30 Sun

BODINNICK SX1352 Map 1
Old Ferry ★ 🛏

Across the water from Fowey; coming by road, to avoid the ferry queue turn left as you go down the hill – car park on left before pub

Readers enjoy staying in this friendly 16th-c inn all year round, and from most of the bedrooms there are fine views of the pretty Fowey river; there are binoculars and a telescope in the guest lounge, and seats outside on the terrace all looking over the water. The three simply furnished little rooms have quite a few bits of nautical memorabilia, a couple of half model ships mounted on the wall, and several old photographs, as well as wheelback chairs, built-in plush pink wall seats, and an old high-backed settle; there may be several friendly cats and a dog. The family room at the back is actually hewn into the rock; piped music. Decent bar food includes home-made soup (£3.25), sandwiches (from £2.35; toasties 35p extra), ploughman's (from £5.50), quite a few dishes with chips (from £4.10; home-cooked ham and egg £5.10), home-made cream cheese and broccoli pasta bake (£6.50), curry of the day (£6.75), home-made steak and kidney pie (£6.95), fresh smoked haddock with scrambled egg (£7.95), puddings (from £3.25), and popular evening daily specials like fresh crab and prawn cocktail (£5.50), wild mushroom and brandy sauce puff pastry parcel (£8.75), local rack of lamb with honey and ginger sauce (£10.25), sirloin steak (£10.95), and fresh scallops, king prawns and monkfish in tomato sauce (£12.95). The restaurant is no smoking. Sharps Own on handpump, kept under light blanket pressure; darts and TV. *(Recommended by Dave Braisted, David and Anthea Eeles, Dr and Mrs M W A Haward, Prof and Mrs Tony Palmer, Michael Dandy, Simon, Jo and Benjamin Cole, M Benjamin, Nick Lawless, Tony and Maggie Bundey, Jayne Capp, John and Judy Saville)*

Free house ~ Licensees Royce and Patricia Smith ~ Real ale ~ Bar food (12-2.30, 6-9) ~ Restaurant ~ (01726) 870237 ~ Children in family room ~ Dogs allowed in bar and bedrooms ~ Open 11-11; 12-10.30 Sun; 11.30-2.30, 6.30-10.30 weekdays in winter; closed 25 Dec ~ Bedrooms: /£55(£65S)(£70B)

Stars after the name of a pub show exceptional quality. One star means most people (after reading the report to see just why the star has been won) would think a special trip worth while. Two stars mean that the pub is really outstanding – many that for their particular qualities cannot be bettered.

BOSCASTLE SX0990 Map 1
Napoleon

High Street; up at the top of the village

New licensees had just taken over this 16th-c thick-walled white cottage as we went to press but are keeping most of the staff, so we are hoping that not much will change. Several little flagstoned rooms ramble around up and down, with oak beams, slate floors, log fires, an exposed oven, an interesting and unusual collection of prints and memorabilia of Napoleon, pottery boots, walking sticks and lots of other knick-knacks. Well kept St Austell Tinners, HSD and seasonal ales tapped from casks behind the bar, and decent wines. Bar food now includes home-made soup with herb scones, garlic mushrooms or home-made hummous (£2.95), filled focaccia (from £4.95), home-made seafood or vegetable quiche (£6.95), beef and mushroom casserole with herb dumplings and saffron mash or italian chicken (£7.25), gammon steak (£7.50), rump steak (£8.50), and puddings like home-made treacle and orange tart or bread and butter pudding (£2.95). Piped music, shove-ha'penny, cribbage, and dominoes. There are seats on a covered terrace and in the large sheltered garden. The pub is at the top of this steep, quaint village, and there are splendid views on the way up. *(Recommended by David Cartwright, G Walsh, Dr and Mrs M W A Haward, Bob and Sue Hardy, JCW, the Didler, JP, PP, W F C Phillips, Canon Michael Bourdeaux, Keith and Margaret Kettell)*

St Austell ~ Tenants Liam and Jacquie Flynn ~ Real ale ~ Bar food (12-2.30, 6.30-9.30) ~ Restaurant ~ (01840) 250204 ~ Children in eating area of bar ~ Dogs allowed in bar ~ Live blues and folk Tues evening, folk and blues Fri evening ~ Open 11-11; 11-11 Sat; 12-10.30 Sun ~ Bedrooms: /£45

CADGWITH SW7214 Map 1
Cadgwith Cove Inn

Down very narrow lane off A3083 S of Helston; no nearby parking

It's best to park at the top of the village and walk down the steep slope to reach this old-fashioned and friendly thatched local set in a working fishing cove. Its two snugly dark front rooms have plain pub furnishings on their mainly parquet flooring, a log fire in one stripped stone end wall, and plenty of locals chatting around the serving counter; there are lots of local photographs including gig races, cases of naval hat ribands and of fancy knot-work, a couple of compass binnacles, and ship's shields on some of its dark beams – others have spliced blue rope hand-holds. Well kept Flowers IPA, Greene King Abbot and Ruddles County, Sharps Own, and Wadworths 6X on handpump. A plusher pink back room has a huge and colourful fish mural. The daily specials tend to be the things to go for in the food line: local crab soup (£5.95), moules marinière (£5.95 or £9), skate wing with capers (£7.95), super local cod and chips or sole meunière, monkfish tail in a light creamy curry sauce (£8.95), and hake in a tangy cheese sauce (£9.95). Other dishes include sandwiches and baguettes (from £4.25; the crab are particularly good), filled baked potatoes (from £3.95), ploughman's (£5.95), home-made curry or home-made lasagne (£6.95), steak (£10.45), and puddings like home-made blackberry and apple pie with clotted cream (£3.85); best to check food times in winter. The left-hand room has darts. There may be 1960s piped music, and a folk club on Tuesdays and Cornish singing on a Friday. A good-sized front terrace has green-painted picnic-sets, some under a fairy-lit awning, looking down to the fish sheds by the bay. Coast Path walks are superb in both directions. *(Recommended by Malcolm and Jennifer Perry, Lawrence Pearse, Di and Mike Gillam, P R and S A White, Jeanne and Paul Silvestri, Sue Holland, Dave Webster, Cathy Robinson, Ed Coombe, Mr and Mrs McKay, R G Price, Mrs B M Smith)*

Pubmaster ~ Lease David and Lynda Trivett ~ Real ale ~ Bar food ~ Restaurant ~ (01326) 290513 ~ Children in restaurant ~ Dogs welcome ~ Folk club Tues, Cornish singing Fri ~ Open 12-11; 12-11 Sat; 12-10.30 Sun; 12-3, 7-11 in winter ~ Bedrooms: £19.75/£39.50

CONSTANTINE SW7229 Map 1

Trengilly Wartha ★ (🏠) ♖ 🍺 🛏

Simplest approach is from A3083 S of Helston, signposted Gweek near RNAS Culdrose, then fork right after Gweek; coming instead from Penryn (roads narrower), turn right in Constantine just before Minimarket (towards Gweek), then pub signposted left in nearly 1 mile; at Nancenoy, OS Sheet 204 map reference 731282

Tucked away down steep narrow lanes, this popular inn continues to please a wide range of customers. The long low-beamed main bar has a woodburning stove and attractive built-in high-backed settles boxing in polished heavy wooden tables, and at one end, shelves of interesting wines with drink-in and take-out price labels (they run their own retail and wholesale wine business). The bright no smoking conservatory has an area leading off that houses pool, shove-ha'penny, dominoes, cribbage, shut the box, and a TV; they run their own cricket team. Popular bar food includes soup, chicken liver and port pâté with home-made chutney (£5.60), king prawns in garlic and chilli oil (£5.80), pasties (£6.20), lunchtime ploughman's with home-made breads and pickles (£6.70), their own sausages with mustard mash and onion gravy (£7.20), big salads such as roast vegetable and goats cheese or thai chicken (from £7.80), leek and cheese soufflé (£8.60), ham hock with a stout and honey glaze (£9.50), king prawn tails in a coconut curry sauce (£11.50), plenty of daily specials like local white crab meat in olive oil, garlic and chilli with spinach pasta (£5.90), big local scallops with local asparagus and lemon grass butter (£8), free-range local chicken supreme stuffed with sage and garlic sausage meat on a bubble and squeak cake with crispy pancetta (£12.80), and local spring lamb with rosemary-braised broad beans and parsnip cream (£13), with puddings like white chocolate and Grand Marnier crème brûlée, rhubarb crumble or sticky toffee pudding (£3.50); they offer many dishes in helpings for smaller people. Well kept Skinners Knocker, Sharps Cornish, and a local guest on handpump or tapped from the cask. Over 50 malt whiskies (including several extinct ones), up to 20 wines by the glass (from a fine list of over 250), and around 10 armagnacs. The pretty landscaped garden has some tables under large parasols, an international sized piste for boules, and a lake; lots of surrounding walks. *(Recommended by DRH and KLH, Andy and Yvonne Cunningham, Dr Paull Khan, David Rule, Hazel Morgan, M G Hart, Roger and Jenny Huggins, Ruth and Andrew Crowder, Mr R P Brewer, the Didler, R and S Bentley, Nigel and Olga Wikeley, Comus and Sarah Elliott, Dr and Mrs M E Wilson, Eamonn and Natasha Skyrme, Patrick Hancock, Jenny and Brian Seller, JP, PP, Neil and Angela Huxter, Bernard Stradling, M A Borthwick, Tom McLean)*

Free house ~ Licensees Nigel Logan and Michael Maguire ~ Real ale ~ Bar food (12-2.15(2 Sun), 6.30(7 Sun)-9.30; not 25 Dec) ~ Restaurant ~ (01326) 340332 ~ Children in restaurant and family room ~ Dogs welcome ~ Open 11-3, 6.30-11; 12-3, 7-10.30 Sun ~ Bedrooms: £49B/£78B

CRACKINGTON HAVEN SX1396 Map 1

Coombe Barton

Off A39 Bude—Camelford

This much-extended old inn benefits from a setting that's hard to beat, directly opposite a splendid craggy bay that's a favourite with surfers and walkers. A side terrace has plenty of tables to enjoy the view. It's a popular spot in summer, but the spacious, modernised bar easily has enough room to cope. Smartly uniformed young staff efficiently serve a wide range of food, including fresh crab sandwiches, changing specials such as beef and Guinness pie, local steaks (from £12), and plenty of fresh fish such as bass (£15); children's menu. Booking is recommended for the Sunday carvery. The three real ales typically include brews from Sharps and St Austell. A glass screen helps break up the huge room, separating the pool table from the eating areas; lots of local pictures on the walls, and a surfboard hangs from the wood-planked ceiling. Fruit machines, piped music, darts, TV. The restaurant and big, plain family room are no smoking. The car park fills quickly, though there's a big pay and display next door. We haven't had any reports on the bedrooms. *(Recommended by Mrs C Noble, Keith and Margaret Kettell, Tim and Sue Halstead, Mr and Mrs R B Hayman)*

Free house ~ Licensee Nick Cooper ~ Real ale ~ Bar food (not 25 Dec) ~ (01840) 230345 ~ Children in restaurant and family area ~ Dogs allowed in bar ~ Open 11-3, 6-11; 11-11 school hols and Sat; 12-10.30 Sun ~ Bedrooms: /£70B

DULOE SX2358 Map 1
Olde Plough House
B3254 N of Looe

One reader was delighted to find that despite not visiting this bustling and popular neatly kept place for some years, things were as enjoyable as ever. The two communicating rooms have a lovely dark polished Delabole slate floor, some turkey rugs, a mix of pews, modern high-backed settles and smaller chairs, foreign banknotes on the beams, three woodburning stoves, and a restrained décor – some prints of waterfowl and country scenes, a few copper jugs and a fat china pig perched on window sills. The public side (just as comfortable) has darts. Well liked and reasonably priced food at lunchtime includes home-made soup (£2.75), filled baguettes (from £3.75), a roast of the day (£5.45), ploughman's (from £5.45), local pork sausage with mash (£5.75), home-cooked ham and egg (£5.95), and vietnamese sweet chilli chicken or vegetable lasagne (£6.25), with evening dishes like thai-style fishcakes (£9.25), chicken wellington (£9.95), half slow-roasted duck with oriental sauce (£10.95), and fillet steak with bubble and squeak and madeira sauce (£12.95), and daily specials such as fillet of salmon and scallops with a leek, bacon and mushroom cream sauce (£10.25) or fillets of bass with avocado and cherry tomato salsa (£11.45); the evening dining room is no smoking. Well kept Bass and Sharps Cornish Coaster and Doom Bar on handpump, sensibly priced wines, and good attentive service. There is a small more modern carpeted dining room, and a few picnic-sets out by the road. The two friendly jack russells are called Jack and Spot, and the cat, Willow. *(Recommended by J M Tansey, Prof and Mrs Tony Palmer, Nick Lawless, Mayur Shah, John and Shelia Brooks, Theocsbrian, R G Price, Mrs B M Smith, P R and S A White, Mrs M E Lewis, J A Lewis, Dr and Mrs M W A Haward, B J Harding, Bob Turnham, Ian Phillips)*

Free house ~ Licensees Gary and Alison Toms ~ Real ale ~ Bar food (not 25 Dec) ~ Restaurant ~ (01503) 262050 ~ Children in restaurant ~ Dogs allowed in bar ~ Open 12-2.30, 6.30-11; 12-2.30, 7-10.30 Sun; closed evenings 25-26 Dec

EDMONTON SW9672 Map 1
Quarryman
Village signposted off A39 just W of Wadebridge bypass

You can be sure of a friendly welcome and a good meal in this unusual pub, built around a carefully reconstructed slate-built courtyard of former quarrymen's quarters, and part of a holiday complex; there's now a gas-heated area for outside evening meals. The three beamed rooms (one is no smoking) have simple pleasant furnishings, a set of interesting old brass spirit optics above the fireplace nestling among some fine old whisky advertising figurines, fresh flowers on tables, a woodburner, and a couple of bow windows (one with a charming stained-glass quarryman panel) looking out to a distant wind farm; there are some Roy Ullyett menu cartoons for British Sportsman's Club Savoy lunches for visiting cricket and rugby international teams. As well as lunchtime snacks such as sandwiches (£5.50), home-made burgers (£6), and ploughman's (from £6), the enjoyable dishes might include oven-roasted vegetable soup (£3.90), moules marinière (£6.50), hand dived scallops seared with chorizo and basil oil (£7), local cod fillet on chargrilled courgettes with caper sauce or slow braised lamb shank with port and marsala gravy (£12.50), and monkfish curry with crispy noodles or whole roasted bass with ginger marmalade (£13.90). Well kept Sharps Eden and Skinners Coastliner, with a couple of guests like Timothy Taylors Landlord or one from the Cottage Brewery on handpump; pool, cribbage and dominoes. The dog is called Floyd. There's a cosy no smoking bistro on the other side of the courtyard. *(Recommended by Geoff Calcott, Dr S J Shepherd, Simon, Jo and Benjamin Cole, Mrs S Wiltshire, Alan and Paula McCully, DRH and KLH, Pete and Rosie Flower, Cynthia and Stephen Fisher, M A Borthwick)*

Free house ~ Licensees Terry and Wendy De Villiers Kuun ~ Real ale ~ Bar food (12-2.30, 6-9; not 25 Dec) ~ (01208) 816444 ~ Well behaved children in eating area of bar, but not late in the evening ~ Dogs allowed in bar ~ Open 12-11; 12-10.30 Sun

EGLOSHAYLE SX0172 Map 1
Earl of St Vincent £
Off A389, just outside Wadebridge

It's worth popping into this pretty pub – if you can find it tucked away in a narrow quiet back street behind the church – to look at the 162 antique clocks, all in working order (it is pretty noisy at midday); they also have some golfing memorabilia, art deco ornaments, and all sorts of rich furnishings. Well kept St Austell Dartmoor Best, Tinners, HSD, and Tribute on handpump; piped music. Bar food includes soup (£3), sandwiches (from £3.50), ploughman's (from £4.50), mushroom and broccoli au gratin, liver and bacon or ham and egg (£6), fish dishes (from £7), and grills (from £11). The snug is no smoking. In summer, there are picnic-sets in the lovely garden and marvellous flowering baskets and tubs. *(Recommended by the Didler, JP, PP, Brian and Bett Cox, Ted George, Jayne Capp, Keith and Margaret Kettell, Mrs M Griffin, Mr and Mrs B Hobden, Pete and Rosie Flower, R J Herd)*

St Austell ~ Tenants Edward and Anne Connolly ~ Real ale ~ Bar food (not Sun evening) ~ Restaurant ~ (01208) 814807 ~ Children in eating area of bar ~ Open 11-3, 6.30-11; 12-3, 7-10.30 Sun

GURNARDS HEAD SW4338 Map 1
Gurnards Head Hotel ⇐
B3306 Zennor—St Just

In outstanding bleak National Trust scenery, this isolated hotel is surrounded by glorious walks, both inland and along the cliffy coast. There's an unpretentiously pubby bar with log and coal fires at each end, masses of local pictures (some for sale) on plank panelling, a good mix of chatty locals and visitors, and well kept Flowers Original, Fullers London Pride and Skinners Cornish Knocker on handpump; a good wine list, amd friendly licensees and staff. Enjoyable bar food at lunchtime includes sandwiches (from £2.80), vegetarian soup of the day (£3.95; seafood broth £4.95), pork rillettes (£4.75), ploughman's (£5.50), ham and eggs with home-made chips (£6.50), pasta with pesto sauce and parmesan (£7.50), and a fish of the day (£7.95); in the evening, there might be roasted aubergine and red pepper on seasonal leaves (£4.95), smoked fish medley (£6.50), chicken breast with apple slices, flamed with calvados and deglazed with dry cider and cream (£10.95), confit of duck with a puy lentil and rich madeira sauce (£11.95), and a trio of local fish with pickled marsh samphire and lemon rondelle (£12.95), with puddings such as bread and butter pudding with clotted cream or chocolate truffle cake (from £3.50). The two-room carpeted dining bar and straightforward family room are no smoking. There are tables in the garden behind, and bedrooms either have views of the rugged moors or of the Atlantic. *(Recommended by Stuart Turner, Anthony Rickards Collinson, John and Tricia Parker, John and Gillian Scarisbrick, Mrs Roxanne Chamberlain, David Crook)*

Free house ~ Licensees Ray and Joy Kell ~ Bar food (12-2.15, 6.30-9.15) ~ Restaurant ~ (01736) 796928 ~ Children in restaurant ~ Dogs allowed in bar ~ Irish and blue grass Weds evening, folk/celtic Fri evening ~ Open 12-3, 6-11; 12-4, 7-11 Sun; closed evening 25 Dec ~ Bedrooms: £32.50S/£55S

HELFORD SW7526 Map 1
Shipwrights Arms
Off B3293 SE of Helston, via Mawgan

In good weather, this thatched pub gets very busy as there are seats on the terrace that look down over the pretty wooded creek (at its best at high tide), and plenty of surrounding walks, including a long distance coastal path that goes right past the door. There's quite a nautical theme inside, with navigation lamps, models of ships, sea pictures, drawings of lifeboat coxswains, and shark fishing photographs. A dining area has oak settles and tables; winter open fire. Well kept Castle Eden and Sharps Doom Bar on handpump, and bar food such as home-made soup (£3.60), buffet lunch platters (from £4.95), summer evening barbecue dishes such as marinated lamb fillet (£9.25), steaks (from £9.40), and monkfish marinated with chilli, lime and coriander (£12.25), and home-made puddings (£4.80); piped music. The pub is quite a walk from the nearest car park but there's also a foot ferry from Helford Passage. *(Recommended by Paul Humphreys, Tim and Jan Dalton, Andrea Rampley, JP, PP, R J Herd, Alan and Paula McCully, Geoff Pidoux, Maggie and Tony Harwood, P R and S A White, Brian Skelcher, the Didler, Jenny and Brian Seller, John Martin, Veronia Banting)*

Greenalls ~ Lease Charles Herbert ~ Real ale ~ Bar food (not Sun or Mon evenings in winter) ~ (01326) 231235 ~ Children in eating area of bar ~ Dogs welcome ~ Open 11-2.30, 6-11; 12-3, 7-10.30 Sun; closed Sun and Mon evenings

HELSTON SW6522 Map 1
Halzephron 🍽 � ⇌

Gunwalloe, village about 4 miles S but not marked on many road maps; look for brown sign on A3083 alongside perimeter fence of RNAS Culdrose

'A real gem' is how one of our readers describes this former smugglers' haunt – and a great many other customers agree. It is deservedly extremely popular (and does get packed at the height of the season) but Mrs Thomas and her attentive staff somehow seem to cope admirably. There's a really friendly feeling in the bustling, spotlessly clean bar, with comfortable seating, copper on the walls and mantelpiece, and a warm winter fire in the big hearth; there's also a quite a small no smoking family room. Using the best of local produce, the particularly enjoyable food might include lunchtime sandwiches (from £3.15; super crab £7.95), home-made soup (£4), ploughman's (from £5), pâté of the day with home-made toasted brioche (£5.20), local smoked fish selection (£7.60), tagliatelle bolognese (£8), and crab platter (£13.40), with specials like seafood chowder or duck leg confit on red onion, rocket and parmesan salad (£6.50), cep risotto topped with wild mushrooms and herbs (£9.50), lasagne or thai chicken curry (£10.50), lamb, lemon and honey tagine with chilli and apricot couscous (£11), black bream with a rosemary butter, fennel and herbs (£12.50), and caramelised gressingham duck breast on butternut squash purée with a redcurrant and juniper sauce (£15); home-made puddings such as hot chocolate mousse, treacle tart or fruit crumbles (from £4). All the eating areas are no smoking. Well kept Sharps Special, Own and Doom Bar, St Austell Tribute, and a beer named for the pub on handpump, a good wine list, lots of malt whiskies, and around 25 liqueurs; dominoes and cribbage. This is a smashing place to stay with sea views in some rooms and good breakfasts. There are lots of lovely surrounding unspoilt walks with fine views of Mount's Bay, Gunwalloe fishing cove is just 300 yards away, and there's a sandy beach 1 mile away at Church Cove. The church of St Winwaloe (built into the dunes on the seashore) is also only 1 mile away, and well worth a visit – as is the nearby herb shop that grows its own herbs and makes them into sauces and dips. *(Recommended by Pete and Rosie Flower, John and Gloria Isaacs, Brian Skelcher, Andrea Rampley, Andy and Yvonne Cunningham, David Crook, Jayne Capp, Eamonn and Natasha Skyrme, R and S Bentley, John and Judy Saville, Dr Phil Putwain, M G Hart, Stuart Turner, John Bodycote, Sue Holland, Dave Webster, JMC, Maggie and Tony Harwood, Mrs Caroline Siggins, Jenny and Brian Seller, Stephen Hobbs, Paul Humphreys, Nick Lawless, Cliff Blakemore, Jacquie and Jim Jones, Cathy Robinson, Ed Coombe, Derek and Margaret Underwood, Dr and Mrs M W A Haward)*

Free house ~ Licensee Angela Thomas ~ Real ale ~ Bar food (not 25 Dec) ~ Restaurant ~ (01326) 240406 ~ Children in family room, in dining areas if over 10 ~ Open 11-2.30, 6(6.30 winter)-11; 12-2.30, 6-10.30 Sun; closed 25 Dec ~ Bedrooms: £44B/£78B

KINGSAND SX4350 Map 1
Halfway House 🍺

Fore Street, towards Cawsand

As we went to press, we heard that this popular place was up for sale, so we are keeping our fingers crossed that things will not change too much. The present hard-working licensees offer a friendly welcome, and the simply furnished but quite smart bar is mildly Victorian in style, and rambles around a huge central fireplace, with low ceilings, soft lighting, and plenty of locals. Enjoyable bar food using local produce includes daily specials such as asparagus with parma ham and lemon mayonnaise (£4.95), moules marinière (£5.25), chicken supreme with spinach mousseline in a cream sauce (£8.95), liver and bacon on sweet potato mash (£9.75), beef, mushroom and red wine casserole (£9.95), moroccan-style lamb shank with black olives (£10.95), tuna steak with salsa fresca (£11.95), and puddings like banoffi pie, chocolate torte or apple and blackberry crumble; also, filled baguettes (from £2.95), home-made soup (£3.45), filled baked potatoes (from £4.15), ploughman's (from £6), home-cooked ham and egg (£7), red pepper and spinach lasagne (£7.30), curry of the day (£8.25), and steaks (from £11.35). Well kept Courage Best, Sharps Doom Bar, Wadworths 6X, and a guest from Cottage, Exmoor or Smiles on handpump kept under light blanket pressure, and decent wines; cribbage and dominoes. To reach this attractive old inn, you can park and walk through the narrow hilly streets down towards the sea and harbour. The village is well placed for visiting Mount Edgcumbe House and Country Park, and there are marvellous surrounding walks, especially on the cliffs at Rame Head. *(Recommended by Nicholas Regam, Stephen and Judy Parish, B J Harding, Steve Whalley, John and Pat Morris, Mrs J Levinson)*

Free house ~ Licensees Sarah and David Riggs ~ Real ale ~ Bar food ~ Restaurant ~ (01752) 822279 ~ Children welcome ~ Dogs allowed in bar and bedrooms ~ Choir Weds evenings; quiz winter Tues evenings ~ Open 11.30-4, 6.30-11; 12-4, 7-10.30 Sun; open 30 mins later in winter ~ Bedrooms: £28.50S/£57B

LANLIVERY SX0759 Map 1
Crown 🍷

Signposted off A390 Lostwithiel—St Austell (tricky to find from other directions)

This year, the friendly licensees have redecorated this bustling place both inside and out, and laid new carpets. The small, dimly lit public bar has heavy beams, a slate floor, and built-in wall settles and an attractive alcove of seats in the dark former chimney. A much lighter room leads off here with beams in the white boarded ceiling, some settees in one corner, cushioned black settles, a small cabinet with wood turnings for sale, and a little fireplace with an old-fashioned fire; there's another similar small room. No noisy games machines or music. Well liked bar food includes sandwiches (from £1.85), home-made soup (£3.15), sausage and chips (£3.75), ploughman's (from £4.15), home-made curries (from £6.15), daily specials like fresh grilled local mackerel (£6.50), moroccan lamb (£7.95), steak and stilton pie (£8.15), and tuna steak with mango sauce (£9.95), and puddings such as fresh fruit crumble or tiramisu with clotted cream (£3.75). Well kept Sharps Own, Doom Bar, Eden, and a beer named for the pub called Glory on handpump; darts, dominoes, cribbage, table skittles, shove-ha'penny, and an informal quiz on Monday evenings. The slate-floored porch room has lots of succulents and a few cacti, and wood-and-stone seats, and at the far end of the restaurant is a no smoking sun room, full of more plants, with tables and benches. There's a sheltered garden with granite faced seats and white cast-iron furniture. The Eden Project is only 10 minutes away. *(Recommended by Dennis Jenkin, Andy and Yvonne Cunningham,*

Frank Willy, John and Jackie Chalcraft, David M Cundy, M and R Thomas, David Heath, David Rule, Dr and Mrs M W A Haward, Richard and Margaret Peers, Graham and Lynn Mason, Evelyn and Derek Walter, Robyn Turner, Anne and David Robinson, David Crook, Jayne Capp, Prof and Mrs Tony Palmer, Bill and Jessica Ritson, Martin and Karen Wake)

Free house ~ Licensees Ros and Dave Williams ~ Real ale ~ Bar food ~ Restaurant ~ (01208) 872707 ~ Children welcome ~ Dogs allowed in bar ~ Trad jazz once a month ~ Open 11-3, 6-11; 12-3, 6-10.30 Sun ~ Bedrooms: £40S/£60S

LOSTWITHIEL SX1059 Map 1
Royal Oak ◗

Duke Street; pub just visible from A390 in centre – best to look out for Royal Talbot Hotel

Although this old town centre pub is very popular locally, there's a warm welcome for visitors too. The six real ales are quite a draw, with well kept Bass, Fullers London Pride, Marstons Pedigree, Sharps Own, and a couple of changing guests such as Keltek Royal Oak or Tower Tower of Strength on handpump – as well as lots of bottled beers from around the world. Well liked bar food includes lunchtime sandwiches (from £1.95; toasties 25p extra), ploughman's (from £4.50), and fried chicken (£5.50), as well as soup (£2.65), stuffed mushrooms (£4.10), broccoli pie (£7.50), fresh local trout (£8.95), steaks (from £9.95), daily specials like crab au gratin (£7.95), curry or steak and kidney in ale pie (£8.25), fresh whole local plaice (£9.95), and lamb steak with rosemary (£10.95), and puddings such as home-made treacle tart or cherry pie (£2.75). The neat lounge is spacious and comfortable, with captain's chairs and high-backed wall benches on its patterned carpet, and a couple of wooden armchairs by the gas-effect log fire; there's also a delft shelf, with a small dresser in one inner alcove. The flagstoned and beamed back public bar has darts, fruit machine, TV, and juke box, and is liked by younger customers; piped music. On a raised terrace by the car park are some picnic-sets. *(Recommended by Mrs Pam Mattinson, Graham and Lynn Mason, Stuart Turner, David Crook, Alan and Paula McCully, Lee Potter, Jayne Capp, Hazel Morgan, David and Kay Ross, George Atkinson, Brian and Diane Mugford, Ron Shelton, Margaret Mason, David Thompson)*

Free house ~ Licensees Malcolm and Eileen Hine ~ Real ale ~ Bar food (12-2, 6.30-9.15) ~ Restaurant ~ (01208) 872552 ~ Children welcome ~ Dogs allowed in bar ~ Open 11-11; 12-10.30 Sun ~ Bedrooms: £40B/£70B

MALPAS SW8442 Map 1
Heron

Trenhaile Terr, off A39 S of Truro

The creekside position here is lovely and can be enjoyed on a sunny day from seats on the terrace; tables by the window inside enjoy the same view. The spotlessly kept bar is long and narrow with several areas leading off and a raised area at one end, and it is all very light and airy with blue and white décor and furnishings throughout. Two gas fires, mainly wooden floors with flagstones by the bar, modern yacht paintings on the wood-planked walls, some brass nautical items, heron pictures and a stuffed heron in a cabinet, and a chatty brasserie-type atmosphere; half the pub is no smoking. Bar food includes filled rolls (from £4.50), duck and orange pâté with tangy marmalade (£4.95), whitebait with citrus mayonnaise (£5.50), local venison sausages with mustard mash and onion gravy (£6.35), ham and eggs (£6.50), tomato and basil pasta (£6.95), curries (from £8.55), chicken breast in a creamy mustard sauce (£8.95), and daily specials like home-made cottage pie (£5.95), home-made fish pie (£6.95), home-made crab ravioli with saffron butter sauce (£9.95), and medallions of fillet steak in creamy pepper sauce (£10.95); they keep your credit card behind the bar. Well kept St Austell IPA, HSD, and Tribute on handpump, good wines by the glass, and several malt whiskies; piped music. More reports please. *(Recommended by Pete and Rosie Flower, Dr and Mrs M E Wilson, Norman and Sarah Keeping, Bob Turnham, Gloria Bax, Alan M Pring, Patrick Hancock, Debbie and Neil Hayter)*

St Austell ~ Tenant F C Kneebone ~ Real ale ~ Bar food ~ (01872) 272773 ~
Children in eating area of bar ~ Open 11-3, 6-11; 12-3, 7-10.30 Sun; 11-2.30,
6-10.30 winter

MANACCAN SW7625 Map 1
New Inn
Down hill signed to Gillan and St Keverne

In a lovely setting not far from Helford or St Anthony, this charming old thatched village pub is a neatly kept and friendly place. The double-room bar has a beam and plank ceiling, individually chosen chairs, traditional built-in wall seats, and fresh flowers. Good bar food at lunchtime includes a marvellous choice of up to 30 sandwiches such as crispy bacon and avocado, hot sausage and onion, and cheddar and mango (from £3.50), home-made soup (£4), smoked salmon or stilton and walnut pâté (£5), fresh fish in their own beer batter (£7.50), steak in ale pie (£8.50), and kedgeree (£9), with evening dishes like vegetable stir fry with egg-fried rice (£7), chicken breast stuffed with stilton and wrapped with parma ham or crab cakes with chive butter sauce (£10.50), and roasted lamb loin with redcurrant and thyme sauce or roasted trio of local fish with hollandaise (£11.50), and puddings such as treacle tart, eton mess or crème brûlée (£3.75). Well kept Flowers IPA and Sharps Doom Bar on handpump; cribbage, dominoes and euchre. There are picnic-sets in the rose-filled garden, and a sweet pub dog. This is a lovely setting and not far from Helford and St Anthony. *(Recommended by the Didler, Nicholas Pope, Andrea Rampley, JP, PP, Mike and Linda Boxall, Paul Humphreys, Richard Nicholson, Michael Pashby)*

Pubmaster ~ Tenant Penny Williams ~ Real ale ~ Bar food (12-2.30, 6.30-9.30; not 25 Dec) ~ (01326) 231323 ~ Children welcome ~ Dogs welcome ~ Open 12-3, 6-11; 12-2.30, 7-10.30 Sun

MITCHELL SW8654 Map 1
Plume of Feathers 🍽 🛏
Just off A30 Bodmin—Redruth, by A3076 junction; take the southwards road then turn first right

Cornwall Dining Pub of the Year

The friendly licensees have spent a lot of time and effort making the garden areas here pleasant for children and sun lovers, and there are many more plants and seats than last year. They are hoping to add a conservatory extension to the restaurant, too. The attractive bars have stripped old beams and an enormous open fire, pastel-coloured walls, plenty of seats for either a drink or a meal, and a natural spring well has been made into a glass-topped table. There's a no smoking restaurant with interesting paintings, and an eating area near the main bar for the minority who want to smoke. Good, interesting and well presented food at lunchtime might include sandwiches (from £2.95), smooth chicken liver pâté with red onion jam (£4.25), moules marinière (£5.50), hand-made cornish pasty (£5.60), potato gnocchi in a cheese, spinach and chive cream (£6.95) green thai chicken curry (£6.95), with specials like home-made tomato and red pepper soup (£3.25), home-cooked ham and egg (£5.50), grilled whole mackerel fillets with avocado, mango and spring onion salsa (£7.75), and grilled whole dabs with parsley butter (£8); in the evening choices might be grilled goats cheese with roasted tomatoes, toasted pine nuts and basil and balsamic dressing (£5.15), slow cooked lamb shank with chorizo, chick pea and butter bean salsa (£9.75), duck confit with braised red cabbage (£10.75), and steaks (from £10.75), with specials like duck rilette with courgette and tomato compote (£5.40), chargrilled swordfish, saffron mash, roasted plum tomatoes and herb butter (£12.75), and rib-eye fillet of beef, tournedos rossini (£14.95). They also offer puddings like banana sticky toffee pudding with butterscotch sauce (£4.25), and cream teas (£4.95); friendly, efficient service. Well kept Courage Directors, Greene King IPA, Sharps Doom Bar and Shepherd Neame Spitfire on handpump, a comprehensive wine list, freshly squeezed orange juice and good fresh italian coffees. Juke box, fruit machine, and TV. The bedrooms in the refurbished barns at the back are very well thought of. *(Recommended by Andy Sinden, Louise Harrington, George Atkinson, Patrick Hancock, Rob and Catherine Dunster, Ian Wilson, Mr and Mrs A M Marshall, Simon Priestman, Dr Phil Putwain, Brian and Bett Cox, Mrs Pat Crabb)*

Free house ~ Licensees M F Warner and J Trotter ~ Real ale ~ Bar food (12-10; not evening 25 Dec) ~ Restaurant ~ (01872) 510387 ~ Children in eating area of bar and restaurant ~ Dogs allowed in bar ~ Open 10.30-11; 12-10.30 Sun; closed evening 25 Dec ~ Bedrooms: £41.25S(£48.75B)/£65S(£75B)

MITHIAN SW7450 Map 1
Miners Arms

Just off B3285 E of St Agnes

There's plenty of atmosphere and history in this 16th-c pub – it has been used as a court and a chapel, and a passage behind the fireplace in the sitting room once led to a tunnel connecting it to the manor house. Several cosy little rooms and passages are warmed by winter open fires, and the small back bar has an irregular beam and plank ceiling, a wood block floor, and bulging squint walls (one with a fine old wall painting of Elizabeth I); another small room has a decorative low ceiling, lots of books and quite a few interesting ornaments. The Croust Room is no smoking; piped music. Bar food includes home-made soup (£3), open sandwiches (from £3.95), pork and apple sausages (£6.75), steak and oyster pie (£7.25), specials like home-made beef curry (£8.75), oven-roasted ginger pork (£8.95), stuffed whole bass or local haddock with horseradish aïoli (£11.95), and puddings (from £3.25). Bass, Courage Best and Sharps Doom Bar on handpump, and several wines by the glass. Shove-ha'penny, cribbage, and dominoes. There are seats on the back terrace, with more on the sheltered front cobbled forecourt. *(Recommended by Patrick Hancock, Mr and Mrs P Eastwood, Brian Skelcher, Joe and Marion Mandeville, Pete and Rosie Flower, David Crook, Andrea Rampley, JP, PP, W F C Phillips, Su and Bob Child, Stephen and Judy Parish)*

Inn Partnership (Pubmaster) ~ Lease Andrew Bown ~ Real ale ~ Bar food ~ (01872) 552375 ~ Children in restaurant ~ Dogs allowed in bar ~ Open 12-3(2.30 in winter), 6-11(10.30 Sun); 12-2.30, 6-11 in winter

MOUSEHOLE SW4726 Map 1
Old Coastguard ♀ ⇌

The Parade (edge of village, coming in on coast road from Newlyn – street parking just before you reach the inn); village also signposted off B3315

In summer, the neat and attractive sizeable garden here really comes into its own, with palms and dracaenas, marble-look tables on decking, and a path leading down to the water's-edge rock pools. Inside, the main area of this seaside bar (which is attached to a comfortable hotel but a few steps down from a separate entrance) is light, airy and spacious with modern metal and wicker seats around well spaced matching tables on wood strip flooring, good cheerful modern sea and fish pictures on butter-coloured walls, and palms, potted plants and fresh flowers. Its lower dining part, liked by readers, has a glass wall giving a great view out over the garden to Mounts Bay. A quiet back area is darker, with comfortable art deco leatherette tub chairs. Well kept Bass and Sharps Doom Bar on handpump, a good choice of wines by the glass, good value house wines by the bottle, and a thoughtful choice of fresh juices and pressés. Bar food includes home-made soup (£3.50), sandwiches (from £3.50), grilled local goats cheese with red pepper dressing (£5.50), roasted vegetables, chick peas and local cheese on a potato rösti (£9), chicken pasta with crème fraîche, sun-dried tomato and tarragon or pasta with mussels and scallops (£12), steaks (from £11.50), and puddings like chilled stem ginger and orange pudding (£4); light breakfasts (from £2), and afternoon cream tea (£3.95). More reports please. *(Recommended by Mrs M Griffin, Andy Sinden, Louise Harrington, Mrs W Frost, E G Parish)*

Free house ~ Licensee Amanda Wood ~ Real ale ~ Bar food (12-2.30, 6-9.30) ~ Restaurant ~ (01736) 731222 ~ Children in eating area of bar and restaurant ~ Dogs allowed in bar ~ Open 11-11; 11-10.30 Sun; 11-3, 6-11(10.30 Sun) in winter; closed 25 Dec ~ Bedrooms: £45B/£90B

MYLOR BRIDGE SW8137 Map 1
Pandora ★★ ♀

Restronguet Passage: from A39 in Penryn, take turning signposted Mylor Church, Mylor Bridge, Flushing and go straight through Mylor Bridge following Restronguet Passage signs; or from A39 further N, at or near Perranarworthal, take turning signposted Mylor, Restronguet, then follow Restronguet Weir signs, but turn left down hill at Restronguet Passage sign

As well as driving to this idyllically placed pub, you can reach it by walking along the estuary amongst avenues of wild flowers or arrive (as do many customers) by boat; in fine weather you can sit with your drink on the long floating pontoon and watch children crabbing. Inside, the several rambling, interconnecting rooms have low wooden ceilings (mind your head on some of the beams), beautifully polished big flagstones, cosy alcoves with leatherette benches built into the walls, a kitchen range, and a log fire in a high hearth (to protect it against tidal floods); half the bar area is no smoking – as is the restaurant. Some redecoration this year. Bar food includes home-made soup (£3.95), lunchtime sandwiches (from £4.25, good local crab £7.75), sausages with apple chutney (£6.95), spicy bean goulash (£7.25), chicken curry (£7.50), crab thermidor or chicken strips with a wild mushroom sauce (£9.95), sirloin steak (£12.95), and puddings (£5.50); swift, friendly staff. Well kept Bass, and St Austell HSD and Tribute on handpump, several wines by the glass, and local cider. It does get very crowded in summer, and parking is difficult at peak times. Good surrounding walks. *(Recommended by DRH and KLH, Richard Dixon, JP, PP, Andy and Yvonne Cunningham, Dennis Jenkin, Andy and Ali, P R and S A White, Bob and Sue Hardy, Mr and Mrs K Box, Geoff and Jan Dawson, Emma Kingdon, Tim and Ann Newell, Anne and Paul Horscraft, Geoff Pidoux, David Crook, Bob Turnham, Comus and Sarah Elliott, Andrea Rampley, Peter Meister, Patrick Hancock, Brian Skelcher, Paul Humphreys, the Didler, Richard Fendick, David Rule, S Horsley, Mike Rowan, Di and Mike Gillam, Alison Hayes, Pete Hanlon, John Martin, Veronia Banting)*

St Austell ~ Tenant John Milan ~ Real ale ~ Bar food ~ Restaurant ~ (01326) 372678 ~ Children welcome ~ Dogs allowed in bar ~ Open 11-11; 12-10.30 Sun

PENZANCE SW4730 Map 1
Turks Head

At top of main street, by big domed building (Lloyds TSB), turn left down Chapel Street

There's always a good mix of locals and visitors in this reliably friendly local, and happily, nothing much seems to change. The bustling bar has old flat irons, jugs and so forth hanging from the beams, pottery above the wood-effect panelling, wall seats and tables, and a couple of elbow rests around central pillars; piped music. Popular bar food includes soup (£2.60), lunchtime sandwiches, lasagne (£5.30), mexican hotpot (£5.50), cod in beer batter (£7.20), steaks (from £8.25), white crabmeat salad (£9.50), and daily specials like a roast of the day (£5.95), vegetable moussaka or pie of the day (£6.95), cajun chicken stir fry (£8.95), and scallop and monkfish thermidor (£11.50). Well kept Greene King IPA, Sharps Doom Bar, Youngs Special, and a guest on handpump; helpful service. The suntrap back garden has big urns of flowers. There has been a Turks Head here for over 700 years – though most of the original building was destroyed by a Spanish raiding party in the 16th c. *(Recommended by Dr Phil Putwain, Theocsbrian, Ken Flawn, Andrea Rampley, Peter Meister, Gloria Bax, Neil and Anita Christopher, JP, PP, Helen Flaherty)*

Pubmaster ~ Lease William Morris ~ Real ale ~ Bar food (11(12 Sun)-2.30, 6-10) ~ Restaurant ~ (01736) 363093 ~ Children in downstairs dining room ~ Open 11-3, 5.30-11; 12-3, 5.30-10.30 Sun; closed 25 Dec

PHILLEIGH SW8639 Map 1

Roseland ★ ♀

Between A3078 and B3289, just E of King Harry Ferry

Even when this popular little pub is at its most busy, the genuinely friendly staff still manage to remain cheerful and efficient – not easy to do, given the limited space. There's always a good mix of both locals and visitors, and the two bar rooms (one with flagstones and the other carpeted) have wheelback chairs and built-in red-cushioned seats, open fires, old photographs and some giant beetles and butterflies in glasses, and a relaxed chatty atmosphere; the little back bar is used by locals. Good, interesting, if not cheap, bar food includes cornish pasty (£3.25), lunchtime sandwiches (from £4; fresh local crab £7), home-made hummous with olives or macaroni cheese (£6.50), lunchtime ploughman's (£6.95), thai green chicken curry (£10), whole baked local sole glazed with lemon and herb butter (£11), popular shank of lamb in cranberry, red wine, mint, rosemary and orange on herb mash (£11), rib-eye steak (£12.50), bass fillets with a red onion and mango salsa (£13), daily specials, and puddings; vegetables are extra (£2). You must book to be sure of a table; the restaurant is no smoking. There may be quite a wait at peak times. Well kept Ringwood Best, Sharps Doom Bar, and a guest beer on handpump, a good wine list with quite a few by the glass, and several malt whiskies. Shove-ha'penny, darts, dominoes and cribbage. The pretty paved front courtyard is a lovely place to sit in the lunchtime sunshine beneath the cherry blossom, and the pub is handy for Trelissick Gardens and the King Harry ferry. *(Recommended by Walter and Susan Rinaldi-Butcher, Dr Phil Putwain, J L Wedel, Geoff Palmer, Geoff and Jan Dawson, M Joyner, Jenny and Brian Seller, Anthony Rickards Collinson, Patrick Hancock, Joe and Marion Mandeville, Richard Till, Jack Clark, Deborah Taylor, Mayur Shah, Lorraine and Fred Gill, Paul Boot, Mr and Mrs B J P Edwards, D S Jackson, Stuart Turner, Andrea Rampley, JP, PP, Bob Turnham, Nick Lawless, MDN, the Didler, Alison Hayes, Pete Hanlon)*

Authentic Inns ~ Lease Colin Philips ~ Real ale ~ Bar food ~ Restaurant ~ (01872) 580254 ~ Children in eating area of bar and restaurant ~ Dogs allowed in bar ~ Open 11-11; 12-10.30 Sun; 11-2.30, 6-11 winter ~ Bedrooms: /£80B

POLKERRIS SX0952 Map 1

Rashleigh

Signposted off A3082 Fowey—St Austell

Although the splendid position of this pub comes into its own in good weather – it's just a few steps from an isolated beach with a jetty, and seats on the stone terrace in front of the building enjoy the views towards the far side of St Austell and Mevagissey bays – there are plenty of customers even on wet mid-winter days. The bar is snug and cosy, and the front part has comfortably cushioned seats and up to half a dozen well kept real ales on handpump such as Sharps Doom Bar and a beer named for the pub, Timothy Taylors Landlord, and guests like Blue Anchor Spingo, Butcombe Bitter, Keltek Magik, and St Austell HSD; Addlestone's farm cider in the summer and quite a few wines by the glass. The more simply furnished back area has local photographs on the brown panelling, and a winter log fire. Reasonably priced bar food includes sandwiches (from £2.50; open ones from £5.80), ploughman's (from £4.95), vegetarian shepherd's pie (£5.75), cottage pie (£6.25), daily specials like tuna pasta (£6.50), local plaice (£7.50), wild mushroom and pigeon pie (£7.75), and grilled pink bream (£12.50). Though parking space next to the pub is limited, there's a large village car park, and there are safe moorings for small yachts in the cove. This whole section of the Cornish Coast Path is renowned for its striking scenery. *(Recommended by Simon, Jo and Benjamin Cole, Jenny and Brian Seller, David and Pauline Brenner, Kevin Flack, Mr and Mrs B J P Edwards, David Crook, JP, PP, Mayur Shah, the Didler, Bob and Margaret Holder, Alan and Paula McCully, Jayne Capp, Dave Braisted, DAV, M Benjamin, Prof and Mrs Tony Palmer, M and R Thomas, Brian Skelcher, Charles and Pauline Stride)*

There are report forms at the back of the book.

Free house ~ Licensees Jon and Samantha Spode ~ Real ale ~ Bar food (12-2, 6-9; snacks on summer afternoons) ~ Restaurant ~ (01726) 813991 ~ Children in eating area of bar and restaurant ~ Open 11-11; 12-10.30 Sun

PORT ISAAC SX0080 Map 1
Golden Lion
Fore Street

The hub of the lovely steep village, this is a friendly little local with quite a mix of customers. The cosy, simply furnished rooms have a bustling, chatty atmosphere, and a bar with a fine antique settle among other comfortable seats (those by the window enjoy the view) and decorative ceiling plasterwork; the back room has a fine open fire. Bar food includes sandwiches (lunchtime only, from £2.45), filled baked potatoes (from £3.25), home-made vegetable korma (£6.95), proper fish and chips (£7.50), home-made fish pie (£7.95), home-made steak in ale pie (£8.95), chargrilled sirloin steak (£11.95), and daily specials like fresh crab sandwich (£5.50) or warm goats cheese and bacon salad (£7.95); during the summer, evening meals are also served in the no smoking bistro. Well kept St Austell Tinners, HSD and Tribute on handpump and several malt whiskies. Darts, dominoes, cribbage, a fruit machine in the public bar, and piped music. On a balmy day, you can sit on the terrace and look down on the rocky harbour and lifeboat slip far below. You can park at the top of the village unless you are lucky enough to park on the beach at low tide. *(Recommended by Betsy Brown, Nigel Flook, Tom Evans, MDN, Canon Michael Bourdeaux, DRH and KLH, Mayur Shah, Karen and Graham Oddey, DAV, the Didler, Margaret Mason, David Thompson)*

St Austell ~ Tenants Mike and Nikki Edkins ~ Real ale ~ Bar food ~ Restaurant (evening) ~ (01208) 880336 ~ Children in eating area of bar and restaurant ~ Open 11.30-11; 12-10.30 Sun; closed evening 25 Dec

Port Gaverne Inn ♀ 🛏
Port Gaverne signposted from Port Isaac, and from B3314 E of Pendoggett

The bedrooms in this well liked 17th-c inn were being upgraded as we went to press and readers do enjoy staying here; plenty of splendid surrounding clifftop walks and bird life. There's a bustling atmosphere in the bar which has big log fires and low beams, flagstones as well as carpeting, some exposed stone, and lots of chatty locals. In spring, the lounge is usually filled with pictures from the local art society's annual exhibition, and at other times there are interesting antique local photographs. Bar food includes sandwiches, home-made crab soup (£4.25), home-made chicken liver pâté (£5), ploughman's (from £5.25), creamy vegetable risotto (£6), ham and egg (£6.25), home-made seafood pie (£6.75), daily specials like cottage pie (£6.75) or fishcakes (£6.95), and puddings such as chocolate and brandy mousse or fruit crumble (£3.95); you can eat in the bar, the 'Captain's Cabin' – a little room where everything is shrunk to scale (old oak chest, model sailing ship, even the prints on the white stone walls) or on a balcony overlooking the sea; the restaurant is no smoking. Well kept St Austell HSD, and Sharps Doom Bar and Cornish on handpump, a good wine list, and several whiskies; cribbage and dominoes. There are seats in the garden close to the sea. *(Recommended by John and Jackie Chalcraft, Alan and Paula McCully, MDN, Peter Salmon, Anthony Barnes, Keith Stevens, Betsy Brown, Nigel Flook)*

Free house ~ Licensee Graham Sylvester ~ Real ale ~ Bar food ~ Restaurant ~ (01208) 880244 ~ Children in eating area of bar and restaurant ~ Dogs allowed in bar ~ Open 11-11; 12-10.30 Sun ~ Bedrooms: £35B/£70B

Pubs staying open all afternoon at least one day a week are listed
at the back of the book.

PORTHLEVEN SW6225 Map 1
Ship

Village on B3304 SW of Helston; pub perched on edge of harbour

'A cracking pub' is how one of our many keen readers describes this old fisherman's pub. To reach it, you have to climb a flight of rough stone steps – it's actually built into the steep cliffs, and there are marvellous views over the pretty working harbour and out to sea; at night, the harbour is interestingly floodlit. The knocked-through bar has log fires in big stone fireplaces and some genuine character, and the family room is a conversion of an old smithy, with logs burning in the huge open fireplace. Popular bar food includes sandwiches, toasties and crusties (from £4.95), filled baked potatoes (from £5.50), moules marinière or grilled goats cheese on a pesto crouton with gooseberry sauce (£4.95), ploughman's (from £6.95), home-made chilli or half a barbecue chicken (£8.95), crab and prawn mornay (£11.50), steak (£11.50), local crab claws (£11.95), daily specials like vegetable curry (£8.95), home-made steak and kidney pie (£9.50), monkfish wrapped in bacon or bass with a garlic crumb (£12.95); the candlelit dining room also enjoys the good view. Well kept Courage Best, Greene King Old Speckled Hen, and Sharps Doom Bar on handpump, and several malt whiskies; good, friendly service. Dominoes, cribbage, fruit machine and piped music. There are seats out in the terraced garden. *(Recommended by M G Hart, Mrs Caroline Siggins, the Didler, Tom McLean, Brian Skelcher, Cliff Blakemore, R J Herd, Mr and Mrs McKay, Vivian Stevenson, JMC, John and Gloria Isaacs, Nigel and Olga Wikeley, Tim and Jan Dalton, Geoff Calcott, Andrea Rampley, P R and S A White, Cathy Robinson, Ed Coombe, Giles Francis, Roger and Jenny Huggins, Maggie and Tony Harwood, Di and Mike Gillam)*

Free house ~ Licensee Colin Oakden ~ Real ale ~ Bar food (12-9 in summer) ~ (01326) 564204 ~ Children in family room ~ Dogs allowed in bar ~ Open 11.30-11; 12-10.30 Sun; 11.30-3(3.30 Sun), 6.30-11 winter

SENNEN COVE SW3526 Map 1
Old Success

Off A30 Land's End road

Named after one of the fishing companies that used to operate along this stretch of coast, this well placed old-fashioned seaside hotel boasts marvellous views of the surf of Whitesands Bay, particularly from its terraced garden, up some steps from the busy car park. We arrived late one Saturday night, when a traditional folk band was entertaining a good mix of locals and visitors. The beamed and timbered bar has plenty of lifeboat memorabilia, including an RNLI flag hanging on the ceiling; elsewhere are ship's lanterns, black and white photographs, dark wood tables and chairs, and a big ship's wheel that doubles as a coat stand. Bar food includes good crab sandwiches, soup (£2.95), grilled gammon and egg (from £5.50), lasagne (£7.15), fresh plaice (£8.25), smoked seafood platter (£8.95), children's dishes, and daily specials (sometimes favourites of the Greek chef); they also do local cornish pasties (£2.75), cream teas (£2.25), and home-made saffron cake. Well kept Sharps Doom Bar and Special and Skinners Keel Over on handpump. Service is friendly and efficient, even in the height of summer; it's less hectic out of season. The upper bar and restaurant are no smoking. Piped music, TV; quiz night most Fridays. Bedrooms are basic but comfortable, enjoying the sound of the sea; they also do self-catering suites. Land's End is a pleasant walk away, and the clean beach is very attractive – as well as a big draw for surfers. *(Recommended by Mr and Mrs McKay, Maggie and Tony Harwood, Geoff Calcott, David Crook, Keith Stevens, Stuart Turner, Dr and Mrs A K Clarke, Anthony Barnes)*

Free house ~ Licensee Martin Brooks ~ Real ale ~ Bar food (12-2.30, 6-9.30) ~ Restaurant ~ (01736) 871232 ~ Children welcome ~ Dogs allowed in bar ~ Live music most Sats, quiz Fri ~ Open 11-11; 12-10.30 Sun ~ Bedrooms: £29B/£84B

ST AGNES SV8807 Map 1
Turks Head ◗ 🛏

The Quay

This converted little boathouse is a rather special place and is held dear in the hearts of a great many customers. Although it does get rather swamped by visitors in the summer (the hard-working licensees still cope as efficiently as ever), this is the best time to come as you can sit on the extended area across the sleepy lane or on terraces down towards the sea, and there are steps down to the slipway so you can take your drinks and food and sit right on the shore; the hanging baskets are very pretty. Winter opening hours tend to be quite sporadic, given that only some 70 people live on the island. The simply furnished but cosy and very friendly pine-panelled bar has quite a collection of flags, helmets and headwear, as well as maritime photographs and model ships. The real ale arrives in St Agnes via a beer supplier in St Austell and two boat trips, and as well as Dartmoor Best and a beer named for the pub, they serve Ales of Scilly Scuppered and Natural Beauty from a local microbrewery on handpump; decent house wines, a good range of malt whiskies, and hot chocolate with brandy. At lunchtime, the well liked bar food includes open rolls (from £3.25; local crab £5.05), ploughman's (from £4.65), salads (from £6.25; local crab £8.75), cold ham with chips (£6.50), vegetable pasta bake (£6.75), and puddings (£3.10), with evening fish dishes like crab cakes with dip (£7.25) or fried gurnard on couscous (£10.25); children's meals (from £2.75). Ice cream and cakes are sold through the afternoon, and in good weather they may do evening barbecues. The dining extension is no smoking, and the cats are called Taggart and Lacey, and the collie, Tess. Darts, cribbage, dominoes and piped music. If you wish to stay here, you must book months ahead. *(Recommended by Pete and Rosie Flower, Neil and Anita Christopher, Theocsbrian, Peter Meister, Maureen and Bill Sewell, Dr and Mrs M E Wilson, A J Longshaw, JP, PP)*

Free house ~ Licensees John and Pauline Dart ~ Real ale ~ Bar food (12-2.30, 6.30-9) ~ (01720) 422434 ~ Children in eating area of bar and restaurant ~ Dogs allowed in bar ~ Open 11-11; 12-11 Sun; best to phone for limited opening hours in winter ~ Bedrooms: /£55B

ST BREWARD SX0977 Map 1
Old Inn

Old Town; village signposted off B3266 S of Camelford, also signed off A30 Bolventor—Bodmin

Originally built to house the monks building the church, this old pub is a friendly place, and the spacious middle bar has plenty of seating on the fine broad slate flagstones, banknotes and horsebrasses hanging from the low oak joists that support the ochre upstairs floorboards, and plates on the stripped stonework; two massive granite fireplaces date back to the 11th c. Decent bar food includes home-made soup (£2.95), filled baps or sandwiches (from £3), filled baked potatoes (from £4.95), local ham and eggs (£5.95), ploughman's (from £5.95), all-day breakfast (£6.95), mixed grill (£11.50), and daily specials like fresh beer-battered cod, a home-made pie of the day, home-made nut roast with onion and port gravy, and liver and bacon (£6.95). The newly extended restaurant and family room are no smoking. Well kept Bass, Sharps Doom Bar, Eden and Special Ale, and a guest beer on handpump; quite a few malt whiskies; sensibly placed darts, piped music, and fruit machine. Picnic-sets outside are protected by low stone walls. There's plenty of open moorland behind, and cattle and sheep wander freely into the village. In front of the building is very a worn carved stone; no one knows exactly what it is but it may be part of a Saxon cross. *(Recommended by Roger and Jenny Huggins, JP, PP, Alan and Paula McCully, the Didler, Margaret Mason, David Thompson)*

Free house ~ Licensee Darren Wills ~ Real ale ~ Bar food (11-2, 6-9) ~ Restaurant ~ (01208) 850711 ~ Children in eating area of bar and family room ~ Dogs allowed in bar ~ Open 11-11; 12-10.30 Sun; 11-3, 6-11 Mon-Thurs in winter

ST KEW SX0276 Map 1
St Kew Inn
Village signposted from A39 NE of Wadebridge

Set next to a lovely church, this rather grand-looking old stone building has a really imposing stable yard, now used for parking. The neatly kept bar has winged high-backed settles and varnished rustic tables on the lovely dark Delabole flagstones, black wrought-iron rings for lamps or hams hanging from the high ceiling, a handsome window seat, and an open kitchen range under a high mantelpiece decorated with earthenware flagons. At lunchtime, the good, popular bar food includes soup (£2.75), sandwiches (from £2.75), filled baked potatoes or good ploughman's (£5.75), leeks and bacon in a cheese sauce or plaice and chips (£6.25), and sirloin steak (£12), but it's the daily specials (lunchtime and evening) that people enjoy most: lasagne, ratatouille, parmesan and oregano tart or roasted red pepper and aubergine gratin (£6.50), fried haddock (£7.50), steak and kidney or fish pies (£7.75), and lemon sole with lime butter (£10.50). Well kept St Austell Tinners, HSD, and Tribute tapped from wooden casks behind the counter (lots of tankards hang from the beams above it), a couple of farm ciders, a good wine list, and several malt whiskies; darts, cribbage, dominoes, and shove-ha'penny. The big garden has a small summer marquee, seats on the grass and picnic-sets on the front cobbles. *(Recommended by Tracey and Stephen Groves, M A Borthwick, Andrea Rampley, MDN, Brian Skelcher, Jacquie and Jim Jones, Bob and Sue Hardy, the Didler, JP, PP, Margaret Mason, David Thompson, Bill and Jessica Ritson)*

St Austell ~ Tenant Desmond Weston ~ Real ale ~ Bar food ~ (01208) 841259 ~ Children in dining room ~ Open 11-2.30, 6-11(all day July and Aug); 12-3, 7-10.30 (all day in July and Aug) Sun; closed 25 Dec

ST MAWGAN SW8766 Map 1
Falcon 🛏
NE of Newquay, off B3276 or A3059

As well as being a very nice place to stay, this comfortable and friendly pub, set in a pretty village, is especially popular for its good food. There's a new chef this year and they now have a strong emphasis on fresh seafood which is landed at nearby Newlyn: fresh cod in beer batter (£6.50), Fowey river mussels in cider and cream or fresh haddock with local smoked blue cheese topping (£9.95), scallops grilled in their shells with ginger and coriander (£10.50), whole sea bream with hazelnuts and spring onions (£11.50), and plain grilled whole dover sole with parsley butter (£13.95). Also, sandwiches, garlic mushrooms (£4.25), local goats cheese salad (£4.50), vegetable pasta (£6.25), red thai chicken curry (£6.95), moroccan-style lamb with orange and mint couscous (£7.95), mixed game casserole (£8.95), sirloin steak (£10.50), and puddings like home-made white chocolate and Baileys cheesecake, apple pie or lemon tart (£2.95). The neatly kept big bar has a log fire, small modern settles, large antique coaching prints and falcon pictures on the walls, well kept St Austell Tinners, HSD and Tribute on handpump, and a decent wine list; efficient service even when busy. The restaurant is no smoking and has paintings and pottery by local artists for sale; darts and euchre. Particularly when the fine wisteria is flowering, the cobbled courtyard in front (new outside heaters this year) with its stone tables, is a lovely spot to relax. The peaceful, attractive garden has plenty of seats, a wishing well, and play equipment for children. *(Recommended by Bob Turnham, Neil and Anita Christopher, Suzanne Stacey, Mrs A P Lee, JCW, David and Julie Glover, Robyn Turner, John and Judy Saville, Jane Taylor, David Dutton, Patrick Hancock, Mrs Caroline Siggins, W Ruxton)*

St Austell ~ Tenant Andy Banks ~ Real ale ~ Bar food ~ Restaurant ~ (01637) 860225 ~ Children in restaurant and family room ~ Dogs welcome ~ Open 11-3, 6-11; 12-3, 7-10.30 Sun ~ Bedrooms: £25(£40S)/£52(£70S)

We say if we know a pub allows dogs.

TREBURLEY SX3477 Map 1
Springer Spaniel 🍴 ♀

A388 Callington—Launceston

Since our last edition, new licensees have taken over this bustling, roadside pub. The relaxed, friendly bar has a lovely, very high-backed settle by the woodburning stove in the big fireplace, high-backed farmhouse chairs and other seats, and pictures of olde-worlde stage-coach arrivals at inns; this leads into a cosy room with big solid teak tables. Up some steps from the main bar is the beamed, attractively furnished, no smoking restaurant. Good, popular food now includes bar meals like sandwiches (until 7pm, from £3.50; ciabattas such as steak, mushroom and local brie melt £6.95), local ham and egg (£3.95), steak in ale pie (£5.95), crab pasty (£7.95), and venison and game pie (£8.95), as well as home-made soup (£2.95), wild boar terrine with local chutneys (£4.95), mediterranean tart (£5.50), pasta of the day or mushroom stroganoff (£7.95), chicken breast stuffed with sun-dried tomatoes, mozzarella and olives (£8.95), well liked stilton beef (£10.95), daily specials like loin of lamb forestière (£10.95), and fresh fillet of bass in saffron sauce (£14.95), and puddings such as minted white chocolate cheesecake or fresh lemon mousse (£4.50). Well kept Sharps Doom Bar, Eden, Cornish Coaster, and a beer named for the pub on handpump, a good wine list, and quite a few malt whiskies; dominoes and Sunday evening quiz. More reports please. *(Recommended by C P Baxter, Richard and Margaret Peers, W F C Phillips, Mrs J A Taylar, Brian and Diane Mugford, Brian and Bett Cox, Mike and Sue Loseby, DAV, DRH and KLH, Mr and Mrs J Brown)*

Free house ~ Licensee Andrew Brotheridge ~ Real ale ~ Bar food ~ Restaurant ~ (01579) 370424 ~ Children welcome ~ Dogs allowed in bar ~ Open 11-3, 6-11; 12-3, 7-10.30 Sun

TREGADILLETT SX2984 Map 1
Eliot Arms

Village signposted off A30 at junction with A395, W end of Launceston bypass

Friendly new licensees have taken over this creeper-covered inn, and there's a good bustling atmosphere and a nice mix of locals and visitors. The series of little softly lit rooms is still full of interest: 72 antique clocks (including seven grandfathers), 400 snuffs, hundreds of horsebrasses, old prints, old postcards or cigarette cards grouped in frames on the walls, quite a few barometers, and shelves of books and china. Also, a fine old mix of furniture on the Delabole slate floors, from high-backed built-in curved settles, through plush Victorian dining chairs, armed seats, chaise longues and mahogany housekeeper's chairs, to more modern seats, and open fires; piped music. Straightforward bar food now includes home-made soup (£2.65), sandwiches (from £3.45), ploughman's (from £4.75), spinach and mushroom lasagne (£5.95), home-made steak and stilton pie or ham and egg (£6.25), a curry of the day (£6.95), cod on spinach and topped with cheese (£8.45), a big mixed grill (£10.45), daily specials, and Sunday roast lunch (£4.95). The restaurant is partly no smoking. Well kept Greene King Ruddles County, and Sharps Doom Bar and Eden on handpump; darts, fruit machine, cribbage, and dominoes. There are seats in front of the pub and at the back of the car park; more reports please. *(Recommended by Janet Walters, P R and S A White, Brian Skelcher, the Didler, John and Elizabeth Thomason, David Crook, Brian and Bett Cox, Duncan Cloud, Terry and Linda Moseley, JP, PP, W W Burke, Jacquie and Jim Jones, Mr and Mrs D Lloyd, Louise English, DAV, Charles Gysin, Di and Mike Gillam, W F C Phillips, Mr and Mrs K Box, Liz and Tony Colman)*

J P Leisure ~ Managers Rob and Pat Cox ~ Real ale ~ Bar food (12-2.30, 6.30-9.30) ~ Restaurant ~ (01566) 772051 ~ Children in family room ~ Dogs allowed in bar ~ Open 11.30-3, 6-11; 11.30-11 Sat; 12-10.30 Sun ~ Bedrooms: £35B/£45B

If we know a pub does summer barbecues, we say so.

TRESCO SV8915 Map 1
New Inn ♀ ◑ ⇔

New Grimsby; Isles of Scilly

In a super spot near the harbour, this well run pub is a friendly place. The locals' bar has a good chatty atmosphere, while visitors enjoy the main bar room or the light, airy dining extension. There are some comfortable old sofas, banquettes, planked partition seating, and farmhouse chairs and tables, a few standing timbers, boat pictures, a large model sailing boat, a collection of old telescopes, and plates on the delft shelf. The Pavilion extension has plenty of seats and tables on the blue wooden floors, cheerful yellow walls, and looks over the flower-filled terrace where there's plenty of teak furniture and views of the sea. Well liked bar food at lunchtime includes home-made soup (£3.25), sandwiches (from £4.75; open crab sandwich £8.95), trio of cornish sausages with cheddar and mustard mash (£6.25), ploughman's with home-made bread (£6.75), pasta with roasted peppers, pesto and parmesan or potted local crab with toasted home-made bread (£7.95), fish and chips or chargrilled chicken and artichoke salad (£8.95), and thai fry of fresh fish with rice noodles (£11.95), with evening dishes such as interesting pizzas (from £6.50; local bresaola, mushroom and rocket £8.95), smoked salmon, buckwheat pancakes and sour cream (£6.95), marinated spatchcocked chicken with bombay potatoes and onion bhaji (£11.95), and grilled bass with garlic and parsley crust and saffron mash or mixed grill (£14.95); puddings like a home-made tart of the day or crème brûlée with fruit and nut infusion (£4.25), and all sorts of breakfasts – continental, vegetarian or traditional (£6.25). The five well kept real ales are all Cornish: Ales of Scilly Maiden Scuppered, Skinners Betty Stogs Bitter, Cornish Blonde Wheat Beer, and Tresco Tipple, and Tetleys on handpump; interesting wines (by the large glass), up to 25 malt whiskies, and 10 vodkas; real espresso and cappuccino coffee, piped music, darts, pool, cribbage, dominoes, and euchre. Note that the price below is for dinner, bed and breakfast. *(Recommended by Gloria Bax, John and Jackie Chalcraft, Bernard Stradling, Pete and Rosie Flower, Neil and Anita Christopher, Dr and Mrs M E Wilson, R J Herd)*

Free house ~ Licensee Alan Baptist ~ Real ale ~ Bar food (all day) ~ Restaurant ~ (01720) 422844 ~ Children welcome ~ Dogs allowed in bar ~ Open 11-11; 12-10.30 Sun; 11-3, 6-11 in winter ~ Bedrooms: /£178S

TREVAUNANCE COVE SW7251 Map 1
Driftwood Spars ◑ ⇔

Quay Road, off B3285 in St Agnes

As this 17th-c inn is set just up the road from the beach and dramatic cove and is surrounded by plenty of coastal walks, it does get very crowded in summer, and readers very much enjoy coming here out of high season. It was originally a marine warehouse and fish cellar and is constructed from local slate and granite, and timbered with massive ships' spars – the masts of great sailing ships, many of whom were wrecked along this coast. There's said to be an old smugglers' tunnel leading from behind the bar, up through the cliff. The two bustling lower bars have a good mix of locals and visitors, with a variety of wooden tables and chairs, old ship prints and lots of nautical and wreck memorabilia, and a winter log fire; one bar has a juke box, pool, fruit machine, table football, and TV. Upstairs, the comfortable dining areas offer plenty of space (and residents have the use of a gallery bar). Well liked bar food includes sandwiches (£2.95), filled baked potatoes (£4.90), sausage and egg (£4.50), ploughman's (from £4.60), roast vegetable stroganoff (£5.90), barbecued ribs (£6.60), sirloin steak (£9.85), and daily specials like 12-inch pizza (£6.20), stir-fried beef in black bean sauce (£8.20), smoked duck and cashew nut salad with an orange and Grand Marnier sauce (£8.50), and fish of the day (£9.20). They have their own microbrewery where they produce Cuckoo Ale, and keep six guests from Bass, Fullers, Greene King, Sharps, Skinners and St Austell on handpump; over 100 malt whiskies, Addlestone's cider, and friendly helpful staff. There are seats in the garden, and the summer hanging baskets are pretty. *(Recommended by Mrs M Furness, David Crook, the Didler, JP, PP, Peter Salmon, DRH and KLH, John Martin, Veronia Banting)*

Own brew ~ Licensees Gordon and Jill Treleaven ~ Real ale ~ Bar food (12-2.30, 6.30-9.30; all day during summer school hols) ~ (01872) 552428 ~ Children welcome ~ Dogs allowed in bar ~ Live music Fri/Sat evenings ~ Open 11-11(12 Fri and Sat); 12-10.30 Sun ~ Bedrooms: £36S(£40B)/£72S(£80B)

TRURO SW8244 Map 1
Old Ale House 🍺 £
Quay Street

Happily, very little changes at this bustling and chatty pub. There's still a good mix of customers, a friendly welcome, and of course, a marvellous choice of real ales. Kept on handpump or tapped from the cask, there are a dozen that change regularly from breweries such as Arundel, Batemans, Brakspears, Cottage, Everards, Fullers, Gales, Sharps, Shepherd Neame, and Skinners; 21 country wines. Good, wholesome bar food prepared in a spotless kitchen in full view of the bar includes doorstep sandwiches (from £2.75; hot baked garlic bread with melted cheese, small £1.75, big £3.25), filled oven-baked potatoes or ploughman's (from £3.25), hot meals served in a skillet pan like five spice chicken, sizzling beef or vegetable stir fry (small helpings from £4.95, big helpings from £6.25), daily specials such as cauliflower and broccoli bake, pork and apple casserole or beef bourguignon (from £3.25), and puddings (£2.95). The dimly lit bar has an engaging diversity of furnishings, some interesting 1920s bric-a-brac, beer mats pinned everywhere, matchbox collections, and newpapers and magazines to read. Dominoes, giant Jenga, giant Connect Four, and piped music. *(Recommended by Dr and Mrs M E Wilson, Patrick Hancock, JP, PP, B J Harding, Tim and Ann Newell, Brian Skelcher, Joyce and Maurice Cottrell, Ted George, the Didler)*

Enterprise ~ Tenant Mark Jones ~ Real ale ~ Bar food (12-2.45(5 Sat), 7-8.45; no food Sat or Sun evenings) ~ (01872) 271122 ~ Children in eating area of bar until 9 ~ Live music Mon, Weds, Thurs ~ Open 11-11; 12-10.30 Sun

---

Lucky Dip

Besides the fully inspected pubs, you might like to try these Lucky Dips recommended to us and described by readers (if you do, please send us reports: www.goodguides.com).

ALTARNUN [SX2182]
☆ *Rising Sun* [NW, towards Camelford]: Rough-hewn 16th-c moorland local in attractive spot, with two small traditional flagstoned or tiled-floor rooms, coal fire, six well kept and interesting changing ales, generous cheap simple home-made food from sandwiches, baguettes and pasties up, good house wines, cheerful staff and locals; dogs welcome, open all day wknds and summer, tables outside, bedrooms *(Dennis Jenkin, the Didler, W F C Phillips, JP, PP, Howard Gregory)*
ASHTON [SW6028]
Lion & Lamb [A394 Helston—Penzance]: Welcoming pub with wide range of food and of real ales, occasional mini beer festivals, obliging staff; open all day, lovely hanging baskets and flower beds, handy for SW Coastal Path *(Maggie and Tony Harwood)*
BODMIN [SX0467]
☆ *Borough Arms* [Dunmere (A389 NW)]: Neat and friendly, with partly panelled stripped stone, open fire, lots of railway photographs and posters (by Bodmin—Wenford terminus),

well kept Sharpes ales, decent wines, cheerful efficient staff and plenty of room even when busy, big helpings of good value straightforward food (no sandwiches) inc evening and Sun lunchtime carvery, woodburner; side family room, unobtrusive piped music, fruit machine; picnic-sets out among shady apple trees, on Camel Trail, good walks, open all day *(BB, Alan and Paula McCully)*
Weavers [Honey St]: Flower-decked refurbished local in pedestrian area, welcoming and cosy beamed bar, friendly landlady, wide choice of usual bar food, full St Austell beer range kept well; SkyTV sports; tables outside *(George Atkinson)*
BOLINGEY [SW7653]
Bolingey Inn [Penwartha Rd – no inn sign]: Quiet, picturesque and unspoiled local in small village, cosy atmosphere, well kept local and national beers, small choice of good inexpensive food inc fresh fish, friendly staff; tables outside, handy for Perranporth but away from the tourists *(Pete Hennessey)*

BOSCASTLE [SX0990]

☆ *Cobweb* [B3263, just E of harbour]: Well used local with hundreds of old bottles hanging from heavy beams, two or three high-backed settles, dark stone walls, cosy log fire, real ales such as Dartmoor and St Austell, no smoking area; darts, dominoes, cribbage, pool, fruit machine and juke box, more machines and another fire in sizeable family room; live music Sat, open all day *(P R and S A White, David Eagles, LYM, DAV, Dr D J Groves, JP, PP, the Didler)*

BOTALLACK [SW3632]

Queens Arms: Friendly pub with wide and unusual food choice, well kept local beers, helpful staff, big open fireplace; large pleasant garden, handy for wonderful clifftop walks *(Helen Flaherty)*

BOTUSFLEMING [SX4061]

Rising Sun [off A388 nr Saltash]: Untouched low-ceilinged rural local in same family for many years, rather spartan but cosy, with great atmosphere, welcoming landlord, well kept Bass and a changing guest beer, good coal fire, no food; cl Mon-Thurs lunchtimes, open all day wknds *(the Didler)*

BUDE [SS2006]

Falcon [Falcon Terrace]: 19th-c hotel overlooking canal, old-fashioned furnishings and atmosphere, lots of quick good value food in bar and restaurant inc crunchy veg, daily roast, local fish and good puddings, smiling staff, well kept Bass and St Austell Tinners and HSD, good coffee and herbal teas; big family room with two pool tables, dogs welcome; bedrooms comfortable and well equipped, good breakfast *(Rita Horridge)*

BUDOCK WATER [SW7832]

Trelowarren Arms: Wide range of good value food inc fresh fish, friendly efficient service *(John Wooll)*

CALLINGTON [SX3569]

☆ *Coachmakers Arms* [A388 towards Launceston]: Imposing 18th-c pub, beams and timbers, ceilings with flags from around the world matching clock collection with differing time zones, bric-a-brac and tropical fish, well kept ales inc Sharps Doom Bar and Skinners Cornish Knocker, bar food from baguettes to chargrills, restaurant; piped music, Weds quiz night; children in eating areas, dogs welcome *(Mayur Shah, LYM, Joan and Michel Hooper-Immins, Howard Gregory, Mrs E Hayes)*

CARGREEN [SX4362]

☆ *Crooked Spaniard* [off A388 Callington—Saltash]: Much-altered pub in grand spot by Tamar, with smart river-view dining extension and waterside terrace – always some river activity, esp at high tide; cosy and comfortable panelled bar, huge fireplace in another room, good generous food inc Sun carvery, well kept ales; under same management as Crooked Inn at Trematon *(David M Cundy)*

CHAPEL AMBLE [SW9975]

☆ *Maltsters Arms* [off A39 NE of Wadebridge]: Bright and clean knocked-together rooms with stripped stone, fresh eau de nil paintwork, panelling, big open fire, oak joists, heavy

furnishings on partly carpeted flagstones; well kept Bass, Greene King Abbot, Sharps Cornish Coaster and a beer brewed by them for the pub, good wines, enjoyable if not cheap food in bar and restaurant; dogs welcome in bar, children confined to plain upstairs family room, piped pop music may be loud, service can slow; benches out in sheltered sunny corner *(DAV, Brian and Bett Cox, MDN, A Sadler, R and S Bentley, Liz and Tony Colman, Bob and Sue Hardy, David and Julie Glover, WINN, Jane Taylor, David Dutton, LYM)*

CHARLESTOWN [SX0351]

Harbour Inn [part of Pier House Hotel]: Small well managed somewhat hotelish bar in first-class spot alongside and looking over the classic little harbour, good choice of enjoyable traditional food, well kept Bass and Flowers Original, quick friendly service; interesting film-set conservation village with shipwreck museum *(Duncan Cloud, David Rule)*

Rashleigh Arms [Quay Rd]: Large bar, very big lounge, wide choice of good value food inc fresh fish and popular puddings in unpretentious restaurant, seats out on terrace (dogs allowed there) and separate garden above little harbour and heritage centre; good choice of well kept ales, good coffee, cheery quick helpful service, good canalside family room; piped music may be loud, on the coach circuit; good value bedrooms *(G W A Pearce)*

CHILSWORTHY [SX4172]

White Hart: Well restored and relaxed, with generous enjoyable food, well kept Sharps beers, lots of local activities; nice steep garden, great Tamar valley and Dartmoor views from back terrace *(Nigel Long)*

CONSTANTINE [SW7329]

Queens Arms [Fore St]: Comfortable, friendly and unpretentious, with good value simple food from good cheese or ham sandwiches up, well kept Sharps Doom Bar, decent house wine, interesting collection of ancient tools; dogs allowed, handy for 15th-c church, good walks *(Dennis Jenkin, Jenny and Brian Seller)*

CRAFTHOLE [SX3654]

☆ *Finnygook:* Clean and comfortable much-modernised lounge bar, light and airy, with good baguettes and ploughman's, lots of blackboard dishes, well kept St Austell beers, reasonably priced wines, friendly helpful staff, restaurant; discreet piped music, one car park is steep, and beware of the high pressure taps in the lavatories; tables in yard, good sea views from residents' lounge, low-priced bedrooms *(BB, Dennis Jenkin)*

CRANTOCK [SW7960]

☆ *Old Albion* [Langurroc Rd]: Pleasantly placed photogenic thatched village pub, low beams, flagstones and open fires, old-fashioned small bar with brasses and low lighting, larger more open room with local pictures, informal local feel despite all the summer visitors (and the souvenirs sold here), friendly staff, generous basic home-made bar lunches inc good sandwiches and giant ploughman's, well kept Sharps and Skinners ales, farm cider, decent house wines; dogs welcome, tables out on terrace, open all day *(JP, PP, Patrick Hancock, Dennis Jenkin, Brian Skelcher, LYM, Colin Gooch, Peter Salmon)*

CREMYLL [SX4553]

☆ *Edgcumbe Arms*: Super setting by foot-ferry to Plymouth, with good Tamar views and picnicsets out by water; attractive layout and décor, with slate floors, big settles and other oldfashioned furnishings, old pictures and china, no smoking area, plentiful food from sandwiches up, well kept St Austell ales, friendly staff, games area; children in eating area, bedrooms *(Richard Fendick, LYM, Mr and Mrs Allan Chapman)*

CRIPPLES EASE [SW5036]

Engine [B3311 St Ives—Penzance]: Familyfriendly former tin-mine counting house in superb moorland location, views of the sea on all sides from nearby hill (very popular summer evenings); well kept Greene King Old Speckled Hen, Marstons Pedigree and Sharps Doom Bar, welcoming landlady, enjoyable food, pool; good value bedrooms *(Richard Dixon, Susan and Nigel Wilson)*

CROWN TOWN [SW6330]

Crown: Friendly staff, good atmosphere, fine range of well kept real ales, giant Jenga (great fun) and pool *(Richard Fairweather)*

CUBERT [SW7858]

☆ *Smugglers Den* [village signed off A3075 S of Newquay, then brown sign to pub (and Trebellan holiday park) on left]: Hugely extended open-plan 16th-c thatched pub, lots of well ordered tables, dim lighting, stripped stone and heavy beam and plank ceilings, West Country pictures and seafaring memorabilia, small barrel seats, steps down to no smoking area with enormous inglenook woodburner, another step to big side family dining room; neat helpful friendly staff, fresh generous enjoyable food inc local seafood, well kept ales such as Sharps Eden, Skinners Betty Stogs and St Austell HSD and Tribute, farm cider; well lit pool area, darts; fruit machine, may be loud piped music; picnic-sets in small courtyard and on lawn with climbing frame; has been cl winter Mon-Weds lunchtime *(David Crook, John and Judy Saville, JP, PP, Tim and Ann Newell, BB, Pete and Rosie Flower, P R and S A White, the Didler, Patrick Hancock, Chris Reeve)*

DEVORAN [SW7938]

☆ *Old Quay House* [Quay Rd – brown sign to pub off A39 Truro—Falmouth]: Very pleasant old local at end of coast to coast cycle way, welcoming and relaxing; two small unpretentious rooms, one with food inc good baguettes and some interesting specials, the other with daily papers and big coal fire, boating bric-a-brac, well kept Bass, Flowers Original, Fullers London Pride and Sharps Doom Bar, quick service; no dogs; steeply terraced garden making the most of the idyllic spot – peaceful creekside village, lovely views, walks nearby; good value bedrooms, open all day in summer *(Alan M Pring, David Crook, BB)*

FALMOUTH [SW8033]

Boathouse [Trevethan Hill/Webber Hill]: Interesting two-level pub with plenty of atmosphere, lots of woodwork, nautical theme, log fire, well kept beer, friendly bar staff; jam nights, deck with great estuary views *(JP, PP, Dr and Mrs M E Wilson)*

Chain Locker [Custom House Quay]: Fine spot by inner harbour with window tables and lots outside, welcoming atmosphere and interesting strongly nautical bare-boards décor, real ales such as Sharps Doom Bar and Skinners, well priced food from sandwiches to fresh local fish, friendly service, good separate darts alley; fruit machine, piped music; well behaved children welcome, open all day, selfcatering accommodation *(JP, PP, Kevin Blake, LYM, Patrick Hancock, Dr and Mrs M E Wilson, Joyce and Maurice Cottrell)*

Grapes [Church St]: Spacious family-friendly refurbished pub with fine harbour view (beyond car park) from the back, beams, comfortable armchairs, sofas, lots of ships' crests and nautical memorabilia, plenty of tables, wide range of cheap food esp fish from adjoining servery, helpful friendly young staff, local real ales, games room; piped music, steep stairs to lavatories *(Lorraine and Fred Gill, Geoff Pidoux)*

☆ *Quayside Inn & Old Ale House* [ArwenackSt/Fore St]: Bustling bare-boards dark-panelled bar with well kept Greene King Ruddles County, Sharps Special, Skinners Cornish Knocker, Timothy Taylors Landlord and Wadworths 6X, decent wines, friendly staff, lots of pub games (also juke box or piped music, fruit machine, TV), upstairs harbourview lounge with armchairs and sofas one end, reasonably priced food (all day in summer) from doorstep sandwiches to Sun roasts, more skillets evening (with a younger crowd then – packed Fri/Sat for live music); children welcome, open all day, plenty of waterside picnic-sets *(Alan M Pring, Patrick Hancock, Geoff and Jan Dawson, JP, Jenny and Brian Seller, Dr and Mrs M E Wilson, LYM, David Crook, Andy and Yvonne Cunningham, Richard Fendick, John Martin, Veronia Banting)*

☆ *Seven Stars* [The Moor (centre)]: Classic unchanging and unsmart 17th-c local with wonderfully entertaining vicar-landlord, no gimmicks, warm welcome, Bass, Sharps Own and Skinners tapped from the cask, homemade rolls, chatty regulars, big key collection, quiet back snug; tables on roadside courtyard *(the Didler, Patrick Hancock, JP, PP, BB)*

FLUSHING [SW8033]

Royal Standard [off A393 at Penryn (or foot ferry from Falmouth); St Peters Hill]: Trim and traditional waterfront local with veteran welcoming landlord, plenty of genuine characters, great views from front terrace, neat bar with pink plush and copper, alcove with pool and darts, simple well cooked food inc good baked potatoes and home-made pasties, well kept Bass, Flowers IPA and Sharps Doom Bar; outside gents' *(JP, PP, the Didler,*

Debbie and Neil Hayter)
FOWEY [SX1252]

☆ *Galleon* [Fore St; from centre follow Car Ferry signs]: Superb spot overlooking harbour and estuary, well refurbished with solid pine and modern nautical décor, dining areas off, well kept and priced Bass, Flowers IPA, Sharps Cornish Coaster and a guest beer, generous good value food with plenty of fish, fast friendly service; jazz Sun lunchtime; tables out on attractive extended waterside terrace and in sheltered courtyard, good estuary-view bedrooms *(Michael Dandy, George Atkinson, Andy and Yvonne Cunningham, BB)*

☆ *King of Prussia* [Town Quay]: Large neat upstairs bar in handsome quayside building, bay windows looking over harbour to Polruan, St Austell ales, sensibly priced wines, good friendly service, side family food bar with good value individually cooked food inc fish and seafood; may be piped music, occasional live; seats outside, open all day at least in summer, pleasant bedrooms *(Nick Lawless, LYM, Edward Mirzoeff, M Benjamin, Charles and Pauline Stride, Martin and Karen Wake)*
Lugger [Fore St]: Unpretentious locals' bar, comfortable small dining area, very family-friendly but popular with older people too for good inexpensive food inc lots of seafood, cheap well kept St Austell ales, friendly service, big waterfront mural; piped music; tables outside, bedrooms *(BB, Nick Lawless, the Didler)*
GOLANT [SX1155]

☆ *Fishermans Arms* [Fore St (B3269)]: Plain but charming waterside local, nice garden, lovely views particularly from terrace; good generous straightforward home-made food all day in summer (cl Sun afternoon), well kept Sharps Doom Bar and Ushers Best, friendly landlord, efficient service, log fire, interesting pictures, tropical fish *(Andy and Ali, George Atkinson, Evelyn and Derek Walter, the Didler, M Benjamin, Martin and Karen Wake)*
GOLDSITHNEY [SW5430]

☆ *Crown* [B3280]: Roomy and comfortable local with good value food inc local fresh fish and bargain Thurs and Sun lunches, well kept St Austell ales, decent house wines, good friendly service, L-shaped beamed bar and small attractive no smoking dining room; pretty sun-trap glass-roofed front loggia and pavement tables, masses of hanging baskets *(Brian and Genie Smart, Dr Phil Putwain)*
GRAMPOUND [SW9348]

☆ *Dolphin* [A390 St Austell—Truro]: Main road pub recently refurbished under newish licensees, good value generous food from baguettes and baked potatoes to some interesting dishes, help with special diets, well kept St Austell beers, decent house wines, friendly helpful staff, two-level bar with comfortable atmosphere, interesting prints and log fire; children welcome, handy for Trewithen Gardens *(Mrs M Griffin, Jenny and Brian Seller, Michael Dandy)*
GWEEK [SW7027]
Gweek Inn [back roads E of Helston]: Cheerful

family chain pub, large comfortable open-plan low-ceilinged bar with woodburner, quick good-humoured service, well kept Greene King Old Speckled Hen and Wadworths 6X, reasonably priced standard food inc good puddings choice, decent wines, lots of motoring trophies (enthusiast licensees), roomy pleasant restaurant; live music Fri, children welcome, tables on grass (safe for children), summer kiosk with all-day snacks, short walk from seal sanctuary *(Maggie and Tony Harwood, Ian and Deborah Carrington)*
HELFORD PASSAGE [SW7627]

☆ *Ferry Boat* [signed from B3291]: Extensive recently refurbished family bar in popular spot about a mile's walk from gate at bottom of Glendurgan Garden (NT), by sandy beach with swimming, small boat hire, fishing trips and summer ferry to Helford, suntrap waterside terrace with covered area and barbecues; full St Austell range kept well, very good range of wines by the glass, good generous food from sandwiches and baked potatoes to fresh fish and afternoon teas, no smoking restaurant, efficient cheerful helpful service; may be piped music, games area with pool, juke box and SkyTV, steep walk down from the overflow car park; usually open all day summer (with cream teas and frequent live entertainment); bedrooms *(John Wooll, Maggie and Tony Harwood, David Crook, LYM, Jenny and Brian Seller, Roger Wain-Heapy, Michael Dandy)*
HELSTON [SW6527]

☆ *Blue Anchor* [Coinagehall St]: 15th-c thatched tavern, very popular for the Spingo IPA, Middle and specials they still brew in their ancient brewhouse; quaint rooms off corridor, flagstones, stripped stone, low ceilings and simple old-fashioned furniture, cheap lunchtime food from rolls and sandwiches up, traditional games, family room; would probably be a main entry if current licensees could only be bothered to let us have up-to-date factual details; open all day *(the Didler, Andrea Rampley, Tim and Ann Newell, Sue Holland, Dave Webster, Su and Bob Child, Roger and Jenny Huggins, Giles Francis, Tom McLean, JP, PP, Maggie and Tony Harwood, M G Hart, Di and Mike Gillam, John Martin, Veronia Banting, LYM)*
LAMORNA [SW4424]

☆ *Lamorna Wink* [off B3315 SW of Penzance]: Unspoilt no-frills country local short stroll above pretty cove, with good coast walks; good collection of warship mementoes, sea photographs, nautical brassware and hats, Sharps Own and Doom Bar and Skinners Cornish Knocker, nice house wine, sandwiches and other simple food from homely kitchen area (may not be available out of season), books for sale, coal fire, pool table; children in eating area, benches outside, open all day in summer *(Roger and Jenny Huggins, Bob and Sue Hardy, John and Vivienne Rice, LYM, Duncan Cloud, Peter Wrobbel)*
LANNER [SW7240]

☆ *Fox & Hounds* [Comford; A393/B3298]: Well

run pub, relaxed and rambling, with low black beams, stripped stone, dark panelling, high-backed settles and cottagey chairs on flagstones, warm fires, good choice of generous reasonably priced food from good sandwiches and baguettes through lunchtime ad lib buffet to duck, shark or guinea fowl, well kept St Austell ales tapped from the cask, decent house wines, very friendly helpful staff, children welcome in no smoking dining room; pub games, dogs allowed in bar, piped music; great floral displays in front, neat back garden with pond and play area, open all day wknds *(Dennis Jenkin, P R and S A White, Andy and Yvonne Cunningham, LYM)*

LANREATH [SX1757]

☆ *Punch Bowl* [signed off B3359]: Rambling 17th-c inn with traditional flagstoned public bar and comfortable black-panelled lounge, well kept Sharps Figgys Brew and Skinners Betty Stogs or Cornish Knocker, separate striking panelled medieval restaurant with decent attractively priced food as well as its chandeliers and gargoyles; children welcome, cl Mon lunchtime in winter, bedrooms, pleasant tucked-away village *(LYM, George Atkinson, Dr Paull Khan)*

LAUNCESTON [SX3384]

West Gate [Westgate St]: Well run town pub with bargain food; gents' across the street *(DAV)*

LELANT [SW5436]

Old Quay House [Griggs Quay, Lelant Saltings; A3047/B3301 S of village]: Extensively refurbished and neatly kept large pub in marvellous spot overlooking estuary, car park shared with RSPB; good value wholesome usual food, real ales, good service; up-to-date bedrooms *(John and Jackie Chalcraft)*

Watermill [Lelant Downs; A3074 S]: Converted mill dining pub refurbished after recent floods, working waterwheel behind with gearing in dark-beamed central bar opening into brighter airy front extension and gallery restaurant area with racks of wine, well kept Sharps Doom Bar and Figgys Brew, decent wines (off-sales too), good coffee; dark pink pool room, may be piped nostalgic pop music; tables out under pergola and among trees in pretty streamside garden *(Richard Fendick, BB, John and Gillian Scarisbrick, Joyce and Maurice Cottrell)*

LERRYN [SX1457]

☆ *Ship* [signed off A390 in Lostwithiel; Fore St]: Lovely spot esp when tide's in, nr famous stepping-stones and three well signed waterside walks, picnic-sets and pretty play area outside; wide food choice from proper pasties and good sandwiches to masses of main courses and popular Sun carvery, well kept ales such as Bass, Skinners and Sharps Eden, local farm cider, good wines, fruit wines and malt whiskies, no smoking area, huge woodburner, attractive adults-only dining conservatory (booked quickly evenings and wknds), friendly staff; games room with pool, dogs on leads and children welcome; nice bedrooms in adjoining

building, wonderful breakfast *(George Atkinson, David Crook, Peter and Audrey Dowsett, Simon, Jo and Benjamin Cole, Dr and Mrs B D Smith, Nick Lawless, LYM)*

LINKINHORNE [SX3173]

☆ *Church House* [off B3257 NW of Callington]: Neatly modernised bar, part rustic furniture and flagstones, part plush and carpet, with some decorative china etc, woodburner, darts; well kept Sharps Doom Bar and Skinners Cornish Knocker, low mark-ups on wine, welcoming service, popular home-made food inc some bargains for children, also plush no smoking restaurant (best to book Sun); piped music; nice spot opp church, has been cl Mon *(BB, Rona Murdoch, John and Sarah Perry)*

LIZARD [SW7012]

☆ *Top House* [A3083]: Spotless well run pub particularly popular with older people, in same family for over 40 years; lots of interesting local sea pictures, fine shipwreck relics and serpentine craftwork (note the handpumps) in neat bar with generous good value bar food from sandwiches to local fish and seafood specials, well kept ales such as Flowers IPA, Sharps Doom Bar and Wadworths 6X, reasonably priced wines, roaring log fire, big no smoking area, no piped music (occasional live); tucked-away fruit machine, darts, pool; tables on sheltered terrace, interesting nearby serpentine shop *(Sue Holland, Dave Webster, Mr and Mrs McKay, Alan and Paula McCully, Mrs Roxanne Chamberlain, BB, E G Parish)*

LOOE [SX2553]

Olde Salutation [Fore St, E Looe]: Good welcoming local bustle in big squareish beamed and tiled bar, red leatherette seats and neat tables, nice old-fashioned fireplace, lots of local fishing photographs, side snug with olde-worlde harbour mural and fruit machine, step down to simple family room; good value food from notable crab sandwiches to tasty specials and Sun roasts, fast friendly service, well kept real ale; piped music, forget about parking; open all day, handy for coast path *(BB, Joyce and Maurice Cottrell)*

LOSTWITHIEL [SX1059]

Globe [North St]: Rambling traditional pub with cheerful bustle in roomy unassuming front bar, attractive décor in cosy and comfortable restaurant (worth booking – locally very popular), good food choice, well kept Cotleigh Tawny, friendly landlady and staff, open fire; tables in small attractive courtyard garden *(P G Ashford, David and Kay Ross, Bob and Sue Hardy)*

LUDGVAN [SW5133]

Old Inn [B3309, off A30 at Crowlas]: Reworked by new young landlord, some emphasis on carefully cooked food inc interesting dishes, summer cream teas; tables in restored garden *(anon)*

☆ *White Hart* [Churchtown; off A30 Penzance—Hayle at Crowlas – OS Sheet 203 map ref 505330]: Unpretentious and well worn in beamed and small-roomed 19th-c pub with much appeal to the many readers who like things truly unspoilt; great atmosphere, paraffin lamps, masses of mugs, jugs and pictures, rugs on bare boards, two big woodburners, well kept Bass, Flowers IPA and Marstons Pedigree tapped from the cask, sensibly priced home cooking (not Mon evenings exc high season) from sandwiches up, no piped music; no high chairs *(Brian Skelcher, the Didler, Andrea Rampley, Helen Flaherty, Keith Stevens, P R and S A White, DAV, LYM, Su and Bob Child)*

LUXULYAN [SX0458]

Kings Arms [Bridges]: Friendly open-plan village pub by bridge, simple décor with light oak fittings and beams, friendly helpful staff, good range of enjoyable reasonably priced home-made food, well kept St Austell ales inc Tribute, back games area with pool; tables on small front terrace and in back garden, handy for Eden Project *(George Atkinson)*

MARAZION [SW5130]

Godolphin Arms [West End]: Redeveloped hotel with great views across beach and Mounts Bay towards St Michael's Mount, good food, well kept ales inc Sharps Eden, good service, comfortable and civilised upper lounge bar and no smoking dining room, family room with play area, informal lower bar, roomy terrace; good carefully decorated bedrooms, most with sea view *(Roger Wain-Heapy)*

MEVAGISSEY [SX0145]

☆ *Fountain* [Cliff St, down alley by Post Office]: Welcoming unpretentious harbourside local, low beams, slate floor and some stripped stone, with good value simple food inc good crab sandwiches, good fish in popular upstairs restaurant, well kept St Austell ales, lovely coal fire, lots of old local prints and photographs, cosy back bar with glass-topped cellar; local artist does piano sing-song Fri (may be trombone accompaniment), occasional live music other nights – piped music may be very loud for warm-up; dogs welcome, SkyTV sports in back room; open all day, bedrooms, pretty frontage *(Pete and Rosie Flower, Christopher Wright, the Didler, Bob and Margaret Holder, Colin McKerrow, JP, PP, Mayur Shah, Rona Murdoch, Tim and Ann Newell, BB)*

Kings Arms [Fore St]: Small welcoming local, cheap cheerful food inc wide choice of fresh fish, well kept Bass and Sharps Doom Bar; good local male voice choir Mon, often music Sat too *(Pete and Rosie Flower, Patrick Hancock)*

Sharks Fin [The Quay]: On the pretty working harbour, with snug bar reminiscent of smugglers' cave with part-painted stone walls, ships' timbers and packing cases, reasonable choice of bar food, seafood restaurant; open all day in summer for food (also has large tearoom), good value bedrooms *(Kevin Flack)*

Ship [Fore St, nr harbour]: Lively 16th-c pub with interesting alcove areas in big comfortable open-plan bar, low ceilings, flagstones, nice nautical décor, open fire, friendly helpful staff, good range of generous quickly served food, full St Austell range kept well; fruit machines, piped music, occasional live music;

comfortable bedrooms *(Pete and Rosie Flower, Christopher Wright, Nick Lawless)*

MORVAL [SX2657]

Fox & Hounds: Well decorated modern building, divided beamed bar with real ales such as Nelsons Old Coach and Sharpes, good short wine list, wide choice of enjoyable food, good welcoming service; bedrooms and campsite *(Joyce and Maurice Cottrell)*

MORWENSTOW [SS2015]

☆ *Bush* [signed off A39 N of Kilkhampton; Crosstown]: One of Britain's oldest pubs, quiet, individual and unchanging; part Saxon, with serpentine Celtic basin in one wall, ancient built-in settles, beams and flagstones, and big stone fireplace, upper bar with interesting bric-a-brac, well kept St Austell HSD and Worthington BB tapped from the cask, Inch's cider, friendly service, darts, no piped music; limited lunchtime food (not Sun), no children or dogs, seats out in yard; lovely setting, interesting village church with good nearby teashop, great cliff walks; cl Mon in winter *(the Didler, Mr and Mrs McKay, Tracey and Stephen Groves, Basil Minson, LYM, DAV)*

MOUSEHOLE [SW4626]

☆ *Ship* [Harbourside]: Bustling harbourside local very popular for its lovely setting; beams, panelling, flagstones and open fire, usual food from baguettes up, well kept St Austell IPA, Tinners, HSD and Tribute, evening restaurant area; prominent TV and machines in one part; children and dogs welcome, bedrooms, open all day *(Maggie and Tony Harwood, Patrick Hancock, Colin Gooch, Andrea Rampley, Bob Broadhurst, LYM, Jayne Capp, John and Annabel Hampshire, Alan and Paula McCully, Roger and Jenny Huggins, John and Judy Saville, Keith Stevens, Alison Hayes, Pete Hanlon)*

MULLION [SW6719]

☆ *Old Inn* [Churchtown – not down in the cove]: Extensive thatched and beamed family food pub with central servery doing generous good value food (all day July/Aug) from good doorstep sandwiches to pies and evening steaks, linked eating areas with lots of brasses, plates, clocks, nautical items and old wreck pictures, big inglenook fireplace, no smoking rooms, well kept Sharps Doom Bar, Skinners Cornish Knocker and John Smiths, friendly attentive staff; children welcome, open all day Sat/Sun and Aug; can be very busy (esp on live music nights), darts, fruit machine; open all day, picnic-sets in pretty orchard garden, good bedrooms *(Mrs B Sugarman, LYM, Lawrence Pearse, Richard Fendick, Sue Holland, Dave Webster, Anne and Paul Horscraft, Kevin Blake, Alan and Paula McCully)*

MYLOR BRIDGE [SW8036]

Lemon Arms [Lemon Hill]: Friendly traditional village pub, three well kept St Austell ales, good value mainly blackboard food; handy for start or finish of very pretty walk *(Mrs Diane M Hall)*

NEWQUAY [SW8061]

☆ *Fort* [Fore St]: Massive recently built pub in

magnificent setting high above surfing beach and small harbour, decent food all day from sandwiches, hot baguettes and baked potatoes up through the full price range, open-plan areas well divided by balustrades and surviving fragments of former harbourmaster's house, good solid furnishings from country kitchen to button-back settees, soft lighting and one panelled area, friendly service, well kept St Austell HSD and Tribute, games area with two well lit pool tables, excellent indoor play area; great views from long glass-walled side section and from sizeable garden with terrace and play areas, good bedrooms, open all day *(Mike and Lynn Robinson, BB, Derek and Margaret Underwood, Father David Cossar)*

Lewinnick Lodge [Pentire headland, off Pentire Rd]: Attractively rebuilt and newly furnished in open uncluttered style; outstanding position built into the bluff just above the beach, with big picture windows in bar and restaurant for the terrific views, good interesting if not cheap food, friendly staff *(Brian Skelcher, Father David Cossar)*

Skinners Ale House [East St]: Open-plan bare-boards bar with steps up to back part, good choice of Skinners with some guests tapped from the cask, good value food; live music wknds inc trad jazz Sun night; small front terrace, open all day *(the Didler, Mike and Lynn Robinson, JP, PP)*

PADSTOW [SW9175]

Golden Lion [Lanadwell St]: Pleasant black-beamed front bar, high-raftered back lounge with plush banquettes against ancient white stone walls; cheerful local bustle, reasonably priced simple lunches inc very promptly served good sandwiches, evening steaks and fresh seafood, well kept real ales, coal fire; pool in family area, piped music or juke box, fruit machines; bedrooms *(P R and S A White, the Didler, JP, PP, Harry Thomas, BB)*

☆ *London* [Llanadwell St]: Basic down-to-earth fishermen's local, impressive hanging baskets out in front, lots of pictures and nautical memorabilia, buoyant atmosphere, St Austell beers on sparkler, decent choice of malt whiskies, good choice of wknd lunchtime bar food inc good value crab sandwiches and fresh local fish, more elaborate evening choice (small back dining area – get there early for a table), great real fire; games machines but no piped music – home-grown live music Sun night; open all day, bedrooms good value *(Harry Thomas, Steve Crooke, Ted George, JP, PP, LYM, Brian and Bett Cox, Val Stevenson, Rob Holmes, John and Judy Saville, A Sadler, Brian Skelcher, P R and S A White, Margaret Mason, David Thompson)*

Old Custom House [South Quay]: Large airy open-plan seaside bar with conservatory and big family area, well kept St Austell ales, food from sandwiches and baguettes up, pool, big TV; good spot by harbour, open all day, attractive sea-view bedrooms *(BB, Alan and Paula McCully, John and Judy Saville)*

Old Ship [Mill Sq, just off North Quay/Broad St]: Hotel's bustling open-plan bar with well

kept Flowers IPA, Sharps Doom Bar and St Austell, usual food with plenty of fresh fish, upstairs restaurant; tables in heated front courtyard tucked away just off harbour, open all day summer, 15 bedrooms *(BB, Alan and Paula McCully, Margaret Mason, David Thompson)*

Shipwrights [North Quay; aka the Blue Lobster]: Stripped brick, lots of wood, flagstones, lobster pots and nets in big low-ceilinged quayside bar with quick popular food, St Austell ales, friendly service, upstairs restaurant; busy with young people evenings; a few tables out by water *(BB, MDN, Bob and Sue Hardy)*

PELYNT [SX2054]

Jubilee [B3359 NW of Looe]: Immaculate 16th-c inn with interesting Queen Victoria mementoes and some handsome antique furnishings in relaxed beamed lounge bar and Victoria Bar, good food and atmosphere, well kept ales inc Bass and Skinners Betty Stogs, children welcome in eating areas; separate public bar with sensibly placed darts, pool, fruit machine, and piped music; picnic-sets under cocktail parasols in inner courtyard with pretty flower tubs, good play area, comfortable bedrooms, open all day wknds *(LYM, B J Harding, Prof and Mrs Tony Palmer)*

PENELEWEY [SW8240]

☆ *Punch Bowl & Ladle* [B3289]: Much extended thatched dining pub in picturesque setting, cosy Victorian-feel bar with big settees and rustic bric-a-brac, wide choice of reasonably priced generous food from good sandwiches up (Thurs is very popular with elderly lunchers), friendly efficient service, Bass and St Austell ales; unobtrusive piped music, children and dogs on leads welcome; handy for Trelissick Gardens, small back sun terrace, open all day summer *(David M Cundy, Pat and Robert Watt, Dennis Jenkin, LYM, Joe and Marion Mandeville, Mr and Mrs J Evans, Peter Salmon)*

PENZANCE [SW4730]

☆ *Dolphin* [The Barbican; Newlyn road, opp harbour after swing-bridge]: Roomy welcoming pub with attractive nautical décor, good harbour views, good value food using local produce, well kept St Austell ales, good service, great fireplace, children in room off main bar; big pool room with juke box etc, no obvious nearby parking *(the Didler, Darly Graton, Graeme Gulibert, A J Bowen, LYM, JP, PP)*

☆ *Globe & Ale House* [Queen St]: Well kept Bass, Sharps Own and Skinners Betty Stogs and Bettys Mild with guest beers, some tapped from the cask, in small low-ceilinged tavern, lots of old pictures and artefacts, bare boards and dim lighting, enthusiastic helpful landlord, enjoyable prompt food *(the Didler, JP, PP, A J Bowen)*

Mounts Bay Inn [Promenade, Wherry Town]: Small busy pub nr seafront, welcoming landlord, straightforward food inc local meat and fish, well kept ales inc Sharps Doom Bar and Skinners, pool; no children *(JP, PP,* the Didler, Dr B and Mrs P B Baker)

PERRANARWORTHAL [SW7738]

☆ *Norway* [A39 Truro—Penryn]: Large pub refurbished in traditional style after flood damage, half a dozen areas, beams hung with farm tools, lots of prints and rustic bric-a-brac, old-style wooden seating and big tables on slate flagstones, open fires, tropical fish tank; big helpings of popular food, well kept Bass and St Austell, decent wines, quick friendly service, attractive restaurant; games machine and piped music; tables outside, open all day *(BB, Dr and Mrs A K Clarke, David Crook)*

PERRANUTHNOE [SW5329]

☆ *Victoria* [signed off A394 Penzance—Helston]: Comfortable and relaxed L-shaped pub, cosy low-beamed bar, some stripped stonework, coastal and wreck photographs, freshly baked lunchtime baguettes and doorstep sandwiches, interesting evening specials, friendly efficient service, well kept ales such as Bass and Sharps Doom Bar, nice wine choice, neat coal fire, no smoking and family areas; quiet piped music; seats outside, good bedrooms, handy for Mounts Bay *(Ann and Bob Westbrook, LYM, Neil and Anita Christopher)*

PERRANWELL [SW7739]

☆ *Royal Oak* [off A393 Redruth—Falmouth and A39 Falmouth—Truro]: Welcoming and relaxed village pub with large black-beamed bar, nice décor, cosy seats, buoyant rather upmarket atmosphere, fine choice of food, not cheap but good value, inc sandwiches, well kept Sharps and good wines by the glass from small counter, particularly good landlord and service, good log fire; provision for children, picnic-sets in small garden *(David Crook, LYM)*

PILLATON [SX3664]

☆ *Weary Friar* [off Callington—Landrake back road]: Pretty tucked-away 12th-c pub with four spotless and civilised knocked-together rooms (one no smoking), appealing décor, comfortable seats around sturdy tables, easy chairs one end, log fire, four well kept ales (two usually local), farm cider, nicely presented substantial bar food inc lunchtime sandwiches, children's helpings and good puddings, quick cheerful helpful service; big back restaurant (not Mon), children in eating area; tables outside, Tues bell-ringing in church next door; comfortable bedrooms with own bathrooms *(Richard and Margaret Peers, Ted George, LYM, Jacquie and Jim Jones)*

POLMEAR [SX0853]

Ship [A3082 Par—Fowey]: Good friendly atmosphere, chatty locals and welcoming uniformed staff, good food using fresh produce, nice shipping décor, big stove, back dining area still in keeping with dark furniture, big conservatory opening to tables in sizeable garden; nr holiday camps *(Pete and Rosie Flower, M and R Thomas, Jayne Capp)*

POLPERRO [SX2051]

☆ *Blue Peter* [Quay Rd]: Dark and cosy, in great setting up narrow steps above harbour; unpretentious little low-beamed wood-floored local now doing food again, with well kept St

Austell and guest beers such as Sharps Doom Bar, farm cider, quick friendly service, log fire, nautical memorabilia, traditional games, dogs and children welcome, family area upstairs with video game; can get crowded, and piped music – often jazz or nostalgic pop – can be loudish, may be live music Sat; some seats outside, open all day *(Val Stevenson, Rob Holmes, the Didler, S Creeson, Ted George, LYM, JP, PP, Jackie Evans, Prof and Mrs Tony Palmer, P R and S A White, Phil and Christine Young)*

☆ *Old Mill House* [Mill Hill; bear right approaching harbour]: Stripped pine, bare boards and flagstones, nautical décor, big log fireplace, well kept Sharps Cornish Coaster and Eden Ale, decent bar food, no smoking dining room; quiz nights, games area with darts and pool, piped music, no nearby parking; children in eating areas, picnic-sets out in streamside garden, open all day *(LYM, Bob Broadhurst, Prof and Mrs Tony Palmer)*

☆ *Three Pilchards* [Quay Rd]: Welcoming low-beamed fishermen's local, lots of black woodwork, dim lighting, simple furnishings, open fire in big stone fireplace, enjoyable food from baguettes and pasties to lots of local seafood, well kept real ales, regulars' photographs; piped music, can get very busy; tables on upper terrace (no sea view) up steep steps, open all day *(Mayur Shah, Esther and John Sprinkle, Val Stevenson, Rob Holmes, Prof and Mrs Tony Palmer, BB, Jackie Evans, P R and S A White)*

POLRUAN [SX1251]

☆ *Lugger* [back roads off A390 in Lostwithiel, or passenger/bicycle ferry from Fowey]: Beamed waterside pub with high-backed wall settles, big model boats etc, open fires, good views from upstairs partly no smoking family room, bar food inc local fish and children's, wider evening choice, restaurant, well kept St Austell ales, pub games; children and well behaved dogs welcome, piped music (occasional live), games machine; good walks, open all day *(the Didler, Nick Lawless, Jayne Capp, M Benjamin)*

PORTHLEVEN [SW6325]

☆ *Atlantic* [Peverell Terr]: Friendly local doing well under new licensees, pleasant helpful staff, well kept ales such as Bass, Skinners and St Austell, good reasonably priced food, big open-plan lounge with well spaced seating and cosier alcoves, good log fire in granite fireplace, no smoking dining room with amazing trompe l'oeil mural; stunning setting, good bay views from front terrace, open all day *(Maggie and Tony Harwood)*

Harbour Inn [Commercial Rd]: Large well looked-after pub/hotel notable for outstanding setting with tables out on big quayside terrace; good value simple food in impressive dining area off expansive lounge and bar, quick friendly service, well kept St Austell ales, comprehensive wine list, restaurant, decent bedrooms, some with harbour view *(Dr and Mrs A K Clarke, E G Parish, Richard Fendick)*

PORTHTOWAN [SW6948]

Blue [Beach Rd, East Cliff]: On the beach and recently refurbished, with great surf views, good value food inc a popular burger, good service and wines; keg beers *(Andy Sinden, Louise Harrington)*

PORTLOE [SW9339]

☆ *Lugger*: Under newish management, elegantly refurbished with restaurant not pub licence, but does good bar lunches inc fine crab sandwiches, in comfortable bar or on small terrace looking down on cove; good meals in light and airy restaurant too, friendly staff, decent wines, two fires; bedrooms (not all with sea view) *(LYM, Mrs D W Privett, Pauline and Philip Darley)*

Ship: Comfortable, bright and cosy L-shaped bar, plenty of interesting nautical and local memorabilia and photographs, sensibly priced food inc good pasties, curries and pizzas, children's menu, well kept St Austell ales, staff with a sense of humour; piped music; sheltered and attractive streamside garden over road, pretty fishing village with lovely cove and coast path above, open all day Fri-Sun in summer *(Pete and Rosie Flower, Christopher Wright, Lorraine and Fred Gill, Jeanne and Paul Silvestri, Jenny and Brian Seller, T B, BB)*

PORTREATH [SW6545]

Portreath Arms [by B3300/B3301 N of Redruth]: Friendly helpful staff and real cooking, good choice from open sandwiches to steaks, local fish and good value Sun roast, well kept real ales inc Skinners, decent house wine, tidy and comfortable hotel lounge bar with green plush seating, steps down to no smoking dining room, separate large public bar with pool, darts etc; bedrooms, well placed for coastal walks *(Debbie and Neil Hayter)*

PORTSCATHO [SW8735]

☆ *Plume of Feathers* [The Square]: Comfortable and cheerful pub in pretty fishing village, sea-related bric-a-brac in linked room areas, side locals' bar (can be very lively in the evening), well kept St Austell and other ales, good value pubby bar food inc popular bargain Fri fish night, good staff, restaurant; dogs welcome, very popular with summer visitors but perhaps most welcoming out of season *(Jenny and Brian Seller, P R and S A White, Geoff and Jan Dawson, Malcolm and Jennifer Perry, Dr D J and Mrs S C Walker, Jack Clark, Lorraine and Fred Gill, LYM)*

PRAZE AN BEEBLE [SW6336]

St Aubyn Arms [The Square]: Traditional two-bar country pub, well kept Sharps and Skinners ales, wide choice of enjoyable food inc Fri steak specials and children's (who are warmly welcomed), two restaurants, one upstairs; public bar with games and piped music; large garden *(Colin Gooch, John and Glenys Wheeler, P R and S A White)*

RILLA MILL [SX2973]

Manor House: Friendly pub with wide-ranging food inc local fish and choice of curries, well kept real ales, good house wines, cheerful helpful landlord *(DAV)*

ROCHE [SW9860]

Rock [Fore St]: Roomy originally 14th-c pub with wide choice of enjoyable food from open kitchen in dining and restaurant areas, well kept real ales, welcoming staff and good atmosphere *(G W A Pearce)*

RUAN LANIHORNE [SW8942]

☆ *Kings Head* [off A3078]: Attractive neatly kept pub opp fine old church, beamed bar with hanging china and framed cigarette cards, pleasant family room, standard food inc children's and Sun roast, no smoking dining room, well kept Sharps Cornish, a beer brewed for the pub by Skinners and two guest beers; piped music, traditional games – for children too; suntrap sunken garden, views over the Fal estuary, cl Mon lunchtime (and Mon evening in winter) *(Bernard Stradling, Mike Gorton, Paul Boot, Jenny and Brian Seller, Lorraine and Fred Gill, LYM)*

SALTASH [SX4159]

Ploughboy [Liskeard Rd]: Wide choice of good value home-made food inc local fish, duck and steak, bargain wine *(David Leah)*

Union [Tamar St]: Small real ale pub with good changing choice of well kept local beers; no food, nor children (except at waterfront picnic-sets outside), jazz and folk nights *(David Leah)*

SCORRIER [SW7244]

Fox & Hounds [B3298, off A30 just outside Redruth]: Long partly panelled well divided bar, big log or coal fires each end, red plush banquettes, hunting prints, stripped stonework and creaky joists, large no smoking section, wide choice of generous food, well kept Sharps Doom Bar; unobtrusive piped music; picnic-sets out in front, handy for Portreath—Devoran cycle trail *(David Crook, LYM)*

ST AGNES [SW7250]

☆ *Railway Inn* [Vicarage Rd, via B3277]: Friendly village local with fascinating shoe collection, also splendid original horsebrasses, interesting naval memorabilia and photographs; decent cheap bar food from lunchtime sandwiches to steaks, OAP specials and good value Sun lunch, well kept Bass, Boddingtons and Flowers IPA, no smoking restaurant; juke box; children in eating area, open all day summer, tables on terrace *(John and Glenys Wheeler, P R and S A White, JP, PP, Derek and Margaret Underwood, LYM)*

ST BURYAN [SW4025]

St Buryan Inn: Two-bar local with well kept Sharps Cornish Coaster, friendly landlord, solid-fuel stove, tractor seats by bar, kitchen chairs and a few plain tables, horse collars and brass on modern stone wall; darts, TV, juke box, good karaoke *(Giles Francis)*

ST DOMINICK [SX4067]

☆ *Who'd Have Thought It* [off A388 S of Callington]: Comfortable country pub with plenty of individuality and superb Tamar views, esp from no smoking conservatory; plush lounge areas with antique bric-a-brac and open fires, food from sandwiches and baked potatoes to steaks, children's menu, partly no smoking dining area, well kept Bass,

St Austell HSD, Skinners Betty Stogs and Worthington Best, decent wines, friendly new landlord – too recently arrived for us to confirm the pub's former main entry status; garden tables, handy for Cotehele (NT) *(Dennis Jenkin, LYM, John Evans)*

ST EWE [SW9746]

☆ *Crown* [off B3287]: Attractive cottagey dining pub, smartly traditional, with 16th-c flagstones, church pews and a fine settle, large no smoking back dining room up steps, lovely log fire, voluble parrot, St Austell ales kept well, good service; children in eating areas, picnic-sets on raised back lawn, handy for the Lost Gardens of Heligan, open all day in summer *(Pete and Rosie Flower, LYM, Patrick Renouf, Christopher Wright, Dr and Mrs M W A Haward, JDM, KM, Dennis Jenkin, Jenny and Brian Seller, Brian Skelcher, June and Ken Brooks)*

ST ISSEY [SW9272]

Pickwick [Burgois, signed off A389 at St Issey]: Spacious and comfortable lounge around central bar, good reasonably priced food inc fine steaks, well kept St Austell HSD, decent wines, friendly efficient uniformed staff, log fire, Dickensian memorabilia and dark oak beams, pretty candlelit restaurant, family room; quiet piped music, pool, machines; garden with good play area, bowling green and tennis, bedrooms, lovely setting above Camel estuary *(Alan and Paula McCully)*

☆ *Ring o' Bells* [Churchtown; A389 Wadebridge—Padstow]: Neatly modernised cheerful village local with consistently good freshly made sensibly priced food inc children's helpings in bustling beamed bar or good-sized no smoking side restaurant, well kept Bass and local beers, decent wines, welcoming service, open fire, no piped music; darts and pool one end, no dogs, can get packed in summer, car park across rd; some tables in flowery courtyard, bedrooms *(Theo, Anne and Jane Gaskin, CMW, JJW, John Wooll, LYM, Alan and Paula McCully)*

ST IVE [SX3067]

Butchers Arms [A390 Liskeard—Callington]: Immaculate 16th-c pub with well prepared good value food, prompt service, cosy cottage-style dining lounge, bar with pub games; lovely area *(Nigel Long)*

ST IVES [SW5441]

Castle [Fore St]: Cosy and spotless, low ceilings and lots of dark panelling in one long room, stained-glass windows, old local photographs, maritime memorabilia, well priced ample wholesome bar food, good range of well kept ales such as Greene King Abbot tapped from the cask (beer festivals), good value coffee, friendly staff; unobtrusive piped music, bustling in summer, relaxing out of season *(Roger Wain-Heapy, Ted George, Tim and Ann Newell)*

Lifeboat [Wharf Rd]: Busy harbourside pub, good atmosphere, cosy corners, nautical theme, friendly staff, bar food, good views, bar billiards; open all day *(E G Parish)*

☆ *Pedn Olva* [The Warren]: More hotel than pub, with tasteful modern mediterranean décor and some emphasis on the handsome restaurant's good modern cooking, particularly in the evenings; large bar with well kept St Austell Bitter and Tribute, exemplary friendly service, picture-window views of sea and Porthminster beach, esp from tables on rooftop terrace; comfortable bedrooms *(Ken Flawn, E G Parish, Alan Johnson)*

☆ *Sloop* [The Wharf]: Low-beamed and flagstoned harbourside pub crowded all year (the friendly staff cope well), with bright St Ives School pictures and attractive portrait drawings in front bar, booth seating in panelled back bar, well cooked down-to-earth food from sandwiches and baguettes to lots of fresh local fish, well kept Bass, John Smiths, Greene King Old Speckled Hen and Sharps Doom Bar, good coffee; juke box or piped music, TV; children in eating area, a few seats out on cobbles, open all day, bedrooms, handy for Tate Gallery *(A J Bowen, LYM, Alan Johnson, Dr and Mrs M E Wilson, the Didler, Emma Kingdon, Patrick Hancock, JP, PP, Giles Francis, John and Judy Saville, James Woods, John and Annabel Hampshire, R T and J C Moggridge)*

Union [Fore St]: Spotless friendly pub, roomy but cosy dark interior, low beams, small fire, masses of old local photographs, neatly ordered tables, food from filled baguettes to local fish, well kept ales inc Bass and John Smiths, decent wines, coffee; piped music, can get very crowded *(Alan Johnson, Tim and Ann Newell)*

ST JUST IN PENWITH [SW3631]

Kings Arms [Market Sq]: Friendly local, comfortable and clean, with plenty of character, good value bar meals, well kept St Austell ales, some tapped from the cask; popular live music nights, Sun quiz; reasonably priced bedrooms with own bathrooms, prodigious breakfast *(Jeanne and Paul Silvestri, the Didler)*

☆ *Star* [Fore St]: Harking back to the 60s in customers, style and relaxed atmosphere; interesting and informal dimly lit low-beamed local with good value home-made food from sandwiches and pasties up, well kept St Austell ales, farm cider in summer, mulled wine in winter; traditional games inc bar billiards, nostalgic juke box, local male voice choir usually in late Fri; tables in attractive back yard, simple bedrooms, good breakfast *(the Didler, Jeanne and Paul Silvestri, LYM, Brian Skelcher)*

ST KEVERNE [SW7921]

☆ *Three Tuns* [The Square]: Enthusiastic new licensees in relaxing village pub by church, well kept Greene King Abbot and Sharps Doom Bar, friendly helpful service, generous honest food, handsome high ceilings and lots of old photographs; picnic-sets out by square, attractive sea-view garden with pitch and putt, bedrooms *(Sue Holland, Dave Webster, BB, Helen White, Mrs Roxanne Chamberlain, Nicholas Pope)*

ST MABYN [SX0473]

St Mabyn Inn: Cheerful bustling country pub,

generous appetising restaurant food inc lots of fish, pleasant service, attractive décor, good choice of real ales inc Sharps Coaster and Doom Bar and Skinners, farm cider, interesting wines; darts *(the Didler, Margaret Mason, David Thompson)*

ST MAWES [SW8433]

Idle Rocks [Tredenham Rd (harbour edge)]: Newly extended waterfront hotel with enjoyable food from good sandwiches and bar snacks to brasserie/restaurant dishes (has been more of an evening restaurant out of season, must book), well kept Skinners Betty Stogs, good house wines, attentive welcoming service, superb sea view from bar and terrace tables; bedrooms *(Dennis Jenkin, MDN, E G Parish)*

☆ *Rising Sun* [The Square]: Close-set tables in tidy open-plan hotel bar with dozens of old Cornwall prints, interesting choice of reasonably priced good food here and in restaurant inc proper sandwiches and hugely popular Fri fish and chip night, well kept ales inc Sharps Doom Bar, decent wines, good coffee, efficient, welcoming and helpful staff; pleasant conservatory, slate-topped tables on sunny terrace just across lane from harbour wall of this pretty seaside village; dogs allowed, open all day summer, good value attractive bedrooms *(Jenny and Brian Seller, Lorraine and Fred Gill, Pamela and Merlyn Horswell, Dennis Jenkin, R and S Bentley, MDN, Gordon Stevenson, LYM)*

☆ *Victory* [Victory Hill]: Back on good form after refurbishment, good well served food from sandwiches and pasties to some interesting specials with inventive touches to the cooking in bar and upstairs restaurant, good no smoking area, friendly staff particularly helpful to families, warm log fires, Bass, Greene King Old Speckled Hen and Tetleys; comfortable bedrooms, good breakfast *(Jenny and Brian Seller, LYM, Jack Clark, David Pennington, Cliff Blakemore, Michael Dandy, Richard Till, Mayur Shah, Lorraine and Fred Gill, Geoff and Jan Dawson, Peter Gondris, Geoff Palmer, Alison Hayes, Pete Hanlon)*

ST MERRYN [SW8874]

☆ *Cornish Arms* [Churchtown (B3276 towards Padstow)]: Well kept St Austell ales, friendly efficient service and usual bar food at reasonable prices, also more extensive evening menu, in spotless local with fine slate floor, some 12th-c stonework, RNAS memorabilia; children over 6 may be allowed in eating area, good games room; picnic-sets out under cocktail parasols *(LYM, Alan M Pring, Alan and Paula McCully)*

Farmers Arms: Big busy family dining pub with several rooms, dark beams and panelling, floodlit well, no smoking area, well kept St Austell ales, good value house wine, simple lunches inc baguettes and pasties, wider evening choice inc carvery, quick service; tables on back terrace, bedrooms, open all day – handy for Trevose Head and superb walks *(Alan and Paula McCully)*

ST NEOT [SX1867]

☆ *London* [N of A38 Liskeard—Bodmin]:

Spotless 16th-c beamed country pub on Bodmin Moor, comfortable and airy with almost the feel of an upmarket hotel than a pub; cheerful efficient staff, good home-made food from sandwiches (normal or doorstep) up, Fullers London Pride and Sharps Doom Bar tapped from the cask, decent house wines (choice of glass sizes), two log fires, dining area behind trellis; unobtrusive piped music; attractive village in wooded valley, 15th-c church with outstanding medieval stained glass *(Dr and Mrs M E Wilson, Alan and Paula McCully, R G Price, Mrs B M Smith)*

ST TEATH [SX0680]

☆ *White Hart* [B3267]: Unpretentious flagstoned village pub with warm welcome, reasonably priced food from sandwiches to good steaks and good value Sun roasts, well kept Bass, Greene King Ruddles County and Sharps Doom Bar, decent wines, friendly attentive staff, sailor hat-ribands and ship's pennants from all over the world, coal fire, neat dining room off; games bar, live music wknds, children very welcome, open all day wknds, comfortably refurbished bedrooms, good breakfast *(Dr Paull Khan, LYM, Gloria Bax)*

ST TUDY [SX0676]

Cornish Arms [off A391 nr Wadebridge]: Friendly 16th-c beamed local with largish front bar, pool room and restaurant, good choice of well kept beer inc Sharps, bar food; children welcome *(anon)*

STICKER [SW9750]

Hewas [signed just off A390]: Warmly welcoming ivy-covered pub in pleasant village, flower-filled heated front terrace, good-sized bar with dining area each end (one no smoking), popular reasonably priced home-made food with some more unusual blackboard specials, three St Austell beers; back pool room, weekly entertainment and quiz *(Alan Bowker, Matt Waite)*

STITHIANS [SW7037]

Golden Lion [Stithians Lake, Menherion]: Welcoming pub with lakeside terrace, good sensibly priced food from sandwiches and other bar food to restaurant meals (busy Fri and wknds), well kept St Austell ales, friendly licensees, no smoking area *(Sue Rowland, Paul Mallett)*

STRATTON [SS2306]

Kings Arms [Howells Rd (A3072)]: Lively and friendly 17th-c three-room local with well kept Exmoor, Sharps and several guest beers, reasonably priced food, good service, attractive tiled tables; children welcome; piped music and central fruit machine may obtrude; tables out by car park *(Tracey and Stephen Groves)*

Tree [just E of Bude; Fore St]: Rambling 16th-c inn with cheerful family service, interesting old furniture, great log fires; dimly lit bar rooms get very busy at lunchtimes – or for big-screen sports TV; well kept ales inc Sharps Doom Bar, well priced generous food from soup and sandwiches to Sun carvery, character evening restaurant; children welcome in back bar; seats alongside unusual old dovecote in attractive ancient coachyard, bedrooms *(Tom Evans, BB)*

TREBARWITH [SX0586]

☆ *Mill House* [signed off B3263 and B3314 SE of Tintagel]: Marvellously placed in 12 acres of steep streamside woods above sea, black-beamed bar with fine Delabole flagstones, informal mix of furnishings and interesting local pictures, good rather upmarket food, well kept ales inc Sharps Doom Bar, restaurant; piped music; provision for dogs and children, tables out on terrace and by stream, 12 comfortable bedrooms, open all day *(MB, BB, M A Borthwick, Nick Farrow)*

TREEN [SW3824]

Logan Rock [just off B3315 Penzance—Lands End]: Relaxed local nr fine coast walks, low-beamed traditional bar with inglenook seat by hot coal fire, well kept ales inc Sharps, lots of games in family room, no smoking in small back snug with cricket memorabilia, friendly dogs (others allowed on leads); usual food (all day in summer) from sandwiches and pasties up, may be juke box or piped music, no children inside; tables in small sheltered garden *(Anthony Barnes, David Crook, Mr and Mrs McKay, the Didler, Gloria Bax, LYM, Helen Flaherty, Lucien Perring)*

TREGONY [SW9245]

☆ *Kings Arms* [Fore St (B3287)]: Well run old local, two chatty comfortable bars, well kept Skinners Betty Stogs and Heligan Honey and Tetleys, decent wine, friendly licensees, good value quickly served standard food inc fresh fish and Sun lunch, dining area with no smoking room; tables in pleasant garden, charming village *(Geoff Palmer, M G Hart, Christopher Wright)*

TREMATON [SX3959]

☆ *Crooked Inn* [off A38 just W of Saltash]: A tucked-away surprise, relaxed and friendly, down a long bumpy drive: lots of animal drawings and photographs, a good mix of furnishings in the big stepped bar, conservatory, generous bar food using local produce, well kept Sharps Own and Doom Bar, Skinners Cornish Knocker and St Austell HSD, decent wines, friendly service; great for children, with tame sheep, hens, ducks, rabbits, cats, dog and horses, courtyard tables and more out on the grass with a good play area, tree house and far views; open all day wknds, good bedrooms and breakfast *(Clive, David M Cundy, LYM, Ian Phillips, Esther and John Sprinkle, Laura Wilson)*

TRURO [SW8244]

Barley Sheaf [Old Bridge St, behind cathedral]: Stretches back through linked beamed areas, lots of wood, two chesterfields by the fire, well kept Boddingtons, Sharps Doom Bar and Skinners Cornish Knocker, decent low-priced standard food, conservatory; piped music, big-screen TV; suntrap terrace *(Patrick Hancock, David Crook, Ted George)*

☆ *City* [Pydar St]: Rambling bar with enjoyable food inc light lunchtime dishes, well kept Courage Best, Skinners Betty Stogs, Sharps Doom Bar and a guest beer, genuine character, cosy atmosphere, attractive bric-a-brac, cheerful helpful service, pool in room off;

sheltered back courtyard garden *(Tim and Ann Newell, Patrick Hancock)*

White Hart [New Bridge St (aka Crab & Ale House)]: Good food and beer in tidy efficiently run pub, nautical theme, friendly staff *(Ted George)*

TYWARDREATH [SX0854]

New Inn [off A3082; Fore St]: Friendly, informal and busy conversion of private house in nice village setting, well kept Bass tapped from the cask and St Austell ales on handpump, food (till 8 in evening), games and children's room; secluded garden, bedrooms *(the Didler, BB)*

UPTON CROSS [SX2772]

Caradon [B3254 N of Liskeard]: Pleasant country local with built-in banquettes and dark chairs, carpet over 17th-c flagstones, woodburner, pewter hanging from joists, Castella card collection, decorative plates, fish tank; cheery friendly staff, wide choice of good value generous home-made food, well kept Courage and Sharps Doom Bar and Wills Resolve, airy and comfortable public bar with pool; children welcome, some picnic-sets outside *(DAV, BB, Rona Murdoch)*

VERYAN [SW9139]

☆ *New Inn* [village signed off A3078]: Neat and comfortably homely one-bar beamed local with good value nourishing food inc popular Sun lunch, well kept St Austell ales, good house wines, good coffee, leisurely atmosphere, inglenook woodburner, lots of polished brass and old pictures, no smoking dining area; friendly alsatian and burmese cat; quiet garden behind the pretty house, bedrooms; interesting partly thatched village – nearby parking unlikely in summer *(the Didler, Bernard Stradling, Jeanne and Paul Silvestri, Patrick Renouf, Christopher Wright, John Moulder, Jenny and Brian Seller, Pauline and Philip Darley, BB, John and Joan Calvert)*

WATERGATE BAY [SW8464]

Phoenix: Spectacular coast views from open balcony, good value food inc interesting fish dishes, real ales, decent wines, sensible prices, friendly efficient staff *(Susan Ferris)*

WENDRON [SW6731]

Wendron Inn [B3297]: Village pub reopened under new name (was New Inn), well kept ales such as Greene King Abbot, Oakham JHB and Skinners Cornish Knocker, enjoyable food inc good value roasts, welcoming staff; bedrooms *(Pete and Rosie Flower)*

WIDEMOUTH [SS2002]

Bay View [Marine Drive]: Open-plan, with fine views over beach, good value food, well kept Sharps Doom Bar and Own, Skinners Betty Stogs and a beer brewed for the pub; open all day in summer, bedrooms *(the Didler)*

ZELAH [SW8151]

Hawkins Arms [A30]: Cosy, warm and comfortable 18th-c beamed stone-built local, log fire, generous good value fresh food inc Sun roast, half a dozen real ales inc Skinners, farm cider, copper and brass in bar and dining room; quiet piped music, TV, can be smoky; children and dogs welcome, pub golden

retriever, bedrooms *(CMW, JJW, Dr B and Mrs P B Baker, JP, PP)*
ZENNOR [SW4538]
Tinners Arms [B3306 W of St Ives]: Unaffected and relaxed country local in lovely windswept setting by church nr coast path, usually ales such as Sharps and Wadworths 6X kept well in casks behind bar, Lane's farm cider, decent coffee, friendly licensees, dogs and cats, flagstones, granite and stripped pine, real fires each end, back pool room (where children may be allowed), no music; limited food (all day in summer inc cream teas); tables in small suntrap courtyard, fine long walk from St Ives *(the Didler, Maggie and Tony Harwood, Jacquie and Jim Jones, Peter and Anne Hollindale, Mr and Mrs McKay, LYM, Gloria Bax)*

ISLES OF SCILLY
BRYHER [SV8715]
Fraggle Rock: Tiny friendly waterside local with good pizzas in upstairs eating area; campsite a field away *(Pete and Rosie Flower)*
ST MARTIN'S [SV9215]
Seven Stones [Lower Town]: Stunning location and sea-and-islands view, 11 steps up to big main bar nicely and unpretentiously reworked inside, friendly ex-HGV landlord, well kept Sharps Doom Bar and St Austell Triumph, appealing reasonably priced fresh food inc pizzas, pasta, steaks and local crab, summer teas and sandwiches, bar billiards, nice window seats; terrace tables, limited winter opening *(D and M T Ayres-Regan, Pete and Rosie Flower, Peter Meister, Bernard Stradling)*
ST MARY'S [SV9010]
☆ *Atlantic Inn* [The Strand; next to but

independent from Atlantic Hotel]: Spreading rather dark bar with nice little room at one end, low beams, hanging boat and lots of nautical bits and pieces, flowery-patterned seats, bar food (best to book for sizeable brighter restaurant overlooking harbour – local fish is good), reasonably priced St Austell ales inc XXXX Mild, friendly landlord, efficient service, mix of locals and tourists; darts, pool, fruit machines; little terrace with green cast-iron furniture and wide views, good bedrooms *(Pete and Rosie Flower, Neil and Anita Christopher, Theocsbrian, Kevin Thorpe, BB)*
☆ *Bishop & Wolf* [Hugh St/Silver St (A3110)]: Lively and friendly local atmosphere, interesting sea/boating décor with secluded corners and gallery above road, nets, lots of woodwork and maritime bric-a-brac, lifeboat photographs, friendly helpful staff, well kept St Austell Tinners and HSD, very wide choice of good generous food with plenty of seafood (should book, attractive relaxed upstairs restaurant – no bar food after 7.30); piped music, popular summer live music *(Pete and Rosie Flower, Neil and Anita Christopher, Peter Meister)*
Mermaid [The Quay]: Thorough-going nautical theme, with lots of seafaring relics, rough timber, stone floor, dim lighting, big stove, and amazing antics during the annual world gig-rowing championships, inc dancing on the tables; picture-window all-day restaurant with spectacular views across town beach and harbour, may be Boddingtons and Flowers; cellar bar with boat counter, pool table, TV and music for young people (live wknds) *(Pete and Rosie Flower, Roger and Jenny Huggins)*

'Children welcome' means the pub says it lets children inside without any special restriction. If it allows them in, but to restricted areas such as an eating area or family room, we specify this. Places with separate restaurants usually let children use them, hotels usually let them into public areas such as lounges. Some pubs impose an evening time limit – let us know if you find this.

Cumbria

Top pubs up here these days, most of them in lovely positions, include the quiet and comfortable Barbon Inn (well liked as a place to stay), the smart and civilised Pheasant near Bassenthwaite Lake (lovely food, good wines, super to stay at), the cosy Blacksmiths Arms at Broughton Mills (good food using local supplies), the Pheasant at Casterton (a consistently good all-rounder), the Punch Bowl at Crosthwaite (delicious food in an idyllic setting, fine wine choice), the classic Britannia at Elterwater (very well run, a great favourite), the nicely set Shepherds Arms at Ennerdale Bridge (doing very well under new licensees), the upmarket Drunken Duck near Hawkshead (very good for a smart meal or luxurious stay), the Watermill at Ings (particularly for its great beer choice), the Kirkstile Inn at Loweswater (nice food and particularly helpful staff – they're kind to wet walkers), the Mill Inn at Mungrisdale (another place where the hard-working licensees make all the difference), the Newfield Inn at Seathwaite (a walkers' and climbers' favourite), the Blacksmiths Arms at Talkin (a friendly and well run all-rounder), the interesting Queens Head at Troutbeck, and the restauranty Bay Horse near Ulverston (civilised and smart, with lovely food). This year we also welcome as new entries the Queens Head in Hawkshead (friendly staff and delicious food), the neatly refurbished Herdwick at Penruddock (good all round) and the Masons Arms on Cartmel Fell – back in the Guide after a break, its newish licensees and the changes they are making settling in well now. The Pheasant, Punch Bowl, Drunken Duck, Bay Horse and the Hawkshead Queens Head are all rewarding for a special meal out: for the second year running, the Drunken Duck near Hawkshead takes the title of Cumbria Dining Pub of the Year. From a splendid choice of places in the Lucky Dip section at the end of the chapter, we'd pick out particularly the Olde Fighting Cocks in Arnside, Brook House at Boot, Hole in t' Wall in Bowness, Wheatsheaf at Brigsteer, Manor Arms in Broughton-in-Furness, Dutton Arms at Burton-in-Kendal, Sun at Crook, Royal at Dockray, Stag at Dufton, George & Dragon at Garrigill, Highland Drove at Great Salkeld, Swinside Inn near Keswick, White Horse at Scales, Greyhound at Shap, Eagle & Child at Staveley and Church House at Torver. On average, drinks prices here are comfortably below the national norm. The Blue Bell in Heversham holds the bargain banner for its very low-priced Sam Smiths beer; the Golden Rule in Ambleside and Black Dog in Dalton-in-Furness are also good value. Jennings is the main local brewer, with Yates featuring fairly widely too, and the new Hawkshead brewery beginning to make an impact on the local beer scene; and a bonus is that several pubs here brew their own good beers.

Anyone claiming to arrange or prevent inclusion of a pub in the *Guide* is a fraud. Pubs are included only if recommended by genuine readers and if our own anonymous inspection confirms that they are suitable.

AMBLESIDE NY3804 Map 9
Golden Rule

Smithy Brow; follow Kirkstone Pass signpost from A591 on N side of town

Although this is a straightforward town local, it is made special by the genuine welcome from both the jovial landlord who runs it and the chatty and friendly locals. The bar has lots of local country pictures and a few fox masks decorating the butter-coloured walls, horsebrasses on the black beams, built-in leatherette wall seats, and cast-iron-framed tables; dominoes and cribbage. The no smoking room on the left has darts and a fruit machine, and the one down a few steps on the right has lots of seating. Well kept Hartleys XB and Cumbrian Way, and Robinsons Best, Frederics, Hatters Mild, and Old Stockport on handpump; pork pies (75p), and filled rolls (£2). There's a back yard with tables, and especially colourful window boxes. The golden rule referred to in its name is a brass measuring yard mounted over the bar counter. *(Recommended by Mike and Sue Loseby, Mayur Shah, P Abbott, MLR)*

Robinsons ~ Tenant John Lockley ~ Real ale ~ No credit cards ~ (015394) 32257 ~ Children welcome until 9pm ~ Dogs welcome ~ Open 11-11; 12-10.30 Sun

APPLEBY NY6921 Map 10
Royal Oak

B6542/Bongate is E of the main bridge over the River Eden

This old-fashioned coaching inn has a good open fire in the oak-panelled public bar and a chatty, relaxed atmosphere, and the beamed lounge has old pictures on the timbered walls, some armchairs and a carved settle, and a panelling-and-glass snug enclosing the bar counter; dominoes and cribbage. Bar food includes home-made soup (£2.25), filled baguettes (from £3.75), chicken liver pâté (£3.95), toasted local goats cheese with warm red pepper marmalade (£4.95), local sausages (£5.95), steak in ale pie or red peppers stuffed with couscous and tomato sauce (£6.95), popular chicken topped with bacon, glazed with stilton and served with a barbecue sauce (£7.95), pork medallions in a madeira and cream sauce (£9.95), and steaks (from £9.95). The restaurant is no smoking. Well kept Black Sheep and John Smiths, with a couple of guests such as Barngates Tag Lag or Hop Back Crop Circle on handpump, and a good range of wines and malt whiskies; TV. There are seats on the front terrace, and attractive flowering tubs, troughs and hanging baskets. You can get here on the scenic Leeds/Settle/Carlisle railway (best to check times and any possible delays to avoid missing lunch). *(Recommended by Guy Vowles, Angus Lyon, Greta and Christopher Wells, Paul A Moore, JWAC, Linda Reiterbund , Ron and Mary Nicholson, Brian and Janet Ainscough, David Edwards, MLR, Diane Manoughian, Jeremy Woods)*

Mortal Man Inns ~ Manager Tim Collins ~ Real ale ~ Bar food (12-2.30, 6-9(8 Sun)) ~ Restaurant ~ (01768) 351463 ~ Children in family room ~ Dogs allowed in bar ~ Open 11-11; 12-10.30 Sun ~ Bedrooms: £35B/£69B

BARBON SD6282 Map 10
Barbon Inn 🛏

Village signposted off A683 Kirkby Lonsdale—Sedbergh; OS Sheet 97 map reference 628826

The quiet and comfortable little bedrooms in this friendly 17th-c coaching inn are well liked by our readers, and some overlook the lovely sheltered and prettily planted garden; plenty of surrounding tracks and paths all around to walk along. Several small rooms lead off the simple bar with its blackened range, each individually and comfortably furnished: carved 18th-c oak settles, comfortable sofas and armchairs, a Victorian fireplace. Reasonably priced bar food includes sandwiches or home-made soup (£2.50), home-made pâté (£3.95), morecambe bay shrimps (£4.95), cod and chips or cumberland sausage (£5.95), steak in ale pie or mushroom stroganoff (£6.95), gammon steak (£7.95), and rib-eye steak (£8.95); the restaurant is no smoking. Well kept Theakstons Best and a guest such as

Marstons Pedigree on handpump; dominoes and piped music. *(Recommended by Vivienne and Alan Morland, Mr and Mrs W D Borthwick, R M Corlett, Margaret Dickinson)*

Free house ~ Licensee Lindsey MacDiarmid ~ Real ale ~ Bar food ~ Restaurant ~ (015242) 76233 ~ Children welcome ~ Dogs allowed in bar ~ Open 12-2.30(3 Sat), 6.30-11(10.30 Sun) ~ Bedrooms: £30(£40B)/£65B

BASSENTHWAITE LAKE NY1930 Map 9
Pheasant ★ ⊕ ♀ ⇌

Follow Pheasant Inn sign at N end of dual carriageway stretch of A66 by Bassenthwaite Lake

Civilised and rather smart, this very well run hotel does have customers who drop in for a quick pint, but most people like to make the best of the particularly good food and lovely, comfortable bedrooms. The little bar remains as pleasantly old-fashioned and pubby as ever, with mellow polished walls, cushioned oak settles, rush-seat chairs and library seats, hunting prints and photographs, and well kept Bass, Jennings Cumberland, and Theakstons Best on handpump; a dozen good wines by the glass and over 50 malt whiskies. Several comfortable lounges have log fires, fine parquet flooring, antiques, and plants; one is no smoking – as is the restaurant. Enjoyable lunchtime bar food includes soup with home-made bread (£3.25), salmon mousse (£5.75), open sandwiches with home-made crisps (from £5.45; prawns with guacamole, served with a chilli, mint and mango salsa £6.25), potted silloth shrimps (£6.35), ploughman's (£5.95), pasta with prawns and chargrilled artichokes (£7.75), stir-fried chicken with chilli and ginger (£8.75), braised local venison (£9.95), fillet of smoked haddock on a bed of spinach with a light cheese sauce topped with a poached egg (£10.95), and puddings (from £4.25). There are seats in the garden, attractive woodland surroundings, and plenty of walks in all directions. *(Recommended by Peter F Marshall, Peter Burton, Dr D J and Mrs S C Walker, John Hale, Alan Thwaite, Jack Clark, John and Sheila Lister, David and Ruth Shillitoe; also in the Good Hotel Guide)*

Free house ~ Licensee Matthew Wylie ~ Real ale ~ Bar food (not in evening – restaurant only) ~ Restaurant ~ (017687) 76234 ~ Children in eating area of bar and in restaurant if over 8 ~ Dogs allowed in bar ~ Open 11.30-2.30, 5.30-11; 12-2.30, 6-10.30 Sun; closed 25 Dec ~ Bedrooms: £75B/£140B

BEETHAM SD5079 Map 7
Wheatsheaf ♀ ⇌

Village (and inn) signposted just off A6 S of Milnthorpe

New licensees have taken over this 16th-c coaching inn and have added new soft furnishings and artefacts to the bars. The opened-up front lounge bar has lots of exposed beams and joists, and the main bar is behind on the right, with well kept Jennings Cumberland and 1828, and a fortnightly changing guest beer on handpump, and a fine choice of new world wines by the glass; there's also a cosy and relaxing smaller room for drinkers, and a roaring log fire. Piped music, dominoes, chess and cards. Good lunchtime bar food now includes home-made soup (£2.95), sandwiches (£4.50), ploughman's (£5.25), crab and salmon fishcakes with a sweet and sour dipping sauce (£5.50), chick pea, spring onion and garlic bakes with a coconut cream sauce (£7.50), beef in ale pie or gammon with pineapple (£7.95), and braised lamb shank with red wine and redcurrant gravy (£10.95), with evening dishes like prawns in a chive and lemon dressing wrapped in smoked salmon (£5.95), seared scallops on puréed cauliflower with caviar-filled cherry tomatoes (£6.95), vegetable korma (£7.95), chicken stuffed with white stilton and apricot cheese, wrapped in pancetta with a little chilli oil (£12.95), and gressingham duck in honey, soy and coriander with redcurrant and cranberry sauce (£14.95). *(Recommended by Gerald Wilkinson, John Foord, Chris and Duncan Grant, Mr and Mrs C J Frodsham, Maurice and Gill McMahon, Revd D Glover, Geoff and Angela Jaques, Jean and Douglas Troup, Roger Everett, Jim Bush, David Carr, Mike Green, Tim and Judy Barker)*

Free house ~ Licensees Mark and Kath Chambers ~ Real ale ~ Bar food (12-2, 6-9) ~ Restaurant ~ (015395) 62123 ~ Children in eating area of bar ~ Open 11.30-3, 5.30-11; 12-3, 6.30-10.30 Sun ~ Bedrooms: £55B/£65B

BOUTH SD3386 Map 9
White Hart ♦
Village signposted off A590 near Haverthwaite

The half a dozen or so real ales kept well on handpump in this authentic Lakeland inn certainly draw in customers: Black Sheep, Jennings Cumberland, and Tetleys, and changing guests such as Hawkshead Bitter, Timothy Taylors Landlord, and Yates Bitter. They also have 40 malt whiskies. The sloping ceilings and floors show the building's age, and there are lots of old local photographs and bric-a-brac – farm tools, stuffed animals, a collection of long-stemmed clay pipes – and two log fires, one in a woodburning stove. The games room has darts, pool, dominoes, fruit machine, TV, table football, and juke box; piped music. Bar food includes sandwiches, soups, pizzas (from £6.25), salads (from £7.25), vegetarian chilli (£7.25), sirloin steak (10.95), and daily specials like herdwick lamb (£8.95) or bass with Pernod and fennel (£10.25); there may be quite a wait. The restaurant is no smoking. Seats out in the attractively planted garden, and plenty of surrounding walks. Two more bedrooms have been added this year. *(Recommended by Jane Taylor, David Dutton, JDM, KM, Michael Doswell, Mr and Mrs W D Borthwick, S and R Gray, Dr B and Mrs P B Baker, Sheila and Phil Stubbs, Karen Eliot, Margaret and Roy Randle, Margaret Dickinson)*

Free house ~ Licensees Nigel and Peter Barton ~ Real ale ~ Bar food (12-2, 6-8.45; not Mon or Tues lunchtime) ~ Restaurant ~ (01229) 861229 ~ No credit cards ~ Children in eating areas and family room until 9pm ~ Open 12-2, 6-11; 12-11 Sat; 12-10.30 Sun; closed Mon and Tues lunchtimes (exc bank hols) ~ Bedrooms: £42S/£70S(£50B)

BROUGHTON MILLS SD2190 Map 9
Blacksmiths Arms
Off A593 N of Broughton-in-Furness

After a day on the fells, the thought of the roaring open fires and enjoyable food in this charming little pub is most heart-warming. Three of the four simply but attractively decorated small rooms have open fires; ancient slate floors, and well kept Jennings Cumberland plus Barngates Tag Lag and Dent Aviator on handpump, summer farm cider, and interesting bottled beers. Bar food is very good and they use meat from local farms, and local game and fish: filled baguettes or pitta pockets (from £3.25), cheese, leek and caramelised red onion flan (£6.75), steak and kidney pie or cumberland sausage (£6.95), italian baked fish (£7.95), roast duck with lakeland honey (£9.45), daily specials like pasta with creamy wild mushrooms (£5.95), herdwick lamb or pork chop in a cider and apple sauce (£6.95), local wild brown trout (£7.45), slow-roasted wild venison (£7.95), and steaks (from £10); they sell local organic bread. There are three smallish dining rooms (the back one is no smoking). Darts, dominoes, and children's books and games. Pretty summer hanging baskets and tubs of flowers in front of the building. *(Recommended by Derek Harvey-Piper, JES, S and R Gray, Dave Braisted, Angus Lyon, Julie and Bill Ryan, Margaret Dickinson)*

Free house ~ Licensee Philip Blackburn ~ Real ale ~ Bar food (not winter Mon lunchtime) ~ Restaurant ~ (01229) 716824 ~ Children welcome ~ Dogs allowed in bar ~ Open 12-11; 12-10.30 Sun; 5-11 Mon (cl winter Mon), 12-2.30, 5-11 Tues-Fri in winter; closed 25 Dec

Please tell us if any Lucky Dips deserve to be upgraded to a main entry – and why. No stamp needed: The Good Pub Guide, FREEPOST TN1569, Wadhurst, E Sussex TN5 7BR.

BUTTERMERE NY1817 Map 9
Bridge Hotel 🛏

Just off B5289 SW of Keswick

This chatty, friendly inn is a fine place to stop for lunch while enjoying some of the lovely surrounding walks; Crummock Water and Buttermere are just a stroll away. The flagstoned area in the beamed bar is good for walking boots, and has built-in wooden settles and farmhouse chairs around traditional tables, a panelled bar counter and a few horsebrasses, and there's a dining bar with brocaded armchairs around copper-topped tables, and brass ornaments hanging from the beams; the restaurant and guest lounge are no smoking. Tasty bar food includes lots of interesting sandwiches, filled baguettes and toasties such as cajun chicken with garlic mayonnaise, brie and cranberry or hot cumbrian ham, dijon mustard and melted cheddar, and chicken and peppers with tomato salsa in a tortilla wrap (from £3.25), home-made burgers with different toppings (from £4.50), ploughman's (£4.95), butterbean casserole (£6.65), cumberland sausage with apple sauce and onion gravy (£6.95), and lamb hotpot (£7.20). Well kept Black Sheep, Flowers IPA, and Theakstons Old Peculier on handpump, quite a few malt whiskies, and a decent wine list. Outside, a flagstoned terrace has white tables by a rose-covered sheltering stone wall. The views from the bedrooms are marvellous; please note, the bedroom prices are for dinner, bed and breakfast; self-catering, too. *(Recommended by Tracey and Stephen Groves, Filip Lemmens, Richard J Holloway, Rod Stoneman, Dr D J and Mrs S C Walker)*

Free house ~ Licensee Peter McGuire ~ Real ale ~ Bar food (12-9.30) ~ Restaurant ~ (017687) 70252 ~ Children in eating area of bar and, if over 7, in restaurant ~ Dogs allowed in bedrooms ~ Open 10.30-11; 10.30-10.30 Sun; closed second week Jan ~ Bedrooms: £73B/£146B

CARTMEL FELL SD4288 Map 9
Masons Arms 🍷

Strawberry Bank, a few miles S of Windermere between A592 and A5074; perhaps the simplest way of finding the pub is to go uphill W from Bowland Bridge (which is signposted off A5074) towards Newby Bridge and keep right then left at the staggered crossroads – it's then on your right, below Gummer's How; OS Sheet 97 map reference 413895

An upstairs dining area, similarly furnished to the downstairs bars, has been opened up in this hard-to-find pub, and there are newly refurbished self-catering cottages and apartments behind. The main bar has plenty of character, with low black beams in the bowed ceiling, country chairs and plain wooden tables on polished flagstones, and a grandly Gothick seat with snarling dogs as its arms. A small lounge has oak tables and settles to match its fine Jacobean panelling, there's a plain little room beyond the serving counter with pictures and a fire in an open range, and a family room with an old-parlourish atmosphere. Well kept Black Sheep, Hawkshead Bitter, Timothy Taylors Best and Landlord, and a guest like Jennings Cocker Hoop on handpump. Generous helpings of enjoyable bar food include home-made soup (£3.25), filled baked potatoes (£4.50), sandwiches (from £4.50), barbecued ribs (£5.25), ploughman's (£6.25), meaty or vegetarian lasagne (£7.50), home-made steak and kidney pudding (£8.95), minted lamb shoulder (£9.95), and whole baked bass with an oriental marinade (£10.50). On the front terrace, there are rustic benches and tables with an unrivalled view overlooking the Winster Valley to the woods below Whitbarrow Scar. *(Recommended by John Dwane, Deb and John Arthur, S and R Gray, Mr and Mrs Maurice Thompson, Anthony Rickards Collinson, Malcolm Taylor)*

Free house ~ Licensee Helen Parker ~ Real ale ~ Bar food ~ Restaurant ~ (015395) 68486 ~ Children welcome ~ Dogs allowed in bar ~ Live jazz Weds evenings ~ Open 11.30-11; 12-10.30 Sun

CASTERTON SD6279 Map 10

Pheasant ♀ 🛏

A683 about 1 mile N of junction with A65, by Kirkby Lonsdale; OS Sheet 97 map reference 633796

You can be sure of a warm welcome in this civilised inn, both from the hardworking licensees and from the friendly crowd of locals enjoying the well kept real ales. The neatly kept and attractively modernised beamed rooms of the main bar (some have been redecorated this year) have padded wheelback chairs, cushioned wall settles, newspapers and magazines to read, a woodburning stove surrounded by brass ornaments in a nicely arched bare stone fireplace, and Theakstons Bitter and guests such as Black Sheep Bitter, Dent Aviator or Marstons Pedigree on handpump; over 30 malt whiskies, and a good wine list offering 12 by the glass. There's a further room (which is no smoking) across the passage with a piano. Good bar food includes home-made soup (£2.95), lunchtime sandwiches (from £3.25), chicken liver pâté with fruit coulis (£4.50), smoked salmon and scrambled eggs (£5.95), local cumberland sausage with onion gravy (£6.95), steak in ale pie (£7.25), spinach, feta cheese and mushroom strudel with salsa sauce (£7.95), aberdeen angus steaks (from £12.95), daily specials such as goats cheese on garlic ciabatta with roasted peppers (£5.25), lamb curry (£8.95), honey-baked lamb with redcurrant and minted gravy (£9.50), and red snapper fillet with a sweet chilli sauce (£11.95), and home-made puddings (from £3.95). The restaurant is no smoking. Darts, dominoes, chess, cards, and piped music. There are some tables with cocktail parasols outside by the road, with more in the pleasant garden. The nearby church (built for the girls' school of Brontë fame here) has some attractive pre-Raphaelite stained glass and paintings. *(Recommended by Robert Hill, Brian and Anita Randall, Pierre and Pat Richterich, Deb and John Arthur, Malcolm Taylor, Revd D Glover, Peter Walker)*

Free house ~ Licensees Melvin and May Mackie ~ Real ale ~ Bar food ~ Restaurant ~ (015242) 71230 ~ Children welcome ~ Dogs welcome ~ Open 11-3, 6-11(10.30 Sun); closed 25 and 26 Dec ~ Bedrooms: £42B/£80B

COCKERMOUTH NY1231 Map 9

Bitter End ◖ £

Kirkgate, by cinema

The atmosphere in this interestingly furnished pub is bustling and friendly, helped by a good mix of customers. There's a view of the little brewery through a tiny Victorian-style window where the landlord brews his own Cuddy Luggs, Cocker Snoot and Farmers Ale; he also keeps several Jennings ales, and two or three differing weekly guests on handpump, in good condition; quite a few bottled beers from around the world. The three main rooms have a different atmosphere in each – from quietly chatty to sporty, with the décor reflecting this, such as unusual pictures of a Cockermouth that even Wordsworth might have recognised, to more up-to-date sporting memorabilia, and framed beer mats. Some tables in the front bar are no smoking. As well as simple lunchtime snacks, the good value bar food includes cumberland sausage (£6.15), three cheese pasta and broccoli bake or fish and chips (£6.25), chicken tikka masala (£6.45), lasagne or steak and mushroom in ale pie (£6.45), and daily specials. Service is very welcoming; piped music. The public car park round the back is free after 6. *(Recommended by Edward Mirzoeff, Gerald and Wendy Doyle, Christine and Neil Townend, Kevin Flack, David and Rhian Peters, R M Corlett, MLR)*

Own brew ~ Licensee Susan Askey ~ Real ale ~ Bar food ~ (01900) 828993 ~ Children in eating area of bar ~ Open 12-2.30, 6-11; 11.30-11 Sat; 12-3, 7-10.30 Sun

> Children: if the details at the end of an entry don't mention them, you should assume that the pub does not allow them inside.

CONISTON SD3098 Map 9
Sun ◖

Pub signposted from centre

This 16th-c pub is in a spectacular position, surrounded by dramatic bare fells, and there are seats and tables in front, and in the big tree-sheltered garden, which make the most of the lovely views. Inside, the old-fashioned, classic Lakeland bar has walls stripped back to the stonework, ceiling beams, a flagstoned floor, and a 19th-c range with leaping hare tiles; also, cask seats and cast-iron-framed tables, old Victorian settles, and Donald Campbell photographs (this was his HQ during his final attempt on the world water speed record). Some readers feel a lick of paint might not go amiss. There's a public lounge next to the conservatory. Well liked bar food includes home-made soups such as ham, bean and bacon (from £3.95), sandwiches using home-made bread (from £5.15), pork and apricot terrine (£5.50), lamb hotpot (£8), steak and kidney cobbler or vegetable pie (£8.50), cumberland sausage (£11.50), honey-roast duck breast (£14.50), 16oz T-bone steak (£16), daily specials, and puddings; vegetables are extra (from £2.25). Five well kept real ales on handpump: Coniston Bluebird, Moorhouses Black Cat, and guests from Barngates, Black Sheep, Hawkshead, and Yates, a decent wine list, a growing number of malt whiskies. Darts, cribbage, and dominoes. (*Recommended by Tina and David Woods-Taylor, P Abbott, Jim Abbott, Keith Jacob, Mike and Sue Loseby, Lorraine and Fred Gill, Mr S J Lawton, Neil and Anita Christopher, S and R Gray, John Foord, JDM, KM, K Nicholls, Ewan and Moira McCall*)

Free house ~ Licensee Alan Piper ~ Real ale ~ Bar food (12-2.30, 6-9) ~ Restaurant ~ (015394) 41248 ~ Children in eating area of bar and restaurant ~ Dogs allowed in bar ~ Open 11-11; 12-10.30 Sun ~ Bedrooms: £35S/£70S(£80B)

CROSTHWAITE SD4491 Map 9
Punch Bowl ⏧ ♀

Village signposted off A5074 SE of Windermere

Although customers do pop in to this 16th-c inn – set next to the old church and overlooking a lovely narrow valley – most come to enjoy the excellent and imaginative food. It's also a nice place to stay. There are several separate areas carefully reworked to give a lot of space, and a high-raftered central part by the serving counter with an upper minstrel's gallery on either side; all areas are no smoking except the bar. Steps lead down into a couple of small rooms on the right, and there's a doorway through into two more airy rooms on the left. It's all spick and span, with lots of tables and chairs, beams, pictures by local artist Derek Farman, and an open fire. As well as a set-price lunch (two courses £9.95, three courses £12.95), the menu might include sandwiches, cream of tomato and basil soup (£2.75), chicken liver parfait with warm button onions, sultanas, toasted pine kernels, and a damson balsamic glaze (£5.25), oven-baked goats cheese on filo with roast beetroot and crumbled roquefort (£5.95), baked aubergine filled with ratatouille (£8.95), chargrilled breast of chicken on a fondant potato and buttered spinach with a caramelised orange jus (£8.25), boned and rolled stuffed saddle of rabbit with a tarragon wild mushroom sauce (£14), local fillet steak on horseradish mash with a truffle and madeira sauce (£14.50), daily specials such as chargrilled tuna fillet on spiced sweet potato mash with soy, spring onion and ginger dressing (£6.25), and bass fillet with a sweet red pepper tomato sauce with grilled tiger prawns (£14.75), and puddings like steamed white chocolate and vanilla sponge with seville marmalade ice cream and an orange Grand Marnier anglaise, honey and Drambuie crème brûlée or mango and raspberry sorbet (from £3.95). Well kept Adnams, Black Sheep, and Coniston Bluebird on handpump, a carefully chosen wine list with 21 by the glass, and several malt whiskies. There are some tables on a terrace stepped into the hillside. (*Recommended by RDK, C Tranmer, W K Wood, Derek and Margaret Underwood, John and Sylvia Harrop, Revd D Glover, Margaret and Roy Randle, Maurice and Gill McMahon, Tracey and Stephen Groves, Roger Stock, Gwyneth and Salvo Spadaro-Dutturi, John Saul*)

Free house ~ Licensee Steven Doherty ~ Real ale ~ Bar food (not Sun evening, not Mon) ~ Restaurant ~ (015395) 68237 ~ Children welcome ~ Dogs allowed in bar ~ Open 11-11; 12-3 Sun; closed Sun evening, all day Mon, 1 wk Jan, 1 wk May or June, 1 wk Nov, 1 wk Dec ~ Bedrooms: £37.50B/£60B

DALTON-IN-FURNESS SD2376 Map 7

Black Dog ◄ £

Holmes Green, Broughton Road; 1 mile N of town, beyond A590

On Sunday mornings you can now have a full english breakfast (£3.95, from 9 to 12) in the newly refurbished brasserie of this simple and comfortable local; access is from the terrace in the car park. The unpretentious bar has beer mats and brasses around the beams, two log fires, partly tiled and flagstoned floor, and plain wooden tables and chairs; there may be several dried hams hanging above the bar counter. A side terrace has a few plastic tables and chairs. Good value hearty bar food – all home-made – includes soup (£1.75), sandwiches (from £1.95), omelettes (from £3.95), cumberland sausage or leek and potato bake (£4.50), chicken curry or beef stew (£5.25), poached hake fillets with parsley sauce (£5.95), sirloin steak (£7.95), daily specials like dry-cured ham and eggs (£3.25), black pudding platter (£3.95) or lamb cutlets with garlic and mushroom sauce (£4.95), and puddings such as blackberry and apple crumble or chocolate sponge (£2.20). The seven real ales change constantly but might include Barngates Catnap, Brysons Shrimpers Stout, Dent Aviator, Highgate Mild, Timothy Taylors Landlord, and Yorkshire Terrier on handpump; they also have three or four farm ciders, a farm perry, home-made lemonade, and mulled wine. Table skittles, bar billiards, shove-ha'penny, cribbage, and dominoes. The pub is handy for the South Lakes Wild Animal Park. More reports please. *(Recommended by Richard Gibbs)*

Free house ~ Licensees Jack Taylor and Julia Walker ~ Real ale ~ Bar food (12-2, 5-8; all day weekends) ~ Restaurant ~ (01229) 462561 ~ Children welcome ~ Dogs welcome ~ Open 12-11; 12-10.30 Sun; closed weekday lunchtimes Oct-end April ~ Bedrooms: £17.50(£25B)/£40S

ELTERWATER NY3305 Map 9

Britannia ★ ◄ ⌘

Off B5343

As this thriving inn is so well placed in the heart of the Lake District, close to Langdale and the central lakes, and with tracks over the fells to Grasmere and Easedale, it's not surprisingly very popular with walkers. At peak times, despite the friendly efficiency of the licensees and their staff, there are inevitable queues. As well as a small and traditionally furnished back bar, there's a front one with a couple of window seats looking across to Elterwater itself through the trees on the far side: cosy coal fires, oak benches, settles, windsor chairs, a big old rocking chair, well kept Coniston Bluebird, Jennings, Tetleys, Timothy Taylors Landlord, and Yates Bitter on handpump, lots of malt whiskies, a few country wines, and winter mulled wine; the lounge is comfortable. Good, popular bar food includes lunchtime filled rolls (from £2.90; beef with onion gravy £3.50), home-made soup (£2.95), filled baked potatoes (£3.90), home-made quiche (£4.95) or home-made langdale pie (£7.25), with evening dishes such as home-made pâté with cumberland sauce or deep-fried brie wedges with fruit coulis (£4.25), home-made lamb rogan josh, steak and mushroom pie, grilled trout fillet with lemon and dill butter (£8.95), and puddings like hot banana with butterscotch pancakes or bread and butter pudding (£3.85); super breakfasts and home-baked fruit scones for afternoon cream teas. The main bar, restaurant and residents' lounge are no smoking; dominoes and cribbage. In summer, people flock to watch the morris and step and garland dancers. The bedrooms are to be refurbished. Plenty of seats outside. *(Recommended by Roy and Lindsey Fentiman, Andy and Ali, SLC, Ian and Jane Irving, Neil and Jean Spink, John Foord, Michael Doswell, M S L Webster, Dr S Edwards, S and R Gray, Tina and David Woods-Taylor, Mr and Mrs Maurice Thompson, Dave Irving, Trevor Hosking, Roger and*

Jenny Huggins, David Carr, Steve and Liz Tilley, A Sadler, Richard and Karen Holt, Ewan and Moira McCall, Mayur Shah, Jane Taylor, David Dutton, Margaret Dickinson)

Free house ~ Licensees Clare Woodhead and Christopher Jones ~ Real ale ~ Bar food (all day) ~ Restaurant ~ (015394) 37210 ~ Children welcome ~ Dogs allowed in bar ~ Quiz Sun evenings ~ Open 11-11; 12-10.30 Sun; closed 25 and 26 Dec ~ Bedrooms: /£72(£80S)

ENNERDALE BRIDGE NY0716 Map 9
Shepherds Arms ♀ ◖ ▭

Ennerdale signposted off A5086 at Cleator Moor E of Egremont; it's on the scenic back road from Calder Bridge to Loweswater

The new licensee has hung over 300 pictures since taking over this marvellously placed inn – there are over 80 in the bar alone. This is somewhere that genuinely welcomes walkers, however wet and miserable, and there's a detailed pictorial display of the off-road footpath plans in the porch, a daily updated weather-forecast blackboard, and a bookcase full of interest, including Wainwright books – it's on his popular coast-to-coast path. The friendly bar has its serving counter in a bare-boards inner area up three steps, with a longcase clock and a woodburning stove below a big beam hung with copper and brass objects. Its carpeted main part has an open log fire and a homely variety of comfortable seats; it opens into a small brick-floored no smoking extension with pub tables and objets d'art. Substantial bar food – using local meat and fish and only fresh vegetables – includes home-made carrot and coriander soup (£2.75), sandwiches (from £2.75), home-made chicken liver pâté (£3.95), omelettes (from £6.50), cumberland sausage with fried egg or pineapple (£6.95), several vegetarian dishes such as mixed bean casserole or home-made spinach and wensleydale tart (£5.95), home-made lasagne (£6.50), home-made steak in ale pie (£7.50), sirloin steak (£10.95), daily specials like fresh tiger prawns with a lime and garlic dressing (£5.95), wild rabbit casserole with cider, cream and calvados (£8.95), fresh swordfish with a chardonnay hollandaise sauce (£10.25), and half shoulder of fellside lamb (£10.95), puddings (£3), and children's menu (£2.95); the Georgian panelled dining room is no smoking. Well kept Coniston Bluebird, Jennings, Tetleys, Timothy Taylors Landlord, and other guest beers on handpump, decent coffee, and a good choice of wines by the glass; a couple of daily papers, and maybe piped music. An entrance lounge has sofas, ancestral portraits, and antiques. Plenty of tables under parasols outside. *(Recommended by Angela and Steve Handley, Barry James, Geoff and Angela Jaques; also in the Good Hotel Guide)*

Free house ~ Licensees Val and Steve Madden ~ Real ale ~ Bar food (12.15-2, 6.30-9) ~ Restaurant ~ (01946) 861249 ~ Children welcome ~ Dogs allowed in bar and bedrooms ~ Open 11-11; 12-10.30 Sun ~ Bedrooms: £32S(£37.50B)/£59B

GRASMERE NY3406 Map 9
Travellers Rest

Just N of Grasmere on A591 Ambleside—Keswick; OS Sheet 90 map reference 335089

This 16th-c inn seems to fit in well with its wonderful surroundings, and there's a friendly, cosy atmosphere. The lounge area has settles, sofa benches, and upholstered armchairs, a warming log fire, and local watercolours and old photographs as well as suggested walks and coast-to-coast information, on the walls. Tasty bar food includes home-made soup (£3.25), sandwiches with home-baked bread (from £3.95), feta, onion and pine nut tart (£7.95), steak and kidney in ale pie, whitby scampi and waberthwaite cumberland sausage (all £8.95), daily specials like goats cheese and asparagus puff pastry lattice (£7.95), and seared venison steak with juniper mash or grilled bass with wild mushroom risotto (£9.95), and puddings such as a popular trio of chocolate and sticky date and caramel pudding (£3.95). Well kept Jennings Bitter, Cumberland, and Sneck Lifter, and a guest such as Coniston Bluebird on handpump, and up to 20 malt whiskies. The games room is popular with families: darts, pool, fruit machine, TV, and dominoes. As well as the telephone number listed below, they have a reservations number – 0500 600 725. *(Recommended by Maurice and Gill McMahon, Mr and Mrs Maurice Thompson, Michael Butler, David Heath, Derek and Margaret Underwood, MDN, Stephen Buckley, Tina and David Woods-Taylor, Walter and Susan Rinaldi-Butcher, Roger Thornington, David Edwards, Mr and Mrs W D Borthwick, Roy and Lindsey Fentiman, Jeremy Woods)*

Free house ~ Licensees Lynne, Derek and Graham Sweeney ~ Real ale ~ Bar food (12-9.30; 12-3, 6-9.30 in winter) ~ Restaurant ~ (015394) 35604 ~ Children in eating area of bar and in family room ~ Dogs allowed in bar ~ Open 11-11; 12-10.30 Sun ~ Bedrooms: £48S/£68S

HAWKSHEAD NY3501 Map 9

Drunken Duck ★ Ⓨ ♀ 🍺 🛏

Barngates; the hamlet is signposted from B5286 Hawkshead—Ambleside, opposite the Outgate Inn; or it may be quicker to take the first right from B5286, after the wooded caravan site; OS Sheet 90 map reference 350013

Cumbria Dining Pub of the Year

They've added a fourth own-brewed real ale to their collection in this civilised and friendly 17th-c inn: Barngates Chester's Strong & Ugly, Cracker Ale, Tag Lag, and the new Catnap. Also kept well on handpump are Yates Bitter and a changing guest, and there's a fine wine list with over 20 by the glass. The bar and snug are traditional beamed rooms with good winter fires, cushioned old settles and a mix of chairs on the fitted turkey carpet, pictures, cartoons, cards, fox masks, and cases of fishing flies and lures. All of the pub is no smoking except the bar. There's no doubt that while locals do drop in for just a drink, the emphasis is on the imaginative, restaurant-style meals. From the lunchtime menu, there might be mixed vegetable and herb soup (£3.95), port, stilton and slow roast tomato pâté (£4.95), devilled portland crab cake with caper mayonnaise (£5.50), ploughman's with tomato and red pepper pickle and smoked duck egg (£7.95), beer-battered cod with chunky chips and a salt and vinegar butter sauce (£8.25), roast chicken breast and cumbrian air-dried ham on garlic mash and caramelised red onions or fish pie with green beans provençale (£8.95), and duck breast with roast shallots, chestnuts and shi-itake mushrooms (£12.95), with evening dishes such as smoked haddock with roquefort rarebit on caramelised red onion with truffle oil (£5.25), pigeon breast marinated with liquorice on agen prunes and parmesan risotto (£5.95), stir-fried prawns with garlic, lime and chilli (£6.95), leek and sun-blushed tomato tartlet with grilled goats cheese, wild rocket and truffle oil dressing (£9.95), ginger-marinated pork fillet on sautéed leeks and bacon with roast potatoes and black pudding served with garlic jus (£12.95), and seared scallops on roast beetroot and mustard purée with parisienne potatoes and sultana and caper dressing (£13.95). Puddings might include vanilla and anise scented brûlée with ginger florentine, melting dark chocolate tart with marmalade ice cream or roasted pineapple with lime and basil sorbet and pink peppercorn tuile (from £4.50). There are seats on the front verandah with stunning views and quite a few rustic wooden chairs and tables at the side, sheltered by a stone wall with alpine plants along its top; the pub has fishing in a private tarn behind. This is a lovely place to stay. *(Recommended by M and C Lovatt, John and Gillian Scarisbrick, Edward Jago, A N Caldwell, Karen Eliot, Mark Kenny, John Saul, Dominic Epton, Tracey and Stephen Groves, A Sadler, Jim Abbott, Lorraine and Fred Gill, B H and J I Andrews, Sally Anne and Peter Goodale, Ian S Morley, Maurice and Gill McMahon, Mike and Sue Loseby, Mike Pugh, Michael Doswell, SLC, Jack Clark, MSL Webster, Dr S Edwards, Mrs Jane Kingsbury, Jeremy Woods, Margaret Dickinson)*

Own brew ~ Licensee Steph Barton ~ Real ale ~ Bar food (12-2.30, 6-9; not 25 Dec) ~ Restaurant ~ (015394) 36347 ~ Children in eating area of bar and restaurant ~ Dogs allowed in bar ~ Open 11.30-11; 12-10.30 Sun; closed lunchtime 25 Dec ~ Bedrooms: £63.75B/£85B

Kings Arms ◀ ⇌

The Square

This is a cheerful and bustling place to visit with a friendly atmosphere and a good mix of both locals and visitors. There are traditional pubby furnishings, some fine original Elizabethan beams (including the figure of a medieval king holding up the ceiling, carved recently), and Black Sheep, Coniston Bluebird, Tetleys and Theakstons, and a guest such as Fraoch Heather Ale or Yates Bitter on handpump; several malt whiskies, summer cider, and winter mulled wine. Piped music, darts, fruit machine, dominoes and cribbage. Enjoyable bar food at lunchtime includes home-made soup (£2.95), filled baked potatoes (£4.25), filled focaccia, pitta, ciabatta or tortilla wraps (£4.50), and cumberland sausage, home-made steak in ale pie or home-battered fish and chips (£6.25); in the evening, there might be black pudding and bacon salad (£3.75), home-made pâté with home-made chutney (£4.25), stir-fried hoisin duck (£6.75), a vegetarian dish of the day, local fell-bred minted lamb steaks or roast pheasant breast wrapped in smoked bacon with a cranberry and orange stuffing (£9.25), chargrilled aberdeen angus rump steak (£11.95), and daily specials. The restaurant is no smoking. As well as comfortable bedrooms, they offer self-catering cottages. The square on which this pub sits is glorious. *(Recommended by Deb and John Arthur, John Foord, Dr and Mrs R G J Telfer)*

Free house ~ Licensee Rosalie Johnson ~ Real ale ~ Bar food (12-2.30, 6-9.30) ~ Restaurant ~ (015394) 36372 ~ Children in eating area of bar and restaurant ~ Dogs allowed in bar and bedrooms ~ Open 11-11; 12-10.30 Sun; closed evening 25 Dec ~ Bedrooms: £36(£41S)/£62(£72S)

Queens Head

Main Street

In the heart of the village is this lovely black and white timbered pub with its pretty summer window boxes. Inside, the bustling low-ceilinged bar has heavy bowed black beams, red plush wall seats and plush stools around heavy traditional tables, lots of decorative plates on the panelled walls, and an open fire; a snug little room leads off. Lunchtime food served in either the bar or no smoking restaurant includes home-made soup (£2.95), interesting filled ciabattas, baguettes, bagels, focaccias, and tortillas (from £4.50), chicken liver pâté with orange and tequila (£5.25), club salad of crisp fried bacon and chicken topped with a free range poached egg (£5.75), garlic, thyme and mascarpone risotto (£6.75), haddock and home-made chips (£7.75), organic salmon, haddock and prawns in a lemon and parsley cream sauce (£8.50), chicken and prawn thai green curry (£9.50), and lamb henry with a rosemary scented sauce (£10.50); in the evening, there might be braised leg of guinea fowl on a potato and bacon rösti with a spicy fig chutney (£5.50), dublin bay langoustine with garlic and ginger with an olive-scented crouton (£5.75), fresh tagliatelle with chicken, mushrooms and sweetcorn in a tarragon and cream sauce (£11.25), seared calves liver on crushed potato with a rich onion gravy and crispy bacon (£12.75), marinated pork fillet roasted on rhubarb on a sage and potato rösti or sail fish and arctic char grilled and seved over mustard mashed potato (£13.95), and grilled wild boar steak on beetroot bubble and squeak with a port and black cherry sauce (£14.25); friendly, helpful staff. Well kept Frederics, Old Tom and another couple of beers from Robinsons on handpump, and quite a few whiskies; dominoes, cribbage, and piped music. Walkers must take their boots off. As well as bedrooms in the inn, they have three holiday cottages to rent in the village. *(Recommended by John Foord, Deb and John Arthur, SLC, Michael Doswell)*

Robinsons ~ Tenants Mr and Mrs Tony Merrick ~ Real ale ~ Bar food (12-2.30, 6.15-9.30) ~ Restaurant ~ (015394) 36271 ~ Children in no smoking snug ~ Open 11-11; 12-10.30 Sun ~ Bedrooms: £45(£55B)/£64(£80B)

Pubs brewing their own beers are listed at the back of the book.

HESKET NEWMARKET NY3438 Map 10

Old Crown ◖

Village signposted off B5299 in Caldbeck

As we went to press, we heard that customers were forming a co-operative and hoping to buy this unfussy local with the aim of keeping it exactly as it is at the moment. The good, own-brewed real ales on handpump would also continue: Hesket Newmarket Blencathra Bitter, Great Cockup Porter, Helvellyn Gold, Skiddaw Special Bitter, Old Carrock Strong Ale, and Catbells Pale Ale. Well liked evening curries (meaty ones £7.50 and vegetarian £6.50), plus sandwiches, home-made soup (£2.50), ham and egg (£5), lamb casserole (£6.50), and roast Sunday lunch (£5.60). The dining room is no smoking. The little bar has a few tables, a coal fire, and shelves of well thumbed books, and a friendly atmosphere; piped music, darts, pool, fruit machine, cribbage, and dominoes. They have a self-catering cottage. The pub is in a pretty setting in a remote, attractive village. More reports on the possible changes please. *(Recommended by MLR, Tina and David Woods-Taylor, Gwyneth and Salvo Spadaro-Dutturi)*

Own brew ~ Licensee Kim Mathews ~ Real ale ~ Bar food (12-2, 6.30-8.30; not Mon or Tues, not Sun evening) ~ Restaurant ~ No credit cards ~ (016974) 78288 ~ Children in eating area of bar and restaurant ~ Dogs welcome ~ Folk first Sun of month ~ Open 12-3, 5.30-11; 12-3, 7.30-10.30 Sun; closed Mon and Tues lunchtimes

HEVERSHAM SD4983 Map 9

Blue Bell

A6 (now a relatively very quiet road here)

Civilised and comfortable, this partly timbered 15th-c country hotel is the sort of place you can reliably return to again and again. The lounge bar has warm winter fires, pewter platters hanging from the beams, an antique carved settle, cushioned windsor armchairs and upholstered stools, and small antique sporting prints and a display cabinet with two stuffed fighting cocks on the partly panelled walls. One big bay-windowed area is divided off as a no smoking room, and the long, tiled-floor public bar has darts, pool, cribbage, dominoes, fruit machine, TV, and piped music. Reasonably priced, the tasty bar food includes home-made soup (£2.95), sandwiches (from £3.95), filled baked potatoes (from £4.95), lovely morecambe bay potted shrimps (£5.95), daily specials such as breaded fillet of plaice with chips (£4.95), cumberland sausage in a giant yorkshire pudding with onion gravy (£5.95), chicken breast with a red wine chasseur sauce or ham salad (£6.95), roast beef (£7.95), and sirloin steak (£13.95), and puddings (£2.95); they also do morning coffee and afternoon tea. The restaurant is no smoking. Well kept Sam Smiths OB on handpump kept under light blanket pressure, quite a few malt whiskies, and a fair wine list. Crossing over the A6 into the village itself, you come to a picturesque church with a rambling little graveyard; if you walk through this and on to the hills beyond, there's a fine view across to the estuary of the River Kent. The estuary itself is a short walk from the pub down the country road that runs by its side. *(Recommended by Ray and Winifred Halliday, Sylvia and Tony Birbeck, MLR, Maurice and Gill McMahon, Tony and Ann Bennett-Hughes, Ruth and Paul Lawrence, Michael Doswell, Andy and Ali)*

Sam Smiths ~ Managers Susan and Richard Cowie ~ Real ale ~ Bar food (all day during holidays) ~ Restaurant ~ (015395) 62018 ~ Children in eating area of bar and restaurant ~ Dogs allowed in bedrooms ~ Open 11-11; 12-11 Sun ~ Bedrooms: £37.50B/£75B

INGS SD4599 Map 9

Watermill ◖

Just off A591 E of Windermere

Fell walkers, marathon runners and locals all mingle happily in this well run, busy

pub – most are here to enjoy the marvellous range of up to 16 real ales. Well kept on handpump, there might be Black Sheep Best and Special, Coniston Bluebird, Jennings Cumberland, Lees Moonraker, and Theakstons Best and Old Peculier, with changing guests like Batemans Dark Mild, Brysons Shifting Sands, Hesket Newmarket Doris's 90th Birthday Ale, Hop Back Summer Lightning, Oakham JHB, Orkney Dark Island, Skinners Betty Stogs, and Yates XB; also, lots of bottled beers, farm cider, and up to 50 malt whiskies. The bars have a friendly, bustling atmosphere, and a happy mix of chairs, padded benches and solid oak tables, bar counters made from old church wood, open fires, and amusing cartoons by a local artist. The spacious lounge bar, in much the same traditional style as the other rooms, has rocking chairs and a big open fire; two areas are no smoking. Enjoyable bar food includes home-made soup (£3), lunchtime sandwiches, toasties or filled baguettes (from £3.25), home-made pâté (£4.25), mediterranean pasta bake (£7), battered haddock (£7.25), venison sausage with beer onion gravy (£7.50), chicken pie of the day (£7.75), beef in ale pie (£7.95), 10oz sirloin steak (£12.75), and daily specials like goats cheese tartlet or stuffed mushrooms (£4.25), vegetable parcel with stem ginger and sweet chilli (£7), fresh fish such as local char with lemon, prawns and capers (from around £8), and cumbrian tattie pot (£8.25). Darts, shove-ha'penny, cribbage, and dominoes. There are seats in the front garden. Lots to do nearby. Note that even residents cannot book a table for supper.
(Recommended by MLR, Richard Lewis, Jack Morley, Mr and Mrs D W Mitchell, A N Caldwell, Paul Boot, S and R Gray, Lee Potter, Jim Abbott, MDN, Michael Doswell, Stephen, Julie and Hayley Brown, Mike Pugh, Hugh Roberts, Peter F Marshall, Mayur Shah, Tracey and Stephen Groves, Mr and Mrs Maurice Thompson, John and Gillian Scarisbrick, Maurice and Gill McMahon, SLC, Dr D J and Mrs S C Walker, Julie and Bill Ryan)

Free house ~ Licensees Alan and Brian Coulthwaite ~ Real ale ~ Bar food (12-4.30, 5-9) ~ (01539) 821309 ~ Children in family room ~ Dogs allowed in bar ~ Storytelling club first Tues of month ~ Open 12-11(10.30 Sun); closed 25 Dec ~ Bedrooms: £25S/£50S

KESWICK NY2623 Map 9

George

St Johns Street, off top end of Market Street

The poet Southey used to wait by the good log fire for Wordsworth to arrive from Grasmere in the attractive traditional black-panelled side room of this fine old inn. There's also an open-plan main bar with old-fashioned settles and modern banquettes under Elizabethan beams, pleasant efficient staff, and daily papers. Bar food includes home-made soup (£2.25), sandwiches or filled baguettes (from £2.75), home-made chicken liver pâté (£3.75), beef goulash, breaded haddock, spicy pork curry or home-made steak and mushroom pie (£6.45), and cumberland sausage or gammon and pineapple (£7.45). Well kept Jennings Bitter, Cocker Hoop, Cumberland, and Sneck Lifter on handpump. The restaurant is no smoking; piped music, fruit machine, and dominoes. More reports please. *(Recommended by Gerald and Wendy Doyle, Jim Abbott, David Carr, Stephen Buckley, Chris and Maggie Kent)*

Jennings ~ Lease Ian Pettifrew and Ian Dixon ~ Real ale ~ Bar food (12-2.30, 6-9) ~ Restaurant ~ (017687) 72076 ~ Children welcome away from bar ~ Open 11-11; 12-10.30 Sun ~ Bedrooms: £32.50B/£65B

LANGDALE NY2906 Map 9

Old Dungeon Ghyll 🛏

B5343

From the window seats cut into the thick stone walls here, there are grand views of the Pike of Blisco rising behind Kettle Crag, and this no-nonsense walkers' pub is in a marvellous position at the heart of the Great Langdale Valley and surrounded by fells including the Langdale Pikes flanking the Dungeon Ghyll Force waterfall. The whole feel of the place is basic but cosy – and once all the fell walkers and climbers crowd in, full of boisterous atmosphere. There's no need to remove boots or muddy trousers, and you can sit on the seats in old cattle stalls by the big warming fire, and enjoy the six well kept real ales such as Black Sheep, Jennings Cumberland, and Yates Bitter with guests from Barngates, Coniston or Hawkshead on handpump. Part of the bar is no smoking. Straightforward food includes sandwiches (£2.50, lunchtime), home-made soup (£2.50), filled baked potatoes (£3.50), main meals such as cumberland sausage, a vegetarian dish, battered haddock or half chicken (from around £7), and children's meals (£3.50); darts. It can get really lively on a Saturday night (there's a popular National Trust campsite opposite). *(Recommended by Dave Irving, Sarah and Peter Gooderham, Hugh Roberts, John Wooll, Mayur Shah, Thomas Day)*

Free house ~ Licensee Neil Walmsley ~ Real ale ~ Bar food ~ Restaurant ~ (015394) 37272 ~ Children welcome ~ Dogs allowed in bar ~ Open 11-11; 12-10.30 Sun; closed Christmas ~ Bedrooms: £35(£37.50B)/£74S

LITTLE LANGDALE NY3204 Map 9
Three Shires 🏠

From A593 3 miles W of Ambleside take small road signposted The Langdales, Wrynose Pass; then bear left at first fork

The three shires are Cumberland, Westmorland and Lancashire, which used to meet at the top of the nearby Wrynose Pass. The comfortably extended back bar in this comfortable inn has stripped timbers and a beam-and-joist stripped ceiling, antique carved oak settles, country kitchen chairs and stools on its big dark slate flagstones, Lakeland photographs lining the walls, and a warm winter fire in the modern stone fireplace with a couple of recesses for ornaments; an arch leads through to a small, additional area. Well liked bar food at lunchtime includes soup (£3), sandwiches (£3.25), rustic cobs or soup and sandwich £5), home-made fishcake with lime and cucumber crème fraîche (£5), ploughman's or risotto of beetroot, coriander and crème fraîche (£6), and local cumberland sausage or beef in ale pie (£7.50); more elaborate evening meals such as chicken, walnut and apple terrine (£5), mushroom and mixed nut wellington (£8.95), marinated pork steak with prune compote and sweet cider and mustard sauce (£10.95), fresh cod fillet with spinach and sun-dried tomato (£11.50), and local venison steak with bitter chocolate sauce (£12.95). The restaurant and snug are no smoking. Well kept Jennings Bitter and Cumberland, and a guest such as Coniston Old Man or Hawkshead Bitter on handpump, 40 malt whiskies, and a decent wine list; darts, cribbage and dominoes. From seats on the terrace there are lovely views over the valley to the partly wooded hills below Tilberthwaite Fells, with more seats on a well kept lawn behind the car park, backed by a small oak wood. *(Recommended by Tina and David Woods-Taylor, Dave Irving, Lorna and Howard Lambert, Roger and Jenny Huggins, Mr and Mrs Maurice Thompson, Ewan and Moira McCall, DC, SLC, Jack Clark, Dr and Mrs R G J Telfer)*

Free house ~ Licensee Ian Stephenson ~ Real ale ~ Bar food (12-2, 6-8.45; no evening meals midweek in Dec or Jan) ~ Restaurant ~ (015394) 37215 ~ Children welcome ~ Dogs allowed in bar ~ Open 11-10.30(11 Fri and Sat); 12-10.30 Sun; 11-3, 6-11 (10.30 midweek) in winter; closed 25 Dec ~ Bedrooms: /£74B

LOWESWATER NY1222 Map 9
Kirkstile Inn 🏠

From B5289 follow signs to Loweswater Lake; OS Sheet 89 map reference 140210

As there are plenty of outdoor pursuits on the surrounding peaks and fells, and as this 16th-c inn is situated between Loweswater and Crummock Water, it's not surprising that many of the customers are walkers – and no matter how wet they are, all are dealt with in a very friendly, courteous manner. The bar is low-beamed and carpeted, with a roaring log fire, comfortably cushioned small settles and pews, and partly stripped stone walls; slate shove-ha'penny board. Generous helpings of tasty bar food include home-made soup (£2.75), hot tomato and feta cheese tartlet (£3.75), vegetarian lasagne (£5.75), steak in ale pie (£6.50), lamb cobbler (£7.25), chicken on a wild mushroom risotto with an asparagus and white wine cream

(£7.95), daily specials like slices of smoked halibut with mackerel pâté (£3.75), seared tuna steak with béarnaise sauce (£7.95), braised lamb shoulder with a fennel and root vegetable sauce (£9.50), and puddings such as blackcurrant parfait or toffee, date and walnut sponge pudding with a rich toffee sauce (£3.25); good breakfasts and helpful staff. The restaurant and lounges are no smoking. Well kept Coniston Bluebird, Jennings Bitter, and Yates Bitter with a guest like Tirril Charles Gough's Old Faithfull on handpump; the licensees are hoping to start brewing their own ales. You can enjoy the view from picnic-sets on the lawn, from the very attractive covered verandah in front of the building, and from the bow windows in one of the rooms off the bar. *(Recommended by Guy Vowles, Mr and Mrs D W Mitchell, Mike and Penny Sutton, Sylvia and Tony Birbeck, Simon and Caroline Turner, John Hale, Dr Paull Khan, Kevin Flack)*

Free house ~ Licensees Roger and Helen Humphreys ~ Real ale ~ Bar food (12-2, 6-9) ~ Restaurant ~ (01900) 85219 ~ Children in eating area of bar ~ Dogs allowed in bar and bedrooms ~ Jazz once a month ~ Open 11-11; 11-10.30 Sun; closed 25 Dec ~ Bedrooms: £37B/£60(£64B)

MUNGRISDALE NY3630 Map 10
Mill Inn

Off A66 Penrith—Keswick, a bit over 1 mile W of A5091 Ullswater turn-off

Charmingly placed by a tumbling brook in a little village, this friendly inn is well run by hardworking licensees who have bought it from Jennings and now own it themselves. The simply furnished and neatly kept main bar has a wooden bar counter with an old millstone by it, an open fire in the stone fireplace, and a warm welcome for both locals and visitors. Good, enjoyable bar food includes 11 varieties of home-made pies such as wild venison, pheasant and rabbit, a medley of roasted vegetables in a herby tomato sauce or pork, local cumberland sausage and apple (from £6.25), as well as home-made soup (£2.10), grilled black pudding on herb mash with a grain mustard and bacon sauce (£3.50), home-made fishcakes with roasted red pepper and tomato salsa (£4.25), chicken lasagne (£5.95), ragoût of lamb (£6.70), mushroom stroganoff (£7.30), grilled fresh salmon with a creamy mushroom sauce (£8.55), duck breast with a honey, port and coriander sauce (£9.50), and fillet steak topped with a slice of haggis and served with a whisky sauce (£12.95). The restaurant is no smoking; morning coffee and afternoon tea with their own scones and cakes. Well kept Jennings Bitter and Cumberland, and guests like Black Sheep or Jennings Cocker Hoop on handpump, and quite a few malt whiskies; games room with darts, pool, dominoes, and piped music. There are tables on the gravel forecourt and neat lawn sloping to a little river. Please note that there's a quite separate Mill Hotel here. *(Recommended by Peter and Pat Frogley, Angus Lyon, Mike and Penny Sutton, Jack Morley, Alan and Paula McCully)*

Free house ~ Licensees Jim and Margaret Hodge ~ Real ale ~ Bar food (12-2.30, 6-8(9 Sat)) ~ Restaurant ~ (017687) 79632 ~ Children in eating area of bar and in games room ~ Dogs allowed in bar ~ Open 11-11; 12-10.30 Sun; closed 25-26 Dec ~ Bedrooms: £25(£27.50B)/£50(£55B)

NEAR SAWREY SD3796 Map 9
Tower Bank Arms ◖

B5285 towards the Windermere ferry

Visitors from all over the world come to this little country inn as it features in *The Tale of Jemima Puddleduck*, and Beatrix Potter's Hill Top Farm (owned by the National Trust) backs on to it. It does get very busy at peak times. The low-beamed main bar has a fine log fire in the big cooking range, high-backed settles on the rough slate floor, local hunting photographs and signed photographs of celebrities on the walls, a grandfather clock, and good traditional atmosphere. Well kept Theakstons Best and Old Peculier, Wells Bombardier, and a couple of guests from Barngates or Hawkshead on handpump, as well as lots of malt whiskies, and belgian fruit beers and other foreign beers. Straightforward bar food, and darts, shove-ha'penny, and dominoes. Seats outside have pleasant views of the wooded Claife Heights. This is a good area for golf, sailing, birdwatching, fishing (they have a licence for two rods a day on selected waters in the area), and walking, but if you want to stay at the pub, you'll have to book well in advance. More reports please. *(Recommended by Angus Lyon, Mike Pugh, John Dwane, Mr and Mrs Maurice Thompson, Jason Caulkin, Tina and David Woods-Taylor, Michael Doswell, Gerald and Wendy Doyle, David and Helen Wilkins)*

Free house ~ Licensee Philip Broadley ~ Real ale ~ Bar food (not 25 Dec) ~ Restaurant ~ (015394) 36334 ~ Children in eating area of bar lunchtime but in restaurant only, in evenings ~ Dogs allowed in bar and bedrooms ~ Open 11-3, 5.30(6 in winter)-11; 12-3, 5.30-10.30 Sun; closed evening 25 Dec ~ Bedrooms: £38B/£55B

NEWBY BRIDGE SD3786 Map 9
Swan 🖙
Just off A590

In strict terms, this is not a pub, but a substantial hotel. However, the immaculately kept bar round to the left offers Bass and Boddingtons on handpump, and rambles through various nooks and corners, with flagstones here, carpet there, and bare boards in one inner recess, and has some heavy black beams, Lakeland and country pictures, and a mix of comfortably cushioned seating from country-kitchen to easy chairs and settees; two alcoves off the bar and a lounge are no smoking. Good cafetière coffee and obliging uniformed staff; piped music. As well as nicely presented bar snacks such as home-made soup (£3), and sandwiches, toasties, and filled ciabatta rolls (from £3.45), there are proper meals which are taken in the adjoining brasserie (just a couple of steps from the bar) which has some stripped stone and a raised balustraded bare-boards area: garlic mushrooms (£4.15), smoked salmon and apricot terrine (£4.45), prawn and asparagus quiche or caesar salad with chicken (£7.90), mushroom stroganoff (£8), honey and ginger chicken or beef in ale pie (£8.35), poached fillet of scottish salmon with a cucumber and dill cream sauce (£8.50), steaks (from £14.95), daily specials, and puddings (£4.30). Outside, picnic-sets under cocktail parasols line a pretty inlet at the foot of Lake Windermere (the main body of the lake is just a short stroll away); it's a lovely spot. *(Recommended by Michael Doswell)*

Free house ~ Licensees Paul Roebuck and Jonathan Cowley ~ Real ale ~ Bar food (all day snacks and food all day weekends) ~ Restaurant ~ (015395) 31681 ~ Children in eating area of bar and in restaurant until 9pm ~ Open 11-11; 12-10.30 Sun ~ Bedrooms: £69B/£138B

PENRUDDOCK NY4327 Map 10
Herdwick
Off A66 Penrith—Keswick

Neatly refurbished and well cared for, this 18th-c cottagey inn is a friendly place with helpful, welcoming staff. Plenty of stripped stone and white paintwork, a good cosy atmosphere, well kept Jennings Cumberland and Tetleys on handpump from an unusual curved bar, and a no smoking dining room with an upper gallery (best to book, especially in the evenings). Good bar food includes sandwiches, home-made soup (£2.95), home-made pâté or smoked sausage with cumberland sauce (£4.25), spinach and cheese roulade topped with basil and provençale sauce (£7.75), a daily pasta (£7.85), home-made steak pie (£7.90), spiced herdwick lamb with a home-made scone (£8.45), poached salmon topped with muscat grapes and served with a creamy wine sauce (£10.85), crispy duck with sage and onion stuffing (£11.35), fillet steak (£15.05), daily specials, and home-made puddings (£3.50). Pool, piped music, juke box, darts, and pool. Nearby Dalemain is well worth a visit. *(Recommended by Mike and Penny Sutton, C L Clarkson, Maurice and Gill McMahon, Mike and Sue Loseby, Michael Doswell, Alan and Paula McCully)*

Free house ~ Licensee Ian Hall ~ Real ale ~ Bar food (12-2, 6-9) ~ Restaurant ~ (017684) 83007 ~ Children in eating area of bar ~ Open 12-2.30, 6-11; 12-3, 7-10.30 Sun ~ Bedrooms: £27S/£54S

SANDFORD NY7316 Map 10

Sandford Arms ♀ ◖ ⇌

Village and pub signposted just off A66 W of Brough

With its snug atmosphere and homely furnishings, you feel more like a family friend than a customer in this neat and welcoming little inn. The two sons do the cooking, and the food is good, using local organic ingredients where possible: home-made soup (£2.50), grilled black pudding with mustard sauce (£3.20), sandwiches (from £3.25), salads or home-made pie of the day (£7.20), chicken with mushrooms and bacon in a creamy sauce (£7.75), gammon with egg or pineapple (£7.95), salmon fillet with parsley sauce (£8.25), steaks (from £11.95), and puddings like sticky toffee pudding or highland trifle (from £2.95). The compact and comfortable no smoking dining area is on a slightly raised balustraded platform at one end of the L-shaped carpeted main bar, which has stripped beams and stonework, well kept Black Sheep and a guest like Hesket Newmarket Skiddaw Special Bitter on handpump, a good range of malt whiskies, and nice new world house wines (including ones from the Sandford Estate – no connection); maybe the clatter of dominoes as George licks his team into shape for the local league. There's also a more formal separate dining room (not always in use), and a second bar area with broad flagstones, charming heavy-horse prints, an end log fire, and darts and piped music. There are a few picnic-sets outside. *(Recommended by Phil and Sally Gorton, Dr and Mrs R G J Telfer)*

Free house ~ Licensee Susan Stokes ~ Real ale ~ Bar food ~ Restaurant ~ (017683) 51121 ~ Children in eating area and in restaurant ~ Dogs allowed in bar ~ Open 12-1.45, 7(6.30 Weds-Sat)-11 ~ Bedrooms: £40B/£60B

SANTON BRIDGE NY1101 Map 9

Bridge Inn

Off A595 at Holmrook or Gosforth

In a quiet riverside spot by the bridge, this traditional little black and white Lakeland inn has fell views, picnic-sets in the garden, and more seats out in front by the quiet road. The turkey-carpeted bar has stripped beams, joists and standing timbers, a coal and log fire, and three rather unusual timbered booths around big stripped tables along its outer wall, with small painted school chairs and tables elsewhere. Bar stools line the long concave bar counter, which has well kept Jennings Cumberland, Cocker Hoop, and Sneck Lifter, and a guest such as Greene King Old Speckled Hen or Wells Bombardier on handpump; good big pots of tea, speciality coffees, welcoming service; well reproduced piped nostalgic pop music, darts, and dominoes. Bar food includes filled baguettes, home-made soup (£2.50), salads like caesar or greek (from £3.95), steak and kidney pie or cumberland sausage (£7.50), meaty or vegetable chilli with sour cream and nachos (£7.95), battered haddock (£8.95), chicken riesling (£10.50), steaks (from £11.95), and daily specials. The dining room is no smoking, the small reception hall has a rack of daily papers, and there's a comfortable more hotelish lounge (with an internet café) on the left. More reports please. *(Recommended by Nigel and Sue Foster, Roger Braithwaite)*

Jennings ~ Tenants John Morrow and Lesley Rhodes ~ Real ale ~ Bar food (12-2.30, 6-9.30) ~ Restaurant ~ (01946) 726221 ~ Children welcome ~ Dogs allowed in bar and bedrooms ~ Open 11-11; 12-10.30 Sun ~ Bedrooms: £40(£45S)/£55(£60B)

Food details, prices, timing etc refer to bar food – not to a separate restaurant if there is one.

SEATHWAITE SD2396 Map 9
Newfield Inn
Duddon Valley, near Ulpha (ie not Seathwaite in Borrowdale)

With good walks from the doorstep of this cottagey 16th-c inn, it's not surprising that walkers and climbers crowd in at weekends, and there are tables out in the nice garden with good hill views. Inside, the slate-floored bar has a genuinely local and informal atmosphere, with wooden tables and chairs, and some interesting pictures, and well kept real ales such as Coniston Bluebird, Jennings Bitter, Theakstons Old Peculier, and Wells Bombardier on handpump. There's a comfortable side room and a games room with darts, cribbage, and dominoes. Good value bar food includes sandwiches and filled rolls (from £2.40), home-made soup (£2.45), small helpings of bean casserole, cumberland sausage or haddock (from £3.25), whitebait or free range eggs and chips (£3.45), pâté and cheese with granary bread (£4.50), home-made lasagne (£6.45), home-made steak pie (£6.95), salmon fillet with lime butter (£7.85), steaks (from £9.95), and puddings like home-made pear and chocolate crumble (£2.45). The grill room is no smoking; piped music. The pub owns and lets the next-door self-catering flats. (Recommended by David Heath, Derek Harvey-Piper, Margaret Dickinson)

Free house ~ Licensee Paul Batten ~ Real ale ~ Bar food (12-9) ~ Restaurant ~ (01229) 716208 ~ Children welcome ~ Dogs allowed in bar ~ Open 11-11; 11-10.30 Sun

SEDBERGH SD6692 Map 10
Dalesman
Main Street

This is a popular stop-over for walkers on the Dales Way and Cumbrian Cycle Way as both pass the door of this nicely modernised pub, and there are lots of walks of varying difficulty all around. The various rooms have quite a mix of decorations and styles – lots of stripped stone and beams, cushioned farmhouse chairs and stools around dimpled copper tables, and a raised stone hearth with a log-effect gas fire; also, horsebrasses and spigots, Vernon Stokes gundog pictures, various stuffed animals, tropical fish, and a blunderbuss. Through stone arches on the right, a no smoking buttery area serves generous helpings of bar food such as home-made soup (£2.50), home-made chicken liver pâté with plum chutney (£4), chargrilled flat mushrooms with pesto (£3), a big ploughman's, pork and leek sausage or steak and kidney pie (£7), omelettes (from £7), lamb shank with redcurrant gravy or home-made butternut squash risotto (£8), popular belly of pork with crackling or fresh cod in beer batter (£9), aberdeen angus steaks (from £13), and puddings like orange crème brûlée or chocolate and Baileys terrine (£4); in the winter they hold themed food evenings. Well kept Black Sheep, Tetleys Bitter, and their own Dalesman Bitter on handpump, and several malt whiskies; dominoes and piped music. Some picnic-sets out in front, and a small car park. More reports please. (Recommended by Edward Jago, Tony and Ann Bennett-Hughes)

Free house ~ Licensees Michael and Judy Garnett ~ Real ale ~ Bar food (12-2, 6-9.30) ~ Restaurant ~ (015396) 21183 ~ Children welcome ~ Live music Sun afternoon and one Fri of the month ~ Open 11-11; 12-10.30 Sun ~ Bedrooms: £30B/£60B

STAINTON NY4928 Map 10
Kings Arms
1¾ miles from M6 junction 40: village signposted from A66 towards Keswick, though quickest to fork left at A592 roundabout then turn first right

Handy for the M6, this is a quiet and friendly pub. The pleasantly modernised and neatly kept open-plan bar has a rather cosy feel, leatherette wall banquettes, stools and armchairs around wood-effect tables, brasses on the black beams, and prints and paintings of the Lake District on the swirly cream walls; one room is no smoking during mealtimes. Enjoyable, reasonably priced traditional bar food includes lunchtime snacks such as sandwiches (from £2.45; toasties from £3.05; open ones from £3.90), filled baked potatoes (from £4.10), and ploughman's (£4.45); also, home-made soup (£2.05), crispy mushrooms with garlic dip (£3.20), bacon chop with egg (£4.40), beef in ale casserole in yorkshire pudding (£5.65), lemon and ginger chicken or steak and kidney pie (£6.05), vegetarian lasagne (£6.65), sirloin steak (£9.95), daily specials, roast Sunday lunch, and puddings (£2.95). Members of the Vintage Motorcycle Club receive 10% discount on meals on presentation of their membership card. Well kept Tetleys plus a couple of summer guests such as Courage Directors or Greene King Old Speckled Hen on handpump, and 21 malt whiskies; welcoming staff. Sensibly placed darts, dominoes, and piped music. There are tables on the side terrace, with more on a small lawn. *(Recommended by Darly Graton, Graeme Gulibert, John and Sylvia Harrop, Alistair Forsyth, Alan and Paula McCully)*

Pubmaster ~ Tenants James and Anne Downie ~ Real ale ~ Bar food (not Mon) ~ (01768) 862778 ~ Children in eating area of bar if dining until 9 ~ Open 11.30-3, 6.30-11; 12-3, 7-10.30 Sun; open 7pm evenings in winter; closed Mon exc bank hols and school hols

STONETHWAITE NY2613 Map 9
Langstrath 🍴 🛏

Off B5289 S of Derwent Water

Built around 1590, this civilised little inn – completely no smoking now – is in a lovely spot surrounded by the steep fells above Borrowdale. The first thing you see in the neat and simple bar is the welcoming coal and log fire in a big stone fireplace; it has just a handful of cast-iron-framed tables, plain chairs and cushioned wall seats, and on its textured white walls quite a few walking cartoons and attractive Lakeland mountain photographs. They have well kept Black Sheep and Jennings on handpump with a couple of guest beers such as Hop Back Summer Lightning and Tirril Charles Gough's Old Faithful, and quite a few malt whiskies. A little oak-boarded room on the left reminded us almost of a doll's house living room in style. Enjoyable bar food (they tell us prices have not changed since last year) includes home-made soup (£2.95), sandwiches (from £3.25), mushrooms in creamy garlic sauce (£4.25), morecambe bay potted shrimps (£4.95), mushroom, broccoli and stilton pasta bake (£7.95), local trout poached with tarragon (£8.95), local roast lamb with mint (£10.25), daily specials like cumberland sausage with onion gravy (£8.25), wild boar and duckling pie (£8.90), and fillet of halibut in pastry parcel with lemon butter sauce (£9.25). There is also a separate back restaurant, by the residents' lounge. Outside, a big sycamore shelters a few picnic-sets. More reports please. *(Recommended by Jane Taylor, David Dutton, Mayur Shah, Kevin Flack)*

Free house ~ Licensees Donna and Gary MacRae ~ Bar food (12-2, 6-8.30) ~ Restaurant ~ (017687) 77239 ~ Children in restaurant ~ Open 11-11; 12-10.30 Sun; closed late Dec-early Jan ~ Bedrooms: £27/£54(£64S)(£72B)

TALKIN NY5557 Map 10
Blacksmiths Arms 🍷 🛏

Village signposted from B6413 S of Brampton

Well run and friendly, this former blacksmith's is a popular place for either a drink or a meal. On the right is a warm, neatly kept lounge with upholstered banquettes, tables and chairs, an open fire, and country prints and other pictures on the walls; a couple of rooms are no smoking at lunchtime. Well kept Black Sheep, Jennings Cumberland, and Tetleys on handpump, and over 20 wines by the glass; piped music and dominoes. As well as lunchtime sandwiches and filled baguettes, the good, enjoyable food might include home-made soup (£2.10), chicken and pistachio pâté (£3.45), fresh haddock in home-made beer batter (£5.75), steak and kidney pie or vegetable curry (£6.25), sweet and sour chicken (£7.25), salmon in a light parsley and lemon sauce (£8.65), beef stroganoff (£10.95), steaks (from

£12.25), and daily specials; three-course Sunday lunch (£6.95; children £4.75). The no smoking restaurant on the left is pretty. There are seats outside in the garden. *(Recommended by Mrs Phoebe A Kemp, Dr and Mrs R G J Telfer, David and Julie Glover, JWAC, Michael Doswell)*

Free house ~ Licensees Donald and Anne Jackson ~ Real ale ~ Bar food (12-2, 6-9) ~ Restaurant ~ (016977) 3452 ~ Children welcome ~ Open 12-3, 6-11(10.30 Sun) ~ Bedrooms: £35B/£50B

TIRRIL NY5126 Map 10
Queens Head ★ 🍺 🛏

3½ miles from M6 junction 40; take A66 towards Brough, A6 towards Shap, then B5320 towards Ullswater

Dating from 1719, this bustling inn has four open fireplaces including one roomy inglenook which still has in place its original hooks for smoking meats. The oldest parts of the bar have low bare beams, black panelling, original flagstones and floorboards, and high-backed settles; the little back bar has a lot of character; piped music. Their own beers, brewed at Brougham Hall a couple of miles away, include Bewshers Best (after the landlord in the early 1800s who bought the inn from the Wordsworths and changed its name to the Queens Head in time for Victoria's coronation), Acadamy Ale, Brougham Hall, Old Faithful, and the new 1823, and they keep guest beers from other local breweries on handpump. During the Cumbrian Beer & Sausage Festival during August, there are 20 local real ales. Over 40 malt whiskies, a good choice of brandies and other spirits, and a carefully chosen wine list. As well as lunchtime bar snacks, the enjoyable food includes home-made soup (£2.75), home-made chicken liver pâté or garlic mushrooms (£3.50), a daily fresh pasta dish (£7.75), home-made pie (£7.95), chicken tikka (£8.95), braised shoulder of lamb in redcurrant gravy (£10.50), steaks (from £12.95), daily specials like monkfish and noodles in pesto sauce (£5.75), peach, cashew nut and red pepper tikka (£8.25), cod steak in lime crust or baked local trout stuffed with lemon and herbs (£8.95), and red snapper on mango and spring onion salsa (£13.50), with puddings like chocolate truffle slice or toffee apple bread and butter pudding (from £2.95). The restaurant is no smoking. Pool, juke box, and dominoes in the back bar. The pub is very close to a number of interesting places, such as Dalemain House at Dacre, and is just 2½ miles from Ullswater. *(Recommended by Dr Terry Murphy, Darly Graton, Graeme Gulibert, John Oates, Mike Pugh, Hugh Roberts, Mr and Mrs J Curtis, Ian and Nita Cooper, Andy and Jill Kassube, A White, J Roy Smylie, Steve Whalley, P Abbott, Maurice and Gill McMahon, Sally Anne and Peter Goodale, Mike and Maggie Betton, Christine and Neil Townend, David Heath, Brian and Anna Marsden, Eric Larkham, Geoff and Angela Jaques, Karen Eliot, Michael Doswell, Paul Boot, David and Barbara Knott, Jeremy Woods, Alan and Paula McCully)*

Own brew ~ Licensees Chris Tomlinson and Ian Harris ~ Real ale ~ Bar food (12-2, 6-9.30) ~ Restaurant ~ (01768) 863219 ~ Children in eating area of bar and in restaurant; under 3 or over 13 for accommodation ~ Dogs welcome ~ Open 12-3, 6-11; 12-11 Fri and Sat; 12-10.30 Sun ~ Bedrooms: £35B/£60B

TROUTBECK NY4103 Map 9
Queens Head ★ 🍴 🍷 🍺 🛏

A592 N of Windermere

Although this civilised inn has been considerably extended over the past few years, the alterations fit in well with the parts dating back 400 years. The big rambling original U-shaped bar has a little no smoking room at each end, beams and flagstones, a very nice mix of old cushioned settles and mate's chairs around some sizeable tables (especially the one to the left of the door), and a log fire in the raised stone fireplace with horse harness and so forth on either side of it in the main part, with a woodburning stove in the other; some trumpets, cornets and saxophones on one wall, country pictures on others, stuffed pheasants in a big glass case, and a stag's head with a tie around his neck, and a stuffed fox with a ribbon around his.

A massive Elizabethan four-poster bed is the basis of the finely carved counter where they serve Boddingtons, Coniston Bluebird, and Jennings Bitter, with guests such as Barngates Cracker, Black Sheep Special or Dent Ramsbottom on handpump. The newer dining rooms (where you can also drop in for just a drink) are similarly decorated to the main bar, with oak beams and stone walls, settles along big tables, and an open fire. Imaginative bar food includes home-made soup with home-made bread (£2.75), baked goats cheese topped with roasted pistachio and pesto crumb (£5.25), steak, ale and mushroom cobbler (£7.25), mixed bean and sweet potato cake with fresh chillies, a pear and red onion compote, and coriander and lime yoghurt or supreme of chicken filled with an apple and tarragon forcemeat and served with an onion cream (£9.95), fillet of salmon marinated in lemon grass, ginger and coriander baked on to sautéed mange tout and cherry tomatoes with a sweet chilli dressing or whole shank of lamb on mint mash with a redcurrant and rosemary jus (£10.50), haunch of local venison on braised red cabbage (£14.25); proper food for children (from £3), and a three-course menu £15.50. Piped music. Seats outside have a fine view over the Trout valley to Applethwaite moors. *(Recommended by Roy and Lindsey Fentiman, Ray and Winifred Halliday, Malcolm Taylor, Tony and Ann Bennett-Hughes, Pat and John Morris, Dominic Epton, Mayur Shah, Derek and Margaret Underwood, John and Gillian Scarisbrick, Phil and Heidi Cook, Tina and David Woods-Taylor, Lorraine and Fred Gill, A Sadler, Tracey and Stephen Groves, Barry Robson, Jack Clark, Maurice and Gill McMahon, Mike Pugh, Ian and Jane Irving, Hugh Roberts, Paul Boot, David and Helen Wilkins)*

Free house ~ Licensees Mark Stewardson and Joanne Sherratt ~ Real ale ~ Bar food ~ Restaurant ~ (015394) 32174 ~ Children welcome ~ Dogs allowed in bar ~ Open 11-11; 12-10.30 Sun; closed 25 Dec ~ Bedrooms: £60B/£85B

ULVERSTON SD2978 Map 7
Bay Horse 🏮 ♗ 🛏

Canal Foot signposted off A590 and then you wend your way past the huge Glaxo factory

Civilised and smart, this small hotel stands on the water's edge of the Leven Estuary and has commanding views of both the Lancashire and Cumbrian fells. It's at its most informal at lunchtime when the good, imaginative bar food might include home-made chilled apple, celery and stilton soup with cream and chopped walnuts (£3.25), sandwiches (from £3.50; smoked chicken with curry mayonnaise and toasted coconut £3.95; hot roast beef on onion marmalade with red chilli and spring onions £6.25), home-made cheese and herb pâté with cranberry and ginger purée, tomato and orange salad and garlic and herb bread, baked potatoes with fillings like poached scottish salmon with chive mayonnaise, prawn and vegetable thai curry or beef chilli with ginger and red kidney beans, and button mushrooms in a tomato, cream and brandy sauce on a peanut butter crouton (all £6.25), braised lamb, apricot and ginger puff pastry pie (£8.50), large field mushrooms filled with cream cheese and herb pâté baked with a savoury breadcrumb topping and diced smoked bacon or cumberland sausage with date chutney, cranberry and apple sauce (£9), fresh crab and salmon fishcakes on a white wine and fresh herb cream sauce (£9.50), and home-made puddings (£4.50). Well kept Jennings and Thwaites and a guest on handpump, a decent choice of spirits, and a carefully chosen and interesting wine list with quite a few from South Africa. The bar, notable for its huge stone horse's head, has a relaxed atmosphere despite its smart furnishings: attractive wooden armchairs, some pale green plush built-in wall banquettes, glossy hardwood traditional tables, blue plates on a delft shelf, and black beams and props with lots of horsebrasses. Magazines are dotted about, there's a handsomely marbled green granite fireplace, and decently reproduced piped music; darts, bar billiards, shove-ha'penny, cribbage, and dominoes. The no smoking conservatory restaurant has fine views over Morecambe Bay (as do the bedrooms) and there are some seats out on the terrace. Please note, the bedroom price includes dinner as well. *(Recommended by Sylvia and Tony Birbeck, Tina and David Woods-Taylor, JDM, KM, Derek Harvey-Piper, Philip Vernon, Kim Maidment, Jenny and Chris Wilson; also in the* Good Hotel Guide)

Free house ~ Licensee Robert Lyons ~ Real ale ~ Bar food (lunchtime only; not Mon) ~ Restaurant ~ (01229) 583972 ~ Children in eating area of bar and in restaurant if over 12 ~ Dogs allowed in bar and bedrooms ~ Open 11-11; 12-10.30 Sun ~ Bedrooms: /£125B

Farmers Arms ⑪ ♀ ◀

Market Place

Pretty much unchanged from the outside since it was built in the 16th c, this friendly town pub has been appealingly modernised and extended inside. The original fireplace and timbers blend in well with the more contemporary furnishings in the front bar – mostly wicker chairs on one side, comfortable sofas on the other; the overall effect is rather unusual, but somehow it still feels like the most traditional village pub. A table by the fire has newspapers, glossy magazines and local information, then a second smaller bar counter leads into a big raftered eating area, part of which is no smoking; piped music. Up to six swiftly changing well kept real ales on handpump: Black Sheep, Hawkshead Bitter, Hook Norton, Marstons Brewers Droop, Moorhouses, and Theakstons Best. They specialise in carefully chosen new world wines, with around a dozen by the glass. Good food includes lunchtime hot and cold sandwiches (from £3.95; bacon, sun-dried tomato and goats cheese £4.25) and filled baked potatoes (£5.95), plus home-made soup (£2.50), hot garlic prawns on toast (£3.95), bangers and mash with onion sauce or chicken curry (£6.50), mushroom and sweet pepper stroganoff in a creamy paprika sauce (£6.75), fresh cod with parsley sauce or interesting salads (£6.95), evening steaks (from £9.95), and daily specials like beef in chilli and ginger with stir-fried oriental vegetables (£7.95), red mullet served with a seafood and lime kebab (£8.95), and roast barbary duck on red cabbage chutney (£9.95). In front is a very attractive terrace with plenty of good wooden tables looking on to the market cross, big heaters, and lots of colourful plants in tubs and hanging baskets. If something's happening in town, the pub is usually a part of it, and they can be busy on Thursday market day. More reports please. *(Recommended by Ray and Winifred Halliday, Lesley Bass, David Field)*

Free house ~ Licensee Roger Chattaway ~ Real ale ~ Bar food ~ (01229) 584469 ~ Children in eating area of bar and restaurant ~ Open 11(9.30 for breakfast)-11(10.30 Sun)

WASDALE HEAD NY1808 Map 9
Wasdale Head Inn ⇐

To NE of lake; long detour off A595 from Gosforth or Holmrook

One of the main draws to this three-gabled hotel is the fine choice of real ales including their own-brewed beers from the Great Gable Brewing Company: Great Gable, Wasd' Ale, Wrynose and Scawfell, and there are plans to add a stout called Black Sail and a Christmas porter called Yule Barrow. Also well kept on handpump, there might be guests from Derwent, Hesket Newmarket, and Yates. There's a high-ceilinged, spacious bar with an old-fashioned country-house feel and a fine collection of climbing photographs, mostly from the camera of the famous Abraham brothers showing the early days of climbing. Ritson's Bar (named for the first landlord, Will Ritson, who by his death in 1890 had earned the reputation of being the World's Biggest Liar for his zany tall stories) is mainly no smoking and has old church pews, a good bustling atmosphere, and plenty of customers chatting about their day on the fells. There's also a comfortably old-fashioned residents' bar and lounge, and a snug and restaurant. Bar food includes soup (£2), filled baps (£2.25), and main courses served cafeteria-style from a hot counter like rabbit pie, local herdwick lamb, fresh borrowdale trout, and steak in ale pie (all £6.50); a decent choice of malt whiskies, and good wine list; dominoes, cribbage, and quoits. The drive below the plunging majestic screes by England's deepest lake is quite awesome. Besides the comfortable bedrooms, they offer well equipped self-catering accommodation; nice breakfasts. *(Recommended by John Foord, Mike Pugh,*

Jason Caulkin, Peter Burton, Nigel and Sue Foster, Thomas Day; also in the Good Hotel Guide)

Own brew ~ Licensee Howard Christie ~ Real ale ~ Bar food (all day in summer; more restricted in winter) ~ Restaurant ~ (019467) 26229 ~ Children welcome ~ Dogs allowed in bar ~ Open 11-11(10 in winter); 12-10.30 Sun ~ Bedrooms: £45B/£90B

YANWATH NY5128 Map 9
Gate Inn 🍴

2¼ miles from M6 junction 40; A66 towards Brough, then right on A6, right on B5320, then follow village signpost

If you're after a break from the M6, then this welcoming and unpretentious village local with its reliably good, interesting food is just the place to head for. The simple turkey-carpeted bar, full of chatting regulars, has a log fire in an attractive stone inglenook and one or two nice pieces of furniture and middle-eastern brassware among more orthodox seats; or you can go through to eat in a two-level no smoking restaurant. Carefully prepared, the dishes from the menu might include home-made soup (£2.95), lunchtime sandwiches (from £3.50), mushrooms in stilton cream sauce (£3.95), seafood pancake (£4.25), and chicken korma or pies such as sweet potato or chicken, ham and egg in parsley sauce (£7.25), with daily specials like salmon and smoked haddock fishcakes with parsley cream sauce or roasted mediterranean vegetable tartlet (£8.25), whole bass with warm tomato vinaigrette or fillet of beef in red wine and cream with smoked bacon, mushrooms and rutland cheese (£12.50), and ostrich steak with wild mushroom and green peppercorn sauce (£13.50); piped music. Black Sheep Bitter and Jennings 1828 on handpump, and a decent wine list; darts, dominoes, cribbage, and shove-ha'penny; the friendly border collie is called Domino and is good with children. There are seats on the terrace and in the garden. *(Recommended by Susan and John Douglas, Christine and Neil Townend, JWAC, Richard J Holloway, Karen Eliot, Marcus Byron, Michael Doswell, M S Catling, C M Vipond, David and Julie Glover, Roy and Margaret Jones, Geoff and Angela Jaques, Tina and David Woods-Taylor, Alan and Paula McCully)*

Free house ~ Licensees Ian and Sue Rhind ~ Real ale ~ Bar food ~ Restaurant ~ (01768) 862386 ~ Children welcome ~ Dogs allowed in bar ~ Open 12-3, 6-11(10.30 Sun); evening opening 6.30 in winter; closed middle two weeks of Jan

---

Lucky Dip

Besides the fully inspected pubs, you might like to try these Lucky Dips recommended to us and described by readers (if you do, please send us reports: www.goodguides.com).

ALSTON [NY7146]
☆ *Angel* [Front St]: Friendly 17th-c local on steep cobbled street of charming small Pennine market town, beams, timbers, big log and coal fire, traditional furnishings, prompt service, good value generous quickly served food (not Tues evening) from well filled sandwiches to steaks, well kept Flowers IPA and Wadworths 6X, decent house wines; children welcome in eating area, tables in sheltered back garden; cheap bedrooms *(R T and J C Moggridge, LYM, MLR)*

AMBLESIDE [NY3704]
Salutation [Lake Rd]: Large comfortable hotel bar welcoming to families, friendly service, good menu, Theakstons Best; bedrooms *(D W Stokes)*
Wateredge [Borrans Rd]: Hotel rather than pub, great views from smartly refurbished bar, Coniston Bluebird and Bluebird XB, good value imaginative food, good service,

welcoming log fire; lots of tables in charming lakeside garden, comfortable bedrooms, parking *(D J Hulse, Margaret Dickinson, MDN)*

APPLEBY [NY6820]
A'th Board [Boroughgate]: Welcoming, with well kept ales inc Black Sheep and Everards Tiger, reasonably priced food from good sandwiches up; quiet piped music *(P G Plumridge)*

ARMATHWAITE [NY5046]
☆ *Dukes Head* [off A6 S of Carlisle]: Pleasant village inn with generally helpful licensees, civilised lounge bar with antique hunting prints, oak settles and little armchairs among more upright seats, coal fire, decent food using plenty of local produce, no smoking restaurant, well kept Tetleys and a guest beer such as Jennings, separate public bar; children welcome, tables out on the lawn behind, boules, bedrooms with good breakfast, pretty

village; open all day Sun *(Michael Doswell, Jason Caulkin, Dr and Mrs M W A Haward, Richard J Holloway, Dr T E Hothersall, LYM, Mr and Mrs A Campbell)*

Fox & Pheasant: Cosy, comfortable and neatly kept 18th-c coaching inn overlooking River Eden, enjoyable generous food inc imaginative dishes, helpful staff, Theakstons ales, attractive traditional beamed and flagstoned bar, shining brass, roaring fire; tables outside, bedrooms *(Jackie Moffat, Jean and Douglas Troup)*

ARNSIDE [SD4578]

Olde Fighting Cocks [Promenade]: Comfortably renovated seaside pub, big no smoking lounge and dining area, small restaurant, wide choice of bar food inc lunchtime and early evening bargain meals, well kept Thwaites, fairly priced wines, cheerful, helpful and efficient service, pool table; elevated garden giving magnificent views over estuary, refurbished bedrooms, open all day *(Chloe and Robert Gartery)*

ASKHAM [NY5123]

☆ *Punch Bowl*: Attractive pub reopened after two refurbishments (first after closure, then after a sudden fire), rambling beamed lounge bar, small snug, arches to public bar with juke box and pool room, enjoyable food from good lunchtime sandwiches up, wider evening choice, well kept Barngates Cracker and Black Sheep, lots of whiskies, good coffee, friendly service, two roaring log fires; children really welcome, plastic tables out in front facing green, delightful village *(Stuart Turner, Christine and Neil Townend, Michael Doswell, Hugh Roberts, C M Vipond, C L Clarkson, LYM, Di and Mike Gillam, Angus Lyon)*

Queens Head [lower green; off A6 or B5320 S of Penrith]: Two-room lounge with open fire, lots of beams, copper and brass, good choice of well served food inc good fresh fish and veg, well kept ale, wide choice of wines, friendly staff, nice local feel; children welcome, pleasant garden; bedrooms comfortable with creaking floorboards, good breakfast *(LYM, Peter and Giff Bennett, Steve and Louise Walker)*

BASSENTHWAITE [NY2332]

Sun [off A591 N of Keswick]: Opened-up rambling bar, homely and friendly, with low 17th-c beams, two big log fires, good choice of well kept Jennings ales, quickly served filling food, interesting local photographs, pool; provision for children, tables in pretty front yard looking up to the fells *(Christopher Tull, LYM)*

BLENCOW [NY4630]

Clickham [on B5288]: Comfortably cottagey two-bar local with real fires, quaint alcoves, warmly welcoming efficient service, good value wholesome food in small pretty dining area, Tetleys and Wadworths 6X, pool room with darts *(Gill and Keith Croxton, Alan and Paula McCully)*

BOOT [NY1700]

☆ *Brook House*: Converted small Victorian hotel, warm and welcoming, with obliging family service, wide choice of good generous home-

cooked food inc some interesting dishes on solid timber tables, small no smoking plushly modernised bar, comfortable hunting-theme lounge, log fires, four well kept ales inc Black Sheep and Theakstons, decent wines, peaceful dining room, good views; handy for Ravenglass railway and great walks, eight good bedrooms with own bathrooms – and good drying room *(John Dwane, Christine and Neil Townend, David and Rhian Peters, Tim and Judy Barker, Mike and Penny Sutton)*

Burnmoor [signed just off the Wrynose/Hardknott Pass rd]: Comfortably modernised beamed bar with ever-burning fire, well kept Black Sheep, Jennings Bitter and Cumberland and a guest beer, decent wines and malt whiskies, good mulled wine all year, enjoyable lunchtime bar food from sandwiches and baked potatoes up using carefully chosen ingredients, no smoking restaurant; booked minibus parties may have priority, games room with pool, TV and juke box; children welcome, seats out on sheltered front lawn with play area, open all day, bedrooms, good walks, lovely surroundings *(Dr Paull Khan, LYM, Nicholas Paint)*

Woolpack [Bleabeck, midway between Boot and Hardknott Pass]: Last pub before the notorious Hardknott Pass, a whitewashed beacon for travellers and walkers with generous good value home cooking, well kept Jennings and several summer guest beers, nice garden with mountain views; children welcome, bedrooms and bunkhouse *(John Dwane)*

BORROWDALE [NY2617]

Borrowdale Hotel [B5289, S end of Derwentwater]: A hotel, but very good choice of reasonably priced 'pub lunch' food from sandwiches up, roomy bar, pleasant staff, tables in garden; bedrooms *(Kevin Flack)*

BOWLAND BRIDGE [SD4189]

☆ *Hare & Hounds* [signed from A5074]: The 'new' team taking over this comfortably modernised and pleasantly set pub have done very well at two other Cumbrian pubs (and the landlord had this one some 20 years ago); good up-to-date bar and restaurant food from baguettes up, open fires, helpful service, real ales, children welcome; picnic-sets in spacious side garden *(RDK, LYM)*

BOWNESS-ON-WINDERMERE [SD4097]

☆ *Hole in t' Wall* [Lowside]: Ancient beams and flagstones, stripped stone, lots of country bric-a-brac and old pictures, lively bustle, splendid log fire under vast slate mantelpiece, upper room with attractive plasterwork (and dominoes and juke box), reasonably priced generous food from sandwiches to steak and good curries, well kept Robinsons Frederics, Best and Hartleys XB, may be home-made lemonade or good winter mulled wine; very busy in tourist season; no dogs or prams, sheltered picnic-sets in tiny flagstoned front courtyard *(Mike and Sue Loseby, Ian S Morley, David Heath, Edward Jago, LYM, Jim Abbott, Val Stevenson, Rob Holmes, Richard Lewis, Margaret Dickinson)*

BRIGSTEER [SD4889]
☆ *Wheatsheaf*: Cosy traditional pub in quiet pretty village, comfortable atmosphere and country views; sold as we went to press, but no changes yet – same welcoming efficient staff, good food from interesting sandwiches (using delicious home-made bread) and early-week bargains to plenty of fish, good value Sun lunch, Boddingtons, Theakstons and guests, nice wines; more reports please *(Malcolm Taylor, John Foord, John and Sylvia Harrop, Michael Doswell, Margaret and Roy Randle)*

BROUGHTON-IN-FURNESS [SD2187]
☆ *Black Cock* [Princes St]: Olde-worlde pub dating from 15th c, good range of well kept beers such as Charles Wells Bombardier, enjoyable reasonably priced food, sociable landlord and good service, step down to lounge bar with convivial atmosphere and cosy fireside, spacious comfortable dining room, juke box in games room up steps in former back stables; comfortable pleasantly decorated bedrooms *(Derek Harvey-Piper, G Coates, Cliff Blakemore)*
☆ *Manor Arms* [The Square]: Outstanding choice of well kept ales, several changing award-winners from far and wide as well as regulars such as Coniston Bluebird, Timothy Taylors Landlord and York Terrier in neatly kept and comfortable open-plan pub on quiet sloping square, flagstones and bow window seats, coal fire in big stone fireplace, chiming clocks, good sandwiches, pizzas and bockwurst sausages, winter soup, pool table; children allowed, stairs down to lavatories (ladies' has baby-changing); well appointed good value bedrooms, big breakfast, open all day *(BB, Derek Harvey-Piper, Andrew Jackson, G Coates)*

BURTON-IN-KENDAL [SD5277]
☆ *Dutton Arms* [4 miles from M6 junction 35; just off A6070 N of Carnforth (and can be reached – unofficially – from M6 northbound service area between junctions 35 and 36)]: Stylishly refurbished popular pub/restaurant with two well kept real ales in very small smartly comfortable pre-meal bar, roomy two level restaurant, partly no smoking, with candlelit dark tables, log fire, grand piano, wide choice of good food from baguettes (not cheap) to imaginative hot dishes (the vegetarian ones tempt even meat eaters), good value wines, good young staff, toys for children; smallish back garden with play area and view of Virgin trains; new bedrooms, open all day Sun and summer wkdys *(BB, Glenn and Julia Smithers)*

CALDBECK [NY3239]
☆ *Oddfellows Arms* [B5299 SE of Wigton]: Local bustle in comfortable bar, well cooked generous food from baked potatoes and lunchtime sandwiches to lots of blackboard specials, well kept Jennings Bitter and Cumberland, decent wines, reasonable prices, obliging staff, good-sized no smoking dining room; piped music, games area with pool, juke box and TV; children welcome, open all day wknds and summer, bedrooms, nice village

(Gwyneth and Salvo Spadaro-Dutturi, Mike and Penny Sutton, Dave Braisted, Canon David Baxter)

CARTMEL [SD3778]
Cavendish Arms [Cavendish St, off main sq]: Civilised hotelish bar with open fire, well kept Theakstons, varied menu from good if not cheap sandwiches up, no smoking restaurant, children truly welcome; tables out in front and behind by stream, comfortable bedrooms, good walks, open all day *(R T and J C Moggridge, Hugh Roberts, LYM)*
☆ *Kings Arms* [The Square]: Picturesque and inviting, nicely placed at the head of the attractive town square – rambling and neatly kept heavy-beamed bar, mix of furnishings from traditional settles to banquettes, several well kept real ales, wide choice of generous bar food inc meats from rare breeds, reasonable prices, all-day scones, cakes and so forth, good friendly service and attentive landlord, nice view from small no smoking back dining area; children welcome, sunny seats out on square and in attractive back courtyard by beck, craft and gift shop upstairs *(John Dwane, John Foord, JDM, KM, LYM, Margaret Dickinson)*
Royal Oak [The Square]: Low ceilings, cosy nooks, pleasant décor, generous good value food from baguettes up, well kept real ales such as Wadworths 6X, decent wines, friendly helpful service; nice big garden, bedrooms *(Maggie and Tony Harwood, Gerald and Wendy Doyle, BB)*

CASTLE CARROCK [NY5455]
Weary Sportsman: Unusual reworking of 17th-c building, comfortable sofas and stylish bucket chairs on bare boards of light and airy bar with good prints and wall of glassware and objets, smart conservatory dining room, carefully prepared upmarket food with mediterranean leanings, well kept Black Sheep, interesting wines; back japanese garden, bedrooms being upgraded *(anon)*

CHAPEL STILE [NY3205]
☆ *Wainwrights* [B5343]: Roomy new-feeling slate-floored bar welcoming walkers and dogs, old kitchen range, cushioned settles, well kept Jennings beers, food from sandwiches and baked potatoes up inc children's dishes, no smoking family dining area, darts and dominoes; piped music, Tues quiz night; good views from front picnic-sets, good walks, open all day wknds and summer *(B H and J I Andrews, LYM, Michael Butler, Ewan and Moira McCall)*

CONISTON [SD3098]
☆ *Black Bull* [Yewdale Rd (A593)]: Good Old Man, Coniston and Bluebird brewed here, lots of Donald Cambell water-speed memorabilia, bustling flagstoned back area (dogs allowed), banquettes and open fire in partly no smoking lounge bar (no smoking restaurant too), usual food inc children's and good sandwiches, farm ciders, quite a few bottled beers and malt whiskies; children welcome in eating areas, tables out in former coachyard, bedrooms, open all day *(Michael Doswell, John and Gillian Scarisbrick, Mike and Sue Loseby,*

Neil and Anita Christopher, JDM, KM, J Roy Smylie, Jim Abbott, P Abbott, Edward Jago, Angus Lyon, A N Caldwell, S and R Gray, LYM)

CROOK [SD4795]

☆ *Sun* [B5284 Kendal—Bowness]: Welcoming new licensees doing wide choice of good plentiful food (all day wknds) from unusual sandwiches to enterprising hot dishes and winter game, two comfortable no smoking dining areas off low-beamed bar, roaring log fire, fresh flowers, well kept Coniston Bluebird and Courage Directors, good value wines, cheerful helpful service *(Sue and Geoff Price, Michael Doswell, David and Julie Glover, Leo Horton, Tina and David Woods-Taylor, Karen Eliot, LYM, Sheila and Phil Stubbs, Les and Barbara Owen, Maurice and Gill McMahon, Deb and John Arthur, Dominic Epton, John Foord)*

CROOKLANDS [SD5383]

Crooklands Hotel [A65/B6385, nr M6 junction 36]: Big Best Western hotel dating from 16th c, pubby bar with good atmosphere, exposed brick and stonework, comfortable chairs and settles, log fires, Theakstons Best, pleasant staff, snug brick-floored second bar, good value straightforward food at sensible prices in intimate stable-theme carvery and upstairs bistro, afternoon teas, games area with pool; good new shop doing local produce and crafts (normal shop hours only), comfortable bedrooms *(BB, Margaret Dickinson)*

CULGAITH [NY6029]

☆ *Black Swan* [off A66 E of Penrith]: Well run cheerful 17th-c inn prettily set in quiet Eden Valley village handy for Acorn Bank (NT), jovial landlord, enjoyable food inc Sun lunch, fish specialities, attractive no smoking dining area, real ales such as Black Sheep and Tetleys, open fire, plenty of brasses and old photographs; pleasant bedrooms *(Dr D Parker, Tony and Katie Lewis, Michael Doswell, Alan and Paula McCully, JWAC)*

DACRE [NY4526]

☆ *Horse & Farrier* [between A66 and A592 SW of Penrith]: Cheerful 18th-c black-beamed village local with jovial landlord, wife cooks generous good value straightforward food in dining extension, particularly well kept Black Sheep and a weekly guest beer, friendly helpful staff, elderly stove, darts, dominoes, bridge, quiz and gourmet nights; integral post office *(Geoff and Angela Jaques, Richard Stancomb, Kevin Flack)*

DENT [SD7086]

☆ *Sun* [Main St]: This bustling pub in a picture-book village, very popular with readers for its own Dent ales brewed a few miles up the dale, with a simple and pleasant traditional beamed bar and straightforward sensibly priced food from sandwiches up, was for sale as we went to press – we hope it continues on the same lines as before; children welcome, open all day in summer *(LYM, Gerry and Rosemary Dobson)*

DOCKRAY [NY3921]

☆ *Royal* [A5091, off A66 or A592 W of Penrith]: Bright and immaculate open-plan bar in great spot away from the summer crowds, wide choice of good food from lunchtime rolls and baked potatoes up inc imaginative starters, children's helpings, friendly helpful service, well kept Black Sheep, Boddingtons, Castle Eden, Jennings Cumberland, Theakstons and Timothy Taylors Landlord, decent wines by the glass, two dining areas (one no smoking), walkers' part with stripped settles on flagstones, attractive restaurant; darts, cribbage and dominoes, piped music; picnic-sets in garden, open all day, comfortable bedrooms, good breakfast *(P Abbott, Roger Braithwaite, LYM, Mr and Mrs Richard Osborne, Jim Abbott)*

DUFTON [NY6825]

☆ *Stag*: Small basic pub by peaceful green of lovely unspoilt village on Pennine Way; friendly landlord, good value food inc good lunchtime sandwiches, well kept Black Sheep Best and Flowers IPA, good coffee, sensible prices, splendid early Victorian kitchen range in main bar, room off on left, back dining room; children, walkers and dogs welcome; open all day summer (cl winter Mon lunchtime), picnic-sets in charming front garden, bedrooms in next-door cottage, big breakfast *(Mrs R Somers, Mr and Mrs Maurice Thompson, Guy Vowles)*

ESKDALE GREEN [NY1300]

☆ *Bower House* [½ mile W]: Civilised old-fashioned stone-built inn with good log fire in main lounge bar extended around beamed and alcoved core, well kept ales such as Coniston Bluebird, Jennings, Theakstons XB and Youngs Waggle Dance, friendly staff, bar food, no noisy machines (but may be piped music), no smoking restaurant; nicely tended sheltered garden by cricket field, charming spot with great walks, bedrooms, open all day *(Derek Harvey-Piper, David and Rhian Peters, Tina and David Woods-Taylor)*

FAR SAWREY [SD3795]

☆ *Sawrey Hotel*: Comfortable, warm and welcoming stable bar with tables in wooden stalls, harness on rough white walls, even water troughs and mangers, big helpings of good simple lunchtime bar food inc well presented inexpensive sandwiches, well kept Black Sheep, Jennings and Theakstons, good coffee, pleasant helpful staff, attractive prices; separate hotel bar, evening restaurant; seats on nice lawn, beautiful setting, walkers, children and dogs welcome; bedrooms comfortable and well equipped *(LYM, Mr and Mrs Maurice Thompson)*

FOXFIELD [SD2185]

Prince of Wales [opp station]: Friendly and simple, with wide choice of well kept ales inc beers brewed in the former stables here and at the Tigertops brewery down in Wakefield (same owners), bottled imports and regular beer festivals, enthusiastic licensees, enjoyable simple home-made food, open fire, pub games inc bar billiards, daily papers and beer-related reading matter; children very welcome, games for them; cl Mon/Tues, opens 5 Weds/Thurs, open all day Fri-Sun, reasonably priced bedrooms with own bathrooms

(David Heath, Dr B and Mrs P B Baker)
GARRIGILL [NY7441]
☆ *George & Dragon* [off B6277 S of Alston]: Nicely set small 17th-c village inn flourishing under welcoming new licensees, new range of good food, well kept ales such as Black Sheep, good wines, great log fire in flagstoned bar and attractive stone-and-panelling dining room; pleasant newly decorated bedrooms *(LYM, Mrs Laurie Humble)*
GRASMERE [NY3307]
Tweedies [Dale Lodge Hotel]: Big square bar with settles, tartan panels and TV, family dining room, generous food from baguettes up, prompt friendly service, John Smiths and Theakstons, pool, plenty of young people; big pleasant hotel garden, bedrooms *(Michael Butler)*
GREAT ASBY [NY6712]
Three Greyhounds: Traditional village pub with helpful friendly landlord, usual food; pretty village with a well and good walks *(Jason Caulkin)*
GREAT CLIFTON [NY0429]
Old Ginn House [Moor Rd; just off A66 E of Workington]: Doing well under new management, with welcoming relaxing atmosphere, helpful young staff, enjoyable food, good mix of customers; good value peaceful bedrooms *(David V Carter)*
GREAT SALKELD [NY5536]
☆ *Highland Drove* [B6412, off A686 NE of Penrith]: Neatly kept early 18th-c inn with surprisingly inventive food from unusual sandwiches to innovative main dishes based on local produce, fish and game, also great vegetarian mezze; straightforward bar and plain pool room, large orthodox dining lounge, new hunting-lodge style upstairs dining room with woodburner and Pennine views, well kept Black Sheep, Theakstons and a monthly guest beer, good wine and whisky choice, proper soft drinks; welcoming helpful father-and-son licensees; stone tables out in garden with water feature, good value comfortable bedrooms with own bathrooms *(Kevin Tea, Michael Doswell, Janette, BB, JWAC)*
GREAT STRICKLAND [NY5522]
Strickland Arms: Comfortable and civilised old two-bar village inn, good value food inc original dishes, Black Sheep, Ind Coope Burton, Jennings and Youngs on tap, pool and darts area, may be piped classical music *(Mr and Mrs Maurice Thompson)*
GREAT URSWICK [SD2674]
☆ *General Burgoyne* [Church Rd]: Flagstoned early 18th-c village pub overlooking small tarn; four small cosy rambling rooms with log fires, bustling cheerful country atmosphere, mugs, glasses and hop bines hanging from beams, friendly efficient service, good value generous standard food, Robinsons Hartleys XB and guest beers; board games, piped music *(Andrew Jackson, BB)*
GRIZEBECK [SD2385]
Greyhound: Large warmly welcoming 17th-c local, beams and flagstones, good value food inc good home-made pies, well kept Greene

King Old Speckled Hen, John Smiths and Theakstons XB, good service, woodburners, no smoking dining room; well behaved dogs welcome, tables in pleasant garden behind, good value smart bedrooms with big breakfast *(Brian Dickinson, Margaret and Roy Randle)*
HALE [SD5078]
Kings Arms [A6 S of Beetham]: Immaculate traditional pub with plenty of brass, china and hunting prints, copious satisfying food inc some interesting dishes and free puddings with some, friendly obliging service, well kept Thwaites Lancaster Bomber and Worthington, two open fires *(Michael Doswell)*
HAVERTHWAITE [SD3284]
Anglers Arms [just off A590]: Busy and friendly split-level pub with good choice of generous fresh food from sandwiches to steak, quick courteous service, well kept Jennings and Theakstons, overflow upstairs dining room, lower area with pool *(Sheila and Phil Stubbs)*
HAWKSHEAD [SD3598]
☆ *Sun* [Main St]: Thriving pub with good reasonably priced food using imaginative recipes and local produce, lots of brass, brickwork and beams, friendly staff, well kept beer, sizeable restaurant; children and dogs welcome, tables out in front by small courtyard, bedrooms *(B H and J I Andrews, Karen Eliot)*
KENDAL [SD5288]
Punch Bowl [Barrows Green (A65 about 3 miles S)]: Good value generous freshly made baguettes, starters and main courses in comfortable open-plan pub, usual puddings, well kept Timothy Taylors Landlord and Theakstons, warm décor and button-back banquettes *(Michael Doswell)*
Shakespeare [Highgate]: Upstairs pub through archway to small close, lots of woodwork, wide choice of food all day, Theakstons Best; decent bedrooms *(David Carr)*
KESWICK [NY2623]
☆ *Dog & Gun* [Lake Rd]: Lively and unpretentious town local with some high settles, low beams, partly slate floor (rest carpeted or boards), fine Abrahams mountain photographs, coins in beams and timbers by fireplace, log fire; well kept Theakstons Best and Old Peculier and Yates, open fires, generous straightforward bar food all day from sandwiches up; piped music; children welcome, open all day *(Nigel and Sue Foster, LYM, David Carr, Mr and Mrs G Clay, Gerald and Wendy Doyle, SLC)*
☆ *Swinside Inn* [only pub in Newlands Valley, just SW; OS Sheet 90 map ref 242217]: Attractive neatly modernised but rustic and rambling pub very popular for good value tasty and substantial fresh food from sandwiches, baguettes or soup and warm rolls up in bar and restaurant, no smoking area, welcoming obliging service, well kept Jennings beers, decent wines, good log fires, family room; dogs allowed, plenty of tables outside with play area, open all day Sat and summer; bedrooms, brilliant peaceful valley setting, stunning views across to Catbells

(D J Hulse, Tina and David Woods-Taylor, Rev John Hibberd, LYM, Margaret Dickinson)

KIRKBY LONSDALE [SD6278]

Snooty Fox [B6254]: New manager in rambling partly panelled pub with eye-catching pictures and bric-a-brac, country furniture, two coal fires, no smoking dining annexe, well kept Timothy Taylors Landlord, Theakstons Best and a guest beer, several country wines, and quite a choice of food; piped music in back bar; children in eating areas, tables in pretty garden, bedrooms, open all day *(Angus Lyon, LYM, Dave Braisted)*

KIRKBY STEPHEN [NY7707]

☆ *Croglin Castle* [South Rd]: Stone-built local with basic décor in large comfortable bar, remarkably good interesting food in dining room, friendly staff, good wines, Thwaites and a guest beer *(Guy Vowles, Marcus Byron)*

KIRKOSWALD [NY5541]

Crown: Friendly small renovated 16th-c coaching inn, clean and tidy, beams covered with plates, brasses around fireplace, teapots over bar, good generous reasonably priced food from big sandwiches to innovative dishes using local produce and fish (same menu in bar and small no smoking restaurant, new licensees' Italian father is head chef), pleasant service, well kept Jennings ales *(Kevin Tea, Roy Morrison)*

LANERCOST [NY5563]

☆ *Abbey Bridge Inn* [follow brown Lanercost Priory signs from A69 or in Brampton]: Small newly refurbished pub in secluded riverside position nr 12th-c priory, restrained décor with fresh flowers, dark pub tables in one room, rough-hewn rustic furniture in the other, airy dining room, relaxed atmosphere, usual food from baguettes and baked potatoes up, some interesting dishes, well kept Coniston Bluebird XB, Yates and guest beers, plenty of malt whiskies, good coffee, pleasant obliging service; cl midweek lunchtimes in winter, picnic-sets outside *(LYM, Michael Doswell)*

LANGWATHBY [NY5633]

Shepherds [A686 Penrith—Alston]: Unpretentious and cheerful, good quickly served reasonably priced food, friendly efficient service, well kept beers, decent wine choice, comfortable banquettes, bar down steps from lounge, games room; tables and chairs outside, attractive spot on huge green of Pennines village, play area *(Roy Morrison)*

LOWICK GREEN [SD3084]

☆ *Farmers Arms* [just off A5092 SE of village]: Charming cosy public bar with heavy beams, huge slate flagstones, big open fire, cosy corners and pub games (also piped music, TV; this part may be cl winter), some interesting furniture and pictures in plusher hotel lounge bar across yard, tasty reasonably priced food in bar and restaurant inc daily roast, well kept John Smiths and Theakstons, friendly attentive staff; unobtrusive piped music; children welcome, open all day, comfortable bedrooms *(LYM, Margaret and Roy Randle)*

MELMERBY [NY6237]

Shepherds [A686 Penrith—Alston]: Heavy-

beamed comfortable no smoking room off flagstoned bar, spacious end room with woodburner, straightforward bar food, well kept Badger IPA, Black Sheep Riggwelter, Hesket Newmarket Blencathra and Jennings, quite a few malt whiskies, games area with pool and juke box; children welcome, open all day *(Mr and Mrs Maurice Thompson, Mike and Wendy Proctor, Alan and Paula McCully, LYM)*

METAL BRIDGE [NY3564]

Metal Bridge Hotel [off A74 Carlisle—Gretna, nr Rockcliffe]: Friendly staff, enjoyable bar food, reasonably priced wines by the glass, nice river view from sun lounge *(Richard J Holloway, Michael and Marion Buchanan)*

NETHER WASDALE [NY1204]

Screes: Long friendly plush lounge and character public bar, stunning views of mountains and along Wasdale, particularly well kept ales such as Black Sheep, Yates Best and Derwent Springtime, quick friendly service, good value home-made food inc lunchtime sandwiches and enjoyable vegetarian dishes, interesting piped music; picnic-sets out on large front green, five bedrooms *(John Foord, Tony Hughes)*

OXENHOLME [SD5390]

☆ *Station Inn* [½ mile up hill, B6254 towards Old Hutton]: Spruce and roomy dining pub with good generous home-made food from hearty sandwiches and standard bar meals to interesting specials, well kept Boddingtons, Tetleys and Theakstons, nice wine list, very friendly staff, log fire; large garden with extensive play area, bedrooms, good walks *(Michael Doswell)*

PENRITH [NY5130]

Agricultural [A592 in from M6 junction 40]: Down-to-earth Victorian pub with many original features, comfortable L-shaped beamed lounge with partly glazed panelling, plenty of seating, log fire, curved sash windows over the bar, and a thorough mix of customers; full Jennings range on handpump, over 30 malt whiskies, decent bar food, no smoking restaurant (children allowed), darts and dominoes; piped music; good views from side picnic-sets, bedrooms, open all day *(Richard J Holloway, MLR, LYM)*

POOLEY BRIDGE [NY4724]

Sun: Down-to-earth panelled village pub with good value generous food from sandwiches to nicely cooked main dishes, friendly service, full Jennings range kept well, good wine choice, small lounge bar, steps past servery to bigger bar with games and piped music, restaurant; plenty of garden tables, great views to Catbells *(Hugh Roberts, David Heath, David Edwards)*

RAVENSTONEDALE [NY7203]

Black Swan [just off A685 SW of Kirkby Stephen]: Hotel bar with open fire and some stripped stone, enjoyable food from sandwiches up (meals only by booking at quietest times of year), friendly staff; tables in charming tree-sheltered streamside garden over road, comfortable bedrooms inc some for

disabled, good serious walking country
(BB, Susan and John Douglas)
Fat Lamb [Crossbank; A683 Sedbergh—
Kirkby Stephen]: Remote inn with pews in
cheery bar, log fire in traditional black kitchen
range, good local photographs and bird plates,
friendly staff, perhaps well kept Boddingtons,
food from filled baguettes to enjoyable
restaurant meals; facilities for disabled,
children welcome; bedrooms with own
bathrooms, tables out by sheep pastures, good
walks *(T Pascall, BB)*

SATTERTHWAITE [SD3392]
Eagles Head: This small unpretentious
Grizedale Forest pub, with a big log fire, lots of
local photographs and maps, pool room and
comfortable bedrooms sharing bathroom, has
been popular with readers for well kept
Jennings Cumberland and Theakstons, good
value food and a real welcome for small
children, but changed hands as we went to
press; news please *(Michael Butler,
Michael Doswell, Maeve Brayne, Margaret and
Roy Randle)*

SCALES [NY3426]
☆ *White Horse* [A66 W of Penrith]: Light and
airy beamed pub-restaurant with cosy corners,
interesting farmhouse-kitchen memorabilia and
good open fires, well kept Jennings ales, fairly
priced wines, wide choice of good food inc
some local specialities and good wknd fish,
welcoming landlord; a couple of no smoking
tables, well behaved children welcome (over
5 evening), lovely setting below Blencathra
(David Cooke, Mike and Penny Sutton, LYM)

SEDBERGH [SD6592]
Red Lion [Finkle St (A683)]: Cheerful beamed
Jennings local, down to earth, comfortable and
friendly, with their full beer range kept well,
good value generous tasty food inc bargain Sun
lunch, helpful attentive staff, coal fire, sports
TV *(BB, Malcolm Taylor, Dr D J and
Mrs S C Walker)*

SHAP [NY5615]
☆ *Greyhound* [A6, S end]: Bustling and
unpretentious former coaching inn, current
licensees (former catering college lecturers)
doing good hearty local food esp slow-cooked
meats and memorable puddings in open-plan
bar or restaurant, copious helpings, half a
dozen well kept ales such as Greene King,
Jennings, Wadworths 6X and Youngs, good
wine list, quick service by happy attentive staff;
unobtrusive piped classical music; comfortable
bedrooms, popular with coast-to-coast walkers
*(Michael Doswell, D and B M Clark,
David Edwards, Paul and Anita Holmes)*

SOUTHWAITE [NY4146]
Crown [away from village, towards Gaitsgill]:
Very welcoming, with good reasonably priced
fresh food from sandwiches and home-made
soup up, Theakstons Best and a guest beer,
open fire, brightly decorated light and airy
dining extension; handy for races at Carlisle
(Michael Doswell)

STAVELEY [SD4798]
☆ *Eagle & Child* [off A591 Windermere—
Kendal]: Nicely refurbished L-shaped open-

plan bar with good home-made food inc fresh
fish and veg, imaginative modern dishes,
thoughtful provision for children and generous
Sun lunch, good helpful service, well kept
changing ales such as Coniston Bluebird, Hop
Back Crop Circle, Jennings Crag Rat and Yates
Summer Fever from small bar counter, farm
cider, good wine choice, coal fire, lots of
prints, upstairs barn-style restaurant; neat
riverside garden, comfortably renovated
bedrooms, good breakfast, open all day *(BB,
Jackie Moffat, MLR, S and R Gray, Mr and
Mrs Maurice Thompson, Richard Lewis)*

TEBAY [NY6104]
Cross Keys [very handy for M6 junction 38]:
Comfortable roadside pub with plentiful good
value food from baguettes and baked potatoes
up in separate eating area, prompt friendly
service, well kept Black Sheep, decent wine,
coal fire, darts, pool, cribbage; bedrooms
(Andrew Crawford)

THIRLSPOT [NY3217]
Kings Head [A591 Grasmere—Keswick]: Long
modernised bar with wide choice of food
(much as Travellers Rest, Grasmere) in no
smoking eating area, well kept Jennings,
Theakstons Best, XB and Mild, Yates and a
guest ale, fast polite service, inglenook fires,
games room with pool and big-screen TV; can
be smoky, piped music; walkers and children
welcome, with toy box; tables in garden, good
spot, comfortable bedrooms (the hotel part and
restaurant are separate) *(LYM, Tina and
David Woods-Taylor, Jim Abbott, Roy and
Lindsey Fentiman)*

THRELKELD [NY3225]
☆ *Horse & Farrier*: Comfortably enlarged 17th-c
dining pub, recently renovated and attractively
furnished, with hunt cartoons, imaginative
rather restauranty food, three well kept
Jennings ales, good house wines, good
welcoming service, plenty of space for drinkers;
open all day, dogs allowed when restaurant is
closed, good bedrooms *(Angus Lyon)*

TORVER [SD2894]
☆ *Church House* [A593/A5084 S of Coniston]:
Big rambling place with lots of low beams, fine
log fire in cheerful flagstoned bar with
interesting bric-a-brac, another in comfortable
lounge with dark red walls, splendid hill views
(if weather allows), good value food from good
sandwiches and baguettes to interesting main
dishes, quick pleasant service, well kept
Caledonian Deuchars IPA, Coniston and other
ales such as Bass and Castle Eden, decent
house wines; friendly alsatian and whippet,
children welcome, attractive evening
restaurant; open all day at least in summer,
nice big garden, small caravan/camp site,
bedrooms *(John Foord, Christine and
Neil Townend, Lorraine and Fred Gill,
Neil and Anita Christopher)*

TROUTBECK [NY4103]
☆ *Mortal Man* [A592 N of Windermere; Upper
Rd]: Neatly kept partly panelled beamed hotel
bar with big log fire, mix of seats inc a
cushioned settle, copper-topped tables, cosy
eating room, no smoking picture-window

restaurant, food from sandwiches to steaks with some tempting specials, well kept ales such as Jennings, John Smiths and Theakstons Best, friendly young staff, darts, dominoes, great views from gloriously sited tables outside; piped music, TV room, Sun folk/blues night; children welcome, open all day, comfortable bedrooms – lovely village *(Peter Heaton, Brian and Janet Ainscough, B H and J I Andrews, LYM, D W Stokes)*

Sportsman [B5288, just off A66]: Big rambling bar, Jennings beers, good wine choice, bar food and separate restaurant menu; children welcome, pretty back terrace overlooking valley, open all day *(Alan and Paula McCully)*

UNDERBARROW [SD4692]

Punchbowl: Small friendly open-plan village local, softly lit beamed bar with button-back banquettes and good log fire, good value fresh homely food from sandwiches up, particularly well kept Black Sheep and Jennings Cumberland, quick helpful service even when busy; handy for walkers *(Michael Doswell)*

WARWICK-ON-EDEN [NY4656]

Queens Arms [2 miles from M6, junction 43; signed off A69 towards Hexham]: Reasonably priced enjoyable home-made food inc good Sun roast and puddings in clean unpretentious two-room bar, well kept Thwaites, good choice of good value wines and malt whiskies, warm log fires, nice atmosphere; children welcome, tables in attractive side garden with bright play area, comfortable bedrooms *(Elizabeth Booker, LYM)*

WATERMILLOCK [NY4523]

Brackenrigg [A592, Ullswater]: Opened-up rustic 19th-c inn in lovely spot overlooking Ullswater, good imaginative food, cheery helpful staff, particularly well kept Black Sheep Special, Theakstons and Jennings Cumberland, friendly mix of holidaymakers and locals; bedrooms and self-catering *(Geoff and Angela Jaques)*

WINSTER [SD4193]

☆ *Brown Horse* [A5074 S of Windermere]: Roomy open-plan dining place, light and comfortable, popular esp with older people for enjoyable attractively priced food from soup and sandwiches to some interesting dishes; well spaced tables inc no smoking dining room, cheerful helpful service, well kept Black Sheep and Jennings Bitter and Cumberland, decent wines; children welcome (own menu, toys) *(Dr and Mrs R G J Telfer, Michael Doswell, Malcolm Taylor, LYM)*

WINTON [NY7810]

☆ *Bay Horse* [off A685 N of Kirkby Stephen]: Two low-key and low-ceilinged rooms with Pennine photographs and local fly-tying, very good generous home-cooked food inc local meat and fresh veg, well kept beers such as Black Sheep, Daleside and Rudgate, low prices, games room, children welcome; cl winter afternoons, open from 1.30 (noon wknds) summer but not till 7 Tues; comfortable modestly priced bedrooms, good breakfast, tiny peaceful moorland hamlet *(Karen Eliot, P Abbott, LYM, Comus and Sarah Elliott)*

If a service charge is mentioned prominently on a menu or accommodation terms, you must pay it if service was satisfactory. If service is really bad you are legally entitled to refuse to pay some or all of the service charge as compensation for not getting the service you might reasonably have expected.

Derbyshire

Derbyshire pubs generating particularly enthusiastic reports from readers these days include the intriguing and highly individual Bear at Alderwasley (it wins a Food Award this year), the Waltzing Weasel at Birch Vale (a very good dining pub), the very traditional Olde Gate at Brassington, the friendly Miners Arms at Eyam (nice food), the Bentley Brook at Fenny Bentley (a new entry, brewing its own good beers, good food too), the Coach & Horses in the same village (a welcoming all-rounder; both these serve food all day), the unspoilt Barrel near Foolow (also good all round, with terrific views), and in Foolow itself the Bulls Head (another nice new entry, with well kept beer, nice food and comfortable bedrooms), the rather smart Chequers on Froggatt Edge (very good food), the Hardwick Inn hard by Hardwick Hall (good value food all day), the very foody Plough prettily set on the edge of Hathersage (gaining a Food Award this year for its inventive cooking), the Red Lion at Hognaston (nicely combining really good food with a warm local atmosphere), the Dead Poets in Holbrook (pleasantly idiosyncratic décor, good beers), the splendidly old-fashioned Barley Mow at Kirk Ireton, the Miners Arms in Milltown (a good straightforward dining pub), the Monsal Head Hotel (its Stable Bar is a great favourite), and the chatty Three Stags Heads at Wardlow (a very individual farm pub). Our three entries in Derby are also well liked: the Olde Dolphin for its relaxed traditional style, the other two chiefly for their beers. For a special meal out, we'd head for the Bear at Alderwasley, the Waltzing Weasel at Birch Vale, the Druid at Birchover, the Chequers on Froggatt Edge, the Plough at Hathersage, or the Red Lion at Hognaston. Once again, it's the Waltzing Weasel at Birch Vale which wins the title of Derbyshire Dining Pub of the Year. In the Lucky Dip section at the end of the chapter, pubs scoring high marks are the Bulls Head in Ashford in the Water, Lamb at Chinley, Boat at Cromford, Abbey Inn and Flower Pot in Derby, Old Nags Head in Edale, Duke of York at Elton, Fox House near Hathersage, Wheel in Holbrook, Packhorse at Little Longstone, Colvile Arms at Lullington, Bulls Head at Monyash, Royal Oak at Ockbrook, Malt Shovel in Shardlow and George at Tideswell. Drinks prices in the area are a bit lower than the national average; the John Thompson near Melbourne and Brunswick in Derby (brewing their own) and the Alexandra there had the lowest beer prices we found.

ALDERWASLEY SK3153 Map 7
Bear ★ 🍽 🍷

Village signposted with Breanfield off B5035 E of Wirksworth at Malt Shovel; inn ½ mile SW of village, on Ambergate—Wirksworth high back road

This enchantingly unspoilt pub is not just memorable for its delightful interior and peaceful setting – the food here is enjoyable too. From a daily changing blackboard, interesting dishes (made mostly with ingredients from local farms and growers) could include home-made soup (£2.95), deep-fried haggis and stilton balls with apple and whisky chutney (£4.50), ham, egg and chips, home-made lasagne or caramelised onion and goats cheese tartlet in champagne and asparagus sauce (£7.95), poached smoked salmon with white wine and butter sauce (£8.95) and venison steak with port and cranberry (£12.95), with puddings such as treacle sponge (£3.75); they also do sandwiches (£3.25), and there's a Sunday carvery (£7.95). Service is friendly and helpful. The several small dark rooms, with low beams, bare boards and ochre walls throughout, have a great variety of old tables, with seats running from brocaded dining chairs and old country-kitchen chairs to high-backed settles and antique oak chairs carved with traditional Derbyshire motifs. One little room is filled right to its built-in wall seats by a single vast table. There are log fires in huge stone fireplaces, candles galore, antique paintings and engravings, plenty of Staffordshire china ornaments, and no fewer than three grandfather clocks. Despite the treasures, this is a proper easy-going country local, with dominoes players clattering about beside canaries trilling in a huge Edwardian-style white cage (elsewhere look out for the talkative cockatoos, an african grey parrot, and budgerigars). They have a fine range of interesting wines, as well as Bass, Greene King Old Speckled Hen, Marstons Pedigree, and a guest such as Black Sheep well kept on handpump. There are peaceful country views from well spaced picnic-sets out on the side grass. There's no obvious front door, and you get in through the plain back entrance by the car park. We have not yet heard from any readers who have stayed here. *(Recommended by Richard Cole, Kevin Blake, Derek and Sylvia Stephenson, JP, PP, Andrew Pearson)*

Free house ~ Licensee Nicola Fletcher-Musgrave ~ Real ale ~ Bar food (12-9.30) ~ Restaurant ~ (01629) 822585 ~ Children welcome in family area and restaurant ~ Dogs welcome ~ Open 12-11 ~ Bedrooms: £45S/£70S

BEELEY SK2667 Map 7
Devonshire Arms

B6012, off A6 Matlock—Bakewell

This handsome old stone building was cleverly converted from three early 18th-c cottages to become a prosperous coaching inn by the 19th c – when Dickens is said to have been a regular. There's a big emphasis on the tasty bar food, which is served all day, and could include soup (£3), generously filled baguettes (from £4.35), duck and fig terrine (£5.75), ploughman's (£6.50), steak and ale pie (£7.35), smoked haddock rarebit or chicken and leek suet pudding (£8.50), braised knuckle of lamb in rosemary sauce (£9.50) and steak (from £12.50), with puddings (from £3). They have a Friday fish night, and on Sundays do a Victorian breakfast (£11.50); you'll need to book for both, and at weekends. Big log fires cheerfully warm the cosy black-beamed rooms, which have comfortably cushioned stone seats along stripped walls, and antique settles and simpler wooden chairs on flagstoned floors. Five handpumps serve well kept Bass, Black Sheep Best and Special, Theakstons Old Peculier and a guest such as Marstons Pedigree. They've also decent good value house wine, and about three dozen malt whiskies; shove-ha'penny, cribbage, and dominoes. The restaurant and cocktail bar are no smoking. The pub is beautifully set in a pretty Peak District estate village, and is only about a mile away from Chatsworth House; nearby at Pilsley is the Duchess of Devonshire's excellent produce shop. *(Recommended by M G Hart, Ian S Morley, Mike and Sue Loseby, Keith and Chris O'Neill, Roger and Maureen Kenning, Dr S J Shepherd, Derek and Sylvia Stephenson, Anne and Steve Thompson, the Didler, Ann and Colin Hunt, JP, PP, June and Malcolm Farmer, Bob and Valerie Mawson, Jenny and Peter Lowater)*

Free house ~ Licensee John A Grosvenor ~ Real ale ~ Bar food (12-9.30) ~ Restaurant ~ (01629) 733259 ~ Children welcome ~ Open 10-11; 12-10.30 Sun; closed 25 Dec

> The letters and figures after the name of each town are its Ordnance Survey map reference. *Using the Guide* at the beginning of the book explains how it helps you find a pub, in road atlases or large-scale maps as well as in our own maps.

BIRCH VALE SK0286 Map 7
Waltzing Weasel 🍴 ⛊ 🛏

A6015 E of New Mills

Derbyshire Dining Pub of the Year

High on a hill, this well run dining pub has fine views of Kinder Scout and the Peak District from its charming back restaurant, pretty garden and terrace. The home-made bar food is good and beautifully presented, though prices are high for the area. With quite an italian influence, the interesting menu could include soup (£4.25), sandwiches (from £6.95), black olive pâté (£4.95), scallops in cream sauce (£6.50), pizzas (from £5.75), crayfish tails (£6.25), vegetable crêpe (£8.50), seafood tart (£9.50), casserole of the day (£9.75), a fish dish such as bass or halibut (from £10.50), and the italian platter (£11.95); tasty puddings such as bread and butter pudding or brandy snap baskets with fruit and ice cream (£4.85). On weekday evenings they do a slightly different set menu (£23.50 for two courses), and there's a roast on Sunday (£10.75). As well as a good choice of decent wines and malt whiskies, they've well kept Kelham Gold, Marstons Best and perhaps a guest such as Timothy Taylors on handpump. The bar has a comfortably worn-in pubby atmosphere, with a roaring fire, plenty of houseplants on corner tables, and daily papers on sticks. The licensees' interest in antiques (they're former dealers) is reflected in some of the furnishings, with handsome oak settles and tables among more usual furniture, and there are lots of nicely framed mainly sporting Victorian prints, and a good longcase clock. The bedrooms are spacious, and comfortably furnished; good breakfasts. Bess, the friendly pub dog, likes meeting visitors. *(Recommended by A S and M E Marriott, Kevin Blake, B and M Kendall, Dr T E Hothersall, Mike and Linda Hudson, Frank Gorman, Richard Fendick, Peter F Marshall, Mike and Wendy Proctor, Mr and Mrs C W Widdowson, Anne and Steve Thompson, Bob Broadhurst, Robin and Joyce Peachey, JP, PP, Eddie Edwards, Alison Hanratty)*

Free house ~ Licensee Michael Atkinson ~ Real ale ~ Bar food ~ Restaurant ~ (01663) 743402 ~ Children in eating area of bar, must be over 7 in restaurant ~ Dogs allowed in bar and bedrooms ~ Open 12-3, 5.30-11(10.30 Sun) ~ Bedrooms: £48S/£88B

BIRCHOVER SK2462 Map 7
Druid 🍴

Village signposted off B5056

Candlelit at night, the spacious and airy two-storey dining extension is really the heart of this creeper-clad dining pub, which has been run by the same landlord for more than 20 years. The range of good food is remarkably wide, but could include home-made soup (£3), garlic mushrooms (£5.20), and main dishes (with plenty of well cooked vegetables) such as lamb casserole with mint and rosemary dumplings (£7.80), poached chicken breast with bacon and stilton sauce (£9.90), cod and mushroom bake topped with white wine sauce and grated cheese (£10.20), and steaks (from £12.50), as well as around 10 vegetarian dishes such as vegetable and pasta bake, five bean casserole with vegetarian suet dumplings or fruit and vegetable pasta (£7.90); among the tempting selection of puddings could be apple and marzipan torte or warm bakewell pudding with cream (£3.50). Alongside Druid Ale (brewed for the pub by Leatherbritches), they serve well kept Marstons Pedigree from handpump; there's a good selection of malt whiskies, and the wines are reasonably priced. The small plain bar has plush-upholstered wooden wall benches around straightforward tables, and a big coal fire. The Garden Room, tap room and part of the bar are no smoking; piped music. As we went to press the pub was undergoing a thorough refurbishment with new carpets, curtains, furniture, and even a new bar. There are picnic-sets in front, and this is a good area for walks. *(Recommended by Darly Graton, Graeme Gulibert, the Didler, John Close, Andy and Ali, Mike and Wendy Proctor, T J W Hill, Richard Cole, Roy and Margaret Jones, M G Hart, JP, PP, Patrick Hancock, Bob and Valerie Mawson, Roger Bridgeman, Cliff Blakemore, Stephen and Judy Parish)*

Free house ~ Licensee Brian Bunce ~ Real ale ~ Bar food (not Mon; 12-1.45(1.30 winter), 7-8.45(8.30 winter)) ~ Restaurant ~ (01629) 650302 ~ Children if eating until 8.15 ~ Dogs allowed in bar ~ Open 12-2.30, 7-11; they often close earlier in winter; closed Mon (exc bank hols), 25 Dec and evening 26 Dec

BRASSINGTON SK2354 Map 7
Olde Gate ★

Village signposted off B5056 and B5035 NE of Ashbourne

Carsington reservoir (excellent for water sports and activities) is only a five-minute drive away from this well liked village pub, a good place to stop after a bracing walk. The relaxing public bar is traditionally furnished, with a lovely ancient wall clock, rush-seated old chairs, antique settles, including one ancient black solid oak one, and roaring log fires. Gleaming copper pots sit on a 17th-c kitchen range, pewter mugs hang from a beam, and a side shelf boasts a collection of embossed Doulton stoneware flagons. On the left of a small hatch-served lobby, another cosy beamed room has stripped panelled settles, scrubbed-top tables, and a blazing fire under a huge mantelbeam. From the stone-mullioned windows you can look out across lots of tables in the pleasant garden to small silvery-walled pastures, and in fine weather, the small front yard with a few benches is a nice place to sit (listen out for the village bell-ringers practising on Friday evenings). In summer they do a variety of barbecued dishes including tasty steaks. Otherwise the largely home-made (and not cheap) bar food, from a regularly changing menu, could include well presented open sandwiches and baguettes (from £4.95 to £6.95), ploughman's (£6.25), home-made pies such as ham, leek and stilton or salmon and asparagus (from £7.50), cheese and leek bake with mushrooms (£8.95), home-made curries (£10.50) and seafood lasagne (£11.50), with puddings such as chocolate fudge cake or (highly recommended by readers) lemon pie (£3.50). The dining room is no smoking; the back bar is prettily candlelit at night. Well kept Marstons Pedigree and a guest such as Charles Wells Bombardier on handpump, and a good selection of malt whiskies; cribbage and dominoes. Although the date etched outside the pub is 1874, it was originally built in 1616, of magnesian limestone and timbers salvaged from Armada wrecks, bought in exchange for locally mined lead. *(Recommended by Peter F Marshall, RWC, Stephen and Judy Parish, Di and Mike Gillam, P Abbott, Pat and Roger Fereday, Phil and Heidi Cook, JP, PP, the Didler, Roger Bridgeman, Kevin Blake, John Saul, Anne and Steve Thompson)*

Marstons (W & D) ~ Tenant Paul Burlinson ~ Real ale ~ Bar food (12-1.45(2 Fri/Sat), 7-8.45(9 Fri/Sat), not Sun evening) ~ (01629) 540448 ~ Children over 10 ~ Dogs welcome ~ Open 12-2.30(3 Sat), 6-11; 12-3, 7-10.30 Sun; closed Mon lunchtime except bank hols

BUXTON SK1266 Map 7
Bull i' th' Thorn

Ashbourne Road (A515) 6 miles S of Buxton, near Hurdlow

This intriguing cross between a medieval hall and a straightforward roadside pub has recently been taken over by a new landlady. There's lots to look at inside, and among the lively old carvings that greet you on your way in is one of the eponymous bull caught in a thornbush (the pub's name comes from a hybrid of its 15th-c and 17th-c titles, the Bull and Hurdlow House of Hurdlow Thorn), and there are also images of an eagle with a freshly caught hare, and some spaniels chasing a rabbit. In the hall, which dates from 1471, a massive central beam runs parallel with a forest of smaller ones, there are panelled window seats in the embrasures of the thick stone walls, handsome panelling, and old flagstones stepping gently down to a big open fire. It's furnished with fine long settles, an ornately carved hunting chair, a longcase clock, a powder-horn, and armour that includes 17th-c german helmets, swords, and blunderbusses and so forth. Stuffed animals' heads line the corridor that leads to a candlelit hall, used for medieval themed evening banquets. An adjoining room has pool, and dominoes. A simple no smoking family room opens on to a terrace and big lawn with swings, and there are more tables in a sheltered angle in front. The bar menu includes around 10 different vegetarian dishes (and on Thursday evenings they have over 10 extra) such as vegetable wellington and mushroom and pepper stroganoff (£7.50), as well as soup (£2.25), filled baguettes (from £3.75), a range of salad platters (from £7.25), steak and kidney pie (£7.50), salmon (£8.25), and roast lamb shank with redcurrant and rosemary (£8.75), with puddings such as spotted dick (from £3.25); best to book for their seafood night (Tuesday) and steak night (Wednesday). They serve Robinsons Best on handpump. The pub is handy for the High Peak Trail. *(Recommended by the Didler, G B Longden, JP, PP, Paul and Margaret Baker, Mike and Wendy Proctor, Kevin Blake, Dr Paull Khan, Ann and Colin Hunt, A Sadler)*

Robinsons ~ Tenant Annette Maltby-Baker ~ Real ale ~ Bar food (9.30-9) ~ (01298) 83348 ~ Children in restaurant and family room ~ Dogs welcome ~ Open 9.30-11 (10.30 Sun) ~ Bedrooms: /£60B

CASTLETON SK1583 Map 7
Castle Hotel 🛏

High Street at junction with Castle Street

You can sit out in the pretty garden of this neatly kept historic hotel (which handily serves food all day), and there are good views from the heated terrace. The inviting bar has stripped stone walls with built-in cabinets, lovely open fires, finely carved early 17th-c beams and, in one room, ancient flagstones. Popular and good value bar food includes lunchtime sandwiches (from £3.75), crispy bacon and warm black pudding salad (£3.95), crab and salmon fishcakes (£5.25), gammon steak (£6.35), cod and chips (£6.75), beef and ale pudding (£7.95), rump steak (from £8.75) and ham hock with creamy mustard sauce (£8.95), with puddings such as chocolate brownie or cheesecake (£3.45). Service is very pleasant and efficient. They have well kept Bass and Tetleys on handpump, and over a dozen wines by the glass; freshly squeezed orange juice in summer. A good part of the pub is no smoking, and there's a fruit machine and piped music. There are lots of spooky tales associated with this pub including one about the ghost of a bride who, instead of enjoying her planned wedding breakfast here, died broken-hearted when she was left at the altar. A good day to visit is 29 May, when the colourful procession of the Garland Ceremony, commemorating the escape of Charles II, passes by. *(Recommended by Simon Woollacott, John Hulme, Mark Percy, Lesley Mayoh, Ian S Morley, Paul Hopton, Kevin Blake, JP, PP, Lorraine and Fred Gill, D J and P M Taylor, Mike and Wendy Proctor, Stephen Buckley)*

Vintage Inns ~ Manager Glen Mills ~ Real ale ~ Bar food (12-10(9.30 Sun)) ~ Restaurant ~ (01433) 620578 ~ Children in restaurant ~ Open 11-11; 12-10.30 Sun ~ Bedrooms: £59.95B/£69.95B

DERBY SK3435 Map 7
Alexandra 🍺 £

Siddals Road, just up from station

There's a buoyant chatty atmosphere in the simple bustling bar of this two-roomed Victorian pub, which has good heavy traditional furnishings on dark-stained floorboards, shelves of bottles, breweriana, and lots of railway prints and memorabilia. The big draw is the well kept real ale, and besides Bass, Castle Rock Nottingham Gold and York Yorkshire Terrier, they have around six frequently changing guest beers from all sorts of small breweries around the country such as Becketts, Caledonian, Grainstore, Skinners and Wentworth; the friendly beer-loving landlord is happy to help you make up your mind. They also have up to five continental beers on tap, country wines, cider tapped from the cask, around two dozen malt whiskies; their soft drinks are very good value too. The lounge is no smoking; darts, dominoes and piped music. At lunchtime they serve good value rolls (from £1.60), and on Sundays they do a bargain roast (£3.75, two for £7). Handily, it's just a few minutes from Derby Station. *(Recommended by Richard Lewis,*

David Carr, the Didler, C J Fletcher, JP, PP, Paul and Ann Meyer, Paul Hopton,
Patrick Hancock)

*Tynemill ~ Manager Mark Robins ~ Real ale ~ Bar food (lunchtimes only) ~ No
credit cards ~ (01332) 293993 ~ Dogs allowed in bar ~ Open 11-11; 12-3, 7-10.30
Sun ~ Bedrooms: £25S/£35S*

Brunswick ☜ £

Railway Terrace; close to Derby Midland railway station

Fantastic if you like real ale (there are 17 handpumps), this well liked pub is now
owned by Everards but seems run very much as before, as an independent brewpub.
A jaw-dropping selection on handpump or tapped straight from the cask includes
seven from the Brunswick Brewery, produced in the purpose-built brewery tower
which you can see from a viewing area at the back of the pub: Father Mikes Dark
Rich Ruby, Old Accidental, Second Brew, Railway Porter, Triple Hop, Triple Gold
and Old Accidental. Up to 10 regularly changing guests from far and wide could
include Cairngorm Highland IPA, Everards Tiger, Hook Norton Old Hooky,
Marstons Pedigree, Kelham Island Easy Rider and Timothy Taylors Golden Best
and Landlord; farm cider is tapped from the cask. The welcoming high-ceilinged
serving bar has heavy well padded leather seats, whisky-water jugs above the dado,
and a dark blue ceiling and upper wall, with squared dark panelling below. The no
smoking room is decorated with little old-fashioned prints and swan's neck lamps,
and has a high-backed wall settle and a coal fire; behind a curved glazed partition
wall is a chatty family parlour narrowing to the apex of the triangular building.
They'll gladly provide a bowl of water for your dog; darts, dominoes, cribbage,
fruit machine and TV. Tasty value lunchtime bar food is limited to filled rolls (from
£1.75), soup (£1.95), hot beef, cheese and bacon or sausage cobs (from £2.10), and
a couple of dishes such as quiche, ploughman's, chilli and a vegetarian dish (£3.75)
and lasagne (£4.10); on Sunday they do rolls only. There are two outdoor drinking
areas, including a terrace behind. At the apex of a row of preserved railway
cottages, the pub is said to be the first railwaymen's hostelry in the world (wall
displays tell you about the history and restoration of the building, and there are
interesting old train photographs). *(Recommended by Richard Lewis, Paul Hopton,
Martin Grosberg, Kevin Blake, Keith and Chris O'Neill, the Didler, Paul and Ann Meyer, JP, PP,
C J Fletcher, David Carr, Kevin Thorpe, R T and J C Moggridge, John and Gillian Scarisbrick,
Patrick Hancock)*

*Everards ~ Licensee Graham Yates ~ Real ale ~ Bar food (12-5 Mon-Sat) ~ No credit
cards ~ (01332) 290677 ~ Children in family room ~ Dogs welcome ~ Jazz Thurs
evenings ~ Open 11-11; 12-10.30 Sun*

Olde Dolphin ☜ £

Queen Street; nearest car park King St/St Michaels Lane

The terrace of this quaint little place (Derby's oldest pub) is a nice spot to escape
the bustle of the city centre. Inside, they serve up to 10 real ales on handpump
including Adnams, Bass, Black Sheep, Caledonian Deuchars IPA, Greene King
Abbot and Marstons Pedigree, along with guests from breweries such as Brains,
Hop Back, Hook Norton, Wychwood and Wye Valley; there's a beer festival in the
last week of July. The pub is friendly and well run, with good-humoured uniformed
staff. The four snug old-fashioned rooms (two with their own separate street doors)
have big bowed black beams, shiny panelling, cast-iron-framed tables, opaque
leaded windows, lantern lights, and coal fires; there are varnished wall benches in
the tiled-floor public bar, and a brocaded seat in the little carpeted snug. There's no
piped music or noisy fruit machines to spoil the pleasant chatty atmosphere (though
one or other of the rooms can get smoky), and they get the newspapers every day.
Good value hearty bar food includes soup (£1.95), sandwiches (from £2.10, hot
filled baguettes £3.50), crispy vegetable kiev (£3.50), home-made pie or fish and
chips (£3.95), and 8oz rump steak or spicy cajun chicken breast (£4.95); they do an
all-day breakfast (£3.25), and Sunday lunch (£4.25). A no smoking upstairs

restaurant serves reasonably priced steaks. The pub is just a stroll from the cathedral. *(Recommended by the Didler, David Carr, JP, PP, Kevin Blake, Hazel Morgan, Richard Lewis, Paul Hopton, Paul and Ann Meyer)*

Six Continents ~ Lease James and Josephine Harris ~ Real ale ~ Bar food (10.30-10.30; 12-6 Sun) ~ Restaurant ~ (01332) 267711 ~ Open 10.30-11; 12-10.30 Sun

EARL STERNDALE SK0967 Map 7
Quiet Woman 🍺 £
Village signposted off B5053 S of Buxton

Those who like their pubs basic, old-fashioned and without frills really enjoy this stone-built cottage, and a good time to visit is during their Sunday lunchtime jamming session. It's very simple inside, with hard seats, plain tables (including a sunken one for dominoes or cards), low beams, quarry tiles, lots of china ornaments and a coal fire. There's a pool table in the family room (where you may be joined by two friendly jack russells eager for a place by the fire), cribbage, dominoes and darts. Mansfield Dark Mild and Marstons Best and Pedigree are well kept on handpump along with a couple of guests such as Brakspears Bitter and Moorhouses Black Cat. Bar food is limited to locally made pork pies. There are picnic-sets out in front, and the budgies, hens, turkeys, ducks and donkeys help keep children entertained. You can buy free-range eggs, local poetry books and even silage here; they have a caravan for hire in the garden, and you can also arrange to stay at the small campsite next door. *(Recommended by the Didler, Barry Collett, Bernie Adams, R M Corlett, JP, PP, Ann and Colin Hunt, Rona Murdoch, Dr D J and Mrs S C Walker, Patrick Hancock)*

Free house ~ Licensee Kenneth Mellor ~ Real ale ~ No credit cards ~ (01298) 83211 ~ Children in family room ~ Jamming sessions most Sun lunchtimes ~ Open 12-3, 7-11; 12-5, 7-10.30 Sun

EYAM SK2276 Map 7
Miners Arms 🛏️
Signposted off A632 Chesterfield—Chapel-en-le-Frith

Tremendously cosy in winter, the three little neatly kept plush beamed rooms of this welcoming pub each have their own stone fireplace. Good home-made bar food includes soup (£3.50), sandwiches (from £3.50), ploughman's (£6.95), sausage of the day with onion gravy and mashed potato (£7.95), changing dishes such as home-made steak and ale pie (£8.25), chicken pasta with pesto cream sauce (£8.95) and lamb chops with cranberry jus and mustard mash (£9.95), and puddings such as delicious trifle and bread and butter pudding (around £4.25). It's very well run, and the friendly landlord and helpful chatty staff add to the pleasantly relaxed atmosphere; it becomes more lively in the evening, when locals drop in for a well kept pint. They have Bass, Stones and a guest such as Timothy Taylors Landlord on handpump; cribbage, dominoes and piped music. The bedrooms have recently been redecorated; good breakfasts. It's an excellent base for exploring the Peak District, and there are decent walks nearby, especially below Froggatt Edge. Eyam is famous for the altruism of its villagers, who isolated themselves during the plague to save the lives of others in the area. *(Recommended by the Didler, JES, Revd John E Cooper, R T and J C Moggridge, Roy Morrison, Ann and Colin Hunt, JP, PP, B and M Kendall, Mr and Mrs Gregg Byers, Tim and Jane Shears)*

New Century Inns ~ Tenants John and Michele Hunt ~ Real ale ~ Bar food (12-2.30; 5.30-9, not Sun evening) ~ Restaurant ~ (01433) 630853 ~ Children welcome ~ Dogs allowed in bar and bedrooms ~ Open 12-11(10.30 Sun) ~ Bedrooms: £30B/£60B

Bedroom prices are for high summer. Even then you may get reductions for more than one night, or (outside tourist areas) weekends. Winter special rates are common, and many inns cut bedroom prices if you have a full evening meal.

FENNY BENTLEY SK1750 Map 7

Bentley Brook ◀

A515 N of Ashbourne

This substantial black and white inn, handy for Dovedale, has for some years been well worth knowing for the interesting Leatherbritches ales they brew here, increasingly available in other pubs we list. The range includes Goldings, Ashbourne, Belter, Hairy Helmet and Bespoke. At their May bank holiday beer festival you get a chance to taste the full range (and dozens of other beers), but usually they have just a selection on handpump, attractively priced, along with a guest such as Marstons Pedigree, and local Saxon farm cider. Nowadays it's winning plaudits for its food, too, and the main area is well laid out for this. It has quite an airy feel, thanks to big windows, fairly high ceilings and quite a few mirrors, with well lit pictures, some brassware and decorative plates on the neat white walls, wheelback and other chairs around plenty of dark polished tables on the bare boards, and a log fire in the stone fireplace between the two linked areas. Bar food includes sandwiches (from £2.50), soup (£3.25), prawn cocktail (£4.75), sausage, mash and gravy (£5.25), fisherman's pie (£6.50), mushroom stroganoff (£6.75), chicken breast with white wine and mushroom sauce (£7.50), rolled fillet of lemon sole with light parsley sauce (£7.95), and sirloin steak (£11.95). They use herbs, fruit and some vegetables from their own garden. A separate smarter no smoking restaurant has its own menu; and they sell their own preserves, sausages and so forth (the black pudding is highly recommended). They also have a small nursery producing quite a range of plants. There may be well reproduced piped music; dominoes, chess, cards, Jenga and board games. Picnic-sets under cocktail parasols on a broad terrace look down over a pleasant lawn and proper barbecue area, and they have summer barbecues, boules, croquet, skittles and a good play area. We have not yet heard from readers who have stayed here, but would expect this to be a pleasant place to stay in. The streamside grounds include a wildflower meadow, and room for campers. *(Recommended by Dr R C C Ward, JP, PP, Andy and Ali, Derek and Sylvia Stephenson, Peter Meister)*

Own brew ~ Licensees David and Jeanne Allingham ~ Real ale ~ Bar food (12-9.30) ~ Restaurant ~ (01335) 350278 ~ Children in restaurant and family room ~ Dogs welcome ~ Open 11-11; 12-10.30 Sun ~ Bedrooms: £47.50B/£69.50B

Coach & Horses

A515 N of Ashbourne

Handily, they serve reasonably priced bar food all day at this warmly welcoming 17th-c rendered stone house. The front bar is a good place to relax, with hand-made flowery-cushioned wall settles and library chairs around the dark tables on its flagstone floor, waggon wheels hanging from the black beams, horsebrasses, pewter mugs, and prints on the walls. There are more prints on the stained pine panelling in the little back room, with country cottage furnishings, and a lovely old fireplace (one of three – a real bonus in winter). The dining room and back bar are no smoking. Outside, there are views across fields from picnic-sets in the side garden by an elder tree, and wooden tables and chairs under cocktail parasols on the front terrace. From a changing menu, tasty bar food might include home-made soup (£2.75), lunchtime sandwiches (from £3.25), avocado and prawn salad (£3.75), steak and stilton pie or vegetable korma (£6.50), spicy crab cakes with sweet chilli dip or venison casserole with redcurrants, port and thyme (£7.50) and mouth-watering puddings such as spotted dick and summer pudding (£3.25); they've recently opened a new dining extension. You'll find well kept Marstons Pedigree and a couple of guests such as Oakham JHB and Whim Hartington on handpump, and they've added 24 whiskies. The landlords are friendly; cribbage, dominoes and piped music. *(Recommended by Peter Meister, Duncan Cloud, Eric Locker, Kevin Thorpe, Sue Holland, Dave Webster, Anne and Steve Thompson, JP, PP, R T and J C Moggridge, the Didler, M G Hart, Bernie Adams, Richard and Karen Holt, Ian and Jane Irving, Mr and Mrs John Taylor, John and Gillian Scarisbrick, Cathryn and Richard Hicks)*

Free house ~ Licensees John and Matthew Dawson ~ Real ale ~ Bar food (12-9, not 25 Dec) ~ (01335) 350246 ~ Children in eating area of bar and restaurant ~ Open 11-11; 12-10.30 Sun

FOOLOW SK2077 Map 7
Barrel ★

Bretton; signposted from Foolow, which itself is signposted from A623 just E of junction with B6465 to Bakewell; can also be reached from either the B6049 at Great Hucklow, or the B6001 via Abney, from Leadmill just S of Hathersage

Gains a star this year, not just for the unparalleled views (which stretch right the way over five counties when the weather's kind) but for the happy way the licensees run this old stone turnpike inn. The cosy and peaceful oak-beamed bar keeps an old-fashioned charm, with flagstones, studded doors in low doorways, lots of pictures, antiques and a collection of bottles. Stubs of massive knocked-through stone walls divide it into several areas: the cosiest is at the far end, with a log fire, a leather-cushioned settle, and a built-in corner wall-bench by an antique oak table. The cheery landlord is welcoming and service is friendly and obliging. Aside from interesting daily specials such as rabbit braised with brown ale and herb dumplings (£9.95), halibut with parsley and scallop sauce or lamb shank braised with red wine, garlic, tomatoes and oregano (£12.95), enjoyable bar food could include home-made soup (£2.65), sandwiches (from £3.20, toasted from £3.45), brie, spinach and walnut crêpe (£4.95), beer-battered cod or steak, kidney and Guinness pie (£8.25), and 10oz rump steak (from £12.45), with puddings (£3.95); they do children's meals (£3.95). Alongside well kept Greene King Abbot, Marstons Pedigree and Tetleys, they've a changing guest such as Brains Rev James on handpump; also more than 20 malts. The pub is on the edge of an isolated ridge in excellent walking country; seats out on the front terrace and a courtyard garden give good shelter from the breeze. *(Recommended by Peter F Marshall, the Didler, Keith and Chris O'Neill, Patrick Hancock, David Carr, JP, PP, Gareth and Toni Edwards, IHR, Nick and Meriel Cox, Bill Sykes, Derek and Sylvia Stephenson, A J Law, Alan Cole, Kirstie Bruce, Richard Waller)*

Free house ~ Licensee Paul Rowlinson ~ Real ale ~ Bar food (12-2.30, 6.30-9.30 (9 Sun), not 2 Jan) ~ Restaurant ~ (01433) 630856 ~ Children in eating area of bar ~ Dogs allowed in bar ~ Ceilidh Weds evening ~ Open 11-3, 6-11 weekdays and bank hol Mon; 11-11 Sat; 11-10.30 Sun; closed 25 Dec ~ Bedrooms: £45B/£65B

Bulls Head ● ⇖

Village signposted off A623 Baslow—Tideswell

The enthusiastic couple who have run this pub for the last couple of years have now bought the freehold, and this seems to have given the place a real boost. Service is prompt and cheerful, and there's a really friendly atmosphere in the simply and neatly furnished flagstoned bar, with a couple of quieter areas set more for eating. A step or two takes you down into what may once have been a stables, with its high ceiling joists, some stripped stone, and a woodburning stove. On the other side, a smart no smoking dining room has more polished tables set in cosy stalls. Interesting photographs include a good collection of Edwardian naughties. Black Sheep is well kept alongside three changing guests such as Adnams, Charles Wells Bombardier and Shepherd Neame Spitfire; piped music and darts. The wide range of enjoyable food includes generous sandwiches (from £2.75), soup (£3.25), thai fishcakes with sweet chilli sauce (£3.95), battered cod (£6.95), daily specials such as fried scallops with lemon butter (£4.25), mushroom and spinach filo parcels with mushroom sauce (£6.75), sautéed chicken breast with leek and stilton sauce (£9.95), sea bream fillets with lemon butter (£10.95), braised lamb shank with redcurrant and rosemary (£11.25), puddings such as bread and butter or sticky toffee (£3.95), and three succulent roasts on Sunday (£6.50). The pub, which has fine Victorian etched and cut glass windows, has picnic-sets outside. You can buy basic provisions here (milk, eggs, bread, and so forth); handy, as there's no shop in this upland village. It's an appealing spot, surrounded by rolling stone-walled pastures; the small pretty green has a medieval cross and a pond, and there are good walks. *(Recommended by David Carr, Roy Morrison, Jane Taylor, David Dutton, Susan and Tony Dyer, Derek and Sylvia Stephenson)*

Free house ~ Licensees William and Leslie Bond ~ Real ale ~ Bar food (12-2, 6.30-9; 12-2, 5-8 Sun) ~ Restaurant ~ (01433) 630873 ~ Children welcome away from bar ~ Dogs allowed in bar ~ Live folk or Irish singer Fri evening ~ Open 12-3, 6.30-11; 12-10.30(12-3, cl evening winter) Sun ~ Bedrooms: £40S/£60S

FROGGATT EDGE SK2477 Map 7
Chequers 🍴

A625 off A623 N of Bakewell; OS Sheet 119 map reference 247761

Froggatt Edge is just up through the woods behind this attractively set country inn, a good place for an interesting well cooked meal. The menu changes frequently and, as well as huge tasty sandwiches (from £4.75), might include soup (£3.25 – the spinach and watercress is especially good), warm chicken salad (£7.95), lamb casserole with mint and redcurrant sauce (£8.95), smoked haddock fishcakes or poached chicken breast with creamed leeks and stilton sauce (£9.95), and steaks (from £10.95), with tempting specials such as calves liver on mustard mash or parmesan-crusted cod on wilted spinach with lemon sauce (£13.95), and fried venison with apricot risotto and sherry jus (£14.95); puddings could be banana pancakes or bakewell pudding (£4.10). It's a good idea to book; the dining area is partly no smoking. The bar is fairly smart, with library chairs or small high-backed winged settles on the well waxed boards, an attractive richly varnished beam-and-board ceiling, antique prints on white walls that are partly stripped back to big dark stone blocks, and a big solid-fuel stove; one corner has a nicely carved oak cupboard. There are also seats in the pleasant peaceful back garden (which has recently been upgraded). On handpump, they've well kept Greene King Abbot and Charles Wells Bombardier, and there's a good range of malt whiskies and a changing wine board; piped music. Service is friendly and efficient. *(Recommended by Andrew Stephenson, W K Wood, Mike and Wendy Proctor, Maureen and Bill Sewell, DC, Dr S J Shepherd, Hilary Forrest, B and M Kendall, Mrs M Shardlow, June and Malcolm Farmer, Jane Taylor, David Dutton, M G Hart, Ian S Morley, Mike and Karen England, D L Parkhurst, A J Law, Cathryn and Richard Hicks)*

Pubmaster ~ Lease Jonathan and Joanne Tindall ~ Real ale ~ Bar food (12-2, 6-9.30; 12-9.30 Sat; 12-9 Sun) ~ Restaurant ~ (01433) 630231 ~ Children in eating area of bar ~ Open 12-3, 6-11; 12-11 Sat; 12-10.30 Sun; closed 25 Dec ~ Bedrooms: /£50B

HARDWICK HALL SK4663 Map 7
Hardwick Inn

2¾ miles from M1 junction 29: at roundabout A6175 towards Clay Cross; after ½ mile turn left signed Stainsby and Hardwick Hall (ignore any further sign for Hardwick Hall); at sign to Stainsby follow road to left; after 2½ miles turn left at staggered road junction

Very popular with readers as a refreshing break from the M1, this 17th-c golden stone house serves good value food all day. Enjoyable, generously served dishes could include soup (£2.40), sandwiches (from £2.85), stilton and peppered mushrooms (£3.50), ploughman's (from £5.25), home-made lasagne (£6.25), roast of the day (£6.75), grilled salmon topped with prawns (£7.75) and steaks (from £9.75), with daily specials such as beef and Guinness pie (£6.95) or trout with lemon and black pepper (£7.50), and puddings such as apple and rhubarb crumble (from £2.85); readers enjoy the Sunday carvery. They also do children's meals (from £2.90), and afternoon cream teas (£2.95). The carvery restaurant is no smoking. As well as more than 170 malt whiskies, they've well kept Greene King Old Speckled Hen and Ruddles County, Marstons Pedigree and Theakstons XB and Old Peculier on handpump; they may play piped music. There are plenty of outside tables, and the attractive back garden is a real pleasure in summer. The cosy rooms – one has an attractive 18th-c carved settle – have stone-mullioned latticed windows. The carpeted lounge is the most comfortable, with its upholstered wall settles, tub chairs and stools around varnished wooden tables. It does get very busy (especially on weekends) but service remains friendly and efficient, and the atmosphere is cheerfully bustling. The pub was originally built as a lodge for the nearby Elizabethan Hall, and is owned by the National Trust. *(Recommended by W W Burke, Mrs Anthea Fricker, Susan and John Douglas, Keith and Chris O'Neill, Brian and Janet Ainscough, JES, Roger and Maureen Kenning, June and Ken Brooks, Bill Sykes, Susan and Nigel Wilson, Michael Lamm, Peter F Marshall, the Didler, Dave Braisted, Pat and Tony Martin, Peter and Audrey Dowsett, JP, PP, BKA, Peter and Anne Hollindale, Darly Graton, Graeme Gulibert, Stephen, Julie and Hayley Brown, Irene and Ray Atkin, Mrs G R Sharman, M Borthwick)*

Free house ~ Licensees Peter and Pauline Batty ~ Real ale ~ Bar food (11.30-9.30; 12-9 Sun) ~ Restaurant ~ (01246) 850245 ~ Children in restaurant and three family rooms ~ Open 11.30-11; 12-10.30 Sun

HASSOP SK2272 Map 7
Eyre Arms

B6001 N of Bakewell

There's a fountain in the small garden of this peaceful 17th-c stone-built inn, which has tables looking out over beautiful Peak District countryside. Inside, the Eyre coat of arms, painted above a stone fireplace (which has a coal fire in winter), dominates the beamed dining bar. This has a longcase clock, cushioned settles around the walls, comfortable plush chairs, and lots of brass and copper. A smaller public bar has an unusual collection of teapots, dominoes and another fire; the snug is no smoking too, and there's another small dining area. They have well kept Black Sheep Special, John Smiths and Marstons Pedigree on handpump; piped classical music, cribbage and dominoes. Besides lunchtime sandwiches (from £3.45) and ploughman's (from £5.40), enjoyable dishes might include soup (from £3), thai-style crab cakes with sweet pepper sauce (£3.45), battered cod (£7.15), chicken breast with smoked bacon and mushrooms topped with cheddar (£8.15), and steak (from £9.15), with a decent choice of vegetarian dishes such as mushroom stroganoff or vegetable balti (£7.95). They also do daily specials such as steak and kidney pudding (£7.65) and rabbit pie (£9.95), while puddings could include lemon tart (£3.35); children's meals (£2.65). Colourful hanging baskets, and in autumn virginia creeper brightens up the stonework. There are good walks near here. *(Recommended by JP, PP, Mike and Karen England, the Didler, Ann and Colin Hunt, DC, Patrick Hancock, Trevor and Sylvia Millum, M G Hart)*

Free house ~ Licensee Lynne Smith ~ Real ale ~ Bar food ~ Restaurant ~ (01629) 640390 ~ Children in eating area of bar ~ Open 11.30-3, 6.30-11; 11-3, 7-11 winter; closed 25 Dec

HATHERSAGE SK2380 Map 7
Plough 🍲 ♟ 🛏

Leadmill; B6001(A625) towards Bakewell, OS Sheet 110 map reference 235805

Readers very much like staying at this popular former farmhouse. It's beautifully set by the River Derwent, and tables in the pretty garden run right down to the water. The emphasis is firmly on the imaginative food (drinkers may have trouble finding a seat at busy times), and there's an excellent choice. The menu changes every three months and could include home-made soup (£3.50), fried scallops with squid, chorizo and squid ink dressing (£6.95), wild boar terrine with pancetta and green tomato chutney (£5.95), chilli con carne (£8.25), steak and kidney pudding (£8.95), bagels with roasted pumpkin, spinach, poached eggs and mustardy sauce (£9.95), chicken breast filled with crab with stir-fried greens and ginger and coriander dressing (£13.25), indian spiced monkfish with bombay potatoes, roasted mango and chilli dressing with yoghurt (£14.95), with puddings such as bread and butter pudding (£3.50); they also do sandwiches at lunchtime (from £3.50). It's worth booking for Sunday lunch. Everything is spotlessly kept, and the attractive bar, with good solid tables and chairs, is on two levels, with a big log fire at one end and a woodburning stove at the other. The staff are hardworking, and service is very well organised; piped music and no smoking restaurant. They serve around nine good value wines by the glass, alongside well kept Theakstons Bitter and Old Peculier, and a couple of guests such as Adnams and Jennings on handpump; excellent breakfasts. *(Recommended by Sue and John Harwood, Lynne and Philip Naylor, DC, Keith and Chris O'Neill, Christine and Neil Townend, Mike and Linda Hudson, Ian S Morley, W W Burke, Terry Mizen, Jo Rees, IHR, Rod and Chris Pring, Tom and Ruth Rees, R N and M I Bailey, Barry and Anne)*

Free house ~ Licensee Bob Emery ~ Real ale ~ Bar food (11.30-2.30, 6.30-9.30; 11.30-9.30 Sat; 12-9 Sun) ~ Restaurant ~ (01433) 650319 ~ Children in eating area of bar, and restaurant until 7pm ~ Open 11.30-11; 12-10.30 Sun; closed 25 Dec ~ Bedrooms: £49.50B/£79.50B

HOGNASTON SK2350 Map 7
Red Lion 🍽 🛏

Village signposted off B5035 Ashbourne—Wirksworth

Not just popular for its good food, this welcoming pub also impresses readers with its pleasant local-pub atmosphere and friendly service. From a frequently changing menu, generously served, nicely presented dishes could include home-made soup (£3.95), filled baguettes or home-made smoked salmon pâté (£4.95), tagine of moroccan lamb or salmon and caper fishcakes (£9.95), roast rack of lamb with chargrilled vegetables, pineapple and mint and rosemary jus (£10.95) and grilled fillet steak with green peppercorn, cream and brandy sauce (£11.95), with puddings such as lemon and marmalade bread and butter pudding (£3.95). The open-plan oak-beamed bar is relaxing, with almost a bistro feel around the attractive mix of old tables (candlelit at night) on ancient flagstones, and copies of *Country Life* to read. There are old-fashioned settles among other seats, three open fires, and a growing collection of teddy bears among other bric-a-brac. They've well kept Bass, Greene King Old Speckled Hen and Marstons Pedigree, and perhaps a guest such as Charles Wells Bombardier on handpump, and you can get country wines; piped music, dominoes. It's in a lovely peaceful spot, handy for Carsington Reservoir. *(Recommended by R T and J C Moggridge, M Joyner, Mike and Maggie Betton, John and Gillian Scarisbrick, Jan and Alan Summers, Bernard Stradling, Anne and Steve Thompson, JP, PP, Alan Bowker, Ron and Sheila Corbett, Andrew Scarr, Mrs P J Carroll)*

Free house ~ Licensee Pip Price ~ Real ale ~ Bar food (not Sun evening, not Mon) ~ Restaurant ~ (01335) 370396 ~ Children in restaurant ~ Dogs allowed in bar ~ Open 12-3, 6-11; closed Mon lunchtime except bank hols ~ Bedrooms: £50S/£80S

HOLBROOK SK3644 Map 7
Dead Poets 🍺 £

Village signposted off A6 S of Belper; Chapel Street

Now owned by Everards, and with a new licensee, this low white-painted pub continues to serve a great selection of real ales. Alongside well kept Greene King Abbot Ale and Marstons Pedigree, you'll find at least six guests from brewers such as Burton Bridge, Church End, Dent, Everards, Titanic and Tower on handpump or served by the jug from the cellar; also farm cider and several country wines. Its regular beer festivals are very popular. It's very dark inside, with low black beams in its ochre ceiling, stripped stone walls with some smoked plaster, and broad flagstones. Candles burn on scrubbed tables, there's a big log fire in the end stone fireplace, high-backed winged settles form snug cubicles along one wall, and there are pews and a variety of chairs in other intimate corners and hide-aways. The décor makes a few nods to the pub's present name (it used to be the Cross Keys), and adds some old prints of Derby. Alongside cobs (from £2, nothing else on Sundays), bar food is limited to a few good value hearty dishes such as home-made soup (£2), chilli con carne or casserole (£3.95) and chicken jalfrezi (£3.95). There's a good atmosphere, and a nice mix of customers, male and female; well reproduced piped music. Behind is a sort of verandah room, with lanterns, fairy lights and a few plants, and more seats out in the yard, with outdoor heaters. It's tucked into a quiet street. *(Recommended by the Didler, JP, PP, Derek and Sylvia Stephenson, Bernie Adams, Alan Bowker)*

Everards ~ Licensee William Holmes ~ Real ale ~ Bar food (lunchtimes Mon-Sat) ~ No credit cards ~ (01332) 780301 ~ Well behaved children in snug ~ Dogs welcome ~ Poetry night first Tues in month ~ Open 12-3, 5-11; 12-11 Fri-Sat; 12-10.30 Sun

IDRIDGEHAY SK2848 Map 7
Black Swan
B5023 S of Wirksworth

At lunchtime this very restauranty pub does an excellent value two-course meal for £8.95 (not Sunday). Most of the open-plan space (and indeed the feel of the place) is given over to eating, but there is still a little sitting area by the big bow window on the left, with a rack of daily papers and magazines, a few bar stools, wicker armchairs and padded seats, and snapshots of some very cheery customers. Bass, Marstons Pedigree and John Smiths are well kept on handpump, there's a pleasant unhurried atmosphere, and the staff are polite and efficient. There are well spaced tables with wicker chairs comfortably cushioned in a mix of colours, and a bright and airy simple décor – white ceiling, ragged yellow walls with a few pictures of french restaurants, wine bottles and local scenes. The bare floors make for cheerful acoustics (not too clattery); fairly quiet piped light jazz. Down steps is a similarly furnished no smoking area, given a slight conservatory feel by its high pitched roof light (with rattan blinds) and two narrow floor-to-ceiling windows at the far end, looking out over the neat and pleasant garden to rolling tree-sheltered pastures. The enjoyable bar food is well presented and generously served, and could include lunchtime dishes such as home-made soup (£3.50), filled ciabattas (from £3.95), roasted red pepper pâté with cumberland sauce (£4.55), grilled chicken breast with cajun spices and singapore noodles (£6.95), grilled scotch salmon with fresh apricot sauce (£7.50) and vegetable tagine with lemon-scented couscous and pitta bread (£7.95), with evening dishes such as vegetable balti (£10.95), local pheasant breast with black bean sauce and stir-fried noodles (£14.50), sautéed calves liver with red wine and sage jus (£14.55), and puddings such as spotted dick and treacle sponge (£3.50); on Tuesday evening they do a two-course dinner for £9.95. *(Recommended by Mrs Kathy Barkway)*

Free house ~ Licensee Steve Williams ~ Real ale ~ Bar food (12-2, 7-9.30; 12-4 Sun) ~ Restaurant ~ (01773) 550249 ~ Children welcome ~ Jazz bands alternate Weds ~ Open 11-11; 12-6 Sun

KIRK IRETON SK2650 Map 7
Barley Mow ♦ 🛏
Village signed off B5023 S of Wirksworth

With its dimly lit passageways and narrow stairwells, this tall gabled Jacobean brown sandstone inn has a timeless atmosphere, helped along by traditional furnishings and civilised old-fashioned service. The small main bar has a relaxed pubby feel, with antique settles on the tiled floor or built into the panelling, a roaring coal fire, four slate-topped tables, and shuttered mullioned windows. Another room has built-in cushioned pews on oak parquet and a small woodburning stove, and a third has more pews, tiled floor, beams and joists, and big landscape prints. One room is no smoking. It's a good place to sit and chat in, and the only games you'll find are dominoes and cards; look out for the young newfoundland, Hector – well, you can't really miss him. In casks behind a modest wooden counter are well kept (and reasonably priced) Hook Norton Best and Old Hooky, Leatherbritches, Whim Hartington and possibly a guest from another small brewery such as Cottage or Eccleshall; farm ciders too. Lunchtime filled rolls (75p) are the only food; the good home-made interesting evening meals are reserved for residents. There's a decent-sized garden, and a couple of benches out in front, and they've opened a post office in what used to be the pub stables. Handy for Carsington Water, the pretty hilltop village is in good walking country. *(Recommended by John and Gillian Scarisbrick, Bernard Stradling, Pete Baker, P and S Blacksell, JP, PP, Rob Webster, the Didler, Kevin Thorpe, MLR, P Abbott, Mike Rowan)*

Free house ~ Licensee Mary Short ~ Real ale ~ Bar food (lunchtime) ~ No credit cards ~ (01335) 370306 ~ Children welcome lunchtimes away from bar ~ Open 12-2, 7-11; closed 25 Dec and 1 Jan ~ Bedrooms: £28S/£50B

LADYBOWER RESERVOIR SK1986 Map 7
Yorkshire Bridge 🛏

A6013 N of Bamford

An enjoyable place to stay, this fine roadside hotel is prettily set near the Ladybower, Derwent and Howden reservoirs (immortalised by the World War II Dambusters), so there are plenty of pleasant countryside walks close by. Service is friendly and obliging, and there's a cheerful bustling atmosphere. One area has a country cottage feel, with floral wallpaper, sturdy cushioned wall settles, Staffordshire dogs and toby jugs on a big stone fireplace with a warm coal-effect gas fire, china on delft shelves, a panelled dado and so forth. Another extensive area, with another fire, is lighter and more airy with pale wooden furniture, good big black and white photographs and lots of plates on the walls. The Bridge Room has yet another coal-effect fire and oak tables and chairs, and the small no smoking conservatory gives pleasant views across a valley to steep larch woods. In summer it's a good idea to arrive early, to be sure of a table. The enjoyable menu, which has lots of generously served traditional dishes, includes lunchtime sandwiches (from £3.20), filled baked potatoes (from £3.25), and ploughman's (£6.25), as well as soup (£2.75), prawn cocktail (£4.40), home-made steak and kidney pie (£6.95), barbecued lamb chops (£8.75), and good steaks (from £10.25), with specials such as chicken, mushroom and asparagus pie (£6.95) or halibut steak with stir-fried vegetables (£8.50) and puddings such as lemon meringue pie (from £3.10); children's meals (£3.25). All three dining rooms are no smoking; the restaurant is for residents only. Well kept on handpump are Black Sheep, Stones, Theakstons Best and Old Peculier; darts, dominoes, fruit machine, and piped music; disabled lavatories. *(Recommended by Richard Gibbs, Anne and Steve Thompson, John and Glenna Marlow, Alan J Morton, Irene and Ray Atkin, Mike and Wendy Proctor)*

Free house ~ Licensees Trevelyan and John Illingworth ~ Real ale ~ Bar food (12-2, 6-9(9.30 Fri/Sat); 12-8.30 Sun) ~ (01433) 651361 ~ Children in eating area of bar and family room ~ Dogs allowed in bedrooms ~ Open 11-11(10.30 Sun) ~ Bedrooms: £45B/£64B

LITTLE HUCKLOW SK1678 Map 7
Old Bulls Head

Pub signposted from B6049

A little low door leads you into the two neatly kept, heavily oak-beamed rooms at this friendly old country pub; one room is served from a hatch, the other over a polished bar counter. The low ceilings and walls are packed with brasses, tankards and mining equipment, local photographs, thickly cushioned built-in settles, and a coal fire in a neatly restored stone hearth; darts, dominoes. For years a shaft in the cellar led down to a mine, until an explosion in the shaft blew off a piece of the cellar roof to create the unusual little 'cave' room at the back. The neatly tended garden boasts lovely views over to the Peak District, and if you get tired of looking at that, there's an unusual collection of well restored and attractively painted old farm machinery here too. Well kept John Smiths and Tetleys are served from carved handpumps, and they keep several malt whiskies. Straightforward bar food such as garlic mushrooms (£4.95), scampi, lasagne or stilton and vegetable bake (£8.95) and steaks (from £12.95) with traditional puddings such as spotted dick (from £3.50). Please note the opening times. *(Recommended by Patrick Hancock, Richard Gibbs, Kevin Blake, JP, PP, Doug Christian)*

Free house ~ Licensee Julie Denton ~ Real ale ~ Bar food (not lunchtimes Mon-Thurs) ~ (01298) 871097 ~ Children welcome ~ Open 12-3, 6-11(10.30 Sun); closed lunchtimes Mon-Thurs ~ Bedrooms: /£60B

LITTON SK1675 Map 7
Red Lion

Village signposted off A623, between B6465 and B6049 junctions; also signposted off B6049

The peaceful tree-studded village green in front of this welcoming 17th-c village pub is pretty, and there are good walks nearby. It's very much a proper community local, but the cheerily friendly landlord makes everyone feel like a regular. A good time to visit is during the annual village well-dressing carnival (usually the last weekend in June), when villagers create a picture from flower petals, moss and other natural materials, and at Christmas a brass band plays carols. The two inviting homely linked front rooms have low beams and some panelling, and blazing log fires. There's a bigger no smoking back room with good-sized tables, and large antique prints on its stripped stone walls. The small bar counter has well kept Barnsley Bitter, Black Sheep, Jennings Cumberland and a guest such as Shepherd Neame Spitfire on handpump, with decent wines and 30 malt whiskies; shove-ha'penny, cribbage, dominoes and table skittles. Good value tasty bar food includes hot and cold sandwiches (from £2), soup (£2.60), breaded garlic mushrooms (£3), steak and ale pie, gammon or battered cod (£6.25), 8oz sirloin (£7.90) and daily specials such as rabbit casserole or whitby seafood platter (£6.75) and minted lamb (£8.10). No children under six. *(Recommended by Peter F Marshall, the Didler, Keith and Chris O'Neill, John Watson, Ann and Colin Hunt, Patrick Hancock, Derek and Sylvia Stephenson, JP, PP, Ian S Morley, B and M Kendall, Barry Collett)*

Free house ~ Licensees Terry and Michele Vernon ~ Real ale ~ Bar food (12-2, 6-8(8.30 Thurs-Sat); not Sun evenings) ~ (01298) 871458 ~ Well behaved children over 6 till 8pm ~ Dogs welcome ~ Open 12-3, 6-11; 12-11 Fri-Sat; 12-10.30 Sun

MELBOURNE SK3427 Map 7
John Thompson ◨ £

Ingleby, which is NW of Melbourne; turn off A514 at Swarkestone Bridge or in Stanton by Bridge; can also be reached from Ticknall (or from Repton on B5008)

Well worth trying, the own-brewed real ales (JT Bitter, Summer Gold and Winter Porter) at this converted 15th-c farmhouse are a real bargain. It's a simple but comfortable place; its big modernised lounge has ceiling joists, some old oak settles, button-back leather seats, sturdy oak tables, antique prints and paintings, and a log-effect gas fire; piped music. A couple of smaller cosier rooms open off, with a piano, fruit machine, pool and a juke box in the children's room; there's a no smoking area in the lounge. Outside are lots of tables by flowerbeds on the well kept lawns, or you can choose to sit on the partly covered outside terrace which has its own serving bar. The landlord is warmly welcoming (he's been brewing his own real ales here since 1977). Good value and straightforward home-made bar food consists of sandwiches and rolls (from £1.40, nothing else on Sundays), soup (£2), salads with cold ham or beef (£4), tasty roast beef with yorkshire puddings and gravy (£6, not Mondays), and mouthwatering puddings such as bread and butter pudding or rhubarb crumble (£2). *(Recommended by the Didler, MLR, Bernie Adams, C Herbert, Peter and Patricia Burton, Mrs Kathy Barkway, Dr S J Shepherd, Keith and Chris O'Neill, Peter and Carol Heaton, Theo, Anne and Jane Gaskin)*

Own brew ~ Licensee John Thompson ~ Real ale ~ Bar food (lunchtime) ~ (01332) 862469 ~ Children in eating area of bar and family room ~ Dogs allowed in bar ~ Open 10.30-2.30, 7-11; 12-2.30, 7-10.30 Sun

---

Pubs in outstandingly attractive surroundings are listed
at the back of the book.

MILLTOWN SK3561 Map 7
Miners Arms
Off B6036 SE of Ashover; Oakstedge Lane

It's a good idea to book if you want to enjoy the restaurant-style food at this neatly kept stone-built pub. Listed on a board, the (fairly straightforward) changing dishes are very good value considering the quality, and could include home-made soup (from £2.10), spinach-stuffed mushrooms (£3.65), pork terrine (£3.65), pork, apple and sausage pie (£7.65), turkey escalope with herb butter (£8.95), chicken breast with mustard cream sauce or grilled cod (£9.10), and puddings such as chocolate crumble cheesecake and crème brûlée (£3.25); the vegetables are especially well cooked. Service is friendly and efficient. The layout is basically L-shaped, with a local feel up nearer the door; the dining room is no smoking. They serve good value wines, and two constantly rotating well kept real ales such as Adnams Broadside and Batemans XXXB; at lunchtime there may be quiet piped classical music. Virtually on the edge of Ashover, the pub is in former lead-mining country, with vestiges of the old workings adding interest to attractive country walks right from the door. Please note their opening times. *(Recommended by the Didler, Derek and Sylvia Stephenson, Cathryn and Richard Hicks)*

Free house ~ Licensees Andrew and Yvonne Guest ~ Real ale ~ Restaurant ~ (01246) 590218 ~ Children welcome ~ Open 12-3, 7-11 Weds-Sat; 12-3 Sun; closed Weds evening winter; closed Mon/Tues, and Sun evening

MONSAL HEAD SK1871 Map 7
Monsal Head Hotel 🍺 🛏
B6465

Whether it's the dead of winter (when you can fully appreciate the cosy bar) or the height of summer (sitting outside and soaking up the terrific views is a real pleasure), this busy extended hotel is an enjoyable place to visit. It's in a marvellous setting, perched high above the steep valley of the River Wye. The comfortable stable bar once housed the horses that used to haul guests and their luggage from the station down the steep valley; the stripped timber horse-stalls, harness and brassware, and lamps from the disused station itself, all hint at those days. There's a big warming woodburning stove in the inglenook, and cushioned oak pews around the tables on the flagstones. Eight well kept real ales on handpump include Monsal Best (brewed for them by Lloyds), Timothy Taylors Landlord and Whim Hartington, alongside guests from breweries such as Abbeydale, Kelham Island and Theakstons, and they also keep a very good choice of bottled german beers, and sensibly priced wines; piped music. Good bar food from a reasonably priced menu might include home-made soup (£2.90), crispy duck spring roll (£4.50), spinach and ricotta tart (£7.20), 8oz gammon with two eggs and pineapple, or cod in beer batter (£6.90), lamb mint pudding (£8.90), with specials such as mozzarella and parma ham salad (£4.20), chargrilled halibut (£10.50), fried duck breast with orange and raspberry sauce (£10.50), and puddings such as hot chocolate sponge (£3.90). From 12 to 6, they do sandwiches (from £3.95), and filled baked potatoes (from £3.20); there's also a children's menu (from £2.90). It's very well run, and readers are full of praise for the friendly and helpful staff. The boundary of the parishes of Little Longstone and Ashford runs through the hotel, and the spacious no smoking restaurant and smaller lounge are named according to which side of the line they sit; beer garden. The best place to admire the view is from the big windows in the lounge, and from four of the seven bedrooms; good generous breakfasts. *(Recommended by Anne and Steve Thompson, Nick and Meriel Cox, the Didler, Phil and Heidi Cook, John and Gillian Scarisbrick, Peter F Marshall, G B Longden, Richard Fendick, Dr S J Shepherd, Andrew Wallace, Mike and Wendy Proctor, Ann and Colin Hunt, Professor John Hibbs, Patrick Hancock, Keith and Chris O'Neill, JP, PP, Richard Waller, Andrew Pearson)*

If we know a pub has a no smoking area, we say so.

Free house ~ Licensees Christine O'Connell and Philip Smith ~ Real ale ~ Bar food
(12-9.30) ~ Restaurant ~ (01629) 640250 ~ Children welcome ~ Dogs allowed in bar
and bedrooms ~ Open 11-11(10.30 Sun); closed 25 Dec ~ Bedrooms: £40B/£45B

OVER HADDON SK2066 Map 7
Lathkil

Village and inn signposted from B5055 just SW of Bakewell

This pleasantly unpretentious hotel is very popular with walkers, who can leave
their muddy boots in the pub's lobby, so it's best to arrive early in fine weather.
Steeply down below the pub lies Lathkil Dale, one of the quieter dales with a
harmonious landscape of pastures and copses – the views are spectacular (the
walled garden is a good place to sit and soak them in). They serve five well kept
real ales from handpump, including Charles Wells Bombardier and Whim
Hartington alongside a couple of guests from brewers such as such as Black Sheep,
Burton Bridge and Kelham Island (samples are offered in sherry glasses); select malt
whiskies and a good range of new world wines (not cheap). The airy room on the
right as you go in has a nice fire in the attractively carved fireplace, old-fashioned
settles with upholstered cushions or plain wooden chairs, black beams, a delft shelf
of blue and white plates, original prints and photographs, and big windows. On the
left, the spacious and sunny dining area – partly no smoking – doubles as a
restaurant in the evenings; although it isn't quite as pubby as the bar, they don't
have a problem with shorts or walking gear at lunchtime. The changing blackboard
menu could include tasty home-made soup (£2.30), filled rolls (from £2.45),
smoked mackerel (£5.75), beef and black peppercorn crumble (£6.35), chicken
stuffed with apricot (£6.50), steak and kidney pie (£6.35), dressed crab salad
(£6.95) and venison casserole (£7.75), with puddings (from £2.75). There are darts,
bar billiards, shove-ha'penny, backgammon, dominoes, cribbage, and piped music.
(Recommended by the Didler, Andrew Stephenson, JP, PP, W K Wood, A McCormick, T Powell,
Lorraine and Fred Gill, Peter F Marshall, Hugh A MacLean, Mike and Wendy Proctor,
Doug Christian, Ann and Colin Hunt, Cliff Blakemore, Peter Meister, Derek and
Sylvia Stephenson, Mike Ridgway, Sarah Miles, David and Helen Wilkins, Ian and Liz Rispin)

Free house ~ Licensee Robert Grigor-Taylor ~ Real ale ~ Bar food (lunchtime, not
25 Dec) ~ Restaurant ~ (01629) 812501 ~ Children in dining room, must be eating
in the evening ~ Dogs allowed in bar and bedrooms ~ Open 11.30-3, 6.30(7 winter)-
11; 11.30-11 Sat; 12-10.30 Sun; closed 25 Dec evening ~ Bedrooms: £37.50S/£70B

SHARDLOW SK4330 Map 7
Old Crown 🍺

3 miles from M1 junction 24, via A50: at first B6540 exit from A50 (just under 2 miles) turn
off towards Shardlow – pub E of Shardlow itself, at Cavendish Bridge, actually just over
Leics boundary

The bustling bar of this 17th-c coaching inn is packed with hundreds of jugs and
mugs hanging from the beams, and brewery and railway memorabilia and
advertisements and other bric-a-brac cover the walls (even in the lavatories). The
atmosphere is cheerfully friendly, and the staff go out of their way to make you feel
at home. Seven well kept real ales on handpump could include Bass, Everards Tiger,
Fullers London Pride, Marstons Pedigree and Tower Malty Towers, with guests
such as Everards Tiger or Nottingham Rock Ale, and they have a nice choice of
malt whiskies; fruit machine and piped music. Readers enjoy the tasty bar food
(prices haven't changed since last year), which might be soup (£1.70), sandwiches
(from £2), a good range of baguettes (from £3.25), omelettes (from £4.25),
mediterranean vegetable lasagne (£4.95), cod (£6.95), grilled ham (£7.25) and
steaks (from £8.25), with good specials such as tasty beef and kidney pie (£5.95),
chicken with mustard and cider sauce or grilled lamb chops topped with blue
cheese sauce (£6.95), and puddings such as chocolate sponge and spotted dick
(from £2.25); best to book for Sunday lunch. Handy for the A6 as well as the M1,
the pub was once a deportation point for convicts bound for the colonies. In winter,

they may close early. *(Recommended by Michael and Marion Buchanan, Kevin Blake,* `
John Beeken, Marian and Andrew Ruston, Jenny and Dave Hughes, MLR, the Didler,
Darly Graton, Graeme Gulibert, John and Judy Saville, Dick and Penny Vardy, JHBS, Joy and
Simon Maisey, JP, PP, Roger and Maureen Kenning, Cathryn and Richard Hicks)

*Free house ~ Licensees Peter and Gillian Morton-Harrison ~ Real ale ~ Bar food
(lunchtime) ~ (01332) 792392 ~ Children in eating area of bar ~ Dogs welcome ~
Open 11.30-3.30, 5-11; 12.30-3.30, 7-10.30 Sun; closed evenings 25-26 Dec and
1 Jan ~ Bedrooms: £35S/£45S*

WARDLOW SK1875 Map 7
Three Stags Heads ✇
Wardlow Mires; A623 by junction with B6465

Genuinely traditional, this simple white-painted cottage is a real find if you like
your pubs basic and full of character. Beer-lovers happy to chat with the friendly
locals and landlord over a hearty home-made meal will feel very much at home
here; the four well kept real ales on handpump are Abbeydale Absolution, Black
Lurcher (brewed for the pub at a hefty 8% ABV) and Matins, and Broadstone
Ladywell. They've also lots of bottled continental and english beers (the stronger
ones aren't cheap), and in winter they do a roaring trade in mugs of steaming tea –
there might be free hot chestnuts on the bar. Warmed right through by a cast-iron
kitchen range, the tiny flagstoned parlour bar has old leathercloth seats, a couple of
antique settles with flowery cushions, two high-backed windsor armchairs and
simple oak tables (look out for the petrified cat in a glass case). You can book the
tables in the small no smoking dining parlour, which has another open fire. The
pub is situated in a natural sink, so don't be surprised to find the floors muddied by
boots in wet weather (and the dogs even muddier); cribbage and dominoes, nine
men's morris and backgammon. The front terrace looks across the main road to the
distant hills. The seasonal menu (which they try to vary to suit the weather) might
include pasta (£6.50), steak and kidney pie (£8.50), fried pigeon breasts (£9.50) and
hare pie (£10.50); the hardy plates are home-made (the barn is a pottery
workshop). Please note the opening times. *(Recommended by JP, PP, the Didler, Pete
Baker, Mike and Wendy Proctor, Andrew Stephenson, John Hulme, Trevor and Sylvia Millum)*

*Free house ~ Licensees Geoff and Pat Fuller ~ Real ale ~ Bar food (12.30-4, 7-9.30) ~
No credit cards ~ (01298) 872268 ~ Well behaved children over 8, till 8.30pm ~
Dogs welcome ~ Folk music most Sat evenings ~ Open 7-11 Fri; 12-11 Sat; 12-10.30
Sun; closed weekdays exc Fri evenings and bank hols*

WHITTINGTON MOOR SK3873 Map 7
Derby Tup ✇ £
Sheffield Road; B6057 just S of A61 roundabout

There are plenty of tempting drinks to choose from at this down-to-earth corner
house. Ten handpumps serve Greene King Abbot, Kelham Island Easy Rider,
Theakstons Old Peculier and Whim Hartington, alongside six changing guests from
breweries such as Abbeydale, Batemans, Exmoor, Fullers, Ossett and Roosters.
There's also a selection of continental and bottle-conditioned beers, fruit beers, farm
ciders, perry, and decent malt whiskies; good value soft drinks. The plain but
sizeable rectangular bar, with frosted street windows and old dark brown linoleum,
has simple furniture arranged around the walls (including a tremendously long green
plastic banquette), leaving lots of standing room. There are two more small no
smoking rooms; daily papers, darts, dominoes and cribbage. From a straightforward
but wide-ranging menu, good value bar food might include home-made soup (£2),
savoury mince with herby dumplings or pasta provençale (£3.25), chilli, mushroom
goulash or tuscan bean stew (£4.25), steak and ale pie or lamb steak in mint gravy
(£4.50), and lasagne (£4.95); the tasty sandwiches are made with fresh bread from
the neighbouring bakery (from £2). Despite the name, Whittington Moor is on the
northern edge of Chesterfield, and the pub can get very busy on weekend evenings.
(Recommended by the Didler, Patrick Hancock, Keith and Chris O'Neill, JP, PP)

Tynemill ~ Tenant Peter Hayes ~ Real ale ~ Bar food (12-2.30 Mon-Tues; 12-3 Weds-Sun, plus 5-8 Thurs-Sat) ~ (01246) 454316 ~ Children in two side rooms ~ Dogs welcome ~ Open 11.30-3, 5-11 Mon-Tues; 11.30-11 Weds-Sat; 12-4, 7-10.30 Sun

WOOLLEY MOOR SK3661 Map 7
White Horse
Badger Lane, off B6014 Matlock—Clay Cross

Picnic-sets in the well maintained garden of this attractive old pub have lovely views across the Amber Valley, and there's a very good play area with a wooden train, boat, climbing frame and swings. Still very much in its original state, the bustling tap room has a pleasant chatty atmosphere, and serves well kept real ales such as Adnams Broadside, Greene King Ruddles, Jennings Cumberland and Lakeland and Theakstons Old Peculier; decent wines too, and polite efficient service. There is piped music in the lounge and no smoking conservatory (great views of Ogston reservoir from here). Enjoyable, good value dishes could include soup (£3.25), sandwiches and toasted paninis (from £4.25), broccoli and smoked brie quiche (£5.95), fish and chips (£6.85) and game and ale pie (£7.50), or you can choose from slightly more elaborate dishes such as game terrine (£4.15), duck and apricot salad (£5.15), asparagus and goats cheese filo parcel (£8.30), roast lamb marinated in garlic and thyme with sautéed sweet potatoes and mint and cranberry jus, or steaks (£12). The good children's meals come with a puzzle sheet and crayons. It's best to book for the restaurant. A sign outside shows how horses and carts carried measures of salt along the toll road in front – the toll bar cottage still stands at the entrance of the Badger Lane (a badger was the haulier who transported the salt). The pub is in a delightful spot, and has its own boules pitch. *(Recommended by JP, PP, the Didler, Andy and Ali, Jenny Coates, Ms J Davidson, Bernie Adams, Norma and Keith Bloomfield)*

Musketeers ~ Managers Charlotte Adshead and Keith Hurst ~ Real ale ~ Bar food (12-2, 6-9; 12-8 Sun) ~ Restaurant ~ (01246) 590319 ~ Children in eating area of bar and restaurant ~ Dogs allowed in bar ~ Open 12-3, 6-11; 12-10.30 Sun

Lucky Dip
Besides the fully inspected pubs, you might like to try these Lucky Dips recommended to us and described by readers (if you do, please send us reports: www.goodguides.com).

APPERKNOWLE [SK3878]
☆ *Yellow Lion* [High St]: 19th-c stone-built village local with new licensee keeping good balance between enjoyable food from sandwiches up and a good choice of real ales and wines on the drinks side; realistic prices, comfortable banquettes in L-shaped lounge, no smoking dining room; children welcome, garden with play area, attractively priced bedrooms *(the Didler, Patrick Hancock, Peter F Marshall, Keith and Chris O'Neill, JP, PP)*
ASHBOURNE [SK1746]
Bramhalls [Buxton Rd]: Former coaching inn, now a smart bar and brasserie, simple décor in big dining room on right, smaller rooms and bar on left, Bass, good wine list, good interesting food; reasonably priced bedrooms *(Guy Vowles)*
☆ *Smiths Tavern* [bottom of market place]: Neatly kept traditional pub, chatty and relaxed, stretching back from heavily black-beamed bar to light and airy end no smoking dining room (food generally good value), well kept Banks's, Marstons Pedigree and a guest

beer, lots of whiskies and vodkas, daily papers, traditional games; children welcome, open all day summer Sun *(R T and J C Moggridge, JP, PP, Guy Vowles, T J W Hill, P Abbott, LYM)*
ASHFORD IN THE WATER [SK1969]
☆ *Bulls Head* [Church St]: Comfortable dining pub with cosy and homely lounge, thriving bar, well kept Robinsons Best, Old Stockport and Hartleys XB, well prepared food from good lunchtime sandwiches to adventurous and satisfying recipes, prompt friendly service; may be piped music or radio; children in public bar, tables out behind and by front car park *(DJH, MLR, Patrick Hancock, Dr Emma Disley)*
BARLBOROUGH [SK4777]
De Rodes Arms [handy for M1 junction 30 – A619 Chesterfield Rd roundabout]: Old but modernised chain dining pub useful for all-day food, pleasant friendly atmosphere, two real ales, decent wine and soft drinks choice, no smoking area; music quiz Thurs, children allowed, picnic-sets outside *(CMW, JJW)*
Pebley [A618 towards Killamarsh, nr

Woodhall service area access rds]: Good value blackboard food (not Sun evening or Mon/Tues) inc children's helpings and menu, three real ales in lined glasses, good choice of other drinks, L-shaped lounge with no smoking dining area up two steps; children and dogs welcome, big garden with picnic-sets and swing, open all day (from 3pm Mon/Tues) *(CMW, JJW)*

BARLOW [SK3474]

Old Pump [B6051 towards Chesterfield]: Comfortable lounge and bars with valley views, good choice of enjoyable attractively priced food from well filled rolls to popular Sun lunch, well kept Everards, Mansfield and Marstons Pedigree, good value wines, good polite service, restaurant; bedrooms, good walks *(Keith and Chris O'Neill)*

BASLOW [SK2572]

Devonshire Arms [A619]: Small hotel in pleasant surroundings, footpath to Chatsworth; long L-shaped bar with nice mix of different-sized tables and various seats inc leather chairs, well kept Bass and Marstons Pedigree, well trained young staff, food from decent sandwiches and baguettes to carvery meals, fish nights and evening restaurant with attractive draped ceiling, end games area; may be quiet piped music; bedrooms *(M G Hart, Stephen, Julie and Hayley Brown)*

Robin Hood [A619/B6050]: Fairly modern, well decorated and comfortable, with tidy banquettes, well kept Banks's and Mansfield ales, good reasonably priced food from sandwiches up, friendly landlord; may be soft piped music; big back uncarpeted bar for walkers and climbers (boots and dogs on leads welcome); bedrooms, good walking country nr Baslow Edge *(Ann and Colin Hunt)*

BELPER [SK3547]

Cross Keys [Market Pl]: Two-room pub with Batemans and a guest beer, coal fire, bar billiards; mid-week entertainment, open all day *(the Didler)*

Imperial Vaults [King St]: Town pub with well kept Bass, M&B Mild and a guest beer, helpful barman, small bar with three simple interconnected rooms (one with TV); tables in attractive garden behind *(Martin Grosberg)*

Queens Head [Chesterfield Rd]: Warm and cosy three-room pub with constant coal fire, well kept Greene King IPA, Ind Coope Burton and guest beers, local photographs; quiz and band nights, beer festivals; terrace tables, open all day *(the Didler)*

BONSALL [SK2858]

Barley Mow [off A6012 Cromford—Hartington; The Dale]: Friendly tucked-away pub with particularly well kept Whim Hartington and two or three guest beers, fresh sandwiches and other food, character furnishings; live music wknds inc landlord playing accordion, organises local walks; cl wkdy lunchtimes (may open Fri by arrangement, open all day Sat) *(the Didler, JP, PP)*

Kings Head [Yeoman St]: Cosy and homely 17th-c pub with good village atmosphere,

scrubbed tables in two rooms, log fires, interesting choice of good value food, helpful friendly staff, real ales, good house wines; dogs welcome, handy for Limestone Way and other walks *(Ian and Celia Abbott)*

BUXTON [SK0572]

Bakers Arms [West Rd]: Homely family-run terraced local with well kept Greene King Abbot, Tetleys and guest beers, welcoming comfortable atmosphere, good mix of customers *(the Didler, JP, PP)*

☆ *Old Sun* [33 High St]: Relaxing traditional pub back on form, well kept Banks's and Marstons Best and Pedigree, good choice of reasonably priced wines by the glass, farm cider, decent usual food from sandwiches up, friendly staff, several small softly lit areas off central bar, open fires, low beams, bare boards or tiles, stripped wood screens, old local photographs; piped music, TV; children in back bar, open all day *(Dr W J M Gissane, Barry Collett, Peter F Marshall, the Didler, Andrew Crawford, Mike and Wendy Proctor, JP, PP, Anne and Steve Thompson, LYM, MLR)*

Royal Oak [Hurdlow; just off A515 6 miles S, towards Crowdecote]: Friendly and straightforward country pub with good choice of good value home-made food, esp pies, all day; handy for High Peak/Tissington Trail *(Mike and Wendy Proctor)*

BUXWORTH [SK0282]

☆ *Navigation* [S of village towards Silkhill, off B6062]: Busy bright décor in cheerful extended pub with restored canal basin, linked low-ceilinged flagstoned rooms with canalia and brassware, lacy curtains, coal and log fires, flagstone floors, well kept Marstons Pedigree, Timothy Taylors Landlord, Websters Yorkshire and a guest beer, summer farm ciders, winter mulled wine, games room, generous food (all day wknds); quiet piped music; tables on sunken flagstoned terrace, play area and pets corner; open all day, bedrooms *(Bob Broadhurst, Dr Paull Khan, Anne and Steve Thompson, Keith and Chris O'Neill, Stephen Buckley, Richard Fendick, Bernie Adams, Brian and Anna Marsden, LYM)*

CALVER [SK2474]

Bridge Inn [Calver Bridge, off A623 N of Baslow]: Unpretentious two-room stone-built village local, welcoming if hardly quiet, short choice of good value plain food (not Mon evening or winter Sun evening), small separate eating area, particularly well kept Hardys & Hansons ales, quick friendly service, cosy comfortable corners, coal fires, bank notes on beams, local prints and décor; picnic-sets in nice big garden by River Derwent *(DC, Ann and Colin Hunt, CMW, JJW)*

CASTLETON [SK1583]

☆ *George* [Castle St]: Relaxed atmosphere, good food from nourishing sandwiches to imaginative main dishes, well kept Wadworths 6X, friendly licensees, two good-sized rooms, one mainly for eating, with beams and stripped stone, no music; tables on wide forecourt, lots of flower tubs; popular with young people – nr

YHA; dogs, children and muddy boots welcome *(Liz and John Soden, JP, PP, Lorraine and Fred Gill, Mike and Wendy Proctor)*

CHAPEL-EN-LE-FRITH [SK0581]

Cross Keys [Chapel Milton]: Pleasant atmosphere and good generous fresh food (all day Sun) in popular old local with smartly decorated small restaurant, well kept beers, friendly service; children welcome *(Kevin Blake)*

CHELMORTON [SK1170]

Church Inn [between A6 and A515 SW of Buxton]: Comfortable split bar, ample space for diners, good range of reasonably priced generous food inc fresh veg and delicious puddings, friendly landlord and golden labrador, well kept Adnams and Marstons with a guest such as Mansfield; piped music, outside lavatories; tables out in pleasant sloping garden with terrace, well tended flower boxes, superb walking country, open all day summer wknds *(JP, PP, Mrs P J Carroll, David and Helen Wilkins)*

CHESTERFIELD [SK3871]

Barley Mow [Saltergate]: Former Wards pub with original stained glass, well kept Marstons Pedigree and John Smiths, wide choice of enjoyable food and hot drinks; very active in charity work *(Keith and Chris O'Neill)*

Barrow Boy [Low Pavement]: Real ale pub with Black Sheep, Thwaites and changing guest beers particularly well kept by enthusiastic young landlord, enjoyable food, cellar internet café; open all day from 9.30am (9am Mon, Fri and Sat market days, just 12–4 Sun) *(Keith and Chris O'Neill)*

Calico [Church Way]: Stylish and comfortable upstairs evening bar with great lighting and sound system, modern drinks choice, good service, light meals early evening; cl Mon *(Andrew Crawford)*

Rutland [Stephenson Pl]: Ancient L-shaped pub next to crooked spire church, well kept ales inc Boddingtons and Castle Eden, farm cider, rugs and assorted wooden furniture on bare boards, good value food, pleasant service, darts, old photographs; piped music; children welcome, open all day *(R T and J C Moggridge, Keith and Chris O'Neill)*

Woodside [Ashgate Rd]: Well refurbished, fresh and civilised, with plenty of sofas and wing armchairs, good value traditional food (all afternoon Sun), real ales such as Marstons Pedigree, John Smiths and Charles Wells Bombardier, good choice of wines by the glass; no children, great terrace, open all day *(Andrew Crawford)*

CHINLEY [SK0482]

☆ *Lamb* [just off A624 S of Hayfield]: Profusely decorated three-room stone-built pub tucked below road, current emphasis on enjoyable and good value generous food (all day wknds and bank hols) from lunchtime sandwiches and (not Fri/Sat evening) baguettes to fresh fish and interesting cheffy dishes, very popular OAP lunch and some children's dishes, warmly welcoming service, well kept Bass and other

ales; children welcome, lots of tables out in front with good views *(Jack Morley, JE, Dr and Mrs R E S Tanner, BB, Mrs P J Carroll)*

COMBS [SK0378]

Beehive: Roomy, comfortable and neatly kept, with good generous home cooking (good wkdy lunch deals, bargain suppers Mon, Weds/Thurs steak nights, food all day wknds), well kept ales such as Black Sheep, log fire, pleasant staff; quiet piped jazz, live music Fri, quiz night Tues; bedrooms, tables outside, by lovely valley tucked away from main road *(Anne and Steve Thompson)*

COXBENCH [SK3743]

Fox & Hounds [off B6179 N of Derby; Alfreton Rd]: Entirely no smoking village local with long partly flagstoned bar, attractive raised restaurant area, wide choice of good interesting fresh food, reasonable prices, well kept changing ales such as Fullers London Pride, Marstons Pedigree and Tetleys, good welcoming service; may be piped music *(the Didler, JP, PP, David and Helen Wilkins)*

CRICH [SK3454]

Cliff [Cromford Rd, Town End]: Cosy and unpretentious two-room pub with real fire, well kept Hardys & Hansons Bitter and Mild, good value generous standard bar food inc children's; great views, handy for National Tramway Museum *(Tony Hobden, the Didler, JP, PP)*

CROMFORD [SK2956]

☆ *Boat* [Scarthin, off Mkt Pl]: Traditional 18th-c waterside pub nicely refurbished and doing well under young brother and sister, well kept Marstons Pedigree, Springhead and changing beers from small local breweries, friendly relaxed atmosphere, log fire, good value food, long narrow low-beamed bar with stripped stone, bric-a-brac and books, darts, new restaurant; beer festivals; children welcome, garden, quaint village *(JP, PP, the Didler, Anne and Steve Thompson, C J Thompson, Derek and Sylvia Stephenson)*

CUTTHORPE [SK3373]

Peacock [School Hill (B6050 NW of Chesterfield)]: Neatly kept and comfortable, good straightforward food with separate bookable modest dining area, good service, well kept real ales; space for caravans in garden behind *(Keith and Chris O'Neill)*

DALE [SK4338]

☆ *Carpenters Arms* [Dale Abbey, off A6096 NE of Derby]: Ivy-clad pub with panelling, low beams, country prints, several well kept ales inc Adnams, well priced usual food in bar, lounge (no dogs here) and restaurant, friendly service, real fire, family room, darts, fruit machine; garden with play area (camping ground behind), good walking country – popular with walkers, can get very busy; pleasant village with abbey ruins and unusual church attached to house *(R T and J C Moggridge)*

DENBY [SK3847]

Old Stables [Park Hall Rd, just off B6179 (former A61) S of Ripley]: Raftered former stable barn, with bench seating and sawdust on floor, now tap for Leadmill microbrewery, with their full range, some from the cask, at low prices, and two or three guest beers; friendly atmosphere, fresh filled cobs, visits of the 1800s former mill brewery; open only Fri-Sun initially, all day *(the Didler, B and H)*

DERBY [SK3438]

☆ *Abbey Inn* [Darley St, Darley Abbey]: Unexpected conversion of surviving part of 11th-c abbey into pub, notable for massive stonework remnants; brick floor, studded oak doors, big stone inglenook, stone spiral stair to upper bar with handsome oak rafters and tapestries (and the lavatories with their beams, stonework and tiles are worth a look too); well kept cheap Sam Smiths, decent low-priced lunchtime bar food, children allowed; piped music; opp Derwent-side park, pleasant riverside walk out from centre *(the Didler, JP, PP, Kevin Thorpe, LYM)*

Capt Blake [Agard St]: Comfortably reworked open-plan local with enjoyable food, Adnams, Bass and Marstons Pedigree, flame-effect gas fire; open all day Sat *(the Didler)*

Exeter Arms [Exeter Pl]: Several comfortable and friendly areas inc super little snug with black-leaded and polished brass range, black and white tiled floor, two built-in curved settles, lots of wood and bare brick, HMS *Exeter* and regimental memorabilia and breweriana; friendly staff, well kept Banks's and Camerons Strongarm, fresh rolls and pork pies, daily papers, well reproduced piped music; open all day *(the Didler, David Carr, JP, PP)*

Falstaff [Silver Hill Rd, off Normanton Rd]: Lively and friendly three-room former coaching inn, basic and unsmart, with changing well kept ales such as Greene King Abbot and Marstons Pedigree; right-hand bar with coal fire usually quieter; open all day *(the Didler)*

☆ *Flower Pot* [King St]: Extended real ale pub with great choice of well kept changing beers mainly from small breweries - glazed panels show cellarage, regular beer festivals; friendly staff, three linked rooms inc comfortable back bar with lots of books, side area with old Derby photographs and brewery memorabilia, good value food till early evening, daily papers, pub games; piped music, concert room - good live bands wknds; open all day, tables on cherry-tree terrace; same small group runs the Smithfield *(Richard Lewis, Keith and Chris O'Neill, JP, PP)*

☆ *Old Silk Mill* [Full St]: Attractively decorated and welcoming two-room 1920s pub with old prints and full-scale mural of 1833 Derby turnout, good interesting range of beers under light carbon dioxide blanket, lots of country wines, good value cheap food from sandwiches to steaks all day from 9am on, back dining area, daily papers, real fires, SkyTV sports; open all day, handy for cathedral and Industrial Museum *(the Didler, Richard Lewis, Kay Wheat , JP, PP, David Carr)*

Rowditch [Uttoxeter New Rd (A516)]: Good value local with thriving friendly atmosphere,

well kept Mansfield, Marstons Pedigree and guest beers, country wines, attractive small snug on right, coal fire, quiz and food nights *(the Didler)*

☆ *Smithfield* [Meadow Rd]: Friendly and comfortable bow-fronted pub with big bar, snug, back lounge full of old prints, curios and breweriana, fine choice of well kept changing ales, filled rolls and hearty lunchtime meals, real fires, daily papers; piped music, pub games inc table skittles, board games, TV and games machines, quiz nights, live music; open all day, children welcome, riverside garden *(JP, PP, C J Fletcher, the Didler, Richard Lewis)*

☆ *Standing Order* [Irongate]: Imposing and echoing banking hall converted to vast Wetherspoons, central bar, booths down each side, elaborately painted plasterwork, pseudo-classical torsos, high portraits of mainly local notables; usual popular food all day, good range of well kept ales, reasonable prices, daily papers, neat efficient young staff, no smoking area; good disabled facilities *(Richard Lewis, JP, PP, Kevin Blake, the Didler, BB)*

Station Inn [Midland Rd]: Friendly and bustling basic local with good food lunchtime and early evening in large back lounge, particularly well kept Bass in jugs from cellar, M&B Mild and Marstons Pedigree on handpump, tiled floor bar, side room with darts, pool and TV, ornate façade; piped music, open all day Fri *(the Didler, JP, PP)*

DRONFIELD [SK3378]

Jolly Farmer [Pentland Rd/Gorsey Brigg, Dronfield Woodhouse; off B6056]: Extensive bar done as comfortably rustic ale house, old pine, bare bricks, boards and carpets, alcoves and cosy corners, bric-a-brac and fresh flowers, very friendly staff and atmosphere, no smoking dining area, daily papers, comfortable seats, open fire, real ales from glazed cellarage such as Batemans, Black Sheep, Hook Norton, Robinsons, Tetleys and Timothy Taylors Landlord, good wine choice, enjoyable simple food inc choice of Sun roasts, daily papers; piped music, games area with pool and TV, quiz nights Tues and Sun; children allowed if eating, open all day

(Andrew Crawford, CMW, JJW)

EDALE [SK1285]

☆ *Old Nags Head* [off A625 E of Chapel-en-le-Frith; Grindsbrook Booth]: Popular and friendly well used pub at start of Pennine Way, flagstoned area for booted walkers, food from basic hearty sustenance to more interesting dishes and wknd restaurant, well kept ales such as Grays Best, open fire; children in airy back family room, tables on front terrace and in garden - short path down to pretty streamside cottages; open all day *(C J Fletcher, JP, PP, LYM, Richard Fendick, John Hulme, R T and J C Moggridge)*

EDLASTON [SK1842]

Shire Horse [off A515 S of Ashbourne]: Peaceful spot, good food inc some interesting recipes, friendly attentive service, Marstons Pedigree and Wadworths 6X; tables outside *(Darly Graton, Graeme Gulibert)*

ELMTON [SK5073]
Elm Tree [off B6417 S of Clowne]: Softly lit
and popular low-ceilinged rural pub with good
value bar food, separate no smoking restaurant
Fri/Sat evening and for good Sun lunch, well
kept Adnams, Black Sheep, Greene King Old
Speckled Hen and Tetleys; open all day Weds-
Sun *(Gerry and Rosemary Dobson)*
ELTON [SK2261]
☆ *Duke of York* [village signed off B5056 W of
Matlock; Main St]: Unspoilt old-fashioned
local in charming Peak District village, like
stepping back in time, lovely little quarry-tiled
back tap room with coal fire in massive
fireplace, glazed bar and hatch to corridor,
more fires in the two front ones – one like
private parlour with piano and big dining
table (no food, just crisps); Adnams and
Mansfield, friendly character landlady,
welcoming regulars, darts; lavatories out by
the pig sty; open 8.30-11, and Sun lunchtime
*(Kevin Thorpe, the Didler, JP, PP, RWC,
Pete Baker)*
ETWALL [SK2734]
Seven Wells [Heage Lane]: Consistently
enjoyable food inc snacks all day, well kept
Hardys & Hansons, good wines by the glass,
friendly efficient staff; tables outside
(Ian and Freda Millar)
FROGGATT EDGE [SK2577]
Grouse [Longshaw, off B6054 NE of
Froggatt]: Plush front bar, log fire and wooden
benches in back bar, big dining room, good
home cooking inc imaginative dishes and good
value smaller helpings, good sandwiches too,
Banks's beers (no Mild) with guests such as
Barnsley and McMullens, friendly service,
handsome views; verandah and terrace, clean
bedrooms, good gritstone moorland walking
country *(G B Longden, David and Pam
Wilcox, John Yates, C J Fletcher)*
GLOSSOP [SK0294]
Globe [High St W]: Good choice of well kept
ales, comfortable relaxed atmosphere, friendly
licensees; no food, live blues and jazz nights
(Charles Eaton)
Old Glove Works [Riverside Mill, George St]:
Good real ale pub with regularly changing
choice of well kept beers, lunchtime bar food
and restaurant; occasional live music
(Charles Eaton)
Star [Howard St]: Bare-boards alehouse opp
station, up to a dozen changing real ales inc
small breweries; open all day *(the Didler)*
GREAT HUCKLOW [SK1878]
Queen Anne: Friendly family atmosphere,
beams and gleaming copper, well kept
Mansfield and guest beers such as Adnams,
open fire, walkers' bar, unpretentious
blackboard food (may be just soup and
sandwiches, winter lunchtimes); may be
unobtrusive piped music; french windows to
small back terrace and charming garden with
lovely views, two quiet bedrooms, good walks
(the Didler, JP, PP)
GRINDLEFORD [SK2378]
Sir William [B6001]: Comfortable dining pub
with wide choice of good value food, well kept

ales, good coffee; splendid view esp from
terrace, walking nearby *(DC)*
HASLAND [SK4068]
New Inn [Winsick; B6039 SE of Chesterfield]:
Newly refurbished, large lounge with no
smoking dining area up steps and two or three
other areas (one with pool and games
machines), wide choice of inexpensive
straightforward food inc OAP bargain lunch
(not Sun, when good value carvery may need
booking), two real ales; ice-cream cabinet,
piped pop music, karaoke Fri, live music Sat,
music quiz Sun; big garden with play area
(CMW, JJW)
HATHERSAGE [SK2680]
☆ *Fox House* [A6187/A625 3 miles towards
Sheffield – just inside S Yorks]: Handsome and
well run 18th-c stone-built Vintage Inn with
several linked rooms on different levels, oak-
framed open fireplaces, good value well
presented food from sandwiches up (discounts
for regulars, free transport offer), Bass, good
wine choice, quick friendly service; nice
moorland location, good views from back
terrace, bedrooms with own bathrooms
(BB, Guy Vowles, Richard Fendick)
☆ *Scotsmans Pack* [School Lane, off A625]: Big
clean welcoming open-plan local very popular
with walkers, huge choice of generous nicely
presented imaginative food inc wide vegetarian
choice (best to book Sun lunch), reasonable
prices, well kept Burtonwood beers inc Top
Hat, decent wines, good service even when
very busy; some seats in pleasant side
courtyard by trout stream; four good value
bedrooms, huge breakfast (may be piped radio
then) *(Gill Pennington, Patrick Hancock, Paul
A Moore, DC, Jane Taylor, David Dutton,
David Carr, D I Lucas, C J Fletcher)*
HAYFIELD [SK0388]
☆ *Lantern Pike* [Glossop Rd (A624 N)]: New
licensees doing enjoyable freshly made food inc
bargain Sun lunch, plush seats, lots of brass,
china and toby jugs, well kept Boddingtons,
Flowers IPA and Timothy Taylors Landlord,
good choice of malt whiskies, fine view from
no smoking back dining room and terrace,
darts, dominoes, perhaps piped music; children
welcome, open all day wknds, good value
bedrooms (quieter at back), great spot for
walkers *(JE, John Hulme, LYM, Jack Morley)*
HOLBROOK [SK3644]
Spotted Cow [Town St]: Traditional pub
extended behind, Jennings, good value food inc
generous help-yourself veg, comfortable no
smoking eating area *(Bernie Adams)*
☆ *Wheel* [Chapel St]: Friendly beamed country
local with well kept Courage Directors,
Marstons Pedigree, Theakstons Best and lots of
guest beers, some in jugs from the cellar,
biannual beer festivals, interesting whiskies and
brandies, good value home-made food (not
Sun evening or Mon) from sandwiches and
baguettes to popular Sun lunch, good log fire,
cheerful attentive staff, snug, family room,
attractive conservatory restaurant; pleasant
secluded garden with covered terrace and new
barbecue, open all day Sat, cl Mon lunchtime

(Peter and Sheila Tarleton, the Didler, Bernie Adams, Alan Bowker, JP, PP)

HOLYMOORSIDE [SK3369]

Bulls Head [New Rd]: Village pub with enjoyable food (not Sun-Tues evenings) and appealing little dining room – Sun lunch is good value and particularly popular *(Keith and Chris O'Neill)*

Lamb [Loads Rd, just off Holymoor Rd]: Small, cosy and spotless two-room village pub in leafy spot, Bass, Theakstons XB and up to six guest beers, pub games, tables outside; cl lunchtime Mon-Thurs *(the Didler, JP, PP)*

HOPE [SK1783]

☆ *Cheshire Cheese* [off A625, towards Edale]: 16th-c village pub handy for Pennine Way and Edale Valley, three snug beamed rooms each with a coal fire, no smoking lower dining room, well kept Barnsley Best, Wentworth PA and a couple of guest beers, good choice of house wines and malt whiskies, good staff; piped music; children in eating areas, open all day Sat, attractive bedrooms *(John Hulme, Hilary Forrest, John Close, JP, PP, James Woods, Patrick Hancock, Kevin Blake, Dr and Mrs P Truelove, LYM, Gordon Tong, Jean Kendrick, the Didler)*

ILKESTON [SK4643]

Bridge Inn [Bridge St, Cotmanhay; off A609/A6007]: Two-room local by Erewash Canal, popular with fishermen and boaters for early breakfast and sandwich lunches; low-priced well kept Hardys & Hansons Best and Best Mild, well behaved children allowed, nice back garden with play area, open all day *(the Didler)*

Dewdrop [Station St, Ilkeston Junction, off A6096]: Large three-room Victorian pub in old industrial area, two blazing coal fires, pictures and plates, interesting range of well kept changing guest beers, books to read or borrow, darts and TV in small public bar and impromptu piano sessions in lounge; sheltered outside seating, barbecue; no evening food, has been cl Sat lunchtime, bedrooms, walks by former Nottingham Canal *(Derek and Sylvia Stephenson)*

KILBURN [SK3845]

Travellers Rest [Chapel St]: Two-room 1850s local with Greene King Abbot, Ind Coope Burton, Tetleys and a local Leadmill beer *(the Didler)*

LITTLE LONGSTONE [SK1971]

Packhorse [off A6 NW of Bakewell via Monsal Dale]: Rustic charm in snug 16th-c cottage with old wooden chairs and benches in two homely and appealing well worn in beamed rooms, well kept Marstons Best and Pedigree, simple food from toasties up, welcoming informal service; pub games, Weds folk night; hikers welcome (on Monsal Trail), terrace in steep little back garden, open all day Sun *(the Didler, LYM, Andrew Stephenson, Patrick Hancock, Peter F Marshall, JP, PP, M and H Paiba)*

LULLINGTON [SK2513]

☆ *Colvile Arms* [off A444 S of Burton; Main St]: Very well kept 18th-c village pub with basic

panelled bar, cosy beamed lounge with soft seats and scatter cushions, pleasant atmosphere, friendly staff, piped music, four well kept ales inc Bass, Marstons Pedigree and a Mild, good value filled fresh cobs; picnic-sets on small sheltered back lawn overlooking bowling green, cl wkdy lunchtimes *(LYM, David Gaunt)*

MAKENEY [SK3544]

☆ *Holly Bush* [from A6 heading N after Duffield, take 1st right after crossing R Derwent, then 1st left]: Unspoilt two-bar village pub, cosy and friendly, good choice of well kept changing ales (may be brought from cellar in jugs), beer festivals, lots of brewing advertisements; three roaring open fires (one in old-fashioned range by snug's curved settle), flagstones, beams, black panelling and tiled floors; cheap food from lunchtime rolls up inc Thurs steak night; games lobby; children allowed in rough and ready hatch-served back conservatory, picnic-sets outside, dogs welcome *(Bernie Adams, the Didler, BB, JP, PP)*

MATLOCK [SK2960]

Thorn Tree [Jackson Rd, Matlock Bank]: Superb views over valley to Riber Castle from homely two-room 19th-c stone-built local, esp from front picnic-sets; well kept Bass, Whim Hartington and guest beers, pleasant quick service, chatty licensees, sensibly priced lunchtime food from sandwiches up (Weds-Sun), darts, dominoes; TV, piped nostalgic music, outside gents'; cl Mon/Tues lunchtime *(the Didler)*

MATLOCK BATH [SK2958]

Princess Victoria [South Parade]: Small Batemans pub with three of their beers kept well and guests such as Marstons Pedigree and Timothy Taylors Landlord, good value food in comfortable long beamed and panelled bar and upstairs restaurant, chatty landlady, coal fire; games machine, piped music; open all day, busy wknds *(the Didler, Kevin Blake, Richard Lewis)*

MILFORD [SK3545]

William IV [Milford Bridge]: Stone-built pub with beams, bare boards and quarry tiles, relaxing atmosphere, Bass, Fullers London Pride, Timothy Taylors Landlord, Charles Wells Bombardier and Whim Hartington tapped from casks in back room, blazing coal fire, cheap food inc sandwiches and pork pies most evenings *(the Didler, JP, PP)*

MILLERS DALE [SK1473]

☆ *Anglers Rest* [just down Litton Lane; pub is PH on OS Sheet 119, map ref 142734]: Friendly creeper-clad pub on Monsal Trail, with wonderful gorge views and riverside walks; good value fresh food from cobs up in cosy lounge, ramblers' bar and no smoking dining room, well kept Marstons Pedigree, Tetleys and a guest such as Barnsley, lots of toby jugs, plates and teapots, pool room; children welcomed, attractive village *(Derek and Sylvia Stephenson, A and B D Craig, Roy and Margaret Jones, the Didler, JP, PP)*

MONYASH [SK1566]

☆ *Bulls Head* [B5055 W of Bakewell]:

Welcoming unsmart high-ceilinged two-room local with oak wall seats and panelled settle, horse pictures, shelf of china, roaring log fire, mullioned windows, good value home cooking using local ingredients, sandwiches too, Tetleys Bitter and Mild, Theakstons Black Bull and Whim Hartington, obliging service; plush two-room dining room, darts, dominoes, pool in small back bar, may be quiet piped music; long pews out facing small green, friendly ginger cat, children and muddy dogs welcome; simple bedrooms, attractive village *(JP, PP, A G Thompson, D C Leggatt, BB, Bruce M Drew)*

NEW MILLS [SJ9886]

Fox [Brookbottom; OS Sheet 109 map ref 985864]: Friendly and unchanging old country pub cared for well by long-serving landlord, well kept Robinsons, plain good value food inc sandwiches, log fire, darts, pool; children welcome, handy for walkers (can get crowded wknds); splendid tucked-away hamlet down single-track lane *(John Hulme, the Didler, David Hoult)*

NORWOOD [SK4681]

Angel [Rotherham Rd]: Roomy open-plan pub said to date from 17th c, enjoyable straightforward food all day inc children's and Sun roast, four real ales and good soft drinks choice, dining area (no mealtime smoking) down three steps, games area other end with big-screen TV; quiet piped music, entertainment most nights; garden with play area, handy for Rother Valley country park and Chesterfield Canal *(CMW, JJW)*

OAKERTHORPE [SK3855]

Anchor: Comfortable dining pub (but smoking allowed throughout), with linked rooms and bookable back restaurant area, good choice inc game and lots of puddings, real ales inc Marstons Pedigree and Timothy Taylors Landlord; can be busy wknds *(Gerry and Rosemary Dobson)*

OCKBROOK [SK4236]

Cross Keys [Green Lane]: Small and welcoming, interesting jugs hanging from low beams, well kept Marstons Pedigree, darts – and very friendly to dogs; play area outside *(Mrs J Brewster)*

Queens Head [Victoria Ave]: Locally popular for very wide food choice inc game, fish and other fresh often local ingredients, OAP lunches, new back restaurant extension, Bass, Marstons Pedigree and a couple of changing guest beers, friendly attentive service *(anon)*

☆ *Royal Oak* [village signed off B6096 just outside Spondon; Green Lane]: Quiet 18th-c village local run by same family for half a century, small unspoilt rooms (one no smoking), well kept Bass and several interesting guest beers (Oct beer festival), tiled-floor tap room, turkey-carpeted snug, inner bar with Victorian prints, larger and lighter side room, nice old settle in entrance corridor, open fires, cheap popular lunches from good sandwiches up, evening rolls, traditional games inc darts, no music or machines; band night Sun; tables in sheltered cottage garden, more on cobbled front courtyard, separate play area

(the Didler, Pete Baker, BB, JP, PP)

OWLER BAR [SK2978]

Peacock [A621 2 miles S of Totley]: Attractive Chef & Brewer in moorland setting with panoramic views of Sheffield and Peak District, good food from extensive blackboard menu, big log fires, helpful attentive staff, large no smoking area; open all day *(Frank Gorman, Kathy and Chris Armes)*

PARWICH [SK1854]

Sycamore: Welcoming old unspoilt pub with jovial landlady, lively chat and roaring log fire in simply furnished but comfortable main bar, lots of old local photographs, hatch-served tap room with games and younger customers; plain wholesome fresh food lunchtimes and Weds-Sat evenings, big helpings, well kept Robinsons inc seasonal Old Tom, and Theakstons; tables out in front and on grass by car park, quiet village not far from Tissington *(Pete Baker, the Didler, JP, PP)*

PILSLEY [SK2371]

☆ *Devonshire Arms* [off A619 Bakewell—Baslow; High St]: Welcoming tastefully refurbished local with good value generous home cooking inc interesting fish and Thurs-Sat evening carvery (may need to book), well kept Mansfield Riding and Old Baily and a guest such as Badger, San Miguel on tap, public bar area for walkers and children; no credit cards, quiz and music nights; very handy for Chatsworth farm and craft shops, lovely village *(John Evans, Ann and Colin Hunt, DC)*

REPTON [SK3126]

Mount Pleasant Inn [Mount Pleasant Rd]: Enormous recently refurbished room with very long bar, wide choice of enjoyable reasonably priced food, friendly service; notable village church, attractive countryside *(Theo, Anne and Jane Gaskin)*

RIPLEY [SK3851]

Excavator [Buckland Hollow; A610 towards Ambergate, junction B6013]: Welcoming open-plan pub, family dining area and no smoking area, wide choice of good value food (all day Sun) inc good children's menu, friendly prompt service, well kept Marstons Pedigree, clean modern décor *(John and Judy Saville, Darly Graton, Graeme Gulibert)*

Moss Cottage [Nottingham Rd]: Welcoming atmosphere, enjoyable home-cooking inc choice of joints from good lunchtime carvery, well kept Bass *(Arthur Baker)*

ROWSLEY [SK2565]

☆ *Peacock*: Civilised 17th-c small hotel carefully refurbished under new ownership (the family who had it till 1940), relaxed atmosphere and enjoyable bar food in spacious and comfortable lounge and interesting inner bar, real ales, good wines; separate dining room; attractive riverside gardens, trout fishing, good bedrooms *(LYM, Kathy and Chris Armes)*

SANDIACRE [SK4737]

Blue Bell [Church St]: Friendly tucked-away 1700s former farmhouse, beams and breweriana, well kept Ind Coope Burton, Mallard, Marstons Pedigree, Oldershaws and a Mild *(Tony and Wendy Hobden, the Didler)*

SCARCLIFFE [SK4968]
Horse & Groom [not far from M1 junction 29
– B6417 SE of Bolsover]: Particularly
welcoming two-bar pub – strangers quickly
made to feel they've been regulars for years;
about six well kept ales on handpump; no
music or machines, no food other than pickled
eggs and crisps, dominoes; covered back
verandah with water feature and caged bird,
good-sized garden *(Pete Baker)*

SHARDLOW [SK4330]
☆ *Malt Shovel* [3½ miles from M1 junction 24,
via A6 towards Derby; The Wharf]: Old-world
beamed pub in 18th-c former maltings
attractively set by canal, pretty hanging baskets
etc, interesting odd-angled layout, well kept
Banks's Best and Marstons Pedigree, quick
friendly service, cheap lunchtime food from
baguettes and baked potatoes up (meal orders
stop 2 sharp), good central open fire, farm
tools and bric-a-brac; no small children, lots of
tables out on waterside terrace *(JP, PP,
Tony and Wendy Hobden, the Didler,
Roger and Maureen Kenning, Marian and
Andrew Ruston, LYM, Kevin Douglas, MLR,
John Beeken)*

SHELDON [SK1768]
Cock & Pullet: Light and cheerful cottage
conversion, small and cosy, with helpful staff,
good local atmosphere, well kept Bass and
Timothy Taylors Landlord, busy dining area
with good value tasty food inc Sun roasts and
home-made puddings, morning coffee, open
fire, scrubbed oak tables and pews, poultry
models; unobtrusive piped music, pool in
adjacent room off; welcomes ramblers; picnic-
sets in pleasant courtyard with small water
feature *(Anne and Steve Thompson, DC, Peter
F Marshall, JP, PP, Keith and Chris O'Neill)*

SHOTTLEGATE [SK3247]
☆ *Hanging Gate* [A517 W of Belper]: Charming
Vintage Inn dining pub, above-average sensibly
priced food all day, well kept Bass, decent
choice of sensibly priced wines, friendly helpful
staff, pleasant tidily kept rooms with attractive
settles and lovely views; garden
(Stephen, Julie and Hayley Brown)

SMALLEY [SK4044]
☆ *Bell* [A608 Heanor—Derby]: Small thriving
two-room village pub, dining area with good
reasonably priced changing food, well kept
cheap real ales such as Adnams Broadside,
Fullers London Pride, Whim IPA and
Hartington and one or two guest beers, good
choice of wines, pots of tea or coffee, smart
efficient friendly staff; post office annexe,
tables out in front and on big relaxing lawn
with play area, beautiful hanging baskets, open
all day wknds, attractive bedrooms behind
*(Derek and Sylvia Stephenson, JP, PP,
Bernie Adams, the Didler)*

SOUTH WINGFIELD [SK3755]
Old Yew Tree [B5035 W of Alfreton; Manor Rd]:
Cosy and convivial local with good value food esp
steaks and Sun lunch, well kept Marstons Pedigree
and a couple of interesting guest beers, log fire,
panelling, kettles and pans hanging from beams,
separate restaurant area *(Kevin Blake, Derek and*

Sylvia Stephenson, JP, PP)

SPONDON [SK3935]
☆ *Malt Shovel* [off A6096 on edge of Derby, via
Church Hill into Potter St]: Cheap well
prepared food, well kept Bass and Highgate
Saddlers Best from hatch in tiled corridor with
cosy panelled and quarry-tiled or turkey-
carpeted rooms off, old-fashioned décor, gas
heater in huge inglenook, steps down to big
games bar with full-size pool table, cheerful
efficient staff; lots of picnic-sets, some under
cover, in big well used back garden with rabbit
pens and good play area *(the Didler, JP, PP,
John Beeken, BB)*

STANTON IN PEAK [SK2464]
Flying Childers [off B5056 Bakewell—
Ashbourne; Main Rd]: Cool in summer, warm
in winter with coal fire in cosy and unspoilt
right-hand room, well kept changing ales
usually from Bass, Batemans, Fullers and/or
Whim, very welcoming old-fashioned landlord,
chatty locals, dominoes and cribbage, good
value ready-made filled lunchtime rolls; in
delightful steep stone village overlooking rich
green valley; cl Mon and perhaps Thurs
lunchtimes *(Peter F Marshall, the Didler, JP, PP)*

STARKHOLMES [SK3058]
White Lion [Starkholmes Rd]: Well run, in
exceptional location, with enjoyable
imaginative food at reasonable prices, and well
kept Burtonwood, Marstons Pedigree and
Whim Hartington *(C J Thompson)*

STAVELEY [SK4374]
☆ *Speedwell* [Lowgates]: Attractively refurbished,
brewing its own good keenly priced Townes
beers, fine choice of bottle-conditioned belgian
beers too, friendly staff, no smoking area, no
juke box or machines (nor food); cl wkdy
lunchtimes, open all day wknds *(Keith and
Chris O'Neill)*

STONEY MIDDLETON [SK2375]
Moon [Townend (A623)]: Good sensibly
priced food inc OAP lunchtime bargains, well
kept ales such as Black Sheep, Stones and
Charles Wells Bombardier, reasonably priced
wines, friendly staff, nice décor with old
photographs; handy for dales walks
(Sue Wheeler, Peter F Marshall)

SUTTON CUM DUCKMANTON [SK4371]
Arkwright Arms [A632 Bolsover—
Chesterfield]: Friendly pub with bar, pool
room and dining room, all with real fires,
decent choice of lunchtime food and drinks inc
two real ales; quiet piped music; garden and
play area, open all day *(CMW, JJW)*

TIDESWELL [SK1575]
☆ *George* [Commercial Rd (B6049, between
A623 and A6 E of Buxton)]: Hard-working
and friendly licensees and quick cheerful staff
in pleasantly unpretentious pub/hotel,
traditional L-shaped bar/lounge inc dining area
and linked no smoking room, good value
generous food from bar meals to wide choice
of restaurant dishes, three well kept Hardys &
Hansons ales, modestly priced wines, open
fires; piped music, separate bar with darts,
pool, juke box and machines; children really
welcome, dogs too, live 60s music Fri; by

remarkable church, tables in front overlooking pretty village, sheltered back garden; five comfortable bedrooms (church clock strikes the quarters), pleasant walks *(Derek and Sylvia Stephenson, BB, Peter F Marshall, the Didler, Michael Butler, Roy Morrison, Patrick Hancock, JP, PP, R T and J C Moggridge)*

WENSLEY [SK2661]

Red Lion [B5057 NW of Matlock]: Virtually a pub with no beer (may not even have bottles now), but worth a visit for its unspoilt appeal; friendly two-room no smoking farmhouse with chatty brother and sister owners, an assortment of 1950s-ish furniture, piano in main bar (landlord likes sing-songs), unusual tapestry in second room (usually locked, so ask landlady), no games or piped music, just tea, coffee, soft drinks and filled sandwiches or home-baked rolls perhaps using fillings from the garden; outside lavatories; open all day *(Pete Baker, JP, PP, the Didler)*

WESTON-UPON-TRENT [SK4028]

Old Plough [5 miles SE of Derby]: Rambling village pub with Edwardian décor and surprisingly wide food choice, with good-sized no smoking restaurant; well kept ales such as Adnams and Marstons Pedigree, good choice of wines (take-away sales too), helpful staff, children's/games room; popular Sun quiz night; good back lawns with play area and barbecues *(Dave Braisted)*

WHITTINGTON [SK3875]

Cock & Magpie [Church Street N, behind museum]: Dining pub with no smoking conservatory and good choice of good food inc sandwiches and early evening bargains for two (booking suggested for Sun), friendly service; also has tap room and proper snug, with particularly well kept Banks's, Mansfield and Marstons Pedigree; next to Revolution House museum *(Keith and Chris O'Neill)*

WHITTINGTON MOOR [SK3873]

Donkey Derby [Sheffield Rd]: Large chain pub with usual food, good choice of beers and other drinks; hearty landlord is a Sheffield Wednesday fan, wife is Sheffield United! *(Keith and Chris O'Neill)*

Red Lion [Sheffield Rd (B6057)]: New landlady doing well in small friendly 19th-c stone-built pub tied to Old Mill, with their Bitter, Bullion and a seasonal beer kept well, thriving atmosphere, old local photographs in two rooms *(the Didler, Keith and Chris O'Neill)*

WINSTER [SK2460]

Bowling Green [East Bank, by NT Market House]: Pleasantly traditional refurbished local with friendly staff, well kept beers such as Whim Hartington, wide choice of enjoyable generous home cooking inc good Sun lunch, log fire, dining area and family conservatory; has been cl wkdy lunchtimes, open all day wknds *(the Didler, JP, PP, Theocsbrian)*

Miners Standard [Bank Top (B5056 above village)]: Welcoming 17th-c local, friendly family service, well kept Boddingtons and Marstons Pedigree, attractively priced generous food inc huge pies, big open fires, lead-mining photographs and minerals, ancient well; children allowed away from bar; restaurant, attractive view from garden, interesting stone-built village below; open all day (at least Sun) *(JP, PP, the Didler)*

YOULGREAVE [SK2164]

☆ *George* [Alport Lane/Church St]: Handsome yet unpretentious stone-built 17th-c inn opp church, quick friendly service, welcoming locals, good straightforward home cooking inc game, comfortable banquettes, well kept John Smiths, Theakstons Mild and a guest such as Hartington; flagstoned locals' and walkers' side room, dogs welcome, games room, juke box; attractive village handy for Lathkill Dale and Haddon Hall, roadside tables, open all day *(JP, PP, Maggie and Tony Harwood, the Didler)*

Real ale to us means beer which has matured naturally in its cask – not pressurised or filtered. We name all real ales stocked. We usually name ales preserved under a light blanket of carbon dioxide too, though purists – pointing out that this stops the natural yeasts developing – would disagree (most people, including us, can't tell the difference!)

Devon

This big county has a remarkable variety of good pubs, including lovely unspoilt places with good local beers and ciders, some glorious historic old pubs and inns, and some really sophisticated well run foody pubs (food tends to be generous, and is strong on fresh fish). Throughout, there's very little pretension; it's one of Britain's very best areas for the pub-lover. Pubs on top form here are the Sloop in Bantham (good food, nice to stay at), the Fountain Head nicely set in Branscombe (brewing its own beer, plenty of atmosphere), the smarter Masons Arms there (super food, elegant new restaurant), the Drewe Arms at Broadhembury (a great favourite, with excellent fresh fish), the Drake Manor at Buckland Monachorum (an unassuming little charmer, very friendly, with nice food), the Ring o' Bells in Chagford (good all round), the Churston Court at Churston Ferrers (new entry, a converted manor house complete with lots of armour and portraits), the immaculately kept Five Bells at Clyst Hydon (another favourite, with particularly friendly and helpful staff), the Anchor at Cockwood (pulls the crowds with its fish specialities), the New Inn at Coleford (nice balance between pub and restaurant in this lovely old pub), the Culm Valley at Culmstock (another new entry, already good all round and clearly on the up), the Nobody Inn at Doddiscombsleigh (a great favourite, particularly on the drinks side, and very good indeed all round), the Drewe Arms at Drewsteignton (clever blend of unspoilt front bar with busy back restaurant), the Imperial in Exeter (good beers in an imposing building), the friendly Turf Hotel in its lovely if inaccessible position at Exminster (super barbecues), the Duke of York at Iddesleigh (another favourite, run by smashing people), the restauranty Dartmoor Inn near Lydford (outstanding food), the Church House at Marldon (good all round), the Royal Oak nicely set at Meavy (brought back into the Guide by cheerful licensees who have taken over since it was last in these pages some years ago), the Two Mile Oak near Newton Abbot (the very good licensees gain a Food Award this year), the Ship in its delightful waterside setting at Noss Mayo (another fine all-rounder), the Peter Tavy Inn (an exemplary Dartmoor village pub), the Hare & Hounds near Sidbury (this big well run place is full of interest, with good food too), the Sea Trout at Staverton (friendly caring licensees, proper home cooking), the Kings Arms at Stockland (civilised meals, comfortable weekends away, and a thriving local side – all cleverly balanced by hard-working licensees), the Bridge on the edge of Topsham (a favourite unspoilt pub with lots of real ales), the Start Bay at Torcross (wonderful fish straight off the beach, some caught by the landlord – another crowd-puller), the Kings Arms at Winkleigh (new licensees turning out very well), the Northmore Arms at Wonson (utterly unspoilt yet civilised, with enjoyable food), and the Diggers Rest at Woodbury Salterton (a previous Guide pub, regaining its place under enthusiastic young new licensees who have made a lot of changes). In all these pubs, the friendliness of landlords, landladies and staff is a strong point. In quite a few, we have highlighted the food. It is perhaps best of all at the Dartmoor Inn near Lydford, but for most of our readers the pubbier atmosphere in the Masons Arms at Branscombe would be a big plus; so it is the Masons Arms at

Branscombe which takes the award of Devon Dining Pub of the Year. In the Lucky Dip section at the end of the chapter, current front-runners are the Royal George in Appledore, Watermans Arms at Ashprington, Ship in Axmouth, Exeter Inn at Bampton, Anchor in Beer, White Hart in Buckfastleigh, Sir Walter Raleigh at East Budleigh, Double Locks, Great Western and Ship in Exeter, Rock at Georgeham, Poachers at Ide, Grampus at Lee, Beer Engine at Newton St Cyres, Ring of Bells at North Bovey, Millbrook at South Pool, Tradesmans Arms at Stokenham (despite its restricted opening), Lighter and Passage House in Topsham, Kingsbridge Inn in Totnes, Maltsters Arms at Tuckenhay and Rising Sun at Umberleigh. Drinks prices in Devon are close to the national average. The Imperial in Exeter is a real price-buster, much cheaper than average; the Fountain Head at Branscombe, brewing its own, was the next cheapest we found for beer. A good few local brews such as Teignworthy, Branscombe Vale, Summerskills, Otter, Princetown, Jollyboat and Country Life often take the bargain beer spot on Devon pub price lists.

ASHPRINGTON SX8156 Map 1
Durant Arms

Village signposted off A381 S of Totnes; OS Sheet 202 map reference 819571

Set opposite the church in a pretty village, this neatly kept place is run by friendly licensees. There's now much more emphasis on the good food with many of the tables set for dining, but the beamed open-plan bar still has several open fires, lamps and horsebrasses, fresh flowers, and a mix of seats and tables on the red patterned carpet; there's a lower carpeted lounge too, with another open fire. Enjoyable bar food includes sandwiches (from £2.25), home-made soup (£3.50), home-cooked ham and eggs (£6.45), good liver and onions, tasty spinach and mushroom risotto or cottage pie (all £7.45), steak and kidney pie (£7.95), fish dishes such as grilled salmon steak with a tomato and cucumber salsa (£10.95) or scallops and monkfish in a bacon and cream sauce (£13.45), gressingham duck breast (£13.95), and puddings such as blackberry and apple pie or home-made brûlée (£3.75); best to book if you want to be sure of a table. The no smoking dining room has lots of oil and watercolours by local artists on the walls. Good, attentive service. St Austell Dartmoor Best and Tribute on handpump, and Luscombe cider; no games machines but they do have piped music. The back terrace has wooden garden furniture and there's a water feature. *(Recommended by Mike Gorton, Richard and Margaret Peers, Mrs J L Wyatt, Jay Bohmrich, Mr and Mrs D Barlow, Comus and Sarah Elliott, John Glaze, Ann and Bob Westbrook, E B Ireland)*

Free house ~ Licensees Graham and Eileen Ellis ~ Real ale ~ Bar food ~ Restaurant ~ (01803) 732240 ~ Children in eating area of bar and restaurant ~ Dogs allowed in bar ~ Open 11.30-2.30, 6.30-11; 12-2, 7-10.30 Sun; closed evenings 25 and 26 Dec ~ Bedrooms: £40B/£70B

BANTHAM SX6643 Map 1
Sloop ♀ ⇌

Off A379/B3197 NW of Kingsbridge

This 16th-c pub is the sort of place that quite a few of our readers return to again and again over several years, and enjoy staying overnight. The black-beamed bar has a good bustling atmosphere, country chairs around wooden tables, stripped stone walls and flagstones, a woodburning stove, and easy chairs in a quieter side area with a nautical theme. From a wide choice, the good, interesting bar food includes pasties (from £2.30), sandwiches (from £2.95; fresh crab £5.25), tasty home-made soups (from £2.60), basket meals (from £3.35), hot potted shrimps

(£4.45), ploughman's (£4.80), mediterranean hotpot (£5.65), fresh crab salad (£10.65), daily specials such as laver bread with ham and cockles (£4.45), seared scallop salad (£5.95), tagliatelle with sun-dried tomato pesto (£6.65), steamed fillet of local haddock with a cream and spinach sauce (£7.90), breast of chicken stuffed with apricot mousse (£8.45), barbary duck breast with a creamy green peppercorn and apple brandy sauce (£10.75), and home-made puddings. Part of the dining room is no smoking. Well kept Bass, and Palmers IPA and Copper Ale on handpump, Luscombe farm cider, 25 malt whiskies, 14 wines by the glass from a carefully chosen wine list (including some local ones), and a good choice of liqueurs and West Country drinks like rum and shrub or brandy and lovage. Darts, dominoes, cribbage, and table skittles. There are some seats at the back. The bedrooms in the pub itself have the most character; they also have self-catering cottages. Plenty of surrounding walks. *(Recommended by David Crook, Chris Butt, Lynda and Trevor Smith, H L Dennis, David M Cundy, Jay Bohmrich, Pete and Jo Cole, Alan and Paula McCully, Nick Lawless, Mr and Mrs J Curtis, Alan Cowell, Theocsbrian, Michael Porter, Comus and Sarah Elliott, Ann and Bob Westbrook, Steve Whalley, Jack Clark, Geoff Calcott, Mr and Mrs C R Little, Derek and Caroline Earwood, C A Hall, Dr and Mrs Michael Smith)*

Free house ~ Licensee Neil Girling ~ Real ale ~ Bar food (12-2, 7-10) ~ Restaurant ~ No credit cards ~ (01548) 560489 ~ Children in eating area of bar and restaurant ~ Dogs welcome ~ Open 11-2.30, 6-11; 12-2.30, 6.30-10.30 Sun; closed evenings 25 and 26 Dec ~ Bedrooms: /£72B

BERRYNARBOR SS5646 Map 1
Olde Globe
Village signposted from A399 E of Ilfracombe

The series of dimly lit homely rooms in this bustling and rambling 13th-c pub has low ceilings, curved deep-ochre walls, and floors of flagstones or of ancient lime-ash (with silver coins embedded in them). There are old high-backed oak settles (some carved) and plush cushioned cask seats around antique tables, and lots of cutlasses, swords, shields and fine powder-flasks, a profusion of genuinely old pictures, priests (fish-coshes), thatcher's knives, sheep shears, gin-traps, pitchforks, antlers, and copper warming pans; there's a partly no smoking family room and no smoking dining room. Well kept Bass, St Austell Dartmoor Best, and a guest like Barum Original or Fullers London Pride on handpump; sensibly placed darts, pool, skittle alley, dominoes, piped music, and winter quiz nights every other Sunday evening. Bar food includes sandwiches (from £1.80), ploughman's (from £4), filled baked potatoes (from £4.25), vegetable lasagne or home-made steak and kidney pie (£6.25), steaks (from £7.50), daily specials, children's meals (£2.50), and puddings (from £2.75). The crazy-paved front terrace has some old-fashioned garden seats, and there is a children's activity house. *(Recommended by Canon Michael Bourdeaux, R and J Bateman, Dr D J and Mrs S C Walker, Dr and Mrs P Truelove, Boyd Catling, George Atkinson, Paul and Ursula Randall, Annette Tress, Gary Smith, Maysie Thompson)*

Unique Pub Co ~ Lease Don and Edith Ozelton and family ~ Real ale ~ Bar food (not 25 Dec) ~ No credit cards ~ (01271) 882465 ~ Children in family room or in dining room if over 8 ~ Dogs allowed in bar ~ Open 12-3, 6-11; 12-3, 7-10.30 Sun; 12-2.30, 7-11 in winter

BRANSCOMBE SY1888 Map 1
Fountain Head ◀
Upper village, above the robust old church; village signposted off A3052 Sidmouth—Seaton, then from Branscombe Square follow road up hill towards Sidmouth, and after about 1 mile turn left after the church; OS Sheet 192 map reference SY188889

Looking down a lane lined by thatched cottages, with the steep pastures of the combe beyond, this medieval tiled stone house has a lot of old-fashioned character, and also brews its own beers in the Branscombe Vale Brewery: Branoc, Draymans Best, Jolly Geff (named after Mrs Luxton's father, the ex-licensee), and summer

Summa That, and summer guest beers like Adnams Broadside or Exmoor Fox; they also hold a midsummer weekend beer festival which comprises three days of spitroasts, barbecues, live music, morris men, and over 30 real ales; farm cider, too. The room on the left – formerly a smithy – has forge tools and horseshoes on the high oak beams, a log fire in the original raised firebed with its tall central chimney, and cushioned pews and mate's chairs. On the right, an irregularly shaped, more orthodox snug room has another log fire, white-painted plank ceiling with an unusual carved ceiling-rose, brown-varnished panelled walls, and rugs on its flagstone-and-lime-ash floor; the children's room is no smoking, the airedale is called Max, the new puppy, Chester, and the black and white cat, Casey Jones. Bar food such as sandwiches, filled baked potatoes or ploughman's, sausage and mash with onion gravy (£4.95), good ham and egg, steak and kidney pie or moussaka with greek salad (£6.25), and fresh battered cod (£6.95). Darts, shove-ha'penny, cribbage, and dominoes. There are seats out on the front loggia and terrace, and a little stream rustling under the flagstoned path. They offer self-catering; pleasant nearby walks. *(Recommended by Mike Gorton, Steve Crick, Helen Preston, Dr and Mrs M E Wilson, Roger and Pauline Pearce, the Didler, Dr D E Granger, June and Malcolm Farmer, JP, PP, Mrs Jean Clarke, Maurice Ribbans, David Holloway, Peter Herridge)*

Own brew ~ Licensee Mrs Catherine Luxton ~ Real ale ~ Bar food ~ (01297) 680359 ~ Children in restaurant at lunchtime but must be over 10 in evening ~ Dogs welcome ~ Folk/country & western/rock ~ Open 11.30-3, 6-11; 12-3, 6.30-10.30 Sun

Masons Arms ♈ ♀ 🍺

Main Street; signed off A3052 Sidmouth—Seaton, then bear left into village

Devon Dining Pub of the Year

There have been quite a few changes at this fine 14th-c inn this year. The long-standing licensee found that the restaurant was always fully booked with residents so locals and visitors were unable to eat there, so what was the conference room has now been turned into a new, elegant restaurant; its bar was converted into a kitchen, allowing diners to watch the chefs at work. Nearly all the cottage bedrooms and rooms in the hotel have been updated except the budget rooms which do not have ensuite bathrooms. The wine list has been rewritten with more emphasis on the New World, and they now use local breweries for their real ales. The rambling low-beamed main bar has a massive central hearth in front of the roaring log fire (spit roasts on Tuesday and Sunday lunch and Friday evenings), windsor chairs and settles, and a good bustling atmosphere. The no smoking Old Worthies bar has a slate floor, a fireplace with a two-sided woodburning stove, and woodwork that has been stripped back to the original pine. There's also the original no smoking restaurant (warmed by one side of the woodburning stove). Very good bar food includes lunchtime sandwiches (from £3), ploughman's (from £4.95), omelettes (£5.75), and filled panini such as their own honey roast ham, with tomato, mozzarella and basil or roasted vegetables and pesto (from £5.75), as well as a warm salad of lambs kidneys (£4.95), house pâté (£5), brochette of king prawns and monkfish (£6.95), fresh cod in beer batter (£8.50), spicy root and lentil casserole (£8.95), steak and kidney pudding or popular fresh thai crabcakes (£9.50), cider braised ham hock (£11.95), local estate steaks (from £12.95), rack of lamb with black pudding (£13.95), daily specials, puddings like baked apples with raisins and sultanas or syrup sponge pudding (£3.95), and children's meals (from £3.95). Well kept Bass, Otter Ale, a beer named for the pub, and guests from Barum, Blackdown, Clearwater, Cotleigh, Cottage, Exe Valley, Exmoor, O'Hanlans, Scattor Rock, and so forth on handpump, and they hold a popular beer festival in July; 30 malt whiskies, lots of wines by the glass, and Addlestone's and Lyme Bay cider; polite, attentive staff. Darts, dominoes, and a lovely 200-year-old shove-ha'penny board. Outside, the quiet flower-filled front terrace has tables with little thatched roofs, extending into a side garden *(Recommended by June and Jeff Elmes, JP, PP, Phyl and Jack Street, Alan and Paula McCully, P and J Shapley, the Didler, Dr and Mrs M E Wilson, B and F A Hannam, Cathy Robinson, Ed Coombe, Howard and Margaret Buchanan, Lynn Sharpless, Richard and Margaret Peers, Dr S J Shepherd, John and*

Jane Hayter, Barry Steele-Perkins, Mr and Mrs Allan Chapman, Peter Craske, Michael Doswell, Cathryn and Richard Hicks; also in the Good Hotel Guide)

Free house ~ Licensees Murray Inglis, Mark Thompson, and Tim Manktelow-Gray ~ Real ale ~ Bar food ~ Restaurant ~ (01297) 680300 ~ Children welcome ~ Dogs allowed in bar ~ Open 11-11; 12-10.30 Sun; 11-3, 6-11 in winter ~ Bedrooms: £70B/£50(£100B)

BROADHEMBURY ST1004 Map 1
Drewe Arms ★ 🍽️ ♜

Signposted off A373 Cullompton—Honiton

'Simply could not be bettered' is how a reader described his visit to this pretty thatched 15th-c village pub. Of course, the emphasis remains on the very fresh, excellent fish dishes, but the small bar area has kept its lovely local chatty atmosphere so that anyone walking in for just a drink would not feel at all out of place. The bar has neatly carved beams in its high ceiling, and handsome stone-mullioned windows (one with a small carved roundabout horse), and on the left, a high-backed stripped settle separates off a little room with flowers on the three sturdy country tables, plank-panelled walls painted brown below and yellow above with attractive engravings and prints, and a big black-painted fireplace with bric-a-brac on a high mantelpiece; some wood carvings, walking sticks, and framed watercolours for sale. The flagstoned entry has a narrow corridor of a room by the servery with a couple of tables, and the cellar bar has simple pews on the stone floor; the dining room is no smoking. Unfailingly good, the food might include open sandwiches (from £5.25; gravadlax £5.95; fillet steak and melted stilton £8.25), daily specials such as spicy crab chowder (£6.50), griddled sardines (£7 small helping, £10.50 large helping), smoked haddock and stilton rarebit (£7 small helping, £12.50 large helping), wing of skate with black butter and capers (£13.50), sea bream with orange and chilli (£14.50), half lobster (£16), fillet of brill with horseradish hollandaise (£16.75), and puddings such as spiced pears with stem ginger ice cream or rhubarb compote with vanilla ice cream (£5). Best to book to be sure of a table. Well kept Otter Bitter, Ale, Bright and Head tapped from the cask, and a very good wine list laid out extremely helpfully – including 12 by the glass; shove-ha'penny, dominoes and cribbage. There are picnic-sets in the lovely garden which has a lawn stretching back under the shadow of chestnut trees towards a church with its singularly melodious hour-bell. Thatched and very pretty, the 15th-c pub is in a charming village of similar cream-coloured cottages. *(Recommended by JP, PP, Mr and Mrs H D Brierly, Alan and Paula McCully, Basil Minson, John and Fiona Merritt, John and Joan Nash, Shaun Pinchbeck, the Didler, Patrick Hancock, John and Sonja Newberry, Andy and Jill Kassube, Peter Craske, R T and J C Moggridge, B H and J I Andrews, Bob and Margaret Holder, David and Nina Pugsley, Howard and Margaret Buchanan, Andy Harvey, P M Wilkins, J Coote)*

Free house ~ Licensees Kerstin and Nigel Burge ~ Real ale ~ Bar food (not Sun evening) ~ Restaurant ~ (01404) 841267 ~ Well behaved children in eating area of bar and in restaurant ~ Dogs allowed in bar ~ Open 11-3, 6-11; 12-3 Sun; closed Sun evening, 31 Dec

BUCKLAND BREWER SS4220 Map 1
Coach & Horses

Village signposted off A388 S of Monkleigh; OS Sheet 190 map reference 423206

The helpful staff offer a genuinely friendly welcome to all their customers in this carefully preserved 13th-c thatched house. The attractively furnished and heavily beamed bar has a bustling pubby atmosphere, comfortable seats (including a handsome antique settle), a woodburning stove in the inglenook, and maybe Harding the friendly cat – who is now 17; a good log fire also burns in the big stone inglenook of the cosy lounge. A small back room has darts and pool. Good bar food includes sandwiches (from £2.95), large home-made pasties (£3.50), ploughman's (£4.75), home-made curries (£7.75), daily specials such as bolognese and local cheddar pasta bake (£6.50), steak and mushroom in ale pie (£7.25), pork in honey and mustard sauce or creamy spiced chicken (£7.50), lamb strips in chilli, garlic and olives (£8.50), chicken breast with bacon and stilton (£9.95), skate wing with capers (£10.95), and whole bass (£12.95). The restaurant is no smoking. Well kept Bass and Fullers London Pride on handpump; dominoes, cribbage, fruit machine, skittle alley, and piped music. There are tables on a terrace in front, and in the side garden. The two letting rooms have been converted into a one bedroom self-contained flat, which is also available on a bed and breakfast basis, and they have a cottage to let. *(Recommended by Harry Thomas, Rita Horridge, Bob and Margaret Holder, John and Sonja Newberry, R J Walden, the Didler, Simon Robinson)*

Free house ~ Licensees Oliver Wolfe and Nicola Barrass ~ Real ale ~ Bar food (not evenings 25 or 26 Dec) ~ Restaurant ~ (01237) 451395 ~ Children welcome ~ Dogs allowed in bar ~ Open 12-3, 6-11; 12-3, 7-10.30 Sun ~ Bedrooms: £30B/£60B

BUCKLAND MONACHORUM SX4868 Map 1
Drake Manor

Off A386 via Crapstone, just S of Yelverton roundabout

The floral displays at the front of this delightful and friendly little pub are very attractive all year round, and the sheltered back garden – where there are picnic-sets – is prettily planted. Inside, the heavily beamed public bar on the left has brocade-cushioned wall seats, prints of the village from 1905 onwards, some horse tack and a few ship badges on the wall, and a really big stone fireplace with a woodburning stove; a small door leads to a low-beamed cubby hole where children are allowed. The snug Drakes Bar has beams hung with tiny cups and big brass keys, a woodburning stove in an old stone fireplace hung with horsebrasses and stirrups, a fine stripped pine high-backed settle with a partly covered hood, and a mix of other seats around just four tables (the oval one is rather nice). On the right is a small, beamed no smoking dining room with settles and tables on the flagstoned floor. Shove-ha'penny, darts, euchre, and dominoes. Enjoyable bar food includes soup or lunchtime sausage and chips (£2.75), lunchtime baguettes (from £3.50), home-made brie and broccoli filo parcels on a sweet pepper sauce (£3.75), crispy coated ginger and garlic prawns (£4.25), ploughman's (from £4.25), home-made lasagne or vegetable tagine (£5.95), home-made steak and kidney pie (£6.25), gammon and pineapple (£7.25), and steaks (from £9.25), with daily specials like baked fillet of cod with a creamy seafood and wine sauce (£8.95), and braised lamb shank with fruits, port and rosemary (£9.95). Well kept Courage Best, Greene King Abbot and Sharps Doom Bar on handpump, and they keep nearly 100 malt whiskies, a decent wine list, and Inch's dry cider. The pub is handy for Garden House. *(Recommended by Jacquie and Jim Jones, Sheila Brooks, DAV, Lynn Sharpless, Gordon Stevenson, B J Harding, John Wilson, David Crook)*

Innspired Inns ~ Lease Mandy Robinson ~ Real ale ~ Bar food (12-2, 7-10(9.30 Sun)) ~ Restaurant ~ (01822) 853892 ~ Children in restaurant and family room ~ Dogs allowed in bar ~ Open 11.30-2.30(3 Sat), 6.30-11; 12-3, 7-10.30 Sun

BUTTERLEIGH SS9708 Map 1
Butterleigh Inn

Village signposted off A396 in Bickleigh; or in Cullompton take turning by Manor House Hotel – it's the old Tiverton road, with the village eventually signposted off on the left

New licensees have taken over this bustling and unspoilt village pub, and there are plans to extend the snug to create extra dining space. They also hope to extend the garden, too, adding a summer house with tables and chairs, and a barbecue area. Inside, there is still plenty to look at in its little rooms: pictures of birds and dogs, topographical prints and watercolours, a fine embroidery of the Devonshire Regiment's coat of arms, and plates hanging by one big fireplace. One room has pine dining chairs around country kitchen tables, and another has an attractive elm trestle table and sensibly placed darts; two no smoking areas. Bar food now includes filled lunchtime rolls or home-made soup (£2.95), lunchtime ploughman's

(£4.75), popular home-made burger or asparagus, mushroom and tomato tartlet (£5.95), bacon chops with a plum sauce (£8.75), steaks (from £9.25), and daily specials. Well kept Cotleigh Tawny and Yellowhammer, and a guest such as Cottage Golden Arrow or Fullers London Pride on handpump; darts, fruit machine, TV, shove-ha'penny, dominoes, and piped music, and a skittle alley is to be created. More reports on the changes, please. *(Recommended by B H and J I Andrews, P J Ridley, George Atkinson, Dr and Mrs P Truelove, Jane and Adrian Tierney-Jones, Tom Evans)*

Free house ~ Licensees David and Suzanne Reed ~ Real ale ~ Bar food ~ (01884) 855407 ~ Children in eating area of bar lunchtime only ~ Dogs welcome ~ Open 12-2.30(3 weekends), 6-11; 12-3, 7-10.30 Sun

CHAGFORD SX7087 Map 1
Ring o' Bells
Off A382 Moretonhampstead—Whiddon Down

You can be sure of a warm welcome in this quietly civilised old black and white pub, and it's just the place to enjoy a pint with the daily papers – with no interruptions from noisy games machines or piped music. Dogs are made at home, too, with fresh water and a large jar of free dog biscuits; Coriander the cat keeps visiting dogs under control and Maggie the pub dog is a favourite with customers. The oak-panelled bar has black and white photographs of the village and local characters past and present on the walls, comfortable seats, a big fireplace full of copper and brass, and a log-effect gas fire. There's a small no smoking candlelit dining room. Generous helpings of good food using local produce include sandwiches (from £3.25), ploughman's (£5.95), chip platters with home-cooked ham or local sausages (from £6.50), and hot mixed vegetable platter with rosemary and redcurrant gravy and fruit stuffing (£7.75), with daily specials like garlic, chicken and mushroom soup (£3.50), pâté or stilton, pear, walnut and sweet apple salad (£5), tandoori chicken or mushroom risotto (£8.25), salmon fillet with lemon and tarragon cream sauce (£11.25), half a duckling with orange liqueur sauce (£13.95), and puddings such as Bailey's chocolate cream glace or eton mess (£3.95). Well kept Butcombe Bitter, Exmoor Ale, and St Austell HSD on handpump, Addlestone's cider, and several malt whiskies; smiling, efficient service. Shove-ha'penny, cribbage, dominoes, and darts (if the pub is not busy). The sunny walled garden behind the pub has seats on the lawn, and there are walks on the nearby moorland. *(Recommended by B H and J I Andrews, DAV, Mr and Mrs C R Little, John and Annabel Hampshire, Adrian and Ione Lee, Richard and Margaret Peers, Michael Lamm, Mrs Jean Clarke, Margaret Ross, Nigel Williamson, K Chard, John Wall)*

Free house ~ Licensee Mrs Judith Pool ~ Real ale ~ Bar food (they serve breakfast and snacks from 8.30am) ~ (01647) 432466 ~ Children over 10 in eating area of bar; younger children in restaurant but no pushchairs ~ Dogs welcome ~ Open 11-3, 5-11; 12-3, 6-10.30 Sun; may close earlier if trade is quiet; cl 2 weeks mid-June, 2 weeks mid-Nov, 31 Dec, 1 Jan ~ Bedrooms: £30S/£45(£50S)

CHERITON BISHOP SX7793 Map 1
Old Thatch Inn
Village signposted from A30

A most enjoyable pub for its friendly welcome, well kept beers, and good, popular food. The rambling beamed bar is separated from the lounge by a large open stone fireplace (lit in the cooler months), and has Branscombe Vale Branoc, Otter Ale, and a guest like Adnams Broadside or Palmers IPA on handpump. At the end of May, they hold a weekend beer festival featuring mainly West Country ales from small independent breweries. As well as daily specials like cajun chicken with a spicy peanut sauce or seared fillet of salmon with chorizo, pepper and basil oil (£7.95), and roast breast of duck with red wine jus (£11.95), the menu includes sandwiches (from £2.95), filled baguettes (from £3.80), omelettes (£5.50), ploughman's (from £5.50), pasta with tomato or cheese sauce (£5.95), steak in ale pie or fish and chips with home-made tartare sauce (£7.50), lamb chops (£7.95), and steaks (from £9.95); fresh flowers on the tables, and polite, hard-working staff. The family room is no smoking, and leads on to the terrace with a thatched water well; piped music. *(Recommended by John and Vivienne Rice, M Hounsell, Geoff Pidoux, A Sadler, David Crook, Michael Lamm, Tracey and Stephen Groves, Ian and Deborah Carrington, R J Walden, Jenny and Brian Seller, Peter and Margaret Lodge, Mrs I Charles, Lorraine and Fred Gill, Peter Wrobbel, Colin McKerrow, Anthony Barnes, Dr and Mrs R E S Tanner, Ron Shelton)*

Free house ~ Licensee Stephen James Horn ~ Real ale ~ Bar food ~ Restaurant ~ (01647) 24204 ~ Children in restaurant and family room ~ Dogs allowed in bar ~ Open 11.30-3, 6-11; 12-3, 7-10.30 Sun; closed winter Sun evenings ~ Bedrooms: £39B/£55B

CHURSTON FERRERS SX9056 Map 1
Churston Court 🏠
Village signposted off A3022 S of Torquay; Church Road

In a very pretty spot next to an ancient church, this well converted manor house dates back to Saxon times, and was a favourite with the author Agatha Christie. Its history is full of tales of ghosts and underground passageways (and Bruce Reynolds hid here after the Great Train Robbery); the warren of candlelit rooms leading off the main hall is suitably packed with suits of armour, historic portraits, faded tapestries and darkly evocative corners. The partly flagstoned main bar has plenty of oak beams and long wooden tables, as well as sofas, gilt-framed mirrors, long red curtains, and a huge inglenook fireplace; on our visit it was brimming over with a mix of wedding guests, locals and visitors. Greene King Abbot, Princetown Dartmoor and Jail and a guest such as Badger Tanglefoot on handpump; they may have farm cider in summer, and some of their wines are from a local vineyard. They always have a carvery (£7.95 midweek lunchtimes, £10.95 Saturday evening and Sunday lunch), as well as a choice of other things including sandwiches (£3.95), ploughman's (£5.95), changing specials, and plenty of fresh fish from nearby Brixham such as bass and scallops poached with ginger and lime and seared with fresh herbs and sweet véronique sauce (£14.95). Around half the rooms (including the restaurant) are no smoking; piped classical music. There are lots of tables outside the wisteria-covered building, with more on an attractive walled lawn. Some bedrooms have four posters. The big car park can fill up quickly, and on the busiest summer days you'll sometimes see cars parked right the way up the little lane. Good walks nearby. *(Recommended by D and S Price, J E M Andeville, Neil and Anita Christopher, Roland Curtis, Elaine Thompson)*

Free house ~ Licensee Peter Malkin ~ Real ale ~ Bar food (2-2.30, 7-9.30) ~ Restaurant ~ (01803) 842186 ~ Children welcome ~ Pianist Weds evening ~ Open 11-11; 12-10.30 Sun ~ Bedrooms: /£60B

CLAYHIDON ST1615 Map 1
Merry Harriers ♀ 🍺
3 miles from M5 junction 26: head towards Wellington; turn left at first roundabout signposted Ford Street and Hemyock, then after 1 mile turn left signposted Ford Street; at hilltop T junction, turn left towards Chard – pub is 1½ miles on right

Although it keeps several real ales, most customers come to this welcoming and charmingly laid out dining pub to enjoy the good restaurantly food using fresh local produce. From the menu, there might be home-made soup (£3.50), open sandwiches (from £4), free range local pork and venison pâté with rowanberry jelly (£4.50; main course £8.25), large prawns with sweet chilli dipping sauce (£5; main course £9.25), lightly smoked ham with free range eggs (£6.50), fresh fish in beer batter (£7.50), home-made tortellini stuffed with goats cheese, pine nuts and shallots with tomato and pesto sauce (£11.50), free range organic chicken breast with a tarragon crust and madeira sauce, local lamb casserole or aberdeen angus rump steak (£11.50), and brixham scallops with lemon butter sauce (£16), with puddings such as sticky toffee pudding or exotic fresh fruit salad (from £4). Several small linked green-carpeted areas have comfortably cushioned pews and farmhouse chairs, lit candles in bottles, a woodburning stove with a sofa beside it, and plenty of horsey and hunting prints and local wildlife pictures. Two dining areas have a brighter feel with quarry tiles and lightly timbered white walls. You can smoke only in the bar area. Three well kept ales from breweries like Bishops, Blackdown, Exmoor, Otter, Stonehenge, and Wychwood, 10 wines by the glass, Bollhayes farm cider, and a good choice of spirits. There are two dogs, Annie who likes real ale, and Nipper who only has three legs. Picnic-sets on a small terrace, with more in a sizeable garden sheltered by shrubs and the old skittle alley; this is a good walking area. More reports please. *(Recommended by Brian and Bett Cox, Di and Mike Gillam)*

Free house ~ Licensees Barry and Chris Kift ~ Real ale ~ Bar food ~ Restaurant ~ (01823) 421270 ~ Children over 6 in restaurant lunchtime; no children in evening ~ Dogs allowed in bar ~ Open 12-3, 7-11; 12-3 Sun; closed Sun evening, Mon

CLYST HYDON ST0301 Map 1
Five Bells 🍴

West of the village and just off B3176 not far from M5 junction 28

A favourite with a great many customers, this most attractive thatched pub is particularly well run by friendly and helpful licensees. The partly no smoking bar is spotlessly kept, has a bustling, chatty atmosphere, and is divided at one end into different seating areas by brick and timber pillars; china jugs hang from big horsebrass-studded beams, there are many plates lining the shelves, lots of sparkling copper and brass, and a nice mix of dining chairs around small tables (fresh flowers and evening candles in bottles), with some comfortable pink plush banquettes on a little raised area; what was the restaurant is now part of the bar, and is no smoking. Past the inglenook fireplace is another big (but narrower) room they call the Long Barn with a pine dresser at one end and similar furnishings. As well as sandwiches and more straightforward dishes, the very good, popular daily specials might include smoked venison with a honey and mustard dressing, baked avocado with bacon and brie or prawns and kiln-roasted salmon (£4.95), steak and kidney suet pudding (£8.95), smoked fish platter (£10.75), tenderloin of pork with white wine and pink peppercorns, apricots, and cream or lamb shank braised in honey and rosemary (£11.45), local fillet steak with stilton, mushroom and red wine sauce (£15.45), and puddings like home-made treacle tart or butterscotch sticky meringues (from £4.95). Well kept Cotleigh Tawny, O'Hanlon's Blakeley's Best, and Otter Bitter on handpump, a thoughtful wine list, and several malt whiskies; piped music. The immaculate cottagey front garden is a fine sight with its thousands of spring and summer flowers, big window boxes and pretty hanging baskets; up some steps is a sizeable flat lawn with picnic-sets, a play frame, and pleasant country views. *(Recommended by Anne and David Robinson, Alan and Paula McCully, Malcolm and Jennifer Perry, Jacquie and Jim Jones, R J Walden, Martin Jennings, N and S Alcock, J C Brittain-Long, Dr and Mrs M E Wilson, Tony Dyer, Comus and Sarah Elliott, Maurice Ribbans, Barry Smith, Andrew and Samantha Grainger, Ann and Max Cross, Peter Saville, John and Sonja Newberry, Alison Hayes, Pete Hanlon, Cathryn and Richard Hicks, Dr and Mrs M W A Haward)*

Free house ~ Licensees Robin Bean and Charles Hume Smith ~ Real ale ~ Bar food (till 10pm) ~ (01884) 277288 ~ Well behaved children allowed away from front of bar ~ Dogs welcome ~ Open 11.30-2.30, 6.30-11; 12-2.30, 6.30-10.30 Sun; evening opening 7(6.30 Sat) in winter

COCKWOOD SX9780 Map 1
Anchor 🍴

Off, but visible from, A379 Exeter—Torbay

Although non-fishy dishes do appear on the big menu in this very well run place, nearly everyone comes to enjoy the immensely popular fish and seafood. They now do two sittings in the restaurant on winter weekends and every evening in summer to cope with the crowds – which the staff manage to do with efficient cheerfulness.

They offer 30 different ways of serving mussels (£6.50 normal size helping, £11.50 for a large one), 14 ways of serving scallops (from £5.25 for a starter, from £13.95 for a main course), 10 ways of serving oysters (from £6.95 for a starter, from £13.95 for a main course), and four 'cakes' such as crab cakes or mussel cakes (£5.95 for a starter, £9.95 for a main course), as well as tuna steak in tomato and garlic or whole grilled plaice (£6.50), and a shellfish selection (£15.50), and lots of daily specials like grilled mackerel with gooseberry and elderflower sauce or fried dab (£5.95), and skate wing with black butter or john dory with lemon mayonnaise (£6.50). Non-fishy dishes feature as well, such as home-made soup (£2.85), sandwiches (from £2.95), home-made chicken liver pâté (£3.85), cheese and potato pie (£4.50), home-made steak and kidney pudding (£6.50), rump steak (£8.95), and children's dishes (£3). But despite the emphasis on food, there's still a pubby atmosphere, and they keep six real ales on handpump or tapped from the cask: Bass, Brains, Fullers London Pride, Greene King Abbot and Old Speckled Hen, Otter Ale and Wadworths 6X. Also, a rather good wine list (10 by the glass – they do monthly wine tasting evenings September-June), 30 brandies, over 60 malt whiskies, and West Country cider. The small, low-ceilinged, rambling rooms have black panelling, good-sized tables in various alcoves, and a cheerful winter coal fire in the snug; the cosy restaurant is no smoking. Darts, dominoes, cribbage, fruit machine, and piped music. From the tables on the sheltered verandah you can look across the road to the bobbing yachts and crabbing boats in the harbour. *(Recommended by Ken Flawn, Richard and Margaret Peers, Meg and Colin Hamilton, John and Vivienne Rice, R J Walden, Peter and Jenny Quine, John and Sonja Newberry, Alain and Rose Foote, J F Stackhouse, Canon Michael Bourdeaux, John Beeken, N and S Alcock, Cathryn and Richard Hicks)*

Heavitree ~ Tenants Mr Morgan and Miss Sanders ~ Real ale ~ Bar food (12-3(2.30 Sun), 6.30-10(9.30 Sun)) ~ Restaurant ~ (01626) 890203 ~ Children in eating area of bar and in restaurant ~ Dogs allowed in bar ~ Open 11-11; 12-10.30 Sun; closed evening 25 Dec

COLEFORD SS7701 Map 1

New Inn 🍴 🍷 🛏

Just off A377 Crediton—Barnstaple

In an attractive hamlet of thatched cottages, this 13th-c inn strikes a good balance between a proper old pub and a restaurant. There are several interestingly furnished areas that spiral around the central servery, with ancient and modern settles, spindleback chairs, plush-cushioned stone wall seats, some character tables – a pheasant worked into the grain of one – and carved dressers and chests; also, paraffin lamps, antique prints and old guns on the white walls, and landscape plates on one of the beams, with pewter tankards on another; the resident parrot Captain is chatty and entertaining. The servery itself has settles forming stalls around tables on the russet carpet, and there's a winter log fire. Good, interesting food using local produce includes soup or wild mushroom tart with salsa verde (£3.95), filled baguettes (from £3.95; ciabatta with honey-marinated chicken and smoked bacon £5.95), chicken liver and wild mushroom pâté with hawthorn berry jelly (£4.50), ploughman's (from £5.95), smoked salmon omelette or fishcakes with caper and mustard mayonnaise (£6.95), cider and lentil patties with tomato coulis (£7.50), curry of the day or sweet baked ham with broad beans in parsley sauce (£7.95), coq au vin (£9.95), steaks (from £8.50), and daily specials. The restaurant is no smoking. Well kept Badger Best and Greene King Abbot with a guest like Fullers London Pride or Ring O' Bells Bodmin Boar on handpump, and quite a range of malt whiskies, ports and cognacs. Fruit machine (out of the way up by the door), darts, and piped music. There are chairs, tables and umbrellas on decking under the willow tree along the stream, and more on the terrace. *(Recommended by Mike Gorton, Richard and Margaret Peers, Steve Harvey, R J Walden, Mrs Joy Griffiths, Richard and Judy Winn, DRH and KLH, DAV, Peter and Jenny Quine)*

Soup prices usually include a roll and butter.

Free house ~ Licensees Paul and Irene Butt ~ Real ale ~ Bar food (till 10(9.30 Sun)) ~ Restaurant ~ (01363) 84242 ~ Children in eating area of bar and in restaurant ~ Dogs allowed in bar ~ Open 12-2.30, 6-11; 12-3, 7-10.30 Sun; closed 25 and 26 Dec ~ Bedrooms: £62S(£58B)/£78S(£73B)

COMBEINTEIGNHEAD SX9071 Map 1
Wild Goose 🍺

Just off unclassified coast road Newton Abbot—Shaldon, up hill in village

The garden behind this bustling pub, overlooked by the 14th-c church, has been landscaped this year, with plenty of seats for outside dining, and new outdoor heaters for chillier evenings. Inside, the spacious back beamed lounge has a mix of wheelbacks, red plush dining chairs, a decent mix of tables, and french windows to the garden, with nice country views beyond; the front bar has some red Rexine seats in the window embrasures of the thick walls, flagstones in a small area by the door, some beams and standing timbers, and a step down on the right at the end, with dining chairs around the tables and a big old fireplace with an open log fire. In the main part are standard lamps in corners, a small carved oak dresser with a big white goose, and cribbage, dominoes, chess, and shove-ha'penny; there's also a cosy section on the left with an old settee and comfortably well used chairs. Seven well kept West Country ales from breweries like Blackawton, Exe Valley, Otter, Palmers, Scattor Rock, Sharps, Skinners, Stonehenge, and Teignworthy on handpump, over 40 malt whiskies, and local Luscombe cider. Good, reasonably priced bar food includes lunchtime snacks such as filled baguettes (from £3.50; rump steak and fried onions £5.75), hand-made pasty (£3.75), various omelettes (from £4.95), and ploughman's (£5.95), as well as home-made soup (£3.25), chicken liver pâté (£5.75), ham and egg (£6.25), stilton and vegetable crumble, game sausages with redcurrant gravy and mustard mash or steak and kidney pie (£7.50), barbecue chicken (£8.95), whole rack of ribs with a sweet chilli sauce (£9.95), and steaks (from £10.50). *(Recommended by E B Ireland, Dr and Mrs M E Wilson, JP, PP, B H and J I Andrews, Neil and Beverley Gardner, David and Elizabeth Briggs, Mike and Mary Carter, Owain Ennis, Phil and Heidi Cook, Mr and Mrs B Hobden, the Didler)*

Free house ~ Licensees Jerry and Kate English ~ Real ale ~ Bar food (till 10(9.30 Sun)) ~ (01626) 872241 ~ Well behaved children in eating areas ~ Dogs allowed in bar ~ Local guitarist/singer first Fri of month ~ Open 11.30-2.30, 6.30-11; 12-2.30, 7-10.30 Sun

CORNWORTHY SX8255 Map 1
Hunters Lodge

Off A381 Totnes—Kingsbridge ½ mile S of Harbertonford, turning left at Washbourne; can also be reached direct from Totnes, on the Ashprington—Dittisham road

You can be sure of a genuinely warm welcome – whether you are a local or a visitor – from the genuinely friendly and helpful licensees in this spotlessly kept little pub. The small low-ceilinged bar has two rooms with an engagingly pubby feel and a combination of wall seats, settles, and captain's chairs around heavy elm tables; there's also a small and pretty cottagey dining room with a good log fire in its big 17th-c stone fireplace. Half the pub is no smoking. Good, well presented food at lunchtime includes sandwiches, celery and cheddar cheese soup (£3), country pâté (£3.95), fried egg on smoked bacon on toasted bread (£4.25), salmon and dill fritters (£4.45), smoked duck salad (£4.95; main course £8.95), ploughman's (£5.25), local sausages and mash (£5.25), and steak and kidney pie or moroccan lamb (£7.95), with evening dishes such as smoked salmon and prawn parcels (£5.25), baked avocado and crab (£5.45), chicken breast with camembert and bacon in a carbonara sauce (£10.45), calves liver (£11.95), and steaks (from £11.95), and daily fresh fish like scallops (£5.25; main course £11.95), dressed crab salad (£5.50; main course £12.95), cod fillet with herb and cheese topping (£8.95), and whole bass (£12). Well kept Teignworthy Reel Ale, and a couple of guests from breweries like Cottage or Sutton on handpump, 58 malt whiskies, country wines, a good wine list, and local organic juices. Dominoes, cribbage, and piped music. In summer, there is plenty of room to sit outside, either at the picnic-sets on a big lawn or on the flower-filled terrace closer to the pub. They have two cats, Ollie and Alex, the huge ginger tom, and two dogs, Sam and Sherry. *(Recommended by N and S Alcock, Mr and Mrs N Smith, Doreen and Haydn Maddock , Jeffrey Stackhouse, Mrs A Maslen, Glen Hamill, Joe and Marion Mandeville)*

Free house ~ Licensees Elizabeth and Roger Little ~ Real ale ~ Bar food ~ Restaurant ~ (01803) 732204 ~ Children welcome ~ Dogs welcome ~ Varied live music fourth Thurs of month ~ Open 11.30-2.30, 6.30-11; 12-3, 7-10.30 Sun

CULMSTOCK ST1013 Map 1
Culm Valley ♀ ◖

B3391, off A38 E of M5 junction 27

Though at first glance this village inn looks a bit scruffy, it's actually very rewarding and warmly civilised, gradually being transformed by its keen and chatty landlord. He and his brother import wines from smaller vineyards in France, so you can count on a few of those, as well as some unusual french fruit liqueurs, but the emphasis is more on the excellent range of real ales, straight from the barrel. You'll usually find between four and six mostly local brews, such as Branscombe Vale Draymans, Cotleigh Tawny, Hop Back Crop Circles and Teignworthy Beachcomber, but the choice can swell to 17 during their occasional beer festivals; also better than average bottled beers, and farm cider. The very good bar food usually comes with a choice of helping size, and might include sandwiches, cured herrings (£5/£9), loch fyne mussels (£7/£11), lebanese stuffed flatbread parcels with squash, pistachios and local cheese (£6/£11), hand-dived scallops with pomegranate molasses dressing (£7/£14), leg of lamb with ginger, garlic, cumin and coriander (£9), john dory with quince aïoli (£10/£16) and local cracked crab (from £11); the choice may be more limited on Sunday evenings. They grow their own herbs, and lots of the other locally sourced ingredients are organic. Smoking is strongly discouraged in the eating areas. There's a good thriving mix of locals and visitors in the salmon-coloured bar, which has well worn upholstered chairs and stools, a big fireplace with some china above it, newspapers, and a long stripped wooden bar counter; further along is a dining room with chalkboard menu, and a small room at the front popular with families. Old photographs show how the railway line used to run through what's now the car park. Outside, tables are very attractively set overlooking the bridge and the River Culm. The gents' are in an outside yard. The bedrooms were being done up as went to press; we haven't yet heard from anyone who's stayed here. *(Recommended by Mrs V C Greany)*

Free house ~ Licensee Richard Hartley ~ Real ale ~ No credit cards ~ (01884) 840354 ~ Children welcome away from bar ~ Dogs welcome ~ Open 12-3, 6-11(10.30 Sun); 12-11 Sat; 12-10.30 Sun; 12-3, 6-11(10.30 Sun) weekends winter ~ Bedrooms: /£50

DALWOOD ST2400 Map 1
Tuckers Arms

Village signposted off A35 Axminster—Honiton

Parts of this pretty cream-washed thatched longhouse date back to the 13th c, and after the church, it is the oldest building in the parish. The fine flagstoned bar has a lot of atmosphere, plenty of beams, a random mixture of dining chairs, window seats, and wall settles (including a high-backed winged black one), and a log fire in the inglenook fireplace. The back bar has an enormous collection of miniature bottles. Popular, well liked bar food includes soup (£2.95), filled granary rolls or baps (from £4.25; rib-eye steak £6.95), ploughman's (£4.95), platters of cold meats and pickles or sausages, black pudding and eggs (£6.95), and tossed green salad topped with grilled goats cheese with walnut or seafood medley (from £6.95), sweet potato and pine nut roulade (£7.95), escalope of pork with green ginger wine, lime, chocolate and chilli sauce (£8.95), supreme of chicken filled with pâté and pepper sauce (£9.95), calves liver with port sauce and wild mushroom risotto (£11.95), and steaks (from £11.95). The restaurant is no smoking. Well kept Courage Directors, Otter Ale, and Salopian Firefly on handpump kept under light blanket pressure; skittle alley and piped music. The summer hanging baskets, flowering tubs and window boxes in front of the building are lovely. *(Recommended by Basil Minson, Jenny Cridland, Gordon Cooper, Mike Gorton, Alan and Paula McCully, Andy Harvey, John and Vivienne Rice, Bob and Margaret Holder, R T and J C Moggridge, Andy Sinden, Louise Harrington, James A Waller)*

Free house ~ Licensees David and Kate Beck ~ Real ale ~ Bar food ~ Restaurant ~ (01404) 881342 ~ Children in restaurant and family room ~ Open 12-3, 6.30-11; 12-3, 7-10.30 Sun; closed 26 Dec ~ Bedrooms: £32.50S/£55S

DARTMOUTH SX8751 Map 1
Cherub

Higher Street

In summer particularly, this Grade II* listed 14th-c building is a striking sight with each of the two heavily timbered upper floors jutting further out than the one below, and its very pretty hanging baskets. The bustling bar has tapestried seats under creaky heavy beams, leaded-light windows, a big stone fireplace, and a warm welcome from the friendly staff; upstairs is the fine, low-ceilinged and no smoking restaurant. Four well kept real ales on handpump: Exmoor Gold, Otter Ale, Shepherd Neame Spitfire, and a beer named for the pub from Summerskills, 20 malt whiskies, and 10 wines by the glass; piped music. Bar food includes soup (£2.50), sandwiches (from £3), filled baked potatoes (£4.50), smoked haddock in white wine sauce and topped with cheese (£6), steak, mushroom and Guinness pie (£7.25), curry of the day (£7.50), and steak and chips (£8.50). *(Recommended by Pete and Jo Cole, Christine and Neil Townend, Nick Vernon, Graham and Rose Ive, Steve Whalley, Derek and Sylvia Stephenson, Emma Kingdon, Neil and Beverley Gardner, JP, PP, Tony Middis, Geoff Calcott, John and Laney Woods, Comus and Sarah Elliott, Julie and Bill Ryan, Ann and Bob Westbrook, Graham Lynch-Watson, Margaret and Roy Randle)*

Free house ~ Licensee Laurie Scott ~ Real ale ~ Bar food ~ Restaurant ~ (01803) 832571 ~ Children in restaurant only and must be over 10 ~ Dogs allowed in bar ~ Open 11-11; 12-10.30 Sun; 11-2.30, 5-11 weekdays in winter

Royal Castle Hotel 🛏

The Quay

There's a good welcoming atmosphere and quite a bit of character in this rambling 17th-c hotel, overlooking the inner harbour. There are two ground floor bars, each with their own atmosphere. On the right is the Galleon bar which is more lounge-like, and has some fine antiques, a Tudor fireplace, and a no smoking area. To the left of the flagstoned entrance hall is the Harbour Bar with a nautical theme, leather seats and lots of light wood; TV, cribbage, dominoes, and piped music. Well kept Bass, Courage Directors, Exe Valley Dob's Best Bitter, and Whitbreads on handpump. Well liked bar food includes home-made soup (£2.95), sandwiches (from £3.25; crab £4.25), baked potatoes (from £3.95), good deep-fried brie with a port and orange sauce (£4.95), ploughman's (£5.75), vegetable lasagne (£5.95), home-baked ham with eggs (£5.95), three local sausages (£6.45), popular home-made steak and kidney pudding (£7.45), braised lamb shank in a rich mint and rosemary sauce (£8.55), fresh crab (£10.95), steaks (from £11.75), and puddings (£3.45); they hold regular themed food evenings, and on winter lunchtimes, they serve spit-roasts from their 300-year-old Lidstone range – pork, lamb and beef, all from local suppliers. The inn was originally two Tudor merchant houses (but has a Regency façade); they have their own secure parking. No children. *(Recommended by Neil and Beverley Gardner, Pete and Jo Cole, Joyce and Maurice Cottrell, Tim and Carolyn Lowes, Terry and Linda Moseley, JP, PP, Tony Middis, Gill and Keith Croxton, David and Julie Glover, Tracey and Stephen Groves)*

*Free house ~ Licensees Nigel and Anne Way ~ Real ale ~ Bar food (all day) ~
Restaurant ~ (01803) 833033 ~ Dogs allowed in bar ~ Open 11-11; 12-10.30 Sun ~
Bedrooms: £74.95B/£169.90B*

DODDISCOMBSLEIGH SX8586 Map 1
Nobody Inn ★★ ⊕ ♀ ◀ ⊨

Village signposted off B3193, opposite northernmost Christow turn-off

Extremely popular and well run, this fine old place continues to be a favourite with
many of our readers. The range of drinks is quite extraordinary and the wine list is
probably the best pub wine cellar in the country. There are around 800 by the
bottle and 20 by the glass kept oxidation-free, and they hold tutored tastings (they
also sell wine retail, and the good tasting-notes in their detailed list are worth the
£3.50 it costs – anyway refunded if you buy more than £30-worth). Also, a choice
of 240 whiskies, local farm ciders, and well kept Nobody's (brewed by
Branscombe), Otter Ale, and a guest such as Scattor Rock Teign Valley Tipple on
handpump; friendly, well informed staff. The two rooms of the lounge bar have
handsomely carved antique settles, windsor and wheelback chairs, benches, carriage
lanterns hanging from the beams, and guns and hunting prints in a snug area by
one of the big inglenook fireplaces. Good bar food includes tasty home-made soup
(£3.90), poppy seed briochon bread filled with mushrooms, tomatoes and pesto
(£5), tiger prawn kebab with sweet chilli dip (£5.50), ploughman's (£6.50),
mushroom stroganoff or pork, herb and garlic sausages (£6.90), breast of chicken
in red pepper, orange and fig sauce (£8.50), slow roasted lamb shank in red wine
and basil sauce (£9.50), braised venison steak in port and black cherry sauce
(£9.50), griddled bass on tomatoes with mint dressing (£10.50), and puddings such
as chocolate truffle cake, apple cobbler, and marmalade sponge pudding (£4.50);
half a dozen good West Country cheeses from an incredible choice of around 40
(£5.90; you can buy them to take away as well). The restaurant is no smoking.
There are picnic-sets on the terrace with views of the surrounding wooded hill
pastures. The medieval stained glass in the local church is some of the best in the
West Country. No children are allowed inside the pub. *(Recommended by C A Hall,
MDN, R J Walden, A Sadler, Duncan Cloud, J Wedel, John and Sonja Newberry,
Mrs J H S Lang, J L Wedel, JP, PP, Steve Whalley, DRH and KLH, Lorraine and Fred Gill,
Richard and Margaret Peers, Andrea Rampley, Mr and Mrs Richard Hanks, the Didler, Ann and
Colin Hunt, Andy and Katie Wadsworth, B N F and M Parkin, Kevin Blake, Dr and
Mrs Rod Holcombe, R M Corlett, Peter B Brown, Andrew Shore, Stuart Turner, Betsy Brown,
Nigel Flook, Lynn Sharpless, Terry and Linda Moseley, Dr S J Shepherd, Dr T E Hothersall,
N and S Alcock, Lucy Bishop, Cathryn and Richard Hicks, Bill and Jessica Ritson, J P Marland;
also in the Good Hotel Guide)*

*Free house ~ Licensee Nick Borst-Smith ~ Real ale ~ Bar food (till 10) ~ Restaurant ~
(01647) 252394 ~ Open 12-2.30, 6-11; 12-3, 7-10.30 Sun; closed 25 and 26 and
evening 31 Dec ~ Bedrooms: £33S(£38B)/£55S(£70B)*

DOLTON SS5712 Map 1
Union ⊨

B3217

Readers have very much enjoyed staying in this comfortable village inn recently,
and the breakfasts, using fresh local produce, are good and generous. The little
lounge bar has a cushioned window seat, a pink plush chesterfield, a nicely carved
priest's table and some dark pine country chairs with brocaded cushions, and
dagging shears, tack, country prints, and brass shell cases. On the right, and served
by the same stone bar counter, is another bar with a chatty atmosphere and liked
by locals: heavy black beams hung with brasses, an elegant panelled oak settle and
antique housekeeper's chairs, a small settle snugged into the wall, and various
dining chairs on the squared patterned carpet; the big stone fireplace has some brass
around it, and on the walls are old guns, two land-felling saws, antlers, some
engravings, and a whip. Well liked, tasty bar food includes lunchtime filled

baguettes (£4; toasted ones £4.50) and cold platters (£4.95), as well as home-made soup (£2.95), grilled sardines or burgers (£4.75), omelettes (£5.15), local ham and eggs or local sausages with bubble and squeak topped with an egg (£5.50), and daily specials like moules marinière (£5.50), spinach and feta pie (£5.95), and local plaice fillets in beer batter (£6.75). The restaurant is no smoking. Well kept St Austell Tribute and a guest such as Jollyboat Freebooter, Sharps Doom Bar or Teignworthy Reel Ale on handpump, and decent wines; cribbage and dominoes. Outside on a small patch of grass in front of the building are some rustic tables and chairs. No children. *(Recommended by Mrs E A Brace, A C and B M Laing, R J Walden, Janice and Phil Waller)*

Free house ~ Licensees Ian and Irene Fisher ~ Real ale ~ Bar food (not Weds) ~ Restaurant ~ (01805) 804633 ~ Dogs allowed in bar and bedrooms ~ Open 12-2.30, 6-11; 12-2.30, 7-10.30 Sun; closed Wednesdays and first 2 weeks Feb ~ Bedrooms: /£60S(£75B)

DREWSTEIGNTON SX7390 Map 1
Drewe Arms
Signposted off A30 NW of Moretonhampstead

Thankfully, little changes in this unpretentious and friendly old thatched pub. The small, unspoilt room on the left still has its serving hatch and basic seats; the room on the right with its assorted tables and chairs has a log fire, and is not much bigger. Well kept Bass, Gales HSB, and a guest such as Brakspears kept on racks in the tap room behind, and local cider. At the back is a sizeable eating area, with well liked food such as a huge bowl of soup with a loaf of bread (£3.50), good sandwiches (from £4.50), a proper ploughman's (£5.95), pork and sage sausage with bubble and squeak, a vegetarian dish, big cod fillet in beer batter or crispy belly of pork on tatties and leeks with apple sauce (all £7.95), and shank of lamb with an orange and red wine sauce £12). The restaurant is no smoking. Dominoes, cribbage, darts, shove-ha'penny, and skittle alley. Castle Drogo nearby (open for visits) looks medieval, though it was actually built in the 20th c. *(Recommended by DAV, Barry Steele-Perkins, Anthony Longden, Eddie Edwards, JP, PP, Peter Craske, Di and Mike Gillam, Robert Gomme, Ann and Colin Hunt, the Didler, Jane Parsons, John and Sonja Newberry, Jenny and Brian Seller, D I Lucas, Steve Crooke, Julie and Bill Ryan, Tim and Carolyn Lowes, Rose, Len Banister)*

Whitbreads ~ Lease Janice and Colin Sparks ~ Real ale ~ Bar food (not 25 Dec) ~ Restaurant ~ (01647) 281224 ~ Children in eating area of bar and in restaurant ~ Dogs allowed in bar ~ Open 11-3, 6-11; 12-3, 7-10.30 Sun ~ Bedrooms: /£60B

EXETER SX9292 Map 1
Imperial ◖ £
Crediton/Tiverton road near St Davids Station

Standing in its own six-acre hillside park, this early 19th-c mansion is reached along a sweeping drive; the attractive cobbled courtyard in front has elegant garden furniture, and there are plenty of picnic-sets in the grounds. Inside, it's quite spread out with various different areas including a couple of little clubby side bars, a left-hand bar looking into a light and airy former orangery – the huge glassy fan of its end wall is lightly mirrored – and a glorious ex-ballroom filled with elaborate plasterwork and gilding brought here in the 1920s from Haldon House (a Robert Adam stately home that was falling on hard times). One area is no smoking. The furnishings give Wetherspoons' usual solid well spaced comfort, and there are plenty of interesting pictures and other things to look at. Well kept and very cheap Bass, Blackawton, Courage Directors, Greene King Abbot, Shepherd Neame Spitfire, and Theakstons Best tapped from the cask; friendly, efficient staff. Decent bar food includes filled baps (from £3.05), filled baked potatoes (from £3.55), sausage and mash (£5.25), quite a few burgers (from £5.25), chargrilled vegetable and ricotta cannelloni (£5.55), aberdeen angus pie (£5.65), steaks (from £6.09), and puddings like treacle sponge (from £1.99); there's also an all day every day offer of two meals for £6.25. Silenced fruit machines and video game. *(Recommended by Mike Gorton, Tim and Carolyn Lowes, Steve Crick, Helen Preston, Dr and Mrs A K Clarke, the Didler, JP, PP, C J Fletcher, Joe Green)*

Wetherspoons ~ Manager Val Docherty ~ Real ale ~ Bar food (11-10; 12-9.30 Sun) ~ (01392) 434050 ~ Children in family area until 6pm ~ Open 10-11; 11-10.30 Sun

EXMINSTER SX9487 Map 1
Turf Hotel ★

Follow the signs to the Swan's Nest, signposted from A739 S of village, then continue to end of track, by gates; park, and walk right along canal towpath – nearly 1 mile; there's a fine seaview out to the mudflats at low tide

You cannot reach this isolated and friendly pub by car. You must either walk (which takes about 20 minutes along the ship canal) or cycle, or take a 40-minute ride from Countess Wear in their own boat, the *Water Mongoose* (bar on board; £5 adult, £2 child return, charter for up to 56 people £200). They also operate a 60-seater boat which brings people down the Exe estuary from Topsham quay (15 minute trip, adults £3, child £2), and there's a canal boat from Countess Wear Swing Bridge every lunchtime. Best to phone the pub for all sailing times. For those arriving in their own boat there is a large pontoon as well as several moorings. In fine weather, the decking area, with the outdoor rotisserie for chicken and pig roasts and outside bar, really comes into its own. Inside, the pleasantly airy bar has church pews, wooden chairs and alcove seats on the polished bare floorboards, and pictures and old photographs of the pub and its characters over the years on the walls; woodburning stove and antique gas fire. From the bay windows there are views out to the mudflats (full of gulls and waders at low tide). Good bar food includes a big choice of toasties and filled baked potatoes (from £3.25; chicken and melted brie in ciabatta £5.95), fried calamari with sweet chilli sauce (£4.25), smoked salmon, crème fraîche and watercress or wild Exe salmon open sandwiches (£5.50), roasted aubergine with smoked cherry tomatoes (£6.50), local cheese ploughman's (£7.50), lamb tagine with couscous and sweet potatoes (£8.50), steaks, and puddings like sticky toffee pudding with butterscotch sauce (from £3.25). The dining room is no smoking. Well kept Otter Bitter and Ale, and a guest beer on handpump, Green Valley farm cider, freshly squeezed orange juice, local apple juice, and cappuccino and espresso coffee; cribbage, dominoes, shove-ha'penny, and piped music. The garden has a children's play area built using a lifeboat from a liner that sank off the Scilly Isles around 100 years ago. *(Recommended by Mike Gorton, JP, PP, Minda and Stanley Alexander, Jenny Perkins, Keith Stevens, the Didler, Ken Flawn, John Beeken)*

Free house ~ Licensees Clive and Ginny Redfern ~ Real ale ~ Bar food (12-2.30(3 Sat and Sun), 7-9.30) ~ (01392) 833128 ~ Children welcome ~ Dogs welcome ~ Open 11.30-11; 11.30-10.30 Sun; closed Jan, Feb; open weekends Oct, Nov, Dec, March ~ Bedrooms: £30/£60

HARBERTON SX7758 Map 1
Church House

Village signposted from A381 just S of Totnes

In a tucked away, steep little village, this ancient place was originally built to house the masons working on the church; it then became a chantry house for monks. The open-plan bar has some magnificent medieval oak panelling, and the latticed glass on the back wall is almost 700 years old and one of the earliest examples of non-ecclesiastical glass in the country. Furnishings include attractive 17th- and 18th-c pews and settles, candles, and a large inglenook fireplace with a woodburning stove; one half of the room is set out for eating. The family room is no smoking. Bar food includes soup (£3.50), sandwiches (from £3.95), chicken liver pâté (£4.25), locally made sausages (£4.25), ploughman's (from £5.25), local sausages and chips (£5.50), ham and egg (£6.95), steak in ale pie or broccoli and stilton crumble (£7.95), rabbit casserole (£8.50), and local steaks (from £8.95). Well kept

Cottage Mild and Champflower and Tetleys on handpump, farm cider, quite a few wines by the glass, and several malt whiskies; darts and dominoes. Tabitha the cat is very friendly. *(Recommended by Comus and Sarah Elliott, June and Ken Brooks, John and Sonja Newberry, Alan and Paula McCully, Mr and Mrs C R Little)*

Free house ~ Licensees David and Jennifer Wright ~ Real ale ~ Bar food ~ (01803) 863707 ~ Children in family room ~ Dogs welcome ~ Open 12-2.30(3 Sat), 6-11; 12-3, 6.30-10.30 Sat ~ Bedrooms: £30(£35B)/£50(£60B)

HATHERLEIGH SS5404 Map 1
George

A386 N of Okehampton

The little front bar in this black and white timbered old pub is in the original part of the building and has huge oak beams, stone walls two or three feet thick, an enormous fireplace, and easy chairs, sofas and antique cushioned settles. The spacious L-shaped bar was built from the wreck of the inn's old brewhouse and coachmen's loft, and has more beams, a woodburning stove, and antique settles around sewing-machine treadle tables; piped music, juke box, pool, and fruit machine. There's also the Mad Monk bar with murals of monks on its light gold walls, and a mix of country tables and chairs, and another dining area. Well kept Bass, St Austell Dartmoor Best and a beer named for the pub on handpump, lots of malt whiskies, and farm cider. Bar food includes sandwiches, soup (£2.95), filled baked potatoes (from £4.25), duck liver pâté with red onion marmalade (£4.95), ploughman's (£5.50), home-made lasagne (£5.95), stir-fried vegetables with chinese-style noodles (£6.75), beef curry (£7.95), steaks (from £11), and fresh fish dishes. In summer, the window boxes and hanging baskets in the courtyard are particularly pretty, and there are rustic wooden seats and tables on the cobblestones; there's also a walled cobbled garden. *(Recommended by the Didler, Rita Horridge, R J Walden, JP, PP)*

Free house ~ Licensees Janice Anderson and J Pozzetto ~ Real ale ~ Bar food (12-2.30, 6.30-9.30) ~ Restaurant ~ (01837) 810454 ~ Children in eating area of bar ~ Dogs allowed in bar ~ Open 11-11; 12-10.30 Sun ~ Bedrooms: £48S/£69.50S(£79.50B)

HAYTOR VALE SX7677 Map 1
Rock ★ 🛏

Haytor signposted off B3387 just W of Bovey Tracey, on good moorland road to Widecombe

Although customers do drop in for a drink, most of the emphasis in this neatly kept and civilised place is on the popular food and bedrooms. The two communicating, partly panelled bar rooms have polished antique tables with candles and fresh flowers, old-fashioned prints and decorative plates on the walls, and good winter log fires (the main fireplace has a fine Stuart fireback); most of the pub is no smoking. At lunchtime, the good bar food includes home-made soup (£3.50), sandwiches (£4.25), mussels in chilli, lemon and parsley (£5.95), chicken curry or local sausages with onion gravy (£7.95), steak and kidney suet pudding (£8.95), tomato and mascarpone risotto (£9.50), seafood fishcakes (£9.95), and fresh seafood platter (£10.95), with evening choices like chicken liver parfait with red onion marmalade (£6.95), scallop salad with roasted hazelnut butter (£8.95), duck breast with braised lentils and roasted shallots on a rosemary scented thyme sauce (£13.95), and grilled bass with mediterranean vegetables and a vanilla dressing (£14.95); puddings such as chocolate tart or sticky toffee pudding with pecan nut sauce (£4.25). Well kept Bass, Greene King Old Speckled Hen, and St Austell Dartmoor Best on handpump, and several malt whiskies. In summer, the pretty, large garden opposite the inn is a popular place to sit and there are some tables and chairs on a small terrace next to the pub itself. Parking is not always easy. *(Recommended by Mike Gorton, Di and Mike Gillam, Patrick Hancock, Alan and Paula McCully, Suzanne Stacey, Richard and Margaret Peers, DF, NF, Chris and*

Joan Woodward, J F Stackhouse, Basil Minson, Andrea Rampley, Julie and Bill Ryan,
Margaret Ross, Neil and Beverley Gardner, Alun Howells, H L Dennis, N and S Alcock,
R J Walden, M G Hart, Ian Wilson, Betsy Brown, Nigel Flook, Brian England)

*Free house ~ Licensee Christopher Graves ~ Real ale ~ Bar food (not 25 Dec) ~
Restaurant ~ (01364) 661305 ~ Children in eating area of bar and restaurant ~ Dogs
allowed in bedrooms ~ Open 11-11(10.30 in winter); 12-10.30 Sun; closed 25 Dec ~
Bedrooms: £65B/£85S(£95B)*

HOLBETON SX6150 Map 1
Mildmay Colours ◖

Signposted off A379 W of A3121 junction

There's a good bustling atmosphere in this off-the-beaten-track pub, set in a quiet
village, and a friendly mix of holidaymakers and locals. The bar has various horse
and racing pictures, and the framed racing colours of Lord Mildmay-White on the
partly stripped stone and partly white walls, plenty of bar stools as well as
cushioned wall seats and wheelback chairs on the turkey carpet, and a tile-sided
woodburning stove; an arch leads to a smaller, similarly decorated family area with
pool, fruit machine, TV, pinball, cribbage, dominoes, and a basket of toys. One
area is no smoking. Though the brewery has moved away, they still offer Mildmay
SP and Colours, and a guest beer such as Sharps Cornish Knocker and Eden on
handpump; local farm cider. Tasty bar food includes sandwiches and filled
baguettes (from £3.10), home-made soup (£3.20), home-made chicken liver pâté
(£3.75), ham and egg (£4.10), local sausages and beans (£4.90), ploughman's (from
£4.95), home-made lasagne (£6.55), home-made fruit and nut roast (£6.95), steaks
(from £10.95), and daily specials like pheasant casserole (£7.50), chicken breast
with a spicy salsa sauce (£7.95), and scallops with wine, cream and grapes (£9.95);
some meals are offered in smaller helpings. The well kept back garden has picnic-
sets, a swing, and an aviary, and there's a small front terrace with lots of newly
planted colourful flowers. *(Recommended by John Evans, Laura Wilson, Esther and
John Sprinkle, John and Joan Calvert)*

*Free house ~ Licensee Louise Price ~ Real ale ~ Bar food ~ Restaurant ~ (01752)
830248 ~ Children in family room ~ Dogs welcome ~ Open 11-3, 6-11; 12-3, 7-
10.30 Sun ~ Bedrooms: £32.50B/£50B*

HORNDON SX5280 Map 1
Elephants Nest ◖

If coming from Okehampton on A386 turn left at Mary Tavy Inn, then left after about ½
mile; pub signposted beside Mary Tavy Inn, then Horndon signposted; on the Ordnance
Survey Outdoor Leisure Map it's named as the New Inn

Originally three 16th-c miners' cottages, this isolated pub is surrounded by plenty
of walks and both walkers and their dogs are welcome. Benches on the spacious
lawn in front look over dry-stone walls to the pastures of Dartmoor's lower slopes,
and the rougher moorland above; they have their own cricket pitch. Inside, the bar
has a good log fire, flagstones, and a beams-and-board ceiling; there are two other
rooms plus a dining room and garden room. Well kept Palmers IPA and Copper
and St Austell HSD, and a guest such as Exe Valley Spring Beer or Sharps Eden Ale
on handpump, decent wines, farm cider, and proper tea and coffee; friendly service.
Reasonably priced, good bar food includes starters and snacks (from £3.50) like
home-made soup, sandwiches and ploughman's, caramelised red onion tartlet
topped with goats cheese, ham and egg, crispy duck salad with orange and anise
dressing or scallops in garlic and butter sauce; main courses (from £6.95) such as
sausages with onion gravy, tagliatelle in a three-cheese sauce, Elizabethan pork with
fruits and spices, and whole lemon sole with caper butter, and puddings (£3.95);
two Sunday roasts (£8.95). Darts, cribbage, dominoes, regular quiz nights, and
piped music. *(Recommended by DAV, Peter Craske, Jacquie and Jim Jones, John and
Marion Tyrie, Len Banister)*

Free house ~ Licensee Peter Wolfes ~ Real ale ~ Bar food (12-2.15, 6.30-9) ~ (01822) 810273 ~ Children in dining room and family room ~ Dogs welcome ~ Folk/contemporary music first Weds evening of month ~ Open 12-3, 6.30-11; closed Mon except bank hols and Sun evening Jan-Mar

HORNS CROSS SS3823 Map 1
Hoops
A39 Clovelly—Bideford

Handy for touring Exmoor and the rugged North Devon coast, this picturesque thatched 13th-c inn has plenty of nearby outdoor attractions, and the pub itself offers falconry experience days and golf breaks. The sheltered central courtyard is particularly pretty in summer with lots of flowering tubs and baskets and you can eat out here, too. The oak-beamed bar has an ancient well set into the floor, paintings and old photographs of the pub on the walls, cushioned window seats and oak settles, and logs burning in big inglenook fireplaces; leading off here is a small similarly furnished room with another fireplace. There are several no smoking areas. Six well kept real ales tapped from the cask such as Barum Original, Cottage Norman's Conquest, Exmoor Best, Jollyboat Freebooter and Mainbrace, Ring O' Bells Bodmin Boar, and guests like Bass or Greene King Old Speckled Hen. Farm cider, over 50 malt whiskies, and lots of wines by the glass (including champagne). Popular bar food (using home-grown herbs and salad) at lunchtime includes sandwiches (from £2.50), ploughman's (from £4.50), home-cooked honey-roasted ham and egg (£5.50), and smoked salmon with creamy scrambled egg (£6); from the main menu, there might be home-made soup (£3.90), spiced chick-pea cakes with red onion (£4.70), paprika-dusted whitebait (£4.90), warm salad of pigeon breast with marsala sauce (£5.80), scallops and black pudding on grain mustard mash (£6.90), beef in Guinness stew (£8.50), stilton and apple strudel with spiced pickled pears (£9.50), spiced baked cod with a citrus sauce (£10.50), rabbit casserole or large steak and kidney pudding (£9.75), and pork fillet in smoked bacon filled with sage and spiced apples on sweet potato with a cider and apple brandy sauce (£11.90). Piped music, darts, dominoes, cribbage, and TV. *(Recommended by Tom Evans, the Didler, David Carr, Brian and Bett Cox, Liz Webb, Rita Horridge, John and Judy Saville, Barry Smith, Barbara and Brian Best, David Gibbs)*

Free house ~ Licensee Gay Marriott ~ Real ale ~ Bar food (12-3, 6-9.30; all day weekends and summer school hols) ~ Restaurant ~ (01237) 451222 ~ Well behaved children in eating area of bar ~ Dogs allowed in bar ~ Open 11-11; 12-10.30 Sun; closed 25 Dec ~ Bedrooms: £55B/£90B

IDDESLEIGH SS5708 Map 1
Duke of York ★ ⇐
B3217 Exbourne—Dolton

You can be sure of a warm welcome from the friendly licensees in this old thatched pub – whether you are a local, a visitor, a child or a dog. The bar has a lot of character, with rocking chairs by the roaring log fire, cushioned wall benches built into the wall's black-painted wooden dado, stripped tables, and other homely country furnishings, and well kept Adnams Broadside, Cotleigh Tawny, and a guest such as Exe Valley Dobbs or Sharps Doom Bar tapped from the cask; freshly squeezed orange and pink grapefruit juice. Good bar food includes sandwiches, two home-made soups (£3 small, £3.50 large), chicken liver and brandy pâté (£5.50), scallops wrapped in smoked bacon or crab mayonnaise (£5 small, £8.50 large), grilled or battered fish and chips (£6), spinach, mushroom and brie filo parcel with a tomato and basil sauce, beef in Guinnesss casserole, chicken korma or liver and bacon (all £7), steak and kidney pudding, leg of lamb steak with minted gravy or pork chop with apple gravy (£8.50), sirloin steak (£12), and home-made puddings (£4); it can get a bit cramped at peak times. Cribbage, dominoes, shove-ha'penny, and darts. Through a small coach arch is a little back garden with some picnic-sets. Fishing nearby. This is a nice place to stay with super breakfasts. *(Recommended by*

Mike Gorton, Roy Smith, the Didler, Jane and Adrian Tierney-Jones, Mike Peck, M and D Toms, R J Walden, Steve Crick, Helen Preston, JP, PP, David and Pauline Brenner, Andrew and Samantha Grainger, Anthony Longden, Theo, Anne and Jane Gaskin, Ron and Sheila Corbett, Richard Till)

Free house ~ Licensees Jamie Stuart and Pippa Hutchinson ~ Real ale ~ Bar food (all day) ~ Restaurant ~ (01837) 810253 ~ Children welcome ~ Dogs allowed in bar ~ Open 11-11; 12-10.30 Sun ~ Bedrooms: £30B/£60B

KINGSTON SX6347 Map 1
Dolphin 🍺

Off B3392 S of Modbury (can also be reached from A379 W of Modbury)

Half a dozen tracks lead from this peaceful shuttered 16th-c inn down to the sea, and unspoilt Wonwell Beach, about a mile and a half away. Inside, several knocked-through beamed rooms have a good mix of customers, a relaxed, welcoming atmosphere (no noisy games machines or piped music), amusing drawings and photographs on the walls, and rustic tables and cushioned seats and settles around their bared stone walls; one small area is no smoking. Under the new licensee bar food now includes sandwiches, home-made soup (£2.95), mushrooms with onions and smoked bacon cooked in red wine and garlic (£3.95), cumberland sausage (£5.50), ham and egg (£5.75), home-made steak in ale pie (£6.95), stilton and vegetable crumble (£7.25), crab bake (£7.50), pork medallions in cider with apple sauce and cheese melt (£8.95), lemon sole (£9.95), and home-made puddings with clotted cream such as fruit crumble or treacle and almond tart (£3.50); nice breakfasts. Well kept Bass and Courage Best with a couple of guests like Sharps Doom Bar and Ushers Founders on handpump. Outside, there are tables and swings. *(Recommended by Rod and Chris Pring, Geoff Calcott, Angus Lyon, Darren Le Poidevin, Simon, Jo and Benjamin Cole, Tim and Carolyn Lowes, Nick Lawless, Malcolm Taylor)*

InnSpired ~ Lease Janice Male ~ Real ale ~ Bar food ~ (01548) 810314 ~ Children in eating area of bar and in family room ~ Open 11-3, 6-11; 12-3, 7-10.30 Sun ~ Bedrooms: £39S/£55S

KNOWSTONE SS8223 Map 1
Masons Arms ★

Off A361 Tiverton—South Molton (brown sign to pub), or B3227 Bampton—South Molton

In a lovely quiet position opposite the village church, this unspoilt 13th-c thatched inn is certainly worth driving down country lanes to find. Run by friendly licensees, it has a simple little main bar with heavy medieval black beams, farm tools on the walls, pine furniture on the stone floor, and a fine open fireplace with a big log fire and side bread oven – there is always a fire lit, whatever the weather. Good bar food includes lunchtime rustic rolls and filled panini (from £4.50) and ploughman's (£5), as well as cream of leek and stilton soup (£2.95), prawn and red pepper pâté or crispy toasted goats cheese with cranberry sauce (£4), curried cauliflower and courgette crumble or steak, kidney and Guinness pie (£6.95), chargrilled cajun chicken (£7.95), smoked haddock and prawn pie with leek and potato mash (£8.50), and chargrilled rib-eye steak (£12.50), with puddings (£3.50); the restaurant is no smoking. Well kept Cotleigh and Exmoor Ale tapped from the cask; piped music, dominoes, and cribbage. Although they don't offer bedrooms in the pub itself, they have a very popular cottage a walk from the pub, with an ensuite bedroom and downstairs sitting room with an inglenook fireplace and woodburning stove, and breakfast supplied from the pub. *(Recommended by Bob and Margaret Holder, A Hawkes, Mr and Mrs Richard Hanks, the Didler, R H Down, P Dash, Paul and Karen Cornock, Tom Evans, June and Robin Savage, Frank Shotton, Mr and Mrs J M Lefeaux, JP, PP, David Carr, Brian and Anita Randall)*

Free house ~ Licensees Paul and Jo Stretton-Downes ~ Real ale ~ Bar food (not Sun evening) ~ Restaurant ~ (01398) 341231 ~ Children in family room ~ Dogs allowed in bar ~ Open 12-3, 6-11; 12-3, 7-10.30 Sun; closed 25 Dec ~ Bedrooms: £40S/£60S

LITTLEHEMPSTON SX8162 Map 1

Tally Ho!

Signposted off A381 NE of Totnes

Very much a family affair, this friendly little pub has neatly kept and cosy rooms with two coal fires, low beams and panelling, an interesting mix of chairs and settles (many antique and with comfortable cushions), and fresh flowers and candles on the tables. The bare stone walls are covered with porcelain, brass, copperware, stuffed wildlife, old swords, and shields and hunting horns and so forth. One bar is no smoking. Well liked bar food includes lunchtime snacks such as sandwiches (from £3.25), ploughman's or sausage and chips (£4.95), and lasagne (£6.95), plus a home-made cream soup (£2.95), spicy crab cakes (£4.25), garlic mushrooms or home-made chicken liver pâté with onion marmalade (£4.50), home-made steak and kidney pie (£7.95), gammon topped with cheese and served with egg or pineapple (£8.95), chargrilled lamb chops with redcurrant and rosemary sauce or grilled tuna steak with a crab and brandy cream sauce (£9.95), oven-roasted chicken with butter-fried leeks and a white wine and bacon sauce (£10.95), steaks (from £10.95), and calves liver with onions and mushrooms and a brandy and cream sauce (£11.95); vegetarian dishes, puddings, and children's meals also available. Well kept Barum Jester, Bass, Cains Bitter, and Robinsons on handpump. The four cats are called Monica, Thomas, Ella and Tiggy. The terrace is full of flowers in summer. More reports please. *(Recommended by Pamela and Merlyn Horswell, Derek and Margaret Underwood)*

Free house ~ Licensees P Saint and L Saint ~ Real ale ~ Bar food ~ Restaurant ~ (01803) 862316 ~ Children in eating area of bar ~ Dogs allowed in bar ~ Open 12-3, 6-11(10.30 Sun); closed 25 Dec ~ Bedrooms: £45S/£55S

LOWER ASHTON SX8484 Map 1

Manor Inn ◀

Ashton signposted off B3193 N of Chudleigh

This creeper-covered pub is a popular place and is set in a charming valley with fine views; the summer hanging baskets are pretty. There's a good mix of customers, although the left-hand room with its beer mats and brewery advertisements on the walls is more for locals enjoying the well kept Princetown Jail Ale, RCH Pitchfork, Teignworthy Reel Ale, and a constantly changing guest on handpump; local cider and decent wines by the glass. On the right, two rather more discreet rooms have a wider appeal, bolstered by the good, popular home-made food which might include sandwiches (from £2.60; filled baguettes from £5.50), home-made soup (£2.95), lots of filled baked potatoes (from £3.75), home-made burgers with various toppings (from £4.25), ploughman's (from £5.50), vegetable bake (£5.95), home-cooked ham and egg or steak, mushroom and ale pie (£6.95) and steaks (from £9.95), with a good choice of changing specials such as stilton and mushroom bake (£5.95), bacon, mushroom, onion and cheddar quiche (£6.25), game sausages with creamy onion and butter sauce (£7.25), fruity chicken curry (£7.50), and a variety of grilled or fried fish (from £8.50), and puddings like chocolate biscuit cake with blackcurrant sorbet or treacle tart (£3.50). Shove-ha'penny. The garden has lots of picnic-sets under cocktail parasols (and a fine tall scots pine). No children inside. *(Recommended by R J Walden, Mr and Mrs J and S E Garrett, JP, PP, the Didler, Mike Gorton)*

Free house ~ Licensees Geoff and Clare Mann ~ Real ale ~ Bar food (12-1.30, 7-9.30; not Mon except bank hols) ~ (01647) 252304 ~ Dogs welcome ~ Open 12-2(2.30 Sat and Sun), 6.30(7 Sun)-11; closed Mon (except bank hols)

Looking for a pub with a really special garden, or in lovely countryside, or with an outstanding view, or right by the water? They are listed separately, at the back of the book.

LUSTLEIGH SX7881 Map 1
Cleave
Village signposted off A382 Bovey Tracey—Moretonhampstead

The neat and very pretty sheltered garden runs around this thatched 15th-c building, and the summer hanging baskets and flowerbeds are lovely. Inside, the low-ceilinged no smoking lounge bar has attractive antique high-backed settles, cushioned wall seats, and wheelback chairs around the tables on its patterned carpet, granite walls, and a roaring log fire. A second bar has similar furnishings, a large dresser, harmonium, an HMV gramophone, and prints, and the no smoking family room has crayons, books and toys for children. Good bar food listed on boards might include home-made soup (£3.95), home-made chicken liver pâté (£4.95), ploughman's (£6.50), roast beef and yorkshire pudding (£8.95), and half a honey-roast duckling with orange sauce or fresh fillet of wild bass (£14.95); the dining room is no smoking. Well kept Bass, Otter Ale, and Wadworths 6X on handpump kept under light blanket pressure, quite a few malt whiskies, and several wines by the glass. More reports please. *(Recommended by Wally and Irene Nunn, Jacquie and Jim Jones, Mark and Amanda Sheard, David and Teresa Frost, Di and Mike Gillam, Neil and Beverley Gardner, Andrea Rampley)*

Heavitree ~ Tenant A Perring ~ Real ale ~ Bar food ~ Restaurant ~ (01647) 277223 ~ Children in family room ~ Dogs welcome ~ Open 11-3, 6-11; 11-11 Sat; 12-10.30 Sun; closed Mon

LYDFORD SX5184 Map 1
Dartmoor Inn 🍴 ♀
Downton, on the A386

The small bar in this very well run place certainly does welcome locals and a few weekend walkers, but there's no doubt that most customers come to enjoy the excellent food in one of the other four rooms. At lunchtime, the bar menu might offer a bowl of soup with a nutmeg cream (£4), celeriac fritters with blue cheese cream sauce or steak and kidney pie (£5.75), ploughman's with three farmhouse cheeses and an apricot and walnut chutney or a small omelette with creamed smoked haddock (£6.75), cod and chips with green mayonnaise (£7.75 small, £12.75 large), lambs liver and kidneys with bacon, mushrooms and deep-fried onions (£10.75), and mixed fish with herb butter (£13.75); there's a two-course set lunch for £10.75. Also, butterflied fillets of sardine with bacon, lemon and herb butter (£4.75), marinated goats cheese and avocado salad with hazelnut dressing (£5.75), potted ox tongue with walnuts (£5), escalope of pork in breadcrumbs with a fried egg and caper butter (£10.75), scallops with a prawn bisque sauce or peppered mignon of beef with red wine and celeriac crisps (£15.75), and puddings like honey custard tart with caramelised bananas and cardamom syrup, rhubarb and treacle pudding with vanilla sauce or bitter sweet chocolate torte with chocolate sauce (£4.95). Well kept Bass, St Austell Dartmoor Best, and a guest like Fullers London Pride on handpump, and an interesting and helpfully short wine list with six good wines by the glass. The overall feel is of civilised but relaxed elegance: matt pastel paintwork in soft greens and blues, naïve farm and country pictures, little side lamps supplemented by candles in black wrought-iron holders, basketwork, dried flowers, fruits and gourds, maybe an elaborate bouquet of fresh flowers. You can smoke only in one room. There are tables out on the terrace, with a track straight up on to the moors. *(Recommended by Robin and Clare Hosking, Adrian and Ione Lee, Robin and Nicky Barthorp, Jacquie and Jim Jones, Andy Sinden, Louise Harrington, John and Vivienne Rice)*

Free house ~ Licensees Philip Burgess and Ian Brown ~ Real ale ~ Bar food (12-2.30, 6.30-9.30; not Sun evening or Mon) ~ Restaurant ~ (01822) 820221 ~ Children in restaurant ~ Dogs allowed in bar ~ Occasional live jazz ~ Open 11.30-3, 6-11; 12-2.30 Sun; closed Sun evening, Mon

MARLDON SX8663 Map 1
Church House 🍽 ♟

Just W of Paignton

You can be sure of a consistently enjoyable visit to this charming and attractive inn, and despite being busy, the staff remain friendly and efficient. The spreading bar has a good relaxed atmosphere, and several different areas radiate off the big semi-circular bar counter. The main bar has interesting windows, some beams, dark pine chairs around solid tables on the turkey carpet, and green plush-seated bar chairs; leading off here is a cosy little candlelit room with just four tables on the bare-board floor, a dark wood dado and stone fireplace, and next to this is the attractive, no smoking restaurant with a large stone fireplace. At the other end of the building, a characterful room is split into two parts with a stone floor in one bit and a wooden floor in another (which has a big woodburning stove). Good, interesting bar food includes sandwiches, italian vegetable soup (£4.50; fish soup £6), chicken liver pâté with home-made orange sultana chutney or open mushrooms filled with vegetable ragoût and served with provençale sauce (£5), smoked salmon fishcakes with spicy tomato salsa (£6.50), red thai pork curry (£10), fillet of salmon with seafood and watercress velouté (£10.50), slow cooked lamb shank with tarragon mash and red wine sauce (£11.50), sirloin steak with bordelaise sauce (£13), grilled fillet of brill with lemon and capers (£15), and puddings (£4.75). Well kept Bass, Flowers IPA, Fullers London Pride, St Austell Dartmoor Best, and a guest such as Greene King Old Speckled Hen or Shepherd Neame Spitfire on handpump, and 10 wines by the glass; skittle alley and piped music. There are three grassy terraces with picnic-sets behind. *(Recommended by James Woods, Ken Arthur, John and Sonja Newberry, Pamela and Merlyn Horswell, Gordon Tong, David Hoare, Mr and Mrs Colin Roberts, Darly Graton, Graeme Gulibert)*

Whitbreads ~ Lease Julian Cook ~ Real ale ~ Bar food (12-2, 6.30-9.30) ~ Restaurant ~ (01803) 558279 ~ Children in eating area of bar and restaurant ~ Dogs allowed in bar ~ Open 11.30-2.30, 5-11; 11.30-11 Sat; 12-10.30 Sun ~ Bedrooms: £30B/£50B

MEAVY SX5467 Map 1
Royal Oak

Off B3212 E of Yelverton

The ancient oak from which this partly 15th-c pub gets its name is just close by, and this is an attractive setting with the old church behind the building and the village green in front; there are seats out here. Inside, the heavy-beamed L-shaped and no smoking bar has pews from the church, red plush banquettes and old agricultural prints and church pictures on the walls; a smaller bar – where the locals like to gather – has flagstones, a big open hearth fireplace and side bread oven. Promptly served by friendly staff, the well liked bar food at lunchtime includes soup (£2.95), filled baked potatoes and baguettes (from £3.95), ham and egg (£5.50), ploughman's (£5.95), and cottage or fish pies; in the evening there might be broccoli and cheese bake (£6.95), pork escalope with an apple and cider sauce (£8.50), steaks (from £8.50), baked salmon with a caper and cream dressing (£8.95), lamb shank on minted mash (£10.95), duck breast with black cherry and port sauce (£12.95), and puddings such as eton mess, chocolate truffle torte or jaffa puddle pudding (from £3.95). Well kept Bass, Princetown IPA and Jail Ale, and maybe Sharps Doom Bar on handpump. There are picnic-sets and benches outside or on the green. No children inside. *(Recommended by Mr and Mrs J E C Tasker)*

Free house ~ Licensee Ann Davis ~ Real ale ~ Bar food ~ (01822) 852944 ~ Dogs welcome ~ Open 11-3, 6.30-11; 12-3, 6.30-10.30 Sun

---

If you stay overnight in an inn or hotel, they are allowed to serve you an alcoholic drink at any hour of the day or night.

MOLLAND SS8028 Map 1
London ◖

Village signposted off B3227 E of South Molton, down narrow lanes

There's certainly no piped music or noisy games machines to disturb the informal, chatty atmosphere in this proper Exmoor inn. The two small linked rooms by the old-fashioned central servery have lots of local stag-hunting pictures, tough carpeting or rugs on flagstones, cushioned benches and plain chairs around rough stripped trestle tables, a table of shooting and other country magazines, ancient stag and otter trophies, and darts, table skittles, cribbage, and dominoes; maybe working dogs from local shoots (there is a bowl of water for them by the good log fire). On the left an attractive beamed room has accounts of the rescued stag which lived a long life at the pub some 50 years ago (and is still remembered by at least one reader, from childhood visits); on the right, a panelled dining room with a great curved settle by its fireplace has particularly good hunting and gamebird prints, including ones by McPhail and Hester Lloyd. Good value honest home cooking in the bar includes home-made soup (£2.80), sandwiches (from £3.30), ham and egg (£4.40), ploughman's (£4.50), filled baked potatoes (£4.80), savoury pancakes or local rabbit (£5.20), a dish of the day like game pie or chicken curry (£5.80), steak (£8.80), and puddings (£2.80), with evening choices like venison steak marinated in port and red wine (£8.80) or grilled bass with crunchy lime and coriander coating (£9.20); the cheerful licensees are very welcoming. A small hall with stuffed birds and animals and lots of overhead baskets has a box of toys, and there are good country views from a few picnic-sets out in front. The low-ceilinged lavatories are worth a look, with their Victorian mahogany and tiling (and in the gents' a testament to the prodigious thirst of the village cricket team). And don't miss the next-door church, with its untouched early 18th-c box pews – and a spring carpet of Tenby daffodils in the graveyard. *(Recommended by the Didler, JP, PP, Dr and Mrs M E Wilson)*

Free house ~ Licensees M J and L J Short ~ Real ale ~ Bar food ~ Restaurant ~ No credit cards ~ (01769) 550269 ~ Children in family room ~ Dogs welcome ~ Open 11.30-2.30, 6-11; 12-2.30, 7-10.30 Sun ~ Bedrooms: /£50B

NEWTON ABBOT SX8468 Map 1
Two Mile Oak ⦅¶⦆ ◖

A381 2 miles S, at Denbury/Kingskerswell crossroads

Doing particularly well under the present, warmly friendly licensees, this old coaching inn is a fine place for a drink or enjoyable meal out. There's a relaxed atmosphere, a beamed lounge and an alcove just for two, a mix of wooden tables and chairs, and a fine winter log fire. The beamed and black-panelled bar is traditionally furnished, again with a mix of seating, lots of horsebrasses, and another good log fire. Well kept Bass, Flowers IPA, Greene King Abbot and Otter Ale tapped from the cask, and decent wines. By the time this book is published, the menu will have changed, but dishes have included home-made soup (£3.50), filled baguettes (from £4.50), ploughman's (from £6), goats cheese coated in pink peppercorns and couscous served with a honey and dill dressing (£6.25), hot thai chicken curry (£9.25), roasted lamb shank with sweet redcurrant and ginger sauce or chicken supreme filled with rosemary and mascarpone cheese (£11.50), and daily specials such as venison in red wine and chocolate sauce or skate wing with capers and black butter (£12.50); their puddings, from a daily-changing choice of eight, are pretty special: banoffi pie, raspberry brûlée or chocolate bread and butter pudding (£3.45). Piped music, darts, and cribbage. There are picnic-sets on the terrace where they hold summer barbecues, and a lawn with shrubs and tubs of flowers. *(Recommended by Mrs A P Lee, JP, PP, B J Harding, Mr and Mrs Colin Roberts, the Didler, Ian Phillips, Neil and Beverley Gardner, Joe Green)*

Heavitree ~ Manager Melanie Matthews ~ Real ale ~ Bar food ~ (01803) 812411 ~ Children welcome ~ Dogs allowed in bar ~ Open 11-11; 11-11 Sat; 12-10.30 Sun

NOMANSLAND SS8313 Map 1

Mountpleasant

B3131 Tiverton—South Molton

The long bar in this cosy country pub is divided into three, with huge fireplaces each end, one with a woodburning stove under a low dark ochre black-beamed ceiling, the other with a big log fire. A nice informal mix of furniture on the patterned carpet includes an old sofa with a colourful throw, old-fashioned leather dining chairs, pale country kitchen chairs and wall pews, and tables all with candles in attractive metal holders; there are country prints and local photographs including shooting parties. The bar, with plenty of bar stools, has well kept Bass, Cotleigh Tawny, Flowers Original and Whitbreads, and decent wines, and coffee is particularly well served. A good choice of enjoyable and reasonably priced food (using carefully sourced local produce) includes home-made soup (£2.95), baguettes and toasties (£4.50), filled baked potatoes (£5.50), all-day breakfast (£5.95), ham and egg (£6.50), steak and kidney pie or tortillas filled with chilli con carne, cheese and crème fraîche (£6.95), pasta with mushroom and pesto cream (£7.50), chicken breast cooked in a choice of sauces (£9.95), steaks (from £12.95), and puddings like sticky ginger pudding or chocolate brownie (£3.95). On the left a high-beamed stripped stone dining room with a stag's head over the sideboard was once a smithy, and still has the raised forge fireplace. Games machines, darts, TV, cribbage, dominoes, and maybe piped radio; picnic-sets under smart parasols in the neat back garden, out past the stables. Samuel the spaniel comes in to say hello at closing time. More reports please. *(Recommended by Richard and Anne Ansell)*

Free house ~ Licensees Anne Butler, Karen Southcott and Sarah Roberts ~ Real ale ~ Bar food (all day) ~ Restaurant ~ (01884) 860271 ~ Children welcome ~ Dogs allowed in bar ~ Open 11.30-11; 12-10.30 Sun; closed evening 25 Dec, 1 Jan

NOSS MAYO SX5447 Map 1

Ship 🍺

Off A379 via B3186, E of Plymouth

In good weather, you can sit at the octagonal wooden tables on the sunny terrace here and look over the idyllic inlet; visiting boats can tie up alongside – with prior permission. Parking is restricted at high tide. Inside, the two thick-walled bars have a happy mix of dining chairs and tables on the wooden floors, log fires, bookcases, dozens of local pictures, newspapers to read, and a friendly, chatty atmosphere. All of the first floor is no smoking; Scrabble, draughts, dominoes, cribbage, and chess. Good food (which can be eaten anywhere in the pub and features much local produce) might include leek and potato soup (£4.25), sandwiches (from £4.25; local crab £5.95), wild mushroom and blue cheese tartlet (£4.95), roasted ham hock salad with poached egg (£5.50), local mussels (£5.95; main course £8.95), pork and leek sausages with black pudding, herb mash and gravy or oriental vegetables and goats cheese spring rolls with a sweet chilli dip (£7.95), local cod fillet in ale batter with minted mushy peas (£8.95), shank of devon lamb on rosemary and garlic mash (£11.50), and warm salad of sautéed cornish scallops with crispy smoked bacon (£12.75); cheerful, helpful staff. Well kept Palmers Dorset Gold, Princetown Dartmoor IPA, Summerskills Tamar, and guests like Shepherd Neame Spitfire, and Wadworths 6X on handpump, lots of malt whiskies, and eight wines by the glass. *(Recommended by John Evans, R J Walden, David and Heather Stephenson, Esther and John Sprinkle, Laura Wilson, John and Joan Calvert, Dr and Mrs M E Wilson, Andy and Katie Wadsworth, Charles and Pauline Stride, Margaret and Roy Randle)*

Free house ~ Licensees Lesley and Bruce Brunning ~ Real ale ~ Bar food (12-9.30) ~ Restaurant ~ (01752) 872387 ~ Children welcome before 7pm ~ Dogs allowed in bar ~ Open 11-11; 12-10.30 Sun

PETER TAVY SX5177 Map 1
Peter Tavy Inn
Off A386 near Mary Tavy, N of Tavistock

This attractive old stone inn was once the village blacksmith's – it's now a pleasant and friendly pub with a good bustling atmosphere. The low-beamed bar has high-backed settles on the black flagstones by the big stone fireplace (a fine log fire on cold days), smaller settles in stone-mullioned windows, a snug, no smoking side dining area, and efficient service. As well as lunchtime filled baguettes and baked potatoes, the popular food here might include tomato and basil soup (£3.25), stilton and pear pâté or spicy chicken filo parcels (£4.95), wild mushroom, chestnut and leek pie (£7.95), shank of lamb on garlic mash (£11.45), monkfish wrapped in bacon with pesto dressing, pork tenderloin with stilton sauce or roast duck breast with peking sauce (all £12.95), with puddings such as warm chocolate soufflé or apple and apricot crumble (£3.75). Well kept Fullers London Pride, Princetown Jail Ale, and Summerskills Tamar Best, with a couple of guests from breweries like Blackawton or Sutton on handpump, kept under light blanket pressure; local farm cider, 30 malt whiskies and nine wines by the glass; piped music and darts. From the picnic-sets in the pretty garden, there are peaceful views of the moor rising above nearby pastures. *(Recommended by Neil and Beverley Gardner, Joyce and Maurice Cottrell, Richard and Margaret Peers, John Evans, JP, PP, Jacquie and Jim Jones, Dr and Mrs M W A Haward, DAV, Cathryn and Richard Hicks)*

Free house ~ Licensees Graeme and Karen Sim ~ Real ale ~ Bar food (not 25 Dec) ~ Restaurant ~ (01822) 810348 ~ Children in family room ~ Dogs welcome ~ Open 12-2.30(3 Sat), 6.30(6 Sat)-11; 12-3, 6.30-10.30 Sun; closed 25 Dec and evenings 24, 25 and 31 Dec

POSTBRIDGE SX6780 Map 1
Warren House
B3212 1¾ miles NE of Postbridge

The name of this no-frills but friendly place comes from the fact that there are so many rabbits all around. The cosy bar has a fireplace at either end (one is said to have been kept almost continuously alight since 1845), and is simply furnished with easy chairs and settles under a beamed ochre ceiling, wild animal pictures on the partly panelled stone walls, and dim lighting (fuelled by the pub's own generator); there's a no smoking family room. Good no-nonsense home cooking includes home-made soup (£2.75), locally made meaty or vegetable pasties (£2.95), sandwiches (from £3.50), filled baked potatoes (from £4), good ploughman's (£5.95), home-made rabbit pie or home-made vegetable curry (£7), home-made steak in ale pie (£7.50), daily specials (from £8), and home-made puddings such as chocolate truffle torte or lime posset (£3.75). Well kept Butcombe Gold, Moor Old Freddy Walker, Sharps Doom Bar, and a guest like Shepherd Neame Spitfire or Timothy Taylors Landlord on handpump, local farm cider, and malt whiskies. Darts, pool, cribbage, and dominoes; maybe piped music. There are picnic-sets on both sides of the road that enjoy the views – the pub is set high up on Dartmoor; plenty of surrounding walks. *(Recommended by Robert Gomme, Joyce and Maurice Cottrell, DAV, Doreen and Haydn Maddock, Eddie Edwards, David Crook, Pat and Robert Watt, Neil and Beverley Gardner)*

Free house ~ Licensee Peter Parsons ~ Real ale ~ Bar food (all day summer) ~ (01822) 880208 ~ Children in family room ~ Dogs allowed in bar ~ Open 11-11; 12-10.30 Sun; may be much more restricted weekdays in winter

---

We mention bottled beers and spirits only if there is something unusual about them – imported belgian real ales, say, or dozens of malt whiskies; so do please let us know about them in your reports.

RATTERY SX7461 Map 1

Church House

Village signposted from A385 W of Totnes, and A38 S of Buckfastleigh

The original building here probably housed the craftsmen who built the Norman church, and may then have served as a hostel for passing monks. It is one of Britain's oldest pubs, and the spiral stone steps behind a little stone doorway on your left as you come in date from about 1030. There are massive oak beams and standing timbers in the homely open-plan bar, large fireplaces (one with a little cosy nook partitioned off around it), windsor armchairs, comfortable seats and window seats, and prints on the plain white walls; the no smoking dining room is separated from this room by heavy curtains. Under the friendly landlord who took over just after we had gone to press last year, the good, popular bar food might include home-made soup (£2.95), filled granary rolls (from £3.35), ploughman's (from £4.95), salads (from £5.50), home-made quiche lorraine (£5.75), cold cider-cooked ham with egg (£6.25), a fry up (vegetarian £6.25, meaty £7.25), steak and kidney pie (£6.75), chicken and cranberry curry (£7.50), rump steak (£9.75), daily specials like rabbit casserole, brixham plaice or venison, and puddings such as treacle tart or hazelnut meringue (£3.25). Well kept Adnams Broadside, Greene King Abbot, St Austell Dartmoor Best, and Wells Bombardier on handpump, several malt whiskies, and a decent wine list. Outside, there's a new garden with picnic benches on the large hedged-in lawn, and peaceful views of the partly wooded surrounding hills. *(Recommended by Dudley and Moira Cockroft, D S Jackson, David M Cundy, John and Vivienne Rice, MP, B J Harding, Neil and Beverley Gardner, Ted George, Ian Phillips, Dr and Mrs M E Wilson, Wally and Irene Nunn, Liz and Tony Colman, JP, PP, Mr and Mrs I Bell, Bob Broadhurst, Lee Potter, Dr and Mrs D Woods)*

Free house ~ Licensee Ray Hardy ~ Real ale ~ Bar food ~ Restaurant ~ (01364) 642220 ~ Children welcome ~ Dogs allowed in bar ~ Open 11-3, 6-11; 12-3, 7-10.30 Sun

ROCKBEARE SY0295 Map 1

Jack in the Green 🍴 �

Signposted from new A30 bypass E of Exeter

The food in this reliable and well run dining place is consistently good, but there's also a friendly welcome from the hard-working licensee, a relaxed atmosphere and the drinks choice of a proper pub – Branscombe Vale labelled as JIG for the pub, Otter Ale and Cotleigh Tawny or Greene King Ruddles County on handpump, and 10 good wines by the glass. The neat and comfortable good-sized bar has wheelback chairs, sturdy cushioned wall pews and varying-sized tables on its dark blue carpet, with sporting prints, nice decorative china and a dark carved oak dresser; piped music. The larger no smoking dining side is air-conditioned but similarly traditional in style: some of its many old hunting and shooting photographs are well worth a close look, and it has button-back leather chesterfields by its big woodburning stove. Using fresh local produce, the high standard popular food includes bar snacks such as soup (£3.75), bangers and mash with mustard sauce or rillette of duck with roast garlic, toasted brioche and apple chutney (£7.50), tagliatelle with leeks, pine nuts and mascarpone sauce (£7.95), lamb burger with tomato salsa and focaccia bread (£8.50), chicken supreme with caesar salad or smoked salmon and fresh crab salad with lime dressing (£9.50), and rib-eye steak with peppercorn sauce (£12.50); two-course lunch £18. There are some tables out behind, by a back skittle alley, with more in a garden area. *(Recommended by John and Sonja Newberry, Richard and Margaret Peers, Oliver and Sue Rowell, David Rule, David Jeffreys, Brian and Bett Cox, Andy Millward, Basil Minson, Martin and Karen Wake)*

Free house ~ Licensee Paul Parnell ~ Real ale ~ Bar food ~ Restaurant ~ (01404) 822240 ~ Well behaved children in eating area of bar ~ Open 11-3, 5.30(6 Sat)-11; 12-10.30 Sun; closed 25 Dec-3 Jan

SIDBURY SY1595 Map 1
Hare & Hounds ◨

3 miles N of Sidbury, at Putts Corner; A375 towards Honiton, crossroads with B3174

Even on cold winter weekdays, this very well run roadside pub is full of cheerful customers. It is so much bigger inside than you could have guessed from outside, rambling all over the place, but despite this, the very friendly and efficient staff will make you welcome and serve you promptly. There are two good log fires (and rather unusual wood-framed leather sofas complete with pouffes), heavy beams and fresh flowers throughout, some oak panelling, plenty of tables with red leatherette or red plush-cushioned dining chairs, window seats and well used bar stools too; it's mostly carpeted, with bare boards and stripped stone walls at one softly lit no smoking end. At the opposite end of the pub, on the left, another big dining area has huge windows looking out over the garden. As you come in, the first thing you see is the good popular daily carvery counter, with a choice of joints, and enough turnover to keep up a continuous supply of fresh vegetables (lunchtime £6.25, evening £6.75, children £4.25). Other food includes sandwiches (from £2.95), filled baked potatoes (from £2.60), home-made soup (£2.95), home-made chicken liver pâté (£3.95), vegetarian pie (£5.95), ploughman's (£5.75), lasagne (£5.90), pie of the day or home-made curry (£5.95), steaks (from £10.25), and daily specials such as duck breast carved over apple mash with a calvados and caramelised apple sauce (£10.25), chargrilled red mullet on mediterranean roasted vegetables and pesto (£10.50), and fillet of salmon on fresh spinach (£11.20). Well kept Greene King Abbot and Otter Ale and Bitter on handpump or tapped from the cask; pool in one side room, another with big-screen sports TV. The big garden, giving good valley views, has picnic-sets, a play area enlivened by a pensioned-off fire engine, and a small strolling flock of peafowl. *(Recommended by Brian and Bett Cox, Joyce and Maurice Cottrell, Paul and Annette Hallett, Chris Ray, Alan and Paula McCully, Michael and Marion Buchanan, John Couper, Mike and Wendy Proctor)*

Free house ~ Licensee Peter Cairns ~ Real ale ~ Bar food (all day) ~ Restaurant ~ (01404) 41760 ~ Children in eating area of the bar ~ Dogs allowed in bar ~ Live music Sun lunchtimes in marquee ~ Open 10-11; 12-10.30 Sun

SIDFORD SY1390 Map 1
Blue Ball ◨ ⇌

A3052 just N of Sidmouth

For 75 years, this thatched 14th-c inn has been run by five generations of the same family. The low, partly-panelled and neatly kept lounge bar has heavy beams, upholstered wall benches and windsor chairs, three open fires, and lots of bric-a-brac; the family room and part of the restaurant are no smoking. Bar food includes sandwiches (from £2.50), home-made soup (£2.95), local sausages (£4.25), ploughman's or omelettes (£5.50), wild mushroom lasagne (£6.25), steak and kidney pudding (£8.25), fresh salmon fillet with lime and coriander sauce (£8.50), steaks (from £9.50), and daily specials. Bass, Flowers IPA, Greene King Old Speckled Hen, Otter Ale, and a guest from Adnams, Jennings or Smiles on handpump, kept well in a temperature-controlled cellar. A plainer public bar has darts, dominoes, cribbage, and a fruit machine; piped music. Tables on a terrace look out over a colourful front flower garden, and there are more seats on a bigger back lawn – as well as in a covered area next to the barbecue; see saw and play house for children. *(Recommended by Mike Gorton, JP, PP, Maurice Ribbans, P R and S A White, Steve Crick, Helen Preston, Alan and Paula McCully, John and Jane Hayter, Joyce and Maurice Cottrell, Ian and Deborah Carrington, Tony Radnor, Geoffrey G Lawrance, Mrs Joy Griffiths, the Didler, Joan and Michel Hooper-Immins, Mike and Wendy Proctor)*

Pubmaster ~ Lease Roger Newton ~ Real ale ~ Bar food (11-2, 6.30-9.30 but they also offer breakfast between 8 and 10am) ~ Restaurant ~ (01395) 514062 ~ Children in restaurant and family room ~ Dogs allowed in bar ~ Occasional live entertainment ~ Open 11-11; 12-10.30 Sun ~ Bedrooms: £28(£40B)/£45(£70B)

SLAPTON SX8244 Map 1
Tower ★ ⑪

Signposted off A379 Dartmouth—Kingsbridge

As we went to press, we heard that this fine old place was being sold. We are keeping our fingers crossed that the new licensees will continue in the same vein as the Acfields. The low-ceilinged beamed bar has armchairs, low-backed settles and scrubbed oak tables on the flagstones or bare boards, open log fires, and up to five well kept real ales such as Adnams Best, Badger Tanglefoot, and St Austell Dartmoor Best with guests like Black Sheep, Exmoor Gold or Wells Bombardier on handpump; farm cider and several wines by the glass. The food has been excellent and has included home-made soup (£3.25), sandwiches (from £4.25), crab and prawn tower with a light basil oil (£5.95), duck foie gras terrine with pistachio and wild mushrooms (£6.75), smoked salmon and asparagus risotto or white navarin of rabbit (£8.95), slow cooked lamb shank with a herb sauce (£9.95), marinated venison on creamed savoy, radicchio and carrot with a red wine and chocolate sauce (£13.25), and puddings such as treacle tart or white frozen chocolate and orange terrine with marinated cherries (£4.25). Cribbage, dominoes, chess, backgammon, Scrabble, draughts, and piped music. The lane up to the pub is very narrow and parking is not easy. More reports on the new regime, please.
(Recommended by Tracey and Stephen Groves, the Didler, BOB)

Free house ~ Real ale ~ Bar food ~ Restaurant ~ (01548) 580216 ~ Children in room next to bar ~ Dogs allowed in bar ~ Open 12-3, 6-11; 12-3, 7-10.30 Sun; closed 25 Dec and evening 26 Dec ~ Bedrooms: £40S/£55S

SOURTON SX5390 Map 1
Highwayman ★

A386, S of junction with A30

For over 40 years, Mrs Thomson's parents put huge enthusiasm into the extraordinary décor here – you will be amazed at the sheer eccentricity of it all. The porch (a pastiche of a nobleman's carriage) leads into a warren of dimly lit stonework and flagstone-floored burrows and alcoves, richly fitted out with red plush seats discreetly cut into the higgledy-piggledy walls, elaborately carved pews, a leather porter's chair, Jacobean-style wicker chairs, and seats in quaintly bulging small-paned bow windows; the ceiling in one part, where there's an array of stuffed animals, gives the impression of being underneath a tree, roots and all. The separate Rita Jones' Locker is a make-believe sailing galleon, full of intricate woodwork and splendid timber baulks, with white antique lace-clothed tables in the embrasures that might have held cannons. They now sell real ale on handpump from Teignworthy, and specialise in farm cider and organic wines, and food is confined to sandwiches or pasties (£2.50), and platters (£5.50); service is warmly welcoming and full of character; old-fashioned penny fruit machine, and 40s piped music; no smoking at the bar counters. Outside, there's a fairy-tale pumpkin house and an old-lady-who-lived-in-a-shoe house. You can take children in to look around the pub but they can't stay inside. The period bedrooms with four-posters and half-testers are attractive. A cycle route which incorporates the disused railway line now passes the inn, and there are bunk rooms available for walkers and cyclists.
(Recommended by Kevin Blake, Mayur Shah, the Didler, JP, PP, Ann and Colin Hunt, R J Walden)

Free house ~ Licensees Sally and Bruce Thomson ~ Real ale ~ Bar food ~ No credit cards ~ (01837) 861243 ~ Dogs welcome ~ Open 11-2, 6-10.30; 12-2, 7-10.30 Sun; closed 25 and 26 Dec ~ Bedrooms: £22.50S/£60B

'Children welcome' means the pub says it lets children inside without any special restriction; readers have found that some may impose an evening time limit – please tell us if you find this.

SOUTH ZEAL SX6593 Map 1
Oxenham Arms ★ ♀ 🛏

Village signposted from A30 at A382 roundabout and B3260 Okehampton turn-off

This marvellous building was first licensed in 1477 – though it has grown up around the remains of a Norman monastery, built here to combat the pagan power of the neolithic standing stone that still forms part of the wall in the family room behind the bar (there are actually twenty more feet of stone below the floor). It later became the Dower House of the Burgoynes, whose heiress carried it to the Oxenham family. And Charles Dickens, snowed up one winter, wrote a lot of *Pickwick Papers* here. The beamed and partly panelled front bar has elegant mullioned windows and Stuart fireplaces, and windsor armchairs around low oak tables and built-in wall seats. The small family room has beams, wheelback chairs around polished tables, decorative plates, and another open fire. Well liked bar food includes lunchtime sandwiches (from £2.50), ploughman's (£5), and salads (from £5.50), as well as ham and egg (£6), local pork sausages with mustard and leek mash and onion gravy or prawn curry (£6.50), steak, kidney, mushroom and Guinness pie (£6.75), grilled whole rainbow trout (£9.50), and chargrilled sirloin steak (£9.75), and daily specials like mediterranean chicken breast (£6.75), large pork rib in a spicy ginger, chilli, spring onion and tomato sauce (£8.25), and smoked haddock and asparagus tart (£8.25). Well kept Princetown IPA and Sharps Doom Bar and Eden Ale on handpump or tapped from the cask, and an extensive list of wines. Note the imposing curved stone steps leading up to the garden where there's a sloping spread of lawn. *(Recommended by Pete Baker, Mrs Ursula Hofheinz, Andrea Rampley, DRH and KLH, Brian and Bett Cox, Joyce and Geoff Robson, Jacquie and Jim Jones, MB, Colin and Stephanie McFie, JP, PP, M G Hart, Di and Mike Gillam, Paul Humphreys, Ian and Deborah Carrington, Richard Endacott, Dennis Jenkin, the Didler, Brian Skelcher, Walter and Susan Rinaldi-Butcher, Jenny Cridland, Gordon Cooper, Dr Brian and Mrs Anne Hamilton, Neil and Angela Huxter, Jane and Adrian Tierney-Jones, R J Walden, R T and J C Moggridge, Mayur Shah, Ann and Colin Hunt, Bernard Stradling, John and Sonja Newberry, Peter and Margaret Lodge, Richard and Margaret Peers, Dr D G Twyman, Stuart Turner, Rita Horridge, Betsy Brown, Nigel Flook, Dr and Mrs M W A Haward)*

Free house ~ Licensee Paul Lucas ~ Real ale ~ Bar food ~ Restaurant ~ (01837) 840244 ~ Children in eating area of bar, restaurant and family room ~ Dogs allowed in bar ~ Open 11-2.30, 5-11; 12-2.30, 7-10.30 Sun ~ Bedrooms: £45B/£60S(£70B)

STAVERTON SX7964 Map 1
Sea Trout

Village signposted from A384 NW of Totnes

Run by licensees who care, this is a friendly old village pub with a cheerful mix of locals and visitors. The neatly kept rambling beamed lounge bar has sea trout and salmon flies and stuffed fish on the walls, cushioned settles and stools, and a stag's head above the fireplace; the main bar has low banquettes, soft lighting and an open fire, and there's also a public bar with darts, pool, TV, bar billiards, shove-ha'penny, and a juke box. Enjoyable bar food includes lunchtime sandwiches, home-made soup with home-made crusty bread (£3.50), creamy garlic mushrooms (£4.25), galantine of wild game wrapped in bacon and served with onion marmalade (£4.95), local farm sausages with onion gravy (£7.50), tartlet of broccoli, leek and somerset brie (£7.25), steak in ale pie or chicken breast stuffed with asparagus and served with sorrel cream (£8.75), whole grilled local trout with caper-crushed new potatoes and toasted almond dressing (£8.95), daily specials such as local fresh fish or curries, and puddings like glazed lemon bread and butter pudding with lavender anglaise or bitter chocolate tartlet with clotted cream (£3.95). The restaurant and most eating areas are no smoking. Well kept Palmers IPA, Bridport, Copper, and 200 on handpump, a decent range of wines, quite a few whiskies, and farm cider; efficient, helpful staff. There are seats under parasols on the attractive paved back garden. A station for the South Devon Steam Railway is not too far away. *(Recommended by the Didler, Roger Bridgeman, Joyce and Maurice Cottrell, David M Cundy, Dr and Mrs Rod Holcombe, Comus and Sarah Elliott, Dennis Jenkin, Neil and Beverley Gardner, JP, PP, Chris Butt)*

Palmers ~ Tenants Nicholas and Nicola Brookland ~ Real ale ~ Bar food ~ Restaurant ~ (01803) 762274 ~ Children in eating area of bar and restaurant ~ Dogs allowed in bar ~ Open 11-3, 6-11; 12-4, 7-10.30 Sun ~ Bedrooms: /£58B

STOCKLAND ST2404 Map 1
Kings Arms 🍽 ♀ 🛏

Village signposted from A30 Honiton—Chard; and also, at every turning, from N end of Honiton High Street

The hard-working licensees have struck a clever balance in this spotlessly kept and individually run 16th-c inn, between somewhere with plenty of locals, a good bustling atmosphere, and live music nights, to a civilised place for a special meal out or a comfortable weekend away. The dark beamed, elegant Cotley Bar has solid refectory tables and settles, attractive landscapes, a medieval oak screen (which divides the room into two), and a great stone fireplace across almost the whole width of one end; the cosy restaurant has a huge inglenook fireplace and bread oven. Enjoyable bar food is served at lunchtime only (not Sunday): sandwiches (from £2.50), home-made soup (£3), omelettes (from £4), duck liver pâté (£5), and various pasta dishes (small £4.50, large £7.50), with specials like portuguese sardines (£4), moules marinière or confit of duck with a plum sauce (£5), mushroom stroganoff or pasta carbonara (£7.50), steak and kidney pie (£8.50), guinea fowl (£10.50), king prawn thermidor (£12.50), and puddings such as apple and treacle crumble, crème brûlée or chocolate truffle torte (£5). In the evening, only the restaurant menu is available and diners are invited to the Cotley Bar to have the menu explained in full detail. Well kept Exmoor Ale and Otter Ale, and maybe O'Hanlons Yellowhammer and Port Stout on handpump, over 40 malt whiskies (including island and west coast ones; large spirit measures), a comprehensive wine list, and farm ciders. At the back, a flagstoned bar has cushioned benches and stools around heavy wooden tables, and leads on to a carpeted darts area, another room with dark beige plush armchairs and settees (and a fruit machine), and a neat ten-pin skittle alley; dominoes, TV, and quiet mainly classical piped music. There are tables under cocktail parasols on the terrace in front of the white-faced thatched pub and a lawn enclosed by trees and shrubs. *(Recommended by Andy Harvey, John and Fiona Merritt, Steve Whalley, John and Glenys Wheeler, Wally and Irene Nunn, Jenny and Chris Wilson, Brian and Bett Cox, Ian Wilson, John and Sonja Newberry, Shirley Mackenzie, Derek and Sylvia Stephenson, Dr and Mrs M E Wilson, Douglas Allen, Derek and Margaret Underwood, TOH, Mrs Jean Clarke, Brian and Anita Randall, Alan and Paula McCully, Mrs Sylvia Elcoate, A Sadler, B H and J I Andrews, DRH and KLH)*

Free house ~ Licensees Heinz Kiefer and Paul Diviani ~ Real ale ~ Bar food (12-1.45, not Sun) ~ Restaurant ~ (01404) 881361 ~ Children in eating area of bar and restaurant ~ Dogs allowed in bar ~ Live music Sat and Sun evenings and bank hol Mon ~ Open 12-3, 6.30-11; closed 25 Dec ~ Bedrooms: £40B/£60B

STOKE FLEMING SX8648 Map 1
Green Dragon ♀

Church Road

Popular locally, this friendly, very relaxed place is liked by visitors, too. It is run by Peter Crowther, the long-distance yachtsman, and on the walls are cuttings about him, maps of his races, and accounts of his sinking 800 miles out in the Atlantic. The main part of the flagstoned and beamed bar has two small settles, bay window seats and stools, boat pictures, and maybe Maia the burmese cat or Rhea the german shepherd; down on the right is a wooden-floored snug (recently decorated) with throws and cushions on sofas and armchairs, a few books (50p to RNLI), adult board games, and a grandfather clock. Down some steps is the no smoking

Mess Deck decorated with old charts and lots of ensigns and flags, and there's now a reclaimed pitch-pine floor and winter open fire; piped music, shove-ha'penny, and dominoes. Enjoyable home-made bar food includes home-made soup (£2.30), freshly cooked filled baguettes (£3.50), baked crab and mushrooms in a creamy anchovy sauce, topped with cheese (£4.20), prawn platter (£4.90), steak in ale or fish pies (£6.50), and daily specials such as thai crab cakes, field mushrooms with sun-dried tomato and pepper pesto topped with local goats cheese, venison and cranberry daube, and marinated tuna steak (£6.50-£8), and Friday night fish and chips (£5); winter Sunday lunch. Well kept Bass, Flowers IPA, Otter Ale, and Wadworths 6X on handpump (all except Bass kept under light blanket pressure), big glasses of good house wines, Luscombe's slightly alcoholic ginger beer and organic apple juice, and a decent range of spirits; you can take the beer away with you. There are some seats outside, and outdoor heaters on the front terrace. The church opposite has an interesting tall tower. Parking can be tricky at peak times. *(Recommended by Kim and Jerry Allen, Paul Boot, Barry Smith, Alan Vere, John and Fiona Merritt, J M Law, Val Stevenson, Rob Holmes, Pete and Jo Cole, Laura Wilson, Alan and Paula McCully)*

Heavitree ~ Tenants Peter and Alix Crowther ~ Real ale ~ Bar food (12-2.30, 6.30-9) ~ No credit cards ~ (01803) 770238 ~ Children in eating area of bar and in restaurant ~ Dogs allowed in bar ~ Open 11-3, 5.30-11; 12-3, 6-10.30 Sun

STOKE GABRIEL SX8457 Map 1
Church House

Village signposted from A385 just W of junction with A3022, in Collaton St Mary; can also be reached from nearer Totnes

From the outside of this friendly old local, you can see the priest hole, dating from the Reformation. Inside, there's an exceptionally fine medieval beam-and-plank ceiling in the lounge bar, as well as a black oak partition wall, window seats cut into the thick butter-coloured walls, decorative plates and vases of flowers on a dresser, and a huge fireplace still used in winter to cook the stew; darts. The mummified cat in a case, probably about 200 years old, was found during restoration of the roof space in the verger's cottage three doors up the lane – one of a handful found in the West Country and believed to have been a talisman against evil spirits. Straightforward bar food includes home-made soup (£2.95), a big choice of sandwiches and toasties (from £2.95; ham, cheese, pineapple and onion toastie £3.95), filled baked potatoes (from £3.95), ploughman's (from £4.75), steak and kidney pie, turkey curry or stilton and leek bake (£6.75), and puddings (£3.75). Well kept Bass, Worthington Best, and a weekly guest ale on handpump, and 20 malt whiskies. Euchre in the little public locals' bar. There are picnic-sets on the little terrace in front of the building. No children inside. The church is very pretty. *(Recommended by Dr and Mrs M E Wilson, P Duffield, Mike and Mary Carter, Richard and Margaret Peers, Emma Kingdon, David Hammond, James Woods, Derek and Margaret Underwood)*

Free house ~ Licensee T G Patch ~ Real ale ~ Bar food (11-2.30, 6.30-9.30) ~ No credit cards ~ (01803) 782384 ~ Dogs allowed in bar ~ Open 11-3, 6-11; 11-11 Fri and Sat; 12-4, 7-10.30 Sun

TOPSHAM SX9688 Map 1
Bridge 🍺

2¼ miles from M5 junction 30: Topsham signposted from exit roundabout; in Topsham follow signpost (A376) Exmouth on the Elmgrove Road, into Bridge Hill

This is a favourite with those who love really unspoilt pubs. The utterly old-fashioned layout and character of this 16th-c ex-maltings remains unchanged over the years, and the fifth generation of the same family helps to run it. There are fine old traditional furnishings (true country workmanship) in the little lounge partitioned off from the inner corridor by a high-backed settle; log fire. A bigger lower no smoking room (the old malthouse) is open at busy times. The cosy regulars' inner sanctum keeps up to 10 real ales tapped from the cask: Adnams Broadside, Badger Tanglefoot, Blackawton Westcountry Gold, Branscombe Vale Branoc or Summa'that, Exe Valley Hope, Moor Old Freddy Walker, O'Hanlons Yellowhammer, Otter Ale, RCH Firebox, and Teignworthy Martha's Mild. Local farm cider and elderberry and gooseberry wines; friendly service. Simple, tasty bar food such as pasties (£2), sandwiches (from £2.90; the smoked chicken with elderflower and gooseberry pickle is liked), and various ploughman's (from £5.50); the local hand-fried crisps are excellent. No noisy music or machines – just a chatty, relaxed atmosphere. There are riverside picnic-sets overlooking the weir.

(Recommended by Pete Baker, RWC, Hugh Roberts, Rob and Catherine Dunster, Steve Harvey, the Didler, Tony Radnor, Jenny and Brian Seller, June and Ken Brooks, Michael Rowse, JP, PP, Jenny Perkins, Keith Stevens, Dr and Mrs M E Wilson, Jane and Adrian Tierney-Jones)

Free house ~ Licensee Mrs C Cheffers-Heard ~ Real ale ~ Bar food ~ No credit cards ~ (01392) 873862 ~ Children in room without bar ~ Dogs allowed in bar ~ Occasional live music ~ Open 12-2, 6(7 Sun)-10.30(11 Fri/Sat)

TORCROSS SX8241 Map 1
Start Bay
A379 S of Dartmouth

For those who love fresh fish, this immensely popular dining pub is just the place to head for – but as there are often queues before the pub opens, it does make sense to get there early to be sure of a table. Local fishermen work off the beach right in front of the pub and deliver all kinds of fish, a local crabber drops the crabs at the back door, and the landlord enjoys catching plaice, scallops, and bass: cod (medium £4.70; large £6.50; jumbo £8.50) and haddock (medium £4.80; large £6.60; jumbo £8.60), whole lemon sole (from £6.90), skate (from £7.50), whole dover sole (in four sizes from £8.20), brill (from £8.75), and whole bass (small £9.50; medium £10.50; large £11.50). Other food includes sandwiches (from £2.50), ploughman's (from £4.10), filled baked potatoes (from £3.10), vegetable lasagne (£5.95), gammon and pineapple (£7.25), steaks (from £8.75), and children's meals (£3.90); they do warn of delays at peak times. Well kept Bass and Flowers Original or Otter Ale on handpump, and maybe Heron Valley cider and fresh apple juice, and local wine from the Sharpham Estate. The unassuming main bar (which has a small no smoking area) is very much set out for eating with wheelback chairs around plenty of dark tables or (round a corner) back-to-back settles forming booths; there are some photographs of storms buffeting the pub and country pictures on its cream walls, and a winter coal fire; a small chatty drinking area by the counter has a brass ship's clock and barometer. The winter games room has darts and shove-ha'penny; there's more booth seating in a no smoking family room with sailing boat pictures. There are seats (highly prized) out on the terrace overlooking the three-mile pebble beach, and the freshwater wildlife lagoon of Slapton Ley is just behind the pub.

(Recommended by Tracey and Stephen Groves, Neil and Beverley Gardner, Derek and Margaret Underwood, Laura Wilson, Pete and Jo Cole, Alan and Paula McCully, Tony Middis, Claire Nielsen, Esther and John Sprinkle, Jill Hummerstone, Nigel Long)

Whitbreads ~ Tenant Paul Stubbs ~ Real ale ~ Bar food (11.30(12 Sun)-2(2.15 Sun), 6-10) ~ (01548) 580553 ~ Children in family room ~ Dogs welcome ~ Open 11.30-11; 12-10.30 Sun; 11.30-3, 6-11 in winter

WIDECOMBE SX7176 Map 1
Rugglestone £
Village at end of B3387; pub just S – turn left at church and NT church house, OS Sheet 191 map reference 720765

Although this unspoilt, tucked away local now has new licensees, things seem to be as good as ever. The small bar has a strong rural atmosphere, just four small tables, a few window and wall seats, a one-person pew built into the corner by the nice old stone fireplace, and a rudimentary bar counter dispensing well kept Butcombe Bitter and St Austell Dartmoor Best tapped from the cask; local farm cider and a decent little wine list. The room on the right is a bit bigger and lighter-feeling, and shy strangers may feel more at home here: another stone fireplace, beamed ceiling, stripped pine tables, and a built-in wall bench. There's also a little no smoking room which is used for dining; cribbage, euchre, and dominoes. Tasty simple bar food includes home-made soup or meaty pasties (£2.50), filled baked potatoes (from £2.95), ploughman's (£4.20), and daily specials like various vegetarian meals (from £4.40), prawn pie (£5.95), poached salmon (£6.95), and maybe venison casserole. Outside across the little moorland stream is a field with lots of picnic-sets. Tables and chairs in the garden. *(Recommended by Mike Gorton, the Didler, Andrea Rampley, David and Nina Pugsley, JP, PP, Paul Hopton, Neil and Beverley Gardner, Guy Charrison, Mr and Mrs McKay)*

Free house ~ Licensees Rod and Diane Williams ~ Real ale ~ Bar food ~ Restaurant ~ No credit cards ~ (01364) 621327 ~ Children in dining room and second bar ~ Dogs welcome ~ Open 11-11; 12-10.30 Sun

WINKLEIGH SS6308 Map 1
Kings Arms
Village signposted off B3220 Crediton—Torrington; Fore Street

Whether you are a local or visitor, you can be sure of a friendly welcome in this popular, well run thatched village pub. There's an attractive main bar with beams, some old-fashioned built-in wall settles, scrubbed pine tables and benches on the flagstones, and a woodburning stove in a cavernous fireplace; another woodburning stove separates the bar from the no smoking dining room. Under the new licensees, good bar food includes home-made soup (£2.95), sandwiches (from £2.95; filled baguettes from £3.50), creamy garlic mushrooms (£4.25), ploughman's or filled baked potatoes (£4.50), ham and eggs (£5.50), fish or steak and kidney pies or vegetable roulade in a tomato and basil sauce (£6.50), lamb chops with rosemary and redcurrant gravy or chicken breast wrapped in bacon (£7), and steaks (£7.95). Well kept Butcombe Bitter and Gold, and Wells Bombardier on handpump, local cider, and decent wines. There are seats out in the garden. *(Recommended by R J Walden, M and D Toms, Comus and Sarah Elliott, Pamela and Merlyn Horswell, Dr and Mrs M E Wilson)*

Free house ~ Licensees Chris Guy and Julia Franklin ~ Real ale ~ Bar food (all day) ~ Restaurant ~ (01837) 83384 ~ Children in eating area of bar and restaurant ~ Dogs allowed in bar ~ Open 11-11; 12-10.30 Sun

WONSON SX6789 Map 1
Northmore Arms ♀ ◀
Off A382 ½ mile from A30 at Whiddon Down; turn right down lane signposted Throwleigh/Gidleigh. Continue down lane over hump-back bridge; turn left to Wonson; OS Sheet 191 map reference 674903

It's almost as if time has stood still here. Hidden away down country lanes is this charming secluded cottage run by a warmly friendly landlady. The two small connected beamed rooms – modest and informal but civilised – have wall settles, a few elderly chairs, five tables in one room and just two in the other. There are two open fires (only one may be lit), and some attractive photographs on the stripped stone walls; darts and cribbage. Besides well kept ales such as Adnams Broadside, Cotleigh Tawny and Exe Valley Dobs, they have good house wines, and most enjoyable home-made food such as sandwiches (from £1.75; toasties from £2.25), garlic mushrooms (£2.65), ploughman's (£4.25), filled baked potatoes (from £4.25), ham and egg or liver and bacon (£4.75), roast lamb with garlic potatoes (£5.95), grilled breast of duck (£6.95), steak (£8.25), and puddings such as home-made treacle tart with clotted cream (£2.50); Sunday roast beef (£5.95); Tuesday curries (£6.95), and huge breakfasts. The ladies' lavatory is up steep steps. Tables and chairs sit precariously in the steep little garden – all very peaceful and rustic; excellent walking from the pub (or to it, perhaps from Chagford or Gidleigh Park). Castle Drogo is close by. *(Recommended by Mike Gorton, JP, PP, Keith Stevens,*

R J Walden, Alice Harper, Andrea Rampley, M A Borthwick, the Didler, Karen and Steve Wilson, Anthony Longden, MP, Mike and Wendy Proctor)

Free house ~ Licensee Mrs Mo Miles ~ Real ale ~ Bar food (12-9; 12-2.30, 7-9 Sun) ~ (01647) 231428 ~ Well behaved children away from bar ~ Dogs welcome ~ Open 11-11; 12-10.30 Sun ~ Bedrooms: /£35

WOODBURY SALTERTON SY0189 Map 1
Diggers Rest

3½ miles from M5 junction 30, off A3052 towards Sidmouth

Since this thatched village pub was last in the *Guide*, quite a lot has changed. New licensees have taken over and extensively refurbished the bars adding new lighting, soft furnishings, antique furniture, and local art on the walls; an extra large sofa and armchair provide a cosy seating area by the open fire to enjoy either a morning cappuccino while reading the daily papers or a pre-dinner drink while looking through the menu. But there's also emphasis on the pubby side with well kept Fullers London Pride, and Otter Bitter and Otter Ale on handpump, a well chosen wine list from a local merchant, and local organic soft drinks. Using fresh local and organic produce, the enjoyable home-made food now includes soups such as butternut squash (£3.95), sandwiches and filled baguettes (from £3.95), fried scallops with bacon (£5.75), home-cooked ham and eggs (£6.75), local organic pork sausages (£7.25), steak and kidney pie (£7.65), home-made haddock and herb fishcakes on dressed leaves with a crème fraîche tartare sauce (£7.75), roast chicken, blue cheese and apple salad (£7.95), fresh seasonal crab salad (£8.95), and chargrilled rib-eye steak (£11.95), with daily specials like chicken in tarragon and madeira sauce (£8.25), moroccan lamb tagine with spicy couscous (£8.75), bass with a pine nut and basil crust or slow-cooked lamb shanks (£9.95), and puddings such as sticky toffee pudding or rhubarb crumble pie (£3.95); Sunday roasts (from £7.25), and a good children's menu. All the dining areas are no smoking during mealtimes; piped music. The skittle alley has been refurbished, and the terraced garden has been redeveloped, with contemporary garden furniture under canvas parasols, and lovely countryside views. *(Recommended by Dr and Mrs M E Wilson, Richard and Margaret Peers)*

Free house ~ Licensee Stephen Rushton ~ Real ale ~ Bar food (12-2, 7-9.30) ~ Restaurant ~ (01395) 232375 ~ Children in eating area of bar and restaurant ~ Dogs allowed in bar ~ Open 11-3, 6-11(all day weekdays July/Aug); all day Sat; all day Sun

WOODLAND SX7968 Map 1
Rising Sun ⇐

Village signposted off A38 just NE of Ashburton – then keep eyes peeled for Rising Sun signposts

Half the fun is trying to find this friendly Dartmoor inn – and it's well worth the detour off the A38. Although people do drop in for just a drink, there's quite an emphasis on the good, frequently changing food: home-made soup (£3.50), sandwiches (from £4), smoked chicken and venison platter with marinated peppers or pigeon breast with a watercress and orange salad (£4.95), home-cooked local ham with free range eggs and home-made chips (£5.95), almond risotto with roasted garlic and peppers (£6.50), popular home-made pies (£6.95), local pork chop with a mustard and cream sauce (£8.95), local lamb chump chop with a rosemary and red berry sauce (£10.95), roasted monkfish wrapped in pancetta on a pea and mint purée (£11.95), and home-made puddings such as chocolate marquise or sticky toffee pudding with butterscotch sauce (£3.50); they keep a super choice of West Country cheeses. The dining area is no smoking. There's an expanse of softly lit red plush button-back banquettes and matching studded chairs, partly divided by wooded banister rails, masonry pillars and the odd high-backed settle. A forest of beams is hung with thousands of old doorkeys, and a nice part by the log fire has shelves of plates and books, and old pictures above the fireplace. Well kept Princetown Jail Ale and IPA, and Teignworthy Spring Tide on handpump, and local wines and Luscombe cider; cheerful service. The family area has various toys (and a collection of cookery books). There are some picnic-sets in the spacious garden, which has a play area including a redundant tractor. *(Recommended by Andy Sinden, Louise Harrington, Mrs M E Lewis, John and Vivienne Rice, Ian and Nita Cooper, Dr and Mrs M E Wilson, Neil and Beverley Gardner, Mrs J L Wyatt, Graham and Rose Ive, Daphne and Peter Ross)*

Free house ~ Licensee Heather Humphreys ~ Real ale ~ Bar food (12-2.15(3 Sun), 6(7 Sun)-9.15) ~ Restaurant ~ (01364) 652544 ~ Children in eating area of bar, restaurant and family room ~ Dogs welcome ~ Open 11.45-3, 6-11; 12-3, 7-10.30 Sun; closed Mon lunchtime (except bank hols) and all day Mon in winter; 25 Dec ~ Bedrooms: £30B/£53B

Lucky Dip

Besides the fully inspected pubs, you might like to try these Lucky Dips recommended to us and described by readers (if you do, please send us reports: www.goodguides.com).

ABBOTSHAM [SS4226]
Thatched Inn: Extensively refurbished family pub, friendly staff, well kept Bass, Butcombe, Courage Directors and John Smiths, enjoyable food inc fresh fish and good value Sun lunch, mix of modern seats and older features; tables outside, handy for the Big Sheep *(Dr D J and Mrs S C Walker, R J Walden, Simon Robinson)*

ABBOTSKERSWELL [SX8569]
☆ *Court Farm* [Wilton Way; look for the church tower]: Attractive neatly extended 17th-c former farmhouse under new licensee, various rooms off long crazy-paved main beamed bar, partly no smoking, good mix of furnishings, good helpings of well presented food from sandwiches to steaks and bargain Sun lunch, half helpings for children, friendly helpful service, several real ales, farm cider, decent wines, woodburners; piped music; children in eating area, picnic-sets in pretty garden, open all day *(E B Ireland, John Braine-Hartnell, LYM, Ann and Bob Westbrook)*

APPLEDORE [SS4630]
Beaver [Irsha St]: Great estuary views from raised area in thriving well worn in harbourside pub, good value food esp fish, friendly staff, well kept local ales such as Jollyboat, decent house wines, great range of whiskies; pool in smaller games room; tables on sheltered terrace, children really welcome, disabled access *(Andy and Jill Kassube, Paul and Ursula Randall, Christine and Neil Townend)*
☆ *Royal George* [Irsha St]: Simple but good fresh food inc local fish in no smoking dining room with superb estuary views, well kept ales such as Bass, Greene King Old Speckled Hen and Ind Coope Burton, decent wines, good friendly service, cosy unspoilt front bar (dogs allowed), attractive pictures (sensitive souls should steer clear of the postcards in the gents'); fresh flowers; disabled access, picnic-sets outside, picturesque street sloping to sea *(Christine and Neil Townend, Dr and Mrs P Truelove)*

ASHPRINGTON [SX8156]
☆ *Watermans Arms* [Bow Bridge, on Tuckenhay road]: Bustling quarry-tiled heavy-beamed pub in great waterside spot, comfortable and roomy, with high-backed settles and other sturdy furnishings, stripped stonework, partly no smoking eating area, log fire, wide food choice inc children's, welcoming newish landlord, well kept Bass, Theakstons XB and a beer brewed for the pub, decent wines, local farm cider, darts, dominoes, cribbage; piped music, TV; children and dogs welcome, open all day, comfortable bedrooms, pretty flower-filled garden, and close-set tables over road by creek *(Ann and Bob Westbrook, Dr and Mrs M E Wilson, Tony Harwood, LYM, Comus and Sarah Elliott, Lynda and Trevor Smith, Norman and Sheila Davies, Mike and Mary Carter)*

AVETON GIFFORD [SX6947]
Fishermans Rest [Fore St]: New licensees doing enjoyable food in bar and restaurant, inc succulent fresh fish *(Mrs M W Broad)*

AVONWICK [SX7158]
Avon [off A38 at W end of South Brent bypass]: Italian landlord has left and the food in this comfortable fairly modern dining pub has lost that influence, though it has some interesting dishes instead; well kept Badger Best and Bass, woodburner; may be piped music; picnic-sets in attractive meadow by River Avon, adventure playground *(John Evans, LYM)*

AXMINSTER [SY2998]
Hunters Lodge [A35 nr B3165 junction]: Friendly and well run, with a welcome for coach parties, good value bar and restaurant food inc carvery, pleasant staff, well kept Bass and Worthington; big garden with children's play area, well behaved dogs welcome *(Prof and Mrs Tony Palmer)*

AXMOUTH [SY2591]
Harbour Inn [B3172 Seaton—Axminster]: Prettily set thatched local, beams, flagstones, traditional settles and big log fires, well kept Flowers IPA and Original, Otter and Wadworths 6X, pool and big simple summer family bar, food from sandwiches up, cheerful if not always speedy service, friendly cats;

children in eating area, disabled access and facilities, tables in the neat back flower garden, cl winter Sun evenings *(Gerry and Rosemary Dobson, Richard C Morgan, Michael and Marion Buchanan, LYM)*

☆ *Ship* [Church St]: Comfortable and civilised, good fresh local fish and other food using their own herbs inc children's and interesting vegetarian speciality, well kept Bass and Otter, good wines and coffee, lots of embroidered folk dolls, one room devoted to Guinness memorabilia, friendly staff and samoyeds, computer for customers, no smoking restaurant; skittle alley full of nostalgiamenta, tables in attractive garden with long-established owl rescue home *(LYM, Mike and Cheryl Lyons, Richard C Morgan)*

BAMPTON [SS9520]

☆ *Exeter Inn* [A396 some way S, at B3227 roundabout]: Long low stone-built roadside pub under steep hill overlooking River Exe, several friendly and comfortable linked rooms, mainly flagstoned, huge choice of good food inc local crab, fish and Mon/Tues steak night bargains, large pleasant carvery restaurant, well kept Cotleigh Tawny and Exmoor Ale and Gold tapped from the cask, log fire, friendly landlord, daily papers, no piped music, free-range eggs for sale (lots of double-yolkers); tables out in front, reasonably priced bedrooms with own bathrooms, open all day, fairly handy for Knightshayes Court *(Andy and Jill Kassube, Dr and Mrs M E Wilson, Peter and Audrey Dowsett, Stan Edwards, BB)*

BEER [ST2289]

☆ *Anchor* [Fore St]: Nicely placed sea-view dining pub back on form under new management after complete refit, good choice of well cooked food from baguettes and ciabattas to plenty of fish caught here, friendly helpful service, Greene King IPA, Abbot and Ruddles County, decent wines, old local photographs in bow-windowed front bar, large no smoking eating area; reasonably priced bedrooms, lots of tables in garden opp, balcony harbour views, delightful seaside village – parking may not be easy *(Ken Flawn, Dr and Mrs M E Wilson, John and Judy Saville, Gerry and Rosemary Dobson, LYM)*

Barrel of Beer [Fore St]: Small pub with generous home cooking using fresh local ingredients from simple dishes to good interestingly cooked seafood, real ales such as Exe Valley Devon Glory and Wadworths 6X, small restaurant area; open all day *(Kevin Stokes, Barry and Verina Jones, Paul and Annette Hallett, Chris Powell)*

☆ *Dolphin* [Fore St]: Friendly and lively open-plan local quite near sea, old-fashioned décor, oak panelling, nautical bric-a-brac and interesting nooks inc marvellous old distorting mirrors and antique boxing prints in corridors leading to back antique stalls, Bass and Cotleigh Tawny and Barn Owl, decent wine, popular food from good crab sandwiches up; piped music; children and dogs very welcome, one or two tables out by pavement, bedrooms *(Mike Gorton, John Couper, LYM)*

BEESANDS [SX8140]
Cricket: Friendly local by sea wall, with tables outside; softly lit bar with interesting local photographs, enjoyable food inc good crab sandwiches and good choice of fresh fish, well kept real ales, log fire, family room; unobtrusive piped music; bedrooms, at start of coast path to Hallsands and Start Point *(Tony Middis, Comus and Sarah Elliott, Tracey and Stephen Groves)*

BERE FERRERS [SX4563]

☆ *Old Plough* [long dead-end road off B3257 S of Tavistock]: 16th-c pub with stripped stone and panelling, low beam-and-plank ceilings, slate flagstones, old-fashioned furniture, open fires, good value food, well kept changing ales such as Sharps Doom Bar, local farm cider, warm local atmosphere, steps down to cosy restaurant; garden overlooking estuary, secluded village *(E G Parish, G L Gibson)*

BERRY HEAD [SX9356]
Berry Head Hotel: Large L-shaped pubby bar popular with Torquay businessmen, panoramic Torbay views with the Brixham fishing boats sailing past, enjoyable food inc good carvery in room off, welcoming caring service, Greene King Old Speckled Hen and St Austell Dartmoor Best and Triumph; unobtrusive piped music; children welcome, terrace tables *(John and Laney Woods)*

BICKLEIGH [SS9406]
Fishermans Cot: Greatly extended thatched pub with lots of tables on acres of turkey carpet broken up with pillars, plants and some panelled parts, charming view over shallow rocky race below 1640 Exe bridge, more tables out on terrace and waterside lawn, efficient service, huge food choice inc popular carvery, chilled beers such as Bass and Tetleys, piped music; open all day, bedrooms looking over own terrace to river *(Peter and Audrey Dowsett, Andy and Jill Kassube, Neil and Anita Christopher, BB, John Wilson)*

Trout [A396, N of junction with A3072]: Welcoming and comfortable thatched pub with easy chairs in huge bar and dining lounge, well kept ales such as Blackdown and Exmoor Gold, nice coffee, enjoyable pub food inc good value Sun roasts, efficient friendly service; children welcome, tables on pretty lawn, car park across road; well equipped bedrooms, good breakfast *(Andy and Jill Kassube, LYM)*

BLACKAWTON [SX8050]

☆ *George* [signed off A3122 and A381]: Very welcoming two-bar family pub, rather frayed around the edges, with woodburner in cosy end lounge, enjoyable food (not Mon lunchtime) inc fresh fish and some good specials, Teignworthy Spring Tide and Marthas Mild and a guest beer, good choice of belgian beers (early May and Aug beer festivals with live bands), traditional games; children welcome, nice views from garden picnic-sets, cottagey bedrooms *(Paul Boot, Comus and Sarah Elliott, Steve Dark, LYM)*

Normandy Arms [off A3122 W of Dartmouth]: Low-key partly 15th-c pub in pretty village, good log fire, well kept

Blackawton and a guest beer, enjoyable sandwiches and home cooking (not winter Sun evening), interesting World War II battle gear, traditional games, children allowed in no smoking restaurant; piped music; some garden tables, good value bedrooms, open all day Sat and summer Sun (*Comus and Sarah Elliott, Alan Cowell, C A Hall, LYM*)

BLACKMOOR GATE [SS6443]

☆ *Old Station House* [A39/A399]: Former station on redundant line interestingly converted into big friendly dining pub; decent food inc interesting dishes and popular carvery Sat night/Sun lunch, well kept ales, good personal service, carved pews, plush dining chairs, soft red lighting, lots of bric-a-brac, character no smoking area with grandfather clock; spacious games area with two well lit pool tables, darts, piped music may obtrude; big garden with good views; skittle alley; children allowed (but under-5s in small family room only), open all day (*BB, Peter and Audrey Dowsett, Ian and Sharon Shorthouse*)

BOLBERRY [SX6939]

☆ *Port Light*: Former radar station alone on dramatic NT clifftop, bright, clean, spacious and busy, with superb picture-window views, decent food, well kept Dartmoor ales, friendly efficient service, restaurant and conservatory; well behaved children and dogs welcome (they host dog wknds), tables on quiet terrace and in garden with splendid fenced play area; five bedrooms, nr fine beaches, right on the coast path (*Esther and John Sprinkle, MDN*)

BOVEY TRACEY [SX8178]

Cromwell Arms [Fore St]: Appealing old local, popular and friendly, with reasonably priced generous food inc good value Sun lunch, quick service, well kept well priced Marstons Pedigree and other beers, good wine choice, several areas with high-backed settles, no piped music (*John Wilson, Joyce and Maurice Cottrell*)

BOW [SS7101]

White Hart [A3072 W of Crediton]: Well worn in dark beamed bar with settles and huge inglenook log fire, well kept Scattor Rock Kingfisher, reasonably priced food (not Mon), small dining room; lighter games room with pool, TV, skittle alley, juke box may be loud; tables in big back garden – narrow drive to car park; open all day wknds (*Tom Evans, BB*)

BRAMPFORD SPEKE [SX9298]

Agricultural [off A377 N of Exeter]: Dining pub with their own enjoyable beer as well as huge range of good interesting nicely presented bar food, fair prices, good wine (frequent special events such as tastings), very friendly staff and atmosphere, gallery restaurant (children allowed); picnic-sets on sheltered terrace (*Patrick Tolhurst*)

BRAYFORD [SS7235]

☆ *Poltimore Arms* [Yarde Down; 3 miles towards Simonsbath]: Chatty and pubby 17th-c yellow-painted two-bar local in isolated spot, cheerful staff, enticing good value blackboard food inc good Sun roast, well kept Cotleigh Tawny and Exmoor tapped from the cask, basic traditional

furnishings, fine woodburner in inglenook, interesting ornaments, two attractive restaurant areas (children allowed); picnic-sets in side garden, no dogs inside, has been cl winter lunchtimes (*LYM, Mrs P Burvill, Peter and Audrey Dowsett*)

BRENDON [SS7547]

Rockford Inn [Lynton—Simonsbath rd, off B2332]: Charming homely 17th-c inn well set for walkers (and fishermen) by East Lyn river, generous low-priced food from good sandwiches to fresh fish, cream teas (all day in summer), well kept Cotleigh Tawny and Barn Owl and a guest beer, good choice of malt whiskies, farm cider, lots of local pictures, darts, pool, shove-ha'penny, cribbage, dominoes; restaurant, children in eating areas, dogs welcome, folk night every 3rd Sat, bedrooms; open all day summer (*Andy and Jill Kassube, Peter and Audrey Dowsett, Dr D J and Mrs S C Walker, LYM*)

☆ *Staghunters*: Family-run hotel in idyllic setting with garden by East Lyn river, warmly welcoming neat traditional bar with woodburner, enjoyable freshly prepared food from delicious filled baguettes up, good helpings and low prices, well kept Wadworths 6X and Addlestone's cider, family room with pool table, restaurant; walkers and dogs welcome, can get very busy, good value bedrooms (*Peter and Audrey Dowsett, Lynda and Trevor Smith*)

BRIDESTOWE [SX5287]

Fox & Hounds [A386 Okehampton—Tavistock]: Friendly and old-fashioned well worn in moors-edge pub, good value generous food (all day at least in summer) inc good steaks, good range of real ales; dogs welcome, bedrooms (*BB, Dr D J and Mrs S C Walker*)

BRIXHAM [SX9255]

Blue Anchor [Fore St/King St]: Harbourside pub with well kept Dartmoor Best, Greene King Abbot and a guest such as Exmoor, decent usual food inc local fish in two small dining rooms – one a former chapel, down some steps, good mix of locals and visitors, banquettes and plenty of nautical hardwear; live music Fri/Sat, open all day (*Steve Whalley, JP, PP, Emma Kingdon*)

Vigilance [Bolton St]: Sizeable open-plan Wetherspoons useful for its cheap food, beers inc Exmoor Gold, no smoking area, no music – very busy with locals and families all day; nearby parking difficult (*Emma Kingdon, Mr and Mrs Colin Roberts*)

BROADCLYST [SX9995]

Hungry Fox [Station Rd (was B3185), S of Dog Village – ½ mile off A30 opp airport]: Roomy and popular mock-Tudor dining pub, good home-made food, pleasant atmosphere, Bass, Flowers IPA, Otter and Whitbreads, decent wines, good service (*John and Sonja Newberry*)

New Inn: Well run warm and friendly former farmhouse with stripped bricks, boarded ceiling, low doorways, roaring log fires, country and horsey bygones, good range of reasonably priced bar food, decent wine, small

restaurant, skittle alley *(E V M Whiteway)*
Red Lion [B3121]: Quiet pub with
fine wisteria, not far from Killerton (NT – they
own the pub too); recently extended from
heavy-beamed flagstoned core with cushioned
pews and low tables by old woodburner,
cushioned window seats, some nice chairs
around a mix of oak and other tables, good
service, real ales inc Bass and Fullers London
Pride, generous bar food and separate dining
area with longer menu; picnic-sets on front
cobbles, more in small enclosed garden across
quiet lane *(Dr and Mrs M E Wilson,
Pamela and Merlyn Horswell, LYM)*
BROADHEMPSTON [SX8066]
☆ *Monks Retreat* [The Square]: Black beams,
massive old walls, lots of copper, brass and
china, log fire in huge stone fireplace, well kept
Bass, Butcombe and a guest beer, good
changing attractively priced food using local
materials and unusual vegetables, lunchtime
sandwiches and wide children's choice too,
sizeable no smoking dining area a couple of
steps up (best to book), prompt cheerful
service; by arch to attractive churchyard, a few
picnic-sets out in front *(Keith and Liz Harding,
Mr and Mrs Christopher Warner)*
BUCKFASTLEIGH [SX7466]
☆ *Dartbridge* [Totnes Rd, handy for A38]: Big
dependable family pub prettily placed opp Dart
Valley Railway, good range of generous food
(all day at least in summer) with some
emphasis on fish, good crab sandwiches, choice
of Sun roasts, well kept Otter ales, good house
wines, efficient friendly service even under
summer pressure; reasonable disabled access,
tables on neatly kept front terrace, bedrooms,
open all day *(John Evans, Joyce and Maurice
Cottrell, Alan and Paula McCully)*
☆ *White Hart* [Plymouth Rd]: Simple but
attractive comfortably carpeted open-plan bar
with cheerful homely feel, woodburner one
end, huge log fire the other, stone walls, lots of
pictures, horsebrasses, plates, jugs and so forth;
particularly well kept ales such as Ash Vine
One Way Traffic, Greene King Abbot and
Teignworthy Beachcomber, with a beer brewed
for them by Teignworthy, also Sam's local
farm cider, lots of pumpclips above bar,
friendly licensees, good service, home cooking
with good changing choice, side family dining
room; dogs welcome; bedrooms, tables in
pretty back courtyard with barbecues; open all
day, cl Sun afternoon and Mon lunchtime
(Angus Lyon, Neil and Beverley Gardner)
BUDLEIGH SALTERTON [SY0682]
☆ *Salterton Arms* [Chapel St]: Attractive bar with
well kept Bass, Butcombe and Fullers London
Pride, sensible choice of good low-priced
home-made food inc some interesting country
cooking, happy caring staff, small open fires,
small back restaurant and larger upper dining
gallery; can get very busy summer; children
welcome, has been open all day wknds
*(Dr and Mrs M E Wilson, Dennis and Janice
Chaldecott, LYM, John Beeken)*
BURGH ISLAND [SX6444]
☆ *Pilchard* [300 yds across tidal sands from

Bigbury-on-Sea; walk, or take summer Tractor
– unique bus on stilts]: Great setting high
above sea on tidal island with unspoilt cliff
walks, neatly refurbished but keeping its
ancient beams and flagstones, lanterns,
nautical/smuggling feel and blazing fire;
straightforward food, real ales, good
uniformed service, family room; some tables
down by beach, open all day all year
*(the Didler, Mayur Shah, Keith Stevens,
Comus and Sarah Elliott, JP, PP, Esther and
John Sprinkle, Cathy Robinson, Ed Coombe,
LYM)*
CHAWLEIGH [SS7112]
Royal Oak [B3042, off A377 NW of
Crediton]: Simple bar food well presented by
landlord, three real ales, welcoming landlord
(S C Wicks)
CHITTLEHAMHOLT [SS6521]
☆ *Exeter Inn* [off A377 Barnstaple—Crediton,
and B3226 SW of South Molton]: Spotless old
inn with enjoyable food from sandwiches,
baguettes and baked potatoes to good local
steaks and Sun roast, no smoking restaurant,
well kept Dartmoor Best, Greene King Abbot
and a guest beer, farm ciders, open stove in
huge fireplace, side area with booth seating;
traditional games, piped music, dogs allowed;
children in eating areas, benches out on
terrace, decent bedrooms with showers
*(Paula, Paul and Ella Hawkins, Eddie
Edwards, Dr and Mrs A K Clarke, Crystal and
Peter Hooper, LYM)*
CHRISTOW [SX8384]
Artichoke: Pretty thatched local with
comfortable open-plan rooms stepped down
hill, low beams, some black panelling,
flagstones, reliable food inc fish and game, big
log fire (2nd one in no smoking end dining
room), real ales, warm welcome; tables on
back terrace, pretty hillside village nr
Canonteign Waterfalls and Country Park *(BB,
Ann and Colin Hunt)*
CHUDLEIGH [SX8679]
Bishop Lacey [Fore St, just off A38]: Quaint
partly 14th-c church house with good service,
well kept Branscombe Vale, Flowers IPA,
Fullers London Pride and a guest such as
Princetown Jail, some tapped from casks in
back bar, good strong coffee, two log fires,
good value food, no smoking dining room;
tables in garden, winter beer festival,
bedrooms, open all day *(JP, PP, the Didler,
Dr and Mrs A K Clarke, John and Judy Saville)*
Old Coaching House [Fore St]: Popular
flagstoned country pub with attractively priced
food inc good curries and mixed grill in bar or
restaurant, well kept Greene King Abbot and
Worthington, friendly staff, local jazz Fri *(the
Didler, JP, PP)*
CHUDLEIGH KNIGHTON [SX8477]
☆ *Claycutters Arms* [just off A38 by B3344]:
Friendly and attractive 17th-c thatched two-
bar village pub with well kept ales such as
Fullers London Pride and a hefty Otter, decent
wines, food from good sandwiches and
ploughman's up, good service, stripped stone,
interesting nooks and crannies, pleasant

restaurant; dogs welcome, tables on side terrace and in orchard *(June and Robin Savage, LYM, Dennis Jenkin, Neil and Beverley Gardner)*

CHURCHSTOW [SX7145]

☆ *Church House* [A379 NW of Kingsbridge]: New owners in long character pub with heavy black beams (dates from 13th c), stripped stone, cushioned settles, quickly served generous food from sandwiches to mixed grill and (Weds-Sat nights, Sun lunch) popular carvery, well kept Bass and other ales, decent wines, nice atmosphere, back conservatory with floodlit well feature; well behaved children and dogs welcome, tables outside *(Michael Porter, LYM, Comus and Sarah Elliott, Mrs W Boast)*

CLEARBROOK [SX5265]

☆ *Skylark* [village signed down dead end off A386 Tavistock—Plymouth]: Welcoming old two-room pub in pretty cottage row tucked right into Dartmoor, relaxed and chatty, with plenty of locals, well kept Bass, Courage Best and Greene King Old Speckled Hen, wide choice of good value food from sandwiches up inc good vegetarian dishes, good service, simple furnishings, log fire; quite separate children's room in big back garden with plenty of picnic-sets and other seats, small adventure play area, wandering ponies *(BB, Mayur Shah, Jacquie and Jim Jones)*

COCKWOOD [SX9780]

☆ *Ship* [off A379 N of Dawlish]: Comfortable 17th-c inn overlooking estuary and harbour, partitioned beamed bar with big log fire and ancient oven, decorative plates and seafaring prints and memorabilia, small no smoking restaurant, good value food from open crab sandwiches up inc imaginative evening fish dishes and good puddings (freshly made so takes time), well kept Greene King IPA and Abbot and Sharps Doom Bar, friendly helpful staff; piped music; good steep-sided garden *(John Beeken)*

COLYTON [SY2494]

Gerrard Arms [St Andrews Sq]: Good value open-plan local with well kept Bass and guests such as local Otter, good value home-made food inc Sun roasts; nice garden *(JP, PP, the Didler)*

☆ *Kingfisher* [off A35 and A3052 E of Sidmouth; Dolphin St]: Village local with hearty popular food from good crab sandwiches and baked potatoes up, stripped stone, plush seats and elm settles, beams and big open fire, well kept Badger Best and Tanglefoot and changing guest beers, low-priced soft drinks, friendly family service; pub games, upstairs family room, skittle alley, tables out on terrace, garden with water feature *(LYM, the Didler)*

COUNTISBURY [SS7449]

Exmoor Sandpiper [A39, E of Lynton]: Beautifully set rambling and cheery heavy-beamed pub with antique furniture, several good log fires, well kept Bass and two Exmoor ales tapped from the cask, decent hearty food inc fine ploughman's, friendly service, pewter mugs on old beams, lots of stuffed animals

(and two sandpipers), restaurant; children in eating area, garden tables, good nearby cliff walks, comfortable bedrooms, open all day *(LYM, John and Judy Saville, Richard Gibbs, Beryl and Tim Dawson)*

CREDITON [SS8300]

Crediton Inn [Mill St (follow Tiverton sign)]: Small friendly straightforward local with well kept Sharps Doom Bar and two quickly changing guest beers (150 a year), cheap well prepared food, back games room; open all day Mon-Sat, free skittle alley can be booked *(Pete Baker)*

DARTINGTON [SX7762]

Cott [Cott signed off A385 W of Totnes, opp A384 turn-off]: Picturesque long recently rethatched 14th-c pub, heavy beams, steps and flagstones, big log fires, well kept Greene King IPA and Abbot and Otter, food (not cheap) from lunchtime sandwiches and baked potatoes up; children welcome, picnic-sets in garden and on pretty terrace, bedrooms with own bathrooms, open all day at least in summer *(MDN, Tony and Katie Lewis, Neil and Beverley Gardner, Pat and Robert Watt, Comus and Sarah Elliott, Ian Phillips, Ann and Bob Westbrook, LYM, Nigel Long)*

White Hart Bar [Dartington Hall]: Light bright modern décor and open fires in the college's bar (open to visitors), good low-priced food here and in baronial hall, real ales such as Exmoor and one brewed for the bar; very special atmosphere sitting out in the famously beautiful grounds *(Graham and Rose Ive, Catherine Pitt)*

DARTMOUTH [SX8751]

Dartmouth Arms [Lower St, Bayards Cove]: Thriving friendly local (popular with naval students evening) with well kept beer, good value efficiently served basic bar food inc lots of pizzas, log fire, panelling and boating memorabilia; tables out in prime spot overlooking Dart river estuary *(Esther and John Sprinkle)*

Floating Bridge [Coombe Rd]: Friendly pub by upper ferry, good Dart river views, wide range of food inc good fish and shellfish, well kept real ales, dogs welcome *(J E M Andeville)*

DITTISHAM [SX8654]

☆ *Ferry Boat* [Manor St; best to park in village – steep but attractive walk down]: Very welcoming, in idyllic waterside setting, big windows making the most of it, limited good value food inc baguettes and pies, real ale; no parking, quite a walk down; nr little foot-ferry you call by bell, good walks *(Geoffrey and Karen Berrill, Graham and Rose Ive, LYM)*

DREWSTEIGNTON [SX7489]

Anglers Rest [E of village; OS Sheet 191 map ref 743899]: Idyllic wooded Teign valley spot by 16th-c pack-horse bridge, lovely walks; much extended former tea pavilion, with tourist souvenirs and airy café feel, but has well kept Otter and Sharps Doom Bar and reliable food (not Sun) inc good local cheese ploughman's, children's meals, apple cake and cream teas; friendly helpful service, log fire, waterside picnic-sets; cl winter evenings *(LYM, John and Vivienne Rice)*

DUNSFORD [SX8189]

Royal Oak [signed from Moretonhampstead]: Relaxed village inn with good generous food (home-made so may take a while), Sharps and three other well kept changing ales, local farm ciders, friendly service, light and airy lounge bar with woodburner, steps down to games room, provision for children; quiz nights, piped music; Fri barbecues in sheltered tiered garden, good value bedrooms in converted barn *(R M Corlett, LYM)*

EAST BUDLEIGH [SY0684]

☆ *Sir Walter Raleigh* [High St]: Chattily convivial and attractive local nr interesting church in lovely village, pleasant service under friendly new licensees, enjoyable food, well kept real ales inc local brews, good wines, charming large no smoking dining area; wheelchair access, but parking some way off; bedrooms, handy for Bicton Park gardens *(Pamela and Merlyn Horswell, LYM, Pam Adsley, Dr and Mrs M E Wilson, Mike and Wendy Proctor)*

EAST PRAWLE [SX7836]

Pigs Nose [Prawle Green]: Cheery and homely, with low beams and flagstones, well kept ales such as Golden Celebration tapped from the cask, enjoyable if limited food from good ploughman's and sandwiches up, open fire, easy chairs and sofa, interesting knick-knacks and local pictures, lots of nice dogs, jars of wild flowers and candles on tables, small family area with small box of unusual toys, pool room with darts and bird log; unobtrusive nostalgic piped music, hall for live bands; tables outside, nice spot on village green *(Mr and Mrs M Dalby, Comus and Sarah Elliott, Jill Hummerstone)*

Providence [off A379 E of Kingsbridge]: The former Freebooter, now reopened and back to its original name, simple bare-boards interior with unpretentious food inc fresh fish, model ship, word games; tables in nice small garden, good walks *(LYM)*

ERMINGTON [SX6353]

Crooked Spire [The Square]: Open-plan pub recently refurbished in bright colours, well kept Bass and Otter, enjoyable straightforward food from good sandwiches to Sun roasts with good veg, pleasant service; theme and quiz nights; good heated back courtyard, comfortable bedrooms with shared bathroom *(Keith Richard Waters, Margaret and Roy Randle)*

EXETER [SX9390]

☆ *Double Locks* [Canal Banks, Alphington, via Marsh Barton Industrial Estate; OS Sheet 192 map ref 933901]: Remote waterside hideaway still much enjoyed by many for its character, enduring informality, laid-back atmosphere, great range of real ales and good value plain bar food all day; but it can be on the scruffy side, some would appreciate more deferential service, and they don't let people have tap water (you have to pay for mineral); piped music, frequent live; children in eating areas,

distant view to city and cathedral from seats out on decking, good big play area, open all day *(Mike Gorton, Jayne Capp, Laura Wilson, Kerry Law, Simon Smith, Ruth and Andrew Crowder, Esther and John Sprinkle, Jonathan Smith, Barry Steele-Perkins, LYM, JP, PP, Michael and Marion Buchanan, SH, the Didler, JHBS)*

☆ *Great Western* [St Davids Hill]: Great choice of well kept changing real ales usually inc Adnams, Bass, Exmoor, Fullers London Pride and Teignworthy in large hotel's small sociable public bar, with plenty of regulars, attractively priced honest and generous food all day from sandwiches up (also a restaurant), daily papers, peanuts in the shell, no music; bedrooms fresh and warm *(Philip Kingsbury, the Didler, Phil and Sally Gorton, Catherine Pitt, Colin Gooch, Dr and Mrs A K Clarke, C J Fletcher, JP, PP, Jane and Adrian Tierney-Jones, Joe Green)*

Hour Glass [Melbourne St]: Close to quay, thriving 19th-c city pub with beams, panelling, candles and lots of wood, well kept ales such as Bass, Greene King Abbot and Otter, good house wine, enjoyable reasonably priced food, friendly helpful staff, cellar restaurant *(the Didler)*

Mill on the Exe [Bonhay Rd (A377)]: Good spot by new pedestrian bridge over weir, heated waterside terrace, bar comfortably done out with bare boards, old bricks, beams and timbers, large airy river-view conservatory restaurant, good sensibly priced food inc good value lunchtime light dishes, well kept St Austell ales, good house wines, friendly young staff; children welcome *(John and Vivienne Rice, BB, Joe Green)*

Port Royal [Weirfield Path, off Weirfield Rd]: Along the E bank Exe-side path downstream from The Quay, low gabled pavilion reopened after neat refurbishment, attractive nautical-theme lounge, river-view tables, new licensees doing wide choice of interesting attractively priced food, pleasant service; public bar with games and piped music *(Dr and Mrs M E Wilson, John and Vivienne Rice)*

Prospect [The Quay]: Good quayside spot, with lower beamed bar and upper river-view dining area, new décor in yellows, oranges and reds with modern prints, up-to-date bar food, well kept ales inc Otter, friendly helpful staff; piped music – live some evenings *(Dr and Mrs M E Wilson, Sue and Mike Todd, Alan M Pring, John and Vivienne Rice, P F Willmer, Joe Green)*

☆ *Ship* [Martins Lane, nr cathedral]: Pretty 14th-c proper pub with substantial furniture in bustling well laid out heavy-beamed bar, well kept Boddingtons, Flowers, Greene King Old Speckled Hen and Marstons Pedigree, farm cider, speedy friendly service, generously filled sandwiches only down here, enjoyable meals in comfortable upstairs restaurant with feel of below-decks man-o'-war *(Mr and Mrs Colin Roberts, Dr and Mrs M E Wilson, LYM, DAV, Stephen Hussey)*

Welcome [Haven Banks, off Haven Rd (which is first left off A377 heading S after Exe crossing)]: Old two-room pub near the gasometers and little changed since the 1960s (ditto the juke box), gas lighting and flagstones, very friendly old-school landlady, well kept RCH PG Steam; a few tables out overlooking basin on Exeter Ship Canal, and can be reached on foot via footbridges from The Quay *(the Didler, Dr and Mrs M E Wilson, JP, PP)*

Well House [Cathedral Yard, attached to Royal Clarence Hotel]: Big windows looking across to cathedral in open-plan bar with tables divided by inner walls and partitions, lots of interesting Victorian prints, good choice of well kept real ales with a west country emphasis, quick service, popular bar lunches inc good sandwiches and salads, daily papers; Roman well beneath (can be viewed when pub not busy); piped music can be obtrusive, gets smoky *(John and Judy Saville, BB, Stephen Hussey)*

☆ *White Hart* [South St]: Attractively old-fashioned largely no smoking rambling bar (heavy beams, oak flooring and nice furnishings inc antiques), charming inner cobbled courtyard, Bass, Ind Coope Burton and Tetleys, good wines, efficient cheerful staff, good value bar food inc good sandwich choice; handy reasonably priced central place to stay, with good breakfast and free parking *(JP, PP, Nigel Williamson, Dr and Mrs M E Wilson, Neil and Beverley Gardner, David and Nina Pugsley, LYM, Susan and Nigel Wilson, Clare Pearse, Joan and Michel Hooper-Immins)*

EXMOUTH [SX9980]

Beach [Victoria Rd]: Down-to-earth old quayside local with shipping and lifeboat memorabilia and photographs, beams, posts and panelling, cast-iron framed tables, Bass, Greene King Old Speckled Hen and Otter, food, friendly landlord and staff *(Dr and Mrs M E Wilson)*

Grove [Esplanade]: Roomy panelled Youngs outpost set back from beach with large seafront garden and play area, their beers kept well with a guest such as Smiles, decent house wines, good coffee, good value food inc plenty of local fish and children's menu, young efficient staff, simple furnishings, caricatures and local prints, 1930s replicas, attractive fireplace at back, sea views from upstairs restaurant; live music Fri *(John Beeken)*

Powder Monkey [The Parade]: Wetherspoons with long bar, armchairs in two smaller front rooms (children allowed in one), five real ales; very popular with young people wknds; a few tables on courtyard facing roundabout *(Alan Wilson, Dr and Mrs M E Wilson)*

EXTON [SX9886]

Puffing Billy: Wide choice of good inventive food inc seafood in pristine smartly reworked dining pub, friendly staff *(Samantha Simonitsch, Ken Flawn)*

FILLEIGH [SS6727]

Stags Head [off A361, via B3226 N of S Molton]: Pretty 16th-c thatched and flagstoned pub with reasonably priced home-made food,

well kept Barum Original, Bass and Tetleys, good value wines, welcoming landlord, friendly local bar with crack darts team, banknotes on beams, Corgi toy collection, very high-backed settle, newer and larger cottagey dining room up a couple of steps; old rustic tables out in fairy-lit honeysuckle arbour by big tree-sheltered pond with lots of ducks and fish; bedrooms comfortable and good value, good breakfast *(Tracey and Stephen Groves, BB)*

FROGMORE [SX7742]

Globe [A379 E of Kingsbridge]: Walls papered with maritime charts, lots of ship and yacht paintings, some built-in settles creating corner booths, mix of simple tables, generous usual food from sandwiches and good ploughman's to steak inc children's, well kept Exmoor Ale and Greene King Abbot, local farm cider in summer, country wines, good log fire, games and TV in flagstoned locals' bar; prominent fruit machine, piped music may be loud; tables out on pretty terraces with play area and a bit of a creek view, plenty of walks, bedrooms; cl Mon lunchtime in winter *(Tracey and Stephen Groves, C A Hall, Caroline Raphael, Dr and Mrs Allen, LYM, John and Vivienne Rice)*

GEORGEHAM [SS4639]

☆ *Rock* [Rock Hill, above village]: Well restored oak-beamed pub with well kept ales such as Barum, Cotleigh Golden Eagle and Greene King IPA and Abbot, local farm cider, decent wines, good value food inc speciality baguettes and appealing puddings, quick welcoming service, old red quarry tiles, open fire, pleasant mix of rustic furniture, lots of bric-a-brac, vine-adorned back conservatory great for children; piped music, darts, fruit machine, pool room and juke box; tables under cocktail parasols on front terrace, pretty hanging baskets *(Paul and Ursula Randall, Steve Harvey, Boyd Catling, BB, Derek Harvey-Piper, Simon Robinson)*

GRENOFEN [SX4971]

Halfway House [A386 near Tavistock]: Welcoming, clean and attractive, good choice of reasonably priced home-made food inc local beef, four real ales such as Bass and Sharps, farm cider, decent wines, lounge, restaurant and traditional bar with pool and darts; tables out overlooking Dartmoor, good value bedrooms *(Wally Parson, Brian Cudlip)*

HALWELL [SX7853]

☆ *Old Inn* [A381 Totnes—Kingsbridge, junction with B3207]: Good atmosphere, well kept RCH IPA, Premium and PG Steam, matey landlord, big helpings of low-priced interesting food cooked by his Filipino wife; bedrooms *(Dudley and Moira Cockroft, Comus and Sarah Elliott)*

HATHERLEIGH [SS5404]

☆ *Tally Ho* [Market St (A386)]: Attractive heavy-beamed and timbered linked rooms, sturdy furnishings, big log fire and woodburner, usual food from lunchtime sandwiches up, good real ales brewed for them locally by Clearwater, no smoking restaurant, traditional games; piped music; tables in nice sheltered garden, three cosy and prettily furnished bedrooms *(LYM,*

the Didler, JP, PP, Christine and Neil
Townend, Tom Evans)

HEMERDON [SX5657]

Miners Arms: Friendly and attractive low-
beamed former tin miner's cottage with
internal well, wide range of well kept beers inc
local Sutton Dirty Blond, cheap food; big
attractive garden with good play area, on edge
of pastoral Dartmoor countryside
(Esther and John Sprinkle)

HOLCOMBE [SX9575]

Castle [Fordens Lane, off A379]: Reliable food
using local ingredients, pleasant cheerful
service, well kept Bass and a changing guest
beer, lovely views; refurbished garden
(Mark and Belinda Halton)

HOLNE [SX7069]

☆ *Church House* [signed off B3357 W of
Ashburton]: Country inn well placed for
attractive walks, log fires in both rooms, nicely
served well cooked food from good lunchtime
sandwiches up, children's helpings, several well
kept ales inc Butcombe, Dartmoor and
Wadworths 6X, Gray's farm cider, country
wines, decent house wines, friendly staff, no
smoking areas, traditional games in public bar;
well behaved children in eating area;
comfortable bedrooms, some newly
refurbished, dogs welcome *(D and M T Ayres-
Regan, LYM, Simon and Rachel Dowdy,
Richard and Margaret Peers, Len Banister)*

HOLSWORTHY [SS3408]

Kings Arms [Fore St/The Square]: 17th-c inn
with Victorian fittings, etched windows and
coal fires in three interesting traditional bars,
old pictures and photographs, 40s and 50s
beer advertisements, lots of optics behind
ornate counter, particularly well kept Bass and
Sharps Doom Bar, friendly locals; open all day,
Sun afternoon closure *(JP, PP, the Didler)*

HONITON [SY1198]

Greyhound [Fenny Bridges, B3177 4 miles W]:
Big busy thatched family dining pub with wide
food choice from good open sandwiches and
baked potatoes up, quick friendly service, well
kept Otter beers, old-fashioned heavy-beamed
décor, attractive restaurant with no smoking
area; bedrooms *(Dr and Mrs M E Wilson,
LYM)*

☆ *Red Cow* [High St]: Welcoming local, very
busy on Tues and Sat market days, scrubbed
tables, pleasant alcoves, log fires, well kept
Bass, Courage Directors and local Otter,
decent wines and malt whiskies, good value
no-nonsense food in restaurant part inc
excellent sandwiches and good puddings, fast
service from friendly Welsh licensees (may have
Radio Wales), loads of chamber-pots and big
mugs on beams, pavement tables; bar can get
smoky; bedrooms *(BB, Dr and Mrs M E
Wilson, R G Price, Mrs B M Smith, Sue and
Mike Todd)*

HOPE COVE [SX6640]

Hope & Anchor: Simple inn, friendly and
comfortable, in lovely seaside spot, with good
open fire, kind efficient staff, good value
straightforward food, well kept Bass and a beer
brewed for the pub, reasonably priced wines,

flagstone floor, no piped music; children and
dogs welcome in family room, games room
with pool; good views from tables outside,
bedrooms, open all day *(LYM, Norma and
Keith Bloomfield, Comus and Sarah Elliott)*

HORSEBRIDGE [SX3975]

☆ *Royal* [off A384 Tavistock—Launceston]:
Cheerful slate-floored rooms, interesting bric-
a-brac and pictures, tasty food from baguettes
and baked potatoes up, Bass, Sharps Doom
Bar, Wadworths 6X and guest beers, farm
cider, bar billiards, cribbage, dominoes, no
smoking café-style side room, no music or
machines; no children in evening, tables on
back terrace and in big garden
*(Howard Gregory, Andrea Rampley, LYM,
DAV, John Wilson)*

IDE [SX8990]

☆ *Poachers* [3 miles from M5 junction 31, via
A30; High St]: Good welcoming atmosphere,
reasonably priced generous food, both
traditional and inventive, inc good fish choice,
well kept Branscombe Vale Branoc and Otter,
good value house wines, attentive friendly
service, sofas and open fire; blues night,
attractively decorated bedrooms *(Eamonn and
Natasha Skyrme, R J Walden, John and
Vivienne Rice, Mrs Deborah Phillips,
Dr and Mrs M E Wilson)*

IDEFORD [SX8977]

☆ *Royal Oak* [2 miles off A380]: Friendly and
cosy thatched and flagstoned village local
brightened up by new licensees but still
unspoilt, interesting marine memorabilia, well
kept Flowers IPA and Original, bar food, log
fire *(JP, PP, the Didler)*

ILFRACOMBE [SS5247]

☆ *George & Dragon* [Fore St]: Oldest pub here,
handy for harbour, with good local
atmosphere, proper pubby food inc Sun lunch,
helpful friendly staff, well kept real ale, decent
wines, attractive olde-worlde décor, soft
lighting, lots of ornaments, china etc; may be
piped music, cash machine but no credit cards
*(Gene and Kitty Rankin, Margaret and Roy
Randle, June and Robin Savage, Ken Flawn)*

INSTOW [SS4730]

☆ *Boat House* [Marine Parade]: Airy modern
high-ceilinged café/bar with huge tidal beach
just across lane and views to Appledore, big
old-fashioned nautical paintings on stripped
stone wall, well kept Bass, Flowers IPA and a
local guest beer, good choice of popular food
from sandwiches to steaks inc plentiful fish,
open fire, friendly prompt service even when
crowded, lively family bustle – children
welcome, gets very busy; piped music; roof
terrace *(Janet Walters, John and Judy Saville,
Ken Flawn, LYM)*

Quay Inn [Marine Parade]: Pleasant open-plan
seaside pub just above quay, tables looking out
over estuary, simple reasonably priced food
from baguettes to lobster tails, also afternoon
teas, real ales, friendly staff; disabled access,
open all day *(Andy and Jill Kassube)*

IPPLEPEN [SX8366]

Wellington [off A381 Totnes—Newton Abbot;
Fore St]: Attractively furnished two-bar village

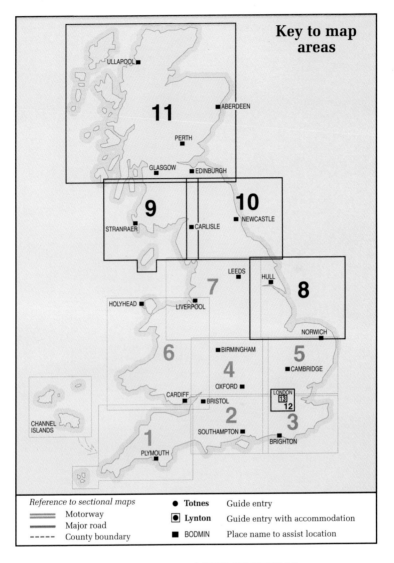

Key to map areas

ULLAPOOL

ABERDEEN

11

PERTH

GLASGOW   EDINBURGH

9

STRANRAER   CARLISLE

10

NEWCASTLE

LEEDS

HULL

7

HOLYHEAD   LIVERPOOL

8

NORWICH

6

BIRMINGHAM

5

CAMBRIDGE

4

OXFORD

CARDIFF   BRISTOL

LONDON
13
12

CHANNEL
ISLANDS

2

SOUTHAMPTON

3

BRIGHTON

1

PLYMOUTH

Reference to sectional maps

≡≡≡ Motorway	● **Totnes** Guide entry
— Major road	◉ **Lynton** Guide entry with accommodation
- - - County boundary	■ BODMIN Place name to assist location

MAPS IN THIS SECTION

For Maps 1 – 7 see earlier colour section

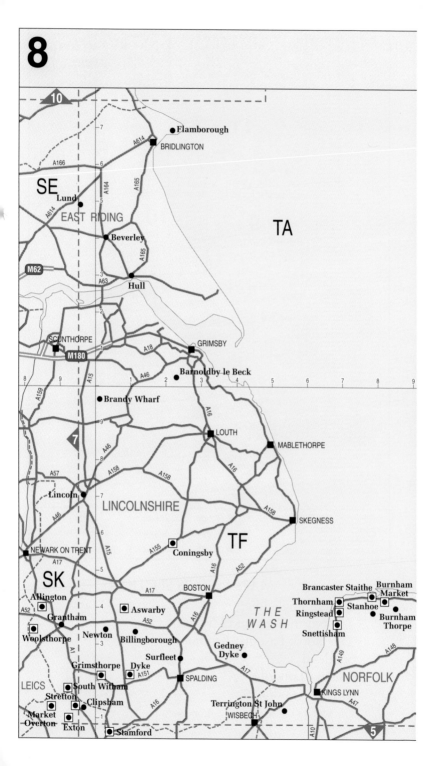

8

10

● Flamborough
BRIDLINGTON

A614
A166

SE
● Lund
EAST RIDING

A164
A165
A614

● Beverley

A165

TA

M62

A63
Hull

SCUNTHORPE
M180

A18
GRIMSBY

A15
A46
● Barnoldby le Beck

A159
● Brandy Wharf

A46
■ LOUTH

A16
● MABLETHORPE

A57
A158
A158

Lincoln
LINCOLNSHIRE

A16

A46
A15
A158

SKEGNESS

A155
● Coningsby
TF

NEWARK ON TRENT
A17

A16
A52

SK
BOSTON

● Allington
A52
A17

THE
WASH

Brancaster Staithe ● Burnham Market
Thornham ● Stanhoe
Ringstead ●
● Burnham Thorpe

● Grantham
● Aswarby
A52

A16

● Snettisham

● Woolsthorpe
● Newton
● Billingborough

A1

● Grimsthorpe
● Surfleet
● Gedney Dyke

A149
A148

LEICS
● Dyke
A151
SPALDING
A17

NORFOLK

● South Witham
● Stretton
● Clipsham

A16

● KINGS LYNN
A47

● Market Overton
● Exton
● Stamford

Terrington St John
WISBECH

A10
5

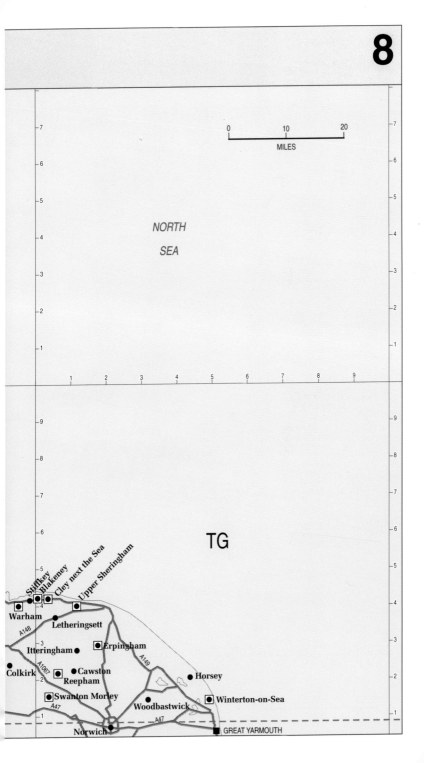

0   10   20

MILES

NORTH

SEA

—7

—6

—5

—4

—3

—2

—1

1   2   3   4   5   6   7   8   9

—9

—8

—7

—6

TG

—5

Stiffkey

Blakeney

Cley next the Sea

Upper Sheringham

Warham

Letheringsett

A148

Erpingham

Itteringham

A149

Colkirk

A1067

Cawston

Reepham

Horsey

Swanton Morley

A47

Woodbastwick

Winterton-on-Sea

Norwich

A47

GREAT YARMOUTH

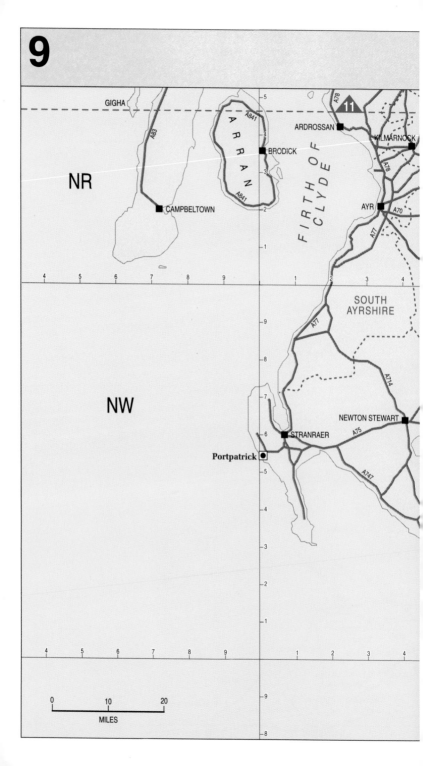

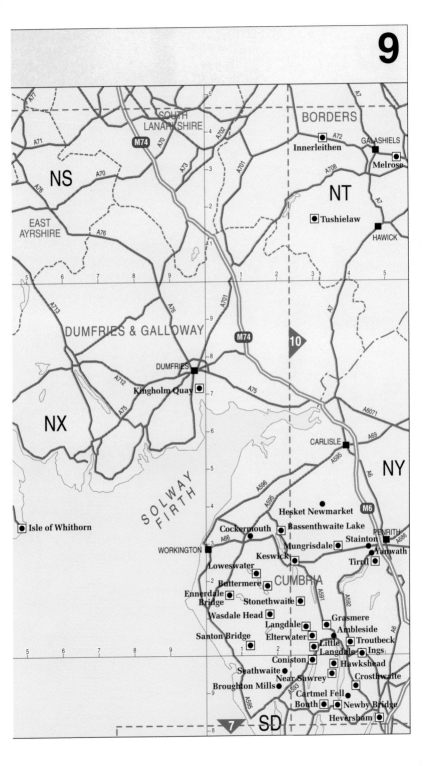

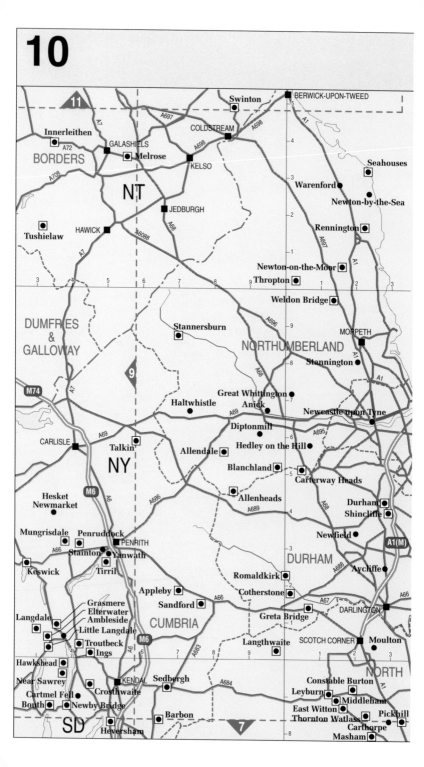

10

11

Swinton

BERWICK-UPON-TWEED

Innerleithen

GALASHIELS

COLDSTREAM

BORDERS

Melrose

KELSO

NT

Seahouses

Warenford

Newton-by-the-Sea

Tushielaw

HAWICK

JEDBURGH

Rennington

Newton-on-the-Moor

Thropton

Weldon Bridge

DUMFRIES & GALLOWAY

Stannersburn

NORTHUMBERLAND

MORPETH

Stannington

M74

9

Great Whittington

Haltwhistle

Anick

Newcastle upon Tyne

CARLISLE

Talkin

Diptonmill

NY

Allendale

Hedley on the Hill

Hesket Newmarket

Blanchland

Carterway Heads

M6

Allenheads

Durham

Shincliffe

Mungrisdale

Penruddock

A1(M)

PENRITH

Newfield

Stainton

Yanwath

Keswick

Tirril

DURHAM

Romaldkirk

Aycliffe

Appleby

Cotherstone

Grasmere

Sandford

CUMBRIA

Elterwater

Ambleside

Greta Bridge

DARLINGTON

Langdale

Little Langdale

Troutbeck

Ings

Langthwaite

SCOTCH CORNER

Moulton

Hawkshead

Near Sawrey

KENDAL

Sedbergh

NORTH

Cartmel Fell

Crosthwaite

Constable Burton

Bouth

Newby Bridge

Leyburn

Middleham

Barbon

East Witton

Pickhill

Thornton Watlass

Heversham

Carthorpe

Masham

SD

7

NU

N O R T H

S E A

0 10 20
MILES

SOUTH SHIELDS

SUNDERLAND

NZ

A19

HARTLEPOOL

MIDDLESBROUGH

A174

A171

A172

Whitby

Egton Bridge

Beck Hole

Robin Hood's Bay

A169

A171

Osmotherly

YORKSHIRE

A19

Blakey Ridge

SE

Fadmoor

Lastingham

TA

Appleton-le-Moors

Levisham

Felixkirk

Kirkbymoorside

Cropton

Scawton

A170

Pickering

A170

Scarborough

Harome

Marton

8

A165

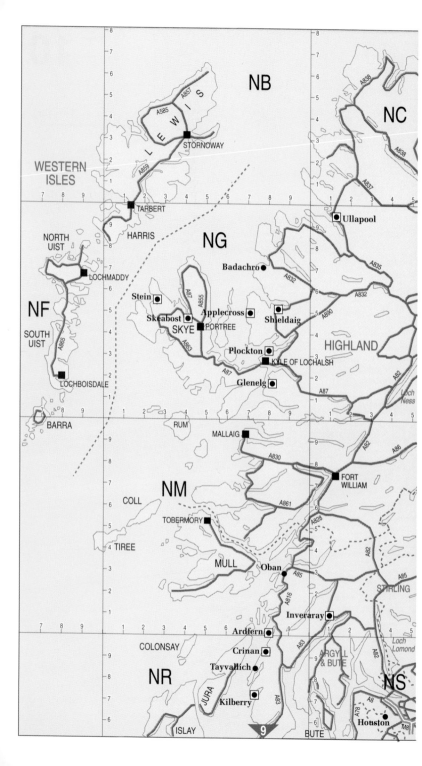

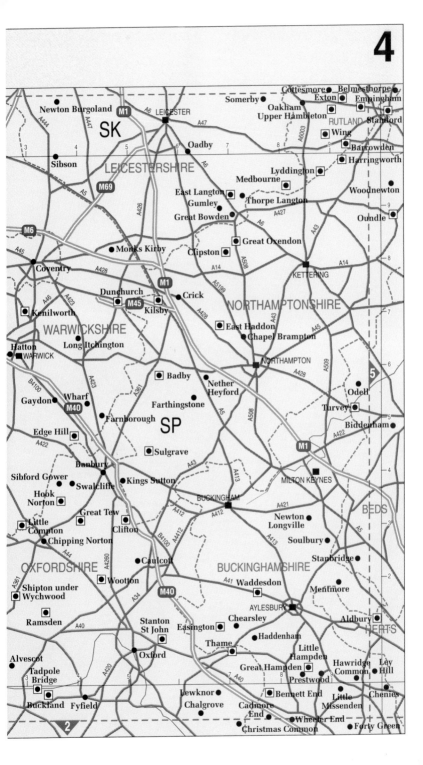

4

Newton Burgoland M1 LEICESTER A6 A47 SK

Cottesmore Belmesthorpe
Somerby Exton Empingham
Oakham
Upper Hambleton RUTLAND Stamford
Wing

Sibson LEICESTERSHIRE A6 Oadby A47 Barrowden
Harringworth
Lyddington
Medbourne
East Langton Thorpe Langton Woodnewton
Gumley
Great Bowden A6 A427 Oundle
A426 Great Oxendon
M69 Clipston A508 A43
Monks Kirby A14 KETTERING A14
M6 A45 Coventry A428 A5199 NORTHAMPTONSHIRE A509
Dunchurch M1 Crick A428
M45 Kilsby A43
Kenilworth East Haddon A45
WARWICKSHIRE Long Itchington Chapel Brampton
Hatton NORTHAMPTON A428 Odell
WARWICK A423 Badby A361 Turvey
Gaydon M40 Wharf Nether Heyford Biddenham
Farnborough Farthingstone SP A5 A508 M1
Edge Hill A422
Sulgrave A43 A413 MILTON KEYNES BEDS
Banbury A5
Sibford Gower Swalcliffe Kings Sutton BUCKINGHAM A421
Hook Norton A412 Newton Longville Soulbury Stanbridge
Little Comton Great Tew Clifton A412 A413
Chipping Norton B4100 BUCKINGHAMSHIRE Mentmore
A44 A4260 Caulcott
Shipton under Wychwood Wootton A41 Waddesdon Aldbury HERTS
A361 A34 M40 AYLESBURY
Ramsden A40 Stanton St John Easington Chearsley Hawridge Ley Hill
Alvescot Thame Haddenham Little Hampden Common Chenies
Tadpole Bridge Oxford A420 Great Hampden Prestwood Little Missenden
Buckland Fyfield Lewknor A40 Bennett End Forty Green
Chalgrove Cadmore End Wheeler End
Christmas Common

2

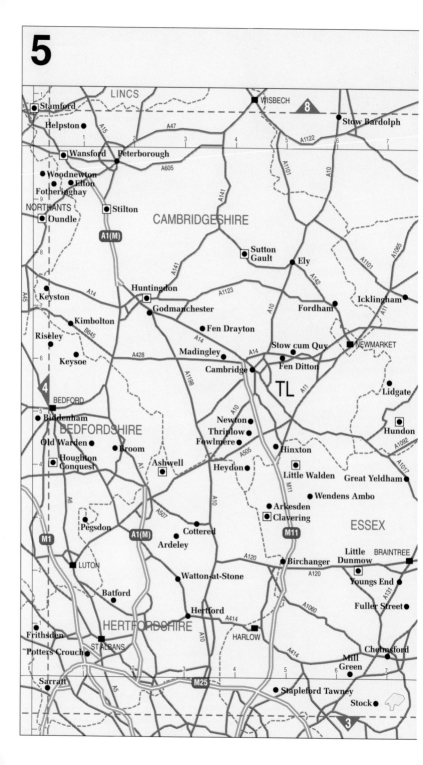

5

LINCS

Stamford
Helpston
WISBECH
Stow Bardolph

Wansford   Peterborough
A47
A1122

Woodnewton
Elton
Fotheringhay
NORTHANTS
Oundle
Stilton

CAMBRIDGESHIRE

A141

Keyston
A14
Huntingdon
Godmanchester
A1123

Sutton Gault
Ely
A142

Fordham
Icklingham

Kimbolton
B645
Riseley
Keysoe
A428
Fen Drayton
A14
Madingley

Stow cum Quy
NEWMARKET
Fen Ditton

Cambridge

TL

A11

Lidgate

BEDFORD
Biddenham
BEDFORDSHIRE
Old Warden   Broom
Houghton
Conquest
Ashwell

Newton
Thriplow
Fowlmere
A505
Heydon
Hinxton
Little Walden

Hundon
A1092

Great Yeldham
A1017

Wendens Ambo

Pegsdon
A1(M)
Cottered
Ardeley

Arkesden
Clavering
M11

ESSEX

Watton-at-Stone

A120
Birchanger
A120
Little
Dunmow
BRAINTREE

Youngs End
A131
Fuller Street

Batford

Hertford
A414
A1060

Frithsden
ST ALBANS
Potters Crouch
HERTFORDSHIRE
HARLOW
A414

Chelmsford
Mill
Green

Sarratt
M25
Stapleford Tawney
Stock

8

4

M1

3

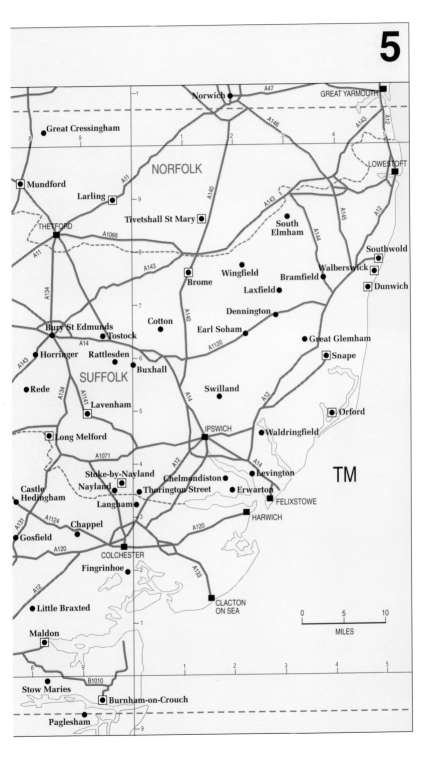

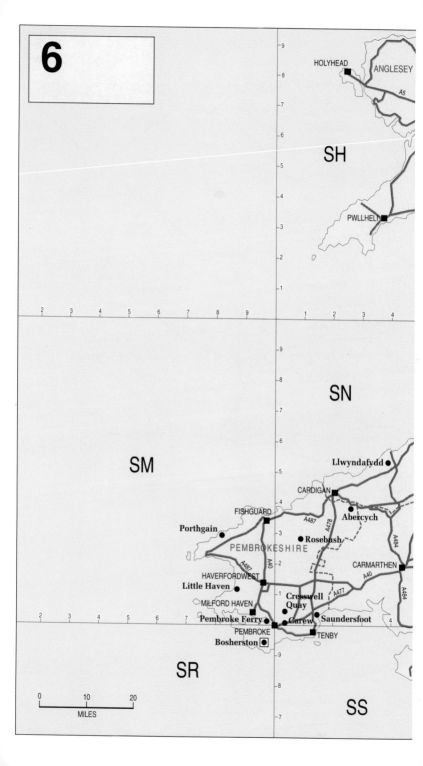

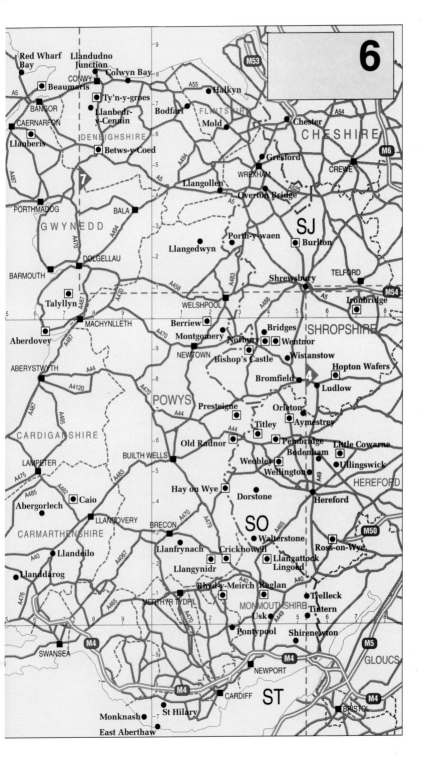

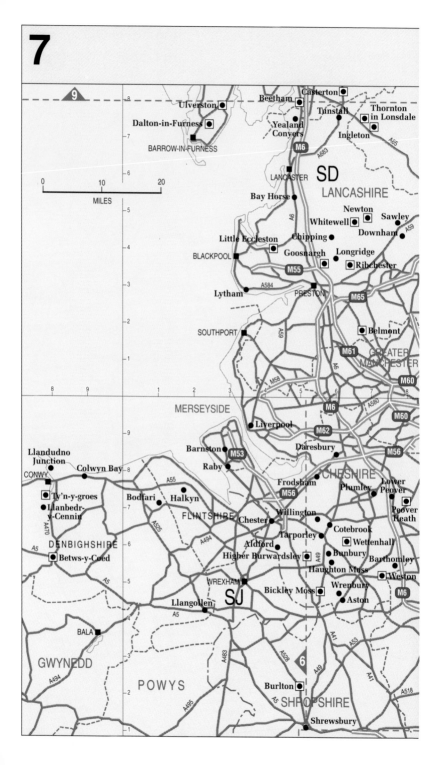

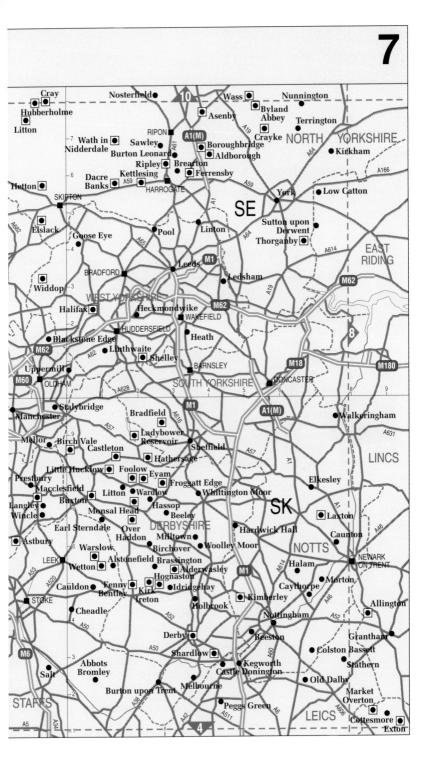

pub popular for good fresh reasonably priced food; helpful staff, picnic-sets outside, pleasant village *(Mr and Mrs N Ward, Gordon Tong)*

KENTISBEARE [ST0606]

Keepers Cottage [not far from M5 junction 28, via A373]: Friendly pub with decent food served with fresh veg, well kept Bass and Otter, good value wines *(Mr and Mrs D Hockley)*

KENTON [SX9583]

Devon Arms [Fore St; A379 Exeter—Dawlish]: Comfortable 16th-c beamed bar with old farm tools, animal photographs and hunting trophies, sound good value food from good filled baguettes and pasties up, well kept Bass, Scattor Rock Teign Valley Tipple and Wadworths 6X, decent wine, friendly helpful service, dining area; small back garden with play area, aviary and caged rabbits; bedrooms with own bathrooms, handy for Powderham Castle *(Dennis Jenkin, Alain and Rose Foote)*

KILMINGTON [SY2698]

New Inn: Old-fashioned pub, originally three cottages, with well kept Palmers IPA, basic food, friendly service, open fire in public bar; large garden with aviaries and guinea pigs *(R T and J C Moggridge)*

Old Inn [A35]: Thatched pub with friendly service and local atmosphere, small character polished-floor front bar (dogs allowed here), back lounge with leather armchairs by inglenook fire, well kept Boddingtons, Flowers IPA, Wadworths 6X and Worthington BB, good value food, small no smoking restaurant, traditional games; children welcome, two gardens *(David Gaunt, Andrea Rampley, LYM)*

KINGSKERSWELL [SX8867]

Hare & Hounds [A386]: Busy extended beamed and timbered food pub with good value fresh food from open kitchen, friendly helpful service, good wheelchair access; good play area *(anon)*

KINGSTEIGNTON [SX8773]

☆ *Old Rydon* [Rydon Rd]: Dining pub with big log fire in small cosy heavy-beamed bar, upper gallery seating, no smoking restaurant with conservatory, food from baked potatoes and toasted muffins to chargrills, children's dishes, well kept Bass, Fullers London Pride and a guest beer such as Greene King Abbot, decent wines; piped music; tables on terrace and in nice sheltered garden *(Pamela and Merlyn Horswell, Mike and Mary Carter, John and Sonja Newberry, Ian Phillips, LYM)*

LAKE [SX5288]

Bearslake [A386 just S of Sourton]: Thatched stone Dartmoor inn with beams, flagstones, inglenook fireplace, pews and plenty of locals in friendly character bar, doing well under newish family, with enjoyable and popular home-made food; picnic-sets in sizeable garden with terrace, six bedrooms *(A McCormick, T Powell)*

LEE [SS4846]

☆ *Grampus* [signed off B3343/A361 W of Ilfracombe]: Attractive and welcoming 14th-c pub short stroll from sea, simple furnishings, wide range of good simple home-made food,

well kept real ales, woodburner, pool in family room, dogs very welcome; two bedrooms, lots of seats in quiet sheltered garden, superb coastal walks *(BB, Lynda and Trevor Smith, Natalie and Chris Sharpe)*

LIFTON [SX3885]

Arundell Arms [Fore St]: Substantial and delightfully run if not cheap fishing hotel in same ownership for many years, rich décor, very agreeable atmosphere, good interesting lunchtime bar food and evening restaurant; can arrange fishing tuition – also shooting, deer-stalking and riding; bedrooms – a pleasant place to stay *(Alain and Rose Foote)*

LUPPITT [ST1606]

Luppitt Inn [back roads N of Honiton]: Unspoilt little basic farmhouse pub, friendly chatty landlady who keeps it open because she (and her cats) like the company; one room with corner bar and a table, another with fireplace and not much else, Otter tapped from the cask, no food or music, lavatories across the yard; a real throwback, may be cl some lunchtimes *(the Didler, JP, PP, RWC)*

LUTTON [SX5959]

Mountain [pub signed off Cornwood—Sparkwell rd]: New owners in simply furnished beamed pub with log fires, some stripped stone, a high-backed settle, well priced traditional food, well kept local ales and farm cider, friendly service, provision for children; seats on verandah and vine-arbour terrace *(LYM, John Poulter, Geoff and Marianne Millin)*

LYDFORD [SX5184]

☆ *Castle Inn* [off A386 Okehampton—Tavistock]: Interestingly furnished and stylishly old-fashioned twin bars, low beams and flagstones, food from sandwiches to steaks inc interesting dishes, friendly generally efficient service (can slow down sometimes), well kept Flowers IPA, Fullers London Pride and Greene King Old Speckled Hen, organic ciders, decent wines, traditional games; children in eating areas, bedrooms, great location by daunting ruined fort and near lovely river gorge, open all day *(Mike Gorton, Ann and Colin Hunt, LYM, Mrs J H S Lang, Simon, Jo and Benjamin Cole, Andrea Rampley, Richard Gibbs, Jacquie and Jim Jones, DAV, Karen and Steve Wilson, Mrs Ursula Hofheinz, James and Hellen Read, Duncan and Lisa Cripps, Dr and Mrs Rod Holcombe, Paul Boot)*

LYMPSTONE [SX9984]

Globe [off A376 N of Exmouth; The Strand]: Roomy dining area with generous food from sandwiches to fresh fish, four real ales, decent house wines, bar with individual local atmosphere – collie dogs, cuckoo clocks and roaring fire; can be smoky; children welcome, some live entertainment, open all day in summer *(LYM, Mrs Jean Clarke, Chris Parsons, Pam Adsley, Ken Flawn)*

☆ *Redwing* [Church Rd]: Friendly two-bar pub well known locally for live music (most wknds, some bank hols, and jazz every Tues); good value well prepared food inc lots of local fish and good puddings, well kept Greene King

Abbot, Palmers and a guest such as Ushers, local farm ciders, good house wines, caring licensees and helpful efficient staff, brightly painted lounge, neat little no smoking dining area with wild flowers, open all day wknds; may be discreet piped music, quiz nights; pretty garden behind (sometimes music here in fine weather), unspoilt village with shore walks *(the Didler, Ken Flawn, Chris Parsons, Michael Rowse, BB)*

LYNMOUTH [SS7249]

☆ *Rising Sun* [Mars Hill, by harbour]: Wonderful position overlooking harbour, good immaculate bedrooms (one very small) in cottagey old thatched terrace stepped up hill; concentration on the upmarket hotel side and the attractive cosy no smoking restaurant (where residents come first), but they have Cotleigh Tawny, Exmoor Gold and Fox and a beer brewed for the pub by Clearview, good limited lunchtime bar food, quick friendly helpful service, and a good fire; may be quiet piped classical music; bedrooms, charming gardens up behind, children may be allowed in eating areas *(C J Fletcher, RB, Tracey and Stephen Groves, Dave Irving, John and Judy Saville, Steve Whalley, George Atkinson, Peter and Audrey Dowsett, LYM, Adam and Tracy Bradbery)*

LYNTON [SS7148]

☆ *Bridge Inn* [B3234 just S]: Good sensibly priced home-made food and decent wines, welcoming new landlady, well kept ales, pleasant straightforward décor, churchy Victorian windows, dining room overlooking West Lyn gorge; glorious coast views from terrace, footbridge to wooded NT walks up to Watersmeet or even the Rockford Inn at Brendon – and there's a lovely short walk from Lynton centre, on the Lynway *(John and Judy Saville, Derek Orgill)*

Hunters [Martinhoe, Heddon's Gate – which is well signed off A39 W of Lynton]: Popular for its glorious Heddon Valley position beside NT information centre, great walks inc one, not too taxing, down to the sea; enjoyable freshly prepared food from soup and baguettes to local seafood (may be a wait when crowded), cheerful young staff, real ale; garden with peacocks *(Theocsbrian, Dr D J and Mrs S C Walker)*

MAIDENCOMBE [SX9268]

☆ *Thatched Tavern* [Steep Hill]: Spotless much extended three-level thatched pub with lovely coastal views, well kept Flowers IPA and Original and a summer guest beer in pubby bar, well priced generous food inc local fish (can be a wait) and tempting puddings in two cosy eating areas, one no smoking, attentive service even when busy, big family room, pleasant restaurant; children allowed, nice garden with small thatched huts (dogs allowed out here but not in pub), small attractive village above small beach *(Geoffrey and Karen Berrill, E G Parish, B and F A Hannam, Alan Garnett)*

MALBOROUGH [SX7039]

Old Inn [Higher Town; just off A381

Kingsbridge—Salcombe]: Good atmosphere in big rather modern-feeling open-plan dining pub, wide choice of food inc fresh fish, quick friendly service, Adnams Broadside and Charles Wells Bombardier, good house wine, pleasant children's room; lovely village *(Mr and Mrs C R Little)*

MANATON [SX7580]

Kestor: Welcoming modern Dartmoor-edge inn in splendid spot nr Becky Falls, attractive dining room with good blackboard range of food inc adventurous children's menu, friendly Yorkshire landlord, good mix of locals and visitors, well kept real ales, farm cider, open fire; piped music; attractive bedrooms *(Joan York, Chris Parsons)*

MARY TAVY [SX5079]

Royal Standard [A386]: Spotlessly comfortable traditional pub with lounge at one end and bar at the other, good choice of well kept ales inc Otter, good generous home-made food inc popular steak nights, friendly attentive staff and locals, open fire; dogs welcome, open all day wknds *(Ifor John Mason)*

MERRIVALE [SX5475]

☆ *Dartmoor Inn* [B3357, 4 miles E of Tavistock]: Well run and sensitively refurbished pub in tranquil spot with high Dartmoor views; generous lunchtime food from sandwiches and good ploughman's up, well kept ales inc Bass and one labelled for the pub, good choice of country wines, water from their 36-metre (120-ft) deep well, open fire, tables outside – very popular summer evenings; good walks, nr bronze-age hut circles, stone rows and pretty river *(David M Cundy, DAV)*

MILTONCOMBE [SX4865]

☆ *Who'd A Thought It* [village signed off A386 S of Yelverton]: Attractive 16th-c black-panelled bar with interesting bric-a-brac, woodburner, barrel seats and high-backed winged settles, separate lounge and dining conservatory, newish licensees doing wider choice of food, friendly staff, well kept real ales and reasonably priced wines; quiet piped music; children welcome, well planted garden with water feature (flaming torches may light your way from the car park on summer nights), more tables out in front; folk club Sun *(LYM, Dr and Mrs Rod Holcombe)*

MONKLEIGH [SS4520]

Bell: Relaxed partly thatched village local with good Civil War pictures by local artist (prints for sale), log fire, well kept Barum Original and XTC, Thatcher's farm cider, bargain down-to-earth home-made food inc some interesting variations, friendly licensees and staff, children and dogs welcome – friendly boxer called Tasha; Fri music night; attached shop with organic meats and local food, pleasant garden, good walks, low-priced bedrooms, open all day *(James Davies, Kevin Beer)*

MORCHARD BISHOP [SS7707]

London [signed off A377 Crediton—Barnstaple]: Open-plan low-beamed 16th-c coaching inn in picturesque village position, big carpeted red plush bar with woodburner in large fireplace, huge helpings of good simple home-made food in bar or small dining room, friendly engaging service, real ales inc Fullers London Pride and Sharps Doom Bar, pool, darts and skittles *(Peter Craske, M and D Toms)*

MORTEHOE [SS4545]

Chichester Arms [off A361 Ilfracombe—Braunton]: Lots of old village prints in busy plush and leatherette panelled lounge and comfortable no smoking dining room, wide choice of good value generous food (not Sun night or Mon/Tues, at least in winter) cooked by landlord inc local fish and meat and good veg and puddings (loudspeaker announcements), well kept ales such as Greene King Old Speckled Hen and local Barum Original, reasonably priced wine, speedy service even on crowded evenings; pubby locals' bar with darts and pool, no piped music; skittle alley and games machines in summer children's room, tables out in front and in small garden, good walks *(Joyce and Maurice Cottrell, Paul and Ursula Randall)*

☆ *Ship Aground* [signed off A361 Ilfracombe—Braunton]: Welcoming open-plan village pub with big family room, three well kept ales inc Cotleigh, Hancock's cider in summer, decent wine, good choice of inexpensive bar food from good crab sandwiches up, big log fires, friendly service; massive rustic furnishings, interesting nautical brassware, pool, skittles and other games; tables on sheltered sunny terrace with good views, by interesting church, wonderful walking on nearby coast footpath *(LYM, Dr and Mrs P Truelove)*

NEWTON ABBOT [SX8571]

Dartmouth [East St]: Relaxing three-room pub with good choice of well kept ales from the area's small breweries, farm cider, log fires, enjoyable food; children welcome till 7, tables and barbecues in nice outside area *(the Didler)*

Golden Lion [Market St]: Friendly and ancient, with good choice of real ales, many tapped from the cask, decent choice of bar food, pleasant atmosphere *(Joe Green)*

Jolly Abbot [East St]: Olde-worlde, with beams, friendly staff and cheerful customers, wide choice of good value home-made food, well kept ales inc guests *(Ken Flawn)*

☆ *Olde Cider Bar* [East St]: Casks of eight interesting low-priced farm ciders and a couple of perries, with more in bottles, in unusual basic cider house, no-nonsense dark stools, barrel seats and wall benches, flagstones and bare boards, pre-war-style décor; good country wines, baguettes, heated pies and venison pasties etc, very low prices; small games room with machines *(JP, PP, the Didler, Joe Green)*

NEWTON FERRERS [SX5447]

☆ *Dolphin* [Riverside Rd E]: Friendly 18th-c pub nicely refurbished with slate floors, good food now from sandwiches up, well kept Bass, Sharps Doom Bar and a Sharps brew for the pub, good service even when crowded, back family room, darts, upstairs restaurant; two terraces across road overlooking yachting harbour, lovely village *(Esther and*

John Sprinkle, Ann and Bob Westbrook, Vivian Stevenson)

NEWTON ST CYRES [SX8798]

☆ *Beer Engine* [off A377 towards Thorverton]: Friendly helpful licensees in cheerful and roomy pub brewing its own good beers, with good home-made bar food, no smoking eating area welcoming children, traditional games; large sunny garden, popular summer barbecues, open all day *(John and Bryony Coles, Gene and Kitty Rankin, Jane and Adrian Tierney-Jones, Dr B and Mrs P B Baker, LYM)*

NEWTON TRACEY [SS5226]

Hunters [B3232 Barnstaple—Torrington]: Extended 15th-c pub with good conventional home-made food inc huge puddings and children's dishes, massive low beams and log fire, four well kept ales inc guests, decent wines and malt whiskies, good friendly service, evening restaurant, themed menu nights; skittle alley/games room, juke box (may be loud) and machines; tables on small terrace behind, play area, usually open all day in summer *(B and F A Hannam, Peter Bakker, Colin Baker, E B Ireland, BB)*

NORTH BOVEY [SX7483]

☆ *Ring of Bells* [off A382/B3212 SW of Moretonhampstead]: Attractive bulgy-walled 13th-c thatched inn, low-ceilinged bar with well kept real ales inc Butcombe, Gray's farm cider and good log fire, enjoyable freshly made bar food inc good ploughman's and notable treacle tart, restaurant, longer more functional room with pool and TV; seats out by lovely tree-covered village green below Dartmoor, good walks from the door, big bedrooms with four-posters *(LYM, Clare West, Mark Percy, Lesley Mayoh)*

NOSS MAYO [SX5447]

Swan [off B3186 at Junket Corner]: Small unpretentious two-room local with lovely waterside views, simple food inc plenty of low-priced fresh fish, well kept Bass and a beer brewed for the pub, old beams, open fire; can get crowded, with difficult parking; dogs on leads and children welcome, tables outside *(Esther and John Sprinkle)*

OAKFORD [SS9121]

Red Lion: 17th-c country coaching inn, partly rebuilt in Georgian times, with large attractive open-plan bar, big fireplace, collection of cigarette cards, rifles, swords, irons, attractively priced food inc steaks and seafood, real ales such as Adnams and Youngs, popular no smoking restaurant areas *(Andy and Jill Kassube)*

OKEHAMPTON [SX5895]

Plymouth [West St]: Pretty pub with friendly helpful landlord and staff, local-feel bar with surprisingly enterprising food at very reasonable prices, well kept real ales from far and wide tapped from the cask (May and Nov beer festivals), no smoking area, provision for children; open all day wknds *(Dr and Mrs A K Clarke, Mr and Mrs M Saunders)*

White Hart [Fore St]: Rambling pub/hotel (quite a few steps) with St Austell Tinners, good value bar food, pleasant atmosphere; clean and comfortable bedrooms, old-fashioned plumbing *(Ron and Sheila Corbett)*

OTTERTON [SY0885]

Kings Arms [Fore St]: Extended open-plan family dining pub in charming village by Ladram Bay, good value quick food inc proper sandwiches and children's helpings, well kept Flowers IPA and Otter, friendly service, TV and darts in lounge; dogs welcome, good skittle alley doubling as family room; bedrooms, beautiful evening view from picnic-sets in good-sized attractive back garden with play area *(Dennis Jenkin)*

OTTERY ST MARY [SY0995]

London [Gold St]: Cosy rambling village pub, beams, timbers and brasses, reasonably priced food from sandwiches and baked potatoes to mixed grill, Butcombe and Otter; large back terrace, bedrooms *(John Beeken)*

PAIGNTON [SX8960]

☆ *Inn on the Green* [Esplanade Rd]: Big brightly comfortable unpubby bar open all day, useful lunchtime for enormous choice of popular keenly priced quick food, well kept real ales, good soft and hot drinks, cheerful service; out-of-the-way family room, live music and dancing nightly, restaurant, big terrace looking out over green to sea *(LYM, Mr and Mrs Colin Roberts)*

Isaac Merritt [Torquay Rd]: Spacious efficiently run open-plan Wetherspoons conversion of former shopping arcade, worth knowing for its low-priced food and drink all day; no music, no smoking area *(Pamela and Merlyn Horswell)*

Ship [Manor Rd, Preston]: Large yet homely mock-Tudor pub with comfortable furnishings inc leather settees, soft lighting, well kept Wadworths 6X from very long bar, enjoyable generous low-priced food easily adaptable to children (dining areas on three floors), quick cheerful service; children welcome, a minute's walk from Preston beach *(Mr and Mrs Colin Roberts)*

Spinning Wheel [Esplanade Rd]: Beamed pub, great out of season with cosy corners and open fires (may be busy with young people in summer); welcoming service, well kept beers, wide choice of bar food *(Colin Gooch)*

PARRACOMBE [SS6644]

☆ *Fox & Goose* [off A39 Blackmoor Gate—Lynton]: Rambling attractively relaxed and informal pub with wide range of good freshly made food from sandwiches through their prized steak and seaweed pie to Exmoor lamb and venison or local fish, well kept local ales such as Cotleigh Barn Owl, local farm cider, decent wines; children welcome *(Paul and Ursula Randall, Annette Tress, Gary Smith, Stan Edwards, David Gibbs)*

PETROCKSTOWE [SS5109]

Laurels [signed off A386 N of Hatherleigh]: Hospitable and well run former coaching inn with good generous freshly made food, well kept real ales such as Sharps and Skinners *(R J Walden)*

PLYMOUTH [SX4755]

☆ *China House* [Sutton Harbour, via Sutton Rd off Exeter St (A374)]: Attractively reworked Vintage Inns conversion of Plymouth's oldest warehouse, super views day and night over harbour and Barbican, great beams and flagstones, bare slate and stone walls, good log fire, great choice of wines by the glass, well kept Bass and Tetleys, food all day from ciabattas and filled baguettes up, well organised welcoming service; piped music; good parking and disabled access and facilities, open all day *(R T and J C Moggridge, LYM, Pamela and Merlyn Horswell)*

Dolphin [Barbican]: Well used lively and unspoilt local, good range of beers inc particularly well kept Bass and Worthington Dark tapped from the cask, coal fire; colourful green and orange décor, Beryl Cook paintings inc one of the friendly landlord; open all day *(John Poulter, JP, PP, David Crook, the Didler)*

Lounge [Stopford Pl, Stoke]: Unspoilt open-plan backstreet pub, Bass and a guest beer from oak-panelled counter, popular lunchtime food, friendly landlord *(the Didler, JP, PP)*

Queens Arms [Southside St, Barbican]: Small cosily Victorian local, spotless and smartly decorated, with comfortable banquettes, well kept Bass, excellent sandwiches inc fresh crab from efficient servery, good friendly staff *(Steve Whalley, Caroline and Michael Abbey)*

Rising Sun [Eggbuckland Rd, Higher Compton]: Well run traditional local, plenty of character, well kept beer inc two or three guests, warm friendly atmosphere, usual food lunchtime and evening *(Martyn Scott)*

Thistle Park [Commercial Rd]: Welcoming pub nr National Maritime Aquarium, good range of well kept beers inc some from next-door Sutton brewery, tasty straightforward food all day, friendly landlady, interesting décor, children welcome; open all day, live music wknds *(the Didler, JP, PP)*

PORTGATE [SX4185]

☆ *Harris Arms* [Launceston Rd (old A30)]: Warmly friendly, bright and comfortable, good food inc superb South Devon steaks and mixed grill, well kept Bass and guest ales such as Sharps Doom Bar, good informal service, prompt and accommodating; wonderful view from dining room *(DAV)*

POSTBRIDGE [SX6579]

☆ *East Dart* [B3212]: Central Dartmoor hotel by pretty river, in same family since 1861; roomy and comfortable open-plan bar with promptly served enjoyable food from large crisp baguettes up, well kept real ale, good wines by the glass, good fire, hunting murals and horse tack, pool room; children welcome, tables out in front and behind, bedrooms, some 30 miles of fishing *(Dennis Jenkin, Di and Mike Gillam, BB, David M Cundy, Nigel Long)*

POUNDSGATE [SX7072]

Tavistock Inn [B3357 continuation]: 13th-c Dartmoor-edge village local with narrow-stepped granite spiral staircase, original flagstones, ancient fireplaces and beams, well kept real ales inc Wadworths 6X, local farm cider, bar food from baguettes up, pub games, family room; tables in quiet back garden, lovely scenery *(LYM, DAV)*

PRINCETOWN [SX5973]

☆ *Plume of Feathers* [Plymouth Hill]: Much-extended local doubling as hikers' pub, cheerful, welcoming and individual, with good value generous food inc good pasties, quick cheerful service even with crowds, well kept ales inc Princetown Jail, good house wines, two log fires, solid slate tables, live music Fri night, Sun lunchtime; big family room with a real welcome for children, play area outside; good value bedrooms, also bunkhouse and camping; open all day *(Joyce and Maurice Cottrell, David and Nina Pugsley)*

PUSEHILL [SS4228]

☆ *Pig on the Hill* [off B3226 nr Westward Ho!]: Family holiday dining pub on farm, with its own good Country Life Bumpkin, Old Appledore, Wallop and other ales; small bar, extensive seating in raised gallery and adjacent room through archways, pig decorations, reasonably priced food from baked potatoes up, games room with table footer and skittle alley; good views, huge playground, small wildlife collection in extensive grounds, small swimming pool, boules *(Andy and Jill Kassube, Tony and Mary Pygott)*

RACKENFORD [SS8518]

Stag [pub signed off A361 NW of Tiverton]: 13th-c low-beamed thatched pub interesting for its ancient layout, with the original flagstoned and cobbled entry passage between massive walls, and a huge fireplace flanked by ancient settles; well kept Cotleigh Tawny and local guest beers, farm cider, cottagey dining room (children allowed), simple bedrooms *(June and Robin Savage, LYM, JP, PP)*

RINGMORE [SX6545]

☆ *Journeys End* [signed off B3392 at Pickwick Inn, St Anns Chapel, nr Bigbury; best to park up opp church]: Old village inn with character panelled lounge, well kept changing ales, some tapped from casks in back room, local farm cider, log fires; varied interesting food inc good fresh fish (lunchtime menu may be limited, but helpful about special diets), friendly locals and staff, pleasant big terraced garden, sunny back add-on family dining conservatory; may be piped radio; attractive setting nr thatched cottages, not far from the sea; bedrooms antique but comfortable and well equipped *(Nick Lawless, JP, PP, the Didler, LYM)*

SALCOMBE [SX7338]

☆ *Fortescue* [Union St, end of Fore St]: Sizeable but homely, popular and welcoming, nautical theme in five interlinked rooms, lots of old local black and white shipping pictures, well kept changing beers such as Banks's, Bass and Courage Directors, decent wines, enjoyable promptly served food inc hot pork rolls, reasonable prices, pleasant service, good woodburner, restaurant, big public bar with pool, darts etc, no piped music; children welcome, picnic-sets in courtyard *(Angus Lyon, Geoff Calcott, Comus and Sarah Elliott, Keith Stevens, Ann and Bob Westbrook, Peter Salmon)*

Victoria [Fore St]: Smartly attractive and tidy yet unpretentious, with bare-boards bar, comfortable lounge, well kept St Austell Tinners and Dartmoor Best, good coffee, generous bar food, cosy stone-walled dining room downstairs; may be unobtrusive piped music, segregated children's room; bedrooms, large sheltered terrace garden behind *(Comus and Sarah Elliott, Dr and Mrs M E Wilson, Pete and Jo Cole)*

SAMPFORD COURTENAY [SS6300]

New Inn [B3072 Crediton—Holsworthy]: Attractive 16th-c thatched pub with hospitable new landlord, good food, well kept Otter, pleasant décor in low-beamed open-plan bar, open fires; nice garden with play area *(R J Walden)*

SANDY GATE [SX9690]

Blue Ball [handy for M5 junction 30; 1st right off A376, towards Topsham]: Dining pub with good rather upmarket food (even the baked potatoes never see a microwave), good helpings, beams, old wood and tile floors, lovely settles, well kept Bass and well priced wine, no smoking section, friendly attentive young staff, nice village atmosphere; good gardens inc good play area *(John and Vivienne Rice, Barry Steele-Perkins)*

SANDY PARK [SX7087]

☆ *Sandy Park Inn* [A382 S of Whiddon Down]: Thatched country local with old-fashioned small bar, stripped pine tables, built-in high-backed wall seats, big black iron fireplace, good food with copious veg here or in small cosy dining room (children allowed there), friendly staff, well kept ales such as Blackawton and Otter, decent wines and farm cider; simple clean bedrooms *(LYM, Mark Percy, Lesley Mayoh, Len Banister)*

SCORRITON [SX7069]

Tradesmans Arms: Good-sized Dartmoor-edge open-plan pub in attractive countryside, welcoming licensees, enjoyable carefully prepared food inc some interesting dishes, real ales, farm cider, open fire, snug one end, big children's room; bedrooms *(J Sumner)*

SHALDON [SX9372]

Ferryboat [Fore St]: Cosy and quaint little waterside local, basic but comfortable, long low-ceilinged bar overlooking estuary with Teignmouth ferry and lots of boats, helpful staff, Dartmoor, Greene King IPA and Old Speckled Hen, interesting wines, big helpings of good value varied home-made food, open fires, seafaring artefacts; tables on small sunny terrace across narrow road by sandy beach *(Ken Flawn)*

London [The Green]: Friendly new landlord in pleasant village pub, enjoyable food, well kept Greene King Abbot, decent wines; children welcome, good value bedrooms with wholesome breakfast, pretty waterside village *(Ken Flawn, J D O Carter, Simon Harris)*

Shipwrights Arms [B3195 to Newton Abbot]: Friendly village pub under new landlady, new chef doing good food, obliging service, well kept ales, real character; pleasant river views from back garden *(LYM, J D O Carter)*

SHEEPWASH [SS4806]

☆ *Half Moon* [off A3072 Holsworthy— Hatherleigh]: A good place for fishermen, with 10 miles of private fishing on the River Torridge (salmon, sea trout and brown trout), rod and drying rooms and fishing supplies; big log fire in beamed bar, good sandwiches and other simple lunchtime snacks, well kept Courage Best, Greene King Ruddles County and a guest beer, fine choice of malt whiskies, evening restaurant, extensive wine list, games room; children in eating areas, comfortable annexe bedrooms *(LYM, Richard Pierce)*

SIDMOUTH [SY1287]

☆ *Old Ship* [Old Fore St]: Partly 14th-c, with low beams, mellow black woodwork and panelling, sailing ship prints, good inexpensive food from huge crab sandwiches to local fish, well kept Flowers Original, Wadworths 6X and a guest beer, prompt courteous service even when busy, friendly atmosphere; close-set tables but roomier raftered upstairs bar with family room, dogs allowed; in pedestrian zone just moments from the sea (note that around here parking is limited to 30 mins) *(Barry Smith, BB, Ann and Bob Westbrook, Meg and Colin Hamilton)*

SILVERTON [SS9502]

☆ *Three Tuns* [Exeter Rd]: Wide choice of appetising and sensibly priced food inc fine vegetarian dishes in 17th-c or older inn's attractively old-fashioned beamed bars or cosy restaurant (where children welcome), comfortable settees and period furniture, efficient friendly staff, well kept ales inc local ones; tables in pretty inner courtyard, handy for Killerton

(Tim and Ann Newell, Michael Rowse)

SLAPTON [SX8245]

Queens Arms: Old village local, modernised but friendly and welcoming, with snug comfortable corners, good value straightforward food, well kept Bass, Exmoor and Palmers, interesting World War II pictures; lovely suntrap back garden with plenty of tables *(Angus Lyon)*

SMALLRIDGE [ST3000]

☆ *Ridgeway* [signed off A358 N of Axminster]: Friendly local with charming décor, fresh flowers, comfortable seating, good value food inc good fish range prepared to order (so may be a wait), well kept Otter, nice choice of wines, attentive service, open fire, family atmosphere; pleasant quiet terrace and garden, lovely spot *(John and Ann Colling, R T and J C Moggridge)*

SOUTH BRENT [SX6958]

Woodpecker [A38]: Pleasant décor, booth tables, no smoking area, very wide choice of enjoyable good value food (should book in season), Bass and Blackawton 44, reasonably priced wines *(Dudley and Moira Cockroft)*

SOUTH POOL [SX7740]

☆ *Millbrook* [off A379 E of Kingsbridge]: Charming little streamside pub with two attractive compact bars and new dining area, tasty good value food from sandwiches up, well kept Bass, Fullers London Pride,

Wadworths 6X and a changing guest beer, local farm cider; children in eating area/family room, covered seating and heaters for front courtyard and waterside terrace, new bedrooms *(Claire Nielsen, B J Harding, Roger Wain-Heapy, LYM, David and Heather Stephenson, Nick Lawless, Mr and Mrs J Curtis, Jack Clark, Jill Hummerstone)*

SOUTH TAWTON [SX6594]

☆ *Seven Stars* [off A30 at Whiddon Down or Okehampton, then signed from Sticklepath]: Unpretentious beamed local in attractive village, remarkable range of food from baguettes to ostrich and perhaps even crocodile, great puddings, welcoming caring licensees, well kept Otter and Sharps Doom Bar, decent wines, fires in cosy bar and large square no smoking restaurant; children welcome, bedrooms *(LYM, Keith and Sally Jackson)*

SPARKWELL [SX5857]

Treby Arms: Warmly olde-worlde atmosphere, very wide choice of good value food with some enterprising specials, friendly helpful service, good range of beers inc unusual guests and one brewed locally for the pub, decent house wines, small dining room; disabled facilities, nearby wildlife park *(John Evans)*

STOKEINTEIGNHEAD [SX9170]

☆ *Church House* [signed from Combeinteignhead, or off A379 N of Torquay]: 13th-c pub with thatch, heavy beams, inglenook fireplace, antique furnishings, ancient spiral stairs and relaxed, informal atmosphere, some emphasis on food from good sandwiches up, well kept Adnams, Bass, and Greene King Abbot or Otter Ale, farm cider, good coffee, obliging staff, no smoking dining room, simple public bar with traditional games and TV; quiet piped music; children in eating area, neat interestingly planted back garden, unspoilt village *(Pamela and Merlyn Horswell, M G Hart, LYM, Comus and Sarah Elliott)*

STOKENHAM [SX8042]

☆ *Church House* [opp church, N of A379 towards Torcross]: Comfortable open-plan pub, enjoyable food from proper generous sandwiches and filled baked potatoes to fresh local seafood and good steaks, real ales inc Bass and Flowers Original, farm cider, hard-working long-serving landlord, no smoking dining room; unobtrusive piped music; attractive garden with enjoyably individual play area and fishpond *(Comus and Sarah Elliott, LYM, C A Hall, Lynn Sharpless, Mr and Mrs M Dalby)*

☆ *Tradesmans Arms* [just off A379 Dartmouth— Kingsbridge]: Charming upmarket 15th-c thatched dining pub with very good inventive cooking by landlord, esp local game and fish, nice antique tables in neat just-so beamed bar and no smoking dining room, well kept Adnams and a more local guest beer, local farm cider, well chosen wines; some garden tables; cl lunchtimes and Sun evening, but open Sun lunchtime (only time children allowed) *(Tracey and Stephen Groves, Roger Wain-*

Heapy, Rev E D Coombes, Mr and
Mrs J Curtis, Pete and Jo Cole, Nick Lawless,
C A Hall, LYM, Paul Boot)
STRETE [SX8446]
Kings Arms: Pleasant service, new chef doing
good choice of really good food esp fresh fish,
more elaborate dishes (Weds-Sat evenings) in
sea-view restaurant *(Susan Pinney)*
TEDBURN ST MARY [SX8193]
Kings Arms [off A30 W of Exeter]: Picturesque
traditional pub, open-plan but comfortable,
with heavy-beamed and panelled L-shaped bar,
lantern lighting and snug stable-style alcoves,
big log fire, lots of brass and hunting prints,
well kept Bass, Sharps Doom Bar and St
Austell Bodmin Boar, local farm cider, friendly
service, end games area, sparkling Christmas
decorations, food from good sandwiches and
baguettes up, modern restaurant; may be piped
pop music; children in eating area, tables on
back terrace, bedrooms *(Alan Wilson,
Gloria Bax, LYM, John Beeken, John and
Vivienne Rice)*
TEIGNMOUTH [SX9372]
Molloys [Teign St]: Town drinking pub
notable for its short choice of good cheap food
inc bargain steaks; no credit cards *(Ken Flawn)*
THELBRIDGE CROSS [SS7912]
Thelbridge Cross Inn [B3042 W of Tiverton]:
Welcoming lounge bar with log fire and plush
settees, good generous food inc some unusual
dishes in extensive dining area and separate
restaurant, friendly helpful service, particularly
well kept Bass and Butcombe, good drinks
prices; reasonable disabled access, bedrooms
smallish but good breakfast *(Mr and
Mrs A Forgie, BB, John Evans)*
TINHAY [SX3985]
Fox & Grapes: Traditional tavern in same
family for generations, beer and farm cider
tapped from the cask, very old-fashioned till;
line dancing Weds, may be cl wkdy lunchtimes
(DAV)
TIPTON ST JOHN [SY0991]
☆ *Golden Lion* [signed off B3176 Sidmouth—
Ottery St Mary]: Enjoyable food from baked
potatoes and ploughman's to good fish and
some interesting dishes, well kept Bass, Greene
King Old Speckled Hen, Otter and Wadworths
6X, roaring log fire, attractive décor and mix
of furnishings, no smoking restaurant; piped
music; children in eating areas, open all day
wknds, seats out on terrace and in garden, two
comfortable bedrooms with showers
*(Barry Smith, Mark Clezy, LYM, Dr and
Mrs M E Wilson)*
TIVERTON [SS9512]
White Ball [Bridge St]: Typical Wetherspoons
with choice of well kept real ales and enjoyable
food inc special offers; large floodlit well
(Andy and Jill Kassube)
TOPSHAM [SX9688]
☆ *Globe* [Fore St; 2 miles from M5 junction 30]:
Substantial traditional inn dating from 16th c,
good solid furnishings in heavy-beamed bow-
windowed bar, good interesting home-cooked
food at reasonable prices, well kept Bass,
Hancocks HB and Sharps Doom Bar, decent

reasonably priced wine, prompt friendly
service, plenty of locals, log-effect gas fire, snug
little dining lounge, good value separate
restaurant, back extension; children in eating
area, open all day, good value attractive
bedrooms *(D J Hulse, LYM, Barry Steele-
Perkins, the Didler, Dr and Mrs M E Wilson)*
☆ *Lighter* [Fore St]: Spacious and comfortable
(with further extension and major
refurbishment in hand), panelling and tall
windows looking out over tidal flats, more
intimate side room, nautical décor, welcoming
efficient staff, well kept Badger Best and
Tanglefoot, food from good sandwiches to
mildly upmarket dishes inc local fish, central
log fire, good children's area; games machines,
piped music; tables out in lovely spot on old
quay, handy for big antiques centre
*(Dr and Mrs M E Wilson, Minda and Stanley
Alexander, E G Parish, Hugh Roberts,
P R and S A White, the Didler, Pam Adsley,
R J Walden, Andy Millward, Dr and
Mrs A K Clarke, BB, Comus and Sarah Elliott)*
Lord Nelson [High St]: Lots of sea prints and
nautical memorabilia inc sails over big dining
area, smaller side one up steps (both no
smoking), wide choice of reasonably priced bar
meals, Bass and Flowers Original, good service;
may be piped music; useful car park
(the Didler)
☆ *Passage House* [Ferry Rd, off main street]:
Attractive foody pub with good fresh fish
choice, other dishes from sandwiches up, well
kept Bass, Greene King IPA, Otter and
Wadworths 6X, good wines, traditional black-
beamed bar and no smoking slate-floored
lower dining area (children welcome here),
quiet terrace looking over river moorings
(lovely at sunset); may be piped music; open all
day wknds and summer *(LYM, Ian Phillips,
the Didler, Comus and Sarah Elliott, Tony
Middis, Dr and Mrs M E Wilson, Howard and
Margaret Buchanan, Ann and Bob Westbrook,
Andy and Yvonne Cunningham, Hugh
Roberts, P R and S A White, Richard and
Margaret Peers, D J Hulse, David Crook,
Mike and Wendy Proctor)*
Steam Packet [Monmouth Hill]: Well priced
bar food, several well kept ales, dark
flagstones, scrubbed boards, panelling, stripped
masonry, a lighter dining room; on boat-
builders' quay *(the Didler, LYM)*
TORBRYAN [SX8266]
☆ *Old Church House* [most easily reached from
A381 Newton Abbot—Totnes via Ipplepen]:
New owners doing wide choice of enjoyable
food in early 15th-c inn by part-Saxon church,
quaint bar on right with benches built into
Tudor panelling, high-backed settle and big log
fire, also rambling series of comfortable and
discreetly lit lounges, one with a splendid
inglenook fireplace, well kept real ales;
children welcome, well equipped character
bedrooms *(John and Glenys Wheeler,
M J Caley, LYM)*
TORQUAY [SX9175]
Crown & Sceptre [Petitor Rd, St Marychurch]:
Friendly two-bar local in 18th-c stone-built

coaching inn, eight real ales inc guests, bar food, interesting naval memorabilia and chamber-pot collection, good-humoured landlord, jazz Tues and Sun, folk first Thurs of month, bands Sat *(the Didler, JP, PP)*

Willow Tree [Condor Way, The Willows]: Comfortable modern chain dining pub in residential area, enjoyable generous food, good friendly service; children welcome, play area *(Mr and Mrs Colin Roberts)*

TORRINGTON [SS4919]

☆ *Black Horse* [High St]: Pretty twin-gabled inn dating from 15th c, overhanging upper storeys, beams hung with stirrups, solid furniture, oak bar counter, no smoking lounge with striking ancient black oak partition wall and a couple of attractive oak seats, oak-panelled restaurant with aquarium, good value generous straightforward food inc OAP wkdy lunchtime bargains, friendly service, well kept Courage Best and Directors, John Smiths and changing guest beers, darts, shove-ha'penny, cribbage, dominoes; well reproduced piped music, friendly cat and dogs; open all day Sat (may close slightly over-promptly other days), handy for RHS Rosemoor garden and Dartington Crystal *(LYM, Gordon Tong, D and S Price, Dr and Mrs M E Wilson)*

TOTNES [SX8060]

King William IV [Fore St]: Warm, spacious and comfortably carpeted Victorian pub, popular (esp with older people) for appealingly priced home-made food from sandwiches to bargain steak and huge mixed grill; Boddingtons, Flowers, Tetleys and Worthington, friendly service; bedrooms with own bathrooms *(Neil and Beverley Gardner, Mr and Mrs Colin Roberts)*

☆ *Kingsbridge Inn* [Leechwell Street]: Attractive and hospitable rambling bar, neat and tidy, with black beams, timbering and some stripped stone, combines well with eating areas inc small no smoking upper part (children allowed here); two log fires, plush seats, good home-made food (not Mon lunchtime) from lunchtime sandwiches, baguettes and baked potatoes to some unusual hot dishes, well kept Bass, Greene King Abbot, Sharps Doom Bar and Theakstons Old Peculier, friendly service, pleasant relaxed atmosphere; may be piped music; children in eating area, some live music and readings *(LYM, David M Cundy, DAV, Mr and Mrs N Ward, John Wilson, Adrian and Ione Lee)*

Smugglers [Steamer Quay Rd]: Comfortable air-conditioned big shining pub divided into various eating areas, huge choice of good value food (small helpings available), friendly well trained staff, well kept beer, decent wine, big family room *(Mrs E Mutum, Joyce and Maurice Cottrell)*

Steam Packet [St Peters Quay, on W bank (ie not on Steam Packet Quay!)]: Well refurbished and welcoming, staff cheerful and efficient even when it's crowded, enjoyable food from tasty lunchtime crab and other sandwiches up, half a dozen real ales inc two guests, good wines and coffee, log fire, restaurant with

spectacular river view from no smoking conservatory; children welcome (books and games for them in leather-seated side area), jazz Sun lunchtime, winter quiz night Mon; tables outside, bedrooms, open all day *(J G S Widdicombe, Dr and Mrs M E Wilson, Joyce and Maurice Cottrell)*

TUCKENHAY [SX8156]

☆ *Maltsters Arms* [Ashprington road out of Totnes (signed left off A381 on outskirts)]: Lovely spot by a peaceful wooded creek with tables out by the water, simple up-to-date décor inside, well kept Princetown Dartmoor IPA and up to three changing guest beers, lots of good wines by the glass and other good drinks, traditional games, dogs welcome in bar; food inc good interesting dishes and thoughtful things for children, but can be on the pricy side for what you get (and a no smoking area would be appreciated), service generally friendly and helpful; children in eating areas, bedrooms (there may be a minimum wknd stay of two nights), open all day *(Mike Gorton, Rebecca Nicholls, Norman and Sheila Davies, John Evans, John and Vivienne Rice, Lynda and Trevor Smith, J M Law, Suzanne Stacey, Richard and Margaret Peers, the Didler, LYM, Joan Thorpe, Comus and Sarah Elliott, Tracey and Stephen Groves, Simon, Jo and Benjamin Cole, JP, PP, Andrew Pearson, Barry and Anne)*

TURNCHAPEL [SX4952]

☆ *Boringdon Arms* [off A379 via Plymstock and Hooe; Boringdon Terr]: Cheerful 18th-c pub at foot of cliffs and built back into them, several well kept ales, farm cider, good value freshly made food all day esp curries and pies, roaring log fire in massive fireplace, RN, RM and other nautical memorabilia, shelves of bottled beers; monthly beer festivals, Sat folk nights; dogs welcome, tables outside, shortish water-taxi ride from central Plymouth; open all day, cheap bedrooms *(the Didler, JP, PP)*

UGBOROUGH [SX6755]

Anchor [off A3121]: Village pub with log fire in unpretentious beamed bar, well kept Bass, Shepherd Neame Spitfire and Suttons XSB, partly no smoking restaurant, small outside seating area; children welcome, bedrooms, open all day wknds *(Trevor Owen, Esther and John Sprinkle, Laura Wilson, David M Cundy, John and Joan Calvert, Alan and Paula McCully, LYM)*

Ship [off A3121 SE of Ivybridge]: Popular open-plan dining pub extended from cosy 16th-c flagstoned core, bright smartish bar, wide choice of enjoyable home-made food, efficient service, well kept Bass and Butcombe; tables outside *(Esther and John Sprinkle, Virginia Walker, John Braine-Hartnell)*

UMBERLEIGH [SS6023]

☆ *Rising Sun* [A377 S of Barnstaple]: Welcoming new owners in comfortable and civilised fishing inn with five River Taw salmon and sea trout beats, lots of stuffed fish and fishing memorabilia in pleasant partly no smoking divided bar with woodburner and flagstones; good food inc lunchtime sandwiches, well kept real ales inc local brews, good wines by the glass and farm cider; children in eating areas, tables outside, good bedrooms *(Mrs P Burvill, LYM, David Gibbs)*

WEMBURY [SX5349]

Odd Wheel [Knighton Hill]: Village pub with largely home-made food from sandwiches to fresh fish in big plush lounge, real ales inc Courage, Princetown, Sutton and guest beers tapped from the cask, traditional front games bar; wheelchair access, children's eating area, tables on back terrace with chicken coop, open all day Sat *(Esther and John Sprinkle)*

WEMBWORTHY [SS6609]

☆ *Lymington Arms* [Lama Cross]: Clean and bright, with current chef doing wide choice of good food (not Mon), friendly service, well kept beers inc Sharps Doom Bar, Inch's cider, decent wines, agreeable restaurant (not Sun/Mon); children welcome, tables in garden, pleasant country setting *(R J Walden, A C and B M Laing, M and D Toms, Val Davies)*

WEST ALVINGTON [SX7243]

☆ *Ring o' Bells*: Very wide choice of good attractively priced food inc children's and half helpings, pleasant efficient staff; children and dogs welcome, comfortable bedrooms with good views and great breakfast – also B&B in licensees' own converted barn *(Mrs S Tatum, Mrs B Sugarman)*

WESTCOTT [ST0204]

Merry Harriers [B3181 S of Cullompton]: Small country pub with very wide range of decent food cooked by landlord, welcoming service by wife and daughter, big log fire, Bass and Flowers, choice of house wines, attractive restaurant *(Ken Flawn)*

WESTLEIGH [SS4728]

Westleigh Inn [½ mile off A39 Bideford—Instow]: Excellent play area in big neat garden overlooking Torridge estuary, inglenook log fire, well kept Bass, usual food from baguettes up, friendly prompt service, no smoking room; fruit machine; Tarka Trail walks *(Dr and Mrs B D Smith, LYM, John and Judy Saville)*

WHIMPLE [SY0497]

☆ *New Fountain* [off A30 Exeter—Honiton; Church Rd]: Attractive and civilised yet extremely friendly beamed village pub with cosy local atmosphere, good inexpensive food inc interesting dishes, well kept changing beers inc one from the village, woodburner *(LYM, Dr B and Mrs P B Baker)*

Thirsty Farmer: Large and rather grand (former substantial private house), transformed by new licensee, good varied menu from snacks to full meals, good cheerful service, well kept real ales, several smaller areas, log fires, spacious restaurant; garden tables *(E V M Whiteway)*

WIDECOMBE [SX7176]

☆ *Old Inn* [B3387 W of Bovey Tracey]: Busy, friendly and comfortable, with 14th-c stonework, big log fires, olde-worlde pubby front bar, some concentration on large restaurant area with wide choice of good value hearty food from well filled granary rolls up, well kept ales inc Wadworths 6X, local farm cider, decent wines, decent friendly service, family room; in pretty moorland village – get there before about 12.30 in summer to miss the tourist coaches; room to dance on music nights, good big garden with pleasant terrace; great walks – the Grimspound one gives spectacular views *(LYM, J C Brittain-Long, Neil and Beverley Gardner, David and Nina Pugsley, Mike Turner, JP, PP, Ian and Nita Cooper)*

WOODBURY [SY0187]

White Hart [3½ miles from M5 junction 30; A376, then B3179; Church St]: Good local atmosphere, good choice of good value food, well kept Bass and Worthington BB, decent wines, plain public bar, comfortable quieter dining lounge, log fire; attractive small walled garden with aviary, skittle alley, nice spot by church in peaceful village *(Dr and Mrs M E Wilson, Mark Clezy)*

WOODBURY SALTERTON [SY0290]

White Horse [A3052 Exeter—Sidmouth]: Modern spacious pub locally popular for good-sized helpings of reasonably priced food (booking essential Sat); well kept ales, comfortably divided dining areas, cheerful service, good children's room and play area; bedrooms *(Meg and Colin Hamilton)*

WRAFTON [SS4935]

Williams Arms [A361 just SE of Braunton]: Attractive modernised thatched family dining pub giving children free rein, two big bars divided into several cosy areas, interesting wall hangings, wide bar food choice, unlimited self-service carvery in busy separate restaurant, children's helpings, quick friendly helpful service, Bass and Courage, decent house wines; pool, darts, piped music, discreet TV; picnic-sets outside with play area and aviary *(Joyce and Maurice Cottrell, David Carr)*

YARCOMBE [ST2408]

☆ *Angel* [A30 2 miles E of A303]: 14th-c thatched pub with Victorian dolls and other bric-a-brac in spotless little front bar, up to eight well kept and interesting ales tapped from the cask which may include ones collected from Scotland, flagstones and ancient stonework, limited choice of attractively priced food all home-made from sandwiches to pastas, pizzas and so forth, helpful informal Scottish landlord, landlady does manicures, separate dining room, handsome old english sheepdog; quiet piped music, dogs allowed; upstairs skittle alley, small back terrace overlooking churchyard *(George Atkinson, Ron Shelton)*

YEALMPTON [SX5851]

Rose & Crown [A379 Kingsbridge—Plymouth]: Friendly pub with enjoyable food, well kept beer, reasonable prices and lots of theme nights *(Simon Batchelor, Margaret and Roy Randle)*

If we know a pub has a no smoking area, we say so.

Dorset

New entries here this year are the New Inn at Church Knowle (back in the Guide after a break, with enjoyable food emphasising fresh fish, and the chance of browsing through their cellar to choose a nice wine), Skippers in Sherborne (cheerful and good value, with a super landlord), the charming little Trooper at Stourton Caundle (the new landlord making some gentle changes without upsetting the unspoilt country feel), and the welcoming Bull in Sturminster Newton with its good value food. Other pubs doing particularly well here this year are the ancient Royal Oak in Cerne Abbas (a cosy and friendly all-rounder), the Countryman at East Knighton (families treated well in this big buoyant pub with its tasty food), the Cock & Bottle at East Morden (another good all-rounder, with an interesting layout), the well run Thimble at Piddlehinton (enjoyable food and drink, and a nice garden), the unchanging Digby Tap in Sherborne (lots of character, great beer), the West Bay in West Bay (its imaginatively prepared fresh seafood is a big draw, gaining it a new Food Award – this year it also gains a Place to Stay Award), and the unspoilt rustic Square & Compass in Worth Matravers (which gains a Star for the special way it keeps to old-fashioned methods and style). New licensees are settling in at the Fishermans Haunt near Christchurch, the Acorn at Evershot (a pubbier bar menu now), the Brace of Pheasants at Plush (useful to have both a pubby menu and a more elaborate food choice), and the rather smart Manor Hotel in seaside West Bexington (a nice place to stay in). Dorset now has quite a few pubs that are rewarding for a special meal out (check out the ones with a Food Award); the current pick of the bunch is the West Bay in West Bay, which takes the title of Dorset Dining Pub of the Year. The Lucky Dip section at the end of the chapter is a rich trawling ground, strong in starred entries. As in the main section, quite a few pubs are showing changes under new licensees this year; and this area has several good family dining pubs tied to Badger, one of the main local brewers (the other is Palmers). Pubs we'd note particularly in the Dip are the Worlds End at Almer, Spyway at Askerswell, White Lion in Broadwindsor, Three Horseshoes at Burton Bradstock, Greyhound in Corfe Castle, Fleur-de-Lys at Cranborne, Poet Laureate on the edge of Dorchester, Elm Tree at Langton Herring, Bottle at Marshwood, Hunters Moon at Middlemarsh, Marquis of Lorne at Nettlecombe, Three Horseshoes at Powerstock, Crown at Puncknowle, Bankes Arms at Studland, Red Lion in Sturminster Marshall, Greyhound at Sydling St Nicholas, Ilchester Arms at Symondsbury, Crown at Uploders, Old Ship and Riverhouse, both at Upwey, and Wise Man at West Stafford. Dorset drinks prices are generally a touch above the national average; the Digby Tap in Sherborne was the cheapest of our main entries.

Post Office address codings confusingly give the impression that some pubs are in Dorset, when they're really in Somerset (which is where we list them).

BURTON BRADSTOCK SY4889 Map 1
Anchor ⑪

B3157 SE of Bridport

Most people visit this bustling little seafood pub, which is prettily set in an attractive village, for the excellent fresh fish; it's best to book well ahead, especially at weekends. Listed on blackboards, the wide (though by no means cheap) selection could include mussels (£6.95/£11.95), salmon (£13.95), scallops (£14.95), brill (£16.95), monkfish in parma ham (£17.95), lobster thermidor (£28) and, good for an expensive treat, a shellfish platter (£55 for two). A lunchtime snack menu has filled baguettes (from £2.95), baked ham and egg, mackerel or salmon fishcakes (£6.95), balti chicken (£7.95), and you can also choose from dishes such as peppered pork loin (£13.95) or leg of lamb or duck (£14.95); puddings (£3.95). On Sunday they do a choice of roasts (£6.95). Fairly straightforward, the lounge bar has pink plush wall seats and some fishy décor. There's usually a good crowd of locals in the public bar, which has big windows, more cushioned seats, darts, table skittles, bar billiards, TV, shove-ha'penny, cribbage and dominoes. Alongside well kept Thomas Hardy Ushers Best and Founders and a seasonal beer such as Spring Fever on handpump, the welcoming Scottish landlord also has over 40 malt whiskies. The two restaurants are no smoking. *(Recommended by TOH, David and Julie Glover, Graham and Rose Ive, Mrs J L Wyatt, Terry Mizen, Comus and Sarah Elliott)*

InnSpired ~ Lease J R Plunkett ~ Real ale ~ Bar food ~ Restaurant ~ (01308) 897228 ~ Children in eating area of bar and restaurant ~ Dogs allowed in bar ~ Open 11-3.30, 6-11.30; 11-11.30 Sat; 12-10.30 Sun

CERNE ABBAS ST6601 Map 2
Royal Oak ⑪ ♀

Long Street

This picturesque creeper-covered Tudor inn is popular for the delicious bar food, and it's just as pleasant to drop in for a drink. From handpumps on the uncommonly long bar counter, they serve well kept Butcombe, Greene King Old Speckled Hen, Quay Weymouth, St Austell Dartmoor and a guest such as St Austell Tribute (you can have a taste beforehand to see which you like best). They also have around 15 wines by the glass, and 15 malt whiskies. Three flagstoned communicating rooms have sturdy oak beams, lots of shiny black panelling, an inglenook with an oven, and warm winter log fires. The stone walls and the ceilings are packed with all sorts of small ornaments from local photographs to antique china, brasses and farm tools, and a nice touch is the candles and pots of herbs on the tables; occasional piped music. It's well run by the enthusiastic licensees, and the staff are friendly. Skilfully prepared using good ingredients, mostly local, the bar food includes lunchtime sandwiches (£3.25) as well as soup (£3.50), whitebait (£5.25), fish and chips (£7.50), venison sausages and mash (£7.75, steak and blue cheese pie (£8.45), fried local pork fillet with white wine sauce (£9.75), and whole bass with pak-choi and asian dressing (£13.95); they do smaller meals for children. The enclosed back garden is very pleasant, with Purbeck stone terracing and cedarwood decking, comfortable chairs, and tables under cocktail parasols, and it has outdoor heaters. If the weather is nice, they may serve drinks and snacks out here on summer afternoons. *(Recommended by Mr and Mrs Bentley-Davies, the Didler, JP, PP, Tracey and Stephen Groves, W W Burke, Jess and George Cowley, Rosanna Luke, Julia and Richard Tredgett, Andrew Shore, Ian and Deborah Carrington, Terry Mizen, M G Hart, Mike and Shelley Woodroffe)*

Free house ~ Licensees David and Janice Birch ~ Real ale ~ Bar food (12-2, 7-9.30 (9 Sun)) ~ Restaurant ~ (01300) 341797 ~ Children welcome ~ Dogs welcome ~ Open 11.30(11 Sat)-3, 6-11; 12-3, 7-10.30 Sun

CHIDEOCK SY4292 Map 1

Anchor 🛏

Seatown signposted off A35 from Chideock

In one of the county's most striking spots, this well liked pub nestles dramatically beneath the 188-metre (617-ft) Golden Cap pinnacle, just a few steps from the cove beach and very near the Dorset Coast Path. Seats and tables on the spacious front terrace are ideally placed for the lovely sea and cliff views, though to bag a place in summer you'll have to get here really early. It's nice too out of season: when the sometimes overwhelming crowds have gone and you've been for a walk by the stormy sea, the little bars feel especially snug, with warming winter fires, some sea pictures and lots of interesting local photographs, a few fossils and shells, simple but comfortable seats around neat tables, and low white-planked ceilings; the family room is no smoking, and the cats are friendly (Billy Boy is over 22 years old). The sweet-natured black labrador is called Oliver. The friendly hard-working licensees have run this pub for more than 17 years, and there's a good welcoming atmosphere, even when it's really busy. They'd like to extend to improve some of the facilities but have sadly been turned down on planning grounds. Efficient helpful staff serve bar food which includes lunchtime sandwiches (from £2.45) and ploughman's (from £4.95), as well as soup (£3.45), burgers (from £5.45), plaice and chips (£6.45), avocado bake (£7.45), beef curry (£8.45), and daily specials such as vegetable and spinach pancakes (£7.25), sausages in cider (£7.25), brill (£8.95) or local lobster (£10.50); the puddings are home-made. Well kept Palmers 200, IPA and Copper on handpump (under light blanket pressure in winter only), freshly squeezed orange juice, and a decent little wine list; piped, mainly classical, music. There are fridges and toasters in the bedrooms (which are simple, and share a bathroom) so you can make your own breakfast while enjoying the sea views. *(Recommended by Doreen and Haydn Maddock, Heather and Dick Martin, Dr and Mrs M E Wilson, Peter Meister, Mike and Cheryl Lyons, Val and Alan Green, John Mitchell, Tracey and Stephen Groves, John Beeken, John and Vivienne Rice, Peter Salmon, Richard Martin, Lynn Sharpless, James Woods, Joan and Michel Hooper-Immins)*

Palmers ~ Tenants David and Sadie Miles ~ Real ale ~ Bar food (usually all day in summer) ~ (01297) 489215 ~ Well behaved children welcome ~ Dogs allowed in bar ~ Jazz, folk and blues Sat evening ~ Open 11-11; 12-10.30 Sun; 11-2.30, 6-11 winter ~ Bedrooms: £25/£50

CHRISTCHURCH SZ1696 Map 2

Fishermans Haunt 🛏

Winkton: B3347 Ringwood road nearly 3 miles N of Christchurch

Aptly named given that the River Avon runs alongside the grounds and the number of fisheries in the area, this well run hotel is also not far from the New Forest. The very neat bar, partly no smoking, is divided into various pleasant areas, with brocaded chairs around tables, stools at a pine-panelled bar counter, and a few pictures on brown wallpaper. At one end big windows look out on the neat front garden, and there are attractive views of the River Avon from the restaurant (open Saturday and Sunday only). Well kept Bass, Gales HSB and GB, Ringwood Fortyniner and possibly a guest on handpump, and lots of country wines. From a fairly straightforward menu generous helpings of reasonably priced bar food include sandwiches (from £2.95), filled baked potatoes (from £4.50), ham, egg and chips (£6.25), steak and kidney pie (£6.50), breaded plaice (£6.70) and a couple of daily specials. The quiet back garden has tables among the shrubs, roses and other flowers; disabled lavatories. *(Recommended by Eddie Edwards, Ian Phillips, W W Burke, David M Cundy, Philip and June Caunt, Colin Fisher)*

Gales ~ Managers Peter and Shirley Palmer ~ Real ale ~ Bar food (all day Sat, Sun) ~ Restaurant ~ (01202) 477283 ~ Children welcome ~ Dogs allowed in bar and bedrooms ~ Open 11-11; 11-10.30 Sun ~ Bedrooms: £49.50B/£66B

CHURCH KNOWLE SY9481 Map 2
New Inn ♀
Village signposted off A351 just N of Corfe Castle

The emphasis at this partly thatched 16th-c inn is fairly firmly on the very good food, and particularly the daily fresh fish which might include moules marinière (£6.75), half a pint of prawns (£6.95), fruits de mer (£8.75), and john dory, turbot, halibut, bass and so on priced at the market rate each day. Other meals include sandwiches (from £3.75), popular blue vinney soup (£3.95), ploughman's (from £5.50), steak and kidney pie (£7.75), and steaks (from £10.75). The pub is prettily set in a nice little village, and has been run by the same friendly licensees for many years. It's restauranty in style, and not really a place to drop in for a drink, though they usually have well kept Flowers Original, Greene King Old Speckled Hen and Wadworths 6X on handpump, farmhouse cider and organic apple juices, and the atmosphere is pleasantly relaxed. The two main areas, linked by an arch, are attractively furnished with farmhouse chairs and tables, with lots of bric-a-brac, and a log fire at each end; one area is no smoking. Readers enjoy choosing wines from an enjoyable display in the wine cellar, which often includes interesting bin ends in their recently opened wine shack (they also do off sales from here), and they serve several wines by the glass (either 175 or 250 ml). Also about a dozen malt whiskies; skittle alley (private hire only) and piped music; disabled facilities, though there is a step down to the gents'. The good-sized garden has plenty of tables and fine views of the Purbeck hills. If you book beforehand you can camp in two fields behind. *(Recommended by Mrs Hazel Blackburn, Tony and Katie Lewis, Pat and Robert Watt, James Woods, Mike and Sue Richardson, John and Enid Morris, JDM, KM, W W Burke, R J Davies, Terry and Linda Moseley, Mr and Mrs P L Spencer)*

Inn Partnership (Pubmaster) ~ Tenants Maurice and Rosemary Estop ~ Real ale ~ Bar food ~ (01929) 480357 ~ Children welcome ~ Open 11-3, 6-11; 12-3, 6-10.30 Sun; closed Mon in winter exc bank hols

COLEHILL SU0302 Map 2
Barley Mow
From roundabout junction of A31 Ferndown bypass and B3073 Wimborne road, follow Colehill signpost up Middlehill Road, pass Post Office, and at church turn right into Colehill Lane; OS Sheet 195 map reference 032024

Part-thatched and part-tiled, this attractive former drovers' cottage is especially striking in summer, when colourful flowers in tubs and hanging baskets are set off vividly against the whitewash. Sheltered by oak trees, there's a pleasant, enclosed big lawn at the back with a boules pitch. Inside, the cosy low-beamed main bar has a good winter fire in the huge brick inglenook, attractively moulded oak panelling, some Hogarth prints, and a relaxed dining atmosphere; the cat is called Misty; piped music and a fruit machine. Home-made bar food is served in generous helpings by attentive staff, and includes soup (£2.75), sandwiches (from £3.95), prawn cocktail (£4.95), ham and egg, lasagne or salmon fishcakes (£5.50), mushroom crumble or turkey, gammon and leek pie (£6.95), smoked haddock with creamy leek sauce and grilled cheese (£7.95), cajun chicken (£8.75), rump steak (£9.95), puddings such as chocolate and cherry sponge pudding (£3.75), and Sunday roast (£5.95). Very well kept Badger Best, Tanglefoot and a seasonal ale on handpump, and a dozen fruit wines. There are some nice country walks nearby. *(Recommended by Nigel and Sue Foster, B and K Hypher, Colin Draper, R J Walden, W W Burke, Peter Burton)*

Badger ~ Manager Bruce Cichocki ~ Real ale ~ Bar food (12-2, 6-9) ~ (01202) 882140 ~ Children in family room ~ Dogs allowed in bar ~ Open 11-3, 5.30-11; 12-3, 7-10.30 Sun

---

Cribbage is a card game using a block of wood with holes for matchsticks or special pins to score with; regulars in cribbage pubs are usually happy to teach strangers how to play.

EAST CHALDON SY7983 Map 2
Sailors Return

Village signposted from A352 Wareham—Dorchester; from village green, follow Dorchester, Weymouth signpost; note that the village is also known as Chaldon Herring; OS sheet 194 map reference 790834

In lovely countryside, this well extended thatched pub is close to Lulworth Cove, and from nearby West Chaldon, a bridleway leads across to join the Dorset Coast Path by the National Trust cliffs above Ringstead Bay. Picnic-sets, benches and log seats on the grass in front look down over cow pastures to the village, and you can wander to the interesting little nearby church or enjoy a downland walk from the pub. Although fairly isolated it gets very busy at weekends, especially in fine weather. The convivial flagstoned bar still keeps much of its original country-tavern character, while the newer part has unfussy furnishings, old notices for decoration, and open beams showing the roof above. A wide range of popular but straightforward bar food, served in generous helpings, might include whitebait (£4.95), steak and kidney pie or rainbow trout (£7.25), local plaice (£8.95), whole gammon hock (£9.25) or half a shoulder of lamb (£9.95). The no smoking dining area has solid old tables in nooks and corners; service is good even when it's busy. Well kept Hampshire Strongs Best and Ringwood and around four guests such as Badger Tanglefoot, Palmers IPA, Quay Steam Beer and Tetleys Imperial on handpump, as well as country wines and several malt whiskies; darts, cribbage, dominoes and piped music. *(Recommended by B and K Hypher, R J Davies, Pat and Robert Watt, Joan and Michel Hooper-Immins, Marjorie and David Lamb, Simon and Jane Williams, Paul and Annette Hallett, W W Burke, Ian and Deborah Carrington, S P Watkin, P A Taylor)*

Free house ~ Licensees Mike and Sue Pollard ~ Real ale ~ Bar food (12-2, 6-9) ~ Restaurant ~ (01305) 853847 ~ Children in restaurant ~ Dogs allowed in bar ~ Open 11-11; 12-10.30 Sun; 11.30-2.30, 6.30-11 winter

EAST KNIGHTON SY8185 Map 2
Countryman 🍴 🍺 🛏

Just off A352 Dorchester—Wareham; OS Sheet 194 map reference 811857

Locals and visitors alike enjoy the buoyant atmosphere at this big bustling pub. Families feel comfortable too, as they are well catered for, with toys inside, play equipment in the garden, and baby-changing facilities. The neat and comfortable long main bar has a mix of tables, wheelback chairs and comfortable sofas, and fires at either end. This room opens into several other smaller areas, including a no smoking family room, a games bar with pool and darts, and a carvery (£12.75 for a good roast and pudding; not Monday, nor lunchtime on Tuesday). They serve well kept real ales such as Courage Best, Greene King Old Speckled Hen and Ringwood Best and Old Thumper on handpump, as well as farm cider, and a good choice of wines; piped music. Generous tasty dishes include sandwiches or filled rolls (from £2.70), home-made soup (£3.50), ploughman's (from £5.75), tomato and lentil lasagne (£7.95), lemon and pepper chicken breast or fried plaice (£8.25), a handful of daily specials such as butternut squash bisque (£3.50), lamb and bacon meatloaf (£7.95), prawns fried with thai spices (£10.75), and home-made puddings such as treacle tart and sorbet (from £3.50); best to book on Sunday, when they have two lunchtime sittings; no smoking restaurant, disabled lavatories.
(Recommended by Brian and Karen Thomas, Peter Neate, Jeff and Wendy Williams, OPUS, Mr and Mrs A Stansfield, Philip and Elaine Holmes, Joyce and Maurice Cottrell, Ian and Deborah Carrington, Guy Masdin, James A Waller, Charles Moncreiffe, MDN, Alain and Rose Foote, M N Pledger, Peter Salmon, Simon and Jane Williams, S P Watkin, P A Taylor)

Free house ~ Licensees Jeremy and Nina Evans ~ Real ale ~ Bar food (till 9.30) ~ Restaurant ~ (01305) 852666 ~ Children welcome ~ Dogs welcome ~ Open 11(12 Sun)-3, 6-11; closed 25 Dec ~ Bedrooms: £54S/£70S

EAST MORDEN SY9195 Map 2
Cock & Bottle 🍽 ♀ ◀

B3075 between A35 and A31 W of Poole

A good all-rounder, this welcoming pub is particularly popular for its well cooked enjoyable food. The interior is divided into several communicating areas (mostly laid out for dining), with heavy rough beams, some stripped ceiling boards, squared panelling, a mix of old furnishings in various sizes and degrees of antiquity, small Victorian prints and some engaging bric-a-brac. There's a roaring log fire, and comfortably intimate corners each with just a couple of tables, and although the emphasis is on dining there's still a pubby wood-floored public bar with piped music, a fruit machine, and a sensibly placed darts alcove. This in turn leads on to yet another individually furnished dining room. Booking is recommended if you do want to eat, and, as well as lunchtime ploughman's (£5.50) and filled baguettes (from £5.55), the good changing bar menu might include starters such as wild mushroom tartlet with mustard hollandaise (£5.25), duck spring rolls with chilli jam (£5.75), main courses such as an unbeatable steak and kidney pudding (£9.50), grilled plaice with parsley butter or calves liver with red onion and sherry sauce (£9.95), pheasant breast braised in cider, apple and chestnut sauce (£11.95), and puddings such as soft chocolate pudding with raspberry cream or orange and Drambuie crème brûlée (from £4). They may do half helpings for children. Most of the restaurant is no smoking, and they have some disabled facilities. Well kept Badger Best, K&B and Tanglefoot on handpump, and a good choice of decent house wines including half a dozen by the glass; service is pleasant, though when it's busy food might take a while to come. There are a few picnic-sets outside, a garden area, and an adjoining field with a nice pastoral outlook. *(Recommended by M G Hart, Ian Phillips, Geoffrey G Lawrance, Mark Clezy, W A Evershed, Malcolm Taylor, DJH, Mr and Mrs A Stansfield, Terry and Linda Moseley, Colin Draper, Howard and Margaret Buchanan, Norman and June Williams, Joan and Michel Hooper-Immins)*

Badger ~ Tenant Peter Meadley ~ Real ale ~ Bar food (12-2, 6(7 Sun)-9) ~ Restaurant ~ (01929) 459238 ~ Children in eating area of bar and restaurant ~ Dogs allowed in bar ~ Open 11-3, 6-11; 12-3, 7-10.30 Sun

EVERSHOT ST5704 Map 2
Acorn ♀ 🛏

Village signposted from A37 8 miles S of Yeovil

This prettily placed former coaching inn is in a charming village with lots of good surrounding walks. Immortalised as the Sow & Acorn in Thomas Hardy's *Tess of the d'Urbervilles*, it is a distinctive place, with thoughtful touches and helpful pleasant service. The Hardy Bar has oak panelling and two hamstone fireplaces carved by local craftsmen, a fine carved and gilded oak sconce, pictures by local artists, re-upholstered chairs, and copies of the inn's deeds going back to the 17th c. Another lounge has a woodburning stove. Their well kept beers on handpump might be Butcombe Bitter and Fullers London Pride, and they have home-made elderflower cordial, damson vodka and sloe gin, and an interesting wine list; pool, darts, skittle alley, dominoes, cribbage, backgammon, chess, and juke box. The format of the food has changed a little this year, in that they've confined their more elaborate menu to the no smoking restaurant, and introduced a much pubbier, and very reasonably priced, menu to the bar: sandwiches (from £2.50), soup (£3.75), pasta of the day (£4.95), smoked salmon salad (£5.50) and mediterranean vegetable tart (£5.95). Outside is a terrace with dark oak furniture. *(Recommended by John and Judy Saville, Peter Neate, Peter and Giff Bennett, John Hale, Andrew Shore, W A Evershed, R J Davies, Ann and Colin Hunt, Helen Whitmore, Mike and Shelley Woodroffe)*

Free house ~ Licensee Todd Moffat ~ Real ale ~ Bar food (12-2, 6.30-9) ~ Restaurant ~ (01935) 83228 ~ Children in eating area of bar and restaurant ~ Dogs allowed in bar and bedrooms ~ Open 11-11; 12-10.30 Sun ~ Bedrooms: £60B/£80B

FARNHAM ST9515 Map 2

Museum 🍴 🍷 ◗ 🛏

Village signposted off A354 Blandford Forum—Salisbury

Attractively extended, this 17th-c thatched building has been opened up into a series of nicely finished interconnecting rooms and bars. The various areas have a bright, fresh feel, thanks to cheery yellow walls and plentiful windows. The flagstoned bar has a big inglenook fireplace, light beams, good comfortably cushioned furnishings and fresh flowers on all the tables. To the right is a dining room with a fine antique dresser, while off to the left is a cosier room, with a very jolly hunting model and a seemingly sleeping stuffed fox curled in a corner. Another room feels rather like a contemporary version of a baronial hall, soaring up to a high glass ceiling, with dozens of antlers and a stag's head looking down on a long refectory table and church-style pews. It leads to an outside terrace with more wooden tables. The choice of wines is excellent, and three real ales come from smaller breweries, such as Exmoor Gold, Hop Back Summer Lightning and Ringwood Best. Promptly served by professional antipodean staff, the contemporary menu might include sandwiches (from £4.50), smoked haddock, leek and potato soup (£4.50), terrine of quail, potatoes, mushrooms and guinea fowl with waldorf salad (£6), wild rocket risotto (£9), roast shoulder of lamb with crushed peas and new potatoes (£13.50), roast turbot fillet with basil, aïoli and balsamic dressing (£14.50), lobster salad (£18), and puddings such as dark chocolate mousse with praline and raspberries (£5.50). They use a lot of local and organic produce, and make their own bread, jams, chutney and marmalades. The stylish restaurant (no smoking till 10pm) is open only for Friday and Saturday dinner and Sunday lunch; it's a good idea to book. Please note that you have to give them five days' warning for a bedroom cancellation or you're likely to be charged in full. *(Recommended by John and Vivienne Rice, Peter Neate, Phil Metcalfe, Phyl and Jack Street, J R Ringrose, Dr L Kaufman, W W Burke, Colin and Janet Roe)*

Free house ~ Licensees Vicky Elliot and Mark Stephenson ~ Real ale ~ Bar food (12-2(3 Sun), 7-9.30) ~ Restaurant (Fri and Sat evening and Sun lunch) ~ (01725) 516261 ~ Children over 8 evenings and in accommodation ~ Dogs welcome ~ Open 12-3, 6-11; 12-11(10.30 Sun) Sat; closed 25 Dec, 31 Dec evening ~ Bedrooms: £65B/£75B

FURZEHILL SU0102 Map 2

Stocks

Village signposted off B3078 N of Wimborne Minster

The older, thatched part of this extended 17th-c pub has the most character, bringing to mind rumours that the original cellar had a tunnel which came out in Smugglers Lane. Two long rooms divide into rather snug low-beamed sections, each with an open fire (brick in one and stone in the other), plush wall and window seats and stools, and timbered ochre walls. A dining area leads off here, with lots of copper and earthenware, an area with nets and a crab pot, and a big wall mirror cleverly creating an illusion of even more space. There are other dining areas with more mirrors, solid farmhouse chairs and tables, low ceilings and soft lighting, and good New Forest black and white photographs, old prints, farm tools, hay sleds, and so forth – even a Rayburn range in one place; piped music, darts and fruit machine. Very friendly helpful staff serve well kept Ringwood Best and Fortyniner and a guest such as Theakstons Old Peculier from handpumps. Popular bar food includes lunchtime sandwiches and hot baguettes (from £3.45, not Sunday), soup (£3.95), breaded camembert with redcurrant dressing (£4.45), ham, egg and chips (£5.95), sausage and mash or battered fish (£6.95), beef and ale pie (£7.50), red thai chicken curry (£8.50) and red pepper, mushroom and brie en croûte with red pepper coulis (£8.95); most of the restaurant is no smoking. There are some green plastic seats out in front, and solid teak furniture under a fairy-lit arbour by the back car park. *(Recommended by Nick and Pam Hancock, Peter Neate, Carol Mills)*

Scottish Courage ~ Manager Emily George ~ Real ale ~ Bar food (12-2.30, 6-9.30) ~

Restaurant ~ (01202) 882481 ~ Children in eating area of bar and restaurant ~ Dogs allowed in bar ~ Open 11-11; 12-10.30 Sun

GODMANSTONE SY6697 Map 2
Smiths Arms £
A352 N of Dorchester

This old-fashioned 15th-c thatched inn has just six tables in its one quaint little bar, which, at only 12 by 4 metres, makes this one of the smallest pubs in the country. It's traditionally furnished with long wooden stools and chunky tables, antique waxed and polished small pews and an elegant little high-backed settle, all tucked against the walls. There are National Hunt racing pictures and some brass plates on the walls, an open fire, dominoes and cribbage and Wadworths 6X on electric pump. The cheap home-made food is simple but tasty, and might include sandwiches (from £2.30), giant sausage (£3.95), ploughman's (from £4.35), chilli or quiche (£4.95), and daily specials such as chicken salsa tortilla pie (£5.20), moussaka (£5.35) and puddings (from £2.25). Seats and tables are very pleasantly set out on a crazy-paved terrace and on the grassy mound by the narrow River Cerne. There's a nice walk over Cowdon Hill to the River Piddle. Note the limited opening times. *(Recommended by the Didler, Peter Neate)*

Free house ~ Licensees John and Linda Foster ~ Real ale ~ Bar food (12-3) ~ No credit cards ~ (01300) 341236 ~ Open 11(12 Sun)-5.30; closed mid-Oct to a week before Easter

PIDDLEHINTON SY7197 Map 1
Thimble
B3143

In one of the county's prettiest valleys, this partly thatched streamside pub is well worth a detour from the main road. Simpler than the exterior suggests, the neatly kept low-beamed bar is nicely spacious and airy, so that in spite of attracting quite a lot of people in the summer, it never feels too crowded. There's a handsome stone fireplace, a deep glassed-over well, and a collection of thimbles. Attractively floodlit at night, the flower-filled garden is pleasant for a summer meal outdoors. Popular reasonably priced bar food served generously might include sandwiches (from £2.50), soup (£2.75), filled baked potatoes (from £3.50), fried whitebait or chicken liver pâté (£4), battered haddock (£5.85), steak and kidney pudding (£6.60), and steak (from £10.50), with daily specials such as lasagne (£6), rabbit pie (£6.60) or grilled bass (£7.50), and puddings such as warm chocolate and raspberry truffle or fresh fruit tartlet (£3.95); Sunday roast (£6.10). The staff are friendly and helpful even when it's busy. Well kept Badger Best and Tanglefoot, Palmers Copper and IPA, and Ringwood Old Thumper on handpump, along with quite a few fruit wines and malt whiskies. Darts, shove-ha'penny, dominoes, cribbage, and piped music. *(Recommended by Greta and Christopher Wells, John and Joan Nash, Joan and Michel Hooper-Immins, H D Wharton, Pat and Robert Watt, R Kendall, Dudley and Moira Cockroft, Dennis Jenkin, Peter Bell, Michael and Ann Cole, Prof Keith and Mrs Jane Barber)*

Free house ~ Licensees N R White and V J Lanfear ~ Real ale ~ Bar food ~ Restaurant ~ (01300) 348270 ~ Children welcome ~ Dogs allowed in bar ~ Open 12-2.30, 7-11(10.30 Sun); closed 25 Dec and evening 26 Dec

PLUSH ST7102 Map 2
Brace of Pheasants
Village signposted from B3143 N of Dorchester at Piddletrenthide

Charmingly placed in a fold of hills surrounding the Piddle Valley, this handsome 16th-c thatched pub used to be two cottages and the village smithy. There's a fairly upmarket but relaxed atmosphere in the airy beamed bar, which has good solid tables, windsor chairs, fresh flowers, a huge heavy-beamed inglenook at one end with cosy seating inside, and a good warming log fire at the other. A usefully pubby bar menu includes good snacks such as soup (£3.50), tomato, mozzarella and basil baguette or smoked salmon and scrambled egg on toast (£4.75), cottage pie (£7) and steak sandwich (£7.95), and a second more elaborate menu might include beer-battered scallops with salsa verde (£6.95), twice-baked cheese soufflé with plum compote (£5.25), venison sausages with mash and red wine gravy (£8.95), turbot fillet in parma ham with tomato and coriander salsa (£14.50), and puddings such as chocolate orange mousse or elderflower meringues with compote of redcurrants and cream (from £4). The restaurant and family room are no smoking. They serve well kept Adnams, Fullers London Pride and a guest such as Butcombe Bitter tapped from the cask. A decent-sized garden and terrace includes a lawn sloping up towards a rockery. The pub lies alongside Plush Brook, and an attractive bridleway behind goes to the left of the woods and over to Church Hill. *(Recommended by Dr and Mrs M E Wilson, the Didler, Ann Evans, Simon and Jane Williams, S P Watkin, P A Taylor)*

Free house ~ Licensees Toby and Suzie Albu ~ Real ale ~ Bar food ~ Restaurant ~ (01300) 348357 ~ Children welcome ~ Dogs allowed in bar ~ Open 12-3, 7-11(10.30 Sun); closed Mon

SHAFTESBURY ST8622 Map 2
Two Brewers ◖ £

St James Street, 150 yards from bottom of Gold Hill

This pubby place is near the bottom of the steep and famously photogenic Gold Hill featured in those famous Hovis TV advertisements. The open-plan turkey-carpeted bar is well divided for a cosily chatty feel, with plush banquettes in small bays, masses of decorative plates running along a delft shelf with more on the walls, and two nicely carved modern fireplaces. Well kept Courage Best, Fullers London Pride, Gales HSB, Greene King Old Speckled Hen and a guest such as Shepherd Neame Spitfire on handpump; the house wines are good value. Under the new licensees good value bar food includes sandwiches (from £2.75), soup (£2.25), ploughman's (from £5.95), vegetarian specials (from £4.75), quiche salad (£4.95), steak and kidney or chicken, ham and mushroom pie (£5.75), mixed grill (£9.95) and puddings such as home-made crumbles (£2.95). The back eating area, with stripped pews, lots of engravings, prints and other pictures, is no smoking. They have a skittle alley, and an attractive good-sized back garden has lovely views from its picnic-sets, some under cocktail parasols. More reports please. *(Recommended by JP, PP, Dr and Mrs M E Wilson, Ron Shelton, Colin and Janet Roe)*

Enterprise ~ Lease Harvey and Tracy Jones ~ Real ale ~ Bar food (12-2, 6-9) ~ Restaurant ~ (01747) 854211 ~ Children in eating area of bar and restaurant ~ Dogs allowed in bar ~ Open 11-3, 6-11; 12-3, 7-10.30 Sun

SHERBORNE ST6316 Map 2
Digby Tap ◖ £

Cooks Lane; park in Digby Road and walk round corner

Not a pub for those seeking sophistication, this old-fashioned town ale house pleases everyone who likes their pubs down-to-earth, interesting and friendly. Two other solid attractions here are the changing real ales, and the straightforward but very good value enjoyable food. They work through around 20 different beers a week, mostly from West Country brewers such as Exmoor, Otter, Sharps and Teignworthy, with four or five on handpump at any one time. Served in huge helpings, bar food includes tasty soup (£1.95), sandwiches or baguettes (from £1.75, toasted from £1.80), filled baked potatoes (from £2.80), and daily specials such as lasagne, sausage casserole, liver and bacon or steak and kidney pie (£3.95). Simple but full of character, the flagstoned main bar is relaxed and friendly with a good mix of customers. Several small games rooms have pool, cribbage, fruit machine, TV and piped music, and there are some seats outside. The pub is handy for the glorious golden stone abbey. *(Recommended by B H and J I Andrews, Stephen,*

Julie and Hayley Brown, Evelyn and Derek Walter, R M Corlett, Dr and Mrs M E Wilson, Basil Minson, W W Burke, Simon and Jane Williams)

Free house ~ Licensees Peter Lefevre and Nick Whigham ~ Real ale ~ Bar food (12-1.45; not evenings or Sun) ~ No credit cards ~ (01935) 813148 ~ Children welcome in eating area of bar at lunchtime ~ Dogs welcome ~ Open 11-2.30, 5.30-11; 11-3, 6-11 Sat; 12-3, 7-10.30 Sun; closed 25 Dec and 31 Jan evenings

Skippers

A352 link road, W of centre; car park, or park around corner, in Horsecastles

Thoroughly cheerful, this place, with the landlord's outgoing and welcoming nature reflected not just by his efficient staff but also in the décor – bright tablecloths in the dining area at the far end, scatter cushions on a window seat, a lively collection of helicopter and other mainly RNAS photographs, puce Anaglypta walls. There is basically a line of three fairly snug rooms, partly separated by knocked-through stone walls, starting with the serving area – which has well kept Butcombe and Wadworths IPA, JCB and 6X on handpump (Old Timer is tapped from a cask in the cellar in winter). Tables on the turkey carpet vary from dark pub style to sturdy varnished pine. Colourful chalk boards list dozens of dishes, which might include sandwiches (from £2.50), soup (£2.50), smoked salmon with prawns (£4.95), beef and red wine casserole or ham egg and chips (£7.95), pheasant breast in bacon with orange and Cointreau sauce (£12.50), with lots of fish fresh daily from Portland and Poole, such as kingfish with asparagus or grilled dover sole (£13.95). A bargain OAP lunch (not Sunday) gives three courses for £5.75. There is a rack of daily papers and a coal-effect gas fire, and may be unobtrusive piped radio. There are tables outside. *(Recommended by Joan and Michel Hooper-Immins)*

Wadworths ~ Tenants Sandra and Chris Frowde ~ Real ale ~ Bar food ~ Restaurant ~ (01935) 812753 ~ Children in eating area of bar ~ Open 11-2.30, 6-11; 12-2.30, 7-10.30 Sun

SHROTON ST8512 Map 2
Cricketers ♀ ◖

Off A350 N of Blandford (village also called Iwerne Courtney); follow signs

Well run and notably welcoming, this red brick pub is prettily set facing the peaceful village green. The bright divided bar, with a big stone fireplace, alcoves and cricketing memorabilia, has well kept changing ales such as Butcombe, a Ringwood seasonal beer, Shepherd Neame Spitfire and Charles Wells Bombardier served from pumps made into little cricket bats, a dozen wines by the glass, and quite a few malt whiskies. With Mrs Cowie in the kitchen, Mr Cowie and his neatly uniformed staff are friendly and attentive as they serve from a well balanced changing menu that might include very fairly priced smoked duck salad with tarragon cream dressing (£4.50), toasted ciabatta topped with passata, peppers and mozzarella (£4.75), black pudding and lambs kidneys in whisky dijon sauce or spicy meatballs with chilli sauce (£7.50), fried red mullet with roasted red pepper, tomato and basil (£9.90) and tiger prawn risotto with stir-fried vegetables (£9.50). The comfortable back restaurant (there's a no smoking area on the way through to here) has a fresh neutral décor, and a sizeable games area has pool, darts and a fruit machine. Secluded and attractive, the garden has big sturdy tables under cocktail parasols and some outdoor heaters, a fairy-lit clematis arbour, well tended shrubs, and a well stocked – and well used – herb garden by the kitchen door. We've not yet had reports from readers on the single well equipped bedroom, which opens on to the garden. There are good walks from here over Hambledon Hill with its fine views (though you will need to leave your boots outside). *(Recommended by Pat and Robert Watt, Paul and Annette Hallett, Dr A Abrahams, J Conti-Ramsden)*

Free house ~ Licensees George and Carol Cowie ~ Real ale ~ Bar food ~ Restaurant ~ (01258) 860421 ~ Children in eating area of bar and restaurant ~ Open 11.30-2.30, 6.30-11; 12-3, 7-10.30 Sun ~ Bedrooms: /£70S

STOURTON CAUNDLE ST7115 Map 2
Trooper
Village signposted off A30 E of Milborne Port

A charming little hideaway, this stone-built pub sits opposite Enid Blyton's former farm, better known as Finniston Farm in one of her *Famous Five* books. There are a few picnic-sets out in front and in its side garden, by a stream which is cut into a deep stone channel along the village lane. Ducks and bantams wander out here among the bygone agricultural machinery, with pheasants confined to a run. Inside, the skittle alley is home to quite a formidable collection of rustic tools built up by the previous landlord and his father, who were both former shepherds (look out for the sheep bells). The tiny low-ceilinged bar on the left has cushioned pews and wheelback chairs, a cabinet of sports trophies, charity bookshelves, over 80 horse bits, and lots of good horsebrasses on their leathers decorating the big stripped stone fireplace, which now has an oak pew built into it. There's another big fireplace in the stripped stone dining room on the right. A short menu of simple lunchtime snacks includes sandwiches (from £3), pasty and chips (£3.50), ploughman's (£4) and sausage, egg and chips (£4.50). As we went to press the new landlord was planning to introduce an evening menu that might include fish pie, pork in cider, and steak and kidney pie at around the £7 mark. *(Recommended by Marjorie and David Lamb)*

Free house ~ Licensee Richard Soar ~ Real ale ~ Bar food (not evenings (but see text), not Sun) ~ No credit cards ~ (01963) 362405 ~ Dogs allowed in bar ~ Open 12-2.30, 7-11(10.30 Sun); closed Mon lunchtime ~ Bedrooms: £15/£30

STRATTON SY6593 Map 2
Saxon Arms ♀ ♣ ◖
Village signposted off A37 bypass NW of Dorchester; The Square

The friendly licensees at this newly built stone, flint and thatched pub have a very good track record in the *Guide* (at their last pub they were our Licensees of the Year), and readers are reporting the same warm welcome here. It's also popular for the very fairly priced food, which includes soup (£2.95), filled ciabatta or baked potatoes (from £3.50), prawn cocktail (£4.50), deep-fried camembert (£4.75), chicken, bacon and tarragon pie (£6.95), warm spinach and feta cheese pie (£6.50), lasagne (£7.50), and daily specials such as fried scallops with smoked bacon and garlic salad (£9.50) or roast duck breast with cumberland sauce (£10.25), with puddings such as sticky toffee pudding and raspberry cheesecake (£3.75). The bright open-plan room has plenty of space, with a fireplace and drinking area to the left, and a large no smoking dining section on the right. The floor has big flagstones, and there are smart curtains, fresh flowers on the light oak tables, and comfortable cushioned settles. Friendly staff serve well kept Fullers London Pride and Palmers Dorset Gold and Saxon Ale and a guest such as Jennings Cumberland from handpump; the very reasonably priced wine list includes about eight wines by the glass, and there are a dozen malt whiskies; soft piped music, cribbage, dominoes, table skittles. The chocolate labrador is called Ed. There are lots of tables outside, overlooking a clutch of similar new buildings and the village green. *(Recommended by Ian and Deborah Carrington, Brian and Bett Cox, Martyn and Nicola Wyatt, Dr C D and Mrs S M Burbridge, Mr and Mrs J R Lyons, J P Humphery)*

Free house ~ Licensees Ian and Anne Barrett ~ Real ale ~ Bar food (11.30-2, 6.30-9) ~ (01305) 260020 ~ Children in eating area of bar ~ Dogs allowed in bar ~ Open 11-2.30, 5.30(6 Sat)-11; 12-3, 6.30-10.30 Sun

STURMINSTER NEWTON ST7813 Map 2
Bull
A357 near junction with B3092, S of village centre

This compact thatched local has a comfortable more or less L-shaped bar with soft lighting and some low beams. The joists by the serving counter are packed with key fobs, others have lots of decorative mugs, and the swirly cream walls have anything from country prints and bull cartoons to snaps of happy regulars; there are charity shelves of readable paperbacks at one end. Service is really friendly, and the food, home-made from fresh ingredients and served in hearty helpings, is good value: good sandwiches (from £2.95), prawn cocktail (£4.25), ploughman's (from £4.95), battered haddock (£6.25), vegetable lasagne or steak and stilton pie (£6.95), braised steak with white wine and mushroom sauce and grilled blue cheese (£8.25) and puddings such as bread and butter pudding or lemon brûlée (£3.50). Well kept Badger IPA, Best and Tanglefoot on handpump, good house wines; there may be piped Classic FM. They have a skittle alley, some picnic-sets out in front by rather totemic wooden statuary (and the busy road), and more in a fenced garden. *(Recommended by Mike and Shelley Woodroffe, Andrew York)*

Badger ~ Tenant H C Edward-Jones ~ Real ale ~ Bar food (till 9.30; not Sun evening) ~ (01258) 472435 ~ Children welcome ~ Dogs allowed in bar ~ Acoustic night first Sun in month ~ Open 11.30-3, 6.45-11; 12-3, 7-10.30 Sun

Swan 🛏

Town signposted off A357 Blandford—Sherborne, via B3092; Market Place

Traditional and very neatly kept, the busy beamed bar at this friendly 18th-c coaching inn has a particularly interesting brick fireplace at one end, its tiny grate sitting incongruously next to an old safe. Close by is a comfortable green leatherette sofa, as well as wooden corner seats, a table with newspapers to read, and the odd stuffed fish or bird in glass cases. Elsewhere there's lots of exposed brickwork, including sturdy brick pillars dividing the room, plenty of panelling, and a good number of tables leading through into a couple of eating areas (one is no smoking). Like everything else at the bar, the well kept Badger Best and Tanglefoot have their prices displayed with admirable clarity; fruit machine, TV, cribbage, dominoes, board games and soft piped music. There are many more tables out on a terrace and lawn behind. Bar food includes lunchtime soup (£2.95), sandwiches (from £2.95), burgers (from £3.45) and pasta carbonara (£5.95), as well as chicken and spinach curry (£6.95) and steaks (from £8.75), with a few more evening and Sunday dishes such as beef stifado (£7.95) and barbary duck breast (£12.75). More reports please. *(Recommended by Andrew York)*

Badger ~ Tenants Roger and Marion Hiron ~ Real ale ~ Bar food (11.30-3.30, 5.30-8.45) ~ Restaurant ~ (01258) 472208 ~ Children over 5 in restaurant ~ Dogs allowed in bar ~ Open 10-11; 11.30-10.30 Sun ~ Bedrooms: £45B/£65B

TARRANT MONKTON ST9408 Map 2
Langton Arms 🍴

Village signposted from A354, then head for church

Run with real care and thought, this pretty 17th-c thatched pub is owned by a farming couple. It's pretty much Mrs Cossins's show, though she sometimes hauls the farmer off his tractor to help behind the bar. Whether you're a family looking for a good lunch or a dog-walker after a quick well kept pint, this should enjoyably fit the bill (and your dog may be lucky enough to be offered a free sausage). Alongside Hop Back Best and Ringwood they serve three quickly changing varied guests from brewers such as Batemans, Butcombe and Moor on handpump (and have a beer festival once a year). The fairly simple beamed bar has a huge inglenook fireplace, settles, stools at the counter and other mixed dark furniture, and the public bar has a juke box, darts, pool, a fruit machine, TV, cribbage, and dominoes; piped music. The no smoking bistro restaurant is in an attractively reworked barn, and the skittle alley doubles as a no smoking family room during the day. The fairly imaginative menu (with one or two almost historically old-fashioned dishes) includes home-made soup (£2.95), filled baguettes (from £3.50), four-bean stew (£6.25), braised wild rabbit with tarragon and mustard (£7.20), chicken breast in oriental spices, breaded scampi or pigeon breast in cranberry and red wine sauce (£7.95), and puddings such as treacle tart, summer pudding or local ice creams (from £3.20). Children enjoy the very good wood-chip play area in the garden. The pub is in a charming village which has a ford that can flow quite fast in wet weather, and is well located for local walks and exploring the area. *(Recommended by Sheila and Robert Robinson, G Coates, John Robertson, Tom Evans, Ron Shelton, Ian Wilson, Stephen and Judy Parish)*

Free house ~ Licensees Barbara and James Cossins ~ Real ale ~ Bar food (11.30-2.30, 6-9) ~ Restaurant ~ (01258) 830225 ~ Children in restaurant and family room ~ Dogs allowed in bedrooms ~ Open 11.30-11; 12-10.30 Sun ~ Bedrooms: £50B/£70B

WEST BAY SY4690 Map 1
West Bay 🍽 🛏

Station Road

Dorset Dining Pub of the Year

Even on a winter midweek evening this seaside pub can get very busy with people turning up for the imaginatively prepared food, and particularly the extensive fresh fish menu, so it's virtually essential to book. Making the most of the freshly landed seafood (they always have at least 10 fish dishes), and using local suppliers wherever possible, the interesting menu might include soup (£3.25), sandwiches (from £3.50, fresh crab £4.25), ploughman's (£5.25), fried scallops with roasted pine nuts and crispy parma ham (£5.95), steak and kidney casserole with mustard dumpling or fettuccine with roasted vegetables, cream and coriander sauce and garlic croutons (£7.95), salmon fillet on seafood linguini with white wine sauce or salt and pepper duck breast on potato rösti with plum and redcurrant sauce (£11.95), monkfish and scallop thai green curry (£14.95) and hot crab and shellfish plate (£15.50). They have occasional gourmet evenings. An island servery separates the fairly simple bare-boards front part with its coal-effect gas fire and mix of sea and nostalgic prints from a cosier carpeted no smoking dining area with more of a country kitchen feel. Friendly hands-on licensees and cheerful service generate a pleasantly relaxed atmosphere. Well kept Palmers IPA, Copper and 200 on handpump, good house wines and whiskies, with decent piped music; they've also a skittles alley, and the local team meets here. A new dining terrace has tables outside; there's plenty of parking. Bedrooms are quiet and homely. *(Recommended by Bob and Margaret Holder, Janet and Julian le Patourel, M G Hart, Prof and Mrs S Barnett, Simon and Jane Williams, Joan and Michel Hooper-Immins)*

Palmers ~ Tenants John Ford and Karen Trimby ~ Real ale ~ Bar food (12-2, 6.30-9.30; 12-2.30, 7-9 Sun) ~ Restaurant ~ (01308) 422157 ~ Children in eating area of bar ~ Dogs allowed in bar ~ Open 11-2.30, 6-11; 12-3, 7-10.30 Sun; closed Sun evening winter ~ Bedrooms: /£60(£70B)

WEST BEXINGTON SY5387 Map 2
Manor Hotel 🛏

Village signposted off B3157 SE of Bridport; Beach Road

At quiet times you can hear waves breaking along the shore from this well run and much liked old stone-built hotel, which is just a short stroll from lovely if tiring walks on Chesil beach and the cliffs above. There are stunning views from the approach road, and you can see the sea from the smart no smoking Victorian-style conservatory (which has airy furnishings and lots of plants), the comfortable lounge with its log fire, the bedrooms, and also the garden, where there are picnic-sets on a small lawn with flower beds lining the low sheltering walls; a much bigger side lawn has a children's play area. The bustling downstairs cellar bar has horsebrasses on the walls, red leatherette stools and low-backed chairs (with one fat seat carved from a beer cask) under the black beams and joists, as well as heavy harness over the log fire; piped music. Very good attractively presented bar food served by smartly uniformed staff includes sandwiches (from £3.15), soup (£3.45), ploughman's (from £5.65), cottage pie and sausage and mash (£6.95), crab cakes (£7.55), vegetable moussaka (£8.55), peppered salmon (£12.65), and steaks (from

£12.95), with puddings such as chocolate roulade (£3.95); there's a good restaurant too, and breakfasts are much enjoyed. Well kept Butcombe Gold and Quay Steam Beer on handpump, quite a few malt whiskies and several wines by the glass. Readers really enjoy staying here, with the helpful, courteous staff going out of their way to make visitors feel welcome, and they are accommodating to families with young children. *(Recommended by R W E Farr, Peter and Giff Bennett, Alan and Paula McCully, W A Evershed, Gerry and Rosemary Dobson, W Seymour-Hamilton, OPUS, Lawrence Pearse)*

Free house ~ Licensees Peter King and Sheree Lynch ~ Real ale ~ Bar food ~ Restaurant ~ (01308) 897616 ~ Children welcome ~ Dogs allowed in bar ~ Open 11-11; 12-10.10 Sun ~ Bedrooms: £70B/£115B

WORTH MATRAVERS SY9777 Map 2

Square & Compass ★ ◀

At fork of both roads signposted to village from B3069

Not to be missed by fans of old-fashioned slightly idiosyncratic classics, this thriving pub has been run by the Newman family for more than 90 years. Hardly anything has changed during that time: it stays completely unspoilt and basic. On a winter's evening with the rain lashing the windows, you wouldn't be that surprised if a smuggler, complete with parrot and wooden leg, suddenly materialised. Well kept Badger Tanglefoot, Ringwood Best and a guest from a brewer such as Hop Back or Palmers are tapped from a row of casks and passed to you in a drinking corridor through two serving hatches – there's no bar counter. A couple of rooms opposite have simple furniture on the flagstones, a woodburning stove, and a staunch band of friendly locals (service is friendly too). The only bar food you can get is home-made pasties (£2.20, served all day); cribbage, shove-ha'penny and dominoes. A little free museum shows local fossils and artefacts, mostly collected by the current landlord and his father. The setting is a peaceful hilltop, and on a clear day gives a fantastic view from benches out in front, looking down over the village rooftops to the sea between the East Man and the West Man (the hills that guard the coastal approach) and out beyond Portland Bill. You may find free-roaming hens, chickens and other birds clucking around your feet. There are good walks from the pub – but limited parking, so it's usually best to park in the public car park 100 yards along the Corfe Castle road. *(Recommended by Pete Baker, A C Nugent, Mary and Dennis Jones, R J Davies, the Didler, Joyce and Geoff Robson, Andrea Rampley, John Roots, James Woods, JP, PP, Simon and Jane Williams, Mike and Sue Loseby, JDM, KM, Peter Meister, Michael and Ann Cole, Patrick Hancock, Bruce Bird)*

Free house ~ Licensee Charlie Newman ~ Real ale ~ Bar food (all day) ~ No credit cards ~ (01929) 439229 ~ Children welcome away from bar ~ Dogs allowed in bar ~ Open 12-3, 6-11; 12-11 Sat; 12-4, 7-10.30 Sun; closed Sun evening winter

Lucky Dip

Besides the fully inspected pubs, you might like to try these Lucky Dips recommended to us and described by readers (if you do, please send us reports: www.goodguides.com).

ABBOTSBURY [SY5785]
Ilchester Arms [B3157]: Busy rambling stone inn done out as themed servants' quarters from cook's sitting room to potting shed, with old pine furniture and lots to look at inc prints of the famous swans; decent food from sandwiches, ciabattas or baked potatoes up, attractive no smoking conservatory restaurant, quick service, Courage-related real ales tapped from the cask, good house wines in three glass sizes, nice views from suntrap terrace tables; darts, winter pool, fruit machine, TV and

piped music; children in eating areas, open all day *(L Elliott, Lawrence Pearse, OPUS, Dennis Jenkin, Tracey and Stephen Groves, David Carr, Gloria Bax, LYM, Ann and Colin Hunt, Mrs J Thomas)*
ALMER [SY9097]
☆ *Worlds End* [B3075, just off A31 towards Wareham]: Attractive open-plan thatched family dining pub, beams, panelled alcoves and soft lighting, very wide choice of food all day (you can choose generous or smaller helpings), well kept Badger ales, good quick friendly

service (lots of tables but so popular you may have to wait for one), restaurant with no smoking area; open all day, picnic-sets out in front and behind, outstanding play area *(Mrs J Slowgrove, BB, D and S Price)*

ASKERSWELL [SY5292]

☆ *Spyway* [off A35 Bridport—Dorchester]: Charming country pub with new licensees doing enjoyable food inc adventurous dishes and good fresh local fish, well kept Greene King Abbot, Palmers and a guest such as Branscombe Vale Branoc, old-fashioned high-backed settles, cushioned wall and window seats, cosy old-world décor, no smoking beamed dining area; children in eating areas, marvellous views from back terrace and garden, bedrooms, good walks *(David and Julie Glover, Mrs A P Lee, Graham and Rose Ive, LYM)*

BEAMINSTER [ST4701]

Hine Bar [Hogshill St]: Enjoyable well served food, well kept beer, decent wine; renamed and themed some years ago for local brandy family *(Simon and Jane Williams, Peter Neate)*

BERE REGIS [SY8494]

Drax Arms [West St; off A35 bypass]: Comfortable and welcoming village local with cheerful helpful service, well kept Badger ales and farm cider, limited choice of good reasonably priced home-made food from sandwiches up, esp pies and casseroles, big open fire on left, small dining area; good walking nearby *(R T and J C Moggridge)*

BISHOP'S CAUNDLE [ST6913]

☆ *White Hart* [A3030 SE of Sherborne]: Nicely moulded dark beams, ancient panelling, attractive furnishings, sizeable no smoking family area with french windows to big prettily floodlit garden with fine play area and all sorts of games; friendly helpful service, well kept Badger Best, K&B and Tanglefoot, wide choice of generous food from reasonably priced lunchtime sandwiches to steaks inc smaller and children's helpings; darts, skittle alley, fruit machine, muted piped music; reasonably priced bedrooms *(LYM, Marjorie and David Lamb, Pat and Robert Watt)*

BLANDFORD FORUM [ST8806]

Crown [West St]: Best Western hotel's well furnished spacious bar areas used by locals as pub, well kept Badger beers from nearby brewery, good range of reasonably priced bar food, separate restaurant; bedrooms *(Colin and Janet Roe, Peter Neate)*

BLANDFORD ST MARY [ST8805]

Hall & Woodhouse: New visitor centre, base for Badger brewery tours (not Sun), their full beer range, popular food; spectacular chandelier made of Badger beer bottles, lots of memorabilia in centre and upper gallery *(Joan and Michel Hooper-Immins)*

BOURNEMOUTH [SZ0691]

Porterhouse [Poole Rd, Westbourne]: Well kept Ringwood ales with a guest such as Rebellion Mutiny and changing farm ciders in welcoming dark-panelled tavern, good choice of malt whiskies, simple cheap bar lunches; disabled access *(G Coates)*

BOURTON [ST7430]

☆ *White Lion* [High St, off old A303 E of Wincanton]: Plushly refurbished stripped stone dining pub, welcoming and nicely lit beamed bars with sporting equipment, well kept real ales, well prepared and sensibly priced hearty food using good fresh ingredients, good range of home-made puddings, friendly service, restaurant; dogs welcome, well spaced tables in pleasant garden, two neat bedrooms *(Michael Yeo, LYM, R J Davies, Colin and Janet Roe)*

BRADFORD ABBAS [ST5814]

☆ *Rose & Crown* [Church Rd]: Popular country local with four linked rooms, two with blond tables set for the enjoyable food, well kept Bass and Wadworths IPA and 6X from thatched counter, pleasant service, interesting collection of old village photographs and clippings; may be quiet piped radio; charming sheltered garden by fine medieval church, bedrooms *(W W Burke, BB)*

BRIDPORT [SY4692]

George [South St]: This Georgian two-bar pub, which has been open all day and a popular main entry for its bargain home-made food (not Sun), Palmers ales, decent wines and informal atmosphere, has now been completely redone inside, too late for us to form a view yet – news please *(LYM)*

BROADWINDSOR [ST4302]

☆ *White Lion* [The Square (B3163/B3164)]: 17th-c stone-built pub/restaurant with friendly new tenants, good choice of generous reasonably priced home-made food using local produce from good sandwiches to popular Sun roasts, Palmers beers, pews and flagstones on left, pine booth seating and big inglenook with woodburner in carpeted area on right, a modicum of china, fresh and dried flowers; unobtrusive piped music, disabled facilities, no machines *(BB, Mrs T A Bizat, Ron Shelton)*

BURTON BRADSTOCK [SY4889]

☆ *Three Horseshoes* [Mill St]: Attractive thatched inn in charming village, with comfortable, homely and roomy carpeted lounge, well kept Palmers real ales, good wines, smiling helpful service, unpretentious quickly served bar food from sandwiches and baked potatoes up, separate no smoking restaurant, unobtrusive piped music (maybe enhanced by the local bellringers); Fri band night; tables out on lawn, pleasant shingle beach a few minutes' drive away (with NT car park), bedrooms *(James Woods, Pat and Tony Martin, LYM, Terry Mizen)*

CATTISTOCK [SY5999]

Fox & Hounds: Tucked-away 16th-c or older pub carefully refurbished and furnished in keeping by new landlord, enjoyable food, good friendly service, good reasonably priced wine choice; comfortable bedrooms *(anon)*

CERNE ABBAS [ST6601]

New Inn [14 Long Street]: Externally handsome Tudor inn with mullioned window seats in unpretentious beamed bar, well kept ales such as Tetleys and Wadworths 6X, no smoking dining room; children welcome, tables on sheltered lawn behind old coachyard, bedrooms, open all day wknds and summer *(Mr and Mrs Bentley-Davies, LYM, Joyce and Geoff Robson, Julia and Richard Tredgett)*

CHARLTON MARSHALL [ST9003]

☆ *Charlton Inn* [A350 Poole—Blandford]: Comfortably extended beamed pub with wide choice of good honest food (may take a while) from doorstep sandwiches up inc fresh fish and plenty of vegetarian dishes, very big helpings, particularly good veg, several carpeted country-style areas inc snug and plenty of dining tables, Badger Best and Tanglefoot, several wines by glass, quick service, no smoking area, unobtrusive piped music; small garden *(BB, Terry and Linda Moseley, David and Elizabeth Briggs)*

CHIDEOCK [SY4292]

☆ *George* [A35 Bridport—Lyme Regis]: Thatched 17th-c pub, welcoming and relaxed, with neat rows of tables in simple front bar, plusher lounge, hundreds of banknotes on beams, lots of ephemera and bric-a-brac, big log fire, well kept Palmers, good value wines and coffee, good value food from good hot-filled baguettes to fresh fish (like the meat all local), friendly helpful service, family room and big restaurant (two no smoking areas); may be quiet piped music; tables in back garden with terrace, bedrooms, open all day *(Ann and Colin Hunt, Peter Salmon, John and Vivienne Rice, LYM, W A Evershed)*

CORFE CASTLE [SY9681]

Castle Inn [East St]: Friendly smallish pub mentioned in Hardy's *Hand of Ethelberta*, good value home cooking inc Sun lunches, well kept Ringwood Best and Fortyniner, two smartly refurbished yet unpretentious rooms with flagstoned floors shown to good effect *(Robert Newton, JP, PP)*

☆ *Fox* [West St]: Old-fashioned take-us-as-you-find-us stone-built local with ancient origins inc pre-1300 stone fireplace, hatch service, tiny front bar, glassed-over well in lounge (many tables reserved for eaters), well kept ales such as Greene King Abbot, Fullers London Pride or Wadworths 6X tapped from the cask, food from sandwiches and baguettes up; dogs allowed in, informal garden *(A C Nugent, Paul A Moore, Mary and Dennis Jones, Patrick Hancock, David Carr, R J Davies, Andrea Rampley, Geoffrey G Lawrance, the Didler, JP, PP)*

☆ *Greyhound* [A351]: Bustling much photographed old pub in centre of tourist village, three small low-ceilinged panelled rooms, several well kept changing ales such as Gales and Hook Norton, traditional games inc Purbeck shove-ha'penny on 5ft board, no smoking family room, food (all day in summer, inc wknd breakfast) from filled rolls and baked potatoes up; piped music may be loud, live Fri; garden with fine castle and countryside views, pretty courtyard opening on to castle bridge, bedrooms, open all day wknds and summer *(LYM, James Woods, JDM, KM, Philip and June Caunt, David Carr, Dave Braisted, Dr D E Granger, Patrick Hancock, JP, PP, the*

Didler, Tracey and Stephen Groves, Andrew York, Darly Graton, Graeme Gulibert)*

CORFE MULLEN [SY9798]

Coventry Arms [A31 W of Wimborne; Mill St]: Two linked low-beamed bars separated by open fire, various nooks and corners, Ringwood and guest ales tapped from the cask, decent clutch of malt whiskies, good unusual food from filled baked potatoes and baguettes up, good service, tables out by small stream; quiet lunchtime but busy evenings, with weekly live music and lots of special events *(Ian and Deborah Carrington)*

Holme Bush [Old Wareham Rd]: Neatly kept country pub with real ales such as Flowers, Gales and Ringwood, decent wines, good value straightforward food inc OAP lunches and fresh fish, friendly service, two bar areas each with a log-effect gas fire, beamed dining extension; piped music; picnic-sets in garden with animals and aviaries, open all day *(B and K Hypher)*

CORSCOMBE [ST5205]

☆ *Fox* [outskirts, towards Halstock]: Quintessential old thatched country pub in attractive setting, roses over the door, big inglenook log fires, beams and flagstones, built-in settles and other assorted furniture, nice country prints and bric-a-brac, Aga in no smoking extra dining room; friendly new licensees, well kept Exmoor and Fullers London Pride, local cider, good wines, ambitious food; well behaved children welcome, tables on streamside lawn over quiet lane on a lawn, good walks, comfortable bedrooms *(Mike Gorton, LYM)*

CRANBORNE [SU0513]

☆ *Fleur-de-Lys* [B3078 N of Wimborne]: Well run and furnished 17th-c inn nicely set on the edge of Cranborne Chase, subject of a witty Rupert Brooke poem about going to the wrong pub (framed above fire in panelled lounge); friendly landlord, simpler beamed public bar with well kept Badger Best and Tanglefoot, farm cider, decent wines, good value bar food from good baguettes and sandwiches up inc children's, evening restaurant; pub games, piped music, TV; comfortable pretty bedrooms *(H D Wharton, Colin and Mary Prior, David Surridge, John and Judy Saville, Mike and Shelley Woodroffe, LYM, Dr D E Granger, W W Burke, Colin and Janet Roe)*

DORCHESTER [SY6890]

☆ *Blue Raddle* [Church St]: Thriving unpretentious sidestreet local popular with older people for its good very attractively priced food inc game, well kept changing ales from small West Country breweries, good wines, obliging landlord; no credit cards, may be quiet piped jazz; disabled access, but one step *(John Beeken, Peter Neate, G Coates, David Carr, Simon and Jane Williams, the Didler, Meg and Colin Hamilton)*

Kings Arms [High East St]: Hotel bar with well kept Bass and Courage Directors, decent wines, food from sandwiches up, pleasant helpful service, open fire; close associations with

Nelson and Hardy's *Mayor of Casterbridge*; bedrooms (the Lawrence of Arabia suite and the Tutankhamen are pretty striking) *(Ian Phillips, the Didler, David Carr, LYM)*

☆ *Poet Laureate* [Pummery Sq, Poundbury]: Recently opened in the Prince of Wales's Poundbury development (two readers found the Prince having a drink there to celebrate Poundbury's 10th anniversary): substantial building, with light and airy L-shaped bar, good range of food from baguettes to enjoyable full meals (meats from named local farms), well kept Bass and Palmers, short choice of decent wines, proper coffee, pleasant restaurant area, quick friendly service, daily papers and a couple of sofas, a hint of regency in the décor, flame-effect stove; unobtrusive piped music, jazz Sun evening; a few picnic-sets on side terrace *(W W Burke, Terry and Linda Moseley, B and K Hypher)*

Tom Browns [High East St]: Small plain bare-boards L-shaped bar notable for very well kept Goldfinch beers such as Tom Browns Best, Flashmans Clout and Midnight Blinder brewed in back microbrewery, wholesome reasonably priced bar food most lunchtimes (not Sun); welcoming staff, friendly locals, traditional games; nostalgic juke box, outside lavatories; open all day Thurs-Sun *(Simon and Jane Williams, G Coates)*

EAST STOUR [ST8123]
Kings Arms [B3095, 3 miles W towards Shaftesbury; The Common]: Large bar with good eating area, new owners doing good value fresh home-made food, wide range of well kept ales inc Bass, decent wines, good friendly service, local paintings and drawings, no piped music; public bar with darts and fruit machine, children welcome; lots of flowers in front, tables in big garden *(Pat and Robert Watt)*

FIDDLEFORD [ST8013]
☆ *Fiddleford Inn* [A357 Sturminster Newton— Blandford Forum]: Comfortable and cheerful, good generous quickly served food from sandwiches up in lounge bar, restaurant area and back family area, well kept real ales such as Scattor Rock, friendly service, three linked smartly refurbished areas (can get full despite all the space), ancient flagstones and some other nice touches; unobtrusive piped music; big pleasant garden with play area *(Tom Evans, B and K Hypher, David Rawlins, LYM)*

HINTON ST MARY [ST7816]
White Horse [just off B3092 1 mile N of Sturminster]: Village local with unusual inglenook fireplace in cheery tiled bar, nicely set dining tables in extended lounge, enjoyable reasonably priced food, well kept real ales inc changing guests, darts; tables in flower garden *(Marjorie and David Lamb)*

KINGSTON [SY9579]
Scott Arms [West St (B3069)]: Busy well run holiday pub with rambling warren-like rooms, panelling, stripped stone, beams, open fires and some fine antique prints, attractive room overlooking garden, decent family extension, well kept Courage Directors and Ringwood

Best, lots of wines, nice staff, generous if not cheap standard food inc summer cream teas, no smoking dining area; darts, dominoes and fruit machine, piped music; attractive garden with superb views of Corfe Castle and the Purbeck Hills *(the Didler, John Roots, LYM, JP, PP)*

LANGTON HERRING [SY6182]
☆ *Elm Tree* [signed off B3157]: Low black beams, lots of copper, brass and bellows, cushioned window seats, windsor chairs and scrubbed pine tables, inglenook, and traditionally furnished extension, good range of food from lunchtime sandwiches and ciabattas up inc some interesting dishes, mainly organic local suppliers, decent house wine, Bass and Flowers or Marstons Pedigree, friendly staff cope well even when busy; no dogs inside; pretty flower-filled sunken garden, track down to Coast Path which skirts Chesil lagoon *(Liz and John Soden, Lawrence Pearse, Peter Neate, J S Davies, James Woods, OPUS, Dave Braisted, LYM, W A Evershed, Joan and Michel Hooper-Immins, S P Watkin, P A Taylor)*

LANGTON MATRAVERS [SY9978]
Kings Arms [High St]: Popular old-fashioned village pub with ancient flagstoned corridor to bar, simple rooms off, one with a fine local marble fireplace, nice pictures, well kept Ringwood Best and Fortyniner and a guest such as Fullers London Pride, friendly locals and staff, generous plain home cooking from tiny kitchen inc good Sun roasts, splendid antique Purbeck longboard for shove-ha'penny; sunny picnic-sets outside, good walks *(B and K Hypher, Richard Burton, LYM)*

LITTON CHENEY [SY5590]
☆ *White Horse*: Relaxed and unpretentious, with good home-made food using fresh local ingredients (some home-grown veg), well kept Palmers Copper, Best and 200, friendly efficient staff, woodburner, pictures on stripped stone walls, some flagstones, country kitchen chairs in dining area, table skittles; good spot on quiet lane into quaint village, picnic-sets on pleasant streamside front lawn *(BB, R J Davies, W A Evershed, Joan and Michel Hooper-Immins, Marjorie and David Lamb)*

LODERS [SY4994]
Loders Arms [off A3066 just N of Bridport]: Comfortably worn in local, welcoming and relaxed, log fire, Palmers real ales, good choice of house wines, good value changing food from huge baguettes to interesting main dishes, no smoking dining room, skittle alley; may be piped music; children in eating areas, pleasant views from tables in small back garden, pretty thatched village, open all day Sun *(LYM, OPUS, Marjorie and David Lamb)*

LONGHAM [SZ0699]
Angel [A348 Ferndown—Poole]: Beamed roadside pub newly refurbished and extended, roomy bar, family room in extension, tables and chairs on wooden floors, wide choice of food from baguettes (no sandwiches now) to

good value unpretentious piping hot dishes inc steaks and children's, good smiling staff, well kept Badger Best and Tanglefoot; big garden with lots of play facilities inc bouncy castle *(John and Vivienne Rice)*

LYME REGIS [SY3492]

Pilot Boat [Bridge St]: Handy food spot, nicely set nr waterfront, plenty of tables in cheery nautically themed bars with no smoking dining area, cheap quickly served generous food all day from sandwiches to steak, Palmers real ales, several wines by the glass, skittle alley; piped music; children and dogs welcome, tables out on terrace, open all day *(Peter Salmon, Quentin and Carol Williamson, Mike and Cheryl Lyons, Tracey and Stephen Groves, James A Waller, LYM, JDM, KM, Joan and Michel Hooper-Immins, Pat and Tony Martin)*

Royal Standard [Marine Parade, The Cobb]: Right on broadest part of beach, with suntrap courtyard (own servery and wendy house); lively bar serving area dominated by pool table and piped pop, but has some fine built-in stripped high settles, and there's a quieter no smoking area with stripped brick and pine; well kept Palmers BB, 200 and Copper, good value food inc sensibly priced sandwiches, plenty of local crab and fish, good cream teas, darts; children welcome *(BB, Joan and Michel Hooper-Immins)*

Victoria [Uplyme Rd]: Enjoyable food in bar and restaurant, well kept beer, welcoming staff *(Mr and Mrs Patrick Fowler)*

☆ *Volunteer* [top of Broad St (A3052 towards Exeter)]: Friendly local atmosphere in long cosy low-ceilinged bar, enjoyable food inc lots of modestly priced fresh local fish in dining room (former lounge – children allowed here), good changing choice of well kept ales and farm ciders, roaring fires; dogs welcome, open all day *(Suzanne Miles, Mike Stephenson, LYM)*

MARNHULL [ST7719]

Blackmore Vale [Burton St, via Church Hill off B3092]: Comfortably modernised pub with large open fire in extended no smoking dining area, cosy smaller bar with settles, sofas and pub games, well kept Badger beers, traditional menu, pleasant service; piped music; children welcome, tables in garden (one of them thatched) *(LYM, Colin and Janet Roe)*

MARSHWOOD [SY3799]

Bottle [B3165 Lyme Regis—Crewkerne]: 16th-c thatched country local with enjoyable food inc interesting dishes, organic ingredients and a good vegetarian choice, well kept ales inc Weymouth, big inglenook log fire in attractive low-ceilinged bar, small games bar, skittle alley; good spacious garden with camp site beyond, pretty walking country *(Tracey and Stephen Groves, Pat and Tony Martin, LYM)*

MIDDLEMARSH [ST6607]

☆ *Hunters Moon* [A352 Sherborne—Dorchester]: Reopened after thorough refurbishment, with plenty of tables in largely no smoking L-shaped bar, good if not cheap food from sensibly limited menu, well kept Bass, Palmers IPA, Sharps Doom Bar and Timothy Taylors

Landlord, proper coffee, low beams, three log fires and pleasant décor; good seats out in nice big garden, attractive bedrooms with own bathrooms *(Joy and Arthur Hoadley, M G Hart, Peter Neate, Joan and Michel Hooper-Immins)*

MORETON [SY7889]

Frampton Arms [B3390 nr station]: Quiet, relaxed and very neatly kept, with good choice of generous good value food from sandwiches and crisp baguettes up inc good fish and seafood, well kept Boddingtons and Flowers IPA, log fire, friendly landlord, good service even on a busy Sun, steam railway pictures in lounge bar, Warmwell Aerodrome theme in public bar, bright and airy conservatory restaurant; tables on front terrace, comfortable bedrooms *(John and Vivienne Rice, D J Ferrett, Mrs Hazel Blackburn)*

MUDEFORD [SZ1892]

☆ *Ship in Distress*: Dining pub very popular for good fresh carefully cooked fish and seafood, and classy puddings, in restaurant (best to book) and bar – two rooms, one plain, one cosy with fun décor inc hops, plants and nautical memorabilia; well kept Bass, Greenalls Original, Marstons Pedigree and Ringwood Best, good house wines, friendly service *(A D Marsh, Julian and Linda Cooke)*

NETTLECOMBE [SY5195]

☆ *Marquis of Lorne* [off A3066 Bridport—Beaminster, via W Milton]: Tucked away in lovely countryside, neat and comfortable panelled main bar, two smarter dining areas, one no smoking, log fires, good food from sandwiches to fresh fish and carefully cooked game, well kept Palmers real ales, decent wines, friendly generally efficient service, public bar with cribbage, dominoes and table skittles; children in eating areas, seven comfortable bedrooms with big breakfast, big pretty garden with rustic-style play area *(R Clark, Keith Barker, Ann and Colin Hunt, David and Julie Glover, Roger Braithwaite, Tracey and Stephen Groves, R M Corlett, Elizabeth Pickard, Dominic and Christiane Zwemmer, Paul and Annette Hallett, Anthony J Woodroffe, Simon and Jane Williams, Philip and Elaine Holmes, Evelyn and Derek Walter, LYM, Michael Graubart and Valerie Coumont Graubart, Joan and Michel Hooper-Immins)*

OSMINGTON MILLS [SY7381]

☆ *Smugglers* [off A353 NE of Weymouth]: Enterprising new young licensees in pretty part-thatched pub, much extended but done well, with cosy dark corners, log stove, shiny black panelling and nautical decorations; well kept Badger Best, Tanglefoot and a guest such as Fursty Ferret, quickly served generous enjoyable food from good filled baps to full meals, partly no smoking restaurant; discreet games area, piped music, can be very crowded in summer (holiday settlement nearby), disabled access tricky; children in eating areas, streamside garden with good play area and thatched summer bar, fine position a short stroll up from the sea, good cliff walks, four comfortable bedrooms, big breakfast, open all day *(the Didler, LYM, Pamela and Merlyn Horswell, John Hale, Kerry and Tricia Thomas, Alain and Rose Foote, Joan and Michel Hooper-Immins, S P Watkin, P A Taylor)*

PIDDLETRENTHIDE [SY7099]

☆ *European:* Unpretentiously old-fashioned oak-beamed pub locally favoured for good generous reasonably priced fresh food (perhaps not Tues, should book wknds) inc fine home-cooked ham and very good value lamb shanks, well kept Courage Directors and Ringwood Best, genuinely friendly and helpful cheery staff, log fire in attractive copper-hooded fireplace, willow-pattern china, stylish chairs; piped music; tables in neatly kept front garden, three bedrooms with own baths and good views *(Dennis Jenkin, BB, R J Townson)*

PIMPERNE [ST9009]

Anvil [well back from A354]: 16th-c thatched pub with bays of plush seating in bright and welcoming modern bar, all clean and shiny, pink walls with some stripped brick, enjoyable home-made food from generous sandwiches to venison, real ales such as Butcombe and Fullers London Pride, friendly staff; fruit machine, piped music; bedrooms with own bathrooms, attractive surroundings *(Ron Shelton, BB)*

POOLE [SZ0190]

Blue Boar [Market Cl]: Comfortable former mansion house opened as a pub in the 1990s, with well kept Cottage Southern, Courage Best and Directors and two guest beers, wide choice of inexpensive lunchtime food, lots of interesting nautical theme pictures and artefacts, cellar bar too with live music wknds and folk club Weds; nearby parking can be difficult *(Dave Way)*

☆ *Guildhall Tavern* [Market St]: Largely restaurant rather than pub, French-run and good (if not cheap), mainly fish; friendly service, small front bar, well kept Ringwood and decent house wine, thorough-going bright nautical décor, thriving atmosphere *(B and K Hypher, LYM, D Cairns)*

☆ *Inn in the Park* [Pinewood Rd, off A338 towards Branksome Chine, via The Avenue]: Pleasantly decorated and cheerful open-plan bar in substantial Edwardian villa (now a small hotel), popular with local residents and business people for well kept Adnams Broadside, Bass and Wadworths 6X and good value generous bar food (not Sun evening) from good 'sandwedges' (sandwiches with chips) to fresh seafood, airy and attractive restaurant (children allowed) and Sun carvery; polite young staff, log fire, oak panelling and big mirrors, tables on small sunny terrace; comfortable bedrooms, quiet pine-filled residential area just above sea *(Mrs V A Goulds, W W Burke, LYM, JDM, KM)*

PORTLAND [SY6872]

George [Reforne]: Particularly well kept Ringwood Best, Greene King Abbot, a guest beer and good value food (not Weds lunchtime) from big filled baps to cheap home-made hot dishes in 17th-c stone-built pub

mentioned by Thomas Hardy and reputed to have smugglers' tunnels running to the cliffs; low beams, flagstones, small rooms, interesting prints and a case of Georgian shillings, children's room *(Joan and Michel Hooper-Immins)*

PORTLAND BILL [SY6768]

Pulpit: Welcoming extended dark-beamed pub in great spot nr Pulpit Rock, short stroll to lighthouse and cliffs, picture-window views; generous quickly served food inc local fish and crab (wide evening choice), well kept Bass, Fullers London Pride, Greene King Old Speckled Hen and Ringwood Best; may be piped music *(Joan and Michel Hooper-Immins)*

POWERSTOCK [SY5196]

☆ *Three Horseshoes* [off A3066 Beaminster—Bridport via W Milton]: Friendly new landlord/chef in attractive country pub with good fires and stripped panelling, appealing fresh food from generous baguettes to full meals inc good fish, well kept Palmers real ales, good wines by the glass, children welcome in no smoking restaurant; open all day, pleasant bedrooms, lovely views towards the sea from tables in big garden behind *(Chris and Ann Coy, S G N Bennett, Michael Graubart and Valerie Coumont Graubart, OPUS, LYM, Ann and Colin Hunt, Philip and Elaine Holmes, Barry and Verina Jones, Richard Gibbs, Simon and Jane Williams, C W Burke)*

PRESTON [SY7082]

Spyglass [Bowleaze Coveway]: Busy bright and airy family dining pub, great views over Weymouth Bay from top of Furzy Cliff, wide choice of enjoyable food with plenty for children, four to six well kept ales such as Courage Directors, Ringwood Fortyniner and Quay JD1742 and Harbourmaster; piped music; tables outside, adventure play area *(Colin and Janet Roe, Joan and Michel Hooper-Immins)*

PUNCKNOWLE [SY5388]

☆ *Crown* [off B3157 Bridport—Abbotsbury]: 16th-c thatched and heavy-beamed inn facing partly Norman church, welcoming log fires in big stone fireplaces, plush stripped stone lounge, neat rambling public bar (darts and table skittles) with no smoking family room, friendly cheerful staff, well kept Palmers Copper, IPA, 200 and seasonal Tally Ho, country wines, straightforward food from sandwiches and baked potatoes up; views from nice peaceful back garden, good walks, bedrooms *(Lynn Sharpless, W W Burke, Alan and Paula McCully, LYM, Ian and Deborah Carrington, David Carr, OPUS, Elizabeth Pickard, Marjorie and David Lamb, Ann and Colin Hunt, Dr Diana Terry, Tim O'Keefe, W A Evershed, Geoffrey G Lawrance, Joan and Michel Hooper-Immins)*

SANDFORD ORCAS [ST6220]

☆ *Mitre* [off B3148 and B3145 N of Sherborne]: Tucked-away country local with flagstones and fresh flowers throughout, welcoming attentive service, good value attractively presented straightforward food, well kept real ales, country wines, small bar and larger pleasantly homely dining area; has been cl Mon lunchtime *(LYM, Debbie and Neil Hayter)*

SHAFTESBURY [ST8622]

Half Moon [Salisbury Rd (A30, by roundabout)]: Pleasantly enlarged family-friendly pub with comfortable restaurant area, wide choice of good value generous food inc popular Sun lunch, quick welcoming service, Badger beers; garden with adventure playground *(Marjorie and David Lamb, Nicholas and Dorothy Stephens)*

☆ **SHAVE CROSS** [SY4198]

Shave Cross Inn: Charming partly 14th-c thatched pub with flagstones and enormous inglenook, recently reopened and attractively furnished under new individualistic landlord, with enjoyable food (just roasts, crab sandwiches or prawns Sun lunchtime), stylish dining room and pretty garden; more reports please *(LYM)*

SHERBORNE [ST6316]

Half Moon [Half Moon St]: Smart and upmarket but relaxed, with clubby alcoves in bar, attractive bright and airy no smoking restaurant, good choice of enjoyable and thoughtful food, also sandwiches, baked potatoes and children's dishes; 16 bedrooms with own bathrooms *(Joan and Michel Hooper-Immins)*

STOKE ABBOTT [ST4500]

☆ *New Inn* [off B3162 and B3163 2 miles W of Beaminster]: 17th-c thatched pub well run by friendly new tenants, reliable generous home-made food inc local fish and OAP lunches, well kept Palmers ales, decent wines; beams, flagstones and brasses, stripped stone alcoves on either side of one big log fireplace, another with handsome panelling, no smoking dining room; children welcome, neat and attractive sizeable garden, unspoilt quiet thatched village, good walks, bedrooms *(LYM, Simon and Jane Williams, Basil Minson, Mrs G Coleman, Marjorie and David Lamb, J S Davies)*

STUDLAND [SZ0382]

☆ *Bankes Arms* [off B3351, Isle of Purbeck; Manor Rd]: Very popular spot above fine beach, outstanding country, sea and cliff views from huge pleasant garden with masses of seating; comfortably basic, friendly and easy-going big bar with raised drinking area, very wide choice of decent food (at a price) all day from baguettes to local fish and good crab salad, well kept beers such as Palmers, Poole, Wadworths 6X and unusual guest beers, local farm cider, good wines by the glass, efficient service, great log fire; big-screen sports TV, darts and pool in side games area; children welcome, just off Coast Path; can get very busy trippery wknds and in summer, parking in season can be complicated or expensive if you're not a NT member; big comfortable bedrooms *(Ron Shelton, Betsy Brown, Nigel Flook, A C Nugent, David and Elizabeth Briggs, Jayne and Peter Capp, Tony and Katie Lewis, JDM, KM, Dr B and Mrs P B Baker, W Ruxton, James Woods, Jenny and Brian Seller, Dr Diana Terry, Tim O'Keefe)*

Manor House [Manor Rd]: Quiet and civilised

hotel with good value food (may have to book – and you can't just come for a drink), quick welcoming service even when busy, comfortable spacious lounge with open fire, conservatory, coast views, attractive garden above beach; attractive bedrooms, handy for walks *(Ron Shelton)*

STURMINSTER MARSHALL [SY9499]

Black Horse [A350]: New tenant doing enjoyable food from particularly good sandwiches up, comfortable long bar, interesting pictures and local artefacts in dining area, well kept Badger ales *(Pat and Robert Watt)*

☆ *Red Lion* [N end of High St, opp handsome church; off A350 Blandford—Poole]: Attractive and well run village pub, clean and pleasant, with old-fashioned roomy U-shaped bar, good friendly relaxed atmosphere, good value home-made food inc substantial interesting starters, bargain OAP two-course lunch, sandwiches on Sun too, smart efficient service, well kept Badger Best and Tanglefoot, log fire, team photographs and caricatures, cabinet of sports trophies, quiet end round corner, roomy no smoking restaurant/family room in skittle alley conversion *(BB, Paul and Annette Hallett, Michael and Ann Cole, John and Joan Nash, David M Cundy, B and K Hypher)*

SWANAGE [SZ0278]

Red Lion [High St]: Stone-built two-bar pub, low beams densely hung with hundreds of keys, real ales such as Flowers, Greene King Old Speckled Hen and Ringwood, Addlestone's cider, decent food, prompt friendly service; piped music; children's games in large barn, picnic-sets in extended garden with partly covered back terrace *(Peter and Audrey Dowsett, the Didler, JP, PP, R J Davies)*

SYDLING ST NICHOLAS [SY6399]

☆ *Greyhound* [High St]: Wide choice of good food from filled crusty rolls to main dishes with plentiful properly cooked veg, good fish and delicious puddings, friendly family service, chatty locals, well kept Palmers and Youngs Special, long brick bar counter, some stripped stonework and flagstones, pleasant bistro-style flagstoned conservatory, restaurant, pool, piped music; good tables in nice small garden with play area, very pretty village *(Anthony Barnes, Simon and Jane Williams, BB, Dr and Mrs D Woods)*

SYMONDSBURY [SY4493]

☆ *Ilchester Arms* [signed off A35 just W of Bridport]: Attractive and popular partly thatched old inn in peaceful village, snugly traditional open-plan low-ceilinged bar with high-backed settle built in by big inglenook, cosy no smoking dining area with another fire, good food choice concentrating on local produce (bistro meals and take-aways too, but they do stick strictly to the menu), well kept Palmers beers, friendly service; pub games, skittle alley; children welcome, tables by pretty brookside back garden, good walks nearby *(Marjorie and David Lamb, Simon and*

Jane Williams, LYM, Stephen, Julie and Hayley Brown, Dr Diana Terry, Tim O'Keefe, Tracey and Stephen Groves)

TOLPUDDLE [SY7994]

Martyrs [former A35 W of Bere Regis]: Relaxed friendly local feel, good fresh food in bar and busy attractively laid out restaurant, hard-working staff, well kept Badger beers; no credit cards; children welcome, nice garden with ducks, hens and rabbits, open all day, quiet bypassed village *(Glenwys and Alan Lawrence, Gerald Wilkinson, Ann and Colin Hunt, R T and J C Moggridge)*

UPLODERS [SY5093]

☆ *Crown* [signed off A35 E of Bridport]: Welcoming new tenants and helpful staff in homely brightly furnished low-beamed village pub, plentiful enjoyable food, well kept Palmers ales, log fires, pretty restaurant; table skittles; tables in attractive two-tier garden, bedrooms *(Simon and Jane Williams, Brian and Bett Cox, Alan and Paula McCully, Mrs A P Lee, LYM)*

UPWEY [SY6785]

Old Ship [off A354; Ridgeway]: Welcoming new licensees in traditional beamed pub with lots of alcoves and log fires each end, well kept changing ales such as Fullers London Pride, food from lunchtime baguettes to some good interesting fish dishes; picnic-sets in garden with terrace *(M G Hart, Mrs J Thomas, Joyce and Geoff Robson, John Beeken, Sean Odell, Cathy Robinson, Ed Coombe, Peter Neate, JDM, KM, Simon and Jane Williams, Alan and Paula McCully, LYM)*

☆ *Riverhouse* [B3159, nr junction A354]: Coal-effect gas fireplace dividing flagstoned bar side from neat carpeted no smoking dining side, main emphasis on wide range of good food from lunchtime baguettes through familiar dishes to italian specialities, children's dishes, well kept Wadworths 6X and a beer brewed for the pub, adventurous wine choice, good coffees, friendly efficient service; well reproduced piped pop music; disabled access, sizeable garden with play area, cl Sun evening *(H Robinson, Tony and Jenny Holland, Peter Neate, L Elliott, BB)*

WAREHAM FOREST [SY9089]

Silent Woman [Wareham—Bere Regis]: New management in deceptively big all-day food pub, lounge bar extended into stripped-masonry dining area with country bygones, well kept Badger ales, more interesting books than usual on walls, military insignia, access for wheelchairs; children welcome, good play area, walks nearby *(Pat and Robert Watt)*

WEST BAY [SY4590]

Bridport Arms: Cheerfully unpretentious 16th-c thatched local on beach of Bridport's low-key holiday village, generous good value food esp soups and fish, well kept Palmers IPA, Copper and 200, two-room lounge and separate basic flagstoned summer bar, back family room facing beach, bright dining room, no music; tables in adjoining hotel with own entrance; tables outside, paying public car park *(Joan and Michel Hooper-Immins,*

E G Parish, BB)

WEST KNIGHTON [SY7387]

New Inn [off A352 E of Dorchester]: Biggish neatly refurbished pub with good value food inc tempting puddings, friendly attentive staff, real ales, country wines, small restaurant, skittle alley, good provision for children; big colourful garden, pleasant setting in quiet village with wonderful views *(Simon and Jane Williams, Terry and Linda Moseley, Bill and Doreen Sawford)*

WEST LULWORTH [SY8280]

Lulworth Cove: Good beer, good range of enjoyable food *(Simon and Jane Williams)*

WEST STAFFORD [SY7289]

☆ *Wise Man* [signed off A352 Dorchester—Wareham]: New licensees doing good food inc local fish (this Thurs-Sat only, out of season) and some inventive cooking in comfortable 16th-c village pub nr Hardy's cottage, very busy in summer; thatch, beams, toby jugs and masses of old pipes, happy staff, well kept Ringwood Best and a couple of guest beers, farm cider, decent wines and country wines, coal and log fire, sensibly placed darts, close-set tables in cottagey stripped-stone restaurant; piped music; reasonable disabled access, dogs on leads welcome, solid tables out in front, picnic-sets in small back garden, lovely walks nearby *(J G Dias, Simon and Jane Williams, Pamela and Merlyn Horswell, BB, R J Davies, Joan and Michel Hooper-Immins)*

WEST STOUR [ST7822]

Ship: Good value very generous food cooked by landlord, friendly landlady, well kept local beer, spotless attractive furnishings, big log fire, lovely views from chatty bar, intimate split-level restaurant; garden behind, comfortable bedrooms *(Pat and Robert Watt, M Chapman, Colin and Janet Roe)*

WEYMOUTH [SY6778]

Boot [High West St]: Largely 18th-c beamed pub nr harbour, beams and stone-mullioned windows even older, well kept Ringwood ales with a guest beer, Cheddar Vale and Thatcher's farm cider, good value filled rolls and cold snacks, welcoming bearded landlord *(Joan and Michel Hooper-Immins, Simon and Jane Williams)*

Dorothy [Esplanade]: Neatly kept real-ale pub in outstanding seafront spot, great views from pavement tables; big plain two-level open-plan bar, carpet and bare boards, interesting changing ales such as Badger Tanglefoot, Bass, Cotleigh Golden Eagle, Exmoor Fox, Palmers Gold, Weymouth Quay Best and one brewed for the pub by Otter, farm cider, good value straightforward food (all day in summer, from breakfast on) inc crab sandwiches and variety sausages, friendly landlady, daily papers; children welcome, some tables outside, open all day, multi-bed bedrooms (may stay open as nightclub till 2am – if so they warn B&B customers) *(the Didler, Joan and Michel Hooper-Immins, Tracey and Stephen Groves)*

Ferrybridge [Portland Rd, Wyke Regis]: Unpretentious pub with new licensees doing reliable food and well kept beers *(OPUS)*

Marquis of Granby [Chickerell Rd (B3157)]: Happily homely and welcoming modern pub, comfortable and softly lit, with well kept Greene King Abbot and Old Speckled Hen, Ringwood Best and Wadworths 6X, enjoyable food with some nice touches, restaurant, good service; tables outside, with covered area *(Joan and Michel Hooper-Immins)*

Old Rooms [Cove Row/Trinity Rd]: Bustling low-beamed pub, well priced food (some all day at least in summer) inc lots of fish, friendly staff, changing real ales, old nautical lamps and maps, unpretentious restaurant; may be piped music, no nearby parking; front terrace with harbour views over part-pedestrianised street *(Liz and John Soden)*

☆ *Red Lion* [Hope Sq]: Lively unsmart bare-boards pub with well kept Courage Best and (brewed at smart touristy Brewers Quay complex in former brewery opp) Silent Knight, JD1742 and Organic Gold, quickly served cheap simple lunches from good crab sandwiches up, interesting RNLI and fishing stuff all over the walls and ceiling (even two boats), open fires, daily papers, friendly family atmosphere, good staff; plenty of tables on sunny terrace (more than inside), open all day in summer (food all day then too) *(the Didler, Simon and Jane Williams, BB, Joan and Michel Hooper-Immins)*

Spa [Dorchester Rd, Radipole; off A354 at Safeway roundabout]: Large open-plan family pub, enjoyable food (all day Sun) from traditional favourites to local and exotic fish and other changing more unusual dishes, good helpings, friendly attentive service, real ales such as Tetleys and Wadworths 6X, peaceful no smoking picture-window back restaurant; open all day, good garden with terrace and play area *(Joan and Michel Hooper-Immins)*

Wellington Arms [St Alban St]: Unpretentious panelled town pub, good value lunchtime food (all day summer wkdys) from toasted sandwiches and baguettes to sensibly priced hot dishes inc daily roasts, well kept Ind Coope Burton, Tetleys and Wadworths 6X, children welcome in no smoking back dining room *(Joan and Michel Hooper-Immins)*

WINFRITH NEWBURGH [SY8085]

Red Lion [A352 Wareham—Dorchester]: Comfortable and welcoming family dining pub with wide range of reasonably priced food, enthusiastic manager, friendly prompt service, Badger ales; TV room, piped music, tables in big sheltered garden (site for caravans), bedrooms *(Marjorie and David Lamb)*

WINTERBORNE KINGSTON [SY8697]

Greyhound [North St]: Good range of food in bar and popular carvery restaurant, efficient service, well kept ales inc Fullers London Pride, plenty of room; may be piped radio *(Marjorie and David Lamb, Dudley and Moira Cockroft)*

WINTERBORNE ZELSTON [SY8997]

Botany Bay [A31 Wimborne—Dorchester]: Roomy and attractive restaurant-oriented pub with good range of reasonably priced food, well kept Ringwood, decent house wines and coffee, lots of books, quick friendly service; tables on back terrace *(Marjorie and David Lamb, Miss J F Reay)*

WOOL [SY8486]

Ship [A352 Wareham—Dorchester]: Roomy open-plan thatched and timbered family pub, well decorated and furnished, with good choice of generous locally sourced food all day from baguettes and baked potatoes to seafood inc children's in long low-ceilinged lounge bar and plush back restaurant, friendly quick service, well kept Badger Best, K&B and Tanglefoot, decent wines, good coffee; quiet piped music; picnic-sets overlooking railway in attractive fenced garden with terrace and play area, handy for Monkey World and Tank Museum, pleasant village *(Jenny and Brian Seller, Joan and Michel Hooper-Immins, Mrs Pat Crabb, Terry and Linda Moseley)*

Bedroom prices normally include full english breakfast, VAT and any inclusive service charge that we know of. Prices before the '/' are for single rooms, after for two people in double or twin (B includes a private bath, S a private shower). If there is no '/', the prices are only for twin or double rooms (as far as we know there are no singles).

Essex

*Pubs currently on top form here are the Axe & Compasses at Arkesden
(gaining a Food Award this year for its fish specials), the Three Willows at
Birchanger (good value fresh fish and prompt service – handy for the M11),
the Swan at Chappel (a new Food Award for the fish specialities at this well
run nicely set pub), the immaculately modernised 16th-c Cricketers at
Clavering (imaginative cooking, at a price), the Square & Compasses at Fuller
Street (an appealing and civilised country pub, good all round, with good
individual cooking), the friendly Green Man at Gosfield (good english food –
staff likely to stay though the landlady herself plans to retire), the imposing
White Hart at Great Yeldham (not cheap, but good ambitious cooking that
hits the mark), the interesting Bell in Horndon-on-the-Hill, the Blue Boar in
Maldon (a new entry, an ancient inn made over with great individuality by its
new owner – and brewing its own beer), the gently idiosyncratic Mole Trap
out in the country near Stapleford Tawney, and the cheerful Prince of Wales at
Stow Maries (interesting beers and enjoyable food including unusual fish
barbecues). We have mentioned good food as a strong point at quite a few of
these top Essex pubs. For a special meal out in handsome surroundings, the
White Hart at Great Yeldham wins the accolade of Essex Dining Pub of the
Year; you can eat moderately inexpensively here at lunchtime, but for the best
things on the evening menu be prepared to pay restaurant prices. In the Lucky
Dip section at the end of the chapter, front-runners these days are the
Theydon Oak at Coopersale Street, Griffin in Danbury, Black Bull at Fyfield,
Duck at Newney Green, Eight Bells in Saffron Walden and restauranty Green
Man at Toot Hill. Drinks prices in the county are close to the national
average, with some well flavoured local beers to look out for from Ridleys,
Crouch Vale and the newer Mighty Oak.*

ARKESDEN TL4834 Map 5
Axe & Compasses ★ ⑪ ♀
Village signposted from B1038 – but B1039 from Wendens Ambo, then forking left, is
prettier

Popular for its good food (readers can't resist the puddings), this rambling thatched
country pub has a welcoming and relaxed atmosphere, and friendly staff. Dating
back to the 17th c, the oldest part is the cosy carpeted lounge bar, which has
beautifully polished upholstered oak and elm seats, easy chairs and wooden tables,
a blazing fire, and lots of gleaming brasses. A smaller quirky public bar (which can
get a bit smoky) is uncarpeted, with cosy built-in settles, and darts. The bar food is
home-made and changes regularly, but usually includes half a dozen well prepared
fresh fish dishes such as grilled salmon fillet with asparagus and butter, cream and
white wine (£10.95), skate wing with butter and capers (£11.95), and monkfish on
roasted red pepper sauce (£13.95), as well as dishes such as carrot and coriander
soup (£3.50), sandwiches (from £3.25, weekdays only), prawn and smoked
mackerel roulade (£4.95), moussaka and greek salad (£9.95), chicken supreme with
lemon and tarragon butter or spaghetti and meatballs (£9.95), and duck with
Drambuie (£16.50); on the puddings trolley you might find delicious banoffi pie,

chocolate roulade or raspberry and hazelnut meringue (£4). The no smoking restaurant has a more elaborate menu. They've a very good wine list and over 20 malt whiskies; well kept Greene King Abbot, IPA and maybe Old Speckled Hen on handpump. There are seats out on a side terrace with pretty hanging baskets; parking at the back. It's in a very pretty village, with a crafts centre in the post office opposite. *(Recommended by Angela Gorman, Paul Acton, David R Crafts, H O Dickinson, Adele Summers, Alan Black, Marjorie and Bernard Parkin, Philip and Elaine Holmes, B N F and M Parkin, S Horsley, John and Patricia White, John and Judy Saville, Len Banister)*

Greene King ~ Lease Themis and Diane Christou ~ Real ale ~ Bar food (12-2, 6.45-9.30, not Sun evening in winter) ~ Restaurant ~ (01799) 550272 ~ Children in restaurant and family room ~ Open 11.30(12 Sat)-2.30, 6-11; 12-3, 7-11 Sun

BIRCHANGER TL5022 Map 5
Three Willows

Under 1 mile from M11 junction 8: A120 towards Bishops Stortford, then almost immediately right to Birchanger Village; don't be waylaid earlier by the Birchanger Services signpost!

It's no surprise that this pub fills quickly at mealtimes – not only is the food well cooked and generously served, it's exceptionally reasonably priced too. Alongside a fairly wide choice of standard bar food including sandwiches (from £2.40), filled baked potatoes (from £3.50), ploughman's (£3.95), chilli con carne (£4.95), ham egg and chips (£5.95), and steaks (from £9.95), they serve a good choice of deliciously fresh simply cooked fish (around £8.95 for most fish including paella and crab, £9.95 for whole lemon sole or bass) with chunky chips and plain salads; puddings such as cheesecake (£3.25). It's a good idea to book if you want to eat in the restaurant. The roomily extended carpeted main bar is filled with dark chairs and tables laid for dining; the pub's name refers to cricket bats of the last three centuries, and above a puce dado, the buff and brown ragged walls have a plethora of cricketing prints, photographs, cartoons and other memorabilia. A small public bar has pool and sensibly placed darts, and there's a fruit machine. They serve well kept Greene King IPA, Abbot and Ruddles County on handpump, and there are decent house wines; helpful and prompt family service. There are picnic-sets out on a terrace with heaters and on the lawn behind, with a sturdy climbing frame, swings and a basketball hoop (you can hear the motorway out here). No children are allowed inside. *(Recommended by Charles Gysin, Tina and David Woods-Taylor, Mrs J Ekins-Daukes, Leigh and Gillian Mellor, Stephen and Jean Curtis)*

Greene King ~ Tenants Paul and David Tucker ~ Real ale ~ Bar food (not Sun evening) ~ Restaurant ~ (01279) 815913 ~ Open 11.30-3, 6-11; 12-3, 7-11 Sun

BURNHAM-ON-CROUCH TQ9596 Map 5
White Harte 🛏

The Quay

Warm and cosy in winter, when there's an enormous log fire, this welcoming old hotel has a great outlook over the yachting estuary of the River Crouch. Throughout the partly carpeted bars, with cushioned seats around oak tables, are models of Royal Navy ships, and assorted nautical hardware such as a ship's wheel, a barometer, even a compass in the hearth. The other traditionally furnished high-ceilinged rooms have sea pictures on panelled or stripped brick walls. The atmosphere is cheerful, and the staff are friendly. Tasty, promptly served bar food from the very reasonably priced, straightforward menu could include sandwiches (from £2.10, toasted sandwiches from £2.70), a handful of daily specials such as chilli con carne, lamb casserole, various curries, lasagne, and steak and kidney pie (all £5.80), locally caught skate, plaice or cod (£8.60), and puddings such as apple crumble and fruit pies (£2.80). They serve well kept Adnams and Crouch Vale Best on handpump. You can hear the water lapping against the pub's private jetty (there are seats here and out in front of the pub), and rigging slapping against the masts of boats on moorings beyond. It's popular with boaty types in summer, and can get very busy on Friday and Saturday evenings. Readers enjoy staying here, and the breakfasts are hearty. *(Recommended by G A Hemingway, Lisa Lewis, Ian Phillips, Mr and Mrs M Hayes, Peter Meister, Keith and Chris O'Neill)*

Free house ~ Licensee G John Lewis ~ Real ale ~ Bar food ~ Restaurant ~ (01621) 782106 ~ Children in eating area of bar and restaurant ~ Dogs allowed in bar ~ Open 11-11; 12-10.30 Sun ~ Bedrooms: £19.80(£48B)/£37(£59B)

CASTLE HEDINGHAM TL7835 Map 5
Bell

B1058 E of Sible Hedingham, towards Sudbury

The big walled garden behind this fine old coaching inn is a pleasant place to sit in summer, with an acre or so of grass, trees and shrubs, as well as a sandpit and toys for children; there are more seats on a vine-covered terrace. The unchanging beamed and timbered saloon bar has Jacobean-style seats and windsor chairs around sturdy oak tables, and, beyond standing timbers left from a knocked-through wall, some steps lead up to an unusual little gallery. Behind the traditionally furnished public bar, a games room has dominoes and cribbage; piped music. One bar is no smoking, and each of the rooms has a warming log fire; dogs are welcome but you must phone first. Tapped from the cask, they've well kept Adnams, Greene King IPA and Mighty Oak Oscar Wilde Mild with a guest such as Greene King Old Speckled Hen. From a straightforward menu, reasonably priced bar food includes home-made soup (£2.95), sandwiches (from £3.25), chicken liver pâté (£4), ploughman's (£5.50), liver and bacon casserole (£6.95), steak and Guinness pie or fisherman's pie (£7.50), vegetarian chilli or lasagne (£7.25), and steak (from £9.25), with puddings such as treacle tart or hot cherry pie (£3.50). On Monday night they have fish barbecue: sardines £6.75, swordfish £9.50. The pub has been run by the same friendly family for over 35 years. It's in a pretty village, and the nearby 12th-c castle keep is worth a visit. *(Recommended by Bernie Adams, MLR, Charles Gysin)*

Grays ~ Tenants Penny Doe and Kylie Turkoz-Ferguson ~ Real ale ~ Bar food (not 25 Dec) ~ (01787) 460350 ~ Children welcome ~ Traditional jazz last Sun lunchtime of month, acoustic guitar group Fri evening ~ Open 11.30-3(3.30 Sat), 6-11; 11.30-11 Fri; 12-4, 7-10.30 Sun; closed 25 Dec evening

CHAPPEL TL8927 Map 5
Swan 🍴

Wakes Colne; pub visible just off A1124 Colchester—Halstead

This popular old timbered pub is splendidly set, with the River Colne running through the garden on its way downstream to an impressive Victorian viaduct. Big overflowing flower tubs and french street signs lend the sheltered suntrap cobbled courtyard a continental feel, and gas heaters mean that you can sit out even on cooler evenings. What really impresses readers is the excellent range of deliciously cooked fresh fish including scallops grilled with bacon (£6.95), fried rock eel (£7.95, large £10.25), haddock (£8.95, large £12.95), skate (£9.50) and grilled lemon sole or a mixed fish platter (£13.95). Other well liked, good value bar food includes lunchtime filled baguettes or sandwiches (from £1.95), and ploughman's (from £3.95), as well as chicken curry or gammon and pineapple (£6.95), calves liver and bacon (£9.95), and sirloin steak (from £11.95), with a tempting selection of home-made puddings such as plum crumble (from £3.45). They also do a simple children's menu (from £2.50); service is friendly and prompt. The spacious and low-beamed rambling bar has standing oak timbers dividing off side areas, plenty of dark wood chairs around lots of dark tables for diners, one or two swan pictures and plates on the white and partly panelled walls, and a few attractive tiles above the very big fireplace (which is filled with lots of plants in summer). The central bar area keeps a pubbier atmosphere, with regulars dropping in for a drink; fruit machine, cribbage, dominoes and piped music. The lounge bar is no smoking. Well kept Greene King IPA and Abbot and a guest such as Nethergate on handpump; also wines by the glass, and just under two dozen malt whiskies. Just a few minutes' walk away is the Railway Centre (a must for train buffs). *(Recommended by Malcolm and Jennifer Perry, John and Elspeth Howell, David J Bunter, Colin and Dot Savill, Richard Siebert, Bryan and Mary Blaxall, Ian Phillips, John and Judy Saville, Philip and Elaine Holmes, Mike and Mary Carter)*

Free house ~ Licensee Terence Martin ~ Real ale ~ Bar food (12-2.30, 7(6.30 Sat)-10.30; 12-3, 7-10 Sun, not 25-26 Dec) ~ Restaurant ~ (01787) 222353 ~ Children in eating area of bar and restaurant ~ Dogs allowed in bar ~ Open 11-3, 6-11; 11-11 Sat; 12-10.30 Sun

CHELMSFORD TL7006 Map 5
Alma

Arbour Lane, off B1137 (Springfield Road)

They have regular theme nights at this enthusiastically run pub, and also do a good value two-course bargain meal (£5.99, not Sunday lunch, Saturday evening or on theme nights). With an attractive layout and décor and a civilised country-pub feel, the mainly carpeted beamed bar has a comfortable mix of tables and brocade-cushioned chairs and stools, a central brick fireplace with a club fender, a piano nearby, and a big mirror over another prettily tiled fireplace flanked by bookcases. One cosy alcove has a deeply cushioned button-back leather sofa and armchair, and above a dark dado is a nice collection of old advertising posters on the puce rough-cast walls. There are red-cushioned bar stools on flagstones by the brick-built serving counter – look out for the trompe l'oeil on the wall opposite. Well kept Greene King IPA and a couple of guests such as Nethergate Suffolk County and Shepherd Neame Spitfire on handpump, and decent house wines; a TV in one corner, piped music and fruit machine. Besides the bar dining area, a comfortable no smoking restaurant is prettily decorated in creams and blues, with an inglenook fireplace. Lunchtime dishes served Monday to Saturday include sandwiches (from £2.95), ploughman's (£5.50), home-made beef lasagne (£6.95) and breaded scampi (£7.95), along with regularly changing specials such as scallops on wilted spinach wrapped in bacon (£6.95), peppered duck breast on thai noodles (£11.95), chargrilled sirloin steak (£12.95) and seared beef fillet with roquefort crème fraîche (£14.95); they also do three-course Sunday lunch (£8.95). There are picnic-sets out on a crazy-paved terrace at the front and in a small garden at the back. More reports please. *(Recommended by Robert Swanborough, Rebecca Nicholls)*

Free house ~ Licensees David and Sheila Hunt ~ Real ale ~ Bar food (12-2.30, 7-9; 12-6 Sat; 12-8 Sun) ~ Restaurant ~ (01245) 256783 ~ Children welcome ~ Dogs allowed in bar ~ Open 11-11; 12-10.30 Sun

CLAVERING TL4731 Map 5
Cricketers 🍴 🛏

B1038 Newport—Buntingford, Newport end of village

This smart, immaculately modernised 16th-c dining pub is an excellent place for a special meal. Prices are certainly not cheap (it attracts a well heeled set), but the food is imaginative and very well prepared. The spotlessly kept and roomy L-shaped beamed bar has standing timbers resting on new brickwork, and pale green plush button-backed banquettes, stools and windsor chairs around shiny wooden tables on a pale green carpet, gleaming copper pans and horsebrasses, dried flowers in the big fireplace (open fire in colder weather), and fresh flowers on the tables; one area and the restaurant are no smoking; piped music. They serve Adnams Broadside, Tetleys and a guest on handpump; specialist teas. The attractive front terrace has picnic-sets and umbrellas among colourful flowering shrubs. During busy lunchtimes, when you may have to wait for the freshly prepared bar food, there can be a really lively atmosphere, and the staff are friendly and professional. As well as sandwiches (from £3.75), the seasonally changing menu might include generous starters such as tomato and onion soup (£4), sardine fillets coated in parmesan cheese and breadcrumbs with tomato sauce (£5.75), pigeon breasts sautéed with apple, celeriac and hazelnut dressing (£5.90), and main courses such as roasted vegetable tower with herb couscous and red pepper sauce (£12.75), roast lamb rump with rösti potato and rosemary and onion gravy (£15.90), slices of salmon and halibut with herb butter sauce (£16.25), and bass fillet with beetroot and watercress with lemon oil (£17.50); tempting puddings (£4.75). They do children's meals (£4.50), or (a real bonus) they can have a half helping of some main meals. The bedrooms are in the adjacent cottage. The pub is run by the parents of TV chef Jamie Oliver. *(Recommended by Derek Thomas, David Twitchett, Maysie Thompson, Adele Summers, Alan Black, Gordon Theaker, Angela Gorman, Paul Acton)*

Free house ~ Licensee Trevor Oliver ~ Real ale ~ Bar food (12-2, 7-10) ~ Restaurant ~ (01799) 550442 ~ Children welcome ~ Open 10-11; closed 25-26 Dec ~ Bedrooms: £70B/£100B

FINGRINGHOE TM0220 Map 5
Whalebone

Follow Rowhedge, Fingringhoe signpost off A134, the part that's just S of Colchester centre; or Fingringhoe signposted off B1025 S of Colchester

Although the main focus is the inventive, well presented food, this civilised and relaxing pub is an enjoyable place to come even if you just want a coffee. Pleasant in summer (when they sometimes have plays), the back garden, with gravel paths winding through the grass around a sizeable old larch tree, has picnic-sets with a peaceful valley view. The pale yellow-washed interior has been very nicely done out, its three room areas airily opened together, leaving some timber studs; stripped tables on the unsealed bare boards have a pleasant mix of chairs and cushioned settles. Roman blinds with swagged pelmets, neat wall lamps, a chandelier and local watercolours (for sale) are good finishing touches. Besides tasty breakfasts (10-11.30am), and lunchtime sandwiches and baguettes (from £2.75 – you can choose your own fillings), a good choice of dishes, listed on a blackboard over the small but warming coal fire, could include home-made soup (£3.75), honey and thyme roasted beetroot with crème fraîche (£4.75), sardines with garlic butter (£5.95), wild mushroom risotto with parmesan shavings or chicken breast with green thai sauce (£9.95), braised lamb shank with mustard mash and sweet onion sauce (£11.50), griddled bass filled with fresh herbs (£14.25), and delicious home-made puddings such as pancakes with honeycomb ice cream or sticky fig and ginger pudding (from £4); children's meals (from £3.95). Four well kept ales such as Adnams Broadside, Greene King IPA and Old Speckled Hen, and Mighty Oak on handpump, as well as decent house wines; piped music. *(Recommended by Andrew Morgan, M and G Rushworth, MDN)*

Free house ~ Licensee Vivien Steed ~ Real ale ~ Bar food (10-2.30, 6.30-9.30) ~ Restaurant ~ (01206) 729307 ~ Children in family room ~ Dogs allowed in bar.~ Open 10-3, 5.30-11; 10-11 summer Sat/Sun

FULLER STREET TL7416 Map 5
Square & Compasses 🍴

From A12 Chelmsford—Witham take Hatfield Peverel exit, and from B1137 there follow Terling signpost, keeping straight on past Terling towards Great Leighs; from A131 Chelmsford—Braintree turn off in Great Leighs towards Fairstead and Terling

Along with the stuffed birds, traps and brasses which adorn the L-shaped beamed bar of this small, civilised country pub, you'll find otter tails, birds' eggs and old photographs of local characters, many of whom still use the pub. Comfortable and well lit, this carpeted bar has a woodburning stove as well as a big log fire; shove-ha'penny, table skittles, cribbage, dominoes and a fruit machine. The staff are very friendly and efficient, the licensees cheerful, and there's a welcoming atmosphere. Very well kept Nethergate Suffolk County and Ridleys IPA are tapped from the cask, and they've also decent french regional wines. The food here is home-made and very good (readers especially like the chips), and aside from lunchtime sandwiches (from £3.50), soup (£3.75), ham and eggs (£8.25) and fish pie (£10), they do interesting, regularly changing specials such as venison sausages with bubble and squeak (£12.50), pork medallions (£13), fresh fish such as swordfish with roasted peppers (£13.50) or chargrilled butterfish with asparagus (£14), and precisely cooked rib-eye steak (£14), with home-made puddings such as double chocolate sponge and lemon curd cheesecake (from £3.75); limited menu Sunday evenings. There are gentle country views from tables outside; disabled lavatories. *(Recommended by Philip and Elaine Holmes, Adrian White, Colin and Dot Savill, Sherrie Glass, Tina and David Woods-Taylor, Nick Mattinson, John and Judy Saville)*

Free house ~ Licensees Howard Potts and Ginny Austin ~ Real ale ~ Bar food (12-2.15, 7-9.30(10 Fri/Sat)) ~ Restaurant ~ (01245) 361477 ~ Well behaved children welcome in eating area of the bar ~ Dogs welcome ~ Open 11.30-3, 6.30(7 in winter)-11; 12-3, 7-10.30 Sun; closed Mon (exc bank hols)

GOSFIELD TL7829 Map 5
Green Man 🍽 🍷

3 miles N of Braintree

Not long after the *Guide* comes out, the welcoming landlady of this smart dining pub plans to retire, but her excellent friendly staff are likely to stay on. At lunchtime, it's worth trying to catch the help-yourself cold table, where you can choose from home-cooked ham and pork, turkey, tongue, beef and poached or smoked salmon, as well as game pie, salads and home-made pickles (from £7.65). Otherwise, served generously, a choice of mostly traditional english bar food could include soups such as game or asparagus (from £3), sandwiches (from £3.45), filled baked potatoes (from £3.50), soft roe on toast (£4.25), and main courses (served with fresh vegetables and home-made chips) such as steak and kidney pudding (£7.65), trout baked with almonds (£7.75), calves liver and bacon or pork chops marinated in dill and mustard (£8.95), and half a roast duck with orange and red wine sauce (£12.50), with puddings such as fruit pie and treacle tart (£3.50). Booking is advisable even midweek. You can get many of the decent nicely priced wines by the glass. There's a laid-back sociable atmosphere in the two little bars, and they serve very well kept Greene King IPA and Abbot on handpump; they've got pool and a juke box. *(Recommended by David Twitchett, I D Greenfield, George Atkinson, David and Christine Vaughton, John and Patricia White, Richard Siebert)*

Greene King ~ Lease Janet Harrington ~ Real ale ~ Bar food (not Sun evening) ~ Restaurant ~ (01787) 472746 ~ Children in eating area of bar and restaurant ~ Dogs allowed in bar ~ Open 11-2.30, 6.30-11; 12-2.30, 7-10.30 Sun

GREAT YELDHAM TL7638 Map 5
White Hart 🍽 🍷

Poole Street; A1017 Halstead—Haverhill

Essex Dining Pub of the Year

Watch your head as you come into this popular black and white timbered dining pub: the door into the bar is very low. The ambitious food is what most people come here for, so it's a good idea to book, but there's also a very good wine list with about 12 by the glass, and aside from well kept Adnams, they serve two continually changing guests such as Mighty Oak Oscar Wilde and Orkney Dark Island. Also, they've a good choice of belgian bottled beers, organic fruit juices and cider. The building is one of only a small handful of pubs to be Grade I* listed, and the main areas inside have stone and wood floors with some dark oak panelling, especially around the fireplace. In fine weather, the attractive landscaped garden is a pleasant place to sit, with well tended lawns and pretty seating. The same menu is available in the bar or in the no smoking restaurant. Beautifully prepared by the landlord (though by no means cheap, and you have to pay extra for vegetables), dishes could include lunchtime sandwiches (from £3.25), leek, celery and pea soup (£4.25), kedgeree fishcakes with light curry sauce (£6.25), turkey and ham pie with creamy mash and spring greens (£10.50), calves liver with bubble and squeak cake, crispy bacon and honey roast parsnips (£14.75), grilled bass with warm greek salad and parsley mash (£16), and beef medallion on roast cocotte potatoes with wild mushroom, mustard and tarragon jus (£16.50), while puddings could be home-made apple pie with vanilla custard (£4.75). They do a lunch special (two-courses £10.50, not Sunday), and smaller helpings are available for children. *(Recommended by Richard Siebert, Marjorie and Bernard Parkin, RWC, I D Greenfield, Mrs Roxanne Chamberlain, Derek Thomas, Pam and David Bailey, M and G Rushworth, Adele Summers, Alan Black)*

Free house ~ Licensee John Dicken ~ Real ale ~ Bar food (12-2, 6.30-9.30) ~ Restaurant ~ (01787) 237250 ~ Children in eating area of bar and restaurant ~ Regular dinner dances ~ Open 11-11; 12-11 Sun

HORNDON-ON-THE-HILL TQ6683 Map 3
Bell 🍺 ♀ ◀ 🛏

M25 junction 30 into A13, then left into B1007 after 7 miles, village signposted from here

They stock over a hundred well chosen wines from all over the world, including 16 by the glass, at this bustling medieval hall, and you can buy very fairly priced bottles off-sales. They're also keen on supporting local brewers, and three swiftly rotating guests such as Mauldons Suffolk Pride, Mighty Oak Burntwood and Charles Wells Bombardier are well kept on handpump alongside Bass, Crouch Vale Brewers Gold and Greene King IPA; they hold occasional beer festivals. The heavily beamed bar has some antique high-backed settles and benches, rugs on the flagstones or highly polished oak floorboards, and a curious collection of ossified hot cross buns hanging from a beam. Available in the bar and no smoking restaurant, the frequently changing menu includes ambitious, carefully presented dishes such as cauliflower soup with oysters (£3.95), scallop and avocado ravioli with curried onions and crab jus (£6.95), fried asparagus with wheat grass, pea and broad bean sauté or braised bacon loin with pea risotto and mustard (£11.50), roast monkfish tail with veal and snail fritters or roast organic pork with cider, pea sauce and english mustard (£11.95), and tasty puddings such as glazed lemon and juniper tart with lemon bicarbonate of soda jelly (£5). There's also a separate bar menu with dishes such as smoked haddock fishcakes with hollandaise (£6.25), roast lamb kidneys with mash and mustard jus (£7.50), and fried salmon with basil (£7.95); they also do sandwiches (from £4.95). You may need to book, and when it's busy service can sometimes slow (though they are good about giving some priority to people such as business luncheers who can't tarry). Centuries ago, many important medieval dignitaries would have stayed here, as it was the last inn before travellers heading south could ford the Thames at Highams Causeway. *(Recommended by Malcolm and Jennifer Perry, Suzie Gibbons, Simon Pyle, Stephen, Julie and Hayley Brown, Evelyn and Derek Walter, Adrian White, Bob and Maggie Atherton, Bernie Adams, R T and J C Moggridge, John and Judy Saville, Kevin Flack, John and Enid Morris, Ian Phillips, Sarah Markham Flynn, Alan Cole, Kirstie Bruce, Len Banister)*

Free house ~ Licensee John Vereker ~ Real ale ~ Bar food (12-2, 6.30-9.45; not bank hol Mon or 25-26 Dec) ~ Restaurant ~ (01375) 642463 ~ Children in eating area of bar and restaurant ~ Dogs allowed in bar and bedrooms ~ Open 11-2.30(3 Sat), 5.30(6 Sat)-11; 12-4, 7-10.30 Sun; closed evenings 25-26 Dec ~ Bedrooms: /£65B

LANGHAM TM0233 Map 5
Shepherd & Dog ♀

Moor Road/High Street; village signposted off A12 N of Colchester

Readers very much enjoy the food at this welcoming village pub. The spick and span L-shaped bar embraces an engaging hotch-potch of styles, with interesting collections of continental bottled beers and brass and copper fire extinguishers. Chalked on boards around the bar, hearty home-made dishes (they use fresh local produce wherever possible) change every day, but might include sandwiches (from £2.30), soup (£2.95), chicken liver pâté (£3.95), ploughman's (from £4.20), chicken in filo pastry with tarragon and asparagus sauce, steak and ale pie or 8oz rump steak (£8.95), with a good choice of fresh fish such as butterfish (£8.95), brill (£9.95), and bass (£11.95), with home-made puddings such as apple and apricot crumble or cheesecake (£3.25); they also do children's meals (£3.95), and a Sunday roast (£6.95). Service is very friendly and helpful. The wine list is short but thoughtful, and you'll find well kept Greene King IPA, Abbot and Ruddles County on handpump, along with a monthly changing guest such as Nethergate Suffolk County; piped music. In summer, there are very pretty window boxes, and a shaded bar in the enclosed side garden; tables outside. Their regular theme weeks and activity nights are very popular. *(Recommended by John and Judy Saville, John McDonald, R M Corlett, Ian Phillips, Philip Denton, Shirley Mackenzie)*

Free house ~ Licensee Julian Dicks ~ Real ale ~ Bar food (12-2.15, 6-9.30(10 Fri); 12-10 Sat; 12-9 Sun) ~ Restaurant ~ (01206) 272711 ~ Children welcome ~ Dogs allowed in bar ~ Open 11-3.30, 5.30-11; 11-11 Sat; 12-10.30 Sun; closed 26 Dec

LITTLE BRAXTED TL8314 Map 5
Green Man

Kelvedon Road; village signposted off B1389 by NE end of A12 Witham bypass – keep on patiently

Tucked away down an isolated country lane, this pretty brick house is a great place to come for a peaceful drink. The welcoming little lounge (especially cosy in winter when there's an open fire) has an interesting collection of bric-a-brac, including 200 horsebrasses, some harness, mugs hanging from a beam, and a lovely copper urn. The recently redecorated tiled public bar has books, darts, shove-ha'penny, cribbage, dominoes and a video machine. You'll find well kept Ridleys IPA, Rumpus and Old Bob on handpump, along with several malt whiskies. Generous helpings of enjoyable bar food, from a straightforward menu, include sandwiches (from £2.55), ploughman's (£5.25), cottage pie (£3.95), a couple of daily specials such as steak and ale pie (£7.25), and minted lamb shank (£7.95), with puddings such as treacle tart or apple pie (£2.95); service is friendly. The sheltered garden behind the pub has picnic-sets and a pond. *(Recommended by Ian Phillips, John and Elspeth Howell, Mary and Dennis Jones, John and Judy Saville, Len Banister)*

Ridleys ~ Tenant Neil Pharaoh ~ Real ale ~ Bar food ~ (01621) 891659 ~ Dogs allowed in bar ~ Open 11.30-3, 6-11; 12-3.30, 7-10.30 Sun

LITTLE DUNMOW TL6521 Map 5
Flitch of Bacon 🛏

Village signposted off A120 E of Dunmow, then turn right on village loop road

Under 10 miles from Stansted airport, this unchanging country pub attracts a comfortable mix of visitors and locals, and although it's quietly relaxing on weekday lunchtimes, in the evenings it can get quite bustling. The small timbered bar is simply but attractively furnished, with flowery-cushioned pews and ochre walls; piped music. A back room has french windows looking out on to the terrace. On handpump, they've well kept Greene King IPA and a couple of guests from brewers such as Crouch Vale and Mauldons, and they do several wines by the glass, along with 10 or so malt whiskies; the Scottish licensees are welcoming. Reasonably priced bar food from a fairly short, straightforward menu could include sandwiches (from £2.30), local ham, egg and chips (£6.50), beef and ale casserole (£6.75), lamb in redcurrant and rosemary (£7.50), and sirloin steak (£9.50), with puddings such as chocolate fudge cake or cherry and apple pudding (£2.75); service can slow at times. The back eating area is no smoking. There are views across a quiet lane to a broad expanse of green with a few picnic-sets on the edge. Nearby, the church of St Mary is well worth a visit (the pub has a key). The bedrooms are basic, but clean and comfortable. *(Recommended by Stephen and Jean Curtis, Ian Phillips, Tony Beaulah, Philip and Susan Philcox)*

Free house ~ Licensees David and Teresa Caldwell ~ Real ale ~ Bar food (not Sun evening) ~ Restaurant ~ No credit cards ~ (01371) 820323 ~ Children in restaurant ~ Dogs allowed in bar ~ Open 12-3, 6-11(7-10.30 Sun) ~ Bedrooms: £40S/£55S

LITTLE WALDEN TL5441 Map 5
Crown ◀

B1052 N of Saffron Walden

The friendly staff at this 18th-c low white cottage serve around six well kept real ales tapped straight from the cask, and alongside Adnams, Greene King IPA and Abbot are a couple of changing guests such as City of Cambridge Boathouse and Mauldons Bitter. The cosy low-beamed bar has a good log fire in the brick fireplace, bookroom-red walls, flowery curtains and a mix of bare boards and navy carpeting. Seats, ranging from high-backed pews to little cushioned armchairs, are spaced around a good variety of closely arranged tables, mostly big, some stripped. The small red-tiled room on the right has two little tables; piped local radio (which can be intrusive). Huge helpings of tasty bar food such as sandwiches (from £2.25), soup (£3.50), ploughman's (from £4.25), home-made lasagne (£6.95) and steak and ale pie (£7.95), with daily specials on blackboards such as vegetable curry (£7.50), smoked haddock mornay (£7.95), chicken cacciatore (£8.95), cold seafood platter (£9.75), and beef stroganoff (£10.25); puddings could include delicious apple crumble or bread and butter pudding (from £3.50). As we went to press, they had almost finished building an extension which will have a new restaurant, and three bedrooms with their own bathrooms – we'd like to hear how readers find these. The walk from the car park in the dark can be tricky. *(Recommended by B N F and M Parkin, Mr and Mrs T B Staples, MLR, Margaret and Allen Marsden)*

Free house ~ Licensee Colin Hayling ~ Real ale ~ Bar food (not Mon evening) ~ (01799) 522475 ~ Children in eating area of bar and restaurant ~ Dogs welcome ~ Trad jazz Weds evening ~ Open 11-3, 6-11; 12-10 Sun ~ Bedrooms: /£75S

MALDON TL8407 Map 5
Blue Boar

Silver Street; go on round behind to find the car park

The new owner (a local farmer) has injected a good deal of ironic and individualistic humour into the elaborate refurbishment of this former coaching inn; it's well worth having a look around the hotel part on the right, as well as the simpler and more informal separate bars on the left of the coach entry. The obliging and friendly staff are happy to bring you a drink in the main lounge – entertainingly luxurious with its gilt and chenille love-seats, its seductive paintings, and its Canova-look marble figures. The dining room now has a mass of chandeliers, pewter, more paintings and at least one formidable antique refectory table to go with its beams and panelling. Over the coach way the bars proper are much simpler, nice and relaxed: two smallish rooms with dark oak beams and timbers, dark pub furniture (also a Jacobean carved oak dresser in the front one), a woodburning stove, quite a few sailing ship paintings. Regrettably we didn't see the newly restored upper room there, which is said to have a spectacular vaulted ceiling. Besides well kept Adnams tapped from the cask, they now brew their own Farmers Pucks Folly in a former back stables building; the coffee is good, too. Enjoyable bar food (made mostly with local ingredients) includes sandwiches, baguettes or baked potatoes (£4.50), beef stroganoff, moroccan flatbread with salsa and goats cheese, beef strips cooked in spicy tomato coulis with melted cheese or chargrilled minute steak (all £6), and specials such as local mullet with thai noodles or lasagne (£6), with puddings such as home-made apple crumble and trifle (£4); the restaurant menu (which can also be eaten in the bar) has dishes such as field mushrooms and roasted fennel au gratin (£5), chargrilled pork medallions with creamy sauce and rum and peppers (£11), and gigot of lamb with port and cranberry sauce (£12). We have not heard from any readers who have stayed here since it changed hands, but would expect it to be a nice place to stay in. *(Recommended by Oliver Hylton)*

Free house ~ Licensee John Wilsdon ~ Real ale ~ Bar food (12-2.30, 6.30-9.30) ~ Restaurant ~ (01621) 855888 ~ Children in eating area of bar and family room ~

Dogs allowed in bar and bedrooms ~ Jazz on Thurs, pianist in restaurant on Sat ~ Open 11-11.30; 12-11 Sun; closed 3-5pm winter ~ Bedrooms: £55B/£80B

MILL GREEN TL6401 Map 5
Viper ◀ £

The Common; from Fryerning (which is signposted off north-east bound A12 Ingatestone bypass) follow Writtle signposts

There's an easy-going welcoming atmosphere at this charmingly uncomplicated little pub – the kind of place where it's easy to fall into casual conversation with the friendly locals or amiable landlord. It's peacefully set in the middle of a wood, and tables on the lawn overlook a carefully tended cottage garden which is a dazzling mass of colour in summer (when the front of the pub is almost hidden by pretty overflowing hanging baskets and window boxes). The two timeless cosy lounge rooms have spindleback seats, armed country kitchen chairs, and tapestried wall seats around neat little old tables, and there's a log fire. Booted walkers are directed towards the fairly basic parquet-floored tap room, which is more simply furnished with shiny wooden traditional wall seats, and beyond that another room has country kitchen chairs and sensibly placed darts; shove-ha'penny, dominoes, cribbage. From an oak-panelled counter you can get well kept Mighty Oak Oscar Wilde Mild and Ridleys IPA on handpump, along with three weekly changing guests from more or less local breweries such as Crouch Vale, Mighty Oak and Nethergate; farm cider too. Served only at lunchtime, very simple tasty bar snacks include sandwiches (from £2.25, toasted from £2.50), soup (£2.95), hawaiian toast (£3.25), chilli con carne (£3.75), and ploughman's (from £4.95); on Saturday and Sunday, they also do real ale sausages with fried onions in a baguette (£3). Cheerful service even when busy; no children in pub. The friendly dog is called Ben. *(Recommended by Pete Baker, Ian Phillips, Phil and Sally Gorton, Sarah Davis, Rod Lambert, Kevin Thorpe, Anthony Rogers)*

Free house ~ Licensees Roger and Sharon Beard ~ Real ale ~ Bar food (lunchtime) ~ No credit cards ~ (01277) 352010 ~ Dogs allowed in bar ~ Open 12-3, 6-11(7-10.30 Sun); closed 25 Dec evening

PAGLESHAM TQ9293 Map 3
Punchbowl

Church End; from the Paglesham road out of Rochford, Church End is signposted on the left

In a secluded spot down long country lanes, this pretty white weatherboarded pub has a peaceful outlook over the fields. The cosy beamed bar is beautifully kept, with pews, barrel chairs and other seats, and lots of bric-a-brac. Well kept Adnams and Ridleys Old Bob and a couple of guests from brewers such as Elgoods and Nethergate on handpump; piped music. The bar food is good value, and enjoyable dishes could include rolls, sandwiches and filled baguettes (from £2.30), soup (£2.25), filled baked potatoes or prawn cocktail (£3.50), ploughman's (£4.25), vegetable jambalaya or battered haddock (£5.25), cajun chicken or gammon steak (£6.95), and daily specials such as venison in red wine (£8.25) or good fresh fish such as plaice (£5.95), salmon (£6.25), and skate (£7.50); puddings could be bread pudding or raspberry pavlova (from £2.75). There are some tables in the little garden, with a couple more out by the quiet road. More reports please. *(Recommended by George Atkinson)*

Free house ~ Licensees Bernie and Pat Cardy ~ Real ale ~ Bar food ~ Restaurant ~ (01702) 258376 ~ Children in restaurant ~ Open 11.30-3, 6.30-11; 12-3, 6.30-10.30 Sun

---

Post Office address codings confusingly give the impression that some pubs are in Suffolk, when they're really in Essex (which is where we list them).

STAPLEFORD TAWNEY TL5001 Map 5

Mole Trap ◗

Tawney Common, which is a couple of miles away from Stapleford Tawney and is signposted off A113 just N of M25 overpass – keep on; OS Sheet 167 map reference 500013

There is quite a tribe of resident animals at this appealing country pub, many rescued and most wandering around outside, including very friendly cats, rabbits, a couple of dogs, hens, geese, a sheep, goats and horses. Although it's tucked away in what seems like the back of beyond, it's usually humming with customers; the piped radio tends to be almost inaudible over the contented chatter. The smallish carpeted bar (mind your head as you go in) has black dado, beams and joists, brocaded wall seats, library chairs and bentwood elbow chairs around plain pub tables, and steps down through a partly knocked-out timber stud wall to a similar area. The pub is run with considerable individuality by forthright licensees; the three blazing coal fires are a huge treat in winter. There are a few small pictures, 3-D decorative plates, some dried-flower arrangements and (on the sloping ceiling formed by a staircase beyond) some regulars' snapshots, with a few dozen beermats stuck up around the serving bar. They have three constantly changing guests such as Crouch Vale Brewers Gold, Hop Back Summer Lightning and Moorhouses Black Cat on handpump, alongside Fullers London Pride. Enjoyable home-made dishes include tasty lamb curry, chilli and lasagne (all £5.95), steak (from £7.50), and fresh daily fish such as plaice, cod or salmon (all £6.95); they also do sandwiches, and a roast on Sunday (£5.95). Outside are some plastic tables and chairs and a picnic-set. Do make sure children behave well here if you bring them. *(Recommended by H O Dickinson, Ian Phillips, Bruce M Drew, Paul A Moore, Bernie Adams, David Twitchett, Derek Thomas, Philip and Elaine Holmes, Evelyn and Derek Walter, LM)*

Free house ~ Licensees Mr and Mrs Kirtley ~ Real ale ~ Bar food (not Sun evening) ~ No credit cards ~ (01992) 522394 ~ Well behaved children in family room ~ Open 11.30-3, 6.30-11; 12-4, 6.30-10.30 Sun

STOCK TQ6998 Map 5

Hoop ◗

B1007; from A12 Chelsmford bypass take Galleywood, Billericay turn-off

Prettily bordered with flowers, the large sheltered back garden of this enjoyably unmodern village pub has picnic-sets, a covered seating area, and in fine weather an outside bar and weekend barbecues. Although it's very popular with locals, the atmosphere in the cosy, bustling bar is cheerfully inclusive, and the staff are friendly and accommodating. Undisturbed by fruit machines or piped music, you can choose from around six well kept changing ales tapped from the cask or on handpump, from breweries such as Adnams, Crouch Vale, Hop Back, Mighty Oak, Old Kent, Shepherd Neame and Woodfordes, and they also serve changing farm ciders and perries, and mulled wine in winter; they hold a popular May beer festival. Reasonably priced tasty bar food from a mostly traditional menu includes soup (£3.25), sandwiches (from £2), omelettes (from £3.50), ploughman's (from £5), home-baked ham and eggs (£6.25), sausage pie (£6.50), a couple of daily specials such as cod fillet, irish stew, good fish pie or curry (£6.50), and home-made puddings such as apple pie or crème brûlée (£3); vegetables are £1.25 extra. There's a coal-effect gas fire in the big brick fireplace, brocaded wall seats around wooden-top tables on the left, and a cluster of brocaded stools on the right; sensibly placed darts (the heavy black beams are pitted with stray flights), dominoes and cribbage. Over-21s only in the bar; the two collies are called Colly and Boots. *(Recommended by Evelyn and Derek Walter, Ian Phillips, John and Enid Morris, Kevin Thorpe, Glenwys and Alan Lawrence, Adrian White, B and M Kendall, Peter Hagler, Mrs Roxanne Chamberlain)*

Free house ~ Licensees Albert and David Kitchin ~ Real ale ~ Bar food (11-2.30, 6-9; 11-9 Fri-Sat; 12-8 Sun) ~ (01277) 841137 ~ Open 11-11; 12-10.30 Sun

STOW MARIES TQ8399 Map 5
Prince of Wales ◨
B1012 between S Woodham Ferrers and Cold Norton Posters

On some summer Sundays at this laid-back welcoming pub, they barbecue unusual fish such as saupe, mahi-mahi and black barracuda (as well as steaks for the less adventurous), while on Thursday evenings in winter they fire up the old bread oven to make pizzas in the room that used to be the village bakery. Otherwise, generously served enjoyable dishes (with good fish specials) might include mexican chilli wrap (£5.95), steak and kidney pie (£6.45), tuna steak (£7.95), beer-battered cod or haddock (£8.25), and lamb shank (£8.45), with puddings such as spotted dick and sticky toffee pudding (£2.75); they also do sandwiches (from £2.95). The well kept beers win further praise from readers (the cheery landlord is a real ale fanatic), and you'll find five interesting, frequently changing beers on handpump from brewers such as Dark Star, Hambleton, Mauldons, RCH and Titanic; they've also two draught belgian wheat beers, several bottled beers, farm cider, and vintage ports. It's worth trying to catch one of their beer festivals, and on most bank holidays and some Sundays, there are live bands. Although the cosy and chatty low-ceilinged rooms appear unchanged since the turn of the last century, they've in fact been renovated in a traditional style. Few have space for more than one or two tables or wall benches on the tiled or bare-boards floors, though the room in the middle squeezes in quite a jumble of chairs and stools. There are seats and tables in the back garden, and between the picket fence and the pub's white weatherboarded frontage is a terrace with herbs in Victorian chimney pots; they've a marquee for summer weekends. *(Recommended by Adrian White, Sarah Davis, Rod Lambert, Paul A Moore, Ian Phillips, Kevin Thorpe)*

Free house ~ Licensee Rob Walster ~ Real ale ~ Bar food (12-2.30, 7-9.30, 12-9.30 Sun) ~ No credit cards ~ (01621) 828971 ~ Children in family room ~ Dogs welcome ~ Open 11-11; 12-10.30 Sun

WENDENS AMBO TL5136 Map 5
Bell
B1039 just W of village

The extensive back garden and terrace of this village local (handy for Audley End) have plenty to keep children entertained, with a wooden wendy house, proper tree swing, crazy golf (£1), a sort of mini nature-trail wandering off through the shrubs, and a big tree-sheltered lawn; look out for Reggie and Ronnie the goats. Inside, the small cottagey low-ceilinged rooms have brasses on ancient timbers, wheelback chairs around neat tables, comfortably cushioned seats worked into snug alcoves, quite a few pictures on the cream walls, and an inviting open fire. Bar food includes filled rolls (from £2.75), ploughman's (£4.25), sausages and mash (£5.50), steak and kidney pie (£6.95), home-made fish pie (£7.95), and sirloin steak (£10.95), with puddings such as apple pie, sherry trifle or spotted dick (£3); the dining room is no smoking. Well kept real ales include Adnams Bitter and Broadside on handpump, along with a couple of changing guests, and the new landlord plans to hold two beer festivals a year; piped music. *(Recommended by S Horsley, Ian Wilson, Eddie Edwards)*

Free house ~ Licensee Shaun Fetzer ~ Real ale ~ Bar food (not Sun or Mon evenings) ~ Restaurant ~ (01799) 540382 ~ Children welcome away from bar ~ Dogs allowed in bar ~ Open 11.30-3, 6-11; 11.30-11 Sat; 12-10.30 Sun

---

Please keep sending us reports. We rely on readers for news of new discoveries, and particularly for news of changes – however slight – at the fully described pubs. No stamp needed: The Good Pub Guide, FREEPOST TN1569, Wadhurst, E Sussex TN5 7BR or send your report through our web site: www.goodguides.com

YOUNGS END TL7319 Map 5
Green Dragon
A131 Braintree—Chelmsford, just N of Essex Showground

The neat back garden of this bustling dining pub has lots of picnic-sets under cocktail parasols, and a budgerigar aviary. Although lots of people come here to eat, there's quite a pubby atmosphere in the two bar rooms, which have ordinary pub furnishings, and in the little extra low-ceilinged snug just beside the serving counter. Greene King Abbot, IPA and perhaps Ruddles County are well kept on handpump; unobtrusive piped jazz music. At lunchtime (not Sunday) you can have bar food in part of the restaurant, where the tables are bigger than in the bar. Reasonably priced dishes include a good choice of seafood specials such as smoked salmon (£6.50), scottish clams in garlic butter or cajun red snapper with yoghurt dressing (£8.50), tuna steak with salsa (£9.50), lobster salad (half £10.95), and fruits de mer for two (£42), as well as sandwiches (from £2.95, filled baguettes from £3.95), home-made soup (£3), ploughman's (from £4.95), cottage pie (£5), curry of the day or steak, kidney and mushroom pie (£7.50), and lamb shank (£9.50). The no smoking restaurant area has an understated barn theme with stripped brick walls, a manger at one end, and a 'hayloft' part upstairs. More reports please. *(Recommended by Paul and Ursula Randall, Mrs P J Pearce, Adrian White, Tina and David Woods-Taylor)*

Greene King ~ Lease Bob and Mandy Greybrook ~ Real ale ~ Bar food (12-2, 6-9(8.30 Sun, 9.30 Sat)) ~ Restaurant ~ (01245) 361030 ~ Children in eating area of bar and restaurant ~ Open 11.30(12 Sat)-3, 5.30-11; 12-10.30 Sun

Lucky Dip
Besides the fully inspected pubs, you might like to try these Lucky Dips recommended to us and described by readers (if you do, please send us reports: www.goodguides.com).

ARDLEIGH [TM0429]
☆ *Wooden Fender* [A137 towards Colchester]: Recently refurbished and extended under new licensees, popular for good value food, three well kept real ales, decent wines, beams and log fires, children welcome in dining area; good-sized family garden with water feature *(LYM, Arthur Baker)*
BANNISTER GREEN [TL6920]
Three Horseshoes [off B1417 nr Felsted]: Small comfortable 15th-c beamed country local with welcoming licensees, well kept Ridleys, good value generous straightforward food inc Sun lunch (booking advised in small no smoking restaurant); children welcome, tables out on broad village green and in garden *(Paul and Ursula Randall, LYM)*
BATTLESBRIDGE [TQ7894]
Barge [Hawk Hill]: White clapboarded local right by waterside antiques and craft centre, chatty bar on right, quieter eating areas on left (decent food all day), real ales inc Adnams and Ind Coope Burton, cheery landlord; piped music; tables out in front *(BB, George Atkinson)*
BILLERICAY [TQ6893]
Duke of York [Southend Rd, South Green]: Pleasant beamed pub with some emphasis on modern restaurant, good choice of food here and in bar, well kept Greene King beers, real fire, longcase clock, local photographs, upholstered settles and wheelback chairs, long-

serving licensees; may be unobtrusive piped music, monthly quiz night, fortnightly ladies' darts *(David Twitchett, John and Judy Saville)*
BLACKMORE [TL6001]
Leather Bottle [The Green]: Comfortable furniture on millstone floors, nice décor, five well kept real ales inc a bargain guest beer, decent food; tables in garden behind *(Len Banister)*
BOREHAM [TL7509]
Grange [B1137 off A12/A130 interchange]: New Chef & Brewer with striking crooked roof, three log fires, Adnams and Greene King Abbot (and happy to do a pot of tea), good range of usual food, cheerful manageress and enthusiastic young staff *(Tina and David Woods-Taylor)*
BROOMFIELD [TL7009]
Angel [B1008 N of Chelmsford]: Partly 16th-c, well refurbished and extended in keeping as Vintage Inn dining pub, well kept Bass and Tetleys, good choice of reasonably priced wines, varied shortish choice of food all day, well trained staff *(Tina and David Woods-Taylor)*
BURTON END [TL5323]
Ash [just N of Stansted airport]: Timbered country pub with dining extension, pleasantly unfussy décor, helpful cheerful staff, two or three real ales, enjoyable reasonably priced food; tables outside with climbing frames *(Keith and Janet Morris)*

CANFIELD END [TL5821]
Lion & Lamb [A120 Bishops Stortford—Dunmow]: Neat and comfortable, with friendly efficient staff, good atmosphere, wide choice of enjoyable generous food inc daily fresh fish in open-plan bar and spacious but cosy dining room, well kept Ridleys, decent wines and coffee; piped music; back garden with terrace, barbecue and play area, open all day *(Linda Lewis, MDN)*

CHELMSFORD [TL7206]
Fox & Raven [Barnes Mill Rd]: Based on former farmhouse, with wide choice of enjoyable food, prompt service *(John and Judy Saville)*

Queens Head [Lower Anchor St]: Lively and welcoming Victorian backstreet local, well run and orderly, with three well kept Crouch Vale real ales and five changing guest beers, summer farm cider, winter log fires, simple and substantial cheap lunchtime food inc filled rolls; open all day from noon (11 Sat) *(Keith and Janet Morris, Bruce M Drew)*

Rose & Crown [Rainsford Rd]: Pleasantly refurbished pub/restaurant with good food choice inc mediterranean-style dishes, well kept Greene King IPA, friendly courteous staff, open fires *(Paul and Ursula Randall, Mrs S Harvey)*

CLAVERING [TL4731]
Fox & Hounds [High St]: Village local with enjoyable food under new regime *(Frank Knowles)*

COGGESHALL [TL8224]
☆ *Compasses* [Pattiswick, signed off A120 W]: Yet another management change in friendly country pub surrounded by rolling farmland, neatly comfortable spacious beamed bars, wide food choice from sandwiches to steaks inc wkdy lunch deals, more elaborate dishes in partly no smoking barn restaurant, well kept Adnams and Greene King IPA and Abbot; children welcome, plenty of lawn and orchard tables, adventure play area, open all day wknds and summer *(LYM, Charles Gysin)*

George & Dragon [Coggeshall Hamlet; B1024 S]: Friendly family-run local, Greene King IPA, warm atmosphere; back garden *(Eddie Edwards)*

COLCHESTER [TM0025]
Dragoon [Butt Rd (B1026)]: Welcoming unpretentious L-shaped local with lounge and public ends, limited very cheap bar food (fry-up recommended), well kept Adnams and a guest beer, friendly staff *(Pete Baker)*

COLNE ENGAINE [TL8530]
Five Bells [signed off A1124 (was A604) in Earls Colne; Mill Lane]: Welcoming traditional village pub with enjoyable home-made food using local produce, modern bistro-style dishes as well as baguettes, sausages, stew, fish, steaks and so forth, well kept Greene King ales, woodburner and old photographs in lounge/dining room, public bar, no music; attractive new front terrace with gentle views *(Cate Gunn, Amanda Eames)*

COOPERSALE COMMON [TL4702]
Garnon Bushes: Welcoming beamed country local, formerly two cottages, popular

reasonably priced food in bar and small restaurant, well kept Greene King, log fires, brasses, fresh flowers, World War II memorabilia from nearby North Weald airfield; quiet piped music; tables on front terrace *(Robert Lester)*

COOPERSALE STREET [TL4701]
☆ *Theydon Oak* [off B172 E of Theydon Bois; or follow Hobbs Cross Open Farm brown sign off B1393 at N end of Epping]: Attractive weatherboarded dining pub with lots of hanging baskets, long convivial beamed bar with lots of brass, copper and old brewery mirrors, decorative antique tills, interesting old maps, well kept Black Sheep and Wadworths 6X, friendly staff, ample good value quickly served food from sandwiches up inc plenty of bargain specials, Sun roasts and puddings cabinet, log fire; no piped music, popular with older lunchers – very busy in summer; no dogs, tables on side terrace and in garden with small stream (maybe ducks), wknd barbecues and separate play area *(H O Dickinson, Robert Lester, BB)*

COXTIE GREEN [TQ5695]
White Horse [3 miles from M25 junction 28, via South Weald]: Pleasant recently refurbished two-room local with good value generous food (not Sun-Weds evenings), six changing ales from small breweries and July beer festival, friendly service, darts; quiet piped music, can get smoky when busy; huge garden with play area *(CMW, JJW, Mrs Roxanne Chamberlain)*

DANBURY [TL7705]
☆ *Griffin* [A414, top of Danbury Hill]: Particularly good Chef & Brewer, spacious but charmingly divided into small homely and congenial sections, 16th-c beams and some older carved woodwork, roaring log fires, splendid friendly service, very wide blackboard choice of flavoursome food, well kept Theakstons Best and Shepherd Neame Spitfire, good choice of wines by the glass, soft lighting and candles at night; no bookings so get there early, subdued piped music, high chairs *(Adrian White, Oliver Hylton)*

DEDHAM [TM0533]
Sun [High St]: Roomy and comfortably refurbished Tudor pub, cosy panelled rooms with big log fires in splendid fireplaces, handsomely carved beams, well kept Greene King Abbot, decent wines, reasonably priced varied food (not Sun evening), cheerful helpful staff, no piped music; tables on back lawn, car park behind reached through medieval arch, wonderful wrought-iron inn sign; comfortable panelled bedrooms with four-posters, good walk to or from Flatford Mill *(LYM)*

DUTON HILL [TL6026]
☆ *Three Horseshoes* [off B184 Dunmow—Thaxted, 3 miles N of Dunmow]: Quiet traditional village pub (doubling as post office) with decent low-priced food inc good value big lincolnshire sausages with choice of mustards in wholemeal baps, well kept Ridleys IPA and one or two guests such as Archers, masses of bottled beers, central fire, aged armchairs by fireplace in homely left-hand parlour,

welcoming licensees, interesting theatrical and 1940s memorabilia and enamel signs; pool in small public bar, pleasant views from garden where local drama groups perform in summer *(BB, Len Banister)*

ELSENHAM [TL5326]

Crown [The Cross; B1051]: Friendly pub with enjoyable home-made food, changing beers such as Adnams Broadside and Youngs; garden tables *(Adrian White)*

EPPING [TL4602]

Black Lion [High St]: Impressive beer range kept well by knowledgeable landlord and good choice of well priced food in nicely set-out little 17th-c pub, beams and horsebrasses, simple furniture on bare floors, roaring log fire; dogs in bar but not eating area *(Len Banister)*

EPPING FOREST [TQ3997]

Owl [Lippitts Hill, nr High Beach]: Big 1930s pub with beams and plates above bar, good cosy atmosphere, McMullens ales, bar food; great Epping Forest views from cypress-shaded terrace, picnic-sets spreading down to paddock, pets corner with plenty of rabbits *(Ian Phillips)*

FEERING [TL8720]

☆ *Sun* [Feering Hill, B1024]: Friendly and easy-going, with half a dozen quickly changing interesting real ales, farm ciders, plenty of malt whiskies, inglenooks and 16th-c beams in open-plan bar divided by standing timbers, daily papers, board games, woodburner, food from sandwiches up; well behaved children allowed, tables out on partly covered paved terrace and in attractive garden, some wknd barbecues *(LYM, Joy and Peter Heatherley, Ian Phillips)*

FELSTED [TL6720]

☆ *Swan* [Station Rd]: Reopened after sensitive refurbishment as comfortable pub/restaurant with three contemporary dining areas off the traditional bar, sofas by central log fire, good food, well kept Ridleys from the nearby brewery, good value wines, welcoming landlord and cordial service; papers *(anon)*

FIDDLERS HAMLET [TL4701]

☆ *Merry Fiddlers* [Stewards Green Rd, 1 mile SE of Epping]: Long low-beamed and timbered 17th-c country pub, lots of copper and brass, chamber-pots, beer mugs and plates, real ales such as Adnams, Bass and Greene King IPA and Old Speckled Hen, good helpings of reasonably priced sensible home-cooked food inc substantial Sun roast and fresh veg, family dining area, attentive friendly staff; may be unobtrusive piped music, occasional live sessions; big garden with good play area (motorway can be heard) *(B N F and M Parkin, Roger and Pauline Pearce, Robert Lester, H O Dickinson)*

FINCHINGFIELD [TL6832]

☆ *Red Lion* [Church Hill – B1053 just E of B1057 crossroads]: Good blackboard choice of sensibly priced food from huffers to some interesting dishes and no-nonsense roast Sun lunch, well kept Adnams and Ridleys, interesting wine choice, chatty enthusiastic landlord, cosy local atmosphere and simple

furnishings, Tudor beams and huge dividing chimney breast, bar billiards, dominoes and cards, small upstairs dining area; attractive garden, three good value bedrooms with own bathrooms, nice spot opp churchyard and 15th-c guild hall *(MDN, Pete Baker)*

FYFIELD [TL5606]

☆ *Black Bull* [B184, N end]: 15th-c pub with heavy low beams and standing timbers, emphasis on popular no smoking country-style dining area with wide range of good if not cheap food; drinkers still very welcome in comfortably modernised pubby bar, well kept Greene King Ruddles and Marstons Pedigree, good service, open fire, traditional games; quiet piped music; tables outside, lots of flower-filled barrels, aviary with budgerigars and cockatiels *(Bernie Adams, LYM, Mary and Dennis Jones, Roy and Lindsey Fentiman)*

Queens Head [off B184; Queen St/Church St]: Welcoming 15th-c local reopened and smartened up by enthusiastic new young owners, low beams and timbers, high-backed settles forming cosy areas, half a dozen interesting well kept changing ales, good wines by the glass inc champagne, good if not cheap food from good sandwiches up; no children inside; small attractive streamside garden *(GL, Mrs L Saunders, Len Banister)*

GREAT EASTON [TL6025]

Swan [2 miles N of Dunmow, off B184 towards Lindsell]: Small, cosy and very friendly old pub in attractive village street, two clean and tidy traditional front rooms, country bygones, comfortable furnishings, good ordinary food, well kept real ales *(Len Banister)*

GREAT TEY [TL8925]

Chequers [off A120 Coggeshall—Marks Tey]: Well kept comfortable old pub with jovial landlord, good reasonably priced food inc daily fresh fish and good Sun roast, puddings and cheeses, efficient service, well kept real ale, traditional games; children and dogs welcome, fine walled garden; quiet village, plenty of country walks *(Marianne and Peter Stevens)*

GREAT YELDHAM [TL7638]

Waggon & Horses [High St]: Cheerful 16th-c timbered inn with attractive oak-beamed bars, well kept Greene King IPA and three other changing ales inc a seasonal Nethergate, decent bar food, welcoming family service, popular restaurant; bedrooms, most in modern back extension *(Maurice Young)*

HASTINGWOOD [TL4807]

☆ *Rainbow & Dove* [¼ mile from M11 junction 7]: Friendly 17th-c rose-covered cottage with cosy fires in three homely little low-beamed rooms off main bar area, reasonably priced standard food from sandwiches up, well kept Courage Directors, Greene King IPA and a guest ale such as Youngs Special; piped music, and pub can come under pressure from motorway escapees; picnic-sets out on the grass with picnic-sets; children in eating areas *(Bob and Margaret Holder, Colin and Janet Roe, David Twitchett, Tony Beaulah, Peter Meister, Ian Phillips, Roy and Lindsey*

Fentiman, LYM, Tony Middis, Adrian White)
HATFIELD HEATH [TL5115]
Thatchers [A1005 towards Bishop's Stortford]:
Neatly refurbished beamed and thatched pub
with well kept Fullers London Pride, Greene
King IPA and Charles Wells Bombardier and
decent house wines from long bar, wide choice
of food from good bacon sandwiches up,
hospitable landlady, woodburner, copper
kettles, jugs, brasses, plates and pictures in
L-shaped bar, back dining area; no children in
bar, may be piped music; at end of large green,
tables out under cocktail parasols *(Marjorie
and Bernard Parkin, George Atkinson)*
HERONGATE [TQ6391]
Boars Head [Billericay Rd, just off A128]:
Picturesque low-beamed dining pub with
pleasant nooks and crannies, wide blackboard
choice of reliable sensibly priced traditional
food all day inc good choice of lunchtime
baguettes, Adnams, Greene King Abbot and
John Smiths, reasonably priced wines, friendly
staff; can get crowded at peak times; garden
tables overlooking big attractive reed-fringed
pond with ducks and moorhens *(Roy and
Lindsey Fentiman, Mark Morgan)*
HEYBRIDGE BASIN [TL8707]
Old Ship [Lockhill]: Good choice of reliable
standard food and changing specials, well kept
Greene King IPA, Abbot and Old Speckled
Hen, malt whiskies, blond wooden furniture
(window tables reserved for diners), more
ambitious upstairs restaurant with estuary
views, good friendly service, daily papers; well
behaved dogs and children welcome; seats
outside, some overlooking water by canal lock
– lovely views of the saltings and across to
Northey Island, pretty window boxes; can be
very busy, esp in summer when parking nearby
impossible (but public park five mins' walk)
(Pam and David Bailey, Peter Butterworth)
HIGH BEACH [TQ4098]
Duke of Wellington [Wellington Hill, nr
Loughton]: Unpretentious pub near popular
forest-edge viewing spot, Bass and Tetleys,
popularly priced usual food inc children's
menu *(Len Banister)*
HIGH ONGAR [TL5903]
☆ *Wheatsheaf* [signed Blackmore, Ingatestone off
A414 just E of Ongar]: Comfortable low-
beamed pub/restaurant with emphasis on good
food (not Sun evening), unusual intimate stalls
in big front bay window, log fires each end,
Greene King IPA; children in side room,
charming big back garden, plenty of play space
and equipment
(LYM, H O Dickinson, Len Banister)
HORSLEY CROSS [TM1228]
Hedgerows [Clacton Rd]: Good choice of
home-cooked food and of beers and wines,
reasonable prices; children welcome
(Pamela Goodwyn)
KIRBY LE SOKEN [TM2221]
Ship [B1034 Thorpe—Walton]: Wide choice of
generous good value food in tastefully
refurbished old pink-washed beamed building
with relaxing atmosphere, well kept Greene
King, good wine list, pleasant staff, rustic

tables outside; unobtrusive piped music,
children in eating area, has been open all day
(Mr and Mrs Staples)
LAYER DE LA HAYE [TL9619]
Donkey & Buskins [off B1026 towards
Colchester]: Friendly old-fashioned country
pub with general mix of furnishings and
ornaments in several rooms, good range of
reasonably priced straightforward food in bar
and dining room esp fresh fish and good Sun
roasts, decent helpings, well kept Adnams, Bass
and Greene King IPA, pleasant service; handy
for Abberton Reservoir's fishermen and birders
(J Strain, Gordon Neighbour, Len Banister)
LITTLE BADDOW [TL7807]
Generals Arms [The Ridge; minor road
Hatfield Peverel—Danbury]: Newly
refurbished and building up the food side, with
friendly service, well kept Shepherd Neame
ales, reasonably priced wines; lawn with tables
and play area *(LYM, Paul and Ursula Randall)*
Rodney [North Hill, towards Hatfield Peverel]:
Attractive low-beamed country local, former
17th-c farmhouse, full of nautical memorabilia,
well kept Greene King IPA and Old Speckled
Hen with an interesting guest beer, good value
food from rolls, sandwiches and baguettes to
low-priced main dishes, small pool room with
unobtrusive piped music; terrace and garden
with well equipped play area *(Paul and
Ursula Randall, Tony Hobden)*
LOUGHTON [TQ4297]
☆ *Gardeners Arms* [York Hill, just off A121
High Rd]: Country feel in traditional pub with
Adnams and Greene King Ruddles in attractive
central bar, big prints and old firearms, two
open fires, friendly service, good
straightforward lunchtime bar food (not Sun)
from sandwiches up with hot dishes all fresh-
cooked (so can be delays), children in back
dining area, sleepy dogs; unexpected views
towards London *(LYM, Len Banister)*
MALDON [TL8407]
White Horse [High St]: Unpretentious, with
several Shepherd Neame ales, good value
straightforward lunchtime food, flourishing
local atmosphere, friendly helpful staff;
unobtrusive piped music and pool *(MLR)*
MANNINGTREE [TM1031]
☆ *Crown* [High St]: Pleasant bare-boards no
smoking mealtime bar on left with plenty of
old local photographs and advertisements, low-
ceilinged lino-floored and ochre-walled front
public bar, estuary views from brightly
carpeted or tiled two-level back area with more
dining tables and nautical stuff under high
pitched ceiling, well kept Greene King IPA,
Abbot and XX Mild, cheerful staff, usual food
inc interesting sandwiches and plenty for
children, super Christmas decorations; picnic-
sets on back terrace, attractively priced
bedrooms, open all day *(Bernie Adams,
Ian Phillips, Ian and Nita Cooper, BB)*
MARGARETTING [TL6701]
Red Lion [B1002 towards Mountnessing]:
Busy but relaxed beamed and timbered local,
all tables laid for good choice of enjoyable
food inc good fish specialities, no smoking

dining area, well kept Ridleys IPA, Bob and Prospect, efficient unrushed service, attractive floral displays; piped radio; good wheelchair access, picnic-sets and play area outside *(John and Judy Saville, Roy and Lindsey Fentiman, Ian Phillips)*

MARGARETTING TYE [TL6801]

White Hart: L-shaped bar with good value food from sandwiches up, good choice of well kept ales inc Adnams, comfortable conservatory-roofed family dining room; may be piped music; robust play area and pets corner in attractive garden by quiet village green, good walks *(Carole and John Smith, Paul and Ursula Randall, Paul Hunkin, Evelyn and Derek Walter)*

MATCHING GREEN [TL5310]

Chequers: Friendly pub/restaurant in quiet spot overlooking pretty cricket green, candles on plain pine tables, lounge with sofas and open fire, sparse decoration, good traditional and mediterranean-style food, american-style central bar with Greene King IPA and Old Speckled Hen and Charles Wells Bombardier, lots of lagers, shiny taps and glistening bottles (good wine choice), relaxed at lunchtime, busy evenings; garden; jazz Tues, cl Mon *(Len Banister)*

MESSING [TL8919]

Old Crown [signed off B1022 and B1023; Lodge Rd]: Attractive late 17th-c country local with well kept Ridleys PA and Prospect, good coffee, enjoyable food in bar and dining room from baguettes to good value Sun lunch, helpful staff, interesting articles about village inc its association with George W Bush; nr fine church *(Michael and Jenny Back)*

MILL GREEN [TL6401]

☆ *Cricketers*: Low beams, lots of interesting cricketing memorabilia and emphasis on generous and popular freshly cooked traditional food, well kept Greene King IPA, Abbot and Old Speckled Hen tapped from the cask, decent wines, friendly attentive service, no smoking area and restaurant, no music; children very welcome, picturesque setting, plenty of picnic-sets on big front terrace and in extensive garden behind, cl wknds Sun evenings *(Eddie Edwards, Len Banister, Piotr Chodzko-Zajko)*

MORETON [TL5307]

Nags Head [signed off B184, at S end of Fyfield or opp Chipping Ongar school]: Attractive array of salvaged rustic beams and timbers still showing their wedges and dowels, comfortable mix of tables, three big log fires, country knick-knacks, wide rather adventurous blackboard choice of good value food, full Ridleys range kept well, restaurant; children welcome, picnic-sets on side grass *(H O Dickinson, Len Banister)*

White Hart [off B184, just N of A414]: Comfortable divided L-shaped lounge bar with log fire, soft lighting, nice prints and lots of woodwork, well kept Adnams, Greene King IPA and Youngs Special, decent house wines, generous if not cheap italian food all day, attractive small timbered dining room; picnic-

sets on small back terrace and in informal garden with play area *(LYM, Len Banister)*

MOUNTNESSING [TQ6397]

Prince of Wales [Roman Rd (B1002)]: New management in rambling beamed pub opp windmill, popular for its food inc fish specialities and well kept Ridleys ales; good wine list *(Roy and Lindsey Fentiman)*

MUCH HADHAM [TL4218]

Old Crown [Hadham Cross]: Unpretentious pub quickly winning friends for its warm welcome, particularly well kept beer and cheap home-made food *(Len Banister)*

NEWNEY GREEN [TL6506]

☆ *Duck* [off A1060 W of Chelmsford via Roxwell, or off A414 W of Writtle – take Cooksmill Green turn-off at Fox & Goose, then bear right]: Comfortable and welcoming dining pub with attractive rambling bar full of hop-hung beams, timbering, panelling and interesting bric-a-brac, comfortable furnishings, enjoyable food inc good value set lunches, well kept Shepherd Neame real ales, decent wines by the glass, attentive and polite young staff; well laid tables out on attractive terrace *(LYM, John and Enid Morris, Paul and Ursula Randall, Mary and Dennis Jones)*

NORTH END [TL6617]

Butchers Arms [A130 SE of Dunmow]: Small attractively unpretentious 16th-c country pub with beams, timbers, log fire and inglenook woodburner, particularly well kept Ridleys, some emphasis on good value straightforward food, cheerful service, dining area; children welcome, sheltered garden and well equipped play area, open all day wknds *(Paul and Ursula Randall)*

NORTH FAMBRIDGE [TQ8597]

☆ *Ferry Boat* [village signed from B1012 E off S Woodham Ferrers; keep on past railway to quay]: Unpretentious 15th-c weatherboarded pub tucked prettily down by the marshes, warmly welcoming chatty landlord, simple traditional furnishings, nautical memorabilia, log fire one end, woodburner the other, good value honest food from sandwiches to Sun lunches, well kept Shepherd Neame Bitter, Spitfire and Bishops Finger, traditional games, children in family room and partly no smoking restaurant; piped music, fruit machine, TV; tables in garden with pond (ducks and carp), bedrooms in barn-like building behind, good lonely walks *(John and Judy Saville, LYM)*

PAGLESHAM [TQ9492]

☆ *Plough & Sail* [East End]: Friendly 17th-c dining pub in pretty spot, beams and big log fires, pine tables, lots of brasses and pictures, enjoyable food from sandwiches through familiar favourites to interesting specials inc fresh fish, well kept Greene King IPA and a guest beer, decent house wines, traditional games; rather relaxed service, unobtrusive piped music; tables and aviary in neat and attractive garden, open all day Sun *(LYM, Tina and David Woods-Taylor)*

PELDON [TM0015]

☆ *Rose* [on B1025 Colchester—Mersea]: Low 17th-c beams and some venerable bar furnishings contrasting with spacious airy no smoking conservatory, lots of good wines by the glass, well kept Adnams Best and Broadside, Greene King IPA and a guest beer, home-made bar food from sandwiches to local Mersea fish, children's helpings, friendly staff; children welcome away from bar, roomy well furnished garden with duck pond, open all day *(R Richards, Gordon Neighbour, Chris Pearson, Robb Tooley, LYM, Rona Murdoch)*

PLESHEY [TL6614]

Leather Bottle [The Street]: Good plain 1940s-style pub with particularly well kept Ridleys IPA and cheap cheerful food *(Len Banister)*

☆ *White Horse* [The Street]: 15th-c beams and timbers, big back extension with two dining rooms, one no smoking (should book wknds), welcoming service, good range of enjoyable bar food from sandwiches to imaginative full meals (freshly made, so may take a while), well kept Youngs Bitter and AAA, decent wines; may be piped music; luncheon club and theme nights, children welcome, tables out on terrace and in garden with small safe play area, pretty village with ruined castle *(LYM, Richard Trim, Len Banister)*

RADWINTER [TL6137]

☆ *Plough* [Sampford Rd (B1053 E of Saffron Walden)]: Congenial and neatly kept red plush open-plan black-timbered beamed bar with some concentration on generous home-made food esp good fresh fish, well kept Greene King IPA and a changing guest beer, good coffee, friendly service, no music; children, and dogs on lead, welcome, very attractive terrace and garden, open countryside; comfortable bedrooms *(DC, Andrew and Samantha Grainger, BB)*

RIDGEWELL [TL7340]

White Horse [Mill Rd (A1017 Haverhill—Halstead)]: Comfortable open-plan low-beamed local, bar covered in old pennies, good value food from sandwiches up, with nicely served real butter and sauces, two changing real ales, good service; tables outside *(MLR)*

ROWHEDGE [TM0321]

Anchor [Quay; follow Rowhedge signpost off A134, the part that's just S of Colchester centre]: Reopened after attractive refurbishment, picture-window views over marshes and tidal River Colne with its swans, gulls and yachts, flagstoned bar, pine furniture in tiled bistro, enjoyable fresh up-to-date food, real ales inc Greene King IPA and Old Speckled Hen, nice house wines; large waterside terrace, cl Mon *(Andrew Morgan)*

SAFFRON WALDEN [TL5438]

☆ *Eight Bells* [Bridge St; B184 towards Cambridge]: Large Tudor pub under friendly new management, obliging young staff, wide choice of enjoyable and interesting food inc good home-made puddings in open-plan rambling bare-boards bars and carpeted handsomely raftered and timbered refurbished restaurant, Adnams and Greene King IPA, children allowed; open all day, tables in garden, handy for Audley End, good walks

(Alain and Rose Foote, LYM, John and Judy Saville, Peter Hagler, Len Banister)

STANFORD RIVERS [TL5300]

☆ *Woodman* [Little End, London Rd (A113 S of Ongar)]: Weatherboarded roadside dining pub, well extended to ramble comfortably and attractively around central bar, with beams, log fire in big inglenook, lots of pictures, brasses and bric-a-brac, well kept Shepherd Neame Bitter, Spitfire and Bishops Finger, food all day, friendly efficient staff; piped music; open all day, big garden with country views, very good play area *(BB, Len Banister)*

STISTED [TL7924]

☆ *Dolphin* [A120 E of Braintree, by village turn]: Well kept Ridleys tapped from the cask in heavily beamed and timbered locals' bar on right, popular well priced straightforward food (not Tues or Sun evenings) inc steak bargains Sat evening, log fire, bright eating area on left (children allowed here); tables outside *(Pete Baker, LYM)*

STOCK [TQ6998]

Bear [Mill Rd, just off B1007]: Charmingly refurbished old building, civilised locals' front bar, enjoyable food inc good Sun roasts, well kept ales such as Adnams and Greene King Abbot, friendly efficient staff, stained glass and bric-a-brac, cosy no smoking restaurant, children's room; nice back garden overlooking pond *(BB, John and Judy Saville)*

STURMER [TL6944]

Red Lion [A1017 SE of Haverhill]: Good new licensees for attractive thatched and beamed pub with freshly cooked food in bar, dining area, nice conservatory and small no smoking dining room, well kept real ales, good service, well spaced tables with solid cushioned chairs, big fireplace, convenient layout if you don't like steps; large pleasant garden *(Adele Summers, Alan Black, BB)*

TOOT HILL [TL5102]

☆ *Green Man* [off A113 in Stanford Rivers, S of Ongar, or A414 W of Ongar]: Simply furnished country pub in appearance though really a good restaurant in style and price (meals rather than bar food), with a long plush dining room alongside the colourful front terrace; very good wine list, real ales such as Crouch Vale Best, Fullers London Pride, Nethergate Winter Warmer and Ridleys PA; may be piped music, no under-10s, tables in back garden *(David and Ruth Shillitoe, LYM, Ian Phillips, Adrian White, John and Judy Saville, John and Enid Morris, Mrs Jill Silversides, Barry Brown, Philip and Elaine Holmes, Len Banister)*

WALTHAM ABBEY [TQ4199]

Volunteer [½ mile from M25 junction 26; A121 towards Loughton]: Roomy extensively refurbished family pub popular for good value generous chinese as well as english food, prompt friendly service, attractive conservatory, McMullens Country and Mild; piped music; some tables on side terrace, pretty hanging baskets, nice spot by Epping Forest *(John and Judy Saville, BB)*

WEST BERGHOLT [TL9627]
Treble Tile [Colchester Rd]: More restaurant than pub, but with good atmosphere, well kept Adnams in proper bar with casual furnishings, and no booking; good reasonably priced food with extra evening choice *(John Prescott)*

WEST TILBURY [TQ6677]
Kings Head [The Green]: Comfortable and homely, with bench seating, pleasant staff and willing landlord, good range of reasonably priced home-made food, nice wines; pleasant setting on small green *(Tina and David Woods-Taylor)*

WIDDINGTON [TL5331]
Fleur de Lys [signed off B1383 N of Stansted]: Unpretentious low-beamed timbered bar with tasty home-made food, Adnams and Greene King, decent wines, inglenook log fire, banknote collection, games in back bar; no credit cards; children in restaurant and no smoking family room, picnic-sets on pleasant side lawn, handy for Mole Hall wildlife park *(Adrian White)*

WITHAM [TL8115]
Albert [B1018, nr stn]: Open-plan town pub, nicely smartened up, with enjoyable cheap food all day from baguettes up, hard-working friendly landlord and staff, five real ales *(Tina and David Woods-Taylor)*

WRITTLE [TL6807]
Horse & Groom [Roxwell Rd (A1060)]: Attractive mock-Tudor Chef & Brewer family dining pub specialising in fresh fish, well kept Theakstons Best, decent wines, cheerful friendly staff, spacious bar, big pine tables in good-sized no smoking area, several log fires, evening candles; unobtrusive piped music; tables outside with country views *(Tina and David Woods-Taylor)*

Inn on the Green [The Green]: Spacious well worn in pub on large attractive green, buoyant atmosphere, half a dozen well kept ales, neat and friendly staff, enjoyable bar food, old advertisements, sepia photographs; end games area popular with young people *(Bruce M Drew)*

Real ale may be served from handpumps, electric pumps (not just the on-off switches used for keg beer) or – common in Scotland – tall taps called founts (pronounced 'fonts') where a separate pump pushes the beer up under air pressure. The landlord can adjust the force of the flow – a tight spigot gives the good creamy head that Yorkshire lads like.

Gloucestershire

One of Britain's best areas for good pubs, the county has a great mix from truly unspoilt gems to places with seriously good imaginative food. Landlords and landladies are friendly and helpful, and free from the pretentiousness which now seems to be afflicting some elsewhere. A lot of the best pubs take you into lovely villages and wonderful countryside, and there are good local beers and plenty of good wines to be found. Pubs new to this edition are the Ostrich at Newland (an unspoilt country pub with good interesting food and a fine beer choice), the Eagle & Child in Stow-on-the-Wold (a relatively new venture in an ancient building – interesting up-to-date food and good wines), the riverside Fleet at Twyning (a good all-rounder, nice for families – especially in summer) and the White Hart in Winchcombe (swedish-run and a bit different, with enjoyable food all day). Other pubs here on fine form include the Boat at Ashleworth Quay (much loved for its unspoilt character), the restauranty Village Pub at Barnsley, the Red Hart at Blaisdon (a friendly and likeable country pub with enjoyable food and beers), the Golden Heart near Brimpsfield (feels just right, thanks to its friendly landlord as much as its enjoyable food and beer), the Eight Bells in Chipping Campden (good all round, in a lovely building), the New Inn at Coln St Aldwyns (clever combination of good smart food and bedrooms with well kept beers and a friendly pubby feel), the Kings Arms at Didmarton (the good imaginative food gains a new Food Award for this tidy and well run pub with its good local beers), the Five Mile House at Duntisbourne Abbots (a favourite unspoilt building, much enjoyed for its food, drink and service), the White Horse at Frampton Mansell (a top-notch dining pub), the chatty and friendly old Bull at Hinton Dyrham (new licensees doing well here), the Masons Arms at Meysey Hampton (a proper village pub, everything just right), the Weighbridge near Nailsworth (super licensees, good food, wines and beers), the Anchor in Oldbury-on-Severn (nice combination of village pub and dining place, very well and kindly run), the Churchill at Paxford (it's the imaginative food that counts here), the Bell at Sapperton (super if pricy food, snacks too, and a welcome for walkers and locals), the George at St Briavels (a good all-rounder, nicely placed), the civilised and restauranty Gumstool near Tetbury, and the remarkably friendly Horse & Groom at Upper Oddington (it could hardly be more welcoming). With so many pubs here doing really good food, there's no shortage of choice for a special meal out; the Bell at Sapperton takes the top title, as Gloucestershire Dining Pub of the Year. In the Lucky Dip section at the end of the chapter, quite a few pubs are jostling for space among the main entries. Ones to note particularly include the Black Horse at Amberley, Fox at Broadwell, Hare & Hounds near Chedworth, Twelve Bells in Cirencester, Colesbourne Inn, Bull in Fairford, Plough at Ford, Glasshouse Inn, Fox at Great Barrington, Ragged Cot at Hyde, Fox at Lower Oddington, Kings Arms at Mickleton, Falcon in Painswick, Boat at Redbrook, Queens Head in Stow-on-the-Wold, Bell at Willersey, Old Corner Cupboard and Plaisterers Arms (both in Winchcombe), Ram and Royal Oak (both in Woodchester). Drinks prices here are close to the national average. The local beers from Donnington, Wickwar and Goffs (who now own the main entry Royal Oak at Gretton) often show up as good value, and other good local beers to look out for include Uley, Freeminer, Stanway and North Cotswold. Hook Norton from over the Oxfordshire border is commonly very pocket-friendly.

ALMONDSBURY ST6084 Map 2
Bowl ⚔

1¼ miles from M5 junction 16 (and therefore quite handy for M4 junction 20; from A38 towards Thornbury, turn first left signposted Lower Almondsbury, then first right down Sundays Hill, then at bottom right again into Church Road

If you want a good break from the M5 – you'd never imagine you were so close – then this well run and popular pub is just the place to head for. The long neatly kept beamed bar has terracotta plush-patterned modern settles, dark green cushioned stools and mate's chairs around elm tables, horsebrasses on stripped bare stone walls, quite a mix of customers, and big winter log fire at one end, with a woodburning stove at the other. Well liked bar food includes filled baguettes (from £4.50), interesting salads such as deep-fried goats cheese with marinated red pepper or battered tiger prawns with sweet chilli sauce (from £4.50 for starter helpings, and from £8.50 for a main course), ploughman's (£4.95), pasta with wild mushrooms, parmesan and crème fraîche (£4.95; main course £8.95), battered cod and chips or sausage and mash with onion gravy (£6.95), roast loin of pork with a wholegrain mustard and cider sauce (£8.95), steak and oyster mushroom pie (£9.95), rib-eye steak (£12.95), and puddings such as warm chocolate pudding with hot chocolate sauce or apple and blackberry crumble with crème anglaise (£3.95); they will serve half helpings for children under 12, and breakfasts are good. Well kept Courage Best, Moles Best, Smiles Best, and a guest from Bath or a seasonal one from Moles or Smiles on handpump; piped music and fruit machine. Seats outside – which get quickly snapped up in good weather – and it all looks very pretty with the church next door and the lovely flowering tubs, hanging baskets, and window boxes. More reports please. *(Recommended by Rod Stoneman, Neil Rose, Ian Phillips, Dr D J and Mrs S C Walker, Peter and Jenny Quine, Rev Michael Vockins, Mrs Jane Kingsbury)*

Free house ~ Licensee Miss E Alley ~ Real ale ~ Bar food (12-2.30, 6-10; not 25 Dec) ~ Restaurant ~ (01454) 612757 ~ Children in eating area of bar and restaurant ~ Dogs allowed in bar ~ Open 11.30-3, 5(6 Sat)-11; 12-10.30 Sun ~ Bedrooms: £44.50S/£71S

AMPNEY ST PETER SP0801 Map 4
Red Lion ◖

A417, E of village

For 27 years, the charming and courteous Mr Barnard has been welcoming a fine mix of locals and visitors into his delightfully unspoilt little roadside pub. It's a great place for a friendly chat, and a central stone corridor, served by a hatch, gives on to the little right-hand tile-floor public bar. Here, one long seat faces the small open fire, with just one table and a wall seat, and behind the long bench an open servery (no counter, just shelves of bottles and – by the corridor hatch – handpumps for the well kept Hook Norton Best and summer Haymaker, and maybe Flowers IPA). There are old prints on the wall, and on the other side of the corridor is a small saloon, with panelled wall seats around its single table, old local photographs, another open fire, and a print of Queen Victoria one could believe hasn't moved for a century – rather like the pub itself. There are seats in the side garden.

(Recommended by the Didler, Dr and Mrs A K Clarke, R Huggins, D Irving, E McCall, T McLean, Giles Francis, Phil and Sally Gorton, Richard Stancomb, Paul and Ann Meyer, RWC, Sue and Jeff Evans)

Free house ~ Licensee John Barnard ~ Real ale ~ No credit cards ~ (01285) 851596 ~ Children in the tiny games room ~ Dogs allowed in bar ~ Open 6-10.30; 12-2.30, 6(7 Sun)-10.30 Sat; closed weekday lunchtimes

ASHLEWORTH SO8125 Map 4

Queens Arms ⓘ ♀ ◧

Village signposted off A417 at Hartpury

This attractive low-beamed country pub is now completely no smoking and it's all kept spotlessly neat and tidy. The comfortably laid out and civilised main bar, softly lit by fringed wall lamps and candles at night, has faintly patterned wallpaper and washed red ochre walls, big oak and mahogany tables and a nice mix of farmhouse and big brocaded dining chairs on a red carpet. Most customers come to enjoy the extensive choice of good, imaginative bar food which includes lunchtime specials such as greek salad (£5.95), filled baguettes (from £5.95), curried pickled fish (a south african dish, £6.50), faggots or boerewors (a south african sausage) with onion and tomato gravy (£6.95), liver and bacon casserole (£7.25), and chicken and mushroom pie (£7.95). There's also pork and duck terrine with cumberland sauce or home-made soup (£3.95), fresh mussels in a mild curry and cream sauce (£5.25), seafood st jacques in a lobster and brandy cream sauce (£6.25), steak and kidney pie, a balti of the day or home-cooked ham and egg (£8.95), steaks (from £11.25), daily specials like bobotie (£10.95), chicken in an italian tomato and olive sauce on pasta (£11.95), braised guinea fowl with port, orange and pickling onions with mashed celeriac (£12.95), and fresh bass fillets topped with oyster mushroom and chablis cream sauce or ostrich fillet steaks with a madagascar green peppercorn, brandy and cream sauce (£13.95), and puddings such as baked chocolate marble cheesecake or walnut and fudge pudding (from £4.25). From a rotating choice of 18 real ales on handpump, there might be Archers Village, Brains Rev James, and Shepherd Neame Spitfire. A thoughtful wine list with quite a few South African choices (the licensees hail from there) and 10 by the glass, and 22 malt whiskies. Piped music, shove-ha'penny, cribbage, dominoes, and winter skittle alley. The little black pub cat Bonnie charms customers with her ping-pong football antics. Two perfectly clipped mushroom shaped yews dominate the front of the building, and there are wrought-iron tables in the sunny courtyard. *(Recommended by Mrs J L Wyatt, EML, Stephen and Jean Curtis, Guy Vowles, P J G Nicholl, Brian and Pat Wardrobe, Rodney and Norma Stubington, Neil and Debbie Cook, Mrs Pam Vanden Bergh, Mrs A Willis, Neil and Anita Christopher, David Carr, Bernard Stradling, James Woods, P J G Nicoll, Ian and Nita Cooper, Mike and Wendy Proctor, Jane Bailey)*

Free house ~ Licensees Tony and Gill Burreddu ~ Real ale ~ Bar food (till 10 Fri and Sat) ~ Restaurant ~ (01452) 700395 ~ Well behaved children welcome ~ Open 12-3, 7-11(10.30 Sun); closed 25 and 26 Dec

ASHLEWORTH QUAY SO8125 Map 4

Boat ★

Ashleworth signposted off A417 N of Gloucester; quay signed from village

This quite unspoilt and rather special pub is the sort of place where you strike up conversations with complete strangers – one reader spent a most enjoyable evening sharing a scrubbed deal table with three elderly gents, all over 80, who were on a pub crawl. It's set in an idyllic spot on the banks of the River Severn, and there's a front suntrap crazy-paved courtyard, bright with plant tubs in summer, with a couple of picnic-sets under cocktail parasols; more seats and tables under cover at the sides. The little front parlour has a great built-in settle by a long scrubbed deal table that faces an old-fashioned open kitchen range with a side bread oven and a couple of elderly fireside chairs; there are rush mats on the scrubbed flagstones, houseplants in the window, fresh garden flowers, and old magazines to read. One small lounge is no smoking; shove-ha'penny, dominoes and cribbage (the front room has darts). A pair of flower-cushioned antique settles faces each other in the back room where daily-changing beers from breweries such as Arkells, Bath, Church End, Cottage, Goffs, Hobsons, Hook Norton, Malvern Hills, RCH, Slaters, and Wye Valley are tapped from the cask, along with a full range of Weston's farm ciders. They usually do good lunchtime rolls (from £1.45) during the week. The same family have run the pub since it was originally licensed by Royal Charter in the 17th c – we believe this is a record for continuous pub ownership. *(Recommended by Pete Baker, Theocsbrian, the Didler, P R and S A White, Ian and Nita Cooper, David Carr, Guy Vowles, Keith Jacob, Richard Stancomb, Peter Scillitoe, James Woods, Tom McLean)*

Free house ~ Licensees Jacquie and Ron Nicholls ~ Real ale ~ Bar food (lunchtime only) ~ No credit cards ~ (01452) 700272 ~ Children welcome until 8pm ~ Open 11-2.30(3 Sat), 6(7 in winter)-11; 12-3, 7-10.30 Sun; evening opening 7pm in winter; closed Mon and Weds lunchtimes Oct-Apr

AWRE SO7108 Map 4
Red Hart ◖
Village signposted off A48 S of Newnham

Nicely placed in an out-of-the-way little farming village between the River Severn and the Forest of Dean, there's a very un-mass-produced feel to the architecture and internal character of this tall 15th-c pub. The neat L-shaped bar, the main part of which has a deep glass-covered illuminated well, has an antique pine bookcase filled with cookery and wine books, an antique pine display cabinet with Worcester china, pine tables and chairs, and a relaxed, friendly atmosphere. The bottom end of the bar has old prints of the village and surrounding area, and the restaurant has some exposed wattle and daub. Enjoyable home-made bar food includes sandwiches, home-made soup (£2.95), chicken liver pâté flavoured with apricots and Southern Comfort and served with red onion marmalade (£3.95), oak-smoked salmon fettuccine (£4.95), ham and egg (£6.75), cod in home-made beer batter or lambs liver and bacon in a red wine and mushroom sauce (£6.95), wild mushroom and pine nut wellington with a tomato and garlic sauce (£7.50), supremes of local pheasant with celeriac purée and parsnip ribbons in a port and juniper sauce (£9.95), steaks (from £11.95), and half a crispy duck with lime, ginger and soy sauce (£12.50). The eating part of the bar is no smoking, as is the restaurant. Well kept Archers Best, Fullers London Pride, and Goffs Jouster plus a guest such as Deuchars IPA or Youngs Special on handpump, and a varied wine list. In front of the building are some picnic-sets. *(Recommended by Bob and Margaret Holder, Revd John E Cooper, David Jeffreys, Mike and Mary Carter, Theocsbrian, Tim and Ann Newell)*

Free house ~ Licensee Jeremy Bedwell ~ Real ale ~ Bar food ~ Restaurant ~ (01594) 510220 ~ Children in eating area of bar until 8.30 ~ Open 12-3, 6.30-11; 12-3, 7-10.30 Sun; closed Mon

BARNSLEY SP0705 Map 4
Village Pub ⊕ ♀
B4425 Cirencester—Burford

Smart and rather civilised, this bustling place is very much somewhere to come for a special meal out. The low-ceilinged communicating rooms (one is no smoking) have oil paintings, plush chairs, stools, and window settles around polished candlelit tables, and country magazines and newspapers to read. Particularly good, if not cheap, food at lunchtime includes sweet potato and chilli soup (£4), devilled lambs kidneys (£6), cold roast beef sandwich with sweet and sour courgettes or guinea fowl and wild mushroom ballotine (£6.25), rabbit cooked with mustard, baby carrots and jersey royals (£12.50), rare grilled tuna with aubergine and cardamom tagine and couscous (£13), and rib-eye steak with béarnaise sauce (£15.50); in the evening there might be crab bisque with rouille and croutons (£4.50), fried squid with chorizo and new potatoes (£6), chicken liver foie gras parfait with pickled figs (£6.50), grilled mackerel with roast tomato, anchovy and parsley salad (£11.50), duck breast with roast beetroot, baby red chard and horseradish (£13.50), and roast fillet of beef, herb polenta and red wine (£16.50), with puddings like chocolate, orange and macadamia nut torte, bramble apple crumble or honey and rosemary ice cream with home-made tuile (£5). Well kept Hook Norton Bitter, and Wadworths 6X with a guest such as Donnington SBA or Shepherd Neame Spitfire on handpump, local cider and apple juice, malt whiskies, and 20 wines by the glass; courteous service. Dominoes, chess, and draughts. The sheltered back courtyard has plenty of good solid wooden furniture under umbrellas, and its own outside servery. *(Recommended by Mrs E V McDonald, Maysie Thompson, John Kane, Anna and Martyn Carey, Alec and Barbara Jones, Dr W I C Clark, Kate and Michael Colgrave, Peter Meister, Mrs Sally Lloyd, R Huggins, D Irving, E McCall, T McLean, Wendy and Bob Needham, Lesley and Peter Barrett, Guy Vowles, Mr and Mrs B Golding, Di and Mike Gillam, Bernard Stradling)*

Free house ~ Licensees Tim Haigh and Rupert Pendered ~ Real ale ~ Bar food (12-2.30, 7-9.30) ~ Restaurant ~ (01285) 740421 ~ Children welcome ~ Dogs allowed in bar ~ Open 11-3, 6-11; 12-4, 7-10.30 Sun ~ Bedrooms: £65S/£80S(£105B)

BISLEY SO9006 Map 4
Bear ◀

Village signposted off A419 just E of Stroud

The landlord in this elegantly gothic 16th-c inn makes a point of warmly welcoming all his customers – locals or first-time visitors. There's a good, relaxed pubby atmosphere, and the meandering L-shaped bar has a long shiny black built-in settle and a smaller but even sturdier oak settle by the front entrance, and an enormously wide low stone fireplace (not very high – the ochre ceiling's too low for that); the separate no smoking stripped-stone area is used for families. Enjoyable home-made bar food includes soup (£3.60), goats cheese toasties (£3.95), lots of baguettes interestingly filled with tuna salad niçoise, brie and grape, roasted ratatouille or lamb steak with redcurrant jelly (mostly £4.75), sautéed potatoes and onions on lettuce with tomato and garlic (£5.95), provençale vegetables (£5.85) or smoked salmon and leek (£6.25), home-made rabbit or steak, kidney and Guinness pies or vegetable pasty (from £7.50), and daily specials like pasta carbonara (£6.95), spicy meatloaf with wine gravy or mild and creamy chicken curry (£7.25), sausages casseroled with bacon, onions and sage (£7.95), and chunky cod roasted with red peppers and cherry tomatoes (£8.95). Well kept Flowers IPA, Marstons Pedigree, Tetleys, and Wells Bombardier on handpump; dominoes, cribbage, and table skittles. A small front colonnade supports the upper floor of the pub, and the sheltered little flagstoned courtyard made by this has a traditional bench; the garden is across the quiet road, and there's quite a collection of stone mounting-blocks. The steep stone-built village is attractive. *(Recommended by Bob and Margaret Holder, R Huggins, D Irving, E McCall, T McLean, Mr and Mrs P Higgins, Dave Irving, P R and S A White, Gaynor Gregory, Richard Gibbs, Guy Vowles, Dick and Mary Pownall, Nick and Meriel Cox, Simon Collett-Jones, Jill Hurley, Margaret Morgan, Di and Mike Gillam)*

Pubmaster ~ Tenants Simon and Sue Evans ~ Real ale ~ Bar food (not Sun evening) ~ (01452) 770265 ~ Children in family room ~ Dogs welcome ~ Occasional Irish music ~ Open 11.30-3, 6-11; 12-3, 7-10.30 Sun ~ Bedrooms: £20/£40

BLAISDON SO7017 Map 4
Red Hart ◀

Village signposted off A4136 just SW of junction with A40 W of Gloucester; OS Sheet 162 map reference 703169

This is the sort of reliable and friendly place that customers tend to return to again and again. The flagstoned main bar has a thoroughly relaxing atmosphere – helped along by well reproduced piped bluesy music, and maybe Spotty the perky jack russell – as well as cushioned wall and window seats, traditional pub tables, and a big sailing-ship painting above the log fire. Well kept Hook Norton Best, Tetleys, and three guests such as Timothy Taylors Landlord, Uley Bitter, and Wickwar

Brand Oak Bitter on handpump, and a decent wine list. On the right, there's an attractive beamed two-room no smoking dining area with some interesting prints and bric-a-brac, and on the left, additional dining space for families. Well liked bar food inlcudes home-made soup (£2.75), sandwiches (from £3.75), fried sardines (£4.75), salmon and coriander fishcakes (starter £4.25, main course £6.50), crab tartlet with dill mayonnaise (starter £4.75, main course £6.50), ham, egg and bubble and squeak (£5.75), lemon chicken stir fry (£9.50), bass with watercress sauce (£10.50), and fillet of lamb with red wine and rosemary sauce (£10.50). Cribbage, dominoes, and table skittles. There are some picnic-sets in the garden and a children's play area, and at the back of the building is a large space for barbecues. *(Recommended by Peter Scillitoe, Geoff and Brigid Smithers, Hugh and Erica Swallow, P and J Shapley, Neil and Jean Spink, Mr and Mrs F J Parmenter, W Ruxton, Rod Stoneman, S P Watkin, P A Taylor)*

Free house ~ Licensee Guy Wilkins ~ Real ale ~ Bar food ~ Restaurant ~ (01452) 830477 ~ Children in eating area of bar ~ Dogs allowed in bar ~ Open 11.30-3, 6-11; 12-3.30, 7-10.30 Sun

BLEDINGTON SP2422 Map 4
Kings Head ♀ ◀
B4450

This classic-looking Cotswold pub is set in a peaceful village and overlooks the village green where there might be ducks pottering about. Inside, the main bar is full of ancient beams and other atmospheric furnishings (high-backed wooden settles, gateleg or pedestal tables), and there's a warming log fire in the stone inglenook (with a big black kettle hanging in it). To the left of the bar a drinking space for locals has benches on the wooden floor, a woodburning stove, and darts, cribbage, TV, and piped music; on Sunday lunchtimes it is used by families. The lounge looks on to the garden. The food in the bar is often of award standard, and might include soup (£3.95), lunchtime toasted paninis filled with tomato, mozzarella and pesto or smoked bacon and brie (£4.95), smooth chicken liver parfait (£5.50), lunchtime ciabattas with fillings like prawn and avocado or roast chicken and chips (from £5.50), duck confit with teriyaki noodle salad (£6.50), lunchtime ploughman's (£6.95), spiced chick pea cakes with tzatziki, red onion and coriander salad (£7.50), gloucester old spot sausages with lightly curried potato and watercress salad, pasta with chilli, basil, sun-blush tomato and mozzarella or home-made haddock and mackerel fishcakes with chive and coriander mayonnaise (all £7.95), lamb skewers (£8.50), puddings like chocolate fudge brownies or lemon mousse with raspberry coulis (£3.95), and interesting cheeses (a choice of three for £4.95). The dining room is no smoking. Well kept Adnams Bitter and Hook Norton Best, and a couple of guests from Archers or Cottage on handpump, an excellent extensive wine list, with 11 by the glass (champagnes also), over 20 malt whiskies, organic cider and perry, and local apple juice. There are seats in the back garden; aunt sally. *(Recommended by Steve Harvey, Stephen Buckley, R Halsey, A S and M E Marriott, Maysie Thompson, David and Anthea Eeles, Richard Greaves, Mr and Mrs John Taylor, Felicity Stephens, John and Jackie Chalcraft, John Kane, P and J Shapley, Les Trusler, David and Nina Pugsley, C A Hall, Walter and Susan Rinaldi-Butcher, Sally Ramsay Patrick, Stephen, Julie and Hayley Brown, Hugh Spottiswoode, Colin Fisher, Victoria Simon, Dr K Roger Wood, Jane McKenzie, Matthew Shackle, Carolyn Price, Paul Hopton, Chloe Selicourt, Angus Lyon, Ian Phillips, Dick and Mary Pownall)*

Free house ~ Licensees Nicola and Archie Orr-Ewing ~ Real ale ~ Bar food ~ Restaurant ~ (01608) 658365 ~ Children in restaurant ~ Dogs allowed in bar ~ Open 11-2.30, 6-11; 12-3, 7-10.30 Sun; closed 25 and 26 Dec ~ Bedrooms: £50B/£65B

> Post Office address codings confusingly give the impression that some pubs are in Gloucestershire, when they're really in Warwickshire (which is where we list them).

BOX SO8500 Map 4
Halfway Inn ♀

Edge of Minchinhampton Common; from A46 S of Stroud follow Amberley signpost, then after Amberley Inn turn right towards Box, then left along common edge as you reach Box; OS Sheet 162 map reference 856003; can also be reached from Brimscombe on A419 SE of Stroud

The licensees here are keen to ensure that this extended tall house remains somewhere for both a casual drink, and a meal. The light and airy open-plan upstairs bar wraps around the central serving bar, and there are simple rush seated sturdy blond wooden chairs around good wooden tables, a built-in wall seat and long pew, a woodburning stove, and stripped wood floors. The bar has yellowy cream walls and ceiling, the dining area is mainly a warm terracotta, there are windows with swagged curtains and views to the common, and an unusual pitched-roof area. A new conservatory is planned. Good, interesting food includes sandwiches, baguettes or ploughman's (from £4.95), salad of maize-fed chicken (£4.95), goats cheese with peppers and tomatoes (£5.15), cornish scallops (£6.45), calves liver (£11.95), perigord duck breast (£12.95), fillet steak (£14.95), and puddings such as sticky toffee pudding or chocolate mousse (£4.25); the restaurant is no smoking. Well kept Hook Norton Best, Smiles, Wickwar BOB, and fortnightly guests on handpump, and decent wines; piped music and fruit machine. There are seats in the landscaped garden and giant chess and Connect Four sets. They hold beer and cider festivals in May and September. More reports please. *(Recommended by Charles and Pauline Stride, R Huggins, D Irving, E McCall, T McLean)*

Free house ~ Licensees Matt Walker and Sarah Lowe ~ Real ale ~ Bar food (12-2, 7-9; not Sun evening, not Mon) ~ Restaurant ~ (01453) 832631 ~ Children in eating area of bar and restaurant ~ Dogs allowed in bar ~ Open 12-11; 12-10.30 Sun; 12-3, 6-11 Tues-Fri in winter; closed Mon

BRIMPSFIELD SO9413 Map 4
Golden Heart ♀ ◀

Nettleton Bottom (not shown on road maps, so we list the pub instead under the name of the nearby village); on A417 after the Brimpsfield turning

A firm favourite with many customers, this bustling place just feels right as soon as you walk through the door. It's run by a friendly, knowledgeable landlord who offers a warm welcome to all, and the main low-ceilinged bar is divided into three cosily distinct areas, with a roaring log fire in the huge stone inglenook fireplace in one, traditional built-in settles and other old-fashioned furnishings throughout, and quite a few brass items, typewriters, exposed stone, and wood panelling. A comfortable parlour on the right has another decorative fireplace, and leads into a further room that opens on to the terrace; two rooms are no smoking. Well presented, popular bar food includes home-made soup (£3.50), sandwiches (from £3.50), home-made pâté (£4.50), filled baked potatoes or ploughman's (from £4.95), omelettes (£6.95), chicken curry (£7.95), mushroom stroganoff (£8.25), and steaks (from £10.95), with daily specials like lemon and black pepper chicken, fried ostrich with water chestnuts or crayfish and prawn cocktail (all £4.95), steak in ale pie (£9.25), navarin of goat (£9.95), and pork tenderloin casserole with cider and apple (£10.95), and puddings like mixed fruit crumble or profiteroles (£3.95). Well kept Archers, Timothy Taylors Landlord and Golden Best, and Youngs on handpump; decent wines. They hold a beer festival during the August bank holiday. There are pleasant views down over a valley from the rustic cask-supported tables on its suntrap gravel terrace, and good nearby walks. *(Recommended by R Huggins, D Irving, E McCall, T McLean, Angus and Rosemary Campbell, Guy Vowles, Neil and Anita Christopher, Rev Michael Vockins, James Woods, John Wheeler, Giles Francis, Dave Irving, W W Burke, Malcolm Taylor, Simon J Barber)*

Free house ~ Licensee Catherine Stevens ~ Real ale ~ Bar food (12-3, 6-10; all day weekends) ~ Restaurant ~ (01242) 870261 ~ Children in eating areas and in family room ~ Dogs welcome ~ Open 11-3, 5.30-11; 11-11 Fri and Sat; 12-10.30 Sun ~ Bedrooms: £35S/£55S

BROAD CAMPDEN SP1637 Map 4
Bakers Arms ◖▮

Village signposted from B4081 in Chipping Campden

What was the kitchen has now been converted into a no smoking dining room here with beams and exposed stone walls, and the same menu as the bar. The part with the most character is the tiny beamed bar with its pleasant mix of tables and seats around the walls (which are stripped back to bare stone), and inglenook fireplace at one end; the atmosphere is chatty and relaxed, and undisturbed by noisy games machines or piped music. The oak bar counter is attractive, and there's a big framed rugwork picture of the pub. Bar food includes lunchtime sandwiches (from £3.25), ploughman's (£4.50), and filled yorkshire puddings (£4.95), as well as home-made soup (£2.75), smoked haddock bake or cheese, leek and potato bake (£5.95), suet pudding of the day or liver and bacon (£6.50), puddings (£3.25), and daily specials. Well kept Donningtons SBA, Hook Norton Best, Stanway Stanney Bitter, Timothy Taylors Landlord, and Wells Bombardier on handpump. Darts, cribbage, dominoes. A terraced area has seats by the play area behind this traditional village pub, and there are more seats under parasols by flower tubs on other terraces and in the back garden. This is a tranquil village. *(Recommended by Yvonne Iley, Maurice Ribbans, John Brightley, Brian and Anna Marsden, P R and S A White)*

Free house ~ Licensees Ray and Sally Mayo ~ Real ale ~ Bar food (all day in summer) ~ No credit cards ~ (01386) 840515 ~ Children welcome ~ Folk music third Tues evening of month ~ Open 11.30-11; 12-10.30 Sun; 11.30-2.30, 4.45-11 weekdays in winter; closed 25 Dec, evening 26 Dec

BROCKHAMPTON SP0322 Map 4
Craven Arms ♀

Village signposted off A436 Andoversford—Naunton – look out for inn sign at head of lane in village; can also be reached from A40 Andoversford—Cheltenham via Whittington and Syreford

This attractive 17th-c inn is a well organised and bustling place, and is set in a pleasant gentrified hillside village with lovely views. There are low beams, thick roughly coursed stone walls and some tiled flooring, and though much of it has been opened out to give a sizeable (and spotlessly kept) eating area off the smaller bar servery, it's been done well to give a feeling of several communicating rooms; the furniture is mainly pine, with some wall settles, tub chairs and a log fire. Well liked, changing bar food using fresh local produce includes chicken liver parfait with tomato chutney (£4.75), home-made salmon fishcake with dill mayonnaise or deep-fried goats cheese with salsa (£4.95), leek and gruyère pie (£8.25), rack of english lamb on redcurrant and port sauce (£11.95), steaks (from £11.95), whole fresh plaice cooked with lemon and butter (£12.95), and puddings (£3.95); popular Sunday roasts. Well kept Fullers London Pride, Hook Norton Best and a weekly guest on handpump; shove-ha'penny. Although there are nice surrounding walks, please note that dogs are not allowed in the garden. *(Recommended by Roy and Lindsey Fentiman, Guy Vowles, Mike and Mary Carter, Peter Burton, Mr and Mrs B J P Edwards, John and Joan Wyatt, Maurice Ribbans)*

Free house ~ Licensee Dale Campbell ~ Real ale ~ Bar food (not Sun evening) ~ Restaurant ~ (01242) 820410 ~ Children in eating area of bar and restaurant ~ Open 11-3, 6-11; 12-4 Sun; closed Sun evening; 25 Dec

---

It is illegal for bar staff to smoke while handling your drink.

CHEDWORTH SP0511 Map 4

Seven Tuns

Village signposted off A429 NE of Cirencester; then take second signposted right turn and bear left towards church

The famous Roman villa is only a pleasant walk away from this little 17th-c pub, and there are other nice walks through the valley, too. Inside, the cosy little lounge on the right has a good winter log fire in the big stone fireplace, comfortable seats and decent tables, sizeable antique prints, tankards hanging from the beam over the serving bar, and a partly boarded ceiling. The public bar on the left down a couple of steps has an open fire, and this opens into a no smoking dining room with another open fire; the upstairs skittle alley also acts as the games room with darts, cribbage, shove-ha'penny, and dominoes. Enjoyable bar food includes sandwiches or baguettes (from £4.75; back bacon and fried mushrooms £5.75; scotch sirloin steak £5.75), ploughman's (£5.95), ham and egg (£6.50), filled baked potatoes (from £6.50), beef or vegetarian lasagne (£8.50), and daily specials such as prawn curry (£7.50), asparagus and chicken casserole (£7.95), fresh poached salmon with parsley butter (£8.95), and fillet steak with pepper sauce (£12.95); piped music. Well kept Hook Norton, Smiles Best, and Youngs Bitter and Waggle Dance on handpump; lots of malt whiskies, and prompt service. Across the road is a little walled raised terrace with a waterwheel and a stream, and there are plenty of tables both here and under cocktail parasols on a side terrace. *(Recommended by Des and Jen Clarke, Derek Carless, Peter and Audrey Dowsett, R Huggins, D Irving, E McCall, T McLean, George Atkinson, Anne Morris, Neil and Anita Christopher, Tim and Carolyn Lowes, J M Law, Guy Vowles, Di and Mike Gillam)*

Youngs ~ Tenant Kevin Dursley ~ Real ale ~ Bar food (12-3, 6-10.30) ~ (01285) 720242 ~ Children in eating area of bar and restaurant ~ Dogs welcome ~ Open 11-11; 12-10.30 Sun; 11-3, 6-11 in winter

CHIPPING CAMPDEN SP1539 Map 4

Eight Bells 🍺

Church Street (which is one way – entrance off B4035)

This is a fine old pub run by friendly, helpful people. There are heavy oak beams with massive timber supports, stripped stone walls, cushioned pews and solid dark wood furniture on the broad flagstones, daily papers to read, and log fires in up to three restored stone fireplaces. Part of the floor in the no smoking dining room has a glass inlet showing part of the passage from the church by which Roman Catholic priests could escape from the Roundheads. Good bar food includes lunchtime (not Sunday) filled baguettes (from £4.95), plus home-made soup (£3.95), smoked salmon fishcakes with wilted chard and chive butter sauce (£5.25), confit of duck leg with fig chutney and pancakes (£5.75), seared scallops with pickled vegetable salad and sweet chilli sauce (£6.75), home-baked ham and egg (£7.95), pasta with mushrooms, onions, garlic and parmesan (£8.75), flaked blackened salmon salad with capers and fennel (£9.75), chicken supreme with smoked cheese and ham sauce (£10.75), roasted pork cutlet with parsley mash and honey-glazed apples (£11), and puddings such as lime and lemon cheesecake with dark chocolate sauce or chunky apple pie with cinnamon syrup and clotted cream (£4.25). Well kept Goffs Jouster, and Hook Norton Best and Old Hooky on handpump from the fine oak bar counter; country wines. Piped music, darts, cribbage, and dominoes. Plenty of seats in the large terraced garden with striking views of the almshouses and church. Handy for the Cotswold Way walk to Bath. *(Recommended by Rodney and Norma Stubington, P R and S A White, Desmond O'Donovan, Grahame Brooks, John Mitchell, Mrs N W Neill, Lynda Payton, Sam Samuells, Ted George, Gillian and Les Gray, Ian Phillips, Di and Mike Gillam, Peter Burton, Dave Braisted, Martin Jones, Jenny and Chris Wilson, W W Burke, Gerry and Rosemary Dobson)*

Free house ~ Licensee Neil Hargreaves ~ Real ale ~ Bar food (12-2.30, 6.30-9.30) ~ Restaurant ~ (01386) 840371 ~ Children welcome ~ Dogs welcome ~ Open 11-3, 5.30-11; 11-11 Sat; 12-10.30 Sun; closed 25 Dec ~ Bedrooms: £45B/£70B

Volunteer ◀

Lower High Street

As well as a friendly welcome, you can find up to half a dozen well kept real ales on handpump in this friendly old local: Hook Norton Best, North Cotswold Brewery Genesis, Stanway Stanney Bitter, and guests such as Goffs Jouster, Wells Bombardier, and Wychwood Shires. Quite a few malt whiskies, too. The little bar by the street has cushioned seats in bay windows, a log fire piled with big logs in the golden stone fireplace with hops, helmets and horse bits above it, proper old dining chairs with sage green plush seats and some similarly covered stools around a mix of tables, old army (Waterloo and WWI) paintings and bugles on the walls, with old local photographs on the gantry, and quite a few brass spigots dotted about. The public bar has modern upholstered wing settles, juke box, darts, pool, fruit machine, cribbage, dominoes. Tasty bar food includes soup (£2.95), goats cheese baked on puff pastry with bacon (£4.95), home-roasted honey glazed ham with egg and chips or battered cod (£6.25), steak and kidney pie (£6.95), calves liver and bacon with balsamic gravy (£7.95), chicken breast flamed with calvados and finished with cream and almonds (£8.75), and 10oz rib-eye pepper steak (£10.75); Sunday roast (£6.50). There are picnic-sets in a small brick-paved ivy courtyard with an arch through to the back garden where there are more seats. *(Recommended by Lawrence Pearse, Steve Whalley, Guy Vowles, Di and Mike Gillam, Ted George, Bruce M Drew)*

Free house ~ Licensee Hilary Mary Sinclair ~ Real ale ~ Bar food ~ (01386) 840688 ~ Children in eating area of bar ~ Dogs allowed in bar ~ Open 11.30-3, 5(6 Sat)-11; 12-3, 7-10.30 Sun ~ Bedrooms: £35B/£60B

COLN ST ALDWYNS SP1405 Map 4

New Inn ⑪ ♀ 🛏

On good back road between Bibury and Fairford

Very cleverly, the licensees here have managed to combine the fairly upmarket bedrooms and particularly good cooking with some character of a village pub selling first class beer; not an easy thing to do but very much appreciated by a lot of customers. The two neatly kept main rooms are attractively furnished and decorated, and divided by a central log fire in a neat stone fireplace with wooden mantelbeam and willow-pattern plates on the chimney breast; there are also low beams, some stripped stonework around the bar servery with hops above it, oriental rugs on the red tiles, and a mix of seating from library chairs to stripped pews. Down a slight slope, a further room has a coal fire in an old kitchen range at one end, and a white pheasant on the wall. Many of the starters on the imaginative menu can also be taken as main courses: soup (£3.25 or £5.50), roast provençale vegetables couscous salad, green olive, mint and lemon vinaigrette (£4.75 or £8.50), and foie gras and chicken liver parfait, pear and apple chutney (£6.25 or £9.95). There's also warm leek, mushroom and gruyère tart (£9.50), cumberland sausages with seed mustard mash and sweet onions (£9.95), poached smoked haddock, welsh rarebit, spring onion potatoes, and chive and tomato butter (£10.25), steak in ale pie with thyme roast new potatoes (£11.25), braised lamb shank with baked vine tomato, olives, rosemary and garlic (£12.75), and puddings such as white chocolate and passion fruit parfait, raspberry and mint bread and butter pudding or steamed chocolate and orange pudding with chocolate sauce and crème fraîche sorbet (£4.50). Lunchtime sandwiches and filled baguettes; the restaurant is no smoking. Well kept Butcombe Best, Hook Norton Best, and Wadworths 6X on handpump, eight good wines by the glass, and several malt whiskies; shove-ha'penny and dominoes. The split-level terrace has plenty of seats, and they have popular day tickets for fly fishing on the river in the water meadows. The peaceful Cotswold village is most attractive, and the riverside walk to Bibury is not to be missed. *(Recommended by Fred Chamberlain, Brian and Anita Randall, Morag McGarrigle, Mrs B Sugarman, George Atkinson, John Urquhart, Doreen and Haydn Maddock, Philip Vernon, Kim Maidment, Paul Humphreys, Glen and Nola Armstrong, Simon Collett-Jones, Peter Sutton, Ted George, Lesley and Peter Barrett, Peter Meister, John Bowdler,*

DRH *and* KLH, *Mr and Mrs G S Ayrton, J H Harris, Tony Brace, Philip and Jenny Grant; also
in the* Good Hotel Guide*)*

*Free house ~ Licensee Brian Evans ~ Real ale ~ Bar food (12-2.30, 7-9(9.30 Fri/Sat))
~ Restaurant ~ (01285) 750651 ~ Children in eating area of bar; must be over 10 in
restaurant ~ Dogs allowed in bar ~ Occasional jazz duo ~ Open 11-11; 12-10.30 Sun
~ Bedrooms: £85S/£115B*

DIDMARTON ST8187 Map 2
Kings Arms ⓦ � ◖

A433 Tetbury road

Everything in this attractively restored and decorated 17th-c coaching inn is neat
and tidy, with good attention to detail. It's a good all-rounder, too – customers very
much enjoy the good food, the local ales, the interesting wine, and the friendly,
helpful staff. The knocked-through rooms work their way around a big central
counter: deep terracotta walls above a dark green dado, a pleasant mix of chairs on
bare boards, quarry tiles and carpet, hops on beams, a big stone fireplace, and a
nice old upright piano. You can eat the same menu in the bar or restaurant which
might include filled baguettes, soup (£3), salmon, cod and dill fishcakes with a light
curry and cumin mayonnaise (£3.95; main course £7.95), duck, orange, honey and
thyme terrine with spicy redcurrant jelly (£5.25; main course £8.65), smoked
chicken, mango and watercress salad with a tarragon and wholegrain mustard
dressing (£5.45; main course £8.95), pork and leek sausages on parsley and
cheddar mash with onion gravy or tagliatelle with smoked bacon and mushrooms
with a sweet tomato and basil sauce (£8.95), steaks (from £8.95), wild mushroom
stroganoff (£9.85), pepper-crusted pork tenderloin with an apple and calvados
sauce (£11.95), whole braised partridge with red wine, baby onion and pâté sauce
(£12.50), and chocolate rum truffle with fresh raspberries, lemon and lime citrus
tart with passion fruit coulis, and Baileys and coffee laced crème brûlée (£4.50).
The restaurant is no smoking. Well kept Badger Best, Uley Bitter, and a couple of
guests (changing four or five times a week) from small brewers or microbreweries
on handpump, a good wine list with half a dozen by the small or large glass, farm
cider in summer, and several malt whiskies; darts, cribbage, and dominoes. Seats in
the pleasant back garden, and they have self-catering cottages in a converted barn
and stable block. *(Recommended by Guy Vowles, Peter and Audrey Dowsett,
Martin Jennings, S H Godsell, Jenny and Brian Seller, Hugh Roberts, Derek Carless, Mike Pugh,
Colin McKerrow, Paul Hopton, Stephen and Jean Curtis, John and Gloria Isaacs, MRSM,
Gaynor Gregory, Philip and Jenny Grant, Mr and Mrs A H Young, Mike and Mary Carter,
Martin and Karen Wake, Di and Mike Gillam, Bernard Stradling, Ian and Nita Cooper)*

*Free house ~ Licensees Nigel and Jane Worrall ~ Real ale ~ Bar food ~ Restaurant ~
(01454) 238245 ~ Children in eating area of bar; must be over 7 in evening
restaurant ~ Dogs allowed in bar ~ Open 12-2.30, 6-11; 12-3, 7-10.30 Sun ~
Bedrooms: £45S/£70S*

DUNTISBOURNE ABBOTS SO9709 Map 4
Five Mile House ◖

From A417, follow directions to the Services; the pub is tucked back from the old road about
300 yards downhill from entrance to the Services

The original part of this popular and relaxed old place was built as a public house
in the 17th c on what was until quite recently Ermine Street, the main Roman road
from Wales to London, and was probably used as a toll station. It's a favourite pub
with many customers, and the front room has a companionable bare-boards
drinking bar on the right, with wall seats around the big table in its bow window
and just one other table; on the left is a flagstoned hallway tap room snug formed
from two ancient high-backed settles by a woodburning stove in a tall carefully
exposed old fireplace; newspapers to read. There's a small cellar bar, a back
restaurant down steps, and a family room on the far side; cribbage and dominoes.
The lounge and cellar bar are no smoking. Well kept Donningtons BB, Timothy

Taylors Landlord, and Youngs Bitter with a local guest on handpump (the cellar is temperature-controlled), and interesting wines (strong on new world ones); cribbage and dominoes. Generous helpings of good, popular bar food (cooked by the landlord) include, at lunchtime, open sandwiches (from £4.45), ploughman's (from £5.50), free range egg omelette (£6.25), home-cooked ham with eggs or deep-fried cod and chips (£7.30), and whole local trout with a prawn and lemon butter (£9), with evening dishes such as home-made soup (£3.75), home-made chicken liver pâté (£5) or chicken breast fillet stuffed with stilton, wrapped in bacon and served with a mushroom and brandy cream sauce (£10.25), and daily specials like home-made faggots or hot avocado filled with apricots, figs, celery, apple and grapes and topped with toasted brie (£7.95), pork loin steaks glazed with honey and mustard (£10), and barbary duck breast with a mulled wine and orange glaze (£11.50); puddings such as white chocolate cheesecake, crème brûlée, treacle tart or fruit crumble (£4.25), children's helpings where possible, and Sunday roast lunch (£8.95). You may have to book some time ahead. Service is thoughtful and friendly. The gardens have nice country views. *(Recommended by Debbie and Neil Hayter, John Holroyd, R Huggins, D Irving, E McCall, T McLean, Dave Irving, R T and J C Moggridge, Peter Scillitoe, Rob Webster, Giles Francis, the Didler, Dennis Jenkin, Rev Michael Vockins, Guy Vowles, Richard Stancomb)*

Free house ~ Licensees Jo and Jon Carrier ~ Real ale ~ Bar food (12-2.30, 6-9.30) ~ Restaurant ~ (01285) 821432 ~ Children welcome if well behaved ~ Dogs allowed in bar ~ Open 12-3, 6-11; 12-3, 7-10.30 Sun

DURSLEY ST7598 Map 2
Old Spot 🐷

By bus station

They keep a fine range of half a dozen real ales in this unassuming town pub: Otter Bitter, Ringwood Old Thumper, Shepherd Neame Spitfire, Uley Old Ric, and a couple of changing guests on handpump; several malt whiskies. The front door opens into a deep pink little room with stools on shiny quarry tiles along its pine boarded bar counter, and old enamel beer advertisements on the walls and ceiling; there's a profusion of porcine paraphernalia, and a cheerful bunch of customers. Leading off here there's a little room on the left with a bar billiards table, shove-ha'penny, cribbage and dominoes, and the little dark wood-floored room to the right has a stone fireplace. From here a step takes you down to a cosy Victorian tiled snug and (to the right) the no smoking meeting room. Bar food includes sandwiches, home-made soup (£2.95), cauliflower cheese (£4.25), cottage pie (£5.25), brunch or sausages with leek mash and onion gravy (£5.50), and daily specials. More reports please. *(Recommended by Hugh Roberts, Comus and Sarah Elliott, P R and S A White)*

Free house ~ Licensees Steve and Belinda Herbert ~ Real ale ~ Bar food (lunchtime only) ~ (01453) 542870 ~ Children in family room ~ Dogs welcome ~ Folk and jazz Weds evenings ~ Open 11-3, 5-11; 11-11 Sat; 12-10.30 Sun

EASTLEACH TURVILLE SP1905 Map 4
Victoria ♀

Village signposted off A361 S of Burford

Although this low-ceilinged old pub is open-plan inside, it is nicely divided, and rambles cosily around a central bar, with sturdy pub tables of varying sizes, and some attractive seats – particularly those built in beside the log fire in the stripped stone chimneybreast. There are some unusual engravings and lithographs of Queen Victoria around the back. Enjoyable freshly made food includes filled baguettes, home-made chicken liver parfait, moules marinière or field mushrooms baked with stilton (£4.25), warm smoked chicken, bacon and brie salad (£6.95), salmon fishcakes with prawn and dill sauce or steak and mushroom pie (£7.25), and calves liver and bacon with red wine sauce (£9.25), with evening extras such as chicken breast with creamy stilton sauce (£8.50), pork medallions with grape, mushroom and tarragon sauce or poached smoked haddock and egg coated with mustard sauce (£9.25), and lamb shank on minty mash topped with caramelised onion and jus (£10.95); part of the restaurant is no smoking. Arkells 2B and 3B on handpump, six or seven nice new world wines by the large glass, well served cafetière coffee, and welcoming service; may be unobtrusive piped music. The right-hand area has more of a public bar feel, with darts, shove-ha'penny, cribbage and dominoes. There are picnic-sets out in front, looking down over a steep bank of daffodils at the other stone-built houses and a couple of churches; more seats at the back behind the car park. It can get very busy on warm days with quite a good mix of customers. *(Recommended by Dr and Mrs M E Wilson, Patrick Hancock, R Huggins, D Irving, E McCall, T McLean, Ted George, Peter and Audrey Dowsett, R M Corlett)*

Arkells ~ Tenants Stephen and Susan Richardson ~ Real ale ~ Bar food ~ Restaurant ~ (01367) 850277 ~ Children in eating area of bar and restaurant ~ Dogs allowed in bar ~ Open 12-3(4 Sat), 7-11; 12-4, 7-10.30 Sun; closed evening 25 Dec

EWEN SU0097 Map 4
Wild Duck ♀
Village signposted from A429 S of Cirencester

From the outside, this actually looks more like an old manor house in part than a typical pub. Inside, there's a high-beamed main bar with a nice mix of comfortable armchairs and other seats, paintings on the red walls, crimson drapes, a winter open fire, candles on tables, and magazines to read; the residents' lounge has a handsome Elizabethan fireplace and antique furnishings, and looks over the garden. Good bar food includes lunchtime ploughman's (£5.95), beer battered fish with chips or burger with cheese and bacon (£7.50), and rump steak open sandwich (£9.95), as well as soup (£3.50), feta, chick pea and chilli salad with avocado and lime dressing (£5.50), prawn and gruyère bake (£5.95), baked chicken with wild mushrooms and olives in a creamy oregano sauce (£10.95), fillet of red bream poached in a seafood laksa with prawns and mussels (£11.50), chargrilled sirloin steak (£12.95), and roast duck breast on a goose liver croûte with a red wine, orange and brandy reduction (£14.95). As well as Duckpond Bitter, brewed especially for the pub, there might be Greene King Old Speckled Hen, Smiles Best and Mayfly, and Theakstons XB and Old Peculier on handpump, good wines, several malt whiskies, and piped music; efficient rather than friendly service. There are wooden tables and seats in the neatly kept and sheltered garden. More reports please. *(Recommended by M Sambidge, Roger and Jenny Huggins, KC, R Huggins, D Irving, E McCall, T McLean, Ian Phillips, Pat and Tony Martin, Matthew Shackle, Richard Gibbs, Anne Morris, Maysie Thompson, Peter B Brown, Rob Webster, Bernard Stradling, Mr and Mrs J McRobert, Nick and Alison Dowson)*

Free house ~ Licensees Tina and Dino Mussell ~ Real ale ~ Bar food (till 10pm) ~ Restaurant ~ (01285) 770310 ~ Children in eating area of bar and restaurant ~ Dogs allowed in bar ~ Open 11-11; 12-10.30 Sun; closed evening 25 Dec ~ Bedrooms: £60B/£80B

FRAMPTON MANSELL SO9201 Map 4
White Horse 🍴 ♀
A491 Cirencester—Stroud

The landscaping of the garden here was just being completed as we went to press, and will offer a relaxing and tranquil place to eat or drink. This is a smart, friendly dining place with attractive furnishings. Alongside the pine tables, rush matting and clean up-to-date décor of the main part, there's a cosy bar area with a large sofa and comfortable chairs for those who want to pop in just for a relaxing drink. Well kept Uley Bitter and a guest such as Arkells Summer Ale or Hook Norton Best on handpump, seven wines by the glass from a well chosen wine list, and quite a few malt whiskies. Maintaining a modern style of British cooking and using good quality ingredients, the changing dishes might include lunchtime snacks like various filled baguettes (£4.95), ham and egg (£7.50), fish and chips (£7.95), and salad

(£8.25), as well as mushroom soup (£3.50), chicken, bacon and pine nut terrine with tomato chutney (£5.25), duck confit with braised red cabbage and thyme jus or tuna carpaccio with fennel seeds, paprika, and soy sauce (£5.75), beetroot risotto with grilled goats cheese and basil pesto (£9.95), pork cutlet with caramelised baby apples and a ginger, soy and balsamic jus (£10.50), black bream with asparagus and a baby artichoke and thyme sauce (£11), rib-eye steak with a cracked black pepper sauce (£13.50), and puddings like dark chocolate and coconut iced terrine with chocolate sauce and caramelised walnuts or sticky toffee pudding with butterscotch sauce (from £4); a good choice of coffee or tea, and friendly staff. *(Recommended by Dr and Mrs C W Thomas, Tom and Ruth Rees, Mike Snelgrove, Eleanor Taylor, John Kane, Mr and Mrs R Drury, Paul Hopton, Mr and Mrs G S Ayrton, Guy Vowles, R Huggins, D Irving, E McCall, T McLean, Evelyn and Derek Walter)*

Free house ~ Licensees Shaun and Emma Davis ~ Real ale ~ Bar food (12-2.30(3 Sun); not evenings) ~ Restaurant ~ (01285) 760960 ~ Children welcome ~ Dogs welcome ~ Open 11-3, 6-11; 12-4 Sun; closed Sun evening; 24-26 Dec

GRETTON SP0131 Map 4
Royal Oak 🍺

Village signposted off what is now officially B4077 (still often mapped and even signed as A438), E of Tewkesbury; keep on through village

Some fine walks surround this well liked pub (and walkers are welcome), and from seats on the flower-filled terrace there are fine views over the village and across the valley to Dumbleton Hills and the Malverns. There are more seats under a giant pear tree, a neatly kept big lawn running down to a play area (with an old tractor and see-saw), and even a bookable tennis court. Inside, the series of bare-boarded or flagstoned rooms has beams hung with tankards, hop bines and chamber-pots, old prints on the walls, a medley of pews and various chairs, stripped oak and pine tables, and a friendly bustle. The no smoking dining conservatory has stripped country furnishings, and a broad view over the countryside. As well as lunchtime bar snacks such as filled baguettes (from £4.95), ham and egg (£6.95), and a pie of the week (£8.95), the enjoyable food might include home-made soup (£3.95), chicken satay (£4), welsh rarebit topped with crispy bacon (£4.50), moules marinière (£4.95), spinach and feta cheese pie with herby tomato sauce (£8.50), rack of ribs, trio of local sausages with mustard mash and onion gravy or chicken breast filled with stilton and bacon in a cider, mushroom and cream sauce (all £8.95), escalope of veal and mozzarella (£9.95), rib-eye steak (£10.95), and fresh tuna steak with a sweet chilli dip (£11.50). Well kept Goffs Jouster, Tournament, and White Knight, and a weekly changing guest on handpump, and a decent wine list. From spring through to the start of winter, the private Gloucestershire/Warwickshire Railway runs along the bottom of the garden. *(Recommended by Ian Phillips, John and Joan Wyatt, Will Hayes, David Rule, Norman and June Williams, Bernard Stradling, Richard and Karen Holt, Hugh Roberts, Ted George, Jenny Matterface, Stuart Turner)*

Free house ~ Licensee Marcus Goff ~ Real ale ~ Bar food (12-2.30, 7-9) ~ Restaurant ~ (01242) 604999 ~ Children in restaurant ~ Dogs allowed in bar ~ Open 12-3, 6-11; 12-3, 7-10.30 Sun

GUITING POWER SP0924 Map 4
Hollow Bottom

Village signposted off B4068 SW of Stow-on-the-Wold (still called A436 on many maps)

This friendly and relaxed 17th-c inn is very much a racing place, and the comfortable beamed bar has lots of racing memorabilia including racing silks, tunics and photographs (it is owned by a small syndicate that includes Peter Scudamore and Nigel Twiston-Davies); there's a winter log fire in an unusual pillar-supported stone fireplace. The public bar has flagstones and stripped stone masonry and racing on TV. Enjoyable bar food includes home-made soup (£3.95), filled baguettes (from £4.95), filled baked potatoes (from £5.95), ploughman's or home-made burger (£7.75), home-made cottage pie or lasagne (£8.20), steaks (from £13.50), and daily specials like stuffed red pepper and mushrooms (£10), calves liver or kangaroo (£12); Sunday carvery. Well kept Fullers London Pride, Hook Norton, and a guest such as Timothy Taylors Landlord on handpump, several malt whiskies, and helpful, pleasant service; piped music, darts, cribbage, dominoes, and Spoof. From the pleasant garden behind are views towards the peaceful sloping fields. Decent walks nearby. *(Recommended by Guy Vowles, Stuart Turner, David Musgrove, Chris Glasson, Stephen, Julie and Hayley Brown, Neil and Anita Christopher, Di and Mike Gillam, Paul and Annette Hallett, Mike and Mary Carter)*

Free house ~ Licensees Hugh Kelly and Charles Pettigrew ~ Real ale ~ Bar food (12-9.30 (snacks during the afternoon rather than meals)) ~ Restaurant ~ (01451) 850392 ~ Children in eating area of bar and restaurant ~ Dogs allowed in bar ~ Live entertainment during Cheltenham Races ~ Open 11-11; 12-10.30 Sun ~ Bedrooms: £45B/£60B

HINTON DYRHAM ST7376 Map 2
Bull

2.4 miles from M4 junction 18; A46 towards Bath, then first right (opposite the Crown)

This pretty 16th-c stone-built pub is a very good diversion from the M4. It's a friendly, chatty place, and the two huge fireplaces with good coal and log fires face each other across the ancient pitted flagstones of the main bar, with a nice window-seat and some massive built-in oak settles and pews as well as dark captain's chairs, and one or two big oriental rugs; even by day candles burn in wall sconces – no surprise the low ceiling is so smoky. A stripped stone back area has some unusual cushioned cast-iron chairs, and there's a family room on the left; piped music. All is glisteningly well kept, as is the Wadworths IPA and 6X, and guest beer on handpump. The interesting and enjoyable food includes bar snacks plus roasted red pepper gazpacho (£3.75), home-smoked corn-fed chicken caesar salad (£4.50), spicy salmon and lime leaf fishcakes with coconut and mustard seed sambal (£4.75), confit duck spring roll with asian salad with toasted sesame and ginger dressing (£4.95), risotto of ceps, roast garlic and fresh herbs (£8.75), twice cooked soy braised pork belly with stir-fried chinese leaf in sherry and anise jus (£10.25), and bass fillet wrapped in rice paper with blackbean salsa and sweet chilli jam (£12.50); the restaurant is no smoking. There are plenty of picnic-sets (and plenty of play equipment) out in a sizeable sheltered upper garden, with more on its sunny front terrace. *(Recommended by Michael Doswell, Andrew Shore, Michael Cooper, Richard and Margaret Peers, Chris and Martin Taylor, Anne Morris, Gerald Wilkinson)*

Wadworths ~ Tenants Ivan Locke and Caroline Robins ~ Real ale ~ Bar food ~ (0117) 937 2332 ~ Children in restaurant ~ Dogs allowed in bar ~ Open 11.30-3, 6-11; 12-3, 7-10.30 Sun

KINGSCOTE ST8196 Map 4
Hunters Hall

A4135 Dursley—Tetbury

For 500 years, this well run and civilised old inn has held a continuous licence, and it still offers a warm welcome to its customers. There is quite a series of bar rooms and lounges with fine high Tudor beams and stone walls, a lovely old box settle, sofas and miscellaneous easy chairs, and sturdy settles and oak tables on the flagstones in the lower-ceilinged, cosy public bar. An airy end room serves the good, enjoyable food which includes lunchtime sandwiches (not Sunday; from £2.25), home-made soup (£3.50), tian of mushrooms marinated in lime and coriander oil with crispy bacon (£4.50), chicken and duck liver pâté with a red onion and orange chutney (£4.95), ploughman's (from £4.95), steak, kidney and Guinness pie or pork and leek sausages (£7.50), liver and bacon (£7.95), tomato, spinach and parmesan risotto (£9.25), chicken supreme wrapped in pancetta with a red wine and sage jus (£10.50), salads with salmon, tuna and cod brochettes or baked goats cheese and red pepper (£10.95), steaks (from £11.25), and braised lamb shank with a pear and rosemary glaze (£12.95); there's more space to eat in the Gallery upstairs. The Retreat Bay and restaurant (where there is piped music) are no smoking. Well kept Greene King IPA, Abbot, and Ruddles Best, and Uley Hogs Head on handpump; friendly, helpful staff. A back room – relatively untouched – is popular with local lads playing pool; darts, cribbage, shove-ha'penny, and juke box. The garden has seats, and a wooden fortress, play house, and swings for children. (*Recommended by John and Marion Tyrie, Peter and Audrey Dowsett, Neil and Anita Christopher, Hugh Roberts, Dr Paull Khan, R Huggins, D Irving, E McCall, T McLean*)

Old English Inns ~ Tenant Stephanie Ward ~ Real ale ~ Bar food ~ Restaurant ~ (01453) 860393 ~ Children welcome ~ Dogs allowed in bar ~ Open 11-11; 12-10.30 Sun ~ Bedrooms: £55B/£85B

LITTLE BARRINGTON SP2012 Map 4
Inn For All Seasons ♈ ♉

On the A40 3 miles W of Burford

A fine haven from the rigours of the A40, this comfortable and civilised place has a friendly, bustling atmosphere, and particularly good food. They specialise in fresh fish and some of the delicious dishes might include irish rock oysters, grilled fresh sardines with garlic and parsley butter sauce, fillet of River Dart salmon with a vermouth, smoked bacon and spinach sauce, grilled fillet of yellowfin tuna on salad niçoise with anchovy dressing, roast bass on a chinese stir fry, and whole grilled dover sole (from £6.50 to £14.95). Other non-fishy dishes include sandwiches, home-made soup (£3.95), free range chicken livers flash fried with smoked bacon, served in a pastry case with a shallot and madeira sauce (£4.95), home-smoked and cured duck breast salad with sesame seed dressing and home-made chutney (£5.25), pasta with field mushrooms, spinach and pine nuts in a creamy pesto sauce or cumberland sausage with an onion and red wine jus (£8.95), roast rack of english lamb with a sweet garlic and thyme jus or grilled hereford rump steak with dijon mustard sauce (£13.95), and puddings such as banana and honey parfait with raspberry coulis, champagne and lemon mousse with a coconut biscuit crust or tiramisu (£4.25). The attractively decorated, mellow lounge bar has low beams, stripped stone, and flagstones, old prints, leather-upholstered wing armchairs and other comfortable seats, country magazines to read, and a big log fire (with a big piece of World War II shrapnel above it); maybe quiet piped classical music. Well kept Bass, Wadworths 6X or Wychwood Shires XXX on handpump, a good wine list with 100 bin ends, and over 60 malt whiskies; cribbage and dominoes. The pleasant garden has tables and a play area, and there are walks straight from the inn. It's very busy during Cheltenham Gold Cup Week – when the adjoining field is pressed into service as a helicopter pad. (*Recommended by Mr and Mrs J McAngus, Simon Collett-Jones, Peter and Audrey Dowsett, Rod Stoneman, Barry Smith, Mrs N W Neill, Les and Barbara Owen, Felicity Stephens, A Bradshaw, Mike and Heather Watson, Mr and Mrs L Hemmingway, Mr and Mrs N Ward, Dick and Madeleine Brown, Mike Horler*)

Free house ~ Licensees Matthew and Heather Sharp ~ Real ale ~ Bar food ~ Restaurant ~ (01451) 844324 ~ Children welcome ~ Dogs welcome ~ Open 11-2.30, 6-11; 12-2.30, 7-10.30 Sun ~ Bedrooms: £54B/£93B

LITTLETON-UPON-SEVERN ST5990 Map 4
White Hart ◀

3½ miles from M4 junction 21; B4461 towards Thornbury, then village signposted

On a cold winter's day when the log fires are roaring away, this 17th-c farmhouse is a cosy, welcoming place. The three atmospheric main rooms have some fine furnishings: long cushioned wooden settles, high-backed settles, oak and elm tables, and a loveseat in the big low inglenook fireplace. There are flagstones in the front, huge tiles at the back, and smaller tiles on the left, plus some old pots and pans, and a lovely old White Hart Inn Simonds Ale sign. By the black wooden staircase are some nice little alcove seats, there's a black-panelled big fireplace in the front room, and hops on beams. A no smoking family room, similarly furnished, has some sentimental engravings, plates on a delft shelf, and a couple of high chairs, and a back snug has pokerwork seats and table football; darts, cribbage, chess, backgammon and Jenga. Bar food includes filled baguettes (from £3.50), popular battered haddock (£7.95), ham and egg, mushroom, nut and bean stroganoff, beef and cashew nut curry or lots of summer salads (all £7.95), and puddings (£3.95). Youngs Bitter, Special, Waggle Dance, and Winter Warmer, and a guest such as Smiles Best on handpump. Picnic-sets on the neat front lawn with interesting cottagey flowerbeds, and by the good big back car park are some attractive shrubs and teak furniture on a small brick terrace. Several walks from the pub itself. *(Recommended by Dr and Mrs C W Thomas, Tom Evans, Ian Phillips, Rob Webster, W F C Phillips, Pat and Derek Roughton, Bob Broadhurst, Mrs B M Spurr, Mike and Mary Carter, Andy Sinden, Louise Harrington, Theocsbrian, Di and Mike Gillam)*

Youngs ~ Managers Howard and Liz Turner ~ Real ale ~ Bar food ~ (01454) 412275 ~ Children in family room ~ Dogs welcome ~ Open 12-2.30(3 Sat), 6-11; 12-4, 7-10.30 Sun ~ Bedrooms: £55B/£75B

MEYSEY HAMPTON SU1199 Map 4
Masons Arms

High Street; just off A417 Cirencester—Lechlade

This is everything a proper village pub should be. There's always a friendly welcome, a good bustling atmosphere, enjoyable beers and food, and a proper mix of customers. The longish open-plan bar has painted brick walls, carefully stripped beams with some hops, solid part-upholstered built-in wall seats with some matching chairs, good sound tables, a big inglenook log fire at one end, daily newspapers, and a few steps up to the no smoking restaurant. Well kept Hook Norton Best and Wickwar Cotswold Way, and a couple of guests from breweries like Cottage, Goffs or Uley on handpump, and decent wines including several ports; dominoes, cribbage, and piped music. Well liked bar food includes sandwiches (from £1.95; filled baguettes from £3.95), home-made soup (£2.65), cajun chicken caesar salad (starter £4.95; main course £6.95), moules marinière (small £5.25; large £7.25), honey-roasted ham with two eggs (£5.95), a pie of the day or vegetable chilli (£6.75), lemon and tarragon chicken (£6.95), braised lamb shank, chinese-style duck or salmon hollandaise (£8.95), and steaks (from £9.45). *(Recommended by P and J Shapley, R T and J C Moggridge, Darly Graton, Graeme Gulibert, R Huggins, D Irving, E McCall, T McLean, Charles Gysin, Geoff Palmer, Anne Morris, James Woods, Des and Jen Clarke, P R and S A White, Peter and Audrey Dowsett, Di and Mike Gillam, Sue and Jeff Evans, Mr and Mrs John Taylor)*

Free house ~ Licensees Andrew and Jane O'Dell ~ Real ale ~ Bar food (not Sun evening) ~ Restaurant ~ (01285) 850164 ~ Children in eating areas until 9 ~ Dogs welcome ~ Open 11.30-2.45, 6-11; 12-4, 7-10.30 Sun; closed Sun evening in winter ~ Bedrooms: £45B/£65S

MISERDEN SO9308 Map 4
Carpenters Arms

Village signposted off B4070 NE of Stroud; also a pleasant drive off A417 via the Duntisbournes, or off A419 via Sapperton and Edgeworth; OS Sheet 163 map reference 936089

You can pop in here for a pint and feel just as welcome as those out for a special meal. The pub is set in an idyllic Cotswold estate village, and the two open-plan bar areas have low beams, nice old wooden tables, seats with the original little brass name plates on the backs, and some cushioned settles and spindlebacks on the bare boards; also, stripped stone walls with some interesting bric-a-brac, and two big log fires; The small no smoking dining room has dark traditional furniture. The sizeable collage (done with Laurie Lee) has lots of illustrations and book covers signed by him. Well kept Greene King IPA and Wadworths 6X, and a guest such as Moles Best or Smiles Bitter on handpump, country wines, and darts. As well as lunchtime filled baguettes or filled baked potatoes (from £4.50), and ploughman's (from £5.25), the bar food might include soup (£3.50), chicken liver pâté (£4.50), spinach and ricotta tortellini in a creamy white wine sauce (£6.95), gammon and egg or cajun chicken (£7.25), and sirloin steak (£8.95); quite a few daily specials like a pie of the day, pork curry, ham quiche or duck with orange sauce. There are seats out in the garden and occasional summer morris men. The nearby gardens of Misarden Park, open midweek summer, are well worth visiting. *(Recommended by BKA, Guy Vowles, Philip Hill, Bernard Stradling, Austin and Lisa Fleming, Neil and Anita Christopher)*

Free house ~ Licensee Johnny Johnston ~ Real ale ~ Bar food (12-2.30, 7-9.30) ~ Restaurant ~ (01285) 821283 ~ Children in eating area of bar and in restaurant until 9 ~ Dogs allowed in bar ~ Occasional country music ~ Open 11-2.30(3 Sat), 6-11; 12-3, 7-10.30 Sun

NAILSWORTH ST8599 Map 4
Egypt Mill 🍽️ 🛏️

Just off A46; heading N towards Stroud, first right after roundabout, then left

This is a stylish conversion of a three-floor stonebuilt mill, which still has working waterwheels and the millstream flowing through. The brick-and-stone-floored split-level bar gives good views of the wheels, and there are big pictures and lots of stripped beams in the comfortable carpeted lounge, along with some hefty yet elegant ironwork from the old mill machinery. Although it can get quite crowded on fine weekends, it's actually spacious enough to feel at its best when it's busy – with good service to cope, and the atmosphere is almost bistro-ish; piped music. There's a civilised upstairs no smoking restaurant. Food is extremely good and very popular, and might include sandwiches, soup with croutons (£3.85), baked portabella mushrooms topped with a spring onion and blue cheese rarebit or a plate of cured meats, marinated vegetables and grilled ciabatta (£5.50), grilled prawns cooked in garlic, ginger and lime butter with a thai dressing (£6.95), steak and kidney suet pudding (£8.95), spinach and ricotta tortellini with tomato, basil, black olives and white wine sauce (£9.50), confit of duck leg with truffle mash and red wine jus (£10.50), roast chump of lamb with mint jus (£12.85), roast tenderloin of pork with chorizo sausage and sage butter (£12.90), and sirloin steak with red wine and shallot sauce (£13.80). Well kept Archers, Tetleys and a guest beer on handpump (they change every two weeks). The floodlit terrace garden by the millpond is pretty, and there's a little bridge over from the car park; boules and croquet. *(Recommended by Lesley and Peter Barrett, John and Patricia White, Rod Stoneman, Dr and Mrs C W Thomas, Andrew Barker, Claire Jenkins, Mike and Mary Carter, Philip and Jenny Grant, Joyce and Maurice Cottrell)*

Free house ~ Licensee Stephen Webb ~ Real ale ~ Bar food (all day) ~ Restaurant ~ (01453) 833449 ~ Children welcome ~ Open 11-11; 12-10.30 Sun ~ Bedrooms: £54.50B/£75B

Weighbridge 🍽️ 🍷

B4014 towards Tetbury

A favourite with quite a few of our readers, this bustling place is run by particularly cheerful and welcoming licensees. The relaxed bar has three cosily old-fashioned rooms (one is no smoking) with stripped stone walls, antique settles and country chairs, and window seats. The black beamed ceiling of the lounge bar is thickly festooned with black ironware – sheepshears, gin traps, lamps, and a large collection of keys, many from the old Longfords Mill opposite the pub. Upstairs is a raftered hayloft with an engaging mix of rustic tables; no noisy games machines or piped music. Their speciality is the very popular 2 in 1 pies which are served in a large bowl – half the bowl contains the filling of your choice and the other is full of home-made cauliflower cheese (or broccoli mornay or root vegetables), and is topped with pastry: steak and mushroom, turkey and trimmings, salmon in a creamy sauce, roast root vegetables, pork, bacon and celery in stilton sauce or chicken, ham and leek in a cream and tarragon sauce (from £7.80; you can also have mini versions from £5.90 or straightforward pies without the cauliflower cheese, from £7). Other choices include home-made soup (£2.75), filled baguettes (from £3.40), filled baked potatoes (from £3.60), coarse chicken liver pâté with red onion chutney (£3.95), cottage pie (£4.75), bangers and mash with rich onion gravy and garlic and rosemary mash (£6.95), daily specials, and puddings such as banana crumble, crème brûlée or lemon cheesecake (£3.75). Well kept Uley Old Spot, Wadworths 6X, and a couple of guests like Black Sheep or Uley Laurie Lee on handpump, 16 wines (and champagne) by the glass, and Weston's cider. Behind is a sheltered landscaped garden with picnic-sets under umbrellas. Good disabled access and facilities. *(Recommended by Bruce Adams, R Huggins, D Irving, E McCall, T McLean, John and Jane Hayter, R Telfer, Mike Snelgrove, Chris and Jan Phillips, Sylvia and Tony Cooper, Paul Weedon, Tom and Ruth Rees)*

Free house ~ Licensees Jane and Simon Hudson ~ Real ale ~ Bar food (all day) ~ (01453) 832520 ~ Children in eating area of bar ~ Dogs welcome ~ Open 12-11; 12-10.30 Sun

NAUNTON SP1123 Map 4
Black Horse 🛏

Village signposted from B4068 (shown as A436 on older maps) W of Stow-on-the-Wold

This L-shaped little inn on a quiet village lane is close to some fine Cotswold walks. The comfortable, neatly kept bar has black beams, stripped stonework, simple country-kitchen chairs, built-in oak pews, polished elm cast-iron-framed tables, and a warming open fire. Decent straightforward bar food includes soup (£3.30), huge baguettes (from £4.50), home-made pâté (£4.75), ploughman's (from £5.95), filled baked potatoes (from £6.50), leek and macaroni cheese bake (£4.75), steak and kidney suet pudding or ham and egg (£7.95), pork hock with fruit compote (£9.95), and daily specials. The dining room is no smoking. Well kept and well priced Donnington BB and SBA on handpump, and sensibly placed darts, cribbage, dominoes, and piped music. Some tables outside. *(Recommended by KC, Pete Baker, Mike and Mary Carter, Norman and June Williams, Di and Mike Gillam, Patricia A Bruce, Guy Vowles, Lynn Sharpless, Lawrence Pearse, Rod Stoneman, Dick and Mary Pownall)*

Donnington ~ Tenant Martin David Macklin ~ Real ale ~ Bar food ~ (01451) 850565 ~ Children in eating area of bar ~ Dogs allowed in bar ~ Open 11.30-3, 6-11; 12-3, 7-10.30 Sun ~ Bedrooms: /£50B

NEWLAND SO5509 Map 4
Ostrich ♀ 🍷

Off B4228 in Coleford; or can be reached from the A466 in Redbrook, by the turn-off at the England-Wales border – keep bearing right

This is a fine example of an unspoilt country pub with a friendly pubby atmosphere, a fine range of real ales, and good, enjoyable food. The spacious but cosily traditional low-ceilinged bar has creaky floors, uneven walls, window shutters, candles in bottles on the tables, and comfortable furnishings such as cushioned window seats, wall settles and rod-backed country-kitchen chairs, and a fine big fireplace; quiet piped jazz. Good, popular food (you can also eat the restaurant menu in the bar) is totally home-made, and might include soup (£4.50), baked figs stuffed with goats cheese and wrapped in parma ham (£4.95), pigeon and foie gras terrine (£5.95), three cheese tart (£6.50), salmon and spinach fishcakes with parsley sauce (£7.50), chicken stuffed with cream cheese, rosemary and garlic and wrapped in puff pastry with a red pepper salsa (£10.50), whole bass thai-style (£11), best end of lamb wrapped in smoked bacon on champ with a rich jus (£12.50), and puddings like sticky toffee pudding or raspberry and amaretti cheesecake; the restaurant is no smoking. They have eight well kept real ales on handpump: Greene King Abbot, Timothy Taylors Landlord, Wye Valley Butty Bach, and five constantly changing others. There are seats outside in front of the partly 13th-c building, and the church is opposite. *(Recommended by Phil and Heidi Cook, LM, Mike and Mary Carter)*

Free house ~ Licensee Catherine Horton ~ Real ale ~ Bar food (not Sun evening or Mon) ~ Restaurant ~ (01594) 833260 ~ Well behaved children welcome ~ Dogs allowed in bar ~ Open 12-3, 6.30(6 Sat)-11; 12-3, 7-10.30 Sun

NORTH CERNEY SP0208 Map 4
Bathurst Arms ♀ 🛏

A435 Cirencester—Cheltenham

New licensees have taken over this handsome old place and are introducing an interesting and reasonably priced wine list and have changed the menu. The beamed and panelled bar has a fireplace at each end (one quite huge and housing an open woodburner), a good mix of old tables and nicely faded chairs, old-fashioned window seats, and some pewter plates. There are country tables in a little carpeted room off the bar, as well as winged high-backed settles forming a few booths around other tables; one of the small dining rooms is no smoking. Bar food now includes sandwiches (from £2.95), freshly baked nachos with guacamole and salsa fresca or home-made soup (£3.50), grilled black pudding, apple and bacon with a mustard and cider sauce (£4.25), ploughman's (£5.95), haddock in their own beer batter or beef and mushroom pie with horseradish suet crust (£7.95), chicken stuffed with ginger and lemon grass with a pineapple and banana sauce or pork tenderloin on spring onion mash with a creamy wild mushroom, sage and apple sauce (£9.95), sirloin steak with brandy and peppercorn sauce (£12.25), and puddings like lime and orange tart or double chocolate mud pie (£3.95); Sunday roast lunch (£8.50), and summer barbecue and boules every Saturday lunchtime. Well kept Hook Norton Best, Wickwar Coopers and Cotswold Way, and a guest like Archers or Wadworths 6X on handpump; piped music. There are picnic-sets outside sheltered by small trees and shrubs; lots of surrounding walks. More reports please. *(Recommended by R Huggins, D Irving, E McCall, T McLean, Neil and Anita Christopher, Andrew Barker, Claire Jenkins, Dave Irving, KC)*

Free house ~ Licensee James Walker ~ Real ale ~ Bar food ~ Restaurant ~ (01285) 831281 ~ Children in family room ~ Dogs allowed in bar ~ Live music last Fri of month ~ Open 11-3, 6-11; 12-3, 7-10.30 Sun ~ Bedrooms: /£65B

NORTH NIBLEY ST7596 Map 4
New Inn 🍺

Waterley Bottom, which is quite well signposted from surrounding lanes; inn signposted from the Bottom itself; one route is from A4135 S of Dursley, via lane with red sign saying Steep Hill, 1 in 5 (just SE of Stinchcombe Golf Course turn-off), turning right when you get to the bottom; another is to follow Waterley Bottom signpost from previous main entry, keeping eyes skinned for small low signpost to inn; OS Sheet 162 map reference 758963; though this is the way we know best, one reader suggests the road is wider if you approach directly from North Nibley

In warm weather, after enjoying one of the nearby walks, you can flop on to one of the many seats on the lawn outside this peacefully set pub and enjoy a pint of Bath Gem Bitter or SPA, Cotleigh Tawny, Greene King Abbot or Wickwar Cotswold Way all well kept and dispensed from Barmaid's Delight (the name of one of the antique beer engines) or tapped from the cask; there's also a neat terrace and boules. Inside, the lounge bar has cushioned windsor chairs and varnished high-backed settles against the partly stripped stone walls, and dominoes, cribbage, TV, and sensibly placed darts in the simple public bar. Served by the warmly friendly landlady, the short choice of home-made bar food includes sandwiches or toasties (from £2), soup (£3), filled baguettes (from £3.30), ploughman's (from £4.20), goats cheese and red onion flan or steak and kidney pie (£6.75), beef and mushroom casserole (£8), and poached plaice with prawn sauce (£8.50); they import their own french wines and hold a beer festival on the last weekend in June; Thatcher's cider. *(Recommended by Patrick Hancock, the Didler, Mrs C McNulty, Phil and Jane Hodson, BKA, Guy Vowles, Lawrence Pearse)*

Free house ~ Licensees Jackie and Jacky Cartigny ~ Real ale ~ Bar food (not Mon

*except bank hols) ~ (01453) 543659 ~ Children welcome ~ Dogs allowed in bar ~
Open 12-2.30, 6(7 Mon)-11; 12-11 Sat; 12-10.30 Sun; closed Mon lunchtime except
bank hols*

NORTHLEACH SP1114 Map 4
Wheatsheaf

West End; the inn is on your left as you come in following the sign off the A429, just SW of
its junction with the A40

Now owned by a pub company who have installed new licensees, this handsomely
proportioned 16th-c stone-built inn has seen quite a few changes; we are keeping
our fingers crossed that things will all be settled by the time this book is published.
There is plenty to see (including a fascinating collection of musical boxes and
clocks, polyphons and automata), and it's all light and airy, with the three big-
windowed rooms lining the street now run together. The central bar part has
flagstones, the dining area open to it on the right has bare boards, and both have
quite high ceilings – so the acoustics are bright and lively. The room on the left,
with comfortable red or green semi-easy chairs on matching carpet matting, has a
less exposed atmosphere which some might prefer. Well kept Hook Norton Best,
Marstons Pedigree, and Wadworths 6X on handpump, and several wines by the
glass. Bar food now includes lunchtime sandwiches and sausages of the day, as well
as home-made soup (£4), duck livers in a warm tartlet with spinach or warm
pigeon salad with crispy bacon (£5), faggots with onion gravy (£7), cod in beer
batter (£8), pot-roasted lamb shank (£10), roast breast of guinea fowl and crushed
parsnip mash (£12), rib-eye steak with peppercorn sauce (£13), and puddings like
chocolate tart or sticky toffee pudding with butterscotch sauce (£4). Behind is a
pretty garden with picnic-sets on tiers of grass among flowering shrubs. This is a
lovely little town. More reports please. *(Recommended by Dr W J M Gissane,
H O Dickinson, David Blackburn, Michael Dandy, W W Burke, Gerald Wilkinson)*

*Punch ~ Lease Caspar and Gavin Harvard-Walls ~ Bar food (12-3,
7(6 Sun)-10(9 Sun); all day Sat) ~ Restaurant ~ (01451) 860244 ~ Children welcome
~ Dogs allowed in bar ~ Open 12-11; 12-10.30 Sun ~ Bedrooms: /£55B*

OLD SODBURY ST7581 Map 2
Dog

Not far from M4 junction 18: A46 N, then A432 left towards Chipping Sodbury

Handy for the M4, this is a bustling village pub with quite a mix of customers. The
two-level bar and smaller no smoking room both have areas of original bare stone
walls, beams and timbering, low ceilings, wall benches and cushioned chairs, and
open fires; best to get here early to be sure of a seat. From a huge menu, the choice
of food might include fresh fish dishes like sole, plaice, halibut, cod, trout, scallops,
shark or tuna, giant prawns, and several different ways of serving mussels and
squid (£5.95-£9.95), as well as sandwiches (from £2.25), smoked mackerel pâté
(£3.95), ploughman's (£4.95), vegetarian moussaka (£6.75), cheese and onion flan
or lasagne (£6.95), home-made steak and kidney pie, prawn curry or mexican tacos
(£7.45), creamy seafood tagliatelle (£7.95), steaks (from £7.95), puddings like
home-made fruit pie, jam roly poly or rhubarb crumble (from £2.75), and
children's meals (from £2.25). Well kept Marstons Pedigree, Wadworths 6X,
Wickwar BOB, and a guest beer on handpump, several malt whiskies, and quite a
few wines. Dominoes, fruit machine, and juke box. There's a large garden with lots
of seating, a summer barbecue area, climbing frames, swings, slides, and football
net. Lots of nearby walks. *(Recommended by Roger and Jenny Huggins, Sebastian Leach,
Jane Taylor, David Dutton, Roy and Lindsey Fentiman, Ian Phillips, W W Burke, Tom Evans,
Dr and Mrs A K Clarke, Matthew Shackle, Simon and Amanda Southwell, David and
Ruth Shillitoe, Colin and Stephanie McFie, George Atkinson, Bob Moffatt)*

Tipping is not normal for bar meals, and not usually expected.

Enterprise ~ Lease John and Joan Harris ~ Real ale ~ Bar food (12-2, 6-9.30) ~ (01454) 312006 ~ Children in eating area of bar until 9 ~ Dogs allowed in bedrooms ~ Open 11-11; 12-10.30 Sun ~ Bedrooms: £28(£40S)(£50B)/£45(£60S)(£65B)

OLDBURY-ON-SEVERN ST6292 Map 2
Anchor ♀ ◀

Village signposted from B4061

This is a rather special place and consistently well run. They've cleverly managed to combine a proper village local with plenty of chatty regulars, and a dining pub with lots of customers enjoying the very good food. The neatly kept lounge has modern beams and stone, a mix of tables including an attractive oval oak gateleg, cushioned window seats, winged seats against the wall, oil paintings by a local artist, and a big winter log fire. Diners can eat in the lounge or bar area or in the no smoking dining room at the back of the building (good for larger groups) and the menu is the same in all rooms. All the food is home-made using local produce, and although they don't do chips, they do offer dauphinois potatoes, and new and baked ones. From the light menu, for those with smaller appetites or in more of a hurry, there might be home-made soup (£2.80), wholemeal bread with pâté, home-cooked beef and ham, sliced smoked chicken breast and fresh orange, and cheeses (from £3.95), and quite a few salads (from £4.60). There's also good home-made faggots with onion gravy (£5.95), vegetable tagliatelle (£6.25), traditional roast beef with yorkshire pudding (£6.25; small helping £4), beef in ale pie (£7.45), chicken breast in a hickory and barbecue sauce (£8.50), breast of guinea fowl stuffed with lemon couscous with a spicy, fruity sauce (£9.25), daily specials like fresh asparagus and smoked salmon in hollandaise sauce (£7.25), and lamb riojana (£8.05), and puddings such as home-made chocolate meringue roulade with hot chocolate sauce or banoffi pie (£3.50). Well kept Bass, Butcombe Bitter, Theakstons Old Peculier, and Wickwar BOB on handpump or tapped from the cask, all well priced for the area. Also over 75 malts, and a decent choice of good quality wines (12 by the glass); darts and cribbage; they have wheelchair access and a disabled lavatory. In fine weather, you can eat in the pretty garden here, and the hanging baskets and window boxes are lovely; boules. Plenty of walks to the River Severn and along the many footpaths and bridleways, and St Arilda's church nearby is interesting, on its odd little knoll with wild flowers among the gravestones (the primroses and daffodils in spring are lovely). *(Recommended by James Morrell, Dr and Mrs C W Thomas, Tom Evans, Andrew Shore, Mike and Mary Carter, Charles and Pauline Stride, Theocsbrian, Mrs M Albery, John and Patricia White, John and Gloria Isaacs)*

Free house ~ Licensees Michael Dowdeswell, Alex de la Torre ~ Real ale ~ Bar food ~ Restaurant ~ (01454) 413331 ~ Children in restaurant only ~ Dogs allowed in bar ~ Open 11.30-2.30, 6.30-11; 11.30-11 Sat; 12-10.30 Sun; closed evenings 25 and 26 Dec

PAXFORD SP1837 Map 4
Churchill ⑪ ♀

B4479, SE of Chipping Campden

This is the sort of friendly place that you pop into for a drink – and end up staying for a meal. They have kept to their policy of not allowing advance table booking, and your name goes on a chalked waiting list if all the tables are full. The simply furnished atmospheric flagstoned bar has low ceilings, assorted old tables and chairs, and a snug warmed by a good log fire in its big fireplace; there's also a dining extension. Well kept Hook Norton and a couple of guests such as Arkells Summer Ale, Goffs Jouster or Wychwood Shires XXX on handpump, and eight good wines by the glass; dominoes. From a constantly changing menu, the very good imaginative food might include soups such as potato and horseradish (£3.50), galantine of duck with bean sprouts, orange and caper sauce (£6), salt and pepper squid with tomato, gherkins and parsley aïoli (£6.75), lambs kidneys wrapped in bacon with saffron sauce and parmesan (£8), chicken, ham and leek pie (£8.50),

skate wing with fennel stuffing, beetroot and vanilla, chervil and tomato butter
(£9.50), cod fillet with star anise sauce and deep-fried ravioli of pecorino and
mushroom (£10), blade of beef with jus and soubise sauce (£11), and puddings like
orange cheesecake or iced white and dark chocolate terrine with dark chocolate
sauce (£4). There are some seats outside; aunt sally. *(Recommended by Susan and
John Douglas, Canon Michael Bourdeaux, Mr and Mrs A H Young, Geoff Palmer,
John Bowdler, Patricia A Bruce, Brian and Pat Wardrobe, Dr John Lunn, Mike and
Sue Richardson, Martin Jones, George Atkinson, Mr and Mrs C W Widdowson)*

*Free house ~ Licensees Leo and Sonya Brooke-Little ~ Real ale ~ Bar food ~
Restaurant ~ (01386) 594000 ~ Children welcome ~ Open 11.30-3, 6-11; 12-3,
7-10.30 Sun ~ Bedrooms: £40B/£70B*

SAPPERTON SO9403 Map 4
Bell 🍽 🍷 🍺

Village signposted from A419 Stroud—Cirencester; OS Sheet 163 map reference 948033

Gloucestershire Dining Pub of the Year

The hard-working licensees here go to a lot of effort to ensure that all their
customers are happy. They count the whole community as welcome customers,
whether just dropping in for a pint, walking to them for a ploughman's or coming
to enjoy the very good food on a special occasion in a less formal atmosphere than
a restaurant. There are three separate, cosy rooms with stripped beams, a nice mix
of wooden tables and chairs, country prints and modern art on stripped stone
walls, one or two attractive rugs on the flagstones, log fires and woodburning
stoves, fresh flowers, and newspapers and guidebooks to browse. Using only the
freshest produce, the very popular and imaginative food might include ploughman's
with carefully chosen cheeses, smoked duck breast, roasted pear and rocket (£6.25),
risotto of wild garlic and jumbo prawns (£6.75), carpaccio of beef fillet with hand-
made buffalo cheese or seared tuna with niçoise-style salad (£7.50), chargrilled
spicy lamb and cheese burger (£9.75), smoked haddock cakes with good chips and
dill mayonnaise or baked moroccan spiced vegetables and couscous with harissa
dressing (£10.95), chicken stuffed with bresaola and smoked mozzarella (£11.75),
chargrilled sirloin of locally reared beef with garlic and herb butter (£14.95), seared
fresh scallops with pancetta and stir-fried greens (£15.95), daily specials such as
roasted garlic and tomato soup (£3.50), steamed mussels in garlic, wine and cream
(£5.75), crispy skinned mackerel fillet with soy and sesame dipping sauce (£6.50),
local gammon and eggs (£9.50), crisp, beer battered cod (£10.75), steamed wild
halibut on samphire and crushed new potato (£14.50), and puddings like rhubarb
and strawberry crumble or rich chocolate torte with Cointreau oranges (£5). A
basket of home-made bread and butter and olives accompanies every meal. Well
kept Uley Old Spot and Hogshead, Wickwar Cotswold Way, and a guest from
Archers, Goffs or Hook Norton on handpump, up to 17 wines by two sizes of
glass, champagne by the glass, and Weston's cider. Harry the springer spaniel likes
to greet everyone. There are tables out on a small front lawn and in a partly
covered and very pretty courtyard, for eating outside. Good surrounding walks,
and horses have their own tethering rail (and bucket of water). *(Recommended by
Evelyn and Derek Walter, Paul Hopton, R Huggins, D Irving, E McCall, T McLean, Di and
Mike Gillam, Dr and Mrs C W Thomas, Michael Doswell, Cyrus I Harvey, Jr, Ronald Harry,
Colin McKerrow, Barry and Victoria Lister, Guy Vowles, Philip and Jenny Grant, John and
Joan Wyatt, Mr and Mrs J Curtis, RJH, M A and C R Starling, Gaynor Gregory, Ian Arthur,
Martin Jennings, Charles and Pauline Stride, John Kane, Marianne and Peter Stevens, Mr and
Mrs G S Ayrton)*

*Free house ~ Licensees Paul Davidson and Pat Le Jeune ~ Real ale ~ Bar food (not
Mon except bank hols) ~ Restaurant ~ (01285) 760298 ~ Children in eating area of
bar but must be over 10 in evening ~ Dogs welcome ~ Open 11-2.30, 6.30-11; 12-3,
7-10.30 Sun; closed 25 Dec and evenings 26 and 31 Dec and 1 Jan*

Please let us know of any pubs where the wine is particularly good.

SHEEPSCOMBE SO8910 Map 4

Butchers Arms ♀

Village signed off B4070 NE of Stroud; or A46 N of Painswick (but narrow lanes)

The views from this bustling 17th-c pub are marvellous and there are teak seats below the building, and tables on the steep grass behind. There's still a good mix of customers, locals and visitors, young and older, and the bar has log fires, seats in big bay windows, flowery-cushioned chairs and rustic benches, and lots of interesting oddments like assorted blow lamps, irons, and plates. They have kept their popular policy of not reserving tables in the bar so casual diners and drinkers have a relaxed area in which to enjoy their drinks. As well as filled rolls, baked potatoes and bar snacks, bar food includes cauliflower and leek lasagne (£7.25), cumberland sausage (£7.75), cajun chicken or pork escalope marinated in cranberries with worcestershire sauce (£8.25), roasted trout fillet with a herb crust (£8.50), lamb shank braised in honey and mustard (£9.95), half a crispy roast duck (£12.95), and a meal for two (£19.95). The restaurant and a small area in the bar are no smoking. Well kept Hook Norton Best, Uley Old Spot, and a guest like Wye Valley Dorothy Goodbodys on handpump, several wines by the glass, country wines, and good soft drinks; darts, cribbage, and dominoes. There's a cricket ground behind on such a steep slope that the boundary fielders at one end can scarcely see the bowler. This pub is part of the little Blenheim Inns group. *(Recommended by R Huggins, D Irving, E McCall, T McLean, BKA, David and Rhian Peters, Andrew Shore, R J Herd, Austin and Lisa Fleming, P R and S A White, Paul Boot, Martin Jennings, Hugh Roberts, Peter Scillitoe, Di and Mike Gillam)*

Free house ~ Licensees Johnny and Hilary Johnston ~ Real ale ~ Bar food (12-2.30, 7-9.30) ~ Restaurant ~ (01452) 812113 ~ Children in eating area of bar and restaurant ~ Occasional morris men and folk music ~ Open 11.30-3, 6-11; 12-3.30, 7-10.30 Sun

ST BRIAVELS SO5605 Map 4

George

High Street

Bustling and friendly, this attractive white painted pub has three rambling rooms with old-fashioned built-in wall seats, some booth seating, cushioned small settles, toby jugs and antique bottles on black beams over the servery, and a large stone open fireplace; a Celtic coffin lid dating from 1070, discovered when a fireplace was removed, is now mounted next to the bar counter. The restaurant is no smoking. Enjoyable home-made bar food includes filled baguettes (£4.95), grilled goats cheese en croûte with a raspberry coulis or garlic prawns (£4.95), five bean cassoulet with garlic bread (£7.95), popular chicken breast stuffed with apricots and brie, wrapped in bacon with a tarragon and sherry sauce (£9.95), and seafood provençale or welsh shoulder of lamb with cranberries and shallots (£12.95). The dining room is no smoking; piped music. Well kept Bath Spa, Freeminer Bitter and Iron Brew, Fullers London Pride, Moles Bitter, and RCH Pitchfork on handpump, farm cider, and country wines. Seats on the flagstoned terrace behind overlook a grassy former moat to the silvery 12th-c castle built as a fortification against the Welsh. There's an ancient escape tunnel connecting the castle to the pub, and a ghost called George. Lots of walks start nearby but muddy boots must be left outside; outdoor chess. *(Recommended by Mr and Mrs P Talbot, Bob and Margaret Holder, Rob Holt, Stephen and Helen Digby, Mr and Mrs F J Parmenter, A S and M E Marriott, Mike and Mary Carter, Jane and Graham Rooth, Neil and Jean Spink, Les Trusler, S P Watkin, P A Taylor)*

Free house ~ Licensee Bruce Bennett ~ Real ale ~ Bar food ~ Restaurant ~ (01594) 530228 ~ Children in eating area of bar and in restaurant ~ Dogs allowed in bar ~ Open 11-2.30, 6.30-11; 12-2.30, 7-10.30 Sun ~ Bedrooms: £35S/£50S

Waterside pubs are listed at the back of the book.

STOW-ON-THE-WOLD SP1925 Map 4
Eagle & Child ♀ 🛏
Attached to Royalist Hotel, Digbeth Street

This appealing pub, opened three years ago, takes the name which in the 13th c was used for a forerunner of the adjacent hotel – itself mainly 17th-c, but with some striking features and parts of great antiquity, using thousand-year-old timbers (there was some sort of inn on the site in 947). This younger offshoot has flagstone floors, dark low beams and joists, terracotta pink walls with a modicum of horsey prints and old school photographs, russet curtains, a woodburning stove, perhaps a friendly black labrador – and a thriving bustling atmosphere. There's a nice mix of individual tables in the main part and a back conservatory, which has humorous horse-racing pictures on its terracotta walls, and french windows to a small courtyard with a couple of picnic-sets and some topiary tubs. Good interesting food from the hotel's Australian chef includes sandwiches, home-made soup (£3.95), local and mediterranean charcuterie with salsa, dips and pickles (£5.50; main course £8.75), confit shallot tatin with gorgonzola and rocket salad (£5.75), local sausages with onion gravy (£7.75), beer battered fresh fish with crushed peas (£8.75), cannelloni of ricotta and grilled vegetables with herb salad (£8.95), smoked chicken, red onion and olive paella (£11.25), seared liver with crispy pancetta and onion marmalade (£11.50), 12oz rib-eye steak with green peppercorn sauce (£14.25), and puddings like banana fritters with toffee sauce, rich chocolate and hazelnut fondue with biscotti, amaretti biscuits and marshmallows or sticky toffee pudding (from £3.95). They have well kept Hook Norton Best on handpump, and good wines by the glass; good service by friendly staff in smart black and white. The bedrooms of course are in the parent hotel. Nearby parking is not always easy, and take note of the old adage 'Stow-on-the-Wold, where the wind blows cold' – it's a lovely small town to wander around. *(Recommended by Sophie Kidd, Guy Vowles, Janet and Philip Shackle)*

Free house ~ Licensees Alan and Georgina Thompson ~ Real ale ~ Bar food (12-2.30 (3 Sun), 6-10(9 Sun)) ~ Restaurant ~ (01451) 830670 ~ Children welcome ~ Dogs allowed in bar ~ Open 11(12 weekends)-11; 12-10.30 Sun ~ Bedrooms: £60B/£90B

TETBURY ST8394 Map 4
Gumstool 🍴 ♀ 🛏
Part of Calcot Manor Hotel; A4135 W of town, just E of junction with A46

Of course this is not a pub – and it is attached to a well thought of country hotel – but it's a civilised place to enjoy the well kept Courage Best, Wickwar BOB, and couple of changing guest beers on handpump while reading the daily papers. The layout is well divided to give a feeling of intimacy without losing the overall sense of contented bustle, the lighting is attractive, and materials are old-fashioned (lots of stripped pine, flagstones, gingham curtains, hop bines) though the style is neatly modern; well chosen pictures and drawings; beyond one screen there are a couple of marble-topped pub tables and a leather armchair by the big log fire; 62 malt whiskies, and a dozen interesting wines by the glass, spanning a wide price range. Good, imaginative food includes several dishes that sensibly come in two sizes: caesar salad with smoked chicken, parmesan, and garlic croûtes (£5.50; generous £7.75), oriental pork and duck spring roll with shi-itaki, pak choi, noodles and plum sauce (£5.75; generous £7.95), pasta with italian prosciutto, tomato, mozzarella and fresh basil pesto (£5.95; generous £7.95), and devilled lambs kidney in a crisp pastry case (£6.25; generous £8.50). They also offer soup (£3.50), baked camembert soufflé with apple and grapes (£5.75), smoked salmon muffin with a poached egg and hollandaise sauce (£6.75), free-range gloucester pork and herb sausages with spring onion mash (£8.95), smoked haddock fishcakes with lemon and dill butter sauce (£9.50), breast of chicken with chestnut mushrooms, dijon mustard, lemon and tarragon (£9.75), chargrilled rib-eye steak with tarragon shallot butter (£12), and puddings like lemon meringue pie, waffles with bananas in caramel sauce and coconut ice cream or steamed viennese chocolate sponge with hot chocolate sauce (£4.25). Extra vegetables £1.95, and several coffees; professional, friendly service. To be sure of a table, you must book beforehand. Most of the restaurant is no smoking; piped music. Westonbirt Arboretum is not far away. *(Recommended by JMC, Ian and Joan Blackwell, Mike Green, B and F A Hannam, Donald Godden, Alec and Barbara Jones, Tom and Ruth Rees, Rod Stoneman, KC, Carol and Dono Leaman, Neil and Debbie Cook, Bernard Stradling, Dr and Mrs C W Thomas)*

Free house ~ Licensees Paul Sadler and Richard Ball ~ Real ale ~ Bar food ~ Restaurant ~ (01666) 890391 ~ Children welcome ~ Open 11.30-2.30, 6-11; 11.30-11 Sat; 12-10.30 Sun ~ Bedrooms: £140B/£165B

Trouble House 🍽 ♀

A433 towards Cirencester, near Cherington turn

Despite the emphasis on the good modern cooking, this is still a nice place to drop in for a pint of beer or a coffee. Furnishings are mainly stripped pine or oak tables with chapel chairs, some wheelback chairs and the odd library chair, and there are attractive mainly modern country prints on the cream or butter-coloured walls. The rush-matting room on the right is no smoking, and on the left there's a parquet-floored room with a chesterfield by the good log and coal fire in the big stone fireplace, a hop-girt mantelpiece, and more hops hung from one of its two big black beams; in the small saggy-beamed middle room, you can commandeer one of the bar stools, where they have well kept Wadworths IPA and 6X on handpump, and a nice selection of wines by the glass. From an interesting menu, the good modern food might include spinach and nutmeg soup (£4; large helping £6), cauliflower cheese soufflé (£5.50), provençale vegetables in a tomato jelly with fennel and rosemary (£6), foie gras ballotine with green bean and hazelnut salad (£7.25), calves liver and bacon with onion gravy (£12), ham hock with white beans, pancetta and sage (£12.50), roasted bass with ratatouille and saffron potato (£13), roasted rack of lamb with tomato and chorizo tart (£13.50), hereford rib-eye steak with béarnaise sauce (£14.50), and puddings like chocolate tart or pineapple strudel (£5); piped music and cribbage. They sell quite a few of their own preserves such as tapenade or preserved tomatoes with onions (the homely packaging would easily let you pass them off as your own work, for point-scoring presents); service is friendly. You can sit out at picnic-sets on the gravel behind, or in a back paddock where there might be wild rabbits hopping around. *(Recommended by Dr and Mrs M E Wilson, Mrs Sally Lloyd, Richard Stancomb, Derek Thomas, Guy Vowles)*

Wadworths ~ Tenants Michael and Sarah Bedford ~ Real ale ~ Bar food (not Sun evening, not Mon) ~ Restaurant ~ (01666) 502206 ~ Children in restaurant only ~ Dogs welcome ~ Open 11-3, 6.30-11; 12-3, 7-10.30 Sun; closed Mon; 25, 26, 31 Dec, 1 Jan, 2 weeks early Jan

TODENHAM SP2436 Map 4
Farriers Arms ♀ 🍺

Between A3400 and A429 N of Moreton-in-Marsh

Run by friendly people, this tucked away pub has fine views over the surrounding countryside from the back garden, and there are a couple of tables with views of the church on a small terrace by the quiet little road. Inside, there's a cosy, relaxed atmosphere, and the main bar has nice wonky white plastered walls, hops on the beams, lovely old polished flagstones by the stone bar counter and a woodburner in a huge inglenook fireplace. A tiny little room off to the side is full of old books and interesting old photographs. Good bar food includes home-made soup (£3.75), grilled goats cheese on a pesto crouton with salad and roasted apple (£4.95), filled baguettes (from £4.95), home-made lamb burger in rosemary focaccia (£6.25), ploughman's or chicken, gorgonzola and pesto on mediterranean olive bread (£6.95), ham and eggs or home-made steak and kidney pie (£7.95), daily specials like whole grilled plaice (£9.95) and seared scallops (£13.75), and puddings (£3.95). The restaurant is no smoking. Well kept Hook Norton Best, and a couple of guests such as Timothy Taylors Landlord or Wye Valley Butty Bach on handpump, and quite a few wines by the glass. Aunt sally. *(Recommended by Martin and Karen Wake, Adam and Joan Bunting, Alan and Gill Bull, Ted George, S Evans, H O Dickinson, John and Hazel Williams, K H Frostick, Neil and Anita Christopher, John Bowdler, Alun Howells, Di and Mike Gillam)*

Free house ~ Licensees Sue and Steve Croft ~ Real ale ~ Bar food (not Sun evening or Mon) ~ Restaurant ~ (01608) 650901 ~ Children in eating area of bar and restaurant ~ Dogs allowed in bar ~ Open 12-3, 6.30-11; 12-3, 6.30-10.30 Sun; closed Sun evening and Mon

TWYNING SO8737 Map 4
Fleet

Just over 1 mile from M50 junction 1; Fleet Inn & Ferry brown sign from westbound A38 slip road

At the end of a quiet lane, this makes the most of its setting above the River Avon (crossed by the M5 in the distance), with two floodlit terraces stepping down alongside an elaborate rockery cascade towards the river, picnic-sets on the waterside grass below, its own ferry across from the opposite bank (which is a fair walk from the B4080 SW of Bredon), and a stop on the Tewkesbury—Bredon summer boat run. The garden's good fun for families, with giant parasols, huge exotic masks on the trunk of a tall yew, little statues of hedgehogs and deer, even live chipmunks and doves. Inside, at quiet times there's a cheery local feel in the blue-carpeted core on the left of the entrance corridor, with regulars clustered around the counter, brocaded wall banquettes, housekeeper's, library and kitchen chairs, cream Anaglypta walls, some dark panelling, a woodburning stove and big TV. The pub stretches out extensively from here with plenty of room for the much busier days of summer, with well spread tables, quite a lot of old local black and white boat photographs, good river views from big windows, a light and airy back restaurant area, and a games room with darts, bar billiards (no children in here while games are being played); a couple of fruit machines, piped music. Adnams Regatta, Banks's, Boddingtons, Greene King Old Speckled Hen and Charles Wells Bombardier on handpump; fairly priced food such as soup (£2.95), sandwiches or filled baguettes (from £3), breaded mushrooms (£3.95), home-made pâté (£4.75), antipasti (£5.95), ham and egg or cod in batter (£7.25), vegetable pasta bake (£7.95), steak in ale pie (£8.45), steaks (from £10.45), and puddings like apple and blackberry pie or chocolate fudge gateau (£3.50). There is disabled access, they also have a tearoom and tuck shop, and there are caravans off to the side. We have not yet heard from readers who have used the bedrooms here. *(Recommended by Dave Braisted)*

Free house ~ Licensees Jack and Bamia Pitcher ~ Real ale ~ Bar food (12-2.30, 6-9) ~ Restaurant ~ (01684) 274310 ~ Children welcome ~ Dogs allowed in bar ~ Live entertainment Fri and Sat evenings ~ Open 11-11; 12-10.30 Sun ~ Bedrooms: /£55B

UPPER ODDINGTON SP2225 Map 4
Horse & Groom

Village signposted from A436 E of Stow-on-the-Wold

It would be hard to find a warmer welcome from such genuinely friendly and helpful licensees, and even when they are really busy (which they often are), they will make time for a chat. The bar has pale polished flagstones, a handsome antique oak box settle among other more modern seats, dark oak beams in the ochre ceiling, stripped stone walls, and an inglenook fireplace. There's quite an emphasis on the popular food which might include lunchtime sandwiches, home-made soup (£3), chicken liver and mushroom parfait (£3.50), leek and bacon tartlet (£4), cajun spiced chicken (£7.50), baked goats cheese and tomato on creamy spinach (£8), breast of guinea fowl with pickled red cabbage and grilled mozzarella (£9.50), grey mullet provençale (£10.50), daily specials like smoked haddock kedgeree or feta cheese and walnut salad (£4), lambs liver and crispy bacon with caramelised onions

(£7.50), grilled bass (£11), and veal milanese (£12), and puddings like toffee and apple crumble (£3.75); Wednesday evening half crispy duck with rosemary and black pepper sauce (£12.50), and good coffee. The no smoking candlelit dining room is pretty. Well kept Flowers IPA, Hook Norton Best, and a guest like Adnams or Bass on handpump; chess, draughts, dominoes, and aunt sally league. There are seats in the pretty garden, a fine play area, and a new vineyard which they hope will produce 100 bottles a year. *(Recommended by John Kane, Mrs N W Neill, Sam Merton, John Bowdler, Colin McKerrow, Robert Gomme, Andrew Carter, Stuart Turner, Mr and Mrs Richard Osborne, P and J Shapley, Adrian and Nicky Hall, Mike Green, Mrs Anthea Fricker, Tom and Ruth Rees, John and Judy Saville, M A and C R Starling, Richard and Karen Holt, Mrs E V McDonald, Christopher White, Rosie Farr, Alun Howells, Tom Evans, Richard Greaves, Mr and Mrs R Tate, Martin Jones, Jo Rees, Bernard Stradling, Bill and Jessica Ritson, Rod Stoneman)*

Free house ~ Licensees Peter and Assumpta Golding ~ Real ale ~ Bar food ~ Restaurant ~ (01451) 830584 ~ Children welcome ~ Live entertainment Sun evening ~ Open 11-11; 12-10.30 Sun; closed 25 Dec ~ Bedrooms: £45S/£60S

WINCHCOMBE SP0228 Map 4
White Hart ♀ ⇐

High Street (B4632)

More café-bar than pub, with well kept Greene King IPA and Old Speckled Hen, Stanney Bitter, and Wadworths 6X on handpump, and a good choice of wines by the glass – brought to your table unless you're sitting at the big copper-topped counter. What marks it out most perhaps is the fact that its friendly staff are, like the landlady, virtually all Swedish, and this influences the food, served on big plates all day, with a good trio of seafood open sandwiches (£5.95), meatballs in a creamy sauce (£8.95), smorgasbord platter (£9.50) and very popular Friday lunchtime smorgasbord buffet, alongside more universal dishes such as tomato and basil soup (£3.95), filled baguettes (from £5.95), home-made american-style burgers (£7.50), cajun chicken (£8.95), sirloin steak (£14.95), rack of lamb on ratatouille (£14.95), and puddings like white chocolate crème brûlée, frozen Dime cheesecake or apple and cinnamon crumble (£4.95); as we went to press, they'd just opened a pizzeria with pizzas from £5.95 (not open Monday or Tuesday). The main area has mate's chairs, dining chairs and small modern settles around dark oak tables on black-painted boards, cream walls, and what amounts to a wall of big windows giving on to the village street – passers-by knock on the glass when they see their friends inside. A smaller no smoking back area has its kitchen tables and chairs painted pale blue-grey, and floor matting. Daily papers, a good relaxed mix of all ages, laid-back piped music; a downstairs bar with black beams, stripped stone above the panelled dado, and pews and pine tables on the good tiles, may be open too at busy times. The back car park is rather small. *(Recommended by Rod Stoneman, Peter King, Di and Mike Gillam)*

Enterprise ~ Lease Nicole Burr ~ Real ale ~ Bar food ~ Restaurant ~ (01242) 602359 ~ Children welcome ~ Dogs allowed in bar and bedrooms ~ Occasional jazz evenings ~ Open 11-11; 12-10.30 Sun ~ Bedrooms: £55B/£65B

'Children welcome' means the pub says it lets children inside without any special restriction. If it allows them in, but to restricted areas such as an eating area or family room, we specify this. Places with separate restaurants usually let children use them, hotels usually let them into public areas such as lounges. Some pubs impose an evening time limit – let us know if you find this.

Lucky Dip

Besides the fully inspected pubs, you might like to try these Lucky Dips recommended to us and described by readers (if you do, please send us reports: www.goodguides.com).

ALDERTON [SP0033]
Gardeners Arms [Beckford Rd, off B4077 Tewkesbury—Stow]: Thatched Tudor pub with decent food from filled baps and baked potatoes to bistro dishes and fresh fish, well kept Flowers IPA, Greene King Abbot and Old Speckled Hen and guests such as Archers and Wye Valley, above-average wines, hospitable landlady, log fire; piped music (turned down on request); dogs and children welcome, tables on sheltered terrace, well kept garden with boules *(George Atkinson, LYM, Andrew Wones, Theocsbrian)*
ALDSWORTH [SP1510]
☆ *Sherborne Arms* [B4425 Burford—Cirencester]: Cheerful extended wayside pub very popular for wide choice of good fresh food from baked potatoes and ploughman's up esp fish; log fire, beams, some stripped stone, smallish bar, big dining area and attractive no smoking conservatory, friendly obliging service and attentive landlord, well kept Greene King IPA, Abbot and Ruddles County; games area with darts, lots of board games, fruit machine, piped music; pleasant front garden, lavatory for disabled *(Derek Carless, Giles Francis, R Huggins, D Irving, E McCall, T McLean, BB)*
AMBERLEY [SO8401]
Amberley Inn [steeply off A46 Stroud—Nailsworth – gentler approach from N Nailsworth]: Beautiful views, comfortable panelled and carpeted lounge bar, reasonably priced food inc generous carvery, real ales; bedrooms *(Mr and Mrs J Brown)*
☆ *Black Horse* [off A46 Stroud—Nailsworth; Littleworth]: Spectacular views and cheerful local atmosphere, friendly staff, well kept changing ales such as Archers Best and Golden and a seasonal Wickwar beer (special prices midweek and early evening), farm cider, interesting wines, good value usual food inc midweek bargains, open fire and daily papers, interesting murals, conservatory, no smoking family bar, games room; tables on back terrace with barbecue and spit roast area, more on lawn (sometimes a parrot out here); open all day summer wknds, has been cl Mon *(R Huggins, D Irving, E McCall, T McLean, LYM, John and Gloria Isaacs, Derek and Margaret Underwood, Mike and Heather Watson, John Davis, David and Carole Chapman, Guy Vowles)*
AMPNEY CRUCIS [SP0701]
Crown of Crucis [A417 E of Cirencester]: Bustling rather hotelish food pub, enjoyable if not cheap food very popular particularly with older people, pleasant lemon and blue décor, split-level no smoking restaurant, real ales; children welcome, disabled facilities, lots of tables out on grass by car park, comfortable modern bedrooms around courtyard, good breakfast, open all day *(Peter and Audrey Dowsett, LYM)*

ANDOVERSFORD [SP0219]
Royal Oak [signed just off A40; Gloucester Rd]: Cosy and attractive beamed village pub, lots of stripped stone, nice galleried dining room beyond big central open fire, well kept ales inc Hook Norton Best, reasonably priced food inc good value light meals, prompt obliging service; popular quiz night, tables in garden *(R Huggins, D Irving, E McCall, T McLean, BB, Guy Vowles)*
APPERLEY [SO8628]
☆ *Coal House* [Gabb Lane; village signed off B4213 S of Tewkesbury]: Airy bar in splendid riverside position, welcoming licensees, well kept Hook Norton Best and Charles Wells Bombardier, plenty of blackboards listing the substantial and enjoyable inexpensive food from baguettes up, walkers welcome; tables and chairs on front terrace and lawn with Severn views, play area, moorings *(Pete and Rosie Flower, Theocsbrian, BB, Andy and Jill Kassube, Rod Stoneman)*
ARLINGHAM [SO7111]
☆ *Old Passage* [Passage Rd]: Roomy upmarket place now more restaurant than pub, nice clean décor, interesting food choice inc good fish and seafood, friendly helpful staff; beautiful setting, french windows to pleasant terrace and big garden extending down to River Severn *(Jane McKenzie, Michael Herman, BB, Jo Rees)*
AUST [ST5789]
☆ *Boars Head* [½ mile from M48 junction 1, off Avonmouth road]: Promising signs that this useful ivy-covered motorway break is back on good form, with wide choice of reasonably priced food in good helpings served efficiently; nice mix of old furnishings in rambling series of linked rooms and alcoves, beams and some stripped stone, huge log fire, well kept real ales, good house wines, children allowed in partly no smoking eating area away from bar; piped music; pretty sheltered garden, dogs allowed on a lead *(Charles and Pauline Stride, LYM, Colin Moore, Ian Phillips, Rob Webster, John and Enid Morris)*
AVENING [ST8898]
Bell [High St]: Comfortable country pub with beams, brasses and stripped stone, good value generous food, Marstons, Wickwar BOB and guest beers, courteous service, real fire, one room no smoking; quiz nights *(R Huggins, D Irving, E McCall, T McLean)*
BIBURY [SP1106]
Catherine Wheel [Arlington; B4425 NE of Cirencester]: Open-plan main bar and smaller back rooms refurbished under new management, low beams, stripped stone, good log fires, no smoking dining area (children allowed), well kept Bass, Courage Best and Wadworths 6X, food from sandwiches up, traditional games; picnic-sets in attractive and spacious garden with play area, famously

beautiful village, handy for country and riverside walks; open all day, children welcome *(P R and S A White, BKA, Joyce and Geoff Robson, Richard Gibbs, Peter and Audrey Dowsett, LYM, Di and Mike Gillam)*

BIRDLIP [SO9214]

Royal George: Big smart two-level bar beyond hotel reception, beams hung with chalked sayings from such savants as Hemingway and Homer Simpson, small area with armchairs and low tables, extensive wine racks in lower part, wide range of reasonably priced bar and restaurant food from sandwiches up, three well kept Greene King ales, pleasant staff, soft lighting; quiet piped music; fine garden, pleasant setting, bedrooms *(R Huggins, D Irving, E McCall, T McLean)*

BLOCKLEY [SP1634]

☆ *Great Western Arms* [Station Rd (B4479)]: Convivial and comfortable village local with straightforward modern-style lounge/dining room, cheery landlord, wide choice of quickly served good value home-made pub food, three well kept Hook Norton ales, no piped music, busy public bar with games room; attractive village, lovely valley view *(George Atkinson, Giles Francis, Alec and Barbara Jones, G W A Pearce)*

BOURTON-ON-THE-WATER [SP1620]

Mousetrap [Lansdown, W edge]: Small comfortable stone pub with well kept Hook Norton and Wadworths 6X in long narrow partly beamed bar, good generous food inc imaginative dishes and particularly good steaks in separate attractive kitchen-style dining area, attentive friendly service, welcoming fire; picnic-sets out in front, bedrooms *(Keith and Chris O'Neill, Helen White)*

BROADWELL [SP2027]

☆ *Fox* [off A429 2 miles N of Stow-on-the-Wold]: Appealing small family-run pub opp neat broad green in pleasant village, friendly service, generous straightforward food from good ploughman's up, well kept Donnington BB and SBA, Addlestone's cider, decent wines, nice coffee, stripped stone and flagstones, beams hung with jugs, log fire, darts, dominoes and chess, plain public bar with pool room extension, plump black cat, nice separate restaurant (locally popular for Sun family lunches); may be piped music; tables out on gravel, good big back garden with aunt sally, meadow behind for Caravan Club members; bedrooms *(Roger and Jenny Huggins, Mr and Mrs Richard Osborne, BB)*

BROOKEND [SO6801]

Lammastide [New Brookend]: Small neatly kept and friendly pub in quiet spot inland from Sharpness, enjoyable usual food, two or three nicely chosen real ales; tables out on decking, play area *(Barbara Ogburn)*

BUSSAGE [SO8804]

Ram: Roomy and recently much modernised Cotswold stone pub, split-level partly flagstoned L-shaped bar with snug corner and pleasant dining area, generous good value wholesome food from sandwiches up, well kept ales such as Brakspears, decent and

unusual wines, friendly and knowledgeable landlord; soft piped music, fruit machine; good valley view esp from deck outside *(June and Ken Brooks, Simon Collett-Jones)*

CERNEY WICK [SU0796]

Crown: Roomy modern lounge bar, comfortable conservatory extension, enjoyable reasonably priced popular food inc good Sun roasts, well kept real ales, coal-effect gas fires; unobtrusive piped music, public bar with pool, darts, fruit machine; children welcome, good-sized garden with swings, small motel-style bedroom extension *(G W A Pearce, BB)*

CHEDWORTH [SP0609]

☆ *Hare & Hounds* [Fosse Cross – A429 N of Cirencester, some way from village]: Rambling dining pub interestingly furnished with modern touches, low beams, soft lighting, cosy corners and little side rooms, two big log fires, small conservatory; good food with some inventive dishes, well kept Arkells 2B, 3B and Kingsdown, good house wines, friendly and helpful landlord, happy staff; children welcome away from bar, disabled facilities, open all day Fri-Sun *(Tim and Carolyn Lowes, KC, Fred Chamberlain, LYM, Phil and Jane Hodson, P R and S A White, R Huggins, D Irving, E McCall, T McLean)*

CHELTENHAM [SO9325]

Kemble Brewery [Fairview St]: Small backstreet local with friendly atmosphere and charming irish landlady, well kept Smiles Best, Timothy Taylors Landlord and Youngs, good value robust lunchtime food; small back garden *(Derek and Sylvia Stephenson, Theocsbrian, Giles Francis)*

CHIPPING CAMPDEN [SP1539]

☆ *Lygon Arms* [High St]: Comfortably worn in stripped-stone bar with welcoming long-serving landlord, helpful staff, very wide choice of enjoyable reasonably priced food till late evening inc interesting dishes, well kept Greene King Old Speckled Hen, Hook Norton Best and Wadworths 6X and JCB (they use sparklers), lots of horse pictures, open fires, small back dining room, raftered evening restaurant beyond shady courtyard with tables; children welcome, open all day exc winter wkdys; good bedrooms *(Geoff Calcott, Michael Porter, LYM, Lynda Payton, Sam Samuells, Peter Meister)*

Noel Arms [High St]: Old inn with polished oak settles, attractive old tables, armour, casks hanging from beams, tools and traps on stripped stone walls, well kept Bass and Hook Norton Best, decent food from sandwiches to some interesting dishes, no smoking restaurant, coal fire; piped music; children welcome, tables in enclosed courtyard, bedrooms *(Susan and John Douglas, Tony Brace, Patricia A Bruce, LYM, Marjorie and Bernard Parkin)*

CIRENCESTER [SP0201]

Bear [Dyer St]: Long bar with cheap well kept Moles, young friendly staff, quiet raised eating end, more lively end with juke box and games machine; lots of pavement tables *(R Huggins, D Irving, E McCall, T McLean)*

☆ *Corinium Court* [Dollar St/Gloucester St]:

Cosy and civilised character inn with welcoming relaxed atmosphere, big log fire, attractive antique coaching prints, good mix of tables, sofas and small armchairs, well kept changing ales, decent wines, food from sandwiches, baguettes and baked potatoes up in bars and nicely decorated restaurant; no piped music; entrance through charming courtyard with tables, attractive back garden, large car park; good bedrooms *(Guy Vowles, R Huggins, D Irving, E McCall, T McLean, BB, David Blackburn)*

Fleece [Market Pl]: Substantial old hotel with wide choice of decent bar food from sandwiches and baked potatoes to scampi and steaks, flagstones and stripped wood, also plusher hotel bar; bedrooms *(BB, Abi Benson)*

Somewhere Else [Castle St]: Two light and airy rooms with pastel walls and café tables, well kept Youngs, decent house wine and cheerful service – bistro-feel café/restaurant by day, with small interesting choice of quickly served food inc interesting tapas, more of a lively pub mood evenings; piped music can be rather loud; lots of tables on heated terrace, games room off with pool *(R Huggins, D Irving, E McCall, T McLean, Betsy and Peter Little, Joyce and Maurice Cottrell)*

☆ *Twelve Bells* [Lewis Lane]: Cheery well worn in backstreet pub with particularly well kept Abbey Bellringer and enterprising choice of five ever-changing beers, small low-ceilinged three-roomed bar, small back dining area with sturdy pine tables and rugs on quarry tiles, good coal fires, pictures for sale, clay pipe collection, friendly forthright hard-working landlord, good food inc local produce, fresh fish and some unusual dishes lunchtime and early evening; can get smoky, piped music may be loud; readers might like to know that the nearby public lavatories are neatly kept; small sheltered back terrace with fountain *(R Huggins, D Irving, E McCall, T McLean, Pete Baker, Paul and Ann Meyer, Giles Francis, Mike Pugh, Ian and Nita Cooper, Nick and Alison Dowson, Peter and Audrey Dowsett, BB, Frank Willy, Edward Longley)*

Waggon & Horses [London Rd]: Comfortably cottagey stone-built pub with lots of bric-a-brac, good choice of well kept changing ales, back dining room *(R Huggins, D Irving, E McCall, T McLean)*

Wheatsheaf [Cricklade St]: Real ales such as Fullers London Pride, Greene King IPA and Abbot and Tetleys Imperial, wide choice of cheap and cheerful food until 4pm inc OAP bargains, quick invariably welcoming service; no piped music but corner TV, and they don't seem to light the two log fires; well used skittle alley, back car park, open all day *(R Huggins, D Irving, E McCall, T McLean, Peter and Audrey Dowsett)*

CLEEVE HILL [SO9826]

Rising Sun [B4632]: Splendid view over Cheltenham to the Malvern Hills from the terrace and lawn, esp as the evening lights come on; decent food, friendly staff, Greene King beers *(Rod Stoneman, Di and Mike Gillam)*

COLD ASTON [SP1219]

☆ *Plough* [aka Aston Blank; off A436 (B4068) or A429 SW of Stow-on-the-Wold]: Tiny 17th-c village pub back on form under welcoming newish licensees, low black beams and flagstones, old-fashioned simple furnishings, log fire, well kept Donnington BB and Hook Norton Best, enjoyable usual food from baguettes up; piped music; well behaved children welcome, picnic-sets under cocktail parasols on small side terraces, good walks, has been cl Mon *(P and J Shapley, LYM, Lawrence Pearse, Martin Jones, Di and Mike Gillam)*

COLESBOURNE [SO9913]

☆ *Colesbourne Inn* [A435 Cirencester—Cheltenham]: 18th-c grey stone gabled coaching inn redecorated in soft colours, beams, panelling and log fires, comfortable mix of settles, softly padded seats, even a chaise longue, good value well presented food, friendly staff, well kept Wadworths IPA, 6X and Farmers Glory, no smoking restaurant; traditional games, no dogs, piped music; views from attractive back garden and terrace, well appointed bedrooms in converted stable block *(P R and S A White, David and Higgs Wood, LYM, R Huggins, D Irving, E McCall, T McLean, Di and Mike Gillam, Denys Gueroult, Malcolm Taylor)*

COMPTON ABDALE [SP0616]

Puesdown Inn [A40 outside village]: Former coaching inn thoroughly smartened up as rather upmarket dining pub by new licensees, wide choice of good food using local sources at reasonable prices from panini up (no sandwiches), pleasantly airy no smoking restaurant, smart and relaxing bar with well padded seats on polished boards, cheerful easy chairs and settees by big log fire, quick hospitable service, two real ales; piped music; nice garden behind, bedrooms *(Derek Carless, Peter and Audrey Dowsett, Mrs Koffman, Anthony Gill)*

COOMBE HILL [SO8827]

Swan [A38/A4019]: Light and airy dining pub, polished boards and no curtains, wide choice of attractively presented freshly cooked good value food, real ales, decent house wine, good informal service *(Theocsbrian)*

COWLEY [SO9614]

☆ *Green Dragon* [off A435 S of Cheltenham at Elkstone, Cockleford signpost]: Two-bar country dining pub in nice spot, enjoyable food from sandwiches up, beams, cream or stripped stone walls, log fires, fresh flowers and candles, tasteful oak furniture and fittings, pine boards or limestone composition floor, well kept Courage Directors, Hook Norton Best, Theakstons Old Peculier and Wadworths 6X, reasonably priced wines, espresso machine, no smoking area; piped music; children allowed; big car park, two terraces, one heated, comfortable bedrooms off courtyard, good breakfast – good walking area *(Guy Vowles, R Huggins, D Irving, E McCall, T McLean, LYM, Bob Moffatt)*

CRANHAM [SO8912]

☆ *Black Horse* [off A46 and B4070 N of Stroud]: Old-fashioned 17th-c pub with good log fire and high-backed wall settles in quarry-tiled public bar, cosy little lounge, well kept Boddingtons, Flowers Original, Greene King IPA, Hook Norton Best and Wickwar BOB, generous food (not Sun evening) from sandwiches and omelettes using their own free range eggs to fish and duck, shove-ha'penny, a couple of pub dogs, no smoking upstairs dining rooms; piped music; children welcome, sizeable garden with good steep view *(Pete Baker, Giles Francis, Nigel and Sue Foster, LYM)*

DOYNTON [ST7174]

Cross House [High St]: Pleasant village pub with good friendly mix of locals and visitors, well kept Bass, Courage Best, Fullers London Pride, Greene King Old Speckled Hen and Smiles Best, good wholesome food, attentive landlord *(Colin and Peggy Wilshire, Pete and Rosie Flower)*

DYMOCK [SO6931]

Beauchamp Arms: Well kept real ales, interesting range of reasonably priced food, friendly obliging staff; small pleasant garden with pond, bedrooms *(Duncan Cloud)*

EBRINGTON [SP1840]

Ebrington Arms [off B4035 E of Chipping Campden or A429 N of Moreton-in-Marsh]: Well refurbished village pub with low beams, stone walls, flagstones and inglenooks, well kept Donnington SBA, Hook Norton Best and Charles Wells Bombardier, sensible wine range, new dining room; children welcome, no dogs at meal times, picnic-sets on pleasant sheltered terrace, handy for Hidcote and Kiftsgate, bedrooms *(John Kane, Michael and Anne Brown, LYM)*

EDGE [SO8509]

☆ *Edgemoor* [Gloucester Rd]: Tidy modernised dining place, ideal for grandma's birthday lunch, with wide choice of good value food inc fine home-made puddings, friendly landlord and quickish helpful service, picture-window panoramic valley view across to Painswick, relaxing atmosphere, well kept Smiles, Uley Old Spot and Wickwar BOB, good coffee; no smoking area, children welcome, pretty terrace, good walks nearby; cl Sun evening *(LYM, Dave Irving, Lawrence Pearse)*

ELKSTONE [SO9610]

☆ *Highwayman* [Beechpike; off northbound A417 6 miles N of Cirencester]: Rambling 16th-c warren of low beams, stripped stone, cosy alcoves, antique settles, armchairs and sofa among more usual furnishings, big log fires, rustic decorations, welcoming new landlord, well kept Arkells ales, good house wines, big back eating area (wide affordable choice); may be quiet piped music; disabled access, good family room, outside play area *(R Huggins, D Irving, E McCall, T McLean, the Didler, P R and S A White, David and Rhian Peters, LYM)*

FAIRFORD [SP1501]

☆ *Bull* [Market Pl]: Civilised and friendly beamed hotel in charming village (church has UK's only intact set of medieval stained-glass windows), large comfortably old-fashioned timbered bar with plenty of character and local RAF

memorabilia, enormous blackboard choice of good value food, happy helpful staff, well kept Arkells 2B and 3B, two coal-effect gas fires, charming restaurant in former stables, no smoking areas, no piped music; children welcome, 22 fresh bright bedrooms, open all day *(Peter and Audrey Dowsett, Des and Jen Clarke, Peter Meister, Stephen and Yvonne Agar)*

Plough [London St]: Lively public bar, plusher yet homely lounge, good welcome, well kept Arkells, sensibly priced food; piped music may obtrude, TV, outside lavatories *(Peter and Audrey Dowsett)*

FORD [SP0829]

☆ *Plough* [B4077]: Newish tenants finding their feet well now in beamed and stripped-stone bar with racehorse pictures (it's opposite a famous stables), cheerful prompt service and wide choice of pub food from baguettes and lunchtime sandwiches up, also seasonal asparagus feasts, old settles and benches around big tables on uneven flagstones, well kept Donnington BB and SBA and Addlestone's cider, four welcoming fires, dominoes, cribbage and shove-ha'penny; TV (for the races), piped music; children allowed in one area, garden tables and play area, open all day, bedrooms *(Sheila and Robert Robinson, Neil and Anita Christopher, Mike Horler, the Didler, Lucien Perring, Peter and Audrey Dowsett, John and Gloria Isaacs, LYM, Denys Gueroult, Paul and Annette Hallett)*

FOREST OF DEAN [SO6212]

Speech House [B4226 nearly 1m E of junction with B4234]: Hotel superbly placed in centre of Forest, warm interior with lots of oak panelling, well kept Bass, afternoon teas, bar food, plush restaurant; comfortable bedrooms, tables outside *(Neil and Anita Christopher, Tom and Ruth Rees)*

FORTHAMPTON [SO8731]

Lower Lode Inn: Brick-built Tudor pub with moorings on River Severn and plenty of waterside tables (prone to winter flooding – hence the stilts for nearby caravan park), enjoyable usual pubby food, friendly landlady, local ales such as Donnington, Goffs and Wickwar, games room; children welcome (swarms with holiday families in summer), good value bedrooms with good breakfast, cl Sun lunchtime and winter Mon to Tues lunchtime *(Peter Scillitoe, Andy and Jill Kassube)*

FOSSEBRIDGE [SP0711]

Fossebridge Inn [A429 Cirencester—Stow-on-the-Wold]: Handsome Georgian inn with quiet and civilised much older two-room bar at the back, beams, arches and stripped stone, pleasant old-fashioned furnishings with more modern side area, roaring log fires, popular food from baguettes up here or in dining area, real ales; children welcome, tables out on streamside terrace and spacious lawn, comfortable bedrooms *(LYM, Joyce and Maurice Cottrell, Meg and Colin Hamilton)*

FRAMPTON ON SEVERN [SO7407]

Bell [The Green]: Georgian dining pub by huge

village cricket green, well kept real ales inc Bass and interesting guests, friendly service, log fire and plush seats, steps up to L-shaped family dining room, separate locals' bar with pool; good small back play area, now open all day *(Dave Irving, Nick and Meriel Cox, Meg and Colin Hamilton, Peter Neate)*

Frampton Arms: Nice spot in middle of the enormous village green, well kept beer, bustling front bar, comfortable back dining room (children welcome) which still feels pub-like *(Steve Crick, Helen Preston)*

GLASSHOUSE [SO7121]

☆ *Glasshouse Inn* [first right turn off A40 going W from junction with A4136; OS Sheet 162 map ref 710213]: Charming ancient country tavern with three well kept ales such as Bass and Butcombe, beams and flagstones, log fire in vast fireplace, good generous honest home cooking (not Sun) from thick sandwiches up, friendly staff, interesting decorations, recent extension carefully toning in; no children inside; darts and quoits, lovely hanging baskets, seats on tidy fenced lawn with interesting topiary inc yew tree seat, fine walks in nearby Newent Woods *(LYM, Guy Vowles, the Didler, Neil and Jean Spink, Mr and Mrs F J Parmenter)*

GLOUCESTER [SO8318]

☆ *Fountain* [Westgate St/Berkeley St]: Friendly and civilised L-shaped bar, plush seats and built-in wall benches, charming helpful service, well kept Brakspears, Boddingtons, Fullers London Pride, Greene King Abbot and Wickwar BOB, good range of whiskies, attractive prints, handsome stone fireplace (pub dates from 17th c), log-effect gas fire; cheap usual food; tables in pleasant courtyard, good disabled access, handy for cathedral, open all day *(BB, Mike and Mary Carter, David Carr, Dave Irving)*

Linden Tree [Bristol Rd; A350 about 1½ miles S of centre, out past docks]: Unpretentious local, low beams and stripped stone, well kept Wadworths and interesting guest beers, usual good value lunchtime food, coal fire, back skittle alley; bedrooms, open all day Sat *(the Didler)*

Tall Ship [Southgate St, docks entrance]: Extended Victorian pub by historic docks, raised dining area with emphasis on wide choice of enterprisingly cooked fresh fish, also good sandwiches, ploughman's and daily roasts, morning coffee and afternoon tea, well kept Wadworths and a guest beer; pool table and juke box (may be loud) on left; terrace, open all day *(David Carr)*

GOTHERINGTON [SO9629]

Shutter [off A435 N of Cheltenham; Shutter Lane]: Pleasant new licensees doing good home-made food inc fish and chips with particularly good batter, well kept Boddingtons, Castle Eden, Flowers IPA, Wickwar Cotswold Way and Youngs, decent house wines, welcoming atmosphere; children welcome, disabled access, garden with good play area *(Mike and Liz Nash)*

GREAT BARRINGTON [SP2013]

☆ *Fox* [off A40 Burford—Northleach; pub

towards Little Barrington]: Charming Cotswold spot in summer, heated terrace by River Windrush (swans and private fishing), orchard with pond, river views from dining area; low-ceilinged small bar with stripped stone and simple country furnishings, well kept Donnington BB and SBA, farm cider, friendly landlord, promptly served food from sandwiches (not Sun) to good seasonal pheasant casserole – all day Sun and summer Sat, not winter Mon night, restaurant in former skittle alley; darts, shove-ha'penny, cribbage, dominoes, juke box, fruit machine, TV; children welcome, open all day *(David and Kay Ross, LYM, Neil and Anita Christopher, Pete Baker, Ted George, Stephen, Julie and Hayley Brown, R M Gibson, the Didler, R Huggins, D Irving, E McCall, T McLean, Les Trusler, Tim and Ann Newell, Joyce and Geoff Robson, Rod Stoneman)*

GREAT RISSINGTON [SP1917]

☆ *Lamb* [off A40 W of Burford, via Gt Barrington]: Partly 17th-c, with civilised two-room bar, well kept Hook Norton Best, decent wines, open fire, interesting if not cheap food, darts, dominoes, and cribbage, no smoking candlelit restaurant with another fire; may be piped classical music; children welcome, sheltered hillside garden, comfortable bedrooms *(LYM, Mr and Mrs I Bell, Pam Adsley, Simon Collett-Jones, Paul Humphreys, Jill Small)*

GUITING POWER [SP0924]

Farmers Arms [Fosseway (A429)]: Stripped stone and flagstones, particularly well kept cheap Donnington BB and SBA, wide blackboard range of unpretentious food from sandwiches and good ploughman's up inc children's dishes, prompt service, good coal or log fire; skittle alley, games area with darts, pool, cribbage, dominoes, fruit machine; piped music; seats (and quoits) in garden, good walks; children welcome, bedrooms, lovely village *(Derek Carless, P R and S A White, LYM, the Didler, Guy Vowles, Lawrence Pearse)*

HANHAM [ST6470]

Elm Tree [Abbots Rd; S, towards Willsbridge and Oldland Common]: Cheerful efficient service, well kept Bass and Courage Diectors, good menu from sandwiches to steaks, a couple of early evening bargains, restaurant; lovely hanging baskets *(M C and Susan Jeanes)*

Old Lock & Weir [Hanham Mills; follow sign to Chequers pub down narrow dead end]: Idyllic setting by River Avon, plain but comfortable inside, good value food from baguettes to full meals inc Sun lunch, real ales with occasional beer festivals, friendly attentive young staff; children in side rooms; extensive waterside gardens and landing stage *(Peter Scillitoe)*

HAWKESBURY UPTON [ST7787]

Fox [High St]: Friendly and attentive licensees, well kept Smiles, lots of local photographs; good value bedrooms with own bathroom, pleasant village *(BB, R Huggins, D Irving, E McCall, T McLean)*

HYDE [SO8801]

☆ *Ragged Cot* [Burnt Ash; off A419 E of Stroud, OS Sheet 162 map ref 886012]: 17th-c pub with comfortably padded seat right round beamed and stripped stone bar, log fire, good value attractive bar food, good choice of well kept real ales, good wine list, dozens of malt whiskies, traditional games, attractive no smoking eating area; picnic-sets (and interesting pavilion) in garden, comfortable bedrooms in adjacent converted barn *(R Huggins, D Irving, E McCall, T McLean, LYM)*

KEMBLE [ST9897]

☆ *Thames Head* [A433 Cirencester—Tetbury]: Stripped stone, timberwork, softly lit cottagey no smoking back area with pews and log-effect gas fire in big fireplace, country-look dining room with another big gas fire, real log fire in front area (enjoyed by Toy the dog), enjoyable generous reasonably priced food, good value wines, Arkells 2B and 3B; skittle alley, seats outside, children welcome, good value four-poster bedrooms, nice walk to nearby source of River Thames (which is not monumentally impressive) *(Gerald Wilkinson, A B and G S Dance, LYM)*

KILCOT [SO6925]

Kilcot Inn [B4221, not far from M50 junction 3]: Renovated and extended, stripped to rustic bare brick, three real ales, no smoking eating area with blackboard food *(Theocsbrian)*

KILKENNY [SP0018]

Kilkeney Inn [A436 W of Andoversford]: Spacious modernised dining pub with log fire and comfortable no smoking conservatory, well kept Bass and Hook Norton; well behaved children allowed in eating areas, tables outside, attractive Cotswold views, open all day wknds *(Joyce and Geoff Robson, Mike and Mary Carter, Rita Horridge, LYM, John and Glenys Wheeler, Brian and Pat Wardrobe, John and Joan Wyatt, Bernard Stradling, Trevor and Sylvia Millum)*

KINETON [SP0926]

☆ *Halfway House* [signed from B4068 and B4077 W of Stow-on-the-Wold]: Unpretentious country local with helpful friendly licensees, baguettes and sensibly priced traditional hot dishes using local ingredients, well kept cheap Donnington BB and SBA from nearby brewery, decent wines, farm cider, pub games (and juke box), restaurant; children allowed lunchtime, no visiting dogs; attractive sheltered back garden, tables on narrow front terrace too, simple comfortable bedrooms, good walks *(LYM, Stephen Williamson)*

KNOCKDOWN [ST8388]

Holford Arms: Popular and comfortable, enjoyable bar lunches, more choice in small dining area, friendly staff, real ales inc Bass, huge fireplace; kitchen radio may make itself heard; neat side garden, handy for Westonbirt *(Meg and Colin Hamilton, Peter and Audrey Dowsett)*

LECHLADE [SU2199]

New Inn [Market Sq (A361)]: Very wide choice of good value generous food from good filled baguettes up, good changing range of well kept ales, helpful staff, huge log fire in big plain lounge with games machine and TV at one end, back restaurant; piped music; play area in big garden extending to Thames, good walks, comfortable bedrooms *(Fred Chamberlain, Peter and Audrey Dowsett, Gerald Wilkinson)*

☆ *Trout* [A417, a mile E]: Low-beamed three-room pub dating from 15th c, with some flagstones, stuffed fish and fishing prints, local paintings for sale, spill-over bar out in converted boathouse, big Thames-side garden with boules, aunt sally; well kept Courage Best, John Smiths and a guest such as Smiles, popular if pricy food from baked potatoes and ploughman's up, no smoking dining room, two fires, board games and magazines; children in eating areas, jazz Tues and Sun, no piped music, fishing rights; may be long waits in summer (open all day Sat then), when very busy, with bouncy castle and fairground swings; large car park, camping *(SLC, P R and S A White, Keith Stevens, JCW, Neil and Anita Christopher, LYM, R Huggins, D Irving, E McCall, T McLean, Paul and Annette Hallett)*

LEIGHTERTON [ST8290]

Royal Oak [off A46 S of Nailsworth]: Unpretentious old stone-built pub, mullioned windows, linked carpeted rooms with pleasantly simple décor in original part and matching extension, emphasis on good value simple food, three well kept ales such as Butcombe; nice garden, quiet village, quite handy for Westonbirt Arboretum *(Guy Vowles, Mrs Sally Lloyd)*

LONGBOROUGH [SP1729]

Coach & Horses: Unpretentious largely flagstoned L-shaped local, good log fire, welcoming service, particularly well kept Donnington inc XXX Mild, walkers and dogs welcome; tables outside *(Pete Baker, Mrs N W Neill)*

LONGFORD [SO8320]

Queens Head [Tewkesbury Rd]: Attractive open-plan bar with no smoking restaurant area, good value lunches from baguettes and baked potatoes up, slightly more upmarket evening meals, well kept ales such as Bass, Fullers London Pride, Greene King Old Speckled Hen and Hook Norton, pleasant efficient service *(Mr and Mrs J Norcott, Neil and Anita Christopher)*

LOWER ODDINGTON [SP2326]

☆ *Fox*: Formerly a prized main entry, sold in 2002; reports under the courteous new owner have been generally very favourable, with some real enthusiasm for the interesting carefully cooked rather restauranty food (the kitchen team has stayed); well kept ales such as Badger Tanglefoot and Hook Norton Best, good wines, efficient service, appealing décor in linked rooms with inglenook fireplace and flagstones; beware, smokers are not segregated – odd these days, in such a foody pub; children welcome, tables on heated terrace with awning, pretty garden, pleasant walks, comfortable bedrooms *(Karen and Graham Oddey, Terry*

and Linda Moseley, Tom Evans, Maurice
Ribbans, John and Judy Saville, Jay Bohmrich,
Dr W I C Clark, LYM, Martin Jones, Michael
and Anne Brown, Rod Stoneman, Mr and
Mrs P Lally, Bernard Stradling)

LOWER SWELL [SP1725]

☆ *Golden Ball* [B4068 W of Stow-on-the-Wold]:
Sprucely unspoilt stone-built beamed local with
well kept Donnington BB and SBA from the
pretty nearby brewery, good range of ciders
and perry, very friendly landlady, well
presented generous home-made food, big log
fire, games area with fruit machine and juke
box behind big chimneystack, small cavernous
restaurant (not Sun evening), conservatory; no
dogs or children; small garden with occasional
barbecues, aunt sally and quoits; three decent
simple bedrooms, pretty village, good walks
*(the Didler, George Atkinson, Roger and
Jenny Huggins, LYM)*

MARSHFIELD [ST7773]

☆ *Catherine Wheel* [High St; signed off A420
Bristol—Chippenham]: Stripped stone pub
bought by a consortium of customers to keep
its village feel, friendly staff, wide choice of
food (not Sun) inc imaginative if not cheap
dishes, good choice of well kept ales, farm
cider, decent wines, plates and prints, medley
of settles, chairs and stripped tables, open fire
in impressive fireplace, cottagey back family
bar, charming no smoking Georgian dining
room, darts, dominoes; flower-decked back
yard, bedrooms, unspoilt village *(LYM,
Pete and Rosie Flower, Susan and
John Douglas, Dr and Mrs A K Clarke)*
Crown [High St (A420)]: Large busy pub, new
management making improvements and
adding bedrooms, efficient friendly staff, big
log fire in well furnished beamed lounge, wide
choice of food, well kept real ales, competitive
prices; pool and machines, live music Sat;
children welcome *(Pete and Rosie Flower)*
Lord Nelson [A420 Bristol—Chippenham;
High St]: Spacious range of beamed rooms
with open fires, wide choice of quickly served
inexpensive food, well kept real ales, bistro
restaurant, games bar with pool and machines;
live music Sun afternoon; charming small
courtyard, bedrooms in cottage annexe
(Pete and Rosie Flower)

MICKLETON [SP1543]

☆ *Kings Arms* [B4632 (ex A46)]: Hard-working
newish management doing well, wide choice of
enjoyable food from toasties up, unusual
puddings and good value OAP lunches, relaxed
and civilised open-plan family lounge and
dining room, soft lighting and comfortable
tables, quick friendly service, well kept Flowers
Original and Marstons Pedigree, decent wines
by the glass, farm cider, small log fire; piped
music; welcoming locals' bar with darts,
dominoes and cribbage; some tables outside,
handy for Kiftsgate and Hidcote *(Ian Phillips,
John Brightley, Martin and Karen Wake, BB,
K H Frostick, Mrs Mary Walters, Martin Jones)*

MINCHINHAMPTON [SO8500]

☆ *Old Lodge* [Nailsworth—Brimscombe – on
common fork left at pub's sign; OS Sheet 162

map ref 853008]: Relaxed and welcoming
dining pub, small snug central bar opening into
eating area with beams and stripped brick, no
smoking area, friendly efficient staff, well kept
Youngs ales; tables on neat lawn with
attractive flower border, looking over common
with grazing cows and horses, has been cl Mon
*(LYM, R Huggins, D Irving, E McCall,
T McLean, Bernard Stradling, Neil and
Anita Christopher)*

MORETON-IN-MARSH [SP2032]

Black Bear [High St]: Unpretentious beamed
pub, stripped stone with hanging rugs and old
village pictures, well kept Donnington
XXX, BB and SBA, good coffee, good value
pub food inc fresh fish, friendly service; public
bar with lots of football memorabilia, darts,
sports TV and games machine, large airy
dining lounge (not Sun evening); may be piped
radio; tables outside, big bedrooms sharing
bathrooms *(Joyce and Maurice Cottrell,
the Didler, Ted George, Joan and Michel
Hooper-Immins, BB)*

Inn on the Marsh [Stow Rd]: Reasonably
priced food from baguettes, fishcakes, burgers
and so forth to more restauranty dishes,
distinctive unpretentious beamed bar with
inglenook woodburner, comfortable armchairs
and sofa, lots of pictures particularly ducks,
Mansfield and Marstons Bitter and Pedigree,
smartly attractive modern candlelit dining
conservatory; can be smoky; bedrooms
*(Pat and Robert Watt, Joyce and
Maurice Cottrell, Tom Evans,
George Atkinson, Mrs N W Neill)*

☆ *Redesdale Arms* [High St]: Fine old coaching
inn with prettily lit alcoves and big stone
fireplace in solidly furnished comfortable
panelled bar on right, well kept ales such as
Courage Directors and Wye Valley, small but
good wine list, cafetière coffee, interesting
choice of generous food, friendly staff, log
fires, spacious back restaurant and dining
conservatory, darts in flagstoned public bar;
piped music, fruit machine, TV; tables out on
heated courtyard decking, comfortable well
equipped bedrooms beyond *(George Atkinson,
Joyce and Maurice Cottrell, BB, Ted George,
Guy Vowles)*

NAILSWORTH [ST8499]

Britannia [Cossack Sq]: Much refurbished,
with bright service and good wines by the glass
(Tom and Ruth Rees)

George [Newmarket]: Traditional pub with
above-average freshly made food, well kept
beer, good welcoming service *(Bruce Adams)*

NETHER WESTCOTE [SP2220]

New Inn [off A424 Burford—Stow]: Cosy and
comfortable 17th-c country pub with log fires
in bar and dining area down a few steps, wide
choice of locally sourced food from baguettes
up, well kept Morrells and several other
changing ales such as Bass, Hook Norton and
Wadworths 6X, friendly helpful service, games
room; may be piped music, some live music;
children and dogs welcome (a couple of pub
dogs), adjoining campsite with showers etc,
pretty village *(anon)*

NEWENT [SO7225]

George [Church St]: Old coaching inn with friendly local feel in partly no smoking L-shaped bar, good value inexpensive lunchtime food from sandwiches up, big log fire, well kept Courage and local beers, restaurant; children welcome, bedrooms, nice location opp Shambles museum *(Neil and Jean Spink)*

Travellers Rest [B4215 E]: Decent pub food, good range of real ales, personable licensees *(Mr and Mrs J Norcott)*

NEWNHAM [SO6911]

Ship [High St]: Character pub being smartened up, friendly young staff, interesting attractively priced menu (no chips or coleslaw), local farm cider; reasonably priced bedrooms *(Caroline and Michael Abbey)*

NORTH NIBLEY [ST7495]

Black Horse [Barrs Lane]: Friendly pleasantly refurbished village pub handy for Cotswold Way, wide range of generous good value home-made food, well kept Flowers Original and Marstons Pedigree, good log fire, restaurant; tables in pretty garden, good value cottagey bedrooms, good breakfast *(Mrs S A Brooks, James Morrell, LYM)*

OAKRIDGE LYNCH [SO9103]

☆ *Butchers Arms* [off Eastcombe—Bisley rd E of Stroud]: Popular unpretentious pub, rambling partly stripped stone bar, food (not Sun evening or Mon) from hot baguettes to steak, well kept Archers Best, Greene King Abbot, Tetleys and Wickwar BOB, three open fires, no smoking restaurant; children welcome away from bar, tables on neat lawn overlooking valley, good walks by former Thames & Severn canal *(R Huggins, D Irving, E McCall, T McLean, LYM, Nick and Meriel Cox, BB, Bernard Stradling)*

PAINSWICK [SO8609]

☆ *Falcon* [New St]: Sizeable old stone-built inn opp churchyard famous for its 99 yews; open-plan and relaxing, largely panelled, with high ceilings, bare-boards bar with stuffed birds and fish, mainly carpeted dining area with lots of prints, high bookshelves and shelves of ornaments by coal-effect fire, wide range of good value food from popular baguettes to some interesting dishes, lots of wines by the glass, well kept Boddingtons, Hook Norton Best and Old Hooky and Wadworths 6X, good coffee, pleasant efficient service, daily papers; big comfortable bedrooms, good breakfast *(R Huggins, D Irving, E McCall, T McLean, James Morrell, Meg and Colin Hamilton, Di and Mike Gillam, Chris Parsons, BB, Neil and Anita Christopher, David Biggins)*

☆ *Royal Oak* [St Mary's St]: Old-fashioned partly 16th-c town pub, some attractive old or antique seats, enjoyable food from filled rolls to interesting main dishes, well kept real ales, decent wines, friendly efficient service, open fire, small sun lounge by suntrap pretty courtyard; children in eating area *(R Huggins, D Irving, E McCall, T McLean, LYM)*

PARKEND [SO6208]

Fountain [just off B4234]: Homely and welcoming, with assorted chairs and settles, real fire, old local tools and photographs, freshly made food inc good range of curries, efficient landlord, well kept local Freeminer and guest beers; children welcome *(Pete Baker)*

☆ *Woodman* [Whitecroft]: Roomy and relaxed stripped-stone bar, two open fires, heavy beams, forest and forestry decorations, mix of furnishings inc some modern seats, smaller back bar and dining room, well presented food (not Sun or Mon evenings) inc good vegetarian range, children's meals and Sun lunch, well kept Greene King Old Speckled Hen and Wadworths 6X, decent wines, pleasant service, evening bistro (Thurs-Sat); picnic-sets on front terrace facing green, more out behind, good walks into Forest of Dean; bedrooms *(Neil and Anita Christopher, BB, Bernard Stradling)*

PERROTTS BROOK [SP0105]

Bear [A435 Cirencester—Gloucester]: Well run and popular beamed roadside pub, plenty of atmosphere, comfortable seating, well kept real ales, enjoyable food *(R Huggins, D Irving, E McCall, T McLean)*

PILLOWELL [SO6306]

Swan Cheesehouse [off B4234 Lydney—Parkend; Corner Rd]: Small carefully run pub, its bar food confined to ploughman's but with choice of several dozen unusual mainly local cheeses, good chutneys and pickles, also remarkable range of bottle-conditioned ales, and local and West Country wines; attentive licensees, cheese/beer shop; no children or dogs, cl lunchtimes Mon/Tues and winter Weds *(Bernard Stradling)*

POULTON [SP1001]

Falcon [London Rd]: Pleasantly redecorated by new owners, good food, well kept real ales, nice choice of wines, good service, big fireplace, long dining room; children welcome, tables outside, pretty village with ancient church *(Fiona Duncan, CMW, JJW, Peter and Audrey Dowsett)*

PRESTBURY [SO9624]

☆ *Plough* [Mill St]: Well preserved thatched village local, cosy and comfortable front lounge with panelling-look wallpaper, service from corridor counter in basic but roomy flagstoned back taproom, grandfather clock and big log fire, consistently friendly service, well kept Greene King Abbot and Charles Wells Bombardier tapped from the cask, homely food from good fresh sandwiches up; lovely flower-filled back garden *(Roger and Jenny Huggins, Di and Mike Gillam)*

Royal Oak [The Burgage]: Small comfortable village local doing good freshly made restaurant food at sensible prices, good service, nice house wines, welcoming atmosphere, well kept ales such as Archers, Timothy Taylors Landlord and Wadworths 6X in low-beamed bar, no fruit machines or small children inside; good-sized garden behind, open all day summer wknds *(Mr and Nrs R L Fraser)*

REDBROOK [SO5410]

☆ *Boat* [car park signed on A466 Chepstow—Monmouth, then 100-yard footbridge over Wye]: Beautifully set laid-back Wyeside walkers' pub, friendly landlord, changing well kept ales such as Black Sheep, Spinning Dog, Wadworths and Wye Valley tapped from casks, good range of country wines and hot drinks, roaring woodburner, a couple of cats and beautiful old english sheepdog, inexpensive usual food inc good value baked potatoes, fresh baguettes and children's dishes; dogs and children welcome, live music Tues and Thurs, rough home-built seats in informal garden with stream spilling down waterfall cliffs into duck pond, open all day wknds *(Keith Stevens, LYM, LM, Mr and Mrs P Talbot, Mr and Mrs R A Newbury, Phil and Heidi Cook, David Carr, Bob and Margaret Holder)*

RODBOROUGH [SO8404]

Bear [Rodborough Common]: Comfortably cosy and pubby beamed and flagstoned bar in smart hotel, friendly staff, pleasant window seats, welcoming log fire, hops hung around top of golden stone walls, interesting reproductions, well kept Bass and Uley, good value food (bar and restaurant); children welcome *(R Huggins, D Irving, E McCall, T McLean, BB)*

SAPPERTON [SO9403]

Daneway Inn [Daneway; off A419 Stroud—Cirencester]: Flagstone-floored local worth tracking down for its tables on terrace and lovely sloping lawn in charming quiet wooded countryside near ambitious canal restoration project with good walks and interesting tunnel; amazing floor-to-ceiling carved oak dutch fireplace, sporting prints, well kept Wadworths IPA, 6X and a guest such as Adnams, Weston's farm cider, food from filled baps up (may be a wait), small no smoking family room, traditional games in inglenook public bar; camping possible *(Richard Gibbs, Dave Irving, R Huggins, D Irving, E McCall, T McLean, Richard Stancomb, LYM)*

SIDDINGTON [SU0399]

☆ *Greyhound* [Ashton Rd; village signed from A419 roundabout at Tesco]: Friendly licensees and enjoyable food from good sandwiches up in two unpretentious linked rooms each with a big log fire, furnishings rearranged making them feel lighter and roomier, well kept Badger Tanglefoot, Wadworths IPA and seasonal beers, public bar with slate floor, darts and cribbage, striking deep well in skittle alley/function room; piped music may be loud and service can slow on busy lunchtimes; garden tables *(LYM, P R and S A White, R Huggins, D Irving, E McCall, T McLean, Peter and Audrey Dowsett)*

SLAD [SO8707]

Woolpack [B4070 Stroud—Birdlip]: Small hillside village pub with lovely valley views, several linked rooms with Laurie Lee photographs, some of his books for sale, good value food (not Sun evening) from sandwiches and baguettes to enjoyable hot dishes inc generous Sun roast, well kept Bass and Uley ales, farm cider and perry, log fire and nice tables, games and cards *(R Huggins, D Irving, E McCall, T McLean, Matthew Shackle, Pete Baker)*

SNOWSHILL [SP0934]

Snowshill Arms: Handy for Snowshill Manor and for Cotswold Way walkers, with friendly service, well kept Donnington BB and SBA, log fire, spruce and airy carpeted bar, neat array of tables, local photographs, stripped stone, quickly served food (fill in your own order form); skittle alley, charming village views from bow windows and from big back garden with little stream and play area, friendly local feel midweek winter and evenings, can be very crowded other lunchtimes – get there early; children welcome if eating, nearby parking may be difficult *(LYM, Maysie Thompson, Martin Jennings, David and Anthea Eeles, C A Hall)*

SOUTH CERNEY [SU0496]

Royal Oak [High St]: Sympathetically extended local, Bass, Greene King and Ushers Founders, lively atmosphere; pleasant garden with big terrace and summer marquee *(R Huggins, D Irving, E McCall, T McLean)*

SOUTHROP [SP2003]

☆ *Swan*: Attractively refurbished low-ceilinged dining lounge with log fire and flagstones, well spaced tables and good generous interesting food, friendly attentive staff, real ales such as Greene King IPA and Marstons Pedigree, good wines, no smoking restaurant (not Sun evening); stripped stone skittle alley, public bar, children welcome; pretty village esp at daffodil time *(Mrs M Milsom, LYM, Mrs Challiner)*

STANTON [SP0734]

Mount [off B4632 SW of Broadway; no through road up hill, bear left]: Gorgeous spot up steep lane from golden-stone village, with views to welsh mountains; heavy beams, flagstones and big log fire in original core, horseracing pictures and trappings and plenty of locals, roomy picture-window extensions, one no smoking with cricket memorabilia; well kept Donnington BB and SBA, farm cider, bar food (not Sun evening) from interestingly filled baguettes up; open all day Sat and summer Sun, well behaved children allowed, tables outside *(Richard and Karen Holt, Di and Mike Gillam, Christopher and Jo Barton, Bruce M Drew, Tim and Carolyn Lowes, Pam Adsley, LYM, Martin Jennings, Lawrence Pearse)*

STAVERTON [SO9024]

☆ *House in the Tree* [Haydon (B4063 W of Cheltenham)]: Pleasantly busy spick-and-span beamed and partly flagstoned pub, friendly efficient service, Fullers London Pride and Tetleys, Bulmer's and Thatcher's farm ciders, good value straightforward food on huge plates in main part's rambling linked areas inc no smoking area, nice little public bar with high-backed settles by big inglenook log fire (and TV for sports); plenty of tables in garden with good play area and pets corner *(BB)*

STOW-ON-THE-WOLD [SP1729]

☆ *Coach & Horses* [Ganborough (A424 N)]: Warmly welcoming beamed and flagstoned country pub alone on former coaching road, cheerful relaxed service, good value

Donnington BB and SBA, very wide choice of popular generous well priced food (all day summer Fri/Sat) from baguettes to some interesting dishes, good fires, steps up to carpeted dining area with high-backed settles, no smoking area; popular skittle alley, children welcome, tables in garden, open all day Sun too *(Mrs N W Neill, A H C Rainier, Giles Francis, LYM, Les and Barbara Owen, John Kane)*

☆ *Kings Arms* [The Square]: Doing well under new management, small choice of reasonably priced good food in pleasant bar and charming upstairs dining room overlooking town, Greene King Old Speckled Hen and Ruddles County, some Mackintosh-style chairs on polished boards, bowed black beams, some panelling and stripped stone; bedrooms, open all day – opens early for coffee *(BB, Peter Burton, Michael and Anne Brown)*

☆ *Queens Head* [The Square]: Good proper pub, chatty and relaxing, with heavily beamed and flagstoned traditional back bar, high-backed settles, big log fire, horse prints, piped classical or opera, usual games; lots of tables in civilised stripped stone front lounge, straightforward fresh food (not Mon evening or Sun), well kept Donnington BB and SBA, decent house wines, mulled wine, friendly helpful service, nice dogs; children welcome, tables outside, occasional jazz Sun lunchtime *(LYM, C A Hall, Guy Vowles, the Didler, Klaus and Elizabeth Leist)*

Roman Court [Fosseway, just S nr A424/A429 junction at foot of Stow Hill]: Restaurardy pub with good authentic italian food in bar eating area and no smoking dining room with small pre-meal seating area *(Mr and Mrs I Bell)*

☆ *Talbot* [The Square]: Light, airy and spacious modern décor, brasserie/wine bar feel, plain tables and chairs on new wood block floor, modern prints, genteel relaxed atmosphere, attractive reasonably priced continental-feel food, three real ales, lots of good value wines by the glass, good coffee, daily papers, big log fire, bright friendly service even when busy; may be piped radio, lavatories upstairs; bedrooms nearby, open all day *(George Atkinson, Guy Vowles, BB, W W Burke)*

STROUD [SO8505]

Queen Victoria [Gloucester St]: Welcoming local with unusual changing ales such as Milton Zeus, Smiles, Springhead Roundheads Gold and Woodfordes Great Eastern, good baps; wknd live music; tables outside *(Dave Braisted)*

SWINEFORD [ST6969]

Swan [A431, right on the Somerset border]: Converted from three cottages, food in bar with no smoking area and restaurant inc popular good value Sun roasts (booked weeks ahead), Bass tapped from the cask and other ales such as Butcombe, friendly attentive staff *(Peter Scillitoe)*

TETBURY [ST8993]

Crown [Gumstool Hill]: Large 17th-c town pub, good value bar lunches, well kept ales such as Black Sheep and Hook Norton Best,

long oak-beamed front bar with big log fire and attractive medley of tables, efficient service; may be unobtrusive piped music; pleasant back no smoking family dining conservatory with lots of plants, picnic-sets on back terrace, comfortable bedrooms *(R Huggins, D Irving, E McCall, T McLean)*

Snooty Fox [Market Pl]: Good unusual food and well kept beer in welcoming high-ceilinged hotel lounge with medieval-style chairs and elegant fireplace, restaurant; bedrooms good value *(Patricia A Bruce, Barry and Anne)*

TEWKESBURY [SO8932]

Berkeley Arms [Church St]: Pleasantly olde-worlde medieval timbered pub (most striking part down the side alley), with well kept Wadworths real ales, friendly new tenant, open fire, wide range of food, separate front public bar (can be smoky), raftered ancient back barn restaurant; open all day summer, bedrooms *(Theocsbrian)*

☆ *Olde Black Bear* [High St]: County's oldest pub, rambling unpretentious rooms with heavy low beams (one with leather-clad ceiling), lots of timbers, armchairs in front of open fires, bare wood and ancient tiles, plenty of pictures and bric-a-brac, well kept beers such as Greenalls and Charles Wells Bombardier, reasonably priced wines, friendly staff, food all day from lunchtime baguettes up, no smoking dining room; piped music, quiz nights Weds and Sun; children welcome, terrace and play area in riverside garden, open all day *(the Didler, David Carr, John Beeken, LYM)*

TOCKINGTON [ST6186]

Swan: Clean, bright and spacious, recovered from 2003 fire damage, with beams, standing timbers, bric-a-brac on stripped stone walls, log fire still, good range of reasonably priced food, friendly staff, Greene King real ales; piped music; good wheelchair access, tables in tree-shaded garden, quiet village *(Pamela and Merlyn Horswell, Charles and Pauline Stride)*

TYTHERINGTON [ST6688]

Swan [Duck St]: Big well furnished family food pub with good choice (all day Sun) from sandwiches, baguettes and baked potatoes to some interesting specials, no smoking area, children's room; huge car park, very busy wknds *(Mr and Mrs P Cowley)*

ULEY [ST7998]

Old Crown [The Green]: Unpretentious pub prettily set by village green just off Cotswold Way, long narrow lounge with settles and wooden floors, friendly staff, enjoyable home cooking from sandwiches and baked potatoes to good fish choice, four well kept changing ales such as Uley and Wye Valley, small games room up spiral stairs with pool, darts etc; dogs welcome; attractive garden, bedrooms *(Di and Mike Gillam, Geoffrey Tyack)*

WHITMINSTER [SO7708]

Fromebridge Mill [A38 nr M5 junction 13]: Large recently done mill-based eatery with attractively extended bar and dining areas, decent reasonably priced food from sandwiches and baked potatoes up inc popular good value lunchtime carvery, Greene King real ales, friendly helpful staff; picnic-sets out behind with play area, lovely setting overlooking weir *(Mike and Mary Carter, Peter Scillitoe, Pauline and Philip Darley)*

Old Forge [A38 1½ miles N of M5 junction 13]: Simple L-shaped beamed pub with small carpeted bar, games room and no smoking dining room, good inexpensive food (not Sun evening or Mon) inc bargain lunch, well kept real ales such as Black Sheep, Exmoor and Wickwar Cotswold Way, happy staff, decent wines; children welcome *(R Huggins, D Irving, E McCall, T McLean, Tony Hobden)*

WICK [ST7072]

Rose & Crown [High St (A420)]: Well run Chef & Brewer, busy and roomy, plenty of character in largely untouched linked 17th-c rooms with low beams, mixed furnishings and candlelight, well kept Courage Best and one or two other ales, interesting wine choice, very wide blackboard food range from good value lunchtime sandwiches and baguettes to unusual fish dishes (only main meals on Sun), efficient, friendly and helpful staff, daily papers; pleasant tables facing village green *(Michael Doswell, Andrew Shore, Dr and Mrs M E Wilson, Ron Shelton, Dr Louise Bawden, Dr Ed Bond)*

WILLERSEY [SP1039]

☆ *Bell* [B4632 Cheltenham—Stratford, nr Broadway]: Attractive stone-built pub, open-plan and much modernised, front part comfortably set for the carefully prepared interesting but unpretentious home-made food, Aston Villa memorabilia and huge collection of model cars in back area past the big L-shaped bar counter with its well kept Hook Norton Best, Tetleys and Wadworths 6X, relaxed atmosphere, friendly helpful service; darts, may be piped music, Thurs evening chess ladder; overlooks delightful village's green and duck pond, lots of tables in big garden, bedrooms in outbuildings *(Alec Hamilton, Alan Cowell, Miss J Brotherton, BB)*

WINCHCOMBE [SP0228]

Old Corner Cupboard [Gloucester St]: Newish licensees doing promising food in attractive golden stone pub, well kept Fullers London Pride, Hook Norton Old Hooky and seasonal local Stanway ales, decent wines, comfortable stripped-stone lounge bar with heavy-beamed Tudor core, traditional hatch-service lobby, small side smoke room with woodburner in massive stone fireplace, partly no smoking restaurant, some nice old furnishings and traditional games; children in eating areas, tables in back garden, open all day *(Di and Mike Gillam, George Atkinson, Joyce and Geoff Robson, Martin Jones, Norman and Sarah Keeping, BB, LYM, Dave Braisted)*

☆ *Plaisterers Arms* [Abbey Terr]: 18th-c pub with stripped stonework, beams, Hogarth prints, bric-a-brac and flame-effect fires, two chatty front bars both with steps down to dim-lit lower back dining area with tables in stalls, rewarding and enterprising cooking by Irish landlady, good service, well kept Goffs Jouster, Greene King Old Speckled Hen and Ushers

Best; dogs very welcome, good play area in charming garden, long and narrow; comfortable bedrooms (up tricky stairs), handy for Sudeley Castle *(BB, George Atkinson, John Whitehead, Di and Mike Gillam, Martin Jones, Neil and Anita Christopher, Joyce and Maurice Cottrell, W W Burke)*

WITHINGTON [SP0315]

Kings Head [Kings Head Lane]: Unpretentious local, well kept Hook Norton Best and a changing Wickwar beer tapped from the cask, friendly service, long narrow bar with darts, shove-ha'penny, table skittles and pool, lounge with piano, may be pork pies and pickled eggs; pleasant garden behind *(Pete Baker)*

☆ *Mill Inn* [off A436 or A40]: Idyllic streamside setting for mossy-roofed old stone inn, with tables out in pretty garden including some on small island, splendid walks all around; beams, flagstones, big stone fireplaces, plenty of character with nice nooks and corners, well kept low-priced Sam Smiths OB, decent wine list, darts and dominoes, no smoking dining room, food from baguettes and baked potatoes up; piped music; children very welcome, bedrooms *(LYM, Rod Stoneman, Nick and Meriel Cox, Susan and Nigel Wilson, Mary Rayner, John and Joan Wyatt, R Huggins, D Irving, E McCall, T McLean, Roger and Pauline Pearce, John Holroyd, Mike and Mary Carter, Martin Jennings, Dick and Mary Pownall)*

WOODCHESTER [SO8302]

☆ *Ram* [Station Rd, South Woodchester]: Attractively priced well kept ales such as Archers Best, John Smiths, Theakstons Old Peculier, Uley Old Spot and several interesting guest beers, in relaxed L-shaped beamed bar with friendly staff, nice mix of traditional furnishings, stripped stonework, bare boards, three open fires, darts, varied menu from good value generous baguettes to steaks, restaurant; children welcome, open all day Sat/Sun, spectacular views from terrace tables *(Gill and Tony Morriss, LYM, R Huggins, D Irving, E McCall, T McLean, Tom and Ruth Rees)*

☆ *Royal Oak* [off A46; Church Road, N Woodchester]: Good-humoured new licensees still doing a good choice of well kept ales such as Bath and Uley, scrubbed tables and chapel chairs in several pleasant areas inc upstairs dining room with great valley view, big log fire in huge fireplace, decent food (not Sun evening or Mon lunchtime) inc baguettes and some interesting specials; big-screen TV, piped music; children and dogs welcome, open all day Sat *(R Huggins, D Irving, E McCall, T McLean, LYM, Alan Bowker)*

WOOLASTON COMMON [SO5900]

Rising Sun [village signed off A48 Lydney—Chepstow]: Unpretentiously old-fashioned village pub on fringe of Forest of Dean, friendly and welcoming, reasonably priced fresh food (not Weds evening) inc curries, well kept Fullers London Pride, Hook Norton and usually a guest beer, darts and piano in side area (folk nights alternate Tues); seats outside, cl Weds lunchtime *(Pete Baker)*

Hampshire

Half a dozen new entries here this year span quite a range of styles: the Vine in Hambledon (a proper traditional country pub of the best sort, good all round), the Kings Head in Lymington (a dim-lit 17th-c town pub, attractively remodelled to make the most of its considerable character), the pretty thatched Black Swan at Monxton (good value food, especially its bargain OAP lunches), the cheerful Castle Inn in Rowland's Castle (good value here too), the cosily low-beamed Chequers at Well (enjoyable food and friendly service) and the highly idiosyncratic Black Boy in Winchester (good fun to look around, and good beers). Another dozen pubs here stand out for the warmth of the reports we have been getting on them in the last few months: the cosy and chatty Sun at Bentworth (great beers, nice home-made food), the Red Lion at Boldre (hearty food in a good part of the New Forest for walks), the civilised Fox at Bramdean (gaining a Food Award this year for the landlord's good cooking), the Flower Pots at Cheriton (an unspoilt village local brewing its own good beers), the Star at East Tytherleigh (great enthusiasm for its food and atmosphere), the simple and cheerful thatched Royal Oak, part of a working farm deep in the New Forest at Fritham (good beers), the Trooper up above Petersfield (good all round under its very welcoming landlord, with particularly enjoyable food), the Wine Vaults in Southsea (despite its name great for beer-lovers, with food all day too), the friendly and well run Plough at Sparsholt (excellent food), the delightfully unspoilt and unchanging Harrow at Steep, the cosy and relaxing little Three Cups in Stockbridge (new to us last year and already becoming a favourite), and the Brushmakers Arms at Upham (another friendly and attractive all-rounder). Good food stands out as a plus in several of these. It's also a major part of the appeal in the interesting rather upmarket Chestnut Horse at Easton (which gains its Food Award this year), the prettily set Bush at Ovington, and the bustling Wykeham Arms in Winchester. The top award of Hampshire Dining Pub of the Year goes to the Plough at Sparsholt. Quite a few pubs in the Lucky Dip section at the end of the chapter are showing particularly well these days: the Globe and Horse & Groom in Alresford, Crown at Arford, Dog & Crook at Brambridge, Three Tuns at Bransgore, Hampshire Arms in Crondall, Hampshire Bowman at Dundridge, George in East Meon, Alverbank House in Gosport, John o' Gaunt at Horsebridge, Trout at Itchen Abbas, Red Shoot at Linwood, Jolly Farmer in Locks Heath, Pilgrim in Marchwood, Trusty Servant at Minstead, Still & West in Portsmouth, Woolpack at Sopley, Cricketers Arms and Fox, both at Tangley, Jekyll & Hyde at Turgis Green and Horse & Groom at Woodgreen. Drinks prices in Hampshire pubs tend to be 10p or so higher than the national average. The Chestnut Horse at Easton (stocking local Itchen Valley beer), Flower Pots at Cheriton (brewing its own) and particularly the Brushmakers Arms at Upham (also with a local beer, from Ringwood) stood out as particularly good value for beers. Gales and Ringwood are the county's main brewers. Smaller ones to look out for include Hampshire, Becketts, Oakleaf and fff.

AXFORD SU6043 Map 2
Crown ♀
B3046 S of Basingstoke

Rambling around a central servery, the three compact rooms at this tucked-away country pub open together enough to build a chatty atmosphere, but each keeps its own character: appealing late 19th-c local villager photographs, cream walls, patterned carpet and stripped boards on the left, for instance, abstract prints on pale terracotta walls and rush carpeting on the right. Furnishings are largely stripped tables and chapel chairs, and each room is candlelit at night, with a small winter log fire; daily papers, and unobtrusive piped music. You'll find well kept Fullers London Pride and Triple fff Moondance on handpump, and the wine list includes a nice choice by the glass. Enjoyable food might be creamy wild mushrooms in paprika sauce (£4.25), grilled goats cheese with onion marmalade (£4.50), filled ciabattas or ploughman's (£5.95), beef and Guinness pie (£8.50), thai chicken curry (£9.95), and 10oz sirloin steak (£13.50), with home-made puddings such as white chocolate and Baileys mousse and tiramisu (£3.95). There are picnic-sets out in the front, and a sloping shrub-sheltered garden behind has a suntrap terrace, and countryside views; the friendly, helpful landlord plans to hold barbecues in summer. Readers tell us there are lovely walks around Moundsmere, and in the woods of Preston Oak Hills (bluebells in May). *(Recommended by Tony and Wendy Hobden, Julian McCarthy, Phyl and Jack Street, Lynn Sharpless)*

Free house ~ Licensee Steve Nicholls ~ Real ale ~ Bar food (12-2.30, 6.30-9.30) ~ Restaurant ~ (01256) 389492 ~ Children in eating area of bar and restaurant, not Fri/Sat nights ~ Dogs allowed in bar ~ Open 12-3, 6-11(10.30 Sun)

BANK SU2807 Map 2
Oak ◖
Signposted just off A35 SW of Lyndhurst

Now with a new landlady, this 18th-c pub is peacefully set, but inside you'll find it bustling with a welcoming mix of customers. Friendly staff serve well kept Bass, Holdens Black Country Special, Ringwood Best, and a couple of guests such as Black Sheep or Hop Back Summer Lightning drawn straight from the barrel; country wines too. On either side of the door in the bay windows of the L-shaped bar are built-in green-cushioned seats, and on the right, two or three little pine-panelled booths with small built-in tables and bench seats. The rest of the bar has more floor space, with candles in individual brass holders on a line of stripped old and blond newer tables set against the wall on bare floorboards, and more at the back; some low beams and joists, fishing rods, spears, and a boomerang, and old ski poles on the ceiling, and on the walls are brass platters, heavy knives, stuffed fish, and guns; a big fireplace. There are cushioned milk churns along the bar counter, and little red lanterns among hop bines above the bar; piped music, shove-ha'penny, and dominoes. Bar food includes tasty lunchtime sandwiches (from £3.95), and ploughman's (from £4.95), as well as home-made soup (£3.95), home-cooked ham and eggs or local sausages (£6.95), home-made pie (£7.95), rib-eye steak (from £10.95), and daily specials such as venison steak (£12.95) with a good choice of fish specials such as sardines (£6.95), plaice (£9.50), and bass (£12.95); puddings such as treacle pudding (£3.95). The side garden has picnic-sets and long tables and benches by the big yew trees. *(Recommended by Diana Brumfit, M Joyner, Jess and George Cowley, D Lamping, I Sachdev, J V Dadswell, Dennis Jenkin, R T and J C Moggridge, David M Cundy, Lynn Sharpless, Tom and Ruth Rees, Prof Keith and Mrs Jane Barber)*

Free house ~ Licensee Karen Slowen ~ Real ale ~ Bar food ~ (023) 8028 2350 ~ Children in eating area of bar ~ Dogs welcome ~ Open 11-3, 6-11; 11-11 Sat; 12-10.30 Sun

---

You can send us reports through our web site: www.goodguides.com

BENTWORTH SU6740 Map 2

Sun 🍷

Sun Hill; from the A339 coming from Alton the first turning takes you there direct; or in village follow Shalden 2¼, Alton 4¼ signpost

The chatty, cosy atmosphere at this especially friendly, tucked away pub isn't spoilt by any noisy games machines or piped music. Pleasant staff serve eight well kept real ales on handpump such as Badger Tanglefoot, Bass, Brakspears Bitter, Cheriton Pots, Fullers London Pride, Ringwood Best, Stonehenge Pigswill, and a beer from Hampshire named after the pub; several malt whiskies. The two little traditional communicating rooms have high-backed antique settles, pews and schoolroom chairs, olde-worlde prints and blacksmith's tools on the walls, and bare boards and scrubbed deal tables on the left; big fireplaces with roaring fires and candles make it especially snug in winter (over Christmas the pub is handsomely decorated). An arch leads to a brick-floored room with another open fire and hanging baskets. Enjoyable home-made bar food includes soup (£2.95), good sandwiches (around £2.95), chicken fajitas, poached salmon or steak and kidney pie (£7.95), lamb cutlets or liver and bacon with onion gravy (£8.95), and dressed crab (£10.95), while puddings could include white chocolate cheesecake (£3.25); they do a good Sunday roast (£7.95). There are seats out in front and in the back garden, and pleasant nearby walks. *(Recommended by Martin and Karen Wake, Ann and Colin Hunt, Simon Fox, R Lake, the Didler, Lynn Sharpless, Mr and Mrs P L Haigh, John Hale, Ian Phillips, Phyl and Jack Street, Andrew Scarr, Tim and Carolyn Lowes, John Davis)*

Free house ~ Licensee Mary Holmes ~ Real ale ~ Bar food ~ (01420) 562338 ~ Children in family room ~ Dogs welcome ~ Open 12-3, 6-11; 12-10.30 Sun

BOLDRE SZ3198 Map 2

Red Lion ★ ♀

Village signposted from A337 N of Lymington

In a fine area for walking, with 1,000 acres of Royden Wood to explore, this warmly welcoming New Forest pub is a great place to stop for a hearty meal. In summer, the flowering tubs and hanging baskets outside are charming, with tables out in the back garden. The four neatly kept black-beamed rooms are filled with heavy urns, platters, needlework, rural landscapes and so forth, taking in farm tools, heavy-horse harness, needlework, gin traps and even ferocious-looking man traps along the way. The central room has a profusion of chamber-pots, and an end room has pews, wheelback chairs and tapestried stools, and a dainty collection of old bottles and glasses in the window by the counter; most of the pub is no smoking. There's a fine old cooking range in the cosy little bar, and two good log fires; staff are friendly and very attentive. Generously served and enjoyable (though not particularly cheap) bar food includes sandwiches (from £3.95; club sandwich £6.50), filling starters such as whitebait or home-made salmon and crab fishcakes (£5.90), ploughman's (£6.50), mushrooms stroganoff or vegetable teriyaki (£8.20), home-made steak and kidney pie (£9.90), and half a crispy gressingham duck (£11.50), with daily specials such as fried chicken breast in garlic, bacon and mushroom sauce (£9.90) and monkfish medallions with prawn and saffron sauce (£12.40); puddings could be pecan and rum tart or fruit trifle (£4.25). They've an extensive wine list, and well kept Bass and Flowers IPA on handpump. No children inside. *(Recommended by Lynn Sharpless, Phyl and Jack Street, JMC, D Lamping, I Sachdev, M Joyner, John Davis, Mrs J L Wyatt, Miss J F Reay, Joan and Michel Hooper-Immins, A D Marsh, Mr and Mrs W D Borthwick, Peter Saville, Prof Keith and Mrs Jane Barber)*

Eldridge Pope ~ Tenant Vince Kernick ~ Real ale ~ Bar food (12-2.30, 6.30-9; 12-2.30, 6.30-9.30 wknds) ~ Restaurant ~ (01590) 673177 ~ Open 11-11; 12-10.30 Sun

---

Pubs staying open all afternoon at least one day a week are listed at the back of the book.

BRAMDEAN SU6127 Map 2
Fox ⓦ

A272 Winchester—Petersfield

With an appealingly civilised atmosphere, this well run dining pub is a popular choice for a relaxed meal. Beautifully cooked by the landlord using lots of fresh ingredients, the food includes a good selection of fish, and lunchtime dishes such as sandwiches (from £2.25), soup (£3.50), baked brie in filo pastry with redcurrant jelly (£5.95), fried scallops with bacon (£6.95), home-made steak and kidney pie (£9.95) and fresh salmon fillet with lime and chilli butter or grilled lamb cutlets (£10.95). Evening choices run to sirloin steak with onions, garlic and tomatoes (£13.95), and monkfish fillet with tarragon sauce or half a roast duck with orange gravy (£14.95); puddings could include apple and almond crumble and summer pudding (£4.25). The carefully modernised open-plan bar has black beams, tall stools with proper backrests around the L-shaped counter, and comfortably cushioned wall pews and wheelback chairs – the fox motif shows in a big painting over the fireplace, and on much of the decorative china. At least one area is no smoking. Well kept Greene King Abbot on handpump; piped music. At the back of the building is a walled-in terraced area, and a spacious lawn spreading among the fruit trees; a play area has a climbing frame and slide. No children inside. Good surrounding walks. *(Recommended by Michael and Robin Inskip, Father Robert Marsh, John Davis, W A Evershed, Phyl and Jack Street, Meg and Colin Hamilton, Betty Laker, Charles and Pauline Stride, Tony and Wendy Hobden, W W Burke)*

Greene King ~ Tenants Ian and Jane Inder ~ Real ale ~ Bar food ~ (01962) 771363 ~ Open 11-3, 6-11; 12-3, 7-10.30 Sun

BURSLEDON SU4809 Map 2
Jolly Sailor ♀

2 miles from M27 junction 8; then A27 towards Sarisbury, then just before going under railway bridge turn right towards Bursledon Station; it's best to park round here and walk as the lane up from the station is now closed to cars

A great place to while away an afternoon watching the boats on the River Hamble, this well run pub has seats in the courtyard under a big yew tree, and on the covered wooden jetty looking over the harbour. Inside is nice too, and the airy front bar has ship pictures, nets and shells, as well as windsor chairs and settles on the floorboards; the window seat gives views of the water. The beamed and flagstoned back bar, with pews and settles by its huge fireplace, is a fair bit older. They serve well kept Badger Best, K&B, Tanglefoot and Gribble Fursty Ferret on handpump, eight wines by the glass, freshly squeezed juice, and country wines; Battleships, Jenga, Connect Four, and piped music. Besides sandwiches (from £3.95), well prepared bar food includes home-made soup (£3.40), prawns and noodles topped with mascarpone and crab cream (£5.50), ploughman's (£6.50), roasted vegetable and goats cheese tart (£7.95), trio of sausages with mash and onion gravy or lime and coriander chicken salad (£8.50), seafood pie (£8.95), moules marinière (£9.95), and sirloin steak (from £11.95), with daily specials such as seafood chowder (£3.40), coriander and chilli marinated pork steak (£8.95), salmon with dill and ginger sauce (£10.50), and chargrilled tuna steak with mustard sauce (£10.95); children's menu (£3.50). The dining area is no smoking. The path down to the pub from the lane is steep (and the steps really rule out disabled access). *(Recommended by Ian Phillips, Colin McKerrow, Alan Thomas, Ann and Colin Hunt, John and Judy Saville, the Didler, Stephen, Julie and Hayley Brown, Charles and Pauline Stride, Roger and Pauline Pearce, Tony and Wendy Hobden, John Davis, Jess and George Cowley)*

Badger ~ Managers Adrian Jenkins and Jackie Cosens ~ Real ale ~ Bar food (12-9.30) ~ (023) 8040 5557 ~ Children in no smoking area ~ Dogs welcome ~ Open 11-11; 12-10.30 Sun

CHALTON SU7315 Map 2
Red Lion

Village signposted E of A3 Petersfield—Horndean

First licensed in 1503, this handsome timbered and thatched pub is Hampshire's oldest (and apparently began life in 1147 as a workshop and residence for the craftsmen constructing St Michael's church opposite). The most characterful part is the heavy-beamed and panelled front bar with high-backed traditional settles and elm tables, and an ancient inglenook fireplace with a frieze of burnished threepenny bits set into its mantelbeam; the lounge and dining room are no smoking. The garden is pretty in summer and the pub is popular with walkers and riders as it is fairly close to the extensive Queen Elizabeth Country Park, and about half a mile from an Iron Age farm and settlement. Good bar food includes sandwiches or filled baguettes (from £3.55), filled baked potatoes (from £4.85), and ploughman's (from £5.25), plus lots of daily specials such as home-made soup (£3.75), oyster mushroom stroganoff (£7.50), mixed game parcels with cranberry and redcurrant gravy (£8.75), slow-roasted lamb shank with mango and ginger (£8.95), pacific kingfish with macadamia nut butter (£9.50), marlin steak (£10.50), and puddings such as treacle tart or strawberry shortbread (£3.50). You are offered a choice of potatoes: colcannon (creamed potato with leeks, cabbage and butter), dauphinoise, cheesy, baked or chips. There are also various toppings for fish: lime, coconut and coriander mayonnaise, tomato, tangy lemon chutney or ginger and sweet pepper glaze. Well kept Gales Butser, GB, HSB, Festival Mild and a couple of guests such as Marstons Pedigree or Wadworths 6X on handpump, country wines, and over 50 malt whiskies; piped music. The car ferry is only about 20 minutes away from here. More reports please. *(Recommended by P R and S A White, Ann and Colin Hunt, Ian Phillips, Tony and Wendy Hobden)*

Gales ~ Managers Mick and Mary McGee ~ Real ale ~ Bar food (not Sun evening) ~ Restaurant ~ (023) 9259 2246 ~ Children in restaurant ~ Dogs allowed in bar ~ Open 11-3, 6-11; 12-3, 7-10.30 Sun; closed evenings 25/26 Dec

CHERITON SU5828 Map 2
Flower Pots ★ ◀ £

Pub just off B3046 (main village road) towards Beauworth and Winchester; OS Sheet 185 map reference 581282

They serve very good value Cheriton beers from the brewhouse beside this charmingly unspoilt village local: well kept Pots, Diggers Gold and Cheriton Best tapped from casks behind the bar. The two little rooms get a good mix of customers – the one on the left is a favourite, almost like someone's front room, with pictures of hounds and ploughmen on its striped wallpaper, bunches of flowers, and a horse and foal and other ornaments on the mantelpiece over a small log fire; it can get smoky in here. Behind the servery is disused copper filtering equipment, and lots of hanging gin traps, drag-hooks, scaleyards and other ironwork. The neat extended plain public bar (where there's a covered well) has cribbage, shove-ha'penny and dominoes. Very useful in fine weather (when the pub can fill up quickly), the pretty front and back lawns have some old-fashioned seats; in summer they sometimes have morris dancers out here. Bar food prices have hardly changed since last year, and on the fairly short straightforward menu, you'll find sandwiches (from £2.20; toasties from £2.50; big baps from £3), winter home-made soup (£3), filled baked potatoes (from £3.90), ploughman's (from £4.30), and hotpots such as lamb and apricot, chilli or beef stew (from £5.20); popular indian dishes on Wednesday evenings; friendly service. The menu may be restricted at weekend lunchtimes, or when they're busy. The pub is near the site of one of the final battles of the Civil War; it got its name through once belonging to the retired head gardener of nearby Avington Park. No children inside. *(Recommended by Lynn Sharpless, Jenny Cridland, Gordon Cooper, Ann and Colin Hunt, Basil Cheesenham, Jess and George Cowley, Phil and Sally Gorton, Simon Collett-Jones, the Didler, Patrick Hancock, P R and S A White, Les Trusler, Colin and Janet Roe, Mark Percy, Lesley Mayoh, Tim and Carolyn Lowes, John Davis, Ron Shelton, John and Annabel Hampshire)*

Own brew ~ Licensees Jo and Patricia Bartlett ~ Real ale ~ Bar food (not Sun evening or bank hol Mon evenings) ~ No credit cards ~ (01962) 771318 ~ Dogs welcome ~ Open 12-2.30, 6-11; 12-3, 7-10.30 Sun ~ Bedrooms: £40S/£60S

DROXFORD SU6018 Map 2
White Horse

4 miles along A32 from Wickham

A lovely place to sit in fine weather, the secluded flower-filled courtyard of this rambling 17th-c inn is comfortably sheltered by the building's back wings. Inside, the lounge bar is made up of several small cosy rooms – low beams, bow windows, alcoves, and log fires, while the public bar is larger and more straightforward: pool, darts, table football, TV, cribbage, dominoes, shove-ha'penny, and a CD juke box. Welcoming staff serve well kept Greene King IPA, Abbot, Old Speckled Hen and Ruddles County on handpump, perhaps with a guest such as Cheriton Pots; they stock several malt whiskies. Besides lunchtime dishes such as sandwiches (from £2), baguettes or filled baked potatoes (from £2.50), ploughman's (from £3.75), and ham, egg and chips (£5), popular bar food could include home-made soup (£2.75), locally smoked salmon pâté (£4), thai red vegetable curry (£7.50), scotch salmon steak with cream and white wine (£7.95), chargrilled gammon steak (£8.25), and steaks (from £9.50), with daily specials such as stuffed chicken breast (£7.50), and tasty steak and game pie (£8.50), while puddings could include gooseberry crumble (from £2.50); they have a children's menu (from £2.75). The two dining rooms are no smoking. One of the cubicles in the gents' overlooks an illuminated well. It's set in rolling country – good for walking; the Southdowns Way is nearby. We had reports of some marked ups and downs in summer 2002, but since then the pub has been thoroughly back on good form. *(Recommended by Phyl and Jack Street, Ann and Colin Hunt, Lynn Sharpless, Prof and Mrs Tony Palmer, W A Eversbed, Ian Phillips)*

Greene King ~ Lease Paul Young ~ Real ale ~ Bar food (not 25/26 Dec or 1 Jan) ~ Restaurant ~ (01489) 877490 ~ Children welcome ~ Dogs allowed in bar ~ Occasional Jazz ~ Open 11(12 Sun)-11 ~ Bedrooms: £25(£40B)/£35(£50B)

EAST STRATTON SU5339 Map 2
Northbrook Arms

Brown sign to pub off A33 4 miles S of A303 junction

Now with new licensees, and open all day, this substantial brick inn looks across a quiet lane to a neat lawn with picnic-sets by an old horse-drawn plough – a nice spot, in a small thatched village. Inside has been opened into an unpretentious L-shaped area: blond wheelback chairs and solid square pale-varnished tables on quarry-tiles on the right, with a log fire, and a carpeted dining area on the left. Big windows, cream walls, a large mirror and fresh flowers give a pleasantly airy, uncluttered feel. Welcoming staff serve cold dishes such as sandwiches (from £3.50) and ploughman's all day, otherwise the enjoyable menu could include soup (£3.50), scampi and chips (£5.95), vegetarian pasta bake (£6.95), steak and ale pie or battered cod (£8.95), and duck breast (£9.95), with puddings such as cheesecake and bakewell tart (£3.50). Well kept Gales HSB and Otter Bitter along with changing mostly local guests such as Hambletons and Hop Back Best on handpump, nice bottled beers and decent house wines; piped local radio, darts, bar billiards and a skittle alley. We would expect this to be a nice place to stay; readers tell us there are fine walks nearby. *(Recommended by Lynn Sharpless, Ann and Colin Hunt)*

Free house ~ Licensees Mr Sheaff and Mr Greaves ~ Bar food (12-3, 6-9) ~ (01962) 774150 ~ Children in eating area of bar, restaurant and family room ~ Dogs welcome ~ Open 11-11; 12-10.30 Sun ~ Bedrooms: £25/£50

We say if we know a pub has piped music.

EAST TYTHERLEY SU2927 Map 2

Star 🅔 🛏

Off B3084 N of Romsey; turn off by railway crossing opp the Mill Arms at Dunbridge

This superbly run and exceptionally popular 16th-c pub wins praise all round from many readers. You can eat from the same menu in the bar or restaurant, and a bonus is that quite a few dishes are available in starter or main course helpings. Beautifully prepared food might typically include home-made soup (£3.25), sandwiches or toasted focaccia (from £3.50), well liked creamed smoked haddock in pastry case with poached egg (£4.95; main course £9.50), smoked venison (£5.95), lamb, rosemary and vegetable pie or faggots with pea and potato purée (£7.95), cumberland sausage with leek and mustard mash and black pudding or lambs liver, mash and bacon (£8.95), linguini with artichokes, french beans, mange tout and roasted tomato oil (£4.50; main course £10), steaks (from £12), and grilled bass with fennel and asparagus and langoustine jus (£16.50); gorgeous (though not cheap) puddings such as bread and butter pudding (£4.25), and pear and almond filo pastry with armagnac and apricot (£5.75). The bar has a mix of comfortable furnishings, log fires in attractive fireplaces, and horsebrasses and saddlery; there's a lower lounge bar, and a cosy and pretty no smoking restaurant. Ringwood Best and a guest such as Gales HSB are well kept on handpump, they've several malt whiskies, and a thoughtful wine list with 10 by the glass; shove-ha'penny, and a popular skittle alley for private dining. You can sit out on a smartly furnished terrace, and a children's play area has play equipment made using local reclaimed wood. The bedrooms overlook the village cricket pitch (which is used every Tuesday and Saturday through the summer); delicious breakfasts. There are good walks nearby. *(Recommended by Phyl and Jack Street, Prof and Mrs Tony Palmer, Nick and Meriel Cox, Dr and Mrs W T Farrington , Mike and Heather Watson, Terry and Linda Moseley, Mrs J A Taylar, Paul Humphreys, Derek Harvey-Piper, Andy Sinden, Louise Harrington, Mrs J Purry, Derek Hayman, Patrick Hall, Peter J and Avril Hanson)*

Free house ~ Licensees Paul and Sarah Bingham ~ Real ale ~ Bar food ~ Restaurant ~ (01794) 340225 ~ No babies in restaurant in evening ~ Dogs allowed in bar ~ Open 11-2.30, 6-11; 12-2.30, 7-10.30 Sun; closed Mon except bank hols, and 26 Dec ~ Bedrooms: £50S/£70S

EASTON SU5132 Map 2

Chestnut Horse 🅔 ♀

Village signposted off B3047 Kings Worthy—Itchen Abbas; bear left in village

A welcoming place to visit whether you're after a well prepared meal or just a civilised drink, this rather upmarket 16th-c dining pub gains a food award in this edition. There are good tables out on a smallish sheltered back terrace with colourful flower tubs and baskets (readers really like it at night when it's very prettily lit). Although inside it's all opened together, the pub manages to retain the cosy feel of small separate rooms, with a really snug décor: candles burning on all the tables even at lunchtime, dark comfortable furnishings, black beams and joists hung with all sorts of jugs, mugs and chamber-pots, lots of attractive waterfowl and other country pictures on the cream or dusky green walls, some panelling, log fires in cottagey fireplaces. The restaurant areas are no smoking. Good (though not cheap) generously served food might include home-made soup (£3.95), sandwiches or grilled open sandwiches on ciabatta (from £4.50), home-made smoked mackerel pâté (£5.95), local ham and free range eggs (£8.95), pork and leek sausages on wholegrain mustard mash with deep-fried leeks and rich onion and red wine jus (£9.95), popular fish in beer batter (£9.95; massive £12.95), steaks (from £12.95), daily specials such as baked scallops with spinach and cheese (£6.95), calves liver on crispy bacon and black pudding (£14.95), and confit of duck with bacon and apple mash and port jus or grilled fillets of sea bream with sweet chilli dressing and fresh lime (£15.95); irresistible puddings could be home-made chocolate mousse or treacle and lemon tart (£4.95). They also do a good value two-course meal (lunchtimes Monday-Saturday and 6-7.30 Monday-Thursday) for £9.95. You must book to be sure of a table at weekends, and as dishes are cooked to order, there may be a wait at busy times. Besides Chestnut Horse (brewed specially for the pub by Itchen Valley), they serve well kept Courage Best, Fullers London Pride and Youngs Special on handpump; also decent wines (10 by the glass), champagne by the glass, and more than 50 malt whiskies. The atmosphere is buoyant yet relaxed, and service is friendly and helpful; cribbage and fairly unobtrusive piped music. This sleepy village is handy for Itchen valley walks. *(Recommended by Tim and Carolyn Lowes, Lynn Sharpless, Keith and Sheila Baxter, Norman and Sheila Sales, Ron Shelton, Phyl and Jack Street, Martin and Karen Wake, Susan and John Douglas)*

Free house ~ Licensee John Holland ~ Real ale ~ Bar food (12-2.30, 6.30-9.30; 12-8.30 Sun in summer) ~ Restaurant ~ (01962) 779257 ~ Children in eating area of bar and restaurant ~ Dogs allowed in bar ~ Open 11-3, 5.30-11; 12-10.30 (6 in winter) Sun

EVERSLEY SU7861 Map 2
Golden Pot
Reading Road, Eversley; B3272

The new landlord of this little brick pub plans to continue holding the popular rösti night on Mondays; you can choose from toppings such as melted cheese and two fried eggs, pork and onion in white wine cream sauce or wild boar in a rich red wine sauce (from £6.95). Other tasty bar food might include soup (£3.95), smoked duck and orange salad or calves liver and bacon with mustard mash and caramelised onion gravy (£8.50), roasted cod with creamed potatoes, bacon, pea and mushroom broth (£8.75), pork schnitzel (£8.95), chicken breast stuffed with brie and wrapped in bacon with asparagus sauce (£10.95), and steak (from £11), with puddings such as fig and almond tart (from £4.25); they also do lunchtime baguettes. There's a comfortable atmosphere in the different spreading areas, bowls of lilies, candles in bottles on the tables, and one particularly snug part by the log-effect gas fire, with two armchairs and a sofa. Well kept Greene King Abbot and Ruddles County, and a guest such as Batemans XXXB on handpump, and eight wines by the glass; piped music. The pretty restaurant is no smoking. There are some picnic-sets under a pergola overlooking fields as well as in front by the car park; the masses of colourful flowering tubs, pots and window boxes carry on through the summer and right into autumn. *(Recommended by Martin and Karen Wake, Mr and Mrs S Felstead, Francis Johnston, Ian Phillips, P J Ridley, Philip and June Caunt, KC)*

Greene King ~ Lease John Calder ~ Real ale ~ Bar food ~ Restaurant ~ (0118) 973 2104 ~ Pianist/vocalist/guitarist Mon evening ~ Dogs allowed in bar ~ Open 11-3, 5.30(6 Sat)-11; 12-3.30, 7-10.30 Sun; closed Sun evening in winter

FRITHAM SU2314 Map 2
Royal Oak ◖
Village signed from exit roundabout, M27 junction 1; quickest via B3078, then left and straight through village; head for Eyeworth Pond

This charming cob and brick-built thatched pub is part of a working farm, with livestock nearby as well as the ponies and pigs out on the green. They serve around half a dozen well kept real ales tapped from the cask, which include Cheriton Pots, Hop Back Summer Lightning and Ringwood Best and Fortyniner, along with guests such as Archers SSB and Palmers Dorset Gold; they hold a beer festival in September. With a proper traditional atmosphere, the three neatly kept, simple bar rooms have antique wheelback, spindleback, and other old chairs and stools with colourful seats around solid tables on the new oak flooring, prints and pictures involving local characters on the white walls, restored panelling and black beams, and two roaring log fires. You'll find darts, dominoes, shove-ha'penny and cribbage, and the back bar has quite a few books. The pub attracts a good mix of customers, and the staff are cheerily friendly. Simple lunchtime food is limited to freshly made winter soup (£3), ploughman's with home-made pâté, smoked mackerel, local cheese or gammon, and home-made quiche or pies (£4.50), and sometimes home-made scotch eggs or sausage parcels; they usually do evening meals on Mondays in winter, best to check. On bank holidays in summer they hold barbecues and hog roasts in the neatly kept big garden (they have a marquee for bad weather). There are gentle views across forest and farmland, and fine surrounding walks. *(Recommended by Philip and Susan Philcox, Pete Baker, the Didler, David M Cundy, Ann and Colin Hunt, Keith Stevens, Tracey and Stephen Groves, Tom and Ruth Rees)*

Free house ~ Licensees Neil and Pauline McCulloch ~ Real ale ~ Bar food (lunchtime – though see text) ~ No credit cards ~ (023) 8081 2606 ~ Children welcome but must be well behaved ~ Dogs welcome ~ Open 11-3(11.30-2.30 in winter), 6-11; 11-11 Sat; 12-10.30 Sun

HAMBLEDON SU6414 Map 2
Vine
West Street, just off B2150

Open-plan and gently smartened up, this remains a proper traditional country pub, even down to a place on the chenille-covered sofa in one bow window for the pub dog – a charmer called Blue. Besides the usual pub tables and chairs there's a winged high-backed settle, tankards and copper kettles (and even an accordion) hang from old brown beams and joists, and the cream or dark red walls have decorative plates, sporting and country prints, some interesting watercolours of early 20th-c regimental badges, and a bit of bric-a-brac – signed cricket bats, banknotes, gin traps, a boar's head, snare drums and a sort of shell-based mandolin on the piano. Besides the central heating there are a couple of log fires and a woodburning stove. It all adds up to a warmly welcoming atmosphere, with a landlord who is prepared to chat, good smiling service, and at lunchtime a nice mix of regular drinkers and older lunchers. Besides good lunchtime sandwiches (from £2.95), the freshly made food, from a daily changing blackboard, might typically include aubergine, leek and tomato bake, home-made steak and kidney pie, and breaded plaice (all £6.95), popular peppered lamb baked with ginger, coriander and red wine (£8.95), with evening dishes such as coq au vin (£8.95), fried sirloin steak with peppercorn sauce (£10.95), and bass poached with butter, dill and parsley (£11.95); mostly home-made puddings could include treacle tart and pecan pie (£3.50). The restaurant is no smoking. Around five well kept real ales such as Charles Wells Bombardier, Gales Butser, Ringwood Best, Cheriton Pots and Green Light on handpump, Addlestone's cider, country wines; shove-ha'penny, darts and cribbage; tables in a small informal back garden. This pretty downland village has good walks nearby. *(Recommended by Ann and Colin Hunt, Val and Alan Green, P R and S A White)*

Free house ~ Licensee Peter Lane ~ Bar food (not Sun evening) ~ Restaurant ~ (023) 9263 2419 ~ Dogs allowed in bar ~ Open 11.30-3, 6-11; 12-4, 7-10.30 Sun

HAWKLEY SU7429 Map 2
Hawkley Inn ◗
Take first right turn off B3006, heading towards Liss ¾ mile from its junction with A3; then after nearly 2 miles take first left turn into Hawkley village – Pococks Lane; OS Sheet 186 map reference 746292

This unpretentious country local is on the Hangers Way Path, and at weekends it's a popular place for walkers to relax with a pint of well kept beer. The half a dozen real ales on handpump are from small breweries (readers have often never even heard of some of them before), and you might find Arundel Castle, Becketts Old Town Bitter, Branscombe Vale BVB, Goffs Fallen Knight, Oakleaf Bitter, and Ringwood Fortyniner; they have their own cider, too. There's a chatty, friendly atmosphere and service is welcoming. The opened-up bar and back dining room have a simple décor – big pine tables, a moose head, dried flowers, and prints on the mellowing walls; parts of the bar can get a bit smoky when it's busy, but there is a no smoking area to the left of the bar. Besides good soups such as bacon and mushroom, stilton and celery or tomato and watercress (£4.85), swiftly served tasty bar food includes filled rolls (£3.75), cheese, leek and potato pie (£7.95), pork and cider sausages or faggots and mash (£8.25), beef stew (£8.50), and puddings such as spotted dick (£3.75). There are tables and a climbing frame in the pleasant garden. *(Recommended by the Didler, Martin and Karen Wake, Tony and Wendy Hobden, Tony Radnor, Stephen Kiley, Lynn Sharpless, Ian Phillips, W A Evershed, Simon Collett-Jones, Simon Fox)*

Free house ~ Licensee Al Stringer ~ Real ale ~ Bar food (not Sun evening) ~ (01730) 827205 ~ Children welcome ~ Dogs allowed in bar ~ Live music every second winter Sat ~ Open 12-2.30(3 Sat), 6-11; 12-3, 7-10.30 Sun

LONGSTOCK SU3537 Map 2
Peat Spade

Village signposted off A30 on W edge of Stockbridge, and off A3057 Stockbridge—Andover

A short stroll from the River Test, this dining pub is in an attractive village on the 44-mile Test Way long-distance path (there are bracing downland walks up around the Danebury Hill Fort path). The roomy and attractive squarish main bar is airy and high-ceilinged, with pretty windows, well chosen furnishings and a nice show of toby jugs and beer mats around its fireplace. A rather elegant no smoking dining room leads off, and doors open on to a big terrace. Although locals do drop in for a pint and a chat, most visitors come for the interesting food (don't expect to pay rock-bottom pub prices). The sensibly short menu (made using lots of organic ingredients) might typically include thai chicken and hot green chilli soup (£4.25), sandwiches (from £4.50), fresh anchovy fillets (£5.75), ham and ricotta tortellini (£7.50), salmon, cod and haddock fish pie with creamed potato top (£8.25), baked smoked haddock with cheese topping (£11.75), and gressingham duck breast with green peppercorn sauce (£13.50), with puddings such as baked fresh orange cheesecake (£4.50). As well as a decent wine list with several by the glass, they've two or three real ales from brewers such as Hampshire, Hop Back and Ringwood well kept on handpump. There are teak seats on the terrace, with more in the pleasant little garden, and perhaps free-ranging chickens, two cats, Cleo the cocker spaniel and Mollie the diabetic dog (who is not allowed to be fed). *(Recommended by J R and J Moon, Jill Franklin, Patrick Hall, Stuart Turner, Alan and Ros Furley, Dennis Jenkin, Derek Harvey-Piper, Margaret Ross, John Hale, John Davis, Lynn Sharpless)*

Free house ~ Licensees Bernie Startup and Sarah Hinman ~ Real ale ~ Bar food ~ Restaurant ~ No credit cards ~ (01264) 810612 ~ Children welcome ~ Dogs welcome ~ Open 11.30-3, 6.30-11; 12-3 Sun; closed Sun evening, all Mon

LYMINGTON SZ3295 Map 2
Kings Head ◖

Quay Hill; pedestrian alley at bottom of High Street, can park down on quay and walk up from Quay Street

A handsome sight at the top of its steep cobbled lane of smart small shops, this 17th-c pub rambles darkly up and down steps and through timber dividers, with tankards hanging from great rough beams. Lighting is dim, and even in daytime they light the candles on the tables – a great mix from an elegant gateleg to a huge chunk of elm, with a nice old-fashioned variety of seating too. It's mainly bare boards, with a rug here or there; the local pictures include good classic yacht photographs. One cosy upper corner past the serving counter has a good log fire in a big fireplace, its mantelpiece a shrine to all sorts of drinking from beer tankards to port and champagne cases: they have well kept Fullers London Pride, Gales HSB, Greene King Old Speckled Hen, Ringwood Porter or True Glory and Wadworths 6X on handpump. The enjoyable food (made using organic meat wherever possible) includes some inventive sandwiches (from £4.50), home-made soup (£3.75), lambs liver and bacon with mashed potatoes and gravy (£8.75), crispy battered haddock with chunky chips (£9.95), half a shoulder of lamb roasted in honey and mint sauce (£11.95), and 8oz sirloin steak (£12.95), with specials such as venison haunch steak with black cherry sauce (£13), and sautéed monkfish and prawns in saffron sauce (£13.75), and puddings such as apple and sultana crumble (£4.25). A wall rack holds daily papers; piped pop music may be on the loudish side but is well reproduced. *(Recommended by Sue and Mike Todd)*

Inn Partnership (Pubmaster) ~ Licensee Paul Stratton ~ Bar food (12-2.10, 6-10) ~ Restaurant ~ (01590) 672709 ~ Children welcome ~ Dogs welcome ~ Open 11-2.30(3.30 Sat), 6-11; 12-3.30, 6-10.30 Sun

MICHELDEVER SU5138 Map 2
Half Moon & Spread Eagle

Village signposted off A33 N of Winchester; then follow Winchester 7 signpost almost opposite hall

Set in a picturesque village, this bustling country local is a good starting point for exploring the Dever Valley, and there are lots of pleasant walks nearby. The simply decorated and beamed bar has heavy tables and good solid seats – a nice cushioned panelled oak settle and a couple of long dark pews as well as wheelback chairs – and a woodburning stove at each end. A no smoking area with lighter-coloured furniture opens off; look out for the fish tank. Good bar food includes sandwiches (from £2.75), warm bacon salad (£4.95), ploughman's or ham and eggs (£6.95), stir-fried vegetables and rice (£7.95), cajun chicken (£7.95), fresh mussels in cream and garlic sauce (£8.95), duck breast with blackberries or fresh scallops (£10.95), and half shoulder of lamb (£11.50), with daily specials, and puddings such as banoffi pie or profiteroles (£3.95); there may be a wait when it's busy. Well kept Greene King Abbot, IPA, and Mild, and a guest such as Cheriton Pots Ale on handpump; darts, pool, fruit machine, cribbage, dominoes and piped music. The landlord plays the saxophone, and they have an alsatian called Brew, and four cats. There are seats on a small sheltered back terrace, and some more widely spaced picnic-sets and a play area on the edge of a big cricket green behind; also, rabbits and chickens and a pony. *(Recommended by Phyl and Jack Street, D S Jackson, Roy and Lindsey Fentiman, Geoff Palmer, DJH, Charles Moncreiffe, Lynn Sharpless, Ian Phillips, John Davis, Prof and Mrs Tony Palmer, Tim and Carolyn Lowes)*

Greene King ~ Tenants Ray Douglas and Belinda Boughtwood ~ Real ale ~ Bar food ~ Restaurant ~ (01962) 774339 ~ Children welcome ~ Dogs allowed in bar ~ Live music usually one Fri evening a month ~ Open 12-3, 6-11; 12-3, 7-10.30 Sun

MONXTON SU3144 Map 2
Black Swan

Village signposted off A303 at Andover junction with A343; car park some 25 metres along High Street

This pretty thatched pub, in a row of rose-covered colour-washed thatched cottages, is very popular with Andoverites for lunch. Besides ample lunchtime sandwiches (£3.75), ploughman's (£4.95), and salads (£7.95), well prepared food (the menu changes every day), made with lots of fresh local ingredients, could include starters such as soup (£3.95), and whitebait (£4.75), and main courses such as ham and eggs (£7.50), lasagne (£7.95), scampi (£8.50), spinach and spring onion tart (£8.95), popular steak and kidney pie or vegetable thai red curry (£9.50), and bass with capers and lemon butter or fried salmon with scallop and saffron cream (£13.50), with puddings such as rich chocolate cake or baked rum and raisin cheesecake (£4.25). They do a good value OAP offer (£5 for two courses Monday-Thursday lunchtimes). Past a lobby with a settee and easy chairs, a couple of steps takes you up to the small mansard-ceiling timbered bar with the menu boards, a log fire, a table of daily papers and just a few pub tables (also Fullers London Pride, Ringwood Best and Timothy Taylors Landlord on handpump, and decent house wines). Angling off behind here is the main action: a triangular room with floor-to-ceiling windows looking out at picnic-sets and a play area in a small sheltered garden by the little slow-flowing Pillhill Brook, and a further good-sized no smoking room, both carpeted, with country-kitchen chairs and tables set for eating.

Service is quick and pleasant, with plenty of neatly dressed staff; no music – just chat and the click of cutlery on plates. *(Recommended by Phyl and Jack Street, W W Burke, Margaret Ross, John Braine-Hartnell)*

Enterprise ~ Lease Matthew McCann ~ Bar food (12-2, 6-9.30; 12-2.30, 6-10 Fri-Sun) ~ Restaurant ~ (01264) 710260 ~ Children in eating area of bar and restaurant ~ Dogs allowed in bar ~ Open 11-11; 12-10.30 Sun

NORTH GORLEY SU1611 Map 2
Royal Oak

Ringwood Road; village signposted off A338 S of Fordingbridge

As we went to press new licensees were just about to take over this 17th-c thatched pub, originally a hunting lodge. They plan to serve food all day, and reasonably priced dishes could include soup (£3.25), good sandwiches (from £3.50; baguettes £5), ploughman's (from £5.50), faggots with onion gravy (£6.50), spinach and mushroom bake (£6.50), steak and kidney pie or chicken curry (£7), gammon with egg or pineapple (£7.25), fresh grilled mackerel or salmon (£8.50), and rump steak (£11). French windows look out on to the neatly kept sheltered back garden, which has plenty of seating, and a new play area. Inside, there's a quiet, comfortable and neatly refurbished no smoking lounge on the left, though we prefer the busier main bar on the right: carpeted too, with a corner gas stove, old engravings and other pictures, and steps down to an attractive L-shaped eating area. This has a mix of dark pine tables and pleasant old-fashioned chairs, with big rugs on bare boards, and a further no smoking part with pine booth seating. Friendly and efficient staff serve well kept Fullers London Pride, Greene King IPA, and Ringwood Best on handpump, decent wines, and several malt whiskies; sensibly placed darts, a fruit machine, TV, piped music and there's now boules too. They've also got a hitching rail for horses. Across the road is a big pond with ducks, and there are usually ponies and cattle roaming around. *(Recommended by Phyl and Jack Street, Ian Phillips, Terry and Linda Moseley, Ann and Colin Hunt, Mrs Sally Kingsbury, W W Burke, John Davis)*

Enterprise ~ Lease Sharon Crush and Tom Woods ~ Real ale ~ Bar food (12-9) ~ Restaurant ~ (01425) 652244 ~ Children in restaurant ~ Dogs welcome ~ Open 11-11; 12-10.30 Sun

OVINGTON SU5631 Map 2
Bush 🍴

Village signposted from A31 on Winchester side of Alresford

A delightful place to unwind on a sunny afternoon, the back garden of this picturesquely set little cottage runs down to the River Itchen. The well prepared bar food is popular (it's a good idea to book on weekends), and besides lunchtime sandwiches (from £4.75) and ploughman's (from £6.50), the menu could include soup (£4.40), home-made chicken liver pâté with brandy and port (£6.45), king prawns in garlic, chilli and ginger butter (£9.75), mediterranean roasted vegetable lasagne (£10.25), home-made beef and ale pie or tempura shrimp, salad and jerk-seasoned chips (£11.50), tasty local trout fillets with hazelnut and coriander butter (£11.80), and venison steak with spiced red cabbage and whisky and sherry vinegar sauce (£13.75), with puddings such as sticky toffee pudding and chocolate and black cherry bread and butter pudding (£4.20); they do a few simple children's meals, and two rooms are no smoking. One bad point: even when not busy, they may ask you to leave your credit card behind the bar. The rooms have a nice old-fashioned décor, and the low-ceilinged bar has cushioned high-backed settles, elm tables with pews and kitchen chairs, masses of old pictures in heavy gilt frames on the walls, and a roaring fire on one side with an antique solid fuel stove opposite. They have well kept Wadworths IPA, JCB and 6X and a couple of guests such as Greene King Old Speckled Hen and Jennings Cumberland on handpump, and several country wines and malt whiskies; cribbage, dominoes, Monopoly, Scrabble and Balderdash. The sociable scottish springer spaniel is called Paddy. It's in a lovely spot with nearby walks, so many of the customers in good weather are cyclists and walkers. Please note that if you want to bring children it's best to book, as there are only a few tables set aside for families. *(Recommended by Michael and Robin Inskip, Val and Alan Green, Tim and Carolyn Lowes, Phyl and Jack Street, A R Hawkins, Mrs J V Leighton, Sylvia and Tony Cooper, Ann and Colin Hunt, Mrs Joy Griffiths, W A Evershed, Lynn Sharpless, John Davis, Giles Francis)*

Wadworths ~ Managers Nick and Cathy Young ~ Real ale ~ Bar food (not Sun evening) ~ (01962) 732764 ~ Well behaved children in small family area ~ Dogs welcome ~ Open 11-3, 6-11; 12-2.30, 7-10.30 Sun

OWSLEBURY SU5123 Map 2
Ship

Whites Hill; village signposted off B2177 between Fishers Pond and Lower Upham; can also be reached from M3 junction 10 via Morestead, or from A272 2½ miles SE of A31 junction

This popular pub has plenty to keep families occupied. As well as a very good children's play area and toddler zone, there's a pets corner, and lots of space to run around; in summer there's even a bouncy castle on the weekends, and a marquee (you might find table tennis in here on wet days). Not just rewarding for children, both garden areas have fine views – one side looks right across the Solent to the Isle of Wight, and the other gives a view down to Winchester. Inside, you'll find plenty of locals, and the old bars on the right of the front entrance have varnished black oak 17th-c ship's timbers as beams and wall props, sporting and naval mementos, wheelback chairs around wooden tables, and a big central fireplace. On the left is a comfortable no smoking dining area, and there's also a no smoking separate restaurant. The enjoyable lunchtime menu includes filled baguettes (from £4.95), steak and Guinness pie, spinach and red pepper lasagne or home-cooked ham and eggs (£6.95), while in the evening you might find well prepared (though not cheap) dishes such as smoked salmon, cream cheese and asparagus parcels with white wine sauce (£5.95), locally made speciality sausages with onion gravy (£7.95), wild mushroom stroganoff (£9.95), chargrilled tuna steak with roasted peppers, couscous, thai sauce and stir-fried vegetables (£10.25), and steaks (from £11.95), with daily specials, and children's meals (£3.75); there can be a bit of a wait if it's busy (when certain things may be taken off the menu). Well kept Cheriton Pots and Greene King IPA, Ruddles County and Morlands Original on handpump, and a decent wine list, with 12 by the glass; cribbage, dominoes, alley skittles, and piped music. On fine weekends and during school holidays (when the pub is open all day), it gets very busy, so booking is a good idea. There are lots of lovely surrounding walks. *(Recommended by Roger and Pauline Pearce, Ann and Colin Hunt, Mike Turner, Lynn Sharpless, Charles and Pauline Stride, Phyl and Jack Street, Michael and Robin Inskip, Prof and Mrs Tony Palmer, Tim and Carolyn Lowes, Val and Alan Green, W A Evershed, P R and S A White, Ed and Jane Pearce, Andrew Shore)*

Greene King ~ Tenants Clive Mansell and Ali Carter ~ Real ale ~ Bar food (all day Sat and Sun) ~ Restaurant ~ (01962) 777358 ~ Children welcome ~ Dogs allowed in bar ~ Open 11-3, 6-11; 11-11 Sat; 12-10.30 Sun

PETERSFIELD SU7227 Map 2
Trooper 🍴 🍺 🛏

From B2070 in Petersfield follow Steep signposts past station, but keep on up past Steep, on old coach road; OS Sheet 186 map reference 726273

With 'very pleasant staff', a 'great atmosphere' and a landlord who 'goes out of his way to welcome' customers, this enjoyable pub is a hit with readers. Many people come for the delicious food, and to be sure of a table you must book. The sensibly short menu could include soup (£4.25), avocado and stilton bake or (highly recommended by readers) mussels poached in coconut milk, lemon grass, coriander and chilli (£5.95), caramelised red onion, balsamic and goats cheese tart with pesto sauce and shaved parmesan (£10.95), wild boar steak with peanut and pepper sauce or delicious roasted half shoulder of lamb with honey and mint gravy (£12.95), and aberdeen angus fillet steaks (from £15.95), with puddings such as apricot and almond torte or marshmallow mud pie (£3.95); they also do lunchtime sandwiches. It's not the kind of place to come if you're in a rush, and there may be quite a wait at peak times. There's an island bar, tall stools by a broad ledge facing big windows that look across to rolling downland fields, blond wheelback and kitchen chairs and a mix of tripod tables on the bare boarded or red tiled floor, little persian knick-knacks here and there, quite a few ogival mirrors, big baskets of dried flowers, lit candles all around, fresh flowers, logs burning in the stone fireplace, and good piped music; newspapers and magazines to read. The raftered restaurant is most attractive. The four well kept real ales change frequently but might include Ballards Nyewood Gold, Burton Bridge Stairway to Heaven, Hop Back Crop Circle, and Ringwood Best on handpump, and they have decent house wines. There are lots of picnic-sets on an upper lawn and more on the partly covered sunken terrace which has french windows to the dining area. The horse rail in the car park ('horses only before 8pm') does get used. The bedrooms in the extension behind are very nice indeed, and they do good breakfasts.

(Recommended by JMC, Simon Collett-Jones, John Davis, Ian Phillips, John and Tania Wood, Roger and Pauline Pearce, Patrick Hancock, Ann and Colin Hunt, Paul and Penny Dawson, Lynn Sharpless, Charles and Pauline Stride, Tony Radnor, George and Brenda Jones, Paul Humphreys, Bruce and Penny Wilkie)

Free house ~ Licensee Hassan Matini ~ Real ale ~ Bar food ~ Restaurant ~ (01730) 827293 ~ Children welcome ~ Open 12-2, 6-11; 12-2, 7-10.30 Sun ~ Bedrooms: £59B/£79B

PILLEY SZ3298 Map 2
Fleur de Lys ♀

Village signposted off A337 Brockenhurst—Lymington

This ancient thatched pub was originally a pair of foresters' cottages, and there is said to have been an inn on this site in 1096; they show a list of landlords that goes back to 1498. The lounge bar has heavy low beams, a collection of brass and copper ornaments, and a huge inglenook log fire; the main bar and family room are no smoking. Outside are garden tables and a children's play area; fine forest and heathland walks nearby. Enjoyable changing bar food could include sandwiches (from £3, filled baguettes from £4), home-made soup (£3.75), home-made pâté (£4.95), ham and eggs (£6.50), tortillas filled with mediterranean vegetables (£7.95), half a shoulder of lamb (£10.95), skate wing with chilli and herb butter (£11.95), and steaks (£12.95), with puddings such as hot chocolate fudge cake (from £3.95). They serve well kept Ringwood Best and Fortyniner on handpump, decent wines, and country wines; piped music and fruit machine. *(Recommended by Betsy Brown, Nigel Flook, Derek and Sylvia Stephenson, Paul A Moore, Lynn Sharpless, John Davis, Alan Finley, Charles and Pauline Stride)*

Whitbreads ~ Lease Neil Rogers ~ Real ale ~ Bar food (not 25 Dec) ~ (01590) 672158 ~ Children in family room ~ Dogs welcome ~ Open 11-2.30, 6-11; 12-3, 7-10.30 Sun; closed evenings 25 and 26 Dec

ROTHERWICK SU7156 Map 2
Falcon

4 miles from M3 junction 5; follow Newnham signpost from exit roundabout, then Rotherwick signpost, then turn right at Mattingley, Heckfield signpost; village also signposted from B3349 N of Hook, then brown signs to pub

Terraces at the front and back of this quietly placed country pub have sturdy tables and benches, and there are picnic-sets in a sizeable informal back garden, which has a pair of swings and pasture views. Inside, the pub has a light and fresh open-plan layout, with quite a mixture of dining chairs around an informal variety of tables on its varnished floorboards, big bay windows with sunny window seats, and minimal decoration on its mainly pale mustard-coloured walls – flowers on the tables, and perhaps a big vase of lilies on the terracotta-coloured central bar counter, give colour. Parts can get smoky, but there is a rather more formal no smoking back dining area round to the right, and on the left an overstuffed sofa and a couple of ornate easy chairs by one log fire. Bar food includes home-made soup (£3.25), unusual sandwiches (from £3.50), crispy duck mixed leaf salad (£5.50), steak and ale pie (£7.95), and rump steak (from £10.95), with specials such as calves liver with caramelised onions and mash (£12.95), and puddings such as home-made bread and butter pudding (£3.75). Well kept Adnams Best, Fullers London Pride and a guest such as Shepherd Neame Spitfire on handpump; maybe piped local radio. There are good easy walks nearby. *(Recommended by Howard Dell, Margaret Ross, John Davis, Anthony Barnes, Norman and Sheila Sales)*

Unique Pub Co ~ Lease Andy Francis ~ Real ale ~ Bar food ~ Restaurant ~ (01256) 762586 ~ Children in eating area of bar and restaurant ~ Dogs allowed in bar ~ Open 11-2.30, 6-11; 12-10.30 Sun; 12-5, 6-10.30 Sun in winter

ROWLAND'S CASTLE SU7310 Map 2
Castle Inn

Village signposted off B2148/B2149 N of Havant; Finchdean Road, by junction with Redhill Road and Woodberry Lane

This cheerful and chatty village pub has two appealing smallish eating rooms on the left. The front one has rather nice simple mahogany chairs around sturdy scrubbed pine tables, one quite long, rugs on flagstones, a big fireplace, and quite a lot of old local photographs on its ochre walls; the back one is similar, but with bare boards, local acrylic landscapes by Noel Bingham for sale, and cases of colourful decorative glassware from nearby Stansted Park. A wide choice of good value food includes sandwiches and baguettes (from £3.25), baked potatoes (from £3.25), ploughman's (£5.50), battered cod or ham, egg and chips (£5.50), beef or vegetable chilli or thai cod and prawn fishcakes (£6), with slightly more elaborate evening dishes from the restaurant menu such as spicy crab cakes (£3.50), salmon fillet with wine, cream and dill sauce or lamb shank with rosemary and garlic (£7.95), and steak (£9.75), and puddings such as chocolate mud pie or bread and butter pudding (£3.50). Well kept Gales Butser, GB and HSB and a monthly guest such as Marstons Pedigree on handpump (no smoking at the bar counter), country wines; friendly helpful neatly dressed staff. There is a small separate public bar on the right; disabled access and facilities are good, and the garden behind has picnic-sets. There are good walks around this pleasant village. *(Recommended by Jess and George Cowley, Ian Phillips, W A Evershed, Ann and Colin Hunt)*

Gales ~ Licensee Jan and Roger Burrell ~ Bar food (12-2(3 Sun), 7-9, not Sun/Mon evenings) ~ Restaurant ~ (023) 9241 2494 ~ Well behaved children welcome ~ Dogs allowed in bar ~ Open 11-3, 5-11; 11-11 Fri-Sat; 12-10.30 Sun

SOUTHSEA SZ6498 Map 2
Wine Vaults ◀

Albert Road, opposite Kings Theatre

Not only does this enjoyably basic pub serve up to 11 well kept real ales on handpump, they also do some good special offers too. If you arrive before 5.30 and are coming to eat, you get a free drink, and they have a double happy hour on any night from Monday to Thursday between 5.30 and 7.30 when the beers are cheaper (in fact on Monday it's £1.25 all night). Friendly staff serve Courage Best and Directors, Fullers London Pride, Hop Back GFB and Summer Lightning, Marstons Pedigree, Ringwood Fortyniner, Young's Bitter, and a beer named for the pub, Offyatrolli. Popular with a good mix of age groups, the busy straightforward bar has wood-panelled walls, a wooden floor, and an easy-going, chatty feel; the raised back area is no smoking. They've got newspapers for you to read or, if you prefer, pool, chess, draughts, backgammon and a football table; piped music. Handily served all day, good portions of reasonably priced bar food include sandwiches (from £2.45; grilled ones £3.95), filled baked potatoes (from £3.95), spinach and mushroom korma or steak and ale pie (£5.50), salads like cajun chicken, greek or brie and avocado (from £6.50), mexican dishes such as vegetable burrito or various nachos (from £6.25), and puddings (£3.25); the partly no smoking Vines brasserie has more elaborate dishes. There are seats in the little garden, and a wooden gazebo. *(Recommended by Tony Hobden, the Didler, Val and Alan Green, W A Evershed, Catherine Pitt, Richard and Gaetana Carey, Ian Phillips)*

Free house ~ Licensees Mike Hughes and J Stevens ~ Real ale ~ Bar food (12-9; not 25 Dec, 1 Jan) ~ (023) 9286 4712 ~ Children allowed upstairs; but under 5s must leave before 7.30 ~ Dogs welcome ~ Open 12-11(10.30 Sun); closed 1 Jan

SPARSHOLT SU4331 Map 2
Plough 🍴 ⅌

Village signposted off A272 a little W of Winchester

Hampshire Dining Pub of the Year

Readers are full of praise for the excellent food at this superbly run village pub and, to be sure of a table, it's definitely best to book. On daily changing blackboards, a good choice of bar food might include lunchtime sandwiches (from £3.95), courgette, tomato and chick pea pancake glazed with cheese or wild mushroom and pepper risotto (£8.95), lamb shank with celeriac mash and rosemary jus (£12.95), venison steak with glazed apple and apricot and brandy sauce (£14.50), baked cod fillet with a parmesan crust with leek and spring onion sauce (£14.95), beef medallions glazed with brie and red wine sauce (£16.95), and home-made puddings such as chocolate tart and fruits of the forest crumble (£4.50). The main bar has a bustling atmosphere, an interesting mix of wooden tables and chairs, and farm tools, scythes and pitchforks attached to the ceiling; two no smoking areas. Everything is neatly kept, and the friendly staff are courteous and hard-working. Well kept Marstons Bitter and Wadworths IPA, JCB and 6X on handpump, and an extensive wine list. There's a children's play fort, and plenty of seats on the terrace and lawn. *(Recommended by Lynn Sharpless, Patrick Hall, John and Joan Calvert, Phyl and Jack Street, Tim and Carolyn Lowes, Eleanor and Nick Steinitz, Marjorie and David Lamb, Mr and Mrs G S Ayrton, Richard and Margaret Peers, Mr and Mrs W D Borthwick)*

Wadworths ~ Tenants R C and K J Crawford ~ Real ale ~ Bar food ~ Restaurant ~ (01962) 776353 ~ Well behaved children welcome in part of the bar ~ Dogs welcome ~ Open 11-3, 6-11; 12-3, 6-10.30 Sun; closed 25 Dec

STEEP SU7425 Map 2
Harrow

Take Midhurst exit from Petersfield bypass, at exit roundabout first left towards Midhurst, then first turning on left opposite garage, and left again at Sheet church; follow over dual carriageway bridge to pub

Run by the same family for over 70 years, this country local is as unspoilt and unchanging as ever. The cosy public bar has hops and dried flowers hanging from the beams, built-in wall benches on the tiled floor, stripped pine wallboards, a good log fire in the big inglenook, and wild flowers on the scrubbed deal tables; dominoes. Well kept Ballards Best, Cheriton Diggers Gold, Pots or Village Elder, and Ringwood Best are tapped from casks behind the counter, and they've local wine. Good helpings of enjoyably unfussy home-made bar food include sandwiches, home-made scotch eggs (£3), lovely generous soups such as ham, split pea and vegetable (£4.10), ploughman's, home-made cottage pie, lasagne or quiches (£7.50), and salads (£10), with mouthwatering puddings such as treacle tart or seasonal fruit pies (£3.50). Readers very much enjoy the timeless atmosphere, and the staff are polite and friendly, even when under pressure. The big garden is left free-flowering so that goldfinches can collect thistle seeds from the grass. The Petersfield bypass doesn't intrude on this idyll, though you will need to follow the directions above to find it. No children inside. *(Recommended by John Davis, the Didler, Stephen Kiley, Lynn Sharpless, Ann and Colin Hunt, A D Marsh, Michael and Ann Cole, Ian Phillips, Mary and Dennis Jones, Tony Radnor, Simon Fox, Simon Collett-Jones, W A Evershed)*

Free house ~ Licensee Ellen McCutcheon ~ Real ale ~ Bar food (limited Sun evenings) ~ (01730) 262685 ~ Dogs welcome ~ Open 12-2.30, 6-11; 11-3, 6-11 Sat; 12-3, 7-10.30 Sun; closed winter Sun evenings, and 25 Dec

STOCKBRIDGE SU3535 Map 2
Three Cups ♀ ◧
High Street

The atmosphere at this 15th-c pub is thoroughly relaxed and easy-going, with daily papers, logs blazing in the woodburning stove, and friendly courteous staff. From the outside it looks inviting, with little dormer windows in a very low tiled roof, and inside – there's a settle and hall chair in a small quarry-tiled hallway, then an old-fashioned leather porter's chair by the telephone in an inner lobby. The snug low-beamed bar on the right is quite narrow and very dimly lit (candles in bottles on all the tables at night), with an engaging mix of furnishings on its turkey carpet, from high-backed settles to a button-back leather sofa, with a variety of mainly oak tables; the dark red walls are packed with old engravings, fishing gear, one or two guns, and a fair bit of taxidermy. They serve several decent wines by the glass, and on handpump they've well kept Fullers London Pride and Ringwood Best, along with a guest; fairly quiet piped music. Interesting freshly cooked bar food might include soup (£3.25), good filled baguettes (from £3.75), croque monsieur (£5.75), steamed mussels in shallot and white wine sauce (£5.95), omelettes (£6.95), fried salmon with leeks or hare casserole with red wine and cognac, carrots and mushrooms (£10.95), and rib-eye steak with red wine and onion sauce or lamb cutlets with rosemary sauce (£11.75), with specials (including lots of seasonal game dishes) such as ratatouille (£7.95), whole lemon sole (£13.50), and fillet steak (£14.95); puddings include profiteroles and strawberry cheesecake (£3.50). There is a no smoking restaurant on the left. Behind the bar, there's a little cottage garden and the terrace next to the stream is a nice place to sit on a fine afternoon. *(Recommended by John Oates, David Hammond, Dennis Jenkin, Nigel and Sue Foster, Mr and Mrs R W Allan)*

Free house ~ Licensee Lucia Foster ~ Real ale ~ Bar food (not winter Sun evenings) ~ Restaurant ~ (01264) 810527 ~ Children in restaurant and family room ~ Dogs allowed in bar ~ Open 12-2, 5-11; 12-2, 7-10.30 Sun ~ Bedrooms: £42(£53B)/ £53(£63B)

TICHBORNE SU5630 Map 2
Tichborne Arms
Village signed off B3047

The warmly welcoming licensees will soon make you feel at home in this neat thatched pub. You can expect to find quite a few walkers here during the day, as the Wayfarers Walk and Itchen Way pass close by, and many fine walks lead off in all directions. The comfortable square-panelled room on the right has wheelback chairs and settles (one very long), a log fire in the stone fireplace, and latticed windows. On the left is a larger, livelier, partly panelled room used for eating. The pictures and documents on the walls inside recall the bizarre Tichborne Case (a mystery man from Australia claimed fraudulently to be the heir to this estate). Home-made bar food includes sandwiches (from £3), ploughman's or stilton mushrooms (£5.50), mushroom, red onion and leek crumble (£7.75), chicken, tarragon and mushroom pie (£7.95), steak, ale and stilton pie (£8.50), confit of duck with red onion marmalade (£9.50), and crab salad (£10.50), with puddings such as hot plum tart or rhubarb and ginger crumble (£3.50). Well kept Ringwood Best and Wadworths 6X, with a couple of guests such as Exmoor Gold, Hop Back Summer Lightning or Otter Bitter, tapped from the cask, a decent choice of wines by the glass, country wines and farm cider; sensibly placed darts, shove-ha'penny, dominoes, cribbage and piped music. There are picnic-sets outside in the big well kept garden, a pétanque pitch, and a pub dog. No children inside. *(Recommended by Lynn Sharpless, W A Evershed, Martin and Karen Wake, the Didler, Michael and Robin Inskip,*

Michael Rowse, Phyl and Jack Street, Ann and Colin Hunt, Ron Shelton, Prof and
Mrs Tony Palmer, Phil and Sally Gorton, Stephen and Jean Curtis, Dr and Mrs D Woods)

*Free house ~ Licensees Keith and Janie Day ~ Real ale ~ Bar food (12-1.45, 6.30-
9.45, not 25-26 Dec) ~ (01962) 733760 ~ Dogs welcome ~ Open 11.30-2.30, 6-11;
12-3, 7-10.30 Sun; closed evening 25 Dec*

UPHAM SU5320 Map 2
Brushmakers Arms

Shoe Lane; village signposted from Winchester—Bishops Waltham downs road, and from
B2177 (former A333)

'A really good all-rounder, with everything a pub needs': that reader's report sums
up this attractive old village local. The comfortable L-shaped bar is divided in two
by a central brick chimney with a woodburning stove in the raised two-way
fireplace. It has comfortably cushioned wall settles and chairs, a variety of tables
including some in country-style stripped wood, a few beams in the low ceiling, and
quite a collection of ethnic-looking brushes; there's also a little snug. The
atmosphere is especially welcoming, and you'll usually find a crowd of regulars
chatting contentedly; dominoes, cribbage, fruit machine, shove-ha'penny and
sensibly placed darts. Reasonably priced well kept real ales on handpump include
Ringwood Best and Charles Wells Bombardier along with a beer named for the
pub; also Addlestone's cider, and country wines. The good value bar food is
deservedly popular, and in generous helpings could include lunchtime snacks such
as sandwiches (from £3.50; filled hot croissants £4.50), filled baked potatoes
(£4.75), ploughman's (from £4.75), and ham and egg (£5.25), as well as sardines in
garlic (£4.50), tasty vegetarian dishes such as mushroom stroganoff or vegetarian
lasagne (£5.95), steak and kidney pie (£7.95), local partridge with stilton and bacon
sauce (£8.50), lamb steak with garlic and red wine or crab and sherry bake (£8.95),
and steaks (from £9.95), with home-made puddings (£3.50). The big garden is well
stocked with mature shrubs and trees, and there are picnic-sets on a sheltered back
terrace among lots of tubs of flowers, with more on the tidy tree-sheltered lawn.
Good walks nearby. *(Recommended by Richard Dixon, P R and S A White, Ann and
Colin Hunt, Lynn Sharpless, Godfrey and Irene Joly, Jenny Cridland, Gordon Cooper, Prof and
Mrs Tony Palmer, Amanda Irvine, Martin and Karen Wake, Michael and Robin Inskip,
Betsy and Peter Little)*

*Free house ~ Licensee Tony Mottram ~ Real ale ~ Bar food ~ (01489) 860231 ~
Children in eating area of bar ~ Dogs welcome ~ Open 11-3, 5.45-11; 11-3.30, 6-11
Sat; 11-3.30, 7-10.30 Sun*

WELL SU7646 Map 2
Chequers

Off A287 via Crondall, or A31 via Froyle and Lower Froyle

The vine-covered terrace at this well liked pub is a very pleasant place to sit in
summer (the spacious back garden has picnic-sets too), while in winter a roaring log
fire makes the low-beamed rooms especially cosy. Inside are lots of alcoves, wooden
pews, brocaded stools and GWR carriage lamps, and the panelled walls are hung
with 18th-c country-life prints and old sepia photographs of locals enjoying a drink;
fruit machine, dominoes, chequers, chess and Jenga. The atmosphere is relaxing and
the staff are friendly and attentive. Aside from sandwiches (£4.95, not Sunday),
generously served bar food includes home-made soup (£2.95), game pâté (£4.95),
good ploughman's (£4.95), home-made burgers (£6.95), tuna steak, plaice or
chicken with bacon and brie (£10.25), and sirloin steak (£11.50), with home-made
puddings such as sticky toffee pudding (£3.95). The restaurant is no smoking. Well
kept Badger Best, Tanglefoot and IPA or Fursty Ferret on handpump, and decent
wines. They provide bowls of water and biscuits for dogs. *(Recommended by
Martin and Karen Wake, Mr and Mrs A Swainson, Mr and Mrs R Walton, Ian Phillips,
Piotr Chodzko-Zajko)*

Badger ~ Managers Clare Baumann and Kieran Marshall ~ Real ale ~ Bar food (12-2.30(4 Sat), 6-9.30; 12-4, 6-8.30 Sun) ~ Restaurant ~ (01256) 862605 ~ Children in restaurant ~ Dogs allowed in bar ~ Open 11-3, 6-11; 11-11 Sat; 12-10.30 Sun

WHERWELL SU3839 Map 2
Mayfly

Testcombe (i.e. not in Wherwell itself); A3057 SE of Andover, between B3420 turn-off and Leckford where road crosses River Test; OS Sheet 185 map reference 382390

The pub's splendid setting makes it very popular in fine weather, so it's a good idea to arrive early if you want to get one of the tables on the decking area beside the River Test (where you can watch the ducks and maybe plump trout). Inside, the spacious, beamed and carpeted bar has fishing pictures on the cream walls, rustic pub furnishings, and two woodburning stoves, and there's a no smoking conservatory overlooking the water. Efficient staff serve Gale's HSB, Marstons Pedigree, Ringwood Best, and Wadworths 6X on handpump; piped music. Handily available all day, tasty bar food comes from a buffet-style servery: they do a choice of hot and cold meats, pies, quiches, and salads, and they've a great selection of cheeses. They also do around half a dozen hot specials such as lasagne (from £7.50), casserole (from £7.95), chilli con carne or tandoori chicken (£8.50), and besides ice cream, puddings could include bread and butter pudding or crumble (£4). *(Recommended by Alec and Barbara Jones, D J and P M Taylor, W W Burke, Mike and Sue Richardson, Jess and George Cowley, John Urquhart, Hugh Roberts, B J Harding, Tim and Jan Dalton, Leigh and Gillian Mellor, Angus and Rosemary Campbell, Tim and Carolyn Lowes, Mrs J Wilson, Norman and Sheila Davies, Susan and John Douglas)*

Whitbreads ~ Managers Barry and Julie Lane ~ Real ale ~ Bar food (11.30(12 Sat)-9) ~ (01264) 860283 ~ Children welcome away from bar area ~ Dogs welcome ~ Open 11-11; 12-10.30 Sat; 11-10 Sun; closed 25 Dec

White Lion

B3420, in village itself

'A first-class village local' write two readers (who really know their Hampshire pubs) of this warmly welcoming 17th-c pub. The amiable landlord is very hands-on, and the staff are pleasant and eager to help; the friendly black labrador is called Sam. The multi-level beamed bar has delft plates, sparkling brass, and fresh flowers, and you'll find well kept Flowers Original, and Ringwood Best on handpump; the Village bar has an open fire, and there are two dining rooms – the lower one is no smoking; piped music. Enjoyable, reasonably priced bar food includes home-made soup (£3.50), ploughman's (from £5.50), pie of the day (£7.95), creamy vegetable kiev, salmon fishcakes or scampi (£8), two pork loin steaks with honey and mustard sauce (£8.30), and steaks (from £11.75), with daily specials such as braised beef in red wine, smoked haddock in cheese sauce or steak and mushroom pie; it's a good idea to book for their Sunday roast. There are plenty of seats in the courtyard and on the terrace. The village is pleasant to stroll through, and there's a nice walk over the River Test and meadows to Chilbolton. They may close early on quiet evenings. *(Recommended by Mike Gorton, John Davis, Leigh and Gillian Mellor, B J Harding, Lynn Sharpless, Tim and Carolyn Lowes, Prof and Mrs Tony Palmer, W W Burke, Brian Root, G W A Pearce, Ann and Colin Hunt)*

Inn Partnership (Pubmaster) ~ Lease Adrian and Patsy Stent ~ Real ale ~ Bar food (12-2, 7-9.30(8.30 Sun)) ~ Restaurant ~ (01264) 860317 ~ Well behaved children in restaurant ~ Dogs welcome ~ Folk first and third Thurs of month ~ Open 10-2.30(3 Sat), 6(7 winter Mon-Tues)-11; 12-3, 7-10.30 Sun ~ Bedrooms: £32.50/£45

Planning a day in the country? We list pubs in really attractive scenery at the back of the book.

WHITSBURY SU1219 Map 2
Cartwheel 🍺

Follow Rockbourne sign off A354 SW of Salisbury, turning left just before Rockbourne itself; or head W off A338 at S end of Breamore, or in Upper Burgate – we got mildly lost trying to find it direct from Fordingbridge!

In good walking country, this cheerfully bustling rather out-of-the-way local is opened up inside, with pitched high rafters in one part, lower beams elsewhere, antlers, military prints, country pictures, what looks like a steam-engine's jockey wheel as a divider, and simple but comfortable cloth-cushioned wall seats and other chairs. There's a snug little room by the door, with a couple of tables either side of the fire; a small side room has darts, pool, fruit machine, dominoes, cribbage, Jenga, Scrabble, shut the box, TV, and piped music. Besides tasty sandwiches (from £2.20), big helpings of reasonably priced bar food include whitebait (£4.50), scrambled eggs and smoked salmon (£5.75), cajun chicken with home-made chips, grilled sardines or steak and kidney pudding (all £6.50), and fresh grilled lemon sole (£7.25). On Tuesday they do home-cooked fish and chips which you can eat here or take away. Adnams Broadside and Ringwood Best, with up to four guests from brewers such as Hop Back, Shepherd Neame and Youngs, are kept in top condition on handpump, and they've ciders, and 10 malts; they hold a beer festival in August. Sheltered by a shrubby steep slope, the garden has weekly summer barbecues, and a play area that children really enjoy. We're surprised that we haven't had more reports from readers on this pleasant place. *(Recommended by Phyl and Jack Street)*

Free house ~ Licensee Patrick James Lewis ~ Real ale ~ Bar food (not Mon evening) ~ Restaurant ~ (01725) 518362 ~ Children welcome ~ Dogs welcome ~ Open 11-2.30(3 Sat), 6-11; 12-3, 7-10.30 Sun

WINCHESTER SU4828 Map 2
Black Boy

1 mile from M3 junction 10 northbound; B3403 towards city then left into Wharf Hill; rather further and less easy from junction 9, and anyway beware no nearby daytime parking – 220 metres from car park on B3403 N, or nice longer walk from town via College Street and College Walk, or via towpath

With a splendidly eccentric décor, this unusual pub is packed with things to see and smile at – so best at a quiet time, when it's easy to look around. Several different areas run from a bare-boards barn room with an open hayloft down to an orange-painted room (they certainly go in for bold colours) with big oriental rugs on red-painted floorboards. There are books from floor to ceiling in some parts, lots of big clocks, mobiles made of wine bottles or strings of spectacles, some nice modern nature photographs in the lavatories and on the brightly stained walls on the way, and plenty of other things that you'll enjoy tracking down. Furnishings are similarly eclectic. Of more practical note, aside from fresh sandwiches (£3.50), there are a couple of home-made dishes such as sausage and mash with onion gravy (£6.50), vegetarian pasta (£7), and lamb hotpot (£7.50); on Sunday they only do roasts (£6.50). The beers on handpump are more or less local – with Cheriton Pots, Ringwood Best, and Hop Back Summer Lightning alongside guests such as Becketts Whitewater and Oakleaf Squirrels Delight; decent wines, two log fires, friendly staff, small dogs and regulars. Well chosen and reproduced piped music; table football, shove-ha'penny, cribbage and dominoes; a couple of slate tables out in front, more tables on an attractive secluded terrace with barbecues. *(Recommended by Val and Alan Green, David and Carole Chapman, Tim and Carolyn Lowes, John and Annabel Hampshire, Phil and Sally Gorton)*

Free house ~ Licensee David Nicholson ~ Bar food (not Mon lunchtime or evenings Fri-Sun) ~ (01962) 861754 ~ Dogs welcome ~ Open 11-3, 5-11; 12-3, 7-10.30 Sun

Wykeham Arms ★ 🍴 🍷 🛏️

75 Kingsgate Street (Kingsgate Arch and College Street are now closed to traffic; there is access via Canon Street)

Although lots of people come to this rather civilised but friendly inn for the interesting food (to be sure of a table, it's necessary to book), this is also a superb place for just a relaxed drink. They've a fine choice of 20 wines by the glass (including sweet wines), quite a few brandies, armagnacs and liqueurs, as well as well kept Bass, Gales Butser, GB and HSB, and a guest such as Leyden Crowning Glory on handpump; good coffees too. A series of stylish bustling rooms radiating from the central bar has 19th-c oak desks retired from nearby Winchester College, a redundant pew from the same source, kitchen chairs and candlelit deal tables and big windows with swagged paisley curtains; all sorts of interesting collections are dotted around. A snug room at the back, known as the Watchmakers, is decorated with a set of Ronald Searle 'Winespeak' prints, a second one is panelled, and all of them have a log fire. Served by neatly uniformed staff, the lunchtime menu might include smoked salmon and prawn sandwich (£5.75), smoked haddock topped with welsh rarebit and tomato, rocket and chive oil salad (£7.50), chicken pie with apple and stem ginger chutney (£7.95), braised lamb shank with bubble and squeak and wok-fried vegetables with rich minted jus (£10.50), and daily specials such as lamb and spinach curry (£6.25), and duck confit (£6.50), while in the evening you might find soup (£3.50), oriental pigeon breast with wilted red chard and a cold noodle salad (£5.25), roasted chicken with bacon and red wine risotto, asparagus and a roquefort cream sauce or grilled bass fillets with stir-fried vegetable noodles and sweet oriental chilli dressing (£13.95), with puddings such as orange tart (£4.50). There are tables on a covered back terrace, with more on a small but sheltered lawn. No children inside. Readers highly recommend staying here, and the lovely bedrooms are thoughtfully equipped; the Saint George, a 16th-c annexe directly across the street (and overlooking Winchester College Chapel) has more bedrooms, a sitting room with open fire, general stores, and a burgundian wine store. *(Recommended by John Oates, P R and S A White, Patrick Hall, Lynn Sharpless, John Davis, Martin and Karen Wake, the Didler, John Evans, Ann and Colin Hunt, Ian Phillips, Mr and Mrs R W Allan, Philip Vernon, Kim Maidment, Jess and George Cowley, John and Annabel Hampshire, John and Jane Hayter, Phil and Sally Gorton, Peter Saville, Felicity Stephens, W A Evershed, Phyl and Jack Street, Keith Barker, Andy and Yvonne Cunningham, Mr and Mrs S Felstead, Penny Simpson, Di and Mike Gillam, Patrick Hancock, Tim and Carolyn Lowes, Susan and John Douglas; also in the Good Hotel Guide)*

Gales ~ Managers Peter and Kate Miller ~ Real ale ~ Bar food (12-2.30, 6.30-8.45; not Sun evening) ~ Restaurant ~ (01962) 853834 ~ Dogs allowed in bar ~ Open 11-11; 12-10.30 Sun; closed 25 Dec ~ Bedrooms: £50S/£90B

Lucky Dip

Besides the fully inspected pubs, you might like to try these Lucky Dips recommended to us and described by readers (if you do, please send us reports: www.goodguides.com).

ALRESFORD [SU5832]
Bell [West St]: Relaxing Georgian coaching inn with extended bar, smallish dining room, well kept beers, friendly staff, wide choice of quickly served good value straightforward food inc children's helpings, log fire, daily papers; attractive back courtyard, comfortable bedrooms (some sharing bathroom), open all day *(G W H Kerby, Geoff Palmer, John Oates)*
Cricketers [Jacklyns Lane]: Large pub with good value fresh straightforward food inc bargain wkdy lunches (book ahead for Sun), well kept real ales, friendly efficient service, pleasant cottagey eating area down steps;

garden with terrace and good play area *(Mr and Mrs R W Allan, Phyl and Jack Street)*
☆ *Globe* [bottom of Broad St (B3046)]: Enjoyable and interesting bar food (all day summer wknds) from sandwiches up, sensible prices, lots of wines by the glass, well kept Brakspears SB, Courage Directors, Fullers London Pride and Wadworths 6X, good service, log fires each end, fresh flowers and candles, unusual pictures; no smoking restaurant (children allowed) and tented Garden Room; lots of picnic-sets in garden looking over historic Alresford Pond, open all day Sun, and summer Sat *(Lynn Sharpless,*

John Evans, I D Greenfield, Paul A Moore,
Craig Turnball, Julie and Bill Ryan,
Ron Shelton, Mr and Mrs R W Allan, Ann and
Colin Hunt, LYM, G Coppen, Neil Rose,
Martin and Karen Wake)

☆ *Horse & Groom* [Broad St; town signed off
A31 bypass]: Warm and welcoming beamed
and timbered bar, open-plan but with cosy
alcoves, stepped levels and good bow window
seats, enjoyable reasonably priced food inc
good puddings, well kept ales such as Bass,
Fullers London Pride and Wadworths 6X,
decent wines by the glass, attentive service,
extended back no smoking restaurant area;
decent piped music, open till midnight Sat –
popular then with young people; children
welcome, open all day Fri/Sat *(Ann and
Colin Hunt, Lynn Sharpless, LYM,
Ron Shelton, Mr and Mrs R W Allan)*

ALTON [SU7138]

☆ *French Horn* [The Butts; S of centre on old
Basingstoke road, by railway line]: Welcoming
dining pub with mugs on beams, old
photographs and inglenook fires in traditional
bar, well kept ales such as Bass, Courage Best,
Greene King Abbot, Ushers Autumn Frenzy
and Youngs, efficient friendly service; sizeable
restaurant with generous pub food and plenty
of regular business lunchers, skittle alley;
bedrooms *(Mick Simmons, D J and P M
Taylor, Martin and Karen Wake, Ron Shelton)*

AMPFIELD [SU4023]

White Horse [A31 Winchester—Romsey]:
Vastly extended open-plan Whitbreads dining
pub, period-effect furniture, interesting décor,
log fire, well kept Ringwood and Wadworths,
good choice of wines by the glass, attentive
service, Victorian prints and advertising posters
in dining room; tables outside, pub backs on to
golf course and village cricket green; handy for
Hillier arboretum, good walks in Ampfield
Woods *(Tim and Carolyn Lowes)*

ARFORD [SU8336]

☆ *Crown* [off B3002 W of Hindhead]:
Unpretentious low-beamed bar with coal and
log fires, steps up to homely eating area, well
kept Adnams, Fullers London Pride, Greene
King Abbot and a guest beer such as fff
Moondance, decent wines by the glass,
welcoming service, enjoyable food from
sandwiches to seasonal game and some
interesting dishes, children's menu, no smoking
restaurant; piped music; children welcome in
eating areas, picnic-sets out in peaceful dell by
a tiny stream across the road *(Ian Phillips,
LYM, Martin and Karen Wake)*

ASHMANSWORTH [SU4157]

Plough: Friendly no-frills pub in attractive
village, two quarry-tiled rooms knocked
together, well kept Archers Village, Best and
Golden and a changing guest tapped from the
cask, simple home-cooked food, good attentive
service, log fire, no piped music; seats outside,
good walks, handy for Highclere Castle
(the Didler, Guy Vowles)

ASHURST [SU3410]

Forest [A35 Lyndhurst—Southampton]:
Pleasantly refurbished main-road pub, pubby

bar with Fullers London Pride, Gales HSB and
Ringwood Best, country wines, darts and good
juke box, no smoking dining area on left with
snug areas off flagstoned main part, decent
food, efficient service; big garden
*(R J Anderson, Phyl and Jack Street, BB,
J A Snell)*

BEAUWORTH [SU5624]

☆ *Milbury's* [off A272 Winchester/Petersfield]:
Attractive ancient pub, beams, panelling and
stripped stone, massive 17th-c treadmill for
much older incredibly deep well, log fires in
huge fireplaces; well kept Cheriton Diggers
Gold and Best, fff Altons Pride, Hop Back
Summer Lightning, Theakstons Old Peculier
and a house beer, Addlestone's cider, country
wines, bar food from lunchtime sandwiches to
steaks with wider evening choice; piped music,
and they may try to get you to leave a credit
card while you eat; children in eating areas,
garden has fine downland views, plenty of
walks, open all day *(the Didler, Charles and
Pauline Stride, P R and S A White, Val and
Alan Green, Ann and Colin Hunt, LYM,
Paul A Moore, S F Parrinder, Ed and
Jane Pearce)*

BENTLEY [SU8044]

Bull [A31 Alton—Farnham dual carriageway,
not in village itself]: Good choice of good food
from sandwiches and baked potatoes to
interesting and exotic dishes, friendly welcome
for drinkers as well as diners, well kept
Courage Best and Hogs Back TEA, log fire,
low beams, lots of local prints *(Mrs M Jagger,
John and Joyce Snell, LYM, Martin and
Karen Wake)*

BIGHTON [SU6134]

Three Horseshoes [off B3046 in Alresford just
N of pond; or off A31 in Bishops Sutton]:
Quiet old-fashioned village local with
reasonably priced standard food, well kept
Gales HSB and BBB and Palmers BB and
Copper, decent house wines, small log fire
dining room, darts in bare-boards stripped-
stone public bar, stove in huge fireplace; may
be piped music; children welcome, good walks
nearby; cl Mon winter lunchtime *(the Didler,
W A Evershed, Lynn Sharpless)*

BISHOP'S SUTTON [SU6031]

Ship [B3047, former A31 on Alton side of
Alresford – now bypassed]: Attractive and
relaxed, with well kept Ringwood Best and
Porter and a guest beer, welcoming obliging
service, good fire, decent straightforward
lunchtime food, attractive small back dining
room; well behaved dogs and children
welcome, tables in garden with a couple of
thatched parasols, handy for Watercress Line,
good walks; has been cl Mon lunchtime
*(Lynn Sharpless, Ron Shelton, LYM, Ann and
Colin Hunt, Phyl and Jack Street, Tom and
Rosemary Hall)*

BISHOP'S WALTHAM [SU5517]

Barleycorn [Lower Basingwell St]:
Comfortably relaxed L-shaped main area with
some panelling, well kept Greene King ales inc
Ruddles Best, log fire, simple food inc two-for-
one lunch bargains Mon to Weds, popular Sun

lunch and children's dishes, TV and games on public side; small back garden and play area *(Ian Phillips, David and Elizabeth Briggs, Phyl and Jack Street)*

☆ *Bunch of Grapes* [St Peters St]: Small and simple unspoilt village local run by the same family for a century, well kept Courage Best and Ushers Best tapped from the cask, good chatty landlord and friendly locals, plenty of character, quaintly furnished snug off main room; attractive medieval street *(Val and Alan Green, the Didler, Ann and Colin Hunt)*

White Horse [Beeches Hill, off B3035 NE]: Long country pub in converted hillside cottages, unspoilt and friendly, well kept ales such as Courage Directors, Greene King Old Speckled Hen and Ringwood Best, reasonably priced fresh and imaginative food inc curry specialities and several fish dishes, long-serving landlord, log fire; picnic-sets on front terrace, small play area *(Val and Alan Green, Ian Phillips)*

BLACKNEST [SU7941]
Jolly Farmer [Binsted Rd]: Modern, light and airy dining pub with good value generous blackboard food inc children's, Gales beers, friendly service, big open fire one end, family room; tables on sheltered terrace and in garden with swings *(John and Joyce Snell)*

BRAISHFIELD [SU3725]
☆ *Newport* [Newport Lane]: Very basic two-bar local, unsmart and unspoilt – quite a 1950s time warp; popular with older people at lunchtime (younger people evenings) for simple huge cheap sandwiches and occasional bargain ploughman's, particularly well kept Gales HSB, Best and Butser, country wines, decent milky coffee, down-to-earth long-serving licensees; piped music, cribbage, wknd piano singsongs; good garden with geese, ducks and chickens *(Phil and Sally Gorton, Lynn Sharpless, the Didler)*

Wheatsheaf [Crooks Hill]: Open plan, with terracotta walls, stripped boards and some individualistic features, interesting cooking, real ales such as Hook Norton, Ringwood Best, Timothy Taylors Landlord and Wadworths 6X, decent wines, side pool area, huge friendly black dog; fine views over meadowland to distant woods from big garden with lots of amusements for children inc field for ball games, pleasant walks; open all day *(Lynn Sharpless)*

BRAMBRIDGE [SU4721]
☆ *Dog & Crook* [village signed off M3 junction 12 exit roundabout, via B3335]: Lots of neat tables under hop-hung beams around central bar, emphasis on enlarged kitchen's good food choice from pub standards to some more unusual and restauranty dishes inc lovely puddings (Sun lunch booked weeks ahead), relaxing atmosphere, quick warmly welcoming young staff, well kept Fullers London Pride, Gales HSB and Ringwood Best, country wines, small smoking area; alloy tables and chairs out on deck and under fairy-lit arbour, grass beyond, Itchen Way walks nearby *(Diana Brumfit, BB, John and Joan Calvert, Ann and Colin Hunt)*

BRANSGORE [SZ1997]
☆ *Three Tuns* [Ringwood Rd, off A35 N of Christchurch]: Pretty 17th-c thatched pub, wide range of above-average imaginative food from ciabattas up, cheerful efficient service, well kept Greene King IPA, Ringwood Fortyniner and Timothy Taylors Landlord, good range of wines and hot drinks, tastefully refurbished olde-worlde bar with stripped brickwork and beamery, comfortable partly no smoking dining area popular with older people at lunchtime, fresh flowers; dogs allowed; pleasant back garden with play area and open country views, large flower-decked front terrace; bedrooms *(A D Marsh, BJSM, John and Vivienne Rice, P J French, W W Burke, P L Jones)*

BROOK [SU2713]
Bell: Really a hotel and restaurant (with thriving golf club), but does good interesting lunches in its neatly kept quiet bar, with prompt friendly uniformed staff, good choice of well kept ales inc Ringwood, and lovely inglenook log fire; plush restaurant, big garden, delightful village, comfortable bedrooms *(David M Cundy)*

Green Dragon [B3078 NW of Cadnam]: Big open-plan new forest dining pub (dating from 15th c) with wide choice of reliable food quickly served, variety of areas with scrubbed pine tables or longer refectory tables, proper bar areas too, with well kept Fullers London Pride, Gales HSB and Ringwood and pool room, smiling young staff; big pleasant garden with good enclosed play area, picturesque village *(Dick and Madeleine Brown, J and B Cressey, Ron Shelton, JWAC)*

BROUGHTON [SU3032]
☆ *Tally Ho* [High St, opp church; signed off A30 Stockbridge—Salisbury]: Open-plan square bar, mainly with pews and mixed pub furniture on big terracotta tiles, but one quarter carpeted, with nice seating, a small coal fire, hunting prints, and local landscapes for sale, and another taken up by the servery; well kept fff Stupidly Happy and Ringwood Best and True Glory, good house wines in two glass sizes, another log fire, darts, generous home cooking and good sandwiches, no piped music; children welcome, tables in charming secluded back garden, good walks; has been cl Tues *(Geoffrey G Lawrance, Prof and Mrs Tony Palmer, BB, Bernie Adams, Geoffrey Kemp)*

BUCKS HORN OAK [SU8041]
Halfway House [A325 Farnham—Petersfield]: Good fresh food inc choice of Sun roasts, sensible prices, good service, thriving atmosphere, well kept beers, big cosy bar with separate restaurant area; good nearby garden centre *(Amanda Irvine)*

BURITON [SU7320]
Five Bells [Village signposted off A3 S of Petersfield]: Several interesting rooms, the low-beamed lounge on the left has terracota walls, hops on beams, and a big log fire; the public side has some ancient stripped masonry, a woodburning stove, and old-fashioned tables;

an end alcove has cushioned pews and board games; well kept Badger beers, and a guest on handpump, decent wines, several by the glass; fruit machine, and piped music; seats on an informal lawn stretch back above the building, with more on sheltered terraces; the converted stables are self-catering cottages *(LYM, Nigel Williamson, John Davis, John and Tania Wood)*

BURLEY [SU2202]

☆ *White Buck* [Bisterne Close; ¾ mile E, OS Sheet 195 map ref 223028]: Huge well run bar in 19th-c mock-Tudor hotel in lovely New Forest setting, emphasis on very wide choice of reasonably priced good generous food, Gales Butser, HSB and GB and Ringwood Best, decent wines and country wines, cheap soft drinks, good coffee, log fire, banquette seating, courteous efficient staff (but service may slow with the wknd crowds), thriving atmosphere, smart and attractive added end dining room (should book – but no bookings Sun lunchtime); may be quiet piped music, dogs welcome, hitching posts, pleasant front terrace and spacious lawn; good value well equipped bedrooms, superb walks towards Burley itself and over Mill Lawn *(Caraline and Richard Crocker, Norman and Sheila Davies, BB, A and B D Craig)*

CADNAM [SU2913]

Bartley Lodge: Hotel with bar open to non-residents, enjoyable lunches, coffee and biscuits all day; bedrooms *(Dennis Jenkin)*

Coach & Horses [Southampton Rd]: Popular for wide choice of good value food from baguettes and baked potatoes to more imaginative dishes, OAP discounts on food and drink, efficient cheerful service *(A D Marsh, Ray Horrocks)*

Compass [Winsor, off Totton—Cadnam road at Bartley crossroads; OS Sheet 195 map ref 317143]: Popular 16th-c bare-boards and beamed local off the beaten track, hard-working helpful licensees, pine tables for honest food from good bacon doorsteps to Mon curry and Tues British beef nights (most tables may be booked), real ales inc Gales and Ringwood, May and Aug bank hol beer festivals, log fires; side garden with decorative arbour, Irish band Thurs, open all day *(Dr A Brookes, Phyl and Jack Street, Dave Hills)*

☆ *Sir John Barleycorn* [Old Romsey Rd; by M27, junction 1]: Picturesque low-slung thatched pub, attractive medieval core on left with dim lighting, low beams and timbers, large more modern extension on right, wide food choice from sandwiches up, not cheap but generous, afternoon cream teas, well kept ales such as Fullers London Pride and Ringwood Fortyniner, reasonably priced wines, two log fires, no smoking restaurant end, prompt and friendly young staff; dogs and children welcome, can be very busy; suntrap benches in front and out in garden, eye-catching flowers, open all day *(Phyl and Jack Street, Roy and Lindsey Fentiman, LYM, Mike and Sue Richardson)*

White Hart [½ mile from M27 junction 1]: Big rambling food-oriented pub, well kept Boddingtons, Greene King Old Speckled Hen, Ringwood Best and Wadworths 6X, good wine choice, pleasant efficient service, spotless simple furnishings and no smoking section; piped music; children in eating area, garden tables, food all day *(Dr and Mrs A K Clarke, Ian Phillips, Tim and Carolyn Lowes, Evelyn and Derek Walter, LYM, Phyl and Jack Street)*

CHARLTON DOWN [SU3549]

Hare & Hounds: Pleasantly unpretentious, with plenty of local regulars, friendly staff and helpful licensees; enjoyable food inc enterprising vegetarian dishes *(BB)*

CHAWTON [SU7037]

Greyfriar [Winchester Rd]: Well run 17th-c village pub with low beams, standing timbers studded with foreign coins, good reasonably priced generous food from very well filled home-baked bread sandwiches to unusual dishes, quick efficient service, well kept Fullers London Pride and a guest beer, good coffee; small garden behind with barbecue, opp Jane Austen's house, good walks *(Ian and Deborah Carrington)*

CHILWORTH [SU4118]

Clump [A27 Romsey Rd]: Busy extended chain eating place, largely no smoking; well kept Boddingtons, Fullers London Pride and Gales HSB, good choice of wines, two log fires, smart décor with sofas and easy chairs in one part, spacious conservatory; unobtrusive piped music, disabled facilities but steps at entrance; open all day, large garden *(Phyl and Jack Street, Jim Bush, B and K Hyper)*

COLDEN COMMON [SU4821]

Fishers Pond: Big refurbished Brewers Fayre open all day, sensibly priced generous food inc children's, decent coffee, polite friendly service; pretty setting by pond with ducks, handy for Marwell Zoo *(Ann and Colin Hunt)*

CRAWLEY [SU4234]

Fox & Hounds [off A272 or B3420 NW of Winchester]: Striking almost Swiss-looking building, mix of attractive wooden tables and chairs on polished floors in neat and attractive linked beamed rooms with three log fires, real ales such as Fullers London Pride, Gales HSB, Ringwood Best and Wadworths 6X, decent wines, new licensees with new chefs; tables in garden, pretty village with duck pond *(LYM, Phyl and Jack Street)*

CRONDALL [SU7948]

☆ *Hampshire Arms* [village signed off A287 S of Fleet; Pankridge St]: Unusual combination of relaxed and friendly unassuming local with good gently upmarket conservatory restaurant (booked well ahead wknds, worth booking wkdy evenings too); cosy L-shaped beamed bar with sturdy furnishings, huge log fire and candles in bottles, bar food from two soup cauldrons and good filled home-baked baguettes (not Sun) to chef/landlord's good enterprising main dishes cooked to order, wider evening choice with plenty of seasonal game; well kept Greene King IPA, Abbot and

Ruddles County and a guest such as Hook Norton Old Hooky, good sensibly priced house wines, enthusiastic young staff; dogs welcome, french windows to fenced garden with picnic-sets and floodlit boules pitch *(Martin and Karen Wake, M J Bastin, Andy and Yvonne Cunningham, Ian Phillips, BB)*

Plume of Feathers [The Borough]: Attractive smallish 15th-c village local, generous enjoyable food from hot filled baguettes, double-decker sandwiches and usual bar dishes to more adventurous menu in smarter restaurant end, beams and dark wood, prints on cream walls, log fire in big brick fireplace, Greene King ales, decent wines by the glass; no piped music, children welcome; two red telephone boxes in garden, picturesque village *(Andy and Yvonne Cunningham, Martin and Karen Wake, M J Bastin)*

CURBRIDGE [SU5211]

Horse & Jockey [Botley road (A3051)]: Two neatly refurbished bars and dining area, decent food, cheerful waitress service, Gales HSB and GB and perhaps a guest such as Greene King Old Speckled Hen, country wines; piped music may obtrude; lovely big waterside garden with small terrace, trees and fenced play area, beautiful setting by River Hamble tidal tributary at start of NT woodland trail *(Val and Alan Green)*

DAMERHAM [SU1016]

☆ *Compasses* [signed off B3078 in Fordingbridge; East End]: Neatly refurbished small lounge bar divided by log fire from pleasant dining room with booth seating (children allowed here), pale wood tables and kitchen chairs, good home cooking from sandwiches up esp soups and shellfish, marvellous cheese choice, well kept ales such as Hop Back Summer Lightning, Ringwood Best, Wadworths 6X and a beer brewed for the pub, good choice of wines by the glass, over a hundred malt whiskies, separate locals' bar with pool and juke box; big pretty garden by quiet village's cricket ground, downland walks, well equipped bedrooms *(Geoffrey G Lawrance, Ann Brown)*

DENMEAD [SU6412]

Fox & Hounds [School Lane, Anthill Common]: Friendly and relaxing open-plan bar with pleasant separate eating area (reasonable prices, generous Sun roasts), friendly staff, four well kept ales such as Boddingtons, Fullers London Pride, Marstons Pedigree and Robinsons Best *(Ann and Colin Hunt)*

Harvest Home [Southwick Rd, Bunkers Hill]: Welcoming local with long bar, eating area off, well kept Gales, good value food; open all day, increasingly suburban area but handy for Creech Wood walks *(Ann and Colin Hunt)*

DOGMERSFIELD [SU7852]

☆ *Queens Head* [village signed off A287 and B3016 W of Fleet]: Masses of menu boards and all tables set for eating in well divided dining bar, dark pink walls, some stripped brickwork, a couple of low beams, new owner

but still the wide choice of attractively priced food from baguettes to restaurany main dishes, well kept Courage Best, Fullers London Pride and Youngs Special, good choice of wines esp new world, swift friendly service; well reproduced piped pop music, booking advised evenings (two sittings); tree-shaded picnic-sets on front grass, pretty setting, cl Mon *(Andy and Yvonne Cunningham, BB, Norman and Sheila Sales, Ian Phillips)*

DOWNTON [SZ2793]

Royal Oak [A337 Lymington—New Milton]: Wide choice of good value food in neat partly panelled family pub, half no smoking, with well kept Whitbreads-related ales, decent wines, jovial atmosphere, quick friendly service; unobtrusive piped music; huge well kept garden with good play area *(A D Marsh)*

DUMMER [SU5846]

Queen [½ mile from M3 junction 7; take Dummer slip road]: Very handy for motorway, with beams, lots of softly lit alcoves, log fire, queen and steeplechase prints, bar food and no smoking restaurant allowing children (they may keep your credit card), well kept Courage Best, Fullers London Pride and Greene King Old Speckled Hen, good service; fruit machine, well reproduced piped music, no mobile phones; picnic-sets under cocktail parasols on terrace and in extended back garden, attractive village with ancient church *(Tim and Carolyn Lowes, LYM, Geoffrey Kemp, Geoff Palmer)*

DUNBRIDGE [SU3126]

Mill Arms [Barley Hill]: Friendly and cosily unpretentious open-plan bars with stripped pine beams, sofas, open fire, no smoking conservatory restaurant, helpful landlady, decent blackboard food inc some interesting dishes, two well kept ales brewed for the pub by Hampshire and Itchen Valley with a guest such as Hook Norton, late Sept beer festival, cafetière coffee, refurbished skittle alley; tables in pleasant two-level garden with wendy house, bedrooms *(Tony Hobden, Margaret Ross, Peter Walters)*

DUNDRIDGE [SU5718]

☆ *Hampshire Bowman* [off B3035 towards Droxford, Swanmore, then right at Bishops W signpost]: Friendly and cosy, smartened up a little under new landlady with some colourful new paintings, but still great for unspoilt atmosphere and mix of customers (children, dogs and walkers welcome, usually some classic cars or vintage motorcycles); well kept Ringwood Best and Fortyniner, a changing Cheriton ale and a guest such as Sharps Cornish Coaster tapped from the cask, decent house wines, country wines, low-priced home-made food, Sun bar nibbles, efficient service; tables on spacious and attractive lawn, good downland walks *(Val and Alan Green, Ann and Colin Hunt, Geoff Palmer, W A Evershed, LYM, the Didler)*

DURLEY [SU5116]

☆ *Farmers Home* [village signed off B3354 and B2177 SE of Colden Common; Heathen St/Curdridge road]: Good choice of popular food inc fresh fish and lovely puddings, log fire in comfortable small bar with two-bay dining area on one side and big newer matching no smoking restaurant on the other, well kept Boddingtons, Flowers Original, Gales HSB and Ringwood Best, decent wine; children welcome, big garden with good play area and marquee, nice walks *(Ann and Colin Hunt, Phyl and Jack Street)*

Robin Hood [Durley Street, just off B2177 Bishops Waltham—Winchester]: Smartly refurbished pub with gently upmarket food in lounge and dining room, log fire, good cheerful service, well kept Greene King ales with a guest such as St Austell Tribute, reasonably priced wines, public bar with darts and two amiable labradors; back terrace and big pleasant garden with fine view and play area, good walks *(Val and Alan Green)*

EAST BOLDRE [SU3700]

☆ *Turf Cutters Arms* [Main Rd]: Small dim-lit New Forest country local, relaxed and quite unpretentious, lots of beams and pictures, sturdy tables, rugs, bare boards and flagstones, log fire, good home cooking from sandwiches and basic dishes to quite a lot of game, Gales HSB, Ringwood Best and Wadworths 6X, several dozen malt whiskies, no smoking room, fish tanks, two big friendly dogs; garden tables, some good heathland walks, three big old-fashioned bedrooms, simple but comfortable, good breakfast *(BB, Charles and Pauline Stride, Ben Stephenson, W W Burke)*

EAST END [SZ3696]

☆ *East End Arms* [back road Lymington—Beaulieu, parallel to B3054]: New Forest country local (which means rather upmarket these days) with log fire in chatty plain bright bar, nice pictures in longish neat candlelit dining lounge, well kept Ringwood Best on handpump and other ales tapped from the cask, good choice of wines by the glass, good value home cooking (Sun lunch often booked up), helpful staff; tables in small pleasant garden, popular with families *(BB, E S Funnell, A D Marsh, JMC)*

EAST MEON [SU6822]

☆ *George* [Church St; signed off A272 W of Petersfield, and off A32 in West Meon]: Rambling and relaxing rustic pub with heavy beams and inglenooks, four log fires, cosy areas around central bar counter, deal tables and horse tack; well kept Badger Best and Tanglefoot, decent wines, country wines, wide choice of good substantial food inc interesting dishes, friendly licensees; children welcome, good outdoor seating arrangements, quiz night Sun; small but comfortable bedrooms (book well ahead), good breakfast; pretty village with fine church, good walks *(Ann and Colin Hunt, LYM, Mark Percy, Lesley Mayoh, Cathy Robinson, Ed Coombe, W A Evershed, Patrick Hancock, Dave and Lesley Walker, Nicholas and Dorothy Stephens)*

EASTON [SU5132]

☆ *Cricketers* [off B3047]: Open-plan village local with well kept ales such as Otter, Ringwood Best, Timothy Taylors Landlord and Wessex Slip, wide choice of good value piping hot pub

food, prompt friendly service, pleasant mix of pub furnishings, small bright restaurant, good wine range; darts and shove-ha'penny one end, jazz duo Weds; well cared for bedrooms *(Ron Shelton, Dr and Mrs A K Clarke, Tim and Carolyn Lowes, Lynn Sharpless, Mr and Mrs R W Allan, J R Ringrose)*

EMERY DOWN [SU2808]

☆ *New Forest* [village signed off A35 just W of Lyndhurst]: Good position in one of the nicest parts of the Forest, with good walks nearby; attractive softly lit separate areas on varying levels, each with its own character, hunting prints, two log fires, good imaginative generous food from filled baps up, well kept Hook Norton and two Ringwood beers, wide choice of realistically priced house wines, proper coffee; children allowed, small but pleasant three-level garden *(Dick and Madeleine Brown, W W Burke, Mike and Sue Richardson, B and K Hypher, LYM)*

EMSWORTH [SU7406]

Coal Exchange [Ships Quay, South St]: Unspoilt but comfortable compact L-shaped Victorian local, low ceilings, lots of locals and yachtsmen, well kept Gales ales, cheerful service, good value lunchtime food inc good crab salad and popular Sun lunch (open all day then), real fire each end; can be smoky when busy; tables outside, handy for Wayfarers Walk and Solent Walk *(Ann and Colin Hunt, Val and Alan Green)*

☆ *Kings Arms* [Havant Rd]: Neat and tidily organised local popular for generous wholesome interesting food cooked by landlady, fresh veg and some organic dishes, good choice of wines, good service, cheerful landlord, well kept Gales and a guest beer such as Everards Gold, good wine choice and coffee, small restaurant area, no mobiles; no children in bar, pleasant garden behind *(Miss J F Reay, Ann and Colin Hunt, Martin and Rose Bonner)*

Lord Raglan [Queen St]: Popular little Gales pub with nice welcoming atmosphere, good range of reasonably priced food esp fish, cheerful long-serving licensees, log fire, restaurant (must book summer wknds); live music Sun evening, children welcome if eating, pleasant sea-view garden behind *(Ann and Colin Hunt)*

ENBORNE [SU4264]

Craven Arms [W, towards Hamstead Marshall]: Pleasantly refurbished, with good choice of around five well kept real ales, welcoming service, enjoyable food; plenty of room in and out, cl Mon *(Ian Walker, Sue and Jeff Evans)*

EVERSLEY [SU7762]

White Hart [B3348]: Proper genuine local, old posters and lots of team photographs, reasonably priced food from snacks up, three different areas suiting darts crowd (with sports TV), smart set and doggie set, back dining area, good long-serving tenant; open all day *(Dick and Madeleine Brown)*

EVERTON [SZ2994]

☆ *Crown* [pub signed just off A337 W of

Lymington]: Good interesting food cooked to order (so may be a wait), attractive prices, tiled central bar, two attractive rooms with sturdy tables on polished boards off tiled-floor bar, log fires, lots of jugs and china, well kept Gales HSB, Hampshire Strongs Best and Ringwood Best, friendly attentive and helpful service; no dogs, picnic-sets on front terrace and back grass, quiet village on edge of New Forest (*David Sizer, Dr and Mrs A K Clarke, BB, Mrs S Hayward, A D Marsh*)

EXTON [SU6120]
☆ *Shoe* [village signed from A32]: New licensees doing enjoyable food (not Sun night) inc good chalkboard specials in rustic bar, attractive light oak-panelled room off and cosy log-fire restaurant (very popular with older people, with small helpings on request); neat bright décor, cheerful helpful service, well kept Wadworths ales, decent house wines, piped music; smart façade, tables on lawn down to River Meon – pretty village, good walks (*Peter B Rea, Cathy Robinson, Ed Coombe, W A Evershed, Stephen and Jean Curtis*)

FAREHAM [SU5806]
Cob & Pen [Wallington Shore Rd, not far from M27 junction 11]: Pleasant pine furnishings, flagstones and carpets, Hook Norton Best and Ringwood ales, good value straightforward food, nice separate games room; large garden (*Ann and Colin Hunt, Val and Alan Green*)
Lord Arthur Lee [West St]: Large open-plan Wetherspoons pub named for the local 1900s MP who presented Chequers to the nation, attractively priced well kept beers, good value food, provision for children (*Val and Alan Green, Lynn Sharpless*)
Parsons Collar [nr M27 junction 9; turn off Whiteley Way at Segensworth roundabout into Rookery Ave, sign to Solent Hotel, pub on left]: Warm and welcoming, new but done up to give old-fashioned impression, helpful landlord and friendly staff, decent buffet-style food in lots of nicely separated eating areas, several good beers, fine terrace (attractive wooded area) (*Graeme Hargreaves*)
White Horse [North Wallington]: Two-bar local, neat and friendly, with pictures of old Fareham, well kept ales such as Bass, Oakleaf (from Gosport) and Tetleys, good blackboard choice of well cooked standard food, pleasant service, restaurant; piped music (different in each bar) may obtrude; terrace and garden (*Charles and Pauline Stride, Val and Alan Green*)

FARRINGDON [SU7135]
Rose & Crown [off A32 S of Alton; Crows Lane – follow Church, Selborne, Liss signpost]: Roomy pub, clean, bright and comfortable, with log fire, fresh flowers, daily papers, neat back dining room, cheerful efficient service, Adnams, Courage Best, Four Marks and Greene King IPA, enjoyable food, decent wines, good value coffee; tables in well kept back garden (*BB, Ron Shelton*)
Royal Oak [Gosport Rd (A32 S of Alton), Lower Farringdon]: Pleasant open-plan

roadside pub, new landlord doing good sensibly priced interesting food inc Sun roasts and using local ingredients, quick friendly service, four well kept real ales, log fire, pictures, brasses and some sturdier bric-a-brac such as smith's bellows; children welcome (*Betty Laker, D Crook*)

FREEFOLK [SU4848]
Watership Down [Freefolk Priors, N of B3400 – sharp lane uphill at W end of village]: Fine choice of changing well kept ales from small breweries in genuine unaffected compact village pub, partly brick-floored, with functional furnishings, popular food from sandwiches to good value Sun roasts, no smoking conservatory; games area with plenty of old-fashioned slot machines and table football; piped music, Sun quiz night; nicely placed above grassy bank, huge attractive garden with play area and rabbit pen, pleasant walks and off-road cycling (*Geoff Palmer, Dr and Mrs A K Clarke, Tim and Carolyn Lowes*)

FROGHAM [SU1712]
☆ *Foresters Arms* [Abbotswell Rd]: Busy and well run extensively refurbished New Forest pub, flagstones and small woodburner, friendly service, well kept Wadworths and guest ales, decent wines, reasonably priced enjoyable blackboard food from sandwiches to very popular Sun lunch, extended dining room; children welcome, pleasant garden and pretty front verandah; small camp site adjacent, nearby ponies and good walks (*Martin and Karen Wake, J and B Cressey, LYM*)

GOODWORTH CLATFORD [SU3642]
Royal Oak: Friendly new young management, efficient service and good food from old favourites and Sun roast to more interesting dishes in comfortable and quite smart modern-looking pub, well kept beer; quiet sheltered garden, large, pleasant and safe for children, with good riverside walks nearby (*Phyl and Jack Street, P R and D C Groves*)

GOSPORT [SZ5998]
☆ *Alverbank House* [Stokes Bay Rd, Alverstoke]: Pleasant lounge with half a dozen well kept interesting changing ales in immaculate hotel in woods at end of Walpole Park, over road from promenade; good interesting choice of food with plenty for vegetarians, Ringwood and four well kept guest beers such as Cottage Wheel Tappers, Oakham Heckler, Orkney Northern Lights and Wychwood Wicked Witch, friendly well trained staff, piped music; nice big mature garden with Solent and Isle of Wight view and play area, bedrooms very well appointed (*Val and Alan Green, Ian Phillips*)
☆ *Clarence* [Mumby Rd (A32)]: Partly 18th-c, incorporating a former chapel from the Isle of Wight, heavy furnishings, old books, prints and other pictures, good-sized no smoking area; wide choice of food in bar and upstairs restaurant, well kept local Oakleaf beers (they don't currently use their own microbrewery, viewed through glass panels in bar and minstrel's gallery), log and coal fires, relaxed atmosphere, Edwardian dining room; dogs

welcome, no games or piped music; medieval evenings, open all day *(Ann and Colin Hunt, Ian Phillips)*

Fighting Cocks [Clayhall Rd, Alverstoke]: Unpretentious local with cheap food, popular Tues live music night; piped music may be loud; big garden with play area *(Peter and Audrey Dowsett)*

Jolly Roger [Priory Rd, Hardway]: Harbourside pub with friendly nautical atmosphere, real ales inc Marstons Pedigree, reasonably priced food, harbour and shipping views *(Peter and Audrey Dowsett)*

Queens [Queens Rd]: Bare-boards pub whose landlady expertly keeps Badger Tanglefoot, Roosters Yankee, Youngs Best and two more changing strong beers, three areas off bar with good log fire in interesting carved fireplace, friendly pyrenean mountain dog; very quick service, Sun bar nibbles, perhaps huge filled rolls and other simple food; sensibly placed darts, family area with TV, no piped music, quiz night Thurs; open all day Sat *(Ann and Colin Hunt)*

GREYWELL [SU7151]

Fox & Goose [nr M3 junction 5; A287 towards Odiham then first right to village]: Two-bar village pub with country-kitchen furniture, food from sandwiches up (inc cream teas), Courage Best, Gales HSB and Oakleaf Bitter; good-sized garden behind, attractive village, handy for Basingstoke Canal walks *(Liz and Brian Barnard)*

HAMBLEDON [SU6716]

☆ **Bat & Ball** [Broadhalfpenny Down; about 2 miles E towards Clanfield]: Extended dining pub opp seminal cricket pitch (matches most summer Sundays), plenty of cricket memorabilia, comfortable modern furnishings in three rooms and panelled restaurant, log fire; good interesting food from modestly priced snacks inc baguettes and toasties to fresh fish, energetic landlord, good service, well kept Gales ales, lovely downs views and walks *(Mrs P Sladen, P R and S A White, W A Evershed, LYM, Phyl and Jack Street)*

Horse & Jockey [Hipley]: Smart biggish dining pub, friendly well trained staff, well kept ales inc Fullers London Pride, wide choice of reasonably priced food inc some imaginative dishes, large garden by stream *(David and Ruth Hollands)*

HAZELEY [SU7459]

Shoulder of Mutton [Hazeley Heath]: Friendly old dining pub with popular bar lunches from ploughman's to good steaks (no snacks just meals on Sun, when many tables are booked), good helpful service, good fire in cosy lounge, no smoking area, well kept Courage ales; quiet piped music; attractive building, terrace and garden *(Francis Johnston, R Lake, Colin McKerrow)*

HECKFIELD [SU7260]

☆ **New Inn** [B3349 Hook—Reading (former A32)]: Big well run rambling open-plan dining pub, good welcoming service, enjoyable food inc good light lunch selection, well kept beers, decent wines, attractive layout with some

traditional furniture in original core, two good log fires, no piped music; restaurant; neat tables on pleasant terrace, bedrooms in comfortable and well equipped extension *(LYM, P and R Wayth)*

HERRIARD [SS6744]

Fur & Feathers [pub signed just off A339 Basingstoke—Alton]: Good value home-made food from filled rolls and baked potatoes up in open-plan pub with stripped pine tables and chairs on bare boards, Cheriton Pots, fff Moondance and Shepherd Neame Spitfire, log fire, lots of jockey cigarette cards; well lit pool table in carpeted area with big prints; picnic-sets out on front tarmac *(Jill Hurley, BB, Tony Radnor)*

HILL HEAD [SU5402]

Osborne View [Hill Head Rd]: Roomy modern red plush clifftop pub with three stepped-back levels and picture windows for stunning views to the Isle of Wight, well kept Badger beers, nautical prints and memorabilia, popular attractively priced food inc children's and evening restaurant, efficient service; may be piped music; open all day (busy wknds), garden and beach access, nr Titchfield Haven bird reserve *(Val and Alan Green, A and B D Craig, Jenny Cridland, Gordon Cooper)*

HOLBURY [SU4203]

Bridge Tavern [Ipers Bridge]: Nicely refurbished, in pleasant spot by New Forest, Gales HSB, interesting choice of reasonably priced above-average food *(Dr Martin Owton)*

HOOK [SU7354]

☆ **Crooked Billet** [about 1 mile towards London]: Wide choice of good attractively presented food all day, swift friendly service under good long-serving licensees, homely log fires, well kept Courage Best and Directors and two guest beers, good range of soft drinks; soft piped music; attractive garden by stream with trout and ducks; children welcome *(David Swann, A Park)*

HORDLE [SZ2996]

☆ **Gordleton Mill** [Silver St]: Popular newish licensees doing good satisfying food in side and back dining bar, good wines, friendly staff, attractive country surroundings; smart comfortable bedrooms *(Donald and Margaret Wood, John and Joan Calvert)*

HORNDEAN [SU7013]

Ship & Bell [London Rd]: Comfortable and spacious pub/hotel adjoining Gales brewery, full range of their beers kept well, good range of wines, reasonably priced standard food, quick friendly service, cheerfully relaxed bar with deep well and real fire, snug lounge with broad low steps up to dining room, interesting quotations and photographs; 14 bedrooms with own bathrooms, nice walk to Catherington church *(Ann and Colin Hunt, Joan and Michel Hooper-Immins)*

HORSEBRIDGE [SU3430]

☆ **John o' Gaunt** [off A3057 Romsey—Andover, just SW of Kings Somborne]: Friendly pub in River Test village, very popular with walkers for good attractively priced home cooking (the game casseroles are a treat), well kept ales such as Itchen Valley Fagins, Palmers BB and Ringwood Best and Fortyniner, decent wines by the glass, welcoming licensees, unpretentious L-shaped bar (the black spaniel enjoys its log fire), interesting prints in small back dining area, no piped music; dogs welcome, picnic-sets out in side arbour *(Prof and Mrs Tony Palmer, A and B D Craig, BB, Ron Shelton, Lynn Sharpless)*

HOUGHTON [SU3432]

Boot [S of Stockbridge]: Quiet country pub with good interesting food in unpretentious bar with log fire or roomy and attractive restaurant on left, attentive service, pleasant long garden running down to lovely (unfenced) stretch of River Test, where they have fishing; good walks, and opp Test Way cycle path *(Phyl and Jack Street, Norman and Sheila Davies)*

HURSLEY [SU4225]

Dolphin [A3090 Winchester—Romsey]: Good relaxed country atmosphere, good value food inc children's helpings, well kept Wadworths 6X, attentive staff; attractive garden, animals for children to watch *(Jim and Janet Brown)*

IBSLEY [SU1409]

Old Beams [A338 Salisbury—Ringwood]: Big busy black and white thatched all-day eatery, largely no smoking, redone with lots of pine furniture under aged oak beams, wide choice of food inc large salad bar, Greene King real ales, conservatory; open all day *(the Didler, David M Cundy, LYM, D and S Price)*

ITCHEN ABBAS [SU5332]

☆ *Trout* [4 miles from M3 junction 9; B3047]: Smallish country pub with unpretentious lounge, pleasantly unfussy no smoking restaurant, proper chatty public bar with traditional games, enjoyable food inc some interesting dishes, well kept Greene King ales with a guest such as Everards, decent wines, generally good efficient service and cheerful young licensees; comfortable bedrooms, tables in sheltered pretty side garden, good river and downland walks nearby *(Lynn Sharpless, Susan and John Douglas, Val and Alan Green, LYM, Tim and Carolyn Lowes, Mrs Joy Griffiths, Phyl and Jack Street, Dr and Mrs D Woods)*

KEYHAVEN [SZ3091]

☆ *Gun*: Busy yet cosy 17th-c pub looking over boatyard and sea to Isle of Wight, low-beamed bar with lots of nautical memorabilia and plenty of character (less in family rooms); good choice of generous food using local produce, well kept beers such as Gales HSB, Greene King Old Speckled Hen, Ringwood and Wadworths 6X, well over a hundred malt whiskies, bar billiards; children in back conservatory, garden with swings and fishpond *(A D Marsh, Colin McKerrow, M G Hart)*

KING'S SOMBORNE [SU3531]

Crown [A3057]: Long low pub opp village church and school, several cosy rooms off, good value generous food, pleasant service; smallish back garden with play area, Test Way and Clarendon Way footpaths nearby *(Phyl and Jack Street)*

LANGSTONE [SU7104]

☆ *Royal Oak* [off A3023 just before Hayling Island bridge]: Charmingly placed pub overlooking tidal inlet and ancient wadeway to Hayling Island, boats at high tide, wading birds when it goes out, spacious simply furnished flagstoned bar, two linked dining areas, winter open fires, well kept Boddingtons, Flowers Original, Gales HSB and beer, good choice of wines by the glass, popular food inc all-day snacks; can get very busy and smoky; children in eating areas, good coastal paths nearby, open all day *(Dennis Le Couilliard, LYM, Ian Phillips, Ann and Colin Hunt, Jess and George Cowley, Charles and Pauline Stride, Irene and Derek Flewin, Mr and Mrs S Felstead, Tracey and Stephen Groves)*

☆ *Ship* [A3023]: Busy waterside 18th-c former grain store, smart and well cared for, plenty of tables on heated terrace by quiet quay, lovely view across to Hayling Island from roomy dimly lit nautical bar with upper deck dining room, good no smoking areas, fast friendly helpful service, full Gales range kept well with a guest beer, good choice of wines by the generous glass, country wines, log fire, wide range of generous food inc fresh fish and platters for two, good no smoking areas; children's room, open all day, good coast walks *(Joan and Michel Hooper-Immins, Val and Alan Green, Charles and Pauline Stride, Tony and Wendy Hobden, W A Evershed, David and Carole Chapman, A and B D Craig, Ann and Colin Hunt, Lynn Sharpless)*

LEE-ON-THE-SOLENT [SU5600]

☆ *Bun Penny* [Manor Way]: Carefully extended, with low beams and flagstones, conservatory and restaurant, pleasant furnishings and bric-a-brac, two log fires, good choice of good food (and free peanuts), well kept Boddingtons, Flowers and Wadworths 6X, decent wines, daily papers, friendly efficient staff; garden, lots of flowers in summer *(Jess and George Cowley, Val and Alan Green, Jenny Cridland, Gordon Cooper)*

LINWOOD [SU1910]

☆ *Red Shoot* [signed from A338 via Moyles Court, and from A31; go on up heath to junction with Toms Lane]: Nice New Forest setting, big picture-window bar with attractive old tables, mixed chairs and rugs on bare boards, country pictures on puce walls, large back dining area with generous good value food inc good sandwiches, interesting children's choice and OAP bargain, friendly atmosphere and staff, well kept Wadworths ales and Forest Gold or Toms Tipple brewed at the pub, Mar and Oct beer festivals; children, dogs and muddy boots welcome, some disabled access, picnic-sets on sheltered side terrace, open all day wknds and summer – very touristy then (by big campsite and caravan park) *(M Blatchly, BB, G Coates, Rev John Hibberd, M Joyner)*

LIPHOOK [SU8330]

Links Hotel [Portsmouth Rd]: Spacious golf-oriented pub with subdued modern décor and good 1880-1920s local photographs, Ballards

Best, Courage Best and Hogs Back TEA, decent wines, enjoyable varied restaurant food inc crab, lobster and game, good atmosphere, friendly staff *(Miss C F Skelton, Ian Phillips)*

LITTLE LONDON [SU6359]

Plough [Silchester Rd, off A340 N of Basingstoke]: Cosy unspoilt tucked-away local with tiled floor, low beams, friendly landlord, limited food inc lots of good value baguettes, well kept Ringwood and interesting guest beers, log fire, darts, bar billiards; attractive garden, handy for Pamber Forest and Calleva Roman remains *(J V Dadswell, Pat and Robert Watt, Mick Simmons)*

LOCKS HEATH [SU5006]

☆ *Jolly Farmer* [2½ miles from M27 junction 9; A27 towards Bursledon, left into Locks Rd, at end T-junction right into Warsash Rd then left at hire shop into Fleet End Rd]: Wide choice of food from filled baps to steaks and good value very popular two-sitting Sun lunch in extensive series of softly lit rooms with nice old scrubbed tables (quite close-set) and a forest of interesting bric-a-brac and prints, coal-effect gas fires, no smoking area, well kept Flowers Original, Gales HSB and Fullers London Pride, decent wines and country wines, interesting landlord, neat friendly staff; two sheltered terraces, one with a play area and children's lavatories; nice bedrooms *(Peter and Audrey Dowsett, Michael and Robin Inskip, Charles and Pauline Stride, Roger and Pauline Pearce, Ann and Colin Hunt, LYM, Val and Alan Green)*

LONGPARISH [SU4344]

Plough [B3048, off A303 just E of Andover]: Comfortable open-plan dining lounge divided by arches, pleasant atmosphere, very wide food choice from sandwiches through speciality sausages to steaks, lobster and plenty of fish, children's dishes, partly no smoking restaurant, smiling service, well kept Boddingtons, Greene King Old Speckled Hen, Wadworths 6X and a guest such as Hampshire King Alfreds, decent house wines; piped music; children in eating areas, tables on terrace and in nice garden, bedrooms *(Lynn Sharpless, Jess and George Cowley, Darren Le Poidevin, Derek Allpass, LYM, Geoff Palmer, KC, Gloria Bax, Jayne Capp)*

LOWER FROYLE [SU7643]

Anchor [signed off A31]: Unassuming 14th-c traditional pub with roomy and brightly lit low-ceilinged bar and dining room, popular with older people lunchtime (esp Weds) for reasonably priced food with wide choice from sandwiches to fish, cheerful family service, well kept Courage and Timothy Taylors Landlord, decent malt whiskies; tables outside, bedrooms *(Ron Shelton)*

LOWER WIELD [SU6339]

☆ *Yew Tree* [off A339 NW of Alton, via Medstead or Bentworth]: Primarily a very good if pricy french restaurant, with good wines and charming service, but also has small central flagstoned bar used by locals and walkers, with real ales tapped from the cask and a good log fire; nice quiet spot by village

cricket pitch, tables out on front terrace and in garden, attractive open walking country *(Michael Huberty, John Hale, Phyl and Jack Street, LYM, Christopher and Elise Way)*

LYMINGTON [SZ3295]

Angel [High St]: Large recently refurbished open-plan pub spreading comfortably around central bar, panelling and black beams, enjoyable food inc children's, well kept Wadworths 6X, reasonable prices, helpful staff, no smoking area; piped music; tables in attractive inner courtyard, bedrooms, open all day *(LYM, Ken Flawn, Tim and Carolyn Lowes)*

☆ *Chequers* [Ridgeway Lane, Lower Woodside – dead end just S of A337 roundabout W of Lymington, by White Hart]: Busy yachtsmen's local with polished boards and quarry tiles, attractive pictures, plain chairs and wall pews; generous good food inc local fish, real ales such as Bass, Ringwood and Wadworths 6X, pleasant young staff, traditional games; may be piped music; well behaved children allowed, tables and summer marquee in neat walled back family garden, attractive front terrace, handy for birdwatching at Pennington Marshes *(JMC, LYM)*

☆ *Fishermans Rest* [All Saints Rd, Woodside]: Wide choice of consistently good interesting food inc very popular Sun lunch, reasonable prices, well kept Ringwood ales, decent wines, friendly staff, pleasant atmosphere, plenty of locals at bar; can get busy, wknd booking recommended *(A D Marsh, Mike and Sue Richardson, Ben Whitney and Pippa Redmond)*

Fusion [Queen St]: Recently transformed into appealing pub with interesting thai/fusion restaurant, two real ales *(Ben Whitney and Pippa Redmond)*

LYNDHURST [SU2908]

Crown [High St]: Best Western hotel, cheerful log fire in cosy traditional panelled bar, obliging efficient staff, well kept Ringwood Best and Porter, good value well served food; bedrooms, fine forest walks *(Phyl and Jack Street, Dr and Mrs A K Clarke)*

MAPLEDURWELL [SU6851]

☆ *Gamekeepers* [off A30, not far from M3 junction 6]: Popular dining pub with dark beams, joists and standing timbers, well spaced prettily set tables, glass-topped well with carp in flagstoned and panelled core, large no smoking dining room, well kept Badger ales inc Best and Tanglefoot, good choice of food; piped music; children welcome, picnic-sets on terrace and back grassy area, lovely thatched village with duckpond, good walks, open all day *(Martin and Karen Wake, Phyl and Jack Street, Derek Harvey-Piper, Andrew Scarr, KC, Thomas Neate, Francis Johnston, LYM)*

MARCHWOOD [SU3810]

☆ *Pilgrim* [Hythe Rd, off A326 at Twiggs Lane]: Beautiful and immaculate thatched pub with red plush banquettes in long L-shaped bar, wide choice of consistently good value home-made food, long-serving landlord and generally good welcoming service, well kept mainstream beers, english wines, open fires, separate more expensive restaurant; can be crowded, handy for otter and owl park at Longdown; neat garden *(A and B D Craig, Lynn Sharpless, Phyl and Jack Street, LYM, Anthony Groves)*

MATTINGLEY [SU7357]

Leather Bottle [3 miles from M3 junction 5; in Hook, turn right-and-left on to B3349 Reading Road (former A32)]: Wisteria-covered tiled dining pub with food all day, well spaced tables in linked areas, black beams, flagstones and bare boards, good inglenook log fire, extension opening on to covered heated terrace, well kept Courage Best and Greene King Abbot with a guest beer such as Charles Wells Bombardier; piped music; picnic-sets in two pretty garden areas, one pleasantly modern *(B and K Hypher, LYM, Tracey and Stephen Groves)*

MEONSTOKE [SU6119]

☆ *Bucks Head* [village signed just off A32 N of Droxford]: Plush banquettes, log fire, rugs on bare boards and well spaced tables in partly panelled L-shaped dining lounge looking over road to water meadows, nice public bar with leather settee by another log fire, darts and juke box, well kept Greene King IPA, Gales HSB and a seasonal beer, decent wines, friendly staff; tables and picnic-sets in small garden, lovely village setting with ducks on pretty little River Meon, good walks, bedrooms with own bathrooms, open all day Sun at least in spring and summer *(Ann and Colin Hunt, W A Evershed, BB)*

MICHELDEVER [SU5142]

Dove [Micheldever Station, off A33 or A303]: Wide choice of well presented food from familiar favourites to more exotic dishes, popular good value OAP lunches, children's dishes, Sun carvery and adventurous theme nights, well kept Flowers Original, Ringwood Best and a guest beer *(Pete Robbins)*

MINLEY [SU8357]

Crown & Cushion [A327, just N of M3 junction 4A]: Attractive small traditional pub with low-priced food from baguettes and ciabattas up, Greene King Abbot and Tetleys, coal-effect gas fire; big separate raftered and flagstoned rustic 'meade hall' behind, very popular wknds (evenings more a young people's meeting place), with huge log fire; children in eating area, heated terrace overlooking own cricket pitch *(Ian Phillips, LYM)*

MINSTEAD [SU2811]

☆ *Trusty Servant* [just off A31 nr M27 junction 1]: Three opened-up rooms inc sizeable restaurant area, ageing furniture and lots of character, nicely varied choice of very good generous food from huge baguettes with chips to imaginative main dishes, fresh fish and game, well kept changing ales such as Fullers London Pride, Ringwood Best and Wadworths 6X, annual beer festival, Thatcher's farm cider, decent house wines and country wines, efficient obliging service; dogs very welcome, may be piped music; open all day, tables in good-sized

garden, pleasant simple bedrooms, good breakfast, pretty New Forest village with wandering ponies, interesting church and easy walks *(Dick and Madeleine Brown, Caraline and Richard Crocker, M Joyner, Phyl and Jack Street, BB, Mike and Sue Richardson, A D Marsh, Tom and Ruth Rees, Mike and Heather Watson)*

MORTIMER WEST END [SU6363]

Red Lion [Church Rd; Silchester turn off Mortimer—Aldermaston road]: Country dining pub with good food from generous doorstep sandwiches up (they don't let you stray from the exact menu – service otherwise good and brisk), well kept Badger and other ales, lots of beams, stripped masonry, timbers and panelling, good log fire; quiet piped music; dogs and children welcome, plenty of seats in pleasant garden with play area, and on small flower-filled front terrace, open all day, handy for Roman Silchester *(LYM, J V Dadswell, Shirley Mackenzie)*

Turners Arms [Fairfield Park, West End Rd, Mortimer Common]: Welcoming open-plan L-shaped Brakspears pub with their beers inc Mild, full range of good value generous bar food inc OAP special in no smoking dining area, prompt pleasant service, log fire; tables in garden *(June and Robin Savage)*

NETHER WALLOP [SU2936]

Five Bells [signed off B3084 W of Stockbridge]: Plain beamed village pub with long cushioned settles, Wadworths IPA and 6X, friendly service, traditional games, spacious back dining area, provision for children; seats outside, pretty thatched village *(Nigel and Sue Foster, LYM, Phyl and Jack Street)*

NEWTOWN [SU6112]

Travellers Rest [off A32 N of Wickham]: Uncomplicated country pub gently enlarged but still cosy, one chatty local bar and another mainly for the straightforward food, warm welcome, three real ales inc Fullers London Pride and Greene King Abbot, traditional furnishings; pretty back garden *(LYM, Ann and Colin Hunt)*

OTTERBOURNE [SU4623]

Old Forge [Main Rd]: Pleasantly reworked and well organised Vintage Inn, their usual decent food all day, good atmosphere, efficient friendly staff, Bass and Tetleys *(Phyl and Jack Street)*

PENNINGTON [SZ3194]

Musketeer [North St]: Popular local with helpful service, short but flexible choice of enjoyable low-priced lunches, children's helpings, well kept Ringwood and guest ales from distant small breweries, log fire, family room; terrace tables *(Andy Sykes)*

PETERSFIELD [SU7423]

☆ *Good Intent* [College St]: Committed landlord and neat staff, well kept Gales BB, GB and Festival Mild and Greene King Abbot, wide choice of decent food from sandwiches to steak inc lots of unusual sausages, 16th-c core with low oak beams, log fire, well spaced good-sized pine tables with flowers, Fullers London Pride and other well kept ales, camera collection, cosy family area; some live music *(W A Evershed, Patrick Hancock, Ian Phillips)*

☆ *White Horse* [up on old downs road about halfway between Steep and East Tisted, nr Priors Dean – OS Sheet 186 or 197 map ref 715290]: Legendary old unspoilt country pub high on the downs, with old-fashioned furnishings in two charming and idiosyncratic parlour rooms (candlelit at night), attractive no smoking family dining room, open fires throughout, up to nine real ales, decent simple food (not Sun evening) from sandwiches and baked potatoes up; it's had its ups and downs recently, with management changes, but is wonderful when on form; rustic tables outside *(Ann and Colin Hunt, W A Evershed, the Didler, John Davis, Ian Phillips, Colin Gooch, Charles and Pauline Stride, LYM)*

PHOENIX GREEN [SU7555]

Phoenix [A30 W of Hartley Wintney]: Enjoyable food inc speciality giant sausages and good choice of puddings, Fullers London Pride, decent wines by the glass *(Mr and Mrs J Brown)*

PORTSMOUTH [SZ6399]

American Bar [White Hart Rd]: Spacious colonial-theme bar with good mix of customers, well kept Courage Directors and Wadworths 6X, reasonably priced lunchtime bar food from sandwiches and baguettes up, evening restaurant (one room no smoking) with some emphasis on fresh fish and seafood, good friendly service; garden behind, handy for IoW ferry *(Colin Moore)*

Connaught Arms [Guildford Rd/Penhale Rd]: Attractive and relaxing Tudor corner local with friendly long-serving licensees, good value straightforward food from lots of pasties to Sun roast, well kept changing ales such as Bass, Cheriton Pots and Fullers London Pride, sensibly placed darts; terrace *(Ann and Colin Hunt)*

Fountain [London Rd, North End]: Fairly large spick and span bar with family room off, nicely polished brass, interesting prints, mirrors each end, well kept Badger Best and Gales HSB; seats outside *(Ann and Colin Hunt)*

George [Queen St, nr dockyard entrance]: Venerable nautical pub with leather seats and panelling in front, more comfortably plush at back, well kept Wadworths 6X and Youngs, friendly staff, log fire, covered well and Nelson pictures, pleasant separate eating area; bedrooms, handy for dockyard and HMS Victory *(Ann and Colin Hunt, Jess and George Cowley)*

☆ *Still & West* [Bath Sq, Old Portsmouth]: Great position by the narrow harbour mouth, with big windows for vibrant views even to the Isle of Wight – but you pay for it; nautical décor, tasty bar food, well kept Gales BB and HSB, friendly attentive service, upper partly no smoking restaurant; fruit machines, piped music; open all day, children welcome, lots of picnic-sets out on waterfront terrace *(LYM, W A Evershed, Mike and Jennifer Marsh, Colin Gooch, David and Carole Chapman,*

LM, Ian and Jacqui Ross, Brenda and Rob Fincham, Ann and Colin Hunt, Ken Flawn)

Surrey Arms [Surrey St]: Comfortable two-bar backstreet local popular lunchtime for good food, good choice of well kept beer; bedrooms, open all day *(Ann and Colin Hunt)*

Toby Carvery [Copnor Rd/Norway Rd, Hilsea]: Popular family dining pub specialising in generous daily carvery, busy on Sun (no booking); quick friendly service inc drinks at tables, real ale, decent value wine, tables in garden *(Peter and Audrey Dowsett)*

PRESTON CANDOVER [SU6041]

Purefoy Arms [B3046]: Cheerful local in attractive village, good range of sensibly priced generous food, quick friendly service, well kept Courage Best, games in public bar; get there early for live jazz Thurs and first Sun in month; big peaceful garden with play area overlooking fields, nearby snowdrop walks, open all day Sun *(Ann and Colin Hunt)*

RINGWOOD [SU1405]

Inn on the Furlong [Meeting House Lane, next to supermarket]: Long flagstoned bar, stripped brick and oak timbering, simple décor, full range of Ringwood beers from nearby brewery kept well, daily papers, good friendly young staff, good value lunchtime food, conservatory dining extension; quiet piped music; open all day (Sun afternoon closure), live music Tues, Easter beer festival *(Bruce Bird)*

ROCKBOURNE [SU1118]

Rose & Thistle [signed off B3078 Fordingbridge—Cranborne]: Attractive thatched 16th-c pub with fresh home-made food (best to book Sun lunch), well kept real ales, good range of wines, civilised bar with antique settles, old engravings and good coal fire, traditional games, log fires in front restaurant with no smoking area; may be piped classical music; children welcome, tables by thatched dovecote in neat front garden, charming tranquil spot in lovely village, good walks *(Terry and Linda Moseley, LYM, L M Parsons)*

ROMSEY [SU3521]

Abbey Hotel [Church St]: Friendly and comfortable plush and mahogany bar with enterprising food choice from sandwiches and baked potatoes to rabbit pie and guinea fowl, fast service, well kept Courage Best and Directors, dining area with Victorian photographs; bedrooms, opp Abbey *(Ron Shelton, John Beeken)*

☆ *Dukes Head* [A3057 out towards Stockbridge]: Attractive 16th-c dining pub festooned with flowering baskets in summer, picturesque series of small linked rooms each with its own quite distinct and interesting décor, well kept Courage Best, Fullers London Pride and Greene King Abbot, decent house wines, good coffee, rewarding choice of popular well presented food from unusual fresh sandwiches up, big log fire; may be quiet piped music; picnic-sets out in front, nicer tables on sheltered back terrace, attractive back garden *(R T and J C Moggridge, Gordon Prince,*

Ian Phillips, Prof and Mrs Tony Palmer, BB)
Old House At Home [Love Lane]: Attractive
16th-c thatched pub under new licensees,
tastefully old-fashioned décor, good freshly
made food (can be a wait), well kept Gales ales
inc a seasonal one; no mobile phones *(Ian Bell,
A and B D Craig, Prof and Mrs Tony Palmer)*
Three Tuns [Middlebridge St]: Attractive bow-
windowed pub with panelling and some low
black beams, tastefully refurbished by new
licensees, good bistro food (rather than
sandwiches or pubby snacks, though they do
have light dishes), starched table linen, well
kept Gales GB and Wadworths IPA;
piped music may obtrude; children allowed at
lunchtime, some seats outside, has been open
all day wknds *(John Davis, LYM,
Peter Walters)*

ROTHERWICK [SU7156]
Coach & Horses [signed from B3349 N of
Hook; also quite handy for M3 junction 5]:
Individual furnishings and roaring fire in two
small beamed front rooms, decent generous
food from lunchtime sandwiches to steaks,
fresh veg, no smoking eating areas, inner
parquet-floored serving area with several
Badger ales and a couple of Gribble guests,
daily papers, relaxed atmosphere, entertaining
parrot; tables in back garden, pretty flower
tubs and baskets *(Susan and Nigel Wilson,
M R Jackson, Charles Moncreiffe,
Debbie Lovely, Anthony Barnes, John and
Joan Calvert, Gordon Stevenson, Norman and
Sheila Sales, Mr and Mrs S Felstead, LYM,
Colin and Sandra Tann)*

ROWLAND'S CASTLE [SU7310]
Robin Hood [The Green]: Modern-style bar,
light and airy, with quarry tiles, bare boards
and some carpet, sturdy pine and other tables,
nice contemporary retro artwork, enjoyable
up-to-date food inc plenty of fish, well kept
Fullers London Pride and Hook Norton Old
Hooky, good wine choice; piped music;
disabled access and facilities, picnic-sets on
heated front terrace, on green of pleasant
village *(Ann and Colin Hunt, BB)*

SELBORNE [SU7433]
☆ **Selborne Arms** [High St]: Hop-festooned
village local with well kept Cheriton Pots,
Courage Best and Directors and Ringwood
Fortyniner, lots of wines, enjoyable fresh food
with good mix of pub standards and more
inventive or sophisticated snacks and main
dishes, dining room off unpretentious bar
(smoking in both) with old photographs, fresh
flowers, log fire in fine inglenook, twinkly
landlord, cheerful polite service even when very
busy, good cream teas in back parlour
doubling as collectables shop; tables in garden
with terrace and good play area, right by walks
up Hanger, and handy for Gilbert White
museum *(Val and Alan Green, Ian Phillips,
Margaret Ross)*

SHEDFIELD [SU5512]
Wheatsheaf [A334 Wickham—Botley]: Busy
little local now under same owners as Flower
Pots at Cheriton, their beers tapped from the
cask, restricted menu initially, impromptu

piano sessions in public bar; garden, handy for
Wickham Vineyard *(Ann and Colin Hunt)*

SHERFIELD ENGLISH [SU3022]
Hatchet [Romsey road]: Traditional beamed
pub, good varied generous food inc fish and
children's dishes (chips as good as in Brussels,
say some), Adnams, good wine choice,
attentive staff, restaurant area; tables outside
(Peter Walters)

SOBERTON [SU6116]
☆ **White Lion** [School Hill; signed off A32 S of
Droxford]: Cheerful Georgian-fronted 16th-c
country pub in nice spot by green, enjoyable
basic lunchtime food and bistro evening menu
in rambling no smoking restaurant, irregularly
shaped bare-boards bar with built-in wooden
wall seats and traditional games, more
comfortable lounge, four well kept ales such as
Greene King Old Speckled Hen, Wadworths
6X and a beer brewed for them by Hampshire,
decent house wine, friendly licensees, locals
and dogs; children in eating areas, small
sheltered pretty garden with suntrap fairy-lit
terrace, open all day, good walks nearby
*(Val and Alan Green, LYM, W A Evershed,
Ann and Colin Hunt)*

SOBERTON HEATH [SU6014]
Bold Forester [Forester Rd]: Comfortable
country pub with well kept ales such as
Ringwood Fortyniner, plentiful
straightforward food, daily papers, friendly
licensees, dogs welcome; garden with fenced
play area, field for camping behind, good
walks *(Ann and Colin Hunt)*

SOPLEY [SZ1597]
☆ **Woolpack** [B3347 N of Christchurch]: Pretty
thatched pub with rambling candlelit open-
plan low-beamed bar, rustic furniture,
woodburner and little black kitchen range,
friendly helpful staff, enjoyable food from
sandwiches and ploughman's to steaks and Sun
roasts, well kept Flowers Original, Ringwood
Best and Wadworths 6X, no smoking
conservatory; piped music; open all day,
children in eating areas, charming garden,
picnic-sets under weeping willows, stream with
ducks and footbridges *(David M Cundy, LYM,
Mrs A Trier, Eddie Edwards, S Horsley,
Ian Phillips, Colin McKerrow)*

SOUTHAMPTON [SU4212]
Cowherds [The Common (off A33)]: Low-
beamed Vintage Inn dining pub in nice setting
by common, welcoming atmosphere, cosy
alcoves and tables in nice little bay windows,
lots of Victorian photographs, carpets on
polished boards, log fires, good generous
unfussy food inc fresh fish, well kept Bass and
Tetleys, good wine choice, cheery caring quick
service; very busy with young people Sun;
tables outside with tie-ups and water for dogs
(50p deposit on glasses taken out) *(Mr and
Mrs R W Allan, Neil Rose, Gill and
Keith Croxton, Mr and Mrs Gordon Turner,
Peter and Anne-Marie O'Malley)*

Crown [Highcrown St, Highfield]: Bustling
warmly relaxed local, well kept Archers,
Flowers Original, Fullers London Pride and
Wadworths 6X, good value substantial food,

helpful staff, open fires – popular with students and academics from nearby Uni; piped music; dogs allowed in main bar (giving country feel in the suburbs), heated covered terrace, Sun quiz night, open all day *(Phyl and Jack Street, Prof and Mrs Tony Palmer)*

Duke of Wellington [Bugle St (or walk along city wall from Bar Gate)]: Ancient timber-framed building on 13th-c foundations, bare boards, log fire, friendly relaxed atmosphere, really helpful service, well kept reasonably priced ales such as Bass, Ringwood Best and JCB and Wadworths IPA, good choice of wines by the glass, decent home-made bar food, no smoking back dining room; front bar can get smoky; very handy for Tudor House Museum *(Val and Alan Green, Ken Flawn)*

South Western Arms [Adelaide Rd, by St Denys stn]: A dozen or so real ales inc Badger, Gales and Wadworths, enthusiastic staff, basic food and décor (bare boards and brickwork, toby jugs and stags head on beams, lots of woodwork, ceiling beer mats), upper gallery where children allowed; popular with students, easy-going atmosphere, juke box; picnic-sets on terrace, live jazz Sun afternoon *(Dr Martin Owton)*

SOUTHSEA [SZ6498]

5th Hampshire Volunteer Arms [Albert Rd]: Popular two-bar backstreet local, Gales beers, military memorabilia; open all day *(the Didler)*

Florist [Fratton Rd, Fratton]: Wadworths real ales in 19th-c pub, same family for 35 years; quiet lounge, bar with pool and juke box *(the Didler)*

Hogshead [Palmerston Rd]: Rather dim-lit and studenty, with some character, food inc decent ciabattas, three real ales inc Marstons Pedigree and Wadworths 6X *(Val and Alan Green)*

Olde Oyster House [Locksway Rd, Milton]: Name recalls Langstone Harbour's oyster beds: two-bar pub with five real ales mainly from small breweries, inc a Mild, and farm cider; busy wknd evenings *(the Didler)*

Red White & Blue [Fawcett Rd]: Busy open-plan local, well kept Gales, food Sat lunchtime; games nights, jazz Weds, open all day *(the Didler)*

Sir Robert Peel [Astley St]: Bright plain no-nonsense local among the tower blocks, worth knowing for its well kept low-priced changing ales such as Bass, local Packhorse Old Pompey, Ringwood and Robinsons, Thatcher's farm cider, friendly regulars and staff *(Catherine Pitt)*

SOUTHWICK [SU6208]

Golden Lion [High St; just off B2177 on Portsdown Hill]: Welcoming two-bar local popular for good value simple food inc Sun lunch; well kept Gales, also distinctive Suthwyk ales, brewed by local farm using its own barley which they malt themselves, friendly staff, antique pine, pleasant restaurant; where Eisenhower and Montgomery came before D-Day, picturesque estate village with scenic walks *(Ann and Colin Hunt, Val and Alan Green)*

Red Lion [High St]: Low-beamed Gales dining pub, mainly no smoking, good choice from good baguettes up, BB and a seasonal beer, friendly prompt service *(Val and Alan Green)*

ST MARY BOURNE [SU4250]

Bourne Valley [Upper Link]: Recently refurbished, with friendly bars and restaurant, enjoyable food, good range of local real ales, gardens backing on to river; nine bedrooms *(Arthur Baker)*

STOCKBRIDGE [SU3535]

☆ *Greyhound* [High St]: Substantial inn reworked as restauranty gastropub (you can, though not cheaply, still have a beer and a simple ploughman's or generous sandwich at the bar), log fires each end of bow-windowed bar, old trestle tables and simple seating on woodstrip floor, dark beams and joists with low-voltage spotlights, lots of good black and white photographs, very civilised atmosphere, good wines inc some costly stars, notable restaurant food, Courage Directors, Greene King IPA and Abbot and Wadworths 6X; tables in charming Test-side garden behind, children and dogs allowed, bedrooms and fly fishing *(Derek Harvey-Piper, BB, Margaret Ross)*

☆ *Grosvenor* [High St]: Quietly luxurious atmosphere and quick cheery service in pleasantly restrained and comfortable old country-town hotel's refurbished bar, decent food inc good soup and sandwiches and reasonably priced specials, well kept Greene King IPA, Abbot and Old Speckled Hen, several wines by the glass, country prints and log fire; piped music; big attractive garden behind, good value bedrooms *(Mrs E A Macdonald, W W Burke, BB, Geoffrey Kemp)*

Vine [High St]: Popular pub/restaurant with good value food inc half helpings for children, helpful landlord/chef, old beams and woodwork, stripped bricks and purple wallpaper, delft shelf of china and pewter, bright floral curtains, Boddingtons, Brakspears and Flowers Original, good wine list, unobtrusive piped music; open all day, tables in nice big garden, wknd barbecues, comfortable bedrooms *(Derek Hayman, LYM, C Whittington)*

☆ *White Hart* [High St; A272/A3057 roundabout]: Good value food from soup and sandwiches to Sun lunch in roomy and welcoming divided bar, oak pews and other seats, attractive décor with antique prints, full range of Gales ales kept well, decent wines, country wines, cheerful service; children allowed in comfortable beamed restaurant with blazing log fire, tables in garden, bedrooms, open all day *(Phyl and Jack Street, Stephen and Jean Curtis, Mrs E A Macdonald, Geoff Palmer, Mr and Mrs S Felstead, LYM)*

SWANMORE [SU5816]

Hunters [Hillgrove]: Much-extended family dining pub, excellent for children, with big plain family room, winding garden with secluded tables and several good play areas for different age groups, plenty under cover and even one for babies; long-serving live-wire landlord, well kept Gales HSB and Charles

Wells Bombardier tapped from the cask, good house wine and country wines, attentive service, plush bar with lots of boxer pictures, bank notes, carpentry and farm tools, no smoking area; very busy wknds, nice walks N of village *(Phyl and Jack Street, Val and Alan Green)*

New Inn [Chapel Rd]: Friendly village local with attentive licensees, Greene King ales, home cooking with some more adventurous dishes; games, darts, cricket team; cl Tues lunchtime *(Val and Alan Green)*

Rising Sun [Hill Pound; off B2177 S of Bishops Waltham]: Comfortable tile-hung pub with smart food from baguettes up (booking advised wknd), Weds theme night, well kept Adnams, Greene King Old Speckled Hen, Marstons Pedigree and Ringwood Best, good value wines, good log fires, quick french service, hops on low beams, scrubbed pine, well separated extended dining area; the cat's called Fritz; pleasant good-sized side garden with play area and perhaps summer bouncy castle, handy for Kings Way long distance path – best to head W *(Geoff Palmer, Val and Alan Green, Phyl and Jack Street)*

SWANWICK [SU5109]

Elm Tree [handy for M27 junction 9]: Neat and comfortable, with two bars and dining room off, several real ales, wide range of home-made food; quiet piped music; children welcome, tables in garden, handy for Hampshire Wildlife Reserve *(Val and Alan Green)*

TANGLEY [SU3252]

☆ *Cricketers Arms* [towards the Chutes]: Tucked away in unspoilt countryside, relaxed atmosphere, character small front bar with tiled floor, massive inglenook, roaring log fire, bar billiards, welcoming licensees and friendly labrador called Pots, bistroish back flagstoned extension with a one-table alcove off, some good cricketing prints, good value food from fresh baguettes to imaginative main dishes, well kept Bass and Cheriton Pots tapped from the cask; tables on neat terrace, new bedroom block *(Darren Le Poidevin, I A Herdman, Bernie Adams, LYM)*

☆ *Fox* [crossroads S of village, towards Andover]: Welcoming little beamed and timbered pub with generous good value imaginative home cooking inc fresh fish, generous veg and fine range of puddings, prompt helpful service, two well kept local ales, good choice of wines, two big log fires, two pleasant no smoking family dining rooms *(Penny Power, Nigel and Sue Foster, Arthur Baker)*

THRUXTON [SU2945]

White Horse [Mullens Pond, just off A303 eastbound]: Very friendly 16th-c thatched local rather dwarfed by A303 embankment, soft lighting, very low beams, horse-racing décor, log fire, well kept Fullers London Pride and Greene King IPA, decent food inc good sandwiches, separate dining area, relaxed informality, obliging landlord *(Hugh Roberts)*

TIMSBURY [SU3525]

☆ *Bear & Ragged Staff* [A3057 towards Stockbridge; pub marked on OS Sheet 185 map ref 334254]: Extensively refurbished beamed country dining pub, attractive choice of enjoyable reasonably priced food all day, quick welcoming service, several well kept ales, lots of wines by the glass, country wines; children in eating area, tables in extended garden with good play area, handy for Mottisfont, good walks *(Phyl and Jack Street, Anthony Evers, J P Humphery, LYM)*

Malthouse [A3057 N of village]: Spacious pub with wide choice of decent blackboard food (best to book wknds), real ales such as Gales, Ringwood and Wadworths, courteous service; good secluded back garden with terrace, pretty fishpond, barbecue house and big well equipped play area; nr fine Norman church, pleasant paths to Michelmersh *(Phyl and Jack Street)*

TITCHFIELD [SU5406]

Fishermans Rest [Mill Lane, off A27 at Titchfield Abbey]: Busy Whitbreads family pub/restaurant in fine riverside position opp Titchfield Abbey, tables out behind overlooking water; hearty food all day in eating area with close-set tables and no smoking family area, well kept ales such as Gales HSB, Greene King IPA and Wadworths 6X, cheerful service, two log fires, daily papers, fishing memorabilia *(Peter and Audrey Dowsett, LYM, Ann and Colin Hunt)*

Queens Head [High St; off A27 nr Fareham]: Ancient pub with good value food esp fish cooked by landlord, changing well kept ales such as Fullers London Pride, Hampshire Strongs Best and Pride of Romsey and Timothy Taylors Landlord, friendly service, Sun bar nibbles, cosy 1930s-feel bar with old local pictures, window seats and central brick fireplace, attractive restaurant, a couple of cats; picnic-sets among lovely flower tubs in small back yard, bedrooms, pleasant conservation village nr nature reserve and walks to coast *(Ian Phillips, E S Funnell, Charles and Pauline Stride)*

Titchfield Mill [A27, junction with Mill Lane]: Large popular Vintage Inn catering well for families in neatly kept converted watermill, olde-worlde room off main bar, smarter dining room, upstairs gallery, stripped beams and interesting old machinery, well kept Bass and Tetleys, good choice of wines by the glass, freshly squeezed orange juice, neat attentive and friendly staff; piped music; open all day, sunny terrace by mill stream with two waterwheels – food not served out here *(Charles and Pauline Stride, Mrs Joy Griffiths, Phyl and Jack Street, Ann and Colin Hunt, Michael and Robin Inskip)*

TURGIS GREEN [SU6959]

☆ *Jekyll & Hyde* [A33 Reading—Basingstoke]: Bustling rambling pub with nice mix of furniture and village atmosphere in black-beamed and flagstoned bar, larger stepped-up three-room dining area with varied food from sandwiches up all day inc breakfast, children's helpings, welcoming prompt service, well kept Badger Best and IPA and Wadworths 6X, some interesting prints; lots of picnic-sets in good

sheltered garden (some traffic noise), play area and various games; disabled facilities *(KC, LYM)*
TWYFORD [SU4724]
Phoenix [High St]: Cheerful open-plan local with lots of prints, bric-a-brac and big end inglenook log fire, wide choice of sensibly priced generous food from sandwiches to steaks and theme nights, friendly enthusiastic landlord, well kept Greene King and guest beers, decent wines, back room with skittle alley, children allowed at one end lunchtime; quiet piped music; garden *(Val and Alan Green, Lynn Sharpless)*
UPPER CLATFORD [SU3543]
Crook & Shears [off A343 S of Andover, via Foundry Rd]: Homely olde-worlde 17th-c two-bar pub, bare boards and panelling, small dining area, Ringwood, Whitbreads and a guest beer, back skittle alley *(the Didler)*
UPTON [SU3555]
Crown [N of Hurstbourne Tarrant]: Linked rooms with pine tables and chairs, a pleasant modicum of sporting prints, horse tack and so forth, good log fires, enjoyable fresh food inc interesting evening dishes, good friendly service, well kept Fullers London Pride and Ringwood Best, good coffee, happy bustling atmosphere; may be piped music in public bar; conservatory, small garden and terrace *(Nigel and Sue Foster, Margaret Ross, BB)*
VERNHAM DEAN [SU3456]
☆ *George*: Rambling open-plan beamed and timbered pub, exposed brick and flint, inglenook log fire, good blackboard food, roomy no smoking eating area (children allowed), well kept Greene King IPA, Abbot and Ruddles County, decent wines; darts, shove-ha'penny, dominoes and cribbage; picnic-sets in pretty garden behind, lovely thatched village, fine walks *(Phyl and Jack Street, LYM, the Didler)*
WALTHAM CHASE [SU5614]
Black Dog [Winchester Rd]: Low-ceilinged two-bar pub covered with hanging baskets; well kept Greene King IPA and Abbot, decent wine, wide menu, efficient service, large log fire, partly no smoking back restaurant extension; garden tables *(Ann and Colin Hunt)*
Chase [B2177]: Comfortable seating like smart lounge, second room with nicely extended no smoking eating area, real ales such as Greene King IPA and Ruddles, generous reasonably priced food from baguettes to french restaurant dishes; jazz nights *(Val and Alan Green, Ann and Colin Hunt)*
WEST END [SU4714]
Southampton Arms [Moorgreen Rd, off B3035]: Thriving local, quite big, with Ringwood ales, enjoyable reasonably priced food, friendly efficient service, comfortable and cosy bar, attractive conservatory restaurant; good garden *(Phyl and Jack Street)*
White Swan [Mansbridge Rd]: Pleasant spot with tables out by River Itchen, good beer range, cosy bar and traditional carvery restaurant; riverside walks *(Phyl and Jack Street)*
WEST MEON [SU6424]
Thomas Lord [High St]: Attractive village pub

with well kept Bass, Gales GB, Greene King Old Speckled Hen and Ringwood Best, good selection of wines, log fire, cricket memorabilia inc club ties and odd stuffed-animal cricket match, pool table tucked around corner, pleasant and popular separate dining area, fresh flowers; soft piped music; tables in big garden with play house, good walks W of village *(Ian Phillips, Phyl and Jack Street, W A Evershed)*
WEST WELLOW [SU2919]
Rockingham Arms [pub signed off A36 Romsey—Ower at Canada roundabout]: Beamed 19th-c pub down forest-edge dead end, good choice of reasonably priced food, several well kept changing ales inc Gales and Ringwood, good sensibly priced wine list, friendly atmosphere, open fire, comfortable and attractive back restaurant, games in public bar, lots of Hants CC memorabilia; children welcome, very good play area in garden opening on to pretty heathland with roaming horses *(Phyl and Jack Street, A D Marsh)*
WHITCHURCH [SU4648]
☆ *Red House* [London St]: 14th-c beams and fireplaces (one an inglenook with ancient flagstones in front), family-friendly lounge with step up to no smoking eating area, good generous cooking by landlord/chef from home-baked rolls to modern european hot dishes inc interesting vegetarian ones, friendly service under on-the-ball landlady, well kept Cheriton Pots and a guest such as Archers Golden, decent house wines, separate public bar on left; attractive terrace with play area *(Ian and Deborah Carrington, LYM, Phyl and Jack Street, Mr and Mrs Robert Jamieson, Bryan and Betty Southwell)*
WICKHAM [SU5711]
Greens [formerly Inn on the Square]: Upmarket feel, with smart dining pub on upper level, Bass, Fullers London Pride and a guest such as Hop Back Summer Lightning, long-serving licensees and friendly staff, steps down to no smoking restaurant; tables out on pleasant lawn overlooking watermeadows, cl Mon exc bank hols *(Val and Alan Green)*
Kings Head [The Square]: Pretty two-bar pub with no smoking restaurant up some steps, good log fire, wide choice of decent sensibly priced food, Gales ales, good coffee, friendly service; tables out on square and in back garden with play area, attractive village *(Val and Alan Green)*
Roebuck [Kingsmead; A32 towards Droxford]: Well appointed, with two dining rooms (one no smoking), wide range of food from decent sandwiches to some less usual things, Fullers London Pride and a house beer, generally good helpful service, lots of prints and plates, library of books, white grand piano (friendly new ex-panto landlord sometimes plays and sings); children in no smoking area, conservatory *(A D Marsh, Charles and Pauline Stride, Mrs M Jagger, Tim and Carolyn Lowes)*
WINCHESTER [SU4728]
Bell [St Cross Rd]: Well kept Greene King ales, decent fresh food (nice baked potatoes with

home-baked ham), welcoming service, separate plain public bar; big garden, handy for St Cross Hospital – lovely water-meadows walk from centre *(Val and Alan Green, Craig Turnbull, Phil and Sally Gorton)*

Crown & Anchor [Broadway (E end)]: Comfortable pub opp Guildhall, old pine furniture, three areas, popular food (can be a wait when busy), Greene King Abbot and Wadworths IPA and 6X *(Craig Turnbull, Val and Alan Green, Roger and Pauline Pearce)*

Jolly Farmer [Andover Rd]: Neatly kept, with decent standard menu, Boddingtons, Hook Norton Old Hooky, Ringwood Best and Wadworths 6X *(Val and Alan Green)*

King Alfred [Saxon Rd, Hyde]: Welcoming Victorianised pub with unfussy traditional décor, wood and opaque glass dividers, enjoyable food from lunchtime baguettes and baked potatoes to imaginative blackboard dishes, Greene King ales inc Ruddles, good wine choice, friendly attentive staff; TV, pool, piped music; pleasant garden with boules and small animals *(Lynn Sharpless)*

Old Gaol House [Jewry St]: Big busy Wetherspoons pub with large no smoking area, food all day, good choice of locally brewed beers, low prices, no piped music *(Ann and Colin Hunt, Val and Alan Green)*

Queen [Kingsgate Rd]: Roomy pub in attractive setting opp College cricket ground, reasonably priced mainstream food inc Sun lunch and children's dishes, well kept Greene King ales, decent wines, cricketing and other prints, bric-a-brac on window sills, central fireplace, darts in public bar; disabled facilities, open all day, tables on front terrace and in large attractive garden *(Lynn Sharpless, M Etherington, the Didler)*

☆ *Royal Oak* [Royal Oak Passage, off upper end of pedestrian part of High St opp St Thomas St]: Cheerful main area doubling as coffee bar, little rooms off (some raised), beams and bare boards, scrubbed tables, no smoking areas, five

or six ales such as Caledonian Deuchars IPA, Greene King Abbot, Hook Norton Old Hooky and Ringwood Best, short choice of good value quick food; piped music, several fruit machines, and packed with young people Fri/Sat nights; the no smoking cellar bar (not always open) has massive 12th-c beams and a Saxon wall which gives it some claim to be the country's oldest drinking spot *(the Didler, Tim and Carolyn Lowes, Ann and Colin Hunt, LYM)*

☆ *Westgate Hotel* [Romsey Rd/Upper High St]: Big-windowed corner pub, good food inc organic produce and excellent meat in smallish white-panelled eating area with cheerful prints, friendly relaxed service from neat staff, well kept ales such as Ansells and Tetleys, small choice of good wines, daily broadsheet papers; jazz Mon, bedrooms with own bathrooms *(Mrs Theresa Gillham, BB)*

☆ *Willow Tree* [Durngate Terr]: Warmly welcoming local with landlord/chef cooking unusually good food inc interesting dishes; well kept Greene King beers, good wines; attractive riverside setting *(Phil and Sally Gorton)*

WOODGREEN [SU1717]

☆ *Horse & Groom* [off A338 N of Fordingbridge]: Nice forest setting, comfortable and friendly linked beamed rooms around servery, nature photographs, log fire in pretty Victorian fireplace, well kept Badger ales, good choice of good value home-cooked food; picnic-sets on front terrace and in spreading back garden *(David M Cundy, LYM, Ian Phillips, Prof and Mrs Tony Palmer)*

WOTTON [SZ2497]

Rising Sun [Bashley Common Rd]: Friendly and roomy family pub with very wide choice of food all day inc good baguettes, adult-only bar with Ringwood beers and a guest such as Shepherd Neame Spitfire; garden with good adventure playground and animals, roaming New Forest ponies; busy school hols *(Christopher and Jo Barton)*

Bedroom prices normally include full english breakfast, VAT and any inclusive service charge that we know of. Prices before the '/' are for single rooms, after for two people in double or twin (B includes a private bath, S a private shower). If there is no '/', the prices are only for twin or double rooms (as far as we know there are no singles). If there is no B or S, as far as we know no rooms have private facilities.

Herefordshire

There is some very good food to be found in Herefordshire pubs these days, and places here have been more successful at developing a good restaurant and accommodation side without losing their pubby informality than in many other parts of Britain. Often, the buildings themselves are attractive, sometimes strikingly venerable. And this is rich territory for truly unspoilt cottagey pubs, not to mention good local beers and fine farm ciders. Pubs that currently stand out in one way or another include the Englands Gate at Bodenham (a new entry, nice food in a fine ancient building), the rather smart Roebuck Inn at Brimfield (new licensees doing well – good provision for dining, overnighting or just chatting over a drink), the grand old Feathers in Ledbury (good food and bedrooms, warmly welcoming atmosphere), the friendly and nicely unpretentious Three Horseshoes tucked away in Little Cowarne (our other new entry here this year, enterprising food very strong on local ingredients, and good bedrooms – likely to become a favourite), the attractive Lough Pool at Sellack (already a favourite dining pub for many), the ancient New Inn at St Owen's Cross (enjoyable food, nice atmosphere), the Stagg at Titley (marvellous food and wines), the Three Crowns at Ullingswick (good imaginative food, and keeping to its pubby roots), the Salutation looking down the green in Weobley (good all round) and the Crown at Woolhope (doing well for food and drink under friendly new licensees). The title of Herefordshire Dining Pub of the Year goes to the pleasantly informal Stagg at Titley. In the Lucky Dip section at the end of the chapter, pubs to note particularly are the Neville Arms at Abbey Dore, Live & Let Live at Brockhampton, Harewood End Inn, Bridge Inn at Michaelchurch Escley, Rhydspence at Whitney-on-Wye and Bell at Yarpole. Drinks are generally rather cheaper than the national average here. The Spinning Dog beer brewed and sold at the Victory in Hereford was the cheapest we found, followed by the local Wye Valley beer in the Crown at Woolhope. Hobsons (from over the Worcestershire border) shows up quite frequently as the cheapest beer stocked by a Herefordshire pub; and you might come across Dunn Plowman (see Lucky Dip entry for Queens Head in Kington), which also produces SP Sporting ales.

AYMESTREY SO4265 Map 6

Riverside Inn 🍴 ♈ 🛏

A4110; N off A44 at Mortimer's Cross, W of Leominster

As well as some nice circular walks that start from this idyllically placed black and white timbered inn, you can look around their vegetable plots – there are little diagrams mapping everything out. Inside, the rambling beamed bar has several cosy areas and a good laid-back atmosphere (walkers and their dogs are just as welcome as diners – there's a big restaurant area). The décor is drawn from a pleasant mix of periods and styles, with fine antique oak tables and chairs, stripped pine country kitchen tables, fresh flowers, hops strung from a ceiling waggon-wheel, horse tack, and nice pictures. There are warm log fires in winter, while in summer big overflowing flower pots frame the entrances; shove-ha'penny, cribbage, and piped music. Well kept Woods Parish Bitter, Wye Valley Dorothy Goodbodys Golden Ale, and a guest such as Spinning Dog Mutleys Springer on handpump, local farm cider, several malt whiskies, and decent house wines. The landlord likes to talk to his customers and service is good. Changing every two weeks, the enjoyable bar food includes filled baguettes, fillets of local trout fried in herb butter (£6.25), local venison sausages on minted pea purée with a red wine and rowanberry jus (£7.25), steak and mushroom in ale pie (£8.95), and hotpot of local lamb (£9.25), with specials such as lasagne or roasted stuffed peppers with local cheese (£6.95), locally smoked loin of pork (£8.25), and local eel pie with herb mash (£9.25). At the back are picnic-sets by a flowing river, and rustic tables and benches up above in a steep tree-sheltered garden, as well as a beautifully sheltered former bowling green. Residents are offered fly-fishing (they have fishing rights on a mile of the River Lugg), and a free taxi service to the start of the Mortimer Trail. It does get busy at weekends, so booking would be wise. *(Recommended by R M Corlett, Paul A Moore, Alan Thwaite, Rev Michael Vockins, Pamela and Merlyn Horswell, John Kane, Eleanor and Nick Steinitz, Stan and Hazel Allen, Mr and Mrs A Swainson, Nigel Bowles, Katherine Ellis)*

Free house ~ Licensees Richard and Liz Gresko ~ Real ale ~ Bar food (not Mon) ~ Restaurant ~ (01568) 708440 ~ Children welcome ~ Dogs welcome ~ Open 11-3, 6-11; 12-3, 6.30-10.30 Sun; closed Mon exc bank hols ~ Bedrooms: £45B/£65B

BODENHAM SO5454 Map 4
Englands Gate

Just off A417 at Bodenham turn-off, about 6 miles S of Leominster

This attractively timbered black and white 16th-c coaching inn has been well opened up inside, rambling around a vast central stone chimneypiece, with a big log fire on one side and a woodburning stove on the other – there's also a coal fire near the entrance. It looks every year of its age, with heavy brown beams and joists in low ochre ceilings, well worn flagstones, sturdy timber props, one or two steps, and lantern-style lighting. One nice corner has a comfortably worn leather settee and high-backed settle with scatter cushions; a cosy partly stripped stone room has a long stripped table that would be just right for a party of eight; a lighter upper area with flowers on its tables has winged settles painted a cheery yellow or aquamarine. A wide choice of enjoyable blackboard food includes good doorstep sandwiches, home-made soup (£2.95), rillette of duck with orange and sherry dressing (£3.95; main course £7.95), cajun chicken with cucumber dip (£4.25; main course £7.95), smoked haddock fishcake with green chillies and lime and coriander dressing (£4.75), stuffed aubergine with pesto sauce or steak and mushroom in ale pie (£6.95), sizzling skillet of chicken, steak or a vegetarian option inside mexican-style tortillas (from £7.95), chargilled lamb steak with stir-fried vegetables and a minted jus (£8.95), salmon fillet roasted with crushed tomatoes and basil (£8.95), and chargrilled steaks (from £11.50). Well kept Marstons Pedigree, Woods Shropshire Lad and Wye Valley Hereford and Butty Bach, Stowford Press cider, friendly staff; piped mellow pop music, and TV. There are tables out in an attractive garden. *(Recommended by Alan and Paula McCully, Lucien Perring, Derek Carless, John and Joan Wyatt)*

Free house ~ Licensee Evelyn McNeil ~ Real ale ~ Bar food (12-2.30, 6-9.30; not bank hol Mon evenings) ~ Restaurant ~ (01568) 797286 ~ Children in eating area of bar but must leave by 9 ~ Dogs allowed in bar ~ Open 11(12 Mon)-11; 12-10.30 Sun

BRIMFIELD SO5368 Map 4
Roebuck Inn ⑪ ♀ 🛏

Village signposted just off A49 Shrewsbury—Leominster

As well as offering first class food and comfortable bedrooms, this smart country dining pub makes good provision in the bars for those only wanting a drink and a chat. The new licensees have introduced lunchtime snacks like sandwiches (£4.25), platters with home-made breads and relishes (£5.75), and roast chicken breast or steamed fillet of salmon (£8), and other excellent food might include home-made soup (£3.50), artichoke, wild mushroom and asparagus ragoût or chicken liver parfait with chilli jam (£5.25); main course £9.90), a sausage of smoked chicken mousse served with sweet potato and a madeira sauce (£5.50), steak and mushroom suet pudding or popular fish pie (£8.95), herb-crusted roast fillet of cod with tomato and basil sauce (£9.95), roast chicken breast on a stir-fry of pak choi and sesame seeds with a sweet and sour pepper sauce (£11.95), delicious rump of lamb with port and redcurrant sauce (£13.95), brill and salmon gateaux with saffron and leek cream sauce (£14.95), and steaks (from £15.95). They have an interesting reasonably priced wine list, a carefully chosen range of spirits, Stowford Press cider, and well kept Tetleys and Woods Parish and a guest such as Adnams Broadside on handpump. Each of the three rambling bars has a different but equally civilised atmosphere. The quiet old-fashioned snug is where you might find locals drinking and playing dominoes, cribbage, table skittles or shove-ha'penny by an impressive inglenook fireplace. Pale oak panelling in the 15th-c main bar makes for a quietly relaxed atmosphere, and the Brimfield Bar with a big bay window and open fire is light and airy. The brightly decorated cane-furnished airy dining room is no smoking; courteous staff. There are seats out on the enclosed terrace. *(Recommended by W H and E Thomas, Rodney and Norma Stubington, W W Burke, FS, Dr W J M Gissane, Richard Cole, J H Jones, KC, Neil and Anita Christopher, Karen Eliot, Pamela and Merlyn Horswell)*

Free house ~ Licensees Mr and Mrs Jenkins ~ Real ale ~ Bar food ~ Restaurant ~ (01584) 711230 ~ Children in eating area of bar until 9 ~ Dogs allowed in bar ~ Open 11.30-3.30, 6.30-11; 12-3, 7-10.30 Sun ~ Bedrooms: /£70S(£70B)

CAREY SO5631 Map 4
Cottage of Content
Village signposted from good road through Hoarwithy

This very pretty, out-of-the-way medieval cottage is in a charming position, with a little lane winding past by a stream, and picnic-sets on the flower-filled front terrace. Inside is a pleasant mix of country furnishings – stripped pine, country kitchen chairs, long pews by one big table, and a mix of other old-fashioned tables on flagstones and bare boards, and there are plenty of beams and prints. Enjoyable bar food at lunchtime includes home-made soup (£3.50), filled baguettes and baked potatoes (from £4.50), various ploughman's or omelettes (£4.95), a vegetarian dish (£6.95), and a pie of the day or yorkshire pudding filled with a casserole of the day (£7.50), with evening choices such as tempura-battered hake with sweet chilli dressing (£4.25), warm goats cheese salad (£4.50), meaty or vegetarian lasagne (£7.50), chicken breast with a spicy tomato and chorizo sauce (£9.25), and duck breast with red wine and kumquat sauce (£12.50); part of the dining room is no smoking. Well kept Hook Norton Best and Wye Valley Bitter on handpump, and quite a few wines by the glass; piped music and darts. A couple of picnic-sets on a back terrace look up a steep expanse of lawn. *(Recommended by Ian and Denise Foster, John, Deborah and Ben Snook, Barry Collett, Di and Mike Gillam, the Didler)*

Free house ~ Licensee John Clift ~ Real ale ~ Bar food (not Sun evening or Mon) ~ Restaurant ~ (01432) 840242 ~ Children in eating area of bar ~ Dogs allowed in bar ~ Open 12-3, 7-11; 12-3, 7-10.30 Sun; closed Mon except bank hols

DORSTONE SO3141 Map 6
Pandy
Pub signed off B4348 E of Hay-on-Wye

This lovely half-timbered pub was built in 1185 by Richard de Brico to house workers constructing a chapel of atonement for his part in the murder of Thomas à Becket. The neatly kept homely main room (on the right as you go in) has heavy beams in the ochre ceiling, stout timbers, upright chairs on its broad worn flagstones and in its various alcoves, and a vast open fireplace with logs; a side extension has been kept more or less in character; no smoking area. Bar food includes lunchtime sandwiches (from £3.10) and ploughman's (£7.35), as well as home-made soup (£3.45), creamy garlic mushroom and cheese bake or home-made chicken liver pâté with cumberland sauce (£4.95), home-made salmon and spinach cannelloni or half a baked aubergine topped with toasted vegetables in tomato sauce with a parmesan crumb (£7.35), home-made lasagne (£7.65), steak and mushroom in ale pie (£8.75), local oak-smoked haddock in a cream, dill and whisky reduction and topped with a poached egg (£9.95), mixed venison and pheasant pie (£14.95), and home-made puddings like sticky toffee pudding with butterscotch sauce or apple and raisin crumble (£3.70). Well kept Wye Valley Butty Bach and a guest like Dorothy Goodbodys on handpump, lots of malt whiskies, farm cider and decent wines; darts, quoits and piped music. The hairy persian tom is Tootsie and the ginger tom, Peanuts. There are picnic-sets and a play area in the neat side garden. More reports please. *(Recommended by Mike and Mary Carter, the Didler, Martin Jones, Cathy Robinson, Ed Coombe, Pam and David Bailey, Alan and Paula McCully, Caroline and Michael Abbey, A C Stone)*

Free house ~ Licensees Paul and Marja Gardner ~ Real ale ~ Bar food (Mon lunchtimes) ~ Restaurant ~ (01981) 550273 ~ Well behaved children welcome ~ Open 12-3, 6-11 Tues-Fri; 12-11 Sat; 12-3, 6.30-10.30 Sun; closed Mon lunchtime except bank hols in summer, all day Mon in winter

HEREFORD SO5139 Map 6
Victory ❤ £
St Owen Street, opposite fire station

We were curious as to why this down-to-earth local called its brewery Spinning Dog. We found out when the phone on the bar counter rang: instantly, Cassie the dog spun insanely round and round like a whipping top! There are eight own brews: Chase Your Tail, Top Dog, Mutleys Bark Mild, Mutleys Revenge, Mutleys Springer, and Mutleys Oatmeal Stout, and a couple of changing guests on handpump. Three farmhouse ciders, too. The front bar counter is like a miniature ship of the line, with cannon poking out of its top, and down a companionway the long back room is well decked out as the inside of a man o' war: dark wood, rigging and netting everywhere, long side benches along sides that curve towards a front fo'c'sle, stanchions and ropes forming an upper crow's nest, appropriate lamps. Very reasonably priced straightforward bar food includes sandwiches (from £2), chilli con carne or chicken curry (£4.50), ploughman's or fish of the day (£5) and 8oz steak (£5.50), with specials such as faggots, mash and peas (£5). Service is friendly and informal (they'll show you around the brewery if they're not busy). There's a pool table at the back; also a juke box, darts, fruit machine, TV, skittle alley, cribbage, shove-ha'penny, and dominoes. There are some tables out behind the pub. *(Recommended by Mike Pugh, R T and J C Moggridge, Dr and Mrs M E Wilson, Bernie Adams)*

Own brew ~ Licensee James Kenyon ~ Real ale ~ Bar food (12-7) ~ Restaurant (Sun only) ~ No credit cards ~ (01432) 274998 ~ Children welcome ~ Dogs welcome ~ Acoustic club Thurs, Sat and Sun ~ Open 11-11; 12-10.30 Sun

LEDBURY SO7138 Map 4
Feathers ⊗ ♀ ⊨
High Street, Ledbury, A417

They've very cleverly managed to combine the hotel and food side in this elegantly striking Tudor timbered inn quite comfortably with the pub part. The rather civilised Fuggles bar has chatty and cheerful locals gathered at one end of the room or at stools by the long bar counter, quite uninhibited by those enjoying the good food and fine wines at the brasserie tables behind them. There are beams and timbers, hop bines, some country antiques, 19th-c caricatures and fancy fowl prints on the stripped brick chimneybreast (lovely winter fire), and fresh flowers on the tables – some very snug and cosy, in side bays. In summer, abundant pots and hanging baskets adorn the sheltered back terrace. Well kept Bass, Fullers London Pride and Worthington and a guest such as Everards Tiger on handpump; various malt whiskies, and farm cider. Particularly enjoyable food from an imaginative – if not cheap – menu at lunchtime might include home-made soup such as cream of sweet potato and ginger (£3.90), baguette with gruyère and smoked bacon or gloucester old spot ham sandwich with roasted red pepper mayonnaise (£4.50), a trio of local cheeses with bread and chutney (£5), thai-style filo wrapped prawns with sweet chilli (£6), mozzarella and basil tortellini in a light tomato and cream sauce (£6.95), smoked chicken caesar salad (£7.90), home-made burgers (£8.50), and lambs liver with melted onions, sage and mustard mash (£12.50); in the evening there might be fresh cornish crab with avocado, lime and mango remoulade (£6.50), home-made natural haddock and chive fishcakes or goats cheese polenta with roasted vegetable ratatouille (£8.50), seared fillet of lamb with cracked black pepper and madeira jus and mustard mash (£15.95), duck breast with a plum, brandy and hoisin sauce with warm pickled cabbage or fresh cornish bass on cider carrots, pancetta and minted new potatoes (£16.95), and puddings such as warm chocolate and pecan brownie, caramel and pear crumble or fresh berry terrine with blackcurrant sorbet and clotted cream (£4.50). Smashing breakfasts, and friendly, helpful staff. They do excellent afternoon teas in the more formal quiet lounge by the reception area, which has comfortable high-sided armchairs and sofas in front of a big log fire, and newspapers to read. *(Recommended by David and Ruth Hollands, John Whitehead, Denys Gueroult, Bob Broadhurst, J M and P M Carver, Derek Carless, Jenny and Dave Hughes, Mrs T A Bizat, A S and M E Marriott, Michael Dandy, Bill and Jessica Ritson)*

Free house ~ Licensee David Elliston ~ Real ale ~ Bar food ~ Restaurant ~ (01531) 635266 ~ Children welcome ~ Dogs allowed in bedrooms ~ Open 11-11; 12-10.30 Sun ~ Bedrooms: £71.50B/£95B

LITTLE COWARNE SO6051 Map 4
Three Horseshoes 🛏

Pub signposted off A465 SW of Bromyard; towards Ullingswick

With the front door open on a quiet spring day, the civilised quarry-tiled bar fills with the song of robins and blackbirds; this is deep country indeed, and there are peaceful views from the terrace tables and chairs, or the unusual fixed tables and benches on the neat prettily planted lawn. Some of the sturdy old kitchen tables are cloth-covered for the dominoes and cribbage players, there are old local photographs above the corner log fire, hops drape black beams in the dark peach ceiling (the walls too are peach). Opening off one side is a skylit no smoking sun room with wicker armchairs around more old tables; the other end has a games room with juke box, fruit machine and games machine. For the good bar food they use local gamekeepers and fishermen, buy local eggs and vegetables (though they grow summer salads themselves), and make their own chutneys, pickles, and jams. As well as noteworthy sandwiches, the menu might include onion and cider soup (£2.25), game terrine with pickled pears or crab and lime fishcakes (£4.25), tomato tarte tatin or steak in ale pie (£7.95), rabbit casserole or spiced lamb with apricots (£8.95), cod in home-cured bacon baked with herby home-grown potatoes (£9.50), crispy duck breast in rhubarb and ginger sauce (£9.95), fillet steak au poivre (£12.50), and home-made puddings like chocolate truffle torte, damson soufflé or toffee and banana cheesecake (£3.25). A few blackboard specials such as devilled kidneys or cider mackerel (£4.50) and pheasant (£8.95), with a popular OAP pie lunch on Thursday. Besides well kept Greene King Old Speckled Hen, Marstons Pedigree and Wye Valley Hereford on handpump, they have decent wines (including local english ones), and Oliver's local farm ciders and perry from named apple cultivars. Service is friendly and obliging, and there is disabled access. A roomy and attractive stripped stone raftered restaurant extension has a lunchtime carvery. *(Recommended by Mr and Mrs J Williams, Dr D J and Mrs S C Walker, Alan and Paula McCully, Denys Gueroult, J R Ringrose)*

Free house ~ Licensees Norman and Jane Whittall ~ Bar food ~ Restaurant ~ (01885)
400276 ~ Children welcome ~ Dogs allowed in bar ~ Open 11-3, 6.30-11; 12-3.30,
7-10.30 Sun; closed Sun evening, 25 Dec, 1 Jan ~ Bedrooms: £28.50S/£48S

LUGWARDINE SO5541 Map 4
Crown & Anchor ♀

Cotts Lane; just off A438 E of Hereford

The several smallish and charming rooms in this attractive black and white
timbered pub have a friendly, relaxed atmosphere, and there are usually a few
locals in the bar, which is furnished with an interesting mix of pieces, and has a big
log fire. Butcombe, Greene King Old Speckled Hen, Hook Norton, and Marstons
Pedigree on handpump, and lots of wines by the glass. As well as a huge choice of
good lunchtime sandwiches (from £2.50), there are at least half a dozen interesting
vegetarian dishes each day: black-eyed bean and seaweed casserole, aduki bean
bake, mushroom, butterbean and basil stew, and mixed bean goulash (all £6.50),
alongside a few equally interesting blackboard specials such as caerphilly cheese
and walnut pâté (£4) and cashew nut and wild mushroom korma (£8.50). There's
also home-made soup (£3), deep-fried brie with beetroot relish (£4.25),
ploughman's (from £6), fish pie or gammon and egg (£7.50), chicken with spinach
and mozzarella in a garlic and tomato sauce (£8.50), duck breast with plum and
port sauce (£10), sirloin steak with brandied blue cheese sauce (£12), and specials
such as terrine of venison and pistachios with raspberry vinaigrette (£4.50), papaya,
tiger prawns and star anise salad (£4.75), sausages with juniper and red wine sauce
(£7.50), fillets of torbay sole with mussels and white wine (£9.50), and roast
pheasant with bacon and barley and armagnac sauce (£12). The main eating area is
no smoking. The garden is pretty in summer. The pub is surrounded by newish
housing, but in ancient times the Lugg flats round here – some of the oldest
Lammas meadows in England – were farmed in strips by local farm tenants, and
meetings with the lord of the manor were held in the pub. *(Recommended by*
Christopher and Jo Barton, Denys Gueroult, Dr and Mrs M E Wilson, MJVK, Jenny and
Dave Hughes, R M Corlett, Bill and Jessica Ritson)

Enterprise ~ Lease Nick and Julie Squire ~ Real ale ~ Bar food (till 10) ~ Restaurant
~ (01432) 851303 ~ Children welcome ~ Live jazz first Weds evening of month ~
Open 12-11; 12-10.30 Sun; closed 25 Dec

ORLETON SO4967 Map 6
Boot

Just off B4362 W of Woofferton

New licensees have taken over this 16th-c partly black and white timbered pub,
with the aim of keeping its proper pubby atmosphere while also serving good food.
Cheerily popular with locals, the traditional-feeling bar has a mix of dining and
cushioned carver chairs around a few old tables on the red tiles, one very high-
backed settle, hops over the counter, and a warming fire in the big fireplace, with
horsebrasses along its bressumer beam. The lounge bar is up a couple of steps, and
has green plush banquettes right the way around the walls, mullioned windows, an
exposed section of wattle and daub, and standing timbers and heavy wall beams.
There's a small and pretty no smoking restaurant on the left. Well kept Hobsons
Best and Town Crier and a local guest on handpump, and local farm cider;
cribbage and dominoes. At lunchtime, the bar food now includes home-made soup
(£2.50), sandwiches (from £2.95), ploughman's (from £4.75), hot baguettes (from
£4.95), lasagne (£6.25), gammon and egg (£6.50), broccoli and stilton pasta bake
(£6.75), and steak in ale pie (£6.95); there's also home-made pâté (£3.75), poached
salmon with dill and mustard cream sauce or pork spare ribs (£7.50), stilton
chicken (£8.25), and steaks (from £9.75), along with daily specials such as deep-
fried brie wedges with raspberry coulis (£3.95), fried lambs kidneys and
mushrooms (£4.25), seafood lasagne (£8.95), rack of lamb with rosemary and
garlic gravy (£9.75), and escalope of veal with a light vermouth sauce (£9.95).

There are seats in the garden under a huge ash tree, a barbecue area, and a fenced-in children's play area. More reports please. *(Recommended by Pamela and Merlyn Horswell, Doreen and Haydn Maddock, R T and J C Moggridge)*

Free house ~ Licensees Philip and Jane Dawson ~ Real ale ~ Bar food ~ Restaurant ~ (01568) 780228 ~ Children in eating area of bar and restaurant ~ Dogs allowed in bar ~ Open 12-3, 6-11; 12-3, 7-10.30 Sun

PEMBRIDGE SO3958 Map 6
New Inn
Market Square (A44)

This ancient place is beautifully set in the centre of an attractive black and white mini-town. Its three simple but comfortable little beamed rooms ooze antiquity, with their oak peg-latch doors and elderly traditional furnishings including a fine antique curved-back settle on the worn flagstones; the log fire is the substantial sort that people needed long before central heating was reinvented. One room has sofas, pine furniture and books; the welcoming homely lounge is no smoking; darts, shove-ha'penny, and quoits. Well kept Black Sheep and Fullers London Pride and perhaps a couple of guests such as Dunn Plowman Kingdom on handpump, 30 malt whiskies, and local wine and apple juice. As well as sandwiches (from £2.75) and ploughman's (from £3.95), the good bar food includes home-made soup (£2.75), home-made pâté (£4.95), crab tartlet (£5.25), home-baked ham with new potatoes (£6.50), fish and chips (£6.95), breast of chicken with prunes and apricots (£7.50), and steak and mushroom pie (£7.95), with daily specials like leek and stilton croustade (£6.50), seafood stew (£9), and salmon with watercress sauce (£10); friendly staff. Tables out on the cobblestones between the pub and the former wool market overlook the church, which has an unusual 14th-c detached bell tower beside it. *(Recommended by Maurice and Gill McMahon, Gill and Tony Morriss, R M Corlett, Kevin Blake, Bill and Jessica Ritson)*

Free house ~ Licensee Jane Melvin ~ Real ale ~ Bar food ~ Restaurant ~ (01544) 388427 ~ Children in eating area of bar till 8.30 ~ Dogs allowed in bedrooms ~ Folk third Thurs of month ~ Open 11-3, 6-11; 12-3, 7-10.30 Sun; 12-2.30, 6-11 in winter; closed first week in Feb ~ Bedrooms: £20/£40

ROSS-ON-WYE SO6024 Map 4
Eagle ♀
Broad Street

Locals enjoy the bar on the right here, which is a fairly typical of a town pub: upholstered pews in booths, turkey carpeting (except in the central flagstoned serving area), darts (which they take seriously here), a well lit pool table and audible fruit machine at the back, and some really entertaining period cigarette cards; also piped pop music, TV, dominoes and cribbage. On the left is a more stylish dining area, with black bentwood chairs around modern tables on bare boards, cream or deep blue walls, steps up to a carpeted section with an open kitchen, spiral stairs to an upper gallery, and a whole wall of wine bottles. Handily served all day, the food is interesting (you can choose from the bar or the restaurant menu), running from fill-your-own sandwiches (from £2.95) to roast pheasant in bacon with chestnuts (£10.95); other dishes could be tomato and basil soup (£3.50), home-pickled mackerel with crunchy vegetables (£4.75), steak and kidney pie, lamb and mint casserole or cod in beer batter (£5.95), pasta with tomato, peppers and pesto (£7.95), chargrilled chicken with cider and onion sauce (£8.95), poached salmon fillet with mushrooms and mussels (£9.50), and 10oz T-bone steak (£15.95). Pleasant service from nicely uniformed waitresses, good wine, and Wye Valley Butty Bach on handpump. *(Recommended by Jean-Claude Ohms, David Carr)*

Enterprise ~ Lease James Arbourne ~ Real ale ~ Bar food (all day) ~ Restaurant ~ (01989) 562652 ~ Children welcome ~ Dogs allowed in bar and bedrooms ~ Open 8.30-11(10.30 Sun) ~ Bedrooms: £21.50/£55B

SELLACK SO5627 Map 4
Lough Pool ★ ⑪ ♀

Back road Hoarwithy—Ross-on-Wye

Set in countryside full of bridleways and walks, this attractive black and white timbered cottage has plenty of picnic-sets on its neat front lawned area, and pretty hanging baskets. Inside, the beamed central room has kitchen chairs and cushioned window seats around wooden tables on the mainly flagstoned floor, sporting prints and bunches of dried flowers, and a log fire at each end. Other rooms lead off, gently brightened up with attractive individual furnishings and nice touches like the dresser of patterned plates. The same interesting menu – which changes daily – is available in the chatty bar as well as the restaurant, and might include rocket and tarragon soup (£3.50), haggis fritters with beetroot relish (£4.95), spanish charcuterie (£5.50), grilled chicken and bacon ciabatta with mustard mayonnaise (£5.95), unmoulded goats cheese soufflé with hazelnut sauce (£5.75), ploughman's (£7.25), slow-cooked pork and foie gras terrine with toasted brioche (£7.50), venison sausages and mash with red wine gravy (£9.50), steak and kidney with Guinness (£11), butternut squash risotto with truffle oil (£11.50), chargrilled rib-eye steak (£12.50), moroccan chicken with chick pea purée (£13), and whole lemon sole with capers and lemon (£13); the restaurant is no smoking. Well kept John Smiths, Wye Valley Butty Bach, and a couple of guest beers from breweries like Freeminer or Spinning Dog, a good range of malt whiskies, local farm ciders and a well chosen reasonably priced wine list. Service is good. The landlord hopes to add bedrooms in 2004. *(Recommended by Pamela and Merlyn Horswell, GSB, John Kane, Guy Vowles, KN-R, Bernard Stradling, Mr and Mrs A Swainson, Anthony Rickards Collinson, Christopher and Jo Barton, Alec and Barbara Jones, Lucien Perring, Joyce and Maurice Cottrell, Stephen Williamson, Jill McLaren, Neil and Jean Spink, Ian and Denise Foster, Mike and Mary Carter, Di and Mike Gillam)*

Free house ~ Licensee Stephen Bull ~ Real ale ~ Bar food ~ Restaurant ~ (01989) 730236 ~ Children in eating area of bar, restaurant and family room ~ Dogs allowed in bar ~ Open 11.30-2.30, 6.30-11; 12-2, 7-10.30 Sun; closed 25 Dec and 26 Dec evenings

ST OWEN'S CROSS SO5425 Map 4
New Inn

Junction A4137 and B4521, W of Ross-on-Wye

In summer, the big enclosed garden at this unspoilt black and white timbered coaching inn really comes into its own, and there are colourful hanging baskets all around the building. The fine views stretch over rolling countryside to the distant Black Mountains. Inside, both the lounge bar (with a buoyant local atmosphere) and the no smoking restaurant have huge inglenook fireplaces, intriguing nooks and crannies, settles, old pews, beams, and timbers. Enjoyable food at lunchtime includes home-made soup (£3.25), sandwiches (from £3.50), home-made chicken liver pâté (£4.95), ploughman's or cumberland sausage with garlic and herb mash and gravy (£5.45), home-made lasagne or ham and egg (£5.95), a curry of the day (£7.25), and home-made steak and kidney pie (£7.45); in the evening there might be extras like thai fishcakes with a sweet chilli sauce (£4.45), garlic mushrooms (£4.75), lamb steak marinated in mint and garlic (£9.95), duckling with an orange and Grand Marnier sauce (£10.95), and steaks (from £10.95). Puddings such as chocolate truffle torte (£3.50) and mid-week lunchtime two-course meal (£5.99); friendly and pleasant service. Well kept Tetleys and Wadworths 6X alongside Adnams Broadside, Brains, and Shepherd Neame Spitfire on handpump, local cider, and a fair choice of malt whiskies; darts, shove-ha'penny, cribbage, dominoes, and piped music. The big doberman is called Tia Maria. More reports please. *(Recommended by Pam and David Bailey, R T and J C Moggridge, Gordon Prince, Neil and Jean Spink, Duncan Cloud, Pamela and Merlyn Horswell, R G Price, Mrs B M Smith)*

If you know a pub's ever open all day, please tell us.

Free house ~ Licensee Nigel Donovan ~ Real ale ~ Bar food ~ Restaurant ~ (01989) 730274 ~ Children welcome ~ Dogs welcome ~ Open 12-2.30(3 Sat), 6-11; 12-3, 7-10.30 Sun ~ Bedrooms: £40S(£45B)/£70S(£80B)

STOCKTON CROSS SO5161 Map 4
Stockton Cross Inn
Kimbolton; A4112, off A49 just N of Leominster

This is the sort of place customers regularly return to – and even plan their routes to include it as a lunchtime stop. It's a spotlessly kept little black and white timbered pub with a good mix of customers, and friendly, helpful service. A comfortably snug area at the top end of the long heavily beamed bar has a handsome antique settle facing an old black kitchen range, and old leather chairs and brocaded stools by the huge log fire in the broad stone fireplace. There's a woodburning stove at the far end too, with heavy cast-iron-framed tables and sturdy dining chairs; up a step, a small no smoking side area has more tables. Old-time prints, a couple of épées on one beam and lots of copper and brass complete the picture. Cooked by the landlady, the good, tasty bar food includes soup (£3.95), black pudding with smoked bacon and melted cheese (£4.50), pancake filled with smoked chicken, bacon and mushrooms in a creamy sauce (£5.50), rack of ribs in home-made barbecue sauce (£8.95), rabbit pie (£10.25), poached salmon fillet with lemon, wine and tarragon sauce (£10.75), tagine of lamb with apricots, honey and flaked almonds (£10.95), and steaks (from £12.95), with specials like home-cooked ham and egg (£6.95), stilton and mushroom pasta (£7.25), and home-made steak and kidney pie (£7.75). Puddings such as treacle tart, chocolate cake with hot fudge sauce, and fruit crumble (£4.50). Well kept Brains Rev James, Wye Valley Butty Bach, and a guest such as Batemans XXXB or Wychwood Hobgoblin on handpump; piped music. There are tables out in the pretty garden. *(Recommended by Nigel Bowles, Katherine Ellis, Rodney and Norma Stubington, John and Judy Saville, R T and J C Moggridge, W W Burke, Mike and Mary Carter, Pamela and Merlyn Horswell, Mr and Mrs P J Fisk, Ian and Liz Rispin)*

Free house ~ Licensee R Wood ~ Real ale ~ Bar food (not Sun or Mon evenings) ~ (01568) 612509 ~ Children over 6 allowed ~ Open 12-3(4 Sat), 7-11; 12-5.30 Sun; closed Sun and Mon evenings

TITLEY SO3360 Map 6
Stagg ⑪ ♀
B4355 N of Kington

Herefordshire Dining Pub of the Year

Of course it's the marvellous food that draws most of the customers to this fairly simple-looking old place, but locals do drop in for a pint and a chat later on in the evening. The landlord/chef uses local suppliers wherever possible, and you can be sure of good, fresh, often organic ingredients. The pubbier blackboard menu (not available Saturday evening or Sunday lunchtime) has at least 10 choices which, besides filled baguettes (from £3.50), could include three-cheese ploughman's (£6.90), gammon with apricot sauce, crispy duck leg with cider sauce, smoked haddock with mustard mash, and chicken and mushroom fricassee (all £7.50). On the more elaborate restaurant menu (which can also be eaten in the bar) you might find soup (£3.50), blue cheese, pear and walnut tart (£4.70), seared scallops with curried celeriac purée (£5.90), foie gras two ways: fried and port marinaded with grapes (£7.90), organic salmon fillet with tomato and ginger sauce or free-range chicken breast with garlic mash, girolle mushrooms and tarragon (£11.50), free-range pork tenderloin with braised pork shoulder and black pudding (£13.50), fillet of local beef glazed with herbs and mustard sauce (£15.90), vegetarian dishes, and puddings such as spiced rhubarb with cinnamon panna cotta, chocolate tart or caramelised lemon tart with cassis sorbet (from £4.30). There's also a choice of up to 20 british cheeses. The food can take quite a while to come and helpings can strike some people as small. The two dining rooms (one quite big, the other intimate), are no smoking. A carefully chosen wine list with 10 wines and champagne by the glass, well kept Hobsons Best and Town Crier, and Timothy Taylors Landlord on handpump, and a fine collection of malt whiskies, and local farm cider and apple juice; cribbage and dominoes. The bar, though comfortable and hospitable, is not large, and the atmosphere is civilised rather than lively. The garden now has chairs and tables on a terrace, and fruit trees have been planted. *(Recommended by RJH, Alan and Paula McCully, Alec and Barbara Jones, Nigel Bowles, Katherine Ellis, Tom Halsall, Chris Flynn, Wendy Jones, Bob and Maggie Atherton, Eleanor and Nick Steinitz, Joyce and Maurice Cottrell, Jean and Richard Phillips, R Cross, Gerry and Rosemary Dobson, Maurice and Gill McMahon, Bernard Stradling)*

Free house ~ Licensees Steve and Nicola Reynolds ~ Real ale ~ Bar food ~ Restaurant ~ (01544) 230221 ~ Children welcome ~ Dogs allowed in bar and bedrooms ~ Open 12-3, 6.30-11; 12-3.30 Sun; closed Sun evening, Mon, 25 and 26 Dec, 1 Jan, first two weeks Nov, one week Feb ~ Bedrooms: /£70B

TRUMPET SO6639 Map 4
Verzons ♀ 🛏

A438 W of Ledbury, just E of junction with A417/A4172

Perhaps more of a roadside hotel than a pub, this well liked place does have an inviting and civilised bar, with attractive dining rooms opening off it. The main bar area, quite brightly lit, has well kept Hook Norton Best and Wye Valley Butty Bach on handpump, good house wines and espresso coffee, served by cheerful young staff from its end counter. This part has a big oriental rug on quarry tiles, a nice mix of country pub furniture including a couple of armchairs, little posies of flowers on its heavy sealed tables, and a woodburning stove in a big brick fireplace. A carpeted front section, with hop bines around its log fireplace, has a nice high-backed settle draped with a rug and lots of scatter cushions as well as other seats; with no piped music, the atmosphere is relaxed and chatty. The dining area off to the right is a series of small snug carpeted rooms. There are two no smoking areas. Popular bar food at lunchtime might include sandwiches (£3.55), home-made potato and watercress soup (£3.95), thai spiced crab and potato croquettes with sweet chilli sauce (£5.95), daube of beef with horseradish mash or gloucestershire old spot pork sausage with creamed red onions and apple sauce (£6.95), and beer-battered cornish cod with home-made tartare sauce (£7.95). There's also soup (£3.95), baked goats cheese with raspberry and hazelnut dressing or grilled home-made black pudding with smoked trout mousse and mustard sauce (£5.25), baked aubergine with marmalade, basil and parmesan pesto (£9.95), roast rack of local lamb with minted apricot sauce, roasted turbot fillet with moules marinière or peppered rib-eye steak (£12.95), and puddings like white chocolate mousse with lemon biscotti and raspberry coulis, creamed rice pudding with honey ice cream or strawberry and pistachio crumble with greek yoghurt sorbet (£4.25). Tables out in extensive neatly kept gardens have broad views to the Malvern Hills. The Vintage Sports Car Club meet here on the last Thursday of each month, and there's a special meeting on New Year's Day. *(Recommended by J H C Peters, Terry and Sheila Snow, P Bottomley, Malcolm Taylor)*

Free house ~ Licensee David Barnett-Roberts ~ Real ale ~ Bar food ~ Restaurant ~ (01531) 670381 ~ Children in eating area of bar and restaurant ~ Dogs allowed in bar ~ Open 11-11; 12-10.30 Sun; closed 26 Dec ~ Bedrooms: £55B/£68B

ULLINGSWICK SO5949 Map 4
Three Crowns 🍴 ♀

Village off A465 S of Bromyard (and just S of Stoke Lacy) and signposted off A417 N of A465 roundabout – keep straight on through village and past turn-off to church; pub at Bleak Acre, towards Little Cowarne

Although most customers come here to enjoy a special meal out, the landlord is quite adamant that this is a pub and not a restaurant, and always has a table kept free for the cribbage team and any drinkers who might want to sit there – though many locals are quite happy to stand and chat with their pint. The charmingly traditional interior has hops strung along the low beams of its smallish bar, a couple of traditional settles besides more usual seats, a mix of big old wooden tables with small round ornamental cast-iron-framed ones, open fires and one or two gently sophisticated touches such as candles on tables, and proper napkins; half the pub is no smoking. Using mostly local and organic products, there's a lunchtime two-course (£10.50) and three-course (£12.50) menu with starters such as locally smoked haddock, potato and parsley soup or chicken liver parfait with beetroot chutney, main courses like scrumpy jack sausages with herb mash and onion gravy or grilled pork chop with ratatouille and sage gnocchi, and puddings such as apple and frangipane tart with butterscotch ice cream or rhubarb crumble with ginger ice cream. Also, steamed mussels with samphire and cider or sautéed scallops with lime and dhal (£5.75), roast hake with sauce verde and spring greens or roast fillet and braised shin of beef with horseradish risotto (£13.75), and puddings like dark chocolate tart with mint syrup and almond milk sorbet (£4.25); local cheeses (£4.25). You must book ahead to be sure of a table. They have quite a few wines by the glass, along with well kept Hobsons Best and maybe Wye Valley Bitter on handpump, and local farm ciders and fruit juice. There are nice summer views from tables out on the attractively planted lawn, and new outside heaters for chillier evenings. More reports please. *(Recommended by Mrs Ursula Hofheinz, Denys Gueroult, Chris Flynn, Wendy Jones, Rodney and Norma Stubington, M S Catling, Sir Nigel Foulkes, Bernard Stradling, Jason Caulkin)*

Free house ~ Licensee Brent Castle ~ Real ale ~ Bar food ~ Restaurant ~ (01432) 820279 ~ Well behaved children welcome ~ Open 12-3, 6(7 in winter)-11; 12-2, 6(7 in winter)-10.30 Sun; closed Mon

UPTON BISHOP SO6527 Map 4
Moody Cow

2 miles from M50 junction 3 westbound (or junction 4 eastbound), via B4221; continue on B4221 to rejoin at next junction

Several separate snug areas in this pleasant pub angle in an L around the bar counter, and there's a pleasant medley of stripped country furniture, stripped floorboards and stonework, a few cow ornaments and naïve cow paintings, and a lovely big log fire. On the far right is a biggish no smoking rustic and candlelit restaurant, with hop-draped rafters, and a fireside area with armchairs and sofas. The far left has a second smaller dining area (also no smoking), just five or six tables with rush seats, green-stained woodwork, shelves of country china; piped music. Home-made and cooked to order, the bar food might include soup (£3.75), onion tartlet topped with melted goats cheese or fishcakes with tangy tomato salsa (£4.95), several pasta dishes (£4.95 starter, £8.95 main course), pork, apple and leek sausages with coriander mash and redcurrant and rosemary gravy (£8.75), fresh battered cod or steak and kidney pie (£8.95), avocado, spinach couscous and feta cheese spring rolls with tomato and fresh basil sauce (£9.95), duck breast with a mixed berry compote (£13.95), fresh fish dishes, and puddings like bread and butter pudding or poached pears with melted belgian chocolate and vanilla ice cream (£4.75). Well kept Bass, Hook Norton and Worthington Best on handpump, with a guest such as Wye Valley Bitter. *(Recommended by Guy Vowles, Mike and Mary Carter, Alain and Rose Foote, Steve Crick, Helen Preston, R Davies, P and J Shapley, Sandra Wright, LM, Jenny and Dave Hughes)*

Free house ~ Licensee James Lloyd ~ Real ale ~ Bar food ~ Restaurant ~ (01989) 780470 ~ Children welcome ~ Open 12-2.30, 6.30-11; 12-3 Sun; closed Sun evening and Mon

'Children welcome' means the pub says it lets children inside without any special restriction. If it allows them in, but to restricted areas such as an eating area or family room, we specify this. Some pubs may impose an evening time limit.

WALTERSTONE SO3425 Map 6
Carpenters Arms

Village signposted off A465 E of Abergavenny, beside Old Pandy Inn; follow village signs, and keep eyes skinned for sign to pub, off to right, by lane-side barn

Though it takes some finding, this charming little unspoilt stone cottage on the edge of the Black Mountains is certainly worth the effort. The chatty landlady will make you very welcome (it's been in the same family for many years) and the interior is delightful. The genuinely traditional rooms have ancient settles against stripped stone walls, some pieces of carpet on broad polished flagstones, a roaring log fire in a gleaming black range (complete with pot-iron, hot-water tap, bread oven and salt cupboard), pewter mugs hanging from beams, and the slow tick of a clock. The snug main dining room (which is no smoking) has mahogany tables and oak corner cupboards, with a big vase of flowers on the dresser. Another little dining area has old oak tables and church pews on flagstones; piped music. The reasonably priced home-made food might include sandwiches (from £2), soup, prawn cocktail, ploughman's or steak roll (all £4), home-made dishes such as fish pie, curry or beef in Guinness pie (all £8), a vegetarian choice, thick lamb cutlets with redcurrant and rosemary sauce (£9), steaks (from £9), and home-made puddings (£4). Well kept Wadworths 6X and perhaps one of their seasonal ales tapped from the cask; farm cider. The outside lavatories are cold but in character. More reports please.
(Recommended by R T and J C Moggridge, Dave Braisted, J Taylor)

Free house ~ Licensee Vera Watkins ~ Real ale ~ Bar food ~ Restaurant ~ No credit cards ~ (01873) 890353 ~ Children in eating area of bar ~ Open 12-11; 12-10.30 Sun

WELLINGTON SO4948 Map 6
Wellington ♥

Village signposted off A49 N of Hereford; pub at far end

Since our last edition, this red brick Victorian roadside pub has new licensees who have refurbished both inside and out. There are big high-backed dark wooden settles, an open brick fireplace with a log fire in winter and fresh flowers in summer, and historical photographs of the village and antique farm and garden tools around the walls; there is stripped brickwork in the former stables which is now a charming candlelit restaurant. Hop bines decorate the bar, which has four well kept real ales such as Hancocks HB, Hobsons, Wye Valley Butty Bach, and a changing guest on handpump, and a farm cider. Well liked bar food now includes soup (£3.50), sausages (made locally to their own recipe; £4.75), filled baguettes (from £4.95), scrambled free-range eggs with smoked salmon (£5.50), ploughman's (£6), and free range chicken caesar, and steak and mushroom in ale pie or roasted vegetables in filo pastry with a rich tomato sauce (£6.95); Sunday lunchtime carvery (no other food then). Service is friendly; piped music. There are tables out in the attractive garden behind, and summer barbecues. More reports please.
(Recommended by Mr and Mrs T Lewis, Joanna Foster, Maurice and Della Andrew)

Free house ~ Licensee Ross Williams ~ Real ale ~ Bar food (not Sun evening or Mon) ~ Restaurant ~ (01432) 830367 ~ Children in eating area of bar and restaurant ~ Dogs allowed in bar ~ Open 12-2.30, 6-11; 12-3, 7-10.30 Sun; closed Mon lunchtime

WEOBLEY SO4052 Map 6
Salutation ♀ ⇌

Village signposted from A4112 SW of Leominster; and from A44 NW of Hereford (there's also a good back road direct from Hereford – straight out past S side of racecourse)

Set in a quaint little medieval village, this heavily beamed inn is popular with a good mix of locals and visitors (many of whom very much enjoy staying in the clean and comfortable bedrooms – good breakfasts, too). The two areas of the comfortable and partly no smoking lounge – separated by a few steps and standing timbers – have a relaxed, pubby feel, brocaded modern winged settles and smaller seats, a couple of big cut-away cask seats, wildlife decorations, a hop bine over the bar counter, and logs burning in a big stone fireplace; more standing timbers separate it from the neat no smoking restaurant area, and there's a separate smaller parquet-floored public bar with sensibly placed darts, juke box, TV and fruit machine. Friendly, obliging staff serve well kept Flowers IPA, Shepherd Neame Bishops Finger, and Wye Valley Butty Bach on handpump; there's an extensive wine list with mainly new world wines, and quite a few malt whiskies. Enjoyable food includes sandwiches, home-made soup (£4.25), smoked turkey and bacon terrine with cranberry and onion marmalade (£4.95), steamed mussels with cider, leeks, prawns, herbs and cream (£6.25), stilton, leek and mushroom strudel (£7.95), baked local ham with oyster mushroom and madeira sauce (£8.75), oak-smoked haddock topped with a poached egg with buttered spinach and a whisky cream reduction (£10.95), braised and marinated lamb shank with red wine and rosemary reduction (£11.95), local sirloin steak (£12.95), daily specials like steak in ale pie or double breast of pheasant in port, mushroom and onion sauce (£8.95), and puddings such as sticky toffee sponge with butterscotch and brandy sauce or summer fruit pudding (£4.25). There are tables and chairs with parasols on a sheltered back terrace. *(Recommended by Denys Gueroult, Gerry and Rosemary Dobson, the Didler, R T and J C Moggridge, Revd D Glover, Brian Root, Alan and Gill Bull, R M Corlett, Mrs T A Bizat, Mr and Mrs W D Borthwick, Mike and Heather Watson, Ann and Max Cross, Glenwys and Alan Lawrence, Stuart Turner, Maurice and Gill McMahon, Alec and Barbara Jones, Bernie Adams; also in the* Good Hotel Guide*)*

Free house ~ Licensee Dr Mike Tai ~ Real ale ~ Bar food ~ Restaurant ~ (01544) 318443 ~ Children in eating area of bar and restaurant ~ Dogs allowed in bar ~ Open 11-11; 12-10.30 Sun; closed 25 Dec (apart from 11-1) ~ Bedrooms: £49B/£74B

WOOLHOPE SO6136 Map 4
Crown ♀
In village centre

Friendly new licensees have taken over this bustling old pub, and have opened a big garden with lots of tables, outdoor heaters, and lighting. The neatly kept lounge bar has plush button-back built-in wall banquettes and dark wood tables and chairs, an open fire, and a timbered divider strung with hop bines. Heavy oak posts support a thick stone wall partly dividing off the no smoking dining area; darts, TV and piped music. Well kept Fullers London Pride, Smiles Best, Timothy Taylors Landlord, a guest from Hook Norton, Ringwood or Woods on handpump. Good, popular bar food includes home-made soup (£3.45), filled baked potatoes (from £3.50), home-made potted stilton with mushrooms (£4.35), bacon, mushroom and cheese open toastie (£4.50; triple decker BLT £4.75), home-made crab cakes (£4.95), ploughman's (from £5.35), a snack and share platter (£6.25), pork and leek sausages with onion gravy (£7.45), nut moussaka with feta cheese topping (£7.50), steak, stout and mushroom pie or lamb and cranberry casserole (£7.70), cajun chicken (£8.45), duck breast with a port and black cherry sauce or stuffed pork fillet (£9.10), local steaks (from £9.95), and home-made puddings such as treacle tart, steamed chocolate sponge with chocolate sauce or toffee apple pancakes (£3.50). *(Recommended by Lucien Perring, Ian and Denise Foster, A H C Rainier, Derek Carless, Geoff and Sylvia Donald, J R Ringrose, MLR)*

Free house ~ Licensees Geoff Green and Gina Williams ~ Real ale ~ Bar food ~ Restaurant ~ (01432) 860468 ~ Children welcome ~ Live music monthly Sat evening ~ Open 12-3, 6.30-11; 12-11 Sat; 12-3, 6.30-10.30 Sun

Post Office address codings confusingly give the impression that some pubs are in Herefordshire when they're really in Gloucestershire or even Wales (which is where we list them).

Lucky Dip

Besides the fully inspected pubs, you might like to try these Lucky Dips recommended to us and described by readers (if you do, please send us reports: www.goodguides.com).

ABBEY DORE [SO3830]

☆ *Neville Arms* [B4347]: Country pub smartened up by newish young licensees, cosy bar with log fire, comfortable no smoking beamed restaurant, interesting real ales such as Spinning Dog Chase Your Tail, wide blackboard choice of good food with many unusual dishes inc delicious puddings, half helpings for children; tables outside, nr Norman abbey church, charming Golden Valley views, bedrooms; cl Mon lunchtime and Tues, perhaps other lunchtimes in winter *(George Atkinson, BB)*

ASHPERTON [SO6441]

Hopton Arms [A417]: Friendly and comfortable, good local atmosphere, short realistic food choice, local real ales, Weston's farm cider; tables and play area in garden, new bedrooms in back stable block *(DC)*

BISHOPS FROME [SO6547]

Five Bridges Inn [Five Bridges; A4103 Hereford—Worcester]: Welcoming 18th-c country pub with old household bric-a-brac, well kept beers; new licensees doing enjoyable food in smart civilised restaurant, good ingredients inc fresh fish daily, their own organic garden produce and local meat inc some from their own small herd *(M A Higgins, Frank Hare)*

BROCKHAMPTON [SO7054]

☆ *Live & Let Live* [off A44 Bromyard—Worcester at Wheatsheaf]: Chatty local landlord and friendly service, well kept Hobsons Best and Wye Valley, enjoyable food from lunchtime sandwiches to speciality steaks, two bars, beams and big log fire, red plush seats and a couple of old settees, darts, big-windowed restaurant; picnic-sets in informal garden with swings, aviary and country views *(BB, Edmund Coan)*

BROMYARD [SO6554]

Rose & Lion [New Rd]: Welcoming local tied to Wye Valley brewery, their full range in top condition from central island servery for simple comfortable lounge and games-oriented public bar with darts, cards etc; tables out in pleasant courtyard *(J A Ellis, Pete Baker)*

BROMYARD DOWNS [SO6755]

☆ *Royal Oak* [just NE of Bromyard; pub signed off A44]: Beautifully placed open-plan low-beamed 18th-c pub with wide views, carpeted bar with lots of pig models and Hook Norton Best, dining room with huge bay window, wide range of home-made food, friendly kind service, flagstoned walkers' bar with woodburner, pool, juke box and TV; picnic-sets on colourful front terrace, swings in orchard, good walks *(Alan and Paula McCully, BB)*

COLWALL [SO7342]

☆ *Crown* [Walwyn Rd]: Welcoming and carefully refurbished, carpeted bar with step up to parquet-floor area with log fire, nice prints and lighting, good honest food from sandwiches,

ploughman's and generous starters to popular Sun lunch, some classier dishes, friendly efficient service, well kept Greene King Old Speckled Hen and Timothy Taylors Landlord, decent wines, daily papers *(Dave Braisted, BB)*

CRASWALL [SO2736]

☆ *Bulls Head* [Hay-on-Wye—Llanfihangel Crucorney Golden Valley rd]: Remote unpretentious stone-built pub, low beams, flagstones, antique settles and elderly chairs, logs burning in an old cast-iron stove, 19th-c engravings, well kept Wye Valley Butty Bach and a local beer brewed for them served from a hatch, table skittles, cribbage and dominoes, generous filled home-baked huffers, may be some inventive hot dishes using local ingredients, partly no smoking dining area; tables outside with play area and room for camping, peaceful walking area, open all day, cl Sun evening, Mon and Tues *(Gwyneth and Salvo Spadaro-Dutturi, the Didler, Darren and Jane Staniforth, Chris Saville, Alan and Gill Bull, Chris and Maggie Kent, LYM, Mike and Mary Carter, JWAC)*

DINMORE [SO5150]

Railway Inn: Warm welcome, good service, well kept ales such as Greene King Ruddles, enjoyable food; splendid views to Malverns *(Eleanor and Nick Steinitz)*

FOWNHOPE [SO5734]

☆ *Green Man*: Striking 15th-c black and white inn with big log fire, wall settles, window seats and armchairs in one beamed bar, standing timbers dividing another, popular well priced food from sandwiches to substantial main dishes inc children's and Sun carvery (no smoking main restaurant is plainer), friendly efficient service, well kept Courage Directors, Hook Norton Best, Marstons Pedigree, John Smiths and Sam Smiths OB, Weston's farm ciders; children welcome, quiet garden with play area; comfortably refurbished bedrooms, good breakfast, back fitness centre *(John Hale, Anne Morris, Barry Smith, MJVK, LYM, J R Ringrose)*

HAREWOOD END [SO5227]

☆ *Harewood End Inn* [A49 Hereford—Ross]: Reopened after comfortable restoration of fire damage, enthusiastic landlady and welcoming staff, attractive panelled dining lounge with very wide range of consistently enjoyable home-made food at attractive prices, well kept Bass and Wye Valley Butty Bach, good value wines; attractive garden, good bedrooms with own bathrooms *(T Pascall)*

HEREFORD [SO5139]

Barrels [St Owen St]: Plain and cheery two-bar local brewing its own good Wye Valley Hereford and Dorothy Goodbodys ales at attractive prices (esp 5-7 happy hour), barrel-built counter also serving guest beers such as Buffys Norwich Terrier, farm ciders from Bulmer's, Stowford Press and Weston's, friendly staff, may have sandwiches and pickled eggs, side pool room with games, juke box and TV sports, lots of modern stained glass; piped blues and rock, live music at beer festival end Aug; picnic-sets out on cobbles by brewery, open all day *(the Didler, Mike Pugh, BB, MLR, Joe Green)*

Queens Arms [Broad St]: Original ancient low beams and posts, bare boards, pubby furnishings, two small side rooms, popular food, reasonably priced Bass and Flowers; games machines, TV *(Dr and Mrs M E Wilson)*

Spread Eagle [King St, nr cathedral]: Busy beamed pub down side alley, well kept real ales such as Shepherd Neame Spitfire, food all day inc sausage specialities, welcoming service *(Dave Braisted, David Carr)*

KINGTON [SO3057]

☆ *Olde Tavern* [Victoria Rd, just off A44 opp B4355 – follow sign to Town Centre, Hospital, Cattle Mkt; pub on right opp Elizabeth Rd, no inn sign but Estd 1767 notice]: Splendidly old-fashioned, with small plain parlour and public bar, dark brown woodwork, big windows, old settles and other antique furniture, china, pewter and curios, welcoming locals and long-serving landlady, well kept Ansells, gas fire, no music, machines or food; children welcome, though not a family pub; cl wkdy lunchtimes, outside gents' *(BB, Norma and Keith Bloomfield, Pete Baker, RWC, the Didler)*

Queens Head [Bridge St]: Friendly unassuming Victorian tavern little changed for a century or so, farm ciders and good remarkably cheap beers from its own Dunn Plowman brewery *(Anne and Tim Locke)*

LAYSTERS POLE [SO5563]

Duke of York [A4112 Leominster—Tenbury]: Like someone's 1940s home, very well kept, stone-built roadside pub with big curved settle facing small bar's coal fire, quoits table in the window, a few old pictures and even flying ducks on the wall, side lounge with grandfather clock, settee, gas fire and piano, darts in another side room; well furnished inc some fine antique furniture, no food or music, keg beer *(Kevin Thorpe)*

LEA [SO6621]

Crown [A40 Ross—Gloucester]: Dark and cosy, with window seats, good range of well kept beers, good coffee, bar food, particularly welcoming landlord, daily papers *(Phil and Sally Gorton)*

LEINTWARDINE [SO4073]

Lion [High St]: Beautiful spot by packhorse bridge over River Teme, good bar food esp fish, popular restaurant, welcoming efficient staff and friendly atmosphere, well kept real ales; very busy in main holiday season; nice safely fenced riverside garden with play area, attractive bedrooms *(Ian and Denise Foster)*

☆ *Sun* [Rosemary Lane, just off A4113]: Unspoilt gem, three bare benches by coal fire in red-tiled front parlour off hallway, venerable landlady brings you well kept Woods tapped from the cask in her kitchen (and may honour you with the small settee and a couple of chairs by the gas fire in her sitting room); no food exc pickled eggs and crisps *(RWC, BB, B and H,*

Pete Baker, Martin Grosberg)

LEOMINSTER [SO4958]

Ducking Stool [South St]: Attractive solid furnishings inc padded pews, decent reasonably priced food, immaculate housekeeping; fairly loud piped music, keg beers *(Joe Green)*

Grape Vaults [Broad St]: Friendly well preserved two-room pub, welcoming and unpretentious, with etched windows, original dark high-backed settles, veteran tables, coal fire, bottle collection, old local prints and posters; wide range of simple freshly cooked food, well kept Banks's, Marstons and a guest ale, no machines or music *(Kevin Thorpe, Peter Truckle, Joe Green)*

LETTON [SO3346]

Swan [A438 NW of Hereford]: Friendly atmosphere, accommodating service, good value home-made food inc some nice recipes, well kept cheap beers inc one brewed for the pub by Wye Valley, cosy beamed bar with sofas and bric-a-brac, games room; well appointed bedrooms, good garden, caravan parking *(Dr B and Mrs P B Baker)*

LINTON [SO6525]

Alma: Rejuvenated local in small village, well kept real ale and good fire; cl wkdy lunchtimes *(Phil and Sally Gorton, Theocsbrian)*

MICHAELCHURCH ESCLEY [SO3133]

☆ *Bridge Inn* [off back road SE of Hay-on-Wye, along Escley Brook valley]: Remote homely black-beamed riverside inn delightfully tucked away in attractive valley, good honest food from lunchtime sandwiches to locally sourced home cooking and Sun lunch, well kept Wye Valley beers, farm ciders, children welcome; seats out on waterside terrace, field for camping, good walks; open all day Sat, can be busy wknds *(LYM, John Anthony)*

MORDIFORD [SO5737]

☆ *Moon* [B4224 SE of Hereford]: Country pub in good spot by Wye tributary, black beams and roaring log fire, Marstons Pedigree, Tetleys and Wadworths 6X, local farm ciders, reasonably priced wines, back bar popular with young locals and students out from Hereford, polite old-fashioned service; children in eating areas when food service restarts (none as we went to press), open all day wknds *(Mike and Mary Carter, Guy Vowles, LYM)*

MUCH MARCLE [SO6533]

☆ *Slip Tavern* [off A449 SW of Ledbury]: Country pub with splendidly colourful gardens overlooking cider orchards (Weston's Cider Farm is close by), well kept Hook Norton Best and local farm cider, attentive service, bar popular with older people at lunchtime, with villagey local evening atmosphere; standard bar food, attractive no smoking conservatory restaurant; folk music first Thurs of month *(A and B D Craig, R T and J C Moggridge, Edward Hughes, Mike and Mary Carter, Kitt Gruseon, Dr and Mrs Jackson, LYM, Bernie Adams)*

ORCOP HILL [SO4727]

Fountain [off A466 S of Hereford]: Small friendly village pub, simple cosy bar with daily papers, big helpings of enjoyable food in back dining room and restaurant inc fresh fish specials and cheap lunchtime deals, Marstons Pedigree and John Smiths; darts, piped music; tables in peaceful pretty front garden *(Ian and Denise Foster, BB)*

SYMONDS YAT [SO5615]

☆ *Saracens Head* [Symonds Yat E, by ferry, ie over on the Gloucs bank]: Riverside beauty spot next to 60p ferry, busy down-to-earth flagstoned bar popular with canoeists, mountain bikers and hikers, cheerful efficient staff, good range of well presented nourishing food from good value sandwiches up, well kept Theakstons Best, XB and Old Peculier and Wye Valley, three farm ciders, pine tables, settles and window seats; cosy carpeted restaurant, games bar with pool, piped jazz and blues, SkyTV, lots of picnic-sets out on waterside terraces, live music Thurs; summer boat trips, super walks, nice good value bedrooms – good place to stay out of season *(David Carr, BB, Abi Benson)*

UPPER COLWALL [SO7643]

Chase [Chase Rd, off B4218 Malvern—Colwall, 1st left after hilltop on bend going W]: Great views from attractive garden and refined and comfortable lounge of genteel and friendly two-bar pub on Malvern Hills, well kept real ales inc Wye Valley Dorothy Goodbodys seasonal ones, limited choice of enjoyable lunchtime bar food inc good filled rolls, no smoking room; cl Tues *(Bruce M Drew, Dr and Mrs Jackson, J R Ringrose)*

WALFORD [SO5820]

☆ *Spread Eagle* [B4234 Ross—Lydney]: Former Mill Race, back to original name under new licensees and largely no smoking (separate snug for smokers, through Norman arch), good value food inc some enterprising hot dishes, well kept Adnams, Greene King Abbot and

Charles Wells Bombardier, Weston's and Stowford Press cider, good wine choice, nice mix of furnishings, some fine old features in open-plan bar with some stripped stone and high rafters; garden and play area, has been cl Mon out of season *(Barry Smith, BB, Lucien Perring)*

WHITNEY-ON-WYE [SO2747]

☆ *Rhydspence* [A438 Hereford—Brecon]: Well run very picturesque ancient black and white country inn right on Welsh border, with attractive old-fashioned furnishings, heavy beams and timbers in rambling spick-and-span rooms, pretty dining room, good interesting food using local produce, generous helpings and nice touches, good service, well kept Bass and Robinsons Best, Dunkerton's farm cider, good wine choice, log fire; tables in attractive garden with fine views over Wye Valley, comfortable bedrooms *(Rodney and Norma Stubington, LYM, Cliff Blakemore, David and Julie Glover, Pam and David Bailey)*

WOOLHOPE [SO6135]

Butchers Arms [off B4224 in Fownhope, then beyond village]: This tucked-away low-beamed 14th-c pub in lovely quiet countryside, a popular main entry in previous editions, was closed for refurbishment under new owners as we went to press; news please *(LYM)*

YARPOLE [SO4664]

☆ *Bell* [just off B4361 N of Leominster]: Neat and tidy picturesquely timbered ancient pub, extended into former cider mill; comfortably smart and warmly welcoming, with brass and bric-a-brac, well kept Greene King Old Speckled Hen, decent wines, good bar food, more restauranty menu in country dining area; tables in sunny flower-filled garden, very handy for Croft Castle *(Dr D E Granger, Mr and Mrs J Bishop, Alan Thwaite)*

Hertfordshire

The charming and stylish Alford Arms at Frithsden – which last year took the county's top food title for its good imaginative cooking – still has no really close rivals, and is again Hertfordshire Dining Pub of the Year. Other pubs on fine form here this year are the rambling Greyhound in attractive Aldbury (good food), the Valiant Trooper there (more local-feeling, good value), the Jolly Waggoner in Ardeley (a popular dining pub), and the immaculate Holly Bush at Potters Crouch (a most relaxing motorway break). The Lucky Dip section at the end of the chapter also has a few places to note particularly: the Bushel & Strike in Ashwell, Clarendon Arms at Chandlers Cross, Two Brewers at Chipperfield, Black Horse in Chorleywood, Crown & Sceptre near Hemel Hempstead, Rose & Crown and Six Bells in St Albans and Plough just outside, Fox & Duck at Therfield and Robin Hood in Tring. On average, Hertfordshire drinks prices tend to be a bit higher than the national norm. London-based Fullers has been extending its domain into the county, and its beers and pubs generally represent good value here. McMullens is the county's own main brewer; Tring is a smaller newer brewery worth looking out for, and you might also come across beers from Green Tye (see Lucky Dip entry for the Prince of Wales there).

ALDBURY SP9612 Map 4
Greyhound

Stocks Road; village signposted from A4251 Tring—Berkhamsted, or reached directly from roundabout at E end of A41 Tring bypass

There's a buoyantly thriving atmosphere throughout the rambling rooms of this spacious old pub, with efficient smiling service, even when it's busy. The beamed interior shows some signs of considerable age (around the copper-hooded inglenook, for example), with plenty of tables in the two rooms off either side of the drinks and food serving areas. A big room at the back overlooks a suntrap gravel courtyard, and it's also well worth a winter visit, when the lovely warm fire and subtle lighting make it really cosy inside. Badger Best, IPA, Tanglefoot and a Badger seasonal guest are kept well on handpump, and there's a weekday early evening happy hour (5-7pm). Generous bar food from a fairly short lunchtime menu includes sandwiches (from £5.50), filled baked potatoes (£4.95), ham and eggs (£5.95), penne with roast peppers and tomatoes, basil and parmesan (£7.50) and poached salmon with chardonnay sauce (£9). The evening menu is a little more elaborate and includes dishes such as beef carpaccio (£5.95) and roast cod with rosemary crumb crust, truffle mash with spinach and red wine jus (£12.95). Very pleasant no smoking conservatory, piped music, cribbage and dominoes. Benches outside face a picturesque village green complete with stocks and lively duckpond. The handsome Georgian façade is especially stunning in autumn when the blazing leaves of its virginia creeper provide a brilliant counterpoint to the backdrop of bronzing Chiltern beechwoods (part of the National Trust's Ashridge Estate). There are plenty of good walks nearby (plastic bags are kept near the entrance for muddy boots), for instance, around the monument to the canal mogul, the 3rd Duke of Bridgewater, up on the escarpment; for the less energetic, the toll road through the Ashridge Estate is very attractive. *(Recommended by M A and C R Starling, Ian Phillips, Mike and Heather Watson, David and Ruth Shillitoe, Ian and Joan Blackwell, J T Pearson,*

B and M Kendall, Peter and Giff Bennett, Brian Root, Howard Dell, Mike Turner, Tim Maddison)

Badger ~ Manager Richard Coletta ~ Real ale ~ Bar food (12-2.30(3 Sun), 7-9; not Sun evening) ~ Restaurant ~ (01442) 851228 ~ Children in restaurant ~ Dogs allowed in bar ~ Open 11-11; 12-10.30 Sun ~ Bedrooms: £45S/£75S

Valiant Trooper ◧

Trooper Road (towards Aldbury Common); off B4506 N of Berkhamsted

Known in early days as the Royal Oak, this partly pink-painted and tiled pub changed its name to the Valiant Trooper in 1803 – legend has it that the Duke of Wellington met his officers here to discuss tactics, and its traditional atmosphere and antique cavalry prints do well in conjuring up those days. The first room is beamed and tiled in red and black, and has built-in wall benches, a pew and small dining chairs around the attractive country tables, and a woodburning stove in the inglenook fireplace. The middle bar has spindleback chairs around the tables on its wooden floor, some exposed brickwork – and signs warning you to 'mind the step'. The far room has nice country kitchen chairs around individually chosen tables, and a brick fireplace. Generously served bar food includes filled baked potatoes or open sandwiches (£4), ciabatta sandwiches (£4.50), ploughman's (£5), and daily specials such as roast field mushrooms with goats cheese (£5), moules marinière (£5/£7.50), roast vegetable lasagne (£7.50), steak and kidney pie (£9), duck with orange sauce (£10) and roasted bass with ratatouille (£11), with puddings such as sticky toffee pudding or white chocolate and raspberry torte (£3.75). The lounge bar is no smoking at lunchtime; pleasant obliging service. Well kept Adnams, Fullers London Pride and three guests from brewers such as Marstons, Thomas Hardy and Tring on handpump. Shove-ha'penny, dominoes, cribbage, bridge on Monday nights. The enclosed garden has a play house for children. *(Recommended by John Roots, Darren Le Poidevin, Brian Root, Colin McKerrow, D J and P M Taylor, Ian Phillips, David and Ruth Shillitoe)*

Free house ~ Licensee Tim O'Gorman ~ Real ale ~ Bar food (12-2(2.30 Sun), 6.30-9.15; not Sun/Mon evening) ~ Restaurant ~ (01442) 851203 ~ Children in eating area of bar, restaurant and family room ~ Dogs allowed in bar ~ Open 11.30-11; 12-10.30 Sun; closed 25 Dec

ARDELEY TL3027 Map 5
Jolly Waggoner

Village signposted off B1037 NE of Stevenage

'A cracker, all that a pub in winter should be – warm with good beer, an open fire, newspapers to read and good food' is how one reader described this pleasant, cream-washed dining pub, which is peacefully set in a pretty tucked-away village. Using fresh local produce where possible, good imaginative food from the bar menu includes sandwiches (from £3), soup (£4.50), ploughman's (£6.50), chicken fillet with creamy mushroom and garlic sauce (£12), and calves liver with sage or roquefort cheese and horseradish (£12.50), with changing specials such as dressed crab (£6.75/£9) and steak and kidney pie (£11). Full of nooks and crannies, the comfortable bar has a relaxed and civilised atmosphere, open woodwork and beams and a window overlooking the garden; one area is no smoking, and they have darts. Decorated with modern prints, the no smoking restaurant has been extended into the cottage next door; they add a 10% service charge here, and booking is essential for their Sunday lunch. Well kept Greene King IPA tapped from the cask and Abbot on handpump, a decent range of wines and freshly squeezed orange juice in summer; the young staff are cheerful and unobtrusive. There may be piped music; £1 credit card surcharge for bills under £10. There's a pleasant garden and terrace; Cromer Windmill is nearby. *(Recommended by Jill McLaren, Roger Everett, Ian Phillips, George Atkinson, B and M Kendall)*

Greene King ~ Tenant Darren Perkins ~ Real ale ~ Bar food (12-2, 6.30-9, not Sun evening) ~ Restaurant ~ (01438) 861350 ~ Children over 7 ~ Open 12-2.30 (3 Sat), 6.30-11; 12-3, 7-10.30 Sun; closed Mon except bank hols, then cl Tues

ASHWELL TL2639 Map 5
Three Tuns
Off A505 NE of Baldock; High Street

This pleasant flower-decked 18th-c hotel has a nicely old-fashioned atmosphere. In a pretty village that nestles at the foot of a hill (with far-reaching views from the top), it's very popular with groups of hikers on summer weekends. There's an air of Victorian opulence in the cosy lounge with its relaxing chairs, big family tables, lots of pictures, stuffed pheasants and fish, and antiques. The simpler more modern public bar has pool, darts, cribbage, dominoes, a fruit machine, SkyTV, and Greene King IPA, Abbot and Ruddles on handpump, and there's a good choice of wines; piped light classical music. Served by friendly attentive staff, changing home-made bar food might include soup (£3.95), chicken liver pâté (£4.50), devilled whitebait (£4.95), ploughman's (from £5.45), vegetarian pasta bake (£6.95), chicken, ham and mushroom pie (£8.45), and salmon with hollandaise sauce or braised venison in port and plum sauce (£10.25); no smoking dining room. The substantial shaded garden has boules, and picnic-sets under apple trees; lavatories are down a steep flight of steps. One of the six bedrooms has a four-poster bed, and another its own dressing room; we still have not heard from readers who have stayed here. *(Recommended by B and M Kendall, Dr Paull Khan, Gordon Neighbour, W W Burke, Ian Phillips, Mike Moden, Joy and Colin Rorke)*

Greene King ~ Tenants Claire and Darrell Stanley ~ Real ale ~ Bar food (12-2.30, 6.30-9.30; 12-9.30 Sat/Sun) ~ Restaurant ~ (01462) 742107 ~ Children welcome ~ Dogs allowed in bar ~ Open 11-11; 12-10.30 Sun ~ Bedrooms: £39(£59B)/£49(£69B)

BATFORD TL1415 Map 5
Gibraltar Castle
Lower Luton Road; B653, S of B652 junction

This useful roadside pub has well kept Fullers Chiswick, ESB, London Pride and a seasonal brew on handpump, a good range of malt whiskies, well made irish coffee, and a thoughtful choice of wines by the glass; piped music. The new landlord's tasty bar food might include club sandwiches or soup (from £3.95), smoked salmon stuffed with prawns and seafood sauce (£5.95), casseroles and pies (£8.95), brie-stuffed chicken wrapped in parma ham (£10.95), rib-eye steak (£13.75), and home-made puddings such as lemon and blueberry cheesecake (£3.95); booking is recommended for their very popular good value Sunday roast (£8.95). A bonus is the interesting collection of militaria, particularly at the end on the right as you go in, which has something of the feel of a hunting lodge; here the low beams found elsewhere give way to soaring rafters, and glass cases show off pristinely kept uniforms, bullets, medals and rifles. There's plenty to look at in the rest of the long carpeted bar, with its nice old fireplace, comfortably cushioned wall benches, and a couple of snugly intimate window alcoves, one with a fine old clock; piped music, fruit machine. There are tables and chairs on a new, safely enclosed decked back terrace, a few tables in front by the road, and pretty hanging baskets and tubs dotted around. *(Recommended by Martin and Karen Wake, Barry and Marie Males, Ian Phillips)*

Fullers ~ Tenant Hamish Miller ~ Real ale ~ Bar food (12-2.30(3 Sun), 6-9, not Sun evening) ~ Restaurant ~ (01582) 460005 ~ Children in eating area of bar ~ Dogs welcome ~ Jam session Tues evening ~ Open 11.30-3, 5-11; 11.30-11 Sat; 12-10.30 Sun

---

Post Office address codings confusingly give the impression that some pubs are in Hertfordshire, when they're really in Bedfordshire or Cambridgeshire (which is where we list them).

COTTERED TL3129 Map 5

Bull

A507 W of Buntingford

There's a pleasantly relaxing atmosphere at this old tree-surrounded inn. The pub faces a row of pretty thatched cottages, and there are benches and tables in the attractive big garden. The airy low-beamed front lounge is nicely laid out and well looked after, with polished antiques on a stripped wood floor, and a good fire. A second bar has darts, a fruit machine, shove-ha'penny, cribbage and dominoes; unobtrusive piped music. They have well kept Greene King IPA and Abbot on handpump, and decent wines. At lunchtime thoughtfully presented bar food includes sandwiches (from £2.65), burgers (from £5.75), ploughman's (£5.95), steak, Guinness and stilton pie (£8), chicken in a cream, wine and garlic sauce (£11) and salmon fillet with cheese and mushroom sauce (£11.50). In the evening the same dishes are about £1 more expensive, and the menu is slightly longer; £1 surcharge for credit card bills under £10; friendly and obliging service. *(Recommended by Peter and Joan Elbra, Mr and Mrs D Barlow)*

Greene King ~ Tenant Darren Perkins ~ Real ale ~ Bar food (12-2, 6.30(7 Sun)-9) ~ Restaurant ~ (01763) 281243 ~ Children over 7 ~ Open 12-2.30(3 Sat), 6.30-11; 12-3, 7-10.30 Sun; closed Tues evening

FRITHSDEN TL0110 Map 5

Alford Arms 🍴

From Berkhamsted take unmarked road towards Potten End, pass Potten End turn on right, then take next left towards Ashridge College

Hertfordshire Dining Pub of the Year

As this is the only pub in this county to qualify for our Food Award (new this year), you will need to book well ahead for a table at the weekend. Fashionably refurbished by thoughtful licensees, this secluded country inn is an elegantly casual place for a very good meal out. The airy interior has simple prints on pale cream walls, with areas picked out in blocks of Victorian green or dark red, and an appealing mix of good furniture from Georgian chairs to old commode stands on bare boards and patterned quarry tiles. It's all pulled together by luxurious richly patterned curtains. Very good and successfully innovative bar food is served by charming staff, and might include rustic bread with roast garlic and balsamic olive oil (£3), soup (£3.75), duck liver and pistachio terrine with toasted brioche (£5.75), crab and avocado salad with parmesan crisp (£6.75), toulouse sausages with spring onion mash and gravy (£9.50), pea, mint and broad bean risotto (£9.75), roast lamb loin with moroccan couscous and citrus juices (£11.75), fried bass with king prawn salad niçoise (£13); extra vegetables (from £2), and puddings such as rhubarb, elderflower and saffron crumble (from £4.25); good sweet wines. Well kept Brakspears, Flowers Original, Marstons Pedigree and Tetleys on handpump; piped jazz, darts. They have plenty of tables out in front. *(Recommended by Mike and Jennifer Marsh, John and Joyce Snell, Keith James, BKA, M Fynes-Clinton, Mike Turner)*

Enterprise ~ Lease Becky and David Salisbury ~ Real ale ~ Bar food (12-2.30(3 Sun), 7-10) ~ Restaurant ~ (01442) 864480 ~ Children welcome ~ Dogs allowed in bar ~ Open 11-11; 12-10.30 Sun

HERTFORD TL3212 Map 5

White Horse 🍺 £

Castle Street

The main attraction at this friendly, unpretentious town-centre pub is the range of 10 perfectly kept beers. Especially impressive considering it's a tied house, the choice can be different every day, but you can expect to find beers from brewers such as Black Dog, Country Life, fff, Scattor Rock and Teignworthy, alongside the Adnams and Fullers London Pride, Chiswick and ESB – so no need to worry if you can't make it here for their May or September beer festivals. They also keep around

20 country wines. Parts of the building are 14th-c, and you can still see Tudor brickwork in the three quietly cosy no smoking rooms upstairs. Downstairs, the two main rooms are small and homely. The one on the left is more basic, with a bit of brewery memorabilia, bare boards, and a few rather well worn tables, stools and chairs; an open fire separates it from the more comfortable right-hand bar, which has a cosily tatty armchair, some old local photographs, beams and timbers, and a red-tiled floor. Service can be quite chatty, and though it's quite a locals' pub, visitors are made to feel welcome; bar billiards, darts, shove-ha'penny, shut the box, cribbage and dominoes. The pub faces the castle, and there are two benches on the street outside. Very good value bar food (lunchtime only) includes sandwiches (from £2.35), soup (£2.45), filled baguettes (from £3.35), as well as hot dishes such as mushroom stroganoff (£3.50), curries and steak and kidney pie (£4.50) and thai fishcakes (£4.75). On Sunday they do a two-course lunch for £6.50, three courses for £7; no children's meals. *(Recommended by Ian Arthur, Pat and Tony Martin, Ian Phillips, R T and J C Moggridge, LM)*

Fullers ~ Tenant Nigel Crofts ~ Real ale ~ Bar food (lunchtime only) ~ (01992) 501950 ~ Well supervised children in upstairs family room ~ Dogs allowed in bar ~ Blues duo Fri/Sat evening ~ Open 12-2.30, 5.30-11; 12-11(10.30 Sun) Fri/ Sat

POTTERS CROUCH TL1105 Map 5

Holly Bush 🍸 £

2¼ miles from M25 junction 21A: A405 towards St Albans, then first left, then after 1 mile turn left (ie away from Chiswell Green), then at T-junction turn right into Blunts Lane; can also be reached fairly quickly, with a good map, from M1 exits 6 and 8 (and even M10)

You wouldn't know it inside this beautifully kept country pub, but it is actually surrounded (at some distance) by three motorways, so it makes a really handy place to break a journey, and relax in delightful surroundings. The meticulously furnished bar has an elegantly timeless feel, and it's not the kind of place where you'll find fruit machines or piped music. Everything is spotless, and shows unusually dedicated attention to detail. Thoughtfully positioned fixtures create the illusion that there are lots of different rooms – some of which you might expect to find in a smart country house. In the evenings, neatly placed candles cast shadows over the mix of darkly gleaming varnished tables, all of which have fresh flowers, and china plates as ashtrays. There are quite a few antique dressers, several with plates on, a number of comfortably cushioned settles, the odd plant, a fox's mask, some antlers, a fine old clock, carefully lit prints and pictures, daily papers, and on the left as you go in a big fireplace. The long, stepped bar counter has particularly well kept Fullers Chiswick, ESB, London Pride and the Fullers seasonal beer on handpump, and the sort of reassuringly old-fashioned till you hardly ever see in this hi-tech age. Service is calm and efficient even when they're busy. Straightforward bar food from a fairly short menu is served lunchtimes only (not Sunday), from a menu that includes sandwiches (from £2.40), burgers (from £3.80), filled baked potatoes (from £4.30), ploughman's (from £5.10), chilli or very good salad platters (£5.60), and apple pie (£2.50). Behind the pretty wisteria-covered white cottagey building, the fenced-off garden has a nice lawn, handsome trees, and sturdy picnic-sets – a very pleasant place to sit in summer. Though the pub seems to stand alone on a quiet little road, it's only a few minutes from the centre of St Albans, and is very handy for the Gardens of the Rose. *(Recommended by Jill McLaren, LM, B and M Kendall, Brian Root, Ian Phillips, Stephen, Julie and Hayley Brown, Peter and Giff Bennett, John and Joyce Snell, Howard Dell, John and Judy Saville, Alan Cole, Kirstie Bruce)*

Fullers ~ Tenant R S Taylor ~ Real ale ~ Bar food (lunchtime only, not Sun) ~ (01727) 851792 ~ Open 11.30-2.30, 6-11; 12-2.30, 7-10.30 Sun

SARRATT TQ0499 Map 5

Boot

The Green

The nice unspoilt feel at this delightful old place is given a real boost by the cheery landlord and his staff, who are really out to please. Coming in generous helpings, blackboard bar meals might include soup (£3.50), good filling sandwiches (from £3.75) and baked potatoes, battered fish (£7.50), salmon and seafood bake, steak and kidney pie or navarin of lamb (£7.95), and prawn or crayfish salad (£9.45). They also have a more elaborate bistro-style restaurant menu, including fresh fish and seasonal game, on Wednesday to Saturday evenings; the supper room is no smoking. The cosy rambling rooms have comfortably cushioned benches along the part-panelled walls, with carpet or dark flooring tiles, and a fine early 18th-c inglenook fireplace with a good winter log fire. Greene King IPA, Abbot, Speckled Hen and Ruddles County are well kept on handpump; darts, cribbage, dominoes, fruit machine and piped music. Going outside, the attractive tiled building faces the charming village green, and has an old-fashioned black wrought-iron bench and picnic-sets under a pair of pollarded century-old lime trees. A pretty, sheltered lawn has a children's play area, and more tables among roses, fruit trees and a weeping willow. *(Recommended by Iain and Joan Baillie, Ian Phillips, Jarrod and Wendy Hopkinson, John and Glenys Wheeler, Peter Saville, Mrs W Mabilat)*

Free house ~ Licensee Richard Jones ~ Real ale ~ Bar food (lunchtime only) ~ Restaurant ~ (01923) 262247 ~ Children in eating area of bar and restaurant ~ Open 11.45-3, 5.30-11; 12-10.30 Sun

Cock

Church End: a very pretty approach is via North Hill, a lane N off A404, just under 1 mile W of A405

Picnic-sets at the front of this beautifully set cosy cream-painted 17th-c country pub look out across a quiet lane towards the churchyard. The terrace at the back gives open country views, and a pretty, sheltered lawn has tables under parasols, with a children's play area. The latched door opens into a carpeted snug with a vaulted ceiling, original bread oven, and a cluster of bar stools. Through an archway, the partly oak-panelled cream-walled lounge has a lovely log fire in an inglenook, pretty Liberty-style curtains, pink plush chairs at dark oak tables, and lots of interesting artefacts and pictures of cocks; piped music, and well kept Badger Best, Sussex, Tanglefoot and a Badger guest; fruit machine and TV. Under new licensees, elaborate bar food might include mushroom risotto with rocket leaves and tomato truffle oil (£10.25), smoked duck on fennel with bitter orange sauce (£11.75), sole fillets with champagne and lobster sauce (£14.95) and beef and pork medallions and lamb fillet stuffed with asparagus spears with tomato and basil olive oil (£15.95). The no smoking restaurant is in a nicely converted barn. *(Recommended by John Hale, Stan Edwards, Peter and Giff Bennett, Peter Saville, BKA, Ian Phillips, Gerald Wilkinson, Jarrod and Wendy Hopkinson)*

Badger ~ Manager Shelley Chase ~ Real ale ~ Bar food (12-2.30, 6-9.30) ~ Restaurant ~ (01923) 282908 ~ Children welcome ~ Dogs allowed in bar ~ Open 12-3, 5-11; 11-11 Sat; 12-6 Sun

WATTON-AT-STONE TL3019 Map 5

George & Dragon ♀

Village signposted off A602 about 5 miles S of Stevenage, on B1001; High Street

This freshly painted country dining pub has kitchen elbow-chairs around attractive old tables, dark blue cloth-upholstered seats in the bay windows, an interesting mix of antique and modern prints on the partly timbered ochre walls, and a big inglenook fireplace. Another room off the main bar has spindleback chairs and wall settles cushioned to match the green floral curtains, and old photographs of the village above its panelled dado. Proper napkins, antiques and daily newspapers add a smart feel. At its best the bar food is very good indeed: sandwiches (from £2.25), soup (£3.45), burger (£5.65), salmon carpaccio (£6.25), chicken breast wrapped in prosciutto with port and rosemary sauce (£9.85), pork fillet en croûte with tarragon and spinach and with oyster mushroom and sherry sauce (£12.25), and daily specials such as fried mushrooms with port and stilton sauce on toasted brioche (£4.85), penne with lemon, thyme and mascarpone (£7.25), beef and oregano meatballs filled with mozzarella with tomato sauce (£8.25), and salmon steak with roasted red pepper and basil crust (£9.25). As well as a good wine list, well kept Greene King IPA and Abbot are served alongside a guest such as Batemans XXXB on handpump; several malt whiskies; fruit machine. The pretty extended shrub-screened garden has outdoor heaters and boules. The pub is quite handy for Benington Lordship Gardens. *(Recommended by Ian Phillips, Gordon Tong, Pat and Tony Martin, Peter Saville, Tina and David Woods-Taylor, John and Judy Saville, Maysie Thompson, Boyd Catling, Enid and Henry Stephens)*

Greene King ~ Tenants Peter and Jessica Tatlow ~ Real ale ~ Bar food (12-2, 7-10; not Sun evening) ~ Restaurant ~ (01920) 830285 ~ Children in eating area of bar and restaurant ~ Open 11-3, 6(5.30 Fri)-11; 11-11 Sat; 12-10.30 Sun

Lucky Dip

Besides the fully inspected pubs, you might like to try these Lucky Dips recommended to us and described by readers (if you do, please send us reports: www.goodguides.com).

ALLENS GREEN [TL4517]
Queens Head: Former pub reopened after 15 years' closure, neat and tidy, with Fullers London Pride, Greene King IPA and a guest such as local Green Tye; large garden *(Ian Arthur)*

AMWELL [TL1613]
☆ *Elephant & Castle* [signed SW from Wheathampstead]: Secluded and spacious floodlit grass garden behind low-beamed ancient pub with relaxed and welcoming local feel, great inglenook log fire, panelling, stripped brickwork, immensely deep covered well shaft in bar; good value hearty bar food (not Sun), well kept ales inc a changing guest, friendly service, no piped music, children in eating area *(LYM, Jill McLaren, Peter Shapland)*

ASHWELL [TL2639]
☆ *Bushel & Strike* [off A507 just E of A1(M) junction 10, N of Baldock, via Newnham; Mill St opp church, via Gardiners Lane (car park down Swan Lane)]: Neat front dining bar with fresh flowers, hunting and coaching prints, local colour photographs, cheery prompt service, enjoyable food from OAP lunches and nice lunchtime sandwiches (not Sun) up, quite a lot of fish in the eating area, sofas in small back drinking area, well kept real ales, freshly squeezed fruit juice, hot toddies, mulled wine and half a dozen wines by the glass, no smoking restaurant (not always open) with 'conservatory' murals; tables on lawn and small terrace, may be summer barbecues *(LYM, Barry and Marie Males, Ruth and Paul Lawrence, Michael Dandy, David Blackburn)*

AYOT GREEN [TL2213]
☆ *Waggoners* [off B197 S of Welwyn]: Friendly pub with three cosy areas: low-ceilinged bar, bigger comfortably furnished extension, and nicely set out eating area with proper napkins; good enterprising food inc lunchtime bar

snacks, three-course meals and Sun roasts, efficient knowledgeable service, six changing real ales; attractive and spacious suntrap back garden with sheltered terrace and play area (some noise from A1M), dogs must be on a lead, wooded walks nearby, open all day *(David and Pauline Loom, BB)*

AYOT ST LAWRENCE [TL1916]
☆ *Brocket Arms* [off B651 N of St Albans]: Peacefully set 14th-c building, one of the county's most distinctive pubs, two simple old-fashioned low-beamed rooms, roaring fire in big inglenook, a dozen or so wines by the glass, Adnams Broadside, Batemans XXXB, Greene King IPA and Abbot and guest beers, traditional games, lunchtime bar food from sandwiches to game pie, wider choice in cosy no smoking evening restaurant, informal service; piped classical music; children welcome, nice suntrap walled garden with outside bar and play area, bedrooms, open all day *(Susan and Nigel Wilson, LYM, Barry and Marie Males, Ian Phillips, Giles Francis, Alistair and Kay Butler, Tim Maddison)*

BARKWAY [TL3834]
Tally Ho [London Rd]: Unspoilt and welcoming, with chatty local public bar, enjoyable home-made food possibly using fruit from the pleasant garden, Nethergate tapped from the cask *(Richard C Morgan)*

BELSIZE [TL0300]
Plough: Welcoming village pub doing well under newish licensees, central bar, barn-like beamed lounge with open fire, good friendly service, Adnams, Courage Directors and Greene King IPA, enjoyable home-made food inc authentic Mon curry night; picnic-sets in nice garden *(Jarrod and Wendy Hopkinson)*

BENINGTON [TL3023]
☆ *Bell* [Town Lane; just past Post Office, towards Stevenage]: Welcoming bustling partly 15th-c pub in very pretty village, generous food from sandwiches to good main dishes, good cheery

service, well kept Greene King IPA, Abbot and Morlands Original and a guest beer, hops with fairy lights hanging from low beams, sloping walls, flowers and candles on tables, unusual faded stag-hunt mural over big inglenook fireplace with woodburner, mix of old furnishings, aircraft memorabilia and enamel signs, separate dining room; no children in bars, piped music, weekly folk night; big pleasant garden with country views, handy for Benington Lordship *(Gordon Neighbour, BB, B and M Kendall)*

BERKHAMSTED [SP9807]

Crystal Palace [Station Rd]: By Regents Canal, good choice of beers, restaurant area, particularly good service *(Eddie Edwards)*

Goat [High St]: Unpretentious bustling pub run by long-serving family, four or five real ales, good wine choice, low-priced standard food, roaring fire; live music Thurs and Sun; well kept back garden with terrace *(MP)*

BRAUGHING [TL3925]

Brown Bear [just off B1368; The Street]: Quiet little low-beamed pub with big log fire, friendly staff, enjoyable simple well cooked food, Greene King IPA and Old Speckled Hen; delightful village *(Len Banister)*

BRICKENDON [TL3208]

☆ *Farmers Boy* [S of Hertford]: Roomy refurbished village pub in attractive spot nr green, wide choice of popular food all day from sandwiches up, friendly service, Adnams and Greene King, dining area; open all day, seats in back garden and over road *(Kate Branston)*

BRICKET WOOD [TL1502]

Moor Mill [off Smug Oak Lane – turn at Gate pub]: Attractive 18th-c restored watermill, now an Out & Out chain eating pub, with central working wheel, beams, brick walls and flagstones, two floors, oak tables and comfortable chairs; no end of picnic-sets in big waterside garden with play area, open all day *(O K Smyth, LYM)*

BUSHEY [TQ1395]

Swan [Park Rd; turning off A411]: Homely atmosphere in rare surviving example of unspoilt single-room backstreet terraced pub, reminiscent of 1920s *(Pete Baker, LYM)*

CHANDLERS CROSS [TQ0698]

☆ *Clarendon Arms* [Redhall Lane]: Friendly traditional pub in attractive country setting, handy for woodland and canal walks, with consistently good value generous home-made food esp Sun lunch and barbecues, particularly pleasant cheerful attentive staff, well kept ales inc Fullers London Pride, wide choice of wines by the glass, log fire; children welcome, live band Thurs, Mon quiz night; pleasant verandah, lots of tables and cocktail parasols *(Mrs W Mabilat, Peter and Giff Bennett, Hans and Thelma Liesner)*

CHAPMORE END [TL3216]

Woodman [off B158 Hertford—Wadesmill]: Small two-bar village local by pond with well kept Greene King IPA and Abbot tapped from the cask, usual lunchtime food (not Sun) from sandwiches up, some curry nights, bare boards,

simple furnishings; annual music festival; dogs welcome, big back garden, small front one, pets corner and play area *(Ian Arthur)*

CHARLTON [TL1728]

Windmill: Wide choice of good value food, friendly helpful staff, well kept beers inc Adnams Broadside and Charles Wells; piped music; garden with ducks and weeping willow, pleasant streamside setting in small village *(Mrs Diane M Hall, B and M Kendall)*

CHIPPERFIELD [TL0400]

Cart & Horses [Commonwood, just S]: Popular small pub with wide blackboard food choice, well kept Greene King beers, welcoming staff; plenty of picnic-sets *(Stan Edwards)*

Royal Oak [The Street]: Friendly relaxed atmosphere and well kept beer in two small neatly kept bars, Youngs Special and guest beers, good wines, limited choice of enjoyable fresh lunchtime food from enterprising sandwiches up, log fire, vintage car photographs; may be soft piped music *(Stan Edwards, David and June Pither)*

☆ *Two Brewers* [The Common]: Attractive country hotel housing good Chef & Brewer with roomy linked areas in bow-windowed bar, two log fires, dark décor; good if not cheap food all day from sandwiches and baked potatoes up, real ales, but no bar stools or bar-propping; provision for children, comfortable bedrooms, nice spot on common *(LYM, John and Joyce Snell, Robert F Smith)*

Windmill [The Common]: Good choice of home-made food (not Sun evening) and of well kept beers, welcoming obliging licensees, no smoking dining area; pleasant garden, bedrooms *(Stan Edwards)*

CHORLEYWOOD [TQ0295]

☆ *Black Horse* [Dog Kennel Lane, the Common]: Very welcoming to families, walkers and even dogs (basket of dog biscuits on mantelpiece), nice seating under low dark beams in attractively divided traditional room with thick carpet, two massive log fires, well kept Adnams, Flowers Original, Theakstons Best and Wadworths 6X, decent wines (and tea and coffee), friendly landlord and staff, usual food (not Mon) from sandwiches to popular good value Sun lunches, no music; family area, separate bar with SkyTV; pretty setting, picnic-sets overlooking common *(Tracy Fern, Darren Le Poidevin, Peter and Giff Bennett)*

Land of Liberty Peace & Plenty [Long Lane, Heronsgate; just off M25 junction 17]: Newish owners doing very wide choice of modestly priced home-made food, also good choice of real ales such as Brakspears, Courage Best, Slaters and Timothy Taylors Landlord *(Comus and Sarah Elliott)*

Stag [Long Lane/Heronsgate Rd, handy for M25 junction 17]: Smart attractive open-plan pub under new management, well kept McMullens ales, wide range of good value bar and restaurant food, friendly attentive staff, large no smoking dining conservatory; quiet piped music, busy wknds; tables on back lawn, play area, good walking area *(Paul A Moore, Tracey and Stephen Groves)*

COLNEY HEATH [TL2006]
Crooked Billet [High St]: Unpretentious pub with four well kept changing ales and lots of unusual bottled beers, series of small rooms with seated alcoves and traditional tiled bar, friendly service, good value food inc fresh baguettes; piped music; garden with barbecues and partly covered terrace (*P Abbott, LYM*)
Plough [just off back road N, between A414 St Albans—Hatfield and A1057]: Popular pleasantly refurbished 18th-c low-beamed local, warm and cosy at front with good log fire and small dining area, good value generous homely food (lunchtime Mon-Sat, and Fri/Sat evening), well kept Greene King Abbot, Fullers London Pride and Tetleys, friendly efficient service; garden overlooking fields (*BG, RG, John Cadge, Monica Cockburn, Mike Jefferies*)
DATCHWORTH [TL2717]
☆ *Horns* [Bramfield Rd]: Weatherboarded Tudor pub facing small green, low beams and big inglenook one end, high rafters and rugs on patterned bricks the other, attractive décor, good food, well kept real ales; tables out on crazy-paved terrace among roses (*LYM, J B Young*)
DIGSWELL [TL2415]
Cowper Arms [Station Rd]: Friendly, with good range of food, real ales inc Bass, Courage Directors and Greene King Abbot (*Stephen, Julie and Hayley Brown*)
FLAMSTEAD [TL0714]
Spotted Dog [High St]: Pleasant furnishings and open fire in small neat bar, larger back eating area, limited good value lunchtime food from sandwiches up, real ales such as Ansells, Fullers London Pride and Robinsons, friendly helpful service; piped music, games machine (*Michael Dandy*)
Three Blackbirds [High St (just off A5)]: Lively and welcoming low-beamed partly Tudor local, much modernised inside, but still with old dark wood and brickwork, pictures, brass, copper, lots of horse tack, roaring fire, well kept Courage Best and Directors and Shepherd Neame Spitfire from central bar, good value straightforward food from sandwiches to good Sun roasts, no smoking area; children's corner, dogs welcome, darts, pool, piped music, SkyTV; tables on terrace by car park behind, lots of flowers (*Ian Phillips, BB, David and Ruth Shillitoe*)
FLAUNDEN [TL0100]
☆ *Bricklayers Arms* [village signed off A41; from village centre follow Boxmoor, Bovingdon road and turn right at Belsize, Watford signpost]: Cottagey and friendly country pub, low beams, log fire, timbered stub walls, attractive décor, enjoyable food from sandwiches to restaurant dishes, several well kept ales such as Brakspears PA, Fullers London Pride and Ringwood Old Thumper, decent wines, good service, no piped music, children in eating areas; nice old-fashioned garden, nearby walks (*Tracey and Stephen Groves, Jarrod and Wendy Hopkinson, LYM, Jill McLaren, Chris Smith*)

GRAVELEY [TL2327]
George & Dragon [High St]: Well run old coaching inn, well kept Greene King ales, good value food inc imaginative dishes, good welcoming service even when busy, restaurant; stairs down to lavatories (*JMC*)
GREAT HORMEAD [TL4030]
Three Tuns: Old timbered country pub with wide range of good imaginative well presented food (just roasts on Sun), small linked areas, huge inglenook (alsatian brings the logs) with another great hearth behind, Greene King IPA and Old Speckled Hen, personable and friendly landlord, big back conservatory extension (*Ian Phillips*)
GREAT MUNDEN [TL3523]
☆ *Plough* [SW, towards Dane End]: Unique full-size working Compton theatre organ in comfortable and lofty lounge extension built specially to house it; decent nicely presented food (Sun lunch with organ recital is worth booking), well kept Greene King IPA and Abbot, friendly landlord, pleasant staff, good facilities for the disabled; nearby walks (*LYM, Gordon Neighbour*)
GREAT OFFLEY [TL1427]
☆ *Green Man* [signed off A505 Luton—Hitchin; High St]: Roomy, comfortable and attractive Chef & Brewer family dining pub open all day, with wonderful country view from large flagstoned conservatory and picnic-sets on pleasant back terrace and garden; roaring winter fires, very wide food choice, good service, Courage Directors and Theakstons Old Peculier; may be unobtrusive piped classical music, very busy wknds; front play area, striking inn-sign (*LYM, Keith and Janet Morris, Ian Phillips*)
GREEN TYE [TL4418]
Prince of Wales: Unpretentious and chatty traditional two-bar village local brewing its own good Green Tye ales such as Union Jack and Wheelbarrow, one guest beer, friendly landlord, usual simple lunchtime food, coal fire; tables in garden (*Ian Arthur, Len Banister*)
HEMEL HEMPSTEAD [TL0411]
☆ *Crown & Sceptre* [Bridens Camp; leaving on A4146, right at Flamstead/Markyate sign opp Red Lion]: Classic country pub, cheerful and cosy communicating rooms, some oak panelling, antique settles among more usual seating, good value filling food from wide range of sandwiches and baguettes up, well kept Greene King IPA and Abbot and a guest such as Jennings, friendly staff, log fires; darts and dominoes, children and dogs welcome; back garden with chickens, ducks and scarecrow, heated front picnic-sets, good walks; open all day summer wknds (*LYM, R T and J C Moggridge, Ian Phillips*)
Swan [Pimlico; A41 just SE of Hemel, between Leverstock Green and Bedmond]: Family pub with good choice of generous reasonably priced food, restaurant and conservatory, Whitbreads-related ales and a local guest beer, friendly staff; large garden (*anon*)
HERTFORD [TL3212]
☆ *Old Cross Tavern* [St Andrew St]: Particularly

well kept Fullers London Pride, Oakham JHB and fine choice of up to half a dozen guest beers, good home-made lunchtime food, friendly olde-worlde feel with brass, china etc (conversion from antiques shop); small heated back terrace, dogs welcome *(Ian Arthur)*

HEXTON [TL1230]

☆ *Raven* [signed off B655]: Large recently refurbished 1920s family dining pub, four neat areas inc long tidy public bar (open fire, pool one end), extensive no smoking areas, plenty of dining tables, oil paintings (some for sale); wide range value food from baguettes and baked potatoes up, two children's menus, well kept ales inc Fullers London Pride and Greene King IPA and Old Speckled Hen, friendly efficient service; children welcome, big garden with heated terrace, barbecue, well segregated play area *(Phil and Heidi Cook)*

HIGH WYCH [TL4614]

Rising Sun: Cosy unspoilt local, serving hatch to carpeted lounge with coal or log fire, central area with Courage Best and good guest beers tapped from casks behind the counter, friendly landlord and locals, bare-boards games room (children allowed) with darts and woodburner; no food, no mobile phones or pagers, no music; tables in small garden *(the Didler, Pete Baker)*

HINXWORTH [TL2340]

☆ *Three Horseshoes* [High St; just off A1(M)]: Thatched, beamed and timbered 18th-c dining pub under new management, good value food (not Sun evening, Mon) inc children's dishes, pews in extended red plush bar, steps up to no smoking high-ceilinged dining area, well kept Greene King IPA, Abbot and Ruddles, decent wines, friendly landlord, woodburner in big brick inglenook, soft lighting; piped music; children welcome, good big garden with play area *(Anthony Barnes, Gordon Neighbour, BB)*

HODDESDON [TL3808]

Fish & Eels [Dobbs Weir]: Spacious chain pub prettily placed opp weir on River Lea, nature reserve behind, long river walks; decent food inc huge sandwiches, Bass and Tetleys, friendly staff; garden with play area, handy for Rye House *(Len Banister)*

HUNSDON [TL4114]

Fox & Hounds: This pub, a find for good fresh food in our last edition, has unfortunately now closed *(LYM)*

ICKLEFORD [TL1831]

Plume of Feathers [Upper Green]: Good mixed choice of enjoyable fresh food from sandwiches to some unusual main dishes, two good landladies, coal-effect gas fires; nice quiet spot overlooking green *(David and Ruth Shillitoe, Mrs Ann Adams)*

KNEBWORTH [TL2320]

Lytton Arms [Park Lane, Old Knebworth]: Several big-windowed rooms around large central servery, Adnams, Fullers London Pride and perhaps other real ales, bar food from sandwiches and ciabattas up, no smoking conservatory; children welcome, picnic-sets on front terrace, back garden with play area, open all day wknds *(LYM)*

LEMSFORD [TL2112]

Crooked Chimney [Cromer Hyde Lane (B653 towards Wheathampstead)]: Big old building handsomely refurbished as Vintage Inn dining pub, good if not cheap food inc children's helpings, well kept Bass and Tetleys, central feature fireplace and two further log fires, hop-hung beams; pleasant garden by fields, play area *(Stephen, Julie and Hayley Brown, LYM, Len Banister)*

Sun: Comfortable, welcoming and rather smart low-beamed and timbered pub nr River Lea, well kept ales inc Bass, Fullers London Pride and Greene King Abbot, good value generous bar food; can be busy evenings *(LYM, Stephen, Julie and Hayley Brown)*

LITTLE HADHAM [TL4322]

Nags Head [Hadham Ford, towards Much Hadham]: 16th-c country dining pub with linked heavily black-beamed rooms, three well kept Greene King beers tapped from the cask in small bar, decent house wines, freshly squeezed orange juice, no smoking restaurant down a couple of steps; children in eating areas, tables in pleasant garden *(Gordon Neighbour, LYM, B N F and M Parkin, A S and M E Marriott)*

LONDON COLNEY [TL1803]

☆ *Green Dragon* [Waterside; just off main st by bridge at S end]: Friendly and immaculate, with good value generous food (not Sun), lots of ancient timbers, beams and brasses, soft lighting, well kept changing ales such as Adnams, Fullers London Pride, Greene King Abbot and York Yorkshire Terrier, decent wine; prettily set riverside picnic-sets *(Ian Phillips, LYM)*

MARSWORTH [SP9114]

Anglers Retreat [Startops End]: Pleasantly unpretentious, with well kept Fullers London Pride and a lighter beer brewed for the pub, decent food inc fresh baguettes, Australian licensees; handy for Tring Reservoirs – special for waterfowl *(Val and Alan Green)*

MUCH HADHAM [TL4219]

☆ *Bull* [High St]: Attractive old pub with well presented food inc speciality sausages, well kept real ales, happy helpful staff, unspoilt inglenook public bar, nicely worn-in comfortable banquettes in roomy dining lounge with farm tools and old pictures, smaller back family dining room; children welcome, unusually big garden *(John and Patricia White, LYM)*

PERRY GREEN [TL4317]

☆ *Hoops* [off B1004 Widford—Much Hadham]: Village pub opp Henry Moore Foundation (guided tours in summer by appointment), stripped brick, terracotta walls and standing timbers, food from sandwiches to all-day Sun lunch, Fullers London Pride and perhaps other ales, cosy no smoking dining area (children allowed); garden tables, some under awnings, open all day Sun *(Ruth and Paul Lawrence, Hugh Roberts, LYM)*

PRESTON [TL1824]

☆ *Red Lion* [The Green]: Lively village-owned local, very neatly kept, with enjoyable home-

made food inc game, fish and choice of Sun roasts, five well kept changing real ales, welcoming service; picnic-sets in gardens front and back, local cricket HQ *(Barry and Marie Males, Alison Jeffers, Richard Beharrell)*
REED [TL3636]
☆ *Cabinet* [off A10; High St]: 16th-c weatherboarded pub, emphasis now on attractive upmarket no smoking restaurant with good imaginative if not cheap food (well behaved children allowed), simpler menu in small bar with inglenook log fire, piped music, darts, shove-ha'penny, dominoes and cribbage, well kept Adnams, Greene King Abbot and IPA and a guest beer; tables in charming big garden with pond *(LYM)*
RICKMANSWORTH [TQ0594]
Pennsylvanian [High St]: Wetherspoons with no smoking family area, and all their usual features *(Tony Hobden)*
RUSHDEN [TL3031]
Moon & Stars [Mill End; off A507 about 1 mile W of Cottered]: Unspoilt cottagey beamed country pub with neatly kept no smoking lounge bar, inglenook log fire, well kept Greene King ales, good choice of good value food (small dining room, worth booking); pleasant garden, peaceful country setting *(Joy and Colin Rorke, LYM, S Horsley)*
SARRATT [TQ0499]
Cricketers [The Green]: Big busy dining pub in attractive spot overlooking large green, good choice of food inc impressive range of fish and seafood in restaurant part, separate bar food menu, good choice of well kept real ales, friendly efficient uniformed staff, pleasant décor; tables out by pond, open all day *(Stan Edwards)*
SAWBRIDGEWORTH [TL4814]
Gate [London Rd (A1184)]: 18th-c pub with good range of quickly changing well kept ales in lined glasses, bank hol beer festivals with live music, cheap fresh lunchtime food, roomy and relaxed front bar, back bar with pool and games *(the Didler)*
ST ALBANS [TL1307]
Blue Anchor [Fishpool St]: Popular dining lounge with good value bar food (not Sun evening) from sandwiches up, well kept McMullens ales inc Mild, attractive prices, welcoming landlord, small locals' bar on left, daily papers, sensibly placed darts, real fire; sizeable garden, handy for Roman remains *(Pam Adsley, the Didler)*
Farmers Boy [London Rd]: Bustling bay-windowed pub with back brewery producing Verulam IPA, Farmers Joy and a monthly special such as Ginger Tom (ask for a taster), also their own lager and 10 continental bottled beers, lots of old prints on smoke-effect walls, imposing clock, real fire, back open kitchen serving straightforward food from sandwiches and baked potatoes up all day, helpful staff, two large friendly dogs; SkyTV; open all day, plenty of suntrap tables out behind *(the Didler, Richard Lewis)*
Farriers Arms [Lower Dagnall St]: Plain but welcoming little local in no-frills old part, well

kept McMullens inc Mild, bar food wkdys *(the Didler)*
Fighting Cocks [Abbey Mill Lane; through abbey gateway – you can drive down]: Odd-shaped former abbey gatehouse, much modernised inside but with sunken area which was a Stuart cockpit, some low and heavy beams, big inglenook fires, pleasant nooks, corners and window alcoves, and well kept real ales (at a price); can be very busy evenings, shame about the piped pop music; children welcome (good family room), attractive public park beyond garden, open all day *(Mr and Mrs John Taylor, the Didler, LYM)*
☆ *Garibaldi* [Albert St; left turn down Holywell Hill past White Hart – car park left at end]: Relaxed Fullers local with well kept Chiswick, London Pride and ESB and a guest beer, good low-priced wholesome lunchtime food (not Mon), good house wines, cheerful staff; may be piped music; children welcome, open all day *(the Didler, LYM)*
Lower Red Lion [Fishpool St]: Relaxing and convivial two-bar local, good chatty atmosphere, interesting changing range of well kept beers, May Day and Aug bank hol beer festivals, home-made food, log fire, red plush seats and carpet; open all day Sat, tables in good-sized back garden, pleasant bedrooms *(Tracey and Stephen Groves, the Didler)*
☆ *Plough* [Tyttenhanger Green; off A414 E]: Spacious and friendly village pub, good-humoured licensees, young staff polite and prompt even when it's packed, lovely longcase clock, good log fire, well kept changing ales, good value straightforward food, fine collection of old beer bottles, other bric-a-brac; conservatory, big garden with play area *(LYM, the Didler, P Abbott, Ian and Joan Blackwell)*
☆ *Rose & Crown* [St Michaels St]: Busy 400-year-old beamed town pub with uneven timbered walls covered with American landlord's impressive collection of sporting memorabilia, big log fires, dominoes, cribbage and darts, well kept Adnams, Fullers London Pride, Tetleys and a guest beer, great speciality american-style sandwiches and other pub standards (lunchtime, not Sun), family room (no smoking at lunchtime); live music Mon/Thurs evenings; lots of tables and benches outside, pretty floral and ivy-hung back yard, handy for Roman Verulam Museum *(LYM, R J Davies, Pat and Tony Martin, Ian Phillips, the Didler, Tracey and Stephen Groves)*
☆ *Six Bells* [St Michaels St]: Well kept timbered and low-beamed food pub on site of a Roman bath house, well kept Adnams, Greene King IPA and Broadside, Fullers London Pride and Tetleys, cheerful helpful service even when bustling with locals, big helpings of good value freshly made food from sandwiches up, quieter no smoking panelled eating area; children welcome, family room, occasional barbecues in small back garden, open all day Fri-Sun *(Mike and Jennifer Marsh, R T and J C Moggridge, LYM, J Silverman, Rita Scarratt, Ian Phillips)*

White Hart Tap [Keyfield, round corner from Garibaldi]: Small but friendly white-panelled pub, well kept real ales, good value quickly served lunchtime food; tables outside, open all day, live band Tues *(Derek R A Field)*

STEVENAGE [TL2324]

Chequers [High St]: Open-plan high-ceilinged Greene King pub, comfortable U-shaped bar, friendly staff, good value food (not Sun) from sandwiches up inc evening steak menu and early-evening bargains, rugby football memorabilia; busy wkdys, juke box; well kept sunny courtyard *(Gordon Tong)*

THERFIELD [TL3336]

☆ *Fox & Duck* [The Green; off A505 Baldock—Royston]: Easy-going beamed village pub with scrubbed oak tables and attractive décor, interesting food inc seasonal game and some thai dishes, well kept ales such as Greene King IPA and Ruddles and Theakstons, decent wines and coffee, courteous staff; bedrooms, a few tables in garden with good play equipment, more on attractive village green, pleasant walks nearby *(Pat and Tony Hinkins, Morris and Jenny Le Fleming)*

THORLEY STREET [TL4818]

☆ *Coach & Horses* [A1184 Sawbridgeworth—Bishops Stortford]: Now a Vintage Inn and much changed; prompt service, good value food, good décor, and on an alternative route to congested part of M11 *(R C Vincent)*

TRING [SP9313]

Grand Junction Arms [Bulbourne; B488 towards Dunstable, next to BWB works]: Small friendly and unspoilt open-plan canalside pub with well kept Flowers and other ales, reasonably priced good curries in raised side eating area (advisable to book in evenings),

canal photographs and memorabilia; children welcome, play area in big waterside garden, barbecues and Sat evening live music out here *(Geoffrey Tyack)*

Kings Arms [King St]: Green décor, pine and pews, no juke box or video screens, simple wholesome home cooking (lunchtime emphasis on this) from hot beef sandwiches up, ethnic and vegetarian leanings, five well kept changing ales usually inc local Tring brews and Wadworths 6X direct from the brewers, friendly welcome; busy with young people evenings *(anon)*

☆ *Robin Hood* [Brook St (B486)]: Well run olde-worlde Fullers local with surprisingly good food esp daily fresh fish such as bass, marlin or black bream (wide choice, but they don't buy much of each, so the blackboard may change as you watch), several small drinking areas, three well kept Fullers beers, comfortable settles, lots of dark wood, slight nautical theme, dining conservatory with woodburner and random collection of prints; piped music; no children or dogs inside, tables on small pleasant back terrace, free public car park nearby *(MP, John Branston, Ken Richards, BB)*

WELWYN [TL2214]

Red Lion [B197 S, by Welwyn Garden City]: Good atmosphere in well run Vintage Inn with well kept Bass and enjoyable food *(Stephen, Julie and Hayley Brown)*

WHITWELL [TL1821]

☆ *Maidens Head* [High St (B651)]: First-class landlord and friendly staff in McMullens local with good value food, well kept ales tapped from the cask, good coffee, interesting key-ring collection; seats in safe children's garden *(Barry and Marie Males)*

People named as recommenders after the main entries have told us that the pub should be included. But they have not written the report – we have, after anonymous on-the-spot inspection.

Isle of Wight

Considering its size and population, this county has a surprising number of good pubs. Top of the heap this year are the Red Lion in Freshwater (good imaginative food in pleasant surroundings, no young children), the very hospitable Seaview Hotel (good food here too, and a nice choice between interesting pubby bar and smart dining atmosphere), and the New Inn at Shalfleet (as so often with pubs under that name it's in fact a really ancient place – nice all round, with notable fresh local fish). All three are rewarding places to visit, for anything from just a drink through a snack to a special meal out. Its flexibility giving it a slight edge, the Seaview Hotel wins the accolade of Isle of Wight Dining Pub of the Year. One pub in the Lucky Dip section at the end of the chapter which on current form looks like joining the main entries soon is the Buddle at Niton; and we'd be particularly interested in readers' views on other pubs in that section which could merit inspection. Drinks prices on the island are a little higher than the national average but just a shade lower than across the Solent in Hampshire; three flourishing small breweries on the island are Ventnor, Yates (see Lucky Dip entry for the St Lawrence Inn) and Goddards.

ARRETON SZ5486 Map 2
White Lion
A3056 Newport—Sandown

This cosy white-painted village pub is popular, especially in summer, for good value straightforward food, and is particularly handy as the food is served all day. Besides sandwiches and baguettes (from £3.25) and baked potatoes (from £3.95), mostly home-made dishes include lasagne, steak and kidney pie or chilli (£5.95), wild rice and spinach bake (£6.45), battered scampi (£6.95) and steaks (from £8.95), as well as specials such as marlin steak with garlic prawns (£7.95) and ostrich steak with plum and red wine sauce (£13.95), and enjoyable puddings with lots of cream or custard; no smoking restaurant and family room. The pleasant beamed lounge bar has shining brass and horse tack on the partly panelled walls, cushioned wheelback chairs on the red carpet, and Badger Best and Flowers Best kept well on handpump. There may be piped music, and the public bar has cribbage, dominoes, darts, fruit machine and TV. You can sit out in front by the tubs of flowers, and the pleasant garden has a small play area. *(Recommended by Nigel B Thompson, JDM, KM, Pete Yearsley, Penny and Peter Keevil)*

Whitbreads ~ Lease Chris and Kate Cole ~ Real ale ~ Bar food (12-9) ~ (01983) 528479 ~ Children in family room ~ Dogs allowed in bar ~ Open 11-11; 12-10.30 Sun

BEMBRIDGE SZ6587 Map 2
Crab & Lobster 🍴
Foreland Fields Road, off Howgate Road (which is off B3395 via Hillgate Road)

Tucked away on a coastal bluff, this clifftop pub is not somewhere you'd stumble across if you weren't in the know. With great sea views from its terrace, bedrooms, garden and window seats it's actually quite an easy walk from the beach. There's more room inside than you'd expect from the frontage, which is prettily bedecked with flower baskets in summer. The attractively decorated interior has a civilised, almost parlourish style, with lots of yachting memorabilia and old local photographs. They serve a very good choice of eight or nine changing fresh local seafood specials every day, from sardines in garlic butter and lemon (£3.95), through moules marinière (from £5.95), tasty home-made crab cakes (£7.25), grilled plaice topped with olives, garlic and basil (£7.50) and bass with garlic butter and lemon (£10.50), to whole lobster (£21.95). Other very well prepared food includes sandwiches (from £3.75), baked potatoes (from £3.95), ploughman's (£4.95), lasagne (£5.95), pork steaks with mozzarella and rosemary (£8.25), fillet steak (£10.50), and puddings such as spotted dick (£2.95); the restaurant is no smoking. Well kept Flowers Original, Greene King IPA and Goddards Fuggle-Dee-Dum on handpump, decent house wines, country wines from the barrel, good coffee; piped music (even in the lavatories), darts, dominoes and cribbage. It does get very popular, so best to get there early or late at lunchtime. *(Recommended by Glyn and Janet Lewis, Pete Yearsley, Gordon Stevenson, Roger and Pauline Pearce, Phil and Heidi Cook, E S Funnell, Ken Flawn, Alain and Rose Foote, Jan and Alan Summers, Pat and Graham Williamson, Richard Dixon)*

Whitbreads ~ Lease Richard, Adrian and Pauline Allan ~ Real ale ~ Bar food (12-2.30, 6-9.30) ~ Restaurant ~ (01983) 872244 ~ Children in eating area of bar and restaurant ~ Dogs allowed in bar ~ Open 11-11; 12-10.30 Sun ~ Bedrooms: /£70B

BONCHURCH SZ5778 Map 2
Bonchurch Inn

Bonchurch Shute; from A3055 E of Ventnor turn down to Old Bonchurch opposite Leconfield Hotel

The layout of this old stone coaching inn and stables has changed very little since it gained its licence in the 1840s. Cut into the side of the hill, its various buildings form the sides to a small cobbled central courtyard. Tables, a fountain and pergola out here are nicely enclosed, giving it a slightly continental feel on warm summer days. The furniture-packed Victorian bar has a good chatty atmosphere, and conjures up images of salvaged shipwrecks, with its floor of narrow-planked ship's decking, and seats like the ones that old-fashioned steamers used to have. There's a separate entrance to the very simple no smoking family room (a bit cut off from the congenial atmosphere of the public bar). As well as Courage Directors tapped from the cask, there are italian wines by the glass, a few bottled french wines, darts, bar billiards, shove-ha'penny, dominoes and cribbage. The welcoming landlord is Italian, and the menu reflects this with dishes such as lasagne, seafood risotto, spaghetti bolognese or cannelloni (from £6), as well as sandwiches (from £3, toasted 30p extra), soup (£4), battered squid (£7.50), chicken cordon bleu (£8.95) and sirloin steak (£9.50); for puddings they have ice creams and sorbets (£3); there may be a small charge for credit cards. The no smoking restaurant is just across the courtyard, and the pub owns a holiday flat for up to six people. *(Recommended by Tom and Ruth Rees, Pete Yearsley, Paul Humphreys)*

Free house ~ Licensees Ulisse and Gillian Besozzi ~ Real ale ~ Bar food ~ Restaurant ~ (01983) 852611 ~ Children in family room ~ Dogs welcome ~ Open 11-3, 6.30-11; 12-3, 7-10.30 Sun; closed 25 Dec ~ Bedrooms: /£60B

FRESHWATER SZ3487 Map 2
Red Lion 🍴 ♀

Church Place; from A3055 at E end of village by Freshwater Garage mini-roundabout follow Yarmouth signpost, then take first real right turn signed to Parish Church

Consistently maintaining its standing as one of the best pubs on the island, this quietly tucked-away pub has a grown-up atmosphere that visitors without smaller children tend to appreciate. It's so popular that if you want to eat here it's a good idea to book ahead. As well as a couple of lunchtime snacks such as baguettes (from £4.25), ploughman's (from £4.75) and fish and chips (£8.50), very well prepared imaginative daily specials are listed on a big blackboard behind the bar, and might include soup (£3.75), wild boar terrine (£4.75), herring roes on toast (£5.25), steak and kidney pie (£7.50), wild mushroom and spinach risotto (£7.95), linguini with crab (£8.75), pork cutlet with bacon mash and mustard cream (£9.25), grilled halibut with chilli and coriander sauce (£9.95), and puddings such as rhubarb crumble or citrus cheesecake (£3.75). Service is thoughtful and warmly attentive, and there's a cheery bustling atmosphere in the comfortably furnished open-plan bar, which has open fires, low grey sofas and sturdy country-kitchen style furnishings on mainly flagstoned floors, with bare boards at one end, and lots of local pictures and photographs and china platters on the walls. Well kept Black Sheep, Flowers Original, Fullers London Pride and Goddards on handpump, and the good choice of wines includes 16 by the glass. Fines on mobile phone users go to charity (they also collect a lot for the RNLI); there's a fruit machine. There are tables on a carefully tended grass and gravel area at the back (some under cover), behind which is the kitchen's herb garden, and a couple of picnic-sets in a quiet square at the front, by the church; nearby are good walks, especially around the River Yar. *(Recommended by Dr and Mrs P Truelove, Mike and Sue Richardson, Miss J F Reay, Derek and Sylvia Stephenson, David and Kay Ross, June and Malcolm Farmer, E S Funnell, Ken Flawn, Peter and Margaret Glenister, Sheila Stothard, Paul Humphreys, Jan and Alan Summers, Penny and Peter Keevil)*

Enterprise ~ Lease Michael Mence ~ Real ale ~ Bar food (12-2, 6-9) ~ (01983) 754925 ~ Children over 10 ~ Dogs allowed in bar ~ Open 11.30-3, 5.30-11; 11-4, 6-11 Sat; 12-3, 7-10.30 Sun

ROOKLEY SZ5183 Map 2
Chequers
Niton Road; signposted S of village

In contrast to the pub described above, there's plenty of entertainment for little people at this former customs and excise house, which has a toboggan run and bouncy castle in the large play area outside, and a Lego table and colouring competitions in the large no smoking family room. Parents can keep an eye on children outside from the new sun lounge and bar which looks out over the garden and play area. There's also a mother and baby room. The comfortable carpeted lounge bar has cottagey ornaments and in winter a good log fire; it gives inland views of rolling downland. The flagstoned public bar beyond has a good lively local character (it's popular with young farmers), sensibly placed darts, fruit machine, TV; perhaps piped music. Five real ales include Courage Best and Directors, Gales HSB, Greene King Old Speckled Hen and Ventnor Golden on handpump. Bar food includes sandwiches (from £2.95), soup (£2.75), deep-fried brie with redcurrant jelly (£4.75), baked potatoes (from £5.45), ploughman's (from £5.65), vegetable lasagne (£5.95), chicken curry (£6.95), moules marinière (£7.95), half a roast duck (£9.50), steaks (from £9.95), lobster salad (£10.95), and puddings (from £3.25). *(Recommended by Pete Yearsley)*

Free house ~ Licensees R G and S L Holmes ~ Real ale ~ Bar food (12-9) ~ Restaurant ~ (01983) 840314 ~ Children in eating area of bar, restaurant and family room ~ Dogs allowed in bar ~ Open 11-11; 12-10.30 Sun

SEAVIEW SZ6291 Map 2
Seaview Hotel 🍽 ♀ 🛏
High Street; off B3330 Ryde—Bembridge

Isle of Wight Dining Pub of the Year

Getting quite famous these days for its charming hospitality and warm service, this comfortably bustling little hotel has various reception rooms ranging from pubby to smart dining, and is a lovely place to stay. The relaxingly civilised airy bay-windowed bar at the front has an impressive array of naval and merchant ship photographs, as well as Spy nautical cartoons for *Vanity Fair*, original receipts for Cunard's shipyard payments for the *Queen Mary* and *Queen Elizabeth*, and a line of close-set tables down each side on the turkey carpet. There's a more informal down to earth atmosphere in the simpler nautical back bar, with traditional wooden furnishings on bare boards, lots of seafaring paraphernalia around its softly lit ochre walls, and a log fire. They keep Goddards and Greene King Old Speckled Hen on handpump, and have quite a few malt whiskies and a good wine list (the landlord used to be a director of Corney & Barrow, the wine merchants); darts, cribbage, dominoes, shove-ha'penny and piped music. Using local ingredients wherever possible and fish fresh from the sea, very good well presented and generously served bar food includes soup (£3.95), smoked haddock and prawn chowder (£4.20), a hot crab ramekin that's been a favourite here for years (£5.95), scampi and chips (£7.95), grilled rib-eye steak with peppercorn sauce or local chicken breast with oak-smoked garlic and rosemary risotto (£9.95), and puddings such as steamed treacle pudding or iced lemon brûlée (£3.95); the smart formal restaurant is no smoking. Tables on the little terraces on either side of the path to the front door look down to the sea and along the coast, and some of the attractive bedrooms also have a sea view. *(Recommended by Geoffrey Kemp, JDM, KM, Derek and Sylvia Stephenson, E S Funnell, N Bayley, June and Malcolm Farmer)*

Free house ~ Licensee N W T Hayward ~ Real ale ~ Bar food ~ Restaurant ~ (01983) 612711 ~ Children welcome (over 5 in restaurant) ~ Dogs allowed in bar and bedrooms ~ Open 10.30-2.30, 6-11; 12-3, 7-10.30 Sun; closed three or four days at Christmas ~ Bedrooms: £65S/£80S(£100B)

SHALFLEET SZ4189 Map 2
New Inn 🍽 ♀ 🍺

A3054 Newport—Yarmouth

Don't miss this welcoming former fishermen's pub – just a short walk from the fish quay – if you enjoy fresh fish. Well known for their crab or lobster salad (from £11.95) and seafood platter (£50 for two), they also have a great choice of up to 16 fresh fish dishes a day, such as grilled sardines with garlic and black pepper butter (£3.95), moules marinière (£5.95/£8.95), hake fillets with lemon and tarragon (£9.95) and bass in lemon (£13.95). A little crab shack in the garden sells potted shrimps, dressed crab and local lobster, which you can snack on at the pub or take away. Other dishes include smoked venison with green fig chutney (£4.95), steak and ale pie (£7.95) and chicken breast with honey and cream (£8.95), alongside a short menu with sandwiches (from £2.95), filled baguettes (from £3.75) and ploughman's (from £5.25). You will need to book, and there may be double sittings in summer. The partly panelled flagstoned public bar has yachting photographs and pictures, a boarded ceiling, scrubbed deal tables, windsor chairs, and a roaring log fire in the big stone hearth, and the carpeted beamed lounge bar has more windsor chairs, boating pictures, and a coal fire. The snug and gallery (with slate floors, bric-a-brac and windsor chairs at scrubbed pine tables) are no smoking. Well kept Flowers Original, Greene King IPA, Marstons Pedigree and Ventnor Golden on handpump, and around 60 wines; piped music. *(Recommended by Jan and Alan Summers, Geoffrey Kemp, Tom and Ruth Rees, Dr and Mrs P Truelove, Peter and Margaret Glenister, Joyce and Geoff Robson, Gordon Stevenson, Pat and Graham Williamson, Ian and Gail Isted, Derek Hayman, Paul Humphreys)*

Whitbreads ~ Lease Mr Bullock and Mr McDonald ~ Real ale ~ Bar food (12-2.30, 6-9.30) ~ Restaurant ~ (01983) 531314 ~ Children welcome ~ Dogs welcome ~ Open 12-3, 6-11(10.30 Sun)

SHORWELL SZ4582 Map 2
Crown

B3323 SW of Newport

During the summer months crowds head for the tree-sheltered garden – with picnic-sets and white garden chairs and tables by a little stream that broadens out into a small trout-filled pool – at this country pub. A decent children's play area blends in comfortably. Inside, four rooms spread pleasantly around a central bar. The beamed two-room lounge has blue and white china in an attractive carved dresser, old country prints on the stripped stone walls, other individual furnishings, and a winter log fire with a fancy tile-work surround. Black pews form bays around tables in a stripped-stone room off to the left, with another log fire; it's largely no smoking. Bar food includes sandwiches (from £2.75), soup (£2.95), lasagne or fisherman's pie (£6.95), and daily specials such as beef in stout (£7.95) and seafood platter (£11.50), with puddings (from £2.75) and children's meals. Well kept Boddingtons, Flowers Original and Wadworths 6X, with a guest such as Badger Tanglefoot on handpump; piped music and TV. *(Recommended by Peter and Margaret Glenister, Jan and Alan Summers, Lynn Sharpless)*

Whitbreads ~ Lease Mike Grace ~ Real ale ~ Bar food (12-2.30, 6-9.30(9 in winter)) ~ (01983) 740293 ~ Children in eating area of bar and family room ~ Dogs welcome ~ Open 10-11; 12-10.30 Sun; 10-3, 6-11 Mon-Sat; 12-3, 6-10.30 Sun in winter

VENTNOR SZ5677 Map 2
Spyglass

Esplanade, SW end; road down very steep and twisty, and parking nearby can be difficult – best to use the pay-and-display (free in winter) about 100 yards up the road

On a nice sunny day you'd be hard pushed to find yourself basking in a better spot than this terrace which is perched on top of the sea wall right next to the sea. If it's too wet to appreciate the view, there's plenty to look at inside. Among the really interesting jumble of mainly seafaring memorabilia are wrecked rudders, ships' wheels, old local advertisements, rope-makers' tools, stuffed seagulls, an Admiral Benbow barometer and an old brass telescope. The bustling mainly quarry-tiled interior is snug and pubby, and the atmosphere is buoyant; fruit machine, piped music. Usefully served all day, generous helpings of good, very fairly priced bar food are promptly served and include sandwiches (from £3.25, baguettes from £4.25), filled baked potatoes (from £4.95), whitebait or calamari (£5.95), ploughman's or spinach and ricotta cannelloni (£6.25), cottage pie or chilli (£6.50) with daily specials such as seafood chowder (£4.50), steak and ale pie (£6.95) and seafood casserole (£8.75). They usually have well kept Badger Best, Tanglefoot and Gribble Fursty Ferret, Ventnor Golden and possibly a guest on handpump. They don't mind muddy boots; no smoking area. *(Recommended by Peter and Margaret Glenister, Roger and Pauline Pearce, Dr and Mrs P Truelove, Pete Yearsley, Jan and Alan Summers, M Joyner, Paul Humphreys)*

Free house ~ Licensees Neil and Stephanie Gibbs ~ Real ale ~ Bar food (12-9.30 (9 Sun)) ~ (01983) 855338 ~ Children in family room ~ Dogs allowed in bar ~ Live entertainment most nights ~ Open 10.30-11; 12-10.30 Sun ~ Bedrooms: /£50B

Lucky Dip

Besides the fully inspected pubs, you might like to try these Lucky Dips recommended to us and described by readers (if you do, please send us reports: www.goodguides.com).

CHALE [SZ4877]
☆ *Clarendon (Wight Mouse)* [off A3055/B3399]: Popular rambling family pub with plenty to keep children occupied inc indoor play area for under-12s (admission charge); traditional core with log fire, woody extension with high pitched ceiling, lots of bric-a-brac, well kept Badger ales and Ventnor Gold, cheerful service, bar food from sandwiches, baguettes and baked potatoes to steaks, games room with pool and pews, no smoking dining area; good bedrooms in adjoining hotel *(LYM)*
COWES [SZ5092]
☆ *Folly* [Folly Lane – which is signposted off A3021 just S of Whippingham]: The splendid

estuary setting is the attraction here, with big windows and seats on a waterside terrace; very yachtie-oriented, with wind speed indicator, barometer and chronometer among the bric-a-brac and old pictures and books on the timbered walls of the opened-out bar, moorings, showers and breakfast service (call the water taxi on Channel 7); straightforward bar food most of the day from sandwiches up, Flowers IPA and Original and Goddards, no smoking area; pool, TV and piped music; children welcome, garden with summer bouncy castle (very busy then), open all day *(LYM, Joyce and Geoff Robson, Eddie Edwards)*
Union [Watch House Lane]: Small Gales local

with good atmosphere, log fire, cosy side room, good choice of beers inc interesting guest, good value nicely prepared food inc fine crab sandwiches, good fish and OAP bargain lunches, farm cider and proper ginger beer shandies, dining room and conservatory; bedrooms *(Penny and Peter Keevil)*

☆ **FISHBOURNE** [SZ5592]
Fishbourne Inn [from Portsmouth car ferry turn left into Fishbourne Lane no through road]: Hospitable, spacious and neatly kept recently renovated pub, comfortable wall settles, good choice of food from ploughman's to grills and local seafood, friendly staff, good range of real ales; attractive well kept outdoor area *(D and S Price, Roger and Pauline Pearce, Nick and Sylvia Pascoe)*

FRESHWATER [SZ3387]
Colwell Bay Inn [Colwell Rd]: Pleasantly refurbished, with decent food, helpful staff, good coffee, bar billiards; piped music; informal garden behind *(Geoffrey Kemp)*

HULVERSTONE [SZ3984]
Sun [B3399]: Picture-book thatched pub under new licensees, smart tables under cocktail parasols in charming flower-filled garden, even village stocks; unpretentious local feel inside, with stripped brickwork – has had well kept real ales and decent food; may be piped music; peaceful setting, sea views *(Nick and Sylvia Pascoe, Mrs J Thomas, Paul Humphreys)*

NITON [SZ5075]
☆ *Buddle* [St Catherines Rd, Undercliff; off A3055 just S of village, towards St Catherines Point]: Pretty former smugglers' haunt, heavy black beams, big flagstones, broad stone fireplace, no smoking areas, enjoyable reasonably priced food inc generous ploughman's, seafood, griddle dishes and Sun lunches, good service even when busy, family dining room/games annexe, up to half a dozen real ales, friendly dogs; views from well cared for sloping garden and terraces, good walks; open all day, some live jazz *(Peter and Margaret Glenister, Brian Root, LYM, Pete Yearsley, Carol and Dono Leaman, Paul Humphreys)*

SANDOWN [SZ5984]
Clancys [Beachfield Rd]: Spacious bright

modern bar/restaurant with imaginative menu leaning towards friendly owners' antipodean origins, also good home-made pizzas – and they do their best to meet special wishes; may be cl winter Sun/Mon evenings *(Colin Moore)*
Old Comical [St Johns Rd]: Homely local, flagstones and bare boards in beamy front bar, well kept Greene King Abbot, Ushers and summer guest beers, cheerful welcoming service, big back bar with pool; live music Fri (plus Weds night and Sun afternoon in holidays); well behaved children and dogs welcome, garden with play area, boules and summer Sun and bank hol barbecues *(Colin Moore)*

ST LAWRENCE [SZ5376]
St Lawrence Inn [Undercliffe Drive/Steephill Rd (A3055)]: Two well kept and attractively priced Yates beers brewed in adjacent building, good choice of enjoyable food, big partly no smoking split-level dining room (former stables) with much wood, good value wines; piped music, local singer Fri; sea-view tables out on decking *(Jeanne and Paul Silvestri, Pete Yearsley, Paul Humphreys)*

VENTNOR [SZ5677]
Crab & Lobster [Grove Rd]: Comfortable old-fashioned local full of interesting memorabilia, cask tables, straightforward low-priced bar food lunchtime and wknd evenings, bargain lunch deals, well kept Ventnor and guest ales, decent house wines, thoughtful service, wknd bar nibbles; dogs allowed, open all day, bedrooms *(Liz and John Soden)*
☆ *Mill Bay* [Esplanade]: Seafront pub with light airy décor, large conservatory, good choice of reasonably priced generous food, Badger Best and local Ventnor Gold, good welcoming service, darts and cribbage; quiz nights, good live music; big beachside terrace with play area *(Liz and John Soden, BB)*
☆ *Volunteer* [Victoria St]: Small old-fashioned local with interesting customers and involved landlord, six well kept ales such as Badger, Ringwood, Ventnor Wight Spirit and Yates, reasonable prices, coal fire, darts, the local game of rings, no machines or juke box, no food, friendly cat called Rosie; no children, open all day, quiz nights *(Liz and John Soden, Hywel Bevan)*

Kent

Kent has a great many sound pubs, but you have to know where to look if you want to track down its real treasures – the handful of memorably good proper unspoilt pubs, and the equally small and select band of places that do super food. Pubs which do stand out these days include the cheerfully unchanging Gate by the marshes at Boyden Gate, the Woolpack down at Brookland (new licensees doing well in this traditional charmer), the Dove at Dargate (exceptional food and good atmosphere), the Crown at Groombridge (a fine all-rounder), the Harrow at Ightham Common (much enjoyed for its food), the civilised Hare at Langton Green (interesting food and good wines), the friendly old George at Newnham (good all round, gaining its Food Award this year), the Bottle House out in the country above Penshurst (another well liked all-rounder, with a great food choice), the Clarendon in Sandgate (a surprising wine choice in this unchanging little local), the Rose & Crown near Selling (a charming country pub with a lovely garden), the Chequers at Smarden (a nice place to stay, with good food and local beers), the idiosyncratic and cheerfully civilised Red Lion at Stodmarsh, Sankeys in Tunbridge Wells (splendidly relaxed pubby atmosphere, lovely fish and seafood), and the Swan on the Green in West Peckham (imaginative modern food and a fine range of beers brewed on the spot). Against stiff competition, the Dove at Dargate takes the top title of Kent Dining Pub of the Year. In the Lucky Dip section at the end of the chapter, pubs that currently stand out are the Harbourmasters House in Chatham, Griffins Head at Chillenden, Fountain at Cowden, Kentish Rifleman at Dunks Green, Junction Inn at Groombridge, Green Cross near Goudhurst, restaurant y Plough at Ivy Hatch, Bell at Smarden, Padwell Arms at Stone Street, White Lion in Tenterden and Grove Ferry near Upstreet. Drinks prices tend to be rather higher than the national norm in Kent pubs. The local Goachers we bought at the Lord Raglan near Staplehurst, and the beers brewed at the Swan on the Green in West Peckham, were much more comfortably priced. The main local brewer, Shepherd Neame, prices its beers competitively in most of its tied pubs. Other smaller and newer local brewers to look out for here include Larkins (becoming widely available in Kent these days), Hopdaemon, Swale and Flagship.

BIDDENDEN TQ8538 Map 3
Three Chimneys 🍴 ♀

A262, 1 mile W of village

This pretty ochre-coloured country pub is well worth visiting before or after a visit to nearby Sissinghurst Gardens. There's a rambling, low-beamed series of small, very traditional rooms with plain wooden furniture and old settles on flagstones and coir matting, some harness and sporting prints on the stripped brick walls, and good log fires. The simple public bar has darts, dominoes and cribbage. As well as a good wine list, local Biddenden cider and several malt whiskies, they have well kept Adnams Best, Harveys Best, and Shepherd Neame Bishops Finger and Spitfire tapped straight from the cask. Well presented, but not cheap, dishes can be eaten in the bar or restaurant (though they'll serve you a ploughman's in the garden): soup (from £3.95), chicken liver pâté (£5.50), crab and salmon fishcakes with thai-style sweet and sour sauce (£7.95), sun-dried tomato couscous topped with roasted red peppers, caramelised red onions and grilled goats cheese or lambs liver and bacon with port and red onion gravy (£10.95), wild boar and apple sausages topped with chutney with a rich port jus (£12.95), king scallops on roasted red peppers and wilted spinach with roasted cherry tomatoes and sweet chilli dressing (£16.95), and fillet steak with garlic butter (£18.95); there may be a wait if they are busy, and food service may stop before 2pm then. French windows in the civilised candlelit bare board restaurant open on to the garden, which has picnic-sets (some nice and shady on a hot day), and a smart terrace area has tables and outdoor heaters. *(Recommended by Peter Meister, the Didler, John Evans, Anthony Longden, Michael Clementson, Glenwys and Alan Lawrence, Alan Cowell, Stephen and Jean Curtis, Mrs Catherine Draper, Bob Pike, Cathryn and Richard Hicks)*

Free house ~ Licensee Craig Smith ~ Real ale ~ Bar food ~ Restaurant ~ (01580) 291472 ~ Children allowed if not encouraged ~ Dogs allowed in bar ~ Open 11-2.40, 6-11; 12-2.40, 7-10.30 Sun; closed 25 Dec and evening 31 Dec

BOUGH BEECH TQ4846 Map 3
Wheatsheaf ♀ ◗

B2027, S of reservoir

There's plenty of history and lots of interesting things to look at in this popular pub, and the older part is thought to have been a hunting lodge belonging to Henry V. The neat central bar and the long front bar (with an attractive old settle carved with wheatsheaves, shove-ha'penny, dominoes, and board games) have unusually high ceilings with lofty oak timbers, a screen of standing timbers and a revealed king post. Divided from the central bar by two more rows of standing timbers – one formerly an outside wall to the building – is the snug, and another bar. Other similarly aged features include a piece of 1607 graffito, 'Foxy Holamby', thought to have been a whimsical local squire. There are quite a few horns and heads, as well as a sword from Fiji, crocodiles, stuffed birds, swordfish spears, and the only matapee in the south of England on the walls and above the massive stone fireplaces. Thoughtful touches such as piles of smart magazines to read, tasty nibbles, chestnuts to roast and mulled wine in winter, summer Pimms, and a range of local fruit juices. Well kept Fullers London Pride, Greene King Old Speckled Hen, Harveys and Shepherd Neame Bitter on handpump, a decent wine list, and several malt whiskies. Besides lunchtime snacks such as an open sandwich of spiced chicken and plum sauce, and ploughman's, salmon and broccoli fishcakes with lemon and parsley butter sauce or minced beef and onion pie (all £5.95), a large choice of bar food from an ambitious menu could include broccoli and stilton soup (£4.95), duck and orange pâté or grilled goats cheese ciabatta with pesto and caramelised red onion (£5.95), vegetarian sausages and mash (£7.95), hoki fish with mild curry sauce or beef goulash with dumplings (£9.95), lambs liver, bacon and black pudding (£10.95), sirloin steak or crispy duck with mash and plum sauce (£14.95), and puddings such as chocolate sponge with hot chocolate sauce or apricot tart (£4.25); you may have to wait when they are busy. There are plenty of seats, and flowerbeds and fruit trees in the sheltered side and back gardens; shrubs help divide it into various areas, so it doesn't feel too crowded even when it's full. *(Recommended by Bob and Margaret Holder, Douglas and Pamela Cooper, Tony Brace, Jim Bush, Debbie and Neil Hayter, Jane Cross, A Sadler)*

Whitbreads ~ Lease Elizabeth Currie ~ Real ale ~ Bar food (12-10) ~ (01732) 700254 ~ Children in part of bar ~ Dogs welcome ~ Folk and country Weds 8.30 ~ Open 11-11; 12-10.30 Sun

---

Pubs with attractive or unusually big gardens are listed at the back of the book.

BOYDEN GATE TR2265 Map 3
Gate Inn ★ ♀ ◖

Off A299 Herne Bay—Ramsgate – follow Chislet, Upstreet signpost opposite Roman Gallery; Chislet also signposted off A28 Canterbury—Margate at Upstreet – after turning right into Chislet main street keep right on to Boyden; the pub gives its address as Marshside, though Boyden Gate seems more usual on maps

There's always lots going on in this bustling old-fashioned pub, and the long-standing licensee (28 years now) is a genial host with a cheerful personality that is an important part of the pubby atmosphere. The winter inglenook log fire serves both quarry-tiled rooms, and there are flowery-cushioned pews around tables of considerable character, hop bines hanging from the beam and attractively etched windows. Where possible they use organically grown local produce to prepare their tasty straightforward bar meals, which include a fine choice of sandwiches (from £2.75), burgers (from £2.95), home-made soup (£3.25), filled baguettes (from £3.30), lots of filled baked potatoes (from £3.95), quite a few different ploughman's (£5.25), omelettes or spicy hotpots (from £5.95), and a mega grill (£6.75). The eating area is no smoking at lunchtime. Well kept Shepherd Neame Bitter and Spitfire and a seasonal ale are tapped from the cask; they've also interesting bottled beers, a fine range of 17 wines by the glass, and country wines. Shove-ha'penny, dominoes, and cribbage. On fine summer evenings, you can sit at the picnic-sets on the sheltered side lawn and listen to the contented quacking of a multitude of ducks and geese, coots and moorhens out on the marshes (they sell food inside – 10p a bag). More reports please. *(Recommended by Ian Phillips, Kevin Thorpe, Andrea Rampley, Bruce Eccles)*

Shepherd Neame ~ Tenant Christopher Smith ~ Real ale ~ Bar food ~ No credit cards ~ (01227) 860498 ~ Well behaved children welcome ~ Dogs welcome ~ Open 11-2.30, 6-11; 12-4, 7-10.30 Sun

BROOKLAND TQ9724 Map 3
Woolpack £

On A259 from Rye, as you approach Brookland, take the first right turn where the main road bends left, just after the expanse of Walland Marsh; OS Sheet 189 map reference 977244

When news spread that the long-standing licensees were to leave this early 15th-c cottage, there were quite a few worried customers, but all is well. Mr and Mrs Morgan have gently refurbished the place with a lick of paint here and there but it remains a genuine country pub with just the right atmosphere, local beer, and proper home cooking. The ancient entrance lobby has an uneven brick floor and black-painted pine-panelled walls, and on the right, the simple but homely main bar has basic cushioned plank seats in the massive inglenook fireplace (a lovely log fire on chilly days), a painted wood-effect bar counter hung with lots of water jugs, and some ships' timbers that may date from the 12th c in the low-beamed ceiling. On the quarry-tiled floor is a long elm table with shove-ha'penny carved into one end, other old and newer wall benches, chairs at mixed tables, and photographs of the locals on the walls. To the left of the lobby is a sparsely furnished little room, and an open-plan games room with central hearth, modern bar counter, and young locals playing darts or pool; dominoes, cribbage, shove-ha'penny, fruit machine, and piped music. Friendly staff serve well kept Shepherd Neame Bitter and Spitfire by handpump. Very reasonably priced, enjoyable bar food includes sandwiches (from £2), good home-made soup (£2.75), baked potatoes (from £4.25), ploughman's (£4.95), ham and egg, vegetable lasagne or home-made steak pie (all £5.45), and home-made daily specials like beef cobbler, liver and bacon or chicken curry (£4.95), and game pie or breast of chicken with stilton and bacon (£5.95); the proper steak and kidney pudding on winter Tuesdays goes down a treat. *(Recommended by John Davis, Peter and Joan Elbra, David and Rhian Peters, Jan and Alan Summers, Gill and Tony Morriss)*

Shepherd Neame ~ Tenants Barry and Sandra Morgan ~ Real ale ~ Bar food ~ (01797) 344321 ~ Children in family room ~ Dogs welcome ~ Open 11-3, 6-11; 11-11 Sat; 12-10.30 Sun

CHIDDINGSTONE TQ4944 Map 3
Castle Inn ♀

Village signposted from B2027 Tonbridge—Edenbridge

The licensees publish three circular walks from this National Trust village which are proving very popular. It's worth walking around the village itself as well, to look at the picturesque cluster of unspoilt Tudor houses, and in fine weather, there are tables in front of the building facing the church, with more in the pretty secluded vine-hung garden. Inside, a handsome, carefully modernised beamed bar has well made settles forming booths around the tables, cushioned sturdy wall benches, an attractive mullioned window seat in one small alcove, and latticed windows (a couple of areas are no smoking); darts, shove-ha'penny, dominoes and cribbage. From the bar menu, there might be open sandwiches (from £4.75, ciabatta baguettes £5.55), filled baked potatoes (from £4.75), curry, chilli or pasta with tomato and basil sauce (£5.75), sausages (from £5.95), and puddings like warm date and ginger sponge (£3.95); in the evening they do more elaborate (though not cheap) dishes such as seared pigeon breast with onions glazed in molasses with a broad bean and tomato salsa or terrine of corn-fed chicken, duck foie gras and herbs with pear and cardamom chutney (£9.35), pavé of salmon on braised baby fennel with white wine and sorrel sauce (£13.25), and roasted rump of lamb with rosemary and puy lentils (£14.35). Afternoon tea, and two-course Sunday lunch (£19.50). You may have to wait when they're busy and service can be variable. Well kept Fullers London Pride, Harveys Best, and Larkins Traditional (it's brewed in the village, and in winter they have Porter too), along with an impressive wine list, and a good range of malt whiskies. *(Recommended by Colin McKerrow, Anthony Longden, Alan and Paula McCully, Eve Samsow, Mrs Romey Heaton, Pat and Robert Watt, Alison Hayes, Pete Hanlon)*

Free house ~ Licensee Nigel Lucas ~ Real ale ~ Bar food (11.30-9.30) ~ Restaurant ~ (01892) 870247 ~ Children in eating area of bar and restaurant ~ Dogs welcome ~ Open 11-11; 12-10.30 Sun

DARGATE TR0761 Map 3
Dove ⊕ ♀

Village signposted from A299

Kent Dining Pub of the Year

Down a network of narrow lanes in a quiet hamlet, this tucked-away dining pub offers exceptionally good restaurant-style food in a relaxed atmosphere. As well as lunchtime dishes such as filled baguettes (£4.25), salt cod with flageolet beans and chorizo (£6.50), and marinated chicken salad with mint or caramelised pork with stir-fried vegetables (£7.25), the menu could include bacon, avocado and rocket salad (£5.75), crab and spring onion risotto (£6.75), prawns with garden herbs and pickled ginger (£6.99), roast shank of lamb with wild mushrooms (£14.95), confit of duck with roasted black pudding or roast free range guinea fowl (£14.99), tuna with sun-dried tomatoes and green beans (£15.50), whole bass on fennel and red peppers (around £16.50), and puddings like orange and passion fruit crème brûlée or baked chocolate pudding (from £4.75); you have to book some time in advance. The charmingly unspoilt rambling rooms have photographs of the pub and its licensees throughout the past century on the walls, a good winter log fire, and plenty of seats on the bare boards; piped music. Well kept Shepherd Neame on handpump. The sheltered garden has roses, lilacs, peonies and many other flowers, picnic-sets under pear trees, a dovecote with white doves, a rockery and pool, and a swing. A bridlepath leads up from the pub (along the quaintly-named Plumpudding Lane) into Blean Wood. *(Recommended by Sean and Sharon Pines, KN-R, Guy Vowles, Kevin Thorpe, David and Betty Gittins, John Davis, Richard Siebert)*

Shepherd Neame ~ Tenants Nigel and Bridget Morris ~ Real ale ~ Bar food (not Sun and Tues evenings or all day Mon) ~ (01227) 751360 ~ Well behaved children in eating area of bar ~ Dogs allowed in bar ~ Open 11.30-3, 6-11.30; 12-3, 7-11 Sun; closed Mon except bank hols

DEAL TR3752 Map 3
Kings Head

Beach Street, just off A258 seafront roundabout

Just across the road from the promenade and the sea, this handsome three-storey Georgian inn is festooned in summer with pretty hanging baskets and window boxes, and there are picnic-sets out on a broad front paved terrace side area. You'll find a nice mix of locals and visitors in the four comfortable bar rooms which work their way round a central servery. The walls, partly stripped masonry, are decorated with marine architectural drawings, maritime and local pictures and charts, and other material underlining connections with the Royal and Merchant navies, and another area has an interesting collection of cricket memorabilia. There are a couple of flame-effect gas fires; quiet piped music and TV. Well kept Fullers London Pride, Shepherd Neame Bitter and Spitfire, and a guest such as Greene King IPA on handpump. Straightforward bar food includes sandwiches and filled baguettes (from £2.20), omelettes (from £4), filled baked potatoes (from £4.25), ploughman's, roast vegetable tart or fish pie (£4.95) and sirloin steak (£9.50) with daily specials on a blackboard; two-course Sunday lunch (£6.95). Beware that traffic wardens here are vigilant during the week; there's pay-and-display (two-hour limit) parking opposite, and another (three-hour limit) just a few minutes' walk away. *(Recommended by JMC, David Gregory, Jan and Alan Summers, Paul A Moore, P Goodson, Nigel B Thompson, Father Robert Marsh)*

Courage (S & N) ~ Lease Graham Stiles and Shirley Russell ~ Real ale ~ Bar food (11-2.30, 6-9) ~ (01304) 368194 ~ Children in eating area of bar and family room ~ Dogs welcome ~ Open 10-11; 12-10.30 Sun ~ Bedrooms: £40S/£58B

FORDCOMBE TQ5240 Map 3
Chafford Arms

B2188, off A264 W of Langton Green

In summer, this friendly tile-hung old pub is quite a sight, when it is covered with flowers against a backdrop of cascading creepers and carefully tended shrubs and perennials. Most of the flowers are in front but there's a pleasant sheltered lawn behind with an attractive shrubbery and arbours. The welcoming landlord tells us that bar food prices have not changed and dishes might include sandwiches (from £2.65), home-made soup (£2.95), smoked salmon pâté (£4.65), ploughman's (£4.95), creamy vegetable and cheese kiev (£5.45), moules marinière (£5.95), grilled trout or gammon steak (£7.95), steaks (from £9.45) and enjoyable skate wing or dressed crab and prawn salad (£9.95); they do a Thursday evening curry and a pint for £6. There's plenty of room between neat tables and comfortable seats on a turkey carpet, and an uncluttered décor; the quite separate public bar, full of sporting memorabilia and trophies, often gets much busier towards the close of the evening as the dining side winds down; darts, shove-ha'penny, dominoes, TV, and fruit machine. Well kept Larkins and Shepherd Neame Spitfire on handpump, local farm cider, and decent house wines. Just up the steepish lane is an archetypal village cricket green. *(Recommended by Mr and Mrs H D Brierly, Colin Draper, Peter Meister, Peter and Patricia Burton, Richard Gibbs, John Davis, Geoffrey G Lawrance, Ken Arthur)*

Enterprise ~ Lease Barrie Leppard ~ Real ale ~ Bar food (not Sun and Mon evenings (except bank hols)) ~ Restaurant ~ (01892) 740267 ~ Children welcome ~ Dogs welcome ~ Jazz third Sun evening of month ~ Open 11.45-3, 6.30-11; 11-11 Sat; 12-4, 7-10.30 Sun

---

It is illegal for bar staff to smoke while handling your drink.

GROOMBRIDGE TQ5337 Map 3
Crown
B2110

Once the haunt of smugglers en route between London and Rye, this tile-hung old place is picturesquely set at the end of a row of pretty cottages overlooking the steep village green; there are picnic-sets in front on a sunny brick terrace. Inside, the beamed rooms are snug, with a jumble of bric-a-brac including old teapots, pewter tankards, and antique bottles, and there's a fine winter log fire in the big brick inglenook. The walls, mostly rough yellowing plaster with some squared panelling and timbering, are decorated with small topographical, game and sporting prints, and a circular large-scale map with the pub at its centre. The no smoking end room (normally for eaters) has fairly close-spaced tables with a variety of good solid chairs, and a log-effect gas fire in a big fireplace. Decent bar food includes soup (£3.50), lunchtime baked potatoes (from £5.50) or ploughman's (£5.90), grilled cumberland sausages with onion gravy or vegetable lasagne (£7.80), home-made steak in ale pie (£7.90), fish stew (£8.90), and grilled rib-eye steak (£11.50). Served from the long copper-topped bar counter, there might be Greene King Abbot, Harveys, and Larkins on handpump; shove-ha'penny, dominoes, cribbage and Scrabble. Across the road a public footpath beside the small chapel leads across a field to Groombridge Place Gardens. The bedrooms have been upgraded this year. *(Recommended by Peter Meister, Andrea Rampley, John Davis, Will Watson, Joyce and Geoff Robson, Mrs J Ekins-Daukes, P and J Shapley, Derek Thomas, Quentin and Carol Williamson)*

Free house ~ Licensee Peter Kilshaw ~ Real ale ~ Bar food (12-3, 7-9; not Sun evening) ~ Restaurant ~ (01892) 864742 ~ Children welcome ~ Dogs allowed in bar ~ Open 11-3, 6-11; 11-11 Fri and Sat; 12-10.30 Sun; 11-3, 6-11 Sat and Sun in winter ~ Bedrooms: £40/£45(£60S)

HAWKHURST TQ7630 Map 3
Queens
Rye Road (A268 E)

The civilised interior of this wisteria-covered Georgian-faced building is sensitively opened up and appealingly decorated in keeping with its age. Light filters in through creeper tendrils that threaten to cover the old sash windows of the more pubby area at the front, which is pleasantly chatty, with locals on stools along the extensive counter, and sofas by the big brick inglenook fireplace; piped pop, fruit machine, pool. The mood becomes more like that of a wine bar further in: terracotta, sand or pea-green colourwashes give an airy feel despite the heavy low beams, and there's a nice mix of old pine tables on bare boards with plenty of scattered rugs. At night it's pleasantly candlelit. Starting with breakfast at 8.30am, the food is usefully served all day and might include filled baguettes or home-made soup (£4.95), ploughman's (£5.50), pizzas (from £6.50), chicken liver parfait, pasta carbonara or ham and egg (£6.95), chargrilled chicken burger (£8.50), steak in ale pie or haddock in beer batter (£9.95), lambs liver with pancetta and baby onion jus (£10.95), braised lamb shank (£13.95), puddings like treacle tart or warm chocolate fudge cake (£3.95), and daily specials such as grilled tuna steak on egg noodles with chargrilled vegetables (£10.95); Sunday carvery (£8.99). Two eating rooms are no smoking. Well kept Fullers London Pride and Harveys Best on handpump. There are outdoor heaters in the courtyard. *(Recommended by Colin and Janet Roe, Alan and Paula McCully, Jason Caulkin, Mike Gorton)*

Enterprise ~ Lease Janelle Tresidder ~ Real ale ~ Bar food (all day) ~ Restaurant ~ (01580) 753577 ~ Children in eating area of bar and family room ~ Open 11-12; 12-12(10.30 Sun) Sat ~ Bedrooms: £55B/£75B

HODSOLL STREET TQ6263 Map 3
Green Man
Hodsoll Street and pub signposted off A227 S of Meopham; turn right in village

Next to the village green and with pretty summer tubs and hanging baskets, this is a popular pub with friendly licensees. There's a relaxed atmosphere in the big airy carpeted rooms which work their way round a hop-draped central bar, neat tables are spaced tidily around the walls, interesting old local photographs and antique plates on the walls, and a warm winter log fire. Well liked bar food includes a light lunchtime menu with sandwiches (from £3; baguettes from £3.50; tortilla wraps £6), and ploughman's (£4.50), as well as home-made soup (£3), deep-fried camembert (£4), goats cheese and sun-blush tomato tart (£8.50), beer-battered cod (£9), salmon fillet with hollandaise or chicken stuffed with prawns and wrapped in filo pastry (£10), lamb shank with red wine jus (£11), veal escalope with a mushroom and marsala sauce or roast loin of rabbit (£12), calves liver with bubble and squeak (£13), and puddings; Sunday roast (£6), and Tuesday curry night (£8). Well kept Flowers, Fullers London Pride, Youngs Bitter and a guest such as Harveys or Larkins on handpump, and decent wines; piped music and Monday evening quiz night. Outside, there are seats on a well tended lawn. Look out for morris dancers who practise here regularly. The nearby North Downs have plenty of walks. *(Recommended by Roger and Pauline Pearce, Annette Tress, Gary Smith, Peter Scillitoe, S Collins, GHC, Peter and Joan Elbra, Mr and Mrs R A Newbury , Jan and Alan Summers, Pat and Tony Martin, Ian Phillips, Bev and Jeff Brown, Ian and Barbara Rankin)*

Enterprise ~ Lease John, Jean and David Haywood ~ Real ale ~ Bar food (12-2 (4 Sun), 6.30-9.30) ~ No credit cards ~ (01732) 823575 ~ Children welcome ~ Dogs welcome ~ Open 11-2.30, 6-11; 11-11 Fri and Sat; 12-10.30 Sun

ICKHAM TR2257 Map 3
Duke William ♀
Village signposted off A257 E of Canterbury

The inside of this comfortable pub is bigger than its little street front exterior suggests. The open-plan carpeted bar extends on either side of the serving counter, and there's a pleasant lived-in feel in the front part, helped by the gas lighting and big inglenook fireplace, longcase clock and all the brasses, copper and other bric-a-brac. There's more formal seating behind, with a rather smart air-conditioned restaurant area and then a well shaded no smoking Victorian-style conservatory which overlooks the attractive neatly kept garden and fields beyond. From a large menu, the well liked food might include home-made soup (£3.50), deep-fried brie with redcurrant dip (£4.25), filled baguettes or filled baked potatoes (from £4.50), sausage and mash (from £4.95), lots of pasta dishes (from £5.45), ploughman's (from £5.50), 10 pizzas (from £5.95), steak and kidney pie or chicken curry (£6.95), butter-fried trout on leeks, fennel and sun-dried tomatoes (£7.95), and cold meats with salad and bubble and squeak (£9.95). Polite, friendly staff serve the well kept Adnams, Fullers London Pride, Shepherd Neame and guest such as Wells Bombardier on handpump, and there's an extensive wine list and freshly squeezed orange juice; darts, pool, shove-ha'penny, dominoes, fruit machine and juke box. This is a picturesque village. *(Recommended by Tina and David Woods-Taylor, Peter Scillitoe, Ian Phillips, Grahame Brooks)*

Free house ~ Licensees Mr and Mrs A R McNeill ~ Real ale ~ Bar food (11-2, 6-10) ~ Restaurant ~ (01227) 721308 ~ Children in eating areas and conservatory ~ Dogs allowed in bar ~ Open 11-3, 6-11; 12-5, 7-10.30 Sun

---

Most pubs in this book sell wine by the glass. We mention wines if they are a cut above the average. Please let us know of any good pubs for wine.

IDEN GREEN TQ8031 Map 3
Woodcock

Iden Green is signposted off A268 E of Hawkhurst and B2086 at W edge of Benenden; in village at crossroads by bus shelter follow Standen Street signpost, then fork left at pub signpost – beware that there is an entirely different Iden Green just 10 miles away near Goudhurst

On the edge of Standen Wood, this is a bustling and friendly little country pub with an unaffected local atmosphere, and a welcoming landlord. The small flagstoned bar is snugly comfortable, with stripped brick walls and very low ceilings bearing down heavily on a couple of big standing timbers; it has a comfortable sofa and armchairs by a warming woodburning stove, and chunky big old pine tables tucked snugly into little nooks; darts, shove-ha'penny, fruit machine, and piped local radio. Four well kept real ales on handpump could be Greene King IPA, Abbot, and Old Speckled Hen, and maybe Harveys Best. Served in generous helpings, the well liked bar food includes pâté (£3.75), filled baguettes (from £4.50), smoked salmon (£5.75), ham, egg and chips (£6.50), scampi or steak and kidney pie (£8.95), daily specials, and puddings such as treacle sponge or lemon meringue (£3.50); it can get very busy at weekends, so you may need to book. The partly panelled dining area opens on to a verandah, and there are seats in the pretty side garden. The car park is across the road. *(Recommended by Peter and Joan Elbra, Tina and David Woods-Taylor, Colin and Janet Roe, Grahame Brooks, Kevin Thorpe)*

Greene King ~ Lease Frank Simmons ~ Real ale ~ Bar food ~ Restaurant ~ (01580) 240009 ~ Children in eating area of bar ~ Dogs allowed in bar ~ Open 11-11; 12-10.30 Sun

IGHTHAM COMMON TQ5755 Map 3
Harrow 🍽️ ♀

Signposted off A25 just W of Ightham; pub sign may be hard to spot

There's no doubt that most customers come to this civilised country pub to enjoy the particularly good food, though it does have a nice mix of customers and they do keep Greene King IPA and Abbot on handpump. Constantly changing, the enjoyable bar food might include deep-fried camembert with gooseberry compote (£5.95), moules marinière with saffron (£6.95), lincolnshire sausages with onion gravy (£7.95), rich leek tart with garlic and chive mayonnaise (£8.95), goan chicken with pineapple, coconut and chilli, lasagne or salmon and chive fishcakes with citrus sauce (all £9.95), roast shank of lamb with red wine jus (£10.95), and puddings like strawberry and marsala trifle, rhubarb crumble or chocolate and praline gateau (£4.25). The decent sensibly priced wine list has plenty of rewarding wines by the glass. Assorted country furniture stands on nice old brick flooring or black and white squared vinyl in two simply but attractively decorated rooms, both warmed by log fires in winter. The straightforward traditional public bar is painted a cheerful sunny yellow above its dark green dado, and there is appealing attention to detail – daily papers, fresh flowers, candles on the tables. A lush grapevine grows around the delightful little antiquated conservatory which leads off an elegant no smoking dining room laid with white cloths; piped music; tables and chairs on a pretty little pergola-enclosed back terrace. Ightham Mote is nearby. *(Recommended by Andrea Rampley, T Dunbar, David Twitchett, David R Crafts, Pat and Tony Martin, Tim and Pam Moorey, B and M Kendall, Nigel and Olga Wikeley, Mary Ellen Cummings, Uta and John Owlett, Oliver and Sue Rowell, Bob and Margaret Holder, Derek Thomas, Ian Phillips, Bob White, Nicky Mayers, Richard Gibbs, Alan Cowell)*

Free house ~ Licensees John Elton and Claire Butler ~ Real ale ~ Bar food (12-2, 6-9.30; not Mon or evening Sun) ~ Restaurant ~ (01732) 885912 ~ Children in restaurant (not Sat evening) ~ Open 12-3, 6-11; 12-3 Sun; closed Sun evening and Mon

---

If we know a pub has an outdoor play area for children, we mention it.

LANGTON GREEN TQ5538 Map 3
Hare 🍴 ♀
A264 W of Tunbridge Wells

Although many customers come to this civilised Edwardian roadside pub to enjoy the good, interesting food, the front bar is well liked by drinkers, and the four real ales are well kept. The knocked-through rooms have big windows and high ceilings giving a pleasant feeling of space: dark-painted dados below light walls, oak furniture and turkey carpets on stained wooden floors, old romantic pastels, and plenty of bric-a-brac (including a huge collection of chamber-pots). Interesting old books, pictures and two big mahogany mirror-backed display cabinets crowd the walls of a big chatty room at the back, which has lots of large tables (one big enough for at least a dozen) on a light brown carpet. From here french windows open on to a sheltered terrace with picnic-sets looking out on to a tree-ringed green. Service is very pleasant and efficient, and the atmosphere is pubby and sociable. From quite a choice, the bar food might include home-made soup (£3.75), filled baguettes or granary bread (from £3.95; hot roast beef topped with stilton mayonnaise and fried onions £5.50; smoked trout, prawn and taramasalata wrap with lemon, black pepper and crème fraîche £6.25), cheese, onion and Guinness rarebit with apple and celery salad (£4.95), cajun salmon, mango and rocket filo tart with vanilla dressing (£5.50), green herb omelette filled with garlic chestnut mushrooms and cream cheese (£7.25), tarragon chicken, orange and chicory salad with tahini dressing (£9.95), crispy baked bream on rice noodle and green vegetable stir fry and red curry sauce (£13.95), and puddings such as banoffi pie, ginger sponge pudding, and strawberry and Drambuie cheesecake (from £4.25); best to book to be sure of a table. Greene King IPA and Abbot, and a couple of guests on handpump, lots of wines by the glass, and over 40 malt whiskies; piped music in the front bar area, shove-ha'penny, cribbage and dominoes. At peak times, parking is not easy unless you get here early. *(Recommended by Mrs J Thomas, Derek Harvey-Piper, Mrs Catherine Draper, Comus and Sarah Elliott, Derek Thomas, R T and J C Moggridge, B J Harding, Joyce and Geoff Robson, Ian and Barbara Rankin, Gillian Rogers)*

Brunning & Price ~ Tenant Brian Whiting ~ Real ale ~ Bar food (12-9.30(9 Sun)) ~ (01892) 862419 ~ Well behaved children in restaurant lunchtime ~ Dogs allowed in bar ~ Live acoustic music bank hols ~ Open 11-11; 12-10.30 Sun

NEWNHAM TQ9557 Map 3
George 🍴 ♀
44 The Street; village signposted from A2 just W of Ospringe, outside Faversham

This is a very well run pub with a friendly welcome from the licensees, an enjoyable choice of drinks, and particularly good food. There are several atmospheric spreading rooms with plenty of look at – dressers with teapots, prettily upholstered mahogany settles, dining chairs and leather carving chairs around candlelit tables, table lamps and gas-type chandeliers, and rugs on the waxed floorboards; open fires, fresh flowers, quite a few pictures, and hop bines hanging from the beams. Nicely presented food includes lunchtime sandwiches or baguettes (from £2.50), filled baked potatoes (from £3.95) and ploughman's (from £5.50), along with dishes such as home-made soup (£3.50), chicken liver parfait with red onion marmalade or home-made thai fishcakes with a sweet chilli, ginger and garlic dressing (£4.95), sautéed wild and exotic mushrooms tossed in a rich port sauce and topped with puff pastry (£5.50), vegetable curry (£7.95), steak and kidney pudding (£8.95), chicken curry with mango chutney (£9.25), lightly spiced cod (£11.95), steaks (from £11.50), and daily specials like seared duck with a ginger and cherry sauce or half shoulder of lamb with redcurrant, rosemary and red wine sauce (£12.95), and fresh fillets of bass with fresh asparagus and hollandaise (£14.95). The restaurant is no smoking. They've a dozen wines by the glass, well kept Shepherd Neame Bitter, Spitfire, Bishops Finger and seasonal beers on handpump, and good coffee; piped music. The spacious sheltered garden has some picnic-sets, and there are pleasant nearby walks. *(Recommended by Roger and*

Pauline Pearce, Philip Denton, Peter Scillitoe, J D M Rushworth)

Shepherd Neame ~ Tenant Marc Perkins ~ Real ale ~ Bar food ~ Restaurant ~ (01795) 890237 ~ Children welcome ~ Dogs allowed in bar ~ Open 11-3, 6.30-11; 11-4, 6.30-11 Sun; closed evenings 25 and 26 Dec

OARE TR0163 Map 3
Shipwrights Arms 🍺

S shore of Oare Creek, E of village; coming from Faversham on the Oare road, turn right into Ham Road opposite Davington School; or off A2 on B2045, go into Oare village, then turn right towards Faversham, and then left into Ham Road opposite Davington School; OS Sheet 178 map reference 016635

Splendidly unspoilt, this 17th-c tavern is situated in the middle of marshland, 3ft below sea level; plenty of surrounding birdlife. The three simple little bars are dark and cosy, and separated by standing timbers and wood part-partitions or narrow door arches. There's a medley of seats from tapestry cushioned stools and chairs to black wood-panelled built-in settles forming little booths, pewter tankards over the bar counter, boating jumble and pictures, flags or boating pennants on the ceilings, several brick fireplaces, and a good woodburning stove. They serve only Kent-brewed beers tapped from the cask such as Goachers Gold Star, Mild and Shipwrecked and Hopdaemon Golden Braid and IPA. Reasonably priced straightforward bar food includes sandwiches (from £2.75), filled baked potatoes (from £3.95), ploughman's (from £4.95), home-baked ham and egg (£5.45), sausage and mash (£5.25), cod in crispy batter (£5.95), smoked haddock and spring onion fishcakes (£6.25), and puddings; part of the eating area is no smoking. Piped music, cribbage, and dominoes. Parking can be difficult at busy times. An interesting approach is a walk from the village through the tangle of boatyard; or you can moor a boat in the creek which runs just below the Saxon Shore Way (up a bank from the front and back gardens of the pub). *(Recommended by Kevin Thorpe, the Didler, Richard Gibbs, Keith and Chris O'Neill, Simon and Sally Small)*

Free house ~ Licensees Derek and Ruth Cole ~ Real ale ~ Bar food (not Sun evening, not Mon) ~ No credit cards ~ (01795) 590088 ~ Children in dining room ~ Dogs allowed in bar ~ Open 11-3(4 Sat), 6-11; 12-4, 6-10.30 Sun; closed Mon

PENSHURST TQ5243 Map 3
Bottle House 🍽️

Coldharbour Lane, Smarts Hill; leaving Penshurst SW on B2188 turn right at Smarts Hill signpost, then bear right towards Chiddingstone and Cowden; keep straight on

This is the sort of friendly place that customers come back to again and again. The neatly kept low-beamed front bar has a well worn brick floor that extends behind the polished copper-topped bar counter, and big windows look on to a terrace with climbing plants and hanging baskets around picnic-sets under cocktail parasols, and beyond to views of quiet fields and oak trees. The unpretentious main red-carpeted bar has massive hop-covered supporting beams, two large stone pillars with a small brick fireplace (with a stuffed turtle to one side), and old paintings and photographs on mainly plastered walls; quite a collection of china pot lids, with more in the no smoking low-ceilinged dining room. Several cosy little areas lead off the main bar – all can be booked for private parties; one room is covered in sporting pictures right up to the ceiling, and another has pictures of dogs. There's a very large choice of changing and enjoyable bar food: garlic bread topped with prawns, chilli and cheese (£3.50), home-made leek and potato soup (£3.75), chicken ballotine stuffed with mushroom and roasted papper with herb dressing or wild boar terrine with caramelised onion chutney (£4.95), good speldhurst sausages with garlic mash (£6.95), double cheeseburger (£7.50), spinach, roquefort and onion tart, chilli topped with sour cream and cheese or honey and mustard home-baked ham and egg (£7.95), home beer-battered cod (£8.95), chicken satay (£9.95), moroccan lamb en croûte with tomato jam (£10.95), and calves liver with bacon and garlic mash (£13.95). Helpful staff serve well kept Harveys and Larkins on handpump, and

they have local wine; unobtrusive piped music. Good surrounding walks.
(Recommended by Tina and David Woods-Taylor, LM, Jeff Cameron, Alan M Pring, Father Robert Marsh)

Free house ~ Licensees Gordon and Val Meer ~ Real ale ~ Bar food (all day) ~ Restaurant ~ (01892) 870306 ~ Children welcome ~ Dogs allowed in bar ~ Open 11-11; 12-10.30 Sun; closed 25 Dec

PLUCKLEY TQ9243 Map 3
Dering Arms 🍽 �
Pluckley Station, which is signposted from B2077

Most people come to this striking old dutch-gabled pub – built originally as a hunting lodge on the Dering estate – to enjoy the particularly good seafood. The licensee/chef loves fish, and there's quite a range of fresh dishes to choose from: provençale fish soup with cheese, rouille and croutons or soft herring roes (£4.85), crab newburg or moules marinière (£4.95), half a dozen oysters (£5.95), salmon fishcakes with sorrel sauce (£12.95), skate wing with capers and black butter (£13.95), and fillet of black bream with marsh samphire and butter sauce or monkfish with bacon, orange and cream (£14.95). Non fishy choices might include soup (£3.65), chicken livers with bacon, mushrooms and a brandy and cream sauce (£4.85), a pie of the day (£8.45), confit of duck with bubble and squeak potato cake and wild mushroom sauce (£13.95), and rib-eye steak (from £13.95), with puddings like chocolate fudgecake with warm walnut sauce or oranges in caramel with Grand Marnier (from £4.45). The stylishly plain high-ceilinged main bar has a variety of good solid wooden furniture on stone floors, and a roaring log fire in the great fireplace; dominoes, cribbage and shove-ha'penny. A smaller panelled back bar with wood floors has similar dark wood furnishings with some more comfortable chairs, and a lot of classic car pictures. They've a very good extensive wine list, well kept Dering Ale (made for the pub by Goachers), home-made lemonade, local cider and quite a few malt whiskies; friendly and accommodating service. The big simple bedrooms have old ad hoc furnishings. *(Recommended by Ken Arthur, Robert Coomber, Mr and Mrs Robert Jamieson, Kevin Thorpe, Peter Meister, Oliver and Sue Rowell, Guy Consterdine, Sarah Davis, Rod Lambert, Philip Hill, Jenny and Peter Lowater, Dick and Sue Ward)*

Free house ~ Licensee James Buss ~ Real ale ~ Bar food ~ Restaurant ~ (01233) 840371 ~ Children welcome ~ Dogs allowed in bar and bedrooms ~ Open 11.30-3.30, 6-11; 12-3.30, 7-10.30 Sun; closed 26-28 Dec ~ Bedrooms: £30/£40

Rose & Crown
Mundy Bois – spelled Monday Boys on some maps

There's a welcoming new owner at this quietly set pub which is popular for its enjoyable food. If you prefer not to eat in the cosy candlelit restaurant, you can eat from this menu in the bar, which has its own more pubby menu. This would give you a choice such as soup of the day (£3.50), grilled portuguese sardines or goats cheese salad (£4.50), ham, egg and chips (£4.95), spaghetti bolognese or burger (£5.50), cod and chips (£6.95), baked squash stuffed with vegetables (£8.95), chicken breast stuffed with tomato, feta and cream cheese (£9.95), rump steak with shrimp and bacon sauce (£12.95) and puddings such as malva pudding or tiramisu (£3.75). A fireplace separates the knocked through ends of the carpeted lounge bar, and there's pool and a TV in the smallish bare boards public bar. Well kept Greene King IPA and Shepherd Neame Masterbrew, sensibly priced wines, country wines, plenty of malt whiskies, and farm cider; may be piped classical music. There are seats in the garden, with a play area. *(Recommended by Colin and Janet Roe, Jenny and Peter Lowater)*

Free house ~ Licensees Peter and Helen Teare ~ Real ale ~ Bar food (12-2.30, 6.30-9.30) ~ Restaurant ~ (01233) 840393 ~ Children welcome ~ Dogs allowed in bar ~ Open 11.30-3(3.30 Sat); 12-3 Sun

SANDGATE TR2035 Map 3
Clarendon

Head W out of Sandgate on main road to Hythe; about 100m after you emerge on to the seafront, park on the road across from a telephone box on the right; just back from the telephone box is an uphill track.

A good mix of customers come to enjoy this small and simple local, and there's a friendly welcome from the landlord. The big-windowed, recently refurbished lounge on the left gives a view of the sea (and even, in the right conditions, the coast of France). It has a few pictures of the pub and a full display of the 1950s and 1970s Whitbreads inn sign miniatures, as well as some period advertising and Shepherd Neame posters. Popular with locals, the straightforward pubby right-hand bar has a chatty atmosphere, and lots of old photographs of the pub and of Sandgate; both bars have coal fires in winter. Well kept Shepherd Neame Bitter, Spitfire and seasonal ales on handpump from a rather nice Victorian mahogany bar with a mirrored gantry, as well as 15 wines by the glass, over 20 malts, and home-made sloe gin; shove-ha'penny, cribbage, dominoes, and backgammon. Straightforward food includes sandwiches or baguettes (from £2.10; crab in season £3.25), ploughman's (from £4.25), fillet steak (£6.45), and fish or steak in ale pie (£6.55); the dining room is no smoking. Halfway up a steep lane from the sea, the pub has pretty summer hanging baskets and window boxes, and a few benches at the front have views of the water. They may close early if it's quiet. The Eurotunnel is only 10 minutes away. *(Recommended by David and Betty Gittins, Kevin Thorpe, Ian Phillips, Peter Meister, John Davis, Keith Reeve, Marie Hammond)*

Shepherd Neame ~ Tenants Keith and Shirley Barber ~ Real ale ~ Bar food (till 8.30; not Sun evening) ~ No credit cards ~ (01303) 248684 ~ Well behaved children in dining area ~ Dogs allowed in bar ~ Folk/blues Thurs evening ~ Open 12-3, 6-11; 12-5 Sun; closed Sun evening

SELLING TR0456 Map 3
Rose & Crown ★

Signposted from exit roundabout of M2 junction 7: keep right on through village and follow Perry Wood signposts; or from A252 just W of junction with A28 at Chilham follow Shottenden signpost, then right turn signposted Selling, then right signposted Perry Wood

Once again, the cottagey garden behind this popular 16th-c pub has won a national award; there are lots of picnic-sets, and it's charmingly planted with climbers, ramblers and colourful plants, and there's a fairy-lit apple tree, a neatly kept children's play area, bat and trap, and a small aviary. The flowering tubs and hanging baskets in front are pretty too, and the terrace has outdoor heaters. Inside, the friendly and attentive licensees offer a welcome to all their customers. Around the central servery there are pretty fresh flowers by each of the sturdy corner timbers, hop bines strung from the beams, and an interesting variety of corn-dolly work – more in a wall cabinet in one cosy side alcove, and much more again down steps in the comfortably cottagey no smoking restaurant. Apart from a couple of old-fashioned housekeeper's chairs by the huge fireplace (filled in summer with an enjoyably colourful mass of silk flowers interlaced with more corn dollies and so forth), the seats are very comfortably cushioned; smashing winter log fire. Enjoyable bar food includes home-made soup (£3.50), spinach and feta cheese filo parcel (£3.95), filled rolls (from £4.25), ploughman's (£4.95), filled baked potatoes (from £4.95), hearty steak and kidney pie (£6), and chicken tikka masala or cod and smoked haddock mornay (£8), and daily specials like steak and mushroom suet pudding, stilton and asparagus herb pancake, chicken breast in apple and cider, and moroccan lamb (£8.50); on show in a cold cabinet down steps in a small family room are lots of puddings such as italian white chocolate caramel and amaretto (£3.25). Sunday roast (£7.50). Well kept Adnams, Goachers Mild and Harveys Best, on handpump, with a guest from brewers such as Cottage or Humpty Dumpty, local cider, a good range of malts and decent wines in good measures; cribbage, shove-ha'penny, dominoes and piped music. The pub is surrounded by natural woodland – good walking. *(Recommended by Kevin Thorpe, Basil Wynbergen, Peter Scillitoe, Will Watson, Guy Vowles, Mike Gorton)*

Free house ~ Licensees Richard and Jocelyn Prebble ~ Real ale ~ Bar food (not Sun or Mon evenings) ~ Restaurant ~ (01227) 752214 ~ Children in restaurant and family room ~ Dogs allowed in bar ~ Open 11-3, 6.30-11; 12-3, 7-10.30 Sun; closed evenings 25/26 Dec and 1 Jan

SMARDEN TQ8842 Map 3
Chequers 🏠

Off A20 in Charing, via Pluckley; or off A274 at Standen just under 1 mile N of its junction with A262; The Street

As well as being a nice place to stay (first class breakfasts, too), this 14th-c inn also offers local ales, enjoyable food, and a friendly welcome. The cosy and comfortable bar has a pleasantly relaxed atmosphere and plenty of chatty locals, and there are elegant reproduction tables and chairs in the dining area. Using fresh local produce, the well liked bar food (not served on Saturday evening – only restaurant meals then) includes home-made soup (£3.50), filled baguettes with chips (from £4.95), ploughman's (£5.95), ham and egg (£5.95), sausage and mash or omelettes (£6.95), battered cod or fish pie (£7.95), home-made chicken curry (£8.25), and home-made steak and kidney pie (£9.50); or you can choose from the restaurant menu – grilled goats cheese with red onion marmalade (£4.50), tempura prawns with sweet chilli dip (£5.50), chargrilled rib-eye steak with pepper sauce (£12.95), and whole herb-roasted bass or lamb cutlets with minted gravy (£13.95). The no smoking restaurant has lots of beams, an enormous fireplace, and a flagstone floor. Helpful staff serve well kept Adnams, Bass, Harveys Best, and maybe Old Kent Fine Edge or Rother Valley Level Best on handpump, they've several malt whiskies, and a decent wine list; piped music. A walkway in the attractive landscaped garden leads to a pond with fish and waterfowl, and there's an arbour with climbing plants; the terrace has nice green metal tables and chairs on the york stone. This is an attractive village. *(Recommended by Mr and Mrs P L Haigh, Richard and Margaret Peers, Colin and Janet Roe, Sarah Davis, Rod Lambert, Nick Smith, Tina and David Woods-Taylor, Mr and Mrs H D Brierly)*

Free house ~ Licensee Lisa Bullock ~ Bar food (12-2.30(3 Sun lunch), 6-9.30(10 Sat evening, but see text)) ~ Restaurant ~ (01233) 770217 ~ Children in eating area of bar and restaurant ~ Dogs allowed in bar ~ Open 11-11; 12-10.30 Sun ~ Bedrooms: £40B/£70S(£70B)

SNARGATE TQ9928 Map 3
Red Lion ★ 🍺

B2080 Appledore—Brenzett

Known locally as Doris's, this is a completely unspoilt village local which was last modernised in 1890. It's been in the same family for 90 years, and the three perfectly simple little rooms still have their original cream tongue and groove wall panelling, a couple of heavy beams in a sagging ceiling, dark pine Victorian farmhouse chairs on bare boards, lots of old photographs and other memorabilia, and a coal fire; outdoor lavatories, of course. One charming little room, with a frosted glass wall through to the bar and a sash window looking out to a cottage garden, has only two dark pine pews beside two long tables, a couple more farmhouse chairs and a nice old piano stacked with books. Cheerful groups of regulars catch up on local news and play toad in the hole. As well as Double Vision cider from nearby Staplehurst, and country wines, they serve Goachers Light and up to three well kept real ales from small brewers such as Black Sheep, Hop Back, and Hopdaemon tapped straight from casks on a low rack behind an unusual shop-like marble-topped counter (little marks it as a bar other than a few glasses on two small shelves, some crisps and half a dozen spirits bottles). Although they don't serve food, you're welcome to bring your own. Darts, shove-ha'penny, cribbage, dominoes, nine men's morris and table skittles. *(Recommended by Pete Baker,*

R E Davidson, Andrea Rampley, Peter Scillitoe, Richard Pitcher, the Didler, Ron Shelton, Professor and Mrs J Fletcher, Gill and Tony Morriss, Kevin Thorpe)

Free house ~ Licensee Mrs Jemison ~ Real ale ~ No credit cards ~ (01797) 344648 ~ Children in family room ~ Dogs allowed in bar ~ Open 12-3, 7-11(10.30 Sun)

STAPLEHURST TQ7847 Map 3
Lord Raglan

About 1½ miles from town centre towards Maidstone, turn right off A229 into Chart Hill Road opposite Cross at Hand Garage; OS Sheet 188 map reference 785472

Everywhere you look on the low beams in this unpretentious and simple yet quite civilised country inn are masses of hops, and the mixed collection of comfortably worn dark wood furniture on quite well used dark brown carpet tiles and nice old parquet flooring is mostly 1930s; don't miss the rather battered life-size effigy of Lord Raglan (a general in the Crimean War) propped in a chair in the corner. The interior is quite compact, with a narrow bar – you walk in almost on top of the counter and chatting locals – widening slightly at one end to a small area with a big log fire in winter. In the other direction it works its way round to an intimate area at the back, with lots of wine bottles lined up on a low shelf. Nicely presented on willow pattern plates, the hearty bar food is served generously. Blackboard menus behind the bar include a few pubby staples such as sandwiches (from £2.75), filled baguettes (from £4.95), ploughman's, chilli con carne or sausage, egg and chips (£5.95), as well as more elaborate dishes like marinated anchovies with apple and potato salad (£5.25), smoked duck and orange salad or smoked venison and pickled walnut (£5.50), pasta with tomatoes, olives, peppers and cheese (£7.50), duck breast with port and orange sauce, guinea fowl breast in red wine, and poached salmon with lemon and herbs (all £9.95), king prawns with garlic and ginger (£10.95), grilled fillet steak (£14.50), and puddings such as treacle sponge pudding, banoffi pie or apple crumble (£3.95). Well kept Goachers Light and Harveys Best, with a guest such as Exmoor Fox or Timothy Taylors Landlord, summer farm cider, and a good wine list. No piped music or games machines here, just nice little conversational nooks. Small french windows lead out to an enticing little high-hedged terraced area with white plastic tables and chairs, and there are wooden picnic-sets in the side orchard; wheelchair access is reasonable. More reports please. *(Recommended by Colin and Janet Roe, Ian Phillips, Tony Hobden)*

Free house ~ Licensees Andrew and Annie Hutchison ~ Real ale ~ Bar food (12-2.30, 7-10; not Sun) ~ (01622) 843747 ~ Children welcome ~ Dogs welcome ~ Open 12-3, 6-11; closed Sun

STODMARSH TR2160 Map 3
Red Lion

High Sreet; off A257 just E of Canterbury

Several idiosyncratic rooms in this little pub wrap themselves around the big island bar and are full of character and interest. There are hops all over the place, wine bottles (some empty and some full) crammed along mantelpieces and along one side of the bar, all manner of paintings and pictures, copper kettles and old cooking implements, well used cookery books, big stone bottles and milk churns, trugs and baskets, old tennis racquets and straw hats, a collection of brass instruments in one area with sheet music all over the walls, and some jazz records; a couple of little stall areas have hop sacks draped over the partitioning. There are green-painted, cushioned mate's chairs around a happy mix of nice pine tables, lit candles in unusual metal candleholders, fresh flowers on every table and big arrangements on the bars, and high bar stools on which cheery locals sit chatting to the particularly friendly landlord. The atmosphere is convivial and very relaxed, and large cats sit snoozily by the big log fire. Piped jazz, and bat and trap. Well kept Greene King IPA, Old Speckled Hen, and a seasonal guest, a good wine list with several by the glass, excellent summer Pimms and winter mulled wine, and cider. Good bar food using local produce might include filled baguettes with steak, avocado and bacon, and so forth (£4.95), asparagus wrapped in smoked salmon (£5.95), pigeon breast and partridge fillet with chutney (£6.50), a mixed platter of meat, fish and cheese (£7), crab with basil mayonnaise (£7.25), mussels with sweet chilli and coconut milk (£7.95; main course £10.95), pies such as winter game, chicken, leek and cider or smoked haddock, cornish yarg, and potato (all £9.95), giant vol-au-vent filled with lasagne with a light cheese sauce (£11.95), poached wild salmon wrapped in horseradish leaves and fresh fennel (£14.75), local lamb stuffed with rosemary and garlic (£14.95), and puddings like banoffi pie or bread and butter pudding with Tia Maria (£3.95); jazz and curry (£12). They sell eggs and chutneys. There are picnic-sets under umbrellas in the back garden, pretty flowerbeds, and perhaps some chickens. More reports please. *(Recommended by Allan and Toni Jones, Kevin Thorpe)*

Free house ~ Licensee Robert Whigham ~ Real ale ~ Bar food (not Sun evening) ~ Restaurant ~ (01227) 721339 ~ Well behaved children welcome ~ Dogs welcome ~ Live jazz first Weds in month ~ Open 10.30-11; 12-10.30 Sun ~ Bedrooms: /£60B

TUNBRIDGE WELLS TQ5639 Map 3
Beacon ♀

Tea Garden Lane; leaving Tunbridge Wells westwards on A264, this is the left turn-off on Rusthall Common after Nevill Park

In warm weather, the best place to sit at this airy Victorian pub is out on the pergola-covered wooden deck which has good hillside views. Inside, you'll usually find a nice mix of customers chatting at the sweeping bar counter with its ranks of shiny bottles, or on the comfortable sofas by the fine old wood fireplace. The dining area and spreading bar run freely into each other, with stripped panelling, lovely wood floors, ornately built wall units and glowing lamps giving a solidly comfortable feel. As well as lunchtime sandwiches (from £4.75) or baked potatoes (from £5.50) with interesting fillings such as bacon, brie and mango chutney or roasted vegetable and red pepper hummous, enjoyable bar food includes home-made soup (£4.25), moules marinière or smoked bacon and wild mushroom tartlet glazed with melted goats cheese (£6.50), real ale and chive-battered hake fillet (£7.50), pasta with a pine nut carbonara sauce (£7.75), cumberland sausage with onion marmalade (£8.95), lamb, apricot and chorizo casserole (£10.50), confit of duck on bubble and squeak with red wine jus (£10.75), and roasted monkfish fillet with lemon olive oil and watercress (£14). Well kept Harveys Best, Larkins, and Timothy Taylors Landlord on handpump kept under light blanket pressure, and nine wines by the glass; piped music, shove-ha'penny, cribbage, dominoes, and in the summer volleyball, boules and (very rare for a pub these days) even rounders. More reports please. *(Recommended by Sarah Davis, Rod Lambert, D Charry, Mrs Catherine Draper, Comus and Sarah Elliott)*

Free house ~ Licensee John Cullen ~ Real ale ~ Bar food (12-2.30, 6.30-9.30) ~ Restaurant ~ (01892) 524252 ~ Children in eating area of bar and restaurant ~ Dogs allowed in bar ~ Folk club second and fourth Mon of month ~ Open 11-11; 12-10.30 Sun ~ Bedrooms: £68.50S/£97B

Mount Edgcumbe Hotel ♀ ⇔

The Common

This handsome tile-hung and weatherboarded hotel stands on top of one of the several large rocky outcrops on the common. As you enter the small cosy bar, which has lots of exposed brick and old photographs of the town on the walls, there's a mini waterfall feature on the right, with a few tables (candlelit at night) in an unusual grotto-like snug built into the rock. In the evenings subdued wall lighting and the chatty buzz of customers make for a welcoming atmosphere; piped music and board games. An attractive small two-room restaurant (no smoking) has views out over the common, and tables out on a pleasant side terrace have a similar outlook, reaching over the grass to the town beyond. As well as tasty lunchtime filled baguettes (from £3.75, not Sunday), the fairly short bar menu might include a snack basket (£4.95), moules frites or vegetable pasta (£6.50), toulouse sausages and mash in rich onion gravy (£6.95), crispy hot duck salad with hoi sin sauce (£7.25), and sirloin steak (£10.25); you must book for Saturday evening. They've an extensive wine list, well kept Harveys Best on handpump, fresh orange juice and good coffee; service is cheerful. More reports please. *(Recommended by Derek Thomas)*

Free house ~ Licensees Iain and Darren Arthur ~ Real ale ~ Bar food (12-2.30, 7-10; 12.30-6 Sun) ~ Restaurant ~ (01892) 526823 ~ Children welcome ~ Dogs welcome ~ Jazz Sun evenings ~ Open 11.30-11; 12-11(10.30 Sun) Sat ~ Bedrooms: £45S/£70B

Sankeys 🍴 ♀

Mount Ephraim (A26 just N of junction with A267)

By the time this book is published, this bustling pub/wine bar will have been opened up and rearranged. What was the ground floor restaurant will become similar to the downstairs cellar bar, with open fires, comfortable seating, and a relaxed, chatty atmosphere. The dimly lit bar has pews around closely spaced sturdy old pine tables, and old mirrors, prints, enamel advertising signs, antique beer engines and other bric-a-brac (most of which has been salvaged from local pub closures); french windows lead to a suntrap terrace with teak tables and chairs under cocktail parasols. They specialise in good fresh fish dishes which might include morecambe bay potted shrimps (£5.75), moules marinière (£6.50), queen scallops grilled with garlic and breadcrumbs (£6.75), home-made salmon and cod fishcakes with parsley sauce or fresh scottish beer-battered cod and chips (£8.50), scottish salmon with basil, garlic and lemon crust with olive mash (£9.50), fillets of bass with ginger, spring onion and soy (£14.50), and delicious cornish cock crab (£16.50); there are poultry and game choices, too, lunchtime baguettes, and daily specials. You need to book or get there early for a table in the bar, and half of the ground floor is no smoking. Service is friendly and efficient. Although most people take advantage of the very good wine list, they've well kept Harveys Best and Larkins on handpump, and a selection of interesting bottled beers; also quite a choice of unusual teas. More reports please. *(Recommended by Jeff Cameron, David and Lynne Cure)*

Free house ~ Licensee Guy Sankey ~ Real ale ~ Bar food (all day) ~ Restaurant ~ (01892) 511422 ~ Children in eating area of bar ~ Dogs allowed in bar ~ Open 12-11(10.30 Sun)

ULCOMBE TQ8550 Map 3

Pepper Box 🍺

Fairbourne Heath; signposted from A20 in Harrietsham, or follow Ulcombe signpost from A20, then turn left at crossroads with sign to pub

The name of this cosy old country inn refers to the pepperbox pistol – an early type of revolver with numerous barrels. It's a friendly, bustling place, and the homely bar has standing timbers and low beams hung with hops, copper kettles and pans on window sills, some very low-seated windsor chairs and wing armchairs, and two armchairs and a sofa by the splendid inglenook fireplace with its lovely log fire. A side area is more functionally furnished for eating, and there's a very snug little no smoking dining room; piped music. Well kept Shepherd Neame Bitter, Spitfire and a seasonal guest beer tapped from the cask, and local apple juice. Served by helpful young staff, the enjoyable bar menu includes home-made soup (£3.50), sandwiches (from £3.50), ploughman's (from £4.50), local sausages and onion gravy (£7.50), and braised beef and onions (£8.50), and you can also eat in the bar from the more elaborate restaurant menu, which includes dishes such as duck and orange pâté or chicken satay (£5.50), rump of lamb with apple, mint and calvados (£9.50), sizzling singapore beef (£9.80), and fillet of monkfish with chilli, ginger and spring onion (£10.50). Views from the terrace stretch over a great plateau of rolling arable farmland, and if you're in the garden, with its small pond, shrubs and flowerbeds, you may be lucky enough to catch a glimpse of deer; the tabby tom is called Fred, and there are two more cats and a collie called Rosie. No children inside. *(Recommended by Jan and Alan Summers, Peter Scillitoe, Philip Hill, John Branston, Sarah Davis, Rod Lambert, Colin and Janet Roe)*

Shepherd Neame ~ Tenants Geoff and Sarah Pemble ~ Real ale ~ Bar food (12-2, 7-9.45; not Sun or Mon evenings) ~ Restaurant ~ (01622) 842558 ~ Dogs allowed in bar ~ Open 11-3, 6.30-11; 12-3, 7-10.30 Sun

WEST MALLING TQ6857 Map 3
Swan

Swan Street

This is a stylish brasserie/bar just off the main street of this most attractive little town. They don't serve real ale (but do keep St Peter's bottled beers) so in the strictest sense it is not a pub, but it is a lively bustling place to come for a drink and a chat or for an enjoyable meal. It's all open-plan and very light and airy with stripped pale wood flooring throughout, a chatty, relaxed atmosphere, and lots of efficient and friendly young staff darting about in black clothing. Drinkers tend to congregate around the modern counter where there are a few cream low basketweave armchairs, nice black and white photographs of old local scenes, plants, and mirrors. This leads on to an informal drinking and eating part with a long wall seat at one end with big beige cushions, and elegant, modern dining chairs around slate-topped tables, which in turn spreads into the restaurant: wicker dining chairs around pale wood tables, huge flower arrangements, a flat-screen television showing old silent movies, and a huge contemporary 'chandelier' of exposed bulbs, angel wings and wire. As well as some unusual fruity lagers and good wines, they offer attractively presented imaginative food from a frequently changing menu. At lunchtime you might find chicken caesar salad (£6) or crab linguini (£8) while in the evening dishes might include braised lamb shank with minted pea mash (£11.50), roast salmon with hollandaise (£12), roast chicken with foie gras and porcini mushrooms (£12.50) and puddings such as panna cotta with raspberries and grappa or fresh fruit sorbet of the day (from £4). *(Recommended by Wendy Arnold)*

Free house ~ Licensee Peter Cornwall ~ Bar food (12-2.30, 6-10(10.30 Sat); 12-4, 6-9 Sun) ~ Restaurant ~ (01732) 521910 ~ Children in eating area of bar ~ Open 12-2.30, 6-11; 12-4, 6-10.30 Sun; closed 26-27 Dec 1-2 Jan

WEST PECKHAM TQ6452 Map 3
Swan on the Green ♟

Off B2016, second turning left heading N from A26 (Swanton Road)

Despite a snow blizzard, one reader found the car park at this little tucked-away country pub full, and there's always a good mix of customers from suited office workers out to lunch to friendly locals chatting to the amiable licensee at the bar. Of course, one draw is the half a dozen own-brewed ales: Bewick, Chinook, Ginger Swan, Swan Mild, Port Side, Trumpeter and Whooper Pale. There's an emphasis on the enjoyable enterprising bar food too, which from a daily changing menu, might include lunchtime dishes such as filled ciabatta flutes (£4.75), ploughman's (£5.95), home-made stilton and red onion burgers (£7.50), warm chicken breast and chargrilled bacon salad or butternut squash and courgette risotto (£8.95), fresh cromer crab (£9.25), and seared tuna with niçoise salad (£9.75); evening choices like mixed roasted pepper and spinach soup (£4.75), roast baby squid stuffed with chorizo, anchovies and capers with a warm chilli oil (£6.50), lebanese bread salad with cauliflower, tomatoes, fresh mint and coriander (£9.25), mixed fish tagine (£12.75), and fillet steak with a stew of black pudding, chilli, capers and herbs (£16.50). They may add an 'optional' 10% surcharge to the bill. The bar is light, airy, and open-plan, with rush-seated dining chairs and cushioned church settles around an attractive mix of refectory and other pale oak tables on the wood strip floor, lovely big bunches of flowers (one placed in the knocked-through brick fireplace), hops and beams, some modern paintings at one end, black and white photographs of locals at the other end, and good aztec-patterned curtains; piped music. There are picnic-sets under parasols in front of the building, and more on the charming cricket green opposite; they take a £10 deposit for a rug if you want to eat outside. The nearby church is partly Saxon. *(Recommended by Bob and*

Margaret Holder, Lesley and Peter Barrett, Simon and Sally Small, Hugh Roberts, Kevin Thorpe, Paul Hopton, Gerry and Rosemary Dobson, B and M Kendall)

Own brew ~ Licensee Gordon Milligan ~ Real ale ~ Bar food (not Sun evening) ~ Restaurant ~ (01622) 812271 ~ Children welcome ~ Dogs allowed in bar ~ Regular live entertainment ~ Open 11-3(4 Sat), 6-11; 12-10.30 Sun; 11-3, 6-9 winter Mon, 12-5 Sun in winter

Lucky Dip

Besides the fully inspected pubs, you might like to try these Lucky Dips recommended to us and described by readers (if you do, please send us reports: www.goodguides.com).

ADDINGTON [TQ6559]
Angel [just off M20 junction 4; Addington Green]: 14th-c pub in classic village green setting, plenty of well spaced tables, wide choice of up-to-date food from sandwiches up, Thurs pasta night, quick friendly service; live music Weds (anon)
APPLEDORE [TQ9529]
Black Lion [The Street]: Unpretentious village pub, cosy and warm, with huge range of good value generous food all day esp local fish, partitioned eating area, friendly helpful staff, three or four changing ales such as Greene King; tables out by attractive village street (J P Humphery, Richard Fendick, CJ)
BADLESMERE [TR0154]
Red Lion [A251, S of M2 junction 6]: Attractive, spacious country pub where time stands still, well kept Fullers London Pride, Greene King Abbot, Shepherd Neame and changing guests from small breweries, Johnson's farm cider from Sheppey, enjoyable food (not Sun pm) using local produce; pleasant garden, paddock for caravans and tents, summer beer and folk festivals, live music Fri pm, open all day Fri and wknds (Kevin Thorpe)
BARFRESTONE [TR2650]
☆ *Yew Tree* [off A256 N of Dover; or off A2 at Barham]: Country local tucked away behind huge yew tree, hospitable licensees, good value blackboard food (not Mon) from baguettes, ciabattas and baked potatoes to local game, five well kept changing ales inc a Mild, farm cider, 12 good value wines by the glass, chatty atmosphere, log fire, mix of old pine furniture on bare boards, cosy little dining room with another open fire, games in family room; may be quiet piped music; pub serves as 'shop' for the famous next-door church with its wonderful Norman carvings; open all day Fri-Sun (Kevin Thorpe, LYM, I J and S A Bufton)
BARHAM [TR2050]
Duke of Cumberland [The Street]: Open-plan country dining pub, good traditional range, well kept Adnams and other ales, welcoming staff, bare boards and flagstones, open fire; bedrooms (Peter Heaton, Vanessa Young)
BENOVER [TQ7048]
Woolpack: Pretty tile-hung pub with well kept Shepherd Neame real ales, flagstoned main area set for the good value tasty food, with prints on stripped brickwork, beamed and partly panelled smaller bar, friendly landlord

and nice traditional atmosphere; may be piped local radio; tables on big lawn (Peter Meister, LYM)
BISHOPSBOURNE [TR1852]
☆ *Mermaid* [signed off A2]: Traditional welcoming unspoilt country local in same family for many years, simple lunchtime food (not Sun) inc good filled rolls or sandwiches and bargain hot dishes, well kept Shepherd Neame beers, friendly regulars, coal fire, darts and old books in small back public bar, no music or machines; dogs and walkers welcome, lovely unspoilt village nr Pilgrims Way (Kevin Thorpe, Peter Heaton, Guy Vowles)
BLUETOWN [TQ9175]
Red Lion [High St]: Solitary blitz survivor opp dockyards, lovingly preserved Victorian interior with masses of nautical memorabilia; Fullers London Pride, Shepherd Neame and three changing guest beers, simple food inc good value special sandwiches, pleasant staff; piped music; rooftop garden, tables outside, open all day (Kevin Thorpe)
BRABOURNE [TR1041]
Five Bells [East Brabourne]: Big popular open-plan bar with comfortable banquettes, efficient friendly service, wide choice of good value fresh food, well kept ales, log fire; tables in garden with play area (Lawrence Mitchell)
BRASTED [TQ4654]
White Hart [High St (A25)]: Roomy largely no smoking Vintage Inn, several snug areas taking their mood from the original Battle of Britain bar with signatures and mementoes of Biggin Hill fighter pilots, beams and log fires, helpful staff, well kept Bass and Tetleys, good choice of wine and fresh orange juice; children welcome, big neatly kept garden with well spaced tables and play area; bedrooms, pretty village with several antiques shops (LYM, Tina and David Woods-Taylor, B J Harding, Alan M Pring, GHC)
BREDHURST [TQ7962]
Bell [The Street]: Good range of beers such as Courage Directors, Greene King Ruddles, Shepherd Neame and John Smiths, wholesome food, good staff, cheerful locals, quiz night (J I Davies)
BRENCHLEY [TQ6741]
Bull [High St]: Warm and inviting Victorian pub with enjoyable food, good service, well kept beer (Dr M Mannion)
BRIDGE [TR1854]
Plough & Harrow [High St]: Small friendly

17th-c village local with well kept Shepherd
Neame ales and good wine choice, coal fire
and lots of sporting prints in open-plan brick-
walled lounge, public bar with darts and games
(over 30 clubs and teams call this home); no
food, open all day Sat *(Kevin Thorpe,
Roger Mardon)*
White Horse [High St]: Old dining pub opened
up into comfortable single bar, huge fireplace,
good fresh food from doorstep sandwiches up,
five well kept changing real ales, fine choice of
wines by the glass, friendly efficient service,
dining area and civilised restaurant; attractive
village *(Vanessa Young, Roger Mardon)*
BROADSTAIRS [TR3967]
Neptunes Hall [Harbour St]: Friendly early
19th-c two-bar local with attractive bow
windows and original shelving and panelling,
well kept Shepherd Neame beers, carpeted
back lounge with open fire, lunchtime snacks,
friendly staff and locals; occasional live folk
(daily during Aug folk festival); enclosed
terrace, open all day *(Kevin Thorpe)*
CANTERBURY [TR1458]
Millers Arms [St Radigunds St]: Welcoming
pub with several pleasantly refurbished rooms,
well kept Shepherd Neame ales, good wine
choice; decent bedrooms, quiet street nr river
and handy for Marlow Theatre *(David and
Betty Gittins, Richard Waller)*
New Inn [Havelock St]: Friendly bustle in
unspoilt Victorian terraced local, elderly
furnishings, bare boards, gas fire, good
beermat collection, changing ales such as
Brakspears and Greene King, simple food,
modern back conservatory; juke box popular
with students, nearby parking difficult
(James Woods)
Old Gate [New Dover Rd (A2050 S)]: Big
reliable Vintage Inn, several distinct areas,
stripped brick and beams, open fires,
bookshelves, old prints, dried flowers, old
wooden table and chairs, reasonably priced
food all day, fine wine choice, Bass and
Tetleys, well trained staff, daily papers; some
piped music; bedrooms, picnic-sets in small
back garden *(Kevin Thorpe)*
☆ *Olde Beverlie* [St Stephens Green; A290 from
centre, then right at Tyler Hill/Univ sign]:
16th-c pub with heavy beams, flagstones,
wattle and daub walls and old prints in open-
plan front part, new room off, enjoyable food
(not Sun evening) from good value interesting
sandwiches up, Shepherd Neame ales inc a
seasonal one that's tapped from the cask, good
wine choice, good mix of customers, new
carpeted back dining extension; piped music,
some machines, Mon quiz night; disabled
facilities now, nicely restored walled courtyard
garden with bat and trap *(Kevin Thorpe)*
Simple Simons [Church Lane, St Radigunds]:
Step down into basic pub in 14th-c building,
great beams, broad floorboards and flagstones,
two woodburners, dim-lit upstairs banqueting
hall, well kept Bass and up to five guest beers,
impressive pump clip collection, simple
lunchtime food inc good value sandwiches and
speciality pies, more studenty evening; good

piped classical music in the daytime, live blues
Tues, jazz Thurs; tables in courtyard, open all
day *(Kevin Thorpe)*
Three Tuns [Watling St, opp St Margaret St]:
Interesting 15th-c building with nice old-
fashioned décor, well kept Shepherd Neame
Spitfire, friendly service, enjoyable well priced
food; shame about the piped music
(Richard Waller)
White Hart [Worthgate Pl, opp tree-shaded
square off Castle St]: Three well kept Shepherd
Neame real ales, enjoyable food; large garden
behind – one of very few in the city *(Keith and
Chris O'Neill)*
CAPEL [TQ6444]
☆ *Dovecote* [Alders Rd; SE of Tonbridge]:
Attractive rustic pub in pleasant tucked-away
hamlet, bare bricks, hop-hung beams, smaller
no smoking dining end with pitched ceiling,
generous good value standard food from
ploughman's and baguettes to popular Sun
lunch, well kept beers tapped from the cask
such as Adnams, Badger K&B, Harveys,
Larkins and Marstons Pedigree, Chiddingstone
farm cider; picnic-sets in back garden with
terrace, doves and play area *(Peter Meister)*
CHARING [TQ9551]
Bowl [Egg Hill Rd]: Popular neatly kept 16th-c
pub high on downs nr Pilgrims Way, well kept
Fullers London Pride and other changing ales
such as Adnams, Courage, Harveys and
Wadworths 6X, soup, sandwiches and other
low-priced snacks, log fire, welcoming
licensees, games room with hexagonal pool
table; July beer festival, frequent entertainment;
big garden (room for camping and caravans),
cl lunchtime Mon-Thurs, open all day Fri-Sun
(Peter Scillitoe, Nigel B Thompson)
Royal Oak [High St]: Friendly old village pub,
enjoyable generous food, well kept beer
(Stephen and Jean Curtis)
CHARTHAM HATCH [TR1056]
☆ *Chapter Arms* [New Town St]: Sizeable 18th-c
pub overlooking orchards, flowers and candles
on tables, heavily hop-hung ceiling with brass
instruments and fairy lights, Harveys Best and
Shepherd Neame Bitter and Goldings, decent
wine, friendly service, restaurant through
doorway decorated in lilac, green and silver;
quiet piped music, jazz Mon; nice teak garden
furniture, lots of flower tubs etc *(Peter Dixon,
BB)*
CHATHAM [TQ7569]
☆ *Harbourmasters House* [Historic Dockyard]:
Right in the dockyard World Heritage Site,
handsome little two-room building overlooking
Medway, refurbished and run by nearby
Flagship Brewery, their beers (to take away
too), sandwiches and rolls, old prints and naval
items, no music; seats out by river wall; open
to public 11-6 (members only later) *(R WC,
Kevin Thorpe, Richard Gibbs, Gerry and
Rosemary Dobson)*
CHILLENDEN [TR2653]
☆ *Griffins Head*: Good-sized helpings of
consistently appealing food in attractive
beamed, timbered and flagstoned 14th-c pub
with three comfortable rooms, Shepherd

Neame real ales, good choice of house wines, big log fire, local regulars; small children not welcome; pleasant garden surrounded by wild roses, super Sun barbecues, attractive countryside *(F T Cardiff, R J Davies, S Keens, Peter and Patricia Burton)*

CHIPSTEAD [TQ5056]

George & Dragon [nr M25 junction 5]: Attractive country dining pub with heavy black beams and standing timbers, very wide choice of enjoyable fresh food, reasonable prices, good value wines, relaxed friendly service, children welcome in most areas; tables in pleasant garden *(Peter Rozée, LYM)*

COWDEN [TQ4640]

☆ *Fountain* [off A264 and B2026; High St]: Small unpretentious country local in pretty village with sensibly short choice of unusually good interesting food inc good Sun roast, well kept Harveys, Larkins and guests, decent wines, friendly licensees, darts, woodburner in small beamed back dining room; walkers and dogs welcome, annual flower show *(Derek Thomas, BB, Jason Caulkin)*

☆ *Queens Arms* [Cowden Pound; junction B2026 with Markbeech rd]: Unspoilt and warmly welcoming two-room country pub like something from the 1930s, with splendid landlady, well kept Brakspears, darts; may be cl wkdy lunchtimes *(RWC, R E Davidson, Pete Baker, the Didler, Kevin Thorpe)*

CRANBROOK [TQ7735]

White Horse [Carriers Rd]: Recently reworked local, main bar in modern colours of green or sienna red, smart leatherette dining chairs in yellow, green or brown around new dark wood tables on dark stripped wood floor, brown leatherette banquettes; one end has comfortable smart sofas by open fire, stylish flower arrangements; huge projection screen plus another TV showing pop videos or sport with very loud music or sports; plenty of young locals; two small back dining rooms with contemporary décor; efficient, friendly young staff dressed in black; Greene King IPA, Ruddles Best, Morland Original and a guest like Wells Bombardier, smoothies, lots of good wines by the glass; new chef doing enjoyable up-to-date food using local ingredients; modern aluminium seats in front on the street and at the back by car park; four bedrooms *(Carrie Grey, BB)*

CROCKHAM HILL [TQ4450]

Royal Oak: Well kept village pub with friendly new landlord, good range of well kept beers inc Shepherd Neame Spitfire, wide choice of enjoyable home-made food from sensibly priced baguettes up; handy for walks *(Christopher Wright, G T Brewster, Len Banister)*

DARTFORD [TQ5675]

Wharf [Galleon Bvd, Crossways; just off A206 NE of centre]: Pleasant waterside spot for summer, with tables outside, usual food from sandwiches and baked potatoes up, carvery with early evening bargains Mon-Thurs, Shepherd Neame real ales *(Alan M Pring)*

DENTON [TR2147]

Jackdaw [A260 Canterbury—Folkestone]:

Imposing brick and flint pub with comfortable open-plan bar decorated in cream and book-room red with RAF photographs and books, five well kept changing ales such as Shepherd Neame Spitfire and Charles Wells Bombardier, good value food, friendly young staff, large back restaurant; quiet piped music; children welcome, tables in pleasant garden, open all day *(Kevin Thorpe, Peter Scillitoe)*

DETLING [TQ7958]

☆ *Cock Horse* [The Street]: Pretty tiled and weatherboarded village pub with buoyant atmosphere and enjoyable food in bars and back dining room, friendly licensees, real ales such as Adnams, Bass and Greene King; tables in yard behind, handy for North Downs Way *(Robert Gomme, David Gregory, Richard Gibbs)*

DOVER [TR3141]

Mogul [Chapel Pl, off York St South roundabout]: Three constantly changing well kept ales tapped from the cask, simple food all day inc good sandwiches, open-plan main bar with sea views and slight continental-café feel, separate back public bar with woodburner and traditional pub games; may be piped jazz; tables outside, open all day *(Pete Baker, Kevin Thorpe, R E Davidson)*

DUNGENESS [TR0916]

Pilot [Battery Rd]: Small original bar, modern extension with second bar and family area, good generous fish and chips, well kept Greene King IPA and Abbot *(Peter Meister)*

DUNKS GREEN [TQ6152]

☆ *Kentish Rifleman*: Cosy early 16th-c timbered pub (the big stone-arched vaulted cellar may even be Roman), small public bar welcoming dogs, large lounge/dining area, good traditional menu inc plenty of sandwiches and baguettes and choice of Sun roasts, chirpy landlord and good welcoming service, well kept ales such as Greene King Abbot, Harveys and Charles Wells Bombardier, decent wine and coffee, plenty of character, no machines; tables in well designed garden behind *(GHC, Peter Meister, Carl and Jackie Cranmer, Martin Jennings, BB)*

DYMCHURCH [TR1029]

Ship [High St]: Welcoming atmosphere, enjoyable food in bar and restaurant; bedrooms with own bathrooms *(Bryan R Shiner)*

ELHAM [TR1743]

Rose & Crown [High St]: Small friendly inn, partly 16th-c, quiet and unpretentious, with comfortable sofa by stove, pub cat and dogs, well kept ales, reasonably priced wines, enjoyable food with good menu in evening restaurant; tables in garden, bedrooms *(John and Joan Calvert, Robert Coomber, GHC)*

EYNSFORD [TQ5365]

☆ *Malt Shovel* [Station Rd]: Neatly kept spacious old-fashioned dining pub, child-friendly and handy for castles and Roman villa, dark panelling, good food choice from some good value straightforward pubby dishes to more costly things inc quite a few fish and seafood dishes (lobster tank), well kept Fullers London Pride and Greene King IPA, good choice of wine by the glass, quick helpful service, nice atmosphere; car park across busy road *(Jim and Maggie Cowell, Simon and Gillian Wales, GHC, LM)*

FAIRSEAT [TQ6361]

Vigo [A227]: Unspoilt, basic free house dating from 15th c, stripped stonework and open fire, well kept Harveys and changing ales such as Flagship and Youngs, no food; still has daddlums table in use; cl wkdy lunchtimes *(Kevin Thorpe)*

FARNINGHAM [TQ5467]

Chequers: Good choice of beers such as Fullers ESB, Greene King Abbot and Timothy Taylors Landlord, friendly staff; picturesque village *(Paul and Ann Meyer)*

FAVERSHAM [TR0161]

Albion [Front Brents]: Attractively light and airy pub in improving waterside area, solid pine furnishings and nautical decorations on pale green walls, food from sandwiches up inc summer cream teas, well kept Shepherd Neame ales inc seasonal from the nearby brewery, friendly smiling staff; children welcome in restaurant area, disabled lavatories, picnic-sets out on riverside walkway (Saxon Shore long-distance path), open all day summer *(Tina and David Woods-Taylor, LYM, Kevin Thorpe)*

Anchor [Abbey St]: Smallish friendly two-bar local in attractive 17th-c street nr quay and station, several well kept Shepherd Neame ales, good quiet relaxed atmosphere, bare boards, open fires, settles and part-panelling, low-priced food all day, candlelit tiled eating area; piped radio; music nights, a couple of picnic-sets outside, pretty garden, open all day *(the Didler, Kevin Thorpe)*

Bear [Market Pl]: Friendly carefully refurbished local dating from 16th c (front rebuilt last century), lounge, snug and public bar off side corridor, well kept Shepherd Neame ales from the nearby brewery, basic good value lunchtime home cooking; tables outside, lively musical following, open all day Sat *(the Didler)*

Crown & Anchor [The Mall]: Friendly open-plan local dating from 19th c, wkdy lunchtime food inc Hungarian landlord's authentic goulash, Shepherd Neame real ales, games area with darts and pool *(the Didler)*

Elephant [The Mall]: Picturesque flower-decked terrace town pub now with two well kept Flagship ales, three guests inc a Mild, belgian beers, local farm cider, simple bar food and (with pianist) Sun roasts, thoughtful staff, unpretentiously attractive furnishings on stripped boards, central fireplace, no smoking dining room; beer festivals, back pool room, punk rock juke box, perhaps piped music, darts; suntrap terrace with fishpond and summer barbecues, open all day *(Kevin Thorpe, the Didler, Kevin Flack, BB)*

Sun [West St]: Roomy and rambling old-world 15th-c weatherboarded town pub with good unpretentious atmosphere in small low-ceilinged partly panelled rooms, good value

low-priced lunchtime food, well kept Shepherd Neame beers inc seasonal one from nearby brewery, good service; piped music; open all day, tables in pleasant back courtyard, interesting street *(the Didler)*

FOLKESTONE [TR2335]

Guildhall [The Bayle, nr churchyard]: Bright clean atmosphere, well kept ales such as Gales HSB and Greene King Abbot, very welcoming staff and regulars; soft piped music, laid-back alsatian *(Colin Gooch)*

FORDWICH [TR1759]

George & Dragon [off A28 at Sturry]: Friendly chain dining pub, huge choice of food, well kept real ales; pleasant garden leads down to River Stour, character bedrooms, handy for Stodmarsh nature reserve *(Keith and Chris O'Neill)*

FOUR ELMS [TQ4748]

Four Elms [B2027/B269 E of Edenbridge]: Large busy open-plan dining pub, welcoming and comfortable, wide choice of good value food from sandwiches and baguettes to grills, rota of well kept ales inc Fullers London Pride, Greene King Abbot and Shepherd Neame Spitfire, decent wine and coffee, friendly service, several rambling rooms, two big log fires, huge boar's head, family room, no music; tables outside, handy for Chartwell *(GHC)*

GILLINGHAM [TQ7768]

Frog & Toad [Burnt Oak Terr]: Busy and welcoming backstreet local with three or four well kept real ales, fine choice of mainly belgian bottled beers, occasional beer festivals, cheap sandwiches; pool, darts, TV *(Peter Scillitoe)*

GOATHURST COMMON [TQ4952]

Woodman: Large mainly no smoking Chef & Brewer, decent all-day food and wine, Courage Directors and guest beers, polite helpful young staff, woodburner; delightful walking country *(Tina and David Woods-Taylor)*

GOUDHURST [TQ7037]

☆ *Green Cross* [Station Rd (A262 W)]: Good interesting food, particularly fish and seafood, well kept Harveys and Larkins, good wines, roomy and attractive back restaurant with good napkins, tablecloths etc, contrasting simple two-room bar with good fire and TV, pleasant informal service; bedrooms light and airy, good value; very handy for Finchcocks *(R D Moon, BB, Derek Thomas, Mrs Joan Hall, Peter Meister, W W Burke)*

☆ *Star & Eagle* [High St]: Striking medieval inn with settles and Jacobean-style seats in attractive heavily beamed open-plan bar, well kept Whitbreads-related ales, wide choice of enjoyable food from filled baguettes up, polite efficient service, children welcome; tables out behind with pretty views, lovely character bedrooms, well furnished and comfortable, open all day *(LYM, Joyce and Geoff Robson, Uta and John Owlett)*

GROOMBRIDGE [TQ5337]

☆ *Junction Inn* [Station Rd, off B2110]: Chattily relaxed bar with plenty of fresh flowers, candles in modern wall sconces and pleasantly up-to-date décor, similar small room off, friendly staff, good generous food inc interesting dishes, well kept Harveys, Fullers London Pride and a guest such as Theakstons, good wines, big airy carpeted dining room; skittle alley, picnic-sets out in front and in small pleasant back garden *(Lachlan Milligan, Anne Stephen, BB)*

HEADCORN [TQ8344]

George & Dragon [High St]: Good atmosphere and service, open fires, enjoyable food lunchtime and evening, separate dining room *(Jennifer Vandepeer)*

HEAVERHAM [TQ5758]

Chequers [Watery Lane]: Cottagey old pub with friendly locals' bar, enjoyable food from interesting baguettes up in attractive main bar, well kept Shepherd Neame, popular Sun lunch, attached beamed restaurant; pleasant tables outside *(Uta and John Owlett, Lynn Sharpless, Gwyn Jones)*

HERNE [TR1765]

First & Last [Herne Common (A291)]: Welcoming family-run pub with lots of locals, daily changing food inc popular Sun lunch, well kept real ales, nostalgic décor inc cigarette cards, motoring prints and team photographs; friendly alsatian *(Brian Skelcher)*

HERNE BAY [TR1768]

Rose [Mortimer St]: Spick and span small traditional pub with simple good value freshly made food (not Sun evening), reasonably priced well kept Shepherd Neame; can get crowded wknds *(David and Betty Gittins)*

HORSMONDEN [TQ7040]

☆ *Gun & Spitroast* [The Heath]: Pleasantly furnished clean and polished 1930s pub on village green, friendly and welcoming, wide choice of sensibly priced food from big filled baguettes to some interesting hot dishes, pretty inglenook dining room, obliging helpful staff, well kept ales inc Fullers London Pride and Harveys, log fire; dogs and walkers welcome, picnic-sets out behind with play area, newly done comfortable bedrooms in converted coach house *(Mr and Mrs H D Brierly)*

HORTON KIRBY [TQ5568]

Fighting Cocks [The Street]: Country pub with comfortable saloon, good food inc take-away pizzas Mon; big riverside garden with goats and ducks *(Kevin Flack)*

IDE HILL [TQ4851]

Cock [off B2042 SW of Sevenoaks]: Pretty village-green pub with well kept Greene King, straightforward food (not Sun evening) from sandwiches and ploughman's up, fine log fire, bar billiards; piped music, no children; some seats out in front, handy for Chartwell and nearby walks – so gets busy *(LYM, DJH, GHC)*

IGHTHAM [TQ5956]

☆ *George & Dragon* [A227]: Wonky early 16th-c black and white timbered pub under new management, sofas among other furnishings in long sociable main bar, cottagey and heavy-beamed end room, woodburner and open fires, well kept Shepherd Neame Bitter, Spitfire and seasonal ales, decent wines, good choice of fruit juices, short menu from open sandwiches

(all day till 6.30, not Sun) up, partly no smoking restaurant; children in family/restaurant areas, back terrace, open all day *(LYM, Kevin Flack)*

IVY HATCH [TQ5854]

☆ *Plough* [off A227 N of Tonbridge]: Restaurant rather than pub, often fully booked, with wide choice of consistently good food, fastidious french cooking, near attentive staff, impressive range of reasonably priced wines (and well kept Greene King IPA), attractive dark candlelit décor – upmarket in a friendly informal style, and priced to match; delightful conservatory and garden *(Christopher and Elise Way, Mary Ellen Cummings, Martin Jennings, LYM, Terence Boley, I D Greenfield)*

KEMSING [TQ5659]

Rising Sun [Cotmans Ash Lane; about 1 mile N of Heaverham on the back road to Eynsham, OS Sheet 188 map ref 563599]: Like something out of one of H E Bates's lighter works, dark beamed bars with well worn furniture on red tiled floor, inglenook fireplaces (one with a parrot in a cage), brocaded built-in wall benches and stools, chatty locals and a plump, friendly jack russell, changing mostly kentish beers, low prices, two simple, tatty end rooms with darts; informal, overgrown garden with picnic-sets and children's play things *(Guy Vowles, GHC, John and Elspeth Howell, BB)*

KILNDOWN [TQ7035]

Globe & Rainbow [signed off A21 S of Lamberhurst]: Small cheerful local bar with well kept Harveys and Fullers London Pride, friendly helpful service, fair range of wines by the glass, outer room with piano, home cooking for simple bare-boards dining room; pleasant country views from picnic-sets out on decking *(BB)*

KINGSGATE [TR3971]

Fayreness [Marine Dr/Kingsgate Ave]: Good setting above shingle beach, channel views from bar and modern conservatory, welcoming service, pub food inc ploughman's, Bass, Courage Directors, Websters and Youngs Special; separate games bar with piped music and pool *(Chris B)*

KIPPINGS CROSS [TQ6439]

Blue Boys [A21 just S of Pembury bypass]: Welcoming and properly pubby, with well organised good value bar food, friendly helpful staff, sedate bars with plenty of china and brass, small dining room; tables out behind with play area and country views, reasonably priced bedrooms, open all day (from 7 for breakfast) *(E G Parish)*

KNOCKHOLT [TQ4658]

Crown [Main Rd]: Attractive and cheerful, old-fashioned and unpretentious, popular at lunchtime with older diners – good value food inc sandwiches and sensibly priced home-made hot dishes; dark ochre décor, well kept Adnams Bitter and Broadside, friendly relaxed service, second bar good for walkers; picnic-sets on lawn with fishpond, colourful flowers, path to North Downs Way *(LM)*

Tally Ho [Cudham road]: Well kept Flowers,

Greene King IPA and Larkins, good coffee, wide range of good value blackboard food, welcoming efficient service and good housekeeping, brown panelling and timbering, big woodburner; disabled access *(LM)*

LAMBERHURST [TQ6735]

Brown Trout [B2169, off A21 nr entrance to Scotney Castle]: Popular dining pub specialising in briskly served fish, lots of steaks too, biggish extension off small beamed bar, well kept Fullers London Pride and Harveys, fair choice of decent wines, friendly staff, good log fire, children in eating areas; can be very busy wknds; picnic-sets in large safe garden with play area, pretty window boxes and flower tubs in summer, open all day Sun and summer *(Jeff Cameron, Roy and Margaret Jones, BB, Gordon Neighbour, Chris Pelley)*

Elephants Head [Hook Green; B2169 towards T Wells]: Ancient rambling timber-framed country local, heavy beams, brick or oak flooring, big inglenook log fire, plush-cushioned pews etc, well kept Harveys ales inc seasonal Old, usual food; darts and fruit machine in small side area, may be quiet piped music; picnic-sets by front green and in big back garden with terrace and impressive play area (peaceful view), nr Bayham Abbey and Owl House *(Peter Meister, LYM)*

LANGTON GREEN [TQ5538]

Langton Arms [A264]: Attractive building set well back, light and roomy bar with secluded alcoves and nice garden outlook, enjoyable good value food from tasty baked potatoes to more upmarket dishes; stairs down to lavatories *(Gloria Bax)*

LEIGH [TQ5646]

☆ *Plough* [Powder Mill Lane/Leigh Rd, off B2027 NW of Tonbridge]: Attractive Tudor building much modified inside, enjoyable food from generous baked potatoes and good ciabattas to more adventurous dishes, well kept Badger Best, K&B, Tanglefoot and Fursty Ferret, prompt friendly service; pleasant walks *(BB, Mark Percy, Lesley Mayoh)*

LITTLEBOURNE [TR2057]

☆ *King William IV* [High St]: Good fresh food from well filled sandwiches to good value Sun lunch and imaginative meals inc fish collected daily from landlord's fishing family, well kept beer, fair choice of wines by the glass, spotless roomy straightforward bar with restaurant area; children welcome, handy for Howletts Zoo *(Bev and Jeff Brown)*

LOOSE [TQ7552]

Chequers [Old Loose Hill]: Neatly kept and pretty 17th-c riverside pub, dark tables and chairs in partly panelled bar with flame-effect fire, friendly attentive service, good freshly made lunches, well kept Flowers, Fullers London Pride, Harveys Best and Shepherd Neame Spitfire, nice atmosphere; small walled garden, good walks *(Comus and Sarah Elliott, Sarah Davis, Rod Lambert, Peter Meister)*

LUDDESDOWN [TQ6667]

☆ *Cock* [Henley Street, N of village – OS Sheet 177 map reference 664672; off A227 in Meopham, or A228 in Cuxton]: Tucked-away

early 18th-c country pub, homely bay-windowed lounge, quarry-tiled bar with pews, woodburner and traditional games inc bar billiards and four different darts boards, log fires, half a dozen well kept changing ales, perhaps four farm ciders, modestly priced generous food (not Sun) from sandwiches up; open all day, no children allowed in, tables in big secure garden, boules *(LYM, Kevin Thorpe)*

MAIDSTONE [TQ7656]

Pilot [Upper Stone St (A229)]: Busy old roadside inn, enjoyable low-priced home-made simple food (not Sun), well kept Harveys Bitter, Mild and in season Old, whisky-water jugs hanging from ceiling, darts and pool; tables outside, boules *(Father Robert Marsh, the Didler, Sarah Davis, Rod Lambert)*

Rifle Volunteers [Wyatt St/Church St]: Unspoilt quiet backstreet pub with good attractively priced home-made food, chatty long-serving landlord, local Goachers Light, Mild and seasonal ales, two gas fires, darts, no machines; tables outside *(the Didler, Kevin Thorpe, Gill and Tony Morriss)*

MARDEN THORN [TQ7643]

☆ *Wild Duck* [Pagehurst Lane; off A229 in Staplehurst or B2079 in Marden]: Neat and welcoming country pub with wide choice of interesting well presented food, not over-priced, in attractive bar and big smart dining room, four well kept ales inc Fullers London Pride and Harveys, interesting wines, obliging service, plenty of atmosphere *(John and Joan Calvert, BB)*

MINSTER [TR3164]

Bell [High St; the one near Ramsgate]: Good range of well kept beers and of reasonably priced enjoyable fresh food *(Professor and Mrs J Fletcher)*

New Inn [Tothill St]: Early 19th-c village local with popular food (not Sun evening or Mon), Greene King IPA and Abbot and a changing guest beer (lots of pump clips), old prints and photographs, separate games area with juke box and pool; garden with aviary, rabbits and play area, open all day Fri/Sat *(Kevin Thorpe)*

NEWENDEN [TQ8327]

White Hart [A268]: Long beamed bar, attractive range of food (no sandwiches Sun lunchtime), fast attentive service, well kept real ales, dining area, small public bar with big stone fireplace; children welcome, small roadside garden *(BB)*

OSPRINGE [TR0060]

Ship: Attractive décor with hops on black beams, bare boards, terracotta walls and naughty antique print over log fire, enjoyable nicely served traditional and mexican food *(Melville Summerfield)*

OTFORD [TQ5359]

☆ *Bull* [High St]: Attractively laid out 15th-c Chef & Brewer, their usual huge food choice from sandwiches and baguettes up all day, four real ales such as Courage Best and Ridleys Old Bob, decent wines, several quietly spacious rooms (one no smoking), log fires in two enormous fireplaces, friendly staff; nice garden

(Tina and David Woods-Taylor, Ken Arthur, B J Harding, Alan M Pring)

PENSHURST [TQ5243]

Leicester Arms [B2178]: Cosily well worn old bars and original country-view dining room up steps, well kept Fullers London Pride, Larkins and Wadworths 6X, new management doing food all day inc good bruschetta sandwiches, bargain steak night Fri, friendly helpful service, back extension eating area; lavatories down steps, but a disabled one in car park opp; children and dogs welcome (pub dog too), tables in pretty back garden *(Sarah Davis, Rod Lambert)*

☆ *Spotted Dog* [Smarts Hill, off B2188 S]: Quaint old tiled pub, half no smoking, with tables out on tiered back terrace (the great views recently hidden in summer by over-luxuriant growth), seats on front terrace, too; neatly kept, heavy low beams, timbers, antique settles and more straightforward furnishings, rugs and tiles, cosy inglenook log fire, attractive moulded panelling, Harveys Best and Larkins Best and Traditional; new licensees doing ambitious bar food, no smoking restaurant; children welcome till 7, open all day summer Thurs-Sun *(John and Judy Saville, Sarah Davis, Rod Lambert, Dr T E Hothersall, LYM, B and M Kendall, Father Robert Marsh)*

PETT BOTTOM [TR1652]

Duck [off B2068 S of Canterbury, via Lower Hardres]: Long bare-boards room with pine panelling and wine racks, good blackboard choice of usual food (all day but not Mon afternoon) from sandwiches and baked potatoes up, well kept Greene King IPA and Abbot with three mainly local guest beers tapped from the cask, decent wines, welcoming attentive service, two log fires; piped music (different in bar and restaurant); children and dogs welcome, tables in sizeable pretty garden, attractive spot, open all day, bedrooms *(Kevin Thorpe, LYM)*

PLAXTOL [TQ6054]

☆ *Golding Hop* [Sheet Hill (½ mile S of Ightham, between A25 and A227)]: Secluded country pub, good for families in summer with suntrap streamside lawn; small and simple inside, with well kept changing ales on handpump or tapped from the cask, local farm ciders (sometimes even their own), limited basic bar food (not Mon evening), woodburner; portable TV for big sports events, bar billiards, game machine; well fenced play area *(the Didler, LYM, Peter Hayward)*

RAMSGATE [TR3865]

Artillery Arms [West Cliff Rd]: Chatty open-plan corner local with Charles Wells Bombardier and four adventurous changing guest beers, two farm ciders, doorstep sandwiches all day, daily papers, straightforward two-level bar with artillery prints, cannons and recently restored stained-glass windows dating from Napoleonic wars; juke box (free on Sun) can be intrusive, fruit machine; children and dogs welcome, open all day *(Kevin Thorpe, Ian Phillips)*

Ramsgate Royal Harbour Brewhouse & Bakery [Harbour Parade]: Belgian-style café-bar brewing two beers of their own (you can look round the back brewery), also six belgian imports on tap, over 100 in bottles, and Biddenden farm ciders; table service, bread, pastries and cakes baked all day, ploughman's and simple snacks and light meals too, open from 9 for tea and coffee (from 10 for alcohol); piped music; children welcome, tables out under cocktail parasols *(Kevin Thorpe, Peter Meister)*

ROCHESTER [TQ7468]

Coopers Arms [St Margarets St]: Jettied Tudor building behind cathedral, cosy and quaint inside, bustling local atmosphere, friendly staff, two comfortable bars, generous cheap wkdy bar lunches, well kept Courage Best and Directors *(Tony Hobden)*

Golden Lion [High St]: Good choice of well kept beers inc two changing guests in nicely decorated Wetherspoons with their usual food, various bargains, friendly staff; children welcome in back no smoking area, picnic-sets in big back garden, open all day *(Richard Lewis)*

Man of Kent [John St]: Small bare-boards backstreet pub with well kept Goachers and other local real ales such as Hop Daemon and Swale, also four local farm ciders, draught and bottled continental beers, various schnapps, friendly landlord, log fire, daily papers; back garden, barbecues and themed beer wknds, open all day *(Richard Lewis)*

ROMNEY STREET [TQ5561]

Fox & Hounds [back rd Eynsford—Heaverham]: Four well kept ales such as Adnams Best and Stonehenge Old Smoky, plentiful reasonably priced straightforward food (not Sun-Weds evenings), long bar with attractive low beams, log fire, traditional games; good-sized garden, cl Mon lunchtime, open all day wknds *(Len Banister)*

SANDWICH [TR3358]

Red Cow [Moat Sole; 100 yds from Guildhall, towards Woodnesborough]: Carefully refurbished open-plan pub with separate dining room, old beams and pictures, five well kept ales such as Boddingtons, Fullers London Pride, and Greene King Abbot and Old Speckled Hen, good value food, good atmosphere, friendly staff, lovely log fire, old local pictures; soft piped music, guide dogs only, picnic-sets outside with garden bar and hanging baskets *(Kevin Thorpe, Vanessa Young)*

SEASALTER [TR0864]

☆ *Sportsman* [Faversham Rd, off B2040]: Busy dining pub in caravan land, just inside the sea wall; three starkly furnished linked rooms (two allowing children), wooden floor, big modern photographs, pine tables, wheelback and basket-weave dining chairs, good if pricy contemporary cooking (not Sun evening or Mon), Shepherd Neame Bitter and Spitfire, well chosen wines, no smoking area; must book to get a table; perhaps outside could do with a tidy-up; open all day Sun *(Mayur Shah, Vanessa Young, Guy Vowles, Paul A Moore, Chris Parsons, LYM)*

SEVENOAKS [TQ5555]

Bucks Head [Godden Green, just E]: Picnic-sets out on front terrace by informal green and duckpond, welcoming service and atmosphere, neatly kept bar and restaurant area, full Shepherd Neame range inc a seasonal beer kept well, log fire, decent food from sandwiches up; children welcome away from bar, no dogs or muddy boots; quiet enclosed back garden with bird fountain and pergola (dogs allowed in front one), attractive country behind Knole *(Eddie Edwards)*

Kings Head [Bessels Green; A25 W, just off A21]: Popular local with warm welcome for drinkers and diners, attentive staff, enjoyable home-made food in restaurant, bar and spacious garden (traffic noise here) *(Charles Gray)*

SHOREHAM [TQ5162]

Crown [High St]: Pleasantly old-fashioned, with good value food, mainstream beers, walkers and dogs welcome; note there's a different Crown & Anchor along the street *(Ken Arthur)*

Kings Arms [Church St]: Pretty and popular, with civilised bar, pleasant service, wide choice of decent usual food from good value ploughman's to roast of the day, plates and brasses, bookable restaurant; picnic-sets outside, quaint unspoilt village on River Darent, good walks *(Gloria Bax, Alan M Pring)*

Olde George [Church St]: Limited bar food and large popular restaurant, well kept beer, pleasant welcome; tables outside *(Gloria Bax)*

Two Brewers [High St]: Busy unpretentious local with good choice of substantial value food, friendly efficient staff, wide choice of beers and ciders; good for walkers, but no dogs *(Ken Arthur, GHC)*

SMARDEN [TQ8743]

☆ *Bell* [from Smarden follow lane between church and Chequers, then left at T-junction; or from A274 take unsignposted turn E 1 mile N of B2077 to Smarden]: Pretty rose-covered 17th-c inn with striking chimneys, dim-lit snug low-beamed little rooms, ancient brick and flagstones or quarry tiles, pews and the like, warm inglenooks; no smoking room, end games area with pool; enjoyable bar food, wide choice of real ales, local cider, country wines, winter mulled wine; picnic-sets in very pleasant mature garden, simple bedrooms *(Peter Meister, Philip Hill, the Didler, LYM)*

SOLE STREET [TR0949]

☆ *Compasses* [note – this is the Sole Street near Wye]: Unspoilt 15th-c country pub, easy-going low-ceilinged rambling bars with bare boards or flagstones, antique or reclaimed furnishings, massive brick bread oven, enamel advertisements, well kept Fullers ESB and London Pride and Swale Indian Summer, Biddenden farm cider, fruit wines, well presented hearty food, cheery landlord; children welcome in extended garden room; bar billiards, piped music; big neatly kept garden with rustic tables, play area and various pets, good walks *(LYM, Peter Meister)*

ST MARGARET'S AT CLIFFE [TR3544]

Smugglers [High St]: Friendly staff in tiny bar, cosy welcoming atmosphere, enjoyable reasonably priced food inc good value baguettes, pizzas and mexican dishes, attractive dining room and conservatory; tables in garden *(John and Elspeth Howell, W Glover, F T Cardiff, Wombat)*

ST NICHOLAS AT WADE [TR2666]

Bell [just off A299]: Thriving olde-worlde 16th-c pub, four beamed rooms, well kept Greene King and Marstons Pedigree, reasonably priced food from baguettes to fresh fish and good Sun lunch in bar and restaurant, friendly staff, open fires *(David and Betty Gittins)*

STALISFIELD GREEN [TQ9552]

Plough [off A252 in Charing]: Well presented food from filled baguettes theme evenings, friendly Italian family, peaceful atmosphere, four real ales, farm cider, big but tasteful side extension; tables in big pleasant garden, attractive village green setting, good view and walks *(Andrew Scarr)*

STONE STREET [TQ5754]

☆ *Padwell Arms* [off A25 E of Sevenoaks, on Seal—Plaxtol by-road; OS Sheet 188 map ref 569551]: Spotlessly kept, well run country pub reopened after early 2003 fire damage, airy new back extension giving much more room for the good choice of mainly straightforward home-cooked food (may stop promptly at 1.45pm), sensible prices and generous helpings, efficient, friendly service, particularly well kept Badger, Hook Norton Old Hooky and lots of changing guest beers, nice wines, two local farm ciders, good coffee, red plush banquette seating against dark half-panelled walls with cream wallpaper above, and little local prints; lots of chatty locals; long tables on front terrace (lovely flowering baskets and window boxes) overlooking orchards, more in nice back garden, plenty of shade, good walks *(Gloria Bax, John Branston, the Didler, Peter and Joan Elbra, GHC, BB)*

TENTERDEN [TQ8833]

☆ *White Lion* [High St]: 16th-c inn, beams and timbers, open fires, books and fishing memorabilia, efficient chatty staff, wide choice of generous popular food, Bass and changing ales such as Shepherd Neame Spitfire and Wadworths 6X, sensibly priced wines, smart back panelled restaurant; dogs welcome, wknd nights bar can get crowded with young people; tables on heated terrace overlooking street, 15 comfortably creaky beamed bedrooms, good breakfast, open all day *(Douglas and Pamela Cooper, Nigel B Thompson, Alan and Paula McCully, E G Parish, Pamela and Merlyn Horswell, John Beeken)*

William Caxton [West Cross; top of High St]: Cosy and friendly 15th-c local, big inglenook log fire, beams and bare boards, wide choice of enjoyable food made by licensees in two-room bar or pleasant dining area, well kept Shepherd Neame beers inc seasonal; children welcome, tables in attractive front area, open all day, bedrooms *(Colin and Janet Roe, Alan and Paula McCully, the Didler)*

THURNHAM [TQ8057]

Black Horse [not far from M20 junction 7; off A249 at Detling]: Popular restauranty dining pub, huge choice of enjoyable food inc lunchtime snack meals, friendly service, small bar where dogs but not children allowed; live music Weds; partly covered back terrace, nice views, by Pilgrims Way, bedrooms *(John and Joyce Snell, Nigel B Thompson, Carl and Jackie Cranmer)*

TROTTISCLIFFE [TQ6460]

George [Taylors Lane]: Well preserved unspoilt pub of character, friendly service, well kept Greene King Old Speckled Hen and Shepherd Neame Spitfire, reasonably priced plentiful food *(Robert Gomme)*

TUNBRIDGE WELLS [TQ5839]

Beau Nash [Mount Ephraim, behind Royal Wells Hotel]: Friendly licensees, good value food *(D Charity)*

Bull [Frant Rd]: Bistro-style scrubbed boards and well spaced tables, three Shepherd Neame beers, good value home-made food from filled baked potatoes and ciabattas up, cheeseboard as well as puddings *(Tony Hobden)*

UNDER RIVER [TQ5551]

White Rock [SE of Sevenoaks, off B245]: Pretty village pub, small comfortable bar with hop-hung beams and back extension, well kept Bass, Fullers London Pride and Harveys, decent pub food, no piped music, dining area; children welcome, picnic-sets on back lawn, handy for Greensand Way (walkers asked to use side door) *(John and Elspeth Howell, Jenny and Brian Seller)*

UPNOR [TQ7570]

Kings Arms [High St]: Old pub with good inexpensive food, friendly service and well kept beer; delightful riverside village nr Upnor Castle, good walks *(Janet Box, Bev and Jeff Brown)*

UPPER UPNOR [TQ7570]

Tudor Rose [off A228 N of Strood; High St]: Olde-world 16th-c pub overlooking Medway, next to castle, dim-lit rambling beamed rooms with old mismatched furniture, lots of hanging jugs etc, two log-burning ranges, old local pictures, well kept Youngs Bitter and Special and four guest beers, friendly locals and staff, simple food (not Sun/Mon evenings); piped music, games room; large enclosed garden with play area, open all day *(Kevin Thorpe)*

UPSTREET [TR2363]

☆ *Grove Ferry* [off A28 towards Preston]: Open-plan refurbishment with modern pictures on warm pastel walls, comfortable chairs and table with papers and magazines in front of central bar, bare-boards dining area behind with candles on tables, shortened choice of enjoyable food all day inc good children's choice, four Shepherd Neame ales, good wines by the glass, pleasant uniformed staff, log fire in big fireplace; quiet piped music; french windows to heated deck with lots of tables overlooking river, play area, bedrooms, handy for Stodmarsh national nature reserve

(Keith and Chris O'Neill, John Beeken, Kevin Thorpe)

WAREHORNE [TQ9832]

☆ *Woolpack* [off B2067 nr Hamstreet]: Big neatly kept 16th-c dining pub with very wide choice of good value food in rambling bar and big candlelit restaurant, popular carvery Weds evening (booking essential), elaborate puddings, well kept Greene King ales, decent wines, welcoming landlord, quick attentive service, huge inglenook, hops on heavy beams, plain games room; picnic-sets out overlooking quiet lane and meadow with lovely big beech trees, lots of flower tubs and little fountain *(I D Greenfield, Paul and Barbara Temple, Lawrence Mitchell, BB)*

WEST WICKHAM [TQ3865]

Coney [Coney Hall Parade, Kingsway]: Smartly refurbished as young-at-heart bar, with attractively priced mainstream food inc Sun roast, pleasant service, good housekeeping; pool tables, TV, piped pop music *(Alan M Pring)*

WHITSTABLE [TR10166]

East Kent [Oxford St]: Unpretentious, with good choice of well kept Shepherd Neame beers, good comfortable bare-boards atmosphere, nice snug, good juke box; garden *(Edmund Lamb)*

Old Neptune [Marine Terr]: Seafront pub, busy, friendly and relaxed, real ales inc Greene King Old Speckled Hen, enjoyable food; dogs and children welcome, tables out on beach *(Keith and Chris O'Neill, Kevin Flack)*

Pearsons [Sea Wall]: What people go for is the plain fresh fish and seafood in the cheerful little upstairs restaurant (with oblique sea view), where smoking is allowed; bar (no view) has nautical décor, decent wines, Greene King IPA, and a huge lobster tank in its lower flagstoned part, but also piped pop music and sports TV, and can be smoky; children welcome in eating areas, open all day wknds, just above shingle beach *(LYM, Keith and Chris O'Neill, Kevin Flack, Gordon Neighbour)*

Royal Naval Reserve [High St]: Friendly, comfortable and cosy, much roomier than it looks from outside, well kept Shepherd Neame, nice house wines, good fresh local fish and other good value home cooking, spotless and attractive upstairs dining room *(John and Glenys Wheeler, David and Betty Gittins)*

WORMSHILL [TQ8757]

Blacksmiths Arms [handy for M20 junction 8]: Attractive old low-beamed pub reopened under new licensees after 2002 closure, small bar area with well worn tiles, big log fire and old prints, two other similar no smoking rooms mainly for eating and candlelit, small choice of decent chip-free food from baguettes up, changing real ales such as Archers, Brakspears and Youngs; no children *(Kevin Thorpe)*

WORTH [TR3356]

Blue Pigeons [The Street]: Victorian village pub, large front bar and separate restaurant, small local room, friendly staff, well kept changing ales such as Adnams Broadside, Marstons Pedigree and Youngs Winter

Warmer, reasonably priced standard food; children welcome, good value bedrooms *(Mike Ridgway, Sarah Miles)*

☆ *St Crispin* [signed off A258 S of Sandwich]: Stripped brickwork, bare boards, low beams, pews and central log fire, real paraffin lamps, good value generous home-made food from good baguettes to some imaginative dishes, cheerful service, well kept changing ales, some tapped from the cask, such as Gales HSB, Greene King Old Speckled Hen, Marstons Pedigree, Shepherd Neame and Charles Wells Bombardier, belgian beers, local farm cider, evening restaurant; bedrooms (inc some chalet-style), charming big garden with barbecue,

lovely village position *(Vanessa Young, David and Ruth Shillitoe)*

WYE [TR0546]

☆ *New Flying Horse* [Upper Bridge St]: Comfortably modernised 17th-c beamed inn, pleasantly light, with two or three rooms, wide choice of good interesting fresh bar food (a regular stop for French long-distance drivers), friendly considerate service, well kept Shepherd Neame ales, decent pots of tea, inglenook log fires, bric-a-brac inc carousel horse, no smoking dining area; attractive good-sized garden with boules, pleasant bedrooms, good breakfast *(Tina and David Woods-Taylor, Jan and Alan Summers, Jayne Robinson)*

Bedroom prices normally include full english breakfast, VAT and any inclusive service charge that we know of. Prices before the '/' are for single rooms, after for two people in double or twin (B includes a private bath, S a private shower). If there is no '/', the prices are only for twin or double rooms (as far as we know there are no singles).

Lancashire
(with Greater Manchester
and Merseyside)

The great strength of pubs here is their no-nonsense approach to value. There is plenty of bargain pub food, particularly in the big cities, and drinks prices are far lower than the national average. No doubt a contributing factor is the keen competition between flourishing rival local brewers. The main regional brewers are Robinsons and Thwaites, with Holts, Hydes and Lees particularly prominent around Manchester. Many smaller breweries are active in the area: ones that in-the-know local readers tend to look out for include Bank Top, Cains, Moorhouses and Phoenix. We also found some real bargains at pubs brewing their own beers here. And all this flourishing competition means that the big national brews have to come down in price too, and often offer great value here. As far as individual pubs are concerned, ones to note particularly this year are the very foody Bay Horse at Bay Horse, the cheerful Cartford by the river at Little Eccleston (well liked food, good beers including its own brew), the stunning Philharmonic in Liverpool, the Derby Arms near Longridge (an enjoyable all-rounder), the Spread Eagle at Sawley (we enjoyed the food at this civilised and nicely set dining pub so much that this new entry wins the title of Lancashire Dining Pub of the Year), the cheerful Lunesdale Arms up at Tunstall (enjoyable food using local produce), the exceptionally well run Inn at Whitewell (great food, wines and atmosphere, and a lovely place to stay), and the bustling New Inn at Yealand Conyers (enjoyable food all day). Some establishments in the Lucky Dip section at the end of the chapter deserve a special mention: the Plough at Eaves near Broughton, North Euston in Fleetwood, Stags Head at Goosnargh, Aspinall Arms at Great Mitton, Hest Bank Hotel, Irby Mill at Irby, Ship at Lathom, White Hart at Lydgate, Peveril of the Peak in Manchester and Red Lion at Mawdesley.

BARNSTON SJ2783 Map 7
Fox & Hounds ◗

3 miles from M53 junction 3: A552 towards Woodchurch, then left on A551

The half a dozen well kept real ales on handpump – not to mention over 50 whiskies – are quite a draw here: Bass, Theakstons Best and Old Peculier, Websters Yorkshire, and a couple of guest beers from breweries like Cottage, Hanby or Weetwood. Tucked away opposite the serving counter is a charming old quarry-tiled corner with an antique kitchen range, copper kettles, built-in pine kitchen cupboards, and lots of earthenware or enamelled food bins. With its own entrance at the other end of the pub, a small quarry-tiled locals' bar is worth a peek for its highly traditional layout – not to mention a collection of hundreds of metal ashtrays on its delft shelf; beside it is a snug where children are allowed. Enjoyable lunchtime bar food includes home-made soup (£2.45), open sandwiches (from £2.75), filled baked potatoes (from £3.50), quiche (£4.75), ploughman's (£5.25) and changing specials such as steak and kidney pie (£5.75), chicken cooked in cider and apples (£5.95), and lamb shank (£6.50); service is efficient and well groomed. The main part of the roomy bay-windowed lounge bar has red plush button-back built-in banquettes and plush-cushioned captain's chairs around the solid tables on its green turkey carpet, and plenty of old local prints on its cream walls below a delft shelf of china, with a collection of police and other headgear. Darts, TV, and dominoes. There are some picnic-sets under cocktail parasols out in the yard behind, below a dairy farm. More reports please. *(Recommended by Maurice and Gill McMahon)*

Free house ~ Licensee Ralph Leech ~ Real ale ~ Bar food (lunchtime) ~ Restaurant ~ (0151) 6487685 ~ Children in family area ~ Dogs allowed in bar ~ Open 11-11; 12-10.30 Sun

BAY HORSE SD4952 Map 7
Bay Horse ⑪

1¼ miles from M6 junction 33: A6 southwards, then off on left

To be sure of a table, you must get to this quietly set, upmarket dining pub promptly – or book a table in advance. Beamed and comfortable throughout, it has a warm and cosy atmosphere in its attractively decorated red-walled bar, with a good log fire, cushioned wall banquettes in bays, a friendly cat, gentle lighting including table lamps on window sills, and well kept Boddingtons, Moorhouses Pendle Witches Brew and Thwaites Lancaster Bomber on handpump; lots of fruit wines and decent fairly priced wine list. There are usually fresh flowers on the counter, and may be piped music (anything from pop to classical) or perhaps cricket or racing on TV. The main emphasis though is on the food, with a series of small no smoking dining areas rambling around – the feel of a civilised country restaurant, with a gentle purple décor, another log fire, candle-flame-effect lights and nice tables, including one or two good-sized ones having an intimate corner to themselves. With a good blackboard choice including some unusual sandwiches, starters or light dishes might include soup (£2.95), pressed terrine of chicken, stilton and italian ham with chutney (£5.25), potted morecambe bay shrimps (£5.75), salad of seared scallops, smoked salmon, and fresh coriander with a sweet chilli dressing (£7.95), roast aubergine with couscous and goats cheese with balsamic syrup or lamb, rosemary and garlic sausages with mint mash (£9.25), braised shank of lamb, grain mustard mash, ale and thyme sauce, slow cooked goosnargh duck, potato purée and elderberry wine and honey reduction or roast chicken breast wrapped in prosciutto with potato purée and creamy wholegrain mustard sauce (all £11.95), bass with asparagus, blush tomato and vanilla dressing (£15.95), and puddings such as chocolate marquise with Baileys ice cream, lemon tart with lemon fruit ice or sticky toffee pudding (£4.50); good teas and coffee. There are tables out in the garden behind (peaceful, though the railway is not far off). *(Recommended by Malcolm Taylor, Karen Eliot, Mrs P J Carroll, Margaret Dickinson, Revd D Glover, Deb and John Arthur, Roy Morrison, Steve Whalley)*

Mitchells ~ Tenant Craig Wilkinson ~ Real ale ~ Bar food (not Sun evening, not Mon) ~ Restaurant ~ (01524) 791204 ~ Children in restaurant ~ Open 12-3, 6.30-11; 12-5, 8.30-10.30 Sun; closed Mon; closed bank hol Mon evening (open lunchtime) and Tues following bank hol

BELMONT SD6716 Map 7
Black Dog 🛏

A675

The dining room, games room, kitchen and lavatories here have all been newly refurbished, but the cosy and atmospheric rooms around the bar remain largely untouched except for a new plush blue banquette in the bay opposite the bar. These original cheery and traditional small rooms are packed with antiques and bric-a-brac, from railwaymen's lamps, bedpans and chamber-pots to landscape paintings. There are also service bells for the sturdy built-in curved seats, rush-seated mahogany chairs, and coal fires. Pool, fruit machine and piped music. Very good value and well kept Holts Bitter and Mild on handpump, and generous helpings of reliably good straightforward bar food such as home-made soup (£1.30), sandwiches (from £2.30, baguettes from £2.70), tasty local black pudding (£3), ploughman's (from £4.40), battered cod (£4.80), barbecued spare ribs (£4.90), three cheese and broccoli pasta bake (£4.95), chicken rogan josh (£5.30), and daily specials like breaded garlic mushrooms (£3.75), steak and kidney pie, liver and onion or moussaka (£5.50), cumberland sausage (£5.95), and peppered steak (£7.50); they don't take bookings, so get there early for a table as it does tend to fill up quickly. A small orchestra plays viennese music on New Year's Day at lunchtime, and performs on several other evenings throughout the year. Two long benches on the sheltered sunny side of the pub give delightful views of the moors above the nearby trees and houses. A track leads from the village up Winter Hill and (from the lane to Rivington) on to Anglezarke Moor, and there are paths from the dam of the nearby Belmont Reservoir; the bedrooms are homely and reasonably priced. *(Recommended by MLR, Michael and Marion Buchanan, Pat and Tony Martin, Jim Abbott, Gordon Tong, Ian Phillips, Collin and Julie Taylor, P Abbott, Steve Whalley)*

Holts ~ Tenant Heino Chrobok ~ Real ale ~ Bar food (12-2, 6-8(not Mon or Tues evening); 12-6 Sun and bank hol) ~ (01204) 811218 ~ Children in family room ~ Open 12-11(10.30 Sun) ~ Bedrooms: £32.50S/£42.50S

BLACKSTONE EDGE SD9716 Map 7
White House £
A58 Ripponden—Littleborough, just W of B6138

High up on the bleak and moody moors with panoramic views stretching for miles into the distance is this imposing 17th-c pub. It's a cosy haven for walkers (the Pennine Way crosses the road outside), and the bustling main bar has a cheery atmosphere, a turkey carpet in front of a blazing coal fire, and a large-scale map of the area. The snug Pennine Room opens off here, with brightly coloured antimacassars on its small soft settees; there's also a dining extension. A spacious room on the left has comfortable seating, and a big horseshoe window has impressive moorland views. The enjoyably unpretentious bar food, served in huge helpings (prices have not changed for a couple of years now), includes good soup (£2), sandwiches (from £3), cumberland sausage with egg, steak and kidney pie or vegetable quiche (£4.75), roast chicken breast (£5), chilli con carne, beef curry or lasagne (£5.50), steaks (from £7.50), puddings such as home-made apple pie and sticky toffee pudding (from £2) and daily specials. Service is prompt and friendly. Well kept real ales on handpump include Black Sheep Special, Theakstons Best and one or two guests such as Exmoor Gold and Moorhouses Pendle Witches Brew, also farm cider and malt whiskies; fruit machine. Muddy boots can be left in the porch. *(Recommended by Ian Phillips, Jo and Iain MacGregor, Bob Broadhurst, Michael and Marion Buchanan, Guy Vowles)*

Free house ~ Licensee Neville Marney ~ Real ale ~ Bar food ~ (01706) 378456 ~ Children welcome ~ Open 12-3, 6.30-11; 12-11 Sun

CHIPPING SD6243 Map 7
Dog & Partridge ♀
Hesketh Lane; crossroads Chipping—Longridge with Inglewhite—Clitheroe

Although parts of this neatly kept dining pub date back to 1515, the pub has been much modernised and extended since, with the eating space now spreading over into a nearby stable. The comfortable main lounge has small armchairs around fairly close-set low wood-effect tables on a blue patterned carpet, brown-painted beams, a good winter log fire, and multicoloured lanterns. Served by friendly and well trained staff, the enjoyable lunchtime bar food (not Sunday) includes home-made soup (£3.20), duck and orange pâté (£4.50), sandwiches (from £4.50), home-made steak and kidney pie or roast chicken with stuffing (£8.30), roast duckling with apple sauce and stuffing (£11.75) and grilled sirloin steak with mushrooms (£13), as well as around four vegetarian dishes such as curried nut roast with spicy tomato chutney or mushroom stroganoff (£8.50), daily specials, and puddings such as home-made fruit pie and raspberry shortcake (£3.60). As well as a decent wine list, they have well kept Tetleys Bitter and Mild with a weekly changing guest such as Black Sheep Bitter on handpump, and a good range of malt whiskies. Smart casual dress is preferred in the restaurant – open evenings and Sunday lunchtime; dining areas are no smoking, and you may need to book. More reports please. *(Recommended by Mike Schofield, Norma and Noel Thomas, Margaret Dickinson)*

Free house ~ Licensee Peter Barr ~ Real ale ~ Bar food (12-1.45) ~ Restaurant (7-9 Mon-Sat; 11.45-8.30 Sun) ~ (01995) 61201 ~ Children welcome ~ Open 11.45-3, 6.45(6 Sat)-11; 11.45-10.30 Sun

DOWNHAM SD7844 Map 7
Assheton Arms

From A59 NE of Clitheroe turn off into Chatburn (signposted); in Chatburn follow Downham signpost

This pleasant dining pub is charmingly set in a sloping stone-built village, and window seats and picnic-sets outside look across to a church. Inside, a massive stone fireplace helps divide the separate areas of the rambling beamed bar which has plush-cushioned winged settles around attractive grainy oak tables, some cushioned window seats, and two grenadier busts on the mantelpiece; part of the bar is no smoking. Quite a choice of bar food includes home-made ham and vegetable broth (£3.25), sandwiches (from £3.95, not Saturday evening or Sunday lunchtime), ploughman's or smooth chicken liver pâté (£4.95), morecambe bay shrimps (£5.25), vegetarian chilli (£6.95), home-made steak and kidney pie (£7.50), venison, bacon and cranberry casserole (£8.50), battered haddock (£9.25), steaks (from £13.50), daily specials, and puddings (£3.95). Marstons Pedigree, and 18 wines by the glass; piped music. The pub is featured as the Signalman's Arms in the BBC drama series *Born and Bred*. More reports please. *(Recommended by Pierre and Pat Richterich, Bob Broadhurst, Norma and Noel Thomas, Mike Schofield, Keith Berrett)*

Enterprise ~ Lease David Busby ~ Real ale ~ Bar food (12-2, 7-10) ~ (01200) 441227 ~ Children welcome ~ Dogs welcome ~ Open 12-3, 7-11; 12-10.30 Sun; 12-3, 7-10.30 in winter; closed first week Jan

GOOSNARGH SD5839 Map 7
Horns ♀ 🛏

Pub signed from village, about 2 miles towards Chipping below Beacon Fell

Older than its brightly mock-Tudor façade suggests, this civilised hotel is attractively set in the foothills of the Pennines. The neatly kept snug rooms have colourful flower displays and winter log fires, and beyond the lobby, the pleasant front bar opens into attractively decorated middle rooms; the dining rooms are no smoking. The atmosphere is relaxing, and the young staff are very welcoming and helpful; piped music. The emphasis here is on the enjoyable homely food which includes home-made beef and vegetable soup (£3.50), well presented sandwiches (from £3.50; the pheasant are good), ploughman's (£4.95), home-made steak and kidney pie (£7.95), grilled gammon and egg (£8.50), roast local pheasant (£8.75), and sirloin steak with mushrooms (£10.95), with home-made puddings like fruit pies or sticky toffee pudding (£3.95), and daily specials, all nicely served with freshly cooked, piping hot chips. They don't keep real ales, but there's an extensive wine list with quite a few by the glass, and a fine choice of malt whiskies. *(Recommended by DJH, Gerald Wilkinson, W W Burke, Neville Kenyon)*

Free house ~ Licensee Mark Woods ~ Bar food (not Mon lunchtime) ~ Restaurant ~ (01772) 865230 ~ Children welcome ~ Open 11.30-3, 6-11; 11-11 Sat; 12-3, 6.30-10.30 Sun; closed Mon lunchtime (except bank hols) ~ Bedrooms: £55B/£75B

LITTLE ECCLESTON SD4139 Map 7
Cartford 🍺 🛏

Cartford Lane, off A586 Garstang—Blackpool, by toll bridge

A good mix of customers from real ale enthusiasts to cyclists and walkers enjoy this friendly, well run pub for both its popular food and fine choice of up to seven very well kept real ales on handpump. These include a couple from Hart (their own good microbrewery behind the pub, with brewery tours by arrangement), Boddingtons, Fullers London Pride and up to four changing ales from interesting brewers such as Goose Eye, Moorhouses, Phoenix and Rooster; also decent house wines and several malt whiskies. The attractive rambling interior has oak beams, dried flowers, a lovely log fire and an unusual layout on four different levels, with pleasantly uncoordinated cosy seating areas. Two levels are largely set for dining (the upstairs part is no smoking). Service is friendly and obliging, and the atmosphere is nicely relaxed. Reasonably priced enjoyable food includes soup (£2.20), sandwiches (from £2.95), evening pizzas (from £5, you can take them away), home-made steak and mushroom pie (£4.95), lemon sole (£5.90), curries (from £6.35) and 10oz sirloin steak (£8.95); the blackboard adds specials such as cod and prawn crumble (£5.95), peppered pork steak or lamb dijonnaise (£6.95), and changing puddings (from £2.75); efficient hard-working staff. They've pool, darts, fruit machine, TV and piped music. It's peacefully placed by a toll bridge over the River Wyre (tidal here), and they have fishing rights along 1½ miles; there are tables out in a garden (not by the water), with a play area. *(Recommended by Steve Whalley, David Green, Dr Paull Khan, Andy and Jill Kassube, MLR, Richard Lewis, Harry Gleave, Rob and Catherine Dunster, Keith and Chris O'Neill, Ian and Nita Cooper)*

Own brew ~ Licensee Andrew Mellodew ~ Real ale ~ Bar food (12-9 Sun) ~ Restaurant ~ (01995) 670166 ~ Children in eating area of bar ~ Dogs welcome ~ Open 12-3, 6.30-11; 12-10.30 Sun ~ Bedrooms: £36.95B/£48.95B

LIVERPOOL SJ4395 Map 7
Baltic Fleet 🍺

Wapping

This basic place is a fairly unusual triangular end-of-terrace building with nice big arched windows and a bright green, burgundy and white painted exterior. An abundance of interior woodwork and stout mahogany board floors adds to its nautical feel, as do the interesting old Mersey shipping prints. There's also a good mix of old school furniture and dark wood tables; piped music. Their own-brewed and reasonably priced Wapping beers include Wapping Bitter, Baltic Extra, Summer Ale, and Stout, and guests such as Cambrinus Deliverance or Moorhouses Black Cat, all on handpump, served through a sparkler. At lunchtime they do just soup, sandwiches and toasties made with various types of bread (from £2.95), while in the evening there might be mushroom, goats cheese and spinach soup (£2.95), chicken liver, smoked bacon and thyme pâté (£3.25), pork sausages on leek mash with onion gravy (£6.25), vegetarian stuffed filo pastry parcels with a rich sun-dried tomato, red onion and basil sauce (£6.95), fresh tuna fishcakes with pesto crème fraîche (£7.95), slow cooked lamb shank on minted mash (£9.95), and puddings such as home-made chocolate and orange cheesecake (£2.95); best to book for their popular Sunday roast: roast lamb studded with apricots, garlic and rosemary, roast welsh black beef with yorkshire pudding or parmesan pastry tartlets filled with mushrooms, red onions and brie with a port and redcurrant sauce (all from £6.95). The small back room is no smoking. More reports please. *(Recommended by the Didler, David Field, Mike Pugh, John Dwane)*

Own brew ~ Licensees Simon Holt and Julie Broome ~ Real ale ~ Bar food (12-2.30(4 Sun), 6-8.30(9.30 Fri/Sat); no food Sun or Mon evenings) ~ Restaurant ~ (0151) 709 3116 ~ Children in eating area of bar and restaurant ~ Dogs allowed in bar ~ Open 12(11.30 Sat)-11; 12-10.30 Sun

Philharmonic Dining Rooms ★

36 Hope Street; corner of Hardman Street

A must for any visitor to Liverpool, this fantastic place is a late Victorian gin palace of stunning opulence, from its smart marble façade to the elegant original fittings. The heart of the building is a mosaic-faced serving counter, from which heavily carved and polished mahogany partitions radiate under the intricate plasterwork high ceiling. The echoing main hall is decorated with stained glass including contemporary portraits of Boer War heroes such as Baden-Powell and Lord Roberts, rich panelling, a huge mosaic floor, and copper panels of musicians in an alcove above the fireplace. More stained glass in one of the little lounges declares 'Music is the universal language of mankind', and backs this up with illustrations of musical instruments; there are two plushly comfortable sitting rooms. The famous gents' (ladies are allowed a look if they ask first) are original 1890s Adamant: all pink marble and glinting mosaics. Throughout the pub there's a nice blend of customers, with theatre-goers, students, locals and tourists making up the contented bustle. Real ales on handpump could include well kept Bass, Cains Traditional, and Tetleys, and a couple of guests such as Fullers London Pride, Greene King Old Speckled Hen, and Orkney Dark Island; fruit machine, TV and piped music; the grand lounge is a smart restaurant. Straightforward bar food from a short menu includes soup (£2.75), sandwiches (from £3.95, hot sandwiches from £4.50), ploughman's, leek and gruyère parcel or sausage and mash (£5.50), steak pie or fish and chips (£5.75) and barbecue chicken (£5.95); puddings (£2.50); two areas are no smoking. No children inside. *(Recommended by Patrick Hancock, R T and J C Moggridge, the Didler, David Field, John Dwane, Joe Green, MLR)*

Mitchells & Butlers ~ Manager Marie-Louise Wong ~ Real ale ~ Bar food (12-3 Mon-Sat, 12-5.30 Sun; in winter, 12-6 Mon-Fri, 12-3 Sat/Sun) ~ Restaurant ~ (0151) 707 2837 ~ Open 12-11; 12-10.30 Sun; closed bank hols

LONGRIDGE SD6039 Map 7
Derby Arms 🍴 ♍

Chipping Road, Thornley; 1½ miles N of Longridge on back road to Chipping

The same family have run this warmly welcoming old stone-built country pub for over a century – the current licensee's great-grandmother was married from here in 1898, and readers very much enjoy their visits. There's something of a hunting and fishing theme in the main bar, with old photographs commemorating notable catches, some nicely mounted bait above the comfortable red plush seats, and a stuffed pheasant that seems to be flying in through the wall. To the right is a smaller room with sporting trophies and mementoes, and a regimental tie collection, while off to the left are a couple of no smoking dining areas. Using fresh local ingredients, the well liked bar food might include sandwiches (from £2.95), soup (£3.30), leek and mushroom crumble (£7.95), tasty steak and kidney pudding (£8.95), steaks (from £9.25), roast lamb shank with redcurrant gravy (£11.95), daily specials, and puddings such as hot chocolate fudge cake (£3.50); potatoes and vegetables come in separate dishes. Along with a good range of wines including several half-bottles and a dozen or so by the glass (they're particularly strong on south african), they serve well kept Marstons Pedigree and Tetleys on handpump. The gents' has dozens of riddles on the wall; you can buy a sheet of them in the bar (the money goes to charity). A few tables out in front, and another two behind the car park enjoy fine views across to the Forest of Bowland. *(Recommended by Kevin and Barbara Wilkinson, Margaret Dickinson, Diane Manoughian, Norma and Noel Thomas, Ann and Bob Westbrook, Maurice and Gill McMahon)*

Inn Partnership (Pubmaster) ~ Lease Mrs G M Walme ~ Real ale ~ Bar food ~ Restaurant ~ (01772) 782623 ~ Children in eating area of bar and restaurant ~ Open 12-3, 6-11.30; 12-4, 5-12 Sat; 12-11 Sun

Pubs with outstanding views are listed at the back of the book.

LYTHAM SD3627 Map 7
Taps 🍺 £

A584 S of Blackpool; Henry Street – in centre, one street in from West Beach

A view-in cellar lets you admire the choice of around eight real ales on offer in this bustling pub, and alongside Boddingtons, the weekly changing guests on handpump might include Barnsley IPA, Kelham Island Pale Rider, Taps (brewed for the pub by Titanic), Titanic Mild and Stout, and York Stonewall and Yorkshire Terrier; there are seat belts on the bar and headrests in the gents' to help keep you out of harm's way if you have one too many. They also usually serve some country wines and a farm cider. The Victorian-style bare-boarded bar has a really sociable unassuming feel, with plenty of stained-glass decoration in the windows, depictions of fish and gulls reflecting the pub's proximity to the beach, captain's chairs in bays around the sides, open fires, and a coal-effect gas fire between two built-in bookcases at one end; you are lucky if you get a seat. There's also an expanding collection of rugby memorabilia with old photographs and portraits of rugby stars on the walls; shove-ha'penny, dominoes and a fruit machine. Quickly served by attentive, uniformed staff, the cheap, straightforward bar food includes sandwiches (from £2.25; hot roast beef £3.95), filled baked potatoes or burgers (from £2.50), and curry (£3.95). There are a few seats outside. Parking is difficult near the pub so it's probably best to park at the West Beach car park on the seafront (free on Sunday), and walk. *(Recommended by Margaret Dickinson, Steve Whalley, Maggie and Tony Harwood, J F M and M West, Dr and Mrs A K Clarke)*

Laurel Pub Company ~ Manager Ian Rigg ~ Real ale ~ Bar food (lunchtime only, not Sun) ~ (01253) 736226 ~ Children in eating area of bar ~ Open 11-11; 12-10.30 Sun

MANCHESTER SJ7796 Map 7
Britons Protection ♀ £

Great Bridgewater Street, corner of Lower Mosley Street

After a concert at Bridgewater Hall, this deservedly popular pub is just the place to head for (and it is well known to many orchestral players). It's really well run, and the licensees, who have been here for years themselves, employ a proper career barlady; service is friendly and accommodating, and there's a sociable welcoming atmosphere. The rather plush little front bar has a fine chequered tile floor, some glossy brown and russet wall tiles, solid woodwork and elaborate plastering. A tiled passage lined with battle murals leads to two inner lounges, one served by hatch, with attractive brass and etched glass wall lamps, a mirror above the coal-effect gas fire in the simple art nouveau fireplace, and again good solidly comfortable furnishings. As something of a tribute to Manchester's notorious climate, the massive bar counter has a pair of heating pipes as its footrail. As well as 205 malt whiskies, and an interesting range of spirits, they serve very well kept Jennings, Robinsons and Tetleys and a regularly changing guest on handpump; they also have good wines. Generous helpings of reasonably priced tasty bar food include home-made soup (£1.85), sandwiches (from £2), ploughman's (£4), ham and egg (£4.50, leek and mushroom crumble (£4.75), unusual pies such as wild boar, turkey, hare and pigeon in red wine and brandy sauce (£4.95), and home-made daily specials (from £3.95); piped music. Although it's busy at lunchtime, it's usually quiet and relaxed in the evenings. There are tables out on the terrace behind, and it's handy for the GMEX centre. *(Recommended by Doug Christian, Ken Richards, Stephen and Jean Curtis, Mr and Mrs J G Smith, Beryl Hearman, John Hulme, Stephen, Julie and Hayley Brown, GLD, P G Plumridge, the Didler, P Abbott, Nick Holding, B and M Kendall, Patrick Hancock, JES, Stephen Buckley)*

Punch ~ Lease Peter Barnett ~ Real ale ~ Bar food (11-2.30 only) ~ Restaurant ~ (0161) 236 5895 ~ Children welcome ~ Live entertainment first Tues of month and Weds evening ~ Open 11-11; 12-10.30 Sun

---

Prices of main dishes usually include vegetables or a side salad.

Dukes 92 £

Castle Street, below the bottom end of Deansgate

The setting here is great – this tastefully converted cavernous former stables is near locks and railway arches in the rejuvenated heart of old industrial Manchester, with tables out by the canal basin which opens into the bottom lock of the Rochdale Canal. Inside, black wrought-iron work contrasts boldly with whitewashed bare plaster walls, the handsome bar is granite-topped, and an elegant spiral staircase leads to a no smoking upper room and balcony. Down in the main room the fine mix of furnishings is mainly rather Edwardian in mood, with one particularly massive table, elegantly comfortable chaises-longues and deep armchairs. You can choose from an excellent range of over three dozen cheeses and several pâtés with a generous helping of granary bread (£4.20), and other good value bar food includes filled baked potatoes (from £2.50), soup (£2.80), sandwiches (from £3.75, toasties from £2.75), tagliatelle and roasted vegetables or ham and leek pasta bake (£4.50), salmon and cod fishcakes, cajun chicken or moussaka (£5.50), mezze (£8.95) and oriental platter (£9.95). Well kept Boddingtons and a guest such as Timothy Taylors Landlord on handpump, with the belgian wheat beer Hoegaarden on tap; decent wines and a wide choice of malt whiskies; piped jazz. There's a function room theatre with temporary exhibitions of local artwork. More reports please. *(Recommended by Andrew York, Mike and Linda Hudson, Stephen, Julie and Hayley Brown, P Abbott)*

Free house ~ Licensee James Ramsbottom ~ Real ale ~ Bar food (12-3, 5-8 Mon-Thurs; 12-6 Fri-Sun) ~ (0161) 839 8646 ~ Children welcome ~ Dogs welcome ~ Live bands bank hol weekends ~ Open 11.30-11(12 Fri/Sat); 12-10.30 Sun

Lass o' Gowrie ◧ £

36 Charles Street; off Oxford Street at BBC

A new licensee has taken over this lively and traditional Victorian pub; it is now owned by the Laurel Pub Company and no longer brews its own ales. But they do keep Black Sheep, Boddingtons, Greene King Old Speckled Hen, a beer named after the pub brewed for them by Titanic, and guests on handpump. Behind its richly tiled arched brown façade, the simple big-windowed long bar has gas lighting, bare floorboards, lots of stripped brickwork, and hop pockets draped from the ceiling. At weekends during term time, it's full of cheery university students, with the pavement outside pressed into service for extra room; piped pop music adds to the youthful buzz. At quieter times during the day, the music might be switched off to suit an older crowd of chatty locals. Although it might take some while to get served at busy periods, the staff are friendly and cheerfully obliging. Straightforward bar food includes filled baguettes (from £2.25), filled baked potatoes (£2.45), double egg, chips and beans (£3.25), sausage and mash (£3.45), battered cod (£3.95), steak and kidney pudding (£4.25), and rump steak (£4.95). The snug is no smoking; fruit machine and satellite TV. More reports please. *(Recommended by Sue Holland, Dave Webster, Catherine Pitt, Paul Hopton, Patrick Hancock, Richard Lewis, B and M Kendall, Ian Phillips)*

Laurel Pub Company ~ Manager Ellie Owen ~ Real ale ~ Bar food (12-5 Mon-Fri; 12-3 Sat and Sun) ~ (0161) 273 6932 ~ Children in eating area of bar ~ Open 11-11; 12-10.30 Sun

Marble Arch ◧ £

73 Rochdale Road (A664), Ancoats; corner of Gould Street, just E of Victoria Station

Though the striking décor inside this Victorian pub is a major draw in its own right, the fine choice of own-brew beers has long been an impressive feature. From windows at the back, you can look over the brewery (tours by arrangement) where they produce the distinctive hoppy Cloudy Marble, Lagonda IPA, Manchester Bitter, N/4, Uncut Amber and Marble Ginger Ale; guests could be Hop Back Druids Draft, Oakham Mompessons Gold, Ossett Mistral, Poachers Jocks

Trap, and Stonehenge Danish Dynamite. There's a magnificently restored lightly barrel-vaulted high ceiling, and extensive marble and tiling – the frieze advertising various spirits, and the chimneybreast above the carved wooden mantelpiece, particularly stand out. The pub is furnished with leather sofas, cushioned settles and deep armchairs, and all the walls are stripped back to the glazed brick; bar billiards, fruit machine, pinball and a juke box. The sloping mosaic floor in the bar can be a bit disconcerting after a few pints. Generous sandwiches have interesting fillings such as hot chicken with peanut and ginger sauce or roasted leek and wild mushroom with mint and garlic (£3.75), while other very reasonably priced bar food includes soup (£2.50), and a few daily specials such as breakfast in bread (£4.25), tagliatelle carbonara (£4.50), and barbecued chicken breast (£4.75); friendly staff. The Laurel and Hardy Preservation Society meet here on the third Wednesday of the month and show old films. There's a little garden. *(Recommended by the Didler, Catherine Pitt, Richard Lewis, Peter F Marshall)*

Own brew ~ Licensee Christine Baldwin ~ Real ale ~ Bar food (11.30-2.30, 4.30-8; Sat and Sun 12-3) ~ No credit cards ~ (0161) 832 5914 ~ Children in eating area of bar until 6 ~ Open 11.30-11; 12-11(10.30 Sun) Sat

MELLOR SJ9888 Map 7
Oddfellows Arms 🍽

Heading out of Marple on the A626 towards Glossop, Mellor is the next road after the B6102, signposted off on the right at Marple Bridge; keep on for nearly 2 miles up Longhurst Lane and into Moor End Road

Most customers come to this civilised old pub to enjoy the good food, and it's best to get here early to be sure of a table – and to secure a parking space which can be tricky when they are busy. Alongside specials such as fried black pudding with sweet chilli sauce (£3.95), malaysian chicken or poached smoked haddock with noodles and roasted peppers (£8.95), rib-eye steak with a roquefort cream and puy lentils cooked in red wine (£11.95), and an authentic and popular catalan fish stew (£14.95), the popular bar food might include soup (£2.50), sandwiches (from £4.25; spicy chicken tikka tortilla £4.45), creamy garlic mushrooms (£4.45), crab au gratin (£4.95), bangers with spring onion mash and onion gravy (£7.25), artichoke and cheery tomato pasta with a mustard cream sauce (£7.45), glazed lamb cutlets in a mint and mango marinade (£10.45), thai duck with lychees (£10.95), steaks (from £10.95), and puddings like rich chocolate torte, sticky toffee pudding with toffee sauce or summer pudding (£3.75). The pleasant low-ceilinged flagstoned bar has nice open fires and a cosy, chatty atmosphere; no piped music or games. Well kept Adnams Best, Marstons Best and Pedigree and a weekly changing guest from Brakspears, Cottage or Phoenix on handpump, served with or without a sparkler; several wines by the glass. There's a small no smoking restaurant upstairs, and a few tables out by the road. *(Recommended by Bob and Lisa Cantrell, Mike and Linda Hudson, P Abbott, Hilary Forrest, David Hoult, John Hulme, Brenda and Stuart Naylor)*

Free house ~ Licensee Robert Cloughley ~ Real ale ~ Bar food (12-2.30, 6.30-9.30; not Sun evening or Mon) ~ Restaurant ~ (0161) 449 7826 ~ Children in eating area of bar and restaurant ~ Dogs allowed in bar ~ Open 12-3, 5.30-11(7-10.30 Sun); closed Mon

NEWTON SD6950 Map 7
Parkers Arms

B6478 7 miles N of Clitheroe

From the big front garden of this pretty cream and green painted pub, there are lovely unspoilt views down over the River Hodder and its valley; they keep lots of pets – pygmy goats, rabbits, guinea pigs, hens, pheasants, parrots, two playful black labradors and a turkey. Inside, it's comfortable and well run, with a cheerful atmosphere and welcoming staff, and red plush button-back banquettes, a mix of chairs and tables, stuffed animals, prints, and an open fire. Beyond an arch is a similar area with sensibly placed darts, a log fire, cribbage, dominoes, fruit machine, and TV. Well kept Black Sheep, Boddingtons, and Flowers IPA on handpump, with a good range of malt whiskies and around 55 wines (nine by the glass). Enjoyable bar food includes sandwiches, cumberland sausage (£5.95), steak and kidney in ale pie (£6.50), ploughman's (£6.75), roast lamb or beef or vegetable stuffed pancake (£6.95), honey-roast duck (£10.95), and daily specials such as home-made pâté (£3.95), stilton mushrooms (£4.50), chilli and garlic crayfish (£5.50), lambs liver and onions (£7.95), exotic smoked fish pie (£8.50), beef stroganoff or chicken with black pudding and mustard sauce (£9.95), ostrich with butter, toffee and onion (£15.50), and king and queen scallops in a cream, smoked bacon and mushroom sauce (£15.95); the charming restaurant is no smoking. *(Recommended by Melanie Lawrenson, Steve Whalley, Norma and Noel Thomas, W W Burke, Mike Turner, Bernard Stradling, Margaret Dickinson)*

Enterprise ~ Lease Barbara Clayton ~ Real ale ~ Bar food (12-2.30, 6-9; all day Sat and Sun) ~ Restaurant ~ (01200) 446236 ~ Children welcome ~ Open 11-11; 12-10.30 Sun; 11-2.30, 5.30-11 Mon-Fri in winter ~ Bedrooms: £38S/£55S

RABY SJ3180 Map 7
Wheatsheaf

From A540 heading S from Heswall, turn left into Upper Raby Road, village in about 1 mile; The Green, Rabymere Road

In a quietly picturesque village, this timbered and whitewashed country cottage is known just as the Thatch. The nicely rambling rooms are simply furnished, with an old wall clock and homely black kitchen shelves in the cosy central bar, and a nice snug formed by antique settles built in around its fine old fireplace. A second, more spacious room has upholstered wall seats around the tables, small hunting prints on the cream walls, and a smaller coal fire. It's a popular place, attracting a good mix of customers. Good straightforward lunchtime bar food includes soup (£2.50), sandwiches and a huge range of toasties (from £2.50), ploughman's (£4.75), omelettes (£5.50), spicy chicken breast (£5.95), steak in ale pie (£6), mixed grill (£6.40) and braised knuckle of lamb or poached salmon (£6.95); three-course Sunday lunch (£12.50). The spacious restaurant (Tuesdays to Saturday evening) is in a converted cowshed that leads into a larger no smoking conservatory; piped music is played in these areas only. Up to 11 real ales are kept on handpump: Cains, Greene King Old Speckled Hen, Tetleys, Theakstons Best, Old Peculier and XB, Wells Bombardier and three or four weekly guests such as Dent Aviator, fff Stairway to Heaven and Weetwood Old Dog. A good choice of malt whiskies, and quite a few wines. There are picnic-sets on the terrace and in the pleasant garden behind, with more seats out front. More reports please. *(Recommended by E G Parish, MLR, Mr and Mrs R A Newbury)*

Free house ~ Licensee Wes Charlesworth ~ Real ale ~ Bar food (lunchtime only) ~ Restaurant (evenings 6-9.30, Tues-Sat; not Sun and Mon) ~ (0151) 336 3416 ~ Children in restaurant and family room ~ Dogs allowed in bar ~ Open 11.30-11; 12-10.30 Sun

RIBCHESTER SD6435 Map 7
White Bull 🛏

Church Street; turn off B6245 at sharp corner by Black Bull

In an interesting Roman village by the River Ribble, this popular dining pub has some remains of a Roman bath house scattered behind the building, and the Tuscan pillars that support the entrance porch have stood here or nearby for nearly 2,000 years; there's a small Roman museum nearby. Inside, the spacious main bar has comfortable old settles, Victorian advertisements and various prints, and a stuffed fox in two halves that looks as if it's jumping through the wall. Most areas are set out for eating during the day, and in summer you can also eat out in the garden behind; the dining area is no smoking. Under the new licensee, the well liked bar food includes home-made soup (£1.90), filled baps (from £3), spicy chicken pieces with minty yoghurt dip (£3.45; main course £6.80), home-made chicken liver pâté

(£3.50), home-made steak and kidney pie or vegetable lasagne (£5.55), gammon and egg (£6.25), pork steak topped with creamy stilton and bacon sauce (£6.95), steaks (from £7.95), and mini joint of lamb shoulder braised in rich gravy (£8.95). Well kept Black Sheep, Boddingtons, and Greene King Abbot on handpump; also several wines, and a good range of malt whiskies. Darts, TV, pool, and dominoes in the games room; piped music. *(Recommended by Pat and Tony Martin, Norma and Noel Thomas, MLR, Abi Benson)*

Whitbreads ~ Lease Jill Meadows ~ Real ale ~ Bar food (11.30-9;12-8 Sun) ~ Restaurant ~ (01254) 878303 ~ Children in eating area of bar and restaurant ~ Open 11.30-11; 12-10.30 Sun ~ Bedrooms: /£45.50S(£50.50B)

SAWLEY SD7746 Map 7
Spread Eagle 🍷 ♟
Village signposted just off A59 NE of Clitheroe

Lancashire Dining Pub of the Year

There's no doubt that this professionally run dining pub places firm emphasis on its particularly good, imaginative food, but there is a welcome for drinkers, too. The light and airy continental-feeling main bar (partly no smoking) has comfortable banquette seating, plenty of paintings and prints and lovely photographs of local views on the walls, a roaring winter coal fire, and well kept Black Sheep, Jennings and Tetleys on handpump, 40 malt whiskies and well chosen wines. The highly thought of food might include lunchtime sandwiches, plus exceptionally good creamed cauliflower and mussel soup flavoured with curry oil (£3.25), chicken liver and foie gras parfait with onion jam, port wine sauce and sage and onion toast or caramelised red onion, black olive and dried tomato tart topped with lancashire cheese (£5.25), mosaic of lobster, chicken and spinach with a mango and citrus dressing (£6.95), casserole of spiced chick peas (£8.25), baked smoked haddock with watercress and nutmeg sauce and coddled egg (£9.95), grilled duck breast with duck leg hash, beetroot flavoured sauce and sour cream or slow-cooked boneless shank of lamb with lemon, caper and parsley paste (£10.50), flash roasted venison haunch steak with sweet red cabbage and purée of dates (£11.50), and puddings like orange and cardamom burnt cream with cardamom ice cream and citrus and sesame tuile, rich terrine of dark and white chocolate or white wine poached pear with almond-scented panna cotta and fresh lemon jelly (from £3.95); midweek two-course set menu (£8.50) and two-course Sunday lunch (£12.50). Efficient and attentive smartly dressed staff. The building faces 12th-c Cistercian abbey ruins. The River Ribble is nearby, and the pub is very handy for the Forest of Bowland. *(Recommended by Norman Stansfield, K Ogden, G Hunt, Margaret Dickinson)*

Free house ~ Licensees Nigel and Ysanne Williams ~ Bar food ~ Restaurant ~ (01200) 441202 ~ Children in eating area of bar and restaurant ~ Open 12-3, 6-11; 12-3 Sun; closed Sun pm and all day Mon

STALYBRIDGE SJ9698 Map 7
Station Buffet 🍺 £

Happily, nothing has changed here at all since last year – even the food prices are the same. This is a classic Victorian platform bar – not smart – but comfortably nostalgic, and the bar has a welcoming fire below an etched-glass mirror, newspapers and magazines to read, and old photographs of the station in its heyday and other railway memorabilia; there's a little conservatory. An extension along the platform leads into what was the ladies' waiting room and part of the station-master's quarters, with original ornate ceilings and a dining/function room with Victorian-style wallpaper; dominoes, cribbage, draughts. They serve an impressive range of up to 20 guest ales a week, and such is their reputation for showcasing new real ales that they are continually being approached by interesting microbreweries to stock their latest brews. You'll also find well kept Boddingtons, Flowers IPA and Wadworths 6X, and they have farm cider, and belgian and other foreign bottled beers. As well as good coffee and tea made freshly by the pot, they do cheap old-fashioned snacks such as black peas (50p) and sandwiches (from £1.50), and three or four daily specials such as home-made pie with peas (£1.50), bacon casserole (£2.20) and all day breakfast (£2.25). They hold good beer festivals in early May and late November. On a sunny day you can sit out on the platform. *(Recommended by Tony Hobden, Andrew York, Pete Yearsley, the Didler, John Hulme, Bernie Adams, Tim Butterworth, Nick Holding, Mike and Linda Hudson, Brenda and Stuart Naylor)*

Free house ~ Licensees John Hesketh and Sylvia Wood ~ Real ale ~ Bar food (all day) ~ Restaurant ~ (0161) 303 0007 ~ Children welcome ~ Dogs welcome ~ Folk music Sat evenings, quiz Mon night ~ Open 11-11; 12-10.30 Sun; closed 25 Dec

TUNSTALL SD6173 Map 7
Lunesdale Arms ♀

A683 S of Kirkby Lonsdale

The very good food is undoubtedly the main focus in this civilised and brightly opened-up dining pub, but they do keep a couple of real ales and serve wine by the large glass, and the atmosphere is friendly and relaxed. There's a cheerful bustle in the bars – aided by bare boards and lively acoustics – and shades of blue and yellow: on yellow walls the big unframed oil paintings (some for sale) are often of bluebells, some of the pews and armchairs have blue and/or yellow upholstery, and the blinds for most of the big windows are also blue and yellow. On one side of the central bar part, a white-walled area (where the pictures are framed) has a good mix of stripped and sealed solid dining tables, and sofas around a lower table with daily papers, by a woodburning stove which has a couple of orchids on the stone mantelpiece. At the other end, an airy games section has pool, table football and TV, and a snugger little flagstoned back part has another woodburning stove. With good home-baked bread, and using meat from local farms only, and a lot of local organic produce, the enjoyable food might include lunchtime open sandwiches such as chicken with lime and coriander mayonnaise or salmon with home-made rocket pesto mayonnaise (£3.50), as well as celery and puy lentil soup (£3), morecambe Bay potted shrimps (£4.25), lasagne (£5.50 or £7), sausage and mash with red wine gravy and caramelised onions (£5.50 or £8), vegetable goulash (£7.25), steak and kidney pie (£8.50), lamb with cannelloni bean stew (£9.25), sirloin steak with gremolata sauce (£10.50), and puddings like caramel orange and kumquat crack, sticky toffee pudding and armagnac parfait with prunes and earl grey syrup (£3.75). They do small helpings for children. Service is helpful, and besides well kept real ales such as Black Sheep and a changing guest on handpump they have a good range of sensibly priced wines by the glass (in a choice of sizes), summer Pimms, and winter mulled wine; piped music. This pretty Lune Valley village has a church with Brontë associations. *(Recommended by John and Sylvia Harrop, Malcolm Taylor, Dr K Roger Wood, Michael Doswell, Karen Eliot)*

Free house ~ Licensee Emma Gillibrand ~ Bar food (11-2(2.30 weekends), 6-9; not Mon except bank hols) ~ Restaurant ~ (01524) 274203 ~ Children welcome ~ Dogs allowed in bar ~ Occasional live piano and jazz ~ Open 11-3(2.30 Sat), 6-11; 11-2.30, 6-10.30 Sun; closed Mon exc bank hols

UPPERMILL SD9905 Map 7
Church Inn ☕

From the main street (A607), look out for the sign for Saddleworth Church, and turn off up this steep narrow lane – keep on up!

It's the eight own-brewed Saddleworth real ales that are the main draw to this ancient, isolated local: Saddleworth More, Ayrtons, Bert Corner, Hopsmacker, Robyn's Bitter and Shaftbender, along with seasonal ales. They also keep a couple of guests like Boggart Hole Clough Boggart Bitter or Dark Star on handpump, several malt whiskies and farm cider. The big unspoilt L-shaped main bar has high beams and some stripped stone; one window at the end of the bar counter looks down over the valley, and there's also a valley view from the quieter no smoking dining room. The comfortable furnishings include settles and pews as well as a good individual mix of chairs, and there are lots of attractive prints, staffordshire and other china on a high delft shelf, jugs, brasses and so forth; TV and occasional unobtrusive piped music. The horse-collar on the wall is worn by the winner of their annual gurning (or face-pulling) championship (part of the lively Rush Cart Festival, usually held over the August bank holiday), and handbells here are the church bellringers' practice set. Children and dogs are given an especially warm welcome (if the dogs dare to brave an ever-increasing army of rescued cats). Outside, seats on a small terrace look up towards the moors, with more out in a garden – and anything from rabbits, ducks and geese to horses and a couple of peacocks. *(Recommended by Revd D Glover, the Didler, Bob Broadhurst)*

Own brew ~ Licensee Julian Taylor ~ Real ale ~ Bar food (12-2.30, 5.30-9; 12-9 Sat/Sun) ~ Restaurant ~ (01457) 872415 ~ Children welcome ~ Dogs welcome ~ Open 12-11; 12-10.30 Sun

WHITEWELL SD6546 Map 7
Inn at Whitewell ★★ ⑪ ♀ ⇌

Most easily reached by B6246 from Whalley; road through Dunsop Bridge from B6478 is also good

This is such a lovely, peaceful and cosseting place to stay, that you now have to book quite a long way ahead to secure a room. It's a particularly well run inn set deep in the Forest of Bowland and surrounded by wooded rolling hills set off against higher moors; plenty of fell walking, and they own several miles of trout, salmon and sea trout fishing on the Hodder; with notice they'll arrange shooting. Furnishings are impressive: the old-fashioned pubby bar has antique settles, oak gateleg tables, sonorous clocks, old cricketing and sporting prints, roaring log fires (the lounge has a very attractive stone fireplace), and heavy curtains on sturdy wooden rails; one area has a selection of newspapers and magazines, dominoes, local maps and guide books, there's a piano for anyone who wants to play, and even an art gallery. In the early evening, there's a cheerful bustle but once the visitors have gone, the atmosphere remains tranquil and relaxing; the staff are courteous and friendly. Very good bar food at lunchtime includes home-made soup (£3.20), sandwiches (from £3.90), crispy confit leg of duck with bubble and squeak (£5.50), potted prawns (£6.25), grilled norfolk kipper (£6.50), ploughman's (£6.75), haddock in beer batter (£8.50), fish pie (£8.50), and home-made burger (£8.75), with evening choices such as well liked chicken liver pâté (£4.90; main course £5.90), toasted brioche with creamed field mushrooms and glazed shallots (£5), salad of home-smoked chicken with avocado purée and confit tomatoes (£5.65), cumberland sausages with white onion sauce and champ (£7.50), grilled barnsley chop glazed with minted yoghurt, goats cheese mash and courgette relish (£11.50), and sirloin steak (£12.25), with home-made puddings and home-made farmhouse cheeses (£3.50). You can get coffee and cream teas all day, they sell jars of home-made jam, and if you're staying they'll do you a picnic hamper. Their good wine list contains around 180 wines (including a highly recommended claret), and they've well kept Boddingtons and Marstons Pedigree or Timothy Taylors Landlord on handpump. Down a corridor with strange objects like a stuffed fox disappearing into the wall is the pleasant suntrap garden, with wonderful views down to the valley. *(Recommended by Andrew Stephenson, Peter and Giff Bennett, Comus and Sarah Elliott, Anthony Longden, Norman Stansfield, Paul Humphreys, Jim Abbott, Rob and Catherine Dunster, Mrs P J Carroll, Mike Schofield, Louise English, Sally Anne and Peter Goodale, J F M and M West, Derek and Sylvia Stephenson, Di and Mike Gillam, Stephen Buckley, Bernard Stradling; also in the Good Hotel Guide)*

Free house ~ Licensee Richard Bowman ~ Real ale ~ Bar food (12-2, 7.30-9.30) ~ Restaurant ~ (01200) 448222 ~ Children welcome ~ Dogs welcome ~ Open 11-3, 6-11; 12-2, 7-11 Sun ~ Bedrooms: £66B/£89B

> Post Office address codings confusingly give the impression that some pubs are in Lancashire when they're really in Yorkshire (which is where we list them).

YEALAND CONYERS SD5074 Map 7
New Inn

3 miles from M6 junction 35; village signposted off A6

As this friendly 17th-c ivy-covered village pub is handy for the M6, there's always a good bustling atmosphere and plenty of locals and visitors. The simply furnished little beamed bar on the left has a cosy village atmosphere, with its log fire in the big stone fireplace, and cribbage and dominoes. On the right, two communicating no smoking cottagey dining rooms have dark blue furniture, shiny beams and an attractive kitchen range. Well kept Hartleys XB and Robinsons seasonal beer on handpump, around 30 malt whiskies, winter mulled wine and maybe summer home-made lemonade; piped music. Enjoyable bar food includes soup (£2.90), sandwiches or filled baked potatoes (from £3.45), garlic mushrooms (£4.70), good filled warm baguettes (from £4.85), lentil and red pepper curry (£8.50), chicken breast stuffed with bacon and stilton with a rich madeira sauce (£9.50), steaks (from £12.50), and specials like recommended calves liver with caramelised shallots and bacon, guinea fowl with home-made bacon and apricot stuffing with ale gravy or tasty fresh halibut in white wine and chive sauce (all £10.95). The same menu runs through the dining rooms and bar. Service is courteous and efficient. A sheltered lawn at the side has picnic-sets among roses and flowering shrubs. *(Recommended by John Watson, Jack Clark, Mike Schofield, Eric Locker, Richard Greaves, David Carr, MLR, John Foord, Deb and John Arthur, R T and J C Moggridge, Michael Doswell, Karen Eliot, Stan and Hazel Allen, Brenda and Stuart Naylor)*

Robinsons ~ Tenants Bill Tully and Charlotte Pinder ~ Real ale ~ Bar food (11.30(12 Sun)-9.30) ~ Restaurant ~ (01524) 732938 ~ Children welcome ~ Dogs allowed in bar ~ Open 11.30-11; 12-10.30 Sun

---

Lucky Dip

Besides the fully inspected pubs, you might like to try these Lucky Dips recommended to us and described by readers (if you do, please send us reports: www.goodguides.com).

AFFETSIDE [SD7513]
Pack Horse [Watling St]: Attractive neatly kept moorland local on Roman road, particularly well kept Hydes ale, big helpings of lunchtime bar food, snug pool room, restaurant early evenings (not Sun); good walking country, open all day wknds *(P Abbott, Norma and Noel Thomas, DJH)*
ALTHAM [SD7732]
Walton Arms [Burnley Rd (A678)]: Attractive pub, relaxed and friendly, with wide range of reasonably priced food from good filled rolls and dim sum up, early evening bargains, well kept Jennings, good service *(Andy and Jill Kassube, Derek and Sylvia Stephenson)*
ARKHOLME [SD5872]
Bay Horse [B6254 Carnforth—Kirkby Lonsdale]: Neatly kept and homely old three-room country pub popular for cheap generous food inc good value sandwiches, good service, well kept Boddingtons and a guest such as Everards Tiger, lovely inglenook, good pictures of long-lost London pubs; own bowling green, handy for charming Lune Valley walks *(Steve Whalley, Jane Taylor, David Dutton)*
BACUP [SD8623]
Queens [Yorkshire St]: Unspoilt, with back main bar, homely front room on left with coal fire, darts, cards, dominoes and shove-

ha'penny, friendly efficient service, well kept John Smiths, pool on right *(Pete Baker)*
BALDERSTONE [SD6131]
Myerscough Hotel [Whalley Rd, Samlesbury; A59 Preston—Skipton, just over 2 miles from M6 junction 31]: Solid traditional furnishings in cosy and relaxed softly lit dark-beamed bar, four well kept Robinsons ales, good soft drinks choice, traditional games, good basic home-made food from sandwiches up, no smoking front room (children allowed there, mealtimes); darts, quiz night, no dogs; disabled access, picnic-sets in garden, bedrooms *(CMW, JJW, LYM)*
BARROW [SD7337]
Spread Eagle [Clitheroe Rd]: Comfortably refurbished, good friendly service, very wide choice of enjoyable reasonably priced food, well spaced tables, no smoking area; quiet piped music *(KC)*
BEBINGTON [SJ3385]
Travellers Rest [B5151, not far from M53 junction 4; Higher Bebington]: Friendly semi-rural corner pub with several areas around central bar and separate no smoking room, all laid for enjoyable reasonably priced bar lunches from sandwiches to mixed grill (not Sun; orders stop 1.45), up to eight well kept ales inc some from small breweries, efficient staff, alcoves, beams,

brasses etc; no children, open all day *(MLR)*

BELMONT [SD6915]

Wrights Arms: Large but cosy, warm and friendly, high on the moors, good value food such as hot beef sandwiches and home-made meatballs, well kept Tetleys, helpful staff, separate large restaurant; children's play area behind *(Andrew Scarr)*

BIRKENHEAD [SJ3289]

Crown [Conway St]: Interestingly tiled alehouse with Cains and a couple of guest beers, Weston's farm cider, good value generous food, several rooms; open all day, cl Sun lunchtime *(the Didler, MLR)*

Dispensary [Chester St]: Well kept Cains ales, good value lunchtime food, handsome glass ceiling; handy for ferry, open all day *(the Didler)*

Stork [Price St]: Early 19th-c, carefully done up without being spoilt; Threlfalls tiled façade, four rooms around island bar, polished original floor, old dock and ferry photographs, several well kept real ales, wkdy lunches; open all day (not Sun) *(MLR, the Didler)*

BISPHAM GREEN [SD4813]

☆ *Eagle & Child* [Parbold—Croston rd, off B5246]: Striking pub, largely open-plan, well divided by stubs of walls, attractively understated old furnishings, no smoking snug, and oriental rugs on flagstones in front of the fine old stone fireplaces; has been a popular main entry for its style, imaginative food, six changing real ales, farm cider and lots of malt whiskies, but new licensee again, too recently for us to give a firm rating; piped music; children in eating areas, neat bowling green outside, nice wild garden with nesting moorhens, open all day Sun with food all day then *(Revd D Glover, John Kane, Jack Clark, LYM)*

BLACKO [SD8541]

☆ *Moorcock* [A682 towards Gisburn]: Beautifully placed moorland dining pub, roomy and comfortable, with big picture windows for breathtaking views, tables set close for the huge range of popular and often enterprising food inc lamb from their own flock and excellent beef, very friendly helpful staff, decent wine, Thwaites Bitter and Mild under top pressure; tables in hillside garden with various animals, open all day for food Sun, children and dogs welcome, bedrooms *(Norma and Noel Thomas, Patrick Hancock, LYM)*

BLACKPOOL [SD3136]

Ramsden Arms [Talbot Rd, opp Blackpool North station]: Large local with several areas, masses of old prints and mainly beer-related bric-a-brac, friendly helpful staff, no smoking area, well kept Boddingtons, Marstons Pedigree, Thwaites and several guest ales, over 40 whiskies, lunchtime food; CD juke box, games; good value bedrooms *(Kevin Blake, the Didler, Patrick Hancock, Richard Lewis)*

Shovels [Common Edge Rd (B5261 S)]: Large Steak & Ale pub with sensibly priced

popular food, food order point, no smoking eating area, real ales from small breweries; unobtrusive piped music *(Ian and Nita Cooper)*

Wheatsheaf [Talbot Rd, opp Blackpool North station]: Friendly traditional pub with well kept Theakstons and good choice of guest beers, food all day, old pictures and bric-a-brac inc flags and lots of 60s pop music memorabilia; pianist Tues, tables on small terrace, open all day *(the Didler, Patrick Hancock)*

BOLTON [SD7109]

Howcroft [Pool St]: Friendly backstreet local serving as tap for local Bank Top ales, also guest beers and Addlestone's cider; lots of small screened-off rooms around central servery with fine glass and woodwork, cosy snug with coal fire, good value lunches in lounge, plenty of games inc pinball, darts, bar billiards; bowling green, occasional live music, open all day *(the Didler)*

Olde Man & Scythe [Churchgate]: Interesting 17th-c local with cellar dating from 12th c, lively corridor-style drinking area, two quieter rooms popular for bargain lunchtime food from sandwiches up, good range of real ales from Holts to Fullers London Pride, two or more farm ciders; handy for shopping area, delightful back terrace, open all day *(Collin and Julie Taylor)*

BOLTON BY BOWLAND [SD7849]

Coach & Horses [Main St]: Pleasant open-plan bar/dining area, flagstones and traditional décor, good fresh food using local produce from sandwiches up, friendly licensees, well kept Black Sheep and Boddingtons, log fires, separate dining room, darts and pool; big comfortable bedrooms with own bathrooms, good breakfast, lovely streamside village with interesting church, open all week *(Mr and Mrs I W Clough, Hilary Forrest)*

BROUGHTON [SD4838]

☆ *Plough at Eaves* [A6 N through Broughton, 1st left about 1 mile after traffic lights, then bear left after another 1½ miles]: Two linked very low-beamed carpeted front rooms with coal fire, back extension toning in, consistently enjoyable home-made food (all day wknds), well kept Thwaites Bitter and Lancaster Bomber, lots of malt whiskies, good uniformed staff, plenty of old-fashioned charm; may be piped music; picnic-sets out in front, well equipped play area behind *(LYM, John and Elspeth Howell, Jackie and Martin Smith, Steve Whalley)*

BURNLEY [SD8332]

Inn on the Wharf [Manchester Rd]: Well organised pub by Leeds—Liverpool Canal, handy for centre, clean and spacious, with smart décor of beams, stripped stone and flagstones, good choice at good value food bar, real ales; waterside terrace *(Margaret Dickinson)*

BURY [SD8012]

Garsdale [Woodhill Rd]: Welcoming

traditional beamed pub with good value generous fresh food, all wines available by the glass, good attentive service, no smoking restaurant *(Kevin and Barbara Wilkinson)*

☆ *Lord Raglan* [off A56 N under 1 mile E of M66 junction 1; Mount Pleasant, Nangreaves, down cobbled track]: Welcoming ivy-covered cottage row in lonely moorside location, with great views, brewing its own good Leydens Raglan Sleeve and Nanny Flyer; carefully made food from sandwiches to good meals using fresh ingredients inc a monthly diners' club, pleasant young staff, good wines and interesting foreign bottled beers, lots of bric-a-brac in traditional front bar, big open fire in cosy back room, plainer blond-panelled dining room (where children allowed; crudités as you wait to go in); open all day Sun *(Gordon Tong, DJH, P Abbott, LYM)*

CATON [SD5364]

Ship [Lancaster Rd]: Roomy open-plan dining pub, immaculately kept with interesting range of nautical bric-a-brac, good fire in charming antique fireplace, good choice of reasonably priced food from sandwiches to generous fresh fish and Sun lunch, properly cooked veg, no smoking dining room, well kept Thwaites ales, interesting wines of the month, efficient friendly staff, magazines; subdued piped music, can be busy wknds; tables in garden, handy for Lune valley and Forest of Bowland *(Margaret Dickinson, Michael Doswell)*

CHIPPING [SD6243]

☆ *Sun* [Windy St]: Charming stone-built country local with three small snug panelled rooms, good value hearty simple food, well kept Boddingtons and guest beers such as Coniston Bluebird and Timothy Taylors Landlord (an underground stream cools the cellar), quick friendly service, coal fire, papers and magazines, interesting local photographs and ironstone china, games room with pool and darts; very busy wknds, tables in courtyard, attractive village, good walks *(Margaret Dickinson, Mike and Alison Leyland, Steve Whalley)*

CHORLEY [SD5817]

Yew Tree [Dill Hall Brow, Heath Charnock – out past Limbrick towards the reservoirs]: Tucked-away restaurary pub with good value enjoyable food from open kitchen, friendly staff *(Gordon Tong)*

COLNE [SD9242]

Golden Ball [Burnley Rd (A56)]: Pleasantly refurbished pub with horseshoe bar, lounge side with alcove tables and no smoking area beyond, food all day, Cains, Greene King Old Speckled Hen, Timothy Taylors Landlord and Tetleys; under same management as popular nearby Boundary Mill outlet store – china, glass, designer clothes *(Jim and Maggie Cowell)*

Hare & Hounds [Skipton Old Rd, Black Lane Ends – NE, towards Lothersdale]: Wide choice of food all day inc some

unusual dishes, reasonable prices, good service, relaxed unhurried atmosphere, Timothy Taylors ales *(F J Robinson, Alison Keys)*

CONDER GREEN [SD4556]

Stork [just off A588]: Fine spot where River Conder joins the Lune estuary among bleak marshes, friendly bustle and good fire in rambling newly refurbished panelled rooms; new management still doing generous popular standard food (all day Sun) from sandwiches up, young staff, mainstream real ales; pub games inc pool, juke box or piped music can obtrude; children welcome, handy for Glasson Dock, comfortable bedrooms, open all day *(LYM, Margaret Dickinson)*

DARWEN [SD7222]

☆ *Old Rosins* [Pickup Bank, Hoddlesden, off B6232 Haslingden—Belthorn opp Grey Mare]: Isolated open-plan moorland inn with comfortable banquettes and good log fire, mugs and jugs hanging from beams, picture-window views from no smoking dining end, decent food from sandwiches to steaks, friendly young new managers, Courage Directors, Theakstons Old Peculier and Worthington Best, plenty of malt whiskies; fruit machine, piped music; children welcome, picnic-sets on big crazy-paved terrace, bedrooms with own bathrooms, open all day *(Pat and Tony Martin, H W Roberts, Bob Broadhurst, LYM)*

DENTON [SJ9395]

Lowes Arms [Hyde Rd (A57)]: Smart pub brewing its own LAB real ales, good waitress-served food in end dining area, separate large games room; tables outside, open all day wknds *(Tony Hobden)*

DOBCROSS [SD9906]

☆ *Swan* [The Square]: Low beams, flagstones and traditional settles, three interesting areas (one no smoking) off central bar, several real ales such as Moorhouses and Phoenix, enjoyable sensibly priced food inc children's, attentive young staff; tables outside, attractive village below moors *(Bill Sykes, Richard and Ruth Dean, Tony Hobden)*

DOLPHINHOLME [SD5153]

Fleece [back roads, a couple of miles from M6 junction 33]: Friendly hotel with tasty bar food, well kept real ales, dining area off comfortable beamed lounge, bar with darts and table skittles, open fire; bedrooms *(Kate Coulling)*

ECCLES [SJ7798]

Grapes [Liverpool Rd, Peel Green; A57 ½ mile from M63 junction 2]: Edwardian local with superb glass and tiling, lots of mahogany, brilliant staircase, cheap Holts Bitter and Mild, fairly quiet roomy lounge and smoke room, pool room, vault with Manchester darts (can get quite loud and smoky), drinking corridor; open all day *(the Didler, Pete Baker)*

Lamb [Regent St (A57)]: Gorgeous handsomely preserved Edwardian three-room local, splendid etched windows, fine woodwork and furnishings, extravagantly tiled stairway, admirable trophies in display case; cheap well kept Holts Bitter and Mild, bargain lunchtime sandwiches, full-size snooker table in original billiards room; popular with older people, open all day *(the Didler, GLD, JES, Nick Holding)*

Queens Arms [Green Lane (B5231), Patricroft]: Said to have been the world's first railway pub; basic bar, comfortable lounge, delightful snug, Boddingtons and guest beer, many photographs of old Eccles (inc the original Eccles cake shop); tables outside, open all day wknds, cl wkdy lunchtimes *(the Didler, Bernie Adams)*

Royal Oak [Barton Lane]: Large unspoilt Edwardian pub on busy corner, several rooms, handsome tilework, cheap Holts Bitter and Mild, organ singalongs in back lounge; open all day *(the Didler, Nick Holding)*

Stanley Arms [Eliza Ann St/Liverpool Rd (A57), Patricroft]: Busy mid-Victorian corner local with cheap Holts Bitter and Mild, lunchtime sandwiches, popular front bar, hatch serving two back rooms, drinking corridor *(the Didler)*

White Lion [Liverpool Rd, Patricroft, 1 mile from M63 junction 2]: Welcoming unchanging Edwardian local, clean, tidy and popular with older people, in lively traditional public bar, tiled side drinking corridor with separate smoke room (wknd pianist) and quiet lounge off, great value Holts Bitter and Mild *(the Didler, Pete Baker)*

ECCLESTON [SD5117]

☆ *Farmers Arms* [Towngate (B5250, off A581 Chorley—Southport)]: Big cheery low-beamed pub/restaurant, wide choice of consistently good generous food all day, wkdy bargains and some unusual twists to familiar themes; modernised but keeping character – black cottagey furniture, brocaded wall seats, quotations on stencilled walls, plates, pastoral prints, clocks and brasses; well kept Boddingtons, Tetleys and a guest such as Timothy Taylors Landlord, friendly helpful service, darts, interesting choice of piped music; parking can be tight when busy; good value bedrooms some with own bathroom, open all day *(Margaret Dickinson, Alan Bowker, J A Hooker, Richard Smerdon)*

EDGWORTH [SD7316]

Black Bull [Bolton Rd, Turton]: Busy three-room dining pub in moorside village, good value food from sandwiches and baguettes to hearty main dishes (all day wknds), five well kept changing ales, friendly efficient service, open fire, hill and reservoir views from light and airy restaurant extension, lovely summer floral displays; live music Thurs, Tues quiz night, good walks *(Michael and Marion Buchanan, P Abbott, Norma and Noel Thomas, Gordon Tong)*

ENTWISTLE [SD7217]

☆ *Strawbury Duck* [signed off Edgworth—Blackburn road; by station]: New licensees

for this tucked-away traditional beamed and flagstoned country pub; dimly lit L-shaped bar, Victorian pictures, some bare stone, up to six real ales, bar food all day; pool, fruit machine, TV and piped music; children welcome, tables outside, good for Pennine walks (leave muddy boots in the porch), open all day *(LYM)*

EUXTON [SD5518]

Euxton Mills [A49 S, 3 miles from M6 junction 28]: Roomy pub with wide food choice inc good sandwiches and daily roasts, popular wkdy lunchtime OAP deals, good pleasant service, three real ales inc Burtonwood and Everards *(Margaret Dickinson)*

Plough [Runshaw Moor; 1 mile from A49/B5252 junction]: Charming spotless black-beamed country dining pub with good atmosphere, enjoyable food inc upmarket dishes, well kept real ales, sympathetic extension; big sheltered back lawn with tables and small play area *(Margaret Dickinson)*

FENCE [SD8337]

Bay Horse [Wheatley Lane Rd]: Small, friendly and spotless, with well kept Marstons Pedigree, Theakstons and Charles Wells Bombardier, efficient service, decent food in all price ranges, restaurant *(Norman Stansfield, Norma and Noel Thomas, Margaret Dickinson)*

☆ *Forest* [B6248 Brierfield road, off A6068]: Civilised Pennine-view dining pub with wide choice of food (all day Sun) inc some small helpings for children, real ales such as Greene King Old Speckled Hen and Ruddles, Marstons Pedigree and Theakstons Best, good choice of wines, friendly helpful service, plush banquettes in nicely lit open-plan bar, oak-panelled dining room, lots of paintings, vases, plates and books, no smoking front conservatory; unobtrusive piped music; children welcome, open all day *(Norman Stansfield, LYM, Tony and Caroline Elwood)*

FLEETWOOD [SD3247]

☆ *North Euston* [Esplanade, nr tram terminus]: Big comfortably refurbished bar in massive architecturally interesting Victorian hotel with great sea and hill views, long railway connections (was LMS terminal, with ferry to Scotland); a real oasis, with decent lunchtime food esp in nice back Mediterranean Bar and Spinnaker coffee bar, well kept Moorhouses Black Cat Mild and Pendle Witches Brew and a couple of other changing ales, consistently good service, big no smoking family area (till 7), two restaurants, seats outside; comfortable bedrooms, open all day (Sun afternoon break) *(Margaret Dickinson, Richard and Margaret Peers, Richard Lewis, Dr B and Mrs P B Baker, Keith and Chris O'Neill)*

Thomas Drummond [London St]: Light and airy Wetherspoons with pastel décor, comfortable seats, good value generous food, 10 well kept real ales, friendly staff, no smoking area; tables outside, open all day *(Richard Lewis)*

Wyre [Marine Hall, Esplanade]: Part of exhibition/entertainment centre, quiet and comfortable, good views of beach, Morecambe Bay, boats and ships; well kept Moorhouses Pendle Witches Brew and several other real ales (landlord is an enthusiast), plenty of country wines and malt whiskies; children welcome, seats outside *(Richard Lewis)*

FRECKLETON [SD4328]

☆ *Ship* [towards Naze Lane Ind Est, then right into Bunker St]: Genuinely old, big windows looking out over the watermeadows from roomy nautical-theme main bar, good value generous bar food, four real ales, games area with big-screen TV; children allowed, tables outside *(CMW, JJW, LYM)*

GARSTANG [SD4944]

Bradbeer Bar [Garstang Country Hotel & Golf Club; B6430 S]: Relaxed and spacious bar overlooking golfing greens, good value imaginative food, helpful well trained staff, huge woodburner; tables outside, bedrooms *(Margaret Dickinson)*

Crown [High St]: Sympathetically modernised Thwaites pub, their full beer range kept well, roaring coal fire, particularly friendly licensees *(Steve Whalley)*

☆ *Royal Oak* [Market Pl]: Typical small-town inn in same family for nearly 50 years, cosy yet roomy and comfortably refurbished, with attractive panelling, several eating areas inc charming snug, generous consistently above-average food (all day Sun) inc imaginative specials, small helpings for children or OAPs, pleasant staff, Robinsons real ales, good value coffee, spotless housekeeping; restaurant, disabled access, comfortable bedrooms, open all day Sun *(Margaret Dickinson)*

☆ *Th'Owd Tithebarn* [off Church St]: Rustically converted barn with big flagstoned terrace overlooking Lancaster Canal, thorough-going Victorian country life theme with antique kitchen range, masses of farm tools, stuffed animals and birds, flagstones and high rafters, even waitresses in period costume and a 9-metre (30-ft) central refectory table; simple food all day from filled baguettes up, Flowers IPA and Tetleys, lots of country wines; piped music, can get very busy; children in dining room, open all day summer *(Roy Morrison, Abi Benson, LYM)*

GOOSNARGH [SD5636]

☆ *Stags Head* [B5269]: Reminiscent of a good Vintage Inn (it's actually an S&N franchise), with lots of separate mainly old-world areas rambling around a central servery, plenty of nice features (even proper old-fashioned radiators), good value freshly made food inc imaginative dishes, friendly well trained staff, Flowers IPA, popular restaurant (may be fully booked); well reproduced contemporary chart music, live music Fri *(Margaret Dickinson, BB, Mike and Linda Hudson)*

GREASBY [SJ2587]

☆ *Greave Dunning* [Greasby Rd (off B5139)]: Nicely refurbished extended pub with quiet alcoves in homely flagstoned bar, lofty main lounge with upper gallery, comfortable seating inc a sofa, enjoyable well presented food inc light dishes, polite helpful staff, well kept real ales, decent wines *(E G Parish, LYM)*

GREAT MITTON [SD7138]

☆ *Aspinall Arms* [B6246 NW of Whalley]: Dual bars with red plush wall banquettes, comfortable chairs, settees and bar stools, old-world prints, well kept Greene King IPA and Abbot, Timothy Taylors Landlord and a guest beer, enjoyable food from good cold or hot sandwiches up, cheerful efficient service, coal fire, papers, books and magazines to read, no music or machines; children welcome away from bar; nice surroundings, picnic-sets on flagstoned terrace and in big informal garden with play area just above River Ribble, bedrooms, usefully opens earlier than most pubs around here *(Derek and Sylvia Stephenson, Mike Turner, Mr and Mrs J G Smith, BB, KC)*

GRINDLETON [SD7545]

Duke of York [off A69 via Chatburn; Brow Top]: Smart, cheery and bright old upmarket village local in attractive Ribble Valley countryside, personable landlady, husband does good if not cheap food from sandwiches up inc lovely puddings, well kept Boddingtons and Castle Eden, friendly attentive staff, various areas inc one with open fire, separate dining room; tables in front, garden behind *(RJH)*

HAMBLETON [SD3741]

Shard Bridge [off A588 towards Poulton, next to toll bridge]: Attractive whitewashed pub on Wyre estuary by former toll bridge; small smartly refurbished lounge with restaurant tables beyond, wide choice of reasonably priced freshly cooked waitress-served food from soup and ploughman's up, well kept Marstons Pedigree; nice outdoor tables overlooking water *(Abi Benson, Margaret Dickinson)*

HAWKSHAW [SD7515]

Red Lion [Ramsbottom Rd]: Attractively renovated pub/hotel, good value generous home cooking in big main bar and separate restaurant, well kept Jennings Best and Cumberland with a local microbrew guest beer, enthusiastic friendly licensees, cheerful efficient staff; comfortable bedrooms, quiet spot by River Irwell *(P Abbott, Jim Abbott)*

HELMSHORE [SD7820]

White Horse [Holcombe Rd]: Big stone-built inn opened into large sympathetically modernised low-ceilinged lounge bar, the big tables set for eating but plenty of people just enjoying the well kept Boddingtons and Timothy Taylors Landlord; Irwell valley views from the front *(Jane Taylor, David Dutton)*

HEST BANK [SD4666]

★ *Hest Bank Hotel* [Hest Bank Lane; off A6 just N of Lancaster]: Picturesque and welcoming three-bar coaching inn, good for families, with wide range of good freshly made generous food all day from sandwiches up inc fresh local fish and potted shrimps, also children's dishes, bargain set menus and special food nights, well kept Boddingtons, Cains, Timothy Taylors Landlord and a monthly changing guest beer, decent wines, friendly efficient service, separate restaurant area, lively history, Weds quiz night; plenty of garden tables by Lancaster canal, attractive setting close to Morecambe Bay *(Margaret Dickinson, Derek and Sylvia Stephenson, Denise Dowd, BB)*

HEYSHAM [SD4161]

Royal [Main St]: Two-bar pub dating from 1502, Boddingtons, Everards Beacon, Tetleys, Thwaites Lancaster Bomber and a guest beer, well priced wines, enjoyable changing food in bars and dining room; quiz nights Tues and Thurs, theme nights; tables out in front and good-sized sheltered garden *(Maggie and Tony Harwood)*

HOLDEN [SD7749]

★ *Copy Nook* [the one up by Bolton by Bowland]: Spick-and-span roomy and well renovated pub, wide choice of good reasonably priced food, particularly beef, lamb and fish, in two linked bar rooms and small restaurant behind, well kept Marstons Pedigree and Tetleys, decent wines, efficient obliging staff, friendly atmosphere; six bedrooms *(W W Burke, Geoffrey and Brenda Wilson)*

HORNBY [SD5868]

Castle [Main St]: Small tastefully refurbished hotel, armchairs and sofas in comfortable bar with well kept changing real ale and daily papers, wide range of enjoyable local-flavoured food with imaginative touches, popular pricier restaurant; bedrooms *(Karen Eliot)*

HURST GREEN [SD6838]

★ *Bayley Arms* [off B6243 Longridge—Clitheroe, towards Stoneyhurst Coll]: Sympathetically renovated carpeted bar with attractive mix of old furniture, sporting and music memorabilia, brasses, log fire; enjoyable good value bar food inc children's, inventive menu in more formal restaurant, friendly licensees, smart staff; comfortable bedrooms, attractive Ribble Valley village *(Dr and Mrs D E Awbery)*

Shireburn Arms [Whalley Rd]: Quiet comfortable 17th-c hotel in idyllic setting with panoramic Ribble Valley views, good reasonably priced food, Thwaites and other ales; separate tea room, lovely neatly kept back garden and terrace, safe low-key play area, bedrooms *(Margaret Dickinson)*

IRBY [SJ2586]

★ *Irby Mill* [Irby Mill Hill, off Greasby rd]: Two low-beamed largely flagstoned rooms, one largely set for eating, good value food all day (no sandwiches), well kept Cains FA and Wundshaft, Marstons Pedigree, Timothy Taylors Landlord, Theakstons and changing guest beers, decent house wines, helpful friendly staff, comfortable pub furniture, coal-effect gas fire, interesting old photographs and history of the former mill; can get very busy; a few tables outside *(MLR, Tony Tollitt, BB)*

LANCASTER [SD4761]

Brown Cow [Penny St]: Long narrow unpretentious bar, generous bargain home-made lunches in simple back dining area, Thwaites Bitter and Lancaster Bomber, friendly new landlord *(MLR)*

LANESHAW BRIDGE [SD9341]

Hargreaves Arms [A6068 towards Keighley]: Small open-plan pub with above-average food (not Mon/Tues) inc early lunches, well kept Timothy Taylors, reasonably priced wines, friendly landlord, china collection, dining room *(M S Catling)*

LATHOM [SD4511]

★ *Ship* [off A5209 E of Burscough; Wheat Lane]: Big well run pub tucked below embankment at junction of Leeds & Liverpool and Rufford Branch canals, several separate recently redecorated beamed rooms, some interesting canal memorabilia and naval pictures and crests, some parts set for the good value simple food from good lunchtime sandwiches up (small helpings of some dishes available), prompt friendly service even when busy, up to nine well kept changing ales inc smaller breweries such as Bank Top, Moorhouses and Phoenix; games room with pool; tables outside, open all day *(BB, Andy and Jill Kassube, MLR, Nick Holding)*

LEYLAND [SD5422]

Midge Hall [Midge Hall Lane]: Wide choice of good value popular food from sandwiches and baked potatoes up, friendly helpful staff, Tetleys; children welcome, some live music, seats outside *(Margaret Dickinson, Frank Tomlinson)*

LIVERPOOL [SJ4395]

Cains Brewery Tap [Stanhope St]: Well restored Victorian pub with nicely understated décor, wooden floors, plush raised side snug, lots of old prints and breweriana, handsome bar, flame-effect gas fire, newspapers; cosy relaxing atmosphere, friendly efficient staff, good well priced food, four well kept attractively priced Cains ales with four guest beers from other small breweries; popular brewery tour ending here with buffet and singing; sports TV, open all day *(the Didler)*

Carnarvon Castle [Tarleton St]: Neat city-centre pub next to main shopping area, long and narrow, with one main bar and comfortable back lounge, welcoming chatty atmosphere, well kept Cains Bitter and Mild and a guest such as Caledonian 80/-, lunchtime bar snacks, cabinet of Dinky toys and other eclectic collections, no music; open all day, cl Sun evening *(the Didler, Joe Green)*

Cracke [Rice St]: Attractively basic, bare boards and pews, walls covered with posters for local events and pictures of local buildings, unusual Beatles diorama in largest room, juke box and TV, very cheap lunchtime food and Thurs curry night, well kept Cains, Marstons Pedigree and several guest microbrews; popular mainly with young people; open all day, sizeable garden *(MLR, the Didler, Patrick Hancock, Joe Green)*

☆ *Dispensary* [Renshaw St]: Small chatty local-feeling central pub with well kept Cains ales and three or four interesting guest beers, decent wkdy food 12-7, friendly staff, lots of polished wood and glass inc marvellous etched windows, bare boards, comfortable raised back bar, Victorian medicine bottles and instruments; open all day *(the Didler, David Field, Joe Green)*

☆ *Doctor Duncan* [St Johns Lane]: Neatly kept classic Victorian tiled pub with full Cains range and guest ales kept well, belgian beers on tap, enjoyable reasonably priced food till 7, impressive friendly service, several rooms inc no smoking family room (piped music in bar may be a little loud); open all day *(the Didler, Peter F Marshall, David Field, John Dwane, Joe Green)*

Excelsior [Dale St]: Good value food 11-6 (and breakfast from 9), Cains Bitter and Mild and guest beers; open all day, cl Sun *(the Didler)*

Globe [Cases St]: Welcoming crowded bustle in well appointed comfortably carpeted local, pleasant staff, well kept Cains Bitter and Dark Mild and a guest beer, good port, lunchtime filled baps, tiny sloping-floor lounge, lots of prints of old Liverpool; may be piped 1960s pop music; open all day *(Peter F Marshall, the Didler, MLR, Joe Green)*

Grapes [Mathew St]: Lively and friendly, with well kept Cains and Tetleys, good value lunchtime bar food, open-plan but pleasantly well worn cottagey décor (flagstones, old range, wall settles, no two chairs the same, gas-effect lamps); open all day, can get crowded Fri/Sat, cl Sun *(David Field, the Didler, Patrick Hancock)*

Head of Steam [Lime St Station]: Well restored old railway buildings, several rooms with plenty of character and railway memorabilia, lots of well kept ales such as Caledonian Deuchars IPA, impressive staff, decent food all day; open all day till midnight (2am Fri/Sat) *(David Field, Joe Green)*

Lion [Moorfields, off Tithebarn St]: Splendidly preserved ornate Victorian alehouse, sparkling etched glass and serving hatches in central bar, two small back lounges, unusual wallpaper, big mirrors, panelling and tilework, fine domed structure behind, friendly atmosphere and landlord interested in the history, well kept Lees and other changing ales such as Timothy Taylors, cheap lunchtime sandwiches and baguettes, coal fire; open all day *(the Didler, Pete Baker, Joe Green)*

Ma Boyles [Tower Gardens, off Water St]: Much modernised backstreet pub with good value bar food (all day Sat) from dim sum and pies to seafood specialities, well kept Hydes and guest beers; jazz Weds, open all day, cl Sat night and Sun *(the Didler, John Dwane)*

Midland [Ranelagh St]: Attractive and neatly kept Victorian pub with original décor, ornate lounge, long corner bar, nice etched glass and mirrors; keg beers *(the Didler)*

Roscoe Head [Roscoe St]: Three tiny unspoilt rooms, friendly, quiet and civilised, with particularly well kept Jennings, good value wkdy lunches, amusing cartoons, tie collection; open all day *(the Didler, David Field, Patrick Hancock, Joe Green)*

Ship & Mitre [Dale St]: Friendly gaslit local with up to a dozen well kept changing unusual beers served in oversized lined glasses, two farm ciders, cheap basic lunches, pool, occasional beer festivals; popular with university people (and a visiting music-critic guide dog – showing discomfort when the piped music turns to Elvis Costello or the Police), open all day, cl Sun lunchtime *(MLR, the Didler, Patrick Hancock, John Dwane, Joe Green)*

Vernon Arms [Dale St]: Tap for Liverpool Brewery with six of their beers in top condition (but yes, the bar floor does slope), pleasant service, good value meals till 7, plush banquettes in smarter back room; open all day, cl Sun *(the Didler, Joe Green)*

Vines [Lime St]: Big traditional pub, comfortable and friendly, with mosaic tilework, high-ceilinged room on right with stained glass; may not always have real ale, can get very busy *(the Didler)*

White Star [Rainford Gdns, off Matthew St]: Welcoming traditional local with well kept changing ales such as Cains, good service, lots of woodwork, prints, White Star shipping line memorabilia, magnificent Bass mirror and big-screen sports TV in back room; open all day *(the Didler, Patrick Hancock, John Dwane, Joe Green)*

LOWER BARTLE [SD4832]

Sitting Goose [off B5411 just NW of Preston; Lea Lane]: Attractive, neat olde-worlde country pub, very popular with older people for good value cheap and cheerful lunches, partly no smoking dining room, enthusiastic friendly and chatty licensees, good service, well kept Thwaites ales; conservatory, pleasant outdoor eating area overlooking trees and fields with adjacent play area *(Margaret Dickinson)*

LYDGATE [SD9704]

☆ *White Hart* [Stockport Rd]: 200-year-old stone-built inn overlooking Saddleworth Moor, well refurbished keeping beams and traditional character, main bar and one side room now a largely no smoking brasserie with wide choice of good food from chicken and pesto sandwiches or home-made sausages up, two other rooms for drinkers (well kept Boddingtons, Moorhouses Pendle Witches Brew and Timothy Taylors Landlord, good wine and malt whisky range), modern-style back restaurant; 12 nice bedrooms, pretty village *(Andrew Crawford, Bob and Lisa Cantrell, Edward Leetham)*

LYDIATE [SD3604]

Scotch Piper [Southport Rd]: Medieval white-painted thatched pub with heavy black beams, flagstones and thick stone walls, Burtonwood Bitter and Top Hat, coal fire in front room, darts in middle room off corridor, carpeted back room, no food, music or machines; picnic-sets in large garden with aviary, hens, donkey and abundant flower baskets, open all day wknds *(the Didler)*

MANCHESTER [SJ8284]

☆ *Ape & Apple* [John Dalton St]: Uncharacteristic big open-plan Holts pub with their great value beer kept well and monthly guest beer festival, bargain hearty bar food, comfortable seats in bare-boards bar with nice lighting and lots of old prints and posters, armchairs in upstairs lounge; piped music, TV area, games machines; good mix on busy wknd evenings (unusually for city centre, over-25s won't feel out of place), quieter lunchtime or midweek; unusual brick cube garden, bedrooms, open all day *(Stephen, Julie and Hayley Brown, the Didler, Catherine Pitt, Dr and Mrs A K Clarke, Richard Lewis)*

Bar Centro [Tib St]: Continental-style two-floor café-bar, pale woodwork, well kept Hydes and a couple of local guest beers, continental draught beers, up-to-date food, daily papers, friendly helpful staff, local paintings for sale, frequent live music and DJs; open all day (till 1am Thurs-Sat) *(the Didler, Richard Lewis)*

Bar Fringe [Swan St]: Light and airy continental café-style bare-boards bar specialising in beers from the low countries, also well kept Bank Top Gold Digger and a couple of interesting guest ales, farm cider, friendly staff, food till 7, daily papers, cartoons, prints and bank notes, polished motorcycle hung above door; games inc pinball, good music; tables out behind, open all day *(the Didler, Richard Lewis)*

Beer House [Angel St, off Rochdale Rd]: Lively basic open-plan pub with half a dozen changing well kept ales, also Thatcher's and a guest farm cider, several belgian beers on tap, good range of bottled foreign beers and country wines; bare boards, friendly landlady, old local prints, robust cheap bar food lunchtime and Thurs/Fri evening inc Mon bargain lunch; darts, good CD juke box (may be loud), games machine, more comfortable upstairs bar with bar billiards, table footer and SkyTV, ceilidh band Tues; tables out in small area behind, open all day *(Richard Lewis, Peter F Marshall, Doug*

Christian, Catherine Pitt, the Didler, SLC)

Castle [Oldham St, about 200 yards from Piccadilly, on right]: Unspoilt traditional front bar, small snug, full Robinsons range kept well from fine bank of handpumps, games in well worn back room, nice tilework outside; no food, children allowed till 7, blues Thurs, open all day (Sun afternoon closure) *(the Didler, Patrick Hancock)*

Circus [Portland St]: Great atmosphere in two tiny rooms, back one panelled with leatherette banquettes, very well kept Tetleys from minute corridor bar, friendly landlord, celebrity photographs, no music or machines; often looks closed but normally open all day wkdys (you have to knock) *(Stephen, Julie and Hayley Brown, the Didler, P G Plumridge, Patrick Hancock)*

City Arms [Kennedy St, off St Peters Sq]: Five well kept changing beers, belgian bottled beers, occasional beer festivals, popular bar lunches inc sandwiches and baked potatoes, quiet evenings; coal fires, bare boards, prints and panelling, wheelchair access but steps down to back lounge; good piped music, TV, games machine; open all day (cl Sat lunchtime, Sun) *(P G Plumridge, Richard Lewis, the Didler, Pete Yearsley, John Hulme)*

Coach & Horses [Old Bury Rd, Whitefield; A665 nr Besses o' the Barn Station]: Coaching inn built around 1830, little changed and keeping several separate rooms, very popular and friendly, with well kept Holts, table service, darts, cards; open all day *(the Didler)*

Crescent [The Crescent (A6), Salford – opp Salford Univ]: Three 18th-c houses converted into beer house in 19th, unusual layout and homely unsmart décor, buoyant local atmosphere (popular with students and university staff), up to eight interesting guest ales, farm ciders, lots of foreign beers, good value food (not Sun), friendly staff, pool room, juke box; small enclosed outside area, open all day *(the Didler)*

Didsbury [Wilmslow Rd, Didsbury]: Roomy yet with intimate alcoves and soft lighting inc candles, hop bines on oak beams, mixed old oak and pine furniture, well spaced tables, roaring log fire in stone fireplace, old Didsbury prints on dark panelling, old bottles and copper platters; well kept Courage Directors and Tetleys, decent wines, wide choice of enjoyable food from sandwiches and ciabattas to steaks and popular Sun lunch, daily papers, friendly efficient service; quiet piped music; open all day *(Peter and Andrea Jacobs)*

Eagle [Collier St, off Greengate, Salford]: Old-fashioned basic backstreet local, well kept Holts Bitter and Mild at old-fashioned prices, friendly service, cheap filled rolls, bar servery to tap and passage with two smoke rooms, old Salford pictures; open all day *(the Didler)*

Egerton Arms [Gore St, Salford; A6 by

station]: Several rooms, chandeliers, art nouveau lamps, excellent value Holts Bitter and Mild, also Boddingtons and Marstons; open all day *(the Didler)*

Grey Horse [Portland St, nr Piccadilly]: Cosy traditional Hydes local, welcoming and busy, with timbering, pictures and plates, well kept Bitter and Mild, some unusual malt whiskies, popular lunchtime food; no juke box or machines, open all day *(John Hulme, P G Plumridge, Patrick Hancock, the Didler)*

Hare & Hounds [Shudehill, behind Arndale]: Long narrow bar linking front snug and comfortable back lounge (with TV), notable tilework, panelling and stained glass, well kept Holts, Lees and Tetleys, sandwiches, friendly staff; games and machine, piano singalongs, upstairs Fri folk club; open all day *(Pete Baker, the Didler)*

Jolly Angler [Ducie St]: Plain backstreet local, long a favourite, small and friendly, with well kept Hydes Bitter and a seasonal beer, coal or turf fire; darts, pool and TV, informal folk singing some nights; open all day Sat *(Pete Baker, the Didler, BB, Patrick Hancock)*

Kings Arms [Bloom St, Salford]: Big busy old local, not smart and in a decayed area, but friendly, with ten or more well kept ales inc new local Bazens; small snug with a deep corridor and pinball machines; open all day, handy for Central station *(the Didler)*

Kro Bar [Oxford Rd, opp univ faculty buildings]: Lively and airy modern danish-theme bar favoured by students, scandinavian snacks and full meals, well kept Boddingtons, Marstons Pedigree, Timothy Taylors Landlord and guests such as Gales HSB and Jennings, mainly counter-seating with high stools; picnic-sets under cover on front terrace, open all day *(Ian Phillips, Catherine Pitt)*

Lloyds [Wilbraham Rd, Chorlton cum Hardy]: Former Conservative Club reopened as Lees flagship after costly refurbishment, their full beer range kept well, good coffees and choice of teas, food from enterprising sandwiches and light dishes to pubby favourites and grills, open-plan bare-boards lounge with sofas, armchairs and something of a 1930s feel, smoking area with board games and books, carpeted dining area overlooking crown bowling green; open all day *(Pete Yearsley)*

☆ **Mr Thomas Chop House** [Cross St]: Long bustling Victorian city pub, bare boards, panelling and original gas lamp fittings in front bar with stools at wall and window shelves, back eating area with crisp tilework, interesting period features inc wrought-iron gates, good very popular traditional lunchtime food with innovative touches, Sun lunch too now, proper waiters and waitresses, efficient and friendly, well kept Boddingtons, Timothy Taylors Landlord and guests such as Archers Gold and Smiles Best, decent wines, no smoking area; open all day *(Crystal and Peter Hooper, Steve Whalley, the Didler, Stephen, Julie and Hayley Brown, GLD)*

Old Monkey [Portland St]: Traditional Holts pub, built 1993 but you'd never guess from the etched glass and mosaic tiling; interesting memorabilia, bargain generous tasty food, well kept cheap Bitter and Dark Mild, quick friendly service even when busy, upstairs lounge, wide mix of customers *(Dr and Mrs A K Clarke, the Didler, C J Fletcher, Stephen, Julie and Hayley Brown)*

Old Wellington [Cathedral Gates, off Exchange Sq]: Tudor pub moved from Old Shambles Sq during Arndale rebuild, original flagstones, panelling and 16th-c gnarled oak beams and timbers, new bar fittings; open-plan downstairs with small bar and food area, partly no smoking restaurant on two floors above, well kept Bass, afternoon tea; trendy piped music; lots of tables out overlooking new Exchange Sq *(BB, SLC, Stephen, Julie and Hayley Brown, Mike and Cheryl Lyons, R T and J C Moggridge)*

Olde Nelson [Chapel St, Salford (A6 opp cathedral)]: Lots of brewery and whisky mirrors in drinking corridor linking front sliding-door snug and back lounge – more mirrors and brass here; Boddingtons and Lees, darts, dominoes, cards; live entertainment Sat, open all day *(the Didler, Pete Baker)*

☆ **Peveril of the Peak** [Gt Bridgewater St]: Three very welcoming traditional rooms around central servery, lots of mahogany, mirrors and stained or frosted glass, splendidly lurid art nouveau green external tilework; busy lunchtime but friendly and homely evenings, with cheap basic lunchtime food (not Sun), family service, log fire, well kept Boddingtons, Tetleys and Websters, sturdy furnishings on bare boards, interesting pictures, pub games inc pool, table football, juke box; seats outside, children welcome, cl wknd lunchtimes *(the Didler, Patrick Hancock, John Hulme, Stephen, Julie and Hayley Brown, Doug Christian, P Abbott, LYM)*

Plough [Hyde Rd (A57), Gorton]: Superb tiling, windows and gantry in basic local with TV and wooden benches in large public bar, two quieter back lounges, small pool room, Robinsons on electric pump – handpumps kept for emergencies *(the Didler)*

Pot of Beer [New Mount St]: Small refurbished pub with bare boards, stripped bricks and panelling, four well kept interesting changing beers (some tapped from casks projecting from temperature-controlled chamber), Thatcher's farm cider, good value generous Polish wkdy lunchtime food (and beers), friendly licensees, coal fire; music nights, tables outside, open all day, cl Sun evening *(Richard Lewis, the Didler)*

☆ **Queens** [Honey St, Cheetham; off Red Bank, nr Victoria Station]: Well preserved Empress Brewery tiled façade, well kept Phoenix Bantam, Timothy Taylors Landlord and several guest beers from small breweries, belgian imports, Weston's farm cider, simple enjoyable food (all day wknds), coal fire, bar billiards, backgammon, chess, good juke box; children welcome, quiz night Tues; unexpected views of Manchester across the Irk Valley and its railway lines from large back garden with good play area, worth penetrating the surrounding viaducts, scrapyards and industrial premises; open all day *(the Didler)*

☆ *Rain Bar* [Gt Bridgewater St]: Appealing umbrella works conversion, lots of woodwork and flagstones, full range of Lees beers kept well, decent wines, good value food from 9am breakfast, warmly friendly service, daily papers, great canal views, large upstairs bar too; no under-21s, good canalside terrace, open all day *(Stephen, Julie and Hayley Brown, the Didler, Chrissie Pickering)*

Sams Chop House [Back Pool Fold, Chapel Walks]: Sister pub to Mr Thomas Chop House, with identical good value food in small restaurant off bar, proper waitresses and waiters, Boddingtons and guest beers, good wine choice, thriving atmosphere *(Ken Richards, GLD)*

☆ *Sinclairs* [2 Cathedral Gates, off Exchange Sq]: Largely 18th-c low-beamed and timbered pub reopened after being dismantled, moved a short distance, and re-erected brick by brick, as part of the city centre reconstruction; cheap food, bargain Sam Smiths Bitter and Stout, friendly service, great atmosphere, upstairs bar with snugs and Jacobean fireplace; plastic glasses for the tables out by ultra-modern Exchange Sq *(LYM, Catherine Pitt, the Didler, P G Plumridge)*

Smithfield [Swan St]: Open-plan family-run local tracking down unusual well kept changing beers, regular beer festivals, enjoyable bargain food from sandwiches up from open kitchen servery, TV in back lounge/eating area, daily papers, friendly staff and landlady; pool on front dais, games machine, juke box; open all day, good value bedrooms in nearby building *(Richard Lewis, the Didler, BB)*

Waldorf [Gore St]: Modernised but still quietly old-fashioned, with soft lighting, bare boards and brickwork, alcove areas off central bar, well kept Boddingtons and other real ales, busy friendly staff, wide food choice; games machines, music nights *(the Didler, Dr and Mrs A K Clarke)*

White Lion [Liverpool Rd, Castlefield]: Busy but friendly Victorian pub, tables for eating up one side of three-sided bar, home-made food all day till 10 inc children's helpings, several changing ales, decent house wine, good tea, friendly service, real fire, lots of prints and Man Utd pictures, shelves of bottles and jugs; sports TV, disco Fri; children welcome, tables out among excavated foundations of Roman city overlooking fort gate, handy for Museum of Science and Industry and Royal Exchange Theatre, open all day *(the Didler)*

MARPLE [SJ9488]
Railway [Stockport Rd]: Popular, with good value lunchtime food (children allowed then) from toasties to Sun roasts, well kept Robinsons beers; open all day *(Tony Hobden)*

MAWDESLEY [SD4914]
☆ *Red Lion* [off B5246 N of Parbold]: Busy village pub with darkly traditional bars, colourful dining room and brightly painted conservatory, popular and often rewarding food (all day Sun; not Mon/Tues) inc good value set meals, huge helpings, friendly attentive service, well kept Black Sheep, Theakstons Best and Websters, decent wines by the glass; piped music may obtrude; children in eating areas, tables in courtyard behind, more in front, open all day *(Michael Doswell, Nick Holding, Jack Clark, Norma and Noel Thomas, Mike and Linda Hudson, LYM, Revd D Glover)*

MELLOR [SD6530]
Millstone [this is the Mellor up near Blackburn]: Stone-built village pub, pleasant panelled bar with comfortable lounge one side, modern dining extension the other, obliging friendly staff, well kept Thwaites Bitter, Mild and Lancaster Bomber, decent food from bar snacks to popular substantial Sun lunch, big log fire; bedrooms *(Steve Whalley)*

MELLOR BROOK [SD6431]
Feildens Arms [Whalley Rd]: Three linked areas done up in terracotta and ochre, pine and flagstones, books, old signs and pictures, quick friendly bar service, good choice of wines by the glass, Boddingtons, good if pricy restaurant dishes (attractive bar meals too), pleasant dining room *(Steve Whalley, RJH)*

NETHER BURROW [SD6175]
Highwayman [A683 S of Kirkby Lonsdale]: Attractive 17th-c inn with well kept Thwaites ales, good value home-made blackboard food from sandwiches up, some small helpings available, friendly staff, comfortable banquettes and highwayman theme in civilised bar with coal fire, pleasant back restaurant; children welcome, french windows to big terrace and lovely gardens with play area, pretty Lune Valley countryside *(Gwyneth and Salvo Spadaro-Dutturi, MLR)*

OLDHAM [SD9605]
Peels Arms [Den Lane]: Two welcoming beamed rooms, well kept Greenalls, good value food, committed licensees and switched-on staff *(Jack Clark)*

OVER HULTON [SD7005]
Watergate Toll [just off A6 by M61 junction 4]: Popular pub with changing Whitbreads-related beers, pleasant staff and good choice of reasonably priced food; wheelchair access, karaoke nights *(Michael Tack)*

OVERTON [SD4357]
Globe: Large and attractive, with good range of decent bar food, lunchtime carvery

(all day Sun), Jennings ales, pleasant service, conservatory; safely fenced garden with play area, bedrooms – quiet spot, handy for Sambo's Grave at Sunderland Point *(Margaret Dickinson)*

PENDLETON [SD7539]

☆ *Swan With Two Necks*: Welcoming olde-worlde village pub below Pendle Hill, simply furnished, warm and tidy, with good value generous home cooking, friendly service, well kept local Moorhouses and changing ales such as Evesham and Phoenix; large garden, open all day Sun, cl Mon/Tues lunchtimes *(LYM, Mike Turner)*

PRESTON [SD5330]

Black Horse [Friargate]: Thriving friendly untouched pub in pedestrian street, full Robinsons ale range kept well, inexpensive lunchtime food, unusual ornate curved and mosaic-tiled Victorian main bar, panelling, stained glass, mosaic floor and two quiet cosy enclosed snugs off, upstairs 1920s-style bar; pictures of old town, lots of artefacts, good juke box; no children, open all day *(Pete Baker, the Didler)*

☆ *Fleece* [Liverpool Rd, Penwortham Hill]: Good value pubby food inc imaginative dishes, real ales, good service, happy atmosphere, comfortable no smoking area; large garden with play area *(Norman Revell, Margaret Dickinson)*

RINGLEY [SD7605]

Horseshoe [Fold Rd, Stonehouse; right off A667 at sign for Kidds Garden Centre]: Good imaginative food, wider choice evenings (with advance warning do game, seafood and imaginative vegetarian dishes); friendly landlord, cheap well kept Thwaites, three areas off main bar, open fire, interesting local pictures, pleasant back garden; well behaved children lunchtime *(DC)*

ROBY MILL [SD5107]

Fox [not far from M6 junction 26; off A577 at Up Holland]: Nicely placed big traditional two-roomed black and white village pub, well kept Marstons Pedigree and Timothy Taylors Landlord, wide range of good value food in bar and restaurant, tasteful antiquey décor, friendly staff *(Jack Clark)*

SCOUTHEAD [SD9605]

Three Crowns [Huddersfield Rd]: Wide choice of enjoyable menu and blackboard food, Boddingtons, Marstons and a guest beer, good thriving atmosphere, pleasant welcoming staff; children welcome, inoffensive piped music, no games *(T Pascall)*

SLAIDBURN [SD7152]

☆ *Hark to Bounty* [B6478 N of Clitheroe]: Old stone-built inn in charming Forest of Bowland village, straightforwardly comfortable rather modern décor inside though some older chairs by open fire, wide choice of good value generous food (lots of tables) inc children's and old-fashioned puddings, welcoming efficient service, full Theakstons range kept well, decent wines

and whiskies; bedrooms, open all day, pleasant garden behind, good walks *(Diane Manoughian, LYM)*

SLYNE [SD4765]

Slyne Lodge [Main Rd]: Popular well run hotel, interesting décor, well kept Jennings ales, friendly helpful staff, good value food in imaginative mediterranean-style dining room, open fire, welcoming bar, conservatory; terrace tables, bedrooms with own bathrooms *(Margaret Dickinson, Anthony Rickards Collinson)*

SOUTHPORT [SD3315]

Falstaff [King St]: Roomy and fresh, with enjoyable food and well kept mainly Courage-related beers; open all day *(Keith Jacob)*

Wetherspoons [Lord St]: Well placed, with good choice of food all day and well kept cheap beer, efficient service even when busy *(Derek and Sylvia Stephenson)*

ST ANNE'S [SD3228]

Trawl Boat [Wood St]: Typical Wetherspoons with good lively atmosphere and usual good value food *(Margaret and Roy Randle)*

STOCKPORT [SJ8889]

Alexandra [Northgate Rd]: Large backstreet pub, reputedly haunted, with preserved interior, well kept Robinsons; pool room *(the Didler)*

☆ *Arden Arms* [Millgate St, behind Asda]: Good inventive lunchtime food and well kept Robinsons in welcoming pub with traditional layout inc old-fashioned snug through servery, two coal fires; tables out in courtyard sheltered by the original stables, open all day *(the Didler, John Wildman, Pete Baker)*

Armoury [Shaw Heath]: Small unspoilt locals' bar, comfortable lounge, Robinsons Best and Hatters Mild, perhaps Old Tom from a cask on the bar, lunchtime family room upstairs; open all day *(the Didler)*

Blossoms [Buxton Rd (A6)]: Busy traditional main-road local, very friendly, with well kept Robinsons Best and Hatters Mild, perhaps Old Tom tapped from the cask, superb back room; open all day wknds *(Stephen, Julie and Hayley Brown, the Didler, Bernie Adams)*

Crown [Heaton Lane, Heaton Norris]: Partly open-plan local under arch of vast viaduct, three cosy lounge areas (one no smoking) off gaslit bar, stylish décor, Bank Top and several other well kept ales, farm cider, good value lunchtime bar food, pool, darts, TV; some live music; seats outside, open all day Sat *(the Didler)*

Nursery [Green Lane, Heaton Norris; off A6]: Friendly efficient service, enjoyable lunchtime food from servery on right with visible kitchen, popular set Sun lunch, big bays of banquettes in panelled front room, brocaded wall banquettes in back room, cheap well kept Hydes Bitter and Mild, all very neat and clean; children welcome if eating, on narrow cobbled lane at E end of

N part of Green Lane, bowling green behind, open all day wknds *(BB, the Didler)*

Porters Railway [Avenue St (just off M63 junction 13, via A560)]: Very cheap Porters Bitter, Dark Mild, Rossendale, Porter, Sunshine, Young Tom and Timmys Ginger Beer kept well in comfortable L-shaped bar with old Stockport prints, bottles and memorabilia, friendly staff, decent straightforward home-made food (not Sun), lots of foreign beers, farm cider, no music or machines; tables out behind, open all day *(the Didler)*

Queens Head [Little Underbank (can be reached by steps from St Petersgate)]: Long narrow late Victorian pub with delightful separate snug and back dining area; good friendly bustle, reasonable bar food, well kept Sam Smiths, daily papers, rare brass cordials fountain and old spirit lamps, old posters and adverts; no smoking area, some live jazz, open all day; famous narrow gents' *(Bernie Adams, Stephen, Julie and Hayley Brown, the Didler)*

☆ *Red Bull* [Middle Hillgate]: Friendly well run beamed and flagstoned local, well kept Robinsons Best and Best Mild from nearby brewery, good value home-cooked bar lunches (not Sun), substantial settles and seats, open fires, impressive bar with lots of pictures, brassware and traditional island servery; quiet at lunchtime, can get crowded evening, open all day (Sun afternoon closure) *(the Didler, LYM)*

Swan With Two Necks [Princes St]: Traditional panelled local, comfortable bar, back lounge and drinking corridor, skylight ceiling, Robinsons Mild and Bitter, lunchtime food; handy for shops, open all day, cl Sun *(the Didler)*

SUMMERSEAT [SD7814]

Footballers [Higher Summerseat]: Friendly village local with well kept ales inc Black Sheep, Moorhouses and Timothy Taylors, popular darts, dominoes and quiz nights (free pie for participants), local football team photographs *(P Abbott)*

SWINTON [SD7602]

Morning Star [Manchester Rd, Wardley (A6)]: Busy Holts local, well kept ales, good value basic food wkdy lunchtime, lively games-oriented lounge, usually some Sat entertainment in lounge *(Pete Baker)*

THURSTASTON [SJ2484]

Cottage Loaf [A540]: Picturesque and comfortable, with well kept Cains and a guest such as Wadworths 6X, enjoyable food inc starters and light dishes, pleasant uniformed staff, open fires *(E G Parish, Rita and Keith Pollard)*

TYLDESLEY [SJ6999]

Cart & Horses [Manchester Rd, Astley]: Traditional Holts local with excellent value beer, late Victorian décor, welcoming service; small garden *(Collin and Julie Taylor)*

Mort Arms [Elliott St]: Mature two-room pub, mahogany, etched glass and panels, comfortable lounge, low-priced Holts Bitter and Mild, friendly landlord, crowds huddled around TV for Sat horseracing; open all day *(the Didler)*

UPPERMILL [SE0006]

☆ *Cross Keys* [Church Rd, off Runninghill Gate]: Homely low-beamed moorland local up long steep lane, flagstones and original cooking range, big fires, local pictures for sale, bargain basic well cooked food (all day wknds), quick service even when busy, well kept Lees Bitter and Mild, lots of malt whiskies; pub games, TV in tap room; children in side rooms, tables out on terraces with adventure playground, lovely setting, lots of walks *(Pat and Tony Martin, LYM)*

WEST KIRBY [SJ2186]

White Lion [A540 Chester rd]: Interesting small 17th-c sandstone pub, several small beamed areas on different levels, simple bar lunches inc wide choice of sandwiches, well kept Courage Directors, John Smiths, Theakstons and a guest beer, friendly staff, coal stove; attractive secluded back garden, no children *(MLR)*

WHEELTON [SD5921]

Top Lock [Copthurst Lane]: Cosy pub in picturesque canalside spot, friendly hard-working staff, canal-related décor, good choice of beers such as Cains and Coniston Bluebird, wide range of food – new chef specialising in asian cooking *(Collin and Julie Taylor)*

WIGAN [SD5805]

Swan & Railway [Wallgate, opp Wigan NW Stn]: Appealing traditional local that reverberates with passing trains, several rooms, high ceilings, mosaic tiling of swan and railway lion, lovely swan stained-glass window, welcoming service, cheap basic lunchtime food (not wknds), Banks's and related ales, friendly staff, dominoes, TV; bedrooms, open all day *(Pete Baker, Nick Holding)*

WREA GREEN [SD3931]

☆ *Grapes* [Station Rd]: Busy but roomy open-plan Chef & Brewer with enjoyable food from good sandwiches to some imaginative specials, pleasant clean dining area, well kept Boddingtons, Marstons Pedigree and Theakstons, good choice of wines by the glass, good service, open fire; tables out overlooking village green, picturesque church *(Maurice and Gill McMahon, M S Catling, Margaret and Roy Randle)*

WRIGHTINGTON BAR [SD5011]

Rigbye Arms [3 miles from M6 junction 27; off A5209 via Robin Hood Lane and High Moor Lane]: 16th-c moorland inn popular for good value straightforward food, well kept ales inc Greene King Old Speckled Hen and Timothy Taylors Landlord, nice relaxed atmosphere, pleasant country setting *(Andy and Jill Kassube)*

Leicestershire
and Rutland

*Two nicely contrasting new entries here this year are the interesting Cow &
Plough in Oadby (quite a shrine to beer), and the relaxed Red Lion at Stathern
(great for food, wine and beer – coming straight in with Awards for all three).
Other pubs on top form here this year are the Olive Branch at Clipsham (the
Red Lion's parent pub – very good imaginative food in nice surroundings, and
wins a Star this year for its overall appeal), the Fox & Hounds at Exton
(doing well all round under new Italian licensees – they gain it a Place to Stay
Award), the charmingly placed Nevill Arms at Medbourne (a splendid all-
rounder), the ancient Belper Arms at Newton Bergoland (its enthusiastic
newish landlord settling in well), the Grainstore in Oakham (now has a few
hot dishes to go with its own most enjoyable real ales), the interesting and very
cheerful unspoilt New Inn at Peggs Green, the Old Brewery at Somerby
(bargain food and good value distinctive beers), and the handsome old Kings
Arms at Wing (another fine all-rounder, with good food and well kept beers).
Besides places already noted for good food, the Exeter Arms at Barrowden,
the Nags Head in Castle Donington, the Old White Hart at Lyddington and
the Bakers Arms at Thorpe Langton are all rewarding for a special meal out.
However, it is the Olive Branch at Clipsham which for the second year
running takes the title of Leicestershire and Rutland Dining Pub of the Year.
The Lucky Dip section at the end of the chapter has some current stars to
note: the Barnsdale Lodge at Barnsdale (a hotel, but very welcoming and
relaxed), Wheatsheaf at Greetham, Three Swans in Market Harborough,
Chandlers Arms at Shearsby and Bulls Head at Wilson. Drinks prices are
closely in line with the national average. Several pubs here help their
customers' pockets by brewing their own good beers (or, in the case of the Old
Brewery at Somerby, having Parish beers brewed nearby by a former
landlord). Grainstore beers are also quite widely available at attractive prices
here, as well as at their parent brewpub in Oakham; other small breweries to
look out for include Brewsters and Wicked Hathern. The big Leicester brewer
is Everards.*

BARROWDEN SK9400 Map 4
Exeter Arms 🍽 🍺

Main Street, just off A47 Uppingham—Peterborough

Tucked away in a Rutland stone village, this peaceful 17th-c coaching inn has
picnic-sets on a narrow terrace, overlooking the pretty village green and ducks on
the pond, with broader views stretching away beyond. The pretty setting is not the
only reason to visit, and in an old free-standing barn behind, the pub brews its own
Blencowe beers. Served from up to six handpumps, these might include Beach Boys,
Bevin Boys, Farmer Boys, Four Boys, Fun Boys, and Young Boys (and perhaps a

seasonal brew such as Choir Boys, Lover Boys or Fruity Boys), as well as a couple of guests such as Black Sheep Special and Marstons Pedigree. Painted a cheery yellow, the simple long open-plan bar stretches away either side of a long central counter. It's quite straightforwardly furnished with wheelback chairs at tables at either end of the bar, on bare boards or blue patterned carpet; there's quite a collection of pump clips, beer mats and brewery posters. The blackboard menu changes every day, but good home-made bar food served in generous helpings might typically include soup (£3.75), sandwiches (from £3.75), ploughman's or stilton and black pudding (£4.75), lambs liver stroganoff (£8.50), venison pie (£9.50), grilled bass with herby butter (£10.50), half a crispy duck (£11.50), and fillet steak (£14.50), with home-made puddings such as lemon sponge or fruit crumble (£3.50). There are more well spaced picnic-sets in a big informal grassy garden at the back. They've cribbage, dominoes, shove-ha'penny and piped music, and outside boules and horseshoe pitching. *(Recommended by Stephen, Julie and Hayley Brown, Barry Collett, John, Gwen and Reg, Tom and Ruth Rees, Richard Lewis, DC, Eric Locker, Bob and Maggie Atherton, Susan and John Douglas, Norma and Keith Bloomfield, JWAC, Mike and Sue Loseby, Steve Whalley)*

Own brew ~ Licensees Pete and Elizabeth Blencowe ~ Real ale ~ Bar food (not Sun evening or Mon) ~ Restaurant ~ (01572) 747247 ~ Children (and dogs) welcome away from the bar till 7.30 ~ Blues band alternate Sun evenings, folk club alternate Mon evenings ~ Open 12-2(3 Sat/Sun), 6-11(7-10.30 Sun and bank hols); closed Mon lunchtime ~ Bedrooms: £30S/£60S

BELMESTHORPE TF0410 Map 8
Blue Bell

Village signposted off A16 just E of Stamford

Originally three cottages that have been knocked through into one, this attractive old building is on two levels: so you peer down into the bar counter, and a slope winds down round the counter to another area. The atmosphere is very homely, particularly in the first little beamed cottagey room, which has gleaming brass platters, and an open fire in a huge stone inglenook which opens through to the games room; the new licensees plan to replace the old sofas with pews and settles, and add extra tables for diners. The enjoyable menu includes soup (£3.35), sandwiches (£3.45), filled ciabattas (from £4.45), ploughman's or home-made lincolnshire sausages with chilli mash and tomato gravy (£5.95), and scampi and chips or gammon (£6.45); they've also more elaborate, seasonally changing dishes such as deep-fried king prawns with thai orange sauce (£5.95), roast chicken breast stuffed with cream cheese with asparagus risotto (£10.45), roast rack of lamb with rosemary cream potatoes (£10.95), cinnamon roast duck breast with red onion marmalade and madeira sauce (£11.25), and fresh fish specials. Well kept Bass and Hop Back Summer Lightning with guests such as Fullers London Pride and Charles Wells Bombardier on handpump, and a good choice of wines by the glass; darts, piped music, pool. *(Recommended by Roy Bromell, Bob and Maggie Atherton, Stephen, Julie and Hayley Brown, Bill and Sheila McLardy, Rona Murdoch)*

Free house ~ Licensees Lee Thompson and Angeline Hennessy ~ Real ale ~ Bar food (not Sun evenings) ~ Restaurant ~ (01780) 763859 ~ Children welcome ~ Open 12-2.30, 6-11; 12-10.30 Sun

CASTLE DONINGTON SK4427 Map 7
Nags Head 🍴 ♀

Hill Top; A453, S end

The top-notch food is the reason most people come to this civilised low-beamed dining pub, which is handy for Donnington Race Track. The little bar area as you enter is the simplest part, with quarry tiles, dark green dado and dark tables and wheelback chairs. A step takes you up into a small intimate dining room with simple pressed and punctured iron wall lamps and nice signed french prints on fresh cream walls, three chunky old pine candlelit tables on seagrass, and a little turkey rug in front of a pretty art deco slate fireplace. The other end of the bar takes you into a second much bigger and similarly decorated yellow-washed dining area, its well spaced tables giving it a more elegantly informal feel (from here through an opening to the kitchen you can watch the chefs at work). To be sure of a table, it's a very good idea to book; you order at the bar and are then shown to your table by the waitress when your food is ready. The changing menu could include sandwiches (from £4.95 lunchtime and early evening), soup and baguette (£4.50), tomato and mozzarella with pesto (£4.95), smoked salmon with cream cheese and chives (£6.95), leek and potato bake with cheese sauce (£10.50), beef, mushroom and red wine casserole (£13.50), and lamb shank with mustard mash or halibut steak with garlic and prawn sauce (£14.50); puddings such as chocolate whisky trifle and sticky toffee pudding. Well kept Banks's Mild, Marstons Pedigree and Mansfield on handpump, around 30 malt whiskies and quite a few wines by the glass; they've boules outside. *(Recommended by George and Brenda Jones, Wendy and Bob Needham, the Didler, Ian and Jane Irving, Gillian and Peter Moore, JP, PP, J F Stackhouse, Theo, Anne and Jane Gaskin)*

Marstons (W & D) ~ Tenant Ian Davison ~ Real ale ~ Bar food (not Sun) ~ Restaurant ~ (01332) 850652 ~ Children in restaurant ~ Dogs allowed in bar ~ Open 11.30-2.30, 5.30-11; 12-2.30, 7-10.30 Sun; closed 26 Dec-2 Jan

CLIPSHAM SK9616 Map 8

Olive Branch ★ 🍴 🍷 🍺

Take B668/Stretton exit off A1 N of Stamford; Clipsham signposted E from exit roundabout

Leicestershire and Rutland Dining Pub of the Year

Greatly enjoyed by readers, this well run stone-built country pub has a good choice of drinks and delicious food. The enticing selection of blackboard wines includes interesting bin ends, old clarets and unusual sherries – the friendly obliging staff are happy to help you choose. They've also well kept Grainstore Olive Oil with a guest such as Timothy Taylors Landlord on handpump, freshly squeezed fruit juices, home-made lemonade, good coffee, and winter mulled wine. The emphasis though is on the food, and it's worth booking or arriving early for a table, especially at lunchtime when they do a good value two-course meal (£9.50, not Sunday when they do three courses for £15). Carefully made, using lots of fresh local produce, imaginative dishes change daily, but might include soup (£3.95), sandwiches (from £4.50), game terrine with cumberland sauce (£5.25), excellent honey-roast confit of duck leg with sweet potato and spring onions (£5.50), sausage cassoulet with crispy vegetables (£8.95), braised lamb shoulder with ratatouille and herb crust (£11.25), and roast local partridge with game chips and honey-roast vegetables or fried red mullet with roasted fennel potatoes and sweet pepper sauce (£12.95), with irresistible puddings such as praline parfait or treacle tart with yoghurt ice cream (£4.95); a nice touch is the board of home-baked bread they bring for you to slice yourself, and we liked the cheeseboard (£4.95). There are dark joists and beams in the various smallish attractive rambling room areas, a cosy log fire in the stone inglenook fireplace (they use old menus to light it), and an interesting mix of pictures, some by local artists, country furniture and books (many bought at antique fairs by one of the partners – ask if you see something you like, as much is for sale). The atmosphere is relaxed and civilised. Two of the dining rooms are no smoking; shove-ha'penny, and there may be unobtrusive piped music. Lovely in summer, there are picnic-sets out on a heated terrace, with more on the neat lawn sheltered in the L of its two low buildings. *(Recommended by JWAC, Bob and Maggie Atherton, RB, Mike and Sue Loseby, Barry Collett, Roy Bromell, D F Clarke, Anna and Martyn Carey, Bernie Adams, Jill Franklin, Sally Anne and Peter Goodale, Duncan Cloud, Derek and Sylvia Stephenson)*

Free house ~ Licensees Sean Hope, Ben Jones and Marcus Welford ~ Real ale ~ Bar food (12-2(3 Sun), 7-9, not Sun evening) ~ Restaurant ~ (01780) 410355 ~ Children welcome ~ Dogs allowed in bar ~ Open 12-3, 6-11; 12-11 Sat; 12-5 Sun; 12-3, 6-11 Sat winter; closed Sun evening

COTTESMORE SK9013 Map 7
Sun ♀

B668 NE of Oakham

Most people come to this 17th-c thatched and stone-built village pub for the good value food, and as there aren't many tables in the rooms off the bar, it pays to get here early in winter, or even book; in fine weather, you can also eat out on the terrace. Well prepared food, served by friendly and efficient staff, might include soup (£2.75), scallops (£4.75), baguettes (from £4.50), calves liver or lamb shank (£8.50), and roast gressingham duck breast (£10.50), with specials such as cajun chicken caesar salad (£6.50), and salmon, cod and prawn fishcakes on chilli cream with chilli jam (£7.50), and puddings such as home-made sticky toffee pudding (£3.25). Along with stripped pine furnishings, there's a winter log fire in the stone inglenook, and pictures on the olive and terracotta walls; piped music, and boules outside. Besides decent wines, they serve Adnams and Everards Tiger along with a guest such as Badger Tanglefoot on handpump; generous coffee too. *(Recommended by Paul and Sue Merrick, Barry Collett, Ruth Kitching, Anthony Barnes, Peter and Patricia Burton)*

Everards ~ Tenant David Johnson ~ Real ale ~ Bar food (not Sun evening) ~ Restaurant ~ (01572) 812321 ~ Children welcome till 9pm ~ Dogs allowed in bar ~ Open 11.30-2.30, 6.30-11; 12-3, 7-10.30 Sun; closed Mon

EAST LANGTON SP7292 Map 4
Bell ★ ◧ 🛏

The Langtons signposted from A6 N of Market Harborough; East Langton signposted from B6047

The long stripped-stone beamed bar of this creeper-covered pub is 'a delightful haven on a miserable day' according to readers, with a good log fire and plain wooden tables, while in summer the garden is a pleasant place to sit. The well kept Langton ales are another great draw and, produced in a converted outbuilding, they include Caudle Bitter and Bowler Strong Ale, which are served alongside Greene King Abbot and IPA on handpump, with a couple of guests such as Bass and Timothy Taylors Landlord tapped straight from the cask; there's a £1 discount on a four-pint pitcher. As well as a good choice of lunchtime sandwiches (from £2.95, baguettes from £4.50), home-made bar food might typically include soup (£3.60), pheasant and port pâté or wild mushroom pancake (£4.95), chicken balti (£9.50), fish pie (£9.75), pork stroganoff (£10.95), and minted lamb casserole (£11.25), with puddings (£3.50); they also do a Sunday carvery and weekday OAP lunches. The green-hued dining room is no smoking; cribbage, dominoes. The pub is in an attractive village in peaceful countryside. *(Recommended by M Robinson, Wendy and Bob Needham, Bernie Adams, Philip Atkins, Mrs P Sarson, Gerry and Rosemary Dobson, David Field, R T and J C Moggridge, JP, PP, Mike and Sue Loseby, Eric Locker, John Cook, Howard and Margaret Buchanan, Duncan Cloud, Jim Farmer, Angus Lyon, O K Smyth, Anthony Barnes)*

Own brew ~ Licensee Alastair Chapman ~ Real ale ~ Bar food ~ Restaurant ~ (01858) 545278 ~ Children welcome ~ Dogs allowed in bar and bedrooms ~ Open 11.30-2.30, 7(6.30 Sat)-11; 12-3, 7-10.30 Sun; closed 25 Dec ~ Bedrooms: £39.50S(£39.50B)/£55S(£55B)

EMPINGHAM SK9408 Map 4
White Horse

Main Street; A606 Stamford—Oakham

Handily open all day, this attractive and bustling old dining pub is near Rutland Water. They've well kept Courage Directors and Greene King Old Speckled Hen and Ruddles Best on handpump, along with a guest such as Grainstore Cooking, and up to 10 wines by the glass; they also do morning coffee and afternoon tea. The open-plan carpeted lounge bar has a big log fire below an unusual free-standing chimney-funnel, and lots of fresh flowers, while outside are some rustic tables among urns of flowers. Tasty bar food might include soup (£2.95), filled baguettes (from £3.95), brie, pesto and cherry tomato filo tart (£5.25), vegetable and five bean pasta (£7.95), seafood pancake (£9.95), cajun roast duck breast with smoked bacon, forest berry and wild mushroom sauce (£10.25), and daily specials such as roast leg of lamb with button mushroom and mint gravy (£8.75), and supreme of salmon with white wine and herb marinière sauce (£8.95); puddings (from £3.50), and simple children's meals (£3.95). The restaurant and the Orange Room are no smoking; TV, fruit machine and piped music. Bedrooms are in a converted stable block, and in case any of their residents manage to catch anything they offer freezing facilities. *(Recommended by Neil Skidmore, Eric Locker, Mrs Sally Kingsbury, Rona Murdoch, John and Sylvia Harrop, C J Cox, A Monro, Barry Collett, Mike and Wendy Proctor)*

Courage (S & N) ~ Lease Roger Bourne ~ Real ale ~ Bar food ~ Restaurant ~ (01780) 460221 ~ Children in eating area of bar and restaurant till 8pm ~ Dogs allowed in bedrooms ~ Open 11-11(10.30 Sun) ~ Bedrooms: £50S(£50B)/ £65S(£65B)

EXTON SK9211 Map 7
Fox & Hounds 🛏

Signposted off A606 Stamford—Oakham

On the pleasant well kept back lawn of this handsome former coaching inn, seats among large rose beds look out over paddocks, and the tranquil village green with its tall trees out in front is most attractive. Inside is civilised and comfortable: the high-ceilinged lounge bar has some dark red plush easy chairs as well as wheelback seats around lots of dark tables, maps and hunting prints on the walls, fresh flowers, and a winter log fire in a large stone fireplace. The quite separate public bar has a more pubby atmosphere; cribbage, dominoes and piped music. Under the influence of the new Italian licensees, the good well presented bar food now includes quite a few dishes reflecting their nationality. As well as home-made soup (£3.50), sandwiches (from £3.50), and fresh ciabattas or grilled paninis (from £4.25), you might find mediterranean seafood salad (£5.95), tasty pasta dishes such as fusilli with gorgonzola and spinach or tagliatelle with mushrooms and parmesan (£7.25), rack of lamb with rosemary or home-made steak and kidney pie (£9.95), and grilled halibut steak with mediterranean vegetables (£11.25), with daily specials such as green lip mussels in butter and cider sauce (£6.95), and puddings (£3.50); children's meals (£3.95). The dining room is no smoking. Friendly and attentive staff serve well kept real ales such as Grainstore Cooking and Ten Fifty, and Greene King IPA, with perhaps a guest such as Brewsters Hophead on handpump; they specialise in italian wines, and the coffees are excellent. Only a couple of miles away from Rutland Water, and the pub is a useful stop for walkers on the Viking Way. *(Recommended by Mr and Mrs P L Spencer, Jim Farmer, John and Judy Saville, Angus Lyon, Norma and Keith Bloomfield, F J Robinson, Eric Locker, Barry Collett, C J Cox, A Monro, Graham Holden, Julie Lee, Mike and Sue Loseby, Carol and Dono Leaman, Mike and Wendy Proctor, Roy Bromell)*

Free house ~ Licensees Valter Floris and Rachel Serio ~ Real ale ~ Bar food ~ Restaurant ~ (01572) 812403 ~ Children in eating area of bar and restaurant ~ Dogs allowed in bar ~ Open 11-3, 6-11; 12-4, 7-10.30 Sun ~ Bedrooms: £28/£42

GREAT BOWDEN SP7488 Map 4
Red Lion

Village signposted off A6 just N of Market Harborough; Main Street

On fine weekends in summer, they often hold barbecues at this friendly pub, and have regular wine-tasting evenings and theme nights here too. The four dark brown leather button-back chesterfields in the lounge bar on the left strike a comfortable chord, while other seats around well spaced tables on the polished boards are more orthodox, except perhaps for the group of ultra-tall seats around two unusually lofty tables; the walls too are dark red, and have old-fashioned prints (some of them genuinely old) and a huge mirror. The central bar counter, perhaps with a big vase of flowers, serves up to four well kept real ales such as Adnams Broadside, Fullers London Pride, Greene King IPA and Charles Wells Bombardier on handpump; TV, and piped music may obtrude. On the right is a simply furnished turkey-carpeted dining area. Changing weekly, a short choice of reasonably priced, generously served dishes might include soup or lunchtime sandwiches (£3.50), lamb hotpot and breaded scampi and chips (£5.50), steak, mushroom and Guinness pie or beef lasagne (£6), and specials such as home-made lasagne or curry (around £6); puddings (from £3.50), and Sunday lunch (£7.95, two courses £10.95). The licensees are friendly and enthusiastic, and service is cheerful and obliging. They hold a beer festival around the first summer bank holiday, and they have live bands on some summer Sundays. The well planted green garden has tables out behind; look out for their friendly dog. *(Recommended by Stephen, Julie and Hayley Brown, Duncan Cloud, Eric George, Wendy and Bob Needham)*

Pubmaster ~ Tenants Mandy and Richard Kitson ~ Real ale ~ Bar food (till 10 Fri/Sat, not Sun evening) ~ (01858) 463106 ~ Children in eating area of bar and restaurant till 9pm ~ Dogs allowed in bar ~ Live bands on bank hol Sun ~ Open 12-2.30, 5.30-11; 12-11 Sat; 12.10.30 Sun; closed evening 25 Dec

GUMLEY SP6790 Map 4
Bell

Off A6 Market Harborough—Kibworth, via Foxton; or off A5199 via Laughton; Main Street

Look out for the cricketing prints and cartoons, and the miniature bat collection in the lobby of this cheerful neatly kept village pub. The almost L-shaped bar on the right, with typical pub furnishings, has lots of hunting prints on its cream walls, game bird plates above the bar, china jugs and mugs and horsebrasses on some of its black beams and joists, more china on a delft shelf, and ornaments on the window sills, with perhaps a big flower arrangement in the corner; darts, cribbage, dominoes and piped music (but no mobile phones). Tasty bar food includes sandwiches (from £2.50), home-made soup (£2.75), ploughman's (£4.95), battered cod (£5.95), steak and kidney pie (£6.50), fresh fillet of salmon mornay (£7.95), and steaks (from £8.95), with home-made puddings such as bread and butter pudding or trifle (£2.75); they also do a good value two-course OAP lunch (£3.95). The no smoking dining room fills quickly at lunchtime, so get there early if you want to eat. Bass, Batemans XB and Greene King IPA are well kept on handpump, alongside a guest beer; service is pleasant and attentive. The pretty terrace garden behind is not for children or dogs. More reports please. *(Recommended by George Atkinson, Eric Locker, Gerry and Rosemary Dobson)*

Free house ~ Licensee David Quelch ~ Real ale ~ Bar food (not evenings Sun or Mon) ~ (0116) 2792476 ~ Children over 5 in no smoking eating area, and not in garden ~ Dogs allowed in bar ~ Open 11-3, 6-11; 12-3 Sun; closed Sun evening

KEGWORTH SK4826 Map 7
Cap & Stocking

A mile or so from M1 junction 24: follow A6 towards Loughborough; in village, turn left at chemists' down one-way Dragwall opposite High Street, then left and left again, into Borough Street

A handy retreat from the M1, the three rooms of this town local are an intriguing throwback to another age. The brown paint and etched glass in the right-hand room make it seem as if little has changed since the 1940s, and they still serve Bass from an enamelled jug; you'll also find Greene King IPA and a guest such as Fullers London Pride on handpump. The two determinedly simple but cosy front rooms both have their own coal fire and an easy-going feel, and furnishings include big cases of stuffed birds and locally caught fish, fabric-covered wall benches and heavy cast-iron-framed tables, and a cast-iron range; cribbage, dominoes, fruit machine, trivia and piped music. The back room has french windows to the pretty, secluded garden, where there may be floodlit boules and barbecues in summer. Straightforward bar food includes filled rolls (from £1.60), soup (£2.15), burgers (from £2.70), ploughman's and pizzas (from £5), beef casserole (£6.25), and daily specials such as thai chicken (£6.50). *(Recommended by Simon Collett-Jones, Bernie Adams, the Didler, F J Robinson, Pete Baker, Pauline and Philip Darley, Gillian and Peter Moore, J V Dadswell, Patrick Hancock, David Carr, Steve and Liz Tilley, Mike Turner, D L Parkhurst, Alison Hayes, Pete Hanlon)*

Punch ~ Tenants Graham and Mary Walsh ~ Real ale ~ Bar food (11.30-2.15, 6.30-9) ~ No credit cards ~ (01509) 674814 ~ Children welcome ~ Dogs welcome ~ Open 11.30-2.30, 6.30-11; 12-2.30, 7-10.30 Sun

LYDDINGTON SP8797 Map 4
Old White Hart ⊞
Village signposted off A6003 N of Corby

As you make your way through the passage to the cosy bar at this civilised country inn, notice the original 17th-c window – a discreet reminder that the pub was once part of the Burghley Estate. The softly lit low-ceilinged bar has just three close-set tables in front of its roaring log fire, and heavy bowed beams. The bar opens into an attractive restaurant, and on the other side is another tiled-floor room with some stripped stone, cushioned wall seats and mate's chairs, and a woodburning stove; this second part is no smoking. Most people come here for the excellent food, and the seasonally changing menu might include home-made soups (£3.25), fried sardines with lemon and herb couscous (£4.95), rack of lamb with roast gravy or fried calves liver with crispy bacon and sage jus (£11.95), half a roast duck with orange and clove sauce (£13.95), with lots of daily specials such as toad in the hole with home-made sausages (£8.95), home-made salmon and cod fishcakes (£9.95), and roast monkfish with lemon butter sauce (£11.95), and puddings such as spotted dick or strawberry and vanilla cheesecake (from £4.75). Friendly and efficient staff serve well kept Greene King IPA, Abbot and a guest such as Timothy Taylors Landlord on handpump; shove-ha'penny, cribbage and dominoes, and 12 floodlit boules pitches. The pretty walled garden is a pleasant place for a civilised drink, and if you sit outside on Thursday evening you'll probably hear the church bell-ringers. Set in a picturesque village with good nearby walks, the pub is handy for Bede House. *(Recommended by Bob and Maggie Atherton, Rona Murdoch, Barry Collett, David and Helen Wilkins, Eric Locker, Alan and Gill Bull, Les and Barbara Owen, John Cook, Mike and Sue Loseby)*

Free house ~ Licensee Stuart East ~ Real ale ~ Bar food ~ Restaurant ~ (01572) 821703 ~ Children in eating area of bar and restaurant ~ Open 12-3, 6.30-11(7-10.30 Sun); closed 25 Dec ~ Bedrooms: £50S(£50B)/£75S(£75B)

MARKET OVERTON SK8816 Map 7
Black Bull ⇔
Village signposted off B668 in Cottesmore

With a cheerfully bustling atmosphere, the low black-beamed bar of this friendly old thatched stone-built pub has raspberry mousse walls, red plush stools and cushioned spindleback chairs at dark wood pub tables, and flowers on the sills of its little curtained windows. You'll probably have trouble choosing from the tremendous variety of well cooked reasonably priced dishes on the menu, but if you have any special requests they're happy to try and accommodate them; some of the daily specials are on a blackboard – ask the cheerfully helpful landlord or friendly staff for others. At lunchtime, besides filled ciabattas (from £4.25), there could be home-made burgers (£6.95), tuna salad, sizzling chicken or steak, mushroom and ale pie (£7.95), with evening dishes such as liver and bacon with caramelised onions and creamed potatoes (£8.95), chicken with creamy stilton and bacon sauce, lamb steak with leeks and stilton in redcurrant sauce, or chinese sizzling vegetables (all £9.95), with around six fish dishes such as battered haddock with chips (£10.95), bass with king prawns and scallops with honey and sweet chilli (£13.95), even unusual fish such as nile perch and zander; tempting home-made puddings could be strawberry pavlova or crème brûlée (£3.50). The main dining room has a no smoking area. They serve well kept Fullers London Pride, Greene King IPA, Hook Norton Best and Charles Wells Bombardier from handpump; piped music, darts, fruit machine, TV, cribbage and dominoes. *(Recommended by RB, Barry Collett, Comus and Sarah Elliott, Rodney and Norma Stubington, Keith and Sarah Burrluck, Revd John E Cooper, June and Malcolm Farmer, Eric Locker, Patrick Hancock)*

Free house ~ Licensees John and Val Owen ~ Real ale ~ Bar food ~ Restaurant ~ (01572) 767677 ~ Children in eating area of bar ~ Dogs allowed in bar ~ Open 11-2.30, 6-11; 12-3, 7-10.30 Sun ~ Bedrooms: £35S/£48S

MEDBOURNE SP7993 Map 4
Nevill Arms ★ ◖ ⇌

B664 Market Harborough—Uppingham

You're sure to receive a warm welcome from the hard-working licensees at this excellently run old pub. It's attractive, with handsome stonework and imposing latticed mullioned windows, and it's in a peacefully picturesque village – you reach it by a footbridge over the little duck-filled River Welland. The inviting main bar has a buoyant atmosphere, two log fires in stone fireplaces at either end, chairs and small wall settles around its tables, and a lofty dark-joisted ceiling; piped music. Much needed at busy times, a spacious back room by the former coachyard has pews around more tables, and some toys to amuse children. In summer most people prefer to eat at the tables out on the grass by the dovecote. Enjoyably hearty home-made food from a short but reasonably priced menu includes sandwiches (from £2.50), panini with hot fillings such as mozzarella and chargrilled peppers or chicken and smoky bacon (£3.95), and blackboard specials such as beery beef, tomato and goats cheese tart, lamb with apricots, and pork with cream and mustard (all £5.95), and steak (£7.95). They have well kept Adnams, Fullers London Pride and Greene King Abbot on handpump, with two changing guests such as Black Sheep Bitter and Youngs Bitter, and about two dozen country wines. A wide choice of games includes darts, shove-ha'penny, cribbage, dominoes, table skittles, and on request other board games and even table football; look out for Truffles the cat, and the two inquisitive great danes, Cleo and her son Bertie. The bedrooms are in two neighbouring cottages, and the first-class breakfasts are served in the pub's sunny conservatory. The church over the bridge is worth a visit. *(Recommended by David Carlile, J and C J Dean, John Saul, Stuart and Alison Ballantyne, David Field, Eric Locker, Norma and Keith Bloomfield, Duncan Cloud, George Atkinson, the Didler, Mrs M Smith, Angus Lyon, Tracey and Stephen Groves, Mike and Sue Loseby, Rona Murdoch, Mrs K J Betts, JP, PP, W W Burke, R Pring, Barry Collett, Wendy and Bob Needham, Richard Gibbs, Mrs Phoebe A Kemp, R N and M I Bailey, Janet and Peter Race)*

Free house ~ Licensees Nicholas and Elaine Hall ~ Real ale ~ Bar food (12-2, 7-9.45, not 25 Dec) ~ (01858) 565288 ~ Children in family room ~ Dogs allowed in bar ~ Open 12-2.30(3 Sat), 6-11; 12-3, 7-10.30 Sun; closed 25 Dec evening and 31 Dec ~ Bedrooms: £45B/£55B

NEWTON BURGOLAND SK3708 Map 4
Belper Arms

Village signposted off B4116 S of Ashby or B586 W of Ibstock

From a suit of old chain mail, to a collection of pewter teapots and some good antique furniture, this interesting roadside pub has plenty for you to look at. It's quite a big place, knocked through, with ancient features – heavy beams, changing floor levels and separate areas with varying floor and wall materials – all reflecting the various stages in its development (they help give it a cosy intimate feel). Parts are said to date back to the 13th c, and much of the exposed brickwork certainly looks at least three or four hundred years old. A big freestanding central chimney has a fire one side and a range on the other, with chatty groups of captain's chairs. Look out for the story of the pub ghost (Five to Four Fred) framed on the wall.

Readers enjoy the popular bar food which includes soup (£2.95), baguettes or ciabattas (from £3.95), smoked haddock rarebit with tomato salad (£3.95), vegetable medley with apricots, almonds and couscous (£7.25), steak and ale pie (£7.35), gammon steak with grilled tomato, mushrooms and a fried egg (£7.85), and sirloin steak (£9.95), with specials such as salmon fillet (£8.95), and puddings (from £3); three-course Sunday lunch (£10.75). Up a step on one side of the bar, the big square restaurant is no smoking. Adnams, Hook Norton Best, Marstons Pedigree, and a couple of guests such as Burton Bridge Bitter and Timothy Taylors Landlord are well kept on handpump, and there are 10 wines by the glass. The landlord is very hands-on, and there's a good pubby atmosphere; pleasant piped music and dominoes. A rambling garden has boules, cricket nets and children's play area, and works its way round the pub to white tables and chairs on a terrace, and a steam-engine-shaped barbecue; there's a good campsite here too. *(Recommended by Ian and Jane Irving, Gillian and Peter Moore, JP, PP, the Didler, I J and S A Bufton, Joyce and Maurice Cottrell)*

Mercury Taverns ~ Manager Guy Wallis ~ Real ale ~ Bar food ~ Restaurant ~ (01530) 270530 ~ Children welcome ~ Dogs allowed in bar ~ Open 12-3, 6-11; 12-11 Sat; 12-10.30 Sun

OADBY SK6200 Map 4
Cow & Plough ◖

Gartree Road (B667 N of centre)

A must for anyone interested in real ale and its history, this unique beer house was created from the former milking sheds of what's still a working farm. The best part is undoubtedly the two dark back rooms known as the Vaults, packed with an extraordinary and ever-expanding collection of old brewery memorabilia lovingly assembled by the landlord. Almost every item has a story behind it, from the enamel signs and mirrors advertising long-forgotten brews, through the aged brass cash register, to the furnishings and fittings salvaged from pubs and even churches (there's some splendid stained glass behind the counter). The pub first opened about 15 years ago with just these cosily individual rooms, but it soon tripled in size when an extensive long, light, flagstoned conservatory was added to the front; it too has its share of brewery signs and the like, as well as plenty of plants and fresh flowers, a piano, beams liberally covered with hops, and a real mix of traditionally pubby tables and chairs, with lots of green leatherette sofas, and small round cast-iron tables. One section has descriptions of all Leicester's pubs. The whole of the conservatory is no smoking. Blackboards list the daily changing range of between six and eight often rather unusual beers, which as well as Steamin' Billy brewed for them by Grainstore might typically include things like Batemans XB, Greene King Abbot, Roosters June Buggy, Shardlow Cavendish Dark, and Wye Valley Butty Bach. They also have farm ciders, and country wines; lots of pub games like shove-ha'penny, unobtrusive piped music. Bar food is currently limited to lunchtime sandwiches, but they hope to start doing full meals soon, and perhaps even by the time this edition of the *Guide* reaches the shops. Opening times are unusual (they're not currently open most weekday lunchtimes, and they close at 10), but this may change now that the surrounding farm no longer has any animals. In the days before foot & mouth when it did, it was one of Britain's best-known farm parks – a legacy of which is the huge car park, which gives the Cow & Plough that rare honour of being a pub where you should always be able to park and find a table without any trouble. There are picnic-sets outside. *(Recommended by Rona Murdoch)*

Free house ~ Licensee Barry Lount ~ Real ale ~ Bar food (sandwiches lunchtime only (but see above)) ~ No credit cards ~ (0116) 272 0852 ~ Children welcome except in vaults ~ Dogs welcome ~ Live music Mon ~ Open 12-3 Fri only; 5-10 Mon-Fri; 12-10 Sat/Sun; closed lunchtimes Mon-Thurs

> It's very helpful if you let us know up-to-date food prices when you report on pubs.

OAKHAM SK8508 Map 4
Grainstore ◥

Station Road, off A606

As popular as ever for its excellent own-brew beers, this converted three-storey Victorian grain warehouse now serves food as well. As soon as you arrive, you get the feel of a working brewery, and you can see the vats of beer through glass doors in the functional open-plan bar. The brewery is a traditional tower brewhouse, with raw materials starting on the upper floor and the finished beer coming out on the bottom floor. The interior is very simple, with wide well worn bare floorboards, bare ceiling boards above massive joists (and noises of the workings above) which are supported by red metal pillars, a long brick-built bar counter with cast-iron bar stools, tall cask tables and simple elm chairs. Their fine beers (Grainstore Cooking, Rutland Panther, Steamin' Billy, Triple B and Ten Fifty) are served traditionally at the left end of the bar counter, and through swan necks with sparklers on the right; the friendly staff are happy to give you samples. At lunchtimes alongside soup (£3), good baguettes (from £2.85), and ploughman's (£4.25), they serve dutchman's breakfast (three eggs, ham, cheese and bread – the chef's Dutch), as well as a few reasonably priced dishes such as lasagne (£5.50) and beef and ale pie, with perhaps a special such as mushroom and mustard puff (£4.25); they hope to eventually serve food in the evenings too. In summer they open huge glass doors on to a terrace stacked with barrels, and with picnic-sets; sporting events on TV, fruit machine, bar billiards, cribbage, dominoes, darts, giant Jenga and bottle-walking. Loading trucks used to pass right through the building; disabled access. You can tour the brewery by arrangement, and they do take-aways. It's very handy for the station. *(Recommended by Barry Collett, Bernie Adams, June and Malcolm Farmer, the Didler, Mike and Sue Loseby, Stephen, Julie and Hayley Brown, JP, PP, Rona Murdoch, Ian and Eileen Johnson)*

Own brew ~ Licensee Tony Davis ~ Real ale ~ Bar food (11.30-2.15, not evenings or Sun) ~ (01572) 770065 ~ Children welcome ~ Dogs allowed in bar ~ live bands second Sun evening in month, afternoon jazz third Sun in month ~ Open 11-11; 12-10.30 Sun

OLD DALBY SK6723 Map 7
Crown

By school in village centre turn into Longcliff Hill

This smart, tucked-away creeper-covered former farmhouse now has new licensees. Its three or four intimate little rooms have black beams, one or two antique oak settles, a mix of carvers and wheelback chairs, hunting and other rustic prints, and open fires; the snug is no smoking. Outside, you'll find cast-iron furniture and rustic tables and chairs on the terrace, hanging baskets and urns of flowers; steps lead down through the sheltered sloping lawn where you can practise your boules with the pub's two teams. They've Theakstons Black Bull and Hook Norton with a couple of guests such as Belvoir Beaver or Courage Directors either on handpump or tapped straight from the cask, and two dozen or more malt whiskies; darts and cribbage. Freshly prepared (though not cheap) with mostly local produce, seasonally changing dishes could include lunchtime sandwiches (£3.95, not Sun), chicken waldorf salad (£5.95), spinach and ricotta tartlet, steak and ale pie or moroccan chicken (£9.95), marinated slow-cooked beef (£10.95), and fish such as bass, monkfish and brill (£16.95); puddings such as summer pudding or dutch apple pie (£4.50). The dining room has a pleasantly relaxed bistro feel. *(Recommended by B and J Shurmer, the Didler, JP, PP, Gillian and Peter Moore, Brian Skelcher, John and Sylvia Harrop, A J Bowen, David Carr, J M Tansey)*

Free house ~ Licensees Mr and Mrs Hayle ~ Real ale ~ Bar food (not Sun evening or Mon lunchtime) ~ Restaurant ~ (01664) 823134 ~ Children in family room ~ Dogs allowed in bar ~ Open 12-3, 6-11(7-10.30 Sun); 12-2.30, 6.30-11(7.30-10.30 Sun) in winter; closed Mon lunchtime

PEGGS GREEN SK4117 Map 7
New Inn £

Signposted off A512 Ashby—Shepshed at roundabout, then Newbold sign down Zion Hill

An incredible collection of old bric-a-brac covers almost every inch of the walls and ceilings of the two cosy tiled front rooms at this appealingly quirky village pub. The little room on the left, a bit like a kitchen parlour, has china on the mantelpiece above a warm coal fire, lots of prints and photographs and little collections of this and that, three old cast-iron tables, wooden stools and a small stripped kitchen table. The room to the right has quite nice stripped panelling, and masses of the sort of bric-a-brac you can spend ages trawling through. The little back lounge, with a stripped wooden floor, has a really interesting and quite touching display of old local photographs including some colliery ones. The pub is in the second generation of the same family, and the cheerful and friendly Irish licensees like to think of it as an extension of their home; you're likely to find a cluster of regulars around the old-fashioned booth bar, and the atmosphere is welcoming and relaxed. They serve filled cobs all day (from £1.40), but otherwise, note the limited food serving times. The short and very good value menu could include faggots and peas (£3.50), corned beef hash (£3.95) and two smoked haddock fillets (£4.45); children's meals (£1.95). Well kept Bass, Marstons Pedigree and a weekly guest on handpump; piped music, dominoes, TV, board games and various special events throughout the year. *(Recommended by the Didler, Bernie Adams, CMW, JJW, George and Brenda Jones, R T and J C Moggridge, JP, PP, Mr and Mrs John Taylor)*

Enterprise ~ Lease Maria Christina Kell ~ Real ale ~ Bar food (12-2; 6-8 Mon; not Tues-Sat evenings; not Sun) ~ No credit cards ~ (01530) 222293 ~ Children in eating area of bar ~ Dogs welcome ~ Open 12-2.30, 5.30-11; 12-3, 6.30-11 Sat; 7-10.30 Sun

SIBSON SK3500 Map 4
Cock

A444 N of Nuneaton

As it's such a fine old building and has been such a favourite with readers, we're keeping our fingers crossed that this interesting pub will continue to please, though we've not yet had news of the new regime. Some parts date back as far as the 13th c, and proof of its age can still be seen in the unusually low doorways, ancient wall timbers, heavy black beams and genuine latticed windows of the neatly kept interior. A room on the right has comfortable seats around cast-iron tables, and more seats built in to what was once an immense fireplace (fabled as a highwayman's hideaway, of course). The room on the left has country kitchen chairs around wooden tables, and there's a no smoking dining area. A little garden (there used to be a cock-fighting pit here) and courtyard area has tables, summer hanging baskets and a flower-filled dray cart in front. They serve Bass, Hook Norton Best and a guest such as Marstons Pedigree on handpump; fruit machine and piped music. The new people plan on specialising in fish such as salmon en croûte (£9.95), bass with chilli and garlic salsa (£12.95), and daily offers like baked swordfish with lemon and garlic butter or half a lobster (£9.95); other dishes might typically include soup (£2.95), sandwiches (from £3.50), steak and kidney pie or vegetarian quiche (£8.75), and specials such as beef stroganoff (£9.95). The restaurant was converted from a former stable block, and the pub is handy for Bosworth battlefield. *(Recommended by Susan and John Douglas, Phil Mason, Mike Horler, John Cook, W and P J Elderkin, Christopher and Jo Barton, I J and S A Bufton, JP, PP, Joan and Tony Walker)*

Punch ~ Lease Mrs Champion ~ Real ale ~ Bar food ~ Restaurant ~ (01827) 880357 ~ Children in eating area of bar ~ Open 11-3, 6-11; 12-3, 7-10.30 Sun

---

Real ale to us means beer which has matured naturally in its cask – not pressurised or filtered.

SOMERBY SK7710 Map 4
Old Brewery ▮ £

Off A606 Oakham—Melton Mowbray, via Cold Overton, or Leesthorpe and Pickwell; can also be reached direct from Oakham via Knossington; High Street

The interesting Parish real ales here are quite a draw (they're brewed locally by the pub's former landlord Barrie Parish), and they're very reasonably priced too. If you're feeling particularly strong-headed you can try Baz's Bonce Blower (a whopping 11%), or there's Poachers Ale and Special which are well kept on handpump alongside a few guests such as Batemans XXXB, Bass and Greene King IPA. The comfortable L-shaped main bar has red plush stools and banquettes and plush-cushioned captain's chairs, a sofa in one corner, and a good log fire in the big stone fireplace; another bar has bays of button-back red seating. The straightforward good value bar menu includes soup (£2.25), sandwiches (from £2.95), garlic mushrooms (£3.75), ploughman's or home-made vegetable curry (£4.95), and home-made steak and Parish ale pie (£5.95), with puddings such as fruit pies (£2.50); they do a bargain three-course lunch (£5.95, not Monday), and on Tuesday and Friday lunchtimes you can get two meals for £6. The dining area and part of the restaurant are no smoking. Fruit machine, TV and piped music; they hold a beer festival in May. A fenced-off area by the car park has white plastic tables, and in summer they have a children's bouncy castle. *(Recommended by Dave Irving, O K Smyth, Richard Lewis, Barry Collett, CMW, JJW, Bernie Adams, JP, PP, Rona Murdoch)*

Own brew ~ Licensees Wendy and Mick Farmer ~ Real ale ~ Bar food (not Mon, or Sun evening) ~ (01664) 454777 ~ Well behaved children till 9pm ~ Dogs allowed in bar ~ Live bands first Sat in month ~ Open 12-2.30, 6.30-11; 12-10.30 Sun; closed Mon lunchtime

Stilton Cheese ▮

High Street; off A606 Oakham—Melton Mowbray, via Cold Overton, or Leesthorpe and Pickwell; can also be reached direct from Oakham via Knossington

The hop-strung beamed bar/lounge of this welcoming 16th-c pub has lots of country prints on its stripped stone walls, a collection of copper pots, a stuffed badger and plenty of restful seats. Well cooked (there are three chefs in the family) and reasonably priced dishes might include sandwiches (from £2.15), soup (£2.50), prawn cocktail (£2.90), ploughman's (£4.75), local sausages and mash or chilli con carne (£5.95), battered cod or home-made steak and kidney pie (£6.25), rump steak (£9.25), and tasty specials such as stilton-stuffed mushrooms (£3.95), sliced duck breast with ginger and orange sauce or home-made venison and mushroom pie (£7.45), monkfish provençale (£7.95), and whole lemon sole with lemon and parsley butter (£10.95); children's meals (£3.75). From five handpumps they serve well kept local Grainstore Ten Fifty, Marstons Pedigree, and Tetleys along with two changing guests such as Brewsters Hophead and Oakham JHB, and they've a good choice of wines, and about two dozen malt whiskies. It's a comfortable place, with an enjoyably thriving relaxed atmosphere; shove-ha'penny, cribbage, dominoes, board games and piped music. The restaurant is no smoking. The terrace has wooden seating and outdoor heaters. More reports please. *(Recommended by RB, Eric Locker, Rona Murdoch, Duncan Cloud, JP, PP)*

Free house ~ Licensees Carol and Jeff Evans ~ Real ale ~ Bar food (12-2, 6-9, not evening 25 Dec) ~ Restaurant ~ (01664) 454394 ~ Children in eating area of bar and restaurant ~ Open 12-3, 6-11(10.30 Sun)

> Post Office address codings confusingly give the impression that some pubs are in Leicestershire, when they're really in Cambridgeshire (which is where we list them).

STATHERN SK7731 Map 7
Red Lion 🍴 ♀ ◀

Off A52 W of Grantham via the brown-signed Belvoir road (keep on towards Harby – Stathern signposted on left); or off A606 Nottingham—Melton Mowbray via Long Clawson and Harby

It looks ordinary from the outside, but don't be fooled: this thriving village pub is now run by the team behind the Olive Tree in Clipsham, and has the same enjoyable mix of excellent food, well chosen wines, and a comfortably quirky and casual atmosphere. There's a particularly laid-back feel to the yellow room on the right, a relaxing lounge with sofas, a fireplace, and a big table with books, papers and magazines; it leads off the smaller, more traditional flagstoned bar, with terracotta walls, another fireplace with a pile of logs beside it, and lots of beams and hops. Dotted around are various oddities picked up by one of the licensees on visits to Newark Antiques Fair: some unusual lambing chairs for example, and a collection of wooden spoons. A little room with tables set for eating leads to the long, narrow main dining room in what was once the pub's skittle alley, and out to a nicely arranged suntrap garden, with good hardwood furnishings spread over its lawn and terrace. With an emphasis on local ingredients, the very good bar food might include pork and home-made black pudding terrine with apple and mustard relish (£4.95), melton mowbray pork pie (£5.95), tomato, red onion and mozzarella tart with mixed leaves (£8.25), fish and chips (£9), and sirloin steak with home-made chips, onion rings, garlic mushrooms and a peppercorn or béarnaise sauce (£14.95). At lunchtimes they do a popular set menu; on Sundays this is usually a treat of a roast, and otherwise a typical choice might be lamb terrine, pan-fried salmon, and fresh fruit salad (two courses £9.50, three courses £11.50). The dining room is no smoking; piped music. Blackboards list several bar snacks, from olives to a bowl of chips (£1.50). The splendid range of drinks takes in well kept Brewsters Hophead from just down the road, Grainstore Cooking Bitter, a couple of changing guest beers such as Flowers IPA or Fullers London Pride, draught belgian beer, freshly squeezed orange and grapefruit, several ciders and fruit punches, and an interesting and rewarding wine list with plenty by the glass and the odd half bottle. An extra surprise is the unusually big play area behind the car park, with swings, climbing frames and so on; it's likely to be refurbished over the next few months. *(Recommended by David and Elaine Shaw, Jill and Keith Wright, Derek and Sylvia Stephenson)*

Free house ~ Licensees Sean Hope, Ben Jones, Marcus Welford ~ Real ale ~ Bar food (12-2, 7(6 Fri)-9.30; 12-3 Sun (possibly Sun evening too)) ~ (01949) 860868 ~ Children welcome ~ Dogs allowed in bar ~ Open 12-3, 6-11; 12-11 Fri/Sat; 12-10.30 Sun

STRETTON SK9416 Map 8
Ram Jam Inn ♀ 🛏

Just off A1: heading N, look out for warning signs some 8 miles N of Stamford, turning off at big inn sign through service station close to B668; heading S, look out for B668 Oakham turn-off, inn well signed on left ¼ mile after roundabout

Although it's not exactly a pub, this popular place comes closer than almost anywhere else to being the true modern equivalent of a coaching inn, and is very useful if you're on the A1. As readers say, 'an excellent place to break a journey', whether you're after a quick snack or an overnight stop. As you go in, the first part of the big stylish open-plan bar/dining area has terracotta-coloured walls decorated in one place with a spread of old breadboards, big ceramic tiles on the floor, bentwood chairs and café tables, and sofas in a cosy panelled alcove with daily papers and a standard lamp. The bar on the left here has Fullers London Pride and John Smiths on handpump, good house wines, freshly squeezed orange juice and excellent fresh-ground coffee; faint piped music. This area spreads on back to a no smoking oak-boarded part with old prints and maps, more of the bentwood chairs, dining chairs, and (by a woodburning stove) another sofa and some wicker armchairs. On the right is a more formal dining layout, also no smoking, with big solid tables and attractive mediterranean photoprints by Georges Meris. Swiftly served by the friendly staff, enjoyable (though not cheap) dishes might include soup (£3.50), chicken liver pâté (£6.25), grilled stuffed camembert with garlic, rosemary, peppers and onions (£6.95), chargrilled minute steak with toasted ciabatta and fried onions (£7.25), and specials such as smoked trout mousse (£4.95), fried salmon with noodles and stir-fried vegetables with soy dressing (£9.75), and king prawns fried in garlic butter (£10.95), while puddings could be jam sponge or chocolate and orange mousse (from £4.25); good children's dishes (£3.95). The bread is baked on the premises and comes with proper butter; they also do cream teas (£3.95), breakfasts (from 7 to 11.30; £6.50) and Sunday roasts (from £7.95). *(Recommended by B and M Kendall, John Coatsworth, Peter and Patricia Burton, Paul and Ursula Randall, Anne and David Robinson)*

Free house ~ Licensees Mike Littlemore and Mrs Margaret Cox ~ Real ale ~ Bar food (12-9.30) ~ Restaurant ~ (01780) 410776 ~ Children welcome ~ Dogs allowed in bedrooms ~ Open 11-11; 12-10.30 Sun; closed 25 Dec ~ Bedrooms: £53.50B/ £63.50B

THORPE LANGTON SP7492 Map 4
Bakers Arms ⏻

Village signposted off B6047 N of Market Harborough

As this thatched pub is the kind of place you'd visit for a civilised meal rather than a quick drink, it's a good idea to book. Stylishly simple old-fashioned furnishings in the knocked-through cottagey beamed interior include stripped pine tables and oriental rugs on bare boards, and nice black and white photographs; the atmosphere is pleasantly relaxed, and there are no games or piped music. Popular, very well prepared dishes could include home-made soup (£3.95), smoked duck salad with artichokes, green beans and sherry dressing (£5.50), fried scallops with prawns, smoked bacon and spaghetti (£7.95), wild mushrooms and spinach in puff pastry (£9.25), pork fillet filled with mozzarella and sage served with tomato jus (£11.95), and (a current favourite with readers) lamb chump with a parsley and garlic crust with spiced butternut squash (£13.95); puddings could be glazed lemon tart with warm blueberry compote or bread and butter pudding (£3.75). They've a good wine list (though not cheap) with around five by the glass, well kept Tetleys on handpump, and in winter they do mulled wine too; the staff are friendly and attentive. The Bakers Arms is tucked away in a little village, and has picnic-sets in the garden. It's worth checking the opening times below carefully. *(Recommended by Wendy and Bob Needham, Duncan Cloud, Mike and Sue Loseby, Rob and Catherine Dunster, Eric Locker, Gerry and Rosemary Dobson)*

Free house ~ Licensee Kate Hubbard ~ Real ale ~ Bar food (12-2 Sat/Sun only; 6.30-9.30; not Sun evening, or Mon) ~ Restaurant ~ (01858) 545201 ~ Open 6.30-11; 12-2.15, 6.30-11 Sat; 12-2.15 Sun; closed Mon, lunchtime Tues-Fri, Sun evening

UPPER HAMBLETON SK9007 Map 4
Finches Arms 🛏

Village signposted from A606 on E edge of Oakham

In summer the suntrap hillside terrace of this stone-built dining pub is a delightful place to sit and enjoy the delightful views over Rutland Water. Both the bar and modern no smoking restaurant (good views from here too) have stylish cane furniture on wooden floors, and you'll find well kept Grainstore Cooking and Greene King Abbot along with a guest such as Timothy Taylors Landlord on hand or electric pump; piped music, dominoes and cards. The bar menu changes frequently but includes home-made soup (£3.50) and filled ciabattas (from £4.95), along with enjoyable dishes such as lime and coriander marinated chicken with sweet chilli dipping sauce or baked goats cheese and red onion tart (£4.50), wild mushroom and herb omelette with rocket, pine kernels and chips (£6.75), cumberland sausages with mash and onions (£7), and confit of lamb shoulder with bacon with mascarpone and chive mash or moules marinière (£7.95); home-made puddings such as lemon and lime tart (£3.95). There are good walks around the reservoir (the twin village of Lower Hambleton is beneath the water). No children inside. If you stay, they do good breakfasts. *(Recommended by Mike and Sue Loseby, Anthony Barnes, John Cook, J F M and M West, Michael Doswell, Roger and Maureen Kenning, Roy Bromell, Michael Dandy, Rona Murdoch, Ruth Kitching)*

Free house ~ Licensees Celia and Colin Crawford ~ Real ale ~ Bar food (12-2.30, 7-9; 12-9 Sun) ~ Restaurant ~ (01572) 756575 ~ Open 11-11; 12-10.30 Sun ~ Bedrooms: £55B/£65B

WING SK8903 Map 4

Kings Arms ⑪ ⇐

Village signposted off A6003 S of Oakham; Top Street

This relaxing 17th-c inn continues to please readers with its good food and welcoming atmosphere. Freshly prepared from good ingredients, the changing bar menu could include soup (£3.90), salmon and prawn fishcakes (£4.75), filled ciabattas (from £3.95), sausages and mash (£6.95), ravioli (£7.50), and steak and kidney pie (£7.95), or you can choose from the more elaborate restaurant menu, which includes dishes such as baked ricotta cheese and walnuts (£4.75), pork fillet wrapped in parma ham with baby vegetables (£10.95), monkfish fillet with cajun spices (£12.95), and beef fillet in madeira jus (£14.95), with mouthwatering puddings such as chocolate torte. The charming bar has a traditional feel, with beams, some stripped stone and a flagstone floor, pine tables, old local photographs and a collection of tankards and old-fashioned whisky measuring pots. Two large log fires, one in a copper-canopied central hearth, make it very cosy in winter; they've also a snug. Friendly, helpful staff serve well kept Grainstore Cooking and Ten Fifty, and Marstons Pedigree, and a guest on handpump; piped music. The restaurant (and bedrooms) are no smoking. Outside are colourful hanging baskets in summer, and the sunny yew-sheltered garden has seats, swings and slides. There's a medieval turf maze just up the road. *(Recommended by Norma and Keith Bloomfield, I J and S A Bufton, David and Brenda Tew, Susan and John Douglas, Stephen, Julie and Hayley Brown, Dr Phil Putwain, Robert F Smith, Duncan Cloud, Barry Collett, Rob Powys-Smith, JP, PP, Mike and Sue Loseby, Dennis and Gill Keen, Eric Locker, Wendy and Bob Needham, Tracey and Stephen Groves, Bob and Maggie Atherton, M and G Rushworth)*

Free house ~ Licensees Jason Allen and Richard Page ~ Real ale ~ Bar food ~ Restaurant ~ (01572) 737634 ~ Children welcome ~ Open 12-3, 6-11(10.30 Sun) ~ Bedrooms: £50B/£60B

Lucky Dip

Besides the fully inspected pubs, you might like to try these Lucky Dips recommended to us and described by readers (if you do, please send us reports: www.goodguides.com).

BARKBY [SK6309]
Brookside Inn [Brookside, towards Beeby; off A607 6 miles NE of Leicester]: Warmly welcoming unpretentious two-bar local in pretty village by little stream with intriguing footbridges to houses opposite; well kept Burtonwood and guest ales such as Jennings Cocker Hoop, food from sandwiches and hot baguettes up, roaring fire, lots of toby jugs, brass and copper, extended dining area *(Rona Murdoch)*
BARNSDALE [SK9008]
☆ *Barnsdale Lodge* [just off A606 Oakham—Stamford]: Extensive conservatory dining bar with good food choice, inventive, generous and attractively presented;

charming décor, comfortable sitting-roomish coffee lounge, cream teas, friendly attentive staff, Courage Directors, Grainstore Ten Fifty and Greene King Old Speckled Hen and Ruddles; prices on the high side; pleasant gardens, bedrooms comfortable and attractive, with good breakfast, adjacent antiques centre and handy for Barnsdale Gardens *(BB, Gerry and Rosemary Dobson, David Coleman, George Atkinson)*
BARROW UPON SOAR [SK5717]
Hunting Lodge [South St]: Recently renovated, with two pleasantly decorated rooms, hunting pictures, friendly staff, good value varied food esp mixed grill, children welcome; big garden with swings, boules

and barbecues, six comfortable bedrooms *(F Swann)*

Navigation [off South St (B5328)]: Extended split-level pub based on former barge-horse stabling, attractive and comfortable, with lovely canal view from small back terrace with moorings; good value freshly made food (may be limited winter) inc interestingly filled baguettes and Sun roast, unusual bar top made from old pennies, central open fire, friendly staff, family room; several well kept ales such as Marstons Pedigree and Tetleys, good prices, daily papers, old local photographs, darts, skittle alley; piped music, SkyTV, games machine; open all day *(CMW, JJW, Bernie Adams, Tony and Wendy Hobden)*

BELTON [SK4420]

Queens Head [off A512/A453 between junctions 23 and 24, M1; Long St]: Former coaching inn with two pleasant bars and large dining room, above-average imaginative blackboard food, welcoming efficient service, well kept Bass, good wines and proper coffee; bedrooms, attractive village *(John and Sylvia Harrop)*

BILLESDON [SK7102]

Queens Head [Church St]: Another change of management in this beamed and thatched pub, now very popular for home-made food inc Sun carvery lunch; well kept Everards and a guest beer, decent wines, comfortable lounge bar with warm log fire, unspoilt public bar, small conservatory eating area and no smoking upstairs dining room; children welcome, pretty stone village *(Duncan Cloud, Anna and Martyn Carey)*

BOTCHESTON [SK4805]

Greyhound [Main St, off B5380 E of Desford]: Traditional two-bar village pub with welcoming service, good freshly made food inc bargain lunches and wide evening choice, children's food, Sun carvery, well kept Burtonwood Top Hat, small no smoking restaurant *(Bernie Adams, Rod Weston, Barbara Barber)*

BRAUNSTON [SK8306]

Blue Ball [off A606 in Oakham; Cedar St]: Pretty thatched and beamed dining pub in attractive village, country pine in linked rooms inc no smoking room and small conservatory, enjoyable if not cheap food inc children's helpings, good range of well kept ales and wines, woodburner; dominoes, shove-ha'penny; children welcome, open all day Sun *(Barry Collett, LYM)*

Old Plough [off A606 in Oakham]: Cheery welcome and good range of bar food and of well kept real ales in straightforward but clean and pleasant black-beamed pub, appealing back dining conservatory (where children allowed); tables in sheltered garden *(Derek and Sylvia Stephenson, Barry Collett, LYM, Wendy and Bob Needham)*

BREEDON ON THE HILL [SK4022]

Three Horse Shoes [A453]: Two bars, popular restaurant with good value Sun carvery (worth booking), well kept Banks's

and Mansfield, friendly landlady; motel-style bedrooms *(Stan and Dot Garner)*

BUCKMINSTER [SK8822]

Tollemache Arms [Main St]: Big rambling stone-built pub, central bar between comfortable lounge and plainer dining area, large restaurant, wide range of fresh food, Greene King Ruddles and Charles Wells Bombardier, friendly staff; bedrooms with own bathrooms, pretty village *(Barry Collett)*

BURBAGE [SP4492]

Chequers [Lutterworth Rd]: Open-plan refurbished village pub with tiled floor, open fires, well kept Charles Wells Eagle and Bombardier, good value home-made food (not Sun/Mon), pool room, fortnightly music quiz; pleasant courtyard and excellent family garden, pet animals and even a pony behind; open all day, three twin bedrooms *(Bernie Adams)*

CATTHORPE [SP5578]

Cherry Tree [Main St, just off A5 S of M1/M6/A14 interchange]: Attractive country local with good value food, well kept Bass, Frankton Babby and Hook Norton Best, quick service, dark panelling, lots of plates and pictures, woodburner, hood skittles; cl wkdy lunchtimes *(Bernie Adams)*

CHURCH LANGTON [SP7293]

Langton Arms [B6047 about 3 miles N of Mkt Harborough; just off A6]: Extended village pub with wide choice of good value nicely presented food, good mix of customers, good service even when busy, well kept Greene King IPA and Ruddles County, reasonably priced house wines, no smoking restaurant; piped music; garden with play area *(V Green, Gerry and Rosemary Dobson)*

CROXTON KERRIAL [SK8329]

Peacock [A607 SW of Grantham]: 17th-c former coaching inn with good value generous home cooking in long bar and small restaurant inc speciality fish and chips and fine choice of puddings, pleasant service, real ales, decent wines, hops on beams, real fire partitioned off at one end, some bric-a-brac, good new garden room; well behaved children welcome, picnic-sets in garden, new bedroom block with own bathrooms *(Richard and Liz Dilnot)*

DISEWORTH [SK4524]

Bull & Swan [handy for M1 junction 23A; first left off A453 after East Midlands airport main entrance]: Friendly village pub with Bass, Courage Directors, Marstons Pedigree and Theakstons, good choice of straightforward inexpensive food, fish and chips night Fri *(Alan Bowker)*

EARL SHILTON [SP4697]

Branagans [A47]: Good home-made food from sandwiches up inc OAP bargains and entertaining children's menu, well kept Bass, Marstons Pedigree and guest beers (OAP happy prices at times), good friendly service, two comfortable lounges, one with TV and celebrity photographs, another no smoking and music-free; bare-boards public bar with singer photographs, darts, machines and TVs; open all day, disabled access *(Bernie Adams)*

FOXTON [SP6989]

Black Horse [Main St]: Two roomy bars and sumptuous no smoking dining conservatory with sweeping views, reasonably priced enjoyable food from good sandwiches up inc bargain lunches, well kept Greene King Abbot and Old Speckled Hen; big garden with sheep and goats, short walk from locks, evening vintage car rallies last Thurs Apr-Aug *(Howard and Margaret Buchanan)*

GLOOSTON [SP7595]

☆ *Old Barn* [off B6047 in Tur Langton]: Extensively restored 16th-c village pub with beams, stripped kitchen tables, country chairs and log fire, cheery young licensees, changing real ales from smaller breweries, no smoking dining area (well behaved children allowed); tables out in front, bedrooms with compact shower cabinets, good breakfast, cl Mon lunchtime *(Bernie Adams, LYM, Jim Farmer, Patrick Hancock, Stephen, Julie and Hayley Brown)*

GREAT DALBY [SK7414]

Royal Oak [B6047 S of Melton Mowbray]: Low-beamed and timbered 17th-c village pub, snug and cosy, with enjoyable home cooking inc wide evening choice and Sun lunch, quick service, good range of beers, farm tools; tables in garden with play area *(P Tailyour)*

GREAT GLEN [SP6598]

Yews [A6]: Attractively refurbished and roomy Chef & Brewer, spreading series of softly lit and relaxing separate areas, wide range of enjoyable freshly made food, well kept Greene King Old Speckled Hen, Marstons Pedigree and a guest beer, good house wines, coal fires; piped music; good disabled access and facilities, big attractive garden with terrace; open all day *(John and Judy Saville, BB)*

GREETHAM [SK9214]

Plough [B668 Stretton—Cottesmore]: Tied to Grainstore of Oakham, with their beers inc a Mild and a seasonal beer kept well, interesting home-made food (baguettes sold by the inch), keen pricing, friendly helpful licensees and staff, coal-effect gas fire dividing cosy lounge from eating area, lots of prints and comic verses, exhilarating variety of pub games; games machine, tables out behind (with quoits), open all day Fri-Sun *(Dr and Mrs R Booth, Bernie Adams)*

☆ *Wheatsheaf* [B668 Stretton—Cottesmore]: Comfortable and welcoming L-shaped communicating rooms, country prints and plates on dining room walls, odd pivoted clock, roaring woodburner, wide choice of good value generous food served till 11 from baguettes through bargain wkdy lunches and specials to lots of chargrills, well kept John Smiths and Tetleys, polite, cheerful speedy service, pool and other games in end room; soft piped music; wheelchair access, picnic-

sets out in front and in tidy garden by back car park beside pretty little stream (may be a kingfisher or water vole); bedrooms in annexe *(Michael and Jenny Back, Mr and Mrs J Brown, BB)*

HALLATON [SP7896]

☆ *Bewicke Arms* [off B6047 or B664]: Old thatched pub, prettily set and smartened up with pine furnishings, orange paintwork, and extra seating off the corridor to the bar, well kept beers such as Flowers IPA and Grainstore Cooking, sensibly priced food from sandwiches to gammon, scampi and steak, inventive specials, log fires, some interesting memorabilia about the ancient local Easter Monday inter-village bottle-kicking match; darts, shove-ha'penny, piped music; children in eating areas, stables tearoom across yard, big terrace overlooking paddock and lake, open all day Sun *(Norma and Keith Bloomfield, David Field, LYM, Barry Collett, J M Tansey)*

Fox [North End]: Comfortable and well organised very English country pub with welcoming Spanish-born landlord adding an imaginative continental touch to the good value menu (also Sun carvery); well kept Marstons Pedigree and Tetleys, good value wine inc half-bottles and third-bottles; children welcome, tables out by village duckpond *(O K Smyth)*

HATHERN [SK5032]

Three Crowns [Wide Lane, just off A6]: Busy three-room village local with real fires, Bass, M&B Mild and local Wicked Hathern; skittle alley, nice garden *(the Didler)*

HEMINGTON [SK4527]

Jolly Sailor [Main St]: Welcoming village local with candlelit newish back restaurant and enjoyable freshly made food (not wkdy evenings or Sun), friendly service, well kept Bass, Greene King Abbot, Marstons Pedigree and two guest beers, summer farm cider, decent wines by the glass, good range of malt whiskies and other spirits; good open fire each end, big country pictures, bric-a-brac on heavy beams and shelves, table skittles, pub dog; quiet piped music, games machines; beautiful hanging baskets and picnic-sets out in front, open all day wknds *(Rona Murdoch, the Didler, CMW, JJW)*

HOSE [SK7329]

☆ *Black Horse* [Bolton Lane]: Friendly and pubby little two-room local, part of Tynemill group, with four or five well kept real ales such as Cotleigh Golden Eagle and attractively priced soft drinks, good value food inc interesting dishes, quarry tiles, darts, open fire, amiable landlord *(Darly Graton, Graeme Gulibert, the Didler, JP, PP)*

☆ *Rose & Crown* [Bolton Lane]: Unpretentious Vale of Belvoir pub with four or five well kept and well priced real ales from far and wide, very friendly attentive service, pub games, generous nicely priced standard food (not Sun evening) from baguettes to Sun lunch, no smoking areas in lounge and dining room (children allowed), pub games; piped music; tables on fairy-lit back terrace, fenced family area, cl lunchtimes Mon-Weds *(JP, PP, LYM, the Didler)*

HOUGHTON ON THE HILL [SK6703]
Old Black Horse [Main St (just off A47 Leicester—Uppingham)]: Comfortably refurbished dining pub, very hospitable, with good value home-made food (no hot food Mon lunchtime), friendly helpful staff, good sensibly priced wines by the glass, well kept Everards and guest beers, partly no smoking bare-boards dining area; big attractive garden with boules *(P Tailyour)*

HUNGARTON [SK6907]
☆ *Black Boy* [Main St]: Wide choice of good home-made food (wknd booking advised), pleasant young licensees *(Bernie Adams, S J Robinson)*

ILLSTON ON THE HILL [SP7099]
☆ *Fox & Goose* [Main St, off B6047 Mkt Harboro—Melton]: Welcoming and idiosyncratic unspoilt chatty two-bar local, plain but comfortable and convivial, with interesting pictures and assorted oddments, well kept Everards ales with a guest beer, table lamps, good coal fire; no food, but bedrooms sometimes available *(Eric Locker, Rona Murdoch, LYM, JP, PP)*

KEGWORTH [SK4826]
Britannia [London Rd]: Good value food inc bargain Sun lunch 12-9 *(the Didler)*
Red Lion [1 mile from M1 junction 24, via A6 towards Loughborough; High St]: Very traditional brightly lit village local with four plainish rooms around small servery, well kept Adnams, Banks's Original and several guest beers, limited choice of good wholesome food, good prices; assorted furniture, coal and flame-effect fires, delft shelf of beer bottles, daily papers, darts and cards; picnic-sets in small back yard, garden with play area, open all day *(the Didler, JP, PP, BB, Pete Baker)*
☆ *Station Hotel* [Station Rd towards West Leake, actually just over the Notts border (and its postal address is in Derbyshire!)]: Busy well refurbished pub with bare brick and woodwork, coal fires, two rooms off small bar area, well kept Bass, Courage Directors, Worthington and guest beers, upstairs restaurant with good home cooking; big back lawn, play area; simple good bedrooms, sharing bathroom *(Tony and Wendy Hobden, the Didler, JP, PP)*

KIBWORTH BEAUCHAMP [SP6893]
☆ *Coach & Horses* [A6 S of Leicester]: Congenial turkey-carpeted local with friendly efficient staff, good home-made food (mainly roasts on Sun), good range of well kept beers such as Ansells and Bass, heartening log fire in huge end inglenook, relaxed atmosphere, decent wines, china and pewter mugs on beams, cosy candlelit restaurant *(Eric Locker, Duncan Cloud, Rona Murdoch, BB)*

KIBWORTH HARCOURT [SP6894]
Horseshoes [Main St]: This pub has closed

and reopened as a largely no smoking italian restaurant, though it still has well kept Everards; good pasta and two- and three-course prix fixe meals, plush seating, armchairs in conservatory, tables on attractive back terrace, cl wkdy lunchtimes *(Duncan Cloud, LYM, Rona Murdoch, Gerry and Rosemary Dobson)*

KILBY [SP6295]
Dog & Gun [Main St, off A5199 S of Leicester]: Much-extended pub particularly popular with older people for its wide choice of enjoyable and temptingly priced food; very friendly attentive service, well kept Greene King Abbot and Websters (also the name of the lovely white cat), good wine choice, coal fire *(Rona Murdoch)*

KIRBY MUXLOE [SK5104]
Royal Oak [Main St]: Unassuming 1960s exterior, bar and sizeable no smoking restaurant recently comfortably refurbished, good food inc fish specialities, early evening bargains and wide range of filled baguettes, good friendly service, well kept Adnams and Everards, good wine list; handy for nearby 15th-c castle ruins *(Gerry and Rosemary Dobson)*

KNOSSINGTON [SK8008]
Fox & Hounds [off A606 W of Oakham; Somerby Rd]: Unspoilt small beamed village pub, very welcoming, with coal fire in cosy comfortable lounge, well kept Courage with guests such as Bass and Boddingtons, huge choice of malt whiskies, reasonably priced food inc unusual dishes, small restaurant (best to book), darts, pool room for younger customers; summer barbecues in big garden *(Bernie Adams)*

LANGHAM [SK8411]
☆ *Noel Arms* [Bridge St]: Beams, flagstones and lots of pictures in long pleasant low-ceilinged bar/dining area, friendly service, a welcome for children, generous good value food, well kept Greene King Abbot and Tetleys, central log fire; may be piped music, well behaved dogs allowed; good tables on front terrace, new bedrooms *(Jim Farmer, JES, LYM, David and Helen Wilkins)*

LEICESTER [SK5804]
Ale Wagon [Rutland St/Charles St]: Basic two-room 1930s interior, with changing ales inc those brewed for Hoskins & Oldfield by Everards, also Weston's perry; open all day, handy for station *(the Didler)*
Gateway [The Gateway]: Tynemill pub in old hosiery factory (ladies' underwear on show), bare boards except in no smoking area, five interesting changing ales (one at bargain price), good range of sandwiches and hot dishes till 8 (6 Sun) inc good vegetarian/vegan range, friendly knowledgeable service; piped music, TV; quiz Sun, open all day *(the Didler)*
☆ *Globe* [Silver St]: Well refurbished 18th-c town pub, lots of woodwork in four old-fashioned uncluttered areas off central bar, charming more peaceful upstairs dining room, wrought-iron gas lamps, well kept

Everards ales, nicely priced honest food, keen young landlord and knowledgeable friendly staff, children allowed in some parts; shame about the piped music, very popular with young people wknd evenings – doorman then *(the Didler, Dave Irving, Rona Murdoch, LYM, Val and Alan Green)*

Hat & Beaver [Highcross St]: Basic two-room local handy for Shires shopping centre, good value well filled rolls, Hardys & Hansons Best, Best Mild and Classic; TV *(the Didler, CMW, JJW)*

Hogshead [Market St]: Bare boards and flagstones, panelling, old local photographs, up to 10 changing real ales, bottled beers, lots of country wines, no smoking area, friendly young staff, daily papers, food all day *(the Didler)*

Swan & Rushes [Oxford St/Infirmary Sq]: Well kept Oakham JHB and changing guest beers, several imported beers on tap and many dozens in bottle, farm cider, beer festivals, enjoyable food; open all day *(the Didler)*

Talbot [Thurcaston Rd]: Roomy open-plan pub, Ansells Bitter and Mild and Marstons Pedigree, wide choice of basic good value lunchtime food (not Sun); tables in courtyard and on lawn down to river *(Tony and Wendy Hobden)*

Vaults [Wellington St]: Very basic concrete-floored cellar bar with interesting quickly changing microbrews, some tapped from the cask by friendly landlord – a great place for beers; friendly staff, filled rolls, Sunday cheeses, low ceiling with iron pillars (can get smoky), tall settles forming booths, stripped brick walls with old signs rather reminiscent of a railway station; may be entrance fee for Sun live bands; open all day Fri-Sun, cl Mon-Thurs lunchtime *(the Didler, JP, PP)*

LOUGHBOROUGH [SK5319]
Albion [canal bank, about ¼ mile from Loughborough Wharf]: Down-to-earth little old canalside local with emphasis on well kept changing ales such as Mansfield Bitter and Riding Dark Mild, Sam Smiths OB and local Wicked Hathern; friendly owners, cheap straightforward home-made food, coal fire; children welcome, occasional barbecues, budgerigar aviary in pleasant big courtyard *(Bernie Adams, the Didler, JP, PP)*

Swan in the Rushes [A6]: Good range of well kept ales tapped from the cask and plenty of foreign bottled beers in down-to-earth bare-boards town local; low-priced straightforward food (not Sat/Sun evenings), daily papers, traditional games, open fire, three smallish high-ceilinged rooms – can get crowded; children in eating areas, tables outside, open all day *(Pete Baker, Gillian and Peter Moore, the Didler, David Carr, LYM, BB, JP, PP)*

Tap & Mallet [Nottingham Rd]: Fairly plain pub distinguished by five or six changing microbrews, farm cider, occasional beer festivals; back garden, open all day Sat/Sun

(the Didler, JP, PP)

LUTTERWORTH [SP5484]
Unicorn [Church St]: Cosy and welcoming to all, low-priced food from sandwiches and filled rolls up inc good OAP bargain lunches and children's dishes, nice log fire, Bass and M&B Brew XI; no credit cards *(P Tailyour)*

MARKET BOSWORTH [SK4003]
Black Horse [Market Pl]: 18th-c, with several beamed rooms, wide choice of enjoyable plentiful food, cheerful helpful service, well kept Adnams and Greene King, good house wines and coffee, cosy local bustle, log fire, comfortable restaurant; tables outside – nice setting next to almshouses in attractive village not far from Bosworth Field *(anon)*

MARKET HARBOROUGH [SP7387]
Sugar Loaf [High St]: Popular Wetherspoons, good choice of real ales and good value food, no piped music – just a silenced juke box *(Stephen, Julie and Hayley Brown)*

☆ *Three Swans* [High St]: Comfortable and handsome coaching inn renovated as Best Western conference hotel, with beams and old local prints in plush and peaceful panelled front bar, comfortable no smoking back dining lounge and fine courtyard conservatory (also no smoking) in more modern part, wide range of food inc good value bar lunches and sandwiches, decent wines, well kept ales such as Everards, good coffee, friendly helpful staff, more formal upstairs restaurant; piped music; attractive suntrap courtyard, good new bedrooms in extension *(George Atkinson, Barry Smith, Angus Lyon, Michael Tack, Gerry and Rosemary Dobson)*

MELTON MOWBRAY [SK7519]
Anne of Cleves [Burton St, by St Mary's Church]: Basic-feel pub in former monks' chantry attached to parish church, stripped tables on flagstones, Tudor beams and stonework, cheery staff, separate snug for smokers, well kept Everards Tiger and a guest beer, popular usual food, small end dining room and no smoking room; may be piped music, no under-7s; open all day, Sun afternoon closure *(Angus Lyon, Paul and Sue Merrick, Tony and Wendy Hobden)*

George [High St]: Popular for varied blackboard food, smallish restaurant; can be crowded on market days *(W and P J Elderkin)*

NEWBOLD VERDON [SK4402]
☆ *Windmill* [Brascote, via B582 (off A447 Hinckley—Coalville)]: Country pub based on former mill house, cobbled back way into airy open-plan two-part bar with small snug and upper no smoking restaurant, good food choice (not Sun evening) from baguettes through good value main dishes to Sun roasts, relaxed friendly service, lots of local pictures, darts; children welcome, games machines; open all day wknds, roomy garden with pretty hanging baskets *(Bernie Adams)*

OAKHAM [SK8508]
Horseshoe [Braunston Rd]: 1960s pub with pleasant open-plan lounge bar, smaller lounge leading to restaurant, Everards and guest beers, generous bar food, welcoming staff; some picnic-sets out in front, garden behind *(Barry Collett)*
Normanton Park [off A606 E, S of Rutland Water nr Empingham]: Refreshingly informal waterside hotel's bar and dining area in former stable block, good choice of food inc good Sun lunch, well kept Greene King Old Speckled Hen and Ruddles and Tetleys, helpful pleasant staff; bedrooms, fine views, Rutland Water walks straight from extensive gardens *(BB, Roy Bromell)*
Wheatsheaf [Northgate]: Nicely refurbished three-room 17th-c local nr church, good furnishings and plenty of bric-a-brac, well kept ales such as Batemans Mild, Everards and John Smiths, enjoyable lunchtime pub food, friendly attentive service, open fire, back family room/conservatory; pretty suntrap back courtyard *(Rona Murdoch, Bernie Adams, Norma and Keith Bloomfield, Barry Collett, Michael and Jenny Back, Steve Whalley)*
☆ *Whipper-In* [Market Pl]: Busy stone-built coaching inn with creaky boards, oak-beamed and panelled lounge opening into spotless and attractive bistro area, good interesting food from sandwiches up, friendly staff, real ales, decent wines; comfortable bedrooms *(O K Smyth, LYM)*

QUENIBOROUGH [SK6412]
Horse & Groom [School Lane]: Wide choice of good value food from baguettes to cheap traditional and more exotic dishes, very popular two-for-one bargains, well kept Ansells, Greene King Old Speckled Hen and Tetleys, welcoming fires, lots of brass and World War II aircraft prints; pool in small back public bar, skittle alley *(Mr and Mrs R W Monk, Neil Rose)*

REDMILE [SK8036]
Windmill [off A52 Grantham—Nottingham; Main St]: Comfortable lounge and dining room, well kept Boddingtons and Wadworths 6X, good house wines, enjoyable good value home-made food from baguettes to steaks inc all the usual favourites and children's dishes *(Mrs P J Pearce, W and P J Elderkin, Bernie Adams)*

RYHALL [TF0310]
Millstone [Bridge St]: Neatly kept and quite spacious, with comfortable plush seats, friendly landlord, helpful service, interesting choice of generous freshly made food, both familiar favourites and inventive up-to-date dishes, choice of roasts on Sun, well kept Mansfield and Marstons ales, good wine choice, lots of malt whiskies, proper coffee, small no smoking restaurant, separate bar with pool and juke box, well behaved children welcome *(Kathryn and Richard Wells, Tim and Rosemary Wells)*

SADDINGTON [SP6591]
Queens Head [S of Leicester between A5199 (ex A50) and A6]: Dining pub popular for bargain OAP wkdy lunches, wide choice of other promptly served blackboard food (not Sun evening) from baguettes up, well kept Adnams and three Everards ales, decent wines, quick polite service, daily papers, lots of knick-knacks and plastic plants; no under-5s; country views from dining conservatory and tables in long sloping garden *(Bernie Adams, Eric Locker, LYM, Gerry and Rosemary Dobson, George Atkinson)*

SCALFORD [SK7624]
Kings Arms [King St]: Good competitively priced food inc plenty of fresh fish and well kept real ale in hospitable country inn with old-world values and small intimate eating area; two comfortable bedrooms with own bathrooms *(Eddie Pearson)*

SEATON [SP9098]
George & Dragon [Church Lane, off B672 Caldecott—S Luffenham]: Two bars, one for dining with pine furniture and generous attractively priced food cooked to order, friendly helpful landlord, quick service, well kept Greene King IPA, Marstons Pedigree and Theakstons Best, good wine choice; juke box, pool; tables outside, unspoilt village, good views of famous viaduct *(Miss Joan Morgan, Norma and Keith Bloomfield)*

SHARNFORD [SP4891]
Countryman [Leicester Rd]: 18th-c beamed and timbered village local with world-wide range of good value food inc OAP bargains in new dining extension, three real ales, darts; children allowed, garden may have bouncy castle, handy for Fosse Meadows nature park, open all day wknds *(Bernie Adams)*

SHAWELL [SP5480]
White Swan [Main St; village signed down declassified road (ex A427) off A5/A426 roundabout – turn right in village; not far from M6 junct 1]: Attractive 17th-c beamed and panelled pub, open fire, good range of restaurant food inc Thurs/Fri evening fish specials and good Sun lunch, well kept Greene King IPA, Abbot and Ruddles County, good house wines, service chatty and helpful even when busy, no smoking restaurant (best to book at wknds); tables out in front, bedrooms (plans for more), cl Sun evening, and lunchtime exc Sun *(Gerry and Rosemary Dobson)*

SHEARSBY [SP6290]
☆ *Chandlers Arms* [Fenny Lane, off A50 Leicester—Northampton]: Comfortable and friendly pub with brocaded wall seats, wheelback chairs, flowers on tables, house plants, swagged curtains, candlemaker pictures, well kept Marstons, no smoking bar on left, interesting food choice (not Sun evening) with imaginative vegetarian and vegan dishes, plenty of locals; may be piped music; tables in secluded raised garden, attractive village *(Bernie Adams, Rona Murdoch, Jim Farmer, David Coleman, Mr and Mrs R W Monk, BB)*

SILEBY [SK6015]

☆ *White Swan* [Swan St]: Bright, cheerful and relaxed, with imaginative attractively priced home-made food (not Sun evening or Mon lunchtime) from snacks up inc wkday bargains, well kept Marstons Pedigree, nice house wines, good friendly service, comfortable and welcoming dining lounge, small tasteful book-lined restaurant (booking needed) *(K D J Slowe, Joe Brown)*

SNARESTONE [SK3510]

Odd House [Bosworth Rd]: Former 17th-c coaching inn with enjoyable blackboard food, Fullers London Pride, Greene King Abbot, Marstons Pedigree and Charles Wells Bombardier, traditional games in one bar, pool room, restaurant (not Sun/Mon evenings); tables outside with boules and big sturdy play area, eight good value bedrooms with own bathrooms, open all day wknds, has been cl wkdy lunchtimes *(Kevin and Bruna Lovelack)*

STAPLETON [SP4398]

Nags Head [A447 N of Hinckley]: Two smallish congenial rooms served by same bar, all no smoking at lunchtime, friendly helpful service, good value food from sandwiches and baguettes up, wider evening choice though still straightforward, Everards Tiger and Marstons Bitter and Pedigree, no music *(Gerry and Rosemary Dobson)*

SUTTON CHENEY [SK4100]

☆ *Hercules* [off A447 3 miles S of Market Bosworth]: Attractive old local with darts and dominoes in cheerfully comfortable long bar, frequently changing well kept guest ales and two brewed for the pub, good choice of home-made bar lunches, evening restaurant (not Mon; also Sun lunch), friendly staff (landlord was a Wolves footballer), open fire; piped music; Sun quiz night, children welcome, cl Mon lunchtime *(Bernie Adams, LYM)*

SWITHLAND [SK5413]

☆ *Griffin* [Main St; between A6 and B5330, between Loughborough and Leicester]: Good value local, with well kept Everards, enjoyable straightforward food from sandwiches up (not Sun-Tues evenings), friendly staff, pleasant décor in two cosy arch-linked rooms with old-fashioned woodburners, separate restaurant and pool room; back skittle alley, Weds quiz night, quiet piped music; gardens by stream, nice setting, plans for bedrooms in stable block *(Pete Baker, LYM, CMW, JJW, Wendy and Bob Needham)*

THORNTON [SK4607]

Bricklayers Arms [S of M1 junction 22; Main St]: Nicely refurbished traditional village local with roaring fire and old photographs in beamed bar, Everards Tiger, Beacon and Mild and Greene King Old Speckled Hen, friendly landlord and good staff, good value food, cosy restaurant; piped radio, quiz nights; large back garden with play area, handy for reservoir walks *(Bernie Adams)*

THRUSSINGTON [SK6415]

Blue Lion [off A46 N of Leicester; Rearsby Rd]: Pleasant 18th-c two-bar village pub, beams, oak tables and comfortable settles, country bric-a-brac inc lots of teapots, good value standard food (not Sun evening) served till late, three well kept ales, proper coffee, friendly landlord; may be piped music; garden with play area, ducks and hens *(CMW, JJW)*

TILTON ON THE HILL [SK7405]

Rose & Crown [B6047]: Friendly old place with reasonably priced appetising fresh food, well kept Bass and Boddingtons, good coffee, good pubby atmosphere; unobtrusive piped traditional jazz; garden with boules *(Mr and Mrs J Brown, Bernie Adams, Jim Farmer)*

TUGBY [SK7600]

Fox & Hounds [A47 6 miles W of Uppingham]: Refurbished two-bar beamed pub overlooking green, separate restaurant, lots of decorative china, local caricatures, copper pans and other bric-a-brac, generous home cooking using good fresh local ingredients, well kept real ales, friendly helpful staff, open fire; tables in good-sized garden with terrace *(Mrs Caroline Newton)*

TWYFORD [SK7210]

Saddle [Main St; off B6047 E of Leicester]: Friendly family-run local with comfortable L-shaped knocked-through bar, well kept Mansfield and John Smiths, open fire, reasonably priced usual food, charming little beamed dining area; pool, piped music and TV in games end *(Bernie Adams)*

UPPINGHAM [SP8699]

Vaults [Market Pl]: Attractive pub next to church with some tables out overlooking picturesque square, well kept Marstons ales, popular reasonably priced fresh food, comfortable banquettes; piped music; bedrooms *(Barry Collett)*

WALCOTE [SP5683]

☆ *Black Horse* [1½ miles from M1 junction 20 towards Market Harborough]: Unpretentious pub noted for authentic thai food (not Mon or Tues lunchtime) cooked by the landlady, in good value big helpings, also half a dozen good well kept real ales, interesting bottled beers and country wines, no smoking restaurant; no dogs *(LYM, Mike Pugh)*

WHETSTONE [SP5597]

Bulls Head [Victoria Rd]: Two bars and cosy no smoking area (used for Sun lunches), pleasant décor, Everards and a guest beer, friendly landlady; pub games and juke box, entertainment Fri, garden with play area and barbecue *(Bernie Adams)*

WHITWELL [SK9208]

Noel Arms [Main Rd]: Roomy and comfortable, with wide choice of enjoyable food (till 10) in spaciously extended light pine restaurant and smart carpeted bar with lower side room, well kept Courage and Marstons Pedigree, table drinks service; piped music, can get busy; children welcome, suntrap tables outside with play area and occasional barbecues, handy for Rutland Water, bedrooms *(C J Cox, A Monro, LYM, Janet and Peter Race)*

WHITWICK [SK4316]

Three Horseshoes [Leicester Rd]: Still gives the friendly feel of an unspoilt and utterly unpretentious miners' local, two rooms, one with darts, dominoes and cards, well kept Bass and M&B Mild, no food – the sort of place that has raffles, loan clubs and trips to the races; outdoor lavatories *(Pete Baker)*

WILSON [SK4024]

☆ *Bulls Head* [side road Melbourne—Breedon on the Hill]: Welcoming and comfortable dining pub with cosy alcoves, enjoyable reasonably priced food (not Mon evening) inc lebanese specialities and good Sun lunch, well kept Marstons Pedigree, friendly staff *(Douglas Keith, LYM, Stan and Dot Garner)*

WING [SK8903]

Cuckoo [Top St]: Smart thatched and beamed open-plan pub, good generous food from baked potatoes up, attentive, cheerful and welcoming licensees, well kept ales such as Grainstore Cooking and Triple B, nice log fires each end, cuckoo clock, darts and pool at one end, dining area with small fishtank the other; may be piped music, wknd live music, midsummer beer festival; children and dogs welcome, plenty of tables on neat lawn behind, cl Tues *(Bernie Adams, George Atkinson, Norma and Keith Bloomfield, JP, PP)*

WOODHOUSE EAVES [SK5214]

☆ *Pear Tree* [Church Hill; main street, off B591 W of Quorndon]: Attractive upper flagstoned food area with pitched roof and pews forming booths, open kitchen doing wide choice of food (not Sun night) from sandwiches to grills, helpful welcoming staff; hunting prints in simply furnished lower pub part with conservatory, log fire, Bass, Greene King IPA and Marstons Pedigree, good choice of malt whiskies, decent wines; may be piped radio; children welcome, two large friendly dogs, open all day bank hol wknds, picnic-sets and summer bar with barbecue area outside, good nearby walks *(JP, PP, George Atkinson, David and Helen Wilkins, Roger and Maureen Kenning, Michael and Jenny Back, LYM)*

☆ *Wheatsheaf* [Brand Hill; beyond Main St, off B591 S of Loughborough]: Plush and busy open-plan beamed country pub with light and airy upstairs dining area, smart customers, good interesting home-cooked food from sandwiches to chargrills and other upmarket dishes, changing ales such as Greene King Abbot, Hook Norton Best, Timothy Taylors Landlord and Tetleys, good house wines, friendly landlord, attentive helpful service, log fire, motor-racing memorabilia; floodlit tables outside, dogs welcome but no motor-cyclists or children *(JP, PP, Margaret Jack, Doug Christian, the Didler, George Atkinson, LYM)*

WYMESWOLD [SK6023]

Three Crowns [45 Far St]: Snug village pub with welcoming chatty atmosphere, good value basic lunchtime food, well kept Adnams, Marstons, Tetleys and usually a local guest beer, pleasant character furnishings in beamed bar and split-level lounge, a couple of dogs *(the Didler, Derek and Sylvia Stephenson, Ian and Eileen Johnson)*

'Children welcome' means the pub says it lets children inside without any special restriction. If it allows them in, but to restricted areas such as an eating area or family room, we specify this. Places with separate restaurants usually let children use them, hotels usually let them into public areas such as lounges. Some pubs impose an evening time limit – let us know if you find this.

Lincolnshire

A couple of new entries here this year are the cosily old-fashioned and warmly welcoming Fortescue Arms at Billingborough, and the attractively individual 17th-c Chequers at Woolsthorpe in the Vale of Belvoir. Other pubs on top form here this year are the bustling Welby Arms at Allington (flourishing under enthusiastic new licensees), the ancient Lea Gate Inn near Coningsby (particularly good service at even the busiest times), the Chequers at Gedney Dyke (good imaginative food in this fenland hideaway), the stylish Wig & Mitre in Lincoln (not cheap, but very popular for its inventive food served all day), the individualistic Blue Cow at South Witham (the friendly landlord will show you his own microbrewery), and the smart and interesting old George of Stamford (good food, fine wines and a nice place to stay). As one reader said, this last establishment is rather like stepping back into a world of abundant staff and elegance; for the second year running, the George of Stamford takes the title of Lincolnshire Dining Pub of the Year. The Lucky Dip section at the end of the chapter includes quite a few places well worth looking out; we'd particularly note the Five Horseshoes at Barholm, Blue Pig in Grantham, Bell at Halton Holegate, Willoughby Arms at Little Bytham, White Swan at Scotter, Vine in Skegness and Cross Keys at Stow. Drinks prices are close to the national average, with the main local brewer, Batemans, doing their bit to keep prices down. Among plenty of smaller ones, Oldershaws, Highwood and Newby Wyke crop up quite often and are well worth looking out for.

ALLINGTON SK8540 Map 7

Welby Arms 🍴 🛏

The Green; off A1 N of Grantham, or A52 W of Grantham

Doing very well under its new owners, this bustling pub offers a good meal and hospitable break from the nearby A1. Cheerful obliging waitresses serve really good home-cooked food (with good crunchy chips), which might include soup (£2.95), filled baguettes and ploughman's (from £3.95, lunchtime only), garlic mushrooms (£3.95), fried brie wedges (£4.45), battered haddock (Tues-Fri £7.45), fish pie (£8.95), brie and bacon chicken (£9.95), and puddings such as cherry cheesecake and boozy tiramisu (£2.95). Booking is advisable, especially at weekends. The civilised back no smoking dining lounge (where they prefer you to eat) looks out on to tables in a sheltered walled courtyard with pretty hanging baskets in summer. The large bar area is divided by a stone archway and has black beams and joists, log fires (one in an attractive arched brick fireplace), red velvet curtains and comfortable burgundy button-back wall banquettes and stools. Half a dozen ales include Bass, John Smiths, Timothy Taylors Landlord and three guests such as Adnams Broadside, Jennings Cocker Hoop and Phoenix Wobbly Bob, kept well but served through a sparkler; they have decent wines including eight by the glass, and a good range of country wines; piped music, cribbage and dominoes. A back courtyard formed by the restaurant extension and the bedroom block beyond has tables, with more picnic-sets out on the front lawn. *(Recommended by Michael and Jenny Back, Mr and Mrs W D Borthwick, Peter and Patricia Burton, MJVK, Peter F Marshall, Kevin Thorpe, Mrs J Caunt, the Didler, Mr and Mrs Staples, Brian Clapham, Barry Collett, P W Taylor, Michael Doswell, H Bramwell, Michael Hicks, Peter Hallinan, W and P J Elderkin,*

Derek and Sylvia Stephenson, JP, PP, J R Ringrose, A D Jenkins, Jenny and Dave Hughes,
M and G Rushworth, Gerry and Rosemary Dobson)

*Free house ~ Licensees Matt, Rose and Anna Cavanagh ~ Real ale ~ Bar food (12-2,
7-9) ~ Restaurant ~ (01400) 281361 ~ Children in eating area of bar (over 12 after 7)
and restaurant ~ Open 12-2.30(3 Sat), 6-11; 12-4, 6-10.30 Sun ~ Bedrooms:
£48S/£60S*

ASWARBY TF0639 Map 8
Tally Ho ♀
A15 S of Sleaford (but N of village turn-off)

Locals chatting at the bar and the comfortably worn-in furnishings combine to give
this 17th-c farm manager's house an easy-going relaxed atmosphere – though it's all
very civilised. Probably at its best at night, the fairly small bar is more or less
divided in two by an entrance lobby stacked full with logs, giving the feel of two
chatty little rooms, each with its own stripped stone fireplace, candles on a nice mix
of chunky old pine tables and small round cast-iron-framed tables, big country
prints on cream walls, and big windows; daily papers, piped music. Real ales on
handpump include well kept Bass, Batemans XB and a guest such as Marstons
Pedigree, and they have good house wines. Bar food includes soup (£2.95), filled
baguettes (from £3.95), ploughman's (£4.95), lincolnshire sausage (£5.25), and
blackboard specials such as smoked mackerel pâté (£3.85), vegetable lasagne
(£6.95), lambs liver and bacon in red wine gravy, salmon and spinach fishcakes or
beef and ale pie (£6.95), chicken breast with garlic and mushroom sauce (£7.25),
rump steak (£10.25) and home-made puddings might include crème brûlée and
blackberry sponge (£3.25). It's worth booking if you want to eat in the attractive
no smoking pine-furnished restaurant. There are tables out behind among the fruit
trees, and over the road, the pretty estate church, glimpsed through the stately oaks
of the park, is worth a visit. *(Recommended by Mrs Caryn Paladina, Dr and
Mrs R G J Telfer, Bill and Sheila McLardy, R and M Tait, Steve Whalley)*

*Free house ~ Licensees Christine and Peter Robertson ~ Real ale ~ Bar food (12-2.30,
6.30-9.30) ~ Restaurant ~ (01529) 455205 ~ Children welcome ~ Dogs welcome ~
Open 12-3, 6-11(7-10.30 Sun) ~ Bedrooms: £35B/£50B*

BARNOLDBY LE BECK TA2303 Map 8
Ship ♀
Village signposted off A18 Louth—Grimsby

The collection of Edwardian and Victorian bric-a-brac at this beautifully kept and
rather genteel little pub is quite delightful, and worth a short detour in itself. Heavy
dark-ringed drapes and net curtains swathe the windows, throwing an opaque light
on the carefully laid out nostalgic collection of half-remembered things from the
past like stand-up telephones, violins, a horn gramophone, bowler and top hats, old
racquets, crops and hockey sticks, a lace dress, and grandmotherly plants in ornate
china bowls. Comfortable dark green plush wall benches have lots of pretty
propped-up cushions, and there are heavily stuffed green plush Victorian-looking
chairs on a green fleur de lys carpet. Only the piped music is slightly incongruous.
Many of the tables are booked for dining. Good bar food could include mushrooms
with cream and garlic sauce (£3.45), sandwiches (from £3.45), smoked salmon and
prawns (£4.95), fish pie (£7.45), salmon wrapped in filo pastry with prawn sauce
(£8.95), beef stroganoff (£9.95) and mixed grill (£11.95). Well kept Black Sheep
and Timothy Taylors Landlord on handpump, and an extensive wine list with
plenty by the glass. Out behind are a few picnic-sets under pink cocktail parasols,
next to big hanging baskets suspended from stands. *(Recommended by Dr D Parker)*

*Inn Business ~ Tenant Michele West ~ Real ale ~ Bar food (12-2(12.30-2.30 Sun),
7-9.30) ~ Restaurant ~ (01472) 822308 ~ Children in eating area of bar and
restaurant ~ Dogs allowed in bar ~ Open 12-3, 6-11(10.30 Sun)*

BILLINGBOROUGH TF1134 Map 8
Fortescue Arms
B1177, off A52 Grantham—Boston

Low beams, pleasant mainly Victorian prints and big log fires in two see-through fireplaces give a cosily old-fashioned feel to this line of linked turkey-carpeted rooms. There are nice bay window seats, fresh flowers and pot plants, brass and copper, a stuffed badger and pheasant with various quiz books in one place, and attractive dining rooms at each end, one with stripped stone walls, flagstones and another open fire. Unusually, a long red and black tiled corridor runs right the way along behind the serving bar, making it an island: here they have well kept Batemans XB, Greene King IPA and Ind Coope Burton on handpump, decent wines and a particularly good choice of spirits. Well prepared generous food, where possible using local ingredients, includes soup (£2.25), chicken pâté (£3.95), salad (£5.95), game pie or vegetable curry (£7.25), and baked haddock (£7.50), with a good choice of good fresh vegetables; on some days there may be a cheerful influx of older lunchers (who happily call themselves either the geriatrics or the rejuvenated teenagers). Service is friendly and efficient. The car park is more like the gravelled drive of a country house; on one side are picnic-sets on a lawn under apple trees, and on the other a sheltered courtyard with flowers planted in tubs and a manger. This is a nice village. *(Recommended by William and Elizabeth Templeton, Bill and Sheila McLardy)*

Free house ~ Licensees John and Sharon Cottingham ~ Real ale ~ Bar food ~ Restaurant ~ (01529) 240228 ~ Children in eating area of bar and restaurant ~ Open 11.30-3, 6-11; 12-3, 7-10.30 Sun

BRANDY WHARF TF0197 Map 8
Cider Centre
B1205 SE of Scunthorpe (off A15 about 16 miles N of Lincoln)

One of only a handful of cider taverns left in Britain, this beautifully located canalside inn was built in the 18th c to serve the needs of canal-building navvies and bargemen. They still stock a huge range of ciders, with up to 15 on draught, eight tapped from casks, and the rest kept in stacks of fascinating bottles and small plastic or earthenware kegs on shelves behind the bar. There's also a good range of country wines and meads. The main bar is fairly down-to-earth, with wheelback chairs, brown plush wall banquettes and cheery customer photographs. The dimly lit lounge bar has all sorts of cider memorabilia and humorous sidelights on cider-making and drinking – watch your head for the foot of 'Cyril the Plumber' poking down through the ceiling; piped folk music completes the light-hearted rustic mood. A simple glazed verandah looks on to the river, where there are moorings and a slipway. Generous good value tasty bar food (with wonderful real chips) includes sandwiches (£2.20, £2.60 toasted), burgers (from £3.20), ploughman's or pork and cider sausages (from £3.60), broccoli and cream cheese bake (£5.80) and chicken curry or chilli (£5.90). The whole place is no smoking. Children have lots of space to play out in the meadows (which have tables and chairs), along the water banks, or in the four acres of orchard where you can pick your own fruit when available. On top of that, they also plan to add a dedicated play area; caravan site; quite a few appropriate special events. *(Recommended by Marlene and Jim Godfrey, Neil and Anita Christopher, Paul and Ursula Randall, David and Ruth Shillitoe, WAH, JP, PP, the Didler, Patrick Hancock, Christopher Turner)*

Free house ~ Licensees David and Catherine Wells ~ Bar food (12-2.30, 6-9.30) ~ No credit cards ~ (01652) 678364 ~ Children in eating area of bar ~ Open 12-3, 6-10.30; 11-11 Sat; 12-10.30 Sun; closed Tues

---

The details at the end of each main entry start by saying whether the pub is a free house, or if it's tied to a brewery or pub group (which we name).

CONINGSBY TF2458 Map 8
Lea Gate Inn 🛏️
Leagate Road (B1192 southwards, off A153 E)

Readers are full of praise for the very good service at this friendly 16th-c inn – even on busy bank holidays it's notably efficient. The pleasant interior consists of three separate cosy, softly lit areas that are linked together around the corner bar counter, and have heavy black beams supporting ochre ceiling boards. It's attractively furnished, with a cabinet holding a collection of ancient bottles, a variety of tables and chairs, including antique oak settles with hunting-print cushions, and two great high-backed settles making a snug around the biggest of the fireplaces. Another fireplace has an interesting cast-iron fireplate depicting the Last Supper. Well kept Marstons Pedigree, Theakstons XB and possibly a guest such as Adnams on handpump; piped jazz or pop music. Served in generous helpings, good value tasty bar food includes soup (£2.30), nicely presented lunchtime sandwiches (from £2.65), garlic mushrooms (£2.95), lunchtime ploughman's (£4.95), lincolnshire sausages or spinach lasagne (£6.95), smoked chicken breast (£7.95), steaks (from £9.95), very good beef wellington (£11.95), and specials such as game pie (£7.95) and crab salad (£8.50); no smoking restaurant. The appealing garden has tables and an enclosed play area. The pub once stood by one of the perilous tracks through the marshes before the fens were drained, and you can still see the small iron gantry that used to hold a lamp to guide travellers safely through the mist. Bedrooms are in a newish block.
(Recommended by Bill and Sheila McLardy, Dr John Lunn, Peter J Royle, the Didler, John Bailey, JP, PP, Michael and Marion Buchanan, Pat and Tony Martin)

Free house ~ Licensee Mark Dennison ~ Real ale ~ Bar food ~ Restaurant ~ (01526) 342370 ~ Open 11.30-2.30, 6.30(6 Sat)-11; 12-3, 6-10.30 Sun ~ Bedrooms: £49.50B/£65B

DYKE TF1022 Map 8
Wishing Well 🍺
Village signposted off A15 N of Bourne; Main Street

Families are very welcome at this big bustling black and white village inn, with most people here for the straightforward but good value bar food: soup (£2.50), sandwiches (from £2.80), starters such as prawn cocktail and chicken wings (from £4), home-made lasagne or steak and ale pie (£6.50), breaded scampi (£6.95), steaks (from £7.95), and puddings such as apple pie or carrot cake (from £2.50); no smoking restaurant. A notably interesting choice of five real ales on handpump includes well kept Everards Tiger and Greene King Abbot, alongside three regularly changing guests such as Broughton Greenmantle, Hop Back Crop Circle and Shepherd Neame Spitfire. Don't miss the wishing well at the end of the heavily beamed long, rambling front bar, which has dark stone walls, lots of shiny brasswork, a cavern of an open fireplace, and evening candlelight. The carpeted lounge area has a chesterfield settee, green plush button-back low settles and wheelback chairs around individual wooden tables. The big restaurant is no smoking. Popular with locals for a drink, the quite separate smaller and plainer public bar has sensibly placed darts, pool, fruit machine, video game and TV. There's a small conservatory, and the garden has tables and a play area.
(Recommended by JP, PP, Richard Lewis, Roy Bromell)

Free house ~ Licensee Theresa Gallagher ~ Real ale ~ Bar food (11.30-3, 6.30-9; 11.30(12 Sun)-9 Sat) ~ Restaurant ~ (01778) 422970 ~ Children welcome ~ Open 11-3, 6-12; 11-12 Sat; 12-10.30 Sun ~ Bedrooms: £35B/£65B

GEDNEY DYKE TF4125 Map 8
Chequers 🍴 🍷

Village signposted off A17 Holbeach—Kings Lynn

This friendly fenland pub stands a few feet below sea level. It's fairly simple inside, spotlessly kept, with an open fire in the bar, a rather old-fashioned restaurant area at one end, and, overlooking a garden with picnic-sets, a no smoking dining conservatory; piped music. Seasonally changing bar food might include sandwiches (from £2.75), leek and potato soup (£3.95), prawn cocktail (£5.75), asparagus wrapped in parmesan (£5.95), tomato, cheese and courgette lasagne with tomato dressing (£7.95), lamb chop with wild mushroom risotto and mint pesto (£10.95), good fresh fish such as tuna marinated in five spices on potato and coriander salad (£11.50), seared halibut with pink peppercorn butter (£11.95) and tasty home-made puddings such as brandy snap basket with locally made ice cream or cinnamon meringues with butterscotch cream (£3.95); roast Sunday lunch. Well kept Adnams Bitter and Greene King Abbot on handpump, and a decent wine list with about 10 by the glass. *(Recommended by Charles Gysin, June and Ken Brooks, Jamie and Sarah Allan, R C Wiles, W M Paton, JP, PP, Roger Everett, Baden and Sandy Waller, Mr Ken Marshall, Alison Hayes, Pete Hanlon)*

Free house ~ Licensees Simon and Linda Rattray ~ Real ale ~ Bar food ~ Restaurant ~ (01406) 362666 ~ Children welcome ~ Open 12-2, 7-11(10.30 Sun); closed Mon winter

GRANTHAM SK9135 Map 7
Beehive £

Castlegate; from main street turn down Finkin Street opposite St Peter's Place

Two things give this its special appeal. First, its remarkable claim to fame – the unique pub sign which is a hive full of living bees mounted up in a lime tree. It's been here since at least 1830, and probably a hundred years before that, making this one of the oldest populations of bees in the world. And secondly, it's the buoyant local atmosphere that makes this unpretentious place so popular. The comfortably straightforward but lively L-shaped bar is partly divided by a wall and fireplace, with a coal fire, and has tables on bare boards, and plenty of comfortable seating. A back room has a fruit machine, juke box, pool, TV, piped music, cribbage and dominoes, and there's a good-sized garden. Two or three well kept real ales on handpump come from a good nearby microbrewery, Newby Wyke (see Lucky Dip entry for Willoughby Arms, Little Bytham). A simple choice of good value bar food includes sandwiches (from £1.75), burgers (from £2), filled baked potatoes (£2.50), scampi or gammon and egg (£4.75), 8oz rump steak (£5.50) and a daily special such as lasagne (£3.50). *(Recommended by Richard Lewis, Bernie Adams, the Didler, JP, PP, Derek and Sylvia Stephenson, Rona Murdoch)*

Free house ~ Licensee Andy Glackin ~ Real ale ~ Bar food (12-9(5 Sun)) ~ (01476) 404554 ~ Children welcome till 7.30pm ~ Open 12-11; 12-10.30 Sun

GRIMSTHORPE TF0422 Map 8
Black Horse 🍴 🍷

A151 W of Bourne

There's a quietly composed eating-out mood in the neat rooms of this handsome grey stone coaching inn. Customers are here for the attractively presented food, which is of a standard rare for this part of the world – so readers do feel it's worth the extra couple of pounds. The menu changes every now and then, but might include soup of the day (£3.25), mushroom filled with stilton and mushroom pâté (£4.25), thai fishcake with bean sprout and vegetable stir fry and sweet chilli dressing (£4.35), fish and chips (£7.85), sausage and mash (£8.95), salmon fillet with saffron and nero spaghetti and cream sauce (£9.95), braised lamb shank (£10.95), puddings such as lemon tart with orange sorbet and orange coulis or banoffi pie (£4.25), and Sunday roast (£9.25). A cosy window seat and a nice round oak table stand on oak flooring just as you go in. The narrowish room then stretches away past the oak-timbered bar counter and bar stools down one side, and a row of tables, some of which are quite intimate in their own little booths, down the other. A warming coal fire in a stripped stone fireplace, lamps, fresh flowers and patterned wallpaper give it all a homely feel. They serve well kept Black Horse Bitter and Grimsthorpe Castle which are both brewed for the pub by Oldershaws, and stock some decent wines. Some tables may have notices reserving them for parties of four or six so it's best to book; piped music. *(Recommended by Dr T E Hothersall, Walter and Susan Rinaldi-Butcher, John and Daphne Lock Necrews, Tony Gayfer, Derek and Sylvia Stephenson, David and Ruth Hollands)*

Free house ~ Licensees Brian and Elaine Rey ~ Real ale ~ Bar food (12-1.45, 7-9.30(8.30 Sun)) ~ Restaurant ~ (01778) 591247 ~ Children in eating area of bar ~ Open 11.30-2.30, 6.30(6 Sat)-11; 12-3, 7-10.30 Sun; closed Sun evening, Mon lunchtime ~ Bedrooms: £50B/£69B

LINCOLN SK9771 Map 8
Victoria 🍺 £

Union Road

This tucked-away early Victorian local is a proper ale house with no pretensions and a chatty, buoyant atmosphere (typical of the pubs in this excellent little pub group), and is well worth the short walk up a steep back street behind the castle. The simply furnished little tiled front lounge has a coal fire and pictures of Queen Victoria. It attracts a good mix of ages and is always bustling, especially at lunchtime and later on in the evening. A good range of well kept real ales includes Batemans XB, Castle Rock Hemlock and Timothy Taylors Landlord, and up to five guests from brewers such as Black Sheep, Newby Wyke and Oldershaws, as well as foreign draught and bottled beers, around 20 country wines, a farm cider on tap, and cheap soft drinks. Limited but good value lunchtime food includes filled cobs (from £1.30, huge bacon ones £2.75), toasted sandwiches (£1.95), all-day breakfast and basic home-made hot dishes such as beef stew, sausage and mash, chilli, curry or ploughman's (£3.95). Children are welcome in the restaurant which is only open on Sunday lunchtimes (Sunday roast £5). You can sit in the small conservatory or out in the gravelled side garden, which has good views of the castle. They hold beer festivals in the last week in June and the first week in December. *(Recommended by Darly Graton, Graeme Gulibert, Patrick Hancock, Andy and Jill Kassube, JP, PP, Di and Mike Gillam, Richard Lewis, the Didler, Nick and Pam Hancock, Joe Green)*

Tynemill ~ Manager Neil Renshaw ~ Real ale ~ Bar food (12(11 Sat)-2.30; 12-2 Sun) ~ (01522) 536048 ~ Dogs allowed in bar ~ Open 11-11; 12-10.30 Sun

Wig & Mitre ★ ♀

Steep Hill; just below cathedral

This bustling café-style pub is the sort of place where you can pop in for anything from a coffee up – and at almost any time of the day. They serve freshly squeezed orange juice, and were one of the first pubs to put in proper espresso machines. Food works its way up the spectrum from an extensive breakfast menu (full english £8.50) to a very elaborate restaurant menu. With prices at the higher end of the spectrum, dishes might include soup (£4.50), open sandwich (£6), snail and parsley spring rolls with aïoli (£6.50), baked cheese soufflé with roast red pepper compote and rocket (£6.95), fried skate (£14.95), roast sausages with garlic and black pudding mash and apple cream sauce (£9.50), roast tournedos of beef with sauté globe artichoke and red wine jus (£16.50), puddings such as chocolate orange tart with bitter chocolate sauce and chocolate ice cream (£4.75) and cheese (£6.50). Or you could go for something from the caviar menu (from £38). They have well kept Greene King Ruddles Best or Marstons Pedigree, an excellent selection of over 95 wines, many of them available by the glass, and lots of liqueurs and spirits. Spreading over a couple of floors, the building itself dates from the 14th c, and has plenty of period features. The big-windowed beamed downstairs bar has exposed stone walls, pews and Gothic furniture on oak floorboards, and comfortable sofas in a carpeted back area. Upstairs, the calmer dining room is light and airy, with views of the castle walls and cathedral, shelves of old books, and an open fire. The walls are hung with antique prints and caricatures of lawyers and clerics, and there are plenty of newspapers and periodicals lying about – even templates to tempt you to a game of noughts and crosses. *(Recommended by Paul Humphreys, David and Ruth Hollands, Andy and Jill Kassube, Patrick Hancock, Dr and Mrs M E Wilson, Irene and Ray Atkin, Helen Whitmore, June and Ken Brooks, Anthony Barnes, Fiona McElhone, JP, PP, Richard Jennings)*

Free house ~ Licensees Valerie and Toby Hope ~ Real ale ~ Bar food (8am-11pm) ~ Restaurant ~ (01522) 535190 ~ Children welcome ~ Dogs allowed in bar ~ Open 8am-12pm

NEWTON TF0436 Map 8
Red Lion

Signposted from A52 E of Grantham; pub itself also discreetly signed off A52

A very popular feature at this welcoming old pub is the fine row of carvery roasts (£7.95), available on Friday and Saturday evening and Sunday lunchtime. Other good value bar food includes soup (£2.95), fried whitebait (£3.95), courgette bake (£5.95), battered haddock (£7.50), steak and ale pie (£7.95), fillet steak (£12.95), and daily specials such as leg of lamb steak in rosemary and garlic (£8.95) or chicken fillet with white wine sauce (£9.95). It's comfortable and civilised here, with old-fashioned seating, partly stripped stone walls covered with old farming tools, stuffed creatures, well kept Batemans XB and a guest such as Shepherd Neame Spitfire on handpump, a no smoking dining room, fruit machine and perhaps piped music. A neat, sheltered back garden has some seats on the grass and on the terrace, and there's a good play area. According to local tradition this village is the highest point between Grantham and the Urals – when an east wind isn't blowing in thoughts of Siberia, the countryside makes for pleasant walks. *(Recommended by JP, PP)*

Free house ~ Licensee Mr Blessett ~ Real ale ~ Bar food ~ Restaurant ~ (01529) 497256 ~ Well behaved children away from bar ~ Open 12-3, 6-11; 12-4, 7-10.30 Sun

SOUTH WITHAM SK9219 Map 8
Blue Cow ◀

Village signposted just off A1 Stamford—Grantham (with brown sign for pub)

A gently appealing individuality characterises this welcoming old stone-walled country pub. Just inside the entrance lobby you pass an endearing little water feature on floodlit steps that go down to the cellar. Two enjoyably relaxing bars are separated by a big central open-plan counter. One dark-beamed room has bentwood chairs at big indonesian hardwood tables, wickerwork and panelling, and prettily curtained windows. The second room has big black standing timbers and beams, partly stripped stone walls, shiny flagstones and a dark blue flowery carpet; piped music, darts, TV, cribbage, table skittles and dominoes. The two real ales they serve here, Thirlwells Best (named after the licensees) and Witham Wobbler, are brewed by the very friendly landlord in the building next door – if he's around he'll happily give you a little tour, and sell you some to take home (perhaps even in a recycled Coke bottle). Good value food includes sandwiches (from £3.25), ploughman's (£5.60), chilli (£6.75), pie of the day (£6.95), battered haddock (£7.30), sweet and sour pork (£8.95) and rump steak (£9.50). The garden has tables on a pleasant terrace. We still haven't heard from anyone who has stayed here, but they will even stable your horse overnight. *(Recommended by the Didler, Paul Humphreys, Rona Murdoch, Susan and Tony Dyer, JP, PP)*

Own brew ~ Licensees Dick and Julia Thirlwell ~ Real ale ~ Bar food (12-2.30, 6-9.30) ~ Restaurant ~ (01572) 768432 ~ Children welcome ~ Dogs allowed in bar ~ Open 12-11 ~ Bedrooms: £40S/£45S

STAMFORD TF0207 Map 8

Daniel Lambert ◀

St Leonards Street

The comfortably appealing low-key atmosphere first drew our attention to this nice town pub, and the new landlady seems thoroughly in tune with the feel of the place. The pub's namesake, a 19th-c prison warden, weighed more than 330 kg (52 stone) when he died suddenly during an overnight stop in Stamford. He's buried in St Martin's churchyard, and you can see items of his clothing in the Stamford Museum in Broad Street: a lot to see, as he measured nearly 3 metres – to be exact, 9 ft 4 in – round the body. There's a big picture of Lambert and other bits and pieces about him in the simply decorated and unpretentious smallish bar, which has maroon plush stools and chairs on a green carpet, and a winter log fire. As well as a dozen wines by the glass they have well kept Adnams, Courage Directors, Timothy Taylors Landlord and Tetleys, with a guest from a brewer such as Jennings on handpump. Bar food includes sandwiches (from £2.75), soup (£2.95), chicken liver pâté (£3.25), hot filled baguettes (from £3.50), burgers (from £4.50), honey and mustard chicken (£6.50), battered haddock or stilton and vegetable crumble (£6.95), steaks (from £7.95), mussels (£8.50), three or four daily specials such as seared tuna (£7.25), puddings such as banoffi pie or jam roly-poly (from £3.50), and Sunday roast (£6.95); no smoking restaurant, fruit machine, cribbage, dominoes and piped music. The thoughtfully planted little terraced back garden is neat and tidy, with aluminium tables and chairs, and, with its subtle lighting, looks nice at night. *(Recommended by Beryl and Bill Farmer, Lorraine and Fred Gill, the Didler, Tina and David Woods-Taylor, Comus and Sarah Elliott, MLR, John Moulder, JP, PP)*

Punch ~ Lease Anita Morris ~ Real ale ~ Bar food (not Sun evening) ~ Restaurant ~ (01780) 755991 ~ Children welcome ~ Dogs allowed in bar ~ Open 12-2.30, 6.30-11; 11.30-11 Sat; 12-4, 7-10.30 Sun

George of Stamford ★ ⑪ ♀ ⇌

High Street, St Martins (B1081 S of centre, not the quite different central pedestrianised High Street)

Lincolnshire Dining Pub of the Year

In grand contrast to the Daniel Lambert above, the atmosphere at this elegant old coaching inn is smartly relaxed, its labyrinth of rooms filled with comfortably conversing customers and busy attentive staff. Built in 1597 for Lord Burghley (though there are visible parts of a much older Norman pilgrims' hospice, and a crypt under the cocktail bar that may be 1,000 years old), this hotel has kept its considerable character, while adding a good deal of modern style and comfort. Seats in its beautifully furnished series of rooms range through leather, cane and antique wicker to soft settees and easy chairs, while the central lounge has sturdy timbers, broad flagstones, heavy beams, and massive stonework. If you look hard enough, a ghostly face is supposed to appear in the wooden panelling of the London Room (used by folk headed that way in coaching days). The other front room making up the surprisingly pubby bar is the York Room. Snacks served here include soup (from £4.55), sandwiches (from £4.95), chicken liver pâté with hot bread (£6.25), sausage and mash (£6.95), and a pudding of the day (£3.95). Our Food Award however is for the not cheap but most enjoyable more elaborate meals served in the oak-panelled restaurant (jacket and tie) and less formal Garden Lounge restaurant (which has well spaced furniture on herringbone glazed bricks around a central tropical grove). Using carefully sourced ingredients, food in the Garden Lounge takes on a continental tilt (one of the licensees is Italian). As well as several pasta dishes such as tagliatelle with salmon (£10.95) and half a lobster with spaghetti (£15.95), the menus might include parma ham with sliced fennel salad (£7.95), moules marinière (£9.95), braised lamb shank (£11.45), dressed crab or fish and chips (£11.95), marinated salmon fillet on wok-fried ginger noodles (£13.50), an attractively set out cold buffet (£13.45), seafood platter (£26), and puddings (£4.95). Well kept Adnams Broadside, Fullers London Pride and Greene

King Abbot and Ruddles on handpump, but best of all are the wines, many of which are italian and good value, with about 18 by the glass; there's also freshly squeezed orange juice, and good coffees. The staff are friendly and very professional, with waiter drinks service in the charming cobbled courtyard at the back – a delightful place for a summer afternoon tea (£11.95), with comfortable chairs and tables among attractive plant tubs and colourful hanging baskets on the ancient stone buildings. There's also a neatly kept walled garden, with a sunken lawn where croquet is often played. *(Recommended by J F M and M West, Barry Collett, H Paulinski, JP, PP, Charles Gysin, Tina and David Woods-Taylor, Lorraine and Fred Gill, Roy Bromell, John and Judy Saville, the Didler, R C Wiles, A J Bowen, S F Parrinder, Steve Whalley, John and Enid Morris, Sherrie Glass, B and M Kendall, Mike and Sue Loseby, Gerry and Rosemary Dobson; also in the* Good Hotel Guide*)*

Free house ~ Licensees Chris Pitman and Ivo Vannocci ~ Real ale ~ Bar food (11-11) ~ Restaurant ~ (01780) 750750 ~ Children welcome ~ Dogs allowed in bar and bedrooms ~ Open 11-11; 12-11 Sun ~ Bedrooms: £78B/£105B

SURFLEET TF2528 Map 8
Mermaid

Just off A16 N of Spalding, on B1356 at bridge

Much of this genuinely old-fashioned dining pub looks unchanged since the 70s, but it's still absolutely pristine and fresh-looking inside. A small central glass-backed bar counter (complete with original Babycham décor) serves two high-ceilinged rooms, which have huge netted sash windows, green patterned carpets, beige Anaglypta dado, brass platters, navigation lanterns and horse tack on cream textured walls, and a mixture of banquettes and stools; piped music, cribbage and dominoes. Two steps down, the restaurant is decorated in a similar style. Friendly helpful staff serve home-made bar food which includes lunchtime snacks such as sandwiches (from £2), filled ciabatta (from £3.25) and chilli (£4.95), as well as soup (£2.50), black pudding tower (£3.75), cottage pie or vegetable, mixed bean and soya casserole (£6.75), tuna steak on chilli noodles (£8.95), oriental duck breast with noodles and spicy orange and Cointreau sauce (£10.95), and daily specials such as beef bourguignon (£6.95). Well kept Adnams Broadside and John Smiths and possibly a guest such as Fullers London Pride on handpump. The pretty garden has lots of seats and a terrace with thatched parasols, and a children's play area is safely walled from the River Glen which runs beside the pub. *(Recommended by Michael and Jenny Back, Beryl and Bill Farmer, W M Paton, Derek and Sylvia Stephenson, Mr Ken Marshall)*

Free house ~ Licensee J Bell ~ Real ale ~ Bar food (12-2.30, 6.30-9.30(6-10 Fri/Sat); 12-4, 6.30-9 Sun) ~ Restaurant ~ (01775) 680275 ~ Children in eating area of bar and restaurant ~ Dogs welcome ~ Open 11-11; 12-10.30 Sun

WOOLSTHORPE SK8435 Map 8
Chequers

The one near Belvoir, signposted off A52 or A607 W of Grantham

Up a short dead-end off the main street, part of this 17th-c coaching inn was once the village bakery. It has a mix of chairs around stripped tables in its main dining area, rather light and airy, with a lot of hunting and Victorian prints on the ragged blue walls. On the left, under the heavy beams is a huge boar's head above a good log fire in the big brick fireplace, some stripped sandstone, and handsome leather seats around one massive oak table. Round to the right is a homely area with well used big blue sofas, squashy armchairs and an unusual 1920s-ish dresser; piped music and dominoes. Served by friendly well trained staff, good freshly made food, changing daily and using quite a lot of local produce, includes seasonal game as well as dishes such as salad (£6.95), sausage and mash (£7.50), steak and kidney pie (£8.95) and pot roast rolled beef (£12.50); they will do small helpings on request, and there are two no smoking areas. Three well kept beers on handpump might be Banks's Original, Fullers London Pride and Marstons Pedigree. Also decent house wines, around 50 single malts, organic drinks and local fruit pressés. There are nice teak tables, chairs and benches outside, and beyond some picnic-sets on the edge of the pub's cricket field; boules too, and views of Belvoir Castle. We have not yet heard from readers who have stayed here. *(Recommended by June and Malcolm Farmer, JP, PP)*

Free house ~ Licensee Justin Chad ~ Real ale ~ Bar food ~ Restaurant ~ (01476) 870701 ~ Children welcome ~ Dogs allowed in bar and bedrooms ~ Open 12-3, 5-11; 12-4.30 Sun; closed Sun evening ~ Bedrooms: £40S/£50S

Lucky Dip

Besides the fully inspected pubs, you might like to try these Lucky Dips recommended to us and described by readers (if you do, please send us reports: www.goodguides.com).

ASLACKBY [TF0830]
Robin Hood & Little John [A15 Bourne—Sleaford]: Comfortable timbered pub with attractive olde-worlde décor, lots of polished brass and copper, pot plants, friendly, helpful and efficient service, enjoyable low-priced plain cooking, Marstons and other beers, side restaurant area *(William and Elizabeth Templeton)*

AUBOURN [SK9262]
Royal Oak: Partly 16th-c village pub with generous straightforward food, five well kept real ales, friendly service, pleasantly decorated bar with open fire, recently extended dining room, darts; picnic-sets in nice small front garden *(CMW, JJW)*

BARHOLM [TF0810]
☆ *Five Horseshoes*: Old-fashioned relaxed village local, three rooms just right for a chat, clean, cosy and friendly, with well kept Adnams, Batemans and interesting guest beers, mini beer festivals, good range of wines, comfortable seats, rustic bric-a-brac; children welcome, charming small garden, tables out under shady arbour, wknd barbecues, paddocks behind *(Andy West, LYM)*

BECKINGHAM [SK8753]
Pack Horse [Sleaford Rd; off A17]: Friendly village local with good licensees, home cooking and well kept John Smiths *(James Finch)*

BELCHFORD [TF2975]
Blue Bell [Main Rd; E of A153 Horncastle—Louth]: Reopened late 2002, cosily refurbished bar, well kept Bass, Timothy Taylors Landlord and a guest beer, good choice of reasonably priced wines, enjoyable enterprising food, polite friendly service; handy for wolds walks *(Jill and Keith Wright)*

BOSTON [TF3244]
Carpenters Arms [Witham St]: Lively traditional bare-boards local, well kept Bass, Batemans Mild and XB and guest beers, enterprising home-cooked lunchtime food inc good cheap rolls; reasonably priced bedrooms *(the Didler, JP, PP)*
Coach & Horses [Main Ridge]: Friendly traditional one-bar pub with well kept Batemans XB and good coal fire *(the Didler)*

Eagle [West St, towards station]: Basic cheery local with well kept Batemans, Castle Rock, Timothy Taylors Landlord and three guest beers at low prices, cheap soft drinks too, good value food, quick friendly service even when it's busy, children in eating area lunchtime; Mon folk club, live music Sat, open all day Sat *(BB, Andrew York, the Didler, JP, PP)*
Ropers Arms [Horncastle Rd]: Batemans corner local in nice spot by river and windmill, quiet and unassuming – gets lively for big-screen TV football Sun; some live entertainment; open 2-11, all day wknds and summer *(JP, PP, the Didler)*

BRIGG [SE9907]
Yarborough Hunt [Bridge St]: Closed for some decades and now reopened after restoration to traditional chatty four-room layout, Batemans XXB, Greene King IPA, Tom Woods and two guest beers, old Brigg memorabilia, no piped music; no food; tables out behind *(Chris and Elaine Lyon)*

CASTLE BYTHAM [SK9818]
Castle Inn [off A1 Stamford—Grantham, or B1176]: Cosy black-beamed village pub with good log fire, helpful and friendly new licensees, well kept Adnams, Ansells Mild, John Smiths and Oakham JHB *(LYM)*

CLEETHORPES [TA3108]
Kings Royal [Kingsway]: Well run, with good choice of real ales *(Dr Bongo)*
No 2 Refreshment Room [Station Approach]: Tiny basic 60s-throwback bar almost on platform, real ales inc a Mild and usually a good guest beer from a small brewery, no food; open all day *(the Didler)*
☆ *Willys* [Highcliff Rd; south promenade]: Open-plan bistro-style seafront pub with café tables, tiled floor and painted brick walls; brews its own good beers, also well kept Batemans and guest beers and good value basic lunchtime home cooking; friendly staff, quiet juke box, panoramic Humber views; popular beer festival Nov, open all day *(the Didler, JP, PP)*

DUNSTON [TF0663]
Red Lion [Middle St; ½ mile off B1188 SE of Lincoln]: Appealing tucked-away village pub, big beamed lounge and restaurant very popular midweek with older lunchers, good

value generous home cooking inc plenty of blackboard dishes and very good puddings, good choice of well kept beers, nice house wines, pleasant efficient service *(Mr and Mrs J Brown, Bill and Sheila McLardy)*

EAST KIRKBY [TF3362]

☆ *Red Lion* [Fen Rd]: Lots of chiming clocks, jugs, breweriana and interesting old tools (some for sale behind), well kept Bass and a guest beer, good value standard food, friendly staff, open fire, family room, traditional games; wheelchair access, tables outside (and more machinery), camping; handy for Air Museum *(the Didler, JP, PP)*

EPWORTH [SE7804]

White Bear [Belton Rd]: Bar and three linked well furnished eating areas, enjoyable food with help-yourself veg etc, sensible prices, enthusiastic staff *(Alistair and Kay Butler)*

FROGNALL [TF1610]

☆ *Goat* [B1525, off A16 NE of Mkt Deeping]: Friendly pub with low beams and stripped stone, particularly well kept quickly changing ales such as Arundel Long Willie, Batemans XB, Clarks Treble Hop, Harviestoun All Black and Winters Norwich Revenge, enjoyable usual food from sandwiches and baked potatoes (lunchtime, not Sun) to fish and grills, log fires, two dining rooms (one no smoking where children welcome), helpful landlord, books for sale; games machine, may be piped music; good wheelchair access, big garden with terrace and play equipment, separate area for under-5s – also a hop garden *(Richard Lewis)*

GAINSBOROUGH [SK8189]

Eight Jolly Brewers [Ship Court, Silver St]: Bustling unpretentious pub with beams, bare bricks and brewery posters, up to eight well kept well priced changing ales and one brewed for them by Highwood, quieter bar upstairs, simple lunchtime food (not Sun), friendly staff and locals; folk club, open all day Fri-Sun *(the Didler, JP, PP)*

GRANTHAM [SK9135]

Blue Bull [Westgate]: Two-bar local with four well kept ales mainly from interesting smaller breweries, partly no smoking back dining room with good value food (not Sun or Mon evenings); darts, pool and juke box in side room; tables out behind, handy for station *(the Didler, Richard Lewis)*

☆ *Blue Pig* [Vine St]: Pretty jettied Tudor pub, low beams, panelling, stripped stone and flagstones, lots of pig ornaments, friendly bustle, helpful staff, well kept changing ales such as Bass, City of Cambridge, Timothy Taylors Landlord and York Yorkshire Terrier, good simple lunchtime food, open fire, daily papers, lots of prints and bric-a-brac; piped music, juke box, games machines, no children or dogs; tables out behind, open all day *(JP, PP, Richard Lewis, BB, Tony and Wendy Hobden, Rona Murdoch, the Didler)*

Lord Harrowby [Dudley Rd, S of centre]:

Friendly 60s-feel pub in residential part, lots of RAF pictures and memorabilia in pleasant lounge (with pianist Sat and great atmosphere then), well kept Bass, Worthington and a guest beer, games-oriented public bar; no food, cl lunchtime exc Sun *(Pete Baker)*

Muddle Go Nowhere [main Nottingham road, nr A1/A52]: Large comfortable Tom Cobleigh family pub, lots of beams, woodwork and bare brick, country décor with range fireplaces, no smoking area, their usual generous food inc Sun roasts and Mon/Tues bargains, well kept Flowers IPA, Marstons Pedigree, Tetleys and Theakstons XB, quick helpful service even when busy; outside and inside play areas, baby changing and disabled facilities, Mon quiz night, picnic-sets outside, open all day *(R C Vincent, Richard Lewis)*

Nobody Inn [Watergate]: Friendly bare-boards open-plan local with five well kept changing ales inc cheap Sam Smiths OB and two or three from local Newby Wyke and Oldershaws; back games room with pool, table footer, good juke box, SkyTV; open all day *(the Didler, Mike Turner, JP, PP, Richard Lewis)*

GREATFORD [TF0811]

Hare & Hounds: Large beamed bar, smaller dining room, well kept ales such as Adnams Broadside, Oakham and Charles Wells Bombardier, wide choice of enjoyable fresh food inc bargain lunch; picnic-sets in small back garden, attractive village *(LYM, Barry Collett)*

HAGWORTHINGHAM [TF3469]

George & Dragon [High St]: Hard-working new licensees, Black Sheep and Greene King IPA, attractively priced wines, good value generous food inc Fri fresh fish and bargain Sun lunch, conservatory; unobtrusive piped music; tables outside *(Paul Humphreys)*

HALTON HOLEGATE [TF4165]

☆ *Bell* [B1195 E of Spilsby]: Unchanging pretty village local, simple but comfortable and consistently friendly, with wide choice of decent generous home-made food inc Sun lunches and outstanding fish and chips, tempting prices, well kept Batemans XB, Tetleys and Highwood Bomber County, Lancaster bomber pictures, pub games; children in back eating area (with tropical fish tank) and restaurant *(JP, PP, the Didler, Michael and Jenny Back, Derek and Sylvia Stephenson, LYM)*

HORNCASTLE [TF2669]

Admiral Rodney [North St]: Comfortable hotel with wide range of well kept beers and wines, helpful staff, sensibly priced food inc carvery in courtyard restaurant, no smoking area; bedrooms, good parking *(David and Ruth Hollands)*

INGHAM [SK9483]

Inn on the Green [The Green]: Wide choice of quickly served good fresh home-made food from good sandwich range to steaks, venison and duck in well modernised pub on village green; well kept changing ales such as Black Sheep, Fullers London Pride and Timothy Taylors Landlord, wide-ranging wine list, lots of brass and copper in spacious beamed lounge bar, good fire, locals' bar, downstairs and upstairs dining rooms; children welcome *(C A Hall)*

IRNHAM [TF0226]

Griffin [Bulby Rd]: Small old stone-built village pub with well kept changing beers such as Adnams Broadside, Fullers London Pride and Theakstons Old Peculier, up to three dozen in early July beer festival (lots of room for tents and caravans); home-made food, log fires, lounge, back snug, restaurant, friendly staff; darts, dominoes and pool; nice village setting, cl Mon-Thurs winter *(Richard Lewis)*

KIRKBY ON BAIN [TF2462]

Ebrington Arms [Main St]: Generous good value food inc cheap Sun lunch, five or more well kept changing ales from small breweries far and wide, prompt welcoming service, daily papers, low 16th-c beams, two open fires, nicely set out dining areas each side, copper-topped tables, wall banquettes, jet fighter and racing car pictures; games area with darts, restaurant, may be piped music; beer festivals Easter and Aug bank hols, wheelchair access, tables out in front, swings on side lawn, camp site behind, open all day *(JP, PP, the Didler)*

KIRMINGTON [TA1011]

Marrowbone & Cleaver [High St]: Good pub food, Bass and Black Sheep, nice welcome *(Bruce M Drew)*

LINCOLN [SK9871]

Adam & Eve [Lindum Rd (towards Wragby)]: Civilised pub, one of the oldest here, opp gate to cathedral close; good value food, well kept John Smiths and Theakstons, friendly cheerful staff; boules, tree-shaded play area *(JP, PP, Mr and Mrs G Baker)*

Golden Eagle [High St]: Cheerfully busy basic two-bar town pub, well kept and attractively priced changing ales inc Batemans, Castle Rock and Everards, good choice of country wines, cheap soft drinks, good value lunchtime food; open all day Fri/Sat *(the Didler, JP, PP, Andy and Jill Kassube)*

Morning Star [Greetwellgate]: Unpretentious well scrubbed local handy for cathedral, friendly atmosphere, enjoyable cheap lunches esp Fri specials, well kept reasonably priced ales such as Greene King Ruddles, Marstons Pedigree and Charles Wells Bombardier, coal fire, aircraft paintings, sofas in cosy back snug; piano night Sat; nice outside area, open all day exc Sun *(the Didler, David and Ruth Hollands, JP, PP, Patrick Hancock, Pete Baker, Joe Green)*

Pyewipe [Saxilby Rd; off A57 just S of bypass]: Much extended 18th-c pub popular for wide range of good food inc good fish choice and memorable ginger pudding, well kept real ales such as Timothy Taylors Landlord, friendly atmosphere; comfortable reasonably priced bedrooms, on Roman Fossdyke Canal, pleasant walk out from centre, bedrooms *(Paul Humphreys, Gwen Kahan)*

☆ *Queen in the West* [Moor St; off A57 nr racecourse]: Well kept changing ales such as Bass, Marstons Pedigree, Theakstons XB and Old Peculier and reasonably priced simple bar lunches in busy and welcoming old backstreet pub below cathedral; military prints and miniatures in well decorated lounge, interesting sporting prints in public bar with TV, darts, games; open all day Fri/Sat *(JP, PP, the Didler, Joe Green)*

Sippers [Melville St, opp bus station]: Popular two-bar lunchtime pub with good food (not wknd evenings), Courage Directors, Greene King Old Speckled Hen, Marstons Pedigree and guest beers, friendly licensees; quieter evenings, cl Sun lunchtime *(JP, PP, the Didler)*

Strugglers [Westgate]: Small refurbished local with well kept Bass, Marstons Pedigree and a guest such as Fullers London Pride, coal-effect fire in small back snug; no under-18s, can be smoky; open all day Fri-Sun *(the Didler, David and Ruth Hollands, Alison Keys, JP, PP, Andy and Jill Kassube, Joe Green)*

LITTLE BYTHAM [TF0118]

☆ *Willoughby Arms* [Station Rd, S of village]: Good value substantial food from sandwiches to venison, friendly staff and local atmosphere, good Newby Wyke beers from back microbrewery, enterprising guest beer policy, belgian beers, Weston's farm cider, specialist fruit juices and different coffees, simple bar with wall banquettes, newly stripped tables and coal fire, pleasant old-fashioned end dining room, airy pool room with TV; faint piped music, live music in cellar bar wknds, frequent folk and beer festivals; children welcome, picnic-sets out behind with quiet country views, open all day wknds *(Richard Lewis, June and Malcolm Farmer, Bill and Sheila McLardy, JP, PP, the Didler, BB, Kevin Thorpe)*

LOUTH [TF3387]

Kings Head [Mercer Row]: Large unpretentious bar, well kept beer, good range of good value bar food inc roasts and traditional puddings *(the Didler, JP, PP)*

☆ *Masons Arms* [Cornmarket]: Light and airy, with plush seats, big sunny bay window, good mix of different-sized tables, panelled back bar, good friendly family service, well kept full Batemans range, Marstons Pedigree, Timothy Taylors Landlord and guest beers, farm cider, decent coffee, good home-made food from big hot sandwiches up, good upstairs dining room (remarkable art deco former masonic lodge meeting room); piped radio; good bedrooms, open all day exc Sun *(the Didler, JP, PP, Roy and Lindsey Fentiman, BB)*

Olde Whyte Swanne [Eastgate]: Popular and friendly, ancient low beams, comfortable front bar with open fire, decent soup, Bass and guest beers *(JP, PP, the Didler)*

Wheatsheaf [Westgate]: Cheerful well kept early 17th-c inn, real fires in all three bars, Boddingtons, Flowers and a guest such as Timothy Taylors Landlord, decent lunchtime food; can be crowded; tables outside, open all day Sat *(the Didler, JP, PP)*

Woolpack [Riverhead Rd]: 18th-c wool merchant's house popular for good home cooking (not Sun or Mon evenings) and Batemans ales inc a Mild, Marstons Pedigree and guest ales; bar, lounge, snug, two real fires; cl Mon lunchtime, open all day Sat *(the Didler, JP, PP)*

LUDFORD [TF1989]
Black Horse [A631 Mkt Rasen—Louth]: Keen licensees doing good imaginative food *(K C Girling)*

NORTH KELSEY [TA0401]
Butchers Arms [Middle St; off B1434 S of Brigg]: Busy village local, opened up but not too modern, low ceilings, flagstones, bare boards, dim lighting, with five well kept Highwood beers (brewed by owner on his farm), good value cold lunches, enthusiastic cheerful service, woodburner; pub games, no juke box, tables outside, opens 4 wkdys, open all day wknds *(the Didler, JP, PP)*

NORTH THORESBY [TF2998]
New Inn [Station Rd]: Consistently good food, fine friendly service, roomy restaurant; attractive terrace *(P Norton)*

NORTON DISNEY [SK8859]
☆ *St Vincent Arms* [Main St, off A46 Newark—Lincoln]: Attractive and welcoming village pub with well kept Batemans XXXB or Marstons Pedigree, guest beers sometimes, open fire, good cheap generous plain food from sandwiches up inc beautifully cooked veg, pleasant landlord, appropriately decorated family room (Walt Disney's ancestors came from here) and adults' dining room; tables and big adventure playground out behind *(the Didler)*

ROTHWELL [TF1499]
☆ *Blacksmiths Arms* [off B1225 S of Caistor]: Attractive heavy-beamed old pub reopened by new owners after long closure, pleasant bar divided by arches and warm central coal fire, spacious dining area, enjoyable food from sandwiches and ploughman's to local duck, well kept changing ales such as Courage Directors, Marstons Pedigree, St Austell and Theakstons; tables outside *(John Branston, BB)*

SCAMPTON [SK9579]
Dambusters [High St]: Beams, hops and masses of interesting Dambusters and other World War II memorabilia, reasonably priced simple food (not Sun/Mon evenings), pleasant nostalgic atmosphere, well kept Greene King IPA, Abbot and Ruddles and guest beers, log fire; adjoining post office *(J D M Rushworth)*

SCOTTER [SE8800]
☆ *White Swan* [The Green]: Expansive well kept pub comfortably laid out for dining,

varied well prepared generous food inc fish board and bargain three-course special, five real ales inc Black Sheep and Timothy Taylors Landlord, snug panelled area by one fireplace, friendly landlady and neat pleasant staff; trad jazz Mon, may be piped music; big-windowed restaurant looking over lawn with picnic-sets to duck-filled River Eau; 14 comfortable bedrooms in modern extension *(BB, Jenny and Dave Hughes, Mr and Mrs J R Ward)*

SKEGNESS [TF5660]
☆ *Vine* [Vine Rd, off Drummond Rd, Seacroft]: Unspoilt extended hotel based on late 18th-c country house, calm and comfortable well run bar overlooking drive and own bowling green, imposing antique seats and grandfather clock in turkey-carpeted hall, juke box in inner oak-panelled room; well kept Batemans XB, Mild and XXB, good value food using local produce in bar and restaurant, friendly staff, welcoming fire; tables on big back sheltered lawn with swings, good reasonably priced bedrooms, peaceful suburban setting not far from beach and birdwatching *(the Didler, BB, JP, PP, Derek and Sylvia Stephenson)*

SKENDLEBY [TF4369]
☆ *Blacksmiths Arms* [off A158 about 10 miles NW of Skegness]: Some concentration on good imaginative generous food in big busy back restaurant extension, very generous one-price main courses, also old-fashioned two-room bar, cosy and quaint, with view of cellar, deep 17th-c well, well kept Batemans XB and XXXB tapped from the cask, friendly staff, open fire *(the Didler, JP, PP)*

SKILLINGTON [SK8925]
Cross Swords [The Square]: Small, homely and pleasant, with good food using local produce from ploughman's and other bar snacks to restaurant dishes such as game and ostrich, hospitable service and sociable landlord, Highwood Best and a guest such as Shepherd Neame Spitfire, public bar with coal fire, darts and wall settles; piped music; delightful village, cl Mon lunchtime *(Kevin Thorpe, John Roots)*

SOUTH ORMSBY [TF3675]
☆ *Massingberd Arms* [off A16 S of Louth]: Small welcoming refurbished 17th-c pub, helpful and obliging landlord, well kept John Smiths Magnet and a couple of guest beers such as Buffys, short choice of enjoyable freshly made food inc Sun lunch, restaurant Thurs-Sun evenings; pleasant garden, good wolds walks, cl Mon lunchtime in winter *(Derek and Sylvia Stephenson, JP, PP, the Didler, Dr John Lunn)*

SOUTH THORESBY [TF4077]
☆ *Vine* [about 1 mile off A16 N of Ulceby Cross]: Large two-room village inn with small pub part – tiny passageway servery, steps up to three-table lounge, wide choice of good food inc aberdeen angus steaks in nicely panelled no smoking dining room, well kept Batemans XB and a guest beer, fine choice of malt whiskies, good value

wines, separate pool room; bedrooms, tables in pleasant big garden *(the Didler, JP, PP)*

STAMFORD [TF0207]

Crown [All Saints Pl]: Good reasonably priced english country cooking inc summer rabbit in three-mustard sauce, perhaps springtime rook pie, wkdy two-course lunch deals, in large rambling stone-built hotel's panelled country bar and no smoking dining rooms, changing beers such as Adnams, Bass, Roosters and Timothy Taylors Landlord, decent wines and coffee, polite friendly staff; dogs welcome, comfortable quiet bedrooms, open all day *(the Didler, Roy Bromell)*

Green Man [Scotgate]: Comfortable L-shaped bar with good choice of well kept ales (dozens at Easter beer festival), good value food (not Sun), friendly staff, real fire; TV in raised area, tables in garden, open all day, bedrooms *(Richard Lewis, the Didler)*

Lord Burghley [Broad St]: Old pub with several neat rooms, stripped stone, good atmosphere and service, well kept Bass, Fullers London Pride and Greene King IPA, farm cider, food (not Sun evening) inc good steak and kidney pie and steamed puddings; pleasant small walled garden, open all day *(the Didler, Des and Jen Clarke, Barry Collett)*

Periwig [Red Lion Sq/All Saints Pl]: Gallery above narrow split-level bar, well kept Courage Directors, Oakham JHB, John Smiths and Theakstons XB, well filled good value baguettes, baked potatoes, ploughman's and salads (not Sun), chequered tablecloths in bistro-style eating area; unobtrusive piped music; open all day *(the Didler)*

STOW [SK8881]

☆ *Cross Keys* [B1241 NW of Lincoln]: Modernised and extended, with pleasant dining areas and emphasis on interesting prettily presented food inc unusual vegetarian choices, cheap lunchtime specials and good puddings, several well kept ales, good range of wines, quick courteous service, big woodburner; may be piped music; Saxon minster church just behind; cl Mon lunchtime *(BB, David and Ruth Hollands, Nigel Clifton)*

SUSWORTH [SE8301]

Jenny Wren [East Ferry Rd]: Traditional country pub with good enterprising food at reasonable prices inc lots of fish in large dining area overlooking River Trent, panelling, stripped brickwork, low beams and brasses, various nooks and crannies, three well kept real ales, reasonable wine choice, two open fires, polite service; some tables out by water *(Chris and Elaine Lyon)*

TEALBY [TF1590]

☆ *Kings Head* [Kingsway, off B1203 towards bottom of village]: Mossy-thatched recently redecorated beamed pub in quiet wolds village famous for its cottage gardens; generous low-priced food inc sandwiches, meaty home-made pies and Fri-Sun fish

nights, well kept real ales, farm cider, friendly service, local country pictures; restaurant, wheelchair access, picnic-sets in attractive garden, handy for Viking Way walk *(the Didler, Paul Humphreys, BB, JP, PP)*

Olde Barn [Cow Lane (B1203)]: Neatly kept two-bar pub handy for Viking Way, cheerfully served good straightforward food inc fresh fish in bars and restaurant, well kept ales inc Highwood Best, big attractive back garden with lawn *(Alun Jones)*

TETFORD [TF3374]

White Hart [East Rd, off A158 E of Horncastle]: Early 16th-c pub with interesting layout, old-fashioned settles, slabby elm tables and red tiled floor in pleasant quiet inglenook bar, no smoking snug, basic games room, well kept real ales, lots of whiskies, usual food (not Sun evening); seats and swings on sheltered back lawn, simple bedrooms *(LYM, JP, PP, the Didler)*

WELTON HILL [TF0481]

Farmers Arms [A46 Lincoln—Market Rasen]: Well run comfortable no smoking pub with panelling and some stripped brickwork, houseplants and fresh flowers, hearty helpings of good freshly made food from baguettes to popular Sun lunch, Boddingtons, Castle Rock Gold and Theakstons Mild, good house wines (with a wine theme to décor), prompt service from helpful friendly licensees and neat staff; disabled access, with very shallow steps to upper dining room *(Michael and Jenny Back, Mr and Mrs D Wellington, Patrick Hancock)*

WEST DEEPING [TF1009]

Red Lion [King St]: Long low-beamed partly stripped stone bar with plenty of tables, very popular lunchtime for wide choice of generous food from appetising baguettes and baked potatoes up, OAP lunch Thurs; friendly new young licensees, well kept ales such as Adnams, Fullers London Pride, Hop Back Summer Lightning and Marstons Pedigree, good coffee, roaring coal fire, no smoking other end, brassware and pictures, big pool room; disabled access (best by front door), tables in back garden with attractive play area, open all day *(Michael and Jenny Back)*

WILLOUGHBY [TF4771]

Willoughby Arms [Church Lane]: Wide choice of freshly made competitively priced food, well kept real ales inc a changing guest beer, good individual service; quiet village *(R J Malkin, Anthony Groves, R E Gibbs)*

WOODHALL SPA [TF1962]

☆ *Abbey Lodge* [B1192 towards Coningsby]: Unchanging family-run roadside inn with bustling discreetly decorated bar, Victorian and older furnishings, World War II RAF pictures, well kept Bass, Worthington and a guest such as Greene King IPA, friendly staff, good straightforward bar food from sandwiches to local-breed steak, good service; children over 10 in restaurant, may be piped Radio 1; cl Sun *(John Branston, JP, PP, Paul Humphreys, LYM, Pat and Tony Martin)*

Village Limits [Stixwould Rd]: New licensees, good choice of enjoyable food, changing real ales and pleasant service in smallish bar with plush banquettes and aeroplane prints; nine bedrooms in separate back motel block *(Bill and Sheila McLardy)*

WOOLSTHORPE [SK8435]

Rutland Arms [off Sedgebrook Rd N of village]: Comfortable family pub in quiet spot below Belvoir Castle, by disused Grantham Canal (7-mile restored towpath walk from town); popular reasonably priced generous food in bars and back restaurant,

well kept changing ales such as Bass and Beer Seller Davenports, decent coffee, friendly long-serving landlord, button-back banquettes, hunting prints, brasses and bric-a-brac; big separate games room with video juke box and two pool tables, muddy boots allowed here; picnic-sets outside, huge grassy play area, field for caravans and camping (shower room), open all day wknds *(BB, Richard Lewis)*

WRAGBY [TF1378]

Turnor Arms [Market Pl (A158 Lincoln—Skegness)]: Good stop-off, with well kept Highwood Best and Bomber County, food inc good value Sun lunch *(Derek and Sylvia Stephenson)*

Real ale may be served from handpumps, electric pumps (not just the on-off switches used for keg beer) or – common in Scotland – tall taps called founts (pronounced 'fonts') where a separate pump pushes the beer up under air pressure. The landlord can adjust the force of the flow – a tight spigot gives the good creamy head that Yorkshire lads like.

Norfolk

Norfolk's pubs are flourishing these days, with a good many serving good individual food and drink in interesting and welcoming surroundings. Ones which shine particularly are the carefully expanded White Horse by the sea at Brancaster Staithe (imaginative food, a nice place to stay), the restaurant Ratcatchers at Cawston (good food here too), the Crown at Colkirk (nice all round, and gains a Wine Award this year for its splendid choice by the glass), the warmly welcoming Angel at Larling (better than ever since the A11 bypass has opened), the Fat Cat in Norwich (magnificent choice of well kept beers), the welcoming and nicely laid out Rose & Crown at Snettisham (good imaginative food), the appealing and leisurely Red Lion in Stiffkey (gaining a Food Award this year, for letting the freshness of its local ingredients shine through so well), the interesting old Lifeboat at Thornham (gains a Place to Stay Award now), the unchanging and splendidly old-fashioned Three Horseshoes at Warham, the warm-hearted and unpretentious Fishermans Return at Winterton-on-Sea, and the thatched Fur & Feather at Woodbastwick (tap for the excellent Woodfordes beers, enjoyable food too). Three to add to these are new entries this year: the very interestingly laid out Windmill at Great Cressingham, the good value, welcoming and unassuming Crown at Stanhoe, and the Woolpack at Terrington St John, quickly winning many new friends under its outgoing new landlady. Really on a roll at the moment, the pub which takes the title of Norfolk Dining Pub of the Year is the Rose & Crown at Snettisham. Pubs climbing to the top of the tree in the Lucky Dip section at the end of the chapter include the Chequers at Binham, Buckinghamshire Arms at Blickling, Lord Nelson in Burnham Market, Feathers in Holt, Olde Buck at Honingham, Goat at Skeyton, Chequers at Thompson and Bell at Wiveton. Drinks prices tend to be a little above the national average, with the Fat Cat in Norwich making a splendid exception. Woodfordes, doubling its brewing capacity recently, uses only a veteran low-yield high-quality variety of barley, grown only in Norfolk – you may pass signs showing the fields that produce it. There are several other smaller local breweries to look out for, such as Wolf, Iceni and Reepham.

BLAKENEY TG0243 Map 8

Kings Arms 🍺

West Gate Street

The three simply furnished, knocked-through pubby rooms at this bustling 18th-c pub have low ceilings, some interesting photographs of the licensees' theatrical careers, other pictures including work by local artists, and what must be the smallest cartoon gallery in England – in a former telephone kiosk. Look out for the brass plaque on the wall that marks a flood level. Two small rooms are no smoking, as is the airy garden room; darts, fruit machine, shove-ha'penny, bar billiards and dominoes. The large garden has lots of tables and chairs and a separate, well equipped children's area. There's a good mix of chatty locals and visitors, and the pub has been run by the same licensees for almost 30 years. Well kept Greene King Old Speckled Hen, Marstons Pedigree, Theakstons Best and a couple of changing guests often from Adnams and Woodfordes on handpump. From a good value menu, the well prepared bar food includes sandwiches (from £1.80; toasties from £2.20), soup (£2.95), grilled prawns in garlic butter (£5.25), ploughman's (from £5.50), vegetable pancake rolls (£5.75), battered cod, haddock or plaice (£7.25), grilled gammon and egg (£7.95), and steaks (from £10.50); children's meals (£3.50). The pub is just a short stroll from the harbour. *(Recommended by MDN, Keith and Chris O'Neill, Patrick Hancock, Maureen and Bill Sewell, Paul and Ursula Randall, Klaus and Elizabeth Leist, Jim Abbott)*

Free house ~ Licensees John Howard and Marjorie Davies ~ Real ale ~ Bar food (12-9.30(9 Sun)) ~ (01263) 740341 ~ Children welcome ~ Dogs welcome ~ Open 11-11(10.30 Sun) ~ Bedrooms: £35S/£60S

White Horse

Off A149 W of Sheringham; High Street

The atmosphere in this bustling little hotel is buoyant in season, with locals, holidaymakers and sailing folk mingling happily, and cheerful friendly staff. The chatty long main bar is predominantly green with a venetian red ceiling, and restrained but attractive décor, including watercolours by a local artist. Outside, you'll find tables in a suntrap courtyard and a pleasant paved garden. Enjoyable bar food includes lunchtime sandwiches or filled ciabattas (from £3.50), home-made soup (£3.50), delicious deep-fried soft herring roes on toast (£4.50), home-made smoked haddock and prawn pie or pork and leek sausages with mash, red cabbage and onion gravy (£7.50), and home-made steak and kidney suet pudding (£7.95), with specials such as local asparagus (£4.95) and fresh local mussels (£8.25), and home-made puddings such as treacle tart (£3.50); children's meals (from £4.25). There's also a good no smoking conservatory restaurant. Adnams Best and Broadside, Woodfordes Nelsons Revenge and Wherry are well kept on handpump, and they have a wide choice of reasonably priced wines, and home-made elderflower cordial in summer; cribbage, dominoes and piped music. *(Recommended by Minda and Stanley Alexander, MDN, Basil Minson, Eric Locker, B N F and M Parkin, Pamela Goodwyn, Mrs J Ekins-Daukes, Brian Haywood, David Field, Eleanor and Nick Steinitz)*

Free house ~ Licensees Dan Goff and Simon Scillitoe ~ Real ale ~ Bar food (12-2, 6-9) ~ Restaurant ~ (01263) 740574 ~ Children in family room ~ Open 11-3, 6-11; 12-3, 6-10.30 Sun; closed second and third weeks in Jan ~ Bedrooms: £40B/£60B

BRANCASTER STAITHE TF7743 Map 8
White Horse 🍴 ♟ 🛏

A149 E of Hunstanton

The sun deck is a pleasant place for a relaxing drink or well prepared meal at this popular inn, but even if the weather's not so good, you can enjoy the wide views of the tidal marshes and Scolt Head Island beyond from the big conservatory, well designed so as to stay fresh and cool when the sun does deign to shine. Inside, it's all open-plan, with the main area, at the back and merging into this conservatory, now devoted to the good food and entirely no smoking. Well spaced furnishings here are in unvarnished country-style wood, with some light-hearted seasidey decorations. The considerable extensions back here have freed space in the front part for people who just want a drink, with well kept Adnams Bitter, Fullers London Pride, Greene King IPA and a guest such as Adnams Regatta on handpump from the handsome counter, manned by exceptionally friendly young staff; they also have 15 malt whiskies and about a dozen wines by the glass from an extensive and thoughtful wine list. In this front part there are good local photographs on the left, with bar billiards and TV; on the right is a quieter group of cushioned wicker armchairs and sofas by a table with daily papers, and local landscapes for sale; piped music. The good menu changes twice a day, and as well as a few lunchtime bar snacks such as home-made soup (from £3.75), ploughman's (£5.95), and dressed local crab (£6.10), you might find seafood risotto (£6.10), confit of guinea fowl legs with wild mushroom risotto and parsley pesto (£11.10), and baked black bream fillet with cassoulet of puy lentils, pancetta, root vegetables and jus oil (£11.75), with evening dishes such as beef carpaccio with lemon, garlic and thyme dressing (£6.50), flash-fried squid dusted in semolina and lemon oil (£6.75), confit of grey mullet with baked gnocchi, chorizo sausage and red pepper tapenade (£11.95), and rib-eye steak with bravas potatoes, aïoli and crispy onions (£13.50). The coast path runs along the bottom of the garden, and if you stay they do an excellent breakfast. *(Recommended by John Wooll, Tracey and Stephen Groves, Dr T E Hothersall, M J A Switzer, Pamela Goodwyn, Jamie and Ruth Lyons, O K Smyth, Mike and Sue Loseby, Eric Locker, A Sadler, Comus and Sarah Elliott, John Beeken, Paul and Ursula Randall, Michael Dandy, Neil and Angela Huxter, Peter Rozée; also in the* Good Hotel Guide*)*

Free house ~ Licensees Cliff Nye and Kevin Nobes ~ Real ale ~ Bar food (lunchtime only) ~ Restaurant ~ (01485) 210262 ~ Children in eating area of bar and restaurant ~ Dogs allowed in bar ~ Open 11.30-11; 12-10.30 Sun ~ Bedrooms: £48B/£96B

BURNHAM MARKET TF8342 Map 8
Hoste Arms 🍽 � 🛏
The Green (B1155)

This smart 17th-c inn has so much to offer that even on a Monday lunchtime you may find it humming. Although it's a civilised place, it attracts a nice variety of customers from gentry and shoppers to farmers and fishermen, and the atmosphere is welcoming. The panelled bar on the right has a series of watercolours showing scenes from local walks, there's a bow-windowed bar on the left, a nice sitting room, a little art gallery in the staircase area, and massive log fires. The lovely walled garden has dark wooden tables, chairs and benches (you can enjoy full restaurant service here), or you can eat in the airy conservatory with its comfortable sofas. A good choice of imaginative food, served by friendly staff, includes soup (£4.25), lunchtime sandwiches (from £4.95), rocket, goats cheese and black olive pizza (£5.50), salmon and chilli fishcakes with roasted peanuts and satay dressing (£5.95; £9.95 main course), roasted king scallops with parsnip purée and asparagus tips (£8.25; £15.25 main course), mixed vegetable tempura with sticky rice and citrus dressing (£8.95), chargrilled rump steak and chips (£13.50), and a good choice of fish such as grilled lemon sole with polenta fries and asparagus velouté (£13.25), and baked halibut with crisp pancetta risotto and light pea broth (£14.25), with puddings such as banana and honey pancakes or tiramisu (£5.25). The good wine list has plenty of big names, and includes champagne by the glass; they also have well kept Greene King IPA and Abbot, Woodfordes Nelsons Revenge and Wherry, perhaps a guest from Adnams, a decent choice of malt whiskies, and freshly squeezed orange juice; dominoes. A big awning covers a sizeable eating area in the garden; the inn has its own business centre. *(Recommended by David Carr, I Louden, Mr Bishop, Gillian and Peter Moore, Enid and Henry Stephens, B N F and M Parkin, Comus and Sarah Elliott, Ian Phillips, Gerry and Rosemary Dobson, DF, NF, J Strain, Mike Ridgway, Sarah Miles, Robert M Warner, Roger Wain-Heapy, Shirley Mackenzie)*

Free house ~ Licensees Paul and Jean Whittome and Christopher Bensley ~ Real ale ~ Bar food ~ Restaurant ~ (01328) 738777 ~ Well behaved children in restaurant and family room ~ Dogs welcome ~ Open 11-11; 12-10.30 Sun; closed evenings 25 and 31 Dec ~ Bedrooms: £74S(£102B)/£92S

BURNHAM THORPE TF8541 Map 8
Lord Nelson 🍺
Village signposted from B1155 and B1355, near Burnham Market

The new licensees who have just taken over this friendly pub don't plan to make any great changes. As Nelson was born in this sleepy village it's no surprise to find lots of pictures and memorabilia of him lining the walls, and the recipe for an unusual rum concoction called Nelson's Blood has been handed down from landlord to landlord, though if that doesn't take your fancy you can also choose from well kept Greene King IPA and Abbot, and Woodfordes Nelsons Revenge and Wherry, which are tapped from the cask in a back stillroom. The little bar has well waxed antique settles on the worn red flooring tiles and smoke ovens in the original fireplace, and an eating room has flagstones, an open fire, and more pictures of Nelson; there are two no smoking rooms. Using lots of fresh local ingredients, the interesting, regularly changing menu might typically include parsnip and apple soup (£3.75), filled baguettes (from £4.95), seared pigeon breast with crisp potatoes (£4.50), sweet potato and pea risotto with mixed oils (£7.95), fried plaice with warm tomato and black olive salad (£8.25), braised lamb with beetroot and smoked spanish black pudding with warm jus oil (£8.75), confit of guinea fowl with goats cheese mash and tapenade oil (£9.50), and duck breast with celeriac and bacon risotto and balsamic vinegar (£12.95), with puddings such as toffee and banana cake with toffee sauce or vanilla rice pudding with raspberry coulis (£3.10); the restaurant is no smoking. The staff are friendly and obliging; shove-ha'penny, cribbage and dominoes. There's a good-sized play area in the very big garden. *(Recommended by John Wooll, the Didler, O K Smyth, Anthony Barnes, Ian Phillips, Sue and Geoff Price, Dr Andy Wilkinson, Rosemary and Jeremy Jessel, Neville Kenyon, Barry Collett, Derek and Sylvia Stephenson, Phil and Sally Gorton, Guy Vowles, Mike and Shelley Woodroffe, David and Rhian Peters)*

Greene King ~ Lease David Thorley ~ Real ale ~ Bar food (not Sun evening) ~ Restaurant ~ (01328) 738241 ~ Children in eating area of bar and restaurant ~ Dogs allowed in bar ~ Open 11-3, 6-11; 12-3, 7-10.30 Sun

CAWSTON TG1422 Map 8

Ratcatchers 🏨 ♀

Eastgate, S of village – on B1149 from Norwich turn left towards Haveringland at crossroads ½ mile before the B1145 Cawston turn

They do up to 20 imaginative specials a day at this well run restauranty pub, which is now open all day on the weekends. Starters (£3.45 to £4.95) might include home-made local mussel soup with crunchy garlic crouton, scallops poached in white wine with a breadcrumb and fresh sage crust, lenwade pike, and salmon and prawn wrapped in a herb pancake and served in a vermouth sauce, and main courses (£7.95-£14.95) run from wild boar sausages to braised local rabbit with herbs, vegetables and a pastry lid, sautéed monkfish flamed in vodka with pink peppercorns and cream, or pot-roasted local guinea fowl in a rich burgundy sauce with suet and herb dumplings. At lunchtime they also do sandwiches (not Sunday), ploughman's or sausage and mash with an onion and red wine gravy (£6.25), vegetable stroganoff (£8.25), chicken stir fry (£9.50), and steaks (from £10.95), and puddings might include raspberry crème brûlée and toffee apple crumble (£3.75); they do children's dishes (£4.85). The L-shaped beamed bar has an open fire, nice old chairs, and a fine mix of walnut, beech, elm and oak tables; there's a quieter and cosier candlelit dining room on the right, and a conservatory. There are several no smoking areas. As well as a good wine list with about half-a-dozen by the glass, and 25 malt whiskies, they've well kept Adnams Bitter, Hancocks HB, and a guest from a brewer such as Mauldons on handpump; dominoes, cribbage, and piped music. The terrace has heaters for outdoor dining in cooler weather. *(Recommended by Anthony Barnes, David Twitchett, Neville Kenyon, Philip and Susan Philcox, Roy Bromell, Maureen and Bill Sewell, Dr and Mrs R G J Telfer, Jim Mansfield, Mr and Mrs W T Copeland, Roger and Maureen Kenning, SH, John Beeken, Bill and Lisa Copeland, I Louden, Mr Bishop)*

Free house ~ Licensees Peter and Denise McCarter ~ Real ale ~ Bar food (12-2, 6-10) ~ Restaurant ~ (01603) 871430 ~ Children welcome ~ Open 12-3, 6-11; 12-11 Sat-Sun; closed 26 Dec

---

Post Office address codings confusingly give the impression that some pubs are in Norfolk when they're really in Suffolk (which is where we list them).

CLEY NEXT THE SEA TG0443 Map 8

Three Swallows ⚏

Off A149 E of Blakeney; in village, turn into Holt Road and head for church at Newgate Green

Below the handsome flint church tower, the big garden of this take-us-as-you-find-us village local has picnic-sets on two grass terraces, and is prettily planted with flowering shrubs; there's a prominent water feature with a surprisingly grandiose fountain, and the wooden climbing frame, budgerigar aviary and goat pen help keep children entertained. Inside, the unpretentious carpeted bar on the right has a mix of pubby furnishings including long green leatherette benches around high leathered tables, a good log fire in the small fireplace at one end, and team photographs and pictures of local old boys above its dark dado; they have various board games, and there may be wandering tabby cats. Well kept Adnams and Greene King IPA and Abbot are served from a counter richly carved with fantastical figures and faces, with a handsome carved mirror backing; a couple of steps lead up to a small family eating area. You'll find a second log fire in the informal no smoking stripped pine restaurant on the left. Promptly served, home-made bar food includes sandwiches (from £2.75), home-made soup (£3.25), filled baked potatoes (from £4.50), ploughman's (from £5.50), home-made lasagne (£6.95), large haddock (£7.25), steaks (from £10.75), daily specials such as deep-fried brie with filo pastry and cranberry sauce (£4.50), stilton and broccoli quiche or plaice (£6.95), and crab salad or cajun chicken (£7.50), with puddings such as cherry tart (£3.25); children's meals (£3.95). Handy for the salt marshes, the pub is a favourite with birdwatchers. The bedrooms are simple and comfortable, and they do good breakfasts. *(Recommended by Peter and Pat Frogley, Barry Collett, Eleanor and Nick Steinitz, Charles Gysin, Tracey and Stephen Groves)*

Pubmaster ~ Tenants Jean and James Walker ~ Real ale ~ Bar food (12-2, 6-9) ~ (01263) 740526 ~ Children in restaurant and family room ~ Dogs welcome ~ Open 11-11; 12-10.30 Sun; closed 25 Dec ~ Bedrooms: £40B/£55B

COLKIRK TF9126 Map 8

Crown ♀

Village signposted off B1146 S of Fakenham; and off A1065

In an attractive and peacefully prosperous village, this red brick local has a particularly welcoming atmosphere, and enjoyable food. Besides daily specials such as baked cinnamon duck leg with cumberland sauce, salmon and broccoli cheese bake, steak and ale pie and grilled skate wing (all £8.50), you might find home-made soup (£3), lunchtime baguettes (from £3.45), prawn cocktail (£4.65), chicken fillet with creamy pesto sauce (£8.50), and steaks (from £9.45), with good puddings such as lemon and lime cheesecake or dutch apple tart (£3.50); their tasty Sunday roasts are popular (£7.25; they'll do smaller helpings for children). Spotlessly kept, the public bar and small lounge both have open fires, solid straightforward country furniture, and rugs and flooring tiles; the no smoking dining room leading off is pleasantly informal. As well as around 25 different wines by the glass, the cheerful staff serve well kept Greene King IPA, Abbot, XX Mild and a guest such as Old Speckled Hen on handpump. Darts, fruit machine, cribbage and dominoes; good disabled access. There's a garden and suntrap terrace with picnic-sets. *(Recommended by R C Vincent, J V Nelson, Barry Collett, I Louden, Mr Bishop, R Cross, Jim Mansfield, Bill and Doreen Sawford, Malcolm and Hilary Leeves, R Clark)*

Greene King ~ Tenant Roger Savell ~ Real ale ~ Bar food ~ Restaurant ~ (01328) 862172 ~ Children in eating area of bar and restaurant ~ Dogs allowed in bar ~ Open 11-2.30, 6-11; 12-3, 7-10.30 Sun

---

Bedroom prices include full english breakfast, VAT and any inclusive service charge that we know of.

ERPINGHAM TG1732 Map 8
Saracens Head ♀ 🛏

At Wolterton – not shown on many maps; Erpingham signed off A140 N of Aylsham, keep on through Calthorpe, then where road bends right take the straight-ahead turn-off signposted Wolterton

This gently civilised dining pub was built in the early 19th c by Lord Walpole as a coaching inn for his estate. The two-room bar is simple and stylish, with high ceilings, terracotta walls, and red and white striped curtains at its tall windows – all lending a feeling of space, though it's not actually large. There's a mix of seats from built-in leather wall settles to wicker fireside chairs as well as log fires and flowers, and the windows look out on to a charming old-fashioned gravel stableyard with picnic-sets. A pretty little five-table parlour on the right, in cheerful nursery colours, has another big log fire. Well kept Adnams Bitter and perhaps a beer from Woodfordes on handpump, an interesting wine list, and decent malt whiskies; the atmosphere is enjoyably relaxed, and service is friendly and good-humoured. The imaginative bar food is so popular, you must book to be sure of a table. The changing menu could include red onion and goats cheese tart (£5.50), local mussels with cider and cream (£5.95; £9.50 main course), and main courses such as avocado with sweet pear and mozzarella (£9.50), roast local pheasant with calvados and cream or baked scottish salmon with mango and cream (£9.75), roast leg of lamb with red and white beans (£9.95), scallops with bacon and white wine (£13.50), and puddings such as mulled wine and red fruit pudding (£3.50). The Shed next door (run by Mr Dawson-Smith's daughter Rachel) is a workshop and showcase for furniture and interior pieces. They plan to add three more bedrooms and a new conservatory bar by early 2004, and have recently finished redecorating the existing bedrooms. *(Recommended by Comus and Sarah Elliott, M and G Rushworth, John Wooll, Peter and Pat Frogley, David Field, J F M and M West, Anthony Barnes, Irene and Ray Atkin, Minda and Stanley Alexander, Roger and Maureen Kenning, David Twitchett, Wombat)*

Free house ~ Licensee Robert Dawson-Smith ~ Real ale ~ Bar food ~ Restaurant ~ (01263) 768909 ~ Children welcome ~ Dogs allowed in bedrooms ~ Open 12-3.30, 6-11; 12-3.30, 7-10.30 Sun; closed 25 Dec ~ Bedrooms: £45B/£70B

GREAT CRESSINGHAM TF8401 Map 8
Windmill 🍺

Village signposted off A1065 S of Swaffham; Water End

This popular family pub has been extended so carefully from its black-beamed 17th-c core that you get no impression of add-ons – it all seems part and parcel. All sorts of rooms and side areas ramble cosily around the island servery, with a variety of pubby furniture from pews and wheelback chairs to red leatherette or plush settles, and masses of mainly rustic bric-a-brac and pictures, particularly big sentimental Victorian lithographs. There is some stripped brick and flint, but the walls are mainly painted a warm terracotta pink, and big log fireplaces are re-equipped with electric look-alikes in warmer weather. There is a separate more formal dining room, and a conservatory. A wide choice of generously served food includes sandwiches (from £2.25), soup (£2.55), home-made vegetable pie or spicy turkey curry (£6.50), home-made spicy steak and ale pudding (£6.75), lemon and black pepper chicken fillet (£7.50), rump steak (from £9.25), braised lamb shank with red wine and rosemary gravy (£12.75), and specials such as mushroom stroganoff (£6.95), and hake fillet with hollandaise sauce (£9.90), with puddings such as treacle sponge and custard (£3.25); they also do Sunday roasts (£7.75), and children's meals (from £2.95). Well kept Adnams Bitter and Broadside, Greene King IPA and Windy Miller Quixote (brewed for the pub) on handpump, with a couple of guest beers such as Brains SA and Youngs Special, decent sensibly priced wines, friendly attentive staff. Off a back corridor with a fruit machine is a neat well lit pool room, and one side snug has a big sports TV; also darts, shove-ha'penny, table skittles, cribbage, dominoes, and faint piped music. A good-sized stretch of neatly kept grass behind has picnic-sets and a play area, including a sandpit; a caravan site almost opposite is well screened by trees. It's been run by the same family for 50 years. *(Recommended by Nick and Alison Dowson, George Atkinson, Charles Gysin, Kevin Thorpe)*

Free house ~ Licensee M J Halls ~ Bar food (12-2, 6-10) ~ Restaurant ~ (01760) 756232 ~ Children welcome in five family rooms ~ Country and Western on Tues nights ~ Open 11-3, 6-11; 12-3.30, 6-10.30 Sun

HORSEY TG4522 Map 8
Nelson Head

Signposted off B1159 (in series of S-bends) N of Great Yarmouth

The landlord of this enjoyably simple pub obviously cares a great deal about his customers, who range from ramblers and birdwatchers (Horsey Mere is just down the road) to yachtsmen and holidaymakers. The two homely unpretentious little rooms are furnished with straightforward but comfortable seats (including four tractor-seat bar stools), bits of shiny bric-a-brac, small local pictures for sale, a good fire and geraniums on the window sill. The garden has picnic-sets and an outside marquee. Woodfordes Wherry, and (of course) Nelsons Revenge are very well kept on handpump; darts, cribbage, dominoes and piped music. Enjoyable, carefully prepared bar food includes home-made soup, scampi or garlic mushrooms (£3.95), vegetable chilli (£5.95), chicken in lemon and tarragon with baby new potatoes and broccoli (£7), good home-made steak and kidney pie (£7.50), fresh local cod (£8.95), and fillet steak (£12.75); they also do filled baguettes, and children's meals. The restaurant is no smoking. The pub sign is often hidden by trees in summer; Horsey Windmill and the beach (pleasant walks from here to Winterton-on-Sea) are just down the road. *(Recommended by Ian Martin, Ian Phillips, Derek and Sylvia Stephenson, Shirley Mackenzie, Jestyn Phillips)*

Free house ~ Licensee Reg C Parsons ~ Real ale ~ Bar food ~ Restaurant ~ No credit cards ~ (01493) 393378 ~ Children in family room ~ Dogs allowed in bar ~ Open 11-3, 6-11; 12-3, 6-10.30 Sun

ITTERINGHAM TG1430 Map 8
Walpole Arms 🍺

Village signposted off B1354 NW of Aylsham

The biggish open-plan bar of this red brick dining pub has a good bustling friendly atmosphere, little windows, stripped brick walls, exposed beams, and a mix of dining tables. You probably won't hear the faint piped music over the sound of contented chat. Made with fresh, mostly local ingredients, the food here is good and imaginative, and as well as a few popular snacks such as half a pint of shell-on prawns with tomato mayonnaise (£6), and interesting sandwiches with fillings such as gorgonzola, prosciutto ham and pickled fig (£7), the changing inventive menu could include norfolk crab bisque with chantilly dill cream (£5.25), crayfish tails with russian salad (£5.75), calzone with grilled vegetables, basil and mozzarella (£10.50), pork saltimbocca with potato salad, peppers, green beans, oil and basil or braised cod with chick pea, tomato and spinach stew with lemon oil (£12.75), and calves liver with butter beans, leeks and morcilla (£14.25), with puddings such as saffron poached pear with orange flower rice pudding or date and walnut bread and butter pudding with cream (from £4.75); the no smoking restaurant is attractive. Well kept Adnams Bitter and Broadside, and a beer brewed for the pub by Woodfordes, along with a guest on handpump; they've also a well chosen wine list, with a dozen available by the glass, and local cider. Behind the pub is a two-acre landscaped garden. More reports please. *(Recommended by Philip and Susan Philcox, Anthony Barnes, A D Cross, Michael Williamson, Stephen, Julie and Hayley Brown, Roger and Maureen Kenning, Wombat)*

Free house ~ Licensee Richard Bryan ~ Real ale ~ Bar food (not Sun evening) ~ Restaurant ~ (01263) 587258 ~ Children welcome ~ Dogs allowed in bar ~ Open 12-3, 6-11; 12-11(10.30 Sun); 12-3, 6-11(10.30 Sun) Sat in winter

LARLING TL9889 Map 5
Angel 🍺 🛏

Just off A11 (which now bypasses it) S of Attleborough

The comfortable, well equipped bedrooms at this neatly kept pub (which is handily open all day) are good value, and readers are full of praise for the delicious breakfasts. You can expect a genuine welcome from the friendly, helpful landlord; the pub has been in the same family since 1913, and his great-grandfather used to stable the horses and host the coach travellers here (they still have the original visitors' books with guests from 1897 to 1909). Hearty, reasonably priced bar food includes soup (£2.50), lots of sandwiches and toasties (from £2.50), hot smoked mackerel fillets or home-made pâté (£3.95), ploughman's or sausage, egg and chips (£5.95), home-made burgers (from £5.95), broccoli and cream cheese bake (£6.95), local trout glazed with parsley butter and lemon juice (£8.25), and steaks (from £10.95), with daily specials such as home-made lasagne, steak and kidney pie or (highly recommended by readers) fresh cod in beer batter (£7.50), and home-made puddings such as hot fudge cake (£2.95); children's meals (£3.25). The comfortable 1930s-style lounge on the right has cushioned wheelback chairs, a nice long cushioned and panelled corner settle, some good solid tables for eating and some lower ones, squared panelling, a collection of whisky-water jugs on the delft shelf over the big brick fireplace which houses a big woodburner, a couple of copper kettles, and some hunting prints; there are two dining rooms (one of which is no smoking). Besides well kept Adnams Best and Wolf, they've three changing guests from brewers such as Iceni, Tetleys or Timothy Taylors on handpump, and around 100 malt whiskies. The quarry-tiled black-beamed public bar has a good local atmosphere, with darts, dominoes, cribbage, juke box and fruit machine, and piped music. A neat grass area behind the car park has picnic-sets around a big fairy-lit apple tree, and a safely fenced play area. Peter Beale's old-fashioned rose nursery is nearby. *(Recommended by Anthony Barnes, Beryl and Bill Farmer, Laura and Stuart Ballantyne, Steve Whalley, Peter and Barbara Ayre, James Morton, Stuart and Alison Ballantyne, J F M and M West, Stephen, Julie and Hayley Brown, I A Herdman, M J Caley, Tony Middis, John and Judy Saville)*

Free house ~ Licensee Andrew Stammers ~ Real ale ~ Bar food (till 10 Fri and Sat) ~ Restaurant ~ (01953) 717963 ~ Children in eating area of bar and restaurant ~ Karaoke last Thurs of month ~ Open 10-11; 12-10.30 Sun ~ Bedrooms: £30B/£50B

LETHERINGSETT TG0538 Map 8
Kings Head

A148 just W of Holt

It's not surprising that this busily unpretentious pub is so popular with families. Children enjoy the play castle, living willow tunnel, toys, bikes and games, and a spacious lawn has plenty of tables; there's a very good children's menu with plenty of choices, and they do home-made baby food. The pub is pleasantly set, in grounds well back from the road, opposite a church with an unusual round tower, and it's not far from an interesting working water mill. Inside, the carpeted bar has metal-legged tables, a couple of armchairs and log fires, with various interesting prints, pictures and other items, including a signed poem by John Betjeman. There's also a small plush lounge, and a separate games room with darts, pool, shove-ha'penny, dominoes, cribbage, fruit machines, and piped music; the garden has a summer marquee, and they hold good live music events on most weekends throughout the year. Tasty bar food from the straightforward, reasonably priced menu includes soup (£2.95), sandwiches, baps or baguettes (from £2.95), garlic mushrooms (£3.65), ploughman's (from £6.10), baked pepper with nuts, rice and dates, home-made steak and kidney pie or lasagne (£6.90), lamb cutlets (£7.10), and steaks (from £10.95), with puddings such as home-made apple pie (£3.10); there's also a braille menu. Friendly and efficient staff serve well kept Greene King Abbot and IPA, and a couple of guests from brewers such as Elgoods and Wolf on handpump, local apple juice, and cocktails (including non-alcoholic ones for children). The pub does get a lot of hard family use, and shows plenty of signs of that – at times the cleaners must find it hard to keep up. *(Recommended by Mike Ridgway, Sarah Miles, R C Vincent, John Wooll)*

Free house ~ Licensees David and Pamela Watts ~ Real ale ~ Bar food (11-10; 12-9.30 Sun) ~ (01263) 712691 ~ Children welcome ~ Dogs welcome ~ Live music Sat evenings Sept-June, Sun afternoons June-Aug ~ Open 11-11; 12-10.30 Sun

MUNDFORD TL8093 Map 5
Crown 🍴

Village signposted off A1065 Thetford—Swaffham; Crown Street

Useful for a quick snack or a relaxing drink after a walk in nearby Thetford Forest, this attractive 17th-c former posting inn looks over a peaceful village square. The beamed lounge bar has a friendly bustle, a huge open fireplace in a flint wall, captain's chairs around highly polished tables, and interesting local advertisements, newspaper cuttings and other memorabilia. If the pub is full, a spiral iron staircase with *Vanity Fair* cartoons beside it leads up to the club room, an elegant restaurant and the garden. There are more heavy beams in the separate red-tiled locals' bar on the left, which has cast-iron-framed tables, another smaller brick fireplace with a copper hood, sensibly placed darts, cribbage, dominoes, fruit machine, TV, juke box (which can sometimes be quite loud), and a screened-off pool table. Friendly staff serve well kept Courage Best and Marstons Pedigree, along with one or two frequently changing guests from brewers such as Iceni and Woodfordes on handpump, and they've around 50 malt whiskies. Well liked reasonably priced bar food might include sandwiches (from £2.50, baguettes from £4.75), home-made soup (£3.35), burgers (from £3.95), ploughman's (£5.95), local herb sausage (£5.75), lasagne or local trout (£6.95), vegetable and cashew stroganoff (£7.25), and steak (from £10.95), with daily specials such as poached salmon supreme with penne pasta and lime and tarragon cream (£8.50), medallions of pork with apple, cider and coriander sauce (£9.95), and home-made puddings such as plum and almond tart (£3.50); as well as a children's menu (£3.95), they do children's helpings of most meals. The garden behind has a wishing well; there are limited spaces for cars outside the pub. *(Recommended by Neil Skidmore, G Coates, A Sadler, Darly Graton, Graeme Gulibert, Charles Gysin, Ian Phillips, Pamela Goodwyn, SH, Anthony Barnes, Dr Paull Khan)*

Free house ~ Licensee Barry Walker ~ Real ale ~ Bar food (12-3, 7-10) ~ Restaurant ~ (01842) 878233 ~ Children welcome ~ Dogs welcome ~ Open 11(12 Sun)-11 ~ Bedrooms: £37.50B/£59.50B

NORWICH TG2308 Map 5
Adam & Eve ♀ £

Bishopgate; follow Palace Street from Tombland, N of cathedral

Really pretty in summer with its colourful tubs and hanging baskets, this is Norwich's oldest pub. It's thought to date back to at least 1249 (when it was used by workmen building the cathedral), and even has a Saxon well beneath the lower bar floor, though the striking dutch gables were added in the 14th and 15th c. The little old-fashioned bars quickly fill at lunchtime with a good mix of customers, and have antique high-backed settles (one handsomely carved), cushioned benches built into partly panelled walls, and tiled or parquet floors; the snug is no smoking. Good value straightforward bar food such as sandwiches or granary baps (from £2.75, not Sunday), soup (£3.25; tasty cheese and ale soup £3.85), ploughman's (£5.50), spinach and feta goujons with honey and ginger dip (£4.95), chicken or beef curry (£5.45), chicken and ham pie or cod and chips (£5.95), with daily specials such as home-made cottage pie (£4.95), chilli prawns in filo pastry (£5.25), and lasagne (£5.45). As well as over 60 malt whiskies, they've Adnams Bitter, Greene King IPA, Theakstons Old Peculier and Charles Wells Bombardier well kept on handpump; you'll also find about a dozen decent wines by the glass, and Addlestone's cider. There are wooden picnic-sets out in front. *(Recommended by*

Peter F Marshall, A S and M E Marriott, Anthony Barnes, Shaun and Diane, Jim Abbott, J F M and M West, the Didler, David Carr, Su and Bob Child, Tim and Ann Newell, Alison Hayes, Pete Hanlon, John and Judy Saville, Richard Jennings)

Unique Pub Co ~ Lease Rita McCluskey ~ Real ale ~ Bar food (12-6.45; 12-2.30 Sun) ~ (01603) 667423 ~ Children in snug until 7 ~ Open 11-11; 12-10.30 Sun; closed 25-26 Dec, 1 Jan

Fat Cat ◥

West End Street

'How can they keep so many beers in such good condition?' marvels one reader, and at any one time you might find more than 25 different real ales at this classic town pub. About half of their beers are on handpump, while the rest are tapped from the cask in a still room behind the bar – big windows reveal all: Adnams Bitter, Caledonian 80/-, Dark Star Red Ale, Durham White Bishop, Fullers ESB and an organic one, Honeydew, Greene King Abbot and Ruddles County, Hop Back Summer Lightning, Kelham Island Pale Rider, Leatherbritches Bespoke, North Yorkshire Flying Herbert, Oakham Bishops Farewell, Orkney Dark Island, RCH Old Slug Porter, Salopian Lemon Dream, Timothy Taylors Landlord, Tipperary Carlo Red Ale and Dwan Black Pearl Stout, and Woodfordes Norfolk Nog. You'll also find four draught belgian beers (two of them fruit), draught lagers from Germany and the Czech Republic, up to 15 bottled belgian beers, 15 country wines, and local farm cider. Open all day, with a good mix of customers, and a lively bustling atmosphere at busy times, with tranquil lulls in the middle of the afternoon. The no-nonsense furnishings include plain scrubbed pine tables and simple solid seats, lots of brewery memorabilia, bric-a-brac and stained glass. Bar food consists of a dozen or so rolls (60p) and pies (£1.60) at lunchtime (not Sunday). There are tables outside. *(Recommended by Tim and Ann Newell, Kit Ballantyne, Su and Bob Child, the Didler, David Twitchett, Ian Phillips, Alison Hayes, Pete Hanlon)*

Free house ~ Licensee Colin Keatley ~ Real ale ~ No credit cards ~ (01603) 624364 ~ Open 12(11 Sat)-11; 12-10.30 Sun; closed 25 Dec evening

REEPHAM TG0922 Map 8
Old Brewery House

Market Square; B1145 W of Aylsham

Overlooking an old-fashioned town square, this Georgian hotel has picnic-sets on the front terrace, and (lovely on a sunny afternoon), the gardens at the back have a pond and fountain. Inside, you'll find a good pubby atmosphere in the big high-ceilinged bar, which has a nice mix of oldish pub tables, lots of farming and fishing bric-a-brac and old enamel advertisements on its pale ochre walls, a piano and a dark green dado. A step down from this main seating area takes you to a tiled-floor serving part with well kept Adnams, Greene King Abbot, local Reepham, and a guest such as Greene King Ruddles County on handpump, and several malt whiskies. There's also a red-carpeted lounge leading off, with dark panelling and sturdy brocaded armchairs; piped music, fruit machine, and a roaring fire in cold weather. Besides lunchtime sandwiches (from £3.25; not Sunday), filled baked potatoes (from £3.95), and ploughman's (£5.95), enjoyable food includes soup (£1.95), deep-fried plaice goujons with tartare sauce (£3.75), sausage and mash with crispy onions and ale gravy (£5.50), chargrilled chicken with bacon and mushroom sauce (£6.75), beef and ale pie, hot thai prawn salad or whitby wholetail scampi (£6.95), and rump steak (£7.95), with tasty daily specials, and children's meals (£2.95). The dining room and conservatory are no smoking. *(Recommended by Ian Phillips, the Didler, Brian Haywood, Su and Bob Child, John Wooll, Wombat)*

Free house ~ Licensee David Peters ~ Real ale ~ Bar food ~ Restaurant ~ (01603) 870881 ~ Children welcome ~ Dogs allowed in bar and bedrooms ~ Open 11-11; 12-10.30 Sun ~ Bedrooms: £47.50B/£85B

RINGSTEAD TF7040 Map 8

Gin Trap

Village signposted off A149 near Hunstanton; OS Sheet 132 map reference 707403

Now under new licensees (who've cleared out most of the bric-a-brac, and added new tables and chairs), this village pub is close to the Peddar's Way. The well kept chatty bar has beams, a woodburning stove, captain's chairs and cast-iron-framed tables, while the small no smoking dining room is candlelit in the evening, and has new pine furniture (you can book a table in here). Outside, a handsome spreading chestnut tree shelters the car park, and the neatly kept back garden has seats on the grass or small paved area, and pretty flowering tubs. Adnams Best, Greene King Abbot, Woodfordes Norfolk Nog and Nelsons Revenge are well kept on handpump, along with Gin Trap Bitter (brewed for the pub by Woodfordes). Besides lunchtime sandwiches (from £3.50) and ploughman's (from £4.50), swiftly served generous dishes might include lasagne or steak and kidney pie (£7.50), grilled toulouse sausage in savoury pastry (£4.25), cherry peppers stuffed with cheese with chilli dressing (£7.50), lamb shank (£10.50), monkfish with cream and Pernod sauce (£12.50), and sirloin steak (from £12.50), with home-made puddings such as baked american cheesecake or toffee brûlée (from £3.50). There's an art gallery next door, and self-catering accommodation. They plan to stay open all day in the summer. More reports please on the new regime. *(Recommended by Mrs M A Mees, Ian Phillips, Tracey and Stephen Groves, Pat and Derek Roughton, Pat and Tony Martin)*

Free house ~ Licensees Margaret Greer and Susan Little ~ Real ale ~ Bar food ~ Restaurant ~ (01485) 525264 ~ Children in eating area of bar ~ Dogs allowed in bar ~ Open 11.30-3, 6-11; 12-3, 6-10.30 Sun ~ Bedrooms: /£75S(£80B)

SNETTISHAM TF6834 Map 8

Rose & Crown 🍽 🍷 🛏

Village signposted from A149 King's Lynn—Hunstanton just N of Sandringham; coming in on the B1440 from the roundabout just N of village, take first left turn into Old Church Road

Norfolk Dining Pub of the Year

This popular dining pub is doing exceptionally well all round these days, with readers delighted by the imaginative food, prompt pleasant service, engagingly chatty atmosphere, and comfortable bedrooms. Using fresh local produce, the menu changes around once a month, but at lunchtime might include well presented home-made soup (£4.25), sandwiches (from £5.25), organic bean and tortilla cake with avocado salsa and lime peel yoghurt (£8.25), lamb and stilton sausages with irish champ mash and Guinness gravy (£8.75), and coq au vin with roasted fennel and rosemary spiced potatoes (£1.75), with evening dishes such as salt and pepper crispy squid salad with chilli and ginger (£5.50), linguini with piri-piri chicken and roasted bell peppers (£9.25), and fried bass with turnip, white bean and fennel broth (£13), with specials such as paella with pancetta, rouille and smoked garlic oil (£11.50) or salmon fillet with aubergine tandoori, wilted spinach and banana yoghurt (£11.75); puddings could include chocolate jaffa cake (£4.50). The interior has been very thoughtfully put together, with several separate areas each with its own character: an old-fashioned beamed front bar with black settles on its tiled floor, and a great log fire; another big log fire in a back bar with the landlord's sporting trophies and old sports equipment; a no smoking bar with a colourful but soothing décor (this room is favoured by people eating); and another warmly decorated room, lovely for families, with painted settles and big old tables, leads out to the garden. Some nice old pews and other interesting furniture sit on the wooden floor of the main dining room, and there are shelves with old bottles and books, and old prints and watercolours. One of the restaurants is no smoking. They've 30 wines by the glass, and on handpump you'll find well kept Adnams and Bass,with guests such as Fullers London Pride and Greene King IPA, and local organic fruit juices. The colourful enclosed garden has picnic-sets among herbaceous borders and flowering shrubs, and two spectacular willow trees; there's also a great wooden fort, swings, a playhouse and chipmunks. *(Recommended by Tracey and Stephen Groves, John Wooll, Jenny and Peter Lowater, Richard Cole, Pat and Roger Fereday, David Eberlin, Jamie and Ruth Lyons, Ian Phillips, Pippa Brown, Gordon Tong, J F M and M West, M Borthwick, David and Rhian Peters, David and Helen Wilkins, Mr and Mrs C W Widdowson, Mrs J Thomas, Dave Braisted; also in the Good Hotel Guide)*

Free house ~ Licensee Anthony Goodrich ~ Real ale ~ Bar food (12-2(till 2.30 wknds), 6.30-9(9.30 Fri, Sat)) ~ Restaurant ~ (01485) 541382 ~ Children welcome ~ Dogs welcome ~ Open 11-11; 12-10.30 Sun ~ Bedrooms: £65B/£100B

STANHOE TF8036 Map 5
Crown

B1155 towards Burnham Market

This open-plan country local isn't big, so as it's a popular place it can fill quite quickly. It's clean and bright inside, and aircraft pictures on the white walls give a clue to the welcoming landlord's background – he's ex-RAF. There are upholstered wall seats and wheelback chairs around dark tables on the carpet, a central log fire, and beams and joists overhead – one beam densely studded with coins. Gas masks, guns and various military headgear hang behind the bar, which often has a big bunch of flowers and dispenses well kept Elgoods Cambridge and Wisbech from handpump, and decent house wines and coffee. A sensibly short choice of good value home-made food might include sandwiches (from £3.80), sausages, chips and beans (£5.50), tasty fishcakes, crab salad or poached salmon (£6.80), jugged hare, lamb chops, locally caught bass or steak and kidney pie (£7), and puddings such as treacle sponge and lemon brûlée (£3.50). Service is friendly, and the atmosphere is good-hearted and relaxed. There are tables on a side lawn with a couple of apple trees, and a bigger lawn behind with room for caravans; fancy breeds of chicken may be running free, often with baby chicks. *(Recommended by John Wooll, Joyce and Maurice Cottrell, M J A Switzer)*

Elgoods ~ Licensees Page and Sarah Clowser ~ Bar food (not Sun evening exc bank hol wknds) ~ No credit cards ~ (01485) 518330 ~ Well behaved children away from bar ~ Dogs allowed in bar ~ Open 12-3.30, 6-11; 12-3.30, 7-10.30 Sun

STIFFKEY TF9743 Map 8
Red Lion 🍴

A149 Wells—Blakeney

Across the road from a stream with ducks and swans, in an unspoilt village, this popular pub is warmly welcoming. The oldest parts of the simple bars have a few beams, aged flooring tiles or bare floorboards, big open fires, a mix of pews, small settles and a couple of stripped high-backed settles, a nice old long deal table among quite a few others, and oil-type or lantern wall lamps. Although it gets busy (especially in summer), service remains friendly and efficient. Well kept Adnams, Greene King Abbot and Woodfordes Wherry on handpump, a nice choice of wines, and Stowford Press cider; dominoes, cribbage, and board games. Made with fresh mostly local ingredients, enjoyable dishes might include generous sandwiches (from £3.50), steak and kidney pie or steak and ale pudding (£8.50), and lots of well cooked fish such as delicious local whitebait (£4.95), local moules marinière (£7.95), and sea trout (£8.50); good puddings such as blackberry and apple pie (£3.95), and a popular Sunday roast (£8.95, not August). The back restaurant leads into a no smoking conservatory. A back gravel terrace has proper tables and seats, with more on grass further up beyond; there are some pleasant walks nearby. *(Recommended by John Millwood, Maureen and Bill Sewell, Peter and Pat Frogley, Martin Jennings, Brian Haywood, Chris and Anna Rowley, MDN, Tracey and Stephen Groves, the Didler, Su and Bob Child, Richard Cole, Dr Andy Wilkinson, J F M and M West, John Wooll, Barry Collett, Fiona Wynn, Pete Stroud, Peter Meister)*

Free house ~ Licensee Matthew Rees ~ Real ale ~ Bar food ~ (01328) 830552 ~ Children in family room ~ Dogs welcome ~ Open 12-3, 6(7 in winter)-11

STOW BARDOLPH TF6205 Map 5

Hare Arms ♀

Just off A10 N of Downham Market

Under the same licensees for 27 years, this neatly kept creeper-covered pub has a timelessly traditional village atmosphere. The welcoming bar is decorated with old advertising signs, fresh flowers and bric-a-brac, with plenty of tables around its central servery, and a good log fire. This bar opens into a spacious heated and well planted no smoking conservatory; look out for the friendly cats (a tabby and grey one). Enjoyable bar food includes lunchtime sandwiches (from £2.75), filled baked potatoes (from £4.75), and ploughman's (from £7.25), ham salad or home-made beef lasagne (£8.25), as well as daily specials such as mackerel fillet topped with garlic, smoked paprika, parsley and lemon, wild mushroom lasagne or steak and peppercorn pie (£8.25), swordfish steak with red thai curry sauce (£9.25), and lamb shank with red wine, garlic and rosemary gravy (£9.50); they also do a Sunday roast (£8.25) and children's meals (from £3.75). Friendly, helpful staff serve well kept Greene King IPA, Abbot and Old Speckled Hen, and a guest such as Bass or Batemans XXXB on handpump, a decent range of wines, and quite a few malt whiskies; perhaps cockles and whelks on the bar counter; fruit machine. There are plenty of seats in the large garden behind, and in the pretty front garden too, and chickens and peacocks roam freely. The local church contains an effigy of Lady Sarah Hare, who is reputed to have died as a consequence of sewing on a Sunday and pricking her finger. *(Recommended by John Wooll, Dr Andy Wilkinson, R C Wiles, Pamela Goodwyn, Mike Ridgway, Sarah Miles, Mr and Mrs Richard Hanks)*

Greene King ~ Tenants David and Trish McManus ~ Real ale ~ Bar food (12-2, 7-10) ~ Restaurant ~ (01366) 382229 ~ Children in family room ~ Open 11-2.30, 6-11; 12-2.30, 7-10.30 Sun; closed 25-26 Dec

SWANTON MORLEY TG0117 Map 8

Darbys ◀

B1147 NE of Dereham

They serve up to eight well kept real ales at this creeper-covered brick pub, a careful conversion of two derelict farm cottages. Alongside Adnams Best and Broadside, Badger Tanglefoot, Marstons Pedigree and Woodfordes Wherry on handpump, you'll find guests such as Brakspears, Everards Tiger and Fullers London Pride; piped music, darts, shove-ha'penny, and perhaps papers to read. It's well run, with helpful young staff, and a friendly, bustling atmosphere. The long bare-boarded country-style bar has a comfortable lived-in feel, with lots of gin traps and farming memorabilia, a good log fire (with the original bread oven alongside), tractor seats with folded sacks lining the long, attractive serving counter, and fresh flowers on the big stripped pine tables. A step up through a little doorway by the fireplace takes you through to the no smoking dining room. The children's room (also no smoking) has a toy box and a glassed-over well, floodlit from inside. Enjoyable bar food includes filled baguettes and baked potatoes (from £3.75), salmon, spinach and prawn gratin or a tasty cheeseburger (£5.75), curries (from £6.75), cajun tuna steak (£9.45), steak and mushroom pudding (£9.85), chargrilled lamb steak with rosemary and garlic (£9.95), and steaks (from £11.65); they do a children's menu (from £3.75). The garden has a really good play area; the two dogs are called Boots and Dillon. Bedrooms are in carefully converted farm buildings a few minutes away (they usually run a free pre-booked taxi service to and from the pub for residents), and there's plenty to do if you're staying, as the family also own the adjoining 720-acre estate, and can arrange clay pigeon shooting, golf, fishing, nature trails, and craft instruction. More reports please. *(Recommended by Michael and Jenny Back, David and Ruth Hollands, David Field, MDN)*

Free house ~ Licensees John Carrick and Louise Battle ~ Real ale ~ Bar food (12-2.15, 6.30-9.45; 12-(9.15 Sun)9.45) ~ Restaurant ~ (01362) 637647 ~ Children in family room, restaurant and eating area of bar till 9.15 ~ Dogs allowed in bar ~ Open 11.30-3, 6-11; 11.30-11 Sat; 12-10.30 Sun ~ Bedrooms: £35B/£50B

TERRINGTON ST JOHN TF5314 Map 8
Woolpack
Village signposted off A47 W of King's Lynn

The landlady's vivid personality perks up the atmosphere in this roomy and airy roadside pub, decorated with her bright modern ceramics and cheerful contemporary prints – we'd guess she also set the colour schemes in the striking lavatories. The bar has red plush banquettes and matching or wheelback chairs around its dark pub tables, a patterned red carpet, and terracotta pink walls; the large new back dining room (which looks out on to the garden) has comfortable green seating, an art deco décor punctuated by Mondrian prints, and on our inspection visit a big blackboard shouting 'Yippeeee it's Andrew's birthday'. This is not the place for an anniversary you want to pass unnoticed: Lucille leads the other customers in a rousing celebratory chorus, snapping happily away with her camera – the pictures go up on a board for collection on your next visit. But it's the reliably good value food, with friendly efficient waitresses, which underpins the pub's popularity. At lunchtime you might find sandwiches (from £2.25, baguettes from £2.75), soup (£2.50), ploughman's (£3.75), along with more substantial meals such as large cod and chips or seafood medley (£6.95), lamb steak with mint gravy, pork fillet with stilton sauce and gammon and pineapple (all £7.25), salmon in lemon butter sauce (£7.75), and steaks (from £9.50), with specials such as spicy chargrilled marlin steak with coriander and blueberry salsa, and mixed fish thai green curry or roasted pork tenderloin with apricot and green peppercorn sauce (all £7.25); they do children's meals (£3). Puddings are a strong point, and besides a tempting display in the cold cabinet there are usually hot ones such as spotted dick or treacle sponge and custard (£3). Greene King IPA, Charles Wells Eagle and a guest such as Woodfordes Wherry on handpump; fruit machine, piped music; good disabled access. There are picnic-sets on neat grass by a herb garden and the car park (which has recycling bins including Planet Aid clothes and shoes), and a side bowling green. *(Recommended by Michael and Jenny Back, Carole and Mick Hall)*

Free house ~ Licensees Lucille and Barry Carter ~ Bar food ~ Restaurant ~ (01945) 881 097 ~ Children in eating area of bar and restaurant ~ Open 11.30-11; 12-10.30 Sun

THORNHAM TF7343 Map 8
Lifeboat 🛏
Turn off A149 by Kings Head, then take first left turn

A nice and very popular place to stay, this rambling old white-painted stone pub faces half a mile of coastal sea flats, and there are lots of lovely surrounding walks. The main Smugglers bar is atmospherically lit with antique paraffin lamps suspended among an array of traps and yokes on its great oak-beamed ceiling, and is cosily furnished with low settles, window seats, pews, carved oak tables and rugs on the tiled floor; there are also masses of guns, swords, black metal mattocks, reed-slashers and other antique farm tools. A couple of little rooms lead off here, and all in all there are five open fires. No games machines or piped music, though they still play the ancient game of 'pennies' which was outlawed in the late 1700s, and dominoes. Up some steps from the bustling verdant conservatory is a sunny terrace with picnic-sets, and further back is a good children's playground with fort and slide. Although it draws the crowds in summer, it's still very much a place where locals drop in for a pint. Generously served, enjoyable bar food includes home-made soup (£3.85), filled baguettes (from £4.95), salmon and dill fishcakes (£5.25; £8.95 main), ploughman's (from £6.25), cromer crab salad (£8.50), hickory pork ribs (£9.50), steaks (from £12.95), and daily specials such as steamed local asparagus with hot garlic butter (£5.25), roast leg of lamb with mint sauce (£8.95), and baked grey mullet with sweet chilli sauce (£9.95), with home-made puddings such as chocolate and Guinness sponge or american cheesecake (£3.75); children's dishes (from £3.65). Promptly served by pleasant staff, they've well kept Adnams, Greene King IPA and Abbot, Woodfordes Wherry and a guest such as Youngs on handpump, and several malt whiskies. Most of the bedrooms have sea views. *(Recommended by Keith and Margaret Kettell, Tracey and Stephen Groves, John and Marion Tyrie, John Wooll, O K Smyth, Dr D Parker, David Twitchett, Gillian and Peter Moore, David Eberlin, Mike and Shelley Woodroffe, Derek and Sylvia Stephenson, Mr and Mrs J Curtis, Ian Phillips, the Didler, Mike and Sue Loseby, Sue and John Harwood, I Louden, Mr Bishop, Mrs J Thomas, Dr Andy Wilkinson, Mr and Mrs Broadhurst; also in the Good Hotel Guide)*

Free house ~ Licensee Charles Coker ~ Real ale ~ Bar food (12-2.30, 6.30-9.30) ~ Restaurant ~ (01485) 512236 ~ Children welcome ~ Dogs allowed in bar and bedrooms ~ Open 11-11; 12-10.30 Sun ~ Bedrooms: £62B/£84B

TIVETSHALL ST MARY TM1686 Map 5
Old Ram ♀ ⇌

A140 15 miles S of Norwich, outside village

The sheltered flower-filled terrace of this much extended pub is very civilised, with outdoor heaters and big green parasols. There's quite an emphasis on the food here (which is handily served all day), and they do Over Sixty Club two-course meals (from £7.50 Monday-Friday, until 6pm). A good choice of bar food includes soup (£3.75, with a sandwich £5.95), ricotta and spinach parcels with tomato and basil dressing (£5.25), lasagne or sausages and mash (£8.95), fish pie with mashed potatoes and cheese (£9.95), duck breast with brandy and scorched orange sauce (£13.95), and steaks (from £14.50), with puddings such as toffee pudding or belgian apple pie (£3.95). The spacious country-style main room has lots of stripped beams and standing timbers, antique craftsmen's tools on the ceiling, a huge log fire in the brick hearth, a turkey rug on rosy brick floors, and a longcase clock. It's ringed by smaller side areas, and one no smoking dining room has striking navy walls and ceiling, swagged curtains and an open woodburning stove; this leads to a second comfortable no smoking dining room and gallery. Unobtrusive fruit machine, TV, cribbage, dominoes, and piped music. Well kept Adnams, Bass, Woodfordes Wherry and a guest such as Hancocks HB on handpump, around two dozen wines by the glass, carafe or bottle, freshly squeezed juices and milkshakes. More reports please. *(Recommended by Graham Holden and Julie Lee, Mike and Wendy Proctor)*

Free house ~ Licensee John Trafford ~ Real ale ~ Bar food (all day) ~ Restaurant ~ (01379) 676794 ~ Children in restaurant; under-7s must leave by 8pm ~ Open 11-11; 12-10.30 Sun; closed 25-26 Dec ~ Bedrooms: £49B/£57B

UPPER SHERINGHAM TG1441 Map 8
Red Lion

B1157; village signposted off A148 Cromer—Holt, and the A149 just W of Sheringham

By spring 2004 they plan to add six new bedrooms and a conservatory dining area to this traditional-looking flint cottage. Most people come here to eat and the tables in the main bar are set aside for dining, so you might have to sit outside if all you want is a drink. The two modest but charming little bars have stripped high-backed settles and country-kitchen chairs on the red tiles or bare boards, terracotta-painted walls, a big woodburning stove, and newspapers to read; the red-walled snug is no smoking. It's best to book for the good bar food, which might include home-made soup (£3.50), sandwiches (from £4), home-made pâté or stilton-stuffed mushrooms (£4.50), sweet and sour chicken (£6.50), lasagne (£7.25), vegetable curry, lambs liver in port and orange gravy (£6.75), steak and ale pie (£7.75), and around 10 fresh fish dishes such as plaice, sole, cod, haddock, halibut, trout, and salmon, done with a variety of sauces you can choose from. The restaurant gets very busy (especially at weekends during the holiday season). Well kept Greene King IPA, Woodfordes Wherry and a guest on handpump, with around 12 malt whiskies and decent wines; dominoes and card games. They may stay open all day in summer. *(Recommended by Roger and Maureen Kenning, Shirley Mackenzie, Jim Abbott, Anthony Gill, Michael Porter, Neville Kenyon, Mr and Mrs W M Thomas)*

Free house ~ Licensee Sue Prew ~ Real ale ~ Bar food (12-2, 6.30(8.30 winter)-9) ~ Restaurant ~ No credit cards ~ (01263) 825408 ~ Children in restaurant and family room ~ Dogs welcome ~ Open 11.30-3.30, 6.30-11; 12-5, 6.30-10.30 Sun ~ Bedrooms: /£45

WARHAM TF9441 Map 8
Three Horseshoes 🍺 🛏

Warham All Saints; village signposted from A149 Wells-next-the-Sea—Blakeney, and from B1105 S of Wells

'No visit to North Norfolk is complete without a visit to this delightful village pub', writes one reader of this happily unspoilt local. The simple interior with its gas lighting looks little changed since the 1920s, and parts of the building date back to the 1720s. There are stripped deal or mahogany tables (one marked for shove-ha'penny) on a stone floor, red leatherette settles built around the partly panelled walls of the public bar, royalist photographs, and open fires in Victorian fireplaces. An antique American Mills one-arm bandit is still in working order (it takes 5p pieces), there's a big longcase clock with a clear piping strike, and a twister on the ceiling to point out who gets the next round; darts, cribbage, shove-ha'penny, and dominoes. Well liked home-made bar food (no chips) includes filled baked potatoes (from £3.60), ploughman's (from £5.90), vegetable and cheese bake (£6.20), steak and kidney pudding or cod in cheese sauce (£7.50), and local game and wine pie (£8.70), with interesting specials such as rabbit and wild mushroom soup (£2.95), mushroom, nut and wine pie (£7), cod in shellfish sauce or pot-roast pheasant (£7.50), and puddings such as syrup and coconut tart or spotted dick (£2.95); they do lunchtime rolls and sandwiches (not at weekends), and half-size helpings for children. They don't take bookings, so it's a good idea to arrive early at busy times; the dining room is no smoking. Greene King IPA, Woodfordes Wherry, and a weekly guest such as Iceni Snowdrop are well kept on handpump or tapped from the cask; they also do country wines, local summer cider, and delicious home-made lemonade. The staff are friendly, and the atmosphere is appealingly pubby. One of the outbuildings houses a wind-up gramophone museum – opened on request. They have now opened a courtyard garden with flower tubs and a well. *(Recommended by John Wooll, Philip and Susan Philcox, Paul and Ursula Randall, Barry Collett, I Louden, Mr Bishop, Dr Andy Wilkinson, John Beeken, Anthony Barnes, Brian Haywood, Simon Chell, Peter Meister, Phil and Sally Gorton, the Didler, Pam and David Bailey, Roger Wain-Heapy, Maureen and Bill Sewell, Mike and Shelley Woodroffe, Su and Bob Child, Anthony Longden)*

Free house ~ Licensee Iain Salmon ~ Real ale ~ Bar food (12-1.45, 6-8.30; not 25-26 Dec) ~ No credit cards ~ (01328) 710547 ~ Children welcome ~ Dogs welcome ~ Open 11.30-2.30, 6-11; 12-3, 6-10.30 Sun ~ Bedrooms: £24/£48(£52S)

WINTERTON-ON-SEA TG4919 Map 8
Fishermans Return 🍺 🛏

From B1159 turn into village at church on bend, then turn right into The Lane

'Is there anything better after a walk by the sea than a visit to this lovely, welcoming pub' wonders one reader. It's particularly pleasant in fine weather, when you can sit on the attractive wrought-iron and wooden benches on a pretty front terrace with lovely views, or in the sheltered garden. Inside, everything's spotlessly kept, and the cosily attractive white-painted no smoking lounge bar has vases of fresh flowers, neat brass-studded red leatherette seats and a roaring log fire. The panelled public bar has low ceilings and a glossily varnished nautical air (good fire in here too); the family room and dining room are no smoking. It's been well run by the same hospitable licensees for almost 30 years, and the staff are friendly and courteous. It's a charming place to stay, and the cosy bedrooms (be careful going up the steep curving stairs) have low doors, uneven floors and individual furniture; they do tasty generous breakfasts. The short but enjoyable bar menu includes toasties (from £2.50), ploughman's (£5), delicious fish pie (£5.75), chilli con carne or roast chicken breast (£7.25), seafood platter (£8.25), and steak (£11.50). There are regularly changing specials such as vegetable filo parcels with tomato and mascarpone sauce (£7.75), pork loin stuffed with bacon and wild mushrooms (£8.25), fresh salmon and plaice in herb and lemon sauce (£9.75), and puddings such as toffee crunch pie and chocolate truffle torte (£3.50). Well kept Adnams Best, Greene King IPA and Woodfordes Wherry, and a couple of guests such as Burton Bridge or Mauldons White Adder on handpump, decent wines, around 30 malt whiskies, and farm cider; darts, piped music, dominoes, cribbage, pool, fruit machine and juke box. The lovely sandy beach is nearby. *(Recommended by Shirley Mackenzie, Roger Everett, Shaun and Diane, Ian Martin, Mike and Sue Loseby, Keith and Chris O'Neill, Mike and Wendy Proctor, Steve Whalley, Mike and Shelley Woodroffe, Colin McKerrow, Ian Phillips, JDM, KM)*

Free house ~ Licensees John and Kate Findlay ~ Real ale ~ Bar food ~ (01493) 393305 ~ Children in family room ~ Dogs welcome ~ Open 11-2.30, 6.30-11; 11-11 Sat; 12.10.30 Sun ~ Bedrooms: £45B/£70B

WOODBASTWICK TG3315 Map 8
Fur & Feather 🍺
Off B1140 E of Norwich

Although Woodfordes brewery is next door, the style and atmosphere are not what you'd expect of a brewery tap (it's set out more like a dining pub), but you can still be sure of getting a superb pint at this carefully converted thatched cottage. They keep all eight of their beers on at the same time, on handpump or tapped from the cask; readers also enjoy visiting the brewery shop. The pub forms part of a very attractive estate village, and has tables out in a very pleasant garden. Friendly staff serve huge helpings of enjoyable bar food, such as soup (£3.50), sandwiches or filled baguettes (from £3.25), whitebait or game pâté (£4.50), vegetable stir fry (£7), lambs liver and bacon or scampi (£8.50), steak and kidney pudding or chicken breast with crispy bacon in a creamy mushroom and wholegrain mustard sauce (£8.75), and steaks (from £11), with puddings such as steamed jam pudding and custard (from £3.95); fried fish on Fridays, a roast on Sundays, and children's menu (£3.50). The cosy restaurant and part of the bar are no smoking; piped music. *(Recommended by the Didler, Keith and Chris O'Neill, Geoffrey and Brenda Wilson, Simon Pyle, Stephen, Julie and Hayley Brown, R C Vincent, Meg and Colin Hamilton, Klaus and Elizabeth Leist, Philip and Susan Philcox, Alison Hayes, Pete Hanlon)*

Woodfordes ~ Tenants Tim and Penny Ridley ~ Real ale ~ Bar food (12-2, 6-9) ~ Restaurant ~ (01603) 720003 ~ Children in eating area of bar and restaurant ~ Open 11.30-11(11.30-3, 6-11 in winter); 12-10.30 Sun

Lucky Dip

Besides the fully inspected pubs, you might like to try these Lucky Dips recommended to us and described by readers (if you do, please send us reports: www.goodguides.com).

BACTON [TG3433]
Duke of Edinburgh [Coast Rd]: Enjoyable food inc good value generous Sun carvery *(Samantha Frost)*
BANNINGHAM [TG2129]
Crown [Colby Rd]: Interesting building (which includes a post office), consistently friendly welcome, well kept Greene King ales, decent wines, nice choice of enjoyable food *(David Twitchett, Roger and Maureen Kenning)*
BARFORD [TG1107]
Cock [B1108 7 miles W of Norwich]: Attractively refurbished, with relaxed atmosphere, brewing its own good Blue Moon beers inc Sea of Tranquillity and

Hingham High, friendly landlord and chef, good interesting food *(Chris Pelley)*
BAWBURGH [TG1508]
☆ *Kings Head* [off B1108 just W of Norwich; Harts Lane]: Four comfortable and attractive linked low-beamed rooms, log fire and inglenook woodburner, wide food choice from lunchtime sandwiches to quite a few ambitious dishes, no smoking restaurant, well kept Adnams, Woodfordes Wherry and a guest beer, quite a few wines by the glass; children in eating areas, garden with rustic tables on heated terrace, open all day *(John and Elizabeth Cox, LYM)*
BEACHAMWELL [TF7505]
☆ *Great Danes Head* [off A1122 Swaffham—

Downham Mkt]: Cosy and friendly open-plan dark-beamed pub, good varied food using local produce inc game and good steaks, helpful licensees, Greene King Abbot and Marstons Pedigree, good house red, big log fire; children and dogs welcome, small separate public bar with dominoes and pool, no smoking restaurant; facing green of small village *(Sally Anne and Peter Goodale, BB)*

BILLINGFORD [TM1673]

Horseshoes [A143]: Friendly local nr windmill, well kept beer inc Tindalls Best from over by Bungay, good generous bargain food in quaint and homely smallish no smoking restaurant, quick friendly service; pool *(David Oakley)*

BINHAM [TF9839]

☆ *Chequers* [B1388 SW of Blakeney]: 17th-c, with coal or log fires each end of long civilised low-beamed bar, inglenook, sturdy plush seats, well kept Adnams Best and Regatta, Greene King IPA or Abbot, Nethergate Painted Lady and Woodfordes Wherry, decent house wines, landlord cooks enterprisingly using local produce, very popular Sun lunch (no bookings taken – get there early), good rolls and sandwiches, small no smoking dining area, prompt cheerful service, good coal fires each end, some nice old local prints, no piped music (but may be sports TV); picnic-sets out in front and on grass behind, open all day, two bedrooms, interesting village with huge priory church *(John Wooll, John Beeken, BB, Barry Collett, Robert M Warner, George Atkinson, ML)*

BLAKENEY [TG0244]

Blakeney Hotel [The Quay]: Well run hotel nicely set nr bird marshes, good food, well kept Adnams, attentive pleasant staff, good atmosphere, games room; dogs welcome, bedrooms very comfortable, swimming pool, well set up for family breaks *(MDN, Robert M Warner)*

☆ *Manor* [The Quay]: Attractive hotel in own grounds with decorous bar, popular esp with older people for good enterprising waitress-served bar food, not expensive, from well filled crab sandwiches to attractive puddings; well kept Adnams Best and Broadside, decent house wines, friendly helpful and attentive staff, conservatory, good restaurant; sunny tables in fountain courtyard and walled garden with bowling green, good bedrooms; opp wildfowl reserve and sea inlet *(John Beeken, Paul and Ursula Randall, Robert M Warner, George Atkinson, BB, Tony Middis)*

BLICKLING [TG1728]

☆ *Buckinghamshire Arms* [B1354 NW of Aylsham]: Handsome Jacobean inn by gates to Blickling Hall (NT), neat pews around stripped pine tables in lounge, banquettes in small front snug, enjoyable food from baguettes and baked potatoes up, well kept Adnams Best and Broadside and Woodfordes Wherry, local cider, good range of wines, helpful service; well behaved children in restaurant, lots of tables out on big lawn with summer food servery, perhaps all-day opening in summer if busy, bedrooms with own bathrooms (two nights minimum stay at wknds) *(Beryl and Bill Farmer, Maureen and Bill Sewell, M Borthwick, John Wooll, Dr Andy Wilkinson, Peter and Pat Frogley, LYM, Mike and Shelley Woodroffe, J H Bell, Dave Braisted)*

BRANCASTER STAITHE [TF7944]

☆ *Jolly Sailors* [Main Road (A149)]: New management in old-fashioned pub popular with birdwatchers, three simply furnished beamed rooms, log fire, prompt friendly service, well kept Adnams and Woodfordes Wherry, decent wines, food (all day in summer) from baguettes up, no smoking restaurant; piped music, fruit machine, TV; children in eating areas, sheltered tables in nice garden with terrace and play area, open all day wknds and summer *(Comus and Sarah Elliott, Richard Cole, John Beeken, LYM)*

BURGH ST PETER [TM4893]

Waveney [Waveney River Centre, Staithe Rd]: Spotless riverside pub and restaurant with enjoyable food from attractively priced bar meals to fresh fish grills and a hefty Sun lunch, real ales such as Adnams, Elgoods, Greene King Abbot and Woodfordes, swift friendly service, great boating views; children welcome, good disabled access, in large leisure centre with swimming pool, among boatyards *(M J Winterton, Quentin and Carol Williamson)*

BURNHAM MARKET [TF8342]

☆ *Lord Nelson* [Creake Rd]: Recently refurbished, with small unpretentious no smoking restaurant behind one bar, pool and juke box in the other, some Nelson memorabilia, Courage Directors, Greene King IPA and Tetleys, good choice of enjoyable food from baguettes to lots of fish and seafood, friendly and helpful quick service; two attractive bedrooms with own bathrooms in former outbuilding *(John Wooll, LYM, A D Cross, Michael Dandy)*

CAISTER-ON-SEA [TG5211]

Ship [Victoria St, off Tan Lane]: Busy welcoming local notable for its riot of magnificent hanging baskets and spectacular flower tubs and other less likely containers on front terrace and small back garden; modern furnishings, spacious family room (with pool table closed off at lunch), well kept competitively priced Greene King IPA and Old Speckled Hen, decent house wines, heaps of good value cheap satisfying food inc fresh local fish, coal fire; nostalgic piped pop music, darts, euchre, big screen TV and games machines in side areas, no dogs; not far from long sandy beach *(Mr and Mrs A Medlar, H McKay, BB)*

CASTLE ACRE [TF8115]

Albert Victor [Stocks Green]: Big farmhouse tables and chairs, plush sofas, old prints and maps, tasty and interesting changing blackboard food and children's dishes, Greene King IPA and Abbot Ale; piped music; large attractive back garden and pergola *(Mike Ridgway, Sarah Miles)*

Ostrich [Stocks Green]: Ungentrified pub prettily placed overlooking the tree-lined green, individual mix of utilitarian furnishings and fittings with some ancient beams, masonry and huge inglenook fireplace, well kept Greene King ales, cheap food with vegetarian emphasis, dominoes, cribbage; piped music, fruit machine, family room (but children run pretty free); jazz 2nd and 3rd Weds of month, folk last Weds; picnic-sets in sheltered informal garden with doves and aviary, cheap plain bedrooms sharing shower (good breakfast), attractive village with castle and monastery remains *(Ron and Sheila Corbett, John Wooll, LYM, John Saul)*

CATFIELD [TG3821]

Crown [The Street]: Archetypal village inn, clean and well appointed without being luxurious, four real ales inc Adnams, good choice of attractively priced bar food; bedrooms with own bathrooms, handy for Hickling Broad *(Tony Middis)*

COLTISHALL [TG2719]

☆ *Red Lion* [Church St (B1354)]: Modernised family pub with soft play area now, decent generous home-made food inc good puddings, friendly helpful service, good range of well kept beers inc Weasel brewed for them by Woodfordes, several attractive split-level rooms esp cellar bar, restaurant; away from water but pleasant setting, tables out under cocktail parasols by fountain *(Meg and Colin Hamilton)*

DENVER SLUICE [TF6101]

☆ *Jenyns Arms* [signed via B1507 off A1122 Downham Mkt bypass]: Extensive well laid out roadhouse-style pub in fine spot by spectacular hydraulic sluices controlling Great Ouse, tables out by water, generous usual food (not Sun evening) from good sandwiches to roasts and tempting puddings, friendly, helpful and efficient staff, well kept ales such as Greene King IPA and Old Speckled Hen and M&B Mild; children welcome, big light and airy games area with pool, piped music; bedrooms *(Gerry and Rosemary Dobson, BB, Jestyn Phillips)*

DOCKING [TF7637]

Railway Inn [Station Rd]: Wide choice of enjoyable home cooking from doorstep sandwiches up, Tues bargains for two, quick friendly service, well kept local Buffys Bitter and Norwegian Blue, good house wines, lounge bar and compact panelled dining room, fresh flowers, model train chuffing along under ceiling, some rail prints and posters (station closed 50 years ago), smaller chummy public bar with room in annexe; usually open all day *(M J A Switzer, John Beeken, Chris Rogers, John Wooll)*

DOWNHAM MARKET [TF6103]

Castle [High St]: Old-fashioned market-town inn, unchintzy, friendly and comfortable, with interesting local photographs, cartoons and cuttings in small cosy bar, above-average bar food inc roast of the day (separate restaurant menu), Bass, good value wines, helpful staff; piped music; good bedrooms *(George Atkinson)*

EAST BARSHAM [TF9133]

White Horse [B1105 3 miles N of Fakenham]: Attractively done extended pub, big log fire in long beamed main bar, steps to other areas, well kept ales such as Adnams Bitter and Broadside, Everards Lazy Daze and Greene King IPA, decent wine, good coffee, friendly attentive staff, generous reasonably priced meals (rather than snacks, no sandwiches) inc children's, OAP lunches and steak nights, two small attractive dining rooms; piped music, darts; children welcome, bedrooms – a pleasant quiet place to stay *(R C Vincent, George Atkinson)*

ERPINGHAM [TG1931]

Spread Eagle: Brick-built local with a true welcome for children and dogs (even from the pub's own dog), snug bar with comfortable sofa, Adnams Best, Fullers London Pride, Greene King IPA and Woodfordes Nelsons Revenge, pool table; live music Sun lunchtime and Sat; neat garden *(Robert M Warner)*

GAYTON [TF7219]

☆ *Crown* [B1145/B1153]: Attractive flower-decked pub, comfortably relaxed, with some unusual old features, good choice of well cooked food inc good value sandwiches and snacks, well kept Greene King IPA and Abbot, limited but good wine choice, hospitable landlady and pleasant staff, games room; tables in sheltered garden *(DC, Robert M Warner, John Wooll, David and Rhian Peters, LYM)*

Rampant Horse [Lynn Rd]: Locally popular food all day inc good value Sun lunch, three real ales, pleasant service; big garden with good play equipment, Fri night barbecue and perhaps live music *(R C Vincent)*

GELDESTON [TM3991]

☆ *Locks* [off A143/A146 NW of Beccles; off Station Rd S of village, obscurely signed down long rough track]: Remote pub alone at the navigable head of the River Waveney, recently gently smartened up around ancient tiled-floor core with its big log fire and assorted seating, Woodfordes and very local Tindalls ales tapped from casks, friendly informal service; big extension for summer crowds and wknd music nights, summer evening barbecues, meadow camping; may be cl winter wkdys *(the Didler, LYM, Neil Powell)*

Wherry [The Street]: Enjoyable food from good ploughman's up, well kept Adnams; pleasant garden *(Neil Powell)*

GREAT BIRCHAM [TF7632]

Kings Head [B1155, S end of village (called and signed Bircham locally)]: Unassuming lounge bar (two room areas), mix of high and low tables suiting both diners and drinkers, log fires, some good italian food specialities and lots of seafood, no smoking dining area, well kept Adnams, Bass and Greene King IPA, malt whiskies, good italian wines; big side lawn with picnic-sets and play things, attractive village with Houghton Hall and striking windmill nearby, good value bedrooms *(LYM, Robert M Warner, John Wooll, Mr Biggs)*

GREAT RYBURGH [TF9627]

Boar [Station Rd]: Friendly and comfortable, pleasantly down-to-earth licensees, well kept real ales inc Adnams and one brewed for the pub, wide choice of tasty home-made food in bar and recently refurbished airy dining room (should book Sat night, when service may slow); bedrooms, nice setting opp church *(R C Vincent)*

GREAT YARMOUTH [TG5207]

Mariners [Howard St S]: Popular with real ale fans for its four well kept changing beers and regular beer festivals *(the Didler)*

Red Herring [Havelock Rd]: Welcoming relaxing backstreet pub, nice Victorian décor, at least six well kept changing ales, farm ciders, good value food inc wide choice of good local sausages, may have eggs for sale, rock collection, old local photographs, books to read *(the Didler)*

HAINFORD [TG2219]

Chequers [Stratton Rd]: Comfortable and friendly rebuilt thatched cottage in charming setting, well prepared food from filled baguettes up, good choice of real ales, big airy bar area and rooms off, pleasant licensees; well arranged gardens with play area, children welcome *(M J Bourke)*

HARPLEY [TF7825]

Rose & Crown [off A148 Fakenham—Kings Lynn; Nethergate St]: Unassuming neatly kept cheery village local with modest good value home cooking inc fresh veg, lots of good puddings and children's meals, well kept Greene King IPA and Abbot, decent wine, efficient service, log fire, pool room, small dining room – high chairs provided; good tables in attractive garden with play equipment *(P J and R D Greaves, BB, R C Vincent)*

HEACHAM [TF6737]

Fox & Hounds [Station Rd]: Unpretentious spacious bar with charming friendly service, attractive choice of good generous food (not Sun evening); now brewing its own good real ales, also farm cider and well kept guest beers; open all day *(Peter H Stallard)*

HEMPSTEAD [TG1137]

☆ *Hare & Hounds* [towards Baconsthorpe]: Cottagey country pub, two beamed rooms with wide choice of enjoyable food in huge helpings, log fire in one broad fireplace, well kept Greene King IPA and Abbot and a guest such as Hop Back Summer Lightning, welcoming service; lots of picnic-sets and play area on side grass by pond and rockery *(P J and R D Greaves, Mr and Mrs P Thompson, LYM, Anthony Barnes)*

HOLKHAM [TF8943]

Victoria [A149 near Holkham Hall]: We have reluctantly come round to the management's own view that this place is too hotelish for the main entries, but it's well worth a look, despite its high prices, for the engagingly up-to-date style of its vibrant and popular main bar with its sprawling sofas and eclectic furnishings and décor; good wines, well kept beers such as Adnams, Fullers London Pride and Woodfordes Wherry (with a stiff premium for half-pints), friendly hard-working young staff; children welcome, appealing terrace and lawn (and a play area), charmingly individual bedrooms, open all day *(MDN, Keith and Chris O'Neill, John Wooll, Ian Arthur, Minda and Stanley Alexander, Tessa Rose, I Louden, Mr Bishop, David and Anne Culley, Simon Menzies, LYM)*

HOLT [TG0738]

☆ *Feathers* [Market Pl]: Bustling yet thoroughly relaxed and good-humoured town hotel, locals' bar comfortably extended around original panelled area with open fire, attractive entrance/reception area with antiques, helpful service from friendly staff, good value promptly served generous food, well kept Greene King IPA and Abbot, decent wines, good coffee; piped music, dogs welcome, can get smoky, busy on Sat market day; decent roomy bedrooms *(June and Perry Dann, Blaise Vyner, Robert M Warner, BB, George Atkinson)*

HONINGHAM [TG1011]

☆ *Olde Buck* [just off A47]: Ancient pub with four beamed rooms, some emphasis on wide choice of good food inc huge sandwiches and lunchtime bargains; helpful and friendly service, well kept Greene King IPA and Flowers IPA, relaxing candlelit atmosphere *(Mrs J A Trotter, M J Caley, O K Smyth)*

HORSTEAD [TG2619]

☆ *Recruiting Sergeant* [B1150 just S of Coltishall]: Spacious pleasantly refurbished village pub, enjoyable and generous meals and snacks inc good fish choice, welcoming obliging service, real ales, big open fire, brasses and muskets *(Alan M Pring, M J Bourke, T and A Wyatt, R L Worsdall)*

KELLING [TG0942]

Pheasant [A149 Sheringham—Blakeney]: Beautifully placed small hotel locally very popular for moderately priced lunchtime and evening bar meals inc good interesting specials and bargain lunches in large comfortable lounge, partly no smoking bar, Adnams and Greene King IPA, friendly attentive staff; quiet piped music; tables on small sheltered lawn, bedrooms *(Paul and Ursula Randall, George Atkinson, David Cosham)*

KENNINGHALL [TM0386]

Red Lion [B1113 S of Norwich; East Church St]: Stripped beams, old pictures and floor tiles, small panelled snug, open fires, back stable-style restaurant area with woodburner, comprehensive food choice from good baguettes up, Greene King IPA, Abbot and Ruddles Best and Woodfordes Mild and Wherry, helpful friendly staff, pub cat called Topsy; bedrooms in former stable block *(Michael and Jenny Back)*

KING'S LYNN [TF6120]

Lloyds No 1 [King St/Tuesday Market Pl]: Spacious bar, a Wetherspoons, in former Globe, good value food and good beer choice, impressive service; very busy at times, with doormen; attractive back garden, pleasant bedrooms *(R C Vincent, Joe Green)*

Stuart House [Goodwins Rd]: Well kept beer, good pub atmosphere, obliging young staff, enjoyable if not cheap food in bar and restaurant, occasional live music *(Joe Green)*

☆ *Tudor Rose* [St Nicholas St (just off Tuesday Market Pl)]: Lively 15th-c town pub back on form under hospitable current landlady, smiling efficient service, well kept ales such as Adnams Broadside, Badger Tanglefoot, Bass, Batemans XB and Timothy Taylors Landlord, good choice of other drinks, reliable and plentiful good value bar food from sandwiches up, no smoking upstairs restaurant; back bar can be smoky; sensibly priced bedrooms *(John Wooll, Andrew and Samantha Grainger, Baden and Sandy Waller, J F M and M West, LYM, Alison Hayes, Pete Hanlon)*

LANGHAM [TG0041]

Bluebell [Holt Rd]: Neatly refurbished, with cheerful welcoming licensees, good value quickly served home-made food inc popular OAP wkdy lunches, well kept real ales, no smoking eating area; good disabled access and facilities, quiz night; charming garden with apple trees, bluebells inc roses, set well away from road looking up to church tower *(Robert M Warner)*

LESSINGHAM [TG3928]

Swan [School Rd]: Small and inviting, with two open fires, comfortable armchairs, good beer and wine choice, good side restaurant where chef/landlord uses only local produce *(Steve Toomey)*

MORSTON [TG0043]

Anchor [The Street]: Pleasantly old-fashioned, several rooms with local prints and photographs, Greene King real ales, decent wines, food from sandwiches and rolls to quite a lot of fresh fish, daily papers *(John Wooll)*

NEATISHEAD [TG3421]

White Horse [The Street]: Warm and welcoming multi-roomed pub popular with boaters (free mooring nearby), lots of old broads pictures, welcoming family service, well kept Adnams and Tetleys, popular basic food *(I Louden, Mr Bishop)*

NORTH CREAKE [TF8538]

Jolly Farmers [Burnham Rd]: Two cheerfully rustic small bars, good log fire, well kept Woodfordes Wherry, Nelsons Revenge and Admirals Reserve tapped from the cask, good friendly service, good gently upmarket food inc good value puddings in cosy tasteful dining room; children in eating area, tables in sheltered garden, charming village *(Jim Mansfield, Mike and Shelley Woodroffe)*

NORTH ELMHAM [TF9920]

Railway [Station Rd]: Snug L-shaped bar, settees and easy chairs by log fire at end by small restaurant, reasonably priced food inc bargain grill using local produce such as gloucester old spot, several well kept real ales, lots of papers, magazines and books; tables in garden, open all day *(Chris Rogers)*

NORWICH [TG2108]

Alexandra [Stafford St]: Welcoming, comfortable and efficient two-bar local, well kept real ales such as Chalk Hill and Exmoor Gold, cheap interesting food, open fire; pool, classic juke box *(MP)*

Coach & Horses [Thorpe Rd]: Light and airy tap for Chalk Hill brewery, with their own Bitter, Flint Knappers Mild, CHB, Dreadnought and Old Tackle, also guests such as Boddingtons and Timothy Taylors, friendly service, good choice of generous home cooking 12-9 (8 Sun), also breakfast with limitless coffee; bare-boards L-shaped bar with open fire, lots of dark wood, posters and prints, pleasant back dining area; disabled access possible (not to lavatories), picnic-sets on front terrace, may be summer barbecues, open all day *(the Didler, G Coates, Dr B and Mrs P B Baker)*

Gardeners Arms [Timber Hill]: Small attractive rooms converted from some of the last original shops and houses in old part of town, neatly themed inc convincing kitchen, more room in glassed-over former yard, relaxed friendly staff, real ales inc Murderer (recalling pub's former name), good value food inc sandwiches from breakfast on (not Mon evening), lots of bric-a-brac, no smoking and air-conditioned areas; families welcome, more of a young people's pub evenings *(Shaun and Diane, Gordon Prince)*

Kings Arms [Hall Rd]: Traditional pub with Adnams, Greene King, Wolf and 10 changing east anglian guest beers, beer festivals, 70 malt whiskies, 20 wines, good atmosphere; unobtrusive sports TV, no food but bring your own or order out – plates, cutlery provided; vines in courtyard *(Mrs N J Howard)*

☆ *Ribs of Beef* [Wensum St, S side of Fye Bridge]: Warm and welcoming high-ceilinged old pub, well kept ales such as Adnams, Boddingtons, Fullers London Pride and Woodfordes Wherry, farm cider, decent wine; deep leather settees and small tables upstairs, attractive smaller downstairs room with river view and some local river paintings, generous cheap reliable food (till 5 Sat/Sun), quick friendly service, long-serving licensees; can be studenty evenings *(John Wooll, David Carr)*

Steam Packet [Crown Rd, behind Anglia TV]: Popular and friendly two-bar Adnams pub, no smoking at lunchtime, good pork pies, open all day; great for music *(the Didler)*

Take Five [St Andrews St, next to Cinema City]: Not a pub (in the evenings you can get in only through the next-door cinema for which it serves as the cafeteria), but very pleasant relaxed atmosphere, with well kept Woodfordes Wherry and a guest beer, two farm ciders, mainly organic wines by the glass, good value cheerful food, changing local art, some no smoking tables; piped classical music; tables in nice old courtyard *(Peter and Pat Frogley)*

Whalebone [Magdalen Rd]: Friendly two-bar real ale pub, usually five or six, sometimes more, occasional beer festivals, reasonable prices for the area; TV in back seating area, lots of tables outside *(Sue Rowland, Paul Mallett)*

Wig & Pen [St Martins Palace Plain]: Partly modernised old beamed bar opp cathedral close, lawyer and judge prints, roaring stove with horsebrasses on overmantel, prompt generous bar food, good range of real ales, good value wine, staff who take a genuine interest; piped music *(Evelyn and Derek Walter, Richard and Karen Holt)*

OLD BUCKENHAM [TM0691]

☆ *Gamekeeper* [The Green]: 16th-c pub, welcoming and pretty, good atmosphere with blazing log fire, dried hops and church candles, good seasonal food in cosy bar or larger dining room, Sun lunch 12-5, well kept ales such as Adnams, local Wolf and one brewed for the pub, good wine list, no machines; children welcome *(anon)*

OLD HUNSTANTON [TF6842]

Ancient Mariner [part of L'Estrange Arms Hotel, Golf Course Rd]: Large bar, relaxed and cheerful, well done up with lots of dark wood, bare bricks and flagstones, several little areas inc conservatory and upstairs gallery, pleasant furnishings, four well kept ales such as Adnams Broadside and Youngs Special, good wines by the glass, friendly service, open fires, papers and magazines; hotel has nice bedrooms, long sea-view garden down to dunes, play area *(Peter Rozée, Mike Ridgway, Sarah Miles, David and Rhian Peters)*

RANWORTH [TG3514]

Maltsters [signed from B1140 Norwich—Acle]: Fine position across quiet lane from Ranworth Broad, rather nautical décor, decent food, friendly prompt service, well kept Woodfordes; superb nature trail nearby, ferry to wildlife centre *(LYM, Dave Braisted)*

REEDHAM [TG4001]

☆ *Ferry Inn* [B1140 Beccles—Acle, beside ferry]: Popular with boaters (refundable mooring and showers if you eat here), with well spaced tables on the waterside terrace, long front bar with big picture windows, comfortable banquettes and some robust rustic tables carved from slabs of tree-trunk, secluded back bar with antique rifles, copper and brass, and a fine log fire, well kept Adnams Bitter and Broadside, Woodfordes Wherry and a guest beer, quite a few malt whiskies, country wines, cheerful staff, no smoking restaurant and family room; piped music; open for food all day Sun *(LYM)*

REEPHAM [TG0922]

Kings Arms [Market Pl]: 17th-c coaching inn, pleasant décor with several areas, stripped brickwork, open fire and farm tools, well kept ales such as Adnams, Reepham and Woodfordes Wherry, three open fires, wide choice of reasonably priced good food from sandwiches up, cheerful willing service, games area one end, steps to restaurant; tables outside front and back, bedrooms *(Mike and Lynn Robinson, Tony Middis)*

ROCKLAND ST MARY [TG3204]

New Inn [New Inn Hill]: Over road from staithe, views from attractive barn-style restaurant extension, well kept Marstons Pedigree, reasonably priced generous home-made food inc cheap children's dishes, daily papers for sale from 9.30 (pub doubles as local shop); dogs welcome, bar can be a bit smoky; good disabled access, front terrace tables, back garden, good walks to Rockland Broad and bird hides *(M J Winterton)*

ROYDON [TF7022]

Three Horseshoes [the one nr Kings Lynn; Lynn Rd]: Two-bar pub with new landlord putting more emphasis on wide choice of good value food running up to big mixed grill, pleasant décor in bar and restaurant, Greene King and other ales, attentive service; tables outside *(R C Vincent)*

RUSHALL [TM1982]

Half Moon [The Street]: Spotless extended 16th-c coaching inn popular for generous and competitively priced straightforward food inc plenty of fish and big puddings, in beamed and flagstoned bar or back dining room; well kept Adnams and Woodfordes, friendly service, dolls and bric-a-brac for sale; bedrooms in adjacent modern chalets *(Alan M Pring, Ian and Nita Cooper)*

SALTHOUSE [TG0743]

☆ *Dun Cow* [A149 Blakeney—Sheringham]: Extensively refurbished well run airy pub overlooking salt marshes, decent usual food all day from sandwiches and baked potatoes to fresh crab salad and steak, friendly service, well kept Adnams, Greene King and other ales, open fires, stripped beams and cob walls in big barn-like bar; piped radio, blues nights; children welcome (games in family room), big attractive walled garden with sheltered courtyard, figs and apples, separate family garden with play area, good walks and birdwatching nearby (may get sightings blackboard); bedrooms *(Mrs M A Mees, Rodney and Norma Stubington, Eleanor and Nick Steinitz, BB, David Carr)*

SCOLE [TM1478]

Crossways [Bridge Rd]: Pleasant atmosphere in unpretentious 16th-c inn with impressive fireplaces, well kept Adnams and Greene King Abbot, unusually good wines, generous enjoyable food and good service in restaurant, children's room; dogs welcome (they have a cat and dog), bedrooms *(R C Vincent)*

☆ *Scole Inn* [off A140 bypass just N of A143; Ipswich Rd]: Stately old coaching inn of outstanding architectural interest, with a real sense of history, antique settles, old oak chairs and tables, two impressive inglenook log fires, old prints and collectables and other old-fashioned features in lounge and bare-boards public bar used by locals; decent bar food from baguettes to steak, more elaborate menu in large no smoking restaurant, well kept Greene King IPA and XX Mild; cribbage, dominoes; children and dogs welcome, open all day, comfortable bedrooms in former stable block *(P G Plumridge, Mike and Wendy Proctor, LYM, Ian Phillips, M and G Rushworth)*

SCULTHORPE [TF8930]
Horse & Groom [The Street]: Comfortably refurbished and kept spotless by new owners, friendly service, enjoyable reasonably priced food, well kept Greene King IPA and Abbot; wheelchair access *(Chris Rogers)*

☆ *Sculthorpe Mill* [inn signed off A148 W of Fakenham, opp village]: Converted 18th-c mill reopened after 2002 fire and rebuilding, beamed bar with several comfortable rooms, real ales such as Greene King, decent house wines, enjoyable food from sandwiches and snack menu to full meals, helpful prompt service; children in eating areas, spacious streamside garden, open all day wknds and summer, comfortable bedrooms, good breakfast *(Sue and Geoff Price, LYM, Michael Porter)*

SHERINGHAM [TG1543]
Robin Hood [Station Rd]: Busy central pub, open-plan bar with dining area, smaller side room, Adnams, Bass and Greene King, good value generous food, efficient service; children very welcome, tables outside *(Jim Abbott, B N F and M Parkin)*
Sherry 'n' Ham [Beech Ave]: Enjoyable well presented food at reasonable prices, good drinks range inc Adnams *(D and M T Ayres-Regan)*
Wyndham Arms [Wyndham St]: Comfortable low-beamed lounge bar with big no smoking area and real fire, real ales inc Adnams and Woodfordes, cheap house wine, quick cheerful service, good fresh straightforward home-cooked food inc good range of local fish, busy public bar with pool and piped music, no smoking restaurant; picnic-sets out in courtyard, open all day *(Dr B and Mrs P B Baker, B and H, Peter Salmon)*

SKEYTON [TG2524]
☆ *Goat* [off A140 N of Aylsham; Long Rd]: Convivial extended thatched and low-beamed pub with good food in bar and restaurant (best to book Sat evening), well kept Adnams and Woodfordes ales, good value wines, first-rate service by enthusiastic cheerful staff, log-effect gas fire; pleasant terrace and garden *(Dr and Mrs R G J Telfer, Chris and Jan Harper)*

SOUTH CREAKE [TF8635]
Ostrich [B1355 Burnham Mkt—Fakenham]: Popular local with pine tables in long narrow bar and lounge, enjoyable food from home-made burgers to guinea fowl, well kept Greene King IPA and Abbot and Woodfordes Nelsons Revenge, good wine choice, friendly hard-working owners, side pool table; children welcome *(John Wooll, Mrs A Burton)*

SOUTH LOPHAM [TM0481]
White Horse [A1066 Diss—Thetford]: Beamed pub with good choice of enjoyable home-made food inc bargain OAP roast lunch, good staff (holiday visitors treated like regulars), Adnams, Greene King IPA and Marstons Pedigree, big garden; bedrooms, handy for Bressingham Gardens *(Alan M Pring)*

SOUTH WALSHAM [TG3613]
Ship [B1140]: Small village pub with good fresh home cooking, friendly landlord, well kept Adnams and Woodfordes Wherry, stripped bricks and beams; piped music; tables on front elevated terrace and more in back garden; children's room, play area *(Ms Gaye Mayger)*

SOUTH WOOTTON [TF6422]
Farmers Arms [part of Knights Hill Hotel, Grimston Rd (off A148/A149)]: Olde-worlde conversion of barn and stables, good value food all day in bar and restaurant, puddings cabinet, good changing choice of real ales, good wines, abundant coffee, friendly prompt service; children welcome, comfortable motel bedrooms, health club, open all day *(R C Vincent)*

SPORLE [TF8411]
☆ *Squirrels Drey* [The Street]: Open fire in comfortable lounge, enormous antique round table in bar, well kept real ales (regular beer festivals), friendly young landlord, wide choice of above-average food inc good game and puddings, candlelit restaurant *(Dick and Sue Ward)*

STALHAM [TG3725]
Kingfisher [High St]: Sizeable helpings of good reasonably priced food in small bar and restaurant, well kept Adnams; bedrooms *(Meg and Colin Hamilton)*

SWAFFHAM [TF8209]
George [Station St]: Comfortably modern market-town hotel with small well kept old-fashioned bar, wide choice of reasonably priced decent food inc good seafood, Greene King IPA and Abbot, friendly fast service; children welcome, car park useful on Sat market day; bedrooms *(Robert M Warner, John Cadge)*

THOMPSON [TL9296]
☆ *Chequers* [Griston Rd, off A1075 S of Watton]: Long, low and picturesque 15th-c thatched dining pub with good interesting food inc local game and lots of fresh fish in series of olde-worlde quaint rooms, well kept Adnams, Fullers London Pride, local Wolf and occasional guest beers, good modestly priced wine list, friendly service

and atmosphere, low beams, inglenooks, some stripped brickwork, antique tools and traps; games machines; tables outside, good bedroom block *(R Cross, LYM, Mike and Karen England, Robert M Warner)*

THURNE [TG4016]

Lion [The Street]: Wide food choice, children welcome in family room; looks like former big private house extended to include village shop etc, nearby moorings, open all day *(Meg and Colin Hamilton)*

TILNEY ST LAWRENCE [TF5516]

Coach & Horses [Lynn Rd, off A47]: Neatly refurbished partly 17th-c pub with glowing oak tables, dark wood chairs and settles, lots of brasses, four well kept Elgoods ales, huge helpings of usual blackboard food, no music; children welcome in eating area, picnic-sets in garden behind *(Howard Dell)*

TITCHWELL [TF7543]

☆ *Titchwell Manor* [A149 E of Hunstanton]: Reopened after careful refurbishment as comfortable upmarket hotel, with good often enterprising food and pretty bedrooms overlooking the RSPB bird marshes towards the sea; friendly staff, well kept Greene King IPA, roaring fire in big lounge, airy no smoking restaurant, children welcome, tables in charming walled garden *(S Street, LYM)*

WALSINGHAM [TF9336]

Black Lion [Friday Market Pl]: Dates from 14th c, with three panelled rooms, cast-iron stove in one, open fire in another, various alcoves and small restaurant; well kept beers, wide choice of well presented bar food, Greene King IPA and Abbot, decent wines, quick pleasant service; comfortable bedrooms *(John Wooll)*

WELLS-NEXT-THE-SEA [TF9143]

Bowling Green [Church St]: Attractively refurbished L-shaped bar, flagstone and brick floor, simple furnishings, hearty freshly made food at dining end, friendly efficient service even when busy, two log fires, well kept Greene King IPA and Abbot and Woodfordes Wherry; tables out on terrace *(John Beeken, Peter and Anne Hollindale, Mike and Shelley Woodroffe)*

☆ *Crown* [The Buttlands]: 16th-c coaching inn reworked a couple of years ago with bold colours, stylish modern furnishings and nice conservatory, more as largely no smoking hotel/restaurant (with pleasantly light and airy bedrooms) than as pub; initially a favourite with readers for its inventive cooking (and good bar with Adnams Bitter and Broadside and a guest beer as well as good wines), but recent management changes call for more reports please; children welcome, open all day *(Charles Gysin, LYM)*

WEST BECKHAM [TG1339]

☆ *Wheatsheaf* [off A148 Holt—Cromer; Church Rd]: Gently renovated separate beamed areas, roaring log fire in one part, a smaller coal one in another, comfortable

chairs and banquettes, usually good generous food (not Sun evening) from sandwiches up, two no smoking dining rooms, well kept Woodfordes ales perhaps with a guest such as Robinsons, good wine choice, local country wines, enormous black cat; darts, bar billiards, shove-ha'penny, dominoes, piped music, and service can suffer when busy; children welcome, partly terraced front garden with restored gipsy caravan *(Derek R A Field, Jim Abbott, Derek and Sylvia Stephenson, Philip and Susan Philcox, LYM, Peter and Pat Frogley)*

WEST SOMERTON [TG4719]

☆ *Lion* [B1159/B1152]: Friendly welcome in airy and comfortable modernised pub with keenly priced popular bar food, well kept Greene King and guest ales; children in family room, handy for Martham Broad *(LYM, Jestyn Phillips)*

WEYBOURNE [TG1043]

Maltings: Cosy and comfortably old-fashioned hotel, small bar (dogs allowed) with well kept Wolf beers and friendly helpful staff, relaxing lounges, enjoyable reasonably priced restaurant food; bedrooms *(David Cosham)*

WIMBOTSHAM [TF6205]

Chequers [Church Rd]: Friendly local with enjoyable food (not Tues) inc steak bargains Weds, fish specials Fri lunchtime, OAP lunch Thurs; good log fire *(S Street)*

WIVETON [TG0342]

☆ *Bell* [Blakeney Rd]: Big welcoming open-plan dining pub, Danish landlord cooking wide choice of enjoyable food for bar and restaurant inc some Danish dishes and interesting specials, Adnams Broadside and Bass, good wines, efficient helpful service even under pressure, no music or machines; large carpeted no smoking conservatory, picnic-sets on lawn and garden behind *(BB, John Wooll, John Beeken, Paul and Ursula Randall, Charles Gysin, Brian Haywood)*

WROXHAM [TG3018]

Hotel Wroxham [Bridge Precinct]: Modern building with large bar and dining area, picture windows and terrace overlooking River Bure, waterfowl hoping for food, good value generous carvery with children's prices, well kept ales such as Adnams and Woodfordes; 18 recently refurbished bedrooms, waterside balconies *(Alan M Pring)*

WYMONDHAM [TG1101]

☆ *Green Dragon* [Church St]: Very picturesque heavily timbered jettied 14th-c inn, bulky beams, log fire (Tudor mantelpiece), well kept Adnams and Greene King, friendly relaxed service, welcoming locals, good food from sandwiches to attractively priced main dishes, small back bar, bigger no smoking turkey-carpeted dining area, some interesting pictures; children and dogs welcome; modest bedrooms, nr glorious 12th-c abbey church *(the Didler, M S Catling, BB)*

Northamptonshire

A good newcomer this year is the White Horse at Kings Sutton, a stylishly reworked old place, with good interesting food. Other pubs on top form here are the Windmill at Badby (good fresh food in this civilised country pub), the welcoming Red Lion at Crick (excellent value lunches), the smartly old-fashioned Red Lion at East Haddon (not cheap, but much enjoyed), the Falcon at Fotheringhay (a rewarding place for a special meal out, and the set lunches are good value), the George at Kilsby (its hard-working landlady is the heart of its success), the Old Sun at Nether Heyford (packed with interest, and its new bargain lunches are a great success), and the attractive Star at Sulgrave (newish licensees settling in well, and their up-to-date food is well on the way to a Food Award). For several years on the trot now the Falcon has been our top choice for food here. It's at least as good as ever, a real favourite. However, this year people have been enjoying the Red Lion at East Haddon so much for their meals out that it takes over the title of Northamptonshire Dining Pub of the Year. Notable pubs in the Lucky Dip section at the end of the chapter are the Olde Coach House at Ashby St Ledgers, Old Crown at Ashton, Montagu Arms at Barnwell, Queens Head at Bulwick, Falcon at Castle Ashby, Royal Oak at Eydon, Dusty Fox at Harlestone, Tollemache Arms at Harrington, Woolpack at Islip, Old Saracens Head at Little Brington, Greyhound at Milton Malsor, Navigation at Stoke Bruerne, Kings Head at Wadenhoe and Narrow Boat at Weedon. Drinks prices here are quite close to the national average; the Batemans at the simple and spotlessly kept White Swan at Woodnewton was the cheapest beer we found at our main entries, and the Old Sun at Nether Heyford was also very good value for beers. Local ales well worth looking out for are those from Frog Island, based in Northampton.

BADBY SP5559 Map 4
Windmill 🍽 ⇐
Village signposted off A361 Daventry—Banbury

Lunchtime brings a pubby but civilised bustle to this old thatched inn, so it may be worth booking. The main attraction is the very good freshly cooked bar food from a well balanced menu. It's served promptly by good-natured efficient staff, and might include swede and coriander soup (£2.95), potato skins with yoghurt and mint dip (£3.75), grilled goats cheese on garlic bread with basil and tomato (£4.95), nut roast with cranberry and chilli sauce or steak and kidney pie (£7.95), venison burgers with creamy peppercorn sauce (£8.75), fresh crab salad (£9.75), wild boar steak with whisky and mushroom sauce (£11.95), brill topped with crab and prawn sauce (£12.50), and puddings (from £3.50). Two beamed and flagstoned bars have a nice country feel with an unusual white woodburning stove in an enormous white-tiled inglenook fireplace, simple country furnishings in good solid wood, and cricketing and rugby pictures. There's also a comfortably cosy lounge. The snug and the more modern-feeling, brightly lit carpeted restaurant are no smoking. Well kept Bass, Flowers Original, Greene King Old Speckled Hen, Wadworths 6X and a guest such as Fullers London Pride on handpump, and good fairly priced wines by the bottle; quiet piped music. The bedrooms are in an unobtrusive modern extension, well tucked away at the back, with a couple of new ones in a pretty cottage next door. There are a few seats out in front by the green; this is a pretty village, with lots of nearby woodland walks. *(Recommended by George Atkinson, Maysie Thompson, Robin and Sheila Pitt, Di and Mike Gillam, Dr T E Hothersall, Paul Humphreys, Anthony Barnes, Sheila and Gerry McGrady, Bob Arnett, Judy Wayman, Miss E J Berrill, P Tailyour, John Bramley, R M Corlett)*

Free house ~ Licensees John Freestone and Carol Sutton ~ Real ale ~ Bar food ~ Restaurant ~ (01327) 702363 ~ Children in eating area of bar and restaurant ~ Dogs welcome ~ Open 11.30-3(4 Sat/Sun), 5.30-11(6.30-10.30 Sun) ~ Bedrooms: £59.50B/£69.50B

CHAPEL BRAMPTON SP7266 Map 4
Brampton Halt
Pitsford Road; off A5199 (was A50) N of Northampton

Now part of a small local pub group, this pretty red brick Victorian inn was built as a stationmaster's house, and stands alone by the little Northampton & Lamport Railway, with pleasant meadow views. A visit here makes part of a good day out for the family, as there are train rides at weekends with additional bank holiday and Santa specials, and the Nene Valley Way – a 14-mile walk and cycle-way – runs along an adjacent converted old track through attractive countryside. It's a friendly, relaxed place, with Victorian-style floral wallpaper throughout, matching swagged curtains, and sturdily comfortable furniture. One low-ceilinged area has a woodburning stove and wash drawings of steam trains, and by the bar counter, a high-raftered dining area has old farm tools. Windows at the back overlook the garden and fenced-off rolling stock, and a small sun lounge has a few more tables. Straightforward bar food includes sandwiches (from £3.25), pâté (£3.65), prawn cocktail (£3.95), scampi (£6.75) and steak pie or gammon and egg (£6.95). Well kept Adnams, Everards Old Original and Tiger, Fullers London Pride and Greene King IPA on handpump; decent wines; friendly service; trivia, perhaps piped music. *(Recommended by J Attwood, Bernie Adams, Ian Phillips, Gerry and Rosemary Dobson, Rona Murdoch)*

Free house ~ Licensee Tim Rama ~ Real ale ~ Bar food (12-2, 6-9; 12-9(5 Sun) Sat; not Sun evening) ~ Restaurant ~ (01604) 842676 ~ Children welcome ~ Open 12-3, 5.30-11; 12-11(10.30 Sun) Fri/Sat; closed 25 Dec evening

CLIPSTON SP7181 Map 4
Bulls Head ◀
B4036 S of Market Harborough

Cracks in the heavy low black beams at this nice old village inn are jammed with hundreds of coins. The tradition was started by US airmen based nearby during World War II, who would leave their money wedged in the ancient woodwork ready for their return and their next round – though they certainly didn't have the amazing choice of over 610 whiskies now on offer. Also well kept Bass, Greene King IPA and Abbot and a guest such as Everards Tiger from handpump, and half a dozen wines by the glass. The carpeted bar is divided into three cosily dim areas leading down from the servery, with comfortable seats, sturdy small settles and stools upholstered in red plush, some harness and tools, and a log fire. A back dining area has oak settles and high-backed chairs; the walls are hung with china meat platters. Reasonably priced bar food includes home-made soup (£2.95), sandwiches (from £3.25), garlic mushrooms (£3.50), battered haddock (£4.95), sausage and mash (£5.50), spinach and ricotta cannelloni or steak and kidney pie (£6.95) and mixed grill (£9.50). One of the bars and the restaurant are no smoking; table skittles, darts, TV, fruit machine, dominoes, piped music and newspapers. Slightly saucy pin-ups decorate the gents' and ladies'. Outside, a terrace has tables under cocktail parasols. *(Recommended by George Atkinson, Neil Skidmore, Rona Murdoch, Sally Anne and Peter Goodale, Graham and Lynn Mason, Bernie Adams, Sir Clive Rose)*

Free house ~ Licensees George, Sue and Jo Price ~ Real ale ~ Bar food ~ Restaurant ~ (01858) 525268 ~ Children in eating area of bar and restaurant ~ Dogs allowed in bar ~ Open 11.30-3, 5.30-11; 12-3, 7-10.30 Sun; closed Mon lunchtime ~ Bedrooms: £29.50S/£45S

CRICK SP5872 Map 4
Red Lion ◖ £

1 mile from M1 junction 18; A428

The very good value lunchtime menu at this pretty stone and thatched pub is so popular you may find customers waiting outside in eager anticipation of opening time. You can't help but be impressed by the prices and generous helpings: sandwiches (from £1.75), ploughman's (from £2.90), and straightforward hearty main courses such as chicken and mushroom pie, leek and smoky bacon bake, plaice or vegetable pancake rolls (all £4.10). Prices go up a little in the evening when they do a wider range of dishes, including wild mushroom lasagne (£6.50), stuffed salmon fillet (£7.25), roast duck (£12) and steaks (from £10), as well as puddings such as lemon meringue pie (from £2.20); Sunday roast (£4.50). Service is quick and friendly. The cosy low-ceilinged bar is relaxed and welcoming, with lots of comfortable seating, some rare old horsebrasses, pictures of the pub in the days before it was surrounded by industrial estates, and a tiny log stove in a big inglenook. The snug is no smoking. Four well kept changing beers on handpump might be Greene King Old Speckled Hen, Marstons Pedigree, Theakstons Best and Websters Yorkshire. There are a few picnic-sets under cocktail parasols on grass by the car park, and in summer you can eat on the terrace in the old coachyard, which is sheltered by a Perspex roof; lots of pretty hanging baskets. *(Recommended by Ian Phillips, G R Sharman, Steve Riches, W W Burke, Humphry and Angela Crum Ewing, Ted George, V Green, Darly Graton, Graeme Gulibert, Basil Minson, Wendy and Bob Needham, Roger and Pauline Pearce, Pat and Derek Roughton, F J Robinson, R T and JC Moggridge, B and M Kendall, George Atkinson, David and Ruth Shillitoe, Roger and Jenny Huggins, Nigel Williamson, Mr and Mrs J McRobert, Michael Cross, Keith Reeve, Marie Hammond)*

Wellington ~ Lease Tom and Paul Marks ~ Real ale ~ Bar food (till 9.30 Sat, not Sun evening) ~ (01788) 822342 ~ Children welcome lunchtimes only ~ Dogs welcome ~ Open 11-2.30, 6.15-11; 12-3, 7-10.30 Sun

EAST HADDON SP6668 Map 4
Red Lion ◖ ⇌

High Street; village signposted off A428 (turn right in village) and off A50 N of Northampton

Northamptonshire Dining Pub of the Year

This elegantly substantial golden stone hotel is one of the *Guide's* smarter entries. The neat lounge bar has some attractive antique furniture, including panelled oak settles, library chairs and a mix of oak, mahogany and cast-iron-framed tables. Little kegs, pewter, brass pots, swords and so forth are hung sparingly on a couple of beams, and there's attractive white-painted panelling with recessed china cabinets and old prints. Emphasis throughout is on dining, and though a meal here might be a little more expensive than elsewhere, the good food, generous helpings and excellent service make it worth that little bit extra. The seasonally changing menu might include soup (£3.50), sandwiches (£4), smoked trout and horseradish pâté (£8), vegetable bake or pie of the day (£10), smoked haddock strudel or coq au vin (£11), half a roast duckling with apple and ginger sauce (£13) and puddings, including gateaux from the trolley (£4.50). The pretty no smoking restaurant overlooking the garden has a more elaborate menu. They serve very well kept Adnams Broadside and Charles Wells Bombardier and Eagle, and perhaps a guest such as Greene King Old Speckled Hen on handpump, and decent wines; piped music. The walled side garden is pretty, with lilac, fruit trees, roses and neat flower beds, and leads back to the bigger lawn, which has well spaced picnic-sets. A small side terrace has more tables under cocktail parasols, and a big copper beech shades the gravel car park. *(Recommended by Gerry and Rosemary Dobson, Michael Dandy, Sarah Markham, Anthony Barnes, Alain and Rose Foote, R M Corlett, Tony Lauf, Dr Brian and Mrs Anne Hamilton, Maysie Thompson, W W Burke, Lady Heath, Maurice Ribbans, Geoffrey and Penny Hughes)*

Charles Wells ~ Lease Ian Kennedy ~ Real ale ~ Bar food (12-2, 7-9.30, not Sun evening) ~ Restaurant ~ (01604) 770223 ~ Children in eating area of bar and restaurant ~ Open 11-2.30, 6-11; 12-2.30, 7-10.30 Sun; closed 25 Dec ~ Bedrooms: £60S/£75S

FARTHINGSTONE SP6155 Map 4
Kings Arms 🍺

Off A5 SE of Daventry; village signposted from Litchborough on former B4525 (now declassified)

Do check the limited opening and food serving times below before you head out to visit this traditional old country pub. Built in the 18th c, its handsome gargoyled stone exterior is nicely weathered, and very pretty in summer, with lots of hanging baskets. The timelessly cosy little flagstoned bar has a huge log fire, comfortable homely sofas and armchairs near the entrance, whisky-water jugs hanging from oak beams, and lots of pictures and decorative plates on the walls. A games room at the far end has darts, dominoes, cribbage, table skittles and board games. Hook Norton is well kept on handpump alongside up to three guests such as Adnams, Robinsons and Timothy Taylors Landlord, the wine list is quite decent, and they have a few country wines. The tranquil terrace is charmingly decorated with flower and herb pots and plant-filled painted tractor tyres; the outside gents' has an interesting newspaper-influenced décor. When it comes to food a nice little touch here is the good choice of british cheeses that are listed on a board – you can have your choice served in a filled baguette (£2.80) or as a platter (£4.95). They've recently supplemented this with a few more dishes which are prepared using carefully sourced regional ingredients such as cumberland sausage and mash (£5.75), loch fyne smoked salmon and cheese (£5.95) and yorkshire pudding filled with wild argyll venison casserole (£6.35). If you weren't quite hungry enough to eat when you visited but fancy something for later they do retail quite a few of the things on their menu, including the cheeses, wines and olive oil. Also local crafts for sale. The village is picturesque, and there are good walks including the Knightley Way. *(Recommended by Pete Baker, George Atkinson)*

Free house ~ Licensees Paul and Denise Egerton ~ Real ale ~ Bar food (Sat/Sun lunchtime only) ~ No credit cards ~ (01327) 361604 ~ Children welcome ~ Dogs allowed in bar ~ Open 7-11; 12-3.30, 7-11(9-11 Sun) Sat; closed Mon and Weds, also lunchtime Mon-Fri

FOTHERINGHAY TL0593 Map 5
Falcon ★ 🍽 ♟

Village signposted off A605 on Peterborough side of Oundle

We like the way they keep their feet on the ground at this very civilised dining pub. It is smart and gently stylish, probably the sort of place you'd pick for a special occasion, but what they do here is done naturally, though with tremendous attention to detail. A very high standard is maintained as a matter of course rather than as anything to make a fuss about. So although the menu is very good it's in plain English, and the genuinely welcoming service will have you feeling just as welcome if you're here for a three-course meal or just a sandwich. The very well presented, inventive food from the seasonally changing bar menu is not cheap, but it's worth the money, particularly the very good two-course bargain lunch menu (£11, not Sunday), which might include onion bhaji with mint yoghurt and guacamole, fishcake with parsley sauce, and raspberry cheesecake with raspberry ripple ice cream. Other dishes include rosemary and garlic focaccia with warm olives (£2.50), pea and mint soup with crushed parma ham and crème fraîche

(£4.75), warm couscous and green bean salad with toasted goats cheese and salsa verde (£9.75), stir-fried gressingham duck with chinese vegetables, noodles and plum sauce (£12.75), and roast fillet steak with truffle oil mash, kale creamed mushrooms and thyme sauce (£19.50). The very decent children's menu might include salmon fillet, and they will do smaller helpings of most dishes. Quiet conversation fills the neatly kept bar, which is comfortable, with cushioned slatback armchairs and bucket chairs, good winter log fires in a stone fireplace, and fresh flower arrangements. The conservatory restaurant is pretty, and if the weather's nice the attractively planted garden is particularly enjoyable. The dining room and conservatory are no smoking. A very good range of drinks includes well kept Adnams and Greene King IPA on handpump, alongside a guest, usually from Nethergate or Potton, good wines with about 15 (including a champagne) by the glass, organic cordials, and fresh orange juice. Locals gather in the much smaller tap bar, which has darts. The vast church behind is worth a visit, and the ruins of Fotheringhay Castle, where Mary Queen of Scots was executed, are not far away. *(Recommended by Oliver and Sue Rowell, Mike and Sue Loseby, Alan and Gill Bull, Roger and Maureen Kenning, Maysie Thompson, Bob and Maggie Atherton, Miss Joan Morgan, R C Wiles, Lorraine and Fred Gill, David and Mary Webb, O K Smyth, Mr and Mrs J E C Tasker, Mrs Catherine Draper)*

Free house ~ Licensees Ray Smikle and John Hoskins ~ Real ale ~ Bar food (12-2.15, 6.30-9.30) ~ Restaurant ~ (01832) 226254 ~ Children welcome ~ Dogs allowed in bar ~ Open 12-3, 6-11(10.30 Sun)

GREAT OXENDON SP7383 Map 4

George ♀ 🛏

A508 S of Market Harborough

A great deal of care has gone into the furnishings and décor of this comfortable dining pub, from the welcoming lobby with its overstuffed chairs, former inn-sign, and lavatories entertainingly decked out with rather stylish naughty pictures, through the attractive prints and engravings in the two opened-together rooms of the main beamed bar, to the Portmeirion plates, and the turkey-carpeted no smoking conservatory overlooking the shrub-sheltered garden. The bar is cosy and clubby, with rather luxurious dark wallpaper, panelled dark brown dado, green leatherette bucket chairs around little tables, daily papers on poles, and a big log fire (with a nice club fender); there may be piped easy-listening classical music. They put quite an emphasis on the food, which is very popular with older lunchers (you might want to book), and includes soup (£3.35), filled rolls (from £4.50), pork and leek sausages and mash (£7.65), open steak sandwich (£7.95), beef and Guinness pie or smoked salmon and haddock fishcakes (£8.25), grilled haddock (£8.50), honey-roast lamb shank (£9.85), and puddings such as lemon tart or chocolate fruit and nut truffle cake (£3.35). The evening menu is slightly more elaborate. Well kept Adnams, Greene King Old Speckled Hen and a guest such as Bass on handpump, and around 10 wines by the glass. *(Recommended by Anthony Barnes, Bernie Adams, Jeff and Wendy Williams, Duncan Cloud, Gerry and Rosemary Dobson, Mr and Mrs D J Nash, G A Hemingway, David and Barbara Knott, Mrs J Purry)*

Free house ~ Licensee Allan Wiseman ~ Real ale ~ Bar food (12-2, 7-10) ~ Restaurant ~ (01858) 465205 ~ Children in eating area of bar and restaurant ~ Dogs allowed in bedrooms ~ Open 11.30(12 Sun)-3, 6.30-11; closed Sun evenings ~ Bedrooms: /£55.50B

Please keep sending us reports. We rely on readers for news of new discoveries, and particularly for news of changes – however slight – at the fully described pubs. No stamp needed: The Good Pub Guide, FREEPOST TN1569, Wadhurst, E Sussex TN5 7BR or send your report through our web site: www.goodguides.com

HARRINGWORTH SP9298 Map 4
White Swan 🍺

Seaton Road; village SE of Uppingham, signposted from A6003, A47 and A43

A daylight visit gives you the bonus of a proper look at the attractive exterior of this imposing limestone Tudor inn, with its striking gable and arched window lights. Look carefully and you can also make out the blocked-in traces of its former carriage-entry. There's plenty of exposed stone inside, too. The neatly kept central bar area has good solid tables, a hand-crafted oak counter with a mirror base and an attractive swan carving, an open fire, pictures relating to the World War II Spanhoe airfield nearby, among a collection of old village photographs (in which many of the present buildings are still recognisable), and well kept Fullers London Pride, Greene King IPA and Timothy Taylors Landlord on handpump; darts and piped music. The roomy and welcoming lounge/eating area has comfortable settles, while a quieter no smoking dining room has a collection of old jugs, craft tools, dried flower arrangements and locally painted watercolours. Beautifully presented and imaginative bar food includes sandwiches (from £3.25), cream of broccoli and stilton soup (£3.95), hot baguettes (from £4), chicken liver and black olive pâté (£3.95), seafood and leek risotto (£4.95), basil and tomato tagliatelle or venison sausages, bubble and squeak and onion gravy (£8.95), roast chicken breast with tarragon sauce (£9.95), braised lamb shank with red wine and rosemary sauce (£10.95) and puddings such as strawberry jam sponge pudding and hot chocolate brownies (£4.25); good Sunday lunch. There are tables out on a little terrace. This pretty village is famous for its magnificent 82-arch railway viaduct, and Rockingham race track is just 4 miles away. *(Recommended by Lorraine and Fred Gill, Norma and Keith Bloomfield, Mike and Sue Loseby, David and Mary Webb)*

Free house ~ Licensees Stephen and Lara Hobbs ~ Real ale ~ Bar food ~ Restaurant ~ (01572) 747543 ~ Children in restaurant ~ Open 11.30-2.30, 6.30-11; 12-3, 7-10.30 Sun ~ Bedrooms: £45S/£65S

KILSBY SP5671 Map 4
George

2½ miles from M1 junction 18: A428 towards Daventry, left on to A5 – look out for pub off on right at roundabout

Keeping things simple but really good, the hard-working hands-on landlady at this substantial pub extends a heartwarmingly hospitable welcome to all, making it a relaxing refuge from the motorway. One of the highlights here is the very good value wholesome bar food – you will have to book if you go for Sunday lunch (£5.95). The rest of the week, the lighter lunch menu includes sandwiches (£2), soup (£3), filled baguettes (from £3.75) and ploughman's (£5.50), while the evening menu is less snacky with dishes such as battered cod (£5.90), steak and kidney pudding (£6.90) and puddings such as chocolate fudge cake or a particularly good home-made bread and butter pudding (£2.50). Well kept Bass, Greene King IPA and Abbot and a guest such as Hook Norton Old Hooky on handpump, a splendid range of malt whiskies in generous measures, and decent wines in big glasses. A high-ceilinged bar on the right, with plush banquettes, dark panelling, a coal-effect gas stove and a big bay window, opens on the left into a cheerful and attractive dining area with solidly comfortable furnishings. A long brightly decorated back public bar has a juke box, darts, a good pool table, fruit machine, table football and a huge TV. There are wood and metal picnic-sets out in the back garden, by the car park. *(Recommended by Ian Phillips, Roger and Jenny Huggins, George Atkinson, Ted George, Mr and Mrs J Williams)*

Punch ~ Lease Maggie Chandler ~ Real ale ~ Bar food (12-2.30(3 Sat), 6.30-9; not Sun evening) ~ Restaurant ~ (01788) 822229 ~ Children in eating area of bar ~ Dogs allowed in bar ~ Live music first and third Sat in month, quiz Sun ~ Open 11.30-3, 5.30-11; 12-10.30 Sun ~ Bedrooms: £30/£50

KINGS SUTTON SP4936 Map 4
White Horse ♀

The Square

In a lovely setting beside the village green and its striking church, this attractive village pub has been stylishly modernised under its current licensees, who are also gaining quite a reputation for good fresh food. With beams, timbers and some exposed brickwork around the fireplace, the knocked-through front rooms still have a traditional feel, but with a definite contemporary twist; the walls and ceilings are painted cream, there are light wooden floors and chunky tables, spotlights and other modern lighting, the occasional rug, and some excellent pictures, offering a modish take on the usual country scenes. Ducks drawn on some of the low beams remind you what to do as you approach. At the back are two no smoking rooms for eating in, both with flagstoned floors and substantial wooden tables with thick candles and perhaps a reserved sign; the red room on the right has high rafters and an old stove. An inspection visit confirmed the high praise readers have given the food in recent months: snacks like hand-cut chips (£1.75) and a ramekin of cocktail sausages or spiced green olives with chilli, thyme and cumin (£1.95), a choice of soups from cream of mushroom (£3.95) to rocket and potato with truffle cream (£4.25), lunchtime sandwiches and ciabattas (from £4.25), seared calves liver with mash and onion jus or home-ground beef burger (£6.95), tagliatelle with fried vegetables and pesto rosso sauce (£7.95), more elaborate dishes such as rump of lamb with buttered spinach and fondant potato (£13.50) or fried bass fillet with creamed potato and chive velouté (£13.95), and home-made puddings such as Pimms jelly with lavender ice cream or coffee crème brûlée (£4.50). Service is obliging and attentive; piped music. Three well kept changing real ales such as Shepherd Neame Spitfire and Theakstons XB on handpump, and a carefully chosen wine list with around 10 by the glass; good coffees. Picnic-sets in front overlook the green. *(Recommended by B H and J I Andrews)*

Free house ~ Licensee Craig Williamson ~ Real ale ~ Bar food ~ Restaurant ~ (01295) 810843 ~ Children welcome ~ Dogs welcome ~ Open 12-3, 6-11; 12-10.30 Sun

NETHER HEYFORD SP6558 Map 4
Old Sun ◀ £

1¾ miles from M1 junction 16: village signposted left off A45 westbound; Middle Street

The family who run this mainly 18th-c golden stone pub are welcoming and chatty, and have filled it with a mass of enjoyable and sparklingly kept bric-a-brac. The old cash till is stuck at one and a ha'penny; OK, so your pint and meal won't be that cheap, but the prices here are very reasonable. Wholesome lunchtime bar food includes sandwiches (£2.75) and hot steak roll, lamb casserole or chicken in creamy sauce (£3.95). In the evening, food is served by waitresses at one end of the pub and in the restaurant only, and the menu is a little pricier: steak pie (£7.95), cod and peas (£8.25), ricotta cannelloni with spinach and goats cheese (£8.50), and daily specials. Nooks and crannies in the several small linked rooms are packed with all sorts of curiosities, especially gleaming brassware (one fireplace is a veritable grotto of large brass animals), but lots more too, such as colourful relief plates, 1930s cigarette cards, railway memorabilia and advertising signs, World War II posters and rope fancywork. There are beams and low ceilings (one painted with a fine sunburst), partly glazed dividing panels, steps between some areas, rugs on parquet, red tiles or flagstones, a big inglenook log fire – and up on the left a room with full-sized hood skittles, a fruit machine, darts, TV, table skittles, cribbage, dominoes and sports TV. Furnishings are mostly properly pubby, with the odd easy chair; piped music. Well kept Banks's, Greene King Ruddles, Marstons Pedigree and a weekend guest such as Brakspears are served on handpump from two counters. A fairy-lit front terrace has picnic-sets behind a line of blue-painted grain kibblers and other antiquated hand-operated farm machines, some with plants in their hoppers. *(Recommended by George Atkinson, Gerry and Rosemary Dobson, CMW, JJW, Ian Phillips, B and M Kendall)*

Free house ~ Licensees Geoffrey and James Allen ~ Real ale ~ Bar food (12-2.30, 7-9.30; not Sun/Mon evening) ~ Restaurant ~ (01327) 340164 ~ Children welcome ~ Open 12-3(5 Sat), 6-11; 12-5, 7-10.30 Sun

OUNDLE TL0487 Map 5
Mill

Barnwell Road out of town, off South Road; or follow Barnwell Country Park signs off A605 bypass

On the banks of the River Nene, this mill was fully working and milling flour until 1947 – it's the great setting and the novelty of the building (and the good friendly welcome) that earn it a main entry. There are records of a mill on this site well before the Domesday Book, and the waterwheel of the present building dates partly from the early 17th c. It's been well restored, and you can watch the stream race below the building through a big glass panel by the entrance. A ground-floor bar (open all day in summer, but evening and weekends only in the winter) has red leatherette button-back built-in wall banquettes against its thick stripped-stone walls, and views of boats navigating the lock on the river. They serve bar food in the upstairs Trattoria, which has stalls around tables with more banquettes in bays, stripped masonry and beams, another mill race feature, small windows which look down over the lower millpond and river. In summer they open up the terrace, which has the same views. Up in the roof, the granary restaurant has high ceilings and beams; both restaurants are no smoking; piped music. Straightforward food includes quite a few tex-mex dishes such as nachos (£9.95) or hickory ribs (£9.55), as well as soup (£2.95), calamari (£4.55), lasagne or fish and chips (£7.95), smoked haddock fishcakes or steak, ale and mushroom pie (£8.95), and indonesian halibut (£13.95). Well kept Theakstons and a couple of guests on handpump such as Courage Directors and Nethergate Summer Breeze, and they do quite a few liqueur coffees. There are picnic-sets under cocktail parasols on a bricked area in front, and on a grassy area at the side. More reports please. *(Recommended by H W Roberts, Michael Tack)*

Free house ~ Licensees Neil Stewart and Peter Bossard ~ Real ale ~ Bar food (12-2, 6.30-9(9.30 Sat)) ~ Restaurant ~ (01832) 272621 ~ Children welcome ~ Open 12-3, 6.30-11(10.30 Sun)

Ship

West Street

The well used interior of this relaxed local is testimony to its thriving communal character – particularly evident on nights when a DJ is in. It's a nice old building, brought to life by its cheery bustling but relaxed atmosphere, and friendly smiling service. The heavily beamed lounge bar is made up of three rooms that lead off the central corridor, one of them no smoking at lunchtime. Up by the street there's a mix of leather and other seats, with sturdy tables and a log fire in a stone inglenook, and down one end a charming little panelled snug has button-back leather seats built in around it. The wood-floored public side has darts, dominoes, fruit machine and a juke box. Changing beers might include well kept Adnams Broadside, Bass, Hop Back Summer Lightning, Oakham JHB and possibly a guest on handpump, as well as a good range of malt whiskies (and cocktail specials on some evenings). Bar food includes soup (£3), sandwiches (from £3.50), chicken liver pâté (£4), ham and egg (£5.50), steak and ale pie (£6), and lunchtime specials such as barnsley lamb chop or home-made seafood pie (£6); puddings might include raspberry meringue or home-made fruit crumble (£3). The wooden tables and chairs out on the series of small sheltered terraces are lit at night. *(Recommended by Rona Murdoch, George Atkinson, Tom and Ruth Rees)*

Free house ~ Licensees Andrew and Robert Langridge ~ Real ale ~ Bar food (till 3 Sun) ~ (01832) 273918 ~ Children in eating area of bar and restaurant ~ Dogs welcome ~ Jazz last Sun in month and DJs Weds, Fri, Sat evenings ~ Open 11-11; 12-10.30 Sun; closed 25 Dec evening ~ Bedrooms: £25(£30S)(£40B)/£40(£50B)

SULGRAVE SP5545 Map 4

Star 🍺

E of Banbury, signposted off B4525; Manor Road

Things are going very well at this lovely old creeper-covered stone-built inn, with the bar food on particularly good form. From a seasonally changing menu you could expect dishes such as roast tomato and fennel soup with grilled goats cheese crouton (£3.95), warm squid salad (£5.95), scotch beef burger (£6.95), salmon, leek and bacon fishcakes (£8.95), pork chop with pineapple and mustard seed salsa and sweet potato chips (£9.50), grilled tuna with niçoise salad (£12.50), leg of lamb for two (£24), and home-made puddings such as caramelised apple tart or panna cotta with blueberries and almond biscuits (£3.95). Their Sunday roast (£8.50) is very popular; no smoking back restaurant. The beamed farmhouse-style interior is furnished with small pews, cushioned window seats and wall benches, kitchen chairs and cast-iron-framed tables, with polished flagstones in an area by the big inglenook fireplace, and red carpet elsewhere. Look out for the stuffed back end of a fox, seeming to leap into the wall; or you can browse memorable framed newspaper front pages, recording events such as Kennedy's assassination and the death of Churchill; alley skittles, Jenga, cribbage and dominoes. Well kept Hook Norton Best, Old Hooky, a Hook Norton seasonal beer and a monthly changing guest such as Fullers London Pride on handpump. In summer you can eat outside at wooden tables under a vine-covered trellis, and there are benches in the front and back gardens. The pub is a short walk from the ancestral home of George Washington, and is handy for Silverstone. *(Recommended by J D M Rushworth, R T and J C Moggridge, Mrs J Poole, Morris Bagnall, Malcolm Taylor, Mrs A Cardwell, Patrick Hancock, Comus and Sarah Elliott, Rona Murdoch, Joy and Colin Rorke)*

Hook Norton ~ Tenants Jamie and Charlotte King ~ Real ale ~ Bar food (12-2, 6.30-9; 12.30-3 Sun; not Sun evening, Mon (exc bank hols)) ~ Restaurant ~ (01295) 760389 ~ Children in restaurant ~ Open 11-2.30, 6-11; 12-5 Sun; closed 25 Dec evening, 26 Dec ~ Bedrooms: £40S/£65S

WOODNEWTON TL0394 Map 5

White Swan £

Main Street; back roads N of Oundle, easily reached from A1/A47 (via Nassington) and A605 (via Fotheringhay)

It's quite possible that the very helpful landlord at this friendly pub picked Otter Bright as his guest beer because he's such an otter lover – you will see lots of otter prints dotted around; the house beers are well kept Adnams, Batemans 12 Bore and Marstons Pedigree. Hidden behind an unremarkable frontage is a surprisingly capacious and spotlessly kept interior, where the main focus is on the pleasantly simple no smoking dining area. The other end has a woodburner, space for drinkers, and perhaps local radio. Straightforward but very nicely presented, and very good value bar food includes soup (£3), smoked mackerel (£3.50), ploughman's (£4.50), lasagne (£6.50), steak and ale pie (£7.50), and puddings such as chocolate fudge cake (£3). On Friday night they serve only fish and chips (£5.50); service is cheerfully unruffled. The back lawn has tables and a boules pitch (league matches Tuesday evenings). *(Recommended by George Atkinson, David and Mary Webb, Rona Murdoch)*

Free house ~ Licensees Susan and David Hydon ~ Real ale ~ Bar food (12-1.45(2.30 Sun), 7(6 Fri, 6.30 Sat)-9) ~ Restaurant ~ (01780) 470381 ~ Open 12-2, 7(6 Fri)-11; 12-2.30, 6.30-11 Sat; 12-3 Sun; closed Sun evening, Mon

---

'Children welcome' means the pub says it lets children inside without any special restriction. If it allows them in, but to restricted areas such as an eating area or family room, we specify this. Some pubs may impose an evening time limit.

Lucky Dip

Besides the fully inspected pubs, you might like to try these Lucky Dips recommended to us and described by readers (if you do, please send us reports: www.goodguides.com).

ABTHORPE [SP6446]
New Inn [signed from A43 at 1st roundabout S of A5; Silver St]: Tucked-away partly thatched real country local, rambling dim-lit bars, beams, stripped stone, inglenook log fire, masses of pictures and old family photographs, attractively priced home cooking from sandwiches to Sun lunch, well kept Hook Norton, good choice of malt whiskies, hospitable landlord; nice big garden with goldfish, rabbits and aviary, quiet village (*BB, CMW, JJW*)

ASHBY ST LEDGERS [SP5768]
☆ *Olde Coach House* [off A361]: Rambling softly lit rooms with high-backed winged settles on polished black and red tiles, lots of atmosphere, old kitchen tables, harness and hunting pictures, big log fire, half a dozen or so changing ales inc unusual ones, good choice of decent wines (generous measures), generally good service, wide food choice, front games room; big-screen TV, piped music; tables out among fruit trees and under a fairy-lit arbour, barbecues, play area, interesting church nearby – see the skeleton; children welcome, disabled access, comfortable bedrooms, open all day in summer (*Wendy and Bob Needham, LYM, M J Caley, Bruce Bird, Alain and Rose Foote, Howard and Margaret Buchanan, Patrick Hancock, Susan and John Douglas, Rob and Catherine Dunster, Keith Jacob, Ian Phillips*)

ASHTON [SP7649]
☆ *Old Crown* [the one off A508 S of M1 junction 15]: 18th-c beamed stone-built pub recently refurbished for dining, rather upmarket choice, roomy no smoking area, Charles Wells Eagle and Bombardier with a guest such as Everards Tiger, good wines, notably courteous and attentive staff; tables out on lawn (*George Atkinson, Alan Sutton, Gerry and Rosemary Dobson*)

AYNHO [SP5133]
☆ *Great Western Arms* [B4031 W, towards Deddington]: Unpretentious welcoming creeper-covered pub by what used to be station on main Oxford—Banbury rail line, good generous cheap food in roomy informal dining areas, clubby lounge with log fire, well kept Hook Norton Bitter and Mild, pleasant staff, interesting GWR memorabilia inc lots of steam locomotive photographs; small games area with darts and bar billiards, children's room; enclosed garden by Oxford Canal with moorings, flower-decked back courtyard (*Pete Baker*)

BARNWELL [TL0484]
☆ *Montagu Arms* [off A605 S of Oundle, then fork right at Thurning, Hemington sign]: Attractive unspoilt stone-built pub in pleasant streamside village, two bars with low beams, flagstones or tile and brick floors, not smart but warm, cosy and

welcoming; good interesting food running up to swordfish, hearty helpings, well kept Adnams Bitter and Broadside, Flowers IPA and a guest beer, decent wines, helpful cheerful staff, log fire, neat back dining room; games room off yard, big garden with good well equipped play area, barbecue and camping; open all day wknd, comfortable bedrooms in separate block (*George Atkinson, Rita Horridge, G A Hemingway, BB, Oliver and Sue Rowell*)

BLISWORTH [SP7253]
Royal Oak [off M1 junction 15, off A508; Chapel Lane/High St]: 17th-c thatched and beamed open-plan stone-built pub, carpeted no smoking dining areas off tiled bar, enjoyable home-made usual food (not Mon) from sandwiches up, also take-aways, well kept Adnams Broadside, Flowers, Hook Norton, Charles Wells Bombardier and a guest beer, winter mulled wine, good soft drinks choice, hospitable licensees, lots of wood (and steps), games room with darts, pool, skittles and juke box; no dogs; big garden with play area, nr Grand Union canal, open all day Fri-Sun (*Kevin Thorpe, CMW, JJW*)

BOUGHTON [SP7565]
Whyte-Melville [off A508 N of Northampton; Church St]: Reasonably priced food from good open sandwiches and baked potatoes up, three or four real ales such as Greene King IPA and Morlands Original, bare boards and carpeting, blazing coal fire, beams, lots of brasses and Victorian pictures, friendly attentive service, piped music; spacious, but can get very busy lunchtime (*George Atkinson*)

BRACKLEY HATCH [SP6441]
Green Man [A43 NE of Brackley]: Large Chef & Brewer dining pub on busy dual carriageway nr Silverstone, comfortable beamed lounge area and conservatory, big no smoking family restaurant, wide range of food all day from baguettes and baked potatoes up, relaxed atmosphere, quick, friendly and helpful service, Courage beers, good wines, log fires; tables on lawn, bedrooms in Premier Lodge behind, open all day (*JHBS, Mr and Mrs G S Ayrton, BB*)

BRAUNSTON [SP5465]
Admiral Nelson [Dark Lane, Little Braunston, overlooking Lock 3 just N of canal tunnel]: New licensees doing well in friendly and popular 18th-c ex-farmhouse in peaceful setting by Grand Union Canal Lock 3 and hump bridge, with pleasant waterside garden over bridge; tiled floors in bar and lounge, well kept Courage Directors and John Smiths, good cheery service, enjoyable food with interesting as well as basic dishes, restaurant, games room with skittles; bedroom overlooking lock, towpath walks (*Mike Roberts*)

BRIXWORTH [SP7470]
Coach & Horses [Harborough Rd, just off
A508 N of Northampton]: Welcoming
17th-c stone-built inn nr Pitsford Water,
good helpful staff, generous and enjoyable if
not cheap food from wide choice of good
sandwiches to fresh fish and popular Sun
lunches, well kept ales such as Adnams,
Frankton Bagby Old Chestnut and Marstons
Pedigree, decent house wines, friendly
helpful service, beams and lots of pictures,
small no smoking restaurant; piped music;
children welcome, attractive village with
famous Saxon church (*Gordon Neighbour,
CMW, JJW, George Atkinson, Gerry and
Rosemary Dobson*)
BUCKBY WHARF [SP6066]
☆ *New Inn* [A5 N of Weedon]: Simple 17th-c
pub with picnic-sets out on terrace
by busy Grand Union Canal lock, several
rooms radiating from central servery, inc
small dining room with nice fire, big-screen
TV in back room, parakeets; good range of
decent sensibly priced food from baguettes
and baked potatoes up, Greene King IPA
and Old Speckled Hen and Marstons
Pedigree, friendly licensees and attentive
young staff; live music Sat, quiz Sun, open
all day (*LYM, George Atkinson, CMW,
JJW*)
BUGBROOKE [SP6757]
Five Bells [Church Lane]: Cheerful recently
refurbished pub in attractive village, some
stripped brick in comfortable low-ceilinged
areas off bar, one no smoking, sensibly
priced usual food inc Sun roasts, three real
ales, coal-effect gas fire; pool in games area;
disabled access, children welcome, garden
with play area, open all day wknds (*CMW,
JJW*)
☆ *Wharf Inn* [The Wharf; off A5 S of
Weedon]: Spotless pub in super spot by
canal, plenty of tables on big lawn with
moorings and summer boat trips; emphasis
on big water-view restaurant, also bar and
lounge with pleasant informal small raised
eating area on either side, lots of stripped
brickwork, good choice of generous food
from good value baguettes up, four or five
well kept ales inc Courage Best, Greene King
Old Speckled Hen and local Frog Island,
farm cider, speedy friendly service, nice fire;
weekly quiz and music night; children very
welcome, garden with boules
(*George Atkinson, Hilary Edwards, BB*)
BULWICK [SP9694]
☆ *Queens Head* [just off A43 Kettering—
Duddington]: 17th-c stone-built pub with
shortish changing choice of good interesting
fresh food from sandwiches and unusual
starters or snacks to popular Sun roasts and
imaginative puddings in neat and
unpretentious partly beamed two-room bar
or restaurant, small fire each end, friendly
service, well kept ales such as Adnams,
Fullers London Pride, Greene King,
Hancocks HB and Marstons Pedigree, good
wine choice; live folk music Mon, when

menu may be limited; nice garden, attractive
village, interesting church, red kites often
seen nearby (*Anthony Barnes, BB, JWAC,
Lorraine and Fred Gill, John, Gwen and
Reg*)
CASTLE ASHBY [SP8659]
☆ *Falcon*: Smart hotel in attractive preserved
village, nice log fire in small lounge, 16th-c
cellar bar (not always open, down tricky
steps) with stone walls and hop-hung dark
beams, limited choice of enjoyable bar food
inc imaginative sandwiches, welcoming
landlord and helpful service, Greene King
IPA and Ruddles County; restaurant
overlooking pretty gardens, nicely decorated
bedrooms in nearby cottages, good
breakfast (*Colin and Janet Roe,
George Atkinson, Michael Dandy*)
CHACOMBE [SP4943]
☆ *George & Dragon* [2½ miles from M40
junction 11: A361 towards Daventry, then
village signposted on right; Silver Street]:
Peaceful respite from M40, beams,
flagstones and log fire in massive fireplace,
Courage Directors, Theakstons Best and
perhaps a guest beer, wide (though not
cheap) range of food from a fortnightly
changing menu, sandwiches all afternoon,
Sun roast, no smoking area in restaurant;
darts, dominoes, TV and piped music;
children in eating areas, bedrooms, open all
day (*Bob and Laura Brock, Howard and
Margaret Buchanan, Rod Stoneman,
Bob and Maggie Atherton, Martin and
Karen Wake, John Robertson, Jim Bush,
Comus and Sarah Elliott*)
CHAPEL BRAMPTON [SP7266]
Windhover [A5199/Pitsford Rd]: Large well
done newly opened Vintage Inn on site of
former cold store, Bass and Tetleys, good
choice of wines and soft drinks, food all day
inc lunchtime sandwiches, log fire; piped
music; picnic-sets on terrace, pleasant
Brampton Valley Way walks (*CMW, JJW*)
CLAY COTON [SP5976]
Fox [off B5414 nr Stanford Hall]: Popular,
friendly and relaxed, tucked away in small
village, with two log fires, interesting choice
of well kept ales, summer farm cider, nice
range of reasonably priced well prepared
generous food inc good sandwiches in dining
area; simple but comfortable furnishings,
pleasant garden, dogs and cats, chatty
licensees, occasional piped music – landlord
chooses by clientele; skittle alley
(*Mike Roberts*)
CLIPSTON [SP7181]
Old Red Lion [The Green]: Quiet brightly lit
lounge bar with log fire, wide choice of
blackboard food and back dining tables,
well kept Charles Wells Eagle and
Bombardier and a guest beer, welcoming
staff, locals' bar on left with skittles; piped
music (*Rona Murdoch*)
CRANFORD ST JOHN [SP9276]
Red Lion [3 miles E of Kettering just off
A14; High St]: Attractive two-bar stone-built
pub with good value food inc children's

meals, wider evening choice and Sun lunch, three real ales inc Marstons Pedigree; piped music; pleasant small garden with play area, quiet village, nearby walks *(Eric Locker)*

CULWORTH [SP5447]

Red Lion [off B4525 NE of Banbury]: Done-up 17th-c pub with good value straightforward food and well kept Marstons Pedigree, lots of highly polished brassware in cosy and comfortable well heated lounge *(R M Corlett)*

ECTON [SP8263]

Worlds End [A4500 Northampton—Wellingborough]: Extended 17th-c pub, part of a small group, with two or three real ales, good choice of other drinks, reasonably priced food inc children's; piped music; garden with terrace and play area *(CMW, JJW)*

EYDON [SP5450]

☆ *Royal Oak* [Lime Ave; village signed off A361 Daventry—Banbury, and from B4525]: Old-fashioned extended late 17th-c local, several rooms with stripped stone and assorted old furnishings on polished flagstones, thriving informal atmosphere, enjoyable food (not Sun evening or Mon), Hook Norton Best, Theakstons Black Bull and Timothy Taylors Landlord, friendly young South African staff, inglenook log fire, daily papers, games room with darts, hood skittles and TV; piped music may be rather loud; children welcome, tables out in partly covered back courtyard, picnic-sets in front *(Alan Sutton, CMW, JJW, Lady Heath, LYM, Michael Jones, George Atkinson)*

FARTHINGHOE [SP5339]

Fox [just off A422 Brackley—Banbury; Baker St]: Quiet village local with stone fireplace, floors part tiled and part carpet, big helpings of enjoyable food from good baguettes up, friendly licensee happy to do smaller ones for elderly, Charles Wells ales; garden *(Hugh Spottiswoode)*

GAYTON [SP7054]

Queen Victoria [High St]: Spotless and comfortable village pub, several areas off central bar, light panelling, beams, lots of pictures, books and woodburner, no smoking dining area, decent food from baguettes up, Charles Wells Bombardier and a guest such as Badger, good wine choice, attentive friendly staff; piped music *(LYM, George Atkinson)*

GRAFTON REGIS [SP7546]

☆ *White Hart* [A508 S of Northampton]: Thatched pub in thatched village, several linked rooms, good home-made bar food (not Sun evening) inc lots of splendid winter soups, also bookings-only restaurant with open fire – very popular for flamboyant chef's good imaginative cooking; well kept Greene King IPA and Abbot, many decent wines by the glass, friendly hard-working helpful staff, pensive african grey parrot; piped music; good-sized garden (food not served there), cl Mon exc bank hols *(George Atkinson, BB)*

GREAT BILLING [SP8162]

Elwes Arms [High St]: Thatched stone-built 16th-c village pub, two bars and pleasant no smoking dining room, wide choice of good value fresh food inc tempting Sun lunch, three well kept real ales; may be piped music, Thurs and Sat quiz nights, no dogs; children welcome, wheelchair access to top level, garden with play area *(CMW, JJW)*

GREAT BRINGTON [SP6664]

☆ *Fox & Hounds/Althorp Coaching Inn* [off A428 NW of Northampton, nr Althorp Hall]: Charming thatched stone-built pub with fine log fires in quaint low-beamed flagstoned bar with lots of atmosphere and bric-a-brac, several interesting changing ales, decent wines, wide choice of traditional and mediterranean food, friendly service, small restaurant with no smoking area; children welcome, open all day wknds and summer, tables in attractive courtyard and side garden with play area, nice setting *(Gerry and Rosemary Dobson, James Beeby, Rob and Catherine Dunster, Peter and Giff Bennett, Mrs I Jones, LYM)*

GREAT HOUGHTON [SP7959]

Old Cherry Tree [Cherry Tree Lane; a No Through Road off A428 just before the White Hart]: Early 19th-c, several rooms, stripped stone, low beams and dark panelling, wide range of good value food from sandwiches, baguettes and baked potatoes up, well kept Charles Wells Eagle and Bombardier, friendly service, open fire, no smoking area; piped music, no dogs; picnic-sets in good back garden, quiet village spot *(George Atkinson)*

GREAT OAKLEY [SP8685]

Spread Eagle [Oakley Hay; loop off A6014 S of Corby]: Large former coaching inn open all day for reasonably priced food inc bargain meals and carvery, three real ales, wine offers; children welcome away from bar, large garden with play area *(CMW, JJW)*

GREATWORTH [SP5542]

Inn [Chapel Rd, off B4525]: Partly 16th-c village pub, several blackboards of food, four or five real ales, inglenook log fire, two linked areas and small no smoking family dining room; cl Mon/Tues lunchtimes *(CMW, JJW)*

GREENS NORTON [SP6649]

Butchers Arms [High St]: Large comfortably refurbished lounge, four well kept changing ales, some emphasis on wide choice of good value food from sandwiches up, welcoming service; separate bar, games room with darts, pool, machines and TV, piped pop music; disabled access, picnic-sets out in front, pretty village nr Grafton Way walks *(Edward Leetham, R M Corlett)*

HARDINGSTONE [SP7657]

Sun [High St]: Busy open-plan pub with real ales such as Courage Directors, Theakstons and Youngers, wide food choice, some 18th-c beams and stripped stone; piped music, games machine, TV, no dogs;

children welcome, barn bar/function room, tables on attractive heated back terrace with play area *(CMW, JJW)*

HARLESTONE [SP7064]

☆ *Dusty Fox* [A428, Lower Harlestone]: Nicely redone Vintage Inn, relaxed atmosphere, small front bar and lounge, pleasant furnishings, hops on beams, local photographs, mainly no smoking dining area and conservatory-style barn; enjoyable food all day from separate servery, some nouvelle-ish dishes, Bass and Tetleys, decent wines, friendly speedy highly attentive service, two log fires, no piped music; children welcome, some tables in nice garden, open all day *(David Blackburn, CMW, JJW, George Atkinson, David and Julie Glover, Michael Dandy)*

HARRINGTON [SP7779]

☆ *Tollemache Arms* [High St; off A508 S of Mkt Harboro']: Pretty thatched Tudor pub in lovely quiet ironstone village, very low ceilings in compact red-ceilinged bar with log fire and cask seats and in pleasant partly stripped stone no smoking eating area with books and bric-a-brac, wide food choice from sandwiches and baguettes up, well kept Charles Wells Eagle and Bombardier with two changing guest beers, cheap house wines, friendly staff, lively locals, candlelit restaurant; may be piped music; children welcome, small back garden with country views, attractive and comfortable bedrooms in converted barns, good breakfast *(Mr and Mrs Peter Cazalet, Glenn Foard, George Atkinson, BB, Gerry and Rosemary Dobson)*

HELLIDON [SP5158]

☆ *Red Lion* [Stockwell Lane, off A425 W of Daventry]: Good popular Tues/Weds OAP lunch in small wisteria-covered inn, wide choice of other good value food too inc some interesting dishes, softly lit no smoking low-ceilinged stripped stone dining area with lots of hunting prints, well kept Bass, Greene King IPA and Hook Norton Best, two farm ciders, very helpful cheerful staff, cosy and comfortable lounge, two friendly labradors by woodburner in bar, hood skittles, separate pool room; picnic-sets in front, beautiful setting by green of unspoilt village, good bedrooms, windmill vineyard and pleasant walks nearby *(George Atkinson, CMW, JJW, P Tailyour, J J and B Dix, Di and Mike Gillam)*

ISLIP [SP9878]

☆ *Woolpack* [Kettering Rd, just off A14, by bridge into Thrapston]: Old inn refurbished in attractive contemporary style, small smartish front bar with beams and stripped stone, comfortable armchairs, Greene King ales inc Old Speckled Hen and perhaps a guest, lots of wine by the glass, good coffee, broad steps up to sofas and big popular brasserie dining area, partly no smoking, with wide food choice inc daily fresh fish and pizzas from wood-fired oven, friendly young uniformed staff, bold orange modern

prints, separate bar counter, games room; piped music; children welcome (high chairs), picnic-sets in small garden and on front terrace, simple bedrooms in chalet block behind, Nene Way Walks *(CMW, JJW, Peter Scillitoe, BB)*

KISLINGBURY [SP6959]

Old Red Lion [High St, off A45 W of Northampton]: Wide choice of enjoyable fresh food from snacks to game and fresh fish, Tues/Thurs OAP lunch, well kept Fullers London Pride and Greene King IPA, good choice of other drinks, beamed lounge/restaurant (lower part no smoking) and games room; may be loud piped music; picnic-sets on suntrap back terrace with swings and slide *(George Atkinson, David Robinson)*

Sun [off A45 W of Northampton; Mill Rd]: Thatched stone-built village pub, four small cosy linked rooms with beams, lots of brasses and pictures, three real ales, low-priced generous food (not Sun evening or Weds), real and gas fire, charity book swap; games machine, quiet piped local radio, no dogs; back terrace and small suntrap front garden with waterfall and fish pond, barbecues, river walks nearby *(CMW, JJW)*

LITTLE BRINGTON [SP6663]

☆ *Old Saracens Head* [4½ miles from M1 junction 16, first right off A45 to Daventry; also signed off A428; Main St]: Appealingly individual pub doing well under new management, roomy U-shaped lounge with good log fire, flagstones, alcoves and lots of old prints, no smoking in book-lined eating room off and extended restaurant, enjoyable food from tasty baguettes to full meals with plenty of choice and interesting dishes, well kept Fullers London Pride, Greene King IPA and Timothy Taylors Landlord, telephone in genuine red kiosk; tables in neat back garden, handy for Althorp House and Holdenby House *(BB, Gerry and Rosemary Dobson, R M Corlett)*

LODDINGTON [SP8178]

Hare [Main St]: Emphasis on wide choice of enjoyable good value food inc game specialities in two eating areas, one no smoking; small bar with well kept Adnams, Greene King IPA and Fullers London Pride or Youngs Special, decent house wines *(Stephen, Julie and Hayley Brown, Gerry and Rosemary Dobson)*

LOWICK [SP9780]

☆ *Snooty Fox* [signed off A6116 Corby—Raunds]: Attractive and interesting two-room lounge with handsome 16th-c beams, log fire in huge stone fireplace, neat dining tables, enjoyable food from well filled baguettes up, Banks's Bitter and Original and Marstons Pedigree, helpful service, restaurant; piped music, live Fri, Mon quiz night; children welcome, disabled access, floodlit picnic-sets out on front lawn *(Michael and Jenny Back, Richard Till, LYM, Fiona McElhone)*

MAIDWELL [SP7477]

☆ *Stags Head* [A508 Northampton—Mkt Harboro]: Nice pubby atmosphere in small comfortable beamed front bar with log fire and well kept Fullers London Pride, Greene King and Hook Norton Best, friendly and very attentive service, well chosen pictures, emphasis on food in three attractively light and airy further sections – two no smoking; tables on back lawn with paddock beyond, bedrooms (*Stephen, Julie and Hayley Brown, George Atkinson, P Tailyour*)

MEARS ASHBY [SP8466]

☆ *Griffins Head* [Wilby Rd]: Pleasantly refurbished country pub very popular for substantial OAP bargain wkdy lunches, also bargain midweek suppers and other enjoyable food from sandwiches to good value Sun roasts; smart front lounge, small dining room with no smoking area, cosy back locals' bar, attractive views and hunting prints, log fire in huge fireplace, friendly courteous service, five well kept ales; games room with darts, skittles and machine, piped music; children welcome, seats out in small garden, on edge of attractive thatched village, open all day (*CMW, JJW, George Atkinson*)

MILTON MALSOR [SP7355]

☆ *Greyhound* [2¼ miles from M1 junction 15, via A508]: Big busy but friendly Chef & Brewer, well refurbished in olde-worlde mode, lots of cosy corners, 15th-c beams, old pictures and china, pewter-filled dresser, candlelit pine tables, good log fire, well kept John Smiths, Theakstons Best and Old Peculier, good range of wines, wide choice of food all day from filled rolls up, prompt service; piped music; open all day, well behaved seated children welcome, spreading front lawn with duck/fish pond (*George Atkinson, Pamela and Merlyn Horswell, Mrs G R Sharman, LYM, Stephen, Julie and Hayley Brown, Ted George*)

NASSINGTON [TL0696]

☆ *Black Horse* [Fotheringhay Rd – 2½ miles S of A1/A47 interchange W of Peterboro]: Civilised olde-worlde 17th-c beamed and panelled dining pub in nice village, splendid big stone fireplace, easy chairs and small settees in two rooms linked by bar servery, well kept real ales, good varied wine list, good value food, very attentive quick service; attractive garden, open all day summer wknds (*Roy Bromell, LYM, Rona Murdoch*)

NORTHAMPTON [SP7560]

Britannia [3¾ miles from M1 junction 15; Old Bedford Rd (off A428)]: Rambling refurbished Chef & Brewer with massive beams, mix of flagstones and carpet, attractive 18th-c kitchen, three or four real ales, wide choice of popular food all day from baguettes up, polite attentive young staff, no smoking area, conservatory; may be piped jazz or light classics, Tues quiz night; picnic-sets by River Nene, open all day (*Dr Alan Sutton, LYM, CMW, JJW,*

Gerry and Rosemary Dobson)

☆ *Malt Shovel* [Bridge St (approach road from M1 junction 15); best parking in Morrisons opp back entrance]: Long pine and brick bar opp Carlsberg Brewery, well kept Banks's, Frog Island Natterjack, Fullers London Pride, Tetleys and several interesting changing guests inc a Mild, Rich's farm cider, belgian bottled beers, over 50 malt whiskies, country wines, occasional beer festivals, daily papers, good value home-made usual food from hot baguettes up lunchtime and early evening (not Sun, can take a while), breweriana, open fire, darts, live music Weds; piped music and/or mobile phones may be obtrusive; picnic-sets on small back terrace, back disabled access (*CMW, JJW, Stephen, Julie and Hayley Brown, Bruce Bird, Martin Grosberg*)

Moon on the Square [The Parade, Market Pl]: Popular Wetherspoons, with some café-style furnishings, masses of books, around nine real ales from long bar, good value prompt food all day inc bargains, good coffee, efficient helpful staff, steps up to partly no smoking back conservatory (and stairs up to lavatories); no music, open all day (*Ted George, Michael Tack*)

OLD [SP7873]

White Horse [Walgrave Rd, N of Northampton between A43 and A508]: Wide choice of enjoyable sensibly priced food from good low-priced baguettes to interesting main dishes and popular Sun lunch, thriving atmosphere in cosy and comfortable lounge with good log fire, lots of pictures and plates, friendly service, well kept Banks's and Marstons Pedigree, decent wines, good coffee, restaurant, unusual theme nights; piped radio; lovely garden overlooking 13th-c church (*Pat and Derek Roughton*)

ORLINGBURY [SP8572]

Queens Arms [signed off A43 Northampton—Kettering, A509 Wellingborough—Kettering; Isham Rd]: Stone-built pub with half a dozen or more changing ales, wide choice of appealingly priced fresh food in bar and evening/wknd restaurant, cheerful if sometimes short-handed service, welcoming atmosphere, large comfortable airy lounge with banquettes, stools, bright carpet and beamery, side no smoking area; may be piped music; nice garden with play area, open all day wknds (*Anthony Barnes, Howard Dell, O K Smyth, Peter D B Harding*)

OUNDLE [TL0488]

Rose & Crown [Market Pl]: Armchairs, sofas and lots of old photographs and brasses in friendly stripped-stone beamed front bar, Banks's, Mansfield and Marstons Pedigree, quick friendly service, back public bar, good imaginative food in conservatory beyond; fine view of superb church from suntrap back terrace (*George Atkinson, Guy Vowles, Steve Whalley*)

RAVENSTHORPE [SP6670]

Chequers [Chequers Lane]: Refurbished beamed pub with wide range of good value bar food up to grills and individual roasts, well kept Greene King IPA, Jennings, Thwaites and a guest beer, good service, mainly no smoking restaurant (not Sun night or Mon/Tues – best to book wknds); TV, fruit machine, piped music, monthly quiz night; open all day Sat, quiet garden with terrace and play area *(Gerry and Rosemary Dobson, Michael Tack)*

ROCKINGHAM [SP8691]

Sondes Arms: Nicely set beamed pub with friendly staff, enjoyable blackboard bar food, well kept Charles Wells Eagle and Bombardier and a guest beer, slightly different menu in large separate dining areas; super views, tables out on terrace *(Peter Scillitoe)*

ROTHWELL [SP8181]

Greyhound [High St]: Music-theme décor, with album covers on walls, also frequent live music; well kept ales such as Fullers London Pride and Hop Back Summer Lightning *(Stephen, Julie and Hayley Brown)*

Rowell Charter [Sun Hill (A6)]: Ancient pub with two open fires, friendly service, good atmosphere, well kept Everards Beacon and Greene King Old Speckled Hen, good house wines, wide choice of home-made food at sensible prices *(Stephen, Julie and Hayley Brown, P Tailyour)*

SHUTLANGER [SP7249]

Plough [Main Rd, off A43 N of Towcester]: Out-of-the-way 17th-c pub popular for good value food esp good fresh cornish fish, small no smoking restaurant area, simple bar with lots of hanging jugs, mugs and tankards, stuffed animals, horse pictures and brasses, nice atmosphere, well kept Charles Wells Eagle and Bombardier, darts and hood skittles; piped music; garden with picnic-sets, play area and boules, attractive walks *(R M Corlett, Hilary Edwards)*

SIBBERTOFT [SP6782]

☆ *Red Lion* [Welland Rise, off A4303 or A508 SW of Mkt Harboro]: Cosy and civilised extended dining pub, lounge tables set for generous food with good veg selection, well kept Everards Tiger and guest beers such as Adnams and Bass, decent wines, welcoming landlord, good service, magazines, comfortably cushioned wall seats, some dark panelling, attractive no smoking beamed dining room, covered tables outside; cl Mon/Tues lunchtimes, two self-contained holiday flats *(P Tailyour, Gerry and Rosemary Dobson, George Atkinson)*

SPRATTON [SP7170]

Kings Head [Brixworth Rd]: Large stone-built village pub with flagstoned and carpeted L-shaped bar, three real ales, good soft drinks choice, good choice of enjoyable food inc children's and OAP menus, Thurs curry night, daily papers, woodburner and flame-effect fire, evening restaurant Weds-Sat; TVs, games machines and hood skittles,

separate pool and darts area, Sun quiz night; picnic-sets by car park, open all day Fri-Sun *(CMW, JJW)*

STOKE BRUERNE [SP7449]

☆ *Navigation*: Large clean canalside family pub in rambling stone-built former farmhouse, several levels and cosy corners, sturdy wood furniture inside and out, good value generous usual food inc Sun lunch till 5, good choice of well kept ales such as Marstons Pedigree, decent wines, quick friendly young staff; big play area, open all day *(Hilary Edwards, E J and M W Corrin)*

SYRESHAM [SP6341]

Kings Head [off A43 Brackley—Towcester; Abbey Rd]: Family dining pub with enjoyable food (not Sun evening or Mon lunchtime) from good sandwiches up, friendly Lancashire landlord, well kept Banks's and Marstons Pedigree, inglenook log fire hogged by the cat (two dogs too), no smoking restaurant, beams, brasses, pictures, motor-racing memorabilia – also toys, high chairs, baby-changing; piped music, games area; children welcome, picnic-sets in garden, bedrooms *(CMW, JJW)*

THORPE MANDEVILLE [SP5344]

Three Conies [off B4525 E of Banbury]: This attractive 17th-c stone-built pub, with its appealing two-room flagstoned bar, well kept Hook Norton beers and enjoyable food, has been closed for a spell, reopening too late for us to form a view; reports please *(LYM)*

THORPE WATERVILLE [TL0281]

Fox [A605 Thrapston—Oundle]: Pleasantly extended old pub with lots of fox pictures, wide range of decent straightforward food, well kept Charles Wells ales with a guest such as Greene King Old Speckled Hen, several wines by the glass, log-effect fire, no smoking dining area; piped music, children allowed, no dogs, small garden with play area *(Anthony Barnes)*

TOWCESTER [SP6654]

Peggottys [Fosters Booth (A5 3m N)]: Bar/restaurant rather than pub, but has changing well kept ales such as Batemans XB and Everards Beacon, good value bar food inc sandwiches and light dishes, genial landlord, welcoming service, light and airy flagstoned room with settees and armchairs as well as table seating; fuller meals at slightly higher price in no smoking restaurant *(George Atkinson, Gerry and Rosemary Dobson)*

WADENHOE [TL0083]

☆ *Kings Head* [Church Street; village signposted (in small print) off A605 S of Oundle]: Beautifully placed two-bar 17th-c country pub with picnic-sets on sun terrace and among trees on big stretch of grass by River Nene, pretty village, good walks; solid pine furniture, enjoyable food, well kept Adnams Bitter and Broadside and Badger IPA, good selection of books, no smoking areas, beamed dining room, games room with skittles; children in eating areas, has been cl Mon lunchtime *(Michael Tack, John*

Please use this card to tell us which pubs *you* think should or should not be included in the next edition of *The Good Pub Guide*. Just fill it in and return it to us – no stamp or envelope needed. Don't forget you can also use the report forms at the end of the *Guide*, or report through our web site: www.goodguides.com

ALISDAIR AIRD

In returning this form I confirm my agreement that the information I provide may be used by The Random House Group Ltd, its assignees and/or licensees in any media or medium whatsoever.

YOUR NAME AND ADDRESS (BLOCK CAPITALS PLEASE)

☐ *Please tick this box if you would like extra report forms*

REPORT ON *(pub's name)*

Pub's address

☐ **YES MAIN ENTRY**   ☐ **YES** *Lucky Dip*   ☐ **NO don't include**
Please tick one of these boxes to show your verdict, and give reasons and descriptive comments, prices etc

☐ Deserves FOOD award   ☐ Deserves PLACE-TO-STAY award

REPORT ON *(pub's name)*

Pub's address

☐ **YES MAIN ENTRY**   ☐ **YES** *Lucky Dip*   ☐ **NO don't include**
Please tick one of these boxes to show your verdict, and give reasons and descriptive comments, prices etc

☐ Deserves FOOD award   ☐ Deserves PLACE-TO-STAY award

The Good Pub Guide

The Good Pub Guide
FREEPOST TN1569
WADHURST
E. SUSSEX
TN5 7BR

Saul, Eric Locker, Sir Clive Rose, LYM)

WALGRAVE [SP8072]

Royal Oak [Zion Hill, off A43 Northampton—Kettering]: Old ironstone building under new licensees, well kept ales such as Adnams Bitter and Broadside, Fullers London Pride and Greene King Old Speckled Hen, wide choice of good value food (not Sun evening) inc some interesting dishes, bar split into smaller areas, part no smoking, no smoking dining room too; children welcome, tables outside, play area *(George Atkinson, Gerry and Rosemary Dobson)*

WATFORD [SP5968]

Stags Head [Watford Gap; B4036 towards Daventry]: Attractive and welcoming boat-shaped bar with open fire, enjoyable bar food, smarter restaurant with some unusual and exotic dishes, long-serving Portuguese licensees, cellar public bar; white cast-iron tables on terrace overlooking garden by Grand Union Canal *(Mr and Mrs P Bland)*

WEEDON [SP6359]

Globe [High St; junction A5/A45]: Attractive, tidy and roomy hotel with good value straightforward fresh food inc some light dishes, friendly obliging staff, well kept Marstons Pedigree and often honeyed Enville, log fire, restaurant open for coffee from breakfast on, cream teas; may be piped music or TV; picnic-sets outside, bedrooms *(George Atkinson)*

Heart of England [A45; handy for M1 junction 16]: Big family pub much enlarged around 18th-c core, partly no smoking panelled eating area, busy attractively refurbished lounge bar with small areas off, Banks's, Mansfield and Marstons Pedigree, wide choice of enjoyable food from sandwiches and baked potatoes up, recently extended conservatory restaurant, cheerful young staff, games room with pool; piped pop music; big garden leading down to Grand Union Canal moorings, good value pine-furnished bedrooms *(CMW, JJW, George Atkinson)*

☆ *Narrow Boat* [Stowe Hill (A5 S)]: Very popular in summer for spacious terrace and big garden running down to canal, barbecues; plain décor with canal prints, low bar tables, high-raftered back restaurant extension with canal views, two no smoking rooms, reliable food from ciabatta sandwiches to popular good value Sun lunch (served all afternoon) and tempting puddings, friendly helpful service, well kept Charles Wells ales, decent wines, open fire; fruit machine, skittles, quiet piped music; bedrooms in back motel extension, narrowboat hire next door *(LYM, George Atkinson, Gerry and Rosemary Dobson, Roger and Pauline Pearce, B Allen)*

Plume of Feathers [Bridge St/West St, Weedon Bec, off A5/A45]: Beams, stripped brickwork, pine furniture, candles and old books, reasonably priced food cooked to order (not Sun evening), largely no smoking dining area, attentive service, three well kept real ales inc Greene King IPA and Charles Wells Eagle; quiz night, piped music (some live), TV, pool, hood skittles and games machines; children welcome, picnic-sets and play area in garden, lovely hanging baskets, canal and walks nearby *(Wendy and Bob Needham, CMW, JJW)*

WELLINGBOROUGH [SP8866]

Priory [Bourton Way, by A45/A509 roundabout]: Large bright local with popular food inc Mon-Thurs bargains, good choice of beers, side children's playroom *(Michael Tack)*

WESTON [SP5846]

Crown [the one N of Brackley; Helmdon Rd]: No-frills three-room 17th-c stone-built ex-farmhouse, log fires, beams, flagstones and bare boards, welcoming family service, three or four well kept ales, good coffee, promptly served home-made food (not Sun evening), unusual long room (former skittle alley) with cubicle seating; pool room, darts alcove, no smoking room; children welcome, bedrooms, handy for NT Canons Ashby and Sulgrave, cl Mon lunchtime and winter Sun evening *(CMW, JJW)*

YARDLEY GOBION [SP7644]

Coffee Pot [High St (off A508)]: Pretty village local with cheerful welcome, well kept ales such as Caledonian Deuchars, Fullers London Pride and Tetleys, flame-effect fires each end of roomy low-beamed L-shaped bar, assorted furniture, stripped brick, boards and carpet; landlord does good value generous food with a nice choice for children (allowed in dining room); games room with pool, fruit machine, piped music, TV, live music most wknds, challenging quiz nights, no dogs; small back garden with play area and good value barbecues *(Hilary Edwards)*

YARDLEY HASTINGS [SP8656]

☆ *Red Lion* [High St, just off A428 Bedford—Northampton]: Pretty thatched stone-built local doing well under current licensees, good value food (not Sun/Mon evenings) esp pasta cooked by Italian landlord, sandwiches and ciabattas too, well kept Charles Wells Eagle and Bombardier and perhaps a guest beer, decent wines, good coffee and range of soft drinks, friendly efficient service, cosy lounge with beams and stripped stone (can be smoky), lots of pictures, plates and interesting brass and copper, tiled-floor bar and small carpeted dining area; piped music, no dogs or credit cards; tables in nicely planted sloping garden, and in front *(CMW, JJW, George Atkinson, Marina Pearce, BB)*

Rose & Crown [just off A428 Bedford—Northampton]: Relaxed and spacious 18th-c pub in pretty village, flagstones, beams, stripped stonework and quiet corners, lots of pictures and brasses, step up to big comfortable no smoking family dining room, good value freshly made food, Charles Wells ales, cheerful staff; quiet piped music; picnic-sets in courtyard and garden *(CMW, JJW)*

Northumbria (County Durham, Northumberland and Tyneside)

This area has a fine spread of really worthwhile pubs, from lively city bars of great character to delightful country hideaways. Ones on top form these days include the appealing Rat at Anick (a most enjoyable all-rounder), the smart County in Aycliffe (good stylish modern food), the Manor House Inn at Carterway Heads (doing its good imaginative food all day), the relaxed Fox & Hounds at Cotherstone (nice home cooking using very local produce), the Dipton Mill Inn at Diptonmill (a charming place, lots of local cheeses, and its own beers), the friendly Victoria in Durham (unspoilt Victorian layout), the Queens Head at Great Whittington (delicious food in this dining pub), the Cluny in Newcastle (a new entry, in an interesting warehouse conversion – fine beer range), the Crown Posada there (good beer range here too, in one of the city's oldest pubs, magnificently preserved), the cheerful Cook & Barker Arms at Newton-on-the-Moor (nice all round, with good value most enjoyable food), the spotless and very friendly Masons Arms at Rennington, the lovingly run Rose & Crown at Romaldkirk (great to stay in, good imaginative food), and the Ridley Arms at Stannington (another new entry, just off the A1 – would that there were more motorway and trunk-road stop-offs of this quality). As we have pointed out, good food is a high point at quite a few of Northumbria's best pubs; the stylish cooking at the County in Aycliffe stands out, gaining it the award of Northumbria Dining Pub of the Year. Pubs to note particularly in the Lucky Dip section at the end of the chapter are the Saddle in Alnmouth, Old Well in Barnard Castle, Angel in Corbridge, Jolly Fisherman at Craster, Tankerville Arms at Eglingham, Ship on Holy Island, Carts Bog Inn near Langley on Tyne, Bridge Hotel in Newcastle, Badger at Ponteland and Boathouse at Wylam. Drinks prices here are comfortably below the national average, and in most places a pint of beer has not yet breached the £2 mark. Plenty of local breweries make pub visits particularly interesting for the beer lover up here, such as Mordue, Castle Eden & Camerons, Hadrian & Border, Durham, Wylam, Big Lamp and Darwin.

ALLENDALE NY8355 Map 10
Kings Head £
Market Place (B6295)

The pleasant interior of this quietly welcoming former coaching inn is neat and cosy, with lemon walls, navy curtains and a tartan carpet. The spacious bar/lounge has a lovely warming log fire and some interesting bric-a-brac. Dating from the early 18th c, the pub, in the rambling square of a very attractive small town, is popular with locals; it gets particularly busy on market days. Up to seven (though sometimes down to three) real ales are well kept in a temperature-controlled cellar and could include Jennings Bitter, Cumberland and Sneck Lifter alongside changing guests such as Adnams, Everards Tiger and Timothy Taylors Landlord, all on handpump; also a good choice of just under 80 malt whiskies. Darts, TV and quiet piped pop music. Hearty reasonably priced bar food could include soup (£1.60), sandwiches (from £2), fish and chips or beef and ale pie (£4.95), lasagne or venison sausage (£5.95), and half a roast duck with cherry sauce (£9.50), with blackboard specials such as cumberland sausage with onion sauce (£4.95) and grilled tuna steak (£7.95), puddings (£2.50) and Sunday roast (£5.95); small upstairs no smoking dining room. There are good walks in the area, and the road through the valley is a fine scenic drive. *(Recommended by Patrick Hancock, Jack and Heather Coyle, Peter F Marshall, Michael Doswell, CMW, JJW)*

Jennings ~ Lease Tracy Thompson and Lenny Slater ~ Real ale ~ Bar food (12-2.30, 6.30-9) ~ (01434) 683681 ~ Children welcome ~ Live entertainment second and fourth Fri ~ Open 11-11; 12-10.30 Sun ~ Bedrooms: £25S/£45S

ALLENHEADS NY8545 Map 10
Allenheads Inn £ 🛏
Just off B6295

A bric-a-brac lover's dream, this cheerfully run, welcoming pub certainly doesn't leave you short of things to look at. All available space on the walls, ceilings and counter is covered with thousands of interesting collectables. In any of the loosely themed rooms you might find stuffed animals, mangles, old radios, typewriters, long-silenced musical instruments, an engine-room telegraph, brass and copper bygones, a plastic lobster, aeroplane propellers, brooms, birdcages and even shoes – the list is endless, and it's all well cared for. The games room (with darts, pool, cribbage, dominoes and an antique juke box) has perhaps the most effervescent collection, and the car club discs and number plates on the panelling echo the efforts by members of a classic car club to try to persuade their vehicles to wend their way up here. Tables outside are flanked by more hardware – the sort of machinery that wouldn't fit inside. The Forces room and the dining room are no smoking. Enjoyably straightforward pubby food in hearty helpings includes toasted sandwiches (from £1.75), vegetarian chilli or curry (£4.75), cod (£5.25), steak or chicken pie (£5.75), and puddings such as fudge cake or rice pudding (from £2.25). They usually have well kept Greene King Abbot, Timothy Taylors Landlord and a couple of guests from northern brewers such as Black Sheep and Mordue on handpump; decent coffee, real fire, piped music. The pub is on the Sustrans C2C cycle route; it's particularly peaceful here in winter, and if you're staying the night they do good breakfasts. *(Recommended by Michael Doswell, Mrs K H Clark, G D Marsh, Christopher J Darwent, Michele D'Lemos, Brian Root, Comus and Sarah Elliott)*

Free house ~ Licensee Stephen Wardle ~ Real ale ~ Bar food (12-2.30, 7-9) ~ (01434) 685200 ~ Children in eating area of bar and pool room ~ Open 12-4, 7-11; 12-11 Fri/Sat; 12-10.30 Sun ~ Bedrooms: £27.50B/£48B

We checked prices with the pubs as we went to press in summer 2003. They should hold until around spring 2004 – when our experience suggests that you can expect an increase of around 10p in the £.

ANICK NY9665 Map 10

Rat ◖ £

Village signposted NE of A69/A695 Hexham junction

Readers really enjoy the snugly welcoming atmosphere at this unspoilt country pub, which is comfortably run by really friendly licensees. A coal fire blazes invitingly in the blackened kitchen range, and soft lighting gently illuminates lots of interesting knick-knacks: antique floral chamber-pots hanging from the beams, china and glassware, maps and posters, framed sets of cigarette cards, and quite a lot of Laurel and Hardy memorabilia, from figurines to a signed photograph. Furnishings keep up the cosy relaxed traditional mood, with brocaded chairs around old-fashioned pub tables; piped music, daily papers and magazines. Besides the two small eating areas, a conservatory gives lovely views of the North Tyne valley. Tables out on the terrace and in a charming garden, with dovecote, statues and even flowers sprouting unexpectedly from boots, share the same views. The helpful landlord is happy to chat about the beers, which are well kept on handpump, and include Big Lamp, Greene King Ruddles County and Old Speckled Hen, Mordue Workie Ticket, John Smiths and a guest such as Theakstons Rocketeer. Generous helpings of pubby food from a changing blackboard menu might include soup (£2.50), hot sandwiches (from £3.50), ploughman's (£3.95), plaice and chips (£5.50), lambs liver casserole (£5.95), rabbit stew or mince and dumplings (£6.15), beef and ale pie (£6.25), and puddings such as banana and Amaretto cheesecake (£2.95). Parking is limited. *(Recommended by Kevin Thorpe, C A Hall, Mike and Lynn Robinson, A D Jenkins, Jack and Heather Coyle, Andy and Jill Kassube, John Foord, Peter Burton, Pat and Stewart Gordon)*

Free house ~ Licensees Joan and Donald D'Adamo ~ Real ale ~ Bar food (not Sun evening) ~ Restaurant ~ (01434) 602814 ~ Children in restaurant and family room ~ Open 11-3, 6-11; 12-3, 7-10.30 Sun

AYCLIFFE NZ2722 Map 10

County ⓎⓅ◖

The Green, Aycliffe village; just off A1(M) junction 59, by A167

Northumbria Dining Pub of the Year

Andrew Brown, the talented chef/landlord here, has now been able to buy this stylish pub, which as tenant he's made so popular with visitors from far and wide for his high quality cooking. Using mostly local produce, the pubby bar menu (served at lunchtime and in the early evening only) includes soup (£3.80), smoked salmon and scrambled egg muffin (£5.95), sausage and mash (£7.95), rib-eye sandwich (£8.25) and battered haddock (£8.40). You can also eat from the more elaborate bistro menu in the bar: perhaps savoury bread and butter pudding with red onion and blue cheese mustard cream and white wine sauce (£5.85), duckling breast with sweet potato purée and cranberry and port sauce or grilled tuna with fennel, pepper and tomato ragoût (£13.95), with puddings such a chocolate orange crème brûlée (£4.95). Dishes are cooked from fresh, so there might be a bit of a wait. Furnishings in the extended bar and no smoking bistro are light and modern, definitely geared to dining, and the minimalist décor gives a fresh feel; the atmosphere is friendly and civilised. As well as a good choice of wines by the glass, four well kept real ales on handpump include John Smiths Magnet, Charles Wells Bombardier and a couple of guests from Castle Eden & Camerons. Good swift service by friendly young staff; there may be piped music. The green opposite is pretty. *(Recommended by Jenny and Dave Hughes, Liz and Brian Barnard, Pat and Tony Martin, M Borthwick, Brian and Anna Marsden, Keith Mould, Gerry and Rosemary Dobson)*

Free house ~ Licensee Andrew Brown ~ Real ale ~ Bar food (12-2, 6-9.15; not Sun evening) ~ Restaurant ~ (01325) 312273 ~ Children in eating area of bar and restaurant ~ Open 12-3, 5.30(6 Sat)-11; 12-4 Sun; closed Sun evening, 25 Dec

BLANCHLAND NY9750 Map 10
Lord Crewe Arms ⇌
B6306 S of Hexham

Premonstratensian monks founded this isolated and very attractive old stone village, building it robustly enough to resist most border raiding parties. It is still separated from the rest of the world by several miles of moors, rabbits and sheep. The tremendous age of the fine old inn is evident everywhere. Originally part of the 13th-c monastery guest-house, it then became home to several distinguished families after the dissolution in 1536. The narrow bar is housed in an unusual stone barrel-vaulted crypt, its curving walls being up to eight feet thick in some places. Plush stools are lined along the bar counter and next to a narrow drinks shelf down the opposite wall. Upstairs, the Derwent Room has low beams, old settles, and sepia photographs on its walls, and the Hilyard Room has a massive 13th-c fireplace once used as a hiding place by the Jacobite Tom Forster (part of the family who had owned the building before it was sold in 1704 to the formidable Lord Crewe, Bishop of Durham). You can now eat in the lovely walled garden which was formerly the cloisters. Bar food includes soup (£2.50), filled rolls (from £3.45), ploughman's (from £5), pasta dish of the day (£6.50), cumberland sausage with black pudding and mash (£6.75), daily specials, and puddings (£3.50). Well kept Wylam Gold Tankard on handpump. *(Recommended by John Hale, Rona Murdoch, Kevin Thorpe, Alan Cole, Kirstie Bruce, Andy and Jill Kassube, Greta and Christopher Wells, Tracey and Stephen Groves, Anthony Longden, David and Betty Gittins, Bill and Jessica Ritson)*

Free house ~ Licensees A Todd, Peter Gingell and Ian Press, Lindsey Sands ~ Real ale ~ Bar food ~ Restaurant ~ (01434) 675251 ~ Children welcome ~ Dogs welcome ~ Open 11-11.30; 12-10.30 Sun ~ Bedrooms: £80B/£110B

CARTERWAY HEADS NZ0552 Map 10
Manor House Inn �ّ ♈ ◀ ⇌
A68 just N of B6278, near Derwent Reservoir

Though quite a few pubs now helpfully serve food all day, it's very rarely as good as at this bustling slate-roofed stone house. The enticing choice of well prepared dishes (with especially tasty sauces) includes soup (£2.60), chicken liver pâté with onion marmalade (£3.95), local smoked kippers (£4.35/£7.95), king prawns with sweet and sour sauce or herb butter (£4.95/£9.75), mediterranean vegetables en croûte (£7.75), roast duck breast with sugar roasted plums (£11.95), and specials such as ploughman's (£5.50) and pigeon breast with mushroom and juniper (£11.50). Puddings (£3.60) are home-made, and they do a local cheese platter (£4.95). Welcoming service by cheery young staff, and part of the restaurant (which has a large collection of jugs and lovely views) is no smoking. The locals' bar has an original boarded ceiling, pine tables, chairs and stools, old oak pews, and a mahogany counter. The comfortable lounge bar has a woodburning stove, and picture windows give fine views over moorland pastures. Well kept Courage Directors, Theakstons Best, Charles Wells Bombardier and a guest from a local brewer such as Mordue on handpump, farm cider, around 70 malt whiskies, and decent wines with about eight by the glass; darts, dominoes, TV and piped music (only in the bar). There are rustic tables out on a small side terrace and lawn. They do good breakfasts. *(Recommended by John and Sylvia Harrop, Peter and Patricia Burton, Michael Doswell, Andy and Jill Kassube, Liz and Brian Barnard, Brian and Anna Marsden, Andrew and Samantha Grainger, Dr and Mrs P Truelove, J F M and M West, Jack and Heather Coyle, Pat and Derek Roughton, John Oddey, John Poulter, Stephen, Julie and Hayley Brown, Graham Clarke)*

Free house ~ Licensees Moira and Chris Brown ~ Real ale ~ Bar food (12-9.30 (9 Sun)) ~ Restaurant ~ (01207) 255268 ~ Children welcome ~ Dogs welcome ~ Open 11-11; 12-10.30 Sun; closed 25 Dec evening ~ Bedrooms: £38B/£60B

Soup prices usually include a roll and butter.

COTHERSTONE NZ0119 Map 10
Fox & Hounds ⊨

B6277 – incidentally a good quiet route to Scotland, through interesting scenery

There's an enjoyably relaxing atmosphere at this friendly 200-year-old country inn – it's the sort of place where walkers are welcome. The simple but cheery beamed bar has a good winter log fire, comfortable furnishings such as thickly cushioned wall seats, and local photographs and country pictures on the walls in its various alcoves and recesses. Don't be surprised by the unusual lavatory attendant – an african grey parrot called Reva. Black Sheep Best, Hambleton Stud and possibly a guest are well kept by the hospitable landlord, while the very good generously served bar food is freshly prepared by the landlady. Using lots of local ingredients (notably the beef and lamb), well presented dishes could include lunchtime ploughman's (£5.40), sausage and mash (£5.75), battered whitby cod (£6.30), and ham, cheese and prawn salad (£6.50), with evening dishes such as scampi (£4.40), aubergine and cashew nut loaf with cucumber and mint salsa (£7.30), roast salmon fillet on watercress mash with lemon and lime dressing (£9.40), roast duckling breast with apricot and orange sauce (£10.80), and rack of lamb with cranberry, orange and rosemary sauce (£12.15), while tempting puddings could be fresh fruit fondue with dark chocolate sauce or sticky toffee pudding (£3.75), with local cheeses (£4.30); both of the dining rooms are no smoking. The pub is in a pretty spot overlooking the village green, with good nearby walks, and it's fairly handy for the Otter Trust North Pennine Reserve. *(Recommended by Mrs Phoebe A Kemp, Michael Doswell, Lesley and Peter Barrett, Tim and Carolyn Lowes, Phil Heys)*

Free house ~ Licensees Nichola and Ian Swinburn ~ Real ale ~ Bar food ~ Restaurant ~ (01833) 650241 ~ Children in restaurant ~ Open 12-2.30, 6.30(7 Sun)-11; closed 25-26 Dec ~ Bedrooms: £42.50B/£65B

DIPTONMILL NY9261 Map 10
Dipton Mill Inn ▰ £

Just S of Hexham; off B6306 at Slaley, Blanchland and Dye House, Whitley Chapel signposts (and HGV route sign); not to be confused with the Dipton in Durham

This very appealing little two-roomed pub is tucked away in a peaceful wooded valley hamlet and surrounded by steep hills, with plenty of easy-walking footpaths nearby. It's a good all-rounder, and particularly interesting because the chatty landlord is a brewer in the family-owned Hexhamshire Brewery: Hexhamshire Shire Bitter, Devils Water, Devils Elbow, Old Humbug and Whapweasel are all well kept on handpump and served alongside a guest such as Hambleton Nightmare; also two dozen malt whiskies, and Weston's Old Rosie cider. Freshly prepared by the landlady, bar food is very good value and comes in generous helpings. A nice touch is the choice of a dozen northumbrian cheeses which you can choose from to make up your ploughman's or have after your meal (from £4.50). Other well presented dishes include soup (£1.75), sandwiches (from £1.60), and salads (£5), with specials such as tagliatelle with basil cream sauce and parmesan (£4.50), steak and kidney pie or haddock baked with tomato and basil (£5.65), and chicken breast in tarragon sauce (£6.50). Puddings might include syrup sponge and custard or chocolate rum truffle torte (from £1.60). The snug little bar is very relaxed and friendly, with dark ply panelling, red furnishings, a dark red carpet and the gentle smell of woodsmoke from the open fires. The back games room has darts, bar billiards, shove-ha'penny and dominoes. In summer, it's nice to head for the seats on the sunken crazy-paved terrace by the restored mill stream, or in the attractively planted garden with its aviary. *(Recommended by Karen and Graham Oddey, Patrick Hancock, Andy and Jill Kassube, Kevin Thorpe, JWAC, Tracey and Stephen Groves, Jenny and Brian Seller, Michael Doswell)*

Own brew ~ Licensee Geoff Brooker ~ Real ale ~ Bar food (12-2.30, 6.30(7.30 Sun)-8.30) ~ No credit cards ~ (01434) 606577 ~ Children welcome in back room ~ Quiz night Weds ~ Open 12-2.30, 6-11; 12-4, 7-10.30 Sun; closed 25 Dec

DURHAM NZ2742 Map 10
Victoria ♀ ◧ ⇔

Hallgarth Street (A177, near Dunelm House)

The interior of this down-to-earth cosy local is little altered since it was built in 1899. It's been in the same family for 27 years, and is run with considerable individuality; though there is evidence of generations of wear and tear, it's neat and carefully kept. Built in the closing years of Queen Victoria's reign, it celebrates her life with lots of period prints and engravings, and staffordshire figurines of her and the Prince Consort. A very traditional layout means three work-a-day rooms lead off a central bar, with mahogany, etched and cut glass and mirrors, colourful William Morris wallpaper over a high panelled dado, some maroon plush seats in little booths, some worn leatherette wall seats, long narrow leather-topped drinkers' tables, handsome iron and tile fireplaces for the coal fires, a piano, and some photographs and articles showing a very proper pride in the pub. The main source of income here is the well kept real ales: local Darwins Ghost, Durham, Marstons Pedigree and McEwans 80/- and a frequently changing guest from a brewer such as Exmoor or Mordue on handpump, good cheap house wines, around 40 malts and a remarkable collection of 30 irish whiskeys. In one room they've dominoes, a veteran space invaders game, a Trivial Pursuit machine and a TV; at lunchtime they do toasties (from £1). The good value bedrooms are simple but pleasant, and you get a hearty breakfast in the upstairs dining room. *(Recommended by Eric Larkham, A Reeves, Andy and Jill Kassube, the Didler, Barry Collett, Pete Baker, Tracey and Stephen Groves, Oliver Drerup)*

Free house ~ Licensee Michael Webster ~ Real ale ~ (0191) 386 5269 ~ Children welcome ~ Dogs welcome ~ Open 11.30-3, 6-11; 12-2, 7-10.30 Sun ~ Bedrooms: £40B/£54B

GREAT WHITTINGTON NZ0171 Map 10
Queens Head ⑪ ◧

Village signposted off A68 and B6018 just N of Corbridge

In keeping with the smart stone-built village that forms the setting for this attractive old building, the atmosphere here is sophisticated and civilised. Modern furnishings alongside some handsome carved oak settles and log fires give its two fairly simple beamed rooms a stylishly comfortable feel. The room nearest the bar counter has a mural over its fireplace. Emphasis is on the very good creative food, cooked using local meat and fish fresh from the quay. Aside from tasty lunchtime sandwiches, the bistro menu (which you can eat in the bar) could include soup (£4.50), home-made ravioli filled with seafood mousse with cheese and shellfish sauce (£6.50), vegetable strudel with tomato coulis, roast garlic and basil oil (£9.95), pork tenderloin on orange and onion marmalade with black pudding fritters and cider and sage jus (£11.95) and grilled cod fillet with mussel and prawn ragoût and saffron and herb butter (£13.95). The restaurant is no smoking. Very well kept Hambleton Bitter and Queens Head (brewed for them by Hambleton) on handpump, 30 malt whiskies, and an extensive wine list; perhaps unobtrusive piped music. The small front lawn has half a dozen picnic-sets, and the pub is surrounded by partly wooded countryside. *(Recommended by Peter and Patricia Burton, Barry Robson, R Macfarlane, Colin McKerrow, KN-R)*

Free house ~ Licensee Ian Scott ~ Real ale ~ Bar food (not Sun evening) ~ Restaurant ~ (01434) 672267 ~ Well behaved children in restaurant at lunchtime ~ Open 12-2.30, 6-11; 7-10.30 Sun; closed Mon except bank hols

> Cribbage is a card game using a block of wood with holes for matchsticks or
> special pins to score with; regulars in cribbage pubs are usually happy
> to teach strangers how to play.

GRETA BRIDGE NZ0813 Map 10

Morritt Arms ♀ ⇔

Hotel signposted off A66 W of Scotch Corner

Looking a little like a grand country house, this civilised hotel is a lovely place to stay in, and well worth a stop even if you're just after an enjoyable meal or a relaxing drink. The charming pubby bar is named after Charles Dickens, who stayed here in 1838 on his way to start his research for *Nicholas Nickleby*, and a jolly larger-than-life Dickensian mural runs round its walls. It was painted in 1946 by J V Gilroy – more famous for his old Guinness advertisements, six of which are displayed on the walls here too. Big windsor armchairs and sturdy plush-seated oak settles cluster around traditional cast-iron-framed tables, and big windows look out on the extensive lawn. Flowers brighten up the rooms, and there are nice open fires. Well kept Black Sheep, Timothy Taylors Landlord and a guest such as Jennings Cumberland on handpump, quite a few malt whiskies, and an extensive wine list with about two dozen by the glass. There's a proper old shove-ha'penny board, with raisable brass rails to check the lie of the coins, cribbage and dominoes, and a TV. Freshly prepared well presented bar food, served by obliging professional staff, includes filled baguettes (from £2.95, there's a good coronation chicken one £3.75), soup (£3.50), steak and kidney pie or fish and chips (£6.75), scampi or tasty ploughman's (£6.95) and braised lamb shank (£8.25). The adjacent no smoking bistro, with a more elaborate menu, has wood floors and wrought iron, and is densely hung with paintings and prints by local artists (which you can buy). The attractively laid out garden has some seats, with teak tables in a pretty side area looking along to the graceful old bridge by the stately gates to Rokeby Park, and swings, a slide and a wendy house at the far end. *(Recommended by Pat and Tony Martin, JHBS, Greta and Christopher Wells, Darly Graton, Graeme Gulibert, Peter Burton, Peter and Ruth Burnstone, Barry Collett, Susan and John Douglas, Jack and Heather Coyle)*

Free house ~ Licensees Peter Phillips and Barbara Johnson ~ Real ale ~ Bar food (12-9) ~ Restaurant ~ (01833) 627232 ~ Children welcome ~ Dogs allowed in bar and bedrooms ~ Jazz Fri night in the restaurant ~ Open 11-11; 12-10.30 Sun ~ Bedrooms: £59.50B/£87.50B

HALTWHISTLE NY7166 Map 10

Milecastle Inn

Military Road; B6318 NE – OS Sheet 86 map reference 715660

On the old roman road from Newcastle, this 17th-c pub is in a famously bleak and scenic part of the county. It's very handy for Hadrian's Wall and, although fairly isolated, it can get very busy – so get here early. The snug little rooms of the beamed bar are decorated with brasses, horsey and local landscape prints and attractive dried flowers, and have two winter log fires; at lunchtime the small comfortable restaurant is used as an overflow. Two changing well kept real ales on handpump might include Big Lamb Prince Bishop, Greene King Old Speckled Hen or Tetleys, and they have a fair collection of malt whiskies and a good wine list; no games or music. Generous helpings of bar food include well filled lunchtime sandwiches (£3) and ploughman's (£5.25), and soup (£2.50), vegetable spring rolls (£3.75), breaded plaice (£6.25) and steak and kidney pie (£7.25), with daily specials such as shepherd's pie with cheese and leeks (£6.50) and wild boar and duckling pie (£7.25). The tables and benches out in a pleasantly sheltered walled garden with a dovecote are popular in summer; there's a large car park and walkers are welcome (but no rucksacks). *(Recommended by Tom McLean, Michael Doswell, Andy and Jill Kassube, Peter Scillitoe, A Sadler)*

Free house ~ Licensees Ralph and Margaret Payne ~ Real ale ~ Bar food (12-2, 6.30-9) ~ Restaurant ~ (01434) 321372/320682 ~ Children over 5 if eating ~ Open 12-3, 6.30-11

HEDLEY ON THE HILL NZ0859 Map 10
Feathers 🍴

Village signposted from New Ridley, which is signposted from B6309 N of Consett; OS Sheet 88 map reference 078592

The fairly short but interesting and very sensibly priced menu at this attractive old stone pub changes around twice a week. All dishes are home-made, and the vegetarian choice is particularly imaginative. There might be a soup such as spiced sweet potato, squash and coriander (£3.75), tortilla filled with spiced sweet potato and puy lentils or leek, mushroom, parsnip and almond croustade (£6.75), spiced lamb with ginger, coriander and sweetcorn filled pancakes (£6.95), salmon fillet with lemon and dill butter (£7.75), greek beef casserole (£7.95), and tempting puddings such as brown sugar and cinnamon meringue with cream and soft fruit compote or ginger pudding with ginger wine and brandy sauce (£3.75). Although the emphasis is on the food there's still a good pubby atmosphere in the three well kept turkey-carpeted traditional bars, with beams, open fires, stripped stonework, solid brown leatherette settles and old black and white photographs of local places and farm and country workers. They've well kept Boddingtons and Mordue Workie Ticket and a couple of guest beers from brewers such as Fullers and Yates on handpump; also decent wines and around 30 malt whiskies. Shove-ha'penny, table skittles, cribbage, and dominoes. They hold a mini beer festival at Easter with over two dozen real ales and a barrel race on Easter Monday. Picnic-sets in front provide a nice place to sit and watch the world drift by. *(Recommended by C A Hall, Norman Stansfield, Andrew and Samantha Grainger, Patrick Hancock, Andy and Jill Kassube, Jenny and Dave Hughes, David Lowes Watson, Peter Burton)*

Free house ~ Licensee Marina Atkinson ~ Real ale ~ Bar food (not wkdy lunchtimes or Mon except bank hols) ~ No credit cards ~ (01661) 843607 ~ Children in eating area of bar and family room till 9pm ~ Open 6-11; 12-3, 6-11 Sat; 12-3, 7-10.30 Sun; closed wkdy lunchtimes except bank hols and 25 Dec

NEWCASTLE UPON TYNE NZ2563 Map 10
Crown Posada 🍺

The Side; off Dean Street, between and below the two high central bridges (A6125 and A6127)

One reader told us this marvellously unspoilt place hadn't changed a bit in the 20 years since he'd last visited – we doubt it's changed for many many years more than that. It's the second-oldest and one of the most architecturally interesting pubs in the city. A golden crown and magnificent pre-raphaelite stained-glass windows add grandeur to an already imposing carved stone façade. The interior overflows with architectural charm, such as an elaborate coffered ceiling, stained glass in the counter screens, a line of gilt mirrors each with a tulip lamp on a curly brass mount matching the great ceiling candelabra, and Victorian flowered wallpaper above the brown dado. Fat low level heating pipes make a popular footrest when the east wind brings the rain off the North Sea. It's a very long and narrow room, making quite a bottleneck by the serving counter; beyond that, a long soft green built-in leather wall seat is flanked by narrow tables. There's a fruit machine, and an old record player in a wooden cabinet provides mellow background music when the place is quiet. The building is not the only attraction here. Even when it's busy, you'll get a warm welcome from the friendly barmen, and the atmosphere is easy-going and chatty. It's best to visit during the week when regulars sit reading the papers in the front snug – at the weekend it's usually packed. From half a dozen handpumps, they serve superbly kept Bass and Jennings with continually changing guests from brewers such as Batemans, Godiva, Mordue and Roosters. They don't do food, but at lunchtime you can get a sandwich with a packet of crisps for £1. It's only a few minutes stroll to the castle. *(Recommended by John W Allen, Kevin Thorpe, Andy and Jill Kassube, the Didler, Tracey and Stephen Groves, Peter and Patricia Burton, Pete Baker, Stephen, Julie and Hayley Brown, Karen and Graham Oddey, Val Stevenson, Rob Holmes)*

*Free house ~ Licensee Malcolm MacPherson ~ Real ale ~ No credit cards ~
(0191) 232 1269 ~ Well behaved children over 12 allowed ~ Dogs allowed in bar ~
Open 11(12 Sat)-11; 7-10.30 Sun; closed Sun lunchtime*

Head of Steam @ The Cluny ◀

Lime Street (which runs between A193 and A186 E of centre)

Still known to everyone locally as the Cluny, opposite the Ship on Lime Street look
out for a cobbled bank leading down to the Ouseburn, by the Byker city farm.
Stretching down here, below the clutch of bridges, is this early 19th-c former
bonded whisky warehouse. The Cluny shares this impressively refurbished space
with several dozen artists and craftsmen who have studios here. Its back area
functions as an interesting gallery for changing exhibitions of their paintings,
sculptures and pottery, and for work by visiting artists. The friendly L-shaped bar is
trendy and gently bohemian-feeling despite its minimalist décor, with slightly
scuffed bare boards, some chrome seating and overhead spotlights. It serves well
kept Caledonian Deuchars IPA, Holts, Timothy Taylor Landlord and, as they pride
themselves in having a relationship with every North East independent brewer, up
to half a dozen guest beers on handpump might be from Big Lamp, Camerons,
Durham, Hadrian & Border, Mordue and Wylam; also rotating continental beers
on tap, lots of bottled world beers, a good range of soft drinks including belgian
fruit juices and a fine row of rums. Enjoyable simple food includes very popular
soup such as chick pea, parsley, celery and tomato (£2.50), vegetarian chilli or
pasta with red peppers and mozzarella (£4) and steak and mushroom pie or chicken
breast with red wine and mushrooms (£5); it's all home-made so there may be a
wait. The staff are cheerful, and a raised area looking down on the river (with
much redevelopment work afoot) has comfortable seating including settees, with
daily papers and local arts magazines. Piped music is well reproduced, and a
separate room has a stage for live bands and comedy nights. Disabled access and
facilities, fruit machine and bar billiards. *(Recommended by
Kevin Thorpe, Tracey and Stephen Groves, GSB, Eric Larkham, Andrew York, Mike and
Lynn Robinson, John Foord)*

*Head of Steam ~ Manager Dave Campbell ~ Real ale ~ Bar food (12-9(snacks till
closing)) ~ (0191) 230 4475 ~ Children in family room ~ Dogs welcome ~ Live
bands up to 6 nights a wk ~ Open 12-11(1 Fri/Sat)*

NEWFIELD NZ2033 Map 10
Fox & Hounds ♀

Turn off A688 at 'Willington, Newfield' signpost, or off A690 in Willington, into aptly
named Long Lane; Newfield signposted off this, then turn left at Queens Head into
Stonebank Terrace

Although the emphasis here is very much on dining, this still keeps a pub layout
with its serving bar in the single main room, and they do welcome you if all you
want is a drink – there's a cosy carpeted ante-room with a three-piece suite in
brown velour by an old cream-coloured kitchen stove in a high stone fireplace
(good fires in winter). But the appealing food is the reason for coming. The very
reasonably priced lighter lunch menu includes baguettes (£3.50), scrambled eggs
with smoked salmon and chorizo sausage, chicken korma or pasta with cannellini
beans, roast aubergine and red pesto sauce (£4.95), with more elaborate evening
dishes such as ham knuckle and vegetable broth (£2.75), smoked salmon (£4.95),
basil pancakes with asparagus, pine nuts and ricotta filling (£8.75), halibut steak
with prawn butter sauce or venison steak with orange, cranberry and red wine
sauce (£14.50), and puddings such as apricot and marsala wine syllabub or
pistachio ice cream profiteroles with warm chocolate sauce (£3.75). The
comfortable and gently lit no smoking main area has a polished wood-strip floor,
with candles and flowers on the neatly laid tables all around its sides, big brass
platters on its dark pink timbered walls, and mugs, tankards and whisky-water jugs
hanging from beams skeined with fairy-lights. Big windows look down over steeply

rolling countryside. The house wines are good; they do aim to keep a real ale such as Tetleys on handpump, but may not always have one on; service is friendly and thoughtful. Saturday night gets fully booked well ahead. *(Recommended by BOB)*

Free house ~ Licensee William Thompson ~ Real ale ~ Bar food ~ Restaurant ~ (01388) 662787 ~ Children over 11 in restaurant ~ Open 12-3, 7-11; 12-3 Sun; closed Sun evening, Mon

NEWTON-BY-THE-SEA NU2424 Map 10
Ship

Village signposted off B1339 N of Alnwick; Low Newton – paid parking 200 metres up road on right, just before village (none in village)

It's easy to see why the landlady, who never thought she'd want to run a pub, fell in love with this exquisitely positioned place, which is tucked into the top corner of a National Trust courtyard of low white-painted stone cottages. This simple refuge looks down over the sloping grassy square to the broad beach, and beyond to off-shore rocks packed with seabirds and sometimes seals. It's very quiet here in winter (when opening times are complicated, so it might be best to ring), when they have just one or two real ales including Black Sheep. In contrast, queues can build up on hot summer days, when the beer range extends to two or three guests from brewers such as Border, Mordue and Wylam; also decent wines, an espresso machine (colourful coffee cups, good hot chocolate), and good soft drinks. The plainly furnished bare-boards bar on the right has nautical charts on its dark pink walls, beams and hop bines. Another simple room on the left has some bright modern pictures on stripped stone walls, and a woodburning stove in its stone fireplace; daily papers. Out in the corner of the square are some tables among pots of flowers, with picnic-sets over on the grass. Enjoyable lunchtime snacks include local crab sandwiches (£3.25), warm ciabattas with enterprising fillings (around £3.75), fishcakes and salad (£4.35), ploughman's with local cheddar cheese (£4.95) and crab-filled stotties (£5.45). You must book for the appealing evening meals made with fresh local produce: the short daily-changing menu could include kipper pâté (£3.25), roasted vegetables on almond rice (£5.95), grilled red mullet with herb salsa (£9.95), and venison rump steak with red wine and peppercorn sauce (£10.95) or local lobster (June to October). There's no nearby parking. *(Recommended by Michael Doswell, Ruth and Paul Lawrence, Pat and Tony Martin, Mike and Lynn Robinson, John Foord, Keith and Janet Morris, Comus and Sarah Elliott)*

Free house ~ Licensee Christine Forsyth ~ Real ale ~ Bar food ~ No credit cards ~ (01665) 576262 ~ Children welcome ~ Dogs welcome ~ For opening times it's best to ring

NEWTON-ON-THE-MOOR NU1605 Map 10
Cook & Barker Arms 🍽 🛏

Village signposted from A1 Alnwick—Felton

The atmosphere at this buoyantly run stone inn is lively and bustling. Though most people are here for the generously served food, the relaxed and unfussy long beamed bar is cheerfully pubby, with stripped stone and partly panelled walls, brocade-seated settles around oak-topped tables, brasses, a highly polished oak servery, and a coal fire at one end with a coal-effect gas fire at the other. A no smoking eating area has tables, chairs, an old settle, scrubbed pine furniture, and french windows leading on to the terrace; the top bar area is no smoking, too; piped music. The inviting choice of changing food, served by enthusiastic young staff, might include sandwiches (from £2.75), broccoli and stilton soup (£2.95), rocket, pear and goats cheese salad (£3.95), moules marinière (£4.95), smoked salmon (£5), wild mushroom risotto (£6.50), steak and onion pie (£6.95), grilled sardines with tomato ragoût (£7.50), duck confit (£7.95), braised lamb shank with mustard mash (£8.95), and puddings such as summer pudding (£3.95). Their home-made bread is delicious. Three or four well kept rotating ales on handpump might include Black Sheep, Mordue Workie Ticket and Timothy Taylors Landlord. They also have local bottled beer, quite a few malt whiskies, an extensive wine list, and a dozen wines by the glass. *(Recommended by Mike and Wendy Proctor, Jill and Keith Wright, Dr and Mrs R G J Telfer, Malcolm Taylor, Peter and Jean Hoare, Paul and Annette Hallett, R M Corlett, David J M Taylor, Tony and Wendy Hobden, Dave and Sue Mitchell, Jenny and Dave Hughes, Robin and Joyce Peachey, Alison Hayes, Pete Hanlon, Clare Pearse)*

Free house ~ Licensee Phil Farmer ~ Real ale ~ Bar food (12-2, 6-9) ~ Restaurant ~ (01665) 575234 ~ Children welcome ~ Open 11-3, 6-11; 12-3, 6-10.30 Sun ~ Bedrooms: £45B/£90B

RENNINGTON NU2119 Map 10
Masons Arms 🛏
Stamford Cott; B1340 NE of Alnwick

This jolly friendly pub is quite spotless, and has a relaxed atmosphere in its thoughtfully modernised and comfortable beamed lounge bar, which has wheelback and mate's chairs around solid wood tables on a patterned carpet, plush bar stools, and plenty of brass, pictures and photographs. The dining rooms (one is no smoking) have pine panelling and wrought-iron wall lights. Served by really courteous and helpful staff, the reasonably priced home-made bar food is tasty, and includes lunchtime sandwiches (from £2.75), soup (£2.65), mushrooms in stilton sauce (£4.25), pâté made from craster kippers (£4.35), italian sausage with basil and tomato sauce or spicy lentil lasagne (£6.95), game casserole (£7.25), steaks (from £12.45), daily specials such as scampi (£6.50) or pork, lemon and ginger casserole (£7.20), and puddings such as chocolate fudge gateau (from £3.15); their good value Sunday lunch is understandably popular (£5.75). Two changing well kept beers might be Hadrian & Border Gladiator and Secret Kingdom; shove-ha'penny, dominoes, darts and piped music. There are sturdy rustic tables on the little front lavender surrounded terrace. Only children over five are allowed to stay overnight; the bedrooms are in an adjacent stable block and annexe, and they do good breakfasts – and have a kennel for dogs. This is quite well placed for exploring the nearby coast. *(Recommended by W K Wood, H D Whitham, Mrs Jane Orbell, Mr and Mrs W D Borthwick, Lynette and Stuart Shore, Mike and Wendy Proctor)*

Free house ~ Licensees Paul and Carol Forster ~ Real ale ~ Bar food (12-2(2.30 Sun), 6.30-9; not 25 Dec or 1 Jan evenings) ~ Restaurant ~ (01665) 577275 ~ Children in two no smoking dining rooms ~ Open 12-11(10.30 Sun); 12-2(2.30 Sun), 6.30-11 (10.30 Sun) winter ~ Bedrooms: £39B/£59B

ROMALDKIRK NY9922 Map 10
Rose & Crown ★ 🍽 ♀ 🛏
Just off B6277

Run by Christopher and Alison Davy with loving care and enthusiastic attention to detail, this 18th-c coaching inn is doing really well these days. They put all sorts of effort into getting things just right, such as making their own marmalades, jams, chutneys and bread. The imaginative bar menu changes every week (it's very popular, so you will need to book), and as well as lunchtime baps (from £3.95) and ploughman's (£6.95), delicious food might include home-made soup (£3.50), smoked trout mousse (£4.50), steak, kidney and mushroom pie or roast ratatouille risotto (£9.75), confit of duck leg with orange sauce (£10), grilled bass with smoked bacon and leek purée and red wine jus (£11.95), and puddings such as sticky toffee pudding or crème caramel with winter fruit (£3.50). The traditional cosy beamed bar has old-fashioned seats facing a warming log fire, a Jacobean oak settle, lots of brass and copper, a grandfather clock, and gin traps, old farm tools, and black and white pictures of Romaldkirk on the walls. Black Sheep and Theakstons Best are well kept on handpump alongside about a dozen wines, all of which you can have by the glass. The smart brasserie-style Crown Room (bar food is served in here) has large cartoons of French waiters on dark red walls, a grey carpet and smart high-back chairs. The hall has farm tools, wine maps and other interesting prints, along with a photograph (taken by a customer) of the Hale Bopp comet over Romaldkirk church. There's also a no smoking oak-panelled restaurant. Tables outside look out over the village green, still with its original stocks and water pump. The village is close to the superb Bowes Museum and the High Force waterfall, and has an interesting old church. They do very good breakfasts, if you're staying. *(Recommended by Graham Banks, S J Heaton, Alan Thwaite, Robin and Joyce Peachey, Margaret and Roy Randle, Comus and Sarah Elliott, Tim and Carolyn Lowes, Hans and Thelma Liesner, Barry Robson, Mrs Phoebe A Kemp, Greta and Christopher Wells, Jill and Keith Wright, Michael Doswell, Alan and Mandy Maynard, Mr and Mrs W D Borthwick, Di and Mike Gillam, Alison Hayes, Pete Hanlon; also in the* Good Hotel Guide*)*

Free house ~ Licensees Christopher and Alison Davy ~ Real ale ~ Bar food (12-1.30, 6.30-9.30) ~ Restaurant ~ (01833) 650213 ~ Children welcome, must be over 6 in restaurant ~ Dogs allowed in bar and bedrooms ~ Open 11-3, 5.30-11; 12-3, 7-10.30 Sun; closed 24-26 Dec ~ Bedrooms: £70B/£96B

SEAHOUSES NU2232 Map 10
Olde Ship ★ 🍺 🛏

Just off B1340, towards harbour

If you've been here before you'll have fun trying to spot the new nautical artefacts that are continually being added to the already fascinating treasure-trove of genuine seafaring memorabilia at this nice stone harbour hotel. The entire bar is a tribute to the sea and seafarers – even the floor is scrubbed ship's decking, and, if it's working, an anemometer takes wind speed readings from the top of the chimney. Besides lots of other shiny brass fittings, ship's instruments and equipment, and a knotted anchor made by local fishermen, there are sea pictures and model ships, including fine ones of the North Sunderland lifeboat, and Seahouses' lifeboat the *Grace Darling*). There's also a model of the *Forfarshire* (the paddle steamer that Grace Darling went to rescue in 1838 – you can read more of the story in the pub), and even the ship's nameboard. The bar is gently lit by stained-glass sea picture windows, and it has an open fire in winter. One clear window looks out across the harbour to the Farne Islands, and as dusk falls you can watch the Longstones lighthouse shine across the fading evening sky. The low-beamed Cabin Room is no smoking; possibly piped music. The choice of four well kept ales on handpump – Bass, Greene King Old Speckled Hen and Ruddles, and Theakstons Best – is doubled in summer months with the addition of guests such as Black Sheep and Timothy Taylors Landlord; also some 30 malt whiskies and a good choice of wines. Bar food might include leek and potato soup (£3), chicken liver pâté or grapefruit and mandarin cocktail (£3.60), fish stew, stuffed whiting, liver and onion casserole or beef stroganoff (£7.20), with puddings such as lemon meringue pie or white and dark chocolate sponge with chocolate sauce (£3.60). The pub is not really suitable for children though, along with walkers, they are welcome on the battlemented side terrace (you'll even find fishing memorabilia out here). This and a sun lounge look out on the harbour. You can book boat trips to the Farne Islands Bird Sanctuary at the harbour, and there are bracing coastal walks, particularly to Bamburgh, Grace Darling's birthplace; dominoes, putting and quoits. *(Recommended by Brian England, Rona Murdoch, Filip Lemmens, the Didier, Daphne and Peter Ross, David and Ruth Hollands, D J Hulse, Brian Root, Keith and Janet Morris, KN-R, Anna and Martyn Carey, Paul and Ursula Randall, Comus and Sarah Elliott, Dr and Mrs R G J Telfer, Ruth and Paul Lawrence, Ian and Nita Cooper)*

Free house ~ Licensees Alan and Jean Glen ~ Real ale ~ Bar food (12-2, 7-8.30; not 25 Dec) ~ Restaurant ~ (01665) 720200 ~ Children in family room, over 10 in bedrooms ~ Open 11-11; 12-10.30 Sun ~ Bedrooms: £43S/£90B

We mention bottled beers and spirits only if there is something unusual about them – imported belgian real ales, say, or dozens of malt whiskies; so do please let us know about them in your reports.

SHINCLIFFE NZ2941 Map 10

Seven Stars 🍺

High Street North; A177 1 mile or so S of Durham

Buzzing with customers from early in the evening on, this 18th-c village inn is popular for its very good food, though at the same time it does manage to keep a nice local atmosphere going. From a changing menu, interesting dishes might include soup (£3.50), sandwiches (from £3.50), seafood chowder (£4.50), mexican chicken on a tortilla with guacamole (£4.50), steak and ale pie (£7.50), toulouse sausage with herb mash and soubise sauce (£9), monkfish medallions wrapped in pancetta with lemon and thyme risotto (£12.50), daily specials such as lemon sole stuffed with crayfish with creamy mash and chive butter (£11), and mouth-watering puddings such as white chocolate and blueberry brûlée (£3.50); extra vegetables are billed. It's worth booking for their very good value Sunday roast (£7.50). Friendly staff serve well kept Black Sheep and Castle Eden and a guest such as Courage Directors from handpump, and they've 25 malt whiskies. The comfortable interior is civilised but still largely unspoilt: the lounge bar has a coal fire in its handsome Victorian fireplace, with a pair of big staffordshire dogs on the mantelpiece below a big mirror, old brewery advertisements, copper kettles and a small collection of miners lamps hanging from the beams, and cushioned wall banquettes and stools around cast-iron-framed tables. The romantic candlelit dining room and half the lounge are no smoking; cribbage, chess, draughts, dominoes and piped music. There are pretty window boxes, creepers, and seats outside at the end of the attractive village street. Parking can be a problem but it's just 10 minutes' or so drive from central Durham, with fairly frequent buses passing the door. *(Recommended by Pat and John Morris, Peter Burton, SH, Darly Graton, Graeme Gulibert, Jim Abbott, Keith Mould, R M Corlett, R T and J C Moggridge, Bob and Valerie Mawson, Jenny and Dave Hughes, Peter and Patricia Burton, M Borthwick)*

Mortal Man Inns ~ Manager Feargus Ryan ~ Real ale ~ Bar food (12-2.30, 6-9.30 (9 Sun)) ~ Restaurant ~ (0191) 384 8454 ~ Children in eating area of bar and restaurant ~ Dogs allowed in bar ~ Open 11-11(10.30 Sun); closed evening 25 Dec/1 Jan ~ Bedrooms: £40S/£55S

STANNERSBURN NY7286 Map 10

Pheasant 🍺

Kielder Water road signposted off B6320 in Bellingham

Impeccably kept, the cosy interior of this homely old village pub gleams with polished brass and wood. The traditionally comfortable lounge has stools ranged along the counter, and lots of old local photographs on stripped stone and panelling. A separate public bar is similar but simpler, and opens into a further cosy seating area with beams and panelling (until recently this was a games room). The evening sees a good mix of visitors and locals, when the small no smoking dining room can get quite crowded, and the landlord and staff are particularly friendly. Listed on blackboards, enjoyable home-made bar food could include lunchtime sandwiches (from £2.80) and ploughman's (£5.95), garlic chicken breast salad (£6.75), and game and mushroom pie or roast lamb with redcurrant jus (£6.95), as well as a few more elaborate evening dishes such as grilled salmon with herb mayonnaise or fried marinated chicken with honey-roast peppers (£9.25), and duck confit (£11.95), with puddings such as home-made sticky toffee pudding or lemon and lime cheesecake (£3.35); prices for the same dishes go up by a couple of pounds in the evenings. They do a roast Sunday lunch (£6.95), and if you're staying the breakfasts are good. Building up to four in the summer months, real ales might include well kept Black Sheep, Timothy Taylors Landlord and Wylam Gold Tankard and Bohemia Pilsner on handpump, around 36 malt whiskies, and a decent reasonably priced wine list. A streamside garden has picnic-sets, and a pony paddock behind. This is a peaceful valley, with quiet forests all around, and Kielder Water just up the road. *(Recommended by Ron and Mary Nicholson, John Poulter, Michael Doswell, David and Heather Stephenson, Kate and Byron Davies, GSB)*

Free house ~ Licensees Walter and Robin Kershaw ~ Real ale ~ Bar food ~ Restaurant ~ (01434) 240382 ~ Children in eating area of bar and restaurant ~ Open 11-3, 6-11; 12-3, 7-10.30 Sun; 12-2, 7-10.30 in winter; closed Mon/Tues Nov-Mar ~ Bedrooms: £40S/£70S

STANNINGTON NZ2279 Map 10
Ridley Arms

Village signposted just off A1 S of Morpeth

The Sir John Fitzgerald pub group, which took over this handily placed dining pub fairly recently, is a smallish group, based in the north east but extending from there, which has our respect for thoughtful and interesting pub design and refurbishment. They have certainly done well here. It's a big place, extended and more or less open-plan, but cleverly laid out in a way that gives the feel of several separate relaxing areas, each slightly different in mood and style from its neighbours. The front is a proper bar area, with darts and a fruit machine, and stools along the counter that serves well kept Black Sheep and Timothy Taylors Landlord and up to seven guests from brewers such as Brakspears, Everards, Mordue, Ridley and Ruddles, from handpump. The beamed dining areas, largely no smoking, lead back from here, with a second bar counter, comfortable armchairs and upright chairs around shiny dark wood tables on polished boards or carpet, with portraits and cartoons on cream, panelled or stripped stone walls, careful lighting and some horsey statuettes. Good food served generously includes starters such as soup (£2.95), wild mushroom ravioli (£3.50), black pudding with garlic mash (£3.95), and main courses such as mushroom tart (£5.95), sausage and mash (£6.95), steak and ale casserole (£7.50) and rack of lamb with rosemary garlic potatoes (£8.50); they do a popular family Sunday lunch. Service is quick, and despite the size of the place the friendly landlord is very much in evidence, his staff neatly turned out and cheerful. Disabled access is good; unobtrusive piped music. There are tables outside. *(Recommended by David and Heather Stephenson, John Oddey, Tony and Wendy Hobden, Paul and Ursula Randall, M Borthwick, John Foord, Gerry and Rosemary Dobson)*

Sir John Fitzgerald ~ Manager Lyn Reilly ~ Real ale ~ Bar food (12-9.30(9 Sun)) ~ (01670) 789216 ~ Children welcome ~ Open 11.30-11; 12-10.30 Sun

THROPTON NU0302 Map 10
Three Wheat Heads

B6341

There's a fairly sedate dining atmosphere at this comfortable stone-built 17th-c village hotel, locally popular with older folk for meals out; in summer it tempts a wider range of visitors, with its good position in the heart of Coquetdale, and its attractive garden with lovely views towards the Simonside Hills, a play area and a dovecote. The carpeted bar on the right and the pleasant and roomy flock-wallpapered dining area have good coal fires (one in a fine tall stone fireplace), which you might find lit even when it's not that cold, wheelback chairs around neat rows of dark tables, more heavily cushioned brocaded seats, comfortable bar stools with backrests, and an elaborate longcase clock; darts and piped music. Emphasis is on the enjoyable food, which might include soup (£2.75), breaded crab claws (£4.50), fresh battered cod (£6.50), pork stroganoff (£7.70), steak and mushroom pie or nut roast (£7.75), braised lamb shank (£7.95), sirloin steak (£11.95), and puddings (£2.95); no smoking restaurant. Staff are friendly and efficient, and the Marstons Pedigree and Theakstons on handpump are well kept. *(Recommended by Comus and Sarah Elliott, Kevin Thorpe, Tony and Wendy Hobden, A and B D Craig, Barry Collett, Keith Mould)*

Pubmaster ~ Lease Danny Scullion ~ Real ale ~ Bar food (12-2, 7-9; 12-9 Sat/Sun/ bank hols) ~ Restaurant ~ (01669) 620262 ~ Children welcome ~ Dogs allowed in bar and bedrooms ~ Open 11-3, 6-11(11-11 Sat/Sun) ~ Bedrooms: £39B/£59B

WARENFORD NU1429 Map 10

Warenford Lodge

Off A1 3 or 4 miles S of Belford

Quite simple 60s décor at this slightly quirky stone house makes the partly stripped stone bar look less old than it actually is. It has cushioned wooden seats around pine tables, and a warm fire in the big stone fireplace; steps lead up to an extension with comfortable dining tables and chairs, and a big woodburning stove. They serve a decent selection of wines and malt whiskies, farm-pressed fruit juices, a good choice of teas, and keg John Smiths. You'll need to keep your eyes open to find the pub as there's no sign outside, and do check their limited opening times before you set out. Readers particularly like their interesting local cheese platter (£5.75). Using quite a few local ingredients and served by friendly staff, other well presented home-made dishes could include stottie sandwiches (£2.50), soup with turkestan bread (£2.80), wild mushroom risotto or northumbrian fish soup (£4.60), spinach and ricotta cannelloni (£6.50), lamb hotpot (£7.20), sea bream with chilli jam (£9.50), thai green curry with monkfish and prawns (£10.50), and puddings such as apple and red fruit crumble or dark chocolate flan (£3.30). *(Recommended by Hans and Thelma Liesner, Sam and John Pallett)*

Free house ~ Licensees Ray and Marion Matthewman ~ Bar food (Sun lunchtime only; 7-9.30) ~ Restaurant ~ (01668) 213453 ~ Children in eating area of bar and restaurant ~ Open 7-11; 12-2, 7-11(10.30 Sun) wknds; cl Sun evening, Mon/Tues in winter; closed Mon, Tues-Fri lunchtimes, 25/26 Dec, 1 Jan and 3 weeks in Jan

WELDON BRIDGE NZ1399 Map 10

Anglers Arms

B6344, just off A697; village signposted with Rothbury off A1 N of Morpeth

The nicely lit and traditionally comfortable turkey-carpeted bar at this substantial hotel is divided into two parts: cream walls on the right, and oak panelling and some shiny black beams hung with copper pans on the left, with a grandfather clock and sofa by the coal fire, staffordshire cats and other antique ornaments on its mantelpiece, old fishing and other country prints, some in heavy gilt frames, a profusion of other fishing memorabilia, and some taxidermy. Some of the tables are lower than you'd expect for eating, but their chairs have short legs to match – different, and rather engaging. Greene King Old Speckled Hen and Timothy Taylors Landlord are well kept on handpump alongside a guest such as Adnams, also decent wines and an espresso machine; there may be almost imperceptible piped music. The no smoking side restaurant in a former railway dining car is more formal but light and airy, with crisp white linen and a pink carpet. Bar food includes soup (£2.75), prawn and smoked salmon cocktail (£5.45), battered cod and chips or steak and ale pie (£7.25), grilled rainbow trout with lemon butter stuffed with prawns (£7.95), mixed grill (£12.95) and puddings such as sticky toffee pudding and strawberry pavlova (£4.45); Sunday roast (£7.75). There are tables in an attractive garden with a good play area, and they have rights to fishing on a mile of the River Coquet just across the road. *(Recommended by Keith Mould, Paul and Sue Merrick, Dr Ben Green, Anne Evans)*

Free house ~ Licensee John Young ~ Bar food (12-2, 6-9.30) ~ Restaurant ~ (01665) 570271 ~ Children welcome ~ Dogs allowed in bedrooms ~ Open 11-3, 6-11; 12-3, 6-10.30 Sun ~ Bedrooms: £35S/£55S

Bedroom prices normally include full english breakfast, VAT and any inclusive service charge that we know of. Prices before the '/' are for single rooms, after for two people in double or twin (B includes a private bath, S a private shower). If there is no '/', the prices are only for twin or double rooms (as far as we know there are no singles).

Lucky Dip

Besides the fully inspected pubs, you might like to try these Lucky Dips recommended to us and described by readers (if you do, please send us reports: www.goodguides.com).

ACOMB [NY9366]

Miners Arms [Main St]: Charming small 18th-c pub under newish licensees, well kept Durham Magus, Jennings Cumberland and Mordue, simple cheap home cooking by landlady (not wkdy lunchtimes) from sandwiches to good value Sun lunch, comfortable settles, huge fire in stone fireplace, children in dining room; small garden behind, has been open all day Sun and summer *(Michael Doswell)*

ALNMOUTH [NU2410]

Red Lion [Northumberland St]: Welcoming 16th-c inn in quiet coastal village, log fire in bar full of theatre bills and memorabilia, local real ale, food from good sandwiches to local fish and other restaurant dishes, children's menu – children and dogs welcome *(Dr and Mrs P Truelove)*

☆ *Saddle* [Northumberland St (B1338)]: Unpretentious but hospitable stone-built hotel rambling through several areas inc spacious dining area, wide choice of good attractively priced generous pubby food inc particularly good cheeseboard, popular Sun lunch (small or large helpings), well kept real ales such as Greene King Old Speckled Hen and Theakstons Best, games room with ping pong as well as pool etc, no smoking restaurant; unobtrusive piped music; children welcome, open all day Sat, tables outside, comfortable bedrooms, attractive beaches, good coastal walks *(Richard and Karen Holt, A and B D Craig, Alan Melville, Myke and Nicky Crombleholme, Mrs M Granville-Edge, LYM)*

ALNWICK [NU1813]

Tanners Arms [Hotspur Pl]: Small appealingly basic single-bar pub with flagstones and stripped stones, quick friendly service, well kept Belhaven 80/- and Theakstons Black Bull, bargain lunchtime toasties and pizzas *(Rona Murdoch)*

BAMBURGH [NU1834]

☆ *Victoria* [Front St]: Good cooking in substantial hotel's interesting refurbished no smoking brasserie (shame about the piped music), well kept Castle Eden Nimmos XXXX and Mordue Radgie Gadgie, caring young staff, young children's playroom, pool in public bar; comfortable bedrooms, lovely setting *(Peter and Jean Hoare, Anna and Martyn Carey, Comus and Sarah Elliott)*

BARNARD CASTLE [NZ0516]

☆ *Old Well* [The Bank]: Interesting Tudor coaching inn with big helpings of good food from sandwiches and baked potatoes to gourmet evenings, two bars and three pleasant dining areas (two no smoking, well behaved children allowed), friendly helpful staff, well kept Black Sheep, Courage Directors and Theakstons Best, decent wines; secluded terrace over town walls, big comfortable bedrooms – a good base for

Bowes Museum; cl Mon and Thurs lunchtime *(Tim and Ann Newell, Paul A Moore, Jack and Heather Coyle, M Borthwick)*

BELFORD [NU1033]

☆ *Blue Bell* [off A1 S of Berwick; Market Pl]: Old-fashioned lounge bar in substantial and attractive old coaching inn, decent bar food from sandwiches up inc children's meals, log fire, extensive wine list, around 20 malt whiskies, perhaps John Smiths on handpump, no smoking restaurant; piped music, games in public bar; children welcome, big neatly kept garden, bedrooms *(Peter and Patricia Burton, Mrs Jane Orbell, LYM, Mrs J Ekins-Daukes, John and Sylvia Harrop, John Hale, Dr and Mrs R G J Telfer, GSB)*

BELLINGHAM [NY8383]

Riverdale Hall: Biggish Victorian hotel on River North Tyne, in same family for 25 years; two smart bars, well kept Jennings, interesting bar food here, overlooking swimming pool or cricket field, or out on the lawn, long-serving welcoming staff, asian touches to restaurant menu, good wine list; bedrooms, lots of facilities, salmon fishing *(Guy Vowles, Peter Scillitoe)*

BELSAY [NZ1079]

☆ *Highlander* [A696]: Comfortable and roomy country dining pub, good range of food from good lunchtime sandwiches up in extensively refurbished side bar and open-plan dining area, nice plain wood tables, plenty of nooks and corners for character, reasonable prices, welcoming helpful service, well kept Scottish Courage ales, good log fires, unobtrusive piped music, separate locals' bar; open all day, handy for Belsay Hall *(Michael Doswell, J A Hooker)*

BERWICK-UPON-TWEED [NT9952]

Angel [Brewery Bank, Tweedmouth]: Victorian-style refurbishment with low-priced Cowie, Mordue and other changing ales, welcoming atmosphere, pool and TV; popular with Berwick Rangers supporters, can get crowded wknds; open all day wkdys *(Ian and Nita Cooper)*

Foxtons [Hide Hill]: Cheerful welcoming two-floor bar with slightly frenchified bistro atmosphere, casual and lively, wide choice of good imaginative food, well kept changing ales such as Caledonian 80/- and Timothy Taylors Landlord (happy hour 5.30-6.30), good range of wines and whiskies, friendly service; side restaurant; busy, so worth booking evenings *(Paul and Ursula Randall)*

☆ *Rob Roy* [Dock View Rd/Dock Rd, Spittal (Tweedmouth)]: Quiet and cosy seaview restaurant (rather than pub, though they do bar meals too) with good fresh local fish and outstanding speciality fish soup, dark fishing-theme rustic bar with roaring fire and polished wood floor, pleasant dining room, friendly landlord; keg beers but decent wines and good fresh coffee; bedrooms *(Peter Burton, Paul and Ursula Randall)*

BIRTLEY [NZ2756]

Millhouse [Blackfell; handy for A1 southbound, just S of Angel, off A1231 Sunderland/Washington slip road]: Popular extended dining pub with new chef doing enjoyable food all day, olde-barn décor, alcoved eating areas, Theakstons Best and XB, good service and atmosphere, no smoking restaurant *(Jenny and Dave Hughes)*

CHATTON [NU0528]

Percy Arms [B6348 E of Wooller]: Stone-built inn with neat lounge bar extending through arch, public bar with games, juke box or piped music, Theakstons and around 30 malt whiskies, attractive panelled dining room, cheerful efficient staff, generous straightforward bar food from lunchtime filled baguettes and baked potatoes up; children in family area and dining room, picnic-sets on small front lawn, bedrooms (12 miles of private fishing) *(LYM)*

CHESTER-LE-STREET [NZ2649]

Church Mouse [A167 S, Chester Moor]: Enjoyable food, good drinks choice *(Jenny and Dave Hughes)*

CONSETT [NZ1151]

Grey Horse [Sherburn Terr]: Welcoming two-bar beamed 19th-c pub brewing its own Derwent Rose beers in former back stables, inc Paddy named for the pub dog, and Red Dust, Steel Town and The Works recalling the former steel works here; also a guest beer, lots of malt whiskies, occasional beer festivals, very friendly licensees, cheap bar lunches inc toasties, baguettes and all-day breakfast (may be evening toasties too), good range of customers, pool; pavement tables, open all day *(Andy and Jill Kassube, Brian and Anna Marsden, Kevin Thorpe)*

CORBRIDGE [NY9964]

☆ *Angel* [Newcastle Rd]: Small 17th-c hotel with fresh food from good sandwiches to imaginative blackboard dishes in large simply decorated bar and adjoining plush panelled lounge, three well kept ales inc Black Sheep and Wylam, decent wines, good coffees, friendly if not always speedy service, carefully refurbished restaurant; bedrooms *(Michael Doswell, Peter and Jean Hoare, John Foord, Jenny and Dave Hughes, Robert M Warner, LYM, GSB, Jenny and Brian Seller)*

☆ *Black Bull* [Middle St]: Roomy unpretentious pub, old-fashioned and low-ceilinged, with comfortable mix of seating inc traditional settles in stone-floored bar, four changing well kept ales such as Boddingtons, Caledonian Deuchars IPA, Castle Eden and Flowers Original, good attractively priced wine choice, polite attentive staff, roaring fire, decent food all day inc popular Sun roasts, large no smoking restaurant; good atmosphere even on crowded Fri/Sat night, open all day

(John Foord, Peter Burton, Liz and John Soden)

☆ *Robin Hood* [East Wallhouses, Military Rd (B6318 5 miles NE)]: Unpretentious pub popular for generous wholesome food inc good steak baguettes (choice widest in good-sized candlelit back restaurant); beamed lounge with blazing fires, lots of bric-a-brac and interesting carved settles, great views from bay window, quick friendly service even when busy, daily papers; Greene King Old Speckled Hen, Marstons Pedigree and Tetleys, piped music *(Pat and Derek Roughton)*

Wheatsheaf [Watling St/St Helens St]: Big refurbished stone-built village hotel, popular esp with older lunchers for wide choice of generous food (all day wknds) from sandwiches to seasonal game, quick service, well kept ales such as Jennings Cumberland, Marstons Pedigree and Worthington 1744, good choice of wines and malt whiskies, pleasant Victorian décor in dining lounge and big warm conservatory restaurant with distant hill views; pub games, piped music, some picnic-sets outside; bedrooms *(Jack and Heather Coyle, Hilary Forrest, John Foord, Michael Doswell, LYM)*

COTHERSTONE [NZ0119]

Red Lion: Traditional beamed 18th-c pub with good food (not Mon-Thurs) in bar and no smoking restaurant from sandwiches through familiar things to some interesting dishes, Jennings Cumberland and JJ and Charles Wells Bombardier, log fire, snug; children, boots and dogs welcome, garden tables, bedrooms *(Peter and Eva Lowes)*

CRAMLINGTON [NZ2576]

Beacon Farm [Beacon Lane]: Cheap beer, decent food inc good veg; good for children *(Sherrie Glass)*

Snowy Owl [Blagdon Lane]: Large character Vintage Inn dining pub, beams, flagstones, hop bines, stripped stone and terracotta paintwork, soft lighting and an interesting mix of furnishings and decorations (you'd never guess it was formerly a warehouse), enjoyable food, good choice of wines, well kept Bass, friendly efficient service, daily papers; may be piped music; bedrooms *(Michael Doswell)*

CRASTER [NU2620]

☆ *Jolly Fisherman* [off B1339, NE of Alnwick]: Simple well worn in local, a favourite of many for its crab sandwiches, crab soup and picture-window harbour and sea views, with well kept ales such as Caledonian Deuchars IPA and Marstons Pedigree; imperative to get there early in season; dogs welcome, games area with pool and juke box; picnic-sets on grass behind, lovely clifftop walk to Dunstanburgh Castle. *(the Didler, Anna and Martyn Carey, Barry Collett, W K Wood, Keith and Janet Morris, KN-R, A and B D Craig, LYM, Pat and Tony Martin, Robin and Joyce Peachey, Mr and Mrs Richard Osborne, Des and Jen Clarke)*

CRAWCROOK [NZ1363]
Rising Sun [Bank Top]: Roomy and well refurbished, bright and welcoming, with huge choice of hearty popular food in dining area and conservatory, well kept and priced Black Sheep, Mordue Workie Ticket and three guest beers from long bar, cheerful staff, steps up to lounge, separate pool room; neatly kept garden, open all day *(John Foord, John Oddey)*

DUNSTAN [NU2419]
☆ *Cottage* [off B1339 Alnmouth—Embleton]: Big family dining pub with low beams, some stripped brickwork, banquettes and dimpled copper tables, usual lunches and evening meals, all-day sandwiches and snacks, well kept Belhaven, Wylam and a guest beer, neat friendly young staff, no smoking conservatory, medieval-theme restaurant, games area, children welcome, tables out on flowery terrace and lawn, good adventure play area, modern bedrooms *(W K Wood, Brian Root, Tim and Sue Halstead, Mike and Wendy Proctor, LYM, A and B D Craig, J A Hooker, Michael Doswell, Ian and Barbara Rankin, GSB)*

DURHAM [NZ2642]
Colpitts [Colpitts Terr/Hawthorn Terr]: Basic friendly two-bar local with particularly cheap Sam Smiths, sandwiches, open fires, pool, TV and machines; perhaps the country's smallest beer garden in yard *(the Didler, Eric Larkham)*
Court Inn [Court Lane]: Good generous home-made food all day from sandwiches to steaks and late-evening bargains in unpretentious traditional town pub's extensive no smoking stripped brick eating area, real ales such as Hancocks HB and Worthington 1744, no mobile phones; bustling in term-time with students and teachers, piped pop music; seats outside, open all day *(BB, Eric Larkham, Andy and Jill Kassube, Pete Baker, Tim and Ann Newell)*
☆ *Dun Cow* [Old Elvet]: Unsmart and very welcoming traditional town pub in pretty 16th-c black and white timbered cottage, tiny chatty front bar with wall benches, corridor linking it to long narrow back lounge with machines etc (can be packed with students), real ales inc particularly well kept Castle Eden, cheap soup and sandwiches etc, friendly staff; piped music; children welcome, open all day Mon-Sat, Sun too in summer *(the Didler, Tracey and Stephen Groves, LYM, Pete Baker, Eric Larkham, Richard Lewis)*
Old Elm Tree [Crossgate]: Big busy pub on steep hill opp castle, two-room main bar and small lounge, prompt cheerful service, open fires, several real ales, farm cider; TV, machines, juke box; seats outside, good value bedrooms *(the Didler)*
Swan & Three Cygnets [Elvet Bridge]: Comfortably refurbished Victorian pub in good bridge-end spot high above river, city views from big windows and picnic-sets out

on terrace, bargain food from hot filled baguettes up, cheap well kept Sam Smiths OB; open all day *(Andy and Jill Kassube, BB, Dave Braisted)*

EACHWICK [NZ1069]
Plough [S of village, extension of B6324 NW of Newcastle]: Large family chain dining pub, children welcome (toys and high chairs), reasonably priced food inc popular Sun lunch, well kept Black Sheep, standard décor and furnishings, lots of young staff; garden with wishing well *(Jenny and Brian Seller)*

EARSDON [NZ3272]
Cannon [Front St]: Busy pub, good choice of bar meals and beers, helpful staff *(Robert M Warner)*

EBCHESTER [NZ1055]
☆ *Derwent Walk* [Ebchester Hill (B6309 outside)]: Friendly pub by the Gateshead—Consett walk for which it's named, walkers welcome, fine Derwent Valley views from conservatory and pleasant heated terrace, enterprising choice of good generous home-made food inc interesting hot-filled cobblers, full Jennings range kept well and a guest such as Ridleys or Charles Wells Bombardier, good wine range, good log fire *(Andy and Jill Kassube)*

EGGLESCLIFFE [NZ4213]
☆ *Blue Bell* [Yarm Rd (A67)]: Open-plan John Barras pub with good choice of cheap food all day in spacious and comfortable big-windowed bar, four real ales, good value wines by the glass, friendly service, tables out on deck by goat-cropped grass sloping down to the River Tees with fine view of the great 1849 railway viaduct (and boat trips to Stockton); children's room, no dogs *(LYM, JHBS)*

EGLINGHAM [NU1019]
☆ *Tankerville Arms* [B6346 Alnwick—Wooler]: Pleasant long stone village pub with good value food using local ingredients from good sandwiches to interesting main dishes and Sun roasts (best to book esp Tues), early evening bargains Mon-Thurs, well kept ales such as Black Sheep, Courage Directors, Hadrian & Border and Mordue, decent choice of wines, malt whiskies and of teas and coffees, courteous service, black joists, some stripped stone, plush banquettes, captain's chairs and turkey carpet, coal fires each end, snug no smoking lounge, two dining rooms; dominoes, piped music; children welcome, garden tables *(C A Hall, Jenny and Peter Lowater, Darly Graton, Graeme Gulibert, Mrs Jane Orbell, Tim and Sue Halstead, Dr and Mrs R G J Telfer, Lynne and Philip Naylor, Robert M Warner, LYM)*

ELWICK [NZ4533]
Spotted Cow [¼ mile off A19 W of Hartlepool]: Nicely refurbished old two-bar pub facing village green, Camerons Strongarm, good food inc fresh fish from Hartlepool in pleasantly plush lounge and dining room; open all day *(JHBS)*

EMBLETON [NU2322]

☆ *Dunstanburgh Castle Hotel*: Enjoyable dining room meals at bar prices inc game and fresh fish in comfortable hotel attractively placed nr magnificent coastline, nice bright bar, pleasant staff, several malt whiskies and well priced wines; keg beers; bedrooms clean and well furnished *(Nigel Williamson)*

ETAL [NT9339]

Black Bull [off B6354 SW of Berwick]: Pretty white-painted cottage, the only thatched pub in Northumberland, spacious unpretentious open-plan lounge bar with glossily varnished beams, two well kept real ales, 30 malt whiskies, farm cider, quick service; children in eating area, games room with darts, dominoes, pool, TV, juke box and piped music; open all day Sat, a few picnic-sets out in front; nice spot nr castle ruins and light railway *(Mike and Lynn Robinson, LYM)*

FELTON [NU1800]

☆ *Northumberland Arms* [village signed off A1 N of Morpeth]: Good generous food all day from bargain Tues lunch to interesting specials, also children's dishes; roomy and comfortable open-plan bar with beams, stripped stone and good coal fires, nice mix of furnishings inc big blue settees, elegant small end restaurant; pleasant atmosphere, well kept Bass and Black Sheep Best, good coffee and wines, laid-back service; well reproduced piped music, esp in conservatory pool room, monthly live music 1st Weds; five bedrooms, steps down to bench by River Coquet, open all day *(Michael Doswell, BB)*

GATESHEAD [NZ2758]

Waggon [Galloping Green Rd, Eighton Banks]: Extended refurbished local, good value generous straightforward food (can be ordered ahead) from sandwiches and baked potatoes to Sun lunch, comfortable airy eating areas inc no smoking conservatory overlooking old Bowes Railway, well kept changing beers, friendly prompt service *(M Borthwick)*

HALTWHISTLE [NY7064]

Black Bull [just off Market Sq, behind indian restaurant]: Half a dozen particularly well kept changing ales inc ones brewed at the pub, welcoming landlord and locals, beams, stripped stone, two log fires, darts and monthly quiz night; no music or food, cl Mon-Weds lunchtimes *(Michele D'Lemos, Eric Larkham, Andy and Jill Kassube)*

Twice Brewed [B6318 NE]: Busy pub handy for the wall (and for Once Brewed youth hostel), well kept Mordue and a beer brewed for the pub, enjoyable reasonably priced hearty food, kindly landlord; open all day, tables outside *(Dave Braisted, Jenny and Brian Seller)*

☆ *Wallace Arms* [Rowfoot, Featherstone Park]: Unpretentious and relaxed linked rooms of rambling former farmhouse, beams, dark woodwork, some stripped stone, good log fire, generous simple food from sandwiches

to bargain Sun lunch, well kept Batemans XB and Charles Wells Bombardier, three dozen malt whiskies, games room with another fire; children in eating areas and family room, fairly good disabled access, picnic-sets with lovely fell views, play area and quoits, walks on South Tyne Trail, open all day wknds *(GSB, LYM, Guy Vowles)*

HARTLEPOOL [NZ5233]

Harbour of Refuge [Croft Terrace, The Headland]: Comfortable two-bar pub and restaurant overlooking harbour entrance, panoramic coastal views and interesting local port photographs, good local fish as well as traditional lunchtime pub food, all cheap, coal fire; keg beers; open all day Fri/Sat *(JHBS)*

Jacksons Wharf [Marina Way/The Highlight]: New but looks 18th-c, with attractive maritime interior and no music, decent straightforward food (beware the incendiary madras curry), well kept Camerons; next to Historic Quay Museum *(Nigel Williamson)*

King Johns [South Rd]: Wetherspoons with photographs and diagrams giving a good introduction to local history – trams, ships, the German bombardment; enjoyable food, bargain wine *(JHBS)*

White House [Wooler Rd]: Ember Inn in converted school, six rooms, some with leather armchairs, two log fires and one flame-effect, four changing real ales, good choice of wines by the glass, attractively priced food all day; open all day *(JHBS)*

HAWTHORN [NZ4145]

Stapylton Arms: Carpeted bar with lots of old local photographs, well kept changing ales such as Hydes, chatty ex-miner landlord and wife – she produces enjoyable food from sandwiches to steaks; dogs on leads allowed, may be open all day on busy wknds, nice wooded walk to sea (joins Durham Coastal Path) *(JHBS)*

HAYDON BRIDGE [NY8364]

☆ *General Havelock* [A69]: Civilised and individually furnished dining pub with good food from interesting baguettes to imaginative hot dishes using fresh local ingredients prepared in open-view kitchen, well kept changing beers such as Bass and Wylam, good wines by the glass and coffee, welcoming service and relaxing atmosphere, open fires, more upmarket evening set menus in smart Tyne-view stripped stone restaurant; children welcome, tables on terrace *(Michael Doswell, John Oddey, LYM)*

HEXHAM [NY9464]

Tap & Spile [Battle Hill/Eastgate]: Congenial open-plan bare-boards pub with half a dozen quickly changing well kept ales from central bar, country wines, good filling low-priced food from hot filled stotties up, open fire, expert smiling service; children welcome, no dogs, regular live music, open all day *(John Foord, Andy and Jill Kassube, Patrick Hancock)*

HIGH FORCE [NY8728]

☆ *High Force Hotel* [B6277 about 4 miles NW of Middleton-in-Teesdale]: Beautifully placed high-moors hotel, named for England's highest waterfall nearby and doubling as mountain rescue post, with interestingly basic décor to suit; brews its own good value hoppy Teesdale Bitter, Cauldron Snout and Forest, also Theakstons and good choice of bar food (and of malt whiskies), helpful service, friendly atmosphere; quiz night Fri, usually open all day summer (when it can get busy) but may be cl quiet lunchtimes out of season; children very welcome, comfortable bedrooms, pleasant garden (LYM, Liz and John Soden, Mr and Mrs Maurice Thompson)

HOLY ISLAND [NU1241]

Crown & Anchor: Comfortable and welcoming straightforward pub/restaurant with emphasis on enjoyable quickly served food though bar much used by locals, well kept Caledonian Deuchars IPA, good fresh coffee, pleasant décor inc interesting rope fancy-work; three bedrooms (Paul and Ursula Randall, R E and E C M Pick)

☆ *Ship* [Marygate; causeway passable only at low tide, check times (01289) 330733]: Nicely set summer pub, spotless bar with no smoking eating area off, beamery, wooden furniture, bare boards, panelling, maritime/fishing memorabilia and pictures; good value straightforward food (may be a wait even for sandwiches) esp local seafood and fish, well kept real ales in summer such as Hadrian & Border Blessed, good choice of whiskies, cheerful service; no dogs, even in garden; three comfortable Victorian-décor bedrooms, may close for a while Jan/Feb (Rosemary and Tom Hall, Anna and Martyn Carey, Keith and Janet Morris, Nigel Williamson, Anne Evans)

HORSLEY [NZ0966]

☆ *Lion & Lamb* [B6528, just off A69 Newcastle—Hexham]: Plentiful reasonably priced food (not Sun evening) from sandwiches to daily roast, Mon steak night, bargains for two Tues/Weds, four well kept changing ales inc local ones, cafetière coffee, good service, two main rooms, small smart restaurant, no smoking area, stripped stone, flagstones, panelling, untreated tables and chairs; Tyne views from attractive garden with roomy terrace and particularly good adventure play area, open all day (John Foord, John Oddey, Andy and Jill Kassube, Gerry and Rosemary Dobson)

HUMSHAUGH [NY9171]

Crown: Old village pub with enjoyable generous home-made food, comfortable separate dining room, welcoming staff, decent wines; dogs allowed if it's quiet, bedrooms (Robert M Warner)

KIELDER [NY6393]

Anglers Arms: Big pub (former village club) with good range of popular food served quickly, real ales such as Lubilee Jubilee and Wylam Hedonist; handy for Kielder Water

and castle, open all day summer wknds (Dave Braisted)

LAMESLEY [NZ2557]

Ravensworth Arms [minor road S of Gateshead western bypass, A1, Team Valley junction]: Stone-built pub well refurbished as Chef & Brewer, largely no smoking and given rustic feel by stripped brick and recovered timber dividers, competitively priced popular fresh food inc fish and game, cheerful helpful service even when busy (food can slow then); may be piped music; children welcome, play area and picnic-sets outside, open all day (Jenny and Dave Hughes, Alan Thwaite)

LANGDON BECK [NY8531]

Langdon Beck Hotel [B6277 Middleton—Alston]: Unpretentious isolated pub, wonderful views from dining room with good food choice, helpful landlord; bedrooms (Mrs Roxanne Chamberlain)

LANGLEY ON TYNE [NY8160]

☆ *Carts Bog Inn* [A686 S, junction B6305]: Warmly welcoming new owners in comfortable rambling black-beamed moorside pub, good range of reasonably priced food from sandwiches to good blackboard dishes, huge helpings, well kept Jennings Cumberland and Yates, helpful service, blazing central log fire, some stripped stone and flagstones, side games lounge, lots of malt whiskies – and glasses of milk (very family-friendly place now); tables out on big lawn with high views, quoits (LYM, Andy and Jill Kassube, GSB, John Oddey, R T and J C Moggridge, A H C Rainier, Di and Mike Gillam)

LESBURY [NU2311]

Coach: Nicely furnished clean and comfortable small bar with cheerful licensees, enjoyable food from bar snacks to Fri steak suppers and Sun lunch in restaurant, interesting well kept real ales, good choice of wines; dogs allowed (Robert M Warner)

LONGFRAMLINGTON [NU1301]

☆ *Granby*: Attractive and comfortably modernised two-room bar with wide choice of good generous food inc good value set meals, good collection of malt whiskies, decent wines, welcoming service, restaurant; bedrooms in main building good (but it's a busy road), with big breakfast (Keith and Janet Morris, LYM)

LOWICK [NU0139]

☆ *Black Bull* [Main St (B6353, off A1 S of Berwick-upon-Tweed)]: Friendly bustle in nicely decorated country local with comfortable main bar, small back bar, big back dining room popular for good choice of plentiful good value food (take-aways too), well kept McEwans 80/-, good welcoming service; three attractive bedrooms, on edge of small pretty village (KN-R)

LUCKER [NU1631]

☆ *Apple* [village (and pub) signed off A1 N of Morpeth]: Refurbished village pub with surprisingly good food cooked by youngish landlord, from inventively filled baguettes and enterprising light lunches to creative evening meals and good Sun lunch, with thoughtful children's dishes or half-price small helpings; stripped stone, bare boards or carpet, solid pub furnishings, woodburner, keg beers but well priced wines and good coffee, friendly landlady, pleasantly fresh and airy décor in roomy side restaurant extension (must book for this); piped radio; cl Mon lunchtime *(John and Sylvia Harrop, BB, Michael Doswell)*

MATFEN [NZ0372]
Black Bull [off B6318 NE of Corbridge]: Well placed by green of attractive out-of-the-way 18th-c estate village, tables out on terrace; the part of the pub containing the original attractive dining room has now been hived off as a private house, and it may take time for the refurbished remainder to regain its former appeal (it was a popular main entry); usual food, perhaps a real ale such as Theakstons Black Bull, a good few malt whiskies, log fires; games area, no dogs; has been open all day wknds *(LYM)*

MELDON [NZ1185]
Dyke Neuk Inn: Comfortable banquettes, gentle lighting, fox mask and stuffed fish, reasonably priced mainly standard food from lunchtime sandwiches to choice of Sun roasts, midweek bargain lunches, well kept Marstons Pedigree; big garden *(Mike and Lynn Robinson, Michael Doswell)*

MICKLEY [NZ0761]
Blue Bell [Mount Pleasant, off A695 Prudhoe—Stocksfield]: Cosy little pub with friendly bustling landlady and rural feel (though on edge of built-up area), very popular for low-priced food cooked to order – may have to book wknds *(John Oddey, Jenny and Brian Seller)*

MILBOURNE [NZ1275]
Waggon [Higham Dykes; A696 NW of Ponteland]: Popular greatly extended open-plan bar with soft lighting, comfortable banquettes, beams, stripped stone and panelling, huge fire each end, generous food from lunchtime sandwiches to restaurant dishes (small helpings available), friendly attentive staff, well kept Tetleys and Wylam Haugh *(Michael Doswell)*

MORPETH [NZ2085]
Joiners Arms [Wansbeck St]: Old-fashioned local with well kept changing ales from small breweries, stuffed birds above the bar, what looks like a lamp post holding up the ceiling, comfortable back river-view lounge; quiz night Tues, no food, open all day *(A H C Rainier)*

NETHERTON [NT9807]
Star [off B6341 at Thropton, or A697 via Whittingham]: Unspoilt local in superb remote countryside, spartan but clean, many original features, well kept Castle Eden tapped from cellar casks and served in small entrance lobby, large high-ceilinged room with panelled wall benches, charming

landlady and welcoming regulars; no food, music or children; open evenings and Sun lunch *(RWC, the Didler, Kevin Thorpe)*

NEW YORK [NZ3269]
☆ *Shiremoor Farm* [Middle Engine Lane/Norham Rd, off A191 bypass]: Handsome conversion of former derelict farm buildings, stylish and mildly ironic modern take on rustic décor, good lighting, relaxed civilised atmosphere, well kept very local Mordue Workie Ticket, Timothy Taylors Landlord, Theakstons Best and a guest beer, decent wines by the glass, computer-ordered food all day, no smoking granary extension; children welcome away from main bar, heated covered terrace, open all day *(Brian Taylor, Michael Butler, Michael Doswell, LYM)*

NEWBURN [NZ1665]
☆ *Keelman* [Grange Rd, by Tyne Riverside Country Park]: Shares attractive granite-built former 19th-c pumping station with good Big Lamp Brewery (which you can visit), their full range at attractive prices; high ceiling, lofty windows, wooden gallery, no smoking area, plenty of neat and cheery well trained staff; quick straightforward food (not Sun evening), fruit machine, piped music; open all day, very popular with families in summer, lots of picnic-sets outside, bedrooms in new block, handy for walks *(John Foord, Karen and Graham Oddey, John Oddey, Mike and Lynn Robinson, Andy and Jill Kassube)*

NEWCASTLE UPON TYNE [NZ2665]
Blue Bell [Jesmond Vale]: Keg beer and no food, but good entertainment most nights inc blues Sat, buskers Sun, jazz Mon, modern jazz Tues *(Mike and Lynn Robinson)*
Bodega [Westgate Rd]: Edwardian drinking hall, well restored colourful walls and ceiling with two magnificent original stained-glass domes (has been a mosque), boards, tiles and a handsome rug, cosy alcove banquettes; well kept Big Lamp Prince Bishop, Durham Magus, Mordue Geordie Pride (sold here as No 9) and three guest beers tapped from the cask, lunchtime food; table football now, also juke box or piped music (can be obtrusive), machines, TV, Tues quiz night, busy evenings (and if Newcastle Utd at home or on TV); open all day, next to Tyne Theatre *(Mike and Lynn Robinson, Eric Larkham, the Didler, Michael Doswell)*
☆ *Bridge Hotel* [Castle Sq, next to high level bridge]: Big cheery high-ceilinged room divided into several areas leaving plenty of space by the bar with replica slatted snob screens, particularly well kept Black Sheep, Boddingtons, Mordue Workie Ticket and three guest beers, decent lunchtime food and Sun afternoon teas, magnificent fireplace, great views of river and bridges from raised back no smoking area; sports TV, piped music, fruit machines, very long-standing Mon folk club upstairs; tables on flagstoned back terrace overlooking section of old town wall, open all day *(John Oddey, John Foord,*

John W Allen, the Didler, LYM,
Eric Larkham, Mike and Lynn Robinson,
CMW, JJW)

Chillingham [Chillingham Rd, Heaton]:
Two big rooms, fine panelling and
furnishings, well kept Black Sheep, Mordue
Workie Ticket, Theakstons Best and two
guest beers, occasional beer festivals, good
cheap food lunchtime and (not wknd) early
evening; piped music or juke box in bar with
TV and pool room with two tables and
darts; children in quieter lounge; Tues music
quiz, Weds general quiz, open all day
(Eric Larkham, Mike and Lynn Robinson)

Collingwood Arms: Hard-working young
couple with up to eight well kept ales inc
exemplary Timothy Taylors Landlord in
long narrow chatty bar, relaxed atmosphere
– no TV now *(P Elliott)*

☆ **Cooperage** [The Close, Quayside]: One of
city's most ancient buildings, great
atmosphere in stripped stone bar and cosy
beamed lounge, good waterfront setting,
well kept Bass, Fullers London Pride,
Timothy Taylors Landlord and one from
Mordue (good prices Mon-Thurs and till
9 Fri/Sat), hearty fresh sensibly priced
lunchtime food; upstairs night club Mon
(student night) and Thurs-Sat, pool, juke
box, quiz night Tues; disabled facilities,
cl Sun lunchtime, open all day Fri *(LYM,
Eric Larkham, Chris Doyle, the Didler,
Stephen, Julie and Hayley Brown)*

Cumberland Arms [Byker Buildings]:
Traditional pub doing well under new
landlord, three local real ales (tapped
straight from the cask if you prefer); folk
music Tues, irish folk Weds, blues and jazz
Thurs, open microphone night Sun, also
music and dance rehearsals and other live
bands; cl lunchtime *(Eric Larkham)*

Fitzgeralds [Grey St]: Handsomely
refurbished Victorian pub in elegant street
on fringe of Bigg Market, lots of levels and
alcoves (two short sets of steps between
entrance, main area and lavatories), discreet
lighting, red mahogany and polished brass,
Black Sheep, Mordue Workie Ticket and
two guest beers, wide range of good value
lunchtime food (not Sun) inc freshly baked
baguettes; can get very busy wknds, piped
music, machines; open all day, cl Sun
lunchtime *(Michael Doswell, Eric Larkham)*

Forth [Pink Lane]: Comfortable open-plan
pub, lounge area behind main bar, well kept
Adnams, Fullers London Pride and Mordue
Workie Ticket, food all day (not Sun
evening); piped music, juke box, TV, Sun
quiz night *(Eric Larkham)*

Free Trade [St Lawrence Rd, off Walker Rd
(A186)]: Chattily friendly atmosphere in
artfully basic split-level pub with big
windows for grandstand river and bridge
views, well kept ales (usually two each) from
Hadrian & Border, Mordue and Wylam,
guest beers too, good wkdy early lunchtime
sandwiches, real fire, original Formica
tables; cricket radio, eclectic free CD juke

box, quiz Weds, Sun open mike night, steps
down to back room and lavatories (high-
standard gents' graffiti); tables out on terrace
a bit like a Buddhist pebble garden (or sit on
grass overlooking Tyne), open all day
*(Eric Larkham, Kevin Thorpe, Tracey and
Stephen Groves, Mike and Lynn Robinson)*

Harrogate House [Gosforth St]: Warmly
welcoming local with bargain beers, real ales
now too, big-screen sports TV, great juke
box *(Lynda Stout)*

Head of Steam [Neville St]: Well kept
changing ales, two floors, bare boards and
carpet, some railway prints, reasonably
priced lunchtime food upstairs inc two-
course Sun lunch, friendly staff; very popular
with students, frequent live music; children
allowed, open all day *(Andrew York)*

Hotspur [Percy St]: Cheerful open-plan
Victorian pub with big front windows and
decorated mirrors, well kept Courage
Directors, McEwans 80/-, Theakstons Best
and Old Peculier and guests such as Badger,
Mordue, Robinsons and Charles Wells, farm
cider, lots of bottled belgian beers, good
value wine; sandwiches and hot snacks all
day, machines, big-screen sports TV, piped
music, can get packed, esp pre-match,
upstairs ladies'; open all day *(John Foord,
Eric Larkham, Michael Doswell)*

New Bridge [Argyle St]: Large comfortably
refurbished bar, separate areas and alcoves,
photographs of Tyne Bridge building,
enjoyable home-made lunchtime food inc
telephone take-aways, three well kept
changing beers inc one from Mordue; darts,
piped music, Weds quiz night; open all day,
view of Millennium Bridge from side
entrance *(Eric Larkham)*

Newcastle Arms [St Andrews St]: Open-plan
pub on fringe of chinatown, well kept Black
Sheep, Fullers London Pride or ESB and
guest beers, occasional mini beer festivals,
friendly staff, decent food till 6 inc
sandwiches, interesting old local
photographs; piped music, big-screen sports
TV, can get very busy esp on match days;
open all day *(Eric Larkham, Mike and
Lynn Robinson)*

Pitcher & Piano [Quayside]: Stylish and
roomy modern bar in revitalised riverside
area opp Millennium Bridge, great views of
Tyne and other bridges, good range of
lunchtime food and of beer, Sun night drinks
bargains *(Michael Doswell)*

Quayside [The Close]: Wetherspoons in
floodlit Tyneside warehouse, linked rooms
with small areas up and down stairs, food
all day till 10, Theakstons Best and three
guest beers such as Shepherd Neame Spitfire;
disabled facilities with baby-changing, open
all day, tables out in central courtyard
(Eric Larkham)

Ship [Stepney Bank]: Unchanging traditional
local by Byker city farm, particularly well
kept Boddingtons and Castle Eden Bitter and
Nimmos XXXX, unusual toasted
sandwiches (normally all day), very friendly

locals, pool and juke box in lounge, darts and TV in bar; seats outside and picnic-sets on green opp, open all day *(Eric Larkham, Mike and Lynn Robinson, John W Allen)*
Tilleys [Westgate Rd]: Large old-fashioned well worn in bar next to Tyne Theatre and nr performing arts college, so interesting mix of customers; scores of classic film stills, bar food inc good lunchtime soup, ploughman's with up to 16 cheeses and six pâtés, full Jennings beer range kept well, keen friendly manager and staff; big TV, juke box, machines, pool table in the small mirrored snug, can get very busy; open all day (not Sun lunchtime unless Newcastle playing at home) *(Michael Doswell, Eric Larkham)*
Tyne [Maling St]: Busy single-room pub at confluence of Ouseburn and Tyne, plastered with band posters and prints – frequent live music upstairs; Black Sheep, Durham Magus, a Mordue beer and a guest, exotic hot or cold sandwiches all day, free interestingly stocked CD juke box; fruit machine, sports TV, stairs up to lavatories; usefully placed at end of quayside walk, fairy-lit garden (loudspeakers out here too) under an arch of Glasshouse Bridge, barbecues Sun lunch, early Fri evening; open all day *(Kevin Thorpe, Mike and Lynn Robinson, Eric Larkham, GSB, Dave Braisted)*
NORTH SHIELDS [NZ3470]
☆ *Magnesia Bank* [Camden St]: Lively well run refurbished Victorian pub overlooking Tyne, well kept Durham, Mordue and guest beers in lined glasses, good coffee, vast choice of cheerful home-made lunchtime food inc ciabattas and potatoes done ten different ways, good value all-day breakfast from 8.30am, friendly staff, intriguing mix of customers, open fire; quiet piped pop music, TV, machines; children welcome, tables outside, open all day, live music Thurs and Sun often featuring members of Lindisfarne *(Michael Doswell, Mike and Lynn Robinson)*
☆ *Wooden Doll* [Hudson St]: Bird's-eye view of fish quay and outer harbour – get there early for a table in the largely no smoking glass-fronted extension; full Jennings range kept well, enjoyable food inc fresh fish priced by size, helpful welcoming service, informal mix of furnishings in bare-boards bar, lots of paintings by local artists for sale; disabled facilities, children welcome till 8, some live music, open all day Sat *(John Oddey, Mike and Lynn Robinson, LYM, Robert M Warner)*
PONTELAND [NZ1871]
☆ *Badger* [Street Houses; A696 SE]: Well done Vintage Inn (unexpectedly sharing approach with main road garden centre), more character than most pubs in the area, relaxing rooms and alcoves, old furnishings and olde-worlde décor, flagstones, carpet or bare wood, timbered ceilings, stripped stone, brick and timbering, real fires, Bass and Tetleys, good choice of wines by the glass

and good hot drinks, generous reasonably priced food all day inc imaginative good value light dishes and interesting lunchtime sandwiches (most people here to eat – can get busy Sun lunchtime), pleasant attentive uniformed staff; quiet piped music; open all day *(GSB, Jenny and Dave Hughes, John Foord, Keith Mould, Michael Doswell, BB)*
RENNINGTON [NU2118]
☆ *Horseshoes*: Neat and comfortable flagstoned pub, welcoming licensees, good helpings of enjoyable food freshly cooked by cheerful landlady, well kept Bass, Black Sheep and Courage Directors, good service, simple bar with lots of horsebrasses, spotless compact restaurant with blue and white china; children welcome, tables outside, attractive quiet village nr coast *(Michael Doswell, Tom McLean)*
RIDING MILL [NZ0161]
☆ *Wellington* [A695 just W of A68 roundabout]: Good 17th-c Chef & Brewer, carefully refurbished in tune with its age, beams and candlelight, two big log fires and mix of tables and chairs, some upholstered, some not; very wide good value blackboard food choice from hot ciabatta sandwiches to nice puddings, Courage Directors and Theakstons Bitter and Black Bull, good choice of wines by the glass, friendly service; piped classical music, can get busy; disabled access, children welcome, play area and picnic-sets outside, pretty village with nearby walks and river *(Peter Burton, R J Herd, Stephen, Julie and Hayley Brown, Andy and Jill Kassube)*
ROMALDKIRK [NY9922]
Kirk: Cosy local under friendly new licensees, well kept Castle Eden and a guest beer, good coffee and log fire, wide food choice, 18th-c stonework; darts, may be piped music; picnic-sets out by green of attractive moorland village *(Di and Mike Gillam)*
SEAHOUSES [NU2131]
Lodge [Main St, N Sunderland]: Scandinavian-style hotel with lots of stripped pine, marine and diving decoration, comfortable atmosphere, wide choice of good bar food inc seafood, friendly staff, restaurant; keg beer, unobtrusive piped music, pool and darts; pleasant chalet-style bedrooms behind *(Roger and Christine Hyde)*
SEATON CAREW [NZ5230]
Charters [Staincliffe Hotel, The Cliff]: Nautical bric-a-brac, cheap doubles, decent wine choice (keg beers), full-size snooker table, evening food from sausages and mash up, sea view to Boulby Cliffs; quiz night Thurs, open all day wknds, bedrooms *(JHBS)*
SEATON SLUICE [NZ3376]
Waterford Arms [A193 N of Whitley Bay]: Dining pub with good value food all day, double doors between restaurant and homely bar, tables here likely to be laid for food too (esp fish), several real ales; games area with juke box, pool etc, live

entertainment Thurs/Fri; children welcome,
open all day, simple good value bedrooms,
nice cliff walks *(Robert M Warner, LYM)*
SEDGEFIELD [NZ3528]
☆ **Dun Cow** [Front St]: Large village inn,
friendly and attractive, with wide choice of
good interesting food inc game, fresh whitby
fish and unusual puddings in two bars and
restaurant, good service, Castle Eden and
several guest beers, good range of whiskies,
pleasantly upmarket feel; children welcome;
good bedrooms sharing bathrooms
(Malcolm M Stewart)
SLALEY [NY9757]
Rose & Crown: Early 18th-c village pub
newly tied to Jennings with their beers kept
well, good home-made standard food from
sandwiches to restaurant meals inc good
value roast, welcoming service, comfortable
dark-beamed lounge hung with lots of mugs
and jugs, public bar with darts, fruit
machine, juke box; tables in small neat
garden, quiet village with views behind,
bedrooms attractive and well equipped
*(Andy and Jill Kassube, Robert M Warner,
Michael Doswell, Jack and Heather Coyle)*
SOUTH SHIELDS [NZ3668]
Beacon [Greens Pl]: Welcoming and
pleasantly refurbished pub overlooking river
mouth, with pictures and bric-a-brac, central
bar, stove in back room, obliging service,
three well kept real ales, good value
lunchtime food, two raised eating areas; fruit
machine, quiet piped music *(Kate Arscott)*
Steamboat [Mill Dam/Coronation St]:
Masses of interesting nautical bric-a-brac esp
in split-level back room, friendly landlord,
well kept ales such as Courage Directors,
Greene King Old Speckled Hen and Charles
Wells Bombardier, cheap sandwiches, pool
in central area; usually open all day, nr river
and market place *(Brian and Anna Marsden)*
STOCKTON-ON-TEES [NZ4419]
Sun [Knowles St]: Friendly town local
specialising in particularly well kept Bass,
well served at tempting price; folk night
Mon, open all day *(the Didler)*
SUNDERLAND [NZ3956]
Fitzgeralds [Green Terr]: Busy city pub with
two bars, one rather trendy (nr University),
friendly atmosphere, generous cheap food
from toasties, baguettes and ciabattas to
basic hot dishes, eight well kept ales inc
several from local Darwin; children welcome
lunchtime *(Andy and Jill Kassube)*
THROPTON [NU0302]
☆ **Cross Keys** [B6341]: Friendly young couple
in attractive little three-room village local,
decent pub food, well kept Bass, open fires
in cosy beamed main lounge, darts, satellite
TV; nice terraced garden looking over village
to the Cheviots, open all day at least in
summer *(LYM, Pat and Stewart Gordon)*
TOW LAW [NZ1238]
Old Station [High St]: Completely renovated
under new licensees, enjoyable food inc
bargain Sun lunch, well priced drinks
(D and M T Ayres-Regan)

TYNEMOUTH [NZ3669]
Grand [Grand Parade]: Large hotel, but
worth knowing for its good bar meals and
choice of beers and wines, also good Sun
lunch in restaurant; bedrooms
(Robert M Warner)
WACKERFIELD [NZ1523]
Sun: Well run, locally popular for ample
good value food from generous ploughman's
up, prompt service, John Smiths and
Theakstons Best, pleasant separate dining
room; piped music may obtrude *(David and
Brenda Tew)*
WALL [NY9269]
☆ **Hadrian** [Hexham—Bellingham/Rothbury
Rd]: Two-room beamed lounge with new
chef doing enjoyable generous food, well
kept Jennings and guest beers, good house
wine and whisky range, attentive service,
interesting reconstructions of Romano-
British life, woodburner, airy no smoking
dining room; children welcome, unobtrusive
piped music, games in public bar; neat
garden, roomy comfortable bedrooms –
back ones quieter, with good views
*(Brian Root, Anna and Martyn Carey,
Jack and Heather Coyle, BB)*
WARKWORTH [NU2406]
Black Bull [Bridge St]: Simple and
individual, with wide choice of enjoyable
home-made food mixing traditional with
imaginative dishes, small helpings for
children, no music, well kept Black Sheep
and Theakstons; friendly husband and wife
do all cooking and serving; *(Michael and
Janice Gwilliam)*
☆ **Hermitage** [Castle St]: Rambling local with
interesting quaint décor, old range for
heating, well kept Jennings and John Smiths,
good value generous food from sandwiches
to fresh local fish, quick service, dry-
humoured landlord and staff, dining area
and small plush upstairs restaurant; TV or
piped music; bedrooms, tables out in front,
attractive setting *(Keith and Janet Morris,
BB, Eric Locker, Peter Burton, Des and
Jen Clarke, A and B D Craig)*
Masons Arms [Dial Pl]: Thriving village pub,
quick friendly service, good value generous
food inc fish and bargain lunch, well kept
beers, good coffee and wine choice, local
pictures; dogs welcome, attractive back
flagstoned courtyard *(Robert M Warner,
Des and Jen Clarke, A and B D Craig)*
Warkworth House [Bridge St]: Hotel not
pub, but unusual in having a proper bar
with darts, bar billiards and a real ale such
as Greene King Old Speckled Hen; friendly
atmosphere, comfortable sofas, helpful staff,
good choice of spirits, enjoyable food, decent
wines and coffee; dogs welcome; bedrooms
comfortable *(Robert M Warner, Paul and
Ursula Randall, A C Fieldhouse)*
WEST BOLDON [NZ3460]
☆ **Red Lion** [Redcar Terrace]: Small
comfortable rooms on each side of main bar,
dining room opening on to large deck with
attractive metal tables and chairs, good

generous food (all day) from wide menu inc adventurous fish choice, welcoming helpful service *(Margaret and Brian Sanderson, David and Iris Hunter)*

WHITFIELD [NY7857]

Elks Head [off A686 SW of Haydon Bridge]: Recently refurbished open-plan pub with some stripped stone, helpful service, enjoyable straightforward food, real ales such as Marstons Pedigree, John Smiths and Websters, good coffee, games area and piano; occasional live entertainment; children welcome, picnic-sets in small pretty front garden with quoits, bedrooms, lovely scenic area *(CMW, JJW)*

WOOLER [NT9928]

Tankerville Arms [A697 N]: Pleasant hotel bar in tastefully modernised old building, good choice of local meat and fish, small helpings on request, well kept Hadrian & Border Farne Island and other ales (knowledgeable barman helps you choose), smart restaurant (may have local folk music Sun lunchtime); pleasant setting, nice garden, bedrooms *(Darly Graton, Graeme Gulibert, Jack and Heather Coyle, David Ions)*

WYLAM [NZ1164]

Black Bull [Main Rd]: Transformed by massive refurbishment, good range of real ales inc bargain Boddingtons, enjoyable food inc good specials; new bedrooms *(John Oddey)*

☆ *Boathouse* [Station Rd; across Tyne from village]: Warm and comfortable riverside pub with masses of well kept reasonably priced real ales (the local Wylam Gold Tankard is the hot pick), good choice of malt whiskies, succulent generous lunchtime sandwiches, early evening pizzas, kebabs, curries etc, clean bright lounge with roaring coal or log fire, evening dining room (and for popular Sun lunch); children welcome, Sat afternoon impromptu folk/blues sessions, small garden, open and busy all day *(John Foord, Andy and Jill Kassube, Mr and Mrs Maurice Thompson, Jenny and Brian Seller, Clare Pearse)*

'Children welcome' means the pub says it lets children inside without any special restriction. If it allows them in, but to restricted areas such as an eating area or family room, we specify this. Places with separate restaurants usually let children use them, hotels usually let them into public areas such as lounges. Some pubs impose an evening time limit – let us know if you find this.

Nottinghamshire

Three new entries here this year are the nicely individualistic Black Horse at Caythorpe (brewing its own Caythorpe beers, also available elsewhere), the Waggon & Horses in Halam (young licensees doing good imaginative food), and the interesting and ancient Bell in Nottingham (thriving under its new owners, the Hardys & Hansons brewery). Other pubs on fine form here these days are the chatty Victoria in Beeston (great range of drinks), the civilised Caunton Beck in Caunton (good food all day, and excellent wine choice), the Robin Hood at Elkesley (a good value A1 break), the cheerful Nelson & Railway opposite Hardys & Hansons brewery in Kimberley, the Dovecote at Laxton (another agreeable A1 diversion, good value generous food and kind licensees), and the friendly and intriguing Olde Trip to Jerusalem in Nottingham. For a special meal out the Caunton Beck at Caunton is Nottinghamshire Dining Pub of the Year – taking this prestigious title for the second year running. Quite a few pubs in the Lucky Dip section at the end of the chapter are making a claim for main entry space, notably the Horse & Plough in Bingham, Old Ship in Lowdham, Beehive at Maplebeck, Plough in Nottingham (and we like the Via Fossa there, too), Olde Red Lion at Wellow and Stratford Haven in West Bridgford. This area stands out as much cheaper than average for drinks. Fellows Morton & Clayton in Nottingham, brewing its own, is particularly cheap, and pubs tied to the small local Tynemill group sell their own Castle Rock ales at bargain prices. Plenty of other local breweries add to the fun for beer drinkers here: the major one is Hardys & Hansons, and others to look out for include Springhead, Maypole, Mallard, Alcazar and Broadstone.

BEESTON SK5338 Map 7
Victoria 🍽 ♀ 🍺

Dovecote Lane, backing on to railway station

Readers really enjoy the down-to-earth welcoming atmosphere, impressive choice of drinks and enjoyable food in this unpretentious converted railway hotel. The lounge and bar back on to the railway station, and a covered heated area outside has picnic-sets overlooking the platform, with trains passing a few feet below. The three downstairs rooms have kept their original long narrow layout, and have simple solid traditional furnishings, very unfussy décor, stained-glass windows, stripped woodwork and floorboards (woodblock in some rooms), newspapers to read, and a chatty atmosphere; dominoes, cribbage, piped music. There's usually an impressive range of 12 very well kept real ales, including Bass, Batemans XB, Castle Rock Hemlock and Rylands Gold and Everards Tiger, alongside changing guests such as Abbeydale Matins, Kelham Island Easy Rider and Oakham JHB; they've also farm ciders, over 100 malt whiskies, 20 irish whiskeys, and even over two dozen wines by the glass. Very fairly priced tasty dishes are listed on a daily changing blackboard which might include filled rolls (from £1.60), pâté (£4.75), shepherd's pie or very tasty lincolnshire sausages (£6.50), roast pork, vegetable burritos or pasta (£6.95) and puddings from (£2.95). (*Recommended by Michael Doswell, Revd D Glover, Kevin Blake, Darly Graton, Graeme Gulibert, Sue Holland, Dave Webster, David Eberlin, Blaise Vyner, the Didler,*

Stephen Buckley, Paul and Ann Meyer, JP, PP, Andrew Crawford, Andy and Jill Kassube, Andy and Ali, C J Fletcher, Tony Hobden)

Free house ~ Licensees Neil Kelso and Graham Smith ~ Real ale ~ Bar food (12-8.45(7.45 Sun)) ~ Restaurant ~ (0115) 925 4049 ~ Children in eating area of bar and restaurant till 8pm ~ Dogs allowed in bar ~ Live music Sun and jazz Mon evenings Oct-May ~ Open 11-11; 12-10.30 Sun

CAUNTON SK7460 Map 7
Caunton Beck 🍴 ♟

Main Street; village signposted off A616 Newark—Ollerton

Nottinghamshire Dining Pub of the Year

Unanimous praise from readers confirms the continuing quality of this pleasantly placed and civilised dining pub. Almost new, but not new-looking, it was reconstructed, using original timbers and reclaimed oak, around the skeleton of the old Hole Arms. Scrubbed pine tables, clever lighting, an open fire and country-kitchen chairs, low beams and rag-finished paintwork in a spacious interior make for a relaxed atmosphere. With lots of flowers and plants in summer, the terrace is a nice place to sit when the weather is fine. The main focus is on the good well presented (though not cheap) food, which is served all day. As well as delicious sandwiches (from £5.25) and a hearty english breakfast (£6.50), the menu changes every couple of months, but might include carrot and coriander cream soup (£4.50), thai mussel curry (£5.95), roasted sweet pepper and zucchini frittata with italian cheeses (£10.50), chinese marinated duck breast with bok choy, egg noodles and bean sprouts (£12.95), fried salmon fillet with crab and shallot tartare and truffled risotto cakes (£13.50), puddings such as vanilla panna cotta with rhubarb and custard ice cream (£4.75), and cheeses (£4.95). They also do reasonably priced two- and three-course set menus (£10/£12.95, not Saturday evenings or lunchtime Sunday). About half the wines on the very good wine list are available by the glass, and they've well kept Greene King Ruddles Best, Springhead, Charles Wells Bombardier and a guest such as Broadstone Best on handpump; also freshly squeezed orange juice and espresso coffee. Service is pleasant and attentive; daily papers and magazines, no music. *(Recommended by Neville Kenyon, Derek and Sylvia Stephenson, Stephen Woad, Kevin Thorpe, David and Ruth Hollands, JP, PP, Roger and Maureen Kenning, Blaise Vyner, Ray and Winifred Halliday, David and Helen Wilkins, Michael Doswell, June and Malcolm Farmer, John Brightley, Tim and Sue Halstead, Lorraine and Fred Gill, Margaret and Roy Randle, Richard Cole, Bob Arnett, Judy Wayman, Alison Hayes, Pete Hanlon, Comus and Sarah Elliott)*

Free house ~ Licensees Toby Hope and Julie Allwood ~ Real ale ~ Bar food (8am-10.30pm) ~ Restaurant ~ (01636) 636793 ~ Children welcome ~ Dogs allowed in bar ~ Open 8am-12 midnight

CAYTHORPE SK6845 Map 7
Black Horse ◧

Turn off A6097 450 metres SE of roundabout junction with A612, NE of Nottingham; into Gunthorpe Road, then right into Caythorpe Road and keep on

Run by the same family for many years, this small 300-year-old local naturally mixes an unspoilt and uncluttered country feel with a certain civilised poise. The carpeted bar has just four tables, with brocaded wall banquettes and settles, a few bar stools hosting cheerful evening regulars, a warm woodburning stove, decorative plates on a delft shelf, a few horsebrasses on the ceiling joists, and the landlady herself presiding over the well kept Caythorpe Dover Beck (brewed here), besides two changing guest beers such as Greene King Abbot and Oldershaws Athanum Gold; there may be a plate of interesting bar nibbles. Off the front corridor is a partly panelled inner room with a wall bench running right the way around three unusual long copper-topped tables, and quite a few old local photographs; down on the left an end room has just one huge round table, and a cabinet of sports trophies. We have heard of a bigger tap room across the yard, but not seen it open ourselves.

Enjoyable food includes soup (£2), prawn cocktail (£3.25), dim sum (£3.50), king prawns in garlic and cream sauce (£4.75), scampi (£8), seafood salad (£8.85), fillet steak (£11.50) and puddings such as banana ice-cream cake and sticky toffee pudding (from £2.50). Tuesday to Friday are fresh fish days: cod, haddock or plaice (£6 lunchtimes, £7 evenings). There are some plastic tables outside, and the River Trent is fairly close, for waterside walks. *(Recommended by the Didler, Norma and Keith Bloomfield, JP, PP)*

Own brew ~ Licensee Sharron Andrews ~ Real ale ~ Bar food (not Mon) ~ Restaurant ~ No credit cards ~ (0115) 966 3520 ~ Dogs welcome ~ Open 12-2.30, 5(6 Sat)-11; 12-4, 7(8 winter)-10.30 Sun; cl Mon in winter; closed Mon lunchtimes exc bank hols

COLSTON BASSETT SK7033 Map 7
Martins Arms ♀ ◖

Village signposted off A46 E of Nottingham; School Lane, near market cross in village centre

Although this smart country dining pub is very restauranty (with prices to match), they do stock a good range of around eight well kept real ales on handpump: Bass, Batemans XB, Greene King IPA and Marstons Pedigree, alongside guests such as Adnams, Timothy Taylors Landlord and Woodfordes Wherry. Imaginative food could include soup (£4.50), lunchtime sandwiches (from £4.50), chargrilled lamb steak with red peppers and hummous ciabatta (£8.50), ploughman's or smoked fishcake (£9.50), spaghetti with garlic, clams, chilli and rocket or caramelised duck breast salad (£12), puddings such as citrus panna cotta with balsamic strawberries or chocolate hazelnut torte (£5.50), and cheeses (£7). You are getting into quite an elaborate affair if you choose to eat in the elegant no smoking restaurant, which is smartly decorated with period fabrics and colourings; service is formal, and neatly uniformed, and it's the sort of place where they expect you to pay for bottled water rather than have tap water. Antique furnishings, hunting prints and warm log fires in the Jacobean fireplaces give an upmarket air to the comfortable bar, and there's a proper no smoking snug. They've a good range of malt whiskies and cognacs, and an interesting wine list; cribbage and dominoes. The sizeable attractive lawned garden backs on to estate parkland, but you might be asked to leave your credit card behind the bar if you want to eat out here. You can play croquet in summer, and they've converted the stables into an antiques shop. Readers recommend Colston Bassett Dairy just outside the village, which sells its own stilton cheese. *(Recommended by Doug Christian, JP, PP, the Didler, Roger and Maureen Kenning, Derek and Sylvia Stephenson, Philip Atkins, A C Nugent, Gerry and Rosemary Dobson)*

Free house ~ Licensees Lynne Strafford, Bryan and Salvatore Inguanta ~ Real ale ~ Bar food (12-2, 6-10; not Sun evenings) ~ Restaurant ~ (01949) 81361 ~ Children in restaurant and family room ~ Dogs allowed in bar ~ Open 12-3, 6-11(7-10.30 Sun)

ELKESLEY SK6975 Map 7
Robin Hood

High Street; village well signposted just off A1 Newark—Blyth

Readers have been more than happy to break their journey on the A1 for a meal or good cup of coffee at this friendly village local – their good value two-course meal (£9) is a particular favourite. Other well presented changing bar food might include sandwiches (from £3), delicious bacon and brie baguettes (£5.50), ploughman's (£5.60), salmon fishcakes with lemon butter sauce (£5.80), roast tuscan vegetable tart (£7.50), roast confit of leg of lamb with mint and caper gravy (£10.50), and puddings (£4). The welcoming roomy carpeted dining room and lounge area are both decorated in a traditional style, and non-smokers have plenty of room; darts, TV, quiz machine, unobtrusive piped music. Staff are friendly and efficient, and they have Boddingtons, Flowers IPA and Marstons Pedigree on handpump. The garden (which is moderately well screened from the A1) has picnic-sets and a play area. *(Recommended by Peter Scillitoe, D L Parkhurst, Lorraine and Fred Gill, D and M T Ayres-Regan, Gordon Tong, Stuart Paulley, Peter Walker, Rita and Keith Pollard,*

Mrs Anthea Fricker, Irene and Ray Atkin, Mrs P J Pearce, G A Hemingway, Hazel and Michael Duncombe, Peter Wrobbel, Jenny and Brian Seller, Mr and Mrs J E C Tasker, Mr and Mrs Broadhurst)

Enterprise ~ Lease Alan Draper ~ Real ale ~ Bar food (not Sun evening) ~ Restaurant ~ (01777) 838259 ~ Dogs allowed in bar ~ Open 11.30-2.30, 6.30-11; 12-3, 7-10.30 Sun

HALAM SK6754 Map 7
Waggon & Horses
Off A612 in Southwell centre, via Halam Road

The friendly attentive young licensees in this heavily oak-beamed dining pub are doing a wide choice of enjoyable and often inventive food: lunchtime filled rolls such as parma ham and goats cheese (from £3.95), soup (£3), goats cheese and red onion tartlet with beetroot and orange salad (£4.75), seared marinated king scallops with greek salad (£7.50), and roast chicken breast stuffed with herb crust and asparagus and cherry tomato broth or braised shin of beef with salsa verde (£10). On our spring inspection visit the interesting specials included cod baked with a herb and parmesan crust and roasted cherry tomato sauce (£10), grilled gurnard with an unusual avocado, crème fraîche and basil dressing (£12), and bass with butternut squash mash gently spiced up by red pepper dressing (£12.50). We liked the really sturdy high-back rush-seat dining chairs around the mix of solid mainly stripped tables; there are various wall seats, smaller chairs and the odd stout settle too, with lots of pictures from kittens to Spy cricketer caricatures on walls painted sky blue, terracotta or mustard. The open-plan area is well divided into smallish sections (an appealing black iron screen dividing off the no smoking part is made up of tiny african-style figures of people and animals); candles throughout give a pleasant night-time glow. The pub has recently been taken over by Thwaites of Blackburn, and has their Bitter, Thoroughbred and Lancaster Bomber well kept on handpump, with a quickly changing guest beer such as Hambleton Goldfield; piped jazz. Out past a piano and grandfather clock in the lobby are a few roadside picnic-sets by the pretty window boxes. *(Recommended by Colin Fisher, Derek and Sylvia Stephenson, Alan Thwaite, B Clayton)*

Thwaites ~ Tenants Rebecca and William White ~ Real ale ~ Bar food (12-2.30, 6-9.30) ~ Restaurant ~ (01636) 813109/816228 ~ Children welcome ~ Dogs welcome ~ Open 11.45-3, 5.30-11; 11.45-11.30 Sat; 12-10.30 Sun

KIMBERLEY SK5044 Map 7
Nelson & Railway ▩ £
1¾ miles from M1 junction 26; at exit roundabout take A610 towards Ripley, then signposted Kimberley, pub in Station Road

After 33 years of pulling pints here, Mick has handed the tenancy of this bustling two-roomed Victorian pub over to his son Harry – but as he's planning to carry on behind the counter we're sure the atmosphere will be just as traditional and cheery as ever. Popular with locals, the snugly beamed bar and lounge have a mix of Edwardian-looking furniture, with interesting brewery prints and railway signs on the walls. The pub's name comes from a shortening of its original title the Lord Nelson Railway Hotel, in the days when it stood yards away from two competing stations. The Hardys & Hansons brewery is directly opposite, and they've well kept Kimberley Best and Classic and a seasonal ale on handpump; darts, alley and table skittles, dominoes, chess, cribbage, Scrabble, fruit machine, juke box and piped music. Good value straightforward but satisfying bar food includes soup (£1.50), sandwiches (from £1.40), hot rolls (from £1.70), garlic chicken goujons (£2.90), cottage pie (£3.30), ploughman's (£4.70), steak and ale pie or mushroom stroganoff (£4.90), breaded scampi or chicken tikka masala (£5.40), and blackboard specials such as mexican avocado (£3.90) and shark (£4.95); puddings are £1.90, and they do a good Sunday lunch (£4.75); the dining room is no smoking at meal times. There are tables and swings out in a good-sized cottagey garden. *(Recommended by Bernie Adams, JP, PP, Pete Baker, Roger and Maureen Kenning, Peter F Marshall, Roger Noyes, Dr and Mrs A K Clarke, the Didler, Derek and Sylvia Stephenson, Pat and Derek Roughton, Mr and Mrs J McRobert, David Carr, Karen Eliot)*

Hardys & Hansons ~ Tenants Mick and Harry Burton ~ Real ale ~ Bar food (12-2.30, 5.30-9; 12-6 Sun) ~ Restaurant ~ (0115) 938 2177 ~ Children in lounge till 9pm ~ Dogs allowed in bar ~ Open 11.30-11; 12-10.30 Sun ~ Bedrooms: £24S/£39S

LAXTON SK7267 Map 7
Dovecote
Signposted off A6075 E of Ollerton

The really nice welcome, friendly courteous service and honestly priced enjoyable food are what make this redbrick house such an agreeable place – and it's usefully close to the A1. The central lounge has dark wheelback chairs and tables on wooden floors, and a coal-effect gas fire. This opens through a small bay (the former entrance) into a carpeted no smoking room. Around the other side, another little lounge leads through to a pool room with darts, TV, fruit machine, pool, dominoes and piped music; they have well kept Batemans XXXB, Everards Tiger and Charles Wells Bombardier on handpump. Served in big helpings, bar food includes soup (£3.25), sandwiches and baguettes (from £3.50), steak and kidney pie (£6.75) mushroom stroganoff (£7.50) and sweet and sour battered chicken (£8.50), with specials such as chicken and mushroom cream pie (£7.25), battered cod (£7.50) and bass stuffed with prawns (£9.25). The puddings, such as cheesecake (£3.25), are made by Aunty Mary, the landlord's aunt, who lives in the village. There are wooden tables and chairs on a small front terrace by a sloping garden, which has a disused white dovecote and a children's play area. As well as the two bedrooms, they have a site and facilities for six caravans. Laxton is one of the few places in the country still farmed using the traditional open field system – the pub stands next to three huge medieval open fields. Every year in the third week of June the grass is auctioned for haymaking, and anyone who lives in the parish is entitled to a bid – and a drink. You can find out more at the visitor centre behind the pub. *(Recommended by Keith and Chris O'Neill, Nick and Pam Hancock, JP, PP, JWAC, Derek and Sylvia Stephenson, Dave and Sue Mitchell, Marcus Byron, Patrick Hancock, Dr Michael Denton)*

Free house ~ Licensees Stephen and Betty Shepherd ~ Real ale ~ Bar food (12-2, 6.30(7 Sun)-9) ~ Restaurant ~ (01777) 871586 ~ Children in eating area of bar and restaurant ~ Dogs allowed in bar ~ Open 11.30-3, 6.30-11.30(7-10.30 Sun) ~ Bedrooms: £35B/£50B

MORTON SK7251 Map 7
Full Moon £
Pub and village signposted off Bleasby—Fiskerton back road, SE of Southwell

You can enjoy a very pleasant good value meal at this popular beamed dining pub – especially if you qualify for the £6.25 two-course OAP bargain. Their bargain award – new this year – is for the very reasonably priced lunchtime snack menu, which includes soup and sandwiches (£4.50), liver and bacon (£4.75) and fish and chips (£4.95). The main menu lists soup (£2.50), home-made pâté with cumberland sauce (£3.95), caesar salad (£6.75), steak and kidney pie or nut roast (£7.95), salmon fillet with basil mayonnaise (£8.75), lamb tagine (£9.25) and puddings such as lemon brûlée or treacle sponge pudding (£3.75). Basically L-shaped, the main part has pink plush seats and cushioned black settles around a variety of pub tables, with wheelback chairs in the side dining area, and a couple of fireplaces. Fresh flowers and the very long run of Christmas plates on the walls add a spot of colour; look out for the two sociable pub cats. Well kept Dover Beck, Greene King Ruddles (which they call Full Moon), Charles Wells Bombardier and a changing guest on handpump, and friendly service; there may be piped music. A peaceful back terrace has picnic-sets, with more in a sizeable garden, and some sturdy play equipment. This out-of-the-way hamlet is not far from the River Trent. *(Recommended by JP, PP, Derek and Sylvia Stephenson, the Didler, Andrew Stephenson, W W Burke)*

Free house ~ Licensees Clive and Kim Wisdom ~ Real ale ~ Bar food (12-2; 6.30-9.30(10 Fri/Sat); 12-2.30, 7-9.30 Sun) ~ Restaurant ~ (01636) 830251 ~ Children welcome ~ Open 11-3, 6-11(10.30 Sun); closed 26 Dec evening and 1 Jan

NOTTINGHAM SK5640 Map 7
Bell ▮ £

Angel Row, off Market Square

This quaint and very popular 15th-c pub, dwarfed by the office tower next door, is now owned by Hardys & Hansons. Its great age is evident throughout – some of the original timbers have been uncovered, and in the front Tudor bar you can see patches of 300-year-old wallpaper (protected by glass). This room is perhaps the brightest, with french windows opening (in summer) to tables on the street outside, and bright blue walls. The room with the greatest feeling of age is the very pubby and sometimes quite smoky low-beamed Elizabethan Bar, with its half-panelled walls, maple parquet floor, and comfortable high-backed armchairs. Food is served in a larger no smoking room at the back. Upstairs, at the back of the heavily panelled Belfry (usually open only at lunchtime, when it functions as a family restaurant), you can see the rafters of the 15th-c crown post roof, and you can look down on the busy street at the front. Very good value bar food includes soup (£1.45), sandwiches (from £2.49), smoky bacon, chicken and mushroom pie (£3.99), cod and chips or mushroom stroganoff (£4.99), beef and ale pie (£5.99), and puddings such as apple pie and chocolate pudding (£2.45). A rather different range of beers from those that regulars here might have been used to now includes Hardys & Hansons Best, Old Kim and a changing Hardys & Hansons beer, as well as guests from local brewers such as Castle Rock and Nottingham. The cellars are about 10 metres down in the sandstone rock – groups may be able to arrange tours; about eight wines by the glass and quite a few malt whiskies. Fruit machine and piped music. *(Recommended by Derek and Sylvia Stephenson, C J Fletcher, the Didler, Maggie and Tony Harwood, Rona Murdoch, Patrick Hancock, JP, PP)*

Hardys & Hansons ~ Manager Brian Rigby ~ Real ale ~ Bar food (11(12 Sun)-8(toasties till 10.30)) ~ Restaurant ~ (0115) 947 5241 ~ Children in eating area of bar and restaurant ~ Live music three-five nights a week ~ Open 10.30-11; 12-10.30 Sun

Fellows Morton & Clayton ▮

Canal Street (part of inner ring road)

If you find yourself in the city on a hot sunny day, the large terrace out at the back by the canal is a great place for a relaxing drink. On not so sunny days, this carefully converted old canal building is especially worth visiting if you like real ale. From a big window in the quarry-tiled glassed-in area at the back you can see the little brewery where they brew the tasty Samuel Fellows and Post Haste, which are served alongside five or so other ales that might be from brewers such as Castle Eden, Fullers, Mallard or Oakham. There's a really buoyant atmosphere in the softly lit bar, which has dark red plush seats built into alcoves, wooden tables, more seats up two or three steps in a side gallery, and bric-a-brac on the shelf just below the glossy dark green high ceiling; a sympathetic extension provides extra seating. Piped pop music, fruit machine, big TV, and a rack of daily newspapers; service is prompt and friendly. Popular reasonably priced bar food might include soup (£1.95), filled baguettes (from £4.95), battered haddock (£5.75), thai vegetable curry (£7.25), steak and kidney (£6.50), scampi (£7.95), and puddings such as bread and butter pudding or cherry baked alaska (£3.25); the no smoking restaurant does a bargain two-course lunch (£5.99). At lunchtime it's popular with local workers, while in the evenings (when it can get smoky) you'll find a younger set. *(Recommended by Patrick Hancock, Maggie and Tony Harwood, JP, PP, C J Fletcher, Rona Murdoch, Derek and Sylvia Stephenson, the Didler, David Carr)*

Own brew ~ Licensees Les Howard and Keely Willans ~ Real ale ~ Bar food (11.30-9.30; 12-6 Sun) ~ Restaurant ~ (0115) 950 6795 ~ Children in restaurant ~ Open 11.30-11; 12-10.30 Sun

Lincolnshire Poacher ♦ £

Mansfield Road; up hill from Victoria Centre

The very impressive range of about a dozen real ales at this popular town pub
includes Batemans XB and XXXB, Castle Rock Poachers Gold and Oakham JHB,
kept well alongside guests from some interesting brewers such as Abbeydale,
Brewsters, Burton Bridge, Kelham Island, Newby Wyke and Phoenix; also
continental draught and bottled beers, good farm cider, around 80 malt whiskies
and 10 irish ones, and typically of this small chain, very good value soft drinks. The
short bar menu includes hummous and olives (£2.95), ploughman's (£3.25), goats
cheese bruschetta (£3.75), potato and halloumi roast (£4.95), sausage and mash or
pork in cream and cider (£5.50), warm chicken salad (£5.75) and a couple of daily
specials such as moroccan lamb tagine (£5.50). The traditional big wood-floored
front bar has wall settles and plain wooden tables, and is decorated with
breweriana; it opens on to a plain but lively room on the left, from where a corridor
takes you down to the chatty panelled back snug, with newspapers, cribbage,
dominoes, cards and backgammon; piped music; no smoking area at lunchtime.
It can get very busy in the evening, when it's popular with a younger crowd. A
conservatory overlooks tables on a large terrace behind. *(Recommended by
Patrick Hancock, JP, PP, the Didler, Doug Christian, Derek and Sylvia Stephenson)*

*Tynemill ~ Manager David Whitaker ~ Real ale ~ Bar food (12-8(7 Fri/Sat, 4 Sun)) ~
(0115) 941 1584 ~ Children in conservatory till 8pm ~ Dogs allowed in bar ~ Open
11-11; 12-10.30 Sun*

Olde Trip to Jerusalem ★ ♦ £

Brewhouse Yard; from inner ring road follow The North, A6005 Long Eaton signpost until
you are in Castle Boulevard, then almost at once turn right into Castle Road; pub is up on
the left

The name is a reference to the 12th-c crusaders who used to meet on this site on the
way to the Holy Land. The siting of the current building can be attributed to the
days when a brewhouse was established here to supply the needs of the castle above
– parts of the pub are built into caverns burrowing into the sandstone rock below
the castle. The panelled walls of the unusual upstairs bar (thought to have served as
cellarage for that earlier medieval brewhouse) soar narrowly into a dark cleft
above, and also mainly carved from the rock, the downstairs bar has leatherette-
cushioned settles built into dark panelling, tables on flagstones, and snug
banquettes built into low-ceilinged rock alcoves; there's also a no smoking
parlour/snug, and two more caves open to visitors. Service is prompt and friendly,
and the pub attracts a good mix of people, with tourists, conversational locals and
students all adding to the chatty atmosphere. They keep their real ales in top
condition, and you'll find Hardys & Hansons Kimberley Best, Best Mild, a beer
brewed for the pub and William Clarke, alongside Marstons Pedigree on
handpump. Attractively priced straightforward bar food includes soup (£1.20), a
very good chip butty (£1.80), sandwiches (from £1.99), burgers (from £2.29), giant
filled yorkshire pudding, liver and bacon, steak and ale pie and cod and chips
(£4.99), scampi (£5.29) and rump steak (£5.99), with puddings (from £1.99).
They've ring the bull and a fruit machine, and there are some seats outside.
*(Recommended by Richard Fendick, Kevin Blake, R T and J C Moggridge, Rona Murdoch,
Patrick Hancock, the Didler, Stephen Buckley, David Carr, CMW, JJW, Peter F Marshall,
John W Allen, JP, PP, Joe Green)*

*Hardys & Hansons ~ Manager Claire Underdown ~ Real ale ~ Bar food
(11(12 Sun)-6) ~ (0115) 9473171 ~ Children in family area during food service times
~ Open 11-11; 12-10.30 Sun*

Stars after the name of a pub show exceptional character and appeal. They
don't mean extra comfort. And they are nothing to do with food quality, for
which there's a separate knife-and-fork symbol. Even quite a basic
pub can win stars, if it's individual enough.

Pit & Pendulum

Victoria Street

A novelty *Guide* entry, this theatrical theme place is worth seeing for its entertaining gothic horror film décor. Dark and dramatic, it's lit by heavy chandeliers and (electronically) flaring torches, with flashes of colour from an overhead tangle of Frankenstein-laboratory glass tubing and wiring. Dark seating runs from gothick thrones to spooky red-padded side booths with a heavy bat's-wing hint, tables are inset with ancient documents and arcane jewellery – even the cups and saucers have a spider's web design (the coffee is good). There is plenty of ghoulish carving and creeping ivy, and old horror movies run in silence on the TV above the bar counter – where a tortuous web of piping replaces the usual beer taps. Good wheelchair ramps add cleverly to the design, with their curves and heavy black balusters, and the disabled lavatory is through a false bookcase. Downstairs (and that is indeed a shackled skeleton looming through the distorted glass) there's more of the same, with clearly separated areas, and some more conventional seating; well reproduced piped music, fruit machine and friendly staff. Bar food includes pizza ciabatta (£2.80), frogs legs (£3.75), burgers (from £4.50), coriander chicken or brie and broccoli bake (£6.40) and puddings such as apple pie or cinnamon waffles (£2.75). *(Recommended by Kevin Blake)*

Scottish Courage ~ Licensee Ian Povey ~ Bar food (11-10; 12-9 Sun) ~ (0115) 950 6383 ~ Open 11-11; 12-10.30 Sun; closed 25 Dec

Vat & Fiddle ▣ £

Queens Bridge Road, alongside Sheriffs Way (near multi-storey car park)

For many readers the simplicity of this plain brick pub makes it their preferred option in Nottingham. Down to earth but chatty and relaxed, the fairly functional open-plan interior has quite a strong 1930s feel, with cream and navy walls and ceiling, varnished pine tables and bentwood stools and chairs on parquet and terrazzo flooring, patterned blue curtains, and some brewery memorabilia; there are magazines and newspapers to read, piped music and sometimes TV. The Castle Rock beers here are kept in very good condition (as one would expect given that the pub is right next to the brewery) and served alongside mostly quite full-bodied real guests (often including a Stout) from brewers such as Caledonian, Newby Wyke and Oakham; occasional beer festivals. They also have around 70 malt whiskies, farm cider, continental bottled beers and several polish vodkas; good value soft drinks too. Aside from a decent choice of rolls (from £1.60), a concise choice of straightforward but hearty dishes might include soup (£2.45), chilli (£3.75) and sausage and mash (£4.25). A back terrace has picnic-sets, with more out in front by the road; the train and bus stations are both just a short walk away. *(Recommended by Richard Lewis, C J Fletcher, JP, PP, the Didler, David Carr, Joe Green)*

Tynemill ~ Managers Julian Grocock and N Trafford ~ Real ale ~ Bar food (12-3, 6-8, not Sun evening) ~ (0115) 985 0611 ~ Children in secluded area away from bar ~ Dogs allowed in bar ~ Open 11-11; 12-10.30 Sun

WALKERINGHAM SK7792 Map 7

Three Horse Shoes

High Street; just off A161, off A631 W of Gainsborough

The landlord here is quite a gardener. In summer, using 9,000 plants, he puts on a spectacular display of blazing hanging baskets and tubs, and the japanese-style millennium garden up by the top car park is interesting. All the flowers provide a charmingly vivid contrast with the simple old-fashioned décor inside, where you'll find well kept Bass, Stones, Worthington Best and a guest beer such as Timothy Taylors Landlord on handpump; also darts, dominoes, fruit machine, video game, and piped music. Served by cheerfully welcoming staff, a good choice of enjoyable food could include sandwiches or soup (£1.95), fried mushrooms stuffed with garlic cheese or pâté (£3.50), steak pie, mushroom, cheese, leek and nut pie or gammon and pineapple (£6.50), sirloin steak (£8.95), and – a favourite with readers – beef medallions in a brandy and stilton sauce (£10.50); puddings such as sticky toffee pudding (£2.50). *(Recommended by Walter and Susan Rinaldi-Butcher, WAH, JP, PP, Derek and Sylvia Stephenson, CMW, JJW)*

Free house ~ Licensee John Turner ~ Real ale ~ Bar food (till 9.30 Fri/Sat; not Sun evening) ~ Restaurant ~ (01427) 890959 ~ Children welcome ~ Open 11-3, 6-11; 12-4, 7-10.30 Sun

Lucky Dip

Besides the fully inspected pubs, you might like to try these Lucky Dips recommended to us and described by readers (if you do, please send us reports: www.goodguides.com).

AWSWORTH [SK4844]
Gate [Main St, via A6096 off A610 Nuthall—Eastwood bypass]: Friendly old traditional local with Hardys & Hansons Best and Mild, coal fire in lounge, small pool room; nr site of once-famous railway viaduct – photographs in passage *(the Didler, JP, PP)*
BAGTHORPE [SK4751]
Dixies Arms [2 miles from M1 junction 27; A608 towards Eastwood, then first right on to B600 via Sandhill Rd, then first left into School Rd; Lower Bagthorpe]: Well kept real ales in quaint 18th-c beamed and tiled-floor local, entrance bar with tiny snug next to bar, small part-panelled parlour with fine fireplace, longer narrow room with toby jugs and darts, friendly landlord and labrador; unobtrusive fruit machine, rarely used juke box; jazz or folk Sat, quiz night Sun, big garden with wknd barbecues, play area and football pitch, own flock, gun and morris dancing clubs; open 2-11, all day wknds *(the Didler, JP, PP)*
BINGHAM [SK7039]
☆ *Horse & Plough* [off A52; Long Acre]: Low beams, flagstones and stripped brick, prints and old brewery memorabilia, comfortable open-plan seating inc pews, good value generous lunchtime baguettes, melts, baked potatoes and three or four hot dishes, well kept Charles Wells Bombardier and several guest beers, good wine choice, popular upstairs grill room (Tues-Sat, and Sun lunch – bargain steaks Tues/Weds) with polished boards, hand-painted murals and open kitchen; piped music; open all day *(the Didler, JP, PP, Hugh Roberts, BB)*
BLEASBY [SK7149]
Waggon & Horses [Gypsy Lane]: Comfortable banquettes in carpeted lounge, open fire in character bar, Banks's and Marstons Pedigree, reasonably priced fresh lunchtime food from snacks up, Fri fish and chips night, chatty landlord; piped music; back lobby with play area and comfortable chairs to watch over it, tables outside, small camping area behind *(the Didler, JP, PP)*
BLYTH [SK6287]
☆ *Angel* [Bawtry Rd]: Cheerful bustle in much-modernised coaching inn, nice coal fire, assorted furniture, full range of Hardys &

Hansons ales kept well, usual food inc good value Sun lunch (rare around here so get there early – they don't take bookings), good friendly service, partly no smoking lounge/dining area; piped music, smaller public bar and pool room; children welcome, garden with play area, simple bedrooms *(Duncan Cloud, LYM, Derek and Sylvia Stephenson)*
BRINSLEY [SK4649]
☆ *Yew Tree* [Cordy Lane]: Large well appointed pub doing well under friendly newish tenants, wide-ranging nicely presented food inc good Thurs fresh fish day, well kept Hardys & Hansons ales, good service, lots of copper and brass and coal fire in attractive lounge, restaurant *(Derek and Sylvia Stephenson, Kevin Blake)*
CLIPSTONE [SK6064]
Dog & Duck [B6030 Mansfield—Ollerton]: Three-roomed extended pub with comfortable blue plush seating, pictures for sale in small no smoking dining area, reasonably priced home-made food (not Sun evening), several well kept real ales, friendly service, conservatory; children very welcome, play area and high chairs; quiet piped music, TV, quiz and live music nights; disabled facilities though some steps, some tables outside *(CMW, JJW)*
COLLINGHAM [SK8362]
Grey Horse [Low St]: Enjoyable reasonably priced food inc children's all week; tables outside with play area *(David and Ruth Hollands)*
Kings Head [High St]: Modernised Georgian building, three real ales inc Timothy Taylors Landlord, ad lib coffee, bar sandwiches, good food with unusual touches and properly cooked veg in restaurant *(David and Ruth Hollands)*
COSSALL [SK4843]
Gardeners [Awsworth Lane (A6096, Cossall Marsh)]: Open-plan local with cheap well kept Hardys & Hansons Bitter, Mild and seasonal beers, good value lunchtime food, end games area with pool and sports TV *(the Didler)*
DUNHAM [SK8174]
Bridge Inn [Main St]: Nr toll bridge, well kept ales such as Black Sheep and local Broadstone, enjoyable blackboard food,

friendly landlord and locals, L-shaped beamed room with lots of bric-a-brac, prints and posters, good log fire, small no smoking dining room; piped music, large TV; well behaved children welcome, wheelchair access, a few tables outside, open all day wknds *(Kevin Thorpe, the Didler, JP, PP, Kevin Blake)*

EASTWOOD [SK4846]
Foresters Arms [Main St, Newthorpe]: Cosy two-room village inn, Hardys & Hansons on electric pump, relaxing lounge, TV and old local photographs in bar, darts, dominoes and skittles, piano sing-along wknds; nice garden, occasional barbecues *(the Didler)*

EPPERSTONE [SK6548]
Cross Keys [Main St]: Friendly and comfortable old two-bar village pub, locally popular for hearty reasonably priced home-cooked food (not Sun or Mon) inc cheap OAP lunch Tues-Fri; well kept Hardys & Hansons beers, good value house wine, cheerful efficient young staff; pretty village, pleasant countryside *(Colin Fisher)*

EVERTON [SK6991]
Blacksmiths Arms [Church St]: L-shaped bar with no smoking dining area down step opening into well heated conservatory, real ales such as Barnsley, John Smiths and Theakstons, wide food choice inc bargain family Sun lunches, friendly chatty service, pool in games room; quiet piped music, dogs welcome; smallish garden with play area, open all day wknds *(Ian and Freda Millar, CMW, JJW, Derek and Sylvia Stephenson)*

FARNSFIELD [SK6456]
Plough [E end]: Attractive L-shaped beamed lounge, lunchtime and early evening food, well kept Mansfield beers, good fireplace, bar with TV and video games *(Kevin Blake)*

GOTHAM [SK5330]
Cuckoo Bush [Leake Rd]: Welcoming 19th-c local with comfortable L-shaped lounge bar, pictures, plates etc, three other rooms each with its own atmosphere, limited good value food (not Sat-Weds nights), well kept Bass, very friendly staff, sensibly segregated darts and TV (with sofa), quiet piped music – and don't sit under the cuckoo clock; picnic-sets and barbecue in small garden *(Des and Jen Clarke)*

GRANBY [SK7436]
Marquis of Granby [Dragon St]: Reopened in 2002 and specialising in half a dozen quickly changing guest beers alongside its regular Brewsters Marquis *(R Wilkins)*

KIMBERLEY [SK5044]
Stag [Nottingham Rd]: Friendly 16th-c traditional local run by devoted landlady, two cosy rooms served by small central counter, low beams, dark panelling and settles, well kept changing ales, vintage working penny slot machines and Shipstones brewery photographs; attractive back garden with play area, cl wkdy lunchtimes (opens 5; 1.30 Sat, 12 Sun) *(B and H, the Didler, JP, PP)*

KIRKBY IN ASHFIELD [SK5056]
Countryman [Park Lane (B6018 S)]: Lively traditional atmosphere in upgraded former miners' local, attractive bas relief murals of shooting scenes in cottagey beamed lounge bar, decorative plates and mining memorabilia, well kept Bass, Theakstons and usually two guests, beer festivals, good value generous bar food (not Sun, Mon evening), public bar with pool; popular with walkers, play area, good live folk, rock and blues Fri; open all day *(Kevin Blake, the Didler, JP, PP)*

LAMBLEY [SK6345]
☆ *Woodlark* [Church St]: Well preserved and interestingly laid out two-room village local, careful extension into next house giving extra lounge/dining area, good value lunches and more ambitious evening meals (not Sun evening or Mon), cheerful welcome, three well kept ales, roaring coal fire, darts and pool room, table skittles and skittle alley, no machines or piped music; children in annexe *(BB, CMW, JJW, B and H)*

LANGAR [SK7234]
Unicorns Head [Main St]: Dining pub popular with business and older people, children's menu too, sensible prices, order in the bar then they take you to your table when the meal's ready *(W and P J Elderkin)*

LINBY [SK5351]
Horse & Groom [Main St]: Friendly staff, well kept local ales and enjoyable honest food in unpretentious pub with big play area; attractive village nr Newstead Abbey *(Richard Naish)*

LOWDHAM [SK6646]
☆ *Old Ship* [nr A612/A6097; Main St]: Friendly beamed country pub with comfortable furnishings from traditional built-in settles to plush banquettes, several areas up and down steps inc attractive dining area with big round tables, above-average imaginative blackboard food in extended split-level lounge/bar, well kept Courage Directors, John Smiths and a guest beer such as Ridleys Prospect, friendly service, coal fire, lots of pictures, plates, copper and brass, separate public bar; quiz nights; picnic-sets on neat sheltered back lawn, bedrooms, pleasant walks nearby *(W M Paton, BB)*
Worlds End [Plough Lane]: Small and friendly old beamed village pub with log fire at one end of long room, dining area the other, fresh flowers, some original features, popular reasonably priced straightforward bar and restaurant food, small-helping OAP lunches, well kept Marstons Pedigree; piped music, smoking allowed throughout; good window boxes, picnic-sets in garden *(David and Phyllis Chapman, Rona Murdoch, Alan Bowker)*

MANSFIELD [SK5260]
Nell Gwynne [A38 W of centre]: Former gentlemen's club, cosy country-house décor, warm and welcoming with log-effect gas fire, old colliery plates and mementoes of old

Mansfield pubs; two changing real ales, 1960s piped music, SkyTV sports in one room, Weds quiz night; cl Mon-Thurs lunchtimes, nearby parking difficult *(the Didler)*

Railway Inn [Station St; best approached by viaduct from nr market pl]: Friendly traditional pub with divided main bar and separate room, bargain home-cooked lunches, well kept attractively priced Batemans XB; handy for Robin Hood Line stn, normally open all day but may be cl Sun evening *(Pete Baker)*

MANSFIELD WOODHOUSE [SK5463]

Greyhound [High St]: Two-room village local with Courage, Theakstons and interesting guest beers, darts and pool *(the Didler)*

MAPLEBECK [SK7160]

☆ **Beehive** [signed down pretty country lanes from A616 Newark—Ollerton and from A617 Newark—Mansfield]: Cosy and unspoiled beamed country tavern in nice spot, excellent landlady, tiny front bar, slightly bigger side room, traditional furnishings, open fire, free antique juke box, well kept local Maypole and Rudgate ales, log fires, tables on small terrace with flower tubs and grassy bank running down to little stream, play area with swings, barbecues; no food, may be cl wkdy winter lunchtimes, very busy wknds and bank hols *(LYM, B and H, the Didler, JP, PP, Molly and Arthur Aldersey-Williams, Bernie Adams, Keith and Janet Morris)*

MOORGREEN [SK4847]

Horse & Groom [Church Rd (B600)]: Open-plan, with no smoking area, wide choice of food all day inc (not Sun) OAP lunch, well kept Hardys & Hansons ales; TV and games machine; big back garden with picnic-sets, covered terrace and play area *(CMW, JJW)*

NEWARK [SK7953]

Castle & Falcon [London Rd]: Former coaching inn with local atmosphere, John Smiths and guest beers, two bars and family area, spacious games area with darts and pool; skittle alley, evening opening 7 *(the Didler)*

Fox & Crown [Appleton Gate]: Comfortably unpretentious Tynemill pub, nooks and corners inc no smoking back family areas, stone or wood floors, big brewery mirrors and other breweriana, well kept changing real ales, Inch's cider, dozens of malt whiskies, continental draught and bottled beers, flavoured vodkas, good choice of wines, freshly made food from sandwiches up, friendly efficient staff; good wheelchair access, occasional live music, open all day *(the Didler, JP, PP, David Carr)*

☆ **Mail Coach** [London Rd, nr Beaumont Cross]: Friendly open-plan Georgian local, attractive décor in three candlelit separate areas, lots of chicken pictures, big fire and comfortable chairs, well kept Boddingtons, Flowers IPA and Original and local guests such as Maypole Mad Mild and Oldershaws

Grantham Dark and Newtons Drop, enjoyable home-made lunchtime food inc some unusual dishes, pleasant staff; pub games, jazz, blues or folk wknds, upstairs ladies'; tables outside *(Kevin Blake, the Didler, JP, PP, Keith and Janet Morris)*

Wing [Bridge St, just off Market Pl]: Tucked-away character tavern down paved area beside magnificent church, well kept Theakstons Best, XB and Old Peculier, two small plain rooms, one with games; tables outside *(the Didler)*

Woolpack [Stodman St, off Castlegate]: Ancient pub with three small rooms, good home cooking (inc breakfast from 9am), John Smiths and guest beers; back terrace, skittle alley *(the Didler)*

NEWSTEAD [SK5252]

Station Hotel [Station Rd]: Busy basic red-brick village local opp station on Robin Hood rail line, bargain well kept Barnsley Bitter and Old Tom Mild, old railway photographs; no food Sun *(JP, PP, the Didler)*

NORMANTON ON THE WOLDS [SK6232]

Plough [off A606 5m S of Nottingham]: Unspoiled local with wide choice of good value home-made food in small dining room, friendly service, well kept Bass, John Smiths Magnet and Theakstons; large garden, attractive village *(Neil and Jenny Dury, Gerry and Rosemary Dobson)*

NOTTINGHAM [SK5139]

Canal House [Canal St]: Big alehouse conversion of wharf building by Tynemill, bridge over indoors canal spur complete with narrowboat, lots of bare brick and varnished wood, huge joists on studded steel beams, long bar with Castle Rock Hemlock, Timothy Taylors Landlord and several changing guest beers, good choice of house wines (two glass sizes), lots of standing room; good upstairs restaurant and second bar, masses of solid tables out on attractive waterside terrace; piped music (live Sun), student nights, open all day – till midnight Thurs, 1am Fri/Sat *(the Didler, JP, PP, Richard Greenwood, BB, Richard Lewis)*

Coopers Arms [Porchester Rd, Thornywood]: Solid Victorian local with three unspoilt rooms, real ales inc Theakstons XB; small family room in skittle alley; cl Weds lunchtime *(JP, PP, the Didler)*

Elwes Arms [Oakdale Rd, Carlton]: Comfortable and attractive, with huge range of home-cooked food, good beer range; unobtrusive piped music; nice garden *(Richard Greenwood)*

Falcon [Canning Circus/Alfreton Rd]: Ancient pub redecorated by new owners, two small rooms with old pictures and coal fire in attractive fireplace, well kept Adnams Bitter and Broadside and Charles Wells Bombardier, good choice of wines, new chef doing enjoyable food inc some interesting specials in pleasant upstairs restaurant lined with benches; pavement tables and barbecues, open all day *(the Didler, JP, PP)*

Forest [Mansfield Rd]: Tynemill pub with a difference, varied rather mediterranean food all day inc dishes with pick-list of ingredients, well kept Castle Rock Hemlock, Greene King Abbot, Woodfordes Wherry and a guest such as Batemans XB, low prices for soft drinks too, two smallish rooms knocked together, prints and beer posters on tiled and panelled walls; cl Mon/Tues lunchtime *(the Didler, Derek and Sylvia Stephenson)*

Fox & Crown [Church St/Lincoln St, Old Basford]: Open-plan local refurbished in bright pine, back microbrewery producing its own Alcazar Vixens Vice, Brush Bitter, New Dawn and Maple Magic winter ale, brewery tours Sat, perhaps a guest from another pub brewery; wide choice of pizzas and other dishes inc sandwiches, helpful staff and canadian landlord; good piped music, games machines, Tues quiz night, big-screen sports TV; disabled access possible (lavatories difficult), tables out behind, open all day *(the Didler, JP, PP, G Coates)*

Gladstone [Loscoe Rd, Carrington]: Traditional backstreet two-room alehouse, comfortable seats and reading matter in cosy lounge, darts in basic bar, up to four real ales inc a changing guest, lots of atmosphere – esp on weekly folk nights *(B and H)*

Globe [London Rd]: Real ales such as Mallard, Nottingham, Oakham JHB and three changing guests, farm cider, good food all day; handy for Trent Bridge *(the Didler)*

Hard Rock Café [King St]: New pub in impressive old building, pillars, high ceiling, lots of guitars and other instruments, pictures of rock artistes, John Smiths beers, american-style food in dining area; adjoining souvenir shop *(Kevin Blake)*

Hemlockstone [Bramcote Lane, Wollaton]: Good beer range inc Castle Rock Hemlock Best and a guest beer along with Courage Directors and Home *(Alan Bowker)*

Horse & Groom [Radford Rd, New Basford]: Popular and well run partly open-plan local next to former Shipstones brewery, with their name over door and other memorabilia; nice snug, several changing well kept ales, good value fresh food from sandwiches to Sun lunches, daily papers; jazz, folk, blues or skiffle nights Fri in converted back stables; open all day *(the Didler, JP, PP, Malcolm Taylor)*

Limelight [Wellington Circus, nr Playhouse]: Convivial bar and restaurant attached to Playhouse theatre, several well kept real ales, decent food (not Sun lunchtime), pleasant efficient staff, theatre pictures, attractive continental-style outside seating area; open all day, live blues and jazz *(Patrick Hancock, JP, PP, the Didler, Kevin Blake)*

Lion [Lower Mosley St, New Basford]: Up to 10 well kept ales inc Batemans and local Mallard from one of city's deepest cellars (glass viewing panel – and can be visited at quiet times), farm cider, wide choice of good

wholesome food inc doorstep sandwiches, sensible prices, bare bricks and boards, log fire, daily papers, live folk, jazz and blues Fri-Sun; summer barbecues, open all day *(the Didler, JP, PP)*

News House [Canal St]: Friendly two-room Tynemill pub with attractive blue exterior tiling, eight very well kept ales inc bargain Castle Rock, belgian and czech imports on tap, lots of flavoured vodkas, enjoyable fresh food inc Sun lunch, mix of bare boards and carpet, one room filled with local newspaper front pages spanning years of events and personalities *(C J Fletcher, the Didler, JP, PP)*

Old Moot Hall [Carlton Rd, Sneinton]: Brand new but thoroughly traditional, with eleven well kept and priced ales from small breweries, czech Budvar on tap, foreign bottled beers, good wine choice, polished boards, nice pictures, wooden furniture, coal-effect gas fire, upstairs room; plans for food, Sun quiz night; open all day *(the Didler)*

☆ *Plough* [St Peters St, Radford]: Unpretentious two-room local brewing its own interesting Nottingham ales, also a guest beer and farm ciders, good bargain food inc popular Sun lunch (live jazz then), bargain curries Tues evening, may be free chilli Thurs evening, two coal fires, traditional fittings and nice windows, bar billiards and other traditional games (competitions Weds); open all day Thurs-Sun *(the Didler, B and H, JP, PP)*

Punchbowl [Porchester Rd, Mapperley]: Comfortable and thorough-going refit wearing in well now, good choice of food and of real ales inc Fullers London Pride and a changing guest beer *(Richard Greenwood)*

☆ *Salutation* [Hounds Gate/Maid Marion Way]: Up to a dozen or more well kept changing ales and lots of bottled beers, ancient lower back part with beams, flagstones and well worn cosy corners inc two small quiet rooms and a no smoking area, plusher modern front lounge, helpful staff, speedily served enjoyable plain food till 7; piped music, games machine, can get busy – but a haven in the centre, increasingly dominated by designer bars; open all day *(BB, Des and Jen Clarke, Derek and Sylvia Stephenson, Patrick Hancock, Richard Lewis, JP, PP)*

Stick & Pitcher [University Boulevard, Dunkirk]: Tynemill pub next to city tennis courts and overlooking Highfields hockey club; comfortable upstairs bar with highly polished woodwork, three Castle Rock ales and two guests, enjoyable food, sports TV; open all day *(the Didler)*

Toll Bar [Maid Marion Way/Tollhouse Hill]: Below office block, interesting and surprisingly cosy, with bargain beer, simple good value food inc sandwiches; can be very busy and a bit smoky *(Andrew Crawford)*

☆ *Via Fossa* [Canal St]: Surreal take on mock-medieval in striking warehouse conversion, winding staircases and wandering passages, galleries and balconies, even a chapel – fun to explore, with plenty of cosy corners, six bar counters, enjoyable food all day from toasted baguettes up, John Smiths, decent wines, daily papers, well reproduced piped music, DJs Fri/Sat; wall of french windows to big canalside terraces (children allowed here only), open all day *(the Didler, Andrew Crawford, David Carr, JP, PP, Andy and Ali, LYM)*

Wheelhouse [Russell Dr, Wollaton]: Nicely refurbished by Hardys & Hansons, their full beer range kept well, good value food *(Alan Bowker)*

ORSTON [SK7741]

Durham Ox [Church St]: Welcoming country local opp church, well kept Marstons Pedigree, John Smiths, Theakstons and a guest beer, wine fresh from sensible small bottles, good value beef, ham and other rolls (no hot food); comfortable split-level open-plan bar with interesting RAF/USAF memorabilia, collection of whisky bottles; tables outside (may be hitching rail for ferrets as well as for horses) *(Bernie Adams, the Didler, JP, PP)*

RADCLIFFE ON TRENT [SK6439]

Black Lion [A52]: Friendly bar, big comfortable lounge, good choice of food from beef cobs to full meals, three or four well kept changing ales; big garden and play area, Oct charity steam fair *(the Didler)*

Royal Oak [Main Rd]: Three cosy and friendly comfortably worn in rooms, well kept Greene King Old Speckled Hen, Timothy Taylors Landlord and a guest beer; no food *(Des and Jen Clarke)*

RETFORD [SK7080]

☆ *Market Hotel* [off West Carr Rd, Ordsall; follow Leisure Centre signs from A620, then just after industrial estate sign keep eyes skinned for pub sign on left]: In same family for over 40 years, with eight well chosen and kept changing ales (up to 40 in autumn beer festival), comfortable plush banquettes, generous good value straightforward food (not Sun evening) from sandwiches and rolls up, popular Sun carvery lunch, friendly helpful service; children welcome till early evening, very busy Fri/Sat night, jazz 3rd Sun in month; bedrooms, tables outside, open all day Sat *(Richard Lewis, LYM, JP, PP, Mike and Sue Loseby)*

Whitehouses Inn [A638 London Rd]: Three real ales, fair choice of cheap generous food inc children's meals; quiet piped music, TV and games, quiz night; garden with attractive flowers and play area, bedrooms *(CMW, JJW)*

SELSTON [SK4553]

Horse & Jockey [just off M1 junction 27]: Three carefully refurbished main rooms on three levels, cosy snug off lower bar area, beams, flagstones and coal fire in cast-iron range, well kept Bass, Greene King Abbot, Timothy Taylors Landlord and other ales on handpump or in jugs direct from the cellar,

good value bar lunches (not wknds) inc good baguettes and a hot dish, bar billiards in top room; open all day Sat *(the Didler, JP, PP, Derek and Sylvia Stephenson)*

SOUTH CLIFTON [SK8270]

Red Lion: Being gently refurbished by enthusiastic new young licensees, guest beers, reasonably priced food inc good steaks; juke box, pool; small garden *(David and Ruth Hollands)*

SOUTH LEVERTON [SK7881]

Plough [Town St]: Tiny pub doubling as morning post office, little changed under new owners; basic trestle tables and benches, real fire, Greene King Ruddles Best and a guest beer, traditional games, tables outside; open 2-11 (all day Sat, 12-4, 7-10.30 Sun) *(JP, PP, the Didler, Mike and Sue Loseby)*

SOUTHWELL [SK6953]

☆ *Bramley Apple* [Church St (A612)]: Friendly new landlord, good value enjoyable food from simple lunch choice to more elaborate evening dishes, well kept Springhead and other changing ales, attentive service, light and airy bar *(John Bramley, BB, the Didler, JP, PP, Richard Jennings, Tony and Wendy Hobden)*

Old Coaching House [Easthorpe]: Beams and old-world nooks around central bar, up to six changing well kept ales, roaring coal fires, bar billiards, shove-ha'penny and other traditional games; tables on terrace, may be cl wkdy lunchtimes, open all day wknds *(Blaise Vyner, the Didler, JP, PP)*

THURGARTON [SK6949]

☆ *Red Lion* [Southwell Rd (A612)]: Cheery 16th-c inn with good unusual freshly cooked food (all day Sat, Sun and bank hols) inc fresh fish in brightly decorated split-level beamed bars and restaurant, lots of nooks and crannies, comfortable banquettes and other seating, smart friendly service, well kept ales inc Black Sheep and Mansfield, flame-effect fire, big windows to attractive good-sized two-level back garden with well spaced picnic-sets (dogs on leads allowed here); unobtrusive fruit machine, quite a walk back up to car park; children welcome, comfortable bedrooms *(Richard Greenwood, Andrew Crawford, BB)*

UNDERWOOD [SK4751]

Red Lion [Church Lane; off B600, nr M1 junction 27]: Character 17th-c split-level beamed village pub, spacious open-plan bar with open fire, some cushioned settles, pictures and plates on dressers, good value family food inc OAP lunches, well kept Marstons Pedigree and an interesting local guest beer, good friendly service, penny arcade machine, no piped music; children welcome, picnic-sets and large adventure playground in big garden with terrace, attractive setting; open all day wknds *(Kevin Blake, Derek and Sylvia Stephenson, JP, PP, the Didler)*

UPTON [SK7354]

French Horn [A612]: Friendly licensees in

neatly comfortable open-plan bar with wall banquettes and glossy tables, wide choice of generous food (all day Sun) inc some interesting dishes as well as lunchtime sandwiches, baguettes and baked potatoes, well kept Charles Wells Bombardier; piped music; children welcome, picnic-sets in big sloping back paddock, open all day *(W M Paton, LYM, Darly Graton, Graeme Gulibert)*

WATNALL CHAWORTH [SK5046]

☆ *Queens Head* [3 miles from M1 junction 26: A610 towards Nottingham, left on B600, then keep right; Main Rd]: Cosy and tastefully extended three-room old pub with wide range of good value food, well kept ales inc Nottingham and Theakstons, efficient friendly service; intimate snug, dining area, beams and stripped pine, coal fires; fruit machine, piped music; picnic-sets in spacious and attractive back garden with big play area, open all day Fri/Sat *(the Didler, JP, PP)*

WELLOW [SK6766]

☆ *Olde Red Lion* [Eakring Rd, just off A616 E of Ollerton]: Friendly low-beamed and panelled 16th-c pub by green with towering maypole, good value fresh food from sandwiches to bargain Sun roasts, three well kept changing beers, quick service, no smoking restaurant and dining area, no piped music; children welcome, picnic-sets outside *(DC, LYM, CMW, JJW)*

WEST BRIDGFORD [SK5838]

Southbank [Trent Bridge]: Bright and airy, with polished wood floors, sofas, wide choice of beers, lagers and soft drinks, coffee, good food choice from baguettes to mixed grills; lots of sports TV screens, handy for cricket ground and Notts Forest FC *(the Didler, Andrew Crawford)*

☆ *Stratford Haven* [Stratford Rd, Trent Bridge]: Busy and chatty Tynemill pub, bare-boards front bar, well kept changing ales such as Batemans XB, Caledonian Deuchars IPA, Castle Rock Bitter and Stratford Gold, Everards Tiger, Hook Norton Old Hooky and Marstons Pedigree, farm ciders, good choice of whiskies and wines, relaxed local atmosphere in airy and skylit carpeted yellow-walled back part, good value home cooking, daily papers, tables outside; can get crowded and smoky; handy for cricket ground and Nottingham Forest FC; open all day *(Andy and Ali, the Didler, JP, PP, Andrew Crawford, Des and Jen Clarke, Derek and Sylvia Stephenson, BB)*

Test Match [Gordon Sq, West Bridgford]:

Handsome art deco décor with revolving door, high ceiling and sweeping staircase (to the lounge and lavatories), unpretentious furnishings, big cricketing prints, some signed bats, full range of Hardys & Hansons beers kept particularly well *(Andrew Crawford)*

WEST LEAKE [SK5226]

☆ *Star* [Melton Lane, off A6006]: Comfortable oak-panelled dining lounge with good central log fire, pewter mugs, china, pictures and attractive table lamps, traditional beamed and quarry-tiled country bar on left with wall settles, plenty of character and traditional games, good value home-made food from substantial baps to cheap steaks, well kept Bass and two or three changing guest beers, good choice of malt whiskies, good coffee, welcoming licensees and friendly helpful service, ginger cat called Cracker, no piped music or machines; children in eating area, picnic-sets on front terrace (quiet spot) and in garden with play area *(the Didler, Michael and Jenny Back, LYM, JP, PP)*

WEST MARKHAM [SK7273]

Mussel & Crab [Sibthorpe Hill; B1164 nr A1/A57/A638 roundabout N of Tuxford]: Pub/restaurant specialising in fish and seafood fresh daily from Brixham, other enjoyable dishes on vast array of blackboards, two roomy dining areas (beams and stripped stone, or more flamboyant pastel murals), welcoming attentive staff, real ale, decent wines, good coffee; good disabled access, picnic-sets on terrace, play area, views over wheatfields *(Rita and Keith Pollard)*

WIDMERPOOL [SK6429]

Pullman [1st left off A606 coming towards Nottingham from A46 junction; Kinoulton Lane]: Thriving family dining pub in well converted and extended station building, friendly efficient service, generous above-average food inc good vegetarian dishes, fish nights and Sun carvery, real ale *(Darly Graton, Graeme Gulibert, John and Sylvia Harrop)*

WORKSOP [SK5879]

Mallard [Station, Carlton Rd]: Friendly local feel in idiosyncratic station building handy for Mr Straw's House (NT); quickly changing beers from small breweries and wide range of foreign bottled beers, coal fire, traditional games; wheelchair access, seats outside, parking in station pay-and-display, open all day (Sun afternoon closure) *(the Didler, JP, PP, R T and J C Moggridge)*

If a service charge is mentioned prominently on a menu or accommodation terms, you must pay it if service was satisfactory. If service is really bad you are legally entitled to refuse to pay some or all of the service charge as compensation for not getting the service you might reasonably have expected.

Oxfordshire

Pubs that have been showing particularly well here over the last few months include the 17th-c Plough at Alvescot (a new main entry, friendly, good value and nicely old-fashioned), the restauranty Lamb at Buckland (very enjoyable if not cheap meals, and obliging service), the Lamb in Burford (a classic Cotswold inn, as popular as ever under its new owners, great all round), the cheerful and prettily set Red Lion at Chalgrove (owned by the parish church), the enjoyably pubby Chequers in Chipping Norton (a fine all-rounder), the Fox & Hounds at Christmas Common (gaining a Food Award this year, brought nicely up to date without losing its traditional appeal), the impressive medieval White Hart at Fyfield (enjoyable food, good beer, nice garden), the Gate Hangs High near Hook Norton (good food in this tucked-away country pub), the Sun actually in Hook Norton (a favourite proper pub), the Plough in its attractive spot at Kelmscott (back in these pages after quite break, with its current owners striking a nice balance between its pubby bars and a flourishing food side), the Kings Arms and the Turf Tavern in Oxford (both lively places, each with a different style of appeal), the pretty thatched Stags Head at Swalcliffe (good home cooking, and a nice choice of wines), and the Trout by the river at Tadpole Bridge (charming friendly service, and gaining both a Food Award and a Place to Stay Award this year). For a special meal out here, the Lamb in Burford is an excellent choice, with bags of character and atmosphere as well as really good cooking; its new owners win it the title of Oxfordshire Dining Pub of the Year. The Lucky Dip section at the end of the chapter now contains many notable pubs and inns; we'd particularly pick out the Plough in Bodicote, Lord Nelson at Brightwell Baldwin, foody Bull in Charlbury, Crown at Church Enstone, Wheatsheaf at East Hendred, Five Alls at Filkins, Trout at Godstow, Bird in Hand at Hailey, King William IV at Hailey (same name, two different villages), Lamb at Little Milton, Jersey Arms at Middleton Stoney, Eagle & Child and Rose & Crown in Oxford, Lamb at Shipton-under-Wychwood, restauranty Crooked Billet at Stoke Row and Fish in Sutton Courtenay, Swan at Swinbrook and Hare at West Hendred. Drinks prices here are rather above the national norm. Rather more than half the pubs we looked at here offered a beer from the local Hook Norton brewery, and in almost all of these it was the cheapest beer on offer – a proud record for a relatively small brewery.

ALVESCOT SP2704 Map 4
Plough

B4020 Carterton—Clanfield, SW of Witney

Pleasantly relaxed and easy-going, this partly 17th-c village pub has a nicely old-fashioned feel. The carpeted bar has plenty of cottagey pictures, china ornaments and house plants, a big antique case of stuffed birds of prey, an old harmonium, sundry bric-a-brac, a good log fire, and comfortable seating including cushioned settles, a nice armchair, and of course the bar stools bagged by cheerful regulars in the early evening. A two-part dining area, bare boards at the back, is snug and intimate at night, with its soft wall lights, table candles, and puce walls and ceiling. Good value food in big helpings includes lunchtime filled rolls (from £3.20), baked potatoes (from £3.50), and ploughman's (from £4.80), as well as soup (£3.25), smoked trout fillets (£6.50), cajun butterfly chicken breast, brie, almond and courgette crumble or steak and kidney suet pudding (£6.95), plaice stuffed with prawns and mushrooms or beef and orange casserole (£7.25), and steaks (from £10.25); they also do children's meals (£3.50), and two meals for £10 (Monday-Friday lunchtimes only). The Wadworths IPA and 6X on handpump are kept well, and they have decent wines and good coffee; service is welcoming and helpful. A proper public bar has pool and a fruit machine (and rather surprisingly a big needlework of tropical birds on its patterned green wallpaper); darts, TV, bar billiards, alley skittles and piped music. There are a couple of picnic-sets out in front below colourful hanging baskets by the quiet village road, with more behind under trees, by a bird table and play area; look out for the friendly black cat, Dino. *(Recommended by Peter and Audrey Dowsett, Marjorie and David Lamb, R M Gibson, KN-R, Mrs Challiner)*

Wadworths ~ Tenant Kevin Robert Keeling ~ Real ale ~ Bar food ~ (01993) 842281 ~ Children in eating area of bar, under 10s till 8pm ~ Dogs allowed in bar ~ Open 11.30(11 Sat)-3, 6-11; 12-3, 7-10.30 Sun

BANBURY SP4540 Map 4

Reindeer £

47 Parsons Street, off Market Place

Well worth a visit if you're in town, this fine old pub (now under new licensees) is full of character, and the food here is good value too. The long front room has heavy 16th-c beams, very broad polished oak floorboards scattered with rugs, a magnificent carved overmantel for one of the roaring log fires, and traditional solid furnishings; there's a second log fire. The attractively proportioned Globe Room, with its original wonderfully carved 17th-c panelling, is where Cromwell held court before the Battle of Edgehill. The little back courtyard has picnic-sets under parasols, aunt sally, and pretty flowering baskets. Served only at lunchtime, straightforward bar food in generous portions might include soup (£2.50), sandwiches (from £2.50), omelettes or good filled baked potatoes (from £3.90), all day breakfast (£3.95), shepherd's pie, bubble and squeak or mushroom florentine (£4.50), home-made fishcakes (£5.20), breaded plaice (£6), and rump steak (£6.25), with puddings (£2.50). Well kept Hook Norton Best, First Light, Old, and Mild, and a couple of guests such as Palmer Copper Ale and Wadworths JCB on handpump, country wines, winter mulled wine, a decent selection of whiskies, and even snuffs and clay pipes for the more adventurous; shove-ha'penny, cribbage, dominoes and piped music. A smaller back room up steps is no smoking at lunchtime. No under-21s (but see below). *(Recommended by Ian and Nita Cooper, Leigh and Gillian Mellor, the Didler, Derek and Sylvia Stephenson, George Atkinson, Jennie Hall, Bruce Bird, Arnold Benett, Ted George)*

Hook Norton ~ Tenants Mr and Mrs Puddifoot ~ Real ale ~ Bar food (11-2.30, not Sun) ~ (01295) 264031 ~ Children in family room ~ Open 11-11; 12-3, 7-10.30 Sun

BLEWBURY SU5385 Map 2

Blewbury Inn ♀

London Road (A417)

Beautifully cooked by the French landlord, the imaginative food is the reason to come to this small downland dining pub. There are two-course (£19.50) and three-course (£24.50) meal options, otherwise a sensibly short (though not cheap) choice of food could include smoked salmon and leek tartlet (£5.90), confit of duck with mushroom and white bean vinaigrette (£6.90), roast cod pavé (£13.90), and beef fillet marinated in Guinness with mustard and chorizo mash and thyme jus (£14.90), with puddings such as mango and passion fruit crème brûlée with guava sorbet (£5). The bar on the left has an attractive wood-effect floor, a tremendous mix of simple furnishings from a blue director's chair to a big box settle, and French art and period advertising posters on the dusky red walls, with a good log fire. They've good house wines, and well kept Fullers London Pride and Hook Norton Best on handpump; piped music. The carpeted dining room has wheelchair chairs around pub tables, and just one or two carefully chosen plates and pictures on its stencilled cream walls above a green dado. As we went to press, proposals for redevelopment were being discussed so there may well be changes during the currency of this edition. *(Recommended by Doreen and Haydn Maddock, Robert Hill, Mike and Heather Watson, Mrs M P Owen, Jane Buekett)*

Free house ~ Licensees Franck and Kally Peigne ~ Real ale ~ Bar food ~ Restaurant ~ (01235) 850496 ~ Children welcome ~ Dogs allowed in bar ~ Open 12-3, 6-11; 12-3 Sun; closed Mon, Sun evening, 25 Dec

BROADWELL SP2504 Map 4
Five Bells
Village signposted off A361 N of Lechlade, and off B4020 S of Carterton

In the spacious flower-filled garden of this attractive former coaching inn, they play aunt sally, and grow some of the vegetables used in the kitchen. Inside, the spotlessly kept and well furnished series of rooms has two big, warming log fires, a pleasant mix of flagstones and carpeting, low beams, antique pistols, and plates and rural pictures on the walls. With views of the garden, the sizeable dining room and the small conservatory are both no smoking; the public bar has darts, and dominoes. They serve well kept Bass along with a guest beer such as Archers Village on handpump, and decent house wine; the licensees are friendly and helpful. From a straightforward menu, reasonably priced bar food includes sandwiches (from £1.75), soup (£3.25), stilton mushrooms (£4.50), ham, egg and chips (£5.25), fish and chips (£5.95), salmon and prawn gratin or chicken breast in wine and mushrooms (£6.50), bird pie (£6.95), almond roast or gammon and pineapple (£6.95), and steaks (from £9.95) with puddings such as ginger pudding (from £3.25); best to book for Sunday lunch. Wheelchair access. *(Recommended by Des and Jen Clarke, W M Paton, Rev Michael Vockins, Marjorie and David Lamb, KN-R, Alun Howells, Mr and Mrs D Lines, Dick and Madeleine Brown)*

Free house ~ Licensees Trevor and Ann Cooper ~ Real ale ~ Bar food (12-1.45, 7-9; not Sun evening, not Mon) ~ Restaurant ~ (01367) 860076 ~ Well behaved children if eating in dining rooms only; not Sat evening ~ Dogs allowed in bar ~ Open 11.30-2.30, 7-11; 12-3, 7-10.30 Sun; closed Mon (except Easter Mon and Aug bank hol lunchtimes) ~ Bedrooms: /£55S

BUCKLAND SU3497 Map 4
Lamb 🍽 ♀ 🛏
Village signposted off A420 NE of Faringdon

Of restaurant quality (with prices to match), the delicious food is what draws people to this smart but friendly 18th-c stone pub – it's not really the kind of place you drop into for a quick drink. Pleasant, obliging staff serve lunchtime dishes such as home-made soup (from £3.95), sandwiches (from £3.25), welsh rarebit or mushroom pot (£4.95), ploughman's (£6.75), grilled cornish mackerel with mustard sauce (£6.95), and black pudding or tagliatelle carbonara (£8.95), with evening choices such as monkfish and prawn ragoût (£15.95), dover sole (£18.50), best end of english lamb (£18.25), and roast saddle of venison (£19.95), with puddings such as irresistible sticky date and toffee pudding or bakewell tart (£3.50); they do a two-course Sunday lunch (£19.95). The restaurant is no smoking. Opening off a hallway, and divided in two by dark painted timbers, the civilised neatly kept little bar has plush blue furnishings, potted plants around the windows, and a few carefully chosen sheep and lamb pictures and models around the cream-painted walls. On a piano are newspapers to read, and examples of their own chutneys and jams; it's popular with older visitors at lunchtime. As well as a dozen or so wines by the glass, and carefully mixed Pimms or Bucks Fizz, they've Hook

Norton Best on handpump with an occasional guest; piped music. There are a couple of white plastic tables on a terrace, and a good few wooden picnic-sets in the very pleasant tree-shaded garden; good walks nearby. *(Recommended by John Hale, R M Gibson, the Didler, Richard and Margaret Peers, Peter B Brown, J F M and M West, Mr and Mrs G S Ayrton, Betsy and Peter Little, Ian Phillips)*

Free house ~ Licensees Paul and Peta Barnard ~ Real ale ~ Bar food ~ Restaurant ~ (01367) 870484 ~ Children welcome ~ Open 11-11; 11-3 Sun; closed Sun evening, Mon ~ Bedrooms: /£95B

BURFORD SP2512 Map 4

Lamb ★ ⊕ ♀ ◀ ⇌

Sheep Street; village signposted off A40 W of Oxford

Oxfordshire Dining Pub of the Year

Although it's been taken over by new owners, this civilised 500-year-old stone inn remains a great favourite with readers. The roomy beamed main lounge is charmingly traditional, with distinguished old seats including a chintzy high winged settle, ancient cushioned wooden armchairs, and seats built into its stone-mullioned windows, bunches of flowers on polished oak and elm tables, oriental rugs on the wide flagstones and polished oak floorboards, and a winter log fire under its fine mantelpiece. Also, a writing desk and grandfather clock, and eye-catching pictures, shelves of plates and other antique decorations. The public bar has high-backed settles and old chairs on flagstones in front of its fire. It's best to get there early if you want a table in the bar, where enjoyable daily changing food could include soup (£5), sandwiches and ciabattas (from £6), smoked salmon platter with lime salsa (£6.50), liver, bacon and mash (£10.50), chicken strips with chilli noodles and hoi sin sauce (£10.75), wild mushroom risotto and parmesan wafers (£10.95), fried salmon with buttered asparagus (£13.50), and chargrilled rib-eye steak with fries and béarnaise sauce (£14.95); home-made ice creams (£5), and puddings such as lavender panna cotta with honey-roasted figs or maple cranberry parfait with roast pecan sauce (£5.25). They do a set menu on Sundays (£22.50 for three courses) but no bar meals. The recently refurbished peaceful formal restaurant is no smoking. Well kept Hook Norton Best, Wadworths 6X and a guest such as Badger IPA are dispensed from an antique handpump beer engine in a glassed-in cubicle (you'll be given the choice between straight glass or handle when you order); good wines. A pretty terrace with teak furniture leads down to small neatly-kept lawns surrounded by flowers, flowering shrubs and small trees, and the garden itself is a real suntrap enclosed as it is by the warm stone of the surrounding buildings. *(Recommended by David Rule, Maysie Thompson, Lynn Sharpless, C A Hall, Paul Humphreys, R Huggins, D Irving, E McCall, T McLean, Ian Phillips, Simon Collett-Jones, Mike and Alison Leyland, Karen and Graham Oddey, I D Barnett, the Didler, A P Seymour, Anthony Longden, Tina and David Woods-Taylor, Patrick Hancock, Paul Hopton, Nigel Williamson, Gordon Stevenson, Robin and Joyce Peachey, Michael Dandy, Michael and Ann Cole, Mr and Mrs J McRobert, Don Bryan, Ted George, Colin and Stephanie McFie, Jay Bohmrich, Felicity Sity Stephens, Sarah Markham Flynn, Alison Hayes, Pete Hanlon)*

Free house ~ Licensee Ashley James ~ Real ale ~ Bar food (12-2.30, 7-9.30; not Sun) ~ Restaurant ~ (01993) 823155 ~ Children welcome ~ Dogs allowed in bar and bedrooms ~ Open 11-3, 5.30-11; 12-3, 7-10.30 Sun ~ Bedrooms: £80B/£125B

CAULCOTT SP5024 Map 4

Horse & Groom ◀

Lower Heyford Road (B4030)

They serve a good selection of O'Hagan speciality sausages at this creeper-covered and partly thatched cottage: you can choose from flavours such as spanish chorizo, pork and red wine, somerset scrumpy, creole, and drunken duck (all £7.50). An L-shaped red-carpeted room angles around the servery, with plush-cushioned settles, chairs and stools around a few dark tables at the low-ceilinged bar end, a polo cap collection, framed racehorse cigarette cards, and a blazing fire in the big inglenook with masses of pump clips under its long bressumer beam; shove-ha'penny and cribbage. The far end, up a shallow step, is set for dining (and is no smoking), with lots of decorative jugs hanging on black joists, and some decorative plates. There are some lovely watercolours and original drawings dotted around including a charming one of Harvey the west highland terrier who greets everyone on arrival; look out too for the nice old poster of the auction of the pub in 1899. There's a good village pub atmosphere (it's very popular with locals), and the hard-working licensees are cheerful. Three quickly changing interesting guest beers from brewers such as Butts, Black Sheep, and Spinning Dog are well kept alongside Hook Norton Best on handpump; decent house wines. Bar food includes sandwiches and toasties (from £3.40), home-made soup (£3.75), filled baked potatoes (from £3.90), ham, egg and chips (£6.25), with daily specials such as a pint of jumbo prawns (£7.95), chicken breast (£9.25), steaks (from £10.95), and beef wellington (£13.95), with puddings (£3.95). There is a small side sun lounge, with picnic-sets under cocktail parasols on a neat side lawn. *(Recommended by John Branston, Ian Phillips, W W Burke, Paul and Ann Meyer, D C T and E A Frewer, Peter Neate, Stuart Turner, Dave Braisted, Susan and John Douglas, Simon Collett-Jones)*

Free house ~ Licensees Chris and Celestine Roche ~ Real ale ~ Bar food ~ Restaurant ~ (01869) 343257 ~ Children in restaurant ~ Open 11-3, 6-11; 12-3, 7-10.30 Sun; closed evenings 25 Dec and 1 Jan

CHALGROVE SU6396 Map 4
Red Lion

High Street (B480 Watlington—Stadhampton)

Ever since it first appeared in written records in 1637, this appealing pub has been owned by the local church (worth a look for the interesting medieval wall paintings). It's prettily set opposite the village cross, and behind the little stream that runs right along the partly thatched main street; behind the pub there's a good big garden, which has a pergola, and an aunt sally. Inside, the décor has a smartly contemporary twist – all the walls are painted a crisp white which contrasts strikingly with the simple dark furnishings, the windows have neatly chequered green curtains and fresh flowers, and there's an old woodburner and a log fire. Across from the fireplace is a painting of the landlady's aunt, and there are a few carefully collected prints and period cartoons. The back dining room (sometimes used for functions) is no smoking; piped music, cribbage, shove-ha'penny and darts in the tiled public bar. The menus change regularly (there's quite an emphasis on the food), but could include well prepared sandwiches and baguettes (from £4.50), soup (£3.75), chargrilled haggis with whisky and shallot cream sauce (£4.75), beer battered haddock with chips and mushy peas or fresh linguini with wild mushroom and parmesan (£9.95), lamb shank braised in red wine with broccoli and dauphinoise potatoes (£12.95), sirloin steak (£13.75), and puddings such as steamed treacle pudding or rhubarb crumble (from £3.75); their Sunday lunch is popular, and they serve small helpings for children at reduced prices. Well kept Adnams, and Fullers London Pride with a guest such as Wadworths 6X on handpump, and a decent wine list; the licensees are cheerful and friendly, and the atmosphere is warmly welcoming. *(Recommended by Dick and Madeleine Brown, Paul Hopton, Susan and John Douglas, Bob Turnham, R J Chenery, Ian Phillips, Colin and Sandra Tann)*

Free house ~ Licensees Jonathan and Maggi Hewitt ~ Real ale ~ Bar food (not Sun evening; restricted menu Mon and Tues) ~ Restaurant ~ (01865) 890625 ~ Well behaved children welcome ~ Dogs allowed in bar ~ Open 12-3, 6-11; 12-3, 7-10.30 Sun; closed a few days between 25 Dec and 1 Jan

Bedroom prices normally include full english breakfast, VAT and any inclusive service charge that we know of. Prices before the '*/*' are for single rooms, after for two people in double or twin (B includes a private bath, S a private shower).

CHECKENDON SU6684 Map 2
Black Horse

Village signposted off A4074 Reading—Wallingford; coming from that direction, go straight through village towards Stoke Row, then turn left (the second turn left after the village church); OS Sheet 175 map reference 666841

Full of appeal for those who like their pubs basic and unspoiled, this traditional country local has been run by the same family for many decades. There's a refreshingly relaxed atmosphere in the back still room, where West Berkshire Good Old Boy and Old Father Thames are tapped from the cask. The room with the bar counter has some tent pegs ranged above the fireplace, a reminder that they used to be made here; a homely side room has some splendidly unfashionable 1950s-look armchairs, and there's another room beyond that. They keep pickled eggs and usually do fresh filled rolls (from £1.20). It's tucked away in fine walking country (and popular with walkers and cyclists), and there are seats out on a verandah and in the garden. *(Recommended by Ian Phillips, Pete Baker, the Didler)*

Free house ~ Licensees Margaret and Martin Morgan ~ Real ale ~ No credit cards ~ (01491) 680418 ~ Children allowed but must be well behaved ~ Open 12-2(2.30 Sat/Sun), 7-11(10.30 Sun); closed 25 Dec evening

CHIPPING NORTON SP3127 Map 4
Chequers ◖

Goddards Lane

Readers are as delighted as ever with the 'good old fashioned atmosphere and welcome' at this unpretentious pub. Perhaps best in winter when you can really appreciate the blazing log fires; the three softly lit beamed rooms have no frills, but are clean and comfortable, with low ochre ceilings, plenty of character, and a lively evening atmosphere. Friendly efficient staff serve very well kept Fullers Chiswick, London Pride, ESB and seasonal brews on handpump – unusual to have the full Fullers range around here – and they have good house wines (with 14 by the glass), espresso and cappuccino coffee; cribbage, dominoes, and board games. Carefully prepared with fresh local ingredients, good bar food at lunchtime includes home-made soup (£3.20), sandwiches (from £2.50), goats cheese, cherry tomato and basil filo tart (£4.25), ploughman's (£4.95), thai curry or spinach and mushroom lasagne (£7.45), and chicken breast and cashew nut stir fry (£7.95), with evening dishes such as crab and Pernod fishcakes (£4.50), braised lamb shank on colcannon mash with roast fennel and rosemary redcurrant gravy (£10.50), bass fillets with herb couscous, red onion marmalade and basil pesto (£11.45); daily specials too. The no smoking restaurant at the back (quiet piped music) was converted from an old barn adjacent to the courtyard. It's very handy for the town's Victorian theatre. *(Recommended by Chris Glasson, M Benjamin, R Huggins, D Irving, E McCall, T McLean, Steve Dark, Richard Greaves, Mike and Jennifer Marsh, Michael Jones, Robert Gomme, Stephen, Julie and Hayley Brown, Val and Alan Green, Mrs N W Neill, Paul and Ann Meyer, Mary and Dan Robinson, Derek Harvey-Piper, Andy and Jill Kassube, the Didler, Paul Hopton, Charles and Pauline Stride, Graham Gage, Simon Collett-Jones)*

Fullers ~ Tenants Josh and Kay Reid ~ Real ale ~ Bar food (12-2.30, 6-9.30; 12-5 Sun; not 25-26 Dec, 1 Jan) ~ Restaurant ~ (01608) 644717 ~ Children over 12, before 7.30 ~ Open 11-11; 12-10.30 Sun; closed 25 Dec

CHRISTMAS COMMON SU7193 Map 4
Fox & Hounds ♔

Village signposted from B480 at junction with B481; or follow Fox & Hounds Hill Road from B4009 in Watlington

In lovely Chilterns countryside (and handily open all day in summer), this friendly pub is a popular lunch stop for walkers and cyclists, and this year gains a food award. The cosy beamed bar on the left is plainly furnished with just a few tables and wooden wall benches or bow-window seats, red and black flooring tiles, a big inglenook – which has a fire burning even in summer – and a framed Ordnance Survey walker's map on one cream wall. The snug room to the left of that is popular with locals and pretty much for drinking only, though you may also see Boris the cat. The barn extension houses a restaurant, open-plan kitchen, a couple of bars and inside lavatories (curiously named Richard and Judy). Good (but not cheap) bar food at lunchtime includes generous doorstep sandwiches (from £5), soup (£5.50), ploughman's (from £6.50), and half a roast ham hock caramelised with brown sugar and thyme (£7), as well as interesting dishes such as wild mushroom risotto (£6; main course £11), coconut curried fish (£13.50), roasted lamb chump with roasted mediterranean vegetables (£14), and scottish rib-eye steak with rich red wine sauce (£14.50), with puddings such as vanilla cheesecake or sticky toffee pudding with caramel sauce (£5.50); helpful service from the pleasant uniformed staff. The restaurant is no smoking. Well kept Brakspears Bitter, Special, and a seasonal ale are tapped from the cask in a back still room, good coffee too; dominoes, cribbage, and card games. Outside are rustic benches and tables; you can buy free range eggs, honey, chutney and marmalade here. *(Recommended by John Hale, Susan and John Douglas, Mayur Shah, Andrew French, Phoebe and Duncan Thomas, the Didler, Tracey and Stephen Groves, Kevin Thorpe, Derek Harvey-Piper, Mr and Mrs M Renton)*

Brakspears ~ Tenant Judith Bishop ~ Bar food (12-2.30(3 Sun), 7-9; not Mon evening, or 25 Dec) ~ Restaurant ~ (01491) 612599 ~ Children in eating area of bar ~ Dogs allowed in bar ~ Open 11-11(11.30-3, 6-11 in winter); 11.30-11 Sat; 12-10.30 Sun; closed 25 Dec exc 12-2

CLIFTON SP4831 Map 4
Duke of Cumberlands Head ♀ 🛏

B4031 Deddington—Aynho

There are plenty of wines to choose from at this peaceful pub, just a short stroll from the canal, and they have more than 30 malt whiskies too. Most of the tables are in the spacious if rather reserved lounge which has a big log fireplace, and there are more in the cosy yellow-painted no smoking restaurant. The emphasis is on the interesting bar food, which might include soup (£3.50), smoked mussels with cream and white wine sauce or avocado and prawn salad (£5), goan prawn curry, wild mushroom stroganoff, lamb in garlic cream and mint sauce or steak and kidney pie (all £7; main £10), smoked salmon steak (£10), and 10oz sirloin steak (£14), with puddings such as honey and ginger cheesecake and summer pudding (£3.50); they do a two-course Sunday lunch (£15), and decent breakfasts. Friendly staff serve well kept Black Sheep and Hook Norton Best, alongside a guest such as Adnams Southwold on handpump. *(Recommended by Marcelle Bowman, Miles and Deborah Protter, Sir Nigel Foulkes, Hugh Spottiswoode, Mr and Mrs J A Phipps, Gerald Wilkinson, Robert Coates, Stuart Turner, Gerry and Rosemary Dobson)*

Free house ~ Licensee Nick Huntington ~ Real ale ~ Bar food ~ Restaurant ~ (01869) 338534 ~ Children in eating area of bar and family room ~ Dogs allowed in bar and bedrooms ~ Open 12-2.30(3 Sat), 6.30-10.30(11 Sat); 12-3 Sun; closed Sun evening ~ Bedrooms: £40S(£50B)/£65B

FIFIELD SP2318 Map 4
Merrymouth

A424 Burford—Stow

The simple but comfortably furnished L-shaped bar of this 13th-c stone inn has nice bay-window seats, flagstones, horsebrasses and antique bottles hanging from low beams, some walls stripped back to the old masonry, and an open fire in winter. Except for five tables in the bar, the pub is no smoking; backgammon and piped classical music. The Domesday Book mentions an inn on this site and its name comes from the Murimuth family, who once owned the village in which it is set. Lots of people come here to eat, and enjoyable bar food might include home-made soup (£3.25), lunchtime baguettes (from £4.95), smoked chicken and sweet onion wrap (£5.25), chicken pieces with bacon, mushrooms, cheese and cream

(£8.95), steaks (from £9.95), lamb noisettes with rosemary and redcurrant (£10.75), and pork tenderloin with black pudding and mustard sauce (£10.95), with specials such as twice baked cheese soufflé (£4.95), guinea fowl with orange sauce (£8.95), and hake with cheese and tomato topping (£9.75); readers recommend the home-made puddings which might include chocolate and almond torte and banana cake with toffee sauce (£3.95). Adnams Broadside and Hook Norton Best are well kept on handpump, and they've decent wines; it's family-run, and service is friendly and prompt. There are tables on a terrace and in the back garden (there may be a little noise from fast traffic on the road). The quaint bedrooms are well cared for. *(Recommended by KN-R, Mr and Mrs J Brown, Martin Jennings, Susan and John Douglas, Martin Jones, Bernard Stradling, George Atkinson, Gill and Keith Croxton, A Sadler, Robert Gomme, Peter and Audrey Dowsett, Paul and Penny Rampton)*

Free house ~ Licensees Andrew and Timothy Flaherty ~ Real ale ~ Bar food (not Sun evening) ~ Restaurant ~ (01993) 831652 ~ Children welcome ~ Dogs allowed in bar and bedrooms ~ Open 11-3, 6-10.30; 12-3, 7-10 Sun; closed Sun evening in winter ~ Bedrooms: £45S/£60S(£60B)

FYFIELD SU4298 Map 4
White Hart

In village, off A420 8 miles SW of Oxford

Once you've finished marvelling at the inside of this impressive pub (originally built for Sir John Golafre in about 1450 to house priests who would pray for his soul), it's well worth wandering out through the heavy wooden door to the rambling, sheltered back lawn, which has a children's playground. Inside, the bustling main room is a grand hall with huge stone-flanked window embrasures and an attractive carpeted upper gallery. A nice contrast is the cosy low-ceilinged side bar which has an inglenook fireplace with a huge black urn hanging over the grate, and a framed history of the pub on the wall. The restaurant and gallery are no smoking. There's quite an emphasis on the good food which, besides lunchtime sandwiches (from £4.95), and ploughman's (6.50), includes dishes such as grilled vegetables with parma ham and feta cheese (£5.50), steak, mushroom and ale pie (£8.95), seared salmon escalope in orange butter sauce (£11), fried sirloin steak with green peppercorn sauce and shallot confit (£12.95), and braised lamb shank with leek and potato gratin and rosemary jus (£13.95), and specials such as cottage pie (£5.50), sausages and mash (£8.50), and blackened swordfish steak with coconut rice, orange and rum sauce and fried plantain (£10.50), while puddings could include lemon meringue pie (£3.95); service may be slow at busy times, but the staff are very helpful and engaging. Well kept Hook Norton Best, Fullers London Pride, Theakstons Old Peculier, and Wadworths 6X on handpump along with a monthly guest from a brewer such as West Berkshire; darts, fruit machine and piped music. *(Recommended by Simon Collett-Jones, Tina and David Woods-Taylor, JCW, Ian Phillips, Stephen, Julie and Hayley Brown, Giles Francis, MP, Alison Hayes, Pete Hanlon, Mark and Ruth Brock)*

Free house ~ Licensee Ian Mintrim ~ Real ale ~ Bar food (till 10pm) ~ Restaurant ~ (01865) 390585 ~ Children welcome ~ Dogs allowed in bar ~ Live band on Sun every 5/6 weeks ~ Open 12-3, 6-11; 11.30-11 Sat; 12-4, 7-10.30 Sun; closed 25 Dec

GREAT TEW SP3929 Map 4
Falkland Arms 🚩

Off B4022 about 5 miles E of Chipping Norton; The Green

Along with well kept Wadworths IPA, 6X and a seasonal ale such as Summersault, they serve up to four guests on handpump at this lovely inn, and they hold an annual summer beer festival. It's set in a charming village of untouched golden-stone thatched cottages, and there are tables outside in front of the pub, with picnic-sets under umbrellas in the garden behind (where there's a dovecote). Inside, the partly panelled bar has high-backed settles and a diversity of stools around plain stripped tables on flagstones and bare boards, one, two and three-handled mugs hanging from the beam-and-board ceiling, dim converted oil lamps, shutters for the stone-mullioned latticed windows, and a fine inglenook fireplace with a blazing fire in winter. The bar counter is decorated with tobacco jars and different varieties of snuff which you can buy, and you'll also find 60 malt whiskies, quite a few country wines, and farm cider; darts, cribbage, and dominoes. Lunchtime bar food includes soup (£3.50), filled baguettes (from £3.95), ploughman's (£5.95), steak and kidney pie, bangers and mash or a vegetarian dish (from £6.50), with more sophisticated evening restaurant meals (you must book); home-made puddings might include sticky toffee pudding (£4.25). The dining room is no smoking. You have to go out into the lane and then back in again to use the lavatories. Small good value bedrooms (no under-14s). *(Recommended by Martin Jennings, Barry Collett, the Didler, C A Hall, Robert Coates, Chris Glasson, Jenny and Chris Wilson, Paul Boot, John and Gloria Isaacs, Kevin Blake, Giles Francis, Guy Vowles)*

Wadworths ~ Managers Paul Barlow-Heal and S J Courage ~ Real ale ~ Bar food (lunchtime) ~ Restaurant ~ (01608) 683653 ~ Children in restaurant lunchtimes only ~ Dogs allowed in bar ~ Live folk Sun night ~ Open 11.30-2.30, 6-11; 11.30-11 Sat; 12-10.30 Sun; 11.30-3, 6-11 Sat in winter; 12-3, 7-10.30 Sun in winter ~ Bedrooms: £40S/£65S(£80B)

HENLEY SU7882 Map 4
Anchor 🍺

Friday Street; coming in over bridge, first left towards A4155 then next right

Informally run by a friendly and obliging landlady, this homely and old-fashioned local (a pleasing contrast to the rest of this rich little town) is handily open all day. In the two main rooms, you'll find a well worn in mix of elderly traditional pub furnishings with throw rugs, scatter cushions, chintz curtains, some venerable wall boarding and dim lighting adding to the cottagey feel. The beams in the dark ochre ceiling are thickly hung with chamber-pots, steins, whisky-water jugs, copperware and so forth, and there are interesting pictures: mainly local river photographs in the left room, a mix of antique sporting, ship and comical prints on the right, which has a piano and TV; shove-ha'penny, backgammon, cribbage, dominoes, and winter darts. A simply furnished back dining room has lots of rowing photographs, and a cage with a chatty cockatiel; behind is a charming informal terrace surrounded by lush vegetation and hanging vines. Besides an impressive choice of sandwiches (from £3), generously served bar food includes baked potatoes (from £4.50), and baguettes, ciabattas or ploughman's (£5), and steak and kidney pudding, spinach and red pepper lasagne, curries and chicken and seafood paella (all £7). Well kept Brakspears Bitter and Special with a seasonal ale on handpump, and a good range of malt whiskies and new world wines by the glass. The friendly chocolate labrador is called Ruger. More reports please. *(Recommended by Roy and Lindsey Fentiman, the Didler, Ian Phillips)*

Brakspears ~ Tenant G A Ion-Savage ~ Bar food (not 25 Dec) ~ (01491) 574753 ~ Well behaved children in restaurant until 8.30 ~ Open 11-11; 12-10.30 Sun; closed 25 Dec

HIGHMOOR SU6984 Map 2
Rising Sun

Witheridge Hill, signposted off B481; OS Sheet 175 map reference 697841

This pretty black and white pub is in a nice quiet spot, by a rough sloping green, and in fine weather the fairy-lit terrace is a pleasant place to sit (there are also tables on the grass among the trees). Most people come here to eat, and you may find it difficult to get a table for just a drink (it's a good idea to book at busy times). At lunchtime the menu could include ciabattas (£5.50), salmon salad (£5.75), and wild boar and apple sausages with mash and onion rings (£8.25), with evening dishes such as home-made seafood paella (£9.25), and 10oz rump steak (£12.95), and specials such as shellfish with spaghetti in saffron cream sauce (£10.95), and pork shank with cider sauce and sweet potatoes (£11.95); puddings could be home-made rhubarb crumble or banana fritters with vanilla pod ice cream (£3.80). There are seats around a few simple tables in a smallish carpeted area on the right, by the bar, with some bar stools too, and a log-effect stove in a big brick inglenook fireplace. The main area spreading back from here has shiny bare boards and a swathe of red carpeting, with well spaced tables, attractive pictures on cream or dark salmon walls, and a side bit with a leather settee, low games table and shove-ha'penny, liar dice, chess and so forth. The very friendly, helpful staff serve well kept Brakspears PA and SB on handpump. *(Recommended by Ian Phillips, John Hale, Bob and Margaret Holder, Chris Glasson)*

Brakspears ~ Licensees Bill and Beryl Farrell ~ Real ale ~ Bar food (12-2.30, 7-9.30) ~ Restaurant ~ (01491) 641455 ~ Children welcome ~ Dogs allowed in bar ~ Open 11-3, 6-11; 12-7.30 Sun; 12-3, 6.30-10.30 Sun in winter

HOOK NORTON SP3533 Map 4
Gate Hangs High ♀ 🍽

Banbury Road; 1 mile N of village towards Sibford, at Banbury—Rollright crossroads

In summer, there are flowering tubs and wall baskets around the picnic-sets in front of this tucked-away country pub, and the broad back lawn is a nice place for a drink, with holly and apple trees, and fine views. Inside, the bar has joists in the long, low ceiling, a brick bar counter, stools and assorted chairs on the carpet, baby oil lamps on each table, a gleaming copper hood over the hearth in the inglenook fireplace, and hops over the bar counter. Well kept Hook Norton Best and a guest such as First Light on handpump, a good wine list, and a range of malt whiskies; piped music. Interesting dishes might include home-made soup (£3.25), duck liver and brandy pâté with melba toast (£3.95), excellent braised rabbit in mustard sauce (£8.50), steak and wine pie (£8.95), pork fillet with mushrooms, cream and sherry (£11.95), poached chicken breast with sage stuffing and fresh asparagus with ginger and soy sauce or roasted half a duck with prune and rum sauce (£12.95), and beef fillet with wild mushrooms, red wine and garlic (£14.95), and delicious home-made puddings such as banoffi pie or apple and blackberry crumble (£3.95); they have a good children's menu (from £3.50), and they do a two-course weekday set menu (£9.95; three courses £12.95). You'll need to book for Saturday evening and Sunday lunch. By spring, they plan to convert the old barns at the back of the pub into bedrooms; this will also create a courtyard garden. *(Recommended by Andy and Jill Kassube, Andrew MacLeod, M Benjamin, Stuart Turner, Mike and Mary Carter, John Robertson, Malcolm Taylor, Martin Jones, Ted George, John Mason, Sir Nigel Foulkes, Mike and Sue Richardson, Matthew Shackle, JHBS)*

Hook Norton ~ Tenant Stephen Coots-Williams ~ Real ale ~ Bar food (12-2, 6-10) ~ Restaurant ~ (01608) 737387 ~ Children in eating area of bar and restaurant ~ Dogs allowed in bar ~ Open 12-3, 6-11; 12-4, 7-10.30 Sun

Pear Tree ◀

Village signposted off A361 SW of Banbury

This well liked little pub is barely 100 yards away from the Hook Norton brewery, so you'll find the full range of their ales on handpump including excellently kept Hook Norton Best, Old Hooky, Generation, Mild, and seasonal ales; they do country wines too. The chatty knocked together bar area has country-kitchen furniture on the nicely timbered floor, some long tables, a well stocked magazine rack, and a welcoming log fire; there's a good country pub atmosphere and the staff are friendly. In the attractive, sizeable garden, there's plenty of seating as well as an outdoor chess set, wendy house, swings and slides. A short choice of simple bar food includes sandwiches, soup (£2.95), filled baked potatoes (from £4.95), ploughman's (from £5.50), home-cooked ham and eggs (£6.50), beef in ale or fish pie (£6.75), and puddings such as lemon meringue pie (£2.95). It does get busy at weekends; dominoes, and Jenga. *(Recommended by Chris Glasson, the Didler, Michael Jones, Dick and Madeleine Brown, GSB, JHBS, Barry Collett, Guy Vowles, Derek and Sylvia Stephenson, C A Hall, Robert Gomme, MP, Andy and Jill Kassube)*

Hook Norton ~ Tenant J Sivyer ~ Real ale ~ Bar food (not Sun evening) ~ (01608)
737482 ~ Children in eating area of bar ~ Dogs allowed in bar ~ Open
11.30-2.30(3 Sat), 6-11; 12-4, 7-10.30 Sun ~ Bedrooms: £36S/£50S

Sun 🍴 🛏

High Street

Readers are united in their praise of this bustling place, and the 'good mix of
drinkers and eaters' and 'friendly young staff' make it the kind of pub you'd feel
happy going to on your own. The flagstoned front bar has a buoyant and relaxed
local atmosphere, a huge log fire, and hop-strung beams; there's even a table
reserved for domino players. Hook Norton Best, Mild, Generation, Old Hooky and
a seasonal ale are superbly kept on handpump, and the good value wines include
nine by the glass; darts, alley skittles. Behind the central servery, a cosy carpeted
room with comfortable banquettes and other seats leads into the attractive no
smoking green-walled restaurant. Enjoyable food could include home-made soup
(£3.50), good filled baguettes (from £3.25), mussels in white wine, garlic and
shallots with cream and herbs (£4.75), ploughman's (£5.50), beef and red wine pie
(£7.50), lamb shank with mustard mash and mint and redcurrant sauce or salmon
and cod fishcakes with lemon and butter sauce (£9.95), with specials such as cod
fillet with spinach and mediterranean tomato sauce (£8.95), or sirloin steak with
mushroom and brandy sauce (£10.95); tempting puddings could include peach and
pear crumble (£3.75). Tables out on a back terrace with more on the street in front
create a pleasantly continental feel on summer evenings; good wheelchair access
and disabled facilities. *(Recommended by Susan and John Douglas, Simon Collett-Jones,*
Martin Jones, John Bowdler, Dick and Madeleine Brown, Sir Nigel Foulkes, Pete Baker,
Chris Glasson, K H Frostick, Martin Jennings, MP, Jennie Hall, JHBS)

Hook Norton ~ Tenants Richard and Jane Hancock ~ Bar food ~ Restaurant ~
(01608) 737570 ~ Children in restaurant ~ Dogs allowed in bar ~ Open 12-3.30,
6-11.30; 12-3.30, 7-11 Sun ~ Bedrooms: /£50S(£50B)

KELMSCOTT SU2499 Map 4
Plough 🛏

NW of Faringdon, off A417 or A4095

This is a lovely spot in a peaceful hamlet by the upper Thames (even the council
houses have dormer windows and old tiled roofs), and the landlord is happy to talk
about nearby riverside walks. The small traditional beamed front bar has ancient
flagstones and stripped stone walls, a good log fire and the relaxed chatty feel of a
real village pub. The comfortable main lounge bar is carpeted, with interesting
prints, and there's a second lounge. The pleasant recently expanded back dining
area, with attractively plain and solid furnishings, has good interesting fresh home
cooking, and readers like the way that many lunchtime dishes are available in small
or large portions. Good, friendly staff serve sandwiches (from £4.75), soup (£2.75;
large £4.50), black pudding, egg and bacon salad or traditional pork pie with
potato salad (£4.50; large £7.50), devilled lambs kidneys and fried bread or hot
smoked eel fillets with bacon and mash (£4.50; £8.50), and grilled salmon with
chive cream sauce (£8.50), with evening dishes such as roast duck breast with
cabbage and smoked bacon potato cake, sweet roasted beetroot, shallots and green
peppercorn sauce (£13.50) or roast monkfish medallions wrapped in smoked bacon
with fried scallops, creamed potatoes, buttered spinach and chive cream sauce
(£15.50); puddings could include toffee and banana pudding with butterscotch
sauce or white and dark chocolate torte (from £3.75). Well kept Bass, Hook
Norton Best and perhaps a guest beer such as Hop Back Summer Lightning, Black
Rat farm cider; piped music, darts and an aunt sally. The garden is pretty, with
seats among plantings of unusual flowers, and there are picnic-sets under cocktail
parasols out in front. The bedrooms are named after patterns designed by William
Morris, whose former summer home, the Manor House, is just a short walk away
(for a while the pub itself was also called the Manor – source of some confusion,

sensibly solved by reverting to its present humbler name). There is both fresh and coarse fishing available locally, and boat moorings too. The Oxfordshire cycleway runs close by. *(Recommended by R Huggins, D Irving, E McCall, T McLean, Eleanor and Nick Steinitz, JCW, Sue Dyson, Robert and Anne Dillon)*

Free house ~ Licensee Martin Platt ~ Real ale ~ Bar food ~ Restaurant ~ (01367) 253543 ~ Children in eating area of bar and restaurant ~ Dogs allowed in bar ~ Open 11-3, 6-11.30; 12-3, 6-10.30 Sun; closed Mon, and two weeks in Jan ~ Bedrooms: £45S/£75S(£75B)

LEWKNOR SU7198 Map 4
Olde Leathern Bottel
Under 1 mile from M40 junction 6; just off B4009 towards Watlington

Set in a charming village, this busy country pub is a handy place to stop if you're on the M40. Cheerfully served tasty bar food includes lunchtime filled baguettes or ploughman's (from £4.95), ham and eggs or all-day breakfast (£5.95), and daily specials such as beef and Guinness pie with suet topping or chicken and bacon caesar salad (£6.95), and wok-fried king prawns (£9.95), with home-made puddings such as apple and mincemeat pie or chocolate cake (£2.95). The two bar rooms have heavy beams in the low ceilings, rustic furnishings, open fires, and an understated décor of old beer taps and the like. The no smoking family room is separated only by standing timbers, so you won't feel segregated from the rest of the pub. All their wines are sold by the glass, and you can also get well kept Brakspears Bitter and Special, and occasionally a guest on handpump; dominoes and piped music. The attractive sizeable garden has a children's play area. *(Recommended by Stuart Turner, B and M Kendall, Patrick Hancock, MLR, John and Glenys Wheeler, Jack Clark, Brian Skelcher, Colin and Sandra Tann)*

Brakspears ~ Tenant Mr L S Gordon ~ Real ale ~ Bar food (12-2, 7-9.30; 12-2, 6-10 Fri/Sat) ~ (01844) 351482 ~ Children in restaurant and family room ~ Dogs welcome ~ Open 11-2.30(3 Sat), 6-11; 11-3, 7-10.30 Sun

MAIDENSGROVE SU7288 Map 2
Five Horseshoes ♀
W of village, which is signposted from B480 and B481; OS Sheet 175 map reference 711890

Nicely placed high up in the Chiltern beechwoods, this little 17th-c brick house serves 15 wines by the glass. The rambling main bar is furnished with mostly modern wheelback chairs around stripped wooden tables (though there are some attractive older seats and a big baluster-leg table), and there's a proper log fire in winter; the low ceiling in the main area is covered in bank notes from all over the world, mainly donated by customers. The airy dining conservatory is no smoking (no mobile phones in here either). Each of the three areas outside gives lovely views over the wooded Chiltern Valley (look out for red kites). Interesting food includes home-made soup (£4.45), smoked salmon (£6.45), chargrilled rib-eye steak, baked chicken breast with orange and king prawn risotto or grilled salmon fillet with thai king prawn, strawberry and basil salad (£11.45), and honey-roasted duck breast (£13.95). They also hold summer barbecues, when you can choose from dishes such as tuna steak marinated in lime, ginger and coriander (£9.95), swordfish, salmon and king prawn skewers with lemon (£11.25), and half shoulder of spring lamb (£14.95); children's meals (£4.95). On handpump, they've well kept Brakspears Bitter and Special as well as a seasonal ale; piped music. *(Recommended by Joan Thorpe, Tracey and Stephen Groves, Brian Root, Michael Porter, Tony Harwood, Paul Hopton, John Hale, Andrew Barker, Claire Jenkins, M Borthwick)*

Brakspears ~ Tenants Mr and Mrs Hills ~ Real ale ~ Bar food (12-2, 6.30-9(9.30 Fri-Sat)) ~ Restaurant ~ (01491) 641282 ~ Children welcome ~ Dogs allowed in bar ~ Open 11-3(4 Sat), 6-11; 12-4 Sun; closed Sun evening

OXFORD SP5106 Map 4
Kings Arms £
40 Holywell Street

Opposite the Sheldonian theatre (where the students graduate), this 16th-c pub is nearly always busy with a good mix of students, dons and tourists. There's a big rather bare main room, with a no smoking coffee room just inside the Parks Road entrance, and several cosy and comfortably worn-in side and back rooms, each with a different character and customers. An extra back room has a sofa and more tables, and there's a tiny room behind that. They keep a dictionary for crossword buffs in the Dons Bar, with its elderly furnishings and tiled floor, mix of old prints and photographs of customers, and sympathetic lighting; daily newspapers, fruit machine, video game and cribbage. The hardworking staff are friendly and obliging, and there's a good relaxed atmosphere. Six well kept real ales include Youngs Bitter, Triple A, Special and Waggle Dance with guests such as Smiles Bristol IPA and Wadworths 6X on handpump, they've a fine choice of wines with 20 by the glass, and up to 20 malt whiskies. Bar food includes soup (£2.25), sandwiches (from £2.95), sausages and mash or all day breakfast (£5.25), vegetarian lasagne (£5.65), beer battered fish and chips (£5.95), and steak and ale pie (£6.25). *(Recommended by R Huggins, D Irving, E McCall, T McLean, Dick and Madeleine Brown, Mrs E A Macdonald, Kevin Blake, Derek and Sylvia Stephenson, Tracey and Stephen Groves, Dr and Mrs M E Wilson, the Didler, M Joyner, DRH and KLH)*

Youngs ~ Manager David Kyffin ~ Real ale ~ Bar food (11.30-9(8 Sun)) ~ (01865) 242369 ~ Children in no smoking room till around 9 ~ Open 10.30-11(10.30 Sun)

Turf Tavern ◖
Tavern Bath Place; via St Helen's Passage, between Holywell Street and New College Lane

The little dark-beamed and low-ceilinged rooms of this tremendously enjoyable pub have an infectious lively atmosphere and a fine range of up to 11 well kept ales on handpump. Friendly young bar staff serve Hook Norton Old Hooky and Archers Golden, alongside continually changing guests such as Badger Tanglefoot, Cains Sundowner, Coach House Dick Turpin, Exmoor Fox, Nethergate Wild Goose, Orkney Dark Island, Robinsons Young Tom, Shepherd Neame Early Bird, Titanic Rule Britannia, and Woodfordes Great Eastern; they also stock Hoegaarden belgian beer, Weston's Old Rosie cider, and in winter mulled wine; quiz machine. The cellar is open to the public and they are happy to show people around. On long summer evenings it's especially nice to sit out at the tables in the three attractive walled-in flagstoned or gravelled courtyards (one has its own bar); in winter, they have coal braziers and you can roast chestnuts and toast marshmallows, and there are canopies with lights and heaters. Although it's cut off from the modern bustle of the city by the high stone walls of some of its oldest buildings (including part of the ancient city wall), the pub is usually overflowing with quite a mix of customers – in the evenings, when it's very popular with students, you may have difficulty bagging a seat. Straightforward bar food includes baguettes (from £2.75), filled baked potatoes (from £2.95), caesar salad (£3.95), sausage and mash (£4.45), steak and ale pie (£5.95), grilled salmon (£6.45), and fish and chips (£6.95), with puddings such as apple and blackberry crumble (£2.45); the top food area is no smoking. *(Recommended by Mr and Mrs J McRobert, Dr and Mrs M E Wilson, the Didler, David and Carole Chapman, Paul Hopton, Dick and Madeleine Brown, Tina and David Woods-Taylor, Tracey and Stephen Groves, Kevin Blake, Paul and Ann Meyer, R Huggins, D Irving, E McCall, T McLean, Howard Dell)*

Laurel Pub Company ~ Manager Darren Kent ~ Real ale ~ Bar food (12-7.30) ~ (01865) 243235 ~ Children in family room ~ Dogs welcome ~ Open 11-11; 12-10.30 Sun

---

Pubs with particularly interesting histories, or in unusually interesting buildings, are listed at the back of the book.

RAMSDEN SP3515 Map 4
Royal Oak 🍷 🍺 🛏

Village signposted off B4022 Witney—Charlbury

A good all-rounder, this unpretentious village inn is extremely popular with readers and locals alike. Using mostly local suppliers (and organic when possible), the enjoyable bar food might include lunchtime ploughman's (£5.25) and sausages and mash (£6.95), as well as freshly prepared soup (£3.25), scottish haddock cooked with whisky and cream topped with cheese (£4.95; main course £9.50), stilton, leek and mushroom puff (£8.95), mediterranean-style lamb casserole, crab and smoked salmon fishcakes or 8oz rump steak (£10.95), and daily specials such as coq au vin (£10.50), and confit of duck with puy green lentils (£11.95), with puddings (£3.95); on Thursday evenings they do steak, fries and salad, a home-made pudding and glass of house wine for £12.95; roast Sunday lunch (£8.95). There's a genial relaxing pubby atmosphere, and the basic furnishings are comfortable, with fresh flowers, bookcases with old and new copies of *Country Life* and, when the weather gets cold, a cheerful log fire; service is friendly and attentive, and the licensees are welcoming. The dining room is no smoking. Well kept real ales on handpump include Adnams Broadside and Hook Norton Best along with a guest such as West Berkshire Good Old Boy; they serve 20 wines by the glass (with a large selection of ones from New Zealand). There are tables and chairs out in front and on the terrace behind the restaurant (folding back doors give easy access); outdoor heaters. The spacious bedrooms are in separate cottages; good breakfasts. *(Recommended by John Kane, Dick and Madeleine Brown, MP, Neil Woodcock, Simon Reynolds, Richard Greaves, George Cowie, P W E Sheldon, Simon Collett-Jones, Rainer Zimmer, Chris Wood, Guy Vowles, Ronald Harry, Nigel and Sue Foster, Andrew Shore, Derek and Sylvia Stephenson, Tony Duley, Mr Ronald, Les and Barbara Owen, Mr and Mrs P Dolan, Stephen Buckley, Di and Mike Gillam, J P Marland)*

Free house ~ Licensee Jon Oldham ~ Real ale ~ Bar food (12-2, 7-10) ~ Restaurant ~ (01993) 868213 ~ Children in restaurant ~ Dogs allowed in bar ~ Open 11.30-3, 6.30-11; 12-3, 7-10.30 Sun; closed 25-26 Dec, 1 Jan ~ Bedrooms: £35S/£50S

ROKE SU6293 Map 2
Home Sweet Home

Village signposted off B4009 Benson—Watlington

In fine weather, the low-walled front garden of this traditional, rather smart pub is a lovely place to enjoy a well cooked meal. From a wide-ranging menu, popular dishes (promptly served by welcoming staff) could include sandwiches, toasties, and club sandwiches (from £3.25), stilton and mushroom pancakes (£4.35), lots of ploughman's (from £4.50), filled baked potatoes (from £5.50), delicious battered cod (£6.50), fresh salmon fishcakes with parsley sauce or steak and kidney pudding (£7.25), pork in cider (£9.25), calves liver and crispy bacon (£9.50), and chicken chasseur (£10); puddings such as home-made bread and butter pudding or jam tart (from £3.75). The two smallish bar rooms have a pleasantly relaxed atmosphere, a lovely big log fire, heavy stripped beams, leather armed chairs on the bare boards, a great high-backed settle with a hefty slab of a rustic table in front of it, and a few horsey or game pictures such as a nice Thorburn print of snipe on the stone walls. On the right, a carpeted room, with low settees and armchairs and an attractive corner glass cupboard, leads through to the restaurant. Well kept Wadworths 6X on handpump, and a good choice of malt whiskies. There are lots of flowers around the tables out by the well. *(Recommended by Mrs E A Macdonald, Mayur Shah, John and Glenys Wheeler, C A Hall, Marjorie and David Lamb)*

Free house ~ Licensees Jill Madle, Peter and Irene Mountford ~ Real ale ~ Bar food ~ Restaurant ~ (01491) 838249 ~ Well behaved children in eating area of bar and in restaurant ~ Dogs allowed in bar ~ Open 11(12 Sun)-3, 6-11; closed Sun evening

---

Pubs brewing their own beers are listed at the back of the book.

SHIPTON-UNDER-WYCHWOOD SP2717 Map 4
Shaven Crown 🍺

High Street

Pleasantly lit up at night (when the gas heaters are a welcome addition), the courtyard of this grand old inn is a peaceful place to sit in summer. The imposing building has quite a history: Elizabeth I is said to have used parts of it as a hunting lodge, while as far back as the 14th c it was a hospice for the monastery of Bruern. There's a magnificent double-collar-braced hall roof, lofty beams and a sweeping double stairway down the stone wall, and the beamed bar has a relief of the 1146 Battle of Evesham, as well as seats forming little stalls around the tables and upholstered benches built into the walls. A wide choice of good bar food might include soup (£3.75), sandwiches (from £3.50), fried goats cheese with grape chutney (£4.75), spinach and ricotta pancake with red pepper glaze, lamb shank with rosemary and garlic or grilled bass with butternut risotto (£9.45), duck breast with sage and plum sauce (£10.50), and sirloin steak (£11.20), with specials such as fried red snapper coated with sesame seeds with white wine sauce or chicken burritos with guacamole, sour cream and mexican salsa (£8.95); they do children's meals (£5.50) and smaller portions of some main meals. The restaurant is no smoking. Well kept Hook Norton Best, and a couple of guests such as Eccleshall Slaters Original and Fullers London Pride on handpump, and several wines by the glass; shove-ha'penny, dominoes, cribbage, piped music, and the pub has its own bowling green. The bedrooms are full of character. *(Recommended by Ian Phillips, Chris Glasson, John Bowdler, Mike and Mary Carter, JMC, Bob and Valerie Mawson, G A Hemingway)*

Free house ~ Licensees Robert and Jane Burpitt ~ Real ale ~ Bar food (12-2, 5.30-9.30) ~ Restaurant ~ (01993) 830330 ~ Children welcome ~ Dogs welcome ~ Open 11.30-3, 5-11; 11.30-3, 6-10.30 Sun ~ Bedrooms: £55B/£85S(£95B)

SIBFORD GOWER SP3537 Map 4
Bishop Blaize

Village signposted just off B4035 W of Banbury; Burdrop

With a magnificent garden, particularly welcoming licensees, and an appealingly unspoilt 17th-c bar, this stone-built local is an understandably popular choice. The heavily beamed partly tiled bar has big windows overlooking the garden, some panelling, cosy and comfortable country furnishings, a few framed cartoons, and leaflets advertising local concerts and events. There's an unusual curved wooden counter, opposite which is a very snug inglenook, once used for wakes, but now squeezing in a couple of tiny tables and chairs by an ancient stove. Down a step is a small area with a fruit machine; soft piped music, darts, cribbage and dominoes. The attractively planted garden has a splendid view down over the sheep-strewn hillside and across the surrounding fields, on a clear day stretching into Gloucestershire and Warwickshire; there are plenty of seats out here (perhaps more than inside), as well as swings in the corner. Attentive and thoughtful staff serve enjoyably straightforward home-made bar food such as soup (£2.75), filled baked potatoes (£5.45), thai vegetable schnitzel (£5.25), ham and egg or battered haddock and chips (£5.75), with specials such as tasty chicken, leek and mushroom or steak, mushroom and ale pie (£6.95) or giant filled yorkshire pudding (£7.45); children's menu (£2.95). They serve well kept Vale Best and a couple of guests from brewers such as Archers and Jennings on handpump. There are quite a few steps down from the car park; it's a flatter entrance from the front. Morris dancers occasionally visit in summer; there are good walks nearby. *(Recommended by Arnold Benett, Giles Francis, Ted George, Dave Braisted)*

Free house ~ Licensees Sam and Sheila Merchant ~ Real ale ~ Bar food (12-2, 7(6 Mon)-9; 12-2, 7-8.30 Sun May-Oct; not Sun evening Nov-Apr) ~ (01295) 780323 ~ Children welcome away from bar ~ Open 12-2.30, 6-11; 12-3, 7.10.30 Sun

STANTON ST JOHN SP5709 Map 4
Star

Pub signposted off B4027; village is signposted off A40 heading E of Oxford (heading W, you have to go to the Oxford ring-road roundabout and take unclassified road signposted to Stanton St John, Forest Hill etc); bear right at church in village centre

'Well worth the tortuous route from the East to get to' writes one reader of this pleasant old pub. It's interestingly arranged over two levels, with an attractive extension on a level with the car park. There are old-fashioned dining chairs, a pleasant mix of dark oak and elm tables, rugs on flagstones, pairs of bookshelves on each side of an attractive inglenook fireplace (good blazing fires in winter), shelves of good pewter, terracotta-coloured walls with a portrait in oils, and a stuffed ermine; down a flight of stairs are little low-beamed rooms – one has ancient brick flooring tiles and the other quite close-set tables. Tasty bar food includes sandwiches (£2.60, soup and sandwich £4.45), chicken liver pâté (4.20), ploughman's (from £4.20), mexican bean hotpot, venison pie or moussaka (£7.50), red thai chicken curry (£8.50), and fillet of beef wellington (£10.95), with puddings such as spotted dick (£3.25). Well kept Wadworths IPA and 6X and JCB on handpump, and country wines; service is friendly and helpful. The family room and conservatory are no smoking; piped music, darts, shove-ha'penny, cribbage and dominoes. The walled garden has seats among the rockeries and children's play equipment. *(Recommended by Susan and John Douglas, Ian Phillips, Paul Humphreys, George Atkinson, Marjorie and David Lamb, K H Frostick, Martin Jones, Keith Reeve, Marie Hammond)*

Wadworths ~ Tenant Michael Urwin ~ Real ale ~ Bar food (not Sun evening) ~ (01865) 351277 ~ Children welcome ~ Dogs welcome ~ Open 11-2.30, 6.30-11; 12-2.30, 7-10.30 Sun

Talk House ♀ ⇌

Wheatley Road (B4027 just outside village)

A nice place for a relaxing lunch, this peacefully set 17th-c pub handily stays open all day in summer. The various capacious rooms have lots of oak beams, flagstoned and tiled floors, stripped original stonework, simple but solid rustic furnishings, and attractive pictures and other individual and often light-hearted decorations. While most of the tables are set for dining, there's enough room for those just wanting a sociable drink, and there's a pleasant drinkers' area with comfortable leather sofas around the fireplace. Friendly staff serve well kept Hook Norton Best, Wadworths 6X and a guest such as Everards Tiger on handpump, good house wines, and several malt whiskies; piped music (which readers tell us can be obtrusive). Enjoyable bar food might typically include tasty home-made soup (£3.95), good baguettes or chicken satay skewers (£5.50), scotch smoked salmon (£6.50), steak and ale pie, tandoori chicken or beef medallions with black bean sauce (£10.95), roast pork loin with honey and mustard sauce (£11.95), and bass fillets with lemon and herb butter or chargrilled organic sirloin steak (£12.95); they add a 10% service charge to tables of more than six people. The barn section of the restaurant has been recently re-thatched. There are tables in the sheltered courtyard. *(Recommended by Tim and Ann Newell, Jane Taylor, David Dutton, Mrs Catherine Draper, M E C Comer, Bob Turnham, Mike and Mary Carter)*

The Post Office makes it virtually impossible for people to come to grips with British geography, by using a system of post towns which are often across the county boundary from the places they serve. So the postal address of a pub often puts it in the wrong county. We use the correct county – the one the pub is actually in. Lots of pubs which the Post Office alleges are in Oxfordshire are actually in Berkshire, Buckinghamshire, Gloucestershire or Warwickshire.

Traditional Freehouses ~ Manager Anne-Marie Carlisle-Kitz ~ Real ale ~ Bar food (12-2, 7-9(10 Fri); all day Sat/Sun) ~ Restaurant ~ (01865) 351648 ~ Children in restaurant ~ Open 12-11(12-3, 5.30-11 in winter); 12-10.30 Sun ~ Bedrooms: £40B/£60B

STOKE ROW SU6982 Map 2

Grouse & Claret

Village signposted from B481 S of Nettlebed; from village centre follow signpost to Kingwood Common, 1 mile S; OS Sheet 175 map reference 692825

A good deal of red velvet, low black beams, dark ceilings, the red and black carpet, and plenty of candles give this Chilterns hideaway the feel of somewhere which would be perfect for alluring assignations – particularly perhaps the two softly lit small side rooms, one decorated virtually in black. Everything seems geared to relaxation, with padded stools and a leather elbow-rest along the serving counter, perhaps a huge bunch of flowers there, a table of magazines and daily papers, a variety of comfortable seats around the well mixed tables, and good unobtrusively welcoming and helpful service. The main dining area, nicely divided, is on the left. A wide range of good freshly made food runs from lunchtime filled baguettes and sandwiches (£5.50) to dishes such as home-made soup (£4.50), fresh salmon fishcakes or spicy couscous with roasted mediterranean vegetables (£8.50), slow-roasted pork with apricot compote and colcannon potatoes and buttered leeks (£9), and steak and kidney log with creamed potatoes and marrowfat peas or trout fillets on a bed of courgettes, rocket and potatoes with a light lime and coriander dressing (£9.50), while the puddings such as chocolate torte (£5.50) can be outstanding; no bar snacks Saturday night or Sunday lunchtime. They have a well chosen wine list, and Adnams Broadside and Hook Norton Best on handpump. The sweet little garden, with a terrace and green plastic garden furniture, is surrounded by woodland. *(Recommended by B H and J I Andrews)*

Free house ~ Licensee Robin Gladman ~ Real ale ~ Bar food (12-2.30, 7-9.30) ~ Restaurant ~ (01491) 628359 ~ Children, if eating, in eating area of bar and restaurant ~ Open 12-3, 6-11.30; 12-6 Sun; closed Sun evening

SWALCLIFFE SP3737 Map 4

Stags Head

Bakers Lane, just off B4035

Tables in front of this charmingly picturesque, old thatched village pub look down over a peaceful, steeply winding little lane opposite the church. Behind is a series of neatly terraced gardens with palm trees, a small fountain, several tables under a pergola, and a sensibly segregated play area. Inside, there's a big woodburner at the end of the low-beamed bar and next to it a standard lamp, and high-backed wooden pews and cushioned seats beside the stone walls. Lots of little jugs hang from the ceiling, and the 'head' of a master of foxhounds rather than the fox. A lighter room has lots more tables, and a tiled fireplace, along with newspapers to read, plenty of books, and lists of various local events and activities; there are candles on all the tables in the evening, and it's all very snug and welcoming (the licensees are very friendly too). The top bar area is no smoking. Readers enjoy the home-made bar food which might include lunchtime baguettes (£4.95), brie and smoked bacon melt with cranberry relish (£5.50), tuna and lime fishcakes (£8.95), porcini mushroom and chive risotto (£9.50), thai green chicken curry or lime and chilli chicken (£9.95), and steaks (from £11.95), with specials such as fisherman's platter (£8.95), and pork with camembert, cider and herb sauce (£9.95), with puddings such as belgian white chocolate fondue with dipping fruit (4.25); children's menu (£4.95) and Sunday roast (£8.95). They've well kept Brakspears, Batemans XB, and a guest from a brewer such as Cottage or Spinning Dog, a good changing wine list, with six by the glass, port (by the glass, half pint or pint); piped easy listening music, darts, shove-ha'penny, cribbage, a dominoes team, and two quiz teams. There's a letting bedroom with its own kitchenette. They've two cats, a dog and 10 chickens. More reports *please. (Recommended by George Atkinson, Martin Jones, John and Janet Davey, John Bowdler)*

Free house ~ Licensees Ian and Julia Kingsford ~ Real ale ~ Bar food (12-2.15, 7-9.30) ~ Restaurant ~ (01295) 780232 ~ Children welcome ~ Dogs welcome ~ Open 11.30-2.30(3 Sat), 6.30-11; 12-4 Sun; closed Sun evening and all day Mon ~ Bedrooms: £35S/£60S

TADPOLE BRIDGE SP3300 Map 4
Trout 🍴 � 🛏

Back road Bampton—Buckland, 4 miles NE of Faringdon

The charming landlord of this enjoyable, well-liked place will happily open any bottle of wine (under £25) from the comprehensive, interesting wine list and only charge you for the amount you drink. Peacefully set by the Thames, the pub is popular with walkers and those arriving by boat (bargees taking coal up the river used to stop here), and the atmosphere is cheerfully bustling, with a nice mix of drinkers and diners. The L-shaped bar has plenty of seats on flagstones, and friendly staff serve well kept Archers Village, Youngs Bitter, and a guest or two from Hook Norton or West Berkshire Brewery, along with home-made sloe gin, cherry plum brandy and elderflower cordial; darts, dominoes, cribbage, backgammon, and piped music. The well kept garden is a lovely place to sit in summer with small fruit trees, attractive hanging baskets, and flower troughs. Good, popular food from a changing menu might typically include home-made soup (£3.95), lunchtime sandwiches (£4.75), carpaccio of beef with rocket and parmesan (£4.95), grilled goats cheese salad (£5.25), terrine of chicken foie gras with chestnut mushrooms or spicy meatballs with tagliatelle (£6.95), chargrilled pork steak (£7.50), tomato and black olive risotto with roast vegetables (£8.95), plaice fillet with black pudding cake, spinach and poached egg (£12.95), chargrilled aberdeen angus steak or roast monkfish wrapped in parma ham with leek risotto (£13.95), and roast local lamb rump with bacon dauphinoise potatoes, puy lentils with carrot and celery (£14.95), with puddings such as summer pudding or rhubarb crumble (£4.95); the restaurant is no smoking. Readers have enjoyed staying here, and some of the comfortable rooms overlook the river. The pub sells day tickets for fishing on a 2-mile stretch of the river, and you can also camp here. *(Recommended by Alan Wilson, Mr and Mrs E Mason, Mary Rayner, R M Gibson, J F M and M West, Harold Copeman, Matthew Shackle, Tina and David Woods-Taylor, Bob and Margaret Holder, Di and Mike Gillam, Adrian Savage, Georgina Courtenay-Evans, David and Hazel Lee)*

Free house ~ Licensee Christopher J Green ~ Real ale ~ Bar food ~ Restaurant ~ (01367) 870382 ~ Children welcome ~ Dogs welcome ~ Open 11.30-3, 6-11; 12-3 (plus 7-10.30 July-Aug) Sun; closed Sun evening Sept-June, Christmas and New Year and first week in Feb ~ Bedrooms: £55B/£80B

THAME SP7005 Map 4
Swan ◀

Upper High Street

Readers feel very comfortable at this friendly, civilised 16th-c hotel, which overlooks the market square in the centre of town. There's an interesting mix of furnishings, and although nothing seems to match, it all blends together perfectly: the tables in the main bar are either chests, trunks or a butcher's block, and there's an assortment of well worn armchairs and comfortable old sofas, several grouped together around the stone fireplace. Brightly painted tiles cover the bar counter and the wall behind, and there are beams, timbers, faded rugs, old-fashioned saucy seaside postcards and a handsome clock. Cushioned sofas meander along a passageway, then down a step is an odd but cosy low-ceilinged room with paintings of erstwhile locals on the walls. Well kept Brakspears, Hook Norton and a couple of guests such as Shepherd Neame Spitfire and Timothy Taylors Landlord on handpump, and quite a few wines by the glass; piped classical music (which can sometimes be quite loud), newspapers to read, dominoes, cribbage, chess, and backgammon. Besides sandwiches (from £2.95), tasty, well presented bar food could include soup (£3.95), smoked cheddar and asparagus salad or mushroom and blue cheese omelette (£5.95), pork and leek sausages with mash and red onion gravy (£6.95), lamb and chorizo hotpot (£7.25), and peppered fillet steak (£8.95). The upstairs restaurant still has its medieval ceiling. There are a few tables at the back, in a small shopping arcade. It can get very busy in the evening and parking is quite tricky on market days – the Farmers' Market is held on Tuesdays. *(Recommended by Torrens Lyster, Susan and John Douglas, Giles Francis, Tim and Ann Newell, M Joyner, Ian Phillips)*

Free house ~ Licensee Sue Turnbull ~ Real ale ~ Bar food (12-2.30, 7-9; not 25-26 Dec) ~ Restaurant ~ (01844) 261211 ~ Children away from bar, till 8pm ~ Dogs allowed in bar and bedrooms ~ Open 11-11; 12-10.30 Sun ~ Bedrooms: £50S(£65B)/£90S(£90B)

WOOTTON SP4419 Map 4
Kings Head 🍴 ♀

Chapel Hill (which is near the church and marked by a wooden triangle in the road covering the old well); off B4027 N of Woodstock

All the food at this attractive 17th-c Cotswold stone house is home-made – they even make their own bread and ice cream. The spacious and formal no smoking restaurant is pretty much the focal point, although you can choose to eat in the bar or garden instead. Very well prepared (though not cheap) dishes could include soup (£3.95), warm duck salad (£4.95), muscovado and lime cured scottish salmon (£5.50), wild mushroom risotto (£8.95), chargrilled pork fillet medallions with orange and juniper sauce (£10.95), bass fillets with red onion marmalade (£12.95), and cantonese braised duck with sherry gravy (£14.95), with puddings such as caramelised citrus tart with raspberry coulis and bread and butter pudding (£4.95). The civilised and relaxing beamed no smoking lounge bar has a nice mix of old oak settles and chairs around wooden tables, comfortable armchairs and chintzy sofas, an open log fire, and old prints and ceramics on the pale pink walls. Along with a good wine list with up to seven by the small glass, they've Greene King Ruddles County and Hook Norton Old Hooky on handpump. Although they are allowed in the no smoking restaurant, this is not really a place geared towards children, and they don't do children's meals. *(Recommended by Robin and Joyce Peachey, Sir Nigel Foulkes, Arnold Bennett, Miles and Deborah Protter)*

Free house ~ Licensees Tony and Amanda Fay ~ Real ale ~ Bar food (not Sun evening) ~ Restaurant ~ (01993) 811340 ~ Children over 12 and only if very well behaved ~ Open 12-2.30, 6.45-11; 12-3 Sun; closed Sun evening ~ Bedrooms: £65B/£80B

Lucky Dip

Besides the fully inspected pubs, you might like to try these Lucky Dips recommended to us and described by readers (if you do, please send us reports: www.goodguides.com).

ABINGDON [SU4896]
White Horse [Ock St/Spring St]: Stone-built pub with pretty walled garden, Greene King Old Speckled Hen and Morlands Original, reasonably priced food; fruit machines *(Ian Phillips)*
ADDERBURY [SP4635]
☆ *Bell* [High St; just off A4260, turn opp Red Lion]: Unpretentious largely unspoilt beamed village local with chiming grandfather clock, some panelling, relaxed atmosphere, generous good fresh food, well kept Hook Norton inc seasonal ales; homely front room with armchairs and sofa by huge log fire, sewing

machines and standard lamp, smaller back music room with two pianos, old settles, and folk nights 1st and 3rd Mon of month; candlelit restaurant *(BB, Pete Baker)*
☆ *Red Lion* [The Green; off A4260 S of Banbury]: Smart and welcoming, with big inglenook, panelling, high stripped beams and stonework, Victorian and Edwardian pictures, good blackboard food in bar and cosy rooms off behind, well kept Greene King ales, good wine range, quick friendly service, daily papers, games area on left; piped music; children in eating area, tables out on well kept terrace, comfortable bedrooms, open all day summer

(D C T and E A Frewer, Paul and Penny Rampton, George Atkinson, M Joyner, LYM)

ARDINGTON [SU4388]

Boars Head [signed off A417 Didcot—Wantage]: Restauranty food at one end of low-beamed pub with attractively simple country décor and plainer no smoking extension, good wines; more local atmosphere at the other end, with well kept Arkells 3B, Brakspears and a guest beer, darts, shove-ha'penny, cribbage, dominoes, board games, TV and piped music; children welcome, cl Sun evening, peaceful attractive village *(Dick and Madeleine Brown, LYM, O Richardson, Peter B Brown)*

ASHBURY [SU2685]

☆ *Rose & Crown* [B4507/B4000; High St]: Relaxing, roomy and comfortable open-plan beamed bar, part of old-fashioned hotel, with highly polished woodwork, traditional pictures, chesterfields, deep armchairs and pews, lovely view down pretty village street of thatched cottages, raised section with further oak tables and chairs, lots of wines, well kept Arkells 2B and 3B, nice range of other drinks, friendly helpful staff, sensibly priced usual food, charming restaurant, separate public bar with pool and juke box; tables out in front; 11 bedrooms, attractive village nr Ridgeway *(Marjorie and David Lamb, CMW, JJW, Peter and Audrey Dowsett, BB, Dick and Madeleine Brown)*

BABLOCK HYTHE [SP4304]

Ferryman [off B4449 S of Stanton Harcourt, W of Cumnor]: Cheery and roomy thoroughly refurbished big-windowed Thames-side eating area and tables out on terrace (may be a bouncy castle), wide choice of reasonably priced food, real ales such as Greene King Ruddles County, friendly efficient service, displays of old ferry equipment (the steel ferry-boat for walkers and cyclists, worked by the landlord, was suspended last year for repairs); open all day (and specialises in group events eg OAP teas with entertainment), cl Tues, well equipped bedrooms with river-view balconies, moorings *(Peter and Audrey Dowsett)*

BAMPTON [SP3103]

Morris Clown [High St]: Folies Bergère-style murals in former coaching inn with well kept cheap sensibly priced changing ales, farm cider, darts, bar billiards; garden with old mangle collection, morris dancing late spring bank hol; open all day wknds, cl wkdy lunchtimes *(R M Gibson, the Didler)*

BANBURY [SP4540]

Church House [North Bar St]: Big dining pub showing interesting signs of its ecclesiastical past, well kept Greene King beers, wide range of wines, reasonably priced food inc generous starters (enough for a main meal), particularly helpful staff *(W W Burke)*

Wine Vaults [Parsons St]: Rambles through lots of room areas and partitioned snugs, carpeting, bare boards and some flagstones, plenty of mirrors and pictures from reproduction advertisements to MOMA prints, soft lighting and dark ceilings, row of keg taps

and drinks offers (eg on shooters for Thurs ladies' night), Greene King IPA, cheap food; central games area, well reproduced up-to-date music, popular evening/wknd young meeting place; disabled access and facilities, sheltered back terrace, partly covered and fairy-lit, open all day *(BB, Ted George)*

BARNARD GATE [SP4010]

Boot [Village signposted off A40 E of Witney]: More than 100 items of celebrity footwear at this stone-tiled dining pub, stout standing timbers and stub walls with latticed glass break up the main area, huge log fire, solid country tables and chairs on bare boards; good food, well kept Hook Norton Best and Wadworths 6X on handpump, and decent wines; tables out in front are out of earshot of the nearby road *(Tim Brierly, Simon Collett-Jones, D and M T Ayres-Regan, Ian Phillips, LYM)*

BENSON [SU6191]

Three Horseshoes: Busy village pub, wide choice of generous fresh food in bar and neat dining room, good welcoming service, well kept real ales; big garden *(Franklyn Roberts)*

BINFIELD HEATH [SU7478]

☆ *Bottle & Glass* [off A4155 at Shiplake; between village and Harpsden]: Lovely thatched black and white timbered Tudor cottage, scrubbed wooden tables, low beams and flagstones, fine fireplace, black squared panelling, welcoming landlord, three well kept Brakspears ales, blackboard bar food from sandwiches to big Sun lunch, no smoking dining area, shove-ha'penny, dominoes; no children or dogs inside; big attractive garden with tables under little thatched roofs *(Anthony Longden, Michael Dandy, the Didler, Peter B Brown, Mike and Sue Richardson, LYM, Wombat)*

BLETCHINGDON [SP5017]

Blacks Head [Station Rd; B4027 N of Oxford]: Cosy stripped-stone lounge with woodburner, enjoyable food here and in extended upmarket dining area with conservatory, well kept ales, games room; pleasant garden, good value simple bedrooms *(Jo Morley)*

BLEWBURY [SU5385]

Load of Mischief [South St (off A417)]: Comfortable pub/restaurant with friendly new young South African tenants, Greene King real ales, enjoyable food in bar or dining room; tables on small attractive back terrace *(Franklyn Roberts)*

BLOXHAM [SP4235]

☆ *Joiners Arms* [off A361; Old Bridge Rd]: Good welcoming service, beamed woodblock-floor bar, well kept real ales, good choice of wines, good service, open fires, above-average food inc interesting blackboard dishes here or in smart restaurant down steps (fire door gives disabled access from car park) *(BB, Mr and Mrs J Cooke, Chris Glasson, Paul Kirkham)*

BODICOTE [SP4537]

☆ *Plough* [Goose Lane/High St; off A4260 S of Banbury]: 14th-c pub in same family for 50 years, usually brewing its own cheap ales such as Bodicote Bitter, No 9, Porter and Life Sentence, guests such as Greene King IPA and

Worthington, country wines, wide choice of well cooked straightforward food from good value sandwiches and baguettes to steaks and Sun roast (cooking as well as service may be by the friendly landlord); low heavy beams, stripped stone, hops, pictures and brasses, no music, small open fire; darts, TV and fruit machine in public bar, children and dogs welcome (pub retriever called Daisy), twice-yearly beer festivals; no credit cards (BB, Dr B and Mrs P B Baker, Kevin Thorpe, the Didler, Pete Baker)

BRIGHTWELL BALDWIN [SU6594]
☆ *Lord Nelson* [off B480 Chalgrove—Watlington, or B4009 Benson—Watlington]: Civilised and friendly, with snug armchair area, good log fire, dining chairs around country-kitchen tables, wide range of enjoyable food, plenty of atmosphere, good service, real ales and decent house wines, no smoking restaurant; front verandah, back terrace and attractive garden (David and Ruth Shillitoe, LYM)

BROUGHTON [SP4238]
Saye & Sele Arms [B4035 SW of Banbury]: Enjoyable food in bar and larger restaurant, friendly staff, well kept real ales inc Wadworths 6X (Chris Glasson)

BUCKNELL [SP5525]
Trigger Pond [handy for M40 junction 10; Bicester Rd]: Neat stone-built pub opp the pond, emphasis on popular good value home cooking inc old-fashioned puddings (must book Sun lunch); piped music; pleasant terrace and garden (D C T and E A Frewer, Marjorie and David Lamb)

BURFORD [SP2512]
Angel [Witney St]: Long heavy-beamed dining pub in attractive ancient building, good brasserie food (LYM)
Cotswold Arms [High St]: Cosy bar with welcoming log fire, good sensibly priced food in busy dining area, beautiful stonework, pleasant efficient service, no piped music (Peter and Audrey Dowsett)
Golden Pheasant [High St]: Small early 18th-c Greene King hotel with sofas and comfortable chairs in pleasant front bar, enjoyable imaginative bar food from interesting sandwiches up, wider restaurant menu available here too, well kept Greene King IPA and Abbot, daily papers, flagstoned dining room down some steps, coffee and cream teas; comfortable bedrooms, pleasant sets outside (Michael Dandy, Derek and Sylvia Stephenson, W W Burke)
☆ *Mermaid* [High St]: Handsome jettied Tudor pub under new licensees, attractive long narrow bar, beams, flagstones, panelling and stripped stone, bay seating around the row of tables, enjoyable food in airy dining room and no smoking upstairs restaurant, well kept Greene King IPA, Old Speckled Hen and Ruddles County; piped music, fruit machine; children in eating areas, picnic-sets under cocktail parasols outside, open all day (Peter Sutton, Martin Jones, LYM)

☆ *Royal Oak* [Witney St]: Neat 17th-c stripped stone local with Wadworths real ales, wide range of simple food, efficient friendly service, masses of beer mugs and steins hanging from beams, pine tables and chairs, antlers over log-effect gas fire, bar billiards, back dining room; tables out on terrace, sensibly priced bedrooms off garden behind (Patrick Hancock, R Huggins, D Irving, E McCall, T McLean, Stan Edwards)

CANE END [SU6879]
Fox [A4074 N of Reading]: Good choice of food inc interesting dishes, helpful staff, separate area for drinkers (Hugh Spottiswoode)

CHARLBURY [SP3519]
☆ *Bull* [Sheep St]: Very good bistro-style atmosphere and surroundings, interesting range of well presented good generous food from imaginative baguettes and light dishes (mussels recommended by many) to delicious aberdeen angus Sun roast, restaurant on left, freshly furnished dining bar on right with armchairs and magazines, well kept Greene King IPA, Abbot and Ruddles County, good wines and coffee, friendly jolly staff; attractive sunny back terrace, bedrooms, cl Mon (Michael and Anne Brown, Mrs P Burvill, BB, Nigel and Sue Foster, Caroline Shenton, Janet and Philip Shackle)
Rose & Crown [Market St]: Town pub with good range of well kept beers inc guests, real pubby feel; tables out behind (Nigel and Sue Foster)

CHARLTON-ON-OTMOOR [SP5615]
Crown [signed off B4027 in Islip; High St]: Quiet unassuming two-room local, good value straightforward lunchtime food inc wkdy OAP specials, evening chinese menu inc takeaways, well kept Morrells Oxford, welcoming service, games-oriented public bar; good folk night Thurs (Pete Baker)

CHARNEY BASSETT [SU3794]
☆ *Chequers*: Bustling 18th-c two-room village-green local, spacious and rambling beamed interior with more space for dining room than bar, decent sensibly priced popular food from sandwiches up (may be snacks only, Sat lunchtime), well kept ales such as Archers Golden and Greene King IPA and Ruddles Best (good value pitchers), decent wines, cheerful licensees and good service, daily papers; pool, piped music; mall garden, children welcome, has been cl Mon (Dick and Madeleine Brown, Edward Longley, Debbie and Neil Hayter, BB)

CHILDREY [SU3687]
Hatchet: Friendly old beamed pub, games area one end, dining the other, four or five real ales, wide choice of lunchtime food, pub dog; children welcome, picnic-sets out in front, garden and play area, attractive village, Ridgeway walks (CMW, JJW)

CHISLEHAMPTON [SU5998]
Coach & Horses [B480 Oxford—Watlington, opp B4015 to Abingdon]: Small comfortable 16th-c hotel with two beamed bars, homely but civilised, with good choice of well prepared food in sizeable dining area (polished oak tables and wall banquettes), well kept ales inc

Flowers and Hook Norton, big log fire, welcoming cheerful staff; piped music; well kept terraced gardens overlooking fields by River Thame, comfortable bedrooms in back courtyard *(George Atkinson, Marjorie and David Lamb)*

CHURCH ENSTONE [SP3724]

☆ *Crown* [Mill Lane; from A44 take B4030 turn-off at Enstone]: Popular and attractive old pub with good fresh food (not Mon night) cooked by licensees' son, good lunchtime baguettes, pleasant cottagey bar, good-sized light modern dining area and conservatory, log fire in brass-fitted stone fireplace, beams and stripped stone, welcoming service, real ales such as Hook Norton Best, Shepherd Neame Spitfire and Wadworths 6X, decent wines by the glass, plenty of atmosphere; may be piped music, may be cl Mon lunchtime *(Pam Adsley, Stuart Turner, Chris Glasson, Angus Lyon, Andy and Jill Kassube, LYM)*

CHURCH HANBOROUGH [SP4212]

☆ *Hand & Shears* [opp church; signed off A4095 at Long Hanborough, or off A40 at Eynsham roundabout]: Attractively done open-feeling pub/restaurant, long gleaming bar, steps down into spacious back eating area, another small dining room, wide choice of good reasonably priced brasserie-style food from simple bar dishes to fish and grills inc good thai curries, attentive young staff, well kept Boddingtons, Fullers London Pride and Hook Norton Best, decent wines, open fires, good atmosphere, smartish customers; soft piped music *(Tim Brierly, BB)*

CLANFIELD [SP2802]

Clanfield Tavern [A4095 S of Witney]: Pretty, extended pub with series of small beamed, flagstoned and stripped-stone rooms, nice prints, attractive restaurant and no smoking conservatory; Brakspears and Greene King IPA and Ruddles County, big log fire, wide food choice; piped music may be loud, jazz nights, children welcome, picnic-sets under cocktail parasols in pleasant front garden *(Peter and Audrey Dowsett, LYM, Ian Phillips)*

CLIFTON HAMPDEN [SU5495]

Barley Mow [towards Long Wittenham, S of A415]: Interesting and attractively refurbished thatched Chef & Brewer, very low ancient beams, oak-panelled family room, well kept Courage Best and Directors, efficient friendly service, log fire, usual food all day from sandwiches up, restaurant; piped music; tables on pleasant terrace and in well tended waterside garden with doves and fancy fowls, short stroll from the Thames; bedrooms, open all day *(Chris Glasson, David H T Dimock, LYM, I D Greenfield)*

☆ *Plough* [A415]: Entirely no smoking thatched pub run by a very welcoming turkish family, with low beams, panelling and dim lighting, simple antique furniture on tiled floor, wide range of mainly restauranty food all day (but sandwiches too), popular Sun lunch, well kept Courage Best and Directors and John Smiths, good wines, light and airy restaurant; open all day, children in eating areas, tables outside,

comfortable bedrooms in converted building across courtyard *(the Didler, Mayur Shah, C A Hall, Nigel Williamson, LYM, Wombat)*

COMBE [SP4115]

Cock [off A4095 at Long Hanborough; The Green]: Spick and span classic country pub facing green in charming village, two pleasant bars, friendly landlord and helpful staff, real ale, enjoyable food from good home-made soup and baguettes up *(J A Ellis)*

COTHILL [SU4699]

Merry Miller: Large comfortably olde-worlde pub/restaurant based on 17th-c granary, stripped stone and flagstones, wide food choice from sandwiches up, friendly efficient staff, well kept real ales, good choice of wines, log fires; disabled access *(Franklyn Roberts)*

CRAYS POND [SU6380]

White Lion [B471 nr junction with B4526, about 3 miles E of Goring]: Welcoming pub recently reopened after refurbishment, low ceilings and good traditional atmosphere, open fire, attractive conservatory, enjoyable honest food from good value fresh baguettes to good fish choice, well kept beer, hands-on licensees; big garden with play area, lovely setting *(Pat and Robert Watt, Mr Ronald, Justin Winstanley)*

CROPREDY [SP4646]

☆ *Red Lion* [off A423 N of Banbury]: Rambling old thatched stone-built pub charmingly placed opp pretty village's churchyard, low beams, inglenook log fire, high-backed settles, brass, plates and pictures; reasonably priced food from baguettes up (two rooms set for eating, children allowed in restaurant part), good choice of well kept changing ales, games room; piped music, picnic-sets under cocktail parasols on back terrace by car park *(George Atkinson, LYM, Kevin Blake)*

CROWELL [SU7499]

Shepherds Crook [B4009, 2 miles from M40 junction 6]: Honest traditional pub tastefully refurbished with stripped brick, timber and flagstones, imaginative changing food inc good fresh fish and local meat and game, carpeted raftered dining area, well kept beers from good small breweries, decent wines, friendly straight-talking landlord, no music or machines; views from tables out on green *(Torrens Lyster)*

CUDDESDON [SP5902]

☆ *Bat & Ball* [S of Wheatley; High St]: Walls covered with cricketing programmes, photographs, porcelain models in well lit cases, score books, cigarette cards, pads, gloves and hats, and signed bats, bails and balls; low beams, some flagstones, Banks's LBW, Marstons Pedigree and a guest beer, decent wines, well liked food from baguettes to elaborate dishes (evening concentration on this, big new no smoking dining extension); cribbage, dominoes, piped music; children welcome, pleasant back terrace with good views, aunt sally, comfortable bedrooms, open all day *(Mr and Mrs Richard Osborne, Mayur Shah, Ian Phillips, LYM)*

CULHAM [SU5095]

Waggon & Horses [A415 Abingdon—

Dorchester]: Reasonably priced popular food, smaller helpings on request, Morrells ales, good value wine, log fires; piped music may obtrude; spacious grassy outdoor seating area with play equipment, bouncy castle and barbecues *(Marjorie and David Lamb)*

CUMNOR [SP4603]

Vine [Abingdon Rd]: Restaurany modernised pub with wide choice of enjoyable food from good baguettes to Sun family lunches (must book these), good friendly service despite wknd bustle, three well kept guest ales, good wine range, back dining extension, no smoking area in conservatory; picnic-sets in attractive back garden *(Dick and Madeleine Brown, Colin and Janet Roe)*

CURBRIDGE [SP3208]

Lord Kitchener [Lew Rd (A4095 towards Bampton)]: Comfortably refurbished, with good value food inc generous Sun lunch in smart no smoking end dining area, old local photographs, big log fire, well kept real ales, happy atmosphere, quick efficient service by informal NZ family; piped music may be obtrusive; garden with play area *(R M Gibson, Peter and Audrey Dowsett)*

CUXHAM [SU6695]

Half Moon [B480]: As we went to press, and contrary to expectations, there was little sign of progress on repairs to the serious fire damage suffered by this smashing little 17th-c low-beamed thatched country pub in 2002; we still look forward to its eventual reopening – news please *(LYM)*

DEDDINGTON [SP4631]

☆ *Deddington Arms* [off A4260 (B4031) Banbury—Oxford; Horse Fair]: Welcoming and relaxed beamed and timbered hotel with mullioned windows, some emphasis on enjoyable food from good if rather pricy sandwiches up, sizeable eating area (allowing children) and restaurant, well kept ales such as Caledonian Deuchars IPA, Coach House Squires Gold, Greene King IPA and Wadworths 6X, good choice of wines by the glass, good log fire, friendly attentive largely french young staff, rather modern décor with much ochre paintwork; open all day, comfortable chalet bedrooms around courtyard, good breakfast, attractive village with lots of antiques shops *(Chris Glasson, Charles Moncreiffe, LYM, Gill and Keith Croxton, George Atkinson, Paul and Penny Rampton)*

☆ *Unicorn* [Market Pl]: Busy and friendly 17th-c inn, clean and pleasant modernised bar, inglenook fireplace, very big helpings of usual food inc inexpensive set lunch in oak-beamed restaurant (children welcome), three real ales, morning coffee, quick helpful service; cobbled courtyard leads to lovely walled back garden, with smartly matching tables, chairs and deckchairs; bedrooms *(BB, Pam Adsley, R C Vincent)*

DORCHESTER [SU5794]

☆ *Fleur de Lys* [High St]: Carefully preserved coaching inn opp abbey, dating from 16th c, comfortably traditional two-level interior, wide

choice of good value home cooking, all fresh, Greene King IPA, Old Speckled Hen and Ruddles, friendly helpful service, interesting old photographs of the pub; children very welcome, unobtrusive piped music *(CMW, JJW, Len Banister)*

☆ *George* [just off A4074 Maidenhead—Oxford; High St]: Handsome timbered hotel on good form, with good cooking again, well kept Brakspears and a guest beer, good wines, fine old furnishings in smart beamed bar, roaring log fire; open all day, children in restaurant, bedrooms *(Sheila and Gerry Mc Grady, LYM, Mrs E A Macdonald)*

DRAYTON [SU4794]

Red Lion [B4017 S of Abingdon]: Simple and unpretentious, with good home cooking – a real steal at their generous prices; Morlands ale, games room *(anon)*

DUCKLINGTON [SP3507]

☆ *Bell* [off A415, 1 mile SE of Witney; Standlake Rd]: Pretty thatched local with wide choice of reasonably priced home-made food (not Sun eve) inc particularly good sandwiches, well kept Greene King Old Speckled Hen and Ruddles, good house wines, friendly service; big stripped stone and flagstoned bar with scrubbed tables, log fires (and glass-covered well), old local photographs, farm tools, hatch-served public bar, roomy and attractive well laid out back restaurant (its beams festooned with bells); cards and dominoes, no piped music; folk night 1st Sun of month, regular events such as morris dancing or raft races; small garden behind with play area, colourful hanging baskets, nine bedrooms *(Peter and Audrey Dowsett, BB, Pete Baker)*

Strickland Arms [off A415 SE of Witney; Witney Rd]: Welcoming and cosy old-world pub, low beams and flooring tiles in smart bar partly set for dining, enjoyable traditional food, well kept Adnams and Wadworths 6X, good value wines, compact no smoking restaurant, no music or machines; small pretty garden with skittles and aunt sally *(Geoff Pidoux, Mr and Mrs P Lally)*

EAST HAGBOURNE [SU5288]

Fleur de Lys [Main Rd]: Attractive black and white timbered pub with clean and tidy open-plan bar – half drinking place with cards and darts (lots of trophies in cabinet), half lounge with more emphasis on good value fresh food; well kept Greene King ales, quite a few stuffed fish; ceilidhs 3rd Weds, tables in neat small garden behind *(Mr and Mrs I Bell, Pete Baker, J J and B Dix)*

EAST HENDRED [SU4588]

Plough [off A417 E of Wantage; Orchard Lane]: Big beamed village pub with usual public bar and airy and lofty-raftered main room, interesting farming décor and wartime news, vast blackboard range of enjoyable food (booking advised for restaurant Sun lunch), Greene King IPA, copes well with anything from small leisurely family parties to dozens of walkers; occasional folk nights; pleasant garden with good play area, attractive village *(Dick and Madeleine Brown, BB, Ian Phillips)*

☆ **Wheatsheaf** [signed off A417; Chapel Sq]: Attractive 16th-c black and white timbered village pub with high-backed settles in quarry-tiled bar with big inglenook log fire, booth seating up steps, well kept ales such as Greene King IPA and Abbot and Charles Wells Bombardier, reasonably priced usual food from sandwiches and baked potatoes up, dominoes, shove-ha'penny; piped music; open all day wknds, tables in colourful back garden with aviary *(LYM, Ian Phillips, R Huggins, D Irving, E McCall, T McLean, Chris Glasson)*

ENSTONE [SP3724]

Harrow [A44 Chipping Norton—Woodstock]: Attractive family-friendly village pub, softly lit bar, brasses, pictures and lots of basket and cane work in spacious beamed back dining lounge, wide choice of straightforward enjoyable home-made food inc basket meals, Hook Norton and Morrells Oxford Blue; steps from car park; tables in flower-filled back courtyard and on large lawn *(Meg and Colin Hamilton, George Atkinson)*

EWELME [SU6491]

Shepherds Hut [off B4009 about 5 miles SW of M40 junction 6; High St]: Cosy and relaxed beamed local with good choice of fresh food (worth booking wknds) inc lovely puddings, cheerful helpful service, well kept Greene King ales, decent coffee, rowing memorabilia, Formula 1 photographs, pot plants, darts, small restaurant; may be piped music, fruit machine; children welcome, tables and swing in small pleasant garden *(Geoff and Teresa Salt)*

EXLADE STREET [SU6582]

Highwayman [Signposted just off A4074 Reading—Wallingford]: Rambling mainly 17th-c pub (though parts date back to the 14th c) in lovely countryside; two beamed bar rooms have an unusual layout, with an interesting variety of seats around old tables and even recessed into a central sunken inglenook; an airy no smoking conservatory dining room has more seats (mainly for eating) and overlooks the garden (fine views from here); well kept Fullers London Pride and IPA, and Wadworths 6X on handpump, several malt whiskies, decent wines (by the large and small glass as well as bottle), freshly squeezed orange juice, and champagne and kirs; piped music *(the Didler, Dr M Mills, Andy Sinden, Louise Harrington, Bob and Margaret Holder, Philip Kingsbury, Mrs E A Macdonald, Nigel Williamson, A P Seymour, Robert Hill, LYM)*

EYNSHAM [SP4309]

Newlands [Newland St]: Cosily unpretentious beamed and flagstoned bar, wide choice of generous enjoyable food, quick friendly service, real ales, decent wine, big inglenook log fire, stripped early 18th-c pine panelling, pretty restaurant on left; very busy and bustling wknds, may be piped music *(Geoffrey Hart, P W E Sheldon)*

FARINGDON [SU2895]

Bell [Market Pl]: Red leather settles, inglenook fireplace with 17th-c carved oak chimney-piece, interesting faded mural in inner bar, well kept Wadworths ales, wide choice of food inc plenty of fish in bar and restaurant, friendly staff and customers; children and dogs allowed, tables out among flowers in heated cobbled back coachyard, character beamed bedrooms *(Dave Irving, LYM, Rona Murdoch)*

FILKINS [SP2304]

☆ *Five Alls* [signed off A361 Lechlade—Burford]: Welcoming Cotswold stone pub with particularly friendly staff and locals in light and functional bar, comfortable and relaxing stripped-stone lounge (doubling as ante-room for bookable nicely furnished restaurant) with settees, armchairs and rugs on polished boards, good choice of well presented food, well chosen house wines, well kept Hook Norton beers, good coffee, log fire, daily papers, lots of cartoons; unobtrusive piped music; plenty of tables on terrace and neat lawns, garden chess, attractive well-equipped bedrooms, nice village *(BB, R Huggins, D Irving, E McCall, T McLean, Marjorie and David Lamb)*

FINSTOCK [SP3616]

Plough [just off B4022 N of Witney]: Rambling thatched and low-beamed village local, long divided well worn in bar with armchair by open woodburner in massive stone inglenook, entertaining pub dogs, well kept ales such as Adnams, Brakspears and Hook Norton, small choice of decent wines, enjoyable food from generous sandwiches up, pleasant service, crates of lending books, separate games area with bar billiards, stripped-stone dining room; children in eating areas, dogs allowed in public bar; sizeable garden with old-fashioned roses and aunt sally, good walks, good value bedroom with own bathroom *(R M Gibson, Stuart Turner, Rob and Catherine Dunster, R Naish, LYM, Lynn Sharpless)*

GODSTOW [SP4809]

☆ *Trout* [off A34 Oxford bypass northbound, via Wytham, or A40/A44 roundabout via Wolvercote]: Creeper-covered medieval pub which has slipped comfortably into its Vintage Inn garb, with old-fashioned furnishings in several linked rooms (all but one no smoking), log fires in three huge hearths, hop-hung beams, carvings and shiny ancient flagstones, attractive pictures and country bric-a-brac; decent food all day inc good lunchtime sandwiches, well kept Bass and Fullers London Pride, a good choice of wines by the glass, friendly young well trained staff; can be very busy, quiet piped music; charming in summer with lovely flagstoned heated terrace by a stream full of greedily plump perch, long restored footbridge to island (owned by pub) with ducks and peacocks, abbey ruins opp; in winter they serve mulled wine and hand out blankets for roasting chestnuts out here *(LYM, P R and S A White, Alicia Coates, Eleanor and Nick Steinitz, Denzil Martin, Chris Glasson, Simon Pyle, R M Gibson, Sue Dyson, Mrs M Shardlow, Ian Phillips, Roger and Pauline Pearce, P and J Shapley, Andy Brown)*

GORING [SU6080]

☆ *Catherine Wheel* [Station Rd]: Good value

home cooking inc lots of fish, Brakspears full range kept well, Stowford Press cider, decent wine, good informal atmosphere, very friendly landlord, staff and locals, two cosy bars, good log fire, restaurant; notable door to gents'; nice courtyard and garden, bedrooms, handy for Thames Path, attractive village *(the Didler)*

☆ *John Barleycorn* [Manor Rd]: Endearing and well kept low-beamed cottagey local in pretty Thames village, prints in cosy little lounge bar, good choice of well priced generous home-made food in adjoining eating area, well kept Brakspears, pool in end room, friendly helpful service; children welcome, dogs too (so long as they get on with Harvey the resident pyrenean); bedrooms clean and simple, good breakfast *(the Didler, Fiona McElhone)*

GREAT BOURTON [SP4545]

Bell [just off A423, 3 miles N of Banbury; Manor Rd, opp church]: Friendly local by church, basic bar and more comfortable dining area, decent food inc good soup and sandwiches, well kept Hook Norton, darts, lots of trophies; small garden *(Bob and Laura Brock)*

HAILEY [SP3414]

☆ *Bird in Hand* [Whiteoak Green; B4022 Witney—Charlbury]: Greatly extended old beamed and timbered Cotswold pub, smart and spotless, good choice of carefully cooked food (just set meals on Sun), quick friendly service, well kept ales such as Adnams and Brakspears, subdued lighting (inc candles on tables), large open fire, stone walls, comfortable armchairs, cosy corners in attractive spreading restaurant, nice views; piped music; tables in garden, good value comfortable quietly set cottage-style bedrooms, huge car park *(Peter and Anne-Marie O'Malley, George Atkinson, Nigel and Sue Foster, BB, Richard Marjoram)*

HAILEY [SU6485]

☆ *King William IV* [the different Hailey nr Ipsden, off A4074 or A4130 SE of Wallingford]: Attractive 16th-c pub in charming peaceful countryside, some concentration on wide choice of good generous mainly traditional food, friendly landlord and helpful staff, thriving atmosphere, full Brakspears range kept well, beams, bare bricks and tiled floor (carpet in middle room), big inglenook log fire, clean fresh décor and well kept traditional furnishings, extended dining room; outstanding views from pub and tables on front terrace *(Susan and John Douglas, the Didler, John Hale, John and Glenys Wheeler, Colin McKerrow, LYM, J A Ellis)*

Lamb & Flag [B4022 1 mile N of Witney; Middletown]: Pretty stone-built village local under attentive new licensees, friendly and helpful; good value fresh food, well kept Greene King IPA and Abbot, some ancient flagstones and woodburner in big fireplace, bright lighting, darts, bar billiards; some Sun quiz nights; good garden for children *(BB, Deborah Gee, K H Frostick)*

HANWELL [SP4343]

Moon & Sixpence: Friendly dining pub, wide choice of above-average food in comfortable bar and dining area (often booked up), efficient service, decent wines by the glass; small terrace, pretty location *(anon)*

HEADINGTON [SP5407]

Butchers Arms [Wilberforce St]: Welcoming backstreet local with long narrow seating area, good value wkdy lunchtime food, well kept Fullers beers, lots of sports trophies and memorabilia, games corner with darts, bar billiards and sports TV; pleasant garden with barbecues *(Pete Baker)*

HENLEY [SU7882]

☆ *Three Tuns* [Market Pl]: Heavy-beamed front bar with old-fashioned seating inc traditional settles, coal-effect gas fire, well kept Brakspears and decent wines; back dining area crisply rustic with big Hovis sign on cream-painted panelling and neat table linen, fresh imaginative cooking, friendly young staff; may be piped music; civilised cane furniture under awning in attractively reworked back courtyard *(Susan and John Douglas, Ian Phillips, the Didler, LYM, Rona Murdoch)*

HIGHMOOR [SU6984]

☆ *Dog & Duck* [B481 N of Reading, off A4130 Henley—Oxford]: Cosy and cottagey low-beamed country pub with chintzy curtains, floral cushions, lots of pictures; relaxing bar on left, dining room on right, log fire in each, smaller dining room behind, fine choice of good generous food inc good vegetarian dishes, hard-working licensees, well kept Brakspears PA, SB and Old; tables in garden *(the Didler)*

KIDLINGTON [SP4914]

Kings Arms [The Moors, off High St (not the Harvester out on the Bicester Rd)]: Welcoming local with enjoyable wkdy lunchtime food from sandwiches to a few basic hot meals and good value daily roast, well kept Greene King IPA, Ind Coope Burton and a guest beer, homely lounge, proper public bar; occasional barbecues in courtyard *(Pete Baker)*

KINGSTON BAGPUIZE [SU4098]

Hinds Head [Witney Rd]: Small welcoming country pub, two unpretentious rooms with good value meals in no smoking bar and restaurant from toasties and baguettes up, well kept Greene King beers, quick service; plenty of picnic-sets in good-sized garden with two water features and play area *(Mr and Mrs G S Ayrton, Marjorie and David Lamb)*

LITTLE COXWELL [SU2893]

Eagle [just off A420 SW of Faringdon]: Pleasantly refurbished airy bar, comfortable sofa and armchairs among other furnishings on polished boards, friendly service, well kept Archers and Bass, well chosen wines, new chef doing enjoyable generous food inc good value Sun lunch in bar and attractive no smoking restaurant, dogs welcome in bar; 10 bedrooms with own bathrooms, charming thatched village *(Andrea Houghton, Peter and Audrey Dowsett, Charlie Harman)*

Plough [A420 just SW of Faringdon]: Quick kind friendly service, nice old stone-built core with big log fire, good blackboard choice of reasonably priced food, two or three well kept ales, daily papers, large back dining extension; pool, games machines, piped music; children allowed in conservatory with bowls, swings in big garden, no dogs *(Gill and Keith Croxton, Peter and Audrey Dowsett, CMW, JJW)*

LITTLE MILTON [SP6100]

☆ *Lamb* [3 miles from M40, junction 7: A329 Thame—Wallingford]: Pretty 17th-c thatched pub with beams, stripped stone, low windows, soft lighting, lots of tables on two levels for wide choice of food (all day Sun – very busy then) from sandwiches to good specials and steaks, well kept Adnams, Castle Eden and Marstons Pedigree, decent wines; no piped music, children in eating area (good choice for them), peaceful and attractive garden with swings, pleasant countryside *(Franklyn Roberts, Ian Phillips, BB)*

LONG WITTENHAM [SU5493]

Vine [High St]: New French landlords adding gallic flair in food and wine to traditional pub atmosphere in cosy and comfortable two-level beamed bar, plenty of pictures and bric-a-brac, prompt friendly service, well kept Greene King ales *(Philip Kingsbury)*

LONGWORTH [SU3899]

☆ *Blue Boar* [Tucks Lane]: Cosy beamed and thatched country local with plenty of character, firmly wooden furnishings inc scrubbed tables and traditional settle by one of the two good log fires, good value food inc good puddings and evening and wknd specials, well kept Morrells Oxford Blue, friendly quick service, charming Australian landlady; may be piped music; quiet village *(Franklyn Roberts)*

Lamb & Flag [off A420 Faringdon—Kingston Bagpuize]: New tenants doing good choice of good value food inc all-day carvery, open fire, friendly service; children welcome, tables outside *(Marjorie and David Lamb)*

LOWER HEYFORD [SP4824]

Bell [Market Sq]: Friendly uncluttered refurbished rooms around central beamed bar, good range of generous enjoyable food inc some interesting dishes, well kept Adnams Broadside, Bass and Greene King Abbot; disabled access and facilities, charming creeper-clad building in small village square of thatched cottages, bedrooms, nearby Oxford Canal walks *(Denzil Martin, Ian Phillips, Mrs Roxanne Chamberlain)*

MIDDLE BARTON [SP4425]

Carpenters Arms [North St]: Thatched village inn, open-plan bar of some character with chamber-pot collection, wide choice of generous popular food, Greene King Abbot, Marstons Pedigree and Theakstons Best, no smoking restaurant; bedrooms *(Steve Harvey)*

MIDDLETON STONEY [SP5323]

☆ *Jersey Arms* [Ardley Rd (B430/B4030)]: Successful combination of small 19th-c stone-built country hotel with friendly pub; relaxing atmosphere in pleasantly 'rusticated' bar, beams, oak flooring and some stripped stone, nice tables, sofa and daily papers, good inglenook log fire, good range of interesting if not cheap home-made fresh food from well filled baguettes up, friendly owner and staff, efficient service, well kept Boddingtons, good wine list and coffee, attractive largely no smoking two-level

dining room; piped music, popular for business lunches, car park across road; tables in courtyard and garden, comfortable bedrooms *(George Atkinson, BB, Maysie Thompson, Simon J Barber, Barry and Anne Cooper)*

MILCOMBE [SP4034]

☆ *Horse & Groom* [off A361 SW of Banbury]: Bustling beamed and flagstoned village local with friendly Australian licensees, nice atmosphere with settee and pub parrot, landlady does good reasonably priced bar food from sandwiches to steaks, well kept Greene King IPA and Ruddles, and good largely Australian wine choice, separate coffee menu, inglenook woodburner, new restaurant; occasional live music; children welcome, lots of tables out in front, bedrooms (they can organise fishing) *(Mrs C Watson, Chris Glasson, BB)*

MINSTER LOVELL [SP3211]

Old Swan [just N of B4047 Witney—Burford]: Old inn's interesting bar with cheery welcome, secluded seating areas in variety with deep armchairs and rugs on flagstones, well kept Hook Norton Old Hooky, log fire, enjoyable lunchtime snacks and light meals, restaurant; tables in lovely garden, bedrooms, attached to Old Mill Conference Centre *(LYM, Nigel and Sue Foster)*

MURCOTT [SP5815]

Nut Tree [off B4027 NE of Oxford]: Charming beamed and thatched medieval building, opened into one big space inside; well kept ales such as Batemans XB, Hook Norton Best, Timothy Taylors Landlord and West Berkshire Mr Chubbs, decent wines, log fire, small back conservatory-style no smoking restaurant; rather expensive food (not Mon), piped music, no children inside; pretty garden with terrace, pond and aunt sally, cl Sun evening *(LYM)*

NORTHMOOR [SP4202]

Red Lion [B4449 SE of Stanton Harcourt]: Refurbished 15th-c stone-built village pub with thriving local atmosphere, good choice of enjoyable low-priced down-to-earth food inc good value Sun lunch, well kept ales such as Batemans XXXB, friendly landlord and locals, heavily beamed bar and small dining room off, welcoming log fire; walkers welcome, no dogs, Thurs morning post office; garden *(Dick and Madeleine Brown, Geoff Pidoux, T R and B C Jenkins)*

OXFORD [SP5006]

Albion [Hollybush Row]: Friendly local doing well under newish landlord, well kept real ales, back games room *(Chris Glasson)*

☆ *Bear* [Alfred St/Wheatsheaf Alley]: Intimate low-ceilinged and partly panelled 16th-c rooms, not over-smart and often packed with students; thousands of vintage ties on walls and beams, simple lunchtime food most days inc sandwiches (kitchen may be cl Weds), well kept changing ales such as Adnams, Fullers London Pride and Hancocks HB from centenarian handpumps on recently renewed pewter bar counter, no games machines; upstairs ladies'; tables outside, open all day summer *(LYM, R Huggins, D Irving, E McCall, T McLean)*

Chequers [off High St]: Narrow pub with several interesting areas on three floors, from smart new lounge part with leather armchairs to some interesting gothic sculpture, woodwork and stained glass; five well kept real ales, games room with two pool tables, table footer and balcony; juke box; walled garden with water feature *(R Huggins, D Irving, E McCall, T McLean)*

Crown [Cornmarket St]: Remaining part of former coaching inn with medieval origins, well kept Bass, good choice of usual food from toasted baps and baked potatoes up, pleasant service, long bare-boards bar; piped music; tables out in courtyard *(Kevin Blake, Neil and Anita Christopher)*

☆ *Eagle & Child* [St Giles]: Busy pub with nice panelled front snugs, tasteful stripped-brick modern back extension with no smoking conservatory, well kept Greene King Abbot and Old Speckled Hen, Ind Coope Burton, Marstons Pedigree and Wadworths 6X, plentiful quickly served food, newspapers, events posters, tiny mid-bars full of actors' and Tolkien/C S Lewis memorabilia; piped music *(R Huggins, D Irving, E McCall, T McLean, Chris Glasson, Meg and Colin Hamilton, BB, GHC)*

Grapes [George St]: Traditional pub, some original features, lots of theatrical posters and memorabilia, bar snacks, well kept Morrells *(Patrick Hancock, Kevin Blake)*

Harcourt Arms [Cranham Terr]: Friendly local with proper landlord and some character, pillars dividing it, good value snacks, well kept Fullers ales, open fires, well reproduced piped jazz, good choice of board games *(Jonathan Ives, Pete Baker)*

Hobgoblin [St Aldates]: Small interesting pub with friendly welcome and good atmosphere, three well kept Wychwood ales and up to four guest beers; open all day, good value food till 6pm (may be a wait), wkdy student discount till 8, special beer price Tues *(Tim and Ann Newell, M Joyner, Keith Reeve, Marie Hammond)*

☆ *Isis Tavern* [off Donnington Bridge Rd; no car access]: Early 19th-c former farmhouse in charming waterside spot, log fire, lots of mainly nautical bric-a-brac hanging from high ceiling and covering the walls; well kept real ales, daily papers, sensibly placed darts and bar billiards in one corner, other traditional games; may be piped pop music, TV; children in all-day eating areas, bowling alley, picnic-sets out on heated terrace and in garden, swings, slide, aunt sally by arrangement, open all day (unless winter weather poor) *(R M Gibson, LM, Tim and Ann Newell, LYM)*

Jude the Obscure [Walton St]: Decent food from snacks, wraps and baguettes up, Greene King IPA, Ruddles County and Abbot and two guest beers; no under-18s *(Tim and Ann Newell)*

Lamb & Flag [St Giles/Banbury Rd]: Attractive old pub owned by nearby college, modern in front with big windows over street, more atmosphere in back rooms with exposed stonework and panelled ceilings, well kept real ales, good value well served food, cheerful service; can be packed with students *(Chris Glasson, R Huggins, D Irving, E McCall, T McLean, GHC)*

☆ *Rose & Crown* [North Parade Ave]: Lots of atmosphere, good honest well priced lunchtime home cooking inc Sun roasts and particularly well kept Adnams and Ind Coope Burton in friendly and unspoilt old local; decent wine, prompt service from long-serving enthusiastic and concerned bearded landlord and wife; reference books for crossword buffs, no piped music, machines or mobile phones, jazz piano Tues; traditional small rooms, pleasant back yard with little end eating room, also motorised awning and huge gas heater – children not allowed here or inside unless with friends of landlord *(R Huggins, D Irving, E McCall, T McLean, Torrens Lyster, BB, R E M Lawson)*

Three Goats Heads [Friars Entry, St Michaels St]: Steps up to charming little upper bar, clean and sparkling, with light panelling, ceiling plasterwork and booths of elegant bench seats, political prints and architectural drawings showing details of the work, well kept cheap Sam Smiths, good choice of quick generous food, friendly helpful service; cheery downstairs bar (cl afternoons) with bare boards, TV, fruit machine and piped music *(Dr and Mrs M E Wilson, Kevin Blake)*

Watermans Arms [South St, Osney]: Unpretentious riverside pub nr Osney Lock, well kept Greene King ales, good value home cooking, tables outside *(Alan Kilpatrick)*

☆ *White Horse* [Broad St]: Bustling and studenty, squeezed between bits of Blackwells bookshop; single small narrow bar with snug one-table raised back alcove, mellow oak beams and timbers, ochre ceiling, beautiful view of the Clarendon building and Sheldonian, good lunchtime food (the few tables reserved for this), good range of well kept beers, Addlestone's cider, friendly licensees *(R Huggins, D Irving, E McCall, T McLean, BB)*

PISHILL [SU7389]
☆ *Crown* [B480 Nettlebed—Watlington]: Wisteria-covered ancient building with black beams and timbers, restful décor, log fires and candlelight, good home-made food from filled baguettes inc carefully chosen ingredients and local venison, well kept ales such as Fullers London Pride and Hook Norton; children welcome in restaurant, pleasant bedroom in separate cottage, picnic-sets on attractive side lawn, pretty country setting – lots of walks *(Susan and John Douglas, Dr and Mrs M W A Haward, LYM, the Didler)*

PLAY HATCH [SU7476]
Crown: Good choice of enjoyable food changing monthly in spacious rambling olde-worlde 16th-c pub, very popular with families (though no high chairs); two bars and several rooms inc barn extension restaurant and big no smoking conservatory, well kept Brakspears PA, SB and Old tapped from the cask, decent wines, welcoming service with hi-tech aids

(wireless computer food orders to kitchen); pleasant garden with play area *(J and B Cressey, Joan Thorpe)*

RADCOT [SU2899]

Swan [A4095 2½ miles N of Faringdon]: Welcoming Thames-side pub with enjoyable food from generous baguettes up, friendly newish landlord, well kept Greene King (not so cheap), log fire, lots of stuffed fish; children in eating area; pleasant waterside garden, summer boat trips (lift to bring wheelchairs aboard), four good value bedrooms *(LYM, P Michelson)*

ROTHERFIELD PEPPARD [SU7181]

Dog [Peppard Common]: Small low-beamed 17th-c pub nr green, big fireplace, horsebrasses, dog prints, well kept Bass and Greene King Old Speckled Hen, very quickly served good food from sandwiches, baguettes and generous filled baked potatoes up, pleasant staff and landlord, small restaurant; may be piped music; tables out in front and in attractive side garden *(John Roots)*

SATWELL [SU7083]

☆ *Lamb* [2 miles S of Nettlebed; follow Shepherds Green signpost]: Cosy and attractive 16th-c low-beamed cottage, very small, with tiled floors, pine furniture, family photographs, friendly licensees, huge log fireplace, fresh generous lunchtime food from filled baguettes up, well kept Brakspears, traditional games, small carpeted family room; a couple of cats, a bit twitchy – perhaps because of the very active poltergeist; tables outside, occasional barbecues *(Susan and John Douglas, LYM, Mr and Mrs M Renton)*

SHENINGTON [SP3742]

☆ *Bell* [off A422 W of Banbury]: 17th-c two-room village pub in style and mood (heavy beams, part with flagstones, some stripped stone and pine panelling, coal fire, friendly dogs and informal service), though functioning largely as a restaurant these days, mainly wholesome home cooking by the landlady – often booked solid on Sun; good sandwiches too, low-priced Hook Norton Best, relaxed atmosphere, cribbage, dominoes; children in eating areas, tables out in front, small attractive back garden, bedrooms, good surrounding walks, cl Mon lunchtime *(Sir Nigel Foulkes, LYM, Karen and Graham Oddey, John Kane, Don and Val Brace, Martin Jones, Dr John West, John Bramley, Theocsbrian, David and Helen Wilkins)*

SHILTON [SP2608]

Rose & Crown [off B4020 S of Burford]: Mellow 17th-c low-beamed stone-built village local, small beamed bar with tiled floor, woodburner and inglenook, neat small dining area, good choice of reasonably priced food (should book for Sun roasts), well kept Greene King beers, quick friendly service, darts; tables in garden, nice setting opp pond in pretty village *(Marjorie and David Lamb, Peter and Audrey Dowsett, Barry Collett)*

SHIPLAKE [SU7476]

☆ *Flowing Spring* [A4155 towards Play Hatch and Reading]: Well kept Fullers ales in pleasantly countrified pub, open fires in small

traditional two-room bar, good value food from good fresh sandwiches up, friendly staff, children welcome in bright modern sun room with floor-to-ceiling windows overlooking the water meadows; no mobile phones, steps up from car park; picnic-sets out on heated deck and on lawn *(June and Robin Savage, LYM, Martin and Karen Wake)*

SHIPLAKE ROW [SU7478]

White Hart [off A4155 W of Shiplake]: Relaxed and friendly, three connecting rooms mainly set for good unchanging choice of food (just roasts Sun lunchtime), cheerful staff, well kept Brakspears, decent house wines, log fires; interestingly planted back garden, nice location, fine views, boules, good walks *(June and Robin Savage, Wombat)*

SHIPTON-UNDER-WYCHWOOD [SP2717]

☆ *Lamb* [off A361 to Burford]: Small welcoming dining pub with stylish décor and furnishings, exotic flower displays and elegant candle holders, some stripped stone and log fire, ambitious food (not cheap, and vegetables extra) from enterprising bar snacks to daily fresh brixham fish, Greene King IPA, Ruddles Best and County and perhaps a guest beer, no smoking restaurant in Elizabethan core; piped music, children and dogs welcome, jazz Sun night; tables outside, charming bedrooms at a price, good breakfast *(John Bowdler, Mrs Citroen, Chris Glasson, Arnold Benett, Maysie Thompson, LYM)*

SHUTFORD [SP3840]

☆ *George & Dragon* [Church Lane]: Ancient stone-built pub comfortably refurbished by new licensees and doing well, vaulted flagstoned bar and oak-panelled beamed dining room, good enterprising fresh food with flexible menu and Sun lunches, Fullers London Pride, Hook Norton Best and a guest beer, fine choice of wines by the glass; children and dogs welcome, small garden, cl Mon, open all day Sun *(Mr and Mrs G Olsson, JHBS)*

SOUTH MORETON [SU5588]

☆ *Crown* [off A4130 or A417 E of Didcot; High St]: Rambling old open-plan village pub with friendly licensees and atmosphere, well kept beers, some tapped from the cask, such as Badger Tanglefoot and Wadworths 6X, decent wines and coffee, wide range of good fresh home-made food from sandwiches up (OAP discounts), good service; piped music, Mon quiz night; children allowed, small garden *(Marjorie and David Lamb, DMH, Dudley and Moira Cockroft)*

SOUTH STOKE [SU5983]

☆ *Perch & Pike* [off B4009 2 miles N of Goring]: Relaxing brick and flint dining pub just a field away from the Thames, comfortable cottagey low-beamed bar with open fires and well kept Brakspears and a guest beer, enjoyable home-made bar food, also more elaborate menu where children allowed, friendly staff; may be piped music; tables out on terrace and flower-bordered lawn *(Franklyn Roberts, Derek Harvey-Piper, LYM, John Hale, Dave Braisted)*

SPARSHOLT [SU3487]
☆ *Star* [Watery Lane]: Comfortable 16th-c country pub, tidy and smart but relaxed, short choice of good freshly made food, well kept beers inc a guest, daily papers, log fire, attractive pictures, horse-racing talk; may be subdued piped music; back garden, pretty village – snowdrops fill churchyard in spring *(John Brightley, Marjorie and David Lamb)*

STANDLAKE [SP3902]
Black Horse [High St]: Several real ales, huge food choice from sandwiches hot or cold to imaginative blackboard dishes, three large rooms (one no smoking for families), chatty friendly landlady and smiling service, no piped music *(Peter and Audrey Dowsett, Mr and Mrs J S Roberts)*

STANTON HARCOURT [SP4105]
Harcourt Arms [Main Rd]: Restauranty pub doing well since recent reopening under new management, plenty of room around the bar as well as welcoming, attractive, simply furnished and pleasantly informal dining areas with huge fireplaces, well kept real ales; children welcome *(Franklyn Roberts, Peter and Audrey Dowsett, LYM)*

STEEPLE ASTON [SP4725]
☆ *Red Lion* [off A4260 12 miles N of Oxford]: New landlord keeping up standards in refreshed but still comfortably traditional beamed and panelled bar, well kept Hook Norton Best and Everards Tiger, above-average wines, malt whiskies and brandies, enjoyable food (not Sun evening or Mon) from sandwiches and some good lunchtime dishes to evening no smoking restaurant (children allowed here); suntrap front terrace *(JHBS, Michael Jones, LYM)*

STEVENTON [SU4791]
Cherry Tree [B4017 (High St); village signed off A34 S of Abingdon via A4130]: 18th-c pub with well kept Wadworths IPA, JCB and 6X, perhaps a guest beer, decent wines, generous quickly served well priced food inc sophisticated dishes and good vegetarian choice, open-plan beamed areas around island bar, flagstones and bare boards, mix of furniture inc heavily carved settles and brocaded dining chairs, dark green walls, open fires, old prints and stuffed creatures; fruit machine, may be unobtrusive piped music in public bar; tables out on terrace, open all day Fri-Sun *(Marjorie and David Lamb, BB)*
North Star [Stocks Lane, The Causeway, central westward turn off B4017]: Charmingly unspoilt pub partly destroyed in a bizarre incident with a JCB digger on New Year's Night 2002/3; being rebuilt as we go to press to match its original Grade I listed layout, with tiled entrance corridor, built-in settles, parlourish lounge and simple dining room; when it reopens, expect Greene King ales tapped from casks in a side room, cheap wkdy lunchtime bar food; tables on side grass, front gateway through living yew tree *(LYM)*

STOKE LYNE [SP5628]
☆ *Peyton Arms* [from minor road off B4110 N of Bicester fork left into village]: Largely unspoilt stone-built pub with friendly landlord, simple home-made lunchtime food as well as filled cobs, well kept Hook Norton beers (full range) tapped from casks behind small corner bar in sparsely decorated front snug, tiled floor, inglenook log fire, hops on beam, bigger refurbished room with darts, dominoes and cribbage, charity book store; well behaved children and dogs welcome, no mobile phones, pleasant garden with aunt sally; cl Mon/Tues lunchtimes *(Susan and John Douglas, Pete Baker, the Didler, Paul and Ann Meyer)*

STOKE ROW [SU6784]
Cherry Tree [off B481 at Highmoor]: Unspoilt basic village local in pretty tiled cottage, some low heavy black beams and flagstones, small coal or log fires, couple of steps up to homely parlour with shelves of china, children allowed here and in carpeted games room with pool, darts and fruit machine, well kept Brakspears BB, Mild and SB tapped from casks in back stillage room, well priced sandwiches and soup; piped pop music; picnic-sets out on pleasant green *(the Didler, Ian Phillips, BB)*

☆ *Crooked Billet* [Nottwood Lane, off B491 N of Reading – OS Sheet 175 map ref 684844]: Rustic pub layout with heavy beams, flagstones, antique pubby furnishings and great inglenook log fire, but in practice a restaurant – good, with wide choice of well cooked interesting meals inc good value lunch, attentive welcoming service, well kept Brakspears tapped from the cask (no bar counter), decent wines, relaxed homely atmosphere – like a French country restaurant; children welcome, occasional live music, big garden by Chilterns beechwoods *(Chris Doyle, James Alcock, Stewart Tyler, LYM, D and M T Ayres-Regan, Mrs E A Macdonald, John Hale, the Didler)*

STOKE TALMAGE [SU6899]
Red Lion [signed from A40 at Tetsworth]: Basic old-fashioned country local, very friendly and cheerful; small bare-boards public bar (can get crowded), well kept Hook Norton and lots of changing guest beers from small corner servery, chatty landlord, open fire, prints, posters, darts, shove-ha'penny and other games, carpeted modern lounge; tables under cocktail parasols in pleasant garden, cl lunchtime Mon-Thurs *(Pete Baker, Torrens Lyster, the Didler)*

STONOR [SU7388]
Stonor Hotel [B480, off A4130 NW of Henley]: Upmarket 18th-c small hotel, stylish and sophisticated, with thoroughly modern décor, welcoming young South African staff, cool leather banquettes, pouffes and other smart seating in bar with daily papers, Brakspears PA, good wines by the glass (though cocktails may spring to mind) and lamps like Cork St sculptures, well reproduced piped pop music, good inventive food here or in elegant restaurant in shades of silver and biscuit, long back conservatory looking over appealing garden; good bedrooms *(Susan and John Douglas, BB)*

SUTTON COURTENAY [SU5094]

☆ *Fish* [Appleford Rd]: Civilised well run restaurant rather than pub, small front bar opening into attractive three-part dining room, nice prints (and even the hopeful labrador's collar) toning in with the dark green décor, good fresh-cooked food with some emphasis on fish, starters that can double as interesting bar snacks, good attractively priced house wines, cheerful landlord and pleasant well trained staff, stylish back conservatory; children welcome, tables out in terrace arbour and on neat lawn *(T R and B C Jenkins, Dr W J M Gissane, C A Hall, BB, Peter B Brown)*

☆ *George & Dragon* [Church St]: Chatty upmarket 16th-c local in same family as the Fish, with attractive mix of furnishings, dark beams, candles and nice log fire in main bar, good choice of fair-priced home-made food from thick sandwiches up inc popular Sun lunch, well kept Greene King IPA, Morlands and Old Speckled Hen and Ruddles, good wine choice, welcoming landlord, two further rooms; no dogs, restaurant, big back terrace overlooking graveyard where Orwell is buried – church worth a visit but may be locked *(David H T Dimock, Tom Shebbeare, BB)*

SWERFORD [SP3731]

Masons Arms [A361 Banbury—Chipping Norton]: Spotlessly kept smartly refurbished dining pub, brightly modernised bar with light wooden floors, rugs, stone fireplace, spotlighting, and comfortable blue armchairs around big round tables in light wood, doors open on to a small terrace, and steps lead down into a plank-walled room with chunky tables and big mirrors; round the other side of the bar is a roomy candlelit dining room, with great views; well kept Hook Norton Best, and a decent wine list; hard-working staff; behind is a neat square lawn with picnic-sets, and countryside views *(Robert Gomme, David Gough, LYM)*

SWINBROOK [SP2811]

☆ *Swan* [back road 1 mile N of A40, 2 miles E of Burford]: Softly lit little beamed and flagstoned 16th-c pub prettily set by a bridge over the Windrush, antique settles, sporting prints and woodburner in friendly tap room with flagstones (even so, no muddy shoes allowed) and back dining bar, good attractively presented food (all day wknd) inc interesting specials, well kept Archers Best, Greene King IPA or Old Speckled Hen, Hook Norton Best and Wadworths 6X, farm ciders, decent wines, cheery laid-back service, traditional games, magazines, no piped music; can get very busy on sunny wknds; seats by the lane and in small pretty side garden *(Matthew Shackle, R Huggins, D Irving, E McCall, T McLean, Martin and Karen Wake, Lawrence Pearse, R and S Bentley, LYM, John Kane)*

SYDENHAM [SP7201]

☆ *Crown* [off B4445 Chinnor—Thame]: Relaxed low-beamed village local popular for good home-made food inc Fri/Sat fresh fish, welcoming attentive service, well kept Greene King beers, above-average wines, open fires in

long narrow bar; may be quiet piped music, dominoes, darts, quiz and dress-up theme nights; children welcome, small garden with roses and climbing frame, views of lovely church, picturesque village *(Howard Dell, Rodney Baker-Bates, BB, John and Glenys Wheeler, Marjorie and David Lamb)*

TACKLEY [SP4720]

Gardeners Arms [Medcroft Rd, off A4260]: 17th-c village pub with wide choice of food from sandwiches and baguettes up, efficient service even when busy, comfortable spick and span lounge bar with beams, brasses and coal-effect gas fire in inglenook, well kept Morrells, prints, brasses, old photographs and cigarette cards; separate public bar with darts, TV and fruit machine, piped music, bookable skittle alley; picnic-sets on sunny terrace, handy for Rousham House *(Marjorie and David Lamb)*

TETSWORTH [SP6801]

Red Lion [A40, not far from M40 junction 7]: Friendly local refurbished under new landlord, something of a bistro feel with plenty of candles, but drinkers feel comfortable here too, with good beer choice inc well kept Greene King IPA, decent wines, increasingly popular food with some imaginative dishes, log fire *(Torrens Lyster, B Allen)*

THAME [SP7006]

Old Trout [High St]: Attractive timbered and thatched building, upmarket restaurant not pub, but it does have a small bar with ancient flooring tiles and big inglenook log fire, and something of a pubby atmosphere in its nice collection of small higgledy-piggledy heavily beamed dining rooms; French chef doing good food inc good value set lunches and interesting dishes, good choice of wines and coffee; young canadian staff, keg beer, piped pop music; six bedrooms *(Richard and Margaret Peers, BB, Betty Hampton, B H and J I Andrews)*

Rising Sun [High St]: Nicely freshened up under good new management, three linked rooms with flagstones and bare boards, Brakspears real ales inc a seasonal one, good wines by the glass, new kitchen majoring on an incredible range of sausages from old favourites to exotic novelties (not Mon evening); open all day *(Tim and Ann Newell)*

THRUPP [SP4815]

☆ *Boat* [off A4260 just N of Kidlington]: Stone-built local in lovely surroundings by Oxford Canal (can get very busy), good value decent food from good baguettes up, well kept Morrells, decent wine, coal fire, old canal pictures and artefacts, bare boards and stripped pine, no piped music; good folk night 2nd Sun, occasional theatre; restaurant, nice garden behind with plenty of tables, some in shade *(Denzil Martin, M Joyner, Pete Baker)*

WALLINGFORD [SU6089]

Royal Standard [St Marys St]: New regime in refurbished town pub with contemporary airy décor and modern art, enjoyable food and wines, attentive service *(Alan Reavill)*

WANTAGE [SU4087]

☆ *Royal Oak* [Newbury St]: Welcoming take-us-as-you-find-us two-bar local with lots of ship photographs and naval hatbands, particularly well kept ales such as Bass or Marstons Pedigree, Wadworths 6X and two beers brewed for the pub by West Berkshire, landlord really knows his beers, lunches Fri-Sat; table football, darts, cribbage; has been cl wkdy lunchtimes, bedrooms *(BB, Dick and Madeleine Brown, the Didler)*

Shoulder of Mutton [Wallingford St]: Friendly and chatty local, sympathetically refurbished to keep its character, coal fire and racing TV in bar, passage to two small snug back rooms, well kept Greene King and guest beers, popular food; tables outside, bedrooms *(Pete Baker, the Didler)*

WARBOROUGH [SU6093]

Six Bells [The Green S; just E of A329, 4 miles N of Wallingford]: Low-ceilinged thatched pub facing cricket green, attractive country furnishings in interconnecting seating areas off bar, well kept Brakspears and a guest beer, decent wines, welcoming efficient service, enjoyable food; big log fire, antique photographs and pictures; tables in back orchard *(Franklyn Roberts, LYM, Marjorie and David Lamb)*

WATLINGTON [SU6994]

Carriers Arms [Hill Rd]: Good choice of cheap well cooked food in giant helpings from sandwiches through enormous bargain omelettes to full meals (free range eggs for sale too); genial landlord, friendly efficient young staff, well kept Adnams and Black Sheep, thriving local atmosphere; garden tables looking up to Chilterns, high kite-feeding table (plenty of them circling), good walks *(Dick and Madeleine Brown)*

Chequers [3 miles from M40 junction 6, via B4009; Love Lane]: Attractive rambling bar with character seating and a few good antique oak tables, low beams and candles, well kept Brakspears PA, SB and a seasonal beer, very wide choice of nicely presented food from sandwiches through extremely hot chilli to steaks and popular Sun lunch, steps down to further eating area, vine-hung conservatory (children allowed here); picnic-sets in very pretty garden, nice walks nearby; more reports please *(LYM, D and M T Ayres-Regan, Wombat)*

WEST HENDRED [SU4489]

Hare [A417, outside village]: Civilised and welcoming open-plan pub, low-ceilinged main bar with bare boards and big terracotta tiles, partly divided by timber studding, pleasantly individual seating as well as wheelback and captain's chairs, a good mix of dark heavy tables, comfortable parquet-floor dining area, enjoyable food; well kept Greene King IPA, Abbot and Morlands Original on handpump, decent wines by the glass, efficient friendly service, piped music; there's a long seat in a colonnaded verandah, and picnic-sets are among small trees in side garden *(Canon Michael Bourdeaux, Peter B Brown, LYM)*

WESTCOTT BARTON [SP4325]

Fox [Enstone Road; B4030 off A44 NW of Woodstock]: Spacious stone-built village pub, low beams and flagstones, pews and high-backed settles, well kept Greene King Abbot, Hook Norton, John Smiths and guest beers, log fires, usual food from sandwiches to steaks, small no smoking restaurant (children allowed here); piped music, steps down to lavatories; open all day Thurs-Sun, pleasant garden with water feature, play area and peaceful view *(Dave Braisted, Steve Harvey, LYM)*

WITNEY [SP3510]

☆ *Three Horseshoes* [Corn St, junction with Holloway Rd]: Friendly and attractive 16th-c stone-built pub with heavy beams, flagstones, log fires, simple comfortable well polished old furniture, consistently good home-made food from filled baguettes, ciabattas and other pubby lunchtime choices to more imaginative restaurantry dishes, well kept Greene King Abbot and Morlands Original and a guest beer, decent house wines, separate dining room *(LYM, George Cowie, John and Janet Davey)*

WOLVERCOTE [SP5009]

☆ *Plough* [First Turn/Wolvercote Green]: Lots of comfortably well worn in pubby linked areas, warm and friendly, with bustling atmosphere, armchairs and Victorian-style carpeted bays in main lounge, good varied inexpensive food esp soups and fresh seafood in flagstoned ex-stables dining room and library (children allowed here), well kept real ales, decent wines, traditional snug, woodburner; picnic-sets on front terrace looking over rough meadow to canal and woods *(Franklyn Roberts, BB, Peter and Audrey Dowsett)*

WOODSTOCK [SP4416]

Feathers [Market St]: Formal Cotswold hotel with attractive period furnishings, no smoking restaurant, nice bedrooms; relaxed unstuffy atmosphere and log fire in old-fashioned back Courtyard Bar with stylish bar food (not Sat evening) and good drinks choice, opening on to charming sunny courtyard garden; children welcome, piped music, high prices *(John Bowdler, LYM, Robin and Joyce Peachey, Ian Phillips)*

Star [Market Pl]: Big cheerful beamed town pub, decent food all day from good filled baguettes up, lunchtime salad bar and popular family Sun lunch, well kept beers inc Wadworths 6X, bare boards, some stripped stone, daily papers, open fires; piped music, quiz machine, TV; bedrooms clean and spacious, good breakfast *(BB, Mr and Mrs J McRobert, Ian Phillips, Geoff Pidoux)*

WOOLSTONE [SU2987]

☆ *White Horse* [village signed off B4507]: Plushly refurbished partly thatched 16th-c pub with steep Victorian gables, two big open fires in spacious beamed and part-panelled room with quite a variety of décor styles, wide choice of decent quickly served food, friendly relaxed staff and black labrador, well kept Wadworths 6X and a guest such as Hook Norton Best, decent wines, lots of whiskies, good coffee, log fire; quiet piped music, no visiting dogs; children allowed in eating area, sheltered garden, four charming good value bedrooms, big breakfast, secluded interesting village handy for walkers to White Horse and Ridgeway *(BB)*

WOOTTON [SP4320]

☆ *Killingworth Castle* [Glympton Rd; B4027 N of Woodstock]: Striking three-storey 17th-c coaching inn, good local atmosphere, well kept Greene King ales, decent house wines, friendly service, wide choice of generous food, long narrow main bar with pine furnishings, parquet floor, candles, lots of brasses and log fire with books above it, bar billiards, darts and shove ha'penny in smaller games end, pleasant garden; Fri folk night, jazz 1st and 3rd Weds, music some other nights too; bedrooms *(Pete Baker, BB, JHBS)*

WROXTON [SP4141]

☆ *North Arms* [Mills Lane; off A422 at hotel, pub at back of village]: Pretty thatched stone pub nicely placed in peaceful corner of lovely village, with attractive quiet garden (and you can walk in the abbey gardens opposite during term time); good fresh well prepared food, well kept Greene King, log fire, nice wooden furnishings, character restaurant; may be unobtrusive piped music *(LYM, K H Frostick)*

WYTHAM [SP4708]

☆ *White Hart* [off A34 Oxford ring road]: More restaurant than pub, modern food all day, rather expensive but generous and good value with delicious puddings, busy no smoking dining area (children allowed here), log fire in gently updated bar with handsome panelling and flagstones, helpful staff, well kept real ales, good value house wines; open all day, pretty garden with big tables and solid fuel stove in covered eating area, may be summer barbecues, unspoilt preserved village *(Mark and Maggie Selinger, LYM, Ian Phillips)*

The letters and figures after the name of each town are its Ordnance Survey map reference. *Using the Guide* at the beginning of the book explains how it helps you find a pub, in road atlases or large-scale maps as well as in our own maps.

Shropshire

Shropshire has an interesting range of pubs, from stylish town pubs to chatty country taverns in beautiful scenery, and from old-world charm to up-to-date modernity. You can find some very good food, and great local beer. Pubs on particularly fine form these days include the Burlton Inn (careful enlargement under way, and very good food), the lively Malthouse in Ironbridge (excellent staff, good music nights, and gaining a Place to Stay Award this year), the Sun at Norbury (a new entry, surprisingly elegant for such remote walking country – good food, and a nice place to stay), the Armoury in Shrewsbury (imaginative food and a great range of drinks in this civilised and interesting warehouse conversion), and the good value Three Fishes there (a fine old building, much enjoyed for its entirely no smoking policy). It is the Armoury in Shrewsbury that wins the title of Shropshire Dining Pub of the Year. A couple of other pubs to mention for good food are the Crown at Hopton Wafers, and the appealing little Lime Kiln at Porth-y-waen, which gains its Food Award this year. In the Lucky Dip section at the end of the chapter, pubs to note particularly are the Yew Tree at All Stretton, restauranty Pheasant in Broseley, Coalbrookdale Inn in Coalbrookdale, foody Old Gate at Heathton, Bear in Hodnet, Church Inn in Ludlow and George & Dragon in Much Wenlock. Drinks prices tend to be comfortably below the national average here, with pubs brewing their own beer (the Six Bells in Bishop's Castle) or having it brewed next door (the Plough at Wistanstow) standing out as good value, and a proliferation of interesting and sensibly priced local brews such as Hobsons, Woods, Salopian, Hanby and Worfield.

BISHOP'S CASTLE SO3289 Map 6

Castle Hotel 🛏

Market Square, just off B4385

This substantial early 18th-c stone coaching inn at the top of the town is neatly kept and attractively furnished. There is an immediate sense of welcome in the clubby little beamed and panelled bar glazed off from the entrance, with a good coal fire, old hunting prints and sturdy leather chairs on its muted carpet. It opens into a much bigger room, with maroon plush wall seats and stools, big Victorian engravings, and another coal fire in an attractive cast-iron fireplace. The lighting in both rooms is gentle and relaxing, and the pub tables have unusually elaborate cast-iron frames; they have shove-ha'penny, dominoes, cribbage and board games, and no piped music. On our most recent inspection visit they had well kept Hobsons Best, local Six Bells Big Nevs and Worthington 1744 on handpump, and around 40 malt whiskies. A short choice of enjoyable bar food includes soup (£3), liver pâté (£4.50), filled baguettes (from £4.75), very tasty steak and kidney pie (£7.45), cheese, leek and mushroom sausages with sun-dried tomato sauce (£8.45), salmon fillet poached in white wine (£8.50), and venison in port and Guinness (£8.95). The handsome no smoking panelled dining room is open in the evening and on Sunday lunchtime. In summer the pub is festooned with pretty hanging baskets, and there are a couple of picnic-sets in the reworked back garden, which has two terraces on either side of a large formal raised fish pond, pergolas and climbing plants, and stone walls; it looks out over the town rooftops to the surrounding gentle countryside. The old-fashioned bedrooms are spacious; good breakfasts, and kind friendly service. *(Recommended by Paul A Moore, the Didler, Steve Whalley, Kevin Thorpe, Christopher and Jo Barton, Tim Maddison, MDN, Mrs S Butcher)*

Mitchells & Butlers ~ Licensees David and Nicky Simpson ~ Real ale ~ Bar food (12-1.45, 6-8.45) ~ (01588) 638403 ~ Children welcome ~ Dogs allowed in bar ~ Open 11(12 Sun and in winter)-2.30, 6-11 ~ Bedrooms: £37.50B/£65S

Six Bells ◖

Church Street

Although the no-frills interior of this former coaching inn is quite well worn, the cheery bustle of chatty locals (it can be packed here at the weekend) and busy bar staff generate a good heart-warming atmosphere. Perhaps the main attraction is the excellent beer brewed here – so well liked that some are stocked by other pubs in the area. Big Nevs is most people's favourite, and you'll also find Marathon, Cloud Nine and Duck & Dive. You can arrange a tour of the brewery, and they have a beer festival once a year. They also keep a wide range of country wines. The pub consists of just two simple rooms. One bar is really quite small, with simple furniture and old local photographs and prints; this is no smoking at meal times. The second, bigger room has bare boards, some stripped stone, a roaring woodburner in the inglenook, plenty of locals on the benches around plain tables, darts and lots of board games (they have regular Scrabble nights). Bar food might include soup (£2.50), hearty sandwiches (from £2.50), fidget pie (£6), sausage and mash (£6.50), filo basket filled with ginger stir-fried vegetables (£7.50), medallions of lamb with tarragon, parsley and red wine sauce or grilled halibut with asparagus and cream sauce (£9), and good home-made puddings; they use organic suppliers wherever possible. More reports please. *(Recommended by J Taylor, the Didler, Jane and Adrian Tierney-Jones, Pauline Davies, Kevin Thorpe, Steve Whalley, Ron and Val Broom)*

Own brew ~ Licensees Neville and Colin Richards ~ Real ale ~ Bar food (12-2, 6.30-9; not Sun evening or Mon) ~ Restaurant ~ No credit cards ~ (01588) 630144 ~ Children welcome ~ Folk third Fri in month and live music first Mon in month ~ Open 12-2.30, 5-11; 12-11 Sat; 12-10.30 Sun; closed Mon lunchtime

Three Tuns ◖

Salop Street

You can't miss the four-storied Victorian brewhouse across the yard from this friendly pub. As we went to press it was not functioning (though it is likely to restart), so the beers were being brewed for them by Hobsons, still using their flavoursome recipes: well kept Three Tuns XXX, Offa, Sexton and a seasonal ale with the odd guest beer such as Hobsons itself are served by old-fashioned handpumps. They also do bottled Clerics Cure, Little Tun and Bellringer; you can get carry-out kegs, and there are sales by the barrel or cases of Clerics Cure. An annual beer festival takes place in July, with morris dancers in the yard. Popular with chatty locals, the no-frills beamed rooms are very simply furnished with low-backed settles and heavy walnut tables, and there are newspapers, cribbage, shove-ha'penny, dominoes, backgammon and cards. Served by sociable staff, changing bar food might include sandwiches from (£3.50), various home-made pâtés (£4.25), grilled goats cheese with onion marmalade (£4.25/£8), fish soup (£4.50), pork and ale sausages (£7), well liked beef in ale (£7.50), daily fresh fish (around £9) and good organic steaks (£12), with puddings such as summer pudding (£4); they use locally grown vegetables. There's a small garden and terrace, which has been renovated with new seating. The outside gents' is not suitable for disabled people. The bedrooms are in converted stables: you have to stay for two nights, and breakfast is self-catering. *(Recommended by Barry Lane, Pat and Tony Martin, the Didler, Kevin Thorpe, Jane and Adrian Tierney-Jones, Christopher and Jo Barton, Margaret and Andrew Leach, G Coates, Karen and Graham Oddey, Chris and Maggie Kent, MDN)*

Free house ~ Licensee Jan Cross ~ Real ale ~ Bar food (not Mon/Tues or Sunday evening) ~ Restaurant ~ (01588) 638797 ~ Children in eating area of bar and restaurant ~ Dogs allowed in bar ~ May be live music in function room Fri or Sat ~ Open 12-3, 5-11; 12-11(10.30 Sun) Sat ~ Bedrooms: £50B/£50B

BRIDGES SO3996 Map 6
Horseshoe ✦

Near Ratlinghope, below the W flank of the Long Mynd

This nicely tucked away country pub is just the place for a good pint after a refreshing walk on the Long Mynd which rises up behind. The picturesque streamside setting among deserted hills in good walking country is the draw for many, particularly walking groups, though you'll find locals here too. Warmed by a cosy fire and the chatty landlord's welcome, the down-to-earth yet comfortable bar has interesting windows, lots of pictures and toby jugs, and well kept Adnams Bitter, Shepherd Neame Spitfire and Timothy Taylors Landlord on handpump, as well as several malt whiskies and farm and bottled cider; a small dining room leads off from here; darts and piped music. Served in very generous helpings, straightforward tasty bar food includes sandwiches (from £2.10), soup (£2.75), ploughman's (£5.50), gammon, egg and pineapple, scampi or steak and kidney pie (£6.50), specials such as vegetable and stilton bake (£5.95), and puddings (from £2.75); the chips are particularly good. Tables are placed out by the little River Onny, and the pub is handy for Stiperstones. *(Recommended by Karen and Graham Oddey, Kevin Thorpe, Gloria Bax, Keith Jacob, Tim Maddison, John and Jenny Pullin, MLR)*

Free house ~ Licensee Colin Waring ~ Real ale ~ Bar food (12-3, 6-9; 11-9 Sat/Sun) ~ (01588) 650260 ~ Children welcome ~ Dogs welcome ~ Open 11(12 Sun)-11; closed 25 Dec

BROMFIELD SO4877 Map 6
Cookhouse ♀

A49 2 miles NW of Ludlow

From the outside this handsome brick house looks like an immaculately maintained Georgian home; inside is a rather interesting contemporary take on the traditional inn. The front section has been brightly modernised in minimalist city style, but the back part is more traditional – though still with a modern edge. During the day the focus is on the dining room, café-bar in style, with modern light wood tables, and a big open kitchen behind the end stainless steel counter. A door leads through into the bar, sparse but neat and welcoming, with round glass tables and metal chairs running down to a sleek, space-age bar counter with fresh flowers, newspapers and spotlights. Then it's down a step to the pubbier part, where traditional features like the huge brick fireplace, exposed stonework, and soaring beams and rafters are appealingly juxtaposed with wicker chairs, well worn sofas and new glass tables. Friendly staff serve well kept Hobsons Best and Town Crier on handpump, and the good wine list includes eight by the glass; they also have a good choice of coffees and teas. Some areas are no smoking; piped jazz, daily papers. Very good well presented bar food includes sandwiches, baguettes or soup (from £3.95), salmon with tagliatelle and dill and mushroom sauce or pizza topped with roast vegetables (£7.95), venison and pork sausages with elderberry wine sauce and bubble and squeak (£8.95), and duck breast on red cabbage with plum sauce (£10.95); you can have two courses for £11.50. An attractive secluded terrace has tables under cocktail parasols and a fish pond. By the time this *Guide* is in the shops 15 new bedrooms will be open. More reports please. *(Recommended by Kevin Thorpe, John Whitehead, Christopher and Jo Barton)*

Free house ~ Licensee Paul Brooks ~ Real ale ~ Bar food (11-3, 6-10; 11-10 Sat/Sun) ~ Restaurant ~ (01584) 856565 ~ Children welcome ~ Open 11-11; 12-10.30 Sun ~ New bedrooms, see above

BURLTON SJ4626 Map 6

Burlton Inn ⓨ ◖ ⟷

A528 Shrewsbury—Ellesmere, near junction with B4397

Fairly major alterations were due to start at this well run inn just as we were going to press. The continued conscientious effort these welcoming licensees have put in over the years has seen its reward – they need more room to keep their customers as happy as ever. There will be a new snug and garden room, and a bigger kitchen can only be good news on the food side, which is already flourishing. Everything here seems meticulously arranged and cared for, from the pretty flower displays in the brick fireplace or beside the neatly curtained windows, to the piles of *Country Living* and interior design magazines left seemingly casually in the corner. There are a few sporting prints, spurs and brasses on the walls, open fires in winter and dominoes and cribbage. Well liked bar food from an interesting menu could include home-made soup (£3.25), mushrooms in garlic cream with brandy sauce on toasted brioche (£5.50), venison terrine with red onion and beetroot chutney (£5.95), steak and kidney pie or spiced lentil and tomato moussaka (£8.75), lemon sole fillet with thyme, leeks and white wine and cream of mussel sauce (£13.50), beef medallions with wild mushroom, madeira and crème fraîche (£15.95), and a good choice of home-made puddings. There may be two set-time evening sittings in the restaurant. Well kept Banks's and three continually changing guests from brewers such as Cottage, Greene King and Wye Valley. There are tables on a small lawn behind, with more on a strip of grass beyond the car park, and smart wooden furniture on the pleasant terrace. If you are staying, they do good breakfasts. *(Recommended by Mr and Mrs F Carroll, Mike and Mary Carter, A J Bowen, Janet and Peter Race, John and Caroline, S Horsley, Maurice and Della Andrew, I D Greenfield, R N and M I Bailey, Jason Caulkin)*

Free house ~ Licensee Gerald Bean ~ Real ale ~ Bar food (12-2, 6.30-9.45(7-9.30 Sun)) ~ Restaurant ~ (01939) 270284 ~ Children in eating area of bar and restaurant ~ Dogs allowed in bar and bedrooms ~ Open 11-3, 6-11; 12-3.30, 7-10.30 Sun; closed bank hol Mon lunchtimes; 25/26 Dec and 1 Jan ~ Bedrooms: £45B/£80B

CARDINGTON SO5095 Map 4

Royal Oak

Village signposted off B4371 Church Stretton—Much Wenlock, pub behind church; also reached via narrow lanes from A49

It's well worth the detour to this nice old place, which is tucked away in a lovely spot. In summer the frontage is ablaze with hanging baskets, and tables in the rose-filled front courtyard have lovely views over hilly fields. Licensed for longer than any other pub in Shropshire, the rambling, low-beamed bar has a roaring winter log fire, cauldron, black kettle and pewter jugs in its vast inglenook fireplace, the old standing timbers of a knocked-through wall, and red and green tapestry seats solidly capped in elm; darts, dominoes, and perhaps piped music. Hobsons and a couple of guests such as Cottage Golden Arrow and Salopian Heaven Sent are kept under light blanket pressure. As well as lunchtime snacks such as tasty filled baguettes (from £3.25), filled baked potatoes (from £3.50) and ploughman's (from £4.50), reasonably priced bar food includes soup (£2.50), home-made pâté (£3), vegetable kiev (£7), lasagne or grilled trout with buttered almonds (£7.50), steak and onion pie (£8), steaks (from £9.95), and puddings such as lemon sponge (from £2.65). A comfortable no smoking dining area has exposed old beams and studwork. A mile or so away – from the track past Willstone (ask for directions at the pub) – you can walk up Caer Caradoc Hill, which has great views. More reports please. *(Recommended by Mike and Heather Watson, Pete Yearsley, Patrick Hancock, Kerry Law, Simon Smith, TOH)*

Free house ~ Licensee Michael Carter ~ Real ale ~ Bar food (not Sun evening or Mon) ~ Restaurant ~ (01694) 771266 ~ Children in restaurant and eating area of bar during meal times ~ Open 12-2, 7(6 Fri)-11; closed Mon except bank hols

HOPTON WAFERS SO6476 Map 6
Crown 🍽 ♀ 🛏
A4117 Kidderminster—Ludlow

The streamside garden at this attractive creeper-covered inn is lovely in summer, with tubs of bright flowers and a duck pond, and pleasant terrace areas with tables under cocktail parasols. Inside, the emphasis is on the wide range of freshly prepared food, from a changing menu which could include soup (£3.50), prawn cocktail or stilton pâté (£4.75), roasted mediterranean vegetables with provençal sauce (£7.95), venison casserole (£8.75), thai chicken (£9.95), half a shoulder of lamb with mint and mango (£11.95), puddings such as bakewell tart or fruit crumble (£3.75), and blackboard specials. The restaurant menu is more elaborate (with prices to match). Neatly kept with an understated atmosphere, the cosy cream-painted beamed bar has a large inglenook fireplace, dark wood furniture, oil paintings, and fresh flowers. The restaurant has another impressive inglenook and pretty table settings, and is no smoking; piped music. Well kept Banks's, Hobsons and Woods Shropshire Lad alongside a guest such as Timothy Taylors Landlord on handpump, and ten wines by the glass. *(Recommended by John Hale, Barry Smith, Dr T E Hothersall, Gill and Tony Morriss, Joe Green, Steve Whalley, Neil Skidmore, Ian and Nita Cooper)*

Free house ~ Licensee Howard Hill-Lines ~ Real ale ~ Bar food (12-2.30, 6.30-9.30) ~ Restaurant ~ (01299) 270372 ~ Children in eating area of bar ~ Open 12-3, 6-11; 12-11(10.30 Sun) Sat ~ Bedrooms: £47.50B/£75B

IRONBRIDGE SJ6704 Map 6
Malthouse ♀ 🛏
The Wharfage (bottom road alongside Severn)

Plenty goes on at this big lively eating and music place. The live music (every night except Monday and Tuesday) is mostly jazz, but may also be funk, latin or world music. The lobby and stairwell are exhibition spaces for interesting local artists – the only criteria for showing here is that the owner likes the pictures and that the artist helps hang the paintings. A nice touch is that they don't charge the artist a commission. Readers are very impressed by the happy, hard-working staff, who are obviously inspired by the enthusiastic young licensees – between them they generate a very cheery atmosphere. We are all praise too for a place that is flexible enough to do you a sandwich on a Sunday, even if their Sunday menu doesn't actually include them. Spotlessly kept, the spacious bar is broken up by pine beams and concrete pillars, and has lots of scrubbed light wooden tables with candles; piped music. An appropriately informal menu includes home-made soup or potato wedges (£3.25), chilli and goats cheese fritter with red pepper dressing (£4), chorizo tortilla (£4.75), cheese and bacon burger (£6.25), pork spare ribs with honey and ginger sauce (£6.95), thai fishcakes (£7.25), moroccan beef stew (£7.50), grilled plaice with parsley butter (£9.95), and puddings such as chocolate bread and butter pudding (£3.95). The atmosphere is quite different in the restaurant, most of which is no smoking, and which has a much more elaborate menu. Well kept Boddingtons, Flowers Original and a guest such as Hook Norton Old Hooky on handpump, and a wide choice of wines including about eight by the glass. There are a few tables outside in front. *(Recommended by Mr and Mrs G S Ayrton, Mike and Linda Hudson, M Joyner, Ron and Val Broom, Sue and Geoff Price, Tony Ounsworth, Mike and Wendy Proctor)*

Free house ~ Licensees Alex and Andrea Nicoll ~ Real ale ~ Bar food (12-2.30, 6.30-9.30) ~ Restaurant ~ (01952) 433712 ~ Children in eating area of bar and restaurant ~ Dogs allowed in bar ~ Live jazz and world music Weds-Sat evenings ~ Open 11-3, 6-11; 11-11 Sat; 12-10.30 Sun; closed 25 Dec ~ Bedrooms: £55B/£65B

Places with gardens or terraces usually let children sit there – we note in the text the very few exceptions that don't.

LONGVILLE SO5393 Map 4
Longville Arms

B4371 Church Stretton—Much Wenlock

Friendly service and a warm welcome engender a very comfortable feel at this pleasant pub. The two neatly kept spacious bars have stripped beams and original stone, and the lounge bar on the left has dark plush wall banquettes, cushioned chairs and some nice old tables. The room on the right has oak panelling, and a large no smoking dining room (with disabled access) overlooks the terrace. The shortish bar menu includes tasty dishes such as soup (£2.25), home-made pâté or fried brie wedges (£3.50), stuffed tuscan peppers (£6.95), steak and ale pie (£7.25), salmon with herb crust (£8.75) and home-made puddings such as spotted dick (£2.50). Three well kept real ales might include Courage Directors, Timothy Taylors Landlord and Charles Wells Bombardier on handpump; also several malt and irish whiskies. A games room (no children in here) has a juke box, darts, pool and dominoes, and there's piped music. A terraced side garden has picnic-sets next to two big trampolines in an entertaining children's play area. The countryside around here is really quite beautiful. *(Recommended by TOH, DJH, David Field, Maurice and Della Andrew, Gene and Kitty Rankin, John Whitehead, Dr D Parker)*

Free house ~ Licensees Chris and Wendy Davis ~ Real ale ~ Bar food (12-2.30, 7(6 Sat and summer Suns)-9.30) ~ Restaurant ~ (01694) 771206 ~ Children in eating area of bar and restaurant ~ Dogs welcome ~ Open 12-3, 7-12; 12-4, 6(7 Sun in winter)-12 Sat/Sun ~ Bedrooms: £30S/£48S

LUDLOW SO5175 Map 4
Unicorn

Corve Street – the quiet bottom end, beyond where it leaves the main road to Shrewsbury

The solidly beamed and partly panelled bar with its huge log fire in a big stone fireplace gives this busy 17th-c inn a real feel of age, and a nice mix of friendly locals and visitors generates an appealingly sociable atmosphere. Well kept Greene King Old Speckled Hen, Hancocks HB and a guest such as Timothy Taylors Landlord are served on handpump, and under new licensees bar food includes home-made soup (£3.25), sandwiches (from £3.75), garlic mushrooms (£4.25), tortilla wraps (£6.25), ploughman's (£6.50), chilli (£6.95), pistachio nut pasta or ham in parsley sauce (£7.25), and puddings such as apple crumble (£3.50); the timbered candlelit restaurant is no smoking; cribbage and dominoes. Tables outside shelter pleasantly among willow trees on the pretty little terrace right next to the modest River Corve. Parking in this picturesque town may be tricky. *(Recommended by Amanda Eames, Joe Green, Nick Holding, Karen and Graham Oddey, Alan Thomas, Mr and Mrs P Lally, Mr and Mrs R Wilson, Roland Curtis, Elaine Thompson, James Morrell, David Twitchett, Jo Rees, MLR, Mrs S Butcher, Dick and Madeleine Brown, W W Burke)*

Free house ~ Licensees Mike and Rita Knox ~ Real ale ~ Bar food (12-2.15, 6(7 Sun)-9.15) ~ Restaurant ~ (01584) 873555 ~ Children in eating area of bar and restaurant ~ Dogs allowed in bar ~ Open 12-3, 6-11; 12-3.30, 7-10.30 Sun; closed 25 Dec

MUCH WENLOCK SO6299 Map 4
Talbot 🛏

High Street

Known in a previous life as Abbott's Hall, this ancient place dates back in part to 1360, and was once part of Wenlock Abbey. A flower-festooned coach entry leads off the High Street to a little courtyard with green metal and wood garden furniture and pretty flower tubs – then on into the bar, where friendly licensees, cheery locals and two big log fires in inglenooks all contribute to the warmly inviting atmosphere. The several neatly kept areas have low ceilings, and comfortable red tapestry button-back wall banquettes around their tables. The walls are decorated with prints of fish and brewery paraphernalia, and there are art deco-style lamps and gleaming brasses. They usually serve well kept Bass and a guest from Enville or Woods on handpump, and they've several malt whiskies; quiet piped music. Served in large helpings, tasty bar food includes sandwiches with nice fresh salad (from £3.20), filled baked potatoes (from £4.50), steak sandwich (£5.50), thai fishcakes (£7.50) and poached salmon (£8.95) at lunchtime. The evening menu is more elaborate (and not as cheap) and includes dishes such as smoked salmon (£5.95), pork done with calvados (£12.95) and cumberland duck (£13.95); the dining area is no smoking. There is a cheap car park behind the pub. *(Recommended by John and Judy Saville, John Oates, Tim Maddison, Andrea and Guy Bradley, Nigel B Thompson, Gill and Tony Morriss, Mike and Heather Watson, Mike and Wendy Proctor)*

Free house ~ Licensees Mark and Maggie Tennant ~ Real ale ~ Bar food (12-2.30, 7-9.30) ~ Restaurant ~ (01952) 727077 ~ Children welcome ~ Open 10-3, 6-11; 10-11 Sat; 12-10.30 Sun; 10-3, 6-11 Sat winter; 12-3, 6-10.30 Sun winter; closed 25 Dec ~ Bedrooms: £35B/£70B

NORBURY SO3692 Map 6
Sun 🛏

Off A488 or A489 NE of Bishop's Castle; OS Sheet 137 map reference 363928

This quiet Shropshire village, tucked away in remote walking country below the Stiperstones (there's a good unusual route up from here), is an unexpected place to find such a civilised and soigné dining pub. The restaurant side has a charming lounge with button-back leather wing chairs, easy chairs and a chesterfield on its deep-pile green carpet. The log fire, nice lighting, willow-pattern china on the dark oak dresser, fresh flowers, candles and magazines quickly make you feel at home. The elegantly furnished dining room serves a shortish choice of good food, and a separate bar menu is also short: baguettes (£3.95), cumberland sausage (£5.60), vegetable samosa (£5.95), smoked trout (£6.50), scampi (£6.95) and rump steak (£7.50). A proper tiled-floor bar has brocaded wall seats, cushioned stone seats along the wall by the flame-effect stove, and a few of those mysterious implements that it's fun to guess about on its neat white walls. Alongside is a tiled pool room with shove-ha'penny; gentle piped music. Well kept Wye Valley Hereford and a guest such as Woods Shropshire Lad on handpump, and decent house wines; friendly service. *(Recommended by John and Angela Main, Dr T E Hothersall)*

Free house ~ Licensee Carol Caham ~ Real ale ~ Bar food (7-9; 12-2 summer Sats and Sun) ~ Restaurant ~ (01588) 650680 ~ Children in the bar lunchtimes only ~ Dogs allowed in bar ~ Open 7-11; 12-3, 7-11 Sat/Sun; cl Sat lunchtime and Sun evening in winter; closed Mon exc bank hol lunchtimes, Tues-Fri lunchtimes ~ Bedrooms: £35S/£70S

NORTON SJ7200 Map 4
Hundred House ♀ 🛏

A442 Telford—Bridgnorth

Hops and huge bunches of dried flowers and herbs hang from beams, and bunches of fresh flowers brighten the tables and counter in the neatly kept bar of this immaculately restored old brick pub. Handsome fireplaces have log fires or working coalbrookdale ranges (one has a great Jacobean arch with fine old black cooking pots), and a variety of interesting chairs and settles with some long colourful patchwork leather cushions are set out around sewing-machine tables. Steps lead up past a little balustrade to a partly panelled eating area, where the stripped brickwork looks older than that elsewhere; the main dining room is no smoking; shove-ha'penny, cribbage, dominoes. A good range of drinks includes Heritage Bitter (brewed for them by a small brewery) which is well kept alongside a couple of guests such as Highgate Mild, Old and Saddlers and Robinsons Best on handpump, an extensive wine list with house wines by the carafe, half carafe and big or small glass, farm cider and lots of malt whiskies. The outstanding cottagey gardens (with old-fashioned roses, trees, herbaceous plants, and a big working herb garden that supplies the kitchen – you can buy bags of their herbs for £1 and the money goes to charity) are well worth a visit in themselves. Bar food includes soup (£3.95), chicken liver pâté with brioche and chutney (£4.95), local pork sausages and mash (£7.95), steak and kidney pie or chargrilled cajun chicken with sweet red pepper coulis, mint yoghurt and fennel salad (£8.95), daily specials such as pork, apple, leek and ham pie (£9.95) and puddings such as treacle tart or tiramisu (from £4.95). You must book for the restaurant, though you can eat from its menu in the bar: griddled scallops with sweet pepper coulis, bacon and jerusalem artichoke sandwich and caesar salad (£7.95) and duck breast with orange sauce, confit duck and black pudding (£17.95). *(Recommended by David Field, Peter and Patricia Burton, Lynda and Trevor Smith, Alun Howells, Patrick Hancock, Mike and Wendy Proctor)*

Free house ~ Licensee the Phillips family ~ Real ale ~ Bar food (12-2.30, 6-9.30) ~ Restaurant ~ (01952) 730353 ~ Children welcome ~ Open 11-11(10.30 Sun) ~ Bedrooms: £85B/£125B

PORTH-Y-WAEN SJ2623 Map 6
Lime Kiln 🍴

A495, between village and junction with A483, S of Oswestry

Attention to detail and their natural flexibility when it comes to customers' needs should bring the licensees at this good-natured pub the success they deserve. Good inventive blackboard food (using lots of local produce) might include leek and potato soup (£2.25), duck livers wrapped in bacon with hot and sour beetroot (£3.95), thai crab cakes with cucumber relish (£4.50), grilled bass on crispy noodles with roasted pepper dressing (£8.95), fillet steak medallions with shallot and red wine jus (£12.95), and puddings such a sticky toffee pudding with butterscotch sauce (£3.75). The carefully opened up interior is simple but neat and tidy with some stripped joists and pine dado, a mix of small chairs and cushioned pews and settles around big scrubbed deal tables on quarry tiles, and warm coal fires. A bare-boards no smoking corner has a big photograph of the local lime quarry a century ago, and throughout there are attractive mainly local photographs on the apricot walls – with a big photograph of the Beatles in their earliest days (who may also feature in the quiet piped music). Fullers London Pride and Wadworths 6X are well kept on handpump, they have a good value wine list, and the coffee in big mugs is good. There are picnic-sets out in a side garden with a boules pitch and terraced lawn; the sociable dog is called Blue. More reports please. *(Recommended by Margaret and Andrew Leach, Mrs Suzy Miller)*

Free house ~ Licensees Ian and Jane Whyte ~ Real ale ~ Bar food (12-2, 6-9; 12-3, 5.30-9 Sat; 12-4 Sun) ~ Restaurant ~ (01691) 831550 ~ Children in eating area of bar and restaurant ~ Open 12-3, 5.30-11; 12-11(10.30 Sun) Sat; closed Mon

SHREWSBURY SJ4912 Map 6
Armoury 🍴 ♀ 🍺

Victoria Quay, Victoria Avenue

Shropshire Dining Pub of the Year

This grand 18th-c warehouse didn't start life on this site, but was moved from the Armoury Gardens in 1922. Long runs of big arched windows in the uniform red brick frontages have views across the broad river at the back, and are interspersed with brick columns, hanging baskets and smart coach lights at the front. The open-plan interior is spacious and light, with a mix of wood tables and chairs on expanses of stripped wood floors, a dominating display of floor-to-ceiling books on two huge walls, a grand stone fireplace at one end, and masses of old prints mounted edge to edge on the stripped brick walls. Colonial fans whirr away on the ceilings, which are supported by occasional green-painted standing timbers, and glass cabinets display collections of explosives and shells. The long bar counter has an eye-catching range of drinks, including well kept Boddingtons, Wadworths 6X, Woods Shropshire Lad and up to five changing guest beers from brewers such as Potton, Roosters and Thwaites on handpump, a good choice of wines (with 15 by the glass), around 50 malt whiskies, a dozen different gins, lots of rums and vodkas, a variety of brandies, and some unusual liqueurs. As well as sandwiches with interesting fillings (from £3.75), the bar menu might include soup (£3.25), smoked haddock and salmon fishcake with tomato and onion salad or ham hock, herb and mustard terrine (£3.95), local sausages and mash (£6.45), grilled bass fillet with rocket, spinach, potato and orange salad (£6.50), black olive, goats cheese and sun-dried tomato pasta with sautéed leeks and herb butter (£7.45), baked chicken breast with banana and bacon, sweet potato mash and sweetcorn (£9.95), braised lamb shank with redcurrant gravy (£11.25), and puddings such as lemon tart with raspberry sauce, bread and butter pudding, tiramisu, and crushed meringue and fresh strawberries (from £3.95). Tables at one end are laid out for eating. It gets busy here in the evening, particularly at weekends, when there may even be queues outside. The pub doesn't have its own parking but there are metered spaces up nearer the Quarry. *(Recommended by Dave Irving, I D Greenfield, Tony Ounsworth, Mrs Jean Clarke, Michael Butler, Darly Graton, Graeme Gulibert, Kevin Blake, Mike and Mary Carter, M Joyner, SLC, Geoffrey and Penny Hughes)*

Brunning & Price ~ Manager Jill Mitchell ~ Real ale ~ Bar food (12-2.30, 6-9.30; 12-9.30(9 Sun) Sat) ~ (01743) 340525 ~ Children welcome ~ Open 12-11(10.30 Sun)

Three Fishes

Fish Street

Totally no smoking, this extensively refurbished timbered and flagstoned town pub has been an inn since the 16th c – you can feel its age in the slope of the flagstones under its carpeting. The bar has hops on its profusion of heavy beams, lots of interesting photographs, posters and prints on white walls, dark wood tables and chairs and brocaded wall banquettes. They serve well kept Adnams, Fullers London Pride and Timothy Taylors Landlord, alongside a couple of guest beers from brewers such as Cottage and Oakham; decent house wines. Good value simple robust food includes soup (£2.75), filled baked potatoes (from £3.75), ratatouille and cheese (£5.75), sausage and mash or lambs liver (£5.95), steak and ale pie (£6.10) and salmon fillet (£6.95). Service is quick, cheerful and warmly welcoming, and at lunchtime the pub is popular with an older set enjoying the smoke-free atmosphere and no mobile phones rule; piped music. The ancient Bear Steps area is just around the corner. *(Recommended by Michael Butler, Tony Ounsworth, Sue and Geoff Price, Kevin Thorpe, the Didler, John Lunt, Janet and Peter Race, Derek and Sylvia Stephenson)*

Enterprise ~ Lease Adam Paul Wardrop ~ Real ale ~ Bar food (12-2(3 Sun), 6-8.30; not Sun evening) ~ (01743) 344793 ~ Children in eating area of bar ~ Open 11.30-3, 5-11; 11.30-11 Fri/Sat; 12-10.30 Sun

WENTNOR SO3893 Map 6

Crown 🛏

Village and pub signposted (not very clearly) off A489 a few miles NW of junction with A49

In lovely countryside, this village pub gives a fine view of the Long Mynd from seats on the neat back lawn. The location and the pretty bedrooms (which are very fairly priced) make this a nice place for a night's stay. Beams and standing timbers testify to the age of the building, which has been an inn since it was built in 1640. Much of the main bar area is laid for eating; one end has a snug area with pictures and two sofas, and there are good log fires. They serve well kept Hobsons Best, Greene King Old Speckled Hen, Salopian Shropshire Gold and Worthington Best on handpump, and have decent wines and a good choice of malt whiskies; piped music, dominoes. Under new licensees, bar food might include sandwiches (from £2.75), soup (£2.40), smoked salmon and dill quiche (£5.50), curry or home-made steak and ale pie (£6.50), chicken with leek and stilton sauce (£6.95), pork and apple casserole (£9.75), and home-made puddings such as lemon cheesecake or chocolate and ginger truffle slice (£2.95); the cosy beamed restaurant is no smoking. *(Recommended by Mike and Shelley Woodroffe, Barry and Verina Jones, Collin and Julie Taylor, Tim Maddison, John and Angela Main, DJH, Mrs P Antlett, MDN, John and Brenda Bensted)*

Free house ~ Licensees Mike and Chris Brown ~ Real ale ~ Bar food (12-2, 6-9) ~ Restaurant ~ (01588) 650613 ~ Children in eating area of bar and restaurant ~ Open 12-3, 7-11; 12-11(10.30 Sun) Sat ~ Bedrooms: £30S/£53S

WISTANSTOW SO4385 Map 6

Plough 🍴 🍺

Village signposted off A49 and A489 N of Craven Arms

This agreeable pub is simply furnished and spotlessly kept, with high rafters and cream walls, and a russet turkey carpet, oak or mahogany tables and chairs and welsh dressers to give the modernised bar a more homely feel; service is warm and friendly. Woods beers are brewed next door, so the Woods Parish, Plough Special, Shropshire Lad and seasonal ales are very well kept on handpump; also Addlestone's and Weston's cider and about 15 wines by the glass, including a rosé. The Hardings use local suppliers for their enjoyable english cooking which, from a nicely varied, seasonally changing menu, could include dishes such as soup (£3.20), terrine with home-made chutney (£5.75), steak and kidney suet pudding (£8.95), venison and red wine casserole (£9), baked salmon fillet with local asparagus and home-made mayonnaise (£10.25), grilled lamb steak with red wine jus (£10.95), and puddings such as coffee and walnut sponge with hot chocolate and espresso sauce or crème brûlée (£3.80). On Sundays, the menu is limited to two roasts, a fish and a vegetarian option. You can buy bottles of Woods beer to take away, and they also sell home-made chutney and marmalade. The games area has darts, pool, juke box, and fruit machine and piped music. There are some tables under cocktail parasols outside. *(Recommended by Ruth and Andrew Crowder, TOH, Debbie and Neil Hayter, Revd D Glover, C R Harrison, B and M Kendall, John Whitehead, Keith Berrett)*

Own brew ~ Licensee Denis Harding ~ Real ale ~ Bar food (12-2, 6.30-9; not Mon or Sun evenings) ~ Restaurant ~ (01588) 673251 ~ Children in eating area of bar ~ Dogs allowed in bar ~ Open 11.30-2.30, 6.30-11; 12-2.30, 7-10.30 Sun; closed Mon

Lucky Dip

Besides the fully inspected pubs, you might like to try these Lucky Dips recommended to us and described by readers (if you do, please send us reports: www.goodguides.com).

ALL STRETTON [SO4595]
☆ *Yew Tree* [Shrewsbury Rd (B4370)]: Comfortable beamed bars and dining room, houseplants and lots of pictures, good value food inc interesting vegetarian choice and some dishes in smaller helpings, cheerful service, well kept Hobsons Best and Wye Valley Butty Bach, good log fire, bookable dining room, lively public bar; children welcome, small village handy for Long Mynd, cl Tues *(TOH, Sarah and Peter Gooderham, C J Cox, A Monro)*
ASTON ON CLUN [SO3981]
Kangaroo [Clun Rd]: Large open-plan pub with central fireplace in main bar, front public bar with railway memorabilia inc a large model train over the fireplace, side games room with darts and pool, Roo (brewed for them by Six Bells in Bishop's Castle) and Charles Wells Bombardier, annual beer festival, food lunchtime and evening; juke box can be loud, can get smoky; open all day Fri-Sun, tables in large back garden *(Kevin Thorpe)*

ATCHAM [SJ5409]
Mytton & Mermaid: Comfortable and friendly, with good traditional food in bar and relaxed easy-going restaurant, well kept Greene King Ruddles and Woods Shropshire Lad, good wine choice, helpful staff, some theme nights; pleasant Severn-view bedrooms, nice setting opp entrance to Attingham Park (NT) *(Revd D Glover, Mr and Mrs P Lally)*
BONINGALE [SJ8102]
Horns [A464 S of Albrighton]: Three friendly bars with several well kept changing ales inc local brews such as Enville White and Salopian, wide choice of wholesome nicely presented food inc midweek specials, sizzling steaks and good quickly served Sun lunch, open fires, attractive panelled dining room; children welcome *(Andy and Jill Kassube, Arthur Baker)*
BRIDGNORTH [SO7293]
Bear [Northgate (B4373)]: Former coaching inn with well kept Adnams, Fullers London

Pride, Greene King IPA and Timothy Taylors Landlord, attractively priced pubby lunchtime food (not Sun) from sandwiches up, decent wines by the glass, helpful licensees, two unpretentious bars with wall banquettes and a mix of other furnishings, french windows to small sheltered lawn with picnic-sets; needs a no smoking area; bedrooms *(Theo, Anne and Jane Gaskin, LYM, MDN, Bruce M Drew)*

Golden Lion [High St]: Pleasantly decorated friendly traditional two-bar pub with well kept Banks's and a guest such as Woods Shropshire Lad, decent coffee, hearty helpings of standard bar food from basic sandwiches up; saucy pictures in gents', no music *(Gill and Tony Morriss)*

Habit [E Castle St]: Light and airy bistro atmosphere, big modern paintings on blue walls, welcoming staff, good unusual generous food (all day Sun) attractively served, enterprising children's choice, keenly priced wines by the glass, nice fireplace on upper level, clearly marked smoking area; piped jazz; nr top of Cliff Railway *(Mr and Mrs G S Ayrton)*

☆ *Railwaymans Arms* [Severn Valley Stn, Hollybush Rd (off A458 towards Stourbridge)]: Good interesting more or less local ales inc a Mild in converted waiting-room at Severn Valley steam railway terminus, bustling on summer days; coal fire, station nameplates, superb mirror over fireplace, tables out on platform; may be simple summer snacks, children welcome, wheelchair access; the train to Kidderminster (another bar there) has an all-day bar and bookable Sun lunches *(Kerry Law, Simon Smith, the Didler, Gill and Tony Morriss, LYM)*

BROOME [SO4081]

☆ *Engine & Tender*: Homely bar with well kept Woods from art deco servery, railway memorabilia and other bric-a-brac, cosy corners with tables for eating, also quite extensive restaurant with interesting collection of pottery inc teapots and shelves of jugs, good freshly made food (not Mon) inc generous Sun roast and lovely puddings, good value wines, cheerful unhurried service, forest of good-sized plants in conservatory, games room with pool and glassed-over well; caravan site with hook-up points and showers, nice countryside *(Mr and Mrs Robert Cooper, TOH, Pete Yearsley)*

BROSELEY [SJ6701]

☆ *Pheasant* [Church St]: Smartly done-up dining pub with small choice of good imaginative restaurant food inc seasonal game, small friendly bar, two rooms with sturdy seats, big stripped tables on oak boards, large oil paintings, log fires, candles and gas lamps, real ales, good wines; tasteful bedrooms; cl lunchtimes exc Sun, also Sun/Mon evenings *(Mr and Mrs P Lally, Sally Downes, Mike and Natasha Coussens, Mr and Mrs P Grant)*

BUCKNELL [SO3574]

☆ *Baron of Beef* [Chapel Lawn Rd; just off B4367 Knighton Rd]: Big log fire in front bar, spotless pleasantly refurbished back lounge with fresh flowers, interesting prints, rustic memorabilia inc grindstone and cider press,

good bar food inc enterprising dishes, largish upstairs restaurant with own bar and popular wknd carvery, well kept Greene King IPA, Hobsons and Woods Governors, farm cider, decent house wines, good welcoming service; live entertainment Sat, games bar with pool etc; views from big garden with play area *(Neil and Anita Christopher)*

BURWARTON [SO6185]

Boyne Arms [B4364 Bridgnorth—Ludlow]: Imposing Georgian coaching inn, generous good value straightforward home cooking, attractive prices, changing well kept ales such as Bass and local Hobsons and Woods, cheerfully unassuming local atmosphere, friendly helpful staff, public bar with pool; tables in large garden with good timber adventure playground, bedrooms *(Theo, Anne and Jane Gaskin, John Oates, Michael Mellers)*

CALVERHALL [SJ6037]

Old Jack [New St Lane]: Hard-working and friendly newish licensees, chef/landlord doing enjoyable home-made food changing monthly, log fire in bar with beams and button-back banquettes, arches to separate dining area opening on to terrace *(Nicchi Cannon)*

CLEOBURY MORTIMER [SO6775]

Kings Arms [A4117 Bewdley—Ludlow]: Warmly decorated open-plan bar with pews, bare boards and well spaced tables (some rather bright chairs, too), well kept log fire, enjoyable food using fresh local produce in beamed dining area stretching beyond island servery, welcoming hard-working young staff, well kept ales such as Hobsons; piped music, very popular with young people evenings; open all day, children welcome, garden with water feature, reasonably priced comfortable bedrooms *(R E and E C M Pick, LYM, Joe Green)*

CLUN [SO3081]

☆ *Sun* [High St]: Tudor beams and timbers, some well used but sturdy antique furnishings, interesting prints, enormous open fire in flagstoned public bar with cards and dominoes, good value generous food in larger carpeted lounge bar, well kept Banks's Bitter, Hobsons Best and a guest such as Marstons Pedigree; children allowed in eating area, tables in sheltered well planted back garden with terrace; lovely village, nice bedrooms, hearty breakfast, open all day wkdys *(A H C Rainier, Abi Benson, MLR, Kevin Thorpe, BB, the Didler)*

COALBROOKDALE [SJ6704]

☆ *Coalbrookdale Inn* [Wellington Rd, opp Museum of Iron]: Long flight of steps up to handsome dark brick 18th-c pub, simple, cheerful and bustling tiled-floor bar with local pictures, six well kept changing ales such as Adnams, Brains and Fullers London Pride from square counter also serving rather smaller room set more for the huge platefuls of good value often imaginative food (not Sun) from sandwiches to steaks; good log fire, farm cider, country wines, good mix of people, piano, remarkable bottled beer collection and amusing pub bric-a-brac, no piped music, naughty beach murals in lavatories; dogs welcome, opens noon *(DC, the Didler, BB)*

COALPORT [SJ6903]

☆ *Boat* [Ferry Rd, Jackfield; nr Mawes Craft Centre]: Cosy 18th-c quarry-tiled bar, coal fire in lovely range, good food inc meat, game and cheeses and good value Sun lunch, well kept Banks's Bitter and Mild and Marstons Pedigree, Weston's farm cider, darts; summer barbecues on big tree-shaded lawn, in delightful part of Severn Gorge, footbridge making it handy for Coalport China Museum *(BB, the Didler, G A and G V M A Taylor)*

CORFTON [SO4985]

☆ *Sun* [B4368 Much Wenlock—Craven Arms]: Unpretentious country local with well kept Corvedale ales such as Normans Pride, Dark & Delicious, Junior, Secret Hop and Divine Inspiration from brewery behind (tours available), well kept guest ales, friendly chatty landlord, wide choice of good value home-made blackboard food from generous baguettes to bargain Sun lunch, children's dishes, refurbished lounge with interesting prints, lively beamed bar, and dining room with no smoking area, beer bottle collection and covered well; tables on terrace and in good-sized garden with good play area; piped music; open all day, tourist information, particularly good disabled access throughout *(Pete Yearsley, BB, Michael and Jenny Back)*

CRESSAGE [SJ5904]

☆ *Riverside* [A458 NW]: Spacious upmarket pub with lovely Severn views from big conservatory and garden tables, pleasant mix of furnishings inside, relaxed atmosphere, lunchtime baguettes and more expensive hot dishes, interesting wine choice, real ales such as Hobsons Town Crier, Salopian Golden Thread and one brewed for the pub; comfortable bedrooms (steep stair to top floor), open all day wknds *(Mike and Mary Carter, Mr and Mrs G S Ayrton, Bill Fillery, Mr and Mrs M Stratton, Dave Irving, LYM, Chris Flynn, Wendy Jones)*

ELLESMERE [SJ3934]

☆ *Black Lion* [Scotland St; back car park on A495]: Good value simple cheap substantial food all day inc popular OAP bargains (also for children), pleasantly relaxed and well run beamed bar off tiled entrance corridor, interesting décor and some nice unusual features, quiet and comfortable roomy dining room, cheery enthusiastic young staff, well kept Marstons Bitter and Pedigree, restaurant; piped music; bedrooms, not far from canal wharf *(BB, Lynda Payton, Sam Samuells, John Andrew)*

GRINSHILL [SJ5223]

☆ *Inn at Grinshill* [off A49 N of Shrewsbury]: Recently renovated early Georgian inn, comfortable and welcoming bar (dogs allowed), no piped music or machines, good choice of beers and of enjoyable interesting food, well thought out selection of reasonably priced wines, good service, attractive restaurant with evening pianist and kitchen view, great views from garden; plans for

bedrooms, pretty village in popular walking/riding area *(Mr and Mrs P Lally)*

HADNALL [SJ5220]

Saracens Head [A49 6 miles N of Shrewsbury]: Snug and friendly, with interesting old photographs, enjoyable changing food, good service and wine choice, Burtonwood ales, restaurant with feature well *(Mr and Mrs F Carroll)*

HALFWAY HOUSE [SJ3411]

Seven Stars [A458 Shrewsbury—Welshpool]: Spotless and unspoilt, like a private house; very small bar with two high-backed settles by the gas fire, well kept cheap Burtonwood Best and Mild tapped from casks in the friendly owner's kitchen area, no food or music *(the Didler, RWC)*

HAMPTON LOADE [SO7486]

Lion: This fine riverside pub, a main entry in our 2003 edition, closed in Apr 2003 *(LYM)*

HEATHTON [SO8192]

☆ *Old Gate* [off B4176 W of Wombourn]: 17th-c, very popular for fresh well prepared food from lunchtime baguettes (not Sun, no food Sun evening) to traditional favourites and some interesting specials; plenty of tables packed into the two small main rooms (when these are all booked you may not be allowed to sit down for just a drink), two open fires, reddish décor (reflecting landlord's enthusiasm for Manchester United), friendly service, well kept Enville, Greene King Abbot, Olde Swan Entire and perhaps a guest beer, farm cider, wines from their own burgundy vineyard, golden retriever called Cromwell; children very welcome, colourful garden with picnic-sets and play equipment, cl Mon *(LYM, Mike and Mary Carter, Ian and Nita Cooper)*

HODNET [SJ6128]

☆ *Bear* [Drayton Rd (A53)]: Relaxing refuge from the busy road, small beamed quarry-tiled bar with log fire and Courage Directors, Theakstons Best and Youngs Special, broad arch to rambling open-plan carpeted main area with blond seats and tables set for eating (good range of reasonably priced well presented food from sandwiches up, well filled puddings cabinet), snug end alcoves with heavy 16th-c beams and timbers, friendly helpful service; may be faint piped radio; open all day, children welcome (high chairs and child-size cutlery), six good value comfortable bedrooms, opp Hodnet Hall gardens and handy for Hawkstone Park *(D L Mayer, BB, Mrs B M Needham, Neil Skidmore)*

IRONBRIDGE [SJ6703]

Golden Ball [Newbridge Rd/Wesley Rd, off Madeley Hill]: Interesting partly Elizabethan local at the top of the town, with good atmosphere, helpful landlord and friendly staff, well kept mainstream and more local beers, good choice of competitively priced substantial food from sandwiches to Sun roasts, real fire, quietish lunchtime, more lively evenings; children welcome, pleasant terraced walk down to river, comfortable bedrooms *(M Joyner, Gill and Tony Morriss)*

Horse & Jockey [Jockey Bank, off Madeley

road]: Cosy and welcoming, with plenty of atmosphere, good range of beers inc local Worfield Hopstone, enjoyable sensibly priced proper food inc real steak and kidney pie (none of your puff pastry floaters); should book evenings *(Pat and Sam Roberts)*

Robin Hood [Waterloo St]: Popular Severnside pub, five comfortable and attractive connecting rooms with various alcoves inc barrel-vaulted dining room, lots of gleaming brass and old clocks, well kept interesting changing ales, Stowford Press and Weston's Old Rosie ciders, food from lunchtime sandwiches to Sun carvery; attractive seating area out in front, nice setting handy for museums, bedrooms, good breakfast *(Andy and Jill Kassube, DC, Mike and Wendy Proctor)*

LEEBOTWOOD [SO4798]

☆ *Pound* [A49 Church Stretton—Shrewsbury]: Thatched 16th-c pub, extensively modernised inside, with banquettes and log-effect gas fire in roomy carpeted main bar, good value blackboard food from sandwiches to fresh fish, big no smoking restaurant area (good local roasts for Sun carvery), well kept ales such as Black Sheep, Greene King Old Speckled Hen and Timothy Taylors Landlord, Addlestone's cider, special offers on alcopops, good wine list (occasional tastings), friendly efficient staff, pool and juke box in brightly lit public bar, well reproduced piped pop music; tables in garden *(Dave Irving, TOH, BB)*

LEINTWARDINE [SO4175]

Jolly Frog [Toddings]: Distinctive yellow-green building with emphasis on enjoyably imaginative food esp fish, sensible prices and early evening bargains, cosy rural atmosphere, mix of table sizes, log fire, a beer brewed for the pub, good wine list, relaxed friendly and informative service; may be unobtrusive piped jazz *(Pete Yearsley, Christopher Woodward)*

LINLEY [SO6897]

☆ *Pheasant* [pub signed off B4373 N of Bridgnorth; Britons Lane]: Charming black and white country local in lovely spot, small choice of enjoyable straightforward home-made food, well kept changing ales such as Archers Summer and Wye Valley Hereford, hatch service to back room with pool, individual landlord; three steps down to back lavatories *(LYM, Ian and Nita Cooper)*

LITTLE STRETTON [SO4392]

☆ *Green Dragon* [village well signed off A49]: Well kept Bass, Wadworths 6X, Woods Shropshire Lad and quickly changing guest beers, reasonably priced food from good interesting baguettes up, cheap house wine, malt whiskies, helpful staff, children in eating area and restaurant; tables outside, handy for Cardingmill Valley (NT) and Long Mynd *(Margaret and Andrew Leach, DAV, Pamela and Merlyn Horswell, LYM)*

LLYNCLYS [SJ2823]

White Lion [junction A483/A495]: Good choice of food all day from baguettes up, Boddingtons and Worthington, friendly helpful young landlady, plush seats and pine tables, two small eating areas, games up on right; open all day *(Michael and Jenny Back)*

LOPPINGTON [SJ4729]

☆ *Dickin Arms* [B4397]: Warmly welcoming two-bar country local, comfortably plush banquettes, shallow steps to neat back dining room with good food inc inventive dishes and popular Sun lunch, good service, three real ales, open fire, pool and dominoes; babies and dogs welcome, play area outside, pretty village *(BB, Pamela and Merlyn Horswell)*

LUDLOW [SO5174]

Blue Boar [Mill St]: Big friendly rambling inn, lots of linked areas (one no smoking), bright and airy at the front, darker further back, country bygones and boar memorabilia, food from lunchtime sandwiches, baguettes and baked potatoes up, Greene King IPA and Abbot, hard-working staff; big bedrooms, open all day *(Joe Green, Martin Grosberg)*

☆ *Church Inn* [Church St, behind Butter Cross]: Cheerful and welcoming, nice décor with banquettes in cosy alcoves off central bar, pews and stripped stonework from church (even pulpit as part of bar), well kept ales such as Brains, Hook Norton Old Hooky, Weetwood Eastgate and Wye Valley, roaring trade in tea and coffee, helpful prompt service, enjoyable food inc good sandwiches and top-quality meats, no smoking restaurant; quiet piped music, car parking some way off; children welcome, open all day, nine comfortable bedrooms with further extension under way as we go to press, good breakfast *(Amanda Eames, J M and P M Carver, Joe Green, LYM, Martin Grosberg, P and D Carpenter, Mrs M M Westwood, Kevin Thorpe)*

Queens [Lower Galdeford]: Long town bar with tables and banquettes, pine tables in rather smartly mediterranean-feel dining area with decent food, friendly welcome, Greene King IPA *(Val and Alan Green, Joe Green)*

Wheatsheaf [Lower Broad St]: Traditional welcoming 17th-c beamed pub spectacularly built into medieval town gate, spotless housekeeping, generous usual food, good service, well kept ales inc Woods Shropshire Lad, choice of farm cider, restaurant; attractive bedrooms, warm and comfortable *(Karen and Graham Oddey, Alan Thomas, W W Burke, P and D Carpenter, Joe Green)*

MARSHBROOK [SO4489]

☆ *Station Hotel* [Marshbrook Industrial Estate signed over level crossing by B4370/A49, S of Church Stretton]: Solidly refurbished and comfortably traditional bar on right with well kept Boddingtons, Flowers Original and Salopian Shropshire Gold from high-gloss counter, prompt attentive service, log fire, some stripped stone; extensive eating areas on left, centred on separate modern glass-fronted café-bar with elegant metal-framed furniture on limestone flooring and a popular good value food counter with a good choice from warm baguettes through interesting light dishes up; piped music *(John Whitehead, BB, TOH)*

MUCH WENLOCK [SO6299]

Gaskell Arms [High St (A458)]: 17th-c beams, brasses, pubby décor and big brass-canopied log fire dividing the two rooms; good value food using local produce from generous baked potatoes and ploughman's to good Sun lunch in busy bars and civilised old-fashioned restaurant, friendly service, well kept Courage Directors and John Smiths, banknote collection; subdued piped music, fruit machine in lobby; immaculate roomy garden, bedrooms *(Pete Yearsley, Gloria Bax, John Whitehead)*

☆ *George & Dragon* [High St]: Lots of pictures, even a mural, timbering and beams with hundreds of jugs, antique settles among more conventional seats, snug old-fashioned no smoking rooms leading back past inglenook, popular food (not Sun or Weds evenings) from sandwiches up inc Sun roast, four well kept changing ales, country wines and fruit pressés; well behaved children welcome away from bar, open all day in summer *(LYM, Pete Yearsley, Steve Whalley, Mike and Wendy Proctor, Ian and Nita Cooper)*

Raven [Barrow St]: Small friendly hotel, welcoming landlord, good food and wines; bedrooms simple but comfortable, with own bathrooms *(G M Simon)*

MUNSLOW [SO5287]

Crown [B4368 Much Wenlock—Craven Arms]: Tudor beams, broad flagstones and cosy nooks and crannies in split-level dining lounge and stripped stone eating area, some emphasis on generous enjoyable food from baguettes up, friendly staff, good log fire, another in traditional snug, real ales; may be piped music; children welcome, attractive bedrooms, tables outside *(LYM, Debbie and Neil Hayter)*

NEENTON [SO6387]

Pheasant [B4364 Bridgnorth—Ludlow]: Charming village pub, well kept real ale, good reasonably priced food, quick friendly service, open fires in panelled lounge, plenty of regulars; restaurant *(Joyce and Geoff Robson)*

NESSCLIFFE [SJ3819]

Old Three Pigeons [off A5 Shrewsbury—Oswestry (now bypassed)]: Feeling its years (dates from 16th c), with two well worn in bar areas, brown sofas, mix of tables, log fires, well kept Moles real ale, very attentive staff, dining room with wide range of enjoyable and popular food inc bargains for two; juke box (not always switched on); children welcome, some tables outside, opp Kynaston Cave, good cliff walks *(John A Barker, David Heath, Graham and Lynn Mason, LYM, R Michael Richards)*

NEWCASTLE [SO2482]

☆ *Crown* [B4368 Clun—Newtown]: Friendly and pretty village pub with good mix of locals and campers, good value usual food inc tasty soups (just roast or good sandwiches on Sun) in quiet lounge bar, smart and spacious, with log fire and piped music; lively locals' bar with basic settles and flagstones, darts, pool and so forth in games room, well kept Tetleys, good coffee, efficient service, friendly great dane called Bruno; tables outside; charming well equipped bedrooms, good breakfast, attractive views and walks *(LYM, A N Bance)*

NORTHWOOD [SJ4633]

Horse & Jockey: Low-beamed country pub with simple décor, friendly and helpful young licensees, Banks's Bitter and Original and John Smiths, wide choice of popular straightforward food inc Tues-Fri lunchtime bargains for two, huge mixed grill (free if you finish it all) and good children's dishes in central lounge and plain dining area, nice fire, games room, lots of horse and jockey memorabilia; children and dogs welcome, play area *(Michael and Jenny Back)*

OSWESTRY [SJ2528]

Old Mill [Candy; minor road 3 or 4 miles W]: Country dining pub on Offa's Dyke path, good value food from soup and a roll to some inventive dishes (sells own sauces and pickles), well kept Bass and Greene King Old Speckled Hen, decent wine, welcoming service; steep narrow access; tables in garden, camping *(J Roy Smylie)*

PICKLESCOTT [SO4399]

☆ *Bottle & Glass* [off A49 N of Church Stretton]: Warmly welcoming unspoilt early 17th-c country local tucked away in delightful spot below N end of Long Mynd, pleasant quarry-tiled bar and lounge/restaurant, two log fires, good service, well kept Woods real ales, good value food esp home-made pies; quiet in winter, busy summer – wise to book for food then, esp Sun lunch; cl wkdy lunchtimes, bedrooms *(MDN)*

PRIORSLEE [SJ7109]

Lion [off B5061 at roundabout]: Cosy and well run, with beams, brasses and an inglenook, friendly staff and locals with a good mix of age-groups, limited choice of good value food, well kept real ales, small comfortable dining room *(Nigel B Thompson)*

QUEENS HEAD [SJ3326]

Queens Head [just off A5 SE of Oswestry, towards Nesscliffe]: Emphasis on wide choice of good value food (all day Fri and wknds) from speciality sandwiches inc good steak baguettes to lots of fish and steaks, well kept reasonably priced Theakstons Best, XB and Old Peculier with a guest such as Shepherd Neame Spitfire, prompt helpful service, two dining areas with roaring coal fires, one no smoking with nice conservatory (may need to book); garden by restored Montgomery Canal, country walks *(Mike Schofield, Bill Sykes, John Andrew)*

SHIFNAL [SJ7508]

White Hart [High St]: Consistently good value friendly timbered 17th-c pub, quaint and old-fashioned, separate bar and lounge, comfortable but without frills, good range of interesting changing well kept ales such as Bathams and Enville, wide range of sandwiches, promptly served reasonably priced home-made hot dishes, welcoming staff; lively evenings *(Gill and Tony Morriss, Andy and Jill Kassube)*

SHREWSBURY [SJ4812]

Bellstone [Bellstone]: Friendly bar with good wine list, good value food, restaurant and courtyard tables *(Mr and Mrs F Carroll)*

Boat House Inn [New St/Quarry Park; leaving centre via Welsh Bridge/A488 turn into Port Hill Rd]: Comfortably modernised unpretentious pub in lovely position by footbridge to Severn park, river views from long lounge bar, tables out on sheltered terrace and rose lawn; well kept ales such as Black Sheep, Boddingtons and Fullers London Pride, standard food, friendly staff, bare boards, low ceilings, darts in smaller bar; children welcome, summer barbecues, popular with young people evening; open all day *(M Joyner, Nigel B Thompson, LYM)*

Coach & Horses [Swan Hill/Cross Hill]: Welcoming unspoilt Victorian local, panelled throughout, with main bar, cosy little side room and back dining room, good value food inc daily roasts and some unusual dishes, well kept Bass, Goodalls Gold (brewed for pub by Salopian) and a guest beer, relaxed atmosphere, prompt helpful service even when busy, interesting prints; pretty flower boxes outside *(the Didler, Pete Baker)*

Cromwells [Dogpole]: Good affordable fresh food from baguettes to world-wide variety of dishes inc inventive puddings in smallish dim-lit bar, warm, clean, cosy and friendly; well kept ales inc Hobsons and Slaters, good house wines, pleasant staff, attractive panelled restaurant (same menu); well chosen piped music; raised garden and heated terrace behind, open all day Sat, nice bedrooms sharing bathrooms *(Margaret and Andrew Leach, John Whitehead, Dennis and Gill Keen)*

Dolphin [A49 ½ mile N of station]: Early Victorian pub with its own Dolphin ales from back brewhouse, changing guest beers, foreign bottled beers and perhaps farm ciders, friendly staff, two small gas-lit rooms; cl lunchtime Mon-Sat but opens 3 Fri/Sat *(the Didler)*

Golden Cross [Princess St]: Attractive partly Tudor hotel with two snug quiet bars, one with a comfortable no smoking area, short choice of good sensibly priced lunchtime food, well kept Greene King Abbot and Tetleys, pleasant helpful staff; four good value bedrooms *(Michael Butler)*

Lion [follow City Centre signposts across the English Bridge]: Grand largely 18th-c coaching inn with cosy oak-panelled bar and sedate series of high-ceilinged rooms opening off, civilised service, real ale, reasonably priced bar lunches inc succulent sandwiches, tea or coffee and cakes other times; children welcome, bedrooms comfortable *(Gloria Bax, LYM)*

☆ *Loggerheads* [Church St]: Small old-fashioned pub, panelled back smoke room with flagstones, scrubbed-top tables, high-backed settles and real fire, three other rooms with lots of prints, flagstones and bare boards, quaint linking corridor and hatch service of Banks's Bitter and Mild, Bass, Mansfield, Marstons Pedigree and a guest beer, friendly staff and locals, wide choice of bargain lunchtime food (not Sun), darts, dominoes, poetry society; open all day *(the Didler, Kevin Thorpe, Pete Baker, John Whitehead, MLR)*

TELFORD [SJ6910]

Crown [Market St, Oakengates (off A442,

handy for M54 junction 5)]: Bright bare-boards town local dating from 17th c, up to 10 or so changing real ales from small breweries inc Hobsons Best as a regular, frequent beer festivals, lots of foreign bottled beers, helpful knowledgeable staff, friendly locals, basic front bar, tables and barrels in side room, back room (no smoking, not after 8 Thurs-Sat) with darts and pool, coal fire, interesting home-made food sometimes; live music Thurs; tables outside *(Gill and Tony Morriss)*

UPPER FARMCOTE [SO7792]

☆ *Lion o' Morfe* [off A458 Bridgnorth—Stourbridge]: Country pub with good very reasonably priced food, well kept beer, log fire in plush lounge, coal fire in traditional public bar, carpeted pool room, conservatory; attractive garden spreading into orchard *(Theo, Anne and Jane Gaskin, LYM)*

WALL UNDER HEYWOOD [SO5092]

Plough [B4371]: Good helpings of reliable food in large, clean and comfortable bars and separate restaurant extension, service friendly and efficient despite the bustle, good range of well kept beers; tables in garden *(Gordon Tong)*

WELLINGTON [SJ6611]

Bucks Head [A442 towards Whitchurch]: Refurbished and extended dining pub with good value foods (not Sun evening) inc wkdy OAP lunches, Banks's, Marstons Pedigree and Tetleys from nice long bar, enthusiastic and efficient young staff, conservatory; bedrooms *(Gill and Keith Croxton)*

WENLOCK EDGE [SO5796]

Wenlock Edge Inn [B4371 Much Wenlock—Church Stretton]: Charmingly placed country dining pub, pleasant two-room bar (dogs allowed) with open fire and inglenook woodburner, more modern no smoking dining extension, home-made food from baguettes up, well kept local Hobsons Best and Town Crier; children welcome in eating areas, tables out on terraces, cosy attractive bedrooms (plans for more), lots of walks; cl Mon/Tues lunchtime at least in winter *(LYM, B and H, Alan and Gill Bull, A Sadler, Ron and Val Broom, Paul and Margaret Baker, R Michael Richards)*

WESTON HEATH [SJ7713]

Countess Arms [A41 S of Newport]: Stylish modern purpose-built two-level pub with well kept ales such as Enville and Woods, 30 wines by the glass, wide choice of good interesting largely modern food reasonably priced (and served from 11), obliging unhurried service, great feeling of space; children's area, barbecue, disabled facilities, open all day till midnight *(Ian and Liz Rispin)*

WESTON RHYN [SJ2935]

Plough [Station Rd; off A5/B5070 roundabout S of Chirk, signed to Rhoswiel]: Two-bar 1950s-style local with cheap real ale and equally low-priced good fresh sandwiches and basic hot dishes *(KC)*

WHITCHURCH [SJ5345]

☆ *Willey Moor Lock* [signed off A49 just under 2 miles N]: Picturesque spot by Llangollen Canal, low beams, countless teapots, two log

fires, cheerful chatty atmosphere, well kept
Theakstons Best, three or four well kept guest
beers from small breweries, around 30 malt
whiskies, straightforward quickly served food
from sandwiches and baked potatoes up; fruit
machine, piped music, several dogs and cats;
children welcome away from bar, terrace
tables, garden with big play area *(LYM,
Amanda Eames, MLR, Joyce and
Geoff Robson)*
WOORE [SJ7342]
Swan [London Rd (A51)]: Neat convivial bar,
popular food from simple bar lunches to festive
dinner dances, real ales, good value wines,
smart friendly service *(E G Parish)*
WORFIELD [SO7595]
☆ *Dog* [off A454 W of Bridgnorth; Main St]:

Pretty pub in beautiful unspoilt stone-built
village, three sprucely decorated areas with
emphasis on food from good value baguettes
to plenty of seafood, well kept real ales inc a
guest beer, good house wines, log fire
*(Brian and Carole Polhill, Andy and
Jill Kassube, Pat and Sam Roberts)*
YORTON [SJ5023]
Railway: Same family for over 60 years,
friendly and chatty mother and daughter,
unchanging atmosphere, simple tiled bar with
coal fire and settles, big comfortable lounge
with fishing trophies, well kept ales such as
Hanby, Salopian, Wadworths 6X, Woods
Shropshire Lad and Worfield, simple
sandwiches if you ask, darts and dominoes –
no piped music or machines *(the Didler)*

Bedroom prices normally include full english breakfast, VAT and any inclusive
service charge that we know of. Prices before the '/' are for single rooms, after
for two people in double or twin (B includes a private bath, S a private shower).
If there is no '/', the prices are only for twin or double rooms
(as far as we know there are no singles).

Somerset

In this chapter we include Bristol, as well as Bath. The area has a great many good pubs to track down, from some unspoilt favourites to altogether smarter places, with plenty of good food, some buildings of tremendous character, and other pubs lifted out of the ordinary by really good landlords and landladies. There is still plenty of farm cider to be found here too, though we have the impression (from our own inspections and from the nearly 2,000 reports on Somerset pubs which we have on file from readers this year) that this quintessential country tipple is getting a lot rarer. In the last few months people have been showing particular enthusiasm for the Globe at Appley (good food and wine in this appealing country pub), the Three Horseshoes at Batcombe (gaining its Food Award this year), the little Old Green Tree in Bath (a great favourite, for its fine beer range, enjoyable food and helpful service), the Star there (a nice old alehouse), the villagey Queens Arms at Bleadon (a popular all-rounder), the Cat Head at Chiselborough (a new entry, new licensees doing good food in attractive traditional surroundings), the unspoilt Crown at Churchill (a fine beer range, good value home cooking), the chatty Black Horse at Clapton-in-Gordano (making the M5 seem a century away), the Crown at Exford (another new entry, smart coaching inn flourishing under new management), the Ring o' Roses at Holcombe (very good food, helpful service), the Rose & Crown at Huish Episcopi (little changed in the 135 years this family have had it, and its perky landlady would put many a quarter her age to shame), the pretty little Kingsdon Inn (enjoyable food), the attractively traditional Three Horseshoes at Langley Marsh (a good all-rounder), the Bird in Hand at North Curry (nice food, cheerful atmosphere), the largely no smoking Royal Oake at Oake (yet another new entry, popular for food under its new licensees), the Montague Inn at Shepton Montague (a friendly all-rounder, its upgraded bedrooms putting it in line for a Place to Stay Award), the Rose & Crown at Stoke St Gregory (another good all-rounder, flourishing under a new generation), the Blue Ball at Triscombe (a particular favourite, friendly and helpful, good if restauranty food, great wine-by-the-glass policy), the Crown in Wells (contemporary food and décor in this old coaching inn – the last of our new entries here this year), and the Royal Oak at Withypool (interesting food and lots of atmosphere). As you can see from all this, plenty of pubs here stand out for their food. The one which takes the title of Somerset Dining Pub of the Year is the Blue Ball at Triscombe; really good meals in a lovely building. Pubs which these days are shining brightly in the Lucky Dip section at the end of the chapter include the Coeur de Lion in Bath, Commercial Rooms in Bristol, Manor House at Ditcheat, Faulkland Inn, George in Ilminster, Old Crown at Kelston, Hope & Anchor at Midford, Ship in Porlock, Masons Arms in Taunton, Cotley Inn at Wambrook, Fountain in Wells, Crossways at West Huntspill, Woolpack in Weston-Super-Mare and Ring o' Bells at Wookey. Drinks prices here are not far off the national norm. Local beers to look out for include Butcombe, Exmoor, Cotleigh, RCH, Smiles, Cottage, Abbey and Bath, with interlopers from Devon such as Otter and Teignworthy quite often turning up as the cheapest beer on offer in a pub here.

APPLEY ST0621 Map 1
Globe 🍽

Hamlet signposted from the network of back roads between A361 and A38, W of B3187 and W of Milverton and Wellington; OS Sheet 181 map reference 072215

Particularly well run, this 15th-c country pub is a friendly place and much enjoyed by our readers. The simple beamed front room has benches and a built-in settle, bare wood tables on the brick floor, and pictures of magpies, and there's a further room with easy chairs and other more traditional ones, open fires, and a collection of model boats, art deco items and *Titanic* pictures; skittle alley. A stone-flagged entry corridor leads to a serving hatch from where Cotleigh Tawny and guests such as Palmers IPA or 200 are well kept on handpump. Very good bar food includes sandwiches, home-made soup (£2.95), mushrooms in cream, garlic and horseradish (£4.25), chicken liver pâté (£4.95), a light cold egg pancake filled with prawns, celery and pineapple in marie rose sauce (£6.95), home-made steak and kidney in ale pie (£7.95), thai vegetable curry (£8.25), steaks (from £9.95), chicken breast stuffed with mozzarella and parma ham with a tomato, basil and cream sauce (£10.25), crispy duckling with madeira sauce (£11.95), daily specials like lamb curry (£8.95), medallions of pork fillet with a calvados, apple, wild mushroom and shallot sauce (£10.95), and whole bass with walnut oil and lime (£11.95), and puddings such as chocolate mousse or home-made treacle tart (from £3.95). The restaurant is no smoking. Seats, climbing frame and swings outside in the garden; the path opposite leads eventually to the River Tone. *(Recommended by P Duffield, Glenwys and Alan Lawrence, Paul and Annette Hallett, the Didler, Ian Phillips, RWC, Su and Bob Child, Lorraine and Fred Gill, Dr and Mrs M E Wilson, Michael Rowse)*

Free house ~ Licensees Andrew and Liz Burt ~ Real ale ~ Bar food (till 10) ~ Restaurant ~ (01823) 672327 ~ Children welcome ~ Open 11-3, 6.30-11; 12-3, 7-10.30 Sun; closed Mon except bank hols

ASHILL ST3116 Map 1
Square & Compass

Windmill Hill; off A358 between Ilminster and Taunton; up Wood Torad for 1 mile behind Stewley Cross service station; OS Sheet 193 map reference 310166

In a nicely remote setting, this bustling and unassuming country pub has an open fire and simple, comfortable furnishings in the bar, and well kept Exmoor Ale and Wicked Hathern Bitter, and a guest from breweries such as Branoc or Otter. Generous helpings of enjoyable bar food include home-made soup (£2.50), sandwiches (from £2.95), filled baked potatoes (from £3.95), deep-fried brie (£4.50), ploughman's (£5.50), omelettes (£5.75), tuna pasta bake (£5.95), thai chicken curry or mushroom stroganoff (£6.50), seafood crêpes (£6.95), steaks (from £7.50), large mixed grill (£11.95), and daily specials like liver and bacon or beef stew with dumplings (£6.95), thai crab cakes (£7.95), and chicken with creamy stilton and bacon sauce (£9.95); Sunday roast (£6.95). Piped classical music at lunchtimes; the cats are called Daisy and Lilly. There's a terrace outside and a garden with picnic-sets, views over the Blackdown Hills, and a children's play area. *(Recommended by Mr and Mrs Colin Roberts, S Palmer, Mark Clezy, Graham and Rose Ive, Mrs Sally Lloyd, Dr and Mrs M E Wilson, Malcolm Taylor)*

Free house ~ Licensees Chris, Janet and Beth Slow ~ Real ale ~ Bar food (not Tues, Weds or Thurs lunchtimes) ~ (01823) 480467 ~ Children welcome ~ Dogs welcome ~ Open 12-2.30, 6.30(7 Sun)-11; closed Tues, Weds and Thurs lunchtimes

AXBRIDGE ST4255 Map 1
Lamb

The Square; off A371 Cheddar—Winscombe

The market square on which this ancient inn stands is most attractive. Inside, the big rambling bar is full of heavy beams and timbers, cushioned wall seats and small settles, an open fire in one great stone fireplace, and a collection of tools and utensils including an unusual foot-operated grinder in another. Well kept Butcombe Bitter and Gold, and maybe Wychwood Hobgoblin on handpump from a bar counter built largely of bottles, and local cider; shove-ha'penny, cribbage, dominoes, table skittles and skittle alley. Reasonably priced bar food includes lunchtime sandwiches and filled baguettes (from £2.95), as well as home-made soup (£2.50), deep-fried brie with redcurrant jelly (£3.95), filled baked potatoes (from £4.25), home-cooked ham and eggs (£5.95), home-made leek and potato bake (£6.25), home-made curry or beef in ale pie (£6.95), steaks (from £8.25), and daily specials such as lamb steak in a mint and cranberry sauce (£7.25) or chicken breast with bacon and mushroom with dijon sauce (£8.25). The dining room is no smoking; efficient rather than friendly service. Though the sheltered back garden is not big, it's prettily planted with rock plants, shrubs and trees. The National Trust's medieval King John's Hunting Lodge is opposite. *(Recommended by Mike Gorton, Richard and Helene Lay, Hugh Roberts, S H Godsell, P M Wilkins, J Coote)*

Butcombe ~ Manager Alan Currie ~ Real ale ~ Bar food (12-2.30, 6.30-9; not Sun evenings) ~ (01934) 732253 ~ Children in eating area of bar ~ Dogs allowed in bar ~ Open 11.30-3, 6-11; 11.30-11 Sat; 12-10.30 Sun ~ Bedrooms: £30S/£50B

BATCOMBE ST6838 Map 2
Three Horseshoes 🍴
Village signposted off A359 Bruton—Frome

With well kept real ales and chatty locals, the bar area in this honey stone place keeps its relaxed, pubby feel. But there's no doubt that the good interesting food plays a big part in drawing in customers: spiced tomato and pesto soup (£3.75), chicken liver, smoked pork and ham pâté with spiced chutney or good mozzarella, roast tomato and basil tart with spring onion salsa (£4.95), filo parcel of goats cheese, garlic, spinach and baby leeks on a provençale tomato coulis (£11.95), baked chicken breast with cheddar and parma ham on sun-dried tomato mash and burgundy sauce, calves liver and crispy bacon on flageolet bean mash and red wine gravy or lamb chump steak on spring onion mash with wild mushroom and rosemary sauce (£13.95), and duck breast on sautéed courgette and bacon with gratin potatoes and honey and red wine jus (£14.50). The longish narrow main room has cream-painted beams and planks, local pictures on the lightly ragged dark pink walls, built-in cushioned window seats and solid chairs around a nice mix of old tables, a couple of clocking-in clocks, and a woodburning stove at one end with a big open fire at the other; there's a plain tiled room at the back on the left with more straightforward furniture. The no smoking, stripped stone dining room is pretty. Well kept Butcombe and a changing guest on handpump, and decent wines by the glass. The back terrace has picnic-sets, with more on the grass. The pub is on a quiet village lane by the church which has a very striking tower. *(Recommended by Terry Stewart, Mrs Sally Lloyd, Steve Dark, Mrs Katie Roberts, Mike and Sue Richardson, Michael Doswell, David Gough, S G N Bennett, Paul and Annette Hallett, Paul Hopton, Pippa Rose, Guy Vowles)*

Free house ~ Licensees David and Liz Benson ~ Real ale ~ Bar food (till 10 Fri/Sat) ~ Restaurant ~ (01749) 850359 ~ Children in eating area of bar and restaurant ~ Dogs allowed in bar ~ Open 12-3, 6.30-11; 12-3, 7-10.30 Sun; closed 25 Dec

BATH ST7464 Map 2
Old Green Tree 🍺
12 Green Street

A favourite with a great many customers, this bustling little pub is a smashing place. There are no noisy games machines or piped music to spoil the chatty, friendly atmosphere, and seven real ales are very well kept on handpump: Bath SPA, RCH Pitchfork, Stonehenge Benchmark, and four changing guests; also, 25 malt whiskies, a nice little wine list with helpful notes (and quite a few by the glass), winter hot toddies, a proper Pimms, and good coffee. The three little oak-panelled and low wood-and-plaster ceilinged rooms include a comfortable lounge on the left as you go in, its walls decorated with wartime aircraft pictures in winter and local artists' work during spring and summer, and a no smoking back bar; the big skylight lightens things up attractively. Popular lunchtime bar food includes soup (£4), tasty salads or bangers and mash with cider or beer and onion sauce (£5.50), and daily specials such as enjoyable roast beef baguette (£4), ploughman's with home-made chutney (from £4), home-made pâté (£5.50), and roast duck breast with blueberry salad or mussels in wine and cream (£6.50); if you get there when the pub opens, you should be able to bag a table. Chess, backgammon, shut the box, Jenga. The gents', though good, are down steep steps. No children. *(Recommended by Dr and Mrs M W A Haward, Rona Murdoch, Dr and Mrs A K Clarke, Clive Hilton, Gill and Tony Morriss, Bruce Bird, Roger and Jenny Huggins, Paul Hopton, Val and Alan Green, Mike Pugh, Jack Taylor, Val Stevenson, Rob Holmes, Tim Harper, Jenny and Brian Seller, the Didler, Dr and Mrs M E Wilson, Pete Baker, Susan and Nigel Wilson, David Carr, M V Ward, Nigel Long, Richard Pierce, Tony Hobden, Simon and Amanda Southwell)*

Free house ~ Licensees Nick Luke and Tim Bethune ~ Real ale ~ Bar food (lunchtime until 2.45) ~ No credit cards ~ Open 11-11; 12-10.30 Sun; closed 25-26 Dec, 1 Jan

Star 🍺

23 Vineyards; The Paragon (A4), junction with Guinea Lane

Handy for the main shopping area and set in quiet steep streets of undeniably handsome if well worn stone terraces, this old pub gives a strong sense of the past. Four (well, more like three and a half) small linked rooms are served from a single bar, separated by sombre panelling with glass inserts, and furnished with traditional leatherette wall benches and the like – even one hard bench that the regulars call Death Row. The lighting's dim, and not rudely interrupted by too much daylight. With no machines or music, chat's the thing here – or perhaps cribbage, dominoes and shove-ha'penny. Particularly well kept Bass is tapped from the cask, and they have Abbey Bellringer, and three guests such as Adnams Broadside, Bath Star or Black Sheep, on handpump; 23 malt whiskies. Filled rolls only (from £1.60; served throughout opening hours during the week), and Sunday lunchtime bar nibbles (quail eggs, chopped sausage, chicken wings and so forth); friendly staff and customers. No children inside. *(Recommended by Pete Baker, Dr and Mrs A K Clarke, Clive Hilton, the Didler, Catherine Pitt, Mike and Heather Watson, Paul Hopton, Dr and Mrs M E Wilson, David and Christine Vaughton, R Huggins, D Irving, E McCall, T McLean)*

Punch ~ Lease Terry Langley and Julie Schofield ~ Real ale ~ Bar food (see text) ~ (01225) 425072 ~ Children in family room ~ Dogs welcome ~ Open 12-2.30, 5.30-11; 12-11 Sat; 12-10.30 Sun

BLEADON ST3357 Map 1
Queens Arms 🍺

Village signposted just off A370 S of Weston; Celtic Way

Whether you are a regular or visitor, you will get a warm welcome in this 16th-c pub. It's been opened up but with carefully divided separate areas that still let the comfortably chatty and convivial atmosphere run right through. Plenty of distinctive touches include the dark flagstones of the terracotta-walled restaurant and back bar area (both no smoking), candles in bottles on sturdy tables flanked by winged settles, old hunting prints, a frieze of quaint sayings in Old English print, and above all the focal servery where up to eight well kept changing ales such as Archers, Badger Tanglefoot, Bass, Butcombe Bitter, Otter Bitter, Palmers IPA, Ringwood Old Thumper, and Thwaites Lancaster Bomber are tapped from a stack of casks behind the counter; they have Thatcher's farm cider too, and good coffee. Well liked home-made food at lunchtime includes home-made soup (£2.95), sandwiches (from £2.95), home-made pâté (£3.25), filled baguettes (from £3.25), ploughman's (from £3.95), ham and egg (£5.25), and chicken and chips (£5.95), with evening choices like caesar salad (£3.95; main course £4.95), moules marinière (£5.95), vegetable lasagne (£7.25), fillet of plaice (£7.95), steaks (from £8.95), and daily specials. You may be asked to leave your credit card behind the bar. Service is quick and friendly, and there is a big cylindrical solid fuel stove in the main bar, with another woodburning stove in the stripped-stone back tap bar. They have a quiz night on Sunday, and piped music, TV, and skittle alley. Some benches and picnic-sets out on the tarmac by the car park entrance. *(Recommended by R F Hedges, Gaynor Gregory, Anne and David Robinson, Guy Wilkins, Ken Jones, P M Wilkins, J Coote, Comus and Sarah Elliott, B I Evans)*

Free house ~ Licensees C and A Smith and M Sanders ~ Real ale ~ Bar food (not Sun evening) ~ Restaurant ~ (01934) 812080 ~ Children in eating area of bar and restaurant ~ Dogs allowed in bar ~ Open 11.30-2.30, 5.30-11; 11.30-11 bank hols and Sat; 12-10.30 Sun

CATCOTT ST3939 Map 1
Crown ⬧

Village signposted off A39 W of Street; at T junction turn left, then at war memorial turn off northwards into Brook Lane and keep on

On a quiet country lane in a farming community, this former cider house offers a friendly welcome, and has been decorated this year. To the left of the main door is a pubby little room with built-in brocade-cushioned settles, a church pew and red leatherette stools around just four rustic pine tables, a tall black-painted brick fireplace with dried flowers and a large cauldron, and working horse plaques; around the corner is a small alcove with a really big pine table on its stripped stone floor. Most of the pub is taken up with the roomy, more straightforward dining area with lots of wheelback chairs around tables, and paintings on silk of local views by a local artist on the cream walls. From the menu, there might be sandwiches (from £1.70), soup (£2.30), stuffed mushrooms (£3.50), ploughman's (from £4.25), ham and egg (£5.60), vegetable lasagne, beef curry or home-made steak and kidney pie (£5.95), trout with almonds (£8.45), steaks (from £9.55), and daily specials. Well kept Butcombe Bitter and Smiles Best, and a guest such as Badger Tanglefoot or Shepherd Neame Spitfire on handpump, and piped old-fashioned pop music; fruit machine and skittle alley. The original part of the pub is white-painted stone with black shutters and is pretty with window boxes and tubs. Out behind are picnic-sets and a play area for children with wooden equipment. *(Recommended by D Thomas, Mark Weber, Dr and Mrs C W Thomas, Theo, Anne and Jane Gaskin, the Didler, KC, George Atkinson)*

Free house ~ Licensees C R D Johnston and D Lee ~ Real ale ~ Bar food (12-2, 6(7 Sun)-10) ~ (01278) 722288 ~ Children welcome ~ Open 11.30-2.30, 6-11; 12-3, 7-10.30 Sun; closed 25 Dec

CHISELBOROUGH ST4614 Map 1
Cat Head

Signposted off B3165 between A3088 and A30, W of Yeovil

The licensees at this relaxing country pub are no strangers to these pages, earning high praise in the late 1990s when they ran the Kingsdon Inn. In the year they've been back in Somerset they've already made quite an impression, winning a national food award and drawing enthusiastic reports from readers. The pub often gets busy in the evenings (particularly at weekends), but at lunchtime you may have its peaceful charms almost to yourself; the Gordons quickly make you feel at home and, if you're in the mood, draw you into conversation. The very good bar food might include lunchtime sandwiches, soups such as celeriac and stilton (£2.80), a variety of proper tapas such as meatballs with vegetable and tomato sauce (£2.95) or chorizo sausage fried in red wine (£3.20), baked cornish crab and scallops mornay (£4.80), chicken schnitzel with tomato, mascarpone and basil sauce (£9.20), salmon and prawn fishcakes with lime and coriander mayonnaise (£9.80), half a crispy duck with scrumpy sauce (£10.20), and fresh fish specials such as bass (£10.40). Butcombe, Otter and Marstons Pedigree on handpump; good wine list, farm cider. The neatly traditional flagstoned rooms have plenty of flowers and plants, a woodburning stove, light wooden tables and chairs, some high-backed cushioned settles, and curtains around the small mullioned windows. A carpeted area to the right is no smoking. Soft piped music, darts, alley skittles, cribbage and dominoes. Behind is a very attractive lawned garden with picnic-sets and colourful summer plants (real gardeners these – they go to the length of getting their manure from Paignton Zoo); nice views over the peaceful village. *(Recommended by Mr and Mrs J B Pritchard, Kate Francis)*

Enterprise ~ Lease Duncan and Avril Gordon ~ Real ale ~ Bar food (not 25 Dec) ~ (01935) 881231 ~ Children in eating area of bar ~ Open 12-3, 6-11(10.30 Sun); closed 25 Dec evening

CHURCHILL ST4560 Map 1

Crown 🍺 £

The Batch; in village, turn off A368 into Skinners Lane at Nelson Arms, then bear right

No mod-cons, noisy games machines or piped music here – it's an unspoilt little stone-built cottage with a marvellous range of up to 10 real ales, and a good mix of customers. Tapped from the cask, the real ales might include Bass, Cotleigh Tawny, Hop Back GFB, Otter Bitter, Palmers IPA, P G Steam, and RCH Hewish IPA. The small and local stone-floored and cross-beamed room on the right has a wooden window seat, an unusually sturdy settle, and built-in wall benches; the left-hand room has a slate floor, and some steps past the big log fire in a big stone fireplace lead to more sitting space. Enjoyable bar food using fresh local produce includes good home-made soups (small £2.90, large £3.50), excellent rare beef sandwich (£2.90), ploughman's (£4.65), chilli cauliflower cheese or quiche (£4.50), various casseroles or summer salmon (£6.50), and puddings such as treacle pudding or spotted dick. They do get busy at weekends, especially in summer. There are garden tables on the front and a smallish back lawn, and hill views; the Mendip Morris Men come in summer. Good walks nearby. *(Recommended by Mike and Mary Carter, John Urquhart, Brian Root, Tom Evans, Rob Webster, Catherine Pitt, P M Wilkins, J Coote, the Didler, Chris Flynn, Wendy Jones, Alan and Paula McCully, Jane and Graham Rooth, Paul Hopton, Kerry Law, Simon Smith, Ian Phillips, R J Walden, Matthew Shackle, Peter Herridge)*

Free house ~ Licensee Tim Rogers ~ Real ale ~ Bar food (lunchtime) ~ No credit cards ~ (01934) 852995 ~ Children in eating area of bar ~ Dogs welcome ~ Open 11.30(12 Sun)-11

CLAPTON-IN-GORDANO ST4773 Map 1

Black Horse

4 miles from M5 junction 19; A369 towards Portishead, then B3124 towards Clevedon; in N Weston opposite school turn left signposted Clapton, then in village take second right, maybe signed Clevedon, Clapton Wick

It's well worth leaving the M5 to visit this interesting old place, tucked away down a country lane. There's a welcoming atmosphere and plenty of character, and the partly flagstoned and partly red-tiled main room has winged settles and built-in wall benches around narrow, dark wooden tables, window seats, a big log fire with stirrups and bits on the mantelbeam, and amusing cartoons and photographs of the pub. A window in an inner snug is still barred from the days when this room was the petty-sessions gaol; high-backed settles – one a marvellous carved and canopied creature, another with an art nouveau copper insert reading East, West, Hame's Best – lots of mugs hanging from its black beams, and plenty of little prints and photographs. There's also a simply furnished room just off the bar (where children can go), with high-backed corner settles and a gas fire; piped music. Straightforward bar food includes soup (£2.95), tasty filled baguettes (from £3.50), and a few hot dishes like corned beef hash or chilli (from £4.75). Well kept Courage Best, Shepherd Neame Spitfire, and Smiles Best on handpump or tapped from the cask, and Thatcher's farm cider; friendly, chatty staff. In summer, the flower-decked building and little flagstoned front garden are exceptionally pretty;

there are some old rustic tables and benches, with more to one side of the car park and a secluded children's play area. Paths from the pub lead up Naish Hill or along to Cadbury Camp. *(Recommended by the Didler, Tom Evans, George Atkinson, June and Ken Brooks)*

Inntrepreneur ~ Tenant Nicholas Evans ~ Real ale ~ Bar food (not evenings, not Sun lunchtime) ~ No credit cards ~ (01275) 842105 ~ Children in family room ~ Dogs welcome ~ Live music Mon evening ~ Open 11-2.30, 5-11; 11-11 Fri and Sat; 12-3, 7-10.30 Sun

COMPTON MARTIN ST5457 Map 2
Ring o' Bells ◆ £
A368 Bath—Weston

This is the sort of place that customers like to come back to again and again. There's a happy, bustling atmosphere, and good value beer and food, and no matter how busy they are, the landlord and his staff remain friendly and helpful. The cosy, traditional front part of the bar has rugs on the flagstones and inglenook seats right by the log fire, and up a step is a spacious carpeted back part with largely stripped stone walls and pine tables; the lounge is partly no smoking. Popular, reasonably priced bar food includes sandwiches (from £1.50; toasties from £2.50; BLT in french bread £3.50), soup (£2.50), stilton mushrooms (£3.75), filled baked potatoes, ploughman's or tasty omelettes (from £3.80), ham and eggs (small £4.30, large £5), lasagne, mushroom, broccoli and almond tagliatelle or tasty beef casserole (from £5.50), generous mixed grill (£11), daily specials like various fresh local trout (£5.95), home-made pies or curries (£5.95), good lamb chops (£7.25), and puddings (£2.50); best to get here early to be sure of a seat. On handpump or tapped from the cask, there might be Butcombe Bitter and Gold, Fullers London Pride, and a guest from maybe Adnams, Bath or Timothy Taylors; malt whiskies. The public bar has darts, cribbage, dominoes, and shove-ha'penny; table skittles. The family room is no smoking, and has blackboards and chalks, a Brio track, and a rocking horse; they also have baby changing and nursing facilities, and the big garden has swings, a slide, and a climbing frame. Blagdon Lake and Chew Valley Lake are not far away, and the pub is overlooked by the Mendip Hills. *(Recommended by Tom Evans, Keith Stenner, Leigh and Gillian Mellor, Ian and Rose Lock, John and Gloria Isaacs)*

Free house ~ Licensee Roger Owen ~ Real ale ~ Bar food ~ Restaurant ~ (01761) 221284 ~ Children in family room ~ Dogs allowed in bar ~ Open 11.30-3, 6.30-11; 12-3, 7-10.30 Sun

CONGRESBURY ST4464 Map 1
White Hart
Wrington Road, which is off A370 Bristol—Weston just E of village – keep on

Even when pushed, the staff in this companionable country pub remain friendly and efficient. The L-shaped carpeted main bar has a few heavy black beams in the bowed ceiling of its longer leg, brown country-kitchen chairs around good-sized tables, and a big stone inglenook fireplace at each end, with woodburning stoves and lots of copper pans. The short leg of the L is more cottagey, with teddy bears and other bric-a-brac above yet another fireplace and on a delft shelf, lace and old-gold brocaded curtains, and brocaded wall seats. A roomy family Parlour Bar, open to the main bar, is similar in mood, though with lighter-coloured country-style furniture, some stripped stone and shiny black panelling, and big bright airy conservatory windows on one side; the restaurant is no smoking. There's quite a choice of reasonably priced tasty food including home-made soup (£2.95), deep-fried cheese with cranberry sauce (£4.25), ham and eggs (£5.95), vegetarian dishes like cauliflower cheese or stilton, leek and walnut pie (£6-£7), home-made lasagne (£7.50), home-made steak and kidney pie (£7.95), chicken in stilton or tomato sauce (£9.25), andalucian shoulder of lamb (£12.50), and puddings such as home-made fruit crumbles (£3.75). Well kept Badger Best, Tanglefoot, and Sussex on handpump; perhaps faint piped pop music. There are picnic-sets under an arbour on the terrace behind, and on grass out beyond; the hills you see are the Mendips. *(Recommended by Stan Edwards, Anthony Barnes, James Morrell, Comus and Sarah Elliott, M G Hart, Andy Sinden, Louise Harrington)*

Badger ~ Tenant Ken Taylor ~ Real ale ~ Bar food ~ Restaurant ~ (01934) 833303 ~ Children in restaurant ~ Dogs welcome ~ Open 11-2.30, 6-11; 12-3, 7-10.30 Sun

CROWCOMBE ST1336 Map 1
Carew Arms 🍺 🛏

Village (and pub) signposted just off A358 Taunton—Minehead

A few careful changes to this unspoilt 17th-c beamed village this year, but all in keeping with the original building. The old skittle alley has been turned into a bar and dining room with french windows leading on to a big terrace with country views, and a new skittle alley has been built at the front. More bedrooms are being opened up, too. The front bar has long benches and a couple of old long deal tables on its dark flagstones, a high-backed antique settle and a shiny old leather wing armchair by the woodburning stove in its huge brick inglenook fireplace, and a thoroughly non-PC collection of hunting trophies to remind you that this is the Quantocks. A back room behind the bar is a carpeted and gently updated version of the front one, and on the right is a neat little grey-carpeted dining room decorated with hunting prints and plates; dominoes. Lively conversation is lubricated by well kept Exmoor tapped from the cask and a guest beer such as Black Sheep, Butcombe Gold or Otter Ale on handpump – or likely by Lane's strong farm cider, or the whiskies. Decent bar food at lunchtime includes home-made soup (£3.75), filled baguettes (£3.75), ploughman's (£5.50), and spinach and tomato pudding, breaded cod or steak and kidney pie (£5.95), with evening dishes such as fried mushrooms and grilled bacon (£4.75), mixed cold meats (£7.50), steaks (from £10), braised shoulder of lamb (£11.50), and guinea fowl with puy lentils (£11.95), and home-made puddings like sticky toffee pudding or orange trifle (£3.75). Picnic-sets out on the back grass look over rolling wooded pasture, and the attractive village at the foot of the hills has a fine old church and church house; this is a good value place to stay, in a quiet spot. *(Recommended by P M Wilkins, J Coote, Richard Gibbs, the Didler, Andy and Jill Kassube, Hugh Roberts, Tom Evans, Catherine Pitt)*

Free house ~ Licensees Simon and Reginald Ambrose ~ Real ale ~ Bar food ~ Restaurant ~ (01984) 618631 ~ Children in eating area of bar and restaurant ~ Dogs allowed in bar ~ Light entertainment dinners ~ Open 11-3.30(4 winter Sat/Sun), 6-11; 11-11 Sat; 12-10.30 Sun ~ Bedrooms: £39B/£69B

DOULTING ST6445 Map 2
Waggon & Horses 🍷

Doulting Beacon, 2 miles N of Doulting itself; eastwards turn off A37 on Mendip ridge N of Shepton Mallet, just S of A367 junction; the pub is also signed from the A37 at the Beacon Hill crossroads and from the A361 at the Doulting and Cranmore crossroads

There's a good mix of customers in this attractive 18th-c inn from local farmers who drop in for a drink, city people out to enjoy a meal, and those coming to view the exhibitions of local artists' work or to listen to some of the remarkable classical music and other musical events during the spring and autumn that take place in a big raftered upper gallery to one side of the building. The rambling bar has studded red leatherette seats and other chairs, a homely mix of tables including antiques, and well kept Courage Best and Ushers Founders on handpump, a small, carefully chosen wine list, and cocktails. Two rooms are no smoking. Bar food includes sandwiches (from £3.50), filled baguettes (from £5.90), leek and mushroom bake (£7.50), ham and eggs (£7.90), salmon fishcakes with dill mayonnaise (£8.90), chicken breast topped with ham, cheese and tomato (£11.50), ambitious daily specials, and puddings such as sticky toffee pudding with pecan nut sauce or crème brûlée (£4.20). The big walled garden (with summer barbecues) is lovely: elderly tables and chairs stand on informal terracing, with picnic-sets out on the grass, and perennials and flowering shrubs intersperse themselves in a pretty and pleasantly informal way. There's a wildlife pond, and a climber for children. Off to one side is a rough paddock with a horse (horses are one passion of Mr Cardona, who comes from Colombia and who has bred an olympic horse, Sir Toby) and various fancy fowl, with pens further down holding many more in small breeding groups – there are some really quite remarkable birds among them, and the cluckings and crowings make a splendidly contented background to a sunny summer lunch. They often sell the eggs, too. More reports please. *(Recommended by Colin and Janet Roe, Jacquie and Jim Jones, Guy Vowles, MRSM, Dr and Mrs J F Head, Nigel Long, Ian Phillips, Richard Stancomb, Prof Keith and Mrs Jane Barber)*

InnSpired ~ Lease Francisco Cardona ~ Real ale ~ Bar food ~ Restaurant ~ (01749) 880302 ~ Children tolerated but must be well behaved and quiet ~ Dogs allowed in bar ~ Classical concerts and some jazz ~ Open 11.30-2.30, 6-11; 12-3, 7-11 Sun

EAST LYNG ST3328 Map 1
Rose & Crown
A361 about 4 miles W of Othery

Popular locally (always a good sign), this unchanging coaching inn has an open-plan beamed lounge bar with a winter log fire (or a big embroidered fire screen) in the stone fireplace, a corner cabinet of glass, china and silver, a court cabinet, a bow window seat by an oak drop-leaf table, copies of *Country Life*, and impressive large dried flower arrangements. Well liked bar food includes sandwiches (from £2.20), soup (£2.70), ploughman's (from £4.50), ham and egg (£5), omelettes (from £5.50), steaks (£10.25), roast duckling with orange sauce (£12.50), puddings like home-made treacle tart or fruit crumble (£3.25), and daily specials such as mushroom and red pepper stroganoff, liver and bacon casserole and pork chop with mustard sauce (£6.50); the dining room is no smoking. Well kept Butcombe Bitter and Gold, and Palmers 200 on handpump; skittle alley and piped music. There are lots of seats in the pretty back garden (largely hedged off from the car park) and lovely rural views. More reports please. *(Recommended by G Coates, Bob and Margaret Holder, Ian and Rose Lock, Ian Phillips)*

Free house ~ Licensee Derek Mason ~ Real ale ~ Bar food (not 26 Dec) ~ (01823) 698235 ~ Children in restaurant ~ Open 11-2.30, 6.30-11; 12-3, 7-10.30 Sun ~ Bedrooms: £30S/£50S

EAST WOODLANDS ST7944 Map 2
Horse & Groom ♀ ◀
Off A361/B3092 junction

Many customers come to this small civilised place on a regular basis, and visitors often drop in after or before a visit to the safari park – the pub is set on the edge of Longleat. The pleasant little bar on the left has stripped pine pews and settles on dark flagstones, well kept Branscombe Vale Branoc, Butcombe Bitter, Wadworths 6X, and a guest such as Brakspears Bitter or Butcombe Gold tapped from the cask, and an extensive wine list with six by the glass. The comfortable lounge has a relaxed atmosphere, an easy chair and settee around a coffee table, two small solid dining tables with chairs, and a big stone hearth with a woodburning stove. Well liked bar food includes home-made soup (£2.95), baguettes with interesting fillings like garlic basted chicken with cheese coleslaw or stir-fried beef with oriental vegetables (from £3.60), ploughman's (from £4.75), omelettes (£5.95), curry of the day, lambs liver and bacon in onion gravy, stilton and broccoli bake or sausages of the day (all £6.80), gammon with pineapple and cheesy mushrooms (£7.90), daily specials such as a popular breakfast (£6.95), steak and kidney casserole with dumplings (£7.50), and chicken, prawn and prosciutto paella (£8.50), and puddings like rhubarb and custard crumble pie or tiramisu with balsamic strawberries (£3.90). Cribbage, shove-ha'penny, and dominoes. There are picnic-sets in the nice front garden by five severely pollarded limes and attractive hanging baskets, troughs, and mini wheelbarrows filled with flowers; more seats behind the big no smoking dining conservatory. *(Recommended by P Duffield, Pat and Tony Martin, the Didler, Jack Taylor, Richard Gibbs)*

Free house ~ Licensees Rick Squire and Kathy Barrett ~ Real ale ~ Bar food (not Sun evening or Mon) ~ Restaurant ~ (01373) 462802 ~ Children in lounge and restaurant ~ Dogs welcome ~ Open 11.30-2.30(3 Sat), 6.30-11; 12-3, 7-10.30 Sun; closed Mon lunchtime

EXFORD SS8538 Map 1
Crown ♀
The Green (B3224)

One of the chief joys of this comfortably upmarket Exmoor coaching inn is the delightful water garden behind – a lovely summer spot with a trout stream threading its way past gently sloping lawns, tall trees and plenty of tables. A smaller terraced garden at the side overlooks the village and the edge of the green. Inside, the brightly refurbished two-room bar has a very relaxed feel, plenty of stuffed animal heads and hunting prints on the cream walls, and some hunting-themed plates (this has been the local hunt's traditional meeting place at New Year). There are a few tables fashioned from barrels, a big stone fireplace (with a nice display of flowers in summer), old photographs of the area, and smart cushioned benches; piped music, chess. Exmoor Ale and Gold and a changing guest such as St Austell Tribute on handpump; good wine list (with some available by the half-carafe). Home-made bar food might include sandwiches, soup (£3.95), spinach and parmesan risotto (£4.75), thai fishcakes with tomato salsa (£5.50), tagliatelle with tomato and basil sauce (£7.50), seared salmon with crushed pesto potato (£9.25), lamb shank with herb mash (£9.75), medley of fish with lemon and thyme couscous (£10.25), and calves liver with crispy pancetta (£10.95). They have stabling for horses. We imagine this would deserve our Place to Stay Award, but have yet to hear from anyone who's stayed here (the bedrooms were about to be upgraded as we went to press). *(Recommended by Jane and Adrian Tierney-Jones, Brian and Anita Randall)*

Free house ~ Licensee Hugo Jeune ~ Real ale ~ Bar food ~ Restaurant ~ (01643) 831554 ~ Children welcome ~ Dogs allowed in bar ~ Open 11-2.30, 6-11; 11-11 Sat; 12-10.30 Sun ~ Bedrooms: £55B/£95B

White Horse 🛏
B3224

The long-standing barman in this sizeable creeper-covered inn keeps the place spick-and-span and offers a genuinely warm welcome to all his customers. The more-or-less open-plan bar has windsor and other country kitchen chairs, a high-backed antique settle, scrubbed deal tables, hunting prints, photographs above the stripped pine dado, and a good winter log fire. Well kept Exmoor Ale and Gold, and Greene King Old Speckled Hen, with summer guests like Cotleigh Tawny and Marstons Pedigree on handpump, and over 100 malt whiskies. Well liked honest bar food includes home-made soup (£1.95), sandwiches (from £1.95; baguettes from £2.95), ploughman's (from £3.75), sausage, egg, beans and chips (£4.55), cauliflower cheese (£5.45), home-made lasagne (£5.75), home-made steak and kidney pie (£5.95), daily specials, puddings (£2.95), and popular Sunday carvery (£6.25). The restaurant and eating area of the bar are no smoking; fruit machine, TV, cribbage, dominoes, and winter darts. The village green with children's play equipment is next to the pub. This is a pretty village set beside the River Exe in the heart of the Exmoor National Park. *(Recommended by Tracey and Stephen Groves, Simon Chell, Richard Gibbs, Lynda and Trevor Smith, Dr and Mrs P Truelove, Bob and Margaret Holder, Roger and Jenny Huggins, Andy and Jill Kassube, John Brightley, Jane and Adrian Tierney-Jones, Mike and Mary Carter)*

Free house ~ Licensees Peter and Linda Hendrie ~ Real ale ~ Bar food (11.30-2.30, 6-9.30) ~ Restaurant ~ (01643) 831229 ~ Children welcome ~ Dogs allowed in bar ~ Open 11-11; 12-10.30 Sun ~ Bedrooms: £35B/£55B

FAULKLAND ST7354 Map 2

Tuckers Grave ★ £

A366 E of village

Luckily, nothing ever changes at this warmly friendly and basic cider house. It is a very special place and still claims the title of Smallest Pub in the *Guide*. The flagstoned entry opens into a teeny unspoilt room with casks of well kept Bass and Butcombe Bitter on tap and Thatcher's Cheddar Valley cider in an alcove on the left. Two old cream-painted high-backed settles face each other across a single table on the right, and a side room has shove-ha'penny; dominoes. There's a skittle alley and tables and chairs on the back lawn, as well as winter fires and maybe newspapers to read. Food is limited to sandwiches and ploughman's at lunchtime. There's an attractive back garden. *(Recommended by John Poulter, the Didler, Paul Boot, Dr and Mrs M E Wilson, CMW, JJW, R Huggins, D Irving, E McCall, T McLean, Pete Baker)*

Free house ~ Licensees Ivan and Glenda Swift ~ Real ale ~ Bar food ~ No credit cards ~ (01373) 834230 ~ Children in family room ~ Open 11-3, 6-11; 12-3, 7-10.30 Sun; closed evenings 25 and 26 Dec

GLASTONBURY ST5039 Map 2

Who'd A Thought It

Northload Street (off A39/B3151 roundabout)

There are several linked areas in this pleasant place that make nice use of mellow reclaimed brick, relaid flagstones and pine panelling, and have coal fires, black beams, and a mix of furnishings from built-in pews to stripped country tables and chairs. The walls (and even the ceiling of the no smoking eating area) are profusely decorated with blue and white china, lots of photographs including aerial ones of old Glastonbury, and bygones from a shelf of earthenware flagons and another of old bottles to venerable enamel advertising signs; above an old-fashioned range are fly-fishing rods and a gun. Well liked bar food includes lunchtime sandwiches, various vegetarian dishes (from around £6.95), italian-style chicken or home-made thai fishcakes with chilli dipping sauce (£7.50), lamb shank in a rich rosemary and red wine gravy with mustard mash (£9.50), chicken breast wrapped in parma ham stuffed with goats cheese and spinach in a creamy mustard sauce (£9.95), quite a few fish dishes in various sauces (£10-£15), and duck breast with a port and cranberry gravy (£10.95). Well kept Palmers IPA, Gold and 200 on handpump, 13 wines by the glass, and daily papers. The lavatories are worth a look (the gents' has all you don't need to know, from what to do in a gas attack to a history of England from the Zulu Wars to World War II; the ladies' is more Beryl Cook). The outside of the pub is attractive. *(Recommended by David and Gilly Wilkins, J M Hill, Ken Flawn, H O Dickinson, Liz and Jeremy Baker, Michael Hicks)*

Palmers ~ Tenants Andrew and Irene Davis ~ Real ale ~ Bar food (12-2.30, 6-9.30) ~ Restaurant ~ (01458) 834460 ~ Children in restaurant and family room ~ Dogs allowed in bar ~ Monthly jazz, Irish or blue grass ~ Open 11-11; 12-10.30 Sun ~ Bedrooms: £45B/£60S(£65B)

HOLCOMBE ST6649 Map 2

Ring o' Roses 🍴 🛏

Village signposted off A367 by War Memorial in Stratton-on-the-Fosse, S of Radstock

Readers enjoy their visits to this quietly placed, extensively modernised country pub. There's a friendly welcome from the helpful staff, a relaxed and comfortably civilised feel, and good, popular food. The good-sized dining area on the left, nicely divided by balustrades and so forth, has blue and white plates and some modern prints on the walls. The handsome central bar faces attractively cushioned window seats, with a woodburning stove in a free-standing stone fireplace flanked by bookshelves. There are some orthodox cushioned captain's chairs around cast-iron-framed pub tables in this part, and behind is a gently lit parlourish area with sofas and cushioned chairs around low tables; there are more easy chairs in a pleasant panelled lounge on the right. Using only local suppliers, the well liked bar food at lunchtime includes starters like home-made pâté, home-made soup and deep-fried brie with raspberry coulis (all £3.25), sandwiches (from £3.50; hot steak and red onion £4.25), ploughman's (from £5.50), lambs liver and crispy bacon (£5.95), pork cutlet coated in a cider cream sauce or lamb loin chops with mint sauce (£6.25), roasted vegetable and five bean bake (£6.95), cold poached salmon with lemon mayonnaise (£7.50), and warm chicken breast and bacon salad with roasted pine kernels and walnut dressing (£7.95), with evening choices like twice baked goats cheese soufflé with balsamic onions and chargrilled aubergine (£4.75), cornish crab and crème fraîche mousse on cucumber raita dressed with avocado cream (£5.75), poached breast of guinea fowl and roasted leg with apple brandy and english mustard (£11.25), and half a roast crispy duck with a sweet kumquat and orange sauce (£12.95). The restaurant is no smoking. Blindmans Firken Dog and Otter Ale on handpump, a variety of local bottled ciders, daily papers, and perhaps faint piped radio. There are peaceful farmland views from picnic-sets on a terrace and on the lawn around the side and back, with nice shrub plantings and a small rockery. The chocolate labrador is called Sam. *(Recommended by Susan and Nigel Wilson, M G Hart, DRH and KLH, Angela Gorman, Paul Acton, Jack Taylor)*

Free house ~ Licensee Richard Rushton ~ Real ale ~ Bar food ~ Restaurant ~ (01761) 232478 ~ Children welcome ~ Dogs allowed in bar ~ Open 11.30-11; 11.30-2.30, 7-11 Sat; 11.30-2.30, 7-10.30 Sun ~ Bedrooms: £55B/£85B

HUISH EPISCOPI ST4326 Map 1
Rose & Crown
A372 E of Langport

There's a real sense of family history in this marvellous place. Both Mrs Pittard's father and grandfather held the licence for 55 years each, and the pub has been owned by the family for well over 135 years. Happily, the atmosphere and character remain as determinedly unpretentious and welcoming as ever. There's no bar as such – to get a drink (prices are very low), you just walk into the central flagstoned still room and choose from the casks of well kept Teignworthy Reel Ale or guests such as Butcombe Bitter or Hop Back Summer Lightning; also, several farm ciders (and local cider brandy). This servery is the only thoroughfare between the casual little front parlours with their unusual pointed-arch windows; genuinely friendly locals. Food is home-made, simple and cheap and uses local produce (and some home-grown fruit): generously filled sandwiches (from £2), broccoli and stilton or tomato and lentil soup (£2.80), a wide choice of good filled baked potatoes (from £3), ploughman's (£4.40), cottage pie or stilton and broccoli tart (£5.95), chicken breast in a creamy white wine and tarragon sauce, pork, apple and cider cobbler or steak in ale pie (£6.25), and puddings such as bread and butter pudding or apple pie (£2.95); good helpful service. Shove-ha'penny, dominoes and cribbage, and a much more orthodox big back extension family room has pool, darts, fruit machine, and juke box; skittle alley and popular quiz nights. One room is no smoking at lunchtimes and early evening. There are tables in a garden outside, and a second enclosed garden with a children's play area. The welsh collie is called Bonny. The local folk singers visit regularly, and on some summer weekends you might find the pub's cricket team playing out here (who always welcome a challenge); good nearby walks, and the site of the Battle of Langport (1645) is close by. *(Recommended by R T and J C Moggridge, Su and Bob Child, the Didler, A C Nugent, Comus and Sarah Elliott, Leigh and Gillian Mellor, Pete Baker, Richard Stancomb, Esther and John Sprinkle, OPUS, Bill and Jessica Ritson, Douglas Allen)*

Free house ~ Licensee Mrs Eileen Pittard ~ Real ale ~ Bar food (12-2, 5.45-7.45; sandwiches throughout opening hours) ~ No credit cards ~ (01458) 250494 ~ Children welcome ~ Dogs welcome ~ Open 11.30-2.30, 5.30-11; 11.30-11 Fri and Sat; 12-10.30 Sun

---

Pubs close to motorway junctions are listed at the back of the book.

KINGSDON ST5126 Map 2
Kingsdon Inn

At Podimore roundabout junction of A303, A372 and A37 take A372, then turn right on to B3151, right into village, and right again opposite post office

Although things have changed since one reader visited this pretty thatched cottage 53 years ago (and enjoyed his cider mulled by a red hot poker taken from the grate), there's still a friendly bustle in the four charmingly decorated, low-ceilinged rooms. On the right are some very nice old stripped pine tables with attractive cushioned farmhouse chairs, more seats in what was a small inglenook fireplace, a few low sagging beams, and an open woodburning stove with colourful dried and artificial fruits and flowers on the overmantel; down three steps through balustrading to a light, airy room with cushions on stripped pine built-in wall seats, curtains matching the scatter cushions, more stripped pine tables, and a winter open fire. Another similarly decorated room has more tables and another fireplace. At lunchtime, good, reasonably priced food includes filled baguettes, home-made soup (£3.60), home-made duck liver pâté (£4.60), deep-fried whitebait or ploughman's (£4.80), and lambs liver, bacon and onions, steak and kidney pie or smoked haddock and prawn mornay (all £6.50), with evening dishes like mushroom filled with cambozola and stilton (£4.90), grilled goats cheese with onion marmalade (£5.40), vegetable and parmesan risotto (£8.90), venison marinated in juniper berries, thyme and red wine (£11.90), and half a roast duck in scrumpy cider sauce (£12.80); daily specials such as warm scallop and smoked bacon salad (£5.80), and seared tuna steak with tomato and pepper sauce (£11.90); two dining areas are no smoking. Well kept Butcombe Bitter, Cotleigh Barn Owl, Otter Bitter, and maybe a guest from Cottage or Exmoor on handpump, decent wines, and 20 malt whiskies; piped music. Picnic-sets on the grass. The Lytes Cary (National Trust) and the Fleet Air Arm Museum are nearby. *(Recommended by P Duffield, Terence Boley, JCW, R and S Bentley, Tom Evans, Paul Hopton, Dr and Mrs M E Wilson, Theo, Anne and Jane Gaskin, Jack Taylor)*

Free house ~ Licensees Leslie and Anna-Marie Hood ~ Real ale ~ Bar food ~ Restaurant ~ (01935) 840543 ~ Well behaved children away from main bar; under 12s to leave by 8pm ~ Open 12-3, 6.30-11; 12-3, 7-10.30 Sun

LANGLEY MARSH ST0729 Map 1
Three Horseshoes ◥

Village signposted off B3227 from Wiveliscombe

Tucked away in the Somerset hills, this is a proper traditional local with all that goes with that – the landlady doing the cooking and the landlord looking after the beer. The back bar has low modern settles and polished wooden tables, dark red wallpaper, planes hanging from the ceiling, banknotes papering the wall behind the bar counter, a piano, and a local stone fireplace. Well kept Fullers London Pride, Otter Bitter, Palmers IPA, and Youngs tapped from the cask, and farm cider. Genuinely home-made, good value food includes large baps or sandwiches (from £2.75; soup and a sandwich £4.25), chicken liver pâté (£3.95), scrambled egg and smoked salmon or filled baked potatoes (£4.25), pizzas (from £4.50), steak and kidney pie (£6.50), fish pie (£7.25), steaks (from £8.95), daily specials like cheesy leek pancakes (£5.50), scallops with peppers and cream (£8.75), and venison in red wine and garlic (£9.50), and puddings like raspberry and almond cream or lemon sponge (from £3.25). The dining area has antique settles and tables and benches, and the lively front room has sensibly placed shove-ha'penny, table skittles, darts, dominoes, and cribbage; separate skittle alley, and piped music. You can sit on rustic seats on the verandah or in the sloping back garden, with a fully equipped children's play area; in fine weather there are usually vintage cars outside. They offer self-catering (and maybe bed and breakfast if they are not already booked up). *(Recommended by Bob and Margaret Holder, Tom Evans, M G Hart, Brian Monaghan, Jan MacLaran, the Didler, Julian Hosking, James Greenwood, Stephen, Julie and Hayley Brown, Tony and Maggie Bundey, Ian Phillips)*

Free house ~ Licensee John Hopkins ~ Real ale ~ Bar food (not winter Mon) ~ Restaurant ~ (01984) 623763 ~ No children under 8 inside ~ Open 12-2.30, 7-11(10.30 Sun); closed winter Mon ~ Bedrooms, see above

LOVINGTON ST5930 Map 2
Pilgrims Rest ❤️🍷

B3153 Castle Cary—Keinton Mandeville

Although there is quite an emphasis on the very good food in this quietly placed and civilised country bar/bistro, there are a few bar stools (and a frieze of hundreds of match books) by a corner counter with nice wines by the glass and well kept Cottage Champflower on handpump, from the nearby brewery. There's a chatty, relaxed feel, and a cosy little maroon-walled inner area has sunny modern country and city prints, a couple of shelves of books and china, a cushioned pew, a couple of settees and an old leather easy chair by the big fireplace. With flagstones throughout, this runs into the compact eating area, with candles on tables, heavy black beams and joists, and some stripped stone; piped music. The landlord cooks using all fresh ingredients including local meat and cheeses and daily fresh fish: a daily open sandwich like bacon and camembert on home-made focaccia bread or chicken liver and green peppercorn pâté (£5), crab cakes with piquant tomato salsa or charcuterie (£6), pasta with home-made pesto sauce, sunblush tomatoes and buffalo mozzarella (£9), beer-battered haddock with hand-made chips (£10), salmon with soy, garlic and fresh chilli sauce or sirloin steak with wild mushroom and red wine sauce (£14), roast rack of lamb or fillet of beef (from £14), chicken with bacon lardons, cider, cream and local apple brandy (£15), and puddings like sticky toffee pudding or chocolate mousse (£5); there is also a separate more formal carpeted no smoking dining room. The landlady's service is efficient and friendly, and there's a rack with daily papers. Picnic-sets and old-fashioned benches on the side grass, and the car park exit has its own traffic lights. More reports please. *(Recommended by BOB)*

Free house ~ Licensees Sally and Jools Mitchison ~ Real ale ~ Bar food ~ Restaurant ~ (01963) 240597 ~ Children welcome ~ Dogs allowed in bar ~ Open 12-3, 7-11; closed Sun evening, Mon and Tues lunchtimes; two weeks some time over winter

LUXBOROUGH SS9837 Map 1
Royal Oak

Kingsbridge; S of Dunster on minor roads into Brendon Hills – OS Sheet 181 map reference 983378

The atmospheric bar rooms in this country inn have beams and inglenooks, good log fires, flagstones in the front public bar, a fishing theme in one room, and a real medley of furniture; two characterful dining rooms (one is no smoking). Well kept real ales such as Cotleigh Tawny, Exmoor Gold, and Palmers 200 on handpump, local farm cider, and country wines. Bar food includes lunchtime filled baguettes, smooth chicken liver parfait with a sweet green tomato jam (£5.95), steak in ale pie (£6.95), artichoke and borlotti bean paella or rib-eye steak with stilton sauce (£11.95), risotto of smoked salmon (£13.25), loin of lamb with a mint and yoghurt crust (£14.75), and home-made puddings (£3.95). Dominoes and cribbage – no machines or music. Tables outside, and lots of good surrounding walks. In season, The Shoot will take precedence over any casual callers. More reports please. *(Recommended by Stephen, Julie and Hayley Brown, G F Couch, J M Hill, Suzanne Stacey, Mike and Shelley Woodroffe, Simon Chell, Ken and Jenny Simmonds, Richard Gibbs, the Didler, Andy and Jill Kassube, Jane and Ross Pascoe, Mrs Katie Roberts, Lynda and Trevor Smith, Anthony Barnes, Mrs P Burvill, Steve Whalley, Dr Paull Khan, R and J Bateman, Andy Sinden, Louise Harrington, Neil and Anita Christopher, Dr and Mrs P Truelove, John Dwane, Mike and Mary Carter, Tracey and Stephen Groves, Norman and Sarah Keeping, George Atkinson, Gaynor Gregory)*

Free house ~ Licensees James and Sian Waller and Sue Hinds ~ Real ale ~ Bar food ~ Restaurant ~ (01984) 640319 ~ Children in eating area of bar ~ Dogs allowed in bar

~ Folk every second Fri evening ~ Open 11-2.30, 6-11(10.30 Mon-Weds in winter);
12-2.30, 7-10.30 Sun; closed 25 Dec ~ Bedrooms: £55S/£60(£75B)

MELLS ST7249 Map 2
Talbot ¶ ◧ ⊨

W of Frome; off A362 W of Buckland Dinham, or A361 via Nunney and Whatley

Surrounded by lovely countryside, this is an interesting building, and although
many customers do come to eat, there are a couple of bars in which drinkers are
welcomed, and at weekends there is a 15th-c tithe barn with a high beamed ceiling
which is opened up: well kept Butcombe and Fullers London Pride tapped from the
cask. Taken in the restaurant, the well liked lunchtime food might include home-
made soup (£3.95), chicken liver parfait with spiced apple chutney (£4.95),
ploughman's (£6.95), open ciabatta sandwich with roast chicken, grilled bacon,
and malted brie (£7.25), ham and free range eggs (£7.65), grilled sausages with
garlic mash and mustard sauce (£7.95), steamed steak and kidney pudding (£8.25),
and tagliatelle with smoked salmon and asparagus in a tarragon cream sauce
(£8.75), with evening dishes like moules marinière (£5.95), wild mushroom and
asparagus tartlet (£6.95), calves liver with bacon and onion gravy (£11.95), chicken
breast filled with mushroom stuffing and rosemary sauce (£12.95), and whole
brixham lemon sole (£15.95); the restaurant is no smoking. The attractive main
room has stripped pews, mate's and wheelback chairs, fresh flowers and candles in
bottles on the mix of tables, and sporting and riding pictures on the walls, which
are partly stripped above a broad panelled dado, and partly rough terracotta-
colour. A small corridor leads to a nice little room with an open fire; piped music,
darts, TV, shove-ha'penny, cribbage and dominoes. There are seats in the cobbled
courtyard and a vine-covered pergola. The village was purchased by the Horner
family of the 'Little Jack Horner' nursery rhyme and the direct descendants still live
in the manor house next door. The bedrooms have been newly refurbished. More
reports please. *(Recommended by Gaynor Gregory, H E Wynter, Susan and Nigel Wilson,
John Coatsworth, Jack Taylor, Dr M Mills, David and Christine Vaughton, Richard Stancomb)*

*Free house ~ Licensee Roger Stanley Elliott ~ Real ale ~ Bar food ~ Restaurant ~
(01373) 812254 ~ Children welcome ~ Dogs allowed in bar ~ Open 12-2.30, 6.30-
11; 12-3, 7-10.30 Sun; closed 25 Dec evening ~ Bedrooms: £55B/£75B*

MONKSILVER ST0737 Map 1
Notley Arms ★ ¶

B3188

To be sure of a table here, you must arrive promptly as, in proper pub fashion, they
don't take reservations. The beamed and L-shaped bar has small settles and kitchen
chairs around the plain country wooden and candlelit tables, original paintings on
the ochre-coloured walls, fresh flowers, a couple of woodburning stoves, and
maybe a pair of cats. Popular bar food includes sandwiches or filled pitta breads,
home-made soup (£2.95), country-style pâté (£4.75), home-made tagliatelle with
bacon, mushrooms and cream (£5.25), aubergine tagine with dates and almonds
with couscous (£6.25), bacon, leek and cider pudding (£6.75), teriyaki-style chicken
(£7.95), lamb shanks with rosemary and red wine, beef and Guinness pie or fresh
cod fillet with lemon and parsley butter (£8.50), locally reared sirloin steak (£8.95),
and puddings such as treacle tart with clotted cream, lemon tart or fresh fruit
crumble (from £2.95); winter Sunday lunch. Well kept Exmoor Ale, Smiles Best,
and Wadworths 6X on handpump, farm cider, and country wines; cribbage,
dominoes, and alley skittles; good cheerful staff. Families are well looked after, with
colouring books and toys in the bright no smoking little family room. There are
more toys outside in the immaculate garden, running down to a swift clear stream.
This is a lovely village. *(Recommended by Rob Webster, Tracey and Stephen Groves,
Anthony Barnes, Stephen, Julie and Hayley Brown, John Dwane, Bob and Margaret Holder,
Brian and Bett Cox, the Didler, J M Hill, P Duffield, Andy and Jill Kassube, Peter and
Audrey Dowsett, Mrs Katie Roberts)*

Inn Partnership (Pubmaster) ~ Lease Alistair and Sarah Cade ~ Real ale ~ Bar food (11.30-2, 7-9.30) ~ (01984) 656217 ~ Children in family room ~ Dogs welcome ~ Open 11.30-2.30, 6.30-11; 12-2.30, 7-11(10.30 in winter) Sun; closed 2 weeks end Jan/beg Feb

NORTH CURRY ST3225 Map 1
Bird in Hand
Queens Square; off A378 (or A358) E of Taunton

There's a cheerful, friendly atmosphere in this village pub – which is also popular for its enjoyable food. The bustling but cosy main bar has pews, settles, benches, and old yew tables on the flagstones, original beams and timbers, and some locally woven willow work; there's a log fire in the inglenook fireplace. From an interesting menu, the well liked meals might include sandwiches, baked garlic field mushrooms topped with grilled goats cheese (£4.75), ploughman's or tasty mushroom omelette (£4.95), moules marinière (£6.50), pasta carbonara (£6.75), chinese chicken stir fry (£6.75), fillet steak baguette (£7.25), steaks (from £11.95), fresh fish from Plymouth such as bream or lemon sole (£12.95), bass (£13.95), and dover sole (£16.95), venison in port and orange sauce (£13.95), and puddings such as ginger and lime crunch cheesecake, meringues with coffee ice cream or raspberry brûlée; Sunday roast lunch. More formal dining is available in the separate no smoking restaurant area. Well kept Butcombe Gold, Hop Back Summer Lightning, and Otter Ale on handpump, Rich's farm cider, and half a dozen wines by the glass; good service. Piped music and fruit machine. *(Recommended by Patrick Hancock, Mike and Sue Loseby, Mandy and Simon King, Ian Phillips, Christine and Neil Townend, Tony and Maggie Bundey, Alan and Paula McCully, JCW, Dr and Mrs J F Head, Dr and Mrs A J Edwards, Andrew Barker, Claire Jenkins, Dr Martin Owton)*

Free house ~ Licensee James Mogg ~ Real ale ~ Bar food ~ Restaurant ~ (01823) 490248 ~ Children in eating area of bar and restaurant ~ Dogs allowed in bar ~ Open 12-3(4 Sat), 6(7 Sat)-11; 12-10.30 Sun; closed 25 Dec evening

NORTON ST PHILIP ST7755 Map 2
George ★ 🛏
A366

It is worth visiting this exceptional building to take in the fine surroundings of a place that has been offering hospitality to locals and travellers for over 700 years. The central Norton Room, which was the original bar, has really heavy beams, an oak panelled settle and solid dining chairs on the narrow strip wooden floor, a variety of 18th-c pictures, an open fire in the handsome stone fireplace, and a low wooden bar counter. Well kept Wadworths IPA, 6X, and a guest on handpump, decent wines with a good choice by the glass, and pleasant service. As you enter the building, there's a room on the right with high dark beams, squared dark half-panelling, a broad carved stone fireplace with an old iron fireback and pewter plates on the mantelpiece, a big mullioned window with leaded lights, and a round oak 17th-c table reputed to have been used by the Duke of Monmouth who stayed here before the Battle of Sedgemoor – after their defeat, his men were imprisoned in what is now the Monmouth Bar. The Charterhouse Bar is mostly used by those enjoying a drink before a meal: a wonderful pitched ceiling with trusses and timbering, heraldic shields and standards, jousting lances, and swords on the walls, a fine old stone fireplace, high backed cushioned heraldic-fabric dining chairs on the big rug over the wood plank floor, and an oak dresser with some pewter. Lunchtime bar food includes sandwiches, home-made soup (£3.95), warm chicken and bacon salad with coarse grain mustard (£5.25), home-cooked ham and egg (£5.50), terrine with chutney or leek, mushroom and potato gratin (£5.95), steak and kidney pudding, liver and bacon or chicken and ham pie (£6.95), and rump of lamb with mint and redcurrant sauce or chicken supreme with stilton and asparagus sauce (£8.95). The no smoking dining room (a restored barn with original oak ceiling beams, a pleasant if haphazard mix of early 19th-c portraits and hunting prints, and the same mix of vaguely old-looking furnishings) has a good relaxing, chatty atmosphere. The bedrooms are very atmospheric and comfortable – some reached by an external Norman stone stair-turret, and some across the cobbled and flagstoned courtyard and up into a fine half-timbered upper gallery (where there's a lovely 18th-c carved oak settle). A stroll over the meadow behind the pub (past the picnic-sets on the narrow grass pub garden) leads to an attractive churchyard around the medieval church whose bells struck Pepys (here on 12 June 1668) as 'mighty tuneable'. *(Recommended by John and Glenys Wheeler, the Didler, R Huggins, D Irving, E McCall, T McLean, J and B Cressey, Richard Stancomb, Su and Bob Child, Paul Boot, Joan and Brian Pickering, Michael Doswell, J F M and M West, George Atkinson, Graham Holden, Julie Lee, Alison Hayes, Pete Hanlon)*

Wadworths ~ Managers David and Tania Satchel ~ Real ale ~ Bar food ~ Restaurant ~ (01373) 834224 ~ Children in restaurant ~ Dogs allowed in bar ~ Open 11-2.30, 5.30-11; 11-11 Sat; 12-3, 7-10.30 Sun; closed evenings 25 Dec and 1 Jan ~ Bedrooms: £60B/£80B

OAKE ST1526 Map 1
Royal Oak
Hillcommon, N; B3227 W of Taunton

The licensees at this refurbished country pub arrived only about a year ago, but have quickly established a good reputation for food; when we arrived just before an evening opening, quite a few people were already waiting in the car park. They do sandwiches, lasagne and so forth, but the more interesting meals are the changing specials, with dishes such as chicken stuffed with asparagus wrapped in bacon in stilton sauce (£10.95), lemon sole fillets stuffed with prawns with a mushroom sauce (£11.95), duck with redcurrant, orange and port sauce (£12.95), and grilled bass with home-made red onion marmalade (£13.95). As we went to press, on Tuesday and Thursday lunchtimes pensioners could get their carvery and a pudding for £5.95. Most of the pub is no smoking. Completely redecorated over the last year, the spacious bar has several separate-seeming areas around the central servery; on the left is a neat little tiled fireplace, with a big woodburning stove on the other side. The windows have smart curtains, there are plenty of fresh flowers, and lots of brasses on the beams and walls. At the back is a long dining area popular with families; it leads out to a pleasant sheltered garden. Tables are candlelit in the evenings. Three well kept real ales such as Bass, Cotleigh Tawny, and Wadworths 6X on handpump; cheerful service. They have a skittle alley in winter; piped music. *(Recommended by Bob and Margaret Holder, Andy and Jill Kassube)*

Free house ~ Licensees John and Judy Phripp ~ Real ale ~ Bar food (12-2, 6.30-9.30) ~ Children welcome ~ Open 11-2.30, 6-11; closed Mon lunchtime exc bank hols; 25 Dec

PITNEY ST4428 Map 1
Halfway House 🚩
Just off B3153 W of Somerton

With a fine range of up to 10 real ales, it is not surprising that this old-fashioned and friendly pub is popular with quite a mix of customers. There's a bustling, chatty atmosphere in the three rooms which all have good log fires, and a homely feel underlined by a profusion of books, maps, and newspapers. As well as six regular ales tapped from the cask such as Butcombe Bitter, Cotleigh Tawny, Hop Back Summer Lightning, and Teignworthy Reel Ale, there might be guests like Archers Golden, Hop Back Crop Circle, and RCH Pitchfork. They also have 20 or so bottled beers from Belgium and other countries, Wilkins's farm cider, and quite a few malt whiskies; cribbage and dominoes. Good simple filling food includes sandwiches (from £2.50; smoked salmon and cream cheese £3.95), soup (£3.25), filled baked potatoes (from £2.95), and a fine ploughman's with home-made pickle (from £4.50). In the evening they do about half a dozen home-made curries (from £7.95). There are tables outside. *(Recommended by Evelyn and Derek Walter,*

Andrea Rampley, the Didler, Su and Bob Child, Paul Hopton, Theo, Anne and Jane Gaskin, Jane and Adrian Tierney-Jones, Richard Stancomb, OPUS, Ian and Nita Cooper, Richard Gibbs)

Free house ~ Licensees Julian and Judy Lichfield ~ Real ale ~ Bar food (not Sun) ~ (01458) 252513 ~ Well behaved children welcome ~ Dogs welcome ~ Open 11.30-3, 5.30-11; 12-3.30, 7-10.30 Sun

PORTISHEAD ST4777 Map 1
Windmill ◖

3.7 miles from M5 junction 17; A369 into town, then follow 'Sea Front' sign off left and into Nore Road

In fine weather, a big plus here is the great view over the Bristol Channel to Newport and Cardiff (with the bridges on the right), from the wall of picture windows on the top and bottom floors – the bottom a simple easy-going no smoking family area, the top a shade more elegant with its turkey carpet, muted green and cream wallpaper and dark panelled dado. The middle floor, set back from here, is quieter and (with its black-painted ceiling boards) more softly lit. A third of the building is no smoking; piped music and fruit machine. This is quite different from most of the pubs in this book, and started life as a golf club-house but re-opened as a three-level all-day family dining pub: to eat, you find a numbered table, present yourself at the order desk (by a slimline pudding show-cabinet), pay for your order, and return to the table with a tin (well, stainless steel) tray of cutlery, condiments and sauce packets. It works well: the good value generous food then comes quickly, and unexpectedly they have six quickly changing real ales on handpump, such as Bass, Butcombe Gold, Courage Best, RCH Pitchfork, and two guest beers on handpump; Thatcher's cider. The food includes sandwiches (from £2.95), filled baked potatoes (from £3.75), ploughman's (£4.75), steak and kidney pie (£6.75), steaks (from £9.95), and puddings (£3.50); there are dishes for smaller appetites (from £2.95) and early bird offers. Out on the seaward side are picnic-sets on three tiers of lantern-lit terrace, with flower plantings and a play area. *(Recommended by S H Godsell, Dr and Mrs M E Wilson, W R Miller, Ian Phillips, Tom Evans)*

Free house ~ Licensee J S Churchill ~ Real ale ~ Bar food (all day) ~ (01275) 843677 ~ Children in family area ~ Dogs allowed in bar ~ Open 11-11; 12-10.30 Sun

ROWBERROW ST4558 Map 1
Swan

Village signposted off A38 ¾ mile S of junction with A368

In a quiet village, this sizeable olde-worlde pub has picnic-sets by a pond in the attractive garden, and a tethering post for horses; good surrounding walks. Inside, there are low beams, some stripped stone, warm red décor, comic hunting and political prints, an ancient longcase clock, and a good chatty atmosphere; huge log fires. Well liked bar food includes lunchtimes sandwiches or filled baguettes (from £2), as well as soup (£2.40), stuffed mushrooms (£3.95), chicken liver and garlic mushroom pâté (£4.25), ploughman's (from £4.50), filled baked potatoes (from £4.85), ham and egg (£5.95), cider pork (£6.95), beef in ale pie (£7.50), a daily curry (£7.60), wild mushroom and brandy strudel (£7.95), aylesbury duck and cherry pie (£7.95), steaks (from £10.95), and puddings like treacle tart or apple and raspberry crumble (£3.95). Well kept Bass, Butcombe Bitter and Gold, and a guest from Bath, RCH or Charles Wells on handpump, and Thatcher's cider. No children inside. *(Recommended by Bob and Margaret Holder, Gaynor Gregory, Ken Flawn, MRSM, Matthew Shackle, K H Frostick, Michael Doswell, Ian and Rose Lock, Colin and Janet Roe, Ian Phillips, Roger and Jenny Huggins, Lucien Perring)*

Butcombe ~ Managers Elaine and Robert Flaxman ~ Real ale ~ Bar food (not 25 Dec, evenings 26 Dec and 31 Dec) ~ (01934) 852371 ~ Dogs welcome ~ Open 12-3, 6-11; 12-3, 7-10.30 Sun

SHEPTON MONTAGUE ST6731 Map 2
Montague Inn
Village signposted just off A359 Bruton—Castle Cary

Very pleasant little country pub with a warm welcome from the friendly licensees. The rooms are simply but tastefully furnished with stripped wooden tables, kitchen chairs and a log fire in the attractive inglenook fireplace, and there's a no smoking candlelit restaurant – which has new french windows overlooking the gardens. Using fresh organic produce where possible, the interesting food might include pâté (£5), ciabatta with bacon, brie and caramelised peppers, ham and egg, sausages and mash with onion gravy, smoked duck breast and mango salad, and ploughman's (all £7), mixed antipasti or steak and kidney pie (£8), a daily changing vegetarian dish (from £8), seafood gratin or pork tournedos with apple and cider sauce (£10), steaks (from £12), chicken stuffed with stilton wrapped with bacon on a wild mushroom sauce (£13), and bass with salsa verde (£14); best to book to be sure of a table. Well kept Greene King IPA with maybe a guest like Butcombe Gold tapped from the cask, and local cider; shove-ha'penny, cribbage and dominoes. The pretty back garden and terrace have good views. The bedrooms have been upgraded this year – we'd be grateful for reports from readers. *(Recommended by Simon Collett-Jones, S G N Bennett, DF, NF, Brian and Anita Randall, Paul and Annette Hallett, Robert Newton, Steve Dark, Paul A Moore, Kerry Milis, OPUS, Mrs J H S Lang, John A Barker, M G Hart)*

Free house ~ Licensees Julian and Linda Bear ~ Bar food (not Sun evening, Mon) ~ Restaurant ~ (01749) 813213 ~ Children in restaurant and family room ~ Dogs allowed in bedrooms ~ Open 11-2.30, 6-11; 12-2.30 Sun; closed Sun evening, Mon ~ Bedrooms: /£70S

SPARKFORD ST6026 Map 2
Sparkford Inn
High Street; just off A303 bypass W of Wincanton

Useful for the nearby Fleet Air Arm Museum at Yeovilton and Haynes Motor Museum, this rambling old coaching inn can get very busy (they do take coach parties), though you can usually find plenty of small areas to tuck yourself away in. The rather low-beamed, dimly lit rooms have good dining chairs around a nice mix of old tables in varying sizes, a colour scheme leaning towards plummy browns and dusky pinks, and plenty of worthwhile prints and other things to look at; some areas are no smoking, piped music. Bar food includes sandwiches, home-made soup (£3.25), creamy garlic mushrooms (£4.45), home-cooked ham and egg (£5.95), home-made chilli (£6.95), half rack of barbecued pork ribs (£7.95), steaks (from £9.75), and daily specials such as cottage pie (£6.95), smoked haddock and bacon au gratin or chicken and leek casserole (£7.45); lunchtime carvery (£6.95). The restaurant is no smoking. Well kept Bass, Butcombe Bitter, and Otter Ale on handpump. Tables outside, with a decent play area, and pretty tubs of flowers. *(Recommended by Peter and Audrey Dowsett, M G Hart, Alan and Paula McCully, John and Glenys Wheeler, Ian and Nita Cooper, Guy Consterdine, Richard and Judy Winn, Minda and Stanley Alexander, Doreen and Haydn Maddock , Dr and Mrs R E S Tanner, Jayne Capp, Mrs D W Privett, OPUS, Dr and Mrs M E Wilson, Margaret Mason, David Thompson)*

Free house ~ Licensee Paul Clayton ~ Real ale ~ Bar food ~ Restaurant ~ (01963) 440218 ~ Children in eating area of bar and restaurant ~ Dogs allowed in bar ~ Open 11-11; 12-10.30 Sun ~ Bedrooms: £40S/£65B

STANTON WICK ST6162 Map 2
Carpenters Arms ♀ ⇌
Village signposted off A368, just W of junction with A37 S of Bristol

Converted from a row of old miners' cottages, this long and low tile-roofed inn is set in peaceful countryside with pretty flowerbeds and picnic-sets on the front terrace. Inside, the Coopers Parlour is on the right and has one or two beams, seats around heavy tables with fresh flowers, and attractive curtains and plants in the windows; on the angle between here and the bar area there's a fat woodburning stove in an opened-through corner fireplace. The bar has wood-backed built-in wall seats and some red fabric-cushioned stools, stripped stone walls, and a big log fire. Diners are encouraged to step down into a snug inner room (lightened by mirrors in arched 'windows'), or to go round to the sturdy tables angling off on the right. Bar food includes home-made soup (£3.50), chicken liver and mushroom pâté with spiced apple chutney (£4.95), sandwiches (from £4.95), fettucine with smoked salmon and dill cream (£5.50; main course £8.95), steak, mushroom and ale pie or wild mushroom risotto (£8.95), thai green chicken curry (£10.95), roast duck breast and baby spinach with thyme and sherry vinegar jus (£12.95), and daily specials like moules marinière (£6.50), and pork stir fry with sweet chilli sauce (£10.95). Well kept Bass, Butcombe Bitter, Courage Best, and Wadworths 6X on handpump, a decent wine list, and several malt whiskies; fruit machine and TV. More reports please. *(Recommended by Michael Doswell, Nigel and Sue Foster, Ken Flawn, Dr T E Hothersall, Tom Evans)*

Buccaneer Holdings ~ Manager Simon Pledge ~ Real ale ~ Bar food (till 10) ~ Restaurant ~ (01761) 490202 ~ Children in eating area of bar and restaurant ~ Dogs allowed in bar ~ Pianist Fri/Sat evenings ~ Open 11-11; 12-10.30 Sun ~ Bedrooms: £62B/£84.50B

STOKE ST GREGORY ST3527 Map 1
Rose & Crown 🍴 🍷 🛏

Woodhill; follow North Curry signpost off A378 by junction with A358 – keep on to Stoke, bearing right in centre, passing church and follow lane for ½ mile

The long-standing licensees have now handed over the running of this friendly country pub to their two sons and their wives. It's been in the same family for 25 years and apart from newly decorated dining rooms and a few changes to the well liked bedrooms, not much is different – readers are quick to report cheerful, welcoming service and enjoyable food. The bar is decorated in a cosy and pleasantly romanticised stable theme: dark wooden loose-box partitions for some of the interestingly angled nooks and alcoves, lots of brasses and bits on the low beams and joists, stripped stonework, and appropriate pictures including a highland pony carrying a stag; many of the wildlife paintings on the walls are the work of the former landlady, and there's an 18th-c glass-covered well in one corner. Good bar food includes home-made soup (£3.50), lunchtime sandwiches (from £3.75; chorizo, egg mayonnaise and watercress £4) and ploughman's (from £4.50), local home-cooked smoked ham and eggs (£5.50), home-made steak and kidney pie (£6.50), lambs liver and bacon or scrumpy chicken (£8), prawn stir fry (£8.50), steaks (from £10), grilled brixham plaice fillets (£12.50), grilled skate wings (£13.50), and puddings such as rhubarb crumble or banoffi pie (£3.25). Plentiful breakfasts, and a good three-course Sunday lunch. The attractive dining room is no smoking. Well kept Exmoor Ale, Gold and Fox, and a guest ale on handpump, and a new wine list; unobtrusive piped classical music. Under cocktail parasols by an apple tree on the sheltered front terrace are some picnic-sets; summer barbecues and a pets corner for children. The pub is in an interesting Somerset Levels village with willow beds still supplying the two basket works. *(Recommended by Mike Gorton, Nigel Williamson, Ann and Max Cross, Ken Flawn, Richard and Margaret Peers, Dr and Mrs J F Head, Mrs J L Wyatt, Ian Phillips, Alan and Gill Bull, Mark and Amanda Sheard, Comus and Sarah Elliott, Theo, Anne and Jane Gaskin, Mrs A P Lee, JCW, Steve Dark, John and Fiona Merritt, Bob and Margaret Holder, JWAC)*

Free house ~ Licensees Stephen, Sally, Richard and Leonie Browning ~ Real ale ~ Bar food ~ Restaurant ~ (01823) 490296 ~ Children in eating area of bar and restaurant ~ Dogs allowed in bar ~ Open 11-3, 7-11; 12-3.30, 7-10.30 Sun; closed 25 Dec evening ~ Bedrooms: £36.50(£46.60B)/£53(£73B)

Pubs in outstandingly attractive surroundings are listed at the back of the book.

TRISCOMBE ST1535 Map 1
Blue Ball 🍴 ♀

Village signposted off A358 Crowcombe—Bagborough; turn off opposite sign to youth
hostel; OS Sheet 181 map reference 155355

Somerset Dining Pub of the Year

Very much enjoyed by readers, this rather smart place is on the first floor of a
lovely 15th-c thatched stone-built former coaching stables. The long, low building
slopes gently down on three levels, each with its own fire, and cleverly divided into
seating by hand-cut beech partitions; all the work was carried out with old-
fashioned craftsman's skills, and there is plenty of space. Well kept Cotleigh
Tawny, and a couple of guests such as Otter Head, and Sharps Doom Bar on
handpump; there are 400 wines on the list and they will open any under £20 for
just a glass; old cognacs and armagnacs, farm ciders, and home-made damson gin
or elderflower pressé. There's quite an emphasis on the particularly good,
interesting food which might include lunchtime filled crusty rolls with fillings like
duck and quince or cheese, hummous and sunblush tomatoes (£4.95), proper
ploughman's with good cheese and home-made pickles (£6.95), and super cod in
beer batter (£8.50), as well as watercress, potato and almond soup (£4.25), bang
bang chicken or pork terrine with apple and cider chutney (£5.75), crab and mango
salad (£6.25), seared scallops with sweet chilli and crème fraîche (£7.50), tarte tatin
of tomatoes, taleggio cheese and basil (£9.50), moroccan lamb tagine with couscous
and tzatziki (£11.50), indonesian spiced chicken with coconut and turmeric
(£11.95), duck breast and confit leg, onion marmalade and spiced orange butter
(£13.95), and wild bass with slow roast tomatoes, rosemary and garlic (£16.95),
with puddings like chocolate and praline tart with caramel ice cream, bread and
butter pudding or italian lemon tart (£4.25); good coffee. All dining areas are no
smoking; friendly, helpful staff. They have two tortoiseshell cats, whippets, and a
lurcher. The decking at the top of the woodside, terraced garden makes the most of
the views. *(Recommended by Paul and Annette Hallett, Bob and Margaret Holder, John and
Joan Calvert, John Kane, John and Judy Saville, M G Hart, Sylvia and Tony Birbeck, Brian and
Bett Cox, Anthony Barnes, Rob Webster, Richard and Margaret Peers, Mrs Katie Roberts,
J M Hill, Comus and Sarah Elliott, Ron and Val Broom, John and Jane Hayter, Tracey and
Stephen Groves)*

*Free house ~ Licensee Patrick Groves ~ Real ale ~ Bar food ~ Restaurant ~ (01984)
618242 ~ Well behaved children welcome ~ Dogs welcome ~ Open 12-2.30, 7-11;
12-3, 7-10.30 Sun*

WELLS ST5545 Map 2
City Arms 🍺

High Street

This is the sort of bustling place that many customers like to come back to. They
keep six real ales on handpump: Greene King Abbot, Morlands Original, and
Ruddles County, and three guests like Moles Barley Mole, Palmers Dorset Gold,
and Timothy Taylors Landlord. Also, quite a few wines by the glass, 25 malt
whiskies, and maybe farm cider. It's rather like a cellar bar (and refurbished this
year) with arched doorways and double baluster-shaped pillars, cushioned mate's
chairs, a nice old black settle, and a Regency-style settee and a couple of sofas; up a
step is a similar room with pictures and Wills Grand National cigarette cards on the
walls, big tables and solid chairs, and beyond that, a separate bar with neat sturdy
settles forming booths around tables; plenty of Victorian and Victorian-style
engravings. One area and the fine open-beamed upstairs restaurant are no smoking
while people are eating. Under the present chef, bar food is good, and includes
sandwiches, minestrone (£2.95), chicken liver and cognac pâté (£3.95), field
mushrooms stuffed with gruyère and pesto (£3.95; main course £6.95), aberdeen
angus steaks (from £6.75), lambs liver on garlic and herb mash with onions and
bacon or chicken tikka masala (£7.50), and daily specials like pork chops with
roasted pear and red wine sauce (£7.50), beef and oyster pie (£8.50), and whole

bass with fennel, orange and mustard dressing (£10.95). Friendly service; piped pop music, dominoes and cribbage. It does get crowded at peak times. To get to the pub, you walk through the award-winning cobbled courtyard with metal seats and tables, trees and flowers in pots, and attractive side verandah. *(Recommended by Sarah Money, Paul Hopton, Mr and Mrs R A Newbury , Michael Hicks, Jane Taylor, David Dutton, Derek and Sylvia Stephenson, Guy Consterdine, Darly Graton, Graeme Gulibert, Geoff Calcott, Gwyn Jones, B H and J I Andrews)*

Free house ~ Licensee Jim Hardy ~ Real ale ~ Bar food (all day until 10(9 Sun)) ~ Restaurant ~ (01749) 673916 ~ Children in family room ~ Dogs welcome ~ Open 9-11; 9-10.30 Sun

Crown
Market Place

In the heart of this appealing small city, this former coaching inn has been brightly refurbished and modernised in recent years, and is a useful place to pop in for coffee, lunch or afternoon tea. Despite the building's age, the various bar areas have a very clean, contemporary feel, with the walls painted white or blue, light wooden flooring, and plenty of matching chairs and cushioned wall benches; up a step is a comfortable area with a sofa, and newspapers. A sunny back room has an exposed stone fireplace, GWR prints, and a couple of fruit machines; it opens on to a small courtyard with a few tables. Reliable lunchtime meals include sandwiches and paninis (from £3.75), and ham, egg and rösti, cod and chips or lasagne (£5.95), with evening extras such as baked mozzarella wrapped in parma ham, rocket, balsamic vinegar and olive oil (£5.95), salmon with braised ratatouille (£6.95), chargrilled 6oz rib-eye steak (£7.50), supreme of corn-fed chicken with braised puy lentils and smoky bacon and mushroom sauce (£11.95), roast best end of english lamb with assorted beans (£13.95), and puddings such as double chocolate terrine laced with Baileys or baked apple and raspberry crumble (£3.95). Butcombe, Oakhill Best and Smiles on handpump; helpful service from polite young staff. Part of the restaurant and part of the Penn Bar are no smoking. The music can be a little loud at times. Though there are usually lots of tourists (William Penn is said to have preached from a window here), there are generally a few young locals too. We've yet to hear from readers who have stayed overnight here. *(Recommended by Mr and Mrs Richard Hanks, David Carr, Peter and Audrey Dowsett)*

Free house ~ Licensee Adrian Lawrence ~ Real ale ~ Bar food (12-2, 6-8) ~ Restaurant ~ (01749) 673457 ~ Children welcome ~ Open 11-11; 12-10.30 Sun ~ Bedrooms: /£60B

WINSFORD SS9034 Map 1
Royal Oak ♀ ⇌

In Exmoor National Park, village signposted from A396 about 10 miles S of Dunster

Civilised and rather smart, this is a lovely thatched inn in fine surroundings with good nearby walks. The attractively furnished lounge bar has a cushioned big bay-window seat from which you can look across the road towards the village green and foot and packhorse bridges over the River Winn, tartan-cushioned bar stools by the panelled counter (above which hang horsebrasses and pewter tankards), armed and cushioned windsor chairs set around little wooden tables, and a gas-fired stove in the big stone hearth. Another similar bar offers more eating space with built-in wood-panelled seats creating booths, fresh flowers, and country prints; there are several pretty and comfortable lounges. Served by friendly staff, lunchtime bar snacks include home-made soup (£3.95), sandwiches (with salad and crisps, from £4.25), home-made chicken liver parfait with red onion marmalade (£4.95), and ploughman's (from £5.95), with evening dishes such as pork and leek sausages with creamy mash and onion gravy (£8.95), lamb shank on bacon and spring onion mash or wild mushroom and white wine risotto (£9.25), whole grilled plaice with lemon and herb butter (£10.50), sirloin steak (£12.95), and home-made puddings (£3.50). Well kept Brakspears Bitter and Butcombe Bitter on handpump.

(Recommended by Tracey and Stephen Groves, Andy and Jill Kassube, Jane and Adrian Tierney-Jones, Bob and Margaret Holder, Colin Fisher, Ron and Val Broom, Mike and Mary Carter)

Free house ~ Licensee Charles Steven ~ Real ale ~ Bar food ~ Restaurant ~ (01643) 851455 ~ Children in eating area of bar and restaurant ~ Dogs allowed in bar ~ Open 11-2.30, 6-11; 12-3, 7-11 Sun ~ Bedrooms: /£120B

WITHYPOOL SS8435 Map 1
Royal Oak ♀ 🛏
Village signposted off B3233

R. D. Blackmore stayed in this country village inn while writing *Lorna Doone* and today, it is still a comfortable place to spend the night. The beamed lounge bar has a fine raised log fireplace, comfortably cushioned wall seating and slat-backed chairs, and stags heads, stuffed fish, several fox masks, sporting prints and paintings and various copper and brass ornaments on its walls. The locals' bar (named after the barman Jake who has been here for over 25 years) has some old oak tables, and plenty of character. Enjoyable bar food includes sandwiches, home-made soup (£3.50), smoked trout pâté or home-cured Pernod and parsley gravadlax with citrus crème fraîche (£5.75), risotto of courgette and sun-dried tomatoes with pesto and parmesan dressing (£9.95), cherry and apple wild boar sausages with red onion gravy (£10.50), grilled lamb cutlets with rosemary jus and fine ratatouille (£11.50), seared tuna on niçoise salad with chilli and lime dressing (£12.95), daily specials such as home-baked ham and eggs (£7.95), roast loin of pork with garlic and rosemary sauce (£8.50), and strips of beef fillet in a brandy, cream and mushroom sauce (£11.95), and puddings like sticky toffee pudding with butterscotch sauce or raspberry cheesecake with mango coulis (£4.50). Well kept Exmoor Ale and Gold on handpump, quite a few malt whiskies, and a decent wine list. It can get very busy (especially on Sunday lunchtimes), and is popular with the local hunting and shooting types; cribbage and dominoes; piped music in the restaurant only. There are wooden benches on the terrace, and just up the road, some grand views from Winsford Hill. The River Barle runs through the village itself, with pretty bridleways following it through a wooded combe further upstream. *(Recommended by Bob and Margaret Holder, Jane and Adrian Tierney-Jones, V Green, John Brightley, R M Corlett, Colin and Stephanie McFie, Tracey and Stephen Groves, P R Morley)*

Free house ~ Licensee Gail Sloggett ~ Real ale ~ Bar food (12-2, 6.30-9.30) ~ (01643) 831506 ~ Children in bottom bar and restaurant ~ Dogs allowed in bar and bedrooms ~ Open 11(12 Sun)-2.30, 6-11 ~ Bedrooms: £65B/£100B

WOOKEY ST5145 Map 2
Burcott ◖
B3139 W of Wells

Neatly kept and friendly, this little roadside pub has two simply furnished small front bar rooms that are connected but different in character. There's a square corner bar counter in the lounge, fresh flowers at either end of the mantelpiece above the tiny stone fireplace, Parker-Knollish brocaded chairs around a couple of tables, and high bar stools; the other bar has beams (some willow pattern plates on one), a solid settle by the window and a high backed old pine settle by one wall, cushioned mate's chairs and fresh flowers on the mix of nice old pine tables, old-fashioned oil-type wall lamps, and a hunting horn on the bressumer above the fireplace. A little room on the right has darts, shove-ha'penny, cribbage and dominoes, neat built-in wall seats, and small framed advertisements for Schweppes, Coke, Jennings and Oakhill, and there's a roomy back no smoking restaurant with black joists, stripped stone walls and sea-green check tablecloths; piped music. Tasty bar food includes home-made soup (£2.95), sandwiches (from £3.25 for 1½ rounds), filled baked potatoes (from £3.45), creamy garlic mushrooms (£3.75), ploughman's (£4.95), ham and eggs (£5.95), vegetable and cashew nut bake (£6.25), home-made steak in ale pie (£7.25), roasted duck breast flamed in whisky with a fresh orange marmalade sauce (£9.95), steaks (from £10), and daily specials. Well kept Cotleigh Barn Owl, RCH Pitchfork, Teignworthy Old Moggie, and a beer named for the pub brewed for them by Sharps on handpump, and several wines by the glass. The window boxes and tubs in front of the building are pretty in summer, and the sizeable garden is well spread and has picnic-sets, plenty of small trees and shrubs, and Mendip Hill views; there's a paddock beyond. *(Recommended by Comus and Sarah Elliott, Hugh Roberts, Phil and Sally Gorton, Su and Bob Child, Tom Evans, Mrs Louise Wilkes, Ian and Nita Cooper)*

Free house ~ Licensees Ian and Anne Stead ~ Real ale ~ Bar food (not Sun or Mon evenings) ~ Restaurant ~ (01749) 673874 ~ Children in straightforward family room and restaurant ~ Open 11.30(12 Sat)-2.30(3 Sat), 6-11; 12-3, 7-10.30 Sun; closed 25 and 26 Dec, 1 Jan

---

Lucky Dip

Besides the fully inspected pubs, you might like to try these Lucky Dips recommended to us and described by readers (if you do, please send us reports: www.goodguides.com).

ABBOTS LEIGH [ST5473]
George [A369, between M5 junction 19 and Bristol]: Popular main-road dining pub, tidy and comfortable, with huge choice of attractively presented reasonably priced food from snacks up, well kept ales inc Marstons Pedigree, friendly staff, two log fires; no children, good-sized enclosed garden *(LYM, Rex Miller)*
ASHCOTT [ST4436]
Pipers [A39/A361, SE of village]: Large welcoming beamed lounge, well kept ales such as Butcombe, Greene King Old Speckled Hen, Oakhill, John Smiths, Tetleys, Wadworths and Youngers, wide choice of good reasonably priced food from sandwiches to steaks inc children's, prompt pleasant service, woodburner, leather armchairs, pictures for sale and potted plants, prettily set no smoking beamed dining area; unobtrusive piped music; pleasant roadside garden *(Dr and Mrs C W Thomas, Anne and David Robinson)*
☆ *Ring o' Bells* [High St; follow Church and Village Hall signs off A39 W of Street]: Neatly kept comfortably modernised local, steps up and down making snug areas (at least for the able-bodied), well kept local Moor Merlins Magic and two interesting guest beers, Wilkins's farm cider, wide choice of good value wholesome home-made food from good sandwiches and rolls to unusual dishes and sturdy puddings, separate no smoking stripy pink dining room, decent wines, chatty landlord and helpful service, inglenook woodburner; piped pop music, fruit machines, skittle alley; attractively planted back garden with play area, camping *(Richard and Margaret Peers, Dr and Mrs C W Thomas, Dr and Mrs J F Head, BB)*
ASHILL [ST3217]
Ashill Inn: Family pub with enjoyable bar food, well kept beers, popular carvery Fri night and Sun lunchtime; bedrooms *(Mrs B Larcombe)*
BATH [ST7564]
Ale House [York St]: Cosy and relaxed city-centre local with big windows to street, well kept Courage, Fullers London Pride and

Charles Wells Bombardier, flame-effect fire, food in cellar bar, more seating upstairs, Bath RFC memorabilia *(Susan and Nigel Wilson, Dr and Mrs M E Wilson)*
Bell [Walcot St]: Long narrow studenty musicians' pub, with up to nine well kept changing ales mainly from small breweries, hops hanging from dark ceiling, lots of pump clips and notices, good value baguettes (bargain sell-off end of evening), friendly efficient informal service; calm at lunchtime, lively with loud piped music evenings, frequent live music *(LM, R Huggins, D Irving, E McCall, T McLean, Dr and Mrs A K Clarke)*
Boaters [Argyle St, by Pulteney Bridge]: Good location near river and weir, main bar upstairs, neat cellar bar mainly for younger people, well kept Bass and Courage, enterprising filled rolls, friendly staff; no children inside; tables in good-sized floodlit courtyard *(Esther and John Sprinkle)*
Boathouse [Newbridge Rd]: Large unpubby but attractive riverside establishment nr Kennet & Avon marina on outskirts, rugs on wooden floor, apple-theme and riverside decorations, good value food from filled ciabattas to steaks and restaurant dishes, efficient courteous service, decent house wines, Greene King IPA and Old Speckled Hen; children very welcome, wicker furniture and potted plants in conservatory on lower level, picnic-sets out in neat garden with labelled herbs and steps up to waterside balcony *(Ian Phillips, Anne and David Robinson, Dr and Mrs M E Wilson)*
☆ *Coeur de Lion* [Northumberland Pl; off High St by W H Smith]: Tiny single-room pub (twelve's a crowd), not smart but perhaps Bath's prettiest, cosy and friendly, with well kept Adnams and Charles Wells Bombardier, candles and log-effect gas fire, good mulled wine at Christmas, lunchtime filled rolls in summer; may be piped music, stairs to lavatories; open all day, tables out in charming flower-filled flagstoned pedestrian alley *(LYM, Rona Murdoch, Dr and Mrs A K Clarke, the Didler, Dr and Mrs M E Wilson, SLC, Val and Alan Green)*

☆ *Cross Keys* [Midford Rd (B3110)]: Well refurbished dining lounge with smarter end restaurant (best to book, high chairs for children), good cheap food cooked to order from home-made burgers and sausages up inc popular pies and great choice of puddings, three real ales, friendly service, locals' bar; big garden with prettily populated aviary – great attraction for children *(Meg and Colin Hamilton)*

Curfew [Clevedon Pl W]: Busy low-ceilinged bar, big table on landing down stairs, pool table as well as comfortable seating upstairs, real ales such as Bass and Wadworths 6X; can be smoky; open all day wknds *(R Huggins, D Irving, E McCall, T McLean)*

George [Mill Lane, Bathampton (off A36 towards Warminster or A4 towards Chippenham)]: Busy creeper-covered dining pub distinguished by its nice canalside position, attractive upstairs no smoking family dining room overlooking water, and tables on quiet waterside terrace, safe and spacious, with garden bar; has been popular for a wide choice of enjoyable food, well kept mainstream ales and good log fires, but no reports since its recent takeover by a chain – news please *(anon)*

Olde Farmhouse [Lansdown Rd]: Pleasant setting on hill overlooking Bath, well kept Abbey Bellringer (from neighbouring microbrewery), Butcombe and Wadworths, real fire, perhaps filled cobs, L-shaped parquet-floor bar with wall seats, panelling, stained-glass lamps and bar gantry, big jazz pictures; juke box, big-screen TV; jazz some evenings, open all day *(the Didler, SLC)*

Pig & Fiddle [Saracen St]: Small lively pub tied to Ash Vine, their full range kept well at sensible prices, perhaps guests such as Abbey and Bath, two big open fires, clocks set to different time zones, bare boards and cheery red and yellow walls and ceiling, good value home-made food, steps up to darker bustling servery and little dining area, takeaways too, games area and several TVs; lots of students at night, good if loud piped trendy pop music; picnic-sets on big heated front terrace *(Dr and Mrs A K Clarke, Dr and Mrs M E Wilson, BB, SLC)*

Porter [George St/Miles's Buildings]: Entirely vegetarian food, reasonably priced, largely organic and inc vegan dishes in lively informal pub with well kept Abbey Bellringer, Marstons Pedigree and Smiles, wide choice of other drinks, games room with two pool tables, music area with its own bar and DJs or live bands (admission charge only on comedy nights) *(Christopher and Jo Barton)*

Pulteney Arms [Daniel St/Sutton St]: Small, with well kept Bass, Smiles, Wadworths 6X and a guest tapped from the cask, good chip baps and other food, jugs and lots of rugby posters and Bath RFC memorabilia; unobtrusive piped music; pavement tables *(Colin and Peggy Wilshire, Pete Baker)*

Rising Sun [Grove St]: Small lively pub with well kept ales, good sherries, fresh sandwiches lunchtime and evening, traditional flock wallpaper décor, darts and skittle alley *(Richard Pierce)*

☆ *Salamander* [John St]: Traditional pub tied to Bath Ales, full range of their beers and guests kept well, bare boards and black woodwork, three rooms inc no smoking, no pool, juke box or machines; upstairs is open-kitchen restaurant with good sensibly priced food, decent wines *(Colin and Peggy Wilshire, Dr and Mrs M E Wilson, Geoff and Jan Dawson, Clive Hilton)*

Sam Weller [Upper Borough Walls]: Well kept changing ales, moderately priced wholesome food cooked to order inc all-day breakfast, cheap house wines, no smoking area, friendly young staff, lively mix of customers *(Colin and Peggy Wilshire, Dr and Mrs A K Clarke)*

BATHFORD [ST7866]

Crown [Bathford Hill, towards Bradford-on-Avon, by Batheaston roundabout and bridge]: Spacious and attractively laid out family pub, several distinct but linked areas inc no smoking garden room, good log fire, interesting fairly priced food, well kept real ales, decent wines; tables on terrace, nice garden *(Dr and Mrs A K Clarke, LYM)*

BATHPOOL [ST2525]

Bathpool Inn [A38]: Welcoming neatly kept family pub with plenty to entertain children away from the bar, lots of cosy seating in several linked rooms, each in a different style, friendly helpful staff, fresh food from sandwiches and chips up, high chairs, real ales such as Wadworths 6X, big glasses of wine; safe garden with bark-covered play park and bouncy castle *(Dennis Jenkin, Joe Green)*

BAYFORD [ST7228]

Unicorn: Beams and flagstones, cosy snug beyond fireplace (which now has a log fire again, instead of the water feature that claimed it for a while), friendly welcome, wide choice of food, well kept Butcombe, Fullers London Pride and guest ales, end restaurant area; four good simple bedrooms with own bathrooms, good breakfast *(David Kirkcaldy)*

BECKINGTON [ST8051]

☆ *Woolpack* [off A36 Bath—Warminster]: Well refurbished old inn much improved since village bypass, with big log fire and candlelit tables in flagstoned bar, smarter attractive no smoking dining room and conservatory, enjoyable if not cheap food, well kept ales such as Batemans, Greene King Old Speckled Hen and Wadworths 6X, decent wines, helpful staff; children welcome, comfortable period bedrooms with own bathrooms (but avoid the attic), open all day *(Lady Heath, Dr Diana Terry, Tim O'Keefe, LYM, Dr and Mrs M E Wilson, Philip Irons)*

BLACKFORD [ST4147]

☆ *Sexeys Arms* [B3139 W of Wedmore]: Pleasant village pub dating from 1400s, cosy beamed lounge with big fireplace and unobtrusive piped music, basic tiled floor public bar, friendly landlord well up in local history, enjoyable meals all cooked to order in two sizes of helpings, cheerful service, evening restaurant; picnic-sets in garden, cl Mon at

least in winter (when wkdy hours are a bit
restricted) *(KC)*

BLAGDON [ST5058]

New Inn [off A368; Park Lane]: Old-fashioned
beamed pub with some comfortable antique
settles among more modern furnishings, two
inglenook log fires, enjoyable bar food from
filled rolls up (but just roasts on Sun – and they
simply stop serving early if busy), no smoking
dining area, well kept Butcombe and
Wadworths IPA and 6X; piped music, no
children or dogs; nice views from tables outside
looking down to Blagdon Lake and beyond
*(B and F A Hannam, Jane and Graham Rooth,
LYM, Ian and Rose Lock, M G Hart)*

Queen Adelaide [High St]: Quiet clean one-bar
local in lovely spot overlooking Blagdon Lake,
traditionally decorated, plenty of candlelit
tables, wide choice of well cooked generous
food, well kept beers inc Butcombe, coal-effect
gas fire *(Comus and Sarah Elliott, W R Miller)*

BLAGDON HILL [ST2118]

Lamb & Flag [4 miles S of Taunton]: Doing
well under new licensees, homely country
décor with beams and settles, decent food, well
kept real ales, log fire *(John and Fiona Merritt)*

BRADFORD-ON-TONE [ST1722]

☆ *White Horse*: Well furnished and neatly kept
stone-built local in quiet village, staff helpful
and eager to please, wide choice of enjoyable
reasonably priced food in bar eating area and
restaurant, three well kept ales inc Cotleigh,
decent wines; well laid out side garden, skittle
alley *(Pamela and Merlyn Horswell,
Christine and Neil Townend, Bob and
Margaret Holder)*

BRADLEY GREEN [ST2438]

Malt Shovel [off A39 W of Bridgwater, nr
Cannington]: New licensees here, and no
longer has bedrooms; beamed main bar with
straightforward furniture and woodburner,
little beamed snug, no smoking restaurant and
family room, decent bar food, Butcombe Bitter,
Exmoor Fox and two guest beers, wines by the
glass, traditional games and sizeable skittle
alley; piped music; children in eating areas,
picnic-sets in garden *(LYM)*

BRISTOL [ST5773]

Alma [Alma Vale Rd, Clifton]: Cheerful
extensively refurbished town pub, real ales
such as Greene King Abbot, Theakstons XB
and Wadworths 6X, good plain cheap food,
friendly service, no music; popular upstairs
theatre Tues-Sat – best to book; small back
garden (not late evening) *(Simon and Amanda
Southwell, Dr Diana Terry, Tim O'Keefe)*

Avon Packet [Coronation Rd, Southville]:
Cheerful old-fashioned pub with well kept
Courage Best, Smiles Best and two local ciders,
bridge over cellar access yard to small garden
with picnic-sets and play area; handy for SS
Great Britain *(Ian Phillips)*

Bag o' Nails [St Georges Rd, Hotwells]: Small
shop front for cosy but airy room, well worn
benches and small tables along its length, bare
boards and panelling, soft gas lighting,
inglenook seat by gas fire, glazed portholes
into cellar, old local pictures, well kept Bass,

Burton Bridge, Wye Valley and changing ales
such as RCH and Smiles from long bar, lots of
bottled beers, friendly informative landlord,
helpful staff, good soup and cheeses; piped jazz
*(the Didler, Simon and Amanda Southwell,
Catherine Pitt, Mike Pugh)*

☆ *Brewery Tap* [Upper Maudlin St/Colston St]:
Tap for Smiles brewery, their beers kept well
and sensibly priced, also unusual continental
bottled ones, interesting unpretentious décor,
good chattily relaxed atmosphere even when
packed, log fire in no smoking room, good
value food from filled rolls up, no piped music;
open all day *(Simon and Amanda Southwell,
Matthew Shackle, the Didler, Neville and
Anne Morley, Stephen and Jean Curtis)*

Bridge Inn [Passage St]: Neat tiny one-bar city
pub nr floating harbour, good friendly service,
lots of film stills and posters, well kept Bath
ales, popular lunchtime snacks *(the Didler)*

☆ *Commercial Rooms* [Corn St]: One of
Wetherspoons' best, vast busy conversion of
impressive former merchants' club, hall with
lofty domed ceiling and snug cubicles along
one side, gas lighting, comfortable quieter no
smoking room with ornate balcony; wide
changing choice of good real ales, food all day
inc super granary bread sandwiches,
reasonable prices; good location, very busy
wknd evenings, side wheelchair access
*(G Coates, Peter Scillitoe, Dr and
Mrs A K Clarke, Tony and Wendy Hobden,
Joyce and Maurice Cottrell, the Didler,
Andrew Shore)*

Cornubia [Temple St]: 18th-c backstreet pub
hidden away in concrete jungle, well kept ales
such as local Nursery and RCH, interesting
bottled beers, farm cider, good value home-
cooked food inc Sun roasts, small woody
seating areas in oranges, browns and reds;
benches outside *(Catherine Pitt, the Didler,
Simon and Amanda Southwell)*

Cottage [Baltic Wharf, Cumberland Rd]:
Attractive converted stone-built customs house
on southern bank of Floating Harbour, nr
Maritime Heritage Centre, with fine views of
Georgian landmarks and Clifton suspension
bridge from terrace; comfortable, roomy and
civilised, with big helpings of wholesome plain
home-made food from sandwiches up all day,
well kept Flowers IPA, Smiles Best and
Wadworths 6X, friendly service; may be piped
music; open all day, access through sailing
club, on foot along waterfront, or by round-
harbour ferry *(Colin and Peggy Wilshire,
Ian Phillips, Peter Scillitoe)*

Highbury Vaults [St Michaels Hill, Cotham]:
Nice series of small rooms with old-fashioned
furniture and prints, well kept Youngs and
Smiles, cheap bar food (not Sat/Sun evenings),
bar billiards, dominoes, cribbage; attractive
back terrace with heated arbour, open all day,
busy with Univ students and teachers, children
welcome *(LYM, Simon and Amanda Southwell)*

Hope & Anchor [Jacobs Wells Rd, Clifton]:
Bare-boards 18th-c studenty pub with large
shared pine tables, well kept changing ales
from small breweries, fast pleasant service,

reliable substantial cheap food inc lots of sandwiches, interesting dishes and sumptuous ploughman's – very popular lunchtime; piped music may be loud, can get crowded and smoky late evening; disabled access, summer evening barbecues on good back terrace with interesting niches, occasional live music *(Simon and Amanda Southwell, Matthew Shackle)*

☆ *Kings Head* [Victoria St]: Narrow 17th-c pub lightened by big welcoming front window and splendid mirrored bar back, corridor to cosy panelled back snug with serving hatch, well kept Bass, Courage Best and Smiles, toby jugs on joists, old-fashioned local prints and interesting gas pressure gauge, friendly relaxed atmosphere, generous reasonably priced food inc filling toasties and good yorkshire puddings wkdy lunchtimes; pavement tables, cl Sat lunchtime, open all day Weds-Fri *(Di and Mike Gillam, the Didler, BB, Pete Baker)*

Llandoger Trow [off King St/Welsh Back]: By docks, interesting as the last timber-framed building built here, and making the most of its picturesque past in very cosy collection of cleverly lit small alcoves and rooms with original fireplaces and carvings; reasonably priced simple bar food, draught sherries, eclectic array of liqueur coffees, friendly staff, good mix from students to tourists *(Val Stevenson, Rob Holmes, Richard Pierce)*

Myrtle Tree [Hotwells]: Single unspoilt room, so small it has no cellar and barrels of well kept Bass stand at the end of the bar *(the Didler)*

Old Fish Market [Baldwin St]: Imposing red and cream brick building converted to roomy and airy pub, good mural showing it in 1790s along one wall, lots of wood inc rather ornate counter, parquet floor, relaxed friendly atmosphere, good value lunchtime food from sandwiches through home-baked pies to Sun lunch, well kept Fullers London Pride, ESB and seasonal and guest beers, good coffee, daily papers; quiet piped music, sports TV *(Joyce and Maurice Cottrell, Simon and Amanda Southwell, Nick Elliott, Richard Pierce)*

Palace [West St/Old Market St]: Old-fashioned décor with high-backed settles, fancy chandelier, sloping floor, intricate plasterwork and paint, spiral columns, interesting (!) photographs; now has Bath Spa and Gem and Hop Back Summer Lightning *(the Didler)*

Robin Hood [St Michaels Hill]: Genuine local with a real welcome for strangers, Wadworths beers, food from baguettes and baked potatoes up lunchtime and Mon-Thurs early evening, rock star photographs especially Elvis; small heated garden *(Simon and Amanda Southwell)*

White Lion [Quay Head, Colston Ave]: Small simple bare-boards bar with well kept Wickwar ales such as Coopers, BOB and the hefty Station Porter, a guest such as Tring Colleys Dog, tasters offered and one of the beers at bargain price, very friendly service, wide choice of sandwiches, log fire; a couple of tables out by road, garden with wrought-iron furniture *(BB, Catherine Pitt)*

BURNHAM-ON-SEA [ST3049]

Dunstan House [Love Lane]: Well run busy

food-based Youngs pub in converted hotel, wide choice from sandwiches to fresh fish, efficient service, large thoughtfully divided two-level seating area, conservatory looking over well equipped play area *(MP)*

BUTLEIGH [ST5133]

Rose & Portcullis: Welcoming unpretentious country pub, good generous reasonably priced food inc children's, OAP discounts, well kept Butcombe, Flowers and Wadworths 6X; tables in pretty back garden with play area *(Rev John Hibberd)*

CANNINGTON [ST2539]

Friendly Spirit [Brook St]: Well appointed pub with usual food, friendly atmosphere, well kept Butcombe and Wadworths 6X *(John A Barker)*

CHARD [ST3208]

Phoenix [Fore St]: Enjoyable food from bargain OAP lunches to their speciality belly-busters, busy and lively; good value bedrooms *(Stephen Dowell)*

CHEDDAR [ST4653]

☆ *Gardeners Arms* [Silver St]: Friendly and old-fashioned 16th-c beamed pub with some emphasis on wide choice of enjoyable freshly made food from lunchtime sandwiches and baguettes to unusual main dishes, local beers inc Butcombe, good choice of reasonably priced wine, log fire in handsome fireplace, nice atmosphere, cosy bar with interesting old local photographs; children welcome, garden *(Gill and Keith Croxton, Bob and Margaret Holder)*

Kings Head [Silver St]: Interesting 16th-c thatched and stripped stone local, open ranges in bar and cosy lounge, enjoyable food inc good puddings, well kept Bass, lots of chicken bric-a-brac, darts in public bar; picnic-sets in pleasant covered passageway and on small back lawn *(Guy Consterdine, Alan and Paula McCully)*

CHEW MAGNA [ST5763]

☆ *Bear & Swan* [South Parade]: Good interesting food at sensible prices, good choice of wines, attentive but unfussy friendly service, long bar with good choice of real ales, attractive redecoration strong on timber and local stone; book well ahead wknds *(John Urquhart, Mr and Mrs Jeremy Watkins, Ken Marshall)*

CHEWTON MENDIP [ST5953]

Waldegrave Arms [High St (A38)]: Cheerful, with good pub food from local cheddar sandwiches to fresh Fri fish, well kept Badger Best *(David Hoult)*

CHILCOMPTON [ST6451]

Redan [Frys Well (B3139)]: Friendly recently decorated local, simple and comfortable, with four well kept ales such as Fullers London Pride and Wadworths 6X, good bar food range, no smoking eating area, pool *(Susan and Nigel Wilson)*

Somerset Wagon [B3139; Broadway]: Cosy and friendly, with enjoyable food inc good range of home-made pies, well kept Wadworths IPA, 6X and other ales, pleasant olde-worlde areas off central bar, lots of settles, log fire; small front garden *(Susan and Nigel Wilson)*

CLEVEDON [ST3971]
Little Harp [Elton Rd (seafront)]: Recently completely renovated promenade pub, views towards Exmoor and the Welsh hills from terrace and two dining conservatories, pleasant no smoking family area with mezzanine floor, decent food all day served quickly to the numbered tables, friendly staff, well kept Greene King ales *(W R Miller)*
Moon & Sixpence [The Beach]: Substantial seafront Victorian family dining pub, balconied mezzanine floor with good view of magnificently restored pier and over to Brecon Beacons, well kept Greene King IPA and Abbot, some enjoyable home-made dishes, no smoking area; may be piped music *(Dr and Mrs B D Smith, Richard Fendick, Tom and Ruth Rees)*
Regent [Hill Rd (B3130 off front)]: Simply furnished light and roomy bistro bar looking out on Victorian shopping street, cheap generous light meals inc sandwiches and baked potatoes, good staff, well kept Badger Best, K&B and Tanglefoot, wide wine choice, winebar feel on lower floor with lounges and restaurant; small pretty sunken garden with lilies and jasmine *(Comus and Sarah Elliott, Alan and Paula McCully)*

COMBE HAY [ST7359]
Wheatsheaf [off A367 or B3110 S of Bath]: Under new licensee, pleasantly old-fashioned rooms with low beams, rustic furnishing and décor, big log fire, bar food, Courage Best, Greene King Old Speckled Hen and John Smiths tapped from the cask, children in eating areas, tables on spacious terraced lawn overlooking church and steep valley, dovecotes built into the walls, plenty of good nearby walks, bedrooms, open all day in summer *(LYM)*

CONGRESBURY [ST4363]
Old Inn [Pauls Causeway, off main road]: Low-beamed tucked-away family local, smartened up without being spoilt, deep-set windows with pretty curtains, huge fireplaces, one with ancient stove opening to both bar and no smoking dining area, well kept ales inc Bass and Youngs Special tapped from the cask, limited tasty bar food (not Sun or evenings in winter); tables in back garden, open all day *(Alan and Paula McCully)*
Plough [High St (B3133)]: Old-fashioned flagstoned local with well kept Bass, Butcombe and interesting guest beers tapped from the cask, welcoming staff, three cosy areas off main bar, two log fires, old prints, farm tools and sporting memorabilia, lunchtime sandwiches, darts, table skittles, shove-ha'penny and cards; small garden with boules and aviary, occasional barbecues and other excitements, open all day Sat *(the Didler, Hugh Roberts)*

CORFE [ST2319]
White Hart [B3170 S of Taunton]: New landlord, decent food from sandwiches up, good choice of real ales, lounge with small stools, attractive small no smoking dining room; children welcome *(Bob and Margaret Holder)*

COXLEY [ST5243]
Pound: Young couple doing good choice of well cooked food with fresh veg in unassuming local with good beer range inc Butcombe and Palmers, bar games and interesting bric-a-brac *(James Morrell)*

CREWKERNE [ST4508]
Old Stagecoach [Station Rd]: Enjoyable food inc beer-based belgian dishes, well kept beer inc fine range of belgian beers, good-humoured Belgian landlord keen on classic motor-cycles; comfortable motel-style bedrooms behind *(Annemieke Blondeel, Lyn and Ron Bennett, Patrick, Bob Smith)*
White Hart [Market Sq, opp post office]: Dating from 15th c, cosy, quiet and peaceful, with comfortable plain wooden furniture, fresh food, Bass and Greene King Old Speckled Hen, welcoming staff *(John A Barker)*

CROSCOMBE [SG5844]
George [Long St]: Refurbished by interesting and friendly newish owners, good home-made food from sandwiches up, a couple of real ales and good short choice of sensibly priced wines, locals at bar *(Sylvia and Tony Birbeck)*

CROSS [ST4154]
White Hart [not far from A38]: Attractive and relaxing old two-bar pub, beams, pillars and big log fires, good choice of generous bar food, good service, nice wines *(P M Wilkins, J Coote, Alan and Paula McCully)*

DINNINGTON [ST4013]
Dinnington Docks [Fosse Way]: Good cheery atmosphere in attractive unspoilt and welcoming country local with good inexpensive genuine home cooking, well kept Branscombe Vale, Butcombe and Cottage, log fire, friendly attentive staff, lots of memorabilia to bolster the myth that there was once a railway line and dock here, sofas in family room; garden behind with solid climber *(Dr and Mrs M E Wilson, Malcolm Taylor)*

DITCHEAT [ST6236]
☆ *Manor House* [signed off A37 and A371 S of Shepton Mallet]: Pretty village pub with decent reasonably priced bar food inc unusual hot sandwiches and thoughtful light dishes, first-class service, well kept Butcombe tapped from the cask, interesting wines, open fires, unusual arched doorways linking big flagstoned bar to comfortably relaxed lounge and restaurant (should book for evening meals at busy times); children welcome, skittle alley, tables on back grass *(Jack Taylor, BB, Nick Mann, Cathryn and Richard Hicks)*

DOULTING [ST6443]
Abbey Barn [A361]: Well kept Oakhill Best, simple pub food such as bacon baguettes, coal fire, clock collection *(Susan and Nigel Wilson)*
☆ *Poachers Pocket* [Chelynch Rd, off A361]: Cheerful and popular modernised black-beamed local, log fire in stripped-stone end wall, lots of stripped pine, gundog pictures, welcoming efficient staff, good generous reasonably priced straightforward food from sandwiches to Sun roasts, well kept Butcombe, Oakhill Best, Wadworths 6X and a guest beer, local farm cider, pub games, children in eating

area and large family room/skittle alley, friendly but well behaved cat and dog, back garden with country views *(Mrs Hazel Blackburn, Alan and Paula McCully, LYM)*

DOWLISH WAKE [ST3712]

New Inn [off A3037 S of Ilminster, via Kingstone]: Neatly refurbished and attractive village pub with dark beams and woodburner in stone inglenook, food (not Sun evening) from sandwiches, baguettes and baked potatoes up, well kept Bass, Butcombe, Otter, perhaps a guest beer, and very local farm cider, games area and family room; has suffered rather from speed of management changes recently, the latest too recently for us to form a firm view, but staff friendly; pleasant garden *(LYM)*

DULVERTON [SS9127]

Bridge Inn [Bridge St]: Old pub with *Lorna Doone* connections, wide choice of good value food from good sandwiches to popular Sun carvery, quick friendly service, well kept real ales; riverside garden *(Peter and Audrey Dowsett)*

Rock House [Jury Rd]: Comfortably unpretentious, with good range of real ales such as Butcombe and Cotleigh, cheap standard food, pool room, no piped music *(Andy and Jill Kassube)*

DUNSTER [SS9943]

☆ *Luttrell Arms* [High St; A396]: Interesting bar menu from hotel's new management, old-fashioned back bar in 15th-c timber-framed abbey building, high beams hung with bottles, clogs and horseshoes, stag's head and rifles on walls above old settles and more modern furniture, big log fires, well kept Bass and Exmoor Gold, friendly efficient service, ancient glazed partition dividing off small galleried and flagstoned courtyard, upstairs access to quiet attractive garden with Civil War cannon emplacements and great views; comfortable bedrooms *(Colin and Janet Roe, LYM, H O Dickinson, Derek and Sylvia Stephenson)*

EAST COKER [ST5412]

☆ *Helyar Arms* [off A37 or A30 SW of Yeovil; Moor Lane]: Good fresh well presented food in well decorated spotless and roomy open-plan lounge, low beams, woodburner, lots of brass and pictures, dark-stained traditional furnishings, world map with pushpins for visitors, well kept Bass, Boddingtons and Flowers, reasonably priced wines, sparkling old-fashioned high-raftered dining room, friendly helpful staff; no dogs, comfortable bedrooms with own bathrooms, attractive setting *(Anthony J Woodroffe)*

EASTON-IN-GORDANO [ST5175]

Rudgleigh Inn [A369 1 mile from M5 junction 19]: Spotlessly modernised two-bar roadside pub with popular promptly served food, well kept Courage and Smiles, extension restaurant suiting families; open all day wkdys, big enclosed garden with willows, tamarisks, play area and cricket-field view *(Tom Evans, J Osborn-Clarke, LYM)*

EVERCREECH [ST6538]

Bell [Bruton Rd (B3081)]: Stone-built pub with wide choice of enjoyable home-made food

from sandwiches and baguettes to several fish dishes, Adnams and Butcombe, cafetière coffee, pleasantly restrained décor in high-ceilinged linked rooms, watercolours above panelled dado, mix of solid furnishings, woodburner and log-effect gas fire; quiet piped music; nice rustic garden furniture, open view, quiet village handy for Bath & West Showground *(B and K Hypher)*

EXEBRIDGE [SS9224]

☆ *Anchor* [B3222 S of Dulverton; pub itself actually over the river, in Devon]: New owners in comfortable rather hotelish pub in idyllic spot on edge of Exmoor, some attractive furnishings, oak panelling and pictures, three well kept ales such as Exmoor and Wadworths 6X, local farm cider, above-average wines, woodburner, huge blackboard food choice, low prices and popular carvery, friendly attentive staff, family eating area and no smoking restaurant; children welcome, smaller back games bar, skittle alley; open all day at least in summer, nice big riverside garden with plenty of tables and play area, comfortable bedrooms, good breakfast, fishing rights *(Peter and Audrey Dowsett, Dr and Mrs M E Wilson, George Atkinson, LYM)*

FAILAND [ST5171]

Failand Inn [B3128 Bristol—Clevedon]: Simply furnished old coaching inn, popular for good straightforward reasonably priced food in ample helpings, friendly efficient service, well kept ales inc Courage, comfortable dining extension; 60s piped music *(Rex Miller)*

FARLEIGH HUNGERFORD [ST7957]

Hungerford Arms [A366 Trowbridge—Norton St Philip]: Relaxed local atmosphere, well kept real ales inc Otter, farm cider, enjoyable sensibly priced food, snug alcoves, stained glass and hunting prints, heavy dark beams, carved stone fireplaces, steps down to brighter no smoking family restaurant with nice country view inc ruins of Hungerford Castle; darts, fruit machine; back terrace with same view, open all day wknds *(LYM, Roger Wain-Heapy, Mrs J H S Lang)*

FARMBOROUGH [ST6660]

Butchers Arms [Timsbury Rd]: Comfortable two-bar village pub with welcoming landlord, friendly atmosphere, three well kept real ales, varied food inc good value Sun lunch; popular Tues night quiz, children and dogs welcome *(Mandy and Phil Jones)*

FAULKLAND [ST7354]

☆ *Faulkland Inn*: Friendly country tavern with well kept changing beers such as Greene King Ruddles and Shepherd Neame Spitfire, Cheddar Valley cider, accommodating local feel, amiable dog Lucy, beams and flagstones, brightly painted walls, lighter more contemporary dining room off – in such a pubby local it's quite a surprise to find landlord's son-in-law cooking such very good inventive food (takeaways available); piped music may be loudish; children welcome, small informal back garden, four good value bedrooms, pretty village *(John and Glenys Wheeler, Andy Bates, Dr Diana Terry, Tim*

O'Keefe, Catherine Pitt, N G A Chambers, BB)

FRESHFORD [ST7960]

☆ *Inn at Freshford* [off A36 or B3108]: Picturesque stone-built beamed pub, comfortably modernised, with new management still concentrating on reliable tasty food from sandwiches up inc several fish specials, no smoking restaurant (not Sun evening), well kept Bass, Courage Best, Marstons Pedigree and Wadworths 6X, open fire; piped music, some jazz nights; children in eating areas, pretty gardens, nice spot by River Frome, walks to Kennet & Avon Canal *(Meg and Colin Hamilton, LYM, B and K Hypher)*

FROME [ST7748]

Griffin [Milk St]: Proper civilised pub brewing its own good beer, friendly landlord, easy-going mixed crowd; occasional live music *(Adam Manolson)*

GLASTONBURY [ST5038]

Riflemans Arms [Chilkwell St (A361, SE of centre)]: Chatty popular local with several real ales, farm cider, good games room, live music Sat; play area, sunny terrace *(LYM)*

HALSE [ST1428]

New Inn [off B3227 Taunton—Bampton]: 17th-c traditional inn with good range of well kept real ales, local farm ciders, enjoyable generous home cooking, friendly family service, woodburner in big inglenook, no smoking candlelit dining room, separate games area and skittle alley, no piped music; tables in garden, homely bedrooms with own bathrooms and good breakfast, lovely village *(anon)*

HASELBURY PLUCKNETT [ST4711]

Haselbury Inn [North St]: Thriving two-bar roadside pub popular with older lunchers for enjoyable and enterprising inexpensive food inc set lunches, Otter from proper bar counter, decent wines, chintz armchairs and sofas by the log fire, some heavy red-cushioned cask seats, candles at night, friendly service, no smoking restaurant; children welcome, picnic-sets in garden, has been cl Mon *(Paul and Annette Hallett, Bob and Margaret Holder)*

Haselbury Mill [Merriott Rd; off A30 E of Crewkerne towards Merriott, away from village]: Very modernised country dining pub in quiet spot, big picture windows looking over duck pond, good inexpensive food inc carvery, well spaced tables in comfortable light and airy dining lounge, snug low-ceilinged bar on right, tables out on informal lawn by pretty stream; open all day exc Sun afternoon, bedrooms *(BB, Bob and Margaret Holder)*

HINTON CHARTERHOUSE [ST7758]

Rose & Crown [B3110 about 4 miles S of Bath]: Roomy partly divided pub with nice panelling, ornate stone fireplace, rugby memorabilia, well kept Bass, Butcombe and Smiles tapped from casks, wide choice of good value generous home-made food inc plenty of fish, restaurant, skittle alley; open all day Sat *(BB, Dr and Mrs M E Wilson, Meg and Colin Hamilton, Dr and Mrs A K Clarke)*

☆ *Stag* [B3110 S of Bath; High St]: Attractively furnished ancient pub with good sensibly priced home-made food in bar and stripped-stone dining area, well kept ales such as Bass and Butcombe, smiling helpful service even when busy, log fire, provision for children, no piped music; tables outside, has been open all day *(Meg and Colin Hamilton, Dr and Mrs M E Wilson, LYM)*

HORFIELD [ST5976]

Wellington [off A38 Gloucester Rd]: Roomy 1920s pub newly done up by Bath Ales, their Barnstormer, Gem and Spa kept well, comfortable bar seating, no smoking room, freshly cooked food inc generous Sun roasts; open all day Sun *(Matthew Shackle)*

HOWLEY [ST2609]

Howley Tavern: Comfortable and popular, in attractive spot, with enjoyable sensibly priced food inc imaginative dishes, attentive service, well kept real ales, decent wines *(Malcolm Taylor)*

ILCHESTER [ST5222]

Dolphin [High St]: Two high-ceilinged bars with dark wood and lighter prints, practical food inc mexican dishes such as tuna wrap and tortillas, Bass and Worthington *(MP)*

ILMINSTER [ST3614]

☆ *George* [North St]: Small bar and restaurant now attractively refurbished and run by Mrs Phelps (who with her late husband made such a huge success of the Strode Arms at Cranmore), with the really enjoyable sensibly priced food and good friendly service that readers enjoyed so much there *(Douglas Allen)*

KELSTON [ST7067]

☆ *Old Crown* [Bitton Rd; A431 W of Bath]: Four small friendly traditional rooms with hops on beams, carved settles and cask tables on polished flagstones, logs burning in ancient open range, two more coal-effect fires, well kept ales such as Bass, Butcombe, Smiles and Wadworths 6X tapped from the cask, Thatcher's cider, well priced wines, cheap wholesome bar food (not Sun or Mon evenings) inc two-steak bargains, small restaurant (not Sun), no machines or music; dogs welcome (biscuit tub behind bar), children in eating areas, open all day wknd, picnic-sets under apple trees in sunny sheltered back garden *(Ian and Rose Lock, Colin and Peggy Wilshire, LYM, Meg and Colin Hamilton, Mandy and Phil Jones)*

KENN [ST4169]

Drum & Monkey [B3133 Yatton—Clevedon]: Neatly kept village pub, thriving local atmosphere, brasses and copper-topped tables, open fires, good value food, well kept real ales *(W R Miller)*

KEWSTOKE [ST3263]

Commodore [Beach Rd]: Hotel at end of Sand Bay, beach and dune walks, attractive beamed bar with no smoking part, welcoming service, Courage and John Smiths from small counter, reasonably priced food, two for one lunches popular with older people (younger customers evenings); bedrooms *(Dr and Mrs C W Thomas)*

KEYNSHAM [ST6568]

Brassmill [Avon Mill Lane]: Large and comfortably stylish Brewers Fayre conversion of former brass foundry, wide range of standard food inc midweek bargains, well kept Flowers Original, Fullers London Pride and Wadworths 6X, relaxed atmosphere, several eating areas; pleasant terrace out overlooking River Chew *(Michael Doswell)*

☆ *Lock-Keeper* [A4175]: Lovely spot on Avon island with big garden, lock, marina and weir; small room by bar, arches to main divided room with rust and dark blue décor, black beams and bare boards, barrel-vaulted lower area, well kept Youngs and Smiles, wide range of decent food from baguettes and baked potatoes to more upmarket dishes, friendly helpful young staff, three nicely decorated yet unpretentious areas; boules *(M G Hart, Dr and Mrs M E Wilson, JCW, Nigel Long)*

KINGSBURY EPISCOPI [ST4320]
Wyndham Arms: Attractively unspoilt flagstoned country pub with roaring log fire, attentive helpful licensees, good range of enjoyable attractively priced home-made food inc good big steaks and impressive choice of puddings, well kept Bass and Fullers London Pride, farm cider; tables in garden, two nearby self-catering cottages *(Theo, Anne and Jane Gaskin)*

KNOLE [ST4825]
Lime Kiln [A372 E of Langport]: Very wide choice of good value food, friendly service, three well kept real ales and log fire in large uncluttered bar with dark furnishings, restaurant behind; good modern bedrooms *(Guy Vowles)*

LITTON [ST5954]
☆ *Kings Arms* [B3114, NW of Chewton Mendip on A39 Bath—Wells]: Interesting partly 15th-c pub rambling more extensively than you'd have thought, low heavy beams, polished flagstones, nice old-fashioned settles, huge fireplace with plenty of copper and brass, large family room; some emphasis on appealing food from sandwiches up, well kept ales such as Bass and Wadworths 6X; picnic-sets in neat sloping streamside gardens with good play area *(Michael Doswell, LYM, Thomas Neate, Alan and Paula McCully)*

LONG ASHTON [ST5570]
Angel [Long Ashton Rd]: Two-level lounge bar attractively hung with pewter tankards, well kept Courage Best and Smiles, comfortable seating and blazing log fire, local memorabilia inc old balloon prints, fresh flowers, front smoking room and two other rooms (children allowed there), imaginative well presented food from baked potatoes and baguettes up, friendly sophisticated service; tolerable piped music; tables in quiet courtyard *(P and D Carpenter, Simon and Amanda Southwell)*

LONG SUTTON [ST4625]
Devonshire Arms [B3165 Somerton—Martock, just off A372 E of Langport]: Tall gabled stone inn with settees on right, partly no smoking restaurant area on left, lots of sporting and country prints, well kept real ale, quite a few wines by the glass, friendly staff, bar food from sandwiches up, cream teas, homely flagstoned back bar with darts and TV; may be piped

music; children in eating areas, open all day, bedrooms *(LYM, John and Judy Saville, A C Nugent)*

MARTOCK [ST4619]
Nags Head [East St]: Three well kept real ales (wkdy happy hour 6-7), enjoyable food (not Mon) inc good local steaks and early-evening bargains, separate room with pool and juke box; bedrooms in self-contained flat *(Miss N J Wild)*

MIDFORD [ST7660]
☆ *Hope & Anchor* [Bath Rd (B3110)]: Good attractively presented interesting food running to ostrich, barbary duck and imaginative puddings in bar and separate flagstoned restaurant end, well kept Bass, Butcombe and Smiles, good house wines, proper coffee, friendly service, cosy furnishings, log fire; tables outside, pretty walks along River Frome *(Michael Doswell, Gaynor Gregory, Roger Wain-Heapy)*

MIDSOMER NORTON [ST6654]
White Hart [The Island]: Chatty Victorian local with several rooms, Bass and Butcombe tapped from the cask; open all day *(the Didler)*

MILBORNE PORT [ST6718]
Queens Head [A30 E of Sherborne]: Friendly licensees and staff, quick service, wide range of enjoyable food inc bargain nights, good range of well kept ales such as Greene King Old Speckled Hen, Smiles and Wadworths 6X, farm ciders, friendly service, neat beamed lounge, games in public bar, skittle alley, restaurant; live music nights, children welcome away from bars, reasonable disabled access, tables in sheltered courtyard and garden with play area, three cosy good value bedrooms *(Gerry Hollington, LYM, Pamela and Merlyn Horswell)*

MINEHEAD [SS9646]
Queens Head [Holloway St]: Nicely modern interior with alcove seating, good range of well kept ales, wide choice of decent food, good helpings, quick service, low prices, bar billiards; quiet piped music, nearby parking difficult *(Peter and Audrey Dowsett)*

MONKTON COMBE [ST7761]
Wheelwrights Arms [just off A36 S of Bath; Church Cottages]: Small country inn with attractively laid-out bar, wheelwright and railway memorabilia, candles and big log fire, friendly service, wide choice of good reasonably priced straightforward home-made food, well kept ales such as Adnams, Butcombe and Wadworths 6X, decent house wines, tiny darts room at end; fruit machine, quiet piped music, no children or dogs; garden with valley view, well equipped small bedrooms in separate block *(LYM, J F M and M West)*

MONTACUTE [ST4916]
☆ *Kings Arms* [Bishopston]: Extended partly 16th-c hotel doing well since existing managers bought the lease in 2002, pleasantly furnished stripped stone lounges (one no smoking), blazing log fires, cheerful helpful staff, enjoyable food from interestingly topped toasted bagels up, well kept Greene King IPA and Abbot, good house wines and coffee,

magazines and broadsheet papers, no smoking restaurant; children welcome, pleasant garden, comfortable bedrooms *(Dennis Jenkin, Dr and Mrs J F Head, A C Nugent, LYM, Colin and Janet Roe, Theo, Anne and Jane Gaskin)*

NAILSEA [ST4670]

☆ *Blue Flame* [West End]: Small traditional 19th-c farmers' local with old-fashioned take-us-as-you-find-us feel, several intriguing rooms, well kept Abbey, Bass, Bath, RCH and three guest beers tapped from the cask, Thatcher's farm cider, filled rolls, cosy open fires, great mix of all ages; folk and Thurs cards and pasty nights, pub games, children's room, sizeable informal garden with barbecue *(Catherine Pitt, the Didler, John and Felicity Ford)*

NEWTON ST LOE [ST7064]

☆ *Globe*: Roomy bar attractively split into smaller areas by dark wood partitions, pillars and timbers giving secluded feel, good atmosphere, friendly efficient service (can slow when very busy), enjoyable food all day, well kept beer, large no smoking area *(Roger Wain-Heapy, Dr and Mrs M E Wilson)*

NORTH PERROTT [ST4709]

Manor Arms [A3066 W of Crewkerne; Middle St]: Attractive 16th-c inn on pretty village green, concentrating on restaurant and bedroom side now – good value imaginative freshly made meals rather than snacks inc plenty of fish and fresh veg, bargain three-course lunches, small but good wine choice, good coffee, friendly staff; long tidily restored bar, beams and mellow stripped stone, log fire and plenty of character, does have well kept Butcombe but more hotel feel than pub; simple comfortable bedrooms, good breakfast, pleasant garden with adventure play area *(John A Barker, Chris and Ann Coy, Mr and Mrs D Gould Smith)*

NORTON FITZWARREN [ST1925]

Cross Keys [A358 roundabout]: Stone-built 19th-c pub extended as Chef & Brewer, friendly staff, enjoyable well prepared food inc good hot baguettes, log fires, good wine list *(Andy and Jill Kassube, Bob and Margaret Holder, Ian Phillips)*

NORTON ST PHILIP [ST7755]

☆ *Fleur de Lys* [High St]: 13th-c stone cottages joined centuries ago, steps and pillars giving cosy feel of separate rooms in the beamed and flagstoned areas around the central servery, unspoilt chatty local atmosphere, good value home-made food from baguettes through sausages and mash etc to steak, well kept Wadworths beers, friendly landlord, huge fireplace; children very welcome, skittle alley; car park can be awkward *(Colin McKerrow, Susan and Nigel Wilson, Colin and Peggy Wilshire, the Didler, Dr and Mrs M E Wilson, Dr and Mrs A K Clarke, BB)*

OAKHILL [ST6347]

Oakhill Inn [A367 Shepton Mallet—Radstock]: Good atmosphere, well kept local Oakhill and guest ales, enjoyable honest food inc filled baguettes *(Susan and Nigel Wilson)*

PITMINSTER [ST2219]

Queens Arms [off B3170 S of Taunton (or

reached direct); nr church]: Cosy unspoilt village pub with enterprising new landlord, midweek low season special food offers, well kept ales inc Cotleigh and Otter, interesting wines, log fire, simple wooden bar furniture, pleasant dining room; no music, dogs allowed, bedrooms with own bathrooms *(John and Fiona Merritt)*

PORLOCK [SS8846]

☆ *Ship* [High St]: Picturesque thatched partly 13th-c pub on good form these days, with a warm welcome, well kept Cotleigh ales, guest beers such as Oakhill, farm cider, food from good sandwich range to theme nights, low beams, flagstones and big inglenook log fires, small locals' front bar, back dining room, pub games and pool; children very welcome, attractive split-level sunny garden with decking, nearby nature trail to Dunkery Beacon, bedrooms *(Richard Gibbs, C J Fletcher, Kate and Stuart Clow, LYM, Andy and Jill Kassube, Tracey and Stephen Groves)*

PORLOCK WEIR [SS8547]

Ship [separate from but run in tandem with neighbouring Anchor Hotel]: Prettily restored old inn in wonderful spot by peaceful harbour, with tables in terraced rose garden and good walks (but no views to speak of from bars); nets and chalked beams in busy Mariners Bar with friendly relaxed atmosphere, well kept ales at a price, Taunton cider, huge log fire, usual food inc generous baked potatoes; piped music, dogs welcome, back family room; attractive bedrooms; little free parking, but pay & display opposite *(John and Judy Saville, H O Dickinson, Dave Irving, LYM, Lynda and Trevor Smith, George Atkinson, John and Joan Calvert)*

PORTBURY [ST4975]

Priory [Station Rd, ½ mile from A369 (just S of M5 junction 19)]: Spotless much extended Vintage Inn dining pub, several beamed rooms with nice mix of solid furnishings in alcoves, good wide choice of enjoyable food inc some light dishes, well kept Bass, good range of house wines; piped music; bedrooms, open all day *(Tom Evans, S H Godsell, Comus and Sarah Elliott, James Morrell, J Osborn-Clarke, Dr and Mrs C W Thomas)*

PORTISHEAD [ST4675]

Albion [Old Bristol Rd]: Hungry Horse dining pub popular for filling food from sandwiches up, L-shaped carpeted bar with two log fires, brasses, beamery, bric-a-brac and old photographs, Greene King IPA and Abbot, restaurant; some tables out on front lawn *(W R Miller)*

Poacher [High St]: Popular with regular older lunchers for wide range of freshly cooked low-priced food with real veg, well kept ales such as Courage Best and Smiles (still has a proper part for village beer-drinkers), friendly staff, no smoking restaurant area; cl Sun pm *(Tom Evans)*

Ship [the one on Down Rd (coast rd to Walton in Gordano)]: Quiet and relaxing, good value usual lunchtime food, real ales inc Bass and Butcombe, lovely Severn estuary views esp at sunset *(Tom Evans)*

PURITON [ST3141]
Puriton Inn [just off M5 junction 23; Puriton Hill]: Friendly character pub, clean and tidy, with good value straightforward food, well kept beer, good polite service even when busy; good disabled access, large garden *(B and F A Hannam, Geoff Pidoux)*

RADSTOCK [ST6954]
Radstock Hotel [Market Pl (A367)]: Completely refurbished, with several Smiles ales, plentiful food in bar and dining area, pool room; big garden behind *(Susan and Nigel Wilson)*

RIMPTON [ST6021]
White Post Inn: Small pub straddling Dorset border, well kept Butcombe and Greene King IPA, several blackboards with Swedish and more traditional pub food from good soups up, smaller helpings for children, jolly Swedish landlord, small dining area with pretty view over fields *(Joan and Michel Hooper-Immins, Marjorie and David Lamb)*

RODE [ST8053]
Bell [Frome Rd (A361)]: Comfortable, spotless and roomy, nicely balanced choice of good reasonably priced food, warm welcome, good service, well kept ales such as Butcombe and Courage *(Peter and Audrey Dowsett, Ted George, Ken and Barbara Turner)*

RODNEY STOKE [ST4850]
Rodney Stoke Inn [A361 Wells—Weston]: Wall banquettes, plush stools and dimpled copper tables, bigger nicely set back no smoking restaurant, good imaginative well presented and well priced food, good wine list, well kept Bass and Butcombe, cheery landlord; well lit pool table, fruit machine and juke box or piped pop music, skittle alley, very busy holidays and wknds; picnic-sets out on roadside terrace, camp site *(BB, Ken Flawn, John A Barker, Colin and Janet Roe)*

RUDGE [ST8251]
☆ *Full Moon* [off A36 Bath—Warminster]: Unspoilt black-beamed 17th-c inn with some emphasis on food (simple at lunchtime, more elaborate evenings), well kept Butcombe Bitter, Wadworths 6X and a house beer, local ciders, nice mix of furnishings, inglenook fireplace, flagstoned tap room, small private no smoking dining room with polished furniture, more formal back no smoking restaurant, traditional games and skittle alley; children welcome, pretty gardens with plenty of seats, bedrooms and new self-catering cottages, open all day *(Dr and Mrs M E Wilson, Michael Hicks, Edmund Coan, Andrew Barker, Claire Jenkins, Gloria Bax, Dr and Mrs A K Clarke, LYM)*

SOMERTON [ST4828]
☆ *Globe* [Market Pl]: Chatty and bustling old stone-built local with log fire, good interesting reasonably priced home-made bar food, attentive landlord and friendly staff, well kept ales inc Bass, Boddingtons and Butcombe, good choice of wine, two spacious bars, dining conservatory, back pool room; no music, skittle alley, tables in garden *(Joyce and Geoff Robson, Ken Flawn, Dr and Mrs J F Head, Theo, Anne and Jane Gaskin)*
Unicorn [West St]: Good buoyant atmosphere,

enjoyable sensibly priced food, well kept beer, good wine choice, friendly helpful licensees proud of their pub; bedrooms *(Karen Roskilly, Richard and Helene Lay)*

SOUTH PETHERTON [ST4316]
Brewers Arms [St James St]: Useful diversion off A303, substantially refurbished 17th-c stone-built inn with enjoyable interesting food at pine tables in elegant russet-walled dining lounge, well kept Fullers London Pride, Otter, Ventnor and Worthington, decent wines, games in big public bar; unobtrusive piped music; picnic-sets in neat garden *(Dr and Mrs M E Wilson)*

SOUTH STOKE [ST7461]
☆ *Pack Horse* [off B3110, S edge of Bath]: Intriguing medieval pub, a former priory (central passageway still a public right of way to the church); heavy beams, handsome inglenook log fire, antique settles, well kept Courage Best, Ushers Best and Wadworths 6X, farm cider, shove-ha'penny tables, very wide food choice; piped music, winter quiz nights; children welcome, tables in spacious back garden, boules, open all day wknds *(Liz and Jeremy Baker, MRSM, Ian Phillips, LYM, Richard Stancomb)*

STAPLE FITZPAINE [ST2618]
☆ *Greyhound* [off A358 or B3170 S of Taunton]: Rambling country pub with flagstones, inglenooks, pleasant mix of settles and chairs, log fires throughout, olde-worlde pictures, farm tools and so forth, well kept changing ales, decent house wines, good food choice (high chairs available), friendly service; good bedrooms in modern extension *(Mr and Mrs Colin Roberts, LYM, Mark and Ann Evans)*

STAR [ST4358]
Star [A38 NE of Winscombe]: Reliable extended roadside pub with tasty food, well kept Courage Best, friendly service, good log fire in huge inglenook fireplace, nice mix of tables, big fish tank, enthusiastic Sun lunchtime raffle (bar nibbles then); country views from picnic-sets in field behind *(Bob and Maggie Atherton, Tom Evans)*

STOGUMBER [ST0937]
White Horse [off A358 at Crowcombe]: Little whitewashed local facing church, under new landlord (after threat of closure), long neat bar, old village photographs with more recent ones for comparison, good log fires, straightforward bar food, Cotleigh Tawny, Greene King Old Speckled Hen and Marstons Pedigree, no smoking dining area, games room and skittle alley; children welcome away from bar, quiet garden, bedrooms, open all day wknds and summer *(LYM)*

STOKE ST MARY [ST2622]
Half Moon [from M5 junction 25 take A358 towards Ilminster, 1st right, right in Henlade]: Roomy much-modernised village pub, five neat open-plan main areas, enjoyable food from sandwiches to steaks, one no smoking restaurant, pleasant staff, well kept real ales inc Butcombe, nice coffee, quite a few malt whiskies; bar billiards, may be piped music; children welcome, picnic-sets in well tended

garden (Bob and Margaret Holder, R T and J C Moggridge, LYM)

STRATTON-ON-THE-FOSSE [ST6554]

White Post Inn [A367 S of Midsomer Norton, by B3139 roundabout]: Comfortable Victorian pub with friendly helpful landlord, four well kept ales inc Bass and Butcombe tapped from casks behind the bar, good value traditional food very popular lunchtime with businessmen and older people; varied live entertainment, open all day (the Didler, Susan and Nigel Wilson, Jacquie and Jim Jones)

TAUNTON [ST2525]

☆ *Hankridge Arms* [Hankridge Way, Deane Gate (nr Sainsbury's); very handy for M5 junction 25]: 16th-c former farm restored a few years ago as well appointed old-style dining pub in modern shopping complex, buoyant atmosphere and quick friendly service, good value generous food from interesting soups and sandwiches up in bar and largely no smoking restaurant, Badger Best, K&B and Tanglefoot, big log fire; piped music, can be hard for older people to get to when surrounding shops busy; plenty of tables outside (Andy and Jill Kassube, Ian Phillips, Gill and Keith Croxton, Pamela and Merlyn Horswell, Joe Green)

Harpoon Louie's [Station Rd]: Particularly well kept Otter and guests such as Hop Back and Skinners, attractive panelled front part with quiet early evening happy hour, popular sensibly priced food in back room; piped jazz, cl lunchtime (Catherine Pitt)

☆ *Masons Arms* [Magdalene St, opp St Mary's church]: Traditional town pub with old-fashioned genial chef/landlord and atmosphere, quick freshly home-made food (not Sun but served late other evenings) from interesting soup to sizzling steaks and a good daily special, particularly well kept Bass, Otter and two changing guest beers, reasonable prices, comfortably basic furnishings, cricketing links and cartoons, no music (a veteran TV may emerge for rugby matches); pin-ups in gents', good bedrooms (Andy and Jill Kassube, Brian and Li Jobson, Mrs J James, Douglas Allen, Poppy Howard, Bob and Margaret Holder, Darrell Bendall, Joe Green)

☆ *Vivary Arms* [Middleway, Wilton; across Vivary Park from centre]: Quiet and pretty pub dating from 18th c, good value distinctive freshly made food inc good soup and plenty of fish, in snug plush lounge and small dining room; prompt friendly young staff, relaxed atmosphere, well kept ales such as Smiles Best, John Smiths and Charles Wells Bombardier, decent wines, interesting collection of drinking-related items, no music; bedrooms with own bathrooms in Georgian house next door, easy street parking (Frank Willy, Joe Green)

White Lodge [Bridgwater Rd]: Comfortable Beefeater around older core, welcoming service, well kept ales such as Marstons Pedigree, decent food; adjacent Travel Inn (Mr and Mrs Colin Roberts)

THURLOXTON [ST2730]

Maypole [A38 Taunton—Bridgwater]: Attractively refurbished beamed pub with

several traditional areas, well kept real ales, log fire, biggish no smoking area, wide food choice; soft piped music, no dogs, skittle alley; enclosed garden with play area, lovely flowers, peaceful village (Bob and Margaret Holder, June and Robin Small)

TINTINHULL [ST4919]

Lamb [Vicarage St]: Village pub with friendly helpful staff, good value straightforward food inc bargain lunches (must book for no smoking restaurant), well kept Courage Directors, good choice of other drinks; nice garden, handy for Tintinhull Manor (NT) (John A Barker, Dr and Mrs M E Wilson, Theo, Anne and Jane Gaskin)

TRUDOXHILL [ST7443]

White Hart [off A361 SW of Frome]: Beams, stripped stone, very welcoming service, enjoyable food from good open sandwiches and baguettes up, off-peak bargains, real ales, Thatcher's farm cider, country wines, mainly table seating with a couple of easy chairs by one of the two log fires; children in eating area, restaurant, no dogs, picnic-sets in flower-filled sheltered side garden (Gill and Keith Croxton, the Didler, LYM)

TRULL [ST2122]

Winchester Arms [Church Rd]: Welcoming lively small local, good varied food, well kept Butcombe, obliging service, cosy atmosphere, small dining room; bedrooms (Bob and Margaret Holder)

UPTON [ST0129]

☆ *Lowtrow Cross Inn*: Isolated but very welcoming country inn with nice low-beamed bar, enormous inglenook, consistently good value fresh home-made bar food, local real ale; children welcome (LYM)

VOBSTER [ST7049]

Vobster Inn [Lower Vobster]: Roomy old stone village inn transformed into dining pub particularly popular with older people (children welcomed too), good food choice from sandwiches to fish fresh daily from Cornwall and range of local cheeses in three comfortable open-plan areas, friendly licensees and staff, well kept Fullers London Pride, good new world wines by the glass; tables on side lawn with boules, peaceful views, adventure playground behind (H E Wynter, Edward Mirzoeff, BB)

WAMBROOK [ST2907]

☆ *Cotley Inn* [village signed off A30 W of Chard; don't follow the small signs to Cotley itself]: Stone-built pub in quiet spot with plenty of surrounding walks; smart but unpretentious, with simple flagstoned entrance bar opening on one side into small plush bar, several open fires, good inexpensive food inc generous small-helpings choice, Otter and Wadworths 6X, popular two-room no smoking dining area (best to book, children allowed here); pool, piped music, skittle alley; seats and play area in garden, well refurbished bedrooms (Nigel and Teresa Traylen, Bob and Margaret Holder, LYM)

WASHFORD [ST0441]

Washford Arms: Tidy pub with three real ales

inc Bass and Smiles Best, separate dining area; children welcome, play area, eight bedrooms, next to West Somerset Railway *(Geoff Calcott)*

WATERROW [ST0525]

Rock [A361 Wiveliscombe—Bampton]: Well kept ales such as Cotleigh Tawny and Exmoor Gold, wide choice of food, log fire in smallish bar exposing the rock it's built on, couple of steps up to dining room; good well equipped bedrooms, charming setting in small valley village *(Tom Evans)*

WELLINGTON [ST1420]

Eight Bells [High St]: Well kept Cotleigh beers, warm welcome, attractively priced food, several small rooms; pleasant garden *(Lorraine and Fred Gill)*

WELLS [ST5545]

☆ *Fountain* [St Thomas St]: Comfortable dining pub, good wholesome choice from wkdy lunchtime bargains to fresh fish and interesting dishes in homely downstairs bar with roaring log fire, or popular more formal restaurant up steep stairs (worth booking wknd, good Sun lunch); quick service, well kept Courage Best, Greene King IPA and a guest beer, good choice of wines, good coffee; can get very full wknd lunchtimes, may be piped music; right by cathedral – popular with choir, and you may even be served by a Vicar Choral; children welcome *(Rebecca Davidson, Alan and Gill Bull, Mr and Mrs Richard Hanks, Ken Flawn, Colin and Janet Roe, Mr and Mrs R A Newbury, Michael Collier)*

WEST BAGBOROUGH [ST1733]

Rising Sun: Welcoming 16th-c pub in tiny village below Quantocks, rebuilt after severe fire damage in 2002, attractive décor inc quite an art gallery, enjoyable fresh generous home-cooked food, good service, well kept local ales, wide choice of wines *(Alannah Hunt)*

WEST CAMEL [ST5724]

Walnut Tree [off A303 W of Wincanton; Fore St]: Extended upmarket dining pub/hotel, comfortable grey plush banquettes and red plush cushioned wicker chairs, enjoyable food (not Sun evening or Mon lunchtime) esp fresh fish and puddings, friendly efficient uniformed staff nicely flexible over menus, well kept Bass and Butcombe; neatly kept garden, good bedrooms, pretty village *(Theo, Anne and Jane Gaskin)*

WEST HATCH [ST2719]

Farmers Arms [signed off A380 and B3170]: Spacious 16th-c pub newly refurbished combining bleached wood furniture and unassumingly modern décor with beams, open fires and so forth, friendly atmosphere, well kept Cotleigh Tawny and guest beers, generous reasonably priced usual food in bar or dining room, Sun lunch, welcoming service; piped music, quiz and live music nights; children welcome, garden with small terrace and play area *(A J and C D Stodgell, Andy Harvey)*

WEST HUNTSPILL [ST3044]

☆ *Crossways* [A38 (between M5 exits 22 and 23)]: Informal and comfortably worn in, with variety of places to sit inc a family room, interesting decorations and log fires, good

choice of well kept real ales, notable local farm cider, decent wines, enjoyable piping hot sensibly priced food, friendly staff, no piped music; skittle alley and pub games, picnic-sets among fruit trees in sizeable informal garden *(John and Elizabeth Cox, LYM, Tom Evans, Tim and Sue Halstead, B J Harding)*

WEST PENNARD [ST5639]

Apple Tree [A361 towards Pilton]: Well renovated good value food pub, good choice inc proper pies, thoroughly cooked veg and good Sun lunch; flagstones, exposed brickwork, beams, good woodburner, comfortable seats, thatch above main bar, second bar and two eating areas; well kept real ales inc Cotleigh, good coffee, friendly service; can get crowded lunchtime; tables on terrace, caravan parking *(Stuart Paulley)*

Lion [A361 E of Glastonbury; Newtown]: Enjoyable quickly served food using some local ingredients in three neat dining areas opening off small flagstoned and black-beamed core with settles and woodburner in big stone inglenook, log fire in stripped-stone family area, well kept Ushers ales, reasonable prices, pool in back room; tables on big forecourt, bedrooms comfortable and well equipped, in neatly converted side barn *(K H Frostick, BB)*

WEST QUANTOXHEAD [ST1141]

Windmill [A39 Bridgwater—Minehead]: Large pub, clean and tidy, with well cooked reasonably priced food inc daily fresh fish, well kept beers inc Courage Directors and Exmoor, keen staff; fenced garden for children *(Ian and Sharon Shorthouse)*

WESTBURY-SUB-MENDIP [ST5048]

Westbury Inn: Pleasant mellow interior with some character, dozens of old local photographs, pretty dining room, reasonably priced food from good sandwiches up, well kept Bass and guest beers, sociable Zimbabwean licensees and young terrier, dogs welcome; enclosed garden behind *(Dennis Jenkin)*

WESTON-IN-GORDANO [ST4474]

White Hart [B3124 Portishead—Clevedon, between M5 junctions 19 and 20]: Cheerful highly polished bar with lots of old photographs in lower room, decent usual food, Courage and John Smiths; Gordano valley views from fine back lawn with play area *(B Weeks)*

WESTON-SUPER-MARE [ST3062]

Captains Table [Birnbeck Road]: Good unpretentious local atmosphere, enjoyable food inc fish specials, Tetleys, bay views; terrace *(A C Stone, D and S Price)*

Claremont Vaults [Birnbeck Rd; seafront, N end]: Large well used low-priced dining pub included for wonderful views down the beach or across the bay, well kept Bass, decent wine, cheerful friendly service; pool, quiet piped music, no food Mon *(Comus and Sarah Elliott, Peter and Audrey Dowsett)*

☆ *Woolpack* [St Georges, just off M5, junction 21]: Olde-worlde 17th-c coaching inn with friendly relaxing local atmosphere, good varied well priced food inc some sophisticated dishes and lots of fresh fish, pleasant window seats and library-theme area, well kept changing beers such as Butcombe, Oakhill and Palmers, good house wines, keen efficient service, small but attractive restaurant; skittle alley *(Comus and Sarah Elliott, Brian Root)*

WHEDDON CROSS [SS9238]

Rest & Be Thankful [A396/B3224, S of Minehead]: Spotless comfortably modern two-room bar with wide range of generous home-cooked food from good fresh sandwiches up, cheerful service, well kept ales such as Bass, Exmoor and Greene King Old Speckled Hen, two good log fires, huge jug collection, no smoking restaurant, games area, skittle alley; piped music, no dogs; tables out in courtyard, public lavatory for the disabled, bedrooms *(LYM, Michael Rowse)*

WIDCOMBE [ST2216]

☆ *Holman Clavel*: Simple but comfortable old-fashioned deep-country pub dating from 14th c and named after the massive holly chimney-beam over its huge log fire; good home cooking, friendly informal staff, well kept Cotleigh and Flowers Original, colourful wine list, nice atmosphere; dogs welcome, handy for Blackdown Hills *(BB, John and Fiona Merritt)*

WILLITON [ST0741]

Masons Arms [on outskirts via B3191 for Watchet; pub on corner]: Cosy-looking thatched pub with cheerful atmosphere, good value food in bar and restaurant, real ales inc Fullers London Pride and a local guest, quick friendly service; small well fenced play area, bedrooms *(Ian and Sharon Shorthouse)*

WINCANTON [ST7128]

Red Lion [Market Pl]: Unpretentious bare-boards single bar with helpful licensees, enjoyable fresh inc fish fresh from West Bay, well kept Wadworths real ales, woodburner in big inglenook, comfortable chairs and benches, interesting mottoes on beams *(Neville and Anne Morley)*

WITHAM FRIARY [ST7440]

Seymour Arms [signed from B3092 S of Frome]: Welcoming unspoilt local, two simple rooms off hatch-service corridor, one with darts, the other with central table skittles; well kept Ushers Best, Rich's local farm cider, cards and dominoes – no juke box or machines; attractive garden by main rail line *(the Didler, Adam Manolson, Pete Baker)*

WIVELISCOMBE [ST0827]

Bear [North St]: Good range of well priced home-cooked food from sandwiches and burgers up, well kept local Cotleigh and other real ales (wknd brewery visits, beer festival with music and morris dancers), farm ciders, very attentive friendly landlord; play area, good value bedrooms *(the Didler, Andy and Jill Kassube)*

White Hart [The Square]: Small welcoming country hotel, local real ales, lunchtime snacks and good evening meals reflecting its links with the local farming community, friendly caring service; bedrooms *(David Clark)*

WOOKEY [ST5145]

☆ *Ring o' Bells* [High St]: Welcoming and comfortable proper village local, dark wood

tables and settles, log fire each end, well kept Butcombe and Smiles, enjoyable generous sensibly priced food from sandwiches up inc children's meals in bar and dining room, cribbage; may be piped music *(Tom Evans, Alan and Paula McCully)*

WOOKEY HOLE [ST5347]

Wookey Hole Inn: Usefully placed family pub with unusual cool and trendy décor, relaxed atmosphere, four changing real ales and several belgian beers, enjoyable and innovative realistically priced food, nice staff; jazz Sun lunchtime, pleasant garden, comfortable bedrooms *(W R Taylor)*

WOOLVERTON [ST7954]

☆ *Red Lion* [set back from A36 N of village]: Roomy recently refurbished pub, beams, panelling, flagstones and lots of stripped wood, candles and lovely log fire, well kept Wadworths real ales, wide choice of decent wines by the glass, generous enjoyable food from popular filled baked potatoes and good value children's meals to more upmarket dishes, welcoming attentive service; open all day, plenty of tables outside *(Chris and Ann Coy, LYM)*

WRAXALL [ST4971]

New Battleaxes [Bristol Rd]: Large neatly kept rambling pub with good value food inc soup and daily carvery bargain, well kept real ale; handy for Tyntesfield (NT) *(W R Miller)*

Old Barn [just off Bristol Rd (B3130)]: Traditionally done gabled barn conversion with scrubbed tables, school benches and soft sofas under the oak rafters, stripped boards, flagstones and festoons of dried flowers; wide choice of good home-made food, five well kept beers inc Bass and local brews tapped from the cask, friendly service; Sun quiz night, garden with good play area and barbecues on cobbled terrace *(the Didler, R W Broomfield, Alan and Paula McCully)*

WRINGTON [ST4762]

Plough [2½ miles off A370 Bristol—Weston, from bottom of Rhodiate Hill]: Large friendly pub with good value well cooked bar food inc tapas, well kept Smiles and Youngs, interesting wine list, open fire, lots of dark wood, good atmosphere, small pleasant no smoking dining area; pretty front and side garden, open all day *(John Urquhart, Comus and Sarah Elliott, Alan and Paula McCully)*

YARLINGTON [ST6529]

☆ *Stags Head*: Proper family-run country pub, two bars (the border collie has a peep-hole in door of the left one), homely rustic décor, good choice of good sensibly priced fresh food using local produce and game here and in restaurant, well kept Glastonbury (actually from Somerton) and a couple of other real ales *(Steve Culverhouse, Neville and Anne Morley)*

YATTON [ST4167]

Bridge Inn [B3133 Clevedon—Congresbury]: More tidy roadside restaurant than pub, but good value food served quickly, plenty of seating inc baby chairs, a real ale; children's play room and outside playground, bedrooms *(W R Miller)*

Staffordshire

Three new entries here this year: the handsome old Goats Head in Abbots Bromley (doing well under its new young landlord), the Boat near Lichfield, down towards Walsall (good food in this appealingly modernised pub), and the friendly Fox out by the woods near Stourton (good value food in its rambling rooms). Other pubs on good form here are the welcoming George in Alstonefield (a proper traditional pub), the Watts Russell Arms there (another walkers' favourite), the bustling Burton Bridge Inn in Burton upon Trent (brewing its own good beers), the amazing Yew Tree at Cauldon (unique for its remarkable collections, its ebullient landlord and its very low prices), the Greyhound at Warslow (good value bedrooms, and new licensees settling in well), and the convivial Olde Royal Oak in National Trust walking country at Wetton. Though it is unusual for a new entry to take this top award on its first appearance in the Guide, *the Boat near Lichfield gains the title of Staffordshire Dining Pub of the Year. A few pubs to note particularly in the Lucky Dip section at the end of the chapter are the Black Lion at Consall, George in Eccleshall, Cat at Enville, Manifold Valley Hotel at Hulme End, Den Engel in Leek, Horseshoe at Tatenhill and Olde Dog & Partridge in Tutbury. Drinks prices are comfortably below the national average here, with the Yew Tree, the Fox at Stourton and with its own brews the Burton Bridge Inn all particularly good value for beer. Marstons, part of the Wolverhampton & Dudley group and the main regional brewer, brews in Burton (Britain's brewing capital, the Trent's water having been prized for this). Burton is also the UK HQ of Coors, the US brewer which now owns the Hancocks, M&B and Worthington beer brands, though not all these beers are currently produced at Burton. Coors has also been brewing Bass here for its new owners, Interbrew of Belgium (who own Boddingtons and Flowers, too). Besides Burton Bridge, smaller local breweries to look out for include Enville, Eccleshall, Old Cottage and (another based in Burton) Tower.*

ABBOTS BROMLEY SK0824 Map 7
Goats Head
Market Place

Overlooking the quiet centre of this peaceful and attractive village, the black and white timbered Goats Head fits in well. It is comfortably relaxed inside, with some heavy Tudor beams in the three linked parts of its main lounge bar and dining area. Furniture runs from traditional oak settles to solid dining tables and chairs on turkey carpet, and a big inglenook has a small coal and log fire. The young landlord has some interesting recipes, and does two special dutch meals, frikandell (£5.75), and home-made chicken satay (£6.85) as well as his usual menu, which might include sandwiches (from £2.70; toasties from £2.90), baked potatoes (from £3), smooth chicken liver pâté (£3.90), cumberland sausages with mint mash or home-made lasagne (£5.95), braised lamb shank (£8.15), sirloin steak (from £9), specials such as pork medallions with cream, brandy and pink peppercorn sauce (£9.90), and bass fillet with tangy lemon sauce (£10.75), and puddings (£2.95); vegetables come in rich variety. They have a good range of wines by the glass (from

Tanners of Shrewsbury), and well kept Greene King Abbot and Marstons Pedigree on handpump, and service is friendly and efficient; cribbage, darts, and there may be piped radio. A panelled public bar on the right has darts, and out on a neat sheltered lawn picnic-seats and teak tables and seats look up to the church tower behind. *(Recommended by Guy Vowles, Gordon Oakes)*

Pubmaster ~ Tenant Kristian Hine ~ Real ale ~ Bar food ~ (01283) 840254 ~ Children in eating area of bar ~ Open 12-3 6-11; 12-4 7-10.30 Sun; closed Mon lunchtime exc bank hols, 25 Dec

ALSTONEFIELD SK1355 Map 7
George
Village signposted from A515 Ashbourne—Buxton

All sorts of people enjoy this charming and simple stone pub, from locals and campers, to cyclists and walkers (though no muddy boots); its atmosphere is particularly welcoming and villagey. It's in a peaceful farming hamlet, by the village green, and in fine weather it's a real pleasure to sit out on the stone seats beneath the inn-sign, and watch the world go by. The unchanging straightforward low-beamed bar has pewter tankards hanging by the copper-topped bar counter, a collection of old Peak District photographs and pictures, and a roaring coal fire in winter. The spacious no smoking family room has plenty of tables and wheelback chairs. Friendly staff serve well kept Burtonwood Bitter and a guest such as Jennings Cocker Hoop on handpump; darts, cribbage and dominoes. The down-to-earth home-made food is good value, with prices unchanged since last year. It includes sandwiches (from £2.20), soup (£2.40), ploughman's (from £4.85), meat and potato pie (£5.95) chicken breast, lasagne or breaded plaice (£6.75), a couple of daily specials, and delicious home-made puddings such as fudge and walnut pie and meringue glaze (£2.60); you order from the staff at the kitchen door. The big sheltered stableyard behind the pub has picnic-sets by a pretty rockery, and you can arrange with the landlord to camp on the croft. *(Recommended by Matthew Shackle, John Beeken, Dr P S Fox, Peter F Marshall, Sarah Day, Mark Timms, Roger Bridgeman, the Didler, Mike and Wendy Proctor, John Brightley, Richard Cole, I J Thurman, Mrs J Thomas, Mark Percy, Lesley Mayoh)*

Burtonwood ~ Tenants Richard and Sue Grandjean ~ Real ale ~ Bar food (not 25 Dec) ~ (01335) 310205 ~ Children in family room ~ Open 11-3, 6-11; 11-11 Sat; 12-10.30 Sun

Watts Russell Arms
Hopedale

Prettily set in a little lane outside the village in a deep leafy valley, this 18th-c shuttered stone house is a pleasant spot for a refreshing break after a long walk. The cheerful beamed bar has brocaded wall banquettes and wheelback chairs and carvers, an open fire below a copper hood, a collection of blue and white china jugs hanging from the ceiling, bric-a-brac around the roughcast walls, and an interesting bar counter made from copper-bound oak barrels; there's a no smoking area. You'll find well kept Black Sheep, Timothy Taylors Landlord and a summer guest such as Batemans XB on handpump, about a dozen malts, and a decent range of soft drinks; darts, TV, dominoes and piped music. Outside there are picnic-sets under parasols on the sheltered tiered terrace, and in the garden. Straightforward bar food includes sandwiches (£2.95), home-made soup or creamy garlic mushrooms (£3.45), filled baked potatoes or baguettes (from £3.95), chilli con carne, stilton and vegetable crumble (£6.95), and battered cod (£7.25), with daily specials such as chicken with leek and stilton sauce (£7.95), and lamb shank (£9.75); puddings such as rhubarb and ginger crumble and apple pie (£3.95); they do children's helpings for £3 less. Close to Dovedale and the Manifold, it gets very busy on the weekends. *(Recommended by Ken Richards, Doug Christian, Matthew Shackle, Mike and Wendy Proctor, the Didler)*

Free house ~ Licensee George Tunney ~ Real ale ~ Bar food ~ (01335) 310126 ~ Children welcome ~ Open 12-3, 7-11; closed Mon exc bank hols, and Sun evening in winter

BURTON UPON TRENT SK2423 Map 7
Burton Bridge Inn ★ £

Bridge Street (A50)

Home to the Burton Bridge Brewery, this enjoyably straightforward, bustling brick local serves its own well kept Bitter, Festival, Golden Delicious, Gold Medal and Porter on handpump alongside a guest such as Timothy Taylors Landlord; they also have around 25 whiskies and over a dozen country wines. The simple little front area leads into an adjacent bar, separated from a no smoking oak-panelled lounge by the serving counter. The bar has wooden pews, plain walls hung with notices, awards and brewery memorabilia, and the lounge has oak beams, a flame-effect fire and old oak tables and chairs. Simple hearty bar snacks include cobs (from £1.40), toasties (£2), giant yorkshire puddings with fillings such as roast beef, ratatouille or faggots and mushy peas (from £3.20), and ploughman's (£3.50); the panelled upstairs dining room is only open at lunchtime. A blue-brick patio overlooks the brewery in the long old-fashioned yard at the back. *(Recommended by David Carr, C J Fletcher, the Didler, Pete Baker, Suzanne Miles, Dr S J Shepherd, Tony Hobden, Kevin Douglas, Bernie Adams, Theo, Anne and Jane Gaskin, D L Parkhurst)*

Own brew ~ Licensees Kevin and Jan McDonald ~ Real ale ~ Bar food (lunchtime only, not Sun) ~ No credit cards ~ (01283) 536596 ~ Children in eating area of bar ~ Dogs welcome ~ Open 11.30-2.15, 5-11; 12-2.15, 7-10.30 Sun; closed bank hol Mon lunchtime

CAULDON SK0749 Map 7
Yew Tree ★★ £

Village signposted from A523 and A52 about 8 miles W of Ashbourne

Readers are as happy as ever with this fascinating place: 'we cannot understand why we haven't visited this place sooner' writes one couple, while another feels that 'no holiday in Derbyshire is complete without a visit'. Don't be put off by the plain exterior, or the fact that the pub is tucked unpromisingly between enormous cement works and quarries, and almost hidden by a towering yew tree – inside is a veritable museum's-worth of curiosities all lovingly collected by the lively landlord himself. The most impressive pieces are perhaps the working Polyphons and Symphonions – 19th-c developments of the musical box, often taller than a person, each with quite a repertoire of tunes and elaborate sound-effects; take plenty of 2p pieces to work them. But there are also two pairs of Queen Victoria's stockings, ancient guns and pistols, several penny-farthings, an old sit-and-stride boneshaker, a rocking horse, swordfish blades, a little 800BC Greek vase, and even a fine marquetry cabinet crammed with notable early staffordshire pottery. Soggily sprung sofas mingle with 18th-c settles, plenty of little wooden tables and a four-person oak church choir seat with carved heads which came from St Mary's church in Stafford; above the bar is an odd iron dog-carrier (don't ask how it works!). As well as all this there's an expanding choir of fine tuneful longcase clocks in the gallery just above the entrance, a collection of six pianolas (one of which is played most nights) with an excellent repertoire of piano rolls, a working vintage valve radio set, a crank-handle telephone, a sinuous medieval wind instrument made of leather, and a Jacobean four-poster which was once owned by Josiah Wedgwood and still has his original wig hook on the headboard. The drinks here are very reasonably priced, and you'll find well kept Bass, Burton Bridge and Titanic Mild on handpump or tapped from the cask, along with some interesting malt whiskies; piped music, darts, shove-ha'penny, table skittles, dominoes and cribbage. Simple good value snacks include hot pork pies (70p), meat and potato pies, chicken and mushroom or steak pies (85p), hot big filled baps and sandwiches (from £1.50), quiche, smoked mackerel or ham salad (£3.50), and home-made puddings (£1.50).

(Recommended by C J Fletcher, the Didler, D C Leggatt, Sarah Day, Mark Timms, Mike and Wendy Proctor, Graham and Lynn Mason, Ann and Colin Hunt, Kevin Thorpe, Bernie Adams)

Free house ~ Licensee Alan East ~ Real ale ~ Bar food (12-2, 6-9) ~ No credit cards ~ (01538) 308348 ~ Children in Polyphon room ~ Dogs welcome ~ Folk music first Tues in month ~ Open 10-3, 6-11; 12-3, 7-10.30 Sun

CHEADLE SK0342 Map 7
Queens at Freehay

1 mile SE of Cheadle; take Rakeway Road off A522 (via Park Avenue or Mills Road), then after 1 mile turn into Counslow Road

With a pleasantly thriving atmosphere, this dining pub is an enjoyable place to come for a meal. The comfortable lounge bar is attractively decorated with small country pictures, and pretty curtains with matching cushions. It opens through an arch into a light and airy dining area, with neatly spaced tables. The food is mainly familiar, but all cooked carefully with good flavours, and nicely presented; swift attentive service. Besides lunchtime sandwiches (from £3.25), hoi sin duck in a tortilla wrap (£3.95), and ploughman's (£4.50), other dishes might include soup (£2.95), home-made duck and orange pâté or local black pudding with crispy bacon and cheddar (£3.95), vegetable bake, beef and Guinness pie or battered cod and chips (£7.95), moroccan lamb tagine or sweet and sour pork (£8.95), and sirloin steak (£10.95), with blackboard specials such as half a roast duckling (£9.95), and roasted monkfish (£10.95); as well as various sundaes, puddings might be home-made apple torte or sherry trifle (from £3.25). Bass and Worthington are well kept on handpump, and they do a good range of liqueur coffees; piped music. *(Recommended by Dr T E Hothersall, John and Gillian Scarisbrick, Mike and Wendy Proctor)*

Free house ~ Licensee Adrian Rock ~ Real ale ~ Bar food ~ Restaurant ~ (01538) 722383 ~ Children in restaurant ~ Open 12-2.30, 6-11; 12-3, 6.30-10.30 Sun; closed 25-26 Dec, evenings 31 Dec and 1 Jan

LICHFIELD SK0705 Map 4
Boat 🍽

A461 3 or 4 miles SW of town, just SW of A5 roundabout

Staffordshire Dining Pub of the Year

A relaxed refuge from the nearby trunk roads, this well run modern pub has blue and russet café furniture, a couple of potted palms and bright waterside prints and photoprints in a cheerful area opening straight on to the kitchen, and dominated by big floor-to-ceiling food blackboards. The choice and quality are good, and might include home-made soup (£2.95), sandwiches (from £2.95), wild boar terrine with lime and apple chutney (£4.50), king prawns in garlic sauce (£5.50), caramelised onion tart with rocket and plum tomatoes (£6.50), fried duck breast with braised red cabbage and red wine sauce or roast lamb shoulder with redcurrant and mint (£9), red snapper with roasted vegetables and lime dressing (£10.50), fillet steak with wild mushroom sauce (£14.50), and puddings such as toffee and banana crumble or warm chocolate tart (£3.95). On the right are sturdy pale pine dining tables in a quieter pleasantly decorated carpeted area with some attractive traditional and more contemporary water and country prints. Tucked in by a balustrade here is a chattier corner, with a rack of broadsheet newspapers, magazines on a big cask table, and comfortable banquettes upholstered in a William Morris print. The good solid bar counter has two changing real ales such as Everards Original and Timothy Taylors Landlord on handpump, and good coffee is nicely served; there may be faint piped music. We imagine that now work on the new dual carriageway is finishing they will set about making something of the outside areas, which on our spring 2003 inspection were best described as left fallow. *(Recommended by John and Penny Spinks, Peter Hobson)*

Please let us know of any pubs where the wine is particularly good.

Free house ~ Licensee Ann Holden ~ Real ale ~ Bar food (12-2.30, 7-9.45) ~ Restaurant ~ (01543) 361692 ~ Children welcome ~ Dogs allowed in bar ~ Open 12-3, 6-12; 12-12 Sat; 12-10.30 Sun; 12-3, 6-12 Sat in winter; closed 25-26 Dec

SALT SJ9527 Map 7
Holly Bush

Village signposted off A51 S of Stone (and A518 NE of Stafford)

Decked with brightly coloured flowers in summer, this lovely old white-painted thatched house is set in a pretty village. The oldest part of the building dates back to the 14th c, and has a heavy beamed and planked ceiling (some of the beams are attractively carved), a salt cupboard built in by the coal fire, and other nice old-fashioned touches such as an antique pair of clothes brushes hanging by the door, attractive sporting prints and watercolours, and an ancient pair of riding boots on the mantelpiece. Several cosy areas spread off from the standing-room serving section, with comfortable settees as well as more orthodox seats. The room on the left is no smoking, and a modern back extension blends in well, with beams, stripped brickwork and a small coal fire. They serve well kept Bass, Boddingtons and Marstons Pedigree on handpump; shove-ha'penny, cribbage, dominoes, backgammon, Jenga, fruit machine, perhaps piped nostalgic pop music. They use local suppliers wherever possible, and besides lunchtime sandwiches and toasties (from £2.45), and baked potatoes (from £2.25), the menu could include fried calves liver (£3.50), greek lamb (£7.50), home-made steak and kidney pudding or chicken supreme with red wine, raisins and apricots (£7.95), and specials such as chargrilled red snapper with jamaican spiced tomato chutney (£8.95), and fried pork fillet with apples and cider (£9.95), with puddings (from £3.25); it's a good idea to arrive early if you want to eat. The big back lawn has rustic picnic-sets; they may have traditional jazz and a hog roast in summer, and do a fireworks display on 5 November. *(Recommended by Peter and Patricia Burton, Gavin Wells, Brian Kneale, Michael and Jenny Back, Collin and Julie Taylor, Graham and Lynn Mason, Keith John Ryan, Bob and Laura Brock, Darly Graton, Graeme Gulibert, Maurice and Gill McMahon, Alan and Paula McCully, Mr and Mrs R A Newbury, Patrick Hancock, R Davies, Brenda and Stuart Naylor)*

Free house ~ Licensee Geoffrey Holland ~ Real ale ~ Bar food (12-2, 6-9.30; 12-9.30 Sat/Sun) ~ (01889) 508234 ~ Children welcome, if eating, in eating area of bar ~ Open 12-2.30, 6-11; 12-11 Sat; 12-10.30 Sun

STOURTON SO8485 Map 4
Fox

A458 W of junction with A449, towards Enville

If you weren't in the know, you might easily speed straight past this lonely roadside pub. But what a mistake: once you are inside, it quickly grows on you, thanks largely to the atmosphere generated by the warmly friendly family who run it. Several cosily small areas ramble back from the small serving bar by the entrance, with its well kept Bathams Best on handpump (and a noticeboard of hand-written travel offers). Tables are mostly sturdy and varnished, with pews, settles and comfortable library or dining chairs; there is green carpet here, dark blue there, bare boards beyond, with a good positive colour scheme picked up nicely by the curtains, and some framed exotic menus and well chosen prints (jazz and golf both feature). The woodburning stoves may be opened to give a cheery blaze on cold days. They put out big bunches of flowers, and the lighting (mainly low voltage spots) has been done very carefully, giving an intimate bistro feel in the areas round on the right. A smart conservatory has neat bentwood furniture and proper tablecloths. Good value food runs from hot baguettes (from £3.50), and other bar dishes such as baked potatoes (from £4), home-made curries (from £6), and steak and kidney pie, lasagne or battered cod (£6.50), to interesting more restauranty dishes such as lemon sole with spinach and burnt hollandaise (£5.95), fish stew (£5.95; £12.50 main), bass fillets with basil crème fraîche sauce (£12.95), lamb noisettes with sherry and mushroom sauce (£14.95), and fillet steak poached in wine with celeriac purée (£15.95), and puddings (from £3.25); it's a good idea to book if you want to come to one of their fortnightly fish evenings. A big stretch of sloping grass has well spaced picnic-sets, and the pub is surrounded by woodland; it is well placed for Kinver Country Park walks. *(Recommended by Theo, Anne and Jane Gaskin)*

Free house ~ Licensee Stefan Caron ~ Real ale ~ Bar food (12-2.15(5 Sun), 7-9.30; not Mon or Sun evening) ~ Restaurant ~ (01384) 872614 ~ Children welcome ~ Open 11-3, 5-11; 11-11 Sat; 12-10.30 Sun; closed 25 Dec

WARSLOW SK0858 Map 7
Greyhound 🛏

B5053 S of Buxton

The new licensees haven't made any great changes to this slated stone-built pub, which remains popular with readers. It's surrounded by pretty countryside and handy for the Manifold Valley, Dovedale and Alton Towers (the bedrooms are good value). The side garden has picnic-sets under ash trees, with rustic seats out in front where window boxes blaze with colour in summer. Straightforward but cosy and comfortable inside, the beamed bar has long cushioned antique oak settles (some quite elegant), houseplants in the windows, and cheerful fires. Reasonably priced home-made bar food includes lunchtime sandwiches (from £2.25, baguettes from £3.25), filled baked potatoes (from £3.50), sausage, egg and chips (£4.50), and gammon and pineapple (£7.50), as well as filo prawns with plum and ginger dip (£4.25), lasagne (£7.25), and moroccan lamb, steak and ale pie or caribbean chicken (£7.75). They serve well kept Black Sheep, Marstons Pedigree and a weekly changing guest such as Timothy Taylors Landlord on handpump, as well as 20 malt whiskies; TV, fruit machine, pool, darts, dominoes and piped music. *(Recommended by Derek and Sylvia Stephenson, Doug Christian, D C Leggatt, Gareth and Toni Edwards, Mike and Wendy Proctor, Bernard Stradling, Susan and Tony Dyer, Jo and Iain MacGregor, Paul and Margaret Baker, Matthew Shackle, Ken and Barbara Turner)*

Free house ~ Licensees Jan and Andy Livesley ~ Real ale ~ Bar food (12-3, 6-9; all day Sat/Sun in summer) ~ (01298) 84249 ~ Children welcome ~ Dogs allowed in bar ~ Soft rock and Blues every Sat ~ Open 12-3, 6-11; 12-11(10.30 Sun)Sat; 12-3, 6-11(10.30 Sun)Sat in winter ~ Bedrooms: £17.50/£35

WETTON SK1055 Map 7
Olde Royal Oak

Village signposted off Hulme End—Alstonefield road, between B5054 and A515

Even on a wet winter lunchtime, you're likely to find lots of happy customers at this aged white-painted and shuttered stone-built village house, in lovely National Trust walking country. There's a good convivial atmosphere in the bar, which has golf clubs hanging from black beams with white ceiling boards above, small dining chairs around rustic tables, a piano surrounded by old sheet music covers, an oak corner cupboard, and a coal fire in the stone fireplace. It extends into a more modern-feeling area, which in turn leads to a carpeted sun lounge looking out over the small garden; piped music, darts, TV, shove-ha'penny, cribbage and dominoes. The family room is no smoking. You can choose from more than 40 whiskies, and they've well kept Black Sheep, Greene King Ruddles County, and a guest from a brewer such as Leatherbritches on handpump; in summer you'll also find Anklecracker (an ale brewed especially for them to celebrate the official world toe-wrestling championship that takes place here in the first week of July). In generous helpings, reasonably priced bar food includes soup or staffordshire oatcakes filled with cheese (£2.75), brie wedges with redcurrant sauce (£3.75), ploughman's (£5.75), battered haddock or mediterranean vegetable lasagne (£6.95), local rainbow trout (£7.25), and steaks (from £9.95), with puddings such as ginger sponge pudding or cherry cheesecake (from £2.50); children's meals (from £2.75), and Sunday roasts (£6.25). Service is good, and the landlord is friendly. Behind the pub is a croft suitable for caravans and tents, and Wetton Mill and the Manifold Valley are nearby; the pub is popular with walkers. *(Recommended by Rona Murdoch, Mike and Wendy Proctor, the Didler, I J Thurman, Sue and Dave Harris, MLR, Tim and Jan Dalton)*

Free house ~ Licensees Kath and Brian Rowbotham ~ Real ale ~ Bar food ~ (01335) 310287 ~ Children in family room ~ Folk music Sat evening ~ Open 12-3, 7-11; closed Weds ~ Bedrooms: /£50S

Lucky Dip

Besides the fully inspected pubs, you might like to try these Lucky Dips recommended to us and described by readers (if you do, please send us reports: www.goodguides.com).

ACTON TRUSSELL [SJ9318]
☆ *Moat House* [signed from A449 just S of Stafford; handy for M6 junction 13]: Busy timbered canalside food place, partly dating from 1320, attractive grounds with picnic-sets overlooking Staffs & Worcs Canal; comfortable oak-beamed bar with big open fireplace and armchairs, nice décor, lots of friendly and efficient young staff, enjoyable bar food (only restaurant meals on Sun), well kept Banks's Bitter and Original and Marstons Pedigree, good wine list, no smoking restaurant; fruit machine, piped music; children welcome, open all day wknds, bedrooms *(Roger Cass, Dr S J Shepherd, Maurice and Gill McMahon, Karen Eliot, J Attwood, LYM)*
ALREWAS [SK1714]
William IV [William IV Rd, off main st]: Warm and friendly backstreet pub with Marstons Pedigree and monthly guest beers, interesting specials lunchtime and from early evening on (all day Fri-Sun), two for one lunchtime bargains (not Sun) – bookable partly no smoking raised eating area; music nights, sports TV; tables in garden with aviary and chipmunks *(Glenwys and Alan Lawrence, Bob and Laura Brock)*
AMINGTON [SK2304]
Pretty Pigs [Shuttington Rd]: Welcoming and relaxing old inn based on former small manor house, well kept beers, wide choice of quickly served food inc popular and generous Sun roast (restaurant up a couple of steps), attentive staff; piped music; tables outside *(Colin Gooch)*
ANSLOW [SK2024]
Burnt Gate [Hopley Rd]: Pleasant country pub, comfortable lounge with well kept Bass and Marstons Pedigree, good fresh home-made food in separate restaurant *(C J Fletcher)*
BREWOOD [SJ8808]
Bridge Inn [High Green]: Food inc good fresh fish, well kept Burtonwood *(Bob and Laura Brock)*
BURTON UPON TRENT [SK2423]
Alfred [Derby St]: Tied to local small Burton Bridge brewery, their full range and guest beers kept well from central bar serving two spartan rooms, good beer-oriented food too; no smoking area, pool in back games room, friendly landlord, lots of country wines, beer festivals Easter and early Nov; open all day,

cheap bedrooms *(the Didler, Bernie Adams, Tony and Wendy Hobden)*
☆ *Coopers Tavern* [Cross St]: Splendidly traditional under current landlord (but he's talking of retiring), counterless back tap room with notably well kept Bass, Hardys & Hansons Classic and Best and Marstons Pedigree straight from imposing row of casks (no serving counter); barrel tables, cheap nourishing hot filled cobs, pie and chips etc (lunchtime, not Sun), homely no smoking front parlour with piano and coal fire, friendly staff; impromptu folk nights Tues *(Pete Baker, Bernie Adams, LYM, the Didler, C J Fletcher)*
Derby Inn [Derby Rd]: Unspoilt friendly local with brewery glasses collection in cosy panelled lounge, lots of steam railway memorabilia in long narrow bar, well kept Marstons Pedigree, long-serving landlord, local veg, eggs, cheese and even black pudding for sale wknds; sports TV, open all day Fri/Sat *(C J Fletcher, Bernie Adams, the Didler)*
Devonshire Arms [Station St]: Now tied to Burton Bridge, with a good range of their ales and of continental bottled beers, also country wines, decent lunchtime food, lots of snug corners – some no smoking; pleasant back terrace, open all day Fri/Sat *(the Didler)*
Elms [Stapenhill Rd (A444)]: Several recently refurbished rooms, well kept beers inc one from local Tower brewery – usually Malty Towers *(C J Fletcher)*
Old Cottage Tavern [Rangemoor St/Byrkley St]: Local small brewery Old Cottage's first tied pub here, three of their beers such as Oak, Halcyon Daze and Stout, also guest beers, four rooms inc no smoking room, games room and cosy back restaurant – good value food inc bargain specials; open all day *(the Didler, C J Fletcher)*
Roebuck [Station St]: Comfortable Victorian-style alehouse opp former Bass and Ind Coope breweries, a bargain beer brewed for the pub, also Greene King Abbot, Ind Coope Burton, Marstons Pedigree, Tetleys and guest beers, enjoyable cheap lunchtime food inc add-it-up dishes (you choose the ingredients), friendly staff, prints and artefacts; piped music; open all day wkdys, decent bedrooms *(the Didler)*
Thomas Sykes [Anglesey Rd]: In former stables and waggon shed of ex-Everards brewery (latterly Heritage Brewery Museum), two

friendly high-ceilinged rooms with stable fittings and breweriana, wood benches, cobbled floors, well kept Bass and Marstons Pedigree on handpump and guest beers tapped from the cask, fine pump clip collection, good cheap basic food such as filled cobs, small snug; children welcome till 8, outside gents'; open all day Fri *(C J Fletcher, Bernie Adams, the Didler)*

BUTTERTON [SK0756]

Black Lion [off B5053]: Unspoilt low-beamed 18th-c stone inn in Peak District conservation village, traditional furnishings, log fire, kitchen range in inner room, some banquette seating, reasonably priced food from filled rolls up, well kept ales such as Everards Tiger, Marstons Pedigree, Theakstons Best and Charles Wells Bombardier, traditional games and pool room; piped music; children in eating areas, tables on terrace, tidy bedrooms, cl Mon lunchtime *(Mike and Wendy Proctor, Kevin Blake, the Didler, LYM, John Nielsen)*

CANNOCK WOOD [SK0412]

Park Gate [Park Gate Rd, S side of Cannock Chase]: Extended brick pub with cushioned chairs and pews, lots of woodwork, wide choice of blackboard bar food (not Sat evening) from sandwiches and baguettes up, well kept Banks's Mild, Marstons Pedigree and Worthington, friendly young staff, woodburner, extensive restaurant and conservatory; plenty of picnic-sets and play area outside, by Castle Ring Iron Age fort, good Cannock Chase walks *(Alan Cole, Kirstie Bruce)*

CODSALL [SJ8603]

Codsall Station [Chapel Lane/Station Rd]: Pub in simply restored listed waiting room and ticket office (station still used by trains), good range of Holdens beers kept well inc one brewed for the pub, lots of railway memorabilia, good value basic food from sandwiches and baked potatoes up; open all day wknds *(Robert Garner, Gill and Tony Morriss, Keith Jacob)*

CONSALL [SJ8329]

☆ *Black Lion* [Consall Forge, OS Sheet 118 map ref 000491; best approach from Nature Park, off A522, using car park ½ mile past Nature Centre]: Traditional country tavern tucked away in rustic old-fashioned canalside settlement by restored steam railway station, enjoyable unpretentious food freshly cooked by landlord inc good fish choice, good coal fire, well kept Marstons Best and Pedigree, friendly landlady; piped music; children (but not muddy boots) welcome; busy wknds, good walking area *(the Didler, LYM, Bob and Laura Brock, Mike and Wendy Proctor)*

ECCLESHALL [SJ8329]

☆ *George* [A519/B5026]: Good Slaters beers brewed by the licensees' son, such as Bitter, Original, Premium, Ecky Thump, Shining Knight and Supreme, beamed bar with well worn in unassuming rustic modern furnishings, coal fire in big central inglenook, cosy alcoves, good wines by the glass, friendly service, interesting food choice from newish side

restaurant (all day wknds), reasonable prices; may be piped music; children in eating areas, dogs welcome, open all day *(Sue Holland, Dave Webster, LYM, Derek and Sylvia Stephenson, Christine and Neil Townend, Guy Vowles, Kevin Thorpe, Stan and Hazel Allen)*

ENDON [SJ9553]

☆ *Hollybush* [Denford; by-road some way E, off A53 SW of Leek]: Friendly pub in fine spot by Caldon Canal aqueduct, modernised by new landlord without losing its character (or the fine old flagstones in the front bar), wide range of well kept beer, enjoyable home-made food from sandwiches and bar meals to restaurant dishes, alert helpful service, no piped music, good fire; dogs welcome (nice pub dog), very busy in summer *(DC, Bob and Laura Brock)*

ENVILLE [SO8286]

☆ *Cat* [A458 W of Stourbridge]: 17th-c, with heavy beams, timbers and log fire in two appealingly old-fashioned rooms on one side of servery, plush banquettes on the other, well kept local Enville Ale, White and seasonal Phoenix, other beers such as Tetleys, Wicked Hathern and Wychwood Goliath (landlord helpful with the choice), mulled wine, quickly served generous food from imaginative sandwiches to unusual specials, popular upstairs restaurant, tabby cat and quiet collie; nice yard with picnic-sets, popular with walkers (on Staffordshire Way), cl Sun *(BB, Gill and Tony Morriss, the Didler, Lynda and Trevor Smith)*

ETRURIA [SJ8747]

☆ *Plough* [Etruria Rd (off A53 opp Festival site)]: Small two-room pub, very friendly licensees and staff, five well kept Robinsons beers, nice atmosphere and décor, coal fires, wide choice of good value food served till late esp steaks and hot sandwiches, will do anything on request; busy lunchtime and wknds *(Dr John Worthington)*

FRADLEY [SK1414]

☆ *White Swan* [Fradley Junction]: Perfect canalside location, very popular summer wknds; wide choice of quickly served usual food from sandwiches to good value Sun carvery, well kept Tetleys-related ales inc Mild, efficient friendly staff, cheery traditional public bar, quieter plusher lounge and lower vaulted back bar (where children allowed), lots of malt whiskies, real fire, cribbage, dominoes; waterside tables, good canal walks *(LYM, Bob and Laura Brock, Dave Braisted, Ian and Jane Irving)*

HANLEY [SJ8747]

Coachmakers Arms [Lichfield St]: Unpretentious friendly town local, three small rooms and drinking corridor, well kept Bass and Worthington, well filled cobs, popular darts, cards and dominoes, skittles *(the Didler, Pete Baker)*

Golden Cup [Old Town Rd]: Friendly local with imposing Edwardian façade and bar fittings, Bass and Greene King Ruddles County; can be busy wknds; nice garden, open all day (cl Sun afternoon) *(the Didler)*

Unicorn [Piccadilly]: Small pub handy for

Regent Theatre, efficient pleasant staff
(Dr John Worthington)

HARDINGS WOOD [SJ8354]

☆ *Bluebell*: Unpretentious traditional boaters'
tavern between Macclesfield and Trent &
Mersey canals, half a dozen well kept changing
ales from small breweries, belgian beers, farm
cider, filled rolls, friendly landlord and
customers, busy front bar, quieter back room;
impromptu music sessions; may be cl wkdy
lunchtimes, very popular wknds *(C J Fletcher,
Paul and Ann Meyer, Sue Holland,
Dave Webster, Mike and Wendy Proctor)*

HARTSHILL [SJ8745]

Jolly Potters [Hartshill Rd (A52)]: Outstanding
Bass in four-room local, gently smartened-up
but largely unspoilt and very welcoming to
strangers; central bar, corridor to public bar
(with TV) and three small homely lounges
(the Didler, Pete Baker)

HIGH OFFLEY [SJ7725]

Anchor [off A519 Eccleshall—Newport;
towards High Lea, by Shrops Union Canal,
Bridge 42; Peggs Lane]: Unchanged pub on
Shrops Union Canal, in same family for over a
century; two small plain rooms behind
partition, well kept Marstons Pedigree and
Wadworths 6X in jugs from cellar, Weston's
farm ciders, may be lunchtime toasties;
outbuilding with small shop and semi-open
lavatories, lovely garden with great hanging
baskets, caravan/campsite; cl Mon-Thurs
winter *(Bob and Laura Brock, the Didler)*

HILDERSTONE [SJ9437]

Spotgate [Spot Acre; B5066 N]: Friendly
service, well kept Marstons Pedigree,
reasonably priced wines, enjoyable bar food,
also good value meals in two 1930/40s
Pullman dining coaches behind
(Howard Marsden-Hughes)

HOAR CROSS [SK1323]

Meynell Ingram Arms [Abbots Bromley Rd,
off A515 Yoxall—Sudbury]: Friendly
traditional beamed country local, quiet and
relaxing, log fires on cold days and lounge sides of
central bar, separate entrance to little one-table
front snug, good reasonably priced home-made
blackboard food inc popular Sun lunch, well
kept Marstons Pedigree, Timothy Taylors
Landlord and a guest beer, quick cheerful
service, cards and dominoes; tables out in
courtyard, open all day *(Pete Baker)*

HOPWAS [SK1704]

Tame Otter [A51 Tamworth—Lichfield]:
Rustic beamed Vintage Inn with cosy
atmosphere, lots of nooks and alcoves, three
log fires, easy chairs, settles, dining chairs, old
photographs and canalia, friendly service,
reasonably priced food all day, good choice of
wines, well kept Bass *(Colin Gooch)*

HULME END [SK1059]

☆ *Manifold Valley Hotel* [B5054 Warslow—
Hartington]: Comfortable 18th-c country pub
nr river, well kept Whim Hartington,
Mansfield and Marstons Pedigree, wide choice
of generous food from good sandwiches to
main dishes using local produce, helpful
service, clean and tidy lounge bar, log-effect

gas fires, separate light and airy dining room;
children and cyclists welcome; bedrooms in
converted stone smithy off secluded back
courtyard, disabled facilities *(Glenwys and
Alan Lawrence, BB, D C Leggatt,
Derek Manning, Derek and Sylvia Stephenson)*

KINVER [SO8483]

Plough & Harrow [High St (village signed off
A449 or A458 W of Stourbridge); aka the
Steps]: Old split-level local tied to Black
Country brewers Bathams with their Best, Mild
and XXX kept very well, good choice of ciders
and malt whiskies, cheap plain bar food (filled
rolls even Sun lunchtime), low prices, film star
pictures; proper public bar with darts,
dominoes etc, lounge with nostalgic juke box,
SkyTV and fruit machine, folk nights 1st and
3rd Weds; children allowed in some parts,
tables in back courtyard, open all day wknds
(Pete Baker, the Didler, Gill and Tony Morriss)

Vine [Dunsley Rd]: Italian-run canalside pub
with good value flatbreads, focaccia, pasta and
interesting specials as well as huge baguettes,
well kept low-priced ales such as Enville, Lees
and Woods, no smoking eating area *(Gill and
Tony Morriss)*

LEEK [SJ9856]

Bulls Head [St Edward St]: Narrow three-level
town pub, now tap for new Leek Brewery with
their two real ales at attractive price, Weston's
Old Rosie cider; popular with young people –
pool, juke box can be noisy, can get smoky;
open all day *(Kevin Thorpe)*

☆ *Den Engel* [St Edward St]: Belgian-style bar in
high-ceilinged former bank (talk of moving
round the corner, for more room), over 130
beers from there inc six on tap, three or four
changing british real ales, three dozen genevers,
upstairs restaurant with continental dishes inc
flemish beer-based specialities (Fri/Sat lunch,
Thurs-Sat night, bar food Sun night); piped
classical music, very busy Fri/Sat evening, cl
Sun-Thurs lunchtime *(the Didler, Mike and
Wendy Proctor, C J Fletcher, Kevin Thorpe)*

☆ *Swan* [St Edward St]: Comfortable and
friendly old three-room pub with good cheap
lunchtime food from sandwiches, open
sandwiches, baguettes and oatcakes up,
pleasant helpful staff, no smoking lounge, well
kept Bass and guest ales such as Fullers
London Pride, Charles Wells Bombardier and
Youngs, occasional beer festivals, lots of malt
whiskies, choice of coffees; downstairs wine
bar; folk club, seats in courtyard *(the Didler,
C J Fletcher, Mike and Wendy Proctor,
P Abbott)*

☆ *Three Horseshoes* [A53 NNE, on Blackshaw
Moor]: Friendly family-run inn with emphasis
on reliable generous food inc good bar carvery,
brasserie, and candlelit beamed restaurant –
Sat dinner-dance; lots of nooks and crannies,
open fire, no smoking area, good service, good
range of real ales, sensible prices, children's
area; bedrooms *(Lynette and Stuart Shore,
Geoff Palmer, Mike and Wendy Proctor)*

☆ *Wilkes Head* [St Edward St]: Basic convivial
three-room local dating from 18th c (still has
back coaching stables), tied to Whim with their

ales and a guest such as Oakham JHB kept well; welcoming regulars and dogs, friendly landlord happy to chat, lunchtime rolls, home-made stilton for sale, good choice of whiskies, farm cider, pub games, gas fire, lots of pump clips; juke box in back room, Mon music night; children allowed in one room (but not really a family pub), fair disabled access, tables outside, open all day *(Kevin Thorpe, Pete Baker, the Didler, C J Fletcher)*

LICHFIELD [SK1109]

Queens Head [Queen St]: Alehouse-theme pub, self-choice counter of unusual cheeses with sourdough bread or muffins, huge helpings (doggy bags provided) at very reasonable prices, short but interesting range of daily specials, well kept Marstons and guest ales, friendly staff, bare boards and comfortable old wooden furniture *(C J Fletcher, S P Watkin, P A Taylor)*

☆ *Scales* [Market St, one of the central pedestrian-only streets]: Cosy traditional oak-panelled bar with wooden flooring, screens, gas lights, sepia photographs of old Lichfield; welcoming staff, plentiful good value food from generous baguettes up, well kept Bass, Fullers London Pride and Ind Coope Burton, daily papers, darts; piped music, machines; suntrap back courtyard *(LYM, Brian Manders)*

LONGDON [SK0814]

☆ *Swan With Two Necks* [off A51 Lichfield—Rugeley; Brook Lane]: Cosy in winter with five hot coal fires, long friendly low-beamed quarry-tiled bar and two-room carpeted restaurant, food from lunchtime sandwiches up inc generous popular cod and chips, real ales such as Ansells, Fullers, Holdens and Youngs; piped music, no children; picnic-sets and swings in garden with summer servery *(Barry Smith, Roger Bridgeman, Colin Fisher, LYM, Richard Waller)*

LONGNOR [SK0864]

Crewe & Harpur Arms: Good value straightforward food, service coping well with busy nights *(R M Corlett)*

☆ *Olde Cheshire Cheese*: 14th-c building, a pub for 250 years, some emphasis on the two attractive dining rooms full of steam railway models and bric-a-brac with their own separate bar and cosy after-dinner lounge, wide choice of good attractively priced home-made food here and in traditionally furnished main bar, well kept Robinsons ales, friendly staff; hikers welcome, bedrooms *(Bernie Adams, Doug Christian)*

MUCKLEY CORNER [SK0806]

Olde Corner House [A5/A461]: Comfortable hotel-cum-pub with good generous sensibly priced food in two restaurants (the smarter one is no smoking), well kept Marstons Pedigree and Wadworths 6X, wide choice of modestly priced wines, friendly licensees and staff, pleasant décor; good value bedrooms *(Colin Fisher)*

ONECOTE [SK0455]

Jervis Arms [B5053]: Pets corner with pygmy goats, slides and swings, two family rooms (one no smoking) with high chairs, mother and baby room as well as black-beamed main bar,

three interesting guest beers alongside well kept Bass and Whim Arbor Light, usual food (all day Sun) from sandwiches and baked potatoes up; games and piped music; self-catering accommodation in converted barn, open all day Sun *(LYM, Mr and Mrs John Taylor)*

PENKRIDGE [SJ9214]

Littleton Arms [St Michaels Sq/A449]: Substantial pub done out in olde-worlde style, particularly well kept Bass, enjoyable food all day; children welcome *(Colin Gooch)*

☆ *Star* [Market Pl]: Friendly and charming open-plan local with a warm welcome for strangers, lots of low black beams and button-back red plush, well kept cheap Banks's and guest ales, bar food, prompt pleasant service; piped music, sports TV; open all day, tables on terrace *(Colin Gooch, BB)*

RANTON [SJ8422]

Yew Tree: Locally popular brasserie and bistro-style dining pub with recently upgraded restaurant, good international range, friendly atmosphere *(Paul and Margaret Baker)*

REAPS MOOR [SK0861]

Butchers Arms [off B5053 S of Longnor]: Isolated moorland pub, lots of atmosphere in several distinct areas, good value food inc Sun lunch, Marstons Pedigree and a guest beer; free camping for customers *(the Didler)*

RUSHTON SPENCER [SJ9362]

Knott Inn: Large welcoming local opp former railway and station, good fresh standard food, well kept local beer, helpful landlord; on Staffordshire Way *(Guy Vowles, Hugh A MacLean)*

Royal Oak [A523 Leek—Macclesfield]: Inexpensive freshly made sandwiches and other pubby lunches in lounge bar and no smoking restaurant, well kept Burtonwood Bitter and Top Hat *(Gerry and Rosemary Dobson)*

STOKE-ON-TRENT [SJ8745]

Staff of Life [Hill St]: Character city local, welcoming even when packed, unchanging layout of three rooms and small drinking corridor, well kept Bass ales *(the Didler, Pete Baker)*

TAMWORTH [SK2004]

Market Vaults [Market St]: Friendly little pub, one of town's oldest, with lots of brass, dark oak, original fireplaces and even tales of lost secret tunnel; chatty friendly staff, well kept Marstons Pedigree and other ales, usual bar food inc all-day breakfast and Sun roasts *(Colin Gooch)*

TATENHILL [SK2021]

☆ *Horseshoe* [off A38 W of Burton; Main St]: Civilised tiled-floor bar, cosy no smoking side snug with woodburner, two-level restaurant and back family area, good value food (all day Sat) from sandwiches to steaks inc children's, well kept Marstons ales, good wine range with tempting two-glass offer, quick polite service; pleasant garden, good play area *(C J Fletcher, Graham and Lynn Mason, LYM, S P Watkin, P A Taylor)*

TEANFORD [SK0040]

☆ *Ship*: Small local with good choice of enjoyable freshly made food in modest lounge bar and pleasant separate dining room/bistro, welcoming efficient staff, range of well kept real ales *(John and Gillian Scarisbrick, Mike and Wendy Proctor, Keith John Ryan)*

THORNCLIFFE [SK0360]

Mermaid [2 miles NE at N edge of the Morridge; pub named on OS Sheet 119]: Isolated well run moorland pub with good bar food, friendly atmosphere, old well and mermaid pictures, panoramic views from restaurant (Fri/Sat night, good Sun lunch – worth booking); a refuge for wet walkers *(Mike and Wendy Proctor, Nick and Lynne Carter)*

Red Lion: Comfortable and attractive old-world pub under new owners, good choice of well presented food from sandwiches up, Thurs steak night, no smoking dining room, games area with pool; children welcome *(anon)*

TUTBURY [SK2028]

☆ *Olde Dog & Partridge* [High St; off A50 N of Burton]: Handsome and well managed Tudor timbered inn, largely given over to popular carvery with plenty of snug and attractive areas; lunch and early evening bargains, impressive puddings range, friendly service, second small restaurant, well kept Marstons Pedigree and a guest beer, good wine choice; children welcome, comfortable bedrooms in separate block *(M Borthwick, LYM, A Heggs, W and P J Elderkin, Peter and Patricia Burton, Caroline and Gavin Callow, Dr S J Shepherd, Eric Locker)*

UTTOXETER [SK0933]

Vaults [Market Pl]: Unpretentious three-room local with a real welcome for visitors, Bass, Marstons Pedigree and Worthington, no food (just crisps etc), large bottle collection; handy for station *(the Didler, Joe Green)*

WHEATON ASTON [SJ8512]

Hartley Arms [Long St (Canalside, Tavern Bridge)]: Roomy and restful, eclectic choice of decent food inc interesting dishes, well kept Banks's beers, attractive prices, quick friendly service; tables outside, pleasant spot just above canal, nice long view to next village's church tower *(Bob and Laura Brock)*

WOODSEAVES [SJ7925]

Plough [A519 SW towards Newport]: New tenants doing particularly nice fresh food, well kept Shepherd Neame Spitfire, tidy pleasantly furnished main bar, bright and colourful restaurant on right with modern pictures *(Nick and Lynne Carter)*

'Children welcome' means the pub says it lets children inside without any special restriction. If it allows them in, but to restricted areas such as an eating area or family room, we specify this. Places with separate restaurants usually let children use them, hotels usually let them into public areas such as lounges. Some pubs impose an evening time limit – let us know if you find this.

Suffolk

The three new main entries here this year span the range of what this county has to offer, from unspoilt tavern to luxurious civilised comfort, from intriguing antiquity to up-to-date redesign, from no food at all to really enjoyable meals cooked with flair, from busy town pub to riverside peace. They are the interesting old Nutshell in Bury St Edmunds (absolutely minute), the Black Lion in Long Melford (an excellent small hotel that treats its bar visitors very kindly), and the light and airy Anchor in Nayland (a happy mix of drinkers and diners). Both these last two look well in line for a Food Award, and other pubs with notable food which are currently on very good form are the Crown at Buxhall (imaginative cooking, with good drinks), the well run Trowel & Hammer at Cotton, the Beehive at Horringer (very friendly to all, including children – and unusually for a foody place their dog is a special attraction), the bustling Angel in Lavenham (a favourite of many – which still finds favour too with the local dominoes players), the Ship at Levington (lots of fish, and it must be the liver and bacon champion of East Anglia), the prettily set Plough at Rede (gains its Food Award this year), the Crown in Snape (its archetypal heavily beamed front bar the model for the Boar in Britten's Peter Grimes), the Crown in Southwold (good all round, and more room in its bar now), and the Angel at Stoke-by-Nayland (still hugely popular under a new licensee). The Crown in Snape has had a real surge in popularity among readers recently, and gains the title of Suffolk Dining Pub of the Year. Other pubs currently getting enthusiastic support from readers are the Ship in Dunwich (a nice all-rounder, flourishing under its new landlord), the unpretentious Victoria at Earl Soham (good beers from its nearby brewery), the cheerful and immaculately kept Crown at Great Glemham, the interesting old Harbour Inn in Southwold, the individualistic Moon & Mushroom at Swilland, the warmly friendly Rose at Thorington Street, and the cheerful and villagey Gardeners Arms at Tostock. The Lucky Dip section at the end of the chapter is a very strong one, and has some fine places to track down, too, particularly the Ship at Blaxhall, White Hart at Blythburgh, Cock at Brent Eleigh, Old Cannon in Bury St Edmunds, Froize at Chillesford, Bell at Cretingham, Station Hotel in Framlingham, restauranty Fox & Goose at Fressingfield, Swan at Hoxne, Fat Cat in Ipswich, Admirals Head at Little Bealings, Bell at Middleton, Cock at Polstead, Ramsholt Arms, Duke of Marlborough at Somersham, Lord Nelson in Southwold and Kings Head in Woodbridge. Drinks prices here are generally rather higher than the national average, and we found no outstanding bargains on the beer side. Greene King, based in St Edmunds, is the region's main brewer and now owns other beer brands such as Morlands and Ruddles, and a huge chain of pubs spread across the country. Adnams, based in Southwold, is the prize local brewer, and has won the distinction of supplying the lowest-priced beer in a high proportion of our main entries here. Other good local brewers to look out for include St Peters, Earl Soham, Nethergate and Mauldons.

BRAMFIELD TM4073 Map 5
Queens Head 🍴
The Street; A144 S of Halesworth

Although much emphasis is placed on the highly thought of food in this bustling pub, there are plenty of drinking locals who help to make for a relaxed atmosphere. The high-raftered lounge bar has scrubbed pine tables, a good log fire in its impressive fireplace, and a sprinkling of farm tools on the walls; a separate no smoking side bar has light wood furnishings (one side of the pub is no smoking). Much of the food produced uses ingredients collected weekly from small local traditional organic farms – they have printed a list of their suppliers which you can pick up at the bar, but suggest that if you want to visit the farms, it would be best to telephone first as most do not have farm shops. Changing daily, the menu might include sandwiches, spinach and coconut soup (£3.55), mushrooms baked in cream and garlic and topped with cheese or grilled dates wrapped in bacon on mild mustard sauce (£4.95), mackerel with gooseberry sauce (£5.95), rare breed pork and leek sausage with apple chutney, aberdeen angus beef and pork meatloaf with tomato sauce or hand-dressed fresh cromer crab (£6.95), seafood crumble, pasta with rocket and walnut pesto cream sauce or steak and kidney in ale pie (£8.95), lamb steak with rosemary crust and cream and garlic sauce (£10.95), venison steak with redcurrant, port and orange sauce (£14.95), and puddings like rich chocolate and brandy pot, lemon tart or pavlova with banana, coconut and mango sauce (£4.25); special events such as wine tasting, spanish evenings, and so forth. Well kept Adnams Bitter and Broadside, a good wine list, including lots of organic ones and half a dozen good wines by the glass, home-made elderflower cordial, and organic apple juices and cider. There are seats in the pretty garden, a dome-shaped bower made of willow, and a family of bantams. *(Recommended by Tina and David Woods-Taylor, Pat and Roger Fereday, A J Bowen, Pamela and Merlyn Horswell, Comus and Sarah Elliott, Pat and Tony Martin, Maurice and Gill McMahon, MJVK, Evelyn and Derek Walter, Neil Powell, June and Perry Dann, Simon Watkins, Deborah Trentham, Su and Bob Child, Philip and Susan Philcox, David Field, Sir Clive Rose, Ann and Colin Hunt, Neil and Lorna Mclaughlan, David and Rhian Peters, Tracey and Stephen Groves)*

Adnams ~ Tenants Mark and Amanda Corcoran ~ Real ale ~ Bar food (12-2, 6.30-10(7-9 Sun)) ~ (01986) 784214 ~ Children in eating area of bar ~ Dogs welcome ~ Open 11.45-2.30, 6.30-11; 12-3, 7-10.30 Sun; closed 26 Dec

BROME TM1376 Map 5
Cornwallis 🍴 🍷 🛏
Rectory Road; after turning off A140 S of Diss into B1077, take first left turn

To reach this rather civilised largely 19th-c country hotel you wander down a tree-lined drive through 20 acres of grounds. At its heart is a beamed and timbered 16th-c bar where a step up from the tiled-floor serving area takes you through heavy timber uprights to a stylishly comfortable carpeted area; this is attractively furnished with a good mix of old and antique tables, some oak settles alongside cushioned library chairs, a glazed-over well, and a handsome woodburning stove. Interesting changing bar food might include sandwiches, smoky bacon and lentil soup with root vegetable spaghetti (£5.50), cheddar and spring onion in a fried sandwich with pickled beetroot and shallots (£5.95), roulade of smoked ham, fried quails eggs and truffled crisps (£6.95), chicken with harissa on firecracker rice and pickled mooli (£9.25), thai fishcake with stir-fried cabbage and cucumber and tomato salsa (£9.75), steak and kidney pudding (£10), chargrilled liver with spinach and sage croquettes (£10.95), and puddings like jasmine rice pudding with mango salsa or treacle toffee brûlée with chocolate and date finger (£4.25); attentive service. An extensive carefully chosen wine list with over 30 by the glass, organic local juices, bottled beers and champagne, and Adnams, St Peters Best and a guest such as Adnams Broadside on handpump. A nicely planted Victorian-style side conservatory has coffee-lounge cane furniture, and there's an elegant no smoking restaurant; piped music and board games. *(Recommended by Mike and Wendy Proctor, MDN, David Twitchett, J F M and M West)*

Free house ~ Licensees Jeffrey Ward and Richard Leslie ~ Real ale ~ Bar food (12-3, 6-10 weekdays) ~ Restaurant ~ (01379) 870326 ~ Children welcome ~ Dogs allowed in bedrooms ~ Open 11-11(10.30 Sun) ~ Bedrooms: £87.50B/£109.50B

BURY ST EDMUNDS TL8564 Map 5
Nutshell

The Traverse, central pedestrian link off Abbeygate Street

An engaging curiosity, this tiny bare-boards pub is the smallest we have ever seen, inside. Dating from the 17th c, it's been selling beer since 1873, though a precursor is said to have been first licensed by Charles II (and there are tales of a tunnel to the abbey). Quaint and attractive, it has a short wooden bench along its shop-front corner windows, one cut-down sewing-machine table, an elbow rest running along its rather battered counter, and well kept Greene King IPA and Abbot on handpump – and that's it, in terms of creature comforts. There's no room to swing a cat – this thought prompted by the mummified cat (found walled up here) that hangs from the dark brown ceiling, along with stacks of other bric-a-brac from bits of a skeleton through vintage banknotes, cigarette packets and military and other badges to spears and a great metal halberd. The friendly landlord will expand entertainingly on the background. The modern curved inn sign is appealing. *(Recommended by C J Fletcher, Michael Butler, the Didler)*

Free house ~ Licensee Peter Thorogood ~ No credit cards ~ (01284) 764867 ~ Children welcome ~ Open 12-11; 12-4 Sun; closed some Sun evenings

BUXHALL TM0057 Map 5
Crown 🍽 ♀

Village signposted off B1115 W of Stowmarket; fork right by post office at Gt Finborough, turn left at Buxhall village sign, then second right into Mill Road, then right at T junction

Quieter at lunchtime, this welcoming 17th-c timber framed country pub is very popular in the evenings and on Sunday lunchtime – you must book to be sure of a table. Most customers come to enjoy the imaginative food, with the emphasis on fresh seasonal ingredients. As well as lunchtime snacks such as sandwiches, filled baked potatoes, and nice little finger snacks such as marinated olives or hummous with ciabatta bread sticks, the menu might offer cream of asparagus and stilton soup (£3.95), ravioli filled with basil, olives, and mozzarella (£4.95), salad of crayfish tails (£5.75), carpaccio of beef on watercress salad with quails eggs and béarnaise dressing (£7.45), wild mushroom, spinach and coriander lasagne (£9.45), teriyaki fillet of salmon or chicken with sautéed avocado and sun-dried tomato dressing (£10.50), chargrilled lamb chump on a cassoulet of lentils and root vegetables with creamy mustard sauce (£11.25), calves liver with raspberry and juniper jus or plaice fillets on wilted spinach and saffron risotto with a creamy vermouth sauce (£11.95), and steaks (from £12.50). Well kept Greene King IPA and Abbot, Tindalls Best, and Woodfordes Wherry on handpump; good vegetables and bread, a carefully chosen wine list, smart coffees, and friendly, willing service. The intimate little bar on the left has an open fire in a big inglenook, a couple of small round tables on a tiled floor, and low hophung beams. Standing timbers separate it from another area with pews and candles, and flowers in summer on big stripped oak or pine tables, and there's a further light and airy room which they call the Mill Bar. Plenty of seats and picnic-sets under parasols on the heated terrace, a pretty garden, and nice views over gently rolling countryside. *(Recommended by Chris and Sarah Wishlade, Derek R A Field, J F M and M West, MDN, A F Scotford, M and G Rushworth, A Cowell)*

Greene King ~ Lease Trevor Golton ~ Real ale ~ Bar food (not Sun evening or Mon) ~ Restaurant ~ (01449) 736521 ~ Children in eating area of bar and restaurant ~ Dogs allowed in bar ~ Jazz last Weds of month ~ Open 12-3, 6.30-11; 12-3 Sun; closed Sun evening, Mon

CHELMONDISTON TM2038 Map 5
Butt & Oyster

Pin Mill – signposted from B1456 SE of Ipswich

On a warm day, you can sit outside and watch life on the water – ships coming down the River Orwell from Ipswich and lines of moored black sailing barges. If it's colder you can enjoy the same view through the bay windows of this staunchly simple old bargeman's pub. The half-panelled timeless little smoke room is pleasantly worn and unfussy, with model sailing ships around the walls and high-backed and other old-fashioned settles on the tiled floor; ferocious beady-eyed fish made by a local artist gaze at you from the walls. Adnams Best and Broadside, Flowers Original, and Greene King IPA on handpump or tapped from the cask, and decent wines; shove-ha'penny, cribbage, and dominoes. The good value straightforward bar food is popular and space is limited, so you might need to get here early at the weekend: sandwiches, soup (£3.25), burgers (from £5.95), wild mushroom pilaf or chilli (£6.95), fresh local cod in batter (£7.25), beef in Guinness pie (£7.95), steaks (from £9.95), and daily specials. The annual Thames Barge Race (end June/beginning July) is fun. *(Recommended by the Didler, Peter Meister, Richard Gibbs, Rona Murdoch, Pamela Goodwyn, Alistair and Kay Butler, Peter Thomas, Derek and Sylvia Stephenson, Ann and Colin Hunt, MLR, David Stokes)*

Pubmaster ~ Tenant Steve Lomas ~ Real ale ~ Bar food (all day weekends) ~ Restaurant ~ (01473) 780764 ~ Children in restaurant ~ Dogs allowed in bar ~ Open 11-11; 12-10.30 Sun

COTTON TM0467 Map 5
Trowel & Hammer 🍷 ⚲

Mill Road; take B1113 N of Stowmarket, then turn right into Blacksmiths Lane just N of Bacton

Although there's quite a lot of emphasis on the good, enjoyable food at this civilised, wisteria-covered pub, there's a clutch of well kept real ales, and a nice informal atmosphere. The menu changes daily, but might include home-made leek and tomato or mushroom soup (£2.95), deep-fried brie with red onion marmalade or fresh sardines provençale (£4.50), sautéed scallops in garlic butter (£5.75), chicken and mushroom pie or lasagne (£8.25), pork steak with stilton and walnut sauce (£8.75), feta, roasted pepper and walnut puff (£8.95), thai king prawn stir fry (£9.75), and wild boar steak with cider and wholegrain mustard sauce (£10.95). The spreading series of quiet rooms has fresh flowers, lots of beamery and timber baulks, a big log fire (as well as an ornate woodburning stove at the back), and plenty of wheelbacks and one or two older chairs and settles around a variety of tables. Well kept Adnams, Greene King IPA and Abbot, and a guest, probably from Mauldons or Nethergate on handpump or tapped from the cask, an interesting wine list, and lots of unusual spirits; friendly, helpful service. Pool, fruit machine and piped music. A pretty back garden has lots of roses and hollyhocks, neat climbers on trellises, picnic-sets, and a swimming pool. *(Recommended by J D M Rushworth, Comus and Sarah Elliott, Mr and Mrs W T Copeland, Francis Johnston, Paul and Margaret Baker, Glenwys and Alan Lawrence, M and G Rushworth, Charles and Pauline Stride)*

Free house ~ Licensees Simon and Jonathan Piers-Hall ~ Real ale ~ Bar food ~ Restaurant ~ (01449) 781234 ~ Well behaved children in eating area of bar ~ Dogs allowed in bar ~ Open 12-3, 6-11; 12-11(10.30 Sun) Sat

DENNINGTON TM2867 Map 5
Queens Head

A1120

Set in gardens alongside the church, this Tudor pub is one of Suffolk's most attractive pub buildings. The main neatly kept L-shaped room, usually full of happy customers, has carefully stripped wall timbers and beams, a handsomely carved bressumer beam, and comfortable padded wall seats on the partly carpeted and partly tiled floor. Well kept Adnams Bitter and a guest ale on handpump are served from the brick bar counter; piped music. Under the friendly new licensees, bar food now includes calamari strips with lemon and chive mayonnaise (£3.95), smoked salmon and trout mousse (£4.15), thai fishcakes with sweet chilli dip (£4.25), moroccan vegetable curry (£6.50), steak and kidney pie (£6.95), cheesy cod (£7.50), hawaiian chicken (£7.95), normandy pork with cider, apples, mushrooms, coriander and cream (£8.15), and venison in redcurrant, orange and cranberry sauce (£12.50). There are seats on a side lawn, attractively planted with flowers, and sheltered by some noble lime trees, and the pub backs on to Dennington Park, which has swings and so forth for children. *(Recommended by Comus and Sarah Elliott, Sir Clive Rose, A J Bowen, June and Perry Dann, J F M and M West, Francis Johnston, David and Rhian Peters, Neil Powell)*

Free house ~ Licensees Hilary Cowie and Peter Mills ~ Real ale ~ Bar food ~ Restaurant ~ (01728) 638241 ~ Children in family room ~ Open 9am-11pm(10.30pm Sun)

DUNWICH TM4770 Map 5
Ship £ 🛏

St James Street

Customers very much enjoy staying at this deceptively large old brick pub, and the breakfasts are good, with 'squeeze yourself' orange juice. There's plenty to do or look at around here – lots of surrounding walks, lovely coastal scenery, the RSPB reserve at Minsmere, and the nearby Dunwich Museum. The cosy main bar is traditionally furnished with benches, pews, captain's chairs and wooden tables on its tiled floor, a woodburning stove (left open in cold weather) and lots of sea prints and nautical memorabilia; fruit machine, shove-ha'penny, dominoes, and cribbage. The handsomely panelled bar counter has well kept Adnams Bitter and Broadside and a changing beer from Mauldons from antique handpumps; polite and efficient service. They serve simple fresh fish (from Lowestoft harbour) and home-made chips (£6.25 lunchtime, £8.25 in the evening). The lunchtime menu also includes home-made soup (£2.10), sausage and chips (£4.75), ploughman's (£5.25), and a hot dish of the day (£6.25); in the evening there's stuffed garlic mushrooms (£4.95), spinach flan (£7.50), gammon and pineapple (£7.75), steak in ale casserole (£8.95), pork in peach and madeira sauce (£9.50), and home-made puddings (£3.95). The restaurant is no smoking. A simple conservatory looks on to an attractive sunny back terrace, and the large garden is very pleasant, with its well spaced picnic-sets, two large anchors, and enormous fig tree. It's hard to imagine that centuries ago Dunwich was one of England's busiest ports – it's such a charming little place today. *(Recommended by Sarah Davis, Rod Lambert, Nigel and Olga Wikeley, Sue Holland, Dave Webster, Steve Whalley, Tina and David Woods-Taylor, Derek and Sylvia Stephenson, June and Perry Dann, J F M and M West, Steve and Liz Tilley, Comus and Sarah Elliott, Neil Powell, Penny and Fraser Hutchinson)*

Free house ~ Licensee David Sheldrake ~ Real ale ~ Bar food (12-5, 6-9; restaurant evening only) ~ Restaurant ~ (01728) 648219 ~ Children in restaurant and family room ~ Dogs allowed in bar and bedrooms ~ Open 11-11; 12-10.30 Sun; closed 25 Dec evening ~ Bedrooms: £40S/£68S

EARL SOHAM TM2363 Map 5
Victoria 🍺 £

A1120 Yoxford—Stowmarket

Brewed across the road from this charmingly unpretentious little village pub are their own Earl Soham beers which might include Victoria Bitter, Albert Ale, Edward Ale and Empress of India Pale Ale, all well kept on handpump. There's a friendly and easy-going local atmosphere in the bar, which is fairly basic, with stripped panelling, kitchen chairs and pews, plank-topped trestle sewing-machine tables and other simple scrubbed pine country tables with candles, tiled or board floors, an interesting range of pictures of Queen Victoria and her reign, a piano, and open fires; shove-ha'penny, cribbage, and dominoes. Good value home-made bar food includes sandwiches (from £2.50), soup (£3), ploughman's (from £4.25), popular corned beef hash (£4.95), vegetarian pasta dishes (£5.25), meat or vegetable lasagne (£5.75), pork and pineapple or lamb curry (£6.50), feta and onion tart, beef casserole or winter Sunday roast (£6.95). A raised back lawn has seats, and there are more out in front. The pub is quite close to a wild fritillary meadow at Framlingham, and a working windmill at Saxtead. *(Recommended by Glenwys and Alan Lawrence, Pat and Tony Martin, David and Rhian Peters, Comus and Sarah Elliott, J F M and M West, Stuart and Valerie Ray, Barry Collett, Pam and David Bailey)*

Free house ~ Licensee Paul Hooper ~ Real ale ~ Bar food (till 10) ~ Restaurant ~ No credit cards ~ (01728) 685758 ~ Children welcome ~ Dogs allowed in bar ~ Open 11.30-3, 6-11; 12-3, 7-10.30 Sun

ERWARTON TM2134 Map 5
Queens Head ♀ ◖

Village signposted off B1456 Ipswich—Shotley Gate; pub beyond the attractive church and the manor with its unusual gatehouse (like an upturned salt-cellar)

The friendly bar in this unassuming and relaxed 16th-c pub has bowed black oak beams in its shiny low yellowing ceiling, comfortable furnishings, a cosy coal fire, and several sea paintings and photographs; get there early to bag a window table overlooking the fields to the Stour estuary. The conservatory dining area, partly no smoking, is also very pleasant. Adnams Bitter and Broadside and Greene King IPA are well kept on handpump, they have a decent wine list, and several malt whiskies. Well liked bar food includes sandwiches, home-made soup (£2.95), ploughman's (£5.50), ham and eggs (£6.75), home-made moussaka or fruit and vegetable curry (£7.50), chicken breast in peach and almond sauce or steak, kidney and mushroom pudding (£7.95), breaded prawns with lemon and cajun dip (£8.50), daily specials such as somerset pork with herb dumplings or mixed nut risotto (£7.95), fresh crab salad (£8.25) and lamb and apricot casserole (£8.95), and puddings like chocolate truffle torte, key lime pie or lemon meringue (£3.75); it can get busy at the weekends. Darts, bar billiards, shove-ha'penny, cribbage, and dominoes; maybe piped music. The gents' has quite a collection of navigational charts. There are picnic-sets under summer hanging baskets in front. *(Recommended by Pamela Goodwyn, Adele Summers, Alan Black, Colin and Dot Savill, Tom Gondris, Alistair and Kay Butler, David Field, Peter Thomas)*

Free house ~ Licensees Julia Crisp and G M Buckle ~ Real ale ~ Bar food ~ Restaurant ~ (01473) 787550 ~ Children in restaurant ~ Open 11-3, 6.30-11; 12-3, 7-10.30 Sun; closed 25 Dec

GREAT GLEMHAM TM3361 Map 5
Crown ◖

Between A12 Wickham Market—Saxmundham and B1119 Saxmundham—Framlingham

In a particularly pretty village, this is an immaculately kept, smart pub run by friendly, cheerful licensees. Past the sofas on rush matting in the big entrance hall, an open-plan beamed lounge has wooden pews and captain's chairs around stripped and waxed kitchen tables, local photographs and interesting paintings on cream walls, fresh flowers, and some brass ornaments; log fires in two big fireplaces. Well kept Greene King IPA and Old Speckled Hen from old brass handpumps, and good coffee. Well liked, generously served food (it's worth booking) includes sandwiches (from £3.25), soup (£3.25), coarse pâté (£3.75), baked potatoes (from £4.25), ham and eggs (£5.95), ploughman's (£5.50) and daily specials such as whitebait (£4.75), butterfly prawns with lemon mayonnaise (£5.95), mushroom and spinach lasagne or beef rissoles (£7.95), steak and kidney pie or salmon steak with lime and chives (£7.95), and sirloin steak (£9.95); children's menu (£3.95). A tidy, flower-fringed lawn, raised above the corner of the quiet village lane by a retaining wall, has some seats and tables under cocktail parasols; disabled access. *(Recommended by Gill Pennington, MDN, Mr and Mrs T B Staples, D S Cottrell, J F M and M West, Ian Phillips, David Field, Peter Thomas, Comus and Sarah Elliott, David and Rhian Peters, Michael and Jenny Back, Ann and Colin Hunt, David and Gilly Wilkins, June and Perry Dann, Neil Powell, Tracey and Stephen Groves)*

Free house ~ Licensees Barry and Susie Coote ~ Real ale ~ Bar food (not Mon) ~ (01728) 663693 ~ Children welcome ~ Dogs welcome ~ Open 11.30-3, 6.30-11; 12-3, 7-10.30 Sun; closed Mon (except bank hols)

HORRINGER TL8261 Map 5
Beehive ⊗ ♢

A143

To be sure of a table, you must get to this civilised place promptly. The rambling little rooms have a pleasantly cottagey feel as they've refrained from pulling walls down to create the usual open-plan layout. Despite some very low beams, good chalky wall colours keep it light and airy; there are carefully chosen dining and country kitchen chairs on coir or flagstones, one or two wall settles around solid tables, picture-lights over lots of 19th-c prints, and stripped panelling or brickwork. Changing daily, the imaginative food might include smooth chicken liver parfait with home-made chutney (£4.95), twice-baked soufflé with marinated artichokes (£5.50), warm three cheese and broccoli tart or ham with french bread, salad and chutneys or tortellini with a rosemary cream sauce (£7.95), home-made pork, apple and leek sausages (£9.50), fillet of salmon with a herb mustard gratin (£9.95), seared liver with balsamic jus (£10.50), chargrilled rib-eye steak on crushed mushroom potatoes (£14.95), and puddings like spotted dick with syrup and sauce anglaise or chocolate and Grand Marnier mousse (£3.95). Well kept Greene King IPA and a second changing Greene King beer on handpump, and decent changing wines with half a dozen by the glass. An attractively planted back terrace has picnic-sets and more seats on a raised lawn. Their friendly, well behaved dog Muffin is a great attraction, and very good at making friends, although other dogs are not really welcome. *(Recommended by J F M and M West, John and Judy Saville, David Twitchett, Liz Webb, Michael and Marion Buchanan, Dave Braisted, Ian Phillips, D S Cottrell, R C and J M Clark, Reg J Cox)*

Greene King ~ Tenants Gary and Dianne Kingshott ~ Real ale ~ Bar food (not Sun evening) ~ (01284) 735260 ~ Children welcome ~ Open 11.30-2.30, 7-11; 12-2.30, 7-10.30 Sun; closed 25 and 26 Dec

HUNDON TL7246 Map 5
Plough

Brockley Green – nearly 2 miles SW of village, towards Kedington

This remotely set pub has fine views over the Stour valley, 5 acres of lovely landscaped gardens, and a pleasant terrace with an ornamental pool and good wooden furniture under a wisteria-covered pergola; croquet. Inside, the neatly kept knocked-through bar has soft red brickwork, old oak beams and plenty of old standing timbers, cushions on low side settles, pine kitchen chairs and sturdy low tables, and plenty of horsebrasses. Well presented, the very good bar food might include tomato with sweet basil soup (£3.25), smoked salmon roulade (£4.75), cajun chicken strips on beanshoots and cashew nuts (£5.75), goats cheese and asparagus tart or button mushroom and sweet pepper stroganoff (£7.25), smoked ham and brie quiche (£7.75), steak in ale pie (£8.25), and Friday evening seafood dishes like baked pink tilapia with sun-dried tomato stuffing (£10.75) or monkfish tails poached in white wine with a rich creamy mustard sauce (£13.25). Well kept Greene King IPA, Woodfordes Wherry and a guest beer such as Shepherd Neame Spitfire on handpump, and a carefully chosen wine list with 10 by the glass; piped music. Part of the bar and all the restaurant are no smoking. *(Recommended by Adele Summers, Alan Black, Mr and Mrs M Hayes, Derek and Sylvia Stephenson, MLR)*

Free house ~ Licensees David and Marion Rowlinson ~ Real ale ~ Bar food ~ Restaurant ~ (01440) 786789 ~ Children welcome but no under-5s in bar Sat evenings ~ Dogs allowed in bar and bedrooms ~ Open 12-2.30, 6-11; 12-3, 7-10.30 Sun ~ Bedrooms: £50S(£55B)/£70B

ICKLINGHAM TL7872 Map 5
Red Lion ⑩

A1101 Mildenhall—Bury St Edmunds

There's plenty of atmosphere and character in this civilised 16th-c thatched dining pub – particularly in the best part, which is the beamed open-plan bar with its cavernous inglenook fireplace, attractive furnishings, and nice mixture of wooden chairs, big candlelit tables and turkey rugs on the polished wood floor. Another area behind a knocked-through fireplace has closely spaced dark wood pub tables on carpets. Emphasis is on the generously served enjoyable if not cheap bar food, which includes soup (£4.25), pâté (£6.25), sausages and mash with onion gravy (£6.75), lambs liver and bacon (£9.95), pork chops with apple and cider sauce (£11.95), seasonal wild boar fillet steak with red onion and garlic butter (£16.50), and (on a Saturday night) up to 24 fish dishes such as moules marinière (£8.95), king prawns in garlic butter (£9.95), and bass with chilli and paprika butter £15.95); puddings like eton mess or sticky toffee pudding with butterscotch sauce (£4.50). Well kept Greene King IPA and Abbot on handpump, and lots of country wines. There are picnic-sets with colourful parasols on a lawn in front (the pub is well set back from the road), and more behind on a raised terrace facing the fields, with Cavenham Heath nature reserve beyond; giant outside Jenga; handy for West Stow Country Park and the Anglo-Saxon Village. More reports please.
(Recommended by Comus and Sarah Elliott, J F M and M West, David Cosham, Pamela Goodwyn, Mandy and Simon King, Jamie and Ruth Lyons)

Excalibur ~ Lease Jonathan Gates ~ Real ale ~ Bar food (12-2.30, 6-10; 12-2, 7.15-9.30 Sun) ~ Restaurant ~ (01638) 717802 ~ Children welcome ~ Open 12-2.30, 6-11; 12-2.30, 7-10.30 Sun

LAVENHAM TL9149 Map 5
Angel ★ ⑩ ⚑ ◖ ⇌

Market Place

The former market square setting for this busy, well maintained Tudor inn is charming. The long bar area is light and airy, with a pleasant mix of visitors and locals (who may be enjoying a cheerful game of dominoes), plenty of polished dark tables, a big inglenook log fire under a heavy mantelbeam, and some attractive 16th-c ceiling plasterwork – even more elaborate pargeting in the residents' sitting room upstairs. Round towards the back on the right of the central servery is a further dining area with heavy stripped pine country furnishings; everywhere, except one side of the bar, is no smoking. The good, popular food can be eaten in either the bar or the restaurant, and might include lunchtime dishes like ploughman's (£5.95), home-made pork pie with pickles or pasta with smoked chicken and bacon (£6.25) or home-cooked gammon salad (£8.25), as well as starters such as cream of broccoli and stilton soup (£3.75), asparagus and goats cheese tart with lemon and chive crème fraîche (£6.25), steak in ale pie (£8.50), pork casserole with butterbeans and tomatoes (£8.95), glazed duck breast with spring greens and sweet and sour sauce (£10.25), braised shank of lamb with mustard and chive mash or chargrilled tuna steak with slow roast tomatoes (£10.95), and puddings like chocolate neapolitan mousse, pineapple and mango strudel or steamed syrup sponge pudding (£3.75). Well kept Adnams Bitter, Greene King IPA and Broadside and Nethergate Bitter on handpump, quite a few malt whiskies, and eight or so decent wines by the glass or part bottle (you get charged for what you drink). They have shelves of books and lots of board games; classical piped music. There are picnic-sets out in front overlooking the square, and tables under cocktail parasols in a sizeable sheltered back garden; it's worth asking if they've time to show you the interesting Tudor cellar. *(Recommended by Sir Clive Rose, Charles Gysin, Tina and David Woods-Taylor, Matthew Pexton, Jeff and Wendy Williams, Stuart Manktelow, Peter Saville, Chris Flynn, Wendy Jones, the Didler, John Robertson, Mr and Mrs C Quincey, Pamela Goodwyn, Michael and Ann Cole, Maysie Thompson, Harry Gleave, M Sharp, A Sadler, Mr and Mrs C W Widdowson, Derek and Sylvia Stephenson, Pam and David Bailey, Virginia Greay, Marianne and Peter Stevens, George Atkinson, Brian and Janet Ainscough, Fiona Wynn, Pete Stroud, Derek Thomas, Len Banister, Derek and Maggie Washington)*

Free house ~ Licensees Roy Whitworth and John Barry ~ Real ale ~ Bar food (12-2.15, 6.45-9.15) ~ Restaurant ~ (01787) 247388 ~ Children welcome ~ Classical piano Fri evenings ~ Open 11-11; 12-10.30 Sun; closed 25-26 Dec ~ Bedrooms: £50B/£75B

LAXFIELD TM2972 Map 5
Kings Head ★ ◀

Behind church, off road toward Banyards Green

The three charmingly old-fashioned rooms in this thatched 15th-c house have a really friendly, unspoilt atmosphere. For many, the best is the front room, which has a high-backed built-in settle on the tiled floor, and an open fire. Two other equally unspoilt rooms – the card and tap rooms – have pews, old seats, scrubbed deal tables, and some interesting wall prints. There's no bar: the well kept Adnams Best, Broadside, and Regatta and a guest such as Fullers London Pride are tapped straight from the cask in a cellar; cribbage and dominoes. Bar food includes sandwiches (from £2.50), sausages with mash and onion gravy (£5.50), baked aubergine and goats cheese parcel with red pepper dressing (£6.25), lambs liver and bacon (£6.50), various fish dishes (from £8.50), lamb cutlets (£14.95), and puddings such as apple and rhubarb crumble or lemon and lime syllabub (£3.25). The garden has plenty of benches and tables, there's an arbour covered by a grape and hop vine, and a small pavilion for cooler evenings. *(Recommended by A Sadler, Pete Baker, Pippa Brown, the Didler, Pam and David Bailey, Tim Maddison, Mr and Mrs J Brown, Patrick Hancock, Phil and Sally Gorton, Comus and Sarah Elliott)*

Adnams ~ Tenants George and Maureen Coleman ~ Real ale ~ Bar food (not Mon evening) ~ Restaurant ~ No credit cards ~ (01986) 798395 ~ Children in restaurant ~ Dogs allowed in bar ~ Open 12-3, 6-11; 12-3, 7-10.30 Sun

LEVINGTON TM2339 Map 5
Ship ⊕

Gun Hill; village signposted from A14, then follow Stratton Hall sign

It's worth arriving early at this charming old pub prettily placed by a little lime-washed church and surrounded by lovely countryside. There are lots of ship prints and photographs of sailing barges, a marine compass under the serving counter in the middle room, and a fishing net slung overhead, as well as benches built into the walls, comfortably upholstered small settles (some of them grouped round tables as booths), and a big black round stove. The flagstoned dining room has more nautical bric-a-brac and beams taken from an old barn; two no smoking areas. Particularly good food includes italian breads with olives (£2.50), an interesting soup (£3.25), dressed crab (£5.95), platters with pickles (cheese £6.95, meat £7.50), very popular liver and bacon with madeira sauce (£7.25), individual joint of lamb with mint and honey glaze (£8.95), quite a few fresh fish dishes like griddled skate (£9.95) and seared scallops with wild mushroom risotto (£11.95), and puddings such as white chocolate and summer berry mousse, or pear and cinnamon strudel with vanilla sauce (£3.95); polite, attentive staff. Main courses can be a couple of pounds dearer in the evening. Well kept Adnams Bitter and Broadside and Greene King IPA on handpump or tapped from the cask, and decent wines. If you look carefully enough, there's a sea view from the picnic-sets in front. No children inside. *(Recommended by Gill Pennington, Pamela Goodwyn, Ian Phillips, Peter Thomas, J F M and M West, Bill and Lisa Copeland, Charles and Pauline Stride, Ian and Nita Cooper)*

Pubmaster ~ Tenants Stella and Mark Johnson ~ Real ale ~ Bar food (not Sun evening) ~ Restaurant ~ (01473) 659573 ~ Open 11-2.30, 6-11; 12-3 Sun; closed Sun evening

LIDGATE TL7257 Map 5
Star 🍽 ♀

B1063 SE of Newmarket

A friendly Spanish landlady runs this pretty little village pub and there's an easy-going mix of traditional english and mediterranean influences. The cosy main room has lots of pubby character, with handsomely moulded heavy beams, a good big log fire, candles in iron candelabra on good polished oak or stripped pine tables, bar billiards, dominoes, darts and ring the bull, and some antique catalan plates over the bar. Besides a second similar room on the right, there's a cosy little dining room on the left. The relaxed atmosphere, and the changing bar menu with crisp and positive seasoning in some dishes, speak more openly of the south. There might be mediterranean fish soup or prawns in garlic, catalan salad or venison carpaccio (£5.90), spanish omelette, grilled cod or venison sausages, (£6.50), lambs kidneys in sherry, paella, lasagne or roast lamb in garlic and wine (£12.50), stuffed quail in honey or monkfish marinière (£13.50), seafood stew (£15.50), and puddings such as strawberry cream tart or chocolate roulade (£4); two-course lunch £10.50. Greene King IPA, Abbot and Old Speckled Hen on handpump, and enjoyable house wines. Tables on the raised lawn in front, and in a pretty little rustic back garden. More reports please. *(Recommended by Mrs J Hanmer, C W Dix, Gordon Theaker, Wendy Dye, R C Wiles, David Field, Derek Thomas, Shirley Mackenzie, Hywel Bevan)*

Greene King ~ Lease Maria Teresa Axon ~ Real ale ~ Bar food (not Sun evening) ~ Restaurant ~ (01638) 500275 ~ Children in eating area of bar ~ Dogs allowed in bar ~ Open 11-3, 5(6 Sat)-11; 12-3, 7-11 Sun

LONG MELFORD TL8646 Map 5
Black Lion ♀ 🛏

Church Walk

The mellow bar of this comfortable and well run hotel makes a splendidly civilised retreat. One side of the oak serving counter is decorated in ochre, and, besides bar stools, has deeply cushioned sofas, leather wing armchairs and antique fireside settles, while the other, in shades of terracotta, has leather dining chairs around handsome tables set for the good, stylish, daily-changing bar food: red pepper and tomato soup (£3.50), baked brie with red onion chutney (£4.50), crispy fried ham hash cakes on grain mustard and chive sauce (£4.50), cauliflower cheese charlotte on roasted vegetables (£8.50), steamed beef and suet pudding or warm salmon salad (£9.25), lamb steak finished with wild mushroom sauce (£9.25), and bass on a leek, spinach and potato pie with Pernod sauce (£13.95). The restaurant is no smoking. Big windows with swagged-back curtains have a pleasant outlook over the green, and there are large portraits, of racehorses and of people. Service by neatly uniformed staff is helpful and efficient; Adnams on handpump, a fine range of wines by the glass (including champagne), good generous cafetière coffee; there may be piped Radio Suffolk. The Victorian walled garden is most appealing. *(Recommended by Michael and Ann Cole)*

Ravenwood Group ~ Manager Lahsen Ighaghai ~ Real ale ~ Bar food (till 10 Fri/Sat) ~ Restaurant ~ (01787) 312356 ~ Children welcome ~ Dogs allowed in bar ~ Open 11-11; 12-10.30 Sun ~ Bedrooms: £95.50B/£120B

Stars after the name of a pub show exceptional character and appeal. They don't mean extra comfort. And they are nothing to do with food quality, for which there's a separate knife-and-fork symbol. Even quite a basic pub can win stars, if it's individual enough.

NAYLAND TL9734 Map 5
Anchor ♀

Court Street; just off A134 – turn-off S of signposted B1087 main village turn

Recently carefully refurbished, this now majors on enterprising food, but has kept a warmly local feel in its bare-boards front bar. Light and sunny, this has interesting old photographs of pipe-smoking customers and village characters on its pale yellow walls, farmhouse chairs around a mix of tables, and coal and log fires at each end. Behind, a carpeted room with similar furniture, another fire, and cheerful seaside pictures for sale, leads into a small carpeted sun room. They have their own back smokehouse, and good bar food includes soup (£3.50), chicken liver and blueberry salad with almonds and french beans (£4.25), filled ciabatta bread like smoked chicken with a salsa and guacamole filling or chargrilled mediterranean vegetables with melting goats cheese (from £4.95), ploughman's or scallop and monkfish brochette with shaved fennel salad and basil mayonnaise dressing (£5.95), fresh cromer dressed crab salad or wild mushroom and pecorino risotto with a poached free range egg (£6.95), beer battered cod with home-made tartare sauce (£7.50), chicken supreme stuffed with a tomato and tarragon mousse (£7.95), braised lamb shank with stilton mash and beetroot jus (£8.50), tasty five-spice wild duck with noodles and thai broth or honey and sesame duck breast with wild mushrooms and asparagus, celeriac rösti and morel sauce (£11.95), and puddings like chocolate brownie caramel tart with raspberry coulis, rhubarb and sloe gin bavarois or mango tarte tatin with caramel ice cream (from £3.50). Adnams and Greene King IPA, Morlands Original and Ruddles County on handpump (with elegant beer glasses); a nice changing choice of wines by the glass including local ones; perky service; piped music, but not too intrusive, and dominoes. The separate no smoking restaurant, similarly light and airy, is up quite steep stairs. A gravel terrace behind has picnic-sets looking across to the peaceful River Stour and its quacking ducks. Next to the pub is an ongoing Heritage Farming Project. The farmland is being worked throughout the season by suffolk punch horses using traditional farming methods. The suffolk punch is one of the most endangered species in the world and is on the category I extinction list – making it rarer than the giant panda. Visitors are welcome to watch or to try their hand at the reins. *(Recommended by Derek Thomas, John and Judy Saville)*

Free house ~ Licensees Daniel Bunting and Darren Puljic ~ Real ale ~ Bar food (12-2(2.30 Sat, 4 Sun), 6.30-9.30; no food Sun or Mon evenings) ~ Restaurant ~ (01206) 262313 ~ Children in eating area of bar and restaurant ~ Open 11-2.30, 5-11; 11-11 Sat; 12-10.30 Sun

ORFORD TM4250 Map 5
Jolly Sailor £

Quay Street

Although this unspoilt old brick pub makes a good base for walkers, fishermen and birdwatchers, it was once a smugglers' hangout, and was built in the 17th c, mainly from wrecked ships' timbers. The several snugly traditional rooms have lots of exposed brickwork, and are served from counters and hatches in an old-fashioned central cubicle. There's an unusual spiral staircase in the corner of the flagstoned main bar – which also has 13 brass door knockers and other brassware, local photographs, two cushioned pews and a long antique stripped deal table, and an open woodburning stove in the big brick fireplace (with nice horsebrasses above it); a small room is popular with the dominoes and cribbage players. Cheerful friendly staff serve well kept Adnams Bitter and Broadside on handpump, and big helpings of good straightforward pubby food: battered local cod, skate, eel or flounder with chips, home-made steak pie or lasagne, home-cooked ham and egg, local seasonal pheasant, and daily roasts (all £5.50). There are lovely surrounding coastal walks and plenty of outside pursuits; several picnic-sets on grass at the back have views over the marshes. No children. *(Recommended by Dave Braisted, Ann and Colin Hunt, Barry Collett, David and Rhian Peters, Comus and Sarah Elliott, Peter Thomas, Michael and Ann Cole, June and Perry Dann, David and Gilly Wilkins)*

Adnams ~ Tenant Philip Attwood ~ Real ale ~ Bar food (not Mon evening, nor Mon-
Thurs evenings Nov-Easter) ~ No credit cards ~ (01394) 450243 ~ Dogs allowed in
bar ~ Open 11.30-2.30, 7-11; 12-2.45, 7-10.30 Sun; closed evenings 25 and 26 Dec
~ Bedrooms: /£40

RATTLESDEN TL9758 Map 5
Brewers Arms

Signposted on minor roads W of Stowmarket, off B1115 via Buxhall or off A45 via Woolpit

The popular food in this solidly built 16th-c village local has a growing reputation.
As well as lunchtime (not Sunday) sandwiches (from £3.75) and filled baked
potatoes (from £4.95), a good range of bar food might include home-made soup
(£3.25), home-made chicken liver pâté or onion and stilton tartlet (£3.95), moules
marinière (£4.75), home-made lamb and coriander burger (£5.95), pork and herb
sausages on mustard mash with onion gravy (£6.95), steak and kidney pie (£7.95),
chicken caesar salad or vegetable pie (£8.95), lamb shank with rosemary, shallots
and sun-dried tomatoes on mushroom risotto (£10.95), skate wing in rosemary and
caper butter (£11.50), mixed grill (£13.95), and puddings like chocolate fudge
brownies or spiced apple crumble (£3.50); Sunday roast (£6.95). The restaurant is
no smoking; piped music. Well kept Greene King Abbot and IPA, and a guest like
Batemans on handpump. The pleasantly simple beamed lounge bar on the left has
book-lined walls, individually chosen pictures and bric-a-brac. It winds back
through standing timbers to the main eating area, which is partly flint-walled, and
has a magnificent old bread oven and more comfortable seating. French windows
open on to the garden. (Recommended by Derek R A Field, Maureen and Gerry Whittles,
MDN, Pat and Tony Martin, Michael and Marion Buchanan, Helen and Ian Jobson)

Greene King ~ Tenants Mr and Mrs Davies ~ Real ale ~ Bar food ~ Restaurant ~
(01449) 736377 ~ Well behaved children in eating area of bar and restaurant ~
Open 11.30-2.30, 6-11; 12-3, 7-10.30 Sun

REDE TL8055 Map 5
Plough 🍴 ♀

Village signposted off A143 Bury St Edmunds—Haverhill

The food in this quietly set, thatched pink-washed pub is particularly good, so you
may need to book to be sure of a table. The traditionally simple bar has copper
measures and pewter tankards hanging from low black beams, decorative plates on
a delft shelf and surrounding the solid fuel stove in its brick fireplace, and red plush
button-back built-in wall banquettes. From a changing choice, enjoyable dishes
from the menu might include crab au gratin (£9.95), pasta with clams, parsley and
garlic (£10.50), wild boar in madeira sauce (£10.95), chicken basque, lamb, olives
and artichoke stew or venison and pancetta casserole (all £11.50), guinea fowl in
red wine and tarragon sauce (£11.95), fried, marinated monkfish (£12.95), and
puddings (£3.95); friendly service. Adnams, and Greene King IPA, Abbott and
Ruddles are served from electric pumps and kept under light blanket pressure, and
a decent choice of wines; piped pop music. There are picnic-sets in front, and a
sheltered cottagey garden at the back. (Recommended by Philip and Susan Philcox,
Mrs Jane Kingsbury, Mrs M Grimwood, JKW, M and G Rushworth)

Greene King ~ Tenant Brian Desborough ~ Real ale ~ Bar food (not Sun evening) ~
Restaurant ~ (01284) 789208 ~ Children in eating area of bar ~ Open 11-3, 6.30-11;
12-3, 7-10.30 Sun

SNAPE TM3959 Map 5
Crown 🍽 🍷 🛏

B1069

Suffolk Dining Pub of the Year

Many customers come to this bustling inn to enjoy the very good food or to stay overnight, but there's a proper pubby atmosphere, helped by the friendly barman and well kept Adnams Bitter, Broadside and seasonal ale on handpump; a thoughtful wine list, too, with 11 by the glass (including champagne). The attractive bar is furnished with striking horseshoe-shaped high-backed settles around a big brick inglenook with a woodburning stove, spindleback and country kitchen chairs, and nice old tables on some old brick flooring. An exposed panel shows how the ancient walls were constructed, and there are lots of beams in the various small side rooms. Listed on the blackboard, the popular dishes might include courgette, basil and tomato soup (£2.95), coarse game pâté with home-made chutney (£4.50), moules marinière or cromer crab risotto (£4.95), confit of honey-roast duck on red cabbage and apple with wild mushroom jus (£9.50), steak and kidney suet pudding (£9.75), rack of lamb with a herb crust and red wine and mint gravy (£10.95), fillets of bass with celeriac mash and an orange and grain mustard dressing (£11.95), and puddings like prune armagnac tart or sticky toffee pudding (£3.95); breakfasts are good but perhaps the serving staff then could be more friendly. The dining room is no smoking, and during the Festival they do a useful pre-concert short menu. There's a pretty roadside garden with tables under cocktail parasols. The bedrooms, up steep stairs, are quaint, with beamed ceilings, sloping floors, and doorways that you may have to stoop through. *(Recommended by Pat and Roger Fereday, Peter and Pat Frogley, Anthony Barnes, Pamela Goodwyn, MDN, Mrs Diane M Hall, Bryan and Mary Blaxall, Mrs Rosalie Croft, Barry Collett, Philip and Elaine Holmes, Neil Powell, R C Wiles, D S Cottrell, Phil and Heidi Cook, DF, NF, R M Corlett, Maurice and Gill McMahon, Rob and Catherine Dunster, Mrs Fay Cori, Comus and Sarah Elliott, June and Malcolm Farmer, Sir Clive Rose, A Sadler, Gordon Prince, J F M and M West, E J and M W Corrin, Alistair and Kay Butler, Brian and Pam Lamb)*

Adnams ~ Tenant Diane Maylott ~ Real ale ~ Bar food ~ Restaurant ~ (01728) 688324 ~ Open 12-3, 6-11; 12-3, 7-10.30 Sun; closed 25 Dec, 26 Dec evening ~ Bedrooms: /£70B

Golden Key

Priory Lane

For 26 years, Mr and Mrs Kissick-Jones, the cheerful and friendly licensees, have looked after this beautifully kept inn – they are Adnams's longest-serving tenants. The low-beamed and stylish lounge has an old-fashioned settle curving around a couple of venerable stripped tables on the tiled floor, a winter open fire, and, at the other end, some stripped modern settles around heavy pine tables on a turkey carpet, and a solid fuel stove in the big fireplace. The cream walls are hung with pencil sketches of customers, a Henry Wilkinson spaniel and so forth; a brick-floored side room has sofas and more tables. Straightforward bar food and well kept Adnams, Broadside and Old Ale on handpump, as well as a decent wine list, and about a dozen malt whiskies. One dining room is no smoking, and there's good disabled access. Plenty of white tables and chairs on a terrace at the front, near the small sheltered flower-filled garden. *(Recommended by Phil and Heidi Cook, Stuart and Valerie Ray, B and M Kendall, D S Cottrell, Comus and Sarah Elliott, MDN, Gill Pennington)*

Adnams ~ Tenants Max and Suzie Kissick-Jones ~ Real ale ~ Bar food (12-2.30, 6-9.30) ~ Restaurant ~ (01728) 688510 ~ Children in restaurant ~ Dogs allowed in bar ~ Open 12-3, 6-11; 12-3, 7-10.30 Sun; closed 25 Dec ~ Bedrooms: £65B/£75B

The details at the end of each main entry start by saying whether the pub is a free house, or if it's tied to a brewery or pub group (which we name).

SOUTH ELMHAM TM3389 Map 5
St Peters Brewery
St Peter S Elmham; off B1062 SW of Bungay

Although the opening hours in this lovely medieval manor are quite restricted (they are only open three days a week), it is certainly worth making the effort to get here. The hall itself dates back to the late 13th c, but was much extended in 1539 using materials from the recently dissolved Flixton Priory. Genuinely old tapestries and furnishings perhaps make enjoying a drink or a meal in the small main bar feel more like a trip to a historic home than a typical pub outing, but the atmosphere is civilised and welcoming, with candles and fresh flowers on the dark wooden tables, soft classical music, and comfortable seats – from cushioned pews and settles to a 16th-c French bishop's throne. Their own brewed St Peters Best and Strong are served on draught from a little hatch, while the rest of their ales are available by the bottle; also various teas, and coffee. It's best to book for the good waitress-served food, which might include a short lunchtime choice of things like leek and ham hock soup (£4), open sandwiches or wild boar terrine with spiced ale and date and pear chutney (£6), cromer crab, saffron and chive tart (£6; main course £9), and venison sausages with parsley mash and beer-braised onions (£6.50; main course £10), with evening dishes such as white bean and roast garlic purée, grilled bread, and artichokes (£5.50), potted shrimps and toasted rye sourdough (£6.50), pasta with wild mushrooms, herbs and parmesan (£10.50), ginger-baked cod with chilli, coriander and puy lentils (£11.50), roast guinea fowl, baked squash, and cep mushroom sauce (£12.50), and puddings such as rhubarb crumble, walnut tart or chocolate fondant (£5). There's a particularly dramatic high-ceilinged dining hall (no smoking in here), with elaborate woodwork, a big flagstoned floor, and an imposing chandelier, as well as a couple of other appealing old rooms reached up some steepish stairs: one is no smoking, while the other is a light, beamed room with comfortable armchairs and nice big rug. Outside, tables overlook the original moat. The beers are made using water from a 60-metre (200-ft) bore hole, in brewery buildings laid out around a courtyard; they do tours on the hour between 12 and 4pm; there's a gift shop. More reports please. *(Recommended by Mike and Wendy Proctor)*

Own brew ~ Licensees John Murphy and Janet Fogg ~ Real ale ~ Bar food (only served Fri-Sun and bank hols) ~ Restaurant ~ (01986) 782322 ~ Children in eating area of bar and restaurant ~ Open 11-11 Fri/Sat; 12-6 bank hols and Sun; closed Mon-Thurs (but open summer Thurs), two weeks Jan

SOUTHWOLD TM5076 Map 5
Crown ★ ⑪ ♈ ◧
High Street

With a good mix of customers, this rather smart old hotel remains an enjoyable place for either a drink or a particularly good meal. The extended elegant beamed main bar has a relaxed atmosphere, a stripped curved high-backed settle and other dark varnished settles, kitchen chairs and some bar stools, pretty flowers on the mix of kitchen pine tables, a carefully restored and rather fine carved wooden fireplace, and newspapers to read. The smaller back oak-panelled locals' bar has more of a traditional pubby atmosphere, red leatherette wall benches and a red carpet; shove-ha'penny, dominoes and cribbage. There's a separate no smoking restaurant, too. Changing daily, the imaginative bar food might include chilled gazpacho with chopped egg and garlic crumbs (£4), grilled squid, marinated fennel, endive and chilli salad (£4.50), seared chicken livers with celeriac remoulade (£5), country terrine with red onion marmalade (£6.95), rare tuna with niçoise (£7; main course £12.50), salmon fishcakes with tartare sauce (£9.75), baked chicken breast with sage mash and sun-dried tomato relish (£10.50), roast lamb with local potatoes and sherry vinegar (£12.50), crisp bass with pickled cucumber and sauce vierge (£13), roast beef with roast beetroot and horseradish (£13.50), and puddings like chocolate brownie with warm chocolate sauce, english raspberry tart with raspberry coulis or crème caramel (from £4.50). Perfectly kept Adnams beers on handpump, a splendid wine list, with a monthly changing choice of 20 interesting varieties by the glass or bottle, and quite a few malt whiskies. Tables out in a sunny sheltered corner are very pleasant. *(Recommended by Francis Johnston, Marlene and Jim Godfrey, Comus and Sarah Elliott, the Didler, MJVK, Howard James, Richard Pinnington, T R and B C Jenkins, Pam and David Bailey, Tim Maddison, Mike and Sue Loseby, Sue Holland, Dave Webster, Bob and Margaret Holder,Tina and David Woods-Taylor, Mrs Fay Cori, Dr and Mrs A K Clarke, Neil and Lorna Mclaughlan, D S Cottrell, Richard Siebert, Pamela and Merlyn Horswell, Patrick Hancock, Hilary McLean, R C Wiles, J D M Rushworth, Sir Clive Rose, Christopher and Jo Barton, Derek and Sylvia Stephenson, Glenwys and Alan Lawrence, Stanley and Sally Brooks, M and G Rushworth)*

Adnams ~ Tenant Michael Bartholomew ~ Real ale ~ Bar food (12-2, 7-9.30) ~ Restaurant ~ (01502) 722275 ~ Children in eating area of bar ~ Dogs allowed in bar ~ Open 11-3, 6-11; 12-3, 6-10.30 Sun ~ Bedrooms: £75B/£92B

Harbour Inn

Blackshore, by the boats; from A1095, turn right at the Kings Head, and keep on past the golf course and water tower

In good weather, get to this interesting old waterside place early to bag a seat at the front of the building so you can watch all the goings on in the bustling quay. There's still a lot of genuine nautical character – the friendly landlord is a lifeboatman – but it did have even more in the old days, when the lifeboat station was next door and the lifeboat telephone, and needless to say quite often the lifeboat men, were housed in the pub. The tiny, low-beamed, tiled and panelled front bar has antique settles, and in the back bar which has a wind speed indicator, model ships, a lot of local ship and boat photographs, smoked dried fish hanging from a line on a beam, a lifeboat line launcher, and brass shellcases on the mantelpiece over a stove. This room has rustic stools and cushioned wooden benches built into its stripped panelling. Behind here, the dining area is no smoking. Enjoyable food includes soup (£3.25), filled baguettes (from £4.60), half a pint of prawns (£4.95, a pint £7.95), cod in beer batter with chips, wrapped in paper, or ploughman's (£7.35), moules marinière (£7.85), home-made lasagne (£8.35), provençale vegetable ragoût (£8.95), baked cromer crab (£9.25), and chargrilled sirloin steak on bell pepper mash with grain mustard, cream and red wine sauce (£12.95). Well kept Adnams Broadside and Southwold, and a seasonal guest on handpump; piped music. The back garden, on former marshland, has lots of tables. *(Recommended by Howard James, Richard Pinnington, Simon Watkins, Barry Collett, Neil and Lorna Mclaughlan, Ann and Colin Hunt, Sue Holland, Dave Webster, Bob and Margaret Holder, Comus and Sarah Elliott, Tracey and Stephen Groves)*

Adnams ~ Tenant Colin Fraser ~ Real ale ~ Bar food (12-2.30, 6-9) ~ (01502) 722381 ~ Children in eating area of bar and restaurant ~ Dogs allowed in bar ~ Live rock/folk/blues/jazz Fri/Sat (not bank hols) ~ Open 11-11; 12-10.30 Sun

STOKE-BY-NAYLAND TL9836 Map 5
Angel 🍽 ♀ 🛏

B1068 Sudbury—East Bergholt; also signposted via Nayland off A134 Colchester—Sudbury

Although there has been a change of licensee since our last edition, this stylish and elegant place is enjoying continued success. The comfortable main bar area has handsome Elizabethan beams, some stripped brickwork and timbers, a mixture of furnishings including wing armchairs, mahogany dining chairs, and pale library chairs, local watercolours and older prints, attractive table lamps, and a huge log fire. Round the corner is a little tiled-floor stand-and-chat bar – with well kept Adnams Bitter, Greene King IPA and Abbot and a guest such as Old Speckled Hen on handpump, and a thoughtful wine list. One no smoking room has a low sofa and wing armchairs around its woodburning stove, and Victorian paintings on the dark green walls. The imaginative and very popular food might include home-made soup (£3.25), griddled fresh sardines in oregano (£4.75; main course £8.75), steak and kidney pudding or roast lamb with a garlic and rosemary jus (£7.50), griddled liver and bacon with bubble and squeak with a rich madeira sauce or chicken and king prawn brochette with yoghurt and mint dip (£9.95), grilled fresh skate wing (£10.95), seared swordfish on niçoise salad (£12.95), sicilian-style baked bass (£13.95), chargrilled fillet steak on a chorizo potato cake (£14.25), and home-made puddings such as orange panna cotta with an exotic fruit salad, iced dark chocolate bombe with cherry compote or strawberry and vanilla crème brûlée (£4.25); the restaurant is no smoking. There are cast-iron seats and tables on a sheltered terrace. *(Recommended by Ian and Jane Irving, SH, Stephen Buckley, Sherrie Glass, Philip and Elaine Holmes, David Twitchett, Francis Johnston, MDN, Gill Pennington, Philip J Cooper, Richard Siebert, Mary and Dennis Jones, J D M Rushworth, Sir Clive Rose, Sally Anne and Peter Goodale, Jeff and Wendy Williams, Rob Webster, John Prescott, Maysie Thompson, Mrs Jane Kingsbury, A Sadler)*

Horizon Inns ~ Manager Neil Bishop ~ Real ale ~ Bar food ~ Restaurant ~ (01206) 263245 ~ Children over 8 in restaurant ~ Dogs allowed in bar ~ Open 11-2.30, 6-11; 12-10.30 Sun; closed 25, 26 Dec, 1 Jan ~ Bedrooms: £54.50B/£69.50B

SWILLAND TM1852 Map 5
Moon & Mushroom 🍺

Village signposted off B1078 Needham Market—Wickham Market, and off B1077

Both locals and visitors enjoy their visits to this idiosyncratic cosy old place. It's run by cheerful, genuinely helpful people, including the very efficient local ladies who deal with the meals, and there's a bustling but relaxed atmosphere. The homely interior is mainly quarry-tiled, with a small coal fire in a brick fireplace, old tables (with lots of board games in the drawers) arranged in little booths made by pine pews, and cushioned stools along the bar. A really homely touch is the four hearty hotpots in the no smoking dark green and brown painted, no smoking cottagey dining room through a small doorway from the bar. These are served to you from Le Creuset dishes on a warming counter and might include coq au vin, pork with peppers, minted lamb and pheasant au vin (all £7.95). You then help yourself to a choice of half a dozen or so tasty vegetables. Another couple of dishes might include a very good ploughman's (£4.95), summer lunchtime salads (from £6.95), cod in fine herbs or vegetable curry (£7.95), with proper home-made puddings like raspberry and apple crumble, bread and butter pudding and toffee and ginger pudding with butterscotch sauce (£3.50). As it is still a real local, food service does end quite early. Only independent East Anglian beers are kept here – Buffys Hopleaf and Norwich Terrier, Nethergate Umbel, Wolf Bitter and Coyote and Woodfordes Norfolk Nog and Wherry, which are tapped straight from casks functionally racked up behind the long counter; 10 decent wines by the glass, and around 25 malt whiskies. You approach the pub through an archway of grapevines and creepers, and a little terrace in front has retractable awnings and heaters (so you can still eat in not so sunny or warm weather outside), flower containers, trellis and nice wooden furniture under parasols. No children inside. *(Recommended by JKW, Philip and Susan Philcox, Pat and Tony Martin, J F M and M West, D S Cottrell, Peter Thomas, David Field, Dr and Mrs Michael Smith, M and G Rushworth, Roger Bridgeman, MDN, Pam and David Bailey)*

Free house ~ Licensees Clive and Adrienne Goodall ~ Real ale ~ Bar food (12-2, 6.30-8.15; not Sun, Mon) ~ (01473) 785320 ~ Dogs allowed in bar ~ Open 11-2.30, 6-11; 12-3, 7-10.30 Sun; closed Mon lunchtime except bank hols

THORINGTON STREET TM0035 Map 5
Rose

B1068 Higham—Stoke by Nayland

Mrs Jones is a particularly friendly licensee with a warm welcome for all her customers. There's a proper pubby village atmosphere, and the building is partly Tudor, and has been knocked through into a single longish partly divided room, with old beams, pine tables and chairs, and enough pictures, prints and brasses to soften the room without overdoing the décor. Among them are old photographs of the landlady's family, who were in the fishing trade. Frequent fresh fish is delivered, so the fish and seafood are particularly tasty: battered cod (£6.25), whitebait (£8.95), grilled skate with black butter and capers or monkfish (£11.95) and bass (£12.95). Other dishes might include sandwiches (from £2.90), home-made soup (£3.95), ploughman's (from £3.75), baked potatoes (from £4.95), steaks (from £8.95) and puddings such as pineapple upside-down cake, popular melt-in-the-mouth meringues filled with fruit and cream, and blackberry and apple pie (£3.25); carvery only on Sunday (£8.40). The top end of the restaurant is no smoking. Well kept Adnams, Greene King Abbot and IPA, and Woodfordes Wherry on handpump, and decent wines; dominoes, cribbage, darts, and piped music. The two boxers are well behaved and friendly dogs, and the fair-sized garden has picnic-sets and summer barbecues, and overlooks the Box valley. *(Recommended by John and Judy Saville, Mike and Mary Carter, Stephen Kiley, Michael and Ann Cole, M A and C R Starling, MDN, Mr and Mrs C F Turner)*

Free house ~ Licensee Kathy Jones ~ Real ale ~ Bar food ~ Restaurant ~ No credit cards ~ (01206) 337243 ~ Children in eating area of bar ~ Dogs allowed in bar ~ Open 12-3, 7-11(10.30 Sun); closed Mon (open bank hol lunchtime)

TOSTOCK TL9563 Map 5
Gardeners Arms 🏆
Village signposted from A14 (former A45) and A1088

There's always a friendly welcome from the jovial landlord and his wife at this charmingly unspoilt pub; Badger the lurcher and Rupert the schnauzer will greet you too. The cosily smart lounge bar has heavy low black beams and lots of carving chairs around decent-sized black tables, a warming fire, and a bustling villagey atmosphere; the lively tiled public bar has darts, pool, shove-ha'penny, dominoes, cribbage, juke box, and an unobtrusive fruit machine; regular quiz nights. The food is good, popular, and reasonably priced, and might include sandwiches and lunchtime dishes such as steak and kidney pie or smoked haddock and leek tart (£6.50), and papaya and curried prawns (£6.75), with evening choices like chilli in tacos with salsa or vegetable enchilada (£7.50), salmon with niçoise salad (£8.50), and lamb chops with cumberland sauce or thai prawn curry (£9.25); the dining area is no smoking. Very well kept Greene King IPA and Abbot and a guest such as Batemans XXXB or Wells Bombardier on handpump. A pleasantly sheltered lawn has picnic-sets among roses and other flowers. *(Recommended by JKW, Derek R A Field, Mr and Mrs Staples, Mr and Mrs J Brown, Michael and Marion Buchanan, M and G Rushworth)*

Greene King ~ Tenant Reg Ransome ~ Real ale ~ Bar food (not Sun lunchtime, Mon, Tues evening) ~ Restaurant ~ (01359) 270460 ~ Children in eating area of bar ~ Dogs allowed in bar ~ Open 11.30-2.30, 7-11; 12-3, 7-10.30 Sun

WALBERSWICK TM4974 Map 5
Bell
Just off B1387

To get the best out of this very popular old pub in a lovely setting, it's perhaps worth visiting out of season. The charming interior has brick floors, well worn flagstones and oak beams that were here 400 years ago when the sleepy little village was a flourishing port. The rambling traditional bar has curved high-backed settles, tankards hanging from oars above the counter, and a woodburning stove in the big fireplace; a second bar has a very large open fire. They don't take bookings for the enjoyable changing bar food, so there are usually queues (and they call out your number when it's ready): home-made soup (£3.50), sandwiches (from £3.50; BLT £4.75), home-made pâté (£4.25), smoked haddock in cheese sauce (£4.50), ploughman's (£5.50), cumberland sausage with gravy (£6.50), shepherd's pie (£6.95), mushroom roast with onion and juniper berry gravy (£7.25), salmon and smoked haddock fishcakes or lamb tagine (£7.95), home-made puddings such as rhubarb, apple and ginger crumble or rich chocolate and orange liqueur mousse

(£3.50), and children's menu. There may be quite a wait at peak times. Well kept Adnams Bitter, Broadside and Regatta on handpump, shove-ha'penny, cribbage, dominoes, and boules outside. This is a nice spot close to the beach, and the tables on the sizeable lawn are sheltered from the worst of the winds by a well placed hedge. You can take the little ferry from Southwold and walk here. Most of the bedrooms look over the sea or river. *(Recommended by Howard James, Richard Pinnington, Blaise Vyner, RB, Mrs Fay Cori , Comus and Sarah Elliott, David Field, J F M and M West, Jack and Jemima Valiant, the Didler, Tim Maddison, Mike and Sue Loseby, John Hulme, DF, NF, Pam and David Bailey, Su and Bob Child, Rob Kelvey, Neil and Lorna Mclaughlan, David and Anne Culley, Mrs Rosalie Croft, Ann and Colin Hunt)*

Adnams ~ Tenant Sue Ireland Cutting ~ Real ale ~ Bar food (12-2.30, 6-9) ~ Restaurant ~ (01502) 723109 ~ Children in family room ~ Dogs allowed in bar and bedrooms ~ Open 11-11; 12-10.30 Sun; 11-3, 6-11 Mon-Fri in winter ~ Bedrooms: £70S/£75S(£90B)

WALDRINGFIELD TM2844 Map 5
Maybush

Off A12 S of Martlesham; The Quay, Cliff Road

This is a lovely spot, particularly in kind weather when you can sit on the verandah and enjoy a drink overlooking the River Deben; plenty of bird life and maybe the sailing club to watch. There are dozens of well arranged outside tables, too. The spacious bar has quite a nautical theme, with lots of old lanterns, pistols and so forth, as well as aerial photographs, an original Twister board, and fresh flowers; though it's all been knocked through, it's divided into separate areas by fireplaces or steps. A glass case has an elaborate ship's model, and there are a few more in a lighter, high-ceilinged extension. A number of the dark wooden tables are set for eating, and though it can fill quickly at lunchtime (particularly in summer), service remains prompt, efficient and friendly. As well as lunchtime sandwiches, filled baked potatoes (from £3.95) and salads (from £5.45), the generous helpings of food might include home-made soup (£3.25), breadcrumbed king prawns with sweet chilli dip (£4.95), burgers (from £5.95), mushroom stroganoff (£6.95), home-made steak in Guinness pie (£7.25), mustard chicken (£7.45), grilled fillet of fresh plaice (£7.95), lamb cutlets (£8.45), halibut steak topped with garlic butter and prawns (£8.95), and steaks (from £9.95); daily specials and puddings listed on blackboards. The dining rooms are no smoking. Adnams Best and Broadside, and Greene King IPA on handpump, and a good range of wines, with around nine or ten by the glass. Fruit machine, piped music, and cribbage. River cruises are available nearby. *(Recommended by Pamela Goodwyn, Bill and Lisa Copeland, Rev John Hibberd, Francis Johnston, J F M and M West, Mike and Wendy Proctor)*

Pubmaster ~ Tenants Steve and Louise Lomas ~ Real ale ~ Bar food (12-2.30, 6.30-9.30; 12-9.30 Sat, Sun) ~ Restaurant ~ (01473) 736215 ~ Children in eating area of bar and restaurant ~ Dogs allowed in bar ~ Open 11-11; 12-10.30 Sun

WINGFIELD TM2277 Map 5
De La Pole Arms ★ ◖

Church Road; village signposted off B1118 N of Stradbroke

Deliberately simple yet stylish, the décor in this tucked away village inn – one of three pubs owned by St Peters – maximises the appeal of its timbered 16th-c interior. Dark wood tables on quarry-tiled floors, light timbers criss-crossing cream walls and big inglenooks in the two bars combine with a modern light wood counter to give a farmhouse/bistro feel. They keep two St Peters beers on handpump in winter, upped to four in summer, and their entire range of over a dozen bottled beers. Very good bar food is served by courteous friendly staff, and might include filled tortilla wraps, baguettes or sandwiches (£4.95; rib-eye steak in ciabatta £8.75), layered chicken, pork, and bacon terrine (£5.25), leek, gorgonzola and walnut strudel (£5.65), wild mushroom risotto cake (£9.95), tuna steak with feta, prawns, peach and coriander (£11.95), and house specials like home-made soup (£3.95), cod, smoked haddock and salmon fishcakes (£6.95), steaming bowls of seafood (from £6.95), roast vegetable cassoulet (£8.50), rabbit casserole (£8.95), slow roasted greek-style lamb shanks (£9.25), and monkfish wrapped in pancetta and skewered on rosemary sticks on roasted vegetables (£10.50); the restaurant is no smoking. Good disabled access. More reports please. *(Recommended by Tom Gondris, Comus and Sarah Elliott, Neil and Lorna Mclaughlan, Phil, Tina and Harrison Walker, Derek Thomas, Mike and Wendy Proctor, Philip and Susan Philcox, Julie and Bill Ryan)*

St Peters ~ Tenant Sally Prior ~ Real ale ~ Bar food ~ Restaurant ~ (01379) 384545 ~ Children welcome ~ Dogs allowed in bar ~ Open 11.30-3, 6.30(6 Sat)-11; 12-3 Sun; Mon in winter; closed Sun evening

Lucky Dip

Besides the fully inspected pubs, you might like to try these Lucky Dips recommended to us and described by readers (if you do, please send us reports: www.goodguides.com).

ALDEBURGH [TM4656]
☆ *Cross Keys* [Crabbe St]: Busy 16th-c pub extended from low-beamed core with antique settles, Victorian prints, woodburners, well kept Adnams ales (the full range) and wines, brisk friendly service, ample enjoyable food, Sunday papers; can be rather smoky, loudspeaker food announcements, fruit machine; open all day July/Aug, children in eating areas, picnic-sets in sheltered back yard which opens on to promenade and beach; elegant bedrooms with own bathrooms *(Jack and Jemima Valiant, LYM, Gordon Theaker, MJVK, Tony Middis, Rona Murdoch, Michael Butler, Ian Phillips, Comus and Sarah Elliott, Tracey and Stephen Groves, MDN)*
Mill [Market Cross Pl, opp Moot Hall]: Homely 1920s corner pub nr Moot Hall and beach, friendly and relaxing, with good value food cooked to order from good baguettes to local fish and roast of the day, good service (humorous landlord), well kept Adnams ales, decent coffee, locals' bar, lots of pictures, cosy no smoking beamed dining room with *Gypsy Queen* model, sea view and strong RNLI theme, cream teas July/Aug; fruit machine; open all day Fri/Sat and July/Aug, bedrooms *(Rona Murdoch, George Atkinson, David Oakley, June and Perry Dann, Ian Phillips, Comus and Sarah Elliott)*
ALDRINGHAM [TM4461]
☆ *Parrot & Punchbowl* [B1122/B1353 S of Leiston]: Neatly kept beamed pub with good food inc local fish from downstairs servery, dining-room meals Fri-Sun (must book then), good wine choice, well kept Adnams and Greene King IPA, decent coffee, no piped music; children welcome, dogs allowed; pleasant sheltered garden with own servery and a couple of swings, nice craft centre opp *(BB, Ann and Colin Hunt, Francis Johnston)*
BACTON [TM0467]
Bull [Church Rd]: Friendly good-humoured family service, enjoyable food inc sandwiches, light dishes and some good turkish food, well kept Adnams Broadside and Greene King IPA

and Abbot, wheelchair access to dining room; busy wknds *(John F Morton)*
BARHAM [TM1251]
Sorrel Horse [Old Norwich Rd]: Cheerful and attractive pink-washed pantiled 17th-c country pub, nicely refurbished bar with magnificent log fire, lots of beams, lounge and two dining areas off, ample good value food inc interesting specials, prompt friendly service, particularly well kept real ales, decent wines; children welcome, good garden with big play area, summer bouncy castle and barbecue, stables opp; well placed for walks *(J F M and M West)*
BILDESTON [TL9949]
☆ *Crown* [B1115 SW of Stowmarket]: Picturesque if not smart 15th-c timbered pub, neat beamed main bar with inglenook and comfortable banquettes, smaller more modern bar, good value food from soup and sandwiches up, good puddings choice, no smoking dining room, well kept Adnams and Broadside a guest beer such as Mauldons Black Adder tapped from the cask, obliging pleasantly informal service; may be piped music; children and dogs welcome, nice tables out in courtyard, more in large attractive garden with pet owl, quiet comfortable bedrooms due for some renovation *(Eddie Edwards, George Atkinson, I D Greenfield, Mike Moden, O K Smyth, Charles and Pauline Stride, LYM)*
BLAXHALL [TM3656]
☆ *Ship* [off B1069 S of Snape; can be reached from A12 via Little Glemham]: Low-beamed 18th-c village pub doing well under friendly new licensees, good if not cheap food cooked by landlord inc local fish, enterprising vegetarian dishes, small helpings for children, unassuming dining lounge, well kept Adnams and Woodfordes Wherry and Nelsons Revenge, woodburner; piped music, pool in public bar, live folk nights; children in eating area, self-catering cabins available, attractive country setting; cl Mon and winter Tues, two simple annexe bedrooms *(LYM, Comus and Sarah Elliott, Jenny and Brian Seller, Christopher and Jo Barton)*

BLYTHBURGH [TM4575]
☆ *White Hart* [A12]: Friendly and roomy open-plan family dining pub with reliably enjoyable blackboard food inc game and fish at alluring prices, fine ancient beams, woodwork and staircase, full Adnams range kept well, good range of wines in two glass sizes, good coffee, charming efficient service; may be piped music; children in eating area and restaurant, open all day Fri/Sat, spacious lawns looking down on tidal marshes (barbecues), magnificent church over road, and has bedrooms now *(M A and C R Starling, Comus and Sarah Elliott, Ann and Colin Hunt, LYM, Mrs Rosalie Croft, Tracey and Stephen Groves)*

BOXFORD [TL9640]
☆ *Fleece* [Broad St]: Quietly unpretentious partly 15th-c pub with cosy panelled bar on right, airy lounge bar with wonderful medieval fireplace, armchairs and some distinctive old seats among more conventional furnishings; good home cooking, Adnams, welcoming landlord *(Giles Francis, LYM)*

BRANDESTON [TM2460]
☆ *Queens Head* [The Street, towards Earl Soham]: Good new licensees in unpretentiously attractive open-plan country local, leather banquettes and old pews, well kept Adnams ales, enjoyable food (not Sun evening) inc some interesting dishes, family room; shove-ha'penny, cribbage, dominoes, piped music; bedrooms, campsite, big neat garden with good play area *(LYM, Pat and Tony Martin, Mike and Wendy Proctor)*

BRENT ELEIGH [TL9447]
☆ *Cock* [A1141 SE of Lavenham]: Unspoilt thatched local with piano in clean and cosy snug, benches, table and darts in second small room, antique flooring tiles, lovely coal fire, ochre walls with old photographs of local villages, well kept Adnams and Greene King IPA and Abbot, farm cider, no food beyond crisps and pickled eggs; picnic-sets up on side grass with summer hatch service, attractive inn-sign, bedrooms *(the Didler, BB, Giles Francis)*

BROMESWELL [TM3050]
☆ *Cherry Tree* [Orford Rd, Bromeswell Heath]: Comfortably modernised neat beamed lounge, very popular wknds for good value and enjoyable wide-ranging food with plenty for vegetarians; quick friendly service even when busy, open fire, well kept Adnams and Greene King Old Speckled Hen, well spaced tables; tables outside, big adventure playground, charming inn-sign *(Gill Pennington, Christopher and Jo Barton, BB, Gloria Bax)*

BURES [TL9033]
Eight Bells [Colchester Rd]: Pleasant old-fashioned local with good value well served lunchtime food in simple but attractive bar, several real ales inc a guest, smiling service *(MLR)*

BURY ST EDMUNDS [TL8564]
Angel [Angel Hill]: Thriving long-established country-town hotel with good food from bacon butties and other bar snacks to meals inc beautifully presented starters in elegant Regency restaurant and terrace rooms, helpful friendly service, well kept Adnams in rather plush bar, cellar grill room; bedrooms comfortable *(Chris Flynn, Wendy Jones)*
Linden Tree [Out Northgate St/Station Hill]: Buoyant atmosphere and wide choice of good value food from good baguettes up in pleasant family dining pub with stripped pine bar, friendly quick service, well kept Greene King ales, decent wines in two glass sizes, freshly squeezed orange juice, popular no smoking conservatory restaurant (worth booking); good well kept garden *(J F M and M West)*
☆ *Old Cannon* [Cannon St, just off A134/A1101 roundabout N end of town]: Pub/restaurant brewing its own beers such as Cannon Best and Gunners Daughter (two large polished copper brewing kettles right by the bar), also a couple of guest beers and good wine choice by the glass, good imaginative generous food inc thai from integral kitchen/office, good quick service, terracotta walls and crisp white paintwork, interesting décor with modern paintings and china; can get very busy Fri/Sat evenings; small pretty garden, bedrooms, cl Mon lunchtime *(RWC, Wendy Dye, Derek and Sylvia Stephenson)*
Rose & Crown [Whiting St]: Unassuming town local, fairly spartan but comfortable and spotless, with simple excellent value lunchtime food, particularly well kept Greene King ales and a guest beer, pleasant lounge, bric-a-brac, good games-oriented public bar with darts, cards and dominoes, rare separate off-sales counter *(Pete Baker)*

BUTLEY [TM3650]
Oyster [B1084 E of Woodbridge]: Friendly new landlord in unpretentious country local, stripped pine tables and pews, high-backed settles and more orthodox seats on bare boards, good coal fires, well kept Adnams Bitter, Broadside and a seasonal beer, bar food (not Sun evening) from sandwiches up; children welcome *(Mike and Sue Richardson, LYM)*

CAMPSEY ASH [TM3356]
Dog & Duck [Station Rd]: Welcoming and attractive family-friendly pub with enjoyable food inc Sun lunch, well kept beer, helpful service; nice garden with good play area inc mini assault course *(Jon Stanton)*

CAVENDISH [TL8046]
☆ *Bull* [A1092 Long Melford—Clare]: Attractive 16th-c pub under new ownership – no reader reports yet; open-plan beamed interior, heavy standing timbers and fine fireplaces, Adnams Bitter, Broadside and a seasonal ale, bar food (which has included lots of interesting specials – but you may find all tables booked); may be piped music; children in eating areas, tables in garden, summer barbecues, car park (useful in this honeypot village), has been open all day Sun *(LYM)*
George [The Green]: Attractive recently refurbished building, now more restaurant-with-rooms than pub, good inventive modern food (not cheap, though also do lower-price two- and three-course meals), beamed no

smoking room, further large eating area with bar, nice wines, good coffees and teas; bedrooms *(Adele Summers, Alan Black)*

CHILLESFORD [TM3852]

☆ *Froize* [B1084 E of Woodbridge]: Pleasantly decorated dining pub, largely no smoking, back on form under experienced new management, good country food in bar and restaurant inc good value two-course buffet-style lunch (not Mon), local pork and venison, and more elaborate evening meals Thurs-Sat; Adnams, good wines in choice of glass sizes, warmly welcoming service *(DF, NF, Mrs P J Pearce, LYM, Pamela Goodwyn, Tony and Shirley Albert)*

CLARE [TL7645]

☆ *Bell* [Market Hill]: Large timbered inn with local feel in comfortably rambling bar, splendidly carved black beams, old panelling and woodwork around the open fire, side rooms (one with lots of canal and other prints), well kept Nethergate ales inc Mild (this is the brewer's local), also others such as Greene King IPA, decent wines and food from sandwiches up inc children's in dining conservatory opening on to terrace; darts, pool, fruit machine; nice bedrooms off back courtyard (very special village, lovely church), open all day Sun *(Derek and Sylvia Stephenson, Patrick Hancock, Angela Gorman, Paul Acton, LYM, Helen and Ian Jobson)*

☆ *Swan* [High St]: Proper village local, early 17th-c but much modernised, lots of copper and brass and huge log fire in main room (no smoking at lunchtime), public bar with World War II memorabilia and another fire (dogs allowed here), friendly landlord and staff, reasonably priced food from huge bargain huffers up, well kept Greene King ales; no children; lovely flower tubs out behind *(BB, Patrick Hancock, MLR)*

CREETING ST MARY [TM1155]

Highwayman [A140, just N of junction with A14]: Much extended and modernised, pleasantly relaxed atmosphere with welcoming staff, emphasis on enjoyable food inc interesting dishes and popular Sun lunch, three changing real ales, decent wines, gallery overflow; unobtrusive piped music; tables on back lawn with small pond *(Ian and Nita Cooper, George Atkinson)*

CRETINGHAM [TM2260]

☆ *Bell* [The Street]: Comfortable village pub mixing striking 15th-c beams, timbers and glorious log fire in big fireplace with more modern renovations and furnishings, well kept Adnams and changing guest beers, good generous food inc children's, attentive landlord; no smoking lounge and restaurant with Sun lunch, traditional games in public bar, family room; charming beamed bedrooms, good breakfast, may open all day in summer, seats out in rose garden and on front grass *(June and Perry Dann, LYM, Francis Johnston)*

DALHAM [TL7261]

☆ *Affleck Arms* [Brookside]: Thatched pub by stream (dry in some summers), log fire in cosy low-beamed locals' bar, more comfortable and intimate rambling dining bar on right, wide choice of good value generous food with fresh veg inc children's, Greene King and other ales, friendly service, no smoking dining room; picnic-sets out in front, fish pond behind, pretty village *(LYM, Adele Summers, Alan Black)*

EAST BERGHOLT [TM0734]

☆ *Kings Head* [Burnt Oak, towards Flatford Mill]: Well kept attractive beamed lounge with comfortable sofas, interesting decorations, dining area off, good value home-made blackboard food, well kept Greene King ales, decent wines and coffee, quick pleasant service, thriving atmosphere; piped classical music, juke box in plain public bar; lots of room in pretty garden, flower-decked haywain, baskets and tubs of flowers in front *(Tony and Shirley Albert, Alistair and Kay Butler, Mike and Mary Carter)*

EASTBRIDGE [TM4566]

☆ *Eels Foot* [off B1122 N of Leiston]: Helpful new landlord in cheerful and simple country pub, well kept Adnams Best, Broadside and Regatta, light modern furnishings, darts in side area, neat back dining room; walkers, children and dogs welcome, tables and swings outside, pretty village handy for Minsmere bird reserve and heathland walks; open all day in summer, some folk nights *(LYM, David and Rhian Peters, Simon Watkins)*

FELIXSTOWE FERRY [TM3337]

Victoria: Welcoming well refurbished child-friendly riverside pub, generous straightforward food inc local seafood, well kept Adnams and Greene King ales, briskly efficient friendly service, sea views from upstairs dining area *(Pamela Goodwyn, June and Malcolm Farmer, Barry Collett)*

FRAMLINGHAM [TM2862]

☆ *Station Hotel* [Station Rd (B1116 S)]: High-ceilinged big-windowed bar with pine tables and chairs on stripped boards, interesting generous proper home cooking inc good fish dishes (an emphasis on smoked), well kept Earl Soham Victoria, Albert, Gannet Mild and Sir Rogers Porter, good choice of house wines, welcoming service, informal relaxed atmosphere, plenty of train pictures, small tiled-floor back snug; children welcome, picnic-sets in good-sized pleasant garden *(George and Sarah Saumarez Smith, BB, Jack and Jemima Valiant)*

FRAMSDEN [TM1959]

☆ *Dobermann* [signed off B1077]: Charmingly restored tucked-away thatched pub festooned with summer flowers, friendly welcome, lots of doberman and schnautzer pictures in two neatly kept low-beamed linked rooms with central open fire, sofa and armchairs among other seats, enjoyable generous bar food from sandwiches to steak (freshly made so may take a time), well kept Adnams Bitter and Broadside and a guest beer, efficient service; piped radio; sheltered garden with picnic-sets and boules, one bedroom, cl Mon *(LYM, I D Greenfield, Michael Gray, George Atkinson, Marjorie and*

Bernard Parkin, Peter Thomas, Mike and Mary Carter, Comus and Sarah Elliott)

FRESSINGFIELD [TM2677]

☆ *Fox & Goose* [B1116 N of Framlingham; Church St]: Beautifully timbered 16th-c building owned by the church, newly refurbished and now really a restaurant with comfortable armchairs and sofas in lounge for pre-dinner drinks (no bar counter), two no smoking dining rooms, one with beams and modern art, the other cosy with a high-backed settle and log fire; good food inc light lunches, Adnams Best and Regatta tapped from the cask, fine wines; children welcome, cl Mon *(Comus and Sarah Elliott, Neil Powell, LYM)*

HALESWORTH [TM3877]

Angel [Thoroughfare]: Civilised and comfortable 16th-c Adnams coaching inn with their beers very well kept and reasonably priced, obliging service, enjoyable bar food from soup and sandwiches up, good range of coffees and cakes, good italian restaurant, decent wines; interesting inner courtyard with 18th-c clock and vines, seven well equipped bedrooms, open all day *(Guy Morton, Comus and Sarah Elliott)*

HARTEST [TL8352]

Crown [B1066 S of Bury St Edmunds]: Pink-washed pub by church behind pretty village green, new licensees doing very wide choice of enjoyable food inc fish and grills in no smoking dining rooms and conservatory, pleasant interior with big log fire in impressive fireplace, Greene King IPA, Abbot and Old Speckled Hen, decent house wines, quick service; children in eating areas, tables on big back lawn and in sheltered side courtyard, play area; has been cl Sun evening in Jan-Feb *(LYM, Adele Summers, Alan Black)*

HAUGHLEY [TM0262]

☆ *Kings Arms* [off A45/B1113 N of Stowmarket; Old St]: New chef/owners doing interesting varied reasonably priced food inc delicious puddings in 16th-c timbered pub with airy 1950s back part refurbished to match, well kept Adnams Broadside and Greene King Abbot, decent wines, busy public bar with games, log fire; piped music; tables and play house in colourful back garden *(Ian and Nita Cooper, Pam and David Bailey, BB)*

HOLBROOK [TM1636]

Compasses [Ipswich Rd]: Tranquil old place, clean, tidy and spaciously refurbished, well kept Adnams, Greene King IPA and a guest, friendly attentive staff, big log fire, fairly priced food in bar and restaurant; garden with play area, nice spot on Shotley peninsula *(Ken and Brenda Holroyd, Pamela Goodwyn)*

HORRINGER [TL8261]

Six Bells [The Street]: Neatly refurbished, with good choice of generous reasonably priced home-made food, friendly relaxed atmosphere, front dining room and dining conservatory both no smoking, well kept Greene King; neat garden *(Adele Summers, Alan Black)*

HOXNE [TM1877]

☆ *Swan* [off B1118, signed off A140 S of Diss; Low St]: Striking and well restored late 15th-c thatched pub, broad oak floorboards, handsomely carved timbering in the colour-washed walls, armchairs by deep-set inglenook fireplace, no smoking snug, another fireplace in dining room, good log fires, well kept Adnams and guest beers tapped from the cask, enjoyable reasonably priced food inc good fish, friendly atmosphere, relaxed service; children welcome, sizeable attractive garden behind, summer barbecues *(Mrs Jill Silversides, Barry Brown, Sue Anderson, Phil Copleston, Tom Gondris, Nick and Alison Dowson, Mike and Wendy Proctor, LYM)*

ICKLINGHAM [TL7772]

Plough [The Street]: Welcoming service, well kept ales such as Adnams, Greene King IPA and Woodfordes Wherry, good range of home-made food, friendly atmosphere, lots of cricketing memorabilia and books; subdued piped music; big garden with play area *(Comus and Sarah Elliott)*

IPSWICH [TM1844]

☆ *Fat Cat* [Spring Rd, opp junction with Nelson Rd]: Neatly kept reconstruction of basic bare-boards pub outstanding for 15 or more well kept interesting ales mainly from small breweries, belgian imports, farm ciders, helpful friendly service and cheery regulars, snacks such as scotch eggs and filled rolls (or bring your own food), lots of enamel beer advertisements, no music or machines; very little daytime parking nearby; back conservatory and terrace with summer thai barbecues, open all day *(Ian Phillips, the Didler, Diane Manoughian, BB)*

Lord Nelson [Fore St]: Genuinely old, with bare boards and timbering, friendly prompt service, enjoyable generous pub food, three Adnams ales tapped from the cask; handy for waterfront *(Keith and Janet Morris)*

Milestone [Woodbridge Rd]: Open-plan pub with up to a dozen real ales on handpump and twice as many tapped from the cask, farm ciders, several dozen whiskies, home-made food lunchtime and Mon-Weds evening; live bands, large front terrace *(the Didler)*

KERSEY [TM0044]

Bell [signed off A1141 N of Hadleigh; The Street]: Quaint flower-decked Tudor building in picturesque village, low-beamed bar with tiled floor and log fire divided from lounge by brick and timber screen, friendly prompt service, well kept Adnams and Greene King IPA, decent house wines, sandwiches and popular hot dishes; open all day (afternoon teas), children allowed, sheltered back terrace with fairy-lit side canopy *(LYM, David Biggins)*

LAKENHEATH [TL7182]

Half Moon [High St]: Wide choice of enjoyable food inc good vegetarian dishes, small no smoking dining room *(Carol Johansen)*

LAVENHAM [TL9149]

Cock [Church St]: Comfortable and attractive thatched village pub with enjoyable sensibly priced food esp curries (best to book wknds, quiet wkdy lunchtimes), plush lounge, separate family dining room, basic bar, Adnams and Greene King ales, good wine choice, quick friendly service *(Wendy Dye, the Didler, Sir Clive Rose)*

☆ *Swan* [High Street]: Smart, well equipped and by no means cheap hotel incorporating handsome medieval buildings, well worth a look for its appealing network of beamed and timbered alcoves and more open areas, inc peaceful little tiled-floor inner bar with leather chairs and memorabilia of its days as the local for US 48th Bomber Group, well kept Adnams and Greene King IPA, fairly short lunchtime bar menu, morning coffee, afternoon tea, lavishly timbered no smoking restaurant; food service can be slow; children welcome, sheltered courtyard garden *(Fiona Wynn, Pete Stroud, Maysie Thompson, the Didler, Peter Saville, Brian and Janet Ainscough, LYM, W H and E Thomas)*

LAYHAM [TM0340]

☆ *Marquis of Cornwallis* [Upper St (B1070 E of Hadleigh)]: Homely beamed 16th-c local popular lunchtime for nicely prepared generous food inc good ploughman's and fresh veg, plush lounge bar, friendly atmosphere, well kept Adnams and Greene King, good wines and coffee, warm coal fire; good valley views, popular bird table and picnic-sets in extensive riverside garden, open all day Sat in summer; bedrooms handy for Harwich ferries *(C L Kauffmann, Giles Francis)*

LITTLE BEALINGS [TM2247]

☆ *Admirals Head* [off A12 SW of Woodbridge; Sandy Lane]: Stylish and comfortable, with handsome beams, good choice of home-made food inc interesting dishes using good mainly local ingredients such as traditionally hung aberdeen angus beef, well kept ales inc Adnams Bitter and Broadside, decent changing house wines, friendly chatty service, upper-level candlelit raftered dining room, intriguing little cellar room down steps with trap door to one of the pub's two wells, nice Beeken yachting photographs, no music or machines; picnic-sets out on terrace *(J L Wedel, BB, Ian Phillips)*

LITTLE GLEMHAM [TM3458]

Lion [Main Rd]: Well kept Adnams, wide choice of attractively priced food (they are helpful with special diets), good service; garden with animals, bedrooms *(Mr and Mrs T B Staples)*

LONG MELFORD [TL8645]

☆ *Bull* [Hall St (B1064)]: Medieval great hall, now a hotel (not cheap, but very friendly), with beautifully carved beams in old-fashioned timbered front lounge, blazing log fire in huge fireplace, antique furnishings (and games machine), daily papers; more spacious back bar with sporting prints; good range of bar food from good filled huffers to one-price hot dishes inc imaginative salads and fresh fish, no smoking restaurant, well kept Adnams Best, Greene King IPA and Nethergate, helpful staff; children welcome, courtyard tables, open all day Sat/Sun; comfortable bedrooms *(Chris Flynn, Wendy Jones, Maysie Thompson, LYM, Pamela Goodwyn, R C and J M Clark, Derek Thomas)*

LOWESTOFT [TM5390]

Trowel & Hammer [Pakefield St]: Well kept

pub nr sea, modern though dating from 16th c; well kept beers, good eating choice from lunchtime baguettes and baked potatoes to light air-conditioned restaurant, OAP lunches Mon–Weds; play area, live music Sun night, good tables out overlooking green and sea, open all day *(J F M and M West, June and Perry Dann)*

MARKET WESTON [TL9777]

☆ *Mill* [Bury Rd (B1111)]: Opened-up pub with good staple food using local produce inc popular Sun lunch, well kept Adnams, Greene King IPA and an Old Chimneys beer from the village brewery, enthusiastic effective service; children welcome, theme night *(Derek R A Field)*

MELTON [TM2850]

Wilford Bridge [Wilford Bridge Rd]: Light, roomy and well organised, with emphasis on good value food from good sandwiches to local fish in two spacious bars and restaurant, steak nights Mon/Tues (when it's less busy), takeaways, well kept though pricy Adnams and Greene King Old Speckled Hen, good wines by the glass, prompt friendly service even though busy, pleasant décor; nearby river walks *(Comus and Sarah Elliott, Pamela Goodwyn, J F M and M West, Peggy and Alec Ward)*

MIDDLETON [TM4367]

☆ *Bell* [off B1125 Leiston—Westleton; The Street]: Charming little traditional pub, part thatched and beamed, in pretty setting nr church, newly decorated under new licensees; full Adnams range tapped from the cask and kept well, enjoyable cheap food inc children's, woodburner in comfortable lounge, small back dining room, darts and open fire in small low-ceilinged public bar (dogs allowed); impromptu folk nights Weds; picnic-sets in garden, camping, handy for RSPB Minsmere and coast *(Comus and Sarah Elliott, BB, Les Trusler)*

MILL GREEN [TL9542]

White Horse [just E of Edwardstone]: Down-to-earth local atmosphere, character landlord, basic food such as burgers, well kept rotating beers such as Adnams, Cottage Whippet and a Mild *(Giles Francis)*

MONKS ELEIGH [TL9647]

☆ *Swan* [B1115 Sudbury—Stowmarket]: Chef/landlord doing innovative fresh home-made food inc seasonal game, several fish dishes and bargain early supper, real ales inc Adnams and Greene King, good value wines, welcoming efficient service, comfortably modernised lounge bar, open fire, two dining areas; bedrooms *(Derek Thomas, MDN)*

NEEDHAM MARKET [TM0954]

Lion [Ipswich Rd/Lion Lane]: Mossy-tiled roomy local with wide range of usual food (not Sun evening), friendly staff, Adnams, Boddingtons and Greene King IPA, soft lighting; picnic-sets and play area in big garden *(Ian and Nita Cooper)*

NEWBOURNE [TM2643]

Fox [The Street]: Pleasant 17th-c pub, enjoyable food using fresh local produce, well kept Tolly tapped from the cask, cosy unspoilt oak-beamed drinking area around log fire, nice golden retriever (Hector), separate family room, dining extension; beware, they may try to keep your credit card while you eat; pretty hanging baskets, lots of tables out in attractive garden with pond, musical evenings *(Pamela Goodwyn)*

NEWTON [TL9140]

Saracens Head [A134 4 miles E Sudbury]: Comfortable lounge with small log fire, decent reasonably priced food cooked by landlord, Adnams; overlooks village pond and green, may be ducks and geese among the picnic-sets *(Giles Francis)*

ORFORD [TM4249]

Crown & Castle: Well established hotel with interesting if not cheap bar food inc good ploughman's and fresh crab, good atmosphere, busy dining room; pleasant bedrooms in garden block *(Comus and Sarah Elliott)*

PETTISTREE [TM3054]

☆ *Three Tuns* [off A12 just S of Wickham Mkt; Main Rd]: Interestingly reworked roadside pub with comfortably chintzy armchairs and sofas in linked rooms with old-fashioned lamps, decorative china, old master reproductions, carpet or highly polished boards, civilised food, well kept Adnams and Greene King IPA and Abbot, good coffee, pleasant service, log fire, conservatory; piped Dean Martin-ish music, piano one end; bedrooms *(Pamela Goodwyn, BB)*

POLSTEAD [TL9938]

☆ *Cock* [signed off B1068 and A1071 E of Sudbury, then pub signed; Polstead Green]: Interesting reasonably priced food (not Sun evening) from good value big lunchtime rolls up, welcoming landlady, well kept ales such as Adnams Broadside, Greene King IPA and Woodfordes Wherry, good coffee (with warmed shortbread), good choice of wines, black beams and timbers, dark pink walls, woodburner and open fire, random mix of unassuming furniture, plenty of locals, light and airy barn restaurant; piped music; children welcome, picnic-sets out overlooking quiet green, side play area, cl Mon *(BB, Hazel Morgan)*

RAMSHOLT [TM3041]

☆ *Ramsholt Arms* [signposted off B1083; Dock Rd]: Lovely isolated spot, with picture-window nautical bars overlooking River Deben, and handy for the new Sutton Hoo visitor centre; good wholesome food inc plenty of seafood, children's dishes, well kept Adnams and guest beers, several wines by the glass, easy-going contented bar (one of the dogs can let himself in) with good log fire, friendly staff, no smoking restaurant, summer afternoon terrace bar (not Sun); longish steep walk down from car park, busy summer wknds; children very welcome, roomy bedrooms with stunning view, yacht moorings nearby *(LYM, Pamela Goodwyn, J F M and M West, June and Malcolm Farmer, Comus and Sarah Elliott, Mrs E A Shortland-Jones, Tracey and Stephen Groves)*

REDGRAVE [TM0477]

Cross Keys [The Street]: Friendly village local with comfortable lounge bar, well kept Adnams, Greene King and a guest such as Elgoods Mad Dog or Tindalls Best, good value home cooking inc good sandwiches and Tues OAP lunch, daily papers; Sun quiz night *(Francis Johnston, Sarah Day, Mark Timms)*

RISBY [TL7865]

☆ *White Horse* [Newmarket Rd, just off A14]: Attractive and interesting lounge décor and furnishings, relaxed atmosphere, beams, brickwork and panelling, mats on flagstones, log fire, wide choice of sensibly priced bar food from good baguettes up, friendly and helpful prompt service, Adnams; comfortable separate restaurant, piped music in public bar *(W H and E Thomas, LYM)*

ROUGHAM [TL9063]

Ravenwood Hall: Country house hotel with elaborate restaurant, but also worth knowing as charming spot for a drink or bar meal, with blackboard choice inc sandwiches, sausages and mash and fish and chips; lots of interesting touches, well kept beer, good wines by the glass, mulled wine at Christmas; tables outside, goats and geese by the car park, bedrooms *(J F M and M West)*

SAXON STREET [TL6759]

Reindeer [The Street]: Good choice of well kept real ales, friendly service, enjoyable generous food *(M and G Rushworth, Mike and Jennifer Marsh)*

SAXTEAD GREEN [TM2665]

☆ *Old Mill House* [B1119; The Green]: Roomy dining pub across green from windmill, beamed carpeted bar, neat country-look flagstoned restaurant extension, wooden tables and chairs, pretty curtains, friendly service, popular reasonably priced freshly made food inc good puddings and nightly carvery, well kept real ales inc Adnams, decent wines; discreet piped music; children very welcome, attractive and sizeable garden with terrace and good play area *(Ian and Nita Cooper, LYM, D S Cottrell, Gloria Bax)*

SHOTTISHAM [TM3144]

Sorrel Horse [Hollesley Rd]: Simple thatched two-bar Tudor pub in tucked-away village, well kept Adnams tapped from the cask, good value straightforward food lunchtime and early evening (Sun lunch often completely booked even in winter), friendly helpful service, good log fire; quiz nights some Sats, tables out on green *(Mrs Roxanne Chamberlain, the Didler, Pat and Tony Martin)*

SNAPE [TM3957]

☆ *Plough & Sail* [the Maltings]: Much extended, light and airy and not really a pub, more an enjoyable eating place, with a good modern choice from snacks to full meals; original part with log fires, sofas, settles and bar with well kept Adnams Bitter, Broadside and a seasonal ale, decent wines; teak tables out in big enclosed flower-filled courtyard, open all day in summer *(Jeff and Wendy Williams, Pamela Goodwyn, R C Wiles, Ann and Colin Hunt, LYM, Tracey and Stephen Groves)*

SOMERSHAM [TM0848]

☆ *Duke of Marlborough* [off A14 just N of Ipswich; Main Rd]: Sturdy pine tables on fresh stripped boards in big open room with appealing country prints and 16th-c inglenook, light and airy turkey-carpeted dining room, good service and atmosphere, good fresh food from lunchtime baguettes and baked potatoes to some interesting hot dishes, well kept Greene King IPA and Old Speckled Hen, decent wines, good coffee with fresh cream, quick friendly service by neat staff *(Pamela Goodwyn, Mrs Anne Hayward, BB)*

SOUTHWOLD [TM5076]

Kings Head [High St]: Extended homely family dining pub, lots of maroon and pink plush, interesting memorabilia and 1930s detailing, wide range of reliable home-made food from filled rolls up inc local fish, well kept Adnams, good house wines, friendly service, no smoking area; comfortable family/games room with well lit pool table; jazz some Sun nights, decent bedrooms *(BB, Tina and David Woods-Taylor, Sue Holland, Dave Webster)*

☆ *Lord Nelson* [East St]: Lively bustle in cheerful easy-going seaside local with perfectly kept Adnams full range, decent wines, wholesome plain generous lunchtime food from sandwiches up, low prices, ever-present landlord and quick attentive service, air cleaner; low ceilings, panelling and tiled floor, spotless light wood furniture, roaring fire, lamps in nice nooks and crannies, Lord Nelson memorabilia inc fine model of the *Victory*, no music; disabled access (not perfect, but they help), children welcome away from the bar, nice seats in sheltered back garden, open all day *(Sue Holland, Dave Webster, Comus and Sarah Elliott, David and Gilly Wilkins, Derek R A Field, Mrs Jane Kingsbury, Derek and Sylvia Stephenson, Colin and Dot Savill, the Didier, Tim Maddison, David and Rhian Peters, Patrick Hancock, Pam and David Bailey, Dr Andy Wilkinson, BB, Neil and Lorna Mclaughlan, Ann and Colin Hunt, Tracey and Stephen Groves, Gloria Bax)*

Pier Pub [North Parade]: Good food (summer) and well kept beer, lovely sea views and covered terrace; children welcome, part of new pier development *(June and Perry Dann, Sue Holland, Dave Webster)*

Red Lion [South Green]: Big windows looking over green to sea, pale panelling, ship pictures, lots of brassware and copper, prompt service, well kept Adnams Bitter and Broadside, good value food inc good fish, no smoking dining room; children and dogs welcome, tables outside, right by the Adnams retail shop; bedrooms small but comfortable *(George Atkinson, BB, Simon Watkins, Patrick Hancock, Neil and Lorna Mclaughlan, Sue Holland, Dave Webster, Derek and Sylvia Stephenson, Pam and David Bailey, Tim and Ann Newell, M and G Rushworth)*

Sole Bay [East Green]: Bleached café/bar décor and light wood furnishings combined with cheerful local atmosphere, good simple food

from sensibly priced doorstep sandwiches up, well kept Adnams, friendly service, conservatory; live music Fri; tables on side terrace, moments from sea and lighthouse *(P G Plumridge, Dr Andy Wilkinson, Chris Flynn, Wendy Jones, Sue Holland, Dave Webster, LYM, Tim Maddison)*

SUDBURY [TL8741]

White Horse [North St]: Bustling town pub with several linked bare-boards areas, good value lunchtime food from sandwiches to steaks, well kept Greene King IPA, Abbot and a seasonal beer, helpful friendly staff *(MLR)*

THEBERTON [TM4365]

Lion [B1122]: Unpretentious village local with no smoking lounge, comfortable banquettes, lots of old local photographs, pictures, copper, brass, plates and bric-a-brac, fresh flowers, good value freshly made pub food inc children's, welcoming licensees, well kept Adnams, Woodfordes Wherry and a couple of stronger guest beers, amiable dalmatian; piped radio, cribbage, separate part with darts, pool and TV; jazz 1st Sun of month, perhaps flowers for sale; garden with picnic-sets, small terrace and camp site *(Comus and Sarah Elliott, Peter J Holmes)*

THORNHAM MAGNA [TM1070]

Four Horseshoes [off A140 S of Diss; Wickham Rd]: Thatched pub open all day, with dim-lit rambling well divided bar, very low heavy black beams, mix of chairs and plush banquettes, country pictures and farm tools, logs burning in big fireplaces, inside well, no smoking areas; Adnams, Courage Directors, Greene King Old Speckled Hen and Charles Wells Bombardier, winter mulled wine, attentive young staff, food (all day Sun) inc OAP bargains; piped music, fruit machine and TV; bedrooms, picnic-sets on big sheltered lawn, handy for Thornham Walks and thatched church with ancient frescoes and fine retable *(Linda Crisp, E J and M W Corrin, Ian and Nita Cooper, LYM, JKW, Patrick Hancock)*

THORPENESS [TM4759]

Dolphin: Attractive almost scandinavian décor, light and bright, with good choice of enjoyable food (a restaurant feel, but good lunchtime sandwiches too), well kept Adnams, good wine range; service relaxed and helpful, dogs welcome in public bar; three comfortable bedrooms with own bathrooms, sizeable garden with summer bar and barbecue, quaint seaside holiday village with boating lake *(Ann and Colin Hunt, Mrs Romey Heaton, Wendy Dye, Pamela Goodwyn)*

UFFORD [TM2952]

White Lion [Lower St]: Charming unspoilt 16th-c pub tucked away in small village not far from quiet stretch of River Deben, good value home cooking from sandwiches to steaks, Adnams tapped from the cask, good log fire in central fireplace, flagstone floors, friendly service, no music *(Brian and Pam Lamb)*

WESTLETON [TM4469]

☆ *Crown* [B1125 Blythburgh—Leiston]: Extended coaching inn with enjoyable unpretentious bar lunches, some nice old settles and a big log fire, Adnams, Greene King IPA and Abbot and local guest beers, dozens of malt whiskies, carefully chosen wine list, traditional games, carpeted no smoking dining conservatory; piped music; charmingly landscaped gardens with pets corner, good walks nearby *(LYM, Ian Phillips, Neil Powell, J F M and M West, David and Gilly Wilkins, Michael and Ann Cole, Mr and Mrs W D Borthwick, Roy and Lindsey Fentiman, DF, NF, B and M Kendall, Steve and Liz Tilley, Comus and Sarah Elliott, Sir Clive Rose)*

☆ *White Horse* [Darsham Rd, off B1125 Blythburgh—Leiston]: Less smart and cheaper than the Crown, friendly village pub with generous straightforward food (not winter Tues) inc good value sandwiches and OAP bargain lunch in unassuming high-ceilinged bar and attractive no smoking Victorian back dining room; agreeably busy décor, well kept Adnams Bitter and Broadside and seasonal ales, friendly service; quiet piped music, awkward steps down to picnic-sets in cottagey back garden with climbing frame, more out by village duckpond; children in eating area, bedrooms *(June and Perry Dann, George Atkinson, R K Williamson)*

WOODBRIDGE [TM2749]

Bull [Market Hill]: Neatly kept and attractive 16th-c inn with front blinds and window boxes, cosy little bar and other small beamed rooms, wide choice of good food (not cheap but good value), well kept Adnams ales, accommodating landlady and friendly staff; small but comfortable bedrooms, good breakfast *(Klaus and Elizabeth Leist, Keith Reeve, Marie Hammond)*

☆ *Kings Head* [Market Hill]: Handsome Elizabethan beams, flagstones and timbering in nicely opened up town bar, log fire in massive central chimney-breast, good mix of seating and of tables of all sizes, enterprising food from sandwiches up inc lots of fish and other local ingredients in bar and dining room down a couple of steps, well kept Adnams Bitter and Best and Marstons Pedigree, efficient service, some nice local pictures; unobtrusive piped pop music, fruit machine; picnic-sets outside *(Pat and Tony Martin, Gill Pennington, BB, George Atkinson)*

Old Mariner [New St]: Unpretentious olde-worlde pub with good value home cooking, well kept Adnams, good staff; jazz and folk Thurs; tables out behind *(Tony Middis)*

Olde Bell & Steelyard [New St, off Market Sq]: Unusual and unpretentious olde-worlde pub, steelyard still overhanging the street, good friendly mix of drinking and dining in bar, well kept Greene King, short but varied blackboard choice of home-made food from good filled baguettes to local fish, good service *(DF, NF)*

WORLINGWORTH [TM2267]

Swan [Swan Rd]: Cheerful character pub with enjoyable generous food, well kept Adnams tapped from the cask, good wines by the glass, welcoming service; garden tables *(J F M and M West)*

YOXFORD [TM3968]

☆ *Griffin* [High St]: Friendly 14th-c local with good cosy and pleasantly unsmart atmosphere, log fires, good value generous food using local supplies inc generous bargain lunch and children's, well kept Adnams and changing guest beers such as Caledonian Deuchars IPA, decent reasonably priced wines, attentive staff, medieval feasts in log-fire restaurant decorated to match; notable music nights, quiz night Thurs, two pub cats; comfortable beamed bedrooms, good breakfast *(June and Perry Dann, Comus and Sarah Elliott, John Cooke)*

Post Office address codings confusingly give the impression that some pubs are in Suffolk when they're really in Norfolk or Cambridgeshire (which is where we list them).

Surrey

Pubs on top form here this year are the warmly friendly Plough at Blackbrook (enjoyable food, a fine choice of wines by the glass), the attractive old Cricketers nicely placed just outside Cobham, the civilised Withies at Compton (not cheap, but thoroughly rewarding), the Plough at Leigh (lots of pub games as well as its wide food choice), the Hare & Hounds in Lingfield (nice to find such good food in such an unpretentious local – it gains its Food Award this year), and the Inn at West End (this friendly trendily updated place also gains its Food Award now). Joining these are some appealing new entries (or pubs back in the Guide after a break): the Prince Albert in Bletchingley (rambling rooms and a nice little garden), the welcoming Plough in fine walking country at Coldharbour (brewing its own beers), the riverside Stag at Eashing (enjoyable food in civilised traditional surroundings), and the attractively placed Running Horses at Mickleham (a good balance between the bustling bar side and the smart restaurant). For a special meal out, the Inn at West End is Surrey Dining Pub of the Year. In the Lucky Dip section at the end of the chapter, pubs to note particularly include the Drummond Arms at Albury, Wishing Well at East Clandon, Fox & Hounds in Englefield Green, Marneys in Esher, Parrot at Forest Green, Fox & Hounds in South Godstone, Barley Mow at Tilford, Rose & Olive Branch in Virginia Water, Old Crown in Weybridge, Wotton Hatch at Wotton and Bat & Ball in Wrecclesham. Drinks prices here are among the highest in the country, with beer vastly more expensive than up in Lancashire, say; a pint costs you more than £2 in even the cheapest of the main entries here. Hogs Back TEA is a good local beer that crops up quite frequently; it stands for Traditional English Ale.

BETCHWORTH TQ2149 Map 3
Dolphin ♀

Turn off A25 W of Reigate opposite B2032 at roundabout, and keep on into The Street

Usually busy with a good mix of locals, walkers and visitors, this surprisingly unspoilt village pub has a lovely welcoming atmosphere. It's best to arrive early, or book a table beforehand if you want to enjoy the generously served, good value bar food, which includes sandwiches (from £2.45), home-made soup (£2.95), ploughman's (from £5.25), very popular breaded plaice and chips (£6.85), beef or vegetable lasagne (£6.95), and steaks (from £9.20), with daily specials such as steak and mushroom pie or smoked haddock and chips (£7.15), and dressed crab salad (£7.75); puddings might be spotted dick or chocolate fudge cake (from £3.15). The homely neatly kept front room has kitchen chairs and plain tables on the 400-year-old scrubbed flagstones, and the carpeted back saloon bar is black-panelled, with robust old-fashioned elm or oak tables. There are three warming fires, a nice chiming longcase clock, silenced fruit machine, darts, shove-ha'penny, cribbage and dominoes. As well as up to 18 wines by the glass, friendly staff serve well kept Youngs Bitter, Special, Waggle Dance and a seasonal guest on handpump. There are some seats in the small laurel-shaded front courtyard, and behind are picnic-sets on a terrace and lawn by the car park, opposite the church. Parking can be very difficult in summer. No children inside. (Recommended by Mike Gorton, Ian Phillips, DWAJ, B and M Kendall, Geoffrey Kemp, M and N Watson, Dennis Jenkin, Mr and Mrs J G Smith, the Didler, Debbie and Neil Hayter)

Youngs ~ Managers George and Rose Campbell ~ Real ale ~ Bar food (12-2.30, 7-10) ~ (01737) 842288 ~ Dogs welcome ~ Open 11-3, 5.30-11; 11-11 Sat; 12-10.30 Sun

BLACKBROOK TQ1846 Map 3
Plough ♀

On by-road E of A24, parallel to it, between Dorking and Newdigate, just N of the turn E to Leigh

With welcoming staff, good food and a flourishing atmosphere, this neatly kept pub is, according to readers, 'the sort of place you don't really want to leave'. Recently refurbished, the no smoking red saloon bar has fresh flowers on its tables and on the window sills of its large windows (which have new green and gold curtains); down some steps, the public bar has brass-topped treadle tables, old saws on the ceiling, and bottles and flat irons. There are tables and chairs on the terrace, and in the secluded garden a children's swiss playhouse is furnished with little tables and chairs. The food might include goats cheese risotto with chargrilled vegetables (£6.25), salmon and dill lasagne or chilli con carne (£7.95), cornish plaice with steamed mussels, cherry tomatoes and ginger (£11.75), herb-crusted best end of lamb (£14.95), and puddings such as chocolate bread and butter pudding or blueberry pancake (£3.75); they hold three or four popular curry evenings a year. Well kept Badger Best, K&B and Tanglefoot, and a guest such as Gribble Fursty Ferret on handpump, 16 wines by the glass, and several ports; shove-ha'penny, and cribbage. The countryside around here is particularly good for colourful spring and summer walks through the oak woods, and in summer, the pub's white frontage is covered in pretty hanging baskets and window boxes. *(Recommended by Colin Draper, Jeff Hollingworth, Gordon Stevenson, B and M Kendall, John Davis, Cathryn and Richard Hicks)*

Badger ~ Tenants Chris and Robin Squire ~ Real ale ~ Bar food (not Mon evening) ~ (01306) 886603 ~ Children welcome ~ Dogs allowed in bar ~ Open 11-2.30(3 Sat), 6-11.30; 12-3, 7-10.30 Sun; closed 25-26 Dec, 1 Jan

BLETCHINGLEY TQ3250 Map 3
Prince Albert

Outwood Lane

Bustling and welcoming local with cheerful, chatty staff and customers. The main bar has a couple of very low bar stools favoured by regulars, a side part with hatch service and some cushioned chairs around tables, half-panelled walls, and a little brick fireplace. To the right of the bar are a couple of charming rooms, one with lovely panelled walls and a step down to a half-panelled one – cushioned dining chairs around straightforward pubby tables, vintage car photographs and pictures, and another tiny brick fireplace. To the left of the bar are several little partitioned off rooms that run into one another, with similar furnishings and décor; the bottom room has a glass cabinet filled with Guinness memorabilia, and a fish tank. Well kept Hop Back Summer Lightning, and Itchen Valley Fagins and Pure Gold on handpump. Decent bar food includes home-made soup (£3.50), filled baguettes (from £3.50), pâté (£3.95), ploughman's (from £3.95), whitebait (£4.65), macaroni cheese or vegetable curry (around £5.50), ham and egg (£5.95), cumberland sausage (£6.25), steak pie (£7.50), and daily specials like prawn salad (£10.50), and skate wings in caper butter (£13.50); piped pop music (can be loud). The back garden (some traffic noise) is pretty with a terraced and a lawned area, lots of plants and trees in pots, flowering borders, and green plastic furniture under cocktail parasols. A couple of benches in front of the pub catch the evening sun. *(Recommended by Mrs Diane Amis, John Branston, Dick and Madeleine Brown, C and G Fraser)*

Free house ~ Licensees Patrick and Cathy Egan ~ Real ale ~ Bar food (12-2.30, 7-9.30(9 Sun evening)) ~ Restaurant ~ (01883) 743257 ~ Children must be over 8 and must be eating ~ Dogs allowed in bar ~ Open 11-3, 6-11; 12-3, 7-10.30 Sun

CHARLESHILL SU8944 Map 2
Donkey

B3001 Milford—Farnham near Tilford; coming from Elstead, turn left as soon as you see pub sign

There's an emphasis on the enjoyable (though not cheap) food at this beamed cottagey pub – 'an excellent lunchtime stop' according to readers. Charming staff serve lunchtime sandwiches (from £3, toasties £3.50), baked potatoes (£5.95), and omelettes (£6.50), as well as soup (£3.75), fresh cornish crab (£6.95), stilton and asparagus pancake (£9.95), tender roast lamb shank with leek and herb mash (£10.50), cajun swordfish with mango salsa (£12.50), and puddings such as home-made summer pudding or banoffi pie (£4.95); delicious chunky chips and tasty vegetables. The bright saloon has lots of polished stirrups, lamps and watering cans on the walls, and prettily cushioned built-in wall benches, while the lounge has a fine high-backed settle, highly polished horsebrasses, and swords on the walls and beams; the dining conservatory is no smoking. All their wines are available by the glass, and you'll also find well kept Greene King IPA, Abbot and Old Speckled Hen on handpump; piped music. The garden is very attractive, with a terrace, plenty of seats, and a wendy house for children; the two friendly donkeys are called Pip and Dusty. *(Recommended by Simon and Sally Small, Mike and Heather Watson, John Evans)*

Greene King ~ Licensees Lee and Helen Francis ~ Real ale ~ Bar food (12-2.30, 7-9) ~ Restaurant ~ (01252) 702124 ~ Children welcome ~ Dogs allowed in bar ~ Open 11.30-2.30, 6-11; 12-10.30 Sun; closed evenings 25-26 Dec

COBHAM TQ1060 Map 3
Cricketers

Downside Common; 3¾ miles from M25 junction 10; A3 towards Cobham, first right on to A245, right at Downside signpost into Downside Bridge Road, follow road into its right fork – away from Cobham Park – at second turn after bridge, then take next left turn into the pub's own lane

If you like salads, you'll be especially happy at this welcoming pub, as they do a tremendous variety from smoked mackerel and coachman's pie (£6.50), and coronation chicken or avocado, tomato and mozzarella (£6.95) to mixed seafood (£7.25). Other enjoyable, freshly prepared bar food, served by cheerful friendly staff, could include vegetable spring rolls and rice or battered cod (£5.95), pork and leek sausages with onion gravy (£6.50), steak, mushroom and Guinness pie (£7.45), and sugar-baked ham with peaches (£8.50); children's menu (£3.95). It's worth arriving early to be sure of a table – especially on Sunday. The roomy open-plan interior has plenty of atmosphere, with a blazing log fire, and crooked standing timbers – creating comfortable spaces – supporting heavy oak beams so low they have crash-pads on them. In places you can see the wide oak ceiling boards and ancient plastering laths. Furnishings are quite simple, and there are horsebrasses and big brass platters on the walls; the stable bar is no smoking. Well kept Fullers London Pride, Greene King Old Speckled Hen, Theakstons Best and Youngs on handpump, and several wines by the glass; piped music. Tables in the delightful neatly kept garden (with standard roses, dahlias, bedding plants, urns and hanging baskets) have views over the village green. *(Recommended by Dr P J W Young, Mrs Angela Bromley-Martin, Ian Phillips, Kevin Williams, Gee Cormack, Mrs Suzy Miller, Mrs Sally Lloyd, Geoffrey Kemp, Mike and Heather Watson, Colin Draper, Gerry and Rosemary Dobson)*

Inntrepreneur ~ Tenant Wendy Luxford ~ Real ale ~ Bar food (12-2, 6.30-10) ~ Restaurant ~ (01932) 862105 ~ Children in restaurant and family room ~ Dogs allowed in bar ~ Open 11-2.30, 6-11; 12-10(7 in winter) Sun

---

If we don't specify bar meal times for a main entry, these are normally 12-2 and 7-9; we do show times if they are markedly different.

COLDHARBOUR TQ1543 Map 3
Plough 🍺 🛏️

Village signposted in the network of small roads around Leith Hill

There are good walks all round this old coaching inn, run by friendly licensees and peacefully set in a hamlet high in the Surrey hills. The two bars (each with lovely open fires) have stripped light beams and timbering in the warm-coloured dark ochre walls, with quite unusual little chairs around the tables in the snug red-carpeted games room on the left (with darts), and little decorative plates on the walls; the one on the right leads through to the no smoking candlelit restaurant. From the pub's own Leith Hill Brewery, they serve Crooked Furrow, Tallywacker, and new Tickety-boo on handpump, along with three or four well kept real ales such as Palmers IPA, Ringwood Old Thumper, Shepherd Neame Spitfire and Timothy Taylors Landlord; also Biddenden farm cider. Enjoyable (though not cheap) lunchtime bar food might include soup (£3.95), ploughman's (£6.50), pork and leek sausages with mash and onion gravy or garlic mushrooms in a puff pastry parcel (£8.95), with evening dishes such as deep-fried goats cheese and pecan with berry jus (£4.95), seared salmon with hollandaise sauce (£12.95), and chargrilled lamb steak with mint jus or rib-eye steak with mushroom and onion compote (£13.95); puddings such as ginger and lemon pudding or poached pear and shortbread biscuit (£4.50). There are picnic-sets by the tubs of flowers in front and in the terraced garden with its fish pond and waterlilies. They've recently refurbished the bedrooms (and lavatories). *(Recommended by A J Longshaw, Kevin Thorpe, Susan and John Douglas, Barry Steele-Perkins, C and R Bromage)*

Own brew ~ Licensees Richard and Anna Abrehart ~ Real ale ~ Bar food (not evenings 26 Dec or 1 Jan) ~ Restaurant ~ (01306) 711793 ~ Children in family room ~ Dogs allowed in bar ~ Open 11.30-11; 12-10.30 Sun; 11.30(12 Sun)-3, 6-11(10.30 Sun) winter ~ Bedrooms: £55S/£69.50S

COMPTON SU9546 Map 2
Withies

Withies Lane; pub signposted from B3000

This popular and very civilised 16th-c pub is a pleasant walk down the lane from Polsted Manor and Loseley Park. The immaculate garden, overhung with weeping willows, has tables under an arbour of creeper-hung trellises (part of the restaurant), more on a crazy-paved terrace, and others under old apple trees. It's very attractive inside too, with low beams in the little bar, some fine 17th-c carved panels between the windows, and a splendidly art nouveau settle among the old sewing-machine tables; you'll find a good log fire in a massive inglenook fireplace. They do good straightforward pubby bar food such as soup (£3.75), filled baked potatoes (from £4), smoked salmon pâté (£4.25), sandwiches (from £4.25), ploughman's (from £4.75), cumberland sausages with mash and onion gravy (£5.25), and seafood platter (£9.50), as well as a more elaborate (and more expensive) restaurant menu, which is very popular with a well heeled local set. Even when it's busy, the pleasant uniformed staff remain helpful and efficient. Badger K&B, Fullers London Pride, Greene King IPA and Hogs Back TEA are well kept on handpump. The neat lawn in front of the steeply tiled white house is bordered by masses of flowers. *(Recommended by Mrs M Jagger, John Davis, Ian Phillips, John and Judy Saville, Debbie and Neil Hayter, John Evans, Martin and Karen Wake, Susan and John Douglas, John Braine-Hartnell, Kevin Williams, Gee Cormack)*

Free house ~ Licensees Brian and Hugh Thomas ~ Real ale ~ Bar food (12-2.30, 7-10) ~ Restaurant ~ (01483) 421158 ~ Children welcome ~ Open 11-3, 6-11; 12-3 Sun; closed Sun evening

EASHING SU9543 Map 2

Stag

Lower Eashing; Eashing signposted off A3 southbound, S of Hurtmore turn off; or pub
signposted off A283 just SE of exit roundabout at N end of A3 Milford bypass

Tucked down a narrow lane, this attractive pub has a Georgian brick façade, but
dates back in part to the 15th c. It is opened up inside, with a charming old-
fashioned bar on the right: red and black flooring tiles by the counter, which has
well kept Courage Best, Fullers London Pride and Shepherd Neame Spitfire on
handpump, about 15 wines by the glass and good coffee; then a cosy gently lit
room beyond with a low white plank ceiling, a big stag print and stag's head on the
dark-wallpapered walls, some cookery books on shelves by the log fire, and sturdy
cushioned housekeeper's chairs grouped around dark tables on the brick floor. An
extensive blue-carpeted area rambles around on the left, with similar comfortable
dark furniture, some smaller country prints and decorative plates on pink
Anaglypta walls, and round towards the back a big woodburning stove in a
capacious fireplace under a long mantelbeam. It's all rather smart yet cosily
traditional, the thriving atmosphere helped along by attentive and chatty neatly
dressed staff; there is a table of conservative daily papers, and they are kind to
visiting dogs. Lunchtime and early evening bar snacks include open ciabatta
sandwiches (from £5.50) and burgers (£8.95), while a big blackboard lists food
such as mozzarella salad (£6.25), chicken curry (£8.25), seafood poached in dill
sauce or pork loin with apple and stilton glaze (£11.75), puddings such as lemon
cheesecake with berry fruits or sticky toffee pudding (£3.75). A millstream runs
past the garden, which has picnic-sets and other tables under cocktail parasols
among mature trees, and a terrace with some teak furniture, and more picnic-sets in
a lantern-lit arbour. We look forward to hearing from any readers who have stayed
in one of the three bedrooms. *(Recommended by Susan and John Douglas, Vicky Whitfield,
Ian Phillips, Ann and Colin Hunt, Carlos Acuna, Sally Waterfall)*

*Punch ~ Lease Marilyn Lackey ~ Real ale ~ Bar food (12-2.30(3 Sun), 6-9.30; not Sun/
Mon evenings) ~ Restaurant ~ (01483) 421568 ~ Children welcome away from bar ~
Dogs welcome ~ Open 11-11; 12-10.30 Sun; closed 25 Dec ~ Bedrooms: £40B/£55B*

LEIGH TQ2246 Map 3

Plough

3 miles S of A25 Dorking—Reigate, signposted from Betchworth (which itself is signposted
off the main road); also signposted from South Park area of Reigate; on village green

Picnic-sets under cocktail parasols in a pretty side garden (fairy-lit in the evening), and
colourful hanging baskets make this tiled and weatherboarded cottage especially
pleasant in summer. Notices warn you not to bump your head on the very low beams
in the cosy timbered dining lounge, which is decorated with lots of local prints on
white walls, and is on the right as you go in. On the left, a simpler more local pubby
bar has a good bow window seat, lots of different games including darts, shove-
ha'penny, dominoes, table skittles, cribbage, Jenga, backgammon and shut-the-box;
there's also piped music, an alcove fruit machine and occasional TV. Well kept real
ales are Badger Best, Tanglefoot, Sussex, and a guest such as Gribble Fursty Ferret on
handpump, and you can have a glass of anything on the decent wine list. The wide-
ranging menu includes snacks such as soup (£3.95), a big selection of sandwiches
(from £3.95), baked potatoes (from £4.50), and ploughman's (from £5.95), along
with creamy garlic mushrooms (£4.75), smoked haddock fillet mornay, roasted
vegetable mexican-style tortilla wrap or bacon wrapped chicken (£9.95), and steaks
(from £12.95), with puddings such as pavlova or apple pie (from £3.75); you may
need to book at the weekend. The pub is attractively placed by the village green;
nearby parking is limited. *(Recommended by M G Hart, Michael Butler, Mike Snelgrove,
Ian Phillips, B and M Kendall, David Twitchett, John Davis)*

*Badger ~ Tenant Sarah Bloomfield ~ Real ale ~ Bar food (12-10(9.30 Sun)) ~
Restaurant ~ (01306) 611348 ~ Children in eating area of bar and restaurant ~
Dogs allowed in bar ~ Open 11-11; 12-10.30 Sun*

LINGFIELD TQ3844 Map 3
Hare & Hounds ⑪ ◖

Turn off B2029 N at Crowhurst, Edenbridge signpost, into Lingfield Common Road

They make their own soda bread, ice cream and pasta at this country local, popular with readers for its very well prepared food, and relaxed atmosphere. The smallish open-plan bar, light and airy by day, has soft lighting and nightlights burning on a good mix of different-sized tables at night – when it's full of the chatter of happy customers, some drinking, some eating, all mixing comfortably. Partly bare boards and partly flagstones, it has an eclectic variety of scatter-cushioned dining chairs and other seats from pews to a button-back leather chesterfield, black and white pictures of jazz musicians on brown tongue-and-groove panelling, and perhaps unobtrusive piped jazz. It opens into a quieter dining area with big abstract-expressionist paintings. Well presented, daily changing bar food (with an interesting twist on trusted favourites) might include excellent cumberland sausage with cheddar mash or tagliatelle with field mushrooms and olive tapenade (£7.50), chargrilled pork chump with spring onion mash and mustard and cider sauce (£8.50), bacon-wrapped haddock with sautéed potatoes and pea cream or fried salmon with sweet potato, bok choy, crab, lemon grass and coconut bisque (£8.95), and sirloin steak with fried potato cake and shallot and field mushroom tarte tatin (£12.50); the puddings are light and delicious. Friendly efficient staff serve well kept Flowers Original, Greene King IPA and Old Speckled Hen on handpump, and they have decent wines. There are tables out in a pleasant split-level garden, some on decking. This is good walking country near Haxted Mill; walkers can leave their boots in the porch, guarded by a life-size great dane statue. They hold Irish theme nights around every two months. *(Recommended by Dennis Le Couilliard, B and M Kendall, Mrs Sheena Killick, Derek Thomas, Jill Dyer, Cathryn and Richard Hicks, W W Burke)*

Pubmaster ~ Lease Fergus Greer ~ Real ale ~ Bar food (12-2.30, 7-9.30; not Sun evening) ~ Restaurant ~ (01342) 832351 ~ Well behaved children welcome ~ Dogs allowed in bar ~ Open 11-11; 12-10.30 Sun

MICKLEHAM TQ1753 Map 3
King William IV ⑪ ◖

Byttom Hill; short but narrow steep track up hill just off A24 Leatherhead—Dorking by partly green-painted restaurant – public car park down here is best place to park; OS Sheet 187 map reference 173538

This creeper-covered brick pub is cut into the steep hillside, and the snug plank-panelled front bar gives panoramic views over pretty Surrey countryside. The more spacious back bar is quite brightly lit, with kitchen-type chairs around its cast-iron-framed tables, log fires, fresh flowers on all the tables, and a serviceable grandfather clock. There's a friendly atmosphere throughout. It does get busy in summer (when you may have to queue to place your order, but service should be quick enough after that), and they don't take bookings – so you will need to get here early to secure a table. Very enjoyable bar food in huge helpings might include soup (£3.50), stilton and leek baked mushrooms (£3.95), ploughman's (£5.95), filled baked potatoes (from £5.95), steak, mushroom and Guinness pie (£8.95), thai marinated chargrilled salmon with stir-fried vegetables and pak choi (£10.50), fried calves liver with sage and garlic butter (£11.75), and cajun-style rump steak with red onion and mango marmalade (£12.75), with puddings such as hot chocolate fudge cake or treacle, ginger and apple tart (£3.95); the choice is more limited on Sundays and bank holidays, and they don't do sandwiches on weekends. Very well kept Adnams Best, Badger Best, Hogs Back TEA and a monthly changing guest such as Ringwood Fortyniner on handpump; light piped music. The lovely terraced garden at the back is neatly filled with sweet peas, climbing roses and honeysuckle, and plenty of tables (some in an extended open-sided wooden shelter with gas heaters) have good views. A path leads from the garden straight up through woods behind. Parking can be difficult on the lane, so you may have a character-forming walk up from the public car park. *(Recommended by Derek and Sylvia Stephenson, Mr and Mrs Gordon Turner, B and M Kendall, Rosemary and Tom Hall, John and Angela Main, Sarah Davis, Rod Lambert, A Sadler, Christopher and Elise Way, Ron and Sheila Corbett, Ian Jones, John Davis, Joyce and Geoff Robson, Peter Saville, John and Joan Nash, Mrs J R Sillitoe, Paul Boot, Ian Phillips, C and R Bromage)*

Free house ~ Licensees Chris and Jenny Grist ~ Real ale ~ Bar food (12-2, 7-9.30; 12-5 Sun) ~ (01372) 372590 ~ Open 11-3, 6-11; 12-10.30 Sun; closed 25 Dec

Running Horses ♀

Old London Road (B2209)

Our inspection here coincided with one of those rare balmy summer evenings, and most customers were very much enjoying sitting out at the picnic-sets in front of this attractive white painted substantial inn with its big sash windows, and lovely flowering tubs and hanging baskets; the old church with its strange stubby steeple is just across the quiet lane. Inside, the two neatly kept rooms of the bar are more or less open plan with fresh flowers (in summer) in an inglenook at one end, cushioned wall settles and a couple of high-backed ones, Rexine brass-studded bucket seats and other dining chairs around straightforward pubby tables, bar stools, lots of race tickets hanging from a beam, some really good racing cartoons and hunting pictures, and an informal, relaxed atmosphere. Well kept Adnams, Fullers London Pride, Greene King Abbot, and Youngs on handpump, and good, if pricy wines by the glass, from a serious list. As well as bar food such as soup (£3.95), lunchtime chunky sandwiches (from £4.25), ciabatta toasties like seared chicken with coriander and lime, focaccia with parma ham and balsamic olive salad or caesar salad (£6.50), a pair of fishcakes or farmhouse platter (£6.75), mussels and fries (£7.95), and rustic continental hors d'oeuvres (£8.95), you can choose from the restaurant menu and eat in the bar: seared goats cheese with tapenade crust with parsnip and potato rösti and basil dressed mizuna (£5.95), duck liver and foie gras parfait with white grape chutney (£6.25), lovely seared scallops on celeriac cream purée (£7.25), baby vegetable ratatouille tart (£10.95), steak, Guinness and mushroom pudding (£11.50), breast of cajun chicken on a spicy coconut and vegetable gumbo (£12.95), steaks (from £15.25), and fillet of bass with an apricot and honey dressing and topped with crispy seaweed (£18.75). The restaurant area leads straight out of the bar and although it is set out quite formally with crisp white cloths and candles on each table, it shares the thriving atmosphere of the bar; piped music and professional, bow-tied staff, several from abroad. *(Recommended by Susan and John Douglas, Howard Dell, Thomas Neate, Gerald Wilkinson, Stephen and Judy Parish)*

Free house ~ Licensees Steve and Josie Slayford ~ Real ale ~ Bar food (12-2.30(3 Sat and Sun), 7-9.30(9 Sun)) ~ Restaurant ~ (01372) 372279 ~ Children in function room only ~ Dogs allowed in bar ~ Open 11.30-11; 12-10.30 Sun ~ Bedrooms: £94B/£105.75B

NEWDIGATE TQ2043 Map 3

Surrey Oaks ◀

Off A24 S of Dorking, via Beare Green; Parkgate Road

Once a wheelwright's cottage, this small, civilised country pub serves two interesting guest beers from microbreweries such as Bank Top and Dark Star alongside well kept Adnams Southwold and Harveys Sussex Best on handpump; they also do belgian beers and farm cider. The pub is interestingly divided into four areas; in the older part locals gather by a coal-effect gas fire in a snug little beamed room, and a standing area with unusually large flagstones has a woodburning stove in an inglenook fireplace. Rustic tables are dotted around the light and airy main lounge to the left, and there's a pool table in the separate games room; fruit machine, TV, and piped classical music. The atmosphere is pubby, and families feel particularly welcome here. The pleasant and quite elaborate garden has a terrace, and a rockery with pools and a waterfall – the play area, two goats and aviary help keep children amused. Reasonably priced bar food includes filled baguettes (from £4), ploughman's (from £5), ham, eggs and chips or battered cod (£6.50), with specials such as home-made chicken and ham or steak and ale pie, and a fish dish such as red mullet or bass (all £8.50), and rib-eye steak (£11); children's meals (£5). *(Recommended by M Blatchly, Mary and Dan Robinson, Hugh Roberts, Mike Gorton, C and R Bromage, Kevin Thorpe, DWAJ, Jenny and Brian Seller, Ian Phillips)*

Punch ~ Lease Ken Proctor ~ Real ale ~ Bar food (not Sun and Mon evenings) ~ Restaurant ~ (01306) 631200 ~ Children welcome ~ Dogs allowed in bar ~ Open 11.30-2.30, 5.30-11; 11.30-3, 6-11 Sat; 12-3, 7-10.30 Sun

PIRBRIGHT SU9454 Map 2
Royal Oak 🍺
Aldershot Road; A324S of village

No piped music or noisy games machines spoil the relaxed pubby atmosphere in this lovely old Tudor cottage, where you'll find up to 10 real ales superbly kept on handpump. Alongside Flowers IPA and Original and Hogs Back TEA, they serve changing guests such as Batemans Godivas Gold, Fullers Chiswick, Hook Norton First Light, Orkney Dark Island, St Austell Tribute and Youngs Waggle Dance; they also have a good range of wines by the glass and bottle. The series of heavily beamed and timbered rambling snug side alcoves have ancient stripped brickwork, and brasses gleam around the three real fires; furnishings include wheelback chairs, tapestried wall seats, and little dark church-like pews around the trim tables. A bar extension overlooks the pretty flower-filled back garden, and joins the no smoking dining area. The licensees are friendly and cheerful. Reasonably priced bar food includes sandwiches (from £2.95), baguettes (from £3.75), sausage and mash (£5.95), chicken arrabiata (£7.25), chicken breast with bacon and cheese and mushroom sauce (£8.45), rump steak (£8.95), and specials such as lamb shank or steak and dumplings (£8.95), with puddings such as apple and blackberry crumble or sticky toffee pudding (£3.45). The front gardens are very colourful, and look particularly attractive on fine evenings when the fairy lights are switched on. The big back garden leads down to a stream, and is less affected by noise from passing traffic. They have a disabled lavatory. Good walks lead off in all directions. *(Recommended by KC, Stephen Kiley, Mr and Mrs S Felstead, Mr and Mrs A Swainson, LM, Simon Collett-Jones)*

Laurel Pub Company ~ Managers Julia and Geoff Middleton ~ Real ale ~ Bar food (12-2, 6.30-9(8.30 Sun)) ~ (01483) 232466 ~ Children in family room ~ Open 11-11; 12-10.30 Sun; closed 25 Dec evening

REIGATE HEATH TQ2349 Map 3
Skimmington Castle
3 miles from M25 junction 8: through Reigate take A25 towards Dorking, then on edge of Reigate turn left past Black Horse into Flanchford Road; after ¼ mile turn left into Bonny's Road (unmade, very bumpy track); after crossing golf course fork right up hill

This quaint old country pub is especially nice in fine weather, when you can enjoy the lovely views from the crazy-paved front terrace and tables on the grass by lilac bushes; more tables at the back overlook the meadows and the hillocks (though you may find the views blocked by trees in summer). The bar food is good and popular, so you need to get here early for a table as they don't take bookings. Swiftly served dishes could include sandwiches (from £2.85), soup (£3.25), ploughman's (from £4.50), tortilla (£6.50), tasty home-made fish pie (£6.95), fresh cajun salmon (£7.50), pork medallions in garlic and mushroom sauce (£8.50), lamb steak with spicy couscous (£8.95), and sirloin steak with pink peppercorn sauce (£10.50), with irresistible puddings (£3.75). The bright main front bar leads off a small room with a central serving counter, with dark simple panelling and lots and lots of keys hanging from the beams. There's a miscellany of chairs and tables, shiny brown plank panelling, a brown plank ceiling, well kept Greene King IPA and Old Speckled Hen, Youngs Special and a guest such as Charles Wells Bombardier on handpump, with several wines by the glass, farm cider and even some organic spirits. The cosy back rooms are partly panelled too, with old-fashioned settles and windsor chairs; one has a big brick fireplace with its bread-oven still beside it – the chimney is said to have been used as a highwayman's look-out. Steps take you down to just three tables in a small but pleasant no-smoking room at the back; shove-ha'penny, cribbage, dominoes, ring the bull, board games, and piped music. Remotely placed up a bumpy track, the pub is handy for rambles on the North Downs; there's a hitching rail outside for horses. No children. *(Recommended by J F M and M West, B and M Kendall, Ian Phillips, Gordon Stevenson, R Marshall, Geoffrey Kemp, Joy and Peter Heatherley, C and R Bromage, Derek and Maggie Washington)*

Pubmaster ~ Tenants Anthony Pugh and John Davidson ~ Real ale ~ Bar food (12-2.15(2.30 Sun), 7-9) ~ (01737) 243100 ~ Dogs welcome ~ Open 11-3, 5.30(6 Sat)-11; 12-10.30 Sun; closed evenings 25-27 Dec and 1 Jan

WEST END SU9461 Map 2

Inn at West End 🍴 ♀

Just under 2½ miles from M3 junction 3; A322 S, on right

Surrey Dining Pub of the Year

They hold regular wine tastings at this roadside pub (the landlord is a wine merchant), as well as other special events such as golf days, portuguese evenings and quiz nights. There's an emphasis on the good (though not cheap) food, which could include lunchtime sandwiches (from £5), smoked haddock kedgeree with poached egg (£6.75; £11 main), moules à la crème (£7; £11 main), smoked salmon and scrambled eggs (£7.95), cumberland sausages with spinach and mash (£11), goats cheese parcel with spinach and tomato coulis (£12.50), and pork loin with onion and sage sauce (£14), with home-made puddings such as crème brûlée and spiced apple crumble (£4.50); they do a good value two-course lunch (£16.50). The licensees are helpful, and the staff are friendly and efficient. Appealingly up-to-date, the pub is open-plan, with bare boards, attractive modern prints on canary yellow walls above a red dado, and a line of dining tables with crisp white linen over pale yellow tablecloths on the left. The bar counter, straight ahead as you come in, is quite a focus, with chatting regulars on the comfortable bar stools, well kept Courage Best and Fullers London Pride on handpump, good house wines including good value champagne by the glass (they can also supply by the case), seasonal drinks such as Pimms, bucks fizz and kir royale, and good coffee. The area on the right has a pleasant relaxed atmosphere, with blue-cushioned wall benches and dining chairs around solid pale wood tables, broadsheet daily papers, magazines and a row of reference books on the brick chimneybreast above a woodburning stove. This opens into a terracotta-tiled garden room, with a blue overhead awning, which in turn leads into the attractive garden, where paths wind between flowering shrubs to groups of picnic-sets under cocktail parasols on several areas of neat lawn. They've recently enlarged the car park, added a boules pitch and terrace for dining. *(Recommended by Andrea and Shirley Mackenzie, Martin and Karen Wake, S F Parrinder, Dr Martin Owton, Ian Phillips, Nigel and Sue Foster, Guy Consterdine, Susan and John Douglas)*

Free house ~ Licensees Gerry and Ann Price ~ Real ale ~ Bar food (12-2.30, 6-9.30) ~ Restaurant ~ (01276) 858652 ~ Well behaved children welcome in restaurant if eating ~ Dogs allowed in bar ~ Open 12-3, 5-11; 12-11 Sat; 12-10.30 Sun

---

Post Office address codings confusingly give the impression that some pubs are in Surrey when they're really in Hampshire or London (which is where we list them). And there's further confusion from the way the Post Office still talks about Middlesex – which disappeared in 1965 local government reorganisation.

Lucky Dip

Besides the fully inspected pubs, you might like to try these Lucky Dips recommended to us and described by readers (if you do, please send us reports: www.goodguides.com).

ABINGER COMMON [TQ1146]
☆ *Abinger Hatch* [off A25 W of Dorking, towards Abinger Hammer]: Beautifully placed pub under new management, heavy beams, flagstones, log fires, pews forming booths around oak tables in carpeted side area, popular food (not Sun evening), around five real ales; piped music, children now allowed only in extension; nr pretty church and pond in clearing of rolling woods, tables and friendly ducks in nice garden, summer barbecues, open all day (*Ian Phillips, Ian and Barbara Rankin, LYM, Dick and Madeleine Brown*)

ALBURY [TQ0547]
☆ *Drummond Arms* [off A248 SE of Guildford; The Street]: Comfortable and civilised panelled alcovey bar, attractive dining room, conservatory (children allowed here) overlooking pretty streamside back garden with duck island, tables by willows, fountain, covered terrace and barbecue, some emphasis on enjoyable food, well kept ales such as Brakspears, Courage Best, Gales HSB and Greene King Old Speckled Hen, attentive helpful staff; piped music; bedrooms, attractive village, pleasant walks nearby (*LYM, Barry Fenton, Ian Phillips*)

ALBURY HEATH [TQ0646]
William IV [Little London, off A25 Guildford—Dorking – OS Sheet 187 map ref 065468]: Bustling local and walkers' pub, rustic low-beamed flagstoned bar with big log fire, enjoyable sensibly priced food from sandwiches up, well kept local Hogs Back real ales, simple café-style dining area, close-packed tables in upstairs restaurant, shove-ha'penny and cards; children welcome, tables in pretty front garden (*LYM, Jenny and Brian Seller*)

ALFOLD [TQ0435]
Alfold Barn [Horsham Rd]: Handsomely raftered dining pub with good choice of generous good value food inc fish, venison and Sun roasts, good service (*Sheena Baker*)

BETCHWORTH [TQ2150]
Red Lion [Old Rd, Buckland]: Light and airy dining pub under newish management, steps down to stylish long flagstoned room and no smoking rather tuscan-seeming candlelit dining room, modern furnishings, well kept Adnams Broadside and up to three guest beers, bar food from lunchtime sandwiches to rather ambitious dishes; may be piped pop music; children welcome, picnic-sets on lawn with play area and cricket ground beyond, dining terrace, bedroom block, open all day (*LYM, Mrs G R Sharman, Cathryn and Richard Hicks*)

BLETCHINGLEY [TQ3251]
William IV [3 miles from M25 junction 6; Little Common Lane, off A25 on Redhill side of village]: Quaint old country pub down pretty lane, tile-hung and weatherboarded, three bar rooms and comfortable little back no smoking dining room, wide choice of food from sandwiches and baguettes up (extended

hours Sun) and of well kept ales such as Fullers London Pride, Greene King Old Speckled Hen, Harveys Best and Youngs Special, good wines, good atmosphere, lots of bric-a-brac, friendly if not always speedy service; two-level garden with summer barbecues (*LYM, Ian Phillips, Debbie and Neil Hayter*)

BRAMLEY [TQ0044]
☆ *Jolly Farmer* [High St]: Welcoming rambling pub, very popular for wide choice of generous fresh food inc some unusual dishes, five changing well kept ales, czech beers on tap, proper coffee, good service by nice staff, two log fires, beer mat and banknote collections, big restaurant; comfortable bedrooms (*Mike and Heather Watson, LYM, Phil and Sally Gorton*)

BROCKHAM [TQ1949]
Dukes Head: Pleasantly old-fashioned and friendly pub in pretty spot by village green, log fire, wide range of enjoyable food, good choice of well kept real ales, helpful friendly new management; children welcome away from bar (*John Branston, Mike Gorton*)

BURGH HEATH [TQ2458]
Heathside [Brighton Rd]: Chain dining pub next to Premier Lodge, wide range of generous well presented food inc good value Sun lunch, friendly service (*R C Vincent*)

BURROWHILL [SU9763]
Four Horseshoes [B383 N of Chobham]: Friendly and well run old-fashioned cottagey local, dark and cool inside on hot days, log fires in both rooms winter, varied good value food all day from sandwiches to popular Sun lunch, well kept Ansells and Brakspears, good service, busy bar, expanded dining room; lots of picnic-sets out overlooking green (some under ancient yew) (*Ian Phillips*)

BYFLEET [TQ0661]
Plough [High Rd]: Medley of furnishings in friendly local with welcoming licensees, attractively priced straightforward food, well kept Courage Best, Fullers London Pride and guests such as Cottage Swift Express, Glastonbury Holy Thorn, Timothy Taylors Dark Mild and Wessex Wylye Warmer, lots of farm tools, brass and copper, log fire, dominoes; picnic-sets in pleasant back garden (*Ian Phillips*)

CAPEL [TQ1740]
Crown [signed off A24 at Beare Green roundabout; The Street]: Pleasantly rustic 16th-c ivy-covered village pub by interesting church, cosy and comfortable beamed and ochre-walled small-roomed areas and partly no smoking restaurant, well kept Marstons Pedigree and a guest such as Daleside Footslogger, friendly staff, generous food inc warm baguettes and pizzas; family room, dogs welcome; piped radio, TV and machines in bare-boards front bar, games room with pool, occasional live music; picnic-sets and play area in big garden, open all day wknds (*Kevin Thorpe*)

CHERTSEY [TQ0466]

Crown [London St (B375)]: Friendly and relaxed Youngs pub with button-back banquettes in spreading traditionally renovated high-ceilinged bar, tall and very sonorous longcase clock, well kept ales, fine choice of wines by the glass, nicely presented no-nonsense food from doorstep sandwiches and baked potatoes up, courteous attentive staff; neatly placed darts, discreet fruit machines; children and dogs welcome, garden bar with conservatory, tables in courtyard and garden with pond; smart 30-bedroom annexe *(Joyce and Maurice Cottrell, A C Nugent)*

Golden Grove [Ruxbury Rd, St Anns Hill (nr Lyne)]: Busy local with low beam and plank ceiling, bare boards and stripped wood, cheap straightforward home-made food from sandwiches up (not Sat-Mon evenings) in pine-tabled eating area, well kept Ind Coope Burton, Fullers London Pride and Tetleys, cheerful service, coal-effect gas fire; piped music, fruit and games machines; big pretty garden with picnic-sets under grape-laden vine, play area, tree-shaded pond *(Ian Phillips)*

CHIDDINGFOLD [SU9635]

Crown [The Green (A283)]: Picturesque old inn in attractive surroundings, well worth a visit for its fine carving, Elizabethan plaster ceilings, massive beams, lovely inglenook log fire and tapestried panelled restaurant with upmarket menu; enjoyable bar food from fresh sandwiches up in simpler side bar, well kept Badger beers; children allowed, tables out on verandah, has been open all day, good bedrooms *(LYM, Gerry and Rosemary Dobson)*

CHIPSTEAD [TQ2757]

Well House [Chipstead signed with Mugswell off A217, N of M25 junction 8]: Partly 14th-c, cottagey and comfortable, with lots of atmosphere, decent straightforward food (not Sun evening, and may take a time) from good value hefty sandwiches up, efficient friendly staff, log fires in all three rooms (one bar is no smoking), well kept Bass and other ales such as Adnams and Fullers London Pride; dogs allowed; attractive garden with well reputed to be mentioned in Domesday Book (loudspeaker food announcements though), delightful setting *(Jim Bush, LYM, Jenny and Brian Seller)*

COBHAM [TQ1059]

☆ *Plough* [Plough Lane, towards Downside]: Cheerful black-shuttered local with comfortably modernised low-beamed lounge bar partly divided by L-shaped settles, huge log fire dividing it from very popular restaurant area, Courage Best and Directors and Charles Wells Bombardier, decent house wines, helpful staff, pine-panelled snug with darts, good choice of good value quickly served lunchtime food from sandwiches up; tables outside *(Ian Phillips, LYM)*

COMPTON [SU9546]

☆ *Harrow* [B3000 towards Godalming off A3]: Pleasant staff in popular upmarket country local, enjoyable though not cheap home-made food, well kept ales such as Greene King IPA, Hogs Back TEA and Youngs Special, good

house wines, farm décor; children welcome, a few picnic-sets outside, open all day, cl Sun evening, bedrooms *(Ian Phillips, Brian and Genie Smart, Darren Le Poidevin, LYM, Jason Reynolds, Mike and Heather Watson)*

COX GREEN [TQ0734]

☆ *Thurlow Arms* [Baynards signposted off A281 W of Rudgwick or B2128 N]: Tucked-away converted station house in peaceful countryside, easy-going bare-boards bar with big windows, lots of interesting railway, farm and more miscellaneous memorabilia and bric-a-brac on walls and high ceilings, back games area with pool, darts and juke box, plush banquettes in side dining lounge, friendly staff, well kept Badger Best, Hogs Back TEA and Ringwood Best and Fortyniner, good if not cheap food, no music, dogs welcome; picnic-sets on lawn by rose trellis, meadow beyond with timber play fort – by former railway, now Downs Link Path; simple bedrooms by prior arrangement *(BB, Shirley Mackenzie)*

EAST CLANDON [TQ0651]

☆ *Wishing Well* [just off A246 Guildford–Leatherhead; The Street]: Rambling dining pub with new licensees doing four blackboards of good value home-made food from good generous baguettes and baked potatoes to low-priced main dishes, comfortable relaxed atmosphere in small spotless connecting rooms, big inglenook log-effect fire, fine old elm bar counter, well kept ales such as Badger K&B, Hogs Back TEA and Youngs, polite efficient service; no dogs, boots or overalls; children welcome, picnic-sets on front terrace and in quiet side garden, handy for two NT properties, cl Mon *(LYM, John Evans, LM, DWAJ, Sue and Mike Todd, Mrs T A Bizat)*

ELSTEAD [SU9043]

Mill: Converted watermill in large grounds, enjoyable food, Fullers ales *(J A Snell)*

☆ *Woolpack* [B3001 Milford–Farnham]: High-backed settles in long airy main bar, open fires each end, second big room, country décor, children allowed, garden with picnic-sets, open all day wknds; has been popular for wide range of enjoyable inventive food, with well kept Fullers London Pride, Greene King Abbot and a guest beer, but changed hands early summer 2003, too late for us to form a view on the new team *(LYM)*

ENGLEFIELD GREEN [SU9971]

Barley Mow [Northcroft Rd]: Pretty pub in nice spot with café tables out in front overlooking cricket green (summer steam fairs); good value food served with a smile, well kept Courage Best and Directors, Fullers London Pride, Greene King Old Speckled Hen and Marstons Pedigree, usual refurbished interior, back dining area with no smoking section, darts, quiet piped music; pleasant back garden with play area *(Roy and Lindsey Fentiman, Ian Phillips)*

☆ *Fox & Hounds* [Bishopsgate Rd; off A328 N of Egham]: Popular pub in good setting on edge of Windsor Great Park, short walk from Savile Garden, tables on pleasant front lawn and back terrace; well kept Brakspears and

Fullers London Pride, good wines by the glass, good if not cheap food from baguettes up in bar and restaurant, polite friendly service, two handsome log fires, daily papers; piped music, no children; open all day wknds and July-Sept, picnic-sets outside, good big new car park *(Martin and Karen Wake, LYM, Ian Phillips)*

Sun [Wick Lane, Bishopsgate]: Unassuming welcoming local, well kept Bass, Courage Directors, Fullers London Pride and Greene King Abbot, good blackboard wine choice, long-serving landlord and efficient young staff, enjoyable food from good sandwiches and baguettes to Sun lunch, reasonable prices, daily papers, roaring log fire in back conservatory, biscuit and water for dogs, interesting beer bottle collection; quiet garden with aviary *(Ian Phillips, LM)*

ESHER [TQ1566]

☆ *Marneys* [Alma Rd, Weston Green]: Attractive low-ceilinged cottagey pub in pleasant spot with plenty of tables out overlooking church, duck pond, green and golf course, well kept Bass, Courage Best and Flowers Original, sensibly small choice of good interesting if not cheap food (not Sun) from baguettes to dishes reflecting Norwegian landlord's national cuisine, small helpings on request, quick service by friendly uniformed staff, family dining area, decent wines; very small – can get crowded *(Martin and Karen Wake, Ian Phillips, Ian Wilson, Nigel Williamson, Alec and Barbara Jones, Ellen Weld, David London)*

Prince of Wales [West End Lane; off A244 towards Hersham, by Princess Alice Hospice]: Popular Victorian Chef & Brewer dining pub, attractive period décor, cosy candlelit corners, open fires, turkey carpets, old furniture, prints and photographs, well kept Courage Best, Fullers London Pride, Theakstons Best and a guest beer such as Brains SA, good wine choice, daily papers; big shady garden, nr green and pond *(Kevin Williams, Gee Cormack, Stuart and Alison Wallace, Gordon Stevenson, Ian Phillips)*

EWHURST [TQ0842]

Windmill [Pitch Hill; 1 mile N towards Shere]: Spectacular views from picnic-sets on spacious series of hillside lawns and from big conservatory restaurant used as lunchtime bar overflow, lovely walking country; food from toasted sandwiches to popular Sun lunch, well kept Courage Best, Fullers London Pride and Greene King IPA and Old Speckled Hen, central log fire, books and newspapers, bare-boards country décor with big old sofas, large tables, plates and pitchforks on the walls, ceiling hung with lamps and blow-torches, friendly dog; occasional live music, open all day *(Susan and John Douglas, Ian Phillips, Mike and Lynn Robinson, LYM)*

FARLEIGH [TQ3659]

☆ *Harrow* [Farleigh Common, off B269 Limpsfield—Warlingham]: Big welcoming Vintage Inn, busy lunchtimes even midweek (get there early Sun for a table), reliably enjoyable food from sandwiches up, well kept Bass and lots of wines by the glass from large

horseshoe bar, well trained staff, several rooms inc large no smoking area, old farm tools and machinery; plenty of tables outside *(Jim Bush, Jenny and Brian Seller)*

FARNHAM [SU8742]

Duke of Cambridge [Tilford Woods, Tilford Road]: Very rural, with good play area in long tree-shaded garden, picnic-sets on high grassy terrace at one end – so you can keep an eye on the children – pleasant country views; tidy and neatly but cosily renovated inside, with mix of chairs around pine tables, enjoyable food from sandwiches and ciabattas to traditional and more exotic main dishes, well kept beers *(Malcolm Sutcliffe)*

Fox [Frensham Rd, Lower Bourne]: Cheery staff, real ales such as Batemans XXXB, Caledonian 80/- and Greene King IPA and Abbot, good value wines, log fire, deep crimson décor with heavy curtains, prints, some stripped brickwork, nice blend of wooden furniture and raised back area; can be smoky; picnic-sets and small adventure playground outside *(Martin and Karen Wake, Ian Phillips)*

Lamb [Abbey St]: Cheerful local with well kept Shepherd Neame tapped from the cask, enjoyable food (not Sun evening), back pool area, busking nights; tables on terrace, open all day Fri-Sun *(Gordon Tebbutt)*

Spotted Cow [Bourne Grove, Lower Bourne (towards Tilford)]: Plain and welcoming country local with good home-made food inc lots of fresh fish, well kept ales such as fff Moondance, attentive friendly service, reasonable prices; play area in big attractive garden, nice surroundings *(Martin and Karen Wake, Ian Phillips)*

FOREST GREEN [TQ12410]

☆ *Parrot* [nr B2126/B2127 junction]: Rambling beamed country pub with attractive furnishings and secluded extended restaurant, a well kept ale brewed for them by Hogs Back and several others such a Courage Directors, Fullers London Pride and Wadworths 6X, good generous food, helpful Scottish landlady and cheerful Australian service, end bar with inglenook log fire, interesting bric-a-brac and pool; piped music; children welcome, open all day; plenty of tables in garden by cricket green, good walks nearby *(LYM, C and R Bromage, Jenny and Brian Seller)*

GODALMING [SU9643]

☆ *Inn on the Lake* [junction Portsmouth Rd (A3100) and Shackstead Lane]: Large pub divided into cosy sections inc comfortable family bar with good value food, well kept real ales inc guest beers, good choice of decent wines, good cheerful service, log fire, elegant restaurant; rather steep car park; tables out in lovely garden overlooking lake, summer barbecues, bedrooms *(Mr and Mrs C H M Brooks)*

GODSTONE [TQ3551]

White Hart [handy for M25 junction 6; High St]: Beefeater in beamed and timbered former coaching inn opp pretty village pond, decent food and service, real ales such as Boddingtons,

Marstons Pedigree and Wadworths 6X
(Ian Phillips, BB, Tony and Wendy Hobden)
GRAYSWOOD [SU9134]
Wheatsheaf [A286 NE of Haslemere]: Civilised
much modernised pub, light and airy, with
enjoyable food in bar and restaurant, good
range of well kept ales such as Ringwood and
Timothy Taylors Landlord, attentive courteous
service; conference/bedroom extension
*(Derek and Margaret Underwood, Phil and
Sally Gorton)*
GUILDFORD [SU9949]
Kings Head [Quarry St]: Wide choice of
seating from spacious banquettes to discreet
snugs, lots of beams and stripped brickwork,
cosy inglenook fire, well kept Courage Best
and Directors and Greene King Old Speckled
Hen, decent wines, reasonably priced standard
food from baguettes and ploughman's up,
polite service; picnic-sets in back courtyard,
heated marquee *(Ian Phillips)*
Olde Ship [Portsmouth Rd (A3100 S)]: Three
cosy areas around central bar, ancient beams,
flagstones, good log fire in big fireplace,
candles and comfortable mix of furniture, no
smoking zone (no mobile phones), part with
tables and chairs, good range of interesting but
unpretentious and fairly priced bistro-style
food inc good pizzas, well kept ales inc Greene
King, decent wines, service quick and friendly
even when busy; no music *(Jane Thompson,
Edward Longley)*
HAMBLEDON [SU9639]
Merry Harriers [off A283]: Homely and
quietly old-fashioned country local popular
with walkers, huge inglenook log fire, dark
wood with cream and terracotta paintwork,
pine tables, impressive collection of chamber-
pots hanging from beams, well kept Greene
King IPA and Abbot, Hogs Back TEA and
Hop Back Crop Circle, farm cider, decent
wines and coffee, daily papers and classic
motorcycle magazines, reasonably priced fresh
simple food from sandwiches up; pool room,
folk night 1st Sun of month; big back garden
in attractive countryside, picnic-sets in front
and over road – caravan parking *(Phil and
Sally Gorton)*
HASCOMBE [TQ0039]
☆ *White Horse* [B2130 S of Godalming]:
Picturesque old rose-draped pub, expensive,
but a favourite of many, in a pretty village on
the Greensand Way; attractively simple
beamed public bar, traditional games and quiet
small-windowed alcoves, more restauranty
dining bar (children allowed), well kept
Adnams and Harveys, good wine list, generally
friendly helpful staff, log fires or woodburners;
small terrace, spacious sloping back lawn,
handy for Winkworth Arboretum, open all day
wknds *(Martin and Karen Wake, John Davis,
David and Higgs Wood, John and Angela
Main, M Blatchly, Peter Meister, John and
Tania Wood, Ian Phillips, LYM, T R and B C
Jenkins, John Hale, Susan and John Douglas)*
HASLEMERE [SU9032]
Swan [High St]: Useful Wetherspoons, with
decent inexpensive food, bargain coffee and

real ales such as Adnams, Hogs Back TEA and
Ringwood Old Thumper; pleasant garden and
terrace behind *(Ian Phillips)*
HERSHAM [TQ1164]
Bricklayers Arms [Queens Rd]: Friendly and
well kept, back servery doing wide choice of
good value home-made food from sandwiches
and snacks up, good choice of ales such as
Flowers IPA and Hogs Back TEA, decent
wines, separate public bar with two pool
tables; parking down by green in Faulkners
Rd; small secluded garden, comfortable
bedrooms *(Phil and Sally Gorton, Ian Phillips)*
HOLMBURY ST MARY [TQ1144]
Kings Head: Bare-boards 70s-feel pub in
popular walking country, well kept Kings Best
and four changing guest beers, local farm cider,
bar food (not Sun evening), friendly staff, two
open fires; piped music, SkyTV, outside
lavatories; pretty spot with seats out facing
village green, more in big informal sloping
back garden, open all day wknds and summer
(Kevin Thorpe)
Royal Oak: Well run and relaxing low-beamed
17th-c coaching inn in pleasant spot by green
and church, generous usual food from
sandwiches and baked potatoes up, good
choice of well kept ales such as Greene King
IPA, decent wines by the glass, quick friendly
service, log fire; tables on front lawn,
bedrooms, good walks *(Mike and
Lynn Robinson, P and J Shapley, Jenny and
Brian Seller, Barry Steele-Perkins)*
HORSELL [SU9959]
Bridge Barn [Bridge Barn Lane]: Whitbreads
Out & Out dining pub in quiet canalside spot
(picnic-sets outside, towpath walks), decent
food all day in bar and upstairs raftered
restaurant, both divided by beams and
standing timbers, lots of friendly staff, some
sofas and armchairs; piped music may be loud,
keg beer; bedrooms in adjacent Travel Inn
(B and K Hypher)
Cricketers [Horsell Birch]: Friendly local with
long neatly kept bar, comfortable and quieter
end sections, extended back eating area,
carpet and shiny boards, good choice of
straightforward food (all day Sun and bank
hols), Courage Best, Flowers IPA, Fullers
London Pride, Shepherd Neame Spitfire and
perhaps Greene King Old Speckled Hen,
cheerful service, children well catered for; can
be crowded and a bit smoky evenings, with
thumpy music; big well kept garden, and seats
out in front overlooking village green *(Ian
Phillips)*
Red Lion [High St]: Welcoming comfortably
renovated pub with good food, well kept
Courage Best and Fullers London Pride, decent
wines, friendly staff, picture-filled converted
barn where children allowed; pleasant terrace,
good walks nearby *(Ian Phillips)*
IRONS BOTTOM [TQ2546]
Three Horseshoes [Sidlow Bridge, off A217]:
Friendly recently extended country pub with
attractively priced carefully made food inc
some interesting specials, well kept Fullers
London Pride and guest beers, thoughtful

service; quiz or darts night Tues, summer barbecues *(C and R Bromage, Brian Root)*

KNAPHILL [SU9658]

Royal Oak [Anchor Hill]: Welcoming young licensees, plenty of atmosphere, pig and poultry pictures, Courage Best, Fullers London Pride and Shepherd Neame Spitfire, enjoyable food from sandwiches, pittas and baked potatoes to dressed crab, thai stir fry and beef wellington, small restaurant area; no babies *(Ian Phillips)*

LALEHAM [TQ0568]

☆ *Anglers Retreat* [B376 (Staines Rd)]: Big well appointed family pub, pale panelling, big tropical aquarium set into wall, even larger one in smart no smoking restaurant area extended into conservatory, wide choice of food (all day wknds) inc lots of fresh fish, two bright coal fires, Brakspears and a guest beer, decent wines; Sun quiz night, unobtrusive piped music, fruit machine, no dogs; children welcome, seats out in front, play area in back garden, open all day *(John and Glenys Wheeler, Tom McLean, Mr and Mrs S Felstead, LYM, Evelyn and Derek Walter, Susan and John Douglas)*

Feathers [Broadway]: Roomy old local with friendly new management, traditional décor, lots of hanging pewter mugs, well kept real ales, enjoyable food in beamed back dining area with evening roaring log fire; children welcome (dogs too when food not being served); small terrace and garden *(Mayur Shah, Jean Barnett, David Lewis)*

☆ *Three Horseshoes* [B376 (Shepperton Rd)]: Flagstones, heavy beams and interesting history, given welcoming feel by soft lighting and attractively fresh refurbishment, cosy relaxing areas with comfortable sofas and intimate corners off central serving area, wide choice of enjoyable food, well kept real ales, good service, daily papers, fairy-lit dining area and big no smoking conservatory; lots of picnic-sets on terrace, open all day *(LYM, Mayur Shah, Jim Bush, Susan and John Douglas)*

MARTYRS GREEN [TQ0857]

Black Swan [handy for M25 junction 10; off A3 S-bound, but return N of junction]: Extensively enlarged, with a dozen or more well kept ales inc bargains, simple furnishings, well worn back bar, SkyTV, usual food (queue to order), friendly staff, log fires, restaurant; can get crowded with young people evenings, piped pop music may be loud then, frequent discos and theme nights; plenty of tables in big woodside garden with barbecues and good play area – bouncy castle, playground-quality frames, roundabouts etc; dogs welcome, handy for RHS Wisley Garden, open all day *(A C Nugent, Jason Reynolds)*

MOGADOR [TQ2453]

Sportsman [from M25 up A217 past 2nd roundabout, then Mogador signed; edge of Banstead Heath]: Interesting and welcoming low-ceilinged local, quietly placed on Walton Heath, a magnet for walkers and riders; well kept ales, enjoyable popular food, dogs welcome if not wet or muddy; tables out on common, on back lawn, and some under cover *(anon)*

NORWOOD HILL [TQ2342]

☆ *Fox Revived* [Leigh—Charlwood back road]: Good interesting food in spacious bare-boards country pub's large and attractive double dining conservatory, cottagey old-fashioned furnishings, well kept Greene King Old Speckled Hen and Marstons Pedigree, decent wines, friendly well organised service, daily papers and magazines, shelves of books, pleasant atmosphere; spreading garden *(Dr and Mrs M E Wilson, LYM)*

OCKHAM [TQ0756]

☆ *Hautboy* [Ockham Lane – towards Cobham]: Remarkable red stone Gothick folly, crypt bar and character upstairs brasserie bar, darkly panelled and high-raftered, with oil paintings and minstrel's gallery, emphasis on imaginative choice of good food from snacks up, friendly efficient service; tables on cricket-view terrace and in secluded orchard garden with play area, chintzy bedrooms *(John Evans, LYM)*

OCKLEY [TQ1440]

Inn on the Green [Billingshurst Rd (A29)]: Pleasantly refurbished open-plan pub on green of attractive village, wide choice of enjoyable food from generous toasted baguettes to restaurant dishes, well kept Greene King IPA, interesting cricket memorabilia, easy chairs and sofa by one fireplace, nice mix of tables in dining area leading to conservatory, picnic-sets in garden, bedrooms *(Mike and Lynn Robinson, BB, Jenny and Brian Seller)*

☆ *Kings Arms* [Stane St (A29)]: Comfortably old-fashioned 17th-c country inn with inglenook log fire, heavy beams and carved woodwork, generous imaginative fresh food in bar and small restaurant, well kept real ale inc a seasonal beer, decent wines, good welcoming service; discreetly placed picnic-sets in immaculate big back garden, bedrooms with beautifully fitted bathrooms *(Mike and Heather Watson)*

Old School House [Stane St]: Fine school house attractively converted to popular dining pub, good value generous food from sandwiches up inc fresh pasta and fish, pleasant if not always speedy service, well kept Badger ales, good wines, wonderful log fire; one dog problem reported *(C and R Bromage, Barry Steele-Perkins, Gordon Stevenson, M Blatchly)*

☆ *Punchbowl* [Oakwood Hill, signed off A29 S]: Cosy country pub, smart and clean, with several rooms, huge inglenook log fire, polished flagstones, lots of low beams, well kept Badger Best and Tanglefoot and a Gribble guest, good food choice inc separate sandwich and puddings boards, friendly service and welcoming alsatian, traditional games; children allowed in dining area, picnic-sets on side terrace and in pretty front garden, quiet spot *(LYM, Tony Adlard, John and Elizabeth Cox, C and R Bromage, Jim Bush)*

OTTERSHAW [TQ0263]

Castle [Brox Rd, signed off A320 S]: Comfortable and friendly local, lots of farm tools etc, stripped brick and beamery, log fire; wide range of popular home-made food inc interesting dishes (no smoking dining area), hearty log fire, well kept changing ales such as Adnams, Fullers London Pride, Greene King Abbot, Tetleys and Youngs Special, Addlestone's cider; tables with rustic benches in pleasant creeper-hung booths and on front terrace *(Ian Phillips)*

OUTWOOD [TQ3146]

☆ *Dog & Duck* [Prince of Wales Rd; turn off A23 at Station sign in Salfords, S of Redhill – OS Sheet 187 map ref 312460]: Welcoming rambling beamed country cottage under enthusiastic new landlord, with good mix of furnishings, huge log fires, half a dozen well kept Badger and guest ales, popular food all day, lots of board games etc; children in restaurant, tables outside, open all day *(LYM, Graham Tayar, Brian Root)*

OXTED [TQ4048]

Royal Oak [Caterfield Lane, Staffhurst Wood, S of town]: Good choice of real ales inc Larkins, good range of bar food, more in back restaurant inc choice of Sun roasts *(Christopher Wright)*

PIRBRIGHT [SU9455]

Cricketers [The Green]: Chatty welcoming local in good spot, pleasant licensees, good home cooking, well kept real ale *(Shirley Mackenzie)*

PUTTENHAM [SU9347]

Good Intent [The Street/Seale Lane]: Beamed country local, friendly staff, good range of reasonably priced bar food (not Sun/Mon evenings) from sandwiches up, changing well kept ales such as Caledonian 80/-, Courage Best and Youngs Special, farm cider, log fire, pool, old photographs of the pub; dogs allowed, no children, picnic-sets in small garden, good walks, open all day wknds *(Ian Phillips)*

RIPLEY [TQ0556]

☆ *Anchor* [High St]: Tudor inn with old-fashioned cool dark low-beamed connecting rooms, wide choice of enjoyable food with some emphasis on thai dishes, friendly helpful service, well kept Bass and Courage Best, nautical memorabilia and photographs of Ripley's cycling heyday, two dozing dogs, games in public bar; disabled facilities, tables in coachyard *(BB, Philip and Susan Philcox, C and R Bromage, Ian Phillips)*

Jovial Sailor [Portsmouth Rd]: 19th-c pub much extended as popular Chef & Brewer, their usual food all day from reasonably priced sandwiches and ploughman's up inc busy family Sun lunches, Courage Best and Directors and Hogs Back TEA; may be piped music *(Anthony Evers, Ian Phillips)*

Seven Stars [Newark Lane (B367)]: Neatly kept 1930s pub with lots of blackboards showing good value generous food from sandwiches and baked potatoes to good Sun lunches, well kept Fullers London Pride, Greene King IPA, Abbot and Old Speckled Hen and Tetleys, nice efficient service, no smoking area; piped music may obtrude;

attractive garden behind *(LM, Ian Phillips, Tony and Wendy Hobden)*

Talbot [High St]: Beamed coaching inn with welcoming helpful staff, enjoyable food from generous baguettes up, decent wine, Fullers London Pride and Greene King Abbot, nice atmosphere, restaurant; may be piped music; bedrooms, tables in back courtyard *(Gordon Prince, Andy Sinden, Louise Harrington)*

RUNFOLD [SU8747]

Jolly Farmer [off A31 just NE of Farnham]: Wide choice of interesting well cooked food, reasonable prices, welcoming staff, well kept Greene King Abbot, good wine choice, family restaurant; pleasant garden with good play area – nice retreat from trunk road *(Dr and Mrs B T Marsh, LYM)*

SEND [TQ0156]

New Inn [Cartbridge]: Nice spot by Wey Navigation canal, long bar with lots of appropriate old photographs, reasonably priced food from toasted sandwiches to bass, lobster and crayfish, well kept Adnams Broadside, Fullers London Pride and guest beers such as Greene King Abbot and Marstons Pedigree, efficient cheerful service; piped music, smoking throughout; picnic-sets in front by road and in garden by canal path (Tannoy food announcements out here) *(Mark Percy, Lesley Mayoh, Ian Phillips)*

SENDMARSH [TQ0455]

Saddlers Arms [Send Marsh Rd]: Low-beamed local with creeper-covered porch, well kept Adnams, Fullers London Pride and Youngs, usual food, open fire, no smoking area, toby jugs, brassware etc; picnic-sets out front and back *(Gordon Stevenson, Ian Phillips)*

SHACKLEFORD [SU9345]

☆ *Cyder House* [Peper Harow Lane]: Roomy and civilised country pub rambling around central servery, wide blackboard choice of good value interesting food from ciabatta sandwiches to imaginative starters and hot dishes, chatty friendly staff, well kept Badger ales and Hogs Back TEA, decent house wines, log or coal fires, pleasantly bright and airy layout with lots of mellow pine, dining room and separate children's room with toys and small furniture; fruit machine and sports TV in side room, may be piped pop music; picnic-sets on terrace and back lawn, nice leafy village setting, open all day wknds *(MDN, Mr and Mrs S Felstead, BB, Martin and Karen Wake)*

SHALFORD [TQ0047]

Queen Victoria [Station Row]: Local popular with walkers, Greene King IPA, Hogs Back TEA and Wadworths 6X, reasonably priced food, log fires; picnic-sets in sheltered garden *(Ian Phillips)*

Sea Horse [A281 S of Guildford]: Vintage Inn with attractive décor, good range of reasonably priced food till late evening, well kept beer, plenty of young helpful staff; children welcome *(Dick and Madeleine Brown, C L Kauffmann)*

SHEPPERTON [TQ0766]

☆ *Kings Head* [Church Sq, off B375]: Immaculate 17th-c pub in quiet and attractive square, charming flower-framed façade and moving inn sign, highly polished floors and furnishings, oak beams, neat panelling, various discreet little rooms, inglenook coal fire, big conservatory extension; good value unpretentious home-made food (not Sun) inc good toasties, well kept real ales, decent house wines, smart attentive service; children welcome, sheltered back terrace, open all day Sat *(Geoffrey Kemp, LYM)*

Thames Court [Shepperton Lock, Ferry Lane; turn left off B375 towards Chertsey, 100yds from Square]: Huge Vintage Inn well placed by Thames, generous usual food from snacks up all day, good choice of wines by the glass, well kept Bass, galleried central atrium with separate attractive panelled areas up and down stairs, two good log fires, daily papers; children welcome, large attractive tree-shaded terrace with big gas radiant heaters *(Mayur Shah)*

SHERE [TQ0747]

☆ *White Horse* [signed off A25 3 miles E of Guildford; Middle St]: Striking half-timbered pub, extensively enlarged as Chef & Brewer but still full of character, with several rooms off the small busy bar, uneven floors, massive beams, Tudor stonework, oak wall seats, two log fires, one in a huge inglenook, reliable food all day from chunky sandwiches up, well kept beers such as Courage Best and Hogs Back TEA, lots of wines by the glass, good-sized children's area; tables outside, beautiful village, open all day *(Norma and Noel Thomas, Mike and Lynn Robinson, LYM, Mrs G R Sharman, Ian Phillips)*

SHOTTERMILL [SU8832]

☆ *Mill* [Liphook Rd (B2131, off A287 W of Haslemere)]: 17th-c pub with low black beams, log fire in big stone fireplace, pews and scrubbed tables in candlelit main locals' bar, good interesting well priced generous food from sandwiches (Mon-Sat lunchtime) up, well kept ales such as Greene King IPA, Ringwood Fortyniner, Charles Wells Bombardier and Youngs Special, good choice of wines, Addlestone's cider, pleasant quieter carpeted second room and separate lighter and more airy no smoking room; mill ponds with ducks and geese in front, nice terrace and sloping garden behind with good-sized play area *(W W Burke, Martin and Karen Wake, Betty Laker, BB, Derek Harvey-Piper)*

SOUTH GODSTONE [TQ3549]

☆ *Fox & Hounds* [Tilburstow Hill Rd/Harts Lane, off A22]: Current management doing good food inc some memorable seafood and speciality puddings in attractive old-fashioned pub, cosy low-beamed bar with antique high-backed settles, racing prints and woodburner, well kept Greene King IPA, Abbot and Ruddles County from tiny bar counter, friendly service, evening restaurant (not Sun/Mon evenings); may be piped music, children in eating area *(Ian Phillips, Bill Fillery, LYM, Geoffrey Kemp)*

STAINES [TQ0471]

Swan [The Hythe; south bank, over Staines Bridge]: Splendid Thames-side setting, with moorings, tables on riverside verandah, big conservatory, several distinctly different areas

to suit a mix of customers inc a music room, fairly peaceful upstairs restaurant, and calm chatty corridor, enjoyable traditional food, prompt friendly service, well kept Fullers ales inc a seasonal beer; can be very busy Sun lunchtime and packed with under-30s on summer evenings; comfortable bedrooms *(Simon Collett-Jones, LYM)*

SUNBURY [TQ1068]

Magpie [Thames St]: Lovely Thames views from upper bar and small terrace by boat club, bare boards and panelling, good food from ploughman's up, well kept Boddingtons, Greene King and Marstons Pedigree, decent wines, efficient antipodean service, no smoking areas; jazz in lower bar Mon, parking may be restricted; bedrooms *(Mayur Shah, Joyce and Geoff Robson, Dr Martin Owton)*

SUTTON ABINGER [TQ1045]

☆ *Volunteer* [Water Lane; just off B2126 via Raikes Lane, 1½ miles S of Abinger Hammer]: Country pub under welcoming new management, three low-ceilinged linked olde-worlde rooms, big rugs on bare boards or red tiles, good choice of food, not cheap but worth it, no smoking area, real ales such as Badger Best and Harveys Best, decent wines, roaring fire, homely medley of furnishings; restaurant, children welcome away from bar; nice country setting by clear stream, good tables out on flowery terrace and suntrap lawns stepped up behind, has been open all day summer wknds, good walks *(LYM, Ian Phillips, Carla Francis)*

TADWORTH [TQ2354]

Blue Anchor [Dorking Rd (B2032)]: Busy, warm and homely Vintage Inn in nice setting, log fires and candles, cheerful helpful staff, well kept Bass and Tetleys, good wine choice, vast helpings of food inc popular fish and chips; piped music *(Mrs G R Sharman)*

THAMES DITTON [TQ1567]

Fox on the River [Queens Rd, signed off Summer Rd]: Spacious but cosy Vintage Inn in delightful spot, lots of tables on attractive Thames-side terrace and lawn overlooking Hampton Court grounds, food from sandwiches and ploughman's to more inventive dishes, Bass and Gales HSB, good choice of wines by the glass, friendly helpful staff, log fire, daily papers, flagstones, river pictures, lively mix of customers, popular restaurant; moorings, open all day *(Sue and Mike Todd)*

THE SANDS [SU8846]

Barley Mow [Littleworth Rd, Seale; E of Farnham]: Small comfortable village pub neatly redone in the current clean-cut style with polished pine tables and hard chairs, a step or two down to dining area, well kept Brakspears, Fullers London Pride and Greene King, good if not cheap food from lunchtime sandwiches and boccatas through pasta choice to evening fish specialities and great puddings; picnic-sets in secluded garden *(Howard Dell, Giles Francis)*

THORNTON HEATH [TQ3168]

Wheatsheaf [A23]: Friendly pub with resident Thai caterers – a useful stop *(J S Rutter)*

THORPE [TQ0268]

Red Lion [Village Rd/Ten Acre Lane]: Popular and friendly beamed Steak & Ale pub handy for Thorpe Park, other reasonably priced food too, Courage Best, Fullers London Pride and Greene King Old Speckled Hen, log fires; back terrace and orchard garden *(Ian Phillips)*

TILFORD [SU8743]

☆ *Barley Mow* [The Green, off B3001 SE of Farnham; also signed off A287]: Good food inc late Sun lunch (bar snacks earlier till 2 that day), wknd afternoon teas, charming friendly service, well kept Courage Best, Fullers London Pride, Greene King Abbot and Youngs, imaginative wine list, snug little low-ceilinged traditional bar on right with woodburner, nice scrubbed tables in two small rooms set for food on left, interesting cricketing prints and old photographs; darts, table skittles, no children; pretty setting opposite cricket green, tables in good-sized back garden fenced off from small stream *(John and Mary Ling, G D Sharpe, BB)*

VIRGINIA WATER [SU9968]

Rose & Olive Branch [Callow Hill]: Small unpretentious pub with friendly helpful service, wide choice of good home-made food from good lunchtime sandwich range to lots of fish and pastry-wrapped dishes (busy wknds, best to book then), Greene King IPA and Ruddles County and a guest such as Caledonian 80/-, decent wines, matchbox collection; smoking allowed in all parts, quiet piped music; children allowed lunchtime, picnic-sets on grass behind, good walks *(Ian Phillips, Guy Charrison)*

WALTON ON THE HILL [TQ2255]

Blue Ball [not far from M25 junction 8; Deans Lane, off B2220 by pond]: Facing common nr duck pond, cosily refurbished, with wide choice of good value food, good atmosphere, prompt friendly service, several real ales, decent wines, restaurant (open all day Sun) overlooking big garden with barbecue; good walking area *(C and R Bromage)*

WALTON-ON-THAMES [TQ1065]

Ashley Park [Station Approach/Ashley Park Rd]: Pleasantly refurbished as comfortable Ember Inn, well kept real ales, reasonably priced food; open all day, bedrooms in adjoining separately run hotel *(Tony and Wendy Hobden)*

Regent [Church St]: Attractive Wetherspoons cinema conversion, small no smoking area and family room upstairs *(Tony and Wendy Hobden)*

Swan [Manor Rd, off A3050]: Big three-bar riverside Youngs pub, lots of interconnecting rooms, decent reasonably priced food in bar and attractive restaurant, well kept ales and good wine choice, good service; dogs welcome, lots of tables and chairs in huge pretty garden leading down to Thames, wknd barbecues, moorings, riverside walks *(Mayur Shah, A C Nugent, Gordon Prince)*

Weir [off Sunbury Lane]: Nice Thames-side spot, attractive no smoking family room done as part-panelled river-view library, lots of picnic-sets crowded on to big terrace with good view over river and weir (and steel walkway),

wide range of good food from sandwiches up, Badger Best and Tanglefoot, traditional décor, masses of river pictures, candles on tables, good attentive service; open all day Sun, lovely towpath walks *(Roy and Lindsey Fentiman, David and Carole Chapman)*

WEST CLANDON [TQ0452]

☆ *Bulls Head* [A247 SE of Woking]: Friendly and comfortably modernised 16th-c country local, very popular esp with older people lunchtime for good value generous food from sandwiches, ploughman's and baked potatoes through reliable home-made pies to steak, small lantern-lit beamed front bar with open fire and some stripped brick, old local prints and bric-a-brac, steps up to simple raised back inglenook dining area, efficient service, well kept Courage Best, Greene King Old Speckled Hen and Marstons Pedigree, good coffee, no piped music, games room with darts and pool; children and dogs on leads welcome, lots of tables and good play area in garden, convenient for Clandon Park, good walking country *(DWAJ, R Lake, John Evans, Susan and John Douglas)*

☆ *Onslow Arms* [A247 SE of Woking]: Rambling partly 17th-c country pub under good new management, convivial atmosphere, dark nooks and corners, heavy beams, flagstones, warm seats by inglenook log fires, soft lighting, lots of brass and copper; well kept ales, decent wines, enjoyable food (not Sun evening), partly no smoking dining room (popular Sun lunches), great well lit garden; children welcome (and dogs in bar), open all day *(LYM, Shirley Mackenzie)*

WEST HORSLEY [TQ0853]

Barley Mow [The Street]: Tree-shaded village pub with beams, flagstones, leather settees on bare boards, well kept ales such as Greene King IPA, Jennings Cumberland and Youngs Special, decent wines and spirits, good value lunchtime food, comfortable little dining room, cheerful landlord and staff; picnic-sets in garden *(Ian Phillips)*

King William IV [The Street]: Comfortable chain-owned local, red plush banquettes in very low-beamed open-plan bar with pleasantly secluded areas, reasonably priced food from sandwiches up here and in separate restaurant, well kept Adnams, Courage Best and Directors and Shepherd Neame Spitfire, good coffee, log fires; good disabled access, games area with darts, pool and machine; small garden, gorgeous hanging baskets *(Ian Phillips, M and N Watson)*

WESTHUMBLE [TQ1751]

Stepping Stones [just off A24 below Box Hill]: Roomy and friendly, circular bar with good range of beers inc Fullers, Greene King Abbot and Old Speckled Hen and Ringwood, good value generous food, no music; children and walkers welcome in restaurant, terrace and garden with summer barbecue and play area *(Sue and Mike Todd, C and R Bromage)*

WEYBRIDGE [TQ0965]

Badgers Rest [Oatlands Chase]: Several areas divided by pastel 1930s-theme walls with glazed panels, popular with older people for wide food choice from ciabattas and potted crab through pizzas to steak and salmon, well kept Fullers London Pride and Greene King Old Speckled Hen, good wine choice, helpful staff; back area for smokers; tables on front lawn; immaculate bedrooms *(Ian Phillips)*

☆ *Old Crown* [Thames St]: Friendly and comfortable old-fashioned three-bar pub, very popular lunchtime for good platefuls of reasonably priced straightforward food from sandwiches and baked potatoes up esp fresh grimsby fish (served evening too), good specials; well kept Courage Best and Directors, John Smiths, Youngs Special and a guest beer, service good even when busy, no smoking family lounge and conservatory, no music or machines but may be sports TV in back bar; children welcome, suntrap streamside garden *(DWAJ, A C Nugent)*

Prince of Wales [Cross Rd/Anderson Rd off Oatlands Drive]: Congenial and attractively restored, with relaxed country-local feel, reasonably priced generous bar food inc interesting dishes and Sun lunch with three roasts, well kept ales such as Adnams, Boddingtons, Fullers London Pride, Tetleys and Wadworths 6X, 10 wines by the glass, friendly service, coal-effect gas fires, imaginative menu in stripped pine dining room down a couple of steps (candlelit bistro feel there at night) *(Minda and Stanley Alexander)*

WINDLESHAM [SU9464]

☆ *Brickmakers* [Chertsey Rd]: Popular dining pub with flagstones and pastel colours for bistro feel, wide range of freshly made food (thai fishcakes a favourite), cheerfully busy bar, well kept Brakspears, Courage Best, Fullers London Pride and Marstons Pedigree, good choice of wines, nice coffee, welcoming service, log fire, conservatory, no music; well behaved children allowed, attractive garden with boules and barbecues (live music some summer Suns), lovely hanging baskets *(Mr and Mrs A Swainson, A C Nugent)*

☆ *Half Moon* [Church Rd]: Extended pub with all tables laid for reliable food inc family Sun lunch and fresh veg, good service, modern furnishings, log fires, well kept ales such as Cottage Normans Conquest, Courage Directors and Theakstons Old Peculier, Weston's farm cider, interesting World War II pictures; children welcome, piped music, silenced fruit machine; huge well kept garden *(Mr and Mrs S Felstead, Ian Phillips)*

Surrey Cricketers [Chertsey Rd (B386)]: Warm welcome, lots of neat small tables on bare boards, huge choice of good generous food from well filled baguettes to seafood and steaks, Greene King IPA and Old Speckled Hen and Wadworths 6X, many more seats in separate skittle alley; garden *(Ian Phillips, Mr and Mrs S Felstead)*

WITLEY [SU9439]

☆ *White Hart* [Petworth Rd]: Tudor beams, good

oak furniture, log fire in cosy panelled inglenook snug where George Eliot drank, welcoming landlord, fairly priced Shepherd Neame Best and Spitfire, daily papers, public bar with usual games, restaurant; piped music; tables on cobbled terrace, lots of pretty hanging baskets etc, lower meadow with picnic-sets and play area *(Ian Phillips, LYM, Phil and Sally Gorton)*

WOODHAM [TQ0361]

Victoria: Popular food, good atmosphere, Fullers London Pride, Greene King IPA, Shepherd Neame Spitfire and Youngs *(Ian Phillips)*

WOODMANSTERNE [TQ2759]

Woodman: Friendly late 19th-c village pub with wholesome reasonably priced straightforward food in good dining area, well kept Bass; walkers welcome, tables out in front and in back garden with play area *(Jenny and Brian Seller)*

WORPLESDON [SU9854]

Jolly Farmer [Burdenshott Rd, towards Worplesdon Station]: Fresh décor and modern furnishings in roomy beamed pub now owned by Fullers, with new management from summer 2003 (too soon for us to judge); has had well kept real ales and some emphasis on its airy stripped-brick dining extension, with a log fire in the bar; big sheltered garden, pleasant walks on Whitmoor Common *(LYM)*

WOTTON [TQ1247]

☆ *Wotton Hatch* [A25 Dorking—Guildford]: Attractive and neatly kept Vintage Inn family dining pub, welcoming largely no smoking rambling rooms around 17th-c core, interesting furnishings, good changing choice of generous reasonably priced food (all day Thurs-Sun and summer) from hearty sandwiches up, well kept Bass and Fullers London Pride, good choice of decent wines, generous soft drinks inc freshly squeezed orange juice, keen young staff, daily papers; gentle piped music, no dogs; impressive views from neat garden, open all day *(Gordon Prince, M G Hart, Mrs G R Sharman, Jamie and Ruth Lyons, LYM, Lawrence Clancy, Colin and Sandra Tann, R Halsey)*

WRECCLESHAM [SU8344]

☆ *Bat & Ball* [approach from Sandrock Hill and rough unmade Upper Bourne Lane, or park in Short Heath Rd and walk down unmade Bat & Ball Lane]: Cosy old pub taken over by new licensees who made their previous pub Surrey Dining Pub of the Year three times; our summer 2003 anonymous inspection attempt was foiled by building works, but we sneaked in for a quick look round before we were sent packing and it all looked very promising; expect a good choice of country food from sandwiches up, well kept real ales, friendly service, and a good atmosphere; provision for children and dogs, tables out on terrace and in garden with substantial play fort *(BB)*

By law pubs must show a price list of their drinks. Let us know if you are inconvenienced by any breach of this law.

Sussex

Very well supplied with good pubs, Sussex has some that really shine these days: the Rose Cottage at Alciston (a classic country pub, its kitchen supplied very locally), the Fountain at Ashurst (good food and beer, hard-working owners), the Cricketers Arms at Berwick (a smashing country pub, good all round), the unspoilt Blue Ship near Billingshurst, the Blackboys Inn (another good bustling country all-rounder), the Basketmakers Arms in Brighton (well worth tracking down here), the George & Dragon up at Burpham (good food and drink, and nice downland walks), the Fox Goes Free at Charlton (good food and beer, plenty of character), the Coach & Horses at Danehill (a favourite now, for its wide appeal and good imaginative food), the beautifully placed Tiger at East Dean (interesting food, good drinks), the interesting and warmly welcoming old Three Horseshoes at Elsted, the civilised Griffin at Fletching (good all round), the Star at Old Heathfield just outside Heathfield itself (another all-rounder), the well run Queens Head at Icklesham (hard-working smiling staff, good honest food and nice beers), the smart and civilised Halfway Bridge Inn near Lodsworth (good food, a nice if expensive place to stay), and the Giants Rest at Wilmington (enjoyable food – and a wooden puzzle for each table). To these we'd add these new entries: the simply furnished and interesting old Black Horse at Byworth (the new landlord's cooking is a draw here, bringing it back into these pages after an absence), the Horse & Groom at East Ashling (nice mix of chattily traditional country inn with good food and drink), the Kings Arms near Fernhurst (good interesting food, and a good choice of beers and wines, under ancient low beams), and the cheerful little Lamb at Wartling (good popular food). Among the many pubs here which stand out for their good food, the Coach & Horses at Danehill nicely mixes a warm appeal to people who just want a chatty drink with all the qualities that make for a special meal out: it is Sussex Dining Pub of the Year. The Lucky Dip section at the end of the chapter includes a good few top-notch contenders for the main entries, such as the Bridge at Amberley, Black Horse at Apuldram, Gardeners Arms at Ardingly, Bell and Rose & Crown in Burwash, Royal Oak at Chilgrove, Hatch at Colemans Hatch, George & Dragon near Coolham, Royal Oak at East Lavant, Swan at Fittleworth, Shepherd & Dog at Fulking, Sussex Brewery at Hermitage, restauranty Half Moon at Kirdford, John Harvey in Lewes, Well Diggers Arms near Petworth, Three Cups near Punnetts Town, Cock at Ringmer, Ypres Castle in Rye, White Horse at Sutton and Dorset Arms at Withyham. Drinks prices here are markedly higher than the national average. The Cuckmere Haven beer brewed at the Golden Galleon near Seaford is a bargain there. The main local brewer is Harveys, and others to note include Kings (run by the man who ran King & Barnes before that former big Sussex brewery was taken over and closed by Badger), Gribble (beers from this pub at Oving, which is tied to Badger, are widely available at other pubs in the chain), Rother Valley, Old Forge, Dark Star, Ballards, Weltons/Hepworths, and Rectory (set up by the rector of Plumpton, with parishioners as shareholders and income helping to support the parishes in his charge).

ALCISTON TQ5005 Map 3
Rose Cottage
Village signposted off A27 Polegate—Lewes

The same family have owned this bustling country cottage for more than 40 years, and it remains popular with both locals and walkers. There are cosy winter log fires, half a dozen tables with cushioned pews under quite a forest of harness, traps, a thatcher's blade and lots of other black ironware, and more bric-a-brac on the shelves above the stripped pine dado or in the etched-glass windows; in the mornings you may also find Jasper the parrot (it can get a little smoky for him in the evenings). Best to arrive early to be sure of a seat. There's a lunchtime overflow into the no smoking restaurant area. Using a local fishmonger and butcher, and selling local eggs, honey, and seasonal game, they might have home-made soup (£3.25), chicken liver and mushroom pâté (£3.95), lunchtime ploughman's (£5.50), lincolnshire sausages (£5.75) and steaks (from £10.25), with daily specials such as lasagne (£7.25), home-made steak in ale pie or thai-style chicken (£7.50), vegetarian spinach pancakes topped with tomato sauce and parmesan or casserole of wild local rabbit (£7.95), and local plaice with lemon and parsley butter (£8.75) on the bar food menu; roast Sunday lunch (£7.50). Well kept Harveys Best and a guest such as King Horsham Best on handpump, good wines, and Biddenden farm cider; the landlord, whom we have known now for many years, is quite a plain-speaking character; dominoes, cribbage, and maybe piped classical music. There are gas heaters outside for cooler evenings, and the small paddock in the garden has ducks and chickens. Nearby fishing and shooting. The charming little village (and local church) are certainly worth a look. *(Recommended by R and S Bentley, the Didler, Trevor and Sylvia Millum, MLR, Susan May, Jenny and Peter Lowater, Peter Forsyth, Brian and Andrea Potter, Susan and John Douglas, Jane Basso)*

Free house ~ Licensee Ian Lewis ~ Real ale ~ Bar food ~ Restaurant ~ (01323) 870377 ~ Children allowed if over 10 ~ Dogs allowed in bar ~ Open 11.30-3, 6.30-11; 12-3, 7-10.30 Sun; closed 25 and 26 Dec ~ Bedrooms: /£45S

ALFRISTON TQ5203 Map 3
George
High Street

The long bar in this 14th-c timbered inn has massive low beams hung with hops, appropriately soft lighting, and a log fire (or summer flower arrangement) in a huge stone inglenook fireplace that dominates the room, with lots of copper and brass around it. Sturdy stripped tables have settles and chairs around them, and there's well kept Greene King IPA, Abbot, and Old Speckled Hen, and a guest such as Everards Tiger on handpump; decent wines, cribbage, dominoes, board games, and piped music. Bar food includes lunchtime ploughman's (£6.50), sausages with wholegrain mustard mash and onion gravy (£6.50), and ham and free range eggs (£7.50), as well as steak and kidney pudding (£6.95), wild mushroom pancakes with warm tomato sauce (£9.95), slow braised knuckle of lamb (£11.95), roasted cod on spiced fennel with spinach and lemon sauce or rib-eye steak (£12.95), and puddings (£3.95). Besides the cosy candlelit no smoking restaurant, there's a garden dining room; or you can sit out in the charming flint-walled garden behind. The lovely village is a tourist honey-pot; you can escape the crowds on a fine riverside walk down to Cuckmere Haven, and two long-distance paths (South Downs Way and Vanguard Way) cross in the village. *(Recommended by Michael and Ann Cole, John and Judy Saville, Mrs Alison Challis, Paul Humphreys, John Davis, E G Parish, Ann and Colin Hunt, Richard and Margaret Peers, A Sadler)*

Greene King ~ Tenants Roland and Cate Couch ~ Real ale ~ Bar food (12-2.30, 7-9(10 Fri/Sat)) ~ Restaurant ~ (01323) 870319 ~ Children welcome ~ Dogs allowed in bar ~ Open 12-11; 12-10.30 Sun; closed 25-27 Dec

---

If we know a pub does summer barbecues, we say so.

AMBERLEY SO8401 Map 3
Black Horse
Off B2139

Whether you fancy a walk along the banks of the River Arun, an afternoon's hiking on the South Downs Way, or a look around the enjoyable open air Amberley Industrial Museum, this very pretty pub is well placed. The main bar has high-backed settles on flagstones, beams over the serving counter festooned with sheep bells and shepherds' tools (hung by the last shepherd on the Downs), and walls decorated with a mixture of prints and paintings. The lounge bar has many antiques and artefacts collected by the owners on their world travels; there are log fires in both bars and two in the no smoking restaurant. Well liked bar food includes home-made vegetable soup (£2.95), home-made chicken liver pâté (£3.95), deep-fried brie and camembert with cumberland sauce (£4.55), sandwiches with salad and chips or ploughman's (£4.95), lasagne or broccoli and pasta bake (£7.95), steak in ale pie (£8.95), and various curries or chicken with sauces such as bacon and stilton or prawn and lobster (£9.95). Well kept Greene King IPA and Old Speckled Hen, and Wells Bombardier on handpump, and several malt whiskies; piped music. The garden is a restful place. *(Recommended by A Sadler, John Beeken, W A Evershed, John and Judy Saville, Brian and Andrea Potter, Michael Porter, Ian and Barbara Rankin, Jane Basso)*

Pubmaster ~ Tenant Gary Tubb ~ Real ale ~ Bar food (12-3, 6-9.30(10 Fri/Sat)) ~ Restaurant ~ (01798) 831552 ~ Children in eating area of bar and in restaurant (lunchtime) ~ Dogs allowed in bar ~ Open 11-11; 12-10.30 Sun

Sportsmans
Crossgates; Rackham Road, off B2139

As we went to press friendly new licensees had just taken over this village pub. Mr Mahon has been running restaurants for 25 years, so we would expect the food to be rather special. The three bars have something for everyone: the saloon bar is cosily lit with an interesting choice of seating, the pretty little red-tiled conservatory (engagingly decorated with old local bric-a-brac) is for dining, and the back bar is where friendly locals gather to enjoy the well kept Fullers London Pride, Greene King IPA and Abbot, Harveys Best, and guests like Adnams, Marstons Pedigree or Youngs Bitter on handpump; lots of wines by the glass. Although prices had not been set, starters will be around £5 and main courses from £6.50: smoked chicken and orange on mixed leaves with sour cream, thai crab cakes with a sweet chilli sauce or a terrine of the day, filled baked potatoes or ploughman's, calves liver and bacon, layers of red lentil risotto pressed between chargrilled aubergine with a tomato and herb salsa, chicken breast poached in an asparagus and tarragon cream sauce, fillet of turbot in coriander and lime butter, barbary duck breast with peach compote and raspberry vinegar dressing, and puddings like chocolate, rum and truffle mousse or apple pie. The marvellous views from this village pub can be enjoyed from the decked terrace at the back (and many customers take their binoculars to watch the birds) and from inside. More reports please. *(Recommended by Tracey and Stephen Groves, John Davis, Cathy Robinson, Ed Coombe, Ann and Colin Hunt, R T and J C Moggridge, Tony and Wendy Hobden, Helen and Ian Jobson, Dennis Jenkin, John Beeken)*

Free house ~ Licensee Paul Mahon ~ Real ale ~ Bar food ~ Restaurant ~ (01798) 831787 ~ Children welcome ~ Dogs allowed in bar ~ Open 11-3, 5.30-11; 12-3, 6-10.30 Sun; 11-2.30, 6-11 in winter ~ Bedrooms: £30S/£60S

ARLINGTON TQ5407 Map 3
Old Oak
Caneheath, off A22 or A27 NW of Polegate

After a walk in the nearby Abbotswood nature reserve, the seats in the peaceful garden of this 17th-c former set of almshouses are a nice place to relax with a pint of well kept Badger Best, Harveys Best, and a guest such as Adnams Broadside, Fullers London Pride or Hop Back Summer Lightning tapped from the cask; several malt whiskies. The open-plan, L-shaped bar has heavy beams, well spaced tables and comfortable seating, log fires, and a calm, relaxed atmosphere; piped music and dominoes. Straightforward bar food includes filled baguettes, ploughman's or ham and egg (£5.95), mushroom stroganoff (£6.25), chicken tikka masala (£6.50), lasagne (£6.95), cod and chips (£7.50), steak in ale pie (£7.25), and steaks (from £8.95). The dining area is no smoking. More reports please. *(Recommended by J H Bell, Michael and Ann Cole, Ann and Colin Hunt, R J Walden, Tony and Wendy Hobden)*

Free house ~ Licensees Mr J Boots and Mr B Slattery ~ Real ale ~ Bar food (12-2.30, 6.30-9.30) ~ (01323) 482072 ~ Children welcome ~ Dogs allowed in bar ~ Live entertainment monthly Fri evening ~ Open 11-3, 6-11; 11-11 Sat; 12-10.30 Sun

ASHURST TQ1716 Map 3
Fountain 🍴 🍺

B2135 S of Partridge Green

'Always busy and always good' commented one of our many contented readers after visiting this welcoming 16th-c country pub. The neatly kept and charmingly rustic tap room on the right has a couple of high-backed wooden cottage armchairs by the log fire in its brick inglenook, two antique polished trestle tables, and fine old flagstones; there are more flagstones in the opened-up snug with heavy beams, simple furniture, and its own inglenook fireplace. Good, popular bar food includes lunchtime sandwiches (from £4.25) and ploughman's (£6.50), home-cooked ham and free range egg (£6.95), steak, mushroom and ale pie (£8.50), caramelised onion, goats cheese and cranberry tart (£8.95), chargrilled home-made burger with bacon, mozzarella and onion relish (£9.95), chargrilled chicken breast with fresh chilli, lime and coriander dressing (£10.95), fillet of bass with roasted pepper, lemon and dill dressing (£11.95), evening steaks (from £12.95), and puddings like sticky toffee pudding or hot chocolate fudge cake (£4.25). Well kept Harveys Best, King Horsham Best Bitter, Shepherd Neame Bitter, and a guest like Black Sheep or Timothy Taylors Landlord on handpump, and decent wines; an oak-beamed skittle alley that doubles as a function room. Service is friendly and attentive. The garden is prettily planted, there are seats on the front brick terrace, raised herb beds at the back, a growing orchard, and a duck pond. There's a new car park this year. *(Recommended by Cathy Robinson, Ed Coombe, Tony and Wendy Hobden, Bruce Bird, Mr Bannon, J P Humphery, John Beeken, R J Walden, Barry Steele-Perkins, Mr and Mrs Gordon Turner, Alison Milner-Gulland , Karen Eliot, Helen and Ian Jobson, John Hale, Keith Stevens, Ian Jones, Michael Porter, Peter Forsyth, John Davis, Bruce Jamieson, Phyl and Jack Street, Ben Whitney and Pippa Redmond, Ian and Barbara Rankin)*

Free house ~ Licensees Mark and Chris White ~ Real ale ~ Bar food (11.30-2, 6-9.30; cold food and snacks only Sun and Mon evenings) ~ No credit cards ~ (01403) 710219 ~ Children allowed inside if over 10 ~ Dogs allowed in bar ~ Folk harmony singers first Weds of month ~ Open 11.30-2.30(4.45 Sat), 6-11; 12-3, 7-10.30 Sun; closed evenings 25 and 26 Dec

BARNHAM SU9604 Map 3
Murrell Arms £

Yapton Road

Over the 39 years that the long-standing licensees have run this quite unspoilt and old-fashioned pub, they have collected an extraordinary amount of memorabilia: hundreds of jugs, mugs, china plates and old bottles that are jammed together along delft shelves, little prints, pictures and old photographs cover the walls, agricultural artefacts hang from the ceiling, and there's an elderly grandfather clock, a collection of old soda syphons, an interesting Cox's change machine and Crystal Palace clock, and some old horsebrasses. The saloon bar has some nice old farmhouse chairs, a very high-backed settle by the piano, a mix of tables (including a fine circular Georgian one) with candles in bottles on its partly turkey carpeted, very old dark wood parquet floor, and a huge polished half-barrel bar counter. To get to the cheerful public bar, you walk past the stillage room where the barrels of Gales HSB, BBB and a changing guest are stored; lots of country wines and two open fires. The simple tiny snug over a half wall has an enormous bell wheel from the church on the ceiling; darts and shove-ha'penny. Straightforward bar food includes cockles and mussels (90p), ploughman's (from £2), and a couple of daily specials such as bacon hock with crusty bread or kingsize bangers (£4). From the car park, you walk through a pretty flower-filled courtyard with a large cider press on one side, and fine ancient wooden benches and tables under a leafy grape vine on the other – note the huge bellows on the wall; there are picnic-sets on a cottagey little enclosed garden up some steps. More reports please. *(Recommended by Fred Chamberlain, Ann and Colin Hunt, MLR, Ian Phillips, Ruth and Paul Lawrence)*

Gales ~ Tenant Mervyn Cutten ~ Real ale ~ Bar food (not Thurs evening) ~ No credit cards ~ (01243) 553320 ~ Well behaved children in snug ~ Dogs welcome ~ Folk Thurs evening ~ Open 11-2.30, 6-11; 11-11 Sat; 12-11 Sun

BERWICK TQ5105 Map 3
Cricketers Arms
Lower Road, S of A27

Although this little gem is a fine place to visit in winter, it is perhaps at its best in the summer when you can sit in the old-fashioned cottagey front garden, and enjoy a meal or a drink amongst the flowering shrubs and plants; there are more seats behind. The three little similarly furnished rooms have simple benches against the half-panelled walls, a pleasant mix of old country tables and chairs, burgundy velvet curtains on poles, a few bar stools, and some country prints; quarry tiles on the floors (nice worn ones in the middle room), two log fires in little brick fireplaces, a huge black supporting beam in each of the low ochre ceilings, and (in the end room) some attractive cricketing pastels; some of the beams are hung with cricket bats. Service remains helpful and friendly – even when it's busy. Good straightforward bar food includes home-made soup (£3.50), ham and egg, local pork and herb sausages or ploughman's (£5.50), filled baked potatoes (from £6.25), 6oz steak (£6.50), daily specials such as popular filo prawns with chilli dip (£4.95), fresh dressed crab or smoked haddock mornay (£7.50), and fillet of bass with parsley butter (£8.50); best to get here early to be sure of a seat as it does fill up quickly. Well kept Harveys Best and a seasonal ale tapped from the cask, and decent wine; shove-ha'penny, cribbage, dominoes, and an old Sussex coin game called toad in the hole. *(Recommended by Roger Bridgeman, Peter and Joan Elbra, the Didler, Ann and Colin Hunt, J H Bell, Peter Meister, B and M Kendall, Boyd Catling, Jenny and Peter Lowater, M and R Thomas, Derek Hayman, LM)*

Harveys ~ Tenant Peter Brown ~ Real ale ~ Bar food (12-2.15, 6.30-9; all day in summer and winter wknds) ~ (01323) 870469 ~ Children in family room; under 5s under strict parental control ~ Dogs welcome ~ Open 11-11; 12-10.30 Sun; 11-3, 6-11 weekdays but all day weekends in winter; closed 25 Dec, evening 26 Dec

BILLINGSHURST TQ0830 Map 3
Blue Ship 🍺
The Haven; hamlet signposted off A29 just N of junction with A264, then follow signpost left towards Garlands and Okehurst

Tucked away down a country lane, this charmingly unpretentious pub is in an idyllic spot for a summer evening, when you can relax at the tree-shaded side tables or by the tangle of honeysuckle around the front door, and contentedly take in the air of peaceful simplicity. Inside, the cosy beamed and brick-floored front bar has a blazing fire in the inglenook fireplace, scrubbed tables and wall benches, and hatch service dispensing well kept Badger Best And Tanglefoot, and Gribble Fursty Ferret on handpump. A corridor leads to a couple of small carpeted rooms with dark wood tables and chairs, old prints and fresh flowers, where children can sit – one is no smoking. Darts, bar billiards, shove-ha'penny, cribbage, and dominoes. Well liked and reasonably priced traditional bar food includes sandwiches (from £2.60; baguettes £4), filled baked potatoes (£4.50), ploughman's (£4.95), cauliflower cheese, cottage pie or ratatouille au gratin (£5.50), sausages and eggs (£5.85), steak and onion pie (£6.90), and puddings like treacle sponge or chocolate fudge cake (£3). *(Recommended by Phil and Sally Gorton, Mrs Romey Heaton, John Davis, the Didler, John Robertson)*

Badger ~ Tenant J R Davie ~ Real ale ~ Bar food (not Sun or Mon evenings) ~ No credit cards ~ (01403) 822709 ~ Children in eating area of bar, restaurant and family room ~ Dogs welcome ~ Open 11-3, 6-11; 12-3.30, 7-10.30 Sun

BLACKBOYS TQ5220 Map 3
Blackboys Inn
B2192, S edge of village

There's a chatty, happy and properly pubby atmosphere in the locals' bar of this bustling pub, and a string of old-fashioned and unpretentious little rooms with dark oak beams, bare boards or parquet, antique prints, copious curios (including a collection of keys above the bar), and a good log fire in the inglenook fireplace. Enjoyable food includes home-made soup (£3.50), filled baked potatoes, ploughman's or ham and eggs (£4.95), home-made pie (£6.95), thai red chicken curry (£8.75), and 10oz entrecote steak (£10.95), and nice daily specials such as smoked haddock in cheese and wine sauce (£3.50; main course £6.95), asparagus wrapped in parma ham (£5.75), beef bourguignon or vegetable risotto (£8.95), chicken breast stuffed with mediterranean vegetables or crab salad (£11.50), half lobster salad (£12.50), and fillet steak with a mushroom, cream and brandy sauce (£15.95). The restaurant and dining areas are no smoking; obliging, efficient service even when busy. Well kept Harveys Best, Pale Ale, and a monthly guest on handpump; darts, fruit machine and juke box. In summer, the garden is a big plus as there's masses of space and rustic tables overlooking the pond, with more on the front lawn under the chestnut trees. *(Recommended by Sarah Davis, Rod Lambert, Robert M Warner, Alison Milner-Gulland, Michael and Ann Cole, the Didler, John Davis, J H Bell)*

Harveys ~ Tenants Edward and Claire Molesworth ~ Real ale ~ Bar food (not Sun evenings) ~ Restaurant ~ (01825) 890283 ~ Children in restaurant ~ Dogs allowed in bar ~ Open 11-3, 5(6 Sat)-11; 11-11 Fri; 12-10.30 Sun; closed 1 Jan

BODIAM TQ7825 Map 3
Curlew
B2244 S of Hawkhurst, outside village at crossroads with turn-off to Castle

With a relaxed, informal atmosphere, this compact country dining pub manages to appeal to both drinkers and diners alike. The main bar has a heavily carved bar counter with bar stools in front of it (and locals enjoying a pint of well kept Harveys Best and a couple of guest beers on handpump), a woodburning stove, and hops along the beams. Off to the right is a smaller room mainly used for dining, with timbered pink walls, mirrors that give an impression of more space, and a piano. The no smoking restaurant has dark pink walls, black timbers, more hops on beams, and pictures that are mainly trompe-l'oeil ones of life-size wine bottles looking as if they are in wood-framed alcoves; some sunny watercolour landscapes, too, and interesting photographs in the gents'. Good attractively presented lunchtime bar food might include home-made soup (£3.95), baguettes filled with brie and vine tomato or rib-eye steak and onions (from £5.95; all come with chips), grilled goats cheese, garlic croûtes, and mixed leaves or a good cheese plate with (£6.95), fresh pasta with parmesan, basil, garlic and pomodoro sauce or serrano ham, tomatoes, olives and fresh baguette (£8.95), chicken curry with coconut cream (£10.95), fresh fish in tempura batter with garlic mayonnaise (£11.95), calves liver and bacon with garlic mash and caramelised onion gravy (£12.95), and extra mature rib-eye steak with béarnaise sauce (£13.95), with specials like fresh spaghetti with petit pois, basil, fresh parmesan and tomato sauce (£7.95), foie gras terrine with home-made chutney (£8.95), and pigeon breast on rösti potatoes and madeira sauce (£14.95); there is a more elaborate evening restaurant menu, and an extensive wine list. *(Recommended by RDK, Alan Cole, Kirstie Bruce)*

Free house ~ Licensee Andy Blyth ~ Bar food ~ Restaurant ~ (01580) 861394 ~ Children welcome ~ Dogs allowed in bar ~ Open 11.30-3, 6(6.30 Sat)-11; 12-4 Sun; closed Sun evening, Mon, 26 and 27 Dec, 1 and 2 Jan

BRIGHTON TQ3105 Map 3
Basketmakers Arms £

Gloucester Road – the E end, near Cheltenham Place; off Marlborough Place (A23) via Gloucester Street

Both the staff behind the bar and the customers in this bustling backstreet local are chatty and cheerful – and there's a lot of atmosphere (but not a lot of space, so it's best to get here early, especially at weekends). The two small rooms have brocaded wall benches and stools on the stripped wood floor, lots of interesting old tins all over the walls, cigarette cards on one beam with whisky labels on another, and some old photographs and posters; quiet piped music. Good value enjoyable bar food includes lots of sandwiches (from £1.95; chicken and avocado £2.75; hot salt beef on granary £3.25), particularly good home-made meaty and vegetarian burgers (£2.50), baked potatoes with fillings such as beef, chilli and yoghurt (£2.95), ploughman's (£3.50), and specials such as mozzarella, tomato and avocado salad (£4.25), bangers and mash with onion gravy or thai green chicken curry (£4.50), home-cooked beer-battered cod and chips (£4.75, Fridays), and sirloin steak (£5.95). Well kept Gales Bitter, GB, HSB, and seasonal ales, and a guest such as Fullers ESB or Wells Bombardier; good wines by the large glass and over 80 malt whiskies. *(Recommended by R J Walden, Tracey and Stephen Groves, MLR, Neville and Anne Morley, John Beeken, Ann and Colin Hunt, the Didler, Tony and Wendy Hobden)*

Gales ~ Tenants P and K Dowd, A McIlwaine, A Mawer ~ Real ale ~ Bar food (12-3, 5.30-8.30; 12-3.30 Sat; 12-4 Sun; not Sat/Sun evenings) ~ Children welcome until 8pm ~ Dogs welcome ~ Open 11-11; 12-10.30 Sun; closed evening 25 Dec, 26 Dec

BURPHAM TQ0308 Map 3
George & Dragon 🏮

Warningcamp turn off A27 outside Arundel: follow road up and up

Just a short walk away from this popular 18th-c pub, set in a remote hill village of thatch and flint, there are splendid views down to Arundel Castle and the river – plenty of pretty surrounding walks. Many customers come to enjoy the good, enjoyable food which might include soup (£3.50), sandwiches or warm filled baguettes (from £4.75), filled baked potatoes (from £5.70), warm smoked duck and bacon salad (£5.90), ploughman's (£5.95), avocado and seafood timbale (£6.95), breast of chicken with sunblush tomatoes, sweet peppers topped with melted mozzarella cheese or duck leg with red berry and port jus (£9.50), braised lamb shank with mint and apricot sauce (£10.50), whole black bream with lemon and coriander butter (£12.95), and puddings such as white chocolate mousse or banoffi pie (£4.50); the smart restaurant is no smoking in the evening. The neatly kept, spacious open-plan bar has good strong wooden furnishings, lots of interesting prints, well kept King Horsham Best Bitter, and guests like Arundel Stronghold, Cotleigh Barn Owl, and Sharps Doom Bar on handpump, and a decent wine list; piped music. The Norman church has some unusual decoration. *(Recommended by Ian Phillips, Patricia A Bruce, Terry and Linda Moseley, A Sadler, Karen Eliot, Keith Stevens, Dr Brian and Mrs Anne Hamilton, John Davis, Pamela Goodwyn, John Saul, Jenny and Brian Seller, R T and J C Moggridge, MLR)*

Free house ~ Licensees James Rose and Kate Holle ~ Real ale ~ Bar food (not Sun evening) ~ Restaurant ~ (01903) 883131 ~ Well behaved children over 8 in eating areas ~ Open 11-2.30, 6-11; 12-3, 7-10.30 Sun; closed Sun evening Oct-Easter

BYWORTH SU9820 Map 2
Black Horse
Off A283

New licensees have taken over this interesting old country pub and readers have been quick to voice their enthusiasm. The simply furnished though smart bar has pews and scrubbed wooden tables on its bare floorboards, pictures and old photographs on the walls, large open fires, and newspapers to read; no noisy music or games machines to spoil the chatty atmosphere, and perhaps Dexter the golden retriever whose bed is under the stairs. The no smoking back dining room has lots of nooks and crannies, and there's an upstairs restaurant with lovely views of the Downs. Using local produce, the good, daily-changing and generously served food cooked by the landlord might include sandwiches (from £4), ploughman's (from £4.95), filled baked potatoes (from £5.25), home-made duck and orange pâté (£5.75), english asparagus and crayfish (£6.95), lentil bake (£8.95), home-made crab cakes with citrus salad or cajun chicken with tortilla chips and a cheese and herb dip (£9.25), popular steak and kidney pudding or fresh local trout (£9.50), aberdeen angus steaks (from £12.95), and puddings like spicy tipsy bread and butter pudding, banoffi pie or sticky treacle tart (£5.50); they also offer 12 different cheeses (any three, £5.50), and Sunday roasts (£8.75). Well kept Cheriton Pots Ale, and a couple of guests from breweries like Arundel, Hogs Back, and Itchen Valley on handpump. Darts, table skittles, shove-ha'penny, cribbage, and dominoes. The particularly attractive garden is at its best in summer: tables on a steep series of grassy terraces, sheltered by banks of flowering shrubs, look across a drowsy valley to swelling woodland. *(Recommended by Tom and Rosemary Hall, Cathy Robinson, Ed Coombe, David Cosham, John Beeken, Tony and Wendy Hobden)*

Cockerel Inns ~ Managers Dave and Jo Byford ~ Real ale ~ Bar food ~ Restaurant ~ (01798) 342424 ~ Well behaved children in restaurant ~ Dogs allowed in bar ~ Open 11-11; 12-10.30 Sun; 11-3, 5-11 weekdays in winter

CHARLTON SU8812 Map 3
Fox Goes Free
Village signposted off A286 Chichester—Midhurst in Singleton, also from Chichester—Petworth via East Dean

As there is so much to do around here, this cheerful old pub always has a good mix of customers and a bustling atmosphere; it's doing very well at the moment. Goodwood Racecourse is not far away (on race days it does get very busy), it's also handy for the Weald and Downland Open Air Museum, there are some fine surrounding walks, and the Wednesday evening live music night is popular. The first of the dark and cosy series of separate rooms is a small bar with three tables, a few very mixed chairs and an open fireplace. Standing timbers divide a larger beamed bar which has old and new elm furniture, a huge brick fireplace with a woodburning stove, a couple of elderly armchairs, red tiles and carpet, and brasses and old local photographs on the yellowed walls. A dining area with hunting prints looks over the garden and the South Downs beyond. The no smoking family extension is a clever conversion from horse boxes and the stables where the 1926 Goodwood winner was housed; darts, cribbage, dominoes, fruit machine, and piped music. Well kept Ballards Best, Fox Goes Free (brewed for the pub by Ballards), Greene King Old Speckled Hen, and a guest such as Fullers London Pride or Hop Back Summer Lightning on handpump, Pimms and sangria by the jug in summer, farm cider and several wines by the glass. Good, interesting bar food might include sandwiches or filled baguettes (from £4; not Sunday), filled baked potatoes or ploughman's (£5), avocado and stilton bake (£4.50), crab and cheese bake or mushrooms stuffed with goats cheese (£5.50), king prawns fried in ginger (£6.50), steak and kidney pie or wild mushroom stroganoff (£8.25), liver and bacon (£8.50), chicken breast with mushrooms and bacon (£11), venison steak with redcurrant and port (£11.50), duck breast with roquefort and red wine (£12.50), monkfish with bacon, cream and wine or tuna with pesto and pepper

(£12.50), and puddings (£3.95); you can choose between their larger or smaller helpings of vegetables. The attractive secluded garden is the best place to sit in summer, with several terraces, plenty of picnic-sets among fruit trees, and a notable downland view; the barbecue area can be booked. The friendly jack russell is called Wiggles and the black cat, Guinness. More reports please. *(Recommended by Susan and John Douglas, Keith Stevens, W A Evershed, Linda Blair, Rob Dunton, Martin and Karen Wake, Robert M Warner, Neil Rose, W W Burke, Felicity Stephens, John Davis, Michael and Ann Cole, P R and S A White, Prof and Mrs S Barnett, Ian Wilson, Ann and Colin Hunt)*

Free house ~ Licensee Oliver Ligertwood ~ Real ale ~ Bar food (12-2.30, 6.30-10.30 (10 Sun)) ~ (01243) 811461 ~ Children in eating area of bar and restaurant ~ Dogs allowed in bar and bedrooms ~ Live music Weds evening ~ Open 11-3, 5.30-11; 11-11 Sat; 12-10.30 Sun ~ Bedrooms: £40S/£60S(£90B)

CHIDDINGLY TQ5414 Map 3
Six Bells ★ £
Village signed off A22 Uckfield—Hailsham

You can be sure of a genuinely friendly welcome from the cheerful landlord in this old-fashioned pub. There's always a chatty, bustling atmosphere, and solid old wood furnishings include pews and antique seats, log fires, lots of fusty artefacts and interesting bric-a-brac, and plenty of local pictures and posters. A sensitive extension provides some much needed family space; dominoes and cribbage. Particularly for this part of the country, the bar food is a bargain: straightforward but tasty, there might be french onion soup (£1.50), filled baguettes, steak and kidney pie (£2.90), ploughman's (from £3.50), ravioli in spicy sauce (£3.60), baked potatoes (from £3.80), spare ribs in barbecue sauce, tuna pasta bake or chicken curry (£4.80), hock of ham and beans (£6.95), and puddings like treacle tart or banoffi pie (£2.70). Well kept Courage Directors, Harveys Best, and a guest such as King Horsham Best Bitter on handpump. Outside at the back, there are some tables beyond a big raised goldfish pond, and a boules pitch; the church opposite has an interesting Jefferay monument. Vintage and Kit car meetings outside the pub every month. This is a pleasant area for walks. More reports please. *(Recommended by Phil and Sally Gorton, Jenny and Peter Lowater, David and Pam Wilcox, John Beeken)*

Free house ~ Licensees Paul Newman and Emma Bannister ~ Real ale ~ Bar food (12-2.30, 6-10; 12-10 Sat, 12-9 Sun) ~ (01825) 872227 ~ Children in family room ~ Dogs allowed in bar ~ Live music Fri, Sat and Sun evenings, folk and blues club every other Tues ~ Open 11-3, 6-11; 11-12 Sat; 12-10.30 Sun

CHIDHAM SU7804 Map 2
Old House At Home
Off A259 at Barleycorn pub

A new licensee has taken over this bustling country pub but hopes to make few changes. The homely bar has timbering and low beams, windsor chairs around the tables, long seats against the walls, and a welcoming log fire. The menu was changing as we went to press but might include starters (from £3.50), main courses (from £6.95), and puddings (from £3.50): home-made soup, filled baguettes, ploughman's, pâté, smoked salmon with cream cheese and chives, steak and kidney pie, thai curry, chicken carbonara, medallions of beef, and monkfish. Part of the restaurant is no smoking. Well kept Fullers London Pride, Greene King Abbot, Wadworths 6X, and Youngs Waggle Dance on handpump, and several malt whiskies. More reports please. *(Recommended by Ann and Colin Hunt, Peter Meister, W A Evershed, Mr and Mrs R W Allan, Charles and Pauline Stride, Tracey and Stephen Groves, John Davis, Derek and Margaret Underwood, Ian Phillips, P K Hope-Lang)*

Free house ~ Licensee Don Hoare ~ Real ale ~ Bar food ~ Restaurant ~ (01243) 572477 ~ Children in eating area of bar and restaurant ~ Dogs allowed in bar ~ Open 12-3, 6-11; 12-11 Sat; 12-10.30 Sun

COMPTON SU7714 Map 2
Coach & Horses ◀

B2146 S of Petersfield

In a pleasant village with attractively wooded hilly countryside nearby, this neatly kept 15th-c village local caters well for walkers, with an open fire at each end of the roomy front public bar. The Village Bar has pine shutters and panelling, and the original pitched pine block floor has been restored. It is here that the enjoyable food, cooked by the landlord, is served: sandwiches or filled baguettes (from £3.95), home-made soup (£3.10), black pudding, bacon and poached egg salad (£5.25), chicken and mushroom pie (£8.95), baked aubergine with chargrilled peppers and brie (£8.50), and chicken breast with grain mustard and almond sauce (£9.75). The charming little plush beamed lounge bar serves as a relaxing ante-room to the attractive restaurant. Well kept Brewsters Hophead, Cheriton Village Elder, Dark Star, fff Alton's Pride, and maybe Ballards Best on handpump; old-fashioned juke box, bar billiards, cribbage and dominoes. There are tables out by the square in front; it's not far from Uppark (NT). *(Recommended by Ian Phillips, John Evans, John Davis, W A Evershed, Ann and Colin Hunt, Mary and Bill Kemp, Bruce Bird)*

Free house ~ Licensees David and Christiane Butler ~ Real ale ~ Bar food ~ Restaurant ~ (023) 9263 1228 ~ Children in eating area of bar ~ Dogs allowed in bar ~ Open 11.30-2.30(3 Sat), 6-11; 12-3, 7-10.30 Sun; closed one week late Feb

CUCKFIELD TQ3025 Map 3
White Harte ◀

South Street; off A272 W of Haywards Heath

To be sure of a table in this pretty, partly medieval tile-hung pub, you must get here early or book in advance – it is a very popular place for its good value and honest lunchtime food: double egg and chips (£4), ploughman's (£5.20), home-made quiche (£5.90), and daily specials such as lasagne (£5.90), chicken, turkey and bacon pie or chicken curry (£6.20), and lamb shanks (£6.90); the restaurant area is no smoking at lunchtimes. The comfortable beamed lounge has a mix of polished floorboards, parquet and ancient brick flooring tiles, standing timbers, a few local photographs, padded seats on a slightly raised area, and some fairly modern light oak tables. Furnishings in the public bar are sturdy and comfortable with a roaring log fire in the inglenook, and sensibly placed darts. Well kept Badger Best and K&B and a guest beer on handpump; piped music, TV, cribbage, dominoes, and shove-ha'penny. There are seats and tables under parasols and fine downland views in the pretty back garden which is next to the church. More reports please. *(Recommended by W A Evershed, Robert M Warner, DWAJ, Terry Buckland, R T and J C Moggridge, Fred Chamberlain, Jeremy Woods, Glenwys and Alan Lawrence)*

Badger ~ Tenant Andy Felton ~ Real ale ~ Bar food (lunchtime only, not Mon) ~ Restaurant ~ (01444) 413454 ~ Children welcome ~ Dogs allowed in bar ~ Folk music last Sun of month ~ Open 11-3, 6-11; 12-3, 7-10.30 Sun; closed Mon lunchtime

DANEHILL TQ4128 Map 3
Coach & Horses ⑪ ♟

From A275 in Danehill (S of Forest Row), take School Lane towards Chelwood Common

Sussex Dining Pub of the Year

This well run and welcoming cottagey pub manages cleverly to appeal to a wide mix of customers – locals dropping in for a pint and a chat, customers wanting a good meal out, and children who have a nice hedged-off play area and perhaps a horse in the next-door field to keep them amused. There's a little public bar to the right with half-panelled walls, simple furniture on highly polished wooden floorboards, a small woodburning stove in the brick fireplace, and a big hatch to the bar; darts, cribbage, dominoes, and piped music. The main bar is on the left with plenty of locals crowding around the wooden bar counter or sitting at the high wooden bar stools enjoying the well kept Harveys Best, and a couple of guests from Badger, Brakspears or Timothy Taylors on handpump; good wines by the generous glass, and summer champagne-method cider. Leading from this bar is a new terrace (adults only) under a huge maple tree which will catch the evening sun. Drinks are stacked in a nice old-fashioned way on shelves behind the bar, and there's just one table on the stripped wood floor here. A couple of steps lead down to a half-panelled area with a mix of wheelbacks and old dining chairs around several characterful wooden tables on the fine brick floor, a large lantern in the tiny brick fireplace, and some large Victorian prints; candles and flowers on the tables. Down another step to the no smoking dining area (which has been redecorated this year) with stone walls, a beamed vaulted ceiling, hops hanging from other beams, and a woodburning stove; through a lovely arched doorway is a small room with just a couple of tables. Served by friendly staff, the enjoyable bar food includes snacks like sandwiches on granary or ciabatta bread or filled baguettes, a changing soup such as chilled gazpacho with basil pesto (£4.25), parma ham, duck and foie gras roulade with toasted brioche or spicy crab spaghetti with saffron cream (£6.25), antipasti misto (£6.95), pork and leek sausages with onion marmalade and red wine jus (£8.50), wild mushroom risotto with truffle oil (£9.50), seafood panaché or fried salmon with buttered spinach and herb cream (£10.75), honey-roast duck confit with oriental vegetables (£11.95), and puddings such as iced dark chocolate parfait with berry compote, sticky toffee pudding or glazed lemon tart with crème fraîche (£4.25). The big attractive garden has plenty of seats, and fine views of the South Downs. *(Recommended by Mrs Jane Williams, Tony and Wendy Hobden, Simon Lambert, Mrs J R Sillitoe, Miss G Kybert, Miss R Stevens, Neill Barker, Debbie and Neil Hayter, John Murray, Peter Meister, RDK, Derek and Maggie Washington, Dominic Morgan)*

Free house ~ Licensee Ian Philpots ~ Real ale ~ Bar food (till 9.30 Fri and Sat; not Sun evening exc bank hol wknds) ~ Restaurant ~ (01825) 740369 ~ Well behaved, seated children welcome ~ Dogs allowed in bar ~ Open 11.30(4 Sat)-3, 6-11; 12-4, 7-10.30 Sun; closed evening 25 Dec, 26 Dec and evening 1 Jan

DONNINGTON SU8502 Map 2
Blacksmiths Arms

Turn off A27 on to A286 signposted Selsey, then almost immediately left on to B2201

A beacon for real ale fans, this little white roadside cottage offers four constantly changing well kept real ales such as Fullers London Pride, Greene King Abbot, Oakleaf Bitter and Squirrel's Delight, and Youngs Special on handpump. The small low-ceilinged rooms have Victorian prints on the walls, solid, comfortable furnishings, and a relaxed, welcoming atmosphere. Well liked bar food includes sandwiches (from £3.95), filled baguettes (from £4.95), filled baked potatoes (from £5.25), and ploughman's (£5.55), as well as lunchtime one-course (£6.95), two-course (£8.95), and three-course (£10.95) choices: home-made soup, pâté, devilled whitebait with home-made tartare sauce, battered cod and chips, braised beef, Guinness and mushroom pie, mediterranean vegetable bake, and home-cooked honey-baked ham with pickled peaches. In the evening, there might be grilled goats cheese, roast artichoke and olive salad (£4.95), king prawns in garlic butter (£5.25), chargrilled chicken with stroganoff sauce (£9.95), sirloin steak with creamy mushroom and pepper sauce (£10.50), and english lamb cutlets with redcurrant and rosemary jus (£11.50), and they get fresh fish from Portsmouth several times a week – herb-crusted cod (£10.95), wild sea bream with citrus sauce (£11.95), and dover sole with saffron and dill (£14.95). The big garden has a play area with swings, a climbing frame, a rabbit called Barnham, two dogs (Tess and Cleo), a cat (Amber), and four tortoises (only allowed in the garden on special occasions), and plenty of picnic-sets. *(Recommended by Paul A Moore, Felicity Stephens, Mrs J Muirhead, A and B D Craig, Ian Phillips, Val and Alan Green, Bob and Margaret Holder, Keith Stevens, Bruce Bird, Susan and Peter Davies, Christopher and Elise Way, Nick Roberts, Ann and Colin Hunt, Tracey and Stephen Groves)*

InnSpired ~ Tenant Lesley Ward ~ Real ale ~ Bar food ~ Restaurant ~ (01243)
783999 ~ Children welcome ~ Dogs welcome ~ Open 11-3, 5-11; 11-11 Fri and Sat;
12-10.30 Sun; closed Sun evening in Jan and Feb

DUNCTON SU9617 Map 3
Cricketers
Set back from A285

Although a function room has been added to this pretty little white pub, and there's
a new licensee, it remains a friendly place with a mix of customers. The bar has a
few standing timbers giving the room an open-plan feel, there's an inglenook
fireplace at one end with a good winter fire, cricketing pictures and paintings and
bats on the walls, and a mix of country chairs around scrubbed wooden tables;
down a couple of steps a similarly furnished no smoking room is set for eating –
piped music here. Good, popular bar food now includes light bites such as soup
(£3.95), filled baguettes or tortilla wraps (from £3.95; duck and hoi sin wrap
£5.95), ploughman's (from £4.50), spanish-type omelette with tomato and red
onion salad (£5.50), chicken livers and smoked bacon on olive and caper salad with
roasted garlic dressing or antipasti (£5.95), pasta of the day (from £7.95), lamb
kofta kebab with fresh mint yoghurt dressing (£9.95), and cumberland sausage or
honey ham with two eggs (£8.95), with more elaborate choices such as lemon grass
and coriander steamed local mussels with coconut milk or fresh baby squid on pak
choi and seaweed with peppered pineapple and cucumber sambal (£5.95), creamy
vanilla and artichoke linguini with fresh tarragon mascarpone (£9.25), and grilled
pork fillet on chorizo and apple frittata with blue cheese guacamole and home-
made frites (£10.50). Well kept Youngs Bitter and a couple of guests from Ballards,
Harveys or Hogs Back on handpump, and several decent wines by the glass. The
charming garden behind the building has a proper barbecue, picnic-sets, and an
attractive little creeper-covered seating area, and the flowering baskets and tubs at
the front are very lovely. More reports please. *(Recommended by Tracey and
Stephen Groves, David Cosham, Felicity Stephens, Nigel Williamson, Simon and Sally Small,
J A Snell, Jason Caulkin)*

Inn Company ~ Tenant Jonathan O'Riley ~ Real ale ~ Bar food ~ Restaurant ~
(01798) 342473 ~ Children in restaurant ~ Dogs welcome ~ Open 11-3(3.30 Sat),
6-11; 12-3.30, 7-10.30 Sun

EAST ASHLING SU8207 Map 2
Horse & Groom ♀ ◀
B2178 NW of Chichester

This charming country pub mixes a chatty traditional feel with good food and
drink. The front part is a proper bar, with old pale flagstones and a woodburning
stove in a big inglenook on the right, a carpeted area with an old wireless set and
television on the left, nice scrubbed trestle tables, and bar stools along the counter
serving well kept Harveys Best, Hop Back Summer Lightning, Youngs, and a guest
beer such as Fullers London Pride on handpump. They also have a good choice of
wines by the glass, and service nicely balances friendly informality with fast non-
intrusive efficiency. A couple of tables share a small darker-flagstoned middle area
with the big blackboard that lists changing dishes such as carrot and coriander soup
(£3.95), salad niçoise, mushrooms with tomato and mozzarella salad or deep-fried
brie (£5.30), pasta of the day (£8.80), steak and ale pie (£9.25), calves liver and
bacon (£9.90), rack of lamb with honey and rosemary jus (£12.75), various steaks,
lots of fresh fish and seafood such as tuna steak (£9.75), bass on samphire or selsey
crab (£10.50) and garlic king prawns (£10.75), and puddings. They do good fresh
vegetables. The back part of the pub, entirely no smoking and angling right round
behind the bar servery, with a further extension beyond one set of internal
windows, has solid pale country-kitchen furniture on neat bare boards, and a fresh
and airy décor, with a little bleached pine panelling and long white curtains. French
windows lead out to a garden with picnic-sets under cocktail parasols. Always

popular with local people in the know, the pub gets extremely busy on Goodwood race days. We have not yet heard from readers who have stayed in one of the five bedrooms in the adjoining barn conversion, but would expect this to qualify for one of our Place to Stay Awards. *(Recommended by P R and S A White, Ann and Colin Hunt, Jane Basso)*

Free house ~ Licensee Michael Martell ~ Real ale ~ Bar food (not evenings) ~ Restaurant ~ (01243) 575339 ~ Children welcome ~ Dogs allowed in bar and bedrooms ~ Open 12-3, 6-11; 12-6 Sun; closed Sun evening ~ Bedrooms: £40S/£60B

EAST CHILTINGTON TQ3715 Map 3
Jolly Sportsman 🍴 ♀

2 miles N of B2116; Chapel Lane – follow sign to 13th-c church

For a special meal out, this tucked away and civilised Victorian dining pub remains a popular place. The imaginative food includes a fixed price lunch (two courses £11, three courses £14.75): game pâté with onion marmalade or leek and parmesan pappardelle, navarin of lamb or grilled cod fillet with fried polenta cake, and roast pear with vanilla ice cream or macerated figs with crème fraîche. Vegetarian choices like leek, potato and seed mustard soup (£4.85), roast tomato, basil and goats cheese focaccia (£4.90; main course £7.25), and chargrilled peppers, fennel and courgettes, parmesan and rocket (£6.75; main course £9.75), as well as starters such as six irish oysters with red wine shallot vinegar or crispy fried crab pancake with lobster sauce (£6.45), main courses like slow cooked lamb with spiced black beans (£12.45), corn-fed poussin, chorizo and herb polenta cake (£12.95), and roast barbary duck breast, artichoke, st georges mushrooms and peas (£15.45), and puddings such as blueberry and almond tart with vanilla sauce or chocolate tart with crème fraîche (from £5.25). A couple of chairs by the fireplace are set aside for drinkers in the chatty little bar with stripped wood floors and a mix of furniture, but most people head for the smart but informal no smoking restaurant with contemporary light wood furniture, and modern landscapes on green painted walls. Well kept Brewster's Hophead, Dark Star, and Mauldons Best tapped from the cask, a remarkably good wine list, farm cider, up to 30 malts, summer fruit cocktails and good sherries; Scrabble, draughts, cribbage, dominoes, and chess. There are rustic tables and benches under gnarled trees in a pretty cottagey front garden with more on the terrace and the front bricked area, and the large back lawn with a children's play area looks out towards the South Downs; good walks nearby. More reports please. *(Recommended by Alan Cowell, Dr M Mills, J H Bell, Peter Forsyth, B and M Kendall, John Hale)*

Free house ~ Licensee Bruce Wass ~ Real ale ~ Bar food (12.30-3, 7-9.30(10 Fri and Sat)) ~ Restaurant ~ (01273) 890400 ~ Children welcome ~ Dogs welcome ~ Open 12-2.30, 6-11; 12-4 Sun; closed Sun evening, all day Mon (exc bank hols)

EAST DEAN TV5597 Map 3
Tiger ♀

Pub (with village centre) signposted – not vividly – from A259 Eastbourne—Seaford

In summer particularly, this long low tiled pub is a lovely place to visit and you can sit outside beside the pretty window boxes and flowering climbers and look over the delightful cottage-lined green. Inside, there are just nine tables in the two smallish rooms (candlelit at night) so space at peak times is very limited – particularly in winter when you can't stand outside or sit on the grass; they don't, in the best pub tradition, take bookings so you do have to arrive early for a table. There are low beams hung with pewter and china, polished rustic tables and distinctive antique settles, and old prints and so forth. Well kept Harveys Best with guests such as Adnams Best and Brakspears Bitter on handpump, and a good choice of wines with a dozen by the large glass. They get their fish fresh from Hastings, their lamb from the farm on the hill, all vegetables and eggs from another local farm, and meat from the local butcher. From a sensibly short but ever changing menu, the imaginative food might include a choice of 28 different ploughman's (lunchtime only, £5.50), as well as sausage, mash and onion gravy (£5.25), casseroles like burgundy beef with smoked bacon or mediterranean vegetables topped with grilled goats cheese and pesto, thai pork or local plaice (£7.95), chicken breast wrapped in parma ham on sunblush mash with watercress sauce, local crab or roasted fillet of wild scottish salmon with anchovy and caper butter (£8.95), black bream (£9.95), and lobster (£11.95). At lunchtimes on hot days and bank holidays they usually have only cold food. Being on the South Downs Way, it's naturally popular with walkers and the lane leads on down to a fine stretch of coast culminating in Beachy Head. No children inside. *(Recommended by Father Robert Marsh, Susan and John Douglas, Tony and Vivien Smith, Michael and Ann Cole, John Davis, Karen Eliot, Ann and Colin Hunt, Tony and Wendy Hobden, Paul and Penny Dawson, Uta and John Owlett, Phyl and Jack Street)*

Free house ~ Licensee Nicholas Denyer ~ Real ale ~ Bar food (12-2, 6-9(8 Sun)) ~ No credit cards ~ (01323) 423209 ~ Dogs welcome ~ Morris dancers on bank hols, mummers 26 Dec ~ Open 11-3, 6-11; 11-11 Sat; 12-10.30 Sun

ELSTED SU8119 Map 2
Three Horseshoes 🍺

Village signposted from B2141 Chichester—Petersfield; also reached easily from A272 about 2 miles W of Midhurst, turning left heading W

On a wet morning, readers were delighted to be met with lovely log fires, fresh flowers on the tables, and a warm welcome from the friendly landlady. The snug little rooms have ancient beams and flooring, antique furnishings, attractive prints and photographs, candlelight, and a very congenial atmosphere. Enjoyable bar food includes home-made soup (£3.95), a generous ploughman's with a good choice of cheeses (£5.95), avocado and stilton with mushroom sauce and topped with bacon or prawn mayonnaise wrapped in smoked salmon (£6.95), chicken in dijon mustard or tomato and goats cheese tart (£8.95), steak, kidney and Guinness pie (made by Joan for 22 years now) or braised lamb with apples and apricots in a tomato chutney sauce (£9.95), steak and kidney in ale pie (£9.50), fresh seasonal crab and lobster, and delicious home-made puddings such as treacle tart, fruit crumble or summer pudding (£4.75). The dining room is no smoking. Well kept changing ales racked on a stillage behind the bar counter might include Ballards Best, Cheriton Pots, and Timothy Taylors Landlord with guests like Fullers London Pride or Hop Back Summer Lightning; summer cider; dominoes. The lovely garden has free-roaming bantams, plenty of tables, pretty flowers, and marvellous downland views. *(Recommended by P R and S A White, W A Evershed, RDK, J H Bell, John Davis, Tony Radnor, Paul and Penny Dawson, Ann and Colin Hunt, Phil and Sally Gorton, Godfrey and Irene Joly, Tony and Wendy Hobden, John Evans)*

Free house ~ Licensee Sue Beavis ~ Real ale ~ Bar food ~ (01730) 825746 ~ Well behaved children in eating areas ~ Dogs allowed in bar ~ Open 11-2.30, 6-11; 12-3, 7-10.30 Sun

FERNHURST SU8926 Map 2
Kings Arms ♀ 🍺

A286 towards Midhurst

This 17th-c dining pub, with very low heavy black beams virtually throughout, has a relaxed and civilised atmosphere. Besides dishes of the day such as garlic king prawns (£6), rare roast beef (£7.50), skate with caper butter (£10.75), and bass with vanilla and broad bean velouté, the good food includes ploughman's (£6.25), club sandwich with chips (£7.50), sausages and mash (£8.50) and a few other examples of what they call comfort food. The interesting main menu has starters such as crab bisque (£4.75), poached egg, chorizo and asparagus (£6), and warm duck confit salad with beansprouts and mange tout (£6.25), and main dishes such as baked cod with crab and tomato beurre blanc (£11.50), poached chicken breast with wild mushroom mousse (£12), roasted monkfish with scallop and prawn risotto (£14), and fried veal with fondant potatoes and baked vine tomatoes

(£14.25); fresh fish is always a major feature here, and often cooked inventively. On our summer inspection they had some enterprising iced puddings and home-made ice creams as well as summer pudding with clotted cream, banana fritters, and pear tarte tatin with cinnamon cream (all £4.95). They have a nice line in english cheeses (£5.25), and do espresso coffees and so forth. As they warn, because everything is cooked to order your food may take some time to come. The main area, on the left, is all set for dining, but keeps a traditional feel, especially at the far end with its cushioned wall benches and big log fire under a long low mantelbeam. Past here is a smaller no smoking room, with a display of often intriguing bottle openers, as well as the main concentration of the wine-oriented pictures which form the pub's decorative theme. Its choice of wines is good and interesting, with plenty by the glass. People dropping in just for a drink feel entirely at home, with welcoming service, a table of local newspapers, and a pleasantly chatty seating area on the right, including one long table with a big vase of flowers, by the bar counter, which has well kept changing real ales on handpump, such as Caledonian Nectar, Hop Back Hop Garden Gold, Ringwood Best and Tring Side Pocket, as well as a good value beer brewed for the pub by Ventnor. The lavatories are exemplary, and a fair-sized garden has green picnic-sets under cocktail parasols, or shaded by a weeping willow; though it is completely screened from the road, there is some traffic noise. If you are heading S, take particular care leaving the car park. *(Recommended by Mr and Mrs Gordon Turner, Martin and Karen Wake)*

Free house ~ Licensees Michael and Annabel Hirst ~ Real ale ~ Bar food (12-2.30, 7-9.30) ~ Restaurant ~ (01428) 652005 ~ Children till 7, away from bar ~ Dogs allowed in bar ~ Open 11.30-3, 5.30(6.30 Sat)-11; 12-3 Sun; closed Sun evening

FLETCHING TQ4223 Map 3

Griffin ★ ⊕ ☟ ⇌

Village signposted off A272 W of Uckfield

Run by helpful, friendly and professional people, this civilised old inn has beamed and quaintly panelled bar rooms with a good bustling and chatty atmosphere; also, blazing log fires, old photographs and hunting prints, straightforward furniture including some captain's chairs, china on a delft shelf, and a small bare-boarded serving area off to one side. A snug separate bar has sofas and TV. Imaginative food might include hot ciabatta sandwiches (£4.95), grilled lemon-scented sardines with tomato sauce (£5.50), chicken liver parfait with apricot and date chutney or tuscan winter vegetable soup (£5.95), organic veal meatballs with fresh tomato salsa on tagliatelle, beef bourguignon or sweet potato, oyster mushrooms and taleggio tart (£8.50), free range chicken with olives, potatoes, fennel and white wine (£9.50), slow-roast lamb shanks in red wine with herb mash (£8.95), whole grilled local plaice with lemon and parsley butter (£11.50), chargrilled rib-eye steak with home-made chips and fresh horseradish butter (£12.95), and puddings such as raspberry cheesecake, sticky toffee pudding or dark chocolate marquise and poached pear (£4.95); english cheeses and chutney (£5.50). Well kept Badger Tanglefoot, Harveys Best, King Horsham Best Bitter, and Rother Valley Level Best on handpump, and a fine wine list with a dozen (including champagne) by the glass. The two acres of garden behind the pub look across fine rolling countryside towards Sheffield Park, and there are plenty of seats here and on a sheltered gravel terrace where you can enjoy a summer drink or meal. *(Recommended by Mandy and Simon King, Peter Forsyth, Mrs J R Sillitoe, Pierre and Pat Richterich, Colin and Janet Roe, Mike and Heather Watson, Christopher and Elise Way, Derek Thomas, Mrs J Potter, S F Parrinder, Paul A Moore, J H Bell, Dr Paull Khan, M B R Savage; also in the Good Hotel Guide)*

Free house ~ Licensees N Pullan, J Pullan and John Gatti ~ Real ale ~ Bar food (12-2.30, 7-9.30(9 Sun)) ~ Restaurant ~ (01825) 722890 ~ Children welcome ~ Dogs allowed in bar ~ Live music Fri evening and Sun lunchtime ~ Open 12-3, 6-11; 12-11 Sat; 12-10.30 Sun; closed 25 Dec ~ Bedrooms: £60S/£85B

HAMMERPOT TQ0605 Map 3
Woodmans Arms

Pub visible and well signposted on N (eastbound) side of A27 just under 4 miles E of A284 at Arundel; heading W on A27 the turn is about ½ mile beyond the pub

You can expect a warm welcome from the licensees and their smartly dressed staff in this pretty and neatly kept 16th-c pub. The brick-floored entrance area has a cosy armchair by the inglenook's big log fire, lots of brass, pictures by local artists for sale, and old photographs of regulars. On the right a carpeted no smoking dining area with candles on the tables has wheelback chairs around its tables, and cheerfully cottagey decorations, and on the left a small no smoking room has a few more tables. Some of the beams are so low they are strung with fairy lights as a warning. Well presented honest food includes home-made soups (£3.25), sandwiches (from £3.25), home-made lasagne (£6.95), popular home-made steak and kidney pie, sussex pie (spicy sausage meat with herbs and garlic), broccoli and stilton bake or smoked haddock and prawns in a rich cheese sauce (all £7.25), home-made curry (£7.45), extra mature steaks with sauces (from £11.95), and two Sunday roasts (£7.95). Well kept Gales GB, HSB, Butser Bitter and a guest such as Timothy Taylors Landlord or Wadworths 6X on handpump, and country wines. Cribbage, dominoes, and piped music. The yellow labrador is called Tikka. The garden here – despite some road noise – is charming, with picnic-sets and tables on a terrace (they have mobile outside heaters for chillier weather), under a fairy-lit arbour, and on small lawns among lots of roses and tubs of bright annuals. This is good walking country and they offer a free downland walking map. At the end of April, there's a landlords-led bluebell walk with Sunday lunch (£7.50; must book). *(Recommended by Ann and Colin Hunt, Ian Phillips, R T and J C Moggridge, Colin Draper, Dr and Mrs A K Clarke, John Davis, E F Given, Tony and Wendy Hobden, Bruce Bird, Ian and Jane Irving)*

Gales ~ Tenants Malcolm and Ann Green ~ Real ale ~ Bar food (not Sun evening) ~ Restaurant ~ (01903) 871240 ~ Well behaved children in restaurant and family room ~ Dogs allowed in bar ~ Folk every second Sun evening ~ Open 11-3, 6-11; 12-3, 7-10.30 Sun

HEATHFIELD TQ5920 Map 3
Star

Old Heathfield – head E out of Heathfield itself on A265, then fork right on to B2096; turn right at signpost to Heathfield Church then keep bearing right; pub on left immediately after church

Whether you are a local or a visitor, you can expect a good welcome from the helpful staff in this 14th-c pilgrims' inn, tucked away below the Early English tower of the church. The L-shaped beamed bar has a relaxed, chatty atmosphere, a fine log fire in the inglenook fireplace, panelling, built-in wall settles and window seats, and just four or five tables; a doorway leads into a similarly furnished smaller room. The tables are candlelit at night. Chalked up on boards, a decent choice of bar food includes home-made soup (£4.50), home-made chicken liver pâté with cumberland sauce (£5.50), mussels provençale (£6.50; main course £8.50), ploughman's and filled baked potatoes (£6.95), smoked ham with free range eggs (£7.95), home-made beef, ale and potato pie, cumberland sausage with red wine and onion gravy or locally caught fish with chips (£8.50), smoked salmon fillet marinated in brandy and dill with a piquant sweet and sour mayonnaise (£10.95), and popular half a free range duck with a tangy orange and honey sauce (£11.95); efficient, courteous service. Well kept Harveys Best, Shepherd Neame Best Bitter, and a guest such as Hop Back Summer Lightning on handpump, some malt whiskies, farm cider, and a good bloody mary; piped music, shove-ha'penny, and bar billiards. The prettily planted sloping garden with its rustic furniture has lovely views of rolling oak-lined sheep pastures – Turner thought it fine enough to paint. *(Recommended by Uta and John Owlett, Mrs J Thomas, Mrs P E Brown, E G Parish, John Evans, Robert M Warner, Jenny and Peter Lowater, Alan Cowell)*

Free house ~ Licensees Mike Chappell and Fiona Airey ~ Real ale ~ Bar food (12-2.15, 7-9.30) ~ Restaurant ~ (01435) 863570 ~ Children in eating area of bar ~ Dogs allowed in bar ~ Open 11.30-3, 5.30-11; 12-4, 7-10.30 Sun; closed evenings 25 and 26 Dec

HENLEY SU8925 Map 2
Duke of Cumberland Arms 🍺

Village signposted just off A286 S of Fernhurst, N of Midhurst; if coming from Midhurst, take first turn into village, then keep bearing right; OS Sheet 186 map reference 894258

There are just two unpretentious little low-ceilinged rooms in this tucked away 15th-c cottage – each with a log fire; also, gas lamps on white-painted panelled walls, simple seats around scrubbed rough oak tables, and a few wood carvings, plates, old framed documents, and stuffed birds and animals. Decent bar food includes soup (£3.75), twice-baked goats cheese and thyme soufflé (£4.50), sandwiches (from £4.50), terrine of rabbit, pigeon and venison (£4.75), ploughman's (£5.50), salads (from £5.50), calves liver and bacon with onion gravy (£9.95), grey mullet on fine pasta with a rich tomato compote (£10.95), and rosemary-roasted bass or rump steak with peppercorn sauce (£12.50); their speciality english roasts need 24 hours' notice: from £12.75. Well kept Adnams Broadside, Fullers London Pride, Hop Back Summer Lightning, and Youngs with guests like Gribble Fursty Ferret and Hogs Back TEA and Garden Gold tapped from the cask, and Rich's farm cider; no piped music or games. The red and white bulldog is called Jasper and his sister, Sasha. In summer, the three-and-a-half acre garden here is rather special. It's on a slope, and lush and quite big, with lilacs and other shrubs, and willows by a stream running down through a series of three ponds once used for the pre-industrial iron industry here, but now stocked with trout (which you'll find on the menu). Gnarled old benches and more modern seats out here give lovely views over Black Down and the wooded hills south of Haslemere. More reports please. *(Recommended by Martin and Karen Wake, J A Snell, Susan and John Douglas, John Beeken, Ian Phillips, Mike and Sue Richardson)*

Free house ~ Licensees Gaston Duval and Christina Duval ~ Real ale ~ Bar food (12-2.30, 7-9.30; not Sun evening) ~ Restaurant ~ (01428) 652280 ~ Children welcome ~ Dogs welcome ~ Open 11-3, 5-11; 12-3, 7-10.30 Sun

HORSHAM TQ1730 Map 3
Black Jug 🍷

31 North Street

Even when it's really busy, the staff here remain cheerful and friendly. There's a lively, bustling atmosphere in the airy open-plan turn-of-the-century-style room, and a large central bar, a nice collection of heavy sizeable dark wood tables, comfortable chairs on a stripped wood floor, cream walls crammed with interesting old prints and photographs above a dark wood panelled dado, and a warm terracotta ceiling. A spacious no smoking conservatory has similar furniture and lots of hanging baskets; piped music. Well kept Greene King Abbot, King Horsham Best Bitter, Marstons Pedigree, and Wadworths 6X, with a guest such as Weltons on handpump, 40 malt whiskies, a good wine list with 20 by the glass, and eight chilled vodkas from Poland and Russia. Good bar food includes soup (£3.90), open sandwiches or filled baguettes (from £3.95; chicken, bacon, tomato and lettuce in a flour tortilla £5.50), home-made duck liver and orange pâté with rhubarb and red onion marmalade (£4.95), ploughman's (£5.95), smoked haddock and salmon fishcakes with lemon chutney (£6.95), home-baked ham and egg (£7.25), spinach, ricotta and mushroom pasta bake (£7.95), home-made steakburger with bacon and cheese or steak in ale pie (£8.95), fried cod in beer batter with home-made tartare sauce (£10.95), mediterranean spiced chicken on roasted vegetables (£11.95), scotch rib-eye steak with red wine and mushroom sauce (£13.95), and puddings like white and dark chocolate truffle mousse or sticky toffee pudding (£4.50). The pretty flower-filled back terrace has plenty of garden furniture by outside heaters.

More reports please. *(Recommended by Sebastian Leach, J Garrison, Roger and Debbie Stamp, Ian Phillips, Mr Bannon, Sam, Rev Guy Devon-Smith, Wombat)*

Brunning & Price ~ Manager Sam Cornwall-Jones ~ Real ale ~ Bar food (12-10) ~ (01403) 253526 ~ Children in eating area of bar and restaurant ~ Dogs allowed in bar ~ Open 11-11; 12-10.30 Sun; closed 26 Dec

ICKLESHAM TQ8716 Map 3
Queens Head ♀ ◖

Just off A259 Rye—Hastings

This is the sort of friendly place that you can enjoy just as much if you are with friends, children or even the dog – the landlord and his staff work hard to keep everyone happy. The open-plan areas work round a very big serving counter which stands under a vaulted beamed roof, the high beamed walls and ceiling of the easy-going bar are lined with shelves of bottles and covered with farming implements and animal traps, and there are well used pub tables and old pews on the brown patterned carpet. Other areas (two are no smoking and popular with diners) have big inglenook fireplaces. Well kept Cotleigh Tawny, Courage Directors, Greene King IPA and Abbot, Harveys Best, Oakham Bishops Farewell, Ringwood Fortyniner, and Wells Bombardier on handpump; Biddenden cider, and all wines on the list are available by the glass. Generously served, enjoyable bar food includes sandwiches (from £2.45), home-made soup (£3.50), home-made pâté (£4.25), good soft herring roes on toast (£4.95), ham and egg (£5.95), ploughman's (from £5.95), vegetable curry (£6.95), tasty steak, ale and mushroom pie (£7.50), fresh fish like cod, scallops or skate (from £7.50), steaks (from £9.95), and daily specials like courgette and lentil gratin (£6.50), barbecue pork (£7.95), and calves liver (£8.75); prompt service from efficient staff. Shove-ha'penny, dominoes, cribbage, darts, fruit machine, and piped music. Picnic-sets look out over the vast, gently sloping plain of the Brede valley from the little garden, and there's an outside children's play area, and boules. Good local walks. *(Recommended by Kevin Thorpe, S and R Gray, Bruce Bird, John Davis, Peter Meister, Bob and Margaret Holder, Pamela and Merlyn Horswell, E G Parish, Evelyn and Derek Walter, V Brogden, Ruth and Paul Lawrence, Peter and Joan Elbra, B and M Kendall, Wombat)*

Free house ~ Licensee Ian Mitchell ~ Real ale ~ Bar food (12-2.45, 6.15-9.45; all day Sat, Sun) ~ (01424) 814552 ~ Well behaved children in eating area of bar until 8.30pm ~ Dogs allowed in bar ~ Live jazz/blues/folk Tues evening ~ Open 11-11; 12-10.30 Sun

LEWES TQ4110 Map 3
Snowdrop ◖

South Street; off Cliffe High Street, opposite S end of Malling Street just S of A26 roundabout

Things haven't changed too much under the new licensee, and this bustling pub still has a good mix of customers. There's been some gentle tidying up but the unusual maritime theme remains – including figureheads, ship lamps and other objects of interest. There are two spacious areas (with extra seating outside) with the cliffs as a spectacular backdrop, and the corner by the spiral staircase is cosy and sunny; a small part is no smoking. Upstairs there are more seats and a second pool table. Enjoyable good value food now includes tortilla wraps with fillings like roasted lemon chicken with herb mayonnaise (£3.75; steak with horseradish in focaccia, £3.95), soup (£3.95), open bruschetta with avocado, bacon and salsa (£5.95), pizzas (from £5.95; fresh spinach, olives, peppers, onions and pine nuts, and cheese if required, £6.95), pork and spring onion patties with a watercress and roast red pepper salad (£6.75), tasty mezze plate or a cheese plate using local cheeses (£6.95), and tuna and crayfish tail kebab served on stir-fried egg noodles (£7.95); children's menu. Well kept Harveys Best with a couple of guests like Fullers London Pride and Greene King IPA; piped music, and TV. New wooden seats outside. More reports on the new regime, please. *(Recommended by Jason Caulkin, John Davis, Sarah Davis, Rod Lambert, Keith Stevens, MLR, Patrick Hancock, Tracey and Stephen Groves)*

Free house ~ Licensee Tanya Gander ~ Real ale ~ Bar food (12-9) ~ No credit cards ~ (01273) 471018 ~ Children welcome ~ Dogs welcome ~ Live jazz Mon evening, local bands Sat evening ~ Open 11-11; 12-10.30 Sun

LODSWORTH SU9223 Map 2
Halfway Bridge Inn ★ ⑪ ♀ 🍴 🛏

Just before village, on A272 Midhurst—Petworth

There's a bustling, friendly atmosphere in this smartly civilised inn, and a good mix of customers. The three or four bar rooms are comfortably furnished with good oak chairs and an individual mix of tables, and they use attractive fabrics for the wood-railed curtains and pew cushions. Down some steps, the charming no smoking country dining room has a dresser and longcase clock; one of the log fires is contained in a well polished kitchen range, and paintings by a local artist line the walls. A good range of drinks includes well kept beers such as Cheriton Pots Ale, Fullers London Pride, Gales HSB, and guests such as Branscombe Vale Summa'that, Cheriton Village Elder and Hepworths Pullman on handpump, rather special local cider, and a thoughtful little wine list with a changing choice by the glass; dominoes, cribbage, shove-ha'penny, and board games. Good interesting bar food includes lunchtime sandwiches such as BLT (from £4.75), three cheese tortellini with tomato and basil sauce (£4.95), honey-marinated smoked duck, rocket and raspberry salad (£6.95), local organic sausages with grain mustard mash and onion gravy (£7.50), fish pie or honey-roasted ham with pea and mint mash and fried eggs (£7.95), spinach and wild mushroom korma (£8.50), risotto of lemon-roasted chicken and basil (£9.50), steak, kidney, mushroom and Guinness pudding (£9.95), local organic sirloin steak (£15.25), and puddings such as toasted panettone and dark chocolate sandwich or banana toffee pie (£3.95). The friendly jack russell is called Ralph, and the jack-russell cross, Chip (they wear obligatory 'please don't feed me' badges). At the back there are seats on a small terrace. *(Recommended by Cathy Robinson, Ed Coombe, Peter and Audrey Dowsett, Julie and Bill Ryan, John Davis, W A Evershed, John Evans, Mike and Lynn Robinson, Derek and Sylvia Stephenson, Mike and Mary Carter, Sefton Parke, Kate Hillaby, Martin and Karen Wake, David and Rita Liddiard, George and Brenda Jones, Jane Basso, JCW)*

Free house ~ Licensees Simon and James Hawkins ~ Real ale ~ Bar food (12-2(2.30 wknds), 7-10) ~ Restaurant ~ (01798) 861281 ~ Children over 10 in restaurant ~ Dogs allowed in bar ~ Open 11-3, 5.30(6 Sat)-11; 12-3, 7-10.30 Sun ~ Bedrooms: £60.90B/£90.90B

LURGASHALL SU9327 Map 2
Noahs Ark

Village signposted from A283 N of Petworth; OS Sheet 186 map reference 936272

In summer, this charming 16th-c pub is an especially nice place to visit. The flowering baskets are splendid, there's a back garden with seating, and picnic-sets on the grass in front that are ideally placed for watching the local cricket team play on the village green. Inside, the two neatly furnished bars have warm log fires (one in a capacious inglenook), well kept Greene King IPA, Abbot and Old Speckled Hen on handpump, and several well polished trophies. The family room is decorated like the inside of an ark; darts, dominoes, cribbage and piped music. Well liked bar food (with prices unchanged since last year) includes soup (£3.25), sandwiches (from £3.75; wild boar and apple sausage with caramelised onions £4.25), filled baked potatoes (£4.75), ploughman's (£5.25), hot wraps with fillings such as chilli beef strips with onions and sour cream or feta, mushroom and beansprout (£6.45), home-made burger (£6.50), chicken curry or deep fried cod in cider batter (£6.95), steak and mushroom pie (£7.25), chargrilled fillet steak (£11.75), and puddings such as nutty chocolate torte with chocolate sauce or crème brûlée (£3.50). *(Recommended by Mark Percy, Lesley Mayoh, John Beeken)*

Greene King ~ Tenant Bernard Joseph Wija ~ Real ale ~ Bar food (not Sun evening) ~ Restaurant ~ (01428) 707346 ~ Children in family room ~ Dogs allowed in bar ~

Open 10.30-3, 6-11; may open all day when cricket is on Sat; 12-3, 7-10.30 Sun; closed Sun evening

OFFHAM TQ4012 Map 3
Blacksmiths Arms
A275 N of Lewes

There's no doubt that the very good food is one of the main draws to this neatly kept old red brick cottage. The open-plan bar has a huge inglenook fireplace (with logs stacked to one side) at one end of the gleaming central counter – and at the other, an airy dining area; most of the close-set tables are laid for eating. Nice old prints of London, some Spy prints and several old sporting prints decorate the walls above shiny black wainscoting. As well as bar snacks such as ploughman's (from £4.95), filled baked potatoes (from £5.25), and ham and eggs (£5.95), the popular food might include minted pea soup (£3.95), peanut roasted strips of chicken with stir-fried vegetables and a green chilli dressing (£4.95), wild mushroom stroganoff in a filo basket (£5.25), smoked haddock in cheese sauce (£5.50), fresh scallops with bacon and garlic (£6.50; main course £11.50), potato, red onion, tomato, and wensleydale cheese tart or home-made lasagne (£8.25), steak and kidney pie (£8.50), local trout with dill cream sauce (£9.75), chicken breast with forcemeat stuffing and cranberries or fillet of pork with coconut sauce (£10.25), halibut fillet with creole sauce (£10.75), fillet steak rossini (£11.95), and home-made puddings like spiced apple sponge tart with honey butter and almond cream, blueberry and maple frangipane with cinammon anglaise, and various brûlées (£4.25). Well kept Harveys Best on handpump. French windows open on to a tiny little brick and paved terrace with a couple of flowering tubs and picnic-sets under umbrellas; beware of the dangerous bend when leaving the car park. No children inside. *(Recommended by Ian and Barbara Rankin, A Sadler, Peter Craske, Colin Draper, Mr and Mrs J French)*

Free house ~ Licensee Jean Large ~ Real ale ~ Bar food (not Sun evening) ~ Restaurant ~ (01273) 472971 ~ Children in family room ~ Dogs allowed in bar ~ Open 12-3, 6.30-11; 12-3 Sun; closed Sun evening

OVING SU9005 Map 2
Gribble Inn 🍺
Between A27 and A259 just E of Chichester, then should be signposted just off village road; OS Sheet 197 map reference 900050

The fine choice of own-brewed real ales is the main draw to this 16th-c thatched pub, and as the pub is owned by Badger, you can often find them in other pubs owned by the brewery: Fursty Ferret, Gribble Ale, Porterhouse, Pigs Ear, Plucking Pheasant, Reg's Tipple, and winter Wobbler on handpump. Also 20 country wines, and farm cider. There's a cottagey feel in the several linked rooms, and the chatty bar has lots of heavy beams and timbering, and old country-kitchen furnishings and pews. Half the dining room is no smoking, and all of the family room. Bar food includes lunchtime filled baps (from £4.50), and platters (£5.50), as well as ham and eggs (£6.50), pasta choices (from £6.95), aubergine and bean layer bake (£7.50), beer-battered fish (£7.75), steak and mushroom pie (£7.95), and steaks (from £9.95). Sunday lunch is extremely busy and you may find several items (including yorkshire pudding) have run out; service may be under strain, then. Shove-ha'penny, cribbage, dominoes, fruit machine and a separate skittle alley. There's a covered seating area, and more chairs in the pretty garden with apple and pear trees. *(Recommended by Nigel Williamson, Susan and John Douglas, Ann and Colin Hunt, David H T Dimock, John Davis, P R and S A White, Lesley and Peter Barrett, Val and Alan Green, Veronica Brown, Howard Dell, Colin Draper)*

Own brew ~ Managers Brian and Cynthia Elderfield ~ Real ale ~ Bar food (12-2.30, 6-9.30) ~ Restaurant ~ (01243) 786893 ~ Children in family room ~ Dogs allowed in bar ~ Open 11-3, 5.30-11; 11-11 Sat; 12-10.30 Sun; 11-3, 5.30-11 Sat in winter, 12-4, 7-10.30 Sun in winter

PETT TQ8714 Map 3
Two Sawyers ◖

Pett Road; off A259

A new servery has opened in the garden of this cheerful old country local providing
food, and for children, ice creams; there's also a new segregated adventure
playground. A pretty, suntrap front brick courtyard, too. Inside, the meandering
low-beamed rooms are simply but genuinely put together, with black band saws on
the cream walls, handsome iron wall lamps, and stripped tables on the bare boards
in its two simple bars. A tiny low-ceilinged snug has dark wood pub tables and
cushioned banquettes, with a very old painted flint wall on one side; a sloping
passage leads down to a low-beamed no smoking restaurant. As the pub is the
brewery tap to the Old Forge Brewery, you will find their range of beers on
handpump: Pett Progress, and seasonal guests like Brothers Best, Santa Forge, and
Summer Eclipse. Gunthorpe's Double Vision cider; friendly courteous service.
Bar food includes sandwiches or baguettes (from £2.75), home-made soup (£3.45),
pâté with onion marmalade (£3.95), home-made burgers (from £4.25),
ploughman's (from £5.75), vegetarian quiche (£7.25), steak and mushroom in ale
pie (£7.45), curries (from £7.45), fresh cod in beer batter (£8.95), chinese sizzlers
(from £9.50), steaks (from £10.45), and puddings (£3.45). Fruit machine, cribbage,
dominoes, and piped music. An iron gate leads from a pretty suntrap front brick
courtyard to a quiet back garden with shady trees, a few well spaced picnic-sets, a
children's play area, and boules. *(Recommended by Pamela and Merlyn Horswell, Ruth and
Paul Lawrence, Michael and Ann Cole, the Didler, John Davis, Keith and Chris O'Neill,
Kevin Thorpe, B and M Kendall, Gill and Tony Morriss, Peter Meister)*

*Own brew ~ Licensees Clive Soper and Fred Bramble ~ Real ale ~ Bar food (12-2.30,
6.30-9.30) ~ Restaurant ~ (01424) 812255 ~ Children in restaurant until 8.30 ~
Dogs allowed in bar ~ Local groups and bands Fri evenings ~ Open 11-11; 12-10.30
Sun; 11-3, 6-11 Mon-Thurs in winter*

PETWORTH SU9719 Map 2
Badgers ⊗ ♀

Coultershaw Bridge; just off A285 1½ miles S

There's no doubt that most people come here for a meal rather than a quick drink,
although there is a small chatty drinking area with a couple of tables, bar stools and
an attractive antique oak monk's chair by the entrance. The space around the island
bar servery is devoted to dining tables – well spaced, with an attractive mix of
furniture from old mahogany to waxed stripped pine, and there are white walls that
bring out the deep maroon colour of the high ceiling, charming wrought-iron
lamps, winter log fires, stripped shutters for the big Victorian windows, and a
modicum of carefully chosen decorations including a few houseplants and dried
flower arrangements. Well liked changing bar food might include sandwiches (from
£3.50), moules marinière or chicken liver parfait (£5.95), kedgeree of salmon and
dill (£6.95), ploughman's (from £5.95), thai-style chicken (£8.95), good sausage
and mash (£7.95), pasta with scallops, tiger prawn tails, sunblush tomatoes and
fresh basil or haddock with poached egg and spinach (£10.95), pheasant with rösti
(£12.95), baked cod with fine breadcrumbs, coriander and lime zest and basil pesto
or delicious half a shoulder of lamb with garlic and rosemary and vegetable sauce
(£14.95), and puddings like chocolate torte, treacle tart, and popular apple pie
(£4.95). Well kept Badger Best and Sussex on handpump, and quite a range of
wines; maybe faint piped music (the dominant sound is quiet conversation). A
terrace by a waterlily pool has stylish metal garden furniture under parasols, and
some solid old-fashioned wooden seats. *(Recommended by Cathy Robinson, Ed Coombe,
John Evans, Alison Crooks, Dave Heffernan, Martin and Karen Wake, John Robertson,
Patrick Hall, Christopher and Elise Way, David H T Dimock)*

*Free house ~ Licensee Miss Arlette ~ Real ale ~ Bar food (not winter Sun evenings) ~
Restaurant ~ (01798) 342651 ~ Children in eating area of bar if over 5 ~ Open 11-3,
5.30(6.30 Sat)-11; 12-3, 7-10.30 Sun; closed winter Sun evenings ~ Bedrooms: /£80B*

RUSHLAKE GREEN TQ6218 Map 3
Horse & Groom
Village signposted off B2096 Heathfield—Battle

There's a good mix of customers in this busy pub – plenty of regulars dropping in for a pint of well kept Harveys Best and Shepherd Neame Masterbrew and Early Bird on handpump, plus those wanting to enjoy the popular food. On the right is the heavily beamed dining room with guns and hunting trophies on the walls, plenty of wheelback chairs around pubby tables, and a log fire. The little L-shaped bar has more low beams – watch your head – and is simply furnished with high bar stools and bar chairs, red plush cushioned wall seats and a few brocaded cushioned stools, and a brick fireplace with some brass items on the mantelpiece; horsebrasses, photographs of the pub and local scenes on the walls, and fresh flowers. A small room down a step has jockeys' colours and jockey photographs and watercolours of the pub. Listed on boards by the entrance to the bar (so not very easy to read with other customers trying to get into the bar past you or making their way to the restaurant), the large choice of bar food might include soup (£3.95), steak, kidney and Guinness suet pudding (£7.95), scallops sautéed in spring onions and bacon or fresh haddock in crispy beer batter (£8.25), goats cheese, aubergine and red onion tart (£8.95), mixed tagliatelle with seared smoked salmon and cherry tomatoes or chicken breast stuffed with mozzarella and sun-dried tomatoes and wrapped in bacon with a roasted red pepper sauce (£9.95), chump of lamb roasted and sliced on a port wine sauce (£12.95), steamed turbot with samphire and mushroom sauce (£15.50), and puddings like squidgy chocolate meringue, fruit crumble or summer pudding (£4.95); several wines by the glass. They can be extraordinarily strict about timing, and may not take it kindly if you are a few minutes late or can't decide quickly what you want to eat. The setting, by the large village green, is most attractive and there are oak seats and tables in the rustic garden with pretty country views. More reports please. *(Recommended by J H Bell, Jason Caulkin, John Davis, Colin McKerrow, P W Taylor)*

Free house ~ Licensees Mike and Sue Chappel ~ Real ale ~ Bar food (12-2.15, 7-9.30(9 Sun)) ~ Restaurant ~ (01435) 830320 ~ Children welcome ~ Dogs welcome ~ Open 11.30-3, 5.30(6 Sat)-11; 12-3, 7-10.30 Sun

RYE TQ9220 Map 3
Mermaid 🍷 🛏

Mermaid Street

The little bar at the back of this lovely, civilised black and white timbered hotel is where those in search of a light lunch and a drink tend to head for, and there's a mix of quite closely set furnishings such as Victorian gothic carved oak chairs, older but plainer oak seats and more modern ones in character, and a massive deeply polished bressumer beam across one wall for the huge inglenook fireplace; three antique but not ancient wall paintings show old english scenes. Well kept (if not cheap) Courage Best and Greene King Old Speckled Hen on handpump, a good wine list, and a short choice of bar food such as freshly made filled baguettes (from £5), moules marinière (£7), cold fillet of smoked salmon (£8.50), and seafood platter (£14.70). The smart (expensive) restaurant is no smoking; piped music. Seats on a small back terrace overlook the car park – where there are morris dancers on bank holiday weekends. The cellars date back to 1156 – despite a sign outside that says 'rebuilt in 1420'. *(Recommended by D J Penny, the Didler, E G Parish, Rebecca Nicholls, Mr and Mrs S Felstead, Keith and Chris O'Neill, Sarah Davis, Rod Lambert, John Davis, J H Bell, Nicky Mayers, Alan Cole, Kirstie Bruce)*

Free house ~ Licensees Robert Pinwill and Mrs J Blincow ~ Real ale ~ Bar food (not Sat evening) ~ Restaurant ~ (01797) 223065 ~ Children in eating area of bar and restaurant ~ Open 12-11(10.30 Sun) ~ Bedrooms: £80B/£160B

Pubs with attractive or unusually big gardens are listed at the back of the book.

SALEHURST TQ7424 Map 3
Salehurst Halt ♀
Village signposted from Robertsbridge bypass on A21 Tunbridge Wells—Battle Road

Close to the church, this bustling little local is run by courteous, friendly licensees. The L-shaped bar has a pleasant chatty atmosphere, good plain wooden tables and chairs on flagstones at one end, a cushioned window seat, beams, a little open brick fireplace, a time punch clock, olde-worlde pictures, and fresh flowers; lots of hops on a big beam divide this from the beamed carpeted area with its mix of tables, wheelback and farmhouse chairs, and a half wall leads to a no smoking dining area. Cooked by the landlord, enjoyable home-made food at lunchtime includes sandwiches (from £2.75), ploughman's (£5.50), home-made burgers (from £6.50), home-baked ham and egg (£6.95), and beef and mushroom pie (£7.50), with evening dishes such as good country pâté flavoured with oranges and Cointreau (£3.95), sizzling tiger prawns in garlic and parsley butter (£4.95), chicken in cream and red peppercorn sauce with brandy or spicy vegetable jambalaya (£8.95), rump steak (£9.95), monkfish in a tomato, garlic, oregano and olive oil sauce topped with mozzarella or roasted duck breast in a bitter orange and port sauce (£10.95), and puddings like banoffi pie or treacle pudding (£3.25). Well kept Harveys Best on handpump, and good wines. It can get very busy at weekends, so best to book in advance; piped music. The charming and pretty back garden is a suntrap in summer, and has terraces and picnic-sets for outside meals, and the front window boxes and tubs are most attractive. More reports please. *(Recommended by Colin and Stephanie McFie, Tony and Wendy Hobden, Bryan R Shiner, Derek and Maggie Washington)*

Free house ~ Licensees Colin and Sarah Green ~ Real ale ~ Bar food (12-2.30, 7-9.30; not Mon) ~ Restaurant ~ (01580) 880620 ~ Children welcome ~ Dogs welcome ~ Open 12-3, 7-11(10.30 Sun); closed Mon

SEAFORD TV4899 Map 3
Golden Galleon ♀ ◼
Exceat Bridge; A259 Seaford—Eastbourne, near Cuckmere

With such a marvellous position and a fine choice of own-brewed beers, it's no wonder this pub gets so busy at peak times. From the brewery which is on full view for customers come Downland Bitter, Cuckmere Haven Best, Golden Peace, Governor, and Saxon King Stout; they also keep guests such as Dark Star, King Horsham Best Bitter, and Shepherd Neame Spitfire on handpump or tapped from the cask, plus farm ciders, good wines by the glass, a decent choice of malts, continental brandies, italian liqueurs, and cappuccino or espresso coffee. As well as ploughman's and cold salads (from £4.75), the food might include home-made soup (£3.50), filled baked potatoes (from £5.75), deep-fried chicken fillets in a spicy coating (£6.75), pineapple and gammon (£8.75), marinated tuna steak (£9.50), steaks (from £10.75), stincotto (leg shank of pork cooked slowly on the bone, £10.95), and daily specials like sweet and sour chicken or vegetable pasta bake (£7.95), and an italian platter (£10.95); they may try to keep your credit card behind the bar. The spreading main bar has high trussed and pitched rafters creating quite an airy feel, and the river room forms part of the restaurant; smoking is only allowed in the area next to the bar. The pub is perfectly set for several attractive walks – along the river, down to the sea or inland to Friston Forest and the downs, and there are fine views towards the Cuckmere estuary and Seven Sisters Country Park from tables in the sloping garden. More reports please. *(Recommended by John Beeken, Tony Hobden, Ann and Colin Hunt, Bruce Bird, Paul and Penny Dawson, Alistair Forsyth)*

Own brew ~ Licensee Stefano Diella ~ Real ale ~ Bar food (12-2.30, 6-9(9.30 Fri and Sat); they do serve some dishes all day) ~ (01323) 892247 ~ Children welcome ~ Dogs welcome ~ Open 11-11; 12-10.30 Sun; 12-4 in winter; closed Sun evenings

SINGLETON SU8713 Map 2
Fox & Hounds

Just off A286 Midhurst—Chichester; heading S into the village, the main road bends sharp right – keep straight ahead instead; if you miss this turn, take the Charlton road, then first left

You can be sure of an enjoyable visit to this pretty 16th-c pub – there's a friendly welcome, good food, well kept ales, and cheerful service. The partly panelled main bar has cream paintwork, a polished wooden floor, daily papers and books to borrow, and a good winter log fire. There's a second bar with green settles and another fire, a third flagstoned room on the left, and a further seating area off a side corridor; half the pub is no smoking. Smashing bar food includes pâté (£3.95), home-made soup (£4.50), open sandwiches (from £5.50), cheese platter with pickles (£6.95), pasta of the day (£8.75), tasty steak in ale pie, fishcakes or lambs liver and bacon (£8.95), gammon with mustard, mushrooms and melted cheese (£9.25), well liked shank of lamb in garlic and rosemary (£9.95), steaks (from £9.95), and nice puddings like spotted dick or apple and blackberry crumble (£3.95); Sunday roast (£8.50). They keep Fullers London Pride, Greene King IPA, and Ringwood Best on handpump, and decent wines by the glass; no music or machines, but cribbage and dominoes. There are tables on an attractive small back terrace, and beyond that a big walled garden with colourful flowerbeds and fruit trees. The Weald & Downland Open Air Museum is just down the road, and Goodwood Racecourse is not far away. *(Recommended by Tracey and Stephen Groves, Ann and Colin Hunt, Prof and Mrs S Barnett, W A Evershed, John Davis, Glen and Nola Armstrong, Karen Eliot, Jane Basso)*

Enterprise ~ Lease Tony Simpson ~ Real ale ~ Bar food ~ (01243) 811251 ~ Children in family room ~ Dogs allowed in bar ~ Open 11.30-3, 6-11; 12-3, 7-10.30 Sun

TILLINGTON SU9621 Map 2
Horse Guards 🍽 ♀ 🛏

Village signposted off A272 Midhurst—Petworth

New licensees again for this prettily-set 18th-c dining pub. The neatly kept cosy beamed front bar has some good country furniture, a log fire and a lovely view beyond the village to the Rother Valley from a seat in the big black-panelled bow window. There is an emphasis on the good food, but this still remains somewhere for locals to come for a drink and a chat. As well as snacks and lighter meals at lunchtime and through the afternoon, more substantial dishes might include chicken liver parfait with red onion marmalade or tomato tart (£6.25), a salad of peppers, tomatoes and olives layered with ciabatta and topped with grilled goats cheese (£6.95), fresh seasonal marinated baby vegetables served with a smooth cauliflower cream (£9.95), pork cutlets with crispy black pudding and apple mash drizzled with wholegrain mustard sauce or whole poussin stuffed with garlic and lemon thyme potatoes, wrapped in parma ham and served with a pink peppercorn sauce (£14.95), and roasted bass with shaved fennel and white truffle oil dressing (£17.95); the restaurant is no smoking. Well kept Flowers IPA and Fullers London Pride on handpump, and seven wines by the glass; piped music. There's a terrace outside, and more tables and chairs in a sheltered garden behind. The 800-year-old church opposite is worth a look. More reports on the new regime, please. *(Recommended by John Hale, Karen Eliot, Colin Draper, Michael and Ann Cole, Norman and Sheila Sales, Wendy Arnold, Veronica Brown, RDK, Ken Arthur, Sefton Parke, Peter and Audrey Dowsett, J A Snell, W A Evershed, Nick Roberts, J H Bell)*

Free house ~ Licensee Ruth Keane ~ Real ale ~ Bar food (all day) ~ Restaurant ~ (01798) 342332 ~ Children in eating area of bar, restaurant and family room ~ Dogs allowed in bar ~ Open 11-11; 12-10.30 Sun; 11-3, 6-11 in winter ~ Bedrooms: /£65B

If we know a pub has an outdoor play area for children, we mention it.

TROTTON SU8323 Map 2
Keepers Arms 🍴🍺
A272 Midhurst—Petersfield; pub tucked up above road, on S side

Quite a few changes here over the past year. There's now an old oak floor throughout with a few ethnic rugs scattered around, though the beamed L-shaped bar still has timbered walls and some standing timbers, sofas by the big log fire, and walls decorated with some unusual pictures and artefacts that reflect the Oxleys' previous long years of travelling the world. There are a couple of new and unusual adult high chairs at the oak refectory table, two huge Georgian leather high-backed chairs around another table, an interesting medley of old or antique seats, and dining tables decorated with pretty candelabra, and bowls of fruit and chillis. The restaurant extension has been demolished and a big new one built with a lavatory block (including good disabled facilities) incorporated and decorated a vibrant burnt orange and lapis lazuli blue – worth a look in themselves. What was the old lavatories is now a north african-style room with a cushioned bench around all four walls, with a large central table, rare ethnic fabrics and weavings, and a big moroccan lamp hanging in the centre. Interesting piped music (which they change according to the customers) ranges from Buddha bar-type music to classical. This is very much the family home which the licensees see as their living room with guests. Good home-made food includes soup (£4), fine cheese and ham platters that several people can share (£6), whole, slow-cooked gammon hock or thai-style home-made fishcakes with sweet chilli dipping sauce (£8.50), indonesian peanut chicken or crispy duck salad on sautéed potatoes with hoi sin sauce, cucumber and spring onion (£9), chargrilled ostrich medallion with a wild cranberry and balsamic jus (£12.50), seared king scallops on wilted spinach with bacon, onion, and mushrooms topped with parmesan shavings (£13.50), and puddings like home-made sussex pond pudding (£4); in winter they have a special game pie with venison, pheasant, partridge, and wild duck (£8.50), and in summer (by appointment only), a fresh seafood platter with lobster, dressed crab, crab claws, giant crevettes, atlantic prawns, and oysters (£19.50 per person). The no smoking restaurant has a new woodburning stove. Well kept Ballards Best, Cheriton Pots, and Hop Back Summer Lightning on handpump, and decent wines. Plenty of seats on the attractive, almost mediterranean-feeling front terrace. Dogs lunchtime only. More reports on the changes, please. (*Recommended by J A Snell, Paul and Penny Dawson, Martin and Karen Wake, Cathy Robinson, Ed Coombe, Ann and Stephen Saunders, Michael and Ann Cole, Mike and Sue Richardson, W A Evershed, John Davis, J P Humphery, Tracey and Stephen Groves*)

Free house ~ Licensees Steve and Jenny Oxley ~ Real ale ~ Bar food (not Sun evening, Mon) ~ Restaurant ~ (01730) 813724 ~ Children in restaurant lunchtime ~ Dogs allowed in bar ~ Open 12-3, 6.30-11; 12-3 Sun; closed Sun evening, all Mon

WARNHAM TQ1533 Map 3
Sussex Oak ♀
Just off A24 Horsham—Dorking; Church Street

Attractively opened up inside, this nice old pub has several connecting areas served by a carved wooden bar counter. There are heavy beams and standing timbers, an end room with a good mix of dining chairs and solid wooden tables on the partly carpeted and partly stripped wooden floor, a wooden printers' tray, fishing rods, and wall lamps on the cream panelled walls, and little fireplaces at each end. The central room has green and red patterned old sofas in front of the inglenook fireplace, fine old flagstones, bar billiards and darts, and maybe chatting locals sitting at stools by the bar; piped music and fruit machine. Well kept Adnams Bitter, Fullers London Pride, Timothy Taylors Landlord, Youngs Bitter, and a guest such as Caledonian Deuchars IPA or Greene King IPA on handpump, and a good wine list with many by the glass. Using local produce, the enjoyable, popular bar food includes home-made soup (£3.95), sandwiches (from £4.25; two sausages in a baguette with chilli sauce, bacon and melted cheese), ploughman's or filled baked potatoes (from £4.50), chicken liver and mixed herb pâté (£4.95), black olive and sun-dried tomato giant ravioli with tomato, mozzarella and basil sauce or a combo platter to share (ribs, potato wedges, onion rings, garlic bread, chicken crunchies £7.25), mediterranean vegetable and basil lasagne (£7.95), home-cooked ham and eggs (£8.25), home-made steak, mushroom and ale pie (£8.95, though you can have a small helping, £7.45), grilled escolar on wilted rocket with lemon sauce or loin of pork with glazed baby apples (£9.95), and steaks with several sauce options (from £12.95); good children's choices, and puddings (£3.95). The attractive high raftered restaurant is no smoking. Picnic-sets in the garden. *(Recommended by Ian Phillips, John Davis, Phil Savage, Mike and Heather Watson, Mrs Romey Heaton, Tony and Wendy Hobden)*

Free house ~ Licensees Peter and Angela Nottage ~ Real ale ~ Bar food (12-2.30(3 Sun), 6-9.30; not Sun or Mon evenings) ~ Restaurant ~ (01403) 265028 ~ Children in eating area of bar and restaurant ~ Dogs allowed in bar ~ Open 11-11; 12-10.30 Sun

WARTLING TQ6509 Map 3
Lamb ♀

Village signposted with Herstmonceux Castle off A271 Herstmonceux—Battle

Particularly in the evening, this attractive country pub is popular with customers keen to enjoy the good food; best to get there early to be sure of a table or book in advance. It's a smallish place with a cosy, chatty, bustling atmosphere – helped by no piped music – and genuinely friendly, helpful staff. There's a little entrance bar where locals popping in for a drink tend to gather, with brocaded settles and stools and just a few tables on the green patterned carpet, a big blackboard with specials of the day, and a woodburning stove with logs stacked to one side. A narrow tiled floor area runs along the carved bar counter, and leads to the no smoking snug (mind your head on the low entrance beam): a mix of cushioned chairs and more brocaded settles around straightforward pubby tables, beams and timbering, big church candles on every table, and fresh flowers above the brick fireplace. The dining room (no smoking until 9.30pm) has a mix of homely sofas around low tables by the fireplace, lots more big candles and fresh flowers, and plenty of tables set for eating. Doors from here lead up steps to a back terrace with green picnic-sets, climbers on the gazebo, and flowering tubs and pots. Well kept Cuckmere Haven Guvnor, King Horsham Best Bitter, and Rother Valley Hoppers on handpump, and good wines (and champagne) by the glass. From an interesting menu, the lunchtime food might include soup with home-made bread and cheese or marinated peppers (£4.50), avocado and stilton en croûte (£4.95), fresh king scallops or local sausages with bubble and squeak (£5.95), home-made pie of the day (£6.95), lambs liver and bacon (£8.50), and four fresh fish dishes (from £11.95); in the evening there might be crab and cheddar cheese tartlet with sweet chilli sauce (£4.95), locally smoked salmon with fresh prawns and tomato mayonnaise (£5.95), caesar salad with avocado and prawns or ravioli of asparagus with wild mushroom and pesto cream (£7.95), braised shank of local lamb (£9.25), free range chicken stuffed with spinach and stilton (£9.50), breast of duck with madeira jus (£10.95), fillet of red bream with king scallops and pancetta (£11.95), wild bass with parsley mash and roasted pepper coulis (£12.95), and home-made puddings such as vanilla pod crème brûlée, jaffa cake pudding or iced dark chocolate and Kahlua parfait (from £4.50). Freddie the golden retriever is an old softie. There are seats out in front. *(Recommended by Ian Dowding, Barry and Victoria Lister)*

Free house ~ Licensees Robert and Alison Farncombe ~ Bar food ~ Restaurant ~ (01323) 832116 ~ Children in eating area of bar ~ Open 11-3, 6-11; 12-3 Sun; closed Sun evening and Mon (but this may change)

Planning a day in the country? We list pubs in really attractive scenery at the back of the book.

WILMINGTON TQ5404 Map 3
Giants Rest

Just off A27

You can be sure of a warm welcome from the charming licensees in this comfortable Victorian pub. The long wood-floored bar and adjacent open areas, one with a log fire, are simply furnished with old pews and pine tables (each with their own bar game or wooden puzzle and much enjoyed by readers), and have well kept Harveys Best, Hop Back Summer Lightning, and Timothy Taylors Landlord on handpump; orange and grapefruit juice squeezed in front of you, and decent wines. From a changing blackboard, well presented and generously served bar food includes soup (£3.50), pâté (£4.50), avocado and prawns (£4.50), local sausage ploughman's (£6), salmon fishcakes with lemon mayonnaise or rabbit and bacon or beef in ale pies (£8), spinach, sweet potato and peanut stew (£7.50), asparagus and sweetcorn-filled crêpe with melted brie on a tomato and garlic sauce (£8), home-cooked ham with bubble and squeak or whole local plaice (£8.50), lamb in red wine with thyme and orange (£9.50), and puddings such as sticky date pudding or crumbles (£4); on Sunday lunchtime there may not be much space for those just wanting a drink as most of the tables are booked by diners. There's a sizeable no smoking area, and on Friday and Saturday evenings and Sunday lunchtime, all the pub (apart from the bar) is no smoking; piped music, cribbage, dominoes, and shove-ha'penny. Plenty of seats in the front garden, and the pub is watched over by the impressive chalk-carved Long Man of Wilmington at the foot of the South Downs. *(Recommended by Gill and Tony Morriss, Dr P J W Young, Jo Blake, Alan J Miller, Tony and Wendy Hobden, John Beeken, Mike and Shelley Woodroffe, Mr and Mrs S Felstead)*

Free house ~ Licensees Adrian and Rebecca Hillman ~ Real ale ~ Bar food ~ (01323) 870207 ~ Children in eating area of bar and in restaurant ~ Dogs welcome ~ Open 11-3, 6-11; 11-11 Sat; 12-10.30 Sun ~ Bedrooms: /£40

WINEHAM TQ2320 Map 3
Royal Oak £

Village signposted from A272 and B2116

Simply furnished and old-fashioned, this pub remains unchanging over the years, and still has no fruit machines, piped music or even beer pumps. Logs burn in an enormous inglenook fireplace with a cast-iron Royal Oak fireback, and there's a collection of cigarette cards showing old english pubs, a stuffed stoat and crocodile, a collection of jugs, ancient corkscrews decorating the very low beams above the serving counter, and racing plates, tools and a coach horn on the walls; maybe a nice tabby cat, and views of quiet countryside from the back parlour. Well kept Harveys Best with a guest such as Wadworths 6X or Worthingtons tapped from the cask in a still room; darts, shove-ha'penny, dominoes, cribbage. Bar snacks are limited to home-made winter soup (£2.50), simple sandwiches (from £2.25), and ploughman's (from £4.50); courteous service – the pub has been in the same family for over 50 years. There are some picnic-sets outside – picturesque if you are facing the pub. No children inside. More reports please. *(Recommended by Jenny and Brian Seller, Ron Shelton, John Davis, Mike and Lynn Robinson, Mrs J Wild, R E Greenhalgh, RWC)*

Inn Business ~ Tenant Tim Peacock ~ Real ale ~ Bar food (11-2.30, 5.30-10.30) ~ No credit cards ~ (01444) 881252 ~ Children in family room ~ Dogs welcome ~ Open 11-2.30, 5.30(6 Sat)-11; 12-3, 7-10.30 Sun; closed 25 Dec, evenings 26 Dec and 1 Jan

---

The letters and figures after the name of each town are its Ordnance Survey map reference. *Using the Guide* at the beginning of the book explains how it helps you find a pub, in road atlases or large-scale maps as well as in our own maps.

Lucky Dip

Besides the fully inspected pubs, you might like to try these Lucky Dips recommended to us and described by readers (if you do, please send us reports: www.goodguides.com).

ALFRISTON [TQ5103]
☆ *Star* [High St]: Fascinating façade decorated with fine painted medieval carvings, striking figurehead red lion on the corner; stolid heavy-beamed bar (busy lunchtime, quiet evenings) with medieval sanctuary post, fine antique furnishings, big log fire in Tudor fireplace, some no smoking areas, helpful service, bar food from sandwiches and baked potatoes up, well kept Bass, daily papers and magazines, easy chairs in comfortable lounge, restaurant, good modern bedrooms in up-to-date part behind, open all day summer *(Colin and Janet Roe, S F Parrinder, Richard and Margaret Peers, the Didler, LYM, Mr and Mrs S Felstead)*

AMBERLEY [TQ0211]
☆ *Bridge* [B2139]: Attractive and popular open-plan dining pub, comfortable and relaxed even when busy, with pleasant candlelit bar and separate two-room dining area, wide range of good value generous food from sandwiches up, well kept ales such as Badger Tanglefoot, Fullers London Pride, Harveys and Youngs, cheerful staff; children and dogs welcome, piped music; white plastic seating out in front, more tables in side garden, open all day, cl Sun evening *(Mark Percy, Lesley Mayoh, W A Evershed, David Cosham, Prof and Mrs S Barnett, LYM)*

ANGMERING [TQ0604]
Lamb [The Square]: Friendly village pub with lots of bric-a-brac and big fireplace, relaxed atmosphere, pleasant service, good bar food, well kept Fullers London Pride, Youngs Special and a guest beer such as Wychwood *(Bruce Bird)*
☆ *Spotted Cow* [High St]: Friendly and enthusiastic chef/landlord does good generous food (very popular wkdy lunchtimes with older people) from imaginative sandwiches up, well kept Fullers London Pride, Harveys Best, Ringwood Best and a guest beer, good choice of wines by the glass, good service even when busy, smuggling history, sporting caricatures, cool and roomy in summer, two log fires winter, no piped music; children welcome, restaurant, no smoking conservatory, big garden with boules and play area; open all day Sun, afternoon jazz sometimes then, lovely walk to Highdown hill fort *(Cathy Robinson, Ed Coombe, Bruce Bird, Gordon Stevenson, Tony and Wendy Hobden, Pamela Goodwyn)*

APULDRAM [SU8401]
☆ *Black Horse* [A286 SW of Chichester]: Comfortable open-plan pub dating from 18th c, growing reputation for very wide and reasonably priced blackboard food choice running up to good seafood inc huge lobsters, small bar with Courage Directors, Fullers London Pride and Greene King Old Speckled Hen, more tables in neat no smoking dining area opening on to covered terrace, friendly enthusiastic landlady and well trained staff,

decent wines; terrace tables outside, picnic-sets in big orchard garden with slide and swings *(Mr and Mrs A Hynd, Keith Stevens, BB, Mrs M Smith, Jane Basso)*

ARDINGLY [TQ3429]
Ardingly Inn [Street Lane, off B2028]: Spacious and comfortable brightly lit beamed bar, big central log fire, well kept Badger ales with Gribble guests, generous attractively presented food from sandwiches and bar snacks to interesting restaurant dishes and Sun lunch, good service, traditional games; dogs allowed, reasonably priced bedrooms *(David Cosham, Susan and John Douglas)*
☆ *Gardeners Arms* [B2028 2 miles N]: Rambling olde-worlde pub with various areas and rooms divided up by standing timbers and open-beamed doorways; nice old red tiled floor by inglenook fireplace, carpet and terracotta and newer tiles elsewhere, second inglenook in dining room; farming tools, horsebrasses, and hunting horns, a mix of furniture from barrel tables, nice old wooden and more straightforward ones to brocaded wall seating and cushioned dining chairs, and old local photographs; popular food from good baguettes to some interesting hot dishes, lots of customers, Badger Best and Harveys, piped pop music; no children; attractive wooden furniture on pretty terrace, with lots of picnic-sets in side garden – quite a lot of road noise; opp S of England show ground and handy for Borde Hill and Wakehurst Place *(Bruce Bird, Glenwys and Alan Lawrence, G J C Moss, Nigel Williamson, Susan and John Douglas, BB)*
Oak [Street Lane]: Beamed 14th-c dining pub handy for show ground, good reasonably priced menu inc children's, Courage Best and Harveys BB, prompt friendly service, lots of brass and lace curtains, magnificent old fireplace, bright comfortable restaurant extension; tables in pleasant garden, reservoir walks *(Tony and Wendy Hobden)*

ARUNDEL [TQ0208]
☆ *Black Rabbit* [Mill Rd, Offham; keep on and don't give up!]: Long nicely refurbished riverside pub very popular with families – lovely spot nr wildfowl reserve, lots of tables out looking across to water-meadows and castle; wide range of generous enjoyable food, Badger ales with Gribble guests, good choice of decent wines by the glass, log fires; open all day, doubling as summer tea shop, very busy then, with summer boat trips, good walks *(David and Carole Chapman, Val and Alan Green, Paul and Penny Rampton, LYM, Ian and Jane Irving)*
☆ *Swan* [High St]: Smartly refurbished open-plan L-shaped bar with attractive woodwork and matching fittings, beaten brass former inn-sign hanging on wall, friendly efficient young staff, good choice of well presented food from baguettes and baked potatoes to restaurant meals, Gales Butser, GB and HSB and a guest

such as Fullers London Pride; piped music; restaurant, good bedrooms, open all day *(Miss J F Reay, LYM, Patrick Hancock, Theocsbrian, Mr and Mrs S Felstead)*

BALCOMBE [TQ3033]

☆ *Cowdray Arms* [London Rd (B2036/B2110 N of village)]: Roomy main-road pub popular lunchtime for well prepared and presented food from generous sandwiches and ploughman's to some interesting dishes and imaginative puddings, good helpings, polite attentive service, well kept ales such as Black Sheep, Greene King IPA and Abbot and Harveys, occasional beer festivals, L-shaped bar and no smoking restaurant with conservatory; children welcome, large garden with good play area *(Eamonn and Natasha Skyrme, Ian and Joan Blackwell, DWAJ, Mr Bannon, Terry Buckland)*

BALLS CROSS [SU9826]

Stag [signed off A283 N of Petworth]: Unspoilt 16th-c village pub with flagstones and inglenook log fire, wide choice of good value food from filled rolls up, well kept Badger ales; pleasant back garden, bedrooms, good walks *(J A Snell, John Beeken)*

BATTLE [TQ7515]

Chequers [Lower Lake (A2100 SE)]: Big friendly open-plan pub, well kept Fullers London Pride, Harveys and a guest beer, good value food inc wide lunchtime choice of snacks and sandwiches *(Gill and Tony Morriss)*

Squirrel [North Trade Rd (A269 towards Herstmonceux)]: Generous cheap home cooking inc their own hams and evenings with all-you-can eat curry/carvery etc, well kept beers, chatty licensees; children allowed in pool room, large family garden *(John and Judy Saville, Marjorie and Bernard Parkin)*

BECKLEY [TQ8423]

Rose & Crown [Northiam Rd (B2088)]: Character coaching inn, welcoming and unspoilt, cosy eating area with log fire, good value generous standard food from sandwiches, baguettes and baked potatoes up, several well kept changing beers such as Fullers London Pride, Harveys and Hook Norton; children welcome, good views from garden with swing *(Gill and Tony Morriss)*

BODIAM [TQ7825]

Castle Inn: Typical 18th-c country local, very handy for the castle (and owned by National Trust), with Shepherd Neame Bitter, Spitfire and Porter, enjoyable blackboard food (simpler choice at quiet times), plain tables and chairs in bar, smarter restaurant section; tables outside, summer barbecues *(Peter Meister)*

BOSHAM [SU8003]

Anchor Bleu [High St]: Included for its lovely waterside position in a charming village – sea and boat views, little terrace outside massive wheel-operated bulkhead door to ward off high tides (cars parked on seaward side often submerged); plenty of potential inside, open all day *(JDM, KM, Ann and Colin Hunt, LYM, Karen Eliot, Susan and John Douglas)*

Berkeley Arms [just outside old village]: Good atmosphere, cheerfully welcoming landlord

and staff, well kept Gales, lounge with eating area, public bar *(DJC, Ann and Colin Hunt)*

White Swan [A259 roundabout]: Well refurbished open-plan pub with good cheerful mix of customers, well kept Hop Back Summer Lightning and Crop Circle, Youngs Special and an interesting guest beer, enjoyable changing food from toasties and baked potatoes to restaurant dishes, attentive service, good value coffee, log fire; quiet piped music; children welcome, skittle alley/function room, plenty of tables out on terrace *(Ann and Colin Hunt, Bruce Bird)*

BRAMBER [TQ1810]

Castle Hotel [The Street]: Pleasant and roomy olde-worlde quiet lounge, wide choice of reasonably priced food from baguettes and filled baked potatoes up, Adnams, Bass and Fullers London Pride, good service; charming back garden, in nice spot *(John Branston)*

BRIGHTON [TQ3104]

Bath Arms [Union St/Meeting House Lane, The Lanes]: Several high-ceilinged rooms with panelling and old fireplaces, lots of old photographs and cartoon prints, pleasant atmosphere, half a dozen real ales inc Harveys, decent coffee, New World wines, attentive staff, good value bar food from sandwiches up; pavement tables *(Val and Alan Green)*

Battle of Trafalgar [Trafalgar Rd/Guildford Rd, Portslade (B2193)]: Friendly town local with well kept ales such as Adnams, Fullers London Pride, Greene King Abbot and Harveys Best (no coffee), lunchtime side servery doing hearty food from good doorstep sandwiches up, log fire; pub games, piped jazz and blues; lovely big garden, open all day Thurs-Sun *(Richard Lewis, Tony and Wendy Hobden, Mr and Mrs John Taylor)*

☆ *Colonnade* [New Rd, off North St; by Theatre Royal]: Small beautifully preserved Victorian bar, with red plush, shining brass and mahogany, gleaming mirrors, interesting pre-war playbills and lots of signed theatrical photographs, white gloves and canes in top hats peeking over plush curtains, good friendly service even when very busy, particularly well kept Bass, Boddingtons and Harveys (early evening wkdy happy hour), good choice of good value wines, tiny front terrace; internal stairs to Theatre Royal, they take interval orders – and performers like it *(Val and Alan Green, BB)*

☆ *Cricketers* [Black Lion St]: Cheerful down-to-earth town pub, very well run, with ageing Victorian furnishings and lots of interesting bric-a-brac – even a stuffed bear; well kept Bass, Boddingtons, Courage Directors and Greene King Old Speckled Hen tapped from the cask, good coffee, friendly bustle, usual well priced lunchtime bar food with fresh veg in upstairs bar, restaurant (where children allowed) and covered ex-stables courtyard bar; piped music; open all day *(LYM, Ann and Colin Hunt)*

☆ *Evening Star* [Surrey St]: Chatty and appealingly unassuming tap for good Dark Star microbrewery, with several well kept changing beers from other small breweries;

enthusiastic landlord (may let you sample before you buy), changing farm ciders and perries, lots of country wines, good simple food (not evenings Sat-Mon or Thurs), well worn but clean bare boards, plain furnishings, good mix of customers, railway memorabilia; unobtrusive piped music, live music nights, tables outside, open all day *(Peter Jones, Bruce Bird, Richard Lewis, Tracey and Stephen Groves, MLR)*

George [Trafalgar St]: Three linked rooms (the front ones are the best) off main bar, nice mix of furnishings on stripped floor, several big mirrors and nice etchings, mix of youngish customers, well kept ales inc Harveys, lots of wines by the glass, freshly squeezed fruit juice, inexpensive popular organic and vegetarian/vegan food all day, pleasant staff, daily papers; piped pop music; children welcome, small heated back courtyard under marquee *(anon)*

Sussex Cricketer [Eaton Rd, by cricket ground]: Plush seating in warm and comfortable Ember Inn with welcoming layout, well done standard food all day, well kept real ales *(Tracey and Stephen Groves, Tony Hobden)*

BROAD OAK [TQ8220]
☆ *Rainbow Trout* [A28/B2089, N of Brede]: Well run olde-worlde pub with wide range of good value generous food esp fish served by pleasant waitresses in attractive bustling low-beamed bar and big no smoking restaurant extension; gets very crowded but plenty of room for drinkers, with well kept Boddingtons, Flowers and Fullers London Pride, decent wines; tables out on large lawn *(Glenn and Louise Hamilton, E G Parish, Ralph and Jean Whitehouse)*

BUCKS GREEN [TQ0732]
Fox [A281 Horsham—Guildford]: Ancient open-plan inglenook bar, wide choice of enjoyable food esp fish, well kept Badger beers, decent wines by the glass, helpful service by informally dressed staff, restaurant area; play area *(David Cosham, Derek and Maggie Washington)*

BURGESS HILL [TQ3019]
Woolpack [Howard Ave]: Useful Big Steak pub in big 1930s-look roadhouse, several eating areas inc no smoking area, decent food from snacks up, Bass and Tetleys *(Tony Hobden)*

BURWASH [TQ6724]
☆ *Bell* [A265 E of Heathfield]: Pretty tile-hung village pub opp church, picnic-sets out by colourful flower baskets and tubs, L-shaped bar with interesting bric-a-brac and good log fire, well kept Greene King IPA, Ruddles Best and County and Harveys Best, friendly service, decent house wines, pub games, generous home-made food (not Sun evening) from sandwiches up, no smoking dining room; music nights, TV, piped music, children and dogs welcome; bedrooms sharing bathrooms, charming village, open all day wknds *(John Hale, Peter Meister, LYM, D S Cottrell)*
☆ *Rose & Crown* [inn sign on A265]: Low-beamed timbered local tucked away down lane in pretty village, good value home-made food

inc some interesting dishes in bar and attractive restaurant, well kept Harveys, decent wines, good service, fine log fire; music quiz nights, tables out in small quiet garden, bedrooms, limited nearby parking *(BB, J P Humphery, Jason Caulkin, B M Bannerman, Robert M Warner)*

BURWASH WEALD [TQ6523]
Wheel [A265 Burwash—Heathfield]: Friendly open-plan pub under new owners, new chef doing enjoyable food, comfortable sofas by good inglenook log fire, well kept Harveys and other ales, Post Office counter in games bar up a step or two behind, dining room leading out to garden; tables on sunny front terrace too, lovely walks in valley opp *(BB)*

BURY [TQ0113]
☆ *Squire & Horse* [Bury Common; A29 Fontwell—Pulborough]: Sizeable roadside pub with wide range of popular generous home-made food, well kept ales such as Brakspears, Harveys and Shepherd Neame, Sun bar nibbles, neatly kept U-shaped open-plan bar areas split by half walling and timbering, heavy beams, pink plush wall seats, hunting prints and ornaments, gas woodburner, attractive two-level beamed restaurant with fresh flowers and another stove; green tables and chairs on pretty terrace (some road noise); cl Sun evening, Mon *(BB, Mr and Mrs Gordon Turner, John Beeken, J P Humphery)*

BUXTED [TQ4923]
☆ *White Hart* [Station Rd (A272)]: Neatly kept roadside pub well under friendly licensees, lots of interesting food, reasonable prices, well kept Greene King Old Speckled Hen and Harveys, cheery chatty feel with efficient service and quite a few locals, main bar divided by timbering, big brick fireplace, hops and some horsebrasses, red leatherette seats, left-hand dining bar, big light and airy dining conservatory with fairy-lit plants and light wooden furniture on wood-strip floor; may be piped pop music; pleasant garden with plenty of seats *(Michael and Ann Cole, Sue and Mike Todd)*

CHAILEY [TQ3919]
Five Bells [A275 9 miles N of Lewes]: Attractive rambling roadside pub, spacious and well appointed, with lots of different rooms and alcoves leading from low-beamed bar area with fine old brick floor, brick walls and inglenook, a mix of dining chairs and tables, leather sofa by the fire with another under window, dining extension, well kept Fullers London Pride, Greene King Old Speckled Hen and Harveys Best, decent wine choice, smallish but interesting range of well liked food inc OAP lunch discounts, good service; picnic-sets in garden with play area *(John Beeken, Tony and Wendy Hobden, BB, C and R Bromage, Michael Hasslacher, I D Barnett)*

CHELWOOD GATE [TQ4130]
Red Lion [A275, S of Forest Row junction with A22]: Newly refurbished, with airy open-plan bar/dining area, wooden floor, modern pictures and sculptures, pale colourwashed walls, good choice of bar food and more

unusual blackboard dishes (popular for upmarket evening meals), good service by welcoming uniformed staff, fair-priced drinks; big sheltered side garden with well spaced tables, more out in front – handy for Ashdown Forest walks *(Pam Adsley, BB, RDK)*

CHICHESTER [SU8605]

Bell [Broyle Rd]: Good range of beers, interesting wines, good food inc super puddings, pleasant attentive service; handy for theatre *(John Burgess, Jane Basso)*

Coach & Horses [St Pancras]: Comfortable and friendly open-plan local, choice of well kept real ales, good lunchtime bar food from open side kitchen, quick service; quiet piped music; attractive back terrace *(Ann and Colin Hunt)*

Dolphin & Anchor [West St]: Wetherspoons in former hotel opp cathedral, good value food inc good range of curries, six low-priced real ales, cheerful young well trained staff; small family area till 7 (not wknds), very busy with young people Sat night, doorman and queues to get in; pleasant back terrace, open all day *(Craig Turnball)*

Fountain [Southgate]: Attractive front bar with bric-a-brac, wide food choice from sandwiches and baguettes to good hot dishes and generous Sun roast ordered from counter in no smoking dining room (eat anywhere), well kept Badger beers, friendly efficient staff; fruit machines; open all day, live music Tues and Sat, quiz night Thurs *(Keith Stevens)*

Nags Hotel [St Pancras]: Lots of panelling and old books, log fires, substantial good food in bar and recently pleasantly refurbished eating area inc evening and Sun lunch carvery, friendly staff, thriving local atmosphere, good choice of well kept real ales *(Ann and Colin Hunt)*

☆ *Park Tavern* [Priory Rd, opp Jubilee Park]: Comfortable pub in attractive spot opp Priory Park, current helpful licensees putting emphasis on enjoyable lunchtime food using fresh local produce and the day's fish, also baguettes, sandwiches and some thai dishes (and may be authentic thai evening banquets); cheerful service, well kept Gales BB, HSB, a seasonal beer such as Hampshire Glory and a guest such as Wadworths 6X, relaxing smallish front bar (no smoking on right, with huge mirrors) and extensive back eating area with crisp white tablecloths *(Tony Hobden, Ann and Colin Hunt, Jane Basso, BB)*

Toad [West St]: Former church nicely converted into real ale pub, multi-level seating around big central bar, good value straightforward food till 6, real ales, decent coffee; music and constant videos, good mix of customers inc lively young people at night; open all day, opp cathedral *(Jane Basso)*

CHILGROVE [SU8116]

☆ *Royal Oak* [off B2141 Petersfield—Chichester, signed Hooksway down steep single track]: Welcoming and smartly simple two-room country tavern in charming coach-free spot, beams, brick floors, country-kitchen furnishings, huge log fires; well kept guest beers and one brewed for them by Hampshire,

chatty landlord, sensibly priced no-nonsense food inc lunchtime ploughman's, games, provision for children; some live music Fri in summer; tables out in pretty garden, good walks, cl Mon *(Ann and Colin Hunt, Torrens Lyster, Prof and Mrs S Barnett, Mark Percy, Lesley Mayoh, W A Evershed, Martin and Karen Wake, J A Snell, LYM)*

☆ *White Horse* [off B2141, Petersfield—Chichester]: More smart restaurant than pub, good lunches and more expensive evening dishes, remarkable list of outstanding wines with excellent ones by the glass, good friendly service, log fire in pleasant beamed bar area (mind your head); idyllic downland setting with small flower-filled terrace and big pretty garden, lots of fine walks *(RDK, Martin and Karen Wake, Ian Phillips)*

CLAYTON [TQ2914]

Jack & Jill [A273 N of Brighton]: Country pub with good range of food from ploughman's to steak, constantly changing well kept beers *(Father Robert Marsh)*

CLIMPING [SU9902]

Oystercatcher [A259/B2233]: Thatched Vintage Inn dining pub, largely no smoking and pleasantly back-dated with hops and bric-a-brac, friendly young well trained staff, usual food all day from sandwiches through light dishes to mixed grill, Bass and Tetleys, good choice of wines by the glass, nicely served coffee, log fires; disabled lavatories *(Tony and Wendy Hobden, Jane Basso)*

COCKING CAUSEWAY [SU8819]

Greyhound [A286 Cocking—Midhurst]: Pretty tile-hung pub with cosy and welcoming olde-worlde beamed bar, old fireplaces, soft lighting by table lamps, fresh flowers, old prints, pewter pots and woodworking tools; inexpensive home cooking inc lots for children (who are well looked after), welcoming young staff, Ringwood Best; dovecote in side courtyard, picnic-sets on large lawn, play area, pets corner, aviary; open all day *(Ann and Colin Hunt, Susan and John Douglas, Jonathan and Ann Tross)*

COLEMANS HATCH [TQ4533]

☆ *Hatch* [signed off B2026, or off B2110 opp church]: Quaint and attractive weatherboarded Ashdown Forest pub dating from 1430, big log fire in beamed bar, small back restaurant with another log fire, good generous if not cheap food from sandwiches, baked potatoes, giant ploughman's and filled ciabatta bread through imaginative salads to bass and steak, well kept Harveys, Larkins and one or two guest beers, friendly staff, good mix of customers inc families; picnic-sets on front terrace and in beautifully kept big garden *(Peter Meister, Douglas and Pamela Cooper, RDK, LYM, Robert M Warner)*

COOLHAM [TQ1423]

☆ *George & Dragon* [pub signed just off A272]: Low heavy beams and enormous inglenook fireplace, unpretentious furnishings, well kept Badger ales, good generous home-made food from sandwiches to steak, small restaurant, back games room with bar billiards; fruit machine, TV, can get pretty busy; children allowed in games or eating areas, well spaced tables out in big attractive orchard garden, open all day wknds *(Mike and Heather Watson, John Beeken, LYM, Dominic Morgan, Mike and Shelley Woodroffe, Peter Meister)*

COWBEECH [TQ6114]
Merrie Harriers [village signed from A271]: Beamed and panelled village pub doing well under present tenants, inglenook fireplace with snug old-fashioned settle, well kept Harveys Best and a guest beer, decent wines, home-made fresh food (not Mon evening), children welcome in no smoking back restaurant; unobtrusive piped music; rustic seats in terraced garden *(LYM, J H Bell)*

DALLINGTON [TQ6619]
Swan [Woods Corner, B2096 E]: New licensees in pleasant country local with warm log fire in bare-boards low-beamed bar, simple carpeted back dining room with far views to Beachy Head; has had enjoyable food, well kept Harveys BB and Theakstons Best, decent house wines, good coffee; steps down to smallish garden *(Peter Meister, BB)*

DENTON [TQ4502]
Flying Fish [Denton Rd]: Well kept 17th-c village local with hops and brassware, good reasonably priced home cooking, comfortable dining room, Shepherd Neame real ales; attractive garden behind, tables out in front too *(the Didler)*

EARTHAM [SU9409]
☆ *George* [signed off A285 Chichester—Petworth, from Fontwell off A27, from Slindon off A29]: Big popular pub smartly refurbished in light wood, comfortable lounge, attractive pubbier public bar with games, old farm tools and photographs, welcoming helpful service and hands-on landlord, decent home-made food in sensibly manageable helpings, well kept real ales, log fire, no smoking restaurant; piped music; easy disabled access, children welcome in eating areas, large pretty garden, attractive surroundings, open all day summer wknds *(Peter D B Harding, Mrs Jill Silversides, Barry Brown, W A Evershed, Jane Basso, LYM)*

EAST DEAN [SU9012]
Hurdlemakers [signed off A286 and A285 N of Chichester – OS Sheet 197 map ref 904129]: Unpretentious village pub with generous food in softly lit L-shaped bar, well kept ales such as Adnams, Badger and Wadworths, friendly efficient staff, a helpful welcome for wet walkers and children; charming spot on South Downs Way by peaceful green of quiet village, with rustic seats and swing in pretty walled garden *(Jason Caulkin, LYM)*

EAST LAVANT [SU8608]
☆ *Royal Oak* [signed A286 N of Chichester; Pook Lane]: Upscale dining pub with emphasis on food inc good fresh fish, well kept Badger ales, country wines, good house wines, effective friendly service, candlelight and scrubbed tables, rugs on bare boards and flooring tiles, two open fires and a

woodburner, racing prints, extended restaurant; attractively planted gardens inc secluded terrace with bookable tables (quiet exc for wknd light planes using Goodwood airfield), good walks; comfortable new bedrooms, cl Sun pm, Mon *(Ron Shelton, Gerald Wilkinson, Christopher and Elise Way, J A Snell, John Freestone, Sally Burn, Simon and Debbie Gwynn, LYM)*

EASTBOURNE [TV6198]
Buccaneer [Compton St, by Winter Gardens]: Popular open-plan bar shaped like a galleon, raised no smoking side, Ind Coope Burton, Marstons Pedigree, Tetleys and three guest beers, theatre memorabilia; no food Sun, open all day *(the Didler)*

ELSTED [SU8119]
☆ *Elsted Inn* [Elsted Marsh]: New landlord doing well in appealing two-bar country pub with enjoyable home-cooked food, well kept ales such as Ballards, Cheriton Pots and Timothy Taylors Landlord, nice country furniture, wooden floors, original shutters, old railway photographs, traditional games, log fires; lovely enclosed Downs-view garden with big terrace and summer barbecues, well appointed adjacent bedroom block *(Pat and Tony Martin, LYM, Peter Meister, John Mitchell, Christopher and Elise Way, Bob and Valerie Mawson, W A Evershed, David Cosham)*

ERIDGE STATION [TQ5434]
☆ *Huntsman*: Basic country pub popular for limited ever-changing blackboard choice of surprisingly good enterprising home-made food, reasonable prices, friendly knowledgeable service, well kept Badger beers with a guest such as Holdens Mild, farm cider, good range of wines; friendly cat, walkers and their dogs welcome, big garden *(Ken Arthur, Paul A Moore, Father Robert Marsh, RDK)*

FAIRWARP [TQ4626]
☆ *Foresters Arms* [B2026]: Smiling new tenants and welcoming atmosphere in Ashdown Forest local handy for Vanguard Way and Weald Way, comfortable lounge bar, enjoyable food from baguettes to steak and popular Sunday lunch, efficient service, well kept Badger ales and farm cider, woodburner; piped music; children in eating area, tables out on terrace and in garden with some interesting plants, has been open all day summer *(RDK, Michael and Ann Cole, LYM)*

FERNHURST [SU9028]
Red Lion [The Green; off A286, 3 miles S of Haslemere]: Heavy-beamed old pub tucked quietly away by green nr church, friendly attentive staff, good value food inc interesting sandwiches and snacks, well kept Fullers ales, good wines, attractive layout and furnishings, no smoking area, good relaxed atmosphere; children welcome, pretty garden *(Godfrey and Irene Joly, BB, Gerry and Rosemary Dobson)*

FINDON [TQ1208]
☆ *Gun* [High St]: Civilised and pleasantly renovated low-beamed village pub, friendly atmosphere, traditional main bar, large pine-floored part no smoking dining area, good attractively presented food from lunchtime

sandwiches to modern light and main dishes, sensible prices, quick service, well kept Adnams, Fullers London Pride, Gales HSB and Harveys BB, range of foreign beers; attractive sheltered lawn, pretty village in horse-training country below Cissbury Ring *(Alison Milner-Gulland , LYM, Tony Hobden, J P Humphery)*

FIRLE [TQ4607]

☆ *Ram* [village signed off A27 Lewes—Polegate]: Unpretentious and comfortably worn 17th-c village pub, very welcoming to families and booted walkers; big plain tables, log fires, traditional games, large snug, good-sized family room, several well kept ales such as Harveys Best and RCH Pitchfork, farm cider, usual food (all day) from baguettes and baked potatoes up, with three sizes of children's meals and cream teas; play equipment and nicely segregated table area in walled garden behind, open all day *(LYM, the Didler, Peter Meister, LM, Dominic Morgan)*

FISHBOURNE [SU8304]

Bulls Head [Fishbourne Rd (A259 Chichester—Emsworth)]: Interesting, relaxing and welcoming old village pub with pretty window boxes, fair-sized main bar, full Gales range kept well with guest beers such as Fullers London Pride, good varied food often using local produce (not Sun evening – Sun lunch very popular), quick friendly service, log fire, children's area, restaurant with no smoking area; skittle alley, boules pitch *(Ann and Colin Hunt, J A Snell, Jane Basso)*

Woolpack [Fishbourne Rd W; just off A27 Chichester—Emsworth]: Big comfortably refurbished open-plan pub with welcoming landlord, nice variety of seats inc settees, smart no smoking dining area, enjoyable food, well kept ales such as Hop Back Summer Lightning and Youngs Special; parts of bar can get rather smoky; dozy labrador, dogs welcome, big garden with barbecues and spit-roasts, various events inc live music *(Tony and Wendy Hobden, Ann and Colin Hunt)*

FITTLEWORTH [TQ0118]

☆ *Swan* [Lower St]: Prettily placed 14th-c inn with big inglenook log fire in unpretentious low-beamed lounge with used by locals at night, good enterprising home-made food esp fish and popular Sun lunch in attractive beamed and panelled dining room with landscapes by Constable's deservedly less-known brother George, helpful friendly staff, well kept Badger K&B, Fullers London Pride and Wadworths 6X, reasonably priced wines; piped music, games inc pool in public bar; well spaced tables on big sheltered back lawn, good walks nearby; children in eating area, comfortable bedrooms, open all day Thurs-Sat *(LYM, John Evans, John Beeken, Irene and Derek Flewin, Roger Thornington, Mike and Heather Watson)*

FRANT [TQ5935]

☆ *George* [High St, off A267]: Tucked down charming quiet lane by ancient church and cottages, convivial bar with several rooms rambling round servery, low ceiling, mix of seats inc pews, high-backed settles and sofa, coal-effect gas fire in big inglenook, enjoyable

pleasantly served food, well kept real ales, lots of wines by the glass, good coffee, darts in public bar; busy wknds, pleasant restaurant, picnic-sets in pretty walled garden *(H Bramwell, BB)*

FULKING [TQ2411]

☆ *Shepherd & Dog* [off A281 N of Brighton, via Poynings]: Charming partly panelled low-ceilinged country pub beautifully placed below Downs, antique or stoutly rustic furnishings around log fire, attractive bow windows, well kept Badger ales, wide food choice (all day wknds) from sandwiches and baked potatoes up inc lots of ploughman's and summer salads, no piped music; can be packed out (when service and amenities may suffer); dogs and children welcome, pretty streamside garden with upper play lawn (loudspeaker food announcements out here), open all day *(Mrs M Thomas, LYM, Sarah and Huw, C L Kauffmann, Dr M Mills, Jeremy Woods, M and R Thomas, John and Tania Wood)*

FUNTINGTON [SU7908]

Fox & Hounds: Extensively refurbished beamed pub with wide food choice inc popular Sun roasts, cottagey rooms, comfortable and attractive dining extension, welcoming service, well kept Badger Best and Tanglefoot, reasonably priced wines, good coffee, huge log fire, no music; garden behind *(Peter and Audrey Dowsett, Ann and Colin Hunt)*

GLYNDE [TQ4508]

Trevor Arms: Well kept Harveys ales and enjoyable traditional food, small bar with corridor to no smoking rooms and dining room, Glyndebourne posters and photographs; tables in large garden with downland backdrop – busy wknds *(John Beeken, Tony Hobden)*

GODDARDS GREEN [TQ2820]

Sportsman: Enjoyable generous food from open sandwiches and baked potatoes up, no smoking restaurant and second pubbier eating area, waitress service, Badger real ales, decent house wines *(Tony and Wendy Hobden)*

HALNAKER [SU9008]

☆ *Anglesey Arms* [A285 Chichester—Petworth]: Welcoming new landlord and well kept real ales in unpretentious bar with traditional games, simple but smart candlelit dining room with stripped pine and flagstones (children allowed), decent wines; garden tables *(John Davis, Keith Stevens, LYM)*

HANDCROSS [TQ2629]

Red Lion [High St]: Large bar nicely divided, separate no smoking dining room, lively atmosphere, quick pleasant service, Courage-related real ales, good food choice esp fish *(Fred Chamberlain)*

Royal Oak [A279]: Low beams, two smallish rooms, welcoming staff and Harvey the dog, good range of well crafted food from light dishes to adventurous substantial dishes and seasonal game, well kept beer, winter mulled wine, old photographs and curios; tables in sunny forecourt, small garden behind *(Fred Keens)*

Wheatsheaf [B2110 W]: Well kept Badger ales, good range of generous good value food from sandwiches to steaks inc children's, friendly service, two bars with lots of horse tack and farm tools, no smoking dining area; big garden with piped music and play equipment *(Ian and Joan Blackwell, C and R Bromage)*

HARTFIELD [TQ4735]

☆ *Anchor* [Church St]: Welcoming 15th-c local with heavy beams and flagstones, little country pictures and houseplants, inglenook log fire and a woodburner, comfortable dining area, well kept Adnams, Bass, Flowers IPA and Harveys Best, generous reasonably priced food from sandwiches, toasties and baked potatoes up, long-serving licensees, darts in lower room; piped music; children welcome, seats out on front verandah, garden with play area, open all day *(Hazel and Michael Duncombe, Ken Arthur, LYM, Mike Gorton)*

HASTINGS [TQ8209]

First In Last Out [High St, Old Town]: Congenial and chatty beer-drinkers' pub – even the cat is a character, holding his central armchair against all comers; open-plan bar divided by settles, pews forming booths, posts and central raised log fire, reasonably priced beers brewed in their own microbrewery with a couple of guest ales such as Everards Tiger, farm cider, friendly landlord, simple lunchtime food (not Sun), no games or juke box; can be smoky, gents' down a few steps, parking nearby difficult; small covered back terrace *(Peter Meister)*

HENFIELD [TQ2115]

George [High St]: New owners settling in well in roomy beamed coaching inn, good choice of good value food (particularly popular with older lunchers), well kept ales, open fires, children welcome, restaurant *(David Cosham)*

HERMITAGE [SU7505]

☆ *Sussex Brewery* [A259, by Thorney Island turn]: Thriving stripped-brick bar with sawdust and bare boards, immense log fire and flagstoned alcove (this bit food-free Fri/Sat night), full Youngs beer range kept well, incredible range of sausages, cheerful young staff, no smoking red plush dining room up a few steps, no machines or piped music; can get crowded; small walled garden, open all day *(Ann and Colin Hunt, David H T Dimock, RWC, Keith Stevens, Bruce Bird)*

HILL BROW [SU7826]

Jolly Drover [B2070]: Friendly helpful and cheerful hands-on landlord, good log fires, half a dozen well kept beers such as Bass, Black Sheep, Roosters, Timothy Taylors Landlord, Swamp Donkey farm cider, good food from filled baps up, good coffee, daily papers *(Ian Phillips)*

HOLTYE [TQ4538]

White Horse [Holtye Common; A264 East Grinstead—Tunbridge Wells]: Friendly unpretentiously refurbished ancient village pub with enjoyable food, well kept real ales, illuminated aquarium set into floor; good facilities for the disabled, marvellous view from back lawn, bedrooms *(Mr and Mrs J French)*

HORSTED KEYNES [TQ3828]

Crown [The Green]: This comfortable and

congenial 16th-c local, winning warm recent support from readers for its well kept beer, helpful landlord, and enjoyable food in its attractive no smoking dining bar/restaurant, was largely destroyed by fire after a lightning strike in July 2003, and as we went to press we had not yet heard about rebuilding plans – news please *(anon)*

HOUGHTON [TQ0111]

☆ *George & Dragon* [B2139 W of Storrington]: Elizabethan beams and timbers, appealing old-world bar rambling up and down steps (so not good for disabled people), great views from back extension with no smoking restaurant (popular wkdy bargain lunch for over-50s), well kept Fullers London Pride, Harveys Best and Timothy Taylors Landlord, decent wines, smartly dressed staff; may be piped classical music; children welcome, panoramic views of Arun from terraces of charming sloping garden, good walks, open for food all day wknds *(W A Evershed, LYM, Mark Percy, Lesley Mayoh, J H Bell, Ann and Colin Hunt, Martin Buck, J Iorwerth Davies, David Cosham, Tracey and Stephen Groves, Jane Basso, John Beeken)*

HUNSTON [SU8601]

Spotted Cow [B2145 Chichester—Sidlesham]: Flagstoned pub reworked in relaxed contemporary style, bright and welcoming, with big fires in cosy bar, nicely decorated airy restaurant, generous and enjoyable fresh local food esp fish, attentive chef/landlord and friendly efficient service, well kept ales; good disabled access, big garden, handy for towpath walkers *(Cathy Robinson, Ed Coombe, Jane Basso)*

ISFIELD [TQ4516]

☆ *Halfway House* [Rose Hill (A26)]: Comfortable rambling pub, low beams and timbers, dark pub furniture on turkey carpet, well kept Harveys ales inc a seasonal beer, good value home cooking inc Sun lunch and local game in season, genial landlord, quick efficient service, busy restaurant; children welcome, picnic-sets in small back garden *(BB, Michael and Ann Cole, Jenny and Brian Seller)*

Laughing Fish: Welcoming and simply modernised village local with well kept Greene King IPA and Harveys Best, PA and Old, good honest home-made lunchtime food (not Sun/Mon) with wkdy OAP bargains; children welcome, tables in small garden with entertaining enclosed play area, right by Lavender Line *(BB, the Didler, RDK)*

KINGSTON NEAR LEWES [TQ3908]

Juggs [village signed off A27 by roundabout W of Lewes]: Quaint old rose-covered cottage with interesting furnishings, layout and décor, with well kept Shepherd Neame ales, bar food from ploughman's and baked potatoes up, no smoking family room, log fires, dominoes and shove-ha'penny; nice seating areas outside, compact well equipped play area *(Ian Phillips, Ann and Colin Hunt, Kevin Flack, Michael and Ann Cole, LYM)*

KIRDFORD [TQ0126]

Foresters Arms: New landlady perking up

décor and atmosphere of flagstoned bar, lounge and family games room, well kept Badger ales, limited choice of simple but genuinely home-cooked bar food, log fires, restaurant; boules pitches *(C L Kauffmann, H G Williams)*

☆ *Half Moon* [opp church, off A272 Petworth— Billingshurst]: Pretty and charmingly set 17th-c tile-hung bar/restaurant, good interesting british cooking (may be 10% service charge), well kept Fullers London Pride from the curved counter in the partly quarry-tiled bar, good wines by the glass, log fire, friendly attentive staff, immaculate roomy and rambling largely no smoking low-beamed dining area; tables in pretty back garden and out in front *(Jeremy Woods, John Beeken, Mrs S Park, C and R Bromage, Nicholas and Dorothy Stephens, Derek Thomas, Gerry and Rosemary Dobson)*

LEWES [TQ4110]

Brewers Arms [High St]: Neatly kept pub dating from 16th c, back lounge bar, good choice of attractively priced food, well kept Arundel, Cottage, Harveys and Welton real ales, games room, 260-year list of landlords in public bar *(the Didler, Tony and Wendy Hobden)*

Gardeners Arms [Cliffe High St]: Traditional small local, light, airy and quiet, with well kept Harveys and several changing ales such as Rectory, good value lunchtime sandwiches and ploughman's, good friendly service (with helpful opinions on the beers), plain scrubbed tables on bare boards around three sides of bar, daily papers and magazines, Sun bar nibbles *(Pat and Tony Martin, Ian Arthur, MLR, Tony Hobden)*

☆ *John Harvey* [Harveys Brewery, Cliffe High St]: Tap for Harveys brewery opposite, all their beers inc seasonal kept perfectly and tapped from the cask, good value well prepared food from lunchtime sandwiches, baguettes and panini up, flagstones, oak panelling and a modern take on cask seating, sturdy oak furniture in quieter separate dining area; may be piped music *(Anne and Tim Locke, Sue and Mike Todd, Keith Reeve, Marie Hammond)*

Kings Head [Southover High St]: Friendly corner pub with Harveys Best and Shepherd Neame Spitfire from central bar, enjoyable reasonably priced food from ploughman's and baked potatoes up, raised no smoking area with flame-effect fire, monarch portraits and china displays, board games; garden, bedrooms, handy for Southover Grange and Anne of Cleves House *(John Beeken)*

☆ *Lewes Arms* [Castle Ditch Lane/Mount Pl – tucked behind castle ruins]: Chatty unpretentious corner local built into castle ramparts, small front bar with larger lounge, eating area off, and hatchway, well kept Greene King and Harveys ales, good orange juice, very reasonably priced simple lunchtime food from good baguettes and baked potatoes up, friendly service, daily papers, local pictures, toad in the hole, no music; can get smoky; small terrace *(Colin and Janet Roe, MLR, John Beeken, Anne and Tim Locke, Kevin Flack)*

LICKFOLD [SU9226]

☆ *Lickfold Inn* [NE of Midhurst, between A286 and A283]: Handsome old place with Tudor beams, ancient flooring bricks, big log fire in huge inglenook, simple wooden décor in bar and back dining room, smarter restaurant (tablecloths and sofas) upstairs; good changing wine and beer choice, creative pub food, smart upstairs restaurant, friendly staff; no children in main bar; tables on terrace, interestingly laid out garden *(Martin and Karen Wake, LYM)*

LITLINGTON [TQ5201]

☆ *Plough & Harrow* [between A27 Lewes— Polegate and A259 E of Seaford]: Spotless and neatly extended beamed flint pub with dining area done up as railway dining car (children allowed here), quick friendly service, good home cooking, well kept ales such as Badger Best and Tanglefoot, Hardys & Hansons and Harveys BB, decent wines by the glass; back lawn with children's bar, aviary and pretty views; has had live music Fri *(M and R Thomas, Michael and Ann Cole, Robert M Warner, Peter Meister, LYM, RDK)*

LITTLEHAMPTON [TQ0202]

☆ *Arun View* [Wharf Rd; W towards Chichester, opp railway station]: Roomy and comfortable 18th-c inn in lovely spot right on harbour with river directly below windows, well kept ales such as Badger K&B, Ringwood Old Thumper and Youngs Special, good wine list, diligent friendly and helpful service, interesting menu from sandwiches to good fresh fish (very popular lunchtime with older people, a younger crowd evenings), flagstoned back bar with lots of drawings and caricatures, large eating area and flower-filled terrace both overlooking busy waterway and pedestrian bridge; summer barbecues evenings and wknds, winter live music, bright and modest good value bedrooms *(Cannell Benmore, Mrs D W Privett, Caroline and Gavin Callow)*

LODSWORTH [SU9223]

Hollist Arms [off A272 Midhurst—Petworth]: Cheerful pub in attractive village spot, three well kept real ales, enjoyable food from good value generous baguettes up, friendly service, refurbished restaurant area; children welcome, nice garden *(Ron Shelton, Nicholas and Dorothy Stephens)*

LYMINSTER [TQ0204]

Six Bells: Flint-faced dining pub with good-sized helpings of unusual and enjoyable elegantly presented food from sandwiches and baguettes up, evening meals more expensive, friendly helpful efficient service, well kept Greene King Abbot and Youngs Special, no smoking restaurant area; best to book at wknds *(Alison Crooks, Dave Heffernan, Tony and Wendy Hobden, R T and J C Moggridge)*

MAPLEHURST [TQ1924]

White Horse [Park Lane]: Quiet beamed country local, beautiful wisteria in front, four seating areas inc homely cosy corners and sun lounge (no smoking at lunchtime) with redundant church furniture and lots of plants, well kept Harveys BB, Weltons and changing guest beers from small breweries, farm cider, good value basic food inc sandwiches and baked potatoes, efficient staff, no music or machines; children welcome, pleasant garden, car enthusiasts' evenings (*C and R Bromage, Bruce Bird*)

MARESFIELD [TQ4422]

Piltdown Man [A272 Newick Rd]: Welcoming staff, tasty food, pleasant décor; piped music, but not too loud (*RDK*)

MAYFIELD [TQ5827]

Middle House [High St]: Handsome 16th-c timbered inn in pretty village, L-shaped beamed locals' bar with massive fireplace, well kept Adnams, Fullers London Pride, Greene King Abbot, Harveys BB and a guest beer, local cider, decent wines, quiet lounge with leather chesterfields around log fire in ornate carved fireplace, big menu, panelled no smoking restaurant; piped music; afternoon tea in terraced back garden with lovely views, slide and play house; children welcome, open all day (*John Saul, LYM, Robert M Warner, Michael and Ann Cole*)

☆ *Rose & Crown* [Fletching St]: Pretty weatherboarded old inn, nicely worn in, good choice of enjoyable fresh food with international touches, cosy little low-beamed front rooms and pleasant restaurant, big inglenook, well kept Greene King Abbot and Old Speckled Hen and Harveys Best, good friendly service; shove-ha'penny Mon and Fri, piped music; children welcome, four attractive bedrooms, tables outside; open all day Sat (*LYM, Roger Noble*)

MIDHURST [SU8821]

Angel [North St]: Civilised and handsomely refurbished 16th-c coaching inn with pleasant lounge bar, good dining room, polite efficient service; comfortable bedrooms (*Pamela and Merlyn Horswell*)

MILTON STREET [TQ5304]

☆ *Sussex Ox* [off A27 just E of Alfriston]: Attractive country pub, a magnet for families in summer, with magnificent downs views; smallish beamed and brick-floored bar with roaring woodburner, good no smoking family room (book well ahead in summer), separate restaurant, well kept Harveys Best, Hop Back Summer Lightning and Youngs Special; piped music; children in eating areas, big lawn and marvellous play area, adjacent camping area, lots of good walks (*LYM, Tony and Wendy Hobden, Michael and Ann Cole, Neill Barker, Dominic Morgan*)

NEWHAVEN [TQ4500]

☆ *Hope* [follow West Beach signs from A259 westbound]: Big-windowed pub overlooking busy harbour entrance, settles forming booths in long bar, upstairs conservatory room and breezy balcony tables with even better view towards Seaford Head, well kept Flowers IPA, Fullers London Pride and Harveys BB, simple food from baked potatoes up inc children's, decent wines, reasonable prices, unfussy décor with some nautical touches, friendly efficient staff; unobtrusive piped music, darts and pool in airy public bar; waterside terrace

(*John Beeken, LYM, Craig Turnbull*)

Ship [High St]: Unpretentious 1930s-style pub with well kept Courage Directors and Charles Wells Bombardier, good range of food from sandwiches to steaks and mixed grill, using good fresh ingredients (*Father Robert Marsh*)

NUTHURST [TQ1926]

Black Horse [off A281 SE of Horsham]: Welcoming black-beamed 17th-c country pub with flagstones and inglenook, well kept Harveys Best, King, Timothy Taylors Landlord and guest beers, no smoking snug and restaurant; may be piped music; children and dogs welcome, attractive woodland streamside back garden, more seats on front terrace, open for food all day wknds and bank hols (*W Ruxton, Jeremy Woods, LYM, Pam and John Smith, Lisa Moore, Mike and Heather Watson, Mr Bannon, Guy Vowles, Roger and Debbie Stamp*)

NUTLEY [TQ4426]

Nutley Arms [Fords Green (A22)]: Former William IV, reopened under new Greek landlord and French landlady after careful and complete refurbishment, good if not cheap food, efficient unobtrusive service, well kept beer, decent wines; piped music turned down on request; pleasant outdoor area (*Michael and Ann Cole*)

PATCHING [TQ0705]

Fox [A27 just W of Worthing]: Now under same management as Spotted Cow, Angmering, with emphasis on no smoking dining area, enjoyable reasonably priced generous food freshly made from imaginative sandwiches, baguettes and baked potatoes up, popular Sun roasts (book ahead for these), well kept Harveys Best and Shepherd Neame Spitfire, friendly attentive service, daily papers; quiet piped music, nice big tree-shaded garden with play area, open all day wknds (*Tony and Wendy Hobden, Bruce Bird*)

Worlds End [former A27 Worthing—Arundel, off A280 roundabout]: Roomy pub, recently pleasantly refurbished, with large raftered barn-style no smoking family room, enjoyable generous food inc interesting dishes and progressive approach to children's food, well kept Badger beers inc seasonal, attentive friendly staff, daily papers; neat garden with play area, stream and pond, handy for bluebell woods (*Bruce Bird, Mrs Romey Heaton*)

PETWORTH [SU9921]

☆ *Well Diggers Arms* [Low Heath; A283 towards Pulborough]: Very good if not cheap food using fresh ingredients esp fish and seafood, long tables in stylishly simple dining room, picturesquely cluttered low-ceilinged stripped stone bar almost a museum of the rural 1920s, character friendly landlord, well kept Ballards and Youngs, decent wines, no music or machines; plenty of tables on attractive lawns and terraces, lovely views (*C L Kauffmann, LYM, Martin and Karen Wake, John Davis, Gerry and Rosemary Dobson*)

PLAYDEN [TQ9121]

Peace & Plenty [A268/B2082]: Unpretentious welcoming pub with emphasis on enjoyable food all day in two dining areas off attractively homely small bar, roaring open woodburner in big inglenook, well kept Greene King beers with a guest such as Shepherd Neame Bishops Finger, good coffee, friendly cat; children allowed, tables in pretty garden (some traffic noise), open all day *(Paul and Penny Rampton, Adrian White, John and Elspeth Howell, LYM, Alan Cole, Kirstie Bruce)*

Playden Oasts [Rye Rd]: Comfortable bar and restaurant, friendly staff, good choice of food inc lots of fish, well kept real ale *(anon)*

PLUMPTON [TQ3617]

Fountain [Station Rd, Plumpton Green]: Friendly and down to earth, with good value standard food, simple furnishings, log fire, pool in side area; nicely planted terrace, just off South Downs Way *(Amanda Eames)*

POUNDGATE [TQ4928]

Crow & Gate [A26 Crowborough—Uckfield]: Old pub extended as beamed Vintage Inn, their usual food well presented, well kept Bass and Wadworths 6X, lots of wines by the glass, efficient service, no smoking area; good disabled access, children welcome, tables outside, play area *(Ian Phillips)*

PUNNETTS TOWN [TQ6320]

☆ *Three Cups* [B2096 towards Battle]: Friendly new landlady (and eager-to-please young bull terrier called Wilf) in neighbourly and unassuming beamed country local, gently refurbished and recarpeted, with log fire in big fireplace, small partly no smoking back dining room, well kept Greene King beers with a guest such as Caledonian 80/–, traditional games; work on the kitchen has allowed an expanded food range – we have had no reports on this yet; children and dogs welcome, tables outside, great walks, has been open all day wknds *(Jason Caulkin, LYM)*

PYECOMBE [TQ2912]

Plough [A23]: Smartly refurbished but keeping pub character in bar with well kept ales such as Harveys and Shepherd Neame Bishops Finger from long counter, decent house wines, friendly and efficient staff all in black, good largely italian restaurant in back extension, a real welcome for children; handy for South Downs Way *(David Cosham, Terry Buckland)*

RAKE [SU8027]

Sun [Portsmouth Rd (A3 S of Liphook)]: Comfortable dining pub with two sofas and a woodburner in main bar, two dining areas (back one no smoking), wide food choice from lunchtime ciabattas up inc lots of good fish, Greene King IPA and Abbot and a guest beer, quick friendly service; back terrace tables with lovely valley views *(Martin and Karen Wake)*

RINGMER [TQ4412]

☆ *Cock* [Uckfield Rd – blocked-off section of road off A26 N of village turn-off]: Heavy 16th-c beams and flagstones in main bar with big inglenook log fire, pleasant modernised rooms off inc no smoking lounge, huge good value blackboard food choice, well kept Fullers London Pride, Harveys Best and Mild and Youngs Waggle Dance, welcoming landlord and happy efficient staff, lovely flower

arrangements, enterprising back no smoking restaurant; children allowed in overflow eating area; quiet piped music; tables on small terrace and in big sloping fairy-lit garden with shrubs, fruit trees and lots of spring flowers *(Tony and Wendy Hobden, LYM, Alan J Miller, John Beeken, Peter Meister, Michael and Ann Cole, Robert M Warner, P W Taylor)*

RIPE [TQ5010]

☆ *Lamb* [signed off A22 Uckfield—Hailsham, or off A27 Lewes—Polegate via Chalvington; Church Lane]: Interestingly furnished partly panelled rooms around central servery, masses of attractive antique prints and pictures, nostalgic song-sheet covers, automotive memorabilia, Victorian pin-ups in gents'; sound choice of generous home-made food from sandwiches and baked potatoes up, children's menu, well kept ales such as Adnams and Harveys Best and Old, good range of reasonably priced wines, several open fires, small dining room set out as farmyard stalls; bar billiards, TV; pleasant sheltered back garden with play area and barbecues *(John Beeken, BB)*

ROBERTSBRIDGE [TQ7323]

Ostrich [Station Rd]: Cheerful open-plan former station hotel, enjoyable food, Adnams, Harveys BB and a guest beer, games room; tables in attractive garden, bedrooms *(the Didler)*

RODMELL [TQ4105]

Abergavenny Arms [back road Lewes—Newhaven]: Open-plan village local with large lounge area, some interesting bric-a-brac, good range of food from ploughman's to sensible hot dishes, Harveys Best and Charles Wells Bombardier, quick service, open fire, small no smoking section; dogs on leads welcome, large two-level back terrace, good walks and handy for Virginia Woolf's Monks Cottage *(John Beeken)*

ROWHOOK [TQ1234]

☆ *Chequers* [off A29 NW of Horsham]: Attractive 16th-c pub, beamed and flagstoned front bar with inglenook fire, step up to low-ceilinged lounge, well kept real ales, good wine choice, young chef/landlord doing good mainly restaurant food – Sun lunch particularly enjoyed by readers; piped music; children and dogs welcome, tables out on terraces and in pretty garden with good play area, attractive surroundings *(LYM, Dr P E Gower, David and Elizabeth Briggs)*

RUDGWICK [TQ0936]

Wheatsheaf [Ellens Green (B2128 N)]: Enjoyable fresh food, considerate service, neat housekeeping *(Mrs J A Uthwatt, Derek and Maggie Washington)*

RUNCTON [SU8900]

Royal Oak [Pagham Rd, S]: Very popular, with particularly good sizzling steak and mixed grill; well kept Gales HSB, welcoming landlord *(Eric Block, Jane Basso)*

Walnut Tree [Vinnetrow Rd, towards N Mundham]: Good beer choice, friendly efficient staff, open fires and flagstones, nice atmosphere and reasonably priced food in barn-style restaurant with smaller no smoking annexe, good wine list *(John Evans)*

RUSPER [TQ2037]

Plough [signed from A24 and A264 N and NE of Horsham]: Nicely worn in country local dating from 16th c, padded very low beams, panelling and big inglenook with lovely log fire, well kept changing ales such as Fullers London Pride and ESB, Harveys Best, Kings Best and Summer Ale and Theakstons Old Peculier, good value food, quick pleasant service, dining area; children welcome, bar billiards and darts in raftered room upstairs; pretty front terrace, fountain in back garden, occasional live music *(C and R Bromage, LYM, W W Burke)*

RYE [TQ9220]

George [High St]: Pleasant bar in sizeable hotel, friendly staff, five real ales, reasonably priced bar food; lounge more sedate with sofas and log fire; good bedrooms, but no car park *(J A Snell)*

Olde Standard [High St]: Welcoming and interesting cosily dark local with lots of beams and stripped brick, particularly well kept beers inc local ones from Pett, good value generous food, prompt service, good relaxed family atmosphere, darts, log-effect gas fire; piped music; open all day *(Steve Dark, S and R Gray, Keith and Chris O'Neill)*

☆ *Ypres Castle* [Gun Garden; steps up from A259, or down past Ypres Tower]: Traditional local with simple no smoking dining room, well kept Harveys, decent wines, limited choice of good home-made food from baked potatoes to local fish and marsh lamb, cheerful civilised service, traditional games; may be piped music, live Fri; children welcome, fine views from picnic-sets on sizeable lawn, open all day *(Tina and David Woods-Taylor, C F D Moore, David and Elizabeth Briggs, Colin and Janet Roe, LYM, Derek Harvey-Piper, Gwyn Jones, Gill and Tony Morriss, Nicholas Armstrong, Alan Cole, Kirstie Bruce)*

RYE HARBOUR [TQ9220]

☆ *Inkerman Arms*: Friendly and cosy unpretentious local nr nature reserve, wide choice of good food inc lots of fresh local fish, fine home-made pies and old-fashioned puddings, well kept Greene King ales and a couple from local breweries, pleasantly decorated main bar with secluded eating areas; tables in small garden; cl Mon evening and winter Mon lunchtime *(John Beeken, V Brogden, Gill and Tony Morriss, Alan Cole, Kirstie Bruce)*

William the Conqueror: Big beamed lounge and separate public bar with games, good range of Shepherd Neame ales, fair-priced food, friendly and lively local atmosphere; well placed on harbour edge *(BB, Gill and Tony Morriss)*

SCAYNES HILL [TQ3824]

Sloop [Freshfield Lock]: Named for the boats on the adjacent former Ouse Canal, bare-boards public bar, long saloon bar and dining room with no smoking section, well kept Greene King ales with one or two guest beers,

decent wines, bar billiards room and traditional games; may be piped music; children in eating areas, lots of tables in sheltered garden, open for food all day Sun *(R J Walden, LYM, Joyce and Geoff Robson, Susan and John Douglas, C and R Bromage, Richard May)*

SEAFORD [TV4799]

White Lion [Claremont Rd]: Good range of good value food in bar and no smoking conservatory, well kept Fullers London Pride and Harveys; pool, may be piped music or juke box; bedrooms, open all day *(Paul A Moore)*

SELMESTON [TQ5006]

Barley Mow [A27 Eastbourne—Lewes]: Attractive and homely old low-ceilinged pub, four spacious areas (some no smoking), well kept Flowers and Harveys Best, wide blackboard range of enjoyable good value food inc some interesting dishes, good service, flowers on all tables; unobtrusive piped music; garden with play area *(Paul A Moore, Father Robert Marsh, David Cosham)*

SELSEY [SZ8692]

Lifeboat [Albion Rd, nr seafront]: Traditional unpretentious bar (dogs allowed) with dining extension, wide choice of good value food from sandwiches to local crab salad, Courage Directors, Fullers London Pride and Shepherd Neame Spitfire, friendly helpful staff; tables out on big verandah – only main courses served at hatch here *(J A Snell, Tony and Wendy Hobden)*

SHIPLEY [TQ1321]

Countryman [SW of village, off A272 E of Coolham]: Early 19th-c, wide choice of enjoyable food from warm baguettes up, well kept ales such as Fullers London Pride and Kings, friendly staff, lounge bar, large carpeted dining area, welcoming flagstoned locals' bar with inglenook log fire, darts and bar billiards; may be piped music; picnic-sets and play equipment in pretty garden, horse park, handy for Shipley windmill and D-Day Airfield at Coolham *(C and R Bromage)*

SHORTBRIDGE [TQ4521]

☆ *Peacock* [Piltdown; OS Sheet 198 map ref 450215]: Comfortable and welcoming rebuilt beamed and timbered bar, big inglenook, very generous nicely presented bar food served piping hot inc good fish (10% service charge), well kept Harveys and Wadworths 6X, restaurant; piped music (they will turn it down), children may be much in evidence; sizeable garden *(Michael and Ann Cole, BB, Michael Hasslacher)*

SIDLESHAM [SZ8599]

Anchor [Selsey Rd]: Doing well under focused current management, plenty of tables for enjoyable food esp fresh local fish, friendly staff, real ales; nice terrace, handy for wildlife centre, has been open all day *(Ian and Barbara Rankin)*

☆ *Crab & Lobster* [Mill Lane; off B2145 S of Chichester]: Individualistic old country local, log fire in chatty traditional bar, no smoking plusher side dining lounge, pretty back garden looking over to the bird-reserve of silted

Pagham Harbour; limited choice of good home-made food (not Sun evening, starts 7 other evenings) inc fresh seafood, reasonable prices, well kept ales such as Cheriton Pots and Itchen Valley, decent wines, country wines, log fire, traditional games; dogs welcome, no children, music or machines *(E Prince, Gordon Neighbour, Tracey and Stephen Groves, Pamela Goodwyn, LYM, Phil and Sally Gorton, Veronica Brown)*

SLINDON [SU9708]

☆ *Spur* [Slindon Common; A29 towards Bognor]: Popular, roomy and attractive 17th-c pub, welcoming atmosphere, two big log fires, pine tables, good choice of interesting good value food changing daily, well kept Courage Directors and Greene King Ruddles, cheerful efficient staff, large elegant restaurant, children welcome; games room with darts and pool (for over-18s), friendly dogs; pretty garden (traffic noise) *(John Evans, Ann and Sally Kingsbury)*

SOUTH HARTING [SU7819]

Ship [North Lane (B2146)]: Welcoming, unpretentious and thoroughly dependable 17th-c pub, informal and unspoilt, with good choice of good value food inc sandwiches on request in dimly lit main bar, roaring log fire, old photographs, well kept real ales, friendly staff and dogs, simpler locals' bar (dominoes, perhaps chestnuts to roast by its log fire); unobtrusive piped music; nice setting in pretty village *(John Evans, Ann and Colin Hunt, W A Evershed, John and Tania Wood)*

White Hart [B2146 SE of Petersfield]: Cool décor with well spaced tables on polished wood, efficient friendly young staff, well kept Fullers London Pride and ESB, interesting food choice from ploughman's and hot sandwiches up, woodburner; shame about the piped music; well behaved dogs allowed, walkers and children welcome, good walled garden with spectacular Downs views, handy for Uppark *(Ian Phillips)*

ST LEONARDS [TQ8008]

Horse & Groom [Mercatoria]: Friendly bustling traditional town pub in old Maze Hill area, carved curved bar serving front and back rooms, cheap and cheerful home-made food from sandwiches up, real ales such as Adnams, Harveys and Timothy Taylors Landlord, interesting pictures; small garden *(BB)*

STAPLEFIELD [TQ2728]

Jolly Tanners [Handcross Rd, just off A23]: Spotless, quiet and comfortable, good home-made food, well kept Fullers Chiswick and London Pride, Harveys BB and a Mild such as Batemans or Thwaites, prompt service, real log fire, lots of china, brasses and old photographs, no smoking room; piped music may obtrude; attractive garden with lots of space for children, terrace tables under cocktail parasols and picnic-sets on grass, by cricket green, quite handy for Nymans (NT) *(Bruce Bird, Terry Buckland, Jason Caulkin)*

STEYNING [TQ1711]

Star [High St]: Rambling pub with unpretentious front area, back dining areas, cosy alcove full of old farm tools, enjoyable

pub food, real ales such as Badger K&B and Youngs; streamside garden with huge cask tables *(Mark Percy, Lesley Mayoh)*

STOPHAM [TQ0318]

White Hart [off A283 E of village, W of Pulborough]: Interesting old heavily timbered, beamed and panelled pub reopened after refurbishment, well kept beers such as Flowers, Fullers London Pride and Weltons Kid & Bard, hearty helpings of bar food from baguettes to venison, young enthusiastic staff, log fire and sofas in one of its three snug rooms, no smoking restaurant; piped music may obtrude; children welcome, play area over road, tables out by River Arun *(LYM, John Beeken)*

STOUGHTON [SU8011]

Hare & Hounds [signed off B2146 Petersfield—Emsworth]: Comfortably refurbished and brightened up under new management, some emphasis on sensibly priced food inc Sun roast, well kept real ales such as Timothy Taylors Landlord and Youngs, good polite service, airy pine-clad bar and dining area, big open fires; children in eating areas, tables on pretty front terrace and in back garden; nr Saxon church, good walks nearby *(LYM, Keith Stevens, J A Snell, Ann and Colin Hunt, W A Evershed)*

SUTTON [SU9715]

☆ *White Horse* [The Street]: Charming small and civilised country pub in same ownership as Horse Guards at Tillington (see main entries), island servery separating bare-boards bar from two-room barrel-vaulted dining area with stylishly simple furnishings and Rowlandson prints, good food from bar dishes to enterprising restaurant meals inc local game and fish; Courage Best, Fullers London Pride, Shepherd Neame Spitfire and Youngs Special (may have only two of these on), short interesting wine choice, log fire; tables in garden up behind, good value bedrooms with excellent breakfast, quiet little hamlet nr Bignor Roman villa *(John Beeken, BB, Wendy Arnold, Anne and Jeff Peel, C L Kauffmann, Brenda and Rob Fincham)*

TICEHURST [TQ6831]

Bull [Three Legged Cross; off B2099 towards Wadhurst]: Attractive 14th-c hall house with two big log fires in very heavy-beamed old-fashioned simple two-room bar, light and airy dining extension, well kept Fullers London Pride, Harveys Best and local Rother Valley Level Best, friendly service, darts and other traditional games, maybe piped music; charming front garden with fish pond, bigger back one with play area *(LYM, Peter Meister)*

TURNERS HILL [TQ3435]

☆ *Crown* [East St]: Spacious dining pub, very wide choice of consistently enjoyable reasonably priced food, well kept ales such as Fullers and Harveys, good wine choice, helpful service, log fire, pleasant décor with pictures etc, different levels inc attractive restaurant with pitched rafters; soft piped music; tables outside, pleasant valley views from back garden; children welcome, two bedrooms *(Dr P J W Young, Sue and Mike Todd, BB)*

Red Lion [Lion Lane]: Welcoming old-fashioned local with well kept Harveys Pale Ale, Best and seasonal beers, good value imaginative food inc good Sun roast, narrow bar with alcove seating and small fire, steps up to larger dining area with log fire in magnificent inglenook, oak beams and furniture; children and well behaved dogs welcome, pretty garden *(Bill and Rachael Gallagher, Peter Taylor, W Ruxton, Mike Gorton)*

UPPER BEEDING [TQ1910]

Rising Sun [Shoreham Rd (A2037)]: Homely old pub just off South Downs Way, well laid out inside, with cosy softly lit side rooms, character nooks and crannies, and small dining conservatory; good value home-made standard food with good puddings, well kept Adnams Best, Flowers Original, Fullers London Pride and Marstons Pedigree, friendly landlord, efficient staff; unobtrusive piped music; large pleasant garden with downland views *(John Beeken)*

WADHURST [TQ6131]

☆ *Best Beech* [Mayfield Lane (B2100 1 mile W)]: Pleasant dining pub, newly refurbished cosy eating area, lots of pictures, imaginative, modern cooking using some local produce, bar on left with wall seats, plenty of comfortable sofas, coal fire, well kept Adnams, Harveys and Youngs, good choice of wines by the glass, quick service; back restaurant, tables outside, good value bedrooms, good breakfast *(BB, Robert M Warner)*

Greyhound [B2099]: Neatly kept village pub with good value home-made food and set Sun lunch in restaurant or pleasant beamed bar with big inglenook log fire, well kept Bass, Greene King Old Speckled Hen, Harveys and Youngs Special, decent wines by the glass, games area with bar billiards, no piped music (but can be smoky); tables in well kept and attractive sheltered back garden, bedrooms *(BB, Barbara Carter, Neil Rose)*

WALDERTON [SU7910]

☆ *Barley Mow* [Stoughton road, just off B2146 Chichester—Petersfield]: Spacious flagstoned U-shaped bar popular for good choice of good generous food; well kept Ringwood ales, quick cheerful service even on busy wknds, two log fires, country bric-a-brac, no music; children welcome, skittle alley, nice furniture in big pleasant streamside garden with fish pond, aviary and swings, good walks, handy for Stansted House *(W A Evershed, Ann and Colin Hunt, J A Snell)*

WARBLETON [TQ6018]

☆ *Warbil in Tun* [S of B2096 SE of Heathfield]: Pretty dining pub with good choice of good value food esp meat (helpful ex-butcher landlord), nice puddings, well kept reasonably priced Harveys Best, good coffee, welcoming and cosily civilised atmosphere, beams and red plush, huge log fireplace, no music; tables on roadside green, attractive tucked-away village *(R E Greenhalgh, Michael and Ann Cole)*

WEST ASHLING [SU8107]

Richmond Arms [just off B2146; Mill Rd]:

Tucked-away village local in pretty setting nr mill pond, simple but polished and spotless, well kept Greene King IPA and Abbot with a guest such as Charles Wells Bombardier, enjoyable food from sandwiches and baguettes to steaks, open fire, darts, pool and a skittle alley; can get smoky; children allowed, picnic-sets out by pergola, open all day Sun and summer Sat *(Ian Phillips, Ann and Colin Hunt, Tracey and Stephen Groves, LYM)*

WEST CHILTINGTON [TQ0916]

☆ *Five Bells* [Smock Alley, off B2139 SE]: Welcoming landlord an enthusiast for real ales, with four well kept changing ones from small breweries and a Mild from Badger or Harveys, annual beer festival, farm cider, good value fresh food (not Sun evening), log fire, friendly locals, beams and panelling, old photographs, unusual brass bric-a-brac, distinctive conservatory dining room; no piped music, peaceful garden with terrace, new bedrooms *(Bruce Bird)*

WEST DEAN [SU8512]

Selsey Arms [A286 Midhurst—Chichester]: Large late 18th-c village pub reopened after refurbishment as Greene King dining pub under welcoming new management, enjoyable food and real ales, decent wines, roomy no smoking area, log fire *(Ann and Colin Hunt, Jane Basso)*

WEST HOATHLY [TQ3632]

Cat [signed from A22 and B2028 S of E Grinstead; North Lane]: Stylish and relaxing pub/restaurant, fresh flowers and candles, beams and panelling, two roaring log fires, well kept Harveys Best, decent wines, decent food, smiling service, broadsheet newspapers; piped chill-out music, no children, dogs or muddy boots; tables out on small terrace with quiet view of church *(LYM, Penny Power)*

WEST ITCHENOR [SU8001]

Ship [The Street]: Large friendly panelled pub in good spot nr Chichester Harbour, good long walk from W Wittering; generous food from good baguettes to restaurant dishes inc local fish, exemplary service, well kept Ballards Best, Gales HSB, Itchen Valley Godfathers and Ringwood Best, two roaring fires, lots of bric-a-brac inc many chamber-pots, seats made from old boat, children in eating area; tables outside, may be good visiting barbecue in car park; open all day, said to be able to get supplies for yachtsmen (nearest shop is 2 miles away) *(M Blatchly, Tony and Wendy Hobden, Val and Alan Green)*

WEST MARDEN [SU7713]

Victoria [B2146 2 miles S of Uppark]: Good value home-made food inc interesting dishes and good sandwiches in pleasant rustic surroundings, well kept real ales, decent house wines, small dining room *(J A Snell)*

WEST WITTERING [SZ8099]

☆ *Lamb* [Chichester Rd; B2179/A286 towards Birdham]: Several rooms (some no smoking) neatly knocked through with clean smart furnishings, rugs on tiles, blazing fire, well kept Badger ales, decent wines, good choice of good value food from separate servery, cheerful efficient service; dogs on leads allowed, pleasant outside with tables out in front and in small sheltered back garden – good for children; busy in summer *(David Coleman, BB, P R and S A White, Ian and Jane Irving)*

WHATLINGTON [TQ7619]
Royal Oak [A21]: Steps between two long pleasant beamed rooms with stripped pine tables and chairs, feature well edged with flowers, enjoyable food, decent wine, friendly service; tables in back garden *(BB)*

WINCHELSEA [TQ9017]
☆ *New Inn* [German St; just off A259]: Variety of solid comfortable furnishings in bustling rambling beamed rooms, Georgian décor, some emphasis on enjoyable food from sandwiches to good fresh fish, well kept Greene King IPA and Abbot and Harveys, decent wines and malt whiskies, quick friendly service from pleasant landlady and young staff, log fire; separate public bar with darts, children in eating area, pretty bedrooms (some sharing bathrooms), delightful setting *(Dr T E Hothersall, Robert M Warner, J H Bell, LYM)*

WISBOROUGH GREEN [TQ0526]
Cricketers Arms [Loxwood Rd, just off A272 Billingshurst—Petworth]: Very low beams, bare boards and timbering in attractive open-plan old local, two big woodburners, pleasant mix of country furniture, five or six real ales, no smoking stripped brick dining area on left, cheerful service; piped music; tables out on terrace and across lane from green *(Mike and Lynn Robinson, LYM, Mrs Romey Heaton)*
Three Crowns [Billingshurst Rd (A272)]: Big neat pub very popular lunchtime for wide choice of good value food from sandwiches, baguettes and ploughman's up inc children's and small-appetite meals, good Sun lunch, open-plan bar stretching into no smoking dining room, stripped bricks and beams, well kept real ales, quick attentive service, games room; sizeable back garden *(DWAJ)*

WITHYHAM [TQ4935]
☆ *Dorset Arms* [B2110]: Bustling 16th-c pub in pleasant countryside, easy-going well worn in bar with sturdy tables and simple country seats on wide oak floorboards (sometimes a bit uneven – beware of wobbles), good log fire in Tudor fireplace, well kept Harveys PA, Best and a seasonal beer, decent wines inc local ones, attentive friendly service; bar snacks from fresh filled rolls up, best to book for landlady's consistently good home cooking at appealing prices, pretty no smoking restaurant; dogs welcome, darts, dominoes, shove-ha'penny, cribbage, fruit machine, piped music; white tables on brick terrace by small green, handy for Forest Way *(Robert M Warner, Martin Buck, A J Holland, Richard Gibbs, LYM, Peter and Joan Elbra, Peter Meister)*

WORTHING [TQ1503]
Alexandra [Lyndhurst Rd/Selden Rd]: Two smartish bars and no smoking dining room, low-priced food, Harveys Best and Greene King IPA and Abbot, several wines by the glass; garden tables *(Tony and Wendy Hobden)*
Castle Tavern [Newland Rd]: Welcoming landlord and staff, good choice of sensibly priced home-made food (not Sun/Mon evenings) inc Sun roasts, well kept Harveys Best, Hop Back Summer Lightning, Shepherd Neame Bishops Finger and guests from small breweries such as fff, generous coffee, good local atmosphere; live music Mon and Sat, open all day Fri/Sat *(Bruce Bird, Tony and Wendy Hobden)*
Charles Dickens [Heene Rd]: Rambling pub with several rooms (one no smoking), eight changing real ales such as Kings Red River and Shepherd Neame Spitfire, small choice of sensibly priced wines, low-priced pub food; some live music; terrace and garden *(Tony and Wendy Hobden)*
Coach & Horses [Arundel Rd, Clapham (A27 W)]: Welcoming and well worn in 17th-c coaching inn with rather 1970s feel, wide choice of good bar food (freshly made, so can be a wait – can order ahead by phone) in extended dining area, well kept Fullers London Pride, Youngs Special and guests such as Adnams Best and Broadside, quick friendly service, decent coffee, log fire, lots of brass and china, second back bar; can be smoky, piped music; children welcome, Tues quiz night, jazz first Mon, well kept garden with lots of tables *(Tony and Wendy Hobden, Brian Barder, Quentin and Carol Williamson)*
George & Dragon [High St, Old Tarring]: Extended 17th-c pub with four areas inc airy lounge and lunchtime no smoking restaurant (not Sun), good lunchtime food, well kept Hop Back Summer Lightning, Charles Wells Bombardier, Youngs and an interesting guest beer, friendly efficient service, beams and panelling, bric-a-brac, brass platters and old photographs, no piped music; dogs allowed (not in attractive garden) *(Bruce Bird)*
Hare & Hounds [Portland Rd, just N of Marks & Spencer]: Friendly bustling extended pub with well kept ales such as Badger K&B, Fullers London Pride, Greene King Old Speckled Hen and Marstons Pedigree from central brass and oak bar, good value promptly served straightforward food (not Fri-Sun evenings) from sandwiches and baked potatoes up, wide range of customers inc plenty of regulars, canopied courtyard, occasional jazz; no car park but three multi-storeys nearby *(Tony and Wendy Hobden)*
North Star [Littlehampton Rd (A259)]: Comfortably furnished Ember Inn, no smoking area, sensibly priced food noon to 8, Harveys ales *(Tony and Wendy Hobden)*

YAPTON [SU9704]
Maypole [signed off B2132 Arundel road; Maypole Lane]: Quiet country pub doing well under welcoming new landlord, enjoyable bar food now inc generous Sun roasts, well kept Ringwood Best, Skinners Betty Stogs and four changing guests inc a Mild, two log fires in cosy lounge; skittle alley, seats outside, on good circular walk from Buxted, open all day Fri-Sun *(Bruce Bird)*

Warwickshire (with Birmingham and West Midlands)

Four appealing new entries here are the Malt Shovel at Gaydon (nice couple running it, with enjoyable food, good beers and good relaxed atmosphere), the stylishly up-to-date Clarendon House in Kenilworth (brasserie food all day), the Duck on the Pond at Long Itchington (entertaining décor, and all the right pub virtues), and the trendily reworked canalside Wharf Inn at Wharf (food all day – even breakfast from 8am). Food certainly figures strongly in many of this area's best pubs. Foody pubs on particularly good form include the Bell at Alderminster (imaginative menu but keeping its feet sensibly on the ground), the restauranty Fox & Goose at Armscote (rather modern-feeling, with inventive cooking), the handsome old Kings Head at Aston Cantlow (the new landlady, who worked here under the former regime, is getting it all exactly right), the stylish and civilised Inn at Farnborough (both elaborate dishes and good value set menus), and the convivial and beautifully kept Howard Arms at Ilmington (imaginative food at fair prices). The Kings Head at Aston Cantlow, with good food and wine, great service and plenty of atmosphere, is Warwickshire Dining Pub of the Year. Other pubs here doing really well these days include the Old Joint Stock in Birmingham (enjoyable bar food, good beers and good wines by the glass in this impressive bank conversion), the Dun Cow at Dunchurch (an appealing and particularly well run Vintage Inn, with good value food all day, and gaining a Place to Stay Award this year), the splendidly old-fashioned Case is Altered at Five Ways (a favourite of traditionalists, with particularly well kept beer), the cheerful canalside Navigation at Lapworth, the Red Lion at Little Compton (a welcoming and thoroughly reliable all-rounder), the Beacon in Sedgley (beautifully preserved Victorian interior, and brewing its own good distinctive beer), and the Griffin at Shustoke (a thriving country local with a fine range of beers and good value pub lunches). The Lucky Dip section at the end of the chapter has some notable finds too, such as the Bartons Arms in Birmingham, Turf in Bloxwich, Cherington Arms, Town Wall in Coventry, Shakespeare at Harbury, George at Lower Brailes, Old Swan in Netherton, Rose & Crown at Ratley, Blue Boar at Temple Grafton, Plough at Warmington and Great Western in Wolverhampton. Drinks prices are close to the national average in the Warwickshire countryside; the Garrick in Stratford, and the Red Lion at Little Compton (supplied by the small Donnington brewery over in Gloucestershire), stand out for their low-priced beer. Pubs in the major West Midlands urban areas also tend to have particularly low beer prices – most notably, the Vine in Brierley Hill (with Bathams from the neighbouring brewery) and the Beacon in Sedgley (brewing its own Sarah Hughes beers, available elsewhere too).

Banks's of Wolverhampton is the main regional brewer. Besides Bathams, other good value brewers here include Holdens and Highgate (probably the ones you are most likely to come across), and Frankton Bagby, Beowulf, Church End and Warwickshire.

ALDERMINSTER SP2348 Map 4
Bell 🍴 ♀

A3400 Oxford—Stratford

Run with enthusiastic verve by cheery licensees, this civilised dining pub has a good menu which might include soup (£3.75), filled lunchtime baguettes (from £4.95, not Sun), baked spinach and avocado soufflé (£5.25), liver pâté (£5.50), spinach and ricotta tortellini (£6.50), fishcakes with dill and lemon hollandaise (£8.95), curry (£9.50), steak and kidney pudding (£9.95), fried duck with roasted mediterranean vegetables and celeriac and apple mash (£11.95), and home-made puddings such as fruit crumble and steamed pudding of the day or chilled lemon tart (£4.25). Do make it clear if you want to eat in the bar, as one or two readers have been unwittingly ushered into the restaurant. The licensees put great effort into keeping the atmosphere flourishing, by putting on lots of parties, food festivals, and classical and light music evenings. The communicating rooms of the neatly kept spacious bar have plenty of stripped slatback chairs around wooden tables on flagstones and wooden floors, little vases of flowers, small landscape prints and swan's-neck brass-and-globe lamps on cream walls, and a solid fuel stove in a stripped brick inglenook. Well kept Greene King IPA and Abbot on handpump, alongside a good range of wines and champagne by the glass, freshly squeezed juice and cocktails. They have high chairs, and readers with children have felt particularly welcome. A conservatory and terrace overlook the garden and Stour Valley. *(Recommended by John Bowdler, Brian Skelcher, K H Frostick, Carol and David Havard, Joan and Tony Walker, Maysie Thompson, Michael Gray, Mike and Sue Richardson, Mr and Mrs P Lally, M A Borthwick, Bob and Maggie Atherton, Les and Barbara Owen, Keith and Margaret Kettell, David and Ruth Shillitoe, Peter Sutton, Paul and Annette Hallett, Rob and Catherine Dunster)*

Free house ~ Licensees Keith and Vanessa Brewer ~ Real ale ~ Bar food ~ Restaurant ~ (01789) 450414 ~ Children welcome ~ Dogs allowed in bar and bedrooms ~ Open 12-2, 7-11 ~ Bedrooms: £27(£42S)(£50B)/£42(£50S)(£65B)

ARMSCOTE SP2444 Map 4
Fox & Goose 🍴 ♀ 🛏

Off A3400 Stratford—Shipston

Most readers really enjoy the distinctive contemporary décor at this stylishly transformed blacksmith's forge, which hovers between bistro and upmarket pub – an area in the bar is kept unlaid, for drinkers. Walls are a warm red in the small flagstoned bar and cream in the larger eating area, with bright crushed velvet cushions plumped up on wooden pews, a big gilt mirror over a log fire, polished floorboards and black and white etchings. In a quirky tableau above the dining room's woodburning stove a stuffed fox stalks a big goose; piped jazz. Listed on a daily changing blackboard, the food puts together some imaginative and successful combinations of ingredients, and might include soup (£3.75), sandwiches (£4.25), grilled garlic sardines (£5), home-cured gravadlax on buckwheat blinis with dill crème fraîche (£5.50), home-made tagliatelle with goats cheese, roasted peppers, pesto and parsnip crisps (£9.50), baked salmon on wilted spinach with lemon and basil (£11.95), roast lamb shoulder with rosemary and redcurrant jus (£12.50) and rib-eye steak with onions, tomato and chips (£14). Service is charming and helpful. Well kept Brakspears and a guest such as Greene King Old Speckled Hen on handpump, mulled wine in winter, jugs of Pimms in summer, and well chosen wines including a choice of dessert wines. Bedrooms, which are named after characters in Cluedo, are mildly quirky, stylishly decorated and comfortable. Outside, the garden has an elegant vine-covered deck area overlooking a big lawn with tables, benches and fruit trees, and several of the neighbouring houses boast splendid roses in summer. *(Recommended by Angus Sinclair, John Bowdler, M A and C R Starling, Martin Jones, Jennie Hall, Maurice Ribbans, Peter Sutton, Arnold Benett, Nigel and Sue Foster, Will Watson, Brian and Bett Cox, Jenny and Chris Wilson, Bob and Maggie Atherton, Keith and Margaret Kettell, John and Gloria Isaacs, Roger Braithwaite, Susan and John Douglas, Janet and Peter Race; also in the* Good Hotel Guide*)*

Free house ~ Licensee Sue Gray ~ Real ale ~ Bar food ~ Restaurant ~ (01608) 682293 ~ Children in restaurant ~ Dogs allowed in bar ~ Open 12-3, 6-11; 12-11 (10.30) Sat; closed 25/26 Dec, 1 Jan ~ Bedrooms: £45B/£90B

ASTON CANTLOW SP1359 Map 4
Kings Head 🍽 ♀
Village signposted just off A3400 NW of Stratford
Warwickshire Dining Pub of the Year
The last few months have brought us lots of positive reports from readers about this lovely old black and white timbered Tudor pub, a real picture in summer, with wisteria and colourful hanging baskets. There's particular praise for the good often inventive food and the high standard of enthusiastic service from attentive young staff – it is popular, so you will need to book. The creative menu changes very regularly and meals are freshly prepared: maybe soup or rustic breads with olive oil and roast garlic (£3.45), moules marinière (£5.55), smoked haddock rarebit (£5.65), prawn and crab spring roll with pickled ginger and wasabi (£6.25), toulouse sausages with butterbean roast garlic and tomato stew or ricotta, spinach and pine nut cannelloni with chicory, radicchio and gorgonzola salad (£9.95), chicken breast with lime pickle, olives and almonds or salmon with red salsa and basil oil (£11.75), garlic and smoked paprika marinated rump of lamb with roast aubergine and harissa (£12.75), and baked bass with lime pickle, pickled ginger and garlic (£14.75). The clean and comfortable village bar on the right is a nice mix of rustic surroundings with a civilised gently upmarket atmosphere: flagstones, low beams, and old-fashioned settles around its massive inglenook log fireplace. The chatty quarry-tiled main room has attractive window seats and oak tables. Three well kept real ales on handpump, such as Black Sheep, Greene King Abbot and M&B Brew XI, also decent wines; piped jazz. The garden is lovely, with a big chestnut tree. The pub is not far from Mary Arden's house in Wilmcote, and Shakespeare's parents are said to have married in the church next door. *(Recommended by Maysie Thompson, James Murphy, Susan and John Douglas, Peter Sutton, Glenys and John Roberts, John and Hazel Williams, Trevor and Sylvia Millum, Mrs Ursula Hofheinz, Martin Jones, Howard and Margaret Buchanan, Gill and Keith Croxton, John Hale, Brenda and Stuart Naylor)*

Whitbreads ~ Lease Sally Coll ~ Real ale ~ Bar food (12-2.30, 7-10; 12.30-3, 7-9 Sun) ~ Restaurant ~ (01789) 488242 ~ Children welcome ~ Dogs allowed in bar ~ Open 11-3, 5.30-11; 11-11 Sat; 12-10.30 Sun

BIRMINGHAM SP0686 Map 4
Old Joint Stock ♀
Temple Row West
This interesting old building is the only pub we know of N of Bristol to be owned by the London-based brewer Fullers, and is reminiscent of the Old Bank of England in external appearance. Opposite the cathedral, it's a distinctive romanesque building, its sober exterior giving little indication of the flamboyance within: chandeliers hang from the soaring pink and gilt ceiling, gently illuminated busts line the top of the ornately plastered walls, and there's a splendid if well worn cupola above the centre of the room. Drinks are served from a handsome dark wood island bar counter, and big portraits and smart long curtains create an air of unexpected elegance. Around the walls are plenty of tables and chairs, some in surprisingly cosy

corners, with more on a big balcony overlooking the bar, reached by a very grand wide staircase. It can get busy (it's a lunchtime favourite with local office workers), but effortlessly absorbs what seem like huge numbers of people. A separate room with panelling and a fireplace has a more intimate, clubby feel. Fullers Chiswick, ESB, London Pride and one of their seasonal beers are well kept alongside a guest from the local Beowulf, and they have a decent range of about a dozen wines by the glass; helpful friendly service, teas, coffees. Usefully served all day, and up a notch since last year, very fairly priced bar food includes soup (£3.25), sandwiches (from £3.50), ciabattas and foccacias (from £5.50), ploughman's (£5.75), sausage and mash (£5.95), steak, mushroom and ale pie (£7.25), battered cod (£7.50), daily specials such as goats cheese and spinach tartlet with onion marmalade (£5.45), peppered chicken on wilted spinach with lyonnaise potatoes and stilton sauce (£6.50), grilled salmon fillet with rocket mash and sweet chilli sauce (£6.75), and puddings such as treacle sponge with custard (£3.25). Daily papers, perhaps big-screen TV for major sporting events, and piped music (which can be quite loud). A small back terrace has some cast-iron tables and chairs. At busy times there might be a bouncer on the doors. *(Recommended by Joan and Terry O'Neill, John Dwane, Richard Lewis, Paul and Ann Meyer, Dr R C C Ward, C J Fletcher, Susan and John Douglas)*

Fullers ~ Manager Alison Turner ~ Real ale ~ Bar food (12-9) ~ (0121) 200 1892 ~ Open 11-11; closed Sun and bank hols

BRIERLEY HILL SO9187 Map 4
Vine ♦ £

Delph Road; B4172 between A461 and (nearer) A4100

Nothing changes from one year to the next at this genuine no-nonsense warmly welcoming place, which is truly West Midlands in character, with its friendly down-to-earth landlord and staff. It's known in the Black Country as the Bull & Bladder, a reference to the good stained-glass bull's heads and very approximate bunches of grapes in the front bow windows. It's a popular place, full of local characters, and can get crowded in the front bar, which has wall benches and simple leatherette-topped oak stools; the extended and refurbished snug on the left has solidly built red plush seats, and the back bar has brass chandeliers – as well as darts, dominoes, big-screen TV and fruit machine. As it's the tap for the next-door Bathams brewery the Bitter and Mild, and perhaps Delph Strong in winter, are in top condition, and are most appealingly priced. Simple but good fresh lunchtime snacks are very good value too: samosas (65p), sandwiches (from £1), and curry, faggots and peas, or steak and kidney pie (£2.50). *(Recommended by Theocsbrian, the Didler, Gill and Tony Morriss, Theo, Anne and Jane Gaskin)*

Bathams ~ Manager Melvyn Wood ~ Real ale ~ Bar food (12-2 Mon-Fri) ~ No credit cards ~ (01384) 78293 ~ Children in family room ~ Dogs allowed in bar ~ Open 12-11; 12-10.30 Sun

COVENTRY SP3379 Map 4
Old Windmill £

Spon Street

Perhaps not the sort of building that first springs to mind when you think of Coventry, this timber-framed 15th-c inn is known locally as Ma Brown's after a former landlady. Unlike the rest of the buildings in the street (which are an interesting collection of evacuee survivors from the blitz) this friendly unpretentious place stands on its original site. In the nicely battered interior one of the series of rambling tiny old rooms is little more than the stub of a corridor, another has carved oak seats on flagstones and a woodburner in a fine ancient inglenook fireplace, and another has carpet and more conventionally comfortable seats. There are exposed beams in the uneven ceilings, and a back room preserves some of the equipment used when Ma Brown brewed here. Half a dozen well kept real ales include Banks's, Courage Directors, Greene King Old Speckled Hen, Wychwood Hobgoblin and a couple of frequently changing guests from brewers such as

Adnams and Batemans, all kept under light blanket pressure; fruit machine and juke box. Straightforward good value food passed out straight from the kitchen door includes filled toasties (£2.10), filled baked potatoes (from £1.85) and steak and onion pie, vegetable curry or thai green chicken curry (£3.95); part of the restaurant is no smoking. The pub is popular with students, extremely busy on Friday and Saturday evenings, and handy for the Belgrade Theatre. *(Recommended by Pete Yearsley, DC)*

Unique Pub Co ~ Tenant Robin Addey ~ Real ale ~ Bar food (12-2.30) ~ No credit cards ~ (0247) 625 2183 ~ Open 11-11; 12-10.30 Sun

DUNCHURCH SP4871 Map 4
Dun Cow ⏍

1 mile from M45 junction 1: on junction of A45 and A426

In the heyday of the coaching era up to 40 vehicles a day might pass through this pretty village on their way to and from London. The stables at this extensive mainly Georgian coaching inn might have housed 20 pairs of coach horses and up to 40 post horses. These days the coachyard is filled with tables and is a delightful spot to sit out on a sunny day (there are more on a sheltered side lawn). The very reasonably priced food is served all day, but it's worth arriving early for a table during normal meal times, as it is popular. Ordered from a food counter and served by friendly staff, it might include soup (£2.95), spinach and parmesan baked mushrooms (£3.75), chicken terrine with orange chutney (£3.95), lunchtime sandwiches (from £4.25), cod and chips or mushroom risotto (£6.75), hake fillet crusted with lime and coriander (£6.95), beef and ale pie (£7.95) and ham hock with wholegrain mustard sauce (£8.95); Sunday roast (£7.25). The spotlessly kept and handsomely oak-beamed interior, with a good no smoking area, has lots of traditional features, including welcoming log fires, rugs on the wooden and flagstone floors, country pictures and bric-a-brac, and farmhouse furniture. Well kept Bass and Tetleys on handpump, and a good choice of wines by the glass; piped music. *(Recommended by Ian Phillips, Chris Glasson, Anthony Barnes, Roger and Jenny Huggins, Roger and Pauline Pearce, John and Judy Saville, Joy and Simon Maisey, Mike and Mary Carter, Colin Mason, George Atkinson)*

Vintage Inns ~ Manager Florrie D'Arcy ~ Real ale ~ Bar food (12-10(9.30 Sun)) ~ Restaurant ~ (01788) 810305 ~ Children in restaurant and family room ~ Open 11-11; 12-10.30 Sun ~ Bedrooms: /£57.50S

EDGE HILL SP3747 Map 4
Castle

Off A422

Worth a visit for its interesting appearance, this beautifully positioned crenellated octagon tower (also known as the Round Tower or Radway Tower) is a folly that was built in 1749 by an 18th-c Gothic Revival enthusiast to mark the spot where Charles I raised his standard at the start of the Battle of Edge Hill. The big attractive garden (with aunt sally) has glimpses down through the trees of the battlefield, and it's said that after closing time you can hear ghostly sounds of battle – a phantom cavalry officer has even been seen galloping by in search of his severed hand. There are arched doorways, and the walls of the lounge bar, which have the same eight sides as the rest of the main tower, are decorated with maps, pictures and a collection of Civil War memorabilia. Simple bar food includes soup (£2.90), ploughman's (£4.90), bean casserole (£5.90), lasagne (£6.45), mixed grill (£7.50), and puddings (£3.50). Well kept Hook Norton Best, Old Hooky, one of their seasonal beers, and a guest beer on handpump; also country wines, farm cider and around 30 malt whiskies. The public bar, with old farm tools for decoration, has darts, pool, cribbage, dominoes, fruit machine and piped music. Upton House is nearby on the A422, and Compton Wynyates, one of the most beautiful houses in this part of England, is not far beyond. *(Recommended by Susan and John Douglas, Leigh and Gillian Mellor, C D Watson, Nigel Williamson, Dr Paull Khan, Keith Jacob,*

Alison Crooks, Dave Heffernan, Dave Braisted, Jason Caulkin, Maggie and Tony Harwood, Ken Richards, Karen and Graham Oddey, Brenda and Stuart Naylor)

Hook Norton ~ Lease N J and G A Blann ~ Real ale ~ Bar food (all day summer Sat/Sun) ~ (01295) 670255 ~ Children in eating area of bar ~ Dogs allowed in bar ~ Open 11.15-2.30, 6-11; 11-11(11.15-2.30, 6-11winter) Sat; 12-10.30 (12-3, 7-10.30 winter) Sun ~ Bedrooms: /£57.50B

FARNBOROUGH SP4349 Map 4
Inn at Farnborough 🍴 ♀

Off A423 N of Banbury

The emphasis at this stylishly refurbished and civilised golden stone house is very much on the extremely good food. Listed on blackboards, the quite sophisticated changing menu might include creamy shellfish bisque (£5.95), fishcakes with tomato and tarragon beurre blanc (£6.95), saffron and parmesan risotto cake with local asparagus and tomato compote (£10.95), sautéed strips of beef fillet with mushroom and cognac sauce (£12.95), and sautéed king prawns provençale (£13.95). A plus for many readers recently has been the good value two- and three-course lunchtime and early evening menu (£10.95/£12.95; not Sat evening or Sun). Service is usually cheerfully attentive (though a couple of readers felt it could sometimes be a bit snappier). The immaculately kept interior is a pleasant mix of the traditional and contemporary, with plenty of exposed stonework and thoughtful lighting. The beamed and flagstoned bar has neat blinds on its mullioned windows, a chrome hood in the old stone fireplace, plenty of fresh flowers on the modern counter, candles on wicker tables, and smartly upholstered chairs, window seats and stools. A stable door leads out to chic metal furnishings on a new decked terrace. The dining room has a comfortably roomy seat in a fireplace, nice wooden floors, a good mix of mismatched tables and chairs, and well chosen plants. Well kept Hook Norton and Fullers London Pride on handpump, and a good extensive wine list with around 10 by the glass. A machine dispenses Havana cigars; piped jazz. The landscaped garden is really delightful with a lovely sloping lawn, plenty of picnic-sets (one under a big old tree) and wandering hens. A string of white fairy lights around the roof gives the exterior an elegant appearance at night. *(Recommended by Arnold Bennett, John Kane, George Atkinson, Jennie Hall, Andrew MacLeod, Michael Jones, John Bowdler, Mrs L D Poole)*

Free house ~ Licensee Tony Robinson ~ Real ale ~ Bar food (served during all opening hours) ~ Restaurant ~ (01295) 690615 ~ Children welcome ~ Dogs allowed in bar ~ Open 12-3, 6-11; 12-11(10.30 Sun) Sat

FIVE WAYS SP2270 Map 4
Case is Altered ◗

Follow Rowington signposts at junction roundabout off A4177/A4141 N of Warwick, then right into Case Lane

Readers love the peacefully old fashioned atmosphere at this delightful white cottage – there's no food, children, dogs, games machines or piped music, and you can be sure of a very warm welcome from the cheery staff and regulars. With so much focus on the beers it does mean they are very well kept: Greene King IPA, Hook Norton Old Hooky, Jennings Mild and a guest ale from a microbrewery are all served by a rare type of handpump mounted on the casks that are stilled behind the counter. A door at the back of the building leads into a modest little room, usually empty on weekday lunchtimes, with a rug on its tiled floor and an antique bar billiards table protected by an ancient leather cover (it takes pre-decimal sixpences). From here, the simple little main bar has a fine old poster showing the old Lucas Blackwell & Arkwright brewery (now flats) and a clock with its hours spelling out Thornleys Ale – another defunct brewery; there are just a few sturdy old-fashioned tables, with a couple of stout leather-covered settles facing each other over the spotless tiles. The homely lounge (usually open only weekend evenings and Sunday lunchtime) is reached through the front courtyard or back car park. Behind a wrought-iron gate is a little brick-paved courtyard with a stone table under a chestnut tree. *(Recommended by Kevin Thorpe, Paul and Ann Meyer, Jason Caulkin, Brian Skelcher, John Dwane, Kevin Blake, Pete Baker, Bernie Adams, Joan and Tony Walker, Mike Rowan, the Didler)*

Free house ~ Licensee Jackie Willacy ~ Real ale ~ No credit cards ~ (01926) 484206 ~ Open 12(11.30 Sat)-2.30, 6-11; 12-2, 7-10.30 Sun

GAYDON SP3654 Map 4
Malt Shovel

Under 1 mile from M40 junction 12; B4451 into village, then left and right across B4100; Church Road

A good relaxed atmosphere and quite an unusual layout here, with a sort of pathway in mahogany-varnished boards running through bright carpeting to link the entrance, the bar counter on the right and the log fire on the left. This central area has a high pitched ceiling, with milk churns and earthenware containers in a loft above the bar – which has five well kept real ales on handpump such as Adnams, Castle Eden, Everards Tiger, Greene King Old Speckled Hen and Wadworths 6X, decent wines by the glass, and filter coffee. Three steps take you up to a snug little space with some comfortable sofas overlooked by a big stained-glass window and reproductions of classic posters. At the other end is a busy lower-ceilinged dining area with flowers on the mix of kitchen, pub and dining tables. Here, enjoyable unpretentious food cooked by the chef-landlord includes lunchtime sandwiches (from £2.95) and ploughman's or breakfast (£4.95), as well as soup (£2.95), stilton and port mushrooms (£3.95), battered haddock (£5.95), three-cheese vegetable lasagne (£7.35), braised venison sausage with pancetta and garlic mash (£8.45), moroccan lamb shank (£10.95), daily specials such as liver and bacon casserole or home-made shortcrust pie (£6.95) and confit of duck (£10.95), and puddings such as mango sorbet with Grand Marnier, lemon and ginger iced nougat or sticky toffee pudding (from £3.50); Sunday roast. Service is friendly and efficient; on our inspection visit, 1970/80s piped music; darts, fruit machine. The two springer spaniels are Rose and Jack, and the jack russell is Mollie. *(Recommended by Anna and David Pullman, W Ruxton, R T and J C Moggridge, Jennie Hall, M Joyner)*

Enterprise ~ Lease Richard and Debi Morisot ~ Real ale ~ Bar food (12-2, 6.30-9) ~ Restaurant ~ (01926) 641221 ~ Children in restaurant ~ Dogs allowed in bar ~ Open 11-3, 5-11; 11-11 Sat; 12-10.30 Sun

GREAT WOLFORD SP2434 Map 4
Fox & Hounds ★ ⑪ ◀

Village signposted on right on A3400 3 miles S of Shipston-on-Stour

Although the emphasis at this inviting 16th-c stone inn is on the imaginative cooking, there's still a pleasantly pubby atmosphere – they keep a thoughtful range of real ales, and locals pop in for a drink. The cosy low-beamed bar has a nice collection of chairs and old candlelit tables on spotless flagstones, antique hunting prints, and a roaring log fire in the inglenook fireplace with its fine old bread oven. An old-fashioned little tap room serves well kept Hook Norton and three interesting guests from brewers such as Cottage, Frankton Bagby and Wye Valley on handpump, and over 180 malt whiskies. Bar food includes sandwiches (from £3.75) and soup (£3.50), with daily specials such as seared scallops with rocket, parmesan and garlic butter (£6.50), tomato risotto with mozzarella, rocket and herb oil (£9.25), boiled ham hock with broad beans in dill and parsley sauce (£10.95), roast duck breast with sweet potato pureé, sautéed mushrooms and soy, honey and ginger sauce (£12), and puddings such as warm chocolate nut brownies or Pimms jelly with strawberry, apple and mint salad (£4.25); part of the dining area is no smoking. There's a well on the terrace outside. *(Recommended by John Kane, Di and Mike Gillam, Rod Stoneman, H O Dickinson, Peter Sutton, Roger Braithwaite, Mr and Mrs J McRobert, Ted George, John Bowdler, Peter and Anne Hollindale, Sir Nigel Foulkes,*

Mike and Mary Carter, Martin Jones, Andrew Barker, Claire Jenkins, Les and Barbara Owen, Dr and Mrs M E Wilson, MP, Michael Jones, John Robertson)

Free house ~ Licensees Wendy Veale and John Scott-Lee ~ Real ale ~ Bar food (not Sun evening) ~ Restaurant ~ (01608) 674220 ~ Children in eating area of bar ~ Dogs welcome ~ Open 12-2.30(3 Sun), 6-11(10.30 Sun); closed Mon ~ Bedrooms: £40B/£60B

HATTON SP2467 Map 4
Falcon

4½ miles from M40 junction 15; A46 towards Warwick, then left on A4177, and keep on past Hatton; Birmingham Road, Haseley

There's a feeling of spaciousness in the five knocked-together rooms that work their way around a central island bar, with lots of stripped brickwork, low beams, tiled and oak-planked floors. The pub is nicely decorated with good prints and old photographs, big turkey rugs, chairs in variety, a pleasant mix of stripped and waxed country tables, a couple of dark blue walls, and arrangements of pretty fresh flowers. A big barn-style back dining area is no smoking; piped music. Under the new licensee, pubby food might include soup (£2.50), sandwiches (from £3.25), ploughman's (£5.25), chilli, sausage and mash or lasagne (£6.95), steak and kidney pudding, scampi or battered cod (£7.95), tuna steak (£8.25) and lots of puddings (£3.95). Well kept Banks's Original, Hook Norton, M&B Brew XI, Marstons Pedigree and a guest such as Fullers London Pride on handpump, decent wines. A well separated games room has darts, fruit machine and a TV, and there are picnic-sets and a play area out on lawns at the side and behind. *(Recommended by George Atkinson, Bob and Laura Brock, Brian Skelcher, Ian and Nita Cooper, Jack Clark, Claire Robertson)*

English Country Inns ~ Manager Robert Worthington ~ Real ale ~ Bar food (12-2.30, 6-9; 12-9 Sat/Sun) ~ Restaurant ~ (01926) 484737 ~ Children welcome ~ Dogs allowed in bar ~ Open 12-11; 12-10.30 Sun

HIMLEY SO8791 Map 4
Crooked House ★ £

Pub signposted from B4176 Gornalwood—Himley, OS Sheet 139 map reference 896908; readers have got so used to thinking of the pub as being near Kingswinford in the Midlands (though Himley is actually in Staffs) that we still include it in this chapter – the pub itself is virtually smack on the county boundary

When subsidence caused by mine workings underneath this wonky old place threw the pub 15 degrees out of true they propped it up, rehung the doors and straightened the floors. The result leaves your perceptions spinning in a way that can really feel like being at sea. Inside on one table a bottle on its side actually rolls 'upwards' against the apparent direction of the slope, and for a 10p donation you can get a big ball-bearing from the bar to roll 'uphill' along a wainscot. There's a friendly atmosphere in the old rooms, and at the back is a large, level and more modern extension with local antiques. Very reasonably priced Banks's Bitter and Mild and a couple of guest beers on handpump, and farm cider; fruit machine and piped music. Good value bar food includes soup (£2.10), filled baguettes (£2.95), thai fishcakes or jalapeno pepper battered chicken balls with sour cream and chive dip (£3.15), spinach and mushroom filo bundle (£5.95), mixed grill (£6.75), beef, stout and stilton pie (£6.95), daily specials such as lemon sole with lemon and basil oil or duck breast with orange and Cointreau sauce (£7.95), and puddings such as apple and caramel cooking dough pie (£3.50). The conservatory is no smoking at food times, and there's a spacious outside terrace. It can get busy here in summer, with coach trips. *(Recommended by Joyce and Geoff Robson, the Didler, Bernie Adams)*

Banks's (W & D) ~ Lease Louise Pattern ~ Real ale ~ Bar food (12-2, 6-9(9.30 Fri); 12-9.30 Sat; 12-3.30, 5.30-8 Sun) ~ Restaurant ~ (01384) 238583 ~ Children welcome ~ Dogs allowed in bar ~ Open 11.30-11; 12-10.30 Sun

ILMINGTON SP2143 Map 4
Howard Arms 🍴 ♀ 🛏

Village signposted with Wimpstone off A3400 S of Stratford

It's best to book if you're planning a meal at this beautifully kept convivial golden-stone inn. At notably fair prices given the quality, freshly prepared food from an imaginative menu that changes two or three times a week might include soup (£3.50), pork, herb and spinach terrine (£5), smoked salmon with warm potato cake, sour cream and chives (£6.50), aubergine and potato thai curry or beef, ale and mustard pie (£9), roast duck breast with puy lentils, smoked bacon and red wine jus (£12), poached wild salmon trout with wilted spinach and mousseline sauce (£14), puddings such as warm treacle tart with cinnamon and ginger ice cream or baked vanilla cheesecake with strawberry and lime compote (from £4.50), and cheeses (£5.50). The menu is carefully written on boards above a huge stone inglenook (with a log fire that burns most of the year), and service is good-humoured and efficient. The stylishly simple interior is light and airy, with a few good prints on attractively painted warm golden walls, rugs on broad polished flagstones, and a nice mix of furniture from hardwood pews to old church seats. A snug area and upper bar are no smoking. A nice choice of beers includes well kept Everards Tiger, North Cotswold Genesis and a guest from a brewer such as Jennings or St Austell, as well as organic juices and about a dozen wines by the glass. The garden is lovely in summer with fruit trees sheltering the lawn, a colourful herbaceous border, and a handful of tables on a neat york stone terrace. The pub is nicely set beside the village green, and there are lovely walks on the nearby hills (as well as strolls around the village outskirts). *(Recommended by Maurice Ribbans, John Kane, Martin Jennings, Jamie and Ruth Lyons, M A and C R Starling, Arnold Benett, Terry and Linda Moseley, Martin Jones, Brian Skelcher, Janet and Peter Race, Peter Sutton, MP, John Bowdler, Mike and Heather Watson, P and J Shapley, Hugh Spottiswoode, Hugh Bower, Maysie Thompson, Rod Stoneman, Andrew Barker, Claire Jenkins, Mr and Mrs B J P Edwards, Andrew MacLeod, Roy Bromell, Susan and John Douglas, Richard and Margaret Peers, John Robertson, Les and Barbara Owen, Paul and Annette Hallett; also in the* Good Hotel Guide*)*

Free house ~ Licensees Rob Greenstock and Martin Devereux ~ Real ale ~ Bar food (12-2(2.30 Sun), 7-9(9.30 Fri/Sat)) ~ Restaurant ~ (01608) 682226 ~ Children in eating area of bar till 7.30 ~ Open 11-3(12-3.30 Sun), 6-11 ~ Bedrooms: £52B/£84B

KENILWORTH SP2871 Map 4
Clarendon House 🛏

High Street

This has seen many changes in its time. It's based on Kenilworth's oldest domestic building, a timber-framed tavern that started life in 1430, billeted roundhead troops in the Civil War, made combs in the 1800s, became a builders' merchants, a warehouse, then flats, and is now a comfortable hotel, with a separate entrance for this stylish and relaxed modern bar/brasserie. It stretches comfortably back past the serving counter, which has well kept Greene King IPA and Abbot, Hook Norton Best and a couple of guests from brewers such as Brakspears and Wychwood on handpump, decent wines, good coffee and daily papers. Several softly lit areas have comfortable sofas and black-framed cane chairs, with contemporary prints on mainly orange or yellow walls; the 'complaints department' is a deep stone well imprisoning a mock skeleton. A wide choice of snacks, nicely served with linen napkins, includes filled baps (£1.95), baked potatoes (£4.50), sandwiches or baguettes (£4.95) and good value up-to-date light dishes such as garlic prawn or chinese duck wraps and tapas (£4.95); several main dishes, such as pigeon and pancetta salad or lightly curried kedgeree fishcakes with quail eggs (£9.50) and wild mushroom risotto (£9.95), come in smaller snack-price helpings too, though things like steak (from £10.95) and pheasant (£11.95) do not. The Sunday two-course roast lunch is £9.50 (half price for under-10s); no smoking area in restaurant and lounge. Continental staff, efficient and conscientious; piped pop music, TV. *(Recommended by Andy and Jill Kassube, Joan and Tony Walker, Damian Dixon, Brian Kneale)*

Free house ~ Licensee D L Randolph ~ Real ale ~ Bar food (11-10) ~ Restaurant ~ (01926) 857668 ~ Children welcome ~ Dogs welcome ~ Open 11-11; 12-10.30 Sun; closed 25/26 Dec ~ Bedrooms: £57.50B/£79.50B

LAPWORTH SP1970 Map 4
Navigation ◀

Old Warwick Road S of village (B4439 Warwick—Hockley Heath); by Grand Union Canal, OS Sheet 139 map reference 191709

The friendly landlord has been running this bustling local in his own cheery way for 21 years now, all the time studiously ignoring the conglomerates as they hand the ownership of the building around – it's always amusing to ask him who currently owns the pub. Don't be put off by the unassuming exterior, particularly given the gentle improvements this year which are aimed mainly at lightening up the interior. The beamed bar is genuinely rustic, with an undulating flagstoned floor, high-backed winged settles, seats built in around its window bay, a coal fire in its high-manteled inglenook, one or two bits of brightly painted canal ware, the happy chatter of merry locals and canal-users, and cases of stuffed fish. The fish theme is developed in the lounge, which has more cases of stuffed fish, oak and carpet floors, and pews. By the time this *Guide* is in the shops the quieter dining room at the back will have a fresher contemporary feel with modern art on light mushroom walls, high-backed leather chairs on oak floors, and wooden venetian blinds. This room has a pleasant outlook over the sheltered flower-edged lawn, and on down to the busy canal behind. This is a great place in summer when hatch service to aluminium and wicker chairs on the terrace lets you make the most of its pretty canalside setting; they do ice creams then too, and the pub and gardens are prettily lit at night. Served by friendly staff, bar food in generous helpings includes sandwiches (from £3.50), vegetarian quiche or goats cheese salad (£7.50), chicken balti (£7.95), tasty battered cod or beef and ale casserole (£8.50), pork loin with mustard and cider sauce (£8.95), salmon and crab fishcakes with white wine and dill sauce (£9.25), fillet steak with pepper sauce or redcurrant jus (£13.50), and puddings such as chocolate bread and butter pudding (£3.50). Very well kept Bass, M&B Brew XI and a guest or two such as Cottage Mallard IPA and Hook Norton Old Hooky on handpump, alongside a changing farm cider such as Biddenden Dry, and lots of malt whiskies; fruit machine and TV (rarely on). *(Recommended by Lady Freeland, Mike and Mary Carter, John Brightley, Kevin Thorpe, Mandy and Simon King, David and Helen Wilkins, June and Malcolm Farmer, Arnold Benett, DJH, Kevin Blake, Joan and Tony Walker, Andrew Scarr, Dave Braisted)*

Unique Pub Co ~ Lease Andrew Kimber ~ Real ale ~ Bar food (12-2(3 Sun), 6-9) ~ (01564) 783337 ~ Children welcome ~ Dogs allowed in bar ~ Open 11-3, 5.30-11; 11-11 Sat; 12-10.30 Sun

LITTLE COMPTON SP2630 Map 4
Red Lion

Off A44 Moreton-in-Marsh—Chipping Norton

This attractive 16th-c stone local is a good all-rounder, with a pleasantly villagey atmosphere, friendly landlord and tasty food – and it's in a handy spot for exploring the Cotswolds. The food is very popular so you may need to book, especially at weekends: soup (£3.25), very good filled baguettes (from £4.50), tempura prawns with sweet chilli dip (£4.95), ploughman's (£5.25), scampi (£7.50), thai chicken curry (£7.95), seafood pie (£8.95), and daily specials such as fresh salmon and asparagus lasagne (£7.95) and grilled plaice or grilled lamb steak with rosemary, red wine and redcurrant sauce (£10.25). The simple but comfortably civilised low-beamed plush lounge has snug alcoves and a couple of little tables by the log fire. The plainer public bar has another log fire, and darts, pool, cribbage, dominoes, fruit machine and juke box. The restaurant is no smoking. Donnington BB and SBA on handpump, and an extensive wine list; good service. The well maintained garden is pleasant, and we have had no complaints about the simple bedrooms. *(Recommended by M and G Rushworth, K H Frostick, H O Dickinson, Mike Turner, John Bowdler, Bob Broadhurst, John and Johanne Eadie, Roger and Jenny Huggins, Guy Vowles, J D M Rushworth, Brenda and Stuart Naylor)*

Donnington ~ Tenant David Smith ~ Real ale ~ Bar food ~ Restaurant ~ (01608) 674397 ~ Children in restaurant, over 8 if staying ~ Open 12-2.30, 6-11.30(7-10.30 Sun) ~ Bedrooms: £30/£40

LONG ITCHINGTON SP4165 Map 4
Duck on the Pond

Just off A423 Coventry-Southam; The Green

Redone in a darkly decorative style vaguely reminiscent of 1970s french bistros, this spacious and relaxed pub's central bar has a rococo-look leather suite, royal blue banquettes, some barrel tables, dark pine ceiling planks, bacchanalian carvings around its coal fire, a few big wading bird decoys, and wicker panels for the bar counter, which has Charles Wells Eagle and Bombardier and a guest such as Greene King Old Speckled Hen on handpump. On each side is a sizeable dining area (both no smoking) with pine furniture (some tables painted in light red chequers), a wall of wine bottles, big Edwardian prints on sienna red walls, a crystal chandelier and a grandfather clock. Enjoyable food includes breads with olive oil and balsamic vinegar (£2.95), soup (£3.50), sandwiches (from £3.95), smoked haddock and spring onion fishcake (£3.95), penne with mediterranean roasted vegetables (£7.50), grilled chicken and parmesan salad or battered haddock (£8.95), braised ham hock with peking sauce (£13.95), fillet steak with horseradish mash and vegetables in red wine sauce (£14.95). Service is friendly; piped pop or jazzy soul music may be loud but is well reproduced; TV. Picnic-sets out in front look down on a pond which does indeed have ducks; the main road is quite busy. *(Recommended by Suzanne Miles, Claire Procter)*

Charles Wells ~ Lease Andrew Parry ~ Real ale ~ Bar food ~ Restaurant ~ (01926) 815876 ~ Children welcome ~ Dogs allowed in bar ~ Open 11-3, 5-11; 11-11 Sat; 12-10.30 Sun

MONKS KIRBY SP4683 Map 4
Bell 🏠 ♀

Just off B4027 (former A427) W of Pailton; Bell Lane

It's worth visiting this timbered old pub for a meal with a bit of a difference. The Spanish landlord likes to think of it as a corner of Spain in the heart of England – which pretty much sums up its relaxed mediterranean hospitality and tasty spanish food set against a traditional pub backdrop. An extensive printed menu (not especially cheap) includes starters (which you could have as tapas) such as chorizo in white wine and garlic (£4.25), sardines in garlic butter (£4.95), fried squid (£5.25), moules marinière (£5.65) and scallops cooked with white wine, tomato, lemon juice and breadcrumbs (£5.95), and main courses such as battered cod or spanish omelette (£9.95), meatballs in spicy tomato sauce on pasta (£11.25), pollo pimienta (£11.95), hake and shellfish cooked in a clay dish (£14.25), fish paella (£14.75), and lobster and chicken baked with white wine and cream in an iron dish (£17.75). Although the great majority of readers warmly approve of the food, there have been one or two disappointments, and the friendly service which strikes most readers as charmingly insouciant can seem slightly offhand to others. The ancient dark beamed and flagstoned interior is fairly straightforward, with a no smoking dining area and (possibly quite loud) piped music. As well as well kept Bass and Flowers Original on handpump, there's a spanish wine list, ports for sale by the bottle, and a good range of brandies and malt whiskies. A back terrace by a stream has a pretty little view across to a buttercup meadow. *(Recommended by Andrea and Guy Bradley, Susan and John Douglas, G W H Kerby, Comus and Sarah Elliott, the Earl of Denbigh, D C Leggatt, Lisa Worthington, Mark and Amanda Sheard, Mr and Mrs J E C Tasker, Sally Randall)*

Free house ~ Licensee Paco Garcia Maures ~ Real ale ~ Bar food (12-2.30, 7-10.30)
~ Restaurant ~ (01788) 832352 ~ Children welcome ~ Dogs allowed in bar ~
Open 12-3, 7-11(10.30 Sun); closed 26 Dec

SEDGLEY SO9193 Map 4

Beacon ★ 🍺

Bilston Street (no pub sign on our visit, but by Beacon Lane); A463, off A4123
Wolverhampton—Dudley

This plain-looking old brick pub is an appealing piece of Victoriana. When you
arrive it's worth ignoring the side entrance and walking round from the car park to
the front. Up a couple of steps, the front door opens into a plain quarry-tiled
drinking corridor where you may find a couple of locals leaning up against the
walls going up the stairs, chatting to the waistcoated barman propped in the
doorway of his little central serving booth. Go through the door into the little snug
on your left and you can easily imagine a 19th-c traveller tucked up on one of the
wall settles, next to the imposing green tiled marble fireplace with its big misty
mirror, the door closed for privacy and warmth and a drink handed through the
glazed hatch. The dark woodwork, turkey carpet, velvet and net curtains, heavy
mahogany tables, old piano and little landscape prints all seem unchanged since
those times. Another simple snug on the right has a black kettle and embroidered
mantel over a blackened range, and a stripped wooden wall bench. The corridor
then runs round the serving booth, past the stairs and into a big well proportioned
dark-panelled smoking room with red leather wall settles down the length of each
side, gilt-based cast-iron tables, a big blue carpet on the lino, and dramatic sea
prints. Round a corner (where you would have come in from the car park) the
conservatory is densely filled with plants, and has no seats. The beautifully
aromatic Sarah Hughes beers here – Dark Ruby, Pale Amber and Surprise Bitter –
are brewed in the traditional Victorian brewery at the back, which you can arrange
to look round; they are planning a few beer festivals. The only food served is cheese
and onion cobs (80p). A children's play area in the garden has a slide, climbing
frame and roundabout. *(Recommended by the Didler, Theocsbrian, Bernie Adams,*
Pete Baker, Keith Jacob)

Own brew ~ Licensee John Hughes ~ Real ale ~ No credit cards ~ (01902) 883380 ~
Children in family room ~ Dogs allowed in bar ~ Open 12-2.30, 5.30-10.45(11 Fri);
12-3, 6-11 Sat; 12-3, 7-10.30 Sun

SHIPSTON-ON-STOUR SP2540 Map 4

White Bear

High Street

Proudly positioned in the centre of the town, the fine brick Georgian frontage of
this old coaching inn faces the bustling market square. Inside, the long narrow front
bar on the left has massive stripped settles, attractive lamps and interesting pictures
(charming pen and wash drawings of Paris café society, and sporting and other
cartoons from Alken through Lawson Wood to bright modern ones by Tibb) on the
rag-rolled walls. The back lounge is more plainly furnished and decorated, with
comfortable modern furniture, and big Toulouse-Lautrec and other prints of French
music-hall life. A separate bar on the right has a woodburning stove in a big
painted stone fireplace. Well kept Adnams, Bass, Hook Norton Old Hooky and a
guest beer on handpump, with eclectically chosen wines, including bin ends, a good
selection of ports and wines by the glass; polite, knowledgeable service; daily
papers. Food from a very well balanced menu is served in the bar and restaurant,
and might include tomato and basil soup with croutons (£2.90), cheese fritters with
thai dipping sauce (£4.50), sautéed lambs kidneys on a potato cake (£4.95), steak,
onion and Guinness pie (£7.95), moroccan marinated chicken breast with orange,
onion and coriander (£8.75), grilled salmon fillet with watercress and saffron sauce
(£9.20), and fried bass with parma ham and pesto (£10.95); part of the restaurant
is no smoking. They have darts, dominoes and cribbage; also juke box, TV and

fruit machine. There are some white cast-iron tables in a small back yard. *(Recommended by Michael Graubart and Valerie Coumont Graubart, Paul and Ann Meyer, JHBS)*

Punch ~ Lease George Kruszynskyi ~ Real ale ~ Bar food (12-2(2.30 Sat/Sun, 6.30-9.30(10 Fri/Sat); not Sun evening) ~ Restaurant ~ (01608) 661558 ~ Children welcome ~ Dogs welcome ~ Live music Sun evening ~ Open 11-11; 12-10.30 Sun ~ Bedrooms: £30B/£50B

SHUSTOKE SP2290 Map 4
Griffin ◗ £

5 miles from M6 junction 4; A446 towards Tamworth, then right on to B4114 and go straight through Coleshill; pub is at Furnace End, 1 mile E of village

The finest feature at this unpretentious country local is the interesting range of up to 10 real ales. From a servery under a very low heavy beam, Banks's Mild, Bathams, Hook Norton Old Hooky, Marstons Pedigree and RCH Pitchfork are well kept alongside guests from small brewers up and down the country, also country wines, mulled wine and hot punch in winter. Almost always bustling with a cheery crowd, the low-beamed L-shaped bar has two stone fireplaces (one's a big inglenook) with warming log fires, and besides one nice old-fashioned settle the décor is firmly rooted somewhere in the 60s: cushioned café seats (some quite closely packed), sturdily elm-topped sewing trestles, lots of old jugs on the beams, beer mats on the ceiling, and a fruit machine. As well as a choice of 20 warwickshire cheeses (you can buy them to take away), very good value lunchtime bar food includes pie and chips, broccoli bake, lasagne and cod, chips and mushy peas (£5.50-£5.75); you may need to arrive early to get a table. There are old-fashioned seats and tables outside on the back grass, a play area and a large terrace with plants in raised beds. *(Recommended by Roy and Lindsey Fentiman, Kevin Blake, Dr B and Mrs P B Baker, John Dwane, A J Bowen, Mike Turner, Brian and Anita Randall, Keith Jacob)*

Free house ~ Licensee Michael Pugh ~ Real ale ~ Bar food (12-2; not Sun) ~ No credit cards ~ (01675) 481205 ~ Children in conservatory ~ Dogs welcome ~ Open 12-2.30, 7-11(10.30 Sun)

STRATFORD-UPON-AVON SP2055 Map 4
Garrick ♀

High Street

The name of this ancient place commemorates David Garrick the actor-manager, who inaugurated the Stratford Festival in 1769. These days, its charming external and internal appearance and enjoyable atmosphere are exactly what you'd hope for on a visit to this famous old town. The small but high-beamed, heavily timbered and often irregularly shaped rooms are full of secluded little nooks with wonky walls that are either stripped back to bare stone or heavily plastered, and have long upholstered settles and stools made from barrels on bare boards. A small dining room at the back is air-conditioned and no smoking. Flowers Original, Greene King Abbot, Wadworths 6X and a guest such as Hook Norton Old Hooky are well kept on handpump, and attractively priced for this tourist town. It's heartening too to find that the enjoyable bar food is served in such generous helpings and so fairly priced: soup (£2.95), sandwiches (from £3.75), baguettes (from £4.25), scampi or sausage and mash (£5.95), gammon steak (£6.95), steak and ale pie or fish and chips (£7.75), more elaborate daily specials such as lamb shank with redcurrant and mint sauce (£8.95), roast duck with orange and shallot sauce (£10.95), and puddings such as caramel apple pie or sticky toffee pudding (from £3.45). Staff remain good-natured even when it gets busy (and perhaps a bit cramped for some readers). Fruit machine, piped music and a TV. *(Recommended by Val and Alan Green, Stephen, Julie and Hayley Brown, Duncan Cloud, Leigh and Gillian Mellor, Maggie and Tony Harwood, Andrew McHardy, Arnold Benett, Kevin Blake)*

Laurel Pub Company ~ Licensee Vicky Leng ~ Real ale ~ Bar food (12-9) ~ (01789) 292186 ~ Children in restaurant ~ Singer Fri monthly ~ Open 11-11; 12-10.30 Sun

WELFORD-ON-AVON SP1452 Map 4
Bell

Off B439 W of Stratford; High Street

Each of the five comfortable areas in this attractive 17th-c brick pub has its own character, from the cosy terracotta-painted bar to the light and airy terrace room with its peach and terracotta wash. Flagstone floors, stripped, antique or period-style furniture, and three real fires (one in an inglenook) give it quite a pubby feel which makes a nice backdrop to its main emphasis, the imaginative bar food. Using local produce where possible, it's served by obliging staff and might include soup (£2.95), avocado and smoked bacon salad (£3.95), whitebait (£4.25), sandwiches (from £4.25), breaded plaice (£7.75), lasagne (£7.95), beef casserole (£8.75), daily specials such as thai potato, mushroom and spinach curry (£8.95) or paprika baked hake on paella rice (£12.25), puddings such as honey and almond cheesecake or apricot and brandy bread and butter pudding (£4.75), and a good cheeseboard (£5.75); several no smoking areas. Well kept Hobsons, Hook Norton Old Hooky, Greene King Old Speckled Hen, Wadworths 6X and a guest such as Flowers on handpump, malt whiskies and local wine; piped music. In summer the creeper-covered exterior is hung with lots of colourful baskets, and there are seats in the pretty secluded garden area and back courtyard. The riverside village has an appealing church and pretty thatched black and white cottages. (*Recommended by Angus Lyon, Andrew McHardy, Hugh Roberts, John Bramley, John and Johanne Eadie, Arnold Benett, Lawrence Pearse, Brenda and Stuart Naylor*)

Laurel Pub Company ~ Lease Colin and Teresa Ombler ~ Real ale ~ Bar food (11.30-2.30, 6.45-9.30(6.15-10 Fri/Sat); 12-4, 7-9.30 Sun) ~ Restaurant ~ (01789) 750353 ~ Children in eating area of bar and restaurant ~ Open 11.30-3, 6.30(6 Fri/Sat)-12; 12-4, 7-10.30 Sun

WHARF SP4352 Map 4
Wharf Inn

A423 Banbury—Southam, near Fenny Compton

Recently brought thoroughly up to date by its newish owners, this open-plan pub by Bridge 136 of the South Oxford Canal has a smart tall-windowed dining area on the left. This has plain solid tables and high-backed chairs on mainly wood strip or tiled floors, a big oriental rug, walls in canary yellow, eau de nil or purple, modern artwork, and end windows so close to the water that you feel right by it. They serve breakfast (full english £5.50) first thing, and later on frequently changing bar food might include soup (£3.50), sandwiches (from £3.50), thai fishcake (£4.50), rare grilled beef salad (£5), steak and kidney pudding (£7), sweet and sour Quorn with button onions and peppers, breaded scampi or chicken korma (£7.50), 8oz aberdeen angus sirloin (£15.50), daily specials such as seared tuna loin with pickled vegetables (£4.95), chicken with bubble and squeak and leek and mushroom sauce (£10.50), and puddings such as lemon tart with forest fruits, brandy snap basket and ice cream or fruit suet pudding (from £3.50). They do good freshly ground coffee; there may be faint piped pop music. A small central flagstoned bar (full of smokers on our inspection visit) has Adnams, Fullers London Pride and Greene King Abbot on handpump. On the right is a pair of soft white leather settees by a feature coffee table, a few more tables with deco armchairs, a modern woodburning stove, and some appealing mainly water-related pictures; a little snug beyond has a pile of children's books. Lighting throughout is good, and service efficient and friendly; disabled access and facilities. The slightly sloping waterside garden has picnic-sets, a playhouse on high stilts, and a canal shop. They have moorings, and space for caravans. (*Recommended by Arnold Benett, Ted George, Roger and Debbie Stamp, Carol and David Havard*)

Punch ~ Lease Kevin Partridge ~ Real ale ~ Bar food (8-9.30) ~ Restaurant ~ (01295) 770332 ~ Children in eating area of bar ~ Dogs allowed in bar ~ Open 8-11(10.30 Sun)

Lucky Dip

Besides the fully inspected pubs, you might like to try these Lucky Dips recommended to us and described by readers (if you do, please send us reports: www.goodguides.com).

ALCESTER [SP0957]
Holly Bush [Henley St]: Welcoming warren of panelled rooms off central bar, just right for this time-warp town; well kept Cannon Royall Fruiterers Mild, Uley and several guest beers, reasonably priced straightforward food, hard-working landlady; pleasant back garden (*Jill Bickerton, Pete Baker*)

BAGINTON [SP3375]
☆ *Old Mill* [Mill Hill]: Thoughtful Chef & Brewer conversion of old watermill nr airport (and Lunt Roman fort), smart and well run, with good food range, Scottish Courage beers, good wine choice, neat uniformed staff, heavy beams, timbers and candlelight in roomy rustic-theme main bar, restaurant; lovely terraced gardens leading down to River Sower, 28 bedrooms (*Susan and John Douglas, John and Judy Saville, LYM, Ian and Joan Blackwell, Joan and Terry O'Neill, Duncan Cloud*)

BARSTON [SP2078]
☆ *Bulls Head* [from M42 junction 5, A4141 towards Warwick, first left, then signed down Barston Lane]: Attractive partly Tudor village local, comfortable lounge with pictures and plates, dining room, friendly relaxed service, enjoyable and unpretentious food inc good fresh fish, well kept real ales, oak-beamed bar with log fires and a little Buddy Holly memorabilia; good-sized secluded garden alongside, hay barn behind (*Susan and John Douglas, Brian Skelcher, Pete Baker, Hugh Roberts, Mike Begley*)
Malt Shovel [Barston Lane]: Light and airy civilised dining pub, clean, spacious and stylishly country-modern, with generous brasserie-style food inc interesting starters, three well kept real ales, good choice of wines, trendy young staff, converted barn restaurant; pleasant garden (*Roger Braithwaite, Stephen, Julie and Hayley Brown, Andrew Wallace*)

BERKSWELL [SP2478]
☆ *Bear* [off A452 W of Coventry; Spencers Lane]: Rambling timbered 16th-c Chef & Brewer in attractive setting near interesting church, emphasis on all-day dining downstairs, traditional games bar upstairs, lots of cosy areas decorated in their current style – bric-a-brac, log fires and mottoes chalked on beams, an extensive list of blackboard specials, Scottish Courage beers; children welcome, tables on pleasant tree-sheltered back lawn, Crimean War cannon in front, open all day (*Barry Smith, Kevin Blake, John Brightley, Alun Howells, Brian Skelcher, Roger Thornington, Simon and Amanda Southwell, Roger Braithwaite, LYM, David Green, Mandy and Simon King*)

BILSTON [SO9496]
Trumpet [High St]: Holdens and guest beers, good free jazz bands; trumpets and other instruments hang from ceiling, lots of musical memorabilia and photographs (*the Didler, Paul and Ann Meyer*)
White Rose [Temple St]: Great choice of real ales, reasonably priced food inc Sun roasts till 9, long narrow bar, children's area (*Paul and Ann Meyer*)

BIRMINGHAM [SP0786]
Anchor [Bradford St, Digbeth]: Perfectly preserved three-room Edwardian corner pub, carefully restored art nouveau windows, long high-ceilinged bar with basic seating, well kept ales such as Archers Spring, Everards Tiger, Oakham Bishops Farewell and Springhead St Georges, extra beers at wknds, festivals with lots of beers from single brewery, lots of bottled beers; well priced simple food till 6 inc huge chip butties, friendly staff, back games area with pool and sports TV; tables outside, handy for coach station, open all day (*Richard Lewis*)
☆ *Bartons Arms* [High St, Aston]: Magnificent specimen of Edwardian pub architecture in rather a daunting area, reopened by Oakham Brewery after two-year closure and restoration, inventive series of richly decorated rooms from the palatial to the snug, original coloured tiles, stained glass and mahogany, sweeping stairs, snob screens in one bar; well kept Oakham and guest beers, interesting imported bottled beers, good value thai food (not Mon), hard-working managers and young staff; open all day (*BB, Mark Rogers, Dr B and Mrs P B Baker, Matthew Ford*)
Bennetts [Bennetts Hill]: Attractively converted bank like ballroom with Egyptian/French theme, big mural, high carved domed ceiling, side library and board room with lots of old pictures, ironwork and wood, relaxed atmosphere, comfortable seats inc armchair and leather settee, dining area with usual food inc sensibly priced specials, well kept Banks's, Marstons Pedigree and Morrells Graduate, decent house wines, good coffee, friendly staff (*Richard Lewis, Matthew Shackle, Liz and John Soden*)
Black Eagle [Factory Rd, Hockley]: Four-room character late 19th-c pub, cosily furnished, with good value home-made food, good friendly service, particularly well kept Ansells, Marstons Pedigree and good changing real ales, summer beer festival with live music, small back restaurant; open all day Fri, cl Sun evening (*John Dwane, Simon, Jo and Benjamin Cole*)
Brasshouse [Broad St]: Comfortably reworked and roomy former bank very handy for National Sea Life Centre and convention centre, lots of dark oak and brass; enjoyable food from chip butties to steaks, prompt friendly service, well kept Marstons Pedigree and Tetleys, unusual collection of builders' hard hats (*Colin Gooch*)
Briar Rose [Bennetts Hill]: Busy central open-plan Wetherspoons with usual comfortable

décor, menu and drinks offers inc four changing guest beers, friendly staff, children allowed in separate no smoking back family dining room; lavatories down stairs, can get busy lunchtime and late evening; reasonably priced bedrooms, open all day *(Richard Lewis, Michael Tack, Joe Green)*

Bulls Head [Price St, Aston; off A34]: Friendly well run unspoilt side-street local with displays of guns, bullets etc, good value food, real ales such as Adnams, Ansells Mild, Hook Norton and Wadworths 6X, Addlestone's cider; open all day, breakfast from 7am *(Steve Jennings)*

Charlie Hall [Barnabas Rd, Erdington]: Large Wetherspoons conversion of former bingo hall, their usual good value food and ale range; back terrace *(John Dwane)*

Fiddle & Bone [Sheepcote St]: The nightly live bands which featured at this former schoolhouse by the waterbus stop, appealingly converted by two City of Birmingham Symphony players, were banned in 2002, and after struggling on for a few months the pub sadly closed in spring 2003; it was a popular main entry and a great asset to Birmingham, so we hope it reopens soon – news please *(LYM)*

Garden House [Hagley Rd]: Large good value chain pub with good choice of food from good value sandwiches up, good range of real ales such as Courage Directors, wine by the large glass, good polite service; tastefully updated 1870s pub, big garden *(Eddie Edwards)*

Lamp [Barford St, Digbeth]: Friendly two-room beer-lovers' local in industrial area, well kept ales such as Church End Gravediggers, Everards Tiger, Marstons Pedigree, Stanway Best and Wadworths 6X; lunchtime food, TV and games machine, live music some nights, open all day (cl Sun evening) *(Richard Lewis)*

☆ *Metro* [Cornwall St]: Long softly lit chatty bar with bays of banquettes and stylish mirrored panels, good interesting main-course sandwiches here and upmarket meals in light and airy candlelit modern restaurant with abstract art, helpful service; in same hands as Kings Head at Aston Cantlow (see main entries), cl Sun *(Susan and John Douglas)*

Old Fox [Hurst St]: Traditional two-room high-ceilinged pub with island bar and original Victorian features, changing ales such as Ansells Mild, Burton Bridge Up Yours, Marstons Pedigree and Tetleys, good value lunchtime food, friendly staff, interesting old photographs and theatre prints; pavement tables *(Richard Lewis, Joe Green)*

Square Peg [Temple Ct, Corporation St]: Huge Wetherspoons in former department store, high ceilings, two levels, no smoking end, lots of old local prints, good choice of well kept ales from nearly 30-metre bar, farm cider, decent wines, no music, wholesome good value food all day *(Richard Lewis)*

☆ *Tap & Spile* [Gas St]: Nicely placed with picnic-sets by Gas Street canal basin, attractive back-to-basics yet quite cottagey décor, stripped brickwork, bare boards and reclaimed timber, old pine pews and settles, lots of prints, three levels, Adnams, Bass, Fullers London Pride, Greene King Old Speckled Hen and M&B, low-priced bar food till 5.30 from baguettes to scampi; piped music, darts, dominoes, fruit machine, no children, open all day *(Dr R C C Ward, LYM, Colin Gooch, Richard Lewis, Joe Green, Susan and John Douglas)*

Woodman [Albert St]: Victorian pub with friendly and lively L-shaped main bar, hatch service to relaxing back smoke room with superb tiling and coal fire, good fresh warm baguettes, well kept Ansells Mild, Tetleys and a guest beer, friendly unhurried service, interesting juke box *(the Didler, Pete Baker)*

BISHOP'S TACHBROOK [SP3161]

Leopard [nr M40 junction 13, via A452]: Relaxing country pub under same ownership as Antelope at Lighthorne, enjoyable generous food from bar snacks to more sophisticated dishes in spacious back dining room (children welcome here), well kept Greene King IPA and Abbot and Marstons Pedigree, friendly service *(Arnold Benett, Nigel and Sue Foster)*

BLOXWICH [SJ9902]

☆ *Turf* [Wolverhampton Rd; aka Tinky's]: Unspoilt and friendly local in same family for well over 100 years and little changed in that time, two serving hatches to central corridor, large waiting-roomish tiled bar with heating pipe under settles, tiny back parlour with chairs around tiled fireplace, unusual padded wall settles with armrests in left-hand smoking room, original etched windows and fittings, William Morris curtains and wallpaper, cheap well kept ales inc local Holdens Mild and XB or Golden Glow; no food or music, impressive outside lavatories *(Mike Begley, RWC, Pete Baker, the Didler)*

BODYMOOR HEATH [SP1996]

Dog & Doublet [Dog Lane]: Canalside pub right by lock, three storeys but cosy, with friendly helpful service, wide choice of enjoyable bar food from sandwiches, baguettes and baked potatoes through usual pub meals to generous good value Sun lunch, well kept real ales, dark-panelled rooms both sides of bar, beams, brasses, bargees' painted ware, several open fires, tables in pleasant garden; popular with businessmen at lunch, can get a bit crowded wknds; bedrooms, nr Kingsbury Water Park *(S P Watkin, P A Taylor)*

BUBBENHALL [SP3672]

Three Horseshoes [Spring Hill]: Enjoyable food in recently refurbished and extended old village pub *(Joan and Terry O'Neill)*

CHADWICK END [SP2073]

☆ *Orange Tree* [A41]: Former Brewers Fayre now in the same small group as the Kings Head at Aston Cantlow (see main entries), impressive and comfortable recent refurbishment, charming décor and atmosphere, enjoyable food, good service *(Jill Bickerton)*

CHERINGTON [SP2836]

☆ *Cherington Arms* [off A3400]: Old-fashioned creeper-covered stone house with new landlord doing enjoyable food (not Sun evening) inc interesting dishes, well kept Hook Norton and

Ind Coope Burton, farm cider, good value wines, cafetière coffee, efficient friendly service, nice beamed bar with piano and blazing log fire, separate dining room, big garden with trees and tables; dogs welcome, good nearby walks, cl Mon lunchtime *(K H Frostick, JHBS, BB, June and Malcolm Farmer, Carol and David Havard)*

COVENTRY [SP3378]

Browns [Earl St, between Council House and Herbert Art Gallery]: Large modern café-bar with tempting range of freshly cooked hearty food all at £5 all day, many different types of seating area inc terrace, wide range of decent wines, chilly beers (not cheap); strict door policy, live music upstairs some nights, open 9am-11pm (1am Fri/Sat, 10-7 Sun) *(Suzanne Miles)*

☆ *Town Wall* [Bond St, among car parks behind Belgrade Theatre]: Flourishing Victorian pub with well kept Adnams Bitter and Broadside, Bass and M&B Brew XI, farm cider, good generous lunchtime doorstep sandwiches, filled rolls and cheap hot dishes, engraved windows and open fires, smartly refurbished lounge with careful new extension, simple bar with big-screen sports TV, famously tiny and clubby snug; open all day *(Brian and Anita Randall, Ted George, Barrie Clark, Martin Smith, Martin Bache)*

DUDLEY [SO9487]

Park [Chapel St]: Unexpectedly modern décor (inc attractive octagonal conservatory) in tap for adjacent Holdens brewery, their beers well kept and cheap, welcoming staff, good low-priced lunchtime food inc hot beef, pork and chicken sandwiches – very busy then *(Theocsbrian)*

EASENHALL [SP4679]

☆ *Golden Lion* [Main St]: Cottagey 16th-c inn, attractively decorated comfortable lounge, two-room no smoking restaurant area, low beams, dark panelling, settles and inglenook log fire, good generous food inc fresh fish, self-service lunches (two plate sizes), good Sun carvery with freshly cooked veg, efficient welcoming service even when busy, Greene King IPA, Ruddles and Morlands Original, decent wines, good coffee; spacious attractive garden with terrace, barbecue, pet donkey; well equipped bedrooms in new wing, attractive village *(Eleanor and Nick Steinitz, Gerry and Rosemary Dobson)*

EATHORPE [SP3968]

☆ *Plough* [car park off B4455 NW of Leamington Spa]: Big helpings of good value food in long neat split-level lounge/dining area with toning walls, carpets and table linen, good friendly chatty service, good coffee; cl some wkdys *(Bernie Adams)*

ETTINGTON [SP2550]

Houndshill House [A422 towards Stratford; aka Mucky Mongrel]: Civilised dining pub with tasty traditional food in pleasant surroundings, very popular with families and OAPs; stripped stone and beams, friendly efficient service, well kept ales, tables in big attractive garden with play area well away from buildings, good views from front; children welcome, good well equipped bedrooms *(Catherine and Chris Newman)*

FENNY COMPTON [SP4152]

Merrie Lion [Brook St]: Friendly little low-beamed two-bar village pub, old, neatly kept if not smart, and with plenty of cosy character; quick friendly service, well kept beers inc Banks's and Bass, reasonably priced usual food inc good sandwiches; handy for Burton Dassett country park *(John Brightley)*

HALESOWEN [SO9683]

Hawne Tavern [Attwood St]: Traditional sidestreet local, good range of real ales, good value cheap food inc big baguettes, quiet lounge, bar with games *(Gill and Tony Morriss)*

Lighthouse [Coombes Rd, Blackheath]: Quirky nautical-theme pub, outside painted with lighthouse, L-shaped bar, three rooms behind, good helpings of usual food inc mexican and indian, well kept Enville and Greene King IPA and Abbot, friendly atmosphere *(Gill and Tony Morriss)*

Waggon & Horses [Stourbridge Rd]: Unpretentious gently refurbished welcoming bare-boards local, well kept Bathams, a house beer and up to a dozen or so interesting changing ales from small independent brewers – staff well informed about them; snacks, TV, Tues music night, open all day *(G Coates, the Didler, Paul and Ann Meyer)*

HAMPTON IN ARDEN [SP2080]

White Lion [High St; handy for M42 junction 6]: Beamed pub reopened after appealing refurbishment, stripped pine and fresh flowers, well kept Black Sheep and a guest such as Hook Norton, bar food from lunchtime sandwiches up, welcoming staff, separate back dining room; seven bedrooms, attractive village, handy for NEC *(LYM)*

HAMPTON LUCY [SP2557]

Boars Head [Church St, E of Stratford]: Homely décor in low-beamed two-bar local next to lovely church, hard-working and friendly new licensee, good range of food from good value sandwiches up, log fire, lots of brasses, prompt friendly service; picnic-sets in neat and attractive secluded back garden, pretty village nr Charlcote House *(Brian Skelcher, Joan and Tony Walker)*

HARBURY [SP3660]

☆ *Shakespeare* [just off B4451/B4452 S of A425 Leamington Spa—Southam; Mill St]: Popular and comfortable dining pub with linked low-beamed areas, stripped stonework, big central inglenook log fire, horsebrasses, freshly cooked sensibly priced food (not Sun/Mon evenings) inc some adventurous dishes, well kept Flowers IPA, Timothy Taylors Landlord and one or two guest beers, good hospitable service (landlady has great memory for customers), proper flagstoned locals' bar area with TV, games room off with darts and pool, pleasant conservatory; children welcome, tables in back garden with aviaries *(Pete Baker, Nigel and Sue Foster, BB)*

HATTON [SP2467]

Waterman [A4177]: Good-sized pub above

Hatton flight of 21 locks on Grand Union Canal, views as far as Warwick from sunny balcony and huge garden; Bass and Tetleys, friendly efficient service even when very busy (as it can be), generous food inc children's; good circular walks nearby, moorings *(Martin Jennings, Claire Robertson)*

HOCKLEY HEATH [SP1572]

Nags Head [Stratford Rd (A3400)]: Harvester with wide choice of reliable well priced food inc popular lunchtime two-course express menu, well trained staff *(Barry Smith, David Green)*

Wharf [Stratford Rd (A3400)]: Friendly modernised local, open-plan but cosily divided, with lounge extension overlooking canal, quick generous food from hot meat rolls to carvery, attractive prices, Marstons and guest beers, good canal photographs; children welcome, attractive garden with adventure playground by Stratford Canal, interesting towpath walks *(Dr B and Mrs P B Baker)*

KENILWORTH [SP2872]

☆ *Clarendon Arms* [Castle Hill]: Busy traditional pub opp castle, good attractively priced food in several rooms, some no smoking, off long partly flagstoned bar and in largish upstairs dining room, plenty of atmosphere, efficient and friendly obliging staff, good range of well served beers, wines and other drinks; best to book wknds *(Mr and Mrs J Brown, Damian Dixon, Carol and David Havard)*

Green Man [Warwick Rd]: Spacious refurbished Ember Inn, comfortable and friendly, with sofas and armchairs, decent food inc good Sun lunch, popular quiz nights Weds and Fri *(Carol and David Havard)*

KNOWLE [SP1876]

☆ *Herons Nest* [Warwick Rd S]: Former hotel by Grand Union Canal, attractively reworked as Vintage Inn: dining tables in several individual rooms inc no smoking areas, some flagstones and high-backed settles, hops on beams, interesting décor, open fires, wide choice of good value food inc children's helpings, well kept Bass and Tetleys, good wine choice, friendly staff; plenty of tables in garden with moorings, bedrooms, open all day *(R J Herd, Bill Sykes)*

LAPWORTH [SP1670]

Boot [B4439, by Warwickshire Canal]: Waterside dining pub done up in cool modern upmarket rustic style, raised dining area (food confined to here on busy Sat night, but may take up all tables at other times), roaring fire, good atmosphere, enjoyable food (not cheap) from good baguettes to steaks and fish, well kept beers such as Greene King Old Speckled Hen and Wadworths 6X, decent wines (big glasses), good service by smart young staff, daily papers, lots of board games, cartoons; piped nostalgic pop music; good lavatories, nice garden, pleasant walks *(Arnold Benett, Susan and John Douglas, Geoffrey and Penny Hughes)*

LEAMINGTON SPA [SP3165]

Cricketers Arms [Adelaide Rd]: Friendly town local opp bowling greens, with central bar and comfortable banquettes, cheap wholesome

generous food, changing guest beers; pool, SkyTV sports, friendly dog *(Steve and Liz Tilley)*

Hogshead [Warwick St]: Spick and span, with fine range of well kept changing ales, modern wooden flooring and bare brickwork, raised no smoking area with sofas as well as dining tables, good value straightforward food, good helpful staff; can get busy wknds *(Ted George, Andrew Wallace)*

Somerville Arms [Campion Terr]: Neat and cosy character local with tiny unspoilt Victorian back lounge, well kept ales such as Adnams and Greene King IPA, friendly staff; tables out on wide pavement *(Steve and Liz Tilley)*

LONG COMPTON [SP2832]

Red Lion [A3400 S of Shipston-on-Stour]: Stripped stone, bare beams, panelling, flagstones, old-fashioned built-in settles among other pleasantly assorted old seats and tables, old prints and team photographs, good value food from sandwiches and ploughman's up in bar and restaurant, well kept Adnams, Hook Norton, Websters and a guest such as Courage Directors, log fires and woodburners, simple public bar with pool; pub dog and cat, unobtrusive piped music; dogs and children welcome, big garden with picnic-sets and climber, bedrooms *(LYM, Susan and John Douglas)*

LONG ITCHINGTON [SP4165]

Blue Lias [Stockton Rd, off A423]: Well placed on Grand Union Canal, with friendly efficient staff, wholesome and enjoyable reasonably priced food, well kept Everards Tiger *(Steve and Liz Tilley, Joan and Tony Walker)*

LOWER BRAILES [SP3039]

☆ *George* [B4035 Shipston—Banbury]: Handsome and warmly friendly old stone-built inn with ample good freshly made food inc game in season, smart country-style flagstoned restaurant, local feel in roomy flagstoned front bar with dark oak tables, nice curtains and inglenook log fire, darts, panelled oak-beamed back bar with soft lighting and green décor, full Hook Norton range kept well, good sensibly priced wines, welcoming landlord; provision for children, live music most Sat and Mon evenings and Sun afternoon, aunt sally in sizeable neatly kept sheltered garden with terrace and covered area, six comfortable bedrooms, lovely village, open all day *(Pete Baker, LYM, Chris Glasson, JHBS)*

LOWER GORNAL [SO9291]

Black Bear [Deepdale Lane]: Local with plenty of character (18th-c former farmhouse), Shepherd Neame and four guest beers, good choice of whiskies *(the Didler)*

Fountain [Temple St]: Two-room local with keen and helpful landlord and staff, well kept Enville, Everards, Holdens and up to six changing ales (beer festivals Easter and Oct), two farm ciders, country wines, enjoyable inexpensive food, pigs-and-pen skittles *(the Didler, Theocsbrian)*

LOXLEY [SP2552]

☆ *Fox* [signed off A422 Stratford—Banbury]: Cheerful pub very popular evenings for wide range of good value fresh homely cooking; very neat and clean, with panelling, a few pictures and plates, settles, brocaded banquettes, pleasant dining area, five well kept ales such as Bass, Greene King Abbot and Hook Norton, obliging welcoming service, friendly cat; piped music; tables in good-sized garden behind, sleepy village handy for Stratford *(Janet and Peter Race)*

MERIDEN [SP2482]

Bulls Head [Main Rd]: Very wide choice of good value generous home-made food all day in big busy Vintage Inn dating from 15th c, three log fires, beams, bare boards and flagstones, lots of nooks and crannies, good prompt welcoming service, well kept Bass and Tetleys, ancient staircase to restaurant; can get busy evenings, esp wknds; disabled facilities, 13 bedrooms *(Bernie Adams)*

MONKS KIRBY [SP4683]

☆ *Denbigh Arms* [Main St]: 17th-c beamed pub opp church, old photographs and interesting 18th-c pew seating, no smoking family room, big helpings of enjoyable food from sausage and chips through curries to bargain Tues steak night, Greene King real ales, friendly service even when busy; upstairs folk club 2nd Sun of month; play area *(Ian and Nita Cooper, R C Vincent)*

NAPTON [SP4560]

☆ *Folly* [off A425 towards Priors Hardwick; Folly Lane, by locks]: Beamed old-world boaters' pub in lovely spot by Napton locks on Oxford Canal, three bars on different levels, attractive mix of furnishings inc huge farmhouse table in homely front bar, two big log fires, good home-made pies, good friendly staff, real ales such as Hook Norton and Warwickshire Godiva, pool in back games room; very busy wknds, but winter hours may be curtailed; children welcome, good big lawn with play area, wishing well and fine views (also all-day summer shop and small agricultural museum) *(Roger and Debbie Stamp, Roger and Pauline Pearce, Bernie Adams)*

NETHERTON [SO9387]

☆ *Old Swan* [Halesowen Rd (A459 just S of centre)]: Friendly and traditional, brewing its own good cheap beer, also Greene King Old Speckled Hen and occasional guest beers, lots of whiskies, wide choice of cheap food inc Sun lunches in no smoking room on left, nice old solid fuel stove, fine mirrors, decorative swan ceiling, comfortable back snug, cards and dominoes; regular sing-alongs, open all day *(Theocsbrian, LYM, the Didler, Alan Cole, Kirstie Bruce, Pete Baker)*

NEWBOLD ON STOUR [SP2446]

☆ *Bird in Hand* [A3400 S of Stratford]: Neatly kept U-shaped bar with comfortable well spaced tables, bow windows, good log fire, well kept Hook Norton Best and Old Hooky, decent tea and coffee, well presented varied food at low prices, good friendly service *(BB, K H Frostick)*

NORTHEND [SP3952]

Red Lion [off B4100 Warwick—Banbury; Bottom St]: Bright and neat two-room pub

with concentration on landlord's impressive cooking inc unusual starters and lots of fish (no bar snacks Fri/Sat night or Sun lunchtime), OAP lunch Weds, well kept Timothy Taylors Landlord and an interesting guest beer, decent wines, good friendly service, partly no smoking restaurant; piped radio; best to book wknds, cl Mon *(BB, Rona Murdoch, Carol and David Havard, Duncan Cloud)*

NORTON LINDSEY [SP2263]

New Inn: Popular village dining pub, clean and comfortably modern, good home cooking featuring fresh fish, friendly staff, real ale, choice of wines *(John Bramley)*

OLD HILL [SO9685]

Waterfall [Waterfall Lane]: Down-to-earth local, very friendly staff, consistently well kept and well priced Bathams, Enville and other changing ales, farm cider, country wines, cheap plain home-made food from filled rolls to Sun lunch, tankards and jugs hanging from boarded ceiling; piped music; children welcome, back garden with play area, open all day wknds *(the Didler, Dave Braisted, Theocsbrian)*

PRIORS HARDWICK [SP4756]

☆ *Butchers Arms* [off A423 via Wormleighton or A361 via Boddington, N of Banbury; Church End]: Upmarket restaurant in pleasantly reworked 14th-c building, oak beams, flagstones, panelling, antiques and soft lighting (soft voices, too – a refined low murmur); huge choice of food (not cheap) inc fixed price lunches, small bar with inglenook log fire used mainly by people waiting for a table (also simple public bar); keg beer but good wines, very friendly Portuguese landlord, punctilious smartly uniformed staff, country garden *(Hugh Spottiswoode, Arnold Benett, BB, K H Frostick)*

PRIORS MARSTON [SP4857]

☆ *Holly Bush* [follow Shuckburgh sign, then first right by phone box]: Much extended attractive golden stone pub, small rambling rooms, beams and stripped stone, old-fashioned pub seats on flagstones, blazing log fire one end, central woodburner, friendly helpful service, well kept Greene King IPA and Hook Norton Best, decent wines, good fairly priced food from interesting soups and good range of baguettes and paninis up, large restaurant; large friendly dog, unusual cigar humidor, darts, pool, games machines, TV, juke box, piped music; children welcome, tables in sheltered garden, pretty village, bedrooms *(Rob and Catherine Dunster, LYM, George Atkinson)*

RATLEY [SP3847]

☆ *Rose & Crown* [off A422 NW of Banbury]: Helpful new landlord in charming ancient golden stone beamed local, cosy atmosphere, well kept Charles Wells Eagle and Bombardier, decent honest pub food inc good sandwiches, carefully prepared fish and nice sensibly priced puddings, friendly easy-going service, woodburner in flagstoned area on right, big log fireplace in carpeted area on left; dogs and children welcome, tables in small garden,

nr lovely church in small sleepy village
*(Guy Vowles, Derek and Sylvia Stephenson,
Angus Lyon, Joan and Terry O'Neill,
Steve and Liz Tilley, Brenda Range, Brian and
Anita Randall)*

RIDGE LANE [SP2994]

Church End Brewery Tap [2 miles SW of
Atherstone]: Former working men's club, now
the entirely no smoking home of Church End
beers (formerly produced at the Griffin,
Shustoke) – no keg beers at all; tables outside
(Paul and Ann Meyer)

SAMBOURNE [SP0561]

☆ *Green Dragon* [village signed off A448]: Three
low-beamed rooms, rugs on flagstones, open
fires, enjoyable food inc good curries, well kept
real ales; children in eating area, picnic-sets
and teak seats in pretty courtyard, bowls,
comfortable bedrooms *(Martin Jones, LYM)*

SHIPSTON-ON-STOUR [SP2540]

☆ *Black Horse* [Station Rd (off A3400)]: 16th-c
thatched pub with interesting ornaments and
good inglenook log fire in spotless low-beamed
bar, homely and relaxed; reasonably priced
carefully cooked food inc wkdy OAP bargain
lunches, well kept Adnams, Greene King IPA
and Abbot and Charles Wells Bombardier,
friendly staff and locals, small dining room;
back garden with terrace and barbecue
(Geoff Calcott)

SHREWLEY [SP2167]

Durham Ox [off B4439 Hockley Heath—
Warwick]: Spacious well designed makeover of
country pub with enjoyable food from
interesting sandwiches and baguettes through
up-to-date snacks to traditional favourites, good
service; pleasant garden *(BB, Jill Bickerton)*

SHUSTOKE [SP2290]

Plough [B4114 Nuneaton—Coleshill]:
Rambling local cosily done up in olde-worlde
style with brass galore, good value food,
pleasant dining room, good friendly service
(Mrs M P Owen)

SHUTTINGTON [SK2505]

Wolferstan Arms [Main Rd]: Well run family
pub, lots of beams and pewter tankards,
friendly locals and long-serving staff, enjoyable
food, well kept real ales, farm cider; well
behaved children welcome, rolling country
views from restaurant and big garden with
play area *(Colin Gooch)*

SNITTERFIELD [SP2159]

Foxhunter [Smiths Lane/School Rd; off A46 N
of Stratford]: Cheerful and attractive small
village pub, wide range of well presented and
reasonably priced food cooked to order from
tasty baguettes up, Hook Norton Best and
M&B Brew XI, banquettes and hunting
pictures in L-shaped bar/lounge with simple
white décor, friendly dog; children allowed,
tables outside *(Rob and Catherine Dunster)*

STOCKTON [SP4363]

Barley Mow [off A426 Southam—Rugby;
School St]: Unpretentious and welcoming early
19th-c pub, enjoyable food inc wkdy bargain
lunches, friendly attentive service, Greene King
IPA and Abbot, bar and lounge/diner with
steepish steps down to bottom dining area,

stripped brick, lots of brasses and pictures,
coal-effect fire, small back evening restaurant;
pretty hanging baskets, attractive spot by green
opp church *(George Atkinson)*

STOURBRIDGE [SO8983]

Plough & Harrow [Worcester St]: Four well
kept real ales such as Enville White, good
choice of enjoyable generous bar food from
super hot sandwiches up, cosy horseshoe bar
(Gill and Tony Morriss)

STRATFORD-UPON-AVON [SP2055]

Cox's Yard [Avonbridge Wharf, Bridgefoot]:
Modern riverside pub brewing its own Jesters
and other ales, waterside tables for watching
the swans *(Hugh Roberts, the Didler)*

☆ *Dirty Duck* [Waterside]: 16th-c pub nr
Memorial Theatre, lots of signed RSC
photographs, quick friendly service, reasonably
priced food, Flowers IPA, Greene King Old
Speckled Hen and Wadworths 6X, open fire,
bustling public bar (little lounge seating for
drinkers), children allowed in small dining
area; attractive small terrace looking over
riverside public gardens – which tend to act as
summer overflow; properly the Black Swan
*(LYM, Janet and Peter Race, Brian Skelcher,
Maggie and Tony Harwood, Kevin Blake,
Andy, Julie and Stuart Hawkins)*

Falcon [Chapel St]: Substantial timbered
Tudor hotel with big inglenook fireplace and
furnishings reflecting its 17th-c tavern origins
in quiet panelled bar, other rooms inc lighter
more modern ones, well kept Flowers from
small servery, wide range of decent bar food
from sandwiches up, friendly staff, restaurant;
may be piped music; bedrooms (quieter but
more functional in modern wing) *(Ted George,
Val and Alan Green)*

Jester [Cox's Yard, Bridgefoot]: Part of tourist
complex, long light and airy bar with friendly
staff, fairly priced food, well kept real ale, play
area, roomy riverside terrace; brewery tours
available, open all day, good disabled facilities
(John Whitehead)

Pen & Parchment [Bridgefoot, by canal basin]:
Shakespeare theme in L-shaped split-level
lounge and snug, rustic-style beams, balusters,
bare boards and tiles or flagstones, small
alcoves and no smoking area, big open fire in
old fireplace, decent reasonably priced food,
wide wine choice, four well kept real ales,
prompt helpful service; tables out among
shrubs and ivy, pretty hanging baskets, good
canal basin views; busy road *(Ted George)*

West End [Bull St]: Attractively modernised
old pub in quiet part of old town, good value
nicely presented food, good service
(Maurice Ribbans)

Windmill [Church St]: Cosy and relaxing old
pub with town's oldest licence, beyond the
attractive Guild Chapel; unpretentious but
civilised, with low black beams, quarry-tiled
front bar, bare boards in main one, big log fire,
wide choice of good value food from
sandwiches to substantial main dishes, well
kept sensibly priced Flowers Original and
interesting guests, friendly efficient staff,
carpeted dining area; piped music; tables

outside, open all day from noon
*(Lawrence Pearse, Neil Rose, Ted George,
Kevin Blake, Val and Alan Green)*
STRETTON-ON-DUNSMORE [SP4172]
Oak & Black Dog [Brookside]: Friendly village
local, light and airy long room with end dining
area, lots of beams and china, well kept real
ales inc unusual guest beers, fire, wide choice
of good value generous food lunchtimes and
some evenings, cheerful attentive service, open
fire, evening restaurant area; parking not easy;
children welcome, garden *(Suzanne Miles)*
STRETTON-ON-FOSSE [SP2238]
Plough [just off A429]: Olde-worlde 17th-c
village pub under newish licensees, small bar
and larger lounge, jugs and mugs on oak
beams, Ansells Bitter and Mild and Shepherd
Neame Spitfire, attentive staff, wide choice of
generous home-made food inc wknd spit roast
by the log fire in the big fireplace (chain drive
from windscreen wiper motor), small attractive
candlelit dining room on right; darts, sunny
tables outside, cl Mon lunchtime *(Carol and
Dono Leaman, JHBS)*
STUDLEY [SP0764]
Barley Mow [A435]: Good value Vintage Inn
keeping its individuality, friendly efficient
service (may be much quicker than the food
delay board indicates), Bass and decent wines
(Dave Braisted)
SUTTON COLDFIELD [SP1195]
Bottle of Sack [Birmingham Rd (A5127)]:
Popular two-floor Wetherspoons local, usual
reasonably priced food, well kept Shepherd
Neame Spitfire, big side conservatory;
wheelchair access, but limited nearby parking
(Michael Tack)
Station [Station St]: Reasonably priced food,
friendly staff, well kept beers inc Hook
Norton, Oakham JHB and Timothy Taylors,
decent wines; unobtrusive piped music *(anon)*
TEMPLE GRAFTON [SP1255]
☆ *Blue Boar* [a mile E, towards Binton; off A422
W of Stratford]: Extended country dining pub
with beams, stripped stonework and log fires,
good welcome from cheerful attentive
international staff, well kept ales such as
Brakspears, Greene King Old Speckled Hen,
Hook Norton and Theakstons XB, good wine
choice, enjoyable generous food from baked
potatoes to good value Sun lunch, comfortable
restaurant (past glass-top well with golden
carp) with good no smoking section, good
wine choice, traditional games in flagstoned
side room; children welcome, open all day
summer wknds, picnic-sets outside, pretty
flower plantings; comfortable well equipped
bedrooms inc some new ones *(Rick Baker,
Martin Jennings, Joan and Tony Walker,
LYM, Brenda and Stuart Naylor)*
TREDINGTON [SP2543]
White Lion: Comfortably ancient, with mix of
bare boards, quarry tiles and carpet, decent
food all day, two real ales; folk music Sun pm,
open all day *(JHBS)*
UFTON [SP3762]
☆ *White Hart* [just off A425 Daventry—
Leamington, towards Bascote]: Friendly old

pub with big lounge/dining area (several steps
up to back part), beams, brasses and stripped
stone, sporting memorabilia inc polo
equipment, good choice of usual food inc good
value OAP lunches, well kept Adnams Best,
Tetleys and Bass or Wadworths 6X, quick
friendly attentive service; unobtrusive piped
radio; hatch service to hilltop garden with
boules and panoramic views (Tannoy food
announcements out here) *(DC,
George Atkinson)*
UPPER BRAILES [SP3039]
☆ *Gate*: Attractive and tidily old-fashioned low-
beamed village pub, sizeable part-panelled bar,
smaller lounge with stripped stone, old bread
oven and lots of brass, welcoming landlord,
well kept Hook Norton and guest beers, big
log fire, good value food (not Mon or
lunchtime Tues); piped music in stripped stone
restaurant; dogs and well behaved children
welcome, tables in extensive back garden with
wendy house, pretty hillside spot, plenty of
footpaths *(JHBS)*
UPPER GORNAL [SO9292]
Jolly Crispin [Clarence St]: Little old local,
once a cobbler's shop, several interesting
particularly well kept changing ales, beer
festivals, growing food side; open all day
(the Didler)
WALSALL [SP0199]
Tap & Spile [John St]: Victorian backstreet
local, formerly the New Inn (aka Pretty
Bricks), with good changing range of well kept
beers, enjoyable cheap food, friendly staff, real
fires; non-invasive music *(Steve and
Louise Walker)*
Wharf Bar 10 [Gallery Sq/Wolverhampton St]:
Light and airy new building next to New Art
Gallery at end of the cut, lots of pine and
scrubbed wood, big windows, good choice of
well kept local Highgate beers from central
bar, good value tasty sandwiches, ciabattas and
other snacks, pleasant atmosphere
(Dave Braisted, C J Fletcher)
WARMINGTON [SP4147]
☆ *Plough* [just off B4100 N of Banbury]:
Understated little traditional village local,
cheerily unpretentious pubby bar with big
fireplace, ancient settle and nice chairs, new
owners putting more emphasis on the food
side, extending kitchen and dining room,
several well kept real ales, friendly staff; piped
pop music; children in eating area, delightful
village *(K H Frostick, Arnold Benett,
Jennie Hall)*
WARWICK [SP2764]
Old Fourpenny Shop [Crompton St, nr
racecourse]: Cosy and comfortable split-level
pub with up to five well kept changing beers
such as Hook Norton and Marlow Rebellion,
welcoming licensees, good value food in bar
and heavily beamed restaurant, cheerful
service, no piped music; pleasant reasonably
priced bedrooms *(Ian and Nita Cooper,
Andy and Jill Kassube, Jill Bickerton)*
Racehorse [Stratford Rd]: Large comfortable
family dining pub with generous good value
food inc children's and OAP bargains, well

kept Everards Tiger and guest beers, pleasant service, no smoking areas inc conservatory (children welcome); open all day *(Tony and Wendy Hobden, Michael Lamm, Ian and Nita Cooper)*

Roebuck [Smith St]: Timbered and beamed town pub, good value lunches, Theakstons and other real ales, pleasant restaurant at end of lounge bar; warm welcome to dog owners *(D W Stokes)*

Rose & Crown [Market Pl]: Three-room pub newly reworked in up-to-date country style with bare boards and so forth, emphasis on interesting food at sensible prices in bar and restaurant, two well kept ales such as Charles Wells Bombardier and plenty of fancy keg dispensers, good strong coffee, good service by young antipodean staff, open fires; tables out under parasols, comfortable good-sized bedrooms *(Damian Dixon, June and Malcolm Farmer, LYM)*

☆ *Tilted Wig* [Market Pl]: Roomy and airy, somewhere between tearoom and pub, big windows on square, stone-effect floor on left, bare boards on right, carpet behind, brocaded banquettes and kitchen chairs around pine tables, some stripped stone and panelling, well kept Adnams Broadside, Marstons Pedigree, Tetleys and Warwickshire Lady Godiva, good fairly priced wines, wide choice of good reasonably priced home-made bistro food (not Sun evening) from sandwiches and baguettes up, lively bustle (esp on Fri market day), quick friendly service, two coal-effect fires; SkyTV, piped music may be loud; tables in garden, live jazz and folk Sun evening, open all day, four neat well appointed bedrooms with own bathrooms, good breakfast *(Jenny and Chris Wilson, BB, Brian and Anna Marsden)*

☆ *Zetland Arms* [Church St]: Pleasant and cosy town pub with short choice of cheap but good bar food (not wknd evenings), well kept Marstons Pedigree and Tetleys, decent wine in generous glasses, friendly quick service, neat but relaxing small panelled front bar with toby jug collection and sports TV, comfortable larger L-shaped back eating area with small conservatory, fascinating eavesdropping when the nearby court adjourns for lunch; provision for children, interestingly planted sheltered garden, bedrooms sharing bathroom *(LYM, Suzanne Miles)*

WELLESBOURNE [SP2755]
Kings Head: Vintage Inn with contemporary furnishings in high-ceilinged lounge bar, log fire and smaller areas leading off, lively public bar with games room, well kept Bass, wide choice of keenly priced wines, good food choice (inc sandwiches 12-5), friendly staff; piped music may obtrude; picnic-sets in garden facing church, bedrooms (handy for Stratford but cheaper), open all day *(Maggie and Tony Harwood, LYM, G W A Pearce)*

☆ *Stags Head* [old centre, Bridge St/ Walton Way]: Picturesque 17th-c thatched and timbered pub with good atmosphere in small beamed lounge bar, flagstoned passage to larger stone-floored public bar, friendly

licensees, good service, well kept ales such as Badger Best, Bass, Fullers London Pride, Greene King Abbot, Marstons Pedigree, Timothy Taylors Landlord and Warwickshire Ffiagra, generous usual food from baked potatoes up, lots of local history and photographs; picnic-sets in garden and out in front, bedrooms, lovely setting in group of Elizabethan cottages *(BB, John Allchurch)*

WHATCOTE [SP2944]
☆ *Royal Oak*: Dating from 12th c, quaint low-ceilinged small room with Civil War connections and lots to look at; wide choice of freshly cooked food inc venison and good steaks from the Orkneys, welcoming service, well kept Hook Norton, decent wines, good log fire in huge inglenook, restaurant; children welcome, picnic-sets in informal garden *(JHBS, Mrs Mary Walters, LYM)*

WHICHFORD [SP3134]
Norman Knight: Quietly welcoming flagstoned pub with well kept Hook Norton Best and changing microbrew guests, nicely priced lunchtime food (and Fri/Sat evening); nearby pottery, tables out by attractive village green, cl Tues lunchtime *(Chris Glasson, Dick and Madeleine Brown, JHBS)*

WILLEY [SP4984]
☆ *Sarah Mansfield* [just off A5, N of A427 junction; Main St]: As hospitable and welcoming as ever after some refurbishment following fire damage, wide range of enjoyable cheap food from sandwiches and baked potatoes up, attentive young staff, well kept real ales, long comfortable beamed dining area, small bar area with polished flagstones, stripped stone and brick, cosy corners, open fire; pool table at back *(Bernie Adams, George Atkinson)*

WITHYBROOK [SP4384]
Pheasant [B4112 NE of Coventry, not far from M6 junction 2]: Big busy dining pub with lots of dark tables, plush-cushioned chairs, very wide choice of generous food inc good value specials and good vegetarian choice, Scottish Courage ales, good coffee, blazing log fires; piped music; children welcome, tables under lanterns on brookside terrace *(Paul and Sue Merrick, Mr and Mrs J E C Tasker, LYM)*

WIXFORD [SP0854]
Fish [B4085 Alcester—Bidford]: Attractive riverside setting, reasonably priced food inc lots of chargrills and bargain roasts for two, friendly staff, roomy L-shaped bar and snug, beams, polished panelling, carpets over flagstones, log fire, stuffed fish, and quite an art gallery in corridor to lavatories; piped music; a nice spot on a summer's evening *(Caroline and Michael Abbey)*

WOLVERHAMPTON [SO9098]
☆ *Combermere Arms* [Chapel Ash (A41 Tettenhall road)]: Old-fashioned friendly local with three small cosy rooms, well kept Banks's and guest beers, decent wines, very welcoming staff, food from good range of bargain sandwiches to good value Sun lunch, bare boards and quaint touches, Wolves photographs, bar billiards; quiz Tues, tree

growing in gents', nicely kept small secluded garden with summer live music in courtyard *(Mrs D Hardy, S F Bowett, Bernie Adams)*

☆ *Great Western* [Corn Hill/Sun St, behind BR station]: Vibrantly popular, well run and down to earth, tucked interestingly in the hinterland between the GWR low-level and current railway stations, with particularly well kept Bathams, Holdens Bitter, Golden Glow, Special and perhaps Sham Rock Stout, winter mulled wine (no tea or coffee), friendly no-nonsense service, cheap hearty lunchtime food (not Sun) from baguettes up served incredibly promptly, interesting railway and more recent motorcycle photographs, traditional front bar, other rooms inc separate no smoking bar and neat dining conservatory; SkyTV; picnic-sets in yard with good barbecues, open all day *(Peter and Patricia Burton, D Crutchley, BB, Martin Grosberg, the Didler, C J Fletcher, Gill and Tony Morriss, Pete Baker, Joe Green)*

Hogshead [Stafford St]: Chain pub comfortably done in old tavern style, friendly knowledgable staff, good beer choice inc belgians; very popular with young people Fri/Sat nights, with loud piped music then *(Ian and Liz Rispin)*

Posada [Lichfield St]: Ornate tile and glass frontage, three rooms sympathetically refurbished with lots of wood, brass and glass, nooks and crannies, Greene King Abbot, Tetleys and Charles Wells Bombardier from semi-circle central bar, Shelley memorabilia and genuine old Wolverhampton prints, friendly locals, helpful staff, back room with games; open all day *(Martin Grosberg, Joe Green)*

WOOTTON [SP7656]

Yeomen of England [High St]: Comfortable settees and armchairs, flame-effect fire in no smoking area, horseshoe bar with three or four real ales, reasonably priced bar food; piped music, games machines, quiz nights Sun and Tues, occasional marquee beer festival and live music; children welcome, heated terrace with decking, picnic-sets on back lawn *(CMW, JJW)*

WOOTTON WAWEN [SP1563]

Bulls Head [just off A3400 Birmingham—Stratford]: This attractive black and white dining pub with low Elizabethan beams and timbers, popular with readers for its good food and drink and closeness to one of England's finest churches and the Stratford Canal, was closed in spring 2003 for major reworking – news please *(LYM)*

Wiltshire

Pubs which have been showing particularly well here in recent months include the Barford Inn at Barford St Martin (its friendly landlord gaining it a Food Award this year), the welcoming Boot at Berwick St James (another Food Award pub, growing some of its ingredients in its own garden), the Quarrymans Arms tucked away near Box (a rewarding all-rounder), the relaxed and rather continental-feeling Dandy Lion in Bradford-on-Avon, the warm-hearted Compasses at Chicksgrove (its hands-on landlord earning it a Star this year for its all-round appeal), the substantial and old-fashioned Bear in Devizes, the Horseshoe at Ebbesbourne Wake (a charming country pub, with nice bedrooms), the admirably old-fashioned and good value Red Lion at Kilmington, the George in Lacock (another pub earning its Star for exceptional appeal this year), the Barge at Seend (very popular for its canalside position, with a nice waterside garden), the Spread Eagle in its beautiful National Trust surroundings at Stourton (at least some food all day), the Pear Tree at Whitley (imaginative food, great choice of wines by the glass, good beers), and the friendly 14th-c Bell at Wylye (winning its Food Award this year). Two new entries joining this elite group are the cheerful good value Black Horse at Great Durnford (plenty of evidence of its landlord's sailing background), and the Neeld Arms at Grittleton (good all round, with a splendid landlord). If your primary objective is a special meal out, we'd also mention the Red Lion at Axford and the Linnet at Great Hinton; top current choice though is the Compasses at Chicksgrove, earning the title of Wiltshire Dining Pub of the Year. Quite a few pubs in the Lucky Dip section at the end of the chapter call for special mention: the Black Dog at Chilmark, Seymour Arms at East Knoyle, Ivy at Heddington, Lamb at Hindon, Bridge Inn at Horton, Who'd A Thought It at Lockeridge, George at Mere, Lamb at Nomansland, Kings Head at Redlynch, Lamb at Semington, Carriers at Stockton, Bridge Inn at Upper Woodford, White Horse at Winterbourne Bassett, and a pub ruled out of the main entries only by a lack of reports from readers this year, the Wheatsheaf at Ogbourne St Andrew. Drinks prices here average out close to the national norm, with beers from Wadworths of Devizes often cheaper than average; the Toll Gate at Holt and Neeld Arms at Grittleton have beers from further afield at attractive prices. Besides Wadworths, Arkells of Swindon is Wiltshire's other major brewer, and smaller ones to look out for include Hop Back (a favourite of many readers), Stonehenge, Moles and Archers.

ALVEDISTON ST9723 Map 2
Crown 🖼

Village signposted on left off A30 about 12 miles W of Salisbury

Facing a farmyard with ponies and other animals, the attractive garden of this lovely 15th-c thatched inn is nicely broken up on different levels around a thatched white well, with shrubs and rockeries among neatly kept lawns. Inside, the three cosy very low-beamed and partly panelled rooms have deep terracotta paintwork, two inglenook fireplaces, and dark oak furniture; the friendly young staff are very welcoming. Listed on a blackboard, a fairly short choice of good bar food might include lunchtime sandwiches (£4.95, ciabattas £5.50), red pepper and spinach lasagne, cottage pie or ham, eggs and chips (£5.95), with other dishes such as chicken fillet with mushroom and wine sauce (£9.95), calamari poached in cream and butter (£10.25), and duck breast with orange sauce or fillet steak (£11.95). One of the dining areas is no smoking. Well kept Ringwood Best, and a couple of guests such as Fullers London Pride and Shepherd Neame Spitfire on handpump; darts, cribbage, dominoes and piped music. Avoid the bedroom over the bar unless you want to stay up with the late-night chatterers. The pub is peacefully set in a pretty spot. *(Recommended by Peter Shapland, Mr and Mrs W D Borthwick, Colin and Janet Roe, David R Crafts, Mr and Mrs A Stansfield)*

Free house ~ Licensees Lesley and Joan Finch ~ Real ale ~ Bar food ~ Restaurant ~ No credit cards ~ (01722) 780335 ~ Children welcome ~ Dogs allowed in bar ~ Open 12-3, 6-11; 12-3, 7-10.30 Sun ~ Bedrooms: £40S/£65S

AXFORD SU2370 Map 2
Red Lion 🍽 ⏱

Off A4 E of Marlborough; on back road Mildenhall—Ramsbury

The beamed and pine-panelled bar of this pretty flint-and-brick pub has a big inglenook fireplace, and a pleasant mix of comfortable sofas, cask seats and other solid chairs on the parquet floor – the pictures by local artists are for sale. There are lovely views over a valley from good hardwood tables and chairs on the terrace outside the restaurant, and you get the same views from picture windows in the restaurant and lounge. Welcoming, helpful staff serve well kept Hook Norton, Wadworths 6X and an occasional guest on handpump, along with 17 sensibly priced wines by the glass, and around two dozen malt whiskies. Besides lunchtime (not Sunday) filled rolls (from £4.95), and baked potatoes (from £5.25), bar snacks (not Saturday evening or Sunday lunchtime) could include battered haddock or three local sausages and mash (£6.50), goats cheese and ricotta fritters (£7), and home-made steak and kidney pie (£7.25), along with a wide choice of blackboard specials (which change every six weeks or so) such as grilled plaice or salmon and asparagus quiche (£6.95), wild mushroom and herb crèpes with mushroom and cream sauce or venison, woodland mushroom and chestnut casserole with red onion mash (£10.25), grilled bass with vodka, salmon caviar and cream sauce (£13.95), and baked monkfish wrapped in smoked salmon with white wine, tarragon and cream sauce or scotch fillet steak with creamy wensleydale sauce (£15.75); as dishes are cooked freshly to order, there may be a wait. The restaurant and bar eating area are no smoking. The sheltered garden has picnic-sets under parasols and swings. *(Recommended by Mrs Lesley Singleton, Mary Rayner, Alec and Barbara Jones, R Huggins, D Irving, E McCall, T McLean, Dick and Penny Vardy, Andrew Kerr, Bernard Stradling, CMW, JJW, Glenwys and Alan Lawrence, Evelyn and Derek Walter)*

Free house ~ Licensee Seamus Lecky ~ Real ale ~ Bar food ~ Restaurant ~ (01672) 520271 ~ Children welcome ~ Dogs allowed in bar ~ Open 12-3, 6.30-11; 12-3, 7-10.30 Sun; closed 25 Dec

BARFORD ST MARTIN SU0531 Map 2
Barford Inn 🍽 ⏢

Junction of A30 and B3098 W of Salisbury

It's well worth trying to catch the Friday evening Israeli barbecues (March to October, from 7pm) at this pleasantly old-fashioned 16th-c coaching inn, and on Mondays they do a good value three-course meal (£9). The front bar has some interesting squared oak panelling and a big log fire in winter, while the other well looked after chatty interlinking rooms and bars all have dark wooden tables and red-cushioned chairs; good service from the friendly staff and welcoming Israeli landlord. As well as filled ciabattas (from £3.95), and a good salad bar (£7.50), reasonably priced, freshly cooked bar food might include cheddar and leek bake with tomato and red pepper sauce (£7.95), calves liver and smoked bacon, grilled fish with creamy tomato sauce topped with a herb and cheese crust, steak and kidney pie or chargrilled chicken breast with linguini and wild mushroom sauce (all £8.95), and steaks (from £10.95), with specials such as roast poussin with lemon and black pepper or chargrilled lamb steak with wilted leek and peppercorn sauce (£11), while puddings could be chocolate truffle torte and cherry and almond tart (from £3.95). They serve Badger Best on handpump, quite a few country wines, and lots of israeli wines; no smoking restaurant; disabled access and lavatories. There are tables on an outside terrace, and more in a back garden. *(Recommended by Keith and Sheila Baxter, Mr and Mrs R Cox, Ann and Colin Hunt, Monica Cockburn, Mike Jefferies, J and B Cressey, A R Hawkins, Dr and Mrs M E Wilson)*

Badger ~ Tenant Ido Davids ~ Real ale ~ Bar food ~ Restaurant ~ (01722) 742242 ~ Children in eating area of bar and restaurant ~ Dogs allowed in bar ~ Open 11-11; 12-3, 7-10.30 Sun ~ Bedrooms: £50B/£55B

BECKHAMPTON SU0868 Map 2
Waggon & Horses
A4 Marlborough—Calne

The open-plan bar of this attractive old pub is inviting, with beams in the shiny ceiling where walls have been knocked through, shiny wood floors, mustard walls, an old-fashioned high-backed settle on one side of the room with a smaller one opposite, leatherette stools, and comfortably cushioned wall benches. For many years this was a heartwarming sight to coachmen coming in from what was notorious as the coldest stretch of the old Bath road (and even nowadays readers very much appreciate the log fire in winter). Pleasant, welcoming staff serve well kept Wadworths IPA, JCB, 6X and a couple of guests such as Jennings Snecklifter on handpump or tapped straight from the cask, and over a dozen wines by the glass; piped music, darts, pool, dominoes, fruit machine and TV. Straightforward bar food includes soup (£2.25), sandwiches (from £3.25), spicy thai crab cake (£3.75), chilli or breaded cod (£5.95), fillet steak (£8.95), and specials such as mushroom stroganoff (£6.50), and lamb and spinach curry (£6.95), with puddings such as hot chocolate fudge cake (£3.25); it's especially popular with older visitors, and they do an OAP weekday lunch special (£3.95). The dining area is no smoking. Silbury Hill (a vast prehistoric mound) is just towards Marlborough from here, and Avebury stone circle and the West Kennet long barrow are very close too. As we went to press, they were in the process of rethatching the roof. *(Recommended by Sheila and Robert Robinson, Brian and Pat Wardrobe, Gill and Tony Morriss, Esther and John Sprinkle, Pat and Tony Martin, Andrew Shore, John and Glenys Wheeler)*

Wadworths ~ Manager Doug Shepherd ~ Real ale ~ Bar food (not Sun evening) ~ (01672) 539418 ~ Children in eating area of bar ~ Open 11-2.30, 5.30-11; 11-3, 6-11 Sat; 12-3, 7-10.30 Sun

BERWICK ST JAMES SU0639 Map 2
Boot 🍴
B3083, between A36 and A303 NW of Salisbury

This flint and stone pub is a rewarding place to visit, whether you're after a tasty lunchtime snack or a three-course meal. The partly carpeted flagstoned bar has a contented cosy atmosphere, a huge winter log fire in the inglenook fireplace at one end, sporting prints over a smaller brick fireplace at the other, and houseplants on its wide window sills. A charming small back no smoking dining room has a nice mix of dining chairs around four tables, and deep pink walls with an attractively mounted collection of celebrity boots. Wadworths IPA and 6X along with a changing guest such as Marstons Pedigree are well kept on handpump, and they have a few well chosen house wines, half a dozen malts and farm cider. Service is very friendly and helpful; piped jazz. Listed on a frequently changing blackboard, imaginative fairly priced food is made using as much local produce as possible, and vegetables may even come from the garden. Readers very much enjoy the delicious baguettes (from £4.95), while other enjoyable dishes could include soup (£3.95), filo prawns with sweet chilli dip (£5.95), liver and bacon with mash and onion gravy, beef, mushroom and stilton stew or green thai chicken curry (£8.95), warm scallops and crispy smoked bacon salad (£11.50), and steaks (from £12.95), with puddings such as gooseberry and ginger cheesecake (£3.95); they do children's meals (£3.99). Very neatly kept with pretty flower beds, the sheltered side lawn has some well spaced picnic-sets. *(Recommended by Simon Collett-Jones, Charles Moncreiffe, John Evans, Alan and Paula McCully, A E Furley, Sam and Sally Shepherd, KC, Neville and Anne Morley, Keith and Sheila Baxter, Dr D G Twyman, Gerry and Rosemary Dobson, Steve Crooke, Joyce and Geoff Robson, Diana Brumfit, Esther and John Sprinkle, Peter and Audrey Dowsett, Michael Doswell, Fiona Eddleston)*

Wadworths ~ Tenant Kathie Duval ~ Real ale ~ Bar food (12-2.30, 6.30-9.30; not Mon) ~ Restaurant ~ (01722) 790243 ~ Children welcome ~ Dogs welcome ~ Open 12-2.30(3 Sat), 6-11; 12-3, 7-10.30 Sun; closed Mon lunchtime

BERWICK ST JOHN ST9422 Map 2
Talbot

Village signposted from A30 E of Shaftesbury

The single long, heavily beamed bar at this attractive old village pub (now under friendly new licensees) is simply furnished with cushioned solid wall and window seats, spindleback chairs, a high-backed built-in settle at one end, and tables. The huge inglenook fireplace has a good iron fireback and bread ovens, and there are nicely shaped heavy black beams and cross-beams with bevelled corners. Besides daily specials such as tasty steak and ale pie, battered hake, chicken balti or pork with apple and cider (£6.95), reasonably priced bar food includes lunchtime ploughman's (£3.75), baguettes (from £4), sausage and mash with onion gravy or cheese and mushroom omelette (£4.25), as well as home-made lasagne or breaded scampi (£5.95), and grilled cajun chicken or salmon and broccoli mornay (£6.95). Well kept Bass, Ringwood Best, Wadworths 6X and a guest such as Fullers London Pride on handpump, and farm cider; darts, cribbage. They've recently updated the outdoor seating area. *(Recommended by Ann and Colin Hunt, Richard Gibbs, Mrs J H S Lang, Kerry Milis, Colin and Janet Roe, D P and M A Miles)*

Free house ~ Licensees Pete and Marilyn Hawkins ~ Real ale ~ Bar food ~ (01747) 828222 ~ Children in eating area of bar ~ Dogs allowed in bar ~ Open 12-2.30, 6.30-11; 12-4 Sun; closed Sun evening, Mon

BOX ST8369 Map 2
Quarrymans Arms

Box Hill; coming from Bath on A4 turn right into Bargates 50 yds before railway bridge, then at T junction turn left up Quarry Hill, turning left again near the top at grassy triangle; from Corsham, turn left after Rudloe Park Hotel into Beech Road, then third left on to Barnetts Hill, and finally right at the top of the hill

Well worth the sinuous drive down a warren of lanes, this welcoming low stone building has been run by the same licensees for 15 years. The pub is ideally placed for cavers, potholers and walkers, all of whom generate an interesting atmosphere, and as it was once the local of the Bath stone miners, there are quite a lot of mining-related photographs and memorabilia dotted around the interior (they now run interesting guided trips down the mine itself). One pleasant modernised room with an open fire is entirely set aside for drinking, and they serve well kept Butcombe, Moles and Wadworths 6X on handpump, and perhaps a guest from a brewery such as Bath; also good wines, over 60 malt whiskies, and 10 or so old cognacs. Many people, however, come here for the enjoyable bar food, which might include soup (£2.95), stilton and asparagus pancake (£4.50; £7.25 main), moules marinière (£5.25; £8.25 main), home-made pie (£7.95), various stir fries (£8.25), sirloin steak (£9.25), and plenty of daily specials such as oak-smoked haddock salad with poached egg or lamb shank with pork and redcurrant sauce (£8.95), and bass with tomato and basil sauce (£13.95), with puddings such as sticky toffee pudding (from £3.50). Beautiful sweeping views from big windows in the dining area are usually enough to distract visitors from the mild untidiness. The staff are very friendly and efficient; cribbage, dominoes, fruit machine, and piped music. An attractive outside terrace has picnic-sets, and they play boules here (with football and cricket teams, too). *(Recommended by Mrs D Littler, Paul Hopton, Catherine Pitt, N Bayley, Richard Stancomb, Colin and Peggy Wilshire, Gill and Tony Morriss, Ian Phillips, Dr and Mrs C W Thomas, Philip Chow, Susan and John Douglas, Dr and Mrs M E Wilson, Mike and Mary Carter, Dr and Mrs A K Clarke, Guy Vowles)*

Free house ~ Licensees John and Ginny Arundel ~ Real ale ~ Bar food (11(12 Sun)-3, 6-10) ~ Restaurant ~ (01225) 743569 ~ Children welcome ~ Dogs allowed in bar ~ Open 11-3.30, 6-11; 11-11 Fri/Sat; 12-10.30 Sun ~ Bedrooms: £25(£30B)/£45(£60B)

BRADFORD-ON-AVON ST8261 Map 2
Dandy Lion
Market Street

In the day, this thriving town pub has an enjoyably continental feel, and a good mix of customers, while in the evening, it's popular with a young crowd (especially weekends, when parts can get smoky). Big windows look out on to the street, and have a table and cushioned wooden armchair each. Working in, the pleasantly relaxed long main bar has nice high-backed farmhouse chairs, old-fashioned dining chairs, a long brocade-cushioned settle on the stripped wooden floor (there's a couple of rugs, too), sentimental and gently erotic pictures on the panelled walls, an overmantel with brussels horses, and fairy-lit hops over the bar counter. Up a few steps at the back, a snug little bare-boarded room has a lovely high-backed settle and other small ones around sturdy tables, a big mirror on the mulberry walls, and a piano; newspapers to read, and piped jazz. Served only at lunchtime, reasonably priced, well prepared bar food includes soup (£3.50), sandwiches or baguettes (from £3.50), ploughman's (from £4.95), pasta dishes (from £5.25), mushroom and sweet pepper stroganoff (£5.50), and sausage and mash, caesar salad or traditional fish and chips (£5.95), with changing specials such as mild prawn and potato curry with lemon and herb rice or baked mushrooms topped with minced chicken, spices and herbs (£6.50); Sunday roast (£6.95). The upstairs restaurant is candlelit at night, and has an area with antique toys and baskets of flowers. Well kept Butcombe and Wadworths IPA, 6X and JCB on handpump, and good coffee. They have evening poetry readings. *(Recommended by Richard Stancomb, Ian Phillips, Susan and Nigel Wilson, Dr and Mrs A K Clarke, Dr and Mrs M E Wilson, S and N McLean, David and Rhian Peters, David Carr, Richard Pierce)*

Wadworths ~ Tenant Jennifer Joseph ~ Real ale ~ Bar food (lunchtime) ~ Restaurant ~ (01225) 863433 ~ Children welcome ~ Open 10.30-3, 6-11; 11.30-3, 7-10.30 Sun

BRINKWORTH SU0184 Map 2
Three Crowns ♀
The Street; B4042 Wootton Bassett—Malmesbury

Although food is certainly the priority, this popular pub has a good range of real ales including Hook Norton Old Hooky, Fullers London Pride, Tetleys, Wadworths 6X and a guest such as Archers Best on handpump, and they have a long wine list, with at least 10 by the glass, and mulled wine in winter. If you do want to eat, you must get here early as it can get very crowded, and you may have to wait a long time for a table. Covering an entire wall, the elaborate menu (with prices at the top end of the pub range) includes lunchtime snacks such as filled rolls (from £5), and filled baked potatoes (from £7.25), with other dishes such as home-made steak and kidney pie (£13.45), creole-style blue marlin or lemon sole with home-made savoury butter (£15.45), locally smoked chicken with sherry and cream sauce and dijon mustard (£15.95), and rack of lamb topped with garlic breadcrumbs, with red wine and cream sauce (£18.45); all main courses are served with half a dozen fresh vegetables. Most people choose to eat in the no smoking conservatory. The bar part is more traditional (and can get smoky), with big landscape prints and other pictures, some horsebrasses on dark beams, a dresser with a collection of old bottles, tables of stripped deal, and a couple made from gigantic forge bellows, big tapestry-upholstered pews and blond chairs, and log fires; sensibly placed darts, shove-ha'penny, dominoes, cribbage and chess, fruit machine, and piped music. There's a light and airy no smoking garden room and a terrace with outdoor heating to the side of the conservatory. The garden stretches around the side and back, with well spaced tables and a climbing frame, and looks over a side lane to the church, and out over rolling prosperous farmland. *(Recommended by Andrew Shore, Nigel and Sue Foster, Peter and Audrey Dowsett, Mrs Pat Crabb, John and Judy Saville, Dr and Mrs A K Clarke, Brian and Pat Wardrobe, Mary Rayner, Mrs J Smythe, Tom and Ruth Rees)*

Whitbreads ~ Lease Anthony Windle ~ Real ale ~ Bar food (12-2, 6-9.30) ~ Restaurant ~ (01666) 510366 ~ Children in restaurant ~ Dogs allowed in bar ~ Open 11-3(4 Sat), 6-11; 12-5, 6-10.30 Sun

CHICKSGROVE ST9729 Map 2
Compasses ★ ⑪ ♀ 🛏

From A30 5½ miles W of B3089 junction, take lane on N side signposted Sutton Mandeville, Sutton Row, then first left fork (small signs point the way to the pub, in Lower Chicksgrove; look out for the car park)

Wiltshire Dining Pub of the Year
Superbly run by a genuinely welcoming landlord, this pleasantly relaxed old thatched house gains a Star for its imaginative food, good choice of wines, friendly staff and enjoyably traditional atmosphere – it's also a great place to stay. Besides filled onion bread (from £3.95), baked potatoes (from £3.95), and ham, egg and chips (£5.95), the daily-changing menu might include soup or banana wrapped in bacon and baked with rosemary and gruyère sauce (£4.95), steak and kidney pie (£7.95), wild mushrooms with vinney, apple and cider sauce with noodles (£8.95), grilled lemon sole with lemon, prawn and butter glaze, tuna steak with mango salsa or duck breast with chinese jus (£11.95), and lamb fillet with mint and redcurrant jus (£14.95), with puddings such as raspberry, lemon, ginger and coriander tart or brioche bread and butter pudding (£3.95); all meals come with a good choice of vegetables. The bar has old bottles and jugs hanging from beams above the roughly timbered counter, farm tools and traps on the partly stripped stone walls, and high-backed wooden settles forming snug booths around tables on the mainly flagstoned floor. Real ales on handpump include well kept Bass, Chicksgrove Churl (brewed for the pub by Wadworths), Wadworths 6X and perhaps a guest such as Oakham JHB, they also have six wines by the glass; cribbage, dominoes, bagatelle and shove-ha'penny. The quiet garden and flagstoned farm courtyard are very pleasant places to sit, and there's a nice walk to Sutton Mandeville church and back along the Nadder Valley. Be warned, they close on Tuesdays after bank holiday Mondays. *(Recommended by Rachel Cooper, Mr and Mrs Staples, John Braine-Hartnell, J F Stackhouse, Keith and Sheila Baxter, H D Wharton, Paul Boot, Dr and Mrs C W Thomas, L Topping, R Preston, Jeff and Wendy Williams, Peter J and Avril Hanson, Howard and Margaret Buchanan, Bill and Jessica Ritson)*

Free house ~ Licensee Alan Stoneham ~ Real ale ~ Bar food (not Sun evenings) ~ Restaurant ~ (01722) 714318 ~ Children welcome ~ Dogs welcome ~ Open 12-3, 6-11(7-10.30 Sun); closed Mon except bank hols, then cl Tues ~ Bedrooms: £40B/£65B

CORSHAM ST8670 Map 2
Two Pigs ◖

A4, Pickwick
The admirably eccentric feel of this traditional little drinker's pub owes much to the individualistic landlord, who has amassed a zany collection of bric-a-brac in the 15 or so years he's been in charge, including enamel advertising signs on the wood-clad walls, pig-theme ornaments, and old radios. A good mix of customers gathers around the long dark wood tables and benches, and friendly staff provide good

prompt service; piped blues. Always chatty and friendly, the atmosphere is at its headiest on Monday nights, when live blues draws a big crowd into the narrow and dimly lit flagstoned bar. Alongside Hop Back Summer Lightning and Stonehenge Pigswill, you can expect to find a couple of well kept changing guests from small independent brewers such as Barge & Barrel, Bullmastiff and Teignworthy, and they also do a range of country wines. A covered yard outside is called the Sty. Beware of their opening times – the pub is closed every lunchtime, except on Sunday; no food (except crisps) or under-21s. *(Recommended by Catherine Pitt, Dr and Mrs A K Clarke, Dr and Mrs M E Wilson)*

Free house ~ Licensees Dickie and Ann Doyle ~ Real ale ~ No credit cards ~ (01249) 712515 ~ Blues Mon evening ~ Open 7-11; 12-2.30, 7-10.30 Sun

DEVIZES SU0061 Map 2
Bear ♀ 🍺 🛏
Market Place

They serve around a dozen wines by the glass at this charming old coaching inn, a good base for exploring the area. Especially cosy in winter when there are roaring log fires, the big main carpeted bar has black winged wall settles and muted red cloth-upholstered bucket armchairs around oak tripod tables; the atmosphere is chatty and relaxed. Separated from the main bar by some steps and an old-fashioned glazed screen, a room named after the portrait painter Thomas Lawrence (his father ran the establishment in the 1770s) has dark oak-panelled walls, a parquet floor, shining copper pans on the mantelpiece above the big open fireplace, and plates around the walls; part of it is no smoking. They serve well kept Wadworths IPA, 6X and a seasonal guest on handpump, a good choice of malt whiskies, and freshly squeezed juices from a classic bar counter with shiny black woodwork and small panes of glass. Enjoyable, reasonably priced bar food includes home-made soup (£2.95), sandwiches (from £2.75), filled baked potatoes or baguettes (from £4.25), ploughman's or omelettes (from £4.50), ham and egg (£4.95), tasty fish and chips (£5.95), daily specials such as beef in beer casserole with dumplings (£4.95), and fish of the day (£5.25), with home-made puddings (£2.95); there are buffet meals in the Lawrence Room – you can eat these in the bar too. On Saturday nights they have a good value set menu in the old-fashioned restaurant. Only a stone's throw from here at Wadworths brewery, you can buy beer in splendid old-fashioned half-gallon earthenware jars. The inn has provided shelter to distinguished guests as diverse as King George III and Dr Johnson. *(Recommended by Alan and Paula McCully, Mary Rayner, Dr and Mrs A K Clarke, the Didler, Blaise Vyner, Joyce and Maurice Cottrell, Mike Gorton, Richard Pierce, Bill and Jessica Ritson)*

Free house ~ Licensee Andrew Maclachlan ~ Real ale ~ Bar food (11.30-2.30, 7-9.30) ~ Restaurant ~ (01380) 722444 ~ Children welcome ~ Dogs allowed in bar ~ Open 11-11; 12-10.30 Sun ~ Bedrooms: £50S(£50B)/£75S(£75B)

EBBESBOURNE WAKE ST9824 Map 2
Horseshoe ★ 🍺 🛏
On A354 S of Salisbury, right at signpost at Coombe Bissett; village is around 8 miles further on

A good all-rounder with well kept ales, enjoyable home-cooking and friendly service, this delightfully unspoilt old country pub continues to win praise from readers. It's tucked away in fine downland, and there are pleasant views over the steep sleepy valley of the River Ebble from seats in its pretty little garden; look out for the three goats in a paddock at the bottom of the garden, and a couple of playful dogs. There are fresh home-grown flowers on the tables in the beautifully kept bar, with lanterns, a large collection of farm tools and other bric-a-brac crowded along its beams, and an open fire; a conservatory extension seats 10 people. Served with plenty of well cooked seasonal vegetables (and good chips), enjoyable bar food includes lunchtime ham and eggs (£6.75), curry (£8.95), lambs liver and bacon (£9.50), fish bake or beef, bacon and shallots in ale (£9.75), and evening dishes such as lamb cutlets in port sauce or fillet steak (£13.25), and half a honey-roasted duckling in gooseberry sauce (£15); good puddings. Booking is advisable for the small no smoking restaurant, especially at weekends when it can fill quite quickly. Well kept Adnams Broadside, Ringwood Best, Wadworths 6X and a guest such as Stonehenge Pigswill are tapped from the row of casks behind the bar, and they also stock farm cider, country wines and several malt whiskies. The landlord is friendly and accommodating without being intrusive, and the welcoming, attentive staff seem to enjoy their work. The barn opposite is now used as a gymnasium; good walks nearby. *(Recommended by Margaret Ross, Mike and Shelley Woodroffe, John and Jane Hayter, the Didler, Peter and Giff Bennett, Simon Donan, W W Burke, Richard Gibbs, Dr and Mrs J F Head, Di and Mike Gillam, Douglas and Ann Hare, J V Dadswell, Maurice Averay, Richard Harris, Dr D G Twyman, Mr and Mrs W D Borthwick, Penny Simpson, Colin and Janet Roe, Bill and Jessica Ritson)*

Free house ~ Licensees Anthony and Patricia Bath ~ Real ale ~ Bar food (not Sun evenings or Mon) ~ Restaurant ~ (01722) 780474 ~ Children in eating area of bar ~ Open 12-3, 6.30-11; 12-4, 7-10.30 Sun; closed Mon lunchtime ~ Bedrooms: /£60S(£60B)

FONTHILL GIFFORD ST9232 Map 2
Beckford Arms 🛏

Off B3089 W of Wilton at Fonthill Bishop

The smartly informal rooms at this pleasant, unchanging country house are big, light and airy, with stripped bare wood, a parquet floor and a pleasant mix of tables with church candles. In winter, a big log fire burns in the lounge bar, which leads into a light and airy back garden room with a high pitched plank ceiling and picture windows looking on to a terrace. Locals tend to gather in the straightforward public bar; darts, fruit machine, pool, TV and piped music. There's an enjoyably civilised atmosphere, and the courteous staff are very welcoming. Good (if not cheap) bar food, made from local produce wherever possible, could include dishes such as goats cheese, red pepper and oregano tartlet (£5.60), gravadlax with dill and mustard dressing (£5.90), lunchtime filled ciabattas (from £6.20), local ham, egg and chips (£8.50), grilled mixed seafood with cuban mojito glaze (£11.20), cajun-spiced chicken with pineapple and coconut salsa (£11.90), grilled butterfish with prawn and caper salsa (£12.40), and fillet steak (£15.95), with puddings such as treacle sponge and chocolate and rum mousse (£3.95); on Sundays they do roasts (£7.95), and the menu is more limited. Well kept real ales such as Greene King Abbot, Milk Street Gulp, Timothy Taylors Landlord and a guest such as Fullers London Pride on handpump. The pub is on the edge of a fine parkland estate; you can drive through to see its lake and sweeping vistas. *(Recommended by Phyl and Jack Street, John Evans, Stephen Kiley, Stuart Litster, Ann and Colin Hunt, Richard Gibbs, Colin and Janet Roe)*

Free house ~ Licensees Karen and Eddie Costello ~ Real ale ~ Bar food (not 25 Dec) ~ Restaurant ~ (01747) 870385 ~ Well behaved children welcome ~ Dogs allowed in bar and bedrooms ~ Open 12-11; 12-10.30 Sun ~ Bedrooms: £40S/£70B

GREAT DURNFORD SU1338 Map 2
Black Horse

Signposted off A345 Amesbury—Salisbury

This cheerful pub has a lively bustle at lunchtime, with colourful changing menu boards, and plenty of people tucking into dishes such as toad in the hole (£6.95), steak and kidney pie (£7.25), liver and bacon (£7.50), roast cod with lime chilli sauce, guinea fowl or lamb chops with redcurrant and mint sauce (£8.25), chicken breast with stilton cream sauce (£8.50), and puddings such as spotted dick and hot treacle sponge (£3.50); they also do baguettes (from £5.25, not Sunday), and children's meals (£5.75 including ice cream). The brick serving counter has a line of bar stools (and a great line in funny hats), and opposite it, across a narrow brick floor, another row of bar stools facing a shelf wide enough to hold plates, with an entertaining collection of bric-a-brac above this. At one end of this central spine is an alcove with sensibly placed darts, and another with a single long table; at the other, a snug flag-draped area with three tables and a high-backed settle. Steps take you up to a couple of no smoking rooms, one with ship pictures, models and huge ensigns, the other with a big woodburning stove in a big brick inglenook. Friendly service; well kept Ringwood Best, a slightly lighter house beer brewed for them by Ringwood, and a guest such as Hop Back Crop Circle on handpump; piped radio, darts, shove-ha'penny, table skittles, pinball, cribbage, dominoes and ring the bull. A black gravel terrace outside has picnic-sets, with more on grass leading down to the River Avon, past a timber climbing fort, gondola and tyre swings, and a small wendy house; they have pétanque. We look forward to hearing how readers find the bedrooms here. *(Recommended by Edward and Ava Williams, J and B Cressey, I D Barnett)*

Free house ~ Licensee Mike Skinner ~ Real ale ~ Bar food ~ Restaurant ~ (01722) 782270 ~ Children in eating area of bar ~ Dogs allowed in bar ~ Open 12-2.30, 6-10.30(11 Sat); 12-3, 6-10 Sun; closed Sun evening in winter ~ Bedrooms: £35/£45S(£45B)

GREAT HINTON ST9059 Map 2
Linnet 🍴

3½ miles E of Trowbridge; village signposted off A361 opposite Lamb at Semington

The imaginative food at this attractive brick dining pub is very highly regarded by readers, but be warned – it's best to book a few weeks in advance if you want to be sure of a table on the weekend. The set lunch (£10.25 for two courses; £12.95 for three courses) is excellent value, and dishes are freshly prepared by the dedicated chef/landlord. Served in the little bar or restaurant, the changing menu might include at lunchtimes filled focaccia (from £6.50), roasted salmon with warm green bean and sesame seed salad with shellfish sauce (£7.50), and chicken and asparagus casserole (£7.75), with evening dishes such as duck, fried onion and beetroot cake with orange and mustard chutney (£5.25), grilled asparagus and goats cheese in puff pastry with hummous and red pepper sauce (£10.75), baked lemon sole with king prawn and coriander mousse with lemon grass sauce (£12.95), and roasted rack of lamb with sweet potato mash, minted onion rings and port sauce (£13.95); puddings might be raspberry and praline cheesecake or baked lime custard tart with blackberry compote (from £4.25). The bar to the right of the door has a cream carpet and lots of photographs of the pub and the brewery, there are bookshelves in a snug end part; the cosy restaurant is candlelit at night. As well as more than 20 malt whiskies, and quite a few wines, they serve well kept Wadworths 6X, and maybe a seasonal guest on handpump; piped music. In summer, the flowering tubs and window boxes with seats dotted among them are quite a sight. *(Recommended by Denise Drummond, M G Hart, Lady Heath, Michael Doswell, Mr and Mrs J Ken Jones, Roger Bridgeman, J R and J Moon)*

Wadworths ~ Tenant Jonathan Furby ~ Real ale ~ Bar food ~ Restaurant ~ (01380) 870354 ~ Children welcome ~ Dogs allowed in bar ~ Open 11-2.30, 6-11; 12-3, 7-10.30 Sun

GRITTLETON ST8680 Map 2
Neeld Arms ♀ 🍴 🛏

Off A350 NW of Chippenham; The Street

It's great to see a fairly young licensee all set to join that increasingly rare group of classic pub landlords – true characters, enthusiastic, outgoing, convivial and usually mildly eccentric. Certainly, since Mr West took it on a couple of years ago, this 17th-c black-beamed pub has developed a warmly welcoming and companionable atmosphere. The food's good, too, with blackboards changing from day to day. At lunchtime (not Sunday), you can choose from dishes such as ciabattas (from £4.25), ploughman's (£4.95), fish, chips and mushy peas or salmon and dill fishcakes (£6.95), and sausages or pie of the week (£7.50), while in the evening the menu might include fried chicken liver salad (£4.50), baked figs stuffed with goats cheese wrapped in parma ham (£4.95), sweet pepper and vegetable pancakes (£6.95), stilton, leek and walnut pie (£7.50), lamb shank with mint and rosemary sauce or baked swordfish in a lemon and caper sauce (£9.95), with puddings such as treacle tart or pancakes stuffed with vanilla ice cream and chocolate sauce (£4.25); Sunday roast (£6.95). It's largely open-plan, with some stripped stone, a log fire in the big inglenook on the right and a smaller coal-effect fire on the left, flowers on tables, and a friendly mix of seating from windsor chairs through scatter-cushioned window seats to some nice arts and crafts chairs and a traditional settle. The parquet-floored back dining area has yet another inglenook, with a big woodburning stove; back here, you still feel thoroughly part of what's going on. The substantial central bar counter has well kept Brakspears, Buckleys Best, Wadworths 6X and Wickwar BOB on handpump, and a good choice of good value wines by the glass; they've recently acquired a golden retriever, Soaky, who seems to be developing a taste for the slops bucket. People staying enjoy good breakfasts. *(Recommended by Richard Stancomb, Dr and Mrs M E Wilson, Simon Mays-Smith, Richard Pierce)*

Free house ~ Licensees Charlie and Boo West ~ Real ale ~ Bar food ~ Restaurant ~ (01249) 782470 ~ Children welcome ~ Dogs welcome ~ Open 12-3, 5.30-11; 11.30-3.30, 5.30-11 Sat; 12-3.30, 6(7 in winter)-11 Sun ~ Bedrooms: £40S(£40B)/£60S(£60B)

HEYTESBURY ST9242 Map 2
Angel 🍴 🍺 🛏

High Street; just off A36 E of Warminster

In a quiet village just below the Salisbury Plain, this pleasant 16th-c inn is an enjoyable place for a relaxing drink, a well cooked meal or even a comfortable overnight stop. The spacious homely lounge on the right, with well used overstuffed armchairs (great to sink into) and sofas and a good fire, opens into a charming terracotta-painted back dining room, with navy curtains and hand-painted plates from Portugal. This in turn opens on to an attractive secluded courtyard garden. On the left, a long beamed bar has a convivial evening atmosphere, open fire, some attractive prints and old photographs, and straightforward tables and chairs; piped music. As well as lunchtime ciabattas (£5.50), good food could include dishes such as home-made soup (£3.95), baked mushrooms with herbs and stilton (£4.95), warm chicken and bacon salad (£6.95), beer-battered fish and chips (£7.95), braised lamb shank and mash (£8.95), chicken stuffed with avocado and brie wrapped in bacon (£9.95), and local trout stuffed with prawns and herbs (£12.95), with puddings such as apple and cinnamon crème brûlée and summer pudding (£4.95); Sunday roast (£7.50). Alongside well kept Ringwood Best, they've a couple of guest beers such as Greene King Abbot and Marstons Pedigree on handpump; service is excellent. As we went to press, the pub was due to change hands, so some of these details may change. *(Recommended by Dr and Mrs A K Clarke, Keith and Sheila Baxter, Michael Huberty, Jeff and Wendy Williams, James Woods, M G Hart, David R Crafts, Mr and Mrs H D Brierly, Betsy and Peter Little)*

Greene King ~ Lease Brad Rossiter ~ Real ale ~ Bar food ~ Restaurant ~ (01985) 840330 ~ Children welcome ~ Dogs allowed in bar and bedrooms ~ Open 11.30-11; 12-10.30 Sun; closed 25 Dec evening ~ Bedrooms: £50S/£65S

HINDON ST9132 Map 2
Angel 🍴 🍷

B3089 Wilton—Mere

The back courtyard of this 18th-c coaching inn is prettily lit at night, with good teak chairs around tables under cocktail parasols, and big flowering tubs. Inside, the traditional candlelit bar is painted a warm red, and has a good log fire, a nice mix of old tables and chairs on flagstones, Victorian prints and artefacts, and fresh flowers; daily papers. Off the entrance hall a civilised no smoking lounge has another log fire, grey panelling, armchairs, settees, a cushioned antique settle, country magazines and a shelf displaying the landlady's collection of cheese dishes. The long cream dining room has a huge window that lets you glimpse all the goings-on in the kitchen, and big photographs of the surrounding area. Bass and Wadworths IPA and 6X are well kept on handpump, and they have good wines including over a dozen by the glass. There's an emphasis on the imaginative though not cheap daily-changing food, which you can choose to eat in the bar or the restaurant. Carefully prepared dishes might include soup (£3.95), fried herring roes with capers, bacon and lemon butter (£5.25; £8.25 large), lunchtime sandwiches (from £5.50), beer-battered cod with chips and crushed peas (£7.75), baked gnocchi with roasted pine nuts and roquefort with a horseradish crust (£10.50), seared bass on wild mushroom and asparagus risotto with pesto oil, or thai-style king prawn curry with fragrant rice (£12.95), and scotch rib-eye steak with roasted plum tomatoes, garlic-roasted field mushrooms, rocket and home-made chips (£13.50), with puddings such as bread and butter pudding with custard and vanilla ice cream (£4.95), and an interesting cheeseboard (£6.50); they charge extra for added vegetables, and as dishes are cooked fresh there may be a wait when it's busy. *(Recommended by Wally and Irene Nunn, Jill Franklin, Duncan and Lisa Cripps, Edward Mirzoeff, John Evans, Norman and June Williams, KC, P and J Shapley, Lady Heath, Colin and Janet Roe, Joyce and Geoff Robson, Dr and Mrs R E S Tanner, Simon Chell, John Parker, W W Burke, Geoff Palmer, Charles Moncreiffe, Tony Radnor, Mr and Mrs J McRobert, Bill and Jessica Ritson, Neil and Karen Dignan)*

Free house ~ Licensee Penny Simpson ~ Real ale ~ Bar food ~ Restaurant ~ (01747) 820696 ~ Children in eating area of bar ~ Dogs allowed in bar and bedrooms ~ Open 10-11; 10-2.30, 6-11 in winter; closed Sun evening ~ Bedrooms: £50B/£65B

HOLT ST8561 Map 2
Toll Gate ◖

Ham Green; B3107 W of Melksham

Even the bread at this well run dining pub is home-made, and they do an excellent value set lunch (£9.95 two courses; £11.95 three courses), though if you've just dropped in for a drink, there's a good choice, and you'll be made to feel very welcome. Furnished and decorated with real flair, one leg of the relaxed L-shaped bar has cosy settees and a log fire watched over by big stone cats (there are also two pub cats). The other leg is more adapted to eating (one lovely table gleaming in the corner was put together for the pub from three salvaged flooring planks); there are plenty of hunting prints on pinkish walls, some willow-pattern plates on black panelling, one or two beams in the venetian red ceiling, rugs on old quarry tiles, and soft lighting including table lamps. The high-raftered restaurant, up a few steps, is eclectically decorated with bright cushions on sturdy pews and other country furniture, and attractive bric-a-brac including lots of japanese parasols, all interestingly lit through church windows – this part used to be a workers' chapel, when the main building was a weavers' shed. Freshly prepared, well presented food (they name their suppliers) includes lunchtime snacks such as soup (£4), bubble and squeak with poached egg and hollandaise sauce (£5.50), club sandwich or pancakes filled with fish and glazed with mornay sauce (£6.50), and english cheeses (£6.75), as well as more elaborate dishes such as scottish mussels in thai, chilli and saffron broth (£5.50), puff pastry case filled with roasted mediterranean vegetables, pine nuts and feta cheese (£10.50), whole john dory with capers, parsley, melted butter and new potatoes or fried calves liver with garlic potatoes and mustard sauce (£12.50), and fried duck breast with fondant potatoes and black cherry sauce (£14); home-made puddings might include baked german cheesecake with orange crème anglaise or rhubarb and ginger fool (from £4); extra vegetables are £2.50. They have five well kept changing beers on handpump, bought directly from a good range of interesting smaller brewers such as City of Cambridge, Exmoor, Glastonbury, West Berkshire and York; also eight or so wines by the glass, farm cider and good strong coffee. Good, attentive service; piped music. The gents' is worth a look for its colourful murals. There are picnic-sets out on the back terrace. *(Recommended by Dr and Mrs M E Wilson, Mr and Mrs A H Young)*

Free house ~ Licensees Alison Ward-Baptiste and Alexander Venables ~ Real ale ~ Bar food ~ Restaurant ~ (01225) 782326 ~ Dogs allowed in bar ~ Open 11.30-2.30, 5-11; 12-2.30 Sun; closed Sun evening, Mon ~ Bedrooms: /£65S

KILMINGTON ST7736 Map 2
Red Lion £ 🏠

B3092 Mere—Frome, 2½ miles S of Maiden Bradley; 3 miles from A303 Mere turn-off

Well run by the same landlord for more than 25 years, this down-to-earth 15th-c ivy-covered country inn is a good place to enjoy a well kept pint and a chat. The snug low-ceilinged bar has a good local pubby atmosphere (particularly in the evenings), and is pleasantly furnished with a curved high-backed settle and red leatherette wall and window seats on the flagstones, photographs of locals pinned up on the black beams, and a couple of big fireplaces (one with a fine old iron fireback) with log fires in winter. A newer big-windowed no smoking eating area is decorated with brasses, a large leather horse collar, and hanging plates. It's popular with walkers; you can buy locally made walking sticks, and a gate gives on to the lane which leads to White Sheet Hill, where there is riding, hang gliding and radio-controlled gliders. The simple bar food is good value, with prices unchanged since last year. Served only at lunchtime, it includes soup (£1.80), sandwiches (from £2.80; toasted from £3.25), filled baked potatoes (from £2.85), ploughman's (from £3.95) cornish pasties (from £4), steak and kidney or lamb and apricot pie (£4.45), creamy fish pie (£4.50), meat or vegetable lasagne (£6.75), and perhaps one or two daily specials; last orders for food at 1.50pm. Friendly, helpful staff serve well kept Butcombe, Butts Jester and a regularly changing guest on handpump, farm cider, pressés, and monthly changing wines; sensibly placed darts, dominoes, shove-ha'penny and cribbage. There are picnic-sets in the big attractive garden (look out for Kim the labrador). The pub is owned by the National Trust, and Stourhead Gardens are only a mile away. Dogs allowed in bar – but not at lunchtime. *(Recommended by Roger and Jenny Huggins, H D Wharton, Edward Mirzoeff, Michael Doswell, Simon Collett-Jones, Mike Gorton)*

Free house ~ Licensee Chris Gibbs ~ Real ale ~ Bar food (12-1.50; not 25-26 or 31 Dec) ~ No credit cards ~ (01985) 844263 ~ Children welcome till 8pm ~ Open 11.30-2.30, 6.30-11; 12-3, 7-10.30 Sun ~ Bedrooms: £25/£35

LACOCK ST9168 Map 2
George ★

West Street; village signposted off A350 S of Chippenham

In a famously well preserved National Trust village, this unspoilt homely old pub has been licensed continuously since the 17th c. The low-beamed bar is comfortable and relaxing, with upright timbers in the place of knocked-through walls making cosy rambling corners, candles on tables (even at lunchtime), armchairs and windsor chairs, seats in the stone-mullioned windows, and flagstones just by the counter; piped music (which can be quite loud). The treadwheel set into the outer breast of the original great central fireplace is a talking point – worked by a dog, it was used to turn a spit for roasting. Reasonably priced Wadworths IPA, JCB and 6X are well kept on handpump, and there's a decent choice of good value wines. The long-serving landlord and his family are very friendly, and the atmosphere is particularly welcoming. Big helpings of good bar food (with fresh vegetables and tasty chips) include salmon roulade (£4.95), good vegetarian dishes such as wild mushroom lasagne or lemon and thyme risotto (£7.50), breaded scampi (£7.95), chicken breast stuffed with wild mushrooms wrapped in bacon with red wine sauce or 8oz sirloin steak (£9.95), salmon with cream, wine and garlic sauce (£10.95), and duck breast with plum and ginger sauce (£11.95), with home-made puddings such as bread and butter pudding and raspberry and hazelnut roulade (£4.50); they also do snacks such as sandwiches (from £2.50), baguettes (from £4.75), and ploughman's (from £4.95). It does get busy, so you might think of booking. The barn restaurant is no smoking. There are picnic-sets with umbrellas in the lovely back garden (which has plenty of space to run round), as well as a play area with swings; a bench in front overlooks the main street. This is a nice area for walking. *(Recommended by R Huggins, D Irving, E McCall, T McLean, David and Nina Pugsley, Mrs Jean Clarke, P R and S A White, Joan and Michel Hooper-Immins, Robert W Tapsfield, Dr and Mrs M E Wilson, Roger and Jenny Huggins, Mr and Mrs R W Allan, Richard and Margaret Peers, Mr and Mrs C R Little, Alan and Paula McCully, Mrs D Littler, Richard Fendick, Andrew Shore, Dr and Mrs A K Clarke, Penny and Peter Keevil, Fiona Eddleston, Edward Mirzoeff)*

Wadworths ~ Tenant John Glass ~ Real ale ~ Bar food (not Sun) ~ Restaurant ~ (01249) 730263 ~ Children in eating area of bar and family room ~ Open 10-2.30, 5-11; 10-11 Fri/Sat; 10-10.30 Sun

Red Lion

High Street

This imposing Georgian inn is handy for a drink after a visit to nearby Lacock Abbey or the Fox Talbot Museum. Divided into cosy areas by open handrails, the long and airy cream-painted bar has distressed heavy dark wood tables and tapestried chairs. There are turkey rugs on the partly flagstoned floor, a fine old log fire at one end, aged-looking paintings, and branding irons hanging from the ceiling. The snug is very cosy, with comfortable leather armchairs. Wadworths IPA, JCB, 6X and one of their seasonal beers are well kept on handpump, and they've several malt whiskies; fruit machine and piped music. The atmosphere is pubby and lively, especially towards the end of the evening, when the pub is popular with younger visitors. Good friendly staff serve tasty bar food such as soup (£2.50), sandwiches (from £3.55), ploughman's (£5.50), crab cakes (£4.25), nut cutlets (£5.95), chicken kiev (£6.95), poached cod fillet with tomato pesto and chilli sauce or venison steak with red wine sauce (£9.95), daily specials such as beef and stilton pie or lamb and apricot casserole (£6.95), and puddings such as sticky toffee pudding (£3.25); the top dining area is no smoking. The pub is owned by the National Trust. *(Recommended by R Huggins, D Irving, E McCall, T McLean, George Atkinson, John Robertson, Tony and Mary Pygott, Michael Doswell)*

Wadworths ~ Manager Chris Chappell ~ Real ale ~ Bar food (not evenings 24, 26, and 31 Dec) ~ Restaurant ~ (01249) 730456 ~ Children in eating area of bar and restaurant ~ Dogs allowed in bar ~ Open 11.30-2.30, 6-11; 11.30-11 Sat; 12-10.30 Sun; 11.30-2.30, 6-11(10.30)Sat/Sun in winter ~ Bedrooms: £55B/£75B

Rising Sun 🍺

Bewley Common, Bowden Hill – out towards Sandy Lane, up hill past Abbey; OS Sheet 173 map reference 935679

You'll find the full range of Moles beers on handpump at this cheerily unpretentious pub (and if you can't decide which one to have the friendly staff will probably offer you a taster): Moles Tap Bitter, Best, Molecatcher, Molennium and one of their seasonal ales are well kept alongside a guest such as Rebellion IPA, and they stock farm cider too. It's a good place to enjoy the sunset – views from the big two-level terrace extend around 25 miles over the Avon valley; there's also a children's play area. Inside, the three welcoming little rooms have been knocked together to form one simply furnished area, with a mix of old chairs and basic kitchen tables on stone floors, stuffed animals and birds, country pictures, and open fires; darts, cribbage, dominoes, board games and piped music. Good helpings of home-made bar food include baguettes (from £3.50), ploughman's (£3.95), ham and egg (£5.95), cod and chips or cajun chicken (£6.50), with specials such as salmon steak or mixed mushrooms in brandy sauce (£7.95), and beef kebab with pepper sauce (£8.95); readers like their stir fries, and they do children's meals (£3.50). On Sundays, they do only roasts. *(Recommended by R Huggins, D Irving, E McCall, T McLean, Pat and Tony Martin, Dr and Mrs M E Wilson, Martin and Karen Wake, Andrew Barker, Claire Jenkins, Mike Gorton, Richard Pierce)*

Moles ~ Tenants Roger Catte, Peter and Michelle Eaton ~ Real ale ~ Bar food (12-2, 6-9; 12-2.30, 6-8 Sun; not Mon) ~ (01249) 730363 ~ Children welcome ~ Dogs welcome ~ Live entertainment every Weds and alternate Suns ~ Open 12-3, 6-11; 12-11 Sat/Sun; closed Mon lunchtime

LITTLE CHEVERELL ST9853 Map 2

Owl 🍺

Low Road; just off B3098 Westbury—Upavon, W of A360

This cosy little village local is especially nice in summer when you can sit out on the big raised deck, which looks out over a lovely tall ash- and willow-lined back garden, with rustic picnic-sets on a long split-level lawn running down to a brook. The friendly licensees have recently redecorated inside: the bar and a snugger room at the back have black beams, a pleasant jumble of furnishings including a big welsh dresser and bench table, plenty of chairs, stools, high-backed settles and tables, and farm tools on the beige walls. There are fresh flowers on the tables, local papers and guides to read, and a gently ticking clock; piped music. Bar food might include sandwiches and toasties (£4.95), soup (£3.50), ploughman's, salmon and dill fishcakes or pizza (£6.95), stuffed sweet peppers or chicken breast in white wine and stilton sauce (£8.95), seafood pasta (£9.95), and steaks (from £10.95), with specials such as fried skate wing with butter and capers (£14.95), and puddings such as apple and orange pie or home-made treacle tart (from £3.50); Sunday roast (from £6.95). Well kept Brakspeare, Hook Norton and Wadworths 6X with a guest such as Cotleigh Tawny on handpump (they hold around three beer festivals a year), 21 wines by the glass, and 21 malt whiskies. *(Recommended by Dennis Jenkin)*

Free house ~ Licensees Jamie Carter and Paul Green ~ Real ale ~ Bar food (12-3, 7-10; all day in summer) ~ Restaurant ~ (01380) 812263 ~ Children welcome ~ Dogs welcome ~ Quiz first Weds of month ~ Open 11-11; 12-11(10.30 Sun) Sat; 11-3, 6.30-11 Mon-Sat in winter; 12-4, 7-10.30 Sun in winter ~ Bedrooms: /£50S

LOWER CHUTE SU3153 Map 2

Hatchet

The Chutes well signposted via Appleshaw off A342, 2½ miles W of Andover

One of the county's most attractive pubs, this 16th-c thatched cottage has an unchanging, friendly local atmosphere. The very low-beamed bar has a mix of captain's chairs and cushioned wheelbacks around oak tables, and a splendid 17th-c fireback in the huge fireplace (which has a roaring log fire in winter). Helpful staff serve well kept Otter and Timothy Taylors Landlord, with a guest such as Ringwood Best on handpump, and they have a range of country wines; newspapers, cribbage, dominoes; there may be piped music. Tasty bar food includes around six vegetarian dishes such as jambalaya, aubergine and two-cheese ravioli, and spinach and red pepper lasagne (£6.95), as well as baguettes (from £3.95), home-made soup (£3.75), mushrooms in port with mozzarella (£4.75), ploughman's (£5.25), lamb tagine or thai green chicken curry (£7.25), and tiger prawns in filo pastry or smoked salmon salad (£7.50); they also do daily specials, and a good value Sunday roast. Thursday night is curry night, when you can eat as much as you like (£6.95); no smoking restaurant. There are seats out on a terrace by the front car park, or on the side grass, and a children's sandpit. They have only twin bedrooms. *(Recommended by Phyl and Jack Street, James Woods, Ian Phillips, Rob Webster, Lynn Sharpless, Mrs J H S Lang, Mr and Mrs R Davies, Bill and Jessica Ritson)*

Free house ~ Licensee Jeremy McKay ~ Real ale ~ Bar food ~ Restaurant ~ (01264) 730229 ~ Children in eating area of bar and restaurant ~ Dogs allowed in bar ~ Open 11.30-3, 6-11; 12-3.30, 7-10.30 Sun ~ Bedrooms: /£50S

The 🍺 symbol shows pubs which keep their beer unusually well or have a particularly good range.

MALMESBURY ST9287 Map 2
Smoking Dog ◖

High Street

They've recently extended the garden (which has pleasant views out over the town) at this double-fronted mid-terrace 17th-c pub. Seven well kept real ales include Brains Bitter, Revd James and SA and Wadworths 6X either tapped straight from the cask or on handpump, and a couple of guests such as Orkney Red MacGregor and Woodfordes Norfolk Nog; piped music, TV, Scrabble, dominoes and so forth. The two smallish front bars have a good friendly local atmosphere (with a younger crowd on some evenings), with flagstones, dark woodwork, cushioned bench seating, big pine tables and a blazing log fire. A flagstoned corridor with local notices on the walls leads to a bare-boards back bistro. As well as a lunchtime snack menu with baguettes and ciabattas (from £4.95 – the bacon and swiss cheese is a favourite with some readers), home-made beefburger (£6.95) and grilled smoked haddock fillet with cheddar and ale (£7.95), bar food promptly served by friendly, helpful staff might include grilled rib-eye steak with spicy butter (£10.95), red snapper with stem ginger, spring onions and lemon syrup (£11.95), and daily specials such as ham, mushroom and cream pasta (£7.25), and beef medallions with stilton and black pepper (£15.25), with puddings such as apple and blackcurrant crumble or brown sugar pavlova with raspberries and clotted cream (£4.25); on Sunday they do roasts (£6.95), and the menu is more limited. *(Recommended by Dr and Mrs A K Clarke, James Woods, Jenny and Brian Seller)*

Brains ~ Managers Ian and Sara Shackleton ~ Real ale ~ Bar food (12-2, 7-9.30) ~ Restaurant ~ (01666) 825823 ~ Children welcome if eating ~ Dogs allowed in bar ~ Open 11.30-11; 12-10.30 Sun; closed 25 Dec evening

NEWTON TONY SU2140 Map 2
Malet Arms ◖

Village signposted off A338 Swindon—Salisbury

Peacefully placed in a quiet village, this tiled flintstone pub is immediately welcoming, with a pleasant landlord (who's crazy about cricket), efficient cheerful younger staff, and a good log and coal fire in a huge fireplace (as the paintwork between the black beams suggests, it can smoke a bit if the wind's strongly in the east). Nice furnishings include a mix of different-sized tables with high winged wall settles, carved pews, chapel and carver chairs, and there are lots of pictures mainly from Imperial days. The main front windows are said to have come from the stern of a ship. The good food is served in a similar room on the left, or in the attractive and homely back dining room on the right. Listed on a blackboard, interesting, well prepared dishes could include soup (£4.25), stilton rarebit with cherry tomatoes, rocket and walnuts (£5.95), spicy lamb and pea samosas with mango and coriander relish (£6), goats cheese and filo pastry croustade with apricot and pine nuts (£12.50), chicken supreme wrapped in smoked bacon with a toasted muffin and chive butter sauce or steamed mussels and asparagus in white wine, garlic and cream with tagliatelle (£13.50), and roast rack of lamb with aubergines, sun-dried tomatoes and basil oil (£15.50), with home-made puddings (£4); in winter they do Sunday roasts (£7.95), while in summer the menu includes locally smoked food. You'll find well kept Butts Barbus Barbus, Stonehenge Heelstone, Wadworths 6X and a guest beer, usually from a fairly local brewer such as Archers or Ringwood, tapped from the cask or on handpump; as well as decent wines, they've quite a few nice malt whiskies, also an espresso machine. The two pub jack russells are called Badger and Piper, and they've recently acquired an african grey parrot called Steerpike. There are old-fashioned garden seats on the small front terrace, with some picnic-sets on the grass there, and more in a back garden which has a new wendy house. The pub looks over a chalk stream that you ford to drive to it (though it's best to use an alternative route in winter, when it can be quite deep), with a playing field opposite, and chickens and a horse paddock out behind. More reports on this nice pub, please. *(Recommended by Miss M W Hayter, Colin Moore, J R and J Moon, Mike Gorton)*

Free house ~ Licensee Noel Cardew ~ Real ale ~ Bar food (12-2.30, 6.30-10) ~ Restaurant ~ (01980) 629279 ~ Children in restaurant and family room ~ Dogs allowed in bar ~ Open 11-3, 6-11; 12-3, 7-10.30 Sun

NORTON ST8884 Map 2
Vine Tree ⑪ ♀

4 miles from M4 junction 17; A429 towards Malmesbury, then left at Hullavington, Sherston signpost, then follow Norton signposts; in village turn right at Foxley signpost, which takes you into Honey Lane

From an impressive list, they do around 25 wines by the glass at this civilised dining pub, which is housed in an attractively converted 18th-c mill house. The food here is imaginative and popular, so it's best to book, especially at weekends. The wide-ranging, seasonally changing menu could include vegetarian dishes such as melting blue cheese tart (£4.95), woodland mushroom and feta risotto (£8.50), and lemon grass, ginger and fresh parmesan cake with wilted spinach and sweet potato curry (£11.95), as well as smoked eel (£6.50), trio of local sausages with bubble and squeak and grain mustard and honey sauce (£9.95), seared calves liver with grain mustard and tarragon creamed potatoes and raspberry vinegar sauce or venison and juniper pie (£11.95), pot-roast partridge with white bean casserole (£12.95), griddled fresh squid with squid ink tagliatelle and tarragon and porcini mushroom velouté (£10.95), and gilt head bream fillets with lemon grass and sweet basil broth (£12.95); they also bake their own good bread, and do baguettes and a fine Sunday roast. One dining area is no smoking. Although the emphasis is on eating, there's a buoyant atmosphere, and drinkers do pop in for just a pint of well kept Wychwood Fiddlers Elbow or Youngs; service is very friendly and accommodating. Three beautifully kept little rooms open together, with limited edition and sporting prints, a mock-up mounted pig's mask (used for a game that involves knocking coins off its nose and ears), lots of stripped pine, big church candles on the tables (the lighting's very gentle), and some old settles. There are picnic-sets in a two-acre garden which includes a pretty walled terrace with a lion fountain and urns of flowers, a good well fenced separate play area with a fine thatched fortress, and three boules pitches; look out for the friendly pub dog. As it's not the easiest place to find, it feels more remote than its proximity to the motorway would suggest.
(Recommended by R Huggins, D Irving, E McCall, T McLean, Andrew Shore, Esther and John Sprinkle, Betsy and Peter Little, Mike Pugh, Ann Lewis, Jane Legate, Mike Turner, Mrs Sally Lloyd, Dr and Mrs A K Clarke, Simon King)

Free house ~ Licensees Charles Walker and Tiggi Wood ~ Real ale ~ Bar food (12-2(3 Sun), 7-9.30) ~ Restaurant ~ (01666) 837654 ~ Children welcome ~ Dogs welcome ~ Open 12-3, 6-11; 12-10.30 Sun

PITTON SU2131 Map 2
Silver Plough ♀

Village signposted from A30 E of Salisbury (follow brown tourist signs)

There are masses of things to look at in the comfortable front bar of this pleasant country dining pub: hundreds of antique boot-warmers and stretchers, pewter and china tankards, copper kettles, toby jugs, earthenware and glass rolling pins, painted clogs, glass net-floats, and coach horns and so forth hang from the black beams. Seats on the turkey carpet include half a dozen red-velvet-cushioned antique oak settles (one elaborately carved, beside a very fine reproduction of an Elizabethan oak table), and the timbered white walls are hung with Thorburn and other game bird prints, original Craven Hill sporting cartoons, and a big naval battle glass-painting. The back bar is simpler, but still has a big winged high-backed settle, cased antique guns, substantial pictures, and – like the front room – flowers on its tables. They've well kept Badger IPA, Best, Tanglefoot and a guest on handpump under light blanket pressure, a fine wine list including 10 by the glass and some well priced and carefully chosen bottles, a good range of country wines, and a worthy choice of spirits. Generously served home-made food includes baguettes (from £4.50), ploughman's (£5.50), sliced duck breast salad (£5.95; £9.95 main), beef or roasted vegetable lasagne (£7.95), home-made steak and kidney pie (£8.50), with evening dishes such as mushrooms and chorizo in cream sauce (£4.25), cod with a cheese crust and parsley sauce (£9.95), and calves liver with mustard grain mash and pancetta (£11.95), with daily specials, and home-made puddings (£3.95). On Sunday the menu is more limited, and they do a choice of roasts (£8.95); children's meals (from £3.95). The restaurant is no smoking. There's a skittle alley next to the snug bar; cribbage, dominoes, shove-ha'penny, and piped music. A quiet lawn has picnic-sets and other tables under cocktail parasols, and there are good downland and woodland walks nearby. *(Recommended by Ken and Barbara Turner, Phyl and Jack Street, W W Burke, Dennis Jenkin, Gordon Prince, Susan and John Douglas, OPUS)*

Badger ~ Tenant Hughen Riley ~ Real ale ~ Bar food (12-2, 7-9(9.30Fri/Sat); 12-2, 6.30-8.30 Sun) ~ Restaurant ~ (01722) 712266 ~ Children in snug ~ Dogs allowed in bar ~ Open 11-3, 6-11; 12-3.30, 6.30-10.30 Sat; 12-3, 7-10.30 Sun ~ Bedrooms: /£50S

POULSHOT ST9559 Map 2
Raven 🍺

Village signposted off A361 Devizes—Seend

Well kept Wadworths IPA, JCB and 6X are tapped straight from the cask at this classic country pub, which is prettily placed across from the village green. Two intimate black-beamed rooms are well furnished with sturdy tables and chairs and comfortable banquettes, and the attractive dining room is no smoking. Readers enjoy the bar food, which is carefully prepared by the landlord; generously served, it might include sandwiches (from £3.10), home-made soup (£3.20), ploughman's (from £4.25), creamy garlic and herb mushrooms or chicken terrine (£4.45), mushroom stroganoff (£7.45), battered cod or steak and kidney pie (£8), grilled lamb steak with port and redcurrant sauce (£9.95), and daily specials such as fried lambs liver with bacon and onions (£8.15), and delicious lamb and apricots or mexican beef (£8.40), with good puddings such as home-made dutch apple pie or redcurrant and raspberry cheesecake (from £3.40). The gents' is outside.
(Recommended by Mary Rayner, Mr and Mrs J Brown, Keith and Sheila Baxter, Mary and Dennis Jones, John Beeken, Alan and Paula McCully)

Wadworths ~ Tenants Philip and Susan Henshaw ~ Real ale ~ Bar food ~ Restaurant ~ (01380) 828271 ~ Children in restaurant ~ Dogs allowed in bar ~ Open 11-2.30, 6.30-11; 12-3, 7-10.30 Sun; closed Mon except bank hol lunchtime, 25 Dec, evenings 26, 31 Dec and 1 Jan

ROWDE ST9762 Map 2
George & Dragon 🍽 🍷

A342 Devizes—Chippenham

An excellent choice of seafood is delivered fresh from Cornwall to this attractive old dining pub – a great place for a meal after a walk along the nearby Kennet & Avon Canal. The menu changes seasonally (and the quality and price of the meals are what you'd expect of an upmarket restaurant) but might include provençale fish soup (£5), fish hors-d'oeuvres (£7), warm scallop and bacon salad or roasted razor clams with garlic and olive oil (£8; £16 main), steamed skate with capers and black butter (£12) and monkfish with green peppercorns, brandy and cream (£16), and if you don't like fish you can choose from dishes such as aubergine mezze (£4.50), cheese soufflé (£5; £9 main), lamb korma (£8.50), duck breast with roasted butternut squash or fillet steak (£16); puddings such as walnut, pecan and brazil nut tart (£5) or west country cheeses (£6.50). No smoking dining room; if Ralph the ginger tom is around he may try to help you finish your meal. Tastefully furnished with plenty of dark wood, the bar has a log fire with a fine collection of brass keys by it, while the bare-floored dining room has quite plain tables and chairs, and is close enough to the bar to keep a pleasant chatty atmosphere. You'll find a couple of changing well kept real ales on handpump from breweries such as Butcombe and Milk Street, and they have organic cider, and continental beers and lagers; shove-ha'penny, cribbage and dominoes. *(Recommended by Jane and Graham Rooth, Tina and David Woods-Taylor, Pamela and Merlyn Horswell, Neville and Anne Morley, Mary Rayner, Richard Pierce)*

Free house ~ Licensees Tim and Helen Withers ~ Real ale ~ Bar food (not Sun or Mon) ~ Restaurant ~ (01380) 723053 ~ Children in restaurant till 9.30 ~ Dogs allowed in bar ~ Open 12-3, 7-11(10.30 Sun); closed Mon lunchtime, 1 Jan

SALISBURY SU1429 Map 2
Haunch of Venison
Minster Street, opposite Market Cross

The two tiny downstairs rooms of this ancient pub are quite spit-and-sawdust in spirit, with massive beams in the ochre ceiling, stout red-cushioned oak benches built into the timbered walls, genuinely old pictures, black and white floor tiles, and an open fire. A tiny snug opens off the entrance lobby. The quiet and cosy panelled upper dining room has a small-paned window looking down on to the main bar, antique leather-seat settles, a nice carved oak chair nearly 300 years old, and a splendid fireplace that dates back to the building's early years; behind glass in a small wall slit is the smoke-preserved mummified hand of an 18th-c card sharp still clutching his cards. Courage Best and Directors and Wadworths 6X are served on handpump from a unique pewter bar counter, with a rare set of antique taps for gravity-fed spirits and liqueurs. They've also over 50 malt whiskies, decent wines, and a range of brandies; chess, dominoes and piped music. Bar food such as baguettes (£4.25), soup (£2.95), duck and port terrine with red onion marmalade (£4.35), venison sausages and mash (£8.95), chicken breast with bacon, white butter sauce, sautée potatoes and courgettes (£10.55), and beef fillet with black pepper sauce, potato rösti and courgettes (£15.95); children's menu (£4.95). One area in the restaurant is no smoking. The pub was constructed over 650 years ago to house craftsmen working on the cathedral spire. *(Recommended by M and N Watson, Colin and Janet Roe, Ann and Colin Hunt, Gordon Tong, the Didler, Andrea Rampley, Dr and Mrs M E Wilson, Ian Phillips, Susan and John Douglas, Emma Kingdon, Dr and Mrs A K Clarke, John Robertson, Rob Webster, I D Greenfield)*

Scottish Courage ~ Lease Antony and Victoria Leroy ~ Real ale ~ Bar food (12-2, 6-9, not Sun evening in winter) ~ Restaurant ~ (01722) 322024 ~ Children in eating area of bar and restaurant ~ Dogs allowed in bar ~ Open 11-11; 12-10 Sun; closed 1 and 2 Jan

SEEND ST9461 Map 2
Barge
Seend Cleeve; signposted off A361 Devizes—Trowbridge, between Seend village and signpost to Seend Head

This attractive canalside pub gets extremely busy when the weather's fine, and no wonder – the neatly kept waterside garden is an ideal place to watch the bustle of boats on the Kennet & Avon Canal; old streetlamps let you linger there after dark, and moorings by the humpy bridge are very handy for thirsty bargees. Inside, the bar has a big log fire, an unusual barge-theme décor, and intricately painted Victorian flowers which cover the ceilings and run in a waist-high band above the deep green lower walls. A distinctive mix of attractive seats includes milk churns and the occasional small oak settle among the rugs on the parquet floor, while the walls have big sentimental engravings. The watery theme continues with a well stocked aquarium, and there's also a pretty Victorian fireplace, big bunches of dried flowers, and red velvet curtains for the big windows; fruit machine and piped music. The well kept real ales consist of Butcombe, Wadworths IPA and 6X and a guest such as Charles Wells Bombardier on handpump, and they also have lots of malt whiskies, good coffee, around half a dozen wines by the glass, and mulled wine in winter. Changing bar food could include lunchtime sandwiches (£3.50;

soup and a sandwich £5.95), filled baked potatoes (from £5.25), various pies (from £8.50), irish stew (£9), and sirloin steak (£12.50), with evening dishes such as beer-battered brie with caramel and citrus sauce (£5), chicken, ham and mushrooms topped with puff pastry (£9), confit of duck with a herb scone, coated with sweet plum, ginger and port sauce (£11.50), and stuffed lemon sole with white wine and dill sauce (£13.50); service can slow at busy times. The restaurant extension is no smoking. They recommend booking for meals, especially at weekends; at the busiest times you may even find queues to get in the car park. *(Recommended by Pat and Robert Watt, Alan and Paula McCully, Clifford Payton, Susan and Nigel Wilson, John and Elizabeth Cox, Joyce and Maurice Cottrell, P R and S A White, M G Hart, James Woods, Michael Doswell, W F C Phillips, Dr and Mrs M E Wilson, Brian and Anita Randall, Kevin Thorpe)*

Wadworths ~ Tenant Christopher Moorley Long ~ Real ale ~ Bar food (12-2, 7-9.30(10 Fri, Sat)) ~ Restaurant ~ (01380) 828230 ~ Children welcome ~ Dogs allowed in bar ~ Open 11-4, 6-11; 11-11 Sat; 12-10.30 Sun

SEMLEY ST8926 Map 2
Benett Arms ♀

Turn off A350 N of Shaftesbury at Semley Ind Estate signpost, then turn right at Semley signpost

The cheerful, friendly landlord (who's been here for almost 30 years) fosters a welcoming atmosphere at this white-painted country pub. Lovely and cosy in winter, two hospitable rooms are separated by three carpeted steps, and are furnished with one or two settles and pews, a deep leather sofa and chairs, hunting prints, carriage lamps for lighting, a pendulum wall clock, and ornaments on the mantelpiece over the log fire; there's a thatched-roof servery in the flagstoned bar, and a dark panelling dado in the carpeted upstairs area. From a changing menu, enjoyable well presented bar food could include soup (£3.95), home-made chicken liver pâté (£4.95), steak and kidney pie or local sausage on creamy mash with onion gravy (£7.95), chicken breast filled with stilton with creamed leeks (£9.95), and scotch sirloin steak (£12.95), with specials such as courgette, tomato and cheese lasagne (£7.95), baked salmon with lemon sauce (£8.95), and fried duck breast with honey and caramelised red cabbage (£10.95), and puddings such as lemon and ginger crunch or chocolate toffee pecan pie (£3.45); they do a set lunch on Sunday (£9.95 two courses; £12.95 three courses). Half the dining room is no smoking. Real ales on handpump (served by pleasant staff) include Brakspears, Ringwood Best and Youngs, also farm cider, 10 malt whiskies, lots of liqueurs, and a thoughtfully chosen wine list, including a good few by the glass; piped music, juke box, TV, cribbage and dominoes. This is a lovely spot right on the Dorset border; you can sit out at tables on the pretty village green with its millennium pond, just across the road. *(Recommended by P Tailyour, Ann and Colin Hunt, Mrs J H S Lang, Roger and Pauline Pearce, Dr and Mrs J F Head, Colin and Janet Roe, MP, Ian Phillips, Anne Jennings)*

Enterprise ~ Lease Joe and Jill Duthie ~ Real ale ~ Bar food (12-2.30, 7-9.45) ~ Restaurant ~ (01747) 830221 ~ Children welcome ~ Dogs allowed in bar and bedrooms ~ Open 11-11; 11-4, 7-10.30 Sun; closed 25/26 Dec ~ Bedrooms: £38S/£60S(£60B)

STOURTON ST7734 Map 2
Spread Eagle

Church Lawn; follow Stourhead brown signs off B3092, N of junction with A303 just W of Mere

Caring hardworking staff and licensees help create a civilised and welcoming atmosphere at this lovely old pub. Owned by the National Trust, it's in a delightful setting among other elegant National Trust stone buildings at the head of Stourhead Lake. The attractively decorated interior has antique panel-back settles, a mix of new and old solid tables and chairs, handsome fireplaces with good winter log fires, smoky old sporting prints, prints of Stourhead, and standard lamps or brass swan's-neck wall lamps. One room by the entrance has armchairs, a longcase clock and a corner china cupboard. They do a very good choice of sandwiches (from £1.95), ploughman's (from £4.95), and salads (£5.95), while other enjoyable, reasonably priced dishes could include soup (£2.95), spaghetti bolognese (£5.95), steak and kidney pie (£6.50), and a couple of daily specials such as beef stew (£4.95), cottage pie (£5.95), and chicken with leeks and mushrooms (£6.50). The more elaborate evening menu might typically include sautéed mushrooms with bacon, red wine and cream (£4.25), wild mushroom and cashew stroganoff (£9.95), whole baked plaice with garlic and herb butter (£11.95), and rack of lamb with rösti potatoes and honey and lemon sauce (£12.95). Well kept Courage Best and Wadworths 6X on handpump. There are benches in the courtyard behind. *(Recommended by Geoffrey G Lawrance, John and Jane Hayter, John and Glenys Wheeler, Ann and Colin Hunt, John and Joan Nash, Mike and Mona Clifford, Patricia Theodorou, Mr and Mrs McKay, Geoff Palmer, Colin and Janet Roe, S P Watkin, P A Taylor)*

Free house ~ Licensee Andy Martin ~ Real ale ~ Bar food (12-3, 6-9; cold dishes 12-9) ~ Restaurant (evening) ~ (01747) 840587 ~ Children welcome ~ Open 11-11; 12-10.30 Sun ~ Bedrooms: £60B/£90B

UPTON SCUDAMORE ST8647 Map 2
Angel ♀ ◧ ⇁

Village signposted off A350 N of Warminster

Bare boards, pine tables, country-kitchen and other simple chairs, terracotta walls and rather clattery acoustics make for a bustling modern feel throughout this big dining pub, despite the log fire, and the Spy and other cricketing caricatures and naïve farm animal pictures in the bar, with its shiny newish rafters. On each side of the counter, steps take you down to a long two-part dining room, similar in style except that its pictures (lots of them, for sale) are contemporary. There's a big emphasis on the skilfully prepared food (and you can watch the chefs at work in the kitchen). Good lunchtime dishes might include home-made soup (£2.95), grilled sardines with hazelnut and chilli butter or steamed mussels in mild curry sauce (£4.95; £7.95 large), salmon fishcakes with buttered spinach and parsley velouté or green thai chicken curry (£7.50), and deep-fried cod (£7.95), with evening dishes such as smoked cheddar fritters with red chard salad and quince jelly (£4.95), poached smoked haddock with parmesan gratin, poached egg, caper and parsley velouté (£12.75), and roast rack of lamb with baby fennel and black olive jus (£14.75), with specials such as saddle of lamb with aubergine ragoût and chorizo (£13.95), and bass stuffed with smoked salmon mousse (£14.25); puddings could include sticky toffee pudding with caramel sauce (£4.25). Friendly and professional staff serve well kept Butcombe, Wadworths 6X and a frequently changing guest beer on handpump, and there's a good changing wine choice; piped music, TV, cribbage and dominoes. There are teak tables out on a sheltered flagstoned back terrace with a big barbecue. The well equipped bedrooms (even with CD players) are in a separate house across the car park. *(Recommended by Christine and Neil Townend, Ron Shelton, Suzanne, Mike Gorton, Matthew Shackle)*

Free house ~ Licensees Carol and Tony Coates ~ Real ale ~ Bar food (12-2, 7-9.30 (9 Sun)) ~ Restaurant ~ (01985) 213225 ~ Children welcome ~ Dogs allowed in bar ~ Open 11-3, 6-11; 12-3, 7-10.30 Sun ~ Bedrooms: £60B/£75B

WHITLEY ST8866 Map 2
Pear Tree ⑪ ♀

Off B3353 S of Corsham, at Atworth 1½, Purlpit 1 signpost; or from A350 Chippenham—Melksham in Beanacre turn off on Westlands Lane at Whitley 1 signpost, then left and right at B3353

Although the emphasis at this honey-coloured stone farmhouse is on the imaginative food, you'll be made to feel welcome if all you want is a drink – and they've a good choice. They serve around 25 or so decent wines by the glass (including champagne), along with well kept Wadworths 6X, and a couple of changing guests such as Mauldons Moletrap and Stonehenge Pigswill; lots of speciality teas too. The front bar has quite a pubby feel, with cushioned window seats, some stripped shutters, a mix of dining chairs around good solid tables, a variety of country pictures and a Wiltshire Regiment sampler on the walls, a little fireplace on the left, and a lovely old stripped stone one on the right. Candlelit at night, the popular but unhurried big back restaurant (you may need to book) has green dining chairs, quite a mix of tables, and a pitched ceiling at one end with a quirky farmyard theme – wrought-iron cockerels and white scythe sculpture. A bright spacious garden room opens on to a terrace with good teak furniture and views over the carefully maintained gardens, which are prettily lit at night to show features like the ruined pigsty; boules. Skilfully cooked dishes might include crispy pork belly with shaved fennel, rocket, lemon and capers (£5.50), smoked salmon and paprika fishcake with pickled cucumber salad (£5.50; £8.95 main), pork and herb sausages with grain mustard mash and red onion tempura (£9.50), thai monkfish, salmon and mussel curry with bok choi and braised wild rice (£14.95), and lamb rump with garlic mash and roast ratatouille (£16.50), with specials such as tagliatelle with asparagus spears, goats cheese and pine kernels (£8.75), and grilled skate wing with haricot bean and caper cassoulet, mint and lemon oil (£12.50), and puddings such as red berry and chardonnay jelly with rice pudding ice cream or dark chocolate sponge pudding with roasted pistachios and clotted cream (from £4.50); they do a two-course Sunday lunch (£12.50; £14.95 for three courses). There are eight new bedrooms, some in an old barn and some above the pub; we'd expect these to be nice, and would be very interested to hear from readers who have stayed here. (*Recommended by Dr and Mrs M E Wilson, Richard and Judy Winn, Mike and Heather Watson, Mr and Mrs C R Little, Mike and Mona Clifford, Rob Webster, Mrs Sally Lloyd, John Hale, John and Jane Hayter, Alistair Caie, Hilary McLean, Ian Phillips, Paul and Annette Hallett, Bill and Jessica Ritson, Di and Mike Gillam*)

Free house ~ Licensees Martin and Debbie Still and Mark Nacchia ~ Real ale ~ Bar food (12-2, 6.30-9.30(10 Fri/Sat); 12-2.30, 7-9.30 Sun) ~ Restaurant ~ (01225) 709131 ~ Children in restaurant ~ Dogs allowed in bar ~ Open 11-3, 6-11; 12-3, 7-10.30 Sun; closed 25/26 Dec ~ Bedrooms: £55B/£85B

WOODBOROUGH SU1159 Map 2
Seven Stars ♀

Off A345 S of Marlborough: from Pewsey follow Woodborough signposts, then in Woodborough bear left following Bottlesford signposts

A pleasant blend of traditional English pub with a strong gallic influence (the landlord's French), this pretty thatched red brick house is very popular for its food, although locals do pop in for a well kept pint; and there's also an exemplary wine list, with about 10 by the glass (including plenty of french), and interesting bin ends. As well as snacks such as soup (£3.95; fish soup £4.95), sandwiches (from £3.25), ploughman's or croque monsieur (£5.75), and mushroom stroganoff (£8.75), the good bar food includes regularly changing dishes such as smoked trout with horseradish sauce (£5.75), crevettes (£6.75; £12.75 main), fried calves liver with bacon and gravy or pork fillet with plums and armagnac (£12.75), and fillet of beef bourguignon (£15.75), with puddings such as lemon soufflé and raspberry crème brûlée (£3.95), and a french cheeseboard (£5.25); they receive regular deliveries from France, and do smaller helpings for children. The dining room is no smoking. The bar is traditionally furnished, with polished bricks by the bar counter, hunting prints, attractively moulded panelling, a hot coal fire in the old range at one end, a big log fire at the other, a pleasant mix of antique settles and country furniture, cast-iron-framed tables, and cosy nooks here and there. You'll find Badger Best, Fullers London Pride and Wadworths 6X on handpump; sophisticated piped music. There are seven acres of riverside gardens; they've an alsatian, a friendly white west highland terrier and a black cat (who may try to get at milk left on tables). Please note, the pub shuts on Tuesdays following bank holiday Mondays. (*Recommended by Dr and Mrs M E Wilson, Mike and Heather Watson, Peter and Giff Bennett, Adam and Joan Bunting, Aidan MacDonald, W J MacWilliam, Mike and Mary Carter*)

Free house ~ Licensees Philippe and Kate Cheminade ~ Real ale ~ Bar food ~ Restaurant ~ (01672) 851325 ~ Well behaved children in restaurant and family room ~ Dogs allowed in bar ~ Open 12-3, 6-11; 12-3 Sun; closed Sun evening, all day Mon except bank hol lunchtime, then closed Tues

WYLYE SU0037 Map 4

Bell 🍴 ▣ 🛏

Just off A303/A36 junction; High Street

The friendly, attentive staff and charming licensees make readers feel at home in this cosy little 14th-c country pub, prettily set in a peaceful village. With a civilised unhurried atmosphere, the neatly kept, black-beamed front bar has a log fire, and sturdy rustic furnishings that go well with the stripped stonework and neat timbered herringbone brickwork; don't try counting the bells – there are more than 1,100 of them, from all over the world. The comfortably carpeted no smoking restaurant with pristine white linen has a more sophisticated feel. Very good bar food includes sandwiches (from £3.50), soup (£3.95), mussels in white wine and cream or locally smoked trout with haloumi cheese (£6.95), ploughman's, lasagne or pork and leek sausages with cheddar mash and roasted red onions (£7.95), and sirloin steak (£12.95), with specials such as smooth duck terrine (£4.95) or crayfish tails in herb garlic butter (£5.95), and puddings such as baked rice pudding or apple crumble (£4.95); children's meals (£3.95). The four well kept real ales come from far and wide but might typically include Butcombe Gold, Hop Back GFB, Ringwood Best and Stonehenge Danish Dynamite; piped music, cribbage and daily papers. There are seats outside on a pleasant walled terrace and in a back garden, which is attractively flanked by the church's clipped yews. The pub has fine downland walks nearby, and is about 15 minutes' drive from Stonehenge. *(Recommended by Susan and John Douglas, Shirley Mackenzie, John and Judy Saville, Peter Meister, Dr and Mrs M E Wilson, J and B Cressey, Mrs Pam Mattinson, Roger and Pauline Pearce, Mrs P Sarson, Andrea Rampley, Joyce and Geoff Robson, OPUS, Colin and Janet Roe, Pat and Robert Watt, Anthony Barnes, June and Robin Savage, Alan Kilpatrick, David Crook, Hazel Morgan, Stan and Hazel Allen, A S and M E Marriott)*

Free house ~ Licensees Keith and Linda Bidwell ~ Real ale ~ Bar food (12-2, 6-9.30; 12-2.30, 7-9 Sun) ~ Restaurant ~ (01985) 248338 ~ Children in restaurant ~ Dogs allowed in bar and bedrooms ~ Open 11.30-2.30, 6-11; 12-3, 7-10.30 Sun ~ Bedrooms: £35S(£35B)/£50S(£50B)

Lucky Dip

Besides the fully inspected pubs, you might like to try these Lucky Dips recommended to us and described by readers (if you do, please send us reports: www.goodguides.com).

ALDBOURNE [SU2675]
Blue Boar [The Green (off B4192)]: Inexpensive generous food from sandwiches up in nicely placed homely and relaxed pub with seats out facing pretty village green nr church and neatly kept small back country garden; three well kept Wadworths ales, good choice of wines and soft drinks, farm tools, boar's head and flame-effect woodburner in Tudor bar, extensive more modern back lounge/dining area; darts, quiet piped music; children welcome, open all day *(Mary Rayner, Mr and Mrs C F Turner, Peter Barnwell)*
AVEBURY [SU0969]
Red Lion [A361]: Much-modernised and substantially extended from pretty thatched front part, in the heart of the stone circles; quick friendly service, well kept ales such as Stonehenge and Wadworths 6X, open fires,

food bar, no smoking area and restaurant extension – huge choice inc Sun carvery; may be piped music *(LYM, Eleanor and Nick Steinitz, Richard Pierce)*
BADBURY [SU1980]
Plough [A346 just S of M4 junction 15]: Large rambling bar area, light and airy no smoking dining room (children allowed) looking over road to Vale of the White Horse with pianola and papers to read, well kept Arkells 2B, 3B and Kingsdown, decent wines, wide blackboard choice of usual food inc afternoon snacks, friendly efficient service; darts, piped music; children welcome, play area in sunny garden above, open all day *(CMW, JJW, Kevin Thorpe, Michael and Alison Sandy, Mark and Ruth Brock)*
BIDDESTONE [ST8673]
Biddestone Arms [off A420 W of Chippenham;

The Green]: Well kept roomy village pub, mostly set out for eating – simple choice of tasty generous food; good welcoming service, Wadworths 6X, games in cosy public bar, swings in small fairylit garden, attractive village with lovely pond *(Esther and John Sprinkle, BB)*

☆ *White Horse* [The Green]: Busy 16th-c village local, wide choice of sensibly priced well cooked food and filled rolls in unusual stencilled lounge and partly no smoking dining area, well kept Courage and Wadworths 6X, quick friendly service, small hatch-served bar with shove-ha'penny, darts and table skittles, games machine; children welcome; overlooks duckpond in picturesque village, tables in good garden with play area, aviary and rabbits; bedrooms *(Esther and John Sprinkle)*

BISHOPS CANNINGS [SU0364]

☆ *Crown* [Chandlers Lane; off A361 NE of Devizes]: Welcoming and unassuming refurbished two-bar local with wide choice of good value generous food, well kept Wadworths IPA and 6X, decent wines, upstairs dining room; shame about the piped music; dogs welcome, tables in garden behind, next to handsome old church in pretty village, walk to Kennet & Avon Canal *(John Beeken)*

BISHOPSTONE [SU2483]

Royal Oak [the one nr Swindon]: Two-bar local in beautiful village below Ridgeway and White Horse, some beams and oak panelling, wood floors, settles, bookshelves, prints on striped wallpaper; warm and friendly, with Arkells 2B and 3B, home-made food from good value baguettes to game and organic meat and burgers, cribbage, darts and chess, garden; quiz nights; picnic-sets in sizeable garden, bedrooms in outbuildings *(Guy Vowles)*

BRADFORD LEIGH [ST8362]

Plough [B2109 N of Bradford]: Moles and Wadworths 6X, good choice of sensible pub food, smart service, log fire; darts and pool; children welcome, nice seats outside, play area *(Susan and Nigel Wilson)*

BRADFORD-ON-AVON [ST8260]

Barge [Frome Rd]: Pub part (not on canal) with well kept Wadworths 6X, café (no real ale) with relaxing waterside garden and tables on own barge; friendly licensees, a welcome for children, well kept food inc lunchtime baguettes and some interesting dishes; sensibly priced bedrooms *(Esther and John Sprinkle, Peter and Audrey Dowsett, Keith Stevens)*

☆ *Beehive* [A363 out towards Trowbridge]: Simple cheerful old-fashioned L-shaped pub nr canal on outskirts, half a dozen interesting well kept ales on handpump or tapped from the cask, good service (can be delays on busy summer wknds), huge helpings of traditional food esp substantial sandwiches (some hot) with baskets of chips, good range of wines, 19th-c playbills, cricketing prints and cigarette cards, darts; children and dogs welcome, resident cats; attractive good-sized informal back garden, play area, barbecues *(Pete Baker, BB, Dr and Mrs M E Wilson, Gary Crabbe)*

☆ *Cross Guns* [Avoncliff, outside town]: The star is for its great position with floodlit terraced gardens above the bridges, aqueducts and river; the emphasis is on food piled high (with loudspeaker announcements out here) in the stripped-stone low-beamed bar with its 16th-c inglenook, and the upstairs river-view restaurant; well kept Bass, a house beer, Worthington and a guest beer, lots of malt whiskies and country wines; piped music, and the pub can get very busy indeed, when service and housekeeping can come under pressure; children welcome, open all day *(Peter and Audrey Dowsett, Ian Phillips, LYM, Andrew Shore, Richard Stancomb, R Huggins, D Irving, E McCall, T McLean, Roger and Pauline Pearce, Paul Hopton, Richard Pierce, Gloria Bax)*

Riverside [St Margarets St]: Old stone-built riverside pub, huge fireplace in big beamed bar, Badger Tanglefoot, Butcombe and Wadworths 6X, food inc decent baguettes, pool in large games room; tables out on gravel terrace hedged off from river *(Neil and Anita Christopher)*

Three Horseshoes [Frome Rd, by big car park nr station]: Good friendly licensees and staff, well kept mostly local beers, good substantial food, cosy and chatty front bar with plenty of nooks and corners, small restaurant; tables on terrace *(Ted George)*

BROAD CHALKE [SU0325]

Queens Head [Ebble Valley SW of Salisbury; North St]: Roomy, with heavy beams, inglenook with woodburner, padded settles and chairs, some stripped brickwork, wide range of home-made food from good sandwiches and baguettes to reasonably priced fish (very long-serving chef – Mon and Tues off), well kept Greene King IPA and Old Speckled Hen, Wadworths and a guest beer, decent wines, farm ciders and country wines, good coffee; may be piped music; wheelchair access from back car park, tables in pretty courtyard overlooked by comfortable well equipped bedrooms in newish separate block *(David and Elizabeth Briggs)*

BROKENBOROUGH [ST9189]

Rose & Crown: Restaurant popular for generous well cooked food, served well, esp steaks – must book Fri/Sat night; lively pub part *(James Woods)*

BROMHAM [ST9764]

Oliver Cromwell [A342]: Neatly kept pub with good value quickly served home-made bar food (should book for lunch – you can even order lobster), Sun lunch in restaurant, Wadworths real ales, vintage ciders, decent wines, friendly landlord, flowers on tables; fine view over Roundway Down Civil War battlefield – good small museum in bar *(Richard Pierce)*

BROUGHTON GIFFORD [ST8763]

☆ *Bell on the Common* [The Green]: Ancient and picturesque stone-built pub on huge village green, traditional furnishings, friendly service, home cooking using local organic meat, children's dishes and popular Sun roasts, well kept Wadworths and farm cider from handpumps on back wall, big coal fire, dining lounge full of copper and old country prints, bar with local photographs old and new, small pool room with darts and juke box; children welcome, charming garden (occasional pig roasts and live music), bowls club next door *(Dr and Mrs M E Wilson, Simon Heptinstall, Gloria Bax)*

BURCOMBE [SU0631]

Ship: Cosy two-level bar and no smoking dining area, two open fires, low beams, panelling and window seats, good choice of good value food, country wines; unobtrusive piped music; children welcome, tables on front terrace and in delightful riverside garden, beautiful village *(David Cuckney)*

BURTON [ST8179]

Old House At Home [B4039 Chippenham—Chipping Sodbury]: Spacious and attractive upscale stonebuilt dining pub, not cheap but flavoursome, with good-sized helpings and splendid puddings, log fire, well kept Wadworths, good choice of wines by the glass; piped music, cl Tues lunchtime *(Andrew Shore)*

CASTLE EATON [SU1495]

Red Lion [The Street]: Series of rooms, one with gentle lighting and quietly civilised atmosphere, another with juke box for younger customers, impressive new conservatory looking over shrubby garden to Thames, good blackboard choice of reasonably priced food, well kept real ales; children welcome in eating areas, popular with Thames Path walkers *(Peter and Audrey Dowsett, LYM, R Huggins, D Irving, E McCall, T McLean)*

CHARLTON [ST9588]

☆ *Horse & Groom* [B4040 towards Cricklade]: Wide choice of good generous food in smart but friendly stone-built inn's relaxing bar, old firearms, farm tools and log fire, simpler right-hand bar with hops on beams, friendly and considerate staff, well kept Archers and Wadworths, farm cider, decent wines, exotic Pimms; restaurant (good value Sun lunch), tables outside; dogs welcome, comfortable bedrooms *(Michael Doswell, LYM, Margaret and Roy Randle)*

CHILMARK [ST9632]

☆ *Black Dog* [B3089 Salisbury—Hindon]: Comfortably modernised 15th-c beamed pub currently doing well, good food from new chef, well kept ales inc local brews, good value house wines, friendly polite staff, several smallish relaxing rooms, good local atmosphere (regulars turn up on horseback), armchairs by lounge log fire, fossil ammonites in the stone of one attractive dining room; dogs welcome, tables out in good-sized roadside garden *(Arthur Baker, H D Wharton, LYM, David Cuckney)*

CHIPPENHAM [ST9273]

Four Seasons [Market Pl, by Buttercross]: Lively and friendly, with fine range of well kept sensibly priced ales, also farm ciders and malt whiskies, enjoyable bar food inc sports event specials and recommended book-ahead

steak and kidney pie, attractive pictures and decorations, quaint proverbs *(Richard Pierce)*

Kingfisher [Hungerdown Lane]: Lively local with Wadworths 6X, interesting aperitifs and brandies, good lunchtime sandwiches and salads, fine old prints; soft piped music, board games, frequent music and quiz nights; tables outside *(Richard Pierce)*

CHITTERNE [ST9843]

Kings Head [B390 between Heytesbury and Shrewton]: Salisbury Plain oasis, good cheerful service, varied food with good fish menu inc takeaway fish and chips, woodburner, lovely hanging baskets in summer; bedrooms, pretty village, good walks *(Keith and Sheila Baxter, Richard and Liz Dilnot)*

CHRISTIAN MALFORD [ST9678]

Rising Sun [Station Rd]: Small friendly beamed bar with log fire, pleasant dining room, good home-made food (not Sun evening), three real ales, farm cider; may be piped pop music; tables out in garden and on front heated terrace *(Hayley Sales, CMW, JJW)*

CLYFFE PYPARD [SU0776]

Goddard Arms: Unpretentious 16th-c village pub with log fire and raised dining area in split-level main bar, small sitting room with another fire and two old armchairs, down-to-earth chatty and welcoming licensees, well kept Wadworths 6X and guest beers, good value straightforward fresh food, back skittle alley with prints, paintings, sculptures, second-hand books and records for sale (busy music nights, and pool room off, with darts, cribbage etc); no cards taken; open all day wknds, sculpture garden, bedrooms, tiny pretty thatched village in lovely countryside *(Pete Baker, Guy Vowles)*

COLLINGBOURNE KINGSTON [SU2355]

Barleycorn [A338]: Welcoming smartly kept village pub with several well kept ales such as Hook Norton Old Hooky, Charles Wells Bombardier and Wadworths, wide blackboard choice of affordable food from fresh sandwiches up, decent wines, quick friendly service, pool room, attractive restaurant; piped music; tables outside *(Tony and Shirley Albert, Peter and Audrey Dowsett)*

COMPTON BASSETT [SU0372]

White Horse: Good choice of food inc good value two-course wkdy lunch, very effective cheerful service, well kept Wadworths 6X and guest beers *(Tony Beaulah, Mr and Mrs G Ives)*

CORSHAM [ST8770]

Royal Oak [High St]: Well kept Wadworths beers and Bass, good service, friendly staff, simple wkdy food; folk Thurs, jazz and blues Fri, comedy club upstairs Sun *(Catherine Pitt)*

CORSTON [ST9284]

Radnor Arms [A429, N of M4 junction 17]: Friendly new management, good value food inc enjoyably homely dishes, good choice of real ales inc Moles *(R A Watson)*

CRICKLADE [SU1093]

Red Lion [High St]: Welcoming and relaxed, with interesting décor from stuffed birds through candle sculptures to ski stuff, wide range of beers inc Moles, newish dining area; neat garden *(Des and Jen Clarke, R Huggins,*

D Irving, E McCall, T McLean)

Vale [High St]: Pleasant décor in reworked bar adjoining Georgian hotel, beams and stripped bricks and timbers, well kept ales such as Batemans, Greene King IPA, Abbot and Ruddles County, Smiles and Wadworths 6X, up-to-date food from sandwiches, panini and wraps to good blackboard restaurant dishes, friendly owners and efficient young staff, two dining areas with woodburners and local art for sale; newly modernised bedrooms *(Comus and Sarah Elliott, Mr and Mrs G S Ayrton)*

CROCKERTON [ST8642]

Bath Arms [just off A350 Warminster—Blandford]: Attractive old dining pub with good food from expert new chef/landlord, Butcombe Gold and two beers brewed locally for the pub, good wines by the glass, pleasant informal atmosphere with plenty of well spaced tables in several rooms; picnic-sets in garden *(Edward Mirzoeff)*

DERRY HILL [ST9570]

☆ *Lansdowne Arms* [Church Rd]: Striking and stately stone-built pub opposite one of Bowood's grand gatehouses, well opened up inside to give several civilised areas with comfortable period flavour, hearty log fire and candles in bottles, well kept Wadworths IPA, JCB, 6X and Red Shoot Forest Gold, good value wines by the glass, interesting reasonably priced food in bar and restaurant; faint piped music; fine views, picnic-sets in neat side garden, good play area *(BB, David Crook, Richard Pierce, Simon and Amanda Southwell)*

DEVIZES [ST9961]

Artichoke [The Nursery]: Clean, bright and airy, with Wadworths full beer range, reasonably priced food inc sandwiches and baguettes, fast friendly service *(Comus and Sarah Elliott)*

British Lion [A361 Swindon roundabout]: Bare-boards beer-lover's pub with three quickly changing well kept real ales, reasonable prices, brewery posters and mirrors, gas fire, back bar with darts and pool; juke box, can be smoky; garden behind, open all day *(Kevin Thorpe)*

Moonraker [Nursteed Rd]: Imposing and comfortable 1930s pub with enjoyable food, well kept Wadworths IPA and 6X, good whiskies (expert Scottish landlord), friendly service *(Dr and Mrs A K Clarke, Richard Pierce)*

DONHEAD ST ANDREW [ST9124]

Forester [off A30 E of Shaftesbury, just E of Ludwell; Lower St]: Small thatched pub recently reopened by new owner, inglenook log fire in bar, emphasis on interesting choice of food here and in separate dining room, Adnams, Ringwood Best and Wadworths 6X, very good choice of wines by the glass, efficient pleasant service; small garden, nice views, lovely village *(Colin and Janet Roe)*

DURRINGTON [SU1544]

Stonehenge [A345, off A303 nr Amesbury]: Rambling pub with neat tables in large dining area, low-priced menus, John Smiths and Wadworths 6X, friendly service; piped music in bar may obtrude *(Peter and Audrey Dowsett)*

EAST KNOYLE [ST8731]

Fox & Hounds [off A350 S of A303]: Lovely out-of-the-way setting, superb views from green opp, good choice of fairly priced fresh food esp fish in bar and small conservatory restaurant, Smiles and Youngs ales, farm cider, comfortable seats and pleasant layout *(Colin and Janet Roe)*

☆ *Seymour Arms* [The Street; just off A350 S of Warminster]: Roomy creeper-covered stone-built black-beamed pub, Swiss chef/landlord doing good freshly made generous food inc interesting specials, quietly welcoming and comfortable rambling bar areas, cosy part with high-backed settle by log fire, well kept Wadworths IPA, 6X and JCB, cheerful service; tables in garden with play area, good value bedrooms *(Ann and Colin Hunt, BB, H D Wharton, John and Joan Nash)*

EASTERTON [SU0255]

Royal Oak [B3098]: Attractive thatched Wadworths pub, comfortably renovated and hospitable, with low beams, flagstones, alcoves and soft lighting, two dining areas and separate simpler locals' bar, courteous service, good blackboard food choice inc interesting vegetarian options, well kept ales, good choice of wines by the glass, cafetière coffee, log fires; tables in small front garden *(Joyce and Maurice Cottrell, Michael Doswell)*

EASTON ROYAL [SU2060]

Bruce Arms [Easton Rd]: Fine 19th-c unspoilt local, nicely basic, with scrubbed antique pine tables, brick floor, well kept Wadworths 6X and guest ales, Pewsey organic cider, good filled rolls; open all day Sun *(the Didler)*

EDINGTON [ST9353]

Lamb [Westbury Rd]: Friendly village local nicely opened up by new young licensees (he does most of the cooking), expanding range of reasonably priced pub food from doorstep sandwiches up, well kept Fullers London Pride and Wadworths 6X, cosy bar with snug areas, darts, small dining room; garden with picnic-sets and play area *(Andrew Hall, Matthew Shackle)*

FARLEIGH WICK [ST8064]

Fox & Hounds [A363 Bath—Bradford, 2½ miles NW of Bradford]: Well extended low-beamed rambling pub thriving under new landlady, sensibly priced Bass and Marstons Pedigree, interesting choice of enjoyable food; attractive garden *(Dr and Mrs M E Wilson)*

FORD [ST8474]

☆ *White Hart* [off A420 Chippenham—Bristol]: Interesting stone-built country inn in attractive stream-side grounds, cosy heavily black-beamed bar with ancient fireplace; under new management, well kept real ales, decent wines by the glass, wide choice of food (all day Sun); children in restaurant, pleasant bedrooms (summer wknd wedding parties can make for late nights), open all day wknds *(Mrs Sally Lloyd, M G Hart, LYM, Richard Pierce)*

FOXHAM [ST9777]

Foxham Inn [NE of Chippenham]: Small, relaxed and cosy pub/restaurant, friendly new licensees doing wide choice of food from ciabattas and baguettes to sensibly priced main dishes and puddings (with pudding wines), enterprising wine list; extensive views from front, peaceful village *(anon)*

GREAT BEDWYN [SU2764]

Cross Keys [High St]: Friendly and relaxed village pub with comfortable chairs and settles, good range of generous bar food inc good vegetable soups, Wadworths ales, decent wines; tables in garden with terrace, bedrooms – good walking country nr Kennet & Avon Canal *(Alette and Russell Lawson)*

Three Tuns [High St]: Biggish bare-boards village pub, friendly and lively, with helpful staff, well kept Flowers IPA, Fullers London Pride, Tetleys and Wadworths 6X, traditional old-fashioned atmosphere, enterprising food *(Tim Brierly, Steve Price, Alette and Russell Lawson)*

HANNINGTON [SU1793]

Jolly Tar [off B4019 W of Highworth; Queens Rd]: Relaxing beamed bar with big log fire, flagstoned and stripped stone dining area, lots of decorative china, wide food choice, well kept Arkells ales, reasonable prices, quick friendly service, no piped music; tables out in front and in big garden with play area, pretty village *(BB, Peter and Audrey Dowsett)*

HEDDINGTON [ST9966]

☆ *Ivy*: Picturesque thatched 15th-c village pub with good inglenook log fire in plain L-shaped bar, heavy low beams, timbered walls, assorted furnishings on parquet floor, brass and copper, well kept Wadworths IPA and 6X tapped from the cask, good simple freshly prepared home-made food (not Sun-Weds evenings) from great lunchtime club sandwiches up, back family eating room, sensibly placed darts, piano, dog and cat; may be piped music; disabled access, open all day wknds, picnic-sets in front garden, attractively set hamlet *(the Didler, Richard Stancomb, Pete Baker, LYM, Roger and Jenny Huggins, CMW, JJW, Eleanor and Nick Steinitz, Nigel Long)*

HIGHWORTH [SU1891]

Freke Arms [Swanborough; B4019, 1 mile W on Honnington turning]: Airy and friendly, smart but relaxed, four rooms on different levels, well kept ales inc Arkells 2B and 3B, reasonably priced food inc good sandwiches, straightforward hot dishes and good value Sun lunch, quick service; may be quiet piped music; picnic-sets in small garden with play area, nice views *(Peter and Audrey Dowsett)*

Globe [Sheep St]: Cosy two-bar pub with nice log fire, friendly landlord, very reasonable prices; no piped music *(Peter and Audrey Dowsett)*

Saracens Head [High St]: Civilised and relaxed rambling bar under new licensees, several comfortably reworked and interesting areas around great central chimney block, wide choice of bar food inc children's, well kept Arkells 2B and 3B (barrels on display in new bar area), two log fires; piped music; children in eating area, tables in sheltered courtyard, open all day wkdys; comfortable bedrooms *(Peter and Audrey Dowsett, LYM)*

HINDON [ST9132]

☆ *Lamb* [B3089 Wilton—Mere]: Solid attractive old hotel now comfortably settling in under Youngs ownership, their beers kept well, good helpful service, reasonably priced bar food from sandwiches up, slate floors, nice old furniture and big inglenook woodburner in opened-up long bar with thriving pubby atmosphere, smart restaurant; children and dogs welcome, picnic-sets across the road, comfortable bedrooms now all with own bathrooms, open all day *(Mike Gorton, Shirley Mackenzie, Mark Clezy, W W Burke, Terry and Linda Moseley, John Evans, Colin and Janet Roe, B J Harding, LYM, Stuart Litster, OPUS)*

HODSON [SU1780]

☆ *Calley Arms* [not far from M4 junction 15, via Chiseldon; off B4005 S of Swindon]: Relaxed and welcoming big bar with raised no smoking dining area, good well priced food (not Sun/Mon evenings) inc some unusual dishes and half-priced small helpings, cheerful prompt considerate service, well kept Wadworths ales with a guest, dozens of malt whiskies, farm ciders, country wines, darts and open fire one end; piped music may obtrude; children welcome, picnic-sets in garden with dovecote, plenty of good walks *(Sheila and Robert Robinson)*

HONEYSTREET [SU1061]

Barge [off A345 W of Pewsey]: Friendly open-plan pub by Kennet & Avon Canal, charming almost 18th-c atmosphere with Georgian sash windows, Regency striped wallpaper and dark green high ceiling, well kept real ales, usual food from sandwiches up inc children's and ice-cream cabinet, good prices, log fires, pool; may be quiet piped light clasics, live music Sat; pleasant garden with waterside picnic-sets, bedrooms, camping field – nice setting, good downland walks *(Dr and Mrs M E Wilson, CMW, JJW, Mary Rayner)*

HOOK [SU0785]

Bolingbroke Arms [B4041, off A420 just W of M4 junction 16]: Well renovated and opened up with lots of light pine, informal airy feel, good-sized helpings of enjoyable food from sandwiches and baked potatoes to well cooked main dishes with fresh veg, well kept beer, friendly service; nice spot *(Richard Seal, Dave Irving)*

HORTON [SU0363]

☆ *Bridge Inn* [off A361 Beckhampton road on edge of Devizes]: Sturdy pale pine country-kitchen furniture on carpet or reconstituted flagstones, bargee and other photographs on red walls, log fire, and no smoking room, cheerful efficient service, good range of food from filled rolls, baguettes and bar meals to restaurant dishes, Wadworths IPA and 6X tapped from the cask, decent wines, pub cat; quiet piped pop music; disabled lavatories, picnic-sets and doves in garden fenced off from Kennet & Avon Canal below *(BB, John Beeken)*

KINGTON LANGLEY [ST9277]

Hit or Miss [handy for M4 junction 17, off A350 S; Days Lane]: Olde-worlde cottage on little green in attractive village, emphasis on left-hand restaurant with good log fire, also small rather plush cricket-theme bar with no smoking area, appetising and imaginative food from baguettes up, well kept Highgate Davenports, Timothy Taylors Landlord, Tetleys and Youngs, friendly service, darts and pool in room off; tables outside *(Dick and Madeleine Brown)*

LACOCK [ST9268]

Bell [back road, bottom of Bowden Hill]: Friendly pub with wide choice of food from sandwiches to steaks, changing real ales such as Archers Golden, Cottage Rocket, Wickwar Coopers and Wadworths 6X (take-out containers), Bulmer's cider, good wine list, lots of malt whiskies, helpful staff, brocaded banquettes, pretty blue and white restaurant; well kept sizeable garden with good play house and climbers in children's area, open for food all day wknds *(BB, Esther and John Sprinkle)*

LIMPLEY STOKE [ST7861]

☆ *Hop Pole* [off A36 and B3108 S of Bath]: Friendly licensees (but they plan to retire) in largely panelled 16th-c stone-built two-bar pub, with log fire, Bass, Butcombe, Courage Best and a guest beer, wide choice of bar food and traditional games; TV, piped music; children in eating areas, nice enclosed garden behind *(Pat and Robert Watt, LYM, Dr and Mrs M E Wilson, Susan and Nigel Wilson)*

Rose & Crown [A36]: Large main-road pub with beams, log fires and cosy alcove seating, well kept Smiles, good food choice from big sandwiches to hearty main dishes in bar and restaurant inc good local meat and sensible children's choices; picnic-sets out on terrace and in garden with steep valley views, open all day wknds and bank hols *(Meg and Colin Hamilton, Christopher and Jo Barton, Graham Brooks)*

LOCKERIDGE [SU1467]

☆ *Who'd A Thought It* [signed just off A4 Marlborough—Calne just W of Fyfield]: Welcoming pub with red décor in two main linked rooms set for good sensibly priced well presented food inc very popular OAP lunch, small side drinking area, well kept Hook Norton Old Hooky and Wadworths IPA and 6X, good choice of decent wines by the glass, interesting well illustrated and annotated collection of cooperage tools, caring landlord, coal or log fire, family room – good for children; piped pop music; pleasant back garden with play area, delightful quiet scenery, lovely walks *(Jenny and Brian Seller, BB, Jane Basso)*

LOWER WOODFORD [SU1136]

Wheatsheaf [signed off A360 just N of Salisbury]: Prettily set 18th-c dining pub, big helpings, well kept Badger Best, IPA and Tanglefoot, miniature footbridge over indoor goldfish pool; piped music; children welcome, good disabled access, baby-changing, good big tree-lined garden with play area *(John and Judy Saville, I D Barnett, LYM, Mary and David Richards, R J Walden)*

MAIDEN BRADLEY [ST8038]

Somerset Arms [Church St]: Unspoilt high-ceilinged village pub, relaxed and welcoming, with very friendly licensees, good attractively priced food, well kept Wadworths and guest beers, tempting whiskies; bedrooms *(David Clark, Neville and Anne Morley)*

MALMESBURY [ST9287]

Kings Arms [High St]: Popular 16th-c town pub with two warmly friendly bars, good value well presented food from sandwiches and other bar snacks to interesting full meals, Flowers IPA and a guest beer, decent choice of wines by the glass, pleasant restaurant; nice courtyard garden, large well used function room inc jazz last Sat of month, comfortable bedrooms *(Margaret and Roy Randle, K H Frostick, Dr and Mrs A K Clarke)*

MARLBOROUGH [SU1869]

Royal Oak [High St]: Spacious former coaching inn with gleaming new décor, warm and comfortable, good innovative bar food, well kept Greene King Old Speckled Hen; pleasant back garden *(Dr D E Granger)*

MARSTON MEYSEY [SU1297]

Masons Arms: Comfortable relaxed bar with good changing choice of well kept beers, pleasant helpful staff, daily papers, enjoyable food, separate dining room; bedrooms *(R Huggins, D Irving, E McCall, T McLean)*

Old Spotted Cow [off A419 Swindon—Cirencester]: Big well laid out open-plan Cotswold stone pub, good value generous food, well kept ales such as Fullers London Pride and Marstons Pedigree, decent wines, mulled wine on tap, comfortable chairs, raised stone fireplace, plants and pictures; bar billiards, darts, board and children's games, fruit machine, quiet piped music; open all day wknds, spacious garden with picnic-sets on terrace and lots of play equipment *(R Huggins, D Irving, E McCall, T McLean, Peter and Audrey Dowsett)*

MELKSHAM [ST9063]

Kings Arms [Market Pl]: Well run and attractive former coaching inn, Wadworths ales, limited but varied and well cooked food, decent house wines, dogs allowed; good value bedrooms *(Ken Flawn)*

MERE [ST8132]

☆ *George* [The Square]: New owners (and new name) for comfortably modernised 16th-c inn, good enterprising cooking, quick helpful service, well kept Badger IPA and Best, open fire, well spaced tables in attractive restaurant; good bedrooms *(Joan and Michel Hooper-Immins, BB, Mrs Roxanne Chamberlain, Colin and Janet Roe)*

☆ *Old Ship* [Castle St]: Interesting partly 16th-c coaching inn famous for 17th-c carved fireplace with Charles I portrait; cosy panelled hotel bar, short choice of decent bar food, prompt welcoming service even under pressure, well kept real ales inc Bass, good house wines, good value timbered and raftered upstairs restaurant; spacious separate more pubby bar across coach entry divided by standing timbers, mix of old tables and chairs, pub games;

children allowed in eating area, good value comfortable bedrooms (huge breakfast), picturesque village *(Leigh and Gillian Mellor, Val and Alan Green, LYM)*

MINETY [SU0390]

White Horse [Station Rd]: Recently reopened, with unusual upstairs layout – stripped brick and stone bar with well kept real ales such as Youngs and Wadworths 6X from central servery, good baguettes and limited though innovative choice of lunchtime hot dishes, pleasant no smoking evening restaurant with sofas and armchairs on landing; children very welcome, tables on terrace overlooking pond below *(KC)*

MONKTON FARLEIGH [ST8065]

☆ *Kings Arms* [signed off A363 Bradford—Bath]: Attractive 17th-c building in lovely village, good reasonably priced home-made food in beamed lounge and no smoking tapestried restaurant with huge inglenook, Bass, Butcombe and Wadworths 6X, farm cider, unusual wines, quick friendly service; darts, bar billiards, good live music Fri; rustic tables in front partly flagstoned courtyard, aviaries in back garden, open all day summer wknds *(Mr and Mrs T Bennett, Dr and Mrs M E Wilson, Callum and Letitia Smith-Burnett, Keith Berrett)*

NETHERHAMPTON [SU1129]

☆ *Victoria & Albert* [just off A3094 W of Salisbury]: Appealing black-beamed bar in simple thatched cottage under obliging new landlord, nicely cushioned old-fashioned wall settles on ancient floor tiles, real ales such as Hop Back Summer Lightning, Ringwood Best and Old Thumper and Timothy Taylors Landlord, reasonably priced food, no smoking restaurant; playful little dog (not at meal times); children welcome, hatch service for sizeable garden behind, handy for walks to Wilton House and Nadder Valley *(Susan and John Douglas, LYM)*

NOMANSLAND [SU2517]

☆ *Lamb* [signed off B3078 and B3079]: Attractive old-fashioned building in lovely New Forest village-green setting, friendly donkeys and ponies poking their noses in, attentive welcoming service, reasonably priced wholesome homely cooking inc lots of puddings in small dining room and long bar, Hampshire Strongs, Ringwood, Wadworths and Whitbreads ales, end pool table; good walks *(Prof and Mrs Tony Palmer, Phyl and Jack Street)*

NORTH NEWNTON [SU1357]

Woodbridge [A345 Upavon—Pewsey]: Blazing log fire, decent bar food, well kept Wadworths ales, summer farm cider, friendly efficient service, separate restaurant; piped music, no dogs; pleasantly furnished bedrooms (three with own bathroom), plenty of tables and play area in sizeable garden backing on to River Avon, space for tents or caravans, fly fishing passes available *(LYM, Theocsbrian)*

NORTH WROUGHTON [SU1482]

Check Inn [Woodland View (A4361 just S of Swindon)]: Welcoming extended pub with

glossy pine furniture, various comfortable areas inc children's, up to 10 well kept interesting changing ales in oversized lined glasses, lots of bottled imports, farm cider, good soft drinks choice, tasty straightforward food, log fire, large no smoking area; darts, games machine; disabled access, heated front terrace, garden bar (can pitch tent, motorway noise), open all day Fri-Sun *(CMW, JJW, James Woods)*

NUNTON [SU1526]

☆ *Radnor Arms* [off A338 S of Salisbury]: Pretty ivy-clad village pub very popular for consistently good food inc fish and local game, friendly helpful staff, well kept Badger inc Tanglefoot; three pleasantly decorated and furnished linked rooms inc cheerfully busy yet relaxing bar and staider restaurant, log fires, very friendly labrador; can get rather crowded, booking essential at wknds; attractive garden popular with children *(W W Burke, R J Anderson)*

OARE [SU1563]

White Hart [A345 S of Marlborough]: Unassuming respite from busy road or rainy walk, good value home-made food, well kept Wadworths, new landlady from New Zealand; bedrooms, nice village with lovely gardens *(Guy Vowles, Matthew Shackle)*

ODSTOCK [SU1426]

Yew Tree [off A338 S of Salisbury; Whitsbury Rd]: Pretty thatched and low-beamed country dining pub doing well under new management, big blackboard choice of enjoyable good value food, friendly staff, well kept beers and decent wines, log fire, raised seating area at one end; small garden, good walks *(John Wheeler)*

OGBOURNE ST ANDREW [SU1974]

☆ *Wheatsheaf* [A345 N of Marlborough]: The only reason this civilised pub leaves the main entries this year is a lack of reader reports; the central bar servery has a dining area on one side and a more informal area on the other, with an appealing mix of furnishings, subtle lighting and interesting mainly black and white pictures on chalky grey walls, good imaginative food from an open kitchen, well kept Bass, Wadworths 6X and Worthingtons on handpump, and decent wines; children in back restaurant, pretty back terrace, scented garden, bedrooms *(Jenny and Chris Wilson, Dr and Mrs M E Wilson, LYM)*

OGBOURNE ST GEORGE [SU2074]

Old Crown [A345 Marlboro—Swindon]: 18th-c pub in small village off Ridgeway path, consistently enjoyable food from crusty bread lunchtime sandwiches to restaurant meals (one table a deep glass-covered well), well kept Wadworths 6X, brisk service, cosy small bar with very mixed furniture, piano, pleasant décor and pictures; quiet piped music; children welcome, picnic-sets by car park, bedrooms, cl Mon lunchtime *(Barbara Ogburn, CMW, JJW, A H C Rainier, R E Blakeney)*

PEWSEY [SU1561]

☆ *French Horn* [A345 towards Marlborough; Pewsey Wharf]: Old pub entirely refurbished by newish licensees, everything now home-made (from the bread to the ice cream), well kept Wadworths IPA and 6X, good choice of wines by the glass, good welcoming service, two-part back bar divided by log fire open to both sides, steps down to pleasant and rather smart flagstoned front dining area (children allowed here); piped music; picnic-sets on back terrace, many more in well fenced wood-chip area with robust timber play area above barges moored on Kennet & Avon Canal *(BB)*

POTTERNE [ST9958]

☆ *George & Dragon* [A360]: Interesting and attractive old pub with log fire in traditional heavy-beamed bar, well kept Wadworths IPA and 6X, pool and darts in back room, skittle alley and unique indoor .22 shooting range; steep front steps; children welcome in eating area, pleasant garden and suntrap yard, comfortable bedrooms *(LYM, Kevin Thorpe, Mrs E A McClean)*

RAMSBURY [SU2771]

Bell [signed off B4192 NW of Hungerford, or A4 W]: Small airy bay-windowed bar, civilised, quiet and friendly, generous blackboard range here and in no smoking restaurant, Wadworths real ales, two woodburners, friendly landlord and staff; may be piped music, dogs allowed; picnic-sets on raised lawn *(LYM, Keith Stevens, Mark and Ruth Brock)*

REDLYNCH [SU2021]

☆ *Kings Head* [off A338 via B3080; The Row]: Charming low-ceilinged cottagey 16th-c pub with two carpeted bays, one almost a conservatory, off beamed main bar, nice mix of furnishings, fresh flowers and ornaments, interesting blackboard choice of good generous food, quick friendly service, Courage Best and Directors and Wadworths 6X, good house wine and cafetière coffee, log fire and woodburner; dogs welcome, picnic-sets by bird table in side garden, bedrooms *(John and Vivienne Rice, BB)*

ROWDE [ST9762]

Cross Keys [High St]: Attractive timbered pub under new management, fine stone fireplace in carpeted front public bar with pool, darts, TV and piped pop music, nicely laid out no smoking back restaurant, Wadworths real ales, inexpensive bar food and full meals inc OAP lunches Tues and Thurs *(Kevin Thorpe)*

SALISBURY [SU1429]

☆ *Avon Brewery* [Castle St]: Old-fashioned city bar, long, narrow, busy and friendly, with dark mahogany, frosted and engraved bow windows, friezes and attractive pictures, two open fires, sensibly priced food (not Sun evening) from sandwiches up, well kept Boddingtons, Fullers London Pride and Ind Coope Burton, decent wines; may be classical piped music; long sheltered courtyard garden overlooking river, open all day *(J and B Cressey, Dr and Mrs M E Wilson, LYM)*

Hogs Head [Wilton Rd, opposite main police station]: Big windows overlooking river and busy street, high ceiling, bold pastel décor, stripped pine woodwork, big central open fire; wide choice of good value food inc sharing plates, cheerful staff, comfortable seats,

Boddingtons, Brakspears, Greene King Abbot and Hook Norton; lavatories up good broad stairs *(Dr and Mrs M E Wilson)*

New Inn [New St]: Ancient creaky-timbered pub under new management, massive heavy old beams, quiet cosy alcoves, inglenook log fire, well kept real ales, decent house wines, food from sandwiches up; shame about the piped music; children welcome, walled garden with striking view of nearby cathedral spire, open all day summer wknds *(Adam and Joan Bunting, Ian Phillips, Douglas and Ann Hare, LYM)*

Old Ale House [Crane St]: Long open-plan bare-boards pub with hotch-potch of old sofas, seats and tables, cosy lighting, entertainingly cluttered décor, inexpensive lunchtime food (not Sun), real ales such as Courage Best, Ringwood Best and Wadworths 6X tapped from the cask; darts, cribbage, dominoes, big-screen TV, fruit machines, loud juke box; children welcome away from the bar till 5, picnic-sets in small back courtyard, open all day *(Gordon Tong, Ann and Colin Hunt, Dr and Mrs M E Wilson, LYM)*

Old Mill [Town Path, W Harnham]: Charming 17th-c pub/hotel now taken over by a small new group formed by a member of the Eldridge Pope former brewing family, lovely tranquil setting, picnic-sets in small floodlit garden by duck-filled millpond, a stroll across water-meadows from cathedral, with classic view of it from bridge beyond garden; simple beamed bars (can get rather crowded) with prized window tables, friendly staff, well kept real ales, good wines and malt whiskies, decent bar food from sandwiches up, good value restaurant lunch; children welcome, bedrooms *(Martin and Karen Wake, Derek and Sylvia Stephenson, Richard Fendick, Dr D E Granger, LYM)*

☆ *Wig & Quill* [New St]: Low-beamed and subtly lit 16th-c former shop with ornate rugs, open fires, worn leather armchairs, stuffed birds and low arches to connecting rooms; friendly landlord, Wadworths IPA, JCB and 6X and guest beers such as Castle Rock tapped from the cask, interesting long summer drinks, attractively priced standard food (winter lunchtimes) from sandwiches up, tiled back bar with pool and darts; open all day, dogs allowed, nice small courtyard behind with cathedral views *(David and Elizabeth Briggs, Ann and Colin Hunt, Dr and Mrs M E Wilson, Tony and Wendy Hobden)*

Wyndham Arms [Estcourt Rd]: Basic modern corner pub with two rooms off long bar, friendly atmosphere, tap for reasonably priced good Hop Back beers (originally brewed here until their popularity needed larger premises over at Downton), country wines, simple bar food *(the Didler)*

SEEND [ST9562]

Three Magpies [Sells Green – A365 towards Melksham]: Unspoilt partly 18th-c pub with good service by keen and willing licensees, good value straightforward home-made food, well kept Wadworths IPA and 6X, decent choice of wines by the glass; big garden with play area *(Joyce and Maurice Cottrell)*

SEMINGTON [ST9259]

☆ *Lamb* [The Strand; A361 Devizes—Trowbridge]: Consistently good fresh food inc interesting dishes that work (try their unusual cheesy pudding), buoyant atmosphere in series of attractively furnished rooms, helpful friendly service, well kept Butcombe, Ringwood Best and Shepherd Neame Spitfire, carefully chosen wine list (landlord's special interest) and good coffee, woodburner and log fire; children in eating area, helpful to wheelchairs, tables out in attractively remodelled walled garden; cl Sun evening *(LYM, Mr and Mrs F J Parmenter, Mr and Mrs J Ken Jones, Charles Moncreiffe)*

Somerset Arms [A350 2 miles S of Melksham]: Cosy 16th-c coaching inn, heavy-beamed long bar, real and flame-effect fires, high-backed settles, plenty of tables, lots of prints and brassware, wide range of decent food in bar and restaurant from sandwiches and chips to some imaginative dishes (the cheerful service can sometimes slow), Badger beers, good coffee; piped music; pleasant garden behind, short walk on busy road from Kennet & Avon Canal *(Mike Turner, Guy Consterdine)*

SHAW [ST8765]

Golden Fleece [A365 towards Atworth]: Former coaching inn with low-ceilinged L-shaped bar and long sympathetic front dining extension, real ales such as Butcombe and Marstons Pedigree, generous bargain lunches very popular with older people; tables in garden *(Dr and Mrs M E Wilson)*

SHERSTON [ST8586]

Carpenters Arms [Easton (B4040)]: Cosy local with good choice of reasonably priced food, efficient service, well kept beers and interesting wine choice, small rooms with low beams, settles and shiny tables, log fire, modern conservatory and dining rooms; TV in locals' bar, no piped music; tables in pleasant garden with play area *(Peter and Audrey Dowsett, Ian Rushton, Richard Pierce)*

☆ *Rattlebone* [Church St (B4040 Malmesbury—Chipping Sodbury)]: Rambling beamed and stone-walled 17th-c village pub, comfortable mix of pews, settles and country-kitchen chairs, partly no smoking dining area (no food Sun evening), well kept Youngs beers, decent wines, log fire, public bar with pool, table football and other games, also TV and juke box; would benefit if managers stayed longer; children in restaurant, skittle alley, picnic-sets in attractive back garden, open all day *(Mayur Shah, Alec and Barbara Jones, P R and S A White, Dr and Mrs A K Clarke, Andrew Shore, LYM)*

SHREWTON [SU0743]

Royal Oak [Amesbury Rd]: Open-plan pub refurbished by cheery newish owners, dining tables one end and pool the other, food all day till 6, Fullers London Pride and Ringwood Best with plans for a third beer; children welcome, extended garden *(Kevin Thorpe)*

SOUTH MARSTON [SU1987]

Carpenters Arms [just off A420 E of Swindon]: Popular and roomy, with good value generous food in bar and separate restaurant inc OAP wkdy lunch and popular Sun roasts, well kept Arkells beers, friendly staff, pleasant olde-worlde décor; pool room, quiz night Mon; children welcome, play area and animals in big back garden, up-to-date bedrooms, open all day *(Peter and Audrey Dowsett)*

Village Inn: Smart and spacious bar, part of hotel and leisure complex; real ales such as Boddingtons and Fullers London Pride, popular sensibly priced bar food, old Hollywood film posters, no piped music; children welcome, separate restaurant, bedrooms, open all day Sun *(Peter and Audrey Dowsett)*

STEEPLE LANGFORD [SU0437]

Rainbows End [off A36 E of A303 junction]: Attractive pub with large comfortable bar, good varied freshly made food inc fish, big helpings, friendly helpful staff, three well kept changing beers inc local brews (they may give tasters); nice lake and views of Wylye Valley from sunny conservatory and terrace, picnic-sets on lawn *(J and B Cressey, H C Head, Wombat)*

STIBB GREEN [SU2262]

☆ *Three Horseshoes* [just N of Burbage]: Friendly and spotless olde-worlde local with good choice of simple home-made food (not Sun evening) cooked by landlady, sensible prices and quick service, warmly welcoming landlord, well kept Wadworths ales, farm cider, inglenook log fire in comfortable beamed front bar, second no smoking bar, dining room with railway memorabilia and pictures; attractive garden, cl Mon *(Geoff Palmer, James Woods)*

STOCKTON [ST9738]

☆ *Carriers* [just off A36 Salisbury—Warminster, or follow Wylye sign off A303 then turn right]: Attractive smallish village pub with good food, service and atmosphere, soft lighting, log fire and pretty dining extension, well kept Ringwood and Wadworths 6X, nice wines, character landlord; sunny roadside seats, quiet Wylye Valley village *(Charles Moncreiffe, Richard and Liz Dilnot, David R Crafts, BB, Peter Meister, Dr Jack Barrow, Keith and Sheila Baxter)*

SUTTON BENGER [ST9478]

Vintage [Seagry Rd]: Friendly colourful pub in former chocolate factory, straightforward food inc good meats and traditional puddings, well kept Archers and Wadworths, interesting wines, art gallery restaurant *(Richard Pierce)*

Wellesley Arms [High St]: Large attractively furnished beamed Cotswold stone country pub with several Duke of Wellington pictures, good value pub lunches (need to book Sun), well kept real ales, separate dining room *(Richard Pierce)*

SWINDON [SU1584]

Duke of Wellington [Eastcott Hill; off Commercial Road at Regent Circus]: Honest unspoilt local with particularly well kept Arkells 2B and 3B tapped from the cask, coal fire, tiny snug off main bar with darts, dominoes and cribbage *(Pete Baker)*

Foresters Arms [Common Platt, out towards Purton]: Two-bar pub with friendly staff, three real ales, quite a few wines and soft drinks, good choice of reasonably priced food (not Sun evening); quiet piped radio; garden with picnic-sets and play area *(CMW, JJW)*

Victoria [Victoria Rd]: Good young local atmosphere, well kept Bass, good value organic food; frequent live music in back room *(James Woods)*

TISBURY [ST9429]

Boot [High St]: Ancient building, decent menu, three real ales tapped from the cask, friendly staff, smashing fireplace *(Joe Green)*

Crown [Church St]: Attractive extended pub overlooking parish church, wide choice of food inc good baguettes, helpful staff *(Meg and Colin Hamilton)*

TROWBRIDGE [ST8557]

Sir Isaac Pitman [Castle Pl]: Useful two-level Wetherspoons well done out in elm-coloured wood, comfortable alcoves, no smoking area, good value beer and food, pleasant service *(Dr and Mrs M E Wilson)*

UPAVON [SU1355]

☆ *Antelope* [High St; A345/A342]: Friendly and lively village atmosphere, good home cooking esp specials and puddings in bar and pretty back restaurant, log fire, five well kept real ales, proper coffee, small bow-windowed games area with darts, bar billiards and local RAF memorabilia; pretty terrace *(LYM, the Didler, David and Sue Lee, Jane Reynolds)*

UPPER WOODFORD [SU1237]

☆ *Bridge Inn*: Good sensibly priced food from ploughman's with lots of bread (handy for ducks in attractive riverside garden across road) to wide menu and blackboard choice, well spaced country-kitchen tables on new wooden flooring, big flower prints on eau de nil walls, soft lighting, quick friendly service, well kept Bass and a beer brewed for the pub, log fire, broadsheet dailies, rather smart games room with pool and leather chesterfields; best to book wknds *(BB, Annette and John Derbyshire)*

URCHFONT [SU0357]

Lamb [The Green]: Good range of real ales, farm cider, light lunches, evening filled rolls, find old local photographs; large attractive garden with play area *(Richard Pierce)*

WANBOROUGH [SU2083]

Black Horse [2 miles from M4 junction 15; Callas Hill (former B4507 towards Bishopstone)]: Welcoming open-plan refurbished pub, helpful landlord, enjoyable wholesome lunchtime food from sandwiches to good value Sun roast, well kept competitively priced Arkells Bitter, 2B and 3B, good generous coffee, no piped music, some carefully exposed original panelling; picnic-sets in informal elevated garden with play area, caravan parking in adjoining field, lovely

downland views *(Alan and Paula McCully, Mary Rayner)*

WINGFIELD [ST8256]

☆ *Poplars* [Shop Lane]: Attractive and friendly country local very popular for good value interesting food, especially with older people at lunchtime; well kept Wadworths ales, friendly fast service even when busy, enjoyable atmosphere, no juke box or machines; own cricket pitch *(Dr and Mrs M E Wilson, MRSM, Susan and Nigel Wilson, LYM)*

WINTERBOURNE BASSETT [SU0975]

☆ *White Horse* [off A4361 S of Swindon]: Wide choice of good fresh generous food (may be a wait if busy) inc several fish dishes, popular steak and stilton pie, bargain lunches Mon-Sat and good Sun roast, in neat and well cared for open-plan big-windowed pub, comfortable dining room and warm conservatory, chatty efficient service, well kept Wadworths, good wine list and coffee, huge goldfish; quiet piped music; tables on good-sized side lawn, pleasant setting *(James Woods, BB, Geoff Palmer, Sheila and Robert Robinson)*

WOOTTON BASSETT [SU0682]

Five Bells [Wood St]: Friendly local with up to five well kept ales, enjoyable food with some interesting notions like their Weds sausage night, good atmosphere *(Daniel Williams, James Woods)*

Sally Pusseys [A420 just off M4 junction 16]: Generous unpretentious food from baguettes and baked potatoes to plenty of fish and good Sun carvery, helpful friendly staff cope quickly with the lunchtime rush, well kept Arkells 2B, 3B and Kingsdown, good coffee, spacious bar/dining lounge with hops on beams and lots of pictures, good-sized lower restaurant; may be piped music; picnic-sets in sizeable garden (motorway noise) *(Dave Irving, Geoff Palmer, Stephen and Jean Curtis)*

WOOTTON RIVERS [SU1963]

☆ *Royal Oak* [off A346, A345 or B3087]: 16th-c beamed and thatched pub popular for wide range of food from lunchtime sandwiches, ciabattas and baguettes to plenty of specials and full meals (for which they add a 10% service charge), friendly L-shaped dining lounge with woodburner, timbered bar with small games area, well kept Fullers London Pride, Wadworths 6X and perhaps a guest beer, good wine list; children welcome, tables out in yard, pleasant village, bedrooms in adjoining house *(Mrs J H S Lang, Tina and David Woods-Taylor, Phyl and Jack Street, LYM, Thomas Neate)*

YATTON KEYNELL [ST8676]

Bell [B4039 NW of Chippenham]: Clean comfortable local popular for good value food (best to book at busy times); Courage Best, tables out on fenced lawn *(Pete and Rosie Flower)*

Worcestershire

Three contrasting new entries here this year are the airy and extensive Admiral Rodney at Berrow Green, doing well all round under its cheerful newish landlord; the much smaller stylish and restauranty Childswickham Inn, promising very well on the food side; and the Nags Head in Malvern, with good beers, enjoyable food, and a most relaxing atmosphere in its interestingly decorated network of small rooms. Other pubs giving particular pleasure to readers these days include the cheerful and bustling Little Pack Horse in Bewdley (good value), the civilised and welcoming Bear & Ragged Staff at Bransford (good food), the thriving Fountain at Clent (very popular for lunch), the Old Chequers at Crowle (gaining a Food Award this year, and its prompt service is a big plus, given its handiness for the M5), the Boot at Flyford Flavell (good all round, with a particularly warm welcome), the Bell & Cross at Holy Cross (good imaginative food in a traditional layout of small rooms), and the Bell at Pensax (a friendly and properly pubby all-rounder). It is the recently extended Bear & Ragged Staff at Bransford which takes the title of Worcestershire Dining Pub of the Year – though in the coming year we wouldn't be surprised to see one of this year's new entries giving it a real run for its money. Pubs which feature prominently in the Lucky Dip section at the end of the chapter include the Chequers at Cutnall Green, Plough & Harrow at Drakes Broughton, Greyhound at Eldersfield, Peacock at Forhill (losing its place among the main entries only because of a lack of recent feedback from readers), Three Kings at Hanley Castle, Walter de Cantelupe at Kempsey, Talbot at Knightwick (these last three are all particular favourites), Bellmans Cross at Shatterford and Fruiterers Arms at Stonehall Common. Drinks prices are usually slightly lower than the national average. The King & Castle at Kidderminster has exceptionally cheap beer – much cheaper than the other pubs here. Local beers worth looking out for include Wyre Piddle, Cannon Royall and Malvern Hills. This year we found good local apple juice more widely available than in the past, sometimes pressed and bottled from individual named apple varieties; and there are good farm ciders.

BAUGHTON SO8741 Map 4
Jockey

4 miles from M50 junction 1; A38 northwards, then right on to A4104 Upton—Pershore

A good place for a carefully cooked meal, this dining pub is civilised and very neatly kept, open-plan but partly divided by stripped brick and timbering, with candles alight on the mix of good-sized tables and fresh flowers, a few horse-racing pictures on the butter-coloured walls, and a cream Aga in one brick inglenook. Although the young chef/landlord does do a few hearty snacks such as sandwiches (from £3.25, baguettes from £3.95), ploughman's (£6.95), and mushroom and stilton pasta bake (£8.95), the main emphasis is on his generous more restauranty (and not cheap) food such as king prawns in garlic butter (£5.95), lamb shank or steak and kidney pie (£10.95), bass (£12.95), roast duck breast with orange sauce or fillet steak with pepper sauce (£14.95), and puddings such as treacle and orange tart and sticky toffee pudding (£3.95). On Sunday lunchtime they do set meals only

(£9.95 one course, £10.95 two courses, or £11.95 three courses). Friendly staff serve decent wines, and Hook Norton Best and a guest such as Malvern Hills Bitter on handpump. There are picnic-sets out in front, by an antique pump that's the centrepiece of a water feature (out here, but not inside, you can hear the motorway in the distance). *(Recommended by Alan and Paula McCully, Mike and Mary Carter, Andrew and Amanda Rogers, Paul and Annette Hallett)*

Free house ~ Licensee Peter Lee ~ Real ale ~ Bar food (12-2, 6-9; 12-2.30, 7-9 Sun and bank hol Mon) ~ Restaurant ~ (01684) 592153 ~ Open 11-3, 6-11; 12-3, 7-10.30 Sun; closed Mon except bank hols ~ Bedrooms: /£60S

BERROW GREEN SO7458 Map 4
Admiral Rodney 🍺 🛏️

B4197, off A44 W of Worcester

The cheerful hands-on couple who took over this country inn in 2002 have transformed it into a civilised place with considerable all-round appeal. Throughout, the renovation has made it attractively light and roomy, with plenty of space. The bare-boards entrance bar, with high beams and a sunny bow window, has well kept Greene King IPA, Wye Valley and two changing guest beers such as Marstons Pedigree and Spinning Dog Flannerys Liquid Gold on handpump, big stripped kitchen tables and cushioned chairs, a traditional winged settle, and a woodburning stove in a fireplace that opens through to the comfortable no smoking lounge area. This has some carpet on its slate flagstones, dark red settees, a table of magazines and rack of broadsheet newspapers, quite a few board games, and prints of the Battle of the Saints, where Lord Rodney obliterated the French fleet in the Caribbean. Blackboards list the good food, from lunchtime sandwiches (£3.50) and omelettes (from £5.50), to roasted peppers stuffed with mushroom couscous and topped with goats cheese (£6.25), home-made pie or curry of the day (£6.95), and rump steak (£7.75), with a choice of evening dishes such as fried tiger prawns with warm citrus dressing (£4.95), red pepper, spinach and mushroom wellington (£8.95), half a shoulder of braised lamb coated in rich redcurrant and cassis jus (£13.95), and duck breast marinated in oyster sauce and spices with chinese cabbage (£14.95), with good fresh fish specials such as grilled black bream, red mullet and john dory with basil dressing (£12.95), and spiced monkfish medallions with spinach, pine nuts and balsamic vinegar (£13.50); home-made puddings could include white chocolate cheesecake with blueberry sauce or roasted apple and rhubarb crumble (£3.95). They have a good choice of wines, and justly pride themselves on their bloody marys. A rebuilt barn stepping down through three levels forms a charming end restaurant, and a separate skittle alley has pool; also darts, Jenga, cribbage, dominoes, and perhaps piped music; service is very friendly and capable. Out on a terrace and neat green, solid tables and chairs look over the Lower Teme valley (two of the three bedrooms share the views), and this is good walking territory. *(Recommended by Austin and Jean Dance, Roy and Lindsey Fentiman, Lynda and Trevor Smith, Guy Vowles, Nick and Lynne Carter)*

Free house ~ Licensees Gillian and Kenneth Green ~ Real ale ~ Bar food ~ Restaurant ~ (01886) 821375 ~ Children in eating area of bar and restaurant ~ Dogs welcome ~ Open 11-3, 5-11; 11-11 Sat; 12-10.30 Sun; closed Mon lunchtime ~ Bedrooms: /£55B

BEWDLEY SO7875 Map 4
Little Pack Horse 🍺

High Street; no nearby parking – best to park in main car park, cross A4117 Cleobury road, and keep walking on down narrowing High Street; or can park 150 yards away at bottom of Lax Lane

Cosily pubby and bustling, this ancient low-beamed heavily timbered pub has masses of intriguing bric-a-brac, old photographs and advertisements, and a pleasant mix of old furnishings. It's nicely warmed by a woodburning stove in winter, and the atmosphere is welcoming. They do a wide choice of bar food, and you can order most dishes in two sizes. As well as tasty pies (from £4.05), good value, well presented dishes might be sandwiches (from £3.20), faggots, chips and peas (£4.50; £5.70 large), local sausages with mushy peas, mash and onion gravy (£4.95; £6.35), mediterranean vegetable and baked camembert tartlet (£6.45), beer-battered cod and chips (£6.80), chargrilled cajun salmon with roasted peppers and garlic (£9.45), and steaks (from £10.35), with puddings such as hot chocolate fudge cake (£3); they do a more elaborate evening menu. Around three well kept ales on handpump could include Greene King IPA, Marstons Pedigree and a guest such as Charles Wells Bombardier; there may be piped music. Service is cheerful and efficient. The pub nestles into the quiet back streets of this interesting riverside town; it's best to leave your car in the public car park near the river and walk up. *(Recommended by John and Glenys Wheeler, Lawrence Pearse, Keith John Ryan, David Cosham, John and Gloria Isaacs)*

InnSpired ~ Tenant Michael Stewart Gaunt ~ Real ale ~ Bar food (12-2.15, 6-9.30; 12-9.30 Sat; 12-8.30 Sun) ~ Restaurant ~ (01299) 403762 ~ Children in restaurant ~ Dogs allowed in bar ~ Open 12-3, 6-11; 12-11(10.30 Sun) Sat

BIRTSMORTON SO7935 Map 4
Farmers Arms 🍺 £

Birts Street, off B4208 W

Surrounded by plenty of walks, and good for a relaxing drink or hearty home-cooked meal afterwards, this attractive black and white timbered village pub is neatly kept and friendly. The big room on the right, which has a no smoking area, rambles away under very low dark beams, with some standing timbers, and flowery-panelled cushioned settles as well as spindleback chairs; on the left an even lower-beamed room seems even cosier, and in both the white walls have black timbering; darts in a good tiled area, shove-ha'penny, cribbage, and dominoes. Sociable locals gather at the bar for the well kept Hook Norton Best and Old Hooky on handpump, along with a guest from a brewer such as Wye Valley; there's a pleasant bustling atmosphere and service is welcoming. Simple good value bar food includes sandwiches (from £1.70), soup (£2), ploughman's (from £3), macaroni cheese (£3.50), fish and chips (£4.75), chicken and vegetable curry (£4.70), lasagne (£5.15), steak and kidney pie (£5.70), and mixed grill (£9.25), with good puddings such as apple pie or spotted dick (from £2.10). There are seats out on the large lawn. Please treat the opening hours we give below as approximate, as they may vary according to how busy or quiet things are. *(Recommended by the Didler, Pam and David Bailey, Mrs G R Sharman, Jenny and Dave Hughes, Ian and Nita Cooper, Mike and Mary Carter)*

Free house ~ Licensees Jill and Julie Moore ~ Real ale ~ Bar food (11-2, 6-9.30) ~ No credit cards ~ (01684) 833308 ~ Children in eating area of bar ~ Open 11-4, 6-11; 12-4, 7-10.30 Sun

BRANSFORD SO7852 Map 4
Bear & Ragged Staff 🍴 🍷

Off A4103 SW of Worcester; Station Road

Worcestershire Dining Pub of the Year

With its delicious food and welcoming atmosphere, this stylish place is making readers very happy these days. The cheerful interconnecting rooms have recently been comfortably refurbished, and give fine views over rolling country; in winter there's an open fire. An excellent selection of changing bar food might include soup (£3.95), lunchtime sandwiches (from £4.35, not Sunday), avocado and crayfish tail salad (£7.50), beef stroganoff with braised rice (£9.95), chargrilled rib-eye steak (£10.50), and lamb shank with pesto mash (£10.95), with around four fresh fish specials such as bass with dill crème fraîche (£12.95), and grilled lemon sole with parsley butter and lemon (£16.50), while puddings could include french meringue or rhubarb and hazelnut tart (£4.25); friendly and attentive service. There are proper tablecloths, linen napkins, and fresh flowers on the tables in the no smoking restaurant. Bass and a guest such as Hobsons Best are well kept on handpump, they've a good range of wines, lots of malt whiskies, and quite a few brandies and liqueurs; cribbage, and piped music. Good disabled access and facilities. The garden and terrace are enjoyable places to sit in fine weather (pleasant views from here too). *(Recommended by Jay Bohmrich, Ian and Jacqui Ross, John and Lucy Taylor, Ray and Winifred Halliday, Rodney and Norma Stubington)*

Free house ~ Licensees Lynda Williams and Andy Kane ~ Real ale ~ Bar food (not Sat evening) ~ Restaurant ~ (01886) 833399 ~ Children in eating area of bar and restaurant till 9pm ~ Jazz first Sun evening of month ~ Open 12-2, 5.30(6.30 Sat)-11; 12-2, 7-10.30 Sun

BREDON SO9236 Map 4
Fox & Hounds

4½ miles from M5 junction 9; A438 to Northway, left at B4079, then in Bredon follow signpost to church and river on right

This bustling thatched pub is especially pretty in summer, when it's decked with brightly coloured hanging baskets. Comfortably modernised, the carpeted bar has hop-hung beams, stone pillars and stripped timbers, a central woodburning stove, upholstered settles, a variety of wheelback, tub and kitchen chairs around handsome mahogany and cast-iron-framed tables, dried grasses and flowers, a toy fox dressed in hunting scarlet, and elegant wall lamps. There's a smaller side bar, and the restaurant and part of the bar are no smoking. Tasty, well presented bar lunches might include home-made soup (£3.25), ploughman's and sandwiches (from £4.95), home-made fishcakes (£5.25), vegetable risotto bake with cheesy breadcrumbs, battered cod or gammon and eggs (£7.95), as well as dishes such as caribbean chicken or thai-style stir fry (£10.95), and 8oz sirloin steak (£14.50); they also do Sunday roasts. You'll find well kept Banks's Bitter, Marstons Pedigree and Greene King Old Speckled Hen on handpump, several malt whiskies and wines by the glass; piped music. It's attractively placed next to a church by a lane leading down to the river; some of the picnic-sets are under Perspex. *(Recommended by R T and J C Moggridge, Ian and Denise Foster, Mike and Mary Carter, John and Laney Woods, Jack Clark, John and Vivienne Rice)*

Whitbreads ~ Lease Mike Hardwick ~ Real ale ~ Bar food (12-2, 6-9.30) ~ Restaurant ~ (01684) 772377 ~ Children in eating area of bar and restaurant ~ Dogs allowed in bar ~ Open 11.30-2.30, 6-11; 12-3, 6-10.30 Sun; closed 25, 26 Dec evening

BRETFORTON SP0943 Map 4
Fleece ★★ £

B4035 E of Evesham: turn S off this road into village; pub is in centre square by church; there's a sizeable car park at one side of the church

In summer they make the most of the extensive orchard at this fascinating old pub (now under a new landlord), which has seats on the goat-cropped grass that spreads around the beautifully restored thatched and timbered barn, among the fruit trees, and at the front by the stone pump-trough. There's also an adventure playground, and an enclosure with geese, hens, rabbits and goats; there are more picnic-sets in the front courtyard. What makes this place so special, though, is the unspoilt medieval building and its ancient contents. Before becoming a pub in 1848 it was a farm owned by the same family for nearly 500 years, and was left to the National Trust in 1977. Many of the furnishings, such as the great oak dresser that holds a priceless 48-piece set of Stuart pewter, are heirlooms passed down through that family for many generations. The rooms have massive beams and exposed timbers, worn and crazed flagstones scored with marks to keep out demons, and plenty of oddities such as a great cheese-press and set of cheese moulds, and a rare dough-proving table; a leaflet details the more bizarre items. There's a fine grandfather clock, ancient kitchen chairs, curved high-backed settles, a rocking chair, and a rack of heavy pointed iron shafts, probably for spit roasting (though there have been all sorts of esoteric guesses), in one of the huge inglenook fireplaces – there are three warming log fires. The room with the pewter is no smoking. They serve well kept Ansells, Hook Norton, Uley Pigs Ear and a couple of guests such as Pardoes Entire and Wye Valley Dorothy Goodbody's Golden Ale on handpump, along with over a dozen country wines, 20 malt whiskies, and farm cider. Darts, cribbage, dominoes, shove-ha'penny. Straightforward reasonably priced bar food is ordered through a hatch, and includes sandwiches (from £2.95), faggots and mash (£5.50), battered cod, steak and ale pie or chicken and brie salad (£6.50), and steaks (from £8.95), and puddings such as rhubarb and apple crumble (£2.95); you may have to wait a while as the kitchen facilities are limited. They hold the annual asparagus auctions (end of May) and village fête (August bank holiday Monday) here, there's sometimes morris dancing, and the village silver band plays here regularly too. Dogs are allowed in the bar outside food serving times. It gets very busy in summer. *(Recommended by Peter Sutton, the Didler, Gordon Stevenson, Michael Lamm, Ian and Rose Lock, Guy Vowles, June and Robin Savage, Maysie Thompson, Lynn Sharpless, JHBS, Alison Hayes, Pete Hanlon, MLR, S P Watkin, P A Taylor)*

Free house ~ Licensee Nigel Smith ~ Real ale ~ Bar food (12-2.30, 6.30-9; 12-4 Sun; not Sun evening) ~ (01386) 831173 ~ Children welcome ~ Folk every other Thurs ~ Open 11-11; 11-3, 6-11 in winter; 11-11 Sat; 12-10.30 Sun

BROADWAY SP0937 Map 4
Crown & Trumpet ◀

Church Street

A refreshing contrast to the rest of this smartly attractive (and very touristy) village, this golden stone pub is cheerfully down-to-earth. The beamed and timbered bar has antique dark high-backed settles, good big tables and a blazing log fire, while outside there are hardwood tables and chairs among flowers on a slightly raised front terrace. Friendly staff serve well kept Flowers Original, Greene King Old Speckled Hen and Hook Norton Old Hooky on handpump, along with a beer brewed for the pub by the local Stanway Brewery; they also do five wines by the glass, hot toddies and mulled wine in winter, and summer Pimms and kir. A good range of games includes darts, shove-ha'penny, cribbage, dominoes, ring the bull and Evesham quoits, and they've also a fruit machine, TV and piped music. Straightforward bar food includes tortilla wraps (2.95), battered cod, lasagne and chicken curry (£6.95), with puddings (£2.95); also daily specials, and Sunday roasts. *(Recommended by Graham Holden, Julie Lee, Joyce and Maurice Cottrell, John Mitchell, George Atkinson)*

Laurel Pub Company ~ Lease Andrew Scott ~ Real ale ~ Bar food (12-2.15, 6-9.15; 12-3, 5.30-9.15 Sat/Sun) ~ (01386) 853202 ~ Children welcome ~ Dogs allowed in bar ~ live music Sat evening, Blues one Thurs a month ~ Open 11-3, 5-11; 11-11 Sat; 12-10.30 Sun; 12-4, 6-10.30 Sun in winter ~ Bedrooms: £50S/£55S(£58B)

CHILDSWICKHAM SP0738 Map 4
Childswickham Inn ♀

Village signposted off A44 just NW of Broadway

Reopened in 2002 after careful refurbishment and expansion, in style and décor this is surprisingly modern, even trendy, for a country pub in a quiet village. It all works well, and service, in the hands of the son, is friendly and attentive. The main area, largely no smoking, is for eating in, with a mix of chairs around kitchen tables, big rugs on boards or broad terracotta tiles, more or less abstract contemporary prints on walls painted cream and pale violet or mauve, candlesticks in great variety, a woodburning stove and a piano. The good enterprising restaurant food, cooked by the father, changes daily but might include organic goats cheese with pepper, strawberry and pineapple salad (£4.70), home-cured gravadlax (£4.95), rabbit casserole with green noodles and an orange crust (£12.50), and roast baby monkfish tails wrapped in parma ham (£13.50), with traditional puddings such as bread and butter pudding or date and syrup sponge (£4.95). At lunchtime it's particularly popular with older folk, and attracts a broader mix in the evenings and at weekends. Off to the right is a proper bar (no food in here), light and airy, with Hook Norton Best and Old Hooky on handpump (from a counter that seems made from old doors), Bulmer's cider, a short but good choice of sensibly priced wines all available by the glass, and good coffee in elegant cups. This small carefully lit room has a similarly modern colour-scheme moderated by some big horse pictures, a couple of leather armchairs by a log-effect gas fire, just four sturdy tables, a few kitchen and housekeeper's chairs, and another oriental rug on bare boards. The entrance lobby has the biggest doormat we have ever seen – wall to wall – with good disabled access and facilities. A large sunny deck outside has tables. *(Recommended by Miss J Brotherton, Martin Jones, Martin Jennings)*

Punch ~ Lease Guy Justin Brookes ~ Real ale ~ Restaurant ~ (01386) 852461 ~ Dogs allowed in bar ~ Open 12-2, 5.30-11; 12-10.30 Sun

CLENT SO9279 Map 4
Fountain

Off A491 at Holy Cross/Clent exit roundabout, via Violet Lane, then turn right at T junction; Adams Hill/Odnall Lane

As this tucked-away pub is so popular (especially with an older set at lunchtime), it's a good idea to book if you want to eat here. Service is quick and friendly, and the atmosphere is buoyant and thriving; handily it's open all day. As well as good value lunchtime dishes (not Sunday) such as open sandwiches (from £3.95 – there's an interesting choice), lamb chops with port and mint sauce, baked smoked haddock mornay or pork and pineapple pie (£6.95), generous food, from a changing menu, could include home-made soup (£2.95), spicy duck pancake (£5.50), swiss cheese wellington or courgette and pepper rogan josh (£9.95), herb-roasted cod (£12.50), and half a crispy roast duck with orange and brandy sauce (£13.50), with puddings such as banana fritter with rum and butterscotch sauce and home-made apple crumble (from £4.45); Sunday lunch (from £7.95). The long carpeted dining bar – four knocked-together areas – is filled mainly by sturdy pine tables (mostly no smoking) and country-kitchen chairs or mate's chairs, with some comfortably cushioned brocaded wall seats. There are nicely framed local photographs on the ragged pinkish walls above a dark panelled dado, pretty wall lights, and candles on the tables. Well kept Banks's Bitter and Original, Marstons Pedigree and a guest such as Charles Wells Bombardier on handpump, freshly squeezed orange juice, decent wines served in cut glass, over a dozen malts, and a choice of speciality teas and good coffees; any faint piped music tends to be drowned out by the hum of contented conversation; alley skittles. There are a few picnic-sets out in front, and the surrounding Clent Hills are popular walking territory. More reports on this good pub please. *(Recommended by Lynda and Trevor Smith, Mike and Mary Carter, Malcolm Taylor)*

Union Pub Company ~ Lease Richard and Jacque Macey ~ Real ale ~ Bar food (12-2.30, 6-9(9.30 Fri/Sat); Sun 12-5) ~ (01562) 883286 ~ Children in restaurant till 7.30pm ~ Open 11-11; 12-10.30 Sun

CROWLE SO9256 Map 4
Old Chequers ♚ ♉

2½ miles from M5 junction 6; A4538 towards Evesham, then left after ½ mile; turn right to Crowle Green

Readers are full of praise for the friendly and efficient staff at this smoothly run dining pub – a great place to stop for lunch if you're on the motorway. Much modernised, the pub rambles extensively around an island bar, with plush-seated mate's chairs around a mix of pub tables on the patterned carpet, some brass and copper on the swirly-plastered walls, lots of pictures for sale at the back, and a coal-effect gas fire at one end (there's central heating too). A big square extension on the right, with shinily varnished rustic timbering and beamery, has more tables. Outside, there are picnic-sets on the grass behind, among shrubs and small fruit trees – a pleasant spot, with pasture beyond. Generous home-made food includes reasonably priced light lunches such as soup (£2.95), chicken livers with bacon, cream and brandy, home-made pâté or grilled goats cheese ciabatta (£5.95), along with other dishes such as lasagne (£8.95), thai chicken curry (£10.25), and grilled aberdeen angus sirloin steak (£14.50), with specials such as salmon and crab fishcakes with sweet chilli dip (£5.95), baked bass stuffed with lemon grass, lime and chilli (£11), and half a roast duck with black cherry and port sauce (£12.50); puddings such as crème brûlée (from £4.25). Well kept Banks's Bitter and Original and a guest such as Timothy Taylors Landlord are well kept on handpump, and they've good value house wines. Disabled access. *(Recommended by Karen Eliot, M G Hart, Mrs Sally Lloyd, Roger and Pauline Pearce, John Bowdler, Jo and Iain MacGregor, Dr D J and Mrs S C Walker, Martin Jennings, Stuart Paulley, M Joyner)*

Free house ~ Licensees Steven and Ian Thomas ~ Real ale ~ Bar food (12-1.45, 7-9.45) ~ (01905) 381275 ~ Open 12-2.30, 7-11; 12-3 Sun; closed Sun evening, 26 and 31 Dec

DEFFORD SO9143 Map 4
Monkey House

A4104 towards Upton – immediately after passing Oak public house on right, there's a small group of cottages, of which this is the last

The only hint from the outside that this pretty black and white thatched cottage is actually a pub is a notice by the door saying 'Licensed to sell cider and tobacco'. It's a fascinating throwback – a completely traditional cider-house, which has been in the landlord's wife's family for more than 150 years. Very cheap Bulmer's Medium or Special Dry cider is tapped from barrels and poured by jug into pottery mugs (some locals have their own), and served from a hatch beside the door. As a concession to modern tastes, beer is now sold too, in cans. They don't do food (except crisps and nuts), but you can bring your own. In the summer you could find yourself sharing the garden with Tapper the jack russell (as we went to press they were about to get a new rottweiler puppy), and the hens and cockerels that meander in from an adjacent collection of caravans and sheds; there's also a pony called Mandy. Alternatively you can retreat to a small and spartan side outbuilding with a couple of plain tables, a settle and an open fire. The pub's name comes from the story of a drunken customer who, some years ago, fell into bramble bushes and swore that he was attacked by monkeys. Please note the limited opening times. *(Recommended by Pete Baker, the Didler)*

Free house ~ Licensee Graham Collins ~ No credit cards ~ (01386) 750234 ~ Children welcome ~ Open Fri-Mon 11(12 Sun)-2(2.30 Sat); 6-10.30(7-10 Sun) Weds-Sun; closed Mon evening, all Tues, lunchtimes Weds, Thurs

FLYFORD FLAVELL SO9754 Map 4
Boot 🍺

½ mile off A422 Worcester—Alcester; sharp turn into village beside Flyford Arms, then turn left into Radford Road

You can be sure of a warm welcome at this Georgian-fronted country pub (with parts dating from the 13th c), whether you're here for the well kept real ales or the enjoyable home-made food. The heavily beamed and timbered back area is mainly used for dining now (part is no smoking), with fresh flowers on tables, a log fire in the big fireplace, and plates on its walls. The lower end, divided by a timbered part wall, has a glass-topped well, and leads into a modern conservatory with brocaded dining chairs and swagged curtains. A little beamed front bar has hunting prints, antique chairs, and inglenook seats by the small log fire; on its left are darts and a well lit pool table; also piped music, cards, and fruit machine. Fullers London Pride, Greene King IPA and Old Speckled Hen, and Worthingtons are well kept on handpump alongside a changing guest such as Bass; they've nine malt whiskies and a good range of liqueurs. Served on big white plates, reasonably priced dishes include lunchtime sandwiches (from £3.25), and bar snacks (not Saturday evening) such as thai fishcakes, chicken satay or steak and onion baguette (£6.25), with specials such as king prawns in garlic butter (£4.95), beer-battered cod (£8), various home-made pies or wild mushroom and rocket pesto risotto with parmesan crisps (£8.25), lamb shank with red wine and root vegetable sauce or tuna loin with pineapple and chilli salsa (£10.95), and grilled lemon sole or bass (£12.25), with puddings (£3.50); Sunday roast (£6.95). At lunchtime the pub is popular with older people, who particularly appreciate the patience of the very friendly staff. The neatly kept garden has smart furniture, outdoor heating and lighting, and attractive big planted pots. *(Recommended by Theo, Anne and Jane Gaskin, Stephen Buckley, W H and E Thomas, M Joyner, Martin Jennings, Rod Stoneman, David and Barbara Knott, Martin Jones, Leigh and Gillian Mellor, Dr and Mrs A K Clarke)*

Free house ~ Licensee Sue Hughes ~ Real ale ~ Bar food (12-1.55, 6.30(6 Sat)-9.45) ~ Restaurant ~ (01386) 462658 ~ Children in eating area of bar and restaurant ~ Dogs allowed in bar ~ Open 12-2.30, 5-11; 12-10.30 Sun ~ Bedrooms: £50S/£60S

HOLY CROSS SO9278 Map 4

Bell & Cross 🍴 ◖

4 miles from M5 junction 4: A491 towards Stourbridge, then follow Clent signpost off on left

With a classic unspoilt early 19th-c layout, and a comfortably civilised feel, this pub serves good imaginative food, but is also popular with locals just in for an evening drink. The changing menu could include lunchtime snacks (not Sunday) such as sandwiches (from £3.75, baguettes from £3.95), spaghetti with garlic oil and chilli (£4.95; £6.95 large), and poached salmon, rocket and dill penne (£5.25; large £7.50), as well as delicious soups (£3.60), courgette pancakes with double brie and rocket salad (£5.50), poached smoked haddock, warm potato and baby spinach salad with poached egg (£11.95), pot-roasted lamb shoulder with broad beans, spicy sausage and mint (£12.75), and chargrilled fillet steak with oven-dried tomato fries and green peppercorn sauce (£15.95), with specials such as pot-roasted pork tenderloin with garlic mash, wilted leeks and provençale tomato and red wine sauce (£12.95), and grilled john dory, pumpkin, beetroot and spinach charlotte with sea asparagus sauce (£14.95); puddings could include red fruit gratin with raspberry ripple ice cream or vanilla bean panna cotta with poached peppered strawberries (from £4.95). A Sunday menu includes traditional roasts (mains £10.95); friendly service. The five small rooms and kitchen open off a central corridor with a black and white tiled floor: they give a choice of carpet, bare boards, lino or nice old quarry tiles, a variety of moods from snug and chatty to bright and airy, and an individual décor in each – theatrical engravings on red walls here, nice sporting prints on pale green walls there, racing and gundog pictures above the black panelled dado in another room. Two of the rooms have small serving bars, with well kept Banks's Bitter, Marstons Pedigree and a couple of guests such as Hook Norton and Timothy Taylors Landlord on handpump. You'll find decent house wines, a variety of coffees, daily papers, coal fires in most rooms, perhaps regulars playing cards in one of the two front ones, and piped music. The pub cat is called Pumba. There's a terrace, and a neat side lawn has picnic-sets. *(Recommended by Karen Eliot, Richard and Karen Holt, Dave Braisted, Cliff Blakemore, David and Ruth Shillitoe, W H and E Thomas, Gill and Tony Morriss, Mr and Mrs C R Little, Pete Baker, Nigel Long)*

Enterprise ~ Tenants Roger and Jo Narbett ~ Real ale ~ Bar food (not Sun evening) ~ Restaurant ~ (01562) 730319 ~ Children in restaurant ~ Dogs allowed in bar ~ Open 12-3(3.30 Sun), 6-11; 12-4, 7-10.30 Sun; closed 25 Dec, evenings 26, 31 Dec and 1 Jan

Post Office address codings confusingly give the impression that some pubs are in Worcestershire, when they're really in Gloucestershire, Herefordshire, Shropshire, or Warwickshire (which is where we list them).

KIDDERMINSTER SO8376 Map 4
King & Castle ● £
Railway Station, Comberton Hill

Right at the heart of the Severn Valley Railway terminus, this intriguing re-creation of a classic station refreshment room suggests a better-class Edwardian establishment that has let its hair down to embrace more informal modern ways. Furnishings are solid and in character (even to the occasional obvious need for a touch of reupholstery), and there's the railway memorabilia that you'd expect. You can even take your pint out on to the platform and watch the trains steam by. The atmosphere is lively and sometimes noisily good-humoured (and it can get rather smoky), and the good-natured landlady and friendly staff cope well with the bank holiday and railway gala day crowds – when you'd be lucky to find a seat. Bathams, Highgate Mild and Wyre Piddle Royal Piddle are very well kept alongside a couple of changing guests from brewers such as Enville, Hobsons, and Wye Valley on handpump (with at least one at bargain price). Good value, straightforward bar food includes filled rolls (£1.50), filled baked potatoes (from £2.65), breaded plaice, steak or cajun chicken (£4.95), and traditional puddings such as treacle sponge (£2.25), with a couple of weekend specials such as chilli con carne (£3.95), and beef and beer pie (£4.75); they also do Sunday roasts (around £4.50), and children's meals (£2.50). You can use a Rover ticket to shuttle between here and the Railwaymans Arms in Bridgnorth (see Shropshire chapter). More reports please. *(Recommended by Gill and Tony Morriss, Di and Mike Gillam, John and Glenys Wheeler, Bernie Adams)*

Free house ~ Licensee Rosemary Hyde ~ Real ale ~ Bar food (12-2(2.30 Sat/Sun), 6-8 Fri/Sat, 7-9 Sun; not Mon-Thurs evenings) ~ No credit cards ~ (01562) 747505 ~ Children welcome ~ Dogs welcome ~ Open 11-3, 5-11; 11-11 Sat; 12-10.30 Sun

MALVERN SO7845 Map 4
Nags Head ●
Bottom end of Bank Street, steep turn down off A449

Over the last two or three years this has been turned into a charmingly traditional tavern, with a great choice of beers, and good food. A splendid variety of places to sit rambles through a series of snug individually decorated rooms with one or two steps between some, all sorts of chairs including some leather armchairs, pews sometimes arranged as booths, a mix of tables with some sturdy ones stained different colours, bare boards here, flagstones there, carpet elsewhere, and plenty of interesting pictures and homely touches such as house plants and shelves of well thumbed books. The central servery, with a coal fire opposite, has well kept Greene King IPA, Marstons Pedigree and Woods Shropshire Lad on handpump, and several changing guest beers which on our inspection visit consisted of Banks's, Bathams Mild, Cottage Golden Arrow and Wye Valley Hereford; they also keep a fine range of malt whiskies, and have decent wines by the glass. Young friendly staff happily discuss the beers, and may offer tasters. The general mood is relaxed and easy-going, with both a rack of broadsheet newspapers and a good juke box. The food includes a fine ham ploughman's (£4.95), sausages and mash (£6.50), smoked mackerel in an interesting cheese sauce or diced beef in dijon mustard (£9.80), and specials such as stir fries. In the evenings they do only meals in the extension barn dining room, and don't take bookings – so get there early. Outside are picnic-sets and rustic tables and benches on the front terrace and in a garden, both with heaters; it's a pleasant spot, between the great mass of hill swelling up behind and the plain stretching out below. We have not yet heard from readers who have stayed overnight here. The landlord's natural modesty is so great that he'd prefer not to be in the *Guide* at all (ironic, given so many thousands who hope so much to get in), and as a consequence would not give us food prices, so if you do eat here please let us know food prices.
(Recommended by Dr and Mrs Jackson, Guy Vowles, Ian and Nita Cooper)

Free house ~ Real ale ~ Bar food (12-2, 6.30-8.30) ~ (01684) 574373 ~ Open 11-11; 12-10.30 Sun

PENSAX SO7269 Map 4
Bell 🍺

B4202 Abberley—Clows Top, SE of the Snead Common part of the village

A good mix of customers (including welcoming locals) and friendly staff helps to create an enjoyably pubby atmosphere at this homely roadside mock-Tudor inn. Four changing real ales from brewers such as Cannon Royall, Hook Norton, Woods and Wye Valley are well kept on handpump, along with Hobsons. The L-shaped main bar has a restrained traditional décor, with long cushioned pews on its bare boards, good solid pub tables, and a woodburning stove. Beyond a small area on the left with a couple more tables is a more airy dining room, with french windows opening on to a wooden deck that on hot days can give a slightly californian feel; the pub has a log fire for our more usual weather. Picnic-sets in the back garden look out over rolling fields and copses to the Wyre Forest, and you get the same views from some tables inside. Besides generous sandwiches (from £3.50), straightforward reasonably priced bar food, from a changing menu, might typically include filled baked potatoes and omelettes (from £5.50), liver, bacon and onions, or home honey-cured ham and egg or faggots and mushy peas (£6.50), rump steak (£11.95), and Sunday roast (£6.50). *(Recommended by DAV, Theocsbrian, Alan and Paula McCully, Nigel Espley, Liane Purnell, Gill and Tony Morriss, Edmund Coan, Roy and Lindsey Fentiman)*

Free house ~ Licensees John and Trudy Greaves ~ Real ale ~ Bar food (12-2, 6-9; 12-4 Sun) ~ (01299) 896677 ~ Children in eating area and family room ~ Dogs allowed in bar ~ Open 12-2.30, 5-11; 12-10.30 Sun; closed Mon lunch except bank hols

WELLAND SO7940 Map 4
Anchor 🍽️ 🍺 🛏️

A4104 towards Upton (Drake Street)

An especially good time to visit this pretty Tudor cottage is in summer, when the front is festooned with colourful hanging baskets, with a passion flower and roses climbing the walls. There are picnic-sets on the lawn, with flower borders and a big old apple tree, and behind is a field for tents or caravans (readers enjoy staying here), with electric hook-up points. The welcoming L-shaped bar has country prints on the walls, some armchairs around chatty low tables, and more sitting-up chairs around eating-height tables. Beyond is a spreading, comfortably furnished no smoking dining area, nicely set with candles, pink tablecloths and napkins (fine views from here). Six well kept real ales on handpump include Hook Norton, Smiles Anchor and Best and Woods Shropshire Lad, along with guests such as Timothy Taylors Landlord and Charles Wells Bombardier, and you can have any wine on the list by the glass; shove-ha'penny, chess, Jenga, and perhaps unobtrusive piped music. A wide choice of changing food, on blackboards by the bar, might include fried sardines in garlic and herb butter (£3.99), baguettes or baked potatoes (£4.25), salmon teriyaki with grated ginger (£5.25), pork loin stuffed with apple in stilton sauce (£7.95), lamb steak with cranberry and honey (£9.99), trout stuffed with garlic prawns (£10.70), and tasty thai-style beef fillet with basil and chilli (£12.65), with puddings (£4.25); although the staff are attentive, there may be quite a long wait at busy times. The pub is handy for the Three Counties show ground; a new beer garden (no children) should be open by the time we go to press. *(Recommended by Chris Flynn, Wendy Jones, M Joyner, GSB, Bernard Stradling, Jayne and John Fuller, K H Frostick, Alan and Paula McCully, Jenny and Dave Hughes, Brian and Anita Randall, A S and M E Marriott, Steve Whalley, Joyce and Maurice Cottrell)*

Free house ~ Licensees Colin and Caroline Barrett ~ Real ale ~ Bar food ~ Restaurant ~ (01684) 592317 ~ Children in restaurant ~ Open 11.45-3, 6.45-11; 11.45-3, 6.30-11 Sat; 12-3 Sun; closed Sun evening except bank hols ~ Bedrooms: £45B/£60S(£50B)

WYRE PIDDLE SO9647 Map 4
Anchor
Village signposted off A4538 WNW of Evesham

Seats on the spacious back lawn of this 17th-c pub (once a row of boatsmen's cottages) run down to the water, with spreading views out over the Vale of Evesham as far as the Cotswolds, the Malverns and Bredon Hill. The friendly and neatly kept little lounge has a good log fire in its attractively restored inglenook fireplace, comfortably upholstered chairs and settles, and two beams in the shiny ceiling. The dining area has an open fire, rugs on stripped wood floors and wooden tables and chairs. In the big airy back bar (good views of the River Avon if you get here early), they serve Bass, Boddingtons, Marstons Pedigree, local Wyre Piddle and a monthly guest such as Timothy Taylors Landlord under light blanket pressure, seven wines by the glass, 10 malt whiskies, and country wines; fruit machine and piped music. From a reasonably priced menu, generously served dishes could include home-made soup (£3.25), pigeon breast with diced black pudding (£4.50), courgette and aubergine provençale (£6.75), lambs liver and bacon with parsnip mash or steak, kidney and ale pie (£6.95), chargrilled lamb with rosemary and garlic (£8.95), and steaks (from £10.50), with specials such as beef stroganoff with mushroom, dijon mustard and cream sauce (£8.95), and fried skate wings with garlic and Cointreau (£9.50), with tempting puddings (£3.25); they also do lunchtime sandwiches (from £2.95, not Sunday), and a children's menu (from £3.25). *(Recommended by Brian and Anna Marsden, Roy and Lindsey Fentiman, Ian and Denise Foster, Mike Gorton, Brenda and Stuart Naylor)*

Enterprise ~ Lease Nigel and Hilary Green ~ Real ale ~ Bar food (not 26 Dec, 1 Jan) ~ Restaurant ~ (01386) 552799 ~ Children welcome ~ Dogs allowed in bar ~ Open 12-3, 6-11; 12-11(10.30 Sun) Sat; 12-3, 6-11(7-10.30 Sun) weekends in winter

Lucky Dip
Besides the fully inspected pubs, you might like to try these Lucky Dips recommended to us and described by readers (if you do, please send us reports: www.goodguides.com).

ABBERLEY [SO7567]
Manor Arms: Comfortable country inn tucked away in quiet village backwater, façade emblazoned with coats of arms; two bars and restaurant, interesting collection of toby jugs, Courage Directors and Fullers London Pride, good food esp steaks and lots of puddings; 10 reasonably priced bedrooms *(Edmund Coan)*
ALVECHURCH [SP0272]
Red Lion [in village, handy for M42 junction 2]: Beamed Vintage Inn with side snugs that nicely conceal its size, big log fires, soft lighting, reliable reasonably priced generous food all day, good service, well kept Bass and proper pots of tea; quiet piped music, very busy wknds; back garden *(Alan and Margaret Griffiths, Simon, Jo and Benjamin Cole)*
BADSEY [SP0743]
☆ *Round of Gras* [B4035 2 miles E of Evesham]: Warm and comfortable, with substantial well priced fresh food inc seasonal local asparagus feasts, welcoming landlord, well kept ales such as Boddingtons or Flowers IPA, Fullers London Pride, Shepherd Neame Spitfire and Uley Pigs Ear, Weston's farm cider, country wines, log fire, lots of polished wood, panelling and farm tools, raised restaurant section; children welcome, pleasant fair-sized tree-

shaded garden *(K H Frostick, BB, JHBS, KN-R, Pete Yearsley)*
Wheatsheaf [E of Evesham; High St]: Friendly and homely, with well kept ales such as Greene King Old Speckled Hen and Wadworths 6X, good wines in good-sized glasses, well prepared food inc good hot sandwiches, unusual dishes and local asparagus, efficient service even when busy, partly no smoking restaurant off small lounge, separate public bar; garden tables, bedrooms, some quite new *(MRSM, Brenda and Stuart Naylor)*
BERROW [SO7835]
Duke of York [junction A438/B4208]: Two linked rooms, 15th-c beams, nooks and crannies, friendly atmosphere, cheerful young staff, good log fire, enjoyable food from good sandwiches up, well kept real ales, farm cider, friendly staff and locals, dominoes, cribbage; piped music; children welcome, extended back restaurant, part no smoking, picnic-sets in big back garden, handy for Malvern Hills *(Stuart Turner, BB)*
BEWDLEY [SO7875]
George [Load St]: Smart old black and white coaching inn with friendly public bar, large elegant front bar, cosy back bar, restaurant (enjoyable and not too pricy), decent wines,

Tetleys and a guest beer; bedrooms, handy for Severn Valley Railway *(Gill and Tony Morriss)*

BOURNHEATH [SO9474]

☆ *Gate* [handy for M5 junction 3; Dodford Rd]: Attractive country dining pub with wide choice of attractively priced good food inc lots of vegetarian, lunchtime and early evening bargains, good value Sun lunch, well kept Highgate Saddlers Best, long-serving licensees and quick friendly service even though busy, no smoking conservatory area; nice garden *(Simon, Jo and Benjamin Cole, Gerry and Rosemary Dobson)*

Nailers Arms [Doctors Hill, via B4091; 3 miles from M5 junction 4]: Front stylishly modern and open-plan with comfortable light wood chairs and tables on its stripped floors, good food from lunchtime sandwiches through a good up-to-date choice of starters, main dishes and puddings to hefty Sun lunch, Enville White, Greene King Old Speckled Hen and two changing guest beers, country wines, friendly helpful staff, daily papers, country-style locals' bar; children really welcome, some tables out by car park *(Simon, Jo and Benjamin Cole)*

BROAD HEATH [SO6765]

Fox: Comfortable black and white timbered pub with friendly licensees, good changing choice of real ales inc Hobsons, enjoyable thai food, lively atmosphere with separate public bar and pool room; tidy garden *(M and D Toms)*

BROADWAY [SP0937]

☆ *Lygon Arms* [High St]: Stately but expensive Cotswold hotel's adjoining bar/brasserie has good imaginative food, quick very attentive service, nice wines, children allowed; ancient main building is strikingly handsome, with interesting old rooms rambling away from attractive oak-panelled bar; tables in prettily planted courtyard, well kept gardens, smart comfortable bedrooms, open all day in summer *(LYM, Joyce and Maurice Cottrell, Bernard Stradling)*

CASTLEMORTON [SO7837]

Robin Hood [B4208, 1¼ miles S of Welland crossroads]: Charming old timbered and beamed country pub below the Malvern Hills, relaxed atmosphere, medley of cushioned pews etc, big brick fireplace, lots of horsebrasses, hops, jugs, welcoming service, good value food, well kept Bass, Boddingtons and Greene King, Weston's cider; area with fruit machine and darts, separate small dining room; big lawns and space for caravans behind *(Dave Braisted)*

CHADDESLEY CORBETT [SO8973]

Talbot [off A448 Bromsgrove–Kidderminster]: Attractive much restored late medieval timbered pub in quiet village street, helpful friendly staff, well kept Banks's beers (they are happy to remove the sparklers), good choice of bar food *(I D Greenfield)*

CHARLTON [SP0145]

Gardeners Arms [the one nr Pershore; Strand]: Friendly family-run local on green of pretty thatched village, enjoyable fresh

straightforward food, welcoming atmosphere and service, well kept Marstons Pedigree, Wadworths 6X and a guest beer, decent choice of wines, roomy no smoking dining area, plain public bar with darts and pool room; children welcome *(Brian and Anna Marsden)*

CLEEVE PRIOR [SP0849]

Kings Arms [Bidford Rd (B4085)]: Unspoilt 16th-c beamed pub off the tourist track, well run and comfortable, with good imaginative food at reasonable prices, well kept Wadworths 6X and a guest beer, friendly helpful service, no smoking family dining room, no piped music; children welcome, tables outside *(Brenda and Stuart Naylor)*

CLENT [SO9179]

French Hen [Bromsgrove Rd]: Well redone as 'french pub', well kept real ales inc Highgate Mild, interesting food choice from snacks up, chatty areas with comfortable settees, dining room; handy for walks in Clent Hills *(Gill and Tony Morriss)*

COLWALL [SO7440]

Wellington [A449 Malvern—Ledbury]: Neat and bright, with good food inc lots of italian dishes, sensible wine list, good friendly service, real ales such as Greene King Ruddles and local St Georges, most dining areas no smoking *(Stephen Williamson, Dave Braisted)*

CUTNALL GREEN [SO8768]

☆ *Chequers* [Kidderminster Rd]: Comfortable beamed country dining pub in same family as Bell & Cross, Holy Cross (see main entries), with comprehensive choice of similarly good food inc some good italian dishes; scrubbed tables, stylish green and cream décor, Boddingtons and Marstons Pedigree, good wine choice *(W H and E Thomas, P B Venables)*

DRAKES BROUGHTON [SO9248]

☆ *Plough & Harrow* [A44 NW of Pershore]: Reliable dining pub with partly no smoking extended and refurbished restaurant area, comfortable and attractive rambling lounge, sensibly priced food inc cut-price small helpings for the elderly, good friendly helpful service, well kept Bass and guest beers, log fire; may be two sittings on busy days; pleasant terrace, big orchard-side garden with play area *(Caroline and Michael Abbey, Jason Caulkin, DMT, George Atkinson, Mr and Mrs M Pearson, P B Venables)*

DROITWICH [SO8963]

Old Cock [Friar St]: Several distinctive rooms, beams and stained glass, friendly helpful staff, enjoyable generous food from good value baps and sandwiches up in bar and back bistro (they'll do children's helpings), well kept real ales and good house wines, neat housekeeping; garden courtyard with pool and fountain *(Barry Smith, Stuart, Anne and Rowan Wilkie)*

Railway [Kidderminster Rd]: Small traditional local with friendly new mother-and-daughter licensees, railway memorabilia in two-room lounge bar, well kept Marstons Pedigree and two local guest beers, good value straightforward lunches (Sun only if booked ahead), cribbage, dominoes and darts; big balcony with views of Vines Park and canal basin (soon to be reopened, and canal made navigable), open all day *(Dr B and Mrs P B Baker, Di and Mike Gillam)*

DUNHAMPSTEAD [SO9160]

☆ *Firs* [just SE of Droitwich, towards Sale Green – OS Sheet 150 map ref 919600]: Smart and pretty dining pub, with good food from doorstep sandwiches up (hot dishes freshly made so can be a wait), well kept Banks's and Marstons, welcoming service, flowers on tables, comfortable no smoking dining conservatory; booking advised wknd; flower-filled terrace, small grassy garden; nice spot not far from canal – good walks *(Dr and Mrs Jackson, Lynda and Trevor Smith, LYM)*

EARLS CROOME [SO8642]

☆ *Yorkshire Grey* [A38, N of M50 junction 1]: Bustling pub with imaginative décor, charming young cheerful staff, enterprising choice of good visually appealing food (all day wknd) inc fair-priced lunches, well kept Bass and good australian house wines, candlelit restaurant *(Caroline and Michael Abbey)*

ECKINGTON [SO9241]

Anchor [B4080]: Comfortable and convivial, with enjoyable generous reasonably priced food (wise to book wknds) inc good specials, Marstons Pedigree, John Smiths and Tetleys, lots of stripped stone, three dining areas off bar, one with big fish tank; may be piped music; tables out on terraces front and back, five bedrooms with own shower rooms *(R Clark, Neil and Anita Christopher)*

EGDON [SO9053]

Nightingale [A4538]: Well decorated and furnished Vintage Inn, decent reasonably priced food all day, changing seasonally *(Caroline and Michael Abbey)*

ELDERSFIELD [SO8131]

☆ *Greyhound* [signed from B4211; Lime St (don't go into Eldersfield itself), OS Sheet 150 map ref 815314]: Unspoilt country local with welcoming young licensees, good inexpensive country cooking (not Mon) well kept Bass, Butcombe and Woods Parish tapped from the cask, big woodburner and friendly tabby cat in appealing black-beamed ochre-walled public bar, horse-racing pictures in candlelit carpeted no smoking room, lively skittle alley, strikingly modern lavatories with interesting mosaic in gents'; picnic-sets in small front garden, swings and dovecote out behind *(the Didler, Guy Vowles, BB, Theocsbrian)*

ELMLEY CASTLE [SO9841]

Queen Elizabeth [signed off A44 and A435, not far from Evesham; Main St]: Quaint ancient tavern with haphazard medley of periods in decoration and furnishings, huge fireplace, couple of steps up to bar with lots of pictures, fish tank and old books about pubs, cheery service, Banks's Bitter, cheap farm cider; tables out in yard *(LYM, Neil and Anita Christopher)*

EVESHAM [SP0344]

Green Dragon [Oat St, towards library off High St]: Unpretentious 16th-c coaching inn, well worn in, brewing own Asum and Gold

(glass panel shows brewery); small beamed dining lounge with sloping fire, attractive antique prints and fireside table, big comfortable public bar, back pool room and skittle alley, old well in corridor, friendly staff, inexpensive food inc oriental dishes; can be smoky, evening piped music, perhaps TV; good value bedrooms, good breakfast *(George Atkinson, Pete Baker)*

FECKENHAM [SP0061]

☆ *Lygon Arms* [B4090 Droitwich—Alcester]: Welcoming licensees, enjoyable food using fresh ingredients, well kept ales inc Greene King Old Speckled Hen and guest beers, reasonable prices, new dining conservatory *(Peter Williams, Martin Jennings)*

FLADBURY [SO9946]

Chequers [Chequers Lane]: Warm and very welcoming upmarket dining pub dating from 14th c, huge old-fashioned range at end of long bar, lots of local prints, good generous food, charming beamed back restaurant with carvery, well kept Black Sheep, Fullers London Pride, Hook Norton Best and Wyre Piddle Piddle in the Hole at reasonable prices, quick service; large pleasant garden with play area, peaceful pretty village, comfortable well equipped bedroom extension *(Brian and Anna Marsden)*

FORHILL [SP0575]

☆ *Peacock* [handy for M42 junctions 2 and 3; pub at junction Lea End Lane and Icknield St]: Attractive mix of furnishings and rather stylishly simple décor in spacious knocked-through beamed rooms of quietly placed country pub, woodburner in big inglenook, conventional bar food from open kitchen, restaurant allowing children (food all day wknds), nine interesting changing real ales, country wines; may be piped music; picnic-sets on back terrace and front grass, bar open all day Mon-Fri *(B and M Kendall, LYM, Dr and Mrs A K Clarke)*

GORCOTT HILL [SP0968]

☆ *Hollybush* [off A435 3 miles S of M42 junction 3]: Quietly placed country pub, bright and spacious, with wide range of generous good value home-made food inc all the usual favourites, well kept Courage Directors, decent wines, obliging efficient service; no children, busy with office people wkdy lunchtime, walkers welcome *(Michael and Hazel Lyons, Martin Jennings)*

HADLEY [SO8662]

Bowling Green [Hadley Heath; off A4133 Droitwich—Ombersley]: Large cheerful bar in quaint pleasantly refurbished 16th-c inn, wide range of good value food from enterprising filled baguettes to popular Sun carvery (packed with families then), well kept Banks's Bitter and Mild, Marstons Pedigree and Hook Norton, good value wines, big log fire, hops on beams, attractive restaurant; children welcome, dogs welcome in back bar, tables out overlooking its bowling green (UK's oldest), comfortable bedrooms, pleasant walks nearby *(Lynda and Trevor Smith, Denys Gueroult)*

HANBURY [SO9666]

Gate Hangs Well [Woodgate Rd, nr B4091 towards Stoke Prior]: Much extended dining pub reopened under new management, with good value generous food inc carvery, well kept Banks's and Marstons Pedigree, friendly service; open-plan but well divided, with conservatory and country views *(Dave Braisted)*

HANLEY CASTLE [SO8341]

☆ *Three Kings* [Church End, off B4211 N of Upton upon Severn]: Unchanging classic country local, friendly and well worn in, with huge inglenook and hatch service in little tiled-floor tap room, consistently well kept Butcombe, Thwaites and great choice of changing beers from small breweries usually inc a Mild, farm cider, dozens of malt whiskies, two other larger rooms, one with fire in open range, low-priced homely food (not Sun evening – singer then; be prepared for a possibly longish wait other times), seats of a sort outside; family room, bedroom *(M Joyner, Theocsbrian, the Didler, Gill and Tony Morriss, LYM, Alan and Paula McCully, Pete Baker)*

HONEYBOURNE [SP1143]

☆ *Thatched Tavern* [High St]: Attractive thatched and beamed black and white country local dating from 13th c, homely, comfortable and relaxing; soft lighting, well kept ales such as Bass, Greene King Abbot, St Georges War Drum and Tetleys Imperial, good choice of wines by the glass inc champage, varietal apple juices, bar food, bay window seats, leaded lights, beams and flagstones, woodburner in big stone inglenook, end dining room down a step; nostalgic piped music; picnic-sets in garden behind *(Angus Lyon, BB)*

INKBERROW [SP0157]

☆ *Bulls Head* [A422 Worcester—Alcester]: Handsome Georgian inn, steps between levels, good village atmosphere in much older heavily beamed, timbered and partly flagstoned bar with woodburner in big fireplace, comfortable banquettes and other seats, Banks's, Wychwood Goliath and a beer brewed for the pub by Church End, neat helpful staff, lots of pictures and disaster posters, darts; two comfortable dining areas, decent food inc good roasts; garden behind with terrace and play area, bedrooms *(BB, George Atkinson)*

☆ *Old Bull* [off A422 – note that this is quite different from the nearby Bulls Head]: Photogenic Tudor pub with bulging walls, huge inglenooks, flagstones, oak beams and trusses, and some old-fashioned high-backed settles among more modern furnishings; lots of Archers memorabilia (it's the model for the Ambridge Bull), friendly service, home-made food from sandwiches to Sun roast, well kept Bass and Flowers; children allowed in eating area, tables outside *(LYM, Angus Lyon)*

KEMERTON [SO9437]

Crown [back road Bredon—Beckford]: 18th-c pub with refreshingly modern light furnishings in smallish L-shaped lounge bar, good interesting country cooking from sandwiches

up inc plenty of fish and enjoyable puddings, well kept Bass, Courage Directors and Greene King Ruddles, lively and welcoming licensees, daily papers; pretty garden, upmarket village worth a look around, good walks over Bredon Hill *(Martin Jennings, Jonathan and Ann Tross)*

KEMPSEY [SO8648]

Farmers Arms [Bestmans Lane, Kempsey Common]: Cheerful country pub with locals' bar, dining lounge and restaurant, enjoyable food all day inc home-grown veg, well kept Greene King IPA and Abbot, decent wines, log fire; skittle alley, big garden with boules, start for several good circular walks *(anon)*

☆ *Walter de Cantelupe* [A38, handy for M5 junction 7 via A44 and A4440]: Interesting generous food (till 10 Fri/Sat) inc superb ploughman's, good local produce and quite a lot of fresh fish, four well kept ales such as Everards Beacon, Timothy Taylors Landlord and a seasonal beer, good value bin ends and good choice of wines by the glass, nice coffee, enterprising welcoming landlord, informal well worn mix of furniture, good big fireplace, unpretentious no smoking pine-furnished dining area; cribbage, table skittles, friendly labrador called Monti; children in eating area, pretty walled back garden, comfortable reasonably priced bedrooms, good breakfast, open all day Sun in summer, cl Mon *(Michael and Janice Gwilliam, Dr and Mrs W T Farrington , R and J Bateman, Christopher Garrard, Mrs L Mills, Richard and Wendy Harris, George Atkinson, Denys Guéroult, Roger S Kiddier, C P Gill, Jack Clark, JWAC, Pat and Tony Martin, LYM)*

KIDDERMINSTER [SO8376]

Boars Head [Worcester St]: Interesting good value bar lunches (not Sun), central servery for cosy snug and basic bar; small garden and heated covered courtyard with bottle bar for busy nights – can be lively evenings *(Gill and Tony Morriss)*

KNIGHTWICK [SO7355]

☆ *Talbot* [Knightsford Bridge; B4197 just off A44 Worcester—Bromyard]: Nicely placed 14th-c inn of great individuality, superb when on form (as it almost always is – but not quite consistently enough to be a main entry); interesting furnishings and good pictures in opened-up heavily beamed bar; freshly made food not cheap but often exceptional, using local ingredients and some interesting recipes, decent wines, and their own cider and attractively priced and helpfully described ales (also using their own farm produce); children and well behaved dogs welcome, posher restaurant (same menu), tables served outside, comfortable character bedrooms (best away from back public bar which has games and juke box), good breakfast, own fishing on the Teme; open all day, on Three Choirs and Worcestershire Ways, very busy on farmers' market day (2nd Sun of month) *(R J Herd, Mr and Mrs P J Fisk, Bob Arnett, Judy Wayman, Mike and Mary Carter, Martin Jennings, Guy Vowles, Denys Guéroult,*

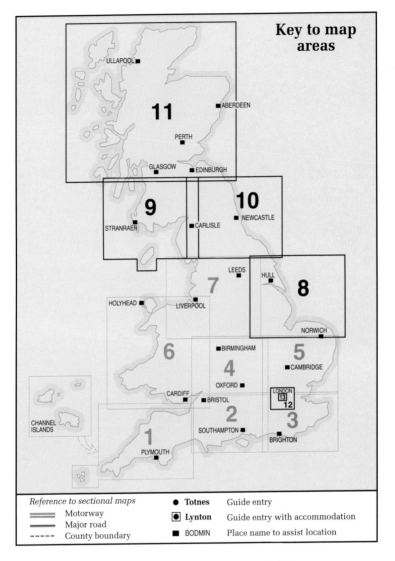

Key to map areas

Reference to sectional maps
- Motorway
- Major road
- County boundary

- ● **Totnes** — Guide entry
- ◉ **Lynton** — Guide entry with accommodation
- ■ BODMIN — Place name to assist location

MAPS IN THIS SECTION

For Maps 1 – 7 see earlier colour section

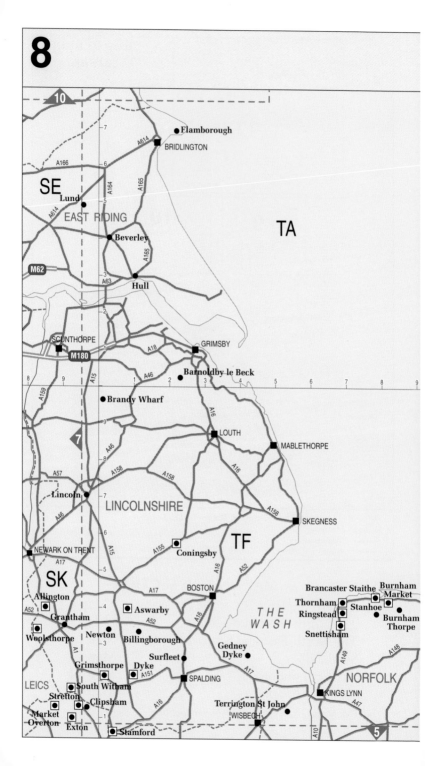

10

Flamborough
BRIDLINGTON
A614
A166
A164
A165

SE
Lund
A614
EAST RIDING

TA

Beverley
A165

M62
Hull
A63
3

2

SCUNTHORPE
M180
A15
1
A18
GRIMSBY

8   9   A46
A159
Barnoldby le Beck
1   2   3   4   5   6   7   8   9

7

9
Brandy Wharf
A46
8
LOUTH
A16
MABLETHORPE
A158
A158
A46
A16
A57
A158

Lincoln
7
LINCOLNSHIRE
A158
SKEGNESS

6
TF
A16
A155
Coningsby
A52

NEWARK ON TRENT
5
A15

SK
A17
A17
BOSTON
Brancaster Staithe   **Burnham Market**

Allington
4
Aswarby
A16
Thornham   **Stanhoe**
A52
Grantham
A52
Ringstead
Burnham Thorpe
THE WASH

Woolsthorpe
Newton
3
Billingborough
Snettisham
A1

Grimsthorpe
Dyke
Surfleet
Gedney Dyke

South Witham
A151
SPALDING
A17
NORFOLK
Stretton
A149   A148
Clipsham
2
A16
Terrington St John
KINGS LYNN
LEICS
Market Overton
WISBECH
A47
Exton
1
Stamford
A10

5

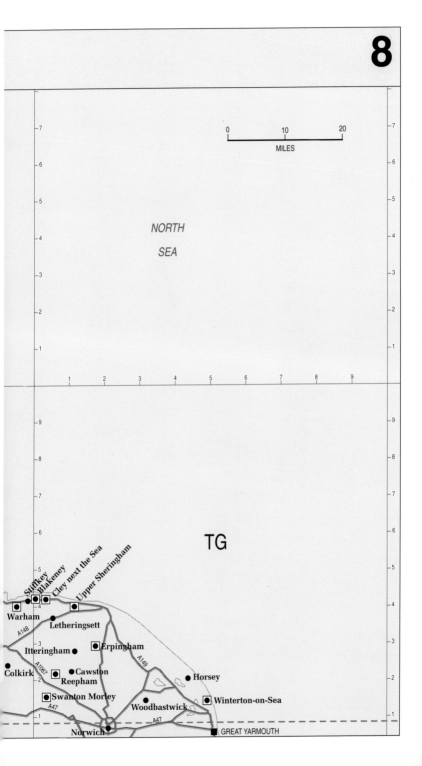

8

0   10   20
MILES

NORTH

SEA

7
6
5
4
3
2
1

1   2   3   4   5   6   7   8   9

9
8
7
6

TG

5

Stiffkey
Blakeney
Cley next the Sea
Upper Sheringham

Warham
Letheringsett
A148

Itteringham ●   ● Erpingham

Colkirk ●
A1067
● Cawston
Reepham
A149
● Horsey

● Swanton Morley
Woodbastwick
● Winterton-on-Sea

A47
Norwich   A47   ■ GREAT YARMOUTH

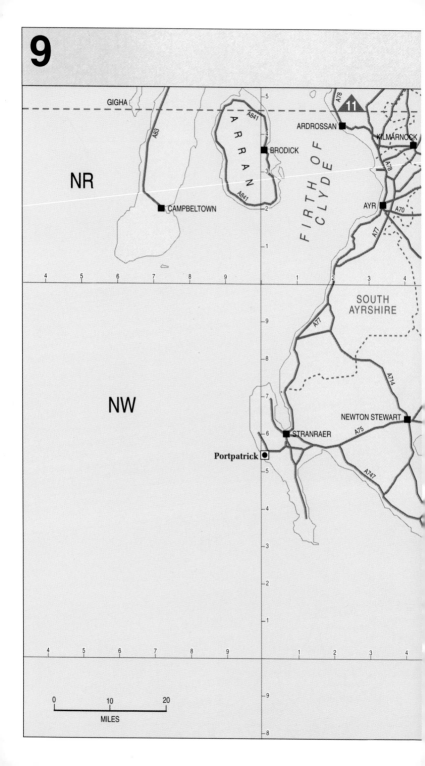

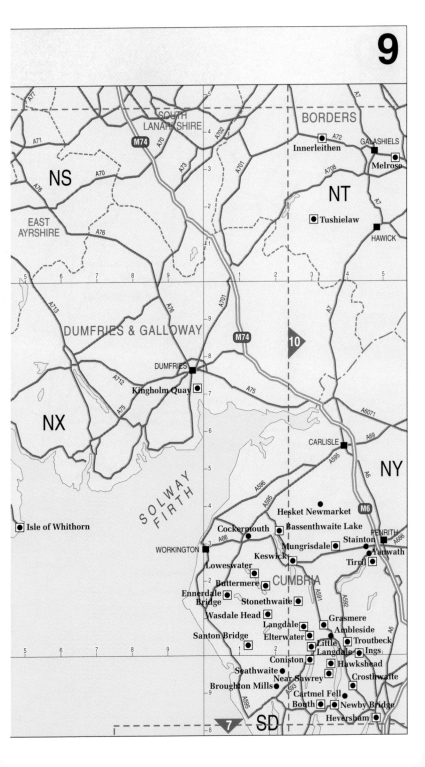

A77
A71
SOUTH LANARKSHIRE
M74
A70
A702
A72
Innerleithen
BORDERS
GALASHIELS
A7
Melrose
A708

NS
A70
A76
A73
A701
NT

EAST AYRSHIRE
A76

Tushielaw
A7
HAWICK

A713
A76
A701
DUMFRIES & GALLOWAY
M74
10

NX
A712
DUMFRIES
A75
Kingholm Quay
A701

NX
A75

SOLWAY FIRTH
A6071
CARLISLE
A69
NY
A6

Isle of Whithorn
A595
M6

Hesket Newmarket
PENRITH
A686
Cockermouth
Bassenthwaite Lake
Stainton
WORKINGTON
A66
Mungrisdale
Yanwath
Keswick
Tirril
Loweswater
CUMBRIA
Buttermere
A591
A592
A6
Ennerdale Bridge
Stonethwaite
Wasdale Head
Grasmere
Langdale
Ambleside
Santon Bridge
Elterwater
Little
Troutbeck
Coniston
Langdale
Ings
Hawkshead
Seathwaite
Near Shwrey
Crosthwaite
Broughton Mills
A593
Cartmel Fell
Bouth
Newby Bridge
Heversham
7
SD
A595
A596

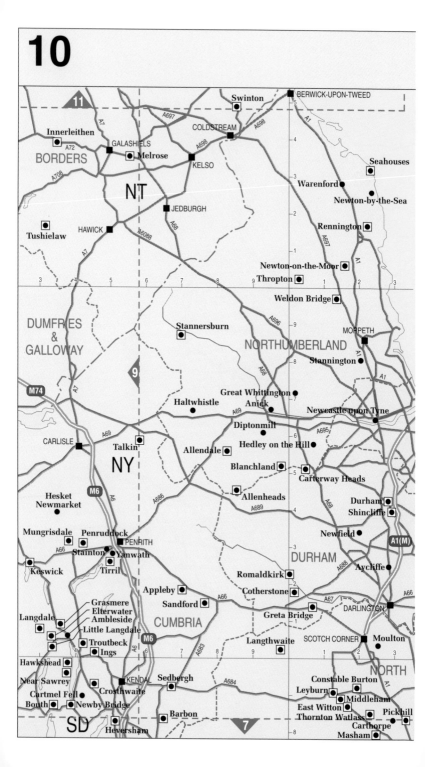

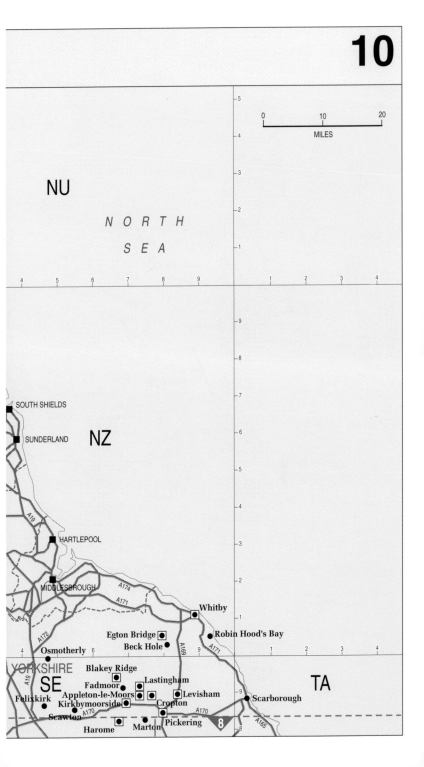

0   10   20
MILES

NU

NORTH

SEA

SOUTH SHIELDS

SUNDERLAND

NZ

HARTLEPOOL

MIDDLESBROUGH   A174

A171

Whitby

Egton Bridge   Robin Hood's Bay
Beck Hole

Osmotherly

YORKSHIRE   Blakey Ridge

SE   Fadmoor   Lastingham   TA

Felixkirk   Appleton-le-Moors   Levisham
    Kirkbymoorside   Cropton   Scarborough

Scawton   A170   A170   A165

Harome   Marton   Pickering   **8**

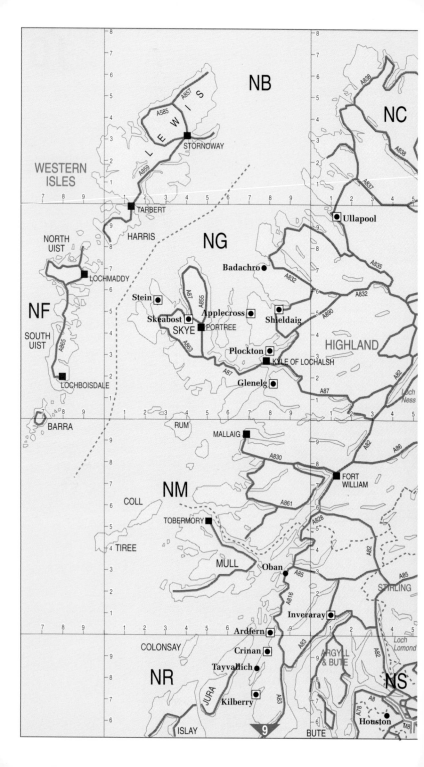

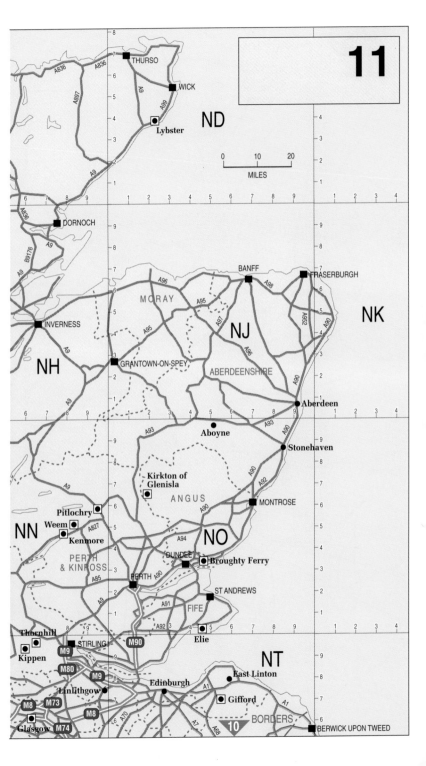

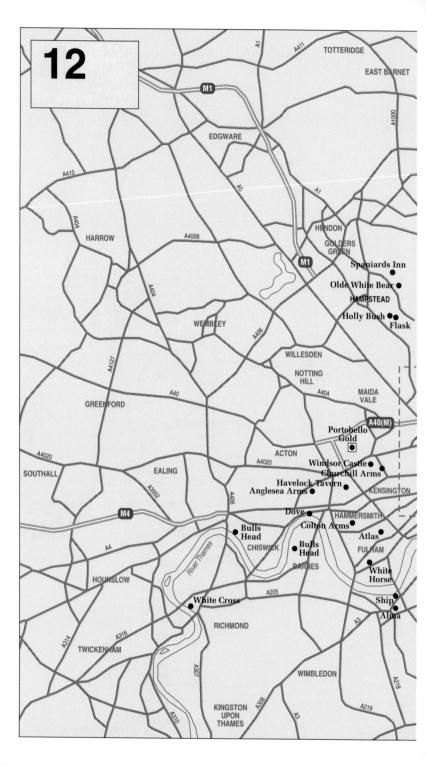

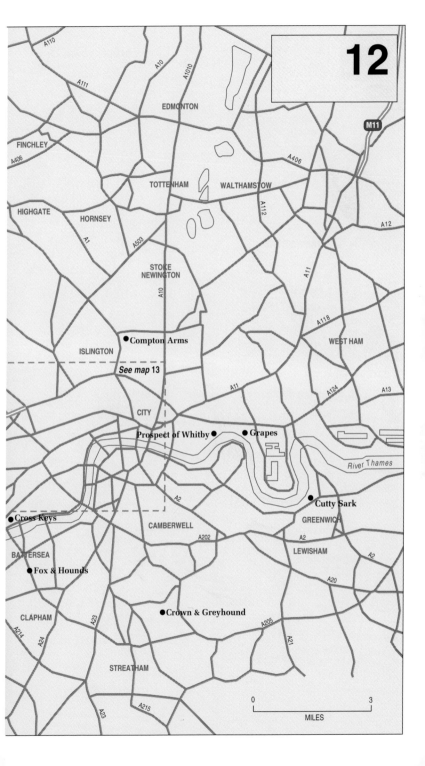

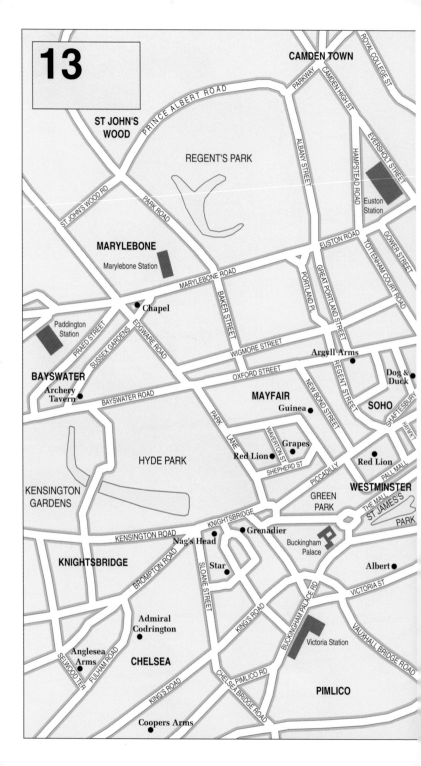

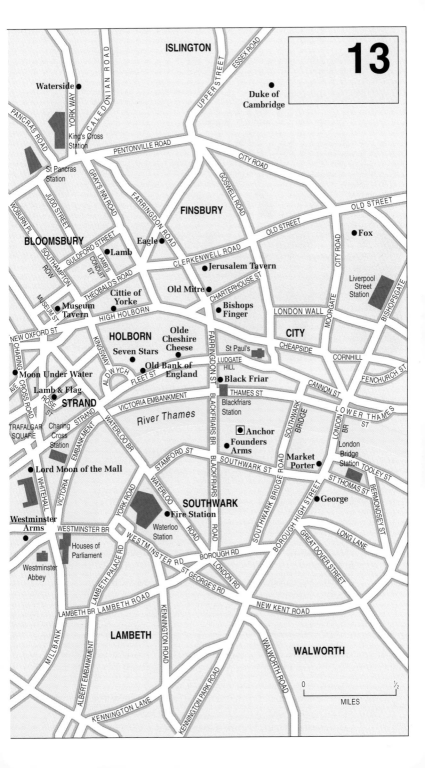

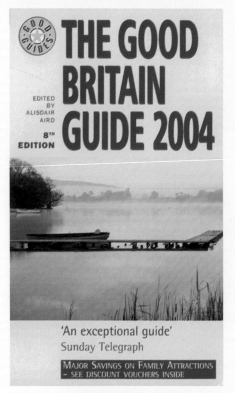

Gill and Tony Morriss, Dr J Kirman, LYM, Dick and Madeleine Brown, Karen Eliot, Alan and Gill Bull, Kevin Thorpe, Dr and Mrs Jackson, Di and Mike Gillam, Cathryn and Richard Hicks)

LINDRIDGE [SO6769]

Nags Head [A443 E of Tenbury Wells]: Friendly and well run, with enjoyable food, well kept Marstons Pedigree, good service, pleasant views of Teme valley *(M and D Toms)*

LOWER BROADHEATH [SO8055]

Plough [off A44 into Crown East Lane W of Worcester (first right, after A4103/A4440 roundabout)]: Village pub next to Elgar's birthplace museum, with emphasis on enjoyable food inc children's; well furnished and decorated lounge bar, welcoming service, Boddingtons, Flowers and Wadworths 6X ales; quiet piped music; garden with play area *(John Whitehead)*

LULSLEY [SO7455]

Fox & Hounds [signed 1 mile off A44 Worcester—Bromyard]: Tucked-away country pub with smallish parquet-floored bar stepping down into neat dining lounge, pretty little restaurant on left, decent food, well kept Bass and a local beer, pleasant wines, open fire; picnic-sets in quiet and colourful enclosed side rose garden *(Denys Gueroult, Lynda and Trevor Smith, BB)*

MALVERN [SO7641]

☆ *Malvern Hills Hotel* [opp British Camp car park, Wynds Point; junction A449/B4232 S]: Red plush banquettes, turkey carpet and open fire in extensive dark-panelled lounge bar with good value filling bar food (very popular wknds), well kept Black Sheep, Hobsons, Greene King Old Speckled Hen and Wye Valley Butty Bach, quite a few malt whiskies, prettily served coffee, good polite service, downstairs pool room, smart more expensive restaurant; well reproduced piped music, live Fri; dogs welcome, picnic-sets outside, bedrooms small but comfortable, open all day – fine position high in the hills *(BB, Bruce M Drew, Denys Gueroult, Joan York)*

Wyche [Wyche Rd]: Comfortable half-timbered pub nr top of Malvern Hills, fine view, Courage Best, Hobsons Best and a guest beer, wide choice of reasonably priced well presented food all day from sandwiches up, quick helpful service, pool in lower area; bedrooms *(Brian and Anna Marsden)*

OMBERSLEY [SO8463]

Cross Keys [A449, Kidderminster end]: Neat and attractive beamed pub, comfortable front bar with well kept beers such as Adnams Broadside and Timothy Taylors Landlord, friendly service; conservatory restaurant specialising in fish *(Mrs Ursula Hofheinz, Chris Flynn, Wendy Jones, Nigel Long)*

☆ *Crown & Sandys* [A4133]: Big open-plan food-oriented bistro pub with imaginative if not cheap food, airy modern décor but keeping beams, flagstones and settles, limestone-floor conservatory leading to terrace with fountain and sizeable garden beyond; landlord is a wine merchant so quite a few wine-theme pictures,

and a fine choice by the glass inc champagnes, also six well kept real ales on handpump; piped music; children welcome, open all day wknds *(Mike and Mary Carter, Alan and Paula McCully, Alun Howells, Lawrence Pearse, Basil Cheesenham, Ian and Jacqui Ross, Alan Cole, Kirstie Bruce, LYM)*

☆ *Kings Arms* [A4133]: Imposing black-beamed and timbered Tudor pub with comfortable rambling rooms, cosy wood-floored nooks and crannies with rustic bric-a-brac, one room with Charles II's coat of arms decorating its ceiling, four open fires; quite restauranty atmosphere and food prices, well kept Banks's Bitter, Marstons Pedigree, and a guest beer; children welcome, colourful tree-sheltered courtyard, open all day Sun *(David and Ruth Shillitoe, Pamela and Merlyn Horswell, Glenys and John Roberts, RJH, Pat and Robert Watt, Rod Stoneman, Mike and Mary Carter, David and Helen Wilkins, Ian and Jacqui Ross)*

PERSHORE [SO9445]

☆ *Brandy Cask* [Bridge St]: Plain high-ceilinged bow-windowed bar, back courtyard brewery producing their own attractively priced Brandysnapper, Whistling Joe and John Bakers Original, well kept guest beers too, Aug beer festival, coal fire, fresh food from sandwiches to steaks inc imaginative salads and some interesting dishes, quaintly decorated no smoking dining room, quick friendly helpful service; well behaved children allowed; long attractive garden down to river (keep a careful eye on the children), with terrace, vine arbour and koi pond *(the Didler, BB, G Coates)*

SEVERN STOKE [SO8544]

Rose & Crown [A38 S of Worcester]: Attractive 16th-c black and white pub, well modernised keeping low beams, knick-knacks and good fire in character front bar, well kept real ales, good value generous food, friendly staff, back room where children allowed; big garden with picnic-sets, playhouse and play area *(anon)*

SHATTERFORD [SO7981]

☆ *Bellmans Cross* [Bridgnorth Rd (A442)]: Neat timber-effect bar popular with business people at lunchtime, interesting and attractively presented bar food from baguettes up, smart tasteful restaurant, French chefs and bar staff, pleasant service with finesse, well kept Bass, Greene King Old Speckled Hen and a guest beer such as Timothy Taylors Landlord, good choice of wines by the glass inc champagne; picnic-sets outside, handy for Severn Woods walks *(Theo, Anne and Jane Gaskin, Martin Jennings, Alan Cole, Kirstie Bruce, BB)*

Red Lion [Bridgnorth Rd (A442)]: Immaculate olde-worlde pub straddling the Shropshire boundary, with gleaming copper and brass, lively coal fire, huge choice of good generous food from sandwiches up, well kept reasonably priced Banks's Best, Bathams and Woods Shropshire Lad, welcoming landlord, friendly efficient staff, smart partly no smoking restaurant extension, fine views; well behaved children welcome, disabled facilities *(Mrs J Poole)*

SHENSTONE [SO8673]
Hare & Hounds [A450]: Welcoming roadside local with log fires, enjoyable fresh generous food inc two-course bargains *(Alan and Pat Newcombe)*

SIX ASHES [SO7988]
Six Ashes Inn [A458 SE of Bridgnorth]: Picturesque whitewashed beamed pub in attractive countryside, good value home cooking inc Mon-Sat OAP specials, friendly service, Banks's real ale *(Theo, Anne and Jane Gaskin)*

STOCK GREEN [SO9959]
Bird in Hand: Proper old-fashioned pub with Banks's, Boddingtons and Enville, good cheap filled rolls *(Dave Braisted)*

STOKE POUND [SO9667]
☆ *Queens Head* [Sugarbrook Lane, by Bridge 48, Worcester & Birmingham Canal]: Plush air-conditioned waterside dining pub with good generous straightforward food inc good value eat-as-much-as-you-can carvery and lots of puddings (Sun lunch very popular, booking advised), Scottish Courage ales, pleasant helpful staff; piped music, rather close-set tables; waterside terrace, camp site, good walk up the 36 locks of the Tardebigge Steps, quite handy for Avoncroft buildings museum *(Di and Mike Gillam, Theo, Anne and Jane Gaskin)*

STOKE WHARF [SO9468]
Navigation [Hanbury Rd (B4091)]: Friendly pub nr Worcs & Birmingham Canal, popular for good food inc Thurs paella night and (by prior arrangement) fantastic seafood platter, real ale inc a guest beer *(Dave Braisted)*

STOKE WORKS [SO9365]
Boat & Railway [Shaw Lane]: Popular and unpretentious, with good old-fashioned atmosphere, well kept Banks's and Hansons, good generous lunchtime snacks; pretty hanging baskets, terrace by Worcester & Birmingham Canal *(Dave Braisted, Dr and Mrs Jackson)*

Bowling Green [1 mile from M5 junction 5, via Stoke Lane]: Attractively and comfortably refurbished, with good value food inc children's, well kept Banks's Bitter and Mild, good atmosphere; big garden with beautifully kept bowling green, handy for Worcs & Birmingham Canal *(Dave Braisted)*

STONEHALL COMMON [SO8848]
☆ *Fruiterers Arms* [S of Norton, via Hatfield]: Civilised country pub with comfortable banquettes, cosy dark-panelled corner with easy chairs, settee and coal fire, extensive back bare-boards or flagstoned dining area with wide blackboard food choice inc winter wkdy bargain meals and lunchtime and early evening carvery, well kept Marstons Best and Worthington 1744, smart helpful staff; piped music; good disabled access, big garden with lots for children and huge timber-and-awning arbour *(Christopher J Darwent, BB)*

STOURPORT ON SEVERN [SO8170]
Angel [Severn Side]: Food inc good baguettes and baked potatoes and bargain lunches for two, Banks's real ales; terrace overlooking Severn by lower basin entrance *(Dave Braisted)*

Steps House [Gilgal]: Friendly new landlord for interesting pub built into town wall, good bar food from baked potatoes up, real ales inc a guest beer, restaurant *(Dave Braisted)*

UPHAMPTON [SO8464]
Fruiterers Arms [off A449 N of Ombersley]: Homely and friendly country local (looks like a private house with a porch) brewing its own Cannon Royall Arrowhead, Kings Shilling, Muzzle Loader and seasonal brews, also farm cider; Jacobean panelled bar serving lounge with beamery, log fire, lots of photographs and local memorabilia, comfortable armchairs; good basic lunchtime food, no music, plain pool room, garden *(Dave Braisted, Gill and Tony Morriss)*

UPPER ARLEY [SO7679]
Harbour [off B4194 NW of Bewdley; or off A442 then footbridge]: Pleasant old-fashioned pub in delightful countryside, good value bar food, restaurant; tables and play area in big field nr Severn, handy for Severn Valley Railway station *(Alain and Rose Foote)*

UPTON SNODSBURY [SO9454]
☆ *Coventry Arms* [A422 Worcester—Stratford]: Hunting prints, fox masks, horse tack and racing gossip in welcoming beamed country inn with good choice of enjoyable food inc daily fresh fish and bargain lunches, well kept Bass, Boddingtons, Greene King Old Speckled Hen and Marstons Pedigree, lots of malt whiskies and ports, cheerful efficient service, cottagey armchairs among other seats, coal fire, two comfortable dining rooms, back conservatory with well spaced cane tables; spacious pleasant lawn (some traffic noise) with well equipped play area, attractive bedrooms *(BB, W H and E Thomas, Martin Jennings)*

☆ *French House* [A422 Worcester—Stratford]: Extensive series of linked carpeted rooms, high-spirited frenchified décor with masses of pictures and bric-a-brac, a lot of it quirkily interesting, ceilings wicker or entirely wine bottles, two grandfather clocks, balustraded no smoking area up three steps, mix of seating from dining tables to leather chesterfields, nice cheerful staff, well kept Tetleys and a couple of guest beers such as Highgate Dark Mild and Charles Wells Bombardier, cheapish wines, sensibly priced generous food; piped music; tables out on terrace and grass, bedrooms, open all day Sun *(M A and C R Starling, Dave Braisted, LYM, Martin Jones, Ian and Denise Foster, Pat and Tony Martin)*

UPTON UPON SEVERN [SO8540]
Little Upton Muggery [Old St, far end main st]: Basic pub with great mug collection, good value generous food, well kept real ales, friendly helpful service, simple furnishings, open fires, pool in third room *(Pat and Derek Roughton)*

Olde Anchor [High St]: Picturesque black and white 16th-c pub, rambling linked rooms with black timbers propping its low beams, good fire in unusual central fireplace, tidy old-fashioned furnishings; helpful service, well kept

Courage Directors, Theakstons and Charles Wells Bombardier, cheap usual food; shame about the piped music and flashing games machines; small back terrace, some tables out in front, open all day summer, can get crowded evenings then *(LYM, Kevin Blake)*

WEATHEROAK HILL [SP0674]

☆ *Coach & Horses* [Icknield St – coming S on A435 from Wythall roundabout, filter right off dual carriageway 1 mile S, then in village turn left towards Alvechurch; not far from M42 junction 3]: Roomy and friendly country pub brewing its own good Weatheroak beers, also good well kept choice of others from small breweries; plush-seated low-ceilinged two-level dining bar, tiled-floor proper public bar, bar food inc lots of baguettes and bargain fish and chips, also modern restaurant with well spaced tables; plenty of seats out on lawns and upper terrace; piped music; children allowed in eating area *(Pete Baker, the Didler, Theocsbrian, LYM)*

WEST MALVERN [SO7645]

Brewers Arms [The Dingle]: Attractive and unspoilt little two-room country local down steep path from the road, with friendly staff, well kept Banks's and Marstons Pedigree, good value fresh lunchtime sandwiches (not Mon), good atmosphere esp on impromptu Tues folk nights; small garden, well placed for walks *(A H C Rainier, GSB)*

WHITTINGTON [SO8752]

Swan [just off M5 junction 7]: Brightly painted country-style bar with lots of pews, changing imaginative reliably good value food, friendly hard-working young staff coping well with the bustle, well kept Banks's and Marstons

Pedigree, good choice of wines, log fire; children welcome, garden with play area *(Chris Flynn, Wendy Jones)*

WORCESTER [SO8455]

Dragon [The Tything]: Lively Georgian alehouse, green décor in simply furnished open-plan bar, half a dozen or so well described unusual changing microbrews inc a Mild and Porter, local Saxon farm cider, welcoming helpful staff, baguettes and light meals wkdy lunchtimes; piped pop music; folksy live bands, partly covered back terrace, open all day wknds *(Kevin Thorpe, Dr B and Mrs P B Baker, Martin Grosberg)*

Old Rectifying House [North Parade]: Flagstoned pub overlooking River Severn, good fish choice, Greene King Old Speckled Hen, decent wines; piped music; jazz Sun afternoon and alternate Weds; open all day *(JHBS)*

Plough [Fish St]: Friendly unpretentious local, two rooms (one with sports TV) off entrance lobby, simple wkdy bar lunches, four well kept changing ales such as Cannon Royall Kings Shilling and Hop Back Summer Lightning, character Spanish landlord; small pleasant back courtyard, cl Mon *(Pete Baker)*

Salmon Leap [Severn St]: Attractive pub opp porcelain museum, unusual pillared porch, comfortable interior, real ales, wide food choice *(Peter and Audrey Dowsett)*

Talbot [Barbourne Rd, The Tything]: Spacious panelled lounge, front bar with small bay window, welcoming service, well kept Greene King IPA, blackboard food, oak-panelled restaurant, fruit machines; bedrooms *(R Michael Richards)*

Real ale to us means beer which has matured naturally in its cask – not pressurised or filtered. We name all real ales stocked. We usually name ales preserved under a light blanket of carbon dioxide too, though purists – pointing out that this stops the natural yeasts developing – would disagree (most people, including us, can't tell the difference!)

Yorkshire

Food features strongly in many Yorkshire pubs, from generous, sometimes even over-generous, helpings of hearty straightforward food at sensible prices in the simpler places, to some extremely good restauranty cooking in the higher reaches of the price range. Another striking Yorkshire theme is the very large number of flourishing local breweries, from well known names like Sam Smiths (with their appealing low-price policy), Timothy Taylors and Black Sheep to brand new start-ups such as Shipton and Wold, with plenty of other good beers to be found here, too. And quite a few pubs have taken to brewing their own. All this helps to keep Yorkshire drinks prices down, with beer normally costing comfortably less than the national average, and sensible wine price levels too (in pubs, these often echo beer price levels). Another big plus is the sheer friendliness of so many Yorkshire pubs. After a mammoth influx of new main entries last year, this year we have limited ourselves to only two newcomers, both excellent, and both warmed by that trademark Yorkshire friendliness: the Tempest Arms at Elslack, on great form under an ex-landlord who ran it in its heyday a few years ago and has now returned to bring it back to the top tier of Yorkshire pubs; and the appealingly updated Appletree at Marton, with its stylish cooking and good drinks. Both these pubs gain a Food Award and Wine Award, and the Appletree takes a Beer Award too. Other pubs on top form this year are the Birch Hall at Beck Hole (a unique mix of sweetie shop and bar, in an enviable spot), the consistently friendly Malt Shovel at Brearton (a fine all-rounder), the Abbey Inn opposite the striking ruin of Byland Abbey (imaginative food, great wine choice, welcoming owners and nice bedrooms), the Star at Harome (exceptional quality all round, without any pretension – one of the handful of places on our personal day-dream list of Pubs We Wish Were Just Up The Road), the restauranty and very popular Angel at Hetton, the Stone Trough in Kirkham (a happy mix of pub and restaurant, good all round, with kind licensees), the Chequers at Ledsham (really good food behind the smokescreen of its menu – a most enjoyable retreat from the A1), Whitelocks in Leeds (a favourite of many readers, for its marvellous old-world décor), the Sawley Arms at Sawley (run with unswerving success by its long-serving landlady, hugely popular despite its lack of real ale), the smart Three Acres in Shelley (more restaurant and hotel than pub, but nice and relaxed), the St Vincent Arms at Sutton upon Derwent (an exemplary welcoming village pub, good food and great beers), the Wombwell Arms at Wass (another very friendly all-rounder, enjoyable food relying entirely on local produce), and the Duke of York in Whitby (one of our favourite town pubs, always bustling and friendly). For a special meal out, the Three Acres in Shelley takes the title of Yorkshire Dining Pub of the Year. The Lucky Dip section at the end of the chapter has a great many pubs which are as appealing for the virtues we mention as many main entries. Among these stars we'd particularly note the restaurant Kaye Arms on Grange Moor, Crown at Great Ouseburn, Maypole at Long Preston, Olde Punch Bowl at Marton cum Grafton, Black Sheep Brewery in Masham (not a pub, but most enjoyable), Millbank at Mill Bank, Grouse at Oakworth and

Royal Oak in York; and three pubs which this year have escaped from the main entry section simply because we have had so few recent reports from readers on them – the White Swan at Ampleforth, Old Bridge in Ripponden and Fox & Hounds at Sinnington.

ALDBOROUGH SE4166 Map 7
Ship 🍺

Village signposted from B6265 just S of Boroughbridge, close to A1

Used as a recruiting post by local regiments during the Napoleonic War, this ivy-clad stone building overlooking the village green has welcoming and attentive new licensees. The heavily beamed bar has some old-fashioned seats around heavy cast-iron tables, lots of copper and brass on the walls, and a coal fire in the stone inglenook fireplace. Well liked bar food includes sandwiches (from £2.50), nice soup (£2.95), filled baked potatoes (from £2.95), large yorkshire pudding with onion gravy and beef £3.95), filled baguettes (from £3.95), ploughman's (from £5.75), tasty steak and kidney pudding (£6.25), and daily specials such as cumberland sausage (£6.95), courgette and aubergine bake or lambs liver with red wine gravy (£7.25), pork chop with cider and apple sauce (£8.25), thai chicken curry or barnsley chop with red wine and rosemary jus (£9.25), baked cod with dill cream sauce (£9.50), and cajun salmon fillet on stir-fried vegetables (£9.95). The restaurant is no smoking. Well kept Greene King Ruddles Best, John Smiths, and Theakstons Best on handpump, a decent wine list, and quite a few malt whiskies; piped music and dominoes. There are seats on the front terrace. The Roman town with its museum and Roman pavements is nearby. *(Recommended by David and Iris Hunter, Jo and Iain MacGregor, Simon Turner, Janet and Peter Race, Carolyn Dixon, John Knighton, W W Burke, Alan Thwaite, Michael Butler, Lawrence Pearse)*

S&N ~ Lease Terry Monaghan ~ Real ale ~ Bar food (12-2, 6-9; 12-2.30, 5.30-7.30 Sun) ~ Restaurant ~ (01423) 322749 ~ Children welcome ~ Open 11.45-2.30, 5.30-11; 11.45-11 Sat; 12-10.30 Sun ~ Bedrooms: £35S/£49S

APPLETON-LE-MOORS SE7388 Map 10
Moors

Village N of A170 just under 1½ miles E of Kirkby Moorside

Almost entirely no smoking, this unassuming little stone-built pub is strikingly neat and fresh, and so bare of the usual bric-a-brac and pub clutter that it almost takes you aback. Sparse decorations include just a few copper pans and earthenware mugs in a little alcove, a couple of plates, one or two pieces of country ironwork, and a delft shelf with miniature whiskies; the whiteness of walls and ceiling is underlined by the black beams and joists, and the bristly grey carpet. Perfect for a cold winter evening, there's a nice built-in high-backed stripped settle next to an old kitchen fireplace, and other seating includes an unusual rustic seat for two cleverly made out of stripped cartwheels; there's plenty of standing space. To the left of the bar, where you'll probably find a few regulars chatting on the backed padded stools, there's a games room with a pool table (the one place you can smoke) and darts; dominoes. Well kept Black Sheep and Tetleys on handpump, and quite a few malt whiskies; efficient service. The wide choice of food in the no smoking dining room could include home-made soup (£2.95), home-made chicken liver pâté (£3.75), pasta with smoked chicken, leek and wholegrain mustard sauce or mushroom quiche (£7.50), pork and tuna rissoles in a cream and caper sauce on tagliatelle (£7.95), pheasant casserole or local trout (£8.25), lamb shoulder with apricot stuffing (£8.95), half a duck in tangy orange sauce (£10.50), creamy peppered steak (£12.95), puddings like apple and raspberry pie (£3.25), and Sunday roast (£6.75). There are tables in the walled garden. The bedrooms are in what used to be a barn behind, and there are moors walks straight from the pub. *(Recommended by Colin and Dot Savill)*

Free house ~ Licensee Janet Frank ~ Real ale ~ Bar food (not lunchtimes exc Sun (will offer food to residents on Mon)) ~ Restaurant ~ No credit cards ~ (01751) 417435 ~ Children welcome ~ Dogs welcome ~ Open 7-11; 12-3, 7-10.30 Sun; closed Mon ~ Bedrooms: /£50B

ASENBY SE3975 Map 7
Crab & Lobster ⓧ ♀ ⇌
Village signposted off A168 – handy for A1

Although this is no longer a free house and has a new licensee, we are keeping our fingers firmly crossed that little will change here. Rambling and L-shaped, the bar has an interesting jumble of seats from antique high-backed and other settles through settees and wing armchairs heaped with cushions, to tall and rather theatrical corner seats; the tables are almost as much of a mix, and the walls and available surfaces are quite a jungle of bric-a-brac, with standard and table lamps and candles keeping even the lighting pleasantly informal. There's also a no smoking dining pavilion with big tropical plants, nautical bits and pieces, and Edwardian sofas. Interesting bar food includes chunky fish soup with cheese croûtes and aïoli (£5.75), pressed terrine of potted beef, ham hock and foie gras with red onion and beetroot marmalade (£6.30), steamed scottish mussels with thyme, garlic, white wine and cream (£6.50), risotto of pea, mint and lemon with griddled asparagus (£11), natural cured haddock with poached egg, black pudding, cheese and bacon potatoes or chicken in bacon, basil, goats cheese, button mushrooms and artichoke mash (£14), slowly braised moroccan spiced lamb shank, dried fruit, couscous and cucumber yoghurt (£14.50), goan fish curry with coconut rice (£15), and puddings like iced white chocolate and raspberry parfait with macerated strawberries and basil syrup, sticky toffee pudding with butterscotch sauce or rhubarb crème brûlée with stem ginger ice cream (£5.25); side dishes £2.75. Well kept Courage Directors and John Smiths on handpump, and good wines by the glass from an interesting wine list; well reproduced piped music. The gardens have bamboo and palm trees lining the paths, there's a gazebo at the end of the walkways, and seats on a mediterranean-style terrace. The opulent bedrooms (based on famous hotels around the world) are in the surrounding house which has three acres of mature gardens, and a 180-metre golf hole with full practice facilities. More reports on the changes, please. *(Recommended by Regine Webster, R F Grieve, Alistair and Kay Butler, Tony Gayfer, Susan and John Douglas, Charles and Pauline Stride, Greta and Christopher Wells, Michael Doswell, G Dobson, Mrs E E Sanders, Mr and Mrs J E C Tasker, Mr and Mrs Allan Chapman)*

Free house ~ Licensee Mark Spenceley ~ Real ale ~ Bar food (12-2.30, 7-9) ~ Restaurant ~ (01845) 577286 ~ Children in eating area of bar and restaurant ~ Dogs allowed in bar and bedrooms ~ Live entertainment Sun lunchtime ~ Open 11.30-11 ~ Bedrooms: /£150B

BECK HOLE NZ8202 Map 10
Birch Hall
Signed off A169 SW of Whitby, from top of Sleights Moor

You can't help but chat to other customers – a good mix of locals and visitors – in this unique and charming pub-cum-village shop. There are two rooms with the shop selling postcards, sweeties and ice creams in between, and hatch service to both sides. Furnishings are simple – built-in cushioned wall seats and wooden tables (spot the one with 136 pennies, all heads up, embedded in the top) and chairs on the floor (flagstones in one room, composition in the other), some strange items such as French breakfast cereal boxes and a tube of Macleans toothpaste priced 1/3d, and well kept ales such as Black Sheep Bitter, Theakstons Black Bull or Best, and guests from local breweries on handpump; several malt whiskies. Bar snacks like butties (£1.95), locally-made pies (£1.30), and home-made scones and cakes including their lovely beer cake (from 80p); friendly, welcoming staff; dominoes and quoits. Outside, an ancient oil painting of the view up the steeply wooded river valley hangs on the pub wall, there are benches out in front, and steep steps up to a little steeply terraced side garden with a moorland view. This is a lovely spot with marvellous surrounding walks – you can walk along the disused railway line from Goathland; part of the path from Beck Hole to Grosmont is surfaced with mussel shells. *(Recommended by Pete Baker, the Didler, Gill and Tony Morriss, JP, PP, Roger and Jenny Huggins, Ron and Mary Nicholson, Rona Murdoch, Anthony Barnes, B and H, JHBS, Alison Hayes, Pete Hanlon, David and Helen Wilkins)*

Free house ~ Licensee Colin Jackson ~ Real ale ~ Bar food (available during all opening hours) ~ No credit cards ~ (01947) 896245 ~ Children in small family room ~ Dogs welcome ~ Open 11-11; 12-10.30 Sun; 11-3, 7.30-11 in winter, 12-3, 7.30-10.30 Sun in winter; closed Mon evenings

BEVERLEY TA0340 Map 8
White Horse £

Hengate, close to the imposing Church of St Mary's; runs off North Bar

Dating from around 1425, this fine unspoilt pub has a carefully preserved Victorian feel – quite without frills – and is known locally as 'Nellies'. The basic but very atmospheric little rooms are huddled together around the central bar, with brown leatherette seats (high-backed settles in one little snug) and basic wooden chairs and benches on bare floorboards, antique cartoons and sentimental engravings on the nicotine-stained walls, a gaslit pulley-controlled chandelier, a deeply reverberating chiming clock, and open fires – one with an attractively tiled old fireplace. They now hold a licence for civil ceremonies to take place here. Well kept and very cheap Sam Smiths OB on handpump. Cheap, simple food includes sandwiches, bangers and mash or pasta provençale (£3.95), steak in ale pie (£4.50), lasagne (£4.95), gammon with parsley sauce (£5.50), lamb shanks (£6.95), and puddings like spotted dick and custard (£2). A separate games room has darts, TV, fruit machine, trivia, juke box, and two pool tables – these and the no smoking room behind the bar are the only modern touches. John Wesley preached in the back yard in the mid-18th c. *(Recommended by Peter and Anne Hollindale, Michael Butler, Paul and Ursula Randall, Barry Smith, Lorraine and Fred Gill, the Didler, Pete Baker, Mark Walker, Arby, JP, PP, Alison Hayes, Pete Hanlon)*

Sam Smiths ~ Manager Anna ~ Real ale ~ Bar food (11-5 Mon-Sat; 12-4.30 Sun) ~ No credit cards ~ (01482) 861973 ~ Children welcome away from bar until 8pm ~ Dogs welcome ~ Live folk Mon, jazz Weds ~ Open 11-11; 12-10.30 Sun

BLAKEY RIDGE SE6799 Map 10
Lion 🍺 🛏

From A171 Guisborough—Whitby follow Castleton, Hutton le Hole signposts; from A170 Kirkby Moorside—Pickering follow Keldholm, Hutton le Hole, Castleton signposts; OS Sheet 100 map reference 679996

On cold, misty days, walkers find this isolated 16th-c inn quite a haven. There are lots of surrounding hikes and the Coast to Coast Footpath is close by; stunning views. The beamed and rambling bars have warm open fires, a few big high-backed rustic settles around cast-iron-framed tables, lots of small dining chairs, a nice leather settee, and stone walls hung with some old engravings and photographs of the pub under snow (it can easily get cut off in winter). Generous helpings of good, standard bar food include sandwiches (from £2.75), ploughman's (£4.95), giant yorkshire pudding and gravy (£2.25), home-cooked ham and egg, and vegetable lasagne or home-made steak and mushroom pie (£6.95), with daily specials such as corned beef pie or mince and dumplings (£6.95), minted lamb chops (£7.50), norfolk duckling with peach and apricot stuffing (£9.45), and 32oz T-bone steak (£12.95), and puddings like spotted dick or apple pie (£2.95). Three restaurants are no smoking. Well kept Greene King Old Speckled Hen, John Smiths, and Theakstons Best, Old Peculier, Black Bull and XB on handpump; piped music, dominoes, and fruit machine. The pub does get very busy in summer. *(Recommended by Walter and Susan Rinaldi-Butcher, Rona Murdoch, Sue Wheeler, Hilary Sargeant, DRH and*

KLH, Tim Newman, JHBS, Geoff and Angela Jaques, R M Corlett, David and Barbara Knott)

Free house ~ Licensee Barry Crossland ~ Real ale ~ Bar food (12-10(10.30 Fri/Sat)) ~ Restaurant ~ (01751) 417320 ~ Children in eating area of bar and restaurant ~ Dogs allowed in bar ~ Live music every other Thurs ~ Open 10-11; 10-10.30 Sun ~ Bedrooms: £17.50(£32.50B)/£50(£58B)

BOROUGHBRIDGE SE3966 Map 7
Black Bull

St James Square; B6265, just off A1(M)

Some redecoration has taken place in this attractive 13th-c inn this year, and the restaurant and bedrooms are shortly to have a makeover. The main bar area, with a big stone fireplace and brown leather seats, is served through an old-fashioned hatch, and there's a cosy and attractive snug with traditional wall settles. Well liked bar food includes soup (£2.65), sandwiches (from £2.85; cajun chicken with sweet salsa tomatoes £3.95), pork sausage with red wine onion gravy (£5.25), home-made pie of the day (£6.25), thai-style stir-fried beef with chilli sauce, mixed vegetables and noodles (£7.25), chargrilled tuna steak or cream cheese and spinach omelette with roasted tomato sauce (£8.95), steaks (from £11.95), and daily specials like chicken breast wrapped in parma ham with wild mushrooms, garlic and port (£10.95), roast bass on a ragoût of prawns and mussels (£11.25), and venison steak topped with fruit purée and stilton cheese (£11.50); three-course Sunday lunch (£10.95).Well kept Black Sheep Bitter, John Smiths, and a guest such as Fullers London Pride or Timothy Taylors Landlord on handpump, enjoyable wines (with 12 by the glass), and quite a few malt whiskies. Service is friendly and attentive, the two borzoi dogs are called Charlie and Sadie, and the two cats Mimi and Cyny; the local mummers perform here three or four times a year. The bedrooms are in a more modern wing. *(Recommended by the Didler, JP, PP, Michael Doswell, Brian and Janet Ainscough, Alistair Forsyth, Nigel Williamson, W W Burke, Tom McLean, Michael Butler, Barbara and Martin Rowbottom, Mike and Linda Hudson, G Dobson, Michael Dandy, Margaret and Roy Randle)*

Free house ~ Licensees Anthony and Jillian Burgess ~ Real ale ~ Bar food (12-2(2.30 Sun), 6-9(9.30 Fri/Sat)) ~ Restaurant ~ (01423) 322413 ~ Children welcome ~ Dogs welcome ~ Open 11-11; 12-10.30 Sun ~ Bedrooms: £42S/£56S

BRADFIELD SK2392 Map 7
Strines Inn

From A57 heading E of junction with A6013 (Ladybower Reservoir) take first left turn (signposted with Bradfield) then bear left; with a map can also be reached more circuitously from Strines signpost on A616 at head of Underbank Reservoir, W of Stocksbridge

Superb scenery surrounds this handsome 13th-c stone inn, and it is right on the edge of the High Peak National Park; fine views from the picnic-sets, and there's a safely fenced in children's playground and some rescued animals. The main bar has a welcoming atmosphere, black beams liberally decked with copper kettles and so forth, quite a menagerie of stuffed animals, homely red-plush-cushioned traditional wooden wall benches and small chairs, and a coal fire in the rather grand stone fireplace; there's a good mixture of customers. A room off on the right has another coal fire, hunting photographs and prints, and lots of brass and china, and on the left, a similarly furnished room is no smoking. Tasty straightforward bar food includes home-made soup, sandwiches (from £1.90; hot panini bread with roast pork and apple sauce £3.50), filled baked potatoes (from £3.25), garlic mushrooms (£3.95), liver and onions (£6.25), roast vegetable and cheese pasta bake (£6.75), filled giant yorkshire puddings or popular pie of the day (£6.95), mixed grill (£9.50), daily specials such as irish mussels in garlic and cream (£4.95), cajun chicken (£6.95), and fresh tuna steak with lime (£8.95), and puddings (£2.95); children's menu. Well kept Marstons Bitter and Pedigree, Kelham Island Pale Rider, and a guest such as Everards Tiger or Morrells Graduate on handpump, several malt whiskies, and good coffees; piped music. The bedrooms have four-poster beds (one has an open log fire), and there's a self-catering cottage. *(Recommended by the Didler, David and Heather Stephenson, James Woods, Peter F Marshall, Norma and Noel Thomas, David and Ruth Hollands, JP, PP, Jo and Iain MacGregor)*

Free house ~ Licensee Jeremy Stanish ~ Real ale ~ Bar food (12-2, 7-9; all day in summer) ~ (0114) 285 1247 ~ Well behaved children in eating area of bar until 9 ~ Dogs welcome ~ Open 11-11; 11-10.30 Sun; 11-3, 6-11 weekdays in winter ~ Bedrooms: £40B/£65B

BREARTON SE3261 Map 7
Malt Shovel 🍴 ♀ 🍺
Village signposted off A61 N of Harrogate

Locals are very fond of this deservedly popular 16th-c village pub, but there's always a warm welcome for visitors too from all the friendly staff. As they don't take bookings, you do need to arrive early, but there is a waiting list system. Several heavily-beamed rooms radiate from the attractive linenfold oak bar counter with plush-cushioned seats and a mix of tables, an ancient oak partition wall, tankards and horsebrasses, an open fire, and paintings by local artists (for sale) and lively hunting prints on the walls; nearly half the pub is no smoking. Reliably good and reasonably priced bar food might include sandwiches, mussels in white wine, garlic, herbs and tomatoes (£3.95; main course £5.95), lasagne, ham and blue wensleydale tart or ploughman's (all £5.50), game or steak in ale pies (£6.50), haddock in crisp beer batter (£6.95), seafood gratin or thai chicken curry (£7.25), lamb shank with garlic and preserved lemons (£7.95), chargrilled steaks (from £8.95), and puddings like banana cheesecake with toffee sauce or lemon tart (£2.95). Well kept Black Sheep Bitter, Daleside Nightjar, and Theakstons Best with a couple of guests such as Durham White Gold or Salamander Axoloti on handpump, real cider, 30 malt whiskies, and a small but interesting and reasonably priced wine list (they will serve any wine by the glass); coffee comes in cafetières. Shove-ha'penny, cribbage, and dominoes. You can eat outside on the small terrace on all but the coldest of days as they have outdoor heaters; there are more tables on the grass. This is an attractive spot off the beaten track, yet handy for Harrogate and Knaresborough. *(Recommended by Pierre and Pat Richterich, Janet and Peter Race, Andrew and Samantha Grainger, Crystal and Peter Hooper, J Roy Smylie, Chloe and Robert Gartery, Robert and Susan Whitehead, G Dobson, P Abbott, Jill and Keith Wright, Michael Doswell, Alison Hayes, Pete Hanlon)*

Free house ~ Licensee Leslie Mitchell ~ Real ale ~ Bar food (not Sun evening, not Mon) ~ No credit cards ~ (01423) 862929 ~ Children welcome ~ Dogs allowed in bar ~ Open 12-2.30, 6.45-11(10.30 Sun); closed Mon

BURTON LEONARD SE3364 Map 7
Hare & Hounds
Village signposted off A61 Ripon—Harrogate (and easily reached from A1(M) exit 48)

Bustling and friendly, this well organised country pub has a good mix of both locals and visitors, and older customers are well looked after by the cheerful staff. The large turkey-carpeted main area is divided by a two-way stone fireplace with a log fire, and the traditional furnishings include flowery-cushioned captain's chairs, wall pews, grey plush stools and so forth; the restaurant and lounge are no smoking. The ceiling has a couple of beech branches strung with white fairy lights, there are some olde-worlde prints and decorative plates, and an eye-catching long bar counter, under gleaming copper and brass pans and measures; well kept Black Sheep, Timothy Taylors Landlord, and Worthington on handpump, a decent choice of wines by the glass, and a couple of dozen malt whiskies. Enjoyable, popular food includes lunchtime sandwiches and filled baguettes (from £2.95), home-made soup (£4.20), creamy garlic mushrooms topped with crispy bacon (£5.85), cajun vegetable curry (£7.95), pork loin with white wine and stilton sauce or poached halibut steak with leek and mushroom sauce (£9.95), rack of lamb with mint and redcurrant sauce (£10.95), steaks (from £12.95), and specials like home-made steak and kidney pie (£7.95), and roast duck breast with port, orange and summer berry sauce (£12.95); three-course Sunday lunch (£13.95). On the left as you go in, a bright little room has a pink sofa and easy chairs, and local village prints and old postcards. In summer, the flowering tubs and window boxes are pretty, and there's a newly extended back garden with new benches. *(Recommended by B and M Kendall, Janet and Peter Race, Michael Doswell)*

Free house ~ Licensees Sarah and Tony Porter ~ Real ale ~ Bar food (12-2, 6-9; not Tues) ~ Restaurant ~ (01765) 677355 ~ Children in eating area of bar and restaurant ~ Open 12-2.30, 5.30-11(10.30 Sun); closed Tues lunchtime

BYLAND ABBEY SE5579 Map 7
Abbey Inn ⑪ 🛏

The Abbey has a brown tourist-attraction signpost off the A170 Thirsk—Helmsley

As well as being a lovely place to stay (and two of the comfortable, individually decorated bedrooms overlook the hauntingly beautiful abbey ruins opposite), this carefully renovated inn is much enjoyed for its excellent food and drink, and for the friendly welcome offered by the hard-working owners. The two no smoking characterful front rooms have big fireplaces, oak and stripped deal tables, settees, carved oak seats, and Jacobean-style dining chairs on the polished boards and flagstones, various stuffed birds, little etchings, and china cabinets, and some discreet stripping back of plaster to show the ex-abbey masonry. The Library has lots of bookshelves and a large single oak table (ideal for a party of up to 10 people), and the big back room has lots of rustic bygones; piped music. At lunchtime, the fine food might include smoked salmon and cream cheese open sandwich (£5.50), duck and fig terrine with caramelised oranges (£7.25), a platter of cold meats and pâté with honey and poppyseed bread (£8.50), warm goats cheese, roasted pepper and sweet apple chutney tart or venison sausages with apple mash and cumberland sauce (£9.25), and fresh warm tuna with orange, mango and lime salsa (£12), with evening dishes such as home-made soup (£3.95), calamari in chilli batter with lemon mayonnaise (£6.75), beef carpaccio with parmesan shavings and home-made horseradish sauce (£7.75), buttered spinach and mushroom crêpes with blue cheese sauce (£8.95), chicken breast filled with mozzarella, wrapped in parma ham with vine tomato, lemon and tarragon sauce (£9.75), roasted monkfish with ginger and chilli sauce (£12.50), and puddings like sticky toffee pudding or rhubarb and clotted cream tart. Well kept Black Sheep Bitter and Tetleys on handpump, and an interesting wine list with 16 (plus champagne) by the glass. Plenty of room outside on the terrace and in the garden. *(Recommended by Ian and Rose Lock, Mr and Mrs J Holroyd, R T and J C Moggridge, John Knighton, J Goodwin, Peter Burton, Mrs D Fiddian, Peter and Anne-Marie O'Malley, Mrs Bramah, G Dobson, Stephen Buckley; also in the Good Hotel Guide)*

Free house ~ Licensees Jane and Martin Nordli ~ Real ale ~ Bar food (not Sun evening or Mon lunchtime) ~ Restaurant ~ (01347) 868204 ~ Children welcome ~ Open 12-3, 6.30-11(midnight Sat); 12-4 Sun; closed Sun evening and Mon lunch ~ Bedrooms: /£90B

CARTHORPE SE3184 Map 10
Fox & Hounds ⑪ �

Village signposted from A1 N of Ripon, via B6285

This is the sort of consistently reliable place that customers come back to on a regular basis. It is a neatly kept and well run extended dining pub with friendly, helpful licensees, and particularly good, enjoyable food; to be sure of a table it's best to book (particularly at weekends). Served by well trained staff, the interesting dishes might include a choice of home-made soups (£3.25), grilled black pudding with caramelised apple and onion marmalade (£4.25), smoked chicken and mango salad (£4.75), fresh crab tartlet topped with mature cheddar cheese (£4.95), chicken breast with creamy coverdale cheese sauce (£9.50), baked haddock with savoury crumb on spinach with cream sauce (£9.75), pheasant breast with pear and thyme stuffing wrapped in bacon with a red wine sauce (£9.95), roast rack of english lamb on a blackcurrant crouton with redcurrant gravy (£11.95), daily specials such as fresh salmon fishcakes or game pâté (£4.75), steak and kidney pie (£9.25), braised lamb shank with root vegetable purée and redcurrant gravy (£10.95), and poached halibut steak with a grain mustard sauce (£11.95), and puddings like white chocolate and irish cream cheesecake, passion fruit tart with passion fruit ice cream or summer fruits in champagne jelly with home-made shortbread biscuits (from £4.25). Three-course Sunday lunch (£12.95; children £6.95). There is some theatrical memorabilia in the corridors, and the cosy L-shaped bar has quite a few mistily evocative Victorian photographs of Whitby, a couple of nice seats by the larger of its two log fires, plush button-back built-in wall banquettes and chairs, plates on stripped beams, and some limed panelling; piped light classical music. An attractive high-raftered no smoking restaurant leads off with lots of neatly black-painted farm and smithy tools. Well kept Black Sheep on handpump, and from their extensive list they will open any wine for you just to have a glass. *(Recommended by Tim and Carolyn Lowes, Ian Cameron, Austin and Marjorie Tushingham, Mr and Mrs C Cameron, Mr and Mrs D Cummings, Mr and Mrs J E C Tasker, Janet and Peter Race)*

Free house ~ Licensees Howard and Bernie Fitzgerald ~ Real ale ~ Bar food (not Mon) ~ Restaurant ~ (01845) 567433 ~ Children in eating area of bar and restaurant ~ Open 12-2.30, 7-11(10.30 Sun); closed Mon, first full week of New Year

CONSTABLE BURTON SE1791 Map 10
Wyvill Arms 🍴 ♀
A684 E of Leyburn

The bar in this creeper-covered ex-farmhouse is decorated with teak and brass, with mirrors along the back of the bar, wine racks, and ornate shelving, and a bar counter which came from a bank 30 years ago. There's a mix of seating (including a 1695 mop-hair engraved-back chair won by the licensee's grandfather in a boxing match), a finely worked plaster ceiling with the Wyvill family's coat of arms, and an elaborate stone fireplace. The second bar where food is served, has semi-circled, upholstered alcoves, a 70s' juke box with music for all ages, hunting prints and a mounted stag's head, and old oak tables; the reception area of this room includes a huge chesterfield which can seat up to eight people, another carved stone fireplace, and an old leaded church stained-glass window partition. Both rooms are hung with pictures of local scenes, most of which are prints done by the local artist, Peter Alice. The restaurant is no smoking. Using local produce and served in generous helpings, the enjoyable home-made food includes light lunches such as soup (£2.95), scrambled egg and smoked salmon (£5.45), lasagne (£7.75), and steak and mushroom pie (£8.45), with evening dishes like pork filled with blackcurrant sauce and cinammon apples (£10.95), tuna steak with provençale sauce (£13.65), halibut with scallops and lemon butter sauce (£13.95), and monkfish wrapped in parma ham with spinach, shi-itake mushrooms and béarnaise sauce (£15.95). Well kept Black Sheep, John Smiths Bitter, and Theakstons Best on handpump, and a thoughtful wine list; cribbage, dominoes, darts and piped music. The white bull terrier is called Tricky. There's a herb and vegetable garden behind the pub, and several large wooden benches with large white parasols for outdoor dining. Constable Burton Gardens are opposite and worth a visit. More reports please. *(Recommended by Michael Doswell)*

Free house ~ Licensee Nigel Stevens ~ Real ale ~ Bar food ~ Restaurant ~ (01677) 450581 ~ Children in eating area of bar and restaurant until 9 ~ Dogs allowed in bar ~ Open 11-3, 6-11; 12-3, 7-10.30 Sun ~ Bedrooms: £34B/£56B

CRAY SD9379 Map 7
White Lion 🍺 🛏

B6160, Upper Wharfedale N of Kettlewell

The highest pub in Wharfedale (1,100 ft up by Buckden Pike) and surrounded by superb countryside, this friendly former drovers' hostelry remains a popular place for a drink or meal. The simply furnished bar has a traditional atmosphere, seats around tables on the flagstone floor, shelves of china, iron tools and so forth, a high dark beam-and-plank ceiling, and a warming open fire; there's also a no smoking dining room. Well liked bar food at lunchtime includes home-made soup (£2.95), filled yorkshire puddings (from £2.95), home-made chicken liver pâté (£3.50), filled baguettes (from £3.50), filled baked potatoes (from £5), home-made steak and mushroom pie or pork in madeira and paprika sauce (£7.95), cashew nut loaf with mushroom and sherry sauce (£8.50), and home-made venison casserole (£9.95), with evening choices such as mushrooms in a rich garlic, cream and mustard sauce (£3.50), slices of black pudding with apple sauce (£3.75), chicken breast fried with smoked bacon with herby vinaigrette or mixed bean casserole (£7.95), whole steamed trout with lemon and dill butter (£8.50), rack of barbecued ribs (£9.95), and steaks (from £10.95); children's meals and puddings. If you eat between 5.45 and 6.15pm you get a 20% discount on some items. Up to four well kept ales like Moorhouses Bitter and Pendle Witches Brew, Timothy Taylors Landlord, and maybe Daleside Blonde or Goose Eye No Eye Deer on handpump; dominoes, shove-ha'penny, ring the bull, and giant Jenga. In fine weather, you can sit at picnic benches above the very quiet steep lane or on the great flat limestone slabs in the shallow stream which tumbles down opposite. *(Recommended by Malcolm and Jennifer Perry, Susan and Tony Dyer, Bill Sykes, Tony and Ann Bennett-Hughes, Mike and Kathryn Budd, Jane Taylor, David Dutton, the Didler, Greta and Christopher Wells, Blaise Vyner, Bob Arnett, Judy Wayman, W A Evershed, Stephen Buckley)*

Free house ~ Licensees Kevin and Debbie Roe ~ Real ale ~ Bar food (12-2, 5.45-8.30) ~ (01756) 760262 ~ Children in family room ~ Dogs allowed in bar ~ Open 11-11; 12-10.30 Sun; closed 25 Dec (but open to residents) ~ Bedrooms: £37.50S/£55S

CRAYKE SE5670 Map 7
Durham Ox 🍽 ♀

Off B1363 at Brandsby, towards Easingwold; West Way

Plenty of locals come to this comfortable pub during the week for a pint and a chat, but at the weekends, much of the space is filled by dining tables. The old-fashioned lounge bar has venerable tables and antique seats and settles on the flagstones, pictures and photographs on the dark red walls, interesting satirical carvings in its panelling (which are Victorian copies of medieval pew ends), polished copper and brass, and an enormous inglenook fireplace with winter log fires (flowers in summer). In the bottom bar is a framed illustrated acount of the local history (some of it gruesome) dating back to the 12th c, and a large framed print of the original famous Durham Ox which weighed 171 stones. Attractively presented, the food might include home-made soup with home-made bread (£3.50), sandwiches (from £5.95; mozzarella melt, roasted peppers and tomatoes £6.25; with chips and coleslaw), lunchtime pizza with toppings like parma ham, rocket and fresh parmesan or fresh seafood of the day (£6.95), caesar salad with seared king prawns or smoked chicken or a platter with cheese, ham, pâté, pickles, boiled egg and their own baked bread (£7.95), and bangers and mash or field mushroom and aubergine stack with beef steak tomatoes and mozzarella (£8.95), with daily specials like goats cheese tartlet with red onion marmalade (£5.25), chicken livers with smoked bacon, pine nuts and rocket or potted shrimps (£5.95), wild mushroom risotto with french brie, chives and cream (£10.95), bacon joint with creamy cherry tomato sauce and chive mash (£11.95), duck breast on red cabbage with rich port jus (£13.95), and puddings such as iced white chocolate and raspberry ripple parfait or warm sticky toffee pudding with butterscotch sauce (from £4.50); good cheeses. The restaurant is no smoking. Well kept John Smiths, Tetleys, Theakstons XB, and Wells Bombardier on handpump, and eight wines by the glass; piped music. There are seats outside on a terrace and in the courtyard, and the comfortable bedrooms are in converted farm buildings. The tale is that this is the hill which the Grand Old Duke of York marched his men up; the view from the hill opposite is marvellous. *(Recommended by Mike Schofield, Pat and Graham Williamson, Pat and Tony Martin, Peter and Anne-Marie O'Malley, Tim and Sue Halstead, Mr and Mrs C Cameron, Michael Doswell, Ian S Morley)*

Free house ~ Licensee Michael Ibbotson ~ Real ale ~ Bar food (12-2.30, 6-9.30(8.30 Sun)) ~ Restaurant ~ (01347) 821506 ~ Children allowed but not in restaurant ~ Dogs allowed in bedrooms ~ Folk/easy listening live music Sun and Thurs evenings ~ Open 11-3, 6-11.30; 12-13, 7-10 Sun; closed 25 Dec ~ Bedrooms: £60B/£80B

CROPTON SE7588 Map 10
New Inn 🍺 🛏

Village signposted off A170 W of Pickering

The day to day running of this comfortably modernised village inn has now been taken over by Mrs Lee's son. The beers brewed in the brewery behind the pub remain a huge draw, and you can arrange a tour: Two Pints, Monkman's Slaughter, Endeavour, and Yorkshire Moors Bitter, which they keep well on handpump, and a guest such as Thwaites. The traditional village bar has Victorian church panels, terracotta and dark blue plush seats, lots of brass, and a small fire. A local artist has designed historical posters all around the no smoking downstairs conservatory. Decent bar food includes soup (£2.95), sandwiches (from £2.95), chorizo salad (£4.25), ploughman's (£5.95), leek and brie tart (£6.95), steak in red wine pie (£7.25), fresh whitby cod or lasagne (£7.50), chicken wensleydale (£9.25), lamb joint (£11.95), and joint of beef for two (£16.95). The elegant no smoking restaurant is furnished with genuine Victorian and early Edwardian pieces. Darts, pool, juke box, fruit machine, TV, and piped music. There's a neat terrace, a garden with a pond, and a brewery shop. More reports please. *(Recommended by Dr Paull Khan, Gill and Tony Morriss, Lorraine and Fred Gill, Peter F Marshall, Su and Bob Child, Malcolm and Jennifer Perry, Barry Smith)*

Own brew ~ Licensee Philip Lee ~ Real ale ~ Bar food (12-2, 6-9) ~ Restaurant ~ (01751) 417330 ~ Children welcome ~ Dogs allowed in bar ~ Open 11-11; 12-10.30 Sun ~ Bedrooms: £39B/£66B

DACRE BANKS SE1962 Map 7
Royal Oak 🍺 🛏

B6451 S of Pateley Bridge

In warm weather you can sit on the terrace or in the garden of this welcoming pub and enjoy the lovely views; boules. Inside, it's basically open-plan, and the two comfortable lounge areas (one is no smoking) have interesting old photographs and poems with a drinking theme on the walls, an open fire in the front part, and well kept Rudgate Yorkshire Dales Bitter, Landlady, and Nidderdale Best on handpump, and a decent wine list. Enjoyable bar food includes sandwiches (from £2.75; bruschetta topped with prawns, garlic and parmesan and served with chips £5.50; filled ciabatta from £5.50), filled yorkshire puddings or salmon and crab fishcake in cajun tomato sauce (£4.95), mussels italian style (£5.75), ploughman's or local sausage in rich beef gravy (£6.95), home-made vegetable cakes on creamy sun-dried tomato and herb sauce or steak, kidney and vegetable in ale pie (£7.50), pigeon breast with red wine, poached apples in a thyme and garlic sauce (£9.95), chicken en croûte (£10.95), steaks (from £11.95), venison steak in black cherry, cranberry and port sauce or grilled loin of cod in prawn and caper butter (£12.95), and king scallops on pesto roasted tomatoes (£13.95). The restaurant is also no smoking. Pool, dominoes, cribbage, TV, and piped music. *(Recommended by Gerald Wilkinson, Norman Stansfield, M and N Watson, Mr and Mrs W D Borthwick, Greta and Christopher Wells, Paul and Ursula Randall, B G Thompson, S D and J L Cooke, Susan and Tony Dyer, Pat and Tony Martin, Alison Hayes, Pete Hanlon)*

*Free house ~ Licensee Stephen Cock ~ Real ale ~ Bar food ~ Restaurant ~ (01423)
780200 ~ Children in eating area of bar and restaurant until 9 ~ Open 11.30-3, 5-11;
12-3, 7-10.30 Sun; closed 25 Dec ~ Bedrooms: £35S/£50S*

EAST WITTON SE1586 Map 10
Blue Lion ★ ⑪ ♀ 🛏

A6108 Leyburn—Ripon

A favourite with many customers, this civilised inn is just the place for a short
break, a fine meal or a chatty drink. The big squarish bar has high-backed antique
settles and old windsor chairs and round tables on the turkey rugs and flagstones,
ham-hooks in the high ceiling decorated with dried wheat, teazles and so forth, a
delft shelf filled with appropriate bric-a-brac, several prints, sporting caricatures
and other pictures on the walls, a log fire, and daily papers; the friendly labrador is
called Archie. By the time this book is published, readers will be pleased to note
that there will be provision for no smokers. Priced more in line with something a bit
special than a basic snack at the end of a walk, the imaginative food might include
sandwiches, home-made soup (£3.65), caesar salad with pancetta and chargrilled
chicken or garlic and wild mushroom on toasted brioche (£5.25), roasted king
scallops with lemon risotto and gruyère cheese (£7.55), terrine of foie gras mousse
with an orange and walnut pickle, apple and orange salad (£7.85), and main
courses such as home-made spaghetti with fresh seafood and tomato (£8.50),
salmon with parma ham, mushrooms and shallots in a grain mustard sauce
(£11.95), venison and Guinness suet pudding (£11.95), slow roast free range belly
pork with honey and apple sauce (£12.20), roast fillet of cod with a pesto and
parsley crust with roast fennel or peppered duck breast with port and blackberry
sauce (£12.95), and individual roast sirloin of beef with horseradish crust and
yorkshire pudding (£16.50). Well kept Black Sheep Bitter and Riggwelter, and
Theakstons Best, and an impressive list of wines with quite a few by the glass.
Picnic-sets on the gravel outside look beyond the stone houses on the far side of the
village green to Witton Fell, and there's a big, pretty back garden. *(Recommended by
Jenny and Dave Hughes, Mrs T C Sweeney, the Didler, E D Fraser, Angus Lyon,
Anthony Longden, Alyson and Andrew Jackson, Tim and Carolyn Lowes, Lynda and
Trevor Smith, JP, PP, Jim Abbott, Greta and Christopher Wells, Margaret and Roy Randle,
Barry and Patricia Wooding, D Clarkson, Jonathan Gibbs, Brian England, Denise Dowd,
Louise English, J Goodwin, Mike and Maggie Betton, Bernard Stradling, Gerry and
Rosemary Dobson)*

*Free house ~ Licensee Paul Klein ~ Real ale ~ Bar food ~ Restaurant ~ (01969)
624273 ~ Children in eating area of bar and restaurant ~ Dogs allowed in bedrooms
~ Open 11-11; 12-10.30 Sun ~ Bedrooms: £53.50S/£69S(£89B)*

EGTON BRIDGE NZ8005 Map 10
Horse Shoe

Village signposted from A171 W of Whitby; via Grosmont from A169 S of Whitby

Everyone is made to feel welcome here by the friendly landlady – and there are
plenty of customers drawn by the charming position, too: comfortable seats on a
quiet terrace and lawn beside a little stream (where there are ducks), and attractive
gardens with pretty roses, mature redwoods, and geese and bantams. Fishing is
available on a daily ticket from Egton Estates; plenty of surrounding walks, too.
Inside, the bar has old oak tables, high-backed built-in winged settles, wall seats
and spindleback chairs, a big stuffed trout (caught near here in 1913), pictures on
the walls, and a warm log fire; the restaurant is no smoking. Nicely presented and
served in generous helpings, the popular food includes lunchtime sandwiches,
home-made soup (£2.95), stilton mushrooms (£3.80), home-made chicken liver
pâté (£4.20), vegetable lasagne (£7.70), gammon topped with egg or pineapple or
fish pie (£8), chicken breast in red wine, mushroom and bacon sauce (£8.20),
braised lamb shank with rosemary and red wine sauce and minted mash (£9.20),
and sirloin of beef (£13). Well kept John Smiths and Theakstons Best, and guests

from local breweries like Durham and Hambleton on handpump, and malt whiskies; darts, dominoes, and piped music. A different way to reach this beautifully placed pub is to park by the Roman Catholic church, walk through the village and cross the River Esk by stepping stones. Not to be confused with a similarly named pub up at Egton. At peak times, single occupancy of bedrooms may be rejected, due to demand. *(Recommended by Ian Piper, Ron and Mary Nicholson, Pete Baker, Dr and Mrs R G J Telfer, Sarah Davis, Rod Lambert, Blaise Vyner, Ian and Jane Irving, John W Allen, Hugh Roberts, Jarrod and Wendy Hopkinson, Michael Doswell, Wendie Huckerby, Peter and Anne-Marie O'Malley, Gill and Tony Morriss, Mr and Mrs P Dix, Mike and Lynn Robinson)*

Free house ~ Licensees Tim and Suzanne Boulton ~ Real ale ~ Bar food ~ Restaurant ~ (01947) 895245 ~ Children in restaurant and separate no smoking back bar area ~ Dogs allowed in bar ~ Open 11.30-3(3.30 Sat), 6.30-11; 12-3.30, 7-10.30 Sun; closed 25 Dec ~ Bedrooms: £30(£38S)/£45(£55S)

ELSLACK SD9249 Map 7

Tempest Arms (knife-and-fork symbol) (wine glass symbol)

Village signposted just off A56 Earby—Skipton

The licensees who have taken over this 18th-c stone pub and put it right back on form are familiar faces to us – they managed it in the late 1990s. There's a lively, welcoming atmosphere and a good mix of customers – especially at weekends. The series of quietly decorated areas has comfortable plum or chocolate plush cushioned armchairs, cushioned built-in wall seats, and stools, and lots of tables; there's also quite a bit of stripped stonework, nice prints on the cream walls, and three log fires (one in a dividing fireplace); Molly the friendly black labrador tends to be sitting in front of one of them. Part of the bar and all of the restaurant are no smoking; piped music in one area only, and winter darts and dominoes. Well kept Black Sheep, Theakstons Best, Timothy Taylors Best and Landlord, and Shipton Brewery Copper Dragon on handpump, eight wines by big or small glass from a good list, several malt whiskies, and good coffees. Very good food from a menu that can be used for both the bar and restaurant might include nibbles like unleavened garlic or cheesy garlic pitta bread (£1.85) or marinated olives with fresh herbs, chilli and capers (£2.65), home-made soup (£2.95), sandwiches with a crisp salad (from £3.50; roasted tomato and hummous £4.15; generous club £5.95), mushrooms in cream and port and topped with melting local blue cheese (£4.50), fresh fishcakes with thai dipping suace (£4.65; main course £7.95), mediterranean prawn pot or roast goats cheese and mushroom with tomato and basil dressing (£4.95), their very popular warm salad (£5.50), bangers and mash with red wine and onion jus (£8.25), chicken caesar salad (£8.99), slow-cooked lamb on the bone with rich mint and redcurrant gravy (£9.50), crispy pork with apple compote, thyme-roasted potatoes and gravy (£9.95), 10oz sirloin steak (£13.50), half a duck with caramelised orange sauce (£13.99), daily specials, puddings like warm lemon sponge with tangy lemon sauce served with red orange ice cream, sticky toffee pudding, and raspberry and rhubarb frangipane (£3.95), and good local and regional cheeses with crackers, fruitcake and celery (£4.95). Tables outside are largely screened from the road by a raised bank. *(Recommended by Karen Eliot, Norman Stansfield, J Taylor, Jim and Maggie Cowell, Robert Hill, Dudley and Moira Cockroft)*

Free house ~ Licensees Martin and Veronica Clarkson ~ Real ale ~ Bar food (12-2.30, 6-9; 12-8 Sun) ~ Restaurant ~ (01282) 842450 ~ Children welcome in several areas away from bar ~ Open 11-11; 12-10.30 Sun ~ Bedrooms: £59.95B/£74.95B

Stars after the name of a pub show exceptional character and appeal. They don't mean extra comfort. And they are nothing to do with food quality, for which there's a separate knife-and-fork symbol. Even quite a basic pub can win stars, if it's individual enough.

FADMOOR SE6789 Map 10
Plough 🍽 ♀
Village signposted off A170 in or just W of Kirkbymoorside

With first-rate food and a warm welcome from the friendly staff, it's not surprising that this neatly kept pub always has a good bustling atmosphere. The elegantly simple little rooms have rugs on seagrass, richly upholstered furnishings, and yellow walls, well kept Black Sheep or Timothy Taylors Landlord on handpump, and an extensive wine list. Excellent food such as home-made soup (£3.50), home-made farmhouse terrine with red onion and mango chutney (£4.50), goujons of fresh haddock with lemon and dill mayonnaise or smoked scottish venison with bramble jelly dressing (£5.95), steamed fresh shetland mussels in cream, white wine and dill (£6.95), braised beef brisket joint with port and shallot sauce (£9.50), chicken breast stuffed with blue stilton and wrapped in bacon with a leek and bacon sauce (£10.50), home-made steak and kidney pudding (£10.95), medallions of monkfish and king scallops in a light creamy curry sauce (£14.50), daily specials such as goats cheese and mixed pepper tartlet with red pepper and garlic chutney (£5.50), slow roasted confit of duck leg on black pudding and apricot couscous with chilled blackberry sauce (£5.95), roast pheasant with pearl barley, parsley, wine and cream sauce (£10.50), and fillets of bass layered with citrus risotto and a tarragon, white wine and cream sauce (£12.50), and puddings like white and dark chocolate marbled cheesecake with strawberry ice cream, ginger and syrup sponge or raspberry crème brûlée with raspberry and mango coulis (£4.25); they offer an early bird menu (6.30-7.30pm, two courses £12.25). The dining areas are no smoking. Dominoes and piped music. There are seats on the terrace. (*Recommended by Peter Burton, Rod Stoneman, Jenny and Dave Hughes, Ian and Rose Lock, Keith Mould, Greta and Christopher Wells, Walter and Susan Rinaldi-Butcher, Geoff and Angela Jaques, Mr and Mrs Maurice Thompson, Jane Gilbert, Beryl and Tim Dawson, Alison Hayes, Pete Hanlon*)

Holf Leisure Ltd ~ Licensee Neil Nicholson ~ Real ale ~ Bar food (12-1.45, 6.30-8.45; 12-2, 7-8.30 Sun) ~ Restaurant ~ (01751) 431515 ~ Children in eating area of bar and restaurant ~ Open 12-2.30, 6.30-11; 12-3, 7-10.30 Sun; closed 25 and 26 Dec, 1 Jan

FELIXKIRK SE4785 Map 10
Carpenters Arms 🍽 ♀
Village signposted off A170 E of Thirsk

In a picturesque small moors-edge village, this warmly inviting place has three or four cosy areas that ramble around the bar counter (made partly from three huge casks), with dark beams and joists hung with carpentry tools and other bric-a-brac, comfortable seats around tables with check tablecloths and little lighted oil burners, and a couple of huge japanese fans by the stone fireplace. Good, enjoyable food at lunchtime includes home-made soups like cream of vegetable and thyme or lightly spiced parsnip and pear (£2.95), quite a few sandwiches (from £3.75; BLT £4.95; chargrilled thai burger £6.50), warm salad of pigeon, crispy bacon and juniper berry dressing (£4.50), pork and leek sausages with onion gravy (£6.95), baked queen scallops with herbs and gruyère (£7.50), home-made steak, ale and mushroom pie (£7.95), beer-battered cod (£8.50), and risotto of cherry tomatoes and chilli with parmesan and basil pesto (£9.50), with evening main courses such as crisp fillet of scottish salmon with baby spinach, mussels and fish cream sauce (£11.95), pork fillet with rocket and red onion salad and dijon and peppercorn sauce (£12.50), and honey-glazed duck breast with stir-fried vegetables, crispy noodles and plum sauce (£14.50), and daily specials like chicken livers with bacon and garlic croutons (£4.50), moules marinière (£5.95), devilled strips of spicy beef with herb rice (£9.95), and whole roast bass with prawn and caper butter (£12.95). Puddings such as banana and Baileys bread and butter pudding or chocolate and coffee torte with Tia Maria cream and mocha glaze (£4.25), and three-course Sunday lunch (£14.50). Friendly staff, well kept Black Sheep, Greene King Old

Speckled Hen, Tetleys, and Timothy Taylors Landlord on handpump, and a good wine list with eight by the glass; piped music. There are three dalmatians, Lucy, George, and Lloyd. The church is prettily floodlit at night. More reports please. *(Recommended by H Bramwell, Janet and Peter Race, C A Hall, Margaret and Mike Iley, Michael Ward)*

Free House ~ Licensee Karen Bumby ~ Real ale ~ Bar food ~ Restaurant ~ (01845) 537369 ~ Children in eating area of bar and restaurant ~ Open 11.30-3, 6.30-11; 12-3, 7-10.30 Sun; closed 25 Dec, evening 31 Dec

FERRENSBY SE3761 Map 7
General Tarleton 🍴 ♀ 🛏
A655 N of Knaresborough

It remains the popular modern cooking that draws customers to this rather smart and comfortable 18th-c coaching inn. The beamed and carpeted bar has brick pillars dividing up the several different areas to create the occasional cosy alcove, some exposed stonework, and neatly framed pictures on the red walls; there's a mix of country kitchen furniture and comfortable banquettes, a big open fire, and a door leading out to a pleasant tree-lined garden with smart green tables. From the menu, the interesting bar food includes cream soup of the day (£4.25), pasta with porcini mushrooms, thyme and tomato (£4.95; main course £9.75), parfait of chicken livers and foie gras (£5.45), lunchtime open sandwiches (from £5.95), local pork sausages with red onion gravy (£7.50), fish and chips with minted mushy fresh peas (£8.95), roast onion stuffed with basil and parmesan served with grilled tuscan vegetables (£9.95), corn-fed chicken with wild forest mushrooms and pancetta (£11.95), seared fillet of bass on a tomato tart with rocket and pesto (£14.25), aberdeen angus rib-eye steak (£15.95), daily specials such as roast cod fillet with pomme purée and chive and prawn butter sauce (£9.95), chargrilled haunch of venison with horseradish mash and mushroom, bacon, and red wine sauce (£12.95) or platter of fruits de mer for two people (£49.95), and puddings like warm chocolate and banana melting pudding or pear and almond frangipane tart with calvados sauce (£4.75). Well kept Black Sheep Best, Timothy Taylors Landlord, and a beer from Hambleton on handpump, over 20 good wines by the glass, and quite a few coffees; service is professional rather than friendly. The courtyard eating area (and restaurant) are no smoking. *(Recommended by Regine Webster, Janet and Peter Race, Peter Burton, Jo and Iain MacGregor, Malcolm and Jennifer Perry, Paul Boot, Guy Vowles, Mrs M Blundell, Kate Arscott, J Roy Smylie, B and M Kendall, Pat and Graham Williamson, Tony Gayfer, H Bramwell, David and Iris Hunter, Robert and Susan Whitehead, Revd D Glover, David and Ruth Hollands, Alan J Morton, Alison Hayes, Pete Hanlon)*

Free house ~ Licensee John Topham ~ Real ale ~ Bar food (12-2.15, 6-9.30(8.30 Sun)) ~ Restaurant ~ (01423) 340284 ~ Children welcome ~ Dogs allowed in bedrooms ~ Open 12-3, 6-11(10.30 Sun); closed 25 Dec ~ Bedrooms: £74.95B/£84.90B

FLAMBOROUGH TA2270 Map 8
Seabirds
Junction B1255/B1229

Although a new licensee has taken over this village pub, the décor seems to have stayed the same. The public bar has quite a shipping theme, and leading off here the comfortable lounge has a whole case of stuffed seabirds along one wall, as well as pictures and paintings of the local landscape, pump labels and beer mats, cups and trophies, and a woodburning stove. Under the new chef, changing, reasonably priced bar food might include sandwiches, deep-fried haddock or cod (from £5.75), home-made steak pie or prawn thermidor (£5.95), home-made curry (£6.25), lamb casserole (£6.50), whole sea bream in lemon and dill butter (£10.25), roast leg of lamb in rosemary and red wine sauce (£10.95), steaks (from £11), and monkfish in a prawn and leek sauce (£11.95). Well kept John Smiths and a weekly changing guest like Jennings Cumberland or Shepherd Neame Spitfire on handpump, and a decent wine list; dominoes and piped music. There are seats in the sizeable garden, and you can eat out here in fine weather. The Chalk Cliffs and lighthouse at Flamborough Head (where there are many spectacular walks) or the seabird colonies at Bempton Cliffs are close by. More reports please. *(Recommended by June and Ken Brooks, Paul and Ursula Randall, DC, Irene and Ray Atkin, Derek and Sylvia Stephenson, M Borthwick)*

Free house ~ Licensee Philip Jones ~ Real ale ~ Bar food (not winter Mon evenings) ~ Restaurant ~ (01262) 850242 ~ Children in eating area of bar and restaurant ~ Dogs allowed in bar ~ Open 12(11.45 Sat)-3, 7(6.30 Sat)-11; 12-3, 7-10.30 Sun; closed Mon evening in winter

GOOSE EYE SE0340 Map 7
Turkey

Just S of Laycock on road to Oakworth and Haworth, W of Keighley; OS Sheet 104 map reference 028406

Friendly and busy, this own brew pub offers a warm welcome from the licensees, and roaring winter log fires. Their own ales remain very popular: Turkey Bitter, Chris Camm, and No-Eyed Deer, and guest beers such as Archers Village or Greene King Abbot on handpump. You can visit the microbrewery – they ask for a donation for Upper Wharfedale Fell Rescue; over 40 whiskies. There are various cosy and snug alcoves, brocaded upholstery, and walls covered with pictures of surrounding areas; the restaurant is no smoking. Decent, straightforward bar food includes home-made soup (£2.10), sandwiches (from £3.50), vegetable lasagne (£5.80), home-made pie (£6), steaks (from £7.20), home-made daily specials (from £6), and puddings (from £2.40); Sunday lunch (£6). Piped music, and a separate games area with pool, fruit machine, and TV. *(Recommended by Matt Waite, Greta and Christopher Wells, Geoffrey and Brenda Wilson, Mr and Mrs P Eastwood)*

Own brew ~ Licensees Harry and Monica Brisland ~ Real ale ~ Bar food (not Mon) ~ Restaurant ~ (01535) 681339 ~ Children in tap room ~ Open 12-3(5 Sat), 5.30(6.30 Sat)-11; 12-11 Sun; closed Mon lunchtime

HALIFAX SE1026 Map 7
Shibden Mill 🕮 ♀

Off A58 into Kell Lane at Stump Cross Inn, near A6036 junction; keep on, pub signposted from Kell Lane on left

At the bottom of a peaceful valley stands this tucked away, restored mill. The rambling, newly refurbished bar has cosy side areas with enticing banquettes heaped softly with cushions and rugs; tables and chairs are well spaced, but candles in elegant iron holders give a feeling of real intimacy. There are old hunting prints, country landscapes and so forth, and a couple of big log fireplaces. The choice of wines by the glass is exceptional and served in nice glasses, and they have John Smiths, a softly flavoured golden beer brewed for them by Moorhouses, Theakstons XB, and a couple of guests like Adnams Bitter or Timothy Taylors Landlord kept well on handpump. Under the new chef, the good, interesting bar food includes light snacks such as corned beef tart with fried egg, macaroni cheese with smoked trout, sausage sandwich with tomato chutney, and basil risotto with warm goats cheese (all £5.25), as well as starters like smoked chicken with wild mushrooms, peas and minted stuffing, ham with potato dumplings and basil salad, crayfish tails with radish and french bean salad (all £5.25), main courses such as organic pork cutlet with green herb mustard mash, roast skate with bubble and squeak, ricotta and spinach cannelloni with lemon butter, and roast lamb with herb risotto (all £14.50), and puddings that include chocolate pot with peanut ice cream or soft meringue with mixed berries in red wine (£4.25); vegetables and salads are £1.95 extra. Piped music. The restaurant has been moved upstairs, and they now have a private dining room. There are plenty of good teak tables and chairs out on an attractive terrace, with lots of heaters; the building is prettily floodlit at night. More reports please. *(Recommended by Lynette and Stuart Shore, Pat and Tony Martin, Derek and Sylvia Stephenson, Andy and Jill Kassube)*

Free house ~ Licensee Glen Pearson ~ Real ale ~ Bar food (12-2, 6-9.30; 12-7.30 Sun) ~ Restaurant ~ (01422) 365840 ~ Children welcome ~ Open 12-2.30, 5.30-11; 12-11 Sat; 12-10.30 Sun ~ Bedrooms: £65B/£80B

HAROME SE6582 Map 10
Star ★ ⑪ ♀ ◧ ⇌
Village signposted S of A170, E of Helmsley

What makes this pretty thatched 14th-c thatched inn so special for this book is that despite the fact the excellent food is obviously the highlight, the very friendly, young licensees have managed to retain a proper pubby atmosphere in the bar. There's a dark bowed beam-and-plank ceiling, well polished tiled kitchen range, plenty of bric-a-brac, interesting furniture (this was the first pub that 'Mousey Thompson' ever populated with his famous dark wood furniture), a fine log fire, and daily papers and magazines. Also, a no smoking dining room, and a popular coffee loft in the eves. For the first-rate, inventive food, fish is delivered daily from Hartlepool, they grow their own herbs and some vegetables, use local hen, duck, and guinea fowl eggs, and three types of honey from the village; they also offer lots of british cheeses. Changing daily, the lunchtime dishes might include home-made soup (£3.50), sandwiches or buns (from £5.95; home-cooked ham with spiced pineapple pickle £6.95), terrine of local wild rabbit with boozy prune and baby leek vinaigrette (£5.95; main course £9.50), grilled asparagus with bubble and squeak, fried quail egg and mustard seed dressing (£7.25; main course £13.50), ploughman's with a selection of cold and cured meats, british cheeses, and chutneys (£8.95), and grilled black pudding with fried foie gras, apple and vanilla chutney and scrumpy reduction (£8.95; main course £11.50); evening main courses such as confit of duck leg with its own cassoulet and home-baked beans (£11.95), calves liver with crispy smoked belly pork, parsnip dauphinoise, and beetroot vinaigrette (£12.50), breast of corn-fed chicken with purée of celeriac, wild mushrooms and truffle shavings (£13.95), roast rump of ryedale lamb with a little shepherd's pie, plum tomato and pearl barley juices (£15.95), and roasted fillet of beef with deep-fried chunky chips and green peppercorn sauce (£16.95); daily specials like seared scallops with deep-fried scarborough woof (£8.95), pot-roast local partridge with beetroot fondant, creamed curly kale and smoked bacon gravy (£13.50), and loin of local lamb with creamed goats cheese, salad of baby leeks, and lavender vinaigrette (£13.95), and lovely puddings – baked ginger parkin with rhubarb ripple ice cream and hot spiced syrup, blood orange burnt cream with its own fruit salad and dark chocolate brownie or caramelised fresh lemon tart with bramble sauce (from £5.25). Particularly good, helpful service from smartly dressed, knowledgeable staff; well kept Black Sheep, John Smiths, Theakstons Best, and a guest on handpump, farm ciders, freshly squeezed juices, home-made rhubarb schnapps, starwberry gin or bramble or thyme vodkas, and quite a few wines by the glass from a fairly extensive wine list; piped music and dominoes. There are some seats and tables on a sheltered front terrace with more in the garden with fruit trees. Eight superbly equipped, stylish bedrooms in converted farm buildings, a private dining room, and open-plan kitchen. Their bakery/delicatessen is called The Corner Shop and sells take-away meals and snacks as well as all manner of delicious goodies from cakes and tarts to fresh truffles and wild mushrooms, local game and fish, and home-made terrines and pies. They have a village cricket team.

(Recommended by John and Daphne Lock Necrews, Terry Mizen, Trevor Hosking, Phil Skelton, Norma and Barry Knaggs, Andrew Scarr, Greta and Christopher Wells, Mr and Mrs C Cameron, Peter and Anne-Marie O'Malley, Derek and Margaret Underwood, Pat and Tony Martin, Ian and Rose Lock, Mike Schofield, Tim Newman, John Coggrave, Sally Anne and Peter Goodale, John Nielsen, Richard Gibbs, Marian and Andrew Ruston, J Goodwin, Brendan Sinnott, Alison Hayes, Pete Hanlon, Comus and Sarah Elliott, Michael Butler; also in the Good Hotel Guide)

Free house ~ Licensees Andrew and Jacquie Pern ~ Real ale ~ Bar food (12-2, 6.30-9.30; 12-6 Sun; not Sun evening, not Mon) ~ Restaurant ~ (01439) 770397 ~ Children in eating area of bar and restaurant ~ Open 11.30-3, 6.30-11; 12-11 Sun; closed Mon lunchtime ~ Bedrooms: £90B/£120B

HEATH SE3519 Map 7
Kings Arms £

Village signposted from A655 Wakefield—Normanton – or, more directly, turn off to the left opposite Horse & Groom

Seats along the front of this old-fashioned pub make the most of the village green setting opposite and the surrounding 19th-c stone merchants' houses; there are picnic-sets on a side lawn, and a nice walled flower-filled garden. Inside, the gas lighting adds a lot to the atmosphere, and the original bar has a fire burning in the old black range (with a long row of smoothing irons on the mantelpiece), plain elm stools and oak settles built into the walls, and dark panelling. A more comfortable extension has carefully preserved the original style, down to good wood-pegged oak panelling (two embossed with royal arms), and a high shelf of plates; there are also two other small flagstoned rooms, and the conservatory opens on to the garden. Served by friendly staff, the good value bar food includes sandwiches (from £1.95; hot sausage and onion £2.25), home-made soup (£2.25), mushroom stroganoff (£4.25), liver and onions in rich gravy, home-made lasagne or beef in ale pie (£5.25), rump steak (£6.95), puddings like treacle sponge and custard (£2.75), and children's meals (£2.55). Well kept Clarks Classic Blonde, Timothy Taylors Landlord, and a couple of guests like Clarks Golden Hornet or Hanby Nutcracker on handpump; quiz night Tuesdays. *(Recommended by the Didler, JP, PP, M and G Rushworth, John W Allen, Mike and Maggie Betton, Geoffrey and Brenda Wilson, Pat and Derek Roughton, Greta and Christopher Wells)*

Clarks ~ Manager Alan Tate ~ Real ale ~ Bar food (12-2, 6-9.30; all day at weekends) ~ (01924) 377527 ~ Children in eating area of bar and restaurant ~ Open 11.30-11; 12-10.30 Sun; 11.30-3, 5.30-11 weekdays in winter

HECKMONDWIKE SE2223 Map 7
Old Hall

New North Road; B6117 between A62 and A638; OS Sheet 104 map reference 214244

As ever, it's the historic building itself that is the main interest here. It dates from 1470, and was once the home of Nonconformist scientist Joseph Priestley. Although it was built in the 15th c, the outer walls were replaced by stone in the 16th c, and inside there are lots of old beams and timbers, latticed mullioned windows with worn stone surrounds, brick or stripped old stone walls hung with pictures of Richard III, Henry VII, Catherine Parr, and Joseph Priestley, and comfortable furnishings. Snug low-ceilinged alcoves lead off the central part with its high ornate plaster ceiling, and an upper gallery room, under the pitched roof, looks down on the main area through timbering 'windows'; one area is no smoking. Bar food is straightforward, with dishes like curry, a pie of the day or three-cheese pasta bake (£5.25). Well kept (and cheap) Sam Smiths OB on handpump; fruit machine, piped music, darts, TV, and dominoes. More reports please. *(Recommended by Michael Butler, Bernie Adams, Ian Phillips, Kevin Blake)*

Sam Smiths ~ Lease Robert Green ~ Real ale ~ Bar food (12-2, 6-8; 12-3 Sun) ~ (01924) 404774 ~ Children welcome ~ Open 11.30-11; 12-10.30 Sun

---

The letters and figures after the name of each town are its Ordnance Survey map reference. *Using the Guide* at the beginning of the book explains how it helps you find a pub, in road atlases or large-scale maps as well as in our own maps.

HETTON SD9558 Map 7
Angel ★ ⑪ ♀

Just off B6265 Skipton—Grassington

A favourite with many of our readers, this is a particularly well run dining pub and most customers do come to enjoy the very good food, rather than using it as a place to drop into for a quick pint after a walk. As it does get very busy, you must book to be sure of a table. From an imaginative menu, there might be little moneybags (seafood baked in filo with lobster sauce, £5.95), terrine of seared chicken livers (£6.50), braised belly pork with black pudding (£8.75), mozzarella cheese and aubergine bake (£10.25), roasted monkfish tail wrapped in sage and pancetta, puy lentils, and fondant potato or wild halibut with english asparagus, crushed new potatoes, and lobster reduction (£14.95), roasted chump of lamb (£15.75), chargrilled aberdeen angus rib-eye steak with thyme jus (£15.95), and puddings like sticky toffee pudding with caramel sauce or chocolate tart with vanilla ice cream (from £4.75). On Friday, there's a fish menu: rustic fish soup with aïoli, gruyère and rouille (£5.95), tuna niçoise (£6.75), roast whitby cod with a light truffle velouté (£12.95), and seared turbot fillets with hollandaise (£15.25). Three-course Sunday lunch (£20.90), and a good value early bird menu – two courses with wine £15.95, three courses with wine £19.25. The restaurant is partly no smoking. Well kept Black Sheep Bitter, Timothy Taylors Landlord, and Copper Dragon from the new Skipton Brewery on handpump, 300 wines (with around 25 by the glass, including champagne), and a good range of malt whiskies. The four timbered and panelled rambling rooms have lots of cosy alcoves, comfortable country-kitchen chairs or button-back green plush seats, Ronald Searle wine snob cartoons and older engravings and photographs, log fires, and in the main bar, a Victorian farmhouse range in the big stone fireplace; part of the bar lounge and part of the restaurant are no smoking. Wooden seats and tables under colourful sunshades on the terrace. *(Recommended by Paul Boot, Robert Hill, Sherrie Glass, Mr and Mrs J E C Tasker, Jim Abbott, Janet and Peter Race, John and Sylvia Harrop, Pierre and Pat Richterich, Norman Stansfield, Karen Eliot, Jane Taylor, David Dutton, Bernard Stradling)*

Free house ~ Licensees Denis Watkins and John Topham ~ Real ale ~ Bar food (12-2.15, 6-9) ~ Restaurant ~ (01756) 730263 ~ Children welcome ~ Open 12-3, 6-11(11.30 Sat; 10.30 Sun); 12-3, 6-9.30 Sun in winter; closed one week Jan ~ Bedrooms: /£125B

HUBBERHOLME SD9178 Map 7
George

Village signposted from Buckden; about 1 mile NW

The two neat and cosy rooms in this remote and unspoilt old Upper Wharfedale building have genuine character: heavy beams supporting the dark ceiling-boards, walls stripped back to bare stone and hung with antique plates and photographs, seats (with covers to match the curtains) around shiny copper-topped tables on the flagstones, and an open stove in the big fireplace. There are seats and tables outside looking over the moors and River Wharfe – where they have fishing rights. Enjoyable wholesome bar food at lunchtime includes filled yorkshire puddings (from £2.60), filled rolls (£2.95), ploughman's (£4.95), gammon and eggs (£6.90), and sirloin steak (£10.95), with evening dishes such as steak and kidney pie or vegetable moussaka (£7.60), breast of duck in a raspberry and red wine sauce or local lamb chops in rosemary and garlic gravy (£10.95), and daily specials like chicken breast in lemon, ginger and honey (£7.95), lamb shank in red wine gravy (£9.95), and bass on wild rice risotto (£12.95). Well kept Black Sheep Bitter and Special, and a changing guest on handpump; cribbage and dominoes. The little village here has just this inn, the ancient church (where J B Priestley's ashes are scattered – this was his favourite pub), a bridge and a handful of stone-built houses. *(Recommended by Maggie and Tony Harwood, B and M Kendall, Walter and Susan Rinaldi-Butcher, RB, John Hale, Jane Taylor, David Dutton, R M Corlett, Mr and Mrs Staples, Tony and Ann Bennett-Hughes, D W Stokes, Dr and Mrs D Woods, Tim Newman, Peter and Ruth Burnstone)*

Free house ~ Licensees Jenny and Terry Browne ~ Real ale ~ Bar food (12-2, 6.30-8.45) ~ (01756) 760223 ~ Children in eating area of bar; no children to stay overnight ~ Dogs welcome ~ Open 11-3, 6-11; 12-3, 6-10.30 Sun; closed one month after first Mon in Jan ~ Bedrooms: £38S(£40B)/£56S(£60B)

HULL TA0927 Map 8

Minerva ♛

Park at top of pedestrianised area at top of Queen's Street and walk over Nelson Street or turn off Queen's Street into Wellington Street, right into Pier Street and pub is at top; no parking restrictions at weekends, 2-hour stay Mon-Fri

Before or after a visit to the nearby The Deep (Europe's deepest aquarium), you can head for this handsome pub for a drink or meal. There are seats out in front of the building, and on the piers on each side, and you can watch the boats in the bustling river and marina. Inside, several rooms ramble all the way round a central servery, and are filled with comfortable seats, quite a few interesting photographs and pictures of old Hull (with two attractive wash drawings by Roger Davis) and a big chart of the Humber; one room is no smoking during mealtimes. A tiny snug has room for just three people, and a back room (which looks out to the marina basin) houses a profusion of varnished woodwork; two coal fires in winter. They hold three beer festivals a year – at Easter, mid-July, and whenever the Sea Shanty Festival is on – August/September. Otherwise, they keep Adnams, Tetleys, and Youngs with guests from Boat, Orkney, Ossett or Roosters on handpump. Good sized helpings of straightforward bar food such as filled baked potatoes (from £2.50), baguettes (from £2.95), ploughman's (£4.50), home-made steak in ale pie (£4.55), cajun chicken or popular huge battered haddock (£5.25), and puddings (£2.50); daily specials, Sunday roast (£4.50), Wednesday curry nights, and Thursday steak nights (best to book in advance). The lounge is no smoking when food is being served. Dominoes, cribbage, fruit machine, TV, and piped music. *(Recommended by the Didler, Lorraine and Fred Gill, Walter and Susan Rinaldi-Butcher, Alistair and Kay Butler, CMW, JJW, JP, PP, Roger and Pauline Pearce, Peter F Marshall, Di and Mike Gillam, Alison Hayes, Pete Hanlon, J R Ringrose)*

Spirit Group ~ Managers Eamon and Kathy Scott ~ Real ale ~ Bar food (11.30-2.30, 6-9; not Fri/Sat/Sun evenings) ~ (01482) 326909 ~ Children in eating area of bar if eating ~ Open 11-11; 12-10.30 Sun; closed 25 Dec

Olde White Harte ★ £

Off 25 Silver Street, a continuation of Whitefriargate; pub is up narrow passage beside the jewellers' Barnby and Rust, and should not be confused with the much more modern White Hart nearby

It's the building and its history that are the reasons for coming to this old place. The six bars have some fine features. The downstairs one has attractive stained-glass windows that look out above the bow window seat, carved heavy beams support black ceiling boards, and there are two big brick inglenooks with a frieze of delft tiles. The curved copper-topped counter serves well kept McEwans 80/-, Theakstons Old Peculier, and a guest beer on handpump, and straightforward bar food; the restaurant is no smoking. It was in the heavily panelled room up the oak staircase that in 1642 the town's governor Sir John Hotham made the fateful decision to lock the nearby gate against Charles I, depriving him of Hull's arsenal; it didn't do him much good, as in the Civil War that followed, Hotham, like the king, was executed by the parliamentarians. There are seats in the courtyard, and outside heaters. *(Recommended by the Didler, Roger and Pauline Pearce, JP, PP, Paul and Ursula Randall, Peter F Marshall, Greta and Christopher Wells, Alison Hayes, Pete Hanlon)*

Scottish Courage ~ Lease Gerry Drew ~ Real ale ~ Bar food (12-7(4 Sat)) ~ Restaurant ~ No credit cards ~ (01482) 326363 ~ Children in eating area of bar and restaurant ~ Dogs welcome ~ Open 11-11; 12-10.30 Sun

INGLETON SD6973 Map 7
Wheatsheaf

High Street

In an attractive village, this pleasant inn is surrounded by great walking country. The long open-plan bar has, at one end, a pool table overlooked by various stuffed birds and animals; at the other, past the good big log fire, there's a family area with an aquarium. Big blackboards list the changing choice of good value home-made food such as filled maize-flour baps, soup (always vegetarian, £2.50), smoked mackerel pâté (£4), moules marinière or spicy king prawns (£4), home-roasted ham and eggs or freshly battered cod with home-made chips (£6.25), leek and pork sausage with bramley apple sauce and rich gravy, roast topside of beef with yorkshire pudding, chicken rogan josh, vegetable strudel or steak in ale pie (all £7.25), fresh salmon and prawn filo parcel with cream of dill sauce (£8.75), sirloin steak (£10.95), and home-made puddings such as steamed chocolate pudding and chocolate sauce or fruit crumble (£3.35); Monday is cheap steak night. Well kept Black Sheep, Tetleys, and Timothy Taylors Landlord on handpump, quite a few whiskies, quick friendly service; piped music and pool. The back garden (keep an eye open for Laurel and Hardy on your way out) has picnic-sets by an aviary with hawks; the black labradors are called Tia and Bella. More reports please. *(Recommended by Darren Le Poidevin, Gerry and Rosemary Dobson)*

Free house ~ Licensees David and Verity Randall and Jeremy and Hayley Thompson ~ Real ale ~ Bar food (12-2.30, 6-9) ~ Restaurant ~ (015242) 41275 ~ Children welcome ~ Dogs allowed in bar ~ Open 12-11(10.30 Sun) ~ Bedrooms: /£60S

KETTLESING SE2256 Map 7
Queens Head ♀ ◖

Village signposted off A59 W of Harrogate

The L-shaped, carpeted main bar in this stone-built pub is decorated with Victorian song sheet covers, lithographs of Queen Victoria, little heraldic shields, and a delft shelf of blue and white china. There's also a quietly chatty atmosphere, and lots of quite close-set elm and other tables around its walls, with cushioned country seats. Nicely presented food, very popular on weekday lunchtimes with older people, includes a special three-course lunch (£7.95), plus home-made soup (£2.95), filled yorkshire puddings (from £2.95), sandwiches (from £2.95), omelettes (£5.50), and home-made battered haddock (£6.95), with evening dishes such as chicken liver pâté with port and smoked bacon (£4.25), steaks (from £11.50), and daily specials like wild boar and apple sausage, salmon fillet with a herb crust and parsley butter (£6.95), chicken breast with mushrooms, bacon and red wine sauce (£9.95), lemon sole with a tomato, caper and lemon butter (£9.50), and medallions of beef with peppercorn sauce (£12); three-course Sunday lunch (£9.95). Coal or log fires at each end and maybe unobtrusive piped radio. A smaller bar on the left, with built-in red banquettes, has cricketing prints and cigarette cards, coins and banknotes, and in the lobby there's a life-size portrait of our present Queen; piped music, dominoes, and table skittles. Well kept Black Sheep Bitter, Theakstons Old Peculier and a quickly changing guest from local breweries on handpump, good house wines, and quick service. There are benches out in front, by the lane. More reports please. *(Recommended by Jim Abbott, Hugh A MacLean, Mr and Mrs Staples, Mr and Mrs W D Borthwick, M and G Rushworth)*

Free house ~ Licensee Glen Garbutt ~ Real ale ~ Bar food ~ (01423) 770263 ~ Children in eating area of bar ~ Open 11-11; 11-3, 6.30-11 Sat; 12-3, 6.30-10.30 Sun; closed 25 Dec and evenings 26 and 31 Dec ~ Bedrooms: £64.62S/£82.25S

Ideas for a country day out? We list pubs in really attractive scenery at the back of the book – and there are separate lists for waterside pubs, ones with really good gardens, and ones with lovely views.

KIRKBYMOORSIDE SE6987 Map 10
George & Dragon 🛏

Market Place

On Wednesdays particularly, this 17th-c coaching inn has a good bustling atmosphere as this pretty, small town has its market day. The pubby front bar has leather chesterfields as well as the brass-studded solid dark red leatherette armchairs set around polished wooden tables, burgundy and cream walls and panelling stripped back to its original pitch pine, horsebrasses hung along the beams, newspapers to read, and a blazing log fire; piped music. There's also an attractive beamed bistro, and a no smoking restaurant. Generously served, the enjoyable bar food includes sandwiches (from £2.95; roast chicken with cajun mayonnaise £3.95), home-made soup (£3.25), chicken liver pâté with plum chutney or wensleydale mushrooms (£4.25), mediterranean vegetable quiche with mango, pawpaw and apple salsa (£6.95), deep-fried whitby haddock in beer batter (£7.25), steak in ale pie or home-made salmon and dill fishcakes with lemon and dill sauce (£7.50), chicken in a cream, smoked bacon and mushroom sauce (£8.50), daily specials, and puddings such as sticky toffee pudding or caramel and walnut tart (£3.95; two courses £9.95). Well kept Black Sheep Bitter, Tetleys, and Timothy Taylors Landlord on handpump, and a good wine list. This is a comfortable place to stay (the bedrooms are in a converted cornmill and old vicarage at the back of the pub), and there are seats under umbrellas in the back courtyard and a surprisingly peaceful walled garden for residents to use. More reports please. *(Recommended by P J Benson, Susan and Nigel Wilson, Mrs Phoebe A Kemp, Pat and Tony Martin, Doreen and Haydn Maddock, Geoff and Angela Jaques, Alison Hayes, Pete Hanlon)*

Free house ~ Licensee Elaine Walker ~ Real ale ~ Bar food (12-2.15, 6.30-9.15) ~ Restaurant ~ (01751) 433334 ~ Children welcome ~ Dogs allowed in bar ~ Open 11-11; 12-10.30 Sun ~ Bedrooms: £49B/£79B

KIRKHAM SE7466 Map 7
Stone Trough 🍽 ♀ 🍺

Kirkham Abbey

This country inn is a very good combination of a proper pub and restaurant, and you can be sure of a friendly welcome from the helpful licensees. The several beamed and cosy rooms have warm log fires, well kept Black Sheep Bitter, Tetleys, Timothy Taylors Landlord, and a couple of guests such as Hambleton Nightmare or Malton Golden Chance on handpump, and an extensive wine list with nine by the glass; one small room and the restaurant are no smoking. From an imaginative menu, the very good bar food might include home-made soup (£3.95), sandwiches (from £4.75; popular hot steak and sautéed onion £5.25), spiced lamb cakes on red onion salad with minted yoghurt dressing (£4.75), terrine or confit shoulder of pork, roast apple and parma ham with sage toast (£4.95), steamed scottish mussels in red thai sauce or smoked chicken and bacon caesar salad (£5.25), pork and herb sausages on thyme mash with rich ale gravy (£6.95), wild mushroom pasta topped with goats cheese crumble (£7.95), chunk of baked cod on garlic mash with smoked cheese sauce (£9.95), moroccan lamb shank on sweet potato mash (£10.50), breast of chicken on a wild mushroom risotto with a light sherry jus (£11.95), daily specials such as truffled chicken liver parfait with pear chutney, breast of mallard on stilton mash with beetroot purée and yorkshire sauce or venison haunch steak on stilton polenta with stewed raisin and orange jus, and puddings like cherry bakewell tart with Amaretto ice cream, hot toffee and pecan sponge with butterscotch sauce and vanilla ice cream or chocolate gateau with spiced oranges (£3.95). The cat is called Crumble. Pool, fruit machine, dominoes, cribbage, shove-ha'penny, and piped music; TV in the pool room. From the seats outside, there are lovely views down the valley, and the inn is handy for Kirkham Abbey and Castle Howard. *(Recommended by Patrick Hancock, Mr and Mrs J Powell, Christopher Turner, Michael Dandy, Mike Ridgway, Sarah Miles, Dr D Parker, Dr and*

Mrs R G J Telfer, John and Sheila Burley, Pat and Graham Williamson, Alison Hayes, Pete Hanlon)

Free house ~ Licensees Sarah and Adam Richardson ~ Real ale ~ Bar food (12-2, 6.30-8.30; not Mon except bank hols) ~ Restaurant ~ (01653) 618713 ~ Well behaved children in eating areas ~ Open 12-2.30, 6-11(12 summer Sat); 11.45-10.30 Sun; closed Mon except bank hols, 25 Dec

LANGTHWAITE NY9902 Map 10
Charles Bathurst 🍴 🍽 🛌

Arkengarthdale, 1 mile N towards Tan Hill; generally known as the CB Inn

For tired walkers, this converted cottage in a lovely – if bleak – spot is a fine place to recharge one's batteries. Appropriately stolid from the outside, it's been knocked through inside to make a long bar with light pine scrubbed tables, country chairs and benches on stripped floors, plenty of snug alcoves, and a roaring fire. The island bar counter has well kept Black Sheep Bitter and Riggwelter, John Smiths, and Theakstons on handpump, and a short but interesting list of wines; darts, pool, TV, and dominoes. Using local ingredients and cooked by the licensee, the well liked food might include lunchtime filled baguettes (from £3.30; hot bacon and melted cheese £3.95), spiced tomato and lentil soup (£3.85), duck liver and pork terrine with cumberland sauce (£4.25), chicken supreme and julienne of ham and mushroom in a cream and masala sauce (£8.95), smoked haddock on leek mash with wholegrain mustard and cream sauce and a poached egg (£9.95), chinese fillet of beef strips with noodles in black bean sauce (£10.50), guinea fowl, boned and stuffed with a lime and ham duxelle with madeira jus (£11.25), and puddings like spiced plum and apple crumble or italian chocolate and almond cake with apricot coulis (£3.75); at lunchtime, the choice might be much more limited. Sunday roast lunch (from £6.95), and children's meals (£3.95). At busy times of year you may need to book a table; the dining room is partly no smoking. The bedrooms are pretty and comfortable, and there are fine views over Langthwaite village and Arkengarthdale. *(Recommended by Jim Abbott, JHBS, Peter and Ruth Burnstone, Lynda and Trevor Smith, Bill and Sheila McLardy, Michael Doswell, Dr Paull Khan, Walter and Susan Rinaldi-Butcher, M S Catling, B and M Kendall, RS, SF, Adrian Savage, Pam Stacey)*

Free house ~ Licensees Charles and Stacy Cody ~ Real ale ~ Bar food ~ (01748) 884567 ~ Children welcome ~ Dogs welcome ~ Open 11-11(3-11 Mon-Thurs Dec-Feb; 12-10.30 Sun ~ Bedrooms: /£65B

LASTINGHAM SE7391 Map 10
Blacksmiths Arms 🍽

Off A170 W of Pickering at Wrelton, forking off Rosedale road N of Cropton; or via Appleton or Hutton-le-Hole

Two hundred years ago it was the church's curate who kept this neat stone inn, saying he needed the money to eke out his stipend and feed his 13 children. It's worth a visit to the church as it has a unique Saxon crypt built as a shrine to St Cedd in 1078. There's a cosily old-fashioned beamed bar with a log fire in an open range, traditional furnishings, and well kept Theakstons Best and Black Bull, and a guest like Marstons Pedigree on handpump; quite a few malt whiskies. Most of the pub (except the bar) is no smoking. Enjoyable home-made bar food includes sandwiches, yorkshire pudding with onion gravy (£2.45), soup (£3.25), crispy garlic mushrooms with garlic mayonnaise (£3.45), roast topside of beef with yorkshire pudding (£6.95), vegetable crumble or steak in ale pie (£7.25), popular beer-battered cod (£7.50), salmon and broccoli bake (£7.95), chicken stuffed with cream cheese and wrapped in bacon (£9.25), half a crispy roast duck with orange sauce (£12.95), and daily specials such as herby sausages with chilli potatoes (£7.50), and slow roasted lamb shank (£9.75). Dominoes. There are seats in the back garden, the village is very pretty, and there are many walks across the moors or more gentle strolls to Hutton-Le-Hole. *(Recommended by James Chatfield, S D and J L Cooke, Malcolm and Jennifer Perry, John Hale, Angus and Rosemary Campbell)*

Free house ~ Licensees Craig and Margaret Miller ~ Real ale ~ Bar food (not winter Tues) ~ Restaurant ~ (01751) 417247 ~ Children in eating area of bar and restaurant ~ Open 12-3, 7-11(10.30 Sun); closed Tues in winter ~ Bedrooms: /£60B

LEDSHAM SE4529 Map 7
Chequers 🍽 🍺

Claypit Lane; 1 mile W of A1, some 4 miles N of junction M62

A very popular and restful break from the busy A1, this friendly stone-built village offers daily newspapers, room for a stroll outside after a stuffy car journey, and interesting food. You'll also get a warm welcome from the licensees, and the old-fashioned little central panelled-in servery has several small, individually decorated rooms leading off with low beams, lots of cosy alcoves, a number of toby jugs, log fires, and a good bustling atmosphere. Enjoyable, rather fancifully described bar food includes home-made soup (£3.95), filled baguettes (from £4.95; steak with fried onions £5.85), smoked chicken breast with sweet chilli dressing (£5.85), tartlet with sherried lambs kidneys, bacon and honeyroast baby onions (£6.45), smoked salmon with scrambled eggs (£6.85), sausage and mash with gravy or home-made steak and mushroom pie (£9.85), baked red pepper with plum tomato, garlic and basil and topped with mozzarella (£12.45), slow cooked lamb shank with mustard mash and berry jus (£12.95), tuna loin on braised celery with asparagus spears (£13.95), and specials such as king scallops with spinach mayonnaise (£6.25), asparagus, spinach and sun-dried tomato risotto with honey and ginger dressing (£11.95), and sirloin steak with three-pepper sauce (£13.95). Well kept Brown Cow Bitter and Simpsons No 4, John Smiths, Theakstons Best, and Timothy Taylors Landlord on handpump; dominoes. A sheltered two-level terrace behind the house has tables among roses, and the hanging baskets and flowers are very pretty. *(Recommended by John and Sheila Burley, Mrs Anthea Fricker, Peter Burton, JHBS, Andy and Jill Kassube, the Didler, MDN, David and Helen Wilkins, Pat and Tony Martin, Patrick Hancock, K M Crook, Blaise Vyner, Greta and Christopher Wells, Michael Doswell, Daphne and Peter Ross, JWAC, M Borthwick, Alison Hayes, Pete Hanlon)*

Free house ~ Licensee Chris Wraith ~ Real ale ~ Bar food (12-2.15, 6-9.15; 12-9.15 Sat) ~ Restaurant ~ (01977) 683135 ~ Children in eating area of bar and restaurant ~ Dogs allowed in bar ~ Open 11-3, 5-11; 11-11 Sat; closed Sun

LEEDS SE3033 Map 7
Whitelocks ★ 🍺 £

Turks Head Yard; alley off Briggate, opposite Debenhams and Littlewoods; park in shoppers' car park and walk

There are few city centre pubs that remain as beautifully preserved as this atmospheric and bustling place – it has hardly changed since Victorian times. The long and narrow old-fashioned bar has polychrome tiles on the bar counter, stained-glass windows and grand advertising mirrors, and red button back plush banquettes and heavy copper-topped cast-iron tables squeezed down one side. And although it might be best to get here outside peak times as it does get packed, the friendly staff are quick and efficient. Under the new licensee, good, reasonably priced bar food includes giant yorkshire puddings (from £1.95), sandwiches (from £2.95; hot filled baguettes from £3.45), and tasty shepherd's pie or home-made steak and potato pie (£4.45). Well kept Greene King Ruddles Best, John Smiths, Theakstons Best and Old Peculier, and four quickly changing guest beers on handpump. *(Recommended by Kevin Blake, Christine and Neil Townend, Patrick Hancock, Matthew Hinkins, JP, PP, R T and J C Moggridge, Ian Phillips, the Didler, David Carr, Alison Hayes, Pete Hanlon, Joe Green)*

Scottish Courage ~ Manager Nicholas James ~ Real ale ~ Bar food (11-7 Mon-Sat, 12-4 Sun) ~ Restaurant ~ (0113) 245 3950 ~ Children in restaurant and family room ~ Open 11-11; 12-10.30 Sun; closed 25 Dec, 1 Jan

LEVISHAM SE8391 Map 10
Horseshoe
Pub and village signposted from A169 N of Pickering

A focal point for this delightful, unspoilt village, and run by friendly licensees, this neatly kept, traditional pub has picnic-sets on the attractive green, and is surrounded by plenty of good walks. The bar has brocaded seats, a log fire in the stone fireplace, bar billiards, well kept Theakstons Best, XB and Old Peculier on handpump, and quite a few malt whiskies. Promptly served enjoyable bar food includes filled buns (from £3), home-made soup (£3.25), creamy garlic mushrooms (£3.75), barbecued spare ribs (£4.50), ploughman's (£5.95), battered whitby haddock or home-made lasagne (£6.50), home-made nut roast with rich tomato and garlic sauce or home-made steak and mushroom pie (£6.95), pork fillet and black pudding or breast of chicken provençale (£7.95), slow cooked lamb joint with rich mint gravy (£8.50; large £10.50), steaks (from £11.50), puddings, and children's menu (£3.50); the restaurant is no smoking. Bar billiards, dominoes, TV, and piped music. *(Recommended by Lorraine and Fred Gill, Ian and Rose Lock, Roger and Jenny Huggins, Jane Gilbert)*

Free house ~ Licensees Brian and Helen Robshaw ~ Real ale ~ Bar food ~ Restaurant ~ (01751) 460240 ~ Children welcome ~ Dogs allowed in bar ~ Open 11-3, 6-11; 12-3, 6.30-10.30 Sun; closed Sun evening and all day Mon in winter ~ Bedrooms: £30/£56(£60S)

LEYBURN SE1191 Map 10
Sandpiper 🍴 ♀
Just off Market Place

Although there is a small bar used by locals, most of the emphasis in this 17th-c little stone cottage is placed firmly on the particularly good food. The bar has a couple of black beams in the low ceiling, antlers, and a few tables and chairs, and the back room up three steps has attractive Dales photographs. Down by the nice linenfold panelled bar counter there are stuffed sandpipers, more photographs and a woodburning stove in the stone fireplace; to the left is the no smoking restaurant. At lunchtime, the enjoyable food might include sandwiches (from £3.85; mozzarella, red onion and avocado toastie £5.50; fish club sandwich £6), seasonal terrine (£4.95), fishcakes with dill and parsley sauce (£5; main course £9.50), omelette arnold bennett (£6.50), sausage and mash with onion gravy (£6.95), fish in beer batter (£7.50), roasted salmon on creamed leeks with pasta (£8.50), breast of chicken on bubble and squeak (£8.95), and crispy duck leg with plum and orange sauce (£10), with evening dishes such as roasted lobster and tomato soup (£4), king prawn and langoustine risotto with wild mushrooms (£8.50), stuffed aubergine topped with herb crust (£9.25), pot-roast rabbit with lemon and thyme (£9.50), breast of chicken topped with smoked bacon on bubble and squeak (£9.95), pork fillet wrapped in parma ham with roasted peppers, sun-dried tomatoes and parmesan macaroni (£12.95), and puddings like terrine of three chocolates and a cappuccino sauce, raspberry and almond tart with clotted cream and sticky toffee pudding with butterscotch sauce (from £3.95). Well kept Black Sheep Bitter and Special, and guests from Daleside, Dent, and Theakstons on handpump, around 100 malt whiskies, and a decent wine list with eight by the glass; piped music. There are green cast-iron tables on the front terrace amidst the lovely hanging baskets and flowering climbers. *(Recommended by Alan J Morton, Maureen and Bill Sewell, K M Crook, Peter Burton, Brian England, E D Fraser, Jim Abbott, Alan Cowell, Greta and Christopher Wells)*

Free house ~ Licensees Jonathan and Michael Harrison ~ Real ale ~ Bar food (12-2.30, 6.30-9(9.30 Fri and Sat)) ~ Restaurant ~ (01969) 622206 ~ Children in eating area of bar but must leave restaurant by 8pm at weekends ~ Dogs allowed in bar ~ Open 11.30-3, 6.30-11; 12-3, 7-10.30 Sun; closed Mon and two weeks Jan ~ Bedrooms: £50S(£55B)/£60S(£65B)

LINTHWAITE SE1014 Map 7

Sair ◀

Hoyle Ing, off A62; 3½ miles after Huddersfield look out for two water storage tanks (painted with a shepherd scene) on your right – the street is on your left, burrowing very steeply up between works buildings; OS Sheet 110 map reference 101143

It's the large choice of own-brewed beers on handpump that draw customers to this old-fashioned and unspoilt pub: Linfit Bitter, Dark Mild, Special, Gold Medal, Cascade, Special, Old Eli, Leadboiler, and the redoubtable Enochs Hammer; occasionally they replace Cascade with Swift, Ginger Beer, Janet St Porter, Smoke House Ale, Springbok Bier or Xmas Ale. Weston's farm cider and a few malt whiskies; weekend sandwiches. The four rooms (with newly planked ceilings) are furnished with pews or smaller chairs (all re-upholstered this year) on the rough flagstones or carpet, and there are bottle collections, beermats tacked to beams, and roaring log fires; one room is no smoking. The room on the left has dominoes, a juke box, and cribbage; piano players welcome. Plenty of seats in front of the pub (and they plan to increase these), and a striking view across the Colne Valley. The Huddersfield Narrow Canal is now restored through to Ashton; in the 3½ miles from Linthwaite to the highest, deepest, and longest tunnel in Britain, are 25 working locks and some lovely countryside. More reports please. *(Recommended by the Didler, Tony Hobden, Patrick Hancock, J R Ringrose, JP, PP)*

Own brew ~ Licensee Ron Crabtree ~ Real ale ~ No credit cards ~ (01484) 842370 ~ Children welcome in three rooms away from bar ~ Dogs allowed in bar ~ Open 7(5 Fri)-11; 12-11 Sat; 12-10.30 Sun

LINTON SE3946 Map 7

Windmill

Leaving Wetherby W on A661, fork left just before hospital and bear left; also signposted from A659, leaving Collingham towards Harewood

The small beamed rooms in this busy dining pub have walls stripped back to bare stone, polished antique oak settles around copper-topped cast-iron tables, pots hanging from the oak beams, a high shelf of plates, and log fires; the restaurant is no smoking. Well liked and attractively presented, the bar food at lunchtime includes sandwiches on granary bread, baguette or folded flat nan and served with salad and potato crisps (from £3.95; prawn and lime fromage frais £4.50; hot smoked bacon with melted swiss cheese £5.75), chicken liver parfait with plum and apple chutney (£4.95), and moules marinière or filled baked potatoes (£5.95), with evening dishes such as spinach, brie and asparagus parcel (£4.50), seared peppered pork fillet salad with apple and cider chutney (£5.95), garlic and lime king prawns with baby spinach and pine nut salad (£6.50), baked chicken and bubble and squeak mash (£7.95), grilled bass fillet with roasted red peppers and basil and tomato dressing or gressingham duck breast with celeriac, smoked bacon and thyme jus (£9.95), steaks (from £9.95), and beef fillet with herb potato rösti and lanark blue cheese sauce (£13.95); daily specials, and puddings (£3.95). Well kept John Smiths, Theakstons Best and a couple of guests from maybe Cropton or Rudgate on handpump; piped music, fruit machine. The pear tree outside was planted with seeds brought back from the Napoleonic Wars and there is a secret passage between the pub and the church next door. More reports please. *(Recommended by John and Sheila Burley, Roger S Kiddier, Michael Doswell)*

Scottish Courage ~ Lease Janet Rowley and John Littler ~ Real ale ~ Bar food (not Sun evening) ~ Restaurant ~ (01937) 582209 ~ Children in eating area of bar and restaurant ~ Dogs allowed in bar ~ Open 11-3, 5-11; 11-11 Sat; 12-10.30 Sun

---

'Children welcome' means the pub says it lets children inside without any special restriction. If it allows them in, but to restricted areas such as an eating area or family room, we specify this. Some pubs may impose an evening time limit.

LITTON SD9074 Map 7
Queens Arms ◗

From B6160 N of Grassington, after Kilnsey take second left fork; can also be reached off B6479 at Stainforth N of Settle, via Halton Gill

As we went to press, they had just opened their own microbrewery at this attractive white-painted inn and were brewing Linfit Ale; they also keep Tetleys on handpump, too. The main bar on the right has a good coal fire, stripped rough stone walls, a brown beam-and-plank ceiling, stools around cast-iron-framed tables on the stone and concrete floor, a seat built into the stone-mullioned window, and signed cricket bats. The left-hand room is an eating area with old photographs of the Dales around the walls. The family room is no smoking. Decent bar food (with prices unchanged since last year) includes home-made soup (£2.60), sandwiches (from £3.50), filled baked potatoes (from £4.50), home-made rabbit pie (£7.60), gammon and egg (£7.95), home-made game pie (£9.10), daily specials such as local blue cheese, onion, mushroom and black olive tart or vegetable pie (£7.50), roast lamb (£7.95), stilton chicken (£8.60), halibut steak in seafood sauce (£10.30), and a massive mixed grill (£15.50), and puddings like rhubarb crumble, bread and butter pudding or syrup tart (£3). Darts, dominoes, cribbage, and piped music. There are seats and a safe area for children in the two-level garden, and the views over the fells are stunning. Plenty of surrounding walks – a track behind the inn leads over Ackerley Moor to Buckden, and the quiet lane through the valley leads on to Pen-y-ghent. Walkers enjoy staying here very much – and there is a walkers' room (price on request). *(Recommended by JWAC, Greta and Christopher Wells, Liam McGreevy, Bob Broadhurst, Tony and Ann Bennett-Hughes, Gill Honeyman, DAV, JAE, Alison Hayes, Pete Hanlon, Jim Abbott)*

Free house ~ Licensees Tanya and Neil Thompson ~ Real ale ~ Bar food (12-2, 6.30-8; not Mon) ~ (01756) 770208 ~ Children welcome ~ Dogs allowed in bar ~ Open 12-3, 7-11; 11.30-3, 6.30-11(10.30 Sun) Sat; closed Mon (except bank hols) ~ Bedrooms: /£56S

LOW CATTON SE7053 Map 7
Gold Cup

Village signposted with High Catton off A166 in Stamford Bridge or A1079 at Kexby Bridge

This comfortable white-rendered house has neatly kept and friendly communicating rooms with a fire at one end, plush wall seats and stools around good solid tables, some decorative plates and brasswork on the walls, and a relaxed atmosphere; the back bar has a woodburning stove in a brick fireplace. Good value bar food using local produce includes lunchtime sandwiches, home-made soup (£2.95), chicken chasseur, popular cajun chicken, home-baked ham with wholegrain mustard sauce or home-made fish pie (from £6.50), roast beef and yorkshire pudding or roast lamb (£6.75), seared salmon steak with lemon and dill hollandaise (£7), and puddings such as lemon posset with home-made shortbread and berries or chocolate swirls with strawberries and cream (£3); children are offered half helpings of adult meals, there are small-appetite dishes for older customers, and Sunday lunch is popular (three courses £9.75). The no smoking restaurant has solid wooden pews and tables, said to be made from a single oak tree, and pleasant views of the surrounding fields. Well kept John Smiths and Tetleys Bitter on handpump; piped music, pool, fruit machine, and dominoes. The garden has a timber climbing frame and grassed area for children, and the back paddock houses Billie the goat and Polly the shetland who are kept in check by Candy the horse; they also now own Boris and Marilyn (retired greyhounds), and have fishing rights on the adjoining River Derwent. More reports please. *(Recommended by Roger A Bellingham, Phil Skelton, P R Morley)*

Free house ~ Licensees Pat and Ray Hales ~ Real ale ~ Bar food (not Mon lunchtime; 12-2.30, 6-9.30; all day weekends) ~ No credit cards ~ (01759) 371354 ~ Children in eating area of bar and restaurant ~ Dogs allowed in bar ~ Open 12-2.30, 6-11; 12-11(10.30 Sun) Sat; closed Mon lunch (except bank hols), evenings 25-26 Dec

LUND SE9748 Map 8
Wellington ⊕ ♀
Off B1248 SW of Driffield

They've sensibly kept the main bar in this smart pub a haven for drinkers only in the evening. Many people do come here to eat, and as well as the restaurant, there is a back dining area where you cannot reserve a table (readers feel this works well). The most atmospheric part is the cosy Farmers Bar, a small heavily beamed room with an interesting fireplace and some old agricultural equipment; the neatly kept main bar (refurbished recently) is much brighter, with a brick fireplace and bar counter, well polished wooden banquettes and square tables, dried flowers, and local prints on the textured cream-painted walls; two areas are no smoking. Off to one side is a plainer flagstoned room, while at the other a york-stoned walkway leads to a room with a display case showing off the village's Britain in Bloom awards. Good enjoyable bar food at lunchtime includes soup of the day (£3.50; with half a sandwich £5.50), smoked haddock fishcakes with mild curried apple sauce or chicken liver parfait with redcurrant and orange sauce (£4.95), sandwiches like mozzarella and chorizo or pork and stuffing and served with chips (from £4.95), greek salad with chicken, avocado and kalamata olives (£7.95), popular fresh filey haddock in beer batter (£8.75), smoked mozzarella, cherry tomato and pesto tartlet (£8.95), chicken breast filled with mild creamed herby goats cheese on fresh tagliatelle with mushroom, marsala and cream sauce (£9.65), and braised lamb shank with mediterranean tomato sauce (£11.95); in the evening there might be extras such as devilled kidney and mushroom hotpot in a filo pastry basket (£4.95), salad of fresh crab, quails eggs and asparagus with bloody mary dressing (£6.25), mixed meat kebab with home-made barbecue sauce (£10.95), king prawn and fresh asparagus risotto with parmesan (£11.95), and calves liver and bacon with onion gravy (£12.95), and puddings like iced toffee and banana parfait, rich white chocolate and amaretto cream or sticky toffee pudding with warm butterscotch sauce (from £4.25). Well kept Black Sheep, John Smiths, and Timothy Taylors Landlord with a changing local guest on handpump, and a good wine list with a helpfully labelled choice for the glass; welcoming, helpful staff. Piped music, darts, pool, TV, and fruit machine. A small courtyard beside the car park has a couple of benches. More reports please. *(Recommended by Ian S Morley, Barrie Meech, Lorraine and Fred Gill, Dr D Parker, Roger A Bellingham)*

Free house ~ Licensees Russell Jeffery and Sarah Warburton ~ Real ale ~ Bar food (not Sun evening or Mon) ~ Restaurant (Tues-Sat evenings) ~ (01377) 217294 ~ Children welcome but must be over 16 in restaurant ~ Open 12-3, 6.30-11; 12-3, 7-10.30 Sun; closed Mon lunchtime

MARTON SE7383 Map 10
Appletree ⊕ ♀ ◧
Village signposted off A170 W of Pickering

This carefully extended four-square stone-built house has been converted into a stylish dining pub. It made its first appearance in our Lucky Dip last year – only we had not realised that not only were there at least two Martons in Yorkshire, but two of them have Appletree pubs, and of course we succeeded in pin-pointing the wrong one. We are very glad to have tracked down the right one now, as it is indeed a splendid find. Throughout there are carefully co-ordinated colour schemes and lighting, all is kept spotless, and service by keen young staff is friendly and personal. The relaxed beamed lounge bar has comfortable settees in red or blue around polished low tables, an open fire in the stone fireplace, and a modicum of carefully placed decorations on the eau de nil walls. The main emphasis is on the terracotta-walled dining room, which has well spaced farmhouse tables, fresh flowers, and masses of candles at night. Meals (using top quality local produce) start with a free bottle of mineral water, and warmly fragrant savoury breads. A typical lunchtime choice might include chips with chive mayonnaise (£2.70), cream of carrot soup (£3), sandwiches (from £4.50), anchovy, lemon and lovage salad or crispy duck and bacon with honey and mustard dressing (£5), miniature fillet beef burger and goats cheese (£5.50), wild garlic and beetroot risotto (£7.50), deep crust lamb and mint pie (£7.90), chicken with mussels, tarragon and chardonnay cream sauce (£8.50), confit belly pork on mustard mash and sage jus (£10), duck breast on fondant sweet potato with strawberry and coriander sauce (£13.90), and beautifully presented puddings such as milk chocolate pyramid filled with Baileys chocolate mousse, treacle tart with lemon curd ice cream or banana and orange cinnamon crumble (from £3.90). Evening extras such as oxtail soup with miniature herb dumplings (£3.90), lamb sweetbreads with egg noodles and spiced szechuan sauce (£4.50), chargrilled sirloin steak with green peppercorn sauce, parsley and deep-fried onion rings (£15), and orange-roasted turbot with braised fennel and Pernod butter sauce (£16.50). They already grow their own herbs, and are working towards growing enough of their own vegetables to use these routinely too. Besides their flavoured breads, they produce quite a few chutneys, preserves, flavoured oils and butters and so forth, and in one corner what might elsewhere have been a small bar counter turns out to be a popular sales counter for their own and some other kitchen produce. They have well kept John Smiths on handpump, alongside three changing guest beers from Hambleton, Rudgate, and York; a good changing choice of a dozen wines by the glass. Despite the emphasis on good food, regulars do drop in for a drink, and perhaps a game of dominoes, giving the bar a properly local atmosphere. There are cast-iron tables and chairs out on a sheltered flagstoned terrace behind, with plant pots and a small water feature, and looking out through young silver birches to an orchard garden with fruit trees. *(Recommended by Peter and Anne-Marie O'Malley, Dr and Mrs P S Fox, Brian and Pat Wardrobe, John Knighton)*

Free house ~ Licensees Melanie Thornton and T J Drew ~ Bar food (12-2(2.30 Sun), 6.30-9.30; not Tues) ~ Restaurant ~ (01751) 431457 ~ Children welcome ~ Open 12-2.30, 6.30-11; 12-3, 7-10.30 Sun; closed Tues, 25 Dec, three weeks Jan

MASHAM SE2381 Map 10
Kings Head ♀ ⇌
Market Square

More bedrooms (including those for disabled customers and families) are to be created in the converted stables, barns and the old smithy of this friendly inn, and there are plans for a new conference room, where they hold a civil wedding licence. The two opened-up rooms of the bar have traditional pine tables and chairs on the wood-stripped floor, a roaring fire in the imposing fireplace, a big clock (from Masham Station), and well kept Theakstons Best, Black Bull, and Old Peculier, and a couple of guests on handpump; extensive wine list with lots by the glass. Good, enjoyable bar food includes home-made soup (£3.45), sandwiches or filled baguettes (from £3.45), filled baked potatoes (from £3.75), pear, walnut and blue cheese salad (£3.95), filled baguettes (from £3.95), black pudding stack with dijon and leek sauce (£4.25), somerset brie tart (£4.75), home-made salmon fishcakes with tarragon crème fraîche (£5.25), steak in ale pie (£7.25), feta risotto with roast butternut squash and pine kernels or asparagus and rocket pasta (£8.95), cod on lemon and chardonnay risotto (£9.95), steaks (from £10.75), chicken breast stuffed with goats cheese and sun-dried tomato wrapped in pancetta and served with mediterranean vegetables (£10.95), and puddings like white and dark chocolate sponge with chocolate sauce, summer pudding or apple and blackberry crumble (from £3.95); helpful, friendly service. The restaurant and some other rooms are no smoking; piped music, fruit machine, TV, cribbage and dominoes. In summer, the hanging baskets and window boxes in front of this friendly inn are very pretty, there are seats on the back terrace (and some in front), and the broad partly tree-shaded market square is just opposite. *(Recommended by Jenny and Dave Hughes, I J and S A Bufton, Greta and Christopher Wells, Janet and Peter Race, Jim Abbott, Angus Lyon, Dave Braisted)*

S&N ~ Manager Philip Capon ~ Real ale ~ Bar food (12-3, 6-9.45; all day Sat/Sun) ~ Restaurant ~ (01765) 689295 ~ Children in eating area of bar and restaurant ~ Open 11-11; 12-10.30 Sun ~ Bedrooms: £56.95B/£78.90B

MIDDLEHAM SE1288 Map 10
White Swan ♀ ⌷

Market Place

In a charming small market town complete with Richard III's castle and lots of racehorses proceeding to their gallops, this village hotel is tastefully decorated in an understated way, and has a good relaxed pubby atmosphere. The beamed and flagstoned entrance bar has a long dark pew built into the big window overlooking the sloping market square, and a mix of chairs around a handful of biggish tables. The curved counter has well kept Black Sheep Best, Special and Riggwelter and John Smiths on handpump, a good choice of wines by the glass, and a couple of dozen malt whiskies, with friendly attentive service and a good inglenook log fire. A second beamed room on the right has a variety of tables and dining chairs, a red oriental rug on its black boards, and like the first is candlelit. There's a third broadly similar room behind. Good bar food includes home-made soup (£2.75), sandwiches (from £3.50), onion and white wensleydale tart with tomato chutney or black pudding and bacon risotto (£3.95), mushroom risotto (£5.75), tarte tatin with mushrooms and leeks topped with blue cheese herb crust (£5.95), tagliatelle tossed with mediterranean vegetables, black olives and tomato sauce (£6.75), home-made fish pie (£8.95), garlic, lemon and tarragon chicken (£9.95), slow roast shoulder of lamb with redcurrant sauce and mustard mash (£10.95), and daily specials like crispy duck and bacon salad (£3.75), fillet of bass with moules marinière dressing or swedish meatballs with creamy sauce (£6.95), and puddings like iced rhubarb parfait or banoffi cheesecake (from £3.65). More reports please. *(Recommended by Gill and Tony Morriss, Angus Lyon, Mr and Mrs Maurice Thompson, Comus and Sarah Elliott)*

Free house ~ Licensees Andrew Holmes and Paul Klein ~ Real ale ~ Bar food (12-2.15, 6.30-9.15) ~ Restaurant ~ (01969) 622093 ~ Children welcome ~ Dogs welcome ~ Open 11-11; 12-10.30 Sun; closed lunchtime 25 Dec ~ Bedrooms: £47.50S/£59(£69B)

MOULTON NZ2404 Map 10
Black Bull ⑪ ♀

Just E of A1, 1 mile E of Scotch Corner

With particularly good food and service, this decidedly civilised place continues to please our readers. The bar has a lot of character – as well as a huge winter log fire, fresh flowers, an antique panelled oak settle and an old elm housekeeper's chair, built-in red-cushioned black settles and pews around the cast-iron tables (one has a heavily beaten copper top), silver-plate turkish coffee pots and so forth over the red velvet curtained windows, and copper cooking utensils hanging from black beams. A nice side dark-panelled seafood bar has some high seats at the marble-topped counter. Good lunchtime bar snacks (with prices unchanged since last year) include lovely smoked salmon in sandwiches (£3.25), on a plate (£5.50), and in pâté (£5.75); they also do very good home-made soup served in little tureens (£2.75), ploughman's or herb crumbed fishcake with tomato and hollandaise sauce (£4.95), welsh rarebit and bacon, feuilletté of smoked haddock, prawns, parsley and mash or tartlet of goats cheese, tomato, olives and parmesan (£5), queenie scallops in garlic with wensleydale and thyme crumb (£5.75), linguini with pancetta, prawns, peas and parmesan or carpaccio of peppered rump with caper and cornichon salad (£5.95), spiced belly pork and spring onion risotto (£6.25), and puddings such as crème brûlée with home-made shortbread, chocolate orange truffle cake or panna cotta with fruit compote (£3.50). In the evening (when people do tend to dress up), you can also eat in the polished brick-tiled conservatory with bentwood cane chairs or in the Brighton Belle dining car. Good wine, a fine choice of sherries, and around 30 malt whiskies, and 30 liqueurs. There are some seats under trees in the central court. *(Recommended by Brian Root, Percy and Cathy Paine, David and Ruth Shillitoe, David and Iris Hunter, Greta and Christopher Wells, Jenny and Dave Hughes, Mr and Mrs J E C Tasker, Mrs A Widdup)*

Free house ~ Licensees Mrs Audrey and Miss S Pagendam ~ Bar food (lunchtime, not Sun) ~ Restaurant (evening) ~ (01325) 377289 ~ Children in eating area if over 7 ~ Open 12-2.30, 6-10.30(11 Sat); closed Sun, 24-26 Dec

NOSTERFIELD SE2780 Map 7
Freemasons Arms ◀

B6267

A new licensee has taken over this lively, chatty pub but is not planning any major changes to the décor. There's lots to look at – low black beams hung with gas masks, steel helmets, miner's lamps, pewter tankards and so forth, big prints of Queen Victoria, many old enamel advertising signs, Union flags propped in corners, and the cosy feel boosted by the warm lighting, the candles on the tables, and the hot coal fires. Well liked bar food now includes home-made soup (£2.50), sandwiches (from £2.95), smoked haddock in creamy cheese sauce or chicken liver pâté (£4.50), moules marinière (£4.95), steak in ale pie (£7), stuffed peppers with cream and stilton sauce (£7.45), liver, bacon and onions (£8), chicken breast on wild mushroom velouté sauce or gammon with egg or pineapple (£8.45), pork fillet with garlic, white wine and paprika cream sauce (£11.45), seared red snapper with sweet red pepper coulis (£12), and puddings like chocolate mousse, raspberry pavlova or sticky toffee pudding with butterscotch and pecan sauce (£3.50). The main bar area has just two or three tables with close wooden booth seating on its flagstones; there are more tables with pews and settles in the carpeted room on the left. Well kept Black Sheep, and Timothy Taylors Best and Golden Best on handpump, decent wines, and piped music. There are a few picnic-sets out in front, with pretty flower tubs and baskets. No children. *(Recommended by Susan and John Douglas, Rona Murdoch, Patrick Hancock, Janet and Peter Race, Pete Baker, James Chatfield)*

Free house ~ Licensee Mr C Stephenson ~ Real ale ~ Bar food ~ (01677) 470548 ~ Open 12-3, 6(7 Sun)-11(10.30 Sun); closed Mon; 25/26 Dec

NUNNINGTON SE6779 Map 7
Royal Oak ⊗

Church Street; at back of village, which is signposted from A170 and B1257

Readers very much enjoy their visits to this neatly kept and attractive little pub. You can be sure of a genuinely warm and friendly welcome, the food is good, and even when busy, service remains efficient and attentive. The bar has carefully chosen furniture such as kitchen and country dining chairs or a long pew around the sturdy tables on the turkey carpet, and a lectern in one corner; the high black beams are strung with earthenware flagons, copper jugs and lots of antique keys, one of the walls is stripped back to the bare stone to display a fine collection of antique farm tools, and there are open fires; the dining room is no smoking. Popular bar food includes sandwiches, vegetable soup with lentil and bacon (£4.15), chicken liver pâté with home-made chutney (£4.75), mushrooms stuffed with garlic butter and stilton (£5.25), seafood hors d'oeuvres (£5.75), ploughman's (£7.95), lasagne or sweet and sour vegetables (£9.50), steak and kidney casserole with herb dumpling or pork fillet in barbecue sauce or chicken breast in cheesy mustard sauce (£9.95), fisherman's pot (£10.50), crispy roast duckling with orange sauce (£12.50), and 12oz sirloin steak (£13.95). Well kept Tetleys, and Theakstons Best and Old Peculier on handpump. Handy for a visit to Nunnington Hall (National Trust). *(Recommended by R Macfarlane, Anthony Barnes, Christopher Turner, J M Pitts, BKA, Geoff and Angela Jaques, Robert and Susan Whitehead, Peter and Patricia Burton, Peter Burton, Michael Dandy)*

Free house ~ Licensee Anthony Simpson ~ Real ale ~ Bar food (not Mon) ~ Restaurant ~ (01439) 748271 ~ Children in family room ~ Open 12-2.30, 6.30-11; 12-2.30, 7-10.30 Sun; closed Mon

OSMOTHERLEY SE4499 Map 10

Golden Lion 🍺

The Green, West End; off A19 N of Thirsk

Even on a mid-week evening, this old stone-built inn is always busy, and it's the sort of place that customers return to again and again. The roomy beamed bar on the left, simply furnished with old pews and just a few decorations on its white walls, has a pleasantly lively atmosphere, candles on tables, well kept Hambleton Bitter, Timothy Taylors Landlord, and maybe Caledonian IPA on handpump, a decent wine list and 40 malt whiskies; piped music. On the right, a similarly unpretentious eating area, brightened up with fresh flowers, has good value generous food, with familiar dishes prepared and presented with real care: sandwiches, soups such as tomato and basil or french onion with gruyère cheese crouton (£3.75), creamy lemon risotto with caramelised onion or rough pâté with onion and apricot relish (£4.95), spicy pork ribs or fresh grilled sardines (£5.25), home-made beef or chilli chicken burgers (£6.50), home-made meaty or vegetarian lasagne (£6.95), steak and kidney pie or lamb casserole (£7.95), salmon fishcake with spinach and creamy sorrel sauce (£8.50), charcoal-grilled poussin with rosemary and garlic (£9.95), 12oz sirloin steak (£13.95), and puddings like middle eastern orange cake with marmalade cream, sticky toffee pudding or raspberry ripple cheesecake with raspberry coulis (£3.75); several teas and coffees. There's also an airy no smoking dining room, mainly open at weekends. Benches out in front look across the village green to the market cross. As the inn is the start of the 44-mile Lyke Wakes Walk on the Cleveland Way, and quite handy for the Coast to Coast Walk, it is naturally popular with walkers. *(Recommended by Peter and Jean Hoare, Jill Franklin, Lorraine and Fred Gill, Geoff and Angela Jaques, David and Ruth Shillitoe, JHBS, Rona Murdoch, Tim Newman, Dr and Mrs R G J Telfer)*

Free house ~ Licensee Christie Connelly ~ Real ale ~ Bar food (12-3.30, 6-10) ~ Restaurant ~ (01609) 883526 ~ Children welcome ~ Dogs allowed in bar ~ Open 12-3.30, 6-11; 12-11(10.30 Sun) Sat; closed evening 25 Dec

PICKERING SE7983 Map 10

White Swan ★ 🍽 ♈ 🛏

Market Place, just off A170

The refurbished restaurant in this former coaching inn now has flagstones, a fine open fire, rich tweed soft furnishings, comfortable settles and gothic screens. What was the snug is now the residents' lounge and what was the lounge is now a private dining room. The bar was about to be freshened up as we went to press, but will keep its charming country atmosphere, panelling, a log fire and just three or four tables. Opposite, a no smoking bare-boards room with a few more tables has another fire in a handsome art nouveau iron fireplace, a big bow window, and pear prints on its plum-coloured walls. Good food using local produce includes soup with home-made bread (£3.95), lunchtime sandwiches and ploughman's (from £4.95), chicken liver pâté with oatcakes and tomato chutney (£4.95), poached whitby bream mousse with cucumber and mint or local goats cheese and chive tart with red onion jam (£5.95), confit of pressed duck, foie gras and black pudding with sauternes sauce (£7.25), seared king scallops with coverdale cheese and parsley gratin and air-dried york ham or sausage and mash with onion gravy (£8.95), fish and chips with home-made tartare sauce or braised ham shank with butterbean stew (£9.95), grilled courgettes with lemon and basil risotto and roast tomatoes (£10.95), juniper marinated venison haunch with bubble and squeak, roast garlic and red wine juices (£15.95), and chargrilled fillet of beef with fresh herb pesto (£16.95), with puddings such as dark chocolate pots with orange and polenta biscuits, glazed lemon tart with double vanilla ice cream or crème caramel with apple crisps and soaked raisins (from £4.50). If you stay, the breakfasts are good. Well kept Black Sheep Bitter and Special and a guest beer like Cropton Yorkshire Moors Bitter or Hambleton Goldfield on handpump, good house wines (by two sizes of glass; superb list of old St Emilions), quite a few malt whiskies, and friendly helpful staff. The old coach entry to the car park is very narrow. More reports please. *(Recommended by Walter and Susan Rinaldi-Butcher, Gerald and Wendy Doyle, Nigel Espley, Liane Purnell, Anthony Barnes, Sue and Alan Addis, Di and Mike Gillam, Alison Keys, Peter Burton; also in the* Good Hotel Guide*)*

Free house ~ Licensees Marion and Victor Buchanan ~ Real ale ~ Bar food ~ Restaurant ~ (01751) 472288 ~ Children in restaurant ~ Dogs allowed in bar ~ Open 10.30-3, 6-11; 10-11 Mon and Sat; 12-5, 7-10.30 Sun ~ Bedrooms: £70B/£110B

PICKHILL SE3584 Map 10
Nags Head 🍴 ♀

Take the Masham turn-off from A1 both N and S, and village signposted off B6267 in Ainderby Quernhow

Very handy for the A1, this bustling place has been professionally run for over 30 years by the Boynton brothers. You can be sure of a friendly welcome from the polite, obliging staff, and there's a relaxed atmosphere that appeals to a wide mix of customers. The busy tap room on the left has beams hung with jugs, coach horns, ale-yards and so forth, and masses of ties hanging as a frieze from a rail around the red ceiling. The smarter lounge bar has deep green plush banquettes on the matching carpet, pictures for sale on its neat cream walls, and an open fire. From a varied menu, the enjoyable food might include sandwiches, soup like asparagus, tomato and vegetable (£3.25), crispy mushrooms filled with ham and stilton (£4.75), roasted red pepper stuffed with feta cheese, cucumber and greek minted yoghurt (£5.50), cottage pie topped with leek and cheese mash (£6.95), tagliatelle with mixed salami, sun-dried red peppers and tomato sauce or a bowl of hot chilli (£7.50), large fish and chips with mushy peas (£7.95), seafood lasagne (£10.95), tenderloin of pork stuffed with apricots and celeriac with spicy mango dressing or crusty topped beef, venison and rabbit pie (£11.95), duck breast with lime, ginger and honey marinade and a crispy roast leg (£13.95), steaks (from £13.95), and puddings like caramelised banana tart with vanilla custard, chocolate and almond praline brûlée basket with crème fraîche or blackberry and mascarpone mousse (£3.95). The library-themed restaurant is no smoking. Well kept Black Sheep Bitter and Special, and Hambleton Bitter on handpump, a good choice of malt whiskies, several vintage armagnacs, and a carefully chosen wine list with several by the glass. One table is inset with a chessboard, and they also have cribbage, dominoes, shove-ha'penny, and faint piped music. There's a front verandah, a boules and quoits pitch, and 9-hole putting green. The bedrooms have been refurbished. More reports please. *(Recommended by George and Brenda Jones, Mr and Mrs C Cameron, Angus Lyon, R T and J C Moggridge, Mrs Roxanne Chamberlain, Trevor and Sylvia Millum, SH, Michael Butler, M Whitfield, G A Hemingway, Blaise Vyner, Stephen Buckley, Alison Hayes, Pete Hanlon)*

Free house ~ Licensees Edward and Raymond Boynton ~ Real ale ~ Bar food (12-2, 6-9.30) ~ Restaurant ~ (01845) 567391 ~ Children in eating area of bar and in restaurant until 7.30pm ~ Dogs allowed in bedrooms ~ Open 11-11; 11-10.30 Sun; closed 25 Dec ~ Bedrooms: £45B/£60B

POOL SE2445 Map 7
White Hart

Just off A658 S of Harrogate, A659 E of Otley

This is a Vintage Inn and therefore similar to others in the chain, but there's a friendly landlord who runs it well, and you can rely on enjoying your visit. The four rooms are carefully reworked, and there are two log fires, a restrained country décor, a relaxing atmosphere, and a pleasant medley of assorted old farmhouse furniture on the mix of stone flooring and carpet; only one area is for smokers. As well as lunchtime sandwiches (from £3.75; chicken caesar wrap £4.25), there's soup (£2.95), creamy wild mushrooms (£3.95), crab and salmon fishcakes with lemon mayonnaise (£5.25), pork, apple and cider sausages with cheddar mash or lemon chicken (£5.95), wild mushroom risotto (£6.75), steaks (from £8.75), ham hock with creamy wholegrain mustard sauce (£8.95), baked bass with lemon and parsley butter (£10.95), and Sunday roast beef or turkey (from £6.55). Well kept Bass and Tetleys on handpump, and all wines on the list sold in two sizes of glass; piped music. There are tables outside, and although the road is quite busy, this is pleasant walking country. More reports please. *(Recommended by R T and J C Moggridge, John and Sylvia Harrop, Marian and Andrew Ruston, Hugh A MacLean, O K Smyth)*

Vintage Inns ~ Manager David Britland ~ Real ale ~ Bar food (12-10(9.30 Sun)) ~ Restaurant ~ (0113) 202 7901 ~ Children welcome ~ Open 11-11; 12-10.30 Sun

RIPLEY SE2861 Map 7
Boars Head 🍽️ 🍷 🍺 🛏️

Off A61 Harrogate—Ripon

In a delightful estate village, this comfortable hotel has a friendly bar that is still very much used by locals – as well as visitors and walkers. It's a long flagstoned room with green checked tablecloths and olive oil on all the tables, most of which are arranged to form individual booths. The warm yellow walls have jolly little drawings of cricketers or huntsmen running along the bottom, as well as a boar's head (part of the family coat of arms), an interesting religious carving, a couple of cricket bats, and well kept Black Sheep, Theakstons Cool Cask and Old Peculier, and a guest such as Daleside Old Leg Over or Hambleton White Boar on handpump; an excellent wine list (with 10 or so by the glass), and a good choice of malt whiskies. Particularly good, interesting bar food includes soup (£3.50), sandwiches (from £4; soup and a sandwich £6.25), warm salad of venison sausage and spicy chorizo with cranberry yoghurt dressing or mousseline of smoked salmon with coriander and cucumber salsa (£5.50; main course £10.50), red pepper mousse with goats cheese salad (£8.95), grilled fillet of cod topped with herb crust on honey glazed vegetables and red pepper coulis, balsamic marinated chicken on rocket and parmesan salad or braised rump of lamb on apricot and thyme crushed new potatoes with madeira jus (£9.95), duck breast on mango and pine nut salad (£10.95), and puddings like vanilla crème brûlée topped with banana ice cream or white chocolate and raspberry ripple parfait with chocolate chew cookies (£3.75); efficient staff even when very busy. The restaurant and part of the bar are no smoking; piped music. Some of the furnishings in the hotel came from the attic of next door Ripley Castle, where the Ingilbys have lived for over 650 years. A pleasant little garden has plenty of tables. More reports please. *(Recommended by Regine Webster, Janet and Peter Race, Kate Arscott, Geoff and Angela Jaques, B and M Kendall, P Abbott, Pat and Tony Martin, Jim Abbott, M and G Rushworth, W W Burke; also in the* Good Hotel Guide*)*

Free house ~ Licensee Sir Thomas Ingilby ~ Real ale ~ Bar food (12-2.30(2 winter), 6.30-9.30) ~ Restaurant ~ (01423) 771888 ~ Children welcome ~ Open 11-11; 11-10.30 Sun; 11-3, 5-11in winter ~ Bedrooms: £99B/£120B

ROBIN HOOD'S BAY NZ9505 Map 10
Laurel 🍺

Village signposted off A171 S of Whitby

Handy for the NT lifeboat station and rock pools by the beach, this delightful little pub is in one of the prettiest and most unspoilt fishing villages on the North East coast. It's at the bottom of a row of fishermen's cottages, and the landlord will welcome visitors as warmly as he does his locals. The beamed and welcoming main bar is neatly kept, and is decorated with old local photographs, Victorian prints and brasses, and lager bottles from all over the world; there's a roaring open fire. They only serve sandwiches (which are good). Well kept John Smiths and Theakstons Cool Cask, Old Peculier and Black Bull on handpump; darts, shove-ha'penny, dominoes, cribbage, and piped music. In summer, the hanging baskets and window boxes are lovely. They have a self-contained apartment for two people.

(Recommended by Margaret Whalley, JP, PP, Michael Doswell, Roger and Jenny Huggins, John and Sheila Burley, Alison Hayes, Pete Hanlon)

Free house ~ Licensee Brian Catling ~ Real ale ~ Bar food (served during all opening hours) ~ No credit cards ~ (01947) 880400 ~ Children in snug bar only ~ Dogs welcome ~ Open 12-11; 12-10.30 Sun

SAWLEY SE2568 Map 7
Sawley Arms ♀

Village signposted off B6265 W of Ripon

Beautifully neat and rather smart, this mostly no smoking dining pub, run by Mrs Hawes for over 33 years now, is deservedly popular. The small turkey-carpeted rooms have log fires and comfortable furniture ranging from small softly cushioned armed dining chairs and settees, to the wing armchairs down a couple of steps in a side snug; maybe daily papers and magazines to read, piped music. The conservatory was almost up and running as we went to press. Genuinely home-made bar food includes soup with croutons (£3.50), lunchtime sandwiches (from £5), salmon mousse or stilton, port and celery pâté (£5.50), home-made steak pie (£7.70), corn-fed chicken breast in a creamy mushroom sauce (£8), plaice mornay (£8.95), daily specials such as roast duckling with orange Curaçao sauce (£7.50), braised lamb chops (£8.50), and fresh whitby cod (£8.95), and puddings such as home-made apple pie or bread and butter pudding (from £4.30); good house wines. There are two stone cottages in the grounds to rent out. In fine weather there are tables and chairs in the pretty garden, and the flowering tubs and baskets are lovely. Fountains Abbey (the most extensive of the great monastic remains – floodlit on late summer Friday and Saturday evenings, with a live choir on the Saturday) – is not far away. *(Recommended by Maysie Thompson, Alan Thwaite, Howard and Margaret Buchanan, JHBS, H Bramwell, Blaise Vyner, Janet and Peter Race, Margaret Dickinson, Hugh A MacLean, Jim Abbott, John Branston)*

Free house ~ Licensee Mrs June Hawes ~ Bar food (not Sun or Mon evenings) ~ Restaurant ~ (01765) 620642 ~ Well behaved children allowed if over 9 ~ Open 11.30-3, 6.30-11; 12-3 Sun; closed Mon and winter Sun evenings

SCARBOROUGH TA0489 Map 10
Hole in the Wall ◖ £

Vernon Road; covered car park at top of road, may be free parking at bottom

The three rooms in this Victorian pub step down alongside the steep road, and are easy-going and down to earth. The bottom one has bare boards and darts, with stools around its cast-iron-framed tables, while the others have carpets and softer seating, with a few brewery advertisements and old local photographs and prints; the overall impression is red. They change the well kept beers on handpump frequently: John Smiths, Theakstons Old Peculier and XB, and maybe Timothy Taylors Landlord. Country wines and Weston's cider. Good value simple bar food includes sandwiches (from £1.80), soup (£2), ploughman's or omelettes (£4.25), filled baked potatoes (£2.95), steak and potato pie or mushroom stroganoff (£4.50), lamb shank in mint sauce (£6.75), steaks (from £7.25), and daily specials like cumberland or vegetarian sausages (£3.95), and liver and bacon casserole (£4.25). Cheerful service; juke box, darts, fruit machine, TV, shove-ha'penny, dominoes, and piped music. *(Recommended by the Didler, Kevin Blake, Mark Walker, Eric Larkham)*

Free house ~ Licensee Cheryl Roberts ~ Real ale ~ Bar food (12-3, 5-8) ~ No credit cards ~ (01723) 373746 ~ Children in eating area of bar until 8 ~ Dogs allowed in bar ~ Open 11-11; 12-10.30 Sun

---

It's very helpful if you let us know up-to-date food prices when you report on pubs.

SCAWTON SE5584 Map 10

Hare 🕮 ♀

Village signposted off A170 Thirsk—Helmsley, just E of Sutton Bank

The bars in this low-built pub are comfortably modernised without losing their cosy and unspoilt feel, and have rag rugs on flagstones and carpet, stripped pine tables, an old-fashioned range and a woodburner, lots of bric-a-brac, simple wall settles, a seat in the bow window, and comfortable eating areas; in the innermost part there's a heavy old beam-and-plank ceiling; shove-ha'penny, cribbage, and dominoes. At lunchtime, bar food includes home-made soup (£3.95), wensleydale cheese and tomato galette (£4.50), filled hot croissants (£5.50), caesar salad (£6.95), deep-fried battered whitby haddock or home-made chicken, mushroom and leek pie (£8.95), and salmon steak with lime and coriander sauce (£10.95), with evening choices such as rillette of duck and green peppercorns with kumquat chutney or grilled king scallops with a fresh tomato and cucumber salsa (£5.50), parsnip, leek and cheese bake topped with parsnip crisps (£8.95), duck breast with raspberry and orange sauce (£12.95), roast monkfish on bubble and squeak cake with mustard and dill sauce (£13.50), and chargrilled sirloin steak (£13.95). The dining rooms are no smoking. Well kept Black Sheep, Timothy Taylors Landlord, and a guest such as Theakstons Old Peculier on handpump, and an extensive wine list with lots by the glass; piped music. A big garden behind has tables, and the pub is attractive with roses against its cream walls and green woodwork, and its pair of inn-signs with naïve hare paintings; handy for Rievaulx Abbey. More reports please. (*Recommended by Colin and Dot Savill, Blaise Vyner, Andrew Scarr, Peter and Anne-Marie O'Malley, Mr and Mrs J Curtis, John Coggrave, R F Grieve, Brendan Sinnott, Wendy Dye, Mr and Mrs J E C Tasker, Pat and Tony Martin, Peter Burton, Lorraine and Fred Gill, Alison Hayes, Pete Hanlon*)

Free house ~ Licensee John Brown ~ Real ale ~ Bar food (not Mon) ~ Restaurant ~ No credit cards ~ (01845) 597289 ~ Children in restaurant ~ Open 12-3, 6.30-11 (10.30 Sun); closed Mon

SHEFFIELD SK3687 Map 7

Fat Cat ◀ £

23 Alma Street

A major draw to this popular pub of course remains the big choice of up to 10 real ales on handpump, including their own, and they have a popular Brewery Visitor's Centre (you can book brewery trips ((0114) 249 4804) with framed beer mats, pump clips, and prints on the walls. As well as their own-brewed and cheap Kelham Island Bitter, Pale Rider, Easy Rider, and another Kelham Island beer, there are six guests on handpump from breweries like Cottage, Daleside, Durham, Glentworth, Moorhouses, Scattor Rock, and so forth, plus belgian bottled beers, two belgian draught beers, fruit gin, country wines, and farm cider. Incredibly cheap, enjoyable bar food includes sandwiches, lentil soup (£2), ploughman's (£3), spinach pasta, courgette and potato pie, pork casserole or quiche (from £3), and puddings such as rhubarb crumble or jam roly poly (£1); well liked Sunday lunch (£3.50). There's always a good, chatty bustle, and the two small downstairs rooms have brewery-related prints on the walls, coal fires, simple wooden tables and cushioned seats around the walls, and jugs, bottles, and some advertising mirrors; the one on the left is no smoking; cribbage and dominoes, and maybe a not-so-fat-cat wandering around. Steep steps take you up to another similarly simple room (which may be booked for functions) with some attractive prints of old Sheffield; there are picnic-sets in a fairylit back courtyard. (*Recommended by Richard Lewis, JP, PP, the Didler, W W Burke, Alison Keys, Patrick Hancock*)

Own brew ~ Licensee Stephen Fearn ~ Real ale ~ Bar food (12-2.30, 6-7.30; not Sat or Sun evening) ~ No credit cards ~ (0114) 249 4801 ~ Children in no smoking room and upstairs room lunchtime and early evening ~ Dogs welcome ~ Open 12-3, 5.30-11; 12-11 Fri and Sat; 12-3, 7-10.30 Sun; closed 25 and 26 Dec

New Barrack 🍺 £

601 Penistone Road, Hillsborough

Sizeable but friendly, this bustling place always has a good crowd of cheerful customers keen to enjoy the fine choice of real ales and regular live music. Served by knowledgeable staff, the well kept beers on handpump might include regulars such as Abbeydale Moonshine, Barnsley Bitter, John Smiths Magnet, and up to six guests from maybe Adnams, Atlas, Oakham, Ossett, Phoenix, Wadworths and so forth; also, seven continental draught lagers, 30 continental bottled beers, and 70 malt whiskies. The comfortable front lounge has red leather banquettes, old pine floors, a woodburning stove, and collections of decorative plates and of bottles, and there are two smaller rooms behind, one with TV and darts – the family room is no smoking. Darts, cribbage, dominoes, and piped music. The good value simple food is all freshly made and might include sandwiches (from £1.50; steak £4.50), ploughman's with home-made chutney, turkey and broccoli casserole, grated carrot and pesto lasagne, spicy vegetable stew, and home-made chilli (all £4.50), with puddings like fresh fruit flan (£1.95); good value Sunday lunch. Daily papers and magazines to read; maybe quiet piped radio. The garden has been newly paved. Local parking is not easy. *(Recommended by Patrick Hancock, Stuart Paulley, Anne and Paul Horscraft, CMW, JJW, the Didler, JP, PP, Andrew Crawford, Richard Lewis)*

Tynemill ~ Manager Steve Bramley ~ Real ale ~ Bar food (12-2.30(3 Sun), 6-8; not Sat or Sun evening) ~ No credit cards ~ (0114) 234 9148 ~ Children in family room ~ Dogs welcome ~ Live music Sat evening and three other times during the month ~ Open 12-11; 12-10.30 Sun

SHELLEY SE2112 Map 7
Three Acres 🍽 🍷 🍺 🛏

Roydhouse (not signposted); from B6116 heading for Skelmanthorpe, turn left in Shelley (signposted Flockton, Elmley, Elmley Moor) and go up lane for 2 miles towards radio mast

Yorkshire Dining Pub of the Year

This civilised and very well run former coaching inn is somewhere for a special occasion, and while there are customers who drop in for a pint by the bar counter, most people come to enjoy the excellent food or to stay overnight. The roomy lounge bar has a relaxed, friendly atmosphere, tankards hanging from the main beam, button-back leather sofas, old prints and so forth, and maybe a pianist playing light music. To be sure of a place, it's best to book (quite a way ahead) – try to get a table with a view. Imaginative and highly enjoyable, the bar food includes a huge choice of interesting sandwiches or filled baguettes (from £3.25; vegetarian club with mozzarella, sun-blush tomatoes, basil, rocket, avocado and pine nuts dressed with sun-dried tomato pesto £3.95; open steak on toasted onion bread with caramelised onions and rocket and topped with blue cheese £7.95), crab and prawn bisque topped with welsh rarebit (£4.50), griddled fresh cornish sardines with chilli, mint and shallot dressing or chicken liver parfait with fruit chutney (£5.95), loch fyne queenies topped with gruyère, garlic and mustard or flash grilled with thai butter (£6.95), roast mushroom and leek shepherd's pie with crispy crumb topping (£9.95), steak, kidney and mushroom pie with cucumber and onion pickle or a lunchtime roast (£10.95), roast stuffed saddle of rabbit, basil, rosemary, black olives, sun-dried tomatoes and fresh pasta (£12.95), leg and shoulder of spring lamb with tempura of sweetbreads with minted roast jus or roast half duckling with sage and onion stuffing, bramley apple purée, and duck jus (£13.95), and tagine of fresh seafood, tomatoes, cumin, lime and coriander served with couscous (£14.95), with puddings such as mocha chocolate tart with praline ice cream, claret and cranberry jelly with orange sauce or sticky toffee pudding with toffee sauce (£5.50). There's a specialist delicatessen next door. Well kept Adnams Bitter, Marstons Pedigree, and Timothy Taylors Landlord on handpump, over 50 whiskies, exceptional (if not cheap) choice of wines, with 10 by the glass, and freshly squeezed orange juice; particularly good, friendly service, even when really pushed. There are fine views across to Emley Moor. *(Recommended by Regine Webster, Julian Heath, W K Wood, Mr and Mrs P Eastwood, P and S Blacksell, J Roy Smylie,*

R N and M I Bailey, P J Benson, Roger Everett, Ian Phillips, Dr and Mrs M W A Haward, Liz Webster, J R Ringrose, Charles Eaton, Brenda and Stuart Naylor)

Free house ~ Licensees Neil Truelove and Brian Orme ~ Real ale ~ Bar food (12-2, 6.45-9.45; Sat bar lunch is soup and sandwiches only) ~ Restaurant ~ (01484) 602606 ~ Children welcome ~ Open 12-3, 6-11; closed 25 and 31 Dec, 1 Jan ~ Bedrooms: £60B/£80B

SUTTON UPON DERWENT SE7047 Map 7
St Vincent Arms 🍴 🍺

B1228 SE of York

Particularly well run, this is a warmly friendly local with cheerful service, good, popular food, and lots of real ales. The parlour-like panelled front bar has traditional high-backed settles, a cushioned bow-window seat, windsor chairs and a gas-effect coal fire; another lounge and separate no smoking dining room open off. To be sure of a seat, it's best to get here early. At lunchtime, the enjoyable dishes might include sandwiches (from £2.50; hot brie and bacon on ciabatta £4.50; crayfish with lemon mayonnaise £4.80), home-made soup (£3.50), large haddock with mushy peas or chicken with garlic and parsley (£7.50), home-made steak and kidney pie (£7.90), and steaks (from £11), as well as baked goats cheese with poached pear and walnut salad (£4.50), seared scallops with basil and tomato and sauce vierge (£4.90), wild mushroom risotto (£5), strips of beef with a spicy cream sauce (£9.50), fillet of salmon wrapped in parma ham with beurre blanc sauce or confit of duck with red wine and peppercorn sauce (£11), rack of lamb with red wine and rosemary sauce (£13), and daily specials like coq au vin (£9.50), fillet of bass with an olive crust (£11.50) or breast of duck with orange and Grand Marnier sauce (£12), and puddings such as jam roly poly (£2.80). Up to eight real ales are well kept on handpump or tapped from the cask: Fullers Bitter, London Pride and ESB, Old Mill Bitter, John Smiths, Timothy Taylors Landlord, Wells Bombardier, and York Yorkshire Terrier; quite a few wines, and several coffees. There are seats in the garden. The pub is named after the admiral who was granted the village and lands by the nation as thanks for his successful commands – and for coping with Nelson's infatuation with Lady Hamilton. Handy for the Yorkshire Air Museum. *(Recommended by Paul and Ursula Randall, Peter and Anne Hollindale, Roger A Bellingham, Hugh A MacLean, Pat and Graham Williamson, W W Burke, Greta and Christopher Wells, John and Sheila Burley, Dr D Parker, John Evans, R T and J C Moggridge, BKA, Pat and Tony Martin)*

Free house ~ Licensees Phil and Enid Hopwood ~ Real ale ~ Bar food ~ Restaurant ~ (01904) 608349 ~ Children welcome ~ Open 11.30-3, 6-11; 12-3, 7-10.30 Sun

TERRINGTON SE6571 Map 7
Bay Horse

W of Malton; off B1257 at Hovingham (towards York, eventually sigposted left) or Slingsby (towards Castle Howard, then right); can also be reached off A64 via Castle Howard, or via Welburn and Ganthorpe

In an unspoilt village on one of the rolling old coach roads that make the most of the Howardian Hill views, this friendly country pub has a peaceful atmosphere. The cosy lounge bar has country prints and a good log fire, there's a handsome dining area and back family conservatory with old farm tools, and well kept Theakstons Black Bull, Timothy Taylors Landlord, and a guest such as Websters on handpump; over 100 whiskies. Well liked bar food includes home-made soup (£2.50), sandwiches (from £2.75; filled baguettes from £3.25), deep-fried king prawns with a tomato and herb dip (£4.95), pies such as steak and kidney (£6.75) and game (£6.95), ham and eggs (£7.95), daily specials like cheese and broccoli bake, italian-style chicken, lemon sole with peppercorn dressing or swordfish steak (from around £5.50), and puddings such as sticky toffee pudding or cheesecakes (£2.95). The restaurant is no smoking; piped music. The traditional public bar has darts, shove-ha'penny, cribbage, and dominoes. There are tables out in a small but attractively planted garden. *(Recommended by Roger and Jenny Huggins, Pat and Tony Martin, John and Sheila Burley, Janet and Peter Race, Christopher and Jo Barton)*

Free house ~ Licensee Michael Wilson ~ Real ale ~ Bar food ~ Restaurant ~ (01653) 648416 ~ Children in eating area of bar and restaurant ~ Open 12-3, 6.30-11(10.30 Sun)

THORGANBY SE6942 Map 7
Jefferson Arms 🍴 🛏
Off A163 NE of Selby, via Skipwith

There's a bistro bar feel here, an impression strengthened by the iron-framed marble-topped tables and bentwood chairs, grey and chrome colours, and large metal bar counter with big urns at either end; readers have been surprised at the radical changes, but quite happy. There's a relaxed and stylish feel, and away from the bar, comfortable sofas and chairs, open fires, heavy draped curtains, and ornate candlesticks; two attractively laid out conservatories, and several no smoking areas. From quite a choice, the well liked bar food includes home-made soup (£3.25), home-made chicken liver pâté (£4.25), fresh salmon and crab fishcakes with spicy tomato salsa (£4.95), steak and kidney pie (£7.95), mushroom stroganoff or toulouse sausage with onion gravy (£8.95), chicken with bacon and stilton sauce (£9.95), creamy garlic and bacon mushrooms (£4.25), goats cheese with port and redcurrant sauce (£4.95), vegetable curry (£7.95), toulouse sausage and mash with onion gravy (£8.95), steaks (from £9.55), and daily specials such as baked black pudding with brie and pesto dressing (£4.95), whole dressed whitby crab (£6.95), roasted peppers filled with ratatouille and topped with melted cheese (£9.95), chicken supreme filled with bacon, mushroom and herbs with creamy mushroom sauce (£12.95), and duck in honey and orange with stir-fried vegetables (£14.95). Well kept Courage Directors, John Smiths, and Theakstons Black Bull on handpump; piped music; friendly, helpful service. The garden has a terrace with a fountain and fish pond. *(Recommended by Paul Boot, Walter and Susan Rinaldi-Butcher, Dr T E Hothersall, John and Sheila Burley, Michael Dandy, Roy Hamnett, Brenda and Stuart Naylor)*

Free house ~ Licensees Clive Bland and Steven Wiper ~ Real ale ~ Bar food (12-2, 6-9) ~ Restaurant ~ (01904) 448316 ~ Children in restaurant ~ Dogs allowed in bedrooms ~ Open 12-2.30, 6-11; 12-3, 6-10.30; may open all day in summer Sun ~ Bedrooms: £45S/£60S

THORNTON IN LONSDALE SD6976 Map 7
Marton Arms 🍺 🛏
Off A65 just NW of Ingleton (or can be reached direct from Ingleton)

It's a real surprise to find such an amazing choice of drinks in this relaxed and quietly set village pub. As well as eight changing guest beers on handpump, they keep Black Sheep Bitter, Special, and Riggwelter, Highgate Mild, Sharps Doom Bar, Timothy Taylors Golden Best, and Wells Bombardier; four-pint take-aways, too. Also, Stowford Press and Weston's farm cider, well over 300 malt whiskies, all sorts of unusual spirits, a decent choice of wines in baby bottles, and an enterprising range of soft drinks, as well as proper tea and coffee. Service is friendly and helpful. The beamed partly no smoking bar is inviting, with stools on black boards by the long counter, and lots of stripped pine tables, pews and built-in wall seats in the carpeted main part – light and airy, with biggish black and white local photographs; some bus and train memorabilia. A curtained-off flagstoned public bar has bar billiards. Using local produce, the nicely prepared food includes home-made soup (£3.10), sandwiches (from £3.60; sirloin steak with onion rings and mushrooms on toasted bun £8.80), quite a few burgers (from £4.10), all-day breakfast (£5.70), lots of home-made pizzas (from £5.70), cumberland sausage (£6.30), chilli (£6.90), mushroom stroganoff (£8), chicken in white wine and cream or steak in ale pie (£8.20), and daily specials such as cajun chicken (£8.10), italian-style red bream (£8.20), beef goulash (£9), marsala lemon sole (£10.40), and seared halibut on spicy red onion relish (£12.10). They offer a take-away service for pizzas and burgers (not Saturday evening or bank holidays). There are picnic-sets out on the front terrace. The bedrooms (two equipped for disabled people) are in an annexe; good breakfasts, which suit this great walking country. *(Recommended by Mr and Mrs Maurice Thompson, Graham Patterson, Andy and Jill Kassube, John Hulme, Peter F Marshall)*

Free house ~ Licensee Colin Elsdon ~ Real ale ~ Bar food (12-2, 6-9; all day weekends and bank hols; not 25 Dec) ~ (01524) 241281 ~ Children welcome ~ Open 11-11; 12-10.30 Sun; closed evening 25 Dec ~ Bedrooms: £32S/£64S

THORNTON WATLASS SE2486 Map 10
Buck 🍺 🛏

Village signposted off B6268 Bedale—Masham

Mr and Mrs Fox have now been welcoming regulars and visitors to their genuine local for over 17 years. The place to head for is the pleasantly traditional right-hand bar with upholstered old-fashioned wall settles on the carpet, a fine mahogany bar counter, a high shelf packed with ancient bottles, several mounted fox masks and brushes, a brick fireplace, and a relaxed atmosphere; piped music. At lunchtime, bar food might include sandwiches, home-made soup (£2.95), smoked haddock fishcakes (£4.25), masham rarebit (wensleydale cheese with local ale topped with bacon, £4.50), ploughman's (£5.50), omelettes (£5.95), vegetable and pasta stir fry (£6.50), beef and beer curry (£6.95), steak and kidney pie (£7.25), and fresh salmon with cream and tarragon (£7.50), and there are daily specials such as goats cheese and tomato tartlet with home-made pear chutney (£4.50), courgette, leek and tuna lasagne (£7.75), baked cod with avocado and tiger prawns (£7.75), and fruit caribbean chicken (£8.95), and home-made puddings like apple pie with wensleydale cheese or chocolate bavarois with Baileys (from £3.95). Well kept Black Sheep Bitter, John Smiths, Theakstons, and a couple of guests from local breweries on handpump, and around 40 malt whiskies. The beamed no smoking dining room (refurbished this year) is hung with large prints of old Thornton Watlass cricket teams, and decorated with signed bats, cricket balls, and so forth; a bigger bar has darts, cribbage, and dominoes. The sheltered garden has an equipped children's play area and summer barbecues, and they have their own cricket team (the pub not only borders the village cricket green – one wall is actually the boundary) and quoits team. *(Recommended by JWAC, Janet and Peter Race, Keith Mould, David and Barbara Knott, RB, Mr and Mrs J E C Tasker, D Roberts, Steve Whalley, Ian Piper, Michael Doswell)*

Free house ~ Licensees Michael and Margaret Fox ~ Real ale ~ Bar food (12-2, 6.15-9.30; 12-9.15 Sat and Sun) ~ Restaurant ~ (01677) 422461 ~ Children welcome ~ Dogs allowed in bedrooms ~ Jazz Sun lunchtimes and occasional Sat evenings ~ Open 11-11; 12-10.30 Sun; closed 25 Dec evening ~ Bedrooms: £45S/£55(£65B)

WASS SE5679 Map 7
Wombwell Arms 🍽 � 🛏

Back road W of Ampleforth; or follow brown tourist-attraction sign for Byland Abbey off A170 Thirsk—Helmsley

The genuinely warm and friendly welcome offered by the hard-working licensees in this bustling pub makes you feel almost more of a house guest than a paying customer. The little central bar is spotlessly kept and cosy, and the three low-beamed dining areas are comfortable and inviting and take in a former 17th-c granary. They use only fresh local produce from local suppliers and producers for the good, enjoyable food: sandwiches, broccoli and leek soup (£3.75), black pudding with wild mushrooms and bacon on a garlic croûte (£5.35), chicken and pork pâté (£5.85), creamy crab mousse (£5.95), beef dijon (£10.45), three-cheese pie, lasagne or wild boar and apple sausages with red onion jam (£8.95), peppered chicken or rabbit with cider and apple and a herb dumpling (£10.95), game casserole (£11.45), king prawns in almond and lemon butter sauce (£11.75), whitby cod with crispy breadcrumbs and cheese topping (£11.85), 10oz steak (£15.50), and puddings (from £4.25); best to book to be sure of a table. Several areas are no smoking. Well kept Black Sheep Bitter, Timothy Taylors Landlord, and a guest from maybe Cropton, Daleside or Hambleton on handpump, decent malt whiskies, and a carefully chosen wine list; cribbage and dominoes.

(Recommended by RJH, Susan and John Douglas, Greta and Christopher Wells, Tim Newman, Walter and Susan Rinaldi-Butcher, Philip and Susan Philcox, J and C J Dean, C Hudd, Mrs Lynn Hepworth, Edward and Deanna Pearce, Robert Gartery, Mike and Linda Hudson, Fergus and Jackie O'Connor, Ian and Rose Lock)

Free house ~ Licensees Andy and Sue Cole ~ Real ale ~ Bar food (12-2(2.30 Sat and Sun), 7-9(9.30 Fri and Sat)) ~ Restaurant ~ (01347) 868280 ~ Children in restaurant and family room ~ Open 11.30-2.30(3 Sat), 6.30-11; closed Sun evening and Mon Jan-March ~ Bedrooms: £42B/£62B

WATH IN NIDDERDALE SE1467 Map 7
Sportsmans Arms 🍽 🍷 🛏

Nidderdale road off B6265 in Pateley Bridge; village and pub signposted over hump bridge on right after a couple of miles

Although this is a civilised restaurant-with-rooms and many customers do come to stay overnight, you can be sure of a genuinely warm welcome from the friendly staff, and locals drop in all the time for a drink and a chat. Using the best local produce – game from the moors, fish delivered daily from Whitby, and nidderdale lamb, pork and beef – the carefully presented and prepared delicious food might include excellent lunchtime sandwiches, fresh soup (£4.50), their special salad with bacon, croutons, olives, anchovies, and parmesan and pecorino cheeses on mixed leaves (£5.20), whitby cod and finnan haddock fishcakes with sauce remoulade (£6.50), roasted scottish salmon with ginger and spring onions (£6.90), salad of seared langoustine tails with mango, melon and mange tout in sesame oil dressing (£7.50), crumbed loin of pork on roasted apples with a creamy plum and calvados sauce (£12.90), breast of chicken on risotto with a mild curry cream sauce (£13.50), fillet of local lamb with asparagus and a roasted garlic and tomato jus or seared and roasted breast of gressingham duckling with sun-dried fruits and nuts and natural jus (£13.95), and puddings such as summer pudding (their most popular pudding over the past 23 years), double chocolate roulade with chocolate ice cream or sticky toffee pudding with toffee sauce (from £3.80). The whole place is no smoking apart from the bar and the lounge. There's a very sensible and extensive wine list, a good choice of malt whiskies, and several russian vodkas; open fires. Benches and tables outside. As well as their own fishing on the River Nidd, this is an ideal spot for walkers, hikers, and ornithologists, and there are plenty of country houses, gardens, and cities to explore. *(Recommended by Di and Mike Gillam, Janet and Peter Race, P R Morley, Mrs S Parker Bowles, Peter Burton, JHBS, Phil Skelton, Geoff and Angela Jaques, P Abbott, Lynda and Trevor Smith, Greta and Christopher Wells; also in the Good Hotel Guide)*

Free house ~ Licensee Ray Carter ~ Bar food ~ Restaurant ~ (01423) 711306 ~ Children welcome ~ Dogs allowed in bar ~ Open 12-2.30, 6.30-11; closed 25 Dec ~ Bedrooms: £50B/£90B

WHITBY NZ9011 Map 10
Duke of York 🍺

Church Street, Harbour East Side

Doing particularly well at the moment, this bustling pub – close to the famous 199 Steps that lead up to the abbey – has a splendid view over the harbour entrance and the western cliff. To be sure of a table, you must arrive early, and the welcoming and comfortable beamed lounge bar has plenty of atmosphere and decorations that include quite a bit of fishing memorabilia – though it's the wide choice of good value fresh local fish on the menu itself which appeals most: there might be delicious fresh crab or prawn sandwiches (£3.50), large fillet of fresh cod or fresh crab salad (£6.50), as well as other sandwiches (from £2.50; filled baguettes from £3.95), vegetable lasagne or chilli (£5.50), steak in ale pie (£5.95), and puddings (£2.95). Well kept Black Sheep Special, Courage Directors, and John Smiths on handpump, decent wines, lots of malt whiskies, hot winter mulled wine, and chilled summer sangria, and quick, friendly service even when busy; piped music, darts, dominoes, TV, and fruit machine. If you stay, several rooms look over the water; breakfast is served from 9am in the bar and costs £4.95. *(Recommended by Colin and Dot Savill, M Borthwick, Roger and Jenny Huggins, Rona Murdoch, David and Ruth Shillitoe, W A Evershed, JP, PP, Gill and Tony Morriss, C J Fletcher, Alain and Rose Foote, Janet and Peter Race, Val Stevenson, Rob Holmes, the Didler, David Carr, Michael Butler)*

Unique Pub Co ~ Lease Lawrence Bradley ~ Real ale ~ Bar food (all day) ~ Restaurant ~ No credit cards ~ (01947) 600324 ~ Children welcome before 9.30 ~ Open 11-11; 11-10.30 Sun ~ Bedrooms: /£45B

WIDDOP SD9333 Map 7
Pack Horse ⬤

The Ridge; from A646 on W side of Hebden Bridge, turn off at Heptonstall signpost (as it's a sharp turn, coming out of Hebden Bridge road signs direct you around a turning circle), then follow Slack and Widdop signposts; can also be reached from Nelson and Colne, on high, pretty road; OS Sheet 103 map reference 952317

Considering its isolation high up on the moors, this traditional pub is surprisingly busy. The bar has warm winter fires, window seats cut into the partly panelled stripped stone walls that take in the moorland view, sturdy furnishings, and well kept Black Sheep Bitter and Special, Greene King Old Speckled Hen, Thwaites Bitter, and a couple of guests such as Greene King Abbot or Timothy Taylors Landlord on handpump, around 130 single malt whiskies, and some irish ones as well, and decent wines; efficient service. Bar food includes sandwiches or baps (from £3.50), home-made steak and kidney pie or mushroom stroganoff (£5.95), steaks (from £8.95), and specials such as garlic mushrooms and stilton (£3.95), queenies in garlic butter and cheese (£4.95; main course £8.95), burger with bacon, pineapple and mango chutney (£4.95), and pecan, broccoli and stilton puffs or pasta napoletana (£5.95). The restaurant is only open on Saturday evenings. There are seats outside. More reports please. *(Recommended by Dr T E Hothersall, Greta and Christopher Wells, Norman Stansfield, Bob Broadhurst)*

Free house ~ Licensee Andrew Hollinrake ~ Real ale ~ Bar food (not Mon or weekday winter lunchtimes) ~ Restaurant ~ (01422) 842803 ~ Children welcome ~ Dogs allowed in bar ~ Open 12-3, 7-11; 12-11 Sun; closed weekday winter lunchtimes and Mon ~ Bedrooms: £39S/£44B

YORK SE5951 Map 7
Maltings ⬤ ■ £

Tanners Moat/Wellington Row, below Lendal Bridge

Always bustling and chatty, this lively small pub fills up quickly with customers keen to try the fine range of real ales. The tricksy décor is entirely contrived and strong on salvaged somewhat quirky junk: old doors for the bar front and much of the ceiling, enamel advertising signs for the rest of it, what looks like a suburban front door for the entrance to the ladies', partly stripped orange brick walls, even a lavatory pan in one corner. There are six or seven particularly well kept changing ales on handpump with Black Sheep and Roosters, and five changing guests, with frequent special events when the jovial landlord adds many more. He also has two or three continental beers on tap, up to four farm ciders, a dozen or so country wines, and more irish whiskeys than you normally see. Generous helpings of good value lunchtime food (get there early for a seat) might include sandwiches (from £2.10), very popular truly home-made chips (£2) with chilli or curry (£2.50), filled baked potatoes (from £2.50), haddock (£4.50), and beef in ale pie or stilton and leek bake (£4.95). The day's papers are framed in the gents'; fruit machine. Nearby parking is difficult; the pub is very handy for the Rail Museum. *(Recommended by*

Richard Lewis, Peter F Marshall, JP, PP, M Benjamin, Jim Abbott, the Didler, Pat and Tony Martin, David Carr, James Woods, Roger A Bellingham, Tony Hobden, Patrick Hancock, Mark Walker, Alison Hayes, Pete Hanlon)

Free house ~ Licensee Shaun Collinge ~ Real ale ~ Bar food (12-2 weekdays, 12-4 weekends; not evenings) ~ No credit cards ~ (01904) 655387 ~ Children allowed after food service and must be well behaved ~ Dogs allowed in bar ~ Jazz Mon, blues Tues ~ Open 11-11.30; 12-10.30 Sun; closed 25 Dec

Lucky Dip

Besides the fully inspected pubs, you might like to try these Lucky Dips recommended to us and described by readers (if you do, please send us reports: www.goodguides.com).

ADDINGHAM [SE0749]

Fleece [Main St]: 18th-c pub doing well under current friendly licensees, good hearty sandwiches and generous well priced blackboard meals using fresh local meat, fish and smoked fish, popular Sun lunch, well kept Black Sheep, Timothy Taylors Landlord and Tetleys, good choice of wines by the glass, low ceilings, flagstones and log fire, separate dining room and tap room with darts and dominoes; very busy wknds; children welcome, tables outside *(Dr and Mrs S Donald, Sarah McGillivary)*

AISLABY [SE8508]

Huntsman [Main Rd, off A171 W of Whitby]: Extended mellow stone beamed pub with lots of pictures, cosy seating, welcoming newish licensee doing enjoyable straightforward food from good sandwiches to whitby fish and steaks, good vegetarian range and children's dishes, very efficient friendly staff and amiable old dog, well kept Black Sheep and John Smiths, decent wines in some bargains; quiet piped music, busy wknds and holidays; children welcome (very baby-friendly), bedrooms *(Mr and Mrs J Powell, Michael Doswell, M Borthwick)*

ALLERTON BYWATER [SE4227]

☆ *Boat* [Main St]: Busy newly extended pub brewing its own refreshing well priced Boat ales such as Boatburger wheat beer, others such as Tetleys, good value food for the heartiest appetites (small helpings also available) inc some interesting specials, friendly staff (landlord an ex rugby league player for Castleford and England, appropriate mementoes); play area, lots of tables out by Aire & Calder Canal, open all day Sun and summer *(Phil and Anne Smithson, Michael Butler, G Dobson, Eric Larkham)*

ALNE [SE4965]

☆ *Blue Bell* [Main St]: New licensees doing wide choice of good enterprising food in upgraded bar and barn restaurant *(Walter and Susan Rinaldi-Butcher, John Knighton)*

AMPLEFORTH [SE5878]

☆ *White Swan* [off A170 W of Helmsley; East End]: Three separate interestingly furnished and decorated rooms, sporting prints, comfortable squashy seating, public bar with darts and dominoes, John Smiths and Tetleys, blazing log fires, no smoking candlelit

restaurant, new chef/landlord cooking promising food – more reports please; children welcome, attractive back terrace *(Liz Clayton, Brendan Sinnott, LYM)*

APPLETON ROEBUCK [SE5542]

Shoulder of Mutton [Chapel Green]: Cheerful and attractive unpretentious bar overlooking village green, wide choice of enjoyable bargain food inc cheap steaks in bar and restaurant, well kept cheap Sam Smiths on all four handpumps, prompt friendly service even on a busy Sun lunchtime (can be crowded with caravanners summer); bedrooms *(Geoffrey and Brenda Wilson, Alan Vere)*

APPLETREEWICK [SE0560]

Craven Arms [off B6160 Burnsall—Bolton Abbey]: Attractively placed creeper-covered 17th-c beamed pub with spartan décor (flagstones and brown-painted ply panelling), well kept Black Sheep Bitter and Special, Tetleys and a guest beer, enjoyable home-made food from good baguettes up, small no smoking dining room, no piped music; nice views from front picnic-sets, more seats in back garden, plenty of surrounding walks *(LYM, Stefanie and Christian Mohr, Andrew and Samantha Grainger, John and Sheila Burley)*

ARNCLIFFE [SD9473]

☆ *Falcon* [off B6160 N of Grassington]: Ideal setting on moorland village green for basic well worn country tavern, no frills, well kept Timothy Taylors Landlord tapped from cask to stoneware jugs in central hatch-style servery, generous plain lunchtime and early evening sandwiches and snacks (from old family kitchen with range and big table that looks used to having a dog tied to its legs), open fire in small bar with elderly furnishings and humorous sporting prints, airy back sunroom (children allowed here lunchtime) looking on to pleasant garden; run very conservatively, same family for generations; cl winter Thurs evenings; plain bedrooms (not all year), good breakfast and evening meal *(JAE, the Didler, JP, PP, Tony and Ann Bennett-Hughes, Neil and Angela Huxter, LYM, Jim Abbott)*

ASKRIGG [SD9591]

Crown [Main St]: Neat and friendly open-plan local, several separate areas off main bar with blazing fires inc old-fashioned range, relaxed atmosphere, cheap generous home-cooked food inc cut-price small helpings, good value

Sun lunch and good puddings choice, well kept Black Sheep and Theakstons XB from swan necks, helpful welcoming staff; children and walkers welcome, tables outside *(Jim Abbott, Michael Butler, W W Burke)*

Kings Arms [signed from A684 Leyburn—Sedbergh in Bainbridge]: Early 19th-c coaching inn in popular James Herriot village, three old-fashioned bars, interesting traditional furnishings and décor, well kept ales such as Black Sheep, John Smiths, Theakstons Best and Old Peculier, good choice of wines by the glass and of malt whiskies, wide food choice (may be a wait when busy), no smoking waitress-served grill room and set-priced restaurant; bedrooms run as part of Holiday Property Bond complex behind – pub side managed separately *(I J and S A Bufton, LYM, Michael Butler, W W Burke, R M Corlett, Gerry and Rosemary Dobson)*

ATLEY HILL [NZ2802]
Arden Arms [B1263 NE of Catterick Bridge, off A1]: Good choice of enjoyable food using fresh local supplies in well organised dining pub stepped up hill, locals' bar with well kept Theakstons Best and Old Peculier, decent wines, good coffee, friendly helpful staff, open fires *(M F Turnbull)*

ATWICK [TA1850]
Black Horse [B1242 N of Hornsea; The Green]: Two friendly comfortable rooms with old photographs, three well kept changing ales, fair-priced food inc local seafood, good landlord; piped music; dogs and children welcome *(Dr W J M Gissane)*

AYSGARTH [SE0088]
George & Dragon [just off A684]: 17th-c coaching inn (on the market as we went to press), small attractive bar with log fire, beams and panelling, well kept Black Sheep Bitter, John Smiths and Theakstons Best, polished hotel lounge with antique china, decent food, no smoking dining areas; children welcome, tables in paved garden, lovely scenery, open all day, bedrooms with own bathrooms *(Jim Abbott, I J and S A Bufton, Janet Walters, Michael Butler, R G Price, Mrs B M Smith, Mr and Mrs M Dalby, Keith Mould, Mike and Maggie Betton, Walter and Susan Rinaldi-Butcher, Lynda and Trevor Smith, Mr and Mrs J E C Tasker, Peter Burton, Bob Broadhurst, LYM)*

Palmer Flatt: Moorland hotel in great scenery nr broad waterfalls, medley of cheerful largely modernised bars but some interesting ancient masonry at the back recalling its days as a pilgrims' inn, decent bar food and well kept beers at competitive prices, restaurant; tables outside, fishing rights, space for caravans, bedrooms *(P Abbott, LYM)*

BAINBRIDGE [SD9390]
☆ *Rose & Crown*: Upgraded inn overlooking moorland village green, more hotel than pub now with prices to match, but pleasantly pubby feel in old-fashioned beamed and oak-panelled front bar with old settles and big log fire, well kept Black Sheep and John Smiths, good coffee, enjoyable food from good

baguettes up in bar and spacious no smoking restaurant; children welcome, busy back extension popular with families, open all day, bedrooms *(P Abbott, LYM, Gerry and Rosemary Dobson)*

BARDSEY [SE3643]
☆ *Bingley Arms* [Church Lane]: Ancient stone-built pub smartly decorated to match, welcoming efficient service, good home-made fresh food inc interesting dishes, two-course lunch and early-supper bargains, spacious lounge divided into separate areas inc no smoking, huge fireplace, well kept Black Sheep, John Smiths and Tetleys, good wines by the glass, hard-working licensees, smaller public bar, picturesque upstairs brasserie, good classical guitarist every other Sat; children welcome, lots of tables in attractively redone terraced garden, lovely Saxon church nearby *(Matthew Hinkins, LYM, Pat and Tony Hinkins, Michael Butler, Roger S Kiddier)*

BEDALE [SE2688]
Old Black Swan: Cheerful local with well kept Theakstons ales, good value lunches; juke box and pool *(Janet and Peter Race)*

BESSACARR [SK6299]
Hare & Tortoise [Bawtry Rd (A638)]: Former surgeon's house redone as relaxed and civilised Vintage Inn pub/restaurant, varying-sized antique tables in eight small rooms off bar, sensibly priced food all day, friendly and efficient young staff, Bass and well chosen wines, log fire *(W W Burke)*

BEVERLEY [TA0339]
☆ *Corner House* [Norwood]: Warm and welcoming, attractive pastel décor, pews, easy chairs and sofas, friendly staff, good fresh restaurant food from baguettes up (no puddings), big good value wknd breakfast from 10, Timothy Taylors and other well kept beers, good wines, wide range of fresh fruit juices, hot beverages, daily papers, air conditioning; tables outside *(Lorraine and Fred Gill)*

Dog & Duck [Ladygate]: Cheerfully busy town local handy for playhouse and market, cheap home-made usual lunchtime food using local produce from sandwiches to bargain Sun lunch, well kept Greene King Abbot, John Smiths and an interesting guest beer, good value wines and good range of malt whiskies, coal fires; piped music, games machine; good value bedrooms up outside iron staircase in courtyard – secure parking *(Lorraine and Fred Gill, Paul and Ursula Randall, Joe Green)*

Moulders Arms [Wilbert Lane]: Warm friendly local with impressive choice of bargain-price fish and seafood lunchtime and early evening (not Sun), generous helpings, well kept Bass and Stones *(Joe Green)*

Sun [Flemingate]: Flagstones, stripped brick and timbers, basic furnishings, changing well kept beers and decent wines, farm cider, cheerful service, good value simple food; some music nights and beer festivals *(Lorraine and Fred Gill, Paul and Ursula Randall)*

BILBROUGH [SE5346]
Three Hares [off A64 York—Tadcaster]:

Quietly upmarket dining pub with beautifully cooked and presented food inc good value two-course Sun lunch, well kept Black Sheep, Timothy Taylors Landlord and a guest beer from end bar with sofas and log fire, minimalist décor; has been cl Mon *(Tony and Wendy Hobden, Nigel and Sue Foster)*
BINGLEY [SE1242]
Dick Hudsons [Otley Rd, High Eldwick]: Reworked as comfortable and appealingly old-world Vintage Inn, with popular food, Bass and Tetleys, good choice of wines by the glass; tables out by cricket field, tremendous views and good walks *(Pat and Graham Williamson)*
BIRSTALL [SE2126]
☆ *Black Bull* [Kirkgate, off A652; head down hill towards church]: Ancient stone pub opp part-Saxon church, dark panelling and low beams in long row of five small linked rooms, traditional décor complete with stag's head and lace curtains, lively local atmosphere, well kept Whitbreads-related ales, perhaps an interesting guest beer, good cheap home-made food inc bargain early meals and good value Sun lunch, good service, upstairs former courtroom (now a function room, but they may give you a guided tour); smoking throughout; children welcome, quiz night Mon, jazz Thurs *(Bernie Adams, BB, Geoffrey and Brenda Wilson, Michael Butler)*
BIRSTWITH [SE2459]
☆ *Station Hotel* [off B6165 W of Ripley]: Welcoming interesting stone-built Dales local, smartly modernised but cosy lounge, good range of good value food inc interesting dishes and quite a lot of seafood, well kept Tetleys and a guest beer, nice china, friendly staff; attractive hanging baskets and tubs in summer, picturesque valley *(Mary and David Richards)*
BISHOP THORNTON [SE2663]
Chequers: Busy traditional pub with good choice of consistently enjoyable food and keg beers, sensible prices, good service; bedrooms, cl Mon/Tues lunchtime *(Dudley and Moira Cockroft)*
BISHOP WILTON [SE7955]
☆ *Fleece* [just off A166 York—Bridlington; Pocklington Rd]: Partly panelled open-plan village inn with generous good value food cooked to order (worth booking) inc wonderful puddings, well kept ales such as Black Sheep, efficient friendly staff, several areas off flagstoned entrance hall, attractive décor with lots of pictures and bric-a-brac, a longcase clock, even a hanging penny-farthing; subdued piped light classics; four compact comfortable bedrooms with own bathrooms, nice spot on the edge of the Wolds nr interesting church *(Paul and Ursula Randall, Marian and Andrew Ruston)*
BISHOPTHORPE [SE5947]
Ebor [Main St]: Popular and welcoming local nr main entrance to Archbishop of York's Palace (hence name), lounge opening into dining area, generous traditional food, helpful attentive staff, Sam Smiths; children welcome, beautiful hanging baskets and big well planted garden *(Pat and Graham Williamson)*

BLUBBERHOUSES [SE1755]
Hopper Lane [A65 Skipton—Harrogate]: Pleasant olde-worlde interior, four linked eating areas, some with low ceilings and/or log and coal fires, lots of bric-a-brac, Black Sheep, Timothy Taylors Landlord, Tetleys and Theakstons, enjoyable varied food from sandwiches to huge mixed grill; bedrooms *(Ian and Freda Millar)*
BOLTON ABBEY [SE0754]
☆ *Devonshire Arms*: Comfortable and elegant hotel in marvellous position, good if pricy food from sandwiches up in attractively furnished brasserie bar with modern paintings, well kept real ales, good wines, smiling staff, tables in garden; handy for the priory, walks in the estate and Strid River valley; smart restaurant, helicopter pad; good bedrooms *(S D and J L Cooke)*
BOROUGHBRIDGE [SE3966]
Crown [Bridge St]: 17th-c hotel (former Great North Road coaching inn), pubby front bar with stripped floor and wooden booths, comfortable lounge, Black Sheep Bitter and Special and John Smiths, good value food from sandwiches to steaks; nicely refurbished comfortable bedrooms *(Michael Dandy)*
Malt Shovel [St James Sq]: Bright and attractively modernised, with enjoyable interesting food from filled baguettes up, well kept Black Sheep *(Rita and Keith Pollard, Janet and Peter Race)*
Three Horseshoes [Bridge St]: Spotless unspoilt 1930s pub/hotel run by same family from the start, character landlord, friendly locals, huge fire in lounge, darts, dominoes and cards in public bar (not always open), original features inc slide-down snob screens, good plain home cooking from sandwiches to steaks in bars and restaurant, well kept Camerons Strongarm and Tetleys, splendidly tiled ladies'; bedrooms, open all day Sun *(the Didler, Pete Baker, JP, PP)*
BRADFORD [SE1633]
Cock & Bottle [Barkerend Rd, up Church Bank from centre; on left few hundred yds past cathedral]: Carefully restored Victorian décor, well kept John Smiths and Tetleys, deep-cut and etched windows and mirrors enriched with silver and gold leaves, stained glass, enamel intaglios, heavily carved woodwork and traditional furniture, saloon with a couple of little snugs (one often with Christian counselling) and a rather larger carpeted music room, open fire in public bar *(BB, the Didler)*
Fighting Cock [Preston St (off B6145)]: Busy bare-floor alehouse by industrial estate, well kept Timothy Taylors Landlord and lots of changing guest beers, also farm ciders, foreign bottled beers, food inc all-day doorstep sandwiches, low prices, coal fires *(the Didler)*
Stansfield Arms [Apperley Bridge; off A658 NE]: Very clean pub with inexpensive tasty food, real ales such as Black Sheep and Timothy Taylors Landlord, friendly efficient staff *(Richard and Karen Holt)*
BRAFFERTON [SE4370]
☆ *Farmers* [between A19 and A168 NW of

York]: Olde-worlde small-roomed village pub with recycled pine country furniture, lots of flowers, nice Yorkshire range with glowing fire, subtle lighting, wide choice of good fair-priced food mixing familiar favourites with some unusual dishes, Tetleys and Theakstons Best, XB and Old Peculier, friendly staff, small restaurant, comfortable games room with fruit machine and darts, tables on back lawn; bedrooms *(Nick and Alison Dowson, John Knighton)*

BRAMHAM [SE4242]
Red Lion [just off A1 2 miles N of A64]: Hospitable former Great North Road coaching inn, well opened up with quiet décor, enjoyable reasonably priced food from good choice of sandwiches up, well kept cheap Sam Smiths OB; children welcome *(Carol and Dono Leaman, J A Ellis)*

BRANDESBURTON [TA1147]
Black Swan [Main St]: Good atmosphere in former farmhouse, helpful service, short choice of enjoyable food inc inventive specials, well kept Banks's and Mansfield Riding, good value wines; children and dogs welcome, garden tables *(Jamie and Sarah Allan, Lorraine and Fred Gill)*
Dacre Arms [signed off A165 N of Beverley and Hornsea turn-offs]: Brightly modernised comfortably bustling pub popular for wide choice of good value food from lunchtime sandwiches (not wknds) to steaks, inc OAP specials and children's; friendly service, well kept Black Sheep, Courage Directors, Tetleys and Theakstons Old Peculier tapped from the cask, darts, restaurant; children welcome, open for food all day wknds *(Brian and Janet Ainscough, LYM)*

BRANTINGHAM [SE9329]
Triton [Ellerker Rd]: Spacious and comfortably refurbished, with good choice of well presented food, conservatory bar, no smoking dining room with french windows to terrace; keg beer; tables in sheltered garden with play area *(Jenny and Dave Hughes, BB)*

BRIDLINGTON [TA1866]
Hook & Parrot [Esplanade]: Modern pub well done out in olde-worlde nautical style, lots of old lamps, snug alcoves, reasonably priced Scottish Courage beers, lunchtime food; pool, TV etc in separate bar *(Kevin Blake)*
Pavilion Bar [Jeromes, Esplanade]: Wicker chairs, modern art, huge lamps, lots of glass and iron pillars in former Floral Hall Theatre, well kept Marstons Pedigree and John Smiths, food lunchtime and early evening; play area, small stage for entertainment *(Kevin Blake)*
Tennyson Bar [Montforte Hotel, Tennyson Avenue]: Smart and comfortable L-shaped bar popular with older people, bar snacks, John Smiths beers, piano with occasional singalongs *(Kevin Blake)*

BRIGHOUSE [SE1323]
Red Rooster [Brookfoot; A6025 towards Elland]: Stone-built alehouse reopened under new management, well kept Caledonian Deuchars IPA, Roosters Yankee, Timothy Taylors Landlord and several other changing

ales, brewery memorabilia, open fire, separate areas inc one with pin table, no food or machines *(Andy and Jill Kassube, JP, PP, the Didler, J R Ringrose)*

BROMPTON [SE9582]
Cayley Arms [A170 W of Scarborough]: Uncluttered pub in pretty village, popular for enjoyable well served food (may be fully booked), well kept ales inc Theakstons; attractively reworked garden, decking with tables under handsome parasols *(Peter Burton, Gloria Bax)*

BUCKDEN [SD9477]
Buck [B6160]: Attractive creeper-covered stone pub in very popular walking spot, under new landlord; modernised and extended open-plan bar, log fire and flagstones in snug original core, local pictures and hunting prints; food from sandwiches (at a price) up, Theakstons Best, Old Peculier and Black Bull, 30 malt whiskies, several wines by the glass; food service stops very promptly; children welcome, terrace with good surrounding moorland views, open all day, bedrooms with own bathrooms *(LYM)*

BURGHWALLIS [SE5311]
☆ *Burghwallis* [signed off A1 southbound, S of Pontefract; Scorcher Hills Lane]: Comfortable former village social club pleasantly refurbished with leather chesterfields, nice china on mahogany sideboards, conservatory, bargain hot food counter inc carvery very popular with older lunchers, well kept nicely priced Old Mill and Tetleys, good choice of wines by the glass, friendly licensees, full-sized pool table *(Andrew Crawford)*

BURLEY WOODHEAD [SE1545]
Hermit: Sympathetically renovated and extended beamed pub, oak panelling and comfortable built-in seats, bay window seat with Wharfedale views, well kept real ales, good value food inc enterprising specials, friendly service, restaurant, no piped music or machines; good walks nearby *(Tim Newman, Fiona Pacey)*

BURN [SE5928]
Wheatsheaf [A19 Selby—Doncaster]: Welcoming landlord, good value usual food, well kept John Smiths, Timothy Taylors Landlord, Tetleys and a guest microbrew, fine whisky choice, eclectic décor inc assorted saws, hops, model lorries, galleon, big rocking horse; pool room, small garden *(J A Ellis)*

BURNSALL [SE0361]
Red Lion [B6160 S of Grassington]: 16th-c inn by River Wharfe, looking across village green to Burnsall Fell, tables out on front cobbles and on big back terrace, attractively panelled sturdily furnished bar, log fire, well kept Greene King Old Speckled Hen, Timothy Taylors Landlord, Theakstons Best and Black Bull and Charles Wells Bombardier, good wine choice by glass or bottle (they import direct), imaginative bar food, no smoking in dining area, bar parlour and conservatory; children welcome, comfortable bedrooms (dogs allowed in some and bar), open all day, fishing permits *(Michael Butler, Mr and Mrs M Porter, B and M Kendall, LYM)*

BURNT YATES [SE2561]

New Inn [Pateley Bridge Rd]: New licensees doing well in appealing pub with enjoyable reasonably priced food inc good value carvery and good puddings, well kept Rudgate, John Smiths and Theakstons, decent wines, friendly service, good atmosphere, interesting décor inc lots of antiques, nicely panelled back room *(M and N Watson, P Abbott, Mary and David Richards, Tim and Ann Newell)*

CADEBY [SE5100]

Cadeby Inn [Main St]: Newly extended as restaurant pub, with attractive furnishings and charming décor in several linked areas with open fires, first-rate service, upmarket food from enlarged kitchen with some emphasis on fresh fish; tables out in sunny garden *(Graham Dobson, LYM)*

CARLTON [NZ5004]

Blackwell Ox [just off A172 SW of Stokesley – the one at NZ5004]: Three relaxing linked rooms off big central bar, good reasonably priced food inc wide choice of toasted baguettes, thai and more traditional dishes, Thai landlady and helpful friendly staff, well kept Bass, Courage and Theakstons, blazing log fire, lots of dark wood, cigarette card collection; garden with big play area, bedrooms, picturesque village location, handy for coast-to-coast and Cleveland Way walkers *(Dr and Mrs R G J Telfer)*

Foresters Arms [off A684 W of Leyburn]: New licensees again for this inn, in a pretty village at the heart of the Yorkshire Dales National Park; log fires, low beams, well kept Black Sheep and John Smiths, several wines by the glass, straightforward bar food (not Sun evening or Tues – exc Tues evening in summer hols), no smoking restaurant; piped music, darts, dominoes; children welcome, bench seats out among tubs of flowers, comfortable bedrooms, lovely views, cl Mon *(LYM)*

CARPERBY [SE0089]

Wheatsheaf [1 mile NW of Aysgarth]: Traditional inn in quiet village, good atmosphere in old-fashioned locals' bar with well kept Black Sheep, John Smiths and Websters, wide bar food choice inc good sandwiches and ploughman's, darts and dominoes, restaurant for residents; bedrooms *(Jim Abbott)*

CAWOOD [SE5737]

☆ *Ferry* [King St (B1222 NW of Selby), by Ouse swing bridge]: Unspoilt neatly kept 16th-c inn, several comfortable areas, well kept ales such as Black Sheep, Mansfield, Timothy Taylors Landlord and a couple of local beers tapped from the cask in corner bar, friendly helpful staff, limited good value food inc bargain steak baguette and lots for children, massive inglenook, stripped brickwork, bare boards; tables out on flagstone terrace and grass by interesting River Ouse swing bridge, good value modest bedrooms with bathrooms, open all day Fri-Sun, cl Mon/Tues lunchtime *(Matt Waite, Janet and Peter Race, Pete Baker, R E and E C M Pick, JP, PP)*

CHAPEL LE DALE [SD7477]

☆ *Hill Inn* [B5655 Ingleton—Hawes, 3 miles N of Ingleton]: Current owners doing good nicely presented food inc lunchtime sandwiches and super puddings (licensee is a pastry chef), cosy bar, warm and welcoming, with flagstones, bare boards, old pine tables and benches, stripped-stone recesses and log fire, separate informal evening dining rooms (best to book), well kept Black Sheep and Theakstons, good coffee; wonderful remote spot, with views to Ingleborough and Whernside *(John and Sylvia Harrop, LYM, Jane Taylor, David Dutton)*

CHURCH FENTON [SE5136]

Fenton Flyer [Main St]: Homely village local with popular home-made food, Mansfield and Sam Smiths real ale, welcoming landlord, L-shaped bar with lots of old photographs and memorabilia of the RAF base opposite, no smoking dining end; TV, darts, Fri music night, no credit cards; garden with play area *(Kevin Thorpe)*

CLOUGHTON [SE9798]

☆ *Falcon* [pub signed just off A171 out towards Whitby]: Big family-run open-plan bar, neatly kept and well divided, light and airy (distant sea view from end windows), with comfortable banquettes and other seats on turkey carpet, good value food inc fine seafood salad (no booking, but worth the wait for a table), well kept John Smiths and Theakstons Best and XB, good friendly service, log fire in big stone fireplace; piped music; picnic-sets on walled lawn, good bedrooms with own bathrooms *(Geoff and Angela Jaques, BB)*

CLOUGHTON NEWLANDS [TA0096]

Hayburn Wyke Hotel [just N of village, which is off A171]: Down very long steep zigzag drive, great spot nr NT Hayburn Wyke, spectacular Cleveland Way coastal path and Scarborough—Whitby path/bicycle trail; monthly karaoke, brightly chalked food and advertising boards, very red furnishings, lowered false ceiling cutting across window tops, rather a take-us-as-you-find-us feel; good value food inc popular Sun carvery, well kept Black Sheep Special and Tetleys, coal fire, pool, table football and video game in bare-boards games area, big café-style dining area; well behaved children welcome, picnic-sets out on terrace and grass, play areas, comfortable recently refurbished bedrooms, good breakfast *(M Borthwick, BB)*

COLTON [SE5444]

☆ *Old Sun* [off A64 York—Tadcaster]: Attractive 17th-c beamed pub with friendly landlady happy to explain the authentic oriental dishes cooked by chef/landlord from Bangkok, familiar dishes too, also well kept ales such as Timothy Taylors Landlord and Tetleys, decent wines, log fires, low doorways, old settles and banquettes, and sparkling brasses; picnic-sets in garden *(Catherine Mason, John and Sheila Burley)*

CONEYTHORPE [SE3958]

Tiger [E of Knaresborough]: Immaculate pretty dining pub on green of charming village, comfortable seats, imaginative choice of good wholesome food from good lunchtime sandwiches and light dishes up, reasonable prices, prompt cheerful service and nice local atmosphere, well kept Marstons Pedigree *(Michael Doswell)*

CONONLEY [SD9846]

New Inn [Main St/Station Rd]: Good value food inc bargain mixed grill (worth booking for food), Timothy Taylors real ales *(Dudley and Moira Cockroft)*

COXWOLD [SE5377]

Fauconberg Arms [off A170 Thirsk—Helmsley]: Attractive old pub in delightful unchanging village, well kept John Smiths and Theakstons Best with a guest such as Black Sheep Special, log fire and pleasant atmosphere in attractively furnished lounge bar, back locals' bar with pub games and TV, bar food from pricy sandwiches to some successfully inventive dishes, no smoking restaurant (Weds-Sat evening and Sun lunch) with own comfortable pre-meal drinks area; dogs and children welcome, open all day in summer *(John Knighton, Norman Stansfield, John Hale, Marian and Andrew Ruston, Mrs Phoebe A Kemp, Ian and Rose Lock, Andrew and Samantha Grainger, LYM, June and Ken Brooks, Peter Walker, Ian and Nita Cooper)*

DALLOW [SE2172]

Drovers [Galphay Moor, Kirkby Malzeard—Pateley Bridge road]: Small and unpretentious single bar with pleasant landlord, reasonably priced generous simple food, well kept Black Sheep, Hambleton and Old Mill – welcome oasis on edge of lonely moorland, good walking; cl Mon lunchtime and all winter wkdys *(Jim Abbott, Janet and Peter Race)*

DANBY [NZ7008]

☆ *Duke of Wellington* [West Lane]: Roomy and popular, with wide choice of good value home-made food inc beautifully cooked veg and praiseworthy puddings, friendly efficient service, well kept ales such as Caledonian Deuchars IPA and Camerons Strongarm, decent wines, good coffee; comfortable bedrooms *(Carolyn Dixon)*

DEWSBURY [SE2523]

Huntsman [Walker Cottages, Chidswell Lane, Shaw Cross – pub signed]: Cosy converted cottages alongside urban-fringe farm, low beams, lots of brasses and agricultural bric-a-brac, friendly locals, wide choice of well kept beers inc Black Sheep and John Smiths, roaring fire, small no smoking front extension; no food evening or Sun/Mon lunchtime, busy evenings *(Michael Butler)*

Leggers [Robinsons Boat Yard, Savile Town Wharf, Mill St E (SE of B6409)]: Friendly if basic wharfside hayloft conversion, low-beamed upstairs bar with two egyptian beers brewed downstairs, and up to four guest beers inc Roosters, snacks and sandwiches or filled rolls all day, real fire, helpful staff, daily papers, lots of old brewery and pub memorabilia; open all day *(JP, PP, the Didler)*

☆ *West Riding Licensed Refreshment Rooms* [Station, Wellington Rd]: Busy three-room early Victorian station bar on southbound platform, well kept changing ales from small breweries, farm ciders, good value interesting wkdy lunchtime food, pie night Tues, curry night Weds, daily papers, friendly staff, coal fire, no smoking area till 6, lots of steam memorabilia inc paintings by local artists; juke box may be loud, jazz nights; disabled access, open all day *(JP, PP, the Didler, Richard Lewis, Joe Green)*

DONCASTER [SE5703]

Corner Pin [St Sepulchre Gate W, Cleveland St]: Well kept beers John Smiths, Charles Wells Bombardier and two interesting changing guest beers, plushly refurbished beamed lounge with old local pub prints, welsh dresser and china, good value traditional food from fine hot sandwiches to cheap Sun roast, friendly landlady, cheery bar with darts, games machine and TV; open all day *(Richard Lewis, the Didler, Patrick Hancock)*

Leopard [West St]: Lively and friendly, with superb tiled façade, well kept John Smiths, one or two local Glentworth beers and an occasional guest, cheap basic lunchtime food; lounge with lots of bric-a-brac, children's games and nostalgic juke box, basic bar area with pool, darts, TV and machine; open all day, disabled access, good live music upstairs, Thurs comedy club; can get very busy, close to railway station *(the Didler, Richard Lewis, Patrick Hancock, Peter F Marshall)*

Plough [W Laith Gate, by Frenchgate shopping centre]: Old-fashioned small local with well kept real ales, old town maps, friendly staff, bustling front room with darts, dominoes and sports TV, quieter back lounge, tiny garden, open all day Tues, Fri, Sat *(Patrick Hancock, the Didler)*

Salutation [South Parade, towards race course]: Bustling divided open-plan alehouse-theme bar with plenty of beams, stone floor and bare boards, several well kept changing ales inc rarities, low-priced food all day, friendly staff; side games area, big-screen sports TV at back, quiet juke box, Tues quiz night; tables on back terrace, open all day *(Richard Lewis, Patrick Hancock, Joe Green)*

DORE [SK3081]

Dore Moor Inn [A625 Sheffield—Castleton]: Busy extended Vintage Inn just outside Sheffield on edge of Peak Park, highly restored for family dining with lots of stripped pine, hard-working helpful staff, superb central log fires and nice flower arrangements, good value ample food, fine choice of wines by the glass, good coffee with refills *(DC, Kathy and Chris Armes)*

DUNFORD BRIDGE [SE1502]

Stanhope Arms [off A628 Barnsley—Manchester]: Cheerful family pub by Trans-Pennine Trail below the moors around Winscar Reservoir, friendly attentive service, good value straightforward food (not Mon) from sandwiches to big Sun lunch, OAP wkdy lunches, afternoon teas summer Suns, well kept

Black Sheep, Timothy Taylors Landlord and Theakstons, pool room (with fruit machine); piped music can be a bit loud, occasional live music; sizeable garden with camping ground, bedrooms, open all day wknds, cl Mon lunchtime *(Charles Harvey, BB, Guy Vowles)*

EAST COWTON [NZ3003]
Beeswing: Good helpings of carefully cooked decent food inc some interesting dishes and good choice of enjoyable puddings, a real ale such as Charles Wells Bombardier; pretty village *(Richard Cole)*

EASTBY [SE0154]
Masons Arms [Barden Rd; back road off A59 between Bolton Bridge and Skipton]: Unpretentious local in pretty village setting among pastures, friendly licensees, good reasonably priced food inc nice puddings, well kept Websters and Charles Wells Bombardier, lots of flowers, no smoking restaurant, lounge, and tap room with four very popular EC-funded computer terminals for community and customer use; back terrace and two bedrooms with nice views *(Rona Murdoch)*

EGTON [NZ8006]
Wheatsheaf: Popular village pub of real character, interesting paintings and prints in simple main bar, enjoyable food inc good Sun lunch, charming family service, new restaurant; bedrooms pretty *(Gloria Bax)*

ELLAND [SE1121]
☆ *Barge & Barrel* [quite handy for M62 junction 24; Park Rd (A6025, via A629 and B6114)]: Large welcoming pub pleasantly refurbished under new management, its own good Eastwood & Sanders ales (now brewed 1 mile away) and changing guest beers such as Timothy Taylors Landlord, pleasant staff, huge helpings of cheapish basic tasty lunchtime food (not Weds), family room (with air hockey); piped radio, live music some Suns; seats by industrial canal, limited parking, open all day *(the Didler, J R Ringrose, Pat and Tony Martin, JP, PP)*

ELSECAR [SE3800]
Milton Arms [Armroyd Lane]: Immaculate pub, comfortable and welcoming, with food cooked to order by landlady, Stones and Theakstons, brassware and toby jugs; front parlour, back lounge and separate dining room, indoor bowls; handy for Elsecar Heritage Centre and several walks *(Ian Phillips)*

EMBSAY [SE0053]
Cavendish Arms [Skipton Rd]: Pleasant pub next to steam railway station, with well cooked good value bar food from sandwiches up, efficient service, real ales inc Theakstons Best *(D W Stokes)*
☆ *Elm Tree* [Elm Tree Sq]: Popular well refurbished open-plan beamed village pub with settles and old-fashioned prints, log-effect gas fire, no smoking dining room, good honest hearty home-made food lunchtime and from 5.30 inc good-sized children's helpings, modest prices, friendly helpful service, well kept Goose Eye No-Eyed Deer and three or four changing guest beers, games area; busy wknds esp

evenings; comfortable good value bedrooms, handy for steam railway *(M S Catling, Ian and Nita Cooper, Margaret Dickinson)*

ESCRICK [SE6442]
Black Bull [E of A19 York—Selby]: Wide choice of good value food inc popular lunchtime and early supper bargains in bustling and neatly polished open-plan pub divided by arches and back-to-back fireplaces, flagstones one side, mix of wooden tables with benches, stools and chairs, small helpings for children and OAPs, good friendly service, well kept John Smiths, Tetleys and a guest such as Elgoods, back dining room *(Joyce and Maurice Cottrell, Roger A Bellingham)*

FEWSTON [SE2054]
Sun [Norwood; B6451 5 or 6 miles N of Otley]: Large 18th-c inn with enjoyable food (inc summer afternoon teas, and may have Fri/Sat evening barbecues), friendly staff, well kept ales inc Black Sheep and Theakstons, several rooms, open fires, games room; tables on balcony and in garden, play area, good walks *(Geoff and Angela Jaques, David Coleman)*

FINGHALL [SE1990]
Friars Head [Akebar, towards Hunton; off A684 E of Leyburn]: Nicely converted barn at entrance to holiday park, popular for enjoyable imaginative fresh blackboard food running up to wild boar, kangaroo and ostrich, attractive stonework and rafters, two dining areas off cosy bar, also charming plant-filled dining conservatory with water feature, looking over bowling green and pay-as-you-play golf; Black Sheep, John Smiths and Theakstons, good coffee, pleasant service, log fire; children welcome till 7.30 *(E D Fraser)*

FLOCKTON [SE2314]
Sun [off A642 Wakefield—Huddersfield at Blacksmiths Arms]: Friendly beamed pub with lots of brasses and open fires in bar and dining area, reasonably priced food (not Sun evening) from sandwiches to cheap Sun roast, three real ales, piano; piped pop music, games machine; children welcome, tables outside, open all day *(CMW, JJW)*

GIGGLESWICK [SD8164]
☆ *Black Horse* [Church St]: Quaint 17th-c village pub crammed between churchyard and pretty row of cottages, smart décor with lots of bric-a-brac and gleaming brasses, good reasonably priced food in bar or intimate dining room, well kept Tetleys, Timothy Taylors and a guest beer, friendly service, coal fire; three recently refurbished bedrooms *(Margaret Dickinson, R Crabtree)*

GLAISDALE [NZ7705]
Mitre: Good choice of guest beers, usually one at a time, short choice of enjoyable food (not Mon) inc Thurs fish and curry night, welcoming staff; tables outside with panoramic view of Esk Valley *(DC)*

GOLCAR [SE0815]
Golcar Lily [Slades Rd, Bolster Moor]: Attractive and unusual building (former Co-op and manager's house), small pastel-shades bar area with comfortable pink wall seats and

stools, swagged curtains, reliable and interesting food in bar and big no smoking restaurant leading off, several well kept ales inc Mansfield and Timothy Taylors, decent wines, pleasant atmosphere, fine valley views; Sun quiz night, luxurious lavatories upstairs; has been cl Mon-Thurs lunchtimes *(John Hillmer, Stuart Paulley)*

GRANGE MOOR [SE2215]
☆ *Kaye Arms* [A642 Huddersfield—Wakefield]: Very good family-run restauranty pub, civilised, friendly and busy, with imaginative proper food (they do sandwiches too), courteous efficient staff, exceptional value house wines, hundreds of malt whiskies, no smoking room; handy for Yorkshire Mining Museum; cl Mon lunchtime *(Michael Butler, Dr and Mrs S Donald, G Dobson, LYM)*

GRANTLEY [SE2369]
Grantley Arms [off B6265 W of Ripon]: Attractive beamed stone pub in quiet Dales village, welcoming coal fires, good food (all day Sun, not Tues lunchtime or Mon) running up to steaks, Black Sheep and John Smiths, music-free no smoking restaurant; children welcome if eating *(Tony and Wendy Hobden)*

GRASSINGTON [SE0064]
Black Horse [Garrs Lane]: Comfortable and cheerful open-plan pub, very popular in summer, with wide choice of enjoyable food from good sandwiches and snacks up inc children's, well kept Black Sheep Bitter and Special, Tetleys and Theakstons Best and Old Peculier, friendly service, modern furnishings, open fires, darts in back room, no smoking area and small attractive restaurant; sheltered terrace, bedrooms comfortable, well equipped and good value, open all day *(BB, the Didler, B and M Kendall, Jim Abbott, Gerry and Rosemary Dobson)*
☆ *Devonshire* [The Square]: Handsome small hotel with good window seats and tables outside overlooking sloping village square, good range of well presented generous food from sandwiches to good Sun lunch in big popular restaurant, interesting pictures and ornaments, beams and open fires, pleasant family room, cheerful chatty staff and nice mix of locals and visitors, well kept Black Sheep Best and Timothy Taylors Landlord, decent wines; comfortable bedrooms *(LYM, JAE, R Gibson, Jim Abbott)*
Foresters Arms [Main St]: Unpretentious old coaching inn with friendly staff, Black Sheep and two changing ales, good value bar food, pool, sports TV; reasonably priced bedrooms, open all day *(the Didler, JAE)*
Grassington House [The Square]: Hotel doing enjoyable varied bar food, well kept beers, decent wines; bedrooms *(JAE)*

GREAT AYTON [NZ5611]
☆ *Royal Oak* [off A173 – follow village signs; High Green]: Wide range of generous good food, well kept Courage Directors and Theakstons, prompt cheerful service, unpretentious convivial bar with good log fire, beam-and-plank ceiling, bulgy old partly panelled stone walls, traditional furnishings inc

antique settles, pleasant views of elegant village green from bay windows, long dining lounge (children welcome), separate appealingly old-fashioned restaurant; comfortable bedrooms *(LYM, Geoff and Angela Jaques, Peter Hacker)*

GREAT HABTON [SE7576]
☆ *Grapes*: Fine cooking by newish chef/landlord, fresh local fish, game and tender meat, delicious imaginative puddings, warm-hearted service, relaxing atmosphere, appealing olde-worlde dining room with interesting bric-a-brac; attractive country walks *(anon)*

GREAT HATFIELD [TA1842]
Woggarth [Station Rd]: Cosy local, friendly new licensees doing cheap simple food all day, well kept Tetleys, comfortably furnished lounge and restaurant, children's room; tables outside, country views, open all day *(Lorraine and Fred Gill)*

GREAT OUSEBURN [SE4562]
☆ *Crown* [off B6265 SE of Boroughbridge]: Cheerful country pub emphasising wide choice of good generous elegantly presented food (all afternoon Sat/Sun) from baguettes to some interesting dishes and big steaks, restaurant quality at sensible prices, early evening bargains, well kept Black Sheep, John Smiths, Theakstons and a local guest beer, good friendly service, lots of Edwardian pictures and assorted bric-a-brac, largely no smoking eating areas; may be piped music; well behaved children welcome, tables in garden with sunny terrace and play area, cl wkdy lunchtimes, open all day wknds and bank hols *(Su and Bob Child, Alison Crooks, Dave Heffernan, LYM, Mr and Mrs C Cameron, Alison Hayes, Pete Hanlon, Mrs A Fletcher)*

GREEN HAMERTON [SE4656]
☆ *Bay Horse* [just off A59 York—Harrogate]: Relaxed village pub with plenty of snug areas and a parrot called Oscar, decent bar food, two dining rooms (one no smoking), Daleside Bitter and Tetleys, good choice of wines, nice big pots of tea, generous food (all day Sun) from sandwiches to steak; children in eating areas, tables in garden, bedrooms in separate block behind, open all day Sun and summer Sats *(Angus Lyon, Michael Doswell, Geoffrey and Brenda Wilson, June and Ken Brooks, Michael Dandy, LYM)*

GREENHOW HILL [SE1164]
Miners Arms [B6265 Pateley Bridge—Grassington]: Good value generous restaurant food, well kept Black Sheep, decent wines, relaxed atmosphere, beams and brasses, woodburner; quiet piped music, anteroom with pool and darts; children welcome, bedrooms, has been cl Mon *(JAE, David)*

GRENOSIDE [SK3394]
Cow & Calf [3 miles from M1 junction 35; Skew Hill Lane]: Refurbished under new licensees, three connected rooms, one no smoking, high-backed settles, stripped stone and beams, reasonably priced lunchtime food, well kept low-priced Sam Smiths OB, tea and coffee; quiet piped music, music quiz nights; children welcome, family room in block across

walled former farmyard with picnic-sets, splendid views over Sheffield, disabled access *(CMW, JJW, LYM, Patrick Hancock)*

GRINTON [SE0598]

Bridge Inn [B6270 W of Richmond]: Unpretentious riverside inn in lovely spot opp Cathedral of the Dales, two well used bars (one with pool), friendly service, straightforward food inc good hot sandwiches and interesting sausage dishes, Jennings ales inc Dark Mild, pleasant restaurant area; children and dogs welcome, attractive tables outside, front and back, bedrooms with own bathrooms; open all day, good walks *(Denise Dowd, E D Fraser, Mr and Mrs Maurice Thompson)*

HACKFORTH [SE2493]

Greyhound: Comfortably refurbished bar and separate dining room *(R J Herd)*

HALIFAX [SE0924]

☆ *Shears* [Paris Gates, Boys Lane; OS Sheet 104 map ref 097241]: Down steep cobbled lanes among tall mill buildings, roomy locals' bar with bays of plush banquettes and plenty of standing space, well kept Timothy Taylors Best, Golden Best, Landlord and Ram Tam and a guest beer, expert landlord (not Tues); very popular for good cheap generous lunchtime food from hot-filled sandwiches to home-made pies, curries, casseroles etc; local sports photographs, big-screen sports TV; seats out above the Hebble Brook *(the Didler, Alan J Morton, J R Ringrose, BB, Tony Hobden)*

Three Pigeons [Sun Fold, South Parade; off Church St]: Welcoming and busy stone-built pub with well kept Black Sheep, Timothy Taylors Best and Landlord and three or four changing more or less local ales, inexpensive popular wkdy lunchtime food from wide range of hot and cold sandwiches up, curry nights, several rooms off bar with interesting ceiling painting, log fire; tables outside, handy for Eureka! Museum, open all day *(Martin Grosberg, Andy and Jill Kassube, J R Ringrose)*

HARDROW [SD8691]

Green Dragon: Promising food under new regime in traditional recently renovated Dales pub, well kept real ales Timothy Taylors Landlord, quick friendly service, big main bar, beamed snug with big coal fire in old iron range; gives access (for a small fee) to Britain's highest single-drop waterfall; children welcome, bedrooms *(LYM, Jane Taylor, David Dutton, Andrew Stephenson)*

HARMBY [SE1289]

Pheasant [A684 about 1½ miles E of Leyburn]: Small comfortable cheery local, well kept Black Sheep and Theakstons, bar with racing photographs, lounge *(Jim Abbott)*

HARROGATE [SE3155]

Coach & Horses [West Park]: Welcoming pub with well kept Black Sheep, Daleside Blonde and Tiger and Tetleys, reasonably priced bar food *(J Roy Smylie)*

Gardeners Arms [Bilton Lane (off A59 either in Bilton itself or on outskirts towards Harrogate)]: Small 16th-c stone-built house converted into good old-fashioned local, totally

unspoilt with tiny bar and three small rooms, tiled floors, panelling, old prints and little else; very cheap well kept Sam Smiths OB, coal fire; tables in nice streamside garden, lovely peaceful setting *(the Didler)*

Old Bell [Royal Parade]: Relaxing pub favoured by Bill Clinton, with eight well kept ales and continental beers from handsome bar counter, friendly staff, enjoyable food, upstairs no smoking evening restaurant; no children, music or machines, open all day *(Dr and Mrs A K Clarke, Mr and Mrs P Eastwood)*

HARTSHEAD [SE1822]

☆ *Gray Ox* [not very far from M62 junction 25]: Popular stone-built moorland dining pub, great views, beams, flagstones and latticed windows, comfortable carpeted areas off inc no smoking room, relaxed country atmosphere, good choice of generous tasty food from good sandwiches to upmarket main dishes and very popular Sun lunch (all afternoon), well kept Black Sheep, Timothy Taylors Landlord, Tetleys and Theakstons, long wine list, helpful attentive staff; open all day Sun, picnic-sets outside *(Pat and Tony Martin, Michael Butler, Geoffrey and Brenda Wilson, BB)*

HAWES [SD8789]

Crown [Market Pl]: Traditional market town local, lively and welcoming, with good range of good value quickly served substantial bar food, well kept Theakstons Best, XB and Old Peculier, quick service, coal fire each end; walkers welcome, children allowed away from bar, seats out on cobbled front forecourt *(W A Evershed)*

Fountain [Market Pl]: Bright and friendly open bar and lounge, quick helpful staff, well kept ales such as Black Sheep and Boddingtons, good value simple food, lots of posters from local operatic society's past productions; may be piped radio; bedrooms *(K M Crook)*

HAWORTH [SE0336]

☆ *Haworth Old Hall* [Sun St]: Friendly open-plan 17th-c beamed and panelled building with valley views, three eating areas off long bar, log fire, stripped stonework, appropriately plain furnishings, up to five well kept Jennings ales, quick service by well trained cheerful staff, generous food from baguettes up in bar and restaurant; piped music; plenty of tables out in front, open all day, bedrooms *(John Foord, Matt Waite)*

HEBDEN [SE0263]

Clarendon: Simple neatly kept country inn notable for consistently good changing food (not Mon) in bar and restaurant using quality local ingredients, well kept Timothy Taylors Best and Tetleys, good well described wines, friendly local licensees and good service, darts; three bedrooms with own bathrooms, close to good walks *(JAE, Greta and Christopher Wells)*

HEBDEN BRIDGE [SE0027]

Hare & Hounds [Billy Lane/Lands End Lane, Wadsworth – above E end of town]: Hospitable new licensees doing enjoyable generous pub food inc Sun roasts, well kept Timothy Taylors Landlord, Best, Golden Best and a seasonal beer, roaring fire in comfortable lounge, playful boxer called George, warmly welcoming atmosphere; well behaved children welcome, tables on terrace with lovely views, plenty of good walks (not to mention the walk up from the town), good bedrooms *(Bruce Bird, MJVK)*

White Lion [Bridge Gate]: Solid stone-built inn with hospitable landlord, comfortable bar and country-furnished bare-boards dining lounge, good choice of sound reasonably priced home cooking all day, fish specialities, well kept Boddingtons, Timothy Taylors Landlord and a guest such as Cottage, pleasant service; attractive secluded riverside garden, comfortable bedrooms *(Derek and Sylvia Stephenson, MJVK)*

HEDON [TA1928]

Shakespeare [Baxtergate, off A1033]: Popular and cheerful village local with open fire in small well worn in L-shaped bar, well kept Tetleys, Theakstons, Worthington and guest beers, decent wines and whiskies, good value generous food from sandwiches up lunchtime and early evening, thousands of beermats on beams, old framed brewery advertisements; darts, games machines, small TV; bedrooms *(Paul and Ursula Randall)*

HELMSLEY [SE6184]

Royal Oak [Market Pl]: Two attractively refurbished and comfortable Victorian rooms, interesting curios, well kept Camerons Strongarm and Marstons Pedigree, good value simple substantial food from sandwiches to Sun lunch, different evening menu, welcoming landlord, quick service even though busy; pool, piped music (may be loud), TV; picnic-sets outside, open all day, good bedrooms, big breakfast *(Andrew Scarr, Pat and Tony Martin, Michael Dandy, Richard Jennings, Michael Butler)*

HEMINGFIELD [SE3901]

Elephant & Castle [not far from M1 junction 36; Tingle Bridge Lane]: Friendly 17th-c waterside stone-built village local with lovely hanging baskets, well kept Eastwood & Sanders and other ales, enjoyable food freshly made so may take a while, small helpings for children, large bar with piano, jugs on beams and delft shelf of teapots, step up to no smoking dining area; piped pop music, games machine; children welcome, benches around small fountain in front, picnic-sets and swing on grass by car park (which has CCTV), nearby walks *(CMW, JJW, Derek and Sylvia Stephenson)*

HEPWORTH [SE1606]

Butchers Arms [off A616 SE of Holmfirth; Towngate]: Friendly L-shaped bar, dark beams, partly panelled stone walls, pine tables on light wood floor, large log fire in dining room, good value food inc popular lunchtime buffet and Sun roasts, well kept Marstons Pedigree, Theakstons XB and Timothy Taylors Landlord, cheerful landlord and good courteous service; pictures for sale, pool and darts one end, dogs welcome; open all day Fri/Sat, good animal sculpture nearby *(Arnold Brill, Carmen Cheetham)*

HOLME [SE1005]

☆ *Fleece* [A6024 SW of Holmfirth]: Cosy pleasant L-shaped bar, lots of lifeboat memorabilia, well kept Theakstons and a guest beer, good coffee, popular fresh pub food inc OAP bargains, warmly welcoming jovial landlord, great staff, real fire; conservatory with nice flowers, pool/darts room, quiet piped music; attractive village setting just off Pennine Way below Holme Moss TV mast, great walks (they have plenty of leaflets) *(Guy Vowles, Norman Revell)*

HOLMFIRTH [SD1108]

Ford [A635 towards Manchester]: New licensees doing enjoyable bar food, and expanding into bistro food in a separate room *(Christine and Neil Townend)*

Huntsman [Greenfield Rd, 1 mile out]: Well run and welcoming country local, well kept Black Sheep, Tetleys and a guest such as Adnams, good value bar food and restaurant *(Ann and Bob Westbrook)*

Rose & Crown [aka The Nook; Victoria Sq]: Friendly family-run pub with tiled floor and low beams, several rooms, half a dozen well kept ales such as Moorhouses Black Cat Mild, Sam Smiths OB and Timothy Taylors Landlord; open all day *(the Didler, Patrick Hancock, Julian Heath, JP, PP)*

HORBURY [SE3018]

Boons [Queen St]: Lively, chatty and comfortably unpretentious, with well kept local Clarks, John Smiths and two or three quickly changing guest beers, simple lunchtime food, some flagstones, bare walls, rugby league memorabilia, back tap room with pool; very popular, can get crowded; no children, tables out in courtyard *(Michael Butler)*

Bulls Head [Southfield Lane]: Large, but well divided into more intimate areas, lots of panelling and wood floors, library room, no smoking snug, popular food in bar and restaurant (busy wknds), Black Sheep and John Smiths, lots of wines by the glass; big car park *(Michael Butler)*

HORSEHOUSE [SE0481]

Thwaite Arms [Coverdale rd Middleham—Kettlewell]: Early 19th-c former farm building in wonderful village setting nr beautiful little church, lots of paths to nearby villages and moors, great drive along dale; good simple food inc fine Sun roast (only a few tables in pretty homely dining room, so worth booking), well kept John Smiths and Theakstons, farm cider, charming friendly landlord, chatty local farmers evening, good coal fire in cosy snug, bigger plainer locals' bar; children welcome, two bedrooms *(Mr and Mrs Maurice Thompson)*

HORTON IN RIBBLESDALE [SD8172]

☆ *Crown* [B6479 N of Settle]: Very well placed for walkers (Pennine Way goes through car park, short walk from Settle—Carlisle line station), small low-ceilinged locals' bar and larger lounge both with dark woodwork, lots of brass and good fires, good value home cooking, well kept Theakstons XB and Old Peculier, welcoming helpful staff, restaurant; good value bedrooms now most with own bathrooms *(R L Johnson, Guy Vowles, John Hulme)*

HUDDERSFIELD [SE1217]

Cherry Tree [John William St]: Well kept Wetherspoons, some alloy seating giving a wine bar appearance, decent food and drink, no smoking area *(Tony Hobden)*

Head of Steam [Station, St Georges Sq]: Railway memorabilia, model trains, cars, buses and planes for sale (and watch the real trains pass, from platform tables), pies, sandwiches, baked potatoes and good value Sun roasts, four rooms inc no smoking eating area, hot coal fire, long bar with well kept changing ales such as Barnsley, Holts, Hop Back Summer Lightning and Tetleys, lots of bottled beers, farm ciders, Gales fruit wines; tables out on platform, jazz nights, can be very busy (bouncers sometimes), open all day *(David Carr, JP, PP, J R Ringrose, Andy and Jill Kassube, Tony Hobden, Richard Lewis, Christine and Neil Townend)*

Royal & Ancient [Colne Bridge; B6118 just off A62 NE]: Large roadside pub with emphasis on good value food, Theakstons ales, log fires, golfing theme bar with extended dining area, popular restaurant; 200 yds from Huddersfield Broad Canal *(Tony Hobden)*

Star [Albert St, Lockwood]: Well kept Eastwood & Sanders, Timothy Taylors and several changing beers inc a Mild, continental beers, farm cider, occasional well organised beer festivals, no juke box, pool or machines – or food (may be pie and peas); growing bric-a-brac collection, customers' paintings; cl Mon, and lunchtime Tues-Thurs *(J R Ringrose)*

HUGGATE [SE8855]

☆ *Wolds Inn* [Driffield Rd]: 16th-c pub cheerfully blending locals' bar and games room with civilised and comfortable panelled lounge and dining room, wide range of good generous food (meats especially well chosen), friendly family service, well kept Greene King Old Speckled Hen, Timothy Taylors Landlord and Tetleys, pool and darts; benches out in front and pleasant garden behind with delightful views; cl lunchtime Mon-Thurs, bedrooms compact but clean and nicely appointed – lovely village, good easy walks, handy for Wolds Way *(Paul and Ursula Randall, C A Hall)*

HULL [TA0927]

Bay Horse [Wincolmlee]: Popular unassuming corner local, Batemans' only tied pub here, their beers kept well, good value basic food, pleasant licensees, open fire, unsmoky lounge, rugby connections; open all day *(JP, PP, Lorraine and Fred Gill, the Didler)*

Olde Black Boy [High St, Old Town]: Little black-panelled low-ceilinged front smoke room, lofty 18th-c back vaults bar with leather seating, interesting Wilberforce-related posters etc, good value food lunchtime (not Sun) and late afternoon (not wknds), also Sun breakfast, friendly service, well kept real ales, country wines, old jugs and bottles, two rooms upstairs (one with pool); darts, piano (live music Thurs), games machine; children allowed, open all day *(BB, the Didler)*

Olde Blue Bell [alley off Lowgate; look out for huge blue bell over pavement]: Friendly traditional 17th-c local with well kept cheap Sam Smiths OB, good value simple lunchtime food, three rooms off corridor, remarkable collection of bells; open all day exc Sun afternoon *(the Didler, BB)*

Pave [Princes Avenue, nr Thoresby St]: Minimalist café-bar with well kept Theakstons and a guest beer such as Roosters, reasonably priced food from all-day breakfast to tapas, pleasant décor, well reproduced piped jazz *(Lorraine and Fred Gill)*

HUSTHWAITE [SE5275]

Roasted Pepper [Low St]: Former Blacksmiths Arms reopened after two-year closure, imaginatively redesigned as tapas and food bar with warm cream and brown décor and stylish dark square tables, welcoming service, up-to-date food, changing Scottish Courage real ales *(Janet and Peter Race)*

ILKLEY [SE1147]

Bar t'at [Cunliffe Rd]: Six real ales, decent wines and good helpings of good value brasserie food lunchtime and (not Tues or Sun) early evening, daily papers, cheerful efficient staff, spiral stairs down to light and airy no smoking bar; tables on back terrace *(Ian and Nita Cooper, David Coleman)*

Cow & Calf [Hangingstone Rd (moors rd towards Hawksworth)]: Vintage Inn with their usual reliable food, olde-worlde décor and fine choice of wines by the glass, lovely views over Ilkley and Wharfedale; good bedrooms *(R M and M J Smith, Geoffrey and Brenda Wilson)*

INGBIRCHWORTH [SE2106]

☆ *Fountain* [off A629 Shepley—Penistone; Welthorne Lane]: Emphasis on generous good value varied bar food inc exotic salads and superb puddings (lunch and very popular early evening bargains); well kept Black Sheep and John Smiths, friendly staff, neat and spacious red plush turkey-carpeted lounge, cosy front bar, comfortable family room, lots of beams, open fires; well reproduced piped music; tables in sizeable garden overlooking reservoir with pretty walks, comfortable bedrooms *(Patrick Hancock, BB, Michael Butler)*

KEIGHLEY [SE0641]

Boltmakers Arms [East Parade]: Split-level open-plan local with affable landlord, particularly well kept Timothy Taylors Landlord, Best, Golden Best and guest beers; enjoyable basic food, open all day, short walk from Worth Valley Railway *(the Didler, Peter F Marshall)*

Globe [Parkwood St]: Refurbished local by Worth Valley steam railway track, wkdy lunches, Timothy Taylors and Tetleys; open all day *(the Didler)*

Roebuck [Skipton Rd]: Doing well under new management, with competitively priced food and two guest beers *(Dudley and Moira Cockroft)*

KETTLEWELL [SD9672]

☆ *Bluebell* [Middle Lane]: Roomy knocked-through pub with snug simple furnishings, low beams and flagstones, cosy welcoming atmosphere, friendly landlord and regulars, well kept Greene King Ruddles County and Theakstons Old Peculier, food from sandwiches up in bar and attractive restaurant; pool room, piped music, children's room, tables on good-sized back terrace; well placed for Upper Wharfedale walks, decent bedrooms *(Maggie and Tony Harwood, Greta and Christopher Wells, D W Stokes, LYM)*

Kings Head: Lively and cheerful old character local away from centre, flagstones and log fire in big inglenook, well kept ales such as Black Sheep and Theakstons, good value food, welcoming landlady, pool room; bedrooms *(BB, Dr and Mrs D Woods)*

☆ *Racehorses* [B6160 N of Skipton]: Friendly newish licensees in comfortable and civilised pub with generous good value food inc lunchtime rolls and baguettes and local game, well kept Black Sheep Best and Special, Timothy Taylors Landlord and Theakstons Old Peculier, good choice of wines, log fires; dogs welcome in front bar, tables on attractive terrace, well placed for Wharfedale walks, good bedrooms with own bathrooms *(BB, D H Ford, DAV, Maggie and Tony Harwood, Lynda and Trevor Smith)*

KILBURN [SE5179]

☆ *Forresters Arms* [between A170 and A19 SW of Thirsk]: Next to Thompson furniture workshops (visitor centre opp) in pleasant village, handsomely furnished by them; big log fire, good home cooking, friendly staff, well kept real ales, side eating area, bar with TV and pool room, restaurant; well behaved children welcome, suntrap seats out in front, good value bedrooms, cheerful and bright, open all day *(LYM, Sue Wheeler)*

KILHAM [TA0664]

Star [Church St]: Quaint old pub in pretty village, warm fires in three of the four small rooms, welcoming landlord and staff, well kept John Smiths, Theakstons and a guest beer, decent fairly priced food (not Sun evening) in bar and popular flagstoned barn restaurant, darts, dominoes *(Barrie Meech, Kevin Blake)*

KILNSEA [TA4015]

Crown & Anchor [Kilnsea Rd]: Great remote location overlooking eroding Spurn Point nature reserve and Humber estuary, with picnic-sets in back garden and out in front; single bar opening into two beamed lounges and linen-set restaurant, prints and bric-a-brac, friendly staff, well kept Tetleys, above-average reasonably priced pub food inc good fresh fish; piped music; four bedrooms with own bathrooms, open all day *(A and B D Craig, Marlene and Jim Godfrey, Susan and Les Hornby, Paul and Ursula Randall)*

KILNSEY [SD9767]

☆ *Tennants Arms*: Beautiful setting in good Wharfedale walking area, views of spectacular overhanging crag from restaurant, good range of good food, well kept Black Sheep, Tetleys and Theakstons Best and Old Peculier, open fires, friendly staff, several rooms, interesting decorations; piped music; comfortable immaculate bedrooms all with private

bathrooms, good value *(JAE, David Findel-Hawkins)*

KIRKBYMOORSIDE [SE6986]

Kings Head [High Market Pl]: 16th-c inn with unpretentious flagstoned walkers' bar (boots allowed), cosy lounge opening into sheltered courtyard and attractive garden, good log fire, well priced food all home-made inc local fish, game and meat, interesting vegetarian menu, friendly service, well kept beer; children welcome, bedrooms *(Sarah Davis, Rod Lambert)*

KNARESBOROUGH [SE3557]

☆ *Blind Jacks* [Market Pl]: Former 18th-c shop now a charming multi-floor traditional tavern, with simple but attractive furnishings, brewery posters etc, well kept changing ales inc Black Sheep, Hambleton and Timothy Taylors, farm cider and foreign bottled beers, bubbly atmosphere downstairs, quieter up; well behaved children allowed away from bar, open all day from noon, cl Mon till 5.30 *(LYM, the Didler, P Abbott)*

KNOTTINGLEY [SE5023]

Winston [Womersley Rd]: Enjoyable sensibly priced food, well kept beers *(Steve Frost)*

LEEDS [SE3033]

Adelphi [Hunslet Rd]: Well restored handsome Edwardian mahogany screens, tiling and cut and etched glass, several rooms, impressive stairway; particularly well kept Tetleys Bitter, Mild and Imperial (virtually the brewery tap), prompt friendly service, good spread of lunchtime cheap food from hot baguettes up, crowded but convivial then; live jazz Sat *(the Didler, Ian Phillips)*

Duck & Drake [Kirkgate, between indoor market and Parish Church]: Two-bar pub with a dozen or more well kept reasonably priced ales inc plenty of Yorkshire ones, farm ciders, basic furniture and beer posters and mirrors; simple substantial low-priced lunchtime food from sandwiches to Sun lunches, friendly staff, games room with hot coal fire and Yorkshire doubles dartboard as well as pool etc; juke box, big-screen sports TV, quiz nights, jazz nights Mon and Thurs; open all day *(the Didler, Pete Baker, Richard Lewis, Patrick Hancock)*

Garden Gate [Whitfield Pl, Hunslet]: Ornate but thoroughly down-to-earth Victorian pub with various rooms off central drinking corridor, intricate glass and woodwork, well kept Tetleys Bitter and Mild, farm cider, no food; open all day, can be boisterous evenings *(BB, the Didler)*

Grove [Back Row, Holbeck]: Well preserved 1930s-feel local, four rooms off drinking corridor, good changing beer range; live music nights; open all day *(the Didler)*

Hogshead [Gt George St, opp Infirmary]: Spacious open-plan pub, minimalist bare-boards décor, some upstairs seating, well kept Black Sheep, Caledonian Deuchars IPA and Timothy Taylors Landlord, pub food from sandwiches up, daily papers, pool room; piped music, open all day *(Ian Phillips, Richard Lewis)*

Horse & Trumpet [The Headrow]: Late Victorian, with period features inc fine façade and separate rooms (superb snug, lovely stained-glass ceiling, comfortable back parlour), lunchtime food, Tetleys and several changing beers often from far afield such as Badger K&B, Harviestoun Ptarmigan, Shepherd Neame Early Bird, Skinners Cornish Blonde, Tetleys and Wye Valley, busy friendly staff, lots of music hall playbills; open all day *(Ian Phillips, Richard Lewis)*

Lloyds No 1 [Gt George St]: One of a Wetherspoons sub-chain, different from their usual pubs – light and airy, with modern mirrors, loud well reproduced piped music and a younger feel; main area below street level, upper gallery bar on three sides, good menu with meal deals, well kept changing beers such as Hydes Autumn Goldings and Springhead; open all day *(Ian Phillips, Richard Lewis)*

Viaduct [Lower Briggate]: Peaceful pub which actively caters for disabled customers; pleasantly furnished long narrow bar, lots of wood, well kept Tetleys-related and guest ales esp Milds, popular lunchtime food, friendly helpful staff, no smoking area; attractive back garden, open all day exc Sun afternoon *(the Didler)*

☆ *Victoria* [Gt George St, just behind Town Hall]: Ornate bustling early Victorian pub with grand cut and etched mirrors, impressive globe lamps extending from the majestic bar, imposing carved beams, booths with working snob-screens, smaller rooms off; well kept Tetleys Best and Mild and three or four good changing guest beers, friendly efficient service by smart bar staff, reasonably priced food all day from sandwiches and light dishes up in luncheon room with end serving hatch, no smoking room; open all day *(Ian Phillips, the Didler, Matthew Hinkins)*

LELLEY [TA2032]
Stags Head [Main St; NE of Preston]: Emphasis on enjoyable enterprising food in lounge bar and restaurant inc popular Sun lunch (food all day then), friendly cheerful family service, well kept Tetleys, decent reasonably priced wines; children welcome, tables outside *(Paul and Ursula Randall)*

LINTON IN CRAVEN [SD9962]
Fountaine [just off B6265 Skipton—Grassington]: Well kept Black Sheep, Timothy Taylors Landlord and Theakstons, good choice of fairly priced food all day from sandwiches up inc interesting light dishes and thoughtful children's ones (same menu throughout pub), welcoming service, character bar with tiny snug, darts and dominoes, smartly organised extended back dining area; charming spot among ancient buildings on neat green running down to little stream, eye-catching hanging baskets, open all day *(Gill Honeyman, S and N McLean, Mr and Mrs Staples, Lynda and Trevor Smith, LYM, Michael Doswell, Jim Abbott)*

LOFTHOUSE [SE1073]
Crown [the one in Nidderdale]: Simple bar food and well kept Black Sheep Bitter and

Special, Daleside and Worthington in small public bar; bedrooms, outside gents' *(Jim Abbott)*

LONG PRESTON [SD8358]
☆ *Maypole* [A65 Settle—Skipton]: Friendly helpful service in two-room pub with sporting prints and plates and stags' heads, solid traditional furnishings, log fires; good choice of good value generous food inc home-made pies, popular Sun lunch and good fresh veg, well kept ales such as Castle Eden, Moorhouses Premier, Timothy Taylors Landlord and Tetleys, good coffee, piano, darts, video game, separate country dining room; good value bedrooms with own bathrooms, good breakfast *(Brian and Janet Ainscough, Andy and Jill Kassube, BB, JAE)*

LOW ROW [SD9898]
Punch Bowl [B6270 Reeth—Muker]: Plain cheery family bar and games area, well kept Theakstons Best, XB and Old Peculier and a guest such as Castle Eden, rows of malt whiskies, decent house wines, wide choice of good value generous food inc enormous cheap baguettes, log fire, two spaniels; piped music; great views of Swaledale from terrace with quoits pitches below; popular tearoom 10-5.30 with home-made cakes, small shop, bicycle and cave lamp hire, folk music Fri; open all day in summer, good simple bedrooms sharing bathrooms, also bunkhouse, big breakfasts *(CMW, JJW)*

LOWER BENTHAM [SD6469]
Punch Bowl [B6480 W of Clapham]: Attractive, welcoming and enjoyable village pub overlooking River Wenning, well kept real ales, good home cooking inc splendid Sun roasts, well kept real ale, personality landlady, open fire, separate dining room and pool room; bedrooms, fishing rights *(Karen Eliot)*

MALHAM [SD9062]
Buck [off A65 NW of Skipton]: Big pub suiting walkers, thriving atmosphere, wide range of quickly served enjoyable generous home-made food from reasonably priced sandwiches up, well kept Black Sheep, Tetleys, Theakstons Best and a guest beer, good value wines, good service, big log fire in plush lounge, roomy basic hikers' bar, separate candlelit dining room, picnic-sets in small garden; attractive building in picture-book village, decent well equipped bedrooms, many good walks from the door *(DAV, Guy Vowles)*

MALTON [SE7871]
Crown [Wheelgate]: In same family for generations, chatty basic town bar with strong horse-racing links (and racing TV on bar), good Malton Crown Double Chance (low price), Golden Chance and a seasonal beer from their back brewhouse, well kept guest beers, popular food (not Sun, sandwiches only Tues, bookings only evenings); lots of local notices, beer festivals Jun and Dec; children welcome in back courtyard nicely redone as conservatory, good value bedrooms *(Patrick Hancock, BB, Mr and Mrs Maurice Thompson, Steve Morris)*

Kings Head [Market Pl]: Ivy-covered pub

reworked in stripped pine and deep blues giving a café-bar feel, limited edition prints for sale, wide choice of good bar food, well kept real ale inc Malton Double Chance from the Crown *(Mark Percy, Lesley Mayoh)*

Wentworth Arms [Town St, Old Malton]: Enjoyable food from well filled baguettes up in bar and big dining room, sensible helpings, well kept ales inc guests such as Daleside and Wold, decent wines, quick friendly service; children welcome *(Sue and Alan Addis, Pat and Tony Martin, Brian and Janet Ainscough)*

MARKET WEIGHTON [SE8741]

Londesborough Arms [High St]: Old-fashioned market-town inn, relaxed and civilised, with quiet bars, friendly efficient staff, interesting food in bars and bistro/restaurant, Black Sheep, decent wine; comfortable good value bedrooms *(LYM, Guy Charrison)*

MARSDEN [SE0411]

☆ *Riverhead* [Peel St, next to Co-op; just off A62 Huddersfield—Oldham]: Basic own-brew pub in converted grocer's, spiral stairs down to microbrewery producing good range of interesting beers named after local reservoirs (the higher the reservoir, the higher the strength) inc Mild, Stout and Porter, farm cider, thriving friendly atmosphere in big ground-floor bar with upstairs overflow, unobtrusive piped music, no food or machines; wheelchair access, cl wkdy lunchtimes, open from 4pm, all day wknds, nice stop after walk by canal or on the hills *(the Didler, Guy Vowles, Tony Hobden)*

Swan [Station Rd]: Well kept Thwaites Bitter and Mild in neat town pub with good bar food inc good value Sun lunches, dining room with waitress service *(Tony Hobden)*

Tunnel End [Reddisher Rd (off A62 via Peel St)]: Four big rooms (one no smoking) refurbished under new licensees and keeping quietly homely feel, large log fire in back room, food inc Sun roasts, real ales; overlooks Standedge Canal Tunnel End Countryside Centre *(Bill Sykes)*

MARTON CUM GRAFTON [SE4263]

☆ *Olde Punch Bowl* [signed off A1 3 miles N of A59]: Comfortable and attractive, with very wide choice of good food from imaginative sandwiches up, not cheap but enterprising, with even more ambitious evening menu, generous helpings, cheerful staff, well kept Black Sheep and Timothy Taylors Landlord, decent wines, roomy heavy-beamed open-plan bar, open fires, brasses, framed old advertisements and photographs, restaurant, no piped music; children welcome, good play area and picnic-sets in pleasant garden *(Comus and Sarah Elliott, Michael Doswell, LYM, John Knighton, F J Robinson)*

MASHAM [SE2381]

☆ *Black Sheep Brewery* [Crosshills]: Not exactly a pub, but well worth a visit; alongside the brewery (interesting tours), this sizeable interesting mill shed has a modern bistro-style café-bar with upper gallery, smart, welcoming and fun, serving good imaginative mediterranean-leaning food all day inc nice puddings, pleasant friendly staff, a sales area with some worthwhile beery tourist trinkets, and on the left the Baa'r with well kept Black Sheep Bitter, Special and Riggwelter and Yorkshire Square – and a good choice of wines; good family facilities inc play area; cl 5 Mon and late winter Sun evenings, can be very busy *(Susan and Nigel Wilson, Tim and Carolyn Lowes, Dr and Mrs Jackson, Steve Whalley, H Bramwell, Bernie Adams, Ian and Nita Cooper, Gerry and Rosemary Dobson)*

☆ *White Bear* [Wellgarth, Crosshills; signed off A6108 opp turn into town]: Appealing pub full of unusual bric-a-brac, plenty of atmosphere, bar food, well kept Black Sheep beers *(the Didler, Patrick Hancock, LYM)*

MEXBOROUGH [SK4799]

Concertina Band Club [Dolcliffe Rd]: Friendly pubby club welcoming visitors, brewing its own good changing ales, also well kept guest beers; large bar with stage and small games area with pool, other games and SkyTV; cl Sun lunchtime *(the Didler)*

MIDDLEHAM [SE1288]

☆ *Black Swan* [Market Pl]: 17th-c stone inn with high-backed settles built in by the heavy-beamed bar's big stone fireplace, racing memorabilia on stripped stone walls, well kept Black Sheep Bitter, John Smiths and Theakstons Best, Old Peculier and XB, wide choice of food from lunchtime sandwiches and baked potatoes to restaurant meals, family room with TV and children's videos; tables out in front and in sheltered back garden, newly refurbished bedrooms with own bathrooms, good walking country *(Greta and Christopher Wells, Angus Lyon, Michael Butler, Margaret and Roy Randle, LYM, Jim Abbott, Roger Bridgeman, K M Crook)*

MIDDLESMOOR [SE0874]

☆ *Crown* [top of Nidderdale road from Pateley Bridge]: Remote inn with beautiful view over stone-built hamlet high in upper Nidderdale, warmly welcoming new landlord, enjoyable food from well made sandwiches and hot filled rolls up, well kept Black Sheep and Theakstons, rich local atmosphere, blazing log fires in cosy spotless rooms, homely dining room, tables in small garden; good value simple bedrooms *(Geoff and Angela Jaques, M and N Watson, Di and Mike Gillam)*

MIDDLETON TYAS [NZ2205]

Shoulder of Mutton [just E of A1 Scotch Corner roundabout]: Friendly warren of small rooms and different-level nooks, dark woodwork, wide choice of enjoyable bar food inc good specials (best to book wknds – serves Sun evening too), well kept real ales, good value coffee, agreeable service *(D G Bayley, V Green, Richard Cole)*

MILL BANK [SE0321]

☆ *Millbank* [Mill Bank Rd, off A58 SW of Sowerby Bridge]: Good dining pub tucked away in the country, clean-cut minimalist modern décor with local touches (eg chapel chairs), small bar area with Timothy Taylors

Landlord, sensibly short dining room menu with interesting cooking successfully combining european and Yorkshire elements, as do the unusual bar snacks (eg suckling pig with cubes of black pudding and mustard mash), good local cheeses; piped music not overwhelming; small terrace with glorious valley views towards old textile mill *(Anne and Tim Locke)*

MUKER [SD9097]

☆ *Farmers Arms* [B6270 W of Reeth]: Unpretentious friendly local in beautiful valley village, well placed both for rewarding walks and interesting drives, warm open fire, decent straightforward food from lunchtime baps and toasties to steaks, Castle Eden Nimmo's XXXX, John Smiths and Theakstons Best and Old Peculier, darts and dominoes; basic gents'; children welcome, self-catering studio flat *(Ron and Mary Nicholson, Ian and Rose Lock, A H C Rainier, LYM, Keith Mould, Jane Taylor, David Dutton, Tony and Ann Bennett-Hughes, Bob Broadhurst)*

NABURN [SE5945]

Blacksmiths Arms [Main St]: Country pub with several linked rooms, pleasant nooks and corners, sizeable dining area, enjoyable straightforward food from sandwiches up, Mansfield and Marstons Bitter and Wicked Witch, fairly priced wines, log fire; TV and juke box in games room *(John and Sheila Burley, Michael Dandy)*

NEWTON-ON-OUSE [SE5160]

☆ *Dawnay Arms* [off A19 N of York]: Attractive comfortably worn-in 18th-c inn nr Beningbrough Hall, with lots of beamery, brass and copper, good log fire, decent bar food from sandwiches to some interesting hot dishes inc early-evening bargains and plenty for vegetarians, friendly and personal family service, well kept Greene King IPA, Old Speckled Hen and Tetleys, dozens of malt whiskies, no smoking river-view restaurant; piped music, no dogs; children in eating area, neat lawn running down to moorings on River Ouse, tables on terrace, play area *(John and Sheila Burley, Roger A Bellingham, Edward Leetham, LYM, E J and M W Corrin, Mr and Mrs J E C Tasker, Michael Dandy)*

NORTHALLERTON [SE3794]

Tithe Bar [Friarage St]: Four quickly changing well kept real ales, masses of continental bottled beers, friendly staff, traditional settle and armchairs in one area, two rooms with tables and chairs on bare boards; restaurant upstairs *(Tim and Carolyn Lowes)*

NORWOOD GREEN [SE1427]

☆ *Olde White Beare* [signed off A641 in Wyke, or off A58 Halifax—Leeds just W of Wyke]: Large 17th-c building well renovated and extended, with character tap room, larger split-level lounge, beams, brasses, good personal service, well kept Boddingtons, Timothy Taylors and Tetleys, limited but interesting choice of enjoyable food in handsome barn restaurant, also bar food, bargain early suppers and popular Sun lunch; tables outside front and back, barbecues *(Michael Butler, Anne and David Robinson)*

OAKWORTH [SE0138]

☆ *Grouse* [Harehills, Oldfield; 2 miles towards Colne]: Comfortable, interesting and spotless old pub in undisturbed hamlet, lots of bric-a-brac, gleaming copper and china, prints, cartoons and caricatures, dried flowers, attractively individual furnishings; locally very popular for well presented good home-made lunchtime bar food (not Mon) from soup and baguettes up, charming evening restaurant, well kept Timothy Taylors, good range of spirits, entertaining landlord, courteous service; fine surroundings and Pennine views *(Neville Kenyon, Andy and Jill Kassube, JAE)*

OGDEN [SE0630]

Moorlands [A629 Denholme—Halifax]: Wide choice of enjoyable food from sandwiches and baked potatoes up inc unusually large vegetarian choice, well kept Black Sheep, Timothy Taylors Landlord and a guest beer, reasonable wine range, quick friendly service, long room with central open fire, raised galleries each end – one comfortably seated for drinks and snacks, the other for more substantial food; another area leads off to further no smoking dining tables, and there's a billiards room; nicely done out with decorative beams and stonework, plates, copper and brass pans, photographs; may be quiet piped music, very busy wknds; disabled access *(Anne and David Robinson, Pat and Tony Martin)*

OLDSTEAD [SE5380]

Black Swan [Main St]: Unpretentious beamed and flagstoned pub in beautiful surroundings, pretty valley views from two big bay windows and picnic-sets outside; reasonably priced good standard food inc Weds steak night and Thurs curry night, well kept Theakstons, friendly landlord, restaurant up steps (level with car park); children welcome, bedrooms in modern back extension *(Sue Wheeler, BB)*

OSMOTHERLEY [SE4597]

Queen Catherine [West End]: Good family pub, welcoming atmosphere, roomy modern décor with old local prints, popular reasonably priced hearty food inc good Sun lunch with proper yorkshire puddings and fresh veg, Tetleys and a well kept guest beer such as Hambleton, fast friendly service; simple but comfortable bedrooms with own bathrooms, good breakfast *(Lorraine and Fred Gill, Debbie Bradley, Geoff and Angela Jaques)*

OSSETT [SE2719]

☆ *Brewers Pride* [Low Mill Rd/Healey Lane (long cul-de-sac by railway sidings, off B6128)]: Warmly friendly basic local brewing its own good beers, four well kept guest beers, cosy front room and bar both with open fires, brewery memorabilia, small games room, lunchtime food (not Sun) and pie or curry night Weds; quiz night Mon, popular folk/country & western night Thurs; open all day wknds, big back garden with local entertainment summer wknds, nr Calder & Hebble Canal *(JHBS, Michael Butler, Bernie Adams, JP, PP, the Didler)*

Red Lion [Dewsbury Rd]: Low-ceilinged stone-built pub with occasional beers brewed behind the pub, as well as Roosters, John Smiths and guest beers, generous food inc popular Sun lunch; open all day *(JP, PP)*

OTLEY [SE2045]

Rose & Crown [Bondgate]: Comfortable olde-worlde beamed stone-built pub, warm and welcoming, with cosy bar and small restaurant, well kept ales inc guests, interesting range of good value fresh generous home-made food (not Fri/Sat evenings) from baguettes up, good service; can be busy lunchtime *(D Hamilton)*

OULTON [SE3628]

Three Horseshoes [Leeds Rd]: Spacious old open-plan dining pub very popular for generous early-evening bargains, real ales such as John Smiths, friendly staff, brass plates and memorabilia; children welcome, lots of hanging baskets outside *(Michael Butler)*

OUTLANE [SE0615]

Lower Royal George [New Hey Rd, Scammonden (A640 towards Denshaw, about 2 miles SW of M62 junction 23)]: L-shaped bar, newly extended but still cosy, with lots of plates, pictures of local landmarks and local TV connections, old and foreign banknotes, red seats and carpets, floral wallpaper, wide choice of attractively priced food from expanded kitchen here or in small dining room, friendly waitresses, Everards Tiger or Charles Wells Bombardier and guest beers, decent range of wines and malt whiskies, good Christmas decorations *(J R Ringrose)*

Swan [just off A640 Huddersfield—Rochdale by M62 junction 23, handy for junction 24 too]: Comfortable open-plan pub doing well after refurbishment under new landlord, good honest home cooking inc hot and cold sandwiches and bargain specials (all afternoon on Sun), well kept Timothy Taylors with guests such as Black Sheep, Caledonian Deuchars IPA and Fullers London Pride, good service; unobtrusive piped music, pool table in side area *(J R Ringrose)*

OXENHOPE [SE0434]

Dog & Gun [Long Causeway; off B6141 towards Denholme]: Beautifully placed roomy moorland pub with beamery, copper, brasses and delft shelves of plates and jugs, big log fire each end, padded settles and stools, a couple of smaller rooms, good varied generous home cooking from sandwiches to lots of fish and Sun roasts in bar and attractive small bistro-style restaurant, full Timothy Taylors beer range kept well, warm welcome, nice views *(A Boss, Andrew and Samantha Grainger)*

PATELEY BRIDGE [SE1565]

Royal Oak [Bridgehouse Gate; B6265 just W]: Plenty of space, attentive new management, popular food, friendly atmosphere; useful spot at the foot of Greenhow Bank *(Janet and Peter Race)*

PATRINGTON [TA3122]

Hildyard Arms [Market Pl]: Cheerful and friendly old coaching inn, tastefully refurbished, with appealing pictures and china in main bar's pleasant dining area, wide range of reasonably priced food inc children's and Fri steak bargain for two, Badger Tanglefoot, Bass and Tetleys *(Alan Thwaite)*

PENISTONE [SE2402]

Cubley Hall [Mortimer Rd, out towards Stocksbridge]: Handsome and rather grand, in big garden with plenty of tables, good playground and distant views; panelling, elaborate plasterwork, mosaic tiling and plush furnishings, roomy conservatory, wide choice of bar food all day, well kept Greene King Abbot and Old Speckled Hen, Marstons Pedigree and Charles Wells Bombardier, decent wines, no smoking room; piped music, fruit machine, TV, often busy with wknd wedding receptions; children welcome, bedrooms with own bathrooms, open all day *(G Dobson, Mike Turner, Derek and Sylvia Stephenson, Graham Dobson, LYM, Charles Harvey)*

PONTEFRACT [SE4521]

Beastfair Vaults [Beastfair]: Spacious and friendly, with good staff, popular food at bargain prices, Stones *(Joe Green)*

POOL [SE2546]

Hunters [A658 towards Harrogate]: Split-level pub with up to eight well kept ales from all over, Saxon farm cider, helpful staff, food inc popular Sun lunch, balcony for warm weather, open fires for cold, pool, dominoes, table skittles; a popular young meeting place, no food evenings or Tues lunchtime; open all day *(Steve Kirby, Mr and Mrs Maurice Thompson, Richard Dixon)*

RAMSGILL [SE1171]

☆ *Yorke Arms* [Nidderdale]: Civilised small hotel, small bar with some heavy Jacobean furniture and log fires, good if pricy food from short interesting choice of light lunches to elegant evening meals (helpings not over-large) in smart no smoking restaurant, well kept Black Sheep Special and Theakstons Best, a fine wine list, good choice of spirits and fresh juices; piped music, cribbage and dominoes, no under-12s even in restaurant; good quiet moorland and reservoir walks *(John Burgess, Lynda and Trevor Smith, LYM, J Roy Smylie, Howard and Margaret Buchanan, Michael Doswell)*

REDMIRE [SE0491]

Bolton Arms [Traditional Yorkshire village pub with small neat bar and dining room, wide choice of good value food inc popular Sun lunch, well kept Black Sheep, John Smiths, Theakstons and a seasonal beer such as Robinsons Robin, friendly licensees, amusing cartoons in gents'; popular with walkers, handy for Bolton Castle *(Mr and Mrs Maurice Thompson, Jim Abbott)*

Kings Arms [Wensley—Askrigg back road]: Tucked away in attractive village, simple welcoming bar with wall seats around cast-iron tables, oak armchair, woodburner, decent bar food, no smoking restaurant, well kept Black Sheep, John Smiths, Theakstons and a guest beer, over 50 malt whiskies; pool, dominoes, cribbage, quoits; children welcome, seats in pretty garden with Wensleydale view, fishing nearby, handy for Castle Bolton *(K M Crook, LYM, Mr and Mrs Maurice Thompson)*

REETH [SE0499]

Buck: Comfortably modernised, with good

varied well priced food in bar and restaurant, sensible prices and good helpings, welcoming atmosphere, efficient, friendly and obliging service even when busy – it's very popular with hikers; bedrooms, good breakfast *(Revd J S B Crossley, Bill and Sheila McLardy)*

Kings Arms [Market Pl (B6270)]: Popular beamed dining pub by green, pine pews around walls, huge log fire in 18th-c stone inglenook, quieter room behind; good reasonably priced food inc adventurous dishes, well kept Black Sheep, full Theakstons range and a guest such as Skipton, friendly efficient service; children very welcome, caged parrot, may be piped music; tables outside, bedrooms *(Denise Dowd, Gill and Tony Morriss, Gerry and Rosemary Dobson)*

RIBBLEHEAD [SD7880]

Station Hotel [B6255 Ingleton—Hawes]: Terrific spot alone on the moors by Ribblehead Viaduct – watch Settle—Carlisle train coming in one window, then going in the other: basic pub furnishings, central pool table, darts, video game and juke box, kind licensees, good log fire in woodburner, well kept Black Sheep and Theakstons XB and Old Peculier (take-aways too), low-priced wine, huge helpings of food from sandwiches to steaks, dining room with viaduct mural (the bar has relevant photographs, some you can buy); open all day in season, some picnic-sets outside, good value simple bedrooms and next-door bunkhouse, good wholesome breakfast *(BB, JHBS)*

RICHMOND [NZ1600]

Buck [Newbiggin]: Welcoming and pleasantly refurbished, Black Sheep – afternoon discount *(Joe Green)*

Holly Hill Inn [Holly Hill]: Friendly pub overlooking castle and River Swale, comfortable lounge, games on upper level, Black Sheep and Timothy Taylors Landlord, bar meals and restaurant *(Mr and Mrs Maurice Thompson)*

RIPON [SE3171]

One-Eyed Rat [Allhallowgate]: No-frills bareboards pub with good choice of interesting well kept ales, Biddenden farm cider, lots of country wines (no food); cigarette cards, framed beer mats, bank notes and old pictures; bar billiards, no juke box, tables in pleasant outside area *(P Abbott)*

Turf [Ripon Spa Hotel, Park St]: Comfortable bar with reliable bar food; bedrooms in parent hotel *(Janet and Peter Race)*

Unicorn [Market Pl E]: Cheerful and popular well used bar with good mix of customers and comfortable seating; hotel bedrooms *(Janet and Peter Race)*

RIPPONDEN [SE0419]

☆ *Old Bridge* [off A58; Priest Lane]: Civilised 14th-c pub in lovely setting by medieval packhorse bridge, considerable atmosphere, oak settles in thick stone walls, rush-seated chairs, a few well chosen pictures and a big woodburner, no smoking areas, some emphasis on rather bistroish food (not Sat/Sun evening) inc popular wkdy lunchtime cold meat buffet, well kept Black Sheep Special, Timothy Taylors

Best, Landlord and Golden and a changing guest beer, 30 malt whiskies, a good choice of foreign beers and interesting wines by the glass; children in eating areas, open all day wknds *(Pat and Tony Martin, Richard and Karen Holt, Bob Broadhurst, Paul Boot, LYM, Tony and Lyn Cassidy, Mike and Linda Hudson)*

ROBIN HOOD'S BAY [NZ9505]

Victoria [Station Rd]: Clifftop Victorian hotel with great bay and sea views, two well kept Camerons ales and two guest beers from curved counter, quick friendly service, wide choice of reasonably priced fresh generous food, solid period décor in bustling bar, large no smoking green-walled family room; children and dogs welcome, useful car park, big garden with play area, nine tidy bedrooms with own bathrooms, good breakfast *(Roger and Jenny Huggins, JP, PP, Jamie and Sarah Allan, Gill and Tony Morriss)*

ROECLIFFE [SE3765]

Crown [about 2 miles W of Boroughbridge]: Thriving pub with good choice of well presented enjoyable food from good sandwiches to interesting starters and main dishes, early evening and wkdy OAP bargains, well kept Black Sheep, Daleside, John Smiths and Timothy Taylors, competent friendly staff, flagstoned bar, lounge with caricatures of famous Yorkshire folk, spacious dining room; front benches overlook quaint village green, lovely village, bedrooms, unobtrusive touring caravan site *(Michael Doswell, Margaret and Peter Brierley)*

ROOS [TA2930]

Roos Arms [just off B1242 N of Withernsea; Main St]: Unpretentious village pub with interesting food from good sandwiches up in bar and restaurant, well kept Tetleys and Youngs, cheerful welcome *(Paul and Ursula Randall)*

ROSEDALE ABBEY [SE7295]

☆ *White Horse* [300 yds up Rosedale Chimney Bank Rd – entering village, first left after Coach House Inn]: Cosy and comfortable farm-based and dog-friendly country inn in lovely spot above the village, character bar with elderly and antique furnishings, lots of stuffed animals and birds, well kept Black Sheep ales and a weekly guest beer, quite a few wines and good choice of malt whiskies, good generous home cooking inc imaginative dishes, sandwiches and ploughman's too, good friendly service, good log fire, great views from terrace (and from restaurant and bedrooms); piped music; children allowed if eating, occasional jazz nights, open all day Sat; attractive bedrooms – a nice place to stay, good walks *(Paul A Moore, LYM, R M Corlett)*

RYEHILL [TA2225]

Crooked Billet [off A1033 Hull—Withernsea]: Family-run local with open fire in relaxed well worn flagstoned bar (which can be smoky), slightly raised dining area, well kept Burtonwood Bitter and Top Hat and guest beers, moderately priced wines, good value fresh unassuming food, hearty Yorkshire landlord, horsey pictures and old prints of the pub *(Paul and Ursula Randall)*

SALTAIRE [SE1437]

Fannys: Former shop converted to cosy and friendly bare-boards alehouse on two floors, gas lighting, log fire, brewery memorabilia, half a dozen well kept real ales, bottled wheat beer, Biddenham farm cider; can be crowded wknd evenings; open all day, cl Mon lunchtime *(Steve Kirby, Richard Lewis)*

SAXTON [SE4736]

☆ *Greyhound* [by church in village, 2½ miles from A1 via B1217]: Charming unchanging medieval stone-built local by church in attractive quiet village, well kept cheap Sam Smiths OB tapped from the cask, three small unspoilt rooms on linking corridor, old prints, open fires and settles, masses of china plates; TV in room on right, no food; a couple of picnic-sets in side yard with attractive hanging baskets, open all day wknds *(LYM, Kevin Thorpe)*

SCARBOROUGH [TA0387]

Cellars [Valley Rd]: Basement of Victorian mansion (now holiday flats), well kept Black Sheep *(C J Fletcher)*

Highlander [Esplanade]: Tartan curtains and carpet, display case of malt whiskies, well kept Tetleys and guest beers such as Fullers Chiswick; bedrooms, close to South Bay *(C J Fletcher)*

Lord Rosebery [Westborough]: Large handsome Wetherspoons in former Co-op (and once the local Liberal HQ), in traffic-free central shopping area; galleried upper bar, well kept beers inc interesting guests, enjoyable food inc Sun roast, good prices, obliging staff; disabled facilities, open all day, very busy and lively evenings *(C J Fletcher, Eric Larkham, David Carr, Derek and Margaret Underwood)*

Scarborough Arms [North Terr]: Comfortable mock-Tudor pub, walls decorated with weaponry, good value filling meals (not Sun evening), well kept Marstons, John Smiths Bitter and Magnet and a guest beer, darts, pool; good outside seating, open all day *(David Carr)*

Tap & Spile [Falsgrave Rd]: Three rooms, one flagstoned, changing well kept ales, farm cider, efficient good-humoured staff, home-made food, no smoking room; jazz Sat, folk night Mon, music Thurs and Sun too *(the Didler, Eric Larkham)*

SCHOLES [SK3895]

Bay Horse [E of M1 junction 35 via A629]: Friendly and chatty old pub with Timothy Taylors Landlord, tasty food evenings not Sun and Sun lunch, no smoking dining area; children welcome, disabled facilities, picnic-sets and play area in garden *(CMW, JJW)*

SCORTON [NZ2500]

Farmers Arms [Northside]: Large blackboard choice of memorable food from French chef/landlord, with a gallic twist to many familiar favourites and interesting specials; good welcoming service, well kept Black Sheep and John Smiths, pubby décor in cosy and comfortable bar, small back restaurant; piped music not too intrusive *(Carol and Dono Leaman, Michael Doswell)*

SCOTTON [SE3259]

Guy Fawkes Arms [Main St]: New tenant and chef putting more emphasis and creative effort into bar and restaurant food in cosy pub with well kept John Smiths and Tetleys *(anon)*

SETTLE [SD8264]

☆ *Golden Lion* [B6480 (main road through town), off A65 bypass]: Old-fashioned market town inn with surprisingly grand staircase sweeping down into spacious high-beamed hall bar, enormous log fireplace, comfortable settles, plush seats, brass, prints and chinese plates on dark panelling; straightforward food (all day wknds), well kept Thwaites Bitter and Mild and a guest beer, decent wines by the glass, public bar with darts, pool, fruit machine, TV and piped music; children in eating area, bedrooms, open all day *(J Roy Smylie, Angus Lyon, Robert Hill, Bob Broadhurst, Mike and Maggie Betton, W W Burke, Margaret Dickinson, LYM)*

SEWERBY [TA2068]

Ship [Cliff Rd]: Welcoming pub overlooking North Sea, lots of sea pictures, good value honest food, well kept Mansfield ales, good service, jugs hanging from beams, small traditional dining room with comfortable wall settles and sea and cricket memorabilia, games/children's room with arcade games; large garden above cliff with big play area, snack bar; very handy for Sewerby Hall, with its land train connection to Bridlington *(John Roots, Kevin Blake, M Borthwick)*

SHEFFIELD [SK3687]

☆ *Cask & Cutler* [Henry St; Shalesmoor tram stop right outside]: Well refurbished small corner pub, six or seven changing real ales mainly from interesting small brewers, occasional Port Mahon beers from its own new back microbrewery, continental beers, frequent beer festivals, farm ciders and perry, coal fire in no smoking lounge on left, friendly licensees, cat and lovable dog, appropriate posters, lunchtime sandwiches and popular cheap Sun lunch (booking advised), daily papers, pub games; open all day Fri/Sat, cl Mon lunchtime, wheelchair access, tables in nice back garden *(Martin Grosberg, the Didler, JP, PP, Richard Lewis)*

☆ *Devonshire Cat* [Wellington Street]: Bright and airy contemporary continental-feel café/bar with plenty of room inc no smoking area, polished light wood, some parquet, big flower pictures, staff knowledgeable about the dozen well kept real ales (it's an offshoot of the Fat Cat – see main entries), more tapped from the cask in glazed stillage (Kelham Island brew one for the pub), masses of bottled beers, two farm ciders, tea and coffee, good value food from end servery, plenty of board games; air conditioning, well reproduced piped music, TV, live music Weds, quiz night Mon; open all day *(the Didler, David Carr, Richard Lewis, Patrick Hancock)*

Gardeners Rest [Neepsend Lane]: Well kept

Timothy Taylors and several guest beers (often the full range from one microbrewery), belgian beers on tap and in bottle, friendly beer-enthusiast landlord, no smoking lounge with old brewery memorabilia, lunchtime food, daily papers, bar billiards (free Mon), changing artwork; frequent live music, poetry/story-telling nights, quiz Sun; disabled access and facilities, conservatory and back garden overlooking River Don, open all day Sun (*JP, PP, Patrick Hancock, the Didler, Richard Lewis*)

☆ *Hillsborough* [Langsett Rd/Wood St; by Primrose View tram stop]: Pub-in-hotel with friendly welcome and five changing well kept ales at attractive prices, also two or three they brew themselves inc a bottle-conditioned real ale, friendly chatty landlord, bare-boards bar, lounge, no smoking room with fire, views to ski slope from attractive back conservatory and terrace tables, daily papers, ginger tom; may have filled rolls, TV, Sun music night; good value bedrooms with own bathrooms, covered parking, real ale bar open only Thurs-Sun evenings, from 4.30 (*CMW, JJW, the Didler, JP, PP, Richard Lewis, Patrick Hancock*)

Kelham Island Tavern [Kelham Island]: Formerly derelict, refurbished by Rutland Arms team as comfortable one-room local with well kept Barnsley Bitter at bargain price, good range of beers from other small brewers, continental imports, farm cider, lunchtime food (not Mon); folk night 1st and 3rd Suns, open all day exc Mon/Tues lunchtimes and Sun afternoon (*the Didler*)

Kings Head [Poole Rd, off Prince of Wales Rd, Darnall; not far from M1 junctions 33/34]: Cheap enjoyable freshly made wkdy lunchtime food (evenings by arrangement) from sandwiches up, real ales such as Courage Directors and Tetleys, friendly hard-working staff, tabloid dailies, comfortable lounge (part no smoking), lots of plants inc big yuccas, brass and copper; big-screen TV, may be quiet piped music; children welcome, covered heated tables in small back floodlit yard with barbecue and small water feature, bedrooms (*CMW, JJW*)

Old Grindstone [Crookes/Lydgate Lane]: Victorian pub very popular with students, food bargains for them, games area with juke box, machines, TV and three pool tables, so can be noisy; but besides the lagers and alcopops it does have several real ales, good soft drinks choice, a raised no smoking area and daily papers; frequent entertainment, open all day (*CMW, JJW*)

Place [Peel St, Broomhill]: Purpose-built new pub with real ales such as Caledonian 80/-, Castle Eden, Fullers London Pride, Greene King Abbot and Stones, good choice of attractively priced wines inc tasters, reasonably priced standard food all day from sandwiches and baked potatoes up (*David Carr*)

Red Deer [Pitt St]: Lively backstreet local surrounded by University buildings, plenty of well kept popular real ales, wide choice of good value lunchtime food, extended lounge

with pleasant raised back area (*the Didler, Roger A Bellingham, Patrick Hancock*)

Red House [Solly St]: Small backstreet pub with charming licensees (and big dog), panelled front room, back snug, comfortable chairs and banquettes, delft shelf of china, well kept ales such as Adnams, Greene King IPA and Jennings, good value wkdy lunchtime food, main bar with pool, darts and cards; occasional folk music (*Pete Baker, DC, the Didler*)

Red Lion [Charles St, nr stn]: Comfortable separate traditional rooms off welcoming central bar, ornate fireplaces and coal fires, attractive panelling and etched glass; well kept Stones and Theakstons, good simple lunchtime food, small back dining room, pleasant conservatory (*the Didler, Pete Baker*)

Rutland Arms [Brown St/Arundel Lane]: Jolly place handy for the Crucible (and station), several sensibly priced changing ales, also bottle-conditioned Wentworth real ales, good wine and soft drinks, plentiful good value food early evening and wknd lunchtimes from cheap basic snacks to more substantial meals, handsome façade; piped music; bedrooms, tables in prettily kept compact garden (*the Didler, CMW, JJW, Tony Hobden, Patrick Hancock*)

Sheaf View [Gleadless Rd, Heeley Bottom]: Friendly and busy no-frills alehouse with wide range of well kept changing ales inc local Abbeydale, Barnsley and Wentworth, spotless unusually shaped bar, pleasant staff; tables outside, open all day, cl Mon lunchtime (*Patrick Hancock, Peter F Marshall*)

Staffordshire Arms [Sorby St, Pitsmoor (A6135)]: Well run local with great atmosphere, Banks's, Stones and Worthington, sandwiches, some seats by bar opening into larger space, cosy snug; two snooker rooms, quiz nights, wknd entertainment; open all day exc Sun (*Bernie Adams*)

Walkley Cottage [Bole Hill Rd]: Chatty 1930s pub popular for good choice of good value generous food (not Sun evening) inc bargain OAP lunch Mon-Thurs and good Sun roast, no smoking dining area, half a dozen well kept real ales, farm cider, good coffee and soft drinks choice, daily papers, friendly black cat and Max the cocker spaniel (not during food service times); piped music, games room with darts, pool (free Mon), machines and big-screen TV, Thurs quiz night; children welcome, views from picnic-sets in small back garden with swings, lovely hanging baskets, open all day (*CMW, JJW, Patrick Hancock*)

SILKSTONE [SE2905]
Ring o' Bells [High St, off A628 W of Barnsley]: Homely 17th-c stonebuilt pub in attractive ex-mining village, lots of copper, old bottles, photographs, cartoons and fish tank in long lounge with no smoking area, limited choice of good inexpensive food (not Sat-Mon evenings) inc bargain fresh Sun lunch, well kept Hardys & Hansons, friendly chatty landlord, daily papers; quiet piped music, TV, games machine; children welcome, side play

area, nearby walks *(CMW, JJW)*

SIMONSTONE [SD8691]

Game Tavern [Simonstone Hall]: Comfortable and tastefully furnished bar attached to country house hotel, carefully cooked reasonably priced bar food inc good hotpot, well kept Theakstons, hunting and fishing trophies, a warm welcome for walkers; terrace tables, lovely garden and fantastic views, good bedrooms *(P Abbott)*

SINNINGTON [SE7485]

☆ *Fox & Hounds* [just off A170 W of Pickering]: Neat 18th-c coaching inn, beamed bar with nice pictures, old artefacts and woodburner, comfortable seating, well kept Black Sheep Special and Camerons, good choice of malt whiskies, good food in bar and no smoking evening restaurant, separate no smoking stables bar; piped music, dominoes, darts; children in eating areas, picnic-sets out in front, pretty village *(Beryl and Tim Dawson, Brian and Pat Wardrobe, Mr and Mrs J Curtis, Norma and Noel Thomas, LYM)*

SKEEBY [NZ1902]

☆ *Travellers Rest* [Richmond Rd (A6108)]: Sparkling long bar, thriving local atmosphere and a welcome for visitors, good well priced fresh food inc children's, bargain breakfast and good vegetarian choice, cheerful service, Theakstons beers, copper and pewter on beams, coal fire; walking parties welcome, tables in garden *(Trevor and Sylvia Millum, Simon and Gillian Wales)*

SKELTON [SE3668]

Black Lion [off B6265]: Popular local with good value low-priced pubby lunches in pleasant dining room, more elaborate evening menu; tables outside, caravan site behind *(M Borthwick)*

SKERNE [TA0455]

Eagle [Wansford Rd]: Fine unspoilt village pub, small front parlour and basic bar either side of hall, low-priced well kept Camerons brought on tray from cellar (ask to see the rare Victorian cash-register beer dispenser), coal fire, friendly landlord and chatty local atmosphere, darts; no food, cl wkdy lunchtimes *(the Didler, JP, PP, RWC, Pete Baker)*

SKIPTON [SD9852]

Black Horse [High St]: Bustling and friendly beams-and-stripped-stone coaching inn opp castle, popular with cavers, climbers and Saturday-market people; good choice of usual food served quickly, real ales, huge low-effect gas fire in big stone fireplace; open all day, children welcome, play barn and small outdoor play area, bedrooms with own bathrooms *(W A Evershed)*

Narrow Boat [Victoria St]: Town pub nr canal, up to half a dozen well kept ales from small breweries such as Dalesman in pleasantly smoke-free bar (smokers confined to upper gallery), lots of bottled belgians, welcoming staff, good plain lunchtime food, home-made chutney and mustard for sale; jazz Tues, quiz Weds; open all day *(John Foord)*

Red Lion [Market Sq]: Well furnished and

bustling (next to the market), with enjoyable home-made food using local produce, lots of game and fish, reasonable prices, real ales, cheerful staff *(Sherrie Glass)*

☆ *Royal Shepherd* [Canal St; from Water St (A65) turn into Coach St, then left after canal bridge]: Busy old-fashioned sociable local in pretty spot by canal, well kept Boddingtons, Castle Eden, Marstons Pedigree and Timothy Taylors Landlord, decent wine, friendly service, unusual sensibly priced whiskies, open fires, low-priced standard quick food, photographs of Yorks CCC in its golden days; big bar (can be rather smoky), snug and dining room, games and juke box; children welcome in side room, tables outside *(John Foord)*

☆ *Woolly Sheep* [Sheep St]: Full Timothy Taylors range kept well in two beamed bars off flagstoned passage, exposed brickwork, stone fireplace, lots of sheep prints and old photographs, old plates and bottles, prompt friendly service, cheap generous plain food inc plenty for children, roomy comfortable dining area; spacious pretty garden, six good value newly refurbished bedrooms, good breakfast *(Roger Bridgeman, Steve Whalley, Lindsay Travis, Tim and Ann Newell)*

SKIPWITH [SE6638]

Drovers Arms [follow Escrick sign off A163 NE of Selby]: Comfortable two-room pub in smart village by Skipwith Common nature reserve, good log fires, welcoming young licensees, well kept beers inc Black Sheep and Shepherd Neame Spitfire, fine range of house wines, enterprising changing food and good Sun roasts, separate dining room; wheelchair access *(Pat and Graham Williamson)*

SLAITHWAITE [SE0513]

Rose & Crown [Cop Hill, up Nabbs Lane then Holme Lane]: Marvellous Colne Valley and moor views, three refurbished rooms off friendly bar, end restaurant, well kept Black Sheep beers, wide choice of malt whiskies, good changing blackboard food inc enormous puddings; good walks *(Andy and Jill Kassube)*

SLEDMERE [SE9365]

Triton [junction B1252/B1253 NW of Gt Driffield]: Simple and comfortable 18th-c inn in attractive spot, friendly chef/landlord doing enjoyable food (not Mon lunchtime) all cooked fresh with good veg, so can take a while, high-backed settles and good log fire in small bar, well kept Tetleys, separate no smoking restaurant with Sun carvery, games in public bar; children welcome, bedrooms *(LYM, Colin and Dot Savill)*

SNAPE [SE2684]

☆ *Castle Arms* [off B6268 Masham—Bedale]: Meticulously clean and comfortably updated low-ceilinged pub with good enterprising food (not Sun night, limited Mon/Tues) in flagstoned bar with big log fire in inglenook, second flagstoned room and attractive small carpeted dining room, friendly licensees and helpful service, well kept Black Sheep. Hambleton Best and John Smiths Magnet, decent wines, country prints; children and dogs welcome, tables in charming courtyard, comfortable bedrooms, pretty village, very handy for Thorp Perrow *(Edward and Deanna Pearce, Janet and Peter Race, Tim and Carolyn Lowes)*

SNEATON [NZ8907]

Wilson Arms [Beacon Way]: Sparkling clean and shiny, with welcoming licensees, good value filling food (not wkdy lunchtime out of season) from sandwiches up, Barnsley, Black Sheep and Theakstons, two good fires, neat staff, pleasant small dining room one end, family room with pool table the other end; bedrooms with fine views *(M Borthwick)*

SOUTH DALTON [SE9645]

☆ *Pipe & Glass* [West End; just off B1248 NW of Beverley]: Friendly dining pub in charming secluded setting, stripped-stone beamed bar with some high-backed settles, old prints, log fires and bow windows, well kept beers inc one brewed for them by Cropton, enjoyable bar food all day, separate ribbon-tied menu for more formal large attractively laid conservatory restaurant overlooking Dalton Park (must book wknds); may be quiet piped music; children welcome, tables in garden with splendid yew tree, three comfortable bedrooms with good huge breakfast, open all day *(LYM, Peter F Marshall, Paul and Ursula Randall)*

SOWERBY BRIDGE [SE0623]

Moorings [canal basin]: Spacious multi-level canal warehouse conversion, big windows overlooking boat basin, cast-iron pillars supporting high beams, stripped stone and stencilled plaster, scatter cushions on good solid settles, canal pictures, Tiffany-style lamps, no smoking family room, enjoyable food (not Sun evening) from baked potatoes up, efficient helpful staff, well kept Black Sheep and Theakstons, lots of bottled beers, good wine choice; unobtrusive piped music, pub games; tables out on terrace, open all day Sat *(LYM, Pat and Tony Martin)*

Puzzle Hall [Hollins Mill Lane, off A58]: Welcoming local with choice of beers, live music in back yard (covered in inclement weather); open all day *(DAV)*

SPOFFORTH [SE3650]

☆ *Railway Hotel* [A661 Harrogate—Wetherby; Park Terr]: Simple little pub made special by friendly hard-working landlord who goes out of his way to make sure everything is right; wide choice of very good value home-made food from sandwiches to steaks, well kept Sam Smiths, straightforward furnishings in basic locals' bar and unfussy no smoking lounge, real fires, no juke box; Weds quiz nights; tables and swing in garden behind *(BB, Stuart Paulley)*

SPROTBROUGH [SE5302]

☆ *Boat* [3½ miles from M18 junction 2, less from A1(M) junction 36 via A630 and Mill Lane; Nursery Lane]: Interesting roomy stone-built ex-farmhouse with lovely courtyard in charming quiet spot by River Don, three individually furnished areas, big stone fireplaces, latticed windows, dark brown beams, lots of old photographs, very wide choice of good value generous usual food (no

sandwiches), well kept Courage Directors, John Smiths Bitter and Magnet and Theakstons, farm cider, prompt helpful service; piped music, fruit machine, no dogs; big sheltered prettily lit courtyard, river walks; restaurant (Tues-Sat evening, Sun lunch); open all day summer Sats *(JHBS, GSB, LYM)*

Ivanhoe [quite handy for A1(M)]: Large mock-Tudor pub, three linked carpeted and panelled rooms with conservatory extension overlooking cricket ground, reasonably priced food (not Sun evening) inc popular Sun carvery, uniformed waitresses, well kept cheap Sam Smiths OB, public bar with pool and TV; children in eating areas, tables out on flagstoned terrace with play area, open all day *(CMW, JJW, JHBS)*

STAMFORD BRIDGE [SE7055]

Three Cups [A166 W of town]: Spacious Vintage Inn family dining pub done up in timbered country style, glass-topped 20-metre well in bar, sound food all day, good range of wines, well kept Bass and Tetleys, friendly manager and staff; children welcome, good play area behind, bedrooms, open all day *(Pat and Graham Williamson, LYM, Guy Charrison)*

STARBOTTON [SD9574]

Fox & Hounds [B6160]: Small inn in pretty and very popular Dales village (so it gets busy, and there may be quite a wait for a meal), big log fire in beamed and flagstoned traditional bar, small no smoking dining room, well kept beer such as Black Sheep, usual bar food, eager-to-please licensees; may be piped music, dogs allowed in bar; children welcome, two good bedrooms, cl Mon *(the Didler, LYM, M and N Watson, Maggie and Tony Harwood, Blaise Vyner)*

STILLINGTON [SE5867]

White Bear [Main St]: Pleasantly olde-worlde village local, friendly service, good value food inc lunchtime and early evening bargains, well kept Black Sheep, John Smiths, Timothy Taylors Landlord and Porter and Tetleys *(Tim and Ann Newell)*

STOCKTON ON THE FOREST [SE6556]

Fox [off A64 just NE of York]: Three cosy linked rooms and separate dining room, good proper home cooking with some adventurous dishes, quick friendly attentive service *(Pat and Graham Williamson)*

STOKESLEY [NZ5209]

☆ *White Swan* [West End]: Friendly country pub with great range of cheeses, home-made pickle and several pâtés for ploughman's, well kept Captain Cook ales brewed at the pub and interesting changing guest beers, welcoming staff, tidy split-level panelled bar, well worn in but clean and comfortable, hat display, friendly ridgeback called Bix and little black dog called Titch; can be a bit smoky; midweek live blues and jazz *(Blaise Vyner, Val Stevenson, Rob Holmes)*

STUTTON [SE4841]

☆ *Hare & Hounds* [Manor Rd]: Pleasantly refurbished stone-built pub with cosy low-ceilinged rooms, very popular for wide choice of enjoyable food (not Sun evening) from light thai dishes to beef and yorkshire pudding, quick pleasant service even when busy, well kept cheap Sam Smiths OB, decent wine, well behaved children in restaurant; may be piped music; cl Mon, long prettily planted sloping garden with playthings *(Geoffrey and Brenda Wilson, Pat and Derek Roughton, LYM, Betsy and Peter Little)*

☆ *Tan Hill Inn* [Arkengarthdale road Reeth—Brough, at junction Keld/W Stonesdale road]: Old stone pub on Pennine Way – Britain's highest, and second most remote, nearly 5 miles from the nearest neighbour, basic, bustling and can get overcrowded, full of bric-a-brac and pictures inc interesting old photographs, simple sturdy furniture, flagstones, ever-burning big log fire (with prized stone side seats); well kept Theakstons Best, XB and Old Peculier (in winter the cellar does chill down – whisky with hot water's good then), big helpings of comforting food inc popular yorkshire pudding, good sandwiches too; often snowbound, with no mains electricity (juke box powered by generator); Swaledale sheep show here last Thurs in May; children and dogs welcome, bedrooms, inc some in extension with own bathrooms, open all day *(Guy Vowles, JHBS, LYM, Jim Abbott, Richard Robinson, Ian and Rose Lock)*

THIRSK [SE4282]

Darrowby [Market Pl]: Friendly open-plan pub with well kept John Smiths, limited choice of enjoyable cheap food, TV in front part, more lounge at the back; tables outside, open all day *(Sue Wheeler)*

THIXENDALE [SE8461]

Cross Keys [off A166 3 miles N of Fridaythorpe]: Unspoilt welcoming country pub in deep valley below the rolling Wolds, single cosy L-shaped room with fitted wall seats, relaxed atmosphere, four or five well kept changing ales, sensible blackboard food; large pleasant garden behind, popular with walkers, handy for Wharram Percy earthworks *(the Didler)*

THORALBY [SE0086]

George: Another change of licensees in prettily set Dales village pub, two smallish cosy linked areas with well kept Black Sheep and another real ale, sensibly priced bar food from sandwiches to steaks, interesting bric-a-brac and solid fuel stove, darts and dominoes; walkers welcome, terrace tables, bedrooms *(Jim Abbott, P Abbott, Michael Butler)*

THORNTON [SE0933]

☆ *Ring o' Bells* [Hill Top Rd, off B6145 W of Bradford]: Spotless 19th-c moortop dining pub very popular for wide choice of well presented good home cooking inc fresh fish, speciality pies, superb steaks, good puddings, bargain early suppers, separate-sittings Sun lunch (best to book), well kept Black Sheep Bitter and Special and Tetleys, crisp efficient service, pleasant bar, popular air-conditioned no smoking restaurant and pleasant conservatory

lounge; wide views towards Shipley and Bingley *(John Unsworth, Andy and Jill Kassube)*

THORNTON-LE-BEANS [SE3990]

Crosby Hotel [just off A168 SE of Northallerton]: Interestingly modernised pub in well hidden village, good inexpensive food inc bargain lunches, welcoming efficient staff, long friendly main bar with beams, brasses and cosy corner, modern front bar room, restaurant; children welcome *(Pat and Derek Roughton, Joanne Keill, A H C Rainier)*

THORNTON-LE-CLAY [SE6865]

☆ *White Swan* [off A64 York—Malton; Low St]: Comfortably old-fashioned beamed dining pub, homely and peaceful, with friendly attentive landlord, good freshly cooked well thought-out food inc imaginative dishes, fresh fish and late suppers, big helpings and reasonable prices, well kept Black Sheep and a local guest beer, decent wines, good log fire, shining brasses, children welcome, plenty of board games, good view from impeccable ladies'; well chosen piped music; tables on terrace, attractive neatly kept grounds with duck pond, herb garden and rescued donkeys, attractive countryside nr Castle Howard; cl Mon lunchtime *(John Knighton, Mr and Mrs P Bland)*

THORPE ARCH [SE4346]

Pax: Useful for A1, wide food choice and good quick service *(R M and M J Smith)*

THORPE HESLEY [SK3695]

Travellers [Smithy Wood Rd, just off A629 Cowley Hill towards Chapeltown at M1 junction 35]: Homely early Victorian two-bar local with no smoking dining room/conservatory, two well kept real ales, bargain straightforward food (not Sun/Mon evenings) from sandwiches up, stuffed birds, brass, pictures and fresh flowers; piped music, high chairs for children; big garden with play area and pets corner, woodland walks *(Ian Phillips)*

THURSTONLAND [SE1610]

Rose & Crown [off A629 Huddersfield—Sheffield, via Thunder Bridge and Stocksmoor]: Spacious and friendly open-plan village pub, banquettes and some stripped stone, five real ales, good soft drinks choice, attractively priced food (all day Sun); some tables out in front *(CMW, JJW)*

TICKHILL [SK5993]

Royal Oak [Northgate]: One long friendly room with central bar, good value OAP lunches Mon and Thurs inc good fresh fish, well kept Black Sheep and other real ales; quiet piped music, TV, quiz nights; garden with play area *(M J Brooks)*

TODMORDEN [SD9223]

Masons Arms [A681/A6033, S of centre]: Welcoming traditional local with particularly well kept Barnsley, Tetleys and one or two guest beers, two knocked-together rooms with darts, cards and pool in popular games end; impromptu folk night Thurs *(anon)*

WAINSTALLS [SE0428]

Cat i' th' Well: Picturesque country pub in fine

spot towards the top of Luddenden Dean (lovely walks), three snug linked areas, fresh and untwee, with 19th-c panelling from nearby demolished hall, nice balance between drinking and dining with new landlord putting more emphasis on above-average food inc good speciality sausages made for them locally, other usual dishes from good sandwich choice up, Timothy Taylors Best and Landlord and guest beers such as Old Mill and Phoenix Navvy, quick friendly service *(Pat and Tony Martin, Anne and Tim Locke)*

WAKEFIELD [SE3320]

Fernandes Brewery Tap [Avison Yard, Kirkgate]: Top floor of 19th-c malt store converted to tap for Fernandes microbrewery, their beers and interesting guests kept well, Biddenden farm cider, good breweriana collection, friendly atmosphere; cl Mon-Thurs lunchtime, open all day Fri-Sun *(the Didler, JP, PP)*

Henry Boons [Westgate]: Well kept Clarks (from next-door brewery) and Black Sheep, Tetleys and Timothy Taylors, in two-room bare-boards local, friendly staff, breweriana; side pool area, machines, live bands; open all day *(the Didler, JP, PP, Patrick Hancock)*

Redoubt [Horbury Rd, Westgate]: Busy traditional city pub, four rooms off long corridor, rugby league photographs, well kept Tetleys Bitter and Mild and Timothy Taylors Landlord, pub games; family room till 8, open all day *(JP, PP, the Didler)*

Wagon [Westgate End]: Busy friendly local specialising in well kept ales mainly from interesting small breweries, lunchtime food, reasonable prices, log fire; side pool table, games machine, juke box; benches outside, open all day *(JP, PP, the Didler, Patrick Hancock)*

Wakefield Labour Club [Vicarage St]: Red wooden shed rather like a works canteen inside, small and inviting – it is a club, but visitors can just sign in; wide changing choice of keenly priced real ales from small breweries such as Ossett, farm cider, belgian beers; picnic-sets outside, cl lunchtime Mon-Thurs and Sun evening *(JP, PP, the Didler)*

WALES [SK4782]

☆ *Duke of Leeds* [Church St]: Comfortable 18th-c stone-faced village pub kept spotless by chatty 3rd-generation landlord, well kept Boddingtons, Castle Eden, Greene King Abbot and a guest beer, good value generous food (not Mon/Tues lunchtimes; may be a wait when busy) inc choice of fresh fish, good soft drinks range, long no smoking lounge and smaller room where smoking allowed, no smoking dining areas, lots of brass and copper, pictures for sale, table fountains, flame-effect gas fire; may be quiet piped music; children welcome lunchtime, no credit cards; nearby walks *(CMW, JJW)*

WALKINGTON [SE9937]

☆ *Ferguson-Fawsitt Arms* [East End; B1230 W of Beverley]: Mock-Tudor bars in 1950s style, good choice of good value meals inc carvery from airy no smoking flagstone-floored food

bar, very popular lunchtime with older people, helpful cheerful service, Courage Directors and John Smiths, decent wine; tables out on terrace, games bar with pool table; delightful village *(June and Ken Brooks, G Dobson, LYM)*

WALSDEN [SD9321]

Cross Keys [Rochdale Rd, S of Todmorden]: Well kept Banks's, Cains, Lees and changing ales mainly from small breweries (often inc a Mild), good generous home cooking (all day Sun), helpful friendly service even when busy, lounge extending into conservatory overlooking restored Rochdale Canal, public bar with pool and big-screen TV; tables outside, lots of good walks (nr Pennine Way), bedrooms, open all day *(Bruce Bird)*

WARLEY TOWN [SE0524]

Maypole [signed off A646 just W of Halifax]: Friendly farmhouse-style pub, country furniture on flagstones, three rooms with two majoring on food – enormous good value choice from substantial lunchtime bar snacks to imaginative evening meals inc seafood, all day Sun, lobster and shellfish festival June/July, well kept beers, good service and wine choice; garden with pleasant seating area, local bands in summer *(Dr T E Hothersall)*

WEAVERTHORPE [SE9771]

Star [village signed off A64 Malton—Scarborough at Sherburn]: Two neatly kept rooms with comfortable maroon plush banquettes and log fires, wide choice of enjoyable home-made food inc game all freshly cooked by landlady (not Tues evening; may be a very long wait on busy nights), well kept Camerons, Tetleys and a weekly guest beer, restaurant; children welcome, no piped music but fruit machine; nice bedrooms, good breakfast, quiet village setting *(John and Joyce Snell, Colin and Dot Savill, BB)*

WENSLEY [SE0989]

Three Horseshoes: Short frequently changing choice of good freshly made food, well kept ales such as Black Sheep, good wines and service *(Terry Mizen)*

WENTBRIDGE [SE4817]

Blue Bell: Several communicating rooms, beams, stripped stone, farm tools and other bric-a-brac, solid wooden tables, chairs and settles; wide choice of good value quick generous food inc interesting dishes, small helpings of some, well kept Bass, Tetleys and Timothy Taylors Landlord, good choice of wines by the glass; family room, good view from garden, bedrooms *(Ian and Freda Millar)*

WEST BURTON [SE0186]

☆ *Fox & Hounds* [on green, off B6160 Bishopdale—Wharfedale]: Friendly local on long green of idyllic Dales village, wide choice of good value generous unpretentious home-made food inc children's and good puddings, well kept Black Sheep and Tetleys, residents' dining room; nearby caravan park; children and dogs welcome, good modern bedrooms, lovely walks and waterfalls nearby *(P Abbott, Roger Bridgeman, Alan J Morton, W A Evershed, Abi Benson)*

WEST TANFIELD [SE2678]
☆ *Bruce Arms* [A6108 N of Ripon]: Thriving
dining pub with good rather upmarket food
inc interesting dishes in intimate log-fire bar or
smallish dining room (often fully booked at
night), friendly service *(Janet and Peter Race,
LYM)*

WEST WITTON [SE0688]
☆ *Wensleydale Heifer* [A684 W of Leyburn]:
Comfortable big-windowed front lounge with
easy chairs, low tables, big log fireplace, small
dimly lit back rooms with nice mix of dark
furniture, horse paintings, another fire in
interesting inlaid fireplace, well kept Black
Sheep Best, John Smiths and Theakstons Best,
decent wines, generous coffee, ample enjoyable
food from sandwiches through good value
early suppers Weds and Sun to fish and game,
tiled-floor bistro, no music; some picnic-sets
outside, nice big bedrooms (back ones
quietest), good big breakfast *(Michael Butler,
BB, Keith Mould)*

WETHERBY [SE4048]
Crown [High St]: Comfortable two-room pub
with cheap Sam Smiths OB *(Joe Green)*

WHISTON [SK4489]
Golden Ball [nr M1 junction 33, via A618;
Turner Lane, off High St]: Extended old pub
remodelled as Ember Inn, meticulously clean,
wide food choice inc good value mixed grill,
real ales such as Bass, Stones and Timothy
Taylors Landlord, Badger Tanglefoot, and
Tetleys, log fire *(Derek and Sylvia Stephenson)*

WHITBY [NZ8911]
Tap & Spile [New Quay Rd]: Three-room
bare-boards local, small no smoking room,
four or so well kept changing ales, country
wines, farm ciders, good value bar food inc
good local fish and chips noon-7, traditional
games; frequent folk nights, open all day
*(the Didler, Damian Dixon, Roger and
Jenny Huggins, JP, PP)*

WHIXLEY [SE4457]
Anchor [New Rd]: Family-friendly village pub,
good value well cooked food, bargain
lunchtime sliced roasts particularly popular
with OAPs, cheery efficient service, well kept
John Smiths and Tetleys, several rooms, coal
fire in small lounge, eccentric teapots on every
surface, sunny conservatory *(Janet and
Peter Race, H Bramwell)*

YORK [SE5951]
Ackhorne [St Martins Lane, Micklegate]: Fine
changing range of well kept ales from small
brewers, four farm ciders, perry, country
wines, foreign bottled beers and good coffee;
beams, leather wall seats, old prints, bottles
and jugs, carpeted snug one end, good value
home-made food (not Mon evening or Sun)
from good choice of sandwiches up, friendly
landlord and family, open fire, daily papers,
traditional games, silenced games machine; Sun
quiz night; tables out behind, open all day
(Jim Abbott, Richard Lewis, the Didler)
☆ *Black Swan* [Peaseholme Green (inner ring
road)]: Marvellous timbered and jettied Tudor
building, well used inside, with serving hatch
to compact panelled front bar, crooked-floored

hall with fine period staircase, black-beamed
back bar with vast inglenook, cheerful service,
low-priced usual food from baked potatoes
and baguettes up, well kept Worthington Best
and guests such as Bass and York Broadcaster
or Yorkshire Terrier, several country wines;
piped music, jazz and folk nights; useful car
park *(the Didler, Paul and Ursula Randall,
Pat and Tony Martin, Patrick Hancock,
R T and J C Moggridge, LYM, David Carr,
Alison Hayes, Pete Hanlon)*
☆ *Blue Bell* [Fossgate]: Unspoilt and warmly
welcoming Edwardian pub with well kept ales
such as Adnams, Camerons Strongarm, Greene
King Abbot, John Smiths and Charles Wells
Bombardier, tiny tiled-floor front bar with
roaring fire, panelled ceiling, stained glass, bar
pots and decanters, corridor to back smoke
room not much bigger, hatch service to middle
bar, lively local atmosphere, good value
sandwiches on counter 11-6, pub games; open
all day, can get very busy *(RWC, David Carr,
Paul and Ursula Randall, the Didler,
Pete Baker, JP, PP, Richard Lewis,
Nick and Alison Dowson)*
Corner Pin [Tanner Row]: Neat and clean,
with linked room areas, low beams and
panelling, lots of prints, well kept Banks's,
Mansfield Bitter and Riding and Marstons
Pedigree, wide food choice, conservatory
opening on to terrace; well reproduced piped
music, TV, games machine; open all day
(Richard Lewis)
Dormouse [Shipton Rd, Clifton Park]:
Purpose-built Vintage Inn, well designed and
given plenty of character and atmosphere, with
their usual food, fairly priced wines, friendly
efficient staff *(John Knighton)*
Fox & Roman [Tadcaster Rd, opp racecourse]:
Large, rambling and welcoming Vintage Inn,
lots of nooks and crannies, good value well
prepared food, good choice of wines by the
glass, quick cheerful helpful service, two log
fires, unrushed atmosphere; relaxing piped
music *(Michael Dandy, Duncan Smart)*
Golden Ball [Cromwell Rd/Bishophill]:
Unspoilt 1950s feel in friendly and well
preserved four-room Edwardian pub,
enjoyable straightforward wkdy lunchtime
food, well kept Marstons Pedigree, John
Smiths and a guest beer, cards and dominoes;
can be lively evenings, live music Thurs and
Sun; small walled garden *(Pete Baker)*
Golden Fleece [Pavement]: Timothy Taylors
Landlord and guest beers often from York
Brewery, long corridor from bar to back
lounge (beware the sloping floors – it dates
from 1503); popular with ghost-hunters
(Eric Larkham)
Golden Slipper [Goodramgate]: Dating from
15th c, recently renovated but keeping a
distinctively old-fashioned almost rustic local
feel in its neat bar and three small rooms, good
cheap plain food from sandwiches, baguettes
and baked potatoes up, Greene King Old
Speckled Hen, John Smiths and Charles Wells
Bombardier, friendly cheerful staff; in the
evenings a different set of customers can make

it seem almost trendy *(Michael Dandy, Pat and Graham Williamson)*

Harkers [St Helens Sq]: Bar rather than pub, former Yorkshire Insurance HQ, with rather upmarket décor (chairman's office intact with panelling and marble fireplace), good new world wines from the long serving counter, food inc all-day breakfast, bangers and mash and fish and chips alongside lamb, steaks etc, welcoming service, spacious smoking room; basement has part of Roman gateway *(E G Parish)*

☆ *Hole in the Wall* [High Petergate]: Rambling open-plan pub handy for Minster, beams, stripped masonry, lots of prints, turkey carpeting, lots of low plush stools, well kept Banks's, Mansfield and Marstons Pedigree, good coffee, very busy lunchtime for good value food noon onwards inc generous Sun lunch, prompt friendly service; juke box, games machines, piped music not too loud, live some nights; open all day *(Michael Dandy, Alan Vere, LYM, Martin Lewis)*

Kennedys [Little Stonegate]: Trendy and pleasantly relaxing café-bar with food inc good bangers and mash, usual lagers *(Hugh A MacLean)*

☆ *Last Drop* [Colliergate]: Former law office dating from 17th c, restored by York Brewery in traditional style, no frills but civilised, several of their own beers with one or two well kept guest beers, decent wines and country wines, reasonably priced lunchtime food from sandwiches and baked potatoes up, friendly staff, bare boards, big barrels and comfortable seats, big windows overlooking pavement, no music, machines or children; attic lavatories; tables out behind, open all day, can get very busy lunchtime *(Richard Lewis, Lorraine and Fred Gill, June and Ken Brooks, Martin Grosberg, Su and Bob Child)*

☆ *Lendal Cellars* [Lendal]: Split-level alehouse down steps in broad-vaulted 17th-c cellars carefully spotlit to show up the stripped brickwork, stone floor, interconnected rooms and alcoves, very well kept Boddingtons, Castle Eden, Marstons Pedigree, Wadworths 6X and a fine choice of guest beers at fair prices, farm cider, country wines, foreign bottled beers, daily papers, cheerful staff, children allowed for good plain food 11.30-7 (5 Fri/Sat), two-for-one bargains; good piped music, popular with students; open all day *(Peter F Marshall, the Didler, JP, PP, Richard Lewis, LYM)*

Olde Starre [Stonegate]: City's oldest licensed pub, and a magnet for tourists, with 'gallows' sign across York's prettiest street, original panelling and prints, green plush wall seats, several other little rooms off porch-like lobby, well kept changing ales such as Caledonian Deuchars IPA, John Smiths, Theakstons Best and York Yorkshire Terrier from long counter, cheerful young staff; separate food servery hatch shuts very promptly, piped music, fruit and games machines; open all day, children welcome away from bar, flower-filled back garden and front courtyard with Minster

glimpsed across the rooftops *(Janet and Peter Race, Dr and Mrs Jackson, Patrick Hancock, Peter F Marshall, Rona Murdoch, LYM)*

Phoenix [George St]: Unpretentious and friendly, with dominoes in proper front public bar, quietly comfortable and sensitively refurbished back horseshoe-shaped lounge, well kept John Smiths, Charles Wells Bombardier and a guest beer, welcoming pub dog *(Pete Baker)*

Postern Gate [Piccadilly]: Wetherspoons in new building, with four regular and six guest beers, food all day inc breakfasts (not Sun) from 10am; family room *(Eric Larkham)*

Punch Bowl [Stonegate]: Bustling family-run local with masses of hanging baskets, friendly helpful service, wide range of good generous lunchtime food from sandwiches up (no smoking area by servery), small panelled rooms off corridor, TV in interesting beamed one on left of food servery, well kept Bass, Worthington and York Yorkshire Terrier; piped music, games machines; open all day, good value bedrooms *(John Clegg, Rona Murdoch, Joyce and Maurice Cottrell)*

Red Lion [Merchantgate, between Fossgate and Piccadilly]: Low-beamed rambling rooms with plenty of atmosphere, some stripped Tudor brickwork, relaxed old-fashioned furnishings, well kept real ales, decent bar lunches, good juke box or piped music; children welcome to eat at lunchtime, tables outside *(Mark Walker, LYM)*

Rook & Gaskill [Lawrence St]: York Brewery's third pub, pleasantly converted (mind the step up to the main bar), with all their beers and lots of guests, also bar food (and some live music) *(Eric Larkham)*

☆ *Royal Oak* [Goodramgate]: Comfortably worn in three-room black-beamed 16th-c pub (remodelled in Tudor style 1934) with warm welcoming atmosphere, cosy corners with blazing fires, good value generous home-made usual food (limited Sun evening) inc fresh veg and home-baked bread served 11.30-8, no sandwiches till 3, speedy service from cheerful bustling young staff, reliably well kept Greene King Abbot, Timothy Taylors Landlord, Tetleys and a guest such as Lees Brooklyn or Jennings Cumberland, wines and country wines, good coffee; prints, swords, busts and old guns, no smoking family room; shame about the piped music; handy for Minster and open all day, can get crowded *(Paul and Ursula Randall, Pete and Kate Holford, Dr and Mrs Jackson, David Carr, BB, Patrick Hancock, CMW, JJW, Joyce and Maurice Cottrell, Pat and Tony Martin)*

Snickleway [Goodramgate]: Snug and comfortable little open-plan pub, cheerful landlord, well kept Greene King Old Speckled Hen and John Smiths, good value fresh well filled doorstep sandwiches, baked potatoes, curry and chilli lunchtimes, good coal fires, cosy nooks and crannies, lots of antiques, copper and brass, unobtrusive piped music, prompt service, splendid cartoons in gents', exemplary ladies' *(Paul and Ursula Randall)*

Swan [Bishopgate St]: Friendly bustle and hatch service to two small rooms off lobby, giving rather a 1950s feel, well kept Timothy Taylors Landlord and local guest beers, helpful staff; small walled garden, nr city walls *(Pete Baker)*

☆ *Tap & Spile* [Monkgate]: Friendly late Victorian two-bar pub with fine choice of around eight well kept real ales, farm cider and 20 country wines, games in raised back area, cheap straightforward lunchtime bar food; tables on heated terrace and in garden; children in eating area, open all day *(the Didler, Richard Lewis, Paul and Ursula Randall, LYM, JP, PP, David Carr, Patrick Hancock)*

☆ *Three Legged Mare* [High Petergate]: Bustling open-plan light and airy café-bar with York Brewery's full beer range and guests such as Castle Rock kept well, attentive cheery young staff, reasonably priced lunchtime snacks inc generous interesting sandwiches and baked potatoes, conservatory; no children, disabled facilities (other lavatories down noisy spiral stairs); tables in back garden, with replica of the original three-legged mare – a local gallows used for multiple executions *(Andy and Jill Kassube, John and Sheila Burley, Paul and Ursula Randall, Pat and Tony Martin, Richard Lewis, Eric Larkham, D W Stokes, Mark Walker)*

York Brewery Tap [Toft Green, Micklegate]: Upstairs lounge at York Brewery, with their own full draught range in top condition, also bottled beers, nice clubby atmosphere with friendly staff happy to talk about the beers, lots of breweriana, comfortable settees and armchairs, magazines and daily papers; no food, brewery tours by arrangement, shop; open 11.30-7, cl Sun, annual membership fee £3 unless you live in York or go on the tour *(the Didler, Michael Dandy, JP, PP, Angus Lyon, Lorraine and Fred Gill, Peter F Marshall)*

London
Scotland
Wales
Channel Islands

London

Two new main entries here this year are both in Central London, and not far from one another: the surprisingly country-feeling Coopers Arms (good food and nice wines), and nearer the river the attractively laid out Cross Keys (interesting bar side, appealing back dining area). Other pubs on particularly good form here are, in Central London, the Argyll Arms (nice old building, good service), the Black Friar (wonderful art nouveau décor, with a wider range of food from its new kitchen), the Cittie of Yorke (remarkable old-fashioned booth-lined bar, great atmosphere), the little Dog & Duck in Soho, the old-fashioned Grapes (full of character, good beer choice), the Lamb (an old favourite, consistently good), the Lamb & Flag (tremendous character and old-fashioned appeal, a great favourite), the Nags Head (a little bit of country charm in a very stylish area), both Red Lions (one for its dazzling décor, the other for its quietly unpretentious welcome), and the interesting little Seven Stars (new licensees doing well, with growing enthusiasm for their food); in North London, the Holly Bush (good food and beer in timeless surroundings); in South London, the Anchor (a fine old place, unspoilt by major refurbishment), the historic George (remarkable survival of a true ancient coaching inn, in the heart of Southwark), and the bustling and friendly Market Porter; and in West London, the Anglesea Arms (SW7: a good all-rounder), the Atlas (very good food, thriving atmosphere, excellent wines), and the White Horse (another fine all-rounder). This year we have noted a growing number of London pubs doing food all day – very handy for visitors. For a special meal out, favourite places are the Atlas (SW6), the Eagle (EC1), the Fox (EC2), the Fox & Hounds (SW11), the Anglesea Arms (W6) and the Havelock Tavern (W14); the Atlas takes the top award of London Dining Pub of the Year. The Lucky Dip section at the end of the chapter has over 170 entries this year, over half of them new to this edition. As it includes so many pubs, we have listed them by postal district, and separated off the outer London suburbs. These come last, after the Central, East, North, South and West numbered postal districts. In this section, pubs to note particularly this year are the Mad Bishop & Bear, W2, Cross Keys, WC2 and Salisbury, WC2 (Central), Head of Steam, NW1 (North), and Mayflower, SE16 and Idle Hour, SW13 (South), though many others have the Star that shows special merit and promise. Drinks prices here are now dreadfully high, averaging over £2.30 for a pint of beer, and wine and spirits prices – and usually even soft drinks prices – following the high-price beer lead. And this is not a question of just small change, either. If you buy a round of drinks for yourself and three friends every day here, by the end of a year you will have spent £686 more than someone doing exactly the same up in Lancashire. The dominant beers in the capital's top pubs are currently the local Fullers London Pride, and Charles Wells Bombardier from Bedfordshire; both Fullers beers and those from the other main London brewer, Youngs, tend to be a little cheaper than many others here.

CENTRAL LONDON Map 13
Admiral Codrington

Mossop Street, SW3; ✸ South Kensington

One of the features that most impresses at this beautifully designed place is the retractable glass roof in the sunny back dining room, which slides open in fine weather. The food in this part is very good indeed, with a changing menu offering a fresh approach to familiar dishes. Particular favourites include their salmon fishcakes (£9.75), cod baked with tomatoes and mushrooms in a soft herb crust (£10.75), and sirloin steak or calves liver (£13.75); good puddings. It's worth booking, particularly at weekends. The more pubby bar is an effective mix of traditional and chic, with comfortable sofas and cushioned wall seats, neatly polished floorboards and panelling, spotlights in the ceiling and lamps on elegant wooden tables, a handsome central counter, sporting prints on the yellow walls, and houseplants around the big bow windows. There's a model ship in a case just above the entrance to the dining room. A separate lunchtime bar menu might include goats cheese and red peppers on ciabatta (£6.25), steak sandwich (£6.95), fish and chips (£7.50) and cottage pie (£7.95); Sunday roasts. Well kept Charles Wells Bombardier and Flowers Original on handpump, and an excellent wine list, with a decent choice by the glass; various coffees, and a range of Havana cigars, with good knowledgeable service from smartly uniformed young staff. There may be piped pop music, and it can seem noisy when busy (the dining room is quieter). At the side is a nice little terrace with tables, benches and heaters. The transformation of the pub's interior was the work of designer Nina Campbell. *(Recommended by MDN, Simon and Jane Williams, BJL, Tracey and Stephen Groves)*

Punch ~ Lease Langlands Pearse ~ Real ale ~ Bar food (12-2.30) ~ Restaurant ~ (020) 7581 0005 ~ Open 11.30-11; closed 25/26 Dec

Albert

Victoria Street, SW1; ✸ St James's Park

A favourite with the Chelsea pensioners from the Royal Hospital, this bustling 19th-c pub was one of the few buildings in this part of Victoria to escape the Blitz (it's now rather dwarfed by the surrounding faceless cliffs of dark modern glass). There's a wonderfully diverse mix of customers, from tourists and civil servants to even the occasional MP: the division bell is rung to remind them when it's time to get back to Westminster. Always busy – especially on weekday lunchtimes and after work – the huge open-plan bar has a surprisingly airy feel, thanks to great expanses of original heavily cut and etched windows along three sides, as well as good solid comfortable furniture, an ornate ceiling, and some gleaming mahogany. Service from the big island counter is generally swift and efficient (particularly obliging to people from overseas), with Charles Wells Bombardier, Courage Best and Directors, Fullers London Pride and Greene King Abbot, and sometimes a more unusual guest on handpump. The separate food servery is good value, offering sandwiches (from £2.75), salads (from £4) and several hearty home-cooked hot dishes such as turkey casserole, fish and chips, sweet and sour chicken and vegetable lasagne (all £5.50); usefully, there's something available all day. The upstairs restaurant does an eat-as-much-as-you-like carvery, better than average (all day inc Sunday, £16.50 for three courses and coffee); it may be worth booking ahead. The handsome staircase that leads up to it is lined with portraits of former Prime Ministers. The back bar is no smoking. Sometimes loudish piped music, fruit machine. Handily placed between Victoria and Westminster, the pub is one of the great sights of this part of London. *(Recommended by Kevin Blake, Mark Walker, Ian Phillips)*

Scottish Courage ~ Manager Roger Swain ~ Real ale ~ Bar food (11(12 Sun)-10) ~ Restaurant ~ (020) 7222 5577 ~ Children in eating area of bar ~ Open 11-11; 12-10.30 Sun; closed 25 Dec

Archery Tavern ◖

Bathurst Street, W2, opposite the Royal Lancaster hotel; ⊖ Lancaster Gate

Changing manager just as we went to press, this welcoming and nicely kept Victorian pub is a useful stop for visitors to this side of Hyde Park. Taking its name from an archery range that occupied the site for a while in the early 19th c, it has plenty of space, and all sorts of types and ages can be found chatting quietly in the several comfortably relaxing, pubby areas around the central servery. On the green patterned walls are a number of archery prints, as well as a history of the pub and the area, other old prints, dried hops, and quite a few plates running along a shelf. Well kept Badger Best, King & Barnes and Tanglefoot on handpump. A big back room has long tables, bare boards, and a fireplace; darts, TV, a big stack of board games, fruit machine, piped music. Bar food has included things like sandwiches, soup, daily specials such as chicken, leek and stilton pie (£5.75), and 8oz rump steak (£6.95); they may do breakfasts on weekend mornings. There's lots more seating in front of the pub, under hanging baskets and elaborate floral displays, and some nicely old-fashioned lamps. A side door leads on to a little mews, where the Hyde Park Riding Stables are based. *(Recommended by Janet and Peter Race, Ian Phillips, Pat and Roger Fereday, Tracey and Stephen Groves, Jarrod and Wendy Hopkinson, Len Banister)*

Badger ~ Manager Nigel Ingram ~ Real ale ~ Bar food (12-2.30(3 Sun), 6-9) ~ (020) 7402 4916 ~ Children welcome ~ Dogs welcome ~ Open 11-11; 12-10.30 Sun

Argyll Arms ◖

Argyll Street W1; ⊖ Oxford Circus, opposite Tube side exit

A useful retreat from the hordes of Oxford Street, this bustling Victorian pub is far nicer and much more individual than its situation might lead you to expect. The most atmospheric and unusual part is the three cubicle rooms at the front, much as they were when built in the 1860s; all oddly angular, they're made by wooden partitions with very distinctive frosted and engraved glass, with hops trailing above. A long mirrored corridor leads to the spacious back room, with the food counter in one corner. Served all day, the blackboard food choice includes good sandwiches and filled baguettes (from £3.95), and hot dishes such as steak and kidney pie, a daily roast, or fish and chips (£6.95). Well kept Adnams, Fullers London Pride and Greene King Old Speckled Hen on handpump; also several malt whiskies. Service is generally prompt and friendly; two fruit machines, piped music (louder in the evenings than at lunch, and very loud indeed at times). Open during busier periods, the quieter upstairs bar overlooks the pedestrianised street – and the Palladium theatre if you can see through the impressive foliage outside the window; divided into several snugs with comfortable plush easy chairs, it has swan's-neck lamps, and lots of small theatrical prints along the top of the walls. The gents' has a copy of the day's *Times* or *Financial Times* on the wall. The pub can get very crowded (and can seem less distinctive on busier evenings), but there's space for drinking outside. *(Recommended by Mayur Shah, Dr and Mrs M E Wilson, Ian Phillips, B and M Kendall, the Didler, Lynn Sharpless, Roger and Jenny Huggins, John and Judy Saville)*

Mitchells & Butlers ~ Managers Kevin Crous and Franco Fernandey ~ Real ale ~ Bar food (11-10; 12-9.30 Sun) ~ (020) 7734 6117 ~ Open 11-11; 12-10.30 Sun; closed 25 Dec

Bishops Finger ♀

West Smithfield, EC1 – opposite Bart's Hospital; ⊖ Farringdon

There are few places in London where you'll find Shepherd Neame beers as well kept as at this swish little pub, in a verdant square beside Smithfield Market. Comfortable and smartly civilised, the well laid-out room has bright yellow walls, big windows, elegant tables with fresh flowers on the polished bare boards, a few pillars, and comfortably cushioned chairs under one wall lined with framed prints. Shepherd Neame Bitter, Spitfire, Bishops Finger and seasonal brews on handpump, with a wide choice of wines (eight by the glass), 10 malt whiskies, and several ports and champagnes; friendly service. Good lunchtime food from an open kitchen beside the bar includes tasty ciabatta sandwiches filled with things like goats cheese, pesto and beef tomato (from £3.35), home-made burgers in focaccia bread (£5.95), a dozen or so types of sausage with mash (from £6.75; they come from a speciality shop nearby), and on Thursday and Friday beer-battered cod and hand-cut chips (£6.95). There are a couple of tables outside. *(Recommended by Ian Phillips)*

Shepherd Neame ~ Manager Paul Potts ~ Real ale ~ Bar food (12-3) ~ (020) 7248 2341 ~ Children welcome ~ Open 11-11; closed Sat/Sun, bank hols

Black Friar

Queen Victoria Street, EC4; ⊖ Blackfriars

This distinctive old favourite now has smart new furniture on its wide forecourt, as well as a new menu with a wider range of food. Of course the main attraction remains its unique décor, which includes some of the best Edwardian bronze and marble art nouveau work to be found anywhere. The inner back room has big bas-relief friezes of jolly monks set into richly coloured florentine marble walls, an opulent marble-pillared inglenook fireplace, a low vaulted mosaic ceiling, gleaming mirrors, seats built into rich golden marble recesses, and tongue-in-cheek verbal embellishments such as Silence is Golden and Finery is Foolish. See if you can spot the opium-smoking hints modelled into the fireplace of the front room. Well kept Adnams, Bass and Fullers London Pride on handpump, and a decent range of wines by the glass; fruit machine. Now served all day, bar food includes sandwiches (from £3.95), pork and herb sausages with mash and onion gravy (£5.75), a vegetarian dish of the day (£5.95), and battered cod and chips or smoked haddock fishcakes (£6.95); Sunday roasts (£6.95). An area around the bar is no smoking. The pub does get busy, and in the evenings lots of people spill out on to the pavement in front, near the approach to Blackfriars Bridge. If you're coming by Tube, choose your exit carefully – it's all too easy to emerge from the network of passageways and find yourself on the wrong side of the street, or marooned on a traffic island. *(Recommended by Mike Gorton, Karen and Graham Oddey, Derek Thomas, I Louden, Mr Bishop, the Didler, Tom McLean, Ian Phillips, Keith Jacob, Patrick Hancock, Alison Hayes, Pete Hanlon)*

Mitchells & Butlers ~ Manager David Tate ~ Real ale ~ Bar food (12-9) ~ (020) 7236 5474 ~ Open 11.30-11; 12-11(10.30 Sun) Sat

Cittie of Yorke ◀

High Holborn, WC1 – find it by looking out for its big black and gold clock; ⊖ Chancery Lane

Like a vast baronial hall, the main back bar of this unique pub takes your breath away when seen for the first time. Vast thousand-gallon wine vats rest above the gantry, big bulbous lights hang from the soaring high-raftered roof, and an extraordinarily extended bar counter stretches off into the distance. It can get packed, especially in the early evening, particularly with lawyers and City folk, but it's at busy times like these when the pub seems most magnificent. Most people tend to congregate in the middle, so you may still be able to bag one of the intimate, old-fashioned and ornately carved booths that run along both sides. The triangular Waterloo fireplace, with grates on all three sides and a figure of Peace among laurels, used to stand in the Hall of Grays Inn Common Room until less obtrusive heating was introduced (thanks to the readers who sent us more thorough notes on its history). Well kept Sam Smiths OB on handpump (appealingly priced at around £1 less than the typical cost of a London pint); friendly service from smartly dressed staff, fruit machine and piped music in the cellar bar. A smaller, comfortable panelled room has lots of little prints of York and attractive brass lights, while the ceiling of the entrance hall has medieval-style painted panels and plaster York roses. Served all day from buffet counters in the main hall and cellar bar, bar food includes sandwiches (from £3.25), and half a dozen daily-changing hot dishes such as steak and kidney pie or lasagne (£4.95). A pub has stood on this site since 1430, though the current building owes more to the 1695 coffee house erected here behind a garden; it was reconstructed in Victorian times, using 17th-c materials and parts. *(Recommended by Ian Phillips, Rona Murdoch, Susan and Nigel Wilson, Tim Maddison, Richard Austen-Baker, BJL, the Didler, Tom McLean, Mayur Shah, Val Stevenson, Rob Holmes, Peter Meister, Richard Lewis, Andrew Barker, Claire Jenkins, Roger and Jenny Huggins, CMW, JJW, R T and J C Moggridge, Patrick Hancock, George Atkinson, David Crook, Barry Collett, Alison Hayes, Pete Hanlon)*

Sam Smiths ~ Manager Stuart Browning ~ Real ale ~ Bar food (12-9) ~ (020) 7242 7670 ~ Children in eating area of bar ~ Open 11.30(12 Sat)-11; closed Sun, bank hols

Coopers Arms

Flood Street; ● Sloane Square, but quite a walk

Relaxed and friendly, this spacious open-plan pub has interesting furnishings that include rush-seated chapel chairs, kitchen chairs and some dark brown plush chairs on the dark stained floorboards, a mix of nice old good-sized tables, and a pre-war sideboard and dresser; also, LNER posters and maps of Chelsea and the Thames on the walls, a stuffed bear in the corner, an enormous railway clock, a fireplace with dried flowers and a tusky boar's head above it, and tea-shop chandeliers. Well kept Youngs Bitter and Special with a guest such as Smiles IPA on handpump, and enjoyable changing bar food reflecting modern tastes alongside familiar favourites changes daily, and might include french onion soup (£3.95), smoked mackerel pâté (£4.95), goats cheese salad (£5.75), seared king scallops (£6.95), bangers and mash (£7.95), shepherd's pie (£8), aberdeen angus steaks (£12), and puddings (£3.50); pleasant helpful staff. *(Recommended by Patrick Hancock, MDN, Derek Thomas, BJL, Mrs V Brown)*

Youngs ~ Tenants Caroline and Simon Lee ~ Real ale ~ Bar food (12.30-3, 6.30-9.30) ~ (020) 7376 3120 ~ Children allowed until 6pm ~ Dogs allowed in bar ~ Open 11-11; 12-10.30 Sun

Cross Keys

Lawrence Street; ● Sloane Square, but some distance away

Attractive outside with foliage and flowers, this bustling Victorian pub has an appealing and roomy high-ceilinged flagstoned bar around the island servery, a roaring fire, all sorts of brassware hanging from the rafters including trumpets and a diver's helmet, lots of atmosphere, and a good mix of customers; there's also a light and airy conservatory-style back restaurant, with an ironic twist to its appealing gardening décor. Well kept Courage Directors and Wadworths 6X on handpump, and a good choice of wines by the glass. Enjoyable bar food includes lunchime baguettes (chicken or steak, £5.50), and sausage and mash or spinach and salmon fishcakes with roasted peppers (£9.50), as well as duck liver parfait on a warm brioche with sweet chutney or mushroom and tarragon risotto with parmesan shavings (£5.95), fried tiger prawns with baby spinach and garlic butter (£7), chicken breast with a blue cheese chunky salad (£12.95), liver and bacon (£15), tuna steak salad niçoise (£15.50), and 9oz rib-eye steak with fondant potatoes (£16.50). Attentive young staff; piped music. *(Recommended by Richard Lippiett, Dr and Mrs A K Clarke, Ian Phillips)*

Free house ~ Licensee Oliver Delestrade ~ Bar food ~ Restaurant ~ (020) 7349 9111 ~ Open 12-11; 12-10.30 Sun; closed bank hols and Christmas

Dog & Duck ◗

Bateman Street, on corner with Frith Street, W1; ● Tottenham Court Road/Leicester Square

A real Soho landmark, this pint-sized corner house is currently very popular with readers, many of whom feel it's stayed essentially unchanged for 40 years. On the floor near the door is an engaging mosaic showing a dog with its tongue out in hot pursuit of a duck; the same theme is embossed on some of the shiny tiles that frame the heavy old advertising mirrors. The main bar really is tiny, though at times it manages to squeeze in a surprisingly large number of people. There are some high stools by the ledge along the back wall, and further seats in a slightly roomier area at one end. The unusual little bar counter serves very well kept Fullers London Pride, Timothy Taylors Landlord, and two changing guests such as Adnams and St Austell Tribute; also Addlestone's cider. There's a fire in winter, and newspapers to read; piped music. They now serve food all day, with bar snacks such as sausage sandwiches (£4.95) and fish and chips (£6.95). In good weather especially, most people tend to spill on to the bustling street, though there's more space in the rather cosy upstairs bar. The pub is said to be where George Orwell celebrated when the American Book of the Month Club chose *Animal Farm* as its monthly selection. Ronnie Scott's jazz club is near by. *(Recommended by Mike Gorton, David Crook, Dr and Mrs M E Wilson, Patrick Hancock, BJL, Ian Phillips, Andrew York, Betsy Brown, Nigel Flook, George Atkinson, Tim Maddison, LM)*

Mitchells & Butlers ~ Manager Liz Maltman ~ Real ale ~ Bar food (12-9) ~ (020) 7494 0697 ~ Open 12-11; 12-10.30 Sun; closed 25 Dec

Eagle 🍴 🍷

Farringdon Road, EC1; opposite Bowling Green Lane car park; ⊖ Farringdon/Old Street

Still packing them in with an excellent and distinctive choice of mediterranean-style meals that rank among the capital's very best, this was the original London gastro-pub. It buzzes with life, and despite the emphasis on eating, always feels chatty and pubby. And though it's often very busy, the atmosphere is so relaxed that readers who've popped in intending to have just a drink find it hard to resist the aromas from the open kitchen. Made with the finest ingredients, typical dishes might include celeriac, ham and potato soup (£5), tuscan bean and bread stew with cavolo nero or spaghetti with asparagus, truffle oil and parmesan cheese (£8), marinated rump steak sandwich (£9), cuttlefish braised with peas, wine and garlic on bruschetta (£10.50), lamb leg chop, roast carrots and jerusalem artichokes with watercress salad (£11), and poached wild sea trout, rocket, french beans and horseradish (£12); they also do unusual spanish, sardinian or goats milk cheeses (£6.50), and portuguese custard tarts (£1); they now take credit cards. On weekday lunchtimes especially, dishes from the blackboard menu can run out or change fairly quickly, so it really is worth getting here as early as you possibly can if you're hoping to eat. Furnishings in the single room are simple but stylish – school chairs, a random assortment of tables, a couple of sofas on bare boards, and modern paintings on the walls (there's an art gallery upstairs, with direct access from the bar). Quite a mix of customers, but it's fair to say there's a proliferation of young media folk (the *Guardian* is based just up the road). It gets particularly busy in the evening (and can occasionally be slightly smoky then), so isn't the sort of place you'd go for a quiet dinner, or a smart night out. Well kept Charles Wells Eagle and Bombardier on handpump, good wines including a dozen by the glass, good coffee, and properly made cocktails; piped music (sometimes loud). There are times during the week when the Eagle's success means you may have to wait for a table, or at least not be shy about sharing; it can be quieter at weekends. *(Recommended by Tim Maddison, Richard and Karen Holt, Andrew Stephenson)*

Free house ~ Licensee Michael Belben ~ Real ale ~ Bar food (12.30-2.30(3.30 Sat/Sun); 6.30-10.30) ~ Restaurant ~ No credit cards ~ (020) 7837 1353 ~ Children welcome ~ Dogs allowed in bar ~ Open 12-11(5 Sun); closed Sun evening, bank hols

Fox 🍴 🍷

Paul Street, EC2; ⊖ Old Street

Wandering into the bare-boards downstairs bar here for the first time, you could be forgiven for assuming it's no more than a basic London boozer, but don't be fooled: the Fox has the same landlord as the Eagle, and a similar emphasis on excellent food. Unpretentious yet relaxed and comfortable, it has lots of stools around a central servery, and small round tables and well-worn furnishings under a dark red ceiling; the first clues that this is something rather unusual are the laid-back jazz and a chalkboard listing the excellent range of well chosen wines (a dozen by the glass). Well kept Charles Wells Bombardier on handpump, and unusual lunchtime bar snacks such as a good hot salt beef sandwich (£5.50), ploughman's with caerphilly, or watermelon with goats curd (both £6). A staircase leads up to the smarter dining room, with its big refectory-style table down the middle, and a very appealing canopied terrace. This is ostensibly the place to enjoy the full menu, though you can have it down in the bar as well. A typical choice might include starters like vichyssoise or serrano ham with broad beans, main courses such as semolina gnocchi, roast tomatoes and rocket, wild salmon and samphire, or neck of lamb and champ, and puddings such as peach and raspberry pavlova or lemon and polenta cake; two courses are £15.50, three courses £19. Service up here is friendly and helpful; they take credit cards. The Fox perhaps takes a bit more effort to seek out than the Eagle, and it will be interesting to see if it causes the same stir. *(Recommended by BOB, Dr and Mrs M E Wilson)*

Unique Pub Co ~ Lease Michael Belben ~ Real ale ~ Bar food (12-3 Mon-Fri) ~ Restaurant ~ (020) 7729 5708 ~ Dogs welcome ~ Open 12-11; closed weekends

Grapes

Shepherd Market, W1; ⊖ Green Park

Well liked by readers for its characterful atmosphere and welcoming coal fire, this chatty and engagingly old-fashioned pub is in the heart of Shepherd Market, one of central London's best-kept secrets. The dimly lit bar has a nicely traditional feel, with plenty of plush red furnishings, stuffed birds and fish in glass display cases, wooden floors and panelling, and a snug little alcove at the back. One small area is no smoking. On sunny evenings smart-suited drinkers spill out on to the square outside. A good range of six or seven well kept (though fairly pricy) beers on handpump usually takes in Boddingtons, Bass, Flowers IPA, Fullers London Pride, Marstons Pedigree and Wadworths 6X; fruit machine. No food, but, very appealingly, they say that customers are welcome to bring in their own. Service can slow down a little at the busiest times; it's much quieter at lunchtimes. *(Recommended by Betsy Brown, Nigel Flook, Roger and Jenny Huggins, Dr and Mrs A K Clarke, Kevin Blake, Ian Phillips, Dr and Mrs M E Wilson)*

Free house ~ Licensees Gill and Eric Lewis ~ Real ale ~ Open 11(12 Sat)-11; 12-10.30 Sun

Grenadier

Wilton Row, SW1; the turning off Wilton Crescent looks prohibitive, but the barrier and watchman are there to keep out cars; walk straight past – the pub is just around the corner; ⊖ Knightsbridge

One of London's most special pubs and, thanks to the active poltergeist said to be its most haunted, this snug and very individual place is well worth the effort it can take to find it. Patriotically painted in red, white and blue, it was once the mess for the officers of the Duke of Wellington. His portrait hangs above the fireplace, alongside neat prints of guardsmen through the ages. The bar is tiny (some might say cramped), but you should be able to plonk yourself on one of the stools or wooden benches; despite the pub's charms it rarely gets too crowded. Well kept Charles Wells Bombardier, Courage Best, Fullers London Pride, and Youngs from handpumps at the rare pewter-topped bar counter; service is friendly and chatty. On Sundays especially you'll find several of the customers here to sample their famous bloody marys, made to a unique recipe. Bar food includes sandwiches, bowls of chips (£2) and nachos (£3.50) – very popular with after-work drinkers – good sausage and mash (£5.55), or hot steak sandwiches (£6.25); Sunday roast (£12.25). There's an intimate back restaurant. The single table in the peaceful mews outside is an ideal spot to dream of owning one of the smart little houses opposite.

(Recommended by Jim Abbott, Dr S J Shepherd, Ian Phillips, MDN, Kevin Blake, Patrick Hancock, Dr and Mrs M E Wilson)

Scottish Courage ~ Manager Debbie White ~ Real ale ~ Bar food ~ Restaurant ~ (020) 7235 3074 ~ Children in restaurant ~ Dogs allowed in bar ~ Open 12-11 (10.30 Sun)

Guinea

Bruton Place; ✆ Bond Street, Green Park, Piccadilly, Oxford Circus

Not to be confused with the quite separate upscale Guinea Grill which takes up much of the same building (uniformed doormen will politely redirect you if you've picked the entrance to that by mistake), this handily-positioned little pub can still impress with its lunchtime bar food: their elaborate grilled ciabattas (from £4.95) and tasty steak and kidney pie (Mon-Fri, £10.50) have both won awards, though it's the latter that's the best known – and which for some is very much the main reason for coming. Dating back in part to the 17th c and with a history that goes back to the 15th, the pub used to cater for the servants and stable hands of the big houses in Mayfair. Like the Grenadier above, it's hidden away in a smart mews, and is pretty much standing room only. Three cushioned wooden seats and tables are tucked to the left of the entrance to the bar, with a couple more in a snug area at the back, underneath a big old clock. Most people tend to prop themselves against a little shelf running along the side of the small room, or stand outside in the street, where there are another couple of tables. Well kept Youngs Bitter, Special, and seasonal brews from the striking bar counter, which has some nice wrought-iron work above it. The look of the place is appealingly simple, with bare boards, yellow walls, old-fashioned prints, and a red-planked ceiling with raj fans, but the atmosphere is chatty and civilised, with plenty of suited workers from Mayfair offices. *(Recommended by Tracey and Stephen Groves, Derek Thomas, Ian Phillips, Patrick Hancock, Sebastian Leach, the Didler)*

Youngs ~ Manager Carl Smith ~ Real ale ~ Bar food (12-2.30 Mon-Fri only) ~ Restaurant ~ (020) 7409 1728 ~ Children over 10 in restaurant ~ Open 11-11; 6.30-11 Sat; closed Sat lunchtime, Sun, bank hols

Jerusalem Tavern ★ 🍺

Britton St, EC1; ✆ Farringdon

There's plenty to recommend at this carefully restored old coffee house, now one of London's very best pubs, but the highlight is undoubtedly the collection of delicious St Peters beers. It's one of only a few pubs belonging to the small, Suffolk-based brewery, and stocks pretty much their full range. Half a dozen are tapped from casks behind the little bar counter: depending on the season you'll find St Peters Best, Fruit Beer, Golden Ale, Grapefruit, Strong, Porter, Wheat Beer, Winter, and Spiced Ales. The rest are usually available in their elegant, distinctively shaped bottles (you may already have come across these in supermarkets); if you develop a taste for them – and they are rather addictive – they sell them to take away. The pub is a vivid re-creation of a dark 18th-c tavern, seeming so genuinely old that you'd never guess the work was done only a few years ago. The current building was developed around 1720, originally as a merchant's house, then becoming a clock and watchmaker's. It still has the shop front added in 1810, immediately behind which is a light little room with a couple of wooden tables and benches, a stack of *Country Life* magazines, and some remarkable old tiles on the walls at either side. This leads to the tiny dimly lit bar, which has a couple of unpretentious tables on the bare boards, and another up some stairs on a discreetly precarious-feeling though perfectly secure balcony. A plainer back room has a few more tables, as well as a fireplace, and a stuffed fox in a case. There's a relaxed, chatty feel in the evenings – though as the pub becomes better-known it's getting harder to bag a seat here then, and it can feel crowded at times. Blackboards list the simple but well liked lunchtime food: soup, good big sandwiches in various breads (from £4.50), and a couple of changing hot dishes such as bangers and mash (£6.50) or lamb shank (£7.50). Prompt, friendly service. A couple of tables outside overlook the quiet street, though take care if standing out here: some readers have found that a neighbouring property's anti-vandalism paint has left a lasting impression on their bags. Note the pub no longer opens at weekends. The brewery also has two main entries in our Suffolk chapter, at Wingfield, and their headquarters at South Elham. *(Recommended by Mike Gorton, Dr and Mrs M E Wilson, the Didler, Val Stevenson, Rob Holmes, John Robertson, Robb Tooley, Andrew York, Giles Francis, Andrew Barker, Claire Jenkins, Alison Hayes, Pete Hanlon)*

St Peters ~ Manager John Murphy ~ Real ale ~ Bar food (12-3; not evenings) ~ (020) 7490 4281 ~ Children welcome ~ Dogs allowed in bar ~ Open 11-11; closed weekends

Lamb ★ ◧

Lamb's Conduit Street, WC1; ⊖ Holborn

One of the capital's most famous pubs, this old favourite has been particularly praised by readers over the last year. Best known for its unique Victorian fittings and atmosphere, it's especially nice after lunch when the crowds have gone and you can better appreciate its timeless charms. The highlight is the bank of cut-glass swivelling 'snob-screens' all the way around the U-shaped bar counter, but sepia photographs of 1890s actresses on the ochre panelled walls, and traditional cast-iron-framed tables with neat brass rails around the rim, all add to the overall effect. Consistently well kept Youngs Bitter, Special and seasonal brews on handpump, along with a guest such as Smiles Best, and around 40 different malt whiskies; thoughtful service. Lunchtime bar food includes a popular hot ham baguette (£4.75), with the meat carved on the counter, as well as ploughman's (£4.75), vegetable curry (£5.75), sausage and mash (£5.95), fish and chips (£6.35), beef and ale pie (£6.95), and lemon and tarragon chicken (£8.50); popular Sunday roasts (£6.75). Shove-ha'penny, cribbage, dominoes; no machines or music. A snug room at the back on the right is no smoking, and there are slatted wooden seats in a little courtyard beyond. It can get very busy, especially in the evenings. Like the street, the pub is named for the Kentish clothmaker William Lamb who brought fresh water to Holborn in 1577. Note they don't allow children. *(Recommended by the Didler, Derek Thomas, Barry Collett, Joel Dobris, Patrick Hancock, Mandy and Simon King, John and Gloria Isaacs, Laura Wilson, Tracey and Stephen Groves, Alison Hayes, Pete Hanlon)*

Youngs ~ Manager Michael Hehir ~ Real ale ~ Bar food (12-2.30, 6-9(not Sun evening)) ~ (020) 7405 0713 ~ Open 11-11; 12-4, 7-10.30 Sun

Lamb & Flag ◧

Rose Street, WC2, off Garrick Street; ⊖ Leicester Square

A Californian reader considers his trips to London complete only after a visit to this ever-popular old place, a pub of great charm and character with an eventful and well documented history: Dryden was nearly beaten to death by hired thugs outside, and Dickens made fun of the Middle Temple lawyers who frequented it when he was working in nearby Catherine Street. Unspoilt and in places rather basic, it's enormously popular with after-work drinkers and visitors; it can be empty at 5pm and heaving by 6, and even in winter you'll find an overflow of people drinking and chatting in the little alleyways outside. Access throughout has been improved in recent years; the more spartan front bar now leads easily into the back, without altering too much the snug feel of the place. The low-ceilinged back bar has high-backed black settles and an open fire, and in Regency times was known as the Bucket of Blood from the bare-knuckle prize-fights held here. Well kept Courage Best and Directors, Charles Wells Bombardier, Youngs Special and changing guests on handpump; as in most pubs round here, the beer isn't cheap, but on weekdays between 11 and 5 you should find at least one offered at a substantial saving. Also, a good few malt whiskies. The bar food – lunchtimes only – is simple but good value, with good sandwiches, filled baked potatoes (£3.50), and half a dozen main courses such as macaroni cheese (£3.95), spicy cumberland sausages or lamb hotpot (£4.25), and a choice of roasts (£5.95). The upstairs Dryden Room is often quieter than downstairs, and has jazz every Sunday evening; there's a TV in the front bar. *(Recommended by Mike Gorton, the Didler, LM, Ted George, BJL, Derek Thomas, Patrick Hancock, Dr and Mrs M E Wilson, Ian Phillips, Val Stevenson, Rob Holmes, David Tindal, David Crook, Peter Scillitoe, Karen and Graham Oddey, Peter Meister)*

Free house ~ Licensees Terry Archer and Adrian and Sandra Zimmerman ~ Real ale ~ Bar food (11(12 Sun)-3) ~ No credit cards ~ (020) 7497 9504 ~ Children in eating area of bar ~ Jazz Sun evenings ~ Open 11-11(10.45 Fri, Sat); 12-10.30 Sun; closed 25 Dec, 1 Jan

Lord Moon of the Mall £

Whitehall, SW1; Charing Cross

More individual than many Wetherspoons pubs, this well converted former bank is a useful pit-stop for families and visitors to the nearby sights. It has frequent special offers on the food, and you'd be hard-pushed to find a cheaper place to eat in the area. The impressive main room has a splendid high ceiling and quite an elegant feel, with smart old prints, big arched windows looking out over Whitehall, and a huge painting that seems to show a well-to-do 18th-c gentleman; in fact it's Tim Martin, founder of the Wetherspoons chain. Once through an arch the style is more recognisably Wetherspoons, with a couple of neatly tiled areas and bookshelves opposite the long bar; silenced fruit machines, trivia. They usually have seven or eight real ales, with the regulars generally Courage Directors, Fullers London Pride, Greene King Abbot, and Shepherd Neame Spitfire; the guests are often very unusual, and the prices always much less than the London norm. They also keep Weston's cider. The good value bar food – served all day – is from the standard Wetherspoons menu: soup (£2.59), sandwiches (from £3.35), bangers and mash (£5.25), five bean chilli (£5.75), aberdeeen angus steak pie (£5.95), and children's meals; they usually have a 2-for-1 meal offer for £6.79. The terms of the licence rule out fried food. Efficient service. The back doors (now only an emergency exit) were apparently built as a secret entrance for the bank's account holders living in Buckingham Palace (Edward VII had an account here from the age of three); the area by here is no smoking. The pub can get busy. As you come out, Nelson's Column is immediately to the left, and Big Ben a walk of 10 minutes or so to the right. *(Recommended by Dr and Mrs M E Wilson, Janet and Peter Race, Ian Phillips, Paul Hopton, Barry Collett, Tracey and Stephen Groves, Len Banister)*

Wetherspoons ~ Manager Mathew Gold ~ Real ale ~ Bar food (10-10; 12-9.30 Sun) ~ (020) 7839 7701 ~ Children welcome till 5 if eating ~ Open 10-11; 12-10.30 Sun

Moon Under Water £

Charing Cross Road, WC2; Tottenham Court Road/Leicester Square

Now opening at 10am for breakfast, this enormous place is another Wetherspoons pub, but rather different from their usual style. It's a conversion of the former Marquee Club, but rather than introducing pseudo-traditional fittings it's been done out in a dramatic, modern style, with remarkable results: big and brash, it's a perfect central London meeting point, attracting an intriguing mix of customers, from Soho trendies and students to tourists and the local after-work crowd. The carefully designed main area is what used to be the auditorium, now transformed into a cavernous white-painted room stretching far off into the distance, with seats and tables lining the walls along the way. It effortlessly absorbs the hordes that pour in on Friday and Saturday evenings, and even when it's at its busiest you shouldn't have any trouble traversing the room, or have to wait very long to be served at the bar; indeed some readers feel the pub is at its best when it's at its most crowded. There are normally up to 10 very nicely priced real ales on handpump: Courage Directors, Fullers London Pride, Greene King Abbot, Shepherd Neame Spitfire, Theakstons Best, and several rapidly changing more unusual guests. They have regular real ale festivals and promotions, also quite a range of coffees, most of which you can buy to take away. Served all day, the good value food is the same as at other Wetherspoons pubs, with the same bargain offers: two meals for £6.49, or special prices on their weekly curry and steak nights. The former stage is the area with most seats, and from here a narrower room leads past another bar to a back door opening on to Greek Street (quite a surprise, as the complete lack of windows means you don't realise how far you've walked). A couple of areas are no-smoking, including the small seating area upstairs, with its birds-eye view of all the comings and goings. If this kind of pub really isn't your thing, at the very least it's a handy shortcut to Soho. *(Recommended by Val Stevenson, Rob Holmes, Tracey and Stephen Groves, Mayur Shah, D J and P M Taylor, B and M Kendall, Patrick Hancock)*

Wetherspoons ~ Manager Nicola Harper ~ Real ale ~ Bar food (10-10.30) ~ (020) 7287 6039 ~ Open 10-11; 12-10.30 Sun

Museum Tavern 🍺

Museum Street/Great Russell Street, WC1; ⊖ Holborn or Tottenham Court Road

Supposed to have been a favourite with Karl Marx, this unspoilt and quietly civilised Victorian pub is directly opposite the British Museum. The single room is simply furnished and decorated, with high-backed wooden benches around traditional cast-iron pub tables, and old advertising mirrors between the wooden pillars behind the bar. Lunchtime tables are sometimes hard to come by, and there can be an initial crush after work, but at other times it can be pleasantly uncrowded in the evenings, with a nicely peaceful atmosphere in late afternoons. A decent choice of well kept beers usually takes in Charles Wells Bombardier, Courage Directors, Fullers London Pride, Theakstons Old Peculier, and Youngs Original and Special; they also have several wines by the glass, a choice of malt whiskies, and tea, coffee, cappuccino and hot chocolate. Good service. From a servery at the end of the room, straightforward bar food might include sandwiches (from £3.45), pie or quiche with salads, fish and chips (£6.75), and Sunday roasts. There are one or two tables out under the gas lamps and 'Egyptian' inn sign. *(Recommended by Peter Meister, Nick Holding, Patrick Hancock, Barry Collett, David Crook, Dr and Mrs A K Clarke, Ian Phillips, Stephen R Holman)*

Scottish Courage ~ Manager Jon Spreadbury ~ Real ale ~ Bar food (11-3.30, 5-9.30) ~ (020) 7242 8987 ~ Open 11-11; 12-10.30 Sun

Nags Head 🍺

Kinnerton Street, SW1; ⊖ Knightsbridge

Minutes from Harrods, but miles away in spirit, this quaint little gem is one of the most unspoilt pubs in London, genuinely characterful and atmospheric, and with the feel of an old-fashioned local in a sleepy country village. Hidden away in an attractive and peaceful mews, it rarely gets too busy or crowded, and there's a snugly relaxed and cosy feel in the small, panelled and low-ceilinged front room, where friendly regulars sit chatting around the unusual sunken bar counter. There's a log-effect gas fire in an old cooking range (seats by here are generally snapped up pretty quickly), then a narrow passage leads down steps to an even smaller back bar with stools and a mix of comfortable seats. The well kept Adnams Best, Broadside and seasonal brews are pulled on attractive 19th-c china, pewter and brass handpumps, while other interesting old features include a 1930s what-the-butler-saw machine and a one-armed bandit that takes old pennies. The piped music is rather individual: often jazz, folk or 1920s-40s show tunes. There are a few seats and a couple of tables outside. Bar food (usefully served all day) includes sandwiches, ploughman's or plenty of salads (from £5.50), sausage, mash and beans, chilli con carne, or steak and mushroom pie (all £5.95), and various roasts (£6); there's a £1.50 surcharge added to all dishes in the evenings, and at weekends. Service is friendly and efficient. Many readers will be delighted to learn they have a fairly hard-line policy on mobile phone use. *(Recommended by Jim Abbott, Patrick Hancock, Tracey and Stephen Groves, Kevin Blake, John and Gloria Isaacs, Ian Phillips, GHC, Pete Baker, the Didler, George Atkinson, Dr and Mrs M E Wilson)*

Free house ~ Licensee Kevin Moran ~ Real ale ~ Bar food (11.30-9.30) ~ No credit cards ~ (020) 7235 1135 ~ Children in eating area of bar ~ Dogs allowed in bar ~ Open 11-11; 12-10.30 Sun

Old Bank of England ♀

Fleet Street, EC4; ⊖ Temple

From the outside, this rather austere Italianate building still looks very much like the subsidiary branch of the Bank of England it once was. But once up the stone steps its spectacular conversion into a pub becomes startlingly clear, and rarely fails to impress first or even second time visitors. In the opulent bar, three gleaming chandeliers hang from the exquisitely plastered ceiling high above the unusually tall island bar counter, and the green walls are liberally dotted with old prints, framed bank notes and the like. Though the room is quite spacious, screens between some of the varied seats and tables create a surprisingly intimate feel, and there are several cosier areas at the end, with more seats in a quieter galleried section upstairs. The mural that covers most of the end wall looks like an 18th-c depiction of Justice (one perhaps over-effusive reader compared it with the Sistine Chapel), but in fact features members of the Fuller, Smith and Turner families. Well kept Fullers Chiswick, ESB, London Pride and seasonal brews on handpump, and around a dozen wines by the glass. Now served all day, good generously served bar food includes soup (£2.75), sandwiches (from £3.50), smoked haddock and salmon fishcakes (£5.75), several pies like leek, mushroom and stilton (£6.25), chicken, red wine and shallot or steak and Fullers Porter (£6.75), pan fried loch duart salmon (£8.25), and steak (£9.75). The piped music is generally classical or easy listening. It can get busy after work. Note they don't allow children, and are closed at weekends. In winter the pub is easy to spot by the Olympic-style torches blazing outside. Pies have a long if rather dubious pedigree in this area; it was in the vaults and tunnels below the Old Bank and the surrounding buildings that Sweeney Todd butchered the clients destined to provide the fillings in his mistress Mrs Lovett's nearby pie shop. *(Recommended by Ian Phillips, D J and P M Taylor, Mayur Shah, Dr and Mrs A K Clarke, Richard Siebert, Barry Collett, Klaus and Elizabeth Leist, Patrick Hancock, the Didler, Tom McLean)*

Fullers ~ Manager Mark Maltby ~ Real ale ~ Bar food (12-9) ~ Restaurant ~ (020) 7430 2255 ~ Open 11-11; closed weekends, bank hols

Olde Cheshire Cheese

Wine Office Court, off 145 Fleet Street, EC4; ⊖ Blackfriars

The succession of dark, historic little rooms at this atmospheric 17th-c former chop house is a joy to explore, and even though it's one of London's most famous old pubs, it doesn't feel as if it's on the tourist route. Over the years Congreve, Pope, Voltaire, Thackeray, Dickens, Conan Doyle, Yeats and perhaps Dr Johnson have called in, and many parts hardly appear to have changed since. The unpretentious rooms have bare wooden benches built in to the walls, sawdust on bare boards, and, on the ground floor, high beams, crackly old black varnish, Victorian paintings on the dark brown walls, and big open fires in winter. A particularly snug room is the tiny one on the right as you enter, but perhaps the most rewarding bit is the Cellar Bar, down steep narrow stone steps that look as if they're only going to lead to the loo, but in fact take you to an unexpected series of cosy areas with stone walls and ceilings, and some secluded corners. There's plenty of space, so even though it can get busy during the week (it's fairly quiet at weekends) it rarely feels too crowded. Usually served all day, bar food includes sandwiches or hot paninis, soup, ploughman's (£4.25), and steak and ale pie, lasagne or various daily specials (£4.75). Sam Smiths OB on handpump, as usual for this brewery, extraordinarily well priced (almost £1 less than other beers can cost at more expensive London pubs); friendly service. Some of the Cellar Bar is no smoking at lunchtimes. *(Recommended by Rona Murdoch, Alan J Morton, Patrick Hancock, Ian Phillips, Val Stevenson, Rob Holmes, Barry Collett, LM, Tom McLean, Richard Siebert, Susan and Nigel Wilson, the Didler, Jim Abbott, Dr and Mrs M E Wilson, Alison Hayes, Pete Hanlon)*

Sam Smiths ~ Manager Gordon Garrity ~ Real ale ~ Bar food (12-9(2 Sun)) ~ Restaurant (Sunday) ~ (020) 7353 6170/4388 ~ Children in eating area of bar and restaurant ~ Open 11-11; 11-3, 5.30-11 Sat; 12-3 Sun; closed Sun evening

Olde Mitre £

Ely Place, EC1; the easiest way to find it is from the narrow passageway beside 8 Hatton Garden; ⊖ Chancery Lane

Nothing seems to change at this carefully rebuilt old tavern, a delightful hidden treasure standing out for its distinctive character and history, and exceptional welcome and service. Unless you approach it from Hatton Garden it can be notoriously difficult to find, but it more than repays the effort; the landlord clearly loves his job, and works hard to pass that enjoyment on to his customers. The cosy dark-panelled small rooms have antique settles and – particularly in the back room, where there are more seats – old local pictures and so forth. It gets good-naturedly packed between 12.30 and 2.15, filling up again in the early evening, but in the early afternoons and by around nine becomes a good deal more tranquil. An upstairs room, mainly used for functions, may double as an overflow at peak periods. Well kept Adnams, Ind Coope Burton and Tetleys on handpump; notably chatty staff. No music, TV or machines – the only game here is darts. Served all day, bar snacks are limited to scotch eggs or pork pies (£1), and really good value toasted sandwiches with cheese, ham, pickle or tomato (£1.75). There are some pot plants and jasmine in the narrow yard between the pub and St Ethelreda's church. Note the pub doesn't open at weekends. The iron gates that guard one entrance to Ely Place are a reminder of the days when the law in this district was administered by the Bishops of Ely. *(Recommended by BJL, the Didler, R T and J C Moggridge, Alison Hayes, Pete Hanlon)*

Spirit Group ~ Manager Don O'Sullivan ~ Real ale ~ Bar food (11-9.15) ~ (020) 7405 4751 ~ Open 11-11; closed weekends, bank hols

Red Lion ◖

Duke of York Street, SW1; ⊖ Piccadilly Circus

Perhaps central London's most perfectly preserved Victorian pub, this busy place has mirrors so dazzling, and gleaming mahogany so warm, that it's hard to believe they weren't put in yesterday. Other notable architectural features squeezed into the very small rooms include the crystal chandeliers and cut and etched windows (readers have been particularly impressed by these this year), and the striking ornamental plaster ceiling. Simple lunchtime snacks such as sandwiches (£2.80) or filled baguettes (£3.50); diners have priority on a few of the front tables, and there's a minuscule upstairs eating area. Well kept Adnams, Bass, Fullers London Pride, Greene King Old Speckled Hen and Tetleys on handpump; friendly efficient service. It can be very crowded at lunchtime (try inching through to the back room where there's sometimes more space); many customers spill out on to the pavement, in front of a mass of foliage and flowers cascading down the wall. No children inside. *(Recommended by BJL, the Didler, Dr and Mrs M E Wilson, Ian Phillips, Tracey and Stephen Groves, P G Plumridge, Alison Hayes, Pete Hanlon)*

Mitchells & Butlers ~ Manager Michael Brown ~ Real ale ~ No credit cards ~ (020) 7321 0782 ~ Open 11.30(12 Sat)-11; closed Sun; bank hols

Red Lion ◖

Waverton Street, W1; ⊖ Green Park

In one of Mayfair's quietest and prettiest corners, this smartly cosy old place is well liked by readers for its very relaxed and distinctly un-London atmosphere. On some evenings after work it can be very busy indeed, but it always keeps its comfortably civilised feel, and has something of the air of a popular country local. The main L-shaped bar has small winged settles on the partly carpeted scrubbed floorboards, and London prints below the high shelf of china on its dark-panelled walls. Well kept beers such as Charles Wells Bombardier, Courage Directors, Fullers London Pride, and Greene King IPA on handpump, and they do rather good bloody marys (with a daunting Very Spicy option); also a dozen or so malt whiskies. Bar food, served from a corner at the front, includes sandwiches (from £3), ploughman's (£4.50), sausage and mash (£4.95), cod and chips, half rack of grilled pork ribs or cajun chicken (all £6.95), and specials such as mushroom stroganoff. Unusually for this area, they serve food morning and evening seven days a week. The gents' usually has a copy of *Private Eye* at eye level (it used to be the *Financial Times*). On Saturday evenings they generally have a pianist. *(Recommended by Tracey and Stephen Groves, Roger and Jenny Huggins, Betsy Brown, Nigel Flook, Ian Phillips, BJL, Patrick Hancock, Kevin Blake, Dr and Mrs M E Wilson, Simon and Amanda Southwell)*

Scottish Courage ~ Manager Greg Peck ~ Real ale ~ Bar food (12-3, 6-9.30) ~ Restaurant ~ (020) 7499 1307 ~ Children in eating area of bar and restaurant ~ Dogs allowed in bar ~ Piano Sat evening ~ Open 11.30-11; 6-11 Sat; 12-3, 6-10.30 Sun; closed Sat am

Seven Stars 🍺

Carey Street, WC2; ⊖ Holborn (just as handy from Temple or Chancery Lane, but the walk through Lincoln's Inn Fields can be rather pleasant)

Long a favourite with lawyers and reporters covering notable trials nearby, this cosy little pub has considerably widened its appeal under the current licensees, who've introduced a greater emphasis on imaginative, home-cooked food. Served all day, the blackboard menu might include things like half a dozen oysters (£6), country scramble (a chunk of sourdough with smoked pork, sliced potato, onion, parsley and thyme, £7.50), chargrilled fresh whole sea bream with lemon wedges and lentil purée (£8), two grilled quails and three merguez sausages with watercress on a sourdough crouton toasted in olive oil (£8), and plenty of seasonal game; at times you may also find vintage port with fruit cake. The two unspoilt rooms have several tables set for eating, as well as plenty of caricatures of barristers and judges on the red-painted walls, posters of legal-themed British films, big ceiling fans, and a relaxed, intimate atmosphere. It can fill up very quickly, and on busy evenings customers sometimes spill on to the quiet road facing the back of the Law Courts. Well kept Adnams Best and Broadside, Fullers Organic Honeydew and Harveys Sussex Best on handpump. Service is prompt and very friendly. The Elizabethan stairs up to the lavatories are rather steep, but the licensees tell us that with the addition of a good strong handrail and some light grey rubber, the trip is now 'a safe and bouncy delight'. *(Recommended by the Didler, LM, Tom McLean, Rona Murdoch, Ian Phillips, B and M Kendall, Richard Gibbs)*

Free house ~ Licensee Roxy Beaujolais ~ Real ale ~ Bar food (12-9) ~ Restaurant ~ (020) 7242 8521 ~ Dogs allowed in bar ~ Open 11-11; 12-11.30 Sat; closed Sun, Easter Mon, 25/26 Dec, 1 Jan, possibly other bank hols

Star 🍺

Belgrave Mews West, SW1, behind the German Embassy, off Belgrave Square; ⊖ Knightsbridge

Said to be where the Great Train Robbery was planned, this nicely traditional pub is one of those timeless places that are such a pleasurable surprise to find in London. A highlight in summer is the astonishing array of hanging baskets and flowering tubs outside, much more impressive than average. Outside peak times it has a pleasantly quiet and restful local feel, and it always impresses with its particularly well kept Fullers Chiswick, ESB, London Pride and seasonal brews. The small entry room, which also has the food servery, has stools by the counter and tall windows; an arch leads to a side room with swagged curtains, well polished wooden tables and chairs, heavy upholstered settles, globe lighting, and raj fans. The back room has button-back built-in wall seats, and there's a similarly furnished room upstairs. Served all day, good value straightforward bar food might include sandwiches (from £3.25), warm roast chicken, bacon and avocado salad, sausage and mash or pasta with sun-dried tomatoes, olives, garlic and cream (£6.25), and rib-eye steak (£9.95). *(Recommended by Patrick Hancock, the Didler, Tracey and Stephen Groves, Kevin Blake, Richard Dixon)*

Fullers ~ Manager T J Connell ~ Real ale ~ Bar food (12-9) ~ (020) 7235 3019 ~ Children in eating area of bar ~ Dogs allowed in bar ~ Open 11.30-11; 12-10.30 Sun

Westminster Arms 🍺

Storey's Gate, SW1; ⊖ Westminster

If during a visit to this unpretentious and friendly Westminster local you see suited gents scrambling to their feet when something a bit like a telephone bell sounds, they are MPs, being chased back across the road by the Division Bell, to vote. The handiest local for the Houses of Parliament and the Abbey, it usually keeps an impressive range of nine real ales, generally including Adnams Best and Broadside, Brakspears PA, Fullers London Pride, Youngs, a beer brewed for the pub, and guests like Batemans, Gales HSB and Greene King Abbot; they also do decent wines, and a dozen or so malt whiskies. Usually packed after work with government staff and researchers, the plain main bar has simple old-fashioned furnishings, with proper tables on the wooden floors, and a good deal of panelling; there's not a lot of room, so come early for a seat. The food is served in the downstairs wine bar (a good retreat from the ground-floor bustle), with some of the tables in cosy booths; typical dishes include filled rolls (from £4), ploughman's (£5.50), steak and kidney pie, fish and chips or scampi (£6.50), and roast beef (£6.95). Piped music in this area, and in the more formal upstairs restaurant, but not generally in the main bar; fruit machine. There is a couple of tables by the street outside. *(Recommended by the Didler, Patrick Hancock, Ian Phillips, Paul Hopton, Stephen, Julie and Hayley Brown)*

Free house ~ Licensees Gerry and Marie Dolan ~ Real ale ~ Bar food (12-8) ~ Restaurant (weekday lunchtimes (not Weds)) ~ (020) 7222 8520 ~ Children welcome at weekends, in restaurant weekdays ~ Open 11-11(6 Sat); 12-6 Sun; closed Sun evening, 25-26 Dec

EAST LONDON Map 12
Grapes

Narrow Street, E14; ⊖ Shadwell (some distance away) or Westferry on the Docklands Light Railway; the Limehouse link has made it hard to find by car – turn off Commercial Road at signs for Rotherhithe tunnel, then from the Tunnel Approach slip road, fork left leading into Branch Road, turn left and then left again into Narrow Street

In a peaceful spot well off the tourist route, this warmly welcoming 16th-c tavern is one of London's most engaging riverside pubs. It was used by Charles Dickens as the basis of his Six Jolly Fellowship Porters in *Our Mutual Friend*, and little has changed since he prophetically wrote 'It had not a straight floor and hardly a straight line, but it had outlasted and would yet outlast many a better-trimmed building, many a sprucer public house'. The back part is the oldest, with the small back balcony a fine place for a sheltered waterside drink; steps lead down to the foreshore. The partly panelled bar has lots of prints, mainly of actors, some elaborately etched windows, and newspapers to read. Well kept Adnams, Bass and Ind Coope Burton on handpump, a choice of malt whiskies, and a good wine list. Good bar food includes soup (£2.95), sandwiches (from £3.25), bangers and mash (£5.75), home-made fishcakes with caper sauce (£5.95), dressed crab (£7.25), and a highly regarded, generous Sunday roast (no other meals then, when it can be busy, particularly in season). They do an excellent brunch on Saturday lunchtimes Booking is recommended for the upstairs fish restaurant, which has fine views of the river (the pub was a favourite with Rex Whistler, who used it as the viewpoint for his rather special river paintings). Shove-ha'penny, table skittles, cribbage, dominoes, chess, backgammon; there may be piped classical or jazz. *(Recommended by Mike Gorton, Tim and Pam Moorey, Bob and Sue Hardy, R T and J C Moggridge)*

Spirit Group ~ Manager Barbara Haigh ~ Real ale ~ Bar food (not Sun evening) ~ Restaurant ~ (020) 7987 4396 ~ Dogs allowed in bar ~ Open 12-3, 5.30-11; 12-11 Sat; 12-10.30 Sun; closed 25/26 Dec, 1 Jan

Prospect of Whitby

Wapping Wall, E1; ✚ Wapping

The view of the Thames from this entertaining old pub can hardly be bettered, and has been a draw since it was a favourite with smugglers and river thieves, back when the pub was known as the Devil's Tavern. It has such a lively history it's no wonder they do rather play on it; the tourists who flock here lap up the colourful tales of Merrie Olde London, and only the most unromantic of visitors could fail to be carried along by the fun. Pepys and Dickens were both frequent callers, Turner came for weeks at a time to study its river views, and in the 17th c the notorious Hanging Judge Jeffreys was able to combine two of his interests by enjoying a drink at the back while looking down over the grisly goings-on in Execution Dock. The pub is an established favourite on the evening coach tours, but is usually quieter at lunchtimes. Plenty of bare beams, bare boards, panelling and flagstones in the L-shaped bar (where the long pewter counter is over 400 years old), and a river view towards Docklands from tables in the waterfront courtyard. Well kept Adnams, Courage Directors, Fullers London Pride and Greene King Old Speckled Hen on handpump, and quite a few malt whiskies. Bar meals are served all day, from a menu including sandwiches and filled baked potatoes (from £3.25), various burgers (from £4.95), ploughman's (£5.25), roasted red pepper lasagne (£7.75), and jamaican jerk spiced chicken (£9.75). One area of the bar is no smoking; fruit machine, golf game. *(Recommended by Roy and Lindsey Fentiman, LM, GHC, Alison Hayes, Pete Hanlon)*

Scottish Courage ~ Manager Christopher Reeves ~ Real ale ~ Bar food (12-9) ~ Restaurant ~ (020) 7481 1095 ~ Children welcome ~ Dogs allowed in bar ~ Open 11.30-11; 12-10.30 Sun

NORTH LONDON Map 13
Chapel 🍴 ♀

Chapel St, NW1; ✚ Edgware Road

Very good, well served and presented food continues to be the hallmark of this much-modernised child-friendly gastropub. The menu changes every day, but might include soups such as cream of pumpkin, tomato and cumin (£3.50) or jamaican chicken and banana (£4), brie, olive and pimientos tartlet (£4.50), ragout of smoked tuna, trout and eel with capers and sun-dried tomato (£5), asparagus tortelli with basil, tomato and gruyère cheese (£8.50), pan-fried calves liver with parma ham, port, mash and rosemary (£11.50), maltese-style braised lamb shank with sweet potato (£12.50), seared swordfish steak with celeriac, potato gratin, lemon and butter sauce (£13), and puddings like chocolate and banana crème brûlée (£3.50). Prompt, charming service from friendly staff, who may bring delicious warm walnut bread to your table while you're waiting. The atmosphere is always cosmopolitan – perhaps more relaxed and civilised at lunchtime, then altogether busier and louder in the evenings. Light and spacious, the cream-painted main room is dominated by the open kitchen; furnishings are smart but simple, with plenty of plain wooden tables around the bar, and more in a side room with a big fireplace. It can fill up quite quickly, so you may have to wait to eat during busier periods. There are more tables on a terrace outside, popular with chic local office workers on fine lunchtimes. Well kept Adnams and Greene King IPA on handpump (both rather expensive, even for London), a good range of interesting wines (up to half by the glass), cappuccino and espresso, fresh orange juice, and a choice of tisanes such as peppermint or strawberry and vanilla. In the evening, trade is more evenly split between diners and drinkers, and the music can be quite noticeable then, especially at weekends. *(Recommended by Sebastian Leach, B and M Kendall)*

Punch ~ Lease Lakis Hondrogiannis ~ Real ale ~ Bar food (12-2.30, 7-10) ~ (020)
7402 9220 ~ Children welcome ~ Dogs welcome ~ Open 12-11(10.30 Sun); closed
some bank hols

Compton Arms ♀ £

Compton Avenue, off Canonbury Road, N1; ⊖ Highbury & Islington

Hidden away up a peaceful mews, this well run tiny local has the unexpected bonus
of a very pleasant crazy-paved terrace behind, with benches and tables among
flowers under a big sycamore tree; there may be heaters in winter, and occasional
barbecues in summer. Inside, the unpretentious low-ceilinged rooms are simply
furnished with wooden settles and assorted stools and chairs, with local pictures on
the walls; it has a very appealing village-local feel, and though there are a TV and
piped music, the only games are things like chess, Jenga and Battleships. Well kept
Greene King Abbot, IPA and Ruddles and a weekly changing guest on handpump,
and around a dozen wines by the glass; friendly service. Good value bar food such
as baguettes, and seven different types of sausage served with mashed potato and
home-made red onion gravy (£4.95); their Sunday roasts come in two sizes, normal
(£4.45) and large (£5.95). The pub is deep in Arsenal country, so can get busy on
match days. *(Recommended by Tim Maddison, R T and J C Moggridge, Ian Phillips)*

Greene King ~ Managers Scott Plomer and Eileen Shelock ~ Real ale ~ Bar food
(12-2.30, 6-8.30; 12-4 Sat/Sun) ~ (020) 7359 6883 ~ Children welcome in family
room till 8pm ~ Open 12-11(10.30 Sun)

Duke of Cambridge 🍴 ♀ ■

St Peter's Street, N1; ⊖ Angel, though some distance away

This well refurbished corner house was London's first completely organic pub, with
an excellent range of impeccably sourced drinks and food. Prices for both are
perhaps higher than you'd pay for a non-organic meal, but it's usually worth the
extra to enjoy choices and flavours you won't find anywhere else. Changing twice a
day, the blackboard menu might include things like pumpkin, pear and celery soup
(£4.50), bruschetta with chicken livers, dandelion leaves, sherry and crème fraîche
(£6), roasted vegetables with parmesan and hazelnut crust (£9), bacon-wrapped
scallops with tartare potato cake and basil crème (£10.50), fried red mullet with
linguini, lemon and chilli sauce (£12), home-smoked lamb fillet with potato,
aubergine and feta gratin (£13), and white chocolate and berry cheesecake (£4.50);
children's helpings. A note explains that though they do all they can to ensure their
game and fish have been sourced from suppliers using sustainable methods, these
can't officially be classed as organic. They make all their own bread, pickles, ice
cream and so on. On handpump are four organic real ales: from London's small
Pitfield Brewery Eco Warrior and Singhboulton (named for the pub's two owners),
St Peters Best, and a guest such as East Kent Goldings or Shoreditch Organic Stout.
They also have organic draught lagers and cider, organic spirits, and a very wide
range of organic wines, many of which are available by the glass; we haven't yet
personally verified the claim that organic drinks are less likely to cause a hangover.
The full range of drinks is chalked on a blackboard, and also includes good coffees
and teas, and a spicy ginger ale. The big, busy main room is simply decorated and
furnished, with lots of chunky wooden tables, pews and benches on bare boards, a
couple of big metal vases with colourful flowers, daily papers, and carefully
positioned soft lighting around the otherwise bare walls. The atmosphere is warmly
inviting, with the constant sound of civilised chat from a steady stream of varied
customers; no music or games machines. A corridor leads off past a few tables and
an open kitchen to a couple of smaller candlelit rooms, more formally set for
eating; there's also a small side terrace. Some areas are no smoking. A couple of
recent reports have detected a slight dip in the usual high standards, which we hope
was only temporary. The licensees run the Crown in Victoria Park (see Lucky Dip
section, under E3) along similar lines. *(Recommended by Dr and Mrs M E Wilson,
Tracey and Stephen Groves, Derek Thomas)*

Free house ~ Licensees Geetie Singh and Esther Boulton ~ Real ale ~ Bar food (12.30-3(3.30 Sat/Sun), 6.30-10.30(10 Sun)) ~ Restaurant ~ (020) 7359 3066 ~ Children welcome ~ Dogs allowed in bar ~ Open 12-11(10.30 Sun); closed 25/26 Dec

Flask ♀ £

Flask Walk, NW3; ⊖ Hampstead

Its name a reminder of the days when the pub distributed mineral water from Hampstead's springs, this properly old-fashioned local is still a popular haunt of Hampstead artists, actors, and characters. The snuggest and most individual part is the cosy lounge at the front, with plush green seats and banquettes curving round the panelled walls, a unique Victorian screen dividing it from the public bar, an attractive fireplace, and a very laid-back and rather villagey atmosphere. A comfortable orange-lit room with period prints and a few further tables leads into a rather smart dining conservatory, which with its plants, prominent wine bottles and neat table linen feels a bit like a wine bar. A couple of white iron tables are squeezed into the tiny back yard. Particularly well kept Youngs Bitter, Special and seasonal brews on handpump, around 20 wines by the glass, and decent coffees – they have a machine that grinds the beans to order. Bar food might include sandwiches (from £2.50), soup, and daily changing specials like chicken casserole, lamb curry or spiced minced beef pie with a cheese and leek mash topping (from £5.50); they do fish and chips at weekends. A plainer public bar (which you can get into only from the street) has leatherette seating, cribbage, backgammon, lots of space for darts, fruit machines, trivia, and big-screen SkyTV. Friendly service from sociable young staff. There are quite a few tables out in the alley. *(Recommended by John Robertson, the Didler, Ian Phillips, Tracey and Stephen Groves)*

Youngs ~ Manager John Cannon ~ Real ale ~ Bar food (12-3(4 Sun), 6-8.30; not Sun/Mon evening) ~ Restaurant ~ (020) 7435 4580 ~ Children in eating area of bar and restaurant ~ Dogs allowed in bar ~ Open 11-11; 12-10.30 Sun

Holly Bush ◀

Holly Mount, NW3; ⊖ Hampstead

A characterful and civilised spot, this cheery Hampstead local is these days winning fans not just for its atmosphere and timeless style, but for its beers and above average food. It's perhaps especially appealing in the evenings, when a good mix of chatty locals and visitors fills the old-fashioned and individual front bar. Under the dark sagging ceiling are brown and cream panelled walls (decorated with old advertisements and a few hanging plates), open fires, bare boards, and cosy bays formed by partly glazed partitions. Slightly more intimate, the back room, named after the painter George Romney, has an embossed red ceiling, panelled and etched glass alcoves, and ochre-painted brick walls covered with small prints; piped music, darts. Well kept Adnams Bitter and Broadside, Fullers London Pride, Harveys Sussex and an unusual guest like Hydes Hubble Bubble on handpump, some unusual bottled beers, plenty of whiskies, and a good wine list; friendly service. Bar food includes soup (£3.50), welsh rarebit (£5), pies like beef and ale or carrot, parsnip, celeriac and cider (from £8), various sausages with cheddar mash and gravy (£8.50), slow roast lamb shank (£9.50), and roasted free-range chicken in smoked paprika sauce (£10), Guinness and mushroom pie (£8.75). An upstairs area is no smoking at weekends. There are tables on the pavement outside. The pub is reached by a delightful stroll along some of Hampstead's most villagey streets. *(Recommended by Tracey and Stephen Groves, the Didler, Ian Phillips)*

Punch ~ Managers Andreas Akerlund and Nicolai Outzen ~ Real ale ~ Bar food (12.30-4, 6.30-10; 12.30-8.30 Sun; not Mon lunchtime) ~ Restaurant ~ (020) 7435 2892 ~ Children welcome ~ Dogs allowed in bar ~ Open 12-11(10.30 Sun)

We say if we know a pub allows dogs.

Olde White Bear

Well Road, NW3; ⊖ Hampstead

Very close to the heath, this neo-Victorian pub is a notably friendly place that attracts a wonderfully diverse mix of people of all ages. The dimly lit knocked-through bar has three separate-seeming areas: the biggest has lots of Victorian prints and cartoons on the walls, as well as wooden stools, cushioned captain's chairs, a couple of big tasselled armchairs, a flowery sofa, a handsome fireplace and an ornate Edwardian sideboard. A brighter section at the end has elaborate brocaded pews and wooden venetian blinds, while a central area has Lloyd Loom furniture, dried flower arrangements and signed photographs of actors and playwrights. Bar food is served all day, from a range including soup (£3.50), good elaborate sandwiches (from £4), ploughman's, japanese tempura prawns or chicken satay (£5), a daily pasta dish (£5.75), pork and leek sausages or thai chicken curry (£6.50), cod in beer batter or beef and Guinness pie (£7), and sirloin steak (£9.50); Sunday roasts. Adnams, Greene King Abbot, Fullers London Pride, and Youngs on handpump. There are a few tables in front, and more in a courtyard behind. Soft piped music, cards, chess, TV, and excellent Thursday quiz nights. Parking may be a problem at times – it's mostly residents' permits only nearby (there are no restrictions on Sundays). *(Recommended by the Didler, Ian Phillips)*

Punch ~ Lease Christopher Ely ~ Real ale ~ Bar food (12-9) ~ (020) 7435 3758 ~ Children welcome ~ Dogs allowed in bar ~ Open 11-11; 12-11 Sat; 12-10.30 Sun

Spaniards Inn 🍺

Spaniards Lane, NW3; ⊖ Hampstead, but some distance away, or from Golders Green station take 220 bus

Tales of ghosts and highwaymen help draw the crowds to this busy former toll house, but to our mind the highlight is perhaps its charming garden, said to be where Keats wrote 'Ode to a Nightingale' in 1820. Nicely arranged in a series of areas separated by judicious planting of shrubs, it has slatted wooden tables and chairs on a crazy-paved terrace opening on to a flagstoned walk around a small lawn, with roses, a side arbour of wisteria and clematis, and an aviary. You may need to move fast to bag a table out here in summer. Inside, the low-ceilinged oak-panelled rooms of the attractive main bar have open fires, genuinely antique winged settles, candle-shaped lamps in shades, and snug little alcoves. Well kept Adnams, Fullers London Pride, Rebellion IPA and a seasonal guest like Hop Back Summer Lightning on handpump – though in summer you might find the most popular drink is their big jug of Pimms; newspapers, fruit machine. Under the new manager food is served all day, from a menu including ciabattas (from £4.95), soup (£3.95), greek salad or spaghetti meatballs in tomato sauce (£6.50), mushroom, parmesan and lemon risotto (£6.95), home-made pork, garlic and herb sausages (£7.50), and steak and kidney pudding (£7.95); they do a paella on Saturdays (£7.50), and a roast on Sundays. The food bar is no smoking at lunchtimes, upstairs, the Georgian Turpin Room is no smoking all day. The pub is believed to have been named after the Spanish ambassador to the court of James I, who had a private residence here. It's fairly handy for Kenwood, and indeed during the 1780 Gordon Riots the then landlord helped save the house from possible disaster, cunningly giving so much free drink to the mob on its way to burn it down that by the time the Horse Guards arrived the rioters were lying drunk and incapable on the floor. Parking can be difficult – especially when people park here to walk their dogs on the heath. *(Recommended by David Carr, John and Judy Saville, Ian Phillips, Trevor Hosking, John Robertson, Tracey and Stephen Groves)*

Mitchells & Butlers ~ Manager Matthew O'Keefe ~ Real ale ~ Bar food (12-10) ~ (020) 8731 6571 ~ Children welcome ~ Dogs allowed in bar ~ Open 11-11; 12-10.30 Sun

Waterside

York Way, N1; ⊖ Kings Cross

A useful place to know if passing through Kings Cross, this handily placed pub benefits from an unexpectedly relaxing outside terrace overlooking the Battlebridge Basin, usually busy with boats. Heaters keep it pleasant all year round. The building is a nicely done pastiche of a 17th-c cider barn, with stripped brickwork, latticed windows, genuinely old stripped timbers in white plaster, lots of dimly lit alcoves, spinning wheels, milkmaids' yokes, and horsebrasses and so on, with plenty of rustic tables and wooden benches. Adnams, Fullers London Pride and a changing guest such as Charles Wells Bombardier on handpump, with cocktails in summer and mulled wine in winter. Bar food (served all day exc Sun) has an emphasis on fairly formidable pizzas (from £4.95), though they also do sandwiches (from £3.25), and hot dishes like fish pie (£5.45), and mushroom ravioli with four cheese sauce or steak in red wine (£5.95); they have a two-for-one meal offer Mon-Thurs. Live jazz Weds evenings. Pool, fruit machine, and sometimes loudish juke box. *(Recommended by Ian Phillips, John Robertson, Janet and Peter Race)*

Laurel Pub Company ~ Manager Farhad Farjad ~ Real ale ~ Bar food (12-9; 12-4.30 Sun) ~ (020) 7713 8613 ~ Children in eating area of bar ~ Live jazz Weds evenings ~ Open 11-11; 12-11 Sat; 12-10.30 Sun; closed 25/26 Dec, 1 Jan

SOUTH LONDON Map 12
Alma ♀

York Road, SW18; ⇌ Wandsworth Town

Feeling lighter and airier since a slight refurbishment last year, this relaxed and comfortable corner pub is very much like a welcoming local, but a rather smart one – and the distinctive food lifts it well out of the ordinary. The furnishings are mostly quite simple: a mix of chairs and cast-iron-framed or worn wooden tables around the brightly repainted walls, and a couple of sofas, with gilded mosaics of the 19th-c Battle of the Alma and an ornate mahogany chimney-piece and fireplace adding a touch of elegance. The popular but less pubby dining room has a fine turn-of-the-century frieze of swirly nymphs, and a new window overlooking an ornamental garden; there's waitress service in here, and you can book a particular table. Youngs Bitter, Special and seasonal brews from the island bar counter, and good house wines (with around 20 by the glass), freshly squeezed juices, good coffee, tea or hot chocolate; newspapers out for customers. Even when it's very full – which it often is in the evenings – service is careful and efficient. The imaginative and generously served bar food might include very good sandwiches (from £3.75), soups such as roasted fennel and parsnip (£3.75), falafels with warm potato, chargrilled courgette and spring onion and cucumber salad (£7.95), spaghetti with english asparagus, salmon and lemon cream (£8.50), and seared lamb with ginger lentils and bok choi (£9.50); the menu is a little different on Sundays, when they do various roasts. Much of the meat is organic, and comes from their own farm in Dorking. If you're after a quiet drink don't come when there's a rugby match on the television, unless you want a running commentary from the well heeled and voiced young locals. Pinball, dominoes. Charge up their 'smart-card' with cash and you can pay with a discount either here or at the management's other pubs, which include the Ship in Wandsworth (see below). Travelling by rail into Waterloo you can see the pub rising above the neighbouring rooftops as you rattle through Wandsworth Town. *(Recommended by Dr Martin Owton, the Didler, Ian Phillips)*

Youngs ~ Tenant Charles Gotto ~ Real ale ~ Bar food (12-4, 6-10; 12-4 Sun) ~ Restaurant ~ (020) 8870 2537 ~ Children welcome ~ Open 11-11; 12-10.30 Sun; closed 25 Dec

---

Food details, prices, timing etc refer to bar food – not to a separate restaurant if there is one.

Anchor

Park Street – Bankside, Southwark Bridge end; ⊖/⇌ London Bridge

The wooden tables on the busy terrace of this old riverside pub offer unrivalled views of the Thames and the City. It's ideally placed for visits to the Tate Modern and the Globe theatre, and happily an almost total refurbishment last year hasn't overly affected the pub's character or appeal. The current building dates back to about 1750, when it was built to replace an earlier tavern, possibly the one that Pepys came to during the Great Fire of 1666. 'All over the Thames with one's face in the wind, you were almost burned with a shower of fire drops,' he wrote. 'When we could endure no more upon the water, we to a little ale-house on the Bankside and there staid till it was dark almost, and saw the fire grow.' It's a warren of dimly lit, creaky little rooms and passageways, with bare boards and beams, black panelling, old-fashioned high-backed settles, and sturdy leatherette chairs; even when it's invaded by tourists it's usually possible to retreat to one of the smaller rooms. Courage Best and Directors on handpump, as well as a dozen wines by the glass, jugs of Pimms, mulled wine in winter, and various teas and coffees; two fruit machines, and occasionally rather loud piped music. Served all day, bar food includes filled baguettes (from £4), and in the upstairs bar hot dishes such as fish and chips, home-baked pies and sausages and mash (£5.50); they do Sunday roasts. Parts of the bar and restaurant are no smoking (other areas can get smoky at times). Morris dancers occasionally pass by, and there are barbecues in summer. We have not yet heard from any readers staying in the new bedrooms, in a Premier Lodge behind. (Recommended by the Didler, BJL, Jim Abbott, Kevin Flack, David Carr, Ian Phillips, Stuart and Alison Wallace, E G Parish, Mayur Shah, John W Allen)

Scottish Courage ~ Manager Ian Robinson ~ Real ale ~ Bar food (12-9) ~ Restaurant ~ (020) 7407 1577 ~ Children in restaurant and family room ~ Open 11-11; 12-10.30 Sun ~ Bedrooms: £78.25B/£84.50B

Bulls Head ♀ £

Lonsdale Road, SW13; ⇌ Barnes Bridge

Top class live jazz is this busy Thames-side pub's main claim to fame. Every night for the last 40 years internationally renowned jazz and blues groups have performed here; you can hear the music quite clearly from the lounge bar (and on peaceful Sunday afternoons from the villagey little street as you approach), but for the full effect and genuine jazz-club atmosphere it is worth paying the admission to the well equipped music room. Bands play 8.30-11 every night plus 2-4.30pm Sundays, and depending on who's playing prices generally range from £4 to around £10. The big, simply furnished and decorated bar has photographs of many of the musicians who've played here, as well as a couple of cosier areas leading off, and an island servery with Youngs Bitter, Special and seasonal beers on handpump. They keep over 70 malt whiskies, and have a particularly impressive wine list, running to 240 bottles at the last count, with around 30 by the glass. A short range of good value bar food (all home-made, with nothing frozen) includes soup (£2), sandwiches (from £3), a hot dish of the day (£4.90), and a daily roast (£5.50); there's usually something available all day, and in the evening they do good thai food in the Stables restaurant. Service is efficient and friendly. Dominoes, cribbage, Scrabble, chess, cards, TV. One room is no-smoking. (Recommended by John Mitchell)

Youngs ~ Tenant Dan Fleming ~ Real ale ~ Bar food (12-11) ~ Restaurant ~ (020) 87876 5241 ~ Children in family room ~ Dogs allowed in bar ~ Jazz and blues every night and Sun lunchtime ~ Open 11-11; 12-10.30 Sun

Crown & Greyhound

Dulwich Village, SE21; ⇌ North Dulwich

A few changes to this big Edwardian pub since our last edition: some parts have been extensively refurbished, and reports since have been ever so slightly mixed, but there's still an impressive welcome for families (with toys, changing facilities, and children's menus), and a good choice of well prepared home-made food. A pleasant garden has lots of picnic-sets under a chestnut tree, and a play area with sandpit. The most ornate room is on the right, with elaborate ochre ceiling plasterwork, fancy former gas lamps, Hogarth prints, fine carved and panelled settles and so forth; it opens into the former billiards room, where kitchen tables on a stripped board floor are set for eating. A big conservatory looks out on the garden. A central snug leads to the saloon with upholstered and panelled settles, a coal-effect gas fire in the tiled fireplace, and Victorian prints. Well kept Adnams, Fullers London Pride and Youngs on handpump (at pretty much central London prices); they have occasional beer festivals with up to 20 different brews. Changing every day, the lunchtime menu might include big doorstep sandwiches and ciabattas (from £2.95), soup (£3.80), and specials such as chicken in mustard sauce, lamb in red wine or cod mornay (all £6.95). Best to arrive early for their popular Sunday carvery (£8.70, or £7.20 for the vegetarian version), as they don't take bookings. Sandwiches are usually available all day, and there are barbecues at weekends. The family room is no smoking, as is the restaurant at lunchtime. Known locally as the Dog, the pub was built at the turn of the century to replace two inns that had stood here previously, hence the unusual name. Busy in the evenings, but quieter during the day, it's handy for walks through the park, and for the Dulwich picture gallery. *(Recommended by Patrick Hancock, Alan M Pring, Tim and Jane Charlesworth, Ian Phillips)*

Mitchells & Butlers ~ Manager Catherine Boulter ~ Real ale ~ Bar food (12-10 (9 Sun)) ~ Restaurant (evenings only) ~ (020) 87299 4976 ~ Children in no smoking area ~ Dogs allowed in bar ~ Open 11-11; 12-10.30 Sun

Cutty Sark

Ballast Quay, off Lassell Street, SE10; ⇝ Maze Hill, from London Bridge; or from the river front walk past the Yacht in Crane Street and Trinity Hospital

It's hard not to imagine smugglers and blackguards with patches over their eyes at every turn in this attractive late 16th-c white-painted house. There are great views of the Thames (and the Millennium Dome) both from the busy terrace across the narrow cobbled lane, or, better still, from the upstairs room with the big bow window (itself striking for the way it jetties over the pavement). The bar has an old-fashioned feel, with flagstones, rough brick walls, wooden settles, barrel tables, open fires, low lighting and narrow openings to tiny side snugs; there's an elaborate central staircase. Changing beers such as Fullers London Pride, Greene King Abbot and Black Sheep on handpump, with a good choice of malt whiskies, and a decent wine list; fruit machine, juke box. Served in a roomy eating area (and available all day during the week), bar food includes sandwiches, and changing hot dishes such as steak and ale pie, fish and chips or liver and bacon (around £6.25); Sunday roasts (£7.50). Service can slow down at busy times, and the pub can be alive with young people on Friday and Saturday evenings. They have jazz festivals two or three times a year, and morris dancers occasionally drop by. *(Recommended by the Didler, D J and P M Taylor, Kevin Flack, Ian and Nita Cooper, Jim Abbott, Roger and Jenny Huggins, Tracey and Stephen Groves, Tim Maddison)*

Free house ~ Licensees Mark and Tina Crane ~ Real ale ~ Bar food (12-9(6 wknds)) ~ Restaurant ~ (020) 87858 3146 ~ Children upstairs ~ Dogs allowed in bar ~ Open 11-11; 12-10.30 Sun

Fire Station ⊕ ♀ ◖

Waterloo Road, SE1; ⊖/⇝ Waterloo

Very handy for the Old Vic and Waterloo Station, this bustling place is a splendid conversion of the former LCC central fire station. Popular with both diners and after-work drinkers, it's something of a cross between a warehouse and a schoolroom, with plenty of wooden pews, chairs and long tables (a few spilling on to the street), some mirrors and rather incongruous pieces of dressers, and brightly red-painted doors, shelves and modern hanging lightshades; the determinedly contemporary art round the walls is for sale, and there's a table with newspapers to read. It can get very noisy indeed in the evenings, which does add to the atmosphere – though if you're after a quiet drink you could find it overpowering. It's calmer at lunchtimes, and at weekends. Well kept Adnams Best, Charles Wells Bombardier, Fullers London Pride, Shepherd Neame Spitfire and Youngs on handpump, as well as a number of bottled beers, variously flavoured teas, several malt whiskies, and a good choice of wines (a dozen by the glass). They serve a range of bar meals between 12 and 5.30, which might include several interestingly filled ciabattas and paninis (from £5.95), salads (from £6), and steamed mussels in coconut milk and thai spices (£10.95), but it's worth paying the extra to eat from the main menu, served from an open kitchen in the back dining room. Changing daily, this has things like baked pear and blue cheese tart with red onion potato salad (£9.95), roast duck breast with sweet potato wedges and sweet soya sauce or blackened kingfish with cornmeal fritters (£11.95), parsley crusted calves liver with bacon and mustard mash (£12.50), and puddings such as peach and almond tart with custard sauce; some dishes can run out, so get there early for the best choice. They also do a set menu at lunchtimes and between 5.30 and 7, with two courses for £10.95, or three for £13.50. You can book tables. Piped modern jazz and other music fits into the good-natured hubbub; there's a TV for rugby matches. Several readers have this year found the service to be efficient rather than friendly – and one considered it to be neither. *(Recommended by Brian Root, Keith and Chris O'Neill, Peter Meister, Jess and George Cowley, Brian and Karen Thomas, Ian Phillips)*

Wizard ~ Manager Philippe Haye Yeung ~ Real ale ~ Bar food (11-10; 12-9.15 Sun) ~ Restaurant ~ (020) 7620 2226 ~ Open 11-11; 12-10.30 Sun

Founders Arms

Hopton Street (Bankside); ⊖/⇌ Blackfriars, and cross Blackfriars Bridge

Like a big, modern conservatory, this efficiently organised place benefits from one of the finest settings of any pub along the Thames, particularly in the City, with fine views of the river, St Paul's, and the Millennium Bridge. Picnic-sets out on the big waterside terrace share the panorama. If you're inside, the lighting is nice and unobtrusive so that you can still see out across the river at night. Also handy for Shakespeare's Globe and the Tate Modern, it can get busy, particularly on weekday evenings, when it's popular with young City types for an after-work drink. Well kept Youngs Bitter, Special and seasonal brews from the modern bar counter angling along one side; also, coffee, tea and hot chocolate. Served pretty much all day, the enjoyable bar food includes sandwiches (from £3.95), paninis from £4.75), soup (£3.95), sausages and mash (£7.45), fresh haddock in beer batter (£7.50), spinach and pumpkin curry (£7.85), steak and kidney pie (£8.45), and daily specials; Sunday roasts. Good, neat and cheerful service. One raised area is no smoking; piped music, and two fruit machines. Like many City pubs, it may close a little early on quieter nights. *(Recommended by the Didler, Mayur Shah, Keith and Chris O'Neill, Mike Turner, Ian Phillips, John W Allen, Dr and Mrs M E Wilson, Roger and Jenny Huggins, David Carr, Gordon Prince, Derek Thomas)*

Youngs ~ Managers Mr and Mrs P Wakefield ~ Real ale ~ Bar food (12-8.30(7 Sun)) ~ (020) 7928 1899 ~ Children in eating area of bar during food service ~ Open 11-11; 12-10.30 Sun

Fox & Hounds 🍽 ♀

Latchmere Road, SW11; ⇌ Clapham Junction

The second of the small chain run by the two brothers who transformed the Atlas (see West London, below), this big Victorian local has a similar emphasis on excellent mediterranean food. But what's particularly nice is that this still feels very much the kind of place where locals happily come to drink – and they're a more varied bunch than you might find filling the Atlas. The bright, spacious bar has bare boards, mismatched tables and chairs, two narrow pillars supporting the dark red ceiling, some attractive photographs on the walls, and big windows overlooking the street (the view partially obscured by colourful window boxes). There are fresh flowers and daily papers on the bar, and a view of the kitchen behind. Two rooms lead off, one rather cosy with its two red leatherette sofas. Changing every day, the bar food might include lunchtime sandwiches, spinach soup with cream, nutmeg and croutons (£3.50), linguini with pancetta, field mushrooms, rosemary, cream and parmesan (£6.50), pan-roast fillet of trout (£8), grilled marinated fillet of salmon with harissa, grilled aubergine and roast tomato salad, and cucumber and yoghurt salsa (£9.50), pan-roast pigeon breasts with grilled polenta, red onions, and rocket and parmesan salad (£10), grilled rib-eye steak with sautéed potatoes, green beans, and salsa verde (£11.50), creamy italian cheese with grilled bread and pear (£5), and chocolate and almond cake (£4). The pub can fill quickly, so you may have to move fast to grab a table. Well kept Bass, Fullers London Pride and a guest like Shepherd Neame Spitfire on handpump; the carefully chosen wine list (which includes around 10 by the glass) is written out on a blackboard. The appealingly varied piped music fits in rather well. There are several tables in a garden behind. The same team have opened a further two similarly organised pubs: the Cumberland Arms near Olympia, and the Swan in Chiswick. *(Recommended by BOB)*

Free house ~ Licensees Richard and George Manners ~ Real ale ~ Bar food (12-2.30 (3 Sat/Sun), 7-10; not Mon lunchtime) ~ (020) 7924 5483 ~ Children welcome till 7 ~ Dogs allowed in bar ~ Open 12-3 5-11; 12-11(10.30 Sun) Sat; closed Mon lunchtime; 24 Dec-1 Jan; Easter Sat/Sun

George ★ 🍺

Off 77 Borough High Street, SE1; ⊖/⇌ Borough or London Bridge

Preserved by the National Trust, this splendid-looking place is probably the country's best example of a 17th-c coaching inn, but it isn't simply playing the heritage card; it's a proper, bustling pub, with a good atmosphere, friendly welcome, and a nice range of beers. Unless you know where you're going (or you're in one of the many tourist groups that flock here in summer) you may well miss it, as apart from the great gates there's little to indicate that such a gem still exists behind the less auspicious-looking buildings on the busy high street. The tiers of open galleries look down over a bustling cobbled courtyard with plenty of picnic-sets, and maybe morris men and even Shakespeare in summer. Inside, the row of no-frills ground-floor rooms and bars all have square-latticed windows, black beams, bare floorboards, some panelling, plain oak or elm tables and old-fashioned built-in settles, along with a 1797 'Act of Parliament' clock, dimpled glass lantern-lamps and so forth. The snuggest refuge is the room nearest the street, where there's an ancient beer engine that looks like a cash register. Two rooms are no smoking at lunchtimes. In summer they open a bar with direct service into the courtyard. Well kept Bass, Fullers London Pride, Greene King Abbot, a beer brewed for the pub and a changing guest on handpump; mulled wine in winter, tea and coffee. Lunchtime bar food might include filled baked potatoes (from £3), soup (£3.25), baguettes (from £3.50), ploughman's (£4.95), sausage and mash or roasted vegetable lasagne (£5.25), various salads (from £5.45), and steak, mushroom and Guinness pie (£5.45); evening meals in the restaurant are broadly similar, but a little more expensive. A splendid central staircase goes up to a series of dining-rooms and to a gaslit balcony; darts, trivia. Their music nights can be quite jolly – anyone can join in the monthly cajun jam sessions. Incidentally, what survives today is only a third of what it once was; the building was 'mercilessly reduced' as E V Lucas put it, during the period when it was owned by the Great Northern Railway Company. *(Recommended by the Didler, Paul Hopton, Ian Phillips, Tim Maddison, I Louden, Mr Bishop, Tony and Wendy Hobden, Dr and Mrs M E Wilson, Dr and Mrs A K Clarke, C J Fletcher, BJL, LM, David Carr, Alison Hayes, Pete Hanlon)*

Laurel Pub Company ~ Manager George Cunningham ~ Real ale ~ Bar food (12-3 (4 weekends)) ~ Restaurant ~ (020) 7407 2056 ~ Children welcome ~ Folk first Mon, Cajun third Mon ~ Open 11-11; 12-10.30 Sun

Market Porter ◖

Stoney Street, SE1; ⊖/⇌ London Bridge

This busily pubby place has perhaps London's best range of real ales. They usually get through 20 different beers each week, with eight on at any one time. You'll always find Courage Best and Harveys Best, along with rapidly changing guests you're unlikely to have heard of before – let alone come across in this neck of the woods: readers have recently enjoyed Archers Dublin Bay, Beowulf Bitter, Milk Street Beer, Skye Brevet Ale, and brews from the nearby London Bridge Brewery, all perfectly kept and served. The main part of the long U-shaped bar has rough wooden ceiling beams with beer barrels balanced on them, a heavy wooden bar counter with a beamed gantry, cushioned bar stools, an open fire, and 20s-style wall lamps. Sensibly priced simple lunchtime bar food includes sandwiches (from £3.25), and paninis (£4.25), home-made pies and pasta (£5.95), and fish and chips wrapped in newspaper (£6.50); Sunday roasts. Obliging, friendly service; darts, fruit machine, TV, and piped music. A cosy partly panelled room has leaded glass windows and a couple of tables. The restaurant usually has an additional couple of real ales. They open between 6.30 and 8.30am for workers and porters from Borough Market. The company that owns the pub – which can get a little full at lunchtimes (it's quiet in the afternoons) – has various others around London; ones with similarly unusual beers (if not quite so many) can be found in Stamford Street and Seymour Place. *(Recommended by BJL, Paul Hopton, Ian Phillips, Catherine Pitt, Dr and Mrs A K Clarke, Richard Lewis, David Carr, the Didler, Tracey and Stephen Groves)*

Free house ~ Licensee Anthony Hedigan ~ Real ale ~ Bar food (12-3(5 Sat/Sun)) ~ Restaurant ~ (020) 7407 2495 ~ Open 6.30am-8.30am, then 11-11; 12-10.30 Sun

Ship ♀

Jews Row, SW18; ⇌ Wandsworth Town

Always packed on sunny days, this relaxed riverside pub has an excellent barbecue every day in summer, and at winter weekends. Serving very good home-made burgers and sausages, marinated lamb steaks, goats cheese quesidillas, and even cajun chicken and lobster; it's all-weather, with plenty of covered areas if necessary. The extensive terrace has lots of picnic-sets, pretty hanging baskets and brightly coloured flower-beds, small trees, and an outside bar; a Thames barge is moored alongside. They do a particularly appealing menu inside too, as at the Alma above (under the same management) relying very much on free-range produce, much of it from Mr Gotto's farm; a typical choice might include poached pear, prosciutto and taleggio cheese (£4.45), spring onion pancake with home-cured gravadlax (£4.95), lemon and garlic corn-fed chicken with chilli rice and wilted spinach (£8.95), fried darne of salmon with chinese leaves, creamed potatoes and parsley and pesto sauce (£8.90), fillet of pork with potato gratin, green beans and stilton sauce (£9.50), and barbary duck breast with fresh mango and cassis gravy (£11.50). You can book tables (except at Sunday lunchtimes), and there's something available all day. Only a small part of the original ceiling is left in the main bar – the rest is in a light and airy conservatory style, with wooden tables, a medley of stools, and old church chairs on the floorboards. One part has a Victorian fireplace, a huge clock surrounded by barge prints, an old-fashioned bagatelle board, and jugs of flowers around the window sills. The basic public bar has plain wooden furniture, a black kitchen range in the fireplace, and a juke box. The atmosphere is laid-back and chatty, and it's a great favourite with smart local twenty-somethings. Well kept Youngs Bitter, Special and seasonal brews on handpump, with freshly squeezed orange and other fruit juices, a wide range of wines (a dozen or more by the glass), and a good choice of teas and coffees. Helpful service from pleasant staff. Alas, their famous fireworks display is no more (not the pub's fault), but they still have a rousing celebration on the last night of the Proms. The adjacent car park can fill pretty quickly. *(Recommended by Ian Phillips, Susan and John Douglas, John and Judy Saville)*

Youngs ~ Tenant C Gotto ~ Real ale ~ Bar food (12-11(10.30 Sun)) ~ Restaurant ~ (020) 8870 9667 ~ Children welcome ~ Dogs allowed in bar ~ Open 11-11; 12-10.30 Sun

White Cross ♀

Water Lane; ⊖/≷ Richmond

The setting of this Thames-side pub is perfect – it's a delightful spot in summer, and has a certain wistful charm in winter as well. On fine days, when it can get rather crowded, the busy paved garden in front can feel a little like a cosmopolitan seaside resort; plenty of tables overlook the water, and in summer there's an outside bar. Inside, the two chatty main rooms have something of the air of the hotel this once was; with local prints and photographs, an old-fashioned wooden island servery, and a good mix of variously aged customers. Two of the three log fires have mirrors above them – unusually, the third is below a window. A bright and airy upstairs room has lots more tables, and a pretty cast-iron balcony opening off, with a splendid view down to the river, and a couple more tables and chairs. Well kept Youngs Bitter, Special and seasonal beers on handpump, and a good range of 15 or so carefully chosen wines by the glass; service is friendly and civilised, even when the pub is at its busiest. Fruit machine, dominoes. From a servery at the foot of the stairs, lunchtime bar food includes good sandwiches (from £2.60), salads (from £5.75), a variety of sausages (£6.50), and good daily-changing home-made dishes such as pasta (£6.25), mixed game pie (£6.75), and a daily roast. Take care if you're leaving your car along the river near the pub, it pays to check the tide times; one reader discovered just how fast the water can rise when on returning to his vehicle he found it marooned in a rapidly swelling pool of water, and had to paddle out shoeless to retrieve it. It's not unknown for the water to reach right up the steps into the bar, completely covering anything that gets in the way. Boats leave from immediately outside for Kingston and Hampton Court. *(Recommended by Ian Phillips, Mayur Shah, Val Stevenson, Rob Holmes, E G Parish, Martin Brunt, the Didler, Dr and Mrs M E Wilson, David and Nina Pugsley)*

Youngs ~ Managers Ian and Phyl Heggie ~ Real ale ~ Bar food (12-4) ~ (020) 8940 6844 ~ Dogs welcome ~ Open 11-11; 12-10.30 Sun

WEST LONDON Map 12

Anglesea Arms ⊗ ♀

Wingate Road, W6; ⊖ Ravenscourt Park

One reader considers the food at this superior gastropub to be the best within a 50-mile radius, so though it's rather off the beaten path, it is well worth tracking down. Changing every lunchtime and evening, the inventive menu might include starters such as asparagus and broad bean soup (£3.95), tomato, aubergine, onion and thyme tartlet (£4.95), breadcrumbed escalope of rabbit, with spinach, lemon, garlic and mustard fruits (£5.25), and moroccan stuffed squid with couscous, raisins and cumin (£5.50), half a dozen irish rock oysters with Guinness bread and shallot relish (£7.25), a short choice of main courses like stuffed globe artichoke, ceps, asparagus, soft duck egg, toasted brioche and rocket (£7.95), monkfish brochette with parma ham, grilled peppers, courgettes and basil (£8.25), pot-roast corn-fed chicken breast with garlic mash and baby vegetables (£8.50), or sautéed calves liver with pancetta, puy lentils, capers, sage and cabernet sauvignon (£9.75), and some unusual farmhouse cheeses (£4.95); they usually do a set menu at lunchtimes, with two courses for £9.95. The bustling eating area leads off the bar but feels quite separate, with skylights creating a brighter feel, closely packed tables, and a big modern painting along one wall; directly opposite is the kitchen, with several chefs frantically working on the meals. You can't book, so best to get there early for a table, or be prepared to wait. It feels a lot more restaurant than, say, the Eagle, though you can also eat in the bar: rather plainly decorated, but cosy in winter when the roaring fire casts long flickering shadows on the dark panelling. Neatly stacked piles of wood guard either side of the fireplace (which has a stopped clock above it), and there are some well worn green leatherette chairs and stools. Courage Best, Fullers London Pride and guest like Adnams Broadside or Shepherd Neame Spitfire on handpump, with a wide range of carefully chosen wines listed above the bar. Several tables outside overlook the quiet street (not the easiest place to find a parking space). *(Recommended by Richard Siebert)*

*Enterprise ~ Lease Fiona Evans and Jamie Wood ~ Real ale ~ Bar food (12.30-2.45
(3 Sat, 3.30 Sun), 7.30-10.30(9.45 Sun)) ~ Restaurant ~ (020) 87749 1291 ~
Children welcome ~ Dogs allowed in bar ~ Open 11-11(10.30 Sun); closed
Christmas for one week, 1 Jan*

Anglesea Arms ◖

Selwood Terrace, SW7; ✪ South Kensington

Managing to feel both smart and cosy at the same time, this genuinely old-
fashioned pub is currently well regarded for its food, as well as its particularly
friendly, chatty atmosphere. In summer the place to be is the leafy front patio (with
outside heaters for chillier evenings), but it's really rather nice in winter, when the
elegant and individual bar seems especially enticing. On busy days you'll need to
move fast to grab a seat, but most people seem happy leaning on the central elbow
tables. There's a mix of cast-iron tables on the bare wood-strip floor, panelling, and
big windows with attractive swagged curtains; at one end several booths with partly
glazed screens have cushioned pews and spindleback chairs. The traditional mood
is heightened by some heavy portraits, prints of London, and large brass
chandeliers. A good choice of real ales takes in Adnams Bitter and Broadside,
Brakspears, Fullers London Pride, Youngs Special and a weekly changing guest like
Greene King Abbot; also a few bottled belgian beers, around 20 whiskies, and a
varied wine list, with everything available by the glass. Downstairs is a separate
eating area, with a Victorian fireplace. The lunchtime menu typically includes
sandwiches and paninis (from £5.55), soup (£3.50), welsh rarebit with crispy bacon
topping (£4.25), scallops wrapped in smoked bacon with a warm sage and olive
dressing (£6.95), steak and kidney pie (£6.95), cumberland sausage and mash with
beer and onion gravy (£7.25), home-made fishcakes (£7.55), and stuffed peppers
with couscous and ratatouille with melted goats cheese (£7.95); in the evening they
add things like mussels in a provençale or white wine and cream sauce (£8.25) and
venison on a bed of rösti and spinach with veal jus (£12.95). Good all-day Sunday
roasts. Service is friendly and helpful. *(Recommended by Tracey and Stephen Groves,
Stephen R Holman, the Didler, BJL, J R Ringrose)*

*Free house ~ Licensees J Podmore and J Brennan ~ Real ale ~ Bar food (12-3, 6.30-
10; 12-10 Sat/Sun) ~ Restaurant ~ (020) 7373 7960 ~ Children in eating area of bar
and restaurant ~ Dogs allowed in bar ~ Open 11-11; 12-10.30 Sun*

Atlas ⊕ ♀

Seagrave Road, SW6; ✪ West Brompton
London Dining Pub of the Year
The first of a burgeoning little chain set up by two brothers, this is a particularly
rewarding food pub, with imaginative reasonably priced meals, an excellent,
carefully chosen wine list, and a good, buzzy atmosphere. If there's a downside it's
simply the place's popularity – tables are highly prized, so if you're planning to eat,
arrive early, or swoop quickly. Listed on a blackboard above the brick fireplace,
and changing every day, the sensibly short choice of food might include pea,
parsnip and mint soup with parmesan crostini (£3.50), very good antipasti (£6),
smoked duck breast salad with green beans, roasted tomatoes and rocket (£7.50),
delicious grilled tuscan sausages with borlotti beans, garlic, rosemary, parsley and
roast red onions (£8), pot-roast half chicken with lemon and thyme, fennel roast
potatoes and tomato chilli jam, or moroccan beef casserole with paprika,
cinnamon, vanilla and cayenne (£10.50), and pan-roast sea bass with vine
tomatoes, basil, black olives and capers (£11.50); they may have a good cake like
lemon and rosemary with whiskey cream (£4), or soft italian cheese with apple and
grilled bread (£5). With a pleasantly bustling feel in the evenings (it's perhaps not
the place for a cosy quiet dinner), the long, simple knocked-together bar has been
well renovated without removing the original features; there's plenty of panelling
and dark wooden wall benches, with a mix of school chairs and well spaced tables.
Smart young people figure prominently in the mix, but there are plenty of locals

too, as well as visitors to the Exhibition Centre at Earls Court (one of the biggest car parks is next door). Well kept Charles Wells Bombardier, Fullers London Pride, and a guest like Brakspears or Greene King IPA on handpump, and a changing selection of around 10 wines by the glass; big mugs of coffee. Friendly service. The piped music is unusual – on various visits we've come across everything from salsa and jazz to vintage TV themes; it can be loud at times. Down at the end is a TV, by a hatch to the kitchen. Outside is an attractively planted narrow side terrace, with an overhead awning; heaters make it comfortable even in winter. Another of their pubs, the Fox & Hounds, is a main entry in the South London section. *(Recommended by Martin and Karen Wake, Jim Bush, Ian Phillips)*

Free house ~ Licensees Richard and George Manners ~ Real ale ~ (020) 7385 9129 ~ Children welcome till 7pm ~ Dogs welcome ~ Open 12-11(10.30 Sun); closed 23 Dec-2 Jan

Bulls Head

Strand-on-the-Green, W4; ⊖ Kew Bridge

Now a Chef & Brewer, this nicely refurbished riverside pub has a greater emphasis on food than it did in the past, but remains an atmospheric place for a cosy drink, in a fine spot by the narrow towpath. There's a comfortably traditional feel to the series of pleasant little rooms rambling through black-panelled alcoves and up and down steps; old-fashioned benches are built into the simple panelling, and small windows look past attractively planted hanging flower baskets to the river. Lots of empty wine bottles are dotted around, and there's plenty of polished dark wood and beams. Served all day, the big menu takes in everything from filled baguettes (£4.99), through fish and chips (£5.95) and beef and ale pie (£6.95), to beef wellington (£15.95); Sunday roasts. Around half the pub is no smoking. Fullers London Pride, Greene King Old Speckled Hen, and Theakstons Best on handpump; newspapers are laid out for customers. The original building served as Cromwell's HQ several times during the Civil War, and it was here that Moll Cutpurse overheard Cromwell talking to Fairfax about the troops' pay money coming by horse from Hounslow, and got her gang to capture the moneybags; they were later recovered at Turnham Green. *(Recommended by Chris Smith, Alan and Paula McCully)*

Scottish Courage ~ Managers Paul and Alex Gibbs ~ Real ale ~ Bar food (11-10; 12-9.30 Sun) ~ Restaurant ~ (020) 8994 1204 ~ Children in eating area of bar ~ Open 11-11; 12-10.30 Sun

Churchill Arms 🍺

Kensington Church Street, W8; ⊖ Notting Hill Gate/Kensington High Street

The wonderfully genial Irish landlord of this busy old favourite continues to be much in evidence, delightedly mixing with customers as he threads his way though the cheery bustle. It always seems jolly and lively (with quite an overspill outside), but they really go to town around Christmas, Hallowe'en, St Patricks's Day and Churchill's birthday (30 November), when you'll find special events and decorations, and more people than you'd ever imagine could feasibly fit inside. One of the landlord's hobbies is collecting butterflies, so you'll see a variety of prints and books on the subject dotted around the bar. There are also countless lamps, miners' lights, horse tack, bedpans and brasses hanging from the ceiling, a couple of interesting carved figures and statuettes behind the central bar counter, prints of American presidents, and lots of Churchill memorabilia. Well kept Fullers Chiswick, ESB, London Pride, and seasonal beers on handpump, with a good choice of wines. The pub can get crowded in the evenings – even early in the week it's not really a place for a quiet pint; it can get a bit smoky too. The spacious and rather smart plant-filled dining conservatory may be used for hatching butterflies, but is better known for its big choice of excellent authentic thai food, such as a very good, proper thai curry, or duck with noodles (all around £5.85); it's no smoking in here. They now do food all day, with other choices including lunchtime sandwiches (from £2.50), ploughman's (£2.50), and Sunday lunch. Fruit machine,

TV; they have their own cricket and football teams. *(Recommended by LM, Derek Thomas, Ian Phillips, Keith Stevens, Klaus and Elizabeth Leist)*

Fullers ~ Manager Jerry O'Brien ~ Real ale ~ Bar food (12-9.30(4 Sun)) ~ Restaurant ~ (020) 7727 4242 ~ Children in restaurant ~ Dogs welcome ~ Open 11-11; 12-10.30 Sun

Colton Arms

Greyhound Road, W14; ⊖ Barons Court

Like a country pub in town, this genuinely old-fashioned little gem is very much a family concern, kept exactly the same by its dedicated landlord for the last 30 years. The main U-shaped front bar has a log fire blazing in winter, highly polished brasses, a fox's mask, hunting crops and plates decorated with hunting scenes on the walls, and a remarkable collection of handsomely carved 17th-c oak furniture. That room is small enough, and the two back rooms are tiny; each has its own little serving counter, with a bell to ring for service. Well kept Caledonian Deuchars IPA, Fullers London Pride and Shepherd Neame Spitfire on handpump (when you pay, note the old-fashioned brass-bound till); the food is limited to sandwiches (weekday lunchtimes only, from £2.50). Pull the curtain aside for the door out to a charming back terrace with a neat rose arbour. The pub is next to the Queens Club tennis courts and gardens. *(Recommended by Susan and John Douglas)*

Unique Pub Co ~ Tenants N J and J A Nunn ~ Real ale ~ Bar food (12-2 Mon-Sat) ~ No credit cards ~ (020) 7385 6956 ~ Dogs welcome ~ Open 12-3, 5.30-11; 12-4, 7-11(10.30 Sun) Sat

Dove

Upper Mall, W6; ⊖ Ravenscourt Park

London has plenty of spots from which to admire its river, but the delightful back terrace of this old-fashioned Thames-side tavern is one of the nicest. The main flagstoned area, down some steps, has a few highly prized teak tables and white metal and teak chairs looking over the low river wall to the Thames reach just above Hammersmith Bridge, and there's a tiny exclusive area up a spiral staircase. If you're able to bag a spot here, you'll often see rowing crews out on the water. By the entrance from the quiet alley, the front bar is cosy and traditional, with black panelling, and red leatherette cushioned built-in wall settles and stools around dimpled copper tables; it leads to a bigger, similarly furnished room, with old framed advertisements and photographs of the pub. They stock the full range of Fullers beers, with well kept Chiswick, ESB, London Pride and seasonal beers on handpump: no games machines or piped music. It's not quite so crowded at lunchtimes as it is in the evenings. Served all day (except Sunday), bar food might include sandwiches, fishcakes, lamb burgers in pitta bread (£5.95), and steak and ESB pie (£7.25), and king prawns with garlic and rice (£7.95). A plaque marks the level of the highest-ever tide in 1928. The pub is said to be where *Rule Britannia* was composed. *(Recommended by D J and P M Taylor, Patrick Hancock, the Didler, Mick Simmons, Dr and Mrs M E Wilson)*

Fullers ~ Manager Alison Harper ~ Real ale ~ Bar food (12-9(4 Sat)) ~ (020) 8748 5405 ~ Children welcome away from bar ~ Dogs welcome ~ Open 11-11; 12-10.30 Sun

Havelock Tavern 🍴 ☟

Masbro Road, W14; ⊖ Kensington(Olympia)

Very classy food is the hallmark of this otherwise ordinary-looking blue-tiled cornerhouse, in an unassuming residential street. Changing every day, the menu might include things like white bean, vegetable and bacon soup with pesto (£4), pork, duck, leek and chorizo terrine (£6), smoked salmon with soft flour tortillas, avocado salsa, coriander and lime (£7.50), asparagus, spring onion and mint omelette or grilled fillets of mackerel with warm bacon, new potato and shallot salad (£8), grilled pork sausages with bubble and squeak and mustard and green peppercorn sauce (£9), pan-fried john dory with sweet and sour red pepper and fennel salad (£10.50), and some unusual cheeses served with apple chutney (£5); you can't book tables. Until 1932 the building was two separate shops (one was a wine merchant, but no one can remember much about the other), and it still has huge shop-front windows along both street-facing walls. The L-shaped bar is plain and unfussy: bare boards, long wooden tables, a mix of chairs and stools, a few soft spotlights, and a fireplace; a second little room with pews leads to a small paved terrace, with benches, a tree, and wall climbers. Well kept (though not cheap) Brakspears, Fullers London Pride and Marstons Pedigree on handpump from the elegant modern bar counter, and a good range of well chosen wines, with around 10 by the glass; mulled wine in winter, and in May and June perhaps home-made elderflower soda. Service is friendly and attentive, and the atmosphere relaxed and easy-going; no music or machines, but plenty of chat from the varied range of customers – at busy times it can seem really quite noisy. Backgammon, chess, Scrabble and other board games. Though evenings are always busy (you may have to wait for a table then, and some dishes can run out quite quickly), it can be quieter at lunchtimes, and in the afternoons can have something of the feel of a civilised private club. On weekdays, parking nearby is metered. *(Recommended by Jack Clark, Evelyn and Derek Walter, Derek Thomas, Paul Hopton, Nigel Williamson)*

Free house ~ Licensees Peter Richnell, Jonny Haughton ~ Real ale ~ Bar food (12.30-2.30, 7-10) ~ No credit cards ~ (020) 7603 5374 ~ Children welcome ~ Dogs welcome ~ Open 11-11; 12-10.30 Sun; closed second Mon in Aug, 22-26 Dec

Portobello Gold ♀

Portobello Road, W11; ⊖ Notting Hill Gate

An enjoyable combination of pub, restaurant, hotel, and even Internet café, this enterprising place has a cheerfully laid-back, almost bohemian atmosphere. Our favourite part is the rather exotic-seeming back dining room, with a profusion of enormous tropical plants (some up to 25 years old); comfortable wicker chairs, stained wooden tables, and a cage of vocal canaries add to the outdoor effect. The big mural has been replaced with an impressive wall-to-wall mirror. In the old days – when we remember this being a Hells Angels hangout – this was the pub garden, and in summer they still open up the sliding roof. The walls here and in the smaller, brightly painted front bar are covered with changing displays of art and photography; the bar also has a nice old fireplace, cushioned pews, daily papers, and, more unusually, several Internet terminals (some of which disappear in the evening). The Gold was the first place in the UK to serve oyster shooters (a shot glass with an oyster, parmesan, horseradish, crushed chillies, Tabasco and lime), and they still have something of an emphasis on oysters and seafood; the salt and pepper sit appealingly in oyster shells. There's an almost bewildering number of menus, with good, thoughtfully prepared meals and snacks available all day: you might typically find big toasted ciabattas (from £4.85), soup (£3.95), cajun jumbo shrimp (from £4.95), half a dozen irish rock oysters (£6.95), mexican fajitas or sausage and parsley mash with red onion and tomato gravy (£7.55), fish and chips or lamb cutlets in cumberland sauce (£9.95), and seafood and pasta specials; the puddings come in two sizes. They do good set menus – at lunchtime offering two courses for £10 and three for £13, and in the evenings, two rather more elaborate courses for £14.50, and three for £19. On Sunday, roasts are served until 8pm. You can eat from the same menu in the bar or dining room (part of which is no smoking). Opening at 10 for coffee and fresh pastries, the bar has well kept Brakspears and Shepherd Neame Spitfire, as well as a couple of draught belgian beers, Thatcher's farm cider, a good selection of bottled beers from around the world, and a wide range of interesting tequilas and other well sourced spirits; the wine list is particularly good (the landlady has written books on matching wine with food), and has around a dozen available by the glass. They also have a cigar menu and various coffees. Polite, helpful young staff; piped music, TV (used only for cricket), chess, backgammon. The landlord has compiled a database of what's sold in each of the surrounding antique shops, for those who'd like their browsing slightly more focused. There are one or two tables and chairs on the pretty street outside, which, like the pub, is named in recognition of the 1769 Battle of Portobello, fought over control of the lucrative gold route to Panama. A lively stall is set up outside during the Notting Hill Carnival. Parking nearby is metered; it's not always easy to bag a space. We've yet to hear from readers who have stayed overnight here; the bedrooms all have free Internet access. *(Recommended by Rebecca Nicholls, Ian Phillips)*

Unique Pub Co ~ Lease Michael Bell and Linda Johnson-Bell ~ Real ale ~ Bar food (12-11(8 Sun)) ~ Restaurant ~ (020) 7460 4910 ~ Children in eating area of bar and restaurant till sundown ~ Dogs allowed in bar ~ Open 10-12; 12-10.30 Sun; closed 25-31 Dec ~ Bedrooms: £30(£75S)/£45(£85S)

White Horse ♀ 🍺

Parsons Green, SW6; ⊖ Parsons Green

Though it's well liked for its food and efficient service, this splendidly organised pub is perhaps best known for its impressively eclectic range of drinks. Six perfectly kept real ales include Adnams Broadside, Bass, Harveys Sussex, Highgate Mild, Oakham JHB, Roosters Yankee, and rapidly changing guests; they also keep 15 Trappist beers, around 50 other foreign bottled beers, a dozen malt whiskies, and a constantly expanding range of good, interesting and reasonably priced wines. Every item on the menu, whether it be scrambled egg or raspberry and coconut tart, has a suggested accompaniment listed beside it, perhaps a wine, perhaps a bottled beer. They're keen to encourage people to select beer with food as you might wine, and organise regular beer dinners where every course comes with a recommended brew. Good bar food might include soup, sandwiches (from £4), ploughman's (with some unusual cheeses, £5), twice-baked cheese soufflé with caramelised onions (£6.25), warm chorizo salad (£6.75), salmon fishcakes with tarragon mayonnaise, or pork sausages and mash (£7.75), beer-battered cod and chips (£8.25), fennel risotto with parmesan and truffle oil (£8.50), fried bass with garlic mash, capers, mint and brown butter (£12.75), and daily specials. There's usually something to eat available all day; at weekends they do a good brunch menu, and in winter they do a popular Sunday lunch. The stylishly modernised U-shaped bar has plenty of sofas, wooden tables, and huge windows with slatted wooden blinds, and winter coal and log fires, one in an elegant marble fireplace. The pub is usually busy (and can feel crowded at times), but there are enough smiling, helpful staff behind the solid panelled central servery to ensure you'll rarely have to wait too long to be served. All the art displayed is for sale. The back restaurant is no smoking. On summer evenings the front terrace overlooking the green has something of a continental feel, with crowds of people drinking al fresco; there may be Sunday barbecues. They have quarterly beer festivals (often spotlighting regional breweries), as well as lively celebrations on American Independence Day or Thanksgiving. *(Recommended by the Didler, Boyd Catling, LM, Paul Hopton, Derek Thomas)*

Mitchells & Butlers ~ Manager Mark Dorber ~ Real ale ~ Bar food (12(11 Sat/Sun)-10.30) ~ Restaurant ~ (020) 7736 2115 ~ Children welcome ~ Dogs allowed in bar ~ Open 11-11; 12-10.30 Sun; closed 25/26 Dec

Windsor Castle

Campden Hill Road, W8; ⊖ Holland Park/Notting Hill Gate

One of the delights of this atmospheric Victorian pub is the big tree-shaped garden behind. There are lots of sturdy teak seats and tables on flagstones (you'll have to move fast to bag one on a sunny day), as well as a brick outside bar, and quite a secluded feel thanks to the high ivy-covered sheltering walls. While that's a huge draw in summer, this is very much a pub with year-round appeal: the inside is particularly cosy in winter , with its time-smoked ceilings and dark wooden furnishings. The series of tiny unspoilt rooms all have to be entered through separate doors, so it can be quite a challenge finding the people you've arranged to meet – more often than not they'll be hidden behind the high backs of the sturdy built-in elm benches. A cosy pre-war-style dining room opens off, and soft lighting and a coal-effect fire add to the appeal. Served all day, bar food includes things like sandwiches (from £4.95), steamed mussels or fish and chips (£7.95), and various sausages with mash and onion gravy (£9); they do a choice of roasts on Sunday (£9.95), when the range of other dishes is more limited. Adnams, Fullers London Pride and a guest like Hook Norton on handpump (not cheap, even for this part of London), along with decent house wines, various malt whiskies, and perhaps mulled wine in winter. No fruit machines or piped music. Usually fairly quiet at lunchtime – when several areas are no smoking – the pub can be packed some evenings, often with (as they think) Notting Hill's finest. *(Recommended by Jill Bickerton)*

Mitchells & Butlers ~ Manager Sally Hemingway ~ Real ale ~ Bar food (12-10) ~ (020) 7243 9551 ~ Dogs allowed in bar ~ Open 12-11(10.30 Sun)

Lucky Dip

Besides the fully inspected pubs, you might like to try these Lucky Dips recommended to us and described by readers (if you do, please send us reports: www.goodguides.com).

CENTRAL LONDON
EC1
Betsey Trotwood [Farringdon Rd]: Tidy and efficient local for *Guardian* newspaper and other nearby offices, Shepherd Neame ales, friendly staff *(Tracey and Stephen Groves)*

☆ *O'Hanlons* [Tysoe St]: Friendly traditional local, bare boards and yellow paintwork, tasty beers from O'Hanlons in Devon, also Brakspears and Fullers London Pride, enjoyable home-made food from baguettes to a few reasonably priced daily specials and usually Sun lunch, with good irish stew in winter; irish folk night Thurs; a couplke of tables outside, open all day *(the Didler, Richard Lewis, Ian Phillips, Richard and Karen Holt, LYM)*

Old Red Lion [St John St]: Theatre bar, simple and atmospherically dark; well kept Adnams Broadside *(Tracey and Stephen Groves)*

Rising Sun [Cloth Fair]: Lofty linked bars in muted browns, with elaborate carved dark woodwork, some nice frosted glass, ornate bookcase, lots of little tables, stools and benches around the edges, relaxed atmosphere, friendly staff, well kept Sam Smiths, good value food from baguettes to Sun lunch, views of church, chess, dominoes, cribbage, upstairs lounge (not always open) up steep stairs; fruit machine, may be piped music *(Tracey and Stephen Groves)*

Sekforde Arms [Sekforde St]: Small and comfortably simple corner Youngs local with friendly licensees, well kept beers and wide range of well priced straightforward food, with nice pictures inc Spy caricatures, upstairs restaurant; pavement tables *(Tracey and Stephen Groves, the Didler, Stephen and Jean Curtis)*

EC2
☆ *Dirty Dicks* [Bishopsgate]: Re-creation of traditional City tavern with barrel tables in bare-boards bar, interesting old prints inc one of Nathaniel Bentley, the original Dirty Dick, Youngs full beer range kept well, decent food inc open sandwiches, baguettes and reasonably priced hot dishes, pleasant service, cellar wine bar with wine racks overhead in brick barrel-vaulted ceiling; loads of character – fun for foreign visitors *(LYM, the Didler, Mike Gorton, Ian Phillips)*

Hamilton Hall [Bishopsgate; also entrance from Liverpool St station]: Big busy Wetherspoons pub, flamboyant Victorian baroque décor, plaster nudes and fruit mouldings, chandeliers, mirrors, upper mezzanine, good-sized upstairs no smoking section (can get crowded and smoky downstairs), comfortable groups of seats, reliable food all day from well filled sandwiches up, interesting changing well kept real ales, decent wines, good prices; silenced machines, no piped music; tables outside, open all day *(Richard Lewis, LYM, Ian Phillips)*

Old Dr Butlers Head [Masons Ave]: 17th-c beamed City pub with more seating than usual, bare boards, dark wood, cream paint, small-paned windows, small tables around big irregularly shaped main room, raised back area with more tables, Shepherd Neame Bitter, Best, Spitfire and Bishops Finger, quick service, lunchtime food, upstairs bar *(Ian Phillips)*

Pacific [Bishopsgate]: Bright US-style brewpub, not cheap, with beer brewed visibly on the premises, wide choice of food in dining room off and upstairs restaurant, good wine choice, friendly often foreign staff *(Richard Lewis)*

EC3
Cock & Woolpack [Finch Lane, off Threadneedle St]: Well done modern pastiche of traditional Victorian pub, more seating than many inc mirrored central saloon and back snug; well kept Shepherd Neame ales *(Tracey and Stephen Groves)*

Crosse Keys [Gracechurch St]: Attractive Wetherspoons in former bank, domed ceiling, marble pillars, ornate wood and plasterwork, panelling, upper gallery, good choice of well kept ales from big oval central bar, their usual menu, friendly helpful staff, silenced games machine, no music; no smoking children's area, open all day bul cl 4pm Sat and all Sun *(Richard Lewis)*

Ship [Talbot Ct, off Eastcheap]: Quaint bare-boards courtyard pub full of City types, well kept Adnams, Fullers London Pride and Greene King IPA, lunchtime snacks; a Nicholsons pub *(Ian Phillips)*

NW1

Metropolitan [Baker St station, Marylebone Rd]: Cool and elegant showpiece Wetherspoons in ornate Victorian hall, lots of tables on one side, very long bar the other; their usual good beer choice and prices, no smoking areas, lack of piped music and so forth *(Tracey and Stephen Groves)*

SW1

☆ *Antelope* [Eaton Terr]: Stylish panelled local, rather superior but friendly; bare-boards elegance in main bar, tiny snug, lots of interesting prints and old advertisements, real ales such as Adnams, Fullers London Pride, Marstons Pedigree and Tetleys, good house wines, sandwiches, baked potatoes, ploughman's and one-price hot dishes; surprisingly quiet and relaxed upstairs wkdy lunchtimes, can get crowded evenings; open all day, children in eating area *(LYM, the Didler, Tracey and Stephen Groves)*

☆ *Buckingham Arms* [Petty France]: Warmly welcoming Youngs local with elegant mirrors and woodwork, unusual long side corridor fitted with elbow ledge for drinkers and SkyTV for motor sports), well kept ales, good value food lunchtime and evening, reasonable prices, service friendly and efficient even when busy; handy for Buckingham Palace, Westminster Abbey and St James's Park, open all day *(LYM, the Didler, Dr and Mrs A K Clarke, Tracey and Stephen Groves)*

Gallery [Lupus St]: Opp Pimlico Underground and handy for the Tate, modern light and airy décor, attractive prints and bric-a-brac, no smoking area, Bass, Courage Best, Greene King Abbot and Shepherd Neame Spitfire, decent food; disabled access and lavatories (conventional ones down stairs) *(George Atkinson, Dr and Mrs M E Wilson)*

Horse & Groom [Groom Pl]: Smart mews-corner pub with plush seats on stripped boards, particularly well kept Shepherd Neame *(Tracey and Stephen Groves)*

Jugged Hare [Vauxhall Bridge Rd/Rochester Row]: Fullers Ale & Pie pub in converted colonnaded bank with balustraded balcony, chandelier, prints and busts; their ales kept well, friendly efficient service, decent food, no smoking back area; fruit machine, unobtrusive piped music; open all day *(BB, the Didler)*

☆ *Morpeth Arms* [Millbank]: Roomy and comfortable nicely preserved Victorian pub, the local for the original Tate, some etched and cut glass, old books and prints, photographs, earthenware jars and bottles, well kept Youngs ales inc Waggle Dance, good range of food from sandwiches up, good choice of wines, helpful well organised service even when it's packed at lunchtime (lots of smokers then), quieter evenings; seats outside (a lot of traffic) *(BB, the Didler, Val and Alan Green, Tracey and Stephen Groves, Meg and Colin Hamilton, Craig Turnbull, Ian and Nita Cooper)*

Red Lion [Parliament St]: Interesting pub nr Houses of Parliament, with Division Bell – used by MPs and Foreign Office staff; parliamentary cartoons and prints, well kept Tetleys, good range of snacks and meals, small narrow no smoking upstairs dining room; also cellar bar *(Craig Turnbull, Dr and Mrs A K Clarke)*

Shakespeare [Buckingham Palace Rd]: Bright and lively since renovations, quick food service, good choice of ales *(Janet and Peter Race)*

Tattershall Castle [off Victoria Embankment]: Converted paddle steamer – marvellous vantage point for watching river traffic and the London Eye opposite; canopied bar serveries, with snacks, barbecues and ice creams too in summer, for both forward and aft decks with picnic-sets; nautical décor with lots of wood and brass in wardroom bar below decks, also restaurant and late-licence wknd nightclub *(Kevin Flack, BB, Dr and Mrs M E Wilson)*

SW3

Builders Arms [Britten St]: Smart bistro-style pub with good food (drinkers welcomed too), attractive street *(Derek Thomas)*

Bunch of Grapes [Brompton Rd]: Splendid Victorian local with some robust wood carving and effusive Victorian decoration; prompt and friendly helpful service, comfortable seats, good if not cheap food from sandwiches up, well kept real ale, very cosmopolitan customers; handy halfway point between Harrods and the V&A *(John Branston, John and Judy Saville)*

Crown [Dovehouse St]: Small modern pub with clear windows and soft pastel colours, smartly comfortable, with particularly well kept Adnams and Fullers, shortish choice of lovingly prepared modestly priced unpretentious food, friendly speedy unobtrusive service; won't appeal to traditionalists – two TVs with different sports events, prominent fruit machine, perhaps piped pop music *(Brian Barder, Tracey and Stephen Groves)*

Hour Glass [Brompton Rd]: Small pub handy for V&A and other nearby museums, well kept Fullers, freshly squeezed orange juice, good value food (not Sun) from speciality toasted sandwiches and baguettes to straightforward hot dishes, welcoming landlady and quick young staff; sports TV, can be a bit smoky; pavement tables *(LM)*

Phoenix [Smith St]: Newly reworked as light and airy comfortably modern two-room bar mixing sofas and low tables with leatherette chairs and dining tables, Battersea beer and good range of wines by the glass, up-to-date food from good lunchtime light dishes such as ciabattas to full menu *(Martin and Karen Wake)*

W1

☆ *Audley* [Mount St]: Classic civilised Mayfair pub, opulent red plush, High Victorian mahogany and engraved glass, clock hanging in lovely carved wood bracket from ornately corniced ceiling, well kept Courage Best and Directors from long polished bar, good food and service, good coffee, upstairs panelled dining room; open all day *(LYM, Kevin Blake)*

☆ *Clachan* [Kingly St]: Neat recently refurbished pub behind Liberty's, lovely wooden bar, ornate plaster ceiling supported by two large fluted and decorated pillars, comfortable screened leather banquettes, smaller drinking alcove up three or four steps, Adnams, Fullers London Pride and Greene King IPA, good service from hard-working smart staff, above-average food inc once-common now-rare pub snacks such as scotch eggs and pork pies; can get busy, but very relaxed in afternoons *(John Harcourt, BB, Dr and Mrs M E Wilson)*

Cock [Great Portland St]: Large corner local with enormous lamps over picnic-sets outside, florid Victorian/Edwardian décor with tiled floor, handsome woodwork, some cut and etched glass, high tiled ceiling, ornate plasterwork, velvet curtains, coal-effect gas fire; well kept cheap Sam Smiths OB with all four handpumps, popular lunchtime food in upstairs lounge with two more coal-effect gas fires *(Ian Phillips, the Didler, Nick Holding)*

Golden Eagle [Marylebone Lane]: Tastefully renovated Victorian pub with traditional features but modern feel, well kept beers such as Brakspears, Fullers London Pride and St Austell, fresh flowers, friendly service; piano singalong Thurs *(Angus Lyon)*

Lamb & Flag [James St/Barratt St]: Pleasant bare-boards pub with panelling and low ribbed and bossed ceiling, friendly staff, Courage Directors, Fullers London Pride, Greene King IPA, Marstons Pedigree and Charles Wells Bombardier from attractive bar counter with barley-sugar pillars supporting coloured leaded glass, decent wines, plain hot dishes *(Ian Phillips)*

Newman Arms [Rathbone St/Newman Passage]: Fullers and Youngs (unusual combination) kept well in small panelled bar with nautical memorabilia and good service, home-made pies in small room upstairs *(Tim Maddison)*

☆ *O'Connor Don* [Marylebone Lane]: Enjoyable and civilised bare-boards pub, genuinely and unobtrusively irish, with good baguettes and other freshly made bar food, waitress drinks service (to make sure the Guinness has settled properly), warm bustling atmosphere, daily papers; good upstairs restaurant with daily fresh galway oysters, folk music Sat *(Richard Gibbs, Ian Phillips, BB)*

☆ *Old Coffee House* [Beak St]: Polished pub with masses of interesting bric-a-brac, unusually wide choice of decent lunchtime food (not Sun) in upstairs food room full of prints and pictures, well kept real ales; fruit machine, piped music; children allowed upstairs 12-3, open all day exc Sun afternoon; very popular with wknd shoppers and tourists *(LYM, Tracey and Stephen Groves)*

Red Lion [Kingly St]: Friendly, solidly modernised without being spoilt, narrow front bar, darts behind, well kept low-priced Sam Smiths, short realistically priced lunchtime food choice in comfortable room upstairs; video juke box *(DC, BB)*

Running Footman [Charles St]: Bow window, dark panelling, ochre ceiling, painting of the eponymous footman over fireplace, real ales inc Shepherd Neame Spitfire, a comfortable crush of happy customers *(Dr and Mrs M E Wilson)*

Toucan [Carlisle St]: Small Guinness pub, five taps for it in relaxed dark and cosy basement bar with toucan paintings and vintage Guinness advertisements, lots of whiskeys and good irish piped music, enjoyable food such as Guinness pie, irish stew, Galway oysters; lighter plainer upstairs bar overflows on to pavement when busy, quiet TV in both bars *(Tim Maddison)*

Waxy O'Connors [Rupert St]: Small ordinary street entry to surprising 3D maze of communicating areas filled with a gothic plethora of reclaimed woodwork; lagers and stouts, friendly young staff, food good if not cheap; a lively crowd of young up-front people *(Dr and Mrs M E Wilson)*

Yorkshire Grey [Langham St]: Small bare-boards corner pub with well kept cheap Sam Smiths OB, lots of wood, bric-a-brac and prints, comfortable seating inc snug little parlour, friendly staff, attractively priced bar lunches; open all day *(Ian Phillips)*

W2

☆ *Mad Bishop & Bear* [Paddington station]: Up escalators from concourse in new part of station, classic city pub décor in cream and pastels, ornate plasterwork, etched mirrors and fancy lamps inc big brass chandeliers, parquet, tiles and carpet, booths with leather banquettes, lots of wood and prints, a guest beer and full Fullers beer range kept well from long counter, good wine choice, friendly smartly dressed staff, wide choice of good value food from breakfast (7.30 on) and sandwiches to Sun roasts, big no smoking area, train departures screen; soft piped music, fruit machine; open all day, tables out overlooking concourse *(Dr and Mrs M E Wilson, Alan Wilson, Simon Collett-Jones, BB, Dr and Mrs A K Clarke, Ian Phillips)*

W8

☆ *Scarsdale Arms* [Edwardes Sq]: Busy Georgian pub in lovely leafy square, keeping a good deal of character, with stripped wooden floors, two or three fireplaces with good coal-effect gas fires, lots of knick-knacks, ornate bar counter; well kept ales such as Fullers London Pride, good wine choice, enjoyable blackboard food inc unusual dishes, pleasant service; tree-shaded front courtyard with impressive show of flower tubs and baskets, open all day *(Gloria Bax, LYM, Craig Turnbull, Alan J Morton, John Davis)*

WC1

Calthorpe Arms [Grays Inn Rd]: Consistently well kept Youngs Bitter, Special and seasonal beer at sensible prices in relaxed and unpretentious corner pub with plush wall seats, big helpings of popular food upstairs lunchtime and evening; nice pavement tables, open all day *(the Didler)*

☆ *Duke of York* [Roger St]: Quietly placed and unpretentious, with Formica-top tables and café chairs on patterned lino downstairs, real ales such as Greene King Old Speckled Hen and Ind Coope Burton, helpful staff, cool and welcoming young atmosphere (big Andy Warhol-style pictures); can be smoky; emphasis on surprisingly good interesting modern food at reasonable prices, upstairs dining room *(Joel Dobris, Roger and Jenny Huggins, BB)*

Pakenham Arms [Pakenham St]: Relaxed unspoilt split-level local, quiet at lunchtime and wknds, well kept real ales, friendly staff, generous food, big open doors making it light and airy in summer; picnic-sets outside, lots of flowers *(Esther and John Sprinkle)*

☆ *Princess Louise* [High Holborn]: Etched and gilt mirrors, brightly coloured and fruity-shaped tiles, slender Portland stone columns, lofty and elaborately colourful ceiling, quiet plush-seated corners, attractively priced Sam Smiths from the long counter, good friendly service, simple bar snacks, upstairs lunchtime buffet; notable Victorian gents'; crowded and lively during the week, with great evening atmosphere – usually quieter late evening, or Sat lunchtime; open all day, cl Sun *(Patrick Hancock, the Didler, Dr and Mrs A K Clarke, LYM, Tracey and Stephen Groves)*

Rugby [Great James St]: Sizeable corner pub with well kept Shepherd Neame ales inc their seasonal beer, usual food, good service; tables outside *(the Didler, Val Stevenson, Rob Holmes, Joel Dobris)*

WC1

Swintons [Swinton St]: Former Kings Head converted to enjoyable dining pub, relaxing ambiance, extensive wine list as well as draught and bottled beer; no TVs or machines *(Martin Ballans)*

WC2

Bierodrome [Kingsway]: One of a small chain specialising in belgian beers, bottled and draught, also lots of genevers, and good choice of wines by the glass; friendly staff, daily papers, open all day *(Richard Lewis)*

☆ *Chandos* [St Martins Lane]: Busy downstairs bare-boards bar with snug booths, more

comfortable upstairs lounge with opera photographs, low wooden tables, panelling, leather sofas, orange, red and yellow leaded windows; well kept cheap Sam Smiths OB, prompt cheerful mainly antipodean service, basic food from sandwiches to Sun roasts, air conditioning, darts and pinball; can get packed early evening, piped music and games machines; note the automaton on the roof (working 10-2 and 4-9); children upstairs till 6, open all day from 9 (for breakfast) *(Susan and Nigel Wilson, Jim Bush, Dr and Mrs M E Wilson, Patrick Hancock, Ian Phillips, LYM)*

Cheshire Cheese [Little Essex St/Milford Lane]: Small cosy panelled pub, leaded bow windows and pretty flower boxes, friendly staff, thriving local atmosphere, cheap food, Courage and more esoteric beers, lots of police badges and shields, basement restaurant *(Dr and Mrs M E Wilson)*

Coach & Horses [Wellington St]: Small friendly and spotless irish pub with imported Dublin Guinness from old-fashioned copper-topped bar, well kept Courage Best, John Smiths and Marstons Pedigree, lots of whiskeys, barman with computer-like drinks order memory, good lunchtime hot roast beef baps; can get crowded, handy for Royal Opera House *(Ian Phillips)*

☆ *Cross Keys* [Endell St/Betterton St]: Friendly and cosy, refreshingly un-Londonish, with masses of of photographs and posters inc Beatles memorabilia, brasses and tasteful bric-a-brac on the dark dim-lit walls, relaxed chatty feel; impressive range of lunchtime sandwiches at sensible prices and a few hot dishes then, well kept Courage Best, Marstons Pedigree and a guest beer, quick service even at busy times; small upstairs bar, often used for functions; fruit machine, gents' down stairs; picnic-sets out on cobbles tucked behind a little group of trees, pretty flower tubs and hanging baskets, open all day *(Dr and Mrs M E Wilson, the Didler, Simon Collett-Jones, John Branston, Tracey and Stephen Groves, LYM)*

Lowlander [Drury Lane]: Smart well run Brussels-style bar with neat long rows of tables (one just for drinking), major beers on tap with some guests and interesting bottled beers *(Tracey and Stephen Groves)*

Marquis of Granby [Chandos Pl]: Small, narrow and high-ceilinged, with high stools by windows overlooking street, cosy parlour-like areas each end through arched wood-and-glass partitions, well kept Adnams and Marstons Pedigree, reasonably priced pub food; open all day *(the Didler, Ted George)*

Nags Head [James St/Neal St]: Etched brewery mirrors, red ceiling, mahogany furniture, some partitioned booths, lots of old local prints, popular lunchtime food from separate side counter, friendly staff, three well kept McMullens ales; piped music, games machine, often crowded; open all day *(P G Plumridge, Richard Lewis)*

Opera Tavern [Catherine St, opp Theatre Royal]: Cheerful bare-boards pub, not too touristy, real ales such as Adnams, Fullers London Pride and Tetleys, reasonably priced snacks from sandwiches and baked potatoes up *(Ian Phillips)*

☆ *Porterhouse* [Maiden Lane]: London outpost of Dublin's Porterhouse microbrewery, shiny three-level maze of stairs, galleries and copper ducting and piping, some nice design touches, their own interesting if pricy unpasteurised draught beers inc Porter and two Stouts (they do a comprehensive tasting tray), also their TSB real ale and a guest, good choice of wines by the glass, reasonably priced food 12-9 from soup and open sandwiches up with some emphasis on rock oysters, sonorous openwork clock, neatly cased bottled beer displays; piped music, Irish bands Weds-Fri and Sun, big-screen sports TV (repeated in gents'); open all day, tables on front terrace *(Christine and Neil Townend, BB, Rona Murdoch, Richard Lewis)*

☆ *Salisbury* [St Martins Lane]: Floridly Victorian with plenty of atmosphere, theatrical sweeps of red velvet, huge sparkling mirrors and cut and etched glass, glossy brass and mahogany; wide food choice from simple snacks to long-running smoked salmon lunches and salad bar (even doing Sun lunches over Christmas/New Year), well kept real ales such as Broughton Ghillie, Courage Directors, Fullers London Pride, Charles Wells Bombardier and Youngs Special, decent house wines, friendly service, no smoking back room *(BB, Mike Gorton, the Didler, Ian Phillips)*

Sherlock Holmes [Northumberland St; aka Northumberland Arms]: Particularly fine collection of Holmes memorabilia, inc complete model of his apartment, also silent videos of black and white Holmes films; Boddingtons, Flowers IPA, Fullers London Pride and Wadworths 6X, usual furnishings, lunchtime pub food from doorstep sandwiches up, young staff, upstairs restaurant; busy lunchtime *(LM, BB)*

Ship [Gate St]: Interesting bare-boards corner pub in narrow alley with painted plaster relief ceiling and upstairs overflow, well kept ales such as Greene King Old Speckled Hen, Theakstons and Charles Wells Bombardier, usual food, friendly service; popular at lunchtime *(Ian Phillips)*

Ship & Shovell [Craven Passage]: Under Charing X station, with four Badger real ales kept well, reasonably priced food, welcoming service and civilised atmosphere, warm fire, bright lighting, pleasant décor inc interesting prints, mainly naval (to support a fanciful connection between this former coal-heavers' pub properly called Ship & Shovel with Sir Cloudesley Shovell the early 18th-c admiral), cosy back section; TV *(Tracey and Stephen Groves, the Didler, Dr and Mrs M E Wilson)*

Welsh Harp [Chandos Pl]: Unpretentious pub with some interesting if not always well executed portraits on its red walls, lovely front stained glass, congenial seating layout with nice high benches around back tables and

along wall counter, unusual ales such as Elgoods, Harveys and York), friendly welcome *(Tracey and Stephen Groves, BB)*

EAST LONDON

E1

Dickens Inn [Marble Quay, St Katharines Way]: Outstanding position above smart docklands marina, oddly swiss-chalet look from outside with its balconies and window boxes, interesting stripped-down bare boards, baulks and timbers interior, wide choice of enjoyable food, well kept Theakstons Old Peculier, friendly prompt service, several floors inc big pricy restaurant extension; popular with overseas visitors, seats outside *(the Didler, John and Judy Saville, LYM)*

E2

Approach Tavern [Approach Rd]: Imposing high-ceilinged Victorian tavern restored as unpretentious food pub, comfortable seating, fairly priced enjoyable food inc good Sun roasts and delicious puddings, well kept Fullers and Ridleys ales, considerate service; good non-contemporary juke box *(Tim Maddison)*

E3

☆ *Crown* [Grove Rd]: Good freshly cooked organic food, fine choice of wines and other drinks inc organic real ales; in attractive Georgian street, dogs and children allowed, nice courtyard tables, open all day, cl Mon lunchtime *(Derek Thomas)*

E4

Plough [Mott St/Sewardstone Rd (A112)]: McMullens pub with beamery and concrete paving, their beers kept well, good choice of decent food; picnic-sets outside with attractive flowers and tubs *(Ian Phillips)*

Good Samaritan [Turner St/Stepney Way]: Spick and span well run pub, reasonably priced food, cheerful prompt service, Courage Directors and Theakstons from central bar, Victorian photographs *(B and M Kendall)*

E14

☆ *Barley Mow* [Narrow St]: Steep steps down into converted dockmaster's house, clean and comfortable, with Victorian-style wallpaper over dark panelled dado, lots of sepia Whitby photographs, candles and ship's lanterns, reasonably priced usual food from sandwiches up, well kept ales such as Greene King IPA, partly panelled conservatory with stained-glass french windows; big heaters for picnic-sets on spacious if breezy terrace with great views over two Thames reaches, swing-bridge entrance to Limehouse Basin and mouth of Regents Canal, still has electric windlass used for hauling barges through; children and dogs welcome, car park with CCTV *(R T and J C Moggridge, Susan and John Douglas)*

George [Glengall Grove]: Cheery East End pub with Courage Best and Greene King Ruddles, good food inc bargain specials and market-fresh fish, bar (Isle of Dogs old guard), lounge (new City types) and conservatory dining room *(Ian Phillips, GHC)*

E17

Flower Pot [Wood St]: Friendly single bar with good atmosphere and particularly well kept Bass and Charles Wells Bombardier; popular with soccer fans *(Len Banister)*

NORTH LONDON
N1

Albion [Thornhill Rd]: Low ceilings, snug nooks and crannies inc cosy back hideaway, some old photographs of the pub, open fires, some gas lighting, no smoking area, reasonably priced straightforward food with plenty of specials, friendly service, well kept Fullers London Pride and Theakstons, interesting Victorian gents'; flower-decked front courtyard, big back terrace with vine canopy *(BB, Dr and Mrs M E Wilson, Tim Maddison)*
Barnsbury [Liverpool Rd]: New food pub, stripped back to original woodwork and fireplaces, with contemporary art for sale, wines inc organic ones, real ales and belgian beers, food all day Sun *(anon)*
Camden Head [Camden Walk]: Reliable standby very handy for the antiques market, enjoyable food inc good specials; tables outside *(Esther and John Sprinkle)*
☆ *Kings Head* [Upper St]: Attractively furnished Victorian pub in good spot opp antiques area, polished boards, coal fire and striking island bar, well kept Adnams, Youngs Best and Special, bar food and popular bistro; an oasis of calm on wkdy lunchtimes, can get packed wknds; live music Sat, good theatre in back room (but hard seats there) *(Tracey and Stephen Groves)*
Wenlock Arms [Wenlock Rd]: Plain and popular open-plan local in a bleak bit of London, warmly welcoming service, central bar serving 10 or so well kept changing ales from small breweries, always inc a Mild, also farm cider and perry, foreign bottled beers, snacks inc good salt beef sandwiches, alcove seating, piano in pride of place, coal fires, darts; piped music; open all day, modern jazz Tues, trad Fri, piano Sun lunch *(Tim Maddison, Tracey and Stephen Groves)*

N4

Grand Parade [Grand Parade, Green Lanes]: Magnificent restored Victorian pub, well kept ales such as Fullers London Pride and Ridleys Old Bob *(Dr and Mrs M E Wilson)*
Salisbury [Grand Parade, Green Lanes]: Grandiose late Victorian former hotel reopened after careful refurbishment of its spacious richly ornamented bars, dark velvet, leather and mahogany, intricate tiling and mirrors, Fullers London Pride and Ridleys ales, food in bar and dining room (not Sun evening); open all day, till 1am Thurs-Sat *(Dr and Mrs M E Wilson)*

N12

Tally Ho [High Rd, N Finchley]: Imposing landmark pub comfortably reworked, with old

local photographs, good value all-day food and beer, large upstairs no smoking room allowing children if eating *(Charles Harvey)*

N20

☆ *Orange Tree* [Totteridge]: Rambling Vintage Inn by duckpond, good value standard food from sandwiches to fish served efficiently even on busy wknds, well kept Bass and Fullers London Pride, good choice of wines by the glass, freshly squeezed orange juice and coffee, friendly staff, light and airy décor with inglenook log fires; welcoming to children (and walkers, who leave boots in porch); tables outside, pleasant surroundings – still a village feel *(LM, John Robertson, LYM, Ian Phillips)*

NW1

☆ *Head of Steam* [Eversholt St]: Large well worn in Victorian-look bar up stairs from bus terminus and overlooking it, lots of railway nameplates, other memorabilia and enthusiast magazines for sale, also Corgi collection, unusual model trains and buses; nine interesting well kept ales (also take-away) changing from session to session, most from little-known small breweries, monthly themed beer festivals, Weston's farm cider and perry, lots of bottled beers and vodkas, kind service, simple cheap bar lunches, no smoking area, downstairs restaurant; TV, bar billiards, games machine, security-coded basement lavatories; open all day *(R T and J C Moggridge, BB, the Didler, Richard Lewis, Dr D J and Mrs S C Walker)*

NW3

Duke of Hamilton [New End]: Attractive family-run Fullers local, good value, with good range of seating, well kept London Pride, ESB and a seasonal beer, Biddenden farm cider; open all day, suntrap terrace, next to New End Theatre *(Tracey and Stephen Groves, the Didler)*
Old Bull & Bush [North End Way]: Attractive Victorian pub, quiet on wkdy lunchtimes with comfortable sofa and easy chairs, nooks and crannies, side library bar with lots of bookshelves and pictures and mementoes of Florrie Ford whose song made the pub famous, enjoyable bar food inc tender filled bagels and good Sun specials, reasonable prices, decent wines, restaurant with no smoking area; evenings piped music may be loud, with trendy lighting; good provision for families, pleasant terrace *(Tracey and Stephen Groves, BB)*

NW6

Corrib Rest [Salusbury Rd/Hopefield Av]: Particularly friendly traditional irish pub, a real welcome for all, good disabled access and facilities; good value *(Jonathan White)*

NW7

☆ *Rising Sun* [Marsh Lane/Highwood Hill, Mill Hill]: Beautiful wisteria-covered local dating from 17th c, doing well under current tenants, small well restored main bar and atmospheric side snug on right with low ceilings, lots of dark panelling, timber and coal fires, big plainer lounge on left, well kept Adnams, Greene King Abbot, Youngs Special and occasional guest ales, good malt whiskies, enjoyable food from sandwiches to interesting hot dishes, polite and helpful well turned out staff; picnic-sets on pleasant back terrace, good walks nearby *(Ian Phillips, Tim Maddison, Steve Merson)*

NW8
Lords Tavern [St Johns Wood Rd]: Next to Lords Cricket Ground, good range of food with thai flavours, well kept real ales, good wine choice and friendly service; tables outside *(BB, Alistair Forsyth)*

SOUTH LONDON
SE1
Barrow Boy & Banker [Borough High St, by London Bridge station]: Large elegant banking hall conversion with upper gallery, full Fullers beer range kept well, decent wines, good manageress and efficient young staff, popular food *(Charles Gysin)*
Bunch of Grapes [St Thomas St]: Pleasant atmosphere, food counter in same good (french) hands since the 1970s, well kept Youngs *(Geoffrey G Lawrance)*
☆ *Horniman* [Hays Galleria, off Battlebridge Lane]: Good stop on Thames walks, spacious, bright and airy, with lots of polished wood, comfortable seating inc a few sofas, no smoking area, Adnams, Bass, Fullers London Pride and Greene King IPA, choice of teas and coffees at good prices, lunchtime bar food from soup and big sandwiches to simple hot dishes, snacks other times; unobtrusive piped music; fine Thames views from picnic-sets outside, open all day *(Ian Phillips, LYM)*
Lord Clyde [Clennam St]: Striking tilework outside, unpretentious panelled L-shaped main bar, small hatch-service back public bar with darts, real ales inc Fullers London Pride, Shepherd Neame Spitfire and Youngs, good value straightforward home-made food wkdy lunchtimes and early evenings, may do toasties etc on request at other times (worth asking), welcoming service *(Pete Baker)*
Mulberry Bush [Upper Ground]: Attractively modernised sympathetically lit Youngs pub, very handy for South Bank complex; open-plan with lots of wood, slightly raised turkey-carpeted balustraded area and small tiled-floor no smoking back conservatory, decent wines, helpful staff, well priced bar food, spiral stairs to bistro *(Stephen R Holman)*
☆ *Royal Oak* [Tabard St]: Small two-bar bare-boards pub carefully refurbished so as to be traditional without being too olde-worlde, standing out for its full range of well kept Harveys ales from the central servery; thriving friendly atmosphere, bargain lunchtime home cooking, open all day, cl wknds *(Giles Francis, Jarrod and Wendy Hopkinson)*
Studio Six [Gabriels Wharf]: South Bank bar/diner in two linked timber-framed

buildings, windows all round, picnic-sets on two terraces (one heated), good menu inc lots of fish, good choice of belgian beers on tap, decent wines, Flowers too, friendly staff; great location opp cycle rickshaw base, open all day *(Ian Phillips, Gillian Rodgers)*
Wellington [Waterloo Rd, opp Waterloo station]: Comfortably refurbished late Victorian pub with large high-ceilinged linked rooms, light wood panelling, enormous stirring Battle of Waterloo murals on wall and ceiling, well kept Adnams, Brakspears, Courage Directors, Youngs and a beer labelled for the pub from ornate bar counter, food all day, plenty of comfortable chairs and sofas, attractive tables, friendly service; can get very crowded despite its size, sports TV; has had deaf people's night every other Fri, bedrooms, open all day *(Giles Francis, Dr and Mrs M E Wilson, John A Barker)*
Wheatsheaf [Stoney St]: Simple bare-boards Borough Market local, Youngs and a guest ale from central servery, decent wine choice, lunchtime food, friendly staff, some brown panelling; sports TV in one bar, piped music, games machine; tables on small back terrace and on pavement by market, open all day, cl Sun *(the Didler, Richard Lewis, Kevin Flack)*

SE3
Hare & Billet [Eliot Cottages, Hare & Billet Rd]: Nicely matured open-plan refurbishment of pub dating from 16th c, panelling, bare boards, good solid furniture and open fire, raised middle section, good value food, real ales such as Adnams, Bass, Fullers London Pride and Wadworths 6X, view over Blackheath *(BB, Roger and Jenny Huggins)*

SE10
Admiral Hardy [College Approach, Greenwich Mkt]: Large recently redesigned open-plan pub keeping some nice portraits and stained glass, changing real ales such as Greene King Old Speckled Hen, Shepherd Neame Spitfire and Vale Black Swan Mild, reopened kitchen doing generous well prepared lunchtime food, attached delicatessen; piped music; backs on to Greenwich Market *(Mr and Mrs A H Young, Tracey and Stephen Groves, Craig Turnbull)*
Coach & Horses [Greenwich Mkt, Blackheath Rd]: Up-to-date food and young helpful staff; heated tables out in covered market *(Dr and Mrs R E S Tanner)*
☆ *Richard I* [Royal Hill]: Quietly old-fashioned pubby atmosphere in friendly no-nonsense traditional two-bar local with well kept Youngs, good staff, no piped music, bare boards, panelling; tables in pleasant back garden with barbecues, busy summer wknds and evenings *(Robert Gomme, the Didler, Peter and Patricia Burton)*
☆ *Trafalgar* [Park Row]: Attractive and substantial 18th-c building with four elegant rooms inc pleasant dining room and central bar with lovely river-view bow window, careful colour schemes, oak panelling, helpful young staff welcoming even when busy (can

get packed Fri/Sat evenings, may have bouncer then), good atmosphere, well prepared usual food inc speciality whitebait and good fresh veg, real ales inc Theakstons, good house wines; piped music in river-view room; handy for Maritime Museum, may have jazz wknds *(Dr and Mrs R E S Tanner, Tracey and Stephen Groves)*

SE11
Doghouse [Kennington Cross]: Large and bright, with reasonably priced food, quieter side bar for locals and diners; may be loud music *(Kevin Flack)*
South London Pacific [Kennington Rd]: Former Cock Tavern converted to polynesian-theme bar, open 6 till late, live music; cl Mon and some Suns *(anon)*

SE13
Watch House [Lewisham High St]: Usual Wetherspoons style, good value special offers, well kept real ales inc three unusual changing guest beers; disabled facilities *(R T and J C Moggridge)*

SE16
☆ **Angel** [Bermondsey Wall E]: Superb Thames views to Tower Bridge and the City upstream, and the Pool of London downstream, esp from balcony supported above water by great timber piles, and from picnic-sets in garden alongside; softly lit simply modernised bar with low-backed settles and old local photographs and memorablilia, food from baguettes to impressive main meals and good Sun roast, well kept cheap Sam Smiths, kind friendly staff, formal upstairs restaurant with waiter service; nr remains of Edward III's palace, interesting walks round Surrey Quays *(LYM, R T and J C Moggridge, Dave Braisted)*
☆ **Mayflower** [Rotherhithe St]: Friendly and cosy riverside pub with thriving local atmosphere despite growing emphasis on decent food (not Sun night) from ciabatta rolls up, black beams, high-backed settles and coal fires, good views from upstairs restaurant (cl Sat lunchtime), well kept Greene King IPA and Abbot and a guest such as Black Sheep, good coffee, quick friendly service; pub's nice jetty/terrace has been undergoing repairs; children welcome, open all day, in unusual street with lovely Wren church *(Susan and John Douglas, LYM, G B Longden, LM, the Didler, M A and C R Starling)*
Ship & Whale [Gulliver St]: Small neatly kept opened-up pub with pleasant bar-style décor, full Shepherd Neame range kept well, welcoming young staff, enjoyable well presented fresh food from sandwiches up, choice of teas and coffees, lots of board games; dogs welcome, small garden behind with barbecue *(LM)*

SE17
Beehive [Carter St]: Unpretentious bare-boards pub/bistro with well kept Courage Best and Directors and Fullers London Pride from island

bar, cushioned pews, bric-a-brac on delft shelf, modern art in candlelit dining room, good choice of home-made food all day from sandwiches to steaks, wide range of wines, friendly service from neat staff; piped music, two TVs; tables outside *(BB, Pete Baker)*

SE20
Dr W G Grace [Witham Rd, Penge]: Themed after the cricketing pioneer, with lots of cricketing memorabilia; food all day, Courage Best and Directors, quiz nights Tues and Thurs, Sat party night, Sun prize box; children (till 7) and well behaved dogs welcome, family tables outside, adult roof terrace *(anon)*

SE26
☆ **Dulwich Wood House** [Sydenham Hill]: Well refurbished and extended Youngs pub in Victorian lodge gatehouse complete with turret, well kept ales, decent wines, attractively priced straightforward food cooked to order popular at lunchtime with local retired people, friendly service; steps up to entrance; lots of tables in big pleasant back garden (no dogs) with old-fashioned street lamps and barbecues *(Alan M Pring, Ian and Nita Cooper)*

SW4
Abbeville [Abbeville Rd]: New dining pub with sturdy furnishings, rugs on dark boards, warm décor, fresh waitress-served food inc mediterranean specials and wknd brunches, Fullers ales and Timothy Taylors Landlord *(anon)*
Coach & Horses [Clapham Park Rd]: Traditionally refurbished and back to its original name, real ales and enjoyable food at reasonable prices, comfortable feel *(James Macdougal)*
☆ **Windmill** [Clapham Common South Side]: Big bustling well restored Victorian pub by the common, particularly worth knowing for its good well equipped bedrooms; civilised bar with sets of four deeply comfortable chairs around each table, plenty of pictures, coal fires and smaller areas opening off inc panelled back no smoking room; decent food (all day wknds) from soup and baguettes up, prompt friendly service, well kept Youngs Bitter, Special and seasonal beers, good choice of wines by the glass; piped music, TV; children in family room, dogs allowed in bar, open all day *(Susan and John Douglas, LYM, Ian Phillips)*

SW8
Canton Arms [South Lambeth Rd]: Recently refurbished, now has good welcoming atmosphere and enjoyable generous proper pub food *(Hannah Bowler)*

SW11
Castle [Battersea High St]: Cosy atmosphere, enjoyable changing food, good short wine list; pretty garden *(Emma Wright, Lesley Henry)*

SW13
Bridge [Castelnau, nr Hammersmith Bridge]:

Stylish conversion of Edwardian pub, three linked rooms one with leather settees by real fire, interesting modern food from open kitchen behind bar, Courage Best and Directors and related guest beers, 10 wines by the glass, friendly service; unobtrusive piped music; tables on decking in back garden, open all day – handy for Thames Path *(Susan and John Douglas)*

☆ *Idle Hour* [Railway Side (off White Hart Lane between Mortlake High St and Upper Richmond Rd)]: Out of the way small local transformed into friendly organic gastropub, very good individually cooked food (may be a wait) inc choice of Sunday roasts, elaborate barbecues, splendid bloody mary, good range of organic soft drinks but only real ale is normal Flowers IPA; nice chunky old tables on bare boards, relaxed atmosphere, daily papers and magazines, piped music, a profusion of wall clocks, small fireplace; tables with candles out in small pretty yard behind, cl wkdy lunchtimes, no children; if driving, park at end of Railway Side and walk – the road quickly becomes too narrow for cars *(Edward Mirzoeff, BB)*

Sun [Church Rd]: Attractive spot with tables over road overlooking duckpond; recently done up inside, with sofas, tuscan wall colours and tracked spotlights, several areas around central servery, real ales, home-cooked food with italian leanings from good paninis up, prompt service even though busy; prices on the high side, piped music may be loud *(Jenny and Brian Seller, Peter Rozée, Gloria Bax)*

SW14

☆ *Victoria* [West Temple Sheen]: Comfortable bar with low chairs, games and wide choice of wines by the glass, good interesting and elegantly presented if not cheap food in restaurant with white-painted boards opening into conservatory, friendly young staff, picnic-sets on back terrace with good-sized play area; service charge added even if you order food and get drinks at the bar; bedrooms *(Martin and Karen Wake)*

SW15

☆ *Dukes Head* [Lower Richmond Rd]: Classic Victorian Youngs pub, spacious and grand yet friendly, light and airy with big ceiling fans, very civilised feel, tables by window with great Thames view, well kept ales, 20 wines by the glass, good value fresh lunchtime food, coal fires; smaller more basic locals' bar, plastic glasses for outside *(Susan and John Douglas, BB)*

Half Moon [Lower Richmond Rd]: Genuine pub with nice atmosphere, well kept Youngs, enjoyable food, good friendly service; popular live music nights *(Martin Brunt)*

☆ *Jolly Gardeners* [Lacy Rd]: Recent remarkable refit of former low-key local, now stylishly redecorated cool bar with draught belgian beers, good wine list, interesting choice of enjoyable food, lots of sofas, trendy artwork, chill-out music; nice tables on tiny back terrace *(BB)*

Olde Spotted Horse [Putney High St]: Large recently refurbished open-plan bar with island servery, good range of food at reasonable prices from on-view kitchen, well kept Youngs, good wine choice, quick efficient service *(Peter Rozée)*

Putney Page [Lower Richmond Rd]: Former Spencer Arms, newly reworked as stylishly modern bar popular with mainly young professionals, light and airy, with pale wood furniture and flooring, matt black marble dining tables, some sofas, pleasant decorations, silenced sports TV screens; enjoyable mainly thai food with some familiar favourites, Courage Directors, Fullers London Pride and Charles Wells Bombardier, pleasant staff; may be quiet piped music *(Susan and John Douglas)*

SW17

Hope [Bellevue Rd]: After a spell as a Firkin, now back to its proper name, heading upmarket with appealing food and Wandsworth Common views *(Chris Parsons)*

SW18

Old Sergeant [Garratt Lane]: Classic homely and unspoilt two-bar local with long-serving landlord, Youngs full range kept well, wkdy lunches, friendly efficient service, good Christmas decorations; open all day *(LM, the Didler)*

SW19

Crooked Billet [Wimbledon Common]: Popular olde-worlde pub by common, lovely spot in summer, open all day; full Youngs range kept well, well cooked generous food, pleasant helpful service, lots of old prints, nice furnishings on broad polished oak boards, soft lighting, daily papers, restaurant in 16th-c barn behind *(Susan and John Douglas)*

Sultan [Norman Rd]: Proper drinking pub emphasising well kept Hop Back ales such as Summer Lightning and Crop Circle; sandwiches and toasties, darts in public bar with trophies in corner, big scrubbed tables inside and out, good courtyard *(LM, Jenny and Brian Seller)*

WEST LONDON

SW5

Blackbird [Earls Court Rd]: Big comfortable bank conversion, dark panelling, plenty of nooks and corners, decent lunchtime food esp home-made pies and freshly carved roasts in barm cakes, full range of Fullers ales kept well, interesting pictures; open all day *(the Didler)*

SW10

Water Rat [Kings Rd]: Small pub specialising in reasonably priced tasty lebanese food; Adnams and Youngs, arty nude photographs, civilised atmosphere (but for SkyTV football and chain-smoking Chelsea fans on match days) *(Mark Percy, Lesley Mayoh)*

W4

Bell & Crown [Strand on the Green]: Big busy Fullers local with their standard beers kept

well, several comfortable areas, local paintings and photographs, good value food inc interesting dishes, efficient friendly staff, log fire, no piped music or machines; great Thames views esp from conservatory and picnic-sets out by towpath (good walks), open all day *(Richard Jennings)*
Bollo House [Bollo Lane]: Spacious modern bar/bistro with sofas, light-coloured furniture and amber walls above pale dado, up-to-date food, Greene King IPA and Abbot, daily papers; tables outside *(Ian Phillips)*

W5
Wheatsheaf [Haven Lane]: Big pleasant flower-decked Fullers pub with cheerful bare-boards bar, their full beer range, friendly service, sandwiches, salads and hot dishes at sensible prices, enormous log fire in back room *(Ian Phillips)*

W6
Black Lion [South Black Lion Lane]: Welcoming and civilised cottagey pub, helpful staff, Courage Best and Directors, decent usual food from baguettes and baked potatoes up, dining area behind big log-effect gas fire; large pleasant heated terrace *(Susan and John Douglas, Ian Phillips, BB)*
☆ *Brook Green* [Shepherds Bush Rd]: Large Victorian pub with energetic licensees, comfortably up-to-date seating, noble high ceilings, ornate plaster, chandeliers, coal fire; good choice of reasonably priced enjoyable home-made food with proper veg, well kept Youngs, friendly atmosphere, good mix of customers; TV for rugby internationals, Thurs blues night and Fri comedy downstairs; 15 comfortably refurbished bedrooms *(Pete Baker, Hywel Bevan)*
Crabtree [Rainville Rd]: Spacious and comfortable conversion, light and airy, with big settees, bookcases, good choice of ciabattas and sandwiches, also hot dishes, good range of wines by the glass; handy for Thames Path and Bishop's Park *(Edward Mirzoeff)*
Thatched House [Dalling Rd]: Spacious Youngs dining pub with their full beer range and enjoyable food (not Mon/Tues, or Sun eve) – though local drinkers still come; stripped pine, modern art, big armchairs, good wine list, welcoming staff and regulars, conservatory; no music; open all day wknds *(Susan and John Douglas, BB)*

W7
Fox [Green Lane]: Friendly open-plan 19th-c pub in quiet cul de sac nr Grand Union Canal, well kept real ales, decent wines, good value wholesome food from good toasties, baguettes and baked potatoes to home-made hot dishes inc Sun roasts, dining area, panelling and stained glass one end, wildlife pictures and big fish tank, farm tools hung from ceiling; smoking throughout, darts end, small side garden, occasional wknd barbecues, towpath walks *(LM, John and Glenys Wheeler, Val Stevenson, Rob Holmes)*

W8
☆ *Britannia* [Allen St, off Kensington High St]: Friendly civilised local opened into single L-shaped bar, relaxed and peaceful, with good value fresh home-cooked lunches, well kept Youngs and no music; attractive indoor back 'garden' (no smoking at lunchtime), open all day *(Susan and John Douglas, Prof and Mrs S Barnett, the Didler)*

W11
☆ *Ladbroke Arms* [Ladbroke Rd]: Good food on big plates, esp pasta, in smartly chatty dining pub, Fullers London Pride and Greene King Ruddles County; tables on front terrace *(Ian Phillips, LYM)*

W14
Beaconsfield [Blythe Rd, Olympia]: Open-plan former Frigate & Firkin reworked with pastel café-bar décor, three well kept real ales and Inch's farm cider, friendly staff, lunchtime food; games machine, big-screen TV; pavement picnic-sets, open all day *(Richard Lewis)*

OUTER LONDON
BARNET [TQ2195]
Gate at Arkley [Barnet Rd (A411, nr Hendon Wood Lane)]: Good friendly service, good value lunchtime baguettes and wide choice of other food, Adnams, Greene King Abbot and Wadworths 6X, reasonably priced wines, several comfortable areas with three blazing log fires, small no smoking conservatory; attractive sheltered garden *(Charles Harvey, BB, Ian Phillips)*
Green Dragon [St Albans Rd (A1081, nr M25)]: All-day bar food (from 8am) using fresh ingredients, restaurant lunch and suppertime, good wine choice, real ales; free internet and fax access *(anon)*

BECKENHAM [TQ3769]
Jolly Woodman [Chancery Lane]: Small traditional local with well kept Bass, Fullers London Pride, Harveys Best and Youngs Best, good value changing lunchtime food, new Yorkshireman landlord; seats out in cosy garden and tiny street *(Gwyn Berry)*

BIGGIN HILL [TQ4159]
☆ *Old Jail* [Jail Lane]: Neatly kept ancient building which was a mainstay for Battle of Britain RAF pilots, with lots of interesting RAF pictures and plates on walls, beams, some painted brickwork, oak floorboards, two large welcoming bar areas, one with a snug and vast inglenook fireplace, friendly efficient service, good sensibly priced quickly served blackboard food cooked by landlord, sandwiches too, well kept Adnams, Fullers London Pride, Greene King IPA and Harveys Best; picnic-sets in attractive shaded garden with good play area *(Ian Phillips, LM, GHC)*

CARSHALTON [TQ2864]
Fox & Hounds [High St]: Picturesque old timbered pub with upper part projecting on

pillars, bare boards and flagstones, well kept changing ales such as Adnams, Bass, Courage Directors, Greene King IPA and Old Speckled Hen, Hook Norton Haymaker, Shepherd Neame Spitfire and Warwickshire Castle, fair-priced usual food; bar billiards and games machines; picnic-sets on back gravel *(Ian Phillips)*

☆ *Greyhound* [High St]: Handsomely refurbished former coaching inn opp ponds in picturesque outer London 'village', several comfortable bars, wide choice of enjoyable food from interesting sandwiches and ciabattas up, well kept Youngs Bitter, Special and Waggle Dance, quick helpful service, easy parking; picnic-sets out by road, bedrooms *(Ian Phillips, Jenny and Brian Seller)*

CHISLEHURST [TQ4570]
Sydney Arms [Old Perry St]: Friendly atmosphere, pleasant quick service even when busy, good range of good value food even on Sun), well kept real ales, big conservatory; pleasant garden good for children, almost opp entrance to Scadbury Park, country walks *(B J Harding)*

CROYDON [TQ3267]
Lion [Pawsons Rd, off A212]: Quiet traditional pub with jovial landlord, Everards Tiger and Flowers IPA, inexpensive food from open kitchen; has its own organ *(anon)*

CUDHAM [TQ4459]
Blacksmiths Arms [Cudham Lane S]: Decent generous reasonably priced food from sandwiches and baguettes up, well kept Greene King IPA, good coffee, friendly helpful staff, cheerfully well worn in low-ceilinged pubby bar, blazing log fires, plenty of tables in no smoking eating area; piped music; big garden, pretty window boxes, good 7-mile circular walk from here *(Tina and David Woods-Taylor, J H Bell, GHC)*

DOWNE [TQ4361]
Queens Head [High St]: Quaint and civilised refurbished village pub, open all day and very comfortable, with Darwin text on walls of unpretentious bar rooms, plush dining room, log fires, good value food from sandwiches to enjoyable Sun roasts, well kept Adnams Bitter and Broadside, good smiling service; big-screen TV in public bar, well equipped children's room; picnic-sets on pavement, more in small back courtyard with aviary, handy for Darwin's Down House *(R T and J C Moggridge, LM)*

EASTCOTE [TQ1089]
Case is Altered [High Rd/Southill Lane, Pinner]: Attractive and authentically old and cottagey local in quiet setting, two homely bars, dark woods and bric-a-brac, well kept mainstream ales, wide choice of food; pleasant garden *(Tracey and Stephen Groves)*

ENFIELD [TQ3399]
King & Tinker [A10 from M25 junction 25, right at 1st lights, right at left-hand bend into

Whitewebbs Lane]: Busy and friendly country pub opp riding stables, not over-modernised, with authentic character and interesting old local photographs, enjoyable food inc big filled rolls and popular Sun lunch, well kept ales inc Greene King IPA, decent wines, quick efficient service; picnic-sets in small attractive garden with fenced play area *(LM)*
Pied Bull [Bullsmoor Lane (A1055); handy for M25 junction 25, by A10]: Red-tiled 17th-c pub with local prints on boarded walls, low beam-and-plank ceilings, lots of comfortable and friendly little rooms and extensions, turkey rugs on bare boards, well priced food, well kept Boddingtons, Flowers Original, Fullers London Pride and Marlow Rebellion Nifty Fifty; conservatory, pleasant garden *(Robert Lester, Ian Phillips)*

FARNBOROUGH [TQ4464]
Woodman [High St]: Welcoming and relaxed beamed pub with three knocked-through rooms, good value usual bar food (not Sun to Tues evening) from sandwiches and baguettes up, friendly staff, Shepherd Neame Bitter and Spitfire, good coffee and afternoon tea; no credit cards, Thurs quiz night, unobtrusive piped music, juke box; reasonable disabled access, well behaved children welcome, picnic-sets on neat back lawn, open all day Thurs-Sun *(Alan M Pring, GHC)*

HAMPTON COURT [TQ1668]
Kings Arms [Hampton Court Rd, by Lion Gate]: On the edge of Hampton Court grounds, with oak panels and beams, stripped-brick lounge with bric-a-brac and open fire one end, public bar the other, relaxed atmosphere, well kept if not cheap Badger beers, good choice of wines by the glass, attractively priced usual food from sandwiches up, pleasant efficient service; piped music; children and dogs welcome (dog biscuits on bar, several doggy regulars such as Ginger and Tilly), picnic-sets on hedged front terrace with camellias in tubs, open all day *(Susan and John Douglas, Colin McKerrow, LYM)*

HAREFIELD [TQ0590]
Coy Carp [Copperhill Lane]: Former Fisheries Inn well done out in olde-worlde Vintage Inn style, with one of their better renamings, their usual wide choice of well cooked food all day, attentive service, good range of wines, Bass beers; lovely spot by Grand Union Canal *(K Drane)*

HARLINGTON [TQ0878]
White Hart [High St S]: Large two-bar Fullers dining pub, good bustling atmosphere, alcoves with good solid furniture, decent food with more sophisticated evening choice, well kept London Pride and ESB; may be piped music *(Tom Evans)*

HEATHROW AIRPORT [TQ0774]
J J Moons [Terminal 4]: Wetherspoons pub, with a branch on the public side and another

in Departures; welcome refuge from this busy and most modern Heathrow terminal, with good range of real ales, decent wine by the glass, good value standard food, aircraft pictures; children welcome *(Sarah Davis, Rod Lambert, B and M Kendall)*

ISLEWORTH [TQ1675]
London Apprentice [Church St]: Large Thames-side pub furnished with character, tables on attractive waterside terrace, and picnic-sets on small riverside lawn; wide choice of bar food from good sandwiches up (light flashes on your table when it's ready to collect), well kept Adnams Broadside, Courage Best and Fullers London Pride, good coffee, log fire, friendly young Australian bar staff, upstairs river-view restaurant (open all Sun afternoon); may be low-key piped music; children welcome, open all day *(Susan and John Douglas, LYM, Ian Phillips, LM)*

KESTON [TQ4164]
Fox [Heathfield Rd]: Roomy and up-to-date open-plan pub with well kept Shepherd Neame, popular traditional food inc a good generous ham ploughman's, and welcoming obliging staff *(Robert Gomme)*

KINGSTON [TQ1869]
Gazebo [Riverside Walk/Kings Passage; alley off Thames St by Entertainer toy shop, or from Kingston Bridge]: Modern style and trendy food, with terrific river view upstairs; lots of tables out on balcony and terrace *(Val Stevenson, Rob Holmes)*

LONGFORD [TQ0576]
White Horse [Bath Rd, off A3044 (and A4)]: Brasses on low 16th-c black beams, fireplace between the two areas, comfortable seats, cosy atmosphere with pot plants in windows and rustic decorations such as antique rifles and equestrian bronzes, enjoyable lunchtime bar food, efficient friendly service, well kept John Smiths and Youngs Special; fruit machine, piped music; flower tubs and picnic-sets outside, one in a little barn, surprisingly villagey surroundings, open all day *(Susan and John Douglas)*

MALDEN RUSHETT [TQ1763]
☆ *Star* [A243 N of M25 junction 9]: Busy family dining pub right on Surrey border, brightened up under new ownership, popular for reliably good value food (same chef has stayed on) from baguettes and baked potatoes to a good range of hot dishes; several areas, good log fire, good friendly service and atmosphere; quiet piped music *(DWAJ)*

MITCHAM [TQ2868]
Ravensbury Arms [Croydon Rd, Mitcham Common]: Reworked as bright and spacious Ember Inn, Adnams Broadside and Fullers London Pride, mainstream food from baked potatoes up, good friendly staff, coal-effect fire in dining area; quiz nights Sun and Tues; picnic-sets on small lawn *(Ian Phillips)*

RICHMOND [TQ1772]
New Inn [Petersham Rd (A307, Ham Common)]: Attractive and comfortable Georgian pub in good spot on Ham Common, with comfortable banquettes and stools, brown décor, good home-made food from ciabattas and other snacks up, pleasant dining area, well kept Adnams, Courage Best and Directors, Charles Wells Bombardier and a guest beer, friendly service, big log fire one side, coal the other; picnic-sets out in front and on back terrace *(Sarah Davis, Rod Lambert, LM)*
Victoria [Hill Rise]: Small, cosy and chatty local, well kept beers inc Youngs; sports TV *(Martin Brunt)*
White Horse [Worple Way, off Sheen Rd]: Large and popular open-plan bare-boards Fullers pub with most tables reserved for eating (but leather settees at one end), imaginative modern food with mediterranean influences, good cheeseboard, friendly staff, well kept London Pride and ESB and good choice of wines from long aluminium bar; may be piped music; small terrace backing on to residential area and playground *(Marie Woods)*
Old Ship [King St]: Bustling Youngs pub close to centre and river, their beers kept well, welcoming service, food inc good Sun roast, three communicating bars with thriving atmosphere, fine panelling in refurbished upper floor; parking almost impossible; open all day *(Klaus and Elizabeth Leist, the Didler)*
Orange Tree [Kew Rd]: Big open-plan room with well kept Youngs from central bar, good food, prompt friendly service; piped music may obtrude, sports TV; open all day, lots of tables out in front, small back covered terrace *(LYM, Mayur Shah)*
Watermans Arms [Water Lane]: Nice friendly atmosphere and helpful licensees in small two-bar local with fresh flowers, Youngs beer, pub games; handy for Thames, nearby parking unlikely *(the Didler)*
White Swan [Old Palace Lane]: Welcoming dark-beamed open-plan plush bar, well kept real ales, good freshly cooked wholesome bar lunches, coal-effect gas fires, upstairs restaurant; children allowed in conservatory, pretty little paved garden below railway, barbecues *(Marie Woods, LYM)*

SUTTON [TQ2562]
Belmont [Brighton Rd, Belmont]: New management doing well in large fairly modern pub with comfortable bar, interesting décor, well kept Courage beers, good value carvery, efficient friendly staff; handy for Banstead Heath walks *(Jenny and Brian Seller)*

TWICKENHAM [TQ1673]
☆ *White Swan* [Riverside; [BR] Twickenham]: Unpretentious take-us-as-you-find-us 17th-c Thames-side house up steep anti-flood steps, little riverside lawn across quiet lane, traditional bare-boards, bar with big rustic tables and blazing fires, back room full of

rugby memorabilia, well kept pricy Courage Directors, Greene King IPA, Shepherd Neame Spitfire and Charles Wells Bombardier, good choice of wines by the glass, winter mulled wine, sandwiches and one or two blackboard hot dishes, summer wkdy lunchtime buffet; backgammon, cribbage, piped blues or jazz, winter Weds folk night; children welcome, open all day summer *(LYM, Ian Phillips)*

UXBRIDGE [TQ0584]
☆ *Load of Hay* [Villier St, off Cleveland Rd opp Brunel University]: Warm and friendly local, with rambling main area and smaller front bar, reliably good value freshly made generous

food, good long-serving landlady, well kept interesting changing beers, thoughtful choice of teas, impressive fireplace in no smoking back part used by diners, more public-bar atmosphere nearer serving bar, local paintings; dogs welcome, flower-filled back garden, pergola with mature vine *(Anthony Longden)*

WEST WICKHAM [TQ3865]
Swan [High St]: Comfortable armchairs and sofas in one bar, bar billiards in the other, smoking allowed in both, pleasant service, popular at lunchtime for food from baguettes and baked potatoes to blackboard specials; conservatory *(Alan M Pring)*

If a service charge is mentioned prominently on a menu or accommodation terms, you must pay it if service was satisfactory. If service is really bad you are legally entitled to refuse to pay some or all of the service charge as compensation for not getting the service you might reasonably have expected.

Scotland

In the last few years Scottish pubs and inns seem to many readers to have become much more visitor-friendly. We can vouch for the fact that it is now a lot easier than it used to be to find enjoyable food, interesting real ales, decent wines and smoke-free places to sit. Bedrooms have been generally upgraded, and there does seem to be more of a feeling of real welcome. Pubs and inns proving particularly popular these days include the pubby Boat at Aboyne (a nice all-rounder), the Applecross Inn (its seaview bedrooms earn it a Place to Stay Award this year, and its fresh seafood is a big draw), the Badachro Inn (a treat to find such good food in such an idyllic and remote spot – it gains a Food Award), the Guildford Arms in Edinburgh (eye-catching Victorian décor and great range of real ales), the very well run harbourside Steam Packet at Isle of Whithorn (a fine all-rounder, with its kitchen upgraded and food side expanded), the cheerful Four Marys opposite the Palace in Linlithgow (an interesting and exemplary town pub), Burts Hotel in Melrose (good inventive food, excellent service, and a nice lively lounge bar), the beautifully placed Plockton Hotel (good value, painstaking licensees, cheerful bustling atmosphere), the Tigh an Eilean Hotel by the sea at Shieldaig (both its civilised hotel side and its simpler bar side earn warm praise), and the Stein Inn on Skye (a particular favourite for its location, pubby bar and nice bedrooms). The Steam Packet at Isle of Whithorn, putting imagination and good fresh ingredients into its dishes of the day, is Scotland Dining Pub of the Year. To help pinpoint places near you, we have divided the Lucky Dip section at the end of the chapter into the counties used as postal addresses (putting Glasgow under Lanarkshire, and Edinburgh under Midlothian). This section has some 165 entries, nearly 90 of them new this year: we hope at least some of these will prove worthy of addition to the main entries, and are very keen to hear your views on which most deserve inspection. To encourage your reactions, we'd note those which currently seem to be showing most promise: the Stag at Falkland (Fife), Letterfinlay Lodge near Spean Bridge (Inverness-shire), Bon Accord and Horseshoe in Glasgow (Lanarkshire), Cawdor Tavern (Nairnshire), Old Inn at Gairloch (Ross-shire), and Cobbles in Kelso (Roxburghshire). We'd also mention the Gordon Arms at Mountbenger (Selkirkshire), a nice pub which loses its place among the main entries this year only because of a lack of reader reports, and the Seafood Restaurant & Bar in St Monance (Fife), which has now become too purely a restaurant for the main entries, but is well worth knowing for its good food. Many Scottish pubs and bars close at midnight, or even later at weekends; we have not mentioned this in the Lucky Dip entries. Drinks prices here tend to be rather higher than in England. The Moulin in Pitlochry and Fox & Hounds in Houston score a point for their customers by selling their own good beers at below-average prices (though our champion pub for low beer prices here was the Counting House in Glasgow, part of the Wetherspoons chain). The Houston beers are now quite widely available elsewhere, too. Other independent Scottish beer brands well worth looking out for, in rough order of how frequently beer-minded readers have been mentioning them to us recently, are Caledonian,

Orkney, Belhaven, Isle of Skye, Harviestoun, Broughton, Atlas, Inveralmond, Isle of Arran and Sulwath; and a south-of-the-border favourite up here is Timothy Taylors.

ABERDEEN NJ9305 Map 11
Prince of Wales ◗ £

St Nicholas Lane

Some say the counter in the middle cosy flagstoned area of this super city centre pub is the longest in Scotland – useful, as they keep a good range of around eight real ales: Caledonian 80/-, Theakstons Old Peculier, a beer named for the pub from Inveralmond and guests from brewers such as Isle of Skye and Orkney. Screened booths are furnished with pews and other wooden furniture, while a smarter main lounge has some panelling and a fruit machine. The cheery atmosphere makes this a popular retreat from the surrounding shopping centre, and at lunchtime a bustling mix of locals and visitors often makes for standing room only. Good value generously served lunchtime food includes sandwiches (from £1.30), filled baguettes or baked potatoes(£3.50), macaroni cheese (£4), steak pie or pork in cream and mustard sauce (£4.50), and breaded haddock or beef stroganoff (£4.80); friendly staff. Fiddlers provide traditional music on Sunday evenings. *(Recommended by Mark Walker, Nick Holding, Roger Huggins, Tom and Alex McLean, the Didler, David and Betty Gittins)*

Free house ~ Licensee Kenny Gordon ~ Real ale ~ Bar food (11.30(12 Sun)-2.30 (4 Sat/Sun)) ~ (01224) 640597 ~ Children in eating area of bar ~ Folk music Sun evening ~ Open 10-12

ABOYNE NO5298 Map 11
Boat ◗

Charlestown Road (B968, just off A93)

The first thing you're likely to notice at this convivial country inn is the model train, often chugging around just below the ceiling, making appropriate noises. Apart from the train, there are scottish pictures and brasses in the two areas downstairs, with well kept Bass and a couple of changing real ales from brewers such as Aviemore and Inveralmond from the bar counter that runs down the narrower linking section, and games along in the public-bar end. The atmosphere is relaxed and pubby, with an openable woodburning stove, and spiral stairs take you up to a roomy additional dining area, which is no smoking. Good fresh food, with more attention to vegetarian cooking than is usual up here, includes soup (£2.25), lunchtime sandwiches (from £3.95), mince and tatties (£6.50), beef steak pie (£7.95), fusilli pasta with tomato, basil and pesto sauce (£7.25) and fresh haddock or stuffed peppers (£7.95); in the evening you can also choose from more elaborate dishes such as duck liver pâté (£4.75), seafood platter (£4.95), chicken supreme stuffed with haggis with whisky and mustard sauce (£8.50) and beef medallions (£9.25), with specials such as mussels or delicious stovies (£4.50), rock turbot (£7.95) and venison (£8.50); puddings could include popular sticky toffee pudding (£3.75) and chocolate and mint cheesecake (£4.25). They use plenty of fresh local produce, and are happy to accommodate special requests; good friendly service. There are tables outside, and they have a self-catering flat. The pub, by the River Dee, used to serve the ferry that it's named for – the original bridge that made the boat redundant, back in the 1820s, was washed away by a flood the following year, but the boat had only the briefest reprieve as the wrecked bridge was quickly replaced by one of the earliest flood-proof suspension bridges. *(Recommended by Sue and Andy Waters, Mick Finn)*

Free house ~ Licensee Wilson Forbes ~ Real ale ~ Bar food (12-2(2.30 Sat/Sun), 5.30-9(9.30 Fri/Sat)) ~ Restaurant ~ (01339) 886137 ~ Children welcome ~ Dogs allowed in bar ~ Open 11-2.30, 5-11; 11-12(11 Sun) Sat; closed 25 Dec, 26 Dec evening, 1-3 Jan

APPLECROSS NG7144 Map 11
Applecross Inn 🍴 🛏

Off A896 S of Shieldaig

This remote but cheerful pub has a splendid waterside setting, looking across to Skye's Cuillin Hills. The drive to the inn over the pass of the cattle (Beallach na Ba), is one of the highest in Britain, and a truly exhilarating experience. The alternative route, along the single-track lane winding round the coast from just south of Shieldaig, has equally glorious sea loch and then sea views nearly all the way. Fresh seafood is a real draw here, and according to the time of year ranges from starters such as haddock and mussel chowder (£2.95), crab bisque (£3.25) or hot-smoked salmon (£5.95) to main course favourites such as curry (£6.95), aubergine and mozzarella bake or crab salad (£7.95), venison casserole or fried monkfish with stir-fried vegetables and noodles (£9.95), halibut fillet with lemon and herbs (£10.95), and puddings such as gooseberry and crème fraîche tart or chocolate bread and butter pudding (£3.25); a good choice of around 50 malt whiskies, and efficient pleasant service. Friendly locals mingle with visitors in the no-nonsense bar with its woodburning stove, exposed stone walls, upholstered pine furnishings on the stone floor, and well kept Isle of Skye Red Cuillin; there's also a no smoking dining area, with lavatories for the disabled and with baby changing facilities. You must book for the small no smoking restaurant. Pool (winter only), TV, dominoes, and juke box (musicians may take over instead). A nice shoreside garden has tables, and expect a great breakfast if you stay. *(Recommended by Brian and Anita Randall, Bruce Jamieson, R E and E C M Pick, Neil Rose, Sarah and Peter Gooderham, Lesley Bass, Anthony Longden, Charles Gysin)*

Free house ~ Licensee Judith Fish ~ Real ale ~ Bar food (12-9; not 25 Dec-1 Jan) ~ Restaurant ~ (01520) 744262 ~ Children welcome until 8.30pm ~ Dogs welcome ~ Open 11-11.30; 12.30-11 Sun; closed 25 Dec, 1 Jan ~ Bedrooms: £25/£50(£60B)

ARDFERN NM8004 Map 11
Galley of Lorne 🛏

B8002; village and inn signposted off A816 Lochgilphead—Oban

Seats out on the sheltered terrace at this welcoming pub have peaceful views of the sea, Loch Craignish and yacht anchorage. The cosy but cheery bar has a warming log fire, big navigation lamps by the counter, an unfussy assortment of furniture, including little winged settles and upholstered window seats on its lino tiles, a decent mix of customers, Caledonian Deuchars IPA and a guest from a local brewery on handpump, and about 50 malt whiskies; darts, dominoes, board games, also fruit machine, TV and piped music. Good interesting home-made bar food includes soup or sandwiches (from £2.75), smoked salmon with cucumber and mint yoghurt (£5.50), creamy vegetable pie, pasta in sun-dried tomato, herb and garlic sauce or fish and chips (£6.50), steak sandwich (£7.75), local lamb shoulder (£7.95), and puddings such as sticky ginger pudding (£3.50). The spacious restaurant, an area of the bar and the bedrooms are no smoking; they do good breakfasts. *(Recommended by Richard Gibbs, Callum and Letitia Smith-Burnett)*

Free house ~ Licensee John Dobbie ~ Real ale ~ Bar food (12-2.30, 6-8.30) ~ Restaurant ~ (01852) 500284 ~ Children welcome except in bar ~ Dogs allowed in bar and bedrooms ~ Open 12-12(1 Fri/Sat); closed 3-5 weekdays winter ~ Bedrooms: £45B/£70B

BADACHRO NG7773 Map 11
Badachro Inn 🍴

2½ miles S of Gairloch village turn off A832 on to B8056, then after another 3¼ miles turn right in Badachro to the quay and inn

It's quite a treat to find such good bar food in this delightfully remote location. This is a tiny village, and the quiet road comes to a dead end a few miles further on at the lovely Redpoint beach. The pub has two moorings (free for visitors), and showers are available at a small charge. The bay is very sheltered, virtually landlocked by Eilean Horrisdale just opposite. A terrace outside, with sturdy tables, virtually overhangs the water, and there are more seats on the attractively planted lochside lawn. With fresh fish featuring quite prominently, daily specials might include half a dozen loch fyne oysters (£6.75), poached halibut fillet with prawn mousse and white wine sauce (£9.50), marinated monkfish with oyster and white wine sauce or venison chops with sweet potato herb mash and wild garlic jus (£13.50), and seafood platter (£12.95), while the regular menu includes soup (£2.35), sandwiches (from £3.40), smoked fish risotto with tomato and basil coulis (£3.95), marinated loch fyne herring fillets or local and locally smoked venison (£4.95), haggis, neeps and tatties (£7.95), roast beef (£8.50), local prawns (£9.95), puddings such as sticky toffee pudding or fried fresh pineapple in pink peppercorn and caramel sauce (£3.10), and highland cheeses (£5.10). A dining conservatory overlooking the bay lets you make the most of this convivial inn's delightful waterside setting, and the charming local atmosphere in the bar is equally rewarding. Gentle eavesdropping within the black and white painted cottagey building suggests that some of the yachtsmen have been calling in here annually for decades, and the talk is still very much of fishing and boats. There are some interesting photographs and collages on the walls, and they put out the Sunday newspapers. The quieter dining area on the left has big tables by a huge log fire, and the conservatory has its own open fire. A couple of changing ales are well kept on handpump, and come from brewers such as Black Isle and Isle of Skye; also around 50 malt whiskies, and a changing wine list; piped music, shove-ha'penny and dominoes. Casper the pub spaniel is friendly. *(Recommended by Bruce Jamieson, Neil Rose, Peter F Marshall, Paul and Ursula Randall)*

Free house ~ Licensee Martyn Pearson ~ Real ale ~ Bar food (12-3, 6-9) ~ Restaurant ~ (01445) 741255 ~ Children welcome till 8pm ~ Dogs allowed in bar ~ Open 12-12(11.30 Sat); 12.30-11.30 Sun

BROUGHTY FERRY NO4630 Map 11

Fishermans Tavern ♀ 🍺 🛏

Fort Street; turning off shore road

This cheery town pub is just yards from the seafront, where there are good views of the two long, low Tay bridges. Changing daily, half a dozen real ales typically include Belhaven St Andrews, Caledonian Deuchars IPA, Timothy Taylors Landlord and guests from brewers such as Fullers, Inveralmond and Orkney, on handpump or tall fount air pressure. They also have a good range of malt whiskies, a dozen wines by the glass, some local country wines, and a draught wheat beer; the choice of wines changes regularly. Most attractive from the outside, the pub has extended into the adjacent cottages. A little brown carpeted snug on the right has nautical tables, light pink soft fabric seating, basket-weave wall panels and beige lamps, and is the more lively bar; on the left is a secluded lounge area with an open coal fire. The carpeted back bar (popular with diners) has a Victorian fireplace; dominoes, TV and fruit machine, and a coal fire. Good value lunchtime bar food includes kedgeree (£4.95), salmon in cream dill sauce or haddock mornay (£6.25) and sole stuffed with prawns (£6.75). Disabled lavatories, and baby changing facilities. The family and breakfast rooms are no smoking. The landlord also runs the well preserved Speedwell Bar in Dundee. On summer evenings, you can sit at tables on the front pavement, and they might have barbecues in the secluded walled garden, where they hold an annual beer festival on the last weekend in May. *(Recommended by David and Heather Stephenson)*

Free house ~ Licensee Jonathan Stewart ~ Real ale ~ Bar food (12-2.30, 7-9) ~ Restaurant ~ (01382) 775941 ~ Children in eating area of bar ~ Dogs allowed in bar ~ Celtic music Thurs night ~ Open 11-12 (1am Thurs-Sat); 12.30-12 Sun ~ Bedrooms: £39B/£62B

It's against the law for bar staff to smoke while handling food or drink.

CRINAN NR7894 Map 11

Crinan Hotel 🍴 🛏

A816 NE from Lochgilphead, then left on to B841, which terminates at the village

This elegant hotel is ideally positioned for taking in the cheering bustle of the Crinan Canal's entrance basin, and picture windows make the most of the marvellous views of fishing boats and yachts wandering out towards the Hebrides. Inside, the cocktail bar has a nautical theme with wooden floors, oak and walnut panelling, antique tables and chairs, and sailing pictures and classic yachts framed in walnut on a wallpaper background of rust and green paisley, matching the tartan upholstery, while the simpler wooden-floored public bar (opening on to a side terrace) has a cosy stove and kilims on the seats. The Gallery bar is done in pale terracotta and creams and has a central bar with stools, Lloyd Loom tables and chairs, and lots of plants. Bar food is sophisticated if not cheap, and includes home-made soup with freshly baked bread (£3.95), blue cheese, broad bean and pea risotto or pork and leek sausages with mustard mash (£8.95), loch crinan stew or organic pork chop (£11.95), and pudding of the day (£3.50). You can get sandwiches and so forth from their coffee shop. There's a good wine list, around 30 malt whiskies, and freshly squeezed orange juice. Breakfasts can be outstanding. Many of the paintings are by the landlord's wife, artist Frances Macdonald. *(Recommended by Nick Holding, Callum and Letitia Smith-Burnett; also in the* Good Hotel Guide*)*

Free house ~ Licensee Nicolas Ryan ~ Bar food (12-2.30, 6.30-8.30) ~ Restaurant ~ (01546) 830261 ~ Children welcome ~ Dogs welcome ~ Open 11(12 Sat)-11; closed 25 Dec, 1 Jan ~ Bedrooms: £95B/£190B

EAST LINTON NT5977 Map 11

Drovers 🍴 🍺

Bridge Street (B1407), just off A1 Haddington—Dunbar

As you enter from the pretty village street, the main bar at this welcoming old inn feels a bit like a cosy living room, with wooden flooring, a basket of logs in front of the woodburning stove, and comfortable armchairs. There's a goat's head on a pillar in the middle of the room, fresh flowers and newspapers, and a mix of prints and pictures on the half panelled, half red-painted walls. A similar room leads off, and a door opens out on to a walled lawn with tables and perhaps summer barbecues. Alongside well kept Adnams Broadside and Caledonian Deuchars IPA on handpump, weekly changing guest beers might include Fullers London Pride, Greene King Old Speckled Hen and Orkney Red MacGregor. Under the new licensees, good helpings of bar food include soup (£2.95), haggis in creamy peppercorn sauce (£4), mussel, onion, dill and lemon stew (£4.25), filled baked potatoes (from £5.25), toasted ciabattas (from £6.25), suckling pig or steak (from £15), and puddings such as sticky toffee pudding or apple pie (£4). Part of the upstairs restaurant is no smoking. *(Recommended by Robert and Susan Whitehead, Jim Bush, R M Corlett)*

Free house ~ Licensees John and Alison Burns ~ Real ale ~ Bar food (all day Sat/Sun) ~ Restaurant ~ (01620) 860298 ~ Children welcome ~ Bands first and third Thurs evening ~ Open 11.30-3, 5-11; 11.30-1 Thurs-Sat; 12.30-12 Sun

EDINBURGH NT2574 Map 11

Abbotsford 🍺

Rose Street; E end, beside South St David Street

Originally built for Jenners department store, this lively single-bar pub is notably friendly, with a pleasingly old-fashioned atmosphere. The refreshingly uncluttered interior is traditional with dark wooden half-panelled walls, a highly polished Victorian island bar counter, long wooden tables and leatherette benches, and a welcoming log-effect gas fire; there are prints on the walls, and a rather handsome plaster-moulded high ceiling. Well kept Caledonian Deuchars IPA and 80/- and interesting guest beers from brewers such as Atlas, Broughton and Crouch Vale are served in the true Scottish fashion from a set of air pressure tall founts. Good reasonably priced lunchtime bar food includes sandwiches (from £1.75), all-day breakfast or steak and kidney pie (£5.95), haggis, neeps and tatties (£6.50), roast of the day or chicken stuffed with haggis (£6.75), and puddings such as coconut-battered ice cream with butterscotch sauce (£3.75). Over 60 malt whiskies, efficient service from dark-uniformed or white-shirted staff; fruit machine, piped music and TV. *(Recommended by C J Fletcher, Joel Dobris, the Didler, Janet and Peter Race, Joe Green, Ian and Nita Cooper)*

Free house ~ Licensee Colin Grant ~ Real ale ~ Bar food (12-3, 5.30-10) ~ Restaurant (12-2.15, 5.30-10) ~ (0131) 225 5276 ~ Children welcome ~ Open 11-11; closed 25 Dec, 1 Jan

Bow Bar ★ ◀

West Bow

Handily tucked away just below the castle, this traditional pub draws visitors from much further away than just the city for its formidable range of drinks and cheery environment. Eight real ales, kept in first-class order by the landlady, are served from impressive antique tall founts made by Aitkens, Mackie & Carnegie, and typically include Belhaven 80/-, Caledonian Deuchars IPA, Timothy Taylors Landlord, and various changing guests from brewers such as Harviestoun, Mordue and Orkney. The grand carved mahogany gantry has quite an array of malts (over 140) including cask strength whiskies, as well as a good collection of rums and gins. Simple, but neat, busy and friendly, the rectangular bar has a fine collection of appropriate enamel advertising signs and handsome antique trade mirrors, sturdy leatherette wall seats and heavy narrow tables on its wooden floor, and café-style bar seats. The only food they serve is filled rolls (from £1) and toasties (from £1.40). *(Recommended by Joe Green, Patrick Hancock, Mark Walker, the Didler, Ruth and Paul Lawrence, Joel Dobris)*

Free house ~ Licensee Helen McLoughlin ~ Real ale ~ Bar food (12-3) ~ No credit cards ~ (0131) 226 7667 ~ Dogs allowed in bar ~ Open 12-11.30; 12.30-11 Sun

Café Royal £

West Register Street

This gem of a city pub is well worth a visit for its superbly ornate Victorian interior. Built in the 19th c as a flagship for the latest in gas and plumbing fittings, the high-ceilinged café rooms have a series of highly detailed Doulton tilework portraits of historical innovators Watt, Faraday, Stephenson, Caxton, Benjamin Franklin and Robert Peel (forget police – his importance here is as the introducer of calico printing). The floor and stairway are laid with marble, chandeliers hang from the fine ceilings, and the big island bar is graced by a new gantry that carefully re-creates the original. Four well kept ales include Caledonian Deuchars IPA, Courage Directors, McEwans 80/-, and a guest such as Orkney Dark Island on handpump, with about 20 malt whiskies, and a decent choice of wines. Served by fast efficient staff, bar food includes sandwiches (from £3.25), soup (£2.95), dips and bread (£3.25), sausage and mash (£4.75), crab and coriander cakes (£5.50), steak and mushroom pie (£6.25), half a dozen oysters (£6.95), braised lamb shank (£7.25), and puddings such as lemon tart and chocolate fudge cake (£2.95); TV, fruit machine and piped music. There are some fine optional fittings in the newly refurbished downstairs gents', and the stained-glass well in the seafood and game restaurant is well worth a look. It can get very busy, and the admirable décor is perhaps best appreciated on quiet afternoons. *(Recommended by C J Fletcher, the Didler, Joe Green, Joel Dobris, Janet and Peter Race, Alistair Forsyth, Doug Christian, Ian and Nita Cooper)*

Scottish Courage ~ Manager Dave Allan ~ Real ale ~ Bar food (11(12.30 Sun)-10) ~ Restaurant ~ (0131) 556 1884 ~ Children in restaurant ~ Open 11(12.30 Sun)-11 (12 Thurs, 1 Fri-Sat); closed 25 Dec

Guildford Arms ⬗

West Register Street

The recently refreshed magnificent décor at this Victorian pub is well worth a look. The main bar has lots of mahogany, glorious colourfully painted plasterwork and ceilings, big original advertising mirrors, and heavy swagged velvet curtains at the arched windows. The snug little upstairs gallery restaurant gives a dress-circle view of the main bar (notice the lovely old mirror decorated with two tigers on the way up), and under this gallery a little cavern of arched alcoves leads off the bar; TV, fruit machine, lunchtime piped jazz or classical music. Up to a dozen beers include well kept Belhaven 80/-, Caledonian Deuchars IPA and 80/-, Fullers London Pride, Harviestoun Bitter & Twisted, Orkney Dark Island, Timothy Taylors Landlord and three guest beers that might be from brewers such as Hop Back, Mordue and Orkney; there's also a good choice of malt whiskies, and 14 wines by the glass. Daytime bar food includes a tasty soup such as chicken and peanut (£2.95), greek salad (£4.95), chicken wrap (£5.75), fried haddock (£6.45), steak casserole (£6.95), and puddings such as crème brûlée and jaffa sponge (£2.50). They serve food in only the Gallery restaurant in the evening. When it's busiest, younger staff occasionally struggle to cope with the crowds. *(Recommended by the Didler, Richard Lewis, Simon and Amanda Southwell, Joel Dobris, Joe Green, C J Fletcher, Mark Walker)*

Free house ~ Licensee Scott Wilkinson ~ Real ale ~ Bar food (12-5.30) ~ Restaurant ~ (0131) 556 4312 ~ Dogs welcome ~ Open 11(12.30 Sun, 12 Fri and Sat)-11; closed 25 Dec

Kays Bar ⬗ £

Jamaica Street W; off India Street

In days past, this busy little backstreet pub was owned by John Kay, a whisky and wine merchant; wine barrels were hoisted up to the first floor and dispensed through pipes attached to nipples which can still be seen above the light rose. Today, a cheerful landlord presides over an interesting range of eight very well kept real ales on handpump, including Belhaven 80/-, McEwans 80/-, Theakstons Best and five guests from brewers such as Isle of Arran, Orkney and Timothy Taylors. The choice of whiskies equally impresses, with around 70 malts between eight and 40 years old, and 10 blended whiskies. Bigger than you might think from the outside, the cosy interior is decked out with various casks and vats, old wine and spirits merchant notices, gas-type lamps, well worn red plush wall banquettes and stools around cast-iron tables, and red pillars supporting a red ceiling. A quiet panelled back room leads off, with a narrow plank-panelled pitched ceiling and a collection of books ranging from dictionaries to ancient steam-train books for boys; lovely warming coal fire in winter. Good, straightforward lunchtime bar food includes soup (£1.25), highly recommended haggis and neeps or mince and tatties, steak pie and filled baked potatoes (£3.25), and lasagne, beefburger and chips and chicken balti (£3.70). Staff are friendly and obliging; TV, dominoes and cribbage. *(Recommended by Percy and Cathy Paine, the Didler, W A Evershed)*

Free house ~ Licensee David Mackenzie ~ Real ale ~ Bar food (12-2.30 (not on rugby international days)) ~ (0131) 225 1858 ~ Children in back room till 6 ~ Dogs welcome ~ Open 11-12(1 Fri, Sat); 12.30-11 Sun

Starbank ♀ ⬗ £

Laverockbank Road, off Starbank Road, just off A901 Granton—Leith

Marvellous views over the Firth of Forth from the long light and airy bare-boarded bar are one good reason to visit this stylish but cheerfully relaxed pub; they also keep a remarkable range of drinks, and the tasty food is very well priced. Around eight well kept real ales from all over Britain include Belhaven 80/- and Sandy Hunters, Caledonian Deuchars IPA, Timothy Taylors Landlord and guest beers from brewers such as Atlas, Badger, Charles Wells and Houston. There's a good choice of wines too (all 23 are served by the glass), and as many malt whiskies. Cheerful friendly staff serve soup (£1.50), herring rollmop salad (£2.50), a daily vegetarian dish (£4.50), ploughman's (£5), seafood salad (£5.50), haddock mornay or chicken supreme with cranberry sauce (£6), poached salmon with lemon butter or minute steak with pepper sauce (£6.50) and puddings (£2.50); conservatory restaurant and sheltered back terrace. There is parking in the adjacent hilly street. *(Recommended by Ken Richards, Peter Burton, Ian and Nita Cooper)*

Free house ~ Licensee Valerie West ~ Real ale ~ Bar food (12-2.30, 6-9; 12(12.30 Sun)-9 weekends) ~ Restaurant ~ (0131) 552 4141 ~ Children welcome ~ Dogs allowed in bar ~ Open 11-11(12 Thurs-Sat); 12.30-11 Sun

ELIE NO4900 Map 11
Ship

The Toft, off A917 (High Street) towards harbour

Readers enjoy the superb setting, friendly welcome and great atmosphere at this harbourside pub. Tables on a terrace enjoy the same shorefront views across Elie's broad sands and along the bay as the upstairs restaurant, both providing ample opportunity to keep an eye on the sports teams based at the pub – in winter you might see the rugby team beefing up on the sand, while on a Sunday in summer you could find yourself supporting their cricket team. The unspoilt, villagey beamed bar has a buoyant nautical feel, with friendly locals and staff, warming winter coal fires, and partly panelled walls studded with old prints and maps; there's a simple carpeted back room. Enjoyable bar food includes soup (£2), lunchtime BLT (£3.25), haggis, neeps and tatties (£3.95), moules (£5), haddock and chips (£7.25), ginger and puy lentils (£7.95), thai green chicken curry (£9), steak and Guinness pie (£8), seafood pie (£8.95), grilled bass (£10), pork fillet with peppercorns (£10.50), and puddings such as chocolate and hazelnut meringues or lemon sorbet (£4). They do a good Sunday lunch, occasional barbecues, and serve food in the garden in summer. Well kept Caledonian Deuchars IPA, several wines by the glass, and half a dozen malt whiskies; cribbage, dominoes, and shut the box. The fairly simple bedrooms are in a neighbouring guesthouse, and an unmanned tourist booth in the garden has leaflets on the local area. *(Recommended by Michael and Marion Buchanan, Kay Wheat, David and Heather Stephenson)*

Free house ~ Licensees Richard and Jill Philip ~ Real ale ~ Bar food ~ Restaurant ~ (01333) 330246 ~ Children in eating area of bar and restaurant ~ Dogs allowed in bar ~ Open 11-12(1 Fri, Sat); 12.30-12 Sun; closed 25 Dec ~ Bedrooms: £30B/£50B

GIFFORD NT5368 Map 11
Tweeddale Arms 🛏

S of Haddington; High Street (B6355)

Probably the oldest building in this appealing Borders village, this comfortable and friendly white-painted hotel looks across a peaceful green to the 300-year-old avenue of lime trees leading to the former home of the Marquesses of Tweeddale. An appealing blend of enjoyable food, cheerfully efficient service and comfortable surroundings keeps the modernised lounge bar busy with customers – new licensees are planning quite a few changes to the décor during the forthcoming year, so we'd be interested to hear what readers think. Bar food now includes soup (£2.50), filled baguettes (£2.75), haggis with whisky sauce or fried brie with redcurrant jelly (£4.25), smoked salmon with prawn marie rose (£4.75), fried haddock (£7.25), cream, leek and mushroom vol au vent (£8), roast of the day (£8.25), smoked haddock with home-cured ham and cheese sauce (£8.65), and puddings from a display cabinet (£3.25). They are planning to serve high teas, too. Well kept Greene King Abbot and Old Speckled Hen and Orkney Dark Island, and quite a few malt whiskies, including the local Glenkinchie. If you're staying (improvements to the bedrooms are lined up too), the tranquil hotel lounge is especially comfortable, with antique tables and paintings, chinoiserie chairs and chintzy easy chairs, an oriental rug on one wall, a splendid corner sofa and magazines on a table; fruit machine,

TV and piped music. *(Recommended by Peter Burton, Howard Bateman, Richard J Holloway)*

Free house ~ Licensees George, Colin, Yvonne and Linda Jarrin ~ Real ale ~ Bar food (12-2, 6-9) ~ Restaurant ~ (01620) 810240 ~ Children away from public bar ~ Dogs allowed in bar ~ Open 11-12(11 Sun) ~ Bedrooms: £49B/£65B

GLASGOW NS5965 Map 11
Auctioneers £

North Court, St Vincent Place

Lively, with a cheery crowd and very audible piped music, the main high-ceilinged flagstoned room at this former auction house has snug little areas around the edges, made out of the original valuation booths. Plenty of eye-catching antiques are dotted about as if they were for sale, with lot numbers clearly displayed. You'd probably be most tempted to bid for the goods in the smarter red-painted side room, which rather than the old lamps, radios, furnishings and golf clubs elsewhere has framed paintings, statues, and even an old rocking horse, as well as comfortable leather sofas, unusual lamp fittings, a big fireplace, and an elegant old dresser with incongruous china figures. Caledonian Deuchars IPA, Orkney Dark Island and perhaps a guest beer such as Timothy Taylors Landlord on handpump, and over two dozen malt whiskies; friendly helpful service; fruit machines, video game, juke box and TV. In the evening a giant sports screen can tend to dominate in the bar, which has lots of old sporting photos, programmes and shirts along one of the panelled walls. Served most of the day, bar food includes soup (£2.75), soup and sandwich (£4.95), haggis, neeps and tatties (£5.25), ploughman's, leek and gruyère parcel or sausage and mash (£5.50), and mixed grill (£9.95). The Counting House (another impressive conversion) is just around the corner. *(Recommended by David and Nina Pugsley, Nick Holding, Christine and Neil Townend)*

Mitchells & Butlers ~ Manager Michael Rogerson ~ Real ale ~ Bar food (12-8.45; 12.30-6.45 Sun) ~ Restaurant ~ (0141) 229 5851 ~ Children welcome 12-5 ~ Open 12(11 Sat)-12; 12.30-11.30 Sun

Babbity Bowster 🍴 🍷 £

Blackfriars Street

Welcoming and cheery, this lively and stylish 18th-c town house has something of the feel of a continental café-bar. A big ceramic of a kilted dancer and piper in the bar illustrates the mildly cheeky 18th-c Lowland wedding pipe tune (Bab at the Bowster) from which the pub takes its name – they'll be delighted to explain further (the landlord is notably enthusiastic, and his friendly staff follow suit). The simply decorated light interior has fine tall windows, well lit photographs and big pen-and-wash drawings of Glasgow, its people and musicians, dark grey stools and wall seats around dark grey tables on the stripped wooden boards, and a peat fire. The bar opens on to a terrace with tables under cocktail parasols, trellised vines and shrubs, and adjacent boules; they may have barbecues out here in summer. Popular well presented bar food includes several hearty home-made soups in two sizes (from £2.50), croques monsieur (from £4.95), haggis, neeps and tatties (£4.95; they also do a vegetarian version), stovies (£5.35), cauliflower and mung bean moussaka (£6.50) and cumberland sausage (£6.95); there are more elaborate meals in the airy upstairs restaurant. Well kept Caledonian Deuchars IPA on air pressure tall fount, a remarkably sound collection of wines, malt whiskies, farm cider, and good tea and coffee. *(Recommended by Nick Holding, Richard Lewis, Callum and Letitia Smith-Burnett, Brian and Anna Marsden, David and Nina Pugsley, Joe Green, Mark and Ruth Brock)*

Free house ~ Licensee Fraser Laurie ~ Real ale ~ Bar food (12-11) ~ Restaurant ~ (0141) 552 5055 ~ Children in restaurant ~ Dogs allowed in bar ~ Open 11(12.30 Sun)-12 ~ Bedrooms: £40S/£60S

Counting House ● £

St Vincent Place/George Square

Converted by Wetherspoons, this busy pub in the heart of Glasgow was once a premier branch of the Royal Bank of Scotland. Typically of Wetherspoons' pubs the building itself is quite a statement, and the low prices set a level that other pubs have to compete with. The astonishingly roomy and imposing interior rises into a lofty, richly decorated coffered ceiling which culminates in a great central dome, with well lit nubile caryatids doing a fine supporting job in the corners. There's the sort of decorative glasswork that nowadays seems more appropriate to a landmark pub than to a bank, as well as wall-safes, plenty of prints and local history, and big windows overlooking George Square. Away from the recently revamped bar, several areas (some no smoking) have solidly comfortable seating, while a series of smaller rooms – once the managers' offices – lead around the perimeter of the building. Some of these are surprisingly cosy, one is like a well stocked library, and a few are themed with pictures and prints of historical characters such as Walter Scott or Mary, Queen of Scots. The central island servery has up to six well kept ales on handpump, regulars being Caledonian 80/- and Deuchars IPA, Courage Directors and Theakstons Best, with a couple of guest beers such as Harviestoun Ptarmigan and Orkney Dark Island, a good choice of bottled beers and malt whiskies, and 12 wines by the glass. The usual Wetherspoons menu is served all day and includes soup (£2.25), sandwiches (from £3.05), wraps (from £3.55), nachos (from £4.25), fish and chips (£4.55), ricotta and grilled vegetable cannelloni (£5.55), chicken balti (£5.75), lamb shank (£6.99) and puddings (from £2.09). Friendly service; fruit machine. *(Recommended by Hugh A MacLean, Simon and Amanda Southwell, David and Nina Pugsley, Richard Lewis)*

Wetherspoons ~ Manager Stuart Coxshall ~ Real ale ~ Bar food (opening-10) ~ (0141) 225 0160 ~ Children in family room till 5 (3 Fri/Sat) ~ Open 7.30(10 Sat, 12.30 Sun)-12

GLENELG NG8119 Map 11
Glenelg Inn ⑪ ⇌

Unmarked road from Shiel Bridge (A87) towards Skye

Getting to this hotel is quite an adventure, with the single-track road climbing dramatically past heather-blanketed slopes and mountains with spectacular views to the lochs below. It's run by an enthusiastic landlord supported by friendly staff, and is the kind of welcoming place where – especially if you've taken full advantage of their good collection of malt and cask strength whiskies – you might find yourself joining in the Saturday night ceilidh with a crowd of locals (the piped music is usually Scottish). Feeling a bit like a mountain cabin (and still decidedly pubby given the smartness of the rest of the place), the unpretentious green-carpeted bar gives an overwhelming impression of dark wood, with lots of logs dotted about, a big fireplace, and only a very few tables and well worn cushioned wall benches – when necessary crates and fish boxes may be pressed into service as extra seating. Black and white photographs line the walls at the far end around the pool table, and there are various jokey articles and local information elsewhere; fruit machine. The very short lunch menu might include a soup such as spiced butternut, sweet potato and coconut soup (£3), home-made hummous and oatcakes (£5), filled ciabatta or granary roll (£5), battered haddock or roast chicken stuffed with garlic mushrooms (£10), with evening dishes such as tuna and salmon fishcakes or vegetable tempura with satay sauce (£8). They also do an outstanding four-course evening meal in the no smoking dining room (£29). Glenelg is the closest place on the mainland to Skye (there's a little car ferry across in summer), and on a sunny day tables in the beautifully kept garden have lovely views across the water (shared by some of the bedrooms). The staff can organise local activities, and there are plenty of enjoyable walks nearby. *(Recommended by Walter and Susan Rinaldi-Butcher, Maurice and Gill McMahon, ML, Lesley Bass, Di and Mike Gillam; also in the* Good Hotel Guide*)*

Free house ~ Licensee Christopher Main ~ Bar food (12.30-2, 6-9; not Sun evening; not winter lunchtimes) ~ Restaurant ~ (01599) 522273 ~ Children welcome ~ Dogs allowed in bar ~ Ceilidh Sat evening ~ Open 12-2.30, 5-11(12.30 Sat); 12-2.30 Sun; cl Sun in winter ~ Bedrooms: £60B/£120B

HOUSTON NS4166 Map 11
Fox & Hounds 🍺

South Street at junction with Main Street (B789, off B790 at Langbank signpost E of Bridge of Weir)

The award-winning Houston beers brewed at this cheery village pub are growing in popularity throughout the region. The four regulars – Barochan, Killellan, Peters Well and Texas – are well kept alongside a couple of seasonal brews. They also keep half a dozen wines by the glass, and around 100 malt whiskies. The clean plush hunting-theme lounge has comfortable seats by a fire and polished brass and copper; piped music; the lively downstairs bar has a TV, pool and fruit machines, and is popular with a younger crowd. Bar food includes soup (£2.50), grilled scallops with sweet chilli sauce (£4.95), steamed mussels with garlic and cream sauce (£4.95), steak and ale casserole (£6.95), apple, celery and mushroom stroganoff with calvados (£7.95), battered fresh scampi or lamb shank (£8.95), salmon fillet with balsamic syrup (£9.95), grilled sirloin (£11.50), and puddings such as warm clootie dumplings and custard (£2.95); friendly staff. The upstairs restaurant has a more elaborate menu; no smoking areas in lounge and restaurant. They host an annual summer beer festival (phone for details). *(Recommended by Graham and Lynn Mason)*

Own brew ~ Licensee Jonathan Wengel ~ Real ale ~ Bar food (12-2.30, 5.30-10; 12-10 weekends) ~ Restaurant ~ (01505) 612448 ~ Children welcome till 8 ~ Dogs allowed in bar ~ Open 11-12(1am Fri, Sat); 12.30-12 Sun

INNERLEITHEN NT3336 Map 9
Traquair Arms 🛏

B709, just off A72 Peebles—Galashiels; follow signs for Traquair House

This attractively modernised inn is in a pretty village, and is a hospitable place, with an easy mix of locals and visitors around the warm open fire in the simple little bar. Bar food is served almost all day, and includes meals such as soup (£2.50), roasted onion and goats cheese tart (£3.65), breaded haddock (£6.85), sausage and mustard mash (£6.95), chicken stuffed with leek and bacon or steak pie (£7.10), grilled lamb chops (£7.75), salmon with ginger and coriander (£9.75), steaks (from £12.45), and puddings such as apple and ginger crumble (£3.10). A pleasant and spacious dining room (all the dining areas are no smoking) has an open fire and high chairs for children if needed; piped music. Three real ales on handpump might include Broughton Greenmantle and Clipper, and one from nearby Traquair House; several malt whiskies and draught cider. Comfortable bedrooms. *(Recommended by Christine and Malcolm Ingram, Kevin Flack)*

Free house ~ Licensee Dianne Johnston ~ Real ale ~ Bar food (12-9) ~ Restaurant ~ (01896) 830229 ~ Children welcome ~ Dogs welcome ~ Open 11(12 Sun)-12; closed 25/26 Dec, 1/2 Jan ~ Bedrooms: £45S/£80B

INVERARAY NN0908 Map 11
George £ 🛏

Main Street E

This comfortably modernised old inn, in the same family for more than 130 years, is nicely placed in the centre of this little Georgian town, stretching along Loch Fyne in front of Inveraray Castle. It's well placed for the great Argyll woodland gardens, best for their rhododendrons in May and early June, and there are good nearby walks – you may spot seals or even a basking shark or whale. The busy flagstoned bar shows plenty of age in its exposed joists, old tiles and bared stone walls, some antique settles, cushioned stone slabs along the walls, nicely grained wooden-topped cast-iron tables, lots of curling club and ships' badges, and a cosy log fire. Good value bar food in big helpings (you order at the table) includes soup (£2.20), prawn cocktail or vegetarian dish of the day (£4.95), steak pie or curry of the day (£5.50), battered haddock (£6.25) and grilled salmon fillet (£7.95). Served by staff who are normally cheerful and helpful (though one or two readers have felt they could sometime be more attentive), two changing real ales might include Caledonian Deuchars IPA or Houston St Peters Well on handpump; lots of malt whiskies; juke box, darts, pool and TV, but no bar games in summer. As we went to press in July work was proceeding on a new conservatory restaurant, using salvaged red pine beams and sandstone pillars. Some of the individually decorated bedrooms (reached by a grand wooden staircase) have antique furnishings and big bathrooms; they are being refurbished one by one, and the latest ones may have higher prices. *(Recommended by Philip and June Caunt, Alain and Rose Foote, A McCormick, T Powell, Mr and Mrs J Curtis, Charles and Pauline Stride)*

Free house ~ Licensee Donald Clark ~ Real ale ~ Bar food (12-9) ~ Restaurant ~ (01499) 302111 ~ Children in eating area of bar and restaurant ~ Dogs welcome ~ Open 11(12 Sun)-12.30; closed 25 Dec-1 Jan ~ Bedrooms: £35B/£60B

ISLE OF WHITHORN NX4736 Map 9
Steam Packet 🍴 ♟ 🛏

Harbour Row

Scotland Dining Pub of the Year

Large picture windows at this well run inn give absorbing views of the picturesque working harbour, where there's usually quite a bustle of yachts and inshore fishing boats (several bedrooms have good views too). Every 1½ to 4 hours there are boat trips from here; or you can walk up to the remains of St Ninian's Kirk, on a headland behind the village. The comfortable low-ceilinged bar is split into two: on the right, plush button-back banquettes and boat pictures, and on the left, green leatherette stools around cast-iron-framed tables on big stone tiles, and a woodburning stove in the bare stone wall. Bar food can be served in the lower-beamed dining room, which has excellent colour wildlife photographs, rugs on its wooden floor, and a solid fuel stove, and there's also a small eating area off the lounge bar. Well prepared meals, imaginative without excessive flights of fancy, might range from filled rolls (from £1.95) and soup (£2.50), to moules marinière (£6.25), sausage ring (£4.95), vegetable tartlet (£5.95), curry of the day (£6.50), seafood platter (£12.50), and specials such as kedgeree (£6.50), grilled sole (£8.95), fried bass with spring onion couscous and vanilla, orange and cardamom sauce (£12.95), and langoustines with ginger, spring onion, lime and lemon grass (£14.95); efficient service from friendly, helpful staff. Well kept Theakstons XB on handpump, with a guest such as tasty local Sulwath Cuil Hill, two dozen malt whiskies and a good wine list; pool and dominoes. White tables and chairs in the garden. The conservatory is no smoking. *(Recommended by Darly Graton, Graeme Gulibert, Pat and Tony Hinkins, MLR, Stan and Hazel Allen, Pam Hall, Christine and Malcolm Ingram, JWAC)*

Free house ~ Licensee John Scoular ~ Real ale ~ Bar food (12-2, 6.30-9) ~ Restaurant ~ (01988) 500334 ~ Children welcome away from bar ~ Dogs welcome ~ Open 11(12 Sun)-11(12 Sat); closed Mon-Thurs 2.30-6 in winter ~ Bedrooms: £35S(£25B)/£70S(£50B)

KENMORE NN7745 Map 11
Kenmore Hotel 🛏

A827 6 miles W of Aberfeldy

Civilised and gently old-fashioned, this small hotel is attractively set in a pretty 18th-c village by Loch Tay; the hotel predates the village by a couple of centuries. Pencilled on the wall above the big log fire in the main front bar, in Burns's own unmistakeable handwriting, is his long poem 'Admiring Nature in her wildest grace' – a tribute to the beauty of the area. This is a comfortable room, with a cosily traditional upmarket feel, armchairs upholstered in a heavy blue and green tartan to match the curtains, and blue and white china with lots of more or less antique fishing photographs on the cream walls above the panelled dado. A newish carpeted light and airy bar at the back has sliding glass doors opening out on to a terrace overlooking the River Tay (the back garden has the same views, and the hotel leases fishing rights from the Kenmore estate), and is furnished in a traditional style, with painted Anaglypta walls, wall lighting and a good mix of upholstered bar stools, captain's chairs and more conventional seating; pool, winter darts, TV, fruit machine and juke box. No real ales but they do keep around 70 malt whiskies. Friendly, helpful staff serve good food including a short range of bar snacks such as sandwiches (from £1.95, baguettes from £3.95), soup (£2.75), cullen skink (£5.25) and smoked salmon or ploughman's (£5.95), steak and ale pie (£8.25), battered haddock (£8.50), duck breast on sage mash with chilli lime salsa or bass stuffed with crayfish mousse with tomato coulis (£12.75); afternoon tea (from around £3.50). *(Recommended by Susan and John Douglas)*

Free house ~ Licensee Mr Hiroz ~ Bar food (11-9) ~ Restaurant ~ (01887) 830205 ~ Children welcome ~ Dogs allowed in bar and bedrooms ~ Entertainment Weds, Sun ~ Open 12(12.30 Sun)-11(12 Fri, Sat) ~ Bedrooms: £59B/£98B

KILBERRY NR7164 Map 11
Kilberry Inn 🛏

B8024

It's quite an expedition to get to this homely whitewashed inn (so remote that local produce often arrives on the school bus), but once you get here the landlord will make you warmly welcome. The road is single-track, so a very leisurely drive lets you make the most of the breathtaking views over rich coastal pastures to the sea and the island of Gigha beyond. You'll know you've arrived when you spot the old-fashioned red telephone box outside, which was inherited from the pub's days as a post office. The small beamed and quarry-tiled dining bar, tastefully and simply furnished, is relaxed and warmly sociable, with a good log fire. No real ale, but a good range of bottled beers and plenty of malt whiskies. The entire pub is no smoking. Enjoyable changing home-made bar food might include starters such as butternut squash and spicy cream soup, warm goats cheese salad or smoked salmon (from £2.95), wild mushroom risotto, venison and game pie or medallions of pork in prune and armagnac sauce (£5.95), and puddings such as sticky toffee pudding with arran ice cream or lemon meringue pie (from £3.25). They appreciate booking if you want a meal. *(Recommended by Callum and Letitia Smith-Burnett, Mrs J Poole, Moira Glover)*

Free house ~ Licensees Mr and Mrs George Primrose ~ Bar food (12-2, 7-8.30) ~ Restaurant ~ (01880) 770223 ~ Dogs allowed in bedrooms ~ Open 11-3, 6.30-11; closed Sun evening, Mon except bank hols; Oct-Easter ~ Bedrooms: £37.50B/£75S

KINGHOLM QUAY NX9773 Map 9
Swan

B726 just S of Dumfries; or signposted off B725

You'll find this well cared-for little hotel in a quiet spot overlooking the old fishing jetty on the River Nith. It would make a handy base for exploring the Caerlaverock nature reserve with its vast numbers of geese. Quickly served in the well ordered lounge or at busy times in the restaurant, a short choice of enjoyable pubby meals ranges from soup (£2.50) and haggis with melted cheese (£3.50), to spinach and ricotta cannelloni or chilli (£6.70), battered haddock (£6.80), and daily specials such as steak pie (£6.25) and lamb braised in red wine (£8.25); half the food service area is no smoking. They also do high teas. The neat and comfortable public bar has well kept Theakstons Best on handpump, and good house wines; quiet piped music. A small garden has tables and a play area. *(Recommended by Michael and*

Marion Buchanan, Christine and Malcolm Ingram, Malcolm Taylor, Richard J Holloway, Lucien Perring)

Free house ~ Licensees Billy Houliston and Tracy Rogan ~ Real ale ~ Bar food (12-2, 5-9) ~ (01387) 253756 ~ Children in eating area of bar and restaurant ~ Dogs allowed in bar ~ Open 11.30-2.30, 5-11; 11.30-11 Sun

KIPPEN NS6594 Map 11
Cross Keys 🍺

Main Street; village signposted off A811 W of Stirling

The unpretentiously cosy atmosphere and friendly hospitality make a visit to this comfortable 18th-c inn particularly enjoyable. The straightforward but welcoming lounge is popular with locals, with a good log fire, and there's a coal fire in the attractive no smoking family dining room; the brightly lit exterior makes a welcoming sight on a cold winter night. From a daily changing menu using fresh local produce, enjoyable generously served food might include home-made pea and mint soup (£2.35), arbroath smokie pâté (£3.50), locally baked ham salad (£6.95), moroccan lamb or breaded haddock (£6.95), beef goulash (£6.75), smoked salmon platter (£7.95), grilled sirloin steak with stilton and cider glaze (£11.50), and puddings such as apple, ginger and nut crumble or chocolate truffle torte (from £3.95); smaller helpings for children. Well kept Belhaven 80/- and Harviestoun Bitter & Twisted on handpump, and around 30 malt whiskies; piped music, and dominoes and TV in the separate public bar. The garden tables have good views towards the Trossachs. *(Recommended by Nick Holding, Sherrie Glass, Sandra and Dave Chadwick, Neil and Jean Spink, Maurice and Gill McMahon)*

Free house ~ Licensees Mr and Mrs Scott ~ Real ale ~ Bar food (12-2, 5.30-9; 12.30-9 Sun) ~ Restaurant ~ (01786) 870293 ~ Children welcome ~ Dogs allowed in bar and bedrooms ~ Open 12-2.30, 5.30-11; 12-12 Sat; 12.30-11 Sun; closed 25 Dec, 1 Jan ~ Bedrooms: £30B/£60B

KIRKTON OF GLENISLA NO2160 Map 11
Glenisla Hotel 🍺

B951 N of Kirriemuir and Alyth

The licensees at this welcoming 17th-c former coaching inn are keen to promote local produce, so the beers, wines, and cheeses all come from nearby suppliers. Two or three real ales might be from Scottish brewers such as Houston and the small Inveralmond brewery in Perth, also local fruit wines and a collection of malt whiskies. With a strong local feel, the simple but cosy carpeted pubby bar has beams and ceiling joists, a roaring log fire (sometimes even in summer), wooden tables and chairs, decent prints, and a chatty crowd of locals; a garden opens off it. The lounge is comfortable and sunny, and the elegant high-ceilinged dining room has rugs on the wooden floor, pretty curtains, candles and fresh flowers, and crisp cream tablecloths; piped music. A converted stable block has darts, dominoes, cribbage, pool, fruit machine and alley skittles. Very good regularly changing bar food might include soup (£2.75), trio of scottish puddings with whisky cream sauce (£3.95), cullen skink or warm goats cheese and vegetable tower (£4.75), thai fishcakes with sweet ginger sauce (£6.95), chicken breast in tarragon sauce (£8.95), filo pastry filled with turkey and ham escalopes stuffed with lanark blue cheese (£9.25), and fried duck breast with orange and Cointreau sauce (£12.95). The pub is attractively situated in one of the prettiest Angus Glens, with some good nearby walks; staff can arrange fishing in local lochs. *(Recommended by Walter and Susan Rinaldi-Butcher, Susan and John Douglas)*

Free house ~ Licensees Steve and Susie Drysdale ~ Real ale ~ Bar food ~ Restaurant ~ (01575) 582223 ~ Children in eating area of bar and restaurant ~ Dogs allowed in bar and bedrooms ~ Live music last Sat in month ~ Open 11-11(1 Sat, 12 Sun); closed 3-5 on weekdays Nov-Easter ~ Bedrooms: £30S/£56B

LINLITHGOW NS9976 Map 11
Four Marys ▉ £

High Street; 2 miles from M9 junction 3 (and little further from junction 4) – town signposted

This bustling place has all you might want from a town pub: a good choice of well kept beer, good generously served bar food, cheery welcoming service, and some points of real interest. The atmosphere is a lot livelier now than during its days as an apothecary's shop, where David Waldie experimented with chloroform – its first use as an anaesthetic. The 16th-c building takes its name from the four ladies-in-waiting of Mary, Queen of Scots, who was born at nearby Linlithgow Palace. Inside are masses of mementoes of the ill-fated queen, such as pictures and written records, a piece of bed curtain said to be hers, part of a 16th-c cloth and swansdown vest of the type she's likely to have worn, and a facsimile of her death-mask. The L-shaped bar also has mahogany dining chairs around stripped period and antique tables, a couple of attractive antique corner cupboards, and an elaborate Victorian dresser serving as a bar gantry. The walls are mainly stripped stone, including some remarkable masonry in the inner area; piped music. Alongside Belhaven 70/-, 80/- and St Andrews and Caledonian Deuchars IPA, four constantly changing guests on handpump might be from brewers such as Atlas, Harviestoun, Orkney and Timothy Taylors. During their May and October beer festivals they have 20 real ale pumps and live entertainment. Simple bar food includes sandwiches (from £2.75), haggis, neeps and tatties (£5.25), lasagne (£5.45), fresh smoked or fried haddock (£5.95), and tasty steak pie (£5.95); part of the restaurant is no smoking. Parking can be difficult. *(Recommended by Pete Yearsley, Nick Holding, Christine and Neil Townend, Peter F Marshall)*

Belhaven ~ Manager Eve Forrest ~ Real ale ~ Bar food (12-3, 5-9; 12(12.30 Sun)-9 Sat) ~ Restaurant ~ (01506) 842171 ~ Children in eating area of bar and restaurant ~ Open 12(12.30 Sun)-11(11.45 Thurs-Sat)

LYBSTER ND2436 Map 11
Portland Arms 🍴 🛏

A9 S of Wick

Our most northerly main entry, this big hotel was built as a staging post on the early 19th-c Parliamentary Road, and is a good base for exploring the spectacular cliffs and stacks of the nearby coastline. One bar area has been attractively laid out as a cosy country kitchen room with an Aga, pine furnishings and farmhouse crockery, and a smart bar-bistro has warm colours and fabrics, solid dark wood furnishings, softly upholstered chairs and a cosy fire. The wide choice of very good meals runs from bar food such as soup (£2.50), sandwiches (£2.50/toasted £3), filled baked potatoes (£4.50), and home-made steak pie (£7.50), to more elaborate specials including sweet herring, smoked salmon and prawns (£4.40), warm mussel and saffron tart (£4.50), vegetable terrine with orange and tomato coulis (£10.40), seafood pie (£11.50), pork medallions in cider cream, duck breast with orange and Cointreau jus on sweet potato and coriander mash or venison saddle topped with blue cheese wrapped in filo (£14), and puddings (£4.50). A good selection of malt whiskies (beers are keg); dominoes, trivia, piped music. Friendly helpful staff can arrange fishing and so forth. *(Recommended by Alan Wilcock, Christine Davidson, Filip Lemmens, Mr and Mrs A Dewhurst, Moira and Margaret Calder; also in the Good Hotel Guide)*

Free house ~ Licensee Robert Reynolds ~ Bar food (12-3, 5-9; 12-9 May-Sept) ~ Restaurant ~ (01593) 721721 ~ Children welcome ~ Open 12(11 Sun)-11(12 Sat); 12-3, 5-11 winter ~ Bedrooms: £50/£75

The knife-and-fork award distinguishes pubs where the food is
of exceptional quality.

MELROSE NT5434 Map 9
Burts Hotel 🍴 🛏

B6374, Market Square

Melrose is perhaps the most villagey of the Border towns, and this comfortably sophisticated hotel is an ideal place to stay in while you explore the area. Always busy and cheerful, the friendly L-shaped lounge bar has lots of cushioned wall seats and windsor armchairs on its turkey carpet, and Scottish prints on the walls; the Tweed Room and the restaurant are no smoking. Well kept Caledonian Deuchars IPA and 80/- and a guest such as Bass or Fullers London Pride on handpump, 80 malt whiskies, and a good wine list. Food here is consistently good, and it's best to arrive early or book. Promptly served by well trained hard-working staff, the inventive bar menu might include soup (£2.75), avocado cheesecake with potato salad and crispy leeks (£4.50), wild mushroom and asparagus strudel (£7.50), scotch smoked salmon, breaded haddock (£7.75), chicken breast poached in creamy coconut curry spices or seared cod on pak choi (£8.95), and puddings such as passion fruit brûlée or ginger and date pudding with butterscotch sauce (£4.50); extremely good breakfasts. There's a well tended garden (with tables in summer). *(Recommended by Mrs J H S Lang, A K and J M Hill, Mike and Lynn Robinson, David and Betty Gittins, Stuart and Roma Crampin, Keith and Janet Morris, John Rahim, Peter Burton, Mark Walker)*

Free house ~ Licensees Graham and Anne Henderson ~ Real ale ~ Bar food ~ Restaurant ~ (01896) 822285 ~ Children in eating area of bar ~ Dogs allowed in bar and bedrooms ~ Open 11-2.30, 5-11; 12-2.30, 6-11 Sun; closed 26 Dec ~ Bedrooms: £53B/£96B

OBAN NM8630 Map 11
Oban Inn

Stafford Street, near North Pier

Even when busy, the atmosphere at this 18th-c harbour-town local is cheerful and welcoming. The beamed downstairs bar is thoroughly pubby and down-to-earth, with small stools, pews and black-winged modern settles on its uneven slate floor, blow-ups of old Oban postcards on the cream walls, and unusual brass-shaded wall lamps. The partly panelled upstairs bar has button-back banquettes around cast-iron-framed tables, a coffered woodwork ceiling, and little backlit arched false windows with heraldic roundels in aged stained glass; the little children's area is no smoking. Well kept Caledonian Deuchars IPA and a guest such as McEwans 80/-, and 45 malt whiskies; fruit machine, juke box, and piped music. Served all day, good value straightforward bar food includes moules marinière (£3.25/£6.50), and three-cheese pasta, haggis, neeps and tatties, beef and ale pie, scampi or cumberland sausage (£5.95). *(Recommended by Dave Braisted, GSB)*

Scottish Courage ~ Manager Erica Mouat ~ Real ale ~ Bar food (12-10) ~ (01631) 562484 ~ Children in restaurant ~ Dogs allowed in bar ~ Open 11(12.30 Sun)-12.45

PITLOCHRY NN9459 Map 11
Moulin 🍺 🛏

Kirkmichael Road, Moulin; A924 NE of Pitlochry centre

Families enjoy the good value food at this bustling pub, and another important feature is the quality of the real ales on handpump, which are brewed in the little stables across the street: Ale of Atholl, Braveheart, Moulin Light, and the stronger Old Remedial; group brewery tours by arrangement. Although the imposing white-painted 17th-c inn has been much extended over the years, the bar, in the oldest part of the building, still seems an entity in itself. Above the fireplace in the smaller room is an interesting painting of the village before the road was built (Moulin used to be a bustling market town, far busier than upstart Pitlochry), while the bigger carpeted area has a good few tables and cushioned banquettes in little booths divided by stained-glass country scenes, another big fireplace, some exposed stonework, fresh flowers, and local prints and golf clubs around the walls; bar billiards, shove ha'penny, cribbage, dominoes and an old-fashioned fruit machine. A wide choice of enjoyable bar food includes soup (£2.50), sandwiches (from £3.95), ploughman's (£4.95), haggis, neeps and tatties (£5.95), steak and ale pie (£6.50), stuffed peppers (£6.75), fish, chips and mushy peas (£6.95), grilled salmon (£7.75), and puddings such as apple pie or honey sponge and custard (from £2.75). They keep around 40 malt whiskies. Picnic-sets outside are surrounded by tubs of flowers, and look across to the village kirk. They offer good value three-night breaks out of season. Rewarding walks nearby. *(Recommended by Christine and Neil Townend, David and Heather Stephenson, Gloria Bax, Sarah Davis, Rod Lambert)*

Own brew ~ Licensee Heather Reeves ~ Real ale ~ Bar food (12-9.30) ~ Restaurant (6-9) ~ (01796) 472196 ~ Children welcome ~ Dogs allowed in bar ~ Open 12-11(11.45 Sat) ~ Bedrooms: £50B/£65B

PLOCKTON NG8033 Map 11
Plockton Hotel ★ 🍴 🛏

Village signposted from A87 near Kyle of Lochalsh

In a lovely National Trust for Scotland village, this stunningly located little hotel forms part of a long, low terrace of stone-built houses. Tables in the front garden look out past the village's trademark palm trees and colourfully flowering shrub-lined shore, and across the sheltered anchorage to the rugged mountainous surrounds of Loch Carron. A stream runs down the hill into a pond in the recently landscaped back garden. Readers really enjoy the cheery bustling atmosphere in the warmly welcoming and comfortably furnished lounge bar, which has window seats looking out to the boats on the water, as well as antiqued dark red leather seating around neat Regency-style tables on a tartan carpet, three model ships set into the woodwork, and partly panelled stone walls. The separate public bar has darts, pool, shove-ha'penny, dominoes, TV and piped music. Very fairly priced, well liked and promptly served bar food includes home-made soup (£2.25, with their own bread), sandwiches (from £3.25), haggis with a tot of whisky (£3.95), fresh prawns (£7.50/£14.95), fish and chips, burger, lasagne or vegetarian dish of the day (£6.95), poached smoked haddock fillet (£7.50), baked lamb shank (£10.95), seafood platter (£17.75) and excellent breakfasts. It's worth booking, as they do get busy, but helpful staff cope well with the numbers; the snug and Courtyard restaurant are no smoking. Well kept Caledonian Deuchars IPA on handpump, bottled beers from the Isle of Skye brewery, a good collection of malt whiskies, and a short wine list. More than half of the no smoking bedrooms in the adjacent building have sea views – one even has a balcony and woodburning stove. A hotel nearby changed its name a few years ago to the Plockton Inn, so don't get the two confused. *(Recommended by Eric Locker, G A Hemingway, Peter F Marshall, H E Wynter, Douglas Keith, Michael and Marion Buchanan, Maurice and Gill McMahon, Olive and Ray Hebson, A McCormick, T Powell, Brian and Anita Randall, Neil Rose, RB, Anthony Longden, Bruce and Penny Wilkie)*

Free house ~ Licensee Tom Pearson ~ Real ale ~ Bar food (12-2.15, 6-9.30; 12.30-2.15, 6-10 Sun) ~ Restaurant ~ (01599) 544274 ~ Children welcome ~ Dogs allowed in bar ~ Live music summer Weds evenings ~ Open 11-12(11.45 Sat); 12.30-11 Sun; closed 25 Dec ~ Bedrooms: £50S(£40B)/£80S

PORTPATRICK NW9954 Map 9
Crown 🛏

North Crescent

Only a stone's throw from the water's edge, this hotel is the focal point of a delightful harbourside village. Tables in front make the most of the evening sun and the comings and goings on the water, especially on a Thursday when the dwindling fishing fleet comes in. Inside, the rambling old-fashioned bar has lots of cosy nooks and crannies, and the partly panelled butter-coloured walls are decorated with old mirrors which have landscapes painted in their side panels. Served by obliging staff, good bar food includes sandwiches (from £2.75), moules marinière (£4.95), crab salad (£5.95), half a grilled lobster (£11.95) and a trio of hot seafood (£15.95). They offer a carefully chosen wine list, and over 70 malt whiskies; TV, fruit machine and perhaps piped music. An airy and very attractively decorated early 20th-c, half no smoking dining room opens through a quiet no smoking conservatory area into a sheltered back garden. *(Recommended by Stan and Hazel Allen, P R Morley)*

Free house ~ Licensee Mr A Schofield ~ Bar food (12-9.30) ~ Restaurant ~ (01776) 810261 ~ Children welcome ~ Dogs welcome ~ Folk and traditional music most Fridays ~ Open 12-11(11.30 Sun) ~ Bedrooms: £43B/£72B

SHIELDAIG NG8154 Map 11
Tigh an Eilean Hotel 🛏

Village signposted just off A896 Lochcarron—Gairloch

Beautifully positioned looking over the forested Shieldaig Island to Loch Torridon and then out to the sea beyond, this welcoming and civilised hotel makes a peaceful escape. Its attached Shieldaig bar, run as a much simpler and pubbier village local, has blue brocaded button-back banquettes in little bays, and picture windows looking out to sea; winter darts, bar billiards and juke box. Its short but enjoyable bar menu includes local fish and seafood, all hand-dived or reel-caught by local fishermen (from £7.50), also sandwiches (from £2), soup (£2.35), shieldaig smoked salmon with home-made bread (starter £5.25, main course £8.95), smoked haddock omelette (£6.25), and daily specials such as crab bisque (£3.50), moules marinière (£4.50), oxtail stew (£6.25), skate wing with black butter sauce (£7.75), grilled bass with basil and crème fraîche (£8), scallops mornay (£8.75), and seafood stew (£10.25). A sheltered front courtyard has five picnic-sets and wall benches. The National Trust Torridon estate and the Beinn Eighe nature reserve aren't too far away. *(Recommended by Peter F Marshall, Dave Braisted, Mrs J Ekins-Daukes, Mr and Mrs J Curtis, Neil Rose; also in the* Good Hotel Guide*)*

Free house ~ Licensee Cathryn Field ~ Bar food (12-8.30) ~ Restaurant ~ (01520) 755251 ~ Dogs allowed in bedrooms ~ Trad music sessions Fri in July/Aug ~ Open 11-11; 12.30-10 Sun; closed 2.30-5 Mon-Fri Nov-March ~ Bedrooms: £52.50B/£115B

SKEABOST NG4148 Map 11
Skeabost House Hotel ★ 🛏

A850 NW of Portree, 1½ miles past junction with A856

Developed from a Victorian hunting lodge, this splendidly grand-looking hotel has 12 acres of secluded woodland and gardens, with glorious views over Loch Snizort. Inside, the bustling high-ceilinged bar has a pine counter and red brocade seats on its thick red carpet, and a fine panelled billiards room leads off the stately hall. A wholly separate public bar has darts, pool, TV, juke box and even its own car park. Well kept Isle of Skye Hebridean Gold, and a fine choice of malt whiskies, including their own and some rare single-year bottlings. Served in the spacious and airy conservatory, bar food includes soup (£2.95), haggis, neeps and tatties with whisky cream sauce (£4.95), baguettes (from £5.95), venison burger or lasagne (£6.95), cod goujons in dill batter (£7.95), liver and bacon casserole (£8.50), and scampi (£8.95). All the eating areas are no smoking; it's best to dress fairly smartly in the main dining room. The hotel is said to have some of the best salmon fishing on the island, and has an 18-hole golf course. *(Recommended by R C Wiles, D S Jackson, Mrs J H S Lang, Dr P D Smart)*

Free house ~ Licensee Michael John Heaney ~ Real ale ~ Bar food (12-2, 6-9) ~ (01470) 532202 ~ Open 12-2, 5-11; 11-12 Sat; 12.30-11 Sun ~ Bedrooms: £54S/£95B

STEIN NG2656 Map 11

Stein Inn 🏠

End of B886 N of Dunvegan in Waternish, off A850 Dunvegan—Portree; OS Sheet 23 map reference 263564

Readers have only praise for this 18th-c inn, and its perfect tranquil setting, in a small untouched village just above a quiet sea inlet. Tables outside (and some of the bedrooms) look over the sea to the Hebrides, and sunsets here can be quite spectacular. The original public bar has great character, with its sturdy country furnishings, flagstone floor, beam and plank ceiling, partly panelled stripped-stone walls and peat fire, and there is a comfortable no smoking lounge and no smoking dining area. The games area has a pool table, and darts, shove-ha'penny, dominoes and cribbage; there may be piped radio. There's a lively children's inside play area, and showers for yachtsmen. The evening crowd of local regulars (where do they all appear from?) and the owners are warmly welcoming, and smartly uniformed service is good. Besides a fine choice of malt whiskies, they have well kept Isle of Skye Red Cuillin and (brewed by Isle of Skye for the pub) Reeling Deck on handpump, a summer guest beer such as Orkney Dark Island, and over 100 malt whiskies. A very short bar food menu uses local fish and highland meat, and includes sandwiches (from £1.65), soup (£2.20) and huge three-cheese ploughman's (£5.50), with a handful of specials such as pork chop with marmalade and ginger, feta spinach parcel or breaded haddock (£5.95), scampi (£7.95), and puddings such as almond praline parfait or profiteroles with chocolate sauce (£3.95).
(Recommended by June and Perry Dann, Richard and Karen Holt, Mike and Kathryn Budd, Walter and Susan Rinaldi-Butcher, John Rahim, Charles and Pauline Stride)

Free house ~ Licensees Angus and Teresa Mcghie ~ Real ale ~ Bar food (12-4, 6-9.30; possibly not Mon) ~ Restaurant ~ (01470) 592362 ~ Children welcome ~ Dogs welcome ~ Open 11-12(12.30 Sat; 12.30-11 Sun; 4-12 weekdays; 12-12 Sat; 12.30-11 Sun in winter; closed 25 Dec, 1 Jan ~ Bedrooms: £24.50S/£49S

STONEHAVEN NO8493 Map 11

Lairhillock ♀ ◧

Netherley; 6 miles N of Stonehaven, 6 miles S of Aberdeen, take the Durris turn-off from the A90

The cheerful beamed bar at this smart extended country pub has a traditional feel, with panelled wall benches and an attractive mix of old seats, dark woodwork, harness and brass lamps on the walls, a good open fire, and countryside views from the bay window; the spacious separate lounge has an unusual central fire. It's a good place to come for a decent meal, with good freshly prepared bar food including soup (£2.75), filled baguettes (£4.65), a changing terrine (£4.75), lunchtime ploughman's (£5.95), home-made wild boar sausages and mustard mash (£7.50), chicken stuffed with haggis in light whisky sauce (£8.95), aberdeen angus or ostrich fillet steaks (from £11.95), and puddings (from £3.15); Sunday buffet lunch (£8.95). A separate thoughtful children's menu includes lasagne and stir-fry chicken (from £2.95). A choice of up to half a dozen well kept ales on handpump might be from brewers such as Belhaven, Courage, Inveralmond and Timothy Taylors on handpump; 65 malt whiskies, and an extensive wine list; darts, cribbage, dominoes, and a nice pub cat. The cosy, highly praised restaurant is in an adjacent building. There are panoramic views from the no smoking conservatory.
(Recommended by Mrs J Ekins-Daukes, John Poulter)

Free house ~ Licensee Roger Thorne ~ Real ale ~ Bar food (12-2, 6-9.30(10 Fri, Sat); 5.30-9 Sun; 4.30-6 winter Sat/Sun) ~ Restaurant ~ (01569) 730001 ~ Children in eating area of bar and restaurant ~ Dogs allowed in bar ~ Open 11-2.30, 5-11(12 Fri); 11-12 Sat; 11-11 Sun; closed 25/26 Dec, 1/2 Jan

SWINTON NT8448 Map 10
Wheatsheaf 🍴 🛏

A6112 N of Coldstream

Friendly professional new licensees are sticking to the successful formula that has made this civilised inn such a favourite with readers in past years. It's nicely set in a pretty village surrounded by rolling countryside, just a few miles away from the River Tweed. The carefully thought-out main bar area has an attractive long oak settle and comfortable armchairs, and sporting prints and plates on the bottle-green wall covering; a small lower-ceilinged part by the counter has pubbier furnishings, and small agricultural prints on the walls – especially sheep. A further lounge area has a fishing-theme décor. Changing daily, a wide range of well cooked and presented food is made from local seasonal ingredients, and at lunchtime might include soup (£2.95), salmon and dill fishcake with tomato and lime salsa (£4.75), avocado and prawn timbale with lemon mayonnaise (£5.65), pork, prune and red onion meatballs in cider gravy with crispy leeks (£6.95), roast chicken breast wrapped in pancetta with garlic, herbs and lemon (£8.90), and evening dishes such as butternut, wild lovage and coriander cream soup (£4.20), sautéed mushrooms and bacon with garlic in filo with melted cheddar (£4.90), peppered duck breast with thyme and pink peppercorn sauce (£15.35), roast rack of border lamb in rosemary and garlic jus with almond polenta (£15.65), and medallions of scotch fillet on roasted shallots and oyster mushroom sauce (£17.45). Booking is advisable, particularly from Thursday to Saturday evening, and they may start serving food on Monday. Caledonian 80/- and a guest, usually from Broughton, on handpump, a decent range of malt whiskies and brandies, a fine choice of wines, and cocktails. Service is helpful, unhurried and genuinely welcoming. The front conservatory has a vaulted pine ceiling and walls of local stone; all the dining areas are no smoking. Good breakfasts with freshly squeezed orange juice. *(Recommended by Carolyn Dixon)*

Free house ~ Licensees Chris and Jan Winson ~ Real ale ~ Bar food (not Mon) ~ Restaurant ~ (01890) 860257 ~ Children in restaurant ~ Dogs allowed in bedrooms ~ Open 11.30-11(4 Sat); closed Sun evening ~ Bedrooms: £58B/£90B

TAYVALLICH NR7386 Map 11
Tayvallich Inn 🍴

B8025, off A816 1 mile S of Kilmartin; or take B841 turn-off from A816 2 miles N of Lochgilphead

You can take in the lovely views over the yacht anchorage and water from the terrace of this simply furnished bar/restaurant, while enjoying seafood freshly brought in by local fishermen from the bay of Loch Sween just across the lane. The small bar has local nautical charts on the cream walls, exposed ceiling joists, and pale pine upright chairs, benches and tables on its quarry-tiled floor; dominoes, cards. It leads into a no smoking dining conservatory, from where sliding glass doors open on to the terrace; there's a garden, too. Service is friendly, and people with children are very much at home here. Bar food might include pâté (£4.25), mussels (£4.75), fried scallops or pasta of the day (£6.50), steak and ale pie (£6.75), battered haddock (£7.95), prawns in garlic (£13.95), and puddings such as crème brûlée and sticky toffee pudding (£3.50). Twenty malt whiskies including a full range of islay malts; they also make fresh milk shakes. *(Recommended by Richard J Holloway, Callum and Letitia Smith-Burnett)*

Free house ~ Licensee Roddy Anderson ~ Bar food ~ Restaurant (from 7) ~ No credit cards ~ (01546) 870282 ~ Children welcome ~ Dogs allowed in bar ~ Open 11-11.30(1 Fri/Sat, 12 Sun); 11-2.30, 5-11, closed Mon in winter, 25 Dec

---

If you report on a pub that's not a main entry, please tell us any lunchtimes or evenings when it doesn't serve bar food.

THORNHILL NS6699 Map 11
Lion & Unicorn
A873

Parts of this attractive building date back to 1635. The open-plan front room has a warm fire, beams and stone walls, and comfortable seats on the wooden floors, with two real ales such as Caledonian Deuchars IPA and Timothy Taylors Landlord on handpump. The beamed public bar has stone walls and floors, piped music, juke box, pool, fruit machine, TV, darts, cribbage and dominoes. Bar food is served all day and includes soup (£2.50), baked potatoes (from £4.25), steak pie (£6.25), scampi (£6.95), gammon steak with cheese or roast parsnip and sweet potato cream bake (£7.25), and puddings such as apple pie and sticky toffee pudding (from £3.25). In the restaurant (half no smoking) you can see the original massive fireplace, almost big enough to drive a car into. Very nice in summer, the garden has a play area, and perhaps barbecues in good weather. We've yet to hear from readers who've used the reasonably priced bedrooms. *(Recommended by W W Burke, Maurice and Gill McMahon, Rosemary and Tom Hall)*

Free house ~ Licensees Fiona and Bobby Stevenson ~ Real ale ~ Bar food (12-9) ~ Restaurant ~ (01786) 850204 ~ Children welcome ~ Open 11-12(1 Sat); 12.30-12 Sun; closed 25 Dec, 1 Jan ~ Bedrooms: £35B/£70B

TUSHIELAW NT3018 Map 9
Tushielaw Inn
Ettrick Valley, B709/B7009 Lockerbie—Selkirk

If you like good meat, choosing a bar meal at this friendly inn by Ettrick Water is simple: depending on your appetite and pocket, go for either the beef baguette (£5.50) or the steaks (from £12), as both use delicious tender pedigree galloway beef. Other dishes include soup (£3), haggis with melted cheese or vegetable or lamb samosas (£3.50), ploughman's (£5.50), lambs liver in garlic, parsley and cream sauce (£6.50), mushroom and nut fettuccine (£6.75), butterfly chicken with lemon and tarragon sauce (£7.50), and puddings such as clootie dumpling or hot chocolate fudge cake (£3.50). Part of the dining room is no smoking. The unpretentious but comfortable little bar draws a mix of customers, from hang-gliders to hikers, and has an open fire, local prints and photographs, and several antiques; decent house wines and a good few malt whiskies, darts, cribbage, dominoes, shove-ha'penny and gaming dice; also piped music and TV. There are tables on an outside terrace. The inn has its own fishing on Clearburn Loch up the B711, and is a useful walking base. *(Recommended by Ralph and Gloria Maybourn, Helen Maynard)*

Free house ~ Licensee Gordon Harrison ~ Real ale ~ Bar food ~ Restaurant ~ (01750) 62205 ~ Children welcome ~ Dogs welcome ~ Open 12-2.30, 6.30-11; closed Tues-Thurs lunchtime, Mon-Weds in winter ~ Bedrooms: £32B/£50B

ULLAPOOL NH1294 Map 11
Ferry Boat ◀
Shore Street; coming from the S, keep straight ahead when main A835 turns right into Mill Street

In summer you can sit on the wall across the road from this welcoming inn and take in the fine views to the tall hills beyond the attractive fishing port, with its bustle of yachts, ferry boats, fishing boats and tour boats for the Summer Isles. The unassuming two-roomed pubby bar is popular with locals and tourists and has big windows with nice views, yellow walls, brocade-cushioned seats around plain wooden tables, quarry tiles by the corner serving counter and patterned carpet elsewhere, a stained-glass door hanging from the ceiling and a fruit machine; cribbage, dominoes and piped music. The more peaceful inner room has a coal fire, a delft shelf of copper measures and willow-pattern plates. Enjoyable bar food includes soup (£2.25), ploughman's (£4.25), haggis, neeps and tatties (£5.75), courgettes stuffed with ricotta and parmesan (£6.50), fried haddock and chips or venison burger (£7.25), puddings such as chocolate and ginger cheesecake (£2.75), and cakes and scones (from 80p); they have well kept Hebridean Islander (from across the water, on Lewis) and Wadworths 6X on handpump. *(Recommended by June and Perry Dann, A and B D Craig, DC, RB, Dr T E Hothersall)*

Free house ~ Licensee Richard Smith ~ Real ale ~ Bar food (all day) ~ Restaurant ~ (01854) 612366 ~ Children in eating area of bar and restaurant till 8 ~ Dogs allowed in bedrooms ~ Thurs evening folk music ~ Open 11(12.30 Sun)-11; closed 24-27 Dec ~ Bedrooms: £37S/£70S

WEEM NN8449 Map 11
Ailean Chraggan ♈ ⇌

B846

Small and welcoming, this family-run hotel is an enjoyable place to stay in, with good food, and chatty locals in the bar. The changing menu, in either the comfortably carpeted modern lounge or the mainly no smoking dining room, might include soup (£2.45), sandwiches (from £2.85), cullen skink (£4.15), gravadlax (£5.25), vegetable and bean curry (£8.65), moules marinière (£9.25), chorizo paella or dover sole (£9.95), poussin stuffed with couscous (£11.95), steamed halibut with ginger, soy and sesame sauce (£13.45), and puddings such as treacle tart and tiramisu (£4.95). Very good wine list, around 100 malt whiskies; winter darts and dominoes. Two terraces outside give lovely views to the mountains beyond the Tay, sweeping up to Ben Lawers (the highest in this part of Scotland) *(Recommended by Callum and Letitia Smith-Burnett)*

Free house ~ Licensee Alastair Gillespie ~ Bar food ~ Restaurant ~ (01887) 820346 ~ Children welcome ~ Dogs allowed in bar and bedrooms ~ Open 11(12.30 Sun)-11; closed 25/26 Dec, 1/2 Jan ~ Bedrooms: £42.50B/£85B

Lucky Dip

Besides the fully inspected pubs, you might like to try these Lucky Dips recommended to us and described by readers (if you do, please send us reports: www.goodguides.com).

ABERDEENSHIRE
ABERDEEN [NJ9305]
Grill [Union St]: Straightforward pub, very old-fashioned (no ladies' till recently), immaculately kept with polished dark panelling, attractive traditional features, well kept Caledonian 80/-, Isle of Skye Red Cuillin and McEwans 80/-, enormous range of malt whiskies, match-strike metal strip under bar counter, basic snacks; open all day *(the Didler)*
☆ *Old Blackfriars* [Castle St]: Welcoming and cosy ancient building on two levels, several well kept mainly scottish changing beers, enjoyable reasonably priced simple food, exemplary waitress service for food and drink, lunchtime no smoking area, plenty of character *(Sue and Andy Waters, Roger Huggins, Tom and Alex McLean, Dr D J and Mrs S C Walker)*

BRAEMAR [NO1591]
Fife Arms: Big tartan-carpeted Victorian hotel balancing catering for coach parties with serving as a local pub, good selection of malt whiskies, reasonably priced self-service pub food, huge log fire, comfortable sofas; children and dogs welcome, piped music; bedrooms warm and comfortable with mountain views, pleasant strolls in village *(Dave Braisted)*

CRATHIE [NO2293]
Inver [A93 Balmoral—Braemar]: Sensitively refurbished 18th-c inn by River Dee, pleasant bar, quiet lounge with open fire, good range of reasonably priced home-cooked food from excellent toasties up, friendly attentive service, well kept beer, decent wine by the glass, lots of whiskies; bedrooms *(J F M and M West)*

GARLOGIE [NJ7905]
Garlogie Inn: Well run dining pub in pleasant setting overlooking Deeside, generous varied food inc good fish, decent wine, reasonable prices, friendly homely atmosphere, attentive staff *(Mrs Jane Kingsbury)*

MUIR OF FOWLIS [NJ5612]
Muggarthaugh [Tough, just off A980 N of Craigievar]: Good friendly service, generous helpings of good value food, some interesting wines; bedrooms, open for most of the day at least in summer *(David and Betty Gittins)*

NEWBURGH [NJ9925]
☆ *Udny Arms* [A975 N of Aberdeen]: Pleasant small hotel with attractively decorated lounge bar opening into sun lounge, good bar lunches, more imaginative than usual, wider choice of evening food esp fish in upstairs

restaurant, real ale; lots of tables on sheltered back lawn, stroll over golf links to sandy beach; comfortable bedrooms *(LYM, Mrs Jane Kingsbury)*

OLDMELDRUM [NJ8128]

☆ *Redgarth* [Kirk Brae]: Good-sized comfortable lounge, traditional décor and subdued lighting, well kept changing ales such as Bass, Castle Eden and Isle of Skye Blaven, good range of malt whiskies, nicely presented satisfying food inc some interesting dishes and good puddings, more intimate restaurant, cheerful and attentive landlord and staff; gorgeous views to Bennachie, immaculate bedrooms *(David and Betty Gittins, Callum and Letitia Smith-Burnett)*

TARLAND [NO4804]

Aberdeen Arms [The Square]: Tidy little family-run hotel in conservation area, flowers on tables and padded banquettes, lively chat one end, no smoking the other, enjoyable food (not Mon) with the current oriental influences, one real ale such as Worthington; bistro and gift shop *(Ian and Nita Cooper)*

ANGUS

DUNDEE [NO3930]

Royal Oak [Brook St]: Pubby bar with stripped stone, old furniture, well kept changing ales, open fire; more like indian restaurant behind, with sombre dark green décor, tasty curries, also wide choice of more general food; wkdy food may stop around 8ish, can be very busy wknds *(Christine and Neil Townend)*

MEMUS [NO4259]

Drovers: Quaint bar interestingly restored with kitchen range, quarry tiles and lots of memorabilia, cosy lounge with duck pictures, real ales such as Orkney Dark Island, wide choice of whiskies, traditional food inc very popular Sunday high teas, pleasantly formal softly lit two-room restaurant divided by woodburner, large dining conservatory looking over charming garden with peaceful country views, impressive adventure play area and Sun barbecues; cl Mon evening *(Susan and John Douglas)*

ARGYLL

ARDUAINE [NM7910]

☆ *Loch Melfort Hotel* [A816 S of Oban]: Gorgeous view of sea and islands from front terrace and picture windows in comfortable hotel's airy modern nautical bar (which now has real ale), good bar food all day from soup and sandwiches to aberdeen angus steak and lots of fresh local seafood, children's menu, no smoking restaurant with good wine list, friendly licensees; children and dogs welcome, good sea-view bedrooms, by Arduaine woodland gardens (lovely late Apr to early June – fun for children, too), open all day *(Mark and Belinda Halton, LYM)*

BRIDGE OF ORCHY [NN2939]

☆ *Bridge of Orchy Hotel* [A82 Tyndrum—Glencoe]: Comfortable bar with nice views, wide choice of good not over-generous food in bar and restaurant, welcoming atmosphere, particularly well kept ales such as Caledonian and Fyne, dozens of malt whiskies, good choice of house wines, interesting mountain photographs; comfortable well decorated bedrooms, good value bunkhouse, spectacular spot on West Highland Way (and if it's on time the sleeper from London gets you here for breakfast) *(Sarah and Peter Gooderham, Mr and Mrs Maurice Thompson, Tina and David Woods-Taylor, Olive and Ray Hebson, John and Sheila Lister)*

CAMPBELTOWN [NR7220]

Ardshiel [Kilkerran Rd]: Attractive and comfortable panelled bar and lounge, great range of malt whiskies inc malt of the month, good choice of reasonably priced food, friendly efficient service; bedrooms *(Christine and Neil Townend, Callum and Letitia Smith-Burnett)*

GLENCOE [NN1058]

☆ *Clachaig* [old Glencoe road, behind NTS Visitor Centre]: Spectacular setting, surrounded by soaring mountains, extended inn doubling as mountain rescue post and cheerfully crowded with outdoors people in season, with mountain photographs in flagstoned walkers' bar (two woodburners and pool), pine-panelled snug, big modern-feeling dining lounge; hearty snacks all day, wider evening choice, lots of malt whiskies, well kept real ales, unusual bottled beers, annual beer festival; children in no smoking restaurant; live music Sat; simple bedrooms, nourishing breakfast, self catering *(LYM, Mr and Mrs Maurice Thompson)*

KILCHRENAN [NN0323]

Kilchrenan Inn [B845]: New management in simple pub fitted out in local pine, window seat and rustic furniture, sandwiches and limited blackboard choice of good food here or in separate dining room, quiet and relaxed atmosphere, friendly staff, one real ale; dogs welcome, tables outside, handy for Loch Awe *(Mr and Mrs J Curtis, Nick Holding)*

OBAN [NM8424]

Barn [off A816 S – follow Ardoran Marine sign]: Friendly converted barn in lovely remote-feeling countryside nr sea, wide choice of good changing chip-free home-made food esp Fri local seafood (great shortbread for sale, too), reasonable prices, wooden tables and settles, Scottish accordion Tues, ceilidh Thurs and folk group Sun; children very welcome, beautiful views from terrace, play area, donkeys, rabbits and hens all around; part of chalet holiday complex *(Mark and Belinda Halton)*

Lorne [Stevenson St]: Well restored friendly Victorian pub with tile decoration and central bar with ornate brasswork; freshly prepared food inc wild salmon, local lamb and seafood

and so forth, well kept McEwans 80/- and
Theakstons *(Sarah and Peter Gooderham)*

SANDBANK [NS1680]

Holy Loch Inn [A815 NW of Dunoon]:
Attractive simply furnished waterside inn, clan
tartans and friendly kilted staff,
straightforward scottish cooking in no smoking
dining room; open all day *(Alan and
Paula McCully)*

BANFFSHIRE

MACDUFF [NJ7064]

Knowes [Market St]: Roomy family-run hotel
with great Moray Firth views, very wide choice
of enjoyable food inc lots of fish, one or two
real ales from small breweries in Scotland or
the south, friendly staff; children welcome,
bedrooms, handy for marine aquarium
(Ian and Nita Cooper)

BERWICKSHIRE

COLDINGHAM [NT9066]

Anchor [School Rd (A1107)]: Two-bar village
pub with friendly helpful landlord and staff,
good range of well kept beers such as Black
Sheep and Orkney Red MacGregor, local sea
memorabilia, good choice of generous food inc
good fish and other local ingredients; handy
for St Abbs *(Malcolm M Stewart, Alan and
Ros Furley)*

LAUDER [NT5347]

Eagle [A68]: Dark wood and beams, pictures,
plates, brass, plants, remarkably ornate bar
counter, stone fireplace, good value bar food,
efficient smiling service and lively atmosphere,
well kept changing real ales, games in public
bar; children welcome, summer barbecues in
old stableyard, bedrooms, open all day *(LYM)*

WESTRUTHER [NT6350]

☆ *Old Thistle*: Superb local aberdeen angus
steaks, besides other food from sandwiches up
to a small range of puddings; a thoroughly nice
pub, with intriguing little 18th-c traditional
bar, games room, thriving local atmosphere,
welcoming service, comfortable two-room
lounge and restaurant; cl wkdy lunchtime but
food all day wknds, children welcome,
refurbished bedrooms *(Dr and Mrs S Donald,
Michael Lamm)*

DUMFRIESSHIRE

CANONBIE [NY3976]

Cross Keys: Attractive 17th-c coaching inn
with River Esk fishing, wide choice of
enjoyable and generous straightforward food
using local produce from sandwiches up in
spacious and comfortably worn in lounge bar,
good carvery Fri-Sun, friendly helpful staff
even when very busy; spacious well equipped
bedrooms, good breakfast *(J A Hooker,
Canon David Baxter)*

Riverside Inn: This aptly named inn, long a
favourite of many readers for its good food
and comfortable bedrooms, was closed and up
for sale as we went to press; we hope to find it

reopened and flourishing again – news please
(LYM)

DUMFRIES [NX9776]

New Bazaar [Whitesands]: Traditional bar
with up to five beers and lots of malt whiskies,
small lounge, inner snug; tables in small yard,
open all day *(Eric Larkham)*

Tam o' Shanter [Queensberry St]: 17th-c
former coaching inn with good choice of
quickly changing beers, two sitting rooms (one
no smoking) off bar; tables in former
coachyard, open all day *(Eric Larkham)*

GLENCAPLE [NX9968]

Nith: Pleasant bar and picture-window dining
room, good quickly served reasonably priced
food, esp smoked salmon and wild salmon;
spacious bedrooms with own bathrooms, good
breakfast *(Dr Michael Denton)*

MOFFAT [NT0805]

☆ *Black Bull* [Churchgate]: Attractive and well
kept, plush softly lit bar with Burns
memorabilia, prompt welcoming service,
generous, enjoyable and sensibly priced hearty
food from sandwiches up, well kept ales such
as Broughton and McEwans 80/-, friendly
public bar with railway memorabilia and good
open fire (may be only bar open out of season),
simply furnished tiled-floor dining room; piped
music, side games bar with juke box, big-
screen TV for golf; children welcome, tables in
courtyard, bedrooms comfortable and good
value, open all day *(LYM, John and
Elspeth Howell, Keith Moss)*

☆ *Moffat House* [High St]: Attractive extended
Adam-style hotel, relaxed and quiet, with
welcoming helpful service, good value food
from quick snack lunches to good Sun roasts,
spacious and relaxing old-fashioned plush
lounge, conservatory coffee lounge, real ales
inc Tetleys; comfortable bedrooms, good
breakfast *(Christine and Neil Townend,
Mr and Mrs Staples)*

MONIAIVE [NX7790]

George [High St]: 17th-c inn with interesting
no-frills old-fashioned flagstoned bar of
considerable character; well kept Belhaven,
decent wine, log fire, reasonably priced
lunchtime food (except sometimes out of
season); can get smoky; simple bedrooms
(Stan and Hazel Allen, LYM)

NEW ABBEY [NX9666]

Abbey Arms [The Square]: Good atmosphere
and neighbourly feel in bar and eating room,
short but good menu esp at lunchtime,
reasonable drinks prices *(Stan and Hazel Allen)*

THORNHILL [NX8795]

☆ *Buccleuch & Queensberry* [this is the
Thornhill in Dumfriesshire]: Pleasantly
refurbished and traditionally solid old red
sandstone inn with comfortable banquettes
and open fire in main beamed bar, friendly
service, food from interesting sandwiches and

baked potatoes to good value main dishes, well kept Caledonian 80/- and a changing guest beer; access to 3 miles of fishing on the River Nith; children welcome, comfortable bedrooms with good breakfast *(LYM, JWAC)*

DUNBARTONSHIRE
ARROCHAR [NN2903]
☆ *Village Inn* [A814, just off A83 W of Loch Lomond]: Fine sea and hill views from informal candlelit all-day dining area with lots of bare wood and big open fire (shame they have to chain down the window-ledge binoculars these days), steps down to bar with generous and enjoyable lunchtime bar food from sandwiches up, well kept changing real ales, several dozen malt whiskies, good coffee, cheerful attentive staff; piped music, juke box, can be loudly busy Sat in summer; children welcome in eating areas till 8, bedrooms with own bathrooms, open all day *(Mr and Mrs Richard Osborne, Michael and Marion Buchanan, LYM, Ian Baillie, Peter and Giff Bennett, Alain and Rose Foote)*

BALLOCH [NS3982]
Balloch Hotel [just N of A811]: Vintage Inn dining pub in superb spot by River Leven's exit from Loch Lomond, good atmosphere in several seating areas (no standing at the bar), helpful young staff, good range of wines by the glass, Bass and Caledonian Deuchars IPA, decent reasonably priced food all day; bedrooms, open all day *(Ian Baillie)*
MV Maid of the Loch: Last paddle steamer built for service in GB, forward café and bar open 10-4, aft restaurant, fine loch views; handy for Loch Lomond Shores *(Dave Braisted)*

FIFE
CERES [NO3911]
Meldrums [Main St]: Small hotel with cottagey parlour bar, pleasant atmosphere, clean and attractive beamed dining lounge with good choice of well prepared and presented reasonably priced bar lunches, prompt friendly service even when busy; well appointed bedrooms, charming village nr Wemyss Pottery *(Peter and Jean Hoare)*

ELIE [NO4900]
Victoria [High St]: Unpretentious Braids Bar with enjoyable food and friendly staff, dogs welcome; also good value smarter restaurant, bedrooms *(Mary and David Richards)*

FALKLAND [NO2507]
☆ *Stag* [Mill Wynd]: Long low 17th-c country pub recently carefully refurbished, making more of its back room; dark wooden pews and stools, stripped stone, copper-topped tables, stone fireplace, limited choice of enjoyable food inc sandwiches made with their good home-baked bread, dining room; bar billiards, fruit machine, TV, unobtrusive piped music, frequent live nights; children welcome, delightful setting opp

charming green, round corner from medieval village square *(Andrew Murphy, Mrs J Ekins-Daukes, Lady Heath, Susan and John Douglas, BB)*

GUARD BRIDGE [NO4518]
Guard Bridge Hotel [Old St Andrews Rd]: Enjoyable homely food all freshly cooked by landlord (so may be a wait) inc fresh fish and good puddings, small unspoilt dark bar with local photographs on claret-coloured walls, river-view dining room, very welcoming service; bedrooms, flower-filled terrace, nice spot by 15th-c bridge over River Eden *(Susan and John Douglas)*

KIRKCALDY [NT2891]
Wheatsheaf [Tolbooth St]: Old-fashioned warm and friendly high-street local with good value generous bar lunches, not Sun, at comfortable tables (a few no smoking), lots of charity work, cheerful service; piped music, keg beers, can get noisy evenings *(Ian and Nita Cooper)*

LIMEKILNS [NT0783]
Ship [Halketts Hall, towards Charlestown; off A985]: Friendly and comfortable blue and yellow lounge with good views over the Forth, mainly nautical décor, good value sandwiches and bar snacks, well kept Belhaven 80/- and perhaps other real ales, no smoking area; piped music (occasional live); children and dogs welcome, open all day, tables outside, interesting waterside conservation area *(Susan and John Douglas, Comus and Sarah Elliott)*

NORTH QUEENSFERRY [NT1380]
Ferrybridge [Main St]: Good varied imaginative food inc popular Sun lunch at attractive prices in hotel snuggled under Forth Bridge, good choice of wine, courteous service; good bedrooms *(Mrs D A Draycott)*

PITTENWEEM [NO5402]
Anchor [Charles St]: Enjoyable food *(Kay Wheat)*

ST ANDREWS [NO5016]
West Port [South St]: Stylish modern bar in handsome Georgian house, continental newspapers, board games, bagels and croissants as well as interesting lunchtime sandwiches, fine range of coffees all day, cheerful efficient staff, enjoyable restaurant, not always open, up a few steps (with Stannah lift for disabled); live music Sun night, large attractive garden *(Susan and John Douglas)*

ST MONANCE [NO5201]
Mayview [Station Rd]: Hotel with good mix of locals and visitors in big public bar, enjoyable food, well kept beer; children welcome, tables outside, bedrooms *(Kay Wheat)*
☆ *Seafood Restaurant & Bar* [West End; just off A917]: Now too purely a restaurant to keep its place in the main entries (they have scrapped

the real ale and bar meals and put sofas there, making it a pre- or post-meal anteroom and not a place for just a drink); but it's well worth knowing for its excellent fish and shellfish, with good value meals deals, friendly service, big windows overlooking the harbour and Forth, and summer terrace tables *(Susan and John Douglas, LYM)*

INVERNESS-SHIRE
ARISAIG [NM6586]
Arisaig Hotel: Cosy and welcoming lounge bar, good reasonably priced food esp fish; bedrooms *(Christine and Neil Townend, Dr P D Smart)*

DRUMNADROCHIT [NH5029]
Fiddlers Elbow: Good real ale choice, enjoyable food, friendly atmosphere, reasonable prices; original little girl effigy at entrance *(Helen Murray, Dr P D Smart)*

FORT AUGUSTUS [NH3709]
Lock [Canalside, just off A82]: Unpretentious pub at foot of Caledonian Canal's climb from Loch Ness to Loch Oich, flagstones, some stripped stone and big open fire, fine choice of malt whiskies, usually a real ale such as Belhaven, Black Isle or Tomintoul, bar food from toasties and filled rolls up, with upstairs restaurant and part of the bar no smoking for people eating; may be piped music; summer folk nights Mon-Weds, and summer barbecues, children in eating areas, open all day *(LYM, A and B D Craig, Alison Hayes, Pete Hanlon)*

FORT WILLIAM [NN1073]
Ben Nevis Bar [High St]: Large beamed bar with friendly efficient staff and pleasant atmosphere, decent food here or in upstairs dining area, Loch Linnhe views from back windows, may have Marstons Pedigree; pool table, fruit machine, pinball and juke box, live music in big lounge *(Sarah and Peter Gooderham)*

GLEN SHIEL [NH0711]
☆ *Cluanie Inn* [A87 Invergarry—Kyle of Lochalsh, on Loch Cluanie]: Welcoming inn in lovely isolated setting by Loch Cluanie (good walks), big helpings of good freshly prepared bar food inc some interesting dishes in three knocked-together rooms with dining chairs around polished tables, overspill into restaurant; friendly efficient staff, good fire, no pool or juke box; children welcome; big comfortable modern bedrooms nicely furnished in pine, stunning views and good bathrooms – great breakfasts for non-residents too *(Sarah and Peter Gooderham, Dave Braisted)*

INVERNESS [NH6945]
☆ *Snow Goose* [Stoneyfield, about ¼ mile E of A9/A96 roundabout]: Vintage Inn dining pub, the most northerly of this chain, with good imaginative well presented bar food at attractive prices in comfortable and relaxing

informal country-feel room areas, beams and flagstones, several log fires, soft lighting, interesting décor, friendly helpful staff, young and enthusiastic; good wine choice *(Alan Wilcock, Christine Davidson, Rod Stoneman)*

KINGUSSIE [NH7500]
Scot House [Newtonmore Rd]: Clean and bright, with good bar food inc sandwiches and baked potatoes, moderate prices, well kept beer, decent wine by the glass, efficient helpful staff, rather pink décor; bedrooms *(J F M and M West)*

LAGGAN [NN2996]
Eagle on the Water [Laggan Locks, NW of Loch Lochy]: Converted dutch barge on Caledonian Canal, small, cosy and friendly, with local microbrew tapped from the cask, Thatcher's farm cider, and (advance booking only) meals using fresh local produce *(R M Corlett)*

MALLAIG [NM6797]
Marine Hotel [Station Rd]: Comfortable hotel lounge bar (up steep stairs) overlooking fishing harbour and beyond to Small Isles and Skye, good lunchtime bar food from sandwiches and baguettes to local seafood, courteous service, no smoking dining room, basic public bar downstairs (notable for its stuffed gannet in full flight) with games room; keg beers, piped music; bedrooms, in centre of fishing village *(Christine and Neil Townend, Olive and Ray Hebson, W and P J Elderkin)*

SPEAN BRIDGE [NN2491]
☆ *Letterfinlay Lodge* [A82 7 miles N]: Warmly welcoming hotel with lovely view over Loch Lochy from big picture-window main bar, wide choice of good food from sandwiches to tender steaks and venison, friendly efficient service, keg beers but good malt whiskies and decent wines, no smoking restaurant, small smart cocktail bar; children and dogs welcome, pleasant lochside grounds, own boats for fishing; clean and comfortable bedrooms, good breakfast, dog baskets available; gents' have good showers and hairdryers – handy for Caledonian Canal sailors *(Dave Braisted, LYM, Walter and Susan Rinaldi-Butcher, A McCormick, T Powell, Dr P D Smart)*

STRUY [NH4240]
Cnoc [A831 just NE of village]: Recently comfortably developed, with charming landlady, bar food such as soup, four-cheese ploughman's, venison sausages and savoury pancakes, good value Sun lunches, pleasant dining room overlooking lawns, afternoon teas; bedrooms *(Dr P D Smart)*

KINCARDINESHIRE
BANCHORY [NO7196]
Scott Skinners [North Deeside Rd, A93 E]: Converted Victorian house with cheerful welcoming staff, simple but comfortable

lounge bar with log fire, cosy locals' bar, wide choice of good value food from small Scottish breweries, decent wine choice inc bin ends; piped music; children very welcome, play area and games room *(Sue and Andy Waters, Ian and Nita Cooper)*

CATTERLINE [NO8778]

☆ *Creel*: Good generous imaginative food esp soups and local fish and seafood in big bar cosy lounge with woodburner, friendly cat and plenty of tables, or small no smoking seaview restaurant (same menu, booking advised); well kept ales such as Caledonian Deuchars IPA and Maclays 70/-, welcoming landladies, small second bar; bedrooms, old fishing village, cl Tues *(Sue and Andy Waters)*

STONEHAVEN [NO8785]

Ship [Shore Head]: Great spot overlooking pretty harbour with plenty going on, simply furnished bar, smarter back dining area, good generous reasonably priced food lunchtimes and all day wknds, well kept Bass and Timothy Taylors Landlord, friendly service, games in side room; children in lounge and restaurant, tables outside *(David and Julie Glover, Mark Walker)*

KINROSS-SHIRE
KINNESSWOOD [NO1702]

Lomond [A911 Glenrothes—Milnathort, not far from M90 junctions 7/8]: Enjoyable fresh food from sandwiches up in bar and restaurant of well appointed and friendly small inn with lovely sunset views over Loch Leven, well kept real ales, decent wines, cheerful helpful staff, log fire; 12 comfortable bedrooms *(Peter F Marshall)*

WESTER BALGEDIE [NO1604]

Balgedie Toll: Attractive old-fashioned décor with lots of wood, interesting food inc starters that do as light dishes, a changing real ale such as Harviestoun Bitter & Twisted; shame about the piped local radio *(Pat and Stewart Gordon, Nick Holding)*

KIRKCUDBRIGHTSHIRE
CASTLE DOUGLAS [NX7662]

Douglas Arms [King St]: Elegant hotel bar, half given over to enjoyable food using local produce at attractive prices, well kept local Sulwath ales, friendly personable staff, pleasant furnishings; good bedrooms *(Pete Yearsley)*

COLVEND [NX8555]

Clonyard House: Attractive small hotel nr Solway coast, said to have enchanted tree; three bar rooms well used by locals, good value food inc particularly enjoyable specials and puddings here and in conservatory, and separate no smoking restaurant, half price for children for most dishes, three-course bargains, decent wines, whiskies and coffee, charming

helpful staff; dogs welcome, bedrooms *(Stan and Hazel Allen, Karen Eliot)*

GATEHOUSE OF FLEET [NX6056]

☆ *Masonic Arms* [Ann St]: Welcoming comfortably refurbished two-room bar, cheerful staff, bustling atmosphere, good choice of reliable generous reasonably priced food served quickly and cheerfully even when busy, well kept Courage Directors; children and dogs welcome, conservatory and garden *(MLR, Stan and Hazel Allen)*

☆ *Murray Arms* [B727 NW of Kirkcudbright]: Pleasantly relaxed inn with wide choice of traditional good value food all day in elegant restaurant and main bar, well kept real ales, lots of malt whiskies, sensible choice of reasonably priced wines, interesting layout with comfortable seating areas inc one with soft easy chairs, friendly attentive service, games in quite separate public bar; children welcome, big comfortable bedrooms *(Maggie and Tony Harwood, Richard J Holloway, LYM)*

HAUGH OF URR [NX8066]

Laurie Arms [B794 N of Dalbeattie]: Warmly welcoming village pub with up to four changing real ales such as Black Sheep, Greene King, Houston and Harviestoun, log fire, enjoyable bar food from sandwiches to good steaks, more adventurous choice in adjacent restaurant with own bar, decent wine; tables outside *(MLR, JWAC)*

KIPPFORD [NX8355]

☆ *Anchor* [off A710 S of Dalbeattie]: Busy waterfront inn in lovely spot overlooking big natural harbour and peaceful hills, red plush banquettes and coal fire in traditional back bar, more plush and stripped stone in no smoking lounge bar, generous usual food from sandwiches up, well kept Theakstons Best with a couple of guest beers, lots of malt whiskies, upstairs summer dining room; piped music, games room with table football and board games, also juke box, TV and machines; children welcome, tables outside, good bedrooms with lovely views, good walks and birdwatching, open all day in summer *(Darly Graton, Graeme Gulibert, LYM, Stan and Hazel Allen, Christine and Malcolm Ingram, JWAC)*

KIRKCUDBRIGHT [NX6850]

Gordon House Hotel [High St]: Wide choice of good reasonably priced food esp fish in comfortable and well decorated bar and restaurant, good beers and wines, welcoming service, log fire; good bedrooms *(Sarah Stokes)*

LANARKSHIRE
GLASGOW [NS5661]

1901 [Pollokshaws Rd]: Pub renamed the year this red sandstone tenement was erected, reworked as bare-boards bar and bistro, with well kept ales such as Atlas Latitude, Black Sheep, Caledonian Deuchars IPA, Houston St

Peters Well and Isle of Arran, Weston's farm cider, enjoyable food, friendly staff, daily papers, lots of old Glasgow prints; open all day *(Richard Lewis)*

Scotia [Stockwell St]: Low beams and panelling, old Glasgow prints, cosy seating around island bar, service friendly even when very busy, low-priced lunchtime food, well kept Caledonian Deuchars IPA; piped music, folk nights; open all day *(Richard Lewis)*

☆ *Bon Accord* [North St]: Welcoming and interesting, fine changing choice of up to 10 well kept scottish and english ales mainly from smaller brewers, good choice of malt whiskies and wines, good value baguettes, baked potatoes and basic hot dishes through the day (perhaps not midweek evenings), daily papers, mixed furnishings from Victorian kitchen to leather sofa, lots of prints and bric-a-brac, traditional games, restaurant; TV with 80s video clips, Weds quiz night; open all day *(Richard Lewis, LYM, Ian Baillie, Nick Holding)*

Clockwork Beer Co [1153 Cathcart Rd]: Comfortable brightly decorated two-level café-bar with microbrewery on view brewing interestingly flavoured beers, also six or more weekly-changing guest beers on tall fount air pressure, excellent range of continental beers, farm cider, dozens of malt whiskies, speciality fruit schnapps, scottish and other country wines, good conventional wines, unusual fruit juices; good reasonably priced food all day, half helpings for children, good vegetarian choice, friendly service, daily papers, spiral stairs to gallery with TV, piano, games tables, books, toys and no smoking area; jazz Tues, disabled facilities and baby-changing, open all day *(Richard Lewis, Nick Holding)*

Crystal Palace [Jamaica St]: Light and airy Wetherspoons in roomy 1850s former warehouse, lovely façade with lots of glass and cast iron, ornate plasterwork, lofty ceiling, inlaid wooden floor, lavish furnishings, small back snug, upper area with long bar, their usual food, well kept beers with bargain prices, friendly staff; open all day *(Richard Lewis, Nick Holding)*

Drum & Monkey [St Vincent St]: Former bank, with good plasterwork and lots of carved mahogany, great atmosphere esp lunchtime with cheap quickly served filling snacks, friendly helpful staff, decent wines *(Nick Holding, Ian Baillie)*

Hogshead [West George St/Dundas St, outside Queen St Stn]: Light and airy two-floor bar with lots of light wood, well kept real ales, friendly staff, no smoking area; nice on warm days, as whole front folds open; open all day *(Richard Lewis, Nick Holding)*

☆ *Horseshoe* [Drury St, nr Central station]: Classic unchanging high-ceilinged pub with enormous island bar, gleaming mahogany and mirrors, snob screens and all sorts of other high Victorian features; friendly jovial staff and atmosphere, well kept Caledonian Deuchars IPA and 80/- and Orkney Red MacGregor, lots of malt whiskies, interesting music-hall era

memorabilia; games machine, piped music; amazingly cheap food in plainer upstairs bar, no smoking restaurant (where children allowed); open all day *(Richard Lewis, Nick Holding, Ian Baillie, LYM, Joe Green)*

Ritz [North St]: Panelling, mirrors, 19th-c plasterwork and cast-iron pillars, leather and other seats, well kept ales such as Caledonian Deuchars IPA and Marstons Pedigree, good choice of wines and coffees, low-priced lunches, daily papers; piped music, silent TV, games machines *(Richard Lewis, Nick Holding)*

State [Holland St]: Handsome oak island servery in high-ceilinged bar with marble pillars, good changing choice of well kept real ales, very cheap enjoyable basic lunchtime food from sandwiches up, friendly staff, armchair among other comfortable seats, coal-effect gas fire in big wooden fireplace, lots of old prints and theatrical posters; piped music, games machine, wknd live music *(Nick Holding, Richard Lewis)*

Three Judges [Dumbarton Rd, opp Byres Rd]: Up to 10 quickly changing real ales from small breweries far and wide (they get through several hundred a year, and will let you sample) in well run open-plan music-free pub with small leather-seat side area, friendly landlady and locals (with their dogs), hundreds of pumpclips on the walls, pork pies, paperback exchange; open all day *(Richard Lewis, R M Corlett)*

Toby Jug [Waterloo St/Hope St]: Bare boards, panelling, barrels and some alcove seating, more tables in slightly raised back area, cask tables in standing part, lots of toby jugs, old Glasgow pictures, good value straightforward lunchtime food, well kept Caledonian Deuchars IPA, Fullers London Pride, Orkney Red MacGregor and Timothy Taylors Landlord, friendly staff, daily papers, shelves of toby jugs; open all day *(Richard Lewis)*

Victoria [Bridgegate]: Comfortably worn in long narrow bar with basic wooden décor, very warm and friendly, plenty of old panelling and wood strip ceiling, lots of musical events posters, well kept Caledonian Deuchars IPA, 80/- and Golden Promise on tall fount from handsome island bar, friendly staff and locals, lounge on left popular with folk musicians, back bar with wonderful historic bottled beer collection; piped music; open all day *(Richard Lewis)*

Waxy O'Connors [West George St]: Fairly irish theme bar (one of a chain), six varied bars on three levels, decent if limited food *(Ian Baillie)*

MIDLOTHIAN
BALERNO [NT1666]

Johnsburn House [Johnsburn Rd]: Lovely old-fashioned beamed bar in 18th-c former mansion with masterpiece 1911 ceiling by Robert Lorimer; well kept interesting changing ales, coal fire, panelled dining lounge with good food inc shellfish and game, more formal evening dining rooms; children welcome, open all day wknds, cl Mon *(the Didler)*

CRAMOND [NT1876]
Cramond Inn [Cramond Glebe Rd (off A90 W of Edinburgh)]: Softly lit little rooms recently nicely refurbished in old-fashioned style, wide range of popular usual food inc some local dishes such as haggis and bashed neeps, two good coal and log fires, friendly service; picturesque waterside village, delightful views from tables out on grass by car park *(Callum and Letitia Smith-Burnett, J F M and M West, Michael and Marion Buchanan, LYM, Jean and Douglas Troup)*

EDINBURGH [NT2574]
☆ *Bennets* [Leven St]: Splendid Victorian bar with wonderfully ornate original glass, mirrors, arcades, panelling and tiles, well kept ales inc Belhaven 70/- and 80/- from tall founts, over a hundred malt whiskies, bar snacks and bargain homely lunchtime hot dishes (children allowed in eating area then), second bar with counter salvaged from old ship; can get smoky; open all day, cl Sun *(Mike Rowan, Nick Holding, LYM, the Didler)*
Berts Bar [William St]: Well done up in traditional style, with well kept Caledonian Deuchars IPA and other ales, good range of tasty straightforward food, long narrow bar, room off with rugby shirt collection *(Callum and Letitia Smith-Burnett, C J Fletcher)*
Caledonian Sample Room [Angle Park Terr/Slateford Rd]: Large simply furnished pub with very long bar counter serving all the Caledonian ales (from the nearby brewery) kept well, also guest beers; welcoming knowledgeable staff, good value food inc popular Andersons pies, thriving atmosphere, rugby and Caledonian Brewery memorabilia; piped music, sports TV – four screens; open all day *(Eric Larkham)*
☆ *Canny Man's* [Morningside Rd]: Great bustling atmosphere, all sorts of interesting bric-a-brac, ceiling papered with sheet music, good bar food inc formidable open sandwiches, huge choice of whiskies, well kept scottish beer, cheap children's drinks, very friendly staff *(Marianne and Peter Stevens)*
Canons Gait [Canongate]: Smart Royal Mile bar with plush booth seating, pleasant atmosphere, attractively priced lunchtime food inc local produce, real ales such as Belhaven St Andrews and Caledonian Deuchars IPA and 80/-, bare-boards basement bar; piped music may obtrude; open all day *(Ian and Nita Cooper)*
Cloisters [Brougham St]: Parsonage turned friendly and interesting alehouse, mixing church pews and gantry recycled from redundant church with bare boards and lots of brewery mirrors; Caledonian Deuchars and 80/-, half a dozen or so interesting guest beers, friendly atmosphere, food till 3 (4 Sat) inc breakfasts and lunchtime toasties; lavatories

down spiral stairs; open all day, folk music Fri/Sat *(the Didler, Eric Larkham)*
Last Drop [Grassmarket]: Bustling friendly pub in old area where public hangings ('the last drop'), took place; lots of atmosphere, decent food till 6.30, well kept beer, good reasonably priced house wine, good service; open all day *(Mark Walker)*
McCowans Brewhouse [Fountainpark, Dundee St]: Part of leisure/entertainment complex on site of former Scottish & Newcastle brewery; brewpub with its own good beers from visible microbrewery (explanatory tours available), the No 3 following the original Youngers recipe without additives, guest beers too, good food, mix of carpet and bare floor, mezzanine (cl on match days) with interesting breweriana inc models and interactive displays; piped music, TV; open all day *(Eric Larkham)*
☆ *Milnes* [Rose St/Hanover St]: Well reworked traditional city pub rambling down to several areas below street level and even in yard; busy old-fashioned bare-boards feel, dark wood furnishings and panelling, cask tables, lots of old photographs and mementoes of poets who used the 'Little Kremlin' room here, wide choice of well kept mostly Scottish Courage beers with unusual guest and bottled ones, open fire, good value lunches inc various pies charged by size; cheerful staff, lively atmosphere, esp evenings *(C J Fletcher, D J and P M Taylor, the Didler, BB)*
☆ *Old Chain Pier* [Trinity Cres, off Starbank Rd]: Attractively restored old pier building jutting right out over the Forth with marvellous water views, bare-boards main room with tables, chairs and a couple of large barrels with high stools, neat and sparkling bar and buffet, no smoking conservatory (children welcome here) and upper gallery with leatherette banquettes; well kept Caledonian Deuchars IPA and two or three guest beers, enjoyable generous varied food; quiet TV, no music; lavatories downstairs *(Joe Green, LYM)*
Oxford [Young St]: Friendly unspoilt pub with two built-in wall settles in tiny bustling front bar, quieter back room, lino floor, well kept Belhaven and scottish guest ales, old-fashioned snacks, lots of interesting characters; lavatories up a few steps *(C J Fletcher)*
Robins Nest [Gilmerton Rd]: Wide choice of generous and enjoyable pub food at very low prices; friendly staff *(Mrs J Matthews)*
☆ *Standing Order* [George St]: Former bank in three elegant Georgian houses, grandly converted by Wetherspoons, imposing columns, enormous main room with elaborate colourful high ceiling, lots of tables, smaller side booths, other rooms inc two no smoking rooms with floor-to-ceiling bookshelves, comfortable green sofa and chairs, Adam fireplace and portraits; civilised atmosphere, friendly helpful staff, good value food (inc Sun evening), coffee and pastries, real ales inc interesting guest beers from very long counter; wknd live music, extremely popular Sat night; disabled facilities, open all day *(Doug*

Christian, Simon and Amanda Southwell, BB, Christine and Neil Townend, Joe Green)

Thomsons [Morrison St]: Carefully and sensitively refurbished, with fine woodwork, interesting glass and bar fittings, eight well kept beers inc some not often seen here, lunchtime food; open all day, cl Sun *(Eric Larkham, C J Fletcher)*

MUSSELBURGH [NT3472]

Volunteer Arms [N High St; aka Staggs]: Same family since 1858, unspoilt busy bar, dark panelling, old brewery mirrors, great gantry with ancient casks, Caledonian Deuchars IPA, 60/- and 80/- and wknd guest beers; open all day (not Tues/Weds, cl Sun) *(the Didler, Joe Green)*

MORAYSHIRE
FINDHORN [NJ0464]

☆ *Kimberley*: Unpretentious wood-floored seaside pub with good generous food inc particularly good fresh seafood, friendly staff, weekly changing guest beers, loads of whiskies, jovial company, log fire, no smoking eating areas; children and dogs welcome, heated terrace tables looking out to sea *(Gwyneth and Salvo Spadaro-Dutturi, Lizzie and Neil)*

NAIRNSHIRE
CAWDOR [NH8450]

☆ *Cawdor Tavern* [just off B9090]: Elegant panelled lounge, nice features in public bar, good lunchtime bar food from sandwiches to seasonally changing hot food with local influences, more restauranty in evening with some stylish upmarket cooking and partly no smoking restaurant, great choice of malt whiskies, well kept Tomintoul Stag and a changing scottish guest beer, efficient hospitable service; pub games, also piped music and TV; children in eating areas, dogs allowed in bar, tables on attractive front terrace, open all day wknds and summer *(Dr D G Twyman, LYM, Mrs J Ekins-Daukes, Mary and David Richards, Sherrie Glass, Paul and Penny Rampton)*

PEEBLESSHIRE
PEEBLES [NT2440]

Neidpath [Old Town]: Typical scottish public bar with pool, darts and nostalgic juke box, Caledonian Deuchars IPA and a guest such as Orkney Dark Island, musical instruments above bar, various toasties, comfortable back saloon with lots of books; Thurs folk club, garden *(Martin Grosberg)*

Park Hotel [Innerleithen Rd]: Hotel not pub, but does good bar meals; bedrooms *(Olive and Ray Hebson)*

Tontine [High St]: Early 19th-c hotel, cosy bar tastefully decorated in muted pinks and blues, attractive stained-glass panels and warm coal fire, wide choice of good bar food, relaxing atmosphere, obliging staff, elegant Adam ballroom now serving as restaurant; tables in cobbled coachyard, bedrooms *(Susan and John Douglas)*

PERTHSHIRE
BRIG O' TURK [NN5306]

☆ *Byre* [A821 Callander—Trossachs, just outside village]: Beautifully placed high-raftered byre conversion reopened in 2002 under former landlady, good interesting cooking, sensible-sized rather than over-large helpings, welcoming service *(LYM, Rosemary and Tom Hall)*

DUNNING [NO0114]

Kirkstyle [B9141, off A9 S of Perth; Kirkstyle Sq]: Olde-worlde streamside pub with log fire in unpretentious bar, good choice of beers and whiskies, friendly efficient staff, good choice of enjoyable home-made food inc interesting dishes, charming back no smoking restaurant with flagstones and stripped stone walls *(Susan and John Douglas, Roy Morrison)*

EAST HAUGH [NN9556]

East Haugh House: Turreted upmarket stone-built country house hotel with very good generous bar food using their own veg and fish and game caught or shot by the chef/landlord, charming fishing-theme small bar with log fire, navy and cream décor and adjoining conservatory, board games, set-price evening restaurant; attractive bedrooms *(Susan and John Douglas)*

ERROL [NO2523]

Old Smiddy [The Cross, High St (B958 E of Perth)]: Attractive compact heavy-beamed bar with assorted old country furniture, farm and smithy tools inc massive bellows, good home cooking using fresh local ingredients and some imagination, well kept Belhaven, lots of country wines, decent coffee, friendly attentive service; pleasant village setting, open all day Sun, cl Mon/Tues lunchtime *(Susan and John Douglas, Callum and Letitia Smith-Burnett, Dave Braisted)*

GLENDEVON [NN9904]

☆ *Tormaukin* [A823]: Plenty of atmosphere in plush softly lit bar with stripped stone, panelling and log fires, Harviestoun Bitter & Twisted, Timothy Taylors Landlord and two guest beers, decent wines, large plainer dining extensions with enjoyable food (all day Sun) inc interesting dishes and good puddings; popular with and well placed for golfers, may be gentle piped music; children and dogs welcome, comfortable if not cheap bedrooms, good walks nearby *(Filip Lemmens, LYM, Jim Bush, Mary and David Richards, O K Smyth, Nick Holding)*

INCHTURE [NO2828]

Inchture Hotel [just off A90 Perth—Dundee by new junction]: Comfortable, airy and elegant lounge bar with big log fire, spacious conservatory restaurant, public bar in separate building *(Susan and John Douglas)*

KILMAHOG [NN6008]

☆ *Lade* [A84 just NW of Callander, by A821

junction]: Proper pub with several small separate areas, beams, panelling, stripped stone and Highland prints, cheerful service, well kept changing ales such as Broughton Greenmantle, Caledonian 80/- and Isle of Skye Red Cuillin, good range of wines by the glass, wide range of food from lunchtime sandwiches to more ambitious restaurant dishes, no smoking room opening on to terrace and pleasant garden with three fish ponds; children in eating area and family room, open all day wknds *(LYM, Jim Bush)*

LOCH TUMMEL [NN8160]

☆ *Loch Tummel Inn* [B8019 4 miles E of Tummel Bridge]: Lochside former coaching inn with great views over water to Schiehallion, lots of local wildlife, big woodburner in cosy partly stripped stone bar with antlers and fishing tackle, gingham-covered tables, well kept local Moulin ales, good choice of wines and whiskies, good food inc home-smoked salmon, welcoming service, no music or machines; attractive bedrooms with log fires, even an open fire in one bathroom, good breakfast, fishing free for residents *(LYM, Jane Holden, Kevin Fagan)*

PITLOCHRY [NN9163]

☆ *Killiecrankie Hotel* [Killiecrankie, off A9 N]: Splendidly placed country hotel with extensive peaceful grounds and dramatic views, attractive panelled bar (may have piped music), airy conservatory extension, food here and in rather formal restaurant, extensive wine list; all no smoking exc bar; children in bar eating area, bedrooms, open all day in summer *(M Whitfield, Sherrie Glass, Hugh A MacLean, Joan and Tony Walker, LYM)*
Old Mill [Mill Lane]: Comfortable and very popular dining stop with enjoyable food inc good venison sausages, Caledonian real ales, draught continental beers, good wine choice, great range of malt whiskies; tables out in courtyard by Moulin Burn *(Dave Braisted, Mike)*

ST FILLANS [NN6924]

☆ *Four Seasons*: Hotel with fabulous views down Loch Earn, welcoming and enthusiastic local landlord and polite cheerful staff, good imaginative food using fresh local ingredients in airy and colourful Tarken Room informal bar/bistro and more formal Meall Reamhar restaurant, flexible cooking (anything to order), nice wines; comfortable well equipped bedrooms, lovely walks *(Mrs Shena McLelland, Robert Stewart Plante-Genet, Alicia McGruer, O K Smyth)*

RENFREWSHIRE
LOCHWINNOCH [NS3558]

Brown Bull [Main St]: Traditional village inn restored with restraint, stripped stone, beams and pews, welcoming landlord, fine range of whiskies and well kept ales such as Belhaven IPA, Caledonian Deuchars IPA, and Auld Simon brewed for the pub, wholesome bar

food, friendly local feel, wknd restaurant; beautiful countryside, nr Castle Semple RSPB reserve *(Angus Lyon)*

PAISLEY [NS4864]

Gabriels [Gauze St]: Comfortable, friendly and cosy local, with well kept Belhaven St Andrews, Harviestoun Schiehallion and Bitter & Twisted and Houston Texas from oval bar, decent food in raised dining area, lots of old signs; children welcome, TV, Sat live music, Tues quiz night *(Richard Lewis)*
Last Post [County Sq]: Fine Wetherspoons conversion of red sandstone former post office epitomising Paisley's heyday a century ago: fine carved woodwork, balcony tables, half a dozen well kept low-priced real ales, comfortable atmosphere with no smoking end; disabled access *(Richard Lewis, Nick Holding)*
Wee Howff [High St]: Small open-plan black-beamed local with comfortable back eating area, well kept beers such as Caledonian Deuchars IPA, Houston Texas and Ind Coope Burton, friendly landlord; well reproduced piped music, games machine, silent TV *(Richard Lewis)*

UPLAWMOOR [NS4355]

Uplawmoor [A736 (Neilston Rd) SW of Neilston]: Comfortable village-inn atmosphere, friendly staff and owners, good well priced bar food using local ingredients, good stock of whiskies, two well kept changing ales, separate cocktail bar and attractive restaurant; tables out on terrace, 14 bedrooms, open all day *(Graham and Lynn Mason)*

ROSS-SHIRE
DORNIE [NG8826]

Dornie Hotel [Francis St]: Friendly and lively locals' bar with McEwans 80/- and good value bar food, attentive staff, pleasant restaurant specialising in good sensibly priced local fish and seafood; simple good value bedrooms, very handy for Eilean Donan castle *(Lesley Bass, Maurice and Gill McMahon, Di and Mike Gillam)*

GAIRLOCH [NG8077]

☆ *Old Inn* [just off A832/B8021]: Well renovated 18th-c inn in nice spot, attractive pictures in comfortable and softly lit two-room lounge, at least four or five well kept interesting changing real ales (the friendly landlord is an enthusiast), good choice of wines by the glass, popular reasonably priced bar food all day using their own herbs and organic veg, also no smoking bistro and restaurant, games in long cheerful public bar; children and dogs welcome, picnic-sets in charming streamside garden, good beach (and Talisker distillery) nearby, comfortable bedrooms, open all day *(Mike and Lynn Robinson, LYM, Paul and Ursula Randall, Paul and Penny Rampton)*

LOCHCARRON [NG9039]

Rockvilla: Light and comfortable bar in small hotel, loch view, quick friendly service, good choice of food inc sandwiches and some local specialities; bedrooms *(Sarah and Peter Gooderham)*

SHIEL BRIDGE [NG9319]
Kintail Lodge: Good food inc local game, wild salmon and own smokings, also children's helpings, in simple front bar or attractive conservatory restaurant with magnificent loch and mountain view, plenty of malt whiskies, decent wines; good value big bedrooms, bunkhouse *(Dave Braisted)*

TORE [NH6052]
Kilcoy Arms [A9 just N of Inverness]: Cosy bar efficiently run by charming NZ couple, welcoming atmosphere, colourful locals, local Black Isle beers and Glen Ord whisky, good range of other malt whiskies, open fire, dining area with good home cooking strong on seafood, large maps of Scotland; three comfortable bedrooms, own bathrooms *(N McAndrew)*

ULLAPOOL [NH1294]
Morefield Motel [A835 N edge of town]: Cheerful mainly no smoking L-shaped lounge bar with generous food strong on local fish and seafood, well kept changing ales such as Black Isle Red Kite and Orkney Red MacGregor, decent wines and a wide range of malt whiskies and ports; piped music, pool and darts; children welcome, terrace tables, simple bedrooms with enjoyable breakfast, open all day *(LYM, A and B D Craig)*

ROXBURGHSHIRE
KELSO [NT7234]
☆ *Cobbles* [Bowmont St]: Small ornate dining pub with well kept McEwans 70/- and 80/- and John Smiths, decent wines and malt whiskies brought on a tray from end bar, enterprising choice of good value home-made food, small helpings for children, very courteous quick service, wall banquettes, some panelling, no smoking room with cheerful log-effect fire; piped music; children very welcome, disabled facilities *(Keith and Janet Morris, Joe Green, Roy and Lindsey Fentiman, David and Heather Stephenson, Mrs M Granville-Edge)*
☆ *Queens Head* [Bridge St (A699)]: Comfortable Georgian coaching inn with roomy refurbished back lounge, unpretentious front bar with lively local feel, wide choice of popular and good value generous home-made food from sandwiches and baked potatoes up, Courage Directors, very good choice of wines by the glass, restaurant, dominoes, pool, fruit machine, TV and juke box; children welcome till 8, good bedrooms, cl Sat evening, open all day Sun *(LYM)*

KIRK YETHOLM [NT8328]
☆ *Border* [The Green]: Welcoming end to 256-mile Pennine Way walk (Pennine Way souvenirs for sale), beams, flagstones, etchings, murals and open fire, pleasant unpretentious atmosphere, friendly management, a well kept

changing ale such as Broughton Greenmantle, wide choice of well cooked generous food in main dining room, small rooms off bar or conservatory; picnic-sets on terrace, good bedrooms *(Keith and Janet Morris)*

TOWN YETHOLM [NT8128]
Plough [High St]: Welcoming unpretentious pub facing green, Greene King Old Speckled Hen and Tetleys, good value food inc very good steaks, nothing too much trouble *(Roy and Lindsey Fentiman)*

SELKIRKSHIRE
MOUNTBENGER [NT3324]
☆ *Gordon Arms* [A708/B709]: Welcoming oasis in these empty moorlands for over 160 years, comfortable public bar with interesting 19th-c letters, poems and photographs, winter fire, well kept Courage Directors, lots of malt whiskies, enjoyable bar food from toasties to local trout and wknd barbecue; children welcome, bedrooms and cheap bunkhouse accommodation, open all day, in winter cl Sun evening and Mon/Tues *(LYM)*

ST MARY'S LOCH [NT2321]
☆ *Tibbie Shiels* [A708 SW of Selkirk]: Down-to-earth inn with interesting literary history (and historic photographs) in wonderful peaceful setting by a beautiful loch, handy for Southern Upland Way and Grey Mares Tail waterfall – quite a few caravans and tents in summer; stone back bar, no smoking lounge bar, homely waitress-served lunchtime bar food inc some local recipes, well kept Belhaven beers, several dozen malt whiskies, traditional games; children welcome, restaurant, open all day (cl Mon/Tues Nov-Mar); bedrooms *(Roy and Lindsey Fentiman, M H Box, LYM)*

STIRLINGSHIRE
BALMAHA [NS4290]
Oak Tree: On Loch Lomond's quiet side, named for the 300-year-old oak cut for its bar counter; enterprising choice of enjoyable food, perhaps a real ale such as Caledonian Deuchars IPA, pleasant tartan décor, restaurant; plenty of tables outside, children welcome, bedrooms, bunkhouse *(Jim and Maggie Cowell)*

BLANEFIELD [NS5279]
Carbeth Inn [A809 Glasgow—Drymen, just S of B821]: Low whitewashed pub with friendly service, enjoyable good value food in lounge and family room, well kept Belhaven 80/-, unusual pine-panelled bar with high fringe of tartan curtains, woodburner or log fires throughout; lots of tables outside, bedrooms, open all day *(Callum and Letitia Smith-Burnett, LYM)*

DRYMEN [NS4788]
Clachan [The Square]: Cottagey pub, licensed since 1734, original fireplace with side salt larder, tables made from former bar tops, former Wee Free pews along one wall,

enjoyable food inc above-average specials in plainer tartan-carpeted lounge with lots of old local photographs, friendly efficient service; piped music, keg beer; on green of attractive village, handy for Loch Lomond and Trossachs *(Callum and Letitia Smith-Burnett, Nick Holding)*

Winnock [The Square]: Big hotel's stripped-stone lounge bar unusual for having four or five well kept real ales; roaring coal fire, friendly staff, decent reasonably priced food, good choice of malt whiskies; ceilidh Sun, big garden with picnic-sets, 48 bedrooms *(Mr and Mrs Maurice Thompson, Brian and Anna Marsden)*

FALKIRK [NS8880]
Behind the Wall [opp Grahamston station]: Brewpub with several interesting guest beers alongside its own Falkirk 400 and a season beer such as Spring Fling, belgian bottled beers, bare-boards and brick top bar with TV in sports-oriented side area, lower bar with decent food in popular eating area, daily papers and large conservatory allowing children *(Richard Lewis)*

MILNGAVIE [NS5573]
West Highland Gate [Main St]: Stylish modern pub with busy Beefeater restaurant, good service and beer range inc Caledonian, comfortable surroundings *(John Knighton)*

STIRLING [NS7993]
Hogshead [Baker St]: Done out in basic alehouse style with stripped wood and mock gaslamps, good choice of well kept ales inc some tapped from the cask, sample trays of four, friendly staff and atmosphere; open all day *(John Watson, Nick Holding)*

THORNHILL [NS6699]
Crown [Main St]: New owners doing well, with enjoyable fresh straightforward food with some more unusual specials at sensible prices, quick efficient service *(Graham Dobson)*

SUTHERLAND
GOLSPIE [NC8300]
Ben Bhraggie [Old Bank Rd (A9)]: Friendly helpful staff, lively public bar, good value food in pleasant conservatory; pipe band practices outside Weds *(Kay Hodge)*

KYLESKU [NC2333]
☆ *Kylesku Hotel* [A894, S side of former ferry crossing]: Useful for this remote NW coast (but in winter open only wknds, just for drinks), rather spartan but pleasant local bar facing the glorious view, with seals and red-throated divers often in sight, friendly helpful staff, short choice of reasonably priced wonderfully fresh local seafood, also sandwiches and soup; three dozen malt whiskies, sea-view restaurant extension, five comfortable and peaceful if basic bedrooms, good breakfast; boatman does good loch trips *(Peter F Marshall)*

ROGART [NC7201]
Pittentrail Inn: Friendly local pub in beautiful Highland crofting valley of River Fleet, deer, eagles and otters nearby, good food such as venison, aberdeen angus beef and cranachan pudding (with oatmeal, whisky and raspberries); over 80 malt whiskies *(Sarah Markham)*

WEST LOTHIAN
QUEENSFERRY [NT1378]
Ferry [High St]: Bustling unpretentious globe-lit bar with well kept beers such as Caledonian Deuchars IPA and Orkney Dark Island, simple snacks; two TVs for sports *(C J Fletcher, Roger and Jenny Huggins)*
Queensferry Arms [High St]: Fine views of both Forth Bridges from the back, enjoyable food inc good chowder and fresh fish; the old street has been well restored, down to the cobbles *(Peter Burton)*
Two Bridges [Newhalls Rd]: No smoking conservatory restaurant giving fine view of the Forth bridges, enjoyable food from sandwiches and baked potatoes to crab and venison, large airy bar, roomy family room, Caledonian Deuchars IPA *(Roger and Jenny Huggins, Nick Holding)*

WIGTOWNSHIRE
CREEBRIDGE [NX4165]
☆ *Creebridge House Hotel* [Minnigaff, just E of Newton Stewart]: Sizeable country house hotel, nice to stay in, with well kept Sulwath Criffel and Cuil Hill and one or two seasonal guest beers, good coffee and comfortably pubby furniture in welcoming and neatly kept carpeted bar, bar billiards, brasserie-style food, no smoking restaurant; unobtrusive piped music; children in eating areas and family room, tables on front terrace by croquet lawn, bedrooms (allowing dogs) *(Darly Graton, Graeme Gulibert, Stan and Hazel Allen, Pat and Derek Roughton, LYM)*

PORTPATRICK [NX0154]
Harbour House [Main St]: Bright and airily spartan modern bar with well kept Houston real ales, good value food, welcoming staff and locals; dogs welcome, cheery Weds winter quiz night; good-sized simple bedrooms overlooking harbour *(Darly Graton, Graeme Gulibert)*

WIGTOWN [NX4355]
Ploughman [Bank St]: Good value food, Courage Directors and pleasant staff, simple café-style surroundings; bedrooms in Wigtown House Hotel, handy for Scotland's book town *(Pete Yearsley)*

SCOTTISH ISLANDS
ARRAN
BRODICK [NS0136]
Brodick Bar [Alma Rd]: Tucked away off seafront, simple refurbished bar and attached restaurant area, remarkably wide choice of enjoyable if not cheap food, friendly attentive service, Isle of Arran and McEwans real ale

(K H Richards, P and D Carpenter, Caroline and Gavin Callow)

BUTE
PORT BANNATYNE [NS0767]
Port Royal [Marine Rd]: Stone-built inn looking across sea to Argyll, reworked with bare boards and timbers to evoke pre-revolution russian tavern (think black and white film versions of *Boris Godunov*), all-day russian food inc good beef stroganoff and chocolate torte, also local fish and seafood, choice of russian vodkas as well as real ales such as Houston and Arran tapped from casks on the bar, Weston's farm cider, cheerful atmosphere, occasional visiting Russian folk musicians; right by beach, deer on golf course behind, four bedrooms *(S V Crooke)*

COLONSAY
SCALASAIG [NR3893]
Isle of Colonsay Hotel: White-walled haven for ramblers and birders, scottish clan décor, enjoyable food with game and venison specialities, real ales at least in summer, lots of malt whiskies; comfortable bedrooms *(Richard Pierce)*

HARRIS
RODEL [NG0483]
Rodel Hotel [A859 at southern tip of South Harris]: Hotel recently comfortabloy refurbished, good bar, enjoyable food and drink; bedrooms *(Jane Taylor, David Dutton)*

ISLAY
BOWMORE [NR3159]
☆ *Harbour Inn* [The Square]: Fine inn with traditional local bar, lovely harbour and sea views from comfortable dining lounge, good food inc local seafood and delicious puddings, good choice of wines and local malts inc attractively priced rare ones, warmly welcoming service; bedrooms *(Alan Cole, Kirstie Bruce, Margaret Marriott)*

LEWIS
STORNOWAY [NB4233]
County [Francis St]: Hotel with locally popular public bar, and one of the few local places where you can get a decent meal and drink on a Sunday; bedrooms *(BB, Jane Taylor, David Dutton)*

NORTH UIST
LANGASS [NF8365]
Langass Lodge [off A867 Lochmaddy—Clachan]: Sporting hotel's relaxing panelled bar open to non-residents, good home-made bar food from sandwiches and other lunchtime snacks to more elaborate evening dishes, all local produce and catches, Isle of Skye Red Cuillin real ale and dozens of malt whiskies; bedrooms, pleasant garden with tables overlooking lochan, RSPB walks to see otters, seals etc *(Michael and Marion Buchanan)*

ORKNEY
TANKERNESS [HY5000]
Quoyburray Inn: Large bar with friendly service and good mix of customers (HQ of local rugby team), enjoyable generous food inc spoots (local razor clams) and more expensive seafood, Orkney bottled beers *(Dave Braisted, Pete Yearsley)*

SKYE
ARDVASAR [NG6303]
☆ *Ardvasar Hotel* [A851 at S of island, nr Armadale pier]: Comfortably modernised white stone inn under hard-working new owner, pleasant staff, lovely sea and mountain views, enjoyable home-made food inc good fish (children welcome in eating areas), prompt service, lots of malt whiskies, well kept beer, two bars and games room; TV, piped music; bedrooms, open all day *(Walter and Susan Rinaldi-Butcher, Richard and Karen Holt, Michael and Marion Buchanan, LYM)*

CARBOST [NG3731]
☆ *Old Inn* [B8009]: Pubby and unpretentious bare-boards bar close to Talisker distillery, friendly staff, simple furnishings, peat fire, darts, pool, cribbage and dominoes, limited bar food; TV, piped traditional music; children welcome, terrace with fine Loch Harport and Cuillin views, sea-view bedrooms in annexe (breakfast for non-residents too if you book the night before), bunkhouse and showers for yachtsmen, open all day, cl afternoons in midwinter *(June and Perry Dann, LYM, Eric Locker, Mike and Kathryn Budd)*

ISLE ORNSAY [NG7012]
☆ *Eilean Iarmain* [off A851 Broadford—Armadale]: Bustling bar as sideline for smart hotel in handsome spot looking out to sea, tantalising choice of vatted (blended) malt whiskies inc its own Te Bheag, bar food from lunchtime sandwiches to steak, open fire; children in eating areas; the hotel side has a charming sea-view restaurant and very comfortable bedrooms *(Maurice and Gill McMahon, Mrs J H S Lang, Walter and Susan Rinaldi-Butcher, LYM)*

UIG [NG3964]
Pier Inn [ferry terminal, A87]: Old pub right on pier, decent reasonably priced food in modern eating extension, Isle of Skye Red Cuillin ale, friendly cream labrador *(Michael and Marion Buchanan)*

SOUTH UIST
ERISKAY [NF7811]
Am Politician [Balla]: Modern bar (only bar on the island) interesting as virtual museum to the sinking of the *Politician* of *Whisky Galore* fame – the boat is still visible at low tide; good quickly served local seafood, original bottles of the salvaged whisky on show – they collect around £1,500 when they come up for sale; pleasant outside table area *(Michael and Marion Buchanan, Jack and Heather Coyle)*

POLLACHAR [NF7514]

☆ *Polochar Inn* [S end of B888]: Comfortably modernised and extended 17th-c shoreside inn in great peaceful spot (though things bound to change with completion of Eriskay causeway), glorious views to Barra and Eriskay, dolphins, porpoises and seals; big public bar with pubby atmosphere, separate dining room, good bar meals running up to aberdeen angus steaks; very helpful friendly staff and locals (all Gaelic speaking); 11 well renovated bedrooms with own bathrooms, good breakfast *(Michael and Marion Buchanan, Jack and Heather Coyle, June and Perry Dann)*

Wales

This year we have been impressed by the large number of pubs here which have made a point of putting good welsh lamb, including light mountain lamb, on their menus; and by the smaller but increasing number which have been highlighting welsh black beef – both tender and tasty. These good trends both look like increasing, with a new body – Huby Cig Cymru – set up specifically to promote welsh red meat. And more generally, many pubs here are making a real effort to track down local sources of fresh ingredients, especially fish, game, cheese, and sometimes rare-bred meats. All this adds interest for anyone searching out good pubs. After a fairly intensive inspection season we have come up with a fair clutch of interesting new main entries: the unpretentious and most appealing Brunant Arms at Caio (good all round, earning our Awards for its food, beer and bedrooms – it was also the cheapest pub we found here for beer), the Pen-y-Bryn looking down on Colwyn Bay (extensive big-windowed foody bar, good drinks too), the White Hart at Llanddarog (fascinating furnishings and things to look at, brewing its own good if not cheap beers), the welcoming and distinctive little Hunters Moon in remote peaceful countryside at Llangattock Lingoed (a nice place to stay, with enjoyable food), the Corn Mill in Llangollen (a stunning riverside conversion of a big watermill, good food, drink and atmosphere), Brickys in Montgomery (top-notch inventive cooking in this simple roadside pub, quite an eye-opener), and the Cross Foxes by the river at Overton Bridge (enjoyable food and drink in an interesting series of attractively furnished rooms). Older stagers which are also on particularly good form these days are the lively Nags Head prettily set at Abercych (generous food, brewing its own good value beer), the waterside Penhelig Arms in Aberdovey (a real favourite, good fresh fish, nice wines, comfortable bedrooms, very friendly staff), the attractively furnished old Ty Gwyn in Betws-y-Coed (a restaurant/hotel licence, but it feels like a pub – friendly, with good food), the Bear in Crickhowell (another great favourite, interesting and attractive, with particularly good food, service and bedrooms), the upmarket Pant-yr-Ochain in Gresford (rather country-house in style, with good food and drink in great variety), the Queens Head near Llandudno Junction (unpretentious and appealing, with consistently good food and nice wines by the glass), the welcoming and idyllically set Harp at Old Radnor (views to the Marches, nice food and bedrooms), and the Nags Head in Usk (the family could hardly be more welcoming, and take great pains to get everything right). As we have said, food is a strong point in many of these top pubs. The one which takes the title of Wales Dining Pub of the Year is the Penhelig Arms in Aberdovey. There are plenty more good discoveries in the Lucky Dip section at the end of the chapter – including over 70 pubs new to it this year. We have divided this section into the major areas, Clwyd, Gwent and so forth – more useful divisions for finding pubs than the new unitary authorities. Pubs which have recently been earning particularly warm praise from readers in this section include the White Lion at Llanelian-yn-Rhos and White Horse at Llangynhafal (Clwyd), Ship in Solva (Dyfed), Raglan Arms at Llandenny, restauranty Walnut Tree at Llandewi Skirrid,

Greyhound at Llantrisant Fawr, Tredegar Arms at Shirenewton and Bell at Skenfrith (Gwent), Grapes at Maentwrog and George III at Penmaenpool (Gwynedd), Prince of Wales at Kenfig (Mid Glamorgan), Farmers Arms at Cwmdu, Griffin at Felinfach and Dragon in Montgomery (Powys), Green Dragon at Llancadle (South Glamorgan), and Joiners Arms in Bishopston (W Glamorgan). Do you agree: are these the best candidates for future promotion to the main entries? Drinks prices in the principality are in general comfortably below the national average; the main local brewers are Brains and Felinfoel, and other local brews to look out for include Tomos Watkins, Swansea (from the Joiners Arms), and Bullmastiff.

ABERCYCH SN2441 Map 6
Nags Head
Off B4332 Cenarth—Boncath

Tucked-away in a little village (and lit by fairy lights in the evening), this picturesque traditional ivy-covered pub is beautifully set next to a river. The dimly lit beamed and flagstoned bar attracts a lively mix of ages and accents, and it's very popular locally. There's a comfortable old sofa in front of the big fireplace, clocks showing the time around the world, stripped wooden tables, a piano, photographs and postcards of locals, and hundreds of bottles of beer displayed around the brick and stone walls – look out for the big stuffed rat. A plainer small room leads down to a couple of big dining areas (one of which is no smoking), and there's another little room behind the bar. Besides the good value beer they brew on the premises (named Old Emrys after one of the regulars), they serve a couple of well kept guests from brewers such as Marstons and Wye Valley; piped music and TV. Popular bar food in huge portions includes soup (£3.25), breaded brie wedges with home-made peach and orange chutney (£3.95), local faggots, chips and mushy peas (£6.50), steak and kidney suet pudding (£7.25), crab salad (£8.75), and rack of lamb with rosemary and redcurrant (£9.95); they do smaller helpings of some dishes (from £4.25), as well as children's meals. Service is pleasant and efficient. Across the peaceful road are tables under cocktail parasols looking over the water, as well as a number of nicely arranged benches, and there's a children's play area; they sometimes have barbecues out here in summer. *(Recommended by R Michael Richards, Malcolm Taylor, Neil and Debbie Cook, Alec and Barbara Jones, David Twitchett, Janice Gillian, John and Enid Morris, Colin Moore)*

Own brew ~ Licensee Steven Jamieson ~ Real ale ~ Bar food (12-2, 6-9) ~ Restaurant ~ (01239) 841200 ~ Children in eating area of bar and restaurant ~ Dogs allowed in bar ~ Open 11.30-3, 6-11.30; 12-10.30 Sun; closed Mon lunchtime

ABERDOVEY SN6296 Map 6
Penhelig Arms 🍴 ♀ 🛏
Opposite Penhelig railway station
Wales Dining Pub of the Year
An excellent all-rounder, this mainly 18th-c hotel is a real favourite with readers. In summer you can sit out by the harbour wall and soak up the lovely views across the Dyfi estuary, while good log fires in the small original beamed bar make it especially cosy in winter. Service is first-class, and there's a good welcoming atmosphere. A highlight is the fresh fish (delivered daily by the local fish merchant), and there are usually around 10 beautifully cooked dishes to choose from such as grilled mullet fillets with chilli, ginger and garlic (£4.95), grilled plaice with lime butter (£9.75), chargrilled tuna with roast peppers and rouille or baked cod with tomatoes, chorizo and mozzarella (£10.50), and mixed fish and seafood platter (£14). Other interesting dishes from the frequently changing menu (which they serve in the bar and restaurant) might include soup (£2.95), lunchtime sandwiches

(from £2.95), fried pork loin with dijon mustard and lemon sauce (£9.75), chargrilled leg of lamb with roasted red onion, garlic, rosemary and cherry tomatoes (£10.50), with puddings such as mango and white chocolate cheesecake or summer pudding (£3.75), and a good selection of british cheeses (£4.75); they do a two-course lunch (£14.50). An excellent expanding wine list includes around 40 half bottles, with 30 by the glass, and they've Tetleys on handpump, along with two well kept changing guests such as Adnams Broadside and Brains SA on handpump. You can also choose from two dozen malt whiskies, fruit and peppermint teas, and a variety of coffees; dominoes. The separate restaurant is no smoking. There are sea views from the bedrooms (some of which have balconies). *(Recommended by Dr and Mrs P Truelove, John and Brenda Bensted, Barry Smith, S D and J L Cooke, M J Park, Lorraine and Fred Gill, Di and Mike Gillam, DHV, V Brogden, Mrs Sylvia Elcoate, Richard Endacott, B and M Kendall, Mike and Mary Carter, E G Parish; also in the* Good Hotel Guide*)*

Free house ~ Licensees Robert and Sally Hughes ~ Real ale ~ Bar food (12-2, 6-9.30) ~ Restaurant ~ (01654) 767215 ~ Children in eating area of bar and restaurant ~ Dogs welcome ~ Open 11-4, 5.30-11; 11-11 Sat; 12-10.30 Sun; 11-3(4 Sat), 6-11; 12.30-3.30, 6-10.30 Sun in winter; closed 25/26 Dec ~ Bedrooms: £39S/£78B

ABERGORLECH SN5833 Map 6
Black Lion £

B4310 (a pretty road roughly NE of Carmarthen)

Delightfully placed in the beautiful Cothi Valley (lots of good walks nearby), with the Brechfa Forest around it, this welcoming little 17th-c coaching inn has recently been taken over by new licensees. The plain but comfortable and cosy stripped-stone bar is traditionally furnished with plain oak tables and chairs, high-backed black settles facing each other across the flagstones by the gas-effect log fire, and has horsebrasses and copper pans on the black beams, and fresh flowers and paintings by a local artist. The dining extension (candlelit at night) has french windows opening on to an enclosed garden. Reasonably priced bar food includes sandwiches (from £2.75), broccoli and stilton crumble (£5.95), fried local trout or beef and ale pie (£6.50), and 8oz sirloin steak (£8.95), with puddings such as sherry trifle and home-made bread and butter pudding (£2.95); on Sunday you can also get roasts (£5.95, £6.95 for three courses), and in summer they do afternoon teas. Brains Rev James is well kept alongside a guest such as Shepherd Neame Spitfire on handpump; daily papers, sensibly placed darts, cribbage, dominoes, draughts, and piped music. There are lovely views from picnic-sets, wooden seats and benches across the quiet road, and the garden slopes down towards the River Cothi where there's a Roman triple-arched bridge. More reports please. *(Recommended by David Brown, Mrs J Horrocks)*

Free house ~ Licensees Michelle and Guy Richardson ~ Bar food ~ (01558) 685271 ~ Children welcome ~ Dogs welcome ~ Open 12-3, 7-11; 12-(10 Sun)11 Sat; closed Mon exc bank hols, 25 Dec evening, 1 Jan

BEAUMARIS SH6076 Map 6
Olde Bulls Head ♀ 🛏

Castle Street

Both Charles Dickens and Samuel Johnson visited this smartly cosy 15th-c inn, and tucked among the snug alcoves of the old-fashioned rambling low-beamed bar, reminders of the pub's interesting past include a rare 17th-c brass water clock, a bloodthirsty crew of cutlasses, and even the town's oak ducking stool. There are also lots of copper and china jugs, comfortable low-seated settles, leather-cushioned window seats, and a good log fire. Quite a contrast, the popular partly no smoking brasserie behind is lively and contemporary (they don't serve food in the bar); the menu includes enjoyable dishes such as home-made soup (£3.10), sandwiches (from £3.95), cured ham terrine with home-made pineapple and apricot chutney (£4.50), mediterranean vegetable lasagne (£5.95), swedish meatballs with linguini (£6.25), roast rack of lamb with chick pea purée, garlic and mint jus or chargrilled swordfish with pea risotto and vierge (£10.25), with puddings such as toasted coconut tart with mandarin sorbet or candied pineapple parfait with dark rum syrup (from £3.55); vegetables are extra; they also do children's meals (from £3.95), and daily specials. They don't take bookings in here, but do for a smart no smoking restaurant upstairs. You'll find 10 wines by the glass, and Bass and Worthington Best are well kept alongside a guest such as Coors Hancocks HB on handpump; freshly squeezed orange juice. The entrance to the pretty courtyard is closed by the biggest simple-hinged door in Britain. Named after characters in Dickens's novels, the bedrooms are very well equipped. *(Recommended by J Roy Smylie, Michael Butler, David Crook, John and Tania Wood, Jack and Jemima Valiant, Richard Harris, David and Higgs Wood, Alison Hayes, Pete Hanlon; also in the* Good Hotel Guide*)*

Free house ~ Licensee David Robertson ~ Real ale ~ Bar food (12-2, 6-9 – but see above) ~ Restaurant ~ (01248) 810329 ~ Children in brasserie, must be over 7 in restaurant ~ Open 11-11; 12-10.30 Sun; closed 25/26 Dec and 1 Jan ~ Bedrooms: £65S/£92S

Sailors Return

Church Street

More or less open-plan, the bar of this bright and cheerful pub has comfortable richly coloured banquettes, and an open fire in winter. There's a quaint collection of china teapots, and maps of Cheshire (maybe where the sailor sailed?) among the old prints and naval memorabilia. It's usually full of contented diners of all ages, especially in the evenings (lunchtimes tend to be quieter), and service is helpful and welcoming. Tasty dishes might include soup (£3.20), sandwiches (from £3.45, readers recommend the toasties), baguettes with chips (£4.75), garlic mushrooms (£3.95), battered cod or lasagne (£6.95), scampi or chicken curry (£6.95), gammon steak with egg and pineapple (£8.45), and fillet steak (£11.95), with daily specials such as bangers and mash (£5.25), grilled salmon fillet (£7.25), and rack of lamb (£7.95), with puddings (£3.20); you can book the tables in the no smoking Green Room dining area. Well kept Bass and a guest on handpump; unobtrusive piped music. Parking can be difficult. More reports please. *(Recommended by Michael Butler, Keith and Chris O'Neill)*

Free house ~ Licensee Mrs E Rigby ~ Real ale ~ Bar food ~ Restaurant ~ (01248) 811314 ~ Children in eating area of bar ~ Dogs allowed in bar ~ Open 11-3, 6-11; 12-3, 6-10.30 Sun ~ Bedrooms: £39S/£60S

BERRIEW SJ1801 Map 6
Lion 🛏

B4390; village signposted off A483 Welshpool—Newtown

In a pretty village (and not far from Powis Castle), this black and white country inn is an enjoyable place to come for something to eat. The black-beamed public bar is thoroughly old-fashioned, with a big woodburning stove in its inglenook, sturdy little plush-cushioned settles and copper-topped tables on its lino; the separate carpeted lounge bar, also beamed, has paintings and old brass between the timbers above its red and gold wall banquettes, and an open fire in one stripped stone wall. The attractive black and white photographs on the walls were taken by the landlord, who used to be a professional photographer. Served in the bar or in the separate restaurant, home-made food might include sandwiches (from £3.25, baguettes from £4.50), soup (£3.25), ploughman's or crevettes in garlic butter (£5.25), steak, mushroom and ale pie or mushroom stroganoff (£7.95), salmon fillet with dill and hollandaise sauce (£8.95), delicious duck breast in red wine, orange and ginger casserole (£10.95), and 8oz fillet steak (£12.95), with home-made puddings (£3.95); children's meals (£3.75). On Sunday they do only roast lunches. Friendly, efficient staff serve Worthington Best and a guest from a brewer such as Shepherd Neame on handpump, and they have decent house wines; piped music, TV and dominoes. There's a lively modern sculpture gallery on the far side of the bridge over the River Rhiew rapids. They've recently refurbished the bedrooms. *(Recommended by MDN, Paul and Margaret Baker, Rodney and Norma Stubington)*

Free house ~ Licensees Tim Woodward and Sue Barton ~ Bar food (not Sun evening) ~ Restaurant ~ (01686) 640452 ~ Children welcome away from main bar ~ Dogs allowed in bar and bedrooms ~ Open 12-3.30, 6(6.45 Sat)-11; 12-3.30, 7-10.30 Sun ~ Bedrooms: £55S(£55B)/£70S(£70B)

BETWS-Y-COED SH7956 Map 6
Ty Gwyn ⓦ

A5 just S of bridge to village

Although the terms of the licence are such that you can't just pop in for a drink (you must eat or stay overnight to be served alcohol), this cottagey coaching inn manages to feel like a proper pub. There's a genuinely welcoming atmosphere in the beamed lounge bar, which has an ancient cooking range worked in well at one end, and rugs and comfortable chintz easy chairs on its oak parquet floor. An interesting clutter of unusual old prints and bric-a-brac reflects the owners' interest in antiques – they used to run an antique shop next door; the staff are friendly and obliging. Good food, from an interesting menu, could include home-made soup (£2.95), stuffed quail with red burgundy and game jus (£4.75), mixed vegetable thai curry or lasagne (£6.50), grilled mackerel with apple and mint (£8.95), excellent roast rack of lamb with red onion and peppercorn marmalade (£12.95), grilled bass with crayfish and spinach velouté (£13.95), and specials such as smoked cod, mushroom and stilton bake (£8.95), monkfish stir fry (£11.95), and thai duck (£12.95); they also do sandwiches. Part of the restaurant is no smoking. Tetleys, and maybe a couple of guests such as Brains Reverend James and Hook Norton Old Hooky are well kept on handpump; piped music; high chair and toys available. *(Recommended by Paul Humphreys, Paul A Moore, David Jeffreys, Alison Hayes, Pete Hanlon, Jarrod and Wendy Hopkinson, Keith and Chris O'Neill)*

Free house ~ Licensees Tim and Martin Ratcliffe and Nichola Bradbury ~ Real ale ~ Bar food ~ Restaurant ~ (01690) 710383 ~ Children welcome ~ Open 12-2, 7-11; closed Mon-Weds in Jan ~ Bedrooms: £20(£28S)/£36(£56S)(£80B)

BODFARI SJ0970 Map 6
Dinorben Arms ♀

From A541 in village, follow Tremeirchion 3 signpost

This attractive black and white inn boasts a choice of over 260 malt whiskies (including the full Macallan range and a good few from the Islay distilleries). It's in a splendid setting, clinging to a hillside next to a church near Offa's Dyke. Outside are lots of tables on the prettily landscaped and planted brick-floored terraces, with attractive sheltered corners and charming views, and there's a grassy play area which (like the car park) is neatly sculpted into the slope of the hills. Inside, three neat and welcoming flagstoned rooms open off the central core of the carefully extended building. There are beams hung with tankards and flagons, high shelves of china, old-fashioned settles and other seats, three open fires, and even a glassed-over old well; there's also a light and airy garden room. They've well kept Banks's, Marstons Pedigree and a guest such as Batemans XB on handpump, plenty of good wines (with several classed growth clarets), vintage ports and cognacs, and unusual coffee liqueurs; darts, pool, fruit machine, TV and piped classical music. Straightforward bar food includes chicken, ham and mushroom pie or breaded scampi (£5.25), vegetable tikka masala (£6.95), seafood mornay (£7.95), and lamb chops or rump steak (£8.95); children's meals (£2.95). *(Recommended by KC, Michael Lamm, Mrs Jane Kingsbury, MLR)*

Free house ~ Licensee David Rowlands ~ Real ale ~ Bar food (12-3, 6-10) ~ Restaurant ~ (01745) 710309 ~ Children welcome ~ Open 12-3.30, 6-11; 12-11 weekends

BOSHERSTON SR9694 Map 6

St Govans Country Inn £

Village signed from B4319 S of Pembroke

Quite close to this comfortably modernised inn, there's a many-fingered inlet from
the sea, now fairly land-locked and full of water-lilies in summer, while some way
down the road terrific cliffs plunge to the 5th-c St Govans Chapel which nestles
near their base by the sea. The spacious bar has stone pillars, and a log fire in its
large stone fireplace; the dining area is no smoking. The pub is popular with
walkers and climbers, and there are lots of good climbing photographs; the south
wall of the bar is decorated with murals of local beauty spots painted by the
landlord's son. Well kept Adnams, Fullers London Pride, Ind Coope Burton,
Tetleys and maybe a guest beer on handpump, and about a dozen malt whiskies;
TV, pool (winter only), dominoes, fruit machine, board games and piped music.
Straightforward bar food might include their speciality cawl (£2.35), ploughman's
(£3.95), cod and chips (£4.95), and minted lamb chops (£5.95), with daily specials
such as steak and kidney pie or faggots in onion gravy (£5.25), and tasty
mushroom stroganoff or fish pie (£5.95), with puddings such as lemon meringue
pie (£2.10); children's meals (£2.25). There are picnic-sets on the small front
terrace. *(Recommended by John Robertson, Barbara and Brian Best, Cliff Blakemore,
George Atkinson, P F Dakin)*

*Free house ~ Licensee Warren Heaton ~ Real ale ~ Bar food (not 25 Dec) ~
Restaurant ~ (01646) 661311 ~ Children welcome till 9pm ~ Dogs allowed in bar ~
Open 12-3.30, 6.30-11; 11-4, 6-11.30 Sat; 12-4, 6.30-11 Sun; 12-3, 7-11 in winter ~
Bedrooms: £27.50S(£27.50B)/£50S(£50B)*

CAIO SN6739 Map 6

Brunant Arms 🍽 🍺 🛏

Village signposted off A482 Llanwrda—Lampeter

A really nice find, this unpretentious place, with a pleasant layout, charming
youngish licensees, good interesting food and a fine choice of real ales and other
drinks. Dishes we or readers have particularly enjoyed recently are potato shells
stuffed with herbs and cheese (from £3.95), braised lamb shank (£7.25), succulent
welsh black steaks (from £9.95), duck on risotto with plum and port sauce and
venison steak with cranberry and cumberland sauce (both £10.50); separate parties
of readers have said that both the venison and their roast veal were the best they
have ever eaten. Other food includes sandwiches (from £2.95), ploughman's
(£4.25), cawl (£4.95 – they do several other vegetarian dishes, at £5.95), home
cider-cooked ham and egg (£5.95), beef and rosemary cobbler or shepherd's pie
(£6.50), and specials such as salmon marinated with basil and lemon; they also do a
roast on Sunday, and breakfasts. It's not a place for a hurried meal, as everything is
cooked freshly for you. As you eat in the smallish blue-carpeted lounge bar, where
locals gather for a chatty drink around at the back on the right, the atmosphere is
convivial and relaxed. High-backed winged settles form booths around some tables,
others have studded leather chairs and dining chairs, a good log fire burns in the
stone fireplace under a big mirror (and an array of china on the mantelpiece,
including some interesting egg cups), house plants line the window, and shelves on
the orange-painted walls hold a few books – and more bagatelle boards than we
have ever seen in one place. Given so few tables, it may be best to book. The well
kept real ales on handpump change frequently and interestingly (as shown by the
proliferation of pumpclips); on our inspection visit they consisted of Breconshire
Ramblers Ruin, Corvedale Normans Pride, Worthington 1744, Wye Valley Crwr
Dewi Sant and Youngs. They also have decent house wines and 25cl mini-bottles,
and two farm ciders. Service is friendly and efficient. The separate stripped stone
public bar on the left has darts, board games, pool, fruit machine, juke box, shove-
ha'penny, table skittles, cribbage, dominoes and TV. The lounge leads out into a
small Perspex-roofed verandah with three old-fashioned garden benches, and a
lower terrace has picnic-sets; judging by the amount of use the long hitching rail

gets, this must be on a pony-trekking route. The big church above is the resting place of Welsh wizard Dr John Harries, and the Dolaucothi gold mines are only a mile up the road; there are good walks all around. *(Recommended by M and D Toms, Hilda and Jim Childs, Jack and Jemima Valiant, Anne Morris, Neil and Anita Christopher)*

Free house ~ Licensees Justin and Jane Jacobi ~ Real ale ~ Bar food ~ Restaurant ~ (01558) 650483 ~ Children welcome ~ Dogs allowed in bar ~ Open 12-3, 6-11; 12-11 Sat(10.30 Sun) ~ Bedrooms: £20/£40S(£40B)

CAREW SN0403 Map 6
Carew Inn
A4075, just off A477

A good time to visit this cheerful old inn is in the summer, when there's a marquee in the garden and, on Thursday and Sunday nights in the school holidays, they hold barbecues. Seats in the pretty little flowery front garden look down to the river (where a tidal watermill is open for afternoon summer visits). Also pleasant, the back garden overlooks the imposing ruins of Carew Castle, beyond a remarkable 9th-c celtic cross nearby; there's a wheelchair ramp and it's safely enclosed, with a wendy house, climbing frame, slide and other toys. Inside, the pub is homely and unpretentious; the little panelled public bar and comfortable lounge have old-fashioned settles, scrubbed pine furniture, interesting prints, and decorative china hanging from the beams. The no smoking upstairs dining room has an elegant china cabinet, a mirror over the tiled fireplace, and sturdy chairs around well spaced tables. Well kept real ales such as Brains Rev James, Worthington and perhaps a guest such as Fullers London Pride on handpump; sensibly placed darts, dominoes, cribbage and piped music. There's a welcoming bustling atmosphere, and the landlady is chatty and attentive. Generously served by friendly staff, reasonably priced bar food includes soup (£2.95), lunchtime sandwiches (from £2.95), smoked mackerel pâté (£3.95), goats cheese and red pepper quiche and thai red curry (£6.95), baked cod with a herb crust or chicken in sweet and sour sauce (£9.95), and lamb with rosemary and red wine or sirloin steak (£10.95), with puddings such as chocolate and orange tart or lemon cheesecake (from £3.25); they do children's meals (from £2.95) as well as smaller portions of main meals; on Sunday lunchtime they do only a choice of three roasts (two courses £7.95). They've recently added outdoor heaters, and there's a new outdoor kitchen. *(Recommended by James Morrell, W W Burke, the Didler, John Robertson, Mr and Mrs M Dalby, Jane and Graham Rooth, Michael Butler, Norman and Sarah Keeping)*

Free house ~ Licensee Mandy Hinchliffe ~ Real ale ~ Bar food (12-2.30, 5.30-9.30) ~ Restaurant ~ (01646) 651267 ~ Children in eating area of bar and restaurant ~ Dogs allowed in bar ~ Live music Thurs evening and summer Sun evening ~ Open 11-11; 11.45-10.30 Sun; 11.30-3, 4.30-11weekdays in winter; closed 25 Dec

COLWYN BAY SH8478 Map 6
Pen-y-Bryn ♀
B5113 Llanwrst Road, on S outskirts; when you see the pub turn off into Wentworth Avenue for its car park

Rather different in appearance from most Brunning & Price pubs, this is really a big modern bar, with plenty of space stretching around the long three-sided bar counter. However, the group's trademark qualities are all present: the mix of seating and of well spaced tables in varying sizes, the oriental rugs on pale stripped boards, the careful lighting, the big pot plants and profusion of pictures, the shelves of books and dark green school radiators – and the thoughtful friendly service, interesting food and good drinks choice. The food includes sandwiches (from £2.95), soup (£3.45), welsh cheddar and leek tartlet with home-made chutney (£4.35), roast vegetable and chick pea curry with braised rice (£7.45), an excellent welsh black burger (though it may be a struggle to persuade them to cook this as rare as it deserves, with the health police breathing down everyone's necks these days) or beef and mushroom pie (£7.95), and oriental salmon with stir-fried vegetables and black bean sauce (£8.95), and puddings such as jam roly poly with custard or dark chocolate tart with white chocolate sauce and cherry ice cream (from £3.95). Besides Flowers Original, Fullers London Pride, Greene King IPA and Ruddles and Thwaites on handpump, they have well chosen good value wines, proper coffee and a freshly squeezed orange machine; two coal fires; cribbage, dominoes, and there may be faint piped music. Big windows look down over the town to the sea (with a telescope); outside are sturdy tables and chairs on a side terrace and a lower one, by a lawn with picnic-sets. (*Recommended by Sheelagh Atwill, W K Wood*)

Brunning & Price ~ Managers Graham Arathoon and Graham Price ~ Real ale ~ Bar food (12-9.30(9 Sun)) ~ Restaurant ~ (01492) 533360 ~ Children allowed till 7.30pm ~ Open 11.30-11; 12-10.30 Sun

CRESSWELL QUAY SN0406 Map 6
Cresselly Arms
Village signposted from A4075

With seats out by the water, this traditional creeper-covered local faces the tidal creek of the Cresswell River, and if the tides are right, you can get here by boat. Although the pub seems an interesting throwback to some period early last century, it's very much alive. There's a relaxed and jaunty air in the two simple comfortably unchanging communicating rooms, which have red and black flooring tiles, built-in wall benches, kitchen chairs and plain tables, an open fire in one room, and a working Aga in the other, and a high beam-and-plank ceiling hung with lots of pictorial china. A third red-carpeted room is more conventionally furnished, with red-cushioned mate's chairs around neat tables. Well kept Worthington BB and a winter guest beer are tapped straight from the cask into glass jugs by the landlord, whose presence is a key ingredient of the atmosphere; there's a fruit machine. (*Recommended by the Didler, Pete Baker*)

Free house ~ Licensees Maurice and Janet Cole ~ Real ale ~ No credit cards ~ (01646) 651210 ~ Open 12-3, 5-11; 11-11 Sat; 12-3, 6(7 winter)-10.30 Sun; closed 25 Dec evening

CRICKHOWELL SO2118 Map 6
Bear ★ ⑪ ♀ ◖ ⇔
Brecon Road; A40

Although you'll be made to feel very welcome if you've come to this excellent old coaching inn just for a drink, you'll probably feel you're missing out if you don't have something to eat too, as the food is excellent. Generously served, changing bar food (made using lots of fresh ingredients) could include sandwiches (from £2.50, baguettes from £3.50), soup (£3.50), deep-fried cockles with capers (£5.50), grilled bacon with bubble and squeak (£6.50), home-made faggots in onion gravy (£6.95), diced lamb with cumin and apricots (£7.95), aubergine and gruyère torte with tomato and olive sauce (£8.95), salmon fillet with a ginger and sultana crust, baked in filo pastry with red pepper coulis (£9.95), and very good welsh black steaks (from £12.50), with specials such as cod and prawn pie or fried lambs liver and bacon with mash (£7.95), and rack of welsh lamb with blue cheese and herb stuffing and creamed leeks (£12.95). As well as mouthwatering puddings such as dark chocolate and orange mousse or bread and butter pudding with brown bread ice cream (£3.50), they do home-made ice creams and sorbets (£3.95). Their Sunday lunch is very popular. There's a calmly civilised atmosphere in the comfortably decorated, heavily beamed lounge, which has lots of little plush-seated bentwood armchairs and handsome cushioned antique settles, and a window seat looking down on the market square. Up by the great roaring log fire, a big sofa and leather easy chairs are spread among the rugs on the oak parquet floor; antiques include a fine oak dresser filled with pewter and brass, a longcase clock, and interesting prints. The family bar is partly no smoking; everything is kept spotless, and they've recently redecorated. Well kept Bass, Brains Rev James, Hancocks HB,

Greene King Old Speckled Hen and a guest beer such as Felinfoel Best on handpump, as well as malt whiskies, vintage and late-bottled ports, unusual wines (with about a dozen by the glass) and liqueurs, with some hops tucked in among the bottles; local apple juice too. The pub is superbly run, and service is particularly friendly and efficient. There are lovely window boxes, and you can eat in the garden in summer; disabled lavatories. This is a great place to stay; the back bedrooms (particularly in the quieter block) are the most highly recommended, with three more bedrooms in the pretty cottage at the end of the garden. *(Recommended by David and Nina Pugsley, Alec and Barbara Jones, M G Hart, A S and M E Marriott, Sebastian Leach, David Carr, Mike Rowan, Di and Mike Gillam, Walter and Susan Rinaldi-Butcher, Pamela and Merlyn Horswell, Filip Lemmens, Dr T E Hothersall, Chris Smith, Graham Holden, Julie Lee, Guy Vowles, Dr Phil Putwain, Keith Barker, Colette Annesley-Gamester, Jonathan Harding, David Jeffreys, Cliff Blakemore, Barry Smith, JWAC, R Michael Richards, Mark and Ruth Brock)*

Free house ~ Licensee Judy Hindmarsh ~ Real ale ~ Bar food (12-2, 6-10) ~ Restaurant ~ (01873) 810408 ~ Children in family room and eating area of bar; no under 12s in restaurant ~ Dogs allowed in bar and bedrooms ~ Open 10-3, 6-11; 12-3, 7-10.30 Sun ~ Bedrooms: £55B/£72B

Nantyffin Cider Mill 🍴 ♀ 🍺

1½ miles NW, by junction A40/A479

In an attractive position facing the River Usk, this handsome, very restauranty, pink-washed inn now does a good value two course special (£10, not Friday-Sunday). A smart and civilised place, it's decorated in brasserie style, with a woodburner in a fine broad fireplace, warm grey stonework, cheerful bunches of fresh and dried flowers, and good solid comfortable tables and chairs. The bar at one end of the main open-plan area has Brains Buckleys IPA and two guests such as Tomos Watkins and Wadworths 6X on handpump, as well as thoughtfully chosen new world wines (a few by the glass or half bottle), and they do Pimms in summer, and hot punch and mulled wine in winter; tasty home-made lemonade. The food is excellent, and wherever possible, they use local and organic meat and vegetables – quite a lot comes from a relative's nearby farm. Beautifully presented dishes, from a changing menu, could include chargrilled moroccan lamb terrine with aromatic couscous (£5.25), baked vegetable tart with leeks, gruyère, mushrooms and home-made spiced apple and tomato relish (£10.50), confit of lamb with herb mash and rosemary and garlic sauce (£10.95), grilled lemon sole with parsley and lemon butter (£12.95), and roast duck supreme with fondant potatoes, rosemary, pancetta, olives and a rich duck sauce (£13.95), with daily specials such as sweetcorn and brie fritters (£4.95), roast guinea fowl supreme with a confit leg and caramelised apples (£12.95), and grilled halibut escalope with chargrilled courgettes, artichokes, tomatoes and red pimiento dressing (£14.50), with puddings such as white truffle and cream torte with Tia Maria chocolate sauce (from £4.75); they do children's meals, and it's very popular with families on Sunday lunchtimes. A raftered barn with a big cider press has been converted into quite a striking no smoking restaurant (which they've recently redecorated). The river is on the other side of a fairly busy road, but there are charming views from the tables out on the lawn above the pub's neat car park; a ramp makes disabled access easy. *(Recommended by LM, Pamela and Merlyn Horswell, Sebastian Leach, Mrs B E Gabriel, David Carr, Neil and Debbie Cook, Bernard Stradling, David and Nina Pugsley)*

Free house ~ Licensees Glyn Bridgeman and Sean Gerrard ~ Real ale ~ Bar food (12-2.30, 6.30-10) ~ Restaurant ~ (01873) 810775 ~ Children welcome ~ Dogs allowed in bar ~ Open 12-3, 6(7 Sun)-11; closed Tues, and Sun evening in winter; closed around a week in early Jan

---

Pubs staying open all afternoon at least one day a week are listed at the back of the book.

EAST ABERTHAW ST0367 Map 6
Blue Anchor ★ ◀

B4265

Full of character and charmingly picturesque, this thatched and creeper-covered stone pub has a warren of snug low-beamed rooms, dating back as far as 1380. There are massive stone walls and tiny doorways, and open fires everywhere, including one in an inglenook with antique oak seats built into its stripped stonework. Other seats and tables are worked into a series of chatty little alcoves, and the more open front bar still has an ancient lime-ash floor; the atmosphere is buoyant. Friendly, helpful staff serve six well kept real ales, and besides a changing guest from a brewer such as Tomos Watkin, you'll find Boddingtons, Brains Buckleys Best, Marstons Pedigree, Theakstons Old Peculier, and Wadworths 6X on handpump; fruit machine, darts and trivia machine. As well as lunchtime sandwiches (from £3.50), and filled baked potatoes (from £4.25), enjoyable bar food might include soup (£2.75), home-made chicken liver terrine (£3.75), daily roast (£6.50), lamb and leek casserole or grilled pork chops with stilton (£6.75), breaded plaice with mushy peas (£6.95), and 8oz rump steak (£8.50), with specials such as pork and apple stroganoff or lamb moussaka (£6.75), and baked cod with tomato and herb sauce (£7.50); children's meals (£3.75). It's best to book for their Sunday roast (no bar food then). Rustic seats shelter peacefully among tubs and troughs of flowers outside, with more stone tables on a newer terrace. From here a path leads to the shingly flats of the estuary. The pub can get very full in the evenings and on summer weekends (it's a shame the front seats are right beside the car park). *(Recommended by Ian Phillips, David Jeffreys, David and Nina Pugsley, Janice Gillian, Roy and Lindsey Fentiman, the Didler)*

Free house ~ Licensee Jeremy Coleman ~ Real ale ~ Bar food (12-2, 6-8; not Sat evening, not Sun) ~ Restaurant ~ (01446) 750329 ~ Children welcome ~ Dogs allowed in bar ~ Open 11-11; 12-10.30 Sun

GRESFORD SJ3555 Map 6
Pant-yr-Ochain 🍽 ♀

Off A483 on N edge of Wrexham: at roundabout take A5156 (A534) towards Nantwich, then first left towards the Flash

In its own attractive grounds with a small lake and lovely trees, this well run place almost seems more like a country house than a typical pub. Thoughtfully refurbished (and with a gently upmarket atmosphere), the light and airy rooms are stylishly decorated, with a wide range of interesting prints and bric-a-brac on walls and on shelves, and a good mix of individually chosen country furnishings, including comfortable seats for relaxing as well as more upright ones for eating. There are good open fires, and the big dining area is set out as a library, with books floor to ceiling. Excellent food, from a menu which changes every day, might typically include soup (£3.45), good sandwiches (from £3.95), roasted aubergine and feta pâté with red onion marmalade and crostini (£4.85), pork and rosemary burger with apple sauce (£7.95), morrocan spiced lamb casserole with lemon and almond couscous and coriander oil (£9.95), chicken and shi-itake mushroom lasagne with tomato salsa (£10.25), and tiger prawns with egg linguini, roasted fennel and asparagus sauce (£11.95), with puddings such as profiteroles with chocolate sauce or waffle with chocolate fudge sauce and rum and raisin ice cream (£4.25); arrive early if you want a seat in the conservatory. Along with well kept Boddingtons, Flowers Original and locally brewed Plassey Bitter on handpump, there are a couple of guests such as Timothy Taylors Landlord and Wye Valley Butty Bach; they have a good range of decent wines (strong on up-front new world ones), and more than 60 malt whiskies. Service is friendly and professional; one room is no smoking. *(Recommended by Paul Boot, John and Vivienne Rice, Jack and Jemima Valiant, Mr and Mrs R A Newbury, Maurice and Gill McMahon, Mrs P J Carroll, Chris Flynn, Wendy Jones)*

Brunning & Price ~ Licensee Lynsey Prole ~ Real ale ~ Bar food (12-9.30(9 Sun)) ~ (01978) 853525 ~ Children welcome in eating area of bar till 6pm ~ Open 12-11(10.30 Sun); closed 25 Dec

HALKYN SJ2172 Map 6
Britannia

Britannia Pentre Road, off A55 for Rhosesmor

Open all day, this old farmhouse is handy if you're driving along the North Wales coast. The views are what make it special and on a clear day, from the terrace and the dining room, you can see as far as Liverpool and the Wirral – you may even be able to pick out Blackpool Tower and Beeston Castle. The snug unspoilt lounge bar has some very heavy beams, with horsebrasses, harness, jugs, plates and other bric-a-brac; a games room has darts, pool, dominoes, a fruit machine, TV, juke box and board games. Tasty bar food includes soup (£1.60), sandwiches (from £3.40), creamy garlic mushrooms (£3.25), stuffed roast salmon or roasted vegetable lasagne (£5.95), lamb balti, caribbean casserole or buffalo braised in ale (£6.25), and rump steak (£7.95); children's meals (from £1.95), and they do smaller helpings for children. The restaurant is no smoking. Well kept Lees Bitter and perhaps a seasonal brew on handpump, and they've a choice of coffees. Outside, there are chickens (you can usually buy fresh eggs here), and buffalo. More reports please. *(Recommended by Maurice and Gill McMahon, MLR, Mike and Wendy Proctor, Michael Butler, KC)*

Lees ~ Tenant Keith R Pollitt ~ Real ale ~ Bar food (12-2.30, 6.30-9) ~ Restaurant ~ (01352) 780272 ~ Children in eating area of bar and restaurant ~ Open 11-11; 12-10.30 Sun

HAY-ON-WYE SO2342 Map 6
Kilverts 🛏

Bullring

With a pleasantly relaxed atmosphere, and a nice mix of visitors and locals, this friendly and informal hotel is a great place for a leisurely lunch. The airy high-beamed bar has an understated civilised feel, with some stripped stone walls, *Vanity Fair* caricatures, a couple of standing timbers, candles on well spaced mixed old and new tables, and a pleasant variety of seating. There are tables out in a small front flagstoned courtyard and in a terraced back garden with a pond. In generous portions, enjoyable bar food could include lunchtime filled baguettes or sandwiches (from £2.95), home-made soup (£3.75), various pizzas or deep-fried calamari (from £4.95), salmon and prawn cakes with a crème fraîche and coriander dip (£5.25), gratinata pasta (£6.95), pork provençale sausages and mash with onion and mustard gravy, or beer battered haddock and chips (£8.50), trout fillets glazed with lime and demerara (£8.95), and braised hock of welsh lamb (£12.95); welcoming service. They've an extensive wine list with about a dozen by the glass, as well as three real ales such as Brains Rev James, Hancocks HB and Wye Valley Butty Bach on handpump, farm cider and good coffees; piped music. There's a £5.50 cleaning charge for dogs in bedrooms. This pretty old town is an excellent place for second-hand books. *(Recommended by Bruce Bird, Steve and Liz Tilley, Rona Murdoch, Cliff Blakemore)*

Free house ~ Licensee Colin Thomson ~ Real ale ~ Bar food ~ Restaurant ~ (01497) 821042 ~ Children welcome ~ Dogs allowed in bar and bedrooms ~ Open 9-11(10.30 Sun); closed 25 Dec ~ Bedrooms: £50S/£70S(£80B)

People named as recommenders after the main entries have told us that the pub should be included. But they have not written the report – we have, after anonymous on-the-spot inspection.

Old Black Lion Ⓨ ◧ ⇌

Lion Street

Dating back in part to the 13th century, this civilised, well run inn is near the site of the former town wall (the gate in this part used to be called the Lion Gate). Spotlessly kept, and with a warmly welcoming atmosphere, the comfortable low-beamed bar has crimson and yellow walls, old pine tables, and an original fireplace. The food here is good (if not cheap), and the restaurant menu can be eaten in the bar too. Besides lunchtime sandwiches (£3.95), carefully prepared dishes could include delicious gloucester old spot sausages and mash (£6.95), thai red chicken curry or chicken and ham pie (£8.95), and sirloin steak (£12.50), as well as more elaborate dishes such as confit of duck leg with chilli plum sauce (£6.25), wild mushroom and leek crêpes with cheese sauce (£10.50), wild boar steak with cider and seed mustard sauce (£13.50), and scottish halibut with vegetable ribbons and wild mushroom sauce (£15.50); tempting puddings such as sticky toffee and date pudding or warm chocolate torte with sour cherries (£4.25). The restaurant is no smoking. As well as Old Black Lion (a good beer brewed for them by Wye Valley) on handpump, they serve a changing Wye Valley real ale, and good value wines; service is very friendly and enthusiastic. There are tables out behind on a sheltered terrace. They can arrange pony trekking and golf, as well as trout and salmon fishing on the Wye. *(Recommended by Bruce Bird, Pam and David Bailey, Mike and Linda Hudson, David and Nina Pugsley, M G Hart, Maurice and Gill McMahon)*

Free house ~ Licensee Vanessa King ~ Real ale ~ Bar food (12-2.30, 6.30-9.30) ~ Restaurant ~ (01497) 820841 ~ Children over 5 away from main bar ~ Open 11-11; 12-10.30 Sun; closed 25/26 Dec ~ Bedrooms: £50S(£42.50B)/£85S(£80B)

LITTLE HAVEN SM8512 Map 6
Swan

Point Road; village signposted off B4341 W of Haverfordwest

In one of the prettiest coastal villages in west Wales, this little pub is a nice place to come for a quiet drink. Seats in the bay window, or on the terrace outside, give good views across a broad and sandy hill-sheltered cove to the sea, and it's right on the coastal path (though no dirty boots). The two communicating rooms have quite a cosily intimate feel, comfortable high-backed settles and windsor chairs, a winter open fire in one and a cast-iron woodburning stove in the other, and old prints on walls that are partly stripped back to the original stonework; look out for the huge ashtray. Well kept Brains Rev James, Worthington Best and perhaps a guest such as Timothy Taylors Landlord on handpump, as well as a good range of wines and whiskies from the heavily panelled bar counter; the landlord is friendly. A short choice of lunchtime bar food includes sandwiches (from £2.50), home-made cawl (traditional welsh lamb and vegetable soup £4.25; £4.75 with cheese), garlic mushrooms (£4.95), crab bake (£5.25), chicken korma (£6.50), and smoked salmon or local crab salad (£8.50), with puddings (from £2.75); you need to book if you want to eat in the Victorian-style restaurant. Parking can be a problem in summer, when you may have to use the public car park at the other end of the village; no children. More reports please. *(Recommended by Michael Butler, John and Enid Morris, W W Burke, P R Morley, Mike Pugh, Barry and Verina Jones)*

Celtic Inns ~ Tenants Glyn and Beryl Davies ~ Real ale ~ Bar food (lunchtime only) ~ Restaurant (Thurs-Sat evenings, also Weds evening in summer) ~ No credit cards ~ (01437) 781256 ~ Open 11.30-3, 6.30-11; 12-3, 7-10.30 Sun

---

Bedroom prices normally include full english breakfast, VAT and any inclusive service charge that we know of. Prices before the '/' are for single rooms, after for two people in double or twin (B includes a private bath, S a private shower). If there is no '/', the prices are only for twin or double rooms (as far as we know there are no singles).

LLANBEDR-Y-CENNIN SH7669 Map 6
Olde Bull

Village signposted from B5106

As it's open all day, this neatly kept little 16th-c drovers' inn (now with a new landlady) is a popular stop for walkers. It's perched on the side of a steep hill, and there are splendid views over the Vale of Conwy to the mountains beyond, especially from seats in the attractive herb garden, which has a big wild area with a waterfall and orchard. Inside, some of the massive low beams in the knocked-through rooms were salvaged from a wrecked Spanish Armada ship, and there are also elaborately carved antique settles, a close crowd of striped stools, brassware, photographs, Prussian spiked helmets, and good open fires (one in an inglenook); the atmosphere is relaxing. Well kept Lees Bitter, and a seasonal guest on handpump, and several malt whiskies; darts, dominoes, and chess. Straightforward bar food includes soup (£2.95), sandwiches (from £3, baguettes from £4.20), beef and Guinness pie or home-made lasagne (£5.95), and gammon steak (£6.95), with puddings such as apple and caramel pie (£2.75); children's meals (£3.50). The lavatories are outside. *(Recommended by David and Higgs Wood, John and Tania Wood, Jane and Adrian Tierney-Jones, Bruce Bird, Alison Hayes, Pete Hanlon)*

Lees ~ Tenant Rachel Hughes ~ Real ale ~ Bar food (in winter not Mon, or Sun night) ~ Restaurant ~ (01492) 660508 ~ Children in restaurant ~ Open 12-11(10.30 Sun)

LLANBERIS SH6655 Map 6
Pen-y-Gwryd £ 🛏

Nant Gwynant; at junction of A498 and A4086, ie across mountains from Llanberis – OS Sheet 115 map reference 660558

High in the mountains of Snowdonia, this hospitable old inn has been a great favourite with mountaineers for generations, and the team that first climbed Everest in 1953 used it as a training base, leaving their fading signatures scrawled on the ceiling. Even today, it doubles up as a mountain rescue post. One snug little room in the homely slate-floored log cabin bar has built-in wall benches and sturdy country chairs to let you gaze at the surrounding mountain landscapes – like precipitous Moel-siabod beyond the lake opposite. A smaller room has a collection of illustrious boots from famous climbs, and a cosy panelled smoke room more fascinating climbing mementoes and equipment. There's a sociable atmosphere, and the landlady is chatty and helpful. Alongside well kept Bass, they've home-made lemonade in summer, mulled wine in winter, and sherry from their own solera in Puerto Santa Maria. Home-made lunchtime bar food (you order it from a hatch) from a short menu could include soup (£2.50), quiche (£4.50), chicken liver pâté with home-made bread, vegetable stew or steak, mushroom and ale pie (£5), with home-made puddings such as pear and blueberry crumble (£2.50); they do excellent traditional breakfasts. Residents have their own charmingly furnished, panelled sitting room, a sauna out among the trees in the attractive garden, and a games room (table tennis, darts, pool, bar billiards, table skittles, and shove-ha'penny); the dining room is no smoking, and beware that there's only one sitting for breakfast and for dinner; dogs £2 a night. The hotel even has its own chapel. Please check the opening times in winter. *(Recommended by Prof and Mrs Tony Palmer, Dr Emma Disley, Gill and Tony Morriss, Tim Maddison, Charlotte Stafford, Tom Buhler, Kevin Thorpe, David Jeffreys, Beti Wyn Thomas, R Michael Richards; also in the* Good Hotel Guide*)*

Free house ~ Licensee Jane Pullee ~ Real ale ~ Bar food (lunchtime) ~ Restaurant (evening) ~ No credit cards ~ (01286) 870211 ~ Children welcome ~ Dogs allowed in bar and bedrooms ~ Open 11-11; closed Nov-Dec, Mon-Thurs Jan-Feb ~ Bedrooms: £27/£54(£64S)(£64B)

LLANDDAROG SN5016 Map 6
White Hart ◖

Just off A48 E of Carmarthen, via B4310; aka Yr Hydd Gwyn

It was a cold grey day when we made our inspection visit, so we made a bee-line for the huge crackling log fire. With a glass of the excellent Coles Cwrw Blasus (brewed here using water from their own bore-hole – they also had Carmarthen Dark Ale and Liquorice Stout), and lounging in one of the heavily carved fireside settles, we spent a happy few minutes just looking around. The place is packed with things to see; a lot more of the 17th-c Welsh oak carving, a tall grandfather clock, stained glass, a collection of hats and riding boots, lots of other bric-a-brac, china, brass and copper on walls and dark beams, antique prints, even a suit of armour. There are steps down to the high-raftered dining room, also interestingly furnished. Food from the servery here includes sandwiches (from £3), toasties and baked potatoes (from £3.25), pizza (£4.95), faggots, peas and gravy (£5.25), ploughman's (from £5.50), home-made pie or curry (£6.50), while the wide-ranging restaurant menu (which you can also eat in the bar) includes smoked mackerel (£3.50), salmon in spanish sauce or chicken chasseur (£11.95), roast duck (£13.50), and steaks (from £12); children's meals (from £3.50). There are picnic-sets out on a terrace by the neatly thatched pub – topped off with a thatch hart. Look out for Homer the great dane; table skittles, shove-ha'penny, cribbage, dominoes and piped music. *(Recommended by Mr and Mrs M Dalby, James Morrell, Mike Pugh, Michael and Alison Sandy, David and Nina Pugsley, Ian and Nita Cooper, Emma Kingdon)*

Own brew ~ Licensee Tricia Coles ~ Real ale ~ Bar food (11.30-2, 6.30-10; 12-2, 7-9.30 Sun) ~ Restaurant ~ (01267) 275395 ~ Children in restaurant ~ Open 11.30-3, 6.30-11; 12-3, 7-10.30 Sun; closed 25/26 Dec

LLANDEILO SN6222 Map 6
Castle ◖ £

Rhosmaen Street (A483)

There's a buoyant atmosphere at this unpretentious town pub, and (as you'd expect of the former home of the Tomos Watkin brewery), the beers here are well kept too. Alongside Tomos Watkins Brewery, OSB and Whoosh, they serve changing guests such as Bass, Greene King Old Speckled Hen and Timothy Taylors Landlord. If there's any space left, the little tiled and partly green-painted back bar is perhaps the most interesting room, with friendly locals sat around the edge chatting, and a big fireplace with stuffed animal heads above it. A comfortably worn in carpeted bar at the front has cosier furnishings, and there's also a side area with a sofa, bookshelves, old maps and prints, and a red-painted dining room with fresh flowers on the tables. Popular, reasonably priced bar food could include sandwiches (from £1.80), soup (£1.95), ham and chips (£2.99), cockles and laverbread (£3.50), steak and stout pie, vegetable crumble or cod and chips (£5.45), and puddings such as sticky toffee pudding and home-made cheesecake (from £2.50); children's meals (£2.95).The friendly new licensees plan to develop the courtyard area, and serve afternoon teas and pastries there. *(Recommended by Anne Morris, Chris and Martin Taylor, R T and J C Moggridge, Mike Pugh, the Didler, Jack and Jemima Valiant, Nigel and Olga Wikeley)*

Celtic Inns ~ Managers Nigel and Kay Carpanini ~ Real ale ~ Bar food (12-2.30, 6.30-9) ~ Restaurant ~ (01558) 823446 ~ Children in restaurant and family room ~ Open 11.30(11 Sat)-11; 12-10.30 Sun; closed 25 Dec

---

Please keep sending us reports. We rely on readers for news of new discoveries, and particularly for news of changes – however slight – at the fully described pubs. No stamp needed: The Good Pub Guide, FREEPOST TN1569, Wadhurst, E Sussex TN5 7BR or send your report through our web site: www.goodguides.com

LLANDUDNO JUNCTION SH8180 Map 6
Queens Head 🍴 ♀

Glanwydden; heading towards Llandudno on B5115 from Colwyn Bay, turn left into
Llanrhos Road at roundabout as you enter the Penrhyn Bay speed limit; Glanwydden is
signposted as the first left turn off this

What draws the crowds to this modest-looking village pub is the good food. They
use lots of fresh local produce and the menu changes every week, but well presented
dishes could include soup (£3.30, tasty fish soup £3.75), open sandwiches (from
£4.95), smoked goose breast (£5.25), mediterranean prawns in garlic butter or a
generous seafood platter (£6.95; £13.95 main), home-made lasagne or jamaican
chicken curry (£7.95), roast pork with crackling, apricot and nut stuffing and roast
potatoes or chicken breast wrapped in smoked bacon with bread sauce and gravy
(£8.25), and roast duck breast with mashed potatoes and black cherry and
cinnamon sauce (£10.95); efficient service. Despite the emphasis on dining, locals
do pop in for a drink, and you'll find well kept Ind Coope Burton, Tetleys and a
weekly guest beer on handpump, as well as decent wines with eight by the glass
(including some unusual ones), 20 malt whiskies, and good coffee. The spacious
and comfortably modern lounge bar has brown plush wall banquettes and windsor
chairs around neat black tables, and is partly divided by a white wall of broad
arches and wrought-iron screens. The dining area has a no smoking section, and
there's also a little public bar; unobtrusive piped music. There are some tables out
by the car park. You can now rent the cottage across the road. *(Recommended by KC,
Mike and Wendy Proctor, Kevin Thorpe, Mr and Mrs Colin Roberts, Mrs Phoebe A Kemp,
John Lunt, Trevor and Sylvia Millum, John and Tania Wood)*

*Punch ~ Lease Robert and Sally Cureton ~ Real ale ~ Bar food (12-2.15, 6-9; 12-9
Sun) ~ Restaurant ~ (01492) 546570 ~ Children over 7 in restaurant and eating area
of bar ~ Open 11-3, 6-11(10.30 Mon in winter); 11-10.30 Sun; closed 25 Dec*

LLANFRYNACH SO0725 Map 6
White Swan ♀

Village signposted from B4558, off A40 E of Brecon – take second turn to village, which is
also signed to pub

The secluded back terrace of this pretty dining pub is charming: with plenty of
stone and wood tables and a good choice of sun or shade, it's attractively divided
into sections by low plantings and climbing shrubs, with views out over peaceful
paddocks. Served only at lunchtime, the imaginative bar menu changes regularly, but
could include skilfully prepared dishes such as mediterranean antipasti with
herb ricotta or oriental salad with teriyaki-marinated beef and crispy noodles
(£5.45), tandoori spiced tiger prawns with sweet and sour cucumber and yoghurt
dressing (£6.95), puff pastry tart with roasted onions, peppers, spinach and slow-
roast tomatoes, local sausages or welsh cheese ploughman's (£7.95), and turbot
fillets with provençale vegetables and a rocket pesto crust (£11.95), with puddings
such as three-layer chocolate terrine or champagne and strawberry mousse (£3.95);
one of the chefs brings out the food, and service is pleasantly brisk. There's a
cheerfully buoyant atmosphere in the bar side, which is on the right as you come in
from the back, the original part stripped stone and flagstones, with sturdy oak
tables and nice carver chairs in a polished country-kitchen style, a woodburning
stove, and leather sofas and armchairs in two groups around low tables. This part
opens into an apricot-walled high-ceilinged extension, light and airy, with bare
boards and different sets of chairs around each table. Well kept Brains and
Hancocks HB on handpump, good wines and coffees; piped music. There's also a
sizeable nicely furnished separate restaurant with heavy beams, modern prints on its
stripped stone walls, a big woodburning stove in a huge fireplace, and a no
smoking area. *(Recommended by David Jeffreys, Charles and Pauline Stride, David and
Silvia Smith, Colette Annesley-Gamester, Jonathan Harding)*

Free house ~ Licensee Richard Griffiths ~ Real ale ~ Bar food (lunchtime) ~ Restaurant ~ (01874) 665276 ~ Children welcome ~ Open 12-3, 7-11; 12-2.30, 7-10.30 Sun; closed Mon (exc bank hols) and Tues

LLANGATTOCK LINGOED SO3620 Map 6
Hunters Moon ⇔

You really need a map to find this; best route is narrow lane off B4521 just E of Llanvetherine, or can be reached off A465 N of Abergavenny

Tucked away in a network of narrow winding country lanes on the edge of the Black Mountains, this ancient unpretentious inn is handy for the Offa's Dyke Path. Thoughtfully run by a helpful, chatty landlady, it sees plenty of locals (the winter skittles nights on Wednesdays are lively affairs). Dark stripped stone walls and deeply worn flagstones predate the nearby church; the two small rooms of the beamed bar are divided by a big woodburning stove. A touch of colour is added by one terracotta wall, some copper-topped tables, a few contemporary prints, a couple of brightly painted exotic masks, and some big cartoons (these give a clue to the landlady's background). Good unpretentious country cooking from a changing blackboard might include baguettes (from £3.50), italian tomato soup (£4), ploughman's or local sausage and chips (£6.50), duck and orange pâté with apricot chutney (£6.75), local ham, eggs and chips or garlic green lip mussels (£7.50), with puddings (£4); it's best to book if you want to eat in the restaurant, which serves more elaborate dishes. The inner room is no smoking. Well kept Wye Valley Crwr Dewi Sant is tapped from a cask behind the bar. The big breakfasts are prettily served on Portmeirion china. There are picnic-sets out on two terraces, with more across the lane in a pretty dell among oak and ash trees; look out for the three sleek pub cats Liberty Belle, Chi Kung and Freja. It's a good idea to phone first in winter if you want to eat here, as they may stop serving food earlier. *(Recommended by Mr and Mrs Ivor Thomas, Chris Parsons)*

Free house ~ Licensee Helene Barratt ~ Bar food (12.30-2.15 Weds-Sat; 7-8 Sun evening) ~ Restaurant ~ (01873) 821499 ~ Children in eating area of bar and restaurant ~ Dogs allowed in bar and bedrooms ~ Open 12-3, 6-11; 12-11 Sat; 12-4, 7-11 Sun; closed Mon-Weds lunchtimes and Sun evening in winter ~ Bedrooms: /£45S(£55B)

LLANGEDWYN SJ1924 Map 6
Green Inn

B4396 ¼ mile E of Llangedwyn

Now under new licensees, this country dining pub (handily open all day on the weekends) is prettily set just opposite the village green. Neatly kept inside, it's nicely laid out with various snug alcoves, nooks and crannies, a good mix of furnishings including oak settles and attractively patterned fabrics, and a blazing log fire in winter. Besides well kept Tetleys, they've around four changing guests such as Boddingtons, Greene King Old Speckled Hen, Charles Wells Bombardier, and Wye Valley; also Somerset farm cider in summer, around 30 malt whiskies, and a decent wine list. You'll find darts, dominoes, cribbage, fruit machine, and piped music. Bar food such as soup (£2.75), lunchtime sandwiches (£3.25), ploughman's (£4.25), steak and kidney pie, breaded plaice or chilli con carne (£5.95), and specials such as grilled lemon sole with lemon and lime butter (£7.45), duck breast with red plum gravy (£9.95), and a bargain OAP special (£4); they do children's meals (£3.50), and a Sunday roast (£6.95). There's an evening no smoking restaurant upstairs. As it's on a well used scenic run from the Midlands to the coast, the pub can get busy in summer – and that's when the attractive garden over the road comes into its own, with lots of picnic-sets down towards the river. The pub has some fishing available to customers (a permit for the day is £4). *(Recommended by Derek and Sylvia Stephenson, Maurice and Gill McMahon, E G Parish, Mr and Mrs A Swainson, David and Judith Stewart, John and Tania Wood)*

Free house ~ Licensees Emma Richards and Scott Currie ~ Real ale ~ Bar food (12-2, 6.30-9) ~ Restaurant ~ (01691) 828234 ~ Children welcome ~ Dogs allowed in bar ~ Open 12-3, 6-11; 11-11 Sat; 12-10.30 Sun

LLANGOLLEN SJ2142 Map 6
Corn Mill ♀

Dee Lane, off Castle Street (A539) just S of bridge

This is a remarkable conversion of a big watermill, handsomely refitted inside with several uncluttered levels of new pale pine flooring on stout beams, a striking open stairway with gleaming timber and tensioned steel rails, mainly stripped stone walls, and quite a bit of the old mill machinery, pulleys and so forth. A great waterwheel turns between the building and external decking cantilevered over the River Dee, rushing broadly over rocks here. This terrace, running along the building and beyond, is a big plus, with lots of good teak tables and chairs, and a superb view over the river to the steam railway station and the embankment of the Llangollen Canal (you may see horse-drawn trip barges). Inside, there is a lively bustling chatty feel, with quick service from plenty of neat young staff, good-sized dining tables, big rugs, nicely chosen pictures (many to do with water) and lots of pot plants. The good changing food could include sandwiches (from £3.95), an excellent ploughman's (£6.75), salmon and chive fishcakes with capers and lemon (£7.25), bacon chop with herb mashed potatoes and parsley sauce (£7.95), southern-style fried chicken with baked potato, corn and a blue cheese dip (£9.25), grilled local trout with lemon and herb butter (£9.75), and braised lamb shoulder with herb gravy (£11.95), with puddings such as bara brith bread and butter pudding with apricot sauce (from £4.25). One of the two serving bars, away from the water, has a much more local feel, with pews on dark slate flagstones, daily papers, and regulars on the bar stools; piped music. Well kept Boddingtons, Plassey, Weetwood Best and a couple of guests such as Archers Golden and Wye Valley on handpump, and a good wine choice that includes pudding wines. *(Recommended by Lynda Payton, Sam Samuells, Mrs J Kent, Mrs J A Uthwatt, Mike Schofield)*

Brunning & Price ~ Manager Andrew Barker ~ Real ale ~ Bar food (12-9.30) ~ Restaurant ~ (01978) 869555 ~ Children in eating area of bar ~ Open 12-11(10.30 Sun); closed 25/26 Dec

LLANGYNIDR SO1519 Map 6
Coach & Horses 🛏

Cwm Crawnon Road (B4558 W of Crickhowell)

Especially pretty in summer when it's decked in flowers, this old coaching inn is welcoming to walkers (it's an ideal base for walking the Newport & Brecon Canal), and handily open all day. The spacious open-plan carpeted lounge has small armchairs and comfortable banquettes against the stripped stone walls, and a nice big open fire. Friendly staff serve well kept Bass, Hancocks HB and a guest such as Fullers London Pride on handpump; pool, fruit machine, video game, TV and piped music. Straightforward bar food (though you can also eat from the restaurant menu in the bar) includes sandwiches (from £2.50), soup (£2.95), ploughman's (from £3.95), chilli con carne (£4.95), pork chop or smoked haddock bake (£5.25), and plaice goujons (£6.50), with specials, and puddings (from £3.75); good breakfasts. There's a no smoking area in the restaurant. Across the road on a well fenced lawn there are plenty of tables running down to a lock and moorings. *(Recommended by Steve and Liz Tilley, Pamela and Merlyn Horswell, Revd John E Cooper, Theocsbrian, Charles and Pauline Stride, N H E Lewis, Neville and Anne Morley)*

Free house ~ Licensee Derek Latham ~ Real ale ~ Bar food (12-2, 6.30-9.30) ~ Restaurant ~ (01874) 730245 ~ Children in eating area of bar and restaurant ~ Dogs allowed in bar and bedrooms ~ Open 11-11; 12-10.30 Sun ~ Bedrooms: £22.50(£28.50B)/£40(£50B)

LLWYNDAFYDD SN3755 Map 6
Crown

Coming S from Newquay on A486, both the first two right turns lead eventually to the village; the side roads N from A487 between junctions with B4321 and A486 also come within signpost distance; OS Sheet 145 map reference 371555

By the side of this attractive white painted 18th-c pub, a lane leads down to a cove with caves by National Trust cliffs – lovely at sunset. A pretty tree-sheltered garden has picnic-sets among carefully chosen shrubs and flowers, and on a terrace above a small pond; there's a good play area for children. Inside, the friendly, partly stripped-stone bar has red plush button-back banquettes around its copper-topped tables, and a big woodburning stove; piped music and winter darts. Tasty bar food includes soup (£2.95), garlic mushrooms (£3.85), pizzas (from £6.55), grilled local rainbow trout (£6.65), steak and kidney pie (£6.85), scampi or chicken curry (£6.95), and steaks (from £10.55), with daily specials such as nut roast with onion gravy (£6.95), and cajun pork steak with tomato and red onion salsa or cod fillet with chilli and white wine cream sauce (£8.25); children's meals (from £2.75). On Sunday lunchtimes they do a roast (the choice of other dishes may be limited then). Welcoming staff serve well kept Flowers IPA and Original on handpump along with one or two guests such as Enville and Greene King Abbot, a decent range of wines and malt whiskies, and a good choice of liqueur coffees. More reports please. *(Recommended by John Brightley, Janice Gillian, Liz and Tony Colman)*

Free house ~ Licensee Ian Green ~ Real ale ~ Bar food (12-2, 6-9) ~ Restaurant ~ (01545) 560396 ~ Children in family room ~ Open 12-3, 6-11(10.30 Sun); closed Sun evening Nov-Easter

MOLD SJ2465 Map 6
Glasfryn 🍽 🍷

Raikes Lane, Sychdyn (the old main road N to Northop, now bypassed by and just off the A5119)

Not only is the food at this bistro-style dining pub (a former farmhouse) interesting and well prepared, but there's a great choice of drinks too. Besides a good variety of generous wines by the glass, and around 100 whiskies, they've well kept Boddingtons, Flowers, Plassey Bitter, Timothy Taylors Landlord and a couple of guests such as Greene King Old Speckled Hen and Shepherd Neame Spitfire on handpump. The rooms which open off have plenty of space and nice quiet corners, with an informal and attractive mix of country furnishings, and interesting decorations; there's a pleasantly relaxed chatty atmosphere, and the attentive young staff are helpful and friendly. Outside, sturdy timber tables on a big terrace give superb views to the Clwydian Hills – idyllic on a warm summer's evening. An inviting range of interesting and reasonably priced bar food could include soup (£3.25), sandwiches (from £3.95), minted lamb samosa with mango chutney (£4.35), ploughman's (£6.95), pork and leek sausage with vegetable mash and onion gravy (£7.95), grilled mackerel fillets with peas, bacon, spring onion and herb butter (£8.50), grilled salmon wrapped in bacon with linguini in a shellfish sauce (£9.50), and braised lamb rump with bubble and squeak mash with mustard and onion gravy (£10.95), with puddings such as milk chocolate and coffee torte with dark chocolate and clotted cream (from £3.95). Theatr Clwyd is just over the road. *(Recommended by Chris Flynn, Wendy Jones, Anne and John, Pat and Tony Hinkins, John Lunt)*

Brunning & Price ~ Manager Duncan Lockhead ~ Real ale ~ Bar food (12-9.30) ~ (01352) 750500 ~ Children welcome away from bar till around 6pm ~ Dogs allowed in bar ~ Open 11.30-11(10.30 Sun)

The 🍺 symbol shows pubs which keep their beer unusually well or have a particularly good range.

MONKNASH SS9270 Map 6
Plough & Harrow ◀

Signposted Marcross, Broughton off B4265 St Brides Major—Llantwit Major – turn left at end of Water Street; OS Sheet 170 map reference 920706

This unspoilt and evocative country pub is in a peaceful spot not far from the coast near Nash Point – it's an enjoyable walk from here down to the sea, where you can pick up a fine stretch of the coastal path. Dating back to the early 12th c, the pub was originally part of a monastic grange, and the stone walls are massively thick. The dark but welcoming main bar (which used to be the scriptures room and mortuary) seems hardly changed over the last 70 years – though after all, that's only a short fraction of its long life. There's a log fire in a huge fireplace with a side bread oven large enough to feed a village, as well as a woodburning stove with polished copper hot water pipes. The heavily black-beamed ceiling has ancient ham hooks, there's an intriguing arched doorway to the back, and on the broad flagstones is a comfortably informal mix of furnishings that includes three fine stripped pine settles. The room on the left has lots of Wick rugby club memorabilia (it's their club room); also daily papers, darts, dominoes, and piped music. Around eight well kept real ales on handpump or tapped from the cask might include Shepherd Neame Spitfire, Tomos Watkin OSB, Worthingtons, and Wye Valley Hereford Pale along with frequently changing, often unusual, guest beers from all over Britain – a typical run might be Bath Ales Gem, Banks, Cottage Dorothy Goodbodies Golden and Taylor Gold Leaf; there's also around 250 different bottled beers, and farm cider. Bar food could include soup (£2.95), filled baguettes (from £4.95), faggots and peas, ham, egg and chips, goats cheese tartlet or home-made steak and Guinness pie (£5.95), with puddings such as rhubarb crumble (£3.95). Although it's very quiet on weekday lunchtimes, the pub can get crowded at weekends, when it's popular with families; the lively landlord is chatty and cheerful, and the staff are friendly. There are picnic-sets in the small front garden, which has a boules pitch, and they hold barbecues out here in summer. More reports please. *(Recommended by David Jeffreys, Ian Phillips, David and Nina Pugsley, Boyd Catling, Tom and Ruth Rees, Janice Gillian)*

Free house ~ Licensee Andrew David Davies ~ Real ale ~ Bar food (all day; 12-2, 6-9 in winter) ~ Restaurant ~ (01656) 890209 ~ Children welcome ~ Live music Sun evening ~ Open 12-11(10.30 Sun)

MONTGOMERY SO2296 Map 6
Brickys 🍴 ♀

Chirbury Road (B4386)

From the road this town pub (the Bricklayers Arms until very recently) looks to be an undistinguished local, one you wouldn't think of stopping at – unless you were in the know. The food here is the special thing, a short but interesting choice, using unusually carefully chosen ingredients cooked with real imagination, and served attractively on big plates. On our inspection visit, we had a very filling creamy parsnip soup, a risotto cake in a spicy tomato sauce cut by pitted black olives, some tender venison from a wild herd on a local estate, and crisply delicious pork belly (from a small local breeder of middle whites). They also search out rare lamb breeds for better taste, and make excellent breads. On a typical day, the choice might include lunchtime dishes such as home-made soup (£3.80, with a sandwich £4.95), baguettes (from £4.25), mushrooms stuffed with caerphilly cheese (£6.20), lamb sausages and mash with spicy salsa (£6.25), and ploughman's (£6.95), as well as dishes such as locally smoked duck with raw baby spinach and warm sugared onions (£5.20), slow-baked chicken breast with red pepper sauce (£10.85), braised lamb shank with shallot and gooseberry gravy (£11.45), and bass fillets fried in butter (£13.85), with home-made puddings (they even make their own ice cream) such as pecan pie and chocolate and hazelnut cheesecake (£4.50). The bar has shiny red flooring tiles throughout. On the left an eating area has seven or eight pub tables, dark kitchen chairs, a few modern prints on ragged print walls, and a bookcase strong on guide books. The two prize tables though are on the right, sharing the small plain bar area with two worn easy chairs by a big woodburning stove in the red-painted fireplace, a varnished pew, and one or two bar stools by the little corner serving counter. This has real ales such as Brains Rev James, and Youngs on handpump, and a short but interesting choice of wines, including good ones by the glass, various whiskies and organic cider; piped music. They also have a linen-set restaurant. Service is friendly and quietly helpful. There are picnic-sets out in front. *(Recommended by Andrew Low)*

Free house ~ Licensee Beverly Legge ~ Real ale ~ Bar food ~ Restaurant ~ (01686) 668177 ~ Children in restaurant ~ Open 12-3, 6-11; closed Tues, and 3 weeks end Jan-beginning Feb

OLD RADNOR SO2559 Map 6
Harp 🛏

Village signposted off A44 Kington—New Radnor in Walton

Although it's set in a peaceful village (which consists almost entirely of the inn itself and its neighbour, a 15th-c turreted church), this welcoming pub does get busy. Chatty locals gather in the old-fashioned brownstone public bar, which has high-backed settles, an antique reader's chair and other elderly chairs around a log fire; cribbage, dominoes. The snug slate-floored lounge has a handsome curved antique settle and another log fire in a fine inglenook, and there are lots of local books and guides for residents. Outside, there's plenty of seating – either under the big sycamore tree, or on the side grass, where there's a play area; good views over the Marches. You'll find two well kept real ales on handpump such as Scattor Rock Golden Valley and Six Bells Big Nevs; friendly, helpful service. Fairly simple, reasonably priced bar food might include soup (£3.25), filled baguettes (from £4.95), ploughman's, home-made faggots or pork and herb sausages and mash (£5.95), lasagne or pasta and stilton bake (£6.50), cod and chips (£7.95), chicken wrapped in bacon with stilton sauce (£8.95), and rump steak (£10.50), with puddings such as home-made sticky toffee pudding (£3.25); on busy evenings, they sometimes don't serve food at all, so best to book. One of the pretty bedrooms has a four-poster, and from spring they hope to rent out a cottage too. The church is worth a look for its interesting early organ screen, and there are good nearby walks. Do check the opening times given below; they don't open on weekday lunchtimes. *(Recommended by the Didler, David Jeffreys, Nick and Meriel Cox, Alan and Gill Bull, Nick Holding, Helen Pickering, James Owen)*

Free house ~ Licensees Erfyl Protheroe and Heather Price ~ Real ale ~ Bar food (7-9 weekdays; 12-2, 7-9 weekends; not 25 Dec) ~ Restaurant ~ (01544) 350655 ~ Children away from bar ~ Dogs allowed in bar ~ Open 6(7 winter)-11; 12-3, 6(7 winter)-11(10.30 Sun) Sat; closed Mon exc bank hols ~ Bedrooms: £30S(£30B)/£58S(£58B)

OVERTON BRIDGE SJ3542 Map 6
Cross Foxes ♀

A539 W of Overton, near Erbistock

Leased from Marstons (Wolverhampton & Dudley) by Brunning & Price, this substantial carefully reworked 18th-c coaching inn has several linked but distinct areas, each with its own character, and all having framed pictures in abundance. Throughout is a good mix of individual tables in varying sizes, with big candles at night, grey carpet here, bare boards there, oriental rugs on quarry tiles elsewhere, mixed dining chairs in some places, built-in padded banquettes in others; they have good log fires, and the lighting is carefully thought out. A large blackboard by the entrance shows a wide choice of consistently good food such as soup (£3.45), salmon and haddock fishcake (£3.95), sandwiches (£4.50), stir-fried prawns with crispy vegetables in pitta bread with chips (£5.25), chicken and mushroom pie (£8.50), marinated cajun chicken with potato wedges and sour cream or grilled salmon with rocket and new potato salad (£8.95), lamb noisettes with crushed potatoes and minted redcurrant gravy (£9.60), and 10oz rib-eye steak (£12.95), with puddings such as rich chocolate and orange tart or apple pie (£3.95), and a cheeseboard (£5.95). They have well kept Banks's, Camerons Strongarm, Mansfield Riding and Marstons Pedigree on handpump, a good changing choice of wines by the glass, and good coffee. Service is kind and efficient. The River Dee sweeps past below, and the end room on the left, with big windows all round its yellow walls, gives a great view of it. This is shared by picnic-sets out on a crazy-paved terrace, and a grassy bank spreads down from here, with a swing and slide – all fenced off from the water. *(Recommended by Tim and Jan Dalton, Rita and Keith Pollard)*

Brunning & Price ~ Licensee Jon Astle-Rowe ~ Bar food (12-(9 Sun)9.30; 12-3, 6-9.30(9 Sun) Mon-Thurs in winter) ~ Restaurant ~ (01978) 780380 ~ Children in eating area of bar and restaurant ~ Dogs allowed in bar ~ Open 12-11; 12-10.30 Sun

PEMBROKE FERRY SM9603 Map 6
Ferry Inn
Nestled below A477 toll bridge, N of Pembroke

Appealing set overlooking the Cleddau estuary, this welcoming old sailors' haunt has daily fresh fish specials such as local black sea bream (£8.50), lemon sole (£9.50), and bass (£10.50). Other generous bar food (from a shortish, fairly simple menu) could include chicken liver pâté (£3.95), vegetable korma (£6.95), gammon and pineapple (£7.25), braised lamb shank with mashed potato and red wine and rosemary sauce (£8.50), and duck breast with black cherry sauce and garlic potatoes (£10.95); children's meals (£3.50). There's quite a nautical feel to the pleasantly pubby bar, which has lots of seafaring pictures and memorabilia, a lovely open fire, and good views over the water. In warm weather, it's nice to sit out on the terrace by the water; friendly, cheerful service. They've well kept Bass, Felinfoel Double Dragon and a weekly changing guest such as Shepherd Neame Bishops Finger on handpump, and a decent choice of malt whiskies; fruit machine, unobtrusive piped music. More reports please. *(Recommended by George Atkinson, Charles and Pauline Stride, Mike Pugh, Keith Barker)*

Free house ~ Licensee Colin Williams ~ Real ale ~ Bar food (12-2, 7-10(9 Sun)) ~ Restaurant ~ (01646) 682947 ~ Children welcome ~ Open 11.30-2.45, 6.30(7 Mon)-11; 12-2.45, 7-10.30 Sun; closed 25/26 Dec

PONTYPOOL ST2998 Map 6
Open Hearth ◀
The Wern, Griffithstown; Griffithstown signposted off A4051 S – opposite main works entrance turn up hill, then first right

Gaining a beer award for its fine choice of up to nine real ales, this pleasant local serves Caledonian Deuchars IPA and Greene King Abbott, with around seven weekly changing guests from brewers such as Archers, RCH, Rebellion, Shepherd Neame, Timothy Taylors, Wychwood and Wye Valley. They also have lots of malt whiskies, and a decent choice of wines; TV, cribbage. The comfortably modernised smallish lounge bar has a turkey carpet and big stone fireplace, and a back bar, while seats outside overlook a shallow stretch of the Monmouthshire & Brecon Canal (the ducks out here like being fed); there's an adventure play area in the garden which has shrubs and picnic-sets. A nice choice of home-made bar food could include filled rolls (from £2, baguettes from £2.50), japanese-style king prawns (£4.50), mushroom stroganoff (£5.95), chicken stir fry (£6.75), gammon (£7.50), and sirloin steak (£11.25), with specials such as tuna steak in tomato and basil sauce (£8.50), and kangaroo steak with port and stilton (£12.50), and puddings (£2.50); there's a downstairs no smoking restaurant. *(Recommended by Bruce Bird, Terry and Linda Moseley, Emma Kingdon, Charles and Pauline Stride)*

Enterprise ~ Lease Emma Bennett ~ Real ale ~ Bar food (12-2, 6.30-10) ~ Restaurant ~ (01495) 763752 ~ Children away from main bar ~ Dogs allowed in bar ~ Open 11.30-11; 12-10.30 Sun

PORTHGAIN SM8132 Map 6

Sloop

Off A487 St Davids—Fishguard

A real bonus in summer, the outside terrace of this tremendously popular long, white-painted old pub has plenty of tables overlooking the harbour (with outdoor heaters for cooler weather), and there are good nearby coastal walks. There's plenty to look at inside too, as the walls of the plank-ceilinged bar are hung with quite a bit of interesting seafaring memorabilia from lobster pots and fishing nets, through ships' clocks and lanterns, to relics from wrecks along this stretch of coast. Down a step another room leads round to a decent-sized eating area, with simple wooden chairs and tables, cushioned wall seats, a help-yourself salad counter, and a freezer with ice creams for children. The staff are particularly welcoming, and the atmosphere is relaxed and friendly. Well kept Felinfoel Double Dragon, Flowers Original, Wadworths 6X, and perhaps a changing guest beer such as Brains Rev James on handpump. Rather than having a number for food service, many of the tables are named after a wrecked ship, and good value, enjoyable dishes could include include soup (£3.10), lunchtime sandwiches (from £2, baguettes from £2.40), moules marinière (£4.50), cod and chips (£5.60), home-made steak, kidney and mushroom pie (£6.70), very good crab salad (£9.80), and steaks (£12.95), with changing specials such as mackerel (£7.95), salmon steak (£10.95), and lamb shank (£10.95), with puddings such as chocolate nut brownie (£3.40); one area is no smoking. There's a well segregated games room (used mainly by children) which has a fruit machine, darts, pool, dominoes, Scrabble; also a TV and piped music. It can get very busy here in summer (when they may extend food serving times). *(Recommended by Ian and Deborah Carrington, Mike Pugh, Cliff Blakemore, Michael Butler, Neil and Debbie Cook, Mr and Mrs M Dalby, Giles Francis, George Atkinson, John and Enid Morris, Collin and Julie Taylor, Stephen Archer, Alec and Barbara Jones)*

Free house ~ Licensee Matthew Blakiston ~ Real ale ~ Bar food (12-2.30, 6-9.30, not 25 Dec) ~ Restaurant ~ (01348) 831449 ~ Children in games room till 9pm, and restaurant ~ Open 11-11; 12-4, 5.30-10.30 Sun

PRESTEIGNE SO3265 Map 6

Radnorshire Arms

High Street; B4355 N of centre

Discreet and well worn-in modern furnishings blend in nicely with venerable dark oak panelling, latticed windows, and elegantly moulded black oak beams (some decorated with horsebrasses) at this rambling, timbered old inn. Although it's part of a small chain of hotels, it's full of individuality and old-fashioned charm – a great place for a morning coffee (or afternoon tea). Some of its history was uncovered during renovations which revealed secret passages and priest's holes, with one priest's diary showing he was walled up here for two years. You'll find well kept Cains and a guest such as Adnams Broadside on handpump, and they've several malt whiskies, and local wine. Friendly, pleasant staff serve tasty bar food such as soup (from £2.95), sandwiches (from £3.45), welsh rarebit (£4.45), with mains such as mushroom stroganoff, salmon and broccoli mornay, oriental sweet and sour pork and thai red chicken curry (all £6.95); in summer they do two courses for £6.95. The separate restaurant is no smoking. There are lots of tables on the sheltered flower-bordered lawn, which used to be a bowling green. Our companion volume *The Good Britain Guide* recommends the nearby Judge's Lodging museum. *(Recommended by Pete Yearsley, Derek Carless, Barry Smith, J R Ringrose)*

Free house ~ Licensee Philip Smart ~ Real ale ~ Bar food ~ Restaurant ~ (01544) 267406 ~ Children in eating area of bar and restaurant ~ Dogs allowed in bar and bedrooms ~ Jazz first Sun in month ~ Open 11-11; 12-10.30 Sun ~ Bedrooms: £59S(£59B)/£72.80S(£72.80B)

> It is illegal for bar staff to smoke while handling your drink.

RAGLAN SO3608 Map 6
Clytha Arms (🍴) 🍺 🛏️

Clytha, off Abergavenny road – former A40, now declassified

The interesting food at this comfortable old country inn is very good value considering the quality, and they've an impressive choice of drinks too. Alongside Bass, Brains SA and Hook Norton, they serve three interesting changing guest beers (around 300 different ones a year) from brewers such as Bullmastiff, Dwan and Everards, and they've an extensive wine list with 10 or so by the glass; also Weston's farm cider and a changing guest cider – even home-made perry. You'll usually find a couple of locals in the spotlessly kept bar, which has solidly comfortable furnishings, a couple of good log fires, and a pleasantly relaxed atmosphere; darts, shove-ha'penny, boules, table skittles, cribbage, dominoes, draughts and chess. Very well prepared bar snacks (not Saturday night or Sunday lunch) could include sandwiches (£3.25, open sandwiches from £5.50), soup (£5.25), half a dozen oysters (£5.50), bacon, laverbread and cockles (£5.95), ploughman's (£6.50), wild boar sausages with potato pancakes (£6.95), and crab and avocado salad or wild mushroom omelette with garlic and rosemary potatoes (£7.20), or you can choose from the restaurant menu which includes dishes such as rabbit and shellfish paella or pork tenderloin with roast peppers and mozzarella (£15), and roast quail with strawberries and balsamic vinegar (£16), with a good choice of puddings such as chargrilled pineapple with coconut sorbet or cinnamon and apple cake with honey ice cream (£4.95); they also do a set menu (£15.95 two courses, £17.95 three courses). As well as an english setter, there are two friendly labradors, Beamish and Stowford. Don't miss the murals in the lavatories. The pub stands in its own extensive well cared-for grounds, which are a mass of colour in spring. Readers recommend their beer and cider festivals. *(Recommended by Terry and Linda Moseley, P R Morley, John and Judy Saville, Mike Pugh, JCW, Gwyneth and Salvo Spadaro-Dutturi, the Didler, David and Nina Pugsley)*

Free house ~ Licensees Andrew and Beverley Canning ~ Real ale ~ Bar food (not Sun evening or Mon) ~ Restaurant ~ (01873) 840206 ~ Children welcome ~ Dogs allowed in bar ~ Open 12-3, 6-11; 12-11 Sat; 12-10.30 Sun; closed Mon lunchtime exc bank hols ~ Bedrooms: £50B/£70B

RED WHARF BAY SH5281 Map 6
Ship ♀ 🍺

Village signposted off B5025 N of Pentraeth

This 18th-c inn is old-fashioned and interesting, with lots of nautical bric-a-brac in big welcoming rooms on each side of the busy stone-built bar counter, both with long cushioned varnished pews built around the walls, glossily varnished cast-iron-framed tables, and roaring fires. Outside, tables on the front terrace are ideally placed to enjoy the view which stretches down along 10 square miles of treacherous tidal cockle-sands and sea, with low wooded hills sloping down to the broad bay. Two rooms are no smoking; piped music and dominoes. They have more than 50 malt whiskies, as well as four changing well kept real ales such as Adnams, Ind Coope Burton, Marstons Pedigree and Tetleys Imperial on handpump, and there's a wider choice of wines than is usual for the area (with a decent choice by the glass). Good changing bar food (which includes quite a few seafood dishes) such as lunchtime sandwiches (from £2.95), potted cockles and shrimps in lime and chilli butter (£5.10), dressed local crab with garlic mayonnaise and lemon (£6.50), chargrilled chicken breast with chilli, spring onion and coconut sauce with fragrant rice (£7.95), roasted cod in pancetta with egg tagliatelle and roasted red pepper dressing (£8.95), and braised lamb shank with crushed potatoes and redcurrant gravy (£9.10), with puddings such as sticky toffee pudding with treacle sauce and cream (£3.65); children's meals (from £4.10). You'll need to arrive early for a table on weekends when it can get quite crowded; service may be slow when it's busy (and they may ask to keep your credit card behind the bar). It's been run by the same friendly family for around 30 years. *(Recommended by J Roy Smylie,*

Michael Lamm, W K Wood, Glenwys and Alan Lawrence, Gill and Tony Morriss, John and Tania Wood)

Free house ~ Licensee Andrew Kenneally ~ Real ale ~ Bar food (12-2.30, 5.30(6.30 winter)-9; 12-9 Sun) ~ Restaurant ~ (01248) 852568 ~ Children welcome away from lounge bar ~ Open 11-11; 12-10.30 Sun; 11-3, 6.30-11 weekdays in winter

RHYD-Y-MEIRCH SO2907 Map 6
Goose & Cuckoo ◀

Upper Llanover signposted up narrow track off A4042 S of Abergavenny; after ½ mile take first left, then keep on up (watch for hand-written Goose signs at the forks)

This remote unspoilt hillside pub is basically one small simply furnished room, with a small picture-window extension making the most of the gorgeous view down the valley. Getting here – particularly if you come on foot, as many do – is part of the pleasure, but what makes it special apart from the setting is the warmth of welcome you get from the friendly licensees. They serve well kept Bullmastiff Best and a couple of guests such as Brains Rev James and Breconshire Ramblers Ruin on handpump, and there are more than 75 whiskies, and good coffees. Also daily papers, and a big woodburner in the arched stone fireplace; cribbage, darts, dominoes, draughts, shove-ha'penny, quoits and boules. A fairly short choice of enjoyably simple home-made food includes home-baked rolls (from £1.70), very good hearty 13-bean soup (£2), a variety of ploughman's (£5.50), baked potatoes or lasagne (£5.50), turkey and ham pie, liver and bacon casserole, spaghetti bolognese or chilli con carne (£6), and home-made puddings (£2.50). There is a variety of rather ad hoc picnic-sets out on the gravel below; the licensees keep sheep, geese and chickens. The bedrooms contain two single beds. More reports please. *(Recommended by Guy Vowles)*

Free house ~ Licensees Michael and Carol Langley ~ Real ale ~ Bar food ~ (01873) 880277 ~ Children in eating area of bar ~ Dogs allowed in bar ~ Open 11.30-3, 7-11; 11.30-11 Fri-Sun; closed Mon exc bank hols ~ Bedrooms: £25S/£50S

ROSEBUSH SN0729 Map 6
Tafarn Sinc

B4329 Haverfordwest—Cardigan

Not your stereotypical pub, this big dark maroon-painted corrugated iron shed used to be a railway halt, left behind when this loop of the line closed over 60 years ago. It's been more or less re-created, even down to life-size dummy passengers waiting out on the platform, and the sizeable garden is periodically enlivened by the sounds of steam trains chuffing through – actually broadcast from a replica signal box. Inside it's not exactly elegant, but really interesting, almost a museum of local history. With an appealingly buoyant atmosphere, the bar has plank panelling, an informal mix of chairs and pews, woodburners, and well kept Cwrw Tafarn Sinc (brewed specially for the pub) alongside a weekly changing guest on handpump; the Welsh-speaking staff and locals are welcoming. Straightforward food includes home-made faggots with onion gravy, glamorgan sausages and chutney, breaded plaice or chicken breast (all £7.50), and steaks (from £9.50), with puddings such as rice pudding (£3.50); children's meals (from £3.90). There's a no smoking dining room. *(Recommended by Gwyneth and Salvo Spadaro-Dutturi, the Didler, Rona Murdoch, Jack and Jemima Valiant, Alec and Barbara Jones, David Twitchett)*

Free house ~ Licensee Brian Llewelyn ~ Real ale ~ Bar food ~ Restaurant ~ 01437 532214 ~ Children welcome ~ Open 12-11(10.30 Sun); closed Mon in winter

---

'Children welcome' means the pub says it lets children inside without any special restriction. If it allows them in, but to restricted areas such as an eating area or family room, we specify this. Some pubs may impose an evening time limit.

SAUNDERSFOOT SN1304 Map 6

Royal Oak ♀ ◧

Wogan Terrace (B4316)

Around 10 fresh fish dishes a day are what draw the crowds to this village pub, and it's a good idea to book if you want a table during the holiday season. Dishes could include a pint of prawns (£5.95), beer-battered haddock (£7.95), tuna steak (£11.95), hake (£13.95), and grilled bass (£14.95); there's a good range of sauces, and prices vary, depending on the catch. If you don't like fish, other choices might be lunchtime sandwiches (from £2.95), local pork and garlic sausages or steak and bacon pie (£7.50), oriental chicken and pork spare ribs (£10.75), rack of lamb with garlic, honey and rosemary or 8oz fillet steak (£14.50), with puddings such as coffee and walnut gateaux (£4.25); they do children's meals (from £2.95), and a two-course Sunday lunch (£7.95, three courses £9.95). Service is pleasant and attentive. There's a cheerful atmosphere in the dining area and carpeted no smoking lounge bar, which has captain's chairs and wall banquettes; piped music. Frequented by chatty locals, the small public bar has a TV and dominoes. Around five well kept real ales on handpump include Ansells Royal Oak, Ind Coope Burton, Greene King Abbot and Old Speckled Hen, Worthington, and a guest such as Marstons Pedigree; they've also 30 malt whiskies, and an interesting choice of wines (lots of new world ones), with a dozen by the glass. It's well placed above the harbour, and in summer the outside tables get snapped up quickly (they have overhead heaters for cooler weather). *(Recommended by Michael Butler, the Didler, John Hillmer, Jane Blethyn, Rob Holt, Keith Barker)*

Free house ~ Licensees R J, T L and T S Suter and D J Kirkpatrick ~ Real ale ~ Bar food (12-2.30, 6-9.30; all day weekends) ~ Restaurant ~ (01834) 812546 ~ Children welcome ~ Dogs allowed in bar ~ Open 11-11; 12-10.30 Sun

SHIRENEWTON ST4894 Map 6

Carpenters Arms ◧

Mynydd-bach; B4235 Chepstow—Usk, about ½ mile N

As well as around 50 different whiskies, they serve six real ales at this appealing country pub (which used to be a smithy). With a proper pubby atmosphere, the series of small interconnecting rooms has lots to look at, from chamber-pots and a blacksmith's bellows hanging from the planked ceiling of one lower room, which has an attractive Victorian tiled fireplace, to a collection of chromolithographs of antique royal occasions under another room's pitched ceiling (more chamber-pots here). Furnishings run the gamut too, from one very high-backed ancient settle to pews, kitchen chairs, a nice elm table, several sewing-machine trestle tables and so forth; it's popular with locals (especially for Sunday lunch). Friendly staff serve well kept real ales such as Bass, Batemans XXXB, Flowers IPA, Fullers London Pride, Youngs Special and Wadworths 6X on handpump; shove-ha'penny, cribbage, dominoes, table skittles, backgammon, bar billiards, and piped pop music. The reasonably priced blackboard menu includes tasty dishes such as hearty sandwiches (from £1.80), home-made soup (£2.60), camembert with cranberry jelly (£2.75), beer-battered cod or ham and egg (£5.25), chicken curry (£6.25), and home-made steak and mushroom pie or chicken in leek and stilton sauce (£6.95). In summer, there's an eye-catching array of hanging baskets outside. The pub is handy for Chepstow. *(Recommended by David and Nina Pugsley, S H Godsell, Dennis Jenkin, Tim and Ann Newell, David and Phyllis Chapman)*

Free house ~ Licensee James Bennett ~ Real ale ~ Bar food (not Sun evening) ~ No credit cards ~ (01291) 641231 ~ Children in family room ~ Dogs welcome ~ Open 11-2.30, 6-11; 12-3, 7-10.30 Sun

ST HILARY ST0173 Map 6

Bush

Village signposted from A48 E of Cowbridge

This genuinely old-fashioned 16th-c thatched pub attracts a pleasant mix of locals and visitors. The enjoyable bar food is good value (prices haven't changed since last year) and might include sandwiches (from £1.95), soup (£2.75), laverbread and bacon (£3.75), ploughman's (£3.95), trout fillet grilled with bacon (£4.95), liver and onion gravy (£5.50), lasagne or chicken curry (£5.95), and sirloin steak (£9.95), with daily specials such as salmon fishcakes, local sausages or faggots and peas (£5.95); puddings might include steamed chocolate pudding (£3.50). The locally popular restaurant is no smoking. Comfortable and cosy, the low-beamed lounge bar (no smoking at lunchtimes) has stripped old stone walls, and windsor chairs around copper-topped tables on the carpet, while the public bar has old settles and pews on aged flagstones; darts, TV, shove-ha'penny, cribbage, dominoes, subdued piped music, and a warming log fire. Service is helpful, and there's a friendly atmosphere; reasonable disabled access. Bass, Greene King Old Speckled Hen and a guest such as Hancocks HB are well kept on handpump or tapped from the cask, and there's a range of malt whiskies and a farm cider. There are tables and chairs in front, and more in the back garden. *(Recommended by Roy and Margaret Jones, Andrew McHardy, Ian Phillips, David and Nina Pugsley, David Jeffreys)*

Punch ~ Lease Sylvia Murphy ~ Real ale ~ Bar food (12-2.15, 7-9.30) ~ Restaurant ~ (01446) 772745 ~ Children welcome ~ Open 11.30-11; 12-10.30 Sun; closed 25 Dec evening

TALYLLYN SH7209 Map 6

Tynycornel 🛏

B4405, off A487 S of Dolgellau

Peacefully nestling below high mountains, this comfortably civilised hotel is in a charming position, with Cadair Idris opposite (splendid walks), while behind is Graig Goch. It's a friendly and relaxed place (though not at all pubby), and in summer, the attractively planted side courtyard is a pleasant place for afternoon tea. Inside it's immaculately kept, with deep armchairs and enveloping sofas around the low tables, a central log fire, and big picture windows looking out over the water, as well as big bird prints, local watercolours, and a good range of malt whiskies (the serving bar, with keg beer, is tucked away behind). Enjoyable bar food includes sandwiches (from £2.50, ciabattas £5.95), soup (£2.95), ploughman's (£6.50), thai red vegetable curry, courgette and vegetable loaf with ratatouille or beer-battered cod and chips (£7.95), and steamed salmon fillet with prawn and parsley sauce or lambs liver casserole (£8.50), and daily specials; courteous service from the uniformed staff. There's a no smoking restaurant and conservatory. Guests have the use of a sauna and fishing facilities, and can hire boats on the lake. More reports please. *(Recommended by Diane Bullock, MDN, Rev Michael Vockins, B and M Kendall)*

Free house ~ Licensee Thomas Rowlands ~ Bar food (lunchtime only, not Sun) ~ Restaurant ~ (01654) 782282 ~ Children welcome ~ Dogs allowed in bedrooms ~ Open 11-11; 12-10.30 Sun ~ Bedrooms: £50S/£100B

TINTERN SO5200 Map 6

Cherry Tree ◧

Pub signed up narrow Raglan road off A446, beside Royal George; parking very limited

As we went to press this white-painted late 16th-c stone cottage was about to gain a new lounge bar and restaurant, and they now have bedrooms too. It's in a quiet and attractive spot, yet only half a mile or so from the honey-pot centre of Tintern. The approach is very promising (though disabled access is difficult): a little stone slab bridge over a tiny stream, then an irregular flight of ancient stone steps up a sort of alley into a beamed and lime-washed bar area, which has a plain serving bar in one area and a good open fire in another. Generous good value food, made using lots of fresh local ingredients, might include lunchtimes snacks such as sandwiches (from £2), baked potatoes (from £3.95), gammon, two eggs and chips or wild mushroom omelette (£4.95), and stir-fried salmon and asparagus with egg noodles and bean sprouts (£5.95), while other dishes could include smoked salmon and cream cheese roulades (£3.50), a good choice of vegetarian dishes such as sweet potato and apple casserole or mushroom and mozzarella ravioli with tomato and basil sauce (£6.95), minted lamb chops or chicken breast in tangy lemon sauce (£7.95), and sirloin steak (£9.95). Up on a blackboard, specials could include home-made sausages and parsley potatoes (£4.95), and various curries (£6.95); they do a Sunday roast (£4.50), and children's meals (from £2.50). Well kept Hancocks HB and a couple of guests such as Cottage Golden Arrow and Greene King Old Speckled Hen are tapped from the cask, and they also serve farm cider, and milk shakes; good service (the young licensees are friendly). There are cribbage, darts, cards, dominoes, and piped music; look out for Guinness the dog. There are tables out in a charming garden, and on a green patio. *(Recommended by the Didler, Tim and Ann Newell, LM, Pete Baker, Steve Hardwick, Emma Kingdon, Piotr Chodzko-Zajko)*

Free house ~ Licensees Jill and Steve Pocock ~ Bar food (12-10) ~ Restaurant ~ (01291) 689292 ~ Children in eating area of bar ~ Dogs allowed in bar ~ Open 12-11(10.30 Sun)

TRELLECK SO5005 Map 6
Lion ◗

B4293 6 miles S of Monmouth

They serve interesting authentic hungarian specialities at this smallish stone-built pub, and the landlord's father regularly brings over ingredients direct from Hungary. Over one fireplace a blackboard hung with dried peppers has a choice of dishes such as peppers filled with minced pork and rice with sweet tomato sauce or potato, hungarian sausage and egg baked with sour cream and cheese (£9.25), and fried pork steak with cream cheese and walnuts with leeks, cream and cheese (£11.75). Other generously served food includes baguettes (from £2.75), baked potatoes (from £3.95), roasted chicken or scampi and chips (£5.75), home-made vegetarian hotpot (£7.30), grilled salmon steak (£7.75), and home-made cottage pie or chicken kiev (£8.25); children's meals (from £3). There's a step up to the dining area. The unpretentious open-plan bar has one or two black beams in its low ochre ceiling, a mix of furnishings including some comfortable brocaded wall seats and tub chairs, old red plush dining chairs, a hop-hung window seat and varying-sized tables, and log fires in two fireplaces facing each other. There's a small fish tank in a wall recess, and another bigger one in the lobby by the lavatories. A colourful galaxy of pumpclips in the porch and another on one wall show the splendid range of the quickly changing well kept guest beers; they keep two alongside Bath SPA and Wye Valley Butty Bach, and they're around 30 malt whiskies. There are some picnic-sets out on the grass. The pub is opposite the church, and handy for the standing stones. They now have bedrooms in a nearby cottage. *(Recommended by LM, Guy Vowles, Charles and Pauline Stride)*

Free house ~ Licensees Deborah and Thomas Zsigo ~ Bar food ~ Restaurant ~ (01600) 860322 ~ Children welcome ~ Dogs allowed in bar ~ Open 12-3, 6(7 Mon)-11; 12-3, 6.30-11 Sat; 12-3 Sun; closed Sun evening

TY'N-Y-GROES SH7672 Map 6
Groes ⑪ ♀ ⇌

B5106 N of village

In a charming spot with magnificent views over the Vale of Conwy and the distant mountains, this old dining pub is said to have been the first Welsh pub to be properly licensed – in 1573. In summer it's a pleasure to sit outside in the pretty back garden with its flower-filled hayricks, and there are also some seats on the flower-decked roadside. Inside (past the hot stove in the entrance area), the spotlessly kept homely series of rambling, low-beamed and thick-walled rooms is nicely decorated with antique settles and an old sofa, old clocks, portraits, hats and tins hanging from the walls, and fresh flowers. A fine antique fireback is built into one wall, perhaps originally from the formidable fireplace in the back bar, which houses a collection of stone cats as well as cheerful winter log fires. There's also an airy verdant no smoking conservatory. The food here is good, and well presented dishes might include soup (£2.95, soup and a sandwich £5.95), sandwiches (from £3.25), grilled mushrooms with stilton, garlic and lemon (£5.50), chicken curry with saffron rice or home-made lasagne (£7.50), tasty steak and kidney pot with thyme dumplings (£8.50), poached salmon and grilled plaice with hollandaise sauce (£11.95), and steaks (from £13), with daily specials such as game casserole (£8.50), local lamb steak (£9.75) and bass (£12.50). As well as puddings such as pecan and syrup tart or lemon and ginger sponge (£3.75), they do delicious home-made ice creams, with a few unusual flavours such as ginger, fragrant rose or honey and lemon. Ind Coope Burton and Tetleys are well kept on handpump, and they've a good few malt whiskies, kir, and a fruity Pimms in summer; light classical piped music at lunchtimes (nostalgic light music at other times). The neatly kept, well equipped bedrooms have fine views (some have terraces or balconies) and good showers. The pub has been run by the same landlady for 18 years; good pleasant service. *(Recommended by KC, Maurice and Della Andrew, Mrs Phoebe A Kemp, Dr Phil Putwain, Sarah and Peter Gooderham, J Roy Smylie, Tim and Sue Halstead, Kevin Thorpe, John and Tania Wood, Chris Smith, David and Higgs Wood, Eric Locker, Alison Hayes, Pete Hanlon, Jarrod and Wendy Hopkinson; also in the Good Hotel Guide)*

Free house ~ Licensee Dawn Humphreys ~ Real ale ~ Bar food ~ Restaurant ~ (01492) 650545 ~ Children in family room ~ Dogs allowed in bedrooms ~ Open 12-3, 6.30(6 Sat)-11; 12-3, 6-10.30 Sun ~ Bedrooms: £75B/£90B

USK SO3801 Map 6
Nags Head 🍽 ♀
The Square

It's worth making a special trip to this relaxed old coaching inn, which has been well run by the same genuinely welcoming family for over 35 years. Generously served, well presented bar food could include home-made soup (£3.80), grilled sardines (£5), home-made steak pie or half a roasted chicken (£6.50), vegetable pancakes filled with mushrooms, broccoli and leeks or glamorgan sausages (£7.25), and delicious rabbit pie or scampi (£7.50), with interesting specials including seasonal game dishes (lovely on a cold winter evening) such as pheasant in port, stuffed partridge, wild boar steak in apricot and brandy sauce, or half a guinea fowl in wine and fig sauce (all £13.50); home-made puddings such as treacle and walnut tart or apple pie (from £3.25). You can book tables, some of which may be candlelit at night; nice proper linen napkins. With a chatty, friendly atmosphere, the traditional main bar has lots of well polished tables and chairs packed under its beams, some with farming tools, lanterns or horsebrasses and harness attached, as well as leatherette wall benches, and various sets of sporting prints and local pictures – look out for the original deeds to the pub. Tucked away at the front is an intimate little corner with some african masks, while on the other side of the room a passageway leads to the pub's own busy coffee bar (open between Easter and autumn). Built in the old entrance to the courtyard, it sells snacks, teas, cakes and ice cream, and tables spill out from here on to the front pavement. A simpler room behind the bar has prints for sale, and perhaps a knot of sociable locals. They do 14 wines by the glass (nice glasses), along with well kept Brains SA, Buckleys Best and Rev James on handpump, and 12 malt whiskies; quiet piped music. The centre of Usk is full of pretty hanging baskets and flowers in summer, and the church is well worth a look. *(Recommended by Peter and Audrey Dowsett, Eryl and Keith Dykes, Neville and Anne Morley, Sue and Ken Le Prevost, Mike and Mary Carter, Dr and Mrs C W Thomas, David and Ruth Shillitoe, David and Nina Pugsley, Dr Oscar Puls, Terry and Linda Moseley, Mike Pugh, Barry Smith, Judith and Ken Smith, Bernard Stradling)*

Free house ~ Licensees the Key family ~ Real ale ~ Bar food ~ Restaurant ~ (01291) 672820 ~ Children in eating area of bar and restaurant ~ Dogs allowed in bar ~ Open 10.30-2.30, 5.30-11; 11.30-3, 5.30-10.30 Sun

Lucky Dip

Besides the fully inspected pubs, you might like to try these Lucky Dips recommended to us and described by readers (if you do, please send us reports: www.goodguides.com).

ANGLESEY
BEAUMARIS [SH6076]
George & Dragon [Church St]: Tudor beams and timbers, welcoming landlord happy to show rare bits of wall paintings and painted beams upstairs, original fireplace and section of wattle and daub wall; good value bar food, well kept Robinsons, friendly staff, nice atmosphere; may be live entertainment *(Michael Butler, Gill and Tony Morriss)*

DULAS [SH4787]
Pilot Boat [A5025 N of Moelfre]: Three-roomed pub, warm, friendly and clean, with wide range of traditional food in good helpings, good service, well kept Robinsons and limited choice of reasonably priced wines, sensible prices; restaurant, garden with playbus *(Gill and Tony Morriss)*

MENAI BRIDGE [SH5572]
Liverpool Arms [St Georges Pier]: Cheerful relaxed four-roomed local, low beams, interesting mostly maritime photographs and prints, panelled dining room, popular conservatory catching evening sun, well kept Flowers, decent wines, welcoming service, usual food from generous sandwiches up; one or two terrace tables *(Gill and Tony Morriss)*

PENTRAETH [SH5278]
Bull: Quick friendly service, good choice of sensibly priced food *(Richard Jowett)*

CLWYD
BRYNFORD [SJ1875]
Llyn y Mawn [B5121 SW of Holywell]: Charming comfortable country pub based on 15th-c coaching inn with sympathetic extension (inc evening restaurant), friendly family service, good sensibly priced food (not Fri evening but all day Sat) from sandwiches and baguettes to mixed grill, best to book Sun lunch, two well kept changing guest beers, summer farm cider; quiz night, good music night 1st Sun of month, open all day wknds *(MLR)*

CILCAIN [SJ1765]
☆ *White Horse* [signed from A494 W of Mold; The Square]: Friendly and homely country local little changed under long-serving landlord, several rooms, low joists, mahogany and oak settles, roaring inglenook log or coal fire, quarry-tiled back bar allowing dogs, two reliably well kept changing ales, pub games, home-made food; no children inside, picnic-sets outside, delightful village *(MLR, LYM)*

DENBIGH [SJ0666]
Brookhouse Mill [Brookhouse, just off A525 Ruthin road]: Friendly pub/restaurant in lovely setting by River Ystrad, enjoyable food in bar and restaurant, well kept beer, decent wines,

good coffee, pleasant young staff; play area outside *(Margaret and Andrew Leach)*

GLYNDYFRDWY [SJ1442]
Berwyn Arms: Good proper home cooking, unpretentious décor, superb sea views from simple bedrooms *(Keith Jacob)*

GRAIANRHYD [SJ2156]
Rose & Crown: [B5430 E of Ruthin]: Delightful two-room local in remote part of Clwydian Hills, filled with interesting bric-a-brac with strong 1950s overtones, all sparklingly kept; two good coal fires, friendly informal young landlord, well kept Flowers IPA, Marstons Pedigree and Wadworths 6X, good value hearty straightforward bar food from sandwiches to steaks; darts, dominoes, pool, fruit machine and well reproduced piped pop music; children welcome, picnic-sets out on rough terrace with pretty hill views, may be cl lunchtimes Mon-Thurs *(anon)*

GWERNYMYNYDD [SJ2161]
Owain Glyndwr [Glyndwr Rd, off A494 at Rainbow Garage W of Mold]: Stone-built pub with several areas, one mainly for eating, Greene King Old Speckled Hen, Marstons Pedigree and Tetleys, enjoyable sensibly priced food, friendly helpful licensees, upstairs restaurant with stunning country views; tables outside sharing the views, good walking area, bedrooms, open all day Sat (may be shorter hours winter) *(MLR)*

GWYDDELWERN [SJ0648]
Ty Mawr: Medieval inn with mix of traditional and sympathetic modern furnishings, erratic sloping floor upstairs, lots of bottled traditional and belgian beers, wide choice of tasty food, good friendly service *(Emma and Will)*

HIGHER KINNERTON [SJ3261]
Royal Oak [Kinnerton Lane, off A55/A5104 SW of Chester; also signed off A483]: Ancient picturesqe coaching inn with good choice of interesting food all day in dining area, decent wines, helpful staff, friendly atmosphere, lots of small rooms, log fires, settles and cosy armchairs, low oak beams hung with jugs, teapots, copper kettles and chamber-pots, interesting collection of soda syphons; tables in small garden, barbecues and play area *(Kevin Blake)*

LLANARMON-YN-IAL [SJ1856]
☆ *Raven* [B5431 NW of Wrexham]: Good value simple lunchtime food and more elaborate evening meals in bar and dining room of 18th-c beamed country local, welcoming service, changing real ales, two woodburners, various pets; seats outside – attractive village, unspoilt countryside *(LYM, Mrs Kirsten Hughes, MLR)*

LLANDEGLA [SJ2051]
Plough [Ruthin Rd]: Cosy and well run locally
popular dining pub, well kept Robinsons, good
value generous home-made food when the
landlord/chef's there inc smaller dishes for
children or OAPs; large dining room; nr Offa's
Dyke Path *(KC)*

LLANELIAN-YN-RHOS [SH8676]
☆ *White Lion* [signed off A5830 (shown as
B5383 on some maps) and B5381, S of Colwyn
Bay]: Family-run 16th-c inn, traditional
flagstoned snug bar with antique settles and big
fire, dining area on left with jugs hanging from
beams, teapots above window, further
comfortable more spacious no smoking dining
area up broad steps, wide choice of good
reasonably priced bar food from sandwiches
and big tureen of home-made soup up, good
friendly staff, well kept Marstons Bitter,
Pedigree and a seasonal beer, good range of
wines, lots of malt whiskies, grotto filled with
lion models; dominoes, cribbage, piped music;
children in eating areas, rustic tables outside,
good walking nearby, comfortable bedrooms
(Michael and Jenny Back, LYM)

LLANFAIR TALHAIARN [SH9270]
Swan [The Square (off A548)]: Two-bar village
pub with well kept Banks's Mild and Marstons
Pedigree, quite extensive menu, friendly
landlord, large back extension with dining
tables and pool table *(Dan White)*

LLANFERRES [SJ1860]
☆ *Druid* [A494 Mold—Ruthin]: Valley and
mountain views from extended 17th-c inn,
civilised plush lounge and larger beamed back
bar with log fire and antique oak settles as well
as more modern furnishings, attractive no
smoking dining area, wide range of generous
changing bar food, well kept Burtonwood Top
Hat and a guest such as Woods Shropshire
Lad, good malt whisky choice, well equipped
games room, also TV and perhaps unobtrusive
piped music; children welcome, tables outside,
comfortable bedrooms, open for food all day
wknds and bank hols *(Chris Flynn,
Wendy Jones, KC, Michael Butler, LYM,
Geoff and Angela Jaques, Mr and
Mrs John Taylor, Alan Cole, Kirstie Bruce)*

LLANGOLLEN [SJ2442]
Sun Trevor [A539 towards Trevor]:
Spectacular views over River Dee and canal,
enjoyable reasonably priced home-made food
from sandwiches up in attractive inglenook bar
and small restaurant, inglenook fireplace,
friendly efficient landlord and staff, well kept
real ales and good wine choice, no piped
music; handy for walkers *(Helen Clarke)*
Wynnstay Arms [Bridge St]: Former partly
16th-c posting inn, cosy bar with several low-
beamed rooms off, friendly staff and locals,
well kept Greene King IPA and Abbot, low-
priced bar food, pool room, restaurant; quiet
piped music, often jazz, outside gents'; tables
on back lawn *(Rona Murdoch, Graham Burns)*

LLANGYNHAFAL [SJ1263]
☆ *White Horse* [Hendrerwydd, off B5429 SE
of Denbigh]: Traditional-looking quietly set
village pub with armchairs and interesting
bric-a-brac in small old-fashioned rustic bar,
opening into three smartly mediterranean-
style bare-boards eating areas with good
unusual changing food; well kept real ale,
relaxed atmosphere, friendly attentive
service *(Steve Cawthray, Alan Cole,
Kirstie Bruce)*

LLANNEFYDD [SH9871]
☆ *Hawk & Buckle* [well signed locally, eg from
B5382/B5429 at Henllan NW of Denbigh]:
Friendly new licensees putting emphasis on
more upmarket food inc interesting dishes in
comfortably modernised hill-village inn's black-
beamed lounge and no smoking dining room,
Brains Arms Park or SA; children in eating
areas, good value bedrooms with remarkable
views, has been cl wkdy lunchtimes exc Weds
out of season *(John Hale, LYM, John and
Joyce Farmer, John Prescott, Dan White)*

MILWR [SJ1973]
Glan-yr-Afon: Four real ales, enjoyable pub
food, warm welcome, log fire *(Bruce M Drew)*

MOLD [SJ2464]
Bryn Awel [A541 Denbigh road nr Bailey Hill]:
Consistently good value dining pub, reliable
choice of satisfying food, big helpings,
attractive prices, attentive service, cheerful
bustling atmosphere, pleasant décor, good no
smoking area; may be piped music *(KC)*

PONTBLYDDYN [SJ2761]
Druid [Wrexham Rd (A541)]: Wide choice of
enjoyable and generous fresh food inc
imaginative dishes in dark, warm and friendly
pub, good service, decent house wines; best to
book wknds; picnic-sets and good play area
out in flower garden *(Nicholas Dawson Paul)*

PONTFADOG [SJ2338]
Swan: Genuine old pub nr river in Ceiriog
valley, good reasonably priced home-made bar
and restaurant food inc imaginative vegetarian
dishes and good value Sun lunch, well kept
Brains and guest beers, welcoming landlord;
children welcome, games room, tables on lawn
(Dr B and Mrs P B Baker)

RHEWL [SJ1744]
☆ *Sun* [off A5 or A542 NW of Llangollen]:
Unpretentious little cottage in lovely peaceful
spot, good walking country just off Horseshoe
Pass, relaxing valley views from terrace and
small pretty garden; simple consistently good
value generous food from sandwiches to good
Sun lunch, a well kept changing real ale, chatty
landlord, old-fashioned hatch service to back
room, dark little lounge; outside lavatories,
portakabin games room – children allowed
here and in eating area; open all day wknds
(John Dwane, LYM, MLR)

TAL-Y-CAFN [SH7871]

☆ *Tal-y-Cafn Hotel* [A470 Conway—Llanwrst]:
Cheerful bustle in comfortable lounge bar with
jugs hanging from ceiling and log fire in big
inglenook, wide choice of consistently good
value satisfying home cooking (may be a wait
when packed), pleasant service, Bass,
Boddingtons and Tetleys; children welcome,
seats in spacious garden, pleasant
surroundings, handy for Bodnant Gardens
*(KC, LYM, Sarah and Peter Gooderham,
J Roy Smylie)*

DYFED
ABERYSTWYTH [SN6777]

Halfway Inn [Pisgah – A4120 right out
towards Devil's Bridge]: Panoramic views, log
fire, beams, stripped stone and flagstones,
scrubbed tables and settles, well kept ales such
as Badger Best, Felinfoel Double Dragon and
Hancocks HB, farm ciders, generous usual
food; pool etc, piped music; children in eating
area, picnic-sets and simple play area outside,
overnight camping, cl winter lunchtimes
(Nick and Meriel Cox, LYM)

Yr Hen Orsaf [Alexandra Rd]: Wetherspoons
in concourse of Cambrian Railways station,
meeting place for students and profs – happy
atmosphere, several different areas, enjoyable
food and drink at appealing prices; terrace
tables by the buffer stops, open all day
(Lloyd Ellis, Joan and Michel Hooper-Immins)

ANGLE [SM8703]

☆ *Old Point House* [signed off B4320 in village;
East Angle Bay]: Idyllic spot overlooking
Milford Haven, dating from 14th c, unspoilt
but comfortable, flagstoned bar with open fire,
small lounge bar, well kept Felinfoel, basic
food strong on good interestingly cooked local
seafood; run by local lifeboat coxswain, many
photographs; plenty of tables and ancient slate
seats out by the seashore *(RWC, D and
G Alderman)*

CILGERRAN [SN1943]

Pendre Inn: This interesting medieval pub with
massive stone walls and broad flagstones
changed hands in the summer of 2003, just as
we went to press *(LYM)*

CROESGOCH [SM8430]

Artramont Arms [A487 Fishguard—St David's,
by Porthgain turn]: Welcoming landlady and
well trained young staff in light bright village
pub handy for camp site, well kept ales inc
Brains Buckleys and Felinfoel Double Dragon,
sensible choice of good value freshly made
food inc good local lamb, fish and seafood,
daily papers, pool, charming conservatory;
dogs welcome, good enclosed garden for
children *(Mike Pugh, Gwyneth and
Salvo Spadaro-Dutturi, Pat and Tony Martin)*

CWM GWAUN [SN0035]

☆ *Dyffryn Arms* [Cwm Gwaun and Pontfaen
signed off B4313 E of Fishguard]: Classic
unspoilt country tavern, very relaxed, basic

and idiosyncratic, with veteran landlady (her
farming family have run it since 1840); 1920s
front parlour with plain deal furniture inc
rocking chair and draughts-boards inlaid into
tables, coal fire, well kept Bass and Ind Coope
Burton served by jug through a hatch, pickled
eggs, time-warp prices, Great War prints and
posters, darts; pretty countryside, open more
or less all day (may close if no customers)
*(Owain Ennis, the Didler, RWC, LYM,
Giles Francis)*

DALE [SM8105]

Griffin: Friendly no-frills waterside pub by
Milford Sound, popular with yachtsmen,
sailboarders and field studies groups; two
smallish rooms, plenty of wood and sailing
pictures, usual food inc seafood, real ales such
as Brains Revd James, welcoming service, good
view of boats in estuary, can sit out on sea
wall; children allowed when eating
(P R Morley, George Atkinson)

FELINDRE FARCHOG [SN0939]

Olde Salutation [A487 Newport—Cardigan]:
Smart, friendly and spacious antiqued pub with
well kept local James Williams and guest beers,
reliable food from toasties and baguettes to
seasonal local sea trout, bass and local beef,
children's meals, good landlord, comfortable
matching seats and tables, separate dining area;
bedrooms, fishing and good walks by nearby
River Nevern *(Blaise Vyner, R Michael Richards)*

FISHGUARD [SM9537]

☆ *Fishguard Arms* [Main St, Lower Town]: Tiny
front bar with a couple of changing real ales
served by jug at unusually high counter, open
fire, rugby photographs; cheap snacks, very
friendly staff, traditional games and
impromptu music in back room with big
window overlooking river *(the Didler, LYM)*

Royal Oak [Market Sq, Upper Town]: Well
worn in beamed front bar leading through
panelled room to big no smoking picture-
window dining extension; stone walls,
cushioned wooden wall seats, woodburner,
welsh dragon carved on bar counter, three well
kept real ales inc Brains Buckley, well priced
generous usual food inc children's, tea, coffee,
hot chocolate; bar billiards, fruit machine;
pictures and mementoes commemorate defeat
here of second-last attempted French invasion
in 1797 *(BB, the Didler)*

HAVERFORDWEST [SM9515]

Mariners [Mariners Sq]: Comfortable hotel
with good fresh varied food in bar and
restaurant; good big quiet bedrooms
(Frank Willy)

HERBRANDSTON [SM8607]

Taberna: New chef doing enjoyable food in
bar and restaurant *(Tracey King)*

LITTLE HAVEN [SM8512]

☆ *St Brides Hotel* [in village itself, not St Brides
hamlet further W]: Pews in compact and

unassuming stripped-stone bar (interesting well in back corner grotto may be partly Roman) and communicating dining area allowing children, welcoming chatty landlord, enjoyable usual food from baked potatoes up, Brains Revd James and Worthington, open fire, TV but no piped music; pay & display parking; big good value bedrooms, some in annexe over road by sheltered sunny terraced garden, short stroll from the sea *(George Atkinson, Michael Butler, LYM)*

LLANDDAROG [SN5016]
☆ *Butchers Arms:* Cheery heavily black-beamed local with three smallish eating areas rambling off central bar, good low-priced generous home cooking from sandwiches through hearty country dishes to some interesting specials and good profiteroles (menu willingly adapted for children), friendly helpful staff, well kept Felinfoel Best and Double Dragon tapped from the cask, decent wines, conventional pub furniture, fairylights and candles in bottles, woodburner in biggish fireplace; piped pop music; tables outside, delightful window boxes *(Emma Kingdon, Carol Mills, Tom Evans, BB)*

LLANDEILO [SN5923]
☆ *Cottage* [Pentrefelin (A40 towards Carmarthen)]: Roomily refurbished open-plan beamed dining pub, huge log fire and lots of horsey prints, plates and brasses, good generous food from sandwiches and baked potatoes to local fish and welsh black beef, well kept ales such as Boddingtons, Flowers IPA and Wadworths 6X, decent house wines, particularly kind friendly service, well appointed back dining room; piped music *(Tom Evans)*
White Horse [Rhosmaen St]: Friendly 16th-c local popular for its particularly well kept changing real ales; occasional live music, tables outside front and back *(Jack and Jemima Valiant, the Didler)*

LLANDOVERY [SN7634]
Red Lion [Market Sq]: One basic but welcoming room with no bar, well kept Brains Buckleys and guest beers tapped from the cask, friendly landlord; cl Sun, may cl early evening if no customers *(RWC, BB, the Didler)*

MATHRY [SM8732]
☆ *Farmers Arms* [Brynamlwg, off A487 Fishguard—St David's]: Carefully renovated homely bar with beams, flagstones and dark woodwork, wide food choice from good crab sandwiches to reasonably priced hot dishes esp fish, well kept ales such as Blackawton Headstrong, Brains Revd James and Felinfoel, fair range of reasonably priced wines, quick friendly and attentive service, children welcome in large no smoking dining conservatory; piped music; tables in small walled garden safe for children, open all day in summer, may be cl wkdy winter lunchtimes, interesting woodworker's opp *(Betsy and Peter Little,*

David and Barbara Davies, George Atkinson, Gwyneth and Salvo Spadaro-Dutturi)

NARBERTH [SN1114]
Angel [High St]: Good choice of fairly priced usual food inc lots of local fish and good value Sun lunch, well kept Brains beers, pleasant relaxed surroundings with almost a hotel feel in lounge bar; pub pianist, fairly handy for Oakwood theme park and other attractions *(Pat and Tony Martin, Mike Pugh)*

NEVERN [SN0840]
☆ *Trewern Arms:* Extended inn in delightful setting nr notable church and medieval bridge over River Nyfer, lively family area merging into appealing dark stripped-stone slate-floored bar, rafters hung with rural bric-a-brac, high-backed settles, plush banquettes, Wadworths 6X, quick friendly service, bar food servery from sandwiches up, restaurant; TV in bar, games room, no dogs; tables in pretty garden, bright comfortable bedrooms, big breakfast *(LYM, Maurice and Della Andrew, T Gripper, George Atkinson, David Twitchett)*

PONT-AR-GOTHI [SN5121]
Salutation [6 miles E of Carmarthen on A40 Carmarthen—Llandeilo]: Friendly roadside pub nicely done out with clean uncluttered décor in pale-painted linked rooms, some stripped stone, new pine tables, well kept Felinfoel Best and Double Dragon, good choice of reasonably priced wines, friendly obliging service, log fire; has had particularly good food inc fish, game and good value Sun lunch, promptly served and plentiful, but a change of chef was in train as we went to press – news please; roadside picnic-sets among flower tubs, cl Mon *(Dr D K M Thomas, LYM)*

RHANDIRMWYN [SN7843]
Royal Oak: Nicely set 17th-c stone inn in remote and peaceful walking country, plenty of hanging baskets and flowering tubs, good views from tables in front garden, comfortable bar with friendly service, two changing real ales, big dining area (can book, quite a few vegetarian dishes); dogs and children welcome, big bedrooms with hill views, handy for Brecon Beacons *(Brian Root, BB, JWAC)*

ROBESTON WATHEN [SN0915]
Bridge Inn [just off A40 – B4314 towards Narberth]: Cottagey and comfortable, large eating area with wide choice of enjoyable reasonably priced food inc good home-made vegetarian dishes and popular Sun lunch, friendly attentive staff, well kept Worthington; children welcome *(Christopher and Jo Barton)*

SOLVA [SM8024]
☆ *Cambrian* [Lower Solva; off A487 Haverfordwest—St Davids]: Attractive and neatly kept civilised stone-built dining pub

much enjoyed by older people; clean and warm, food inc authentic pasta, fresh fish and popular Sun lunch in bar and restaurant, decent italian wines, real ales such as Brains Revd James and local Ceredigion Red Kite, courteous efficient service, log fires; piped music, no dogs or children *(John Hillmer, George Atkinson, John Robertson, Neil Skidmore)*

Harbour Inn [Main St]: Basic three-bar beamed pub worth knowing for delightful setting by small sailing harbour, splendid views and plenty of tables on suntrap terrace; wide choice of reasonably priced food from quickly served sandwiches up, Greene King Old Speckled Hen, attentive service, lots of local pictures; piped music, children's area with pool table; tables on terrace, bedrooms, open all day *(Lawrence Pearse, John Robertson, Betsy and Peter Little, Mike Pugh, George Atkinson)*

☆ **Ship** [Main St, Lower Solva]: Welcoming fishermen's pub quaintly set in attractive harbourside village, interesting low-beamed bar with lots of old photographs, nautical artefacts and bric-a-brac, well kept ales such as Worthington and Wychwood Fiddlers Elbow, enjoyable generous food with emphasis on fish, friendly attentive service, big back family dining room; little garden has play area over stream, public car park just down road *(George Atkinson)*

ST DAVID'S [SM7525]

☆ **Farmers Arms** [Goat St]: Cheerful and busy low-ceilinged pub by cathedral gate, cosy separate areas, wide choice of good value straightforward food from sandwiches to steaks, well kept Brains Revd James, Flowers IPA and Original, Wadworths 6X and Worthington, chatty landlord and locals; pool room, TV for rugby; cathedral view from tables in suntrap back garden, and lack of car park means no tour bus groups *(Chris Smith, John Robertson, J Taylor, W W Burke, Rona Murdoch)*

Old Cross [Cross Sq]: Hospitable hotel, reliable food inc good ploughman's with local cheese, sensible prices, friendly attentive service, nice coffee, good position – get there before the tourist coaches arrive; dogs allowed, pleasant tables on small lawns of flower-filled front garden, bedrooms, own small car park *(George Atkinson)*

STACKPOLE [SR9896]

Stackpole Inn [off B4319 S of Pembroke]: Recently refurbished L-shaped dining pub on four levels, partly no smoking, with good modern cooking, well kept Brains Rev James, Felinfoel Double Dragon and Worthington, neat light oak furnishings, ash beams in low ceilings; piped music, shove-ha'penny and dominoes; children welcome, disabled access and facilities, tables out in attractive gardens, good woodland and coastal walks in the Stackpole estate, open all day (Sun afternoon break) *(Mrs J Bairstow, LYM)*

TENBY [SN1300]

☆ **Plantagenet House** [Quay Hill]: Fascinating well renovated and civilised early medieval building on two levels, with marvellous old chimney, stripped stonework, tile and board floors; downstairs bar with well kept Boddingtons, Flowers IPA and Wadworths 6X; upstairs restaurant with interesting low-priced food inc fine soups, good baguettes, fresh local crab and fish, welsh cheeses, friendly service, cane furniture, candles on tables; piped music, fine Victorian lavatories; open all day in season, but cl lunchtime out of season *(W W Burke, Jane and Graham Rooth)*

WOLFS CASTLE [SM9526]

☆ **Wolfe** [A40 Haverfordwest—Fishguard]: Enjoyable fresh home-made food (not Sun or Mon evenings in winter) from reasonably priced bar lunches to more upmarket restaurant dishes inc authentic italian cooking, comfortable dining lounge, garden room and conservatory, two well kept real ales, well chosen wines, log fire, several board games; pub dog, children welcome, attractively laid-out garden, bedrooms *(CMW, JJW, V Brogden, Mike Pugh, LYM)*

GWENT

ABERGAVENNY [SO3014]

Hen & Chickens [Flannel St]: Simple unpretentious traditional local, relaxed and contented (though very busy on market day), well kept Bass and Brains from bar unusually set against street windows, basic wholesome cheap lunchtime food (not Sun), mugs of tea and coffee, friendly efficient staff, interesting side areas, popular darts, cards and dominoes; TV *(Pete Baker, the Didler, MP, LM)*

Lamb & Flag [Llanwenarth; A40, 2 miles NW]: Brightly refurbished open-plan bars with light oak furniture, pottery, modern art and picture-window hill views, good range of enjoyable food (all day in summer), well kept Brains Bitter, SA and Rev James, conservatory; children welcome, high chairs; open all day in summer, tables on terrace with play area, comfortable bedrooms with own bathrooms *(Joan and Michel Hooper-Immins)*

BRYNGWYN [SO4008]

☆ **Cripple Creek** [off old A40 W of Raglan]: Pleasantly extended and civilised old country pub with wide range of good reasonably priced food from simple things to more elaborate meals inc fresh fish and choice of four Sun roasts, friendly prompt service, real ales such as Adnams Broadside, Brains and Tetleys, teas and coffees, pleasant no smoking dining room; country views from small terrace, play area, open all day *(James Morrell, Eryl and Keith Dykes, Alec and Barbara Jones, Guy Vowles)*

GROSMONT [SO4024]

☆ **Angel**: Pleasant and helpful newish owners in ivy-covered 17th-c village local on attractive steep single street within sight of castle, seats out by ancient market cross beside surprisingly modern little town hall; friendly local atmosphere, several changing well kept ales from Tomos Watkins and (brewed for the pub) Wye Valley, Bulmer's cider, good value food (not Thurs pm) nc speciality sausages; TV, separate room with pool and darts, a couple of tables and boules pitch behind *(BB, R T and J C Moggridge, Mike Pugh)*

LLANDENNY [SO4103]
☆ *Raglan Arms*: Sturdily furnished linked rooms of extensive dining area leading through to conservatory, with good fresh food esp fish and seafood cooked to order, pleasant efficient service and good wine choice (booking advised Fri/Sat evenings and Sun lunchtime); terracotta-walled flagstoned bar with three leather sofas around low table on oriental rug, broadsheet papers and *Country Living*, big log fire in handsome stone fireplace, well kept Felinfoel Double Dragon and a Wye Valley seasonal beer, neat separate public bar with pool and wide-screen TV; garden tables *(Mervyn and Susan Underhill, BB, Pamela and Merlyn Horswell, Colin Mansell)*

LLANDEWI SKIRRID [SO3416]
☆ *Walnut Tree* [B4521]: Restaurant rather than pub, though it does have a small flagstoned bar with fireside seats as well as the airy main dining lounge; excellent inventive food and very good wines (good cider, but no real ale), nice coffee and pleasantly relaxed and individual service; children welcome, cl Sun evening and Mon *(Anthony Rickards Collinson, Bernard Stradling, Pamela and Merlyn Horswell, LYM, Stephen, Julie and Hayley Brown)*

LLANGYBI [ST3797]
White Hart: Friendly village local in delightful 12th-c monastery building, part of Jane Seymour's dowry, above-average straightforward food, good range of well kept real ales inc tip-top Bass, pleasant atmosphere *(Mike Pugh)*

LLANTHONY [SO2928]
☆ *Abbey Hotel* [Llanthony Priory; off A465, back road Llanvihangel Crucorney—Hay]: Terrific setting for plain bar in dim-lit vaulted flagstoned crypt of graceful ruined Norman abbey, with lawns around and the peaceful border hills beyond; well kept Brains and perhaps a guest beer, farm cider in summer, simple lunchtime bar food, no children; occasional live music, open all day Sat (and Sun in summer – much its best time of year); cl Mon-Thurs, Sun evenings in winter; evening restaurant, bedrooms in restored parts of abbey walls, great walks all around *(the Didler, Nick Holding, LYM)*
Half Moon: Basic dog-friendly country inn suiting this unspoilt valley with its great walks and pony-trekking centres, decent plain food, well kept Bull Mastiff beers inc power-packed

Son-of-a-Bitch; bedrooms not luxurious but clean and comfortable *(Eddie Edwards)*

LLANTRISANT FAWR [ST3997]
☆ *Greyhound* [off A449 nr Usk]: Prettily set 17th-c country inn with relaxed homely feel in three linked bar rooms of varying sizes, steps between two, nice mix of furnishings and rustic decorations, well kept Bass, Flowers Original, Greene King Abbot and a weekly guest beer, friendly helpful staff, log fires, wide choice of consistently good home cooking at sensible prices, colourful prints in pleasant grey-panelled dining room; picnic-sets in attractively laid-out garden with big fountain, hill views, adjoining pine shop, good bedrooms in small attached motel *(BB, George and Brenda Jones)*

MAGOR [ST4287]
Wheatsheaf [1 mile from M4 junction 23; B4245]: Welcoming new licensee in traditional pub doing good food inc welsh specialities, reasonable prices, good service *(Mrs C Sleight)*

MAMHILAD [SO3004]
Horseshoe: Pleasant roomy bar with good choice of freshly made food (may take a while) inc generous sandwiches, well kept Bass and Hancocks HB, lots of malt whiskies, friendly and very helpful licensees; play area, lovely views, particularly from tables by car park over road *(Rodney and Norma Stubington)*

MONMOUTH [SO5112]
May Hill [May Hill (A4136)]: Handy for walkers (where Offa's Dyke Path crosses the Wye), with Fullers London Pride and Tetleys, bar food and good pickled eggs; open all day Sun, quiz night then *(Dave Braisted)*

NEWPORT [ST3189]
Lyceum [A4051 just off M4 junction 26, towards centre; Malpas Rd]: Friendly and tastefully modernised Victorian local, several distinct areas around horseshoe bar, popular good value straightforward bar lunches, well kept Courage Best, Greene King Old Speckled Hen and perhaps a guest beer; several quiz nights, Thurs folk club, live music Sat *(Pete Baker)*

PANDY [SO3322]
Lancaster Arms [A465]: Well worn in local right by Offa's Dyke path, welcoming landlady and staff, good service, enjoyable sensibly priced food, small range of well kept beers; dogs welcome, two tidy bedrooms, good breakfast *(Lorraine and Fred Gill, Ian and Nita Cooper, Eddie Edwards)*
Pandy Inn [A465 Abergavenny—Hereford]: Welcoming old slate-built family pub, good reasonably priced bar food inc huge steak pie, friendly staff, changing ales such as Fullers London Pride, comfortable modern settles, 3D Brecons maps, good Sun night nostalgic pianist; adjacent walkers' bunkhouse *(Ian and Nita Cooper, Bob Scott, Lorraine and Fred Gill)*

Park Hotel: Hotel rather than pub, but well worth knowing for food inc authentic austrian and hungarian dishes, decent low-priced wine, a well kept real ale and exotic lager; relaxed atmosphere and service, bedrooms *(Mike Pugh)*

SHIRENEWTON [ST4793]

☆ *Tredegar Arms* [signed off B4235 just W of Chepstow]: Freshly and carefully cooked well presented food in quietly welcoming dining pub, comfortable sofa and chairs in tastefully chintzy lounge bar with big bay window; real ale, games in public bar, children in eating area, small sheltered courtyard, lovely hanging baskets, two good value comfortable bedrooms *(Theocsbrian, Graham and Lynn Mason, LYM)*

SKENFRITH [SO4520]

☆ *Bell*: Attractively reworked inn in beautiful setting by bridge over River Monnow, flagstones and canary walls in linked areas with settees, pews and carved settles among more conventional pub furniture, church candles on tables, log fire in big fireplace, welcoming enthusiastic owners, charming staff, good wines by the glass, Freeminer and Hook Norton Best, interesting if not cheap food inc welsh black beef and entirely using named local suppliers in bar and extensive bareboards restaurant, games room; piped nostalgic pop music; picnic-sets out on terrace, steps up to sloping lawn, bedrooms *(BB, Anthony Rickards Collinson, Pamela and Merlyn Horswell, Theocsbrian, Mrs Kitty Lloyd)*

THE NARTH [SO5206]

Trekkers [off B4293 Trelleck—Monmouth]: Log cabin high in valley, unusual and welcoming, esp for children; big central log fire, helpful licensee, good value generous food (but check that they're serving that day if your walk depends on it: (01600) 860367), well kept changing ales such as Greene King IPA and Ruddles County, good small wine list, furry toy collection, skittle alley family room, disabled facilities; dogs allowed, long back garden, open all day Sun *(LM)*

TINTERN [SO5301]

☆ *Moon & Sixpence* [A466 Chepstow—Monmouth]: Flower-decked small pub, attractively furnished and largely smoke-free, with lots of beams and steps, one room with sofas and wicker armchairs, natural spring feeding indoor goldfish pool, good choice of good value food, well kept ales such as Greene King Abbot, Hook Norton Best and Wye Valley Butty Bach from back bar, friendly helpful service; pleasantly soft piped music; tiny windows, but tables under arbour on terrace look along River Wye to abbey; children welcome, good walks *(A H C Rainier, BB)*

TRELLECK GRANGE [SO5001]

☆ *Fountain* [minor road Tintern—Llanishen, SE of village]: Unassuming inn tucked away on back country road, dark-beamed bar, roomy and comfortable dining room, wide range of good value food inc good fresh sandwiches, fish and popular Sun lunch, cheerful patient staff, well kept Boddingtons and Wadworths 6X, decent malt whiskies and wines; may be nostalgic piped pop music, darts; children allowed away from bar, small sheltered garden with summer kids' bar; bedrooms *(BB)*

USK [SO3801]

☆ *Castle Inn* [Twyn Sq]: Relaxed and jaunty front bar with sofas, locals reading newspapers, interesting carved chair and comfortable window seats, big mirrors, lots of dried hops, wide blackboard choice of generous well served food all day, well organised quick service, changing ales such as Bass, Fullers London Pride and Timothy Taylors Landlord, freshly squeezed orange juice, a couple of cosy little alcoves off back dining room; piped music may be loud; tables in garden behind *(Peter and Audrey Dowsett, BB)*

Kings Head [Old Market St]: Busy pub with fine choice of real ales, superb fireplace; open all day; bedrooms *(Mike Pugh)*

☆ *Royal Hotel* [New Market St]: Popular and unchanging country-town inn with traditional fixtures and fittings, collection of old crockery and pictures, old-fashioned fireplaces, comfortable wooden chairs and tables, filling food inc wider evening choice (not Sun; worth booking Sat and Sun lunch), well kept Bass, Hancocks HB and Felinfoel Double Dragon from deep cellar, friendly service; piped music may obtrude; well behaved children welcome, has been cl Mon lunchtime *(LYM, Chris Flynn, Wendy Jones, Mike Pugh, Peter and Audrey Dowsett)*

GWYNEDD
ABERDOVEY [SN6196]

Britannia [Sea View Terr]: Great harbour and distant mountain views from upstairs bar with balcony; good range of well priced food, friendly bustle, well kept Banks's and Marstons Pedigree, good service, downstairs public bar and small snug; children in side room *(Huw and Patricia Egginton)*

Dovey [Sea View Terr]: Bay-window estuary views, warm friendly helpful service, big helpings of good moderately priced imaginative food inc children's; three terraces, comfortably refurbished bedrooms, good breakfast *(Diane Bullock)*

BANGOR [SH5873]

Union [Garth Rd]: Five friendly areas with lots of entertaining bric-a-brac, much of it nautical, well kept Burtonwood and a monthly guest such as Arundel Gold, reasonably priced food esp steak and kidney pie and local crab, no piped music; terrace tables nr pier, with sound of yards rattling against masts *(Bruce Bird)*

BETWS-Y-COED [SH7956]

Pont y Pair: Welcoming mix of diners and

local drinkers, reasonably priced food from good soup up in small cosy bar and restaurant, separate no smoking room, Tetleys, decent wine, no piped music *(KC)*

Waterloo [A5]: Well served generous food, good obliging service, no piped music; can be smoky; bedrooms *(KC)*

BLAENAU FFESTINIOG [SH7046]

Miners Inn [Llechwedd Slate Caverns]: Part of the good slate mine visitor attraction (entrance fee), unusual site for Victorian pub with coal fire, smallish choice of inexpensive wholesome food, welsh real ales tapped from the cask, several wines and spirits, separate family room *(Gill and Tony Morriss, Peter and Audrey Dowsett)*

Queens [High St]: Small hotel's comfortable lounge bar, clean and smart, with decent food here and in dining room, well kept Bass, Greene King Abbot and Tetleys; may be sports TV *(Mr and Mrs Colin Roberts)*

BONTNEWYDD [SH4859]

Newborough Arms: Welcoming and comfortable dining pub with easy mix of visitors and Welsh-speaking locals, good value food (curries tipped), well kept Burtonwood and other ales; enclosed back garden, bedrooms *(Keith John Ryan)*

CAPEL CURIG [SH7258]

☆ *Bryn Tyrch* [A5 W of village]: Comfortably casual but serious-minded country inn popular with walkers and climbers, Snowdon Horseshoe views from big picture windows, understated furnishings inc homely sofas, hot coal fire, magazines and outdoor equipment catalogues, pool table in plain hikers' bar, generous wholesome food with very strong vegetarian/vegan emphasis, lots of coffee blends and Twinings teas, well kept Castle Eden, Flowers IPA and Wadworths 6X, decent well priced wines; tables outside, steep little streamside garden over road, children welcome, bedrooms, open all day *(Mr and Mrs Colin Roberts, John and Tania Wood, Stuart and Roma Crampin, LYM, David and Higgs Wood)*

CONWY [SH7878]

Bridge Hotel [Rose Hill St]: Well run hotel with Marstons and guest beers, good choice of reasonably priced food inc plenty of vegetarian and even vegan dishes, particularly friendly helpful service, no smoking dining area; bedrooms *(John Andrew, Keith and Chris O'Neill)*

CRICCIETH [SH5038]

☆ *Prince of Wales* [The Square]: Open-plan, but with some individual decorative touches, nice pictures, panelling, open fires and some cosy alcoves – all spick and span; usual bar food inc good steaks, well kept Bass and Marstons Pedigree; TV, children in eating area till 8; open all day Sat summer *(Mr and Mrs Colin Roberts, LYM)*

DOLGARROG [SH7766]

☆ *Lord Newborough* [Conwy Rd (B5106 just S)]: Black-beamed carpeted bar with lots of hanging jugs and other china, Boddingtons, big log fire, welcoming staff, linen-set dining rooms each side specialising in good fish dishes; tables out on two terraces and small lawn with copsey woodland rising steeply behind, cl Tues lunchtime and Sun/Mon *(BB, J Roy Smylie)*

LLANDUDNO [SH7883]

☆ *Kings Head* [Old Rd, behind tram station]: Rambling pretty pub, much extended around 16th-c flagstoned core, spaciously open-plan, bright and clean but with plenty of interesting corners and comfortable traditional furnishings, old local tramway photographs, red wallpaper, dark pine, well kept ales inc a house beer from Phoenix, eclectic choice of wines in friendly-sized glasses, quick friendly service, huge log fire, smart back dining room up a few steps, wide range of generous food (busy at night, so get there early); children welcome, seats on front terrace overlooking quaint Victorian cable tramway's station (water for dogs here), open all day in summer *(Mike and Wendy Proctor, LYM, Kevin Blake, Liz and John Soden, MLR)*

London [Mostyn St]: Interesting welcoming local with lots of London-theme bric-a-brac (even a red pillar box), Burtonwood Mild and Bitter, lunchtime bar food; quiz and occasional music nights; bedrooms *(Kevin Blake)*

Palladium [Gloddaeth Street]: Wetherspoons in beautifully converted former theatre, boxes and seats intact, spectacular ceilings, good value food and drinks inc bargain Shepherd Neame Spitfire *(Liz and John Soden, Kevin Blake, Keith and Chris O'Neill)*

Parade [Church Walks]: Friendly young licensees, decent food, quiz night; good value bedrooms *(Keith and Chris O'Neill)*

LLANDWROG [SH4556]

Harp [½ mile W of A499 S of Caernarfon]: Welcoming lounge bar with irregular shape giving cosy corners, real ales such as Black Sheep and Mutleys Revenge, good value food, helpful landlord and friendly bilingual parrot, daily papers and magazines, cheerful separate dining room, board games and Jenga; picnic-sets among fruit trees, well equipped cottagey bedrooms overlooking quiet village's imposing church, good breakfast, cl Mon *(BB, Prof and Mrs Tony Palmer)*

LLANENGAN [SH2826]

Sun: Friendly and cosy Robinsons pub in small village nr spectacular sandy Hell's Mouth beach, three well kept reasonably priced real ales, enjoyable family food; large partly covered terrace and garden (very popular with children) with outdoor summer bar and pool table, bedrooms *(Keith John Ryan, Mike and Mary Carter, Margaret Mason, David Thompson)*

LLANRWST [SH8464]
Pen y Bont [Bridge St]: Friendly attentive service and enjoyable food; dogs welcome *(Tracy Caddick)*

LLANUWCHLLYN [SH8730]
☆ *Eagles* [aka Eryrod; A494/B4403]: Good home-made food from sandwiches to steaks (cooked to order by landlady so may be a wait), well kept real ale such as Plassey in tourist season, reasonable prices, friendly staff and atmosphere, helpful landlord, small front bar and plush back lounge, neat décor with beams and some stripped stone, panoramic view of mountains with Lake Bala in distance; no music, no smoke, tables out behind *(Michael and Jenny Back)*

MAENTWROG [SH6741]
☆ *Grapes* [A496; village signed from A470]: Rambling old stripped stone inn, very popular with families in summer, with very wide choice of enjoyable reasonably priced generous food, well kept Greene King Old Speckled Hen and two or three changing guest beers such as Hydes, over 30 malt whiskies and decent wine choice, lots of stripped pine (pews, settles, panelling, pillars and carvings), good log fires, intriguing collection of brass blowlamps, lovely views from conservatory dining extension, pleasant back terrace and walled garden; juke box in public bar; disabled lavatories, dogs welcome, open all day *(David Crook, Trevor Swindells, Bruce Bird, Dr and Mrs P Truelove, GSB, D Pratt, Tim Maddison, Myke and Nicky Crombleholme, LYM, Peter and Audrey Dowsett, John and Tania Wood)*

MORFA NEFYN [SH2939]
Bryncynan: Modernised pub concentrating (particularly in summer) on quickly served bar food; quiet in winter with good log fire in the partly tiled bar; well kept Greene King Old Speckled Hen and Wadworths 6X, friendly service, restaurant, rustic seats outside, children allowed; has been cl Sun *(Mr and Mrs Colin Roberts, LYM)*
Cliffs [Lon Bridin]: Practically on beach and coast path, bars set into the cliff, sun room and tables on terrace; decent generous fairly priced food *(Margaret Mason, David Thompson)*

NANT PERIS [SH6058]
Vaynol Arms: Friendly and simple walkers' and climbers' Snowdonia pub, Robinsons beers, good value food; opens 7 *(Gill and Tony Morriss)*

PENMAENPOOL [SH6918]
☆ *George III* [just off A493, nr Dolgellau]: Lovely views over Mawddach estuary from attractive inn with extended no smoking bottom public bar (children allowed), beams, flagstones and stripped stone, well kept ales such as Greene King Ruddles, good choice of wines by the glass, friendly helpful staff, cheerful bar food inc children's; also civilised partly panelled upstairs bar opening into cosy inglenook lounge, with same food, and separate restaurant; open all day, sheltered terrace, good walks, good bedrooms inc some (allowing dogs) in quiet and interesting conversion of former station on disused line *(Dr and Mrs Rod Holcombe, M J Park, Nick and Meriel Cox, MDN, Lorraine and Fred Gill, Dr and Mrs P Truelove, Barry Smith, Dennis Jenkin, Di and Mike Gillam, LYM, MB, John and Tania Wood)*

PORTH DINLLAEN [SH2741]
Ty Coch [beach car park signed from Morfa Nefyn, then 15-min walk]: Stunning spot on curving beach, far from the roads (and quite a long walk from the nearest car park), with great view along coast to mountains; pub itself full of attractive salvage, RNLI memorabilia, lamps and mugs, good prawn and crab salads and other usual lunchtime food, decent coffee; keg beer (and plastic beakers if you drink outside); cl winter exc Sat lunchtimes, but open all day summer and very popular then – on a hot still day this is an idyllic place *(LYM, Peter and Audrey Dowsett, John and Wendy Allin)*

PORTHMADOG [SH5639]
Royal Sportsman [High St]: Extensively refurbished early Victorian hotel with good value lunches from sandwiches and some interesting snacks up in popular log-fire bar and no smoking dining room, slightly more expensive evening meals, local produce, good friendly service, usually a couple of real ales such as Greene King IPA and Timothy Taylors Landlord; tables on terrace, 28 bedrooms *(Mr and Mrs Colin Roberts)*
Ship [Lombard St]: Oldest pub in town, two dimly lit sturdily furnished roomy bars with lots of interesting ship pictures and nautical hardware, well kept ales such as Greene King Old Speckled Hen, Ind Coope Burton and Tetleys, over 80 malt whiskies, big open fire, wide range of bar food (not Mon/Tues in winter); children may be allowed in small no smoking back room, open all day, cl Sun exc summer hol lunchtimes *(LYM)*
Ship & Castle [High St]: Unpretentious pub worth knowing for its low-priced generous food; Ansells Mild and Tetleys, sports TV *(Mr and Mrs Colin Roberts)*
Spooners [Harbour Station]: Decent pub lunches inc good filled baguettes and Thurs-Sat evening meals at reasonable prices, lots of railway memorabilia, particularly well kept Banks's Original, Marstons Pedigree and interesting guest beers such as Spinning Dog Mutleys Pit Stop and Chase Your Tail and Wye Valley Battle; tables out on platform *(Bruce Bird, Tony Hobden, Keith and Chris O'Neill)*
Station Inn: Former railway station nicely converted to popular pub (landlady used to run the refreshment room), by entrance to Welsh Highland Railway *(Peter Duddy)*

RHYD DDU [SH5753]

Cwellyn Arms [A4085 N of Beddgelert]: Basic 18th-c pub with wide choice of good value food from baked potatoes up, up to nine changing ales such as Spinning Dog and Wye Valley; flagstones, log and coal fire in huge ancient fireplace, pleasant restaurant area, small games bar with pool, darts and TV; children and walkers welcome, spectacular Snowdon views from garden tables with barbecue, babbling stream just over wall, big adventure playground; bedrooms, usually open all day (*KC, John Dwane, Bruce Bird, Dr and Mrs P Truelove*)

MID GLAMORGAN

KENFIG [SS8383]

☆ *Prince of Wales* [2¼ miles from M4 junction 37; A4229 towards Porthcawl, then right when dual carriageway narrows on bend, signed Maudlam and Kenfig]: Interesting ancient pub among sand dunes, nicely upgraded without harming character, friendly landlord, wife does good reasonably priced food inc much enjoyed fish specials, well kept Bass, Worthington and often a guest beer tapped from the cask, good choice of malt whiskies and decent wines, stripped stone and log fires, lots of wreck pictures, traditional games, upstairs dining room for summer and busy wknds; handy for nature reserve and walks, children and (in non-carpet areas) dogs welcome (*the Didler, David Jeffreys, Ian Phillips, John and Joan Nash, LYM*)

LLANGYNWYD [SS8588]

☆ *Old House* [off A4063 S of Maesteg; pub behind church, nearly 1 mile W of modern village]: Pretty thatched dining pub, much modernised inside and largely no smoking, with lots of brass and china especially around the huge fireplace and on the beams, more than 350 whiskies, well kept Brains, Worthington and a couple of guest beers, friendly staff, generously priced food all day from filled rolls and baked potatoes to steak, attractive conservatory extension leading to garden with impressive new play area and a soft ice-cream machine; piped music; children welcome, open all day (*Tom Evans, Dave Braisted, LYM*)

Tylers Arms [E of A4063, via Station Rd]: Nice spot between two streams, pleasant seats outside; traditionally pubby, with good value food all day; Cerdin Club sings in back bar Fri (*Andy Sinden, Louise Harrington*)

MACHEN [ST2288]

White Hart [White Hart Lane, off A468 towards Bedwas]: Unusual welcoming bar and lounge full of salvaged ship memorabilia, restored ceiling painting, log fire, wide choice of reasonably priced generous wholesome bar meals (Sun lunches only, but a bargain); brews its own beers, with guest beers too from small servery down panelled corridor, and annual beer festival; garden with play area, bedrooms (*Mike Pugh, Emma Kingdon*)

MISKIN [ST0480]

Miskin Arms [quite near M4 junction 34, via A4119 and B4264]: Friendly and roomy village pub with Everards Tiger, Hancocks HB and guest beers, good value bar food, restaurant Sun lunch and Tues-Sat evenings (*Colin Moore*)

NANT DDU [SO0015]

Nant Ddu Lodge [Cwmtaf; A470 Merthyr Tydfil—Brecon]: Hotel doubling as restaurant and pub, very popular, with wide range of imaginative reasonably priced food, real ale, no smoking lounge, large evening dining room; bright well equipped bedrooms (some in separate block), good walking country by Taff Valley reservoirs (*Pamela and Merlyn Horswell*)

RUDRY [ST2087]

Maenllwyd [off A468 Newport—Caerphilly in Lower Machen, towards Draethen for 2 miles]: Olde-worlde Tudor Chef & Brewer under new management, very comfortably extended and refurnished, but with a real feeling of age and an interesting rambling layout, with low beams, panelling, and logs burning in the lounge bar's huge fireplace; decent food all day, good choice of well kept real ales and of wines, good-sized family dining room; fruit machine, piped music, can be very busy Fri/Sat; nice spot on the edge of Rudry Common, open all day (*LYM*)

THORNHILL [ST1484]

☆ *Travellers Rest* [A469 S of Caerphilly]: Thatched stone-built Vintage Inn dining pub with well kept Bass, good sensibly priced wine choice, prompt friendly service, daily papers and magazines, reasonably priced food all day; huge fireplace and nooks and crannies in low-beamed bar on right, new no smoking extension, great views over Cardiff; children welcome lunchtimes, piped music, very busy wknds, no bookings; open all day, tables out on grass, good walks (*Ian Phillips, David Jeffreys, David and Nina Pugsley, Mr and Mrs M Dalby*)

POWYS

ABEREDW [SO0847]

☆ *Seven Stars* [just off B4567 SE of Builth Wells]: Cosy and attractive local doubling as post office, butcher landlord, good generous honest food inc vegetarian dishes as well as tasty steaks and gammons, well kept Wadworths 6X and two guest beers, efficient friendly service, low beams and stripped stone, log fire, local pictures and antiques, bustling restaurant; disabled facilities, three good newly done bedrooms (*E J C Parker, Hazel and Michael Duncombe, Tom and Katie Parrish*)

CARNO [SN9697]

Aleppo Merchant [A470 Newtown—Machynlleth]: Tapestries in plushly modernised stripped stone bar, small peaceful lounge with open fire, no smoking area, decent reasonably priced food from good sandwiches to steaks, Boddingtons, occasional guest beer, friendly helpful landlord, restaurant (well behaved children allowed here), back games room; piped music; tables in good-sized garden, bedrooms, nice countryside *(S Whaley, LYM, Roy and Margaret Jones, Michael and Jenny Back, John and Tania Wood)*

CRICKHOWELL [SO2119]
Manor [Brecon Rd]: Wonderful Usk Valley views, enjoyable reasonably priced food (it's under the same ownership as the Nantyffin Cider Mill), immaculate table linen and nice ambiance; bedrooms *(N H E Lewis)*
White Hart [Brecon Rd (A40 W)]: Homely bar with stripped stone, beams and flagstones, well kept Brains Bitter, Buckleys Best and Revd James, usual food from lunchtime sandwiches up in eating area (with TV) off one end, or sizeable no smoking restaurant; pub games, may be piped classical music, quiz night Mon; children in eating areas, open all day Sat, some tables outside *(David Carr, LYM)*

CWMDU [SO1823]
☆ *Farmers Arms* [A479 NW of Crickhowell]: Genuine friendly country local, popular with walkers (and with the local farmers on Sat), with helpful welcoming service, unpretentious partly flagstoned bar with attractive prints and stove in big stone fireplace, changing real ales such as Greene King Old Speckled Hen, Shepherd Neame Spitfire and Uley Pigs Ear, good value hearty home cooking inc good local lamb and beef, welsh cheeses and children's dishes, plush restaurant; TV; tables in garden, bedrooms with own bathrooms and good breakfast, campsite nearby – handy for pony-trekkers and Black Mountains *(BB, Mike Stroud, Jenny and Brian Seller)*

DEFYNNOG [SN9228]
☆ *Lion* [aka Tafarn y Llew; A4067]: Nice cottagey décor, good chatty atmosphere and warmly welcoming new owners, with good value generous straightforward food, warm fires and well kept real ale *(Mike and Lynn Robinson, LYM)*
Tanners Arms: Lounge, public bar and restaurant, friendly licensees, wide choice of good value food all freshly made (so may be a wait at busy times); tables out overlooking fields and mountains *(Mike and Lynn Robinson)*

FELINFACH [SO0933]
☆ *Griffin* [A470 NE of Brecon]: Brightly painted opened-up roadside restaurant pub with good unusual food (meals rather than snacks) using only local ingredients in two formally set out bare-boards or flagstoned no smoking front dining rooms with big modern prints, back bar area with stripped furniture and floors, curtainless windows, mustard walls and bright blue dado, may be a spaniel on one of the leather sofas by the log fire on an attractive raised slate hearth; six good house wines in

three glass sizes, may be a real ale, polite service, no smoking area; piped radio; disabled access, comfortable reasonably priced bedrooms, tables outside *(Pamela and Merlyn Horswell, Rodney and Norma Stubington, BB, Dr Clare McGovern, Dr Roger Moss, Leo Horton)*

GLADESTRY [SO2355]
Royal Oak [B4594 W of Kington]: Relaxing unpretentious beamed and flagstoned pub in quiet village handy for Offa's Dyke Path, with refurbished lounge, separate bar, and picnic-sets in lovely secluded garden behind, safe for children; up for sale as we go to press, but has had well kept Bass and Hancocks HB, sandwiches and inexpensive simple lunches, good value bedrooms *(Helen Pickering, James Owen)*

HAY-ON-WYE [SO2342]
Three Tuns [Broad St]: Basic unfussy pub with fireside settle and a few old tables and chairs in tiny dark quarry-tiled bar in one of Hay's oldest buildings, charming veteran landlady (whose parents ran the pub before her) knowledgeable about local history, ciders from barrels on the counter, local apple juice, perhaps a polypin of Wye Valley real ale, Edwardian bar fittings, lots of bric-a-brac, daily papers, interesting old stove, some fresh flowers; no food *(Norma and Keith Bloomfield, the Didler, Pete Baker, RWC, Bruce Bird)*

LIBANUS [SN9926]
Tai'r Bull [A470 SW of Brecon]: Clean and well run, with good helpings of enjoyable food in bar and restaurant, real ales, friendly young licensees, great views out in front; bedrooms well appointed and comfortable, good breakfast – good base for walking *(David Landey)*

LLANDRINDOD WELLS [SO0561]
☆ *Llanerch* [High St/Waterloo Rd; pub signed from station]: New management in cheerful rambling 16th-c inn, nice old-fashioned main bar with big inglenook fireplace and more up-to-date lounges off (one no smoking till 8), well kept real ales, bar food from filled baps and baked potatoes up inc Sun roast; piped music, games room with pool; children welcome, pleasant terrace and orchard garden with play area and boules, 12 bedrooms with own bathrooms, good breakfast, quiet spot with peaceful views, has been open all day wknds *(Martin Grosberg, LYM, Joan and Michel Hooper-Immins)*

LLANGATTOCK [SO2117]
Vine Tree [signed from Crickhowell; Legar Rd]: Small simple pub with generally reliable and generous food in bar and restaurant, pleasant service, well kept Fullers London Pride and Wadworths 6X, good coffee, coal-effect gas fire; children welcome, tables out under cocktail parasols with lovely view of

medieval Usk bridge *(Pamela and Merlyn Horswell, LYM)*

LLANGENNY [SO2417]

☆ *Dragons Head*: Peaceful two-room bar in pretty valley setting, low beams, big woodburner, pews, housekeeper's chairs and a high-backed settle among other seats, two attractive restaurant areas, pleasant landlord and helpful staff, wide choice of enjoyable home-made food from sandwiches up, good choice of well kept reasonably priced real ales inc Brains Buckley Revd James; picnic-sets in garden and over road by stream, open wknd summer afternoons if busy enough *(LYM, Colin McKerrow)*

LLANWENARTH [SO2516]

Pantrhiwgoch: Pleasant for lunch, good service in bar and dining room; due for some refurbishment *(Pamela and Merlyn Horswell)*

LLANWRTYD WELLS [SN8746]

☆ *Neuadd Arms* [The Square]: Comfortably well worn in lounge with big log fire and local pictures, separate small tiled public bar with craft tools and splendid row of old service bells, well kept reasonably priced ales such as Bass, Felinfoel Double Dragon and Robinsons Snowdon, lots of unusual bottled beers, welcoming helpful staff, laid-back atmosphere, popular bar food, restaurant; beer festivals, various other events; tables out on front terrace, bedrooms pleasant and well equipped, engaging very small town – good walking area, mountain bike hire *(BB, Joan and Michel Hooper-Immins)*

LLOWES [SO1941]

☆ *Radnor Arms* [A438 Brecon—Hereford]: Well run and attractive country dining pub with very wide choice of good food served in local pottery (the nearby shop's interesting) from good filled rolls and inventive soups to fine restaurant-style dishes, with dozens of puddings; ancient cottagey bar with beams and stripped stone, very welcoming, with well kept Felinfoel, good coffee, log fire and two small dining rooms; tables in imaginatively planted garden looking out over fields towards the Wye; cl Sun pm, Mon (exc bank hols) *(Rodney and Norma Stubington, Dr Oscar Puls)*

LLYSWEN [SO1337]

Griffin [A470, village centre]: Country pub with uncommercialised local atmosphere, fine log fire in easy-going bar, well kept Brains real ales, decent wines, children in eating areas; piped music; tables out by road, comfortable and attractive bedrooms *(W F C Phillips, Dr and Mrs A K Clarke, LYM, Sebastian Leach, P R Morley, Cliff Blakemore)*

MONTGOMERY [SO2296]

☆ *Dragon* [Market Sq]: Well run tall timbered 17th-c hotel with attractive prints and china in lively beamed bar, good value generous food from toasted sandwiches to steaks inc children's, attentive service, well kept Woods Special and guest beer, good wines and coffee, board games, restaurant; unobtrusive piped music, jazz most Weds; comfortable well equipped bedrooms and swimming pool, very quiet town below ruined Norman castle, open all day *(LYM, Nick Holding, Geoffrey and Penny Hughes)*

PENTRE BACH [SN9032]

Shoemakers Arms [off A40 in Sennybridge]: Individual welcoming local in the middle of nowhere, refurbished and reopened by consortium of local people, enjoyable lunchtime home cooking, restaurant Sun lunchtime and Weds-Sat evenings; good walks *(Mike and Lynn Robinson)*

RHAYADER [SN9768]

Lamb & Flag [North St]: Low-beamed cottagey pub, comfortable furniture inc armchairs, lots of brass, friendly helpful staff, Brains Revd James and Hancocks HB, reasonably priced bar food; bedrooms *(E G Parish)*

Triangle [Cwmdauddwr; B4518 by bridge over Wye, SW of centre]: Interesting mainly 16th-c pub, small and spotless, with enjoyable food from good toasties and ploughman's up lunchtime and early evening, well kept Greene King IPA and Hancocks HB, decent wines, sensible prices, welcoming non-local licensees, quick service, separate dining area with view over park to Wye, darts and quiz nights; tables on small front terrace *(Dennis Jenkin, Pete Yearsley, J A Ellis)*

TALYBONT-ON-USK [SO1122]

☆ *Star* [B4558]: Old-fashioned canalside local with several changing real ales and Weston's Old Rosie farm cider, three bustling plain rooms off central servery inc brightly lit games area, lots of beermats, bank notes and coins on beams; cheering winter fires, low-priced simple food from sandwiches to steak, live band Weds, winter quiz Mon; dogs and children welcome, picnic-sets in sizeable tree-ringed garden below Monmouth & Brecon Canal, bedrooms, open all day Sat *(LYM, the Didler, Di and Mike Gillam, Pete Baker, Neil and Anita Christopher)*

TRECASTLE [SN8729]

Castle Hotel: Pleasantly decorated Georgian inn, neatly kept lounge and dining room up a few stairs from tiled floor bar, Greene King Old Speckled Hen and a choice of coffees, food from good ploughman's and bar snacks to imaginative restaurant dishes; unobtrusive piped music; terrace tables, comfortable bedrooms *(George Atkinson)*

TREFEGLWS [SN9790]

☆ *Red Lion*: Big homely open bar with tiled floor and beams, small lounge area, good interesting food cooked by landlady, Burtonwood, good coffee; pool room, children welcome *(Margaret and Andrew Leach)*

WALTON [SO2559]
Crown [A44 W of Kington]: Good country cooking, real ales inc Brains *(Steve and Liz Tilley)*

SOUTH GLAMORGAN
CARDIFF [ST1776]
Cayo Arms [Cathedral Rd]: Friendly pub tied to Tomos Watkins, five of their ales and guest beers kept well, two areas separated by ironwork, comfortable seats inc fine old wooden armchairs, lots of prints, well priced food all day inc good range of sandwiches, a few hot dishes and Sun lunch, quick service, daily papers; piped music, very busy wknds; tables out in front, open all day *(Andy and Jill Kassube, Meg and Colin Hamilton, Ian Phillips, Mr and Mrs M Dalby, Tony and Wendy Hobden)*
Conway [Conway Rd, Pontcanna]: Popular corner local with small traditional front bar, large comfortable back lounge, well kept ales such as Adnams, Greene King Abbot and Marstons Pedigree, straightforward bar food; pavement picnic-sets *(Mr and Mrs M Dalby, Ian Phillips)*
Cottage [St Mary St, nr Howells]: Proper down-to-earth pub with well kept Brains Bitter, SA and Dark Mild and good value generous home-cooked lunches, long bar with narrow frontage and back eating area, lots of polished wood and glass, good cheerful service, relaxed friendly atmosphere (even Fri/Sat when it's crowded – may be impromptu singing on rugby international days; quiet other evenings), decent choice of wines; open all day *(Ian Arthur, David Carr)*

COWBRIDGE [SS9974]
☆ *Bear* [High St, with car park behind off North St; signed off A48]: Neatly kept old coaching inn with Brains Bitter and SA, Hancocks HB, Worthington BB and a guest beer, decent house wines, friendly young staff, three bars with flagstones, bare boards or carpet, some stripped stone and panelling, big open fires, busy lunchtime for usual bar food from sandwiches up; children welcome; barrel-vaulted cellar restaurant, bedrooms quiet and comfortable, CCTV in car park *(David and Nina Pugsley, LYM)*

LLANCADLE [ST0368]
☆ *Green Dragon* [village signed off B4265 Barry—Llantwit just E of St Athan]: Cheerful traditional bar on left with hunting and other country prints, copper, china and harness, well kept Bass, Brains Revd James and Hancocks HB, farm cider, friendly uniformed staff, good value generous food inc huge mixed grill, comfortably relaxed dining lounge on right with nice pictures; may be piped music; picnic-sets on covered back terrace, bedrooms *(BB, J I Davies)*

LLANTWIT MAJOR [SS9668]
☆ *Old Swan* [Church St]: Unusual medieval building with lancet windows and good log

fires in big stone fireplaces, enjoyable food in bar and restaurant, real ales such as Everards Tiger, Exe Valley Exeter Old and Shepherd Neame Spitfire, lively public bar *(LYM, Ian Phillips)*

SIGINGSTONE [SS9771]
Victoria [off B4270 S of Cowbridge]: Spotlessly well kept neo-Victorian dining pub filled with interesting bric-a-brac, emphasis on good value quickly served food from simple bar meals to more elaborate dishes, popular upstairs restaurant, well kept Bass, good cheerful service, thriving atmosphere *(Alec and Barbara Jones)*

WEST GLAMORGAN
BISHOPSTON [SS5789]
☆ *Joiners Arms* [Bishopston Rd, just off B4436 SW of Swansea]: Thriving local brewing their own good value Swansea beers, also well kept guests such as Charles Wells Bombardier and Marstons Pedigree, decent wines; clean and welcoming, with quarry-tiled floor, old-fashioned décor and furnishings, local paintings and massive solid fuel stove, good generous food, cheap and simple, lunchtime and early evening inc panini, chilli, curries, sizzler dishes and OAP lunches Sat; big-screen TV for rugby – it's the club's local on Sat nights; children welcome, open all day Thurs-Sat; parking can be difficult *(Michael and Alison Sandy, LYM, Anne Morris, Chris and Martin Taylor)*

LLANMADOC [SS4493]
Britannia [the Gower, nr Whiteford Burrows – NT]: Right out on the Gower peninsula with lovely walks nearby, busy summer pub with tables out in front, and plenty more behind in neatly kept big back garden with flowers, lots of play equipment, assorted livestock and birds — and great estuary views; popular standard food with some nice vegetarian dishes, Brains beers, gleaming copper stove in beamed and tiled bar with old tables, a settle, a few farm tools and pool table, steps up to smarter lounge with lots of blowlamps and such, restaurant beyond (accordionist Sat night); children welcome, major caravan sites nearby, open all day Fri/Sat *(BB, Chris and Martin Taylor, Michael and Alison Sandy, Lawrence Pearse)*

MUMBLES [SS6188]
Park Inn [Park St]: Cosy little backstreet pub with wide range of interesting well kept beers inc local Swansea ones, lots of photographs of old Mumbles Railway, attractive plate collection *(A Boss, Michael and Alison Sandy)*

OLDWALLS [SS4891]
Greyhound: Good value food from unusual starters and ploughman's with choice of welsh cheeses to lots of curries and local fish in busy but spacious beamed and dark-panelled plush lounge bar, plush banquettes, half a dozen well kept ales, some tapped from the cask, inc

Bass and Felinfoel, good coffee inc decaf, decent wine, roaring coal fires, friendly service; back bar with display cases; restaurant popular at wknds, folk club Sun; big tree-shaded garden with play area and good views *(Guy Vowles)*

OXWICH [SS4986]
Oxwich Bay Hotel: Large and pleasant food-oriented hotel bar with beautiful bay and beach views, above-average reasonably priced food all day inc good rib of welsh black beef, efficient friendly helpful staff, occasionally a real ale such as Felinfoel Double Dragon; good for families, tables in well kept garden, bedrooms *(Lawrence Pearse, Dr F P Treasure, Mrs J Horrocks)*

PONTARDULAIS [SN6003]
Fountain [handy for M4 junction 47, via A4240/A48 (Bolgoed Rd)]: Popular dining pub under new ownership, good value food in bar and nicely laid out rustic-theme raftered restaurant inc lots of fish, interesting veg, home-made puddings, friendly attentive staff, well kept real ales, old local photographs; comfortable reasonably priced bedrooms with big breakfast, cl Mon *(Michael and Alison Sandy, Brian Green, Roy and Lindsey Fentiman)*

PONTLLIW [SN6002]
Glamorgan Arms [Bryntirion Rd]: Doing well under new landlord, with good food inc pasta and great chargrilled welsh black steaks; very child-friendly, with huge playground *(Andrew Wood)*

PONTNEDDFECHAN [SN8907]
Angel: 16th-c, comfortably opened up and light and airy without losing its interest, friendly staff and atmosphere, well kept ales such as Bass and Brains SA, plenty of dining tables (enjoyable food from good fresh sandwiches and rolls to welsh beef), masses of jugs on beams, old kitchen range, framed

World War II newspapers, separate flagstoned hikers' bar; no dogs inside; lots of flowers in front, venerable tables on terrace; bedrooms, good walks inc the waterfall *(Dave Braisted, Dennis Jenkin, Michael and Alison Sandy)*

REYNOLDSTON [SS4789]
☆ *King Arthur* [Higher Green, off A4118]: Cheery timbered main bar and hall, back family summer dining area (games room with pool in winter), food from lunchtime baguettes to popular Sun lunch, Bass, Felinfoel Double Dragon and Worthington Best, country-house bric-a-brac and log fire, no smoking restaurant; lively local atmosphere evenings, piped music; tables outside with play area, open all day, bedrooms *(Neil Rose, B and F A Hannam, Matthew Shackle, Ian and Nita Cooper, Chris and Martin Taylor, Caroline and Gavin Callow, Lawrence Pearse, David and Nina Pugsley, LYM)*

SWANSEA [SS6592]
No Sign Wine Bar [Wind St, 200 yds below Castle]: Line of four narrow old-fashioned rooms, first parlourish and welcoming, with mahogany cabinets and other fittings, large portrait in oils, cellars under bar; second more of an alcove, third full of church pews, fourth flagstoned and rather bare; some emphasis on decent fairly priced food (can get crowded lunchtimes), good wines, two glass sizes, also three real ales *(Guy Vowles, Dr and Mrs A K Clarke)*

THREE CROSSES [SS5694]
Poundffald Inn [Tirmynydd Rd, NW end]: 17th-c three-roomed beamed and timbered pub popular for generous good value food all day inc tasty welsh black curry, three well kept changing ales such as Greene King Abbot and Wadworths 6X, good coal fires, welcoming efficient staff; tables on side terrace, pretty hanging baskets and raised beds *(Michael and Alison Sandy)*

Post Office address codings confusingly give the impression that some pubs are in Gwent or Powys, Wales when they're really in Gloucestershire or Shropshire (which is where we list them).

Channel Islands

Three main entries which are doing particularly well this year are the Moulin de Lecq at Greve de Lecq (good choice of real ales from far-flung brewers in this converted former mill); the very family-oriented Old Portelet Inn at St Brelade (great clifftop position, lots for children to do); and on Guernsey (both those others are on Jersey) the Fleur du Jardin at King's Mills (consistently good food and a nice place to stay in – it would bear comparison with any mainland pub). It is the Fleur du Jardin which – not for the first time – gains the accolade of Channel Islands Dining Pub of the Year. In the Lucky Dip section at the end of the chapter, another Guernsey pub, the Hougue du Pommier, deserves a special mention; as does the Chambers in St Helier on Jersey, and the Admiral there – losing its place among the main entries this year only through an absence of recent reader reports on it. It's a lot easier than it used to be to find well kept real ale on the islands, with quite a few pubs stocking beers from the mainland, as well as the local brews – Randalls, and (both owned by Jersey Brewery) Guernsey and Tipsy Toad. Drinks prices here are well below the mainland average, though by a much narrower margin than a decade or so ago; indeed, beer in Lancashire pubs (the cheapest mainland area) on average now costs slightly less than it does here.

GREVE DE LECQ Map 1
Moulin de Lecq

During their occupation of the island the Germans commandeered this black-shuttered mill to generate power for their searchlights – you can still see the massive restored waterwheel outside, with its formidable gears in their stone housing behind the bar. Run by a cheery Irish landlady it's popular with visitors and locals alike. The bar has plush-cushioned black wooden seats against white-painted walls, a good log fire in winter, piped music and darts, and well kept changing beers from a broad range of brewers such as Greene King, Guernsey, Ringwood and Tipsy Toad on handpump. Bar food might include soup (£2.50), ploughman's (£5.50), burger or vegetarian lasagne (£5.95), wild mushroom risotto or steak and Guinness pie (£6.25), mussels and chips or fish kebab (£6.95) and daily specials such as grilled jersey plaice (£8.95) and beef wellington (£9.95); summer barbecues. Outside there are picnic-sets under cocktail parasols on the terrace, a children's adventure playground and bouncy castle. The road past here leads down to pleasant walks on one of the only north-coast beaches. *(Recommended by Kevin Flack, Ian Phillips, Stephen R Holman)*

Free house ~ Licensee Caroline Byrne ~ Real ale ~ Bar food (12-2, 6-9) ~ Restaurant ~ (01534) 482818 ~ Children welcome ~ Dogs allowed in bar ~ Open 11-11; cl Mon winter

KING'S MILLS Map 1
Fleur du Jardin 🍴 ♀ 🛏

King's Mills Road
Channel Islands Dining Pub of the Year
Maintaining consistently high standards, this attractive old inn is the sort of place

readers look forward to going back to on their return visit to the island, not least because it's in one of the prettiest parts. It's aptly named, with its good-sized gardens, and picnic-sets among colourful borders, shrubs, bright hanging baskets and flower barrels. Inside, the cosy relaxing rooms have low beams and thick granite walls. A good log fire burns in the public bar (popular with locals), and there are individual country furnishings in the lounge bar on the hotel side. Good interesting bar food includes soup (from £2.75), sandwiches (from £2.95), beef consommé with quail eggs (£4.20), fresh herb omelettes (£5.95), steak baguette (£6.45), fish and chips (£8.25), pork and apple cumberland sausage ring and mash (£8.95), lambs liver with balsamic jus (£10.75) and puddings such as walnut tart and filo basket filled with mixed cherries (from £3.25); part of the restaurant is no smoking. Well kept Bass, Guernsey Sunbeam and a guest, possibly from Tipsy Toad, on handpump, and a good wine list with around 17 by the glass (most by small or large glass); friendly efficient service; unobtrusive piped music. They have a large car park and there is a swimming pool for residents. *(Recommended by Phil and Sally Gorton, Stephen R Holman, B and M Kendall)*

Free house ~ Licensee Keith Read ~ Real ale ~ Bar food (12-2, 6-9.30(6.30-9 Sun)) ~ Restaurant ~ (01481) 257996 ~ Children in eating area of bar and restaurant ~ Open 11-11.45; 12-11.45 Sun ~ Bedrooms: /£88B

ROZEL Map 1
Rozel Bay Hotel

This friendly inn is tucked away at the edge of a sleepy little fishing village just out of sight of the sea. The bar counter and tables in the traditional-feeling and cosy little dark-beamed back bar are stripped to their original light wood finish, and there are dark plush wall seats and stools, an open granite fireplace, and old prints and local pictures on the cream walls. Leading off is a carpeted area with flowers on big solid square tables. Bass and Courage Directors are kept under light blanket pressure. Piped music, and TV, darts, pool, cribbage and dominoes in the games room. The good value short pubby menu in the downstairs bar includes dishes such as soup (£2.50), fish and chips, bangers and mash, and faggots and peas (all £5.95). The upstairs restaurant now concentrates on fresh fish in a relaxed rustic French atmosphere, with up to 10 fish dishes a day and good value specials. The pub has an attractive steeply terraced hillside garden. *(Recommended by Norman and June Williams)*

Randalls ~ Lease Ian King ~ Real ale ~ Bar food (12-2.30, 6-8; not Sun evening) ~ Restaurant (not Sun evening) ~ (01534) 863438 ~ Children welcome ~ Dogs allowed in bar ~ Open 11-11

ST AUBIN Map 1
Old Court House Inn 🛏️

Harbour Boulevard

There are delightful views over the tranquil harbour and on past St Aubin's fort right across the bay to St Helier from the conservatory at this charming 15th-c hotel. The Westward Bar is elegantly constructed from the actual gig of a schooner and offers a restauranty menu with prices to match. The pubby downstairs bar has cushioned wooden seats built against its stripped granite walls, low black beams, joists in a white ceiling, a turkey carpet and an open fire. A dimly lantern-lit inner room has an illuminated rather brackish-looking deep well, and beyond that the spacious cellar room which is open in summer. Enjoyable food (you can eat from the bar or restaurant menu downstairs) includes soup (£2.75), baguettes (from £4.75), vegetable lasagne (£4.95), moules marinière (£5.75), fish and chips or wild mushroom and asparagus risotto (£8.95), local plaice (£10.50), fresh crab (£12.50), fried duck breast with plum sauce (£13.95), local lobster (£30) and shellfish platter for two (£50). Well kept Courage Directors and Theakstons Old Peculier on handpump; TV and piped music. This place has an interesting past – the front used to be the home of a wealthy merchant, whose cellars stored privateers' plunder alongside more legitimate cargo, while the upstairs restaurant still shows signs of its time as a courtroom. It can be difficult to park near the hotel. *(Recommended by Ian Phillips)*

Free house ~ Licensee Jonty Sharp ~ Real ale ~ Bar food (12.30-2, 7-9.45) ~ Restaurant ~ (01534) 746433 ~ Children welcome ~ Open 11-11 ~ Bedrooms: £50B/£100B

ST BRELADE Map 1
Old Portelet Inn
Portelet Bay

This well run 17th-c farmhouse is well placed at the head of a long flight of granite steps, giving views across Portelet (Jersey's most southerly bay) as you go down to a sheltered cove. It's very popular, particularly with families and visitors to the island. Children will be happily occupied in either the supervised indoor play area (entrance 60p) or another one outside, and there are plenty of board games in the wooden-floored loft bar; cribbage, dominoes, and very audible piped music. The low-beamed downstairs bar has a stone bar counter, a huge open fire, gas lamps, old pictures, etched glass panels from France and a nice mixture of old wooden chairs on bare oak boards and quarry tiles. It opens into the big timber-ceilinged no smoking family dining area, with standing timbers and plenty of highchairs. Generous helpings of bar food served by friendly efficient and neatly dressed staff include sandwiches (from £1.95; open ones from £2.99), soup (£1.95), filled baked potatoes (from £3.90), chilli nachos (£4.50), ploughman's (£5.20), moules marinière (£5.85), steak and mushroom pie (£5.99) and sirloin steak (£9.50), with puddings such as chocolate fudge cake (from £2.25). Well kept Boddingtons, Courage Directors and a guest such as Wadworths 6X kept under light blanket pressure, and reasonably priced house wine; they do lots of liqueur coffees and hot chocolates. The picnic-sets on the partly covered flower-bower terrace by a wishing well are a good place to relax, and there are more seats in the sizeable landscaped garden with lots of scented stocks and other flowers; disabled and baby-changing facilities. *(Recommended by Ian Phillips, John Evans, Mrs Catherine Draper, Stephen R Holman, Emma Kingdon, Kevin Blake, Kevin Flack, Roger and Jenny Huggins)*

Randalls ~ Manager Stephen Jones ~ Real ale ~ Bar food (12-2.45, 3-5, 6-9) ~ (01534) 741899 ~ Children welcome ~ Dogs allowed in bar ~ Live music two or three nights a week in the summer, one night in winter ~ Open 9-11

Old Smugglers
Ouaisne Bay; OS map reference 595476

This laid-back pub is a conversion of a row of old fishermen's cottages. It's picturesquely set on a lane just above the beach with interesting views over one of the island's many defence towers from a weatherproof porch. The welcoming bar has thick walls, black beams, log fires, and cosy black built-in settles, also well kept Bass and two guests from brewers such as Ringwood and Shepherd Neame on handpump; sensibly placed darts as well as cribbage and dominoes. Enjoyable bar food includes home-made soup (£2.70), prawn cocktail or ploughman's (£4.95), burgers (from £4.75), filled baked potatoes (from £4.95), steak, Guinness and mushroom pie, or lasagne (£5.95), duck breast with orange and brandy sauce (£7.25), chicken breast filled with banana with coconut crumble in mild curry sauce (£7.50), bass with lemon butter sauce (£7.95), steaks (from £8.25), and king prawns with hot garlic butter (£8.75). A room in the restaurant is no smoking. *(Recommended by Emma Kingdon)*

Free house ~ Licensee Nigel Godfrey ~ Real ale ~ Bar food (12-2, 6-9; not winter Sun evening) ~ Restaurant ~ (01534) 741510 ~ Children welcome ~ Dogs allowed in bar ~ Open 11-11.30

You can send us reports through our web site: www.goodguides.com

ST HELIER Map 1
Town House
New Street

Popular during the day with families (baby-changing facilities and high chairs) the exterior of this 1930s pub is reminiscent of a converted cinema. Two main bars are divided by heavy but airy glass and brass doors. The sports bar on the left has a giant TV screen, darts, pool and a fruit machine. To the right, the lounge area has parquet flooring, some attractive panelling and stained glass, old photographs and solid furnishings; the restaurant has a no smoking area. As we went to press there were murmurings about a refurbishment but no definite plans. Reasonably priced straightforward dishes include soup (£1.80), baguettes (from £1.85), chicken in pitta bread (£3.75), burgers (from £4) and chicken or beef fajitas for two (£12). Well kept Tipsy Toad Jimmys, and sound house wines; piped music. *(Recommended by Ian Phillips, Roger and Jenny Huggins)*

Jersey ~ Managers Jackie and Martin Kelly ~ Real ale ~ Bar food (12.30-2, 6.30-9 (not Mon)) ~ Restaurant ~ (01534) 615000 ~ Children welcome till 5.30 ~ Open 11-11

ST JOHN Map 1
Les Fontaines
Le Grand Mourier, Route du Nord

Deceptively spacious, this former farmhouse is a popular local haunt. The part the tourists miss – where you're likely to hear the true Jersey patois – is the best part, the public bar. To get there, look out for the worn, unmarked door at the side of the building, or as you go down the main entry lobby towards the bigger main bar go through the tiny narrow door on your right. In here you'll find very heavy beams in the low dark ochre ceiling, massively thick irregular red granite walls and old-fashioned red leatherette cushioned settles and solid black tables on the quarry-tiled floor. The big granite-columned fireplace with a log fire warming its unusual inglenook seats may date back to the 14th c, and (a rarity these days) has kept its old smoking chains and side oven; for decoration there are antique prints and staffordshire china figurines and dogs. The carpeted main bar is a marked contrast, with plenty of wheelback chairs around neat dark tables, and a spiral staircase leading up to a wooden gallery under the high pine-raftered plank ceiling. Bass is kept under light blanket pressure, and one large area is no smoking; piped music. A bonus for families is Pirate Pete's, a supervised play area for children (entry 50p for half an hour), though children are also welcome in the other rooms. Bar food includes soup (£2.50), sandwiches (from £2.45), ploughman's (from £5.25), tortellini with ricotta or battered cod (£6.25), sweet and sour chicken (£6.50), cumberland sausage (£6.75), and specials such as baked lamb shank with mash (£8.35), grilled local plaice (£8.80), lobster or crab salad (from £9) and whole bass (£11). Seats on a terrace outside have good views, although lorries from the nearby quarry can mar the atmosphere; close to some good coastal walks. *(Recommended by BOB)*

Randalls ~ Manager Hazel O'Gorman ~ Real ale ~ Bar food (12-2.15(2.45 Sun), 6-9(8.30 Sun) ~ Restaurant ~ (01534) 862707 ~ Children welcome ~ Dogs allowed in bar ~ Open 11-11.30

ST OUENS BAY Map 1
La Pulente
Start of Five Mile Road; OS map reference 562488

There are sweeping views across the endless extent of Jersey's longest beach from the terrace, lounge and conservatory of this welcoming and civilised pub. Cheerful and busy, the public bar has a surfing theme, with photographs and prints on the walls, as well as a juke box, darts, pool, fruit machine and TV. The carpeted eating area upstairs has ragged walls and scrubbed wood tables, and leads off on to the terrace; piped music. Bass and a guest such as Courage Directors are well kept on handpump. Very enjoyable bar food, served by friendly staff, includes sandwiches (from £2.50), baked potatoes (from £3.50), ploughman's (from £5), well liked beer-battered cod (£6.75), and fried chicken breast with asparagus and leek tart and chive mash (£8.95), with daily specials such as guinea fowl with risotto cake, bacon, black pudding and red wine sauce (£8.95), crab salad (£10.50), half a lobster salad (£10.95), and fruits de mer (£30 for two). *(Recommended by J P Corbett, Kevin Flack, Ian Phillips)*

Randalls ~ Manager Rachel Lee ~ Real ale ~ Bar food (12-2.15 6-8.15; not Sun evening) ~ Restaurant ~ (01534) 744487 ~ Dogs allowed in bar ~ Live music Sun afternoon ~ Open 11-11

Lucky Dip

Besides the fully inspected pubs, you might like to try these Lucky Dips recommended to us and described by readers (if you do, please send us reports: www.goodguides.com).

GUERNSEY
CASTEL
Cobo Bay Hotel [Cobo Coast Rd]: Attentive friendly service, good Randalls beer, good well presented food; bedrooms *(C A Hall)*

☆ *Hougue du Pommier* [off Rte de Carteret, just inland from Cobo Bay and Grandes Rocques]: Civilised hotel with roomy partly no smoking beamed bar, sporting prints, trophies and guns, snug area by log fire in big stone fireplace, conservatory with cane furniture, consistently enjoyable food in bar and restaurant; popular with elderly folk (friendly helpful staff) but children welcome, apple trees shading tables on neat lawn, more by swimming pool in sheltered walled garden, and under trees in flower-filled courtyard, pitch-and-putt golf, attractive well appointed bedrooms, good breakfast, no dogs; cl Sun evening *(Bob and Valerie Mawson, Andrew and Amanda Rogers, LYM)*

ST MARTIN
Idle Rocks [Jerbourg Point]: Astonishing views of the island from pleasant lounge bar or terrace, wide choice of generous bar food; bedrooms *(J S Rutter)*

ST PETER PORT
Cock & Bull [Hauteville]: Decent proper pub valuable for its choice of up to six well kept imported real ales; packed on its frequent rollicking irish music nights *(Phil and Sally Gorton, Darly Graton, Graeme Gulibert)*

☆ *Ship & Crown* [opp Crown Pier, Esplanade]: Bustling town pub with bay windows overlooking harbour, very popular with yachting people and smarter locals, sharing building with Royal Guernsey Yacht Club; interesting photographs (esp concerning World War II German Occupation, also boats and ships), good value food from sandwiches through fast foods to steak, well kept Guernsey Bitter, welcoming prompt service even when busy *(Phil and Sally Gorton, Stephen R Holman, LYM)*

JERSEY
ST HELIER
☆ *Admiral* [St James St]: Heavily beamed candlelit pub with lots of shiny dark wood panelling, attractive solid country furniture, plenty of bric-a-brac inc an old penny 'What the Butler Saw' machine and enamel advertising signs (many more in small suntrap back courtyard), reasonably priced bar food (something available all afternoon), perhaps well kept Boddingtons and a monthly guest ale, daily papers, dominoes, cribbage; TV, piped music; children welcome, open all day *(LYM)*

☆ *Chambers* [Mulcaster St]: Impressive heavy-beamed pub with well done décor recalling its days as a court, separate areas, big leather sofas by open fires, candlelit tables, imposing paintings and bookcases, chandeliers, prints and mirrors, longcase clock, massively long bar counter with well kept Marstons Pedigree, Theakstons XB and Old Peculier and guest beers, decent wines, good generous reasonably priced food all day, neat staff, separate gallery dining room; children welcome till 8, quiet and civilised at lunchtime, can be very busy with young people evenings; live music – open till 1 am *(Kevin Blake, LYM, Emma Kingdon)*

Cock & Bottle [Halkett Pl]: Small cosy continental-feel pub, lively but smart, with lots of woodwork, bars upstairs (with zinc-topped counter) and downstairs, well kept Jersey Best and Special and a guest beer, good value lunchtime bar food, fast friendly service; picturesque outside with lots of hanging baskets, tables out on distinguished old leafy square *(Kevin Blake)*

ST MARTIN
☆ *Royal Hotel* [Gde Rte de Faldouet, by church]: Roomy and friendly family local by church in untouristy village, wide choice of generous popular well priced food in large efficiently run no smoking eating area, helpful landlord, well kept Wadworths 6X as well as local beer, decent wines, toys and video games in small children's room off extended lounge, games in public bar, attractive upstairs restaurant, old prints and bric-a-brac; piped music, nightly live music; tables out on big terrace with play area, open all day *(Gill Rowland, Julian Barringer, LYM)*

Overseas Lucky Dip

We're always interested to hear of good bars and pubs overseas – preferably really good examples of bars that visitors would find memorable, rather than transplanted 'British pubs'. A star marks places we would be confident would deserve a main entry.

AUSTRALIA
DALY WATERS
Daly Waters Pub [Stuart Highway, Northern Territory]: Good respite from Darwin—Alice drive, typical corrugated iron outback building said to be Australia's oldest licensed pub, very friendly, with great atmosphere, masses of dusty memorabilia, good outdoor barbecue, guitarists and singalongs; bedrooms, caravan site, locals in for 6.30 log fire breakfast *(Richard Turner)*
ROBE
Caledonian: Like an english pub inside and out – even the inside walls are ivy-covered; log fires, candles on tables, locals drinking at the bar, wonderful food inc top-class steaks, friendly staff, tables in yard and on grass overlooking beach; bedrooms, also two-storey garden flats *(C and R Bromage, John Saul)*
TILBA
Dromedary [Central Tilba]: Friendly traditional pub in picturesque Australian National Trust village, beautiful S coast area; good service, good choice of very cold beers, excellent hot beef rolls *(Peter Meister)*

BELGIUM
ANTWERP
De Grote Witt Arend [17 Reyndersstraat]: Smart café with several rooms and large courtyard with piped classical music, good beer choice, food from lasagne to ostrich steaks *(Mark and Ruth Brock)*
☆ *Het Elfde Gebod* [Torfbrug/Blauwmoezelstr]: Large ivy-clad café behind cathedral, overflowing with mix of religious statues and surreal art; good beer range inc Trappist Westmalle from altar-like bar, good choice of traditional belgian food inc mussels with frites, beef stew and good steaks, overflow upper gallery; piped classical music, can get busy – worth the wait for a table *(Mark and Ruth Brock)*
Paters Vaetje [1 Blaumoezelstraat]: Tall narrow bar by cathedral, interesting old interior with old beer advertisements, small panelled back gallery up steep stairs (occasionally visited by an aloof cat), good beer list, limited food; tables outside ideal for the carillon concerts *(Mark and Ruth Brock)*
Quinten Matsys [Moriaanstraat, off Wolstraat]: Claims to be oldest café here, plenty of character and interesting artefacts,

good shortish beer list and light meals (no snacks) *(Mark and Ruth Brock)*
BRUGES
☆ *Brugs Beertje* [Kemelstraat, off Steenstr nr cathedral]: Small friendly bar known as the Beer Academy, serving 350 of the country's beers, most of them strong ones, in each beer's distinctive glass; table menus, helpful English-speaking staff (and customers), good basic bar food; open from 4, can get a bit smoky later, very popular with tourists *(Mike and Wendy Proctor, Andrew York)*
Cìvière d'Or [Markt 33]: Smart split-level café/restaurant behind crenellated façade, dark panelling, plenty of beers on tap inc Maes and Grimbergen, good wine and authentic local food esp lobsters from live tank – a civilised escape from the touristy market and the other day-tripping Brits (the only blot on this delightful town with its polite locals speaking perfect English); heated and covered tables outside *(Tracey and Stephen Groves, Ian Phillips)*
Craenenburg [Markt]: Large bar with own little turret, quiet and refined, Leffe, Hoegaarden and Jupiter, coffee, cakes and good waffles, daily papers, leather seats, stained-glass window medallions; pavement tables *(Mike and Wendy Proctor, Richard Marjoram)*
Erasmus [Wollestraat 35]: Bustling and welcoming modernish hotel bar, mix of old and new décor inc intricate seasonal decorations, good choice of helpfully described beers, enjoyable food *(Mike and Wendy Proctor)*
Estaminet [Park 5, Astrid Park]: Charming welcoming intimate oak-furnished bar with choice of local beers, good coffee, enjoyable home cooking, attentive relaxed service; well chosen piped blues *(MP)*
☆ *Garre* [1 de Garre, off Breidelstraat]: Attractive and welcoming 16th-c timbered building, stripped brickwork, upper gallery, elegant and civilised but very relaxed and unstuffy, well over 100 mainly local beers inc five Trappists and its own draught beer – each well served in its own glass with cheese nibbles; sensible prices, knowledgeable helpful staff, sandwiches, unobtrusive piped classical music; children welcome *(MP)*
BRUSSELS
Bécasse [11 rue de Tabora]: Rather genteel

brown café, brightly lit by ornate scrolled metal lamps so showing well its dark panelling and beams, wide range of beers inc unblended Lambic (young and old) as well as Kriek served at the table in jugs, good snacks such as croustades made with beer and asparagus; open all day *(R Huggins, D Irving, E McCall, T McLean, Tracey and Stephen Groves)*

Bon Vieux Temps [rue Marché aux Herbes 12]: Classy and relaxing L-shaped brown café down white-tiled passage, beautifully carved dark panelling and stained glass, several unspoiled nooks and crannies, old tables, helpful staff, wide range of beers *(R Huggins, D Irving, E McCall, T McLean, Tracey and Stephen Groves, Mark and Ruth Brock)*

Cirio [20 rue de la Bourse]: Smart fin de siècle bar with impressive art nouveau features, large and full of mirrors but feeling busily cramped in quite a pleasant and very Brussels way; divided into three by panelling and pair of big plants in brass pots, wide choice of food from sandwiches, baguettes and toasties to steaks, good range of belgian beers *(Tracey and Stephen Groves, Roger and Jenny Huggins, Mark and Ruth Brock)*

Falstaff [17 rue Henri Maus]: Large traditional café/restaurant with impressive mix of rococo, art nouveau and art deco, end stained-glass image of Falstaff himself, Hoegaarden and Kriek on draught, bottled beers inc several Trappist ones, reasonably priced food inc moules and beef carbonnade; must pay to use the lavatories *(R Huggins, D Irving, E McCall, T McLean, Mark and Ruth Brock)*

Imaige de Nostre-Dame [Impasse des Cadeaux, off rue du Marché aux Herbes]: Dark, relaxed and intriguing brown bar tucked down alleyway nr Grand Place, two rooms with a right old mix of furniture, wide range of beers, open till midnight; outside lavatories *(Tracey and Stephen Groves)*

☆ *Mort Subite* [R Montagne aux Herbes Potagères; off Grand Place via Galeries St Hubert]: Under same family since 1928, long highly traditional fin de siècle room divided by two rows of pillars into nave with double rows of small polished tables and side aisles with single row, huge mirrors on all sides, leather seats, brisk uniformed waiters and waitresses bustling from lovely mirrored serving counter on dais on right; lots of beers inc their own speciality fruit beers brewed nearby (served by the bucket if you want), good straightforward food inc big omelettes, croques monsieur or madame, and local specialities such as brawn and rice tart, no piped music *(Dave Irving, Andy and Yvonne Cunningham, Roger and Jenny Huggins, Simon and Amanda Southwell, Tracey and Stephen Groves)*

Poechenellekeller [rue de Chêne]: Eccentric three-level bar, dark, cosy and cavern-like, welcoming and civilised; about 45 beers mainly from smaller breweries, strange puppetry collectibles (name means Mannequin Cellar – it's opposite the Mannekin Pis) *(Tracey and Stephen Groves)*

Rose Blanche [Grand Place]: Two-floor bar

overlooking the famous square, huge beer choice, enjoyable traditional food inc enormous helping of moules, waterzooi etc, good friendly service, woodwork galore; tables outside, next to beer museum *(Andy and Yvonne Cunningham, Simon and Amanda Southwell)*

EEKLO
Vreze Gods [6 Kerkplein]: Old-style café, ecclesiastical theme with pews and a pulpit, painted panels on bar showing local worthies, beers inc Westmalle Tripel *(Dr and Mrs A K Clarke)*

VERRE
Flandria [30 Grote Markt]: Modern but with plenty of atmosphere, not to mention 100 beers; friendly efficient service, delightful town square *(Dr and Mrs A K Clarke)*

CANADA
QUEBEC
Maison Serge Bruyère [1200 rue Saint-Jean]: Astonishing place comprising popular irish pub, casual chic bistro, café, and exceptionally good typically french formal restaurant *(Dennis Jenkin)*

TADOUSSAC
Pierre Coquart [off Bord de l'Eau; Quebec]: Enjoyable café food, decent wines, friendly staff; terrace tables, some overlooking bay *(Dennis Jenkin)*

CZECH REPUBLIC
PRAGUE
Dvou Kocek [Helnytrh 10; aka Two Cats]: Good local bar nr old town square clock, good Pilsner Urquell – very cheap if you stand by the bar; also seats in back room, and small area by window *(the Didler)*

Hrocha [opp British Embassy; aka Hippo]: Small backstreet local nr Charles Bridge, good Pilsner Urquell *(the Didler)*

Kalicha [Na Bojisti 12; aka Chalice]: Small parquet-floor bar with graffiti walls, Pilsner Urquell, may be free nuts; open all day *(the Didler)*

Kocovra [Nerudova 2, Mala Strana]: Long narrow three-room pub behind big black door, quiet and relaxing, Budvar beers and good basic czech food *(the Didler)*

☆ *Medvidku* [Na Perstyne 5, Stare Mesto]: Superb busy old bar in red light district, namesake bears etched in stone over entry, lots of copper in left bar, bigger right room more for eating (good low-priced food esp the soups – lots of czech specialities); excellent Budvar Budweiser *(the Didler)*

Milosrdnych [Milosrdnych 11, Stare Mesto]: Busy three-room local nr St Agnes Convent (now an art gallery), good cheap beers inc Pilsner Urquell, Gambrinus and perhaps Primus Pale 10; open all day, cl Sun *(the Didler)*

Pivnice Ruldofine [Klizovnicka]: Busy two-floor local nr Charles Bridge, great value Pilsner Urquell *(the Didler)*

Pivovarsky Dum [Lipova 15]: Brewpub with big windows showing fermentation room and brewing equipment, smart green décor and woodwork, interesting range inc wheat, banana, cherry and even champagne beers as well as classic lager (tempting brewing aromas out on the street), low prices, good choice of english-style food; open all day *(the Didler)*

Sebaracnicka [Rychta Irziste 22]: Narrow sidestreet bar nr British Embassy, comfortable and friendly; good value Pilsner Urquell *(the Didler)*

Snedeneho [1st left over Charles Bridge]: Tiny bar, quiet and friendly, with good value beers inc Budvar Pale, lots of old photographs, old record player in window; downstairs restaurant *(the Didler)*

Vejvodu [Jilska 4]: Carefully rebuilt and extended next door, with good value Pilsner Urquell; roomy but can get busy, handy for old town square *(the Didler)*

FRANCE
CALAIS

John Bull [Cité de L'Europe]: Useful if you can't wait to get back, english-style pub in huge shopping centre nr Eurostar/Shuttle terminal, well kept if rather cold british beers, good range of food inc steak sandwich and generous baguettes, relaxed atmosphere, English-speaking staff (and they take £s) *(Colin Gooch)*

GERMANY
BERLIN

Treffpunkt [Mittelstrasse, off Friedrichstrasse]: Simple and relaxing, pictures of nearby Brandenburg Gate on dark panelling, good beer choice, enjoyable snacks and meals (English menu, not common here), welcoming staff *(Roger and Jenny Huggins)*

HONG KONG
WANCHAI

Coyote [114 Lockhart Rd]: Mexican-themed bar with Samuel Adams and Miller on tap, lots of mexican beers and tequila, friendly atmosphere and helpful English managers, restaurant above with tex-mex wood-smoked and chargrilled steaks and seafood *(Charlie Cooper)*

IRELAND
BELFAST

☆ *Crown* [Gt Victoria St, opp Europa Hotel]: Well preserved bustling 19th-c gin palace with pillared entrance, opulent tiles outside and in, elaborately coloured windows, almost church-like ceiling, handsome mirrors, lots of individual snug booths with little doors and bells for waiter service, gas lighting, mosaic floor – even the graffiti on the pews have atmosphere (but shame about the TV); very wide and sometimes noisy range of customers, good lunchtime meals till 5 upstairs inc oysters, Hilden real ale, open all day; National Trust *(Dr and Mrs A K Clarke, CMW, JJW, Dave Braisted, Joe Green)*

Kitchen [Victoria St]: Friendly pub with impressive staff, decent beer and food,

interesting mix of customers, two long rather narrow bars, one with show business photographs and memorabilia *(Joe Green)*

DINGLE

Long [Strand St; Co Kerry]: Friendly staff, wide choice of food inc good fish; quiet irish piped music, can get very busy *(Angus and Rosemary Campbell)*

Old Smokehouse [Lower Main St; Co Kerry]: Good thoughtful service, friendly English owners, wide food choice inc good fish; unobtrusive irish piped music, can get crowded *(Angus and Rosemary Campbell)*

DUBLIN

Boars Head [Capel St]: Decent moderately priced standard food even Sun evening, in friendly small local *(Joe Green)*

Bruxelles [Harry St, off Grafton St]: Cosy and popular upstairs Victorian bar with dark panelling, mirrors, picture wall tiles and outstanding if rather dear Guinness, quick friendly service even on very busy lunchtimes, plentiful food inc home-made burgers and sausages; another typically Dublin bar downstairs, celtic symbols, grey/black/red décor, seats in alcoves and around central pillars, dim lighting; rock music can be loud, can be smoky; pavement tables *(W W Burke, M Joyner)*

Cassidy's [Campden St, S of centre]: Fine pub extending deeply back from narrow façade, friendly and well kept *(Joe Green)*

Doheny & Nesbitt [Lower Baggot St, by the Shelburne just below St Stephens Green]: Friendly traditional pub, originally a grocer's, close to Parliament; sensitively extended from original core, with Victorian bar fittings, marble-topped tables, wooden screens, old whiskey mirrors etc; mainly drink (inc good Guinness) and conversation, but has good value toasties, paninis, irish stew and so forth; live music, can get very busy but worth the wait *(Joe Green)*

O'Neills [Suffolk St]: Large early Victorian pub with lots of dark panelling and cubby-holes on different levels off big lively bar, good lunchtime carvery (go around 2 to avoid the crush; it's on all day Sun), good value doorstep sandwiches and home-made soup, quick efficient service, good Guinness *(M Joyner, Janet and Peter Race)*

Palace [Fleet St, Temple Bar]: Splendidly unspoilt Victorian bar standing out from the ersatz 'craic' elsewhere in Temple Bar, with snob screens, rooms through etched-glass doors, tiny snug, plainer back room with interesting well preserved cupola; good Guinness *(Joe Green)*

Porter House [Parliament St, nr Wellington Quay]: Vibrant three-storey modern pub, lots of pine and brass for café-bar feel, brewing half a dozen good beers inc Porter (particularly good), Stout, Lager and usually a cask-conditioned real ale, dozens of foreign bottled beers, friendly efficient service; high tables and equally high seats, good food from ciabatta sandwiches to steaks, upstairs restaurant; nightly live music, can be standing room only wknds; see Central London Lucky Dip under WC2 for an offshoot there *(Janet and Peter Race, Steve Harvey)*

ISLE OF MAN
PORT ERIN [SC2069]
☆ *Bay*: Three rooms with bare boards and good furniture, good value enjoyable fresh food, up to half a dozen well kept local Bushys beers (big picture of the old Bushys Bar in lounge) and a guest ale, wide wine choice, lovely spot overlooking sandy beach; flexible opening times *(Andrew Stephenson, David and Judith Stewart)*

LATVIA
RIGA
Alus Seta [6 Tirgonu Iela, by Dome Sq]: Beams, timbers and panelling, sliding windows to pavement tables, cheap Lido (brewed at another establishment in this Lido chain – most of which are more restauranty), Aldaris and excellent Uzavas, also tea and coffee, all-day self-service food bar inc shashliks and local specialities such as garlic toast, beaten pork steak or grey peas with bacon, narrow passage to back drinking hall with own bar, décor of old prints, latvian sayings, bric-a-brac and a constellation of small lights; open all day, very wide range of customers *(Martin Grosberg)*

MADEIRA
FUNCHAL
Prince Albert [off Avenida do Infante, nr Savoy Hotel]: Refuge for home-sick brits, owned by ex-pats, with Victorian-style dark panelling, dark wood furniture inc cast-iron-framed tables on tiled floor, old-fashioned curved bar, lots of advertising mirrors and colonial prints, good value sandwich snacks with chips until midnight, several unusual british bottled beers as well as local lagers and keg beers, darts, TV football, quiz nights, piped local and 60s music; open all day *(Kevin Thorpe)*
Red Lion [Rua do Favila; off main road W, just before Reids – on left, coming from town]: Not the fake-English pub the name suggests, but in fact a pleasant restaurant and bar, doing good reasonably priced local food esp espada (scabbard fish) and espatada (skewered beef); welcoming attentive English-speaking service, cheery bar staff, local Coral beer, excellent wine choice, not expensive; children welcome, tables outside, handy for hotel quarter and Quinta do Magnolia gardens *(Derek Stafford)*
Taska Espanhola [Avenida do Infante, opp Savoy Hotel]: Smart modern café/bar with big comfortable horseshoe bar screened from eating area by display wall of flasks, flagons and decanters, local Coral and Insular beers, food from soup and tacos to good omelettes, pepper beef and scabbard fish; discreet plasma screen TV *(Ian Phillips)*

MAJORCA
SOLLER
Es Guix [C/Baix, Carretera a Lluc; signed off C710 to Pollença]: Mountain bar/restaurant down rough track, handy for Lluc monastery, black beams, copper pans on rough stone walls, tiled floors, good local food inc kid and suckling pig cooked on woodburning range, bread from the monastery, local wines; lush gardens facing waterfall and rock pool, open 12-5, cl winter Tues and all Jan *(Susan and John Douglas)*

MALTA
BUGGIBA
Goodfellas [corner of Trix il Mullet, Qawra]: Stands out among all the tourist bars here as quite a gem, for its so very english décor, atmosphere and appeal; quite dark, with central bar, panelling and bare boards *(Mayur Shah)*

NAMIBIA
WINDHOEK
Joe's Pub: Bierkeller meets african village, german and local Windhoek beers, amazing germano-african food choice from bratwürst and grillhäxi to bushman game kebabs and springbok stir fries; cheap Sun buffet – eat as much as you like *(Richard Lippiett)*

NETHERLANDS
AMSTERDAM
Prins [Prinsengracht 124]: Friendly and appealing brown café on one of the most picturesque canals, well prepared generous food from good lunchtime sandwiches and fashionable snacks to steaks, wider evening choice (can be hard to get a table then), mainly dutch beers with one or two belgians such as La Chouffe, nice local atmosphere; handy for Anne Frank Museum *(Dr and Mrs A K Clarke, Michael Doswell)*
Zotte [Raamstraat 29]: Bustling candlelit belgian bar with good copious flemish food, enormous range of well kept belgian beers, charmingly helpful service; piped jazz *(Michael Doswell)*
DELFT
Locus Publicus [Brabantse Turfmarkt 67]: Dimly lit narrow bar with huge range of european beers, Guinness too, good cheap fresh sandwiches and other snacks, obliging service *(Michael Doswell)*

NEW ZEALAND
AUCKLAND
Fayre & Firkin [Montrose Terr, Mairangi Bay, North Shore]: Not unlike an english pub, with good food and quick pleasant service *(Marianne and Peter Stevens)*
Loaded Hog: Very popular brewpub, friendly and lively, part of a chain of this name, in excellent spot overlooking yacht basin, spacious bare-boards room with central bar open to street, balcony, Loaded Hog, Red Dog and other cold beers in chilled glasses, good quick food in good-sized helpings inc prime burgers, good cheerful service, wide choice of wine by the glass – all cheaper than UK *(Alan Sutton, Tracey and Stephen Groves)*

NORTH CYPRUS
KYRENIA
Harbour Club [Mersin; harbour]: Small downstairs bar with regimental plaques of british units which have served here, good local beer and turkish wines, good service, English-educated manager, great evening atmosphere in upstairs restaurant with verandah tables overlooking harbour, more by harbourside *(Derek Stafford)*

POLAND
WARSAW
Browar Soma [Foksal St 19]: Down passage past massive steel vats, light fresh pilsner brewed here (not cheap), biggish square bar with deep red walls and area off on right under balcony, candlelit tables, contemporary décor and trappings (think Pompidou Centre – except for sumptuous green curtains covering the tall windows), pleasing abstract paintings and beautiful big photographs of people in other cultures, surreal black and white moving images screened behind bar, spotlit rotating silver ball showering coloured stars through the dimness, young staff who make a friendly stab at English, mainly young customers; no food, but superb reasonably priced Restauracja Polska opposite *(Canon Michael Bourdeaux)*

SPAIN
SANTANDER
Prada a Tope [calle Guevara 7]: Smart rustic décor, lots of local wood, slate and sandstone, friendly service, consistently good beer, wines and enjoyable simple organic food such as cheeses, cured meats and sausages, roasted peppers, grilled steaks and lamb chops – all from their own brewery, winery and farms; part of a small local chain *(Steve Whalley)*
SEVILLE
Bar Estrella [Calle Estrella 5]: Plain, but very popular since the 1930s – their tapas win prizes for their originality at the Tapas Fair; in a warren of streets and alleys by the cathedral and Giralda *(Brian Haywood)*
Rinconcillo [Gerona 40]: Oldest bar here, founded 1670, front room with coffered ceiling, smoked hams hanging over ornate counter, towering racks of bottles, tapas with andalucian and mountain specialities; local Cruzcampo beer on tap, dining room open 1pm to 1.30am, smaller private room *(Ian Phillips)*

USA
DIXON
Dawsons [A St/North First St; California]: Proper old-fashioned small-town tavern reminiscent of Norman Rockwell, plenty of locals along the bar stools, food with proper fry-ups from 6am till lunchtime *(Joel Dobris)*
KANSAS CITY
Kelly's Westport Inn [Westport; Missouri]: Landmark building, one of city's oldest, with historic markers inc sign noting the beginning of several of the great western migration trails; friendly and busy, with large selection of inexpensive beer and plenty of local colour – you're encouraged to drop your peanut shells on the floor; another dozen bars and nightclubs within two blocks *(William Maloney)*
LONG BEACH
Rock Bottom [Ocean Blvd/One Pine Ave; California]: Visible microbrewery producing three or four good real ales, wide-ranging food; popular with younger people – can get crowded and noisy; small pavement drinking area *(Peter Scillitoe)*
Yard House [Shoreline Dr; California]: Upmarket pub with wide range of what it calls american fusion cooking (inc good pizzas and fish and chips), some 200 beers on tap from US microbrews to imports; terrace in charming setting overlooking Rainbow Harbour *(Peter Scillitoe)*
NASHVILLE
Big River Grill & Brewing Works [Broadway/2nd Ave; Tennessee]: Big bare-brick brewpub producing six beers; reasonably priced food, friendly service, pool tables, silenced TVs, tables outside *(Roger and Jenny Huggins)*
NEW ORLEANS
Crescent City Brewhouse [527 Decatur St; Louisiana]: Oysters in mirrored bar brewing own beers, copper mash tuns behind counter, T-shirts and pictures for sale, upstairs dining balcony overlooking Mississippi *(Roger and Jenny Huggins)*
ORLANDO
Big River Brewery [Boardwalk, Disney Resort; Florida]: Good bar brewing its own Tilt Pale Ale, Rocket Red and even a cask-conditioned IPA, enjoyable food; pleasant wooden verandah *(Andy and Jill Kassube)*
Shipyard [9333 W Airport Bvd; Florida]: In the airport, useful for its enjoyable food from sandwiches up, and brews its own good beers inc Export, Blue Fin Stout and Old Thumper (even a little heftier than the Ringwood original) *(Andy and Jill Kassube)*
PALO ALTO
Bodeguita del Medio [463 California Ave; California]: Lively antidote to anodyne chains, basic cuban décor, cuban food and beer (good choice on tap), fantastic rum list, lots of locals *(Mrs Jane Kingsbury)*
PASADENA
Lucky Baldwin [California]: Dozens of US and imported beers, esp belgian, many cask-conditioned; reasonably priced sandwiches, cottage pie, fish and chips etc, sports TV *(anon)*
SAN FRANCISCO
Beach Chalet [1000 Gt Highway; California]: Lively pub with good food esp fish and own brewery (taster trays), in old ocean-front Willis Polk building with fascinating 1920s mosaic murals downstairs showing San Francisco history and characters; wonderful view, nr Golden Gate Park *(Mrs Jane Kingsbury)*
ST AUGUSTINE
Rendezvous [St Georges Row, St Georges St; Florida]: 150 bottled beers from around the world, also restaurant food, silenced TV, simple furnishings *(Roger and Jenny Huggins)*

Special Interest Lists

Pubs with Good Gardens

The pubs listed here have bigger or more beautiful gardens, grounds or terraces than are usual for their areas. Note that in a town or city this might be very much more modest than the sort of garden that would deserve a listing in the countryside.

Bedfordshire
Old Warden, Hare & Hounds
Pegsdon, Live & Let Live
Riseley, Fox & Hounds

Berkshire
Aldworth, Bell
Ashmore Green, Sun in the Wood
Crazies Hill, Horns
Frilsham, Pot Kiln
Holyport, Belgian Arms
Inkpen, Crown & Garter
Marsh Benham, Red House
West Ilsley, Harrow
Winterbourne, Winterbourne Arms

Buckinghamshire
Bovingdon Green, Royal Oak
Fawley, Walnut Tree
Hambleden, Stag & Huntsman
Hawridge Common, Full Moon
Hedgerley, White Horse
Mentmore, Stag
Skirmett, Frog
Waddesdon, Five Arrows

Cambridgeshire
Elton, Black Horse
Fowlmere, Chequers
Heydon, King William IV
Madingley, Three Horseshoes
Wansford, Haycock

Cheshire
Aldford, Grosvenor Arms
Bunbury, Dysart Arms
Haughton Moss, Nags Head
Lower Peover, Bells of Peover
Macclesfield, Sutton Hall Hotel
Weston, White Lion

Cornwall
Helford, Shipwrights Arms
Manaccan, New Inn
Mousehole, Old Coastguard
Philleigh, Roseland
St Agnes, Turks Head
St Kew, St Kew Inn
St Mawgan, Falcon
Tresco, New Inn

Cumbria
Barbon, Barbon Inn
Bassenthwaite Lake, Pheasant
Bouth, White Hart

Derbyshire
Birch Vale, Waltzing Weasel
Buxton, Bull i' th' Thorn
Hathersage, Plough
Melbourne, John Thompson
Woolley Moor, White Horse

Devon
Berrynarbor, Olde Globe
Broadhembury, Drewe Arms
Churston Ferrers, Churston Court
Clayhidon, Merry Harriers
Clyst Hydon, Five Bells
Cornworthy, Hunters Lodge
Exeter, Imperial
Exminster, Turf Hotel
Haytor Vale, Rock
Lower Ashton, Manor Inn
Newton Abbot, Two Mile Oak
Sidbury, Hare & Hounds
Sidford, Blue Ball
South Zeal, Oxenham Arms

Dorset
Cerne Abbas, Royal Oak
Christchurch, Fishermans Haunt
Plush, Brace of Pheasants
Shaftesbury, Two Brewers
Shroton, Cricketers, Swan
Tarrant Monkton, Langton Arms
West Bexington, Manor Hotel

Essex
Castle Hedingham, Bell
Chappel, Swan
Great Yeldham, White Hart
Mill Green, Viper
Stock, Hoop
Wendens Ambo, Bell

Gloucestershire
Blaisdon, Red Hart
Brockhampton, Craven Arms
Ewen, Wild Duck
Gretton, Royal Oak
Hinton Dyrham, Bull
Kingscote, Hunters Hall
Nailsworth, Egypt Mill
North Nibley, New Inn
Northleach, Wheatsheaf
Old Sodbury, Dog
Twyning, Fleet
Upper Oddington, Horse & Groom

Hampshire
Bramdean, Fox
North Gorley, Royal Oak
Ovington, Bush
Owslebury, Ship
Steep, Harrow
Tichborne, Tichborne Arms
Whitsbury, Cartwheel

Herefordshire
Aymestrey, Riverside Inn
Sellack, Lough Pool
Trumpet, Verzons
Ullingswick, Three Crowns

Hertfordshire
Ashwell, Three Tuns
Potters Crouch, Holly Bush
Sarratt, Boot, Cock

Isle of Wight
Shorwell, Crown

Kent
Biddenden, Three Chimneys
Bough Beech, Wheatsheaf
Boyden Gate, Gate Inn
Chiddingstone, Castle Inn
Dargate, Dove
Fordcombe, Chafford Arms
Groombridge, Crown
Ickham, Duke William
Newnham, George
Penshurst, Bottle House
Selling, Rose & Crown
Ulcombe, Pepper Box

Lancashire
Newton, Parkers Arms
Whitewell, Inn at Whitewell

Leicestershire
Barrowden, Exeter Arms
Exton, Fox & Hounds
Lyddington, Old White Hart
Medbourne, Nevill Arms
Old Dalby, Crown
Stathern, Red Lion

Lincolnshire
Billingborough, Fortescue Arms

Coningsby, Lea Gate Inn
Lincoln, Victoria
Newton, Red Lion
Stamford, George of
  Stamford

Norfolk
Burnham Thorpe, Lord
  Nelson
Cley next the Sea, Three
  Swallows
Great Cressingham,
  Windmill
Letheringsett, Kings Head
Ringstead, Gin Trap
Snettisham, Rose & Crown
Stanhoe, Crown
Stow Bardolph, Hare Arms
Woodbastwick, Fur &
  Feather

Northamptonshire
East Haddon, Red Lion
Farthingstone, Kings Arms

Northumbria
Anick, Rat
Blanchland, Lord Crewe
  Arms
Diptonmill, Dipton Mill Inn
Greta Bridge, Morritt Arms
Thropton, Three Wheat
  Heads
Weldon Bridge, Anglers
  Arms

Nottinghamshire
Caunton, Caunton Beck
Colston Bassett, Martins
  Arms
Kimberley, Nelson &
  Railway
Walkeringham, Three Horse
  Shoes

Oxfordshire
Broadwell, Five Bells
Burford, Lamb
Chalgrove, Red Lion
Clifton, Duke of
  Cumberlands Head
Fyfield, White Hart
Highmoor, Rising Sun
Hook Norton, Gate Hangs
  High, Pear Tree
Kelmscott, Plough
Maidensgrove, Five
  Horseshoes
Sibford Gower, Bishop
  Blaize
Stanton St John, Star
Stoke Row, Grouse & Claret
Swalcliffe, Stags Head
Tadpole Bridge, Trout

Shropshire
Bishop's Castle, Castle
  Hotel, Three Tuns
Hopton Wafers, Crown
Norton, Hundred House

Somerset
Axbridge, Lamb
Chiselborough, Cat Head
Compton Martin, Ring o'
  Bells
Exford, Crown
Monksilver, Notley Arms
Rowberrow, Swan
Shepton Montague,
  Montague Inn

Staffordshire
Salt, Holly Bush
Stourton, Fox

Suffolk
Brome, Cornwallis
Dennington, Queens Head
Hundon, Plough
Lavenham, Angel
Laxfield, Kings Head
Long Melford, Black Lion
Rede, Plough
Walberswick, Bell
Waldringfield, Maybush

Surrey
Charleshill, Donkey
Coldharbour, Plough
Compton, Withies
Eashing, Stag
Lingfield, Hare & Hounds
Mickleham, King William IV
Newdigate, Surrey Oaks
Pirbright, Royal Oak
West End, Inn at West End

Sussex
Alfriston, George
Amberley, Black Horse
Ashurst, Fountain
Berwick, Cricketers Arms
Blackboys, Blackboys Inn
Byworth, Black Horse
Danehill, Coach & Horses
Elsted, Three Horseshoes
Fletching, Griffin
Hammerpot, Woodmans
  Arms
Heathfield, Star
Henley, Duke of
  Cumberland Arms
Oving, Gribble Inn
Rushlake Green, Horse &
  Groom
Seaford, Golden Galleon
Singleton, Fox & Hounds
Wineham, Royal Oak

Warwickshire
Edge Hill, Castle
Farnborough, Inn at
  Farnborough
Ilmington, Howard Arms
Wharf, Wharf Inn

Wiltshire
Alvediston, Crown
Berwick St James, Boot
Brinkworth, Three Crowns
Chicksgrove, Compasses

Ebbesbourne Wake,
  Horseshoe
Great Durnford, Black Horse
Kilmington, Red Lion
Lacock, George, Rising Sun
Little Cheverell, Owl
Norton, Vine Tree
Seend, Barge
Whitley, Pear Tree
Woodborough, Seven Stars

Worcestershire
Bretforton, Fleece
Welland, Anchor

Yorkshire
East Witton, Blue Lion
Egton Bridge, Horse Shoe
Halifax, Shibden Mill
Heath, Kings Arms
Scawton, Hare
Sutton upon Derwent, St
  Vincent Arms

London
Central London, Cross Keys
East London, Prospect of
  Whitby
North London, Spaniards
  Inn
South London, Crown &
  Greyhound, Founders
  Arms, Ship
West London, Colton Arms,
  Dove, Windsor Castle

Scotland
Ardfern, Galley of Lorne
Badachro, Badachro Inn
Edinburgh, Starbank
Gifford, Tweeddale Arms
Glenelg, Glenelg Inn
Skeabost, Skeabost House
  Hotel
Thornhill, Lion & Unicorn

Wales
Bodfari, Dinorben Arms
Colwyn Bay, Pen-y-Bryn
Crickhowell, Bear, Nantyffin
  Cider Mill
Gresford, Pant-yr-Ochain
Llanbedr-y-Cennin, Olde
  Bull
Llanfrynach, White Swan
Llangattock Lingoed,
  Hunters Moon
Llangedwyn, Green Inn
Llangollen, Corn Mill
Llangynidr, Coach & Horses
Llwyndafydd, Crown
Mold, Glasfryn
Old Radnor, Harp
Presteigne, Radnorshire
  Arms
Raglan, Clytha Arms
Rosebush, Tafarn Sinc
St Hilary, Bush
Tintern, Cherry Tree
Ty'n-y-groes, Groes

Channel Islands
King's Mills, Fleur du Jardin
Rozel, Rozel Bay Hotel

Waterside Pubs
*The pubs listed here are right
beside the sea, a sizeable
river, canal, lake or loch that
contributes significantly to
their attraction.*

Bedfordshire
Odell, Bell

Berkshire
Kintbury, Dundas Arms

Cambridgeshire
Sutton Gault, Anchor
Wansford, Haycock

Cheshire
Chester, Old Harkers Arms
Wrenbury, Dusty Miller

Cornwall
Bodinnick, Old Ferry
Crackington Haven,
  Coombe Barton
Helford, Shipwrights Arms
Malpas, Heron
Mousehole, Old
  Coastguard
Mylor Bridge, Pandora
Polkerris, Rashleigh
Port Isaac, Port Gaverne Inn
Porthleven, Ship
Sennen Cove, Old Success
St Agnes, Turks Head
Tresco, New Inn

Cumbria
Newby Bridge, Swan
Ulverston, Bay Horse

Derbyshire
Hathersage, Plough
Shardlow, Old Crown

Devon
Culmstock, Culm Valley
Dartmouth, Royal Castle
  Hotel
Exminster, Turf Hotel
Noss Mayo, Ship
Torcross, Start Bay

Dorset
Chideock, Anchor

Essex
Burnham-on-Crouch, White
  Harte
Chappel, Swan

Gloucestershire
Ashleworth Quay, Boat
Twyning, Fleet

Hampshire
Bursledon, Jolly Sailor
Ovington, Bush
Wherwell, Mayfly

Herefordshire
Aymestrey, Riverside Inn

Isle of Wight
Bembridge, Crab & Lobster
Seaview, Seaview Hotel
Ventnor, Spyglass

Kent
Deal, Kings Head
Oare, Shipwrights Arms

Lancashire
Little Eccleston, Cartford
Liverpool, Baltic Fleet
Manchester, Dukes 92
Whitewell, Inn at Whitewell

Lincolnshire
Brandy Wharf, Cider Centre

Norfolk
Brancaster Staithe, White
  Horse

Northamptonshire
Oundle, Mill

Northumbria
Newcastle upon Tyne, Head
  of Steam @ The Cluny
Newton-by-the-Sea, Ship

Oxfordshire
Tadpole Bridge, Trout

Shropshire
Ludlow, Unicorn
Shrewsbury, Armoury

Somerset
Churchill, Crown
Compton Martin, Ring o'
  Bells
Portishead, Windmill

Suffolk
Chelmondiston, Butt &
  Oyster
Nayland, Anchor
Southwold, Harbour Inn
Waldringfield, Maybush

Surrey
Eashing, Stag

Warwickshire
Lapworth, Navigation
Wharf, Wharf Inn

Wiltshire
Great Durnford, Black Horse
Seend, Barge

Worcestershire
Wyre Piddle, Anchor

Yorkshire
Hull, Minerva
Whitby, Duke of York

London
East London, Grapes,
  Prospect of Whitby
North London, Waterside
South London, Anchor, Bulls

Head, Cutty Sark,
  Founders Arms, Ship
West London, Bulls Head,
  Dove

Scotland
Aboyne, Boat
Ardfern, Galley of Lorne
Badachro, Badachro Inn
Crinan, Crinan Hotel
Edinburgh, Starbank
Elie, Ship
Glenelg, Glenelg Inn
Isle of Whithorn, Steam
  Packet
Kenmore, Kenmore Hotel
Kingholm Quay, Swan
Plockton, Plockton Hotel
Portpatrick, Crown
Shieldaig, Tigh an Eilean
  Hotel
Skeabost, Skeabost House
  Hotel
Stein, Stein Inn
Tayvallich, Tayvallich Inn
Ullapool, Ferry Boat

Wales
Aberdovey, Penhelig Arms
Abergorlech, Black Lion
Cresswell Quay, Cresselly
  Arms
Little Haven, Swan
Llangedwyn, Green Inn
Llangollen, Corn Mill
Llangynidr, Coach & Horses
Overton Bridge, Cross Foxes
Pembroke Ferry, Ferry Inn
Pontypool, Open Hearth
Red Wharf Bay, Ship
Talyllyn, Tynycornel

Channel Islands
St Aubin, Old Court House
  Inn
St Ouens Bay, La Pulente

**Pubs in Attractive
Surroundings**
*These pubs are in unusually
attractive or interesting
places – lovely countryside,
charming villages,
occasionally notable town
surroundings. Waterside
pubs are listed again here
only if their other
surroundings are special, too.*

Bedfordshire
Old Warden, Hare &
  Hounds
Pegsdon, Live & Let Live

Berkshire
Aldworth, Bell
Frilsham, Pot Kiln

Buckinghamshire
Bovingdon Green, Royal
  Oak

Fawley, Walnut Tree
Frieth, Prince Albert
Hambleden, Stag & Huntsman
Hawridge Common, Full Moon
Little Hampden, Rising Sun
Skirmett, Frog

Cambridgeshire
Elton, Black Horse

Cheshire
Barthomley, White Lion
Bunbury, Dysart Arms
Lower Peover, Bells of Peover
Willington, Boot

Cornwall
Blisland, Blisland Inn
Crackington Haven, Coombe Barton
Gurnards Head, Gurnards Head Hotel
Helston, Halzephron
Manaccan, New Inn
St Agnes, Turks Head
St Breward, Old Inn
St Kew, St Kew Inn
St Mawgan, Falcon
Tresco, New Inn
Trevaunance Cove, Driftwood Spars

Cumbria
Bassenthwaite Lake, Pheasant
Bouth, White Hart
Broughton Mills, Blacksmiths Arms
Buttermere, Bridge Hotel
Coniston, Sun
Crosthwaite, Punch Bowl
Elterwater, Britannia
Ennerdale Bridge, Shepherds Arms
Grasmere, Travellers Rest
Hawkshead, Drunken Duck, Kings Arms
Hesket Newmarket, Old Crown
Ings, Watermill
Langdale, Old Dungeon Ghyll
Little Langdale, Three Shires
Loweswater, Kirkstile Inn
Mungrisdale, Mill Inn
Newby Bridge, Swan
Santon Bridge, Bridge Inn
Seathwaite, Newfield Inn
Stonethwaite, Langstrath
Troutbeck, Queens Head
Ulverston, Bay Horse
Wasdale Head, Wasdale Head Inn

Derbyshire
Alderwasley, Bear
Brassington, Olde Gate

Foolow, Bulls Head
Froggatt Edge, Chequers
Hardwick Hall, Hardwick Inn
Hathersage, Plough
Kirk Ireton, Barley Mow
Ladybower Reservoir, Yorkshire Bridge
Little Hucklow, Old Bulls Head
Litton, Red Lion
Monsal Head, Monsal Head Hotel
Over Haddon, Lathkil
Woolley Moor, White Horse

Devon
Branscombe, Fountain Head
Buckland Monachorum, Drake Manor
Chagford, Ring o' Bells
Churston Ferrers, Churston Court
Culmstock, Culm Valley
Exminster, Turf Hotel
Haytor Vale, Rock
Holbeton, Mildmay Colours
Horndon, Elephants Nest
Iddesleigh, Duke of York
Kingston, Dolphin
Knowstone, Masons Arms
Lower Ashton, Manor Inn
Lustleigh, Cleave
Lydford, Dartmoor Inn
Meavy, Royal Oak
Molland, London
Peter Tavy, Peter Tavy Inn
Postbridge, Warren House
Rattery, Church House
Slapton, Tower
Widecombe, Rugglestone
Wonson, Northmore Arms

Dorset
East Chaldon, Sailors Return
Plush, Brace of Pheasants
Shaftesbury, Two Brewers
Worth Matravers, Square & Compass

Essex
Fuller Street, Square & Compasses
Little Dunmow, Flitch of Bacon
Mill Green, Viper

Gloucestershire
Ashleworth Quay, Boat
Bisley, Bear
Bledington, Kings Head
Brockhampton, Craven Arms
Chedworth, Seven Tuns
Chipping Campden, Eight Bells
Coln St Aldwyns, New Inn
Eastleach Turville, Victoria
Guiting Power, Hollow Bottom

Miserden, Carpenters Arms
Nailsworth, Weighbridge
Newland, Ostrich
North Nibley, New Inn
Northleach, Wheatsheaf
Sapperton, Bell
St Briavels, George
Stow-on-the-Wold, Eagle & Child

Hampshire
East Stratton, Northbrook Arms
East Tytherley, Star
Fritham, Royal Oak
Hawkley, Hawkley Inn
Lymington, Kings Head
Micheldever, Half Moon & Spread Eagle
North Gorley, Royal Oak
Ovington, Bush
Tichborne, Tichborne Arms

Herefordshire
Aymestrey, Riverside Inn
Dorstone, Pandy
Sellack, Lough Pool
Titley, Stagg
Walterstone, Carpenters Arms
Weobley, Salutation

Hertfordshire
Aldbury, Greyhound
Frithsden, Alford Arms
Sarratt, Cock

Kent
Brookland, Woolpack
Chiddingstone, Castle Inn
Groombridge, Crown
Newnham, George
Selling, Rose & Crown
Tunbridge Wells, Mount Edgcumbe Hotel

Lancashire
Blackstone Edge, White House
Downham, Assheton Arms
Little Eccleston, Cartford
Newton, Parkers Arms
Sawley, Spread Eagle
Tunstall, Lunesdale Arms
Uppermill, Church Inn
Whitewell, Inn at Whitewell

Leicestershire
Barrowden, Exeter Arms
Exton, Fox & Hounds
Upper Hambleton, Finches Arms

Lincolnshire
Aswarby, Tally Ho

Norfolk
Blakeney, White Horse
Burnham Market, Hoste Arms
Cley next the Sea, Three Swallows

Horsey, Nelson Head
Thornham, Lifeboat
Woodbastwick, Fur & Feather

Northamptonshire
Chapel Brampton, Brampton Halt
Harringworth, White Swan

Northumbria
Allenheads, Allenheads Inn
Blanchland, Lord Crewe Arms
Diptonmill, Dipton Mill Inn
Great Whittington, Queens Head
Haltwhistle, Milecastle Inn
Newton-by-the-Sea, Ship
Romaldkirk, Rose & Crown
Stannersburn, Pheasant

Nottinghamshire
Laxton, Dovecote

Oxfordshire
Chalgrove, Red Lion
Checkendon, Black Horse
Christmas Common, Fox & Hounds
Great Tew, Falkland Arms
Kelmscott, Plough
Maidensgrove, Five Horseshoes
Oxford, Kings Arms, Turf Tavern
Stoke Row, Grouse & Claret
Swalcliffe, Stags Head

Shropshire
Bridges, Horseshoe
Cardington, Royal Oak

Somerset
Appley, Globe
Axbridge, Lamb
Batcombe, Three Horseshoes
Crowcombe, Carew Arms
Exford, White Horse
Luxborough, Royal Oak
Triscombe, Blue Ball
Wells, City Arms
Winsford, Royal Oak

Staffordshire
Alstonefield, George
Stourton, Fox

Suffolk
Dennington, Queens Head
Dunwich, Ship
Lavenham, Angel
Levington, Ship
Walberswick, Bell

Surrey
Blackbrook, Plough
Cobham, Cricketers
Lingfield, Hare & Hounds
Mickleham, King William IV
Reigate Heath, Skimmington Castle

Sussex
Alfriston, George
Amberley, Black Horse
Billingshurst, Blue Ship
Burpham, George & Dragon
East Dean, Tiger
Fletching, Griffin
Heathfield, Star
Henley, Duke of Cumberland Arms
Lurgashall, Noahs Ark
Rye, Mermaid
Seaford, Golden Galleon
Wineham, Royal Oak

Warwickshire
Edge Hill, Castle
Himley, Crooked House

Wiltshire
Alvediston, Crown
Axford, Red Lion
Ebbesbourne Wake, Horseshoe
Lacock, Rising Sun
Newton Tony, Malet Arms
Stourton, Spread Eagle
Wylye, Bell

Worcestershire
Berrow Green, Admiral Rodney
Broadway, Crown & Trumpet
Kidderminster, King & Castle
Pensax, Bell

Yorkshire
Beck Hole, Birch Hall
Blakey Ridge, Lion
Bradfield, Strines Inn
Byland Abbey, Abbey Inn
Cray, White Lion
East Witton, Blue Lion
Halifax, Shibden Mill
Heath, Kings Arms
Hubberholme, George
Langthwaite, Charles Bathurst
Lastingham, Blacksmiths Arms
Levisham, Horseshoe
Litton, Queens Arms
Lund, Wellington
Masham, Kings Head
Osmotherley, Golden Lion
Ripley, Boars Head
Robin Hood's Bay, Laurel
Shelley, Three Acres
Terrington, Bay Horse
Thornton in Lonsdale, Marton Arms
Thornton Watlass, Buck
Wath in Nidderdale, Sportsmans Arms
Widdop, Pack Horse

London
Central London, Olde Mitre
North London, Spaniards Inn
South London, Crown & Greyhound

Scotland
Applecross, Applecross Inn
Crinan, Crinan Hotel
Kenmore, Kenmore Hotel
Kilberry, Kilberry Inn
Kingholm Quay, Swan
Stein, Stein Inn
Tushielaw, Tushielaw Inn

Wales
Abergorlech, Black Lion
Berriew, Lion
Bosherston, St Govans Country Inn
Caio, Brunant Arms
Carew, Carew Inn
Crickhowell, Nantyffin Cider Mill
Llanbedr-y-Cennin, Olde Bull
Llanberis, Pen-y-Gwryd
Llangattock Lingoed, Hunters Moon
Llangedwyn, Green Inn
Old Radnor, Harp
Red Wharf Bay, Ship
Rhyd-y-Meirch, Goose & Cuckoo
Talyllyn, Tynycornel
Tintern, Cherry Tree

Channel Islands
St Brelade, Old Portelet Inn, Old Smugglers
St John, Les Fontaines

Pubs with Good Views

These pubs are listed for their particularly good views, either from inside or from a garden or terrace. Waterside pubs are listed again here only if their view is exceptional in its own right – not just a straightforward sea view for example.

Cheshire
Frodsham, Ring o' Bells
Higher Burwardsley, Pheasant
Langley, Hanging Gate
Willington, Boot

Cornwall
Crackington Haven, Coombe Barton
Sennen Cove, Old Success
St Agnes, Turks Head

Cumbria
Cartmel Fell, Masons Arms
Hawkshead, Drunken Duck
Langdale, Old Dungeon Ghyll

Loweswater, Kirkstile Inn
Mungrisdale, Mill Inn
Stonethwaite, Langstrath
Troutbeck, Queens Head
Ulverston, Bay Horse
Wasdale Head, Wasdale
Head Inn

Derbyshire
Alderwasley, Bear
Foolow, Barrel, Bulls Head
Idridgehay, Black Swan
Monsal Head, Monsal Head
Hotel
Over Haddon, Lathkil

Devon
Postbridge, Warren House
Sidbury, Hare & Hounds

Dorset
West Bexington, Manor
Hotel
Worth Matravers, Square
& Compass

Gloucestershire
Gretton, Royal Oak
Sheepscombe, Butchers Arms

Hampshire
Owslebury, Ship

Herefordshire
Trumpet, Verzons

Isle of Wight
Bembridge, Crab &
Lobster
Ventnor, Spyglass

Kent
Tunbridge Wells, Beacon
Ulcombe, Pepper Box

Lancashire
Blackstone Edge, White
House
Newton, Parkers Arms
Sawley, Spread Eagle
Uppermill, Church Inn

Norfolk
Brancaster Staithe, White
Horse

Northamptonshire
Kings Sutton, White Horse

Northumbria
Anick, Rat
Newfield, Fox & Hounds
Seahouses, Olde Ship
Thropton, Three Wheat
Heads

Oxfordshire
Sibford Gower, Bishop
Blaize

Somerset
Portishead, Windmill
Shepton Montague,
Montague Inn

Suffolk
Erwarton, Queens Head
Hundon, Plough
Levington, Ship

Surrey
Mickleham, King
William IV

Sussex
Amberley, Sportsmans
Byworth, Black Horse
Elsted, Three Horseshoes
Fletching, Griffin
Henley, Duke of
Cumberland Arms
Icklesham, Queens Head

Wiltshire
Axford, Red Lion
Box, Quarrymans Arms
Lacock, Rising Sun

Worcestershire
Malvern, Nags Head
Pensax, Bell
Wyre Piddle, Anchor

Yorkshire
Blakey Ridge, Lion
Bradfield, Strines Inn
Kirkham, Stone Trough
Langthwaite, Charles
Bathurst
Litton, Queens Arms
Shelley, Three Acres
Whitby, Duke of York

London
South London, Anchor,
Founders Arms

Scotland
Applecross, Applecross Inn
Badachro, Badachro Inn
Crinan, Crinan Hotel
Edinburgh, Starbank
Glenelg, Glenelg Inn
Kilberry, Kilberry Inn
Shieldaig, Tigh an Eilean
Hotel
Stein, Stein Inn
Tushielaw, Tushielaw Inn
Ullapool, Ferry Boat
Weem, Ailean Chraggan

Wales
Aberdovey, Penhelig Arms
Bodfari, Dinorben Arms
Colwyn Bay, Pen-y-Bryn
Halkyn, Britannia
Llanbedr-y-Cennin, Olde Bull
Llanberis, Pen-y-Gwryd
Llangollen, Corn Mill
Mold, Glasfryn
Old Radnor, Harp
Overton Bridge, Cross Foxes
Rhyd-y-Meirch, Goose &
Cuckoo
Talyllyn, Tynycornel
Ty'n-y-groes, Groes

Channel Islands
St Aubin, Old Court House
Inn

Pubs in Interesting Buildings

*Pubs and inns are listed here
for the particular interest of
their building – something
really out of the ordinary to
look at, or occasionally a
building that has an
outstandingly interesting
historical background.*

Berkshire
Cookham, Bel & the Dragon

Buckinghamshire
Forty Green, Royal Standard
of England

Derbyshire
Buxton, Bull i' th' Thorn

Devon
Dartmouth, Cherub
Harberton, Church House
Rattery, Church House
Sourton, Highwayman
South Zeal, Oxenham Arms

Essex
Great Yeldham, White Hart

Lancashire
Liverpool, Philharmonic
Dining Rooms

Lincolnshire
Stamford, George of
Stamford

Northumbria
Blanchland, Lord Crewe
Arms

Nottinghamshire
Nottingham, Olde Trip to
Jerusalem

Oxfordshire
Banbury, Reindeer
Fyfield, White Hart

Somerset
Norton St Philip, George

Suffolk
Laxfield, Kings Head

Sussex
Rye, Mermaid

Warwickshire
Himley, Crooked House

Wiltshire
Salisbury, Haunch of
Venison

Worcestershire
Bretforton, Fleece

Yorkshire
Hull, Olde White Harte

London
Central London, Black Friar, Cittie of Yorke
South London, George

Scotland
Edinburgh, Café Royal, Guildford Arms

Open All Day (at least in summer)
We list here all the pubs that have told us they plan to stay open all day, even if it's only Saturday. We've included the few pubs which close just for half an hour to an hour, and the many more, chiefly in holiday areas, which open all day only in summer. The individual entries for the pubs themselves show the actual details.

Bedfordshire
Old Warden, Hare & Hounds
Pegsdon, Live & Let Live
Stanbridge, Five Bells
Turvey, Three Cranes

Berkshire
Boxford, Bell
Cookham, Bel & the Dragon
East Ilsley, Crown & Horns
Marsh Benham, Red House
Reading, Sweeney & Todd
Windsor, Two Brewers
Woodside, Rose & Crown

Buckinghamshire
Bennett End, Three Horseshoes
Bovingdon Green, Royal Oak
Chearsley, Bell
Easington, Mole & Chicken
Frieth, Prince Albert
Hedgerley, White Horse
Ley Hill, Swan
Mentmore, Stag
Soulbury, Boot
Wheeler End, Chequers
Wooburn Common, Chequers

Cambridgeshire
Cambridge, Eagle
Godmanchester, Exhibition
Kimbolton, New Sun
Peterborough, Brewery Tap, Charters
Wansford, Haycock

Cheshire
Aldford, Grosvenor Arms
Astbury, Egerton Arms
Barthomley, White Lion
Bunbury, Dysart Arms
Chester, Old Harkers Arms
Cotebrook, Fox & Barrel

Daresbury, Ring o' Bells
Higher Burwardsley, Pheasant
Lower Peover, Bells of Peover
Macclesfield, Sutton Hall Hotel
Peover Heath, Dog
Plumley, Smoker
Tarporley, Rising Sun
Wettenhall, Boot & Slipper
Willington, Boot

Cornwall
Blisland, Blisland Inn
Bodinnick, Old Ferry
Boscastle, Napoleon
Edmonton, Quarryman
Lostwithiel, Royal Oak
Mitchell, Plume of Feathers
Mousehole, Old Coastguard
Mylor Bridge, Pandora
Port Isaac, Golden Lion, Port Gaverne Inn
Porthleven, Ship
Sennen Cove, Old Success
St Agnes, Turks Head
Tregadillett, Eliot Arms
Tresco, New Inn
Trevaunance Cove, Driftwood Spars
Truro, Old Ale House

Cumbria
Ambleside, Golden Rule
Bouth, White Hart
Broughton Mills, Blacksmiths Arms
Buttermere, Bridge Hotel
Cartmel Fell, Masons Arms
Cockermouth, Bitter End
Coniston, Sun
Crosthwaite, Punch Bowl
Dalton-in-Furness, Black Dog
Elterwater, Britannia
Ennerdale Bridge, Shepherds Arms
Grasmere, Travellers Rest
Hawkshead, Kings Arms, Queens Head
Heversham, Blue Bell
Ings, Watermill
Langdale, Old Dungeon Ghyll
Little Langdale, Three Shires
Loweswater, Kirkstile Inn
Mungrisdale, Mill Inn
Newby Bridge, Swan
Santon Bridge, Bridge Inn
Seathwaite, Newfield Inn
Sedbergh, Dalesman
Stonethwaite, Langstrath
Tirril, Queens Head
Troutbeck, Queens Head
Ulverston, Bay Horse, Farmers Arms
Wasdale Head, Wasdale Head Inn

Derbyshire
Alderwasley, Bear
Beeley, Devonshire Arms
Buxton, Bull i' th' Thorn
Castleton, Castle Hotel
Derby, Alexandra, Brunswick, Olde Dolphin
Eyam, Miners Arms
Fenny Bentley, Bentley Brook, Coach & Horses
Foolow, Barrel, Bulls Head
Froggatt Edge, Chequers
Hardwick Hall, Hardwick Inn
Hathersage, Plough
Holbrook, Dead Poets
Idridgehay, Black Swan
Ladybower Reservoir, Yorkshire Bridge
Litton, Red Lion
Monsal Head, Monsal Head Hotel
Over Haddon, Lathkil
Shardlow, Old Crown
Wardlow, Three Stags Heads
Whittington Moor, Derby Tup
Woolley Moor, White Horse

Devon
Branscombe, Masons Arms
Churston Ferrers, Churston Court
Cockwood, Anchor
Dartmouth, Cherub, Royal Castle Hotel
Exeter, Imperial
Exminster, Turf Hotel
Haytor Vale, Rock
Horns Cross, Hoops
Iddesleigh, Duke of York
Lustleigh, Cleave
Marldon, Church House
Newton Abbot, Two Mile Oak
Nomansland, Mountpleasant
Noss Mayo, Ship
Postbridge, Warren House
Rockbeare, Jack in the Green
Sidbury, Hare & Hounds
Sidford, Blue Ball
Stoke Gabriel, Church House
Torcross, Start Bay
Widecombe, Rugglestone
Wonson, Northmore Arms
Woodland, Rising Sun

Dorset
Burton Bradstock, Anchor
Chideock, Anchor
Christchurch, Fishermans Haunt
East Chaldon, Sailors Return
Evershot, Acorn
Farnham, Museum
Furzehill, Stocks
Sturminster Newton, Swan

Tarrant Monkton, Langton
  Arms
West Bexington, Manor
  Hotel
Worth Matravers, Square
  & Compass

Essex
Burnham-on-Crouch, White
  Harte
Chappel, Swan
Chelmsford, Alma
Fingringhoe, Whalebone
Little Braxted, Green Man
Little Walden, Crown
Stock, Hoop
Stow Maries, Prince of
  Wales
Wendens Ambo, Bell
Youngs End, Green
  Dragon

Gloucestershire
Almondsbury, Bowl
Barnsley, Village Pub
Bisley, Bear
Brimpsfield, Golden Heart
Broad Campden, Bakers
  Arms
Chedworth, Seven Tuns
Chipping Campden, Eight
  Bells
Coln St Aldwyns, New Inn
Ewen, Wild Duck
Guiting Power, Hollow
  Bottom
Kingscote, Hunters Hall
Nailsworth, Egypt Mill,
  Weighbridge
North Nibley, New Inn
Northleach, Wheatsheaf
Old Sodbury, Dog
Oldbury-on-Severn, Anchor
Sheepscombe, Butchers Arms
Tetbury, Gumstool
Twyning, Fleet
Upper Oddington, Horse
  & Groom
Winchcombe, White Hart

Hampshire
Bank, Oak
Bentworth, Sun
Boldre, Red Lion
Bursledon, Jolly Sailor
Droxford, White Horse
East Stratton, Northbrook
  Arms
Easton, Chestnut Horse
Fritham, Royal Oak
Monxton, Black Swan
North Gorley, Royal Oak
Owslebury, Ship
Rowland's Castle, Castle
  Inn
Southsea, Wine Vaults
Well, Chequers
Wherwell, Mayfly
Winchester, Wykeham Arms

Herefordshire
Bodenham, Englands Gate
Dorstone, Pandy
Hereford, Victory
Ledbury, Feathers
Lugwardine, Crown &
  Anchor
Ross-on-Wye, Eagle
Trumpet, Verzons
Walterstone, Carpenters
  Arms
Weobley, Salutation
Woolhope, Crown

Hertfordshire
Aldbury, Greyhound,
  Valiant Trooper
Ashwell, Three Tuns
Batford, Gibraltar Castle
Frithsden, Alford Arms
Hertford, White Horse
Sarratt, Boot, Cock
Watton-at-Stone, George &
  Dragon

Isle of Wight
Arreton, White Lion
Bembridge, Crab & Lobster
Rookley, Chequers
Shorwell, Crown
Ventnor, Spyglass

Kent
Bough Beech, Wheatsheaf
Brookland, Woolpack
Chiddingstone, Castle Inn
Deal, Kings Head
Fordcombe, Chafford Arms
Groombridge, Crown
Hawkhurst, Queens
Hodsoll Street, Green Man
Iden Green, Woodcock
Ightham Common, Harrow
Langton Green, Hare
Penshurst, Bottle House
Smarden, Chequers
Stodmarsh, Red Lion
Tunbridge Wells, Beacon,
  Mount Edgcumbe Hotel,
  Sankeys
West Peckham, Swan on the
  Green

Lancashire
Barnston, Fox & Hounds
Belmont, Black Dog
Blackstone Edge, White
  House
Chipping, Dog & Partridge
Downham, Assheton Arms
Goosnargh, Horns
Little Eccleston, Cartford
Liverpool, Baltic Fleet,
  Philharmonic Dining
  Rooms
Longridge, Derby Arms
Lytham, Taps
Manchester, Britons
  Protection, Dukes 92, Lass
  o' Gowrie, Marble Arch

Newton, Parkers Arms
Raby, Wheatsheaf
Ribchester, White Bull
Stalybridge, Station Buffet
Uppermill, Church Inn
Yealand Conyers, New Inn

Leicestershire
Belmesthorpe, Blue Bell
Clipsham, Olive Branch
Empingham, White Horse
Great Bowden, Red Lion
Newton Burgoland, Belper
  Arms
Oadby, Cow & Plough
Oakham, Grainstore
Somerby, Old Brewery
Stathern, Red Lion
Stretton, Ram Jam Inn
Upper Hambleton, Finches
  Arms
Wing, Kings Arms

Lincolnshire
Brandy Wharf, Cider Centre
Dyke, Wishing Well
Grantham, Beehive
Lincoln, Victoria, Wig &
  Mitre
South Witham, Blue Cow
Stamford, Daniel Lambert,
  George of Stamford
Surfleet, Mermaid

Norfolk
Blakeney, Kings Arms
Brancaster Staithe, White
  Horse
Burnham Market, Hoste
  Arms
Cawston, Ratcatchers
Cley next the Sea, Three
  Swallows
Itteringham, Walpole Arms
Larling, Angel
Letheringsett, Kings Head
Mundford, Crown
Norwich, Adam & Eve, Fat
  Cat
Reepham, Old Brewery
  House
Snettisham, Rose & Crown
Swanton Morley, Darbys
Thornham, Lifeboat
Tivetshall St Mary, Old Ram
Upper Sheringham, Red Lion
Winterton-on-Sea,
  Fishermans Return
Woodbastwick, Fur &
  Feather

Northamptonshire
Chapel Brampton, Brampton
  Halt
Kilsby, George
Kings Sutton, White Horse
Oundle, Ship

Northumbria
Allendale, Kings Head

Allenheads, Allenheads Inn
Blanchland, Lord Crewe
  Arms
Carterway Heads, Manor
  House Inn
Greta Bridge, Morritt Arms
Newcastle upon Tyne,
  Crown Posada
Newton-by-the-Sea, Ship
Rennington, Masons Arms
Seahouses, Olde Ship
Shincliffe, Seven Stars
Stannington, Ridley Arms
Thropton, Three Wheat
  Heads

Nottinghamshire
Beeston, Victoria
Caunton, Caunton Beck
Halam, Waggon & Horses
Kimberley, Nelson &
  Railway
Nottingham, Bell, Fellows
  Morton & Clayton,
  Lincolnshire Poacher, Olde
  Trip to Jerusalem, Pit &
  Pendulum, Vat & Fiddle

Oxfordshire
Banbury, Reindeer
Buckland, Lamb
Chipping Norton, Chequers
Christmas Common, Fox &
  Hounds
Great Tew, Falkland Arms
Henley, Anchor
Hook Norton, Pear Tree
Oxford, Kings Arms, Turf
  Tavern
Stanton St John, Talk
  House
Thame, Swan
Wootton, Kings Head

Shropshire
Bishop's Castle, Six Bells,
  Three Tuns
Bridges, Horseshoe
Bromfield, Cookhouse
Hopton Wafers, Crown
Ironbridge, Malthouse
Much Wenlock, Talbot
Norton, Hundred House
Porth-y-waen, Lime Kiln
Shrewsbury, Armoury, Three
  Fishes
Wentnor, Crown

Somerset
Axbridge, Lamb
Bath, Old Green Tree
Bleadon, Queens Arms
Churchill, Crown
Clapton-in-Gordano, Black
  Horse
Crowcombe, Carew Arms
Exford, White Horse
Glastonbury, Who'd A
  Thought It
Holcombe, Ring o' Roses

Huish Episcopi, Rose &
  Crown
North Curry, Bird in Hand
Norton St Philip, George
Sparkford, Sparkford Inn
Stanton Wick, Carpenters
  Arms
Wells, City Arms, Crown

Staffordshire
Alstonefield, George
Salt, Holly Bush
Stourton, Fox
Warslow, Greyhound

Suffolk
Brome, Cornwallis
Chelmondiston, Butt &
  Oyster
Cotton, Trowel & Hammer
Dennington, Queens Head
Dunwich, Ship
Lavenham, Angel
Long Melford, Black Lion
Southwold, Harbour Inn
Stoke-by-Nayland, Angel
Walberswick, Bell
Waldringfield, Maybush

Surrey
Betchworth, Dolphin
Charleshill, Donkey
Coldharbour, Plough
Eashing, Stag
Leigh, Plough
Lingfield, Hare & Hounds
Mickleham, Running Horses
Pirbright, Royal Oak
Reigate Heath, Skimmington
  Castle
West End, Inn at West End

Sussex
Alfriston, George
Amberley, Black Horse
Arlington, Old Oak
Barnham, Murrell Arms
Berwick, Cricketers Arms
Charlton, Fox Goes Free
Chiddingly, Six Bells
Donnington, Blacksmiths
  Arms
East Dean, Tiger
Fletching, Griffin
Horsham, Black Jug
Icklesham, Queens Head
Lewes, Snowdrop
Oving, Gribble Inn
Pett, Two Sawyers
Rye, Mermaid
Seaford, Golden Galleon
Warnham, Sussex Oak
Wilmington, Giants Rest

Warwickshire
Armscote, Fox & Goose
Aston Cantlow, Kings Head
Birmingham, Old Joint Stock
Brierley Hill, Vine
Coventry, Old Windmill

Dunchurch, Dun Cow
Edge Hill, Castle
Farnborough, Inn at
  Farnborough
Gaydon, Malt Shovel
Hatton, Falcon
Himley, Crooked House
Kenilworth, Clarendon
  House
Lapworth, Navigation
Long Itchington, Duck on
  the Pond
Shipston-on-Stour, White
  Bear
Stratford-upon-Avon,
  Garrick
Wharf, Wharf Inn

Wiltshire
Barford St Martin, Barford
  Inn
Box, Quarrymans Arms
Devizes, Bear
Fonthill Gifford, Beckford
  Arms
Heytesbury, Angel
Hindon, Angel
Lacock, George, Red Lion,
  Rising Sun
Little Cheverell, Owl
Malmesbury, Smoking Dog
Norton, Vine Tree
Salisbury, Haunch of
  Venison
Seend, Barge
Semley, Benett Arms
Stourton, Spread Eagle

Worcestershire
Berrow Green, Admiral
  Rodney
Bewdley, Little Pack Horse
Bretforton, Fleece
Broadway, Crown &
  Trumpet
Childswickham,
  Childswickham Inn
Clent, Fountain
Flyford Flavell, Boot
Kidderminster, King &
  Castle
Pensax, Bell
Welland, Anchor
Wyre Piddle, Anchor

Yorkshire
Aldborough, Ship
Asenby, Crab & Lobster
Beck Hole, Birch Hall
Beverley, White Horse
Blakey Ridge, Lion
Boroughbridge, Black Bull
Bradfield, Strines Inn
Cray, White Lion
Cropton, New Inn
East Witton, Blue Lion
Elslack, Tempest Arms
Ferrensby, General Tarleton
Goose Eye, Turkey

Halifax, Shibden Mill
Harome, Star
Heath, Kings Arms
Heckmondwike, Old Hall
Hubberholme, George
Hull, Minerva, Olde White
 Harte
Kettlesing, Queens Head
Kirkbymoorside, George
 & Dragon
Langthwaite, Charles
 Bathurst
Ledsham, Chequers
Leeds, Whitelocks
Linthwaite, Sair
Linton, Windmill
Low Catton, Gold Cup
Masham, Kings Head
Osmotherley, Golden Lion
Pickering, White Swan
Pickhill, Nags Head
Pool, White Hart
Ripley, Boars Head
Robin Hood's Bay, Laurel
Scarborough, Hole in the
 Wall
Sheffield, New Barrack
Thornton in Lonsdale,
 Marton Arms
Thornton Watlass, Buck
Whitby, Duke of York
Widdop, Pack Horse

London
Central London, Admiral
 Codrington, Albert,
 Archery Tavern, Argyll
 Arms, Bishops Finger,
 Black Friar, Cittie of
 Yorke, Coopers Arms,
 Cross Keys, Dog & Duck,
 Eagle, Grapes, Grenadier,
 Guinea, Jerusalem Tavern,
 Lamb, Lamb & Flag, Lord
 Moon of the Mall, Moon
 Under Water, Museum
 Tavern, Nags Head, Old
 Bank of England, Olde
 Cheshire Cheese, Olde
 Mitre, Red Lion, Red Lion,
 Seven Stars, Star,
 Westminster Arms
East London, Grapes,
 Prospect of Whitby
North London, Chapel,
 Compton Arms, Duke of
 Cambridge, Flask, Holly
 Bush, Olde White Bear,
 Spaniards Inn, Waterside
South London, Alma,
 Anchor, Bulls Head,
 Crown & Greyhound,
 Cutty Sark, Fire Station,
 Founders Arms, Fox &
 Hounds, George, Market
 Porter, Ship, White Cross
West London, Anglesea
 Arms (both pubs), Atlas,

Bulls Head, Churchill
 Arms, Dove, Havelock
 Tavern, Portobello Gold,
 White Horse, Windsor
 Castle

Scotland
Aberdeen, Prince of Wales
Aboyne, Boat
Applecross, Applecross Inn
Ardfern, Galley of Lorne
Badachro, Badachro Inn
Broughty Ferry, Fishermans
 Tavern
Crinan, Crinan Hotel
East Linton, Drovers
Edinburgh, Abbotsford, Bow
 Bar, Café Royal, Guildford
 Arms, Kays Bar, Starbank
Elie, Ship
Gifford, Tweeddale Arms
Glasgow, Auctioneers,
 Babbity Bowster, Counting
 House
Houston, Fox & Hounds
Innerleithen, Traquair Arms
Inveraray, George
Isle of Whithorn, Steam
 Packet
Kenmore, Kenmore Hotel
Kilberry, Kilberry Inn
Kingholm Quay, Swan
Kippen, Cross Keys
Kirkton of Glenisla, Glenisla
 Hotel
Linlithgow, Four Marys
Lybster, Portland Arms
Oban, Oban Inn
Pitlochry, Moulin
Plockton, Plockton Hotel
Portpatrick, Crown
Shieldaig, Tigh an Eilean
 Hotel
Skeabost, Skeabost House
 Hotel
Stein, Stein Inn
Stonehaven, Lairhillock
Swinton, Wheatsheaf
Tayvallich, Tayvallich Inn
Thornhill, Lion & Unicorn
Ullapool, Ferry Boat
Weem, Ailean Chraggan

Wales
Abercych, Nags Head
Aberdovey, Penhelig Arms
Beaumaris, Olde Bulls Head
Bodfari, Dinorben Arms
Caio, Brunant Arms
Carew, Carew Inn
Colwyn Bay, Pen-y-Bryn
Cresswell Quay, Cresselly
 Arms
East Aberthaw, Blue Anchor
Gresford, Pant-yr-Ochain
Halkyn, Britannia
Hay-on-Wye, Kilverts, Old
 Black Lion
Llanbedr-y-Cennin, Olde

Bull
Llanberis, Pen-y-Gwryd
Llandeilo, Castle
Llandudno Junction, Queens
 Head
Llangedwyn, Green Inn
Llangollen, Corn Mill
Llangynidr, Coach & Horses
Mold, Glasfryn
Monknash, Plough &
 Harrow
Overton Bridge, Cross Foxes
Pontypool, Open Hearth
Porthgain, Sloop
Presteigne, Radnorshire
 Arms
Raglan, Clytha Arms
Red Wharf Bay, Ship
Rhyd-y-Meirch, Goose &
 Cuckoo
Rosebush, Tafarn Sinc
Saundersfoot, Royal Oak
St Hilary, Bush
Talyllyn, Tynycornel
Tintern, Cherry Tree

Channel Islands
Greve de Lecq, Moulin de
 Lecq
King's Mills, Fleur du
 Jardin
Rozel, Rozel Bay Hotel
St Aubin, Old Court House
 Inn
St Brelade, Old Portelet Inn,
 Old Smugglers
St Helier, Town House
St John, Les Fontaines
St Ouens Bay, La Pulente

**Pubs with No Smoking
Areas**
*We have listed all the pubs
which have told us they do
set aside at least some part of
the pub as a no smoking
area. Look at the individual
entries for the pubs
themselves to see just what
they do: provision is much
more generous in some pubs
than in others.*

Bedfordshire
Biddenham, Three Tuns
Broom, Cock
Houghton Conquest, Knife
 & Cleaver
Keysoe, Chequers
Old Warden, Hare &
 Hounds
Pegsdon, Live & Let Live
Stanbridge, Five Bells
Turvey, Three Cranes

Berkshire
Ashmore Green, Sun in the
 Wood
Boxford, Bell

Cookham, Bel & the Dragon
Crazies Hill, Horns
East Ilsley, Crown & Horns
Frilsham, Pot Kiln
Inkpen, Crown & Garter
Kintbury, Dundas Arms
Marsh Benham, Red House
Stanford Dingley, Bull, Old Boot
West Ilsley, Harrow
Winterbourne, Winterbourne Arms
Woodside, Rose & Crown
Yattendon, Royal Oak

Buckinghamshire
Chenies, Red Lion
Fawley, Walnut Tree
Forty Green, Royal Standard of England
Haddenham, Green Dragon
Hawridge Common, Full Moon
Ley Hill, Swan
Little Hampden, Rising Sun
Mentmore, Stag
Newton Longville, Crooked Billet
Prestwood, Polecat
Skirmett, Frog, Boot
Waddesdon, Five Arrows
Wheeler End, Chequers
Wooburn Common, Chequers

Cambridgeshire
Cambridge, Cambridge Blue, Eagle, Live & Let Live
Elton, Black Horse
Fen Ditton, Ancient Shepherds
Fen Drayton, Three Tuns
Fordham, White Pheasant
Fowlmere, Chequers
Godmanchester, Exhibition
Heydon, King William IV
Hinxton, Red Lion
Huntingdon, Old Bridge Hotel
Keyston, Pheasant
Madingley, Three Horseshoes
Newton, Queens Head
Peterborough, Brewery Tap, Charters
Stilton, Bell
Stow cum Quy, White Swan
Sutton Gault, Anchor
Thriplow, Green Man
Wansford, Haycock

Cheshire
Aldford, Grosvenor Arms
Astbury, Egerton Arms
Aston, Bhurtpore
Bunbury, Dysart Arms
Chester, Albion, Old Harkers Arms
Cotebrook, Fox & Barrel

Daresbury, Ring o' Bells
Frodsham, Ring o' Bells
Haughton Moss, Nags Head
Higher Burwardsley, Pheasant
Langley, Hanging Gate
Lower Peover, Bells of Peover
Peover Heath, Dog
Plumley, Smoker
Weston, White Lion
Wettenhall, Boot & Slipper
Willington, Boot
Wincle, Ship
Wrenbury, Dusty Miller

Cornwall
Bodinnick, Old Ferry
Constantine, Trengilly Wartha
Crackington Haven, Coombe Barton
Duloe, Olde Plough House
Edmonton, Quarryman
Egloshayle, Earl of St Vincent
Gurnards Head, Gurnards Head Hotel
Helston, Halzephron
Kingsand, Halfway House
Lanlivery, Crown
Malpas, Heron
Mitchell, Plume of Feathers
Mithian, Miners Arms
Mousehole, Old Coastguard
Mylor Bridge, Pandora
Philleigh, Roseland
Polkerris, Rashleigh
Port Isaac, Golden Lion, Port Gaverne Inn
Porthleven, Ship
St Agnes, Turks Head
St Breward, Old Inn
St Mawgan, Falcon
Treburley, Springer Spaniel
Tregadillett, Eliot Arms
Tresco, New Inn

Cumbria
Ambleside, Golden Rule
Appleby, Royal Oak
Barbon, Barbon Inn
Bassenthwaite Lake, Pheasant
Bouth, White Hart
Broughton Mills, Blacksmiths Arms
Buttermere, Bridge Hotel
Cartmel Fell, Masons Arms
Casterton, Pheasant
Cockermouth, Bitter End
Coniston, Sun
Crosthwaite, Punch Bowl
Elterwater, Britannia
Hawkshead, Drunken Duck, Kings Arms, Queens Head
Hesket Newmarket, Old Crown
Heversham, Blue Bell

Ings, Watermill
Keswick, George
Little Langdale, Three Shires
Loweswater, Kirkstile Inn
Mungrisdale, Mill Inn
Penruddock, Herdwick
Sandford, Sandford Arms
Santon Bridge, Bridge Inn
Seathwaite, Newfield Inn
Sedbergh, Dalesman
Stainton, Kings Arms
Stonethwaite, Langstrath
Talkin, Blacksmiths Arms
Tirril, Queens Head
Troutbeck, Queens Head
Ulverston, Bay Horse, Farmers Arms
Wasdale Head, Wasdale Head Inn
Yanwath, Gate Inn

Derbyshire
Birch Vale, Waltzing Weasel
Birchover, Druid
Brassington, Olde Gate
Buxton, Bull i' th' Thorn
Castleton, Castle Hotel
Derby, Alexandra, Brunswick
Eyam, Miners Arms
Fenny Bentley, Bentley Brook, Coach & Horses
Foolow, Bulls Head
Froggatt Edge, Chequers
Hardwick Hall, Hardwick Inn
Hassop, Eyre Arms
Hathersage, Plough
Hognaston, Red Lion
Idridgehay, Black Swan
Kirk Ireton, Barley Mow
Ladybower Reservoir, Yorkshire Bridge
Melbourne, John Thompson
Milltown, Miners Arms
Monsal Head, Monsal Head Hotel
Over Haddon, Lathkil
Whittington Moor, Derby Tup
Woolley Moor, White Horse

Devon
Ashprington, Durant Arms
Bantham, Sloop
Berrynarbor, Olde Globe
Branscombe, Fountain Head
Broadhembury, Drewe Arms
Buckland Brewer, Coach & Horses
Buckland Monachorum, Drake Manor
Butterleigh, Butterleigh Inn
Chagford, Ring o' Bells
Cheriton Bishop, Old Thatch Inn
Churston Ferrers, Churston Court
Clayhidon, Merry Harriers

Clyst Hydon, Five Bells
Cockwood, Anchor
Coleford, New Inn
Cornworthy, Hunters Lodge
Dalwood, Tuckers Arms
Dartmouth, Cherub
Doddiscombsleigh, Nobody Inn
Dolton, Union
Drewsteignton, Drewe Arms
Exeter, Imperial
Exminster, Turf Hotel
Harberton, Church House
Haytor Vale, Rock
Holbeton, Mildmay Colours
Horndon, Elephants Nest
Horns Cross, Hoops
Kingston, Dolphin
Knowstone, Masons Arms
Littlehempston, Tally Ho!
Lustleigh, Cleave
Lydford, Dartmoor Inn
Marldon, Church House
Meavy, Royal Oak
Nomansland, Mountpleasant
Noss Mayo, Ship
Peter Tavy, Peter Tavy Inn
Rattery, Church House
Rockbeare, Jack in the Green
Sidford, Blue Ball
Slapton, Tower
Sourton, Highwayman
South Zeal, Oxenham Arms
Staverton, Sea Trout
Stockland, Kings Arms
Stoke Fleming, Green Dragon
Topsham, Bridge
Torcross, Start Bay
Widecombe, Rugglestone
Woodbury Salterton, Diggers Rest
Woodland, Rising Sun

Dorset
Burton Bradstock, Anchor
Cerne Abbas, Royal Oak
Chideock, Anchor
Christchurch, Fishermans Haunt
East Chaldon, Sailors Return
East Knighton, Countryman
East Morden, Cock & Bottle
Evershot, Acorn
Farnham, Museum
Furzehill, Stocks
Plush, Brace of Pheasants
Shaftesbury, Two Brewers
Sherborne, Skippers
Shroton, Cricketers
Stratton, Saxon Arms
Sturminster Newton, Swan
Tarrant Monkton, Langton Arms
West Bay, West Bay
West Bexington, Manor Hotel

Essex
Arkesden, Axe & Compasses
Birchanger, Three Willows
Castle Hedingham, Bell
Chappel, Swan
Clavering, Cricketers
Fingringhoe, Whalebone
Gosfield, Green Man
Great Yeldham, White Hart
Horndon-on-the-Hill, Bell
Little Braxted, Green Man
Little Dunmow, Flitch of Bacon
Maldon, Blue Boar
Wendens Ambo, Bell
Youngs End, Green Dragon

Gloucestershire
Ashleworth, Queens Arms
Ashleworth Quay, Boat
Awre, Red Hart
Barnsley, Village Pub
Bisley, Bear
Blaisdon, Red Hart
Bledington, Kings Head
Box, Halfway Inn
Brimpsfield, Golden Heart
Broad Campden, Bakers Arms
Chedworth, Seven Tuns
Chipping Campden, Eight Bells
Coln St Aldwyns, New Inn
Didmarton, Kings Arms
Duntisbourne Abbots, Five Mile House
Dursley, Old Spot
Eastleach Turville, Victoria
Gretton, Royal Oak
Hinton Dyrham, Bull
Kingscote, Hunters Hall
Littleton-upon-Severn, White Hart
Meysey Hampton, Masons Arms
Miserden, Carpenters Arms
Nailsworth, Weighbridge
Naunton, Black Horse
Newland, Ostrich
North Cerney, Bathurst Arms
Old Sodbury, Dog
Oldbury-on-Severn, Anchor
Sapperton, Bell
Sheepscombe, Butchers Arms
St Briavels, George
Stow-on-the-Wold, Eagle & Child
Tetbury, Gumstool, Trouble House
Todenham, Farriers Arms
Upper Oddington, Horse & Groom
Winchcombe, White Hart

Hampshire
Axford, Crown
Boldre, Red Lion
Bramdean, Fox
Bursledon, Jolly Sailor
Chalton, Red Lion
Droxford, White Horse
East Stratton, Northbrook Arms
East Tytherley, Star
Easton, Chestnut Horse
Eversley, Golden Pot
Hambledon, Vine
Hawkley, Hawkley Inn
Longstock, Peat Spade
Lymington, Kings Head
Micheldever, Half Moon & Spread Eagle
North Gorley, Royal Oak
Ovington, Bush
Owslebury, Ship
Petersfield, Trooper
Pilley, Fleur de Lys
Rotherwick, Falcon
Rowland's Castle, Castle Inn
Southsea, Wine Vaults
Sparsholt, Plough
Stockbridge, Three Cups
Well, Chequers
Wherwell, White Lion
Winchester, Wykeham Arms

Herefordshire
Aymestrey, Riverside Inn
Bodenham, Englands Gate
Brimfield, Roebuck Inn
Carey, Cottage of Content
Dorstone, Pandy
Ledbury, Feathers
Little Cowarne, Three Horseshoes
Lugwardine, Crown & Anchor
Orleton, Boot
Pembridge, New Inn
Sellack, Lough Pool
St Owen's Cross, New Inn
Stockton Cross, Stockton Cross Inn
Titley, Stagg
Trumpet, Verzons
Ullingswick, Three Crowns
Upton Bishop, Moody Cow
Walterstone, Carpenters Arms
Wellington, Wellington
Weobley, Salutation
Woolhope, Crown

Hertfordshire
Aldbury, Greyhound, Valiant Trooper
Ardeley, Jolly Waggoner
Ashwell, Three Tuns
Hertford, White Horse
Sarratt, Boot, Cock
Watton-at-Stone, George & Dragon

Isle of Wight
Arreton, White Lion
Bembridge, Crab & Lobster
Bonchurch, Bonchurch Inn

Rookley, Chequers
Seaview, Seaview Hotel
Shalfleet, New Inn
Ventnor, Spyglass

Kent
Boyden Gate, Gate Inn
Chiddingstone, Castle Inn
Groombridge, Crown
Hawkhurst, Queens
Ickham, Duke William
Ightham Common, Harrow
Newnham, George
Oare, Shipwrights Arms
Penshurst, Bottle House
Pluckley, Rose & Crown
Sandgate, Clarendon
Selling, Rose & Crown
Smarden, Chequers
Tunbridge Wells, Mount
  Edgcumbe Hotel, Sankeys
Ulcombe, Pepper Box
West Malling, Swan

Lancashire
Bay Horse, Bay Horse
Belmont, Black Dog
Blackstone Edge, White
  House
Chipping, Dog & Partridge
Downham, Assheton Arms
Goosnargh, Horns
Liverpool, Baltic Fleet,
  Philharmonic Dining
  Rooms
Longridge, Derby Arms
Manchester, Britons
  Protection, Dukes 92, Lass
  o' Gowrie
Mellor, Oddfellows Arms
Newton, Parkers Arms
Raby, Wheatsheaf
Ribchester, White Bull
Sawley, Spread Eagle
Uppermill, Church Inn
Yealand Conyers, New Inn

Leicestershire
Barrowden, Exeter Arms
Belmesthorpe, Blue Bell
Castle Donington, Nags
  Head
Clipsham, Olive Branch
Cottesmore, Sun
East Langton, Bell
Empingham, White Horse
Exton, Fox & Hounds
Great Bowden, Red Lion
Gumley, Bell
Lyddington, Old White Hart
Market Overton, Black Bull
Newton Burgoland, Belper
  Arms
Oadby, Cow & Plough
Old Dalby, Crown
Sibson, Cock
Somerby, Old Brewery,
  Stilton Cheese
Stathern, Red Lion

Stretton, Ram Jam Inn
Thorpe Langton, Bakers
  Arms
Upper Hambleton, Finches
  Arms
Wing, Kings Arms

Lincolnshire
Allington, Welby Arms
Aswarby, Tally Ho
Barnoldby le Beck, Ship
Brandy Wharf, Cider Centre
Coningsby, Lea Gate Inn
Dyke, Wishing Well
Gedney Dyke, Chequers
Lincoln, Wig & Mitre
Newton, Red Lion
South Witham, Blue Cow
Stamford, Daniel Lambert,
  George of Stamford
Surfleet, Mermaid
Woolsthorpe, Chequers

Norfolk
Blakeney, Kings Arms, White
  Horse
Brancaster Staithe, White
  Horse
Burnham Market, Hoste
  Arms
Burnham Thorpe, Lord
  Nelson
Cawston, Ratcatchers
Cley next the Sea, Three
  Swallows
Horsey, Nelson Head
Itteringham, Walpole Arms
Larling, Angel
Letheringsett, Kings Head
Mundford, Crown
Norwich, Adam & Eve
Reepham, Old Brewery
  House
Ringstead, Gin Trap
Snettisham, Rose & Crown
Stiffkey, Red Lion
Stow Bardolph, Hare Arms
Swanton Morley, Darbys
Terrington St John,
  Woolpack
Thornham, Lifeboat
Tivetshall St Mary, Old Ram
Upper Sheringham, Red Lion
Warham, Three Horseshoes
Winterton-on-Sea,
  Fishermans Return
Woodbastwick, Fur &
  Feather

Northamptonshire
Badby, Windmill
Clipston, Bulls Head
Crick, Red Lion
East Haddon, Red Lion
Fotheringhay, Falcon
Great Oxendon, George
Harringworth, White Swan
Kilsby, George
Nether Heyford, Old Sun

Oundle, Mill, Ship
Sulgrave, Star
Woodnewton, White Swan

Northumbria
Allendale, Kings Head
Allenheads, Allenheads Inn
Aycliffe, County
Carterway Heads, Manor
  House Inn
Cotherstone, Fox & Hounds
Great Whittington, Queens
  Head
Greta Bridge, Morritt Arms
Newcastle upon Tyne, Head
  of Steam @ The Cluny
Newton-on-the-Moor, Cook
  & Barker Arms
Rennington, Masons Arms
Romaldkirk, Rose & Crown
Seahouses, Olde Ship
Shincliffe, Seven Stars
Stannersburn, Pheasant
Stannington, Ridley Arms
Thropton, Three Wheat
  Heads
Weldon Bridge, Anglers
  Arms

Nottinghamshire
Caunton, Caunton Beck
Colston Bassett, Martins
  Arms
Elkesley, Robin Hood
Halam, Waggon & Horses
Kimberley, Nelson &
  Railway
Laxton, Dovecote
Morton, Full Moon
Nottingham, Bell,
  Lincolnshire Poacher, Olde
  Trip to Jerusalem

Oxfordshire
Alvescot, Plough
Banbury, Reindeer
Blewbury, Blewbury Inn
Broadwell, Five Bells
Buckland, Lamb
Burford, Lamb
Caulcott, Horse & Groom
Chalgrove, Red Lion
Chipping Norton, Chequers
Christmas Common, Fox &
  Hounds
Clifton, Duke of
  Cumberlands Head
Fifield, Merrymouth
Fyfield, White Hart
Great Tew, Falkland Arms
Highmoor, Rising Sun
Hook Norton, Pear Tree, Sun
Lewknor, Olde Leathern
  Bottel
Oxford, Kings Arms, Turf
  Tavern
Ramsden, Royal Oak
Shipton-under-Wychwood,
  Shaven Crown

Stanton St John, Star, Talk House
Swalcliffe, Stags Head
Tadpole Bridge, Trout
Wootton, Kings Head

Shropshire
Bishop's Castle, Castle Hotel, Six Bells, Three Tuns
Bromfield, Cookhouse
Cardington, Royal Oak
Hopton Wafers, Crown
Ironbridge, Malthouse
Longville, Longville Arms
Ludlow, Unicorn
Much Wenlock, Talbot
Norbury, Sun
Norton, Hundred House
Porth-y-waen, Lime Kiln
Shrewsbury, Armoury
Wistanstow, Plough

Somerset
Appley, Globe
Batcombe, Three Horseshoes
Bath, Old Green Tree
Bleadon, Queens Arms
Chiselborough, Cat Head
Compton Martin, Ring o' Bells
Congresbury, White Hart
Doulting, Waggon & Horses
East Lyng, Rose & Crown
East Woodlands, Horse & Groom
Exford, White Horse
Glastonbury, Who'd A Thought It
Holcombe, Ring o' Roses
Huish Episcopi, Rose & Crown
Kingsdon, Kingsdon Inn
Langley Marsh, Three Horseshoes
Lovington, Pilgrims Rest
Luxborough, Royal Oak
Mells, Talbot
Monksilver, Notley Arms
North Curry, Bird in Hand
Norton St Philip, George
Portishead, Windmill
Shepton Montague, Montague Inn
Stanton Wick, Carpenters Arms
Stoke St Gregory, Rose & Crown
Triscombe, Blue Ball
Wells, City Arms, Crown
Wookey, Burcott

Staffordshire
Alstonefield, George, Watts Russell Arms
Burton upon Trent, Burton Bridge Inn
Cheadle, Queens at Freehay
Lichfield, Boat

Salt, Holly Bush
Stourton, Fox
Wetton, Olde Royal Oak

Suffolk
Bramfield, Queens Head
Brome, Cornwallis
Buxhall, Crown
Dennington, Queens Head
Dunwich, Ship
Erwarton, Queens Head
Hundon, Plough
Lavenham, Angel
Levington, Ship
Lidgate, Star
Long Melford, Black Lion
Nayland, Anchor
Orford, Jolly Sailor
Rattlesden, Brewers Arms
Snape, Crown, Golden Key
South Elmham, St Peters Brewery
Southwold, Crown
Stoke-by-Nayland, Angel
Swilland, Moon & Mushroom
Tostock, Gardeners Arms
Walberswick, Bell
Waldringfield, Maybush
Wingfield, De La Pole Arms

Surrey
Blackbrook, Plough
Bletchingley, Prince Albert
Charleshill, Donkey
Cobham, Cricketers
Coldharbour, Plough
Eashing, Stag
Newdigate, Surrey Oaks
Pirbright, Royal Oak
West End, Inn at West End

Sussex
Alciston, Rose Cottage
Alfriston, George
Amberley, Black Horse, Sportsmans
Arlington, Old Oak
Billingshurst, Blue Ship
Blackboys, Blackboys Inn
Bodiam, Curlew
Burpham, George & Dragon
Byworth, Black Horse
Charlton, Fox Goes Free
Chidham, Old House At Home
Cuckfield, White Harte
Danehill, Coach & Horses
Donnington, Blacksmiths Arms
Duncton, Cricketers
East Ashling, Horse & Groom
East Chiltington, Jolly Sportsman
Elsted, Three Horseshoes
Fernhurst, Kings Arms
Hammerpot, Woodmans Arms

Horsham, Black Jug
Icklesham, Queens Head
Lewes, Snowdrop
Lodsworth, Halfway Bridge Inn
Oving, Gribble Inn
Pett, Two Sawyers
Rye, Mermaid
Salehurst, Salehurst Halt
Seaford, Golden Galleon
Singleton, Fox & Hounds
Tillington, Horse Guards
Trotton, Keepers Arms
Wartling, Lamb
Wilmington, Giants Rest

Warwickshire
Dunchurch, Dun Cow
Edge Hill, Castle
Farnborough, Inn at Farnborough
Gaydon, Malt Shovel
Great Wolford, Fox & Hounds
Hatton, Falcon
Himley, Crooked House
Ilmington, Howard Arms
Kenilworth, Clarendon House
Little Compton, Red Lion
Long Itchington, Duck on the Pond
Monks Kirby, Bell
Shipston-on-Stour, White Bear
Stratford-upon-Avon, Garrick
Welford-on-Avon, Bell

Wiltshire
Axford, Red Lion
Barford St Martin, Barford Inn
Beckhampton, Waggon & Horses
Berwick St James, Boot
Berwick St John, Talbot
Box, Quarrymans Arms
Bradford-on-Avon, Dandy Lion
Brinkworth, Three Crowns
Devizes, Bear
Ebbesbourne Wake, Horseshoe
Great Durnford, Black Horse
Great Hinton, Linnet
Heytesbury, Angel
Hindon, Angel
Holt, Toll Gate
Kilmington, Red Lion
Lacock, George
Lower Chute, Hatchet
Malmesbury, Smoking Dog
Newton Tony, Malet Arms
Norton, Vine Tree
Pitton, Silver Plough
Poulshot, Raven
Rowde, George & Dragon

Salisbury, Haunch of
Venison
Seend, Barge
Semley, Benett Arms
Stourton, Spread Eagle
Whitley, Pear Tree
Woodborough, Seven Stars
Wylye, Bell

Worcestershire
Berrow Green, Admiral
Rodney
Bewdley, Little Pack Horse
Birtsmorton, Farmers Arms
Bransford, Bear & Ragged
Staff
Bredon, Fox & Hounds
Bretforton, Fleece
Clent, Fountain
Crowle, Old Chequers
Flyford Flavell, Boot
Holy Cross, Bell & Cross
Pensax, Bell
Welland, Anchor
Wyre Piddle, Anchor

Yorkshire
Aldborough, Ship
Appleton-le-Moors, Moors
Asenby, Crab & Lobster
Beverley, White Horse
Blakey Ridge, Lion
Boroughbridge, Black Bull
Bradfield, Strines Inn
Brearton, Malt Shovel
Burton Leonard, Hare &
Hounds
Byland Abbey, Abbey Inn
Carthorpe, Fox & Hounds
Constable Burton, Wyvill
Arms
Cray, White Lion
Crayke, Durham Ox
Cropton, New Inn
Dacre Banks, Royal Oak
Egton Bridge, Horse Shoe
Elslack, Tempest Arms
Fadmoor, Plough
Felixkirk, Carpenters Arms
Ferrensby, General Tarleton
Goose Eye, Turkey
Harome, Star
Hetton, Angel
Hull, Minerva, Olde White
Harte
Kirkbymoorside, George &
Dragon
Kirkham, Stone Trough
Langthwaite, Charles
Bathurst
Lastingham, Blacksmiths
Arms
Levisham, Horseshoe
Leyburn, Sandpiper
Linthwaite, Sair
Linton, Windmill
Litton, Queens Arms
Low Catton, Gold Cup
Lund, Wellington

Marton, Appletree
Masham, Kings Head
Nosterfield, Freemasons
Arms
Nunnington, Royal Oak
Osmotherley, Golden Lion
Pickering, White Swan
Pickhill, Nags Head
Pool, White Hart
Ripley, Boars Head
Sawley, Sawley Arms
Scarborough, Hole in the
Wall
Scawton, Hare
Sheffield, Fat Cat, New
Barrack
Sutton upon Derwent, St
Vincent Arms
Terrington, Bay Horse
Thorganby, Jefferson Arms
Thornton in Lonsdale,
Marton Arms
Thornton Watlass, Buck
Wass, Wombwell Arms
Wath in Nidderdale,
Sportsmans Arms
Whitby, Duke of York

London
Central London, Albert,
Black Friar, Grapes, Lamb,
Lord Moon of the Mall,
Moon Under Water, Olde
Cheshire Cheese, Star
North London, Duke of
Cambridge, Holly Bush,
Spaniards Inn, Waterside
South London, Anchor, Bulls
Head, Crown &
Greyhound, Founders
Arms, George
West London, Bulls Head,
Churchill Arms, Portobello
Gold, White Horse,
Windsor Castle

Scotland
Aboyne, Boat
Applecross, Applecross Inn
Ardfern, Galley of Lorne
Badachro, Badachro Inn
Broughty Ferry, Fishermans
Tavern
Crinan, Crinan Hotel
East Linton, Drovers
Edinburgh, Abbotsford,
Starbank
Glasgow, Auctioneers,
Counting House
Houston, Fox & Hounds
Innerleithen, Traquair Arms
Isle of Whithorn, Steam
Packet
Kenmore, Kenmore Hotel
Kilberry, Kilberry Inn
Kingholm Quay, Swan
Kippen, Cross Keys
Linlithgow, Four Marys
Lybster, Portland Arms

Melrose, Burts Hotel
Oban, Oban Inn
Plockton, Plockton Hotel
Portpatrick, Crown
Stein, Stein Inn
Stonehaven, Lairhillock
Swinton, Wheatsheaf
Tayvallich, Tayvallich Inn
Thornhill, Lion & Unicorn
Tushielaw, Tushielaw Inn
Ullapool, Ferry Boat
Weem, Ailean Chraggan

Wales
Abercych, Nags Head
Aberdovey, Penhelig Arms
Abergorlech, Black Lion
Beaumaris, Olde Bulls Head,
Sailors Return
Berriew, Lion
Betws-y-Coed, Ty Gwyn
Bodfari, Dinorben Arms
Bosherston, St Govans
Country Inn
Cresswell Quay, Cresselly
Arms
Crickhowell, Bear, Nantyffin
Cider Mill
Gresford, Pant-yr-Ochain
Halkyn, Britannia
Hay-on-Wye, Kilverts, Old
Black Lion
Llanbedr-y-Cennin, Olde
Bull
Llanberis, Pen-y-Gwryd
Llanddarog, White Hart
Llandeilo, Castle
Llandudno Junction, Queens
Head
Llanfrynach, White Swan
Llangattock Lingoed,
Hunters Moon
Llangedwyn, Green Inn
Llangollen, Corn Mill
Llwyndafydd, Crown
Mold, Glasfryn
Montgomery, Brickys
Old Radnor, Harp
Pembroke Ferry, Ferry Inn
Pontypool, Open Hearth
Porthgain, Sloop
Presteigne, Radnorshire
Arms
Raglan, Clytha Arms
Red Wharf Bay, Ship
Rhyd-y-Meirch, Goose &
Cuckoo
Saundersfoot, Royal Oak
Shirenewton, Carpenters
Arms
St Hilary, Bush
Talyllyn, Tynycornel
Trelleck, Lion
Ty'n-y-groes, Groes
Usk, Nags Head

Channel Islands
King's Mills, Fleur du Jardin
Rozel, Rozel Bay Hotel

St Brelade, Old Portelet Inn
St Helier, Town House
St John, Les Fontaines
St Ouens Bay, La Pulente

Pubs close to Motorway Junctions

The number at the start of each line is the number of the junction. Detailed directions are given in the main entry for each pub. In this list, to help you find the pubs quickly before you're past the junction, we give the name of the chapter where you'll find the text.

M1
16: Nether Heyford, Old Sun (Northants) 1.8 miles
18: Crick, Red Lion (Northants) 1 mile; Kilsby, George (Northants) 2.6 miles
24: Kegworth, Cap & Stocking (Leics) 1 mile; Shardlow, Old Crown (Derbys) 3 miles
26: Kimberley, Nelson & Railway (Notts) 1.7 miles
29: Hardwick Hall, Hardwick Inn (Derbys) 4 miles

M3
3: West End, Inn at West End (Surrey) 2.4 miles
5: Rotherwick, Falcon (Hants) 4 miles
10: Winchester, Black Boy (Hants) 1 mile

M4
9: Holyport, Belgian Arms (Berks) 1.5 miles; Bray, Crown (Berks) 1.75 miles
12: Stanford Dingley, Bull (Berks) 4 miles
13: Winterbourne, Winterbourne Arms (Berks) 3.7 miles
17: Norton, Vine Tree (Wilts) 4 miles
18: Old Sodbury, Dog (Gloucs) 2 miles; Hinton Dyrham, Bull (Gloucs) 2.4 miles

M5
4: Holy Cross, Bell & Cross (Worcs) 4 miles
6: Crowle, Old Chequers (Worcs) 2 miles
9: Bredon, Fox & Hounds (Worcs) 4.5 miles
16: Almondsbury, Bowl (Gloucs) 1.25 miles
19: Portishead, Windmill (Somerset) 3.7 miles; Clapton-in-Gordano, Black Horse (Somerset) 4 miles
26: Clayhidon, Merry Harriers (Devon) 3.1 miles
28: Broadhembury, Drewe Arms (Devon) 5 miles
30: Topsham, Bridge (Devon) 2.25 miles; Woodbury Salterton, Diggers Rest (Devon) 3.5 miles

M6
4: Shustoke, Griffin (Warwicks) 5 miles
16: Barthomley, White Lion (Cheshire) 1 mile; Weston, White Lion (Cheshire) 3.5 miles
19: Plumley, Smoker (Cheshire) 2.5 miles
33: Bay Horse, Bay Horse (Lancs) 1.2 miles
35: Yealand Conyers, New Inn (Lancs) 3 miles
40: Yanwath, Gate Inn (Cumbria) 2.25 miles; Stainton, Kings Arms (Cumbria) 3 miles; Tirril, Queens Head (Cumbria) 3.5 miles

M9
3: Linlithgow, Four Marys (Scotland) 2 miles

M11
8: Birchanger, Three Willows (Essex) 0.8 miles
10: Hinxton, Red Lion (Cambs) 2 miles; Thriplow, Green Man (Cambs) 3 miles

M25
8: Reigate Heath, Skimmington Castle (Surrey) 3 miles
10: Cobham, Cricketers (Surrey) 3.75 miles; Chenies, Red Lion (Bucks) 2 miles
21A: Potters Crouch, Holly Bush (Herts) 2.3 miles

M27
1: Fritham, Royal Oak (Hants) 4 miles
8: Bursledon, Jolly Sailor (Hants) 2 miles

M40
2: Hedgerley, White Horse (Bucks) 2.4 miles; Forty Green, Royal Standard of England (Bucks) 3.5 miles
6: Lewknor, Olde Leathern Bottel (Oxon) 0.5 miles
12: Gaydon, Malt Shovel (Warwicks) 0.9 miles
15: Hatton, Falcon (Warwicks) 4.6 miles

M45
1: Dunchurch, Dun Cow (Warwicks) 1.3 miles

M48
1: Littleton-upon-Severn, White Hart (Gloucs) 3.5 miles

M50
1: Twyning, Fleet (Gloucs) 1.1 miles; Baughton, Jockey (Worcs) 4 miles
3: Upton Bishop, Moody Cow (Herefs) 2 miles

M53
3: Barnston, Fox & Hounds (Lancs) 3 miles

M56
11: Daresbury, Ring o' Bells (Cheshire) 1.5 miles
12: Frodsham, Ring o' Bells (Cheshire) 2 miles

Report Forms

Report forms

Please report to us: you can use the tear-out forms on the following pages, the card in the middle of the book, or just plain paper – whichever's easiest for you, or you can report to our website, **www.goodguides.com**. We need to know what you think of the pubs in this edition. We need to know about other pubs worthy of inclusion. We need to know about ones that should not be included.

The atmosphere and character of the pub are the most important features – why it would, or would not, appeal to strangers, so please try to describe what is special about it. In particular, we can't consider including a pub in the Lucky Dip section unless we know something about what it looks like inside, so that we can describe it to other readers. And obviously with existing entries, we need to know about any changes in décor and furnishings, too. But the bar food and the drink are also important – please tell us about them.

If the food is really quite outstanding, tick the FOOD AWARD box on the form, and tell us about the special quality that makes it stand out – the more detail, the better. And if you have stayed there, tell us about the standard of accommodation – whether it was comfortable, pleasant, good value for money. Again, if the pub or inn is worth special attention as a place to stay, tick the PLACE-TO-STAY AWARD box.

If you're in a position to gauge a pub's suitability or otherwise for **disabled people**, do please tell us about that.

Please try to gauge whether a pub should be a main entry, or is best as a Lucky Dip (and tick the relevant box). In general, main entries need qualities that would make it worth other readers' while to travel some distance to them; Lucky Dips are the pubs that are worth knowing about if you are nearby. But if a pub is an entirely new recommendation, the Lucky Dip may be the best place for it to start its career in the *Guide* – to encourage other readers to report on it.

The more detail you can put into your description of a Lucky Dip pub that's only scantily described in the current edition (or not in at all), the better. A description of its character and even furnishings is a tremendous boon.

It helps enormously if you can give the full address for any new pub – one not yet a main entry, or without a full address in the Lucky Dip sections. In a town, we need the street name; in the country, if it's hard to find, we need directions. Even better for us is the post code. If we can't find out a pub's post code, we no longer include it in the *Guide* – and the Post Office directories we use will not yet have caught up with new pubs, or ones which have changed their names. With any pub, it always helps to let us know about prices of food (and bedrooms, if there are any), and about any lunchtimes or evenings when food is not served. We'd also like to have your views on drinks quality – beer, wine, cider and so forth, even coffee and tea; and do let us know about bedrooms.

If you know that a Lucky Dip pub is open all day (or even late into the afternoon), please tell us – preferably saying which days.

When you go to a pub, don't tell them you're a reporter for the *Good Pub Guide*; we do make clear that all inspections are anonymous, and if you declare yourself as a reporter you risk getting special treatment – for better or for worse!

Sometimes pubs are dropped from the main entries simply because very few readers have written to us about them – and of course there's a risk that people may not write if they find the pub exactly as described in the entry. You can use the forms at the front of the batch of report forms just to list pubs you've been to, found as described, and can recommend.

When you write to The Good Pub Guide, FREEPOST TN1569, WADHURST, East Sussex TN5 7BR, you don't need a stamp in the UK. We'll gladly send you more forms (free) if you wish.

Though we try to answer letters, there are just the four of us – and with other work to do, besides producing this *Guide*. So please understand if there's a delay. And from June till September, when we are fully extended getting the next edition to the printers, we put all letters and reports aside, not answering them until the rush is over (and after our post-press-day late summer holiday). The end of May is the cut-off date for reports for the next edition (we can still cope with reports to our web site during the following weeks). However, the earlier we get them, the more consideration we're able to give them.

We'll assume we can print your name or initials as a recommender unless you tell us otherwise.

I have been to the following pubs in *The Good Pub Guide 2004* in the last few months, found them as described, and confirm that they deserve continued inclusion:

Continued overleaf
PLEASE GIVE YOUR NAME AND ADDRESS ON THE BACK OF THIS FORM

Pubs visited continued...

Your own name and address *(block capitals please)*

Postcode

In returning this form I confirm my agreement that the information I provide may be used by The Random House Group Ltd, its assignees and/or licensees in any media or medium whatsoever.

Please return to
The Good Pub Guide,
FREEPOST TN1569,
WADHURST,
East Sussex
TN5 7BR

IF YOU PREFER, YOU CAN SEND US
REPORTS THROUGH OUR WEB SITE:
www.goodguides.com

I have been to the following pubs in *The Good Pub Guide 2004* in the last few months, found them as described, and confirm that they deserve continued inclusion:

Continued overleaf
PLEASE GIVE YOUR NAME AND ADDRESS ON THE BACK OF THIS FORM

Pubs visited continued...

Your own name and address *(block capitals please)*

Postcode

Please return to
The Good Pub Guide,
FREEPOST TN1569,
WADHURST,
East Sussex
TN5 7BR

IF YOU PREFER, YOU CAN SEND US
REPORTS THROUGH OUR WEB SITE:
www.goodguides.com

REPORT ON _(pub's name)_

Pub's address

☐ **YES MAIN ENTRY**   ☐ **YES** _Lucky Dip_   ☐ NO don't include
Please tick one of these boxes to show your verdict, and give reasons and descriptive comments, prices etc

☐ Deserves FOOD award   ☐ Deserves PLACE-TO-STAY award   2004:1

PLEASE GIVE YOUR NAME AND ADDRESS ON THE BACK OF THIS FORM

REPORT ON _(pub's name)_

Pub's address

☐ **YES MAIN ENTRY**   ☐ **YES** _Lucky Dip_   ☐ NO don't include
Please tick one of these boxes to show your verdict, and give reasons and descriptive comments, prices etc

☐ Deserves FOOD award   ☐ Deserves PLACE-TO-STAY award   2004:2

PLEASE GIVE YOUR NAME AND ADDRESS ON THE BACK OF THIS FORM

Your own name and address *(block capitals please)*

In returning this form I confirm my agreement that the information I provide may be used by
The Random House Group Ltd, its assignees and/or licensees in any media or medium whatsoever.

DO NOT USE THIS SIDE OF THE PAGE FOR WRITING ABOUT PUBS

By returning this form, you consent to the collection, recording and use of the information you submit, by The Random House Group Ltd. Any
personal details which you provide from which we can identify you are held and processed in accordance with the Data Protection Act
1998 and will not be passed on to any third parties. The Random House Group Ltd may wish to send you further information on their
associated products. Please tick box if you do not wish to receive any such information.

IF YOU PREFER, YOU CAN SEND US REPORTS THROUGH OUR WEB SITE:
www.goodguides.com

REPORT ON *(pub's name)*

Pub's address

☐ **YES Main Entry**   ☐ **YES** *Lucky Dip*   ☐ **NO don't include**
*Please tick one of these boxes to show your verdict, and give reasons and
descriptive comments, prices etc*

☐ Deserves Food award   ☐ Deserves Place-to-stay award   2004:3

PLEASE GIVE YOUR NAME AND ADDRESS ON THE BACK OF THIS FORM

REPORT ON *(pub's name)*

Pub's address

☐ **YES Main Entry**   ☐ **YES** *Lucky Dip*   ☐ **NO don't include**
*Please tick one of these boxes to show your verdict, and give reasons and
descriptive comments, prices etc*

☐ Deserves Food award   ☐ Deserves Place-to-stay award   2004:4

PLEASE GIVE YOUR NAME AND ADDRESS ON THE BACK OF THIS FORM

Your own name and address *(block capitals please)*

In returning this form I confirm my agreement that the information I provide may be used by
The Random House Group Ltd, its assignees and/or licensees in any media or medium whatsoever.

DO NOT USE THIS SIDE OF THE PAGE FOR WRITING ABOUT PUBS

✂ ··

Your own name and address *(block capitals please)*

In returning this form I confirm my agreement that the information I provide may be used by
The Random House Group Ltd, its assignees and/or licensees in any media or medium whatsoever.

DO NOT USE THIS SIDE OF THE PAGE FOR WRITING ABOUT PUBS

IF YOU PREFER, YOU CAN SEND US REPORTS THROUGH OUR WEB SITE:
www.goodguides.com

REPORT ON *(pub's name)*

Pub's address

☐ **YES Main Entry**   ☐ **YES *Lucky Dip***   ☐ NO don't include
Please tick one of these boxes to show your verdict, and give reasons and descriptive comments, prices etc

☐ Deserves Food award   ☐ Deserves Place-to-stay award   2004:5

PLEASE GIVE YOUR NAME AND ADDRESS ON THE BACK OF THIS FORM

✂

REPORT ON *(pub's name)*

Pub's address

☐ **YES Main Entry**   ☐ **YES *Lucky Dip***   ☐ NO don't include
Please tick one of these boxes to show your verdict, and give reasons and descriptive comments, prices etc

☐ Deserves Food award   ☐ Deserves Place-to-stay award   2004:6

PLEASE GIVE YOUR NAME AND ADDRESS ON THE BACK OF THIS FORM

Your own name and address *(block capitals please)*

In returning this form I confirm my agreement that the information I provide may be used by The Random House Group Ltd, its assignees and/or licensees in any media or medium whatsoever.

DO NOT USE THIS SIDE OF THE PAGE FOR WRITING ABOUT PUBS

✂ ....

Your own name and address *(block capitals please)*

In returning this form I confirm my agreement that the information I provide may be used by The Random House Group Ltd, its assignees and/or licensees in any media or medium whatsoever.

DO NOT USE THIS SIDE OF THE PAGE FOR WRITING ABOUT PUBS

IF YOU PREFER, YOU CAN SEND US REPORTS THROUGH OUR WEB SITE:
www.goodguides.com

REPORT ON *(pub's name)*

Pub's address

☐ **YES MAIN ENTRY** ☐ **YES** *Lucky Dip* ☐ **NO don't include**
Please tick one of these boxes to show your verdict, and give reasons and descriptive comments, prices etc

☐ Deserves FOOD award ☐ Deserves PLACE-TO-STAY award 2004:7

PLEASE GIVE YOUR NAME AND ADDRESS ON THE BACK OF THIS FORM

✂

REPORT ON *(pub's name)*

Pub's address

☐ **YES MAIN ENTRY** ☐ **YES** *Lucky Dip* ☐ **NO don't include**
Please tick one of these boxes to show your verdict, and give reasons and descriptive comments, prices etc

☐ Deserves FOOD award ☐ Deserves PLACE-TO-STAY award 2004:8

PLEASE GIVE YOUR NAME AND ADDRESS ON THE BACK OF THIS FORM

Your own name and address *(block capitals please)*

In returning this form I confirm my agreement that the information I provide may be used by
The Random House Group Ltd, its assignees and/or licensees in any media or medium whatsoever.

DO NOT USE THIS SIDE OF THE PAGE FOR WRITING ABOUT PUBS

✂ ···

Your own name and address *(block capitals please)*

In returning this form I confirm my agreement that the information I provide may be used by
The Random House Group Ltd, its assignees and/or licensees in any media or medium whatsoever.

DO NOT USE THIS SIDE OF THE PAGE FOR WRITING ABOUT PUBS

IF YOU PREFER, YOU CAN SEND US REPORTS THROUGH OUR WEB SITE:
www.goodguides.com

REPORT ON *(pub's name)*

Pub's address

☐ **YES Main Entry**   ☐ **YES** *Lucky Dip*   ☐ NO don't include
Please tick one of these boxes to show your verdict, and give reasons and descriptive comments, prices etc

☐ Deserves Food award   ☐ Deserves Place-to-stay award   2004:9

PLEASE GIVE YOUR NAME AND ADDRESS ON THE BACK OF THIS FORM

✂

REPORT ON *(pub's name)*

Pub's address

☐ **YES Main Entry**   ☐ **YES** *Lucky Dip*   ☐ NO don't include
Please tick one of these boxes to show your verdict, and give reasons and descriptive comments, prices etc

☐ Deserves Food award   ☐ Deserves Place-to-stay award   2004:10

PLEASE GIVE YOUR NAME AND ADDRESS ON THE BACK OF THIS FORM

Your own name and address *(block capitals please)*

In returning this form I confirm my agreement that the information I provide may be used by
The Random House Group Ltd, its assignees and/or licensees in any media or medium whatsoever.

DO NOT USE THIS SIDE OF THE PAGE FOR WRITING ABOUT PUBS

✂ ··

Your own name and address *(block capitals please)*

In returning this form I confirm my agreement that the information I provide may be used by
The Random House Group Ltd, its assignees and/or licensees in any media or medium whatsoever.

DO NOT USE THIS SIDE OF THE PAGE FOR WRITING ABOUT PUBS

IF YOU PREFER, YOU CAN SEND US REPORTS THROUGH OUR WEB SITE:
www.goodguides.com

REPORT ON *(pub's name)*

Pub's address

☐ **YES MAIN ENTRY**   ☐ **YES** *Lucky Dip*   ☐ **NO don't include**
Please tick one of these boxes to show your verdict, and give reasons and descriptive comments, prices etc

☐ Deserves FOOD award   ☐ Deserves PLACE-TO-STAY award   2004:5

PLEASE GIVE YOUR NAME AND ADDRESS ON THE BACK OF THIS FORM

✂ -

REPORT ON *(pub's name)*

Pub's address

☐ **YES MAIN ENTRY**   ☐ **YES** *Lucky Dip*   ☐ **NO don't include**
Please tick one of these boxes to show your verdict, and give reasons and descriptive comments, prices etc

☐ Deserves FOOD award   ☐ Deserves PLACE-TO-STAY award   2004:6

PLEASE GIVE YOUR NAME AND ADDRESS ON THE BACK OF THIS FORM

Your own name and address *(block capitals please)*

In returning this form I confirm my agreement that the information I provide may be used by The Random House Group Ltd, its assignees and/or licensees in any media or medium whatsoever.

DO NOT USE THIS SIDE OF THE PAGE FOR WRITING ABOUT PUBS

By returning this form, you consent to the collection, recording and use of the information you submit, by The Random House Group Ltd. Any personal details which you provide from which we can identify you are held and processed in accordance with the Data Protection Act 1998 and will not be passed on to any third parties. The Random House Group Ltd may wish to send you further information on their associated products. Please tick box if you do not wish to receive any such information.

IF YOU PREFER, YOU CAN SEND US REPORTS THROUGH OUR WEB SITE:
www.goodguides.com

REPORT ON *(pub's name)*

Pub's address

☐ **YES MAIN ENTRY** ☐ **YES** *Lucky Dip* ☐ **NO don't include**
*Please tick one of these boxes to show your verdict, and give reasons and
descriptive comments, prices etc*

☐ Deserves FOOD award ☐ Deserves PLACE-TO-STAY award 2004:7

PLEASE GIVE YOUR NAME AND ADDRESS ON THE BACK OF THIS FORM

REPORT ON *(pub's name)*

Pub's address

☐ **YES MAIN ENTRY** ☐ **YES** *Lucky Dip* ☐ **NO don't include**
*Please tick one of these boxes to show your verdict, and give reasons and
descriptive comments, prices etc*

☐ Deserves FOOD award ☐ Deserves PLACE-TO-STAY award 2004:8

PLEASE GIVE YOUR NAME AND ADDRESS ON THE BACK OF THIS FORM

Your own name and address *(block capitals please)*

In returning this form I confirm my agreement that the information I provide may be used by
The Random House Group Ltd, its assignees and/or licensees in any media or medium whatsoever.

DO NOT USE THIS SIDE OF THE PAGE FOR WRITING ABOUT PUBS

✂ ···

Your own name and address *(block capitals please)*

In returning this form I confirm my agreement that the information I provide may be used by
The Random House Group Ltd, its assignees and/or licensees in any media or medium whatsoever.

DO NOT USE THIS SIDE OF THE PAGE FOR WRITING ABOUT PUBS

IF YOU PREFER, YOU CAN SEND US REPORTS THROUGH OUR WEB SITE:
www.goodguides.com

REPORT ON *(pub's name)*

Pub's address

☐ **YES MAIN ENTRY**   ☐ **YES** *Lucky Dip*   ☐ NO don't include
Please tick one of these boxes to show your verdict, and give reasons and descriptive comments, prices etc

☐ Deserves FOOD award   ☐ Deserves PLACE-TO-STAY award   2004:9

PLEASE GIVE YOUR NAME AND ADDRESS ON THE BACK OF THIS FORM

✂

REPORT ON *(pub's name)*

Pub's address

☐ **YES MAIN ENTRY**   ☐ **YES** *Lucky Dip*   ☐ NO don't include
Please tick one of these boxes to show your verdict, and give reasons and descriptive comments, prices etc

☐ Deserves FOOD award   ☐ Deserves PLACE-TO-STAY award   2004:10

PLEASE GIVE YOUR NAME AND ADDRESS ON THE BACK OF THIS FORM

Your own name and address *(block capitals please)*

In returning this form I confirm my agreement that the information I provide may be used by
The Random House Group Ltd, its assignees and/or licensees in any media or medium whatsoever.

DO NOT USE THIS SIDE OF THE PAGE FOR WRITING ABOUT PUBS

✂ ....

Your own name and address *(block capitals please)*

In returning this form I confirm my agreement that the information I provide may be used by
The Random House Group Ltd, its assignees and/or licensees in any media or medium whatsoever.

DO NOT USE THIS SIDE OF THE PAGE FOR WRITING ABOUT PUBS

IF YOU PREFER, YOU CAN SEND US REPORTS THROUGH OUR WEB SITE:
www.goodguides.com